BRITISH LIBRARY OF POLITICAL AND ECONOMIC SCIENCE

A London Bibliography of the Social Sciences

Eleventh Supplement

1976

VOLUME XXXIV

MANSELL LONDON 1977

*This Bibliography has been computer typeset from
the machine-readable subject catalogue of the
British Library of Political and Economic Science by*
Mansell Information/Publishing Limited
3 Bloomsbury Place, London WC1A 2QA

ISBN 0 7201 0721 0
ISSN 0076-051X
Library of Congress Card Number 31-9970

*Printed and bound in Great Britain at
The Scolar Press Limited, Ilkley, Yorkshire*

© 1977 *The British Library of Political and Economic Science*

Preface

This annual supplement to *A London Bibliography of the Social Sciences* is the third to be produced by means of computer typesetting.

    Readers are again referred to the 'List of subject headings used in the Bibliography arranged under topics' as an essential guide to related headings in their field. This is to be found at the end of the volume.

D. A. Clarke   *August* 1977

Contents

VOLUMES I-XXXIV

VOLUMES I-IV *Original Compilation*

Holdings up to 1929 of the
British Library of Political and Economic Science
Edward Fry Library of International Law
Goldsmith's Library of Economic Literature,
  University of London
National Institute of Industrial Psychology
Royal Anthropological Institute
Royal Institute of International Affairs
Royal Statistical Society

Special collections in the libraries of
The Reform Club (*political and historical pamphlets*)
University College, London (*the Hume, Ricardo and other economic and political collections*)
The University of London (*works on economics and related subjects*)

VOLUME V *First Supplement*

Additions from 1929 to 1931 to the collections included in Volumes I-IV

VOLUME VI *Second Supplement*

Additions from 1931 to 1936 to the
British Library of Political and Economic Science
Edward Fry Library of International Law
Goldsmith's Library of Economic Literature

VOLUMES VII-IX *Third Supplement*

Additions from 1936 to 1950, other than works in the Russian language, to the
British Library of Political and Economic Science
Edward Fry Library of International Law

VOLUMES X-XI *Fourth Supplement*

Additions from 1950 to 1955 in all languages, and also from 1936 to 1950 in Russian, to the
British Library of Political and Economic Science
Edward Fry Library of International Law

VOLUMES XII-XIV *Fifth Supplement*

Additions from 1955 to 1962 to the
British Library of Political and Economic Science
Edward Fry Library of International Law

VOLUMES XV-XXI *Sixth Supplement*

Additions from 1962 to 1968 to the
British Library of Political and Economic Science
Edward Fry Library of International Law
Volume XXI contains indexes to Volumes XV-XXI

VOLUMES XXII-XXVIII *Seventh Supplement*

Additions from 1969 to 1972 to the
British Library of Political and Economic Science
Edward Fry Library of International Law
Volume XXVIII contains an index to
Volumes XXII-XXVIII

VOLUMES XXIX-XXXI *Eighth Supplement*

Additions from 1972 to 1973 to the
British Library of Political and Economic Science
Edward Fry Library of International Law
Volume XXXI contains an index to
Volumes XXIX-XXXI

VOLUME XXXII *Ninth Supplement*

Additions during 1974 to the
British Library of Political and Economic Science
Edward Fry Library of International Law
with index

VOLUME XXXIII *Tenth Supplement*

Additions during 1975 to the
British Library of Political and Economic Science
Edward Fry Library of International Law
with index

VOLUME XXXIV *Eleventh Supplement*
Additions during 1976 to the
British Library of Political and Economic Science
Edward Fry Library of International Law
with index

PERIODICALS LISTS

An alphabetical list of the periodicals in the British Library of Political and Economic Science in 1929 is given in Volume IV; supplementary lists up to 1936 are given in Volumes V and VI, after which they have been discontinued.

AUTHOR INDEX

Author indexes are given in Volumes IV (for Volumes I-III), V, and VI, but not in later volumes.
Volumes I-XIV were published by the British Library of Political and Economic Science, Houghton Street, London WC2

A London
Bibliography of the
Social Sciences

AARHUS

— Social history.

HAUGAARD JENSEN (JENS) and others. Sociale studier: kriminalitet, prostitution og fattigdom i Århus, ca. 1870-1906. Aarhus, 1975. pp. 483. *bibliogs.*

ABANYAMBO (AFRICAN PEOPLE).

KATOKE (ISRAEL K.) The Karagwe kingdom: a history of the Abanyambo of north western Tanzania, c1400-1915. Nairobi, 1975. pp. 183. *bibliog.*

ABBREVIATIONS.

MONTGOMERY (A.C.) compiler. Acronyms and abbreviations in library and information work: a reference handbook of British usage. London, [1975]. pp. 97.

APELDOORN (C.G.L.) Afkortingen lexicon; medewerking voor België van Remi Sterkens. 2nd ed. Utrecht, 1976. pp. 210.

ABIDJAN

— Religion.

DENIEL (RAYMOND) Religions dans la ville: croyances et changements sociaux à Abidjan. Abidjan, [1975]. pp. 208.

ABILITY, INFLUENCE OF AGE ON

— Finland.

LÄHTEINEN (MARTTI) Ikä ongelmana työelämässä: eri-ikäisten teollisuuden työntekijäin ongelmia kartoittava tutkimus, etc. Helsinki, 1975. pp. 126. *bibliog.* (Finland. Suomen Virallinen Tilasto. Finlands Officielle Statistik. 32. Sosiaalisia Erikoistutkimuksia. 44) With English summary.

ABKHAZIA

— Statistics.

ABKHAZIA. Statisticheskoe Upravlenie. 1973. Narodnoe khoziaistvo Abkhazskoi ASSR: statisticheskii sbornik. Tbilisi, 1973. pp. 439.

ABOLITIONISTS.

McPHERSON (JAMES M.) The abolitionist legacy: from reconstruction to the N.A.A.C.P. Princeton, 1975. pp. 438. *bibliog.*

ABORTION.

DAVID (HENRY PHILIP) ed. Abortion research: international experience. Lexington, Mass., [1974]. pp. 249.

LEE (LUKE TSUNG-CHOU) and PAXMAN (JOHN M.) Pregnancy and abortion in adolescence: a comparative legal survey and proposals for reform. Medford, Mass., 1975. pp. 48. (Tufts University. Fletcher School of Law and Diplomacy. Law and Population Monograph Series. No. 26) Reprinted from Columbia Human Rights Law Review, vol. 6, no. 2.

— Germany.

GLASS (DAVID VICTOR) [Materials for a study of national-socialist population policy and abortion law. 1912, 1931-38]. 1 piece. *Manuscript, typescript, etc.*

— Italy.

CONFERENZA NAZIONALE SULL'ABORTO, ROMA, 1975. Contro l'aborto di classe: [proceedings of a conference sponsored by the Movimento di Liberazione della Donna and the Partito Radicale]; introduzione e cura di Maria Adele Teodori. Roma, 1975. pp. 252.

SÌ o no all'aborto; [by] Adriano Bompiani [and others]; a cura di Piergiorgio Beretta. [Alba, 1975]. pp. 253.

— South Africa.

SYMPOSIUM ON ABORTION, DURBAN, 1973. The great debate: abortion in the South African context; edited by G.C. Oosthuizen [and others]. Cape Town, 1974. pp. 251 (*Human Sciences Research Council (South African Publication Series No. 47*)

— Sweden.

LILJESTRÖM (RITA) A study of abortion in Sweden...: (a contribution to the United Nations World Population Conference). Stockholm, Royal Ministry for Foreign Affairs, 1974. pp. 104. *bibliog.*

— United Kingdom.

WOMAN'S RIGHT TO CHOOSE CAMPAIGN. Why we must fight the Abortion (Amendment) Bill and how to go about it. London, [1975]. pp. 19.

— United States.

McCORMICK (E. PATRICIA) Attitudes toward abortion: experiences of selected black and white women. Lexington, Mass., [1975]. pp. 159. *bibliog.*

— Yugoslavia.

KRAKER (ANA) Gesetz über den Schwangerschaftsabbruch und die rückläufige Entwicklung des Geburtenüberschusses in Jugoslawien; herausgegeben von Hans Harmsen. Hamburg, 1972. pp. 52. (*Akademie für Staatsmedizin in Hamburg. Zur Entwicklung und Organisation des Gesundheitswesens in Sowjetrussland, in Osteuropäischen Volksdemokratien und in der DDR. Band 58*)

ABRUZZI E MOLISE

— Social conditions.

CAVALLARO (RENATO) La sociologia dei gruppi primari: formazione e dinamica dei raggruppamenti sociali di base; con uno studio sulle associazioni volontarie nel Molise. Napoli, 1975. pp. 382. *bibliog.*

ABRUZZO

— Economic conditions.

SANTUCCI (MARIO) ed. L'artigianato in Abruzzo. L'Aquila, 1974. pp. 157. (*Centro Regionale di Studi e Ricerche per lo Sviluppo Economico e Sociale dell'Abruzzo. Collana di Studi Economici. 4*)

ABUSE OF ADMINISTRATIVE POWER

— Russia.

VEREMEENKO (IVAN IVANOVICH) Administrativno-pravovye sanktsii. Moskva, 1975. pp. 192.

ACCIDENT LAW

— United Kingdom.

ATIYAH (PATRICK SELIM) Accidents, compensation and the law. 2nd ed. London, 1975. pp. 646.

ACCIDENTS.

GHOSH (DEBAPRIYA) and others. The economics of personal injury. Farnborough, Hants, [1976]. pp. 137. *bibliog.*

— Prevention.

JONES-LEE (M.W.) The value of life: an economic analysis. London, 1976. pp. 162. *bibliogs.*

ACCOMPLICES

— Russia.

UGREKHELIDZE (NIBLIIA GURAMOVNA) Kriminologicheskaia kharakteristika souchastiia v prestuplenii. Tbilisi, 1975. pp. 112. *With English and German summaries.*

ACCOUNTING.

AMEY (LLOYD RONALD) and EGGINTON (DON A.) Management accounting: a conceptual approach. London, 1973, repr. 1975. pp. 684. *bibliogs.*

PEASNELL (KEN V.) The usefulness of accounting information to investors. Lancaster, [1974]. pp. 29. (*Lancaster. University. International Centre for Research in Accounting. ICRA Occasional Papers. No. 1*)

GLAUTIER (MICHAEL WILLIAM EDGARD) and UNDERDOWN (B.) Accounting in a changing environment: from book-keeping to decision theory. London, 1974. pp. 197. *bibliogs.*

PEASNELL (KEN V.) Accounting objectives: a critique of the Trueblood report. Lancaster, [1974]. pp. 73. *bibliog.* (*Lancaster. University. International Centre for Research in Accounting. ICRA Occasional Papers. No. 5.*)

BEIER (JOACHIM) Zeitraumanalyse: Bindeglied einzel- und gesamtwirtschaftlicher Unternehmensstatistik. Berlin, [1975]. pp. 337. *bibliog.*

MAY (ROBERT G.) and others. A new introduction to financial accounting. Englewood Cliffs, [1975]. pp. 645.

OLDHAM (K. MICHAEL) Accounting systems and practice in Europe. Epping, Essex, 1975. pp. 183.

— History.

SYMPOSIUM INTERNATIONAL DES HISTORIENS DE LA COMPTABILITE, 1ER, BRUXELLES, 1970. La comptabilité à travers les âges: exposition organisée à la Bibliothèque Royale Albert Ier du 2 octobre au 8 novembre 1970; [papers of the symposium organisé par le Collège National des Experts Comptables de Belgique, October, 1970]. Bruxelles, [1970?]. 11 pts. (in 1 vol.). *bibliogs.*

HAVE (O.TEN) The history of accountancy;...translated by A. van Seventer. Palo Alto, Cal., [1976]. pp. 113.

— Law — United Kingdom.

WILLOTT (ROBERT) Current accounting law and practice. London, 1976. pp. 394.

— Research — United Kingdom.

TRICKER (R. IAN) Research in accountancy: a strategy for further work; a research review presented to the S[ocial] S[cience] R[esearch] C[ouncil] Management and Industrial Relations Committee. London, Social Science Research Council, [1975]. pp. 55, xvii. *bibliog.*

— Social aspects.

MINTROP (ANGELIKA) Gesellschaftsbezogene Rechenschaftslegung: Dokumentation "sozialer Verantwortung" der Unternehmen. [Zürich, 1976]. pp. 193. *bibliog.* Dissertation der Universität Zürich zur Erlangung der Würde eines Doktors der Wirtschaftswissenschaft.

— Study and teaching — United Kingdom.

HILTON (KENNETH) Control systems for social and economic management; an inaugural lecture [delivered at the University of Southampton in 1975]. Southampton, 1975. pp. 24.

ACCULTURATION.

WACHTEL (NATHAN) Sociedad e ideologia: ensayos de historia y antropologia andinas. Lima, 1973. pp. 239. *bibliog.* (*Instituto de Estudios Peruanos. Historia Andina. 1*)

ACHIEVEMENT MOTIVATION.

MEDNICK (MARTHA TAMARA SHUCH) and others, eds. Women and achievement: social and motivational analyses. Washington, [1975]. pp. 447. *bibliogs.*

LEICHMAN (GLENN ALAN) The effect of age and educational environment on the development of achievement evaluations and moral judgements. [1976]. fo. 243. *bibliog.* Typescript. Ph.D. (London) thesis: unpublished. This thesis is the property of London University and may not be removed from the Library.

ACHOLI

— Politics and government.

LEYS (COLIN TEMPLE) Politicians and policies: an essay on politics in Acholi, Uganda, 1962-65. Nairobi, 1967 repr. 1972. pp. 107.

ACQUISITION OF TERRITORY.

ACQUISITION OF TERRITORY.

SOLLIE (FINN) and others. The challenge of new territories. Oslo, [1974]. pp. 172. *(Fridtjof Nansen Stiftelsen på Polhøgda. New Territories in International Politics. No. 1)*

SKAGESTAD (ODD GUNNAR) Norsk polarpolitikk: hovedtrekk og utviklingslinjer, 1905-1974. Oslo, 1975. pp. 303. bibliog. *(Fridtjof Nansen Stiftelsen på Polhøgda. New Territories in International Politics. No.4) With English summary.*

ACRONYMS.

MONTGOMERY (A.C.) compiler. Acronyms and abbreviations in library and information work: a reference handbook of British usage. London, [1975]. pp. 97.

ACTING AS A PROFESSION.

LAYDER (DEREK ROY) Occupational careers in contemporary Britain: with special reference to the acting profession. 1976. fo. 376. bibliog. Typescript. Ph.D. (London) thesis: unpublished. *This thesis is the property of London University and may not be removed from the Library.*

ACTION FRANÇAISE.

GUCHET (YVES) Georges Valois: l'Action Française, le Faisceau, la République Syndicale. Paris, [1975]. pp. 249. bibliog.

ACTION RESEARCH.

The USE of action research in developing urban planning policy; report of residential colloquium organised by the Department of the Environment...at the School for Advanced Urban Studies, University of Bristol, from 24 to 27 June 1975. London, Department of the Environment, [1975]. pp. 127.

ACTIONS AND DEFENCES

— United Kingdom.

BULLEN (EDWARD) and others. Precedents of pleadings in the Queen's Bench Division of the High Court of Justice; twelfth edition by I.H. Jacob. London, 1975. pp. 1457.

ADELAIDE

— Poor.

GALE (FAY) and BINNION (JOAN) Poverty among aboriginal families in Adelaide. Canberra, Australian Government Publishing Service, 1975. pp. 52.

ADEN

— Harbour.

ADEN. Port Trust. 1967. The port of Aden handbook, 1967. [Aden, 1967]. pp. 82.

ADENAUER (KONRAD).

ADENAUER (KONRAD) Reden, 1917-1967: eine Auswahl; herausgegeben von Hans- Peter Schwarz. Stuttgart, [1975]. pp. 496.

BERGLAR (PETER) Konrad Adenauer: Konkursverwalter oder Erneuerer der Nation? Göttingen, [1975]. pp. 149. bibliog.

POETTERING (HANS GERT) Adenauers Sicherheitspolitik, 1955-1963: ein Beitrag zum deutsch-amerikanischen Verhältnis. Düsseldorf, [1975]. pp. 240. bibliog. *(Bonn. Universität. Seminar für Politische Wissenschaft. Bonner Schriften zur Politik und Zeitgeschichte. 10)*

POPPINGA (ANNELIESE) Konrad Adenauer: Geschichtsverständnis, Weltanschauung und politische Praxis. Stuttgart, 1975. pp. 296. bibliog.

PUETZ (HELMUTH) ed. Konrad Adenauer und die CDU der britischen Besatzungszone, 1946-1949: Dokumente zur Gründungsgeschichte der CDU Deutschlands; Herausgeber: Konrad-Adenauer-Stiftung. Bonn, [1975]. pp. 882.

KOHL (HELMUT) ed. Konrad Adenauer, 1876/1976. 2nd ed. Stuttgart, 1976. pp. 219.

PIKART (EBERHARD) Theodor Heuss und Konrad Adenauer: die Rolle des Bundespräsidenten in der Kanzlerdemokratie. Zürich, [1976]. pp. 176. bibliog.

ADMINISTRATION.

AFRICAN ADMINISTRATIVE STUDIES (formerly Cahiers africains d'administration publique); ([pd. by] African Training and Research Centre in Administration for Development). [in French and English]. s-a, (formerly irreg.), My 1967 (no.1)- Tangier.

ADMINISTRATION FOR DEVELOPMENT: jl. of the Administrative College of Papua New Guinea. s-a., Ja 1974 (no.1)- Boroko.

BALUTIS (ALAN P.) and HEAPHEY (JAMES J.) Public administration and the legislative process. Beverly Hills, [1974]. pp. 58. bibliog.

OPEN UNIVERSITY. Public Administration Course Team. Social sciences: a third level course: public administration, blocks 1-4, [and] course study guide. Milton Keynes, 1974. 12 parts (in 2 vols) bibliogs. *Bound with The course on public administration in the Open University; [by] William A. Robson.*

BYRD (JACK) Operations research models for public administration. Lexington, Mass., [1975]. pp. 276. bibliog.

MORROW (WILLIAM L.) Public administration: politics and the political system. New York, [1975]. pp. 272. bibliog.

SPIERS (MAURICE) Techniques and public administration: a contextual evaluation. [Lndon] 1975. pp. 250. bibliog.

SWERDLOW (IRVING) The public administration of economic development. New York, 1975. pp. 407.

WHITE (MICHAEL J.) Management science in federal agencies: the adoption and diffusion of a socio-technical innovation. Lexington, Mass., [1975]. pp. 111.

The DYNAMICS of public policy: a comparative analysis; edited by Richard Rose. London, [1976]. pp. 268. bibliogs. *Papers based on a conference of the Comparative Public Policy work group of the Committee on Political Sociology, at Cumberland Lodge, Windsor Great Park, May 6-10, 1974.*

GRIFFITH (JOHN ANEURIN GREY) ed. From policy to administration: essays in honour of William A. Robson. London, 1976. pp. 216.

GUNSTEREN (HERMAN R. VAN) The quest for control: a critique of the rational-central-rule approach in public affairs. London, [1976]. pp. 162. bibliogs.

LEEMANS (ARNE F.) ed. The management of change in government. The Hague, 1976. pp. 361. *(Hague. Institute of Social Studies. Series on the Development of Societies. vol.1)*

CAFRAD NEWS; ([pd. by] African Training and Research Centre in Administration for Development). irreg. Tangier. *Current issues only kept.*

— Bibliography.

U.K. Ministry of Overseas Development. Library. 1976. Public administration: a select bibliography; supplement to the 3rd revised edition. [London], 1976. pp. 103.

ADMINISTRATION OF ESTATES

— United Kingdom.

PARKER (ROBERT ALEXANDER CLARKE) Coke of Norfolk: a financial and agricultural study, 1707-1842. Oxford, 1975. pp. 222.

ADMINISTRATIVE AGENCIES

— Australia.

AUSTRALIA. Social Welfare Commission. Annual report. a., 1975(1st)- Canberra.

— Belgium.

INSTITUT BELGE D'INFORMATION ET DE DOCUMENTATION. The organisational structure of the Belgian economy. Brussels, Ministry of Foreign Affairs, External Trade and Cooperation in Development, 1976. pp. 28. *(Belgian News. No. 3e)*

— Canada.

CANADA. Department of the Secretary of State. 1973. Secretary of State: departmental programmes and affiliated agencies. Ottawa, 1973. pp. 23, 25. *In English and French.*

— Mauritius.

MAURITIUS. Para-Statal Salaries Commission. 1974. Report; [Donald Chesworth, chairman]. Port Louis, 1974. pp. 165.

— United States.

WIRT (JOHN G.) and others. R and D management: methods used by federal agencies. Santa Monica, 1974. pp. 261. *(Rand Corporation. [Rand Reports]. 1156)*

ASHFORD (NICHOLAS ASKOUNES) Crisis in the workplace: occupational disease and injury: a report to the Ford Foundation. Cambridge, Mass., [1976]. pp. 589. bibliog.

BOGART (LEO) Premises for propaganda: the United States Information Agency's operating assumptions in the Cold War;...abridged by Agnes Bogart. New York, [1976]. pp. 250. bibliog.

ADMINISTRATIVE AND POLITICAL DIVISIONS

— Canada — New Brunswick.

NEW BRUNSWICK. Representation and Electoral Districts Boundaries Commission. 1974. Report; [G.E. Graham, chairman]. [Fredericton], 1974. fo. 30, 35. *8 maps in end pocket. In English and French.*

— Germany.

MĚTSK (FRIDO) Die Stellung der Sorben in de territorialen Verwaltungsgliederung des deutschen Feudalismus: ein Beitrag zur Rechts- und Verfassungsgeschichte des deutschen Feudalismus im Sorbenland. Bautzen, 1968. pp. 171. *(Deutsche Akademie der Wissenschaften zu Berlin. Institut für Sorbische Volksforschung in Bautzen. Schriftenreihe. 43)*

— — Saarland.

SAARGEBIET. Statistisches Amt. Einzelschriften zur Statistik des Saarlandes. Nr. 50. Amtliches Gemeindeverzeichnis. 12. Auflage nach dem Stand am 1.1.1974, Neugliederungsgesetz, und am 31.12.1974 mit einer Verwaltungskarte. Saarbrücken, 1975. pp. 64.

— Poland.

POLAND. Biuro do Spraw Prezydiów Rad Narodowych. 1960. Podział administracyjny Polskiej Rzeczypospolitej Ludowej. Warszawa, 1960. pp. 420.

— Uganda.

UGANDA. Electoral Commission. 1970. Report...; under the chairmanship of Ateker Ejalu. [Entebbe, 1970]. pp. 62, 20 maps.

ADMINISTRATIVE COURTS

— United Kingdom.

JUSTICE, discretion and poverty: supplementary benefit appeal tribunals in Britain; edited by Michael Adler and Anthony Bradley. London, 1975. pp. 229. *Papers of a conference held at Edinburgh University on 13th and 14th December 1974, sponsored by the Socio-Legal Studies Committee of the University.*

MICKLETHWAIT (Sir ROBERT) The National Insurance Commissioners. London, 1976. pp. 151. *(Hamlyn Lectures. 28th Series)*

ADMINISTRATIVE DISCRETION

— Europe.

DAVIS (KENNETH CULP) and others. Discretionary justice in Europe and America, [by] K.C. Davis and European associates. Urbana, [1976]. pp. 203.

— United States.

DAVIS (KENNETH CULP) and others. Discretionary justice in Europe and America, [by] K.C. Davis and European associates. Urbana, [1976]. pp. 203.

ADMINISTRATIVE LAW

— Germany.

WOLFF (HANS JULIUS) and BACHOF (OTTO) Verwaltungsrecht: ein Studienbuch. München, 1973-76. 3 vols. *Vol.1 is of the 9th edition, vol.2 of the 4th edition and vol.3 of the 3rd edition.*

— Poland.

STAROŚCIAK (JERZY) Studia z teorii prawa administracyjnego. Wrocław, 1967. pp. 184. *With Russian and French summaries.*

STAROŚCIAK (JERZY) Prawo administracyjne. 3rd ed. Warszawa, 1975. pp. 576.

— Russia.

TARNAPOL'SKII (RUSTEM IL'IASOVICH) Pravovye voprosy upravleniia narodnym khoziaistvom v avtonomnoi respublike: vzaimootnosheniia Soveta Ministrov ASSR s nepodvedomstvennymi organizatsiiami. Kazan', 1974. pp. 120.

KLIUSHNICHENKO (ANATOLII PETROVICH) and SHERGIN (ANATOLII PAVLOVICH) Administrativnye komissii. Moskva, 1975. pp. 111.

— United Kingdom.

BAR (LUDWIK) Sądowa kontrola administracji w Anglii. Warszawa, 1962. pp. 254.

ADOLESCENCE.

FAMILY socialization and the adolescent: determinants of self- concept, conformity, religiosity, and counterculture values; [by] Darwin L. Thomas [and others]. Lexington, Mass., [1974]. pp. 181. *bibliog.*

LEE (LUKE TSUNG-CHOU) and PAXMAN (JOHN M.) Pregnancy and abortion in adolescence: a comparative legal survey and proposals for reform. Medford, Mass., 1975. pp. 48. *(Tufts University. Fletcher School of Law and Diplomacy. Law and Population Monograph Series. No. 26) Reprinted from Columbia Human Rights Law Review, vol. 6, no. 2.*

KONOPKA (GISELA) Young girls: a portrait of adolescence. Englewood Cliffs, [1976]. pp. 176. *bibliogs.*

ADOLESCENT PSYCHOLOGY

— United States.

ADOLESCENT prejudice; [by] Charles Y. Glock [and others] . New York, [1975]. pp. 229. *(California University. Survey Research Center. Five- Year Study of Anti-Semitism in the United States. vol. 7)*

ADULTHOOD.

KIMMEL (DOUGLAS C.) Adulthood and aging: an interdisciplinary developmental view. New York, [1974]. pp. 484. *bibliogs.*

ADVENTISTS.

The RISE of adventism: religion and society in mid-nineteenth- century America; Edwin S. Gaustad, editor. New York, [1974]. pp. 329. *bibliog.*

ADVERTISING.

CONSUMERISM: a threat or a challenge?; speeches at a session...at the 7th national conference of the Institute of Practitioners in Advertising, Eastbourne, 2-4 November 1972; [by] John Crichton [and others]. London, [1973]. pp. 18.

ADVERTISING ASSOCIATION. Advertising expenditure, 1960-73, including an index of media rates 1961-73. London, [1974?]. pp. 12. *(Reprinted from Advertising Quarterly, Nos. 40 and 41)*

BLOOM (PAUL N.) Advertising, competition, and public policy: a simulation study. Cambridge, Mass., [1976]. pp. 203.

LAMBIN (JEAN JACQUES) Advertising, competition and market conduct in oligopoly over time: an econometric investigation in western European countries. Amsterdam, 1976. pp. 312. *bibliog.*

— Social aspects — United States.

EWEN (STUART) Captains of consciousness: advertising and the social roots of the consumer culture. New York, [1976]. pp. 261. *bibliog.*

— Germany.

EUROPEAN BUREAU OF CONSUMERS' UNIONS. A study of advertising in the United Kingdom and the Federal Republic of Germany: a paper prepared...for the Environment and Consumer Protection Service of the E.E.C. Brussels, 1974 repr. 1975. pp. 263.

— United Kingdom.

EUROPEAN BUREAU OF CONSUMERS' UNIONS. A study of advertising in the United Kingdom and the Federal Republic of Germany: a paper prepared...for the Environment and Consumer Protection Service of the E.E.C. Brussels, 1974 repr. 1975. pp. 263.

ADVERTISING and economic behaviour; [by] Keith Cowling [and others]. London, 1975. pp. 202. *bibliogs.*

PIGOTT (STANLEY C.) O[gilvy] B[enson] M[ather]: a celebration: one hundred and twenty-five years in advertising. London, 1975. pp. 84. *bibliog.*

— United States.

ADVERTISING and society; edited by Yale Brozen. New York, 1974. pp. 189. *(Chicago. University. School of Business. Key Issues Lecture Series)*

ADVERTISING AGENCIES

— Accounting — Statistics.

INSTITUTE OF PRACTITIONERS IN ADVERTISING. How much, how many?. London, [1974]. pp. 8.

AERIAL PHOTOGRAPHY IN GEOGRAPHY.

PHOTOGRAPHIE aérienne et urbanisme. [Paris, 1969]. pp. 244. *bibliog.*

AERIAL PHOTOGRAPHY IN GEOLOGY.

ALLUM (J.A.E.) Regional photogeological interpretation of the British Solomon Islands; report;...aerial geophysical surveys project UNSF- BSIP 1965-1968. Honiara, 1967. pp. 78. *bibliog. 10 maps in end pocket.*

AERONAUTICS

— Accidents.

CANADA. Aviation Safety Investigation Division. Synopses of aircraft accidents: civil aircraft in Canada. bi-m., 1975 (no.1)- Ottawa.

— Laws and regulations.

BEREZOWSKI (CEZARY) Międzynarodowe prawo lotnicze. Warszawa, 1964. pp. 286. *With Russian and French summaries.*

WASSENBERGH (H.A.) Public international air transportation law in a new era. Deventer, [1975]. pp. 165. *bibliog.*

— — Bibliography.

LONDON. University. Institute of Advanced Legal Studies. Union Catalogues. No.4. Union list of air and space law literature in the libraries of Oxford, Cambridge and London. 2nd ed. London, 1975. 1 vol. (unpaged).

AERONAUTICS, COMMERCIAL.

TAWIL (EDWIN NESSIM) The economic evaluation of new aircraft types: an analysis of the decision making process for new investment in air transportation. 1975. fo. 128. *Typescript. M.Sc. (Econ.) (London) thesis: unpublished. This thesis is the property of London University and may not be removed from the Library.*

— Passenger traffic.

OPÉRATIONS du tourisme international et transports aériens; par J. David [and others]; colloque dans le cadre du Centre de Transports Aériens. Paris, 1975. pp. 164.

— Canada.

CANADA. Statistics Canada. International air charter statistics. a., 1974(1st issue)- Ottawa. *[In English and French].*

— China.

WIETHOFF (BODO) Luftverkehr in China, 1928-1949: Materialien zu einem untauglichen Modernisierunsversuch. Wiesbaden, [1975]. pp. 380. *bibliog. (Hamburg. Institut für Asienkunde. Schriften. Band 39) With English summary.*

— Europe — Passenger traffic.

GREIG (JOHN ALEXANDER) The rationalisation of airline networks within Western Europe, with special reference to Swissair. 1975. fo. 341. *bibliog. Typescript. Ph.D.(London) thesis: unpublished. This thesis is the property of London University and may not be removed from the Library.*

— France.

FRANCE. Secrétariat Général à l'Aviation Civile. Section Statistique. Bulletin statistique. a., 1972- Paris.

FRANCE. Département des Statistiques des Transports. Enquête annuelle d'entreprise: transports aériens. a., 1973(1st issue)- Paris.

— North Atlantic Ocean.

FRIEDMAN (JESSE J.) A new air transport policy for the North Atlantic: saving an endangered system. New York, 1976. pp. 149.

— United Kingdom.

U.K. Central Office of Information. Reference Division. 1974. British civil aviation. rev. ed. London, 1974. pp. 8. *bibliog.*

— — Freight.

COOPERS AND LYBRAND ASSOCIATES LIMITED and TUCKER (ALISTAIR) ASSOCIATES LIMITED. United Kingdom air cargo; prepared for the Air Cargo Working Party. London, National Economic Development Office, 1975. pp. 18.

U.K. Civil Aviation Authority. 1975. International air freight services; a consultative document. London, 1975. pp. 32. *([Publications]. CAP 379)*

AERONAUTICS, MILITARY

— United States.

KUCERA (RANDOLPH P.) The aerospace industry and the military: structural and political relationships. Beverly Hills, [1974]. pp. 64. *bibliog.*

AEROPLANE INDUSTRY AND TRADE

AEROPLANE INDUSTRY AND TRADE

— **European Economic Community countries.**

EUROPEAN COMMUNITIES. Commission. 1975. Action programme for the European aeronautical sector, etc. [Brussels], 1975. pp. 43. *(Bulletin of the European Communities. Supplements. [1975/11])*

— **Russia.**

IAKOVLEV (ALEKSANDR SERGEEVICH) Sovetskie samolety: kratkii ocherk. 2nd ed. Moskva, 1975. pp. 311.

AEROPLANES

— **Noise.**

ENVIRONMENTAL SCIENCES GROUP. Concorde noise and its effect on London. London, [1975]. pp. 58. *(London. Greater London Council. Research Memoranda. 478)*

— — **Bibliography.**

GOMERSALL (ALAN) compiler. Aircraft noise. London, 1975. pp. 9. *(London. Greater London Council. Research Library. [Research] Bibliographies. No. 68)*

AEROSPACE INDUSTRIES

— **United Kingdom.**

PATTIE (GEOFFREY) Is there a future for the British aerospace industry? London, 1975. pp. 12.

— **United States.**

KUCERA (RANDOLPH P.) The aerospace industry and the military: structural and political relationships. Beverly Hills, [1974]. pp. 64. *bibliog.*

AESTHETICS.

PLEKHANOV (GEORGII VALENTINOVICH) Kunst und gesellschaftliches Leben; herausgegeben von Alexander Uschakow und Pjotr Nikolajew. Berlin, 1975. pp. 463. *bibliog.*

HASKELL (FRANCIS) Rediscoveries in art: some aspects of taste, fashion and collecting in England and France. London, 1976. pp. 246. *bibliog. (New York (City). University. Institute of Fine Arts. Wrightsman Lectures. 1973)*

AFAN VALLEY

— **Economic conditions.**

ALDEN (JEREMY D.) An assessment of community resources in the upper Afan Valley. [Port Talbot, Glamorgan-Glyncorrwg Community Development Project], 1972 [or rather 1973]. fo. 21. *Cover title reads: Community resources and financial self-support.*

GLAMORGAN-GLYNCORRWG COMMUNITY DEVELOPMENT PROJECT. Mobility. [Port Talbot], 1973. fo. 20. *Photocopy.*

AFGHANISTAN

— **History — Sources.**

ARENDARENKO (GEORGII ALEKSEEVICH) Bukhara i Afganistan v nachale 80-kh godov XIX veka: zhurnaly komandirovok G.A. Arendarenko; [redaktsionnaia kollegiia B.G. Gafurov (and others)]. Moskva, 1974. pp. 142.

AFRICA.

OAU REVIEW; (pd. by Information Division, OAU General Secretariat). q., n.s. Ja/Mr 1975 (no.2)- Addis Ababa.

— **Armed forces — Political activity.**

DECALO (SAMUEL) Coups and army rule in Africa: studies in military style. New Haven, 1976. pp. 284. *bibliog.*

OGUERI II (EZE) African nationalism and military ascendancy. Owerri, 1976. pp. 85.

— **Bibliography.**

HARVARD UNIVERSITY. Library. Widener Library Shelflists. No. 2. Africa. Cambridge, Mass., 1965. 1 vol. (various pagings).

ECA INDEX: bibliography of selected ECA documents; [pd. by] Library, Economic Commission for Africa, United Nations. a., 1975- [Addis Ababa]. *[In English and French].*

— **Civilization.**

PAN-AFRICAN CULTURAL FESTIVAL, 1ST, ALGIERS, 1969. News bulletin 1. [Algiers], 1969. pp. 31.

LYCOPS (JEAN PIERRE) L'agression silencieuse ou le génocide culturel en Afrique. Paris, [1975]. pp. 221.

— **Commerce — European Economic Community countries**

EUROPEAN COMMUNITIES. Statistical Office. ACP: yearbook of foreign trade statistics; statistical abstract. a., 1968/1973- Luxembourg. *[In English and French]*

— **Description and travel.**

BRODZKI (STANISŁAW) Księga wielu dżungli. Warszawa, 1953. pp. 232.

— **Economic conditions.**

CAHIERS O.R.S.T.O.M.: série sciences humaines; ([pd. by] l'Office de la Recherche Scientifique et Technique Outre- Mer [France]). 4 a yr., 1963 (v.1)- Paris.

ZAGADNIENIA gospodarcze Afryki: wybór, etc. Warszawa, 1966. pp. 214. *bibliog.*

AFRICAN ECONOMIC INDICATORS; ([pd. by] United Nations Economic Commission for Africa). a., 1968 [1st issue]- Addis Ababa.

CONFERENCE OF DIRECTORS OF SOCIAL AND ECONOMIC RESEARCH INSTITUTES IN AFRICA, UNIVERSITY OF NAIROBI, 1971. Economic independence in Africa; edited by Dharam Ghai. Nairobi, 1973. pp. 235.

WOMEN in Africa: studies in social and economic change; edited by Nancy J. Hafkin and Edna G. Bay. Stanford, 1976. pp. 306. *bibliog. A project of the Committee of the African Studies Association.*

— **Economic policy.**

AFRICAN TARGET: Objectifs africains; pd. q. by United Nations Economic Commission for Africa. [in English and French]. q., D 1968 (v.1, no.3)- Addis Ababa.

DEVELOPMENT policy in Africa: [proceedings of a seminar held in Berlin, 1971]; [Joachim Voss, editor]. Bonn-Bad Godesberg, [1973]. pp. 344. *bibliog. (Friedrich-Ebert-Stiftung. Forschungsinstitut. Schriftenreihe. Band 105)*

LYCOPS (JEAN PIERRE) L'agression silencieuse ou le génocide culturel en Afrique. Paris, [1975]. pp. 221.

TOURNIER (MAURICE) L'échelon régional et la planification nationale. Paris, 1975. pp. 111. *bibliog. (France. Secrétariat d'Etat aux Affaires Etrangères. Méthodologie de la Planification. 3) Refonte complète de "Le travail du planificateur au niveau régional pour l'exécution d'un plan national" publié en 1970.*

DAMACHI (UKANDI GODWIN) and others, eds. Development paths in Africa and China. London, 1976. pp. 251. *bibliog.*

— **Foreign economic relations.**

HORIZONS of African diplomacy; edited by Yashpal Tandon and Dilshad Chandarana. Nairobi, 1974. pp. 259.

— **Foreign relations.**

HORIZONS of African diplomacy; edited by Yashpal Tandon and Dilshad Chandarana. Nairobi, 1974. pp. 259.

See also EUROPEAN ECONOMIC COMMUNITY — Africa.

— — **United States.**

ARKHURST (FREDERICK S.) ed. U.S. policy toward Africa. New York, 1975. pp. 255.

— **Government publications — Bibliography.**

BOSTON, MASSACHUSETTS. University. Libraries. Catalog of African government documents. 3rd ed. Boston, Mass., 1976. pp. 679.

— **History.**

DU BOIS (WILLIAM EDWARD BURGHARDT) The world and Africa: an inquiry into the part which Africa has played in world history;...an enlarged edition, with new writings on Africa...1955-1961. New York, 1965 repr. 1972. pp. 352.

— **Industries.**

AFRICAN TARGET: Objectifs africains; pd. q. by United Nations Economic Commission for Africa. [in English and French]. q., D 1968 (v.1, no.3)- Addis Ababa.

— **Politics and government.**

AFRICAN ADMINISTRATIVE STUDIES (formerly Cahiers africains d'administration publique); ([pd. by] African Training and Research Centre in Administration for Development). [in French and English]. s-a, (formerly irreg.), My 1967 (no.1)- Tangier.

HORIZONS of African diplomacy; edited by Yashpal Tandon and Dilshad Chandarana. Nairobi, 1974. pp. 259.

KILSON (MARTIN) ed. New states in the modern world. Cambridge, Mass., 1975. pp. 254. *bibliog.*

DECALO (SAMUEL) Coups and army rule in Africa: studies in military style. New Haven, 1976. pp. 284. *bibliog.*

KASFIR (NELSON) The shrinking political arena: participation and ethnicity in African politics, with a case study of Uganda. Berkeley, Calif., [1976]. pp. 323. *bibliog.*

CAFRAD NEWS; ([pd. by] African Training and Research Centre in Administration for Development). irreg. Tangier. *Current issues only kept.*

— **Population.**

AFRICAN POPULATION NEWSLETTER (formerly Information sur la population en Afrique): issued by the Population Programme Centre, Economic Commission for Africa, [United Nations] 2 a yr., Ag 1970 (v.1, no.2)- Addis-Abéba.

AFRICAN REGIONAL POPULATION CONFERENCE, 1ST, ACCRA, 1971. Population in African development; [papers presented at the conference]; edited by Pierre Cantrelle [and others]. Dolhain, Belgium, [1974]. 2 vols. *bibliogs.*

— **Rural conditions.**

LELE (UMA J.) The design of rural development: lessons from Africa; published for the World Bank. Baltimore, [1975]. pp. 246. *bibliog.*

— **Social conditions.**

CAHIERS O.R.S.T.O.M.: série sciences humaines; ([pd. by] l'Office de la Recherche Scientifique et Technique Outre- Mer [France]). 4 a yr., 1963 (v.1)- Paris.

WOMEN in Africa: studies in social and economic change; edited by Nancy J. Hafkin and Edna G. Bay. Stanford, 1976. pp. 306. *bibliog. A project of the Committee of the African Studies Association.*

— **Social policy.**

LYCOPS (JEAN PIERRE) L'agression silencieuse ou le génocide culturel en Afrique. Paris, [1975]. pp. 221.

— Statistics.

AFRICAN STATISTICAL YEARBOOK; (pd. by) Economic Commission for Africa, United Nations. a., 1974- Addis Ababa. *[in English and French].* In 4 volumes: pt. 1 North Africa; pt. 2 West Africa; pt. 3 East Africa; pt. 4 Central Africa.

AFRICA, CENTRAL

— Commerce.

UNION DOUANIERE ET ECONOMIQUE DE L'AFRIQUE CENTRALE. Département des Statistiques. 1976. Indices du commerce exterieur des états de l'U.D.E.A.C. sauf le Cameroun, de 1963 à 1971. [Brazzaville], 1976. pp. 108. *(Etudes Statistiques. No. 23)*

— Economic conditions — Statistics.

UNION DOUANIERE ET ECONOMIQUE DE L'AFRIQUE CENTRALE. Département des Statistiques. 1970. Situation économique et sociale des pays membres de l'U.D.E.A.C. [Brazzaville], 1970. fo. 99. *(Etudes Statistiques. No. 19)*

— Social conditions — Statistics.

UNION DOUANIERE ET ECONOMIQUE DE L'AFRIQUE CENTRALE. Département des Statistiques. 1970. Situation économique et sociale des pays membres de l'U.D.E.A.C. [Brazzaville], 1970. fo. 99. *(Etudes Statistiques. No. 19)*

AFRICA, EAST

— History — Sources.

BEACHEY (RAYMOND WENDELL) compiler. A collection of documents on the slave trade of eastern Africa. London, 1976. pp. 140.

AFRICA, NORTH.

INTRODUCTION à l'Afrique du Nord contemporaine; par W.K. Ruf [and others]. Paris, 1975. pp. 449. *bibliog. (Centre de Recherches et d'Etudes sur les Sociétés Méditerranéennes. Collection)*

— Economic conditions.

FOUGEYROLLAS (PIERRE) Le défi de la sécheresse et la lutte des classes en Afrique sahelo-soudanienne. Dakar, African Institute for Economic Development and Planning, 1974. fo. 16.

— Foreign relations.

INDEPENDANCE et interdépendances au Maghreb; par W.K. Ruf [and others]. Paris, 1974. pp. 359. *(Centre de Recherches et d'Etudes sur les Sociétés Méditerranéennes. Collection)*

HUREWITZ (JACOB COLEMAN) ed. The Middle East and North Africa in world politics: a documentary record. 2nd ed. New Haven, 1975 in progress.

— Politics and government.

FOUGEYROLLAS (PIERRE) Le défi de la sécheresse et la lutte des classes en Afrique sahelo-soudanienne. Dakar, African Institute for Economic Development and Planning, 1974. fo. 16.

AFRICA, SUBSAHARAN

— Armed forces — Political activity.

MINOGUE (MARTIN) and MOLLOY (JUDITH) eds. African aims and attitudes: selected documents. London, 1974. pp. 400. *bibliog.*

— Commerce.

MUNRO (JOHN FORBES) Africa and the international economy, 1800-1960: an introduction to the modern economic history of Africa south of the Sahara. London, 1976. pp. 230. *bibliog.*

— Economic conditions.

HARRIS (RICHARD) Ph.D., ed. The political economy of Africa. New York, [1975]. pp. 270.

— — Statistics.

NDONGKO (WILFRED AWUNG) The treatment of subsistence ecnomic activity in the national accounts of African countries. Vienna, 1974. pp. 21. *bibliog. (Wiener Institut für Entwicklungsfragen. Occasional Papers. 74/3)*

— Economic policy.

BADOUIN (ROBERT) Les agricultures de subsistance et le développement économique. Paris, [1975]. pp. 204. *bibliog. (Centre de Recherche, d'Etude et de Documentation sur les Institutions et les Législations Africaines. Collection. 12)*

HARRIS (RICHARD) Ph.D., ed. The political economy of Africa. New York, [1975]. pp. 270.

WORKSHOP ON NATIONAL YOUTH PROGRAMMES AND NATIONAL SERVICE. ACCRA, 1975. Youth for development: an African perspective; report. London, Commonwealth Secretariat, [1975]. pp. 203.

— Foreign relations.

AFRICA RESEARCH GROUP. Race to power: the struggle for southern Africa; [by David Olsen and others]. New York, 1974. pp. 341. *bibliog.*

ARNOLD (GUY) The last bunker: a report on white South Africa today. London, 1976. pp. 286. *bibliog.*

— — Russia.

STEVENS (CHRISTOPHER ANTHONY) The Soviet Union and black Africa. London, 1976. pp. 236. *bibliog.*

— — South Africa.

LEGUM (COLIN) Southern Africa: the secret diplomacy of detente; South Africa at the crossroads. London, 1975. pp. 91.

FRIEDMAN (BERNARD) M.B., Ch.B., D.L.O., R.C.P and S. From...isolation to detente. Johannesburg, 1976. pp. 18. *(South African Institute of Race Relations. Presidential Addresses. 1976)*

— — United States.

UNITED STATES. National Security Council. Interdepartmental Groups for Africa. 1975. The Kissinger study on southern Africa. Nottingham, 1975. pp. 134.

— History.

BECKER (PETER) of Johannesburg. Path of blood: the rise and conquests of Mzilikazi, founder of the Matabele tribe of Southern Africa. London, 1962 repr. 1976. pp. 289. *bibliog.*

SOUTHERN African research in progress; papers given at a conference of the Centre for Southern African Studies, University of York, December 1974; edited by Christopher R. Hill and Peter Warwick. [York, 1976]. pp. 166. *(York University. Centre for Southern African Studies. Collected Papers.1)*

— Military policy.

STOCKHOLM INTERNATIONAL PEACE RESEARCH INSTITUTE. Southern Africa: the escalation of a conflict: a politico- military study. New York, [1976]. pp. 235. *bibliog.*

— Nationalism.

MINOGUE (MARTIN) and MOLLOY (JUDITH) eds. African aims and attitudes: selected documents. London, 1974. pp. 400. *bibliog.*

SMOCK (DAVID R.) and BENTSI-ENCHILL (KWAMENA) eds. The search for national integration in Africa. New York, [1976]. pp. 340.

— Politics and government.

GRANT (STAN) The call of mother Africa. Kingston, Jamaica, 1973. pp. 361.

AFRICA RESEARCH GROUP. Race to power: the struggle for southern Africa; [by David Olsen and others]. New York, 1974. pp. 341. *bibliog.*

AFRICA, SUBSAHARAN

MINOGUE (MARTIN) and MOLLOY (JUDITH) eds. African aims and attitudes: selected documents. London, 1974. pp. 400. *bibliog.*

NYERERE (JULIUS KAMBARAGE) Man and development. Dar es Salaam, 1974. pp. 125.

HARRIS (RICHARD) Ph.D., ed. The political economy of Africa. New York, [1975]. pp. 270.

ARNOLD (GUY) The last bunker: a report on white South Africa today. London, 1976. pp. 286. *bibliog.*

DAVIDSON (BASIL) and others. Southern Africa: the new politics of revolution. Harmondsworth, 1976. pp. 374.

JANKE (PETER F.) Southern Africa: new horizons. London, 1976. pp. 20. *(Institute for the Study of Conflict. Conflict Studies. No 73)*

SMOCK (DAVID R.) and BENTSI-ENCHILL (KWAMENA) eds. The search for national integration in Africa. New York, [1976]. pp. 340.

SOUTHERN African research in progress; papers given at a conference of the Centre for Southern African Studies, University of York, December 1974; edited by Christopher R. Hill and Peter Warwick. [York, 1976]. pp. 166. *(York University. Centre for Southern African Studies. Collected Papers.1)*

STOCKHOLM INTERNATIONAL PEACE RESEARCH INSTITUTE. Southern Africa: the escalation of a conflict: a politico- military study. New York, [1976]. pp. 235. *bibliog.*

— — Bibliography.

BUCHMANN (JEAN) and WEMBI (ANTOINE) compilers. Bibliographie sur les structures politiques en Afrique noire indépendante. Léopoldville, 1972. fo. 32. *(Université Nationale du Zaire. Studia Universitatis "Lovanium": Institut de Recherches Economiques et Sociales. Notes et Documents. vol. 2, no. 5/SP-2)*

— Population.

CALDWELL (JOHN CHARLES) and others, eds. Population growth and socioeconomic change in west Africa. New York, 1975. pp. 763.

MASSER (IAN F.) and GOULD (W.T.S.) Inter-regional migration in tropical Africa. London, 1975. pp. 107. *bibliog. (Institute of British Geographers. Special Publications. No. 8)*

— Race question.

AFRICA RESEARCH GROUP. Race to power: the struggle for southern Africa; [by David Olsen and others]. New York, 1974. pp. 341. *bibliog.*

WEINBERGER (GERDA) An den Quellen der Apartheid: Studien über koloniale Ausbeutungs- und Herrschaftsmethoden in Südafrika, etc. Berlin, 1975. pp. 217. *bibliog.*

STOCKHOLM INTERNATIONAL PEACE RESEARCH INSTITUTE. Southern Africa: the escalation of a conflict: a politico- military study. New York, [1976]. pp. 235. *bibliog.*

— Social conditions.

AFRICA RESEARCH GROUP. Race to power: the struggle for southern Africa; [by David Olsen and others]. New York, 1974. pp. 341. *bibliog.*

CALDWELL (JOHN CHARLES) and others, eds. Population growth and socioeconomic change in west Africa. New York, 1975. pp. 763.

— Social life and customs.

STUDIES in African social anthropology; edited by Meyer Fortes and Sheila Patterson. London, 1975. pp. 267. *bibliogs. Essays presented to Professor Isaac Schapera.*

AFRICA, WEST

AFRICA, WEST
— Commerce.

DAVIES (PETER N.) ed. Trading in West Africa, 1840-1920. London, [1976]. pp. 209.

— Description and travel.

DAVIES (PETER N.) ed. Trading in West Africa, 1840-1920. London, [1976]. pp. 209.

— Economic history.

NDOMA-EGBA (BASSEY) Foreign investment and economic transformation in West Africa 1870-1930, with emphasis on Nigeria. Lund, 1974. pp. 164. *bibliog. (Lund. Ekonomisk-Historiska Föreningen. Skrifter. vol. 15) Ph.D. dissertation - University of Lund.*

— Economic integration.

NIGERIA. Federal Ministry of Economic Development and Reconstruction. 1974. The evolution of a West African economic community; by Adebayo Adedeji, Federal Commissioner for Economic Development and Reconstruction. [Lagos, 1974]. pp. 11.

— History.

AJAYI (JACOB FESTUS ADE) and CROWDER (MICHAEL) eds. History of West Africa. 2nd ed. London, 1976 in progress.

AFRICAN STUDIES.

SOUTHERN African research in progress; papers given at a conference of the Centre for Southern African Studies, University of York, December 1974; edited by Christopher R. Hill and Peter Warwick. [York. 1976]. pp. 166. *(York University. Centre for Southern African Studies. Collected Papers.1)*

— Africa, Subsaharan.

STUDIES in African social anthropology; edited by Meyer Fortes and Sheila Patterson. London, 1975. pp. 267. *bibliogs. Essays presented to Professor Isaac Schapera.*

AFRICANS IN THE UNITED KINGDOM.

The AFRICAN child in Great Britain; report of a seminar... [at] Ibadan...1975 [organised by the Commonwealth Students' Children Society and the Department of Sociology of Ibadan University]. London, [1975]. pp. 64.

AFRO–AMERICAN STUDIES.

ABRAHAMS (ROGER D.) and SZWED (JOHN F.) eds. Discovering Afro-America. Leiden, 1975. pp. 94. *bibliogs.*

AFRO–AMERICANS.

See NEGROES.

AGE (LAW)
— Italy.

BIN (M.) ed. La riforma del diritto di famiglia. Torino, [1975]. pp. 143. *(Turin. Università. Materiali Integrativi per lo Studio del Diritto di Famiglia. 1a Serie. 2)*

AGE AND EMPLOYMENT
— Finland.

LÄHTEINEN (MARTTI) Ikä ongelmana työelämässä: eri-ikäisten teollisuuden työntekijään ongelmia kartoittava tutkimus, etc. Helsinki, 1975. pp. 126. *bibliog. (Finland. Suomen Virallinen Tilasto. Finlands Officiella Statistik. 32. Sosiaalisia Erikoistutkimuksia. 44) With English summary.*

— United Kingdom.

BARR (PAT) Occupation and leisure of the retired and the elderly. London, 1973. pp. 16. *bibliog. (Age Concern England. Manifesto Series. No. 5)*

SHOWLER (BRIAN) Employment in retirement. London, 1974. pp. 12. *bibliog. (Age Concern England. Manifesto Series. No. 19)*

AGE CONCERN ENGLAND. Age Concern on occupation: views of retired people on how and why they spend their time in paid and unpaid work. London, 1975. pp. 24.

CLARKE (KENNETH) and MOCKLER (CHRISTOPHER) An end to the earnings rule?. London, 1976. pp. 22. *(Conservative Political Centre. [Publications]. No. 589)*

AGED AS CONSUMERS
— United Kingdom.

ROBERTS (EIRLYS RHIWEM CADWALADR) The retired as consumers. London, 1974. pp. 12. *bibliog. (Age Concern England. Manifesto Series. No. 13)*

AGENCY (LAW)
— France.

GUYÉNOT (JEAN) The French law of agency and distributorship agreements. London, 1976. pp. 283.

— United Kingdom.

FRIDMAN (GERALD HENRY LOUIS) The law of agency. 4th ed. London, 1976. pp. 341.

AGGRESSION (INTERNATIONAL LAW).

FERENCZ (BENJAMIN B.) Defining international aggression: the search for world peace: a documentary history and analysis. Dobbs Ferry, N.Y., 1975. 2 vols. *bibliog.*

AGGRESSIVENESS (PSYCHOLOGY).

REDL (FRITZ) and WINEMAN (DAVID) Controls from within: techniques for the treatment of the aggressive child. New York, [1952]. pp. 332.

GOLDSTEIN (JEFFREY H.) Aggression and crimes of violence. New York, 1975. pp. 192.

SYMPOSIUM ON COMMUNICATION AND AFFECT, 4TH, ERINDALE COLLEGE, 1974. Nonverbal communication of aggression: (proceedings); edited by Patricia Pliner [and others]. New York, [1975]. pp. 196. *bibliogs.*

AGING.

KIMMEL (DOUGLAS C.) Adulthood and aging: an interdisciplinary developmental view. New York, [1974]. pp. 484. *bibliogs.*

AGRICULTURAL ADMINISTRATION
— Kenya.

CONFERENCE ON COMPARATIVE ADMINISTRATION IN EAST AFRICA, ARUSHA, 1971. Rural administration in Kenya: a critical appraisal: [papers from the conference]; edited by David K. Leonard. Nairobi, 1973. pp. 165. *bibliogs.*

— Poland.

OHRYZKO-WŁODARSKA (CZESŁAWA) Organizacja władz włościańskich w Królestwie Polskim i ich pozostałość aktowa, 1864-1918. Warszawa, 1973. pp. 128.

— Russia.

MARKIN (A.A.) ed. Effektivnost' khoziaistvennykh ob"edinenii. Leningrad, 1974. pp. 191.

PANKRATOV (IVAN FERISANOVICH) Kolkhoznaia demokratiia na sovremennom etape. Moskva, 1974. pp. 190.

AGRICULTURAL COLLEGES
— United Kingdom.

GILES (A.K.) University of Reading, agricultural economics, 1923-73: published on the occasion of the 50th anniversary of the department. Reading, 1973. pp. 92. *bibliog.*

AGRICULTURAL CREDIT
— Australia.

STANDEN (BRUCE JAMES) Some economic implications of monetary and credit policies on rural industries in Australia. 1976. fo. 263. *bibliogs. Typescript. Ph.D.(London) thesis: unpublished. This thesis is the property of London University and may not be removed from he Library.*

— Canada.

CANADA. Statutes, etc. 1959-68. Farm Credit Act...1959, c. 43, as amended...; Farm Credit Act Interest Rates Regulations...established by P.C. 1968- 2094; Farm Credit Regulations...established by P.C. 1968- 2095: (office consolidation). Ottawa, 1969. pp. 39. *In English and French.*

— Germany.

DEENEN (BERND VAN) and ZUREK (ERNST) Die Wirksamkeit zinsverbilligter Mittel in der Dorferneuerung: ein Beitrag zur Darlehenspolitik der Deutschen Siedlungs- und Landesrentenbank. Bonn, 1976. pp. 195. *(Forschungsgesellschaft für Agrarpolitik und Agrarsoziologie. [Publications]. 229)*

— India.

RESERVE BANK OF INDIA. Agricultural Credit Department. Report on financing the crash programme for the development of sericulture in Karnataka; [by B. Venkata Rao]. Bombay, 1974. pp. 132.

— Malaysia.

EDWARDS (ROBERT HOWARD) Public agricultural finance and technological change: a Malaysian case study; [Ph. D. (London) thesis]. 1975. fo. 188. *Typescript: unpublished. This thesis is the property of London University and may not be removed from the Library.*

— Sri Lanka.

MARGA INSTITUTE. The co-operative system and rural credit in Sri Lanka; a study undertaken...for USAID. Colombo, 1974. pp. 174. *(Marga Research Studies. 3)*

— Uganda.

HUNT (DIANA) Ph.D. Credit for agricultural development: a case study of Uganda. Nairobi, 1975. pp. 401. *bibliog.*

— Underdeveloped areas.

See UNDERDEVELOPED AREAS — Agricultural credit.

AGRICULTURAL EDUCATION
— France.

FRANCE. Ministère de l'Agriculture. 1975. Recherche, enseignement, formation, développement: les "investissements intellectuels" qui dépendent du Ministère de l'Agriculture. Paris, 1975. pp. 116. *(Bulletin d'Information. Numéro Spécial)*

— Underdeveloped areas.

See UNDERDEVELOPED AREAS — Agricultural education.

AGRICULTURAL ESTIMATING AND REPORTING
— India — Goa, Daman and Diu.

GOA, DAMAN AND DIU. Bureau of Economics, Statistics and Evaluation. Report on the crop estimation survey in the Union Territory of Goa, Daman and Diu. q., 1974/1975- Panaji.

AGRICULTURE.

AGRICULTURAL EXPERIMENT STATIONS

— **German East Africa.**

BALD (DETLEF) and BALD (GERHILD) Das Forschungsinstitut Amani: Wirtschaft und Wissenscaft in der deutschen Kolonialpolitik, Ostafrika 1900-1918. München, 1972. fo. 115. *bibliog.*

AGRICULTURAL EXTENSION WORK

— **India.**

MYSORE. Department of Agriculture. 1959. Some thoughts on agricultural extension methods and community development programmes in India. [Bangalore], 1959. pp. 57. *(Information Booklets. No. 6)*

— **United States.**

SCOTT (ROY V.) and SHOALMIRE (J.G.) The public career of Cully A. Cobb: a study in agricultural leadership. Jackson, Miss., [1973]. pp. 287. *bibliog.*

AGRICULTURAL GEOGRAPHY

— **Denmark.**

KAMPP (AAGE H.) An agricultural geography of Denmark: (translation revised by Paul A. Compton). Budapest, 1975. pp. 88. *bibliog. (Magyar Tudományos Akadémia. Geographical Research Institute. Geography of World Agriculture. 5)*

AGRICULTURAL INNOVATIONS.

PAPADAKIS (JUAN) The world food problem: another low cost technology is needed: the failure of conventional agronomy. Buenos Aires, 1975. pp. 31. *bibliog.*

VASHANOV (VIACHESLAV ALEKSEEVICH) and LOIKO (PETR FEDOROVICH) Zemlia i liudi: ispol'zovanie zemel'nykh resursov v usloviiakh nauchno-tekhnicheskoi revoliutsii. Moskva, 1975. pp. 199.

— **Ethiopia.**

GREEN (DAVID A.G.) Ethiopia: an economic analysis of technological change in four agricultural production systems. East Lansing, [1974]. pp. 117. *bibliog. (Michigan State University. African Studies Center. Committee on Ethiopian Studies. Occasional Papers Series. Monographs. No.2)*

— **Pakistan.**

KHAN (MAHMOOD HASAN) The economics of the green revolution in Pakistan. New York, 1975. pp. 226.

— **Peru.**

MACDONALD (A.L.) Agricultural technology in developing countries: social factors related to the use of modern techniques in two rural areas in Peru. Rotterdam, 1976. pp. 236. *bibliog.*

— **Russia.**

ZORIN (VISLAVII IVANOVICH) Agrarnoe proizvodstvo v period nauchno-tekhnicheskoi revoliutsii. Alma-Ata, 1975. pp. 159.

AGRICULTURAL LABOURERS

— **Austria.**

BACH (HANS) Berufliche Mobilität und Anpassungshilfen im Agrarbereich. Linz, 1972. pp. 85. *bibliog. (Österreichisches Institut für Arbeitsmarktpolitik. Arbeitsmarktpolitik. Heft 12)*

— **France.**

FRANCE. Ministère de l'Agriculture. Statistique agricole. Supplément. Série Etudes. No. 119. Les agricultures à temps partiel dans l'agriculture française. II. Evolution 1963-1967: quelques enseignements; (étude... rédigée par André Brun [and others]). Paris, 1974. pp. 144.

— **United Kingdom.**

PAGE (WILF) Farming to feed Britain: a policy for farmers, farm workers and consumers. London, [1973?]. pp. 28. *(Communist Party of Great Britain. Communist Party Pamphlets)*

— **United States.**

SCHOB (DAVID E.) Hired hands and plowboys: farm labor in the midwest, 1815-60. Urbana, Ill., [1975]. pp. 329. *bibliog.*

SEAGRAVE (CHARLES EDWIN) The southern negro agricultural worker, 1850-1870. New York, 1975. pp. 119. *bibliog. Ph. D. dissertation-Stanford University, 1971.*

AGRICULTURAL LABOURERS, MIGRANT.
See MIGRANT AGRICULTURAL LABOURERS.

AGRICULTURAL LAWS AND LEGISLATION

— **Algeria.**

GUIN (JEAN PIERRE) Les institutions agricoles algériennes. Paris, 1974. pp. 182. *bibliog. (Centre de Recherches et d'Etudes sur les Sociétés Méditerranéennes. Les Cahiers du CRESM. 2*

— **Czechoslovakia.**

POSPISIL (BOLESLAV) Právní formy kooperace a integrace v agrokomplexu v ČSSR. Praha, 1974. pp. 115. *bibliog. (Československá Akademie Věd. Sudie. 1974, č. 8) With Russian and German summaries.*

— **Russia.**

BYCHKOVA (TSETSILIIA VOLODYMYRIVNA) Pravovi pytannia ahrarno-promyslovoho kooperuvannia. Kyïv, 1974. pp. 120. *With Russian summary.*

PRAVOVOE polozhenie agrarno-promyshlennykh predpriiatii i ob"edinenii. Kishinev, 1974. pp. 744.

AGRICULTURAL MACHINERY

— **Trade and manufacture — Ireland (Republic).**

KENNY (JAMES) The Irish agricultural engineering industry; a report to the National Science Council. Dublin, Stationery Office, [1976]. pp. 48.

AGRICULTURAL RESEARCH

— **France.**

FRANCE. Ministère de l'Agriculture. 1975. Recherche, enseignement, formation, développement: les "investissements intellectuels" qui dépendent du Ministère de l'Agriculture. Paris, 1975. pp. 116. *(Bulletin d'Information. Numéro Spécial)*

— **Mexico.**

ARDITO-BARLETTA (NICOLAS) Costs and social benefits of agricultural research in Mexico. 1971. pp. 214. *bibliog. Ph.D. (Chicago) thesis: unpublished. Microfilm of typescript: 1 reel (2nd item on it).*

— **Poland.**

OSIĄGNIĘCIA nauk ekonomiczno-rolniczych: próba oceny;... Achievements in agricultural-economic sciences: materiały Sesji Naukowej Komitetu Ekonomiki Rolnictwa Wydziału V PAN... 4-6 lutego 1960 r. w Poznaniu. Warszawa, 1961. pp. 271. *bibliog. (Polska akademia Nauk. Wydział 5 Nauk Rolniczyc i Leśnych. Zeszyty Problemowe Postępów Nauk Rolniczych. z.29)*

— **United Kingdom.**

JOINT CONSULTATIVE ORGANISATION FOR RESEARCH AND DEVELOPMENT IN AGRICULTURE AND FOOD [U.K.]. Second reports of the boards of the...Organisation, etc. London, H.M.S.O., 1975. pp. 135.

AGRICULTURAL SOCIETIES

— **European Economic Community countries.**

EUROPEAN COMMUNITIES. Commission. 1974. Directory of non-governmental agricultural organizations set up at community level. [Brussels], 1974. pp. 854.

AGRICULTURAL SURPLUS

— **America, North.**

BROWN (LESTER RUSSELL) The politics and responsibility of the North American breadbasket. Washington, 1975. pp. 43. *(Worldwatch Institute. Worldwatch Papers. No.2)*

AGRICULTURAL WAGES

— **Hungary.**

SCHMIDT (LAJOS) Die Löhne der landwirtschaftlichen Arbeiter in Ungarn. Jena, 1943. pp. 149. *bibliog.*

AGRICULTURAL WASTES

— **United States.**

CORNELL AGRICULTURAL WASTE MANAGEMENT CONFERENCE, 1975. Energy, agriculture and waste management...; edited by William J. Jewell. Ann Arbor, [1975]. pp. 540. *Proceedings of the conference sponsored by Cornell University, New York State College of Agriculture and Life Sciences and the National Science Foundation.*

AGRICULTURE.

CERES: FAO review; (pd. bi-m. by the Food and Agriculture Organization). bi-m., 1968 (v.1)- Rome. *v.1, no.1 entitled FAO review.*

CORBET (HUGH) Agriculture's place in commercial diplomacy; essays on a conference at Ditchley Park,...1973. Enstone, [1974]. pp. 42. *(Ditchley Foundation. Ditchley Papers. No. 48)*

— **Economic aspects.**

BARRONS (KEITH CONVERSE) The food in your future: steps to abundance. New York, 1975. pp. 180. *bibliog.*

EXTERNALITIES in the transformation of agriculture: distribution of benefits and costs from development; edited by Earl O. Heady [and] Larry R. Whiting. Ames, 1975. pp. 341. *bibliogs.*

STABLER (M.J.) Agricultural economics and rural land-use. London, 1975. pp. 95. *bibliog.*

STUHLER (ELMAR A.) and ARTHUR (HENRY B.) Fallstudien zum Agribusiness nach der Harvard-Case-Method: Fallstudien aus der Wirtschafts- und Landwirtschaftsverwaltung, aus den der Landwirtschaft vor- und nachgelagerten Bereichen und landwirtschaftlichen Unternehmen. Hamburg, 1975. pp. 348. *bibliog. (Germany (Bundesrepublik). Bundesministerium für Ernährung, Landwirtschaft und Forsten. Berichte über Landwirtschaft. Neue Folge. Sonderhefte. 189)*

GREENWOOD (DAVYDD J.) Unrewarding wealth: the commercialization and collapse of agriculture in a Spanish Basque town. Cambridge, 1976. pp. 223. *bibliog.*

UPTON (MARTIN) Agricultural production economics and resource-use. London, 1976. pp. 357. *bibliogs.*

— — **Mathematical models.**

HARRISON (S.R.) Biological response curves and their economic interpretation. [Brisbane, 1969]. 1 pamphlet (various pagings). *bibliog. (Queensland. Department of Primary Industries. Economic Services Branch. Technical Bulletins. No. 5)*

— **History.**

DUNMAN (JACK) Agriculture: capitalist and socialist: studies in the development of agriculture and its contribution to economic development as a whole. London, 1975. pp. 256.

AGRICULTURE.(Cont.)

EUROPEAN peasants and their markets: essays in agrarian economic history; edited by William N. Parker and Eric L. Jones. Princeton, [1975]. pp. 366.

WEBER (MAX) The agrarian sociology of ancient civilizations; translated by R. I. Frank. London, 1976. pp. 421. bibliog.

— Indexes.

AGRINDEX; [pd. by] Agris: International Information System for the Agricultural Sciences and Technology, Food and Agriculture Organization. m., 1975 (v.1, no.1)- Rome.

— Social aspects — United States.

BOWERS (WILLIAM L.) The country life movement in America, 1900-1920. Port Washington, N.Y., 1974. pp. 189. bibliog.

— Africa.

AGRICULTURAL ECONOMICS BULLETIN FOR AFRICA; ([pd. by] United Nations Economic Commission for Africa [and] Food and Agriculture Organization of the United Nations Joint Agriculture Division). a. (approx.), Oc 1967 (no.9)- Addis Ababa.

— Africa, East.

AGRICULTURAL planning in East Africa...; G.K. Helleiner, editor. Nairobi, 1968. pp. 183. *Proceedings of a conference held at the University College, Dar es Salaam, April 1967 and organized by the Economic Research Bureau of University College.*

— Africa, Subsaharan.

BADOUIN (ROBERT) Les agricultures de subsistance et le développement économique. Paris, [1975]. pp. 204. bibliog. *(Centre de Recherche, d'Etude et de Documentation sur les Institutions et les Législations Africaines. Collection. 12)*

— America, Latin — Bibliography.

COMMONWEALTH BUREAU OF AGRICULTURAL ECONOMICS. South America: agricultural situation and prospects. [Farnham Royal, 1975]. 4 pts. (in 1 vol.) *(Annotated Bibliographies. Series E. Nos. 1-4) Compiled from World Agricultural Economics and Rural Sociology Abstracts from 1965 to 1974.*

— Argentine Republic.

ZENI (ENRIQUE R.) El destino de la agricultura argentina. Buenos Aires, [1972]. pp. 172.

— Australia.

STANDEN (BRUCE JAMES) Some economic implications of monetary and credit policies on rural industries in Australia. 1976. fo. 263. bibliogs. Typescript. *Ph.D.(London) thesis: unpublished. This thesis is the property of London University and may not be removed from he Library.*

— — Queensland.

AUSTRALIA. Bureau of Agricultural Economics. 1968. The economics of land development in the Belyando-Suttor rivers region, Queensland. Canberra, 1968. pp. 64. bibliog. *Map in end pocket.*

— Belgium.

DELNOY (PAUL) Politique agricole des structures et régimes juridiques d'exploitation du facteur terre. Liège, 1975. pp. 546. bibliog. *(Liège. Université. Faculté de Droit. Collection Scientifique. 38)*

— — Accounting.

BELGIUM. Institut Economique Agricole. Résultats provisoires des comptabilités agricoles pour l'exercice comptable. . a., 1967/68- Bruxelles. *1969/70 in Flemish.*

— — Statistics.

BELGIUM. Institut National de Statistique. 1976- . Recensement général de l'agriculture et des forêts de 1970. Bruxelles, 1976 in progress.

— Bolivia.

WENNERGREN (E.BOYD) and WHITAKER (MORRIS D.) The status of Bolivian agriculture. New York, [1975]. pp. 308. bibliog.

— Brazil — Amazon Valley.

VELHO (OTAVIO GUILHERME) Frentes de expansão e estrutura agraria: estudo do processo de penetração numa area da Transamazônica. Rio de Janeiro, 1972. pp. 178. bibliog.

— Bukhara — History.

ABDURAIMOV (M.A.) Ocherki agrarnykh otnoshenii v Bukharskom khanstve v XVI - pervoi polovine XIX veka. Tashkent, 1966 in progress. bibliog.

— Canada — Statistics.

SELECTED AGRICULTURAL STATISTICS FOR CANADA...; pd. by... Economics Branch, Agriculture Canada. a., 1975- Ottawa. *[In English and French].*

— — Ontario.

MAHANEY (WILLIAM C.) and ERMUTH (FREDERICK) The effects of agriculture and urbanization on the natural environment: a study of human impact in southern Ontario. Toronto, 1974. pp. 152. bibliog. *(York University (Toronto). Department of Geography. Geographical Monographs. No. 7)*

— Caribbean Area — Bibliography.

COMMONWEALTH BUREAU OF AGRICULTURAL ECONOMICS. The Caribbean: agricultural situation and prospects. [Farnham Royal, 1974]. 5 pts. (in 1 vol.) *(Annotated Bibliographies. Series D. Nos. 1-5) Compiled from World Agricultural Economics and Rural Sociology Abstracts from 1965 to 1973.*

— China.

SEL'SKOE khoziaistvo KNR, 1966-1973: "kul'turnaia revoliutsiia" i ee posledstviia. Moskva, 1975. pp. 128. bibliog.

— — Bibliography.

COMMONWEALTH BUREAU OF AGRICULTURAL ECONOMICS. Chinese agriculture and rural society; edited by K.P. Broadbent. [Farnham Royal, 1974]. pp. 37. *(Annotated Bibliographies. No. 30) Compiled from World Agricultural Economics and Rural Sociology Abstracts.*

— Colombia.

COLOMBIA. Oficina de Planeamiento del Sector Agropecuario. Programas de fomento agropecuario. a., 1971- [Bogota].

— Communist countries.

ZAGADNIENIA ekonomicznej efektywności inwestycji w rolnictwie. Warszawa, 1960. pp. 232. *(Polska Akademia Nauk. Wydział 5 Nauk Rolniczych i Leśnych. Zeszyty Problemwe Postępóow Nauk Rolniczych.. z.24)*

KHROMOV (PAVEL ALEKSEEVICH) Tempy razvitiia promyshlennosti i sel'skogo khoziaistva: ekonomiko-statisticheskoe issledovanie. Moskva, 1974. pp. 199.

KURJO (ANDREAS) Agrarproduktion in den Mitgliedsländern des Rates für Gegenseitige Wirtschaftshilfe, RGW. Berlin, 1975. pp. 221. bibliog. *(Giessen. Universität. Zentrum für Kontinentale Agrar- und Wirtschaftsforschung. Giessener Abhandlungen zur Agrar- und Wirtschaftsforschung des Europäischen Ostens. Band 64) With English summary.*

— Cyprus.

CHRYSOMILIDES (G.S.) Productivity standards of export crops in Cyprus, other major Mediterranean producers and the U.S.A.: suggestions for revising agricultural policies in Cyprus. Beirut, 1974. pp. 24. bibliog. *(Reprinted from Anaptyxis, vol. 3-4, June 1974)*

— Czechoslovakia.

EKONOMICKÁ hlediska nové etapy rozvoje zemědělství. Praha, 1975. pp. 207. bibliog.

— East (Near East).

MARTO (MICHEL I.) Food production in the Middle East: tendencies and problems. Amman, [1974]. fo. 27. *(Royal Scientific Society [Jordan]. Economic Research Department. Jordan Economic Studies. 04-07)*

— Egypt.

ABDEL-FADIL (MAHMOUD) Development, income distribution and social change in rural Egypt, 1952-1970: a study in the political economy of agrarian transition. Cambridge, 1975. pp. 157. bibliog. *(Cambridge. University. Department of Applied Economics. Occasional Papers. 45)*

— Ethiopia.

GREEN (DAVID A.G.) Ethiopia: an economic analysis of technological change in four agricultural production systems. East Lansing, [1974]. pp. 117. bibliog. *(Michigan State University. African Studies Center. Committee on Ethiopian Studies. Occasional Papers Series. Monographs. No.2)*

COHEN (JOHN M.) and WEINTRAUB (DOV) Land and peasants in imperial Ethiopia: the social background to a revolution. Assen, 1975. pp. 115.

DEVELOPMENT prospects in the southern Rift Valley, Ethiopia; [by] M.J. Makin [and others]. Tolworth, 1975. pp. 266. bibliog. *(U.K. Ministry of Overseas Development. Land Resources Division. Land Resource Studies. 21) Map sheet in end pocket.*

— Europe.

KONJUNKTURPOLITIK: Zeitschrift für angewandte Konjunkturforschung. Beihefte. Heft 22. Regionalpolitik und Agrarpolitik in Europa: Bericht über den wissenschaftlichen Teil der 38. Mitgliederversammlung der Arbeitsgemeinschaft deutscher wirtschaftswissenschaftlicher Forschungsinstitute...1975. Berlin, [1975]. pp. 135. bibliog. *In German or English.*

— Europe, Eastern.

WAEDEKIN (KARL EUGEN) Sozialistische Agrarpolitik in Osteuropa. Berlin, 1974 in progress. *(Giessen. Universität. Zentrum für Kontinentale Agrar- und Wirtschaftsforschung. Giessener Abhandlungen zur Agrar- und Wirtschaftsforschung des Europäischen Ostens. Band 63) With English summary.*

— European Economic Community countries.

MARTIRANO (GIOVANNI) Agricoltura: risposta europea. Firenze, [1974]. pp. 141.

AGRICULTURAL SITUATION IN THE COMMUNITY, THE: report published in conjunction with the...General report on the activities of the European Communities; (pd. by) [the] Commission. a., 1975- Brussels.

FEDERAL TRUST FOR EDUCATION AND RESEARCH. The CAP and the British consumer; a Federal Trust Study group report; [Tim Josling, chairman]. London,1975]. pp. 28,xv. *With technical annex.*

SWINBANK (ALAN) Some economic consequences of the common agricultural policy of the European Community; [Ph. D. (London) thesis] 1974 [or rather 1975]. fo. 140. bibliog. Typescript: unpublished. *This thesis is the property of London University and may not be removed from the Library.*

DOCUMENTATION EUROPEENNE: série agricole; ([pd. by] Presse et Information, Communautés Européennes). irreg. Bruxelles. *Current issues only kept.*

— — Bibliography.

COMMONWEALTH BUREAU OF AGRICULTURAL ECONOMICS. EEC agricultural policy. Pt. 4. Reform proposals in the enlarged community; compiled by Jean Kestner. [Farnham Royal, 1975]. pp. 23. *(Annotated Bibliographies. No. 29) Compiled from World Agricultural Economics and Rural Sociology Abstracts from 1972 to 1974.*

AGRICULTURE.(Cont.)

— — **Statistics.**

U.K. Ministry of Agriculture, Fisheries and Food. Economics Division. 1974. E.E.C. agricultural and food statistics. [London], 1974. pp. 105.

— **Fiji Islands.**

ANDERSON (A.G.) Indo-Fijian smallfarming: profiles of a peasantry. Auckland, N.Z., [1974]. pp. 199. bibliog.

— **France.**

ANNALES D'ECONOMIE ET DE SOCIOLOGIE RURALES; [pd. by] Institut National de la Recherche Agronomique [France]. [with summaries in English]. s-a., 1972 (v.1)- Paris.

— — **Accounting.**

FRANCE. Institut National de la Statistique et des Etudes Economiques. Les comptes de l'agriculture française. a., 1972- Paris.

— — **History.**

DUBY (GEORGES) and WALLON (ARMAND) eds. Histoire de la France rurale. [Paris, 1975 in progress]. bibliogs.

— — **Statistics.**

FRANCE. Ministère de l'Agriculture. Statistique agricole. Supplément. Série Etudes. No. 109. Approche des résultats économiques des exploitations agricoles en 1967; [par Pierre Greiner et Bernard Périllat]. Paris, 1974. 2 vols.

FRANCE. Ministère de l'Agriculture. Statistique agricole. Supplément. Série Etudes. No. 133. Approche des résultats économiques des exploitations agricoles en 1970. Paris, 1975. 1 vol. (various pagings).

— — **Provence—Côte dAzur.**

REGARDS sur l'espace rural: Provence Côte-d'Azur. Paris, 1974. pp. 525. (Regards sur la France. Février, 1974)

— **Gambia.**

HASWELL (MARGARET ROSARY) The nature of poverty: a case-history of the first quarter-century after World War II. London, 1975. pp. 234. bibliog.

— **Germany.**

STUHLER (ELMAR A.) and ARTHUR (HENRY B.) Fallstudien zum Agribusiness nach der Harvard-Case-Method: Fallstudien aus der Wirtschafts- und Landwirtschaftsverwaltung, aus den der Landwirtschaft vor- und nachgelagerten Bereichen und landwirtschaftlichen Unternehmen. Hamburg, 1975. pp. 348. bibliog. (Germany (Bundesrepublik). Bundesministerium für Ernährung, Landwirtschaft und Forsten. Berichte über Landwirtschaft. Neue Folge. Sonderhefte. 189)

KRUELL (HELMUT) Räumliche Schwerpunktbildung in der Gemeinschaftsaufgabe "Verbesserung der Agrarstruktur und des Küstenschutzes". Bonn, 1976. pp. 119. bibliog. (Forschungsgesellschaft für Agrarpolitik und Agrarsoziologie. [Publications]. 240)

— — **Anhalt — History.**

WALDHAEUSL (F.W.) Der Bodenanbau in der Provinz Sachsen und in Anhalt im Jahre 1913: ein Beitrag zur landwirtschaftlichen Betriebskunde Mitteldeutschlands. Leipzig, 1935. pp. 148. With 12 maps.

— — **North Rhine—Westphalia — Statistics.**

NORTH RHINE-WESTPHALIA. Landesamt für Datenverarbeitung und Statistik. Agrarberichterstattung. bien., 1974/75- Düsseldorf. In three volumes.

— — **Saarland — Statistics.**

SAARGEBIET. Statistisches Amt. Einzelschriften zur Statistik des Saarlandes. Nr. 46, etc. Betriebsverhältnisse der Land- und Forstwirtschaft im Saarland 1971...: Ergebnisse der Landwirtschaftszählung, Grunderhebung 1971. Saarbrücken, 1974 in progress.

SAARGEBIET. Statistisches Amt. Einzelschriften zur Statistik des Saarlandes. Nr. 42, 49. Landwirtschaftliche Betriebe: Ergebnisse der Landwirtschaftszählung 1971: Gemeindestatistik. Saarbrücken, 1975. 2 parts.

— — **Saxony — History.**

WALDHAEUSL (F.W.) Der Bodenanbau in der Provinz Sachsen und in Anhalt im Jahre 1913: ein Beitrag zur landwirtschaftlichen Betriebskunde Mitteldeutschlands. Leipzig, 1935. pp. 148. With 12 maps.

— **Germany, Eastern.**

REUTTER (RUDOLF) Grossgrundbesitzerland wird wieder Bauernland. Weimar, [1946]. pp. 31.

REUTTER (RUDOLF) Die Bauernpolitik der SED. Berlin, [1947]. pp. 32.

REUTTER (RUDOLF) Das deutsche Ernährungsproblem: alte und neue Agrarpolitik. Berlin, [1947]. pp. 48.

— **Guadeloupe — Statistics.**

FRANCE. Ministère de l'Agriculture. Statistique agricole. Supplément. Série Etudes. No. 137. Recensement général de l'agriculture: la constitution du fichier des agriculteurs en Guadeloupe...; étude...rédigée par Jean-Claude Martin. Paris, 1975. pp. 145.

— **Guatemala.**

INTER-AMERICAN COMMITTEE FOR AGRICULTURAL DEVELOPMENT. 1971. Tenencia de la tierra y desarollo socio-economico del sector agricola en Guatemala. Guatemala, 1971. pp. 395. bibliog.

— **India — Taxation.**

INDIA. Committee on Taxation of Agricultural Wealth and Income. 1972. Report; [K.N. Raj, chairman]. [Delhi?], 1972. pp. 169.

— — **Andhra Pradesh.**

NARAYANA (D.L.) Studies in the economics of farm management in Cuddapah district, Andhra Pradesh: combined report for the period 1967-68 to 1969- 70. [Delhi, Manager of Publications, 1974]. pp. 160.

— — **Assam.**

GOSWAMI (PRABHAS CHANDRA) and BORA (C.K.) Studies in the economics of farm management in Nowgong district, Assam: report[s] for the year[s] 1968-69 [and] 1969-70. [Delhi, Controller of Publications, 1974]. 2 vols. (in 1).

— — **Bombay.**

MANN (HAROLD HART) and others. Land and labour in a Deccan village. London, 1917. pp. 184. (Bombay (City). University. Economic Series. No. 1)

— — **Goa, Daman and Diu — Statistics.**

GOA, DAMAN AND DIU. Bureau of Economics, Statistics and Evaluation. 1976. Agricultural census, 1970-71. [Panaji, 1976]. pp. 231.

— — **Gujarat.**

ADHVARYU (J.H.) and PARIKH (GOKUL O.) Studies in the economics of farm management in Surat and Bulsar districts, Gujarat: report for the year 1966-67. [Delhi, Controller of Publications], 1974. pp. 370.

ADHVARYU (J.H.) and PARIKH (GOKUL O.) Studies in the economics of farm management in the I[ntensive] A[gricultural] D[istrict] P[rogramme] region of Surat and Bulsar, Gujarat State: report for the year 1968-69. [Delhi, Controller of Publications], 1976. 2 vols.

— — **Kerala.**

INDIA. Ministry of Agriculture. Directorate of Economics and Statistics. 1973. Studies in the economics of farm management in Kerala: Alleppey and Quilon: combined report for the years 1962-63-- 1964-65. [Delhi], 1973. pp. 118.

— — **Maharashtra.**

KHARA (M. P.) Studies in the economics of farm management in Ahmednagar district, Maharashtra State: report for the year 1967-68. [Delhi, Controller of Publications], 1975. pp. 484.

— — **Orissa.**

MISRA (B.) Studies in the economics of farm management in Cuttack district, Orissa: combined report 1967-70. [Delhi, Controller of Publications, 1975]. pp. 64.

— — **Punjab.**

KAHLON (A.S.) and MIGLANI (SURJIT SINGH) Studies in the economics of farm management in Ferozepur district, Punjab: three-year consolidated report, 1967-68 to 1969-70. [Delhi, Controller of Publications, 1974]. pp. 274.

— — **Tamil Nadu.**

SHANMUGASUNDARAM (VEDAGIRI) Studies in economics of farm management in Thanjavur district, Tamil Nadu: combined report 1967-68 to 1969-70. [Delhi, Controller of Publications, 1974]. pp. 66.

SHANMUGASUNDARAM (VEDAGIRI) Studies in economics of farm management in Thanjavur district, Tamil Nadu: report[s] for the year[s] 1967-68, 1968-69, 1969-70. [Delhi, Controller of Publications, 1974. 3 vols. (in 1).

— — **Uttar Pradesh.**

LAVANIA (GAURI SHANKAR) Studies in economics of farm management in Deoria, Uttar Pradesh: combined report, 1966-69. [Delhi, Controller of Publications, 1974]. pp. 294.

SINGH (ROSHAN) and SINGH (RANBIR) Studies in the economics of farm management in Muzaffarnagar district, Uttar Pradesh: report for the year 1968-69. [Delhi, Controller of Publications], 1974. pp. 577.

SINGH (ROSHAN) and SINGH (RANBIR) Studies in the economics of farm management in Muzaffarnagar district, U.P.: combined report for the years 1966-67 to 1968-69. [Delhi, Controller of Publications], 1975. pp. 266.

— **Ireland (Republic) — Taxation.**

NATIONAL ECONOMIC AND SOCIAL COUNCIL [EIRE]. The taxation of farming profits; (report prepared by A.T.C. McArthur and Ian G. Reid). Dublin, Stationery Office, [1976]. pp. 130. ([Reports]. No. 15)

— **Italy.**

MARTIRANO (GIOVANNI) Agricoltura: risposta europea. Firenze, [1974]. pp. 141.

STEFANELLI (RENZO) L'agricoltura nella crisi italiana. Roma, [1974]. pp. 243. bibliog.

SERENI (EMILIO) La questione agraria nella rinascita nazionale italiana. 2nd ed. Torino, [1975]. pp. 450.

— — **History.**

AMBROSOLI (MAURO) John Symonds: agricoltura e politica in Corsica e in Italia, 1765-1770. Torino, 1974. pp. 165. bibliog. (Fondazione Luigi Einaudi. Studi. 17)

— — **Lombardy.**

LECHI (FRANCESCO) and RICCI (GIUSEPPE) L'agricoltura nella pianificazione delle comunità montane: il caso della Valle Sabbia. Milano, 1974. pp. 122.

— **Japan.**

BOMBAY (STATE). Delegation...to Japan. 1952. Report on agriculture, cottage and small-scale industries in Japan...Pt. 2. Poona, [1952?] repr. 1956. pp. 32.

— — **Statistics.**

JAPAN. Ministry of Agriculture and Forestry. 1972. Report of the 1970 world census of agriculture and forestry in Japan. [Tokyo, 1972]. pp. 77.

AGRICULTURE.(Cont.)

— Jordan.

ARESVIK (ODDVAR) The agricultural development of Jordan. New York, 1976. pp. 375. *bibliog.*

— Kenya.

KENYA. Ministry of Agriculture. Economic Planning Division. Economic review of agriculture. q., Ja/Mr 1974 (v.6, no. 1)- Nairobi.

— Lesotho — Statistics.

LESOTHO. Bureau of Statistics. 1972. 1970 census of agriculture; report. Maseru, 1972. pp. 243.

— Malawi.

MALAWI. Agro-Economic Survey. 1975. Agro-economic survey: report no. 15: Ngabu: a sample farm management survey of cotton and food-crop growers in two villages in the vicinity of Ngabu in Chikwawa district, Malawi. Lilongwe, 1975. fo 57.

— Mexico — Statistics.

MEXICO. Direccion General de Estadistica. Censo Agricola Ganadero y Ejidal, 1970. V Censos agricola ganadero y ejidal, 1970: resumen general. Mexico, 1975. pp. 379.

— Moldavia — History.

DRAGNEV (DEMIR MIRONOVICH) Sel'skoe khoziaistvo feodal'noi Moldavii, konets XVII - nachalo XIX v. Kishinev, 1975. pp. 286.

— New Zealand.

NEW ZEALAND. Ministry of Agriculture and Fisheries. 1974. New Zealand agriculture. Wellington, 1974. pp. 284.

— Nigeria.

ONWUAGBA (BENJAMIN) Problems of agricultural development and change in the East Central State of Nigeria. 1976. fo 254. *bibliog. Typescript. M. Phil. (London) thesis: unpublished. This thesis is the property of London University and may not be removed from the Library.*

— — Statistics.

NIGERIA (WESTERN STATE). Ministry of Economic Planning and Reconstruction. Statistics Division. Digest of agricultural statistics. a., 1971 (2nd)- Ibadan.

— Norway — Statistics.

NORWAY. Statistiske Centralbyrå. 1974. Produksjonsutviklinga i jordbruket, 1925-1972, etc. Oslo, 1974. pp. 223. *(Statistiske Analyser. 8) With English summary.*

— Pakistan.

KHAN (MAHMOOD HASAN) The economics of the green revolution in Pakistan. New York, 1975. pp. 226.

— Panama.

PANAMA'S economic development: the role of agriculture; [by] William C. Merrill [and others]. Ames, Iowa, 1975. pp. 219. *bibliog.*

— Peru — History.

PIEL (JEAN) Capitalisme agraire au Pérou. Paris, 1975 in progress. *(Institute Ffrançais d'Etudes Andines. Travaux)*

— Poland.

IGNAR (STEFAN) and JUSZKIEWICZ (ALEKSANDER) Wieś polska wobec zadań czwartego roku naszej sześciolatki. Warszawa, 1953. pp. 112.

AKTUALNE zadania spółdzielczości zaopatrzenia i zbytu w realizacji programu wy'żywienia narodu oraz rozwoju rolnictwa. Warszawa, 1975. pp. 28.

— — History.

KRASIŃSKI (ADAM) Hrabia. Geschichtliche Darstellung der Bauern-Verhältnisse in Polen und der wirthschaftlich-rechtlichen Reformen im ersten Decennium der Regierung Stanislaus Augustus, 1764-1774. Krakau, 1898. 2 vols (in 1).

WAWRZYŃCZYK (ALINA) Studia nad wydajnością produkcji rolnej dóbr królewskich w drugiej połowie XVI wieku. Wrocław, 1974. pp. 230. *With French summary.*

— — Productivity.

JUSZKIEWICZ (ALEKSANDER) and OZGA-MICHALSKI (JÓZEF) Zjednoczone Stronnictwo Ludowe w walce o podniesienie produkcji rolnej. Warszawa, 1953. pp. 54.

— — Silesia — History.

OLSZEWSKI (BOGUSŁAW) "Osthilfe": interwencjonizm państwowy w rolnictwie śląskim w latach 1919-1939. Wrocław, 1974. pp. 142. *bibliog. With English summary.*

WIATROWSKI (LESZEK) Przemiany gospodarki folwarcznej i chłopskiej na Śląsku w okresie reform agrarnych w XIX w. Wrocław, 1974. pp. 286. *(Wrocław. Uniwersytet. Acta Universitatis Wratislaviensis. No.225. Historia 25) With German summary.*

— Portugal — Mathematical models.

EGBERT (ALVIN CHARLES) and KIM (HYUNG M.) A development model for the agricultural sector of Portugal. [Washington], International Bank for Reconstruction and Development, [1975]. pp. 95. *bibliog. (World Bank Staff Occasional Papers. No.20)*

— — Statistics.

PORTUGAL. Instituto Nacional de Estatistica. Serviços Centrais. Boletim mensal das estatisticas da agricultura e da pesca: continente e ilhas adjacentes (formerly Boletim trimestral das estatisticas da agricultura e da pesca: continente e ilhas adjacentes). m. (formerly q.) Ja/Mr 1975 (ano 1, no.1)- Lisboa. *[In Portuguese and French].*

— Rhodesia — Statistics.

RHODESIA. Central Statistical Office. Agricultural production in African purchase areas: national and provincial totals. a., 1973(5th)- Salisbury.

— Romania — History.

CONSTANTINIU (FLORIN) Relațiile agrare din Țara Românească în secolul al XVIII-lea. București, 1972. pp. 210. *bibliog. (Academia de Științe Sociale și Politice a Republicii Socialiste România. Biblioteca Istorică. 30)*

— Russia.

TIUTIN (V.A.) ed. Ekonomika sotsialisticheskogo sel'skogo khoziaistva. Moskva, 1968. pp. 543.

EMEL'IANOV (ALEKSEI MIKHAILOVICH) ed. Ekonomicheskie i sotsial'nye problemy industrializatsii sel'skogo khoziaistva. Moskva, 1971. pp. 147.

SEMIN (SERGEI IVANOVICH) Ekonomicheskie osnovy agrarno-promyshlennykh kompleksov. Moskva, 1973. pp. 104.

SIVACHENKO (IGOR' IUR'EVICH) Agrokompleks sotsialisticheskogo narodnogo khoziaistva: zakonomernosti formirovaniia i razvitiia. Moskva, 1973. pp. 94.

BODIUL (IVAN IVANOVICH) Sotsial'no-ekonomicheskie otnosheniia v derevne na stadii razvitogo sotsializma. Moskva, 1974. pp. 384.

IGNATOVSKII (PAVEL ARTEM'EVICH) Obshchestvennoe proizvodstvo sovetskoi derevni. Moskva, 1975. pp. 343.

KARLIUK (IPPOLIT IAKOVLEVICH) and MYMRIKOV (NIKOLAI SEMENOVICH) Sel'skoe khoziaistvo SSSR: novye ekonomicheskie usloviia, dostizheniia - pretvorenie v zhizn' reshenii martovskogo 1965 g. Plenuma TsK KPSS. Moskva, 1975. pp. 103.

KURSOM martovskogo Plenuma. Moskva, 1975. pp. 527.

NEGRU-VODE (ALEKSANDR STEPANOVICH) Agrarno-promyshlennoe kooperirovanie v SSSR. Moskva, 1975. pp. 184.

— — Bibliography.

GORBATOV (A.L.) compiler. Agrarno-promyshlennye kompleksy i ob"edineniia: bibliograficheskii ukazatel' otechestvennoi literatury za 1960- 1973 gg. v kolichestve 837 nazvanii i inostrannoi - za 1962-1973 gg. v kolichestve 215 nazvanii. 2nd ed. Moskva, 1973. pp. 190.

— — Costs.

SEBESTOIMOST' i rentabel'nost' proizvodstva sel'skokhoziaistvennoi produktsii. Moskva, 1974. pp. 255.

— — Historiography.

POGUDIN (VASILII IVANOVICH) Put' sovetskogo krest'ianstva k sotsializmu: istoriograficheskii ocherk. Moskva, 1975. pp. 276.

— — History.

SHUNKOV (VIKTOR IVANOVICH) Voprosy agrarnoi istorii Rossii; (redkollegiia A.P. Okladnikov [and others]). Moskva, 1974. pp. 376. *Selected works.*

DUBROVSKII (SERGEI MITROFANOVICH) Sel'skoe khoziaistvo i krest'ianstvo Rossii v period imperializma; [redaktiroval knigu...A.F. Smirnov]. Moskva, 1975. pp. 398.

PROBLEMY istorii sovremennoi sovetskoi derevni, 1946-1973 gg. Moskva, 1975. pp. 508.

SHLIKHTER (OLEKSANDR HRYHOROVYCH) Agrarnyi vopros i prodovol'stvennaia politika v pervye gody Sovetskoi vlasti; [selected works edited by A.M. Rumiantsev and others]. Moskva, 1975. pp. 448.

— — — Bibliography.

STOL'NIKOVA (R.G.) and others, compilers. Istoriia sovetskoi derevni, 1917-1967: ukazatel' literatury, 1945-1967 gg. Moskva, 1975. 4 vols.(in 1).

— — Productivity.

SEBESTOIMOST' i rentabel'nost' proizvodstva sel'skokhoziaistvennoi produktsii. Moskva, 1974. pp. 255.

— — Statistics.

RUSSIA (USSR). Tsentral'noe Upravlenie Narodnokhoziaistvennogo Ucheta. 1939. Sotsialisticheskoe sel'skoe khoziaistvo SSSR: statisticheskii sbornik; [pod redaktsiei I.V. Sautina]. Moskva, 1939. pp. 128.

KOVAL'CHENKO (IVAN DMITRIEVICH) and MILOV (LEONID VASIL'EVICH) Vserossiiskii agrarnyi rynok, XVIII - nachalo XX veka: opyt kolichestvennogo analiza. Moskva, 1974. pp. 412.

— — Daghestan.

BUTAEV (BUTA) Tempy i proportsii razvitiia sel'skogo khoziaistva Dagestana. Makhachkala, 1969. pp. 47.

— — Georgia — History.

PANTSKHAVA (ARCHIL IAKOVLEVICH) Ocherki agrarnoi istorii Gruzii pervoi poloviny XIX veka. Tbilisi, 1969. pp. 122.

— — Lithuania — History.

EFREMENKO (A.P.) Agrarnye preobrazovaniia i nachalo sotsialisticheskogo stroitel'stva v litovskoi derevne v 1940-1941 godakh. Vil'nius, 1972. pp. 264.

KONIUKHOVA (TAT'IANA ALEKSANDROVNA) Gosudarstvennaia derevnia Litvy i reforma P.D. Kiseleva, 1840- 1857 gg.: Vilenskaia i Kovenskaia gubernii. Moskva, 1975. pp. 251.

AGRICULTURE.(Cont.)

— — Moldavian Republic — History.

ROTARU (MIKHAIL FEDOROVICH) Kommunisticheskaia partiia Moldavii v bor'be za pod"em sel'skogo khoziaistva respubliki, 1959-1970; pod redaktsiei...V. P. Seregina. Kishinev, 1974. pp. 188. *bibliog.*

VIZER (BORIS KONSTANTINOVICH) Razvitie sel'skogo khoziaistva Moldavskoi SSR, 1951-1970. Kishinev, 1975. pp. 337.

— — Pskov (Oblast) — History.

SEL'SKOE khoziaistvo Pskovskoi oblasti za 50 let. Leningrad, 1968. pp. 88. *bibliog.*

— — Soviet North.

KHANTIMER (ISMAIL SYDDYKOVICH) Sel'skokhoziaistvennoe osvoenie tundry; Agricultural development of tundra regions. Leningrad, 1974. pp. 226. *bibliog. With brief English summary.*

— — Uzbekistan — History.

ALIMOV (IBRAGIM ABDUGAPPAROVICH) Uzbekskoe dekhkanstvo na puti k sotsializmu: sotsial'no-ekonomicheskie preobrazovaniia v uzbekskom kishlake v 1921-1925 gg. Tashkent, 1974. pp. 239. *bibliog.*

— — White Russia.

MARTINKEVICH (FELIKS STANISLAVOVICH) Sotsial'no-ekonomicheskie problemy sel'skogo khoziaistva Belorussii na etape razvitogo sotsializma. Minsk, 1975. pp. 471.

— — — History.

KUKHAREV (BORIS EFIMOVICH) Sel'skoe khoziaistvo Zapadnoi Belorussii, 1919-1939 gg.; pod. ..redaktsiei...I.N. Shemiakina. Minsk, 1975. pp. 111.

MELESHKO (VASILII IVANOVICH) Ocherki agrarnoi istorii Vostochnoi Belorussii, vtoraia polovina XVII-XVIII v. Minsk, 1975. pp. 247.

— Senegal.

REBOUL (CLAUDE) Causes économiques de la sécheresse au Sénégal: systèmes de culture et calamités naturelles;...document de travail. Paris, Institut National de la Recherche Agronomique, 1975. fo. 59. *bibliog.*

— South Africa — Statistics.

SOUTH AFRICA. Division of Agricultural Marketing Research. Abstract of agricultural statistics. a., 1976- Pretoria. *[in English and Afrikaans].*

— Spain.

ANALES DEL INSTITUTO NACIONAL DE INVESTIGACIONES AGRARIAS: Serie economia y sociologia agrarias. a., 1971 (num. 1)- Madrid.

GREENWOOD (DAVYDD J.) Unrewarding wealth: the commercialization and collapse of agriculture in a Spanish Basque town. Cambridge, 1976. pp. 223. *bibliog.*

— — Seville (Province) — History.

BERNAL (ANTONIO MIGUEL) and DRAIN (MICHEL) Les campagnes sevillanes aux XIXe-XXe siècles: renovation ou stagnation?. [Paris], 1975. pp. 133. *(Madrid. Casa de Velázquez. Publications. Série "Recherches en Sciences Sociales". Fasc. 2)*

— Sri Lanka.

MARGA INSTITUTE. Marga Seminar Papers. 1. Youth, land and employment: [selected papers from a series of seminars held by the Marga Institute]. Colombo, 1974. pp. 185.

— Sweden.

HOLMSTRÖM (SVEN J.R.) Kombinerade skogs- och jordbruksföretag. Stockholm, 1974. pp. 34. *(Jordbrukets Utredningsinstitut. Meddelanden. 1974. Nr. 2) With English summary.*

JORDBRUKETS UTREDNINGSINSTITUT. Meddelanden. 1974. Nr. 4. Energibalans för växtodlingen i svenskt jordbruk. Stockholm, 1974. pp. 65. *With English summary.*

— Switzerland — History.

CLAASSEN (WALTER) Schweizer Bauernpolitik im Zeitalter Ulrich Zwinglis. Berlin, 1899. pp. 168. *bibliog. (Zeitschrift für Social- und Wirtschaftsgeschichte. Ergänzungshefte: Socialgeschichtliche Forschungen. Heft 4)*

— Tanzania.

KNIGHT (C. GREGORY) Ecology and change: rural modernization in an African community. New York, [1974]. pp. 300. *bibliog.*

— Tasmania — Statistics.

TASMANIA. Commonwealth Bureau of Census and Statistics. Tasmanian Office. Agricultural industry. a., 1973/74 (1st)- Hobart.

— Trinidad and Tobago — Statistics.

TRINIDAD AND TOBAGO. Central Statistical Office. Quarterly agricultural report. q., Oc/D 1974 (v.1,no.4)- Port of Spain.

— Turkey.

ASPECTS of modern Turkey; edited by William M. Hale. London, 1976. pp. 129. *bibliog. (Durham. University. Centre for Middle Eastern and Islamic Studies. [Publications. New Series]. 1) Papers of a conference held in April 1973 at the University of Durham, under the auspices of the University's Centre for Middle Eastern and Islamic Studies.*

— Underdeveloped areas.

See UNDERDEVELOPED AREAS — Agriculture.

— United Kingdom.

CROSBIE (GEORGE VERTUE) Observations on the emancipation of industry. London, 1892. pp. 138.

U.K. Study Group on Agricultural Land Classification. 1966. Agricultural land classification; first progress report; [D.J. Griffiths, chairman]. [London], 1966 [repr. 1974]. pp. 27. *bibliog. (U.K. Ministry of Agriculture, Fisheries and Food. Agricultural Land Service. Technical Reports. No. 11)*

AGRICULTURAL LAND PRICES IN ENGLAND AND WALES; [pd. by] Ministry of Agriculture, Fisheries and Food, (Economic and Statistics Group and Agricultural Land Service), [U.K.]. a., 1970 (no.3)- London.

PAGE (WILF) Farming to feed Britain: a policy for farmers, farm workers and consumers. London, [1973?]. pp. 28. *(Communist Party of Great Britain. Communist Party Pamphlets)*

U.K. Central Office of Information. Reference Division. 1974. Agriculture in Britain. rev. ed. London, 1974. pp. 21.

WESTMACOTT (RICHARD) and WORTHINGTON (TOM) New agricultural landscapes: report of a study undertaken on behalf of the Countryside Commission...during 1972. Cheltenham, Countryside Commission, 1974. pp. 98. *bibliog.*

BERESFORD (TRISTRAM) We plough the fields: agriculture in Britain today. Harmondsworth, 1975. pp. 257. *bibliog.*

— — History.

PARKER (ROBERT ALEXANDER CLARKE) Coke of Norfolk: a financial and agricultural study, 1707-1842. Oxford, 1975. pp. 222.

TAYLOR (CHRISTOPHER) 1935- . Fields in the English landscape. London, 1975. pp. 174. *bibliog.*

U.K.[Cabinet Office]. History of the Second World War: United Kingdom Civil Series. Agriculture; by Keith A.H.Murray. rev. ed. London, 1975. pp. 430. *Confidential version with full source references.*

EVANS (ERIC J.) The contentious tithe: the tithe problem and English agriculture, 1750-1850. London, 1976. pp. 185. *bibliog.*

— — — Sources.

YOUNG (ARTHUR) F.R.S. Arthur Young and his times; edited by G.E. Mingay. London, 1975. pp. 264. *bibliog. Selections with introduction and commentary.*

— — Ireland, Northern.

AGRICULTURE IN NORTHERN IRELAND; ([pd by] Department of Agriculture, Northern Ireland]. [title varies]. m., 1932 (v.7)- Belfast.

— — Scotland.

FENTON (ALEXANDER) Scottish country life. Edinburgh, [1976]. pp. 255. *bibliog.*

— — Wales — Statistics.

ANNUAL DIGEST OF WELSH AGRICULTURAL STATISTICS; [pd. by] Welsh Department, Ministry of Agriculture, Fisheries and Food. a., 1969/70- Aberystwyth. *[In English and Welsh]. File includes annual supplement, 1969/70-*

— United States.

BUSE (RUEBEN C.) and BROMLEY (DANIEL W.) Applied economics: resource allocation in rural America. Ames, Iowa, 1975. pp. 623. *bibliogs.*

BREIMYER (HAROLD FREDERICK) Economics of the product markets of agriculture. Ames, Iowa, 1976. pp. 208.

— — History.

SCOTT (ROY V.) and SHOALMIRE (J.G.) The public career of Cully A. Cobb: a study in agricultural leadership. Jackson, Miss., [1973]. pp. 287. *bibliog.*

SCHLEBECKER (JOHN T.) Whereby we thrive: a history of American farming, 1607-1972. Ames, Iowa, 1975. pp. 342. *bibliog.*

— Venezuela — Statistics.

VENEZUELA. Direccion General de Estadistica. Censo agropecuario, 1961. III censo agropecuario 1961: resumen general de la Republica; Parte[s] A [and B]. Caracas, 1967. 2 vols.

VENEZUELA. Ministerio de Agricultura y Cria. Direccion de Planificacion y Estadistica. Division de Estadistica. Produccion agricola de 29 cultivos: resumen del año. a., 1973- Caracas.

VENEZUELA. Ministerio de Agricultura y Cria. Direccion de Planificacion y Estadistica. Division de Estadistica. Produccion agricola: 1 de mayo al 31 de diciembre, periodo de invierno. a., 1974- Caracas.

— Yugoslavia — History.

VUČO (NIKOLA) Agrarna kriza u Jugoslaviji, 1930-1934. Beograd, 1968. pp. 300. *With Russian and English summaries.*

— — Productivity.

YUGOSLAVIA. Savezni Zavod za Statistiku. Studije, Analize i Prikazi. 69. Problemi primene marksove koncepcije utvrdjivanja produktivnosti rada na društvenim poljoprivrednim gazdinstvima Jugoslavije; [by] Katja Vadnal. Beograd, 1974. pp. 95. *bibliog.*

— Zambia.

LAND resources of the Northern and Luapula provinces, Zambia: a reconnaissance assessment; [by] J.E. Mansfield [and others]. Tolworth, 1975-76. 6 vols. *bibliogs. (U.K. Ministry of Overseas Development. Land Resources Division. Land Resource Studies. 19)*

AGRICULTURE, COOPERATIVE.

AGRICULTURE, COOPERATIVE.

RURAL communities: inter-cooperation and development; edited by Yehuda H. Landau [and others]. New York, 1976. pp. 166. *Proceedings of the French-Israeli conference held in Israel, Haifa and Rehovot in May 1973.*

— America, Latin.

FALS BORDA (ORLANDO) El reformismo por dentro en America Latina. Mexico, 1972. pp. 211.

— Denmark.

WEBSTER (F.H.) Agricultural co-operation in Denmark. [London, 1973]. pp. 152. *(Horace Plunkett Foundation. Occasional Papers. No. 39)*

— Germany, Eastern.

MERKER (PAUL) Die Partei in den volkseigenen Gutsbetrieben. Berlin, [1949]. pp. 63. *(Sozialistische Einheitspartei Deutschlands. Schriftenreihe für den Parteiarbeiter. Heft 2)*

DREESSEN (KLAUS) Die Bedeutung der landwirtschaftlichen Produktionsgenossenschaften für die DDR. Tübingen, 1973. pp. 463. *bibliog.*

INDUSTRIEMAESSIGE Produktionsmethoden in der sozialistischen Landwirtschaft der DDR...; (Autorenkollektiv: Kurt Groschoff [and others]). Berlin, 1976. pp. 340.

— Hungary.

HOLÁCS (IBOLYA) Change of the way of living in six transdanubian co-operative villages. Keszthely, 1974. pp. 91. *bibliog. (Keszthelyi Agrártudományi Egyetem. Studies.5)*

— Peru.

BÜCHLER (PETER) Agrarian cooperatives in Peru: a socio-economic survey. Berne, [1975]. pp. 272. *bibliog.* *(Bern. Universität. Institut für Soziologie und Sozio-Ökonomische Entwicklungsfragen. Berner Beiträge zur Soziologie. Band 16)*

— Poland.

SONDEL (JAN) Rezerwy produkcyjne w gospodarstwach rolnych. Wrocław, 1963. pp. 164.

HEGENBARTH (STANISLAWA) Landwirtschaftliche Zirkel und landwirtschaftliche Produktionsgenossenschaften in Polen. Berlin, 1976. pp. 193. *bibliog. (Giessen. Universität. Zentrum für Kontinentale Agrar- und Wirtschaftsforschung. Giessener Abhandlungen zur Agrar- und Wirtschaftsforschung des Europäischen Ostens. Band 72) With English summary.*

— Russia.

OSOFSKY (STEPHEN) Soviet agricultural policy: toward the abolition of collective farms. New York, 1974. pp. 300. *bibliog.*

— — Daghestan.

KALASOV (AIGUM KALASOVICH) Razvitie ekonomiki kolkhozov Dagestana. Makhachkala, 1969. pp. 75.

— — Georgia.

ASATIANI (VLADIMIR ANTIMOZOVICH) Periodicheskaia pechat' Gruzii v bor'be za kollektivizatsiiu sel'skogo khoziaistva i likvidatsiiu kulachestva. Tbilisi, 1974. pp. 92.

— — Lithuania.

EFREMENKO (A.P.) Agrarnye preobrazovaniia i nachalo sotsialisticheskogo stroitel'stva v litovskoi derevne v 1940-1941 godakh. Vil'nius, 1972. pp. 264.

AGRICULTURAL production cooperatives in independent Lithuania, 1920-1940: summary. London, 1974. pp. 80. *In English and German.*

— — Russia (RSFSR).

PANOV (NIKOLAI NIKOLAEVICH) and KAREVSKII (FEDOR ANDRIANOVICH) eds. Kollektivizatsiia sel'skogo khoziaistva v Srednem Povolzh'e, 1927-1937 gg. Kuibyshev, 1970. pp. 670. *(Istoriia Kollektivizatsii Sel'skogo Khoziaistva SSSR: dokumenty i materialy)*

PERMSKAIA OBLASTNAIA KONFERENTSIIA KOLKHOZNIKOV. 1969. Permskaia oblastnaia konferentsiia kolkhoznikov, 17 oktiabria 1969 goda: stenograficheskii otchet. Perm', 1970. pp. 107.

— — Siberia.

KOLLEKTIVIZATSIIA sel'skogo khoziaistva Zapadnoi Sibiri, 1927- 1937 gg. Tomsk, 1972. pp. 333.

AGRICULTURE AND STATE.

DUNMAN (JACK) Agriculture: capitalist and socialist: studies in the development of agriculture and its contribution to economic development as a whole. London, 1975. pp. 256.

EXTERNALITIES in the transformation of agriculture: distribution of benefits and costs from development; edited by Earl O. Heady [and] Larry R. Whiting. Ames, 1975. pp. 341. *bibliogs.*

GREEN (DANIEL) The politics of food. London, [1975]. pp. 220. *bibliog.*

— Africa, East.

AGRICULTURAL planning in East Africa...; G.K. Helleiner, editor. Nairobi, 1968. pp. 183. *Proceedings of a conference held at the University College, Dar es Salaam, April 1967 and organized by the Economic Research Bureau of University College.*

— Algeria.

GUIN (JEAN PIERRE) Les institutions agricoles algériennes. Paris, 1974. pp. 182. *bibliog. (Centre de Recherches et d'Etudes sur les Sociétés Méditerranéennes. Les Cahiers du CRESM. 2*

— Bolivia.

WENNERGREN (E.BOYD) and WHITAKER (MORRIS D.) The status of Bolivian agriculture. New York, [1975]. pp. 308. *bibliog.*

— France.

PUHLE (HANS JUERGEN) Politische Agrarbewegungen in kapitalistischen Industriegesellschaften: Deutschland, USA und Frankreich im 20. Jahrhundert. Göttingen, 1975. pp. 496. *bibliog.*

— Germany.

OLSZEWSKI (BOGUSŁAW) "Osthilfe": interwencjonizm państwowy w rolnictwie śląskim w latach 1919-1939. Wrocław, 1974. pp. 142. *bibliog. With English summary.*

PUHLE (HANS JUERGEN) Politische Agrarbewegungen in kapitalistischen Industriegesellschaften: Deutschland, USA und Frankreich im 20. Jahrhundert. Göttingen, 1975. pp. 496. *bibliog.*

SCHMITT (GUENTHER) and WITZKE (HARALD VON) Ziel- und Mittelkonflikte sektorspezifischer Systeme sozialer Sicherung: das Beispiel der landwirtschaftlichen Sozialpolitik in der Bundesrepublik Deutschland. Berlin, [1975]. pp. 86. *bibliog.*

— Liberia.

LIBERIA. Department of Agriculture. 1968. Crash program for agricultural development, 1968-1971. [Monrovia], 1968. fo. 35. *Xerox copy.*

— Pakistan.

PAKISTAN. Ministry of Food, Agriculture and Rural Development. Agriculture Wing. Planning Unit. 1975. Agricultural development in retrospect and prospect. Islamabad, [1975]. pp. 15.

— Panama.

PANAMA'S economic development: the role of agriculture; [by] William C. Merrill [and others]. Ames, Iowa, 1975. pp. 219. *bibliog.*

— Portugal — Mathematical models.

EGBERT (ALVIN CHARLES) and KIM (HYUNG M.) A development model for the agricultural sector of Portugal. [Washington], International Bank for Reconstruction and Development, [1975]. pp. 95. *bibliog. (World Bank Staff Occasional Papers. No.20)*

— Somali Republic.

SOMALI REPUBLIC. Ministry of Information and National Guidance. 1974. Agriculture in the service of the nation: more production with more efforts. Mogadishu, 1974. pp. 60.

— Spain.

AGRICULTURA ESPAÑOLA, LA: politica y realizaciones; [pd. by] Ministerio de Agricultura, Secretaria General Tecnica [Spain]. a., 1970- Madrid.

— Tanzania.

NYERERE (JULIUS KAMBARAGE) Socialism and rural development. [Dar es Salaam, Government Printer, 1967]. pp. 31.

— United Kingdom.

[STONE (THOMAS) Surveyor] A letter to the right honourable Lord Somerville...late President of the Board of Agriculture, with a view to shew the inutility of the plans and researches of that institution, and how it might be employed in others more beneficial...; by a society of practical farmers. London, G. Cawthorn, 1800. pp. 141.

GREEN (DANIEL) The politics of food. London, [1975]. pp. 220. *bibliog.*

— United States.

PUHLE (HANS JUERGEN) Politische Agrarbewegungen in kapitalistischen Industriegesellschaften: Deutschland, USA und Frankreich im 20. Jahrhundert. Göttingen, 1975. pp. 496. *bibliog.*

AIR

— Pollution — Economic aspects — Mathematical models.

KOHN (ROBERT E.) Air pollution control: welfare economic interpretation. Lexington, [1975]. pp. 155. *bibliog.*

— — Law and legislation — European Economic Community countries.

AMENDOLA (GIANFRANCO) La normativa ambientale nei paesi della Comunità europea: acque, inquinamento atmosferico. Milano, 1975. pp. 254.

— — Canada.

AIR pollution: causes and control; by H. Whaley [and others]. rev. ed. Ottawa, 1970. pp. 25,15. *(Canada. Mines Branch. Information Circulars. 211) In English and French.*

— — Hong Kong.

HONG KONG. Committee on Air Pollution. 1970. A report on air pollution in Hong Kong; [J.L. Marden, chairman]. Hong Kong, 1969 [or rather 1970]. pp. 38. *bibliog.*

— — United Kingdom.

NORTH WEST ECONOMIC PLANNING COUNCIL. Smoke control. [Manchester, 1970]. fo. 16.

— — United States.

BEDNARZ (ROBERT S.) The effect of air pollution on property value in Chicago. Chicago, 1975. pp. 111. *bibliog. (Chicago. University. Department of Geography. Research Papers. No. 166)*

JONES (CHARLES OSCAR) Clean air: the policies and politics of pollution control. Pittsburgh, [1975]. pp. 372. *bibliog.*

AIR LINES

— Rates.

FRIEDMAN (JESSE J.) A new air transport policy for the North Atlantic: saving an endangered system. New York, 1976. pp. 149.

— Europe.

GREIG (JOHN ALEXANDER) The rationalisation of airline networks within Western Europe, with special reference to Swissair. 1975. fo. 341. *bibliog. Typescript. Ph.D.(London) thesis: unpublished. This thesis is the property of London University and may not be removed from the Library.*

THIEL (DIETER) Die Entwicklung des Linien-Luftverkehrs in Europa nach dem Zweiten Weltkrieg. [Berlin?, 1975?]. pp. 293. *bibliog. Inaugural-Dissertation zur Erlangung des Grades eines Doktors der Wirtschaftswissenschaften der Freien Universität Berlin.*

— Switzerland.

GREIG (JOHN ALEXANDER) The rationalisation of airline networks within Western Europe, with special reference to Swissair. 1975. fo. 341. *bibliog. Typescript. Ph.D.(London) thesis: unpublished. This thesis is the property of London University and may not be removed from the Library.*

— United Kingdom — Finance.

FINANCIAL RESULTS - UNITED KINGDOM AIRLINES; (pd. by) Civil Aviation Authority. a., 1968/74(1st)- London.

AIR TRAVEL.

YACOUMIS (JOHN) Air inclusive tour marketing: the retail distribution channels in the U.K. and West Germany. London, 1975. pp. 71. *(International Tourism Quarterly. ITQ Special [Publications]. No. 2)*

AIRPORTS

— Planning.

DE NEUFVILLE (RICHARD) Airport systems planning: a critical look at methods and experience. London, 1976. pp. 201. *bibliog.*

— Price policy.

LENHOFF (MICHAEL) Optimal airport user charges: some models of price, cost and supply of service. [1975]. fo. 394. *bibliog. Typescript. Ph.D. (London) thesis: unpublished. This thesis is the property of London University and may not be removed from the Library.*

— United Kingdom.

U.K. Commission on the Third London Airport. 1969-72. Report, papers and proceedings: [Eustace Roskill, chairman]. London, 1969-72. 33 vols. *Sir Eustace Roskill's own set with his annotations.*

BRITISH AIRPORTS AUTHORITY. 1975 south-east airports origin and destination survey: summary of results. [London], 1975. pp. 34, fo.4.

LENHOFF (MICHAEL) Optimal airport user charges: some models of price, cost and supply of service. [1975]. fo. 394. *bibliog. Typescript. Ph.D. (London) thesis: unpublished. This thesis is the property of London University and may not be removed from the Library.*

U.K. Working Party on General Aviation Facilities in South-East Hampshire and West Sussex. 1975. Report...to the Civil Aviation Authority and local authorities in the area; [J.M. Bowley, chairman]. London, 1975. pp. 10. *(U.K. Civil Aviation Authority. [Publications]. CAP 378)*

— — Planning.

U.K. Civil Aviation Authority. Economics and Statistics Division. 1975. Airport development in south Wales and the south west region of England; a report to the...Authority by a research team of the...Division. London, 1975. pp. 46. *(U.K. Civil Aviation Authority. [Publications]. CAP 377)*

SEALY (KENNETH ROYSTON) Airport strategy and planning. London, 1976. pp. 60. *bibliogs.*

U.K. Civil Aviation Authority. 1976. Future airport development in south Wales and the south-west of England; advice to the Secretary of State for Trade from the...Authority. London, 1976. pp. 13. *([Publications]. CAP 380)*

AIX–EN–PROVENCE.

FRANCE. Direction de la Documentation. La Documentation Française. Notes et Etudes Documentaires. Nos. 4,108-4, 109. Les villes françaises: Aix-en Provence; [par M. Wolkowitsch]. Paris, 1974. pp. 79. *bibliog.*

— Charities.

FAIRCHILDS (CISSIE C.) Poverty and charity in Aix-en-Provence, 1640-1789. Baltimore, [1976]. pp. 197. *bibliog. (Johns Hopkins University. Studies in Historical and Political Science. Series 94. No. 1.)*

— Poor.

FAIRCHILDS (CISSIE C.) Poverty and charity in Aix-en-Provence, 1640-1789. Baltimore, [1976]. pp. 197. *bibliog. (Johns Hopkins University. Studies in Historical and Political Science. Series 94. No. 1.)*

AKWE–SHAVANTE INDIANS.

MAYBURY-LEWIS (DAVID) The savage and the innocent. Boston, 1968 repr. 1971. pp. 270.

GIACCARIA (BARTOLOMEU) and HEIDE (ADALBERTO) Jerônimo Xavante conta: mitos e lendas. Campo Grande, Mato Grosso, 1975. pp. 301.

ALASKA

— Historical geography.

GIBSON (JAMES R.) Imperial Russia in frontier America: the changing geography of supply of Russian America, 1784-1867. New York, 1976. pp. 257. *bibliogs.*

ALBANIA

— Economic policy.

SHEHU (MEHMET) Report on the directives of the 6th Congress of the Party of Labor of Albania for the 5th five-year plan, 1971-1975 of economic and cultural development of the people's republic of Albania; submitted to the 6th Congress of the Party of Labor of Albania, November 4, 1971. Tirana, 1971. pp. 156.

— History.

POLLO (STEFANAQ) and PUTO (ARBEN) eds. Histoire de l'Albanie des origines à nos jours. Roanne, [1974]. pp. 372. *bibliog.*

— Politics and government.

HOXHA (ENVER) Report on the activity of the Central Committee of the Party of Labor of Albania; submitted to the 6th Congress of the Party of Labor of Albania, November 1, 1971. Tirana, 1971. pp. 251.

ALBERTA

— Politics and government.

BARR (JOHN J.) The dynasty: the rise and fall of Social Credit in Alberta. Toronto, [1974]. pp. 256.

ALBIZU CAMPOS (PEDRO).

ALBIZU CAMPOS (PEDRO) La conciencia nacional puertorriqueña...; seleccion, introduccion y notas de Manuel Maldonado-Denis. Mexico, 1972. pp. 218.

ALCOHOLICS

— Rehabilitation — Evaluation.

PROGRAM evaluation: alcohol, drug abuse, and mental health services; edited by Jack Zusman [and] Cecil R. Wurster. Lexington, Mass., [1975]. pp. 278. *Based on papers presented at a Conference sponsored by the Alcohol, Drug Abuse and Mental Health Administration held in Washington in 1974.*

— United States.

CAHN (SIDNEY) The treatment of alcoholics: an evaluative study. New York, 1970. pp. 246. *bibliog.*

ALCOHOLISM.

ROBINSON (DAVID) 1941- . From drinking to alcoholism: a sociological commentary. London, [1976]. pp. 211.

— Treatment — United States.

CAHN (SIDNEY) The treatment of alcoholics: an evaluative study. New York, 1970. pp. 246. *bibliog.*

— United Kingdom.

ALCOHOL dependence and smoking behaviour; edited by Griffith Edwards [and others] on behalf of the Addiction Research Unit, Institute of Psychiatry, University of London. Farnborough, Hants., [1976]. pp. 268. *bibliog.*

ALCOHOLISM AND CRIME.

CHRISTIAN ECONOMIC AND SOCIAL RESEARCH FOUNDATION. Occasional Papers. Series C, No. 2. Alcohol and crime: an exploration of the influence of alcohol on the pattern of crime, and a study of methods whereby changes in the influence may be measured with an approach to scientific accuracy and objectivity. London, 1976. pp. 51.

ALGEBRAIC NUMBER THEORY.

LANG (SERGE) Algebraic number theory. Reading, Mass., [1970]. pp. 345. *bibliog.*

ALGERIA

— Army.

ALGERIA. Ministère de l'Information et de la Culture. 1974. De l'A[rmée de] L[ibération] N[ationale] à l'A[rmée] N[ationale] P[opulaire]: (20e anniversaire de la lutte de libération). Alger, 1974. pp. 171.

— Commerce.

STATISTIQUES DU COMMERCE EXTERIEUR DE L'ALGERIE; (pd. by) Direction des Statistiques. a., 1971- Alger.

— Economic conditions.

VISAGES DE L'ALGERIE. [Algiers, Ministère de l'Information, 1970 in progress].

— — Statistics.

TABLEAUX DE L'ECONOMIE ALGERIENNE; [pd. by] Direction des Statistiques. a., 1971- Alger.

— Economic policy.

ALGERIA. 1970. Plan quadriennal, 1970-1973; rapport général. [Alger, 1970]. pp. 157.

AMMOUR (KADER) and others. La voie algérienne: les contradictions d'un développement national. Paris, 1974. pp. 179.

— History.

VATIN (JEAN CLAUDE) L'Algérie politique: histoire et société. Paris, [1974 in progress]. *(Fondation Nationale des Sciences Politiques. Cahiers. No. 192)*

— — 1945— .

BASTIEN-THIRY (JEAN MARIE) Déclaration du colonel Bastien-Thiry, 2 février 1963. [Paris], [1963]. pp. 54.

ALGERIA (Cont.)

ALGERIA. Ministère de l'Information et de la Culture. 1974. De l'A[rmée de] L[ibération] N[ationale] à l'A[rmée] N[ationale] P[opulaire]: (20e anniversaire de la lutte de libération). Alger, 1974. pp. 171.

— Industries.

ALGERIA. Direction de la Documentation et des Publications. 1969. L'industrie en Algérie. [Algiers, 1969]. pp. 91.

— Nationalism.

LENTIN (ALBERT PAUL) L'histoire de la révolution algérienne: un dossier de France Observateur. [Paris], 1962. pp. 16.

— Politics and government.

VISAGES DE L'ALGERIE. [Algiers, Ministère de l'Information, 1970 in progress].

KOULYTCHIZKY (SERGE) L'autogestion, l'homme et l'état: l'expérience algérienne. Paris, [1974]. pp. 482. bibliog. (Paris. Ecole Pratique des Hautes Etudes. Section des Sciences Economiques et Sociales. Recherches Coopératives. 6)

LECA (JEAN) and VATIN (JEAN CLAUDE) L'Algérie politique: institutions et régime. Paris, [1975]. pp. 501. (Fondation Nationale des Sciences Politiques. Cahiers. 197)

MAHSAS (AHMED) L'autogestion en Algérie: données politiques de ses premières étapes et de son application. Paris, [1975]. pp. 297.

— Population — Bibliography.

DEVILLE (MARTINE) and others, compilers. Démographie algérienne: bibliographie analytique. Paris, Institut National d'Etudes Démographiques, [1973]. pp. 101.

— Social conditions.

VISAGES DE L'ALGERIE. [Algiers, Ministère de l'Information, 1970 in progress].

— Social policy.

ALGERIA. 1970. Plan quadriennal, 1970-1973; rapport général. [Alger, 1970]. pp. 157.

ALGERIANS IN FRANCE.

ETUDES SOCIALES NORD AFRICAINES. Cahiers Nord-Africains. No. 45. Les jeunes Nord-Africains en Métropole. Amsterdam, 1971. pp. 56.

ALGORITHMS.

DOMSCHKE (WOLFGANG) Kürzeste Wege in Graphen: Algorithmen, Verfahrensvergleiche. Meisenheim am Glan, [1972]. pp. 131. bibliog.

LEE (JOHN A.N.) Computer semantics: studies of algorithms, processors and languages. New York, [1972]. pp. 397. bibliog.

WIRTH (NIKLAUS) Algorithms [plus] data structures [equal] programs. Englewood Cliffs, N.J., [1976]. pp. 366. bibliogs.

ALIANZA NACIONAL (PERU).

ALIANZA NACIONAL. El problema economico del Peru: consideraciones esenciales para la elaboracion del programa economico de la Alianza Nacional. [Lima, 1949?]. pp. 95.

ALIEN LABOUR

— Austria.

GEHMACHER (ERNST) Grenzen und Probleme der Beschäftigung von Gastarbeitern im Lande Salzburg;...von der Kammer für Arbeiter und Angestellte für Salzburg. Salzburg, [1974]. fo.154. (Salzburger Institut für Raumforschung. Schriftenreihe. Band 2)

— Europe.

DIMITRAS (ELIE) Enquêtes sociologiques sur les émigrants grecs: deuxième enquête: lors du séjour en Europe occidentale. Athènes, Centre National de Recherches Sociales, 1971. pp. 219.

DIMITRAS (ELIE) and VLACHOS (EVANGELOS C.) Sociological surveys on Greek emigrants: third survey: upon the return to Greece. Athens, National Centre of Social Research, 1971. pp. 131.

ABADAN-UNAT (NERMIN) ed. Turkish workers in Europe, 1960-1975: a socio-economic reappraisal. Leiden, 1976. pp. 424. bibliog.

POWER (JONATHAN) and HARDMAN (ANNA) Western Europe's migrant workers. London, 1976. pp. 40. bibliog. (Minority Rights Group. Reports. No.28)

— France.

COLLECTIF D'ALPHABÉTISATION and GROUPE D'INFORMATION ET DE SOUTIEN DES TRAVAILLEURS IMMIGRÉS. Le petit livre juridique des travailleurs immigrés. 2nd ed. Paris, 1975. pp. 128.

DARIEL (JEAN LOUP) La traite des pauvres: racolage et exploitation des travailleurs étrangers. [Paris, 1975]. pp. 211.

N'DONGO (SALLY) Voyage forcé: itinéraire d'un militant. Paris, 1975. pp. 224.

— Germany.

[HAMBURG. Senat. 1971]. Bericht über die wirtschaftliche und soziale Lage der ausländischen Arbeitnehmer in Hamburg. [Hamburg, imprint, 1971?]. pp. 86.

HOEPFNER (KLAUS) Ökonomische Alternativen zur Ausländerbeschäftigung.. Göttingen, [1975]. pp. 210. bibliog. (Kommission für Wirtschaftlichen und Sozialen Wandel. Schriften. 105)

KOERNER (HELLMUT) Der Zustrom von Arbeitskräften in die Bundesrepublik Deutschland, 1950-1972: Auswirkungen auf die Funktionsweise des Arbeitsmarktes. Bern, 1976. pp. 353. bibliog. (Hamburg. Hansische Universität. Sozialökonomisches Seminar. Schriftenreihe. Band 3)

— Sweden.

OHLSSON (ROLF) Invandrarna på arbetsmarknaden: en undersökning av invandrare i Malmö under perioden 1945-1967. Lund, [1975]. pp. 155. bibliog. (Lund. Ekonomisk-Historiska Föreningens. Skrifter. vol. 16) With English summary.

— Switzerland.

HABICHT (HANS MARTIN) Rickentunnel-Streik und Rorschacher Krawall: St.Gallische Fremdarbeiterprobleme vor dem Ersten Weltkrieg. St. Gallen, 1975. pp. 60. bibliog. (Historischer Verein des Kantons St. Gallen. Neujahrsblatt. 115)

— United Kingdom.

CAMPBELL-PLATT (K.) Workers in Britain from selected foreign countries. London, [1975]. fo. 16.

ALIENATION (SOCIAL PSYCHOLOGY).

THEORIES of alienation: critical perspectives in philosophy and the social sciences; edited by R. Felix Geyer [and] David R. Schweitzer. Leiden, 1976. pp. 305. bibliogs. A revision of papers presented to the Ad Hoc Group on Alienation Theory and Research at the 8th World Congress of Sociology, Toronto, 1974.

WRIGHT (JAMES D.) The dissent of the governed: alienation and democracy in America. New York, 1976. pp. 329. bibliog.

ALIENS

— Africa, East.

DON NANJIRA (DANIEL D.C.) The status of aliens in East Africa: Asians and Europeans in Tanzania, Uganda, and Kenya. New York, 1976. pp. 230.

— Germany.

HELDMANN (HANS HEINZ) Ausländerrecht: Disziplinarordnung für die Minderheit. Darmstadt, 1974. pp. 159.

ALL HALLOWS PARISH, MARYLAND

— History.

EARLE (CARVILLE V.) The evolution of a tidewater settlement system: All Hallow's Parish, Maryland, 1650-1783. Chicago, 1975. pp 239 bibliog. (Chicago. University. Department of Geography. Research Papers. No. 170)

ALLARDT (HELMUT).

ALLARDT (HELMUT) Moskauer Tagebuch: Beobachtungen, Notizen, Erlebnisse. 3rd ed. Düsseldorf, 1974. pp. 424. bibliog.

ALLEGIANCE.

NEUMAN (STEPHANIE GLICKSBERG) ed. Small states and segmented societies: national political integration in a global environment. New York, 1976. pp. 238.

ALLGEMEINER DEUTSCHER ARBEITERVEREIN.

PETRY (LOTHAR) Die Erste Internationale in der Berliner Arbeiterbewegung. Erlangen, 1975. pp. 381. bibliog.

ALLIANCES.

CLINE (RAY S.) World power assessment: a calculus of strategic drift. Boulder, Col., [1975]. pp. 173.

STARR (HARVEY) Coalitions and future war: a dyadic study of cooperation and conflict. London, [1975]. pp. 70. bibliog.

ALLISON (R. BRUCE).

ALLISON (R. BRUCE) Democrats in exile, 1968-1972: the political confessions of a New England liberal. Hinsdale, Ill., [1974]. pp. 147.

ALMSHOUSES AND WORKHOUSES

— United Kingdom — Scotland.

HARVEY (COLIN) Ha'penny help: a record of social improvement in Victorian Scotland. Glasgow, 1976. pp. 197.

— United States.

STATE COMMUNITIES AID ASSOCIATION. [Publications]. No. 12. Hand-book for visitors to the poorhouse. 4th ed. London, 1888. pp. 90.

ALSACE.

SOCIETE D'ETUDES PROSPECTIVE ET AMENAGEMENT. Schéma général d'aménagement de la France: dynamique urbaine et projet régional: un exemple: la région Alsace; (réalisée sous la direction d'Augustin Antunes. Paris, 1975. pp. 141. (France. Délégation à l'Aménagement du Territoire et à l'Action Régionale. Travaux et Recherches de Prospective. 56)

ALSACE–LORRAINE QUESTION.

ROTHENBERGER (KARL HEINZ) Die elsass-lothringische Heimat- und Autonomiebewegung zwischen den beiden Weltkriegen. Bern, 1975. pp. 366. bibliog.

ALTHUSSER (LOUIS).

RANCIÈRE (JACQUES) La leçon d'Althusser. [Paris, 1974]. pp. 277.

CALLINICOS (ALEX) Althusser's Marxism. London, 1976. pp. 133. bibliog.

ALUMINIUM INDUSTRY AND TRADE

— Switzerland.

ALUMINIUM-INDUSTRIE-AKTIEN-GESELLSCHAFT. Geschichte der Aluminium-Industrie-Aktien-Gesellschaft Neuhausen, 1888-1938; [by Walther Meier and others]. [Chippis?], 1942-43. 2 vols.

AMAZON VALLEY

— Economic history.

VELHO (OTAVIO GUILHERME) Frentes de expansão e estrutura agraria: estudo do processo de penetração numa area da Transamazônica. Rio de Janeiro, 1972. pp. 178. *bibliog.*

— Economic policy.

PEREIRA (OSNY DUARTE) A Transamazônica: pros e contras. Rio de Janeiro, 1971. pp. 368. *bibliog.*

AMBOINA

— Nationalism.

WAT moeten ze hier?: Zuidmolukkers op weg naar vrijheid; [by Gerhard Knot and others]. Groningen, [1975]. pp. 96. *bibliog.*

AMERICA

— Antiquities.

PREHISTORIC man in the new world; edited by Jesse D. Jennings [and] Edward Norbeck. Chicago, 1964, repr. 1974. pp. 633. *bibliogs. Papers based on a symposium entitled "Prehistoric Man in the New World", forming part of the fifteenth anniversary festivities of Rice University in 1962.*

— — Bibliography.

GUYOT (MIREILLE) compiler. Bibliographie américaniste: archéologie et préhistoire: anthropologie et ethnohistoire. Paris, 1972. fo. 234.

— History.

JONES (PETER D'ALROY) Since Columbus: poverty and pluralism in the history of the Americas. London, 1975. pp. 282. *bibliog.*

— Race question.

RACE and slavery in the western hemisphere: quantitative studies; edited by Stanley L. Engerman and Eugene D. Genovese. Princeton, N.J., [1975]. pp. 556. *(Mathematical Social Science Board. History Advisory Committee. Quantitative Studies in History). Papers of a conference sponsored by the History Advisory Committee and held at the University of Rochester in 1972.*

AMERICA, LATIN.

HILTON (RONALD) The Latin Americans: their heritage and their destiny. New York, [1973]. pp. 253. *bibliog.*

WILLEMS (EMILIO) Latin American culture: an anthropological synthesis. New York, [1975]. pp. 423. *bibliog.*

— Armed forces — Political activity.

ETCHISON (DON L.) The United States and militarism in Central America. New York, 1975. pp. 150. *bibliog.*

— Bibliography.

GEOGHEGAN (ABEL RODOLFO) Obras de referencia de América Latina: repertório selectivo y anotado de enciclopedias, diccionarios, bibliografías, repertorios biográficos, catálogos, guias, anuarios, indices, etc. [Buenos Aires, 1965]. pp. xxiii, 280.

LATIN AMERICA REVIEW OF BOOKS; ed. by Colin Harding and Christopher Roper. a., 1973 (no.1)- London.

— Biography.

LATIN American government leaders; second edition edited by David William Foster. Tempe, 1975. pp. 130.

— Commerce — Germany.

BROCKSTEDT (JUERGEN) Die Schiffahrts- und Handelsbeziehungen Schleswig-Holsteins nach Lateinamerika, 1815-1848. Köln, 1975. pp. 575. *bibliog. With summaries in English and French.*

— Commercial policy.

TANCER (SHOSHANA B.) Economic nationalism in Latin America: the quest for economic independence. New York, 1976. pp. 251.

— Discovery and exploration.

MORISON (SAMUEL ELIOT) The European discovery of America: the southern voyages, A.D. 1492-1616. New York, 1974. pp. 758. *bibliogs.*

— Economic conditions.

LOCKLEY (LAWRENCE C.) A guide to market data in Central America. Tegucigalpa, Central American Bank for Economic Integration, [1964]. pp. 162. *bibliog.*

KAPLAN (MARCOS) Subdesarrollo y desarrollo de America Latina. Buenos Aires, [1969]. pp. 56. *bibliog.*

MASSES in Latin America; edited by Irving Louis Horowitz. New York, 1970. pp. 608.

BAMBIRRA (VANIA) El capitalismo dependiente latinoamericano. Mexico, 1974 repr.1975. pp. 180.

— Economic history.

CARMAGNANI (MARCELLO) L'America Latina dal '500 a oggi: nascita, espansione e crisi di un sistema feudale. Milano, 1975. pp. 220. *bibliog.*

— Economic integration.

ORGANIZATION OF AMERICAN STATES. Inter-American Economic and Social Council. Committee of Nine. 1966. Report on the Central American national development plans and the process of economic integration; report presented by the Ad Hoc Committee to the governments of the Central American republics. Washington, 1966. pp. 170.

BOLETIN DE LA INTEGRACION: ([pd. by] Institute for Latin American Integration). a., Ag 1968/Ag 1969 - Ag 1971/Ag 1972 (nos. 1-4); ceased pbln. Buenos Aires. *[in English]. Superseded by INTEGRACION LATINOAMERICANA.*

PROCESO DE INTEGRACION DE AMERICA LATINA, EL; [pd. by] Banco Interamericano de Desarrollo, Instituto para la Integracion de America Latina. a., 1972- [Buenos Aires]. *First and second reports separately catalogued.*

BOLETIN DE LA INTEGRACION: ([pd. by] Institute for Latin American Integration). m., Ja 1972-D 1975 (año 7, no.73 - año 10, no.120); ceased pbln. Buenos Aires. *[in Spanish]. Superseded by INTEGRACION LATINOAMERICANA.*

PAZ BARNICA (EDGARDO) Reestructuracion institucional de la integracion centroamericana. [Tegucigalpa], 1972. pp. 534. *bibliog.*

INTEGRACIÓN LATINOAMERICANA: el sistema latinoamericano; ([pd. by] Institute for Latin American Integration). m., Ap 1976 (año 1, no.1)- Buenos Aires. *Supersedes BOLETIN DE LA INTEGRACION and REVISTA DE LA INTEGRACION.*

— Economic policy.

ORGANIZATION OF AMERICAN STATES. Inter-American Economic and Social Council. Committee of Nine. 1966. Report on the Central American national development plans and the process of economic integration; report presented by the Ad Hoc Committee to the governments of the Central American republics. Washington, 1966. pp. 170.

— Foreign economic relations.

TANCER (SHOSHANA B.) Economic nationalism in Latin America: the quest for economic independence. New York, 1976. pp. 251.

— Foreign relations.

CONSEJO LATINOAMERICANO EN CIENCIAS SOCIALES. Asamblea General. Reunion, 2a, Lima, 1968. La dependencia politico-economica de America Latina; por Helio Jaguaribe [and others]. (ponencias presentadas en la Reunion...con la transcripcion de sus discusiones). Mexico, 1970 repr. 1974. pp. 293.

HERRERA OROPEZA (JOSE) America Latina: proceso hacia el socialismo. Caracas, 1972. pp. 224. *bibliog.*

DAVIS (HAROLD EUGENE) and WILSON (LARMAN CURTIS) Latin American foreign policies: an analysis. Baltimore, [1975]. pp. 470. *bibliogs.*

HELLMAN (RONALD G.) and ROSENBAUM (H. JON) eds. Latin America: the search for a new international role. New York, [1975]. pp. 297. *bibliogs. (Center for Inter-American Relations. Latin American International Affairs Series. vol. 1)*

— — Canada.

OGELSBY (J.C.M.) Gringos from the far North: essays in the history of Canadian- Latin American relations, 1866-1968. Toronto, [1976]. pp. 346. *bibliog.*

— — Europe.

RODRIGUEZ O. (JAIME E.) The emergence of Spanish America: Vicente Rocafuerte and Spanish Americanism, 1808-1832. Berkeley, [1975]. pp. 311. *bibliog.*

— — United States.

CORAL (JUAN CARLOS) Indoamerica frente al imperialismo. Buenos Aires, 1966. pp. 76.

SMETHERMAN (BOBBIE BRALY) and SMETHERMAN (ROBERT M.) Territorial seas and inter-American relations, with case studies of the Peruvian and U.S. fishing industries. New York, 1974. pp. 121.

HELLMAN (RONALD G.) and ROSENBAUM (H. JON) eds. Latin America: the search for a new international role. New York, [1975]. pp. 297. *bibliogs. (Center for Inter-American Relations. Latin American International Affairs Series. vol. 1)*

BLASIER (COLE) The hovering giant: U.S. responses to revolutionary change in Latin America. Pittsburgh, [1976]. pp. 315.

— Historiography.

GRAHAM (RICHARD) and SMITH (PETER H.) eds. New approaches to Latin American history. Austin, [1974]. pp. 275.

— History.

GRAHAM (RICHARD) and SMITH (PETER H.) eds. New approaches to Latin American history. Austin, [1974]. pp. 275.

WOODWARD (RALPH LEE) Central America: a nation divided. New York, 1976. pp. 344. *bibliog.*

— Nationalism.

SWANSBROUGH (ROBERT H.) The embattled colossus: economic nationalism and United States investors in Latin America. Gainesville, Florida, 1976. pp. 261. *bibliog. (Florida University. School of Inter-American Studies. Latin American Monographs. 2nd Series. 16)*

— Native races.

INTERNATIONAL CONGRESS OF AMERICANISTS. 39th Congress. Problemas etnicos de la sociedad contemporanea. Mexico, 1970. pp. 340. *(Anuario Indigenista. vol 30) Contains some of the papers presented at the congress with additional contributions.*

— Politics and government.

CALELLO (HUGO) Ciencia social y revolucion en Latinoamerica. Caracas, [1969]. pp. 73.

DIEZ años de insurreccion en America Latina; ([by] Vania Bambirra [and others]). Santiago, Chile, [1971]. 2 vols. (in 1).

LATIN AMERICA REVIEW OF BOOKS; ed. by Colin Harding and Christopher Roper. a., 1973 (no.1)- London.

HARRIS (LOUIS K.) and ALBA (VICTOR) The political culture and behavior of Latin America. Kent, Ohio, [1974]. pp. 221. *bibliogs.*

ETCHISON (DON L.) The United States and militarism in Central America. New York, 1975. pp. 150. *bibliog.*

AMERICA, LATIN.(Cont.)

RUSSELL TRIBUNAL II ON REPRESSION IN BRAZIL, CHILE AND LATIN AMERICA. Repression in Latin America: a report on the first session of the second Russell Tribunal, Rome, April 1974; edited and translated by William Jerman. Nottingham, 1975. pp. 163.

DUFF (ERNEST A.) and McCAMANT (JOHN F.) Violence and repression in Latin America: a quantitative and historical analysis. New York, [1976]. pp. 322. *bibliog.*

— **Population.**

BEAVER (STEVEN E.) Demographic transition theory reinterpreted: an application to recent natality trends in Latin America. Lexington, Mass., [1975]. pp. 177. *bibliog.*

SMITH (THOMAS LYNN) The race between population and food supply in Latin America. Albuquerque, N.M., [1976]. pp. 194.

— **Relations (general) with the United States.**

WELLS (ALAN FRANK) Picture-tube imperialism?: the impact of U.S. television on Latin America. Maryknoll, [1972]. pp. 197. *bibliog.*

— **Relations (military) with the United States.**

ETCHISON (DON L.) The United States and militarism in Central America. New York, 1975. pp. 150. *bibliog.*

— **Rural conditions.**

PEARSE (ANDREW) The Latin American peasant. London, 1975. pp. 289. *bibliog.*

— **Social conditions.**

CALELLO (HUGO) Ciencia social y revolucion en Latinoamerica. Caracas, [1969]. pp. 73.

KAPLAN (MARCOS) Subdesarrollo y desarrollo de America Latina. Buenos Aires, [1969]. pp. 56. *bibliog.*

INTERNATIONAL CONGRESS OF AMERICANISTS. 39th Congress. Problemas etnicos de la sociedad contemporanea. Mexico, 1970. pp. 340. *(Anuario Indigenista. vol 30) Contains some of the papers presented at the congress with additional contributions.*

MASSES in Latin America; edited by Irving Louis Horowitz. New York, 1970. pp. 608.

PIKE (FREDRICK BRAUN) Spanish America, 1900-1970: tradition and social innovation. New York, 1973. pp. 180. *bibliog.*

EDUCATIONAL alternatives in Latin America: social change and social stratification; edited by Thomas J. La Belle. Los Angeles, 1975. pp. 490. *bibliogs. (California University. Latin American Center. Latin American Studies. vol. 30)*

DUFF (ERNEST A.) and McCAMANT (JOHN F.) Violence and repression in Latin America: a quantitative and historical analysis. New York, [1976]. pp. 322. *bibliog.*

— **Social history.**

OLIEN (MICHAEL D.) Latin Americans: contemporary peoples and their cultural traditions. New York, [1973]. pp. 408. *bibliogs.*

PIKE (FREDRICK BRAUN) Spanish America, 1900-1970: tradition and social innovation. New York, 1973. pp. 180. *bibliog.*

— **Social life and customs.**

OLIEN (MICHAEL D.) Latin Americans: contemporary peoples and their cultural traditions. New York, [1973]. pp. 408. *bibliogs.*

— **Social policy.**

ORGANIZATION OF AMERICAN STATES. Inter-American Economic and Social Council. Committee of Nine. 1966. Report on the Central American national development plans and the process of economic integration; report prepared by the Ad Hoc Committee to the governments of the Central American republics. Washington, 1966. pp. 170.

— **Statistics.**

AKADEMIIA NAUK SSSR. Institut Latinskoi Ameriki. Latinskaia Amerika v tsifrakh: statisticheskii sbornik. Moskva, 1971. pp. 394.

AMERICA, NORTH.

WELLS (ROBERT V.) The population of the British colonies in America before 1776: a survey of census data. Princeton, [1975]. pp. 342. *bibliog.*

— **Civilization.**

CRISPO (JOHN H.G.) ed. The public right to know: accountability in the secretive society. Toronto, [1975]. pp. 395. *Includes extensive quotations from books and articles.*

— **Description and travel.**

PATERSON (JOHN HARRIS) North America: a geography of Canada and the United States. 5th ed. New York, 1975. pp. 368. *bibliog.*

— **Economic conditions.**

PATERSON (JOHN HARRIS) North America: a geography of Canada and the United States. 5th ed. New York, 1975. pp. 368. *bibliog.*

— **Economic integration.**

GEIGER (THEODORE) and others. North American integration and economic blocs. London, 1975. pp. 54. *(Trade Policy Research Centre. Thames Essays. No. 7)*

— **Economic policy.**

HANSEN (NILES M.) Public policy and regional economic development: the experience of nine western countries. Cambridge, Mass., [1974]. pp. 351. *bibliog.*

— **Foreign relations — Europe.**

GOODMAN (ELLIOT RAYMOND) The fate of the Atlantic Community. New York, 1975. pp. 583.

— **Population.**

WELLS (ROBERT V.) The population of the British colonies in America before 1776: a survey of census data. Princeton, [1975]. pp. 342. *bibliog.*

— **Social conditions.**

CRISPO (JOHN H.G.) ed. The public right to know: accountability in the secretive society. Toronto, [1975]. pp. 395. *Includes extensive quotations from books and articles.*

AMERICAN LITERATURE

— **Bibliography.**

GUNN (DREWEY WAYNE) compiler. Mexico in American and British letters: a bibliography of fiction and travel books, citing original editions. Metuchen, N.J., 1974. pp. 150.

AMERICAN NEWSPAPERS.

STEWART (DONALD HENDERSON) The opposition press of the Federalist period. Albany, [1969]. pp. 957. *bibliog.*

AMERICAN PERIODICALS.

BRADY (FRANK ROBERT) Hefner. London, 1975. pp. 224.

AMIENS.

FRANCE. Direction de la Documentation. La Documentation Française. Notes et Etudes Documentaires. Nos. 4,144-4, 145-4,146. Les villes françaises: Amiens; par Paul Oudart. Paris, 1974. pp. 84. *bibliog.*

AMIN (IDI).

STRATE (JEFFREY T.) Post-military coup strategy in Uganda: Amin's early attempts to consolidate political support. Athens, Oh., 1973. pp. 58. *(Ohio University. Center for International Studies. Papers in International Studies. Africa Series. No. 18)*

AMMONIA

— **Manufacture — Germany.**

RUHR-STICKSTOFF AG. D[eutsche] A[mmoniak-]V[ereinigung: Geschichte eines Unternehmens und Aspekte seiner Zeit. Bochum, [1974]. pp. 80.

AMNESTY.

DAMICO (ALFONSO J.) Democracy and the case for amnesty. Gainesville, Fla., 1975. pp. 78. *(Florida University. Monographs. Social Sciences. No. 55)*

— **United States.**

DAMICO (ALFONSO J.) Democracy and the case for amnesty. Gainesville, Fla., 1975. pp. 78. *(Florida University. Monographs. Social Sciences. No. 55)*

AMUR (OBLAST')

— **Social history.**

ISAKOV (ANDREI VASIL'EVICH) Razvitie zdravookhraneniia v Amurskoi oblasti. Khabarov, 1967. pp. 86.

ANALYSIS OF VARIANCE.

LINDMAN (HAROLD R.) Analysis of variance in complex experimental designs. San Francisco, [1974]. pp. 352. *bibliog.*

ANARCHISM AND ANARCHISTS.

ROCKER (RUDOLF) Anarchismus und Organisation. Berlin, [192-]. pp. 30.

ROCKER (RUDOLF) Der Kampf ums tägliche Brot. Berlin, [1925]. pp. 43.

TARRIDA DEL MARMOL (FERNANDO) Problemas trascendentales: estudios de sociologia y ciencia moderna. Barcelona, 1930. pp. 202.

GONZALEZ PRADA (MANUEL) Horas de lucha. Buenos Aires, [1946]. pp. 231.

ERNESTAN, pseud. [i.e. Ernest TANREZ] Pages choisies: Valeur de la liberté, Le socialisme contre l'autorité, Socialisme et humanisme. Paris, [1966]. pp. 191.

TULLOCK (GORDON) ed. Further explorations in the theory of anarchy. Blacksburg, [1974]. pp. 70. *(Virginia Polytechnic Institute and State University. Center for the Study of Public Choice. Public Choice Society Book and Monograph Series)*

HOLTERMAN (THOM) Andere staatsopvatting: een anarchistes syndroom. Deventer, [1975]. pp. 89. *bibliog.*

KROPOTKIN (PETR ALEKSANDROVICH) Prince. The essential Kropotkin; edited by Emile Capouya and Keitha Tompkins. London, 1976. pp. 294.

TAYLOR (MICHAEL) Anarchy and cooperation. London, [1976]. pp. 151. *bibliog.*

— **France.**

DEVALDES (MANUEL) Des cris sous la meule; suivi de Fleurs de guerre. Paris, 1927. pp. 159.

DUVAL (CLEMENT) Anarchist. Memorie autobiografiche. Newark, N.J., 1929. pp. 1047.

— **Netherlands.**

DUYN (ROEL VAN) ed. Het beste uit Provo: een bloemlezing uit alle verschenen nummers van het tijdschrift Provo. [Amsterdam, 1967]. pp. 257.

— **Russia.**

LEHNING (ARTHUR) Marxismus und Anarchismus in der russischen Revolution [and] Revolutionär-syndikalistische Bewegung in Russland; [by G.P.] Maximoff. 2nd ed. Berlin, 1971. pp. 146

— Spain.

MAURICE (JACQUES) L'anarchisme espagnol. Paris, [1973]. pp. 159. *bibliog.*

STALINISMUS und Anarchismus in der spanischen Revolution; oder, Bruno Frei und die Methode der Denunziation; ([by] Hans Peter Duerr, Augustin Souchy). Berlin, [1973]. pp. 56.

MUÑOZ (VLADIMIR) Antologia acrata española. Barcelona, 1974. pp. 202.

— United Kingdom.

WARD (COLIN) Housing: an anarchist approach. London, 1976. pp. 182.

— United States.

GOLDMAN (EMMA) and BERKMAN (ALEXANDER) Nowhere at home: letters from exile of Emma Goldman and Alexander Berkman; edited by Richard and Anna Maria Drinnon. New York, [1975]. pp. 282.

KARASEK (HORST) ed. 1886, Haymarket: die deutschen Anarchisten von Chicago; Reden und Lebensläufe. Berlin, [1975]. pp. 190. *bibliog.*

ANDERSON (AGNES ALEXANDRINA) Lady.

MOORE-ANDERSON (ARTHUR PONSONBY) Sir Robert Anderson K.C.B., LL.D. and Lady Agnes Anderson; by their son. London, 1947. pp. 173.

ANDERSON (Sir ROBERT).

MOORE-ANDERSON (ARTHUR PONSONBY) Sir Robert Anderson K.C.B., LL.D. and Lady Agnes Anderson; by their son. London, 1947. pp. 173.

ANDHRA

— Politics and government.

MADRAS. Partition Committee. 1950. Formation of Andhra province; report; [P.S. Kumaraswami Raja, chairman]. [Madras], 1950. pp.64.

ANDHRA PRADESH

— Economic conditions.

ANDHRA PRADESH. 1964. Review of economic trends during 1963. Hyderabad, 1964. pp. 15.

— Economic history.

RAMAN RAO (AJJARAPU VENKATA) Economic development of Andhra Pradesh, 1766-1957. Bombay, 1958. pp. 384.

ANDHRA PRADESH. Planning and Co-operation Department. 1972. Fifth five year plan: technical papers. (1). Review of development. [Hyderabad, 1972]. pp. 141.

— Economic policy.

ANDHRA PRADESH. Planning and Co-operation Department. 1972. Fifth five year plan: approach technical papers. Series 2. [Hyderabad, 1972]. pp. 112.

ANDHRA PRADESH. Planning and Co-operation Department. 1972. Fifth five year plan: technical papers. (1). Review of development. [Hyderabad, 1972]. pp. 141.

— Social policy.

ANDHRA PRADESH. Planning and Co-operation Department. 1972. Fifth five year plan: approach technical papers. Series 2. [Hyderabad, 1972]. pp. 112.

ANDHRA PRADESH. Planning and Co-operation Department. 1972. Fifth five year plan: technical papers. (1). Review of development. [Hyderabad, 1972]. pp. 141.

ANDORRA.

FRANCE. Direction de la Documentation. La Documentation Française. Notes et Etudes Documentaires. No. 4,087. Les vallées d'Andorre; (par Jean-Charles Sacotte). Paris, 1974. pp. 24. *bibliog.*

ANDREOTTI (GIULIO).

ORFEI (RUGGERO) Andreotti. Milano, 1975. pp. 252. *bibliog.*

ANDRIEUX (LOUIS).

ANDRIEUX (LOUIS) Souvenirs d'un préfet de police. Paris, 1885. 2 vols.

ANGER.

NOVACO (RAYMOND W.) Anger control: the development and evaluation of an experimental treatment. Lexington, [1975]. pp. 134. *bibliog.*

ANGERS

— Civic improvement.

FRANCE. Commissariat Général du Plan. 1972. Politiques urbaines. Angers, [1972?]. 6 parts.

ANGOLA

— Foreign relations — United States.

HARSCH (ERNEST) and THOMAS (TONY) Angola: the hidden history of Washington's war;...edited with an introduction by Malik Miah. New York, 1976. pp. 157. *bibliog.*

— History.

MILLER (JOSEPH C.) Kings and kinsmen: early Mbundu states in Angola. Oxford, 1976. pp. 312. *bibliog.*

— Nationalism.

HARSCH (ERNEST) and THOMAS (TONY) Angola: the hidden history of Washington's war;...edited with an introduction by Malik Miah. New York, 1976. pp. 157. *bibliog.*

— Politics and government.

ANGOLA SOLIDARITY COMMITTEE. Angola. London, [1975]. pp. 14. *bibliog.*

ANHYDRITE

— Somali Republic.

SOMALILAND PROTECTORATE. Geological Survey. Mineral Resources Pamphlets. No. 1. Gypsum, anhydrite. Hargeisa, [1954]. fo. 4.

ANIMAL INDUSTRY

— Canada.

CANADA. Department of Agriculture. Economics Branch. Market commentary: animals and animal products. s-a., D 1975- Ottawa.

ANIMAL INTELLIGENCE.

RESTLE (FRANK JOSEPH) Learning: animal behavior and human cognition. New York, [1975]. pp. 330. *bibliog.*

ANIMAL PRODUCTS

— Canada.

CANADA. Department of Agriculture. Economics Branch. Market commentary: animals and animal products. s-a., D 1975- Ottawa.

ANIMALS, HABITS AND BEHAVIOUR OF.

BIOLOGY and politics: recent explorations; [proceedings of a conference held in Paris, 1975; edited by] Albert Somit. Paris, [1976]. pp. 330. *bibliog. (International Social Science Council. Publications. 19)*

ANNUITIES

— Canada.

CANADA. Unemployment Insurance Commission. Annuities: annual report. a., 1973/74- Ottawa. *[in English and French].*

ANTHROPOLOGY.

ANNUNZIO (GABRIELE D').

MEYERS (JEFFREY) A fever at the core: the idealist in politics. London, 1976. pp. 172. *bibliog.*

ANSCHLUSS MOVEMENT, 1918–1938

LUZA (RADOMÍR) Austro-German relations in the Anschluss era. Princeton, [1975]. pp. 438. *bibliog.*

ANSON (HAROLD).

ANSON (HAROLD) Looking forward. London, [1938?]. pp. 295.

ANTHROPOGEOGRAPHY.

CHISHOLM (MICHAEL) Human geography: evolution or revolution?. Harmondsworth, 1975. pp. 207. *bibliog.*

— Canada.

BUNGE (WILLIAM WHEELER) and BORDESSA (RON) The Canadian alternative: survival, expeditions and urban change. Toronto, 1975. pp. 432. *bibliog. (York University (Toronto). Department of Geography. Geographical Monographs. No.2)*

— Greece.

BURGEL (GUY) La condition industrielle à Athènes: étude socio- géographique. Athènes, Centre National de Recherches Sociales, 1970-72. 2 vols. *35 map sheets with each volume, boxed separately.*

— Mohammedan countries.

MIQUEL (ANDRE) La géographie humaine du monde musulman jusqu'au milieu du 11e siècle. Paris, 1967-75. 2 vols. *bibliogs. (Paris. Ecole Pratique des Hautes Etudes. Section des Sciences Economiques et Sociales. Centre de Recherches Historiques. Civilisations et Sociétés. 7, 37)*

— Poland.

POLSKA AKADEMIA NAUK. Instytut Geografii. Geographia Polonica. 31. Warszawa, 1975. pp. 235. *bibliogs. No title: papers mainly concerned with Poland.*

— United States.

DAVIS (GEORGE A.) and DONALDSON (O. FRED) Blacks in the United States: a geographic perspective. Boston, [1975]. pp. 270. *bibliogs.*

GASTIL (RAYMOND D.) Cultural regions of the United States. Seattle, [1975]. pp. 366. *bibliog.*

— — Maryland.

EARLE (CARVILLE V.) The evolution of a tidewater settlement system: All Hallow's Parish, Maryland, 1650-1783. Chicago, 1975. pp. 239 *bibliog. (Chicago. University. Department of Geography. Research Papers. No. 170)*

ANTHROPOLOGY.

POUILLON (JEAN) and MARANDA (PIERRE) eds. Echanges et communications: mélanges offerts à Claude Lévi-Strauss à l'occasion de son 60ème anniversaire. Paris, 1970. 2 vols. *bibliogs.*

AMERICAN ASSOCIATION FOR THE ADVANCEMENT OF SCIENCE. Section L. Annual Meeting, 1969. Philosophical foundations of science: proceedings...; edited by Raymond J. Seeger and Robert S. Cohen. Dordrecht, [1974]. pp. 545. *bibliogs. (Boston Colloquium for the Philosophy of Science. Boston Studies in the Philosophy of Science. vol.11)*

CLASTRES (PIERRE) La société contre l'état: recherches d'anthropologie politique. Paris, [1974]. pp. 187.

COHEN (ABNER) Two-dimensional man: an essay on the anthropology of power and symbolism in complex society. London, 1974. pp. 156. *bibliog.*

MEAD (MARGARET) Ruth Benedict; [with selected papers by Ruth Benedict]. New York, [1974]. pp. 180. *bibliogs.*

ANTHROPOLOGY.(Cont.)

BLOCH (MAURICE E.F.) ed. Political language and oratory in traditional society. London, 1975. pp. 240. *bibliog.*

INTERNATIONAL CONGRESS OF ANTHROPOLOGICAL AND ETHNOLOGICAL SCIENCES. 9th Congress, 1973. Population and social organization: [papers from the Congress]; editor Moni Nag. The Hague, [1975]. pp. 367. *bibliogs.*

PEACOCK (JAMES L.) Consciousness and change: symbolic anthropology in evolutionary perspective. Oxford, [1975]. pp. 264. *bibliog.*

POUILLON (JEAN) Fétiches sans fétichisme. Paris, 1975. pp. 354. *Articles reprinted from various periodicals.*

BELSHAW (CYRIL SHIRLEY) The sorcerer's apprentice: an anthropology of public policy. New York, 1976. pp. 342.

BENNETT (JOHN WILLIAM) The ecological transition: cultural anthropology and human adaptation. New York, [1976]. pp. 378. *bibliog.*

LEWIS (IOAN MYRDDIN) Social anthropology in perspective: the relevance of social anthropology. Harmondsworth, 1976. pp. 386. *bibliog.*

— **Field work.**

WAX (ROSALIE H.) Doing fieldwork: warnings and advice. Chicago, 1971. pp. 395. *bibliog.*

CHAGNON (NAPOLEON A.) Studying the Yanomamö. New York, [1974]. pp. 270. *bibliog.*

— **Methodology.**

BEE (ROBERT L.) Patterns and processes: an introduction to anthropological strategies for the study of sociocultural change. New York, [1974]. pp. 260. *bibliog.*

SARANA (GOPALA) The methodology of anthropological comparisons: an analysis of comparative methods in social and cultural anthropology. Tucson, Az., [1975]. pp. 118. *bibliog. (Wenner-Gren Foundation for Anthropological Research. Viking Fund Publications in Anthropology. No. 53)*

— **Study and teaching — Mexico.**

INTERNATIONAL CONGRESS OF AMERICANISTS. 39th Congress. Problemas etnicos de la sociedad contemporanea. Mexico, 1970. pp. 340. *(Anuario Indigenista. vol 30) Contains some of the papers presented at the congress with additional contributions.*

ANTHROPOMETRY.

ETHNIC variables in human factors engineering: based on papers presented at a symposium...held in Oosterbeek, the Netherlands, 19-23 June 1972, under the auspices of...North Atlantic Treaty Organization; edited by Alphonse Chapanis. Baltimore, [1975]. pp. 290. *bibliogs.*

ANTICLERICALISM

— **Italy — Anecdotes, facetiae, satire, etc.**

MOJETTA (ANNA MARIA) ed. Cento anni di satira anticlericale nei giornali dal 1860 al 1955. Milano, [1975]. pp. 301.

ANTICOMMUNIST MOVEMENTS.

ŁARSKI (ANDRZEJ) Ośrodki antykomunistyczne na Zachodzie. Warszawa, 1970. pp. 179.

BEYER (HANS) Der Antikommunismus: Wesen, Formen und Funktionen. Berlin, 1975. pp. 122.

— **Poland.**

WALICHNOWSKI (TADEUSZ) U źródeł walk z podziemiem reakcyjnym w Polsce. Warszawa, 1975. pp. 347. *bibliog.*

— **Russia — Ukraine.**

PRAVDU ne zdolaty: trudiashchi zakhidnykh oblastei URSR v borot'bi proty ukraïns'kykh burzhuaznykh natsionalistiv u roky sotsialistychnykh peretvoren'. L'viv, 1974. pp. 278.

— **Yugoslavia.**

VODINELIĆ (VLADIMIR) 10 verzija više jedna jednako istina: zapisi o Bonskom i Stockholmskom procesu ustaškim teroristima. Split, 1973. pp. 236.

ANTIFASISTICKO VIJECE NARODNOG OSLOBODJENJA JUGOSLAVIJE.

ANTIFAŠISTIČKO VIJEĆE NARODNOG OSLOBODJENJA JUGOSLAVIJE. Treće zasedanje Antifašističkog Veća narodnog oslobodjenja Jugoslavije; Zasedanje Privremene narodne skupštine, 7-26 avgust 1945: stenografske beleške. Beograd, [1945?]. pp. 708. *In Cyrillic.*

ANTIGUA

— **Statistics.**

ANTIGUA. Statistics Division. Statistical yearbook. a., 1975(1st)- St. Johns.

ANTINAZI MOVEMENT.

LASCHITZA (HORST) Deutschland und die deutsche Arbeiterbewegung, 1939-1945; mit einem Dokumentenanhang. Berlin, 1963. pp. 140.

HOCHMUTH (URSEL) ed. Candidates of humanity: Dokumentation zur Hamburger Weissen Rose anlässlich des 50. Geburtstages von Hans Leipelt. Hamburg, 1971. pp. 74. *bibliog. (Vereinigung der Antifaschisten und Verfolgten des Naziregimes, Land Hamburg. VAN-Dokumentationen. 2)*

HOCHMUTH (URSEL) ed. Fiete Schulze; oder, Das dritte Urteil. Hamburg, 1971. pp. 117. *bibliog. (Vereinigung der Antifaschisten und Verfolgten des Naziregimes, Land Hamburg. VAN-Dokumentationen. 3)*

VEREINIGUNG DER ANTIFASCHISTEN UND VERFOLGTEN DES NAZIREGIMES, LAND HAMBURG. Jacob und Schrübbers: heute wie damals; Dokumentation zum Berufsverbotsbeschluss und zum Fall Ilse Jacob, etc. 2nd ed. Hamburg, 1972. pp. 94. *(VAN-Documentationen. 4)*

GÓRA (WŁADYSŁAW) and OKĘCKI (STANISŁAW) Za nasza i wasza wolność: Für unsere und eure Freiheit: deutsche Antifaschisten im polnischen Widerstandskampf; herausgegeben von Reinhold Jeske; (von Norbert Rösler und Eduard Ullmann ins Deutsche übersetzt). Berlin, [1975]. pp. 562. *bibliog. In German.*

MUELLER (JOSEF) of the Christlich-Soziale Union. Bis zur letzten Konsequenz: ein Leben für Frieden und Freiheit. München, [1975]. pp. 384. *bibliog.*

SBOSNY (INGE) and SCHABROD (KARL) Widerstand in Solingen: aus dem Leben antifaschistischer Kämpfer. Frankfurt/Main, [1975]. pp. 135.

GERHARD (DIRK) Antifaschisten: proletarischer Widerstand, 1933-1945. Berlin, [1976]. pp. 175. *bibliog.*

HINDELS (JOSEF) Österreichs Gewerkschaften im Widerstand, 1934-1945. Wien, [1976]. pp. 435. *bibliog.*

— **Periodicals — Indexes.**

HEINTZ (GEORG) compiler. Index des "Freien/Neuen Deutschland", Mexico, 1941-1946. [Worms, 1975]. pp. 110.

ANTIPATHIES AND PREJUDICES.

ADOLESCENT prejudice; [by] Charles Y. Glock [and others]. New York, [1975]. pp. 229. *(California University. Survey Research Center. Five-Year Study of Anti-Semitism in the United States. vol. 7)*

BETTELHEIM (BRUNO) and JANOWITZ (MORRIS) Social change and prejudice: including Dynamics of prejudice. New York, 1964 repr. 1975. pp. xxxviii, 337. *Dynamics of prejudice first published in 1950. The 1975 reprint contains a new prologue by the authors.*

KIDDER (LOUISE H.) and STEWART (V. MARY) The psychology of intergroup relations: conflict and consciousness. New York, [1975]. pp. 128. *bibliog.*

ANTIQUARIAN BOOKSELLERS

— **Directories.**

GROSE (B. DONALD) The antiquarian booktrade: an international directory of subject specialists. Metuchen, N.J., 1972. pp. 176. *bibliog.*

ANTISEMITISM.

SIMPSON (WILLIAM WYNN) Jews and Christians today: a study in Jewish and Christian relationships. London, 1940. pp. 86. *(Beckly Social Service Lectures. 1940)*

AL-HARDALLO (IBRAHIM) Antisemitism: a changing concept. Khartoum, 1970. pp. 44. *bibliog.*

HERTZBERG (ARTHUR) Anti-semitism and Jewish uniqueness: ancient and contemporary. Syracuse, N.Y., 1973. pp. 20. *(Syracuse University. B.G. Rudolph Lectures in Judaic Studies. 1973)*

— **Germany.**

ANTISEMITEN-Spiegel: die Antisemiten im Lichte des Christenthums, des Rechtes und der Wissenschaft. 2nd ed. Danzig, 1900. pp. 499.

KAHN (SIEGBERT) Antisemitismus und Rassenhetze: eine Übersicht über ihre Entwicklung in Deutschland. Berlin, [1948]. pp. 95. *bibliog.*

REINHARZ (JEHUDA) Fatherland or promised land: the dilemma of the German Jew, 1893-1914. Ann Arbor, [1975]. pp. 328. *bibliog.*

— **Russia.**

FLEGON (ALEC) and NAUMOV (IU.) compilers. Russkii antisemitizm i evrei: sbornik. London, [1968]. pp. 224.

— **United States.**

ADOLESCENT prejudice; [by] Charles Y. Glock [and others]. New York, [1975]. pp. 229. *(California University. Survey Research Center. Five-Year Study of Anti-Semitism in the United States. vol. 7)*

ANTWERP

— **Civilization.**

VOET (LEON) De gouden eeuw van Antwerpen: bloei en uitstraling van de metropool in de zestiende eeuw. Antwerpen, 1974. pp. 487. *bibliog. Maps in end pockets.*

— **Commerce.**

VOET (LEON) De gouden eeuw van Antwerpen: bloei en uitstraling van de metropool in de zestiende eeuw. Antwerpen, 1974. pp. 487. *bibliog. Maps in end pockets.*

— **Social history.**

LAAR (ALBERT VAN) Geschiedenis van de arbeidersbeweging te Antwerpen en omliggende. Antwerpen, 1926; Antwerpen, 1974. pp. 582. *bibliog. Facsimile reprint.*

ANXIETY.

SPIELBERGER (CHARLES DONALD) and SARASON (IRWIN GERALD) eds. Stress and anxiety. Washington, [1975]. 2 vols. *bibliogs.*

APARTMENT HOUSES

— **France.**

CENTRE DE RECHERCHES ET DE DOCUMENTATION SUR LA CONSOMMATION. Contribution sociologique en vue d'une nouvelle législation sur la copropriété dan les grands ensembles immobiliers, etc. Paris, 1975. 2 vols.

APHASIA.

INTELLIGENCE and aphasia; [edited by] Yvan Lebrun and Richard Hoops. Amsterdam, 1974. pp. 139. *bibliog. Based on an international conference held in Brussels in 1973, sponsored by the Contact Group Neurolinguistics of the Belgian Foundation for Medical Scientific Research and others.*

LINGUISTICS: an international review. 154/155. Special issue: linguistic aspects of aphasia. The Hague, 1975. pp. 176. *bibliogs.*

BUCKINGHAM (HUGH W.) and KERTESZ (ANDREW) Neologistic jargon aphasia. Amsterdam, 1976. pp. 100. *bibliog.*

APINAGE INDIANS.

NIMUENDAJÚ (CURT) The Apinaye ; translated by Robert H. Lowie; edited by Robert H. Lowie and John M. Cooper. Oosterhout, 1967. pp. 189. *bibliog. Photomechanic reprint of the 1939 edition.*

APPALACHIAN MOUNTAINS

— Economic policy.

APPALACHIA; [pd. by] Appalachian Regional Commission. bi-m., Je/Jl 1975 (v.8, no.6)- , with gap (Ag/S 1975, v.9, no.1). Washington D.C.

— Social policy.

APPALACHIA; [pd. by] Appalachian Regional Commission. bi-m., Je/Jl 1975 (v.8, no.6)- , with gap (Ag/S 1975, v.9, no.1). Washington D.C.

APPELLATE PROCEDURE

— Austria.

EUROPEAN COMMISSION OF HUMAN RIGHTS. 1965. The Plischke case:...[application No. 1446/62 by Oskar Plischke against Austria]. Strasbourg, Council of Europe, 1965. pp. 36.

APPENZELL

— Social history.

NEF (CLARA) Beten, schaffen, danken: eine Familie erlebt Not und Arbeitslosigkeit. Bern, [1974]. pp. 48.

APPRENTICES

— Austria.

POLLITZER (JOHANN) Die Lage der Lehrlinge im Kleingewerbe in Wien. Tübingen, 1900. pp. 132.

ARAB COUNTRIES

— Economic conditions.

CASADIO (GIAN PAOLO) The economic challenge of the Arabs. Farnborough, Hants., [1976]. pp. 216. *bibliog.*

SHERBINY (NAIEM A.) and TESSLER (MARK A.) eds. Arab oil: impact on the Arab countries and global implications. New York, 1976. pp. 327.

— Economic integration.

AL-HAMAD (ABDLATIF Y.) Towards closer economic cooperation in the Middle East: financial aspects. [Kuwait], 1975. pp. 15.

— Economic policy.

ORGANIZATION OF ARAB PETROLEUM EXPORTING COUNTRIES. General Secretariat. Oil and Arab cooperation. q., current issues only. Kuwait. *[In English and Arabic].*

— Foreign economic relations.

CASADIO (GIAN PAOLO) The economic challenge of the Arabs. Farnborough, Hants., [1976]. pp. 216. *bibliog.*

— — European Economic Community countries.

LIEBER (ROBERT J.) Oil and the Middle East war: Europe in the energy crisis. Cambridge, Mass., [1976]. pp. 75. *(Harvard University. Center for International Affairs. Harvard Studies in International Affairs. No. 35)*

— — United States.

AL-HAMAD (ABDLATIF Y.) The Middle East's economic aspirations and the United States. [Kuwait], 1975. pp. 11.

— Foreign opinion.

RADIO FREE EUROPE. Audience and Public Opinion Research Department. East European sympathies in the Arab-Israeli conflict. [Munich?], 1974. fo. 21.

— Foreign relations.

ABDEL-MALEK (ANOUAR) ed. La pensée politique arabe contemporaine: [readings]. 2nd ed. Paris, [1970]. pp. 384. *bibliog.*

— — Egypt.

DAWISHA (ADHID ISAM) Egypt in the Arab world: the elements of foreign policy. London, 1976. pp. 234. *bibliog.*

— — Israel.

DMITRIEV (E.) and LADEIKIN (VLADIMIR PETROVICH) Put' k miru na Blizhnem Vostoke. Moskva, 1974. pp. 248.

— — United States.

STOOKEY (ROBERT W.) America and the Arab states: an uneasy encounter. New York, [1975]. pp. 298. *bibliog.*

— Nationalism.

ISRAEL and the Palestinians; [papers delivered at a conference organized by the Richardson Institute in London in 1974]; edited by Uri Davis [and others]. London, 1975. pp. 409.

GADHAFI (MOAMMAR) The battle of destiny: speeches and interviews. London, 1976. pp. 137.

— — Bibliography.

CLEMENTS (FRANK) compiler. The emergence of Arab nationalism: from the nineteenth century to 1921; [a bibliography]. London, 1976. pp. 290.

— Politics and government.

ABDEL-MALEK (ANOUAR) ed. La pensée politique arabe contemporaine: [readings]. 2nd ed. Paris, [1970]. pp. 384. *bibliog.*

SOCIETY and political structure in the Arab world; edited by Menahem Milson. New York, [1973]. pp. 336. *Articles originally presented at a series of colloquia at the Van Leer Jerusalem Foundation, 1970-71.*

HAZEN (WILLIAM EDWARD) and MUGHISUDDIN (MOHAMMED) Middle Eastern subcultures: a regional approach; [with contributions by] George N. Atiyeh [and others]. Lexington, [1975]. pp. 215. *bibliog.*

— Relations (general) with the Somali Republic.

SOMALI REPUBLIC. Ministry of Information and National Guidance. 1974. Somalia and the Arab League: a wider role in Afro-Arab affairs. Mogadishu, 1974. pp. 45.

— Social conditions.

SOCIETY and political structure in the Arab world; edited by Menahem Milson. New York, [1973]. pp. 336. *Articles originally presented at a series of colloquia at the Van Leer Jerusalem Foundation, 1970-71.*

— Social policy.

ORGANIZATION OF ARAB PETROLEUM EXPORTING COUNTRIES. General Secretariat. Oil and Arab cooperation. q., current issues only. Kuwait. *[In English and Arabic].*

ARAGO (DOMINIQUE FRANÇOIS JEAN).

MIRECOURT (EUGENE DE) pseud. [i.e. Charles Jean Baptiste JACQUOT] François Arago. Paris, G. Havard, 1855. pp. 96. *(Les Contemporains)*

ARAUCANIAN INDIANS.

STUCHLIK (MILAN) Life on a half share: mechanisms of social recruitment among the Mapuche of southern Chile. London, [1976]. pp. 222. *bibliog.*

ARBITRATION, INDUSTRIAL.

The SETTLEMENT of collective disputes in the public services; [papers for discussion at the congress of Public Services International at Paris in 1967]; rapporteur, H.D. Hughes. London, [1967?]. 1 vol. (various pagings).

INTERNATIONAL LABOUR OFFICE. 1973. Conciliation in industrial disputes. Geneva, 1973. pp. 133.

— Australia.

AUSTRALIA. Commonwealth Bureau of Census and Statistics. 1969. Survey of the incidence of industrial awards, determinations and collective agreements, May 1968. Canberra, [1969]. pp. 12.

AUSTRALIA. Department of Labour and National Service. 1971. Conciliation and Arbitration Act: ministerial statement by the Minister for Labour and National Service. [Canberra], 1971. fo. 31.

AUSTRALIA. Committee of Inquiry on Co-ordinated Industrial Organisations. 1974. Report; [John Bernard Sweeney, chairman]. Canberra, 1974. pp. 59.

— United Kingdom.

ADVISORY CONCILIATION AND ARBITRATION SERVICE [U.K.]. Annual report. a., 1975(1st)- London.

U.K. Central Arbitration Committee. Awards. irreg., 1976 (no.1)- London. *Supersedes U.K. Industrial Arbitration Board. Awards.*

— United States.

AARON (BENJAMIN) The settlement of disputes over rights: a comparative view. Los Angeles, 1974. pp. 422-430. *(California University. Institute of Industrial Relations. [Southern Division]. Reprints. No. 247) (Reprinted from Proceedings of the American Philosophical Society, vol. 118, no. 5. 1974)*

BADERSCHNEIDER (EARL R.) and MILLER (PAUL F.) eds. Labor arbitration in health care: a case book. New York, [1976]. pp. 323.

ARBITRATION, INTERNATIONAL

— Congresses.

INTERNATIONAL CONFERENCE OF WOMEN WORKERS TO PROMOTE PERMANENT PEACE, SAN FRANCISCO, 1915. Women, world war and permanent peace; [edited by May Wright Sewall. San Francisco, 1915; Westport, Conn., 1976. pp. 206.

ARBITRATION AND AWARD

— Yugoslavia.

ARBITRAŽNO rešavanje sporova o arbitraži njenoj pravnoj prirodi i arbitražnom ugovoru, postupak izbranog suda, priznanje i izvršenje stranih arbitražnih odluka. Novi Sad, 1973. pp. 210. *bibliog.*

ARCHAEOLOGY, INDUSTRIAL

— United Kingdom.

GEORGE (ANTHONY DAVID) The industrial archaeology of Preston. [Manchester, 1974]. pp. 8.

BUCHANAN (R.A.) and WATKINS (GEORGE) The industrial archaeology of the stationary steam engine. London, 1976. pp. 199. *bibliog.*

— — Wales.

JOHN (BRIAN S.) Old industries of Pembrokeshire. Lanchester, [1975]. pp. 28. *bibliog.*

ARCHITECTURE

ARCHITECTURE

— Psychological aspects.

DEASY (CORNELIUS MICHAEL) Design for human affairs. New York, [1974]. pp. 183. *bibliog.*

— United Kingdom — Conservation and restoration.

DOCKLANDS JOINT COMMITTEE. Docklands Development Team. Conservation and the role of the river. London, 1975. pp. 48. *(Working Papers for Consultation. 8)*

DEVELOPMENT CONTROL POLICY NOTES. 7. Preservation of historic buildings and areas. [rev. ed.] London, H.M.S.O., 1976. pp. (2). *bibliog.*

ARCHITECTURE, DOMESTIC

— United Kingdom.

DARLEY (GILLIAN) Villages of vision. London, 1975. pp. 152. *bibliog.*

ARCHITECTURE AND SOCIETY.

DEASY (CORNELIUS MICHAEL) Design for human affairs. New York, [1974]. pp. 183. *bibliog.*

TAFURI (MANFREDO) Architecture and utopia: design and capitalist development;... translated from the Italian by Barbara Luigia La Penta. Cambridge, Mass., [1976]. pp. 184.

ARCHIVES

— Canada.

CANADA. Public Archives. 1972. Archives: mirror of Canada past. [Ottawa], 1972. pp. 313. *In English and French.*

— Europe.

THOMAS (DANIEL HARRISON) and CASE (LYNN MARSHALL) eds. The new guide to the diplomatic archives of western Europe. [Philadelphia, 1975]. pp. 441. *bibliogs.*

— Mexico.

GARCIA Y GARCIA (J. JESUS) Guia de archivos: contiene material de interes para el estudio del desarrollo socioeconomico de Mexico. Mexico, 1972. pp. 187. *bibliog.*

— United Kingdom.

NOTTINGHAM. University. Library. Manuscripts Department. Tenth report of the Keeper of the manuscripts [for] October 1971-September 1974. Nottingham, [1974]. pp. 42.

— United States.

CONFERENCE ON THE NATIONAL ARCHIVES AND FOREIGN RELATIONS RESEARCH, WASHINGTON, 1969. The National Archives and foreign relations research: (papers and proceedings of the Conference...sponsored by the National Archives and Records Service); edited by Milton O. Gustafson. Athens, Ohio, [1974]. pp. 292. *(United States. National Archives. National Archives Conferences. vol. 4)*

ARENDARENKO (GEORGII ALEKSEEVICH).

ARENDARENKO (GEORGII ALEKSEEVICH) Bukhara i Afganistan v nachale 80-kh godov XIX veka: zhurnaly komandirovok G.A. Arendarenko; [redaktsionnaia kollegiia B.G. Gafurov (and others)]. Moskva, 1974. pp. 142.

ARENDT (HANNAH).

CANOVAN (MARGARET) The political thought of Hannah Arendt. London, 1974. pp. 136. *bibliog.*

ARGENTINE REPUBLIC

— Economic conditions.

DESARROLLO sin dependencia; [by] Aldo Ferrer [and others]; Tulio R. Rosembuj, compilador. Buenos Aires, 1974. pp. 193. *Consists mainly of contributions to a symposium of the same title held in 1973 in the Facultad de Derecho y Ciencias Sociales [of the University of Buenos Aires?].*

ROFMAN (ALEJANDRO BORIS) Dependencia, estructura de poder y formacion regional en America Latina. Buenos Aires, 1974. pp. 262.

— Economic history.

FERRER (ALDO) The Argentine economy;...translated by Marjory M. Urquidi. Berkeley, 1967. pp. 239.

PINEDO (FEDERICO) La Argentina en un cono de sombra. Buenos Aires, 1968. pp. 248.

ESTUDIOS sobre los origenes del peronismo; [by] Miguel Murmis [and others]. Buenos Aires, 1971-73. 2 vols. (in 1). *Vol. 1 reprinted in 1972.*

CARRETERO (ANDRES M.) Liberalismo y dependencia. Buenos Aires, 1975. pp. 381. *bibliogs.*

— Economic policy.

FERRER (ALDO) The Argentine economy;...translated by Marjory M. Urquidi. Berkeley, 1967. pp. 239.

ARGENTINE REPUBLIC. Ministerio de Economia y Trabajo. 1968. Argentina building for the future: economic programme for 1968. [Buenos Aires], 1968. pp. 102. *Map in end pocket.*

ARGENTINE REPUBLIC. Ministerio de Economia y Trabajo. 1968. La Argentina construye: programa economico para 1968. [Buenos Aires], 1968. pp. 102.

PINEDO (FEDERICO) La Argentina en un cono de sombra. Buenos Aires, 1968. pp. 248.

DESARROLLO sin dependencia; [by] Aldo Ferrer [and others]; Tulio R. Rosembuj, compilador. Buenos Aires, 1974. pp. 193. *Consists mainly of contributions to a symposium of the same title held in 1973 in the Facultad de Derecho y Ciencias Sociales [of the University of Buenos Aires?].*

ARGENTINE REPUBLIC. Statutes, etc. 1973-74. Legislacion economica: (politica economica para la reconstruccion y la liberacion nacional). Buenos Aires, 1975. pp. 225.

— Emigration and immigration.

ALSINA (JUAN A.) La immigracion en el primer siglo de la independencia. Buenos Aires, 1910. pp. 230.

BOURDE (GUY) Urbanisation et immigration en Amérique Latine: Buenos Aires, XIXe et XXe siècles. Paris, 1974. pp. 288. *bibliog.*

— Foreign economic relations.

ROFMAN (ALEJANDRO BORIS) Dependencia, estructura de poder y formacion regional en America Latina. Buenos Aires, 1974. pp. 262.

— Foreign relations.

FITTE (ERNESTO J.) Martin Garcia: historia de una isla argentina. Buenos Aires, [1971]. pp. 209.

— History.

PERELMAN (ANGEL) Como hicimos el 17 de octubre. Buenos Aires, 1961. pp. 80.

HALPERIN DONGHI (TULIO) Politics, economics and society in Argentina in the revolutionary period;...translated by Richard Southern. Cambridge, 1975. pp. 425. *bibliog.*

— — 1860–1910.

CARRETERO (ANDRES M.) Liberalismo y dependencia. Buenos Aires, 1975. pp. 381. *bibliogs.*

— — 1910–1943.

FALCOFF (MARK) and DOLKART (RONALD H.) eds. Prologue to Peron: Argentina in depression and war, 1930-1943. Berkeley, [1975]. pp. 236. *bibliog.*

— Industries.

ACUMULACION y centralizacion del capital en la industria argentina; [by] Elsa Cimillo [and others]. Buenos Aires, [1973]. pp. 191.

ARGENTINE REPUBLIC. Instituto Nacional de Estadistica y Censos. Indicadores industriales. q., 1975(serie 1, no.1)- Buenos Aires.

— Politics and government.

ESTUDIOS sobre los origenes del peronismo; [by] Miguel Murmis [and others]. Buenos Aires, 1971-73. 2 vols. (in 1). *Vol. 1 reprinted in 1972.*

PAVON PEREYRA (ENRIQUE) Peron tal como es. [Buenos Aires], 1973. pp. 341.

PERON (JUAN DOMINGO) Seleccion de sus escritos, conferencias y discursos. Buenos Aires, [1973]. pp. 301.

ALBERTI (BLAS MANUEL) Peronismo, burocracia y burguesia nacional; apendice documental con texto de Marx y Le Duan. [Buenos Aires, 1974]. pp. 248. *Articles originally published in the periodicals Lucha Obrera and Izquierda Nacional.*

HALPERIN DONGHI (TULIO) Politics, economics and society in Argentina in the revolutionary period;...translated by Richard Southern. Cambridge, 1975. pp. 425. *bibliog.*

— Race question.

DICKMANN (ENRIQUE) Contra el odio de razas y la persecucion religiosa. Buenos Aires, 1943. pp. 61.

ARHUACO INDIANS.

FRIEDE (JUAN) La explotacion indigena en Colombia bajo el gobierno de las misiones: el caso de los aruacos de la Sierra Nevada de Santa Marta. 2nd ed. Bogota, [1973]. pp. 184. *bibliog.*

ARHUS.

See AARHUS.

ARID REGIONS

— Spain.

THORNES (JOHN B.) Semi-arid erosional systems: case studies from Spain. London, 1976. pp. 79. *bibliog. (London. University. London School of Economics and Political Science. Department of Geography. Geographical Papers. No. 7)*

ARISTOTLE.

ARISTOTLE. Posterior analytics; translated with notes by Jonathan Barnes. Oxford, 1975. pp. 277. *bibliog.*

ROSEN (FREDERICK) The political context of Aristotle's categories of justice. [Assen], 1975. pp. 12. *(Reprint from Phronesis, vol. 20, no. 3, 1975)*

ARIZONA

— Economic conditions.

MOORE AND WEST ECONOMIC RESEARCH INCORPORATED. The economy of Arizona: a review of Arizona's population, labor force, industries and economic outlook. [Phoenix], Employment Security Commission of Arizona, 1970. pp. 36.

— Economic policy.

ARIZONA. Planning Division. 1969. Comprehensive state planning in Arizona: a concept and work program: summary report;...assisted by Harold F.Wise and Associates, Incorporated. [Phoenix], 1969. pp. 66.

ARIZONA. Planning Division. 1971. Planning coordination in Arizona: a suggested system. [Phoenix], 1971. pp. 39.

ARIZONA. Planning Division. 1971. Status of planning in Arizona. [Phoenix], 1971. pp. 110.

— Social policy.

ARIZONA. Planning Division. 1969. Comprehensive state planning in Arizona: a concept and work program: summary report;...assisted by Harold F.Wise and Associates, Incorporated. [Phoenix], 1969. pp. 66.

ARIZONA. Planning Division. 1971. Planning coordination in Arizona: a suggested system. [Phoenix], 1971. pp. 39.

ARIZONA. Planning Division. 1971. Status of planning in Arizona. [Phoenix], 1971. pp. 110.

ARKHANGEL'SK (OBLAST')

— Statistics.

ARKHANGEL'SK (OBLAST'). Statisticheskoe Upravlenie. Narodnoe khoziaistvo Arkhangel'skoi oblasti v tsifrakh: statisticheskii sbornik. Arkhangel'sk, 1972. pp. 224.

ARMAMENTS.

CONFERENCE OF GOVERNMENT EXPERTS ON THE USE OF CERTAIN CONVENTIONAL WEAPONS, LUCERNE, 1974. Report [of the conference convened by the International Committee of the Red Cross]. Geneva, 1975. pp. 106.

LISTVINOV (IURII NIKOLAEVICH) Obychnoe oruzhie v iadernom veke: amerikanskie kontseptsii vedeniia lokal'nykh voin. Moskva, 1975. pp. 143.

STOCKHOLM INTERNATIONAL PEACE RESEARCH INSTITUTE. Arms uncontrolled...; prepared by Frank Barnaby and Ronald Huisken. Cambridge, Mass., 1975. pp. 232. *bibliog.*

ARMAND (EMILE) pseud.

E. Armand: sa vie, sa pensée, son oeuvre; avec de larges extraits de ses écrits, des essais et commentaires de divers auteurs, de nombreux documents...et une vaste bibliographie. Paris, 1964. pp. 496. *bibliog.*

ARMAND (INESSA FEDOROVNA).

ARMAND (INESSA FEDOROVNA) Stat'i, rechi, pis'ma. Moskva, 1975. pp. 287.

ARMED FORCES.

AMMINISTRAZIONE DELLA DIFESA, L': pubblicazione trimestrale edita dal Servizio Pubblica Informazione del Ministero della Difesa [Italy]. q., Mr 1968 (1)- , with gap (Ja 1971). Roma.

The MILITARY and the problem of legitimacy: edited by Gwyn Harries-Jenkins and Jacques van Doorn. London, [1976]. pp. 213. *bibliog. Papers of sessions of the Research Committee on Armed Forces and Society held during the 8th World Congress of Sociology, Toronto, 1974.*

— Political activity.

SOLDIERS as statesmen; [based on papers presented at a symposium held at the Royal Military College of Canada, Kingston, Ontario in 1975]; edited by Peter Dennis and Adrian Preston. London, 1976. pp. 184. *bibliogs.*

ARMENIA

— History — Sources.

SOVETSKAIA Armeniia v gody Velikoi Otechestvennoi voiny, 1941- 1945: sbornik dokumentov i materialov. Erevan, 1975. pp. 838.

ARMENIAN QUESTION.

CARZOU (JEAN MARIE) Un génocide exemplaire: Arménie 1915. Paris, [1975]. pp. 252.

STEPANIAN (STEPAN SMBATOVICH) Armeniia v politike imperialisticheskoi Germanii, konets XIX - nachalo XX veka. Erevan, 1975. pp. 243. *bibliog.*

ARMENIANS IN THE CRIMEA.

MIKAELIAN (VARDGES ALEKSANDROVICH) Na Krymskoi zemle: istoriia armianskikh poselenii v Krymu. Erevan, 1974. pp. 210.

ARMENIANS IN TURKEY.

CARZOU (JEAN MARIE) Un génocide exemplaire: Arménie 1915. Paris, [1975]. pp. 252.

ARNDT FAMILY.

ARNDT (NIKOLAUS) Die Shitomirer Arndts: eine Familienchronik auf dem Hintergrund hundertfünfzigjähriger Geschichte der westlichen Ukraine. Würzburg, [1970]. pp. 151. *bibliog.*

ARREST

— Canada.

CANADA. [Department of Justice]. 1971. Manual respecting the authority and duties of peace officers in relation to arrest and pre-trial release and detention of accused persons. [Ottawa, 1971]. pp. 23.

— Poland.

MURZYNOWSKI (ANDRZEJ) Areszt tymczasowy oraz inne środki zapobiegające uchylaniu się od sądu. Warszawa, 1963. pp. 293. *bibliog.*

ARSENALS

— Canada.

CANADIAN ARSENALS LIMITED. Canadian Arsenals Limited. Ottawa, 1969. pp. 40.

ART

— Collectors and collecting.

HASKELL (FRANCIS) Rediscoveries in art: some aspects of taste, fashion and collecting in England and France. London, 1976. pp. 246. *bibliog. (New York (City). University. Institute of Fine Arts. Wrightsman Lectures. 1973)*

— History.

GOMBRICH (Sir ERNST HANS) Art history and the social sciences. Oxford, 1975. pp. 60. *(Oxford. University. Romanes Lectures. 1973)*

— Canada — Galleries and museums.

CANADA. Statistics Canada. Cultural Information Section. 1972. Museums, art galleries and related institutions...1970. Ottawa, 1972. pp. 70. *In English and French.*

— Mexico.

SIQUEIROS (DAVID ALFARO) Art and revolution. London, 1975. pp. 224.

ART, BULGARIAN.

VASILIEV (ASEN) Sotsialni i patriotichni temi v staroto bulgarsko izkustvo. Sofiia, 1973. pp. 156. *With French and Russian summaries.*

ART AND SOCIETY.

ZETKIN (CLARA) Über Literatur und Kunst: [selected articles, originally published in "Die Gleichheit", 1906-1911]; zusammengestellt und herausgegeben von Emilia Zetkin-Milowidowa. Berlin, 1955. pp. 115.

VASILIEV (ASEN) Sotsialni i patriotichni temi v staroto bulgarsko izkustvo. Sofiia, 1973. pp. 156. *With French and Russian summaries.*

SIQUEIROS (DAVID ALFARO) Art and revolution. London, 1975. pp. 224.

ART PATRONAGE

— United Kingdom.

REDCLIFFE-MAUD (JOHN PRIMATT REDCLIFFE) Baron Redcliffe-Maud. Support for the arts in England and Wales: a report to the Calouste Gulbenkian Foundation. London, 1976. pp. 201.

— United States.

LEVINE (FAYE) The culture barons. New York, [1976]. pp. 312.

ARTIFICIAL INSEMINATION.

GOA, DAMAN AND DIU. Bureau of Economics, Statistics and Evaluation. 1975. An evaluation of the key village scheme in Goa. Panaji, 1975. pp. 59. *(Evaluation Reports. No. 15)*

ARTIFICIAL INTELLIGENCE.

REPRESENTATION and understanding: studies in cognitive science: [based on a conference in memory of Jaime Carbonell; edited by Daniel G. Bobrow and Allan Collins. New York, 1975. pp. 427. *bibliogs.*

ARTIFICIAL SATELLITES IN TELECOMMUNICATION.

BATTLE (LUCIUS D.) Communications and the economy: communications and peace. Cairo, 1975. pp. 13. *(National Bank of Egypt. Diamond Jubilee Lectures)*

KINSLEY (MICHAEL E.) Outer space and inner sanctums: government, business, and satellite communication. New York, [1976]. pp. 280.

— Economic aspects.

SNOW (MARCELLUS S.) International commercial satellite communications: economic and political issues of the first decade of INTELSAT. New York, 1976. pp. 170. *bibliog.*

ARTISANS

— Finland.

REMESLO i manufaktura v Rossii, Finliandii, Pribaltike: materialy II sovetsko-finskogo simpoziuma po sotsial'no-ekonomicheskoi istorii, 13-14 dekabria 1972 g. Leningrad, 1975. pp. 199. *With Finnish and German summaries and tables of contents.*

— France.

PARTI COMMUNISTE FRANÇAIS. Artisans, commerçants: comment se defendre. Paris, [1954]. pp. 31.

FRANCE. Commission du Commerce, des Services et de l'Artisanat. 1976. Rapport...: préparation du 7e Plan. Paris, 1976. pp. 156.

— Germany — Berlin.

BERGMANN (JUERGEN) Das Berliner Handwerk in den Frühphasen der Industrialisierung. Berlin, 1973. pp. 401. *bibliog. (Historische Kommission zu Berlin. Einzelveröffentlichungen. Band 11)*

— Greece, Ancient.

FRONTISI-DUCROUX (FRANÇOISE) Dédale: mythologie de l'artisan en Grèce ancienne. Paris, 1975. pp. 227.

— Italy.

SANTUCCI (MARIO) ed. L'artigianato in Abruzzo. L'Aquila, 1974. pp. 157. *(Centro Regionale di Studi e Ricerche per lo Sviluppo Economico e Sociale dell'Abruzzo. Collana di Studi Economici. 4)*

— Russia.

REMESLO i manufaktura v Rossii, Finliandii, Pribaltike: materialy II sovetsko-finskogo simpoziuma po sotsial'no-ekonomicheskoi istorii, 13-14 dekabria 1972 g. Leningrad, 1975. pp. 199. *With Finnish and German summaries and tables of contents.*

ARTISANS (Cont.)

— United Kingdom.

ASSOCIATION OF PATTERN MAKERS AND ALLIED CRAFTSMEN. Birkenhead Branch. [Minute book. 1885-91]. 1 vol. *Manuscript.*

ARTS

— Economic aspects.

BLAUG (MARK) ed. The economics of the arts. London, 1976. pp. 272.

— Psychology.

PSYCHANALYSE et sociologie comme méthodes d'étude des phénomènes historiques et culturels: (volume II de Critique sociologique et critique psychanalytique); publié conjointement par l'Institut de Sociologie de l'Université Libre de Bruxelles et l'Ecole Pratique des Hautes Etudes, 6e section. ..; [edited by Brigitte Navelet and Jacques Leenhardt]. Bruxelles, [1973]. pp. 185. *bibliog. (Brussels. Université Libre. Institut de Sociologie. Etudes de Sociologie de la Littérature)*

— Poland.

DYSKURS o tradycji: z zagadnień współczesnej kultury artystycznej w Polsce i ZSRR; materiały wspólnego sympozjum na temat "Znaczenie narodowych i ludowych tradycji we współczesnej sztuce Polski i ZSRR". Wrocław, 1974. pp. 380.

— Russia.

DYSKURS o tradycji: z zagadnień współczesnej kultury artystycznej w Polsce i ZSRR; materiały wspólnego sympozjum na temat "Znaczenie narodowych i ludowych tradycji we współczesnej sztuce Polski i ZSRR". Wrocław, 1974. pp. 380.

— — Kazakstan.

SALIEV (A.) ed. Natsional'noe i internatsional'noe v iskusstve. Frunze, 1973. pp. 253.

— — Kirghizia.

SALIEV (A.) ed. Natsional'noe i internatsional'noe v iskusstve. Frunze, 1973. pp. 253.

— United Kingdom.

KHAN (NASEEM) The arts Britain ignores: the arts of ethnic minorities in Britain;...sponsored by Arts Council of Great Britain, Calouste Gulbenkian Foundation and Community Relations Commission. [London, Community Relations Commission], 1976. pp. 175.

— United States — Management.

LEVINE (FAYE) The culture barons. New York, [1976]. pp. 312.

ARTS AND HISTORY.

GULYGA (ARSENII VLADIMIROVICH) Estetika istorii. Moskva, 1974. pp. 128.

ASBEST.

NIKITIN (PAVEL VASIL'EVICH) and RUBTSOV (NIKOLAI FEDOROVICH) Gorod gornogo l'na: ocherki po istorii Asbesta. 2nd ed. Sverdlovsk, 1970. pp. 164.

ASBESTOS INDUSTRY

— Germany.

PEFFGEN (ELFRIED) Die gummi- und asbestverarbeitende Industrie aus der Sicht der siebziger Jahre. Berlin, [1976]. pp. 98. *(Ifo-Institut für Wirtschaftsforschung. Struktur und Wachstum. Reihe Industrie. Heft 27)*

— Russia.

NIKITIN (PAVEL VASIL'EVICH) and RUBTSOV (NIKOLAI FEDOROVICH) Gorod gornogo l'na: ocherki po istorii Asbesta. 2nd ed. Sverdlovsk, 1970. pp. 164.

ASHTON (THOMAS SOUTHCLIFFE).

ASHTON (THOMAS SOUTHCLIFFE) [Unpublished historical papers and notes. 1927-62]. 20 pieces. *Manuscript, typescript, etc.*

ASIA

— Armed forces — Political activity.

SYMPOSIUM ON MILITARY AND STATE IN MODERN ASIA, JERUSALEM, 1974. Military and state in modern Asia; (Harold Z. Schiffrin, editor). Jerusalem, 1976. pp. 309. *(Hebrew University. Harry S. Truman Research Institute. Truman Institute Studies. Asia Series)*

— Commerce.

APO NEWS (formerly Asian productivity: m. bulletin); pd by Asian Productivity Organization. m., Ja 1969 - My 1971 (v.9, no.1 - v.11, no.5); Je 1971 ([n. s.] v.1, no.1)- with gap (Oc - D 1971; [n.s.] v.1, nos.5- 7). Tokyo.

ASIA and the western Pacific: towards a new international order; edited by Hedley Bull. Melbourne, 1975. pp. 385. *Papers of a conference organized by the Australian Institute of International Affairs at the Australian National University, Canberra, in 1973.*

— — European Economic Community countries.

TULLOCH (PETER) The seven outside: Commonwealth Asia's trade with the enlarged EEC. London, [1973]. pp. 67. *bibliog.*

— Description and travel.

MENDÈS-FRANCE (PIERRE) Face to face with Asia; translated from the French by Susan Danon. New York, [1974]. pp. 255.

— Economic conditions.

ASIAN INDUSTRIAL DEVELOPMENT NEWS; (pd. by] Asian Industrial Development Council, Economic Commission for Asia and the Far East...United Nations). a.(formerly s-a.,) 1967 (no.2)- Bangkok.

INCOME distribution, employment and economic development in Southeast and East Asia: papers and proceedings of the seminar sponsored jointly by the Japan Economic Research Center and the Council for Asian Manpower Studies...1974; with contribution from the ILO World Employment Programme. Tokyo, 1975. pp. 791.

— Economic history.

KRADER (LAWRENCE) The Asiatic mode of production: sources, development and critique in the writings of Karl Marx. Assen, 1975. pp. 454. *bibliog. Including excerpts taken by Marx from the work of M.M. Kovalevskii, with Marx's notes thereon.*

— Economic policy.

ASIAN INDUSTRIAL DEVELOPMENT NEWS; (pd. by] Asian Industrial Development Council, Economic Commission for Asia and the Far East...United Nations). a.(formerly s-a.,) 1967 (no.2)- Bangkok.

APO NEWS (formerly Asian productivity: m. bulletin); pd by Asian Productivity Organization. m., Ja 1969 - My 1971 (v.9, no.1 - v.11, no.5); Je 1971 ([n. s.] v.1, no.1)- with gap (Oc - D 1971; [n.s.] v.1, nos.5- 7). Tokyo.

ASIA and the western Pacific: towards a new international order; edited by Hedley Bull. Melbourne, 1975. pp. 385. *Papers of a conference organized by the Australian Institute of International Affairs at the Australian National University, Canberra, in 1973.*

ASIAN DEVELOPMENT INSITUTE. Quarterly newsletter. q., (formerly bi-m.). Bangkok. *Current issues only kept.*

— Foreign relations.

ASIA and the western Pacific: towards a new international order; edited by Hedley Bull. Melbourne, 1975. pp. 385. *Papers of a conference organized by the Australian Institute of International Affairs at the Australian National University, Canberra, in 1973.*

CHOUDHURY (GOLAM WAHED) India, Pakistan, Bangladesh, and the major powers: politics of a divided subcontinent. New York, [1975]. pp. 276. *bibliog. (Foreign Policy Research Institute. Book Series)*

INTERNATIONAL SYMPOSIUM ON THE INTERNATIONAL ENVIRONMENT IN POSTWAR ASIA, KYOTO, 1974. Papers...prepared for the...symposium...; sponsored by the Ministry of Education [and] the Japan Foundation. Tokyo, [1975?]. 2 vols.(in 1). *(Tokyo Institute of Technology. Basic Studies on the International Environment)*

LACH (DONALD FREDERICK) and WEHRLE (EDMUND S.) International politics in East Asia since World War II. New York, 1975. pp. 388.

SCALAPINO (ROBERT A.) Asia and the road ahead: issues for the major powers. Berkeley, [1975]. pp. 337. *bibliog.*

— — Japan.

LEBRA (JOYCE CHAPMAN) ed. Japan's Greater East Asia Co-Prosperity Sphere in World War II: selected readings and documents. Kuala Lumpur, 1975. pp. 212. *bibliog.*

— — United States.

SIMON (SHELDON W.) Asian neutralism and U.S. policy. Washington, 1975. pp. 111. *(American Enterprise Institute for Public Policy Research. Foreign Affairs Studies. 21)*

— Industries.

ASIAN INDUSTRIAL DEVELOPMENT NEWS; (pd. by] Asian Industrial Development Council, Economic Commission for Asia and the Far East...United Nations). a.(formerly s-a.,) 1967 (no.2)- Bangkok.

— Politics and government.

MENDÈS-FRANCE (PIERRE) Face to face with Asia; translated from the French by Susan Danon. New York, [1974]. pp. 255.

ASIA and the western Pacific: towards a new international order; edited by Hedley Bull. Melbourne, 1975. pp. 385. *Papers of a conference organized by the Australian Institute of International Affairs at the Australian National University, Canberra, in 1973.*

INTERNATIONAL SYMPOSIUM ON THE INTERNATIONAL ENVIRONMENT IN POSTWAR ASIA, KYOTO, 1974. Papers...prepared for the...symposium...; sponsored by the Ministry of Education [and] the Japan Foundation. Tokyo, [1975?]. 2 vols.(in 1). *(Tokyo Institute of Technology. Basic Studies on the International Environment)*

LACH (DONALD FREDERICK) and WEHRLE (EDMUND S.) International politics in East Asia since World War II. New York, 1975. pp. 388.

SCALAPINO (ROBERT A.) Asia and the road ahead: issues for the major powers. Berkeley, [1975]. pp. 337. *bibliog.*

— Population.

UNITED NATIONS. Economic and Social Commission for Asia and the Pacific. Asian Population Studies Series. New York, 1966 in progress.

ASIAN POPULATION PROGRAMME NEWS; [pd. by] Population Division, United Nations Economic Commission for Asia and the Far East. irreg., spring 1971 (v.1[no.1])- Bangkok.

— Religion.

SMITH (BARDWELL L.) ed. Religion and social conflict in south Asia. Leiden, 1976. pp. 115.

— Social conditions.

SYMPOSIUM ON SOCIOLOGY AND SOCIAL DEVELOPMENT IN ASIA, TOKYO, 1973. Sociology and social development in Asia: proceedings of the symposium [organized by the Japan Sociological Society in collaboration with the Japanese National Commission for Unesco]; edited by Tadashi Fukutake [and] Kiyomi Morioka. Tokyo, [1974]. pp. 447.

ASIAN social problems: new strategies for social work education; proceedings of the third Asian regional seminar, "Development of teaching resources and interdisciplinary communication", held August 25-30, 1975, in Hong Kong; [edited by] Mary B. Garcia and Andrij Witiuk. New York, 1976. pp. 168. *Sponsored by the International Association of Schools of Social Work.*

SMITH (BARDWELL L.) ed. Religion and social conflict in south Asia. Leiden, 1976. pp. 115.

— Statistics — Directories.

HARVEY (JOAN M.) Statistics Asia and Australasia: sources for market research. Beckenham, Kent, 1974. pp. 238.

— Statistics, Vital.

UNITED NATIONS. Economic and Social Commission for Asia and the Pacific. Asian Population Studies Series. New York, 1966 in progress.

ASIA, SOUTHEAST.

SPECTRUM; (pd. by) South-East Asia Treaty Organization. q., Ja 1973 (v.1, no.2)- Bangkok.

— Armed forces — Political activity.

HOADLEY (J. STEPHEN) Soldiers and politics in southeast Asia: civil-military relations in comparative perspective. Cambridge, Mass., [1975]. pp. 307.

— Economic conditions.

CONFERENCE ON POLITICS, SOCIETY AND ECONOMY IN THE ASEAN STATES, HAMBURG, 1974. Politics, society and economy in the ASEAN states; [papers presented at the conference]; Bernhard Dahm, Werner Draguhn. eds. Wiesbaden, [1975]. pp. 321. *bibliogs.*

INTERNATIONAL CONFERENCE ON ECONOMIC DEVELOPMENT OF SOUTHEAST ASIA, KYOTO, 1972. The economic development of East and Southeast Asia; edited by Shinichi Ichimura. Honolulu, 1975. pp. 398. *bibliogs. (Kyoto. University. Center for Southeast Asian Studies. Monographs: English Series. 7) Sponsored by Kyoto University Center for Southeast Asian Studies and Kansai Economic Research Center.*

— Foreign relations.

WILSON (RICHARD GARRATT) The neutralization of Southeast Asia. New York, 1975. pp. 206.

— — Portugal.

PFISTER (JAMES W.) The compulsion to war: a quantitative exploration of remote international relations. Beverly Hills, [1974]. pp. 82. *bibliog.*

— — United Kingdom.

TARLING (NICHOLAS) Imperial Britain in South-east Asia; [articles]. Kuala Lumpur, 1975. pp. 273. *Revisions of articles previously published in various journals.*

— History.

CADY (JOHN FRANK) The history of post-war Southeast Asia. Athens, Ohio, [1974]. pp. 720. *bibliog.*

PLUVIER (JAN M.) South-east Asia from colonialism to independence. Kuala Lumpur, 1974. pp. 571. *bibliog.*

— Neutrality.

WILSON (RICHARD GARRATT) The neutralization of Southeast Asia. New York, 1975. pp. 206.

— Politics and government.

BLOODWORTH (DENNIS) An eye for the dragon: South-East Asia observed, 1954-73. Harmondsworth, 1975. pp. 440. *bibliog.*

CONFERENCE ON POLITICS, SOCIETY AND ECONOMY IN THE ASEAN STATES, HAMBURG, 1974. Politics, society and economy in the ASEAN states; [papers presented at the conference]; Bernhard Dahm, Werner Draguhn. eds. Wiesbaden, [1975]. pp. 321. *bibliogs.*

HOADLEY (J. STEPHEN) Soldiers and politics in southeast Asia: civil-military relations in comparative perspective. Cambridge, Mass., [1975]. pp. 307.

— Population.

POPULATION and development in southeast Asia; edited by John F. Kantner [and] Lee McCaffrey. Lexington, Mass., [1975]. pp. 323. *bibliogs. Papers presented at three seminars on population growth and development in southeast Asia organized by the Population Panel of the Southeast Asia Development Advisory Group.*

— Social conditions.

BLOODWORTH (DENNIS) An eye for the dragon: South-East Asia observed, 1954-73. Harmondsworth, 1975. pp. 440. *bibliog.*

CONFERENCE ON POLITICS, SOCIETY AND ECONOMY IN THE ASEAN STATES, HAMBURG, 1974. Politics, society and economy in the ASEAN states; [papers presented at the conference]; Bernhard Dahm, Werner Draguhn. eds. Wiesbaden, [1975]. pp. 321. *bibliogs.*

ASIAN DEVELOPMENT BANK.

FRANCE. Direction de la Documentation. La Documentation Française. Notes et Etudes Documentaires. No. 4,138. La Banque asiatique de développement; (par [Yves] Fievet). Paris, 1974. pp. 39.

ASIAN DEVELOPMENT BANK. Quarterly review (formerly Quarterly newsletter). q. Rizal. *Current issues only kept.*

ASIATICS IN THE UNITED KINGDOM.

TAYLOR (JOHN HENRY) The half-way generation: a study of Asian youths in Newcastle upon Tyne. Windsor, Berks., 1976. pp. 267. *bibliog.*

ASOCIACION CATOLICA NACIONAL DE PROPAGANDISTAS.

SAEZ ALBA (A.) La otra "Cosa Nostra": la Asociacion Catolica Nacional de Propagandistas y el caso de 'El Correo' de Andalucia. Paris, [1974]. pp. 325.

ASPARAGUS.

KING (PATRICIA) The market for asparagus in selected western European countries. London, Tropical Products Institute, 1975. pp. 36. *([Reports]. G101)*

ASQUITH (HERBERT HENRY) 1st Earl of Oxford and Asquith.

ELIAS (FRANK) The Right Hon.H.H. Asquith, M.P.: a biography and appreciation. London, 1909. pp. 248.

ASSASSINATION

— Austria.

WUERTHLE (FRIEDRICH) Die Spur führt nach Belgrad: die Hintergründe des Dramas von Sarajevo, 1914. Wien, [1975]. pp. 352.

— South Africa.

SCHOEMAN (B.M.) Die sluipmoord op Dr. Verwoerd. Pretoria, 1975. pp. 148.

— United States.

MEUNIER (ROBERT F.) Shadows of doubt: the Warren Commission cover-up. Hicksville, N.Y., [1976]. pp. 165. *bibliog.*

ASSAULT AND BATTERY

— United Kingdom.

GILL (TESS) and COOTE (ANNA) Battered women: how to use the law. London, 1975. pp. 23.

ASSEMBLY-LINE METHODS.

GOLDMANN (ROBERT B.) A work experiment: six Americans in a Swedish plant. New York, [1976]. pp. 48.

ASSOCIATION OF CHILD CARE OFFICERS.

JACKA (ALAN ASHBY) The A.C.C.O. story: a personal account of the history of the Association of Child Care Officers...1948-1970, etc. [Birmingham, 1973]. pp. 103.

ASSOCIATION SULLY.

DAVIE (GRACE RIESTRA CLAIRE) Right wing politics among French Protestants, 1900-1944, with special reference to the Association Sully. 1975. fo.323. *bibliog. Typescript. Ph.D.(London) thesis: unpublished. This thesis is the property of London University and may not be removed from the Library.*

ASSOCIATIONS, INSTITUTIONS, ETC.

— Canada — Directories.

LAND (BRIAN) ed. Directory of associations in Canada; Répertoire des associations du Canada. 2nd ed. Toronto, 1975. pp. 550.

— Germany.

PLESSEN (MARIE LOUISE) Die Wirksamkeit des Vereins für Socialpolitik von 1872-1890: Studien zum Katheder- und Staatssozialismus. Berlin, [1975]. pp. 134. *bibliog.*

— Italy.

CAVALLARO (RENATO) La sociologia dei gruppi primari: formazione e dinamica dei raggruppamenti sociali di base; con uno studio sulle associazioni volontarie nel Molise. Napoli, 1975. pp. 382. *bibliog.*

— United Kingdom.

AGE CONCERN ENGLAND. Voluntary organisations and the retired and the elderly. London, 1973. pp. 13. *bibliog. (Age Concern England. Manifesto Series. No. 4)*

— — Directories.

U.K. Countryside Commission. 1973. Countryside information directory. [London, 1973]. *Loose leaf binder.*

COMMUNITY ACTION. Investigators' handbook: a guide for tenants, workers and action groups on how to investigate companies, organisations and individuals. London, [1975]. pp. 55.

SHIPLEY (PETER) ed. The Guardian directory of pressure groups and representative associations; research by Chris Bazlinton and Anne Cowen, etc. London, 1976. pp. 265.

— — Scotland.

HILL (NANCY M.S.) Regional co-operation in Scotland: a report to the Voluntary Organisations Regional Advisory Group (VORAG). Edinburgh, 1975. pp. 35.

ASTRAKHAN'

— History.

GOLIKOVA (NINA BORISOVNA) Astrakhanskoe vosstanie 1705-1706 gg. Moskva, 1975. pp. 328.

ASTRAKHAN' (OBLAST')

— Economic conditions.

RUSSIA (EMPIRE). Ministerstvo Gosudarstvennykh Imushchestv. 1868. Kalmytskaia step' Astrakhanskoi gubernii po issledovaniiam Kumo-Manychskoi ekspeditsii. S.-Peterburg, 1868. 3 pts (in 1).

ASTRONAUTICS

ASTRONAUTICS

— United States.

LEVINE (ARTHUR L.) The future of the U.S. space program. New York, 1975. pp. 198. *bibliog.*

ASTRONAUTICS AND CIVILIZATION.

AMERICAN ASSEMBLY. 20th Assembly, October, 1961. Outer space: prospects for man and society; [background reading] edited by Lincoln P. Bloomfield. rev. ed. Freeport, N.Y., [1968] repr. 1972. pp. 270.

ASTRONOMY.

CANADA'S future in astronomy: (1).The question of a large telescope for Canadian astronomers; report of the Working Group on Astronomy, submitted to the Science Secretariat, August 12, 1968; (2).Astronomy in Canada and Canadian participation in the CAR[negie] S[outhern] O[bservatory] project; a report by the Science Council of Canada to the Minister of Energy, Mines and Resources, September 1969. Ottawa, Queens's Printer, 1970. pp. 33.

ASTURIAS

— History.

DIAZ-NOSTY (BERNARDO) La comuna asturiana: revolucion de octubre de 1934. Bilbao, 1974 repr. 1975. pp. 400. *bibliog.*

ATATÜRK (KEMÂL).

WORTHAM (HUGH EVELYN) Mustapha Kemal of Turkey. London, 1930. pp. 216.

ATHAPASKAN LANGUAGES.

DYEN (ISIDORE) and ABERLE (DAVID F.) Lexical reconstruction: the case of the proto-Athapaskan kinship system. London, 1974. pp. 498. *bibliog.*

ATHEISM.

RELIGIIA, svobodomyslie, ateizm. Frunze, 1967. pp. 96.

ATHENS

— Growth.

BURGEL (GUY) Athènes: étude de la croissance d'une capitale méditerranéenne. Paris, 1975. pp. 612,(165). *Thèse présentée devant l'Université de Paris I.*

— Industries.

BURGEL (GUY) La condition industrielle à Athènes: étude socio- géographique. Athènes, Centre National de Recherches Sociales, 1970-72. 2 vols. *35 map sheets with each volume, boxed separately.*

— Social conditions.

BURGEL (GUY) La condition industrielle à Athènes: étude socio- géographique. Athènes, Centre National de Recherches Sociales, 1970-72. 2 vols. *35 map sheets with each volume, boxed separately.*

ATHLETIC CLUBS

— Hong Kong.

HONG KONG. Advisory Comittee on Private Recreational Leases. 1968. Report; [Sir Albert Rodrigues, chairman]. Hong Kong, 1968. pp. 23, 24. *In English and Chinese.*

ATKINSON (Sir HARRY ALBERT).

BASSETT (JUDITH) Sir Harry Atkinson, 1831-1892. Auckland, 1975. pp. 196. *bibliog.*

ATLANTA, GEORGIA

— Civic improvement.

STONE (CLARENCE NATHAN) Economic growth and neighborhood discontent: system bias in the urban renewal program of Atlanta. Chapel Hill, [1976]. pp. 256. *bibliog.*

ATLANTIC COMMUNITY.

DILEMMAS of the Atlantic Alliance: two Germanys, Scandinavia, Canada, NATO and the EEC; [by] Peter Christian Ludz [and others]. New York, 1975. pp. 252. *(Atlantic Institute. Atlantic Institute Studies. 1)*

GOODMAN (ELLIOT RAYMOND) The fate of the Atlantic Community. New York, 1975. pp. 583.

ATOMIC BOMB

— History.

SHERWIN (MARTIN J.) A world destroyed: the atomic bomb and the grand alliance. New York, 1975. pp. 326. *bibliog.*

YORK (HERBERT FRANK) The advisors: Oppenheimer, Teller, and the superbomb. San Francisco, [1976]. pp. 175.

ATOMIC ENERGY.

NUCLEAR proliferation and the near-nuclear countries; edited by Onkar Marwah and Ann Schulz. Cambridge, Mass., [1975]. pp. 350. *bibliog. Papers presented at a conference held at Clark University in March, 1975.*

UNION OF CONCERNED SCIENTISTS. The nuclear fuel cycle: a survey of the public health, environmental, and national security effects of nuclear power. rev.ed. Cambridge, Mass., [1975]. pp. 291. *bibliogs.*

— Bibliography.

GERMANY (BUNDESREPUBLIK). Deutscher Bundestag. Wissenschaftliche Dienste. 1976. Kernenergie: rechtliche Aspekte, industrielle Anwendung, Risiken: Auswahlbibliographie mit Annotationen; [compiled by Claus-Peter Gerber]. Bonn, 1976. pp. 68. *(Bibliographien. 44)*

ATOMIC ENERGY INDUSTRIES.

UNION OF CONCERNED SCIENTISTS. The nuclear fuel cycle: a survey of the public health, environmental, and national security effects of nuclear power. rev.ed. Cambridge, Mass., [1975]. pp. 291. *bibliogs.*

GUHIN (MICHAEL ALAN) Nuclear paradox: security risks of the peaceful atom. Washington, D.C., 1976. pp. 77. *bibliog. (American Enterprise Institute for Public Policy Research. Foreign Affairs Studies. 32)*

ATOMIC POWER.

IS nuclear power safe?; (an AEI round table held on May 15, 1975...); Melvin R. Laird, moderator, etc. Washington, [1975]. pp. 44. *(American Enterprise Institute for Public Policy Research. Round Tables)*

— International control.

MALININ (SERGEI ALEKSANDROVICH) Mirnoe ispol'zovanie atomnoi energii: mezhdunarodno-pravovye voprosy. Moskva, 1971. pp. 176.

— Law and legislation.

IOIRYSH (ABRAM ISAAKOVICH) Atomnaia energiia: pravovye problemy. Moskva, 1975. pp. 216.

ATOMIC POWER PLANTS

— Environmental aspects.

LOVINS (AMORY BLOCH) and PRICE (JOHN H.) Non-nuclear futures: the case for an ethical energy strategy. San Francisco, [1975]. pp. 223.

— United Kingdom — Location — Bibliography.

TROTMAN (NIGEL) compiler. The siting of hazardous plants in urban areas. London, 1975. pp. 16. *(London. Greater London Council. Research Library. [Research Bibliographies]. No. 60)*

ATOMIC WEAPONS.

ENDICOTT (JOHN E.) Japan's nuclear option: political, technical, and strategic factors. New York, 1975. pp. 289. *bibliog.*

PRANGER (ROBERT JOHN) and TAHTINEN (DALE R.) Nuclear threat in the Middle East. Washington, 1975. pp. 57. *(American Enterprise Institute for Public Policy Research. Foreign Affairs Studies. 23)*

STOCKHOLM INTERNATIONAL PEACE RESEARCH INSTITUTE. Preventing nuclear-weapon proliferation: an approach to the non- proliferation treaty review conference; [by Frank Barnaby]. Stockholm, [1975]. pp. 37.

INTERNATIONAL INSTITUTE FOR STRATEGIC STUDIES. Adelphi Papers. No. 121. Limited nuclear options: deterrence and the new American doctrine; by Lynn Etheridge Davis. London, 1976. pp. 22.

— Testing.

NEW ZEALAND. Ministry of Foreign Affairs. 1973. French nuclear testing in the Pacific: International Court of Justice nuclear tests case, New Zealand v. France. Wellington, 1973. pp. 188. *(Publications. No. 446)*

JÖNSSON (CHRISTER) The Soviet Union and the test ban: a study in Soviet negotiating behavior. Lund, 1975. pp. 221. *bibliog.*

ATOMIC WEAPONS (INTERNATIONAL LAW).

NEW ZEALAND. Ministry of Foreign Affairs. 1973. French nuclear testing in the Pacific: International Court of Justice nuclear tests case, New Zealand v. France. Wellington, 1973. pp. 188. *(Publications. No. 446)*

ATOMIC WEAPONS AND DISARMAMENT.

KAHAN (JEROME H.) Security in the nuclear age: developing U.S. strategic arms policy. Washington, D.C., [1975]. pp. 361.

KELLEHER (CATHERINE McARDLE) Germany and the politics of nuclear weapons. New York, 1975. pp. 372. *bibliog.*

NETTLETON (DICK) If you want peace...: the case for nuclear disarmament. London, [1975]. pp. 30. *bibliog.*

NPT: paradoxes and problems; Anne W. Marks, editor. Washington, D.C., 1975. pp. 106. *bibliogs. Report and working papers of an unofficial international meeting held by the Arms Control Association and the Carnegie Endowment for International Peace, Divonne, France, 1974.*

NUCLEAR proliferation and the near-nuclear countries; edited by Onkar Marwah and Ann Schulz. Cambridge, Mass., [1975]. pp. 350. *bibliog. Papers presented at a conference held at Clark University in March, 1975.*

SIMS (NICHOLAS A.) Approaches to disarmament: an introductory analysis. Panaji, Goa, 1975. pp. 95. *bibliog.*

SMITH (DAN) of the Campaign for Nuclear Disarmament. Insecurity in numbers: the threat of nuclear proliferation. London, [1975]. pp. 35. *bibliog.*

STOCKHOLM INTERNATIONAL PEACE RESEARCH INSTITUTE. Nuclear disarmament or nuclear war?; [by Frank Barnaby]. Stockholm, [1975]. pp. 27.

EPSTEIN (WILLIAM) Secretary of the U.N. Disarmament Commission. The last chance: nuclear proliferation and arms control. New York, [1976]. pp. 341.

GUHIN (MICHAEL ALAN) Nuclear paradox: security risks of the peaceful atom. Washington, D.C., 1976. pp. 77. *bibliog. (American Enterprise Institute for Public Policy Research. Foreign Affairs Studies. 32)*

INTERNATIONAL INSTITUTE FOR STRATEGIC STUDIES. Adelphi Papers. No. 120. The alliance and Europe: part V: nuclear weapons and east- west negotiation; by Uwe Nerlich. London, 1976. pp. 35.

KAPUR (ASHOK) India's nuclear option: atomic diplomacy and decision making. New York, 1976. pp. 295. *bibliog.*

LEGAULT (ALBERT) and LINDSEY (GEORGE) The dynamics of the nuclear balance. rev. ed. Ithaca, 1976. pp. 283.

ATTENTION.

KEELE (STEVEN W.) Attention and human performance. Pacific Palisades, Cal., [1973]. pp. 184. *bibliog.*

ATTERBURY (FRANCIS) Bishop of Rochester.

BENNETT (GARETH VAUGHAN) The Tory crisis in church and state, 1688-1730: the career of Francis Atterbury, Bishop of Rochester. Oxford, 1975. pp. 335. *bibliog.*

ATTITUDE (PSYCHOLOGY).

BEM (DARYL J.) Beliefs, attitudes and human affairs. Belmont, Cal., [1970]. pp. 114. *bibliog.*

TRIANDIS (HARRY C.) Attitude and attitude change. New York, [1971]. pp. 232. *bibliog.*

LISKA (ALLEN E.) ed. The consistency controversy: readings on the impact of attitude on behavior. New York, [1975]. pp. 277. *bibliog.*

BLUMENTHAL (MONICA D.) and others. More about justifying violence: methodological studies of attitudes and behavior. Ann Arbor, 1975. pp. 401. *bibliog.*

ATTITUDE CHANGE.

TRIANDIS (HARRY C.) Attitude and attitude change. New York, [1971]. pp. 232. *bibliog.*

ATTORNEYS–GENERAL.

— United States.

SEYMOUR (WHITNEY NORTH) United States attorney: an inside view of "justice" in America under the Nixon administration. New York, 1975. pp. 248.

AUDITING.

SPICER (ERNEST EVAN) and PEGLER (ERNEST CHARLES) Practical auditing; fifteenth edition by Walter W. Bigg; ([with] Supplement: standard accounting practice). London, 1969, repr. 1972. pp. 700.

AUSTRALASIA

— Statistics — Directories.

HARVEY (JOAN M.) Statistics Asia and Australasia: sources for market research. Beckenham, Kent, 1974. pp. 238.

AUSTRALIA

— Biography.

WHO's who in Australia...; compiled and edited by J.S. Legge. 21st ed. Melbourne, 1974. pp. 1088.

— Emigration and immigration.

RIVETT (KENNETH) ed. Australia and the non-white migrant; edited...for the Immigration Reform Group. Carlton, Victoria, 1975. pp. 327.

— Executive departments.

AUSTRALIA. National Capital Development Commission. 1975. Submission...to the Royal Commission on Australian Government Administration. Canberra, 1975. pp. 117. *(Technical Papers. No. 6)*

— Foreign relations.

AUSTRALIAN FOREIGN AFFAIRS RECORD (formerly Current notes on international affairs); (pd. for the Department of Foreign Affairs [Australia]). m., 1972 (v.43)- Canberra.

AUSTRALIAN INSTITUTE OF INTERNATIONAL AFFAIRS. Annual Conference, 4th, Adelaide, 1974. Advance Australia - where?: [papers read at the conference]; edited by B.D. Beddie. Melbourne, 1975. pp. 222.

— — Netherlands.

LOCKWOOD (RUPERT) Black armada. Sydney, 1975. pp. 352.

— — Papua New Guinea.

HUDSON (W.J.) ed. Australia's New Guinea question. Melbourne, 1975. pp. 163.

— History.

AUSTRALIAN space, Australian time: geographical perspectives; edited by J.M. Powell and M. Williams. Melbourne, 1975. pp. 256. *bibliogs.*

— — Sources.

DAVENPORT-HILL (FLORENCE) and DAVENPORT-HILL (ROSAMUND) [Correspondence about Australia. 1866-1876]. 1 piece. *Manuscript.*

— Industries.

AUSTRALIAN NATIONAL ACCOUNTS: gross product by industry at current and constant prices; (pd. by) Commonwealth Bureau of Census and Statistics. a., 1962-63/1973-74- Canberra.

AUSTRALIA. Commonwealth Bureau of Census and Statistics. 1969. Indexes of factory production, 1949-50 to 1966-67. Canberra, [1969]. pp. 20.

RICHARDS (GRAHAM MARTIN) Labour's share in the value added of Australian manufacturing industry: the post-war experience; [Ph.D.(London) thesis]. 1975. fo. 362. *bibliog.* Typescript: unpublished. This thesis is the property of London University and may not be removed from the Library.

— Parliament — Elections.

OAKES (LAURIE) and SOLOMON (DAVID HARRIS) Grab for power: election '74. Melbourne, 1974. pp. 557.

— Politics and government.

OAKES (LAURIE) and SOLOMON (DAVID HARRIS) Grab for power: election '74. Melbourne, 1974. pp. 557.

GOLLAN (ROBIN) Revolutionaries and reformists: communism and the Australian labour movement, 1920-1955. Richmond, Surrey, 1975. pp. 330. *bibliog.*

RICKARD (JOHN DAVID) Class and politics: New South Wales, Victoria and the early Commonwealth, 1890-1910. Canberra, 1976. pp. 371. *bibliog.*

— Population.

AUSTRALIA. Commonwealth Bureau of Census and Statistics. 1972. Australia: statement prepared for the second Asian population conference, Tokyo, November 1972. Canberra, [1972]. pp. 13.

— Race question.

RIVETT (KENNETH) ed. Australia and the non-white migrant; edited...for the Immigration Reform Group. Carlton, Victoria, 1975. pp. 327.

— Social policy.

LANSBURY (RUSSELL DUNCAN) and others. Social policy: the new frontiers. Melbourne, [1975?]. pp. 13. *(Victorian Fabian Society. Victorian Fabian Pamphlets. [No.] 31)*

AUSTRALIAN ABORIGINES.

AUSTRALIA. Bureau of Agricultural Economics. 1971. Aboriginal pastoral properties, Arnhem Land, Northern Territory. Canberra, 1971. pp. 58.

GALE (FAY) and BINNION (JOAN) Poverty among aboriginal families in Adelaide. Canberra, Australian Government Publishing Service, 1975. pp. 52.

EGGLESTON (ELIZABETH) Fear, favour or affection: aborigines and the criminal law in Victoria, South Australia and Western Australia. Canberra, 1976. pp. 398. *bibliog.* *(Academy of the Social Sciences in Australia. Aborigines in Australian Society. 13)*

AUSTRIA

— Army — History.

SCHMIDT-BRENTANO (ANTONIO) Die Armee in Österreich: Militär, Staat und Gesellschaft, 1848-1867. Boppard am Rhein, [1975]. pp. 547. *bibliog.* *(Militärgeschichtliches Forschungsamt. Militärgeschichtliche Studien. 20)*

— Commerce — Mathematical models.

BREUSS (FRITZ) Komparative Vorteile im österreichischen Aussenhandel. Wien, 1975. pp. 250. *bibliog.* *(Österreichische Akademie der Wissenschaften. Philosophisch-Historische Klasse. Sitzungsberichte. 299. Band. 1. Abhandlung)*

— Constitutional history.

SEIPEL (IGNAZ) Der Kampf um die österreichische Verfassung: [speeches and essays]. Wien, 1930. pp. 379.

HUEMER (PETER) Sektionschef Robert Hecht und die Zerstörung der Demokratie in Österreich: eine historisch-politische Studie. Wien, 1975. pp. 372.

— Economic policy.

WEISSEL (ERWIN) Die Ohnmacht des Sieges: Arbeiterschaft und Sozialisierung nach dem Ersten Weltkrieg in Österreich. Wien, [1976]. pp. 465. *bibliog.* *(Ludwig-Boltzmann-Institut für Geschichte der Arbeiterbewegung. Veröffentlichungen)*

— Foreign relations.

WODAK (WALTER) Diplomatie zwischen Ost und West. Graz, [1976]. pp. 235. *(Österreichische Gesellschaft für Aussenpolitik und Internationale Beziehungen. Österreichische Diplomaten)* Collection of lectures and essays, in German or English. Includes correspondence with Karl Renner.

— — Germany.

LUZA (RADOMÍR) Austro-German relations in the Anschluss era. Princeton, [1975]. pp. 438. *bibliog.*

KATZENSTEIN (PETER J.) Disjoined partners: Austria and Germany since 1815. Berkeley, Calif., [1976]. pp. 263.

— — Italy.

TOSCANO (MARIO) Alto Adige-South Tyrol: Italy's frontier with the German world;...edited by George A. Carbone. Baltimore, [1975]. pp. 283.

— — Russia.

WODAK (WALTER) Diplomatie zwischen Ost und West. Graz, [1976]. pp. 235. *(Österreichische Gesellschaft für Aussenpolitik und Internationale Beziehungen. Österreichische Diplomaten)* Collection of lectures and essays, in German or English. Includes correspondence with Karl Renner.

— — Turkey.

BAYERLE (GUSTAV) Ottoman diplomacy in Hungary; letters from the Pashas of Buda, 1590-1593. Bloomington, Ind., [1972]. pp. 204. *bibliog.* *(Indiana University Graduate School Publications. Uralic and Altaic Series. vol. 101.)*

— History — 1900— .

LUZA (RADOMÍR) Austro-German relations in the Anschluss era. Princeton, [1975]. pp. 438. *bibliog.*

— — 1918—1938.

Das JAHR 1934: 25.Juli; Protokoll des Symposiums in Wien am 8.Oktober 1974; (herausgegeben von Ludwig Jedlicka und Rudolf Neck). Wien, 1975. pp. 154. *(Theodor-Körner-Stiftungsfonds, and Leopold-Kunschak-Preis. Wissenschaftliche Kommission zur Erforschung der Österreichischen Geschichte der Jahre 1927 bis 1938. Veröffentlichungen. Band 3)*

AUSTRIA (Cont.)

JAGSCHITZ (GERHARD) Der Putsch: die Nationalsozialisten 1934 in Österreich. Graz, [1976]. pp. 260. *bibliog.*

— — 1934, Socialist Uprising, February.

DUCZYNSKA (ILONA) Der demokratische Bolschewik: zur Theorie und Praxis der Gewalt; mit einem Vorwort von Friedrich Heer. München, [1975]. pp. 383.

— — 1945—1955, Allied occupation.

WODAK (WALTER) Diplomatie zwischen Ost und West. Graz, [1976]. pp. 235. *(Österreichische Gesellschaft für Aussenpolitik und Internationale Beziehungen. Österreichische Diplomaten) Collection of lectures and essays, in German or English. Includes correspondence with Karl Renner.*

— Industries.

BOBEK (HANS) and STEINBACH (JOSEF) Die Regionalstruktur der Industrie Österreichs. Wien, 1975. pp. 80. *(Österreichische Akademie der Wissenschaften. Kommission für Raumforschung. Beiträge zur Regionalforschung. Band 1) 4 maps in end pocket.*

BOGUSZEWSKI (JAN) and WAGENER (HANS JUERGEN) Zur Industriestatistik der BRD, Österreichs, Polens und Ungarns. Wien, 1975. pp. 58. *(Wiener Institut für Internationale Wirtschaftsvergleiche. Forschungsberichte. Nr.24)*

— Neutrality.

ERMACORA (FELIX) 20 Jahre österreichische Neutralität. 2nd ed. Frankfurt am Main, 1975. pp. 265.

GINTHER (KONRAD) Neutralität und Neutralitätspolitik: die österreichische Neutralität zwischen Schweizer Muster und sowjetischer Koexistenzdoktrin. Wien, 1975. pp. 168. *bibliog.*

— Politics and government.

KREISKY (BRUNO) Politik für Österreichs Zukunft...: Regierungserklärung vom 5.11.1971. [Vienna, 1971]. pp. 63.

BAUER (OTTO) Werkausgabe;...(Redaktion: Hugo Pepper). Wien, [1975 in progress]. *bibliogs.*

HUEMER (PETER) Sektionschef Robert Hecht und die Zerstörung der Demokratie in Österreich: eine historisch-politische Studie. Wien, 1975. pp. 372.

— Social policy.

EBERT (KURT) Die Anfänge der modernen Sozialpolitik in Österreich: die Taaffesche Sozialgesetzgebung für die Arbeiter im Rahmen der Gewerbeordnungsreform, 1879-1885. Wien, 1975. pp. 320. *bibliog. (Österreichische Akademie der Wissenschaften. Kommission für die Geschichte der Österreichisch- Ungarischen Monarchie, 1848-1918. Studien zur Geschichte der Österreichisch-Ungarischen Monarchie. Band 15)*

— Statistics, Vital.

KUHN (DIETMAR) Der Geburtenrückgang in Österreich, etc. Wien, 1975. pp. 103.

AUSTRIA–HUNGARY

— Army — History.

PLASCHKA (RICHARD GEORG) and others. Innere Front: Militärassistenz, Widerstand und Umsturz in der Donaumonarchie, 1918. Wien, 1974. 2 vols. *bibliog. (Österreichisches Ost- und Südosteuropa- Institut. Veröffentlichungen. Bände 8-9)*

— Commerce — Romania.

BINDREITER (UTA) Die diplomatischen und wirtschaftlichen Beziehungen zwischen Österreich-Ungarn und Rumänien in den Jahren 1875-1888. Wien, 1976. pp. 322. *bibliog. (Kommission für Neuere Geschichte Österreichs. Veröffentlichungen. 63)*

— Constitutional history.

GORDON (HAROLD JACKSON) and GORDON (NANCY M.) eds. The Austrian Empire: abortive federation? Lexington, [1974]. pp. 159. *bibliog.*

— Economic history.

STUDIEN zur Geschichte der Österreichisch-Ungarischen Monarchie: [papers of a conference held in Budapest in 1958]; redigiert von V. Sándor und P. Hanák. Budapest, 1961. pp. 524. *(Magyar Tudományos Akadémia. Studia Historica. 51)*

— Foreign relations — Romania.

BINDREITER (UTA) Die diplomatischen und wirtschaftlichen Beziehungen zwischen Österreich-Ungarn und Rumänien in den Jahren 1875-1888. Wien, 1976. pp. 322. *bibliog. (Kommission für Neuere Geschichte Österreichs. Veröffentlichungen. 63)*

— — Russia.

SKAZKIN (SERGEI DANILOVICH) Konets avstro-russko-germanskogo soiuza: issledovanie po istorii russko-germanskikh i russko-avstriiskikh otnoshenii v sviazi s vostochnym voprosom v 80-e gody XIX stoletiia. 2nd ed. Moskva, 1974. pp. 272. *Reproduces the text of the 1st ed. of 1928 with some omissions.*

— History.

PLASCHKA (RICHARD GEORG) and others. Innere Front: Militärassistenz, Widerstand und Umsturz in der Donaumonarchie, 1918. Wien, 1974. 2 vols. *bibliog. (Österreichisches Ost- und Südosteuropa- Institut. Veröffentlichungen. Bände 8-9)*

— Nationalism.

STUDIEN zur Geschichte der Österreichisch-Ungarischen Monarchie: [papers of a conference held in Budapest in 1958]; redigiert von V. Sándor und P. Hanák. Budapest, 1961. pp. 524. *(Magyar Tudományos Akadémia. Studia Historica. 51)*

— Politics and government.

TRUMBIĆ (ANTE) Suton Austro-Ugarske i Riječka rezolucija. Zagreb, 1936. pp. 112.

— Social history.

STUDIEN zur Geschichte der Österreichisch-Ungarischen Monarchie: [papers of a conference held in Budapest in 1958]; redigiert von V. Sándor und P. Hanák. Budapest, 1961. pp. 524. *(Magyar Tudományos Akadémia. Studia Historica. 51)*

AUSTRIANS IN THE UNITED KINGDOM.

MAIMANN (HELENE) Politik im Wartesaal: österreichische Exilpolitik in Grossbritannien, 1938-1945. Wien, 1975. pp. 355. *bibliog. (Kommission für Neuere Geschichte Österreichs. Veröffentlichungen. 62)*

AUTARCHY.

TYNDALL (JOHN) Fascist. The case for economic nationalism. London, [1975]. pp. 14.

AUTHORITY.

DORNBUSCH (SANFORD MAURICE) and SCOTT (WILLIAM RICHARD) Evaluation and the exercise of authority. San Francisco, 1975. pp. 382. *bibliog.*

ECKSTEIN (HARRY HORACE) and GURR (THEODORE ROBERT) Patterns of authority: a structural basis for political inquiry. New York, [1975]. pp. 488.

MEYER (WILLIAM J.) Public good and political authority: a pragmatic proposal. Port Washington, 1975. pp. 147. *bibliog.*

POWER in families; edited by Ronald E. Cromwell and David H. Olson. New York, [1975]. pp. 264. *bibliog. Based on a symposium held in June 1973 at the University of Missouri, Kansas City and sponsored by its Family Study Center.*

NISBET (ROBERT ALEXANDER) Twilight of authority. London, 1976. pp. 287.

SCHONFELD (WILLIAM R.) Obedience and revolt: French behavior towards authority. Beverly Hills, [1976]. pp. 256.

AUTHORS.

The INTERNATIONAL authors and writers who's who; 7th edition, 1976; editor, Ernest Kay. Cambridge, 1976. pp. 676.

AUTHORS, LABOURING CLASS.

EMMERICH (WOLFGANG) ed. Proletarische Lebensläufe: autobiographische Dokumente zur Entstehung der Zweiten Kultur in Deutschland. Reinbek bei Hamburg, 1974-75. 2 vols. *bibliogs.*

AUTHORS, RUSSIAN.

KEMP-WELCH (ANTHONY) The origins and formative years of the Writers' Union of the U.S.S.R., 1932-1936. 1975 [or rather 1976]. fo. 167. *bibliog. Typescript. Ph.D. (London) thesis: unpublished. This thesis is the property of London University and may not be removed from the Library.*

AUTHORS AND PUBLISHERS

— Russia.

SUTULOV (DMITRII MAKAROVICH) Avtorskoe pravo, izdatel'skie dogovory, avtorskii gonorar. 3rd ed. Moskva, 1974. pp. 272.

AUTOMATION.

SCHULZ (ZBIGNIEW) Efektywność ekonomiczna automatyzacji produkcji przemysłowej. Warszawa, 1962. pp. 199. *bibliog. With English and Russian summaries.*

— Social aspects.

KETTERINGHAM (P.J.A.) The human factor in automation. London, 1975. pp. 8.

— France.

FREYSSENET (MICHEL) Schéma général d'aménagement de la France: qualification du travail: tendances et mise en question. Paris, 1975. pp. 195. *bibliog. (France. Délégation à l'Aménagement du Territoire et à l'Action Régionale. Travaux et Recherches de Prospective. 57)*

— Germany.

HOEPFNER (KLAUS) Ökonomische Alternativen zur Ausländerbeschäftigung.. Göttingen, [1975]. pp. 210. *bibliog. (Kommission für Wirtschaftlichen und Sozialen Wandel. Schriften. 105)*

— Underdeveloped areas.

See UNDERDEVELOPED AREAS — Automation.

AUTOMOBILE DRIVERS' LICENCES

— United Kingdom.

SUPPLEMENTARY licensing; [shortened report]; (prepared by a group of officers from the Greater London Council, the Department of the Environment, the Metropolitan Police and the London Boroughs Association). London, Greater London Council, [1974]. pp. 27.

AUTOMOBILE GRAVEYARDS.

BROWN (F. LEE) and LEBECK (A.O.) Cars, cans and dumps: solutions for rural residuals. Baltimore, [1976]. pp. 206. *bibliog.*

AUTOMOBILE INDUSTRY AND TRADE

— Germany.

DORWARD (NEIL MORRISON MACLACHLAN) An analysis of the market areas of the West German motor truck industry; [Ph.D.(London) thesis]. 1975. fo. 432. *bibliog. Typescript: unpublished. This thesis is the property of London University and may not be removed from the Library.*

— Italy.

PUGNO (EMILIO) and GARAVINI (SERGIO) Gli anni duri alla FIAT: la resistenza sindacale e la ripresa. Torino, [1974]. pp. 255.

LOTTA CONTINUA. Commissione Operaia Torinese. La Fiat com'è: la risstrutturazione davanti all'autonomia operaia; a cura di Enrico Deaglio. Milano, 1975. pp. 315.

SAPELLI (GIULIO) Fascismo grande industria e sindacato: il caso di Torino, 1929/1935. Milano, 1975. pp. 260.

— South Africa.

SOUTH AFRICA. Bureau of Statistics. 1976. Census of motor trade and repair services, 1970. [Pretoria, 1976]. pp. 148. *(Reports. No. 04-16-02) In English and Afrikaans.*

— Turkey.

HIÇ (MÜKERREM) Employment and wages in the automotive and other assembly industries in Turkey. Istanbul, 1974. pp. 58. *(Istanbul. Üniversitesi. Iktisat Fakültesi. Institute of Economic Development. Yayinlari. No. 23)*

— United Kingdom.

SOCIETY OF MOTOR MANUFACTURERS AND TRADERS. Statistical Department. The motoring industry of Great Britain 1975. London, [1975]. pp. 272.

ECONOMIST INTELLIGENCE UNIT. Q[uarterly] E[conomic] R[eview] Specials. No. 26. Rubber and the automotive industry in the UK and North America. London, 1976. pp. 54.

— United States.

DEUTSCH (JAN G.) compiler. Selling the people's Cadillac: the Edsel and corporate responsibility. New Haven, 1976. pp. 261.

ECONOMIST INTELLIGENCE UNIT. Q[uarterly] E[conomic] R[eview] Specials. No. 26. Rubber and the automotive industry in the UK and North America. London, 1976. pp. 54.

LEWIS (DAVID LANIER) The public image of Henry Ford: an American folk hero and his company. Detroit, 1976. pp. 598.

AUTOMOBILE INDUSTRY WORKERS.

FORM (WILLIAM HUMBERT) Blue-collar stratification: autoworkers in four countries. Princeton, 1976. pp. 335. *bibliog.*

— Italy.

PUGNO (EMILIO) and GARAVINI (SERGIO) Gli anni duri alla FIAT: la resistenza sindacale e la ripresa. Torino, [1974]. pp. 255.

IMAZIO (ALBERTO) and COSTA (CARLO) L'organizzazione del lavoro alla FIAT: produzione e conflittualità operaia. Venezia, 1975. pp. 175. *bibliog.*

— Sweden.

GOLDMANN (ROBERT B.) A work experiment: six Americans in a Swedish plant. New York, [1976]. pp. 48.

— United States.

MARQUART (FRANK) An auto worker's journal: the UAW from crusade to one-party union. University Park, Pa., [1975]. pp. 162. *bibliog.*

GOLDMANN (ROBERT B.) A work experiment: six Americans in a Swedish plant. New York, [1976]. pp. 48.

AUTOMOBILE PARKING

— Hong Kong.

HONG KONG. Working Party on Parking Offences. 1967. Report. Hong Kong, [1967]. pp. 8, 8. *In English and Chinese.*

— United Kingdom — London.

The CONTROL of private non-residential parking spaces; by a joint working party of the G[reater] L[ondon] C[ouncil] D[epartment] o[f the] E[nvironment]/L[ondon] B[oroughs] A[ssociation]; [W.G. Panther, chairman]. London, [1975]. pp. 24. *(London. Greater London Council. Research Memoranda. 471)*

CARR (R.) Some characteristics of private non-residential parking in Greater London. London, [1976]. pp. 34. *(London. Greater London Council. Research Memoranda. 477)*

AUTOMOBILES

— Apparatus and supplies.

COUNTER INFORMATION SERVICES and TRANSNATIONAL INSTITUTE. Where is Lucas going?. London, [1975?]. pp. 47. *bibliog. (Counter Information Services. Anti-Reports. No. 12)*

— Fuel consumption.

WILDTHORN (SORREL) and others. How to save gasoline: public policy alternatives for the automobile. Cambridge, Mass., [1976]. pp. 324.

— Maintenance and repair.

HONG KONG. Automobile Repairs and Servicing Industrial Committee. 1971. Job standards and specifications for the principal jobs in the automobile repairs and servicing trades. Hong Kong, 1970[or rather 1971]. pp. 28. *In English and Chinese.*

— Service stations.

EIRE. Restrictive Practices Commission. 1975. Report of special review of the operation of Article 3 of the Restrictive Trade Practices Motor Spirit Order, 1972. Dublin, [1975]. pp. 18.

AUTOMOBILES — Trailers.

See CARAVANS (AUTOMOBILE TRAILERS).

AUTONOMY.

INDEPENDANCE et interdépendances au Maghreb; par W.K. Ruf [and others]. Paris, 1974. pp. 359. *(Centre de Recherches et d'Etudes sur les Sociétés Méditerranéennes. Collection)*

AVERNES.

GAROFALO (YOLANDE) and WARNIER (BERTRAND) Un village, paysage et développement: [Avernes]. Paris, La Documentation Française, 1974. pp. 75.

AYERS (BRADLEY EARL).

AYERS (BRADLEY EARL) The war that never was: an insider's account of C.I.A. covert operations against Cuba. Indianapolis, [1976]. pp. 235.

AZERBAIJAN

— Industries.

FARADZHEV (FARID ALIKULU OGLU) Tempy razvitiia i otraslevye proportsii promyshlennosti Azerbaidzhana. Baku, 1975. pp. 294.

GADZHI-ZADE (ABDURAGIM MAMEDIIAEVICH) Azerbaidzhanskii promyshlennyi kompleks. Baku, 1975. pp. 204. *bibliog.*

— Politics and government.

VOPLOSHCHENIE sotsialisticheskogo internatsionalizma. Baku, 1974. pp. 227.

— Social conditions.

GUSHCHIN (SERGEI NIKOLAEVICH) and MEKHTIEV (GIAZENFER GIUSEINOVICH) Sotsializm i blagosostoianie trudiashchikhsia Sovetskogo Azerbaidzhana, 1920-1974 gg. Baku, 1975. pp. 182.

AZORES

— Population.

RAMOS (ANTONIO BRITO) Demografia e emprego nas ilhas adjacentes. Lisboa, 1974. pp. 191. *(Portugal. Ministerio do Trabalho. Gabinete de Planeamento. Serie Estudos. 20) With abstracts in English, French and German.*

BAATH PARTY.

BAATH ARAB SOCIALIST PARTY. Revolutionary Iraq, 1968-1973: [political report delivered to the 8th Regional Congress] by...Ahmad Hassan Al-Bakr. n.p., [1974]. pp. 263.

DEVLIN (JOHN F.) The Ba'th Party: a history from the origins to 1966. Stanford, 1976. *bibliog. (Stanford University. Hoover Institution on War, Revolution and Peace. Hoover Institution Publications. 156)*

BACULARD D'ARNAUD (FRANÇOIS THOMAS MARIE).

DAWSON (ROBERT L.) Baculard d'Arnaud: life and prose fiction. Banbury, 1976. 2 vols. *bibliog. (Studies on Voltaire and the Eighteenth Century. vols. 141-142)*

BADEN

— Politics and government.

STEHLING (JUTTA) Weimarer Koalition und SPD in Baden: ein Beitrag zur Geschichte der Partei- und Kulturpolitik in der Weimarer Republik. Frankfurt/Main, [1976]. pp. 347. *bibliog. Zur Erlangung des akademischen Grades eines Doktors der Philosophie von der Universität Karlsruhe genehmigte Dissertation.*

BAHAYA.

See HAYA (AFRICAN TRIBE).

BAHRAIN

— Politics and government.

NAKHLEH (EMILE A.) Bahrain: political development in a modernizing society. Farnborough, Hants, [1976]. pp. 191. *bibliog.*

BAIL

— United States.

WICE (PAUL B.) Freedom for sale: a national study of pretrial release. Lexington, Mass., [1974]. pp. 212. *bibliog.*

BAILIFFS

— Poland.

POLAND. Statutes, etc. 1960-71. Przepisy dotyczące komorników: zbiór tekstów według stanu prawnego na dzień 1. VII. 1972 r. Warszawa, 1972. pp. 91.

BAKUNIN (MIKHAIL ALEKSANDROVICH).

AVRICH (PAUL HENRY) Bakunin and Nechaev. London, 1974. pp. 32. *bibliog.*

BAKUNIN (MIKHAIL ALEKSANDROVICH) Michel Bakounine et ses relations slaves, -1870-1875; textes établis et annotés par Arthur Lehning. Leiden, 1974. pp. 586. *(International Institute of Social History. Archives Bakounine. 5)*

BALANCE OF PAYMENTS.

BALANCE OF PAYMENTS.

MITTELSTAEDT (AXEL) and others. Unemployment benefits and related payments in seven major countries; Surpluses and deficits in the balance of payments... [by] Erwin Veil; [and] Comparability of consumer prices indices in OECD countries [by] Charlotte Vannereau. [Paris], Organisation for Economic Cooperation and Development, 1975. pp. 56. (*OECD Economic Outlook. Occasional Studies*)

BEENSTOCK (MICHAEL CHARLES) Forward markets, international capital movements and the balance of payments. 1976. fo. 217. *bibliog. Typescript.* Ph.D. (London) thesis: unpublished. *This thesis is the property of London University and may not be removed from the Library.*

FRENKEL (JACOB A.) and JOHNSON (HARRY GORDON) eds. The monetary approach to the balance of payments. London, 1976. pp. 388. *bibliogs.*

— **Mathematical models.**

McKENZIE (GEORGE W.) Shorter-run problems of the balance of payments. [Southampton], 1973. fo. 19. *bibliog.* (*Southampton. University. Discussion Papers in Economics and Econometrics. No.7314*)

FLANDERS (M. JUNE) The Scandinavian model and the balance of payments. [London], 1975. pp. (24). *bibliog.*

KNIGHT (MALCOLM DONALD) and WYMER (CLIFFORD RONALD) A monetary model of an open economy with particular reference to the United Kingdom. [London, 1975]. pp. 24, iii. *bibliog.*

ROTH (JUERGEN) Der internationale Konjunkturzusammenhang bei flexiblen Wechselkursen: eine modelltheoretische Analyse. Tübingen, 1975. pp. 264. *bibliog.* (*Kiel. Universität. Institut für Weltwirtschaft Kieler Studien. 135*)

— **America, Latin.**

SCHINKE (ROLF) Der Zahlungsbilanzausgleich im Gemeinsamen Markt Zentralamerikas: ein Diskussionsbeitrag zur monetären Integration von Entwicklungsländern. Göttingen, [1974]. pp. 168. *bibliog.* (*Göttingen. Universität. Ibero-Amerika- Institut für Wirtschaftsforschung. Arbeitsberichte. Heft 16*)

— **Denmark.**

JOHANSEN (HANS CHR.) Udenrigshandel og betalingsbalance. 2nd ed. København, 1973. pp. 86. *bibliog.*

— **Fiji Islands.**

FIJI. Bureau of Statistics. 1970. Fiji balance of payments, 1965-1968: preliminary estimates. Suva, 1970. fo. 57.

— **Finland.**

FINLAND. Tilastokeskus. Suomen maksutase vuosina: (Finland's balance of payments). a., 1969/1970, 1972/1973- Helsinki. *In Finnish, with Swedish and English headings and notes.*

— **France.**

FRANCE. Comité des Echanges Extérieurs. 1971. Préparation du VIe Plan...: rapport. Paris, 1971. pp. 231.

— **Italy.**

MASERA (FRANCESCO) ed. Bilancia dei pagamenti e sistema monetario internazionale: saggi raccolti. Milano, 1975. pp. 171. (*Rome. Università Internazionale degli Studi Sociali. Pubblicazioni. Studi Economici. 2*)

— **Japan.**

AMANO (AKIHIRO) An econometric model of the Japanese balance of payments, 1961- 1970. Kobe, 1975. pp. 161. (*Kobe. University. School of Business Administration. Monographs. No. 3*)

— **Malaysia.**

CHEW (ALAN) The Malaysian balance of payments, 1960-1970. Kuala Lumpur, 1975. pp. 284. *bibliog.*

— **Singapore.**

SINGAPORE. Statistics Department. 1975. Singapore balance of payments, 1972-1974. Singapore, 1975. fo. 21.

— **United Kingdom.**

FAUSTEN (DIETRICH K.) The consistency of British balance of payments policies. London, 1975. pp. 210. *bibliog.*

— — **Mathematical models.**

JONSON (PETER DAVID) An investigation of the U.K. balance of payments with particular emphasis on the role of monetary factors and disequilibrium dynamics, 1882-1970. 1975. fo. 167. *bibliogs. Typescript.* Ph.D.(London) thesis: unpublished. *This thesis is the property of London University and may not be removed from the Library.*

BALBO (CESARE).

SCAGLIA (GIOVANNI BATTISTA) Cesare Balbo: il Risorgimento nella prospettiva storica del "progresso cristiano". Roma, [1975]. pp. 594.

BALKAN STATES

— **Commerce — Romania.**

RELAȚIILE comerciale ale Țării Românești cu Peninsula Balcanică, 1829-1858. București, 1970. pp. 308. (*Academia Republicii Socialiste România. Institutul de Studii Sud-Est Europene. Biblioteca Istorică. 22*) *With French summary.*

— **Foreign relations.**

TODOROV (KOSTA) Balkan firebrand: the autobiography of a rebel, soldier and statesman. Chicago, [1943]. pp. 340.

— — **United Kingdom.**

BARKER (ELISABETH) British policy in south-east Europe in the Second World War. London, 1976. pp. 320. *bibliog.*

— **Politics and government.**

TODOROV (KOSTA) Balkan firebrand: the autobiography of a rebel, soldier and statesman. Chicago, [1943]. pp. 340.

BARKER (ELISABETH) Truce in the Balkans. London, 1948. pp. 256.

BALTIC, THE

— **Foreign relations.**

LUNTINEN (PERTTI) The Baltic question, 1903-1908. Helsinki, 1975. pp. 252. *bibliog.* (*Academia Scientiarum Fennica. Annales. Ser. B. Tom. 195*)

BALTIC STATES

— **Intellectual life.**

LATVIISKII GOSUDARSTVENNYI UNIVERSITET. Uchenye Zapiski. t.219. Germaniia i Pribaltika. 3. Riga, 1974. pp. 107.

BALUCHISTAN

— **Politics and government.**

PAKISTAN. 1974. White paper on Baluchistan. Rawalpindi, 1974. pp. 55.

BAMBERGER (LUDWIG).

ZUCKER (STANLEY) Ludwig Bamberger: German liberal politician and social critic, 1823-1899. Pittsburgh, [1975]. pp. 343. *bibliog.*

BANANA TRADE

— **United Kingdom.**

BEAVER (PATRICK) Yes! We have some: the story of Fyffes. Stevenage, 1976. pp. 133.

BANCO CENTRAL DE LA REPUBLICA ARGENTINA.

AISENSTEIN (SALVADOR) El Banco Central de la Republica Argentina y su funcion reguladora de la moneda y del credito. 2nd ed. Buenos Aires, 1942. pp. 280. *bibliog.*

BANCO CENTRAL DE VENEZUELA.

MACHADO GOMEZ (ALFREDO) Crisis y recuperacion: la economia monetaria venezolana entre 1961- 1968. Caracas, 1972. pp. 469. (*Banco Central de Venezuela. Coleccion XXX Aniversario*)

BANGLADESH.

BANGLADESH TODAY: a fortn. news bulletin; (pd. by Press and Publicity Division, Bangladesh Mission...London). fortn. London. *Current issues only kept.*

— **Bibliography.**

SCHENDEL (WILLEM VAN) Bangladesh: a bibliography with special reference to the peasantry. Amsterdam, 1976. pp. 227. (*Amsterdam. Universiteit. Antropologisch-Sociologisch Centrum. Afdeling Zuid- en Zuidoost-Azië. Voorpublikaties. Nr.10*)

— **Constitution.**

BANGLADESH. Constitution, 1972. The constitution of the People's Republic of Bangladesh. Dacca, 1973. pp. 83.

— **Description and travel.**

BANGLADESH. Ministry of Information and Broadcasting. 1972. Bangladesh: the youngest republic. [Dacca, 1972]. pp. 34.

— **Economic conditions.**

FAALAND (JUST) and PARKINSON (JOHN RICHARD) Bangladesh: the test case of development. London, [1976]. pp. 203.

— **Economic policy.**

FAALAND (JUST) and PARKINSON (JOHN RICHARD) Bangladesh: the test case of development. London, [1976]. pp. 203.

— **International status.**

INTERNATIONAL COMMISSION OF JURISTS. The events in East Pakistan, 1971: a legal study. Geneva, 1972. pp. 98.

— **Parliament — Elections.**

BANGLADESH. Election Commission. 1973. Report on the first general election to Parliament in Bangladesh 1973. [Dacca], 1973. pp. 105.

— — **Rules and practice.**

BANGLADESH. Parliament. 1974. Rules of procedure of Parliament of the People's Republic o Bangladesh. Dacca, 1974. pp. 102.

— **Population.**

FAALAND (JUST) and PARKINSON (JOHN RICHARD) Bangladesh: the test case of development. London, [1976]. pp. 203.

— **Rural conditions.**

RESEARCH WORKSHOP ON RURAL DEVELOPMENT IN PAKISTAN, MICHIGAN STATE UNIVERSITY, 1971. Rural development in Bangladesh and Pakistan; edited by Robert D. Stevens [and others]. Honolulu, [1976]. pp. 399. *bibliogs. Revised versions of papers presented at the workshop.*

— — **Bibliography.**

SCHENDEL (WILLEM VAN) Bangladesh: a bibliography with special reference to the peasantry. Amsterdam, 1976. pp. 227. (*Amsterdam. Universiteit. Antropologisch-Sociologisch Centrum. Afdeling Zuid- en Zuidoost-Azië. Voorpublikaties. Nr.10*)

BANKS AND BANKING.

— Social conditions.

FAROUK (A.) and ALI (MUHAMMAD) The hardworking poor: a survey on how people use their time in Bangladesh. Dacca, 1975. 1 vol. (various pagings).

BANK HOLDING COMPANIES

— United States.

FRAAS (ARTHUR G.) The performance of individual bank holding companies. [Washington, 1974]. pp. 27. (United States. Board of Governors of the Federal Reserve System. Staff Economic Studies. No. 84)

BANK INVESTMENTS.

BEAZER (WILLIAM F.) Optimization of bank portfolios. Lexington, Mass., [1975]. pp. 180. bibliog.

— Mathematical models.

WOOD (JOHN HAROLD) Commercial bank loan and investment behaviour. London, [1975]. pp. 153. bibliog.

— Canada — Mathematical models.

WHITE (WILLIAM R.) Management by the Canadian banks of their domestic portfolios 1956- 1971: an econometric study. [Ottawa], 1975. pp. 261. bibliog. (Bank of Canada. Staff Research Studies. No.11)

BANK LOANS

— Mathematical models.

WOOD (JOHN HAROLD) Commercial bank loan and investment behaviour. London, [1975]. pp. 153. bibliog.

BANK OF ENGLAND.

SAYERS (RICHARD SIDNEY) The Bank of England, 1891-1944. Cambridge, 1976. 3 vols.

BANK OF JAMAICA.

BANK OF JAMAICA. Report and statement of accounts. a., 1962, 1966- Kingston.

BANKERS

— Europe.

LE GOFF (JACQUES) Marchands et banquiers du Moyen Âge. 5th ed. Paris, 1972. pp. 128. bibliog.

— United Kingdom — Biography.

INSTITUTE OF BANKERS. The first fifty years of the Institute of Bankers, 1879-1929: published under the authority of the Council of the Institute. London, 1929. pp. 69.

BANKING AS A PROFESSION.

INSTITUTE OF BANKERS. Wilde Committee. The Institute of Bankers educational policy review. Part 2. The Institute's post-qualifying activities: a report. London, [1974]. pp. 29.

BANKING LAW

— European Economic Community countries.

INTER-BANK RESEARCH ORGANISATION. Prudential regulation of credit institutions in the EEC;...reports on...the nine member states...[and] a separate summary. London, 1975. 10 vols. (in 1). bibliogs.

— Luxembourg.

LUXEMBOURG. Statutes, etc. 1873-1975. Recueil de la législation sur les banque et bourse: textes coordonnés et jurisprudence; [edited by] (Raymond Weydert). Luxembourg, 1975. pp. 264.

— United Kingdom.

MACAULAY (WALLACE D.) The liability of a banker on a cheque. London, 1953. fo. 116. LL.M. (London) thesis.

REEDAY (THOMAS GEOFFREY) The law relating to banking. 3rd ed. London, 1976. pp. 474.

— United States.

BURNS (HELEN M.) The American banking community and New Deal banking reforms, 1933-1935. Westport, Conn., 1974. pp. 203. bibliog.

BANKRUPTCY.

KELLENS (GEORGES) Banqueroute et banqueroutiers. Bruxelles, [1974]. pp. 212. bibliog.

ARGENTI (JOHN) Corporate collapse: the causes and symptoms. London, [1976]. pp. 193. bibliog.

— Canada.

CANADA CORPORATIONS BANKRUPTCY AND INSOLVENCY: Bulletin (formerly Canada Corporations Act: Bulletin;) [pd. by] Bureau of Corporate Affairs...Canada. [in English and French]. m. Ottawa. Current issues only kept.

— Luxembourg.

LUXEMBOURG. Statutes, etc. 1870-1975. Recueil de la législation sur la faillite: textes coordonnés et jurisprudence; [edited by] (Raymond Weydert). Luxembourg, 1975. pp. 108.

BANKS AND BANKING.

GREGORY (Sir THEODOR EMANUEL GUGENHEIM) [Unpublished economic and personal papers. 1910-34]. 6 pieces. Manuscript, typescript, etc.

SIMPSON (THOMAS D.) Money, banking, and economic analysis. Englewood Cliffs, [1976]. pp. 493. bibliogs.

— Africa, West.

FRY (RICHARD HENRY) Bankers in West Africa: the story of the Bank of British West Africa Limited. London, 1976. pp. 270.

— Australia — New South Wales.

NEW SOUTH WALES. Commonwealth Bureau of Census and Statistics. New South Wales Office. Banking, insurance and other private finance. a., 1972-73/1973-74- Sydney.

— Chile.

CHILE. Superintendencia de Bancos. Boletin estadistico. m., 1966- Santiago. Supersedes bi-m. Estadistica bancaria (1934-1965, with gaps).

— Europe.

HEWSON (JOHN R.) Liquidity creation and distribution in the eurocurrency markets. Lexington, Mass., [1975]. pp. 172. bibliog.

— Europe, Eastern.

BANKING, money and credit in Eastern Europe: main findings of colloquium held 24th-26th January, 1973, in Brussels; [edited by] Yves Laulan. [Brussels], North Atlantic Treaty Organization, [1973?] . pp. 166. In English and French.

— France.

COLLOQUE SUR LES BANQUES ETRANGERES EN FRANCE, PARIS, 1974. L'activité des banques étrangères en France: [proceedings of the colloque]. Paris, [1975]. pp. 118. (Paris. Université de Paris I (Panthéon-Sorbonne). Publications. Série Droit Privé. 2)

GAULLIER (JEAN PIERRE) Le système bancaire français. 2nd ed. Paris, 1975. pp. 126. bibliog.

FRANCE. French Embassy, London. Service de Presse et d'Information. 1976. The French banking system. London, 1976. pp. 22. (France: facts, figures. A/112/2/76)

— Germany.

ROSENBAUM (EDUARD) and SHERMAN (A.J.) Das Bankhaus M.M. Warburg Co., 1798-1938. Hamburg, [1976]. pp. 235. bibliog.

VEREIN FÜR SOZIALPOLITIK. Schriften. Neue Folge. Band 87. Wettbewerbsprobleme im Kreditgewerbe; herausgegeben von Burkhardt Röper. Berlin, [1976]. pp. 283.

— Kenya.

FREDIANI (LORENZO) The liquidity policy of deposit banks in Kenya. Milan, [1975]. pp. 277. bibliog. (Cassa di Risparmio delle Provincie Lombarde. The Credit Markets of Africa. 12)

— Luxembourg.

MEIER (ULRICH) Struktur des Bankwesens in Luxemburg. Frankfurt am Main, [1975]. pp. 148. bibliog. (Berlin. Freie Universität. Institut für Banken und Industrie, Geld und Kredit. Struktur Ausländischer Bankensysteme. Heft 7)

— Sicily.

CUSUMANO (VITO) Storia dei banchi della Sicilia; a cura di Romualdo Giuffrida. [Palermo], 1974. pp. 519. (Fondazione Culturale "Lauro Chiazzese". Biblioteca di Economia e Tecnica Bancaria. 2) Originally published in two volumes, Rome, 1887-92.

— Spain.

SANZ GARCIA (JOSE MARIA) Madrid: capital del capital español?; contribucion a la geografia urbana y a las funciones geoeconomicas de la villa y corte. Madrid, 1975 in progress.

— Sweden.

FRITZ (MARTIN) Ernest Thiel: finansman i genombrottstid. Göteborg, 1974. pp. 51. bibliog. (Göteborgs Universitet. Ekonomisk-Historiska Institutionen. Meddelanden. 33)

— Switzerland.

GYGAX (PAUL) Bank in St. Gallen, 1837-1907: die Geschichte einer schweizerischen Notenbank. St. Gallen, 1907. pp. 398.

CAPAUL (DURI) Graubündner Kantonalbank, 1930-1970: 40 Jahre im Dienste der Bündner Volkswirtschaft. Chur, 1974. pp. 252.

— Thailand — Mathematical models.

CHAIPRAVAT (OLARN) Revenue and cost structures of Thai commercial banks: a cross section-time series analysis, 1963-70. Bangkok, 1974. pp. 18. (Bank of Thailand. Papers. No.1.)

— United Kingdom.

The BANKS and society: based on the [Institute of Bankers'] seminar held at Christ's College, Cambridge... September, 1974. London, [1974]. pp. 84. bibliog.

DENNIS (GEOFFREY EDWIN JAMES) Recent changes in the banking system and their implications. Loughborough, 1974. pp. 32. bibliog. (Loughborough University of Technology. Department of Economics. Loughborough Papers on Recent Developments in Economic Policy and Thought. No. 2)

— — Branch banks.

The BRANCH banker today and tomorrow; based on the seminar held at Christ's College, Cambridge...1975. London, [1975]. pp. 97. bibliog.

— — Ireland.

BARROW (GEORGE LENNOX) The emergence of the Irish banking system, 1820-1845. Dublin, [1975]. pp. 251. bibliog.

— — Ireland, Northern.

SIMPSON (NOEL) The Belfast Bank, 1827-1970: 150 years of banking in Ireland. Belfast, [1975]. pp. 361.

— United States.

KENNEDY (SUSAN ESTABROOK) The banking crisis of 1933. Lexington, Ky., [1973]. pp. 270. bibliog.

BANKS AND BANKING.(Cont.)

BURNS (HELEN M.) The American banking community and New Deal banking reforms, 1933-1935. Westport, Conn., 1974. pp. 203. *bibliog.*

CAMBRIDGE RESEARCH INSTITUTE. Trends affecting the U.S. banking system;...Paul V. Teplitz, principal author. Cambridge, Mass., [1976]. pp. 206. *bibliog.*

— Yugoslavia.

LJUBETIĆ-SIROTKOVIĆ (ECIJA) Mjesto i uloga internih banaka u društvenoj reprodukciji. Zagreb, 1975. pp. 16.

PERIŠIN (IVO) Transformacija monetarnog i bankarsko-kreditnog sistema Jugoslavije; (monetarni sistem i ustavna reforma). Zagreb, 1975. pp. 59. *(Zagreb. Ekonomski Institut. Ekonomska Biblioteka: Aktuelni Problemi. 1/75)*

BANKS AND BANKING, COOPERATIVE

— Germany.

LOESCH (ACHIM VON) Die Bank für Gemeinwirtschaft: Entwicklung, Struktur, Aufgaben. Frankfurt am Main, [1975]. pp. 61. *bibliog.*

— India.

RESERVE BANK OF INDIA. Selected statistics relating to co-operative credit in India: 1960-61, 1965-6 and 1968-9 to 1971-2. 4th ed. Bombay, [1974?]. pp. 52.

— Romania.

USSOSKIN (MOSHE) Struggle for survival: a history of Jewish credit co-operatives in Bessarabia, Old-Rumania, Bukovina and Transylvania. Jerusalem, [1975]. pp. 362. *bibliog.*

— Russia.

USSOSKIN (MOSHE) Struggle for survival: a history of Jewish credit co-operatives in Bessarabia, Old-Rumania, Bukovina and Transylvania. Jerusalem, [1975]. pp. 362. *bibliog.*

— Underdeveloped areas.

See UNDERDEVELOPED AREAS — Banks and banking, Cooperative.

BANKS AND BANKING, INTERNATIONAL.

EHRLICH (BENJAMIN) The world bank of issue; projected by Benjamin Ehrlich. Lisbon, 1972. pp. 275. *bibliog.*

COLLOQUE SUR LES BANQUES ETRANGERES EN FRANCE, PARIS, 1974. L'activité des banques étrangères en France: [proceedings of the colloque]. Paris, [1975]. pp. 118. *(Paris. Université de Paris I (Panthéon-Sorbonne). Publications. Série Droit Privé. 2)*

CROSSLEY (Sir JULIAN) and BLANDFORD (JOHN) The DCO story: a history of banking in many countries, 1925-71. London, 1975. pp. 339.

PERKINS (EDWIN J.) Financing Anglo-American trade: the House of Brown, 1800-1880. Cambridge, Mass., 1975. pp. 323. *bibliog. (Harvard University. Harvard Studies in Business History. 28)*

DAVIS (STEVEN I.) The Euro-bank: its origins, management and outlook. London, 1976. pp. 125. *bibliog.*

STEUBER (URSEL) International banking: the foreign activities of the banks of principal industrial countries. Leyden, 1976. pp. 211. *bibliog.*

BANKS AND BANKING, TRADE UNION

— America, North.

LOESCH (ACHIM VON) North-American worker's banks in the twenties. Francfort, [1974]. p. 38. *(Bank für Gemeinwirtschaft Aktiengesellschaft. Series Commonweal Economy. No. 7)*

BANQUE NATIONALE DE BELGIQUE.

WEE (HERMAN VAN DER) and TAVERNIER (K.) La Banque Nationale de Belgique et l'histoire monétaire entre les deux guerres mondiales; (traduit du néerlandais). [Brussels], 1975. pp. 542. *bibliog.*

BANTUS.

BANTU INVESTMENT CORPORATION OF SOUTH AFRICA LIMITED. Annual report. a., 1969/70-1971/72 (11th-13th), 1974 (15th)- Pretoria. *[in English and Afrikaans].*

SOUTH AFRICA. Bureau of Statistics. National accounts of the Bantu homelands. a., 1969-70/1973-74 (1st)- Pretoria. *[in English and Afrikaans].*

SOUTH AFRICA. Department of Information. 1971. Nutrition and the Bantu. [Pretoria, 1971]. pp. 24.

SOUTH AFRICA. Bureau of Statistics. Statistics of Bantu affairs administration boards. a., 1973/74 (1st)- Pretoria. *[In English and Afrikaans].*

JACKSON (A.O.) The ethnic composition of the Ciskei and Transkei. Pretoria, 1975. pp. 81, 7 maps. *bibliog. (South Africa. Department of Bantu Administration and Development. Ethnological Publications. No. 53)*

SOUTH AFRICA. Parliament. House of Assembly. Select Committee on Bantu Affairs. 1976. First and second reports (with Proceedings) (S.C.6-1976). in SOUTH AFRICA. Parliament. House of Assembly. Select Committee reports.

BARCELONA

— Politics and government.

Les ELECCIONS municipals a Barcelona del 16 d'octubre 1973: assaig de sociologia electoral; [by Ramon M. Canals and other members of the] Facultat de Dret, Universitat Autonoma de Barcelona; estudi i edició patrocinats per la Fundació Jaume Bofill. Barcelona, 1975. pp. 283. *With abstracts in Spanish and English.*

BARCLAY (Sir RODERICK EDWARD).

BARCLAY (Sir RODERICK EDWARD) Ernest Bevin and the Foreign Office, 1932-1969. London, 1975. pp. 166.

BARNES (RON).

BARNES (RON) A licence to live:...scenes from a post-war working life in Hackney. London, [1974] repr. 1976. pp. 76.

BARTER

— Peru.

ALBERTI (GIORGIO) and MAYER (ENRIQUE) eds. Reciprocidad e intercambio en los Andes peruanos. Lima, 1974. pp. 360. *bibliog. (Instituto de Estudios Peruanos. Peru Problema. 12)*

BARTHOU (LOUIS).

HERZOG (WILHELM) Barthou. Zürich, 1938. pp. 328. *bibliog.*

BARTON BLOUNT, DERBYSHIRE

— Antiquities.

BERESFORD (GUY) The medieval clay-land village: excavations at Goltho and Barton Blount. London, 1975. pp. 113. *(Society for Medieval Archaeology. Monograph Series. No. 6)*

BARTOSZEWSKI (WLADYSLAW)

— Bibliography.

BARTOSZEWSKI (WŁADYSŁAW) 1859 dni Warszawy. Kraków, 1974. pp. 835. *bibliog.*

BASQUE PROVINCES

— Economic history.

FERNANDEZ DE PINEDO (EMILIANO) Crecimiento economico y transformaciones sociales del pais vasco, 1100-1850. MExico, 1974. pp. 500. *bibliog.*

SOLOZABAL ECHAVARRIA (JUAN JOSE) El primer nacionalismo vasco: industrialismo y conciencia nacional. Madrid, [1975]. pp. 374.

— History.

DAVANT (JEAN LOUIS) Histoire du Pays Basque: le peuple basque dans l'histoire. Bayonne, [1975]. pp. 165. *bibliog.*

— Nationalism.

ELOSEGI (JOSEBA) Quiero morir por algo. [Bordeaux?, 1971]. pp. 329.

PAYNE (STANLEY G.) Basque nationalism. Reno, Nevada, 1975. pp. 291. *bibliog.*

SOLOZABAL ECHAVARRIA (JUAN JOSE) El primer nacionalismo vasco: industrialismo y conciencia nacional. Madrid, [1975]. pp. 374.

— Social history.

FERNANDEZ DE PINEDO (EMILIANO) Crecimiento economico y transformaciones sociales del pais vasco, 1100-1850. MExico, 1974. pp. 500. *bibliog.*

BATA (THOMAS).

PHILIPP (RUDOLPH) Stiefel der Diktatur. Zürich, 1936. pp. 265.

BATTLES.

KEEGAN (JOHN) The face of battle. London, 1976. pp. 352. *bibliog.*

BAVARIA

— Economic conditions.

BAVARIA. Statistisches Landesamt. 1973- . Die kreisfreien Städte und Landkreise Bayerns in der amtlichen Statistik: [new series]. [Munich], 1973 in progress.

— History.

ZASTENKER (N.) Bavarskaia Sovetskaia Respublika. Moskva, 1934. pp. 160.

— Politics and government.

BEHR (WOLFGANG) Sozialdemokratie und Konservatismus: ein empirischer und theoretischer Beitrag zur regionalen Parteianalyse am Beispiel der Geschichte und Nachkriegsentwicklung Bayerns. Hannover, [1969]. pp. 298. *bibliog. (Friedrich-Ebert-Stiftung. Forschungsinstitut. Schriftenreihe. Band 72)*

ROTH (RAINER A.) ed. Freistaat Bayern: die politische Wirklichkeit eines Landes der Bundesrepublik Deutschland; mit Beiträgen von: Arthur Bader [and others]. Donauwörth, [1975]. pp. 416. *bibliog.*

— Statistics.

BAVARIA. Statistisches Landesamt. 1973- . Die kreisfreien Städte und Landkreise Bayerns in der amtlichen Statistik: [new series]. [Munich], 1973 in progress.

BAYONNE.

FRANCE. Direction de la Documentation. La Documentation Française. Notes et Etudes Documentaires. Nos. 4,174-4, 175. Les villes françaises: Bayonne et la région urbaine côtière; par Pierre Laborde. Paris, 1975. pp. 80. *bibliog.*

BEBEL (AUGUST).

BLEY (HELMUT) Bebel und die Strategie der Kriegsverhütung, 1904-1913: eine Studie über Bebels Geheimkontakte mit der britischen Regierung, etc. Göttingen, 1975. pp. 254.

BECK (JÓZEF).

RAINA (PETER) Stosunki polsko-niemieckie 1937-1939: prawdziwy charakter polityki zagranicznej Józefa Becka. Londyn, 1975. pp. 172.

BECKER (RAYMOND DE).

EUROPEAN COURT OF HUMAN RIGHTS. Publications. Series A: Judgments ad Decisions. A 4. ..."De Becker" case; judgment of 27th March 1962. Strasbourg, Council of Europe, 1962. pp. 33bis. *In English and French.*

BEDFORDSHIRE

— Gentry.

NAUGHTON (KATHERINE S.) The gentry of Bedfordshire in the thirteenth and fourteenth centuries. Leicester, 1976. pp. 90. *(Leicester. University. Department of English Local History. Occasional Papers. 3rd Series. No. 2)*

BEDOUINS.

COLE (DONALD POWELL) Nomads of the nomads: the Al Murrah Bedouin of the Empty Quarter. Chicago, 1975. pp. 179. *bibliog.*

BEEF.

— Prices.

CANADA. Food Prices Review Board. 1974. Report on ground beef. [Ottawa?], 1974. pp. 28.

— Australia — Seasonal variations.

AUSTRALIA. Bureau of Agricultural Economics. 1970. Seasonality in the Australian beef industry. Canberra, 1970. pp. 53. *(Beef Research Reports. No. 7)*

— Japan.

AUSTRALIA. Bureau of Agricultural Economics. 1975. Developments in the Japanese beef market: their implications for production systems in the Australian beef cattle industry, incorporating findings of a B[ureau of] A[gricultural] E[conomics] study tour. Canberra, 1975. pp. 114. *(Beef Research Reports. No. 17)*

— United Kingdom.

WHETHAM (EDITH H.) Beef cattle and sheep, 1910-1940: a description of the production and marketing of beef cattle and sheep in Great Britain from the early 20th century to the Second World War. Cambridge, 1976. pp. 59. *bibliog. (Cambridge. University. Department of Land Economy. Occasional Papers. No.5)*

BEEF CATTLE

— Economic aspects.

HARRISON (S.R.) and CAMPBELL (C.B.) Discounted cash flow analysis of beef development projects. [Brisbane], 1970. pp. 40. *(Queensland. Department of Primary Industries. Economic Services Branch. Technical Bulletins. No. 8)*

AUSTRALIA. Bureau of Agricultural Economics. 1972. Economic principles for increased beef production from butterfat dairy farms. Canberra, 1972. pp. 44. *(Beef Research Reports. No. 9)*

— — Australia.

AUSTRALIA. Bureau of Agricultural Economics. 1975. The Australian beef cattle industry: submissions to the Industries Assistance Commission inquiry. Canberra, 1975. pp. 105. *(Industry Economics Monographs. No. 13)*

AUSTRALIA. Bureau of Agricultural Economics. 1975. Developments in the Japanese beef market: their implications for production systems in the Australian beef cattle industry, incorporating findings of a B[ureau of] A[gricultural] E[conomics] study tour. Canberra, 1975. pp. 114. *(Beef Research Reports. No. 17)*

— — — Northern Territory.

AUSTRALIA. Bureau of Agricultural Economics. 1971. Aboriginal pastoral properties, Arnhem Land, Northern Territory. Canberra, 1971. pp. 58.

— — Australia.

AUSTRALIA. Bureau of Agricultural Economics. 1976. Production systems in the Australian beef cattle industry. Canberra, 1976. pp. 60. *(Beef Research Reports. No. 18)*

— — Feeding and feeds.

AUSTRALIA. Bureau of Agricultural Economics. 1969. The economics of fattening store cattle by dry lot feeding. Canberra, 1969. pp. 46. *(Beef Research Reports. No. 5)*

— — Queensland — Feeding and feeds.

AUSTRALIA. Bureau of Agricultural Economics. 1968. Some factors affecting the profitability of crop fattening beef cattle. Canberra, 1968. pp. 38. *(Beef Research Reports. No. 4)*

BEHAVIOUR MODIFICATION.

SCHWITZGEBEL (RALPH K.) and KOLB (DAVID A.) Changing human behavior: principles of planned intervention. New York, [1974]. pp. 332. *bibliog.*

THOMAS (EDWIN JOHN) ed. Behavior modification procedure: a source book. Chicago, 1974. pp. 323. *bibliogs.*

FISCHER (JOEL) and GOCHROS (HARVEY L.) Planned behavior change: behavior modification in social work. New York, [1975]. pp. 525. *bibliog.*

BEHAVIOUR THERAPY.

GELFAND (DONNA M.) and HARTMANN (DONALD P.) Child behavior analysis and therapy. New York, [1975]. pp. 332. *bibliog.*

NOVACO (RAYMOND W.) Anger control: the development and evaluation of an experimental treatment. Lexington, [1975]. pp. 134. *bibliog.*

BELFAST

— Economic conditions.

EMPLOYERS' PARLIAMENTARY ASSOCIATION. [Correspondence with Sir R.A. Cooper. 1916]. 1 piece. *Typescript.*

BELGIUM

— Commerce.

BELGIUM. Institut National de Statistique. Recensement de l'industrie et du commerce. Recensement de l'industrie et du commerce, 31 décembre 1970. Bruxelles, 1975 in progress.

— Constitution.

SENELLE (ROBERT) La constitution belge commentée. Bruxelles, 1974. pp. 470. *(Belgium. Ministère des Affaires Etrangères et du Commerce Extérieur. Textes et Documents. No. 301)*

SENELLE (ROBERT) The Belgian constitution: commentary. Brussels, Ministry of Foreign Affairs, External Trade and Cooperation in Development, 1974. pp. 493. *(Memo from Belgium. No. 166)* Folded chart in end-pocket.

— Economic conditions.

BELGIUM. Ministère des Affaires Etrangères, du Commerce Extérieur et de la Coopération au Développement. 1973. Foreign policy programme; by Renaat van Elslande, Minister of Foreign Affairs; [and] Chronicles: statements made by Ministers to the press. Brussels, 1973. pp. 82. *(Memo from Belgium. No. 158)*

BELGIUM. Ministère des Affaires Etrangères, du Commerce Extérieur et de la Coopération au Développement. 1973. Statement by the tripartite government [and] political, economical and cultural chronicles. Brussels, 1973. pp. 62. *(Memo from Belgium. No. 157)*

— Economic history — Sources.

MOUREAUX (PHILIPPE) ed. La statistique industrielle dans les Pays-Bas autrichiens à l'époque de Marie-Thérèse: documents et cartes. Bruxelles, 1974 in progress.

— Economic policy.

INSTITUT BELGE D'INFORMATION ET DE DOCUMENTATION. The organisational structure of the Belgian economy. Brussels, Ministry of Foreign Affairs, External Trade and Cooperation in Development, 1976. pp. 28. *(Belgian News. No. 3e)*

— Foreign population.

SPEECKAERT (GEORGES PATRICK) International life in Belgium. Brussels, Ministry of Foreign Affairs, External Trade and Cooperation in Development, 1973. pp. 58. *(Memo from Belgium. No. 156)*

— Foreign relations.

HELMREICH (JONATHAN E.) Belgium and Europe: a study in small power diplomacy. The Hague, [1976]. pp. 451. *bibliog.*

— — United Kingdom.

WAUGH (MAUREEN CRAIGIE) British foreign policy and the security of Belgium's frontiers, 1934-1939. [1976]. fo. 257. *bibliog. Typescript. Ph.D. (London) thesis: unpublished. This thesis is the property of London University and may not be removed from the Library.*

— Industries.

MOUREAUX (PHILIPPE) ed. La statistique industrielle dans les Pays-Bas autrichiens à l'époque de Marie-Thérèse: documents et cartes. Bruxelles, 1974 in progress.

BELGIUM. Institut National de Statistique. Recensement de l'industrie et du commerce. Recensement de l'industrie et du commerce, 31 décembre 1970. Bruxelles, 1975 in progress.

RILEY (RAYMOND CHARLES) Belgium. Folkestone, Kent, 1976. pp. 205. *bibliog.*

— Languages.

EUROPEAN COURT OF HUMAN RIGHTS. Publications. Series A: Judgments and Decisions. [A5]. ...Case relating to certain aspects of the laws on the use of languages in education in Belgium; preliminary objection. 1. Decision of 3rd May 1966. 2. Judgment of 9th February 1967. Strasbourg, Council of Europe, 1967. pp. 20 [bis]. *In English and French.*

EUROPEAN COURT OF HUMAN RIGHTS. Publications. Series B: Pleadings, Oral Arguments and Documents. [B3]. Case "relating to certain aspects of the laws on the use of languages in education in Belgium". vol.1. Pleadings, oral arguments and documents previous to the decision of 9/2/1967: preliminary objection. Strasbourg, Council of Europe, 1967. pp. 531[bis], 533-612. *In English and French.*

EUROPEAN COURT OF HUMAN RIGHTS. Publications. Series A: Judgments and Decisions. [A6]. ...Case relating to certain aspects of the laws on the use of languages in education in Belgium; merits; judgment of 23rd July 1968. Strasbourg, Council of Europe, 1968. pp. 109 [bis]. *In English and French.*

EUROPEAN COURT OF HUMAN RIGHTS. Publications. Series B: Pleadings, Oral Arguments and Documents. [B4]. Case"relating to certain aspects of the laws on the use of languages in education in Belgium". vol.2. Pleadings, oral arguments and documents subsequent to the judgment of 9/2/1967: merits. Strasbourg, Council of Europe, 1968. pp. 270bis, 272-307. *In English and French.*

BELGIUM(Cont.)

— Parliament — Elections.

FROGNIER (ANDRE PAUL) and others. Vote, clivages socio-politiques et développement régional en Belgique. Louvain, [1974]. pp. 149.

— Politics and government.

SOCIÉTÉ D'ÉTUDES POLITIQUES ET SOCIALES. Cahiers. No. 5. La participation politique en Belgique. Louvain, 1966. pp. 57.

— Social conditions.

BELGIUM. Ministère des Affaires Etrangères, du Commerce Extérieur et de la Coopération au Développement. 1973. Foreign policy programme; by Renaat van Elslande, Minister of Foreign Affairs; [and] Chronicles: statements made by Ministers to the press. Brussels, 1973. pp. 82. *(Memo from Belgium. No. 158)*

BELGIUM. Ministère des Affaires Etrangères, du Commerce Extérieur et de la Coopération au Développement. 1973. Statement by the tripartite government [and] political, economical and cultural chronicles. Brussels, 1973. pp. 62 *(Memo from Belgium. No. 157)*

BELIEF AND DOUBT.

BEM (DARYL J.) Beliefs, attitudes and human affairs. Belmont, Cal., [1970]. pp. 114. *bibliog.*

BELINSKII (VISSARION GRIGOR'EVICH).

BEREZINA (VALENTINA GRIGOR'EVNA) Belinskii i voprosy istorii russkoi zhurnalistiki. Leningrad, 1973. pp. 144.

STEPANISHCHEV (SERGEI SEMENOVICH) Razvitie obshchestvennoi mysli v trudakh russkikh revoliutsionerov-demokratov: analiz sotsial'no-politicheskikh, ateisticheskikh i eticheskikh idei A.N. Radishcheva, V.G. Belinskogo, N.P. Ogareva. Minsk, 1975. pp. 478.

BELIZE

— Economic conditions.

BELIZE. Ministry of Finance and Economic Development. Central Planning Unit. Economic survey. a., 1971- Belmopan.

ASHCRAFT (NORMAN) Colonialism and underdevelopment: processes of political economic change in British Honduras. New York, [1973]. pp. 180. *bibliog.*

— Economic history.

ASHCRAFT (NORMAN) Colonialism and underdevelopment: processes of political economic change in British Honduras. New York, [1973]. pp. 180. *bibliog.*

BENEDICT (RUTH FULTON).

MEAD (MARGARET) Ruth Benedict; [with selected papers by Ruth Benedict]. New York, [1974]. pp. 180. *bibliogs.*

BENGAL

— Social history.

INDEN (RONALD B.) Marriage and rank in Bengali culture: a history of caste and clan in middle period Bengal. Berkeley, Calif., [1976]. pp. 161. *bibliog.*

BENGAL, WEST

— Economic policy.

WEST BENGAL. Development Department. 1958. West Bengal second five-year plan, 1956-61. [Alipore, 1958?]. pp. 131.

WEST BENGAL. State Planning Board. 1973. Comprehensive area development programme: a new strategy for development. [Calcutta], 1973. pp. 49.

— Politics and government.

GHOSH (SANKAR) The Naxalite movement: a Maoist experiment. Calcutta, 1974. pp. 183.

— Social policy.

WEST BENGAL. Development Department. 1958. West Bengal second five-year plan, 1956-61. [Alipore, 1958?]. pp. 131.

WEST BENGAL. State Planning Board. 1973. Comprehensive area development programme: a new strategy for development. [Calcutta], 1973. pp. 49.

BEREAVEMENT.

GLICK (IRA OSCAR) and others. The first year of bereavement. New York, [1974]. pp. 311.

BEREAVEMENT: its psychosocial aspects; edited by Bernard Schoenberg [and others]. New York, 1975. pp. 375. *bibliogs.*

BERGSLAGEN

— Population.

NORMAN (HANS) Från Bergslagen till Nordamerika: studier i migrationsmönster, social rörlighet och demografisk struktur med utgångspunkt från Örebro Län, 1851-1915. Uppsala, 1974. pp. 372. *bibliog. (Uppsala. Universitet. Historiska Institutionen. Studia Historica Upsaliensia. 62) With English summary.*

BERKMAN (ALEXANDER).

GOLDMAN (EMMA) and BERKMAN (ALEXANDER) Nowhere at home: letters from exile of Emma Goldman and Alexander Berkman; edited by Richard and Anna Maria Drinnon. New York, [1975]. pp. 282.

BERLIN

— Economic history.

BERGMANN (JUERGEN) Das Berliner Handwerk in den Frühphasen der Industrialisierung. Berlin, 1973. pp. 401. *bibliog. (Historische Kommission zu Berlin. Einzelveröffentlichungen. Band 11)*

— Politics and government.

SOZIALISTISCHE EINHEITSPARTEI DEUTSCHLANDS. Landesvorstand Gross- Berlin. Die Krise der SPD und die Politik der SED. Gross-Berlin, [1947]. pp. 102. *(Material für die Funktionäre der SED)*

ADOMATIS (HANS JOACHIM) Von Berlin aus gesehen: die Springer-Partei. Wuppertal, 1975. pp. 102.

PETRY (LOTHAR) Die Erste Internationale in der Berliner Arbeiterbewegung. Erlangen, 1975. pp. 381. *bibliog.*

HENNIG (OTTFRIED) Die Bundespräsenz in West-Berlin: Entwicklung und Rechtscharakter. Köln, [1976]. pp. 367. *bibliog.*

— Population — Mathematical models.

DEUTSCHES INSTITUT FÜR WIRTSCHAFTSFORSCHUNG. Sonderhefte. [Neue Folge]. 110. Modelle der Bevölkerungsentwicklung in Berlin, West, bis zum Jahre 1990; ([by] Peter Ring und Ingo Pfeiffer). Berlin, 1975. pp. 115. *bibliog.*

— Statistics.

BERLINER STATISTIK; Herausgeber: Statistisches Landesamt Berlin. [West Berlin]. m., 1947 (1.Jg.)- Berlin. *Index: 1947/1964. File includes Sonderhefte and Sonderreihen. To N 1948 statistics included the whole of Berlin.*

BERLIN FREE UNIVERSITY.

BERLIN. Freie Universität. Presse- und Informationsstelle. Auf die Finger gesehen: fünf Informationen zu der Frage: Wo steht die Freie Universität heute?...(Texte: Claus Rietzschel [and others]). Berlin, [1973]. pp. 68.

BERLIN QUESTION (1945—).

GERMANY (BUNDESREPUBLIK). Presse- und Informationsamt. 1971. Die Berlin-Regelung: das Viermächte-Abkommen über Berlin und die ergänzenden Vereinbarungen. [Bonn, 1971]. pp. 348.

HENNIG (OTTFRIED) Die Bundespräsenz in West-Berlin: Entwicklung und Rechtscharakter. Köln, [1976]. pp. 367. *bibliog.*

BERNASCHEK (RICHARD).

KYKAL (INEZ) and STADLER (KARL RUDOLF) Richard Bernaschek: Odyssee eines Rebellen. Wien, [1976]. pp. 317. *bibliog. (Ludwig-Boltzmann-Institut für Geschichte der Arbeiterbewegung. Veröffentlichungen)*

BERNASEK (RICHARD).

See BERNASCHEK (RICHARD)

BERRYER (PIERRE ANTOINE).

MIRECOURT (EUGENE DE) pseud. [i.e. Charles Jean Baptiste JACQUOT] Berryer. Paris, G. Havard, 1855. pp. 96. *(Les Contemporains)*

BERT (PIERRE).

BERT (PIERRE) In vino veritas: l'affaire des vins de Bordeaux. Paris, [1975]. pp. 244.

BERTIE (FRANCIS LEVESON) 1st Viscount Bertie of Thame.

HAMILTON (KEITH ALEXANDER) The embassy of Sir Francis Bertie in Paris during the period 1905-1914. 1975 [or rather 1976]. fo. 447. *bibliog. Typescript. Ph.D.(London) thesis: unpublished. This thesis is the property of London University and may not be removed from the Library.*

BESSARABIA

— Annexation to Russia.

KOPANSKII (IAKOV MIKHAILOVICH) Internatsional'naia solidarnost' s bor'boi trudiashchikhsia Bessarabii za vossoedinenie s Sovetskoi Rodinoi, 1918-1940; otvetstvennyi redaktor...A.M. Lazarev. Kishinev, 1975. pp. 337.

JEWSBURY (GEORGE F.) The Russian annexation of Bessarabia, 1774-1828: a study of imperial expansion. New York, 1976. pp. 199. *bibliog. (East European Quarterly. East European Monographs. 15)*

— Foreign opinion.

KOPANSKII (IAKOV MIKHAILOVICH) Internatsional'naia solidarnost' s bor'boi trudiashchikhsia Bessarabii za vossoedinenie s Sovetskoi Rodinoi, 1918-1940; otvetstvennyi redaktor...A.M. Lazarev. Kishinev, 1975. pp. 337.

— History.

LAZAREV (ARTEM MARKOVICH) Moldavskaia Sovetskaia gosudarstvennost' i bessarabskii vopros. Kishinev, 1974. pp. 910. *bibliog.*

BESTEIRO FERNANDEZ (JULIAN).

BESTEIRO FERNANDEZ (JULIAN) Historia parlamentaria del socialismo: Julian Besteiro...; edicion, guia historica y notas de Fermin Solana. Madrid, [1975 in progress].

BEVIN (ERNEST).

BARCLAY (Sir RODERICK EDWARD) Ernest Bevin and the Foreign Office, 1932-1969. London, 1975. pp. 166.

BHENGU (NICHOLAS).

DUBB (ALLIE A.) Community of the saved: an African revivalist church in the east Cape. Johannesburg, 1976. pp. 175. *bibliog.*

BIBLIOGRAPHY

— Bibliography.

OTTO (FRIEDA) compiler. Bibliographie wirtschafts- und sozialwissenschaftlicher Bibliographien: Zugänge der Bibliothek des Instituts für Weltwirtschaft, Kiel, in den Jahren 1968 bis 1973. Kiel, 1975. pp. 83. *(Kiel. Universität. Institut für Weltwirtschaft. Bibliothek. Kieler Schrifttumskunden zu Wirtschaft und Gesellschaft. 20)*

— Early printed books.

POLLARD (ALFRED WILLIAM) and REDGRAVE (GILBERT RICHARD) A short-title catalogue of books printed in England, Scotland, and Ireland and of English books printed abroad, 1475-1640;... second edition...begun by W.A. Jackson and F.S. Ferguson; completed by Katharine F. Pantzer. London, 1976 in progress.

— Paperback editions.

SMITH (ROGER H.) Paperback Parnassus: the birth, the development, the pending crisis of the modern American paperbound book. Boulder, Co., 1976. pp. 111.

BIBLIOGRAPHY, NATIONAL

— English.

POLLARD (ALFRED WILLIAM) and REDGRAVE (GILBERT RICHARD) A short-title catalogue of books printed in England, Scotland, and Ireland and of English books printed abroad, 1475-1640;... second edition...begun by W.A. Jackson and F.S. Ferguson; completed by Katharine F. Pantzer. London, 1976 in progress.

— Malaysian.

BIBLIOGRAFI NEGARA MALAYSIA: Malaysian national bibliography; [pd. by] Arkib dan Perpustakaan Negara Malaysia. [in Malay and English]. a., 1969 [3rd]- Kuala Lumpur.

— Moroccan.

BIBLIOGRAPHIE NATIONALE MAROCAINE: [index of periodical articles on Morocco]; [pd. by] Bibliothèque Générale et Archives du Maroc. [in French and Arabic]. m., Ja 1969 (n.s., no.73)- Rabat.

BICYCLE INDUSTRY

— Italy.

ATOR CONSULENZA AZIENDALE. Studio sull'evoluzione della concentrazione nell'industria di cicli, motocicli e ciclomotori in Italia. [Brussels, European Communities, Directorate-General for Competition, 1973]. 1 vol. (various pagings).

ATOR CONSULENZA AZIENDALE. Studio sull'evoluzione della concentrazione nell'industria di cicli, motocicli e ciclomotori in Italia 1970-1972. [Brussels, European Communities, Directorate-General for Competition], 1975. pp. 87.

— Netherlands.

AMSTERDAM. Universiteit. Stichting voor Economisch Onderzoek. Studie betreffende de ontwikkeling van de concentratie in de rijwiel- en bromfietsenindustrie in Nederland, etc; [by H.W. de Jong and A.H. Smolders]. [Brussels, European Communities, Directorate-General for Competition, 1973]. pp. 12.

BIESZCZADY.

BIERNACKA (MARIA) Kształtowanie się nowej społeczności wiejskiej w Bieszczadach. Wrocław, 1974. pp. 211. *(Polska Akademia Nauk. Instytut Historii Kultury Materialnej. Biblioteka Etnografii Polskiej. Nr.29)* With English summary.

BIG BUSINESS

— Japan.

CONFERENCE ON JAPANESE ORGANIZATION AND DECISION-MAKING, HAWAII, 1973. Modern Japanese organization and decision-making; edited by Ezra F. Vogel. Berkeley, [1975]. pp. 340. *Proceedings of a conference sponsored by the Joint Committee on Japanese Studies of the American Council of Learned Societies and the Social Science Research Council.*

— Norway.

TANGEN (DAG) Makt og eiendom: hvem styrer norsk industri? Oslo, [1975]. pp. 131.

— United States.

LARGE corporations in a changing society: (the Major Issues Lecture Series...held at the Graduate School of Management of the University of California, Los Angeles; J. Fred Weston, editor. New York, 1974. pp. 187. *(International Telephone and Telegraph Corporation. Major Issues Lecture Series)*

BLUMBERG (PHILLIP I.) The megacorporation in American society: the scope of corporate power. Englewood Cliffs, N.J., [1975]. pp. 188. *bibliogs.*

The FUTURE of the United States multinational corporation: [proceedings of a symposium organized by the John Bassett Moore Society in 1974]; edited by Lee D. Unterman and Christine W. Swent. Charlottesville, 1975. pp. 161.

GALAMBOS (LOUIS) The public image of big business in America, 1880-1940: a quantitative study in social change;...with the assistance of Barbara Barrow Spence. Baltimore, [1975]. pp. 324.

SHEPHERD (WILLIAM G.) The treatment of market power: antitrust, regulation and public enterprise. New York, 1975. pp. 326. *bibliog.*

BIHAR

— Politics and government.

PRASAD (DEVI) The people's resistance in Bihar. London, [1975]. pp. 14.

BILINGUALISM.

TREMAINE (RUTH V.) Syntax and Piagetian operational thought: a developmental study of bilingual children. Washington, [1975]. pp. 131. *bibliog.*

BILLS OF EXCHANGE

— United Kingdom.

RICHARDSON (DUDLEY) Guide to negotiable instruments and the Bills of Exchange Acts. 5th ed. London, 1976. pp. 188.

BIOGRAPHY.

ROBERTS (FRANK C.) compiler. Obituaries from the Times, 1961-1970 including an index to all obituaries and tributes appearing in the Times during the years 1961-1970. Reading, [1975]. pp. 952.

BIOLOGICAL WARFARE.

FINAN (JAMES STUART) Chemical and biological weapons: their potential for nations outside the principal alliances, with special reference to the possibilities open to the Republic of South Africa over the next ten years. 1975. fo. 308. *bibliog.* Typescript. Ph.D. (London) thesis: unpublished. This thesis is the property of London University and may not be removed from the Library.

BIOLOGY.

BIOLOGY and politics: recent explorations; [proceedings of a conference held in Paris, 1975; edited by] Albert Somit. Paris, [1976]. pp. 330. *bibliog.* *(International Social Science Council. Publications. 19)*

— Philosophy.

GRENE (MARJORIE GLICKSMAN) The understanding of nature: essays in the philosophy of biology. Dordrecht, [1974]. pp. 374. *(Boston Colloquium for the Philosophy of Science. Boston Studies in the Philosophy of Science. vol.23)*

BIRDS

— America, Latin.

MEYER DE SCHAUENSEE (RODOLPHE) A guide to the birds of South America. Wynnewood, Penn., [1970]. pp. 470. *bibliog.*

BIRMINGHAM

— Civic improvement.

LLEWELYN-DAVIES WEEKS [AND PARTNERS]. Inner area study: Birmingham: fourth progress report. [London], Department of the Environment, [1975]. pp. 48.

LLEWELYN-DAVIES WEEKS [AND PARTNERS]. Inner area study: Birmingham: interim review. [London], Department of the Environment, [1975]. pp. 38. *bibliog.*

LLEWELYN-DAVIES WEEKS [AND PARTNERS]. Inner area study: Birmingham: Little Green: a case study in urban renewal. [London], Department of the Environment, [1975]. pp. 200. *bibliog.*

LLEWELYN-DAVIES WEEKS [AND PARTNERS]. Inner area study: Birmingham: third progress report. [London], Department of the Environment, [1975]. pp. 94.

— Industries.

BIRMINGHAM COMMUNITY DEVELOPMENT PROJECT. Workers on the scrap-heap: report of meeting held on 15th March 1975 at East Birmingham Trades and Labour Club. [Birmingham, 1975]. pp. 10.

— — Information services.

BIRMINGHAM COMMUNITY DEVELOPMENT PROJECT. Proposals for a trade union research unit in east Birmingham. [Birmingham], 1975. pp. (9).

— Politics and government.

NEWTON (KENNETH) Second city politics: democratic processes and decision-making in Birmingham. London, 1976. pp. 270.

— Social conditions.

LLEWELYN-DAVIES WEEKS [AND PARTNERS]. Inner area study: Birmingham: interim review. [London], Department of the Environment, [1975]. pp. 38. *bibliog.*

SOCIAL AND COMMUNITY PLANNING RESEARCH. Inner area study: Birmingham: Small Heath, Birmingham: a social survey: report...for the consultants, Llewelyn-Davies Weeks Forestier-Walker and Bor; [by Jean Morton-Williams and Richard Stowell]. [London], Department of the Environment, [1975]. pp. 167.

— Social history.

SHERGOLD (PETER ROGER) The standard of life of manual workers in the first decade of the twentieth-century: a comparative study of Birmingham, U.K., and Pittsburgh, U.S.A. 1976. fo. 691. *bibliog.* Typescript. Ph.D. (London) thesis: unpublished. This thesis is the property of London University and may not be removed from the Library.

— Social policy.

LLEWELYN-DAVIES WEEKS [AND PARTNERS]. Inner area study: Birmingham: fourth progress report. [London], Department of the Environment, [1975]. pp. 48.

LLEWELYN-DAVIES WEEKS [AND PARTNERS]. Inner area study: Birmingham: third progress report. [London], Department of the Environment, [1975]. pp. 94.

BIRTH CONTROL.

BIRTH CONTROL.

AMERICAN ASSOCIATION FOR THE ADVANCEMENT OF SCIENCE. Population: dynamics, ethics and policy;...edited by Priscilla Reining and Irene Tinker. Washington, D.C., [1975]. pp. 184. *(Articles reprinted from Science, 1966-1975).*

INTERNATIONAL CONGRESS OF ANTHROPOLOGICAL AND ETHNOLOGICAL SCIENCES. 9th Congress, 1973. Population and social organization: [papers from the Congress]; editor Moni Nag. The Hague, [1975]. pp. 367. *bibliogs.*

INTERNATIONAL PLANNED PARENTHOOD FEDERATION. Family planning in five continents. London, 1975. pp. 28.

RUPRECHT (THEODORE K.) and JEWETT (FRANK I.) The micro-economics of demographic change: family planning and economic well-being. New York, 1975. pp. 153.

SALAS (RAFAEL M.) People: an international choice: the multilateral approach to population. Oxford, 1976. pp. 154.

— Congresses.

SEXUAL REFORM CONGRESS, 3RD, LONDON, 1929. Proceedings...; edited by Norman Haire. London, 1930. pp. 670. *In English, French and German.*

— Law and legislation.

SYMPOSIUM ON LAW AND POPULATION, TUNIS, 1974. Text of recommendations. Medford, Mass., 1974. pp. 49. *(Tufts University. Fletcher School of Law and Diplomacy. Law and Population Monograph Series. No. 20)*

LEE (LUKE TSUNG-CHOU) Legal implications of the world population plan of action. Medford, Mass., 1975. pp. 375-417. *(Tufts University. Fletcher School of Law and Diplomacy. Law and Population Monograph Series. No. 28) (Reprinted from Journal of International Law and Economics, vol. 9, no. 3)*

— — Brazil.

LAW and population in Brazil; [by] Walter Rodrigues [and others]. Medford, Mass., 1975. pp. 46. *(Tufts University. Fletcher School of Law and Diplomacy. Law and Population Monograph Series. No.34)*

— — Chile.

SULBRANDT (JOSE) and FERRERA (MARIA ALICIA) Law and population growth in Chile. Medford, Mass., 1975. pp. 45. *(Tufts University. Fletcher School of Law and Diplomacy. Law and Population Monograph Series. No.31)*

— — Europe.

LAW and fertility in Europe: a study of legislation directly or indirectly affecting fertility in Europe; edited by Maurice Kirk [and others]. Dolhain, [1975]. 2 vols. *Essays and country reports of the Joint Working Group for the Study of Legislation directly or indirectly influencing Fertility in Europe, set up by the European Centre for Co-ordination of Research...in the Social Sciences and the International Union for the Scientific Study of Population.*

— — Ghana.

TURKSON (RICHARD B.) Law and population growth in Ghana. Medford, Mass., 1975. pp. 55. *(Tufts University. Fletcher School of Law and Diplomacy. Law and Population Monograph Series. No. 33)*

— — Iran.

SANEY (PARVIZ) Law and population growth in Iran. Medford, Mass., 1974. pp. 33. *(Tufts University. Fletcher School of Law and Diplomacy. Law and Population Monograph Series. No.21)*

— — Kenya.

UCHE (U.U.) Law and population growth in Kenya. Medford, Mass., 1974. pp. 40. *(Tufts University. Fletcher School of Law and Diplomacy. Law and Population Monograph Series. No.22)*

— Mathematical models.

CHANDRASEKARAN (C.) and HERMALIN (ALBERT I.) eds. Measuring the effect of family planning programs on fertility. Dolhain, Belgium. [1975]. pp. 570. *bibliogs.*

— Religious aspects.

BOUVIER (LEON F.) and RAO (SETHURAMAIAH LAKSHMINARAYANA) Socioreligious factors in fertility decline. Cambridge, Mass., [1975]. pp. 204. *bibliog.*

— Research — United States.

ROBERTO (EDUARDO L.) Strategic decision-making in a social program: the case of family- planning diffusion. Lexington, Mass., [1975]. pp. 182.

— Study and teaching — Singapore.

WAN (FOOK KEE) Communications strategy in the Singapore national family planning programme: a paper prepared for the Seminar in Communication for Family Planning sponsored by the East-West Communication Institute, East-West Centre, Honolulu, Hawaii, August 8th to 20th, 1971. Singapore, Family Planning and Population Board, [1971]. fo. 5. *(FPPB Papers. No.14)*

— America, Latin.

STYCOS (JOSEPH MAYONE) ed. The clinic and information flow: educating the family planning client in four Latin American countries. Lexington, Mass., [1975]. pp. 174.

— Asia.

UNITED NATIONS. Economic and Social Commission for Asia and the Pacific. Asian Population Studies Series. New York, 1966 in progress.

— Canada.

BALAKRISHNAN (T.R.) and others. Fertility and family planning in a Canadian metropolis. Montreal, 1975. pp. 217. *bibliog.*

— Caribbean Area.

SEGAL (AARON LEE) ed. Population policies in the Caribbean. Lexington, Mass., [1975]. pp. 239.

— India.

KARAN SINGH, Maharaja. Population, poverty and the future of India. [New Delhi, National Institute of Family Planning, 1975]. pp. 142,iii.

— Netherlands.

GLASBERGEN (P.) and ZANDANEL (R.) Bevolkingsgroei en welvaartsstaat: een sociologische interpretatie van veranderend fertiliteitsgedrag in Nederland. Assen, 1976. pp. 129. *bibliog.*

— Underdeveloped areas.

See UNDERDEVELOPED AREAS — Birth control.

— United Kingdom.

U.K. Department of Health and Social Security. 1974. Family planning service: memorandum of guidance. [London], 1974. 1 pamphlet in (varying pagings).

PEEL (JOHN) b. 1930, and CARR (GRISELDA) Contraception and family design: a study of birth planning in contemporary society. Edinburgh, 1975. pp. 180.

CARTWRIGHT (ANN) How many children? London, 1976. pp. 202. *bibliog.*

— United States.

BOUVIER (LEON F.) and RAO (SETHURAMAIAH LAKSHMINARAYANA) Socioreligious factors in fertility decline. Cambridge, Mass., [1975]. pp. 204. *bibliog.*

McCORMICK (E. PATRICIA) Attitudes toward abortion: experiences of selected black and white women. Lexington, Mass., [1975]. pp. 159. *bibliog.*

SPILLANE (WILLIAM H.) and RYSER (PAUL E.) Male fertility survey: fertility knowledge, attitudes, and practices of married men. Cambridge, Mass., [1975]. pp. 191. *bibliog.*

BIRTH CONTROL CLINICS

— America, Latin.

STYCOS (JOSEPH MAYONE) ed. The clinic and information flow: educating the family planning client in four Latin American countries. Lexington, Mass., [1975]. pp. 174.

BISMARCK—SCHOENHAUSEN (OTTO EDUARD LEOPOLD VON) Prince.

GRUBBE (JOCHEN) Bismarks Politik in Europa und Ubersee: seine "Annäherung" and Frankreich im Urteil der Pariser Presse, 1883–1885. Bern, 1975 pp. 277. *bibliog.*

BLACK NATIONALISM

— Africa.

OGUERI II (EZE) African nationalism and military ascendancy. Owerri, 1976. pp. 85.

— United States.

CARLISLE (RODNEY P.) The roots of black nationalism. Port Washington, N.Y., 1975. pp. 182. *bibliog.*

PINKNEY (ALPHONSO) Red, black and green: black nationalism in the United States. Cambridge, 1976. pp. 258.

— — Bibliography.

JENKINS (BETTY LANIER) and PHILLIS (SUSAN) compilers. Black separatism: a bibliography. Westport, Conn., 1976. pp. 163.

BLAGODATOV (ALEKSEI VASIL'EVICH).

BLAGODATOV (ALEKSEI VASIL'EVICH) Zapiski o kitaiskoi revoliutsii 1925-1927 gg. 2nd ed. Moskva, 1975. pp. 277.

BLANC (JEAN JOSEPH LOUIS).

MIRECOURT (EUGENE DE) pseudo. [i.e. Charles Jean Baptiste JACQUOT] Louis Blanc. Paris, Chez l'Auteur, 1857. pp. 84. *(Les Contemporains)*

BLANTYRE

— Census.

BLANTYRE. Census, 1972. Blantyre city population sample census, September 11 - October 11, 1972. Zomba, 1974. pp. 117.

BLOOD

— Transfusion.

CANADA. Emergency Health Services Division. 1970. Emergency blood services. Ottawa, 1970. pp. 48.

BLUMER–RIS (HANS).

VEREIN FÜR WIRTSCHAFTSHISTORISCHE STUDIEN. Schweizer Pioniere der Wirtschaft und Technik. 28. Alfred Zellweger, Uster, 1855-1916; Hans Blumer-Ris, Freiburg, 1902-1953; von Hans Rudolf Schmid. Zürich, 1975. pp. 113. *bibliog.*

BLUNT (WILFRED SCAWEN).

MEYERS (JEFFREY) A fever at the core: the idealist in politics. London, 1976. pp. 172. *bibliog.*

BOATMEN

— Russia.

RODIN (FEDOR NIKOLAEVICH) Burlachestvo v Rossii: istoriko-sotsiologicheskii ocherk. Moskva, 1975. pp. 245.

— United Kingdom.

HANSON (HARRY) The canal boatmen, 1760-1914. Manchester, [1975]. pp. 244. *bibliog.*

BOBEK (PAWEŁ).

BOBEK (PAWEŁ) Wspomnienia i zapiski; przygotował do druku i biografią poprzedził Franciszek Serafin. Warszawa, 1974. pp. 143.

BÖCKLER (HANS).

See BOECKLER (HANS).

BOECKLER (HANS).

VETTER (HEINZ OSKAR) ed. Vom Sozialistengesetz zur Mitbestimmung: zum 100. Geburtstag von Hans Böckler. Köln, [1975]. pp. 546. *bibliog.*

BÓJNOWSKI (LUCYAN).

BUCZEK (DANIEL STEPHEN) Immigrant pastor: the life of the Right Reverend Monsignor Lucyan Bójnowski of New Britain, Connecticut. Waterbury, Conn., 1974. pp. 184. *bibliog.*

BOLIVIA

— Economic conditions.

BEYOND the revolution: Bolivia since 1952; James M. Malloy and Richard S. Thorn, editors. Pittsburgh, [1971]. pp. 402. *Based on an interdisciplinary seminar held at the University of Pittsburgh, sponsored by the University's Center for International Studies and Center for Latin American Studies.*

— Economic policy.

BOLIVIA. Secretaria Nacional de Planificacion y Coordinacion, 1963. Plan bienal de desarrollo economico y social, 1963-1964, (Planeamiento, No. 6/8). La Paz, 1963. pp. 327.

— Foreign relations — United States.

BEYOND the revolution: Bolivia since 1952; James M. Malloy and Richard S. Thorn, editors. Pittsburgh, [1971]. pp. 402. *Based on an interdisciplinary seminar held at the University of Pittsburgh, sponsored by the University's Center for International Studies and Center for Latin American Studies.*

— Politics and government.

BEYOND the revolution: Bolivia since 1952; James M. Malloy and Richard S. Thorn, editors. Pittsburgh, [1971]. pp. 402. *Based on an interdisciplinary seminar held at the University of Pittsburgh, sponsored by the University's Center for International Studies and Center for Latin American Studies.*

ZAVALETA MERCADO (RENE). El poder dual en America Latina: (estudio de los casos de Bolivia y Chile). Mexico, 1974. pp. 270.

— Rural conditions.

McEWEN (WILLIAM J.) Changing rural society: a study of communities in Bolivia. New York, 1975. pp. 463. *bibliog. Part of a major research study carried out in Bolivia by the Research Institute for the Study of Man.*

— Rural population.

BOLIVIA. Comision Especial del Seguro Social Campesino. 1972. [Report]. La Paz, 1972. 5 vols.(in 3).

— Social policy.

BOLIVIA. Secretaria Nacional de Planificacion y Coordinacion, 1963. Plan bienal de desarrollo economico y social, 1963-1964, (Planeamiento, No. 6/8). La Paz, 1963. pp. 327.

BOLIVIA. Comision Especial del Seguro Social Campesino. 1972. [Report]. La Paz, 1972. 5 vols.(in 3).

— Statistics.

BOLIVIA. Instituto Nacional de Estadistica. Boletin estadistico. irreg., Jl 1975 (no.1)- La Paz.

BOLIVIANS IN FOREIGN COUNTRIES.

AGUILO (FEDERICO) and LLANO SAAVEDRA (LUIS) El contingente de bolivianos en el exterior. La Paz, 1968. pp. 72.

BOLOGNA (PROVINCE)

— History.

ARBIZZANI (LUIGI) Guerra, nazifascismo, lotta di liberazione nel Bolognese, luglio 1943-aprile 1945: fotostoria. Bologna, 1975. pp. 179.

BOMBERS.

QUANBECK (ALTON H.) and WOOD (ARCHIE L.) Modernizing the strategic bomber force: why and how. Washington, [1976]. pp. 116. *(Brookings Institution. Studies in Defense Policy)*

BOOK INDUSTRIES AND TRADE.

PROBLEMS of the bookworld and how they could be solved: (a digest of recommendations emerging from the seminars organised under the Unesco project on reading materials). Karachi, 1963. pp. 120.

— Canada — Directories.

AMERICAN BOOK TRADE DIRECTORY...: booksellers and publishers in the United States, Great Britain, Ireland and Canada; wholesalers in the United States and Canada; foreign book dealers. trien. 1975/1976 (22nd ed.) New York.

— Ireland (Republic) — Directories.

AMERICAN BOOK TRADE DIRECTORY...: booksellers and publishers in the United States, Great Britain, Ireland and Canada; wholesalers in the United States and Canada; foreign book dealers. trien. 1975/1976 (22nd ed.) New York.

— Netherlands.

HEINSMAN (LOUIS) and TEEFFELEN (WALTER VAN) Concernvorming in de Nederlandse boekenwereld. Amsterdam, 1975. pp. 229.

— Singapore.

BYRD (CECIL K.) Books in Singapore: a survey of publishing, printing, bookselling and library activity in the Republic of Singapore. Singapore, 1970. pp. 161.

— Underdeveloped areas.

See UNDERDEVELOPED AREAS — Book industries and trade.

— United Kingdom.

HUNT (CHRISTOPHER JOHN) The book trade in Northumberland and Durham to 1860: a biographical dictionary of printers, engravers, lithographers, booksellers, stationers, publishers, mapsellers, printsellers, musicsellers, bookbinders, newsagents and owners of circulating libraries. Newcastle, 1975. pp. 116.

— — Directories.

AMERICAN BOOK TRADE DIRECTORY...: booksellers and publishers in the United States, Great Britain, Ireland and Canada; wholesalers in the United States and Canada; foreign book dealers. trien. 1975/1976 (22nd ed.) New York.

— United States.

SMITH (ROGER H.) Paperback Parnassus: the birth, the development, the pending crisis of the modern American paperbound book. Boulder, Co., 1976. pp. 111.

— — Directories.

AMERICAN BOOK TRADE DIRECTORY...: booksellers and publishers in the United States, Great Britain, Ireland and Canada; wholesalers in the United States and Canada; foreign book dealers. trien. 1975/1976 (22nd ed.) New York.

BOOK SELECTION.

BOOK selection in a siege economy; edited by B.H. Baumfield. [London, 1976]. pp. 46. *Proceedings of seminar held by the Working Party on Library and Book Trade Relations in 1975.*

BOOKKEEPING.

YMPYN CHRISTOFFELS (JAN) A notable and very excellente woorke, expressyng and declaryng the maner and forme how to kepe a boke of acco[m]ptes or reconynges... translated...out of the Italian...into Dutche, and out of Dutche, into Frenche, and now out of Frenche into Englische. n.p., 1547; [Kyoto, 1975]. pp. (36),79. *Facsimile reprint of the 1547 edition, with essays by B.S.Yamey and Osamu Kojima.*

BOOKS

— History.

FEBVRE (LUCIEN PAUL VICTOR) and MARTIN (HENRI JEAN) The coming of the book: the impact of printing, 1450-1800. London, 1976. pp. 378.

— — Russia — Tatar Republic.

KARIMULLIN (ABRAR GIBADULLOVICH) Tatarskaia kniga nachala XX veka. Kazan', 1974. pp. 319. *bibliog.*

— Prices.

ERPF (RUEDIGER) Internationale Preisvergleiche wissenschaftlicher Bücher: eine empirische Studie; USA, Grossbritannien, Bundesrepublik Deutschland, Österreich, Schweiz, Frankreich. Hamburg, 1974. 3 vols. *bibliog.*

NIEUWENHUYSEN (JOHN PETER) and OAKLEY (E.E.) Competition in Australian bookselling: resale price maintenance and after. Melbourne, 1975. pp. 82. *bibliog.*

BOOKSELLERS AND BOOKSELLING.

ANDERSON (CHARLES B.) ed. Bookselling in America and the world: some observations and recollections in celebration of the 75th anniversary of the American Booksellers Association. New York, [1975]. pp. 214.

— Directories.

GROSE (B. DONALD) The antiquarian booktrade: an international directory of subject specialists. Metuchen, N.J., 1972. pp. 176. *bibliog.*

— Australia.

NIEUWENHUYSEN (JOHN PETER) and OAKLEY (E.E.) Competition in Australian bookselling: resale price maintenance and after. Melbourne, 1975. pp. 82. *bibliog.*

— Russia.

SOSTOIANIE i perspektivy izucheniia sprosa na knizhnuiu produktsiiu. Moskva, 1974. pp. 61.

— United States.

ANDERSON (CHARLES B.) ed. Bookselling in America and the world: some observations and recollections in celebration of the 75th anniversary of the American Booksellers Association. New York, [1975]. pp. 214.

BORDER PATROLS

— Russia.

POGRANICHNYE voiska SSSR, mai 1945-1950: sbornik dokumentov i materialov. Moskva, 1975. pp. 759.

BORDING (KRISTEN MORTENSEN).

BORDING (KRISTEN MORTENSEN) Dagbog over Danmarks første socialdemokratiske ministerium, 1924- 26; ved Karen Marie Olsen og Hans Sode-Madsen. Aarhus, 1976. pp. 131. *bibliog.*

BOSE (SUBHAS CHANDRA).

CORR (GERARD H.) The war of the springing tigers. London, 1975. pp. 200. *bibliog.*

BOSNIA

— **Description and travel.**

ŠAMIĆ (MIDHAT) Francuski putnici u Bosni na pragu XIX stoljeća i njihovi utisci o njoj; [translated from the French]. Sarajevo, 1966. pp. 312. *bibliog. With German summary.*

— **Nationalism.**

HADŽIJAHIĆ (MUHAMED) Od tradicije do identiteta: geneza nacionalnog pitanja bosanskih Muslimana. Sarajevo, 1974. pp. 263.

BOSTON, MASSACHUSETTS

— **Economic history.**

THERNSTROM (STEPHAN) The other Bostonians: poverty and progress in the American metropolis, 1880-1970. Cambridge, Mass., 1973. pp.345. *(Massachusetts Institute of Technology and Harvard University. Joint Center for Urban Studies. Publications)* .

— **Social conditions.**

GINSBERG (YONA) Jews in a changing neighborhood: the study of Mattapan. New York, [1975]. pp. 214. *bibliog.*

— **Social history.**

THERNSTROM (STEPHAN) The other Bostonians: poverty and progress in the American metropolis, 1880-1970. Cambridge, Mass., 1973. pp.345. *(Massachusetts Institute of Technology and Harvard University. Joint Center for Urban Studies. Publications)* .

BOTANY

— **America.**

SCHLEIFFER (HEDWIG) ed. Sacred narcotic plants of the New World Indians: an anthology of texts from the sixteenth century to date. New York, [1973]. pp. 156.

BOTEV (KHRISTO).

STOIANOVA (RADKA) and ZHECHEV (NIKOLAI) Khristo Botev. Sofiia, 1970. 1 vol. (unpaged). *Album of photographs.*

BOTEV (KHRISTO) Subrani suchineniia v dva toma; pod redaktsiiata na... Mikhail Dimitrov. Sofiia, 1971. 2 vols.

BOTSWANA

— **Economic conditions.**

BOTSWANA. Central Statistics Office. 1974. A social and economic survey in three peri-urban areas in Botswana, 1974. Gaborone, 1974. pp. 110.

— **Executive departments.**

BOTSWANA. Department of Customs and Excise. 1975. Report of the establishment and organisation of the Department of Customs and Excise 1970-1974. Gaborone, 1975. pp. 26.

BOTSWANA. Ministry of Works and Communications. 1975. Duties and responsibilities of the Ministry of Works and Communications. [Gaborone], 1975. fo. 92.

— **Full employment policies.**

BOTSWANA. 1973. Jobs past, present and future: national policy on incomes, employment, prices, and profits. [Gaborone, 1973?]. pp. (7).

— **Industries.**

SELWYN (PERCY) Industries in the southern African periphery: a study of industrial development in Botswana, Lesotho and Swaziland. London, 1975. pp. 156. *bibliog.*

— **Officials and employees — Salaries, allowances, etc.**

BOTSWANA. Directorate of Personnel. 1974. Report of the Salaries Review Commission 1974. Gaborone, 1974. pp. 61. *(Personnel Directives. 1974. No. 12)*

— **Social conditions.**

BOTSWANA. Central Statistics Office. 1974. A social and economic survey in three peri-urban areas in Botswana, 1974. Gaborone, 1974. pp. 110.

— **Statistics.**

BOTSWANA. Central Statistics Office. Statistical bulletin. irreg., Je 1976 (v.1, no. 1)- Gaborone.

— **Statistics, Medical.**

BOTSWANA. Ministry of Health. Medical Statistics Unit. Medical statistics. a., 1974 (1st)- Gaborone.

BOULDING (KENNETH EWART).

KERMAN (CYNTHIA EARL) Creative tension: the life and thought of Kenneth Boulding. Ann Arbor, [1974]. pp. 380. *bibliog.*

FRONTIERS in social thought: essays in honor of Kenneth E. Boulding; edited by Martin Pfaff. Amsterdam, 1976. pp. 386. *bibliog.*

BOUNDARIES.

KLIMENKO (BORIS MIKHAILOVICH) and USHAKOV (NIKOLAI ALEKSANDROVICH) Nerushimost' granits - uslovie mezhdunarodnogo mira. Moskva, 1975. pp. 168.

BOURGUIBA (HABIB).

BOURGUIBA (HABIB) defendant. 9 avril 1938: le "procès" Bourguiba; texte inteégral des interrogatoires et dépositions; articles de presse et correspondance de Bourguiba. Tunis, 1967. 2 vols,(in 1).

BOYCOTT

— **United States.**

LAIDLER (HARRY WELLINGTON) Boycotts and the labor struggle: economic and legal aspects. New York, 1914. pp. 488. *bibliog.*

BOYNE, BATTLE OF THE, 1690.

ELLIS (PETER BERRESFORD) The Boyne water: the battle of the Boyne, 1690. London, 1976. pp. 163. *bibliog.*

BOYS.

BELSON (WILLIAM A.) Juvenile theft: the causal factors: a report of an investigation of the tenability of various causal hypotheses about the development of stealing by London boys, etc. London, 1975. pp. 411.

— **Societies and clubs — United Kingdom.**

AMORY (DEREK HEATHCOTE) 1st Viscount Amory. The service of youth. [London], 1975. pp. 14. *(National Association of Boys' Clubs. Basil Henriques Memorial Lectures. 1975)*

DAWES (FRANK) A cry from the streets: the boys' club movement in Britain from the 1850s to the present day. Hove, 1975. pp. 192.

BRADFORD

— **Description.**

RICHARDSON (C.) of the University of Bradford. A geography of Bradford. Bradford, [1976]. pp. 202.

— **Economic conditions.**

RICHARDSON (C.) of the University of Bradford. A geography of Bradford. Bradford, [1976]. pp. 202.

— **Historical geography.**

RICHARDSON (C.) of the University of Bradford. A geography of Bradford. Bradford, [1976]. pp. 202.

BRADFORD UNIVERSITY.

BOTTOMLEY (J.A.) and others. University of Bradford: costs and potential economies. [Paris], Organisation for Economic Co-operation and Development, 1972. pp. 440. *(Centre for Educational Research and Innovation. Studies in Institutional Management in Higher Education)*

BRAIN.

WARBURTON (DAVID M.) Brain, behaviour and drugs: introduction to the neurochemistry of behaviour. London, [1975]. pp. 280. *bibliog.*

BRAIN DRAIN.

PARTINGTON (MARTIN) The brain drain tax proposal: a lawyer's view. [Oxford], 1975. pp. 717-749. *(Reprinted from World Development, 1975, vol. 3, no. 10)*

VAS-ZOLTÁN (PÉTER) The brain drain: an anomaly of international relations. rev.ed. Leyden, 1976. pp. 151. *bibliog.*

— **Taxation.**

BELLAGIO CONFERENCE ON THE BRAIN DRAIN AND INCOME TAXATION, 1975. The brain drain and taxation: 2: theory and empirical analysis; edited by Jagdish N. Bhagwati. Amsterdam, 1976. pp. 292.

BELLAGIO CONFERENCE ON THE BRAIN DRAIN AND INCOME TAXATION, 1975. Taxing the brain drain: 1: a proposal; edited by Jagdish N. Bhagwati and Martin Partington. Amsterdam, 1976. pp. 222.

BRANDENBURG

— **Prisons and reformatories.**

FRENZEL (MAX) and others. Gesprengte Fesseln: ein Bericht über den antifaschistischen Widerstand und die Geschichte der illegalen Parteiorganisation der KPD im Zuchthaus Brandenburg-Goerden von 1933 bis 1945. Berlin, [1975]. pp. 347.

BRANDT (WILLY).

BRANDT (WILLY) Peace: writings and speeches of the Nobel Peace Prize winner, 1971. Bonn-Bad Godesberg, 1971. pp. 165.

BRANDT (WILLY) Begegnungen und Einsichten: die Jahre 1960-1975. Hamburg, 1976. pp. 655.

BRANTING (GEORG).

PETERS (JAN) Branting und die schwedische Sozialdemokratie:... Hjalmar und Georg Branting in der schwedischen Geschichte. Berlin, 1975. pp. 238.

BRANTING (HJALMAR).

PETERS (JAN) Branting und die schwedische Sozialdemokratie:... Hjalmar und Georg Branting in der schwedischen Geschichte. Berlin, 1975. pp. 238.

BRASILIA.

KUBITSCHEK DE OLIVEIRA (JUSCELINO) Por que construí Brasília. Rio de Janeiro, 1975. pp. 370.

BRASILLACH (ROBERT).

TUCKER (WILLIAM RAYBURN) The fascist ego: a political biography of Robert Brasillach. Berkeley, 1975. pp. 331. *bibliog.*

BRAUN (OTTO).

KUTTNER (ERICH) Otto Braun:...Volksausgabe. Berlin, [1932]. pp. 96.

BRAZIL

— Armed forces — Political activity.

MOREIRA (NEIVA) O exército e a crise brasileira. Montevideo, [1968]. pp. 72.

CARONE (EDGARD) O tenentismo: acontecimentos, personagens, programas. São Paulo, 1975. pp. 518. *bibliog.*

FIECHTER (GEORGES ANDRE) Brazil since 1964: modernization under a military regime; a study of the interactions of politics and economics in a contemporary military regime;... translated from the French by Alan Braley. London, 1975. pp. 310. *bibliog.*

PEDREIRA (FERNANDO) Brasil politica, 1964-1975. São Paulo, 1975. pp. 292.

KEITH (HENRY H.) and HAYES (ROBERT AMES) eds. Perspectives on armed politics in Brazil. Tempe, Arizona, [1976]. pp. 258.

— Biography.

WHO'S who in Brazil: vol. 1, 1968-1969. São Paulo, [1969]. pp. 903. *In English and Portuguese.*

— Commerce.

BRAZIL. Secretaria da Receita Federal. Centro de Informações Economico-Fiscais. Rendas aduaneiras...: arrecadação, regimes de tributação, preços de referência, panta de valor minimo. a., 1973 (v.1)- Brasilia.

HILTON (STANLEY E.) Brazil and the great powers, 1930-1939: the politics of trade rivalry. Austin, [1975]. pp. 304. *bibliog.* (*Texas University. Institute of Latin American Studies. Latin American Monographs. No.38*)

TYLER (WILLIAM G.) Manufactured export expansion and industrialization in Brazil. Tübingen, 1976. pp. 373. *bibliog.* (*Kiel. Universität. Institut für Weltwirtschaft. Kieler Studien. 134*)

— — France.

SCHNEIDER (JUERGEN) Handel und Unternehmer im französischen Brasiliengeschäft, 1815-1848: Versuch einer quantitativen Strukturanalyse. Köln, 1975. pp. 649. *bibliog. With table of contents and summaries in various languages.*

— Commercial policy.

HILTON (STANLEY E.) Brazil and the great powers, 1930-1939: the politics of trade rivalry. Austin, [1975]. pp. 304. *bibliog.* (*Texas University. Institute of Latin American Studies. Latin American Monographs. No.38*)

— Discovery and exploration.

KOMISSAROV (BORIS NIKOLAEVICH) Grigorii Ivanovich Langsdorf, 1774-1852. Leningrad, 1975. pp. 124.

— Economic conditions.

COOPERATIVISMO E NORDESTE: publicação da Secção de Cooperativismo da SUDENE, [Brazil]. 3 a yr. (formerly s-a.). 1966 (ano 1)- Recife.

BRAZIL. Instituto de Planejamento Econômico e Social. Boletim econômico. m., Jl 1969 - Jl/Oc 1970, with gap (S 1969); My 1972 ([n. s.] ano 1, no.1)- ; susp. pbln. N 1970-Ap 1972. [Rio de Janeiro].

EUROPEAN BRAZILIAN BANK. Brazil: land of the present. London, [1972]. pp. 60.

SIMONSEN (MARIO HENRIQUE) Brasil 2002. Rio de Janeiro, 1972. pp. 178.

BRAZILIAN ECONOMIC STUDIES; [pd. by] Instituto de Planejamento Econômico e Social. a., 1975 (no.1)- Rio de Janeiro.

CARRION (FRANCISCO MACHADO) O modelo brasileiro: impasses e alternativas. Porto Alegre, 1975. pp. 153. *bibliog.*

ROBOCK (STEFAN HYMAN) Brazil: a study in development progress. Lexington, Mass., [1975]. pp. 204.

SOARES (ORLANDO ESTEVÃO DA COSTA) Desenvolvimento econômico-social do Brasil y EUA. [Rio de Janeiro, 1975]. pp. 170. *bibliog.*

TAVARES (MARIA DA CONCEIÇÃO) Da substituição de importações ao capitalismo financeiro: ensaios sobre economia brasileira. Rio de Janeiro, 1975. pp. 263.

TYLER (WILLIAM G.) Manufactured export expansion and industrialization in Brazil. Tübingen, 1976. pp. 373. *bibliog.* (*Kiel. Universität. Institut für Weltwirtschaft. Kieler Studien. 134*)

— Economic history.

IANNI (OCTAVIO) Crisis in Brazil; translated by Phyllis B. Eveleth. New York, 1970. pp. 244. *bibliog.*

CARRION (FRANCISCO MACHADO) O modelo brasileiro: impasses e alternativas. Porto Alegre, 1975. pp. 153. *bibliog.*

FERNANDES (FLORESTAN) A revolução burguesa no Brasil: ensaio de interpretação sociologica. Rio de Janeiro, 1975. pp. 413. *bibliog.*

TAVARES (MARIA DA CONCEIÇÃO) Da substituição de importações ao capitalismo financeiro: ensaios sobre economia brasileira. Rio de Janeiro, 1975. pp. 263.

— Economic policy.

BRAZIL. Ministerio do Planejamento e Coordenação Econômica. Escritorio de Pesquisa Econômica Aplicada. 1964. Programa de açao econômica do govêrno, 1964-1966: sintese. [Rio de Janeiro], 1964. pp. 240. (*Documentos EPEA. No.1*)

BELTRÃO (HELIO) Retomada do desenvolvimento e contrôle da inflação. [Rio de Janeiro], Departamento de Imprensa Nacional, 1967. pp. 75.

BRAZIL. Instituto de Planejamento Econômico e Social. Boletim econômico. m., Jl 1969 - Jl/Oc 1970, with gap (S 1969); My 1972 ([n. s.] ano 1, no.1)- ; susp. pbln. N 1970-Ap 1972. [Rio de Janeiro].

BOLETIM INFORMATIVO DO SERFHAU; [pd. by] Serviço Federal de Habitação e Urbanismo [Brazil]. m., Ja-S 1970 (ano 3, nos.22-30); Ja 1971 (ano 4, no.34) - Rio de Janeiro.

BRAZIL. 1971. First national development plan, 1972/74. [Brasilia], 1971. pp. 76.

SIMONSEN (MARIO HENRIQUE) Brasil 2002. Rio de Janeiro, 1972. pp. 178.

BOERGEL (HANNELORE) Abhängige Entwicklung und Inflation in Brasilien. Berlin, 1974. pp. 271. *bibliog.*

BRAZILIAN ECONOMIC STUDIES; [pd. by] Instituto de Planejamento Econômico e Social. a., 1975 (no.1)- Rio de Janeiro.

FIECHTER (GEORGES ANDRE) Brazil since 1964: modernization under a military regime; a study of the interactions of politics and economics in a contemporary military regime;... translated from the French by Alan Braley. London, 1975. pp. 310. *bibliog.*

ROBOCK (STEFAN HYMAN) Brazil: a study in development progress. Lexington, Mass., [1975]. pp. 204.

— Emigration and immigration.

KLARNER (IZABELA) Emigracja z Królestwa Polskiego do Brazylii, 1890-1914. Warszawa, 1975. pp. 169. *bibliog.*

LORENZONI (JULIO) Memorias de um imigrante italiano; traduçao de Armida Lorenzoni Parreira. Porto Alegre, [1975]. pp. 264.

— Foreign economic relations — United States.

SOARES (ORLANDO ESTEVÃO DA COSTA) Desenvolvimento econômico-social do Brasil y EUA. [Rio de Janeiro, 1975]. pp. 170. *bibliog.*

— History.

CARONE (EDGARD) O tenentismo: acontecimentos, personagens, programas. São Paulo, 1975. pp. 518. *bibliog.*

FAORO (RAYMUNDO) Os donos do poder: formação do patronato politico brasileiro. 2nd ed. Porto Alegre, 1975 repr. 1976. 2 vols. (in 1). *Pagination continuous.*

— — 1924–25, Revolution.

MACAULAY (NEILL) The Prestes column: revolution in Brazil. New York, 1974. pp. 281.

— — 1964, Revolution.

BRANCO (CARLOS CASTELLO) Introdução a revolução de 1964. [Rio de Janeiro, 1975]. 2 vols. (in 1).

SILVA (HELIO RIBEIRO DA) 1964: golpe ou contragolpe?. Rio de Janeiro, 1975. pp. 492.

— Industries.

TYLER (WILLIAM G.) Manufactured export expansion and industrialization in Brazil. Tübingen, 1976. pp. 373. *bibliog.* (*Kiel. Universität. Institut für Weltwirtschaft. Kieler Studien. 134*)

— Politics and government.

FARIA (GODOFREDO DE) Marshal. A subversão da ordem social no Brasil: carta aberta em particular ao presidente Costa e Silva e em geral ao clero. Rio de Janeiro, 1968. pp. 54.

MOREIRA (NEIVA) O exército e a crise brasileira. Montevideo, [1968]. pp. 72.

JARBAS CERQUEIRA (JOSE) Rebelion estudiantil brasileña. Montevideo, [1969?]. pp. 63.

IANNI (OCTAVIO) Crisis in Brazil; translated by Phyllis B. Eveleth. New York, 1970. pp. 244. *bibliog.*

PARTIDO COMUNISTA DO BRASIL. Comite Central. La guerra popular en el Brasil. Montevideo, 1970. pp. 57.

BRANCO (CARLOS CASTELLO) Introdução a revolução de 1964. [Rio de Janeiro, 1975]. 2 vols. (in 1).

CARDOSO (FERNANDO HENRIQUE) Autoritarismo e democratização. Rio de Janeiro, 1975. pp. 240.

FAORO (RAYMUNDO) Os donos do poder: formação do patronato politico brasileiro. 2nd ed. Porto Alegre, 1975 repr. 1976. 2 vols. (in 1). *Pagination continuous.*

FIECHTER (GEORGES ANDRE) Brazil since 1964: modernization under a military regime; a study of the interactions of politics and economics in a contemporary military regime;... translated from the French by Alan Braley. London, 1975. pp. 310. *bibliog.*

FORMAN (SHEPARD) The Brazilian peasantry. New York, 1975. pp. 319. *bibliog.*

PEDREIRA (FERNANDO) Brasil politica, 1964-1975. São Paulo, 1975. pp. 292.

SILVA (HELIO RIBEIRO DA) 1964: golpe ou contragolpe?. Rio de Janeiro, 1975. pp. 492.

VIANA FILHO (LUIS) O governo Castelo Branco. Rio de Janeiro, 1975. pp. 572.

KEITH (HENRY H.) and HAYES (ROBERT AMES) eds. Perspectives on armed politics in Brazil. Tempe, Arizona, [1976]. pp. 258.

— Population.

LAW and population in Brazil; [by] Walter Rodrigues [and others]. Medford, Mass., 1975. pp. 46. (*Tufts University. Fletcher School of Law and Diplomacy. Law and Population Monograph Series. No.34*)

BRAZIL (Cont.)

— Rural conditions.

ALBERSHEIM (URSULA) Uma comunidade teuto-brasileira: Jarim. Rio de Janeiro, Centro Brasileiro de Pesquisas Educacionais, 1962. pp. 236. *bibliog.* (*Publicações. Serie VI. Sociedade e Educação. Coleção O Brasil Provinciano. Vol.2*)

FORMAN (SHEPARD) The Brazilian peasantry. New York, 1975. pp. 319. *bibliog.*

— Social conditions.

CARDOSO (FERNANDO HENRIQUE) Autoritarismo e democratizacão. Rio de Janeiro, 1975. pp. 240.

— Social policy.

BOLETIM INFORMATIVO DO SERFHAU; [pd. by] Serviço Federal de Habitação e Urbanismo [Brazil]. m., Ja-S 1970 (ano 3, nos.22-30); Ja 1971 (ano 4, no.34) - Rio de Janeiro.

BRAZIL. 1971. First national development plan, 1972/74. [Brasilia], 1971. pp. 76.

BREMEN

— History.

SCHWARZWAELDER (HERBERT) Geschichte der Freien Hansestadt Bremen. Bremen, [1975 in progress].

— Politics and government.

BRANDT (PETER) Antifaschismus und Arbeiterbewegung: Aufbau, Ausprägung Politik in Bremen 1945/46. Hamburg. [1976]. pp. 446. *bibliog.* (*Hamburg. Forschungsstelle für die Geschichte des Nationalsozialismus in Hamburg, und Hamburger Bibliothek für Sozialgeschichte und Arbeiterbewegung. Hamburger Beiträge zur Sozial- und Zeitgeschichte. Band 11*).

BREST

— Growth.

MICHON (HENRI) Une zone d'activités: Brest-Kergaradec. [Paris, La Documentation Française, 1974]. pp. 50.

BREWING INDUSTRIES

— European Economic Community countries.

RULAND (HEIDEMARIE) Standort und Struktur der Brauindustrie in der Europäischen Gemeinschaft. Berlin, 1975. pp. 274. *bibliog.* 2 maps in end pocket. *Inaugural-Dissertation zur Erlangung des Grades eines Doktors der Wirtschaftswissenschaften der Freien Universität Berlin.*

BREZHNEV (LEONID IL'ICH).

BREZHNEV (LEONID IL'ICH) O kommunisticheskom vospitanii trudiashchikhsia: rechi i stat'i. 2nd ed. Moskva, 1975. pp. 639.

McNEAL (ROBERT HATCH) The Bolshevik tradition: Lenin, Stalin, Khrushchev, Brezhnev. 2nd ed. Englewood Cliffs, [1975]. pp. 210. *bibliog.*

BRIBERY

— Ghana.

GHANA. Commission of Inquiry into Bribery and Corruption. 1975. Final report; [P.D.Anin, chairman]. [Accra], 1975. pp. 161.

BRIGHTON

— Economic history.

DURR (ANDY) ed. A history of Brighton Trades Council and Labour Movement, 1890-1970. Brighton, 1974. pp. 80. (*Brighton Hove and District Trades Council. History Sub-Committee. Pamphlets*)

— History.

TRORY (ERNIE) Brighton and the General Strike. Brighton, 1975. pp. 32.

— Statistics, Vital.

NEWSHOLME (Sir ARTHUR) The Brighton life table: based on the mortality of the ten years, 1881-90. Brighton, 1893. pp. 39.

BRISTOL

— Amusements and recreational activities.

MELLER (HELEN E.) Leisure and the changing city, 1870-1914. London, 1976. pp. 308. *bibliog.*

— Foreign population.

JEFFERY (PATRICIA) Migrants and refugees: Muslim and Christian Pakistani families in Bristol. Cambridge, 1976. pp. 221. *bibliog.*

— History — Sources.

The BRISTOL poll book, being a list of the freeholders and freemen who voted at the general election for members to serve in Parliament for the city and county of Bristol, which commenced at the Guildhall, on...October 6, 1812 and finished...the 16th, etc. Bristol, 1818. pp. 136. *Bound with The poll book of the electors of...Bristol...1832.*

The POLL book of the electors of the electoral district of the city of Bristol, who voted at the general election in December, 1832; with some introductory notes by T.J. Manchee, etc. Bristol, 1833. pp. 195. *Bound with The Bristol poll book...general election...1812.*

— Politics and government.

COSTER (THOMAS) A list of the free-holders and free-men, who voted at the election for members of parliament for the city and county of Bristol, begun Wednesday May 15, MDCCXXXIV...at which election the candidates were, John Scrope, Sir Abraham Elton, Thomas Coster; done from Mr. Coster's original poll-book. Bristol, Felix Farley, [1734?]. pp. 160. *Fly-leaf contains biographical information and list of Coster's agents. This copy was presented to his agent Henry Hart. Some ms. amendments in the text. Title on spine: Bristol poll book, 1734.*

The BRISTOL poll book, being a list of the freeholders and freemen who voted at the general election for members to serve in Parliament for the city and county of Bristol, which commenced at the Guildhall, on...October 6, 1812 and finished...the 16th, etc. Bristol, 1818. pp. 136. *Bound with The poll book of the electors of...Bristol...1832.*

The POLL book of the electors of the electoral district of the city of Bristol, who voted at the general election in December, 1832; with some introductory notes by T.J. Manchee, etc. Bristol, 1833. pp. 195. *Bound with The Bristol poll book...general election...1812.*

BRITISH BROADCASTING CORPORATION.

BRITISH BROADCASTING CORPORATION. The BBC and the Open University: an educational partnership. London, [1975]. pp. 12.

SCHLESINGER (PHILIP RONALD) The social organisation of news production: a case study of BBC radio and television news; [Ph.D. (London) thesis]. [1975]. fo. 393. *Typescript: unpublished. This thesis is the property of London University and may not be removed from the Library.*

BRITISH COLUMBIA

— Economic policy.

BRITISH COLUMBIA. Department of Economic Development. Annual report. a., 1973/74- [Victoria].

— Foreign population.

MORTON (JAMES) In the sea of sterile mountains: the Chinese in British Columbia. Vancouver, 1974. pp. 280.

— Social conditions.

BRITISH COLUMBIA. Department of Rehabilitation and Social Improvement. Annual report. a., 1970/71- Victoria.

— Social policy.

BRITISH COLUMBIA. Department of Rehabilitation and Social Improvement. Annual report. a., 1970/71- Victoria.

BRITISH COLUMBIA. Department of Human Resources. Services for people: annual report... a., 1975 (with fiscal addendum for 1974/75)- Victoria.

BRITISH HONDURAS.

See BELIZE.

BRITISH IN INDIA.

ALLEN (CHARLES) 1940- , ed. Plain tales from the Raj: images of British India in the twentieth century. London, 1975 repr. 1976. pp. 240.

BRITISH IN SOUTH AFRICA.

ENGLISH-speaking South Africa today: proceedings of the National Conference, July 1974; edited by André de Villiers. Cape Town, 1976. pp. 387. *Conference sponsored by the 1820 Settlers National Monument Foundation.*

BRITISH VIRGIN ISLANDS

— Economic conditions.

BRITISH DEVELOPMENT DIVISION IN THE CARIBBEAN. British Virgin Islands: economic survey and projections. [Bridgetown?], 1970. pp. 51.

BROADCASTING POLICY

— Australia — Citizen participation.

AUSTRALIA. Department of the Media. Planning and Research Section. 1974. The public and the media: a discussion paper. [Canberra], 1974. 1 vol. (various foliations). *bibliog. Photocopy.*

— United States — Citizen participation.

GUIMARY (DONALD L.) Citizens' groups and broadcasting. New York, 1975. pp. 170. *bibliog.*

BRODOWICZ (JÓZEF MACIEJ).

MROZOWSKA (KAMILLA) Józef Maciej Brodowicz: z dziejów organizacji nauki i nauczania w Wolnym Mieście Krakowie. Wrocław, 1971. pp. 352. *bibliog.* (*Polska Akademia Nauk. Zakład Historii Nauki i Techniki. Monografie z Dziejów Nauki i Techniki. t.73*) *With Russian and English summaries.*

BROKEN HOMES.

NATIONAL SOCIETY FOR THE PREVENTION OF CRUELTY TO CHILDREN. Training Department. Yo yo children: a study of 23 violent matrimonial cases. London, [1974]. pp. 8. *bibliog.*

BROKERS

— United States.

SHEPARD (LAWRENCE) The securities brokerage industry: nonprice competition and noncompetitive pricing. Lexington, Mass., [1975]. pp. 120. *bibliog.*

BROTHERHOODS.

SCHEID (JOHN) Les Frères Arvales: recrutement et origine sociale sous les empereurs julio-claudiens. Paris, 1975. pp. 431. *bibliog.* (*Paris. Ecole Pratique des Hautes Etudes. Bibliothèque: Section des Sciences Réligieuses. vol. 77*)

SEGALEN (MARTINE) Les confréries dans la France contemporaine: les charités. Paris, [1975]. pp. 257. *bibliog.*

BROWDER (EARL RUSSELL).

JAFFE (PHILIP JACOB) The rise and fall of American communism. New York, [1975]. pp. 236.

BRUENING (HEINRICH).

MORSEY (RUDOLF) Zur Entstehung, Authentizität und Kritik von Brünings "Memoiren, 1918-1934". Opladen, [1975]. pp. 54. (Rheinisch-Westfälische Akademie der Wissenschaften. Geisteswissenschaften. Heft 202)

BRUNEI

— **Commerce — New Zealand.**

NEW ZEALAND. Department of Trade and Industry. 1975. Malaysia and Brunei: handbook. [Wellington], 1975. pp. 87. bibliog.

BRUPBACHER (FRITZ).

LANG (KARL MAX) Kritiker, Ketzer, Kämpfer: das Leben des Arbeiterarztes Fritz Brupbacher. Zürich, [1975]. pp. 361. bibliog. (Studienbibliothek zur Geschichte der Arbeiterbewegung, Zürich. Schriftenreihe. Band 3)

BRUSSELS.

FRANCE. Direction de la Documentation. La Documentation Française. Notes et Etudes Documentaires. Nos. 4,156-4, 157. Les grandes villes du monde: l'agglomération de Bruxelles; [par Jean Comhaire]. Paris, 1975. pp. 82. bibliog.

BUBER (MARTIN).

GUDOPP (WOLF DIETER) Martin Bubers dialogischer Anarchismus. Bern, 1975. pp. 131. bibliog.

BUCA (EDWARD).

BUCA (EDWARD) Vorkuta;...translated from the Polish by Michal Lisinski and Kennedy Wells. London, 1976. pp. 352.

BUCHANAN (JAMES) President of the United States.

SMITH (ELBERT N.) The presidency of James Buchanan. Lawrence, Kan., [1975]. pp. 225. bibliog.

BUCKINGHAMSHIRE

— **Economic conditions.**

BUCKINGHAMSHIRE. County Planning Department. Buckinghamshire County structure plan 1976: report of survey; draft for consultation. Aylesbury, 1976. pp. 283,xi.

— **Economic policy.**

BUCKINGHAMSHIRE. County Planning Department. Buckinghamshire County structure plan 1976: written statement; draft for consultation. Aylesbury, 1976. pp. 96.

— **Social conditions.**

BUCKINGHAMSHIRE. County Planning Department. Buckinghamshire County structure plan 1976: report of survey; draft for consultation. Aylesbury, 1976. pp. 283,xi.

— **Social policy.**

BUCKINGHAMSHIRE. County Planning Department. Buckinghamshire County structure plan 1976: written statement; draft for consultation. Aylesbury, 1976. pp. 96.

BUDGET.

SAWYER (MALCOLM C.) and WASSERMAN (MARK) Income distribution in OECD countries; [and] Public sector budget balances; by Mark Wasserman. [Paris], Organisation for Economic Co-operation and Development, 1976. pp. 51. (OECD Economic Outlook. Occasional Studies)

— **Argentine Republic.**

ARGENTINE REPUBLIC. Direccion Nacional de Programacion e Investigacion. 1975. Presupuestos provinciales y presupuesto nacional: distribuidos por provincias; ejercicio 1971 y 1972. Buenos Aires, 1975. pp. 234.

— **Denmark.**

DENMARK. Finansministeriet. Budget: (om forslag til finanslov). a., Current issue only kept. [København].

— **Europe.**

The POWER of the purse: the role of European parliaments in budgetary decisions: [based on a symposium directed by Political and Economic Planning; papers by] David Coombes et al. London, 1976. pp. 393.

— **European Economic Community countries.**

FRANCE. Direction de la Documentation. La Documentation Française. Notes et Etudes Documentaires. Nos. 4,102-4, 103. La politique budgétaire des pays de la Communauté Européenne; [par Georges Chevallier]. Paris, 1974. pp. 84.

FRANCE. Direction de la Documentation. La Documentation Française. Notes et Etudes Documentaires. Nos. 4,184-4, 185. Les systèmes budgétaires européens; par Joël Molinier et Guy Isaac. Paris, 1975. pp. 62. bibliog.

— **Goa, Daman and Diu.**

GOA, DAMAN AND DIU. Bureau of Economics, Statistics and Evaluation. Budget: an economic and functional classification of the Goa, Daman and Diu. a., 1974/5- Panaji.

— **Hong Kong.**

RABUSHKA (ALVIN) Value for money: the Hong Kong budgetary process. Stanford, Cal., 1976. pp. 176. (Stanford University. Hoover Institution on War, Revolution and Peace. Hoover Institution Publications. 152)

— **India — Goa, Daman and Diu.**

GOA, DAMAN AND DIU. Bureau of Economics, Statistics and Evaluation. 1974. An economic and functional classification of the Goa, Daman and Diu budget, 1969-70 to 1973-74. [Panaji, 1974]. pp. 90.

— **Liberia.**

LIBERIA. Bureau of the Budget. Annual report. a., 1974- Monrovia.

— **Russia.**

HOLZMAN (FRANKLYN DUNN) Financial checks on Soviet defense expenditures. Lexington, Mass., [1975]. pp. 103. bibliog.

— **Underdeveloped areas.**

See UNDERDEVELOPED AREAS — Budget.

— **United Kingdom.**

CONFEDERATION OF BRITISH INDUSTRY. Economic Directorate. Taxation Department. The Finance Act 1975: an explanatory guide. London, 1975. pp. 25.

— **United States.**

WILDAVSKY (AARON BERNARD) The politics of the budgetary process. 2nd ed. Boston, Mass., [1974]. pp. 271. bibliog.

FISHER (LOUIS) Presidential spending power. Princeton, [1975]. pp. 345.

FOSTER (JOHN L.) and others. National policy game: a simulation of the American political process. New York, [1975]. pp. 108.

BUDGET IN BUSINESS.

ABERDEEN. University of Aberdeen. North of Scotland College of Agriculture. Bulletins. [New Series]. No. 10. Budgetary control in farm management. [Aberdeen], 1975. pp. 31.

BUENOS AIRES

— **Growth.**

BOURDE (GUY) Urbanisation et immigration en Amérique Latine: Buenos Aires, XIXe et XXe siècles. Paris, 1974. pp. 288. bibliog.

— **History.**

BOURDE (GUY) Urbanisation et immigration en Amérique Latine: Buenos Aires, XIXe et XXe siècles. Paris, 1974. pp. 288. bibliog.

BUILDING AND LOAN ASSOCIATIONS

— **United Kingdom — Law.**

WURTZBURG (EDWARD ALBERT) and MILLS (JOHN WILLIAM) Building society law: fourteenth edition by John Mills. London, 1976. pp. 610.

BUILDING LAWS AND REGULATIONS

— **United Kingdom.**

SOME implications of statutory controls: [proceedings of a conference organized by the Faculty of Building at Birmingham in 1971]. [Boreham Wood, 1973]. pp. 20.

BUILDING TRADES

— **United Kingdom.**

LAMB (DAVE) The lump: an heretical analysis. Lancaster, 1974. pp. 24. (Solidarity: [for workers' power]. Pamphlets)

BUILDINGS, PREFABRICATED.

COUNCIL FOR THE PROTECTION OF RURAL ENGLAND. Development control: package buildings. London, [1974]. pp. 34.

BUILDINGS, TALL.

See TALL BUILDINGS.

BUKHARA

See also SOVIET CENTRAL ASIA.

— **Economic history.**

ABDURAIMOV (M.A.) Ocherki agrarnykh otnoshenii v Bukharskom khanstve v XVI - pervoi polovine XIX veka. Tashkent, 1966 in progress. bibliog.

— **History — Sources.**

ARENDARENKO (GEORGII ALEKSEEVICH) Bukhara i Afganistan v nachale 80-kh godov XIX veka: zhurnaly komandirovok G.A. Arendarenko; [redaktsionnaia kollegiia B.G. Gafurov (and others)]. Moskva, 1974. pp. 142.

BUKOBA DISTRICT

— **Rural conditions.**

RALD (JØRGEN) and RALD (KAREN) Rural organization in Bukoba district, Tanzania. Uppsala, 1975. pp. 122. bibliog.

BUKOVINA

— **History.**

PIVNICHNA Bukovyna, iï mynule i suchasne. Uzhhorod, 1969. pp. 247. biblog.

BULGARIA

— **Commerce.**

BULGARIA. Tsentralno Statistichesko Upravlenie. 1972. Vutreshna turgoviia. Sofiia, 1972. pp. 141.

— **Economic history.**

30 godini ikonomika na NR Bulgariia. Sofiia, 1974. pp. 560. With Russian and English summaries.

BULGARIA(Cont.)

— Foreign economic relations.

VUNSHNOIKONOMICHESKITE otnosheniia na NR Bulgariia; Les rapports économiques de la RP de Bulgarie avec l'étranger de 1944 à 1974. Sofiia, 1974. pp. 238. *(Sofia. Universitet. Katedra po Politicheska Ikonomiia. Trudove. t.12) With English summary.*

— Foreign relations.

DIMITROV (GEORGI) Selected works. Sofia, 1972. 3 vols.

— — Russia.

BULGARIA. Ministerstvo na Vunshnite Raboti. 1974. Bulgaro-suvetski otnosheniia, 1948-1970: dokumenti i materiali. Sofiia, 1974. pp. 815.

MEL'TSER (DAVID BORISOVICH) Sovetsko-bolgarskie otnosheniia, 1917-1935 gg. Minsk, 1975. pp. 222.

— — United States.

BULGARIA. Ministerstvo na Vunshnite Raboti. 1952. Documents on the hostile and aggressive policy of the government of the United States of America against the People's Republic of Bulgaria. Sofia, 1952. pp. 287.

— History.

RADEV (SIMEON) Stroitelite na suvremenna Bulgariia; predgovor i obshta redaktsiia...Pantelei Zarev [of works first published 1911-12] . Sofiia, 1973. 2 vols.

APRILSKOTO vustanie, 1876-1966: dokladi i izkazvaniia na iubileinata nauchna sesiia v Sofiia; L'insurrection d'avril, 1876-1966: rapports et débats tenus à la session de jubilé à Sofia. Sofiia, 1966. pp. 245. *With French or German summaries and table of contents.*

KHRISTOV (KHRISTO) Osvobozhdenieto na Bulgariia i politikata na zapadnite durzhavi, 1876-1878; La libération de la Bulgarie et la politique des puissances occidentales, 1876-1878. Sofiia, 1968. pp. 256. *With Russian and French summaries.*

— — Sources.

LEVSKI (VASIL) Sviata i chista republika: pisma i dokumenti; sustaviteli Ivan Undzhiev, Nikola Kondarev. [Sofiia], 1971. pp. 222,[xvi].

— — 1923, September Uprising.

KOSEV (DIMITUR) Septemvriiskoto vustanie 1923. 2nd ed. Sofiia, 1973. pp. 785. *With Russian, English and French summaries.*

— Politics and government.

KHRISTOV (KHRISTO) Zakharii Stoianov: obshtestvena i politicheska deinost; Zachari Stoïanov: son activité sociale et politique. Sofiia, 1948. pp. 155. *(Sofia. Universitet. Istoriko-Filologicheski Fakultet. Godishnik. t.44, kn.2) With French summary.*

BOTEV (KHRISTO) Subrani suchineniia v dva toma; pod redaktsiiata na... Mikhail Dimitrov. Sofiia, 1971. 2 vols.

LEVSKI (VASIL) Sviata i chista republika: pisma i dokumenti; sustaviteli Ivan Undzhiev, Nikola Kondarev. [Sofiia], 1971. pp. 222,[xvi].

DIMITROV (GEORGI) Selected works. Sofia, 1972. 3 vols.

ZHIVKOV (TODOR) Modern Bulgaria: problems and tasks in building an advanced socialist society. New York, [1974]. pp. 228.

MILLER (MARSHALL LEE) Bulgaria during the Second World War. Stanford, 1975. pp. 290. *bibliog.*

— Population.

DEMOGRAFIIA na Bulgariia. Sofiia, 1974. pp. 644. *bibliog. With Russian and English summaries and tables of contents.*

RUSSIA (USSR). Ministerstvo Vysshego i Srednego Spetsial'nogo Obrazovaniia. Nauchno-Tekhnicheskii Sovet. Sektsiia Narodonaseleniia. Narodonaselenie. 6. Narodonaselenie zarubezhnykh stran. Moskva, 1974. pp. 93. *With English table of contents.*

— Relations (general) with Russia.

SOTSIALISTICHESKII internatsionalizm v deistvii. Moskva, 1974. pp. 254.

BULGARIAN LITERATURE.

BOTEV (KHRISTO) Subrani suchineniia v dva toma; pod redaktsiiata na... Mikhail Dimitrov. Sofiia, 1971. 2 vols.

BULL (ODD).

BULL (ODD) War and peace in the Middle East: the experiences and views of a U.N. observer. London, 1976. pp. 205.

BUREAUCRACY.

WERNER (LUTZ) Der Kampf der Kommunistischen Parteien in den sozialistischen Staaten gegen Bürokratismus. Kiel, 1974. pp. 152,iv. *bibliog. (Kiel. Universität. Institut für Recht, Politik und Gesellschaft der Sozialistischen Staaten. Manuskripte. 4)*

MOUZELIS (NICOLAS P.) Organisation and bureaucracy: an analysis of modern theories; [reprint with a new introduction of the edition of 1967]. London, 1975. pp. 234.

PRICE (ROBERT M.) Society and bureaucracy in contemporary Ghana. Berkeley, [1975]. pp. 261. *bibliog.*

SHAPIRO (H.R.) The bureaucratic state: party bureaucracy and the decline of democracy in America. New York, [1975]. pp. 366. *bibliogs.*

GOLDWATER (BARRY MORRIS) The coming breakpoint. New York, [1976]. pp. 184.

JAQUES (ELLIOTT) A general theory of bureaucracy. London, 1976. pp. 412. *bibliog.*

KRANZ (HARRY) The participatory bureaucracy: women and minorities in a more representative public service. Lexington, Mass., [1976]. pp. 244.

LAUREN (PAUL GORDON) Diplomats and bureaucrats: the first institutional responses to twentieth-century diplomacy in France and Germany. Stanford, 1976. pp. 294. *bibliog. (Stanford University. Hoover Institution on War, Revolution and Peace. Hoover Institution Publications. 153)*

TULLOCK (GORDON) The vote motive: an essay in the economics of politics with applications to the British economy...with a British commentary by Morris Perlman. London, 1976. pp. 88. *bibliogs. (Institute of Economic Affairs. Hobart Paperbacks. 9.)*

BURGUNDY

— Economic conditions.

DIMENSIONS ECONOMIQUES DE LA BOURGOGNE; revue mensuelle; ([pd. by] Institut National de la Statistique et des Etudes Economiques,...Direction Régionale de Dijon [France]). m., Ja 1972 (no.1)- Dijon.

BABLON (ELISABETH) and others, eds. Bourgogne: aujourd'hui...demain... [Paris], 1973. pp. 135.

BURKE (EDMUND).

BURKE (EDMUND) Edmund Burke on government, politics and society; selected and edited by B.W. Hill. Hassocks, Sussex, 1975. pp. 382. *bibliog.*

BURMA.

LUBEIGT (GUY) La Birmanie. [Paris, 1975]. pp. 127. *bibliog.*

— Armed forces — Political activity.

LISSAK (MOSHE) Military roles in modernization: civil-military relations in Thailand and Burma. Beverly Hills, [1976]. pp. 255. *(Inter-University Seminar on Armed Forces and Society. [Publications]. vol.8)*

— Politics and government.

LISSAK (MOSHE) Military roles in modernization: civil-military relations in Thailand and Burma. Beverly Hills, [1976]. pp. 255. *(Inter-University Seminar on Armed Forces and Society. [Publications]. vol.8)*

BURNS (Sir GEORGE).

HODDER (EDWIN) Sir George Burns, bart.: his times and friends. London, 1890. pp. 528.

BURYAT REPUBLIC

— Economic policy.

RAZVITIE proizvoditel'nykh sil Buriatskoi ASSR. Ulan-Ude, 1968. pp. 187. *(Akademiia Nauk SSSR. Sibirskoe Otdelenie. Buriatskii Filial. Otdel Ekonomicheskikh Issledovanii. Trudy. vyp.5 [being also] vyp.1 [of 1968])*

— Social conditions.

IZ opyta konkretno-sotsiologicheskikh issledovanii. Ulan-Ude, 1972. pp. 198. *(Buriatskii Institut Obshchestvennykh Nauk. Trudy. vyp.17. Seriia Sotsiologicheskaia)*

— Social policy.

VOPROSY preodoleniia perezhitkov proshlogo v bytu i soznanii liudei i stanovleniia novykh obychaev, obriadov i traditsii u narodov Sibiri: materialy nauchno-praticheskoi konferentsii, sostoiavsheisia 22-26 noiabria 1966 g. v g.Ulan-Ude. vyp.2. Ulan-Ude, 1969. pp. 220.

BUSEK (ERHARD).

VODOPIVEC (ALEXANDER) Taus Busek: Persönlichkeit, Konzept und Stil des neuen Führungsteams der ÖVP. Wien, [1975]. pp. 120.

BUSINESS

— Bibliography.

HARVARD UNIVERSITY. Graduate School of Business Administration. Baker Library. Author-title catalogue of the Baker Library, etc. Boston, Mass., 1971 in progress.

VERNON (K.D.C.) ed. Use of management and business literature. London, 1975. pp. 327. *bibliogs.*

— Information services.

VERNON (K.D.C.) ed. Use of management and business literature. London, 1975. pp. 327. *bibliogs.*

BUSINESS AND POLITICS.

PURDIE (WILLIAM K.) and TAYLOR (BERNARD) eds. Business strategies for survival: planning for social and political change. London, 1976. pp. 231.

BUSINESS CONSULTANTS

— Tanzania.

NATIONAL INSTITUTE FOR PRODUCTIVITY [TANZANIA]. N[ational] I[nstitute for] P[roductivity]: management advice, training and on-the-job development. Dar es Salaam, [197-]. fo. 12.

— United States.

GUTTMAN (DANIEL) and WILLNER (BARRY) The shadow government: the government's multi-billion-dollar giveaway of its decision-making powers to private management consultant "experts" and think tanks. New York, [1976]. pp. 354.

BUSINESS CYCLES.

PROBLEMY mirovogo krizisa: diskussiia v Institute mirovogo khoziaistva i mirovoi politiki Komakademii. Moskva, 1932. pp. 210.

WERNER (KURT) Die deutschen Wirtschaftsgebiete in der Krise: statistische Studie zur regional vergleichenden Konjunkturbetrachtung. Jena, 1932. pp. 71.

KALECKI (MICHAŁ) Prace z teorii koniunktury, 1933-1939. Warszawa, 1962. pp. 106.

SZEWORSKI (ADAM) Cykl koniunkturalny a interwencja państwa. Warszawa, 1965. pp. 255. bibliog.

NORTHERN REGION STRATEGY TEAM. Cyclical fluctuations in economic activity in the northern region, 1958-1973. Newcastle upon Tyne, 1975. 1 pamphlet (various pagings). (Technical Reports. No. 1)

GOTTLIEB (MANUEL) Long swings in urban development. New York, 1976. pp. 360. bibliog. (National Bureau of Economic Research. Urban and Regional Studies. 4)

NATIONAL ECONOMIC DEVELOPMENT OFFICE. Cyclical fluctuations in the United Kingdom economy. London, 1976. pp. 40. (Discussion Papers. 3)

— Mathematical models.

BOLTHO (ANDREA) and others. The measurement of domestic cyclical fluctuations. [Paris], Organisation for Economic Cooperation and Development, 1973. pp. 68. (OECD Economic Outlook. Occasional Studies)

SAMUELSON (LEE) and GRAENZER (RANDOLF) A new model of world trade; [and] Cyclical indicators for manufacturing industries; by Randolf Gränzer. [Paris], Organisation for Economic Cooperation and Development, 1973. pp. 55. (OECD Economic Outlook. Occasional Studies)

MASS (NATHANIEL J.) Economic cycles: an analysis of underlying causes. Cambridge, Mass., [1975]. pp. 185. bibliog.

ROTH (JUERGEN) Der internationale Konjunkturzusammenhang bei flexiblen Wechselkursen: eine modelltheoretische Analyse. Tübingen, 1975. pp. 264. bibliog. (Kiel. Universität. Institut für Weltwirtschaft Kieler Studien. 135)

BUSINESS EDUCATION

— United Kingdom.

DODD (L.J.) [Notes of lectures for the degree of B. Comm. at the London School of Economics. 1921-27]. 19 pieces. Manuscript.

BUSINESS ETHICS.

PURDIE (WILLIAM K.) and TAYLOR (BERNARD) eds. Business strategies for survival: planning for social and political change. London, 1976. pp. 231.

BUSINESS FORECASTING.

MORRELL (JAMES) A short guide to business forecasting. London, 1976. pp. 60. (Henley Centre for Forecasting. Occasional Papers. No.2)

WOOD (DOUG) and FILDES (ROBERT) Forecasting for business: methods and applications. London, 1976. pp. 280. bibliogs.

— Mathematical models.

PINDYCK (ROBERT S.) and RUBINFELD (DANIEL L.) Econometric models and economic forecasts. New York, [1976]. pp. 576.

BUSINESS LAW

— East (Near East).

RUSSELL (BRIAN) ed. An introduction to business law in the Middle East. London, 1975. pp. 118.

BUSINESS RELOCATION

— Bibliography.

GOMERSALL (ALAN) compiler. Industrial relocation. London, 1975. pp. 21. (London. Greater London Council. Research Library. Research Bibliographies. No. 61)

BUSINESSMEN

— France.

ENTERPRISE and entrepreneurs in nineteenth- and twentieth-century France; [essays given as lectures in a series sponsored by the Catholic University of America and Johns Hopkins University in 1973]; edited...by Edward C. Carter [and others]. Baltimore, [1976]. pp. 207.

— Japan.

AUSTIN (LEWIS) Saints and samurai: the political culture of the American and Japanese elites. New Haven, 1975. pp. 197. (Yale University. Yale Studies in Political Science. 27)

BRYANT (WILLIAM E.) Japanese private economic diplomacy: an analysis of business- government linkages. New York, 1975. pp. 138. bibliog.

— United States.

AUSTIN (LEWIS) Saints and samurai: the political culture of the American and Japanese elites. New Haven, 1975. pp. 197. (Yale University. Yale Studies in Political Science. 27)

BUTLER (CHRISTINA VIOLET).

TRADITIONS of social policy: essays in honour of Violet Butler; edited by A.H. Halsey. Oxford, [1976]. pp. 285.

BUTLER (JOSEPHINE ELIZABETH).

BUTLER (JOSEPHINE ELIZABETH) Josephine Butler has her say about her contemporaries; selected from...[her] letters...by Margaret Burton. London, 1972. pp. 20.

BYGDEÅ

— Schools.

JOHANSSON (EGIL) En studie med kvantitativa metoder av folkundervisningen i Bygdeå socken, 1845-1873. Umeå, 1972. 2 vols. (in 1). bibliog. With English summary.

BYRON (GEORGE GORDON NOEL) 6th Baron Byron.

HOLDSWORTH (RICHARD JULIAN) Lord Byron's Childe Harold's Pilgrimage as a liberal commentary on European relations around the close of the Napoleonic era. London, 1975. fo. 20. (London. University. London School of Economics and Political Science. Gladstone Memorial Trust Prize Essays. 1975) Typescript.

CAB AND OMNIBUS SERVICE

— United Kingdom.

TAXI CAB SERVICE COMMITTEE. [Report, evidence, minutes. 1952]. 2 pieces. Typescript.

CAEN

— Growth.

PERROT (JEAN CLAUDE) Genèse d'une ville moderne: Caen au XVIIIe siècle. Paris, [1975]. pp. 1157(in 2 vols.). bibliog.

— History.

PERROT (JEAN CLAUDE) Genèse d'une ville moderne: Caen au XVIIIe siècle. Paris, [1975]. pp. 1157(in 2 vols.). bibliog.

CAIRO

— Commerce.

VAN OENEN (J.D.) Cairo as a financial centre and some of its implications. Cairo, 1975. pp. 21. (National Bank of Egypt. Diamond Jubilee Lectures)

CALCULATING MACHINES.

BABBAGE (CHARLES) Charles Babbage and his calculating engines: selected writings by Charles Babbage and others; edited and with an introduction by Philip Morrison and Emily Morrison. New York, 1961. pp. 400.

CALCULUS, OPERATIONAL.

ROTA (GIAN-CARLO) and others. Finite operator calculus. New York, 1975. pp. 159. bibliogs.

CALIFORNIA

— History.

O'FLAHERTY (JOSEPH S.) An end and a beginning: the south coast and Los Angeles, 1850- 1887. New York, [1972]. pp. 222. bibliog.

— Politics and government.

DEWITT (HOWARD A.) Images of ethnic and radical violence in California politics, 1917- 1930: a survey. San Francisco, 1975. pp. 136. bibliog.

— Race question.

DEWITT (HOWARD A.) Images of ethnic and radical violence in California politics, 1917- 1930: a survey. San Francisco, 1975. pp. 136. bibliog.

CALLAGHAN (JAMES).

KELLNER (PETER) and HITCHENS (CHRISTOPHER) Callaghan: the road to Number Ten. London, 1976. pp. 187. bibliog.

CAMBODIA

— Rural conditions.

MARTEL (GABRIELLE) Lovea, village des environs d'Angkor: aspects démographiques, économiques et sociologiques du monde rural cambodgien dans la province de Siem-Réap. Paris, 1975. pp. 359. (Ecole Française d'Extrême-Orient. Publications. vol. 98)

CAMDEN

— Politics and government.

WISTRICH (ENID BARBARA) London government reorganisation: the formation and first years of the London Borough of Camden, 1962-8; [Ph.D.(London) thesis]. [1975]. fo. 431. bibliog. Typescript: unpublished. This thesis is the property of London University and may not be removed from the Library.

CAMEROUN.

CAMEROUN INFORMATIONS: (Cameroon information: bulletin mensuel de la République Unie du Cameroun...édité par le Ministère de l'Information et de la Culture, Direction de l'Information et de la Presse). m., F 1973 (no.3)- Yaoundé.

— Economic history.

EILY (F. ETOGA) Sur les chemins du développement: essai d'histoire des faits économiques du Cameroun. Yaoundé, 1971. pp. 521. bibliog.

— Economic policy.

NDONGKO (WILFRED AWUNG) Planning for economic development in a federal state: the case of Cameroon, 1960-1971. München, [1975]. pp. 203. bibliog. (Ifo-Institut für Wirtschaftsforschung. Afrika- Studien. 85)

— Statistics.

CAMEROUN. Direction de la Statistique et de la Comptabilité Nationale. Note annuelle de statistique [financial year]. a., 1973/74 (1st)- Yaoundé.

CAMEROUN. Direction de la Statistique et de la Comptabilité Nationale. Note annuelle de statistique [calendar year]. a., 1974- Yaoundé.

CAMEROUN. Direction de la Statistique et de la Comptabilité Nationale. Bulletin mensuel de statistique. m., Ja 1975 (2 année, no.1)- ; with gap (Ap-Je 1975, nos 4-6). Yaoundé. Supersedes in part CAMEROUN. Direction de la Statistique et de la Comptabilité Nationale. Note trimestrielle de statistique.

CAMP-MEETINGS.

CAMP-MEETINGS.

BRUCE (DICKSON D.) And they all sang hallelujah: plain-folk camp-meeting religion, 1800-1845. Knoxville, Tenn., [1974]. pp. 155. *bibliog.*

CAMP OF NATIONAL UNITY.
See OBOZ ZJEDNOCZENIA NARODOWEGO.

CAMPAIGN FUNDS.

AMERICAN ACADEMY OF POLITICAL AND SOCIAL SCIENCE. Annals. vol. 425. Political finance: reform and reality; special editor of this volume, Herbert E. Alexander. Philadelphia, 1976. pp. 205.

CAMPAIGN MANAGEMENT.

HERSHEY (MARJORIE RANDON) The making of campaign strategy. Lexington, Mass., [1974]. pp. 164.

STEINBERG (ARNOLD) Political campaign management: a systems approach. Lexington, Mass., [1976]. pp. 292.

— United States.

STEINBERG (ARNOLD) Political campaign management: a systems approach. Lexington, Mass., [1976]. pp. 292.

CAMPBELL (JAMES DUNCAN).

HART (Sir ROBERT) The I.G. in Peking: letters of Robert Hart, Chinese Maritime Customs, 1868-1907...; edited by John King Fairbank [and others]. Cambridge, Mass., 1975. 2 vols. *Letters to his London agent, James Duncan Campbell.*

CAMPBELL—BANNERMAN (Sir HENRY).

O'CONNOR (THOMAS POWER) Sir Henry Campbell-Bannerman. London, 1908. pp. 167.

CANADA

— Appropriations and expenditures.

CANADA. [Parliament]. 1963. Report on supply for the fiscal year ended March 31, 1963. Ottawa, 1963. pp. 71.

— Boundaries — United States.

INTERNATIONAL JOINT COMMISSION, CANADA AND UNITED STATES. Rules of procedure and text of treaty. [Washington, 1968]. pp. 22.

— Civilization.

CANADIAN CONSULTATIVE COUNCIL ON MULTICULTURALISM. Annual report. a., 1974 (1st)- Ottawa. *[In English and French].*

— — American influences.

DICKEY (JOHN SLOAN) Canada and the American presence: the United States interest in an independent Canada. New York, 1975. pp. 202.

— Climate.

LONGLEY (RICHMOND W.) The climate of the prairie provinces. Ottawa, Information Canada, 1972. pp. 79. *bibliog. (Climatological Studies. No. 13)*

— Commerce.

CANADA. Department of Industry, Trade and Commerce. Chemicals Branch. 1971. Chemical import trends, 1965-1966-1967;...to be read and used in conjunction with Chemical import trends 1956-1964. Ottawa, [1971]. pp. 111. *bibliog. In English and French.*

CANADA. Statistics Canada. Trade of Canada commodity classification. irreg., 1975- Ottawa. *In English and French.*

— Constitution.

FORSEY (EUGENE ALFRED) Freedom and order. Toronto, [1974]. pp. 332.

HOCKIN (THOMAS A.) Government in Canada. London, [1975]. pp. 252. *bibliog.*

— Defences.

BURNS (EEDSON LOUIS MILLARD) Defence in the nuclear age: an introduction for Canadians. Toronto, [1976]. pp. 133. *bibliog.*

— Discovery and exploration.

LOWER (J. ARTHUR) Canada on the Pacific rim. Toronto, [1975]. pp. 230. *bibliog.*

— Economic conditions.

ECONOMIC REVIEW: a general review of recent economic developments presented by the...Minister of Finance [Canada]. a., Ap 1972 [1st issue]- Ottawa.

STAGER (DAVID) Economic analysis and Canadian policy. Toronto, [1973]. pp. 482. *bibliogs.*

ARCHER (MAURICE) Canada's economic problems and policies. Toronto, [1975]. pp. 211.

GONICK (CY) Inflation or depression: the continuing crisis of the Canadian economy. Toronto, 1975. pp. 448. *bibliog.*

ROTSTEIN (ABRAHAM) ed. Beyond industrial growth. Toronto, 1976. pp. 131. *Lectures given at Massey College, University of Toronto, 1974-1975.*

— — Statistics.

ECONOMIC REVIEW: a general review of recent economic developments presented by the...Minister of Finance [Canada]. a., Ap 1972 [1st issue]- Ottawa.

— Economic history.

PORTER (GLENN) and CUFF (ROBERT D.) eds. Enterprise and national development: essays in Canadian business and economic history. Toronto, 1973. pp. 138.

— — Sources.

GOURLAY (ROBERT) Statistical account of Upper Canada: abridged [from the original published in 1822] and with an introduction by S.R. Mealing. Toronto, [1974]. pp. 395. *bibliog. (Carleton University. Institute of Canadian Studies. Carleton Library. No. 75)*

— Economic policy.

CANADA. Department of Indian Affairs and Northern Development. 1972. Canada's north, 1970-1980; (statement of the government of Canada on northern development in the 70's). [Ottawa, 1972]. pp. 40. *In English, French and Eskimo.*

DONNER (ARTHUR) and others. Issues in Canadian economic policy. Toronto, 1973. pp. 118.

STAGER (DAVID) Economic analysis and Canadian policy. Toronto, [1973]. pp. 482. *bibliogs.*

ARCHER (MAURICE) Canada's economic problems and policies. Toronto, [1975]. pp. 211.

GONICK (CY) Inflation or depression: the continuing crisis of the Canadian economy. Toronto, 1975. pp. 448. *bibliog.*

ONTARIO. Economic Council. 1976. National independence: issues and alternatives, 1976. [Toronto], 1976. pp. 41.

ROTSTEIN (ABRAHAM) ed. Beyond industrial growth. Toronto, 1976. pp. 131. *Lectures given at Massey College, University of Toronto, 1974-1975.*

— Emigration and immigration.

CANADA MANPOWER AND IMMIGRATION REVIEW (formerly Canada manpower review); [pd. by] Government of Canada Department of Manpower and Immigration. [in English and French]. q., 1970 (v.3)- Ottawa.

CANADIAN LABOUR CONGRESS. Submission...to the Special Joint Committee on Immigration Policy and the Green Paper on Immigration. Ottawa, 1975. fo. 30,5,4.

FERGUSON (TED) A white man's country: an exercise in Canadian prejudice. Toronto, [1975]. pp. 200. *bibliog.*

— Executive departments.

CANADA. Department of Labour. 1968. Vital partner of workers and employers: Canada Department of Labour. [Ottawa, 1968]. 1 pamphlet (unpaged).

CANADA. Department of Labour. 1973. Information on the new Union-Management Services Branch. Ottawa, 1973. 1 pamphlet (unpaged) *In English and French.*

CANADA. Department of the Secretary of State. 1973. Secretary of State: departmental programmes and affiliated agencies. Ottawa, 1973. pp. 23, 25. *In English and French.*

— Foreign economic relations.

CANADA. Parliament. House of Commons. Standing Committee on External Affairs and National Defence. Sub-Committee on International Development. Minutes of proceedings and evidence. irreg., Jl 22 1975 (no.1)- . *In English and French.*

— — America, Latin.

OGELSBY (J.C.M.) Gringos from the far North: essays in the history of Canadian-Latin American relations, 1866-1968. Toronto, [1976]. pp. 346. *bibliog.*

— — United States.

GONICK (CY) Inflation or depression: the continuing crisis of the Canadian economy. Toronto, 1975. pp. 448. *bibliog.*

— Foreign relations.

GRANATSTEIN (J.L.) Canada's war: the politics of the Mackenzie King government, 1939-1945. Toronto, 1975. pp. 436.

PEARSON (LESTER BOWLES) Mike: the memoirs...volume 3, 1957-1968; edited by John A. Munro and Alex I. Inglis. London, 1975. pp. 338.

— — America, Latin.

OGELSBY (J.C.M.) Gringos from the far North: essays in the history of Canadian-Latin American relations, 1866-1968. Toronto, [1976]. pp. 346. *bibliog.*

— — Pacific, The.

LOWER (J. ARTHUR) Canada on the Pacific rim. Toronto, [1975]. pp. 230. *bibliog.*

— — United Kingdom.

BRITAIN and Canada: survey of a changing relationship; edited by Peter Lyon. London, 1976. pp. 191. *Based on papers presented at a conference held at St. Catherine's Cumberland Lodge in 1971.*

— — United States.

CUFF (ROBERT D.) and GRANATSTEIN (JACK LAWRENCE) Canadian-American relations in wartime: from the Great War to the cold war. Toronto, 1975. pp. 205.

DICKEY (JOHN SLOAN) Canada and the American presence: the United States interest in an independent Canada. New York, 1975. pp. 202.

SWANSON (ROGER FRANK) ed. Canadian-American summit diplomacy, 1923-1973: selected speeches and documents. Toronto, [1975]. pp. 314. *(Carleton University. Institute of Canadian Studies. Carleton Library. No.81)*

— — Vietnam.

CANADA. Department of External Affairs. 1973. Viet-nam: Canada's approach to participation in the International Commission of Control and Supervision, October 25, 1972-March 27, 1973. [Ottawa], 1973. pp. 51. *In English and French.*

— History.

LOWER (J. ARTHUR) Canada on the Pacific rim. Toronto, [1975]. pp. 230. *bibliog.*

— — Sources.

CANADA. Public Archives. 1972. Archives: mirror of Canada past. [Ottawa], 1972. pp. 313. *In English and French.*

— — To 1763 (New France) — Bibliography.

ALEXANDRIN (BARBARA) and BOTHWELL (ROBERT) compilers. Bibliography of the material culture of New France. Ottawa, National Museums of Canada, 1970. pp. 32. *(National Museum of Man [Canada]. Publications in History. No.4)*

— — 1841—1867.

CANADA. National Museum of Canada. Human History Branch. 1967. Confederation, 1867. [Ottawa], 1967. pp. 28. *bibliog.*

— — 1866—1870, Fenian invasions.

NEIDHARDT (W.S.) Fenianism in North America. University Park, Pa., [1975]. pp. 164. *bibliog.*

— Industries.

CANADA. Statistics Canada. Domestic and foreign control of manufacturing establishments in Canada. bien, 1969/1970 (1st)- Ottawa.

CANADA. Statistics Canada. Real domestic product by industry. a., 1971/74 (1st)- Ottawa.

— Maps.

NATIONAL MAP COLLECTION [CANADA]. Canada in maps: documents drawn from the...Collection. [Ottawa, 1970]. 1 vol. (unpaged). *In English and French.*

— Maps, Topographic.

SEBERT (L.M.) Every square inch...: the story of Canadian topographic mapping. Ottawa, Queens's Printer, 1970. pp. 26, 5 maps.

— Nationalism.

DICKEY (JOHN SLOAN) Canada and the American presence: the United States interest in an independent Canada. New York, 1975. pp. 202.

ONTARIO. Economic Council. 1976. National independence: issues and alternatives, 1976. [Toronto], 1976. pp. 41.

— Officials and employees.

CANADA. Treasury Board. 1968. Agreement between the Treasury Board and the Council of Graphic Arts Unions of the Public Service of Canada, Printing Operations Group, non-supervisory. [Ottawa, 1968]. pp. 101. *In English and French.*

HODGETTS (JOHN EDWARD) and DWIVEDI (O.P.) Provincial governments as employers: a survey of public personnel administration in Canada's provinces. Montreal, 1974. pp. 216. *(Institute of Public Administration of Canada. Canadian Public Administration Series)*

CANADIAN LABOUR CONGRESS. Submission...to the special joint committee on employer-employee relations in the public service. Ottawa, 1975. fo. 32.

— Parliament.

JACKSON (ROBERT J.) and ATKINSON (MICHAEL M.) The Canadian legislative system: politicians and policy-making. [Toronto], 1974. pp. 196.

MARCH (ROMAN R.) The myth of Parliament. Scarborough, Ont., [1974]. pp. 150. *bibliog.*

— — Elections.

PENNIMAN (HOWARD RAE) ed. Canada at the polls: the general election of 1974. Washington, 1975. pp. 310. *(American Enterprise Institute for Public Policy Research. Foreign Affairs Studies. 24)*

— Politics and government.

ROUSSOPOULOS (DIMITRIOS J.) ed. The political economy of the state: Québec, Canada, U.S.A. Montréal, 1973. pp. 195.

DOERN (G. BRUCE) and WILSON (V. SEYMOUR) eds. Issues in Canadian public policy. [Toronto], 1974. pp. 355. *bibliog.*

FORSEY (EUGENE ALFRED) Freedom and order. Toronto, [1974]. pp. 332.

JACKSON (ROBERT J.) and ATKINSON (MICHAEL M.) The Canadian legislative system: politicians and policy-making. [Toronto], 1974. pp. 196.

DIEFENBAKER (JOHN GEORGE) One Canada: memoirs. Toronto, [1975 in progress].

GRANATSTEIN (J.L.) Canada's war: the politics of the Mackenzie King government, 1939-1945. Toronto, 1975. pp. 436.

HOCKIN (THOMAS A.) Government in Canada. London, [1975]. pp. 252. *bibliog.*

PEARSON (LESTER BOWLES) Mike: the memoirs...volume 3, 1957-1968; edited by John A. Munro and Alex I. Inglis. London, 1975. pp. 338.

PICKERSGILL (JOHN WHITNEY) My years with Louis St Laurent: a political memoir. Toronto, [1975]. pp. 334.

STURSBERG (PETER) Diefenbaker: leadership gained, 1956-62. Toronto, [1975]. pp. 278. *Based on recorded interviews and discussions.*

— Population.

COURCHENE (THOMAS J.) Migration, income and employment: Canada, 1965-68. [Montreal, 1974]. pp. 155. *(Howe (C.D.) Research Institute. Special Studies.1.)*

— Public lands.

CANADA. Statutes, etc. 1952-68. Office consolidation of the Canada Oil and Gas Land Regulations, oil and gas land orders, Public Lands Grants Act, Territorial Lands Act. [Ottawa], 1968. pp. 73.

SYMPOSIUM ON CANADIAN PUBLIC LAND USE IN PERSPECTIVE. OTTAWA, 1973. Canadian public land use in perspective; edited by...J.G. Nelson [and others]. Ottawa, [1974]. pp. 579. *bibliog. Proceedings of the symposium sponsored by the Social Science Research Council of Canada. In English and French.*

— Race question.

FERGUSON (TED) A white man's country: an exercise in Canadian prejudice. Toronto, [1975]. pp. 200. *bibliog.*

— Social conditions.

CRYSDALE (STEWART) and BEATTIE (CHRISTOPHER) Sociology Canada: an introductory text. Toronto, [1973]. pp. 394. *bibliog.*

BEATTIE (CHRISTOPHER) and CRYSDALE (STEWART) eds. Sociology Canada: readings. Toronto, [1974]. pp. 504. *bibliogs.*

FORCESE (DENNIS P.) and RICHER (STEPHEN) eds. Issues in Canadian society: an introduction to sociology. Scarborough, Ont., [1975]. pp. 517. *bibliogs.*

SOCIALIZATION and values in Canadian society; edited by Elia Zureik and Robert M. Pike. Toronto, 1975. 2 vols. *bibliogs.*

— Social history.

CLARK (SAMUEL DELBERT) and others, eds. Prophecy and protest: social movements in twentieth-century Canada. Toronto, [1975]. pp. 437.

FINLAY (JOHN L.) Canada in the North Atlantic triangle: two centuries of social change. Toronto, 1975. pp. 343. *bibliog.*

— Social policy.

CANADA. Department of Indian Affairs and Northern Development. 1972. Canada's north, 1970-1980; (statement of the government of Canada on northern development in the 70's). [Ottawa, 1972]. pp. 40. *In English, French and Eskimo.*

ARMITAGE (ANDREW) Social welfare in Canada: ideals and realities. Toronto, [1975]. pp. 234. *bibliog.*

— Statistics.

GOURLAY (ROBERT) Statistical account of Upper Canada: abridged [from the original published in 1822] and with an introduction by S.R. Mealing. Toronto, [1974]. pp. 395. *bibliog. (Carleton University. Institute of Canadian Studies. Carleton Library. No. 75)*

— Statistics, Medical.

CANADA. Statistics Canada. Health and Welfare Division. Vital Statistics Section. 1973. Cardiovascular-renal mortality...1950-1968. Ottawa, 1973. pp. 96. *In English and French.*

CANADA. Statistics Canada. Public Health Section. 1973. Hospital morbidity: historic summary...Canada, 1964, 1966, 1968 Ottawa, 1973. pp. 17.

— Statistics, Vital.

CANADA. Dominion Bureau of Statistics. Health and Welfare Division. Vital Statistics Section. 1971. Life tables, Canada and provinces...1965-1967. Ottawa, 1971. pp. 55. *In English and French.*

CANADIAN PACIFIC RAILWAY.

CHODOS (ROBERT) The CPR: a century of corporate welfare. Toronto, [1973]. pp. 178.

CANADIANS IN RUSSIA.

MACLAREN (ROY) Canadians in Russia, 1918-1919. Toronto, [1976]. pp. 301. *bibliog.*

CANALS

— United Kingdom.

HANSON (HARRY) The canal boatmen, 1760-1914. Manchester, [1975]. pp. 244. *bibliog.*

CANCER

— Prevention.

HIGGINSON (JOHN) A hazardous society?: individual versus community responsibility in cancer prevention. [Washington], [1975]. pp. 47. *(American Public Health Association. Matthew B. Rosenhaus Lectures. 3rd, 1975)*

— Germany — Saarland.

SAARGEBIET. Statistisches Amt. Einzelschriften zur Statistik des Saarlandes. Nr. 51. Saarländische Krebsdokumentation, 1972-1974. Saarbrücken, 1976. 1 vol.(various pagings).

— New Zealand.

NEW ZEALAND. Department of Health. National Health Statistics Centre. Health statistics report: Cancer data. a., 1972- Wellington. *Formerly included in NEW ZEALAND. Department of Health. National Health Statistics Centre. Health statistics report.*

— Yugoslavia.

YUGOSLAVIA. Savezni Zavod za Statistiku. Studije, Analize i Prikazi. 75. Smrtnost od raka u većim gradovima, 1968-1969; Deaths caused by malignant neoplasm in major towns, 1968-1969; [by] Nevena Stojkov. Beograd, 1975. pp. 71. *With English summary.*

CANNING (GEORGE).

The SUPPRESSED letter to the right honourable George Canning, with Mr. Canning's letter, etc., etc. London, J. Onwhyn, [1818]. pp. 12.

CANNING (GEORGE).(Cont.)

DIXON (PETER) Canning: politician and statesman. London, [1976]. pp. 355. *bibliog.*

CANNING TOWN

— Industries.

CANNING TOWN COMMUNITY DEVELOPMENT PROJECT. Canning Town to North Woolwich: the aims of industry?: a study of industrial decline in one community. London, 1975. pp. 75.

CANNON (JAMES PATRICK).

CANNON (JAMES PATRICK) The Socialist Workers Party in World War II: (writings and speeches, 1940-43); (edited by Les Evans). New York, 1975. pp. 446.

CAPITAL.

LEVER (WILLIAM HESKETH) 1st Viscount Leverhulme. What is capital?...an address delivered at the Lyndhurst Road Congregational Church, Hampstead. [London, imprint, 1920]. pp. 16.

KOSHIMURA (SHINZABURO) Theory of capital reproduction and accumulation, translated by Toshihiro Ataka; edited by Jesse G. Schwartz. Kitchener, Ont., [1975]. pp. 161.

PALLOIX (CHRISTIAN) L'internationalisation du capital: éléments critiques. Paris, 1975. pp. 203. *bibliog.*

ESSAYS in modern capital theory; edited by Murray Brown [and others]. Amsterdam, 1976. pp. 275. *bibliogs.*

HOLLAND (STUART) Capital versus the regions. London, 1976. pp. 328.

HOLLAND (STUART) The regional problem. London, 1976. pp. 179.

KREGEL (J.A.) Theory of capital. London, 1976. pp. 96. *bibliog.*

— Mathematical models.

BIØRN (ERIK) Avskrivningsregler og prisen på bruk av realkapital...: depreciation rules and the user cost of capital. Oslo, 1975. pp. 46. *bibliog.* (Norway. Statistiske Centralbyrå. Artikler. Nr. 74) With English summary.

SARANTIDES (STYLIANOS A.) Foreign trade aspects of capital formation. Piraeus, 1975. pp. 34. (*Reprint from the edition of the Graduate School of Industrial Studies Essays in honour of Professor Andreas Kyrkilitsis*)

STRIGENS (EMIL) Optimale Kapiltalakkumulation: neoklassische Wachstumsmodelle mit exogenem und endogenem Bevölkerungswachstum. Berlin, [1975]. pp. 102. *bibliog.*

SCHAIK (A.B.T.M. VAN) Reproduction and fixed capital. Tilburg, 1976. pp. 306. *bibliog.* (*Tilburg. Katholieke Hogeschool. Tilburg Institute of Economics. Tilburg Studies on Economics. 13*)

— Denmark.

BRINCH (JENS) Kapitalakkumulation i Danmark efter 1940: et forsøg på en konkret konjunkturanalyse. København, [1975]. pp. 112.

— Germany.

GRUNDLAGEN und Formen der Herrschaft des Finanzkapitals; Autorenkollektiv: Peter Hess [and others]. Frankfurt am Main, 1974. pp. 144.

— Kenya.

VAN ZWANENBERG (R.M.A.) Colonial capitalism and labour in Kenya, 1919-1939. Kampala, 1975. pp. 314. *bibliog.*

— Russia.

PAVLOV (VALENTIN SERGEEVICH) Oborotnye sredstva promyshlennosti: formirovanie i ispol'zovanie. Moskva, 1974. pp. 142.

BOIKOV (SERGEI IVANOVICH) Ekonomicheskie funktsii i formy dvizheniia sredstv razvitogo sotsialisticheskogo obshchestva. Leningrad, 1975. pp. 126.

ZHANGERIEV (IURII ABUBOVICH) Zakonomernosti dvizheniia oborotnykh sredstv i kredit. Moskva, 1975. pp. 96.

— United States.

MARCUS (BRUCE W.) Competing for capital: a financial relations approach. New York, [1975]. pp. 265. *bibliogs.*

NEW YORK (CITY). Stock Exchange. Department of Research and Statistics. Demand and supply of equity capital: projections to 1985. New York, 1975. pp. 38.

DOMINGUEZ (JOHN R.) Capital flows in minority areas. Lexington, Mass., [1976]. pp. 164. *bibliog.*

CAPITAL BUDGET.

WHITLAM (G.B.) and others. Methods of evaluation of farm development projects. [Brisbane], 1970. pp. 65. *bibliog.* (*Queensland. Department of Primary Industries. Economic Services Branch. Technical Bulletins. No. 7*)

CAPITAL GAINS TAX

— France.

FRANCE. Commission d'Etude d'une Imposition Généralisée des Plus-Values. Rapport...; rapporteur, Jacques Delmas. Paris, 1975. 2 vols. (in 1).

CAPITAL INVESTMENTS.

INBUCON/AIC MANAGEMENT CONSULTANTS LIMITED. Investment appraisal for the clothing industry; a report prepared...for the Economic Development Committee for the Clothing Industry. London, H.M.S.O., 1973. pp. 80. *bibliog.*

JULIENNE (ROLAND) L'élaboration et l'étude des projets d'investissement. Paris, 1974. pp. 122. *bibliog.* (*France. Secrétariat d'Etat aux Affaires Etrangères. Méthodologie de la Planification. 5*)

— Canada.

CAIRNCROSS (Sir ALEXANDER KIRKLAND) Home and foreign investment, 1870-1913: studies in capital accumulation. Hassocks, 1975. pp. 251. *Originally published in 1953.*

CANADA. Statistics Canada. Service bulletin. Investment Statistics. m., Current issues only. Ottawa.

— Communist countries.

ZAGADNIENIA ekonomicznej efektywności inwestycji w rolnictwie. Warszawa, 1960. pp. 232. (*Polska Akademia Nauk. Wydział 5 Nauk Rolniczych i Leśnych. Zeszyty Problemwe Postępóow Nauk Rolniczych.. z.24*)

— Israel.

ISRAEL. Statutes, etc. 1959. Law for the encouragement of capital investments. Jerusalem, 1961. pp. 49.

— Poland.

BIEŃ (WITOLD) Ewidencja inwestycji i remontów kapitalnych w przedsiębiorstwie. Warszawa, 1963. pp. 204.

CZERWIŃSKA (EL'ZBIETA) Samodzielność finansowa przedsiębiorstwa państwowego. Poznań, 1963. pp. 172. *bibliog.* (*Poznań. Poznańskie Towarzystwo Przyjaciół Nauk. Wydział Historii i Nauk Społecznych. Komisja Nauk Społecznych. Prace. t.11, z.1*) With English summary.

BOGUSZEWSKI (JAN) System finansowy przedsiębiorstw i zjednoczeń. 2nd ed. Warszawa, 1966. pp. 45.

— Russia.

BABAK (VASILII FEDOROVICH) Kredit i tekhnicheskii progress: dolgosrochnyi kredit i kapitalovlozheniia v usloviiakh nauchno-tekhnicheskoi revoliutsii. Moskva, 1975. pp. 168.

PETROV (DMITRII GRIGOR'EVICH) Effektivnost' kapital'nykh vlozhenii v sfere tovarnogo obrashcheniia: voprosy teorii i praktiki. Kiev, 1975. pp. 288.

POLTORYGIN (VIKTOR KUZ'MICH) Effektivnost' tekhnicheskogo perevooruzheniia sotsialisticheskogo proizvodstva: voprosy teorii, metodologii i praktiki. Moskva, 1975. pp. 328.

— United Kingdom.

CAIRNCROSS (Sir ALEXANDER KIRKLAND) Home and foreign investment, 1870-1913: studies in capital accumulation. Hassocks, 1975. pp. 251. *Originally published in 1953.*

NATIONAL ECONOMIC DEVELOPMENT OFFICE. Investment by nationalised industries: relations with suppliers. London, 1975. pp. 41.

NATIONAL ECONOMIC DEVELOPMENT OFFICE. Process Plant Working Party. Process industries investment forecasts: the tenth report by the...Working Party. London, 1975. pp. 27.

HUGHES (JOHN DENNIS) Funds for investment. London, 1976. pp. 20. (*Fabian Society. Research Series. [No.] 325*)

SUMNER (MICHAEL T.) The effect of taxation on corporate saving and investment. London, [1976]. 1 pamphlet (unpaged). *bibliog.* (*Institute for Fiscal Studies. Lecture Series. No.4*)

— Yugoslavia.

BENDEKOVIĆ (JADRANKO) and TEODOROVIĆ (IVAN) Investment project evaluation in Yugoslavia. Zagreb, 1975. pp. 56.

CAPITAL MOVEMENTS.

BEENSTOCK (MICHAEL CHARLES) Forward markets, international capital movements and the balance of payments. 1976. fo. 217. *bibliog.* Typescript. Ph.D. (London) thesis: unpublished. This thesis is the property of London University and may not be removed from the Library.

— United States.

LAFFER (ARTHUR B.) Private short-term capital flows. New York, [1975]. pp. 150. *bibliog.*

CAPITALISM.

PFLUEGER (PAUL) Einführung in die soziale Frage. Zürich, 1910. pp. 200.

WALCHER (JAKOB) Ford oder Marx: die praktische Lösung der sozialen Frage. Berlin, [1925]. pp. 158.

ROCKER (RUDOLF) Die Rationalisierung der Wirtschaft und die Arbeiterklasse. Berlin, 1927. pp. 84.

PROBLEMY mirovogo krizisa: diskussiia v Institute mirovogo khoziaistva i mirovoi politiki Komakademii. Moskva, 1932. pp. 210.

BJORK (GORDON C.) Private enterprise and public interest: the development of American capitalism. Englewood Cliffs, [1969]. pp. xi,243.

CLAUDE (HENRI) Le capitalisme monopoliste d'état: éléments pour une explication théorique;...textes de Lénine. Paris, 1971. fo. 38. (*Centre d'Etudes et de Recherches Marxistes. Cahiers. No. 91*)

BORODAI (IURII MEFOD'EVICH) and others. Nasledie K. Marksa i problemy teorii obshchestvenno-ekonomicheskoi formatsii. Moskva, 1974. pp. 309.

SERENI (EMILIO) Capitalismo e mercato nazionale in Italia. 2nd ed. Roma, 1974. pp. 461.

VARGA (JENO) Izbrannye proizvedeniia. Moskva, 1974. 3 vols.

ARMBRUSTER (BERNT) Transformationsprobleme im Spätkapitalismus: zur Dialektik spätkapitalistischer Reformpolitik am Beispiel der "Vermögensbildung in Arbeitnehmerhand". Heidelberg, 1975. pp. 278. *bibliog. Inauguraldissertation, Wirtschafts- und Sozialwissenschaftliche Fakultät, Universität Heidelberg.*

CHISTOZVONOV (ALEXANDER) Two essays on the origins of capitalism. London, 1975. pp. 28. *(Communist Party of Great Britain. History Group. Our History. No. 63)*

COONTZ (STEPHANIE) and FRANK (CARL) eds. Life in capitalist America: private profit and social decay; [by] Stephanie Coontz [and others]. New York, [1975]. pp. 285. *(Reprinted from International Socialist Review, 1971-74)*

CROSS (PETER) The British business creed: changing ideologies and self images of business elites and management in Britain. [1975]. fo. 488. *bibliog. Typescript. Ph.D. (London) thesis: unpublished. This thesis is the property of London University and may not be removed from the Library.*

DOCKES (PIERRE) L'internationale du capital. [Paris], 1975. pp. 287. *bibliog.*

FRANK (ANDRE GUNDER) On capitalist underdevelopment. Bombay, 1975. pp. 113. *bibliog.*

GRIFONE (PIETRO) Capitalismo di Stato e imperialismo fascista; con i contributi di Giorgio Amendola e Camilla Ravera. Milano, [1975]. pp. 155.

MAGALINE (A.D.) Lutte de classes et dévalorisation du capital: contribution à la critique du révisionnisme. Paris, 1975. pp. 198. *bibliog.*

MANDEL (ERNEST) Late capitalism; translated by Joris De Bres. rev. ed. London, 1975. pp. 599.

PALLOIX (CHRISTIAN) L'économie mondiale capitaliste et les firmes multinationales. Paris, 1975. 2 vols.(in 1).

POLIANSKII (FEDOR IAKOVLEVICH) Kritika reformistskikh kontseptsii sovremennogo kapitalizma. Moskva, 1975. pp. 264.

ROBERTS (DICK) Capitalism in crisis. New York, 1975. pp. 128. *bibliog.*

ROSIER (BERNARD) Croissance et crise capitalistes. [Paris, 1975]. pp. 304. *bibliog.*

STRESS and contradiction in modern capitalism: public policy and the theory of the state; edited by Leon N. Lindberg [and others]. Lexington, Mass., [1975]. pp. 443. *Papers from a conference on "Patterns of change in advanced industrial society: priorities for social science research in the 1970's and 1980's", Monterosso-al-Mare, Genoa, 1973, sponsored by the Council for European Studies and the Giovanni Agnelli Foundation.*

TIULPANOV (SERGEI IVANOVICH) and SHEINIS (VIKTOR LEONIDOVICH) Aktuelle Probleme der politischen Ökonomie des heutigen Kapitalismus; (Übersetzung aus dem Russischen [by] Fredo Müller [and] Günter Wermusch. Berlin, [1975]. pp. 334.

VILLARI (LUCIO) ed. Il capitalismo italiano del Novecento: [an anthology]. 2nd ed. Roma, 1975. 2 vols. *Paged continuously.*

VYGODSKII (SOLOMON L'VOVICH) Sovremennyi kapitalizm: opyt teoreticheskogo analiza. 2nd ed. Moskva, 1975. pp. 518.

POLITISCHE Ökonomie...; ([by] A.M. Alexejewa [and others; edited by] I.D. Schirinski [and others]; Übersetzung: Leon Nebenzahl). Berlin, 1976 in progress.

ALLGEMEINE Krise des Kapitalismus: Triebkräfte und Erscheinungsformen in der Gegenwart; (wissenschaftliche Redaktion: Hans-Heinrich Angermüller [and others]). Berlin, 1976. pp. 624.

ARBEITERKLASSE im Kapitalismus: Klassenkampf und Klassenstruktur; ([by] Hellmuth Kolbe [and others]). Berlin, 1976. pp. 256.

BELL (DANIEL) The cultural contradictions of capitalism. London, 1976. pp. 301.

FUNKEN (KLAUS) Die ökonomischen Voraussetzungen der Oktoberrevolution: zur Entwicklung des Kapitalismus in Russland. Zürich, 1976. pp. 372. *bibliog.*

GAMBLE (ANDREW) and WALTON (PAUL) Capitalism in crisis: inflation and the state. London, 1976. pp. 218.

GORZ (ANDRE) ed. The division of labour: the labour process and class-struggle in modern capitalism. Hassocks, Sussex, 1976. pp. 189.

GUTERMUTH (ROLF) Ausbeutung in der BRD: zur Entwicklung der kapitalistischen Ausbeutung nach dem zweiten Weltkrieg. Berlin, 1976. pp. 256.

HEILBRONER (ROBERT LOUIS) Business civilization in decline. New York, [1976]. pp. 127.

IL'IN (M.A.) and RABINOVICH (MARK ABELEVICH) Politische Ökonomie des Kapitalismus in Fragen und Antworten; (aus dem Russischen übersetzt von Heinz Petrak und Rudolf Thiele). Berlin, 1976. pp. 288.

KUCZYNSKI (JUERGEN) Die Krise der kapitalistischen Weltwirtschaft. Berlin, 1976. pp. 127.

MAERZ (EDUARD) Einführung in die Marxsche Theorie der wirtschaftlichen Entwicklung: Frühkapitalismus und Kapitalismus der freien Konkurrenz, etc. Wien, [1976]. pp. 356.

SCHULZE (HANS) Strategie der Gegenprophetie: zur Kritik der gegenwärtigen bürgerlichen Geschichtsphilosophie. Berlin, 1976. pp. 113.

STRETTON (HUGH) Capitalism, socialism and the environment. Cambridge, 1976. pp. 332.

ZARETSKY (ELI) Capitalism, the family and personal life. London, 1976. pp. 156.

ZUMPE (LOTTE) ed. Wirtschaft und Staat im Imperialismus: Beiträge zur Entwicklungsgeschichte des staatsmonopolistischen Kapitalismus in Deutschland. Berlin, 1976. pp. 313.

— **Congresses.**

COMMUNIST INTERNATIONAL. World Congress, 2nd, 1920. Le monde capitaliste et l'Internationale Communiste: manifeste. Pétrograd, 1920. pp. 47. *(Communist International. Editions. No.63) Not to be consulted without the permission of the Superintendent of Readers' Services.*

CAPITALISM and freedom: problems and prospects: proceedings of a conference in honor of Milton Friedman [held at the University of Virginia in 1972]; edited by Richard T. Selden. Charlottesville, Va., 1975. pp. 331.

CAPITALISTS AND FINANCIERS
— **Iran.**

RABIZADE (MASHALLAKH MIKHAILOVICH) Razvitie kapitalisticheskogo predprinimatel'stva v promyshlennosti Irana v 30-kh godakh XX veka. Baku, 1970. pp. 111. *bibliog.*

— **Russia.**

LAVERYCHEV (VLADIMIR IAKOVLEVICH) Krupnaia burzhuaziia v poreformennoi Rossii, 1861-1900. Moskva, 1974. pp. 252.

ZLOBINA (VERA MAKSIMOVNA) Bor'ba partii bol'shevikov protiv melkoburzhuaznogo vliianiia na rabochii klass v pervye gody nepa, 1921-1925 gg. Moskva, 1975. pp. 168.

— — **Siberia.**

RABINOVICH (GRIGORII KHATSKEL'EVICH) Krupnaia burzhuaziia i monopolisticheskii kapital v ekonomike Sibiri kontsa XIX - nachala XX vv. Tomsk, 1975. pp. 328.

CAPODISTRIA (JOHN) Count.

FLEMING (DAVID C.) John Capodistrias and the Conference of London, 1828-1831. Thessaloniki, 1970. pp. 398. *bibliog. (Hidryma Meleton Chersonesou Tou Haimou. [Publications]. 124)*

CARACAS
— **Social conditions.**

KARST (KENNETH L.) and others. The evolution of law in the barrios of Caracas. Los Angeles, 1973. pp. 125. *(California University. Latin American Center. Latin American Studies. vol. 20)*

CARAVANS (AUTOMOBILE TRAILERS).

DENBIGHSHIRE. County Planning Officer. Caravanners' expenditure in Denbighshire: a technical contribution to the debate on caravans. [Ruthin], 1973. pp. 25.

CARDANO (GIROLAMO).

ORE (OYSTEIN) Cardano: the gambling scholar;...with a translation from the Latin of Cardano's Book on games of chance, by Sydney Henry Gould: [reprint of the work originally published at Princeton, 1953]. New York, 1965. pp. 249. *bibliog.*

CARDENAS (LAZARO).

RODRIGUEZ OCHOA (AGUSTIN) Mexico contemporaneo, 1867-1940: Cardenas en su historia. 2nd ed. Mexico, 1974. pp. 318. *bibliog.*

CARDIOVASCULAR SYSTEM
— **Diseases.**

CANADA. Statistics Canada. Health and Welfare Division. Vital Statistics Section. 1973. Cardiovascular-renal mortality...1950-1968. Ottawa, 1973. pp. 96. *In English and French.*

CARDOSO (FERNANDO HENRIQUE).

KAHL (JOSEPH ALAN) Modernization, exploitation and dependency in Latin America: Germani, González Casanova and Cardoso. New Brunswick, [1976]. pp. 215. *bibliogs.*

CARIB INDIANS.

FARABEE (WILLIAM CURTIS) The Central Caribs. Oosterhout, 1967. pp. 299. *bibliog. (Pennsylvania University. Museum. Anthropological Publications. vol. 10) Photomechanic reprint of the 1924 edition.*

CARIBBEAN AREA
— **Commerce — European Economic Community countries.**

EUROPEAN COMMUNITIES. Statistical Office. ACP: yearbook of foreign trade statistics; statistical abstract. a., 1968/1973- Luxembourg. *[In English and French]*

— **Economic conditions.**

BECKFORD (GEORGE L.) ed. Caribbean economy: dependence and backwardness. Mona, Jamaica, 1975. pp. 181. *bibliogs.*

— **Economic integration.**

MESSINA (MILTON) La integracion economica del Caribe. [Santo Domingo, 1972]. pp. 359. *bibliog.*

— **Economic policy.**

BECKFORD (GEORGE L.) ed. Caribbean economy: dependence and backwardness. Mona, Jamaica, 1975. pp. 181. *bibliogs.*

— **Foreign relations.**

KNEER (WARREN G.) Great Britain and the Caribbean, 1901-1913: a study in Anglo-American relations. Michigan, [1975]. pp. 242. *bibliog.*

— — **United States.**

MUNRO (DANA GARDNER) The United States and the Caribbean republics, 1921-1933. Princeton, [1974]. pp. 394.

CARIBBEAN AREA (Cont.)

— History.

LANGLEY (LESTER D.) Struggle for the American Mediterranean: United States- European rivalry in the Gulf-Caribbean, 1776-1904. Athens, Ga., [1976]. pp. 226. *bibliog.*

— Nationalism.

MINTZ (SIDNEY WILFRED) Caribbean transformations. Chicago, 1974. pp. 355. *bibliog.*

— Politics and government.

AMERINGER (CHARLES D.) The democratic left in exile: the antidictatorial struggle in the Caribbean, 1945-1959. Coral Gables, [1974]. pp. 352. *bibliog.*

— Population policy.

SEGAL (AARON LEE) ed. Population policies in the Caribbean. Lexington, Mass., [1975]. pp. 239.

CARICATURES AND CARTOONS

— Italy.

MOJETTA (ANNA MARIA) ed. Cento anni di satira anticlericale nei giornali dal 1860 al 1955. Milano, [1975]. pp. 301.

— United States.

LEVINE (DAVID) 1926- . No known survivors: David Levine's political plank; introduced and selected by John Kenneth Galbraith. Boston, 1970. pp. 196.

CARITAT (MARIE JEAN ANTOINE NICOLAS) Marquis de Condorcet.

BAKER (KEITH MICHAEL) Condorcet: from natural philosophy to social mathematics. Chicago, 1975. pp. 538. *bibliog.*

CARLISTS.

BLINKHORN (MARTIN) Carlism and crisis in Spain, 1931-1939. Cambridge, 1975. pp. 394. *bibliog.*

CARNAP (RUDOLF).

HINTIKKA (KAARLO JAAKKO JUHANI) ed. Rudolf Carnap, logical empiricist: materials and perspectives. Dordrecht, [1975]. pp. 400. *bibliogs. Includes Rudolf Carnap's Observation language and theoretical language, and his Notes on probability and induction.*

CARPENTERS

— Switzerland.

JAEGER (J.H.) Geschichte der schweizerischen Zimmererbewegung. 1. Band. Basel, 1914. pp. 310. *bibliog.*

CARTULARIES.

SOUTHAMPTON. University. Southampton Records Series. Vols. 19 and 20. The cartulary of God's House, Southampton; edited by J.M. Kaye. Southampton, 1976. 2 vols.

CASAS (BARTOLOMÉ DE LAS) Bishop of Chiapa.

HANKE (LEWIS ULYSSES) All mankind is one: a study of the disputation between Bartolomé de Las Casas and Juan Ginés de Sepúlveda in 1550 on the intellectual and religious capacity of the American Indians. Dekalb, Illinois, [1974]. pp. 205. *bibliog.*

CASEMENT (Sir ROGER DAVID).

MEYERS (JEFFREY) A fever at the core: the idealist in politics. London, 1976. pp. 172. *bibliog.*

REID (BENJAMIN LAWRENCE) The lives of Roger Casement. New Haven, 1976. pp. 532. *bibliog.*

CASH FLOW.

HARRISON (S.R.) and CAMPBELL (C.B.) Discounted cash flow analysis of beef development projects. [Brisbane], 1970. pp. 40. *(Queensland. Department of Primary Industries. Economic Services Branch. Technical Bulletins. No. 8)*

WHITLAM (G.B.) and others. Methods of evaluation of farm development projects. [Brisbane], 1970. pp. 65. *bibliog. (Queensland. Department of Primary Industries. Economic Services Branch. Technical Bulletins. No. 7)*

CASHINAHUA INDIANS.

See KASHINAUA INDIANS

CASTE

— India.

MAYER (ADRIAN CURTIS) Caste and kinship in central India: a village and its region. Berkeley, [1960] repr. 1966. pp. 295. *bibliog.*

— — Bengal.

INDEN (RONALD B.) Marriage and rank in Bengali culture: a history of caste and clan in middle period Bengal. Berkeley, Calif., [1976]. pp. 161. *bibliog.*

— Sri Lanka.

JAYARAMAN (RAJA) Caste continuities in Ceylon: a study of the social structure of three tea plantations. Bombay, 1975. pp. 240. *bibliog.*

CASTELLAMMARE DI STABIA

— History.

BARONE (ANTONIO) Piazza Spartaco: il movimento operaio e socialista a Castellammare di Stabia, 1900-1922. Roma, 1974. pp 237.

CASTELO BRANCO (HUMBERTO DE ALENCAR).

VIANA FILHO (LUIS) O governo Castelo Branco. Rio de Janeiro, 1975. pp. 572.

CASTLEREAGH (HENRY ROBERT STEWART) Viscount, 2nd Marquess of Londonderry.

See STEWART (HENRY ROBERT) Viscount Castlereagh. 2nd Marquess of Londonderry.

CASUAL LABOUR

— United States.

MOREWEDGE (HOSSEINE) The economics of casual labor: a study of the longshore industry. Berne, 1970. pp. 167. *bibliog.*

CATALOGUES, LIBRARY.

HARVARD UNIVERSITY. Library. Widener Library Shelflists. No. 2. Africa. Cambridge, Mass., 1965. 1 vol. (various pagings).

INSTITUT FÜR ZEITGESCHICHTE. Bibliothek. Alphabetischer Katalog; ([with] Erster Nachtragsband). Boston, Mass., 1967-73. 6 vols.

INSTITUT FÜR ZEITGESCHICHTE. Bibliothek. Sachkatalog; ([with] Erster Nachtragsband). Boston, Mass., 1967-73. 8 vols.

INSTITUT FÜR ZEITGESCHICHTE. Bibliothek. Biographischer Katalog. Boston, Mass., 1967. pp. 764.

HARVARD UNIVERSITY. Library. Widener Library Shelflists. [No.] 22. Government. Cambridge, Mass., 1969. pp. 263.

HARVARD UNIVERSITY. Library. Widener Library Shelflists. [No.] 32. General European and world history. Cambridge, Mass., 1970. pp. 959.

HARVARD UNIVERSITY. Graduate School of Business Administration. Baker Library. Author-title catalogue of the Baker Library, etc. Boston, Mass., 1971 in progress.

INSTITUT FÜR ZEITGESCHICHTE. Bibliothek. Erster Nachtragsband: Biographischer Katalog; Länderkatalog. Boston, Mass., 1973. pp. 588.

BRITISH LIBRARY. Catalogue of the Newspaper Library, Colindale. London, 1975. 8 vols.

SIMONI (ANNA ELIZABETH CHARLOTTE) compiler. Publish and be free: a catalogue of clandestine books printed in the Netherlands 1940-1945 in the British Library. The Hague, 1975. pp. 289.

BOSTON, MASSACHUSETTS. University. Libraries. Catalog of African government documents. 3rd ed. Boston, Mass., 1976. pp. 679.

COSTELOE (MICHAEL P.) Mexico state papers, 1744-1843: a descriptive catalogue of the G. R.G. Conway Collection in the Institute of Historical Research, University of London. London, 1976. pp. 153. *(London. University. Institute of Latin American Studies. Monographs. 6)*

SANDERS (IRWIN TAYLOR) and others, compilers. East European peasantries: social relations: an annotated bibliography of periodical articles. Boston, [1976]. pp. 179. *bibliog. A bibliography of a collection of periodical articles at the Mugar Library, Boston University.*

CATALOGUES, PUBLISHERS'

— United Kingdom.

ROSS (DONALD ARMSTRONG) ed. The reader's guide to Everyman's Library. 4th ed. London, 1976. pp. 596.

CATALOGUES, UNION.

The NATIONAL union catalog: a cumulative author list representing Library of Congress printed cards and titles reported by other American Libraries...1968-1972. Vols. 1-104. Ann Arbor, 1973. 104 vols.

POLLARD (ALFRED WILLIAM) and REDGRAVE (GILBERT RICHARD) A short-title catalogue of books printed in England, Scotland, and Ireland and of English books printed abroad, 1475-1640;... second edition...begun by W.A. Jackson and F.S. Ferguson; completed by Katharine F. Pantzer. London, 1976 in progress.

CATALONIA

— Description and travel.

DEFFONTAINES (PIERRE) La Méditerranée catalane. Paris, [1975]. pp. 128. *bibliog.*

CATERERS AND CATERING

— South Africa.

SOUTH AFRICA. Bureau of Statistics. Catering services. a., 1971- Pretoria. *In Afrikaans and English.*

CATHERINE II, Empress of Russia.

RAEFF (MARC) ed. Catherine the Great: a profile. London, 1972. pp. 330. *bibliog.*

CATHOLIC CHURCH

— Relations (diplomatic) with Germany.

KLEIN (CHARLES) Pie XII face aux Nazis. Paris, [1975]. pp. 250.

— Relations (diplomatic) with Russia.

WINTER (EDUARD J.) Die Sowjetunion und der Vatikan: Teil 3 der Trilogie Russland und das Papsttum. Berlin, 1972. pp. 338. *bibliog. (Akademie der Wissenschaften der DDR. Zentralinstitut für Geschichte. Quellen und Studien zur Geschichte Osteuropas. Band 6, Teil 3)*

CATHOLIC CHURCH IN FRANCE.

REARDON (BERNARD MORRIS GARVIN) Liberalism and tradition: aspects of Catholic thought in nineteenth-century France. Cambridge, 1975. pp. 308.

CATHOLIC CHURCH IN GERMANY.

REIFFERSCHEID (GERHARD) Das Bistum Ermland und das Dritte Reich. Köln, 1975. pp. 351. *bibliog.*

METZ (HUBERT) Katholizismus und Wahlen: zum Verhältnis Kirche und Staat in Deutschland. [Mannheim], 1976. pp. 354. *bibliog. Inauguraldissertation zur Erlangung des akademischen Grades eines Doktors der Philosophie der Universität Mannheim.*

CATHOLIC CHURCH IN ITALY.

BEDESCHI (LORENZO) Interpretazioni e sviluppo del modernismo cattolico. Milano, [1975]. pp. 206. *bibliog.*

CATHOLIC CHURCH IN PERU.

DUVIOLS (PIERRE) La lutte contre les religions autochtones dans le Pérou colonial: "l'extirpation de l'idolâtrie" entre 1532 et 1660. Lima, [1972]. pp. 428. *bibliog. (Institut Français d'Etudes Andines. Travaux. 13)*

CATHOLIC CHURCH IN POLAND.

DMOWSKI (ROMAN) Kościół, naród i państwo; [originally published 1927]. Londyn, 1964. pp. 32.

DOBRACZYŃSKI (JAN) Tylko w jednym 'zyciu. [Warszawa], 1970. pp. 431.

PRUS-WIŚNIEWSKI (JÓZEF) Dawne granice Polski i organizacja Kościoła Rzymsko- Katolickego w Polsce po 1945 roku. [Londyn, 1973]. pp. 88.

MARKIEWICZ (STANISŁAW) Kościół rzymskokatolicki a państwa socjalistyczne. Warszawa, 1974. pp. 343.

PIEKARSKI (ADAM) Szkice o kościele w Polsce: fakty, liczby, informacje. Warszawa, 1974. pp. 224. *bibliog.*

CATHOLIC CHURCH IN RUSSIA.

KATOLITSIZM v SSSR i sovremennost': materialy nauchnoi konferentsii, sostoiavsheisia v g. Shiauliai 17-18 dekabria 1969 g. Vil'nius, 1971. pp. 245.

CATHOLIC CHURCH IN THE UNITED STATES.

BUCZEK (DANIEL STEPHEN) Immigrant pastor: the life of the Right Reverend Monsignor Lucyan Bójnowski of New Britain, Connecticut. Waterbury, Conn., 1974. pp. 184. *bibliog.*

CATHOLICS IN FRANCE.

REARDON (BERNARD MORRIS GARVIN) Liberalism and tradition: aspects of Catholic thought in nineteenth-century France. Cambridge, 1975. pp. 308.

BAUMGARTNER (FREDERIC J.) Radical reactionaries: the political thought of the French Catholic League. Genève, 1975 [or rather 1976]. pp. 317. *bibliog.*

CATHOLICS IN GERMANY.

ROSS (RONALD J.) Beleaguered tower: the dilemma of political Catholicism in Wilhelmine Germany. Notre Dame, Ind., [1976]. pp. 218. *bibliog. (Notre Dame. University. Committee on International Relations. International Studies)*

CATHOLICS IN ITALY.

BOSCO NAITZA (G.) and PISU (G.) I cattolici e la vita pubblica in Italia, 1815-1919. Firenze, 1974. pp. 169. *bibliog.*

ACCAME (SILVIO) Gaetano De Sanctis fra cultura e politica: esperienze di militanti cattolici a Torino, 1919-1929. Firenze, 1975. pp. 545.

BIANCHI (SANDRO) and TURCHINI (ANGELO) eds. Gli estremisti di centro: il neo-integralismo cattolico degli anni '70; Comunione e Liberazione. Rimini, [1975]. pp. 172. *bibliog.*

SCOPPOLA (PIETRO) and TRANIELLO (FRANCESCO) eds. I cattolici tra fascismo e democrazia. Bologna, [1975]. pp. 461.

CATHOLICS IN THE UNITED KINGDOM.

BOSSY (JOHN) The English Catholic community, 1570-1850. London, 1975. pp. 446. *bibliog.*

CATHOLICS IN THE UNITED STATES.

DOLAN (JAY P.) The immigrant church: New York's Irish and German Catholics, 1815-1865. Baltimore, [1975]. pp. 221.

FLYNN (GEORGE Q.) Roosevelt and Romanism: Catholics and American diplomacy, 1937- 1945. Westport, 1976. pp. 268. *bibliog.*

CATTANEO (CARLO).

BELLONI (GIULIO ANDREA) Carlo Cattaneo e la sua idea federale; a cura di Giuseppe Armani. Pisa, 1974. pp. 157. *(Domus Mazziniana. Collana Scientifica. 14)*

CATTLE

— Africa, East.

MURMANN (CARSTEN) Change and development in East African cattle husbandry: a study of four societies during the colonial period. Copenhagen, 1974. pp. 125. *bibliog.*

— United Kingdom.

WHETHAM (EDITH H.) Beef cattle and sheep, 1910-1940: a description of the production and marketing of beef cattle and sheep in Great Britain from the early 20th century to the Second World War. Cambridge, 1976. pp. 59. *bibliog. (Cambridge. University. Department of Land Economy. Occasional Papers. No.5)*

CATTLE BREEDING

— India — Goa, Daman and Diu.

GOA, DAMAN AND DIU. Bureau of Economics, Statistics and Evaluation. 1975. An evaluation of the key village scheme in Goa. Panaji, 1975. pp. 59. *(Evaluation Reports. No. 15)*

CATTLE TRADE

— United States.

SKAGGS (JIMMY M.) The cattle-trailing industry: between supply and demand, 1866-1890. Lawrence, Kan., [1973]. pp. 173. *bibliog.*

CAUCASUS

— Commerce.

AKADEMIIA NAUK GRUZINSKOI SSR. Institut Ekonomiki i Prava. Ekonomika. t. 3. [Sbornik statei]. Tbilisi, 1971. pp. 417. *Articles are in Georgian or Russian.*

— Economic policy.

VODOVOZOV (SERGEI ARSEN'EVICH) Problemy razvitiia i razmeshcheniia proizvoditel'nykh sil Severnogo Kavkaza. Moskva, 1975. pp. 232. *bibliog.*

— History.

MEGRELIDZE (SHAMSHE VARFALOMEEVICH) Zakavkaz'e v russko-turetskoi voine, 1877-1878 gg. Tbilisi, 1972. pp. 303.

BOTSVADZE (TEIMURAZ DZHAIDAROVICH) Narody Severnogo Kavkaza v gruzinsko-russkikh politicheskikh vzaimootnosheniiakh XVI - XVIII vekov. Tbilisi, 1974. pp. 106.

— Industries.

ISTORIIA industrializatsii Severnogo Kavkaza, 1933-1941 gg. Groznyi, 1973. pp. 620.

CAUSATION.

ESSAYS on explanation and understanding: studies in the foundations of humanities and social sciences; edited by Juha Manninen and Raimo Tuomela. Dordrecht, [1976]. pp. 440. *bibliogs. Includes papers from the International Colloquium on Explanation and Understanding, Helsinki, 1974.*

CAYAPA INDIANS.

BARRETT (SAMUEL ALFRED) The Cayapa Indians of Ecuador. New York, 1925. 2 vols. *(Museum of the American Indian. Indian Notes and Monographs. No. 40)*

CAYMAN ISLANDS

— Politics and government.

HANNERZ (ULF) Caymanian politics: structure and style in a changing island society. Stockholm, [1974]. pp. 198. *bibliog. (Stockholms Universitet. Socialantropologiska Institutionen. Stockholm Studies in Social Anthropology. 1)*

CECIL (ROBERT ARTHUR TALBOT GASCOYNE) 3rd Marquess of Salisbury.

UZOIGWE (GODFREY N.) Britain and the conquest of Africa: the age of Salisbury. Ann Arbor, [1974]. pp. 403. *bibliog.*

CENSORSHIP

— Russia.

MEDVEDEV (ZHORES ALEKSANDROVICH) Secrecy of correspondence is guaranteed by law. Nottingham, [1975]. pp. 180. *(Medvedev Papers. vol. 2)*

— South Africa.

SOUTH AFRICA. Publications Appeal Board. Report of the... Board and of the Directorate of Publications. 1975 [1st]- Pretoria. *[In English and Afrikaans]. Included in the file of SOUTH AFRICA. Parliament. House of Assembly. Votes and proceedings (with printed annexures). 1st report contains addendum of the former Publications Control Board's archives, January to March 1975.*

CENTRAL AMERICAN COMMON MARKET.

SCHINKE (ROLF) Der Zahlungsbilanzausgleich im Gemeinsamen Markt Zentralamerikas: ein Diskussionsbeitrag zur monetären Integration von Entwicklungsländern. Göttingen, [1974]. pp. 168. *bibliog. (Göttingen. Universität. Ibero-Amerika- Institut für Wirtschaftsforschung. Arbeitsberichte. Heft 16)*

— Honduras.

BUESO (GUILLERMO) La integracion centroamericana y el desarrollo economico de Honduras. Tegucigalpa, 1970. fo. 179.

CENTRAL PLACES.

PAELINCK (JEAN H.P.) and NIJKAMP (PETER) Operational theory and method in regional economics. Farnborough, Hants, [1975?]. pp. 471. *bibliogs.*

REGIONAL analysis...; edited by Carol A. Smith. New York, [1976]. 2 vols. *bibliogs. Papers prepared for a conference held in Santa Fe, New Mexico, in 1973.*

— Denmark.

SONDER (RIC) Graested: reflections on a Danish station-town; based on an investigation...by students of the Royal Academy of Fine Arts and the Polytechnic Institute, Copenhagen. New York, [1955?]. fo. 29.

— Germany — Rhineland—Palatinate.

KOECK (HELMUT) Das zentralörtliche System von Rheinland-Pfalz: ein Vergleich analytischer Methoden zur Zentralitätsbestimmung. [Bad Godesberg], 1975. pp. 204. *bibliog. (Germany (Bundesrepublik). Bundesforschungsanstalt für Landeskunde und Raumordnung. Forschungen zur Raumentwicklung. 2)*

CENTRE FOR EDUCATIONAL RESEARCH AND INNOVATION.

CENTRE FOR EDUCATIONAL RESEARCH AND INNOVATION.

CENTRE FOR EDUCATIONAL RESEARCH AND INNOVATION. 1971. Centre for Educational Research and Innovation: purpose, programmes, progress; (with Supplementary annexes). [Paris], Organisation for Economic Co-operation and Development, [1970-71]. 1 pamphlet (various pagings).

CENTRE PARTIES

— Germany.

MEYER (MAX HERMANN) Die Weltanschauung des Zentrums in ihren Grundlinien. München, 1919. pp. 140. *bibliog.*

SEELIGER (ROLF) ed. SPD offensiv: Beiträge zur Auseinandersetzung mit der CDU/CSU. München, 1974. pp. 107.

ADENAUER (KONRAD) Reden, 1917-1967: eine Auswahl; herausgegeben von Hans- Peter Schwarz. Stuttgart, [1975]. pp. 496.

EISNER (ERICH) Das europäische Konzept von Franz Josef Strauss: die gesamteuropäischen Ordnungsvorstellungen der CSU. Meisenheim am Glan, 1975. pp. 143. *bibliog.*

HACKE (CHRISTIAN) Die Ost- und Deutschlandpolitik der CDU/CSU: Wege und Irrwege der Opposition seit 1969. Köln, [1975]. pp. 151. *bibliog.*

MUELLER (JOSEF) of the Christlich-Soziale Union. Bis zur letzten Konsequenz: ein Leben für Frieden und Freiheit. München, [1975]. pp. 384. *bibliog.*

PUETZ (HELMUTH) ed. Konrad Adenauer und die CDU der britischen Besatzungszone, 1946-1949: Dokumente zur Gründungsgeschichte der CDU Deutschlands; Herausgeber: Konrad-Adenauer-Stiftung. Bonn, [1975]. pp. 882.

HINKELAMMERT (FRANZ JOSEF) Die Radikalisierung der Christdemokraten: vom parlamentarischen Konservatismus zum Rechtsradikalismus. Berlin, [1976]. pp. 142.

LAMMERT (NORBERT) Lokale Organisationsstrukturen innerparteilicher Willensbildung: Fallstudie am Beispiel eines CDU-Kreisverbandes im Ruhrgebiet. Bonn, [1976]. pp. 224. *bibliog. (Institut für Kommunalwissenschaften [Bonn]. Schriftenreihe. Band 5)*

ROSS (RONALD J.) Beleaguered tower: the dilemma of political Catholicism in Wilhelmine Germany. Notre Dame, Ind., [1976]. pp. 218. *bibliog. (Notre Dame. University. Committee on International Relations. International Studies)*

STEHLING (JUTTA) Weimarer Koalition und SPD in Baden: ein Beitrag zur Geschichte der Partei- und Kulturpolitik in der Weimarer Republik. Frankfurt/Main, [1976]. pp. 347. *bibliog. Zur Erlangung des akademischen Grades eines Doktors der Philosophie von der Universität Karlsruhe genehmigte Dissertation.*

— Italy.

CRISI della DC e alternativa socialista: per una trasformazione democratica del paese; ([by] Riccardo Lombardi [and others]). Venezia, 1975. pp. 146. *Proceedings of a conference held by the Partito Socialista Italiano in Trento in 1974.*

TUTTO il potere della DC; ([by] Fernando Vianello [and others]). Roma, 1975. pp. 255.

— Rhodesia.

CENTRE PARTY (RHODESIA). Blueprint for Rhodesia. Salisbury, 1970. fo. 4. *Photocopy.*

CENTRE PARTY (RHODESIA). Working document [summarizing party policy]. Salisbury, 1970. fo. 8. *Photocopy.*

CHABAN—DELMAS (JACQUES).

CHABAN-DELMAS (JACQUES) L'ardeur. [Paris, 1975]. pp. 454.

CHAD

— Economic conditions.

WESTEBBE (RICHARD M.) and others. Chad: development potential and constraints; this report was prepared by the economic mission which visited Chad in...1972, etc. Washington, International Bank for Reconstruction and Development, 1974. pp. 133. *(Country Economic Reports)*

— Economic policy.

WESTEBBE (RICHARD M.) and others. Chad: development potential and constraints; this report was prepared by the economic mission which visited Chad in...1972, etc. Washington, International Bank for Reconstruction and Development, 1974. pp. 133. *(Country Economic Reports)*

CHAMBERS OF COMMERCE

— Austria.

PISECKY (FRANZ) Wirtschaft, Land und Kammer in Oberösterreich, 1851-1976. Linz, 1976 in progress.

— Netherlands.

RAAD VOOR HET MIDDEN- EN KLEINBEDRIJF. Advies inzake de structuur en de werkwijze van de Kamers van Koophandel en Fabrieken. 's-Gravenhage, 1974. pp. 60. *([Publikaties]. 1974, no. 3)*

CHAMPAGNE-ARDENNE

— Economic conditions.

DOUBLE POINT: information économique Champagne-Ardenne: revu mensuelle; ([pd. by] Institut National de la Statistique et des Etudes Economiques...Direction Régionale de Reims [France]). q., (formerly m.), S 1971(no.1)- Reims.

CHANGE (PSYCHOLOGY).

STANSFIELD (RONALD G.) Flux in the factory. London, 1967. pp. 8. *(Hollenden Lectures. No. 15. 1967) (Reprinted from the Clothing Institute Journal, vol. 15, no. 3, 1967)*

CHARITABLE USES, TRUSTS AND FOUNDATIONS.

CIBA FOUNDATION. Symposia. New Series. 30. The future of philanthropic foundations:...symposium...held jointly with the Josiah Macy Jr. Foundation: [proceedings; edited by G.E.W. Wolstenholme and Maeve O'Connor]. Amsterdam, 1975. pp. 240.

— Canada — Ontario.

ONTARIO. Law Reform Commission. 1976. Report on mortmain, charitable uses and religious institutions. [Toronto], 1976. pp. 75.

CHARITIES

— Canada.

CANADA. Statistics Canada. Selected financial statistics of charitable organizations. a., 1971- Ottawa. *In English and French.*

— France.

SEGALEN (MARTINE) Les confréries dans la France contemporaine: les charités. Paris, [1975]. pp. 257. *bibliog.*

— United Kingdom.

WATES FOUNDAION. The Wates Foundation (founded 1965): report on the first phase, 1965-70. [London, 1971?]. pp. 27.

McKEE (CHRISTINE D.) Charitable organisations. Birmingham, 1974. pp. 152.

SEMINAR ON FINANCING THE VOLUNTARY SECTOR, LONDON, 1974. Seminar on financing the voluntary sector: (note of discussion . [London], Voluntary Services Unit, Home Office, [1975 . pp. 23.

— — Directories.

CHARITIES AID FOUNDATION. Directory of grant-making trusts; [edited by] J.D. Livingstone Booth. 4th ed. Tonbridge, [1975]. pp. 1030.

— United States.

LINDEN (EUGENE) The alms race: the impact of American voluntary aid abroad. New York, [1976]. pp. 275.

CHARLES V, Emperor of Germany.

FERNANDEZ ALVAREZ (MANUEL) Charles V: elected emperor and hereditary ruler; (translated from the Spanish by J.A. Lalaguna). London, [1975]. pp. 220. *bibliog.*

CHARTISM.

CADOGAN (PETER) Early radical Newcastle. Consett, [1975]. pp. 153. *bibliog.*

CHASSOT VON FLORENCOURT FAMILY.

See FLORENCOURT FAMILY.

CHAVEZ (CESAR).

LEVY (JACQUES E.) Cesar Chavez: autobiography of La Causa. New York, [1975]. pp. 546.

TAYLOR (RONALD B.) Chavez and the farm workers. Boston, [1975]. pp. 342. *bibliog.*

YINGER (WINTHROP) Cesar Chavez: the rhetoric of nonviolence. Hicksville, N.Y., [1975]. pp. 143. *bibliog.*

CHEMICAL INDUSTRIES.

STRATEGIES des firmes chimiques: perspectives de développement; (par Michel Hors [and others]). Paris, 1975. pp. 173. *(France. Ministère de l'Industrie et de la Recherche. Etudes de Politique Industrielle. 3)*

— Europe.

UNITED NATIONS. Economic Commission for Europe. Annual bulletin of exports of chemical products. a., 1973 (v.1)- Geneva. *In English with summaries in French and Russian.*

— Europe, Eastern.

RAJANA (CECIL) The chemical and petro-chemical industries of Russia and Eastern Europe, 1960-1980. London, 1975. 1 vol. (various pagings). *Includes appendix of 534 tables.*

— Italy.

ATOR CONSULENZA AZIENDALE. Studio sull'evoluzione della concentrazione in alcuni settori dell'industria chimica in Italia: farmaceutico...; fotografico...; prodotti di manutenzione, etc. [Brussels, European Communities, Directorate-General for Competition, 1973]. 1 vol. (various pagings).

— Netherlands.

AMSTERDAM. Universiteit. Stichting voor Economisch Onderzoek. Studie betreffende de ontwikkeling van de concentratie in enkele bedrijfstakken in de chemische industrie in Nederland: farmaceutische industrie...fotochemische industrie... onderhoudsmiddelen, etc; [by H.W. de Jong and A.H. Smolders] . [Brussels, European Communities, Directorate-General for Competition, 1973]. 1 vol. (various pagings).

— Romania.

PETRESCU (ION) Căi de creștere a eficienței economice în industria chimică. București, 1974. pp. 224.

— Russia.

RAJANA (CECIL) The chemical and petro-chemical industries of Russia and Eastern Europe, 1960-1980. London, 1975. 1 vol. (various pagings). *Includes appendix of 534 tables.*

VOLKOV (VLADIMIR AKIMOVICH) V.I. Lenin i razvitie khimicheskoi promyshlennosti SSSR. Moskva, 1975. pp. 285. *bibliog.*

CHILD WELFARE

— — Russia (RSFSR).

PROZOROV (VITALII PETROVICH) Khimicheskaia promyshlennost' Urala v gody dovoennykh piatiletok: iz istorii bor'by partiinykh organizatsii Urala za osushchestvlenie leninskoi politiki sotsialisticheskoi industrializatsii strany. Sverdlovsk, 1969. pp. 76.

— — Ukraine.

MIKULENKO (V.V.) and others. Ordena Lenina Rubezhanskii khimicheskii kombinat: ocherk. Donetsk, 1973. pp. 181.

— — United Kingdom.

FINANCIAL RESULTS OF UK CHEMICAL COMPANIES: [pd. by] Economic Development Commitee for Chemicals. a., 1971-72/1974-75 (1st)- London.

ECONOMIC DEVELOPMENT COMMITTEE FOR CHEMICALS. UK chemicals 1975-85. London, National Economic Development Office, 1976. pp. 100.

CHEMICAL PLANTS

— United Kingdom — Location — Bibliography.

TROTMAN (NIGEL) compiler. The siting of hazardous plants in urban areas. London, 1975. pp. 16. (London. Greater London Council. Research Library. [Research Bibliographies]. No. 60)

CHEMICAL WARFARE.

STOCKHOLM INTERNATIONAL PEACE RESEARCH INSTITUTE. Chemical disarmament: some problems of verification: an examination of the types of data to be reported internationally from economic, statistical and other methods by a national verification organization controlling potential chemical warfare materials; [prepared by John Stares]. Stockholm, [1973]. pp. 184. *(SIPRI Monographs)*

FINAN (JAMES STUART) Chemical and biological weapons: their potential for nations outside the principal alliances, with special reference to the possibilities open to the Republic of South Africa over the next ten years. 1975. fo. 308. *bibliog. Typescript. Ph.D. (London) thesis: unpublished. This thesis is the property of London University and may not be removed from the Library.*

CHEMICALS

— Manufacture and industry — Canada.

CANADA. Department of Industry, Trade and Commerce. Chemicals Branch. 1971. Chemical import trends, 1965-1966-1967;...to be read and used in conjunction with Chemical import trends 1956-1964. Ottawa, [1971]. pp. 111. *bibliog. In English and French.*

CHEMISTS

— United Kingdom — Fees.

ROYAL INSTITUTE OF CHEMISTRY OF GREAT BRITAIN AND IRELAND. R.I.C. remuneration survey 1971: a report on the remuneration of professionally qualified chemists who reside in Great Britain and Ireland and are members of the Royal Institute of Chemistry. London, 1971-1972. 2 pamphlets.

CHEQUES

— United Kingdom.

MACAULAY (WALLACE D.) The liability of a banker on a cheque. London, 1953. fo. 116. *LL.M. (London) thesis.*

CHEREMISSIAN LITERATURE

— History and criticism.

VASIN (KIM KIRILLOVICH) Prosvetitel'stvo i realizm: k probleme genezisa sotsialisticheskogo realizma v mariiskoi literature: istoriko- literaturovedcheskie ocherki. Ioshkar-Ola, 1975. pp. 246. *bibliog.*

CHEREPNIN (LEV VLADIMIROVICH).

OBSHCHESTVO i gosudarstvo feodal'noi Rossii: sbornik statei, posviashchennyi 70-letiiu akademika L'va Vladimirovicha Cherepnina. Moskva, 1975. pp. 351.

CHERNIGOV (OBLAST')

— History — 1917-1921, Revolution — Sources.

CHERNIGOVSHCHINA v gody grazhdanskoi voiny, 1919-1920: sbornik dokumentov i materialov. Kiev, 1975. pp. 455.

CHERNYSHEVSKII (NIKOLAI GAVRILOVICH).

CHERNYSHEVSKAIA (NINA MIKHAILOVNA) N.G. Chernyshevskii i T.G. Shevchenko: vospominaniia, zametki, materialy; (posleslovie E.S. Shablinskogo). Kiev, 1974. pp. 136.

CHICAGO

— Civic improvement.

CONDIT (CARL WILBUR) Chicago, 1910-1929: building, planning, and urban technology. Chicago, 1973. pp. 354. *bibliog.*

— Haymarket Square Riot, 1886.

KARASEK (HORST) ed. 1886, Haymarket: die deutschen Anarchisten von Chicago; Reden und Lebensläufe. Berlin, [1975]. pp. 190. *bibliog.*

— History.

CONDIT (CARL WILBUR) Chicago, 1910-1929: building, planning, and urban technology. Chicago, 1973. pp. 354. *bibliog.*

— Race question.

STAR (SHIRLEY A.) Interracial tension in two areas of Chicago: an exploratory approach to the measurement of interracial tension. 1950. pp. 295. *bibliog. Ph.D. (Chicago) thesis: unpublished. Microfilm of typescript: 1 reel.*

CHICHERIN (BORIS NIKOLAEVICH).

ZOR'KIN (VALERII DMITRIEVICH) Iz istorii burzhuazno-liberal'noi politicheskoi mysli Rossii vtoroi poloviny XIX - nachala XX v.: B.N. Chicherin. Moskva, 1975. pp. 173.

CHILD DEVELOPMENT.

HOLLOS (MARIDA) Growing up in Flathill: social environment and cognitive development. Oslo, [1974]. pp. 166. *bibliog.*

FAMINE and human development: the Dutch hunger winter of 1944- 1945; [by] Zena Stein [and others]. New York, 1975. pp. 284. *bibliog.*

LUCAS (NORMAN BERNARD CHARLES) An experience of teaching. London, [1975]. pp. 196.

SYMPOSIUM ON MORAL DEVELOPMENT, LOYOLA UNIVERSITY OF CHICAGO, 1973. Moral development: current theory and research; [papers] edited by David J. DePalma [and] Jeanne M. Foley. Hillsdale, 1975. pp. 206. *bibliogs.*

EMLER (NICHOLAS PETER) The development of moral reasoning in children: a theoretical and empirical study. [1976]. fo. 385. *bibliog. Typescript. Ph.D. (London) thesis: unpublished. This thesis is the property of London University and may not be removed from the Library.*

FERRI (ELSA) Growing up in a one-parent family: a long-term study of child development. Windsor, Berks., 1976. pp. 196. *bibliog.*

NEWSON (JOHN) and NEWSON (ELIZABETH) Seven years old in the home environment. London, 1976. pp. 436. *bibliog.*

CHILD GUIDANCE CLINICS

— United Kingdom.

WHITMORE (K.) The contribution of child guidance to the community. London, 1974. pp. 22. *bibliog. (National Association for Mental Health. Occasional Papers. No. 2)*

CHILD PSYCHIATRY.

REDL (FRITZ) and WINEMAN (DAVID) Controls from within: techniques for the treatment of the aggressive child. New York, [1952]. pp. 332.

WHITMORE (K.) The contribution of child guidance to the community. London, 1974. pp. 22. *bibliog. (National Association for Mental Health. Occasional Papers. No. 2)*

GELFAND (DONNA M.) and HARTMANN (DONALD P.) Child behavior analysis and therapy. New York, [1975]. pp. 332. *bibliog.*

RUTTER (MICHAEL LLEWELLYN) Helping troubled children. Harmondsworth, 1975. pp. 376. *bibliog.*

CHILD PSYCHOLOGY.

JOSSELYN (IRENE MILLIKEN) Psychosocial development of children. New York, [1948] repr. 1974. pp. 134. *bibliog.*

DEMAUSE (LLOYD) ed. The history of childhood. New York, 1974. pp. 450.

INFANT perception: from sensation to cognition; edited by Leslie B. Cohen and Philip Salapatek. New York, [1975]. 2 vols. *bibliogs.*

CHILD WELFARE

— Canada — Manitoba.

A REVIEW of child welfare policies, programs and services in Manitoba; by Joseph C. Ryant [and others]; a report to the Minister of Health and Social Development; (with Summary). Winnipeg, [Department of Health and Social Development], 1975. 2 pts. *bibliog.*

— Denmark.

WAGNER (MARSDEN) and WAGNER (MARY) The Danish national child-care system: a successful system as model for the reconstruction of American child care. Boulder, Co., 1976. pp. 183.

— Ireland (Republic).

EIRE. Task Force on Child Care Services. 1975. Interim report to the Tanaiste and Minister for Health. Dublin, 1975. pp. 40.

— Underdeveloped areas.

See UNDERDEVELOPED AREAS — Child welfare.

— United Kingdom.

TUNBRIDGE WELLS STUDY GROUP ON NON-ACCIDENTAL INJURY TO CHILDREN. Report and resolutions [of a meeting of the group at Tunbridge Wells, 1973] compiled by Alfred White Franklin. [Edinburgh], 1973. pp. 22.

NATIONAL SOCIETY FOR THE PREVENTION OF CRUELTY TO CHILDREN. Training Department. Yo yo children: a study of 23 violent matrimonial cases. London, [1974]. pp. 8. *bibliog.*

COUNCIL FOR CHILDREN'S WELFARE. Occasional Papers on Child Welfare. No. 3. No childhood: the handicapped child at home and in hospital in the 1970's. London, 1975. pp. 24.

NATIONAL ASSOCIATION FOR MENTAL HEALTH. Assessment of children and their families. London, 1975. pp. 41. *bibliog.*

PACKMAN (JEAN) The child's generation: child care policy from Curtis to Houghton. Oxford, 1975. pp. 200.

CHILD WELFARE (Cont.)

GITTUS (ELIZABETH) Flats, families and the under-fives. London, 1976. pp. 269. *bibliog.*

HOLMAN (ROBERT) Inequality in child care. London, 1976. pp. 38. *(Child Poverty Action Group. Poverty Pamphlets. 26)*

LISTER (RUTH) and EMMETT (TONY) Under the safety net. London, 1976. pp. 39. *(Child Poverty Action Group. Poverty Pamphlets. 25)*

SOCIAL SERVICES RESEARCH AND INTELLIGENCE UNIT [PORTSMOUTH]. First year at Fairfield Lodge: a children's observation and assessment centre in Hampshire. Portsmouth, 1976. pp. 142. *bibliog.*

— United States.

PHADKE (SINDHU VAMAN) Licensing of child care in California, 1911-1961. San Francisco, 1963 repr. 1975. pp. 165. *bibliog. Dissertation (Doctor of Social Work) - University of Southern California.*

SCHORR (ALVIN L.) ed. Children and decent people. London, 1975. pp. 222. *(National Institute for Social Work Training. National Institute Social Services Library. No. 29)*

CHILDREN

— Care and hygiene.

DEMAUSE (LLOYD) ed. The history of childhood. New York, 1974. pp. 450.

— — France.

DAVID (MYRIAM) and LÉZINE (IRENE) Early child care in France. London, [1975]. pp. 148. *bibliog. (International Study Group for Early Child Care. International Monograph Series on Early Child Care. vol. 6)*

— — Israel.

RAPAPORT (CHANAN) and MARCUS (JOSEPH) Early child care in Israel;...in collaboration with Miriam Glikson [and others]. London, [1976]. pp. 199. *bibliog. (International Study Group for Early Child Care. International Monograph Series on Early Child Care. vol. 7)*

— — Sweden.

WALLACE (HELEN M.) ed. Health care of mothers and children in national health services: implication[s] for the United States. Cambridge, Mass., [1975]. pp. 325. *bibliogs.*

— — United Kingdom.

WALLACE (HELEN M.) ed. Health care of mothers and children in national health services: implication[s] for the United States. Cambridge, Mass., [1975]. pp. 325. *bibliogs.*

— — United States.

HAGGERTY (ROBERT J.) and others. Child health and the community. New York, [1975]. pp. 388. *bibliogs.*

— Employment — France.

SOREAU (EDMOND) Note sur le travail des enfants dans l'industrie pendant la Révolution. Paris, [1935]. pp. 7. *(Extrait de la Revue des Etudes Historiques, avril-juin 1935)*

— — Hong Kong.

PORTER (ROBIN) Child labour in Hong Kong. Nottingham, [1975]. pp. 27. *bibliog. (Spokesman, The. Pamphlets. No.50)*

— Hospitals.

DOUGLAS (JAMES WILLIAM BRUCE) Early hospital admissions and later disturbances of behaviour and learning. [London], 1975. pp. 25. *bibliog. (Reprinted from Developmental Medicine and Child Neurology, vol. 17 no. 4, August 1975)*

— Institutional care — United States.

PHADKE (SINDHU VAMAN) Licensing of child care in California, 1911-1961. San Francisco, 1963 repr. 1975. pp. 165. *bibliog. Dissertation (Doctor of Social Work) - University of Southern California.*

— Language.

MAJOR (DIANA) The acquisition of modal auxiliaries in the language of children. The Hague, 1974. pp. 121. *bibliog.*

BEILIN (HARRY) Studies in the cognitive basis of language development. New York, 1975 pp. 420. *bibliog.*

BLOOM (LOIS) and others. Structure and variation in child language:...with commentary by Melissa Bowerman [and] Michael Maratsos and reply by the authors. Chicago, 1975. pp. 97. *bibliogs. (Society for Research in Child Development. Monographs. vol. 40. no. 2)*

CLAUSEN (MARION TANDIWE WHEELER) An anthropological and psychological investigation of use and understanding of kin terms by English children: implications for kinship theory. [1975]. 1 vol. (various foliations). *bibliog. Typescript. M.Phil.(London) thesis: unpublished. This thesis is the property of London University and may not be removed from the library.*

FOUNDATIONS of language development: a multidisciplinary approach; edited by Eric H. Lenneberg [and] Elizabeth Lenneberg. Paris, Unesco Press, 1975. 2 vols. *bibliogs.*

ROGERS (SINCLAIR) ed. Children and language: readings in early language and socialization. London, 1975. pp. 346. *bibliogs.*

TREMAINE (RUTH V.) Syntax and Piagetian operational thought: a developmental study of bilingual children. Washington, [1975]. pp. 131. *bibliog.*

INTERNATIONAL SYMPOSIUM ON FIRST LANGUAGE ACQUISITION, FLORENCE, 1972. Baby talk and infant speech; edited by Walburga von Raffler-Engel and Yvan Lebrun. Amsterdam, 1976. pp. 362. *bibliog.*

MARATSOS (MICHAEL P.) The use of definite and indefinite reference in young children: an experimental study of semantic acquisition. Cambridge, 1976. pp. 144. *bibliog.*

RODGON (MARIS MONITZ) Single-word usage, cognitive development and the beginnings of combinatorial speech: a study of ten English-speaking children. Cambridge, 1976. pp. 163. *bibliog.*

SZAGUN (GISELA) A cross-cultural study of the acquisition of tense forms and time concepts in young children. 1976. fo. 355. *bibliog. Typescript. Ph.D. (London) thesis: unpublished. This thesis is the property of London University and may not be removed from the Library.*

— Law.

SOCIETE JEAN BODIN. Recueils. 35- . L'enfant. Bruxelles, 1975 in progress. *bibliogs. In various languages.*

The CHILD and the law: the proceedings of the first World Conference of the International Society on Family Law, held in Berlin, April 1975; edited by Frank Bates. Dobbs Ferry, N.Y., 1976. 2 vols.

— — Australia.

FOREMAN (LYNNE) Children or families?: an evaluation of the legislative basis for child-protective statutory welfare services in the Australian states and territories. Canberra, Australian Government Social Welfare Commission, 1975. pp. 95. *bibliog.*

— — Russia — Ukraine.

UKRAINE. Statutes, etc. 1973. Zakonodatel'stvo o nesovershennoletnikh: sbornik normativnykh aktov; pod redaktsiei...S.I. Rudika. Kiev, 1974. pp. 636.

— — United Kingdom.

NATIONAL COUNCIL FOR CIVIL LIBERTIES. Reports. The children's ombudsman. London, 1975. pp. 10.

FREEMAN (MICHAEL D.A.) The Children Act 1975: text, with concise commentary. London, 1976. pp. 109.

TERRY (JENNIFER) A guide to the Children Act 1975. London, 1976. pp. 118.

— — United States.

SUSSMAN (ALAN) and COHEN (STEPHAN J.) Reporting child abuse and neglect: guidelines for legislation. Cambridge, Mass., [1975]. pp. 255. *bibliog.*

— Research.

MEDINNUS (GENE ROLAND) Child study and observation guide. New York, [1976]. pp. 183. *bibliogs.*

CHILDREN IN CHINA.

AMERICAN DELEGATION ON EARLY CHILDHOOD DEVELOPMENT IN THE PEOPLE'S REPUBLIC OF CHINA. Childhood in China: [report]; edited by William Kessen. New Haven, 1975. pp. 241.

CHILDREN IN FRANCE.

UNION DES VAILLANTS ET VAILLANTES. L'enfance, notre plus doux espoir. Paris, [1953]. pp. 30. *Not to be consulted without the permission of the Superintendent of Readers' Services.*

CHILDREN IN GERMANY.

HILLEL (MARC) and HENRY (CLARISSA) Lebensborn e.V.: im Namen der Rasse; (berechtigte Übersetzung [from the French] von Annette Lallemand). Wien, [1975]. pp. 352. *bibliog.*

CHILDREN IN NIGERIA.

GOWON (YAKUBU) Broadcast address...on the occasion of the celebration of the Nigerian Children's National Day, May 27, 1973. [Lagos, Government Printer, 1973]. pp. 4.

CHILDREN IN THE UNITED KINGDOM.

NEWSON (JOHN) and NEWSON (ELIZABETH) Seven years old in the home environment. London, 1976. pp. 436. *bibliog.*

CHILDREN OF IMMIGRANTS

— Education — United Kingdom.

CURTIS (SARAH) Don't rush me!: the comic-strip, sex education and a multi- racial society. London, Community Relations Commission, 1975. pp. 52.

COMMUNITY RELATIONS COMMISSION. A second chance: further education in multi-racial areas. London, 1976. pp. 134.

— — — Scotland.

JORDANHILL COLLEGE OF EDUCATION. The immigrant school learner: a study of Pakistani pupils in Glasgow; [by] L. Dickinson [and others for the] Jordanhill College of Education. Windsor, 1975. pp. 200. *bibliog.*

— United Kingdom.

The AFRICAN child in Great Britain; report of a seminar... [at] Ibadan...1975 [organised by the Commonwealth Students' Children Society and the Department of Sociology of Ibadan University]. London, [1975]. pp. 64.

COMMUNITY RELATIONS COMMISSION. Research summaries on the under fives: a critical guide to research on West Indian children under five in Britain. London, [1975]. 1 pamphlet(various pagings).

COMMUNITY RELATIONS COMMISSION. Who minds?: a study of working mothers and childminding in ethnic minority communities; (with Summary). London, 1975. 2 pts.

GARVEY (ANNE) and JACKSON (BRIAN) Chinese children. [Cambridge, 1975]. pp. 64. *bibliog.*

CHILDREN OF WORKING MOTHERS.

LEVITAN (SAR A.) and ALDERMAN (KAREN CLEARY) Child care and ABC's too. Baltimore, [1975]. pp. 125.

CHILE

— Armed forces — Political activity.

ALGUNOS fundamentos de la intervencion militar en Chile, septiembre 1973. 2nd ed. Santiago de Chile, 1974. pp. 137.

NUNN (FREDERICK M.) The military in Chilean history: essays on civil-military relations, 1810-1973. Albuquerque, [1976]. pp. 343. *bibliog.*

— Commercial policy.

STECHER (BERND) Erfolgsbedingungen der Importsubstitution und der Exportdiversifizierung im Industrialisierungsprozess: die Erfahrungen in Chile, Mexiko und Südkorea. Tübingen, 1976. pp. 207. *bibliog. (Kiel. Universität. Institut für Weltwirtschaft. Kieler Studien. 136)*

— Congreso Nacional.

TOHA (JOSE) defendant. Revolucion, Congreso y constitucion: el caso Toha; [edited by] Joan E. Garces. Santiago de Chile, 1972. pp. 415.

— Constitution.

TOHA (JOSE) defendant. Revolucion, Congreso y constitucion: el caso Toha; [edited by] Joan E. Garces. Santiago de Chile, 1972. pp. 415.

— Economic conditions.

CHILE. Oficina de Planificacion Nacional. Informe economico mensual. bi-m., N/D 1973 [covering 1973]- Santiago.

CHILE: politics and society; edited by Arturo Valenzuela and J. Samuel Valenzuela. New Brunswick, N.J., [1976]. pp. 399. *bibliog.*

MAMALAKIS (MARKOS J.) The growth and structure of the Chilean economy: from independence to Allende. New Haven, 1976. pp. 390.

— Economic history.

CARMAGNANI (MARCELLO) Les mécanismes de la vie économique dans une société coloniale: le Chili, 1680-1830. Paris, 1973. pp. 392. *bibliog. (Paris. Ecole Pratique des Hautes Etudes. Section des Sciences Economiques et Sociales. Centre de Recherches Historiques. Monnaie, Prix, Conjoncture. 11)*

MAMALAKIS (MARKOS J.) The growth and structure of the Chilean economy: from independence to Allende. New Haven, 1976. pp. 390.

— Economic policy.

ALLENDE's Chile; edited by Philip O'Brien. New York, 1976. pp. 296. *bibliog.*

— Foreign economic relations — United States.

PETRAS (JAMES FRANK) and MORLEY (MORRIS H.) The United States and Chile: imperialism and the overthrow of the Allende government. New York, [1975]. pp. 217.

— Foreign relations — United States.

PETRAS (JAMES FRANK) and MORLEY (MORRIS H.) The United States and Chile: imperialism and the overthrow of the Allende government. New York, [1975]. pp. 217.

— History.

BAEZA FLORES (ALBERTO) Radiografia politica de Chile. Mexico, 1972. pp. 413.

— Politics and government.

BAEZA FLORES (ALBERTO) Radiografia politica de Chile. Mexico, 1972. pp. 413.

CHILE SOLIDARITY CAMPAIGN. Chile: trade unions and the coup. [London, 1973?]. pp. 12.

BIG FLAME. Brixton Group. Chile si!: the continuing class war. [London, 1974]. pp. 52.

SILVA (RAUL) and others. Evidence on the terror in Chile...; translated by Brian McBeth. London, [1974]. pp. 139.

TARIQ ALI and HEDLEY (GERRY) Chile: lessons of the coup; which way to workers power?. London, [1974?]. pp. 48. *(International Marxist Group. Red Pamphlets. No. 7)*

ZAVALETA MERCADO (RENE). El poder dual en America Latina: (estudio de los casos de Bolivia y Chile). Mexico, 1974. pp. 270.

FLORES OLEA (VICTOR) ed. El golpe de estado en Chile. Mexico, 1975. pp. 324.

The LESSONS of Chile: the Chilean coup and the future of socialism; (a selection of papers and discussion from the proceedings of a conference held in Amsterdam on 22-24 February, 1974...organised by the Transnational Institute); edited by John Gittings. Nottingham, 1975. pp. 91.

ALLENDE's Chile; edited by Philip O'Brien. New York, 1976. pp. 296. *bibliog.*

CHILE: politics and society; edited by Arturo Valenzuela and J. Samuel Valenzuela. New Brunswick, N.J., [1976]. pp. 399. *bibliog.*

NUNN (FREDERICK M.) The military in Chilean history: essays on civil-military relations, 1810-1973. Albuquerque, [1976]. pp. 343. *bibliog.*

— Population.

SULBRANDT (JOSE) and FERRERA (MARIA ALICIA) Law and population growth in Chile. Medford, Mass., 1975. pp. 45. *(Tufts University. Fletcher School of Law and Diplomacy. Law and Population Monograph Series. No.31)*

— Relations (general) with the United States.

HOROWITZ (IRVING LOUIS) ed. The rise and fall of Project Camelot: studies in the relationship between social science and practical politics. rev. ed. Cambridge, Mass., [1974]. pp. 409.

— Rural conditions.

BAUER (ARNOLD J.) Chilean rural society: from the Spanish Conquest to 1930. Cambridge, [1975]. pp. 265. *bibliog.*

LOVEMAN (BRIAN) Struggle in the countryside: politics and rural labor in Chile, 1919-1973. Bloomington, Ind., [1976]. pp. 439. *bibliog. (Indiana University. International Development Research Center. Studies in Development. No. 10)*

— Social conditions.

BIENESTAR y pobreza; edicion preparada por CEPLAN; (edicion a cargo de Raul Gutierrez). Santiago, Chile, 1974. pp. 315. *Includes papers presented to the Seminario Internacional de Distribucion del Ingreso y Desarrollo, 1973, organized by the Centro de Estudios de Planificacion Nacional.*

CHILE: politics and society; edited by Arturo Valenzuela and J. Samuel Valenzuela. New Brunswick, N.J., [1976]. pp. 399. *bibliog.*

— Social history.

BAUER (ARNOLD J.) Chilean rural society: from the Spanish Conquest to 1930. Cambridge, [1975]. pp. 265. *bibliog.*

CHILIYING.

CHU (LI) and TIEN (CHIEH-YUN) Inside a people's commune: report from Chiliying. Peking, 1974. pp. 212.

CHILTERN SOCIETY.

CHILTERN SOCIETY. Sixty-five [to] seventy-five: the Chiltern Society's first ten years. High Wycombe, [1975]. pp. 28.

CHIMNEY-SWEEPS.

SOCIETY FOR SUPERSEDING THE NECESSITY OF CLIMBING BOYS. [Report]. London, annual, 1808 (6th report). pp. 8.

CHINA

— Armed forces — Political activity.

CH'I (HSI-SHENG) Warlord politics in China, 1916-1928. Stanford, 1976. pp. 282. *bibliog.*

JAIN (JAGDISH PRASAD) After Mao what?: army, party and group rivalries in China. London, 1976. pp. 276. *bibliog.*

MAITAN (LIVIO) Party, army and masses in China: a marxist interpretation of the cultural revolution and its aftermath. London, 1976. pp. 373.

— Army.

MAITAN (LIVIO) Party, army and masses in China: a marxist interpretation of the cultural revolution and its aftermath. London, 1976. pp. 373.

— Bibliography.

KAMACHI (NORIKO) and others. Japanese studies of modern China since 1953: a bibliographical guide to historical and social science research on the nineteenth and twentieth centuries: supplementary volume for 1953-1969. Cambridge, Mass., 1975. pp. 603. *(Harvard University. East Asian Research Center. Harvard East Asian Monographs. 60)*

— Commerce.

UNITED STATES. Central Intelligence Agency. 1973. People's Republic of China: international trade handbook. [Washington], 1973. pp. 17. *(Research Aids. N.A73-29) Microfilm : 1 reel.*

UNITED STATES. Central Intelligence Agency. 1974. People's Republic of China: internal trade handbook. [Washington], 1974. pp. 17. *(Research Aids. No.A(ER)74-63) Microfilm: 1 reel.*

CHINA'S changing role in the world economy; edited by Bryant G. Garth and the editors of the Stanford Journal of International Studies. New York, 1975. pp. 222. *Papers presented at a conference held at Stanford University, 1974.*

— — New Zealand.

NEW ZEALAND. Department of Trade and Industry. 1975. The People's Republic of China: handbook. [Wellington], 1975. pp. 70. *bibliog.*

— — United States.

CAHILL (HARRY A.) The China trade and U.S. tariffs. New York, 1973. pp. 161. *bibliog.*

— Constitution.

FRANCE. Direction de la Documentation. La Documentation Française. Notes et Etudes Documentaires. No. 4,223. Les nouvelles institutions chinoises: la Constitution de 1975; par Yves Viltard. Paris, 1975. pp. 39.

— Description and travel.

GOLDWASSER (JANET) and DOWTY (STUART) Huang-Ying: workers' China. New York, [1975]. pp. 404.

— Economic conditions.

CHINA'S changing role in the world economy; edited by Bryant G. Garth and the editors of the Stanford Journal of International Studies. New York, 1975. pp. 222. *Papers presented at a conference held at Stanford University, 1974.*

BURCHETT (WILFRED G.) and ALLEY (REWI) China: the quality of life. Harmondsworth, 1976. pp. 312.

CHINA(Cont.)

— Economic history.

CHINA's modern economy in historical perspective; edited by Dwight H. Perkins. Stanford, 1975. pp. 344. *Papers originally prepared for a conference in Bermuda in 1973 sponsored by the Subcommittee for Research on the Chinese Economy of the Social Science Research Council and the American Council of Learned Societies.*

— Economic policy.

FRANCE-ASIE: revue française des problèmes asiatiques contemporains. 1974. No. 3. Chine: vingt-cinquième anniversaire de la République Populaire, 1949-1974; [by] Jacques Guillermaz [and others]. Paris, 1974. pp. 157.

DAMACHI (UKANDI GODWIN) and others, eds. Development paths in Africa and China. London, 1976. pp. 251. *bibliog.*

— Foreign economic relations.

CHINA'S changing role in the world economy; edited by Bryant G. Garth and the editors of the Stanford Journal of International Studies. New York, 1975. pp. 222. *Papers presented at a conference held at Stanford University, 1974.*

HORVÁTH (JÁNOS) Chinese technology transfer to the third world: a grants economy analysis. New York, 1976. pp. 100. *bibliog.*

— Foreign opinion.

POSPELOV (BORIS VASIL'EVICH) Iaponskaia obshchestvenno-politicheskaia mysl' i maoizm: kritika antimarksistskikh kontseptsii sushchnosti maoizma. Moskva, 1975. pp. 224. *bibliog.*

— Foreign relations.

WOODHEAD (HENRY GEORGE WANDESFORDE) The truth about the Chinese Republic. London, [1925?]. pp. 287.

ADVANCING and contending approaches to the study of Chinese foreign policy; edited by Roger L. Dial. Halifax, 1974. pp. 412. *bibliogs. Papers of a conference held at Lunenburg, Nova Scotia in May 1972.*

IURKOV (S.G.) and PETROV (G.P.) eds. Vneshnepoliticheskie kontseptsii maoizma: pravovye aspekty. Moskva, 1975. pp. 256.

KAPUR (HARISH) China in world politics. New Delhi, 1975. pp. 66.

MUELLER (PETER G.) and ROSS (DOUGLAS A.) China and Japan: emerging global powers. New York, 1975. pp. 218. *bibliog.*

— — Indonesia.

MOZINGO (DAVID) Chinese policy towards Indonesia, 1949-1967. Ithaca, N.Y., 1976. pp. 303. *bibliog.*

— — Japan.

CHOW (JEN HWA) China and Japan: the history of Chinese diplomatic missions in Japan 1877-1911. Singapore, 1975. pp. 317. *bibliog.*

SLADKOVSKII (MIKHAIL IOSIFOVICH) China and Japan, past and present; edited and translated by Robert F. Price. Gulf Breeze, Fla., 1975. pp. 286.

— — Tanzania.

YU (GEORGE T.) China's African policy: a study of Tanzania. New York, 1975. pp. 200. *bibliog.*

— — United Kingdom.

KANE (HAROLD EDWIN) Sir Miles Lampson at the Peking legation, 1926-1933. 1975. fo. 192. *Typescript. Ph.D.(London) thesis: unpublished. This thesis is the property of London University and may not be removed from the Library.*

BOARDMAN (ROBERT) Britain and the People's Republic of China 1949-74. London, 1976. pp. 210. *bibliog.*

— — United States.

KALICKI (JAN HENRYK) The pattern of Sino-American crises in the 1950's: political- military interactions under stress. 1971. fo. 442. *bibliog. Typescript. Ph.D. (London) thesis: unpublished. This thesis is the property of London University and may not be removed from the Library. End pocket contains two offprints from The World Today, April and September 1970.*

SERGEICHUK (S.) Through Russian eyes: American-Chinese relations;... (translation by Elizabeth Cody-Rutter; edited by Philip A. Garon). Arlington, Va., 1975. pp. 220.

FAIRBANK (JOHN KING) China perceived: images and policies in Chinese-American relations. London, 1976. pp. 254.

— — Vietnam.

MURASHEVA (GALINA FEDOROVNA) V'etnamo-kitaiskie otnosheniia XVII-XIX vv. Moskva, 1973. pp. 158. *bibliog.*

LOESCHER (GILBURT DAMIAN) National liberation war in South Vietnam: the perceptions and policies of China and North Vietnam, 1954-1969; [Ph.D. (London) thesis]. 1975. fo. 421. *bibliog. Typescript: unpublished. This thesis is the property of London University and may not be removed from the Library.*

— Gentry.

CONFLICT and control in late imperial China; edited by Frederic Wakeman and Carolyn Grant. Berkeley, California, [1975]. pp. 328. *Papers from a conference sponsored by the Center for Chinese Studies, University of California, and the Committee on Studies of Chinese Civilization of the American Council of Learned Societies.*

— History.

HSÜ (IMMANUEL CHUNG-YUEH) The rise of modern China. 2nd ed. New York, 1975. pp. 1002. *bibliogs.*

— — 1900— .

WOODHEAD (HENRY GEORGE WANDESFORDE) The truth about the Chinese Republic. London, [1925?]. pp. 287.

— — 1912-1949, Republic.

SHERIDAN (JAMES E.) China in disintegration: the Republican era in Chinese history, 1912-1949. New York, [1975]. pp. 338. *bibliog.*

— — 1912-1937.

BLAGODATOV (ALEKSEI VASIL'EVICH) Zapiski o kitaiskoi revoliutsii 1925-1927 gg. 2nd ed. Moskva, 1975. pp. 277.

CH'I (HSI-SHENG) Warlord politics in China, 1916-1928. Stanford, 1976. pp. 282. *bibliog.*

— — 1937-1945.

LI (LINCOLN) The Japanese army in North China, 1937-1941: problems of political and economic control. Tokyo, 1975. pp. 278. *bibliog.*

— — 1945— .

UHALLEY (STEPHEN) Mao Tse-tung: a critical biography. New York, 1975. pp. 233. *bibliog.*

HAN (SUYIN) pseud. [i.e. Elizabeth COMBER] Wind in the tower: Mao Tsetung and the Chinese revolution, 1949-1975. London, 1976. pp. 404.

— Industries.

SLADKOVSKII (MIKHAIL IOSIFOVICH) ed. Problemy i protivorechiia industrial'nogo razvitiia KNR. Moskva, 1974. pp. 240.

UNITED STATES. Central Intelligence Agency. 1974. China: role of small plants in economic development. [Washington], 1974. pp. 18. *(Research Aids. No. A(ER)74-60) Microfilm: 1 reel.*

— Intellectual life.

CHEN(JACK) Inside the cultural revolution. London, 1976. pp. 483. *bibliog.*

The LIMITS of change: essays on conservative alternatives in Republican China; edited by Charlotte Furth. Cambridge, Mass., 1976. pp. 426. *(Harvard University. East Asian Research Center. Harvard East Asian Series. 84) Papers from a conference held in 1972 under the auspices of the Joint Committee on Contemporary China of the Social Science Research Council and the American Council of Learned Societies.*

— Politics and government.

FRANCE-ASIE: revue française des problèmes asiatiques contemporains. 1974. No. 3. Chine: vingt-cinquième anniversaire de la République Populaire, 1949-1974; [by] Jacques Guillermaz [and others]. Paris, 1974. pp. 157.

BAUM (RICHARD) Prelude to revolution: Mao, the party and the peasant question, 1962-66. New York, 1975. pp. 222. *bibliog.*

CHANG (PARRIS H.) Power and policy in China. University Park, Pa., [1975]. pp. 276. *bibliog.*

JOFFE (ELLIS) Between two plenums: China's intraleadership conflict, 1959-1962. Ann Arbor, 1975. pp. 72. *(Michigan University. Center for Chinese Studies. Michigan Papers in Chinese Studies. No. 22)*

KHOLODKOVSKAIA (ADELIIA VLADIMIROVNA) Rabochii klass Kitaia v period "uregulirovaniia", 1961-1965. Moskva, 1975. pp. 157. *bibliog.*

LI (LINCOLN) The Japanese army in North China, 1937-1941: problems of political and economic control. Tokyo, 1975. pp. 278. *bibliog.*

MARKOVA (SVETLANA DANILOVNA) Maoizm i intelligentsiia: problemy i sobytiia, 1956-1973 gg. Moskva, 1975. pp. 245. *bibliog.*

VILTARD (YVES) Le système politique chinois dans le mouvement d'éducation socialiste, 1962-1966. Paris, 1975. pp. 83. *bibliog. (Paris. Université de Paris I (Panthéon-Sorbonne). Publications. Série Science Politique. 4)*

CHEN(JACK) Inside the cultural revolution. London, 1976. pp. 483. *bibliog.*

CH'I (HSI-SHENG) Warlord politics in China, 1916-1928. Stanford, 1976. pp. 282. *bibliog.*

ISRAEL (JOHN) and KLEIN (DONALD WALKER) Rebels and bureaucrats: China's December 9ers. Berkeley, Calif., [1976]. pp. 303. *bibliog. (Columbia University. East Asian Institute. Studies)*

JAIN (JAGDISH PRASAD) After Mao what?: army, party and group rivalries in China. London, 1976. pp. 276. *bibliog.*

LIU (ALAN P.L.) Political culture and group conflict in communist China. Santa Barbara, [1976]. pp. 205. *bibliog.*

MAITAN (LIVIO) Party, army and masses in China: a marxist interpretation of the cultural revolution and its aftermath. London, 1976. pp. 373.

OSNOVNYE aspekty kitaiskoi problemy, 1965-1975. Moskva, 1976. pp. 279.

— Relations (general) with Japan.

POSPELOV (BORIS VASIL'EVICH) Iaponskaia obshchestvenno-politicheskaia mysl' i maoizm: kritika antimarksistskikh kontseptsii sushchnosti maoizma. Moskva, 1975. pp. 224. *bibliog.*

— Relations (general) with other countries.

ANDREEV (MIKHAIL ANDREEVICH) Overseas Chinese bourgeoisie - a Peking tool in Southeast Asia. Moscow, [1975]. pp. 178.

— Relations (general) with Romania.

TRADIȚII ale poporului român de solidaritate și prietenie cu poporul chinez. București, 1973. pp. 478.

— **Relations (general) with the United States.**

FAIRBANK (JOHN KING) Chinese-American interactions: a historical summary. New Brunswick, [1975]. pp. 90. *bibliog.* (University of Puget Sound. Brown and Haley Lectures. 1974)

FAIRBANK (JOHN KING) China perceived: images and policies in Chinese-American relations. London, 1976. pp. 254.

— **Relations (military) with Germany.**

MEHNER (KARL HEINZ LOUIS) Die Rolle deutscher Militärberater als Interessenvertreter des deutschen Imperialismus und Militarismus in China, 1928- 1936. [Leipzig?, 1961]. pp. 226, lxix. *bibliog. Microfilm: 1 reel.*

— **Rural conditions — Bibliography.**

COMMONWEALTH BUREAU OF AGRICULTURAL ECONOMICS. Chinese agriculture and rural society; edited by K.P. Broadbent. [Farnham Royal, 1974]. pp. 37. *(Annotated Bibliographies. No. 30) Compiled from World Agricultural Economics and Rural Sociology Abstracts.*

— **Social conditions.**

BURCHETT (WILFRED G.) and ALLEY (REWI) China: the quality of life. Harmondsworth, 1976. pp. 312.

CHEN(JACK) Inside the cultural revolution. London, 1976. pp. 483. *bibliog.*

— **Social history.**

CONFLICT and control in late imperial China; edited by Frederic Wakeman and Carolyn Grant. Berkeley, California, [1975]. pp. 328. *Papers from a conference sponsored by the Center for Chinese Studies, University of California, and the Committee on Studies of Chinese Civilization of the American Council of Learned Societies.*

CHINESE IN CANADA.

MORTON (JAMES) In the sea of sterile mountains: the Chinese in British Columbia. Vancouver, 1974. pp. 280.

CHINESE IN FOREIGN COUNTRIES.

ANDREEV (MIKHAIL ANDREEVICH) Overseas Chinese bourgeoisie - a Peking tool in Southeast Asia. Moscow, [1975]. pp. 178.

CHINESE IN NEW ZEALAND.

GREIF (STUART WILLIAM) The overseas Chinese in New Zealand. Singapore, 1974. pp. 192. *bibliog.*

CHINESE IN THE UNITED KINGDOM.

GARVEY (ANNE) and JACKSON (BRIAN) Chinese children. [Cambridge, 1975]. pp. 64. *bibliog.*

WATSON (JAMES L.) Emigration and the Chinese lineage: the Mans in Hong Kong and London. Berkeley, [1975]. pp. 242. *bibliog.*

CHINESE—JAPANESE WAR, 1937-1945.

BRICE (MARTIN H.) The Royal Navy and the Sino-Japanese incident, 1937-41. London, 1973. pp. 167.

HU (PU-YU) A brief history of Sino-Japanese war, 1937-1945. Taipei, 1974. pp. 384. *bibliog.*

LINDSAY (MICHAEL FRANCIS MORRIS) 2nd Baron Lindsay. The unknown war: north China 1937-1945. London, 1975. 1 vol. (unpaged) *bibliog.*

CHINESE STUDIES

— **Japan — Bibliography.**

KAMACHI (NORIKO) and others. Japanese studies of modern China since 1953: a bibliographical guide to historical and social science research on the nineteenth and twentieth centuries: supplementary volume for 1953-1969. Cambridge, Mass., 1975. pp. 603. *(Harvard University. East Asian Research Center. Harvard East Asian Monographs. 60)*

CHITA (OBLAST')

— **Economic conditions.**

NEDESHEV (ALEKSEI ALEKSANDROVICH) Oblastnoi ekonomicheskii raion: issledovanie funktsii, struktury i protsessov razvitiia na primere Chitinskoi oblasti; otvetstvennyi redaktor...V.V. Vorob'ev. Novosibirsk, 1975. pp. 162. *bibliog.*

CHOCTAW INDIANS

— **Government relations.**

SATZ (RONALD N.) American Indian policy in the Jacksonian era. Lincoln, Neb., [1975]. pp. 343. *bibliog.*

CHOLULA

— **Social life and customs.**

BONFIL BATALLA (GUILLERMO) Cholula: la ciudad sagrada en la era industrial. Mexico, 1973. pp. 296. *bibliog. (Mexico City. Universidad Nacional Autonoma de Mexico. Instituto de Investigaciones Historicas. Seccion de Antropologia. Serie Antropologica. 15)*

CHOMSKY (NOAM).

HARMAN (GILBERT) ed. On Noam Chomsky: critical essays. Garden City, N.Y., 1974. pp. 345. *bibliogs.*

ROBINSON (IAN) Lecturer in English language in the University College of Swansea. The new grammarians' funeral: a critique of Noam Chomsky's linguistics. Cambridge, 1975. pp. 189.

CHORNOVIL (VIACHESLAV MAKSYMOVYCH).

UKRAÏNS'KA inteligentsiia pid sudom KGB: materiialy z protsesiv V. Chornovola, M. Masiutka, M. Ozernoho ta in.; Ukrainian intellectuals tried by the KGB. [Miunkhen], 1970. pp. 243.

CHOWANETZ (JULIAN FEODOR JOSEPH).

See CHOWNITZ (JULIAN FEODOR JOSEPH).

CHOWNITZ (JULIAN FEODOR JOSEPH).

CHOWNITZ (JULIAN FEODOR JOSEPH) Geschichte der ungarischen Revolution in den Jahren 1848 und 1849, mit Rückblicken auf die Bewegung in den österreichischen Erbländern; in zwei Bänden. Stuttgart, Rieger, 1849. 2 vols. (in 1).

CHRISTIAN VIII, King of Denmark.

NØRREGARD (GEORG) Før stormen: Christian 8.s udenrigspolitik, 1839-48. [Copenhagen, 1974]. pp. 370. *bibliog.*

CHRISTIAN ETHICS.

ELLUL (JACQUES) The ethics of freedom;...translated and edited by Geoffrey W. Bromiley. London, 1976. pp. 517.

CHRISTIAN LIFE.

ESCRIVA DE BALAGUER Y ALBAS (JOSEMARIA) The way. Chicago, 1964. pp. 278.

CHRISTIANITY.

RICOEUR (PAUL) Political and social essays; collected and edited by David Stewart and Joseph Bien. Athens, Ohio, [1974]. pp. 293.

WILSON (BRYAN RONALD) Contemporary transformations of religion. London, 1976. pp. 116. *(Newcastle-upon-Tyne. University. Riddell Memorial Lectures. 45th series)*

— **Controversial literature.**

ROBERTSON (JOHN MACKINNON) What has Christianity done?. Bradford, [1897]. pp. 7. *(Papers for the People. No. 9)*

CHURCH AND ECONOMICS.

CHRISTIANITY AND ECONOMICS.

EDWARDS (DAVID LAWRENCE) The state of the nation: a Christian approach to Britain's economic crisis. London, [1976]. pp. 35. *(Church of England. National Assembly. Board for Social Responsibility. Occasional Papers)*

CHRISTIANITY AND INTERNATIONAL AFFAIRS.

FELLOWSHIP OF RECONCILIATION. [Minute books and papers. 1915-62]. 43 pieces. *Manuscript, typescript, etc.*

CHRISTIANITY AND OTHER RELIGIONS.

SIMPSON (WILLIAM WYNN) Jews and Christians today: a study in Jewish and Christian relationships. London, 1940. pp. 86. *(Beckly Social Service Lectures. 1940)*

CHRISTIANITY AND POLITICS.

BENDER (RYSZARD) Chrześcijanie w polskich ruchach demokratycznych XIX stulecia. Warszawa, 1975. pp. 361. *bibliog.*

DAVIE (GRACE RIESTRA CLAIRE) Right wing politics among French Protestants, 1900-1944, with special reference to the Association Sully. 1975. fo.323. *bibliog. Typescript. Ph.D.(London) thesis: unpublished. This thesis is the property of London University and may not be removed from the Library.*

ECCLESIASTICAL HISTORY SOCIETY. Summer Meeting, 13th, York, 197-. Church, society and politics; papers read at the thirteenth summer meeting and the fourteenth winter meeting...; edited by Derek Baker. Oxford, 1975. pp. 440. *(Ecclesiastical History Society. Studies in Church History. vol. 12)*

HASTINGS (ADRIAN) Southern Africa and the Christian conscience. London, [1975]. pp. 16. *(Catholic Institute for International Relations. Justice Papers. 3)*

MAWHINNEY (BRIAN) and WELLS (RONALD) Conflict and Christianity in Northern Ireland. Berkhamsted, 1975. pp. 127. *bibliog.*

EDWARDS (DAVID LAWRENCE) The state of the nation: a Christian approach to Britain's economic crisis. London, [1976]. pp. 35. *(Church of England. National Assembly. Board for Social Responsibility. Occasional Papers)*

CHRISTMAS MØLLER (JOHN).

CHRISTMAS MØLLER (JOHN) Londonbreve:...korrespondance med hjemlandet, 1942-1945; udgivet af Jørgen Haestrup. [Copenhagen, 1974]. pp. 262.

CHRONICALLY ILL.

STRAUSS (ANSELM LEONARD) Chronic illness and the quality of life. Saint Louis, 1975. pp. 160. *bibliog.*

— **Australia.**

AUSTRALIA. Commonwealth Bureau of Census and Statistics. 1970. Chronic illnesses, injuries and impairments, May 1968. [Canberra, 1970]. pp. 43.

CHRONOLOGY, HISTORICAL.

FREEMAN-GRENVILLE (GREVILLE STEWART PARKER) Chronology of world history: a calendar of principal events from 3000 B.C. to A.D. 1973. London, 1975. pp. 753.

CHULALONGKORN, King of Thailand.

ENGEL (DAVID M.) Law and kingship in Thailand during the reign of King Chulalongkorn. Ann Arbor, 1975. pp. 131. *bibliog. (Michigan University. Center for South and Southeast Asian Studies. Michigan Papers on South and Southeast Asia. No. 9)*

CHURCH AND ECONOMICS.

ELLIOTT (CHARLES) Inflation and the compromised Church. Belfast, 1975. pp. 148. *bibliogs.*

CHURCH AND LABOUR

CHURCH AND LABOUR

— Switzerland.

BRUNNER (JOHANN CASPAR) Soziale Gedanken eines schweizerischen Arbeitgebers vor 40 Jahren; [edited by Ferdinand Buomberger]. Zürich, 1913. pp. 95. *Selected chapters from several pamphlets and passages from "Konkordia", 1871-74.*

— United Kingdom.

HUNT (WILLIAM HENRY) ed. Churchmanship and labour: sermons on social subjects preached at S. Stephen's Church, Walbrook, by H. Scott Holland [and others]. London, 1906. pp. 272.

CHURCH AND RACE PROBLEMS

— South Africa.

HASTINGS (ADRIAN) Southern Africa and the Christian conscience. London, [1975]. pp. 16. *(Catholic Institute for International Relations. Justice Papers. 3)*

CHURCH AND SOCIAL PROBLEMS.

CAMARA (HELDER) Archbishop of Olinda and Recife. Espiral de violencia; (tradujo Alejandro Sierra sobre el original francés). Salamanca, 1970. pp. 81.

NYERERE (JULIUS KAMBARAGE) Man and development. Dar es Salaam, 1974. pp. 125.

ASPEN INTERRELIGIOUS CONSULTATION, ASPEN, 1974. Global justice and development: report of the...consultation...; sponsored by the Overseas Development Council with the support of the Aspen Institute for Humanistic Studies and the Johnson Foundation. Washington, [1975]. pp. 175.

ECCLESIASTICAL HISTORY SOCIETY. Summer Meeting, 13th, York, 197-. Church, society and politics; papers read at the thirteenth summer meeting and the fourteenth winter meeting...; edited by Derek Baker. Oxford, 1975. pp. 440. *(Ecclesiastical History Society. Studies in Church History. vol. 12)*

TAYLOR (JOHN VERNON) Enough is enough. London, 1975 repr. 1976. pp. 120. *bibliog.*

— Catholic Church.

CAMARA (HELDER) Archbishop of Olinda and Recife. La rebelión de los economistas. Madrid, 1969. pp. 46.

— America, Latin — Catholic Church.

CAMARA (HELDER) Archbishop of Olinda and Recife. La iglesia en el desarrollo de América Latina. Madrid, 1969. pp. 44.

— Germany.

GOLDE (GUENTER) Catholics and Protestants: agricultural modernization in two German villages. New York, [1975]. pp. 198. *bibliog.*

— — Catholic Church.

WELTY (EBERHARD) Die Entscheidung in die Zukunft: Grundsätze und Hinweise zur Neuordnung im deutschen Lebensraum. Köln, [1946]. pp. 431.

— Switzerland — Catholic Church.

SPIELER (WILLY) Kirche und Mitbestimmung: der Beitrag der katholischen Soziallehre...in der Schweiz. [Bern, 1976]. pp. 203. *bibliog.*

— United Kingdom — Church of England.

CHURCH OF ENGLAND. Church Congress, Swansea, 1909. The official report of the Church Congress, held at Swansea,...1909; edited by the Rev. C. Dunkley. London, 1909. pp. 575. *Contains the debate on "Socialism from the standpoint of Christianity".*

EDWARDS (DAVID LAWRENCE) The state of the nation: a Christian approach to Britain's economic crisis. London, [1976]. pp. 35. *(Church of England. National Assembly. Board for Social Responsibility. Occasional Papers)*

NORMAN (EDWARD ROBERT) Church and society in England 1770-1970: a historical study. Oxford, 1976. pp. 507. *bibliog.*

CHURCH AND STATE.

EZRIN (GENRIKH IL'ICH) Gosudarstvo i religiia: religioznye organizatsii i politicheskaia struktura obshchestva. Moskva, 1974. pp. 135.

— Catholic Church.

MUSSELLI (LUCIANO) Chiesa Cattolica e comunità politica, dal declino della teoria "potestas indirecta" alle nuove impostazioni della canonistica postconciliare. Padova, 1975. pp. 155. *(Pavia. Università. Istituto di Scienze Giuridiche e Sociali: Studi nelle Scienze Giuridiche e Sociali. Nuova Serie. vol. 15)*

CHURCH AND STATE IN CANADA.

CRUNICAN (PAUL) Priests and politicians: Manitoba schools and the election of 1896 Toronto, [1974]. pp. 369. *bibliog.*

CHURCH AND STATE IN FRANCE.

[BELLOMAYRE (MICHEL DE)] La résistance légale aux décrets du 29 mars: discours prononcé dans une réunion privée tenue à Moulins. n.p. [1880?]. pp. 3-22. *Lacking title-page. Manuscript ascription on p. 3.*

CHESNELONG (PIERRE CHARLES) Les décrets du 29 mars et les devoirs des catholiques: discours prononcé le 23 avril 1880. Paris, [imprint, 1880?]. pp. 3-45.

CHURCH AND STATE IN GERMANY.

REIFFERSCHEID (GERHARD) Das Bistum Ermland und das Dritte Reich. Köln, 1975. pp. 351. *bibliog.*

METZ (HUBERT) Katholizismus und Wahlen: zum Verhältnis Kirche und Staat in Deutschland. [Mannheim], 1976. pp. 354. *bibliog. Inauguraldissertation zur Erlangung des akademischen Grades eines Doktors der Philosophie der Universität Mannheim.*

CHURCH AND STATE IN IRELAND.

LARKIN (EMMET) The Roman Catholic church and the creation of the modern Irish state, 1878-1886. Philadelphia, 1975. pp. 412.

CHURCH AND STATE IN ITALY.

CATALANO (GAETANO) Sovranità dello stato e autonomia della chiesa nella costituzione repubblicana: contributo all'interpretazione sistematica dell'articolo 7 della costituzione. 2nd ed. Milano, 1974. pp. 211.

PORCARO (GIUSEPPE) Chiesa e stato a Napoli dopo l'unità: congiure e processi politici. [Naples, 1974]. pp. 327. *bibliog.*

CHURCH AND STATE IN MEXICO.

OLIVERA SEDANO (ALICIA) Aspectos del conflicto religioso de 1926 a 1929: sus antecedentes y consecuencias. Mexico, 1966. pp. 292. *bibliog. (Instituto Nacional de Antropologia e Historia. Serie Historia. 16)*

CHURCH AND STATE IN POLAND.

DMOWSKI (ROMAN) Kościół, naród i państwo; [originally published 1927]. Londyn, 1964. pp. 32.

MYSŁEK (WIESŁAW) and STASZEWSKI (MICHAŁ T.) eds. Polityka wyznaniowa: tło, warunki, realizacja. Warszawa, 1975. pp. 475. *With Russian and English tables of contents.*

CHURCH AND STATE IN RUSSIA.

McCULLAGH (FRANCIS) The bolshevik persecution of Christianity. London, 1924. pp. 401.

LANE (CHRISTEL OLGA) The impact of communist ideology and the Soviet order on Christian religion in the contemporary U.S.S.R., 1959-1974. 1976. fo. 489. *bibliog. Typescript. Ph.D. (London) thesis: unpublished. This thesis is the property of London University and may not be removed from the Library.*

CHURCH AND STATE IN SPAIN.

GIL DELGADO (FRANCISCO) Conflicto iglesia-estado. Madrid, 1975. pp. 365.

CHURCH AND STATE IN THE UKRAINE.

MYKULA (WOLODYMYR) The gun and the faith: religion and church in Ukraine under the communist Russian rule. London, 1969. pp. 48.

CHURCH AND STATE IN THE UNITED KINGDOM.

BENNETT (GARETH VAUGHAN) The Tory crisis in church and state, 1688-1730: the career of Francis Atterbury, Bishop of Rochester. Oxford, 1975. pp. 335. *bibliog.*

CHURCH AND STATE IN THE UNITED STATES.

SORAUF (FRANK JOSEPH) The wall of separation: the constitutional politics of Church and State. Princeton, [1976]. pp. 394.

CHURCH HISTORY.

ECCLESIASTICAL HISTORY SOCIETY. Summer Meeting, 13th, York, 197-. Church, society and politics; papers read at the thirteenth summer meeting and the fourteenth winter meeting...; edited by Derek Baker. Oxford, 1975. pp. 440. *(Ecclesiastical History Society. Studies in Church History. vol. 12)*

CHURCH LANDS

— Canada — Ontario.

ONTARIO. Law Reform Commission. 1976. Report on mortmain, charitable uses and religious institutions. [Toronto], 1976. pp. 75.

— United Kingdom.

ROBERTS (TED) Housing and ministry: an experiment in the use of church land. London, [1975]. pp. 60.

CHURCH OF ENGLAND

— Congresses.

CHURCH OF ENGLAND. Church Congress, Swansea, 1909. The official report of the Church Congress, held at Swansea,...1909; edited by the Rev. C. Dunkley. London, 1909. pp. 575. *Contains the debate on "Socialism from the standpoint of Christianity".*

— Education.

SILVER (PAMELA) and SILVER (HAROLD) The education of the poor: the history of a National school 1824-1974. London, 1974. pp. 197. *bibliog.*

— History.

MARRIN (ALBERT) The last crusade: the Church of England in the First World War. Durham, N.C., 1974. pp. 303. *bibliog.*

NORMAN (EDWARD ROBERT) Church and society in England 1770-1970: a historical study. Oxford, 1976. pp. 507. *bibliog.*

CHURCH PROPERTY

— France.

[MARTIN DE SALINS (C.C.)] Nécessité et moyens d'établir une loi agraire, d'assurer la subsistance des pauvres, de réformer le clergé et la constitution militaire; par C.C.M. de S...ns. n.p. 1789; repr. Paris, 1966. pp. 49. *Facsimile reprint.*

CHURCH SCHOOLS

— Canada.

CRUNICAN (PAUL) Priests and politicians: Manitoba schools and the election of 1896 Toronto, [1974]. pp. 369. *bibliog.*

CITIES AND TOWNS.

CHURCH WORK WITH THE DEAF.

SPROLL (HEINZ) Studien zur sozio-ökonomischen Struktur von Randgruppen in Baden im 19. und 20. Jahrhundert: die staatliche und verbandliche Fürsorge und kath. Pastoration an Gehörlosen, 1780-1939. Bern, 1975. pp. 489. *bibliog.*

CHURCH WORK WITH YOUTH

— Germany.

SCHELLENBERGER (BARBARA) Katholische Jugend und Drittes Reich: eine Geschichte des Katholischen Jungmännerverbandes, 1933-1939, etc. Mainz, [1975]. pp. 202. *bibliog.* (Kommission für Zeitgeschichte. Veröffentlichungen. Reihe B: Forschungen. Band 17)

CHURCHES

— Secular use — United Kingdom.

ROBERTS (TED) Housing and ministry: an experiment in the use of church land. London, [1975]. pp. 60.

CHURCHILL (JOHN) 1st Duke of Marlborough.

CHURCHILL (JOHN) 1st Duke of Marlborough, and GODOLPHIN (SIDNEY) 1st Earl of Godolphin. The Marlborough-Godolphin correspondence; edited by Henry L. Snyder. Oxford, 1975. 3 vols.

CHURCHILL (Sir WINSTON LEONARD SPENCER).

NEL (ELIZABETH) Mr. Churchill's secretary. London, 1958 repr. 1959. pp. 188.

CHUVASH REPUBLIC

— History — Sources.

CHUVASHSKAIA ASSR v period Velikoi Otechestvennoi voiny, iiun' 1941-1945 gg.: sbornik dokumentov i materialov. Cheboksary, 1975. pp. 528.

— Politics and government.

OCHERKI istorii Chuvashskoi oblastnoi organizatsii KPSS. Cheboksary, 1974. pp. 627.

CIESZYN

— Politics and government.

BOBEK (PAWEŁ) Wspomnienia i zapiski; przygotował do druku i biografią poprzedził Franciszek Serafin. Warszawa, 1974. pp. 143.

CISKEI.

CISKEI. Information Service. 1976. Land of opportunity: Ciskei. [King William's Town, 1976?]. pp. 49.

CITIES AND TOWNS.

LONG (NORTON ENNEKING) Ethos and the city: the problem of local legitimacy. [St. Louis, 1974]. fo. 17.

— Growth.

BOURNE (LARRY S.) Urbn systems: strategies for regulation: a comparison of policies in Britain, Sweden, Australia and Canada. Oxford, 1975. pp. 264. *bibliog.*

CONROY (MICHAEL E.) The challenge of urban economic development: goals, possibilities and policies for improving the economic structure of cities. Lexington, Mass., [1975]. pp. 132. *bibliog.*

GOTTLIEB (MANUEL) Long swings in urban development. New York, 1976. pp. 360. *bibliog.* (National Bureau of Economic Research. Urban and Regional Studies. 4)

KING (ANTHONY D.) Colonial urban development: social power and environment. London, 1976. pp. 328. *bibliog.*

— Planning.

INTERNATIONAL FEDERATION FOR HOUSING AND PLANNING. Standing Committee on Traffic Problems. Urban pattern and transportation system: report for the Tokyo Congress of the IFHP/1966, based on reports...by P.H. Bendtsen [and others]; prepared by S. Dziewulski [and] B. Ledworowski. [Warsaw], 1966. 1 vol. (various pagings).

MEYER-HEINE (GEORGES) Au-delà de l'urbanisme. [Paris, 1968]. pp. 189.

ONTARIO PLANNING SEMINAR, TORONTO, 1970. Ontario planning seminar, 1970, for senior municipal planners: process, model, data; papers and proceedings. Toronto, Queen's Printer, [1971]. 1 vol. (various pagings).

WORLD HOUSING SURVEY: an overview of the state of housing, building and planning within human settlements; [pd. by] Department of Economic and Social Affairs, United Nations. a., 1974(1st)- New York.

REICHARDT (ROBERT) Bedürfnisforschung im Dienste der Stadtplanung: theoretische Konzepte und Forschungsstrategien. Wien, 1974. pp. 89. *bibliog.* (Österreichische Akademie der Wissenschaften. Philosophisch-Historisch Klasse. Sitzungsberichte. 293. Band. 3. Abhandlung)

BOURNE (LARRY S.) Urbn systems: strategies for regulation: a comparison of policies in Britain, Sweden, Australia and Canada. Oxford, 1975. pp. 264. *bibliog.*

CROSS (DONALD) Forecasting in urban and regional planning; a report to the Planning Committee of the S[ocial] S[cience] R[esearch] C[ouncil];...with the assistance of Malcolm Longair and Stephen Grigson. London, Social Science Research Council, [1975]. pp. 94. *bibliog.*

HOUGHTON-EVANS (WILLIAM) Planning cities: legacy and portent. London, [1975]. pp. 203.

RODWIN (LLOYD) The educational perspective of regional science and urban studies. Reading, 1975. pp. 18. *(Reading. University. Department of Geography. Reading Geographical Papers. No.38)*

SMITH (WALLACE FRANCIS) Urban development: the process and the problems. Berkeley, Calif., [1975]. pp. 381. *bibliogs.*

The USE of action research in developing urban planning policy; report of residential colloquium organised by the Department of the Environment...at the School for Advanced Urban Studies, University of Bristol, from 24 to 27 June 1975. London, Department of the Environment, [1975]. pp. 127.

APGAR (MAHLON) ed. New perspectives on community development. London, [1976]. pp. 363.

CURRIE (LAUCHLIN BERNARD) Taming the megalopolis: a design for urban growth. Oxford, 1976. pp. 127.

GREENBIE (BARRIE B.) Design for diversity: planning for natural man in the neo-technic environment: an ethological approach. Amsterdam, 1976. pp. 209. *bibliog.*

TAFURI (MANFREDO) Architecture and utopia: design and capitalist development;... translated from the Italian by Barbara Luigia La Penta. Cambridge, Mass., [1976]. pp. 184.

THORNS (DAVID C.) The quest for community: social aspects of residential growth. London, 1976. pp. 164.

WARD (BARBARA) Baroness Jackson. The home of man. London, 1976. pp. 297.

— — Evaluation — Computer programs.

See also PERP (COMPUTER PROGRAM).

— — Mathematical models.

STEISS (ALAN WALTER) Models for the analysis and planning of urban systems. Lexington, Mass., [1974]. pp. 352.

— Statistics.

INTERNATIONAL INSTITUTE OF STATISTICS. Statistique internationale des grandes villes...1931. [2nd ed.] La Haye, 1931. pp. 708.

INTERNATIONAL INSTITUTE OF STATISTICS. International Statistics of Large Towns. Statistique du tourisme dans les grandes villes, 1929-1934. La Haye, 1938. pp. 89.

INTERNATIONAL INSTITUTE OF STATISTICS. International Statistics of Large Towns. Statistique de l'électricité, du gaz et de l'eau dans les grandes villes, 1934. La Haye, 1939. pp. 97.

INTERNATIONAL INSTITUTE OF STATISTICS. International Statistics of Large Towns. Territoire et population des grandes villes, 1928-1934. La Haye, 1939. pp. 300.

INTERNATIONAL INSTITUTE OF STATISTICS. International Statistics of Large Towns. Statistique du logement dans les grandes villes, 1928-1934. La Haye, 1940. pp. 170.

— Study and teaching.

RODWIN (LLOYD) The educational perspective of regional science and urban studies. Reading, 1975. pp. 18. *(Reading. University. Department of Geography. Reading Geographical Papers. No.38)*

— Africa, East — Growth.

HUTTON (JOHN) ed. Urban challenge in East Africa. Nairobi, 1972. pp. 285.

— Africa, North — — Growth.

VILLES et sociétés au Maghreb: études sur l'urbanisation; par R. Duchac [and others]. Paris, 1974. pp. 233.

— America, Latin.

HARDOY (JORGE) ed. Urbanization in Latin America: approaches and issues. Garden City, N.Y., 1975. pp. 456.

PORTES (ALEJANDRO) and WALTON (JOHN) Urban Latin America: the political condition from above and below. Austin, Texas, [1976]. pp. 217. *bibliog.*

— — Planning.

CASTELLS (MANUEL) ed. Estructura de clases y politica urbana en America Latina. Buenos Aires, 1974. pp. 286.

— America, North.

YEATES (MAURICE H.) and GARNER (BARRY J.) The north American city. New York, [1971]. pp. 536. *bibliog.*

— Asia — Growth.

UNITED NATIONS. Economic and Social Commission for Asia and the Pacific. Asian Population Studies Series. New York, 1966 in progress.

— Australia — Planning.

STILWELL (FRANK J.B.) Australian urban and regional development. Sydney, [1974]. pp. 206.

SANDERCOCK (LEONIE) Cities for sale: property, politics and urban planning in Australia. London, 1976. pp. 260. *bibliog.*

— — New South Wales — Planning.

NEW SOUTH WALES. State Planning Authority. 1972. Planning control of residential development. [Sydney], 1972. pp. 47. *bibliog.*

— Bessarabia — Growth.

ZHUKOV (VIKTOR IL'ICH) Goroda Bessarabii, 1861-1900 gg.: ocherki sotsial'no- ekonomicheskogo razvitiia; otvetstvennyi redaktor...Ia.S. Grosul. Kishinev, 1975. pp. 291.

CITIES AND TOWNS.(Cont.)

— Canada.

BUNGE (WILLIAM WHEELER) and BORDESSA (RON) The Canadian alternative: survival, expeditions and urban change. Toronto, 1975. pp. 432. *bibliog.* (York University (Toronto). Department of Geography. Geographical Monographs. No.2)

PIERCE (JOHN TISDALE) Urban growth in Canada: a study of land conversion, 1966-1971. 1976. fo. 332. *bibliog.* Typescript. *Ph.D. (London) thesis: unpublished. This thesis is the property of London University and may not be removed from the Library.*

— — Ontario — Planning.

ONTARIO PLANNING SEMINAR, TORONTO, 1970. Ontario planning seminar, 1970, for senior municipal planners: process, model, data; papers and proceedings. Toronto, Queen's Printer, [1971]. 1 vol. (various pagings).

— China.

The CHINESE city between two worlds; [including papers presented at a conference held in St. Croix, Virgin Islands, 1968-69]; edited by Mark Elvin and G. William Skinner. Stanford, 1974. pp. 458. *(American Council of Learned Societies and Social Science Research Council. Joint Committee on Contemporary China. Subcommittee on Research n Chinese Society. Studies in Chinese Society)*

— Communist countries.

POLSKA AKADEMIA NAUK. Komitet Przestrzennego Zagospodarowania Kraju. Studia. t.51. Metodologiia izucheniia natsional'nogo dokhoda i gorodskikh aglomeratsii v sotsialisticheskikh stranakh: materialy III Soveshchaniia predstavitelei nauchnykh uchrezhdenii sotsialisticheskikh stran-chlenov SEV po voprosam metodologii regional'nykh issledovanii, Varshava, 4-8 dekabria 1974 g. Varshava, 1975. pp. 270.

— Denmark.

SVALASTOGA (KAARE) Where Europeans meet: a sociological investigation of a bordertown. Copenhagen, 1960. fo. 144. *Lacking section 7, Documents.*

— France.

PHOTOGRAPHIE aérienne et urbanisme. [Paris, 1969]. pp. 244. *bibliog.*

— — Growth.

POTTIER (CLAUDE) La logique du financement public de l'urbanisation. Paris, [1975]. pp. 280. *bibliog.*

— — Planning.

FRANCE. Direction de la Documentation. La Documentation Française. Notes et Etudes Documentaires. No. 3,633. Aménagement du territoire. (1). Métropoles d'équilibre et aires métropolitaines: introduction; par Michel Colot. Paris, 1969. pp. 14.

BUREAU D'ETUDES TECHNIQUES DE L'URBANISME ET DE L'EQUIPEMENT. Grandes surfaces commerciales périphériques: éléments d'information pour les responsables de l'aménagement urbain, septembre 1974; [by A. Fournie and others]. Paris, 1975. pp. 139.

SOCIETE D'ETUDES PROSPECTIVE ET AMENAGEMENT. Schéma général d'aménagement de la France: dynamique urbaine et projet régional: un exemple: la région Alsace; (réalisée sous la direction d'Augustin Antunes. Paris, 1975. pp. 141. *(France. Délégation à l'Aménagement du Territoire et à l'Action Régionale. Travaux et Recherches de Prospective. 56)*

ULLMO (YVES) La planification en France. Paris, 1974 [or rather 1975]. pp. 625. *(Fondation Nationale des Sciences Politiques. Etudes Politiques, Economiques et Sociales)*

— — — Finance.

POTTIER (CLAUDE) La logique du financement public de l'urbanisation. Paris, [1975]. pp. 280. *bibliog.*

— Germany.

TOEPFER (BERNHARD) ed. Stadt und Städtebürgertum in der deutschen Geschichte des 13. Jahrhunderts; im Auftrage des Zentralinstituts für Geschichte an der Akademie der Wissenschaften der DDR, etc. Berlin, 1976. pp. 413.

— — Growth.

GIESBRECHT (ARNO) Die Bauproduktion als Determinante der Stadtentwicklung in der BRD. Hamburg, 1975. pp. 283. *bibliog. Dissertation zur Erlangung des Grades eines Doktors der Wirtschafts- und Sozialwissenschaften der Universität Hamburg.*

HEUER (HANS) Urban economist. Sozioökonomische Bestimmungsfaktoren der Stadtentwicklung. Stuttgart, [1975]. pp. 491. *bibliog.* (Deutsches Institut für Urbanistik. Schriften. Band 50)

— — Saarland.

SAARGEBIET. Statistisches Amt. Einzelschriften zur Statistik des Saarlandes. Nr. 41. Gemeindestatistik 1970: weitere Strukturdaten. Saarbrücken, 1974. pp. 72.

— Ireland (Republic) — Planning.

SHAFFREY (PATRICK) The Irish town: an approach to survival. Dublin, 1975. pp. 192. *bibliog.*

— Italy.

KONFERENTSIIA SOVETSKIKH I ITAL'IANSKIKH ISTORIKOV, 4-aia, RIM, 1969. Rossiia i Italiia: materialy IV Konferentsii sovetskikh i ital'ianskikh istorikov, Rim, 1969; Russkii i ital'ianskii srednevekovyi gorod; Russko-ital'ianskie otnosheniia v 1900- 1914 gg. Moskva, 1972. pp. 477.

— Japan.

KORNHAUSER (DAVID HENRY) Urban Japan: its foundations and growth. London, 1976. pp. 180. *bibliog.*

— Mexico — Growth.

UGALDE (ANTONIO) The urbanization process of a poor Mexican neighbourhood. Austin, 1974. pp. 68. *bibliog.* (Texas University. Institute of Latin American Studies. Special Publications)

— Netherlands — Planning.

MEURS (P.K. VAN) Bestuurlijke kanten van de ruimtelijke ordening in Nederland. 's-Gravenhage, 1965 repr. 1975. pp. 220. *bibliog.*

RAAD VOOR HET MIDDEN- EN KLEINBEDRIJF. Interimrapport: de gevolgen van stadsvernieuwing voor het midden- en kleinbedrijf: een overzicht van zich voordoende knelpunten. 's-Gravenhage, 1974. pp. 40. *([Publikaties]. 1974, no. 1)*

SAAL (C.D.) ed. Woonnood [equals] welzijnsnood. Alphen aan den Rijn, 1975. pp. 154. *bibliogs.*

RAAD VOOR HET MIDDEN- EN KLEINBEDRIJF. Rapport: de participatie van het midden- en kleinbedrijf in het stadsvernieuwingsproces. 's-Gravenhage, 1976. pp. 26. *bibliog. ([Publikaties]. 1976, no.1)*

— New Zealand — Planning.

ENVIRONMENTAL COUNCIL [NEW ZEALAND]. 1975. Urban objectives programme; provisional report. [Wellington], 1975. pp. 36.

— Nigeria — Planning.

AJAEGBU (H.I.) Urban and rural development in Nigeria. London, 1976. pp. 112. *bibliogs.*

— Norway.

RIDENG (ARNE KJELL) Klassifering av kommunene i Norge, 1974...: classification of the municipalities of Norway, 1974. Oslo, 1974. pp. 56. *bibliog.* (Norway. Statistiske Centralbyrå. Artikler. Nr. 67) *With English summary. Map in end pocket.*

— Poland.

BUCZEK (KAROL) Targi i miasta na prawie polskim: okres wczesnośredniowieczny. Wrocław, 1964. pp. 140. *(Polska Akademia Nauk. Oddział w Krakowie. Komisja Nauk Historycznych. Prace. Nr.11) With Russian and French tables of contents.*

DUMAŁA (KRZYSZTOF) Przemiany przestrzenne miast i rozwój osiedli przemysłowych w Królestwie Polskim w latach 1831-1869. Wrocław, 1974. pp. 411. *bibliog. With French summary.*

— — Growth.

RAKOWSKI (WITOLD) Procesy urbanizacji wsi: na przykładzie Woj. Warszawskiego. Warszawa, 1975. pp. 142. *(Polska Akademia Nauk. Komitet Przestrzennego Zagospodarowania Kraju. Studia. t.50) With Russian and English summaries.*

CZY'ZEWSKI (ANDRZEJ) Miasta Wielkopolskie w Polsce Ludowej: ekonomiczno- demograficzne podstawy rozwoju w okresie 1946-1970; the Wielkopolska towns in People's Poland: economic and demographic bases of development during 1946-1970. Poznań, 1976. pp. 151. *bibliog.* (Poznań. Poznańskie Towarzystwo Przyjaciół Nauk. Wydział Historii i Nauk Społecznych, Badania z Dziejów Społecznych i Gospodarczych. nr.52) *With English summary.*

— Russia.

KONFERENTSIIA SOVETSKIKH I ITAL'IANSKIKH ISTORIKOV, 4-aia, RIM, 1969. Rossiia i Italia: materialy IV Konferentsii sovetskikh i ital'ianskikh istorikov, Rim, 1969; Russkii i ital'ianskii srednevekovyi gorod; Russko-ital'ianskie otnosheniia v 1900- 1914 gg. Moskva, 1972. pp. 477.

NESTERENKO (ALEKSEI ALEKSEEVICH) Zakonomernosti sotsial'no-ekonomicheskogo razvitiia goroda i derevni. Kiev, 1975. pp. 311.

STEPIN (ANATOLII PETROVICH) Sotsialisticheskoe preobrazovanie obshchestvennykh otnoshenii gorodskikh srednikh sloev. Moskva, 1975. pp. 235.

DAVIDOW (MIKE) Cities without crisis. New York, [1976]. pp. 240.

HAMM (MICHAEL F.) ed. The city in Russian history. Lexington, Ky., [1976]. pp. 350. *bibliog.*

KRUT'KO (NIKOLAI GRIGOR'EVICH) and KVOCHKIN (M.P.) eds. Sblizhenie goroda i derevni v protsesse stroitel'stva sotsializma i kommunizma: tematicheskii sbornik. Minsk, 1976. pp. 176.

ROZMAN (GILBERT) Urban networks in Russia, 1750-1800, and premodern periodization. Princeton, [1976]. pp. 337. *bibliog.*

— — Growth.

FEDOR (THOMAS STANLEY) Patterns of urban growth in the Russian Empire during the nineteenth century. Chicago, 1975. pp. 245. *bibliog.* (Chicago. University. Department of Geography. Research Papers. No. 163) *With Russian summary.*

KHOREV (BORIS SERGEEVICH) Problemy gorodov: urbanizatsiia i edinaia sistema rasseleniia v SSSR. 2nd ed. Moskva, 1975. pp. 429. *1st ed. has subtitle: ekonomiko-geograficheskoe issledovanie gorodskogo rasseleniia v SSSR.*

— — Planning.

BARKHIN (MIKHAIL GRIGOR'EVICH) Gorod, 1945-1970: praktika, proekty, teoriia. Moskva, 1974. pp. 208. *bibliog.*

— — White Russia.

GRITSKEVICH (ANATOLII PETROVICH) Chastnovladel'cheskie goroda Belorussii v XVI-XVIII vv.: sotsial'no-ekonomicheskoe issledovanie istorii gorodov. Minsk, 1975. pp. 248.

KOPYSSKII (ZINOVII IUL'EVICH) Sotsial'no-politicheskoe razvitie gorodov Belorussii v XVI - pervoi polovine XVII v. Minsk, 1975. pp. 191.

CITIES AND TOWNS.(Cont.)

— Singapore — Planning.

SINGAPORE. Urban Redevelopment Authority. Annual report. a., 1974/75- Singapore.

— South Africa — Planning.

SOUTH AFRICA. Department of Planning and the Environment. 1975. National physical development plan. [Pretoria], 1975. pp. 54, 1 map.

— Sweden — Planning.

ÅHRÉN (PER) Ekonomiska utvärderingsmetoder i samhällsplanering. Stockholm, [1975]. pp. 142. *bibliog. Akademisk avhandling, ekonomie doktorsexamen, Handelshögskolan i Stockholm; with English summary.*

— Underdeveloped areas.

See UNDERDEVELOPED AREAS — Cities and towns.

— United Kingdom.

U.K. Regional Plans Directorate. National Framework Division. 1973. De facto urban areas in England and Wales, 1966. [London, 1973?] repr. 1974. 2 pts. *Map in end pocket.*

CONFERENCE ON ROMANO-BRITISH CANTONAL CAPITALS, LEICESTER UNIVERSITY, 1963. The civitas capitals of Roman Britain: papers given at a conference [organised by the Department of Adult Education]. ..University of Leicester...; edited by J.S. Wacher. Leicester, 1975. pp. 128. *bibliog.*

U.K. Department of the Environment. 1975. Study of the inner areas of conurbations. [London], 1975. 2 vols.

COX (W. HARVEY) Cities: the public dimension. Harmondsworth, 1976. pp. 244.

LONDON. University. London School of Economics and Political Science. Department of Geography. British cities: urban population and employment trends 1951-71; (Part 1 of the final report of a study of Urban change in Britain, 1951-71, undertaken...on behalf of the Urban Affairs and Commercial Property Directorate of the Department of the Environment). [London, 1976]. pp. 69. *(U.K. Department of the Environment. Research Reports. 10)*

MELLER (HELEN E.) Leisure and the changing city, 1870-1914. London, 1976. pp. 308. *bibliog.*

— — Growth.

LEMON (ANTHONY) Postwar industrial growth in East Anglian small towns: a study of migrant firms, 1945-1970. Oxford, 1975. pp. 40. *bibliog. (Oxford. University. School of Geography. Research Papers. No. 12)*

— — Planning.

CAULFIELD (IAN) Urban renewal, densities, infilling and the location of future housing capacity in South Hampshire. [Winchester], 1970. pp. 19. *(South Hampshire Plan Technical Unit. Working Papers. 7)*

HEALTH services in new towns; report of Working Group II: planning health services in new communities: the technical problems; [P.A. Draper, chairman]. [London, Department of Health and Social Security, 1972?]. pp. 47. *bibliog.*

U.K. Department of the Environment. Miscellaneous local government and planning statistics. a., 1973- London.

U.K. Department of the Environment. Development control statistics. a., 1974/75 (1st)- London. *Supersedes U.K. Department of the Environment. Miscellaneous local government and planning statistics, and U.K. Department of the Environment. Statistics for town and country planning, series 1: Planning decisions.*

DENMAN (DONALD ROBERT) Prospects of cooperative planning. Berkhamsted, [1974]. pp. 27. *(Warburton Lectures. 1973)*

LANGLEY (P.E.) Methods of defining and assessing the importance of structure plan objectives. London, Department of the Environment, 1974. fo. 18. *bibliog. (Planning Techniques Papers. 74/2)*

AMBROSE (PETER JOHN) and COLENUTT (ROBERT J.) The property machine. Harmondsworth, 1975. pp. 192. *bibliog.*

HARLOE (MICHAEL) Swindon: a town in transition: a study in urban development and overspill policy. London, 1975. pp. 290.

LICHFIELD (NATHANIEL) and others. Evaluation in the planning process. Oxford, 1975. pp. 325. *bibliog.*

PLANNING and the historic environment: papers presented to a conference in Oxford, 1975; edited by Trevor Rowley and Mike Breakell. Oxford, 1975. pp. 127.

SOARES (MARIA CÂNDIDA MEDEIROS) Alguns aspectos do planeamento regional em Inglaterra: (a experiência das cidades novas). Lisboa, 1975. pp. 79. *(Portugal. Ministerio do Trabalho. Gabinete de Planeamento. Serie Estudos. 29)*

DEVELOPMENT CONTROL POLICY NOTES. 7. Preservation of historic buildings and areas. [rev. ed.] London, H.M.S.O., 1976. pp. (2). *bibliog.*

LEVIN (PETER H.) Government and the planning process: an analysis and appraisal of government decision-making processes with special reference to the launching of new towns and town development schemes. London, 1976. pp. 337.

U.K. Department of the Environment. 1976. The community land scheme. (Booklet) 2. Planning applications and permissions for relevant development. [London, 1976]. pp. 14.

U.K. Welsh Office. 1976. The Dobry report: action by local planning authorities. Cardiff, 1976. pp. (5). *(Circulars. 11/76)*

WOOD (CHRISTOPHER) Town planning and pollution control. Manchester, [1976]. pp. 239. *bibliogs.*

— — — Bibliography.

JOHNSTONE (PAMELA) compiler. Planning controls and planning appeals 1972-75; a select list of references with particular emphasis on the "Review of the Development Control System", [Chairman: George Dobry, Q.C.]. London, 1975. pp. 26. *(U.K. Department of the Environment. Library. Bibliographies. No. 191)*

— — Ireland, Northern — Planning.

SHAFFREY (PATRICK) The Irish town: an approach to survival. Dublin, 1975. pp. 192. *bibliog.*

— — Scotland — Planning.

SCOTLAND. Scottish Development Department. Planning and development in Scotland. a., 1973/74- Edinburgh.

— United States.

CONFERENCE ON PUBLIC POLICY FOR URBAN MINORITIES AND THE POOR IN THE 1970S, NASHVILLE, 1972. The urban scene in the seventies: (proceedings...); edited by James F. Blumstein and Eddie J. Martin. Nashville, 1974. pp. 256. *bibliogs. Proceedings of a conference sponsored by the Urban Affairs Institute of Fisk University and the Urban and Regional Development Center of Vanderbilt University.*

HAUGE (GABRIEL) The quality of citizenship. New York, [1975]. pp. 13.

LINEBERRY (ROBERT L.) and MASOTTI (LOUIS H.) eds. Urban problems and public policy. Lexington, Mass. [1975]. pp. 206. *(Reprinted from Policy Studies Journal, 1975)*

URBAN problems and public policy choices; (edited by Joel Bergsman [and] Howard L. Wiener). New York, 1975. pp. 337. *Papers of a conference held in Washington, 1973, sponsored by the Washington Operations Research Council and the Urban Institute.*

CAPUTO (DAVID A.) Urban America: the policy alternatives. San Francisco, [1976]. pp. 235.

WATSON (JAMES WREFORD) and O'RIORDAN (TIMOTHY) eds. The American environment: perceptions and policies. London, [1976]. pp. 340. *bibliogs.*

— — Growth.

LAMB (RICHARD) 1943- . Metropolitan impacts of rural America. Chicago, 1975. pp. 196. *bibliog. (Chicago. University. Department of Geography. Research Papers. No. 162)*

OTTENSMANN (JOHN R.) The changing spatial structure of American cities. Lexington, Mass., [1975]. pp. 207.

RUST (EDGAR) No growth: impacts on metropolitan areas. Lexington, Mass., [1975]. pp. 241. *bibliog.*

SPEARE (ALDEN) and others. Residential mobility, migration, and metropolitan change. Cambridge, Mass., [1975]. pp. 313. *bibliog.*

URBAN growth management through development timing; [by] David J. Brower [and others]. New York, 1976. pp. 153.

— — Planning.

CONFERENCE ON PUBLIC POLICY FOR URBAN MINORITIES AND THE POOR IN THE 1970S, NASHVILLE, 1972. The urban scene in the seventies: (proceedings...); edited by James F. Blumstein and Eddie J. Martin. Nashville, 1974. pp. 256. *bibliogs. Proceedings of a conference sponsored by the Urban Affairs Institute of Fisk University and the Urban and Regional Development Center of Vanderbilt University.*

BOLAN (RICHARD S.) and NUTTALL (RONALD L.) Urban planning and politics. Lexington, [1975]. pp. 211. *bibliog.*

BRILLIANT (ELEANOR L.) The urban development corporation: private interests and public authority. Lexington, Mass., [1975]. pp. 256. *bibliog.*

FRIEDEN (BERNARD J.) and KAPLAN (MARSHALL) The politics of neglect: urban aid from model cities to revenue sharing. Cambridge, Mass., [1975]. pp. 281. *(Massachusetts Institute of Technology and Harvard University. Joint Center for Urban Studies. Publications)*

OTTENSMANN (JOHN R.) The changing spatial structure of American cities. Lexington, Mass., [1975]. pp. 207.

PUSHKAREV (BORIS SERGEEVICH) and ZUPAN (JEFFREY MICHAEL) Urban space for pedestrians: a report of the Regional Plan Association. Cambridge, Mass., [1975]. pp. 212. *bibliog.*

RUST (EDGAR) No growth: impacts on metropolitan areas. Lexington, Mass., [1975]. pp. 241. *bibliog.*

SCHORR (PHILIP) Planned relocation. Lexington, Mass., [1975]. pp. 227. *bibliog.*

WATTERSON (WAYT T.) and WATTERSON (ROBERTA S.) The politics of new communities: a case study of San Antonio Ranch. New York, 1975. pp. 142. *bibliog.*

WEXLER (HARRY J.) and PECK (RICHARD) Housing and local government: a research guide for policy makers and planners. Lexington, Mass., 1975. pp. 310. *bibliog.*

AWERBUCH (SHIMON) and WALLACE (WILLIAM A.) Policy evaluation for community development: decision tools for local government. New York, 1976. pp. 286. *bibliog.*

BANNON (JOSEPH J.) Leisure resources: its comprehensive planning. Englewood Cliffs, [1976]. pp. 454. *bibliogs.*

FINKLER (EARL) and others. Urban nongrowth: city planning for people. New York, 1976. pp. 227. *bibliog.*

URBAN growth management through development timing; [by] David J. Brower [and others]. New York, 1976. pp. 153.

— — Nebraska.

NEBRASKA. Legislative Council. Committee on the Problems of Local Communities. 1964. Report. [Lincoln], 1964. fo. 13. *(Legislative Council. Committee Reports. No. 137)*

CITIZENS' ADVICE BUREAUX.

ADVICE services in welfare rights; editor, Rosalind Brooke; [by] Paul Burgess [and others]. London, 1976. pp. 36. *(Fabian Society. Research Series. [No.] 329)*

CITIZENSHIP.

BURLET (JACQUES DE) Nationalité des personnes physiques et décolonisation: essai de contribution à la théorie de la succession d'Etats. Bruxelles, 1975. pp. 223. *bibliog. (Louvain. Université. Faculté de Droit. Bibliothèque. 10)*

MITCHISON (NAOMI MARGARET) Sittlichkeit. London, [1975]. pp. 19. *(London. University. Birkbeck College. Haldane Memorial Lectures. 38)*

— Botswana.

WILL (D.D.) The citizenship, immigration, and allied laws of Botswana. [Gaborone, Government of Botswana, 1972]. pp. 19.

— Canada.

CANADA. Statutes, etc. 1952-68. Canadian Citizenship Act, R.S.C., 1952, c. 33, as amended by 1952-53, c. 23, [etc.]; and the Regulations, established by P. C. 1968-1703: (office consolidation). Ottawa, 1969. pp. 35.

— France.

FRANCE. Direction de la Documentation. La Documentation Française. Notes et Etudes Documentaires. No. 4,115. La réforme du droit de la nationalité, loi du 9 janvier, 1973; [par Paule Ascencio]. Paris, 1974. pp. 46. *bibliog.*

LAGARDE (PAUL) La nationalité française. Paris, 1975. pp. 454.

— Germany.

GERMANY (BUNDESREPUBLIK). Statistisches Bundesamt. Staatsangehörigkeit. a., 1970- Wiesbaden. *(Bevölkerung und Kultur. Reihe 1.5)* Supersedes in part GERMANY (BUNDESREPUBLIK). Statistisches Bundesamt. Bevölkerungsstand und -entwicklung.

— Nigeria.

NIGERIA. 1974. Nigerian citizenship. [Lagos, 1974]. pp. 10.

— United Kingdom.

CITIZENSHIP in Britain 1974:...conference deal[ing] especially with Pakistanis and...organised by the (Birmingham) Community Development Project. [Birmingham, Birmingham Community Development Project, 1974]. pp. 28. *Photocopy.*

SOCIETY OF CONSERVATIVE LAWYERS. Towards a new citizenship: a report on British nationality by a Committee of the Society of Conservative Lawyers; members: David Hirst [and others]. London, 1975. pp. 26. *(Conservative Political Centre. [Publications]. No. 566)*

— United States.

HAUGE (GABRIEL) The quality of citizenship. New York, [1975]. pp. 13.

CITY MISSIONS

— America, Latin.

GREENWAY (ROGER S.) An urban strategy for Latin America. Grand Rapids, [1973]. pp. 282. *bibliog.*

CITY NOISE

— Bibliography.

GOMERSALL (ALAN) compiler. Community noise. [London], 1975. pp. 19. *(London. Greater London Council. Research Library. [Research] Bibliographies. No. 67)*

CITY PLANNING AND REDEVELOPMENT LAW

— Europe.

GARNER (JOHN FRANCIS) ed. Planning law in Western Europe. Amsterdam, 1975. pp. 353. *bibliog.*

— United Kingdom.

HEAP (Sir DESMOND) The land and the development; or, The turmoil and the torment. London, 1975. pp. 97. *(Hamlyn Lectures. 27th Series)*

NEWMAN (PHYLLIS E.) Town and country planning casebook. London, 1975. pp. 382. *bibliog.*

ENCYCLOPEDIA of planning law and practice: land development series; [edited by] Desmond Heap [and others]. London, 1976 in progress. *Loose leaf.*

CORFIELD (Sir FREDERICK VERNON) A guide to the Community Land Act. London, 1976. pp. 191[19].

MOORE (VICTOR) Community land: the new Act; a guide to the Community Land Act, 1975. London, 1976. pp. 145.

ROBERTS (NEAL ALISON) The reform of planning law: a study of the legal, political and administrative reform of the British land-use planning system. London, 1976. pp. 305. *bibliog.*

— United States.

McDOUGAL (MYRES SMITH) and HABER (DAVID) Property, wealth, land: allocation, planning and development; selected cases and other materials on the law of real property; an introduction. Charlottesville, Va., 1948. pp. 1213.

CITY TRAFFIC

— Environmental aspects — United Kingdom.

U.K. Department of the Environment. 1975. Road traffic and the environment: summary report of a survey carried out by Social and Community Planning Research. [London, 1975?]. 1 vol. (various pagings).

CIUDAD JUAREZ

— Poor.

UGALDE (ANTONIO) The urbanization process of a poor Mexican neighbourhood. Austin, 1974. pp. 68. *bibliog.* ¶*Texas University. Institute of Latin American Studies. Special Publications)*

CIVICS, EAST AFRICAN.

PREWITT (KENNETH) ed. Education and political values: an East African case study. Nairobi, 1971. pp. 249.

CIVICS, GERMAN.

GIESECKE (HERMANN) and others. Gesellschaft und Politik in der Bundesrepublik: eine sozialkunde. Frankfurt am Main, 1976. pp. 335.

CIVIL ENGINEERING

— France.

FRANCE. Comité du Bâtiment et des Travaux Publics. 1976. Rapport...: préparation du 7e Plan. Paris, 1976. pp. 234.

CIVIL ENGINEERS

— Hong Kong.

HONG KONG. Building Trades Industrial Committee. 1970. Report...on the manpower survey of the building and civil engineering industry conducted during 12th-14th August, 1968. Hong Kong, 1969 [or rather 1970]. pp. 111. *In English and Chinese.*

HONG KONG. Building Trades Industrial Committee. 1972. Minimum job standards and specifications for the principal jobs in the building and civil engineering industry. Hong Kong, 1971 [or rather 1972]. pp. 73. *In English and Chinese.*

CIVIL LAW.

RENNER (KARL) The institutions of private law and their social functions; edited with an introduction and notes, by O. Kahn-Freund; translated by Agnes Schwarzschild. London, 1949 repr. 1976. pp. 307.

— International unification.

INTERNATIONAL ASSOCIATION OF LAW LIBRARIES. Courses in Law Librarianship, 4th, 1972. The unification of private law and law and legal literature in Italy. Marburg, 1974. pp. 120. *bibliog.*

— France.

MAZEAUD (HENRI) and others. Leçons de droit civil; [edited by] Michel de Juglart. Paris, 1969-74. 4 tomes (in 9 vols.). Tome 1, vols. 1-3, and Tome 2, vol. 1, are of the 5th edition; Tome 2, vol.2, and Tome 3, vols. 1-2, are of the 4th edition; Tome 4, vol.1, is of the 3rd edition and Tome 4, vol. 2, is of the 2nd edition.

DALLIGNY (SUZANNE) Essai sur les principes d'un droit civil socialiste. Paris, 1976. pp. 428.

— Poland.

POLAND. Statutes, etc. 1964. Kodeks cywilny oraz przepisy wprowadzające. Warszawa, 1964. pp. 268.

LEIDEN. Rijks Universiteit. Documentation Office for East European Law. Law in Eastern Europe. No. 18. Polish civil law; edited by D. Lasok. Leyden, 1973-75. 4 vols.

— Russia.

PROKURORSKII nadzor po grazhdanskim delam. 2nd ed. Moskva, 1975. pp. 352.

— — Turkmenistan.

MAMEDOVA (OVADAN DURDYEVNA) Grazhdanskii kodeks Turkmenskoi SSR; pod nauchnoi redaktsiei... A.I. Igdyrova. Ashkhabad, 1975. pp. 96.

CIVIL PROCEDURE

— Europe, Eastern.

TRÓCSÁNYI (LÁSZLO) Le droit de procédure en matière de conflits du travail dans les pays socialistes européens; (traduit par Béla Végh). Budapest, 1974. pp. 147.

— France.

FRANCE. Statutes, etc. 1975. Nouveau code de procédure civile. Paris, 1975. pp. 88.

— Poland.

POLAND. Statutes, etc. 1974. Kodeks postępowania cywilnego, z przepisami wykonawczymi i szczególnymi; według stanu prawnego na dzień 1.I.1974 r. 4th ed. Warszawa, 1974. pp. 896.

— Russia.

GRAZHDANSKO-pravovoe polozhenie lichnosti v SSSR. Moskva, 1975. pp. 399.

CIVIL RIGHTS.

EUROPEAN COMMISSION OF HUMAN RIGHTS. 1971. Human rights in prison. Strasbourg, 1971. pp. 46. *(Case-Law Topics. 1).*

PARLIAMENTARY CONFERENCE ON HUMAN RIGHTS, VIENNA, 1971. Parliamentary Conference...[held in] Vienna, 18-20 October 1971. Strasbourg, Council of Europe, 1972. pp. 138.

VEENHOVEN (WILLEM ADRIAAN) and others, eds. Case studies on human rights and fundamental freedoms: a world survey. The Hague, 1975 in progress.

VOGT (HERMANN) ed. Die Wiedergewinnung des Humanen: Beiträge zur gesellschaftlichen Relevanz der Menschenrechte. Stuttgart, [1975]. pp. 243.

CLAUDE (RICHARD P.) ed. Comparative human rights. Baltimore, [1976]. pp. 410.

KLIEMAN (AARON S.) Emergency politics: the growth of crisis government. London, 1976. pp. 19. (Institute for the Study of Conflict. Conflict Studies. No. 70)

— America, Latin.

RUSSELL TRIBUNAL II ON REPRESSION IN BRAZIL, CHILE AND LATIN AMERICA. Repression in Latin America: a report on the first session of the second Russell Tribunal, Rome, April 1974; edited and translated by William Jerman. Nottingham, 1975. pp. 163.

— Austria.

EUROPEAN COURT OF HUMAN RIGHTS. Publications. Series A: Judgments and Decisions. [A 13]. ...Ringeisen case; judgment of 16th July 1971. Strasbourg, Council of Europe, 1971. pp. 56 [bis]. *In English and French.*

EUROPEAN COURT OF HUMAN RIGHTS. Publications. Series A: Judgments and Decisions. [A] 15. ...Ringeisen case: judgment of 22 June /([''; QUESTION OF THE APPLICATION OF aRTICLE 5: OF THE cONVENTION. sTRASBOURG, cOUNCIL of eUROPE, 1972. PP. 12 ?BIS!. iN eNGLISH AND fRENCH.

EUROPEAN COURT OF HUMAN RIGHTS. Publications. Series B: Pleadings, Oral Arguments and Documents. [B11]. "Ringeisen" case, (1970-1971). Strasbourg, Council of Europe, 1972. pp. 299 [bis], 301-371. *In English and French.*

EUROPEAN COURT OF HUMAN RIGHTS. Publications. Series A: Judgments and Decisions. [A] 16. ...Ringeisen case: interpretation of the judgment of 22 June 1972; judgment of 23 June 1973. Strasbourg, Council of Europe, 1973. pp. 13 [bis]. *In English and French.*

EUROPEAN COURT OF HUMAN RIGHTS. Publications. Series B: Pleadings, Oral Arguments and Documents. [B13]. "Ringeisen" case: question of the application of Article 50 of the Convention, (1971-1972). Strasbourg, Council of Europe, 1973. pp. 89 [bis], 91-119. *In English and French.*

EUROPEAN COURT OF HUMAN RIGHTS. Publications. Series B: Pleadings, Oral Arguments and Documents. [B14]. "Ringeisen" case: interpretation of the judgment of 22nd June 1972, (1972-1973). Strasbourg, Council of Europe, 1973. pp. 42 [bis], 43-58. *In English and French.*

— Belgium.

EUROPEAN COURT OF HUMAN RIGHTS. Publications. Series A: Judgments ad Decisions. A 4. ..."De Becker" case; judgment of 27th March 1962. Strasbourg, Council of Europe, 1962. pp. 33[bis]. *In English and French.*

EUROPEAN COURT OF HUMAN RIGHTS. Publications. Series A: Judgments and Decisions. [A11]. ..."Delcourt" case; judgment of 17th January 1970. Strasbourg, Council of Europe, 1970. pp. 21 [bis].

EUROPEAN COURT OF HUMAN RIGHTS. Publications. Series B: Pleadings, Oral Arguments and Documents. [B9]. "Delcourt" case, (1969-1970). Strasbourg, Council of Europe, 1970. pp. 249 [bis], 251-287. *In English and French.*

EUROPEAN COURT OF HUMAN RIGHTS. Publications. Series A: Judgments and Decisions. [A12]. ...De Wilde, Ooms and Versyp cases; "vagrancy" cases. 1. Decision of 28th May 1970. 2. Judgment of 18th November 1970; question of procedure. 3. Judgment of 18th June 1971. Strasbourg, Council of Europe, 1971. pp. 75 [bis].

EUROPEAN COURT OF HUMAN RIGHTS. Publications. Series B: Pleadings, Oral Arguments and Documents.[B10]. "De Wilde, Ooms and Versyp" cases: "vagrancy" cases, 1969-1971. Strasbourg, Council of Europe, 1971. pp. 405 [bis], 407-474. *In English and French.*

EUROPEAN COURT OF HUMAN RIGHTS. Publications. Series A: Judgments and Decisions. [A] 14. ...De Wilde, Ooms and Versyp cases: "vagrancy" cases; judgment of 10 March 1972; question of the application of Article 50 of the Convention. Strasbourg, Council of Europe, 1972. pp. 22 [bis]. *In English and French.*

EUROPEAN COURT OF HUMAN RIGHTS. Publications. Series B: Pleadings, Oral Arguments and Documents. [B12]. "De Wilde, Ooms and Versyp" cases: "vagrancy" cases; question of the application of Article 50 of the Convention, (1971-1972). Strasbourg, Council of Europe, 1973. pp. 97 [bis], 99-126. *In English and French.*

— Europe.

KINSELLA (NOËL A.) The European model for the protection of human rights. [Fredericton], New Brunswick Human Rights Commission, [1971]. pp. 62.

EUROPEAN COMMISSION OF HUMAN RIGHTS. 1972. Bringing an application before the European Commission of Human Rights: (procedure and practice of the Commission). Strasbourg, 1972. pp. 41. *(Case-Law Topics. 3.)*

EUROPEAN COMMISSION OF HUMAN RIGHTS. 1973. Human rights and their limitations. Strasbourg, 1973. pp. 58. *(Case-Law Topics. 4.)*

— France.

LIVET (PIERRE) L'autorisation administrative préalable et les libertés publiques. Paris, 1974. pp. 334. *bibliog.*

ERRERA (ROGER) Les libertés à l'abandon. 3rd ed. Paris, 1975. pp. 320. *bibliog.*

— Germany.

EUROPEAN COMMISSION OF HUMAN RIGHTS. 1968. The Zeidler-Kornmann case: (Application No. 2686/65 by Heinz Zeidler-Kornmann against the Federal Republic of Germany). Strasbourg, Council of Europe, 1968. pp. 120.

SOZIALDEMOKRATISCHE PARTEI DEUTSCHLANDS. Rechtspolitischer Kongress, 4., 1975. Freiheit in der sozialen Demokratie... Dokumentation; herausgegeben von Diether Posser [and others]. Karlsruhe, 1975. pp. 338.

— Ireland (Republic).

EUROPEAN COURT OF HUMAN RIGHTS. Publications. Series A: Judgments and Decisions. [A1]. ..."Lawless" case: preliminary objections and questions of procedure, judgment of 14th November 1960. Strasbourg, Council of Europe, 1961. pp. 20 [bis]. *In English and French.*

EUROPEAN COURT OF HUMAN RIGHTS. Publications. Series A: Judgments and Decisions. [A2]. ..."Lawless" case: judgment of 7th April 1961. Stasbourg, Council of Europe, 1961. pp. 23-24 [bis]. *In English and French.*

EUROPEAN COURT OF HUMAN RIGHTS. Publications. Series A: Judgments and Decisions. [A3]. ..."Lawless" case; merits; judgment of 1st July 1961. Strasbourg, Council of Europe, 1961. pp. 27-67 [bis]. *In English and French.*

— Russia.

CHALIDZE (VALERII N.) Prava cheloveka i Sovetskii Soiuz. N'iu-Iork, 1974. pp. 304. *bibliog.*

CHALIDZE (VALERII N.) To defend these rights: human rights and the Soviet Union;... translated from the Russian by Guy Daniels. New York, [1974]. pp. 340.

GRAZHDANSKO-pravovoe polozhenie lichnosti v SSSR. Moskva, 1975. pp. 399.

— United Kingdom.

NATIONAL COUNCIL FOR CIVIL LIBERTIES. Submissions to the public enquiry...to review the events at Red Lion Square on the 15th June 1974: the Scarman enquiry. London, 1974. pp. 19.

WINSTANLEY (MICHAEL) and DUNKLEY (RUTH) Know your rights. London, [1975]. pp. 123. *bibliogs.*

LABOUR PARTY. United Kingdom charter of human rights: a discussion document for the Labour movement. London, 1976. pp. 11.

LEGISLATION on human rights, with particular reference to the European Convention: a discussion document; [report of an interdepartmental working group]. [London, Home Office, 1976]. pp. 38.

— — Ireland, Northern.

HULL (ROGER H.) The Irish triangle: conflict in Northern Ireland. Princeton, [1976]. pp. 312. *bibliog.*

— United States.

LAMONT (CORLISS) Freedom is as freedom does: civil liberties today. New York, 1956. pp. 322. *bibliog.*

PERKUS (CATHY) ed. Cointelpro: the FBI's secret war on political freedom: [based on material originally prepared for the Militant]. New York, 1975. pp. 190.

SIGLER (JAY A.) American rights policies. Homewood, Ill., 1975. pp. 316. *bibliog.*

CIVIL SERVICE.

The SETTLEMENT of collective disputes in the public services; [papers for discussion at the congress of Public Services International at Paris in 1967]; rapporteur, H.D. Hughes. London, [1967?]. 1 vol. (various pagings).

— Australia — New South Wales.

McMARTIN (SAMUEL THOMAS ARTHUR) The origin and development of the public service of New South Wales, 1788-1856. 1975 [or rather 1976]. fo. 370. *bibliog.* Typescript. Ph.D. (London) thesis: unpublished. *This thesis is the property of London University and may not be removed from the Library.*

— Botswana.

BOTSWANA. Public Service Commission. Report. a., 1970/72- Gaborone.

— Brazil.

FAORO (RAYMUNDO) Os donos do poder: formação do patronato politico brasileiro. 2nd ed. Porto Alegre, 1975 repr. 1976. 2 vols. (in 1). *Pagination continuous.*

— Canada — British Columbia.

BRITISH COLUMBIA. Public Service Commission. Annual report. a., 1974 (56th)- Victoria.

— — Manitoba.

MANITOBA. Task Force on Equal Employment Opportunities in the Civil Service of Manitoba. 1974. Report; [D.A. Duncan, chairman]. [Winnipeg], 1974. pp. 82.

— France.

FRANCE. Direction de la Documentation. La Documentation Française. Notes et Etudes Documentaires. Nos. 4,197-4, 198. Le syndicalisme dans la fonction publique; [by] Yves Saint-Jours. Paris, 1975. pp. 65. *bibliog.*

— Nigeria.

WEY (S.O.) The structure and organisation of the public services. Lagos, 1971. *bibliog.*

NIGERIA. Federal Ministry of Establishments and Service Matters. 1972. Civil service handbook. Lagos, 1972. pp. 67.

— Sierra Leone.

SIERRA LEONE. Public Service Commission. 1965. Public service legislation. [Freetown, 1965]. pp. 59.

— Switzerland.

KLOETI (ULRICH) Die Chefbeamten der schweizerischen Bundesverwaltung: soziologische Querschnitte in den Jahren 1938, 1955 und 1969. Bern, [1972]. pp. 216. *bibliog. (Bern. Universität. Forschungszentrum für Schweizerische Politik. Helvetia Politica. Series B. vol. 8)*

CIVIL SERVICE.(Cont.)

— United Kingdom.

U.K. Civil Service Department. 1974. Civil service pay and conditions of service code. London, 1974 in progress. 4 vols. (loose leaf). Superseded sections boxed and kept at same classification.

LECTURES ON RELATIONS BETWEEN THE CIVIL SERVICE AND THE PUBLIC. [London], Civil Service College, 1975.

— United States.

SHAFRITZ (JAY M.) Public personnel management: the heritage of civil service reform. New York, 1975. pp. 178. *bibliog.*

KRANZ (HARRY) The participatory bureaucracy: women and minorities in a more representative public service. Lexington, Mass., [1976]. pp. 244.

— Zambia.

DRESANG (DENNIS L.) The Zambia civil service: entrepreneurialism and development administration. Nairobi, 1975. pp. 188. *bibliog.*

CIVIL SERVICE PENSIONS

— South Africa.

SOUTH AFRICA. Parliament. House of Assembly. Select Committee on Pensions. 1976. First and second reports (S.C.4-1976). in SOUTH AFRICA. Parliament. House of Assembly. Select Committee reports.

— United Kingdom — Ireland, Northern.

IRELAND, NORTHERN. Department of Finance. Civil Service Management Division. 1975. The principal civil service pension scheme, Northern Ireland, 1975. Belfast, 1975. pp. 109.

— United States.

TILOVE (ROBERT) Public employee pension funds: a Twentieth Century Fund report. New York, 1976. pp. 370.

CIVIL SUPREMACY OVER THE MILITARY.

The MILITARY and the problem of legitimacy: edited by Gwyn Harries-Jenkins and Jacques van Doorn. London, [1976]. pp. 213. *bibliog. Papers of sessions of the Research Committee on Armed Forces and Society held during the 8th World Congress of Sociology, Toronto, 1974.*

— Asia, Southeast.

HOADLEY (J. STEPHEN) Soldiers and politics in southeast Asia: civil-military relations in comparative perspective. Cambridge, Mass., [1975]. pp. 307.

— Chile.

NUNN (FREDERICK M.) The military in Chilean history: essays on civil-military relations, 1810-1973. Albuquerque, [1976]. pp. 343. *bibliog.*

— Germany.

SCHOESSLER (DIETMAR) Der Primat des Zivilen: Konflikt und Konsens der Militärelite im politischen System der Bundesrepublik. Meisenheim am Glan, [1973]. pp. 163. *bibliog.*

HORNUNG (KLAUS) Staat und Armee: Studien zur Befehls- und Kommandogewalt und zum politisch-militärischen Verhältnis in der Bundesrepublik Deutschland. Mainz, [1975]. pp. 448. *bibliog.*

MESSERSCHMIDT (MANFRED) Militär und Politik in der Bismarckzeit und im Wilhelminischen Deutschland. Darmstadt, 1975. pp. 163. *bibliog.*

CIVIL WAR.

BENNOUNA (MOHAMED) Le consentement à l'ingérence militaire dans les conflits internes. Paris, 1974. pp. 235. *bibliog.*

CIVIL wars and the politics of international relief: Africa, South Asia, and the Caribbean; edited by Morris Davis. New York, 1975. pp. 109.

LITTLE (RICHARD) Intervention: external involvement in civil wars. London, 1975. pp. 236.

ZORGBIBE (CHARLES) La guerre civile. [Paris], 1975. pp. 208. *bibliog.*

HULL (ROGER H.) The Irish triangle: conflict in Northern Ireland. Princeton, [1976]. pp. 312. *bibliog.*

CIVILIZATION.

RODO (JOSE ENRIQUE) Motivos de Proteo; [and] Nuevos motivos de Proteo. Mexico, 1969. pp. 245.

— History.

CAMERON (KENNETH NEILL) Humanity and society: a world history. Bloomington, ind., [1973]. pp. 470. *bibliog.*

CIVILIZATION, ANCIENT.

WEBER (MAX) The agrarian sociology of ancient civilizations; translated by R. I. Frank. London, 1976. pp. 421. *bibliog.*

CIVILIZATION, MODERN.

CLARKE (ROBIN) ed. Notes for the future: an alternative history of the past decade. London, [1975]. pp. 230.

TAYLOR (GORDON RATTRAY) How to avoid the future. London, 1975. pp. 340. *bibliog.*

TOFFLER (ALVIN) The eco-spasm report. New York, 1975. pp. 116. *bibliog.*

TRIBE (DAVID) The rise of the mediocracy. London, 1975. pp. 205.

BELL (DANIEL) The cultural contradictions of capitalism. London, 1976. pp. 301.

HEILBRONER (ROBERT LOUIS) Business civilization in decline. New York, [1976]. pp. 127.

SOLZHENITSYN (ALEKSANDR ISAEVICH) Warning to the Western world. London, 1976. pp. 45. *Consists of text of interview with Michael Charlton on BBC television's Panorama, 1 March 1976, and of a BBC radio broadcast, 24 March, 1976.*

TOYNBEE (ARNOLD JOSEPH) and IKEDA (DAISEKU) The Toynbee-Ikeda dialogue: man himself must choose. Tokyo, 1976. pp. 348.

UNION OF INTERNATIONAL ASSOCIATIONS and MANKIND 2000. Year-book of world problems and human potential: a framework for representation of perceptions of interlinked networks of world problems, etc. Brussels, 1976. pp. 1136. *bibliogs.*

CIVILIZATION, ORIENTAL.

DREVNII Vostok: goroda i torgovlia, III-I tys. do n.e. Erevan, 1973. pp. 243. *With English summaries.*

CIVILIZATION, SLAVIC.

GEORGIEV (EMIL) Kiril i Metodii: istinata za suzdatelite na bulgarskata i slavianska pismenost. Sofiia, 1969. pp. 365.

CLANS AND CLAN SYSTEM.

ADAMUS (JAN) Polska teoria rodowa. Łódź, 1958. pp. 348. *bibliog. (Łódź. Łódzkie Towarzystwo Naukowe. Wydział 2 Nauk Historycznych i Społecznych. [Prace]. Nr.23) With French and Russian summaries.*

CLARK (Sir GEORGE NORMAN).

CLARK (Sir GEORGE NORMAN) [Correspondence about the publication of Agenda: a quarterly journal of reconstruction. 1941-43]. 1 folder. *Manuscript, typescript, etc.*

CLASSIFICATION, LIBRARY OF CONGRESS.

OLSON (NANCY B.) compiler. Subject keyword index to the Library of Congress classification schedules, 1974. Washington, D.C., 1974. 6 vols. *(Combined Indexes to the Library of Congress Classification Schedules, 1974. Set 5).*

CLASSROOM MANAGEMENT.

MARTIN (WILFRED B.W.) The negotiated order of the school. [Toronto, 1976]. pp. 191. *bibliog.*

CLAUSEWITZ (CARL VON).

ARON (RAYMOND) Penser la guerre, Clausewitz. [Paris, 1976]. 2 vols. (in 1). *bibliog.*

PARET (PETER) Clausewitz and the state. New York, 1976. pp. 467. *bibliog.*

CLAY

— Zambia.

MACZKA (L.) and CAP (M.) Brick clays in the Kasama area with particular reference to the Lukashya deposit. Lusaka, 1973. pp. 34. *(Zambia. Geological Survey Department. Economic Reports. No. 43) 3 maps in end pocket.*

CLAY (LAURA).

FULLER (PAUL E.) Laura Clay and the woman's rights movement. Lexington, Ky., [1975]. pp. 217. *bibliog.*

CLEATOR MOOR

— Playgrounds.

CUMBRIA COMMUNITY DEVELOPMENT PROJECT. The Big Hill adventure playground, Cleator Moor: (playleader's report for the year June 1974 to June 1975). [Cleator Moor, 1975]. pp. 7.

— Recreational facilities.

CUMBRIA COMMUNITY DEVELOPMENT PROJECT. The report of a study of the needs of young people in Cleator Moor with particular reference to their leisure time; [by] Alan Tweedie [and others]. Cleator Moor, 1973 repr. 1974. pp. 91.

CUMBRIA COMMUNITY DEVELOPMENT PROJECT. Ehenside youth wing: a case study. [Cleator Moor], 1975. 1 pamphlet (unpaged).

CLERGY

— Peru.

APARICIO VEGA (MANUEL JESUS) El clero patriota en la Revolucion de 1814. Cusco, 1974. pp. 355. *bibliog.*

— United Kingdom.

ANSON (HAROLD) Looking forward. London, [1938?]. pp. 295.

CLERKS

— Canada.

FINLEY (JOSEPH E.) White collar union: the story of the OPEIU and its people. New York, 1975. pp. 275.

— France.

MALLET (SERGE) The new working class; translated by Andrée and Bob Shepherd. Nottingham, 1975. pp. 210.

— Sweden.

WHEELER (CHRISTOPHER) White-collar power: changing patterns of interest group behavior in Sweden. Urbana, [1975]. pp. 210.

— United Kingdom.

PESCHANSKII (VALENTIN VLADIMIROVICH) Sluzhashchie v burzhuaznom obshchestve: na primere Anglii. Moskva, 1975. pp. 379.

NORTHERN REGION STRATEGY TEAM. Office activity in the northern region. Newcastle-upon-Tyne, 1976. 1 vol. (various pagings). *(Technical Reports. No.8)*

— **United States.**

FINLEY (JOSEPH E.) White collar union: the story of the OPEIU and its people. New York, 1975. pp. 275.

CLEVELAND, OHIO.

— **History.**

KUSMER (KENNETH L.) A ghetto takes shape: black Cleveland, 1870-1930. Urbana, Ill., [1976]. pp. 305. *bibliog.*

CLIMATIC GEOMORPHOLOGY.

DERBYSHIRE (EDWARD) ed. Geomorphology and climate. London, [1976]. pp. 512. *bibliogs.*

CLIMATOLOGY.

MORTON (F.I.) Evaporation and climate: a study in cause and effect. Ottawa, 1968 [or rather 1969]. pp. 32. *(Canada. Inland Waters Branch. Scientific Series. No. 4)*

SCHNEIDER (STEPHEN HENRY) The genesis strategy: climate and global survival. New York, [1976]. pp. 419.

CLIVE (ROBERT) Baron Clive.

LAWFORD (JAMES PHILIP) Clive, proconsul of India: a biography. London, 1976. pp. 432. *bibliog.*

CLOTHING TRADE

— **Germany.**

BREITENACHER (MICHAEL) Die Bekleidungsindustrie aus der Sicht der siebziger Jahre. Berlin, [1975]. pp. 170. *(Ifo-Institut für Wirtschaftsforschung. Struktur und Wachstum. Reihe Industrie. Heft 26)*

— **United Kingdom.**

STANSFIELD (RONALD G.) Flux in the factory. London, 1967. pp. 8. *(Hollenden Lectures. No. 15. 1967) (Reprinted from the Clothing Institute Journal, vol. 15, no. 3, 1967)*

INBUCON/AIC MANAGEMENT CONSULTANTS LIMITED. Investment appraisal for the clothing industry; a report prepared.. .for the Economic Development Committee for the Clothing Industry. London, H.M.S.O., 1973. pp. 80. *bibliog.*

ECONOMIC DEVELOPMENT COMMITTEE FOR THE CLOTHING INDUSTRY. Unlocking productivity potential: the experience of seven firms in the clothing industry. London, National Economic Development Office, 1975. pp. 58.

CLOTHING WORKERS

— **Hong Kong.**

HONG KONG. Clothing Industrial Committee. 1971. Report...on the manpower survey of the clothing industry, 20th-31st March, 1969. Hong Kong, 1969[or rather 1971]. pp. 126. *In English and Chinese.*

CLOWER (ROBERT W.)

CHEUNG (MICHAEL TOW) A study of the Clower-Leijonhufvud re-interpretation of the Keynesian model. 1975. fo.196. *bibliog. Typescript.* Ph.D. (London) thesis: unpublished. *This thesis is the property of London University and may not be removed from the Library.*

CLUSTER ANALYSIS.

BUSSAB (WILTON DE OLIVEIRA) Hierarchical dichotomous partitions in cluster analysis. 1976. fo. 236. *bibliog. Typescript.* Ph.D. (London) thesis: unpublished. *This thesis is the property of London University and may not be removed from the Library.*

COACHING

— **United Kingdom.**

HIBBS (JOHN ALFRED BLYTH) The bus and coach industry: its economics and organization. London, 1975. pp. 224.

COAL.

COAL AND ENERGY QUARTERLY; ([pd. by] NCB [National Coal Board, U.K.). q., summer 1974 (no.1)- London.

— **European Community countries.**

EUROPEAN COMMUNITIES. Statistical Office. Coal statistics. a., 1974- Luxembourg. *[In Community languages].*

— **South Africa.**

SOUTH AFRICA. Commission of Inquiry into the Coal Resources of the Republic. 1975. Report (R.P.63/1975). in SOUTH AFRICA. Parliament. House of Assembly. Votes and proceedings; (with Printed annexures).

— **United Kingdom.**

COAL AND ENERGY QUARTERLY; ([pd. by] NCB [National Coal Board, U.K.). q., summer 1974 (no.1)- London.

— **United States.**

GORDON (RICHARD L.) U.S. coal and the electric power industry. [Baltimore], [1975]. pp. 213. *bibliog.*

COAL MINE WASTE.

U.K. Working Party on Colliery Waste Tipping on Durham Beaches. 1975. Interim report; [R.T. Scowen, chairman]. [London], 1975. fo. 6.

COAL MINERS

— **Germany.**

ROTHERT (LIEBETRAUT) Umwelt und Arbeitsverhältnisse von Ruhrbergleuten in der 2. Hälfte des 19.Jahrhunderts; dargestellt an den Zechen Hannover und Hannibal in Bochum. Münster, Westfalen, [1976]. pp. 106. *bibliog. (Provinzialinstitut für Westfälische Landes- und Volksforschung. Veröffentlichungen. Reihe 1. Heft 20)*

— **Germany, Eastern.**

FOERSTER (FRANK) Senftenberger Revier, 1890-1914: zur Geschichte der Niederlausitzer Braunkohlenindustrie, etc. Bautzen, 1968. pp. 328. *(Deutsche Akademie der Wissenschaften zu Berlin. Institut für Sorbische Volksforschung in Bautzen. Schriftenreihe. 37)*

— **United Kingdom.**

NATIONAL UNION OF MINEWORKERS. Handbook on the wage structure of the coalmining industry. n.p., 1955-1967. 1 vol. (looseleaf). *Cover title only.*

NOEL (GERARD EYRE) The great lock-out of 1926. London, 1976. pp. 239. *bibliog.*

— — **Wales.**

ARNOT (ROBERT PAGE) South Wales miners: Glowyr de Cymru: a history of the South Wales Miners' Federation, 1914-1926. Cardiff, 1975. pp. 356.

SEWEL (JOHN) Colliery closure and social change: a study of a south Wales mining valley. Cardiff, 1975. pp. 81. *(Wales. University. Board of Celtic Studies. Social Science Monographs. No. 1)*

— **United States.**

ROBERTS (PETER) Graduate of Yale University. Anthracite coal communities: a study of the demography, the social, educational and moral life of the anthracite regions. New York, 1904. pp. 387.

WYNN (DAVID ROBERT) Trade unions and the 'new' immigration: a study of the United Mine Workers of America, 1890-1920. 1976. fo. 452. *bibliog. Typescript.* Ph.D. (London) thesis: unpublished. *This thesis is the property of London University and may not be removed from the Library.*

COAL MINES AND MINING

— **Accidents.**

BRYAN (Sir ANDREW MEIKLE) The evolution of health and safety in mines. [London, 1975] pp. 192.

— **Safety measures.**

BRYAN (Sir ANDREW MEIKLE) The evolution of health and safety in mines. [London, 1975] pp. 192.

— **Germany.**

BOCKHARDT (ANTON) Der Steinkohlenbergbau der Pfalz während der Jahre 1821-1880. ..; bearbeitet, ergänzt und herausgegeben von Wilfried Rosenberger. Bad Kreuznach, 1974. fo. 192.

— **Germany, Eastern.**

FOERSTER (FRANK) Senftenberger Revier, 1890-1914: zur Geschichte der Niederlausitzer Braunkohlenindustrie, etc. Bautzen, 1968. pp. 328. *(Deutsche Akademie der Wissenschaften zu Berlin. Institut für Sorbische Volksforschung in Bautzen. Schriftenreihe. 37)*

— **United Kingdom.**

NATIONAL UNION OF MINEWORKERS. Handbook on the wage structure of the coalmining industry. n.p., 1955-1967. 1 vol. (looseleaf). *Cover title only.*

ANDERSON (DONALD) The Orrell coalfield, Lancashire, 1740-1850. Buxton, [1975]. pp. 208. *bibliog.*

COAL TRADE

— **Germany.**

OLSSON (SVEN OLOF) German coal and Swedish fuel, 1939-1945. Göteborg, 1975. pp. 348. *bibliog. (Göteborgs Universitet. Ekonomisk-Historiska Institutionen. Meddelanden. 36)*

— — **East Prussia.**

RUNGE (HANS) Die Kohlenversorgung Ostpreussens. Jena, 1923. pp. 57. *bibliog. (Kaliningrad. Universität. Institut für Ostdeutsche Wirtschaft. Schriften. 10. Heft)*

— **Ireland (Republic).**

EIRE. Coal Prices Advisory Body. 1975. Report of enquiry into the coal trade. Dublin, [1975]. pp. 137.

— **Sweden.**

OLSSON (SVEN OLOF) German coal and Swedish fuel, 1939-1945. Göteborg, 1975. pp. 348. *bibliog. (Göteborgs Universitet. Ekonomisk-Historiska Institutionen. Meddelanden. 36)*

COALBROOKDALE

— **Economic history.**

TRINDER (BARRIE STUART) The Darbys of Coalbrookdale. Chichester, 1974. pp. 79. *bibliog.*

COALITION GOVERNMENTS.

BUENO DE MESQUITA (BRUCE) Strategy, risk and personality in coalition politics: the case of India. Cambridge, 1975. pp. 198. *bibliog.*

DODD (LAWRENCE C.) Coalitions in parliamentary government. Princeton, [1976]. pp. 283. *bibliog.*

— **Germany.**

ROTH (REINHOLD) Aussenpolitische Innovation und politische Herrschaftssicherung: eine Analyse...am Beispiel der sozialliberalen Koalition, 1969 bis 1973. Meisenheim am Glan, 1976. pp. 380. *bibliog.*

COALITION GOVERNMENTS.(Cont.)

STEHLING (JUTTA) Weimarer Koalition und SPD in Baden: ein Beitrag zur Geschichte der Partei- und Kulturpolitik in der Weimarer Republik. Frankfurt/Main, [1976]. pp. 347. *bibliog. Zur Erlangung des akademischen Grades eines Doktors der Philosophie von der Universität Karlsruhe genehmigte Dissertation.*

— **India.**

BUENO DE MESQUITA (BRUCE) Strategy, risk and personality in coalition politics: the case of India. Cambridge, 1975. pp. 198. *bibliog.*

COASTAL ZONE MANAGEMENT

— **United States.**

KOPPELMAN (LEE E.) and others. A methodology to achieve the integration of coastal zone science and regional planning: detailed work program. New York, 1974. pp. 116. *bibliog.*

BARAM (MICHAEL S.) and others. Environmental law and the siting of facilities: issues in land use and coastal zone management. Cambridge, Mass., [1976]. pp. 255.

RICHARDSON (DAN K.) The cost of environmental protection: regulating housing development in the coastal zone. New Brunswick, N.J., [1976]. pp. 219. *bibliog.*

— — **California.**

MOGULOF (MELVIN B.) Saving the coast: California's experiment in intergovernmental land use control. Lexington, Mass., [1975]. pp. 136. *bibliog.*

SCOTT (ILEY STANLEY) and others. Governing California's coast. Berkeley, 1975. pp. 454. *bibliog.*

COASTS

— **America, North.**

BLACK (WILLIAM ALEXANDER) The view from Water Street. Ottawa, 1973. pp. 43. *bibliog. (Canada. Inland Waters Directorate. Social Science Series. No. 2)*

— **United Kingdom — Scotland.**

SKINNER (DAVID N.) The coast of Scotland: some recently collected survey material; prepared for the Scottish Development Department. [Edinburgh], 1974 [or rather 1976 in progress]. 1 vol. (loose-leaf). *bibliog.*

COBB (CULLY ALTON).

SCOTT (ROY V.) and SHOALMIRE (J.G.) The public career of Cully A. Cobb: a study in agricultural leadership. Jackson, Miss., [1973]. pp. 287. *bibliog.*

COBDEN (RICHARD).

COBDEN (RICHARD) [Letters to Thomas Thomasson. 1850-64]. 23 letters, 1 memorandum. *Manuscript.*

COBOL (COMPUTER PROGRAM LANGUAGE).

CODDINGTON (LEONARD) Quick COBOL. London, [1971]. pp. 265.

ARMSTRONG (RUSSELL M.) Modular programming in COBOL. New York, [1973]. pp. 211.

COCA.

ANDREWS (GEORGE) and SOLOMON (DAVID) 1925- , eds. The coca leaf and cocaine papers. New York, [1975]. pp. 372.

COCAINE.

ANDREWS (GEORGE) and SOLOMON (DAVID) 1925- , eds. The coca leaf and cocaine papers. New York, [1975]. pp. 372.

COCAINE HABIT.

ANDREWS (GEORGE) and SOLOMON (DAVID) 1925- , eds. The coca leaf and cocaine papers. New York, [1975]. pp. 372.

COCKBURN (HENRY) Lord Cockburn.

MILLER (KARL) Cockburn's millennium. London, 1975. pp. 322.

COCOA TRADE

— **Ghana.**

BECKMAN (BJÖRN) Organising the farmers: cocoa politics and national development in Ghana. Uppsala, 1976. pp. 299. *bibliog.*

— **Venezuela.**

NUÑEZ (ENRIQUE BERNARDO) ed. Cacao; ensayo y prologo de Orlando Araujo. Caracas, 1972. pp. 565. *(Banco Central de Venezuela. Coleccion Cuatricentenario de Caracas. 9) A collection of documents.*

CODREANU (CORNELIU ZELEA).

CODREANU (CORNELIU ZELEA) Pentru legionari. v.1. Sibiu, 1936; [Munich, 1968]. pp. 482. *(Colecţia "Omul nou")*

COFFEE

— **Jamaica.**

WILLIAMS (RANDOLPH LAMBERT) The coffee industry of Jamaica: growth, structure and performance. Kingston, Jamaica, 1975. pp. 82. *bibliog.*

— **St. Helena.**

JONES (P.A.) A report upon the prospects of coffee production on the island of St. Helena. [Jamestown, 1962]. fo. (16).

COFFEE TRADE

— **Jamaica.**

WILLIAMS (RANDOLPH LAMBERT) The coffee industry of Jamaica: growth, structure and performance. Kingston, Jamaica, 1975. pp. 82. *bibliog.*

COGNITION.

THEORIES of cognitive consistency: a sourcebook; edited by Robert P. Abelson [and others]. Chicago, [1968]. pp. 901. *bibliog.*

LATVIISKII GOSUDARSTVENNYI UNIVERSITET. Uchenye Zapiski. t.198. Voprosy logiki i metodologii poznaniia. Riga, 1973. pp. 100. *bibliog.*

HANDBOOK of learning and cognitive processes; edited by W.K. Estes. Hillsdale, N.J., 1975 in progress. *bibliogs.*

FODOR (JERRY ALAN) The language of thought. New York, [1975]. pp. 214. *bibliog.*

MANDLER (GEORGE) Mind and emotion. New York, [1975]. pp. 280. *bibliog.*

NORMAN (DONALD A.) and RUMELHART (DAVID E.) Explorations in cognition. San Francisco, [1975]. pp. 430. *bibliog.*

REPRESENTATION and understanding: studies in cognitive science: [based on a conference in memory of Jaime Carbonell; edited by Daniel G. Bobrow and Allan Collins. New York, 1975. pp. 427. *bibliogs.*

COGNITION (CHILD PSYCHOLOGY).

HOLLOS (MARIDA) Growing up in Flathill: social environment and cognitive development. Oslo, [1974]. pp. 166. *bibliog.*

INHELDER (BÄRBEL) and others. Learning and the development of cognition;...translated by Susan Wedgwood. London, 1974. pp. 308. *bibliog.*

BEILIN (HARRY) Studies in the cognitive basis of language development. New York, 1975 pp. 420. *bibliog.*

COHEN (MORRIS RAPHAEL)

HOLLINGER (DAVID A.) Morris R. Cohen and the scientific ideal. Cambridge, Mass., [1975]. pp. 262.

COHN-BENDIT (DANIEL).

COHN-BENDIT (DANIEL) Le grand bazar: entretiens avec Michel Lévy, Jean-Marc Salmon, Maren Sell. Paris, [1975]. pp. 192.

COINAGE

— **Nigeria.**

NIGERIA. Committee on the Decimalization of the Nigerian Currency. 1972. Report; [O. Akinrele, chairman]. Lagos, 1972. pp. 35.

COKE (Sir EDWARD).

BEAUTE (JEAN) Un grand juriste anglais: Sir Edward Coke, 1552-1634: ses idées politiques et constitutionnelles; ou, Aux origines de la démocratie occidentale moderne. Paris, [1975]. pp. 230. *bibliog. (Paris. Université de Paris II. Travaux et Recherches. Série Science Politique. 5)*

COKE (THOMAS WILLIAM) 1st Earl of Leicester of Holkham.

PARKER (ROBERT ALEXANDER CLARKE) Coke of Norfolk: a financial and agricultural study, 1707-1842. Oxford, 1975. pp. 222.

COLLECTIVE BARGAINING.

KAYE (SEYMOUR P.) and MARSH (ARTHUR IVOR) eds. International manual on collective bargaining for public employees. New York, 1973. pp. 389.

INDUSTRIAL RELATIONS RESEARCH ASSOCIATION. Collective bargaining and productivity; authors, Joseph Goldberg [and others]. Madison, Wis., [1975]. pp. 194.

WOLTERS (RUDOLF) Economist. Strategien der Verhandlungsführung: eine Analyse empirischer Tests zur Bargaining-Theorie des Lohnes. Berlin, [1976]. pp. 204. *bibliog.*

— **Canada.**

COLLECTIVE bargaining in the essential and public service sectors: proceedings of a conference held...1975, organized...through the Centre for Industrial Relations, University of Toronto; (Morley Gunderson, editor). Toronto, [1975]. pp. 159.

— **Italy.**

BARTOCCI (ENZO) ed. Sindacato, classe, società: scritti di E. Bartocci [and others]. Padova, 1975. pp. 405.

— **Netherlands.**

CAO'S IN NEDERLAND: een systematische samenvatting van lonen en andere arbeidsvoorwaarden in Nederland, vastgelegd in collectieve arbeidsovereenkomsten en bindende regelingen; [pd. by] Loonbureau [Nederlands]. s-a., Je 1971 (deel 1)- , with gap (Je 1973). 's- Gravenhage.

— **Trinidad and Tobago.**

OKPALUBA (CHUKS) Statutory regulation of collective bargaining, with special reference to the Industrial Stabilisation Act of Trinidad and Tobago. Mona, 1975. pp. 183. *bibliog. (West Indies, University of the. Institute of Social and Economic Research. Law and Society in the Caribbean. No. 5)*

— **United Kingdom.**

VIGENER (MEINOLF) Staatliche Eingriffe in die Autonomie der kollektiven Arbeitgeber-Arbeitnehmer-Beziehungen in Grossbritannien in den Jahren 1965-1972. [Freiburg i. Br.], 1975. pp. 135. *bibliog. Inaugural-Dissertation zur Erlangung der Doktorwürde der Albert-Ludwigs-Universität zu Freiburg i. Br.*

ADVISORY CONCILIATION AND ARBITRATION SERVICE [U.K.]: Draft code of practice: disclosure of information to trade unions for collective bargaining. [London, 1976]. pp. 9.

— **United States.**

COLLINS (JOHN J.) Bargaining at the local level. New York, 1974. pp. 191.

ENCOUNTERING the unionized university; Jack H. Schuster, issue editor. San Francisco, 1974. pp. 106. *bibliogs. (New Directions for Higher Education. No. 5) Papers of a session at the 1973 annual meeting of the American Political Science Association.*

KEMERER (FRANK R.) and BALDRIDGE (J. VICTOR) Unions on campus. San Francisco, 1975. pp. 248. *bibliog.*

WEITZMAN (JOAN) The scope of bargaining in public employment. New York, 1975. pp. 384. *bibliog.*

CHENG (CHARLES W.) Altering collective bargaining: citizen participation in educational decision making. New York, 1976. pp. 179. *bibliog.*

— — **Florida.**

FLORIDA. Legislature. House of Representatives. Committee on Labor and Industry. 1970. Collective bargaining in public employment; a study report. Tallahassee, 1970. pp. 84.

COLLECTIVE LABOUR AGREEMENTS

— **Australia.**

AUSTRALIA. Commonwealth Bureau of Census and Statistics. 1969. Survey of the incidence of industrial awards, determinations and collective agreements, May 1968. Canberra, [1969]. pp. 12.

— **Canada.**

CANADA. Treasury Board. 1968. Agreement between the Treasury Board and the Council of Graphic Arts Unions of the Public Service of Canada, Printing Operations Group, non-supervisory. [Ottawa, 1968]. pp. 101. *In English and French.*

— — **New Brunswick.**

NEW BRUNSWICK. Department of Labour. Labour Market Services Branch. 1974. Collective agreement survey of cost of living adjustment, COLA, clauses (in) various industries in New Brunswick. Fredericton, 1974. pp. 11.

— **Spain.**

CANO VALENTIN (JAIME) Convenios colectivos sindicales y plan de desarrollo economico y social. Madrid, 1965. pp. 87.

— **Sweden.**

JOHANNESSON (CONNY) De centrala avtalsförhandlingarna och den fackliga demokratin: studier över Svenska metallindustriarbetareförbundets förhandlingsorganisation vid förbundsförhandlingar, med samordning. Lund, 1975. pp. 437. *bibliog. Akademisk avhandling, Universitetet i Lund; with English summary.*

— **United States.**

BADERSCHNEIDER (EARL R.) and MILLER (PAUL F.) eds. Labor arbitration in health care: a case book. New York, [1976]. pp. 323.

COLLECTIVE SETTLEMENTS

— **United Kingdom.**

ABRAMS (PHILIP) and McCULLOCH (ANDREW) Communes, sociology and society. Cambridge, 1976. pp. 239. *bibliog.*

COLLEGE DROPOUTS

— **United States.**

COPE (ROBERT G.) and HANNAH (WILLIAM) Revolving college doors: the causes and consequences of dropping out, stopping out, and transferring. New York, [1975]. pp. 190. *bibliog.*

COLLEGE TEACHERS.

See TEACHERS.

COLLINGWOOD (ROBIN GEORGE).

SKAGESTAD (PETER) Making sense of history: the philosophies of Popper and Collingwood. Oslo, [1975]. pp. 118. *bibliog. (Norges Almenvitenskapelige Forskningsråd. Gruppe: Språk og Historie) Based on lectures given at Brandeis University, Spring, 1973.*

COLOGNE

— **Economic history.**

KELLENBENZ (HERMANN) ed. Zwei Jahrtausende Kölner Wirtschaft; mit Beiträgen von Otto Doppelfeld [and others];...herausgegeben im Auftrag des Rheinisch-Westfälischen Wirtschaftsarchivs zu Köln. Köln, 1975. 2 vols. *bibliogs.*

COLOMBIA

— **Economic conditions.**

ARRUBLA (MARIO) Estudios sobre el subdesarrollo colombiano. Medellin, 1969 repr. 1974. pp. 222. *Three articles reprinted, with an introduction, from the journal Estrategia, 1963.*

BELGIUM. Office Belge du Commerce Extérieur. 1972. Colombie. Bruxelles, 1972. pp. 67. *(Un Marché. 9)*

LAURSEN (KARSTEN) Development of the labour surplus economy: essays in theory and case studies of Colombia. Århus, 1972 repr. 1975. 1 vol. (various pagings). *bibliog. (Aarhus. Universitet. Økonomiske Institut. Memos. 1975.2.)*

ROA SUAREZ (HERNANDO) Colombia: dependiente y no participante; aspectos economicos, sociales, culturales y politicos de la participacion; aproximacion a un analisis critico. Bogota, 1973 repr. 1974. pp. 143. *bibliog.*

— **Economic history.**

SAFFORD (FRANK) 1935- . The ideal of the practical: Colombia's struggle to form a technical elite. Austin, [1976]. pp. 373. *bibliog. (Texas University. Institute of Latin American Studies. Latin American Monographs. No. 39)*

— **Politics and government.**

PARTIDO COMUNISTA DE COLOMBIA. Comision Nacional de Educacion. Que es y por que lucha el Partido Comunista. [Bogota,] 1966. pp. 77.

ROA SUAREZ (HERNANDO) Colombia: dependiente y no participante; aspectos economicos, sociales, culturales y politicos de la participacion; aproximacion a un analisis critico. Bogota, 1973 repr. 1974. pp. 143. *bibliog.*

— **Social conditions.**

ROA SUAREZ (HERNANDO) Colombia: dependiente y no participante; aspectos economicos, sociales, culturales y politicos de la participacion; aproximacion a un analisis critico. Bogota, 1973 repr. 1974. pp. 143. *bibliog.*

COLONIAL COMPANIES.

LE COUTEUX (BERNARD) Law et le commerce colonial. Paris, 1921. pp. 100. *bibliog. Thèse (doctorat) - Faculté de Droit de l'Université de Paris.*

COLONIES.

ANTONOWICZ (LECH) Likwidacja kolonializmu ze stanowiska prawa międzynarodowego. Warszawa, 1964. pp. 190. *bibliog.*

ARRUBLA (MARIO) Estudios sobre el subdesarrollo colombiano. Medellin, 1969 repr. 1974. pp. 222. *Three articles reprinted, with an introduction, from the journal Estrategia, 1963.*

BIRNBERG (THOMAS B.) and RESNICK (STEPHEN A.) Colonial development: an econometric study. new Haven, 1975. pp. 347. *bibliog.*

KING (ANTHONY D.) Colonial urban development: social power and environment. London, 1976. pp. 328. *bibliog.*

— **Law.**

HOOKER (M.B.) Legal pluralism: an introduction to colonial and neo-colonial laws. Oxford, 1975. pp. 601. *bibliog.*

LEIBOWITZ (ARNOLD H.) Colonial emancipation in the Pacific and the Caribbean: a legal and political analysis. New York, 1976. pp. 221.

COLONIES (INTERNATIONAL LAW).

LEIBOWITZ (ARNOLD H.) Colonial emancipation in the Pacific and the Caribbean: a legal and political analysis. New York, 1976. pp. 221.

COLONIES IN AFRICA.

LOUIS (WILLIAM ROGER) ed. Imperialism: the Robinson and Gallagher controversy. New York, 1976. pp. 252. *bibliog.*

COLONIES IN THE FAR EAST.

GRUENFELD (ERNST) Hafenkolonien und kolonieähnliche Verhältnisse in China, Japan und Korea: eine kolonialpolitische Studie. Jena, 1913. pp. 239. *bibliog.*

COLOURED PEOPLE (SOUTH AFRICA).

BRINDLEY (MARIANNE) Western Coloured Township: problems of an urban slum. Johannesburg, 1976. pp. 110. *bibliog.*

COLSON (CHARLES W.).

COLSON (CHARLES W.) Born again. London, [1976]. pp. 350.

COMBINATORIAL ANALYSIS.

COMTET (LOUIS) Advanced combinatorics: the art of finite and infinite expansions. rev. ed. Dordrecht, [1974]. pp. 343. *bibliog.*

COMITE PERMANENT INTER—ETATS DE LUTTE CONTRE LA SECHERESSE DANS LE SAHEL.

COMITE PERMANENT INTER-ETATS DE LUTTE CONTRE LA SECHERESSE DANS LE SAHEL. 1974. Statuts: réglement interieur; organisation. Ouagadougou, [1974?]. fo. 13.

COMMERCE.

UNITED NATIONS. Conference on Trade and Development. 1966. Payments arrangements among the developing countries for trade expansion: report of the group of experts. (TD/B/80/Rev.1) (TD/B/C.3/24/Rev.1). Geneva, 1966. pp. 32.

YEUNG (PATRICK P.T.) Toward a pure theory of entrepot trade. [1967]. pp. 108. *bibliog. Ph.D. (Claremont Graduate School) thesis: unpublished. Microfilm of typescript: 1 reel.*

CHISHOLM (GEORGE GOUDIE) Handbook of commercial geography; entirely rewritten by Sir Dudley Stamp; nineteenth edition revised by G. Noel Blake and Audrey N. Clark. London, 1975. pp. 984.

DENTON (GEOFFREY) and others. Trade effects of public subsidies to private enterprise. London, 1975. pp. 293. *bibliog.*

GRIFFITHS (BRIAN) Invisible barriers to invisible trade. London, 1975. pp. 178. *bibliog.*

INTERNATIONAL trade and finance: frontiers for research; edited by Peter B. Kenen. Cambridge, [1975]. pp. 539. *bibliogs. The nine papers in this volume were written for a conference held at Princeton University in March 1973.*

COMMERCE.(Cont.)

EUROPEAN COMMUNITIES. Statistical Office. Trade flows. irreg., 1976 (no.1)- Luxembourg. *[In English, French and German].*

BHATTACHARYA (ANINDYA K.) Foreign trade and international development. Lexington, Mass., [1976]. pp. 107. *bibliog.*

GRAY (HENRY PETER) A generalized theory of international trade. London, 1976. pp. 201.

INFLATION, trade and taxes: essays in honor of Alice Bourneuf; edited by David A. Belsley [and others]. Columbus, Ohio, [1976]. pp. 252. *bibliogs.*

KEMP (MURRAY CHILVERS) Three topics in the theory of international trade: distribution, welfare and uncertainty. Amsterdam, 1976. pp. 327. *bibliogs.*

MAGEE (STEPHEN P.) International trade and distortions in factor markets. New York, [1976]. pp. 140. *bibliog.*

RIJNVOS (C.J.) A new approach to the theory of international trade. The Hague, 1976. pp. 121. *bibliog.*

— **Mathematical models.**

RUMM (ULRICH) Wirtschaftliches Wachstum, Aussenhandel und Preisniveau. Meisenheim am Glan, [1973]. pp. 135, xi. *bibliog.*

SAMUELSON (LEE) and GRAENZER (RANDOLF) A new model of world trade; [and] Cyclical indicators for manufacturing industries; by Randolf Gränzer. [Paris], Organisation for Economic Cooperation and Development, 1973. pp. 55. *(OECD Economic Outlook. Occasional Studies)*

SARANTIDES (STYLIANOS A.) Foreign trade aspects of capital formation. Piraeus, 1975. pp. 34. *(Reprint from the edition of the Graduate School of Industrial Studies Essays in honour of Professor Andreas Kyrkilitsis)*

COMMERCIAL CRIMES

— **United States.**

CLARKE (THURSTON) and TIGUE (JOHN J.) Dirty money: Swiss banks, the Mafia, money laundering, and white collar crime. New York, [1975]. pp. 216.

COMMERCIAL FINANCE COMPANIES

— **Canada — Québec.**

QUEBEC (PROVINCE). Ministère des Institutions Financières, Compagnies et Coopératives. Annual report. a., 1974/75- Québec. *[In English and French].*

— **Denmark.**

DENMARK. Boss-Udvalget. 1971. Betaenkning om finansieringsselskaber og lignende virksomheder. København, 1971. pp. 101. *(Denmark. Betaenkninger. nr. 628)*

— **United States.**

WILSON (WILLIAM L.) Full faith and credit: the story of C.I.T. Financial Corporation, 1908-1975. New York, [1976]. pp. 376.

COMMERCIAL LAW

— **European Economic Community countries.**

EUROPEAN COMMUNITIES. Directorate-General for the Internal Market. 1972. Régime juridique concernant l'accès aux activités non salariées de l'industrie, de l'artisanat, du commerce et des entreprises de services et l'exercice de celles-ci dans les etats membres des Communautés européennes: situation au 31. 12.1970. [Luxembourg, 1972]. pp. 807.

— **India.**

SINGH (NAGENDRA) Commercial law of India. Leyden, 1976. pp. 208.

— **United Kingdom.**

FRANK (WILLIAM FRANCIS) and ROYALL (DAVID V.E.) The legal aspects of industry and commerce. 7th ed. London, 1975. pp. 289. *bibliog.*

RANKING (DEVEY FEARON DE L'HOSTE) and others. Mercantile law, incorporating partnership law and the law of arbitration and awards; fourteenth edition by R.E.G. Perrins and P.R.O. Stuart. London, 1975. pp. 338.

LOWE (ROBERT) Solicitor. Commercial law. 5th ed. London, 1976. pp. 576.

— **United States.**

AMERICAN LAW INSTITUTE and NATIONAL CONFERENCE OF COMMISSIONERS ON UNIFORM STATE LAWS. Uniform commercial code...: 1958 official text, with comments. Philadelphia, [1959]. pp. 713.

COMMERCIAL POLICY.

UNITED NATIONS. Conference on Trade and Development. 1968. Towards a global strategy of development: report by the Secretary-General of the United Nations Conference on Trade and Development to the second session of the Conference. (TD/3/Rev.1). New York, 1968. pp. 76.

SORENSON (VERNON L.) International trade policy: agriculture and development. East Lansing, Mich., 1975. pp. 290. *bibliog. (Michigan State University. MSU International Business and Economic Studies)*

BHATTACHARYA (ANINDYA K.) Foreign trade and international development. Lexington, Mass., [1976]. pp. 107. *bibliog.*

COMMERCIAL PRODUCTS.

ECONOMIST INTELLIGENCE UNIT. World commodity outlook 1975/76: industrial raw materials. London, 1975. pp. 93.

SOTSIALISTICHESKII produkt i ego formy. Moskva, 1975. pp. 183.

ECONOMIST INTELLIGENCE UNIT. World commodity outlook 1976: food, feedstuffs and beverages. London, 1976. pp. 88.

— **Classification.**

MALHOTRA (SAT PAL) Correlation of commodity-industry classifications in the mineral industry. Ottawa, 1971. pp. 23. *(Canada. Mineral Resources Division. Mineral [Information] Bulletins. 116)*

CANADA. Statistics Canada. Trade of Canada commodity classification. irreg., 1975- Ottawa. *In English and French.*

FRANCE. Ministère de l'Economie et des Finances. 1975. Nomenclature d'activités et de produits, 1973: édition avec notes explicatives, 1974. Paris, 1975. pp. 439.

— **Russia.**

AGAFONOV (ALEKSANDR KONSTANTINOVICH) Tovarnoe proizvodstvo i zakon stoimosti pri sotsializme. Kiev, 1975. pp. 240. *bibliog.*

— **Underdeveloped areas.**

See UNDERDEVELOPED AREAS — Commercial products.

COMMERCIAL STATISTICS.

DIRECTION OF TRADE: a suppl. to International financial statistics; [pd. by] International Monetary Fund. 1958/1962 [1st issue], 1961/1964, 1961/1965, 1962/1966; m. and a., 1968- Washington. *Supersedes the a. issue of United Nations Statistical Papers Series T, Direction of international trade (1938, 1948, 1950 - Ja 1963, with gaps).*

HANDBOOK OF INTERNATIONAL TRADE AND DEVELOPMENT STATISTICS; (pd. by) United Nations Conference on Trade and Development. irreg., 1967- Geneva. *[In English and French]. File includes supplements.*

COMMERCIAL VEHICLES.

BELGIUM. Service de Promotion et de Coordination des Communications. Parc des vehicules utilitaires soumis à l'inspection automobile: statistique. a., 1974- [Bruxelles].

SETH-SMITH (MICHAEL) The long haul: a social history of the British commercial vehicle industry. London, 1975. pp. 189. *bibliog.*

COMMODITY CONTROL.

ECONOMIST INTELLIGENCE UNIT. Q[uarterly] E[conomic] R[eview] Specials. No. 27. The potential for new commodity cartels: copying OPEC, or improved international agreements?; by Anthony Edwards. London, 1975. pp. 96.

COMMODITY EXCHANGES.

BILLERBECK (KLAUS) Alternative approaches for the future order of international trade in commodities. Berlin, 1974. pp. 48. *(Deutsches Institut für Entwicklungspolitik. Occasional Papers. No. 25)*

— **France.**

TARDIEU (GEORGES) and PORTEU DE LA MORANDIERE (FRANÇOIS) La Bourse de Commerce de Paris: remisier et clientèle particulière. 2nd ed. Paris, 1974. pp. 254. *bibliog.*

— **Russia.**

PETROV (DMITRII GRIGOR'EVICH) Effektivnost' kapital'nykh vlozhenii v sfere tovarnogo obrashcheniia: voprosy teorii i praktiki. Kiev, 1975. pp. 288.

— **United States.**

TEWELES (RICHARD JACK) and others. The commodity futures game: who wins?, who loses?, why?. New York, [1974]. pp. 638. *bibliog. Edition for 1969 published under title: The commodity futures trading guide.*

COMMON LAW

— **United Kingdom.**

SELDEN SOCIETY. Publications. Vol.91. St. German's Doctor and student; edited...by...T. F.T. Plucknett and J.L. Barton. London, 1974. pp. 346. *In Latin and English.*

COMMONS.

McAREVEY (MARY) compiler. A guide-to definitive maps of public paths: a guide to the preparation of draft, provisional and definitive maps of public paths, revised maps and details of public rights of representation and objection. 3rd ed. London, 1974. pp. 37.

— **Germany.**

KRINGS (WILFRIED) Wertung und Umwertung von Allmenden im Rhein-Maas-Gebiet vom Spätmittelalter bis zur Mitte des 19. Jahrhunderts: eine historisch-sozialgeographische Studie. Assen, 1976. pp. 106. *bibliog. (Stichting "Maaslandse Monografieën". Maaslandse Monografieën. 20)*

— **Netherlands.**

KRINGS (WILFRIED) Wertung und Umwertung von Allmenden im Rhein-Maas-Gebiet vom Spätmittelalter bis zur Mitte des 19. Jahrhunderts: eine historisch-sozialgeographische Studie. Assen, 1976. pp. 106. *bibliog. (Stichting "Maaslandse Monografieën". Maaslandse Monografieën. 20)*

COMMONWEALTH DEVELOPMENT CORPORATION.

RENDELL (Sir WILLIAM) The history of the Commonwealth Development Corporation, 1948- 1972. London, 1976. pp. 294.

COMMUNICABLE DISEASES

— **United Kingdom.**

U.K. Office of Population Censuses and Surveys. Statistics of infectious diseases: notifications of infectious diseases in England and Wales. a., 1974- London.

COMMUNICATION.

POOL (ITHIEL DE SOLA) and others, eds. Handbook of communication. Chicago, [1973]. pp. 1011. *bibliogs.*

WILMOT (WILLIAM W.) Dyadic communication: a transactional perspective. Reading, Mass., [1975]. pp. 196. *bibliog.*

— Social aspects.

McQUAIL (DENIS) Communication. London, 1975. pp. 229. *bibliog.*

— Asia.

UNITED NATIONS. Economic and Social Commission for Asia and the Pacific. Asian Population Studies Series. New York, 1966 in progress.

— Canada — Ontario.

ONTARIO. Ministry of Transportation and Communications. Human, Social and Environmental Factors Research Section. 1974. Communications in Ontario: findings of a survey of public attitudes, 1973. [Toronto, 1974?]. pp. 47.

— Singapore.

WAN (FOOK KEE) Communications strategy in the Singapore national family planning programme: a paper prepared for the Seminar in Communication for Family Planning sponsored by the East-West Communication Institute, East-West Centre, Honolulu, Hawaii, August 8th to 20th, 1971. Singapore, Family Planning and Population Board, [1971]. fo. 5. *(FPPB Papers. No.14)*

— United States.

CHAFFEE (STEVEN H.) and PETRICK (MICHAEL J.) Using the mass media: communication problems in American society. New York, [1975]. pp. 264. *bibliogs.*

COMMUNICATION AND TRAFFIC

— Nigeria.

NIGERIA. [Federal Ministry of Information]. 1972. Building the new Nigeria: transport and communications. [Lagos, 1972]. pp. 22.

— Russia — Uzbekistan.

MANGEL'DIN (DAN'IAR ISKANDEROVICH) Novye rubezhi transporta i sviazi Uzbekistana. Tashkent, 1970. pp. 155.

COMMUNICATION IN MANAGEMENT

— United Kingdom.

ADVISORY CONCILIATION AND ARBITRATION SERVICE [U.K.]. Draft code of practice: disclosure of information to trade unions for collective bargaining. [London, 1976]. pp. 9.

COMMUNICATION IN POLITICS.

CHAFFEE (STEVEN H.) ed. Political communication: issues and strategies for research. Beverly Hills, [1975]. pp. 319. *bibliogs.*

GRABER (DORIS APPEL) Verbal behavior and politics. Urbana, Ill., [1976]. pp. 377. *bibliog.*

COMMUNISM.

MARX (KARL) and ENGELS (FRIEDRICH) Manifeste du Parti Communiste; (traduction de Laura Lafargue, etc). Paris, 1922. pp. 63.

GROTEWOHL (OTTO) Im Kampf um Deutschland: Reden und Aufsätze, [1945-1948] . Berlin, [1948]. 2 vols.(in 1).

ISTORIJA medjunarodnog radničkog i socijalističkog pokreta; po predavanjima održanim na Višoj partiskoj školi "Djuro Djaković" u 1950 51 godini. Beograd, 1952. pp. 636.

MERLEAU-PONTY (MAURICE) Humanism and terror: an essay on the communist problem;... translated and with notes by John O'Neill. Boston, Mass., [1969]. pp. 189.

MOGILEVSKII (SOLOMON ABRAMOVICH) Noveishaia istoriia mezhdunarodnogo kommunisticheskogo i rabochego dvizheniia, 1917-1970 gg. Leningrad, 1971. pp. 160. *bibliog.*

AUCIELLO (NICOLA) Socialismo ed egemonia in Gramsci e Togliatti. Bari, [1974]. pp. 207.

BABICI (ION) Boevaia antifashistskaia solidarnost', 1933-1939 gg.; (perevod s rumynskogo Natalii i Konstantina Unguru). Bukharest, 1974. pp. 244. *(Academia de Ştiinţe Sociale şi Politice a Republicii Socialiste România. Bibliotheca Historica Romaniae. Studies. 49)*

BORODAI (IURII MEFOD'EVICH) and others. Nasledie K. Marksa i problemy teorii obshchestvenno-ekonomicheskoi formatsii. Moskva, 1974. pp. 309.

BRATSTVO narodov i internatsional'noe vospitanie: [materialy respublikanskoi nauchno-teoreticheskoi konferentsii "Torzhestvo leninskikh idei bratstva narodov i internatsional'noe vospitanie trudiashchikhsia"]. Tashkent, 1974. pp. 266.

OPYT sotsialisticheskikh preobrazovanii v SSSR i ego mezhdunarodnoe znachenie: Mezhdunarodnaia nauchnaia konferentsiia v Tashkente, 16-19 oktiabria 1972 g. Moskva, 1974. pp. 336.

SLEPENKOV (IVAN MARKELOVICH) Metodologicheskie printsipy i metodika konkretno-sotsiologicheskogo issledovaniia v nauchnom kommunizme. Moskva, 1974. pp. 128. *bibliog.*

UCHENYE ZAPISKI KAFEDR OBSHCHESTVENNYKH NAUK VUZOV LENINGRADA. Problemy Nauchnogo Kommunizma. vyp.8. Kritika osnovnykh napravlenii sovremennogo antikommunizma; pod red.... A.K. Belykh i ... V.P. Gulina. Leningrad, 1974. pp. 184.

BEYER (HANS) Der Antikommunismus: Wesen, Formen und Funktionen. Berlin, 1975. pp. 122.

BONGIOVANNI (BRUNO) ed. L'antistalinismo di sinistra e la natura sociale dell'URSS: [an anthology]. Milano, 1975. pp. 391. *bibliog.*

BORDIGA (AMADEO) Scritti scelti; a cura di Franco Livorsi. mILANO, 1975. PP. 266.

DALLEMAGNE (JEAN LUC) Construction du socialisme et révolution: essai sur la transition au socialisme. Paris, 1975. pp. 405.

DOBROTIN (EVGENII VLADIMIROVICH) Proletarskii internatsionalizm i edinstvo mirovogo kommunisticheskogo dvizheniia. Moskva, 1975. pp. 63.

INTERNATSIONAL'NYI printsip v stroitel'stve i deiatel'nosti KPSS. Moskva, 1975. pp. 296.

KOSOLAPOV (RICHARD IVANOVICH) Sotsializm: k voprosam teorii. Moskva, 1975. pp. 476.

L'VUNIN (IURII ALEKSANDROVICH) Bor'ba Kommunisticheskoi partii za ukreplenie internatsional'nykh sviazei rabochego klassa SSSR, 1924-1928 gg. Moskva, 1975. pp. 304.

MARKSISTSKO-leninskoe uchenie o sotsializme i sovremennost'. Moskva, 1975. pp. 487.

MATIUSHKIN (NIKOLAI IVANOVICH) Patriotizm i internatsionalizm sovetskogo naroda: istoricheskii opyt i sovremennaia deiatel'nost' KPSS. Moskva, 1975. pp. 416.

PLEBE (ARMANDO) La civiltà del postcomunismo. Roma, [1975]. pp. 646. *Part I consists of the proceedings of the international congress organised by the Associazione Internazionale per la Cultura Occidentale in Rome in March 1975.*

RABOCHII klass v mirovom revoliutsionnom protsesse. Moskva, 1975. pp. 362.

SHEVELEV (ALEKSEI GEORGIEVICH) Sovremennaia epokha i proletarskii internatsionalizm. Leningrad, 1975. pp. 136.

COMMUNISM.

SUSLOV (MIKHAIL ANDREEVICH) Marxism-Leninism: the international teaching of the working class; (translated from the Russian). Moscow, [1975]. pp. 246. *Collected articles and speeches.*

TEORIIA i praktika stroitel'stva sotsializma: iz opyta stran sotsialisticheskogo sodruzhestva. Moskva, 1975. pp. 284.

ZUEV (VLADIMIR IL'ICH) Mirovaia sistema sotsializma: ekonomicheskie i politicheskie aspekty edinstva - metodologicheskie problemy. Moskva, 1975. pp. 302.

AXEN (HERMANN) Sozialismus und revolutionärer Weltprozess: ausgewählte Reden und Aufsätze. Berlin, 1976. pp. 614.

MAVRAKIS (KOSTAS) On Trotskyism: problems of theory and history. London, 1976. pp. 248. *bibliog.*

PELIKÁN (JIŘÍ) Socialist opposition in Eastern Europe: the Czechoslovak example; translated by Marian Sling and V. and R. Tosek. London, 1976. pp. 221.

PROBLEME der kommunistischen Bewegung: einige Fragen zur Theorie und Methodologie; (deutsch [from the Russian] von S. Gorelik). Frankfurt/Main, 1976. pp. 423.

VERNER (PAUL) Für das Wohl der Arbeiterklasse und des ganzen Volkes: ausgewählte Reden und Aufsätze. Berlin, 1976. pp. 507.

— Congresses.

COMMUNIST INTERNATIONAL. World Congress, 2nd, 1920. Le monde capitaliste et l'Internationale Communiste: manifeste. Pétrograd, 1920. pp. 47. *(Communist International. Editions. No.63) Not to be consulted without the permission of the Superintendent of Readers' Services.*

COMMUNIST INTERNATIONAL. Section d'Agitation et de Propagande. Le sens du 5e congrès mondial. Paris, 1924. pp. 35.

— Study and teaching.

BRITISH EMPIRE UNION. Research Department. Danger ahead : socialist and proletarian Sunday schools. London, [1922]. pp. 14.

WIATR (JERZY J.) Współczesny antykomunizm a nauki społeczne: eseje polemiczne, [1967-1969]. Warszawa, 1970. pp. 204. *With Russian and English summaries.*

IAKUSHEVSKII (IGOR' TITOVICH) Dialektika i "sovetologiia": kriticheskii analiz "sovetologicheskikh" interpretatsii materialisticheskoi dialektiki. Leningrad, 1975. pp. 207.

— Albania.

HOXHA (ENVER) Report on the activity of the Central Committee of the Party of Labor of Albania; submitted to the 6th Congress of the Party of Labor of Albania, November 1, 1971. Tirana, 1971. pp. 251.

— Australia.

GOLLAN (ROBIN) Revolutionaries and reformists: communism and the Australian labour movement, 1920-1955. Richmond, Surrey, 1975. pp. 330. *bibliog.*

— Bessarabia.

KOPANSKII (IAKOV MIKHAILOVICH) Internatsional'naia solidarnost' s bor'boi trudiashchikhsia Bessarabii za vossoedinenie s Sovetskoi Rodinoi, 1918-1940; otvetstvennyi redaktor...A.M. Lazarev. Kishinev, 1975. pp. 337.

— Bulgaria.

DIMITROV (GEORGI) Selected works. Sofia, 1972. 3 vols.

ZHIVKOV (TODOR) Modern Bulgaria: problems and tasks in building an advanced socialist society. New York, [1974]. pp. 238.

— Canada.

McEWEN (TOM) The forge glows red: from blacksmith to revolutionary. Toronto, 1974. pp. 260.

COMMUNISM.(Cont.)

— China.

GOLDWASSER (JANET) and DOWTY (STUART) Huang-Ying: workers' China. New York, [1975]. pp. 404.

KHOLODKOVSKAIA (ADELIIA VLADIMIROVNA) Rabochii klass Kitaia v period "uregulirovaniia", 1961-1965. Moskva, 1975. pp. 157. bibliog.

MARKOVA (SVETLANA DANILOVNA) Maoizm i intelligentsiia: problemy i sobytiia, 1956-1973 gg. Moskva, 1975. pp. 245. bibliog.

POSPELOV (BORIS VASIL'EVICH) Iaponskaia obshchestvenno-politicheskaia mysl' i maoizm: kritika antimarksistskikh kontseptsii sushchnosti maoizma. Moskva, 1975. pp. 224. bibliog.

VILTARD (YVES) Le système politique chinois dans le mouvement d'éducation socialiste, 1962-1966. Paris, 1975. pp. 83. bibliog. (Paris. Université de Paris I (Panthéon-Sorbonne). Publications. Série Science Politique. 4)

BURCHETT (WILFRED G.) and ALLEY (REWI) China: the quality of life. Harmondsworth, 1976. pp. 312.

HAN (SUYIN) pseud. [i.e. Elizabeth COMBER] Wind in the tower: Mao Tsetung and the Chinese revolution, 1949-1975. London, 1976. pp. 404.

OSNOVNYE aspekty kitaiskoi problemy, 1965-1975. Moskva, 1976. pp. 279.

— Cuba.

CASTRO RUZ (FIDEL) Socialismo y comunismo: un proceso unico; seleccion y notas: Nicolas Segrate. Montevideo, [1970]. pp. 189.

— Czechoslovakia.

NOVOTNÝ (ANTONÍN) Projevy a stati, 1954-(1964). Praha, 1964. 3 vols.

BIL'AK (VASIL) Pravda zůstala pravdou: projevy a články, říjen 1967 - prosinec 1970. Praha, 1971. pp. 445.

ZA nové Československo: materiály z celoštátnej vedeckej konferencie k 25. výročiu oslobodenia Československa, ktorú usporiadal Ústav marxizmu-leninizmu ÚV KSS v Bratislave, 27., 28. a 29. aprila 1970. Bratislava, 1972. pp. 270. (Komunistická Strana Slovenska. Ústredný Výbor. Ústav Marxizmu-Leninizmu. roč. 12, č. 1)

— Denmark.

KOMMUNISTISK FORBUND. Kampen for arbejdermagt. Aarhus, 1974. pp. 149.

— Europe, Eastern.

INTERNATIONAL CONGRESS ON THE PROBLEMS OF EASTERN EUROPE, 6TH, 197 Reformen und Dogmen in Osteuropa; [papers] herausgegeben von Alfred Domes; Beiträge von Gyula Borbándi [and others]. Köln, [1971]. pp. 269.

RADIO FREE EUROPE. Audience and Public Opinion Research Department. Attitudes toward communism and party preferences in East Europe. [Munich?], 1973. fo. 32.

ŠIK (OTA) Das kommunistische Machtsystem. Hamburg, 1976. pp. 357. bibliog.

— France.

BLUM (LEON) Pour la vieille maison: intervention au Congrès de Tours, 1920. Paris, 1934. pp. 43.

PARTI COMMUNISTE FRANÇAIS. Comité Central. Ecole Elémentaire du Parti Communiste Français. Le front unique. Paris, 1958. pp. 23. bibliog.

La CALOMNIE stalinienne: facteur de division de la classe ouvrière. Paris, [1959?]. pp. 16. (Les Dossiers du Militant. No. 1)

SCHNEIDER (DIETER MARC) Revolutionärer Syndikalismus und Bolschewismus: der Prozess der ideologischen Auseinandersetzung französischer Syndikalisten mit den Bolschewiki, 1914-1922. Erlangen, 1974. pp. 353. bibliog.

VARIN (JACQUES) Jeunes comme J.C.: sur la Jeunesse communiste. Paris, 1975 in progress.

DUPUY (FERNAND) Etre maire communiste. [Paris, 1975]. pp. 254.

FIELD (FRANK) Three writers and the Great War: studies in the rise of communism and fascism. Cambridge, 1975. pp. 212. bibliog.

NAVILLE (PIERRE) L'entre-deux guerres: la lutte des classes en France, 1927-1929 [or rather 1939]. Paris, [1975]. pp. 624. bibliog. Cover title includes the dates 1926-1939.

NAVILLE (PIERRE) La révolution et les intellectuels. new ed. [Paris, 1975]. pp. 214. Articles originally published separately in 1926, 1927 and 1956.

— Germany.

PRATT (JAMES ALEXANDER) The social basis of Nazism and communism in urban Germany. 1948. pp. 277. bibliog. M.A.(Michigan State College of Agriculture and Applied Science) thesis: unpublished. Microfilm of typescript: 1 reel.

RUTIGLIANO (ENZO) Linkskommunismus e rivoluzione in occidente: per una storia della KAPD. Bari, 1974. pp. 281.

BOCK (HANS MANFRED) Geschichte des "linken Radikalismus" in Deutschland: ein Versuch. Frankfurt am Main, 1976. pp. 370. bibliog.

DUPEUX (LOUIS) Stratégie communiste et dynamique conservatrice: essai sur les différents sens de l'expression "National-Bolchevisme" en Allemagne, sous la république de Weimar, 1919-1933. Paris, 1976. pp. 627. bibliog. Thèse-Université de Paris I.

— — Bibliography.

DOWE (DIETER) compiler. Bibliographie zur Geschichte der deutschen Arbeiterbewegung, sozialistischen und kommunistischen Bewegung von den Anfängen bis 1863, etc. Bonn-Bad Godesberg, 1976. pp. 303. bibliog. (Archiv für Sozialgeschichte. Beihefte. 5)

— — Bavaria.

ZASTENKER (N.) Bavarskaia Sovetskaia Respublika. Moskva, 1934. pp. 160.

— Germany, Eastern.

LEMMNITZ (ALFRED) Unser Plan zur Wiederherstellung und Entwicklung der Friedenswirtschaft in der sowjetischen Besatzungszone; nach einem Vortrag, etc. Berlin, [1949]. pp. 55.

Der DIALEKTISCHE Materialismus und der Aufbau des Sozialismus: Konferenz des Instituts für Gesellschaftswissenschaften beim ZK der SED...5. und 6. Mai in Berlin: Diskussionsbeiträge. bERLIN, 1958. PP. 19:.

POLITISCHE Ökonomie des Sozialismus und ihre Anwendung in der DDR: (Tafelwerk; Autorenkollektiv: M. Herold [and others]). Berlin, 1971. 1 vol. (various foliations).

WAGNER (UWE) Vom Kollektiv zur Konkurrenz: Partei und Massenbewegung in der DDR. Berlin, 1974. pp. 232. bibliog.

FIEDLER (HELENE) and others, eds. 30 Jahre volkseigene Betriebe: Dokumente und Materialien zum 30. Jahrestag des Volksentscheids in Sachsen. Berlin, 1976. pp. 255.

SOZIALISTISCHER Staat und staatliche Leitung: aktuelle Probleme der Tätigkeit der Staatsmacht in der DDR; (Autorenkollektiv: Walter Assmann [and others]; Gesamtredaktion: Michael Benjamin [and others]). Berlin, 1976. pp. 439.

— Greece.

PEJOV (NAUM) Makedoncite i graganskata vojna vo Grcija. Skopje, 1968. pp. 212. bibliog.

— Hungary.

KRÁL (VÁCLAV) Intervenční válka československé buržoasie proti Mad'arské sovětské republice v roce 1919. Praha, 1954. pp. 290,32.

HRANCHAK (IVAN MYKHAILOVYCH) and LEBOVICH (MARTIN FARKASHEVICH) Bela Kun - vydaiushchiisia deiatel' vengerskogo i mezhdunarodnogo revoliutsionnogo dvizheniia. Moskva, 1975. pp. 165.

KÁDÁR (JÁNOS) Izbrannye stat'i i rechi, fevral' 1970 g. - dekabr' 1975 g.; [perevod s vengerskogo]. Moskva, 1976. pp. 534.

— India.

GHOSH (SANKAR) The Naxalite movement: a Maoist experiment. Calcutta, 1974. pp. 183.

— Indochina.

COMMUNISM in Indochina: new perspectives; edited by Joseph J. Zasloff and MacAlister Brown. Lexington, Mass., [1975]. pp. 295. Papers originally presented at a seminar held in New York, 1974, sponsored by the Southeast Asia Development Advisory Group.

— Italy.

ORGANIZZAZIONE COMUNISTA AVANGUARDIA OPERAIA. Conferenza Nazionale, 2a, 1972. Documenti. Milano, 1973. 2 vols. (Quaderni. 7)

AUCIELLO (NICOLA) Socialismo ed egemonia in Gramsci e Togliatti. Bari, [1974]. pp. 207.

— Korea.

COMRADE Kim Il Sung: an ingenious thinker and theoretician. Pyongyang, 1975. pp. 160.

KIM (ILPYONG J.) Communist politics in North Korea. New York, 1975. pp. 121.

— Poland.

MARIAŃSKA (ANIELA) Wiklinowe kosz. Warszawa, 1959. pp. 311.

SOKORSKI (WŁODZIMIERZ) Kultura i polityka: szkice i artykuły. Warszawa, 1970. pp. 132.

WERBLAN (ANDRZEJ) Szkice i polemiki; [collected articles, 1958-1969]. Warszawa, 1970. pp. 301.

ARCHIWUM ruchu robotniczego. Warszawa, 1973 in progress.

— Russia.

GALIN (LEO) Sowjet-Russland in der Wirklichkeit. Stuttgart, 1920. pp. 72.

BUXTON (CHARLES RODEN) In a Russian village. London, 1922. pp. 96.

LENIN (VLADIMIR IL'ICH) Will the Bolsheviks maintain power?. London, 1922. pp. 122.

BERDIAEV (NIKOLAI ALEKSANDROVICH) Wahrheit und Lüge des Kommunismus; mit einem Anhang: Der Mensch und die Technik; deutsch von J. Schor. Luzern, 1934. pp. 135.

ALESSANDRI (PIERRE) Le socialisme vainqueur: U.R.S.S. Paris, [1936]. pp. 63. Not to be consulted without the permission of the Superintendent of Readers' Services.

LUXEMBURG (ROSA) Die russische Revolution; eingeleitet und herausgegeben von Ossip K. Flechtheim. Frankfurt am Main, [1963]. pp. 88.

OKTIABR'SKAIA revoliutsiia i formirovanie novykh obshchestvennykh otnoshenii: k 50-letiiu Velikoi Oktiabr'skoi sotsialisticheskoi revoliutsii. Orel, 1967. pp. 221. (Orlovskii Gosudarstvennyi Pedagogicheskii Institut. Uchenye Zapiski. t.37)

PROBLEMY istorii i teorii nauchnogo kommunizma: materialy nauchno- teoreticheskoi konferentsii. Moskva, 1969. pp. 267.

VELIKII Oktiabr' i kommunisticheskoe stroitel'stvo na Srednei Volge: materialy Kuibyshevskoi oblastnoi teoreticheskoi konferentsii, posviashchennoi 50-letiiu Velikoi Oktiabr'skoi sotsialisticheskoi revoliutsii. Kuibyshev, 1969. pp. 495.

UCHENYE ZAPISKI KAFEDR OBSHCHESTVENNYKH NAUK VUZOV LENINGRADA. Istoriia KPSS. vyp.10. Po leninskomu puti. Leningrad, 1970. pp. 141.

LEHNING (ARTHUR) Marxismus und Anarchismus in der russischen Revolution [and] Revolutionär-syndikalistiche Bewegung in Russland; [by G.P.] Maximoff. 2nd ed. Berlin, 1971. pp. 146.

FORMIROVANIE novogo cheloveka - "stroitelia kommunizma. Kishinev, 1973. pp. 127.

KRASNOV (ALEKSANDR VASIL'EVICH) TsKK-RKI v bor'be za sotsializm: rol' TsKK-RKI v osushchestvlenii leninskogo plana postroeniia sotsializma v SSSR, 1923-1934 gg. Irkutsk, 1973. pp. 560. bibliog.

The PLATFORM of the joint opposition, 1927. London, 1973. pp. 117.

IZ-POD glyb: sbornik statei...Moskva, 1974. Paris, [1974]. pp. 281.

KOSICHEV (ANATOLII DANILOVICH) Teoreticheskoe obobshchenie V.I. Leninym opyta Oktiabr'skoi revoliutsii i stroitel'stva sotsializma v SSSR. Moskva, 1974. pp. 314.

MEDVEDEV (ROI ALEKSANDROVICH) K sudu istorii: genezis i posledstviia stalinizma; Let history judge: the origins and consequences of Stalinism. 2nd ed. New York, 1974. pp. 1136.

NIKOLAEVA (LIDIIA VASIL'EVNA) Ob"ektivnye i sub"ektivnye faktory sotsial'nogo progressa i svobody. Moskva, 1974. pp. 259.

OPYT sotsialisticheskikh preobrazovanii v SSSR i ego mezhdunarodnoe znachenie: Mezhdunarodnaia nauchnaia konferentsiia v Tashkente, 16-19 oktiabria 1972 g. Moskva, 1974. pp. 336.

SCHNEIDER (DIETER MARC) Revolutionärer Syndikalismus und Bolschewismus: der Prozess der ideologischen Auseinandersetzung französischer Syndikalisten mit den Bolschewiki, 1914-1922. Erlangen, 1974. pp. 353. bibliog.

GILISON (JEROME MARTIN) The Soviet image of utopia. Baltimore, [1975]. PP. 192.

KALININ (MIKHAIL IVANOVICH) Izbrannye proizvedeniia; (sostaviteli F.G. Vashchenko [and others]). Moskva, 1975. pp. 448.

McNEAL (ROBERT HATCH) The Bolshevik tradition: Lenin, Stalin, Khrushchev, Brezhnev. 2nd ed. Englewood Cliffs, [1975]. pp. 210. bibliog.

POLITIKA i obshchestvo: sotsial'no-politicheskie problemy razvitogo sotsializma. Leningrad, 1975. pp. 191.

SOVETSKII narod - novaia istoricheskaia obshchnost' liudei: stanovlenie i razvitie. Moskva, 1975. pp. 520. bibliog.

TRIFONOV (IVAN IAKOVLEVICH) Likvidatsiia ekspluatatorskikh klassov v SSSR. Moskva, 1975. pp. 406.

TRUKAN (GERMAN ANTONOVICH) Rabochii klass v bor'be za pobedu i uprochenie Sovetskoi vlasti. Moskva, 1975. pp. 303.

PURDY (DAVID) The Soviet Union: state capitalist or socialist?: a Marxist critique of the International Socialists. London, [1976]. pp. 46. bibliog.

SOLZHENITSYN (ALEKSANDR ISAEVICH) Warning to the Western world. London, 1976. pp. 45. Consists of text of interview with Michael Charlton on BBC television's Panorama, 1 March 1976, and of a BBC radio broadcast, 24 March, 1976.

ULAM (ADAM BRUNO) Ideologies and illusions: revolutionary thought from Herzen to Solzhenitsyn. Cambridge, Mass., 1976. pp. 335.

VELIKII Sovetskii narod. Kiev, 1976. pp. 502. bibliog.

— — **Study and teaching — Bibliography.**

KOSYKH (G.T.) compiler. Protiv burzhuaznoi fal'sifikatsii istorii KPSS i sovetskogo obshchestva: ukazatel' literatury; pod redaktsiei...V.V. Privalova. Leningrad, 1974. pp. 118.

— — **Azerbaijan.**

VOPLOSHCHENIE sotsialisticheskogo internatsionalizma. Baku, 1974. pp. 227.

GUSHCHIN (SERGEI NIKOLAEVICH) and MEKHTIEV (GIAZENFER GIUSEINOVICH) Sotsializm i blagosostoianie trudiashchikhsia Sovetskogo Azerbaidzhana, 1920-1974 gg. Baku, 1975. pp. 182.

— — **Daghestan.**

GASANOV (SAID MUSAEVICH) Osushchestvlenie v Dagestane leninskikh idei nekapitalisticheskogo razvitiia ranee otstalykh stran i narodov. Makhachkala, 1970. pp. 209.

— — **Georgia.**

NATMELADZE (MAKVALA VASIL'EVNA) and STURUA (NIKOLAI IVANOVICH) Rabochii klass Gruzii v stroitel'stve material'no- tekhnicheskoi bazy sotsializma i kommunizma v SSSR. Tbilisi, 1975. pp. 97.

— — **Kazakstan.**

TORZHESTVO leninskikh idei proletarskogo internatsionalizma: na materialakh respublik Srednei Azii i Kazakhstana, 1917-1972 gg. Moskva, 1974. pp. 531.

— — **Kirghizia.**

OROZALIEV (KERIMKUL KENZHEVICH) Istoricheskii opyt perekhoda kirgizskogo naroda k sotsializmu, minuia kapitalizm. Frunze, 1974. pp. 377. bibliog.

— — **Moldavian Republic.**

LAZAREV (ARTEM MARKOVICH) Moldavskaia Sovetskaia gosudarstvennost' i bessarabskii vopros. Kishinev, 1974. pp. 910. bibliog.

— — **Soviet Central Asia.**

NARIMANOV (NARIMAN NADZHAF-OGLY) Lenin i Vostok: [sbornik statei, 1924-25; pod redaktsiei Dzh. B. Gulieva]. Baku, 1970. pp. 47.

TORZHESTVO leninskikh idei proletarskogo internatsionalizma: na materialakh Srednej Azii i Kazakhstana, 1917-1972 gg. Moskva, 1974. pp. 531.

— — **Soviet Far East.**

REVKOMY Severo-Vostoka SSSR, 1922-1928 gg.: sbornik dokumentov i materialov. Magadan, 1973. pp. 240.

— — **Ukraine.**

V.I. Lenin i revoliutsiinyi rukh na zakhidnoukraïns'kykh zemliakh. L'viv, 1969. pp. 167.

— — **Uzbekistan.**

ALIMOV (IBRAGIM ABDUGAPPAROVICH) Uzbekskoe dekhkanstvo na puti k sotsializmu: sotsial'no-ekonomicheskie preobrazovaniia v uzbekskom kishlake v 1921-1925 gg. Tashkent, 1974. pp. 239. bibliog.

— **United Kingdom.**

IMPERIALIZM i bor'ba rabochego klassa: sbornik statei pamiati akademika Fedora Aronovicha Rotshteina. Moskva, 1960. pp. 507.

BRITISH AND IRISH COMMUNIST ORGANISATION. The Tories and the left. Belfast, 1974. pp. 11.

— **United States.**

DIGGINS (JOHN P.) Up from communism: conservative odysseys in American intellectual history. New York, [1975]. pp. 522.

— **Vietnam.**

HEMERY (DANIEL) Révolutionnaires vietnamiens et pouvoir colonial en Indochine: communistes, trotskystes, nationlistes à Saigon de 1932 à 1937. Paris, 1975. pp. 524. bibliog.

WOODSIDE (ALEXANDER BARTON) Community and revolution in modern Vietnam. Boston, [Mass., 1976]. pp. 351. bibliog.

— **Yugoslavia.**

VELJIĆ (ANDJELKO) Društveno samoupravljanje u Jugoslaviji: novi oblik demokratije. Sarajevo, 1973. pp. 246. bibliog.

DENITCH (BOGDAN DENIS) The legitimation of a revolution: the Yugoslav case. New Haven, 1976. pp. 254. bibliog.

SINGLETON (FREDERICK BERNARD) Twentieth-century Yugoslavia. London, 1976. pp. 346. bibliog.

— — **Macedonian Republic.**

RAZVOJOT i karakteristikite na Narodnoosloboditelnata vojna i na Revolucijata vo Makedonija: simpozium, Skopje, 9-10 dekemvri 1971 godina. Skopje, 1973. pp. 857. bibliog.

COMMUNISM AND CHRISTIANITY.

BERDIAEV (NIKOLAI ALEKSANDROVICH) Wahrheit und Lüge des Kommunismus; mit einem Anhang: Der Mensch und die Technik; deutsch von J. Schor. Luzern, 1934. pp. 135.

GARAUDY (ROGER) The alternative future: a vision of Christian Marxism;... translated by Leonard Mayhew. Harmondsworth, 1976. pp. 221.

— **Catholic Church — Russia.**

KATOLITSIZM v SSSR i sovremennost': materialy nauchnoi konferentsii, sostoiavsheisia v g. Shiauliai 17-18 dekabria 1969 g. Vil'nius, 1971. pp. 245.

MÍGUEZ BONINO (JOSÉ) Christians and Marxists: the mutual challenge to revolution. London, [1976]. pp. 158. (London Lectures in Contemporary Christianity. 1974)

— **Russia.**

McCULLAGH (FRANCIS) The bolshevik persecution of Christianity. London, 1924. pp. 401.

POWELL (DAVID E.) Antireligious propaganda in the Soviet Union: a study of mass persuasion. Cambridge, [1975]. pp. 206. bibliog.

LANE (CHRISTEL OLGA) The impact of communist ideology and the Soviet order on Christian religion in the contemporary U.S.S.R., 1959-1974. 1976. fo. 489. bibliog. Typescript. Ph.D. thesis: unpublished. This thesis is the property of London University and may not be removed from the Library.

COMMUNISM AND LITERATURE.

IZ istorii Mezhdunarodnogo ob"edineniia revoliutsionnykh pisatelei (MORP). Moskva, 1969. pp. 680. (Akademiia Nauk SSSR. Institut Mirovoi Literatury. Literaturnoe Nasledstvo. t.81) Documents in original languages.

ASADULLAEV (SEIFULLA) Stanovlenie sotsialisticheskogo realizma v rannei sovetskoi literature. Baku, 1969. pp. 295.

MARKOV (DMITRII FEDOROVICH) Problemy teorii sotsialisticheskogo realizma. Moskva, 1975. pp. 352.

MATHEWSON (RUFUS WELLINGTON) The positive hero in Russian literature. 2nd ed. Stanford, 1975. pp. 369.

VASIN (KIM KIRILLOVICH) Prosvetitel'stvo i realizm: k probleme genezisa sotsialisticheskogo realizma v mariiskoi literature: istoriko- literaturovedcheskie ocherki. Ioshkar-Ola, 1975. pp. 246. bibliog.

COMMUNISM AND LITERATURE.(Cont.)

DUNHAM (VERA SANDOMIRSKY) In Stalin's time: middleclass values in Soviet fiction. Cambridge, 1976. pp. 283. *bibliog.*

EAGLETON (TERRY) Marxism and literary criticism. London, 1976. pp. 88. *bibliog.*

COMMUNISM AND MUSIC.

KRIZIS burzhuaznoi kul'tury i muzyka: sbornik statei. vyp.2. Moskva, 1973. pp. 245.

COMMUNISM AND RELIGION.

RELIGIIA, svobodomyslie, ateizm. Frunze, 1967. pp. 96.

MYKULA (WOLODYMYR) The gun and the faith: religion and church in Ukraine under the communist Russian rule. London, 1969. pp. 48.

BAZARBAEV (ZHUMANAZAR) Sekuliarizatsiia naseleniia sotsialisticheskoi Karakalpakii. Nukus, 1973. pp. 181.

MYSŁEK (WIESŁAW) and STASZEWSKI (MICHAŁ T.) eds. Polityka wyznaniowa: tło, warunki, realizacja. Warszawa, 1975. pp. 475. *With Russian and English tables of contents.*

VISSER (A.J.) Karl Marx en Lenin als kerkvaders?. Den Haag, [1975]. pp. 110.

ZYBKOVETS (VLADIMIR FILATOVICH) Natsionalizatsiia monastyrskikh imushchestv v Sovetskoi Rossii, 1917-1921 gg. Moskva, 1975. pp. 205.

COMMUNISM AND SOCIAL SCIENCES.

WIATR (JERZY J.) Współczesny antykomunizm a nauki społeczne: eseje polemiczne, [1967-1969]. Warszawa, 1970. pp. 204. *With Russian and English summaries.*

COMMUNISM AND THE ARTS.

SALIEV (A.) ed. Natsional'noe i internatsional'noe v iskusstve. Frunze, 1973. pp. 253.

PLEKHANOV (GEORGII VALENTINOVICH) Kunst und gesellschaftliches Leben; herausgegeben von Alexander Uschakow und Pjotr Nikolajew. Berlin, 1975. pp. 463. *bibliog.*

COMMUNISM AND ZIONISM.

HAMOL'SKYI (LEONID VOLODYMYROVYCH) Tryzub i "zirka" Davyda. Dnipropetrovs'k, 1975. pp. 191.

COMMUNIST COUNTRIES

— Commerce — United States.

RYANS (JOHN K.) and others, eds. China, the U.S.S.R. and eastern Europe: a U.S. trade perspective. Kent, Ohio, [1974]. pp. 196. *bibliog.*

— Commercial policy.

LOEBER (DIETRICH ANDRE) ed. East-West trade: a sourcebook on the international economic relations of socialist countries and their legal aspects. Dobbs Ferry, N.Y., 1976 in progress. .

HOLZMAN (FRANKLYN DUNN) International trade under communism: politics and economics. New York, [1976]. pp. 239. *bibliog.*

— Economic conditions.

VYSOKÁ ŠKOLA EKONOMICKÁ V BRATISLAVE. Medzinárodná sút'až študentskej vedeckej činnosti, 3., 1972. Zborník: za vyššiu efektívnosť národného hospodárstva v krajinách RVHP. Bratislava, [1973]. pp. 326,[li].

KRITIKA burzuaznykh kontseptsii ekonomiki sotsializma. Moskva, 1974. pp. 159.

PREDMET i metod politicheskoi ekonomii sotsializma; (predislovie A.I. Pashkova). Saratov, 1974. pp. 482.

— — Mathematical models.

PAWŁOWSKI (ZBIGNIEW) Ekonometria. Warszawa, 1966. pp. 417. *bibliog. With English and Russian summaries.*

— Economic integration.

AKTUAL'NYE problemy ekonomicheskoi teorii. Moskva, 1973. pp. 319.

PROBLEMY povysheniia ekonomicheskoi effektivnosti obshchestvennogo proizvodstva v sotsialisticheskikh stranakh. Moskva, 1973. pp. 239.

ROL' transporta v integratsii ekonomiki stran-chlenov SEV. Moskva, 1973. pp. 221. *bibliog. (Institut Kompleksnykh Transportnykh Problem. Trudy. vyp.37)*

INTERNATSIONALIZM i problemy sotsialisticheskoi ekonomicheskoi integratsii. Moskva, 1974. pp. 311.

TIMOSHIN (VIKTOR GRIGOR'EVICH) Razvitie otnoshenii planomernosti v mirovoi sotsialisticheskoi sisteme khoziaistva: na primere stran-chlenov SEV. Moskva, 1974. pp. 173.

VALENTINOVICH (L.S.) and SAVOST'IANOV (V.V.) Metody otsenki ekonomicheskoi effektivnosti mezhdunarodnoi sotsialisticheskoi spetsializatsii i kooperatsii proizvodstva: obzor; pod redaktsiei Iu.F. Kormnova. Moskva, 1974. pp. 47. *bibliog.*

BAUTINA (NINEL' VLADIMIROVNA) ed. Teoriia i praktika sotsialisticheskoi integratsii. Moskva, 1975. pp. 144.

OS'MOVA (MARKIANA NIKOLAEVNA) Formirovanie struktur v promyshlennom proizvodstve v usloviiakh sotsialisticheskoi integratsii. Moskva, 1975. pp. 158.

PUGACHEV (B.M.) Internatsionalizatsiia proizvodstva i sotsialisticheskaia integratsiia: nekotorye voprosy metodologii. Moskva, 1975. pp. 133.

RYBAKOV (OLEG KONSTANTINOVICH) Ekonomicheskaia effektivnosť sotrudnichestva SSSR s sotsialisticheskimi stranami: teoreticheskie i metodologicheskie problemy. Moskva, 1975. pp. 272.

SERGEEV (VITALII PAVLOVICH) and SHEVIAKOV (F.N.) eds. Ekonomicheskaia integratsiia i sovershenstvovanie mekhanizma sotrudnichestva stran-chlenov SEV. Moskva, 1975. pp. 248.

ZUEV (VLADIMIR IL'ICH) Mirovaia sistema sotsializma: ekonomicheskie i politicheskie aspekty edinstva - metodologicheskie problemy. Moskva, 1975. pp. 302.

— Economic policy.

MIKUL'SKII (KONSTANTIN IVANOVICH) ed. Problemy vosproizvodstva v stranakh SEV. Moskva, 1974. pp. 247.

LITVIAKOV (PAVEL PETROVICH) Ekonomicheskaia sistema sotsializma i planirovanie. Moskva, 1975. pp. 279. *bibliog.*

POLSKA AKADEMIA NAUK. Komitet Przestrzennego Zagospodarowania Kraju. Studia. t.51. Metodologiia izucheniia natsional'nogo dokhoda i gorodskikh aglomeratsii v sotsialisticheskikh stranakh: materialy III Soveshchaniia predstavitelei nauchnykh uchrezhdenii sotsialisticheskikh stran-chlenov SEV po voprosam metodologii regional'nykh issledovanii, Varshava, 4-8 dekabria 1974 g. Varshava, 1975. pp. 270.

BETTELHEIM (CHARLES) Economic calculation and forms of property. London, 1976. pp. 151. *bibliogs.*

ECONOMIC analysis of the Soviet-type system; [edited by] Judith Thornton. Cambridge, 1976. pp. 372. *bibliogs.*

NUTTER (GILBERT WARREN) Central economic planning: the visible hand. Washington, D.C., 1976. pp. 23. *(American Enterprise Institute for Public Policy Research. Domestic Affairs Studies. 41)*

— Foreign economic relations.

VNESHNEEKONOMICHESKIE sviazi sotsialisticheskikh stran. Moskva, 1974. pp. 326.

VOINOV (A.M.) and others. Ekonomicheskie otnosheniia mezhdu sotsialisticheskimi i razvitymi kapitalisticheskimi stranami. Moskva, 1975. pp. 195.

LOEBER (DIETRICH ANDRE) ed. East-West trade: a sourcebook on the international economic relations of socialist countries and their legal aspects. Dobbs Ferry, N.Y., 1976 in progress.

HOLZMAN (FRANKLYN DUNN) International trade under communism: politics and economics. New York, [1976]. pp. 239. *bibliog.*

— — Egypt.

USHAKOVA (NATALIIA ALEKSANDROVNA) Arabskaia Respublika Egipet: sotrudnichestvo so stranami sotsializma i ekonomicheskoe razvitie, 1952-1972 gg. Moskva, 1974. pp. 132. *bibliog.*

— — Russia.

LAVROVA (LARISA FEDOROVNA) Internatsionalizm sovetskogo naroda: sotsial'naia aktivnost' narodnykh mass v sfere mezhdunarodnogo sotsialisticheskogo sotrudnichestva. Kiev, 1975. pp. 143.

PETROVA (NINA KONSTANTINOVNA) Mezhdunarodnye proizvodstvennye sviazi rabochego klassa SSSR, 1959- 1970 gg. Moskva, 1975. pp. 304.

RYBAKOV (OLEG KONSTANTINOVICH) Ekonomicheskaia effektivnost' sotrudnichestva SSSR s sotsialisticheskimi stranami: teoreticheskie i metodologicheskie problemy. Moskva, 1975. pp. 272.

— Foreign relations.

SOZIALISTISCHE Diplomatie; ([by] W.N. Belezki [and others]; Redaktionskollegium: I.D. Ostojan-Owsjany [and others]; übersetzt von Wolfgang Eckstein); mit einem Vorwort von A. A. Gromyko. Berlin, 1974. pp. 315.

PETERSON (GORDON LEROY) The rapprochement between the Federal Republic of Germany and the Soviet Union, and the policy of international linkage in east- west relations, 1965-1971; [Ph. D.(London) thesis]. [1975]. fo. 305. *bibliog. Typescript: unpublished. This thesis is the property of London University and may not be removed from the Library.*

SIMON (JEFFREY) Ruling Communist parties and détente: a documentary history. Washington, D.C., 1975. pp. 314. *(American Enterprise Institute for Public Policy Research. Foreign Affairs Studies. 25)*

SOTSIALIZM i mezhdunarodnye otnosheniia. Moskva, 1975. pp. 424.

ŠTRBAC (ČEDOMIR) Jugoslavija i odnosi izmedju socijalističkih zemalja: sukob KPJ i Informbiroa. Beograd, 1975. pp. 231. *bibliog. With English and Russian summaries.*

— Industries.

KHROMOV (PAVEL ALEKSEEVICH) Tempy razvitiia promyshlennosti i sel'skogo khoziaistva: ekonomiko-statisticheskoe issledovanie. Moskva, 1974. pp. 199.

— Politics and government.

GOSUDARSTVO i demokratiia v period postroeniia razvitogo sotsializma. Moskva, 1974. pp. 296.

DALLEMAGNE (JEAN LUC) Construction du socialisme et révolution: essai sur la transition au socialisme. Paris, 1975. pp. 405.

COMMUNIST EDUCATION.

BRATSTVO narodov i internatsional'noe vospitanie: [materialy respublikanskoi nauchno-teoreticheskoi konferentsii "Torzhestvo leninskikh idei bratstva narodov i internatsional'noe vospitanie trudiashchikhsia"]. Tashkent, 1974. pp. 266.

COMMUNIST PARTY

— Russia.

AKADEMIIA OBSHCHESTVENNYKH NAUK. Kafedra Teorii i Metodov Ideologicheskoi Raboty. Voprosy Teorii i Metodov Ideologicheskoi Raboty. vyp.2. [Sbornik statei]. Moskva, 1973. pp. 325.

AKADEMIIA OBSHCHESTVENNYKH NAUK. Kafedra Teorii i Metodov Ideologicheskoi Raboty. Voprosy Teorii i Metodov Ideologicheskoi Raboty. vyp.4. Problemy effektivnosti ideino-vospitatel'noi deiatel'nosti. Moskva, 1975. pp. 333.

BREZHNEV (LEONID IL'ICH) O kommunisticheskom vospitanii trudiashchikhsia: rechi i stat'i. 2nd ed. Moskva, 1975. pp. 639.

POLITICHESKOE obrazovanie: sistema, metodika, metodologiia. Moskva, 1976. pp. 230. *bibliog.*

COMMUNIST ETHICS.

STUDIENTEXTE zur marxistisch-leninistischen Ethik; [edited by Günter Junghänel and Sigrid Tackmann]. Berlin, 1976. pp. 356.

COMMUNIST PARTIES.

PARTIDO COMUNISTA PARAGUAYO. Comite Central. Dos lineas: guerra revolucionaria, compromiso apaciguador; declaracion del C.C. del P.C. Paraguayo en relacion a la Conferencia de Moscu. Montevideo, 1969. pp. 77.

DOROFEEV (SERGEI IVANOVICH) Ekonomicheskaia programma klassovoi bor'by; pod obshchei redaktsiei V.V. Zagladina. Moskva, 1974. pp. 424.

WERNER (LUTZ) Der Kampf der Kommunistischen Parteien in den sozialistischen Staaten gegen Bürokratismus. Kiel, 1974. pp. 152,iv. *bibliog.* (Kiel. Universität. Institut für Recht, Politik und Gesellschaft der Sozialistischen Staaten. Manuskripte. 4)

SIMON (JEFFREY) Ruling Communist parties and détente: a documentary history. Washington, D.C., 1975. pp. 314. (American Enterprise Institute for Public Policy Research. Foreign Affairs Studies. 25)

VODOLAZSKII (ANATOLII FEODOSIEVICH) Zakon zhizni partii: bor'ba Marksa, Engel'sa, Lenina za kollektivnost' partiinogo rukovodstva. Moskva, 1975. pp. 272.

STELTNER (GUENTER) and others. Die Arbeiterklasse der sozialistischen Gemeinschaft in den siebziger Jahren: die Politik der Bruderparteien, etc. Berlin, 1976. pp. 163.

— Party work.

INTERNATSIONAL'NOE znachenie leninskikh printsipov partiinogo stroitel'stva: materialy dvustoronnego nauchnogo simpoziuma, organizovannogo Institutom marksizma-leninizma pri TsK KPSS i Institutom marksizma-leninizma TsK KPCh, Praga, 12-14 dekabria 1972 g. Moskva, 1973. pp. 359.

COMMUNIST PARTY

— Austria.

KOMMUNISTISCHE PARTEI ÖSTERREICHS. Historische Kommission. Beiträge zur Geschichte der Kommunistischen Partei Österreichs. [Vienna, 1976]. pp. 112. *bibliogs.*

— Brazil.

GUEIROS LEITE (ERALDO) O inquérito do P[artido] C[omunista do Brasil] e sua passagem pelo Superior Tribunal Militar. Rio de Janeiro, 1967. pp. 58.

PARTIDO COMUNISTA DO BRASIL. Comite Central. La guerra popular en el Brasil. Montevideo, 1970. pp. 57.

CHILCOTE (RONALD H.) The Brazilian Communist Party: conflict and integration, 1922-1972. New York, 1974. pp. 361. *bibliogs.*

— Bulgaria — Congresses.

BULGARSKA KOMUNISTICHESKA PARTIIA. Kongres, 10-i, 1971. Deseti kongres na Bulgarskata komunisticheska partiia: dokladi, resheniia. Sofiia, 1973. pp. 350.

— Canada.

AVAKUMOVIĆ (IVAN) The Communist Party in Canada: a history. Toronto, [1975]. pp. 309. *bibliog.*

— China.

GUILLERMAZ (JACQUES) Histoire du Parti communiste chinois. [2nd ed.] Paris, [1975]. pp. 473.

WANG (MING) Polveka KPK i predatel'stvo Mao Tsze-duna. Moskva, 1975. pp. 311.

DAVIN (DELIA) Woman-work: women and the party in revolutionary China. Oxford, 1976. pp. 244. *bibliog.*

MAITAN (LIVIO) Party, army and masses in China: a marxist interpretation of the cultural revolution and its aftermath. London, 1976. pp. 373.

— Colombia.

PARTIDO COMUNISTA DE COLOMBIA. Comision Nacional de Educacion. Que es y por que lucha el Partido Comunista. [Bogota,] 1966. pp. 77.

PARTIDO COMUNISTA DE COLOMBIA. Comite Central. Resolución política del Partido Comunista de Colombia (m-l). Montevideo, 1969. pp. 79.

— Czechoslovakia — Party work.

INTERNATSIONAL'NOE znachenie leninskikh printsipov partiinogo stroitel'stva: materialy dvustoronnego nauchnogo simpoziuma, organizovannogo Institutom marksizma-leninizma pri TsK KPSS i Institutom marksizma-leninizma TsK KPCh, Praga, 12-14 dekabria 1972 g. Moskva, 1973. pp. 359.

— — Slovakia — Congresses.

KOMUNISTICKÁ STRANA SLOVENSKA. Zjazd, 1971. Zjazd Komunistickej strany Slovenska, 13.-15. mája 1971. [Bratislava], 1971. pp. 207.

— Denmark.

NIELSEN (MOGENS) ed. Enhed i arbejderbevaegelsen: kilder til belysning af forhandlingerne mellem Danmarks kommunistiske Parti og Socialdemokratiet, 1945. København, [1973]. pp. 47. *bibliog.*

— Dominican Republic.

[PARTIDO COMUNISTA DOMINICANO] Triunfaremos: la lucha revolucionaria en la Republica Dominicana, año 1965. Praga, 1966. pp. 64.

— France.

PARTI COMMUNISTE FRANCAIS. Comment sortir de l'abîme?: programme d'indépendance nationale de progrès social de démocratie et de paix du Parti Communiste Français. Paris, [1951]. pp. 29.

PARTI COMMUNISTE FRANÇAIS. Artisans, commerçants: comment se defendre. Paris, [1954]. pp. 31.

HARRIS (ANDRE) and SEDOUY (ALAIN DE) Voyage à l'intérieur du Parti Communiste. Paris, 1974. pp. 444.

CAMPBELL (IAN R.) The end of the Mitterrand experiment? Coventry, 1975. pp. 57. (University of Warwick. Department of Politics. Working Papers. No. 5)

COMMUNISM in Italy and France; edited by Donald L. M. Blackmer and Sidney Tarrow. Princeton, [1975]. pp. 651. *Papers of a conference held at M.I.T.'s Endicott House, Dedham, Massachusetts, in October 1972.*

VIEUGUET (ANDRE) Français et immigrés: le combat du Parti communiste français. Paris, [1975]. pp. 223.

— Germany.

THAELMANN (ERNST) Volksrevolution über Deutschland: Rede... auf dem Plenum des ZK. der KPD., 15-17. Januar 1931. [Berlin], 1931. pp. 62.

THAELMANN (ERNST) Kampfreden und Aufsätze. Berlin, 1932. pp. 96.

GROTEWOHL (OTTO) Zur politischen Lage Deutschlands: ([Report to the] Parteivorstand der Sozialistischen Einheitspartei Deutschlands...am 22. Januar 1947). Berlin, [1947]. pp. 48.

MAMMACH (KLAUS) Der Kampf der deutschen Arbeiterklasse im August 1930 gegen Imperialismus, Militarismus und Krieg; mit einem Dokumentenanhang. Berlin, 1956. pp. 51. (Institut für Marxismus-Leninismus (Berlin). Beiträge zur Geschichte und Theorie der Arbeiterbewegung. Heft 7)

LASCHITZA (HORST) Deutschland und die deutsche Arbeiterbewegung, 1939-1945; mit einem Dokumentenanhang. Berlin, 1963. pp. 140.

ZUR Geschichte der Kommunistischen Partei Deutschlands: eine Auswahl von Materialien und Dokumenten aus den Jahren 1914-1946. Kiel, [1972]. pp. 462.

BERS (GUENTER) ed. Der Bezirk Mittelrhein/Saar der Kommunistischen Partei Deutschlands, KPD, im Jahre 1922. Wentorf bei Hamburg, [1975]. pp. 156. *bibliogs.*

FRENZEL (MAX) and others. Gesprengte Fesseln: ein Bericht über den antifaschistischen Widerstand und die Geschichte der illegalen Parteiorganisation der KPD im Zuchthaus Brandenburg-Goerden von 1933 bis 1945. Berlin, [1975]. pp. 347.

BAHNE (SIEGFRIED) Die KPD und das Ende von Weimar: das Scheitern einer Politik, 1932-1935. Frankfurt/Main, [1976]. pp. 184. *bibliog.*

— — Bibliography.

GUENTHER (KLAUS) and SCHMITZ (KURT THOMAS) compilers. SPD, KPD/DKP, DGB in den Westzonen und in der Bundesrepublik Deutschland, 1945-1973: eine Bibliographie. Bonn-Bad Godesberg, 1976. pp. 176. (Archiv für Sozialgeschichte. Beihefte. 6)

— — Berlin.

SOZIALISTISCHE EINHEITSPARTEI DEUTSCHLANDS. Landesvorstand Gross- Berlin. Die Krise der SPD und die Politik der SED. Gross-Berlin, [1947]. pp. 102. (Material für die Funktionäre der SED)

— Germany, Eastern.

GROTEWOHL (OTTO) Zur politischen Lage Deutschlands: ([Report to the] Parteivorstand der Sozialistischen Einheitspartei Deutschlands...am 22. Januar 1947). Berlin, [1947]. pp. 48.

SOZIALISTISCHE EINHEITSPARTEI DEUTSCHLANDS. Landesvorstand Gross- Berlin. Die Krise der SPD und die Politik der SED. Gross-Berlin, [1947]. pp. 102. (Material für die Funktionäre der SED)

GROTEWOHL (OTTO) Im Kampf um Deutschland: Reden und Aufsätze, [1945-1948]. Berlin, [1948]. 2 vols.(in 1).

GROTEWOHL (OTTO) Jugend und Partei: (aus einer Rede...des Parteivorstandes der SED, 20 und 21. Juli 1949). Berlin, [1949]. pp. 23.

WAGNER (UWE) Vom Kollektiv zur Konkurrenz: Partei und Massenbewegung in der DDR. Berlin, 1974. pp. 232. *bibliog.*

KIERA (HANS GEORG) Partei und Staat im Planungssystem der DDR: die Planung in der Ära Ulbricht. Düsseldorf, [1975]. pp. 230. *bibliog.*

ARENS (UWE) Die andere Freiheit: die Freiheit in Theorie und Praxis der Sozialistischen Einheitspartei Deutschlands. München, 1976. pp. 291. *bibliog.*

AXEN (HERMANN) Sozialismus und revolutionärer Weltprozess: ausgewählte Reden und Aufsätze. Berlin, 1976. pp. 614.

COMMUNIST PARTY(Cont.)

VERNER (PAUL) Für das Wohl der Arbeiterklasse und des ganzen Volkes: ausgewählte Reden und Aufsätze. Berlin, 1976. pp. 507.

— — Party work.

MITTAG (GUENTER) Aufgaben und Methoden der Parteiarbeit in der Industrie, im Bauwesen und im Handel. Berlin, 1960. pp. 63. *(Sozialistische Einheitspartei Deutschlands. Zentralkomitee. Der Parteiarbeiter. Heft 3)*

— Greece.

WOODHOUSE (CHRISTOPHER MONTAGUE) The struggle for Greece, 1941-1949. London, 1976. pp. 324. *bibliog.*

— Hungary — Congresses.

MAGYAR SZOCIALISTA MUNKÁSPÁRT. Kongresszus, 11., 1975. XI s″ezd Vengerskoi sotsialisticheskoi rabochei partii, Budapesh 17-22 marta 1975g. Moskva, 1975. pp. 278.

— Iran.

Die KOMMUNISTISCHE Bewegung Irans; [translated from the Persian, origininally published in Tudeh No. 15]. [Munich], 1973 in progress. *bibliog.*

— Israel.

NAHAS (DUNIA HABIB) The Israeli Communist Party. London, 1976. pp. 113. *bibliog.*

— Italy.

BRANDIRALI (ALDO) and BOTTINO (GIANMARIO) La linea politica dei comunisti nella Resistenza e nel dopoguerra, 1943-1953. Milano, [1974]. pp. 291. *bibliog.*

BARCA (LUCIANO) and others, eds. I comunisti e l'economia italiana, 1944-1974: antologia di scritti e documenti. Bari, [1975]. pp. 447.

BERLINGUER (ENRICO) La proposta comunista: relazione al Comitato centrale e alla Commissione centrale di controllo del Partito comunista italiano in preparazione del XIV Congresso. Torino, [1975]. pp. 152.

BERLINGUER (ENRICO) La "questione comunista", 1969-1975; a cura di Antonio Tatò. Roma, 1975. 2 vols.

BERLINGUER (ENRICO) Unità del popolo per salvare l'Italia: (il testo integrale del rapporto tenuto al XIV Congresso nazionale del Partito comunista italiano). Roma, [1975]. pp. 111.

BORDIGA (AMADEO) Scritti scelti; a cura di Franco Livorsi. mILANO, 1975. PP. 266.

COMMUNISM in Italy and France; edited by Donald L. M. Blackmer and Sidney Tarrow. Princeton, [1975]. pp. 651. *Papers of a conference held at M.I.T.'s Endicott House, Dedham, Massachusetts, in October 1972.*

HAMRIN (HARALD) Between bolshevism and revisionism: the Italian Communist Party 1944-1947. Stockholm, [1975]. pp. 340. *bibliog. (Utrikespolitiska Institutet. Swedish Studies in International Relations. 5)*

LAJOLO (DAVIDE) Finestre aperte a Botteghe Oscure. Milano, [1975]. pp. 246.

LONGO (LUIGI) Chi ha tradito la Resistenza? Roma, 1975. pp. 373.

MERLI (STEFANO) Fronte antifascista e politica di classe: socialisti e comunisti in Italia, 1923-1939. Bari, [1975]. pp. 355.

RODANO (FRANCO) Sulla politica dei comunisti. Torino, [1975]. pp. 132.

— Netherlands.

BRAUN (MARIANNE) De regeringskommissaris in Finsterwolde: een bijdrage tot de geschiedschrijving van de koude oorlog in Nederland. Amsterdam, 1975. pp. 92. *bibliog.*

— Paraguay.

PARTIDO COMUNISTA PARAGUAYO. Comite Central. Dos lineas: guerra revolucionaria, compromiso apaciguador; declaracion del C.C. del P.C. Paraguayo en relacion a la Conferencia de Moscu. Montevideo, 1969. pp. 77.

— Peru.

PRADO (JORGE DEL) 40 años de lucha: Partido Comunista Peruano, 1928-1968; notas historicas del P.C.P. [Lima?, 1968?]. pp. 58.

— Poland.

GÓRA (WŁADYSŁAW) and OKĘCKI (STANISŁAW) Za nasza i wasza wolność: Für unsere und eure Freiheit: deutsche Antifaschisten im polnischen Widerstandskampf; herausgegeben von Reinhold Jeske; (von Norbert Rösler und Eduard Ullmann ins Deutsche übersetzt). Berlin, [1975]. pp. 562. *bibliog. In German.*

KOWALCZYK (JÓZEF) Komunistyczna Partia Polski w okręgu łom'zyńskim, 1919- 1938. Warszawa, 1975. pp. 312. *bibliog. (Białystok. Ośrodek Badań Naukowych. Seria Rozprawy i Monografie. Nr.4)*

KOWALSKI (JÓZEF) Komunistyczna Partia Polski, 1935-1938: studium historyczne. Warszawa, 1975. pp. 472. *bibliog.*

DZIEWANOWSKI (M.K.) The Communist Party of Poland: an outline of history. 2nd ed. Cambridge, Mass., 1976. pp. 419. *bibliog. (Harvard University. Russian Research Center. Studies. 32)*

NAUMIUK (JAN) Polska Partia Robotnicza na Kielecczyźnie. Warszawa, 1976. pp. 567. *bibliog.*

PRZYGOŃSKI (ANTONI) Z zagadnień strategii frontu narodowego PPR, 1942-1945. Warszawa, 1976. pp. 400. *bibliog.*

RATYŃSKI (WŁADYSŁAW) Lewica Związkowa w II Rzeczypospolitej. Warszawa, 1976. pp. 330. *bibliog.*

— — Party work.

BUDZYŃSKA (CELINA) Krytyka i samokrytyka. Warszawa, 1954. pp. 55.

— Portugal.

WODDIS (JACK) Portugal: support the revolution. London, [1975]. pp. 12. *(Communist Party of Great Britain. Communist Party Pamphlets)*

— Romania.

GILBERG (TROND) Modernization in Romania since World War II. New York, 1975. pp. 261. *bibliog.*

— Russia.

UCHENYE ZAPISKI KAFEDR OBSHCHESTVENNYKH NAUK VUZOV LENINGRADA. Istoriia KPSS. vyp.8. KPSS v bor'be za sotsializm i kommunizm. Leningrad, 1968. pp. 163.

PROZOROV (VITALII PETROVICH) Khimicheskaia promyshlennost' Urala v gody dovoennykh piatiletok: iz istorii bor'by partiinykh organizatsii Urala za osushchestvlenie leninskoi politiki sotsialisticheskoi industrializatsii strany. Sverdlovsk, 1969. pp. 76.

UCHENYE ZAPISKI KAFEDR OBSHCHESTVENNYKH NAUK VUZOV LENINGRADA. Istoriia KPSS. vyp.9. Istoriia KPSS. Leningrad, 1969. pp. 158.

OCHERKI istorii Smolenskoi organizatsii KPSS. Moskva, 1970. pp. 574.

UCHENYE ZAPISKI KAFEDR OBSHCHESTVENNYKH NAUK VUZOV LENINGRADA. Istoriia KPSS. vyp.10. Po leninskomu puti. Leningrad, 1970. pp. 141.

KURS lektsii po istorii Kommunisticheskoi partii Sovetskogo Soiuza. 2nd ed. Leningrad, 1971-75. 3 vols.

URAL'SKII GOSUDARSTVENNYI UNIVERSITET. Uchenye Zapiski. no. 120. Seriia Istoricheskaia. vyp. no.23. Iz istorii partiinykh organizatsii Urala: sbornik statei. Sverdlovsk, 1971. pp. 192.

VALENTINOV (NIKOLAI VLADISLAVOVICH) pseud. [i.e. Nikolai Vladislavovich VOL'SKII] Novaia ekonomicheskaia politika i krizis partii posle smerti Lenina: gody raboty v VSNKh vo vremia NEP; vospominaniia....; The new economic policy and the Party crisis after the death of Lenin: reminiscences of my work at the VSNKh during the NEP; edited by J. Bunyan and V. Butenko, etc. Stanford, 1971. pp. 256.

OCHERKI istorii partiinykh organizatsii Dona, 1898-1920. 2nd ed. Rostov, 1973 in progress.

ZAUZOLKOV (FEDOR NIKOLAEVICH) Kommunisticheskaia partiia - organizator sozdaniia nauchnoi i proizvodstvenno-tekhnicheskoi intelligentsii SSSR. Moskva, 1973. pp. 127.

ANIKEEV (VLADIMIR VSEVOLODOVICH) Deiatel'nost' TsK RSDRP(b)-RKP(b) v 1917-1918 godakh: khronika sobytii: oktiabr' 1917... oktiabr' 1918. Moskva, 1974. pp.557.

ARTOBOLEVSKII (I.I.) and others, eds. Partiia i sovremennaia nauchno-tekhnicheskaia revoliutsiia v SSSR. Moskva, 1974. pp. 336. *bibliog.*

EZHOV (VIKTOR ANATOL'EVICH) and OVSIANKIN (V.A.) eds. Rabochii klass SSSR na sovremennom etape. vyp.3. Leningrad, 1974. pp. 196.

GANIN (NIKOLAI IVANOVICH) Zakonomernosti sotsialisticheskoi revoliutsii i istoricheskii opyt KPSS. Moskva, 1974. pp. 255.

KAPUSTIN (MIKHAIL IVANOVICH) Deiatel'nost' KPSS po sozdaniiu tret'ei metallurgicheskoi bazy strany: rukovodstvo partii razvitiem chernoi metallurgii Sibiri i Dal'nego Vostoka v period mezhdu XX i XXIII s″ezdami KPSS. Irkutsk, 1974. pp. 639.

KOMMUNISTICHESKAIA PARTIIA SOVETSKOGO SOIUZA. Leningradskii oblastnoi Komitet. Institut Istorii Partii. Leningradskaia organizatsiia KPSS v tsifrakh, 1917-1973. Leningrad, 1974. pp. 144.

KPSS i Sovetskoe pravitel'stvo o Sovetskom Kirgizstane: (sbornik dokumentov, 1924-1974). Frunze, 1974. pp. 380.

KUZNETSOVA (LIDIIA SERGEEVNA) Leningradskaia partiinaia organizatsiia v predvoennye gody, 1938 g. - iiun' 1941 g. Leningrad, 1974. pp. 254.

OCHERKI istorii Chuvashskoi oblastnoi organizatsii KPSS. Cheboksary, 1974. pp. 627.

OCHERKI istorii Karel'skoi organizatsii KPSS. Petrozavodsk, 1974. pp. 590.

OCHERKI istorii Penzenskoi organizatsii KPSS. Penza, 1974. pp. 527.

PERMSKAIA oblastnaia organizatsiia KPSS v tsifrakh, 1917-1973: statisticheskii sbornik. Perm', 1974. pp. 191.

TITOV (ALEKSANDR GRIGOR'EVICH) and others. Bor'ba Kommunisticheskoi partii s antileninskimi gruppami i techeniiami v posleoktiabr'skii period, 1917-1934 gg. Moskva, 1974. pp. 359.

UCHENYE ZAPISKI KAFEDR OBSHCHESTVENNYKH NAUK VUZOV LENINGRADA. Istoriia KPSS. vyp.14. Iz istorii sozdaniia i deiatel'nosti partii. Leningrad, 1974. pp. 197.

ANOSHKIN (IVAN FEDOROVICH) Internatsionalizm vnutrennei politiki KPSS: iz teoreticheskogo naslediia V.I. Lenina. Moskva, 1975. pp. 79.

BREZHNEV (LEONID IL'ICH) O vneshnei politike KPSS i Sovetskogo gosudarstva: rechi i stat'i. 2nd ed. Moskva, 1975. pp. 879.

BREZHNEV (LEONID IL'ICH) Ob osnovnykh voprosakh ekonomicheskoi politiki KPSS na sovremennom etape: rechi i doklady. Moskva, 1975. 2 vols.

COMMUNIST PARTY (Cont.)

KOZLOV (NIKOLAI DMITRIEVICH) and ZAITSEV (ALEKSEI DMITRIEVICH) Srazhaiushchaiasia partiia. Moskva, 1975. pp. 271.

LIKHOMANOV (MIKHAIL IVANOVICH) Khoziaistvenno-organizatorskaia rabota partii v derevne v pervyi period Velikoi Otechestvennoi voiny, 1941-1942 gg. Leningrad, 1975. pp. 136.

MATIUSHKIN (NIKOLAI IVANOVICH) Patriotizm i internatsionalizm sovetskogo naroda: istoricheskii opyt i sovremennaia deiatel'nost' KPSS. Moskva, 1975. pp. 416.

OGANESOV (GRANT SAAKOVICH) Vozrastanie rukovodiashchei roli KPSS na sovremennom etape. Erevan, 1975. pp. 346.

OSUSHCHESTVLENIE printsipov internatsionalizma v natsional'noi politike KPSS. Moskva, 1975. pp. 342.

SABUROV (NIKOLAI NIKOLAEVICH) Bor'ba partii za ustanovlenie ekonomicheskoi smychki rabochego klassa s trudiashchimsia krest'ianstvom, 1921-1925 gg.; pod redaktsiei...V.A. Smyshliaeva. Leningrad, 1975. pp. 119.

SIKORSKII (VSEVOLOD MIKHAILOVICH) KPSS na etape razvitogo sotsializma. Minsk, 1975. pp. 334.

TROTSKII (LEV DAVYDOVICH) Tasks before the twelfth congress of the Russian Communist Party; translated by Brian Pearce. London, 1975. pp. 63.

UCHENYE ZAPISKI KAFEDR OBSHCHESTVENNYKH NAUK VUZOV LENINGRADA. Istoriia KPSS. vyp.15. Ispytannyi avangard mass. Leningrad, 1975. pp. 199.

ZLOBINA (VERA MAKSIMOVNA) Bor'ba partii bol'shevikov protiv melkoburzhuaznogo vliianiia na rabochii klass v pervye gody nepa, 1921-1925 gg. Moskva, 1975. pp. 168.

— — Bibliography.

KOSYKH (G.T.) compiler. Protiv burzhuaznoi fal'sifikatsii istorii KPSS i sovetskogo obshchestva: ukazatel' literatury; pod redaktsiei...V.V. Privalova. Leningrad, 1974. pp. 118.

— — Party work.

AKADEMIIA OBSHCHESTVENNYKH NAUK. Kafedra Teorii i Metodov Ideologicheskoi Raboty. Voprosy Teorii i Metodov Ideologicheskoi Raboty. vyp.2. [Sbornik statei]. Moskva, 1973. pp. 325.

NAUCHNYE osnovy partiinoi propagandy. Gor'kii, 1973. pp. 161. (Gor'kii. Universitet. Uchenye Zapiski. vyp.165. Seriia Istoricheskaia)

AKTIVNYE pomoshchniki partiinykh komitetov: iz opyta raboty partiinykh komissii. Moskva, 1974. pp. 287.

BOKAREV (NIKOLAI NIKOLAEVICH) Voprosy sotsiologii v partiinoi rabote. Moskva, 1974. pp. 168. bibliog.

KOMMUNISTICHESKAIA PARTIIA SOVETSKOGO SOIUZA. Pervichnaia partiinaia organizatsiia: dokumenty KPSS; posleoktiabr'skii period. 2nd ed. Moskva, 1974. pp. 527.

AKADEMIIA OBSHCHESTVENNYKH NAUK. Kafedra Teorii i Metodov Ideologicheskoi Raboty. Voprosy Teorii i Metodov Ideologicheskoi Raboty. vyp.4. Problemy effektivnosti ideino-vospitatel'noi deiatel'nosti. Moskva, 1975. pp. 333.

INTERNATSIONAL'NYI printsip v stroitel'stve i deiatel'nosti KPSS. Moskva, 1975. pp. 296.

NOVOE v partiinoi rabote. [vyp.5]. Moskva, 1975. pp. 263.

POLITICHESKOE obrazovanie: sistema, metodika, metodologiia. Moskva, 1976. pp. 230. bibliog.

— — Azerbaijan — Statistics.

KOMMUNISTICHESKAIA PARTIIA AZERBAIDZHANA. Tsentral'nyi Komitet. Institut Istorii Partii. Kommunisticheskaia partiia Azerbaidzhana v tsifrakh: statisticheskii sbornik. Baku, 1970. pp. 161.

— — Kazakstan.

SAPARBAEV (KOISHIBAI) Kommunisticheskaia partiia Kazakhstana v bor'be za sozdanie mashinostroitel'noi promyshlennosti v respublike v gody Velikoi Otechestvennoi voiny. Alma-Ata, 1974. pp. 142. bibliog.

— — Khorezm.

KALANDAROV (NURIDDIN KHODZHAEVICH) Obrazovanie i deiatel'nost' Khorezmskoi Kommunisticheskoi partii, 1920-1924. Tashkent, 1975. pp. 328.

— — Kirghizia — Bibliography.

SHOFLER (ZIGIZMUND GAVRILOVICH) and LI (GENNADII PETROVICH) compilers. Istoriia Kommunisticheskoi partii Kirgizii: annotirovannyi ukazatel' literatury. ch.2. 1946-1967 gg. Frunze, 1969. pp. 403.

— — Latvia.

LATVIISKII GOSUDARSTVENNYI UNIVERSITET. Uchenye Zapiski. t.219. Germaniia i Pribaltika. 3. Riga, 1974. pp. 107.

— — Moldavian Republic.

ROTARU (MIKHAIL FEDOROVICH) Kommunisticheskaia partiia Moldavii v bor'be za pod"em sel'skogo khoziaistva respubliki, 1959-1970; pod redaktsiei...V. P. Seregina. Kishinev, 1974. pp. 188. bibliog.

— — — Congresses.

OLEINIK (KLAVDIIA ELISEEVNA) Dokumenty s"ezdov i plenumov TsK Kompartii Moldavii kak istochnik izucheniia istorii respublikanskoi partorganizatsii, 1941-1951 gg.; pod redaktsiei...M.N. Chernomorskogo. Kishinev, 1974. pp. 135.

— — Ukraine.

MAISTRENKO (IVAN) Storinky 3 istoriï Komunistychnoï partiï Ukraïny. Niu-York, 1967-69. 2 pts (in 1). Reprinted from Suchasnist'.

NARYSY istoriï Kharkivs'koï oblasnoï partiinoï orhanizatsiï. Kharkiv, 1970. pp. 803.

NARYSY istoriï Poltavs'koï oblasnoï partiinoï orhanizatsiï. Khrkiv, 1970. pp. 452.

KOMUNISTYCHNA partiia Ukraïny v rezoliutsiiakh i rishenniakh z"ïzdiv, konferentsii i plenumiv TsK. Kyïv, 1976 in progress.

— — Ukraine, Western.

MASHOTAS (VLADIMIR VLADIMIROVICH) Komunistychna partiia Zakhidnoï Ukraïny. L'viv, 1969. pp. 439.

— — Uzbekistan.

KUDRIAKOV (VLADIMIR MIKHAILOVICH) Za pod"em narodnogo khoziaistva: opyt rukovodstva Kompartii Uzbekistana khoziaistvennym stroitel'stvom v gody semiletki, 1959- 1965 gg. Tashkent, 1969. pp. 192.

OCHERKI istorii Kommunisticheskoi partii Uzbekistana. Tashkent, 1974. pp. 768.

— — White Russia.

PODPOL'NYE partiinye organy Kompartii Belorussii v gody Velikoi Otechestvennoi voiny, 1941-1944: kratkie svedeniia ob organizatsii, strukture i sostave. Minsk, 1975. pp. 270.

ROSMAN (IOSIF SAMUILOVICH) Kompartiia Belorussii v bor'be za uprochenie sotsialisticheskogo obshchestva v predvoennye gody, 1938 - iiun' 1941 gg. Minsk, 1975. pp. 351.

SIKORSKII (VSEVOLOD MIKHAILOVICH) and others, eds. Voprosy istorii KPSS: nekotorye voprosy organizatorskoi i ideologicheskoi deiatel'nosti KPSS, na materialakh Belorusskoi SSR; mezhvedomstvennyi sbornik 5. Minsk, 1975. pp. 216.

VOPROSY istorii KPSS: nekotorye voprosy organizatorskoi i ideologicheskoi deiatel'nosti KPSS; na materialakh Belorusskoi SSR; mezhvedomstvennyi sbornik 4. Minsk, 1975. pp. 238.

— Sweden.

HERMANSSON (CARL HENRIK) För socialismen: (artiklar och tal, 1964-74). Stockholm, 1974. pp. 279.

— United Kingdom.

COMMUNIST PARTY OF GREAT BRITAIN. The N[ational] H[ealth] S[ervice] Co. Ltd.; notes on the health service reorganisation. [London, 1972?]. pp. 16.

POLOZHENIE i bor'ba britanskogo rabochego klassa. Moskva, 1974. pp. 352.

BARNSBY (GEORGE) 1945: year of victory. London, 1975. pp. 37. bibliog. (Communist Party of Great Britain. History Group. Our History. No. 62)

BRENNAN (IRENE) Northern Ireland: a programme for action. London, [1975]. pp. 28. (Communist Party of Great Britain. Communist Party Pamphlets)

COMMUNIST PARTY OF GREAT BRITAIN. Executive Committee. Draft resolutions (for the 34th national congress). London, [1975]. pp. 16.

HINTON (JAMES) and HYMAN (RICHARD) Trade unions and revolution: the industrial politics of the early British Communist Party. London, 1975. pp. 78.

MATTHEWS (GEORGE) Communist. Britain's crisis, cause and cure: the £6 fraud exposed. London, [1975]. pp. 30. (Communist Party of Great Britain. Communist Party Pamphlets)

DEWAR (HUGO) Communist politics in Britain: the CPGB from its origins to the Second World War. London, 1976. pp. 159.

FALBER (REUBEN) Britain needs socialism. London, [1976]. pp. 28. (Communist Party of Great Britain. Communist Party Pamphlets)

MAHON (JOHN A.) Harry Pollitt: a biography. London, 1976. pp. 567. bibliog.

— Ireland.

NOLAN (SEAN) Communist Party of Ireland: outline history. Dublin, [1975]. pp. 64.

— United States.

JAFFE (PHILIP JACOB) The rise and fall of American communism. New York, [1975]. pp. 236.

WEINSTEIN (JAMES) Ambiguous legacy: the Left in American politics. New York, 1975. pp. 179.

— Yugoslavia.

ZOGRAFSKI (TODOR G.) and ZOGRAFSKI (DIMČE A.) KPJ i VMRO (Obedineta) vo Vardarska Makedonija vo periodot 1920-1930. Skopje, 1974. pp. 292.

— — Congresses.

SAVEZ KOMUNISTA JUGOSLAVIJE. Kongres, 5-i, 1948. V kongres Komunističke partije Jugoslavije, 21-28 jula 1948: stenografske beleške. [Beograd], 1949. pp. 909. In Cyrillic.

— — Programme.

SAVEZ KOMUNISTA JUGOSLAVIJE. Nacrt Programa, etc. Beograd, 1958. pp. 230.

— — Slovenia — Congresses.

ZVEZA KOMUNISTOV SLOVENIJE. Kongres, 2-i, 1948. II. kongres Komunistične partije Slovenije. Ljubljana, 1949. pp. 460.

ZVEZA KOMUNISTOV SLOVENIJE. Kongres, 7-i, 1974 7. kongres Zveze Komunistov Slovenije. Ljubljana, 1974. pp. 863.

COMMUNIST PARTY PURGES.

COMMUNIST PARTY PURGES.

CARMICHAEL (JOEL) Stalin's masterpiece: the show trials and purges of the thirties: the consolidation of the Bolshevik dictatorship. London, [1976]. pp. 238. *bibliog.*

COMMUNIST REVISIONISM.

FLOREK (HENRYK) and SZEFLER (STANISŁAW) Dywersja w ekonomice. Warszawa, 1970. pp. 176.

KRAWCZEWSKI (ANDRZEJ) Rewizjonizm a współczesna bur'zuazyjna ekonomia polityczna. Warszawa, 1970. pp. 114. *bibliog. With English and Russian summaries.*

NAMIOTKIEWICZ (WALERY) Myśl polityczna marksizmu a rewizjonizm. 2nd ed. Warszawa, 1970. pp. 295.

ORGANIZZAZIONE COMUNISTA (MARXISTA-LENINISTA). Congresso Nazionale, 1, 1974. Crisi, revisionismo e partito: tesi. Milano, 1974. pp. 115.

MAGALINE (A.D.) Lutte de classes et dévalorisation du capital: contribution à la critique du révisionnisme. Paris, 1975. pp. 198. *bibliog.*

COMMUNIST STATE.

GOSUDARSTVO i demokratiia v period postroeniia razvitogo sotsializma. Moskva, 1974. pp. 296.

TERLETS'KYI (VALENTYN MYKHAILOVICH) Leninskoe ideinoe nasledie i problemy sovetskogo stroitel'stva. Kiev, 1974. pp. 263. *bibliog.*

MUKHINA (GALINA ZOTIKOVNA) Sotsialisticheskaia revoliutsiia i gosudarstvo: razrabotka V.I. Leninym voprosa o gosudarstve diktatury proletariata v period bor'by za Oktiabr' i uprochenie ego zavoevanii, mart 1917 - mart 1918. Moskva, 1975. pp. 277.

ŠIK (OTA) Das kommunistische Machtsystem. Hamburg, 1976. pp. 357. *bibliog.*

COMMUNIST STRATEGY.

PARTIDO COMUNISTA PARAGUAYO. Comite Central. Dos lineas: guerra revolucionaria, compromiso apaciguador; declaracion del C.C. del P.C. Paraguayo en relacion a la Conferencia de Moscu. Montevideo, 1969. pp. 77.

SOKOLOVSKII (VASILII DANILOVICH) Soviet military strategy (third edition); ...edited, with an analysis and commentary, by Harriet Fast Scott. London, [1975]. pp. 494. *bibliog.*

COMMUNISTIC SETTLEMENTS.

RIVERS (PATRICK) The survivalists. London, 1975. pp. 224. *bibliog.*

— China.

CHU (LI) and TIEN (CHIEH-YUN) Inside a people's commune: report from Chiliying. Peking, 1974. pp. 212.

— Israel.

ANDREOU (NICOS) Le collectivisme israélien: étude sociographique. Athènes, Centre National de Recherches Sociales, 1973. pp. 284. *bibliog.*

HELMAN (AMIR) The distribution and allocation of consumer goods in the kibbutz; [Ph.D.(London)thesis]. 1975. fo. 281. *bibliog. Typescript: unpublished. This thesis is the property of London University and may not be removed from the Library.*

TIGER (LIONEL SAMUEL) and SHEPHER (JOSEPH) Women in the kibbutz. New York, [1975]. pp. 334. *bibliog.*

RURAL communities: inter-cooperation and development; edited by Yehuda H. Landau [and others]. New York, 1976. pp. 166. *Proceedings of the French-Israeli conference held in Israel, Haifa and Rehovot in May 1973.*

— United Kingdom.

GORMAN (CLEM) People together: (a guide to communal living). St. Albans, Herts, 1975. pp. 207. *bibliog.*

— United States.

LEWARNE (CHARLES PIERCE) Utopias on Puget Sound, 1885-1915. Seattle, [1975]. pp. 325. *bibliog.*

COMMUNISTS

— Bulgaria.

REVOLIUTSIONNA Sofiia, 1891-1944: spomeni. [Sofiia], 1969. pp. 750.

— Italy.

ANDREUCCI (FRANCO) and DETTI (TOMMASO) Il movimento operaio italiano: dizionario biografico, 1853-1943. Roma, 1975 in progress. *bibliogs.*

— Poland.

DWORKIN (EUZEBIUSZ) Od Manzanares do Oki: wspomnienia dąbrowszczaka. Warszawa, 1974. pp. 119.

COMMUNITY.

GOTTSCHALK (SHIMON S.) Communities and alternatives: an exploration of the limits of planning. New York, [1975]. pp. 169. *bibliog.*

GUSFIELD (JOSEPH R.) Community: a critical response. Oxford, [1975]. pp. 120. *bibliog.*

MOORE (SALLY FALK) and MYERHOFF (BARBARA G.) eds. Symbol and politics in communal ideology: cases and questions. Ithaca, 1975. pp. 245. *bibliogs.*

THORNS (DAVID C.) The quest for community: social aspects of residential growth. London, 1976. pp. 164.

COMMUNITY AND SCHOOL.

CHIARANTE (GIUSEPPE) and NAPOLITANO (GIORGIO) La democrazia nella scuola: (la posizione dei comunisti sui nuovi organi di governo negli istituti e nei distretti scolastici). Roma, [1974]. pp. 137.

MIDWINTER (ERIC CLARE) Education and the community. London, 1975. pp. 163. *bibliog.*

COMMUNITY ANTENNA TELEVISION

— Canada.

BABE (ROBERT E.) Cable television and telecommunication in Canada: an economic ana East Lansing, Mich., 1975. pp. 287. *bibliog. (Michigan State University. MSU International Business and Economic Studies.)*

— United States.

GILLESPIE (GILBERT) Public access cable television in the United States and Canada; with an annotated bibliography. New York, 1975. pp. 157.

COMMUNITY CENTRES

— Canada.

PUBLIC POLICY CONCERN. Community information centres: a proposal for Canada in the 70's; a study prepared for the government of Canada. Ottawa, Information Canada, 1971 repr. 1972. pp. 68. *bibliog.*

— Hong Kong.

RICHES (GRAHAM C.P.) Urban community centres and community development: Hong Kong and Singapore. Hong Kong, 1973. pp. 138. *bibliog. (Hong Kong. University. Centre of Asian Studies. Occasional Papers and Monographs. No. 14)*

— Singapore.

RICHES (GRAHAM C.P.) Urban community centres and community development: Hong Kong and Singapore. Hong Kong, 1973. pp. 138. *bibliog. (Hong Kong. University. Centre of Asian Studies. Occasional Papers and Monographs. No. 14)*

— United Kingdom.

CUMBRIA COMMUNITY DEVELOPMENT PROJECT. Working papers of the C[ommunity] I[nformation and] A[ction] C[entre], 1973/74. Cleator Moor, [1974]. pp. 35.

CUMBRIA COMMUNITY DEVELOPMENT PROJECT. Community information and action centre; report, assessment and recommendations from a community development project in west Cumbria. [York, 1975]. pp. 105. *(Papers in Community Studies. No. 1)*

TWELVETREES (ALAN C.) Community associations and centres: a comparative study. Oxford, 1976. pp. 152. *bibliog.*

COMMUNITY DEVELOPMENT.

APGAR (MAHLON) ed. New perspectives on community development. London, [1976]. pp. 363.

RURAL communities: inter-cooperation and development; edited by Yehuda H. Landau [and others]. New York, 1976. pp. 166. *Proceedings of the French-Israeli conference held in Israel, Haifa and Rehovot in May 1973.*

— Study and teaching.

SARAN (MARY) For community service: the Mount Carmel experiment. Oxford, [1974]. pp. 144.

— Bolivia.

McEWEN (WILLIAM J.) Changing rural society: a study of communities in Bolivia. New York, 1975. pp. 463. *bibliog. Part of a major research study carried out in Bolivia by the Research Institute for the Study of Man.*

— India.

MYSORE. Department of Agriculture. 1959. Some thoughts on agricultural extension methods and community development programmes in India. [Bangalore], 1959. pp. 57. *(Information Booklets. No. 6)*

— Kenya.

ROSS (MARC HOWARD) The political integration of urban squatters. Evanston, 1973. pp. 228. *bibliog.*

MBITHI (PHILIP M.) Rural sociology and rural development: its application in Kenya. Kampala, 1974. pp. 229. *bibliogs.*

— Pacific, The.

SOUTH PACIFIC CONFERENCE. Report [title varies]. a., (formerly trien.), 1950 (1st)- v.p. *[in English and French]. 4th-6th reports published under title Pacific forum. Reports 7-13 also contain Proceedings of the South Pacific Commission.*

— Thailand.

RUBIN (HERBERT J.) The dynamics of development in rural Thailand. [Dekalb, Ill.], 1974. fo. 156. *(Northern Illinois University. Center for Southeast Asian Studies. Special Reports. No. 8)*

— United Kingdom.

VAUXHALL COMMUNITY DEVELOPMENT PROJECT. Notes on the Vauxhall Community Development Project. [Liverpool, 1971]. fo. 5.

COOPER (ROBERT) Ph.D. Managing inner city renewal: Liverpool Corporation and the Vauxhall Community Development Project. [Liverpool, Vauxhall Community Development Project], 1972. fo. 21.

LIVERPOOL. Corporation. Vauxhall Community Development Project Interdepartmental Working Party. The concept of need and the formulation of standards for the provision of services. [Liverpool, 1972]. fo. 4.

VAUXHALL COMMUNITY DEVELOPMENT PROJECT. Interim report of Project Director to David Lane, Minister of State for Home Office. [Liverpool], 1972. fo. 49.

NORTH TYNESIDE COMMUNITY DEVELOPMENT PROJECT. Community development: report to the Home Secretary. [North Shields], 1973. fo. 8.

NORTH TYNESIDE COMMUNITY DEVELOPMENT PROJECT. Community profile. [North Shields], 1973. pp. 34.

VAUXHALL COMMUNITY DEVELOPMENT PROJECT. Report of the Project Director to the Home Secretary. [Liverpool], 1973. fo. 33.

ACTION-research in community development; edited by Ray Lees and George Smith. London, 1975. pp. 202. *bibliog.*

BATLEY (RICHARD) The neighbourhood scheme: cases of central government intervention in local deprivation. London, 1975. pp. 112. *bibliog.* (*Centre for Environmental Studies. Research Papers. 19*)

COMMUNITY DEVELOPMENT PROJECT. The National Community Development Project forward plan, 1975-76. London, 1975. pp. 76.

COVENTRY COMMUNITY DEVELOPMENT PROJECT. C[ommunity] D[evelopment] P[roject] final report. Coventry, 1975. 2 pts.

CUMBRIA COMMUNITY DEVELOPMENT PROJECT. C[ommunity] D[evelopment] P[roject]: what the axe will mean. [Cleator Moor], 1975. pp. 3.

CUMBRIA COMMUNITY DEVELOPMENT PROJECT. Forward plan, 1975/76. [Cleator Moor, 1975]. pp. 6.

CUMBRIA COMMUNITY DEVELOPMENT PROJECT. What has C[ommunity] D[evelopment] P[roject] done?: the facts. [Cleator Moor], 1975. pp. 8.

NORTH TYNESIDE COMMUNITY DEVELOPMENT PROJECT. Annual report, 1974. [North Shields], 1975. pp. 20.

TWELVETREES (ALAN C.) Community associations and centres: a comparative study. Oxford, 1976. pp. 152. *bibliog.*

— **United States.**

FIELD (DONALD R.) and others, eds. Water and community development: social and economic perspectives. Ann Arbor, [1974]. pp. 302. *bibliogs.*

HAMPDEN-TURNER (CHARLES) From poverty to dignity: a strategy for poor Americans. Garden City, N.Y., 1974. pp. 300. *bibliog.*

O'BRIEN (DAVID J.) Neighborhood organization and interest-group processes. Princeton, [1975]. pp. 263. *bibliog.*

COMMUNITY HEALTH SERVICES.

MILIO (NANCY) The care of health in communities: access for outcasts. New York, [1976]. pp. 402.

— **United Kingdom.**

U.K. Department of Health and Social Security. 1974. Community hospitals: their role and development in the National Health Service. [London, 1974]. pp. 13.

— **United States.**

RUSHING (WILLIAM A.) Community, physicians and inequality: a sociological study of the maldistribution of physicians. Lexington, Mass., [1975]. pp. 255. *bibliog.*

The HEALTH gap: medical services and the poor; edited by Robert L. Kane [and others]. New York, [1976]. pp. 321. *bibliog.*

COMMUNITY HEALTH SERVICES FOR CHILDREN

— **United States.**

HAGGERTY (ROBERT J.) and others. Child health and the community. New York, [1975]. pp. 388. *bibliogs.*

COMMUNITY HEALTH SERVICES FOR THE AGED

— **United Kingdom.**

HEALY (PAT) Social and community support for the retired and the elderly. London, 1973. pp. 14. *bibliog.* (*Age Concern England. Manifesto Series. No. 2*)

COMMUNITY LEADERSHIP.

LAUMANN (EDWARD O.) and PAPPI (FRANZ URBAN) Networks of collective action: a perspective on community influence systems. New York, [1976]. pp. 329. *bibliog.*

COMMUNITY LIFE.

ANDERSEN (BO LILLEDAL) and others, eds. Trassige folk: sjølvhjelp og lokaldemokrati i norske småsamfunn. Oslo, 1975. pp. 166.

BALLARD (PAUL H.) and JONES (ERASTUS) ed. The valleys call: a self-examination by people of the South Wales valleys during the 'Year of the valleys, 1974'. Ferndale, Mid-Glam., 1975. pp. 498.

WILLMOTT (PETER) Whatever's happening to London?; an analysis of changes in population structure and their effects on community life. London, 1975. pp. 14. *bibliog.* Paper delivered at the meeting of the London Council of Social Service in London in 1974.

COMMUNITY MENTAL HEALTH SERVICES

— **United Kingdom.**

MITTLER (PETER J.) Mental health services in the community. London, 1968 [repr. 1972]. pp. 12. (*Fabian Society. Fabian Occasional Papers. 4*)

NATIONAL ASSOCIATION FOR MENTAL HEALTH. Mind Reports. No. 11. Community care provisions for mentally ill and mentally handicapped men and women. London, 1973. fo. 9.

ROSENZWEIG (NORMAN) Community mental health programmes in England: an American view. Detroit, 1975. pp. 281. *bibliog.*

ARMISTEAD (NIGEL) Community services for the mentally ill. London, [1976]. pp. 31. *bibliog.* (*London. Greater London Council. Research Memoranda. 476*)

— **United States.**

BAUMAN (GERALD) and GRUNES (RUTH) Psychiatric rehabilitation in the ghetto: an educational approach. Lexington, Mass., [1974]. pp. 177. *bibliog.*

The FUTURE role of the state hospital; edited by Jack Zusman [and] Elmer F. Bertsch. Lexington, Mass., [1975]. pp. 410. *Includes papers presented at a conference organized by the Division of Community Psychiatry of the State University of New York at Buffalo, 1973.*

MONAHAN (JOHN) ed. Community mental health and the criminal justice system. New York, [1976]. pp. 332. *bibliogs.*

— — **Massachusetts.**

MAZER (MILTON) People and predicaments. Cambridge, Mass., 1976. pp. 279. *bibliog.*

COMMUNITY ORGANIZATION.

DUNHAM (ARTHUR) The new community organization. New York, [1970]. pp. 605. *bibliog.*

WARDLE (MICHAEL) The Lordsville project: experimental group work in a deprived area. [Welwyn], 1970. pp. 6. (*Reprinted from Case Conference, vol. 16, no.11, March 1970*)

BAKER (JOHN) of the Association for Neighbourhood Councils and YOUNG (MICHAEL DUNLOP) The Hornsey plan: a role for neighbourhood councils in the new local government. 4th ed. Halstead, Essex, 1973. pp. 20.

LANSLEY (JOHN) Community organisations and local government reform; first interim report [for the Community Councils Development Group]. Liverpool, 1973. pp. 36.

TWELVETREES (ALAN C.) Braunstone neighbourhood project: the first six years. [Leicester, 1973]. pp. 38.

BATLEY (RICHARD) The neighbourhood scheme: cases of central government intervention in local deprivation. London, 1975. pp. 112. *bibliog.* (*Centre for Environmental Studies. Research Papers. 19*)

HALL (DEREK) Residents' concern for community problems: Portsmouth. Portsmouth, 1975. fo. 10. (*Social Services Research and Intelligence Unit [Portsmouth]. Information Sheets. No. 24*)

O'BRIEN (DAVID J.) Neighborhood organization and interest-group processes. Princeton, [1975]. pp. 263. *bibliog.*

RUSHING (WILLIAM A.) Community, physicians and inequality: a sociological study of the maldistribution of physicians. Lexington, Mass., [1975]. pp. 255. *bibliog.*

SOCIOLOGICAL REVIEW, THE; [published by] University of Keele. Monographs. [No.] 21. The sociology of community action; edited by Peter Leonard. [Keele], 1975. pp. 245. *bibliogs.*

VOLUNTEER CENTRE. Current research involving the community in meeting social need. Berkhamsted, [1975]. pp. 13.

JACOBS (SIDNEY) The right to a decent house. London, 1976. pp. 161.

THOMAS (DAVID NICHOLAS) Organising for social change: a study in the theory and practice of community work. London, 1976. pp. 199. (*National Institute for Social Work Training. National Institute Social Services Library. No. 30*)

TWELVETREES (ALAN C.) Community associations and centres: a comparative study. Oxford, 1976. pp. 152. *bibliog.*

COMMUNITY POWER.

COMPARATIVE community politics: [selected papers from three conferences organized by the Committee for Community Research of the International Sociological Association]; edited by Terry Nichols Clark. New York, [1974]. pp. 415. *bibliogs.*

KESSELMAN (MARK) and ROSENTHAL (DONALD B.) Local power and comparative politics. Beverly Hills, [1974]. pp. 53. *bibliog.*

LAMB (CURT) Political power in poor neighborhoods. New York, [1975]. pp. 315. *bibliog.*

STEGGERT (FRANK X.) Community action groups and city governments: perspectives from ten American cities. Cambridge, Mass., [1975]. pp. 105. *bibliog.*

COMMUNITY politics; edited by Peter Hain. London, 1976. pp. 226.

COMMUTING

— **Nigeria.**

OLAYEMI (OLUSEGUN ADEGBOYEGA) Workplace and residence: an analysis of commuting in metropolitan Lagos and its implications for regional planning; [Ph.D. (London) thesis]. 1975. fo. 256. *bibliog. Typescript: unpublished. This thesis is the property of London University and may not be removed from the Library.*

— **United Kingdom.**

FRANCIS (KEITH) Commuting to and from South Hampshire: the present situation and likely trends to 2001. [Winchester], 1969. fo. 14. (*South Hampshire Plan Technical Unit. Working Papers. 2*)

COMORO ARCHIPELAGO

— **Politics and government.**

OSTHEIMER (JOHN M.) ed. The politics of the western Indian Ocean islands. New York, 1975. pp. 260. *bibliog.*

COMPARATIVE LAW

COMPARATIVE LAW.
See LAW, COMPARATIVE.

COMPENSATION (LAW)

— Hong Kong.

HONG KONG. Compensation Board. 1969. Report; [T.L. Yang, chairman]. Hong Kong, 1969. pp. 32.

— United Kingdom.

U.K. Emergency Compensation Committee. 1930. Report; [Sir W.F.K. Taylor, chairman]. London, 1930. pp. 33.

U.K. Department of the Environment. 1973-74. Land compensation: your rights explained. Booklets 1-5. [London, 1973-74]. 5 pts.

ATIYAH (PATRICK SELIM) Accidents, compensation and the law. 2nd ed. London, 1975. pp. 646.

COMPENSATION for compulsory purchase: papers from a conference organised by the Law Society, the Bar Council, and the Royal Institution of Chartered Surveyors [in 1974]. London, 1975. pp. 53. (Journal of Planning and Environmental Law. Occasional Papers)

COMPETITION.

FRIEDMANN (WOLFGANG GASTON) ed. Public and private enterprise in mixed economies. London, 1974. pp. 410.

URBAN (SABINE) Economie de marché et développement des entreprises. [Strasbourg, 1974]. pp. 287. bibliog. (Strasbourg. Université de Strasbourg III. Institut d'Etudes Politiques. Cahiers. Nouvelle Série. 2)

COMPETITION policy in the UK and EEC: [papers presented at a Social Science Research Council conference held at Somerville College, Oxford in 1974]; edited by Kenneth D. George [and] Caroline Joll. Cambridge, 1975. pp. 220.

BLOOM (PAUL N.) Advertising, competition, and public policy: a simulation study. Cambridge, Mass., [1976]. pp. 203.

HARRIS (RALPH) Freedom of choice: consumers or conscripts?. London, [1976]. pp. 9.

SHAW (R.W.) and SUTTON (C.J.) Industry and competition: industrial case studies. London, 1976. pp. 210. bibliogs.

VEREIN FÜR SOZIALPOLITIK. Schriften. Neue Folge. Band 87. Wettbewerbsprobleme im Kreditgewerbe; herausgegeben von Burkhardt Röper. Berlin, [1976]. pp. 283.

— Bibliography.

GERMANY (BUNDESREPUBLIK). Deutscher Bundestag. Wissenschaftliche Dienste. 1975. Wettbewerb und Konzentration: zur Wettbewerbs- und Konzentrationspolitik in der Bundesrepublik Deutschland: Auswahlbibliographie mit Annotationen; [compiled by Bernhard Georg Scheibler]. Bonn, 1975. pp. 109. (Bibliographien. 42)

COMPETITION, INTERNATIONAL.

CHRYSSOMELIDIS (G.S.) The competitiveness of Cyprus in export crops. Thessaloniki, 1974. pp. 25. bibliog. (Reprinted from Hellenic Agricultural Economic Review, vol. 10, no. 1, January 1974)

WIGET (AXEL) Entwicklungstendenzen des Seehafenwettbewerbs zwischen Hamburg, Kopenhagen und dänischen Provinzhäfen. Göttingen, [1975]. pp. 220. bibliog. (Hamburg. Hansische Universität. Institut für Verkehrswissenschaft. Verkehrswissenschaftliche Studien. 27)

COMPETITION, UNFAIR

— European Economic Community countries.

KORAH (VALENTINE) Competition law of Britain and the Common Market. London, 1975. pp. 311. bibliog.

COMPILING (ELECTRONIC COMPUTERS).

LEE (JOHN A.N.) The anatomy of a compiler. 2nd ed. New York, [1974]. pp. 470.

ROHL (JEFFREY SODEN) An introduction to compiler writing. London, [1975]. pp. 307. bibliog.

COMPUTER ASSISTED INSTRUCTION

— United Kingdom.

ANNETT (JOHN) Computer assisted learning: 1969-1975. [London], Social Science Research Council, [1976]. pp. 22. bibliog.

COMPUTER GRAPHICS.

INTERNATIONAL COMPUTER GRAPHICS SYMPOSIUM, BRUNEL UNIVERSITY, 1968. Computer graphics: techniques and applications; edited by R.D. Parslow [and others]. London, 1969. pp. 247. bibliog. Papers from the symposium organized by the Computer Science Department, Brunel University.

NEWMAN (WILLIAM M.) 1939- , and SPROULL (ROBERT F.) Principles of interactive computer graphics. New York, [1973]. pp. 607. bibliog.

COMPUTER INDUSTRY.

MALIK (REX) And tomorrow...the world?: inside IBM. London, 1975. pp. 496. bibliog.

— United Kingdom.

STONEMAN (PAUL) Technological diffusion and the computer revolution: the U.K. experience. Cambridge, 1976. pp. 219. bibliog. (Cambridge. University. Department of Applied Economics. Monographs. 25)

COMPUTER INTERFACES.

MARTIN (JAMES) of the IBM Corporation Systems Research Unit. Design of man-computer dialogues. Englewood Cliffs, N.J., [1973]. pp.559.

COMPUTER NETWORKS.

COMPUTER communication: views from ICCC '74; [a conference] held at Stockholm August 12-14 1974; edited by Nathaniel Macon. Washington, [1975]. pp. 86. bibliogs.

EUROPEAN COMPUTING CONFERENCE ON COMMUNICATIONS NETWORKS, LONDON, 1975. Communications networks. Uxbridge, [1975]. pp. 618. bibliogs. Papers presented at the Conference. This conference was part of the European Computing Congress, 1975.

COMPUTER SIMULATION.

CLARK (JOHN A.) and COLE (SAM) Global simulation models: a comparative study. London, [1975]. pp. 135. bibliog.

COMPUTER STORAGE DEVICES.

PAGE (E.S.) and WILSON (L.B.) Information representation and manipulation in a computer. Cambridge, 1973 repr. 1976. pp. 244. bibliogs.

COMPUTERS.

ACM 70, NEW YORK, 1970. Computers and crisis: how computers are shaping our future; [proceedings of ACM 70, a conference of the Association for Computing Machinery; edited by] R. W. Bemer [and] Susan Brewer. [New York, 1971]. pp. 503.

U.K. National Physical Laboratory. Engineering Sciences Group. 1972-75. Engineering Sciences Group research, 1971(- 1972-4). Vol. 1. Computer science, numerical analysis and computing. London, 1972-75. 2 pts. bibliogs.

INTERNATIONAL SYMPOSIUM ON COMPUTERS IN MEDICINE, 2ND, BLACKBURN, 1971. Computers in medicine: proceedings...; edited by J. Rose. [Bristol], 1972. pp. 166. bibliogs.

GRINDLEY (CHRISTOPHER BRIAN BURROWES) and HUMBLE (JOHN WILLIAM) The effective computer: a management by objectives approach. London, [1973]. pp. 187. bibliog.

ARUTIUNIAN (ARTASHES GALUSTOVICH) and others. Primenenie matematicheskikh metodov i EVM v narodnom khoziaistve. Erevan, 1974. pp. 327. bibliog.

EUROPEAN COMPUTING CONGRESS, 1974. Conference proceedings, Brunel University, England, 13-17 May 1974. [Uxbridge, 1974]. pp. 1208. bibliogs.

COMPUTERS and the educated individual; proceedings of the joint IBM University of Newcastle upon Tyne seminar, held in the University Computing Laboratory, 9th-12th September 1975; edited by B. Shaw. Newcastle upon Tyne, [1975]. pp. 186.

EUROPEAN COMPUTING CONFERENCE ON INTERACTIVE SYSTEMS, LONDON, 1975. Interactive systems. Uxbridge, [1975]. pp. 556. bibliogs. Papers presented at the Conference. This conference was part of the European Computing Congress, 1975.

MINICOMPUTER FORUM, 2ND, 1975. Conference proceedings 1975. [Uxbridge, 1975]. pp. 600. bibliogs.

MUMFORD (ENID) and PETTIGREW (ANDREW M.) Implementing strategic decisions. London, 1975. pp. 241. bibliog.

STATISTIKA i elektronno-vychislitel'naia tekhnika v ekonomike: sbornik statei. vyp.8. Moskva, 1975. pp. 231.

WEIZENBAUM (JOSEPH) Computer power and human reason: from judgment to calculation. San Francisco, [1976]. pp. 300.

— Anecdotes, facetiae, satire, etc.

SCHNEIDER (BEN ROSS) Travels in computerland; or, Incompatibilities and interfaces: a full and true account of the implementation of the London Stage Information Bank. Reading, Mass., [1974]. pp. 244.

— Law and legislation — Europe.

HONDIUS (FRITS WILLEM) Emerging data protection in Europe. Amsterdam, 1975. pp. 282. bibliog.

— Social aspects.

MUMFORD (ENID) and WARD (THOMAS B.) Computers: planning for people. London, 1968. pp. 176. bibliog.

TAVISS (IRENE) ed. The computer impact. Englewood Cliffs, [1970]. pp. 297.

IFIP CONFERENCE ON HUMAN CHOICE AND COMPUTERS, VIENNA, 1974. Human choice and computers: proceedings...; edited by Enid Mumford and Harold Sackman. Amsterdam, 1975. pp. 358. bibliogs.

SIEGHART (PAUL) Privacy and computers. London, 1976. pp. 228. bibliog.

WEIZENBAUM (JOSEPH) Computer power and human reason: from judgment to calculation. San Francisco, [1976]. pp. 300.

— Study and teaching.

SEMINAR ON COMPUTER SCIENCES IN SECONDARY EDUCATION, SÈVRES, 1970. Seminar on computer sciences in secondary education organised by the O.E.C.D.,...at...Sèvres, France, March 9th-14th, 1970. [Paris], Organisation for Economic Co-operation and Development, 1971. pp. 240.

COMTE (ISIDORE AUGUSTE MARIE FRANÇOIS XAVIER).

BARBÉ (CARLOS) Progresso e sviluppo: la formazione della teoria dello sviluppo e lo sviluppo come ideologia; Auguste Comte, Herbert Spencer. Torino, 1974. pp. 241. (Turin. Università. Istituto di Scienze Politiche. Pubblicazioni. vol. 32)

COMTE (ISIDORE AUGUSTE MARIE FRANÇOIS XAVIER) Auguste Comte and positivism: the essential writings; edited and with an introduction by Gertrud Lenzer. New York, 1975. pp. 505. *bibliog.*

COMTE (ISIDORE AUGUSTE MARIE FRANÇOIS XAVIER) Auguste Comte: the foundation of sociology; [extracts from his works, including correspondence with Mill; edited by] Kenneth Thompson. London, 1976. pp. 220. *bibliog.*

CONCENTRATION CAMPS

— Russia.

BUCA (EDWARD) Vorkuta;...translated from the Polish by Michal Lisinski and Kennedy Wells. London, 1976. pp. 352.

CONCORDE (JET TRANSPORTS).

ENVIRONMENTAL SCIENCES GROUP. Concorde noise and its effect on London. London, [1975]. pp. 58. *(London. Greater London Council. Research Memoranda. 478)*

KNIGHT (GEOFFREY EGERTON) Concorde: the inside story. London, [1976]. pp. 174.

CONDUCT OF LIFE.

GARAUDY (ROGER) Parole d'homme. Paris, [1975]. pp. 265.

CONFEDERATE STATES OF AMERICA

— Foreign economic relations — United Kingdom.

LESTER (RICHARD I.) Confederate finance and purchasing in Great Britain. Charlottesville, Va., 1975. pp. 267. *bibliog.*

CONFIDENTIAL COMMUNICATIONS

— Poland.

SAWICKI (JERZY) Tajemnica zawodowa lekarza i dziennikarza w prawie karnym. Warszawa, 1960. pp. 93.

CONFLICT (PSYCHOLOGY).

VÄYRYNEN (RAIMO) Militarization, conflict behavior and interaction: three ways of analyzing the Cold War. Tampere, [1973]. pp. 230. *bibliog. (Tampere Peace Research Institute. Research Reports. No.3)*

BONOMA (THOMAS VINCENT) Conflict: escalation and deescalation. Beverly Hills, [1975]. pp. 84. *bibliog.*

CONFLICT OF INTERESTS (PUBLIC OFFICE).

FRANCE. Direction de la Documentation. La Documentation Française. Notes et Etudes Documentaires. Nos. 4,106-4, 107. Les incompatibilités parlementaires en France et à l'étranger; [par Michel Ceoara]. Paris, 1974. pp. 79. *bibliog.*

— France.

FRANCE. Direction de la Documentation. La Documentation Française. Notes et Etudes Documentaires. Nos. 4,106-4, 107. Les incompatibilités parlementaires en France et à l'étranger; [par Michel Ceoara]. Paris, 1974. pp. 79. *bibliog.*

CONFORMITY

— Mathematical models.

COHEN (BERNARD P.) and LEE (HANS) Conflict, conformity and social status. Amsterdam, 1975. pp. 203. *bibliog.*

CONFUCIUS AND CONFUCIANISM.

HSÜ (LEONARD SHIHLIEN) The political philosophy of Confucianism: an interpretation of the social and political ideas of Confucius, his forerunners, and his early disciples. New York, 1975. pp. 257. *bibliogs. Reprint of the edition published in London, 1932, with a new preface and an updated bibliography.*

CONGO (BRAZZAVILLE)

— Economic policy.

BERTRAND (HUGUES) Le Congo: formation sociale et mode de développement économique. Paris, 1975. pp. 323.

— Politics and government.

NGOUABI (MARIEN) Vers la construction d'une société socialiste en Afrique: écrits et discours du Président du Comité Central du Parti Congolais du Travail, Président de la République Populaire du Congo. Paris, [1975]. pp. 727.

— Social conditions.

BERTRAND (HUGUES) Le Congo: formation sociale et mode de développement économique. Paris, 1975. pp. 323.

CONJUGAL VIOLENCE.

VIOLENCE in the family; [papers presented at two conferences held at Manchester in 1974 and 1975]; Marie Borland, editor. Manchester, 1976. pp. 148.

CONKLIN (HENRY).

CONKLIN (HENRY) 1832-1915. Through "Poverty's Vale": a hardscrabble boyhood in upstate New York, 1832-1862;...edited with an introduction by Wendell Tripp. Syracuse, N.Y., 1974. pp. 264.

CONSCIENTIOUS OBJECTORS.

FELLOWSHIP OF RECONCILIATION. [Minute books and papers. 1915-62]. 43 pieces. *Manuscript, typescript, etc.*

CONSCIOUSNESS.

BOURGUIGNON (ERIKA) ed. Religion, altered states of consciousness, and social change. Columbus, Ohio, 1973. pp. 389.

CONSERVATION OF NATURAL RESOURCES.

HERFINDAHL (ORRIS CLEMENS) Resource economics; selected works...edited by David B. Brooks. Baltimore, [1974]. pp. 316. *bibliog.*

DASMANN (RAYMOND FREDERICK) The conservation alternative. New York, [1975]. pp. 164. *bibliogs.*

SAUVY (ALFRED) Zero growth?; (translator, A. Maguire). Oxford, 1975. pp. 266.

PEARCE (DAVID WILLIAM) Environmental economics. London, 1976. pp. 202. *bibliog.*

— Bibliography.

RUSSELL (VALERIE J.) compiler. Man and resources. London, 1975. pp. 51. *(U.K. Department of the Environment. Library. Bibliographies. No. 181).*

— Study and teaching.

ENVIRONMENTAL education at university level: trends and data; part of this report is based on the results of a workshop on environmental education at university level...Tours...4th to 8th April, 1971, (organised) by CERI, etc. [Paris], Organisation for Economic Co-operation and Development, 1973. pp. 320.

— Canada — Ontario.

SMITHIES (W.R.) The protection and use of natural resources in Ontario. [Toronto], Ontario Economic Council, 1974. pp. 89. *bibliog. (Evolution of Policy in Contemporary Ontario, The. 2)*

— Russia — Latvia — Bibliography.

JAKOBSONE (G.) and PUCE (O.) compilers. Okhrana prirody v Sovetskoi Latvii: ukazatel' literatury. Riga, 1973. pp. 63. *In Latvian and Russian.*

— United States.

BRUBAKER (STERLING) In command of tomorrow: resource and environmental strategies for Americans. Baltimore, [1975]. pp. 177.

CONSERVATISM.

HAYWARD (JACK ERNEST SHALOM) Political inertia. Hull, 1975. pp. 24. *(Hull. University. Inaugural Lectures)*

— China.

The LIMITS of change: essays on conservative alternatives in Republican China; edited by Charlotte Furth. Cambridge, Mass., 1976. pp. 426. *(Harvard University. East Asian Research Center. Harvard East Asian Series. 84) Papers from a conference held in 1972 under the auspices of the Joint Committee on Contemporary China of the Social Science Research Council and the American Council of Learned Societies.*

— Germany.

TREUDE (BURKHARD) Konservative Presse und Nationalsozialismus: Inhaltsanalyse der 'Neuen Preussischen (Kreuz-) Zeitung' am Ende der Weimarer Republik. Bochum, 1975. pp. 195. *bibliog.*

— Sweden.

TORSTENDAHL (ROLF) Mellan nykonservatism och liberalism: idébrytningar inom högern och bondepartierna, 1918-1934. Stockholm, [1969]. pp. 230. *bibliog. (Uppsala. Universitet. Historiska Institutionen. Studia Historica Upsaliensia. 29) With English summary.*

— United Kingdom.

BUCK (PHILIP WALLENSTEIN) How Conservatives think. Harmondsworth, 1975. pp. 185.

— United States.

COSER (LEWIS ALFRED) and HOWE (IRVING) eds. The new conservatives: a critique from the left. New York, [1974]. pp. 343.

BUCHANAN (PATRICK J.) Conservative votes, liberal victories: why the right has failed. New York, [1975]. pp. 184.

EVANS (MEDFORD STANTON) Clear and present dangers: a conservative view of America's government. New York, [1975]. pp. 433.

LAMBRO (DONALD) The conscience of a young conservative. New Rochelle, N.Y., [1976]. pp. 125.

NASH (GEORGE H.) The conservative intellectual movement in America since 1945. New York, [1976]. pp. 463. *bibliog.*

CONSERVATIVE PARTY (CANADA).

LADNER (LEON JOHNSON) The Progressive Conservative Party: its origin and basic principles. [Ottawa, 196-?]. pp. 9. *bibliog.*

MACQUARRIE (HEATH NELSON) A brief record of the Progressive Conservative Party of Canada, 1854-1968. [Ottawa, 1968?]. pp. 20.

MUNRO (JOHN A.) The origins of the Progressive Conservative Party. Ottawa, 1972. pp. 7.

MANTHORPE (JONATHAN) The power and the Tories: Ontario politics, 1943 to the present. Toronto, [1974]. pp. 305.

CONSERVATIVE PARTY (UNITED KINGDOM).

KENNINGTON CONSERVATIVE ASSOCIATION. Executive Committee. [Minute books. 1924-62]. 3 vols. *Manuscript.*

BRIXTON CONSERVATIVE ASSOCIATION. Finance Committee. [Minutes. 1938-51]. 2 pieces. *Manuscript.*

BRITISH AND IRISH COMMUNIST ORGANISATION. The Tories and the left. Belfast, 1974. pp. 11.

AMERY (JULIAN) Towards a solution; [speeches]. London, [1975]. pp. 36.

BOYSON (RHODES) ed. 1985: an escape from Orwell's 1984: a Conservative path to freedom. Enfield, 1975. pp. 146.

CONSERVATIVE PARTY (UNITED KINGDOM).(Cont.)

BUCK (PHILIP WALLENSTEIN) How Conservatives think. Harmondsworth, 1975. pp. 185.

LAYTON-HENRY (ZIG) Reorganisation in the Conservative Party: an analysis of the Chelmer enquiry. Coventry, 1975. pp. 28. *(University of Warwick. Department of Politics. Working Papers. No. 4)*

NORTON (PHILIP) Discipline, dissent and the prevalence of unity: the Conservative party in opposition, 1945-1951. [Sheffield, 1975]. fo. 21.

YOUNG (KENNETH GEORGE) Local politics and the rise of party: the London Municipal Society and the Conservative intervention in local elections, 1894-1963. Leicester, 1975. pp. 255. *bibliog.*

CONSERVATIVE CENTRAL OFFICE. The right approach: a statement of Conservative aims. London, 1976. pp. 71.

The CONSERVATIVE opportunity; edited by Lord Blake and John Patten. London, 1976. pp. 159.

HOWELL (DAVID) 1937- . Time to move on: an opening to the future for British politics. London, 1976. pp. 24. *(Conservative Political Centre. [Publications]. No. 581)*

CONSOLIDATION AND MERGER OF CORPORATIONS.

STEINER (PETER OTTO) Mergers: motives, effects, policies. Ann Arbor, [1975]. pp. 359. *bibliog.*

— European Economic Community countries.

MAZZOLINI (RENATO) European transnational concentrations: top management's perspective on the obstacles to corporate unions in the EEC. London, [1974]. pp. 243. *bibliog.*

— France.

BEAUD (MICHEL) and others. Une multinationale française: Pechiney Ugine Kuhlmann. Paris, [1975]. pp. 288.

— Netherlands.

HEINSMAN (LOUIS) and TEEFFELEN (WALTER VAN) Concernvorming in de Nederlandse boekenwereld. Amsterdam, 1975. pp. 229.

— United Kingdom.

BEAN (D.G.) Financial strategy in the acquisition decision. Epping, Essex, 1975. pp. 175. *bibliog.*

[CITY WORKING PARTY]. The City code on take-overs and mergers: (revised April, 1976). [London], 1976. pp. 67.

DAVIES (P.L.) The regulation of take-overs and mergers. London, 1976. pp. 109.

FIRTH (MICHAEL A.) Share prices and mergers: a study of stock market efficiency. Farnborough, Hants, [1976]. pp. 187. *bibliog.*

HANNAH (LESLIE) The rise of the corporate economy. London, 1976. pp. 243. *bibliog.*

CONSOLIDATION OF LAND HOLDINGS

— Finland.

SCHROWE (YRJÖ JOHANNES VON) Die finnischen Gemeinheitsteilungen im 18. Jahrhundert: Beitrag zur Agrargeschichte Finnlands. Berlin, 1928. pp. 153. *bibliog. (Sozialwissenschaftliche Arbeitsgemeinschaft. Sozialwissenschaftliche Forschungen. Abteilung 2, Heft 4)* 5 maps in end pocket.

CONSTITUTIONAL HISTORY.

BLAUSTEIN (ALBERT P.) and FLANZ (GISBERT H.) eds. Constitutions of the countries of the world: permanent edition: a series of updated texts, constitutional chronologies and annotated bibliographies. Dobbs Ferry, N.Y., 1971 in progress. 14 vols. and supplementary vol. *bibliogs.* Looseleaf.

CONSTITUTIONS.

UNITED STATES. Department of State. 1918-19. The Inquiry handbooks. Wilmington, 1974. 20 vols. *bibliogs.* Reprint of documents originally published in Washington, 1918-19.

BLAUSTEIN (ALBERT P.) and FLANZ (GISBERT H.) eds. Constitutions of the countries of the world: permanent edition: a series of updated texts, constitutional chronologies and annotated bibliographies. Dobbs Ferry, N.Y., 1971 in progress. 14 vols. and supplementary vol. *bibliogs.* Looseleaf.

CONSTITUTIONS, STATE

— United States.

CORNWELL (ELMER ECKERT) and others. State constitutional conventions: the politics of the revision process in seven states. New York, 1975. pp. 212.

CONSTRUCTION INDUSTRY.

WORLD HOUSING SURVEY: an overview of the state of housing, building and planning within human settlements; [pd. by] Department of Economic and Social Affairs, United Nations. a., 1974(1st)- New York.

— Canada.

CANADA. Statistics Canada. The residential general building contracting industry. a., 1973- Ottawa. *[In English and French]*

— China.

UNITED STATES. Central Intelligence Agency. 1974. An index of construction activity in China. [Washington], 1974. pp. 12. *bibliog. (Research Aids. No.A(ER)74-9)* Microfilm: 1 reel.

— France.

FRANCE. Comité du Bâtiment et des Travaux Publics. 1976. Rapport...: préparation du 7e Plan. Paris, 1976. pp. 234.

— — Statistics.

FRANCE. Direction du Bâtiment et des Travaux Publics et de la Conjoncture. Service des Statistiques et des Etudes Economiques. Sous-Direction des Etudes Economiques. 1974. La main-d'oeuvre dans le bâtiment et les travaux publics. Paris, 1974. pp. 61. *(France. Ministère de l'Equipement. Statistiques de la construction. Suppléments. No. 11)*

FRANCE. Direction du Bâtiment et des Travaux Publics et de la Conjoncture. Service des Statistiques et des Etudes Economiques. Sous-Direction des Statistiques. 1974. Statistiques des permis de construire: résultats annuels, 1969- 1970-1971. Paris, 1974. 2 parts. *(France. Ministère de l'Equipement. Statistiques de la construction. Suppléments. Nos. 10,16)*

— Germany.

GIESBRECHT (ARNO) Die Bauproduktion als Determinante der Stadtentwicklung in der BRD. Hamburg, 1975. pp. 283. *bibliog. Dissertation zur Erlangung des Grades eines Doktors der Wirtschafts- und Sozialwissenschaften der Universität Hamburg.*

— — Statistics.

BECKERMANN (THEO) Die Bauwirtschaft: eine vorwiegend statistische Analyse. Berlin, [1976]. pp. 83. *(Rheinisch-Westfälisches Institut für Wirtschaftsforschung, Essen. Schriftenreihe. Neue Folge. 36)*

— Italy.

EDILI senza lavoro, operai senza casa; a cura di Riccardo Roscelli;...scritti di Riccardo Bedrone [and others]. Torino, [1975]. pp. 251.

— Poland.

GORYŃSKI (JULIUSZ) Ekonomika budownictwa. Warszawa, 1970. pp. 324. *With Russian and English summaries.*

— Russia — Soviet North.

AKADEMIIA NAUK SSSR. Sovet po Izucheniiu Proizvoditel'nykh Sil. Mezhduvedomstvennaia Komissiia po Problemam Severa. Problemy Severa. vyp.19. Problemy povysheniia effektivnosti stroitel'stva na Severe. Moskva, 1974. pp. 260.

— United Kingdom.

CONSTRUCTION BOARD NEWS: information from the Construction Industry Training Board [U.K.]. irreg. London. *Current issues only kept.*

THORNE (VIC) Acrow: the success story of achievement through team spirit. [London, 1975]. pp. 108.

ACTION GROUP ON LONDON HOUSING. The public sector housing pipeline in London; fifth report to the Minister for Housing and Construction; [Ernest Armstrong, chairman]. [London], Department of the Environment, 1976. pp. 82.

— — Accounting.

NATIONAL BUILDING AGENCY. Control of capital works programmes; [prepared by W.P. Ridgeway] . London, 1972. pp. 16. *(National Building Agency. Local Government Re- organisation: Management Guides. No. 1)*

— — Management.

NATIONAL BUILDING AGENCY. Control of capital works programmes; [prepared by W.P. Ridgeway] . London, 1972. pp. 16. *(National Building Agency. Local Government Re- organisation: Management Guides. No. 1)*

NATIONAL BUILDING AGENCY. Merging direct labour building organisations; [prepared by W.P. Ridgeway]. London, 1972. pp. 15. *(National Building Agency. Local Government Re- organisation: Management Guides. No. 2)*

— United States.

GOTTLIEB (MANUEL) Long swings in urban development. New York, 1976. pp. 360. *bibliog. (National Bureau of Economic Research. Urban and Regional Studies. 4)*

CONSTRUCTION WORKERS

— France.

FRANCE. Direction du Bâtiment et des Travaux Publics et de la Conjoncture. Service des Statistiques et des Etudes Economiques. Sous-Direction des Etudes Economiques. 1974. La main-d'oeuvre dans le bâtiment et les travaux publics. Paris, 1974. pp. 61. *(France. Ministère de l'Equipement. Statistiques de la construction. Suppléments. No. 11)*

— Hong Kong.

HONG KONG. Building Trades Industrial Committee. 1970. Report...on the manpower survey of the building and civil engineering industry conducted during 12th-14th August, 1968. Hong Kong, 1969 [or rather 1970]. pp. 111. *In English and Chinese.*

HONG KONG. Building Trades Industrial Committee. 1972. Minimum job standards and specifications for the principal jobs in the building and civil engineering industry. Hong Kong, 1971 [or rather 1972]. pp. 73. *In English and Chinese.*

— Italy.

SELLA (DOMENICO) Salari e lavoro nell'edilizia lombarda durante il secolo XVII. Pavia, 1968. pp. 168. *With summaries in English and French.*

EDILI senza lavoro, operai senza casa; a cura di Riccardo Roscelli;...scritti di Riccardo Bedrone [and others]. Torino, [1975]. pp. 251.

— Poland.

POLAND. Statutes, etc. 1954-1960. Zbiór przepisów dotyczących szkolenia i zatrudniania w budownictwie i przemyśle materiałów budowlanych; zebrał i opracował Henryk Ruka. Warszawa, 1960. pp. 271.

CONSUMPTION (ECONOMICS)

— United Kingdom.

NATIONAL BUILDING AGENCY. Merging direct labour building organisations; [prepared by W.P. Ridgeway]. London, 1972. pp. 15. *(National Building Agency. Local Government Re-organisation: Management Guides. No. 2)*

PLANT (J.J.) A survey of labour availability and requirements on London local authority construction sites. London, [1975]. pp. 64. *(London. Greater London Council. Research Memoranda. 468)*

FABIAN SOCIETY. Fabian Tracts. [No.] 445. Changing prospects for direct labour; [by] John Tilley. London, 1976. pp. 15. *(Fabian Society. Initiatives in Local Government. 3)*

SHERMAN (ALFRED V.) Waste in Wandsworth: how direct labour squanders ratepayers' money and the nation's resources. London, [1976?]. pp. 14.

CONSUMER CREDIT

— Law and legislation — United Kingdom.

U.K. Office of Fair Trading. Consumer Credit Division. [Consultative Documents]. London, 1975 in progress.

— Canada.

CANADA. Consumer Services Branch. 1971. Consumer's handbook: consumer credit. rev. ed. Ottawa, 1971. pp. 22.

CONSUMER PROTECTION.

CONSUMERISM: a threat or a challenge?; speeches at a session...at the 7th national conference of the Institute of Practitioners in Advertising, Eastbourne, 2-4 November 1972; [by] John Crichton [and others]. London, [1973]. pp. 18.

— France.

CAS (GERARD) La défense du consommateur. Paris, 1975. pp. 128. *bibliog.*

FRANCE. Comité National de la Consommation. 1975. Un monde en mouvement...:...les organisations de consommateurs. Paris, 1975. pp. 93. *(France. Ministère de l'Economie et des Finances. Dossiers Ouverts)*

— Ireland (Republic).

NATIONAL CONSUMER ADVISORY COUNCIL [EIRE]. Submission to the Minister for Industry and Commerce on proposals for legislation to assure the consumers' interests. Dublin, Stationery Office, [1975]. pp. 31.

— Norway.

ASSUM (TERJE YNGVAR) Hvem har nytte av forbrukerservice?...: to whose benefit is the consumer service?. Oslo, 1974. pp. 22. *(Norway. Statistiske Centralbyrå. Artikler. Nr.64) With English summary.*

— South Africa.

ROELOFSE (EUGENE) Sorry I upset you. Cape Town, 1975. pp. 189.

— United Kingdom.

LONDON ELECTRICITY CONSULTATIVE COUNCIL. Annual report. a., 1974/1975- London. *Formerly included in LONDON ELECTRICITY BOARD. Annual report and accounts, which see also.*

U.K. Department of Prices and Consumer Protection. 1975. The regulation of estate agency: a consultative document. London, 1975. pp. 24.

WINSTANLEY (MICHAEL) and DUNKLEY (RUTH) Know your rights. London, [1975]. pp. 123. *bibliogs.*

— United States.

ANDREASEN (ALAN R.) The disadvantaged consumer. New York, [1975]. pp. 366.

NATIONAL AFFILIATION OF CONCERNED BUSINESS STUDENTS. National Symposium, 2nd, 1974. Protecting the consumer interest: private initiative and public response; edited by Robert N. Katz. Cambridge, Mass., [1976]. pp. 271.

CONSUMERS.

BLOKLAND (JOHANNES) Continuous consumer equivalence scales: item-specific effects of age and sex of household members in the budget allocation model. Leiden, 1976. pp. 176. *bibliog. Proefschrift (doctor) - Erasmus Universiteit Rotterdam.*

— Austria.

RAUTER (ANTON E.) ed. Verbraucherpolitik und Wirtschaftsentwicklung. Wien, [1976]. pp. 475. *bibliogs.*

— Russia.

SOSTOIANIE i perspektivy izucheniia sprosa na knizhnuiu produktsiiu. Moskva, 1974. pp. 61.

— Sweden.

SVERIGES SOCIALDEMOKRATISKA ARBETAREPARTI and LANDSORGANISATIONEN I SVERIGE. Konsumentpolitiska Arbetsgrupp. Socialdemokratisk konsumentpolitik: (rapport; [Kjell-Olof Feldt, chairman]). [Stockholm, 1972]. pp. 38.

— United Kingdom.

HALL (BRYAN D.) Analysis of the results of a survey of shoppers in South Hampshire. [Winchester], 1969. 1 vol. (unpaged). *(South Hampshire Plan Technical Unit. Working Papers. 8)*

SOUTH HAMPSHIRE PLAN TECHNICAL UNIT. Technical Memoranda. A survey of shoppers in South Hampshire: design and response to the survey. 1969. 1 pamphlet (unfoliated). *Xerographic copy.*

BOND (MARIAN ELIZABETH) A structural approach to the demand for imported foods in the United Kingdom, 1950-1969. 1975. fo. 203. *bibliog. Typescript. Ph. D.(London) thesis: unpublished. This thesis is the property of London University and may not be removed from the Library.*

HARRIS (RALPH) Freedom of choice: consumers or conscripts?. London, [1976]. pp. 9.

JAY (PETER) A general hypothesis of employment, inflation and politics; sixth Wincott Memorial Lecture...1975. London, 1976. pp. 34. *(Institute of Economic Affairs. Occasional Papers. 46)*

— United States.

CROSS (JENNIFER) The supermarket trap: the consumer and the food industry. rev. ed. Bloomington, Ind., [1976]. pp. 306. *bibliog.*

EWEN (STUART) Captains of consciousness: advertising and the social roots of the consumer culture. New York, [1976]. pp. 261. *bibliog.*

SCITOVSKY (TIBOR) the Younger. The joyless economy: an inquiry into human satisfaction and consumer dissatisfaction. New York, 1976. pp. 310.

— — Mathematical models.

NATIONAL BUREAU OF ECONOMIC RESEARCH. Conference on Research in Income and Wealth. Studies in Income and Wealth. vol. 40. Household production and consumption: [papers presented in 1973]; Nestor E. Terleckyj, editor. New York, 1975. pp. 669. *bibliogs.*

CONSUMPTION (ECONOMICS)

— Mathematical models.

STEHLING (FRANK) Optimale Konsum- und Investitionsquoten. Meisenheim am Glan, [1972]. pp. 124. *bibliog.*

CARLEVARO (FABRIZIO) Sur la comparaison et la généralisation de certains systèmes de fonctions de consommation semi-agrégées. Berne, 1975. pp. 409. *bibliog. Thèse (docteur ès sciences économiques et sociales) - Université de Genève.*

— Europe, Eastern.

MIECZKOWSKI (BOGDAN) Personal and social consumption in eastern Europe: Poland, Czechoslovakia, Hungary, and East Germany. New York, [1975]. pp. 342. *bibliog.*

— France.

FRANCE. Comité de la Consommation. 1976. Rapport...: préparation du 7e Plan. Paris, 1976. pp. 86.

— Germany.

GERMANY (BUNDESREPUBLIK). Statistisches Bundesamt. 1974. Ausstattung privater Haushalte mit ausgewählten langlebigen Gebrauchsgütern, 1973. Wiesbaden, 1974. pp. 193. *(Preise, Löhne, Wirtschaftsrechnungen. Reihe 18. Einkommens- und Verbrauchsstichproben. 1)*

— — Mathematical models.

RAU (RAINER) Ökonometrische Analyse der Ausgabearten des privaten Verbrauchs:...für die Bundesrepublik Deutschland, 1950-1967. Berlin, [1975]. pp. 153. *bibliog. (Rheinisch-Westfälisches Institut für Wirtschaftsforschung, Essen. Schriftenreihe. Neue Folge. 35)*

— India.

NATIONAL COUNCIL OF APPLIED ECONOMIC RESEARCH. Changes in rural income in India, 1968-69, 1969-70, 1970-71. New Delhi, [1975]. pp. 155.

— Norway.

BJERKE (JUUL) Estimering av konsumfunksjoner på grunnlag av nasjonalregnskapsdata, 1865-1968...: consumption functions from national accounts data, 1865-1968. Oslo, 1972. pp. 60. *(Norway. Statistiske Centralbyrå. Artikler. Nr. 53) With English summary.*

BJØRN (ERIK) Prognoser for de langsiktige endringer i sammensetningen av det private konsum...: long term forecasts for the changes in the composition of the private consumption. Oslo, 1973. pp. 71. *bibliog. (Norway. Statistiske Centralbyrå. Artikler. Nr. 55)*

— — Mathematical models.

BJØRN (ERIK) Estimering av makro-konsumfunksjoner for etterkrigstiden: metodespørsmål og empiriske resultater...: estimating aggregate consumption functions for the post-war period: methodological problems and empirical results. Oslo, 1974. pp. 84. *bibliog. (Norway. Statistiske Centralbyrå. Artikler. Nr. 63) With English summary.*

— Poland.

POLITYKA 'żywnościowa PRL. Warszawa, 1975. pp. 422.

— Russia.

BOROZDIN (IURII VLADIMIROVICH) Tsenoobrazovanie i potrebitel'naia stoimost' produktsii. Moskva, 1975. pp. 144.

UCHENYE ZAPISKI KAFEDR OBSHCHESTVENNYKH NAUK VUZOV LENINGRADA. Politicheskaia Ekonomiia. vyp. 16. Lichnoe potreblenie pri sotsializme. Leningrad, 1975. pp. 151.

— Scandinavia — Mathematical models.

AMUNDSEN (ARNE) Konsumets og sparingens langsiktige utvikling...: consumption and saving in the process of long-term growth. Oslo, 1970. pp. 18. *(Norway. Statistiske Centralbyrå. Artikler. Nr.36)*

— United States.

MANDELL (LEWIS) Economics from the consumer's perspective. Chicago, [1975]. pp. 279. *bibliogs.*

CONSUMPTION (ECONOMICS)(Cont.)

— — Mathematical models.

NATIONAL BUREAU OF ECONOMIC RESEARCH. Conference on Research in Income and Wealth. Studies in Income and Wealth. vol. 40. Household production and consumption: [papers presented in 1973]; Nestor E. Terleckyj, editor. New York, 1975. pp. 669. *bibliogs.*

— Yugoslavia.

YUGOSLAVIA. Savezni Zavod za Statistiku. Studije, Analize i Prikazi. 76. Lična potrošnja stanovništva Jugoslavije, 1952-1972; Personal consumption of population of Yugoslavia, 1952-1972; Lichnoe potreblenie naseleniia Iugoslavii, 1952-1972. Beograd, 1975. pp. 152. *With English and Russian summaries.*

CONTEMPT OF COURT

— United Kingdom.

MILLER (C.J.) Contempt of court. London, 1976. pp. 279.

TEFF (HARVEY) and MUNRO (COLIN R.) Thalidomide: the legal aftermath. Farnborough, [1976]. pp. 154.

CONTRACT LABOUR

— United Kingdom — Commonwealth.

HUTTENBACK (ROBERT A.) Racism and empire: white settlers and colored immigrants in the British self-governing colonies, 1830-1910. Ithaca, N.Y., 1976. pp. 359. *bibliog.*

CONTRACTS

— Netherlands.

RAAD VOOR HET MIDDEN- EN KLEINBEDRIJF. Advies betreffende standaardcontracten. 's-Gravenhage, 1974. pp. 27. *([Publikaties]. 1974, no. 1)*

— Poland.

NOWAKOWSKI (ZYGMUNT KONRAD) Umowa dostawy. Warszawa, 1960. pp. 431.

— Russia.

PETROV (IGOR' NIKOLAEVICH) Otvetstvennost' khozorganov za narusheniia obiazatel'stv. Moskva, 1974. pp. 214.

BYKOV (ANATOLII GRIGOR'EVICH) Plan i khoziaistvennyi dogovor. Moskva, 1975. pp. 158.

— United Kingdom.

CHESHIRE (GEOFFREY CHEVALIER) and FIFOOT (CECIL HERBERT STUART) Law of contract; ninth edition by M.P. Furmston...; historical introduction by A.W.B. Simpson. London, 1976. pp. 694.

CONTRACTS (INTERNATIONAL LAW).

JOURNEES D'ETUDES JURIDIQUES JEAN DABIN, 7es, 1973. Le contrat économique international: stabilité et évolution; travaux des VIIes Journées, etc. Bruxelles, 1975. pp. 586. *bibliog. (Louvain. Université. Faculté de Droit. Bibliothèque. 9)*

CONTRACTS, LETTING OF

— Canada.

CANADA. Restrictive Trade Practices Commission. [Reports]. RTPC No. 49. Road paving in Ontario: report in the matter of an inquiry relating to the supply and transportation of asphalt paving materials in the province of Ontario. Ottawa, 1970. pp. 37.

CONTRACTS, MARITIME

— United Kingdom.

PAYNE (WILLIAM) Barrister-at-Law, and IVAMY (EDWARD RICHARD HARDY) Carriage of goods by sea; tenth edition by E.R. Hardy Ivamy. London, 1976. pp. 312.

CONVENTION PEOPLE'S PARTY.

NKRUMAH (KWAME) The People's Party: text of a speech by President Nkrumah at a rally held in the National Assembly in Accra on June 12th, 1965, to mark the 16th anniversary of the Convention People's Party. [London, Ghana High Commission], 1965. pp. (9). *(Ghana Today. Supplements)*

CONVERSATION.

ALLEN (DONALD E.) and GUY (REBECCA F.) Conversation analysis: the sociology of talk. The Hague, 1974. pp. 284. *bibliog.*

CONVICT LABOUR

— Russia — Estonia.

ESTONIA. Statutes, etc. 1973. Ispravitel'no-trudovoi kodeks Estonskoi SSR: ofitsial'nyi tekst s izmeneniiami i dopolneniiami na 1 oktiabria 1973 goda. Tallin, 1974. pp. 131.

COOK COUNTY, ILLINOIS

— Politics and government.

STETZER (DONALD FOSTER) Special districts in Cook County: toward a geography of local government. Chicago, 1975. pp. 177. *bibliog. (Chicago. University. Department of Geography. Research Papers. No. 169)*

COOMBS (CHARLES A.).

COOMBS (CHARLES A.) The arena of international finance. New York, [1976]. pp. 243.

COOPER (ANTHONY ASHLEY) 7th Earl of Shaftesbury.

HODDER (EDWIN) The seventh Earl of Shaftesbury, K.G., as social reformer. London, 1897. pp. 195.

COOPERATION.

ALLEN (Sir THOMAS) Paper on co-operative principles, and how we may promote their extension...; read at Crystal Palace Conference, August 15th 1900. London, [1900?]. pp. 7.

ENFIELD (ALICE HONORA) The place of co-operation in the new social order. London, 1920. pp. 12.

THUGUTT (STANISŁAW) Spółdzielczość: zarys ideologii; [przedruk z wydania drugiego, Warszawa, 1937]. 2nd ed. Londyn, 1944. pp. 155.

SPAULL (HEBE) and KAY (D.H.) The co-operative movement at home and abroad. London, 1947. pp. 191.

KUEHNE (KARL) Commonweal enterprise a regulative factor in competition: suggestions for a further development of the theory of imperfect competition; with a terminological epilogue by Karl Kühne. Francfort, [1973]. pp. 61. *(Bank für Gemeinwirtschaft Aktiengesellschaft. Series Commonweal Economy. No. 6)*

HERZ (ULRICH) ed. Kooperativa klassiker: dokument ur den svenska konsumentkooperationens idéhistoria. Stockholm, [1974]. pp. 209.

INTERNATIONAL CO-OPERATIVE ALLIANCE. Directory of co-operative libraries and documentation services etc. London, 1974. pp. 69. *In English, French and German.*

HOPPE (MICHAEL) Die klassische und neoklassische Theorie der Genossenschaften: ein Beitrag zur Dogmengeschichte und zur neueren Genossenschaftstheorie. Berlin, [1976]. pp. 186. *bibliog.*

— Africa, East.

HYDEN (GORAN) Efficiency versus distribution in East African cooperatives: a study in organizational conflicts. Nairobi, 1973. pp. 254. *bibliog.*

— America, Latin.

FALS BORDA (ORLANDO) El reformismo por dentro en America Latina. Mexico, 1972. pp. 211.

— Austria.

RAUTER (ANTON E.) ed. Verbraucherpolitik und Wirtschaftsentwicklung. Wien, [1976]. pp. 475. *bibliogs.*

— Belgium.

LAAR (ALBERT VAN) Geschiedenis van de arbeidersbeweging te Antwerpen en omliggende. Antwerpen, 1926; Antwerpen, 1974. pp. 582. *bibliog. Facsimile reprint.*

— Brazil.

COOPERATIVISMO E NORDESTE: publicação da Secção de Cooperativismo da SUDENE, [Brazil]. 3 a yr. (formerly s-a.). 1966 (ano 1)- Recife.

— Germany.

GAERTNER (PAUL) Die Genossenschaftsbewegung. Berlin, [1947]. pp. 171.

— Germany, Eastern.

GAERTNER (PAUL) Die Genossenschaftsbewegung. Berlin, [1947]. pp. 171.

— India — Mysore.

MYSORE. Department of Co-operation. Statistics Branch. 1967. Co-operative movement in Mysore State: important statistics, 1961-65. [Bangalore, 1967]. pp. 50.

— Italy.

GALETTI (VINCENZO) Cooperazione: forza anticrisi. Milano, 1975. pp. 160.

— Netherlands.

NOUWEN (L.J.M.) Heeft de coöperatiewinst een dubbel gezicht?: een tot een beschouwing uitdijende annotatie op het arrest van de Hoge Raad van 14 Mei 1969, etc. Deventer, [1969]. pp. 47.

ECONOMISCH INSTITUUT VOOR HET MIDDEN- EN KLEINBEDRIJF. Bedrijfseconomische Publikaties. De commerciele samenwerking in de kruideniersbranche ontwikkeling in de jaren zestig en zeventig. 's-Gravenhage, 1970. pp. 59.

— Poland.

THUGUTT (STANISŁAW) Wybór pism i autobiografia. Glasgow, 1943. pp. 218. *bibliog.*

KOWALAK (TADEUSZ) Dorobek spółdzielczości w trzydziestoleciu Polski Ludowej. Warszawa, 1975. pp. 164.

— Russia — Daghestan.

BUCHAEV (GAMID AKHMEDOVICH) Leninskii kooperativnyi plan v deistvii: rol' potrebkooperatsii v sotsialisticheskom preobrazovanii ekonomiki i kul'tury Dagestana. Makhachkala, 1969. pp. 145.

— — Latvia.

PUTINTSEV (A.I.) Razvitie kooperativnoi torgovli Latvii. Riga, 1974. pp. 125.

— Sicily.

GIORDANO (CHRISTIAN) and HETTLAGE (ROBERT) Mobilisierung oder Scheinmobilisierung?: Genossenschaften und traditionelle Sozialstruktur am Beispiel Siziliens; mit einer Einführung von Paul Trappe: Aspekte der Massenmobilisierung. Basel, 1975. pp. 103. *bibliogs. (Basel. Universität. Soziologisches Seminar. Social Strategies. vol.1)*

— Spain.

PEREZ TURRADO (MIGUEL) Cooperativismo y politica. Madrid, 1966. pp. 94.

— Sri Lanka.

MARGA INSTITUTE. The co-operative system and rural credit in Sri Lanka; a study undertaken...for USAID. Colombo, 1974. pp. 174. *(Marga Research Studies. 3)*

— Sweden.

HERZ (ULRICH) ed. Kooperativa klassiker: dokument ur den svenska konsumentkooperationens idéhistoria. Stockholm, [1974]. pp. 209.

— Switzerland.

ROSENFELD (LOTTE) Stefan Gschwind: ein Genossenschaftspionier. Basel, 1968. pp. 154. bibliog.

— United Kingdom.

The NEW worker co-operatives; edited by Ken Coates with contributions by Tony Benn [and others]. [Nottingham], 1976. pp. 227. bibliog.

COOPERATIVE SOCIETIES.

WALLRAFF (HERRMANN JOSEF) Present day's workeable commonweal economy; with a terminological epilogue by Karl Kühne. Francfort, [1974]. pp. 22. (Bank für Gemeinwirtschaft Aktiengesellschaft. Series Commonweal Economy. No. 5)

— Colombia.

FISCHER (GERHARD) Genossenschaften in Kolumbien. Bonn-Bad Godesberg, [1973]. pp. 347. bibliog. (Friedrich-Ebert-Stiftung. Forschungsinstitut. Schriftenreihe. Band 104)

— India — Goa, Daman and Diu.

GOA, DAMAN AND DIU. Bureau of Economics, Statistics and Evaluation. 1974. An evaluation study of the working of dairy cooperative societies in Goa, Daman and Diu, 1972-73. Panaji, [1974]. pp. 72. (Evaluation Reports. No. 8)

— Poland — Finance.

SIELICKI (WŁADYSŁAW) and ZMORA (WŁADYSŁAW) System finansowania spółdzielczości zaopatrzenia i zbytu. Warszawa, 1962. pp. 58.

— Sierra Leone.

SIERRA LEONE. Commission of Inquiry on the Sierra Leone Co- operative Marketing Federation of Sierra Leone. 1972. Report; [D.E.M. Williams, chairman]. [Freetown, 1972]. pp. 38.

— Switzerland.

ANGST (EMIL) 1865-1940: zum 75jährigen Jubiläum des Allgemeinen Consumvereins beider Basel: Einzeldarstellungen, etc. Basel, 1940. pp. 182.

— United Kingdom.

SUGDEN (ARTHUR) The co-operative movement in a changing environment; a special paper presented to the 105th co-operative congress at Llandudno, May, 1974. Manchester, 1974. pp. 18.

CO—PARTNERSHIP.

MADDISON (FRED) Should workmen be partners? London, Labour Association, 1901. pp. 8.

COPENHAGEN

— Civic improvement.

COPENHAGEN. Egnsplanrådet. Planlaegningsafdeling. Strukturplan 1972 for hovedstadsregionen. København, 1973. pp. 88.

COPENHAGEN. Egnsplanrådet. Planlaegningsafdeling. Regionplan 1973 for hovedstadsregionen: hovedstruktur og byvaekst. København, 1974. pp. 72. Map in end pocket.

— Harbour.

WIGET (AXEL) Entwicklungstendenzen des Seehafenwettbewerbs zwischen Hamburg, Kopenhagen und dänischen Provinzhäfen. Göttingen, [1975]. pp. 220. bibliog. (Hamburg. Hansische Universität. Institut für Verkehrswissenschaft. Verkehrswissenschaftliche Studien. 27)

COPENHAGEN UNIVERSITY.

JENSEN (ARNE) and others. University of Copenhagen: decision, planning and budgeting. [Paris], Organisation for Economic Co-operation and Development, 1972. pp. 207. (Centre for Educational Research and Innovation. Studies in Institutional Management in Higher Education)

COPPER INDUSTRY AND TRADE.

BILLERBECK (KLAUS) On negotiating a new order of the world copper market. Berlin, 1975. pp. 78. (Deutsches Institut für Entwicklungspolitik. Occasional Papers. No. 33)

NATURAL resources and national welfare: the case of copper; edited by Ann Seidman. New York, 1975. pp. 453. Based on papers presented at a conference held in Lusaka, Zambia, July 3-9, 1974.

TANNER (JOHN) A new deal for the poor: what a new economic order would mean for Britain and the third world. London, 1976. pp. 24. bibliog.

— Chile.

El COBRE en el desarrollo nacional; edicion preparada por Ricardo Ffrench-Davis y Ernesto Tironi. Santiago, Chile, 1974. pp. 271. bibliog. Principal papers presented at a Seminar on Copper, 1973, organized by the Centro de Estudios de Planificacion Nacional.

— Papua New Guinea.

MIKESELL (RAYMOND FRECH) Foreign investment in copper mining: case studies of mines in Peru and Papua New Guinea. Baltimore, [1975]. pp. 143.

— Peru.

MIKESELL (RAYMOND FRECH) Foreign investment in copper mining: case studies of mines in Peru and Papua New Guinea. Baltimore, [1975]. pp. 143.

COPPER MINES AND MINING.

NATURAL resources and national welfare: the case of copper; edited by Ann Seidman. New York, 1975. pp. 453. Based on papers presented at a conference held in Lusaka, Zambia, July 3-9, 1974.

COPROLITES.

GROVE (RICHARD) The Cambridgeshire coprolite mining rush. Cambridge, [1976]. pp. 51. bibliog.

COPYHOLD.

MOGENSEN (MARGIT) Faestebønderne i Odsherred: studier over sociale og økonomiske forhold ca. 1750-1800. København, 1974. pp. 212. bibliog. (Københavns Universitet. Lokalhistorisk Afdeling. Skrifter. Nr. 4)

COPYRIGHT

— Bibliography.

HUANG (TE-HSIEN) compiler. Union list of copyright publications in West European libraries: catalogue collectif, etc. Halifax, N.S., 1974. pp. 621. Title-page also in French and German.

CORDOBA, ARGENTINE REPUBLIC (PROVINCE)

— Politics and government.

RE (ENRIQUE JOSE) Sedicion: cronica de los hechos que produjeron el derrocamiento del gobierno de Cordoba. [Buenos Aires], 1974. pp. 223.

CORITANI.

TODD (MALCOLM) The Coritani. London, 1973. pp. 164. bibliog.

CORMENIN (LOUIS MARIE DE LA HAYE DE).

See LA HAYE (LOUIS MARIE DE) Vicomte de Cormenin.

CORN LAWS

— United Kingdom.

HENDERSON (WILLIAM OTTO) Charles Pelham Villiers and the repeal of the Corn Laws. [Manchester, 1975]. pp. 81.

CORNWALL

— Economic history.

WHETTER (JAMES) Cornwall in the 17th century: an economic history of Kernow. Padstow, 1974. pp. 221.

— — Sources.

GARDINER (DOROTHY M.) A calendar of early Chancery proceedings relating to West Country shipping, 1388-1493. [Exeter], 1976. pp. 131. (Devon and Cornwall Record Society. [Publications]. New Series. vol. 21)

CORONARY HEART DISEASE.

ACTON (JAN PAUL) Evaluating public programs to save lives: the case of heart attacks. Santa Monica, 1973. pp. 136. bibliog. (Rand Corporation. [Rand Reports]. 950)

CORPORAL PUNISHMENT.

COLLINSON (JOSEPH) Facts about flogging. rev. ed. London, 1905. pp. 52.

CORPORATE ENTRY (CATALOGUING).

VERONA (EVA) Corporate headings: their use in library catalogues and national bibliographies; a comparative and critical study. London, 1975. pp. 224.

CORPORATE STATE.

ASSEMBLEA NAZIONALE CORPORATIVA, 1A, 1974. Atti. Roma, [1975]. pp. 356.

MILLER (ARTHUR SELWYN) The modern corporate state: private governments and the American constitution. Westport, Conn., 1976. pp. 269.

CORPORATION LAW

— Europe.

MEINHARDT (PETER) Company law in Europe. Epping, 1975. Loose leaf.

— Luxembourg.

LUXEMBOURG. Statutes, etc. 1868-1975. Recueil de la législation sur les sociétés, associations et syndicats: textes coordonnés et jurisprudence; [edited by] (Raymond Weydert). 2nd ed. Luxembourg, 1975. pp. 233.

— Netherlands.

MEER (S.W. VAN DER) Corporate law of the Netherlands and of the Netherlands Antilles. 5th ed. Zwolle, [1973]. pp. 101.

— Netherlands Antilles.

MEER (S.W. VAN DER) Corporate law of the Netherlands and of the Netherlands Antilles. 5th ed. Zwolle, [1973]. pp. 101.

— New Zealand.

NEW ZEALAND. Special Committee to review the Companies Act. 1973. Final report; [Mr. Justice Macarthur, chairman]. [Wellington], 1973. pp. 246.

— Nigeria.

OROJO (J. OLA) Nigerian company law and practice. London, 1976. pp. 571.

CORPORATION LAW(Cont.)

— Pakistan.

RANJHA (KHALID) Company law and the shareholder. Lahore, 1975. pp. 542. *bibliog.*

— Switzerland.

SWITZERLAND. Statutes, etc. Swiss corporation law: English translation of official text; by the Legal Committee of the American Chamber of Commerce in Switzerland. Zürich, [1974]. pp. 79.

— United Kingdom.

BROWN (W.J.) Cases and statutes on company law. London, 1976. pp. 206.

PALMER (Sir FRANCIS BEAUFORT) Company law; twenty-second edition by Clive M. Schmitthoff [and others]. London, 1976. 2 vols. *vol. 2 is loose-leaf.*

CORPORATIONS.

MEANS (DAVID MACGREGOR) Industrial freedom. New York, 1897. pp. 248.

FRIEDMANN (WOLFGANG GASTON) ed. Public and private enterprise in mixed economies. London, 1974. pp. 410.

ARGENTI (JOHN) Corporate collapse: the causes and symptoms. London, [1976]. pp. 193. *bibliog.*

— Finance.

NATIONAL ECONOMIC DEVELOPMENT OFFICE. Finance for investment: Appendices. London, 1975. 1 vol. (various pagings).

— Canada.

CANADA. Statistics Canada. Domestic and foreign control of manufacturing establishments in Canada. bien, 1969/1970 (1st)- Ottawa.

CLEMENT (WALLACE) The Canadian corporate elite: an analysis of economic power. Toronto, [1975]. pp. 479. *bibliog. (Carleton University. Institute of Canadian Studies. The Carleton Library. No. 89)*

CANADA CORPORATIONS BANKRUPTCY AND INSOLVENCY: Bulletin (formerly Canada Corporations Act: Bulletin;) [pd. by] Bureau of Corporate Affairs...Canada. [in English and French]. m. Ottawa. *Current issues only kept.*

— — Québec.

QUEBEC (PROVINCE). Ministère des Institutions Financières, Compagnies et Coopératives. Annual report. a., 1974/75- Québec. *[In English and French].*

— Europe — Accounting.

OLDHAM (K. MICHAEL) Accounting systems and practice in Europe. Epping, Essex, 1975. pp. 183.

— — Finance.

SAMUELS (J.M.) and others. Company finance in Europe. London, 1975. pp. 341. *bibliogs.*

— European Economic Community countries.

EUROPEAN COMMUNITIES. Commission. 1975. Employee participation and company structure in the European Community. [Brussels], 1975. pp. 107. *(Bulletin of the European Communities. Supplements. [1975/8]).*

— — Finance.

TELLER (ROBERT) Amortissement fiscal et croissance des entreprises dans la C.E.E. Bruxelles, 1974. pp. 289. *bibliog.*

— — Taxation.

EUROPEAN COMMUNITIES. Commission. 1975. Proposal for a council directive concerning the harmonization of systems of company taxation and of withholding taxes on dividends, etc. [Brussels], 1975. pp. 24. *(Bulletin of the European Communities. Supplements. [1975/10])*

— Germany — Taxation.

KOSSOW (BERND HEINRICH) Die Besteuerung der Unternehmung in Deutschland und im Vereinigten Königreich von Grossbritannien und Nordirland: ein Vergleich mit Hilfe der Teilsteuerrechnung. Köln, 1975. pp. 577,370. *bibliog.*

— India.

ROY (S.K.) Corporate image in India: a study of elite attitudes towards private and public industry. New Delhi, [1974]. pp. 343.

— Ireland (Republic) — Taxation.

EIRE. Dail Eireann. Special Committee on the Corporation Tax Bill, 1975. 1976. Parliamentary debates. Dublin, 1976. 6 pts. *(Dail Eireann. Parliamentary Debates: Official Report. 1976. D 21. Nos. 1-6)*

EIRE. Dail Eireann. Special Committee on the Corporation Tax Bill, 1975. 1976. Report...together with the proceedings. Dublin, 1976. pp. (24). *In English and Irish.*

— Mexico.

MICHELSEN TERRY (CARLOS JOSE) A theoretical and empirical study of perceptions of relative power among the staff of some Mexican industrial organizations; [Ph.D. (London) thesis]. 1975. 1 vol. (various foliations). *Typescript: unpublished. This thesis is the property of London University and may not be removed from the Library.*

— Norway — Accounting.

NORWAY. Statistiske Centralbyrå. 1974. Regnskapsanalyse: industri og engroshandel, etc. Oslo, 1974. pp. 131. *(Statistiske Analyser. 12) With summary in English.*

— South Africa.

SOUTH AFRICA. Registrar of Companies. Annual report. a., 1974 (1st)- Pretoria. *Included in the file of SOUTH AFRICA. Parliament. House of Assembly. Votes and proceedings (with Printed annexures).*

— United Kingdom.

FINANCIAL ANALYSIS GROUP. Britain's top 1000 private companies, 1974/5. London, 1974. pp. 77.

ECONOMISTS ADVISORY GROUP. The larger private company in Britain: a study of corporate profitability...directed by Graham Bannock. London, 1975. fo. 68.

THOMAS (RAYMOND ELLIOTT) The government of business. Deddington, Oxford, 1976. pp. 216. *bibliog.*

— — Finance.

NATIONAL ECONOMIC DEVELOPMENT OFFICE. Financial performance and inflation. London, [1975]. pp. 83.

SAMUELS (J.M.) and WILKES (F.M.) Management of company finance. 2nd ed. London, 1975. pp. 580. *bibliogs.*

— — Taxation.

KOSSOW (BERND HEINRICH) Die Besteuerung der Unternehmung in Deutschland und im Vereinigten Königreich von Grossbritannien und Nordirland: ein Vergleich mit Hilfe der Teilsteuerrechnung. Köln, 1975. pp. 577,370. *bibliog.*

SUMNER (MICHAEL T.) The effect of taxation on corporate saving and investment. London, [1976]. 1 pamphlet (unpaged). *bibliog. (Institute for Fiscal Studies. Lecture Series. No.4)*

— United States.

MALIK (REX) And tomorrow...the world?: inside IBM. London, 1975. pp. 496. *bibliog.*

DEUTSCH (JAN G.) compiler. Selling the people's Cadillac: the Edsel and corporate responsibility. New Haven, 1976. pp. 261.

MILLER (ARTHUR SELWYN) The modern corporate state: private governments and the American constitution. Westport, Conn., 1976. pp. 269.

PEARCE (FRANK) Crimes of the powerful: Marxism, crime and deviance. London, 1976. pp. 172.

CORPORATIONS, AMERICAN.

SANTOS (THEOTONIO DOS) Imperialismo y empresas multinacionales. Buenos Aires, 1973. pp. 142.

NEGANDHI (ANANT R.) and PRASAD (S. BENJAMIN) The frightening angels: a study of U.S. multinationals in developing nations. Kent, Ohio, [1975]. pp. 249. *bibliog.*

TORNEDEN (ROGER L.) Foreign disinvestment by U.S. multinational corporations; with eight case studies. New York, 1975. pp. 156. *bibliog.*

— United Kingdom.

DUNNING (JOHN HARRY) U.S. industry in Britain: an EAG business research study. London, 1976. pp. 122.

CORPORATIONS, FOREIGN

— America, Latin.

The NATION-state and transnational corporations in conflict: with special reference to Latin America; edited by Jon P. Gunnemann. New York, 1975. pp. 242. *Papers of the consultation organized by the Council on Religion and International Affairs at Aspen Institute, Colorado, in 1973.*

— Canada.

CANADA. Statistics Canada. Domestic and foreign control of manufacturing establishments in Canada. bien, 1969/1970 (1st)- Ottawa.

— Underdeveloped areas.

See UNDERDEVELOPED AREAS — Corporations, Foreign.

CORPORATIONS, NON-PROFIT.

— United States.

CYERT (RICHARD MICHAEL) The management of nonprofit organizations, with emphasis on universities: (lectures delivered at Hofstra University on the occasion of the inauguration of Robert L. Payton as president; responses by William R. Dill [and others]). Farnborough, Hants, [1975]. pp. 190.

CORPORATIONS, PUBLIC.

FRIEDMANN (WOLFGANG GASTON) ed. Public and private enterprise in mixed economies. London, 1974. pp. 410.

REES (RAY) Public enterprise economics. London, [1976]. pp. 196. *bibliog. (London. University. London School of Economics and Political Science. LSE Handbooks in Economic Analysis)*

WEBB (MICHAEL G.) Pricing policies for public enterprises. London, 1976. pp. 96. *bibliog.*

— Employees.

KAYE (SEYMOUR P.) and MARSH (ARTHUR IVOR) eds. International manual on collective bargaining for public employees. New York, 1973. pp. 389.

— France.

FRANCE. Direction de la Documentation. La Documentation Française. Notes et Etudes Documentaires. Nos. 4,167-4, 168. Un espoir pour les entreprises publiques: les contrats de programme, O.R.T.F., Electricité de France, S.N.C.F., 1970- 1974; par Philippe Comte. Paris, 1975. pp. 70.

— Liberia.

LIBERIAN DEVELOPMENT CORPORATION. Annual report. a., 1974- Monrovia.

COST AND STANDARD OF LIVING.

— **Mauritius.**

MAURITIUS. Para-Statal Salaries Commission. 1974. Report; [Donald Chesworth, chairman]. Port Louis, 1974. pp. 165.

— **Nigeria.**

WEY (S.O.) The structure and organisation of the public services. Lagos, 1971. *bibliog.*

— **Senegal.**

SENEGAL. Commission des Affaires Financières. 1971. Etude sur la structure des établissements publics; [report of a working group]. Dakar, 1971. fo. 48. *Xerox copy.*

— **Spain.**

SPAIN. Instituto de Estudios Fiscales. 1972. La empresa publica en España: aspectos generales; [by Cesar Albiñana Garcia-Quintana and others]. [Madrid, 1972]. pp. 514.

— **United Kingdom.**

NATIONAL ECONOMIC DEVELOPMENT OFFICE. Investment by nationalised industries: relations with suppliers. London, 1975. pp. 41.

CORPORATIONS, RELIGIOUS

— **Canada — Finance.**

CANADA. Statistics Canada. Selected financial statistics of religious organizations. a., 1971 (1st issue)- Ottawa. *[In English and French].*

CORPORATIONS, SWEDISH

— **South Africa.**

LANDSORGANISATIONEN I SVERIGE and TJÄNSTEM ÄNNENS CENTRALORGANISATION. South Africa: black labour - Swedish capital; a report by the LO/TCO study delegation to South Africa 1975; English translation: Jaak Talvend. [Stockholm], 1975. pp. 193. *bibliog.*

CORRUPTION (IN POLITICS).

WERTHEIM (WILLEM FREDERIK) and BRASZ (H.J.) Corruptie. Assen, 1961. pp. 58.

— **Ghana.**

GHANA. 1970. White Paper on the report of the Commission of Enquiry into the affairs of the Sekondi-Takoradi City Council. [Accra], 1970. pp. 11. *(W[hite] P[apers] 1970. No. 6) Bound with the Report.*

GHANA. Commission appointed...to enquire into the affairs of the Sekondi-Takoradi City Council. 1970. Report; [Edmund Brite Gaisie, chairman]. [Accra], 1970. pp. 113. *Bound with the White Paper on the Report.*

GHANA. 1971. White Paper on the report of the Committee of Enquiry on the erstwhile Football Pools Authority. [Accra], 1971. pp. 5. *(W[hite] P[apers]. 1971. No.1) Bound with the report.*

GHANA. Commission of Enquiry into the Diamond Mining Corporation. 1971. Report; [chairman Charles Sterling Acolatse, subsequently Saki Scheck]. Accra, [1971]. fo. 136.

GHANA. Committee of Enquiry on the erstwhile Football Pools Authority. 1971. Report; [P.V. Osei-Hwere, chairman]. [Accra, 1971]. fo. 218. *Bound with White Paper on the report.*

GHANA. Commission of Inquiry into Bribery and Corruption. 1975. Final report; [P.D.Anin, chairman]. [Accra], 1975. pp. 161.

— **Hong Kong.**

HONG KONG. Independent Commission Against Corruption. Annual report on the activities. a., 1974(1st)- Hong Kong.

— **South Africa.**

SOUTH AFRICA. Parliament. Senate. Select Committee on Allegation by Senator. 1975. Report; (with Proceedings and minutes of evidence) (S.C. 1/1975). in SOUTH AFRICA. Parliament. Senate. Reports from the Sessional and Select Committees.

— **Spain.**

KERN (ROBERT W.) Liberals, reformers and caciques in Restoration Spain, 1875-1909. Albuquerque, [1974]. pp. 153. *bibliog.*

— **United Kingdom.**

MURPHY (DAVID) The silent watchdog: the press in local politics. London, 1976. pp. 186. *bibliog.*

— **Venezuela.**

PEREZ JIMENEZ (MARCOS) defendant. Proceso a un ex-dictador...: juicio al general (r) Marcos Perez Jimenez; [edited by] Jose Agustin Catala. Caracas, 1968-69 [or rather 1969]. 2 vols. (in 1).

CORSICA

— **Description and travel.**

AMBROSOLI (MAURO) John Symonds: agricultura e politica in Corsica e in Italia, 1765-1770. Torino, 1974. pp. 165. *bibliog. (Fondazione Luigi Einaudi. Studi. 17)*

— **Economic conditions.**

PERRIER (EDOUARD) Corse: les raisons de la colère; perspectives démocratiques; étude réalisée sous l'égide de la Fédération de la Corse du P.C.F. Paris, [1975]. pp. 228.

— **Politics and government.**

PERRIER (EDOUARD) Corse: les raisons de la colère; perspectives démocratiques; étude réalisée sous l'égide de la Fédération de la Corse du P.C.F. Paris, [1975]. pp. 228.

COSMOLOGY.

SAMBURSKY (SHMUEL) The physical world of the Greeks; translated from the Hebrew by Merton Dagut. London, 1963. pp. 255. *bibliog.*

AMERICAN ASSOCIATION FOR THE ADVANCEMENT OF SCIENCE. Section L. Annual Meeting, 1969. Philosophical foundations of science: proceedings...; edited by Raymond J. Seeger and Robert S. Cohen. Dordrecht, [1974]. pp. 545. *bibliogs. (Boston Colloquium for the Philosophy of Science. Boston Studies in the Philosophy of Science. vol.11)*

COST ACCOUNTING.

DOPUCH (NICHOLAS) and BIRNBERG (JACOB G.) Cost accounting: accounting data for management's decisions. New York, [1969]. pp. 527. *bibliogs.*

COST AND STANDARD OF LIVING.

RUPRECHT (THEODORE K.) and JEWETT (FRANK I.) The micro-economics of demographic change: family planning and economic well-being. New York, 1975. pp. 153.

— **Algeria.**

ASSOCIATION POUR LA RECHERCHE DEMOGRAPHIQUE ECONOMIQUE ET SOCIALE. La consommation des familles d'Algérie; [edited by Alain Darbel]. Paris, 1961. pp. 59.

— **Antigua.**

ANTIGUA. Statistics Division. Cost of living index. irreg., Ja/Ap 1976- [St. John's].

— **Botswana.**

BOTSWANA. Central Statistics Office. 1973. Household expenditure survey, 1968-1970. Gaborone, 1973?]. 1 vol. (unpaged).

— **Canada — New Brunswick.**

NEW BRUNSWICK. Department of Labour. Labour Market Services Branch. 1974. Collective agreement survey of cost of living adjustment, COLA, clauses (in) various industries in New Brunswick. Fredericton, 1974. pp. 11.

— **Europe.**

CONFEDERATION OF BRITISH INDUSTRY. West European living costs, 1976. London, 1976. pp. 32.

— **European Economic Community countries.**

EUROPEAN COMMUNITIES. Statistical Office. Regional statistics: population, employment, living standards. a., 1973/74 [1st]- Luxembourg. *[In Community languages]. Formerly included in EUROPEAN COMMUNITIES. Statistical Office. Regional statistics.*

— **Germany.**

BITTMANN (KARL) Arbeiterhaushalt und Teuerung. Jena, 1914. pp. 181.

FUERTH (HENRIETTE) Der Haushalt vor und nach dem Krieg: dargestellt an Hand eines mittelbürgerlichen Budgets. Jena, 1922. pp. 65.

GERMANY (BUNDESREPUBLIK). Statistisches Bundesamt. 1974. Aufgabe, Methode und Durchführung der Einkommens- und Verbrauchsstichprobe, 1969. Wiesbaden, 1974. pp. 113. *(Preise, Löhne, Wirtschaftsrechnungen. Reihe 18. Einkommens- und Verbrauchsstichproben. 6)*

— **Ireland (Republic).**

EIRE. Central Statistics Office. 1976- . Household budget survey, 1973. Dublin, 1976 in progress.

— **Italy.**

TAGLIACARNE (GUGLIELMO) Livello di vita e tendenze di sviluppo delle aree socio-economiche del Mezzogiorno. [Milano], 1974. pp. 66. *(Associazione per lo Sviluppo dell' Industria nel Mezzogiorno. Centro per gli Studi sullo Sviluppo Economico. Collana di Monografie)*

— **Japan.**

JAPAN. Bureau of Statistics. 1976- . 1974 national survey of family income and expenditures. [Tokyo, 1976], 11 vols. *In English and Japanese.*

— **Norway.**

NORWAY. Statistiske Centralbyrå. 1975. Forbruksundersøkelse, 1973, etc. Oslo, 1975. pp. 231. *bibliog. (Norges Offisielle Statistikk. Rekke A. 705) In Norwegian and English.*

NORWAY. Statistiske Centralbyrå. 1975. Forbruksundersøkelse for skoleungdom og studenter, 1973-1974, etc. Oslo, 1975. pp. 144. *(Norges Offisielle Statistikk. Rekke A. 717) In Norwegian and English.*

NORWAY. Statistiske Centralbyrå. 1975. Levekår, 1973, etc. Oslo, 1975. pp. 139. *(Norges Offisielle Statistikk. Rekke A. 720) In Norwegian and English.*

— **Poland.**

AKTUALNE zadania spółdzielczości zaopatrzenia i zbytu w realizacji zadań wy'zywienia narodu i rozwoju rolnictwa. Warszawa, 1975. pp. 28.

— **Russia.**

ZABOTA partii i pravitel'stva o blage naroda: sbornik dokumentov, oktiabr' 1964-1973. Moskva, 1974. pp. 847.

— — **Azerbaijan.**

GUSHCHIN (SERGEI NIKOLAEVICH) and MEKHTIEV (GIAZENFER GIUSEINOVICH) Sotsializm i blagosostoianie trudiashchikhsia Sovetskogo Azerbaidzhana, 1920-1974 gg. Baku, 1975. pp. 182.

COST AND STANDARD OF LIVING.(Cont.)

— **Singapore.**

SINGAPORE. Statistics Department. 1974. Report on the household expenditure survey, 1972/1973. Singapore, 1974. pp. 69.

— **South Africa.**

POTGIETER (J.F.) The household subsistence level in the major urban centres of the Republic of South Africa: October, 1974. Port Elizabeth, 1974. pp. 85. *bibliog.* (*University of Port Elizabeth. Institute for Planning Research. Research Reports. No. 14*)

— **Tanzania.**

UNITED REPUBLIC OF TANZANIA. Bureau of Statistics. 1974. National consumer price index 1969-1973: basic material, computations and results. Dar es Salaam, 1974. fo. 62.

— **United Kingdom.**

SHERGOLD (PETER ROGER) The standard of life of manual workers in the first decade of the twentieth-century: a comparative study of Birmingham, U.K., and Pittsburgh, U.S.A. 1976. fo. 691. *bibliog.* Typescript. Ph.D. (London) thesis: unpublished. *This thesis is the property of London University and may not be removed from the Library.*

U.K. Central Statistical Office. 1976. Estimates of household expenditure in the United Kingdom at current prices, 1970-1974: comparison between the family expenditure survey and the national accounts. [London, 1976]. pp. (27).

— **United States.**

RAINWATER (LEE) What money buys: inequality and the social meanings of income. New York, [1974]. pp. 242.

SHERGOLD (PETER ROGER) The standard of life of manual workers in the first decade of the twentieth-century: a comparative study of Birmingham, U.K., and Pittsburgh, U.S.A. 1976. fo. 691. *bibliog.* Typescript. Ph.D. (London) thesis: unpublished. *This thesis is the property of London University and may not be removed from the Library.*

COST CONTROL.

ANTHONY (ROBERT NEWTON) and others, eds. Management control systems: text, cases and readings. rev. ed. Homewood, Ill., 1972 repr. 1975. pp. 857. *bibliog.*

COST EFFECTIVENESS.

INDIA. Committee on Plan Projects. Management Group. 1966. Feasibility studies for public sector projects. [New Delhi], 1966. pp. 186. *bibliog.*

McINTOSH (P.T.) and QUARMBY (D.A.) Generalised costs, and the estimation of movement costs and benefits in transport planning. [London], 1970. fo. 38. (*U.K. Department of the Environment. Mathematical Advisory Unit. MAU Notes. 179*)

FLOWERDEW (A.D.J.) and WHITEHEAD (CHRISTINE MARGARET ELIZABETH) Cost-effectiveness and cost-benefit analysis in information science. London, 1974. pp. 71.

CZAMANSKI (DANIEL Z.) The cost of preventive services: the case of fire departments. Lexington, Mass., [1975]. pp. 108. *bibliog.*

IRVIN (G.W.) and others. Roads and redistribution: social costs and benefits of labour-intensive road construction in Iran. Geneva, International Labour Office, 1975. pp. 162.

MACIARIELLO (JOSEPH A.) Dynamic cost-benefit analysis: evaluation of public policy in a dynamic urban model. Lexington, Mass., [1975]. pp. 184. *bibliog.*

MORGAN (R. TRAVERS) AND PARTNERS. Report of the Urban Motorways Project Team to the Urban Motorways Committee: techniques used in the case studies. Technical paper no. 1. Environmental evaluation: the cost-benefit approach. [London], Department of the Environment, 1974 [or rather 1975]. pp. 64.

SELF (PETER J.O.) Econocrats and the policy process: the politics and philosophy of cost-benefit analysis. London, 1975. pp. 212.

JONES-LEE (M.W.) The value of life: an economic analysis. London, 1976. pp. 162. *bibliogs.*

COSTA (JOAQUIN).

SABORIT (ANDRES) Joaquin Costa y el socialismo. Madrid, 1970. pp. 178.

COSTS, INDUSTRIAL

— **Poland.**

AUGUSTOWSKI (ZBIGNIEW) Planowanie kosztów własnych w przemyśle. Warszawa, 1954. pp. 120.

GDAŃSK. Uniwersytet. Wydział Ekonomiki Produkcji. Zeszyty Naukowe. 6. Zagadnienia z finansów i statystyki. Gdańsk, 1975. pp. 179. *bibliog. With English and Russian summaries.*

— **Romania.**

MARINESCU (ILIE) ed. Contribuţii la metodologia de prognoză a costurilor de producţie. Bucureşti, 1976. pp. 188. (*Academia de Ştiinţe Sociale şi Politice a Republicii Socialiste România. Institutul de Cercetări Economice. Biblioteca Oeconomica. 31*) *With English summary and English and Russian tables of contents.*

COSTUME

— **Russia.**

KOSTIUM v Rossii XVIII - nachala XX veka: iz sobraniia Ermitazha; katalog vystavki. Leningrad, 1974. pp. 44,[xxxi].

CÔTE D'AZUR.

See also PROVENCE-COTE D'AZURE.

CÔTES—DU—NORD.

FRANCE. Direction de la Documentation. La Documentation Française. Notes et Etudes Documentaires. Nos . 4,125-4, 126-4,127-4,128. Les départements français. 22. Côtes-du-Nord, Bretagne; [par Daniel Rivière]. Paris, 1974. pp. 132. *bibliog.*

COTTAGE INDUSTRIES

— **Cyprus.**

CYPRUS. Statistics and Research Department. 1973. Cottage industry survey, 1972. [Nicosia, 1973]. pp. 170, iii.

— **Finland.**

REMESLO i manufaktura v Rossii, Finliandii, Pribaltike: materialy II sovetsko-finskogo simpoziuma po sotsial'no-ekonomicheskoi istorii, 13-14 dekabria 1972 g. Leningrad, 1975. pp. 199. *With Finnish and German summaries and tables of contents.*

— **Russia.**

REMESLO i manufaktura v Rossii, Finliandii, Pribaltike: materialy II sovetsko-finskogo simpoziuma po sotsial'no-ekonomicheskoi istorii, 13-14 dekabria 1972 g. Leningrad, 1975. pp. 199. *With Finnish and German summaries and tables of contents.*

— **United Kingdom.**

BENJAMIN (FREDERICK A.) The Ruskin linen industry of Keswick. Beckermet, Cumbria, 1974. pp. 43.

COTTON GROWING AND MANUFACTURE

— **India.**

MEHTA (MADHAVA MAL) Structure of cotton-mill industry of India: a study in the size and location of industrial units in the cotton-mill industry of India. Allahabad, 1949. pp. 328. *bibliog. Ph.D. thesis, University of Allahabad.*

— — **Bombay.**

BOMBAY (STATE). Industrial Conditions Enquiry Committee. Final report...together with suggestions for a labour code, Bombay State; [Purushottam Kanji, chairman]. [Bombay, 1950]. pp. 133.

— **United Kingdom.**

HUTCHINS (ELIZABETH LEIGH) [Correspondence about women's employment in Lancashire. 1914]. 12 letters. *Manuscript.*

COTTON TRADE.

TANNER (JOHN) A new deal for the poor: what a new economic order would mean for Britain and the third world. London, 1976. pp. 24. *bibliog.*

— **South Africa.**

SOUTH AFRICA. Department of the Auditor General. Report...on the accounts of the Cotton Board. a., 1974/75 [1st]- Pretoria. *[In English and Afrikaans]. Included in* SOUTH AFRICA. Parliament. House of Assembly. Votes and proceedings (with Printed annexures).

COUNCIL FOR MUTUAL ECONOMIC ASSISTANCE.

SOZIALISTISCHE ökonomische Integration: Anschauungsmaterial; herausgegeben von der Parteihochschule Karl Marx beim ZK der SED; (Autorenkollektiv...unter Leitung..Otto Raus). Berlin, [1974]. fo.47.

KURJO (ANDREAS) Agrarproduktion in den Mitgliedsländern des Rates für Gegenseitige Wirtschaftshilfe, RGW. Berlin, 1975. pp. 221. *bibliog.* (*Giessen. Universität. Zentrum für Kontinentale Agrar- und Wirtschaftsforschung. Giessener Abhandlungen zur Agrar- und Wirtschaftsforschung des Europäischen Ostens. Band 64*) *With English summary.*

MESHCHERIAKOV (V.V.) and others. SEV: printsipy, problemy, perspektivy. Moskva, 1975. pp. 239.

NYERS (RESZÖ) The C[ouncil for] M[utual] E[conomic] A[ssistance] countries on the road to economic integration. Budapest, 1975. pp. 27. (*Hungarian Scientific Council for World Economy. [Publications]. Trends in World Economy. No. 16*)

SOVET Ekonomicheskoi Vzaimopomoshchi: osnovnye pravovye problemy. Moskva, 1975. pp. 408.

COUNSELLING.

STANDING CONFERENCE FOR THE ADVANCEMENT OF COUNSELLING. Concepts of counselling: papers prepared by a working party of the conference...; edited by T.D. Vaughan. London, [1976]. pp. 95. *bibliogs.*

COUNTRY HOMES

— **United Kingdom — Wales.**

DE VANE (RICHARD) Second home ownership: a case study. Cardiff, 1975. pp. 108. *bibliogs.* (*Wales. University. University College of North Wales. Bangor Occasional Papers in Economics. No. 6*)

COUPS D'ÉTAT.

DECALO (SAMUEL) Coups and army rule in Africa: studies in military style. New Haven, 1976. pp. 284. *bibliog.*

COURT OF JUSTICE OF THE EUROPEAN COMMUNITIES.

PLOUVIER (LILIANE) Les décisions de la Cour de Justice des Communautés Européennes et leurs effets juridiques. Bruxelles, 1975. pp. 310. *bibliog.*

COURT RECORDS

— United Kingdom.

ESSEX. Quarter Sessions of the Peace. Essex Quarter Sessions Order Book, 1652-1661; [edited] by D.H. Allen. Chelmsford, 1974. pp. 236. *(Essex. Records Committee. Essex Record Office Publications. No. 65)*

CAMDEN SOCIETY. [Publications]. 4th Series. vol. 17. Western circuit assize orders, 1629-1648: a calendar; edited... by J.S. Cockburn. London, 1976. pp. 352.

EMMISON (FREDERICK GEORGE) Elizabethan life: home, work and land; from Essex wills and sessions and manorial records. Chelmsford, 1976. pp. 364. *(Essex. Records Committee. Essex Record Office Publications. No. 69)*

GARDINER (DOROTHY M.) A calendar of early Chancery proceedings relating to West Country shipping, 1388-1493. [Exeter], 1976. pp. 131. *(Devon and Cornwall Record Society. [Publications]. New Series. vol. 21)*

LONDON. London Record Society. Publications. vol. 12. The London Eyre of 1276; edited by Martin Weinbaum. London, 1976. pp. 188.

COURTS.

ABRAHAM (HENRY JULIAN) The judicial process: an introductory analysis of the courts of the United States, England and France. 3rd ed. New York, 1975. pp. 543. *bibliog.*

— Germany.

WAGNER (WALTER) Der Volksgerichtshof im nationalsozialistischen Staat. Stuttgart, 1974. pp. 992. *(Institut für Zeitgeschichte. Quellen und Darstellungen zur Zeitgeschichte. Band 16/3)*

KOMMERS (DONALD P.) Judicial politics in west Germany: a study of the Federal Constitutional Court. Beverly Hills, Cal., [1976]. pp. 312.

— United Kingdom.

BRYSON (WILLIAM HAMILTON) The equity side of the Exchequer: its jurisdiction, administration, procedures and records. London, 1975. pp. 217. *bibliog. (Cambridge. University. Yorke Prize Essays. 1973)*

— United States.

JACKSON (PERCIVAL E.) Dissent in the Supreme Court: a chronology. Norman, [1969]. pp. 583.

CARTER (JOHN DENTON) The Warren Court and the constitution: a critical view of judicial activism. Gretna, 1973. pp. 171.

CONANT (MICHAEL) The constitution and capitalism. St. Paul, Minn., 1974. pp. 306.

FEIN (BRUCE E.) Significant decisions of the Supreme Court, 1973-74 term. Washington, D.C., 1975. pp. 152. *(American Enterprise Institute for Public Policy Research. Domestic Affairs Studies. 36)*

COX (ARCHIBALD) The role of the Supreme Court in American government. Oxford, 1976. pp. 118. *(Oxford. University. All Souls College. Chichele Lectures. 1975)*

COURTSHIP.

FERRANDIZ (ALEJANDRA) and VERDU (VICENTE) Noviazgo y matrimonio en la burguesia española. Madrid, 1974 repr. 1975. pp. 283.

COVENANTERS.

COWAN (IAN B.) The Scottish Covenanters, 1660-1688. London, 1976. pp. 191. *bibliog.*

COVENTRY

— Civic improvement.

COVENTRY COMMUNITY DEVELOPMENT PROJECT. C[ommunity] D[evelopment] P[roject] final report. Coventry, 1975. 2 pts.

— Citizen participation.

HUMBLE (STEPHEN) and TALBOT (JENNIFER) A community forum in Coventry?: a document for discussion. [Coventry], Coventry Community Development Project, 1975. pp. 35. *(CDP Occasional Papers. No.14)*

— Social policy.

COVENTRY COMMUNITY DEVELOPMENT PROJECT. C[ommunity] D[evelopment] P[roject] final report. Coventry, 1975. 2 pts.

CRACOW

— Intellectual life.

MROZOWSKA (KAMILLA) Józef Maciej Brodowicz: z dziejów organizacji nauki i nauczania w Wolnym Mieście Krakowie. Wrocław, 1971. pp. 352. *bibliog. (Polska Akademia Nauk. Zakład Historii Nauki i Techniki. Monografie z Dziejów Nauki i Techniki. t.73) With Russian and English summaries.*

CRACOW (PROVINCE)

— Politics and government.

KOZIK (ZENOBIUSZ) Partie i stronnictwa polityczne w Krakowskiem, 1945-1947. Kraków, 1975. pp. 471. *bibliog.*

CRAIGIE COLLEGE OF EDUCATION, AYR.

HIGGS (PETER) and SAVILLE (JOHN) Craigie College of Education: the findings of a commission of inquiry established by the Council for Academic Freedom and Democracy in February 1971. London, [1972?]. pp. 24.

CREATIVE ABILITY.

STEIN (MORRIS ISAAC) Stimulating creativity. New York, [1974-75]. 2 vols. *bibliogs.*

ROEMER (JOACHIM) Ethos und Schöpfertum der Arbeiterklasse im Sozialismus, etc. Berlin, 1975. pp. 168.

CREDIT

— Communist countries.

DEN'GI, kredit i finansy v sotsialisticheskom obshchestve. Moskva, 1975. pp. 263.

— Europe.

REVELL (JACK) Savings flows in Europe: personal saving and borrowing. London, [1976]. pp. 191. *bibliogs. (Wales. University. University College of North Wales. Institute of European Finance. Research Studies)*

— Europe, Eastern.

BANKING, money and credit in Eastern Europe: main findings of colloquium held 24th-26th January, 1973, in Brussels; [edited by] Yves Laulan. [Brussels], North Atlantic Treaty Organization, [1973?] . pp. 166. *In English and French.*

— Netherlands.

RAAD VOOR HET MIDDEN- EN KLEINBEDRIJF. Advies inzake het rapport garantiekredietverlening aan het midden- en kleinbedrijf. 's-Gravenhage, 1974. pp. 18. *([Publikaties]. 1974, no. 3)*

— Russia.

BABAK (VASILII FEDOROVICH) Kredit i tekhnicheskii progress: dolgosrochnyi kredit i kapitalovlozheniia v usloviiakh nauchno-tekhnicheskoi revoliutsii. Moskva, 1975. pp. 168.

KORNEEVA (RAISA VASIL'EVNA) Kreditnye vzaimootnosheniia promyshlennosti s Gosbankom. Moskva, 1975. pp. 223.

ZHANGERIEV (IURII ABUBOVICH) Zakonomernosti dvizheniia oborotnykh sredstv i kredit. Moskva, 1975. pp. 96.

— White Russia.

OCHERKI razvitiia finansov i kredita v Belorussii. Minsk, 1970. pp. 208.

— Sweden.

NYGREN (INGEMAR) Svensk kreditmarknad under freds- och beredskapstid, 1935-1945. Göteborg, 1974. pp. 303. *bibliog. (Göteborgs Universitet Ekonomisk-Historiska Institutionen. Meddelanden. 30)*

— Yugoslavia.

PERIŠIN (IVO) Transformacija monetarnog i bankarsko-kreditnog sistema Jugoslavije; (monetarni sistem i ustavna reforma). Zagreb, 1975. pp. 59. *(Zagreb. Ekonomski Institut. Ekonomska Biblioteka: Aktuelni Problemi. 1/75)*

CREE INDIANS.

BRAROE (NIELS WINTHER) Indian and white: self-image and interaction in a Canadian plains community. Stanford, 1975. pp. 205. *bibliog.*

RICHARDSON (BOYCE) Strangers devour the land: a chronicle of the assault upon the last coherent hunting culture in North America, the Cree Indians of northern Quebec, and their vast primeval homelands. New York, 1976. pp. 342,xiii.

CREMIEUX (ISAAC ADOLPHE).

MIRECOURT (EUGENE DE) pseud. [i.e. Charles Jean Baptiste JACQUOT] Crémieux. Paris, G. Havard, 1858. pp. 92. *(Les Contemporains)*

CREOLES.

WOODS (FRANCES JEROME) Marginality and identity: a colored Creole family through ten generations. Baton Rouge, [1972]. pp. 395.

CRETE

— Foreign relations — United States.

MARCOGLOU (EMMANUEL E.) The American interest in the Cretan revolution, 1866-69. Athens, National Centre of Social Research, 1971. pp. 149. *bibliog.*

— History — 1866-1868, Insurrection of.

MARCOGLOU (EMMANUEL E.) The American interest in the Cretan revolution, 1866-69. Athens, National Centre of Social Research, 1971. pp. 149. *bibliog.*

CRIME AND CRIMINALS.

EUROPEAN COMMITTEE ON CRIME PROBLEMS. Collected Studies in Criminological Research. Strasbourg, Council of Europe, 1967 in progress.

CRIME and delinquency: dimensions of deviance; edited by Marc Riedel, Terence P. Thornberry. New York, 1974. pp. 208. *bibliog. A selection of papers presented at the 1973 annual meeting of the American Society of Criminology.*

McCAGHY (CHARLES H.) Deviant behavior: crime, conflict, and interest groups. New York, [1976]. pp. 400.

McDONALD (LYNN) The sociology of law and order. London, 1976. pp. 340. *bibliog.*

PEARCE (FRANK) Crimes of the powerful: Marxism, crime and deviance. London, 1976. pp. 172.

— Bibliography.

WRIGHT (MARTIN) ed. Use of criminology literature. London, 1974. pp. 242. *bibliogs.*

— Identification.

NASH (W.A.) and IRVING (BARRIE L.) Memorandum of evidence to the Devlin committee on identification parades and procedures. [London], 1974. pp. 38.

— Information services.

WRIGHT (MARTIN) ed. Use of criminology literature. London, 1974. pp. 242. *bibliogs.*

CRIME AND CRIMINALS.(Cont.)

— **Research.**

EUROPEAN COMMITTEE ON CRIME PROBLEMS. Collected Studies in Criminological Research. Strasbourg, Council of Europe, 1967 in progress.

— **Africa.**

CLIFFORD (WILLIAM) Criminologist. An introduction to African criminology. Nairobi, 1974. pp. 226.

— **Canada.**

SILVERMAN (ROBERT A.) and TEEVAN (JAMES J.) eds. Crime in Canadian society. Toronto, [1975]. pp. 455. *bibliog.*

— — **Quebec.**

QUEBEC (PROVINCE). Department of Justice, 1971. The police and public security. [Quebec, 1971]. pp. 176.

— **Denmark.**

HAUGAARD JENSEN (JENS) and others. Sociale studier: kriminalitet, prostitution og fattigdom i Århus, ca. 1870-1906. Aarhus, 1975. pp. 483. *bibliogs.*

— **Europe.**

EUROPEAN COMMITTEE ON CRIME PROBLEMS. 1974. Methods of forecasting trends in criminality. Strasbourg, Council of Europe, 1974. pp. 44.

EUROPEAN GROUP FOR THE STUDY OF DEVIANCE AND SOCIAL CONTROL. Conference, 1st, Impruneta, 1973. Deviance and control in Europe: papers...; edited by Herman Bianchi [and others]. London, [1975]. pp. 209.

MACK (JOHN ALEXANDER) The crime industry: [expanded version of a report to the Council of Europe]. Farnborough, Hants, [1975]. pp. 209. *bibliog.*

— **Kenya.**

MUGA (ERASTO) Crime and delinquency in Kenya: an analysis of crime rate of arrested and convicted persons by racial and ethnic group, sex and age, offences committed and urban and rural differentials. Kampala, 1975. pp. 159. *bibliog.*

— **Russia.**

KRYLOV (IVAN FILIPPOVICH) Ocherki istorii kriminalistiki i kriminalisticheskoi ekspertizy. Leningrad, 1975. pp. 188.

— **South Africa.**

MIDGLEY (JAMES) and others eds. Crime and punishment in South Africa. Johannesburg, [1975]. pp. 261. *bibliogs.*

— **Sweden.**

FÄLLSTRÖM (ANNE-MARIE) Konjunktur och kriminalitet: studier i Göteborgs sociala historia, 1800-1840. Göteborg, [1974]. pp. 168. *bibliog. (Göteborgs Universitet. Historiska Institutionen. Meddelanden. Nr. 8) With English summary.*

— **United Kingdom.**

SOCIAL SURVEYS (GALLUP POLL) LIMITED. Crime and the police: a gallup poll conducted for the Daily Telegraph. London, 1961. pp. 15.

ALBION'S fatal tree: crime and society in eighteenth-century England; [by] Douglas Hay [and others]. London, 1975. pp. 352.

MAYS (JOHN BARRON) Crime and its treatment. 2nd ed. London, 1975. pp. 173. *bibliog.*

THOMPSON (EDWARD PALMER) Whigs and hunters: the origin of the Black Act. London, 1975. pp. 313.

BALDWIN (JOHN) Ph.D., and BOTTOMS (A.E.) The urban criminal: a study in Sheffield;...in collaboration with Monica A. Walker. London, 1976. pp. 262. *bibliog.*

BOTTOMS (A.E.) and McCLEAN (JOHN DAVID) Defendants in the criminal process. London, 1976. pp. 265. *bibliog.*

— **United States.**

AMERICAN ACADEMY OF POLITICAL AND SOCIAL SCIENCE. Annals. vol. 423. Crime and justice in America, 1776-1976; special editor of this volume Graeme R. Newman. Philadelphia, 1976. pp. 227.

CRIME PREVENTION.

GIBBS (JACK P.) Crime, punishment, and deterrence. New York, [1975]. pp. 259. *bibliog.*

ANDERSON (R.W.) The economics of crime. London, 1976. pp. 71. *bibliog.*

CRIMEA

— **History.**

FEODAL'NAIA Tavrika: materialy po istorii i arkheologii Kryma. Kiev, 1974. pp. 216.

— — **Bibliography.**

KRYM za 50 let Sovetskoi vlasti: bibliograficheskii ukazatel' literatury. Simferopol', 1970. pp. 104.

CRIMINAL ACT

— **Poland.**

MAREK (ANDRZEJ) Stopień społecznego niebezpieczeństwa czynu jako podstawa umorzenia postępowania karnego. Toruń, 1970. pp. 199. *bibliog. (Towarzystwo Naukowe w Toruniu. Studia Iuridica. t.10, zeszyt 1) With German summary.*

CRIMINAL ANTHROPOLOGY.

EUROPEAN COMMITTEE ON CRIME PROBLEMS. Collected Studies in Criminological Research. Strasbourg, Council of Europe, 1967 in progress.

CRIMINAL BEHAVIOUR, PREDICTION OF.

EUROPEAN COMMITTEE ON CRIME PROBLEMS. 1974. Methods of forecasting trends in criminality. Strasbourg, Council of Europe, 1974. pp. 44.

FERRACUTI (FRANCO) and others. Delinquents and nondelinquents in the Puerto Rican slum culture. Columbus, Oh., [1975]. pp. 249. *bibliog.*

CRIMINAL INVESTIGATION

— **Russia.**

KRYLOV (IVAN FILIPPOVICH) Ocherki istorii kriminalistiki i kriminalisticheskoi ekspertizy. Leningrad, 1975. pp. 188.

CRIMINAL JUSTICE, ADMINISTRATION OF.

EUROPEAN COMMITTEE ON CRIME PROBLEMS. Collected Studies in Criminological Research. Strasbourg, Council of Europe, 1967 in progress.

— **Economic aspects.**

ANDERSON (R.W.) The economics of crime. London, 1976. pp. 71. *bibliog.*

— **Australia.**

EGGLESTON (ELIZABETH) Fear, favour or affection: aborigines and the criminal law in Victoria, South Australia and Western Australia. Canberra, 1976. pp. 398. *bibliog. (Academy of the Social Sciences in Australia. Aborigines in Australian Society. 13)*

— **China.**

CONFLICT and control in late imperial China; edited by Frederic Wakeman and Carolyn Grant. Berkeley, California, [1975]. pp. 328. *Papers from a conference sponsored by the Center for Chinese Studies, University of California, and the Committee on Studies of Chinese Civilization of the American Council of Learned Societies.*

— **France.**

LANGLOIS (DENIS) Les dossiers noirs de la justice française. Paris, 1975. pp. 221.

— **Mexico.**

MACLACHLAN (COLIN M.) Criminal justice in eighteenth century Mexico: a study of the Tribunal of the Acordada. Berkeley, Calif., 1974. pp. 141. *bibliog.*

— **South Africa.**

MIDGLEY (JAMES) and others eds. Crime and punishment in South Africa. Johannesburg, [1975]. pp. 261. *bibliogs.*

— **United Kingdom.**

NATIONAL ASSOCIATION FOR THE CARE AND RESETTLEMENT OF OFFENDERS. Diversion from criminal justice in an English context: report of a NACRO Working Party under the chairmanship of Michael Zander. Chichester, 1975. pp. 48.

BOTTOMS (A.E.) and McCLEAN (JOHN DAVID) Defendants in the criminal process. London, 1976. pp. 265. *bibliog.*

ZANDER (MICHAEL) Cases and materials on the English legal system. 2nd ed. London, 1976. pp. 492.

— **United States.**

JENNINGS (JOHN B.) Analysis of the night and weekend arraignment parts in the Bronx and Queens Criminal Courts. New York, 1973. pp. 68. *(Rand Corporation. [Rand Reports]. 1236)*

SEYMOUR (WHITNEY NORTH) United States attorney: an inside view of "justice" in America under the Nixon administration. New York, 1975. pp. 248.

AMERICAN ACADEMY OF POLITICAL AND SOCIAL SCIENCE. Annals. vol. 423. Crime and justice in America, 1776-1976; special editor of this volume Graeme R. Newman. Philadelphia, 1976. pp. 227.

MONAHAN (JOHN) ed. Community mental health and the criminal justice system. New York, [1976]. pp. 332. *bibliogs.*

PEPINSKY (HAROLD E.) Crime and conflict: a study of law and society. London, 1976. pp. 159. *bibliogs.*

CRIMINAL LAW

— **Germany.**

MARXEN (KLAUS) Der Kampf gegen das liberale Strafrecht: eine Studie zum Antiliberalismus in der Strafrechtswissenschaft der zwanziger und dreissiger Jahre. Berlin, [1975]. pp. 296. *bibliog.*

— **Poland.**

POLAND. Statutes, etc. 1975. Kodeks karny, przepisy wprowadzające, skorowidz rzeczowy oraz wa'zniejsze ustawy dodatkowe: stan prawny na dzień 1 grudnia 1975 r. Warszawa, 1976. pp. 855.

— **Russia.**

SOVETSKOE ugolovnoe pravo: chast' osobennaia, etc. Moskva, 1973. pp. 576.

— — **Russia (RSFSR).**

RUSSIA (RSFSR). Statutes, etc. 1975. Ugolovnyi kodeks RSFSR: s izmeneniiami i dopolneniiami na 1 ianvaria 1975 goda, s prilozheniem postateino-sistematizirovannykh materialov. Moskva, 1975. pp. 295.

— **United Kingdom.**

ARCHBOLD (JOHN FREDERICK) Pleading, evidence and practice in criminal cases: thirty-ninth edition [by] Stephen Mitchell [and others]. London, 1976. pp. 1823. *With cumulative supplement.*

CROSS (Sir RUPERT) and JONES (PHILIP ASTERLEY) Introduction to criminal law; eighth edition [by] Philip Asterley Jones [and] Richard Card. London, 1976. pp. 474.

MORRIS (TERENCE PATRICK) Deviance and control: the secular heresy. London, 1976. pp. 157.

CRIMINAL LIABILITY

— **Russia.**

BAGRII-SHAKHMATOV (LEONID VASIL'EVICH) Ugolovnaia otvetstvennost' i nakazanie. Minsk, 1976. pp. 383.

CRIMINAL LIABILITY (INTERNATIONAL LAW).

KOLOSOV (IURII MIKHAILOVICH) Otvetstvennost' v mezhdunarodnom prave. Moskva, 1975. pp. 256.

CRIMINAL PROCEDURE

— **New Zealand.**

NEW ZEALAND. Criminal Law Reform Committee. 1974. The power to discharge before arraignment; (report); [R.C. Savage, chairman]. [Wellington, 1974]. pp. 14.

— **Poland.**

MAREK (ANDRZEJ) Stopień społecznego niebezpieczeństwa czynu jako podstawa umorzenia postępowania karnego. Toruń, 1970. pp. 199. *bibliog. (Towarzystwo Naukowe w Toruniu. Studia Iuridica. t.10, zeszyt 1) With German summary.*

— **United Kingdom.**

HARRIS (BRIAN) The criminal jurisdiction of magistrates. 4th ed. London, 1974. pp. 466.

ARCHBOLD (JOHN FREDERICK) Pleading, evidence and practice in criminal cases: thirty-ninth edition [by] Stephen Mitchell [and others]. London, 1976. pp. 1823. *With cumulative supplement.*

CRIMINAL PSYCHOLOGY.

EUROPEAN COMMITTEE ON CRIME PROBLEMS. Collected Studies in Criminological Research. Strasbourg, Council of Europe, 1967 in progress.

CRIMINAL STATISTICS.

EUROPEAN COMMITTEE ON CRIME PROBLEMS. Collected Studies in Criminological Research. Strasbourg, Council of Europe, 1967 in progress.

— **Australia — New South Wales.**

NEW SOUTH WALES. Bureau of Crime Statistics and Research. Court statistics. a., 1974- Sydney.

CRISES.

BANNOCK (GRAHAM) How to survive the slump: a guide to the economic crisis. Harmondsworth, 1975. pp. 170. *bibliog.*

CARLO (ANTONIO) Crisi economica e dialettica storica: saggi di teoria marxista. Roma, [1975]. pp. 234. *bibliog.*

TOFFLER (ALVIN) The eco-spasm report. New York, 1975. pp. 116. *bibliog.*

KUCZYNSKI (JUERGEN) Die Krise der kapitalistischen Weltwirtschaft. Berlin, 1976. pp. 127.

TEMIN (PETER) Did monetary forces cause the Great Depression? New York, [1976]. pp. 201. *bibliog.*

CRISIS INTERVENTION (PSYCHIATRY).

FUNDAMENTALS of crisis counseling; [by] William Getz [and others]. Lexington, Mass., [1974]. pp. 184. *bibliogs.*

CRISTERO REBELLION, 1926-1929.

OLIVERA SEDANO (ALICIA) Aspectos del conflicto religioso de 1926 a 1929: sus antecedentes y consecuencias. Mexico, 1966. pp. 292. *bibliog. (Instituto Nacional de Antropologia e Historia. Serie Historia. 16)*

MEYER (JEAN A.) The Cristero rebellion: the Mexican people between church and state, 1926-1929;...translated by Richard Southern. Cambridge, 1976. pp. 260. *bibliog.*

CRITICISM.

EAGLETON (TERRY) Marxism and literary criticism. London, 1976. pp. 88. *bibliog.*

CROATIA

— **History.**

HORVAT (JOSIP) Ljudevit Gaj: njegov život, njegovo doba. Zagreb, 1975. pp. 399.

— **Nationalism.**

VODINELIĆ (VLADIMIR) 10 verzija više jedna jednako istina: zapisi o Bonskom i Stockholmskom procesu ustaškim teroristima. Split, 1973. pp. 236.

— **Politics and government.**

TRUMBIĆ (ANTE) Suton Austro-Ugarske i Riječka rezolucija. Zagreb, 1936. pp. 112.

BOBAN (LJUBO) Maček i politika Hrvatske seljačke stranke 1928-1941: iz povijesti hrvatskog pitanja. Zagreb, 1974. 2 vols.

CROATS IN THE UNITED STATES.

TRESIĆ-PAVIČIĆ (ANTE) Preko Atlantika do Pacifika: život Hrvata u Sjevernoj Americi; putopisna, estetska, ekonomska i politička promatranja. Zagreb, 1907. pp. 268.

CROCE (BENEDETTO).

BRUNO (ANTONINO) Croce e le scienze politico-sociali. Firenze, 1975. pp. 139.

LABRIOLA (ANTONIO) Lettere a Benedetto Croce, 1885-1904. Napoli, 1975. pp. 423.

CROFTERS.

HUNTER (JAMES) Ph.D. The making of the crofting community. Edinburgh, [1976]. pp. 309. *bibliog.*

CROP YIELDS

— **India — Goa, Daman and Diu.**

GOA, DAMAN AND DIU. Bureau of Economics, Statistics and Evaluation. Report on the crop estimation survey in the Union Territory of Goa, Daman and Diu. q., 1974/1975- Panaji.

CROPS AND CLIMATE

— **South Africa.**

THERON (MARGRIET J.) and others. The economic importance of the weather and weather services to the South African agricultural sector: a Delphi survey. Pretoria, 1973. fo. 134. *(South Africa. Council for Scientific and Industrial Research. CSIR Research Reports. 321)*

CROSSMAN (RICHARD HOWARD STAFFORD).

CROSSMAN (RICHARD HOWARD STAFFORD) The diaries of a cabinet minister. London, 1975 in progress.

YOUNG (HUGO) The Crossman affair. London, 1976. pp. 224.

CROWDING STRESS.

FREEDMAN (JONATHAN L.) Crowding and behavior. San Francisco, [1975]. pp. 177. *bibliog.*

CROWE (Sir EYRE).

COLLIER (Sir LAURENCE) [Impressions of Sir Eyre Crowe: the roots of appeasement. 1960-70]. 1 piece. *Typescript.*

CRUELTY TO CHILDREN.

SMITH (SELWYN M.) The battered child syndrome. London, 1975. pp. 292. *bibliog.*

— **Ireland (Republic).**

EIRE. Committee on Non-Accidental Injury to Children. 1976. Report. Dublin, 1976. pp. 24.

— **United Kingdom.**

STURGESS (JANET) and HEAL (KEVIN) Non-accidental injury to children under the age of 17. [London], Home Office Research Unit, 1975. fo. 14, iv.

AT risk: an account of the work of the Battered Child Research Department, NSPCC; [by] Edwina Baher [and others]. London, 1976. pp. 246. *bibliog.*

— **United States.**

SUSSMAN (ALAN) and COHEN (STEPHAN J.) Reporting child abuse and neglect: guidelines for legislation. Cambridge, Mass., [1975]. pp. 255. *bibliog.*

CUBA

— **Armed forces — Political activity.**

PEREZ (LOUIS A.) Army politics in Cuba, 1898-1958. Pittsburgh, [1976]. pp. 240. *bibliog.*

— **Army — History.**

PEREZ (LOUIS A.) Army politics in Cuba, 1898-1958. Pittsburgh, [1976]. pp. 240. *bibliog.*

— **Census.**

KIPLE (KENNETH F.) Blacks in colonial Cuba, 1774-1899. Gainesville, Fla., 1976. pp. 115. *bibliog. (Florida University. School of Inter-American Studies. Latin American Monographs. 2nd Series. No. 17)*

— **Civilization.**

AGUILAR LEON (LUIS) Pasado y ambiente en el proceso cubano. Havana, [1957]. pp. 85.

— **Description and travel.**

BENEKE (ALFRED) Ein Hamburger auf Kuba: Briefe und Notizen des Kaufmanns... , 1842-1844; ausgewählt und erläutert von Renate Hauschild-Thiessen. Hamburg, 1971. pp. 120.

— **Economic conditions.**

CUBA: the logic of the revolution; edited by David P. Barkin and Nita R. Manitzas. Andover, Mass., [1973]. 1 vol. (various pagings).

— **Economic policy.**

El DEBATE cubano sobre el funcionamiento de la ley del valor en el socialismo; ([by] Ernesto "Che" Guevara [and others]) Barcelona, 1974. pp. 357.

— **Foreign economic relations — Poland.**

LEGOMSKA-DWORNIAK (EWA) Polska - Kuba: gospodarka współpraca. Warszawa, 1975. pp. 280. *bibliog.*

— **Foreign relations — Russia.**

DINERSTEIN (HERBERT SAMUEL) The making of a missile crisis: October 1962. Baltimore, [1976]. pp. 302.

— — **United States.**

BENDER (LYNN DARRELL) The politics of hostility: Castro's revolution and United States policy. Hato Rey, Puerto Rico, 1975. pp. 156. *bibliog.*

CUBA(Cont.)

AYERS (BRADLEY EARL) The war that never was: an insider's account of C.I.A. covert operations against Cuba. Indianapolis, [1976]. pp. 235.

— History — 1933-1959.

BONACHEA (RAMON L.) and SAN MARTIN (MARTA) The Cuban insurrection, 1952-1959. New Brunswick, N.J., [1974]. pp. 451. *bibliog.*

— — 1959— .

AYERS (BRADLEY EARL) The war that never was: an insider's account of C.I.A. covert operations against Cuba. Indianapolis, [1976]. pp. 235.

— Politics and government.

CASTRO RUZ (FIDEL) La historia me absolvera. Havana, 1969. pp. 107.

TIMOSSI (JORGE) El desafio cubano. Montevideo, [1969]. pp. 107.

CASTRO RUZ (FIDEL) Socialismo y comunismo: un proceso unico; seleccion y notas: Nicolas Segrate. Montevideo, [1970]. pp. 189.

CUBA: the logic of the revolution; edited by David P. Barkin and Nita R. Manitzas. Andover, Mass., [1973]. 1 vol. (various pagings).

MESA LAGO (CARMELO) Cuba in the 1970s: pragmatism and institutionalization. Albuquerque, [1974]. pp. 179.

BENDER (LYNN DARRELL) The politics of hostility: Castro's revolution and United States policy. Hato Rey, Puerto Rico, 1975. pp. 156. *bibliog.*

GOODSELL (JAMES NELSON) ed. Fidel Castro's personal revolution in Cuba, 1959-1973. New York, [1975]. pp. 349. *bibliog.*

PEREZ (LOUIS A.) Army politics in Cuba, 1898-1958. Pittsburgh, [1976]. pp. 240. *bibliog.*

— Social conditions.

CUBA: the logic of the revolution; edited by David P. Barkin and Nita R. Manitzas. Andover, Mass., [1973]. 1 vol. (various pagings).

CUBAN MISSILE CRISIS, OCTOBER 1962.

DINERSTEIN (HERBERT SAMUEL) The making of a missile crisis: October 1962. Baltimore, [1976]. pp. 302.

CULTURE.

FRANCE. Direction de la Documentation. La Documentation Française. Notes et Etudes Documentaires. Nos. 4,205-4, 206. Le projet suédois de démocratie culturelle: essai de comparaison avec la situation française; par Claude Fabrizio. Paris, 1975. pp. 72. *bibliog.*

INTERNATIONAL ASSOCIATION FOR CROSS-CULTURAL PSYCHOLOGY. International Conference, 2nd, Kingston, Ont., 1974. Applied cross-cultural psychology: selected papers from the... conference...; edited by J.W. Berry and W.J. Lonner. Amsterdam, 1975. pp. 338. *bibliogs.*

PLEBE (ARMANDO) La civiltà del postcomunismo. Roma, [1975]. pp. 646. *Part 1 consists of the proceedings of the international congress organised by the Associazione Internazionale per la Cultura Occidentale in Rome in March 1975.*

WHITE (LESLIE ALVIN) The concept of cultural systems: a key to understanding tribes and nations. New York, 1975. pp. 192. *bibliog.*

WILLIAMS (RAYMOND) Keywords: a vocabulary of culture and society. London, [1976]. pp. 286. *bibliog.*

CUMBERLAND

— Population.

CUMBRIA COMMUNITY DEVELOPMENT PROJECT. Reports on employment, unemployment and population trends in Cleator Moor and Frizington. [Cleator Moor], 1974. pp. 29.

CUNNINGHAME-GRAHAM (ROBERT BONTINE).

MEYERS (JEFFREY) A fever at the core: the idealist in politics. London, 1976. pp. 172. *bibliog.*

CUNNINGHAM-REID (ALEC STRATFORD).

ELLIS (R.J.) He walks alone...: the public and private life of Captain Cunningham-Reid, D.F.C., Member of Parliament 1922-45. London, [1945]. pp. 292.

CURAÇAO

— Foreign relations — Venezuela.

GOSLINGA (CORNELIS CH.) Curaçao and Guzmán Blanco: a case study of small power politics in the Caribbean. 's-Gravenhage, 1975. pp. 143. *bibliog. (Instituut voor Taal- , Land- en Volkenkunde. Verhandelingen. [Deel] 76)*

— History.

GOSLINGA (CORNELIS CH.) Curaçao and Guzmán Blanco: a case study of small power politics in the Caribbean. 's-Gravenhage, 1975. pp. 143. *bibliog. (Instituut voor Taal- , Land- en Volkenkunde. Verhandelingen. [Deel] 76)*

— Social conditions.

ANDERSON (WILLIAM AVERETTE) and DYNES (RUSSELL ROWE) Social movements, violence and change: the May Movement in Curaçao. Columbus, Ohio, [1975]. pp. 175. *bibliog.*

CUSTOMARY LAW

— Rhodesia.

GOLDIN (BENNIE) and GELFAND (MICHAEL) African law and custom in Rhodesia. Cape Town, 1975. pp. 325.

CUSTOMS ADMINISTRATION

— Botswana.

BOTSWANA. Department of Customs and Excise. 1975. Report of the establishment and organisation of the Department of Customs and Excise 1970-1974. Gaborone, 1975. pp. 26.

— China — History — Sources.

HART (Sir ROBERT) The I.G. in Peking: letters of Robert Hart, Chinese Maritime Customs, 1868-1907...; edited by John King Fairbank [and others]. Cambridge, Mass., 1975. 2 vols. *Letters to his London agent, James Duncan Campbell.*

— European Economic Community countries.

EUROPEAN COMMUNITIES. 1976. European Community customs valuation. [Luxembourg], 1976. 1 vol. (looseleaf).

CUSTOMS UNIONS.

LIBERIA. Treaties. 1973-74. Mano River Declaration, signed in Malema, 3 October, 1973; and protocols to the Declaration, signed in Bo, 3 October, 1974. [Monrovia, 1975]. fo. 14. *Xerox copy.*

CUZCO (PERU)

— History.

APARICIO VEGA (MANUEL JESUS) El clero patriota en la Revolucion de 1814. Cusco, 1974. pp. 355. *bibliog.*

CYBERNETICS.

MACHINE INTELLIGENCE WORKSHOP, EDINBURGH, 5TH, 1970. Machine intelligence 5; edited by Bernard Meltzer and Donald Michie. Edinburgh, [1969]. pp. 588. *bibliog.*

MACHINE INTELLIGENCE WORKSHOP, EDINBURGH, 6TH, 1971. Machine intelligence 6; edited by Bernard Meltzer and Donald Michie. Edinburgh, 1971. pp. 525. *bibliogs.*

MACHINE INTELLIGENCE WORKSHOP, EDINBURGH, 7TH, 1972. Machine intelligence 7; edited by Bernard Meltzer and Donald Michie. Edinburgh, [1972]. pp. 485. *bibliogs.*

YOUNG (JOHN F.) Cybernetic engineering. London, 1973. pp. 153. *bibliogs.*

CYPRUS

— Constitutional history.

POLYVIOU (POLYVIOS G.) Cyprus in search of a constitution: constitutional negotiations and proposals, 1960-1975. Nicosia, 1976. pp. 450. *bibliog.*

— Economic conditions.

KAMINARIDES (JOHN S.) The Cyprus economy: a case in the industrialization progress. Nicosia, [1973]. pp. 304. *bibliog.*

— Economic policy.

CYPRUS. Planning Bureau. 1975. Emergency economic action plan, 1975-1976: revision of the third five-year plan. Nicosia, [1975?]. pp. 67.

— Foreign relations.

For related heading see UNITED NATIONS — Cyprus.

— Industries.

DEMETRIADES (EURIPIDES IOANNOU) An economic evaluation of industrialization policies in Cyprus, 1962-1971. 1975 [or rather 1976]. fo. 504. *bibliog. Typescript. Ph.D. (London) thesis: unpublished. This thesis is the property of London University and may not be removed from the Library.*

— Nationalism.

STAVRINIDES (ZENON) The Cyprus conflict: national identity and statehood. n.p., [1975?]. pp. 134.

— Politics and government.

COMMITTEE OF SCIENTIFIC, EDUCATIONAL AND CULTURAL INSTITUTIONS AND ORGANIZATIONS IN CYPRUS. Appeal to all educational, scientific and cultural organizations of the world. Nicosia, [1974?]. pp. 13. *Also in French and Greek.*

KRANIDIOTIS (NICOS) The Cyprus problem: the proposed solutions and the concept of the independent and sovereign state. Athens, 1975. pp. 78.

STAVRINIDES (ZENON) The Cyprus conflict: national identity and statehood. n.p., [1975?]. pp. 134.

CYPRUS; [by an anonymous journalist and Peter Loizos]. London, 1976. pp. 28. *bibliog. (Minority Rights Group. Reports. No. 30)*

KAROUZIS (GEORGE) Proposals for a solution to the Cyprus problem. Nicosia, 1976. pp. 208. *bibliog.*

PATRICK (RICHARD ARTHUR) Political geography and the Cyprus conflict, 1963-1971;...edited by James H. Bater and Richard Preston. Waterloo, Ont., [1976]. pp. 481. *bibliogs. (University of Waterloo, [Ontario]. Department of Geography. Publication Series. No.4) A collection of major published and unpublished works.*

POLYVIOU (POLYVIOS G.) Cyprus in search of a constitution: constitutional negotiations and proposals, 1960-1975. Nicosia, 1976. pp. 450. *bibliog.*

— Population.

KAROUZIS (GEORGE) Proposals for a solution to the Cyprus problem. Nicosia, 1976. pp. 208. *bibliog.*

— **Race question.**

PATRICK (RICHARD ARTHUR) Political geography and the Cyprus conflict, 1963-1971;...edited by James H. Bater and Richard Preston. Waterloo, Ont., [1976]. pp. 481. *bibliogs.* (*University of Waterloo, [Ontario]. Department of Geography. Publication Series. No.4*) *A collection of major published and unpublished works.*

— **Social policy.**

CYPRUS. Planning Bureau. 1975. Emergency economic action plan, 1975-1976: revision of the third five-year plan. Nicosia, [1975?]. pp. 67.

CYRILLIC ALPHABET.

GEORGIEV (EMIL) Kiril i Metodii: istinata za suzdatelite na bulgarskata i slavianska pismenost. Sofiia, 1969. pp. 365.

CZECHOSLOVAKIA

— **Commerce.**

ČESKOSLOVENSKÁ OBCHODNÍ KOMORA. Facts on Czechoslovak foreign trade, [1975 ed.]. [Prague], 1975. pp. 217.

— **Constitution.**

FLEGL (VLADIMÍR) Ústava Československé socialistické republiky. Praha, 1974. pp. 169.

— **Constitutional history.**

Die DEMOKRATISCH-parlamentarische Struktur der Ersten Tschechoslowakischen Republik; unter Mitarbeit von Stephan Dolezel [and others]; herausgegeben von Karl Bosl; Vorträge der Tagung des Collegium Carolinum in Bad Wiessee...1974. München, 1975. pp. 278.

— **Description and travel.**

TSELISHCHEV (NIKOLAI NIKOLAEVICH) and BRODSKII (IGOR' STEPANOVICH) Marshrutami druzhby. Sverdlovsk, 1969. pp. 115.

— **Economic conditions.**

RADIO FREE EUROPE. Audience and Public Opinion Research Department. Economic expectations in Czechoslovakia; comparison of an internal poll and RFE/APOR findings. [Munich?], 1973. fo. 9.

The DEVELOPMENT of the Czechoslovak economy: materials of a symposium organised by the Central Committee of the Communist Party of Czechoslovakia for members of the Editorial Council of the theoretical and information journal...Problems of Peace and Socialism (World Marxist Review), April-May 1973. Prague, [1974]. pp. 203.

ČESKOSLOVENSKÁ ekonomika v sedmdesátých letech: vybrané problémy. Praha, 1975. pp. 309.

— — **Statistics.**

CZECHOSLOVAKIA. Federální Statistický Úřad. Ekonomický vývoj. a., 1974 (1st)- Praha.

— **Economic policy.**

The DEVELOPMENT of the Czechoslovak economy: materials of a symposium organised by the Central Committee of the Communist Party of Czechoslovakia for members of the Editorial Council of the theoretical and information journal...Problems of Peace and Socialism (World Marxist Review), April-May 1973. Prague, [1974]. pp. 203.

— **Foreign relations.**

BENEŠ (EDVARD) Mnichovské dny: paměti; [with an appendix of documents]. [Praha], 1968. pp. 555.

— — **Treaties.**

WEIGAND (MATTHIAS) Der Vertrag über die gegenseitigen Beziehungen zwischen der Bundesrepublik Deutschland und der Tschechoslowakischen Sozialistischen Republik vom 11. Dezember 1973: eine völkerrechtliche Analyse. Bern, 1975. pp. 127. *bibliog.*

— — **Germany.**

CAMPBELL (F. GREGORY) Confrontation in Central Europe: Weimar Germany and Czechoslovakia. Chicago, 1975. pp. 383. *bibliog.*

WEIGAND (MATTHIAS) Der Vertrag über die gegenseitigen Beziehungen zwischen der Bundesrepublik Deutschland und der Tschechoslowakischen Sozialistischen Republik vom 11. Dezember 1973: eine völkerrechtliche Analyse. Bern, 1975. pp. 127. *bibliog.*

— — **Hungary.**

KRÁL (VÁCLAV) Intervenční válka československé buržoasie proti Maďarské sovětské republice v roce 1919. Praha, 1954. pp. 290,32.

— — **Poland — Bibliography.**

NOWAK (C.M.) compiler. Czechoslovak-Polish relations 1918-1939: a selected and annotated bibliography. Stanford, Ca., 1976. pp. 219. (*Stanford University. Hoover Institution on War, Revolution and Peace. Bibliographical Series. 55*)

— — **Russia.**

RUSSIA (USSR). Ministerstvo Inotrannykh Del. 1975. Sovetsko-chekhoslovatskie otnosheniia, 1961-1971: dokumenty i materialy. Moskva, 1975. pp. 703.

SVEDECTVO dokumentov a faktov. [Bratislava, 1975]. pp. 455.

— — — **Ukraine.**

HODNETT (GREY) and POTICHNYJ (PETER J.) The Ukraine and the Czechoslovak crisis. Canberra, 1970. pp. 154. (*Australian National University. Research School of Social Sciences. Department of Political Science. Occasional Papers. No. 6*)

— **History.**

TOBOLKA (ZDENĚK VÁCLAV) Politické dějiny československého národa od r. 1848 až do dnešní doby. Praha, 1932-37. 4 vols (in 5).

— — **Sources.**

BENEŠ (EDVARD) Mnichovské dny: paměti; [with an appendix of documents]. [Praha], 1968. pp. 555.

SVEDECTVO dokumentov a faktov. [Bratislava, 1975]. pp. 455.

— — **1968— , Intervention.**

TSELISHCHEV (NIKOLAI NIKOLAEVICH) and BRODSKII (IGOR' STEPANOVICH) Marshrutami druzhby. Sverdlovsk, 1969. pp. 115.

HODNETT (GREY) and POTICHNYJ (PETER J.) The Ukraine and the Czechoslovak crisis. Canberra, 1970. pp. 154. (*Australian National University. Research School of Social Sciences. Department of Political Science. Occasional Papers. No. 6*)

HORSKÝ (VLADIMÍR) Prag 1968: Systemveränderung und Systemverteidigung. Stuttgart, [1975]. pp. 534. *bibliog.* (*Evangelische Studiengemeinschaft. Forschungsstätte. Studien zur Friedensforschung. Band 14*)

SVEDECTVO dokumentov a faktov. [Bratislava, 1975]. pp. 455.

— **Intellectual life.**

HORA (JOSEF) Dny a lidé: [výbor z fejetonistiky]. Praha, 1961. pp. 286. (*Dílo Josefa Hory. sv. 16*)

— **Politics and government.**

NOVOTNÝ (ANTONÍN) Projevy a stati, 1954-(1964). Praha, 1964. 3 vols.

BIL'AK (VASIL) Pravda zůstala pravdou: projevy a články, říjen 1967 - prosinec 1970. Praha, 1971. pp. 445.

CZECHOSLOVAKS IN RUSSIA.

ZA nové Československo: materiály z celoštátnej vedeckej konferencie k 25. výročiu oslobodenia Československa, ktorú usporiadal Ústav marxizmu-leninizmu ÚV KSS v Bratislave, 27., 28. a 29. aprila 1970. Bratislava, 1972. pp. 270. (*Komunistická Strana Slovenska. Ústredný Výbor. Ústav Marxizmu-Leninizmu. roč. 12, č. 1*)

Die "BURG": einflussreiche politische Kräfte um Masaryk und Beneš...; unter Mitarbeit von Martin K. Bachstein [and others]; herausgegeben von Karl Bosl; Vorträge der Tagung des Collegium Carolinum in Bad Wiessee...1972 ([and] 1973). München, 1973-74. 2 vols.

BERTSCH (GARY K.) Value change and political community: the multinational Czechoslovak, Soviet, and Yugoslav cases. Beverly Hills, [1974]. pp. 60. *bibliog.*

Die DEMOKRATISCH-parlamentarische Struktur der Ersten Tschechoslowakischen Republik; unter Mitarbeit von Stephan Dolezel [and others]; herausgegeben von Karl Bosl; Vorträge der Tagung des Collegium Carolinum in Bad Wiessee...1974. München, 1975. pp. 278.

HORSKÝ (VLADIMÍR) Prag 1968: Systemveränderung und Systemverteidigung. Stuttgart, [1975]. pp. 534. *bibliog.* (*Evangelische Studiengemeinschaft. Forschungsstätte. Studien zur Friedensforschung. Band 14*)

PRAVDA (ALEX) Reform and change in the Czechoslovak political system: January-August 1968. Beverly Hills, [1975]. pp. 96. *bibliog.*

PELIKÁN (JIŘÍ) Socialist opposition in Eastern Europe: the Czechoslovak example; translated by Marian Sling and V. and R. Tosek. London, 1976. pp. 221.

ZEMAN (ZBYNĚK ANTHONY BOHUSLAV) The Masaryks: the making of Czechoslovakia. London, [1976]. pp. 230.

— **Population.**

RUSSIA (USSR). Ministerstvo Vysshego i Srednego Spetsial'nogo Obrazovaniia. Nauchno-Tekhnicheskii Sovet. Sektsiia Narodonaseleniia. Narodonaselenie. 3. Naselenie i trudovye resursy. Moskva, 1973. pp. 79. *With English table of contents.*

— — **Bibliography.**

BIBLIOGRAFIE ČESKOSLOVENSKÉ STATISTIKY A DÉMOGRAFIE; [pd. by] Výzkumný Ústav Sociálně Ekonomických Informací. a., 1974(9th)- Praha.

— **Relations (general) with Russia.**

TSELISHCHEV (NIKOLAI NIKOLAEVICH) and BRODSKII (IGOR' STEPANOVICH) Marshrutami druzhby. Sverdlovsk, 1969. pp. 115.

— **Relations (general) with Yugoslavia.**

PAULOVÁ (MILADA) Tajný výbor Maffie a spolupráce s Jihoslovany v letech 1916-1918. Praha, 1968. pp. 626. *bibliog.*

— **Statistics.**

CZECHOSLOVAKIA. Federální Statistický Úřad. Knižnice. 1975. Vývoj společnosti ČSSR podle výsledků sčítání lidu, domů a bytů 1970. [Praha, 1975]. pp. 487.

CZECHOSLOVAKIA. Federální Statistický Úřad. Výzkumný Ústav Sociálně Ekonomických Informací. 1975. 30. let ČSSR: dlouhodobé časové řady; zpracoval jako závazek k 30. výročí osvobození kolektiv pracovníků VÚSEI. Praha, 1975. pp. 162. *bibliog.*

PODZIMEK (JAROSLAV) Vývoj československé statistiky v událostech a datech, 1945- 1975. Praha, 1976. pp. 55. *bibliog. With brief Russian, English and German summaries.*

— — **Bibliography.**

BIBLIOGRAFIE ČESKOSLOVENSKÉ STATISTIKY A DÉMOGRAFIE; [pd. by] Výzkumný Ústav Sociálně Ekonomických Informací. a., 1974(9th)- Praha.

CZECHOSLOVAKS IN RUSSIA.

SAJDL (JOSEF) Českoslovenští železničáři v sibiřské anabasi. [Praha]. 1924. pp. 108,[x].

DAGHESTAN

— Economic history.

GASANOV (SAID MUSAEVICH) Osushchestvlenie v Dagestane leninskikh idei nekapitalisticheskogo razvitiia ranee otstalykh stran i narodov. Makhachkala, 1970. pp. 209.

— Politics and government.

DAGHESTAN. Verkhovnyi Sovet. Zasedaniia. Stenograficheskii otchet. sess., D 1971 (8th series, 2nd session)- Makhachkala.

DAHLSTRÖM (HANS).

EUROPEAN COURT OF HUMAN RIGHTS. Publications. Series A: Judgments and Decisions. [A 21]. ...Schmidt and Dahlström case; judgment of 6 February, 1976. Strasbourg, Council of Europe, 1976. pp. 18bis. *In English and French.*

DAHOMEY

— History.

ASIWAJU (ANTHONY IJAOLA) Western Yorubaland under European rule, 1889-1945: a comparative analysis of French and British colonialism. London, 1976. pp. 303. *bibliog.*

DAIRY PRODUCTS

— Cooperative marketing.

WARD (ARTHUR HUGH) A command of cooperatives: the development of leadership, marketing and price control in the cooperative dairy industry of New Zealand. Wellington, New Zealand Dairy Board, 1975. pp. 266.

DAIRY WORKERS

— Denmark.

NIELSEN (SIGURD) Fagforeninger indenfor dansk mejeribrug i tiden 1907-1924. [Horsens, imprint], 1973. pp. 172.

DAIRYING

— Economic aspects.

AUSTRALIA. Bureau of Agricultural Economics. 1972. Economic principles for increased beef production from butterfat dairy farms. Canberra, 1972. pp. 44. *(Beef Research Reports. No. 9)*

— — Australia — Queensland.

— Mathematical models.

BARBELER (MARY T.) and HAMILTON (C.P.) Supply response to price in the southern Queensland dairy industry. I: Darling Downs region. [Brisbane], 1973. pp. 35. *(Queensland. Department of Primary Industries. Economic Services Branch. Research Bulletins. No. 24)*

WHITLAM (G.B.) and HAMILTON (C.P.) Cream and pigs or wholemilk: a study of economic implications at farm level. [Brisbane], 1971. pp. 30. *(Queensland. Department of Primary Industries. Economic Services Branch. Research Bulletins. No. 22)*

— Australia — Queensland — Costs.

VAN HAERINGEN (J.) and BAMFORD (E.J.) Dairy pasture subsidy scheme: report on the first year of its operation. [Brisbane], 1971. pp. 36. *(Queensland. Department of Primary Industries. Economic Services Branch. Research Bulletins. No. 21)*

— India — Goa Daman and Diu.

GOA, DAMAN AND DIU. Bureau of Economics, Statistics and Evaluation. 1974. An evaluation study of the working of dairy cooperative societies in Goa, Daman and Diu, 1972-73. Panaji, [1974]. pp. 72. *(Evaluation Reports. No. 8)*

— New Zealand.

WARD (ARTHUR HUGH) A command of cooperatives: the development of leadership, marketing and price control in the cooperative dairy industry of New Zealand. Wellington, New Zealand Dairy Board, 1975. pp. 266.

— United Kingdom — Scotland.

SCOTLAND. Scottish Milk Marketing Board. Marketing Services Department. 1975. The structure of Scottish milk production at 1975. [Paisley, 1975]. pp. 92. *Summarises the main findings of the 1975 Scottish dairy farm census.*

DAMAGES

— Poland.

WINIARZ (JAN) Ustalenie wysokości odszkodowania. Warszawa, 1962. pp. 199. *bibliog.*

DANGEROUS GOODS

— Transportation.

INTER-GOVERNMENTAL MARITIME CONSULTATIVE ORGANIZATION. 1972- . International Maritime Dangerous Goods Code; (with Supplements). London, 1972 in progress. *List of old IMCO Code page numbers with corresponding new IMCO Code page numbers and UN numbers is bound with the original volume of this set.*

DANISH NEWSPAPERS.

SØNDERGAARD ANDERSEN (JØRGEN) Den danske distriktspresse: udviklingen siden 1900, status i dag, fremtidige udviklingsmuligheder. [Aarhus], 1971. fo. 70,18. *bibliog.*

DANQUAH (JOSEPH BOAKYE).

DANQUAH (JOSEPH BOAKYE) Journey to independence and after: J.B. Danquah's letters, 1947-1965;...compiled by H.K. Akyeampong. Accra, 1970 in progress.

DANUBE, RIVER

— Navigation — Laws and regulations.

ZEMANEK (KARL) Die Schiffahrtsfreiheit auf der Donau und das Künftige Regime der Rhein-Main-Donau-Grosschiffahrtsstrasse: eine völkerrechtliche Untersuchung. Wien, [1976]. pp. 73. *(Österreichische Zeitschrift für öffentliches Recht. Supplementa.4)*

DAR ES SALAAM TECHNICAL COLLEGE.

UNITED REPUBLIC OF TANZANIA. Working Party on Space Utilization at the Dar es Salaam Technical College. 1970. Report...November, 1970; [R.A.H. Mayagila, chairman]. Dar es Salaam, [1970?]. pp. 20.

DARBY FAMILY.

TRINDER (BARRIE STUART) The Darbys of Coalbrookdale. Chichester, 1974. pp. 79. *bibliog.*

DATA BASE MANAGEMENT.

COURANT COMPUTER SCIENCE SYMPOSIUM, 6TH, 1971. Data base systems; edited by Randall Rustin. Englewood Cliffs, N.J., [1972]. pp. 184. *Based on the symposium organized by the Computer Science Department of the Courant Institute of Mathematical Sciences, New York University.*

CAGAN (CARL) Data management systems. Los Angeles, [1973]. pp. 141.

IFIP WORKING CONFERENCE ON DATA BASE MANAGEMENT, CARGESE, 1974. Data base management; proceedings of the...Conference...; edited by J.W. Klimbie and K.L. Koffeman. Amsterdam, 1974. pp. 423. *bibliogs. Conference organized by Technical Committee 2, Programming, of the International Federation for Information Processing.*

SHARE WORKING CONFERENCE ON DATA BASE MANAGEMENT SYSTEMS, MONTREAL, 1973. Data base management systems: proceedings of the...Conference... ; edited by Donald A. Jardine. Amsterdam, 1974 repr.1976. pp. 279. *bibliog.*

DATE (C.J.) An introduction to database systems. Reading, Mass., [1975] repr. 1976. pp. 366. *bibliogs.*

KATZAN (HARRY) Computer data management and data base technology. New York, [1975]. pp. 347. *bibliog.*

MARTIN (JAMES THOMAS) Computer data-base organization. Englewood Cliffs, N.J., [1975]. pp. 558.

DATA LIBRARIES.

BRITISH COMPUTER SOCIETY and CODASYL. Data Description Language Committee. Data Base Administration Working Group. June 1975 report. [London, 1976]. 1 vol. (various foliations).

— Directories.

THOMAS (ANGELA) ed. LUCIS guide to computer-based information services. [London], 1975. 1 vol. (looseleaf). *Prepared for the Central Information Services of the Interim Library Resources Co-ordinating Committee of London University.*

DATA STRUCTURES (COMPUTER SCIENCE).

DAHL (OLE-JOHAN) and others. Structured programming. London, 1972 repr. 1975. pp. 220. *bibliogs. (Automatic Programming Information Centre. Studies in Data Processing. No. 8)*

BERZTISS (A.T.) Data structures: theory and practice. 2nd ed. New York, [1975]. pp. 586. *bibliog.*

HALL (PATRICK A.V.) Computational structures: an introduction to non-numerical computing. London, [1975]. pp. 193. *bibliog.*

WIRTH (NIKLAUS) Algorithms [plus] data structures [equal] programs. Englewood Cliffs, N.J., [1976]. pp. 366. *bibliogs.*

DATA TRANSMISSION SYSTEMS.

MARTIN (JAMES THOMAS) Telecommunications and the computer. Englewood Cliffs, [1969]. pp. 470.

MARTIN (JAMES THOMAS) Introduction to teleprocessing. Englewood Cliffs, N.J., [1972]. pp. 267.

MARTIN (JAMES THOMAS) Systems analysis for data transmission. Englewood Cliffs, [1972]. pp. 910.

BACON (M.D.) and BULL (G.M.) Data transmission. London, [1973] repr. 1974. pp. 135. *bibliog.*

CANADA. Department of Communications. 1973. Computer/communications policy: a position statement by the government of Canada. Ottawa, 1973. pp. 17,17. *In English and French.*

EUROPEAN COMPUTING CONFERENCE ON COMMUNICATIONS NETWORKS, LONDON, 1975. Communications networks. Uxbridge, [1975]. pp. 618. *bibliogs. Papers presented at the Conference. This conference was part of the European Computing Congress, 1975.*

DAY NURSERIES

— Denmark.

WAGNER (MARSDEN) and WAGNER (MARY) The Danish national child-care system: a successful system as model for the reconstruction of American child care. Boulder, Co., 1976. pp. 183.

— United Kingdom.

ARMISTEAD (NIGEL) and others. Children's day care facilities in London, 1966-1974. London, [1975]. pp. (142). *bibliog. (London. Greater London Council. Research Memoranda. 472)*

COMMUNITY RELATIONS COMMISSION. Who minds?: a study of working mothers and childminding in ethnic minority communities; (with Summary). London, 1975. 2 pts.

— **United States.**

LEVITAN (SAR A.) and ALDERMAN (KAREN CLEARY) Child care and ABC's too. Baltimore, [1975]. pp. 125.

DEAF

— **Germany.**

SPROLL (HEINZ) Studien zur sozio-ökonomischen Struktur von Randgruppen in Baden im 19. und 20. Jahrhundert: die staatliche und verbandliche Fürsorge und kath. Pastoration an Gehörlosen, 1780-1939. Bern, 1975. pp. 489. *bibliog.*

DEATH

— **Causes.**

TASMANIA. Commonwealth Bureau of Census and Statistics. Tasmanian Office. Causes of death. a., 1974 (1st)- Hobart.

DEBT

— **Germany.**

GERMANY (BUNDESREPUBLIK). Statistisches Bundesamt. 1975. Vermögensbestände und Schulden privater Haushalte, 1973. Wiesbaden, 1975. pp. 212. *(Preise, Löhne, Wirtschaftsrechnungen. Reihe 18. Einkommens- und Verbrauchsstichproben. 2)*

DEBTS, EXTERNAL — Underdeveloped areas.

See **UNDERDEVELOPED AREAS — Debts, External.**

DEBTS, PUBLIC

— **United Kingdom.**

QUERIES relating to the reduction of the national redeemable debts, from four to three per cent. per ann.; in a letter to ---- ---- Esq. London, J. Purser, 1737. pp. 23.

DEBUGGING IN COMPUTER SCIENCE.

BROWN (ARTHUR ROBERT) and SAMPSON (W. A.) Program debugging: the prevention and cure of program errors. London, [1973]. pp. 166.

DECEMBRISTS.

DZIDZARIIA (G.A.) Dekabristy v Abkhazii. Sukhumi, 1970. pp. 117.

SHATROVA (GALINA PETROVNA) Dekabrist I.I. Gorbachevskii. Krasnoiarsk, 1973. pp. 198.

BARRATT (GLYNN R.V.) The rebel on the bridge: a life of the Decembrist Baron Andrey Rozen, 1800-84. London, 1975. pp. 310. *bibliog.*

BAZANOV (VASILII GRIGOR'EVICH) and VATSURO (V.E.) eds. Literaturnoe nasledie dekabristov. Leningrad, 1975. pp. 400.

LANDA (SEMEN SEMENOVICH) Dukh revoliutsionnykh preobrazovanii...: iz istorii formirovaniia ideologii i politicheskoi organizatsii dekabristov, 1816-1825. Moskva, 1975. pp. 381.

ORLIK (OL'GA VASIL'EVNA) Dekabristy i evropeiskoe osvoboditel'noe dvizhenie. Moskva, 1975. pp. 191. *bibliog.*

PRINTSEVA (GALINA ALEKSANDROVNA) Dekabristy v izobrazitel'nom iskusstve: iz sobraniia Ermitazha. 2nd ed. Leningrad, 1975. pp. 95.

PRINTSEVA (GALINA ALEKSANDROVNA) and BASTAREVA (LIUDMILA IVANOVNA) Dekabristy v Peterburge. Leningrad, 1975. pp. 279. *bibliog.*

SERHIIENKO (HRYHORII IAKOVLEVYCH) Dekabrysty ta ïkh revoliutsiini tradytsiï na Ukraïni. Kyïv, 1975. pp. 183. *With Russian summary.*

SSYLKA i katorga v Sibiri, XVIII - nachalo XX v. Novosibirsk, 1975. pp. 304.

BARRATT (GLYNN R.V.) M.S. Lunin, Catholic Decembrist. The Hague, 1976. pp. 137. *bibliog.*

DECENTRALIZATION IN GOVERNMENT.

GUNSTEREN (HERMAN R. VAN) The quest for control: a critique of the rational-central-rule approach in public affairs. London, [1976]. pp. 162. *bibliogs.*

— **France.**

BOURDOIS (JEAN PATRICK) La réforme administrative dans la "Revue générale d'administration", 1878-1928. Paris, [1975]. pp. 98. *(Paris. Université de Paris II. Travaux et Recherches. Série Science Administrative. 9)*

— **Germany.**

ROCKER (RUDOLF) Zur Betrachtung der Lage in Deutschland: die Möglichkeiten einer freiheitlichen Bewegung; [edited by Helmut Rüdiger]. New York, 1947. pp. 36.

— **Ireland (Republic).**

BARRINGTON (T.J.) From big government to local government: the road to decentralisation. Dublin, [1975]. pp. 238. *Papers reprinted mainly from Administration, 1963-1975.*

— **Nigeria.**

NIGERIA (SOUTH-EASTERN STATE). 1973. Conclusions of the government on the report of the Committee on the Decentralization of South-Eastern State Governmental Functions. Calabar, [1973]. pp. 8. *Bound with the report.*

NIGERIA (SOUTH-EASTERN STATE). Committee on Decentralization of South-Eastern State Governmental Functions. 1973. Report; [E.A. Udoh, chairman]. [Calabar], 1972 [or rather 1973]. pp. 101. *(Nigeria (South-Eastern State). Official Documents. 1973. No.5). Bound with government conclusions on the report.*

— **United States.**

COLE (RICHARD L.) and CAPUTO (DAVID A.) Urban politics and decentralization: the case of general revenue sharing. Lexington, Mass., [1974]. pp. 180.

YIN (ROBERT K.) and YATES (DOUGLAS) Street-level governments: assessing decentralization and urban services. Lexington, Mass., [1975]. pp. 272. *bibliogs.*

DECENTRALIZATION IN MANAGEMENT

— **Europe, Eastern.**

BRYSON (PHILLIP J.) Scarcity and control in socialism: essays on East European planning. Lexington, Mass., [1976]. pp. 202.

DECIMAL SYSTEM.

NIGERIA. Committee on the Decimalization of the Nigerian Currency. 1972. Report; [O. Akinrele, chairman]. Lagos, 1972. pp. 35.

DECISION LOGIC TABLES.

HUMBY (EDWARD) Programs from decision tables. London, [1973]. pp. 91. *bibliog.*

DECISION-MAKING.

AMEY (LLOYD RONALD) ed. Readings in management decision; edited on behalf of the Association of University Teachers of Accounting in the United Kingdom, etc. London, 1973. pp. 272. *bibliogs.*

ARROW (KENNETH JOSEPH) Information and economic behavior. Stockholm, [1973]. pp. 28. *bibliog. (Sveriges Industriförbund. [Nobel Prize] Lectures. 1973)*

ASPLUND (GÖRAN) Strategy formulation: an intervention study of a complex group decision process. Stockholm, 1975. pp. 222. *bibliog. Avhandling (doktor) - Stockholm School of Economics.*

HUMAN judgment and decision processes; edited by Martin F. Kaplan and Steven Schwartz. New York, 1975. pp. 325. *bibliogs. Expanded versions of papers delivered at a conference held at Northern Illinois University in October 1974.*

MUMFORD (ENID) and PETTIGREW (ANDREW M.) Implementing strategic decisions. London, 1975. pp. 241. *bibliog.*

TAWIL (EDWIN NESSIM) The economic evaluation of new aircraft types: an analysis of the decision making process for new investment in air transportation. 1975. fo. 128. *Typescript. M.Sc. (Econ.) (London) thesis: unpublished. This thesis is the property of London University and may not be removed from the Library.*

BOSWELL (JONATHAN S.) Social and business enterprises: an introduction to organisational economics. London, 1976. pp. 216.

BRUNET-JAILLY (JOSEPH) and DALOZ (JEAN PIERRE). Decision-making method in the social action field. Strasbourg, Council of Europe, 1976. pp. 63. *bibliog.*

LOASBY (BRIAN J.) Choice, complexity and ignorance: an enquiry into economic theory and the practice of decision-making. Cambridge, 1976. pp. 242. *bibliog.*

VEREIN FÜR SOZIALPOLITIK. Schriften. Neue Folge. Band 88. Die Bedeutung gesellschaftlicher Veränderungen für die Willensbildung im Unternehmen: (Verhandlungen auf der Arbeitstagung...in Aachen vom 25.-27. September 1975; herausgegeben von Horst Albach und Dieter Sadowski). Berlin, [1976]. pp. 939. *bibliog. In German or English.*

WINBERG (ALAN RONALD) Decision-making theory and the characteristics of crisis; with particular reference to the French reaction to the remilitarization of the Rhineland in 1936. [1976]. fo. 448. *bibliog. Typescript. M.Phil.(London) thesis: unpublished. This thesis is the property of London University and may not be removed from the Library.*

— **Mathematical models.**

FISHBURN (PETER C.) Utility theory for decision making. New York, [1970]. pp. 234. *bibliog. (Operations Research Society of America. Publications in Operations Research. No.18)*

COOPER (MALCOLM J.M.) The industrial location decision making process. Birmingham, 1975. pp. 108. *bibliog. (Birmingham. University. Centre for Urban and Regional Studies. Occasional Papers. No. 34)*

HOWARD (K.) and others. The scope for computer based systems to aid corporate decision- making in the short and medium term in the reorganised local authorities: a feasibility study. Peterlee, 1975. pp. 40. *bibliog. (IBM United Kingdom Limited. UK Scientific Centre. [Technical Reports]. 0074)*

RESEARCH CONFERENCE ON SUBJECTIVE PROBABILITY, UTILITY AND DECISION MAKING, 4TH, ROME, 1973. Utility, probability, and human decision making: selected proceedings...; edited by Dirk Wendt and Charles Vlek. Dordrecht, [1975]. pp. 418. *bibliogs.*

ROUMASSET (JAMES A.) Rice and risk: decision making among low-income farmers. Amsterdam, 1976. pp. 251. *bibliog.*

DECISION-MAKING IN PUBLIC ADMINISTRATION.

WIRT (FREDERICK M.) Power in the city: decision making in San Francisco. Berkeley, [1974]. pp. 417.

BOLAN (RICHARD S.) and NUTTALL (RONALD L.) Urban planning and politics. Lexington, [1975]. pp. 211. *bibliog.*

ROSENTHAL (GLENDA GOLDSTONE) The men behind the decisions: cases in European policy-making. Lexington, Mass., [1975]. pp. 166. *bibliog.*

DECISION-MAKING IN PUBLIC ADMINISTRATION.(Cont.)

AWERBUCH (SHIMON) and WALLACE (WILLIAM A.) Policy evaluation for community development: decision tools for local government. New York, 1976. pp. 286. *bibliog.*

BRUCE-GARDYNE (JOCK) and LAWSON (NIGEL) The power game: an examination of decision-making in government. London, 1976. pp. 204. *bibliog.*

DECLERCQ (GILBERT).

DECLERCQ (GILBERT) Syndicaliste en liberté: entretiens avec A. Besson et J. Julliard. Paris, [1974]. pp. 188.

DE COSMOS (AMOR).

WOODCOCK (GEORGE) 1912- . Amor De Cosmos: journalist and reformer. Toronto, 1975. pp. 177. *bibliog.*

DEFENCE (CRIMINAL PROCEDURE)

— Poland.

PIEKARSKI (MIECZYSŁAW) Pozbawienie strony możości obrony swych praw w postępowaniu cywilnym. Warszawa, 1964. pp. 180. *With Russian and German summaries.*

DEFENCES, NATIONAL.

ROBERTS (EDWARD ADAM) Nations in arms: the theory and practice of territorial defence. London, 1976. pp. 288.

DEFLATION (FINANCE)

— United States.

MYERS (C.V.) The coming deflation: its dangers and opportunities. New Rochelle, N.Y., [1976]. pp. 218.

DEFUNIS (MARCO).

O'NEIL (ROBERT M.) Discriminating against discrimination: preferential admissions and the DeFunis case. Bloomington, [1975]. pp. 271. *bibliog.*

DEGREES, ACADEMIC

— United States.

ADKINS (DOUGLAS L.) The great American degree machine: an economic analysis of the human resource output of higher education...; a technical report sponsored by the Carnegie Commission on Higher Education. Berkeley, Ca., [1975]. pp. 663. *bibliog.*

CARTTER (ALLAN MURRAY) Ph.D.'s and the academic labor market. New York, [1976]. pp. 260. *bibliog. A report prepared for the Carnegie Commission on Higher Education.*

DEGRELLE (LEON).

DANNAU (WIM) Ainsi parla Léon Degrelle;...interviews au magnétophone et conversations avec...Léon Degrelle...recueillies par Wim Dannau de 1965 à 1972, les commentaires de l'auteur, etc. [Strombeek, 1973 in progress].

DEIR EL MEDINEH

— Social history.

MONICA (MADELINE DELLA) La classe ouvrière sous les Pharaons: étude du village de Deir el Medineh. Paris, [1975]. pp. 199. *bibliog.*

DELCEV (GOCE).

DELČEV (GOCE) Pisma i drugi materiali: izdiril i podgotvil za pečat Dino K'osev. Sofiia, 1967. pp. 348.

DELCHEV (GOTSE).

See DELCEV (GOCE).

DELCOURT (EMILE).

EUROPEAN COURT OF HUMAN RIGHTS. Publications. Series A: Judgments and Decisions. [A11]. ..."Delcourt" case; judgment of 17th January 1970. Strasbourg, Council of Europe, 1970. pp. 21 [bis].

EUROPEAN COURT OF HUMAN RIGHTS. Publications. Series B: Pleadings, Oral Arguments and Documents. [B9]. "Delcourt" case, (1969-1970). Strasbourg, Council of Europe, 1970. pp. 249 [bis], 251-287. *In English and French.*

DELEGATION OF POWERS

— United States.

BARBER (SOTIRIOS A.) The constitution and the delegation of Congressional power. Chicago, 1975. pp. 153.

DELHI

— Growth.

KING (ANTHONY D.) Colonial urban development: social power and environment. London, 1976. pp. 328. *bibliog.*

— Social conditions.

MISHRA (VISHWA MOHAN) Communication and modernization in urban slums. New York, [1972]. pp. 128. *bibliog.*

DELINQUENT WOMEN

— United States.

BRODSKY (ANNETTE M.) ed. The female offender. Beverly Hills, 1975. pp. 108. *bibliogs. (Reprint of a special issue of Criminal Justice and Behavior, vol. 1, no. 4, December 1974)*

DELIVERY OF GOODS (LAW)

— Poland.

NOWAKOWSKI (ZYGMUNT KONRAD) Umowa dostawy. Warszawa, 1960. pp. 431.

— Russia.

SHELESTOV (VLADIMIR STEPANOVICH) Dogovor postavki i kachestvo produktsii. Moskva, 1974. pp. 176.

DELMAS (JACQUES CHABAN-).

See CHABAN-DELMAS (JACQUES).

DEMOCRACY.

ZOEPFL (HEINRICH) Die Demokratie in Deutschland: ein Beitrag zur wissenschaftlichen Würdigung von: G.G. Gervinus, Einleitung in die Geschichte des neunzehnten Jahrhunderts. Stuttgart, 1853. pp. 106.

STROHM (GUSTAV) Demos und Monarch: Untersuchungen über die Auflösung der Demokratie. Stuttgart, 1922. pp. 221.

MACPHERSON (CRAWFORD BROUGH) The real world of democracy. New York, 1972 [repr. 1975]. pp. 67.

GALASSO (GIUSEPPE) Da Mazzini a Salvemini: il pensiero democratico nell'Italia moderna. Firenze, 1974. pp. 343. *bibliogs.*

CROZIER (MICHEL) and others. The crisis of democracy...; report on the governability of democracies to the Trilateral Commission. [New York], 1975. pp. 211.

GULIEV (VLADIMIR EVGEN'EVICH) and KUZ'MIN (EDUARD LEONIDOVICH) Gosudarstvo i demokratiia: kritika antimarksistskikh teorii. Moskva, 1975. pp. 215.

MOSS (ROBERT) The collapse of democracy. London, 1975. pp. 300.

SCHULMAN (MICHAEL DAVID) Value consensus and the social cohesion of liberal democracy. 1975. pp. 366. *bibliog. Photocopy of typescript. Ph.D. thesis - Wisconsin University.*

EULAU (HEINZ) and CZUDNOWSKI (MOSHE M.) eds. Elite recruitment in democratic polities: comparative studies across nations. New York, [1976]. pp. 299.

KLIEMAN (AARON S.) Emergency politics: the growth of crisis government. London, 1976. pp. 19. *(Institute for the Study of Conflict. Conflict Studies. No. 70)*

LUCAS (JOHN RANDOLPH) Democracy and participation. Harmondsworth, 1976. pp. 290.

MILL (JOHN STUART) John Stuart Mill on politics and society; selected and edited by Geraint L. Williams. London, 1976. pp. 412. *bibliog.*

— Bibliography.

GERMANY (BUNDESREPUBLIK). Deutscher Bundestag. Wissenschaftliche Dienste. 1974. Systemkritik und Systemstabilisierung: zur Demokratiediskussion in der Bundesrepublik: Auswahlbibliographie mit Inhaltsangaben; [compiled by Günt[h]er Hoherz]. Bonn, 1974. pp. 119. *(Bibliographien. 37)*

DEMOCRATIC PARTY (UNITED STATES).

ALLISON (R. BRUCE) Democrats in exile, 1968-1972: the political confessions of a New England liberal. Hinsdale, Ill., [1974]. pp. 147.

DAVIS (LANNY J.) The emerging Democratic majority: lessons and legacies from the new politics. New York, 1974. pp. 276.

The POLITICS of representation: the Democratic Convention 1972; [by] Denis G. Sullivan [and others]. New York, [1974]. pp. 152.

STEWART (JOHN G.) One last chance: the Democratic Party, 1974-76. New York, 1974. pp. 208.

GROSSMAN (LAWRENCE) The Democratic Party and the negro: northern and national politics, 1868-92. Urbana, [1976]. pp. 212. *bibliog.*

MURRAY (ROBERT KEITH) The 103rd ballot: Democrats and the disaster in Madison Square Garden. New York, [1976]. pp. 336. *bibliog.*

RUBIN (RICHARD L.) Party dynamics: the Democratic coalition and the politics of change. New York, 1976. pp. 203.

DEMOGRAPHY.

UNITED NATIONS. Economic and Social Commission for Asia and the Pacific. Asian Population Studies Series. New York, 1966 in progress.

BOLTE (KARL MARTIN) and KAPPE (DIETER) Struktur und Entwicklung der Bevölkerung. 3rd ed. Opladen, 1967. pp. 98. *bibliog. (Hochschule für Wirtschaft und Politik, Hamburg. Beiträge zur Sozialkunde. Reihe B. Struktur und Wandel der Gesellschaft. 2)*

HUNGARY. Központi Statisztikai Hivatal. Népességtudományi Kutató Intézet. Történeti Demográfiai Tanulmányok. 2. Colloque de démographie historique; Colloqium [sic] on historical demography; Colloquium [sic] der historischen Demographie, Budapest, 23-26 septembre, 1965. Budapest, 1968. pp. 151. *bibliogs. In English, French and German.*

RABB (THEODORE K.) and ROTBERG (ROBERT IRWIN) eds. The family in history: interdisciplinary essays. New York, 1973. pp. 240. *bibliog. (Reprinted from the Journal of Interdisciplinary History)*

LARMIN (OLEG VLADIMIROVICH) Metodologicheskie problemy izucheniia narodonaseleniia. Moskva, 1974. pp. 240.

RUSSIA (USSR). Ministerstvo Vysshego i Srednego Spetsial'nogo Obrazovaniia. Nauchno-Tekhnicheskii Sovet. Sektsiia Narodonaseleniia. Narodonaselenie. 5. Demograficheskii analiz rozhdaemosti. Moskva, 1974. pp. 112. *With English table of contents.*

RUSSIA (USSR). Ministerstvo Vysshego i Srednego Spetsial'nogo Obrazovaniia. Nauchno-Tekhnicheskii Sovet. Sektsiia Narodonaseleniia. Narodonaselenie. 7. Razvitie naseleniia. Moskva, 1974. pp. 94. *With English table of contents.*

ARUTIUNIAN (LIUDMILA AKOPOVNA) Sotsialisticheskii zakon narodonaseleniia. Moskva, 1975. pp. 95.

BEAVER (STEVEN E.) Demographic transition theory reinterpreted: an application to recent natality trends in Latin America. Lexington, Mass., [1975]. pp. 177. *bibliog.*

BOIARSKII (ARON IAKOVLEVICH) Naselenie i metody ego izucheniia: sbornik nauchnykh trudov. Moskva, 1975. pp. 264.

ROBINSON (WARREN C.) ed. Population and development planning. New York, [1975]. pp. 263.

BOURCIER DE CARBON (LUC) Démographie géo-économique. Paris, [1976]. 2 vols. (in 1). *bibliog.*

— **Bibliography.**

UNITED STATES. Smithsonian Institution. Interdisciplinary Communication Program. International Program for Population Analysis. Annotated bibliography. s-a., 1973 (v.1, no.1)- Washington.

— **Mathematical models.**

SHEPS (MINDEL C.) and MENKEN (JANE A.) Mathematical models of conception and birth. Chicago, 1973. pp. 428. *bibliog.*

POPULATION, public policy, and economic development; edited by Michael C. Keeley. New York, 1976. pp. 259. *bibliog.*

DEMONSTRATIONS

— **United Kingdom.**

NATIONAL COUNCIL FOR CIVIL LIBERTIES. Submissions to the public enquiry...to review the events at Red Lion Square on the 15th June 1974: the Scarman enquiry. London, 1974. pp. 19.

DENMARK

— **Boundaries.**

NOACK (JOHAN PETER) Det tyske mindretal i Nordslesvig under besaettelsen. [Copenhagen, 1975]. pp. 213. *bibliog. (Dansk Udenrigspolitisk Institut. Skrifter. 6)*

— — **Germany.**

SVALASTOGA (KAARE) Where Europeans meet: a sociological investigation of a bordertown. Copenhagen, 1960. fo. 144. *Lacking section 7, Documents.*

— **Census.**

DENMARK. Census, 1970. Folke- og boligtaellingen, 9.november 1970. København, 1972 in progress. *(Denmark. Danmarks Statistik. Statistisk Tabelvaerk. 1972. 3, etc.)*

— **Commerce.**

JOHANSEN (HANS CHR.) Udenrigshandel og betalingsbalance. 2nd ed. København, 1973. pp. 86. *bibliog.*

— **Defences.**

EINHORN (ERIC S.) National security and domestic politics in post-war Denmark: some principal issues, 1945-1961. Odense, 1975. pp. 105. *bibliog. (Odense Universitet. Studies in History and Social Sciences. vol. 27)*

— **Economic conditions.**

DENMARK. Økonomiske Sekretariat. Økonomisk oversigt. s-a., Mr 1973- København.

KORST (MOGENS) Industrial life in Denmark: a survey of economic development and production. [Copenhagen, 1975]. pp. 172.

— **Economic history.**

HANSEN (SVEND AAGE) Økonomisk vaekst i Danmark. København, 1972-74. 2 vols. *(Københavns Universitet. Institut for Økonomisk Historie, Publikationer, Nr. 6)*

BRINCH (JENS) Kapitalakkumulation i Danmark efter 1940: et forsøg på en konkret konjunkturanalyse. København, [1975]. pp. 112.

— — **Mathematical models.**

ANDERSEN (ELLEN) En model for Danmark, 1949-1965. København, 1975. pp. 311. *bibliog. (Københavns Universitet. Økonomiske Institut. Studier. Nr. 21) With English summary.*

— **Economic policy.**

DENMARK. Økonomiske Råd. Formandskabet. 1972. Økonomisk demokrati i samfundsøkonomisk belysning. København, 1972. pp. 100.

SCHMIDT (ERIK IB) Dansk økonomisk politik: tidens problemer, og deres baggrund. new ed. [Copenhagen, 1974]. pp. 278.

KRISEN og den statslige planlaegning: muligheder og betingelser for en statslig udviklingspolitik...i Danmark siden 2. verdenskrig; [by] Erik Hannibal Knudsen [and others]. Aarhus, 1976. pp. 283. *bibliog.*

— **Executive departments.**

DENMARK. Arbejdsgruppen vedrørende Centraladministrationens Organisation. 1971. Redegørelse. København, 1971. pp. 99. *(Denmark. Betaenkninger. Nr. 629)*

— **Foreign relations.**

NØRREGARD (GEORG) Før stormen: Christian 8.s udenrigspolitik, 1839-48. [Copenhagen, 1974]. pp. 370. *bibliog.*

See also EUROPEAN ECONOMIC COMMUNITY — Denmark.

— **Historiography.**

SCOCOZZA (BENITO) Klassekampen i Danmarks historie: feudalismen; med et indledende afsnit om den historiske materialisme. [Copenhagen, 1976]. pp. 308. *bibliog.*

— **Industries.**

KORST (MOGENS) Industrial life in Denmark: a survey of economic development and production. [Copenhagen, 1975]. pp. 172.

— **Officials and employees.**

BETAENKNING afgivet af det under 15. oktober 1968 nedsatte udvalg til revision af samarbejdsudvalsvirksomheden inden for statens styrelser m.v. [København], 1971. pp. 53. *(Denmark. Betaenkninger. Nr. 602)*

— **Politics and government.**

NIELSEN (VAGN OLUF) ed. Danmarks første arbejderflertal: kilder til belysning af det parlamentariske samarbejde mellem Socialdemokratiet og Socialistisk Folkeparti, 1966-1967. København, [1974]. pp. 80. *bibliog.*

EINHORN (ERIC S.) National security and domestic politics in post-war Denmark: some principal issues, 1945-1961. Odense, 1975. pp. 105. *bibliog. (Odense Universitet. Studies in History and Social Sciences. vol. 27)*

BORDING (KRISTEN MORTENSEN) Dagbog over Danmarks første socialdemokratiske ministerium, 1924- 26; ved Karen Marie Olsen og Hans Sode-Madsen. Aarhus, 1976. pp. 131. *bibliog.*

— **Relations (military) with Sweden.**

TORELL (ULF) Hjälp till Danmark: militära och politiska förbindelser, 1943-1945. Stockholm, 1973. pp. 385. *bibliog. With English summary.*

— **Rural conditions.**

TO byer i Odsherred...;[by] (Gunnar Viby Mogensen) [and others]. København, 1975. pp. 70. *(Socialforskningsinstituttet. Meddelelser. 12) With English summary.*

— **Social policy.**

DICH (JØRGEN S.) Den herskende klasse: en kritisk analyse af social udbytning og midlerne imod den. 4th ed. [Copenhagen, 1974]. pp. 260.

PEDERSEN (SØREN RISHØJ) ed. Fagbevaegelsen og socialpolitikken. København, 1976. pp. 88. *(Socialpolitisk Forening. Småskrifter. Nr. 46)*

— **Statistics.**

DENMARK. Danmarks Statistik. Statistisk tiårs oversigt. a., 1970, 1972- [København]. *1964-1969, 1971 included in DENMARK. Danmarks Statistik. Statistiske efterretninger.*

DENTAL CARE

— **United States.**

MAURIZI (ALEX R.) Public policy and the dental care market. Washington, 1975. pp. 73. *(American Enterprise Institute for Public Policy Research. evaluative Studies. 24)*

DENTISTS

— **Germany.**

LUBECKI (PAUL) Interaktion und Berufsprestige: eine empirische Untersuchung zur Bewertung von Berufen. [Erlangen-Nürnberg, 1976]. 1 vol.(various pagings). *bibliog. Inaugural-Dissertation zur Erlangung des akademischen Grades eines Doktors der Wirtschafts- und Sozialwissenschaften der Friedrich-Alexander-Universität Erlangen-Nürnberg.*

DEPRECIATION ALLOWANCES.

BIØRN (ERIK) Avskrivningsregler og prisen på bruk av realkapital...: depreciation rules and the user cost of capital. Oslo, 1975. pp. 46. *bibliog. (Norway. Statistiske Centralbyrå. Artikler. Nr. 74) With English summary.*

— **European Economic Community countries.**

TELLER (ROBERT) Amortissement fiscal et croissance des entreprises dans la C.E.E. Bruxelles, 1974. pp. 289. *bibliog.*

DERING (Sir EDWARD).

DERING (Sir EDWARD) The diaries and papers of Sir Edward Dering, Second Baronet, 1644 to 1684; edited by Maurice F. Bond. London, 1976. pp. 237. *(U.K. Parliament. House of Lords. Record Office. Occasional Publications. No.1) Genealogical table in end pocket.*

DESERTION, MILITARY

— **Germany.**

DICKS (HENRY VICTOR) The German deserter: a pyschological study. London, 1944. pp. 30. *(U.K. War Office. Directorate of Army Psychiatry. Research Memoranda. No. 45/03/9)*

DESIGN, INDUSTRIAL

— **Russia.**

HUTCHINGS (RAYMOND FRANCIS DUDLEY) Soviet science, technology, design: interaction and convergence. London, 1976. pp. 320. *bibliog.*

DESPOTISM.

KRIEGER (LEONARD) An essay on the theory of enlightened despotism. Chicago, 1975. pp. 115. *bibliog.*

DETENTE.

CUNY CONFERENCE ON HISTORY AND POLITICS, 1ST, NEW YORK, 1974. Detente in historical perspective:...[proceedings of the] conference...; [edited by] George Schwab...[and] Henry Friedlander, etc. New York, [1975]. pp. 171.

PETROV (VLADIMIR) U.S.-Soviet detente: past and future. Washington, 1975. pp. 60. *(American Enterprise Institute for Public Policy Research. Foreign Affairs Studies. 18)*

DETENTE.(Cont.)

DÉTENTE: (edited versions of interviews originally broadcast, in 1973-75, over Radio Free Europe); edited by G.R. Urban. London, 1976. pp. 368.

INTERNATIONAL SLAVIC CONFERENCE, 1ST, BANFF, ALBERTA, 1974. From the cold war to detente; [selected papers from the conference]; edited by Peter J. Potichnyj [and] Jane P. Shapiro. New York, 1976. pp. 223.

PIPES (RICHARD EDGAR) ed. Soviet strategy in Europe. London, 1976. pp. 316.

DETENTION OF PERSONS

— Austria.

EUROPEAN COURT OF HUMAN RIGHTS. Publications. Series A: Judgments and Decisions. [A8]. ..."Neumeister" case; judgment of 27th June 1968. Strasbourg, Council of Europe, 1968. pp. 48 [bis]. *In English and French.*

EUROPEAN COMMISSION OF HUMAN RIGHTS. 1969. The Köplinger case: (Application No. 1850/63 by Rudolf Köplinger against Austria). Strasbourg, Council of Europe, 1969. pp. 215.

EUROPEAN COURT OF HUMAN RIGHTS. Publications. Series A: Judgments and Decisions. [A9]. ..."Stögmüller case; judgment of 10th November 1969. Strasbourg, Council of Europe, 1969. pp. 47 [bis]. *In English and French.*

EUROPEAN COURT OF HUMAN RIGHTS. Publications. Series A: Judgments and Decisions. [A10]. ..."Matznetter" case; judgment of 10th November 1969. Strasbourg, Council of Europe, 1969. pp. 50 [bis]. *In English and French.*

EUROPEAN COURT OF HUMAN RIGHTS. Publications. Series B: Pleadings, Oral Arguments and Documents. [B6]. "Neumeister" case (1966-1969). Strasbourg, Council of Europe, 1969. pp. 307bis, 309-338. *In English and French.*

EUROPEAN COURT OF HUMAN RIGHTS. Publications. Series B: Pleadings, Oral Arguments and Documents. [B7]. "Stögmüller" case, (1967-1969). Strasbourg, Council of Europe, 1970. pp. 228 [bis], 229-256. *In English and French.*

EUROPEAN COURT OF HUMAN RIGHTS. Publications. Series B: Pleadings, Oral Arguments and Documents. [B8]. "Matznetter" case, (1967-1969). Strasbourg, Council of Europe, 1970. pp. 255 [bis], 257-291. *In English and French.*

EUROPEAN COURT OF HUMAN RIGHTS. Publications. Series A: Judgments and Decisions. [A 13]. ...Ringeisen case; judgment of 16th July 1971. Strasbourg, Council of Europe, 1971. pp. 56 [bis]. *In English and French.*

EUROPEAN COURT OF HUMAN RIGHTS. Publications. Series A: Judgments and Decisions. [A] 15. ...Ringeisen case: judgment of 22 June /([["; QUESTION OF THE APPLICATION OF aRTICLE 5: OF THE cONVENTION. sTRASBOURG, cOUNCIL OF eUROPE, 1972. PP. 12 ?BIS!. iN eNGLISH AND fRENCH.

EUROPEAN COURT OF HUMAN RIGHTS. Publications. Series B: Pleadings, Oral Arguments and Documents. [B11]. "Ringeisen" case, (1970-1971). Strasbourg, Council of Europe, 1972. pp. 299 [bis], 301-371. *In English and French.*

EUROPEAN COURT OF HUMAN RIGHTS. Publications. Series A: Judgments and Decisions. [A] 16. ...Ringeisen case: interpretation of the judgment of 22 June 1972; judgment of 23 June 1973. Strasbourg, Council of Europe, 1973. pp. 13 [bis]. *In English and French.*

EUROPEAN COURT OF HUMAN RIGHTS. Publications. Series B: Pleadings, Oral Arguments and Documents. [B13]. "Ringeisen" case: question of the application of Article 50 of the Convention, (1971-1972). Strasbourg, Council of Europe, 1973. pp. 89 [bis], 91-119. *In English and French.*

EUROPEAN COURT OF HUMAN RIGHTS. Publications. Series B: Pleadings, Oral Arguments and Documents. [B14]. "Ringeisen" case: interpretation of the judgment of 22nd June 1972, (1972-1973). Strasbourg, Council of Europe, 1973. pp. 42 [bis], 43-58. *In English and French.*

EUROPEAN COURT OF HUMAN RIGHTS. Publications. Series A: Judgments and Decisions. [A] 17. ...Neumeister case: judgment of 7 May 1974; question of the application of Article 50 of the Convention. Strasbourg, Council of Europe, 1974. pp. 21 [bis]. *In English and French.*

EUROPEAN COURT OF HUMAN RIGHTS. Publications. Series B: Pleadings, Oral Arguments and Documents. [B15]. "Neumeister" case: question of the application of Article 50 of the Convention, (1971-1974). Strasbourg, Council of Europe, 1974. pp. 142 [bis], 143-170. *In English and French.*

— Germany.

EUROPEAN COURT OF HUMAN RIGHTS. Publications. Series A: Judgments and Decisions. [A7]. ..."Wemhoff" case; judgment of 27th June 1968. Strasbourg, Council of Europe, 1968. pp. 40 [bis]. *In English and French.*

EUROPEAN COURT OF HUMAN RIGHTS. Publications. Series B: Pleadings, Oral Arguments and Documents. [B5]. "Wemhoff" case, (1969). Strasbourg, Council of Europe, 1969. pp. 301bis, 302-361. *In English and French.*

DETROIT

— Industries.

MANDELL (LEWIS) Industrial location decisions: Detroit compared with Atlanta and Chicago. New York, 1975. pp. 120.

DEUTSCHE VOLKSPARTEI.

HUNT (JAMES CLARK) The People's Party in Württemberg and southern Germany, 1890-1914: the possibilities of democratic politics. Stuttgart, [1975]. pp. 203. *bibliog.*

DEVELOPMENT BANKS

— America, Latin.

INSTITUTO LATINOAMERICANO DE INVESTIGACIONES SOCIALES. Seminario Internacional, [5], Lima, 1973. El papel de la banca de fomento en el desarrollo economico de America Latina: seminario internacional realizado en Lima, Peru del 9 al 13 de julio de 1973; Karl-Heinz Stanzick [and] Roberto Keil Rojas, directores. [Santiago de Chile?, 1973?]. pp. 660. *Conference organised jointly by the Instituto and the Direccion General de Asuntos Economicos.*

— Jamaica.

JAMAICA DEVELOPMENT BANK. Annual report. a., 1973- Kingston.

— Underdeveloped areas.

See UNDERDEVELOPED AREAS — Development banks.

DEVELOPMENT CREDIT CORPORATIONS

— Nepal.

NEPAL INDUSTRIAL DEVELOPMENT CORPORATION. Investment Promotion and Publicity Division. Nepal Industrial Development Corporation: an introduction. [Kathmandu, 1971]. pp. 16.

DEVELOPMENTAL PSYCHOLOGY.

BEARD (RUTH M.) An outline of Piaget's developmental psychology for students and teachers. London, 1969 repr. 1974. pp. 128. *bibliog.*

LIFE-SPAN CONFERENCE, 2ND, WEST VIRGINIA UNIVERSITY, 1971. Life-span developmental psychology: methodological issues; edited by John R. Nesselroade and Hayne W. Reese. New York, 1973. pp. 364. *bibliog.*

DEVIANT BEHAVIOUR.

DINITZ (SIMON) and others. Deviance: studies in definition, management, and treatment. 2nd ed. New York, 1975. pp. 641. *bibliogs.*

EUROPEAN GROUP FOR THE STUDY OF DEVIANCE AND SOCIAL CONTROL. Conference, 1st, Impruneta, 1973. Deviance and control in Europe: papers...; edited by Herman Bianchi [and others]. London, [1975]. pp. 209.

GIBBONS (DON C.) and JONES (JOSEPH F.) The study of deviance: perspectives and problems. Englewood Cliffs, 1975. pp. 216. *bibliogs.*

VANDERBILT SOCIOLOGY CONFERENCE, 3RD, NASHVILLE, 1974. The labelling of deviance: evaluating a perspective; [proceedings of the conference]; edited by Walter R. Gove. New York, [1975]. pp. 313. *bibliogs.*

McCAGHY (CHARLES H.) Deviant behavior: crime, conflict, and interest groups. New York, [1976]. pp. 400.

MORRIS (TERENCE PATRICK) Deviance and control: the secular heresy. London, 1976. pp. 157.

DEVONSHIRE

— Economic history — Sources.

GARDINER (DOROTHY M.) A calendar of early Chancery proceedings relating to West Country shipping, 1388-1493. [Exeter], 1976. pp. 131. *(Devon and Cornwall Record Society. [Publications]. New Series. vol. 21)*

— Industries.

DEVONSHIRE. Planning Department. Annual survey of primary industries. a., 1974- [Exeter].

DEWEY (JOHN).

COUGHLAN (NEIL) Young John Dewey: an essay in American intellectual history. Chicago, 1975. pp. 187. *bibliog.*

DIAMONDS.

GHANA. Commission of Enquiry into the Diamond Mining Corporation. 1971. Report; [chairman Charles Sterling Acolatse, subsequently Saki Scheck]. Accra, [1971]. fo. 136.

DIARIES

— Bibliography.

BATTS (JOHN STUART) British manuscript diaries of the nineteenth century: an annotated listing. Totowa, 1976. pp. 345.

DIAZ (PORFIRIO).

HANNAY (DAVID) Diaz. London, 1917. pp. 319. *bibliog.*

DICTATORSHIP OF THE PROLETARIAT.

The DICTATORSHIP of the proletariat. London, [1936?]. pp. 122. *Readings from the works of Marx, Engels, Lenin, Stalin, etc.*

GANIN (NIKOLAI IVANOVICH) Zakonomernosti sotsialisticheskoi revoliutsii i istoricheskii opyt KPSS. Moskva, 1974. pp. 255.

KHESIN (SAMUIL SEMENOVICH) Stanovlenie proletarskoi diktatury v Rossii: voprosy ustanovleniia Sovetskoi vlasti i skladyvaniia proletarskoi gosudarstvennoi sistemy, noiabr' 1917 - mart 1918 g. Moskva, 1975. pp. 471.

MUKHINA (GALINA ZOTIKOVNA) Sotsialisticheskaia revoliutsiia i gosudarstvo: razrabotka V.I. Leninym voprosa o gosudarstve diktatury proletariata v period bor'by za Oktiabr' i uprochenie ego zavoevanii, mart 1917 - mart 1918. Moskva, 1975. pp. 277.

PROBLEMY gegemonii proletariata v demokraticheskoi revoliutsii, 1905 - fevral' 1917 gg. Moskva, 1975. pp. 311.

TRUKAN (GERMAN ANTONOVICH) Rabochii klass v bor'be za pobedu i uprochenie Sovetskoi vlasti. Moskva, 1975. pp. 303.

DIDACTIC LITERATURE, ROMANIAN.

DUȚU (ALEXANDRU) Cărțile de înțelepciune în cultura română. București, 1972. pp. 168. *bibliog.* *(Academia de Științe Sociale și Politice a Republicii Socialiste România. Biblioteca Istorică. 34*

DIDGORA MOUNTAIN, GEORGIA, BATTLE OF, 1121.

MESKHIA (SHOTA AMBAKOVICH) Didgorskaia bitva. Tbilisi, 1974. pp. 124. *Russian colophon gives author's patronymic as 'Ambrosovich'.*

DIEFENBAKER (JOHN GEORGE).

DIEFENBAKER (JOHN GEORGE) One Canada: memoirs. Toronto, [1975 in progress].

STURSBERG (PETER) Diefenbaker: leadership gained, 1956-62. Toronto, [1975]. pp. 278. *Based on recorded interviews and discussions.*

DIESEL MOTOR INDUSTRY

— Russia — Soviet Far East.

AMURSKIE arsenal'tsy: istoriia zavoda "Dal'dizel'". Khabarovsk, 1974. pp. 351.

DIET

— United Kingdom.

The MAKING of the modern British diet; edited by Derek Oddy and Derek Miller. London, [1976]. pp. 235. *bibliogs. Papers read to a research seminar in the Department of Nutrition at Queen Elizabeth College.*

DIFFERENTIAL EQUATIONS, PARTIAL.

COPSON (EDWARD THOMAS) Partial differential equations. Cambridge, 1975. pp. 280. *bibliog.*

DIFFERENTIAL GAMES.

HÁJEK (OTOMAR) Pursuit games: an introduction to the theory and applications of differential games of pursuit and evasion. New York, 1975. pp. 266.

DIFFUSION OF INNOVATIONS.

The DIFFUSION of medical technology: policy and research planning perspectives; edited by Gerald Gordon [and] G. Lawrence Fisher. Cambridge, Mass., [1975]. pp. 210. *bibliog. Based on a conference held at Cornell University in September 1972, and sponsored by the National Institutes of Health.*

STONEMAN (PAUL) Technological diffusion and the computer revolution: the U.K. experience. Cambridge, 1976. pp. 219. *bibliog. (Cambridge. University. Department of Applied Economics. Monographs. 25)*

— Mathematical models.

PAWSON (ERIC) The turnpike trusts of the eighteenth century: a study of innovation and diffusion. Oxford, 1975. pp. 40. *bibliog. (Oxford. University. School of Geography. Research Papers. No. 14)*

— United States.

BINGHAM (RICHARD D.) The adoption of innovation by local government;...with the assistance of Thomas P. McNaught. Lexington, [1976]. pp. 271. *bibliog.*

DIGITAL COMPUTER SIMULATION.

SIEGEL (ARTHUR I.) and WOLF (J.JAY) Man-machine simulation models: psychosocial and performance interaction. New York, [1969]. pp. 177. *bibliog.*

DIMITROV (GEORGI).

KAMENOVA (DORA) Georgi Dimitrov v bulgarskoto izobrazitelno izkustvo. Sofiia, 1972. pp. 155. *With German, Russian, French, English and Spanish summaries and captions to illustrations.*

DIMOV (DIMITUR).

DIMITUR Talev, Svetoslav Minkov, Dimitur Dimov v spomenite na suvremennitsite si. Sofiia, 1973. pp. 755.

DIPLOMACY.

LISKA (GEORGE) Beyond Kissinger: ways of conservative statecraft. Baltimore, [1975]. pp. 159. *bibliog. (Johns Hopkins University. Washington Center of Foreign Policy Research. Studies in International Affairs. No. 26)*

LAUREN (PAUL GORDON) Diplomats and bureaucrats: the first institutional responses to twentieth-century diplomacy in France and Germany. Stanford, 1976. pp. 294. *bibliog. (Stanford University. Hoover Institution on War, Revolution and Peace. Hoover Institution Publications. 153)*

WODAK (WALTER) Diplomatie zwischen Ost und West. Graz, [1976]. pp. 235. *(Österreichische Gesellschaft für Aussenpolitik und Internationale Beziehungen. Österreichische Diplomaten) Collection of lectures and essays, in German or English. Includes correspondence with Karl Renner.*

DIPLOMATIC DOCUMENTS.

THOMAS (DANIEL HARRISON) and CASE (LYNN MARSHALL) eds. The new guide to the diplomatic archives of western Europe. [Philadelphia, 1975]. pp. 441. *bibliogs.*

DIPLOMATIC PRIVILEGES AND IMMUNITIES.

DENZA (EILEEN) Diplomatic law: commentary on the Vienna Convention on Diplomatic Relations. Dobbs Ferry, N.Y., 1976. pp. 348.

DIPLOMATS, AMERICAN.

BURNS (RICHARD DEAN) and BENNETT (EDWARD MOORE) eds. Diplomats in crisis: United States-Chinese-Japanese relations, 1919-1941. Santa Barbara, Ca., [1974]. pp. 346.

PLISCHKE (ELMER) United States diplomats and their missions: a profile of American diplomatic emissaries since 1778. Washington, 1975. pp. 201. *(American Enterprise Institute for Public Policy Research. Foreign Affairs Studies. 16)*

— Correspondence, reminiscences, etc.

NOBLE (HAROLD JOYCE) Embassy at war;...edited with an introduction by Frank Baldwin. Seattle, [1975]. pp. 328. *(Columbia University. East Asian Institute. Studies)*

DIPLOMATS, BRITISH

— Correspondence, reminiscences, etc.

BARCLAY (Sir RODERICK EDWARD) Ernest Bevin and the Foreign Office, 1932-1969. London, 1975. pp. 166.

KIRKBRIDE (Sir ALEC) From the wings: Amman memoirs 1947-1951. London, 1976. pp. 159.

DIPLOMATS, CHINESE.

BURNS (RICHARD DEAN) and BENNETT (EDWARD MOORE) eds. Diplomats in crisis: United States-Chinese-Japanese relations, 1919-1941. Santa Barbara, Ca., [1974]. pp. 346.

DIPLOMATS, FRENCH

— Correspondence, reminiscences, etc.

SEYDOUX (FRANÇOIS) Mémoires d'outre-Rhin. Paris, [1975]. pp. 309.

DIPLOMATS, JAPANESE.

BURNS (RICHARD DEAN) and BENNETT (EDWARD MOORE) eds. Diplomats in crisis: United States-Chinese-Japanese relations, 1919-1941. Santa Barbara, Ca., [1974]. pp. 346.

DIRECTORIES.

INTERNATIONAL ORGANIZATION FOR STANDARDIZATION. Directories of libraries, information and documentation centres. [Geneva, 1972]. fo. 3.

DIRECTORS OF CORPORATIONS

— Switzerland.

BUCHMANN (PETER) Organisation der Verwaltungsräte in 20 der grössten Aktiengesellschaften in der Schweiz. Bern, 1976. pp. 143. *bibliog.*

— United Kingdom.

CROSS (PETER) The British business creed: changing ideologies and self images of business elites and management in Britain. [1975]. fo. 488. *bibliog. Typescript. Ph.D. (London) thesis: unpublished. This thesis is the property of London University and may not be removed from the Library.*

DISARMAMENT.

ARMS LIMITATION AND DISARMAMENT (formerly Arms control and disarmament): notes on current developments; issued by the Foreign and Commonwealth Office [U.K.]. irreg., Ap 1967 [no.1]- London.

NO more armaments for no more Vietnams; [anonymous typescript letter sent to United States student bodies, foreign embassies and sociology departments of British universities]. Upton by Chester, 1970. 1 vol. (unpaged).

BRANDT (WILLY) Peace: writings and speeches of the Nobel Peace Prize winner, 1971. Bonn-Bad Godesberg, 1971. pp. 165.

DISASTER RELIEF

— India — Maharashtra.

SUBRAMANIAN (V.) Parched earth: the Maharashtra drought, 1970-73. Bombay, [1975]. pp. 640.

DISCOURSE ANALYSIS.

SYMPOSIUM ON SUBJECT AND TOPIC, UNIVERSITY OF CALIFORNIA, SANTA BARBARA, 1975. Subject and topic; edited by Charles N. Li. New York, [1976]. pp. 594. *bibliog.*

DISCOVERIES (IN GEOGRAPHY)

— European.

MORISON (SAMUEL ELIOT) The European discovery of America: the southern voyages, A.D. 1492-1616. New York, 1974. pp. 758. *bibliogs.*

DISCRIMINATION.

VEENHOVEN (WILLEM ADRIAAN) and others, eds. Case studies on human rights and fundamental freedoms: a world survey. The Hague, 1975 in progress.

— America.

SYMPOSIUM ON EQUALITY OF OPPORTUNITY IN EMPLOYMENT IN THE AMERICAN REGION, PANAMA, 1973. Equality of opportunity in employment in the American region: problems and policies; report and documents of a regional symposium [held at] Panama, 1-12 October 1973. Geneva, International Labour Office, 1974. pp. 133.

— Canada.

KERR (ROBERT WILLIAM) Legislation against discrimination in Canada; with tables by John Douglas Wallace. [rev. ed.] [Fredericton, New Brunswick Human Rights Commission, 1973?]. pp. 46.

DISCRIMINATION IN EDUCATION

— Law and legislation — United States.

O'NEIL (ROBERT M.) Discriminating against discrimination: preferential admissions and the DeFunis case. Bloomington, [1975]. pp. 271. *bibliog.*

DISCRIMINATION IN EDUCATION (Cont.)

— Rhodesia.

MURPHREE (MARSHALL WARNE) ed. Education, race and employment in Rhodesia. Salisbury, Rhodesia, 1975. pp. 478. *bibliog.*

— United States.

WILLIAMS (ROBERT L.) Educational alternatives for colonized people: models for liberation...; edited by Anne M. St. Pierre. New York, [1974]. pp. 130. *bibliog.*

GLAZER (NATHAN) Affirmative discrimination: ethnic inequality and public policy. New York, [1975]. pp. 248.

DISCRIMINATION IN EMPLOYMENT

— Canada — Manitoba.

MANITOBA. Task Force on Equal Employment Opportunities in the Civil Service of Manitoba. 1974. Report; [D.A. Duncan, chairman]. [Winnipeg], 1974. pp. 82.

— Rhodesia.

MURPHREE (MARSHALL WARNE) ed. Education, race and employment in Rhodesia. Salisbury, Rhodesia, 1975. pp. 478. *bibliog.*

— South Africa.

FOREIGN investment in South Africa: the conditions of the black worker; [by] W.H. Thomas [and others]. [London], 1975. pp. 295. *(Study Project on External Investment in South Africa and Namibia (S.W. Africa). Study Project Papers. [vol. 4])*

— South West Africa.

The ROLE of foreign firms in Namibia: studies on external investment and black workers' conditions in Namibia; [by] Roger Murray [and others]. Uppsala, 1974. pp. 220. *bibliogs.* *(Study Project on External Investment in South Africa and Namibia (S.W. Africa). Study Project Papers. [vol. 3])*

— United Kingdom.

ETHNIC MINORITIES AND EMPLOYMENT; [pd. by] Employment Section, Community Relations Commission. q., D 1975 (no.1)- London.

GRANICK (DAVID) Equality of promotional opportunities in British industry. London, [1975]. pp. 13.

— — Ireland, Northern.

SPJUT (R.J.) The fair Employment (Northern Ireland) Bill: a law to curb religious and political employment in Northern Ireland. London, [1975?]. pp. 19. *(National Council for Civil Liberties. Reports)*

— United States.

FLETCHER (ARTHUR) The silent sell-out: government betrayal of blacks to the craft unions. New York, [1973]. pp. 121.

CARNEGIE COUNCIL ON POLICY STUDIES IN HIGHER EDUCATION. Making affirmative action work in higher education: an analysis of institutional and federal policies with recommendations. San Francisco, 1975. pp. 272. *bibliog.*

GLAZER (NATHAN) Affirmative discrimination: ethnic inequality and public policy. New York, [1975]. pp. 248.

DISCRIMINATION IN HOUSING

— United Kingdom — London.

RUNNYMEDE TRUST. Race and council housing in London: census returns examined by the Runnymede Trust research staff. London, 1975. fo.11. *bibliog.*

LONDON. Greater London Council. Housing Management Committee. Race and council housing: preliminary report of the GLC housing lettings survey; (report by Director of Housing Management and Maintenance). [London], 1976. pp. 15.

— United States — Missouri.

KAIN (JOHN FORREST) and QUIGLEY (JOHN M.) Housing markets and racial discrimination: a microeconomic analysis. New York, 1975. pp. 393. *bibliog.* *(National Bureau of Economic Research. Urban and Regional Studies. 3)*

DISSENTERS

— Netherlands.

DUYN (ROEL VAN) ed. Het beste uit Provo: een bloemlezing uit alle verschenen nummers van het tijdschrift Provo. [Amsterdam, 1967]. pp. 257.

— Russia.

GLAZOV (IURII) Tesnye vrata: vozrozhdenie russkoi intelligentsii; Narrow gates: revival of the Russian intelligentsia. London, 1973. pp. 263.

KIRK (IRINA) Profiles in Russian resistance. New York, [1975]. pp. 299.

MOROZ (VALENTYN IAKOVYCH) Eseï, lysty i dokumenty; essays, letters and documents. Miunkhen, 1975. pp. 288. *bibliog.*

GRIGORENKO (PETR GRIGOR'EVICH) The Grigorenko papers: writings by General P.G. Grigorenko and documents on his case. London, [1976]. pp. 187.

— — Ukraine.

UKRAÏNS'KA inteligentsiia pid sudom KGB: materiialy z protsesiv V. Chornovola, M. Masiutka, M. Ozernoho ta in.; Ukrainian intellectuals tried by the KGB. [Miunkhen], 1970. pp. 243.

DISSENTERS, RELIGIOUS

— United Kingdom — Wales.

REES (D. BEN) Chapels in the valley: a study in the sociology of Welsh nonconformity. Upton, Wirral, [1975]. pp. 222. *bibliog.*

— United States.

GAUSTAD (EDWIN SCOTT) Dissent in American religion. Chicago, 1973. pp. 184. *bibliog.*

DISSERTATIONS, ACADEMIC

— Bibliography.

XEROX UNIVERSITY MICROFILMS. Comprehensive dissertation index, 1861-1972. Ann Arbor, 1973. 5 vols. Library has vols. 17. Social sciences. 25-26. Business and economics. 27. Law and political science. 28. History.

— United Kingdom — Bibliography.

BILBOUL (ROGER R.) ed. Retrospective index to theses of Great Britain and Ireland, 1716-1950. vol.1. Social sciences and humanities. Santa Barbara, [1975]. pp. 393.

— — Wales — Bibliography.

WALES. University. University College of Swansea. Library. University College of Swansea higher degree theses, 1920-1970: supplement no. 4, 1974. [Swansea, 1974]. fo. 8,2.

DISTANCE GEOMETRY.

BILLINGSLEY (PATRICK) Convergence of probability measures. New York, Wiley, [1968]. pp. xiii, 253. *bibliog.*

DISTRIBUTION (ECONOMIC THEORY).

MERKWITZ (JUERGEN) Stationäre Güterverteilungen. Meisenheim am Glan, [1973]. pp. 85. *bibliog.*

DIVERSIFICATION IN INDUSTRY

— United Kingdom.

GORECKI (PAUL KAROL) Enterprise diversification in the manufacturing sector of the United Kingdom, 1958-1963. 1974. fo. 187. *bibliog.* Typescript. Ph.D. (London) thesis: unpublished. *This thesis is the property of London University and may not be removed from the Library.*

— United States.

CONROY (MICHAEL E.) Regional economic growth: diversification and control. New York, 1975. pp. 163. *bibliog.*

DIVIDENDS

— India.

NIGAM (RAJ KUMAR) and JOSHI (N.D.) Corporate dividend trends during the period of industrial growth and planned economic development in India, 1947-57. [Delhi, Manager of Publications, 1962]. pp. 116.

— United Kingdom — Taxation.

WHITTINGTON (GEOFFREY) Company taxation and dividends. London, [1974]. 1 pamphlet (unpaged). *bibliog.* *(Institute for Fiscal Studies. Lecture Series. No.1)*

DIVISION OF LABOUR.

FREYSSENET (MICHEL) Schéma général d'aménagement de la France: qualification du travail: tendances et mise en question. Paris, 1975. pp. 195. *bibliog.* *(France. Délégation à l'Aménagement du Territoire et à l'Action Régionale. Travaux et Recherches de Prospective. 57)*

MAIGNIEN (YANNICK) La division du travail manuel et intellectuel, et sa suppression dans le passage au communisme chez Marx et ses successeurs. Paris, 1975. pp. 130. *bibliog.*

GORZ (ANDRE) ed. The division of labour: the labour process and class-struggle in modern capitalism. Hassocks, Sussex, 1976. pp. 189.

DIVORCE

— France.

Le DIVORCE et les Français. II. L'expérience des divorcés; [by] Louis Roussel [and others]. [Paris,], 1975. pp. 256. *(France. Institut National d'Etudes Démographiques. Travaux et Documents. Cahiers. No. 72)*

FRANCE. Délégation Générale à l'Information. 1975. La réforme du divorce. [Paris, 1975. pp. 32. *(Dossiers de Travail sur les Grands Projets de Loi)*

— Italy.

PALLADINO (ALFONSO) and PALLADINO (VINCENZO) Il divorzio: commento teorico-pratico alla legge sulla disciplina dei casi di scioglimento del matrimonio, legge 1 dicembre 1970, n. 898. 2nd ed. Milano, 1975. pp. 512. *bibliog.*

— New Zealand.

NEW ZEALAND. Property Law and Equity Reform Committee. 1974. Report...on the effect of divorce on testate succession; [C.P. Hutchinson, chairman]. [Wellington, 1974]. pp. 11,2.

— Norway.

NORWAY. Statistiske Centralbyrå. 1975. Skilsmisser, 1971-1973, etc. Oslo, 1975. pp. 59. *(Statistiske Analyser. 16) With English summary.*

— United Kingdom.

RAYDEN (WILLIAM) Law and practice in divorce and family matters in all courts; twelfth edition [by] Joseph Jackson [and others]; (with Supplement). London, 1974. 2 vols.

— **United States.**

HARDY (RICHARD E.) and CULL (JOHN G.) Creative divorce through social and psychological approaches. Springfield, Ill., [1974]. pp. 175. *bibliogs.*

CARTER (HUGH SEIVER) and GLICK (PAUL CHARLES) Marriage and divorce: a social and economic study. rev. ed. Cambridge, Mass., 1976. pp. 508. *(American Public Health Association. Vital and Health Statistics Monographs)*

DIVORCEES.

HART (NICKY) When marriage ends: a study in status passage. London, 1976. pp. 277. *bibliog.*

DOBRACZYNSKI (JAN).

DOBRACZYŃSKI (JAN) Tylko w jednym 'zyciu. [Warszawa], 1970. pp. 431.

DOCK WORKERS

— **United Kingdom.**

AIMS FOR FREEDOM AND ENTERPRISE. The threat to our lifeline. London, [1975]. pp. 10.

CRONJÉ (GILLIAN) Middle class opinion and the 1889 dock strike: a critique of Outcast London. London, 1975. pp. 24. *(Communist Party of Great Britain. History Group. Our History. No. 61)*

BATE (STUART PAUL) Workers' participation in industrial rule-making processes: a theoretical analysis and empirical investigation of a sample of employees in the Port of London. 1976. fo. 430. *bibliog. Typescript. Ph.D. (London) thesis: unpublished. This thesis is the property of London University and may not be removed from the Library.*

HILL (STEPHEN RODERICK) The dockers: class and tradition in London. London, 1976. pp. 252.

— **United States.**

MOREWEDGE (HOSSEINE) The economics of casual labor: a study of the longshore industry. Berne, 1970. pp. 167. *bibliog.*

DOCKS

— **United Kingdom — Bibliography.**

SKINNER (IAN) compiler. Docklands. London, 1976. pp. 39. *(London. Greater London Council. Research Library. Research Bibliographies. No. 73)*

DOERING (WOLFGANG).

DORN (WOLFRAM) and WIEDNER (WOLFGANG) Der Freiheit gehört die Zukunft: Wolfgang Döring; eine politische Biographie. Bonn, [1974]. pp. 265.

DOHERTY (JOHN).

KIRBY (RAY G.) and MUSSON (ALBERT EDWARD) The voice of the people: John Doherty, 1798-1854, trade unionist, radical and factory reformer. Manchester, [1975]. pp. 474.

DOLLAR.

FOUCOU (PHILIPPE) La prééminence du dollar dans le système monétaire international. [Paris, 1974]. pp. 200. *bibliog. With summaries in various languages.*

DOMESTIC ECONOMY.

NERLOVE (MARC) Economic growth and population: perspectives of the "new home economics". New York, 1974. pp. 11. *bibliog. (Agricultural Development Council. Reprints)*

OAKLEY (ANN) The sociology of housework. [London, 1974]. pp. 242.

— **Accounting.**

INTERNATIONAL LABOUR OFFICE. Household Income and Expenditure Statistics. No. 1. 1950-1964. Geneva, 1967. fo. 290.

— **Africa — Accounting.**

INTERNATIONAL LABOUR OFFICE. Household Income and Expenditure Statistics. No. 2. 1960-1972: Africa, Asia, Latin America. Geneva, 1974. fo. 223. *bibliog.*

— **America, Latin — Accounting.**

INTERNATIONAL LABOUR OFFICE. Household Income and Expenditure Statistics. No. 2. 1960-1972: Africa, Asia, Latin America. Geneva, 1974. fo. 223. *bibliog.*

— **Asia — Accounting.**

INTERNATIONAL LABOUR OFFICE. Household Income and Expenditure Statistics. No. 2. 1960-1972: Africa, Asia, Latin America. Geneva, 1974. fo. 223. *bibliog.*

— **Hungary — Accounting.**

HUNGARY. Központi Statisztikai Hivatal. 1962. A családok kulturális kiadásai. Budapest, 1962. pp. 93.

— **Italy.**

COMITATO PER IL SALARIO AL LAVORO DOMESTICO DI PADOVA. Le operaie della casa; a cura del Collettivo Internazionale Femminista. Venezia, 1975. pp. 78. *(Collettivo Internazionale Femminista. Salario al Lavoro Domestico: Strategia Internazionale.1)*

— **Norway.**

NORWAY. Statistiske Centralbyrå. 1975. Tid nyttet til egenarbeid, etc. Oslo, 1975. pp. 77. *(Statistiske Analyser. 19) With English summary.*

— **Russia — Accounting.**

ANDREEV (ALEKSEI KUZ'MIN) Balans denezhnykh dokhodov i raskhodov naseleniia: na primere Kazakhskoi SSR. Moskva, 1975. pp. 111.

— **United States — Accounting.**

NATIONAL BUREAU OF ECONOMIC RESEARCH. Conference on Research in Income and Wealth. Studies in Income and Wealth. vol. 40. Household production and consumption: [papers presented in 1973]; Nestor E. Terleckyj, editor. New York, 1975. pp. 669. *bibliogs.*

DOMESTIC EDUCATION

— **France.**

MARQUART (FRANÇOIS) and others. L'action sociale et l'économie sociale familiale. [Paris], 1974. pp. 302. *bibliog. (Caisse Nationale des Allocations Familiales. Etudes. [17])*

DOMESTIC RELATIONS.

EUROPEAN COMMISSION OF HUMAN RIGHTS. 1972. Family life. Strasbourg, 1972. pp. 43. *(Case-Law Topics. 2).*

SYMPOSIUM ON LAW AND POPULATION, TUNIS, 1974. Text of recommendations. Medford, Mass., 1974. pp. 49. *(Tufts University. Fletcher School of Law and Diplomacy. Law and Population Monograph Series. No. 20)*

The CHILD and the law: the proceedings of the first World Conference of the International Society on Family Law, held in Berlin, April 1975; edited by Frank Bates. Dobbs Ferry, N.Y., 1976. 2 vols.

— **Canada — Ontario.**

ONTARIO. Law Reform Commission. 1969- . Report on family law: [H. Allan Leal, chairman]. [Toronto], 1969 in progress.

— **Italy.**

BIN (M.) ed. La riforma del diritto di famiglia. Torino, [1975]. pp. 143. *(Turin. Università. Materiali Integrativi per lo Studio del Diritto di Famiglia. 1a Serie. 2)*

CARDIA (CARLO) Il diritto di famiglia in Italia. Roma, 1975. pp. 379.

ITALY. Statutes, etc. 1942-1975. Il nuovo codice della famiglia...: vecchie e nuove norme a confronto;...a cura di Giuseppe Branca [and others]. Roma, [1975]. pp. 221.

— **Lesotho.**

POULTER (SEBASTIAN) Family law and litigation in Basotho society. Oxford, 1976. pp. 361. *bibliog.*

— **Poland.**

POLAND. Statutes, etc. 1964. Kodeks rodzinny i opiekuńczy. Warszawa, 1964. pp. 52.

— **Russia — Estonia.**

ANAN'EVA (ZH.) and SALUMAA (E.) Kodeks Estonskoi SSR o brake i sem'e: kommentirovannoe izdanie. Tallin, 1974. pp. 293.

— — **Russia (RSFSR).**

SHAKHMATOV (VLADIMIR PANTELEIMONOVICH) and KHASKEL'BERG (BORIS LAZAREVICH) Novyi Kodeks o brake i sem'e RSFSR. Tomsk, 1970. pp. 324.

— **United Kingdom.**

RAYDEN (WILLIAM) Law and practice in divorce and family matters in all courts; twelfth edition [by] Joseph Jackson [and others]; (with Supplement). London, 1974. 2 vols.

BROMLEY (PETER MANN) Family law. 5th ed. London, 1976. pp. 683.

CRETNEY (STEPHEN MICHAEL) Principles of family law. 2nd ed. London, 1976. pp. 474.

SEAGO (PETER) and BISSETT-JOHNSON (ALASTAIR) Cases and materials on family law. London, 1976. pp. 500.

SWEET AND MAXWELL, LIMITED. Family law statutes; second edition edited by Sweet and Maxwell's legal editorial staff with Jennifer Terry: advisory editor Olive M. Stone. London, 1976. pp. 629.

DOMINICA

— **Parliament — Elections.**

DOMINICA. 1975. Result of the 1975 election held on 24th March, 1975. [Roseau, 1975?]. pp. 3.

— — **Rules and practice.**

PIERRE (MARIE DAVIS) House of Assembly, Dominica: procedure and working methods. [Roseau], 1975. pp. 208,xxviii.

DOMINICAN REPUBLIC

— **Economic history.**

TEJERA (EDUARDO J.) Una decada de desarrollo economico dominicano, 1963-1972: (cuatro ensayos). Santo Domingo, 1975. pp. 243.

— **Emigration and immigration.**

HENDRICKS (GLENN) The Dominican diaspora: from the Dominican Republic to New York City; villagers in transition. New York, [1974]. pp. 171. *bibliog.*

— **History.**

CLAUSNER (MARLIN D.) Rural Santo Domingo: settled, unsettled, and resettled. Philadelphia, 1973. pp. 323. *bibliog.*

— **Politics and government.**

[PARTIDO COMUNISTA DOMINICANO] Triunfaremos: la lucha revolucionaria en la Republica Dominicana, año 1965. Praga, 1966. pp. 64.

DOMINICAN REPUBLIC(Cont.)

— Population.

ANTONINI (GUSTAVO A.) and others. Population and energy: a systems analysis of resource utilization in the Dominican Republic. Gainesville, Fla., 1975. pp. 166. *bibliog.* (Florida University. School of Inter-American Studies. Latin American Monographs. 2nd Series. No.14) With 8 maps in separate case.

— Rural conditions.

CLAUSNER (MARLIN D.) Rural Santo Domingo: settled, unsettled, and resettled. Philadelphia, 1973. pp. 323. *bibliog.*

DOMINICANS (DOMINICAN REPUBLIC) IN THE UNITED STATES.

HENDRICKS (GLENN) The Dominican diaspora: from the Dominican Republic to New York City; villagers in transition. New York, [1974]. pp. 171. *bibliog.*

DOMINICANS IN SILESIA.

KŁOCZOWSKI (JERZY) Dominikanie polscy na Śląsku w XIII-XIV wieku. Lublin, 1956. pp. 356. *bibliog.* (Lublin. Katolicki Uniwersytet Lubelski. Towarzystwo Naukowe. Wydział Historyczno-Filologiczny. Rozprawy. 17) With French summary.

DONCASTER

— Economic conditions.

SOUTH YORKSHIRE. County Council. Doncaster district structure plan: report of survey. [Doncaster, afterwards Barnsley], 1973-5. 9 parts (in 2 vols.).

— Hospitals.

SWANN (GARRY) The Doncaster Royal Infirmary, 1792-1972. Doncaster, [1973]. pp. 172. *bibliog.*

— Social conditions.

SOUTH YORKSHIRE. County Council. Doncaster district structure plan: report of survey. [Doncaster, afterwards Barnsley], 1973-5. 9 parts (in 2 vols.).

DÖRING.

See DOERING.

DORR (THOMAS WILSON).

DENNISON (GEORGE M.) The Dorr War: Republicanism on trial, 1831-1861. Lexington, Ky., [1967]. pp. 250. *bibliog.*

DOUGLAS (THOMAS CLEMENT).

SHACKLETON (DORIS FRENCH) Tommy Douglas. Toronto, [1975] repr. 1976. pp. 333.

DREES (WILLEM).

DREES (WILLEM) Het Nederlandse Parlement: vroeger en nu. Naarden, 1975. pp. 319.

DRINKING AND ROAD ACCIDENTS

— Canada.

CANADA. Road Safety Branch. 1973. The Edmonton study: a pilot project to measure the effectiveness of community public information programs in changing knowledge, attitude and behaviour in relation to driving and the use of beverage alcohols. Ottawa, 1973. pp. 60.

— United Kingdom.

CHRISTIAN ECONOMIC AND SOCIAL RESEARCH FOUNDATION. Occasional Papers. Series C, No.1. Recidivism among drunken motorists, England and Wales, 1964 to 1973. London, 1975. pp. 29.

DRINKING CUSTOMS

— Rhodesia.

MAY (JOAN) Drinking in a Rhodesian African township. Salisbury, Rhodesia, 1973. pp. 94. (University of Rhodesia. Department of Sociology. Occasional Papers. No.8)

— United States.

CAHALAN (DON) and others. American drinking practices: a national study of drinking behavior and attitudes. New Brunswick, N.J., [1969]. pp. 260. *bibliog.* (Rutgers University. Rutgers Center of Alcohol Studies. Monographs. No.6)

DRINKING WATER

— Canada — Standards.

JOINT COMMITTEE ON DRINKING WATER STANDARDS [CANADA]. Canadian drinking water standards and objectives, 1968; [W.M. Walkinshaw, chairman]. Ottawa, Queen's Printer, 1969. pp. 39.

DRÔME (DEPARTMENT).

FRANCE. Direction de la Documentation. La Documentation Française. Notes et Etudes Documentaires. Nos. 4,192-4, 193-4,194. Les départements français. 26. Drôme, Rhône-Alpes; [étude...redigée par Jacques Lambert]. Paris, 1975. pp. 99.

DROPOUTS.

For related headings see COLLEGE DROPOUTS.

DROUGHTS

— Africa, North.

FOUGEYROLLAS (PIERRE) Le défi de la sécheresse et la lutte des classes en Afrique sahelo-soudanienne. Dakar, African Institute for Economic Development and Planning, 1974. fo. 16.

— Africa, Subsaharan.

COPANS (JEAN) ed. Sécheresses et famines du Sahel...; par Yves Albouy [and others]. Paris, 1975. 2 vols (in 1). *(Paris. Ecole des Hautes Etudes en Sciences Sociales. Centre d'Etudes Africaines. Dossiers Africains)*

The POLITICS of natural disaster: the case of the Sahel drought; edited by Michael H. Glantz. New York, 1976. pp. 336. *bibliogs.*

— Australia.

AUSTRALIA. Bureau of Agricultural Economics. 1969. An economic survey of drought affected pastoral properties, New South Wales and Queensland, 1964-65 to 1965-66; (by E.S. Malikides and others). Canberra, 1969. pp. 51. *(Wool Economic Research Reports. No. 15)*

— India — Maharashtra.

SUBRAMANIAN (V.) Parched earth: the Maharashtra drought, 1970-73. Bombay, [1975]. pp. 640.

— Sahel.

FRANCE. Direction de la Documentation. La Documentation Française. Notes et Etudes Documentaires. Nos. 4,216-4, 217. La sécheresse en zone sahélienne: causes, conséquences, études des mesures à prendre. Paris, 1975. pp. 75. *bibliog.*

— Upper Volta.

WASUNGU (PASCAL) Enquête sur les effets de la sécheresse et les mouvements de population en Haute-Volta, 16 février - 30 mars 1974: rapport, 2 avril 1974. Abidjan, United Nations, 1974. 1 vol. (various pagings).

DRUG ABUSE.

CHADEFAUX (MARIE-JOËLLE) ed. Points de vue sur la drogue: extraits de textes. [Paris], 1974. pp. 454. *bibliog.*

KAPLAN (EUGENE H.) and WIEDER (HERBERT) Drugs don't take people, people take drugs. Secaucus, N.J., [1974]. pp. 201. *bibliog.*

ZINBERG (NORMAN E.) and others. Teaching social change: a group approach. Baltimore, Ma., [1976]. pp. 252. *bibliog.*

— Treatment — Evaluation.

PROGRAM evaluation: alcohol, drug abuse, and mental health services; edited by Jack Zusman [and] Cecil R. Wurster. Lexington, Mass., [1975]. pp. 278. *Based on papers presented at a Conference sponsored by the Alcohol, Drug Abuse and Mental Health Administration held in Washington in 1974.*

— France.

CHADEFAUX (MARIE-JOËLLE) ed. Points de vue sur la drogue: extraits de textes. [Paris], 1974. pp. 454. *bibliog.*

— United Kingdom.

SOCIAL MORALITY COUNCIL. Study Group on Education and Drug Dependence. Education and drug dependence. London, 1975. pp. 78.

DRUGS and drug dependence; edited by Griffith Edwards [and others] on behalf of the Addiction Research Unit, Institute of Psychiatry, University of London. Farnborough, Hants., [1976]. pp. 252. *bibliog.*

— United States — Personal narratives.

KIEV (ARI) The drug epidemic. New York, [1975]. pp. 227.

DRUG ABUSE AND CRIME

— United States.

KIEV (ARI) The drug epidemic. New York, [1975]. pp. 227.

DRUG TRADE (PHARMACEUTICAL)

— France.

FRANCE. Direction de la Documentation. La Documentation Française. Notes et Etudes Documentaires. Nos. 4,195-4, 196. Le médicament et l'assurance-maladie; [by] (J.-C. Sournia et Mme. Arsac). Paris, 1975. pp. 88. *bibliog.*

— Italy.

ATOR CONSULENZA AZIENDALE. Studio sull'evoluzione della concentrazione in alcuni settori dell'industria chimica in Italia: farmaceutico...; fotografico...; prodotti di manutenzione, etc. [Brussels, European Communities, Directorate-General for Competition, 1973]. 1 vol. (various pagings).

— Netherlands.

AMSTERDAM. Universiteit. Stichting voor Economisch Onderzoek. Studie betreffende de ontwikkeling van de concentratie in enkele bedrijfstakken in de chemische industrie in Nederland: farmaceutische industrie...fotochemische industrie... onderhoudsmiddelen, etc; [by H.W. de Jong and A.H. Smolders] . [Brussels, European Communities, Directorate-General for Competition, 1973]. 1 vol. (various pagings).

— United Kingdom.

LABOUR PARTY. The pharmaceutical industry. London, 1976. pp. 60.

— United States.

WARDELL (WILLIAM M.) and LASAGNA (LOUIS) Regulation and drug development. Washington, D.C., 1975. pp. 181. *(American Enterprise Institute for Public Policy Research. Evaluative Studies. 21)*

DRUGS.

WARBURTON (DAVID M.) Brain, behaviour and drugs: introduction to the neurochemistry of behaviour. London, [1975]. pp. 280. *bibliog.*

— Laws and legislation.

TEFF (HARVEY) and MUNRO (COLIN R.) Thalidomide: the legal aftermath. Farnborough, [1976]. pp. 154.

— — United States.

AMERICAN CIVIL LIBERTIES UNION. Marijuana. New York, [1973?]. pp. 15.

WARDELL (WILLIAM M.) and LASAGNA (LOUIS) Regulation and drug development. Washington, D.C., 1975. pp. 181. (*American Enterprise Institute for Public Policy Research. Evaluative Studies. 21*)

DRUGS AND MINORITIES

— United States.

HELMER (JOHN) Drugs and minority oppression. New York, [1975]. pp. 192.

DRUGS AND YOUTH.

HARDY (RICHARD E.) and CULL (JOHN G.) eds. Problems of adolescents: social and psychological approaches. Springfield, Ill., [1974]. pp. 278. *bibliogs.*

DRUZHININ (NIKOLAI MIKHAILOVICH).

IZ istorii ekonomicheskoi i obshchestvennoi zhizni Rossii: sbornik statei k 90-letiiu akademika Nikolaia Mikhailovicha Druzhinina. Moskva, 1976. pp. 288.

DU BOIS (WILLIAM EDWARD BURGHARDT).

DU BOIS (WILLIAM EDWARD BURGHARDT) The correspondence of W.E.B. Du Bois...;edited by Herbert Aptheker. Amherst, Mass., 1973 in progress.

DUDLEY (JOHN) 1st Duke of Northumberland.

BEER (BARRETT L.) Northumberland: the political career of John Dudley, Earl of Warwick and Duke of Northumberland. [Kent, Ohio, 1973]. pp. 235. *bibliog.*

DUHEM (PIERRE).

HARDING (SANDRA G.) ed. Can theories be refuted?: essays on the Duhem-Quine thesis. Dordrecht, [1976]. pp. 318. *bibliogs. Reprinted from various sources.*

DUMPING (COMMERCIAL POLICY).

CANADA. Anti-Dumping Tribunal. Annual report. a., 1975 (7th)- Ottawa.

DU PONT FAMILY.

ZILG (GERARD COLBY) Du Pont: behind the nylon curtain. Englewood Cliffs, [1974]. pp. 623.

DUPUY (FERNAND).

DUPUY (FERNAND) Etre maire communiste. [Paris, 1975]. pp. 254.

DURBAN

— Civic improvement.

NATAL. Town and Regional Planning Commission. Natal Town and Regional Planning Reports. Vol. 28. Metropolitan Durban: draft guide plan. Pietermaritzburg, 1974. pp. 93.

— Economic conditions.

DU TOIT (A.S.) and MAHARAJ (M.D.) Socio-economic study of Chatsworth. Durban, 1973. fo. 34. *bibliog.* (*Chatsworth Community and Research Centre. Research Reports. No.2*)

— Social conditions.

DU TOIT (A.S.) and MAHARAJ (M.D.) Socio-economic study of Chatsworth. Durban, 1973. fo. 34. *bibliog.* (*Chatsworth Community and Research Centre. Research Reports. No.2*)

DURHAM (CITY)

— Description.

POCOCK (DOUGLAS CHARLES DAVID) Durham: images of a cathedral city. Durham, 1975. pp. 80. *bibliog.* (*Durham. University. Department of Geography. Occasional Publications (New Series). No.6*)

DURHAM (COUNTY)

— Biography.

HUNT (CHRISTOPHER JOHN) The book trade in Northumberland and Durham to 1860: a biographical dictionary of printers, engravers, lithographers, booksellers, stationers, publishers, mapsellers, printsellers, musicsellers, bookbinders, newsagents and owners of circulating libraries. Newcastle, 1975. pp. 116.

DURKHEIM (EMILE).

NISBET (ROBERT ALEXANDER) The sociology of Emile Durkheim. London, 1975. pp. 293.

POPE (WHITNEY) Durkheim's Suicide: a classic analyzed. Chicago, 1976. pp. 229. *bibliog.*

DUTCH IN THE UNITED STATES.

DE JONG (GERALD FRANCIS) The Dutch in America, 1609-1974. Boston, Mass., [1975]. pp. 326. *bibliog.*

DUTTWEILER (GOTTLIEB).

RIESS (CURT) 1902- . Gottlieb Duttweiler: eine Biographie. Zürich, [1958]. pp. 469.

DUVAL (CLEMENT).

DUVAL (CLEMENT) Anarchist. Memorie autobiografiche. Newark, N.J., 1929. pp. 1047.

DWELLINGS

— United Kingdom — Maintenance and repair.

CLEMENT-EVANS AND WILKINSON. The tenants' brief for the improvement of Bevington and Summer Seat: (appendix to item 3: architect's report on proposed Bevington-Summer Seat rehabilitation). [Liverpool, Vauxhall Project Committee, 1973]. fo.11.

STUDY GROUP ON PROGRAMMES OF SOCIAL OWNERSHIP AND RENOVATION OF COUNCIL DWELLINGS. First report; [Reg Freeson, chairman]. [London, Department of the Environment, 1976]. 1 pamphlet (various pagings).

WILSON (HUGH) AND WOMERSLEY (LEWIS) Firm. Inner area study: Liverpool: housing maintenance project. [London], Department of the Environment, [1976]. pp. 32.

— United States — Maintenance and repair.

HUGHES (JAMES W.) and BLEAKLY (KENNETH D.) Urban homesteading. New Brunswick, N.J., [1975]. pp. 276. *bibliog.*

— — Mathematical models.

JAMES (FRANKLIN J.) ed. Models of employment and residence location. New Brunswick, N.J., [1974]. pp. 339. (*Rutgers University. Center for Urban Policy Research. Survey Series*)

DWORKIN (EUZEBIUSZ).

DWORKIN (EUZEBIUSZ) Od Manzanares do Oki: wspomnienia dąbrowszczaka. Warszawa, 1974. pp. 119.

DYE INDUSTRY

— India.

INDIA. Tariff Commission. Dye-intermediates. Report on the continuance of protection to the dye-intermediates industry. Delhi, 1973. pp. 286.

EAST (FAR EAST)

— Foreign relations.

BURNS (RICHARD DEAN) and BENNETT (EDWARD MOORE) eds. Diplomats in crisis: United States-Chinese-Japanese relations, 1919-1941. Santa Barbara, Ca., [1974]. pp. 346.

EAST (NEAR EAST)

— Bibliography.

ATIYEH (GEORGE NICHOLAS) compiler. The contemporary Middle East, 1948-1973: a selective and annotated bibliography. Boston, Mass., [1975]. pp. 664.

— Defences.

PRANGER (ROBERT JOHN) and TAHTINEN (DALE R.) Nuclear threat in the Middle East. Washington, 1975. pp. 57. (*American Enterprise Institute for Public Policy Research. Foreign Affairs Studies. 23*)

— Description and travel.

BRODZKI (STANISŁAW) Księga wielu dżungli. Warszawa, 1953. pp. 232.

— Economic conditions.

BECKER (ABRAHAM S.) and others. The economics and politics of the Middle East. New York, [1975] repr. 1976. pp. 131. (*Rand Corporation and Resources for the Future, Inc. The Middle East: Economic and Political Problems and Prospects*)

HENLEY CENTRE FOR FORECASTING. Middle east economic prospects: forecasts to 1985. London, [1975]. pp. 274.

The MIDDLE East: oil, politics, and development; edited by John Duke Anthony. Washington, [1975]. pp. 109. *Proceedings of a conference held at the University of Toronto in 1974, sponsored by the Middle East Studies Committee of the International Studies Programme, University of Toronto, and the Canadian Institute of International Affairs.*

— Economic history.

DREVNII Vostok: goroda i torgovlia, III-I tys. do n.e. Erevan, 1973. pp. 243. *With English summaries.*

— Economic policy.

The MIDDLE East: oil, politics, and development; edited by John Duke Anthony. Washington, [1975]. pp. 109. *Proceedings of a conference held at the University of Toronto in 1974, sponsored by the Middle East Studies Committee of the International Studies Programme, University of Toronto, and the Canadian Institute of International Affairs.*

— Foreign relations.

HUREWITZ (JACOB COLEMAN) ed. The Middle East and North Africa in world politics: a documentary record. 2nd ed. New Haven, 1975 in progress.

BECKER (ABRAHAM S.) and others. The economics and politics of the Middle East. New York, [1975] repr. 1976. pp. 131. (*Rand Corporation and Resources for the Future, Inc. The Middle East: Economic and Political Problems and Prospects*)

— — Russia.

CARRERE D'ENCAUSSE (HELENE) La politique soviétique au Moyen-Orient, 1955-1975. Paris, [1975]. pp. 328. (*Fondation Nationale des Sciences Politiques. Cahiers. 200*)

FREEDMAN (ROBERT OWEN) Soviet policy toward the Middle East since 1970. New York, 1975. pp. 198. *bibliog.*

GEORGIEV (VLADIMIR ANATOL'EVICH) Vneshniaia politika Rossii na Blizhnem Vostoke v kontse 30 - nachale 40-kh godov XIX v. Moskva, 1975. pp. 200. *bibliog.*

GLASSMAN (JON D.) Arms for the Arabs: the Soviet Union and war in the Middle East. Baltimore, [1975]. pp. 243. *bibliog.*

EAST (NEAR EAST)(Cont.)

— — United Kingdom.

KEDOURIE (ELIE) In the Anglo-Arab labyrinth: the McMahon-Husayn correspondence and its interpretations, 1914-1939. Cambridge, 1976. pp. 330. *bibliog.*

— — United States.

CONGRESSIONAL QUARTERLY INC. The Middle East: U.S. policy, Israel, oil and the Arabs. Washington, 1974. pp. 100. *bibliog.*

ALROY (GIL CARL) The Kissinger experience: American policy in the Middle East. New York, [1975]. pp. 189.

PRANGER (ROBERT JOHN) and TAHTINEN (DALE R.) Nuclear threat in the Middle East. Washington, 1975. pp. 57. *(American Enterprise Institute for Public Policy Research. Foreign Affairs Studies. 23)*

— History.

ASHTOR (ELIYAHU) A social and economic history of the Near East in the middle ages. London, 1976. pp. 384.

— Nationalism — Bibliography.

CLEMENTS (FRANK) compiler. The emergence of Arab nationalism: from the nineteenth century to 1921; [a bibliography]. London, 1976. pp. 290.

— Politics and government.

LIEBMAN (SEYMOUR B.) The Middle East: a return to facts. [New York, 1974]. pp. 148.

BECKER (ABRAHAM S.) and others. The economics and politics of the Middle East. New York, [1975] repr. 1976. pp. 131. *(Rand Corporation and Resources for the Future, Inc. The Middle East: Economic and Political Problems and Prospects)*

BEN-MEIR (ALON) The Middle East: imperatives and choices. Mount Vernon, N.Y., [1975]. pp. 221.

HASSOUNA (HUSSEIN A.) The League of Arab States and regional disputes: a study of middle east conflicts. Dobbs Ferry, N.Y., 1975. pp. 512. *bibliog.*

LENCZOWSKI (GEORGE) ed. Political elites in the Middle East. Washington, 1975. pp. 227. *(American Enterprise Institute for Public Policy Research. Foreign Affairs Studies. 19)*

The MIDDLE East: oil, politics, and development; edited by John Duke Anthony. Washington, [1975]. pp. 109. *Proceedings of a conference held at the University of Toronto in 1974, sponsored by the Middle East Studies Committee of the International Studies Programme, University of Toronto, and the Canadian Institute of International Affairs.*

TACHAU (FRANK) ed. Political elites and political development in the Middle East. New York, [1975]. pp. 310. *bibliogs.*

— — Dictionaries and encyclopaedias.

SHIMONI (YAACOV) and LEVINE (EVYATAR A.) eds. Political dictionary of the Middle East in the 20th century. rev. ed. New York, 1974. pp. 510.

EAST AFRICAN COMMUNITY.

HAMMOND (ROBERT C.) Fiscal harmonization in the East African Community. Amsterdam, 1975. pp. 134. *bibliog. (International Bureau of Fiscal Documentation. Series on International Fiscal Harmonization. No. 2)*

HAZLEWOOD (ARTHUR DENNIS) Economic integration: the east African experience. London, 1975. pp. 180.

EAST ANGLIA.

U.K. Central Office of Information. Reference Division. Reference Pamphlets. 142. The English regions: East Anglia. London, 1976. pp. 46. *bibliog.*

— Economic policy.

LABOUR PARTY. Eastern Regional Council. Look East: a prospect for the eastern region; report of a working party set up by the...council. [Ipswich], 1976. pp. 24.

U.K. Department of the Environment. 1976. East Anglia regional strategy: government response to Strategic choice for East Anglia. [London], 1976. pp. 14.

— Industries.

LEMON (ANTHONY) Postwar industrial growth in East Anglian small towns: a study of migrant firms, 1945-1970. Oxford, 1975. pp. 40. *bibliog. (Oxford. University. School of Geography. Research Papers. No. 12)*

— Social policy.

LABOUR PARTY. Eastern Regional Council. Look East: a prospect for the eastern region; report of a working party set up by the...council. [Ipswich], 1976. pp. 24.

U.K. Department of the Environment. 1976. East Anglia regional strategy: government response to Strategic choice for East Anglia. [London], 1976. pp. 14.

EAST GHOR CANAL PROJECT.

HAZELTON (JARED E.) The impact of the East Ghor canal project on land consolidation, distribution and tenure. Amman, 1974. fo. 49. *(Royal Scientific Society [Jordan]. Economic Research Department. Jordan Economic Studies. 04-06)*

EAST INDIANS IN COMMONWEALTH COUNTRIES.

TINKER (HUGH) Separate and unequal: India and the Indians in the British Commonwealth, 1920-1950. London, [1976]. pp. 460. *bibliog.*

EAST INDIANS IN NATAL.

RIP (COLIN M.) and others. Socio-economic position of aged Indians in Natal. Pretoria, 1974. pp. 32. *bibliog. (Human Sciences Research Council [South Africa]. Institute for Sociological, Demographic and Criminological Research. Research Findings. No. S-N-45)*

EAST INDIANS IN THE UNITED KINGDOM.

COUPER (KRISTEN) and LAKHANI (HIMAT) The unemployed, homeless and destitute: a report on the situation of British Asians in Uganda, April 1970: second report. London, 1971. fo. 9.

OXFORD (ALEC) Implications of youth work in Asian community: report of a conference organised by the National Association of Indian Youth,...Birmingham...1973. [Leicester], 1973. pp. 49. *(Youth Service Information Centre. Occasional Papers.7)*

CRISHNA (SEETHA) Girls of Asian origin in Britain. London, [1975]. pp. 45.

KUEPPER (WILLIAM G.) and others. Ugandan Asians in Great Britain: forced migration and social absorption. London, 1975. pp. 122. *bibliog.*

WALLACE (TINA) U.K. passport holders in Kenya: the end of an era?. [London], 1975. fo. 38. *bibliog.*

COMMUNITY RELATIONS COMMISSION. Refuge or home?: a policy statement on the resettlement of refugees; (with Summary). London, [1976]. 2 pts.

EAST INDIANS IN UGANDA.

KUEPPER (WILLIAM G.) and others. Ugandan Asians in Great Britain: forced migration and social absorption. London, 1975. pp. 122. *bibliog.*

EAST PRUSSIA

— Religion.

REIFFERSCHEID (GERHARD) Das Bistum Ermland und das Dritte Reich. Köln, 1975. pp. 351. *bibliog.*

EAST SUSSEX

— Economic conditions.

EAST SUSSEX. Planning Department. County structure plan 1975; [and] Report of survey 1975. Lewes, 1975. 2 vols (in 1).

— Economic policy.

EAST SUSSEX. Planning Department. County structure plan 1975; [and] Report of survey 1975. Lewes, 1975. 2 vols (in 1).

— Social conditions.

EAST SUSSEX. Planning Department. County structure plan 1975; [and] Report of survey 1975. Lewes, 1975. 2 vols (in 1).

— Social policy.

EAST SUSSEX. Planning Department. County structure plan 1975; [and] Report of survey 1975. Lewes, 1975. 2 vols (in 1).

EAST-WEST TRADE (1945—).

NAGÓRSKI (ZYGMUNT) 1912- . The psychology of East-West trade: illusions and opportunites. New York, [1974]. pp. 228. *bibliog.*

KROK-PASZKOWSKI (JAN) Między Brukselą a Moskwą: procesy integracyjne w Europie. London, 1975. pp. 159. *bibliog.*

VOINOV (A.M.) and others. Ekonomicheskie otnosheniia mezhdu sotsialisticheskimi i razvitymi kapitalisticheskimi stranami. Moskva, 1975. pp. 195.

ZWASS (ADAM) Monetary cooperation between East and West. White Plains, N.Y., [1975]. pp. 265. *bibliog.*

LOEBER (DIETRICH ANDRE) ed. East-West trade: a sourcebook on the international economic relations of socialist countries and their legal aspects. Dobbs Ferry, N.Y., 1976 in progress.

HOLZMAN (FRANKLYN DUNN) International trade under communism: politics and economics. New York, [1976]. pp. 239. *bibliog.*

QUANTITATIVE and analytical studies in East-West economic relations; edited by Josef C. Brada. Bloomington, Ind., [1976]. pp. 133. *bibliogs. (Indiana University. International Development Research Center. Studies in East European and Soviet Planning, Development and Trade. No. 24) "Papers originally presented at a joint Romanian-American Seminar in Bucharest during June of 1974".*

WILCZYNSKI (JOZEF) The multinationals and East-West relations: towards transideological collaboration. London, 1976. pp. 235. *bibliog.*

WOLYNSKI (ALEXANDER) Western economic aid to the USSR. London, 1976. pp. 12. *(Institute for the Study of Conflict. Conflict Studies. No. 72)*

EASTERN QUESTION (BALKAN).

BARKER (ELISABETH) Truce in the Balkans. London, 1948. pp. 256.

DJORDJEVIĆ (DIMITRIJE) Izlazak Srbije na Jadransko More i Konferencija ambasadora u Londonu, 1912. Beograd, 1956. pp. 160. *bibliog. In Cyrillic.*

AVRAMOVSKI (ŽIVKO) Balkanske zemlje i velike sile, 1935-1937: od italijanske agresije na Etiopiju do jugoslovensko-italijanskog pakta. Beograd, 1968. pp. 354. *bibliog. With English and Russian summaries.*

KHRISTOV (KHRISTO) Osvobozhdenieto na Bulgariia i politikata na zapadnite durzhavi, 1876-1878; La libération de la Bulgarie et la politique des puissances occidentales, 1876-1878. Sofiia, 1968. pp. 256. *With Russian and French summaries.*

PANTEV (ANDREI LAZAROV) Angliia sreshtu Rusiia na Balkanite, 1879-1894. Sofiia, 1972. pp. 307. *bibliog. With Russian and English summaries.*

AKADEMIIA NAUK SSSR. Institut Slavianovedeniia i Balkanistiki. Balkanskie Issledovaniia. [vyp.1]. Mezhdunarodnye otnosheniia na Balkanakh. Moskva, 1974. pp. 331. *bibliog.*

SKAZKIN (SERGEI DANILOVICH) Konets avstro-russko-germanskogo soiuza: issledovanie po istorii russko-germanskikh i russko-avstriiskikh otnoshenii v sviazi s vostochnym voprosom v 80-e gody XIX stoletiia. 2nd ed. Moskva, 1974. pp. 272. *Reproduces the text of the 1st ed. of 1928 with some omissions.*

PAREŽANIN (RATKO) Za Balkansko jedinstvo: osnivanje, program i rad Balkanskog Instituta u Beogradu, 1934-1941. Minhen, 1976. pp. 121.

EASTERN QUESTION (FAR EAST).

OCHERKI mezhdunarodnykh otnoshenii v Iuzhnoi, Iugo-Vostochnoi Azii i na Dal'nem Vostoke posle vtoroi mirovoi voiny, 1945- 1955. Moskva, 1975. pp. 400.

EASTERN QUESTION (NEAR EAST).

ARENDARENKO (GEORGII ALEKSEEVICH) Bukhara i Afganistan v nachale 80-kh godov XIX veka: zhurnaly komandirovok G.A. Arendarenko; [redaktsionnaia kollegiia B.G. Gafurov (and others)]. Moskva, 1974. pp. 142.

DMITRIEV (E.) and LADEIKIN (VLADIMIR PETROVICH) Put' k miru na Blizhnem Vostoke. Moskva, 1974. pp. 248.

GEORGIEV (VLADIMIR ANATOL'EVICH) Vneshniaia politika Rossii na Blizhnem Vostoke v kontse 30 - nachale 40-kh godov XIX v. Moskva, 1975. pp. 200. *bibliog.*

EBERT (FRIEDRICH).

BUSE (DIETER K.) ed. Parteiagitation und Wahlkreisvertretung: eine Dokumentation über Friedrich Ebert und seinen Reichstagswahlkreis Elberfeld-Barmen, 1910-1918. Bonn-Bad Godesberg, [1975]. pp. 135. *(Archiv für Sozialgeschichte. Beihefte. 3)*

ECOLOGY.

RICHARDS (BRYANT N.) Introduction to the soil ecosystem. London, 1974 repr. 1976. pp. 266. *bibliogs.*

WHITTAKER (ROBERT HARDING) Communities and ecosystems. 2nd ed. New York, [1975]. pp. 385. *bibliogs.*

WYNNE-TYSON (JON) Food for a future: the ecological priority of a humane diet. London, 1975. pp. 183. *bibliog.*

FOIN (THEODORE C.) Ecological systems and the environment. Boston, [Mass., 1976]. pp. 591. *bibliogs.*

— **Mathematical models.**

ECOLOGICAL modeling in a resource management framework; Clifford S. Russell, editor. Washington, D.C., 1975. pp. 394. *(Resources for the Future Inc. Working Papers. QE-1) Proceedings of a symposium held at the Brookings Institution, Washington in 1974, sponsored by National Oceanic and Atmospheric Administration and Resources for the Future.*

— **America, Latin.**

BIOGEOGRAPHY and ecology in South America; edited by E.J. Fittkau [and others]. The Hague, 1968-9. 2 vols. *bibliogs. In various languages.*

ECONOMIC ASSISTANCE.

KALECKI (MICHAŁ) and SACHS (IGNACY) Z zagadnień finansowania rozwoju krajów o "gospodarce mieszanej": [trzy prace]. Warszawa, 1967. pp. 147.

PROKHOROV (GRIGORII MIKHAILOVICH) Ekonomicheskoe sotrudnichestvo i razvitie. Budapesht, 1968. pp. 32. *bibliog. (Magyar Tudományos Akadémia. Afro-Ázsiai Kutató Központ. Studies on Developing Countries. No. 15)*

HOWE (JAMES W.) and others. The U.S. and world development: agenda for action 1975; [by] James W. Howe and the staff of the Overseas Development Council. New York, 1975. pp. 274.

JALAN (BIMAL) Essays in development policy. Delhi, 1975. pp. 156. *bibliog.*

ZUM Verhältnis von Aussenwirtschafts- und Entwicklungspolitik; [by] Axel Borrmann [and others]. Hamburg, 1975. pp. 409. *bibliog. (Hamburg. Hamburgisches Welt-Wirtschafts-Archiv. Veröffentlichungen)*

CLINE (WILLIAM R.) International monetary reform and the developing countries. Washington, D.C., [1976]. pp. 126.

COLE (JOHN) Journalist. The poor of the earth. London, 1976. pp. 144.

— **Ghana.**

GHANA. 1969. Ghana's economy and aid requirements, January 1969-June 1970. [Accra, 1969]. pp. 49.

ECONOMIC ASSISTANCE, AMERICAN.

HOWE (JAMES W.) and others. The U.S. and world development: agenda for action 1975; [by] James W. Howe and the staff of the Overseas Development Council. New York, 1975. pp. 274.

TENDLER (JUDITH) Inside foreign aid. Baltimore, [1975]. pp. 140. *bibliog.*

— **Europe.**

GIMBEL (JOHN) The origins of the Marshall Plan. Stanford, 1976. pp. 344.

— **France.**

BETTELHEIM (CHARLES) Le "plan Marshall" et ses conséquences pour l'économie française. [Paris, 1952]. pp. 27-42. *(Extracted from Cahiers Internationaux, 4e année, no. 40)*

— **Poland.**

STASHEVSKYI (DMYTRO MYKOLAIOVYCH) Interwencja pod pozorem pomocy: działalność misji 'żywnościowych Stanów Zjednoczonych w Polsce; [translation from Russian]. Kraków, 1964. pp. 119.

ECONOMIC ASSISTANCE, BRITISH.

U.K. Crown Agents for Overseas Governments and Administrations. Annual review (formerly Report). a., 1971- London.

CROWN AGENTS QUARTERLY REVIEW, THE; pd. by the Crown Agents for Overseas Governments and Administrations. q., Je 1976 (no.1)- London.

ECONOMIC ASSISTANCE, CANADIAN.

COOPERATION CANADA; ([pd. by] Canadian International Development Agency). [in English and French]. bi-m., Mr/Ap 1972 (no.1)- Ottawa.

GERIN-LAJOIE (PAUL) No room for routine; thoughts at the beginning of 1973. [Ottawa, Canadian International Development Agency], 1972. pp. 17, 18. *(Thoughts on International Development. 6) In English and French.*

CANADA. Parliament. House of Commons. Standing Committee on External Affairs and National Defence. Sub-Committee on International Development. Minutes of proceedings and evidence. irreg., Jl 22 1975 (no.1)- . *In English and French.*

ECONOMIC ASSISTANCE, CHINESE.

HORVÁTH (JÁNOS) Chinese technology transfer to the third world: a grants economy analysis. New York, 1976. pp. 100. *bibliog.*

— **Africa.**

WEINSTEIN (WARREN) ed. Chinese and Soviet aid to Africa. New York, 1975. pp. 287.

ECONOMIC ASSISTANCE, COMMUNIST.

LAMM (HANS SIEGFRIED) and KUPPER (SIEGFRIED) DDR und Dritte Welt. München, 1976. pp. 328. *(Deutsche Gesellschaft für Auswärtige Politik. Forschungsinstitut. Schriften. Band 39)*

ECONOMIC ASSISTANCE, DOMESTIC

— **United States.**

HOLMES (MICHAEL S.) The New Deal in Georgia: an administrative history. Westport, Conn., [1975]. pp. 364. *bibliog.*

JAMES (DOROTHY BUCKTON) Analyzing poverty policy. Lexington, Mass., [1975]. pp. 259.

LEVITAN (SAR A.) and TAGGART (ROBERT) The promise of greatness. Cambridge, Mass., 1976. pp. 316.

ECONOMIC ASSISTANCE, DUTCH.

TIJDSCHRIFT VOOR ANTI-IMPERIALISME SCHOLING. Jaargang 8, nr. 1. Nederlandse ontwikkelingshulp in dienst van kapitaalsbelangen. [Amsterdam], 1973. pp. 280.

ECONOMIC ASSISTANCE, GERMAN.

LEMINSKY (GERHARD) and OTTO (BERND) eds. Gewerkschaften und Entwicklungspolitik. Köln, [1975]. pp. 496.

ZUM Verhältnis von Aussenwirtschafts- und Entwicklungspolitik; [by] Axel Borrmann [and others]. Hamburg, 1975. pp. 409. *bibliog. (Hamburg. Hamburgisches Welt-Wirtschafts-Archiv. Veröffentlichungen)*

ECONOMIC ASSISTANCE, JAPANESE.

HASEGAWA (SUKEHIRO) Japanese foreign aid: policy and practice. New York, 1975. pp. 172. *bibliog.*

ECONOMIC ASSISTANCE, RUSSIAN.

POMOSHCH' Sovetskogo Soiuza razvivaiushchimsia stranam. Budapesht, 1968. pp. 74. *bibliog. (Magyar Tudományos Akadémia. Afro-Ázsiai Kutató Központ. Studies on Developing Countries. No. 17)*

— **Africa.**

WEINSTEIN (WARREN) ed. Chinese and Soviet aid to Africa. New York, 1975. pp. 287.

ECONOMIC ASSISTANCE IN AFRICA.

DEVELOPMENT policy in Africa: [proceedings of a seminar held in Berlin, 1971]; (Joachim Voss, editor). Bonn-Bad Godesberg, [1973]. pp. 344. *(Friedrich-Ebert-Stiftung. Forschungsinstitut. Schriftenreihe. Band 105)*

ECONOMIC ASSISTANCE IN ASIA.

COLOMBO PLAN NEWSLETTER, THE; [pd. by] the Colombo Plan Bureau Information Department. m. (formerly bi-m.)., Je 1970 (v.1, no.1)- Colombo.

COLOMBO PLAN FOR CO-OPERATIVE ECONOMIC DEVELOPMENT IN SOUTH AND SOUTH-EAST ASIA, THE. Consultative Committee. Annual report. a., 1971 (18th)- v.p. *18th annual report pd. by H.M.S.O. in London. Earlier reports are included in the file of British Parliamentary Papers.*

COLOMBO PLAN FOR CO-OPERATIVE ECONOMIC DEVELOPMENT IN SOUTH AND SOUTH-EAST ASIA, THE. Consultative Committee. Special topic...papers...of the Consultative Committee meetings. irreg., 1974 (24th meeting)- Colombo. *Special topic papers previously included in Annual report of the Consultative Committee.*

ECONOMIC ASSISTANCE IN LIBERIA.

GORDON (LESTER E.) The prospects for foreign assistance to Liberia. Monrovia, Department of Planning and Economic Affairs, [1969?]. fo. 9. *(Conference on Development Objectives and Strategy, Monrovia, 1969. Documents. 15) Xerox copy.*

ECONOMIC ASSISTANCE IN LIBERIA.(Cont.)

JOHNSON (J. RUDOLF) Foreign aid to Liberia. Monrovia, Department of Planning and Economic Affairs, [1969?]. fo. 61. *bibliog. (Conference on Development Objectives and Strategy, Monrovia, 1969. Documents. 5) Xerox copy.*

ECONOMIC ASSISTANCE IN RUSSIA.

WOLYNSKI (ALEXANDER) Western economic aid to the USSR. London, 1976. pp. 12. *(Institute for the Study of Conflict. Conflict Studies. No. 72)*

ECONOMIC ASSISTANCE IN THAILAND.

The ROLE of foreign financial assistance to Thailand in the 1980s; edited by W. Lee Baldwin [and] W. David Maxwell. Lexington, Mass., [1975]. pp. 167. *Papers presented at a Southeast Asia Development Advisory Group seminar held in June 1974 in Chieng Mai, Thailand.*

ECONOMIC CONDITIONS.

U.K. Economic Advisory Council. Committee on Economic Information. Report. irreg., Oc 1930-Jl 1939 (1st-27th). London.

PROBLEMY mirovogo krizisa: diskussiia v Institute mirovogo khoziaistva i mirovoi politiki Komakademii. Moskva, 1932. pp. 210.

SACHVERSTAENDIGENRAT ZUR BEGUTACHTUNG DER GESAMTWIRTSCHAFTLICHEN ENTWICKLUNG. Währung, Geldwert, Wettbewerb: Entscheidungen für morgen: Jahresgutachten 1971-72. Stuttgart, 1971. pp. 240.

LABORATOIRE DE CONJONCTURE ET PROSPECTIVE. Schéma général d'aménagement de la France: firmes multinationales et division internationale du travail. Paris, 1975. pp. 90. *(France. Délégation à l'Aménagement du Territoire et à l'Action Régionale. Travaux et Recherches de Prospective. 55)*

ECONOMIC DEVELOPMENT.

SACHS (IGNACY) Sektor państwowy a rozwój gospodarczy. Warszawa, 1961. pp. 203.

KALECKI (MICHAŁ) and SACHS (IGNACY) Z zagadnień finanswania rozwoju krajów o "gospodarce mieszanej": [trzy prace]. Warszawa, 1967. pp. 147.

UNITED NATIONS. Conference on Trade and Development. 1968. Towards a global strategy of development: report by the Secretary-General of the United Nations Conference on Trade and Development to the second session of the Conference. (TD/3/Rev.1). New York, 1968. pp. 76.

UNITED NATIONS. Conference on Trade and Development. Expert Group on International Monetary Issues. 1969. International monetary reform and co-operation for development: report, etc. (TD/B/285/Rev.1). New York, 1969. pp. 26.

LEVY (EMANUEL) M.A., Dr. rer.pol. Per capita product and the level of economic development. Basel, 1972. pp. 284. *bibliog.*

INTERNATIONAL LABOUR OFFICE. Employment Research Papers. Strategies for employment promotion: an evaluation of four inter-agency employment missions. Geneva, 1973. pp. 162.

WILBER (CHARLES K.) ed. The political economy of development and underdevelopment. New York, [1973]. pp. 431. *bibliog.*

BECKERMAN (WILFRED) Two cheers for the affluent society: a spirited defense of economic growth. New York, [1974]. pp. 238.

BELIANOVA (ANTONINA MIKHAILOVNA) O tempakh ekonomicheskogo razvitiia SSSR: po materialam diskussii 20-kh godov. Moskva, 1974. pp. 174.

GRANELL TRIAS (FRANCISCO) Las empresas multinacionales y el desarrollo. Barcelona, [1974]. pp. 271. *bibliog.*

HUNKER (HENRY L.) Industrial development: concepts and principles. Lexington, Mass., [1974]. pp. 322. *bibliog.*

KRISTENSEN (THORKIL) Development in rich and poor countries: a general theory with statistical analyses. New York, 1974. pp. 164.

MIKUL'SKII (KONSTANTIN IVANOVICH) ed. Problemy vosproizvodstva v stranakh SEV. Moskva, 1974. pp. 247.

NYERERE (JULIUS KAMBARAGE) Man and development. Dar es Salaam, 1974. pp. 125.

URI (PIERRE) Développement sans dépendance. [Paris, 1974]. pp. 261.

VELEZ GOMEZ (CARLOS) Integration and development. Manizales, 1974. pp. 170.

ACTION-oriented approaches to regional development planning; edited by Avrom Bendavid-Val [and] Peter P. Waller. New York, 1975. pp. 132.

ANNERSTEDT (JAN) and GUSTAVSSON (ROLF) Towards a new international economic division of labor?: patterns of dependence and conditions for liberation in the periphery of capitalism. [Roskilde], 1975. pp. 111.

BIRNBERG (THOMAS B.) and RESNICK (STEPHEN A.) Colonial development: an econometric study. new Haven, 1975. pp. 347. *bibliog.*

ETUDES de doctrine et de droit international du développement; par Alain Colombeau [and others]. Paris, 1975. pp. 385. *bibliog. (Université d'Aix-Marseille. Faculté de Droit et de Science Politique. Travaux et Mémoires. No. 21)*

FOOD aid and international economic growth; ([by] Uma K. Srivastava [and others]). Ames, Iowa, 1975. pp. 160. *bibliog.*

HAGEN (EVERETT EINAR) The economics of development. rev. ed. Homewood, Ill., 1975. pp. 563. *bibliog.*

HILSMAN (ROGER) The crouching future: international politics and U.S. foreign policy; a forecast. Garden City, N.Y. 1975. pp. 666.

HOWE (JAMES W.) and others. The U.S. and world development: agenda for action 1975; [by] James W. Howe and the staff of the Overseas Development Council. New York, 1975. pp. 274.

INTERNATIONAL GEOGRAPHICAL UNION. Regional Conference [in New Zealand], 1974. Proceedings of the International Geographical Union Regional Conference and eighth New Zealand Geography Conference, Palmerston North, December 1974; edited by William Brockie [and others]. [Christchurch], 1975. pp. 380. *bibliogs. (New Zealand Geographical Society. Conference Series. No. 8)*

JALAN (BIMAL) Essays in development policy. Delhi, 1975. pp. 156. *bibliog.*

JOHNSON (HARRY GORDON) Technology and economic interdependence. London, 1975. pp. 187. *bibliog. (Trade Policy Research Centre. World Economic Issues)*

JONES (HYWEL G.) An introduction to modern theories of economic growth. London, 1975. pp. 253. *bibliogs.*

MORGAN (JOSEPH THEODORE) Economic development: concept and strategy. New York, [1975]. pp. 429.

OLSON (MANCUR) and LANDSBERG (HANS H.) eds. The no-growth society: (essays by Mancur Olson [and others]). London, 1975. pp. 259. *bibliog.*

OSAD'KO (MIKHAIL PETROVICH) ed. Protsess sotsialisticheskogo nakopleniia. Moskva, 1975. pp. 140.

PLURALISM and development in island communities; report of the commonwealth seminar held in Mauritius, January 1975. [London], Commonwealth Secretariat, [1975]. pp. 94. *bibliog.*

REHOVOT CONFERENCE, 7TH, 1973. Economic growth in developing countries - material and human resources: proceedings...; edited by Yohanan Ramati. New York, 1975. pp. 501.

ROBINSON (WARREN C.) ed. Population and development planning. New York, [1975]. pp. 263.

ROEMER (MICHAEL) and STERN (JOSEPH J.) The appraisal of development projects: a practical guide to project analysis with case studies and solutions. New York, 1975. pp. 223.

ROSIER (BERNARD) Croissance et crise capitalistes. [Paris, 1975]. pp. 304. *bibliog.*

SAUVY (ALFRED) Zero growth?; (translator, A. Maguire). Oxford, 1975. pp. 266.

SINGH (SATEESH KUMAR) Development economics: some findings. Lexington, Mass., [1975]. pp. 296. *bibliog.*

SWERDLOW (IRVING) The public administration of economic development. New York, 1975. pp. 407.

TAYLOR (JOHN VERNON) Enough is enough. London, 1975 repr. 1976. pp. 120. *bibliog.*

WORKSHOP ON NATIONAL YOUTH PROGRAMMES AND NATIONAL SERVICE, ACCRA, 1975. Youth for development: an African perspective; report. London, Commonwealth Secretariat, [1975]. pp. 203.

BHATTACHARYA (ANINDYA K.) Foreign trade and international development. Lexington, Mass., [1976]. pp. 107. *bibliog.*

CAIRNCROSS (Sir ALEXANDER KIRKLAND) and PURI (MOHINDER) eds. Employment, income distribution and development strategy: problems of the developing countries: essays in honour of H. W. Singer. London, 1976. pp. 264. *bibliog.*

GILBERT (ALAN GRAHAM) ed. Development planning and spatial structure. London, [1976]. pp. 207. *bibliogs.*

GIOTOPOULOS (PANAGIOTES A.) and NUGENT (JEFFREY B.) Economics of development: empirical investigations. New York, [1976]. pp. 478. *bibliog.*

KALECKI (MICHAŁ) Essays on developing economies. Hassocks, Sussex, 1976. pp. 208.

MEIER (GERALD MARVIN) Leading issues in economic development. 3rd ed. New York, 1976. pp. 862.

STRACHAN (HARRY W.) Family and other business groups in economic development: the case of Nicaragua. New York, 1976. pp. 129.

STRATEGY for development; edited by John Barratt [and others]. London, 1976. pp. 324. *Based on a conference held in Johannesburg in 1974, sponsored by the South African Institute of International Affairs and others.*

THIRLWALL (ANTHONY PHILIP) Financing economic development. London, 1976. pp. 95. *bibliog.*

URI (PIERRE) Development without dependence. New York, 1976. pp. 166.

— Abstracts.

U.S. Agency for International Development. A.I.D. research and development abstracts. q., Jl 1973 (v.1,no.1)- Washington, D.C.

— Congresses.

SOCIETÀ ITALIANA DEGLI ECONOMISTI. Riunione Scientifica, 12a, Roma, 1971. Politica monetaria e sviluppo economico. Milano, 1975. pp. 151.

— Mathematical models.

WAN (HENRY Y.) Economic growth. New York, [1971]. pp. 428. *bibliogs.*

STEINMETZ (VOLKER) Zur Existenz von Wachstumsgleichgewichten in Wachstumsmodellen vom von Neumannschen Typ. Meisenheim am Glan, [1972]. pp. 100. *bibliog.*

RUMM (ULRICH) Wirtschaftliches Wachstum, Aussenhandel und Preisniveau. Meisenheim am Glan, [1973]. pp. 135, xi. *bibliog.*

IANCU (AUREL) Modele de creştere economică şi de optimizare a corelaţiei dintre acumulare şi consum. Bucureşti, 1974. pp. 292. bibliog. (Academia de Ştiinţe Sociale şi Politice a Republicii Socialiste România. Institutul de Cercetări Economice. Bibliotheca Oeconomica. 29) With English and Russian tables of contents.

KHROMOV (PAVEL ALEKSEEVICH) Tempy razvitiia promyshlennosti i sel'skogo khoziaistva: ekonomiko-statisticheskoe issledovanie. Moskva, 1974. pp. 199.

SHATILOV (NIKOLAI FILIPPOVICH) Analiz zavisimostei sotsialisticheskogo rasshirennogo vosproizvodstva i opyt ego modelirovaniia; otvetstvennyi redaktor... V.K. Ozerov. Novosibirsk, 1974. pp. 250.

FEIWEL (GEORGE R.) Growth in supply constrained economy. Naples, 1975. pp. 105. (Istituto di Studi per lo Sviluppo Economico. Quaderni d'Istituto. 3)

JONES (DONALD W.) 1948- . Migration and urban unemployment in dualistic economic development. Chicago, 1975. pp. 174. bibliog. (Chicago. University. Department of Geography. Research Papers. No. 165)

KAZINETS (LEV SEMENOVICH) Tempy rosta i absoliutnye prirosty: izmerenie i analiz. Moskva, 1975. pp. 191. bibliog.

KLEIN (LAWRENCE ROBERT) and SCHLEICHER (STEFAN) Techniques of model building for developing economies. Vienna, 1975. pp. 80. (Institut für Höhere Studien und Wissenschaftliche Forschung. Forschungsberichte. No. 91)

STRIGENS (EMIL) Optimale Kapiltalakkumulation: neoklassische Wachstumsmodelle mit exogenem und endogenem Bevölkerungswachstum. Berlin, [1975]. pp. 102. bibliog.

MORGENSTERN (OSKAR) and THOMPSON (GERALD LUTHER) Mathematical theory of expanding and contracting economies. Lexington, Mass., [1976]. pp. 275. bibliog.

POPULATION, public policy, and economic development; edited by Michael C. Keeley. New York, 1976. pp. 259. bibliog.

— **Social aspects.**

SINE (BABAKAR) Impérialisme et théories sociologiques du développement; présentation par Samir Amin. Paris, [1975]. pp. 396. bibliog.

SMELSER (NEIL JOSEPH) The sociology of economic life. 2nd ed. Englewood Cliffs, [1976]. pp. 177. bibliog.

ECONOMIC FORECASTING.

BENTZEL (RAGNAR) and BECKEMAN (JAN) Framtidsperspektiv för svensk industri, 1965-1980. Stockholm, 1966. pp. 184.

BIØRN (ERIK) Prognoser for de langsiktige endringer i sammensetningen av det private konsum...: long term forecasts for the changes in the composition of the private consumption. Oslo, 1973. pp. 71. bibliog. (Norway. Statistiske Centralbyrå. Artikler. Nr. 55)

NEW YORK (CITY). Stock Exchange. Department of Research and Statistics. Demand and supply of equity capital: projections to 1985. New York, 1975. pp. 38.

STEIN (HERBERT) Economic planning and the improvement of economic policy. Washington, D.C., 1975. pp. 33. (American Enterprise Institute for Public Policy Research. Domestic Affairs Studies. 38)

HEILBRONER (ROBERT LOUIS) Business civilization in decline. New York, [1976]. pp. 127.

— **Mathematical models.**

KRELLE (WILHELM) Erfahrungen mit einem ökonometrischen Prognosemodell für die Bundesrepublik Deutschland. Meisenheim am Glan, [1974]. pp. 182.

FRERICHS (W.) Ein disaggregiertes Prognosesystem für die BRD. Meisenheim am Glan, 1975 in progress. bibliog.

CHETYRKIN (EVGENII MIKHAILOVICH) Statisticheskie metody prognozirovaniia. Moskva, 1975. pp. 184.

CLARK (JOHN A.) and COLE (SAM) Global simulation models: a comparative study. London, [1975]. pp. 135. bibliog.

DEUTSCHES INSTITUT FÜR WIRTSCHAFTSFORSCHUNG. Sonderhefte. [Neue Folge]. 109. Verkehrswege und Ersatzbedarf; ([by] Bernd Bartholmai). Berlin, 1975. pp. 125.

METODOLOGICHESKIE voprosy prognozirovaniia proizvoditel'nosti truda. Kiev, 1975. pp. 216. bibliog.

U.K. Treasury. 1976. HM Treasury macroeconomic model: technical manual. London, 1976. 1 vol. (various pagings). Updated to describe model as at 1st October, 1975.

— **European Economic Community countries.**

The FUTURES of Europe; edited...by Wayland Kennet, Director of the Europe Plus Thirty Project; based on a report to the Commission of the European Communities. Cambridge, 1976. pp. 242.

— **United Kingdom.**

NATIONAL PORTS COUNCIL. Economics and Statistics Division. United Kingdom international trade, 1980-1985. London, 1976. pp. 173. bibliog.

ECONOMIC HISTORY.

ASHWORTH (WILLIAM) A short history of the international economy since 1850. 3rd ed. London, 1975. pp. 318. bibliog.

KUCZYNSKI (JUERGEN) Vier Revolutionen der Produktivkräfte: Theorie und Vergleiche; mit kritischen Bemerkungen und Ergänzungen von Wolfgang Jonas. Berlin, 1975. pp. 194.

BLACK (CYRIL EDWIN) ed. Comparative modernization: a reader. New York, [1976]. pp. 441.

— **Historiography.**

SARRAZIN (THILO) Ökonomie und Logik der historischen Erklärung: zur Wissenschaftslogik der New Economic History. Bonn-Bad Godesberg, [1974]. pp. 168. bibliog. (Friedrich-Ebert-Stiftung. Forschungsinstitut. Schriftenreihe. Band 109)

— **Methodology.**

McCLELLAND (PETER D.) Causal explanation and model building in history, economics and the new economic history. Ithaca, 1975. pp. 290. bibliog.

HOWELLS (PETER GRAEME ALLISON) Economic theory in historical explanation: the Hempel explanation schema in economic history. 1976. fo. 239. bibliog. Typescript. Ph.D. (London) thesis: unpublished. This thesis is the property of London University and may not be removed from the Library.

ECONOMIC INDICATORS

— **Africa.**

AFRICAN ECONOMIC INDICATORS; ([pd. by] United Nations Economic Commission for Africa). a., 1968 [1st issue]- Addis Ababa.

— **Canada.**

CANADA. Economic Council. 1973. Shaping the expansion: performance indicators. [Ottawa], 1973. 1 pamphlet (unpaged).

— **India.**

ECONOMIC AND SOCIAL INDICATORS: INDIA; [pd. by] United States Agency for International Development, New Delhi, India. a., 1972- New Delhi.

ECONOMIC INDICATORS FOR INDIA; prepared by the Economic Affairs Division, Office of Development Policy, U.S. Agency for International Development, New Delhi, India. bi-m. New Delhi. Current issues only kept.

ECONOMIC LEGISLATION

— — Madras.

MADRAS. Finance Department. 1971. Tamil Nadu: an economic appraisal, 1971-72. Madras, [1971]. pp. 326.

— Norway.

NORWAY. Statistiske Centralbyrå. 1975. Sesongkorrigering av norske konjunkturindikatorer, etc. Oslo, 1975. pp. 29. (Statistiske Analyser. 18) With English summary.

— Pakistan.

UNITED STATES. Agency for International Development. USAID- Islamabad. Division of Economic Analysis. 1975. Pakistan economic indicators. [Islamabad], 1975. fo. 14.

— Portugal.

PORTUGAL. Ministerio do Trabalho. Gabinete de Estudos, Planeamento e Organização. Relatorio de conjuntura. q., 1974 (no.4)- Lisboa.

— Russia.

KONSTANTINOVA (LIDIIA MIKHAILOVNA) and SOKOLINSKII (ZALMAN VENIAMINOVICH) Ekonomicheskaia effektivnost' obshchestvennogo proizvodstva: analiz statisticheskikh pokazatelei. Moskva, 1974. pp. 160.

SMIRNITSKII (EVGENII KONSTANTINOVICH) Ekonomicheskie pokazateli promyshlennosti: spravochnik. Moskva, 1974. pp. 381. bibliog.

— Turkey.

ECONOMIC AND SOCIAL INDICATORS: TURKEY; [pd. by] United States Agency for International Development, Ankara, Turkey. a., Jl 1970- Ankara.

ECONOMIC LEGISLATION

— **Argentine Republic.**

ARGENTINE REPUBLIC. Statutes, etc. 1973-74. Legislacion economica: (politica economica para la reconstruccion y la liberacion nacional). Buenos Aires, 1975. pp. 225.

— **Belgium.**

DESCHAMPS (CLAUDE) Planification et decentralisation économique en Belgique. Bruxelles, 1973. 1 vol. (loose-leaf).

— **European Economic Community countries.**

EUROPEAN COMMUNITIES. Directorate-General for the Internal Market. 1972. Régime juridique concernant l'accès aux activités non salariées de l'industrie, de l'artisanat, du commerce et des entreprises de services et l'exercice de celles-ci dans les etats membres des Communautés européennes: situation au 31. 12.1970. [Luxembourg, 1972]. pp. 807.

— **Italy.**

BACHELET (VITTORIO) Legge e attività amministrativa nella programmazione economica. Milano, 1975. pp. 224.

— **Romania.**

STĂNESCU (VASILE) and CONSTANTINESCU (MIHAI) Unitatea economică socialistă: raportul dintre gestiunea economică, capacitatea juridică şi subiectul de drept. Bucureşti, 1974. pp. 207. bibliog. With English summary.

— **Russia.**

TARNAPOL'SKII (RUSTEM IL'IASOVICH) Pravovye voprosy upravleniia narodnym khoziaistvom v avtonomnoi respublike: vzaimootnosheniia Soveta Ministrov ASSR s nepodvedomstvennymi organizatsiiami. Kazan, 1974. pp. 120.

BYKOV (ANATOLII GRIGOR'EVICH) Plan i khoziaistvennyi dogovor. Moskva, 1975. pp. 158.

ECONOMIC LEGISLATION(Cont.)

KHOMENKO (VASILII NIKOLAEVICH) Otvetstvennost' v khoziaistvennom prave. Kiev, 1975. pp. 171.

LAPTEV (VLADIMIR VIKTOROVICH) ed. Teoreticheskie problemy khoziaistvennogo prava. Moskva, 1975. pp. 413.

MANOKHIN (VASILII MIKHAILOVICH) Khoziaistvennoe obsluzhivanie organizatsii i grazhdan: organizatsionno-pravovye voprosy. Moskva, 1975. pp. 222.

— Spain.

HILLERS DE LUQUE (SIGFREDO) España: una revolucion pendiente. Madrid, [1975]. pp. 487. *bibliog.*

— United States.

HUGHES (JONATHAN ROBERTS TYSON) Social control in the colonial economy. Charlottesville, Va., 1976. pp. 178.

ECONOMIC POLICY.

LOWITSCH (ALFRED) Energie, Planwirtschaft und Sozialismus. Jena, [1929]. pp. 77. *(Urania: kulturpolitische Monatshefte über Natur und Gesellschaft. Jahrgang 1928/29. Buchbeigaben. 4)*

WARD (BENJAMIN N.) The socialist economy: a study of organizational alternatives. New York, [1967]. pp. 272.

CIBOTTI (RICARDO) and SIERRA (ENRIQUE) El sector publico en la planificacion del desarrollo. Mexico, 1970. pp. 271. *bibliog.*

JUDGE (GEORGE G.) and TAKAYAMA (TAKASHI) eds. Studies in economic planning over space and time. Amsterdam, 1973. pp. 727. *bibliogs.*

OFFICE location and regional development; proceedings of a conference organised by An Foras Forbartha...Dublin, March 1973. Dublin, An Foras Forbartha, 1973. pp. 76.

BRETON (ALBERT) The economic theory of representative government. London, 1974. pp. 228.

HAY (ALAN M.) and others. Government intervention. Milton Keynes, 1974. pp. 110. *bibliogs. (Open University. Social Sciences: a third level course. Regional analysis and development 4: Units 14-16)*

SYSTEME D'ETUDES DU SCHEMA GENERAL D'AMENAGEMENT DE LA FRANCE. Schéma général d'aménagement de la France: Sésame année 5. Paris, 1974. pp. 71. *(France. Délégation à l'Aménagement du Territoire et à l'Action Régionale. Travaux et Recherches de Prospective. 50)*

ECONOMIC planning, east and west; edited and with an introduction by Morris Bornstein. Cambridge, Mass., [1975]. pp. 329. *Revised papers from a conference conducted by the Comparative Economics Program at the University of Michigan in Bellagio, Italy, in 1973.*

GILLINGWATER (DAVID) Regional planning and social change: a responsive approach. Farnborough, Hants., [1975]. pp. 272. *bibliog.*

JURKOVIĆ (PERO) Uvod u teoriju ekonomske politike. Zagreb, 1975. pp. 52.

NOVE (ALEXANDER) Planning: what, how and why. Edinburgh, [1975]. pp. 23. *(Glasgow. University of Strathclyde. Fraser of Allander Institute. Speculative Papers. No. 1)*

OLSON (MANCUR) and LANDSBERG (HANS H.) eds. The no-growth society: (essays by Mancur Olson [and others]). London, 1975. pp. 259. *bibliog.*

QAYUM (ABDUL) Techniques of national economic planning. Bloomington, [1975]. pp. 240. *(Indiana University. International Development Research Center. Studies in Development. 9)*

ROUX (JEAN) La rationalisation des choix politiques. Paris, 1975. pp. 227. *bibliog.*

STIGLER (GEORGE JOSEPH) The citizen and the state: essays on regulation. Chicago, 1975. pp. 209.

STRESS and contradiction in modern capitalism: public policy and the theory of the state; edited by Leon N. Lindberg [and others]. Lexington, Mass., [1975]. pp. 443. *Papers from a conference on "Patterns of change in advanced industrial society: priorities for social science research in the 1970's and 1980's", Monterosso-al-Mare, Genoa, 1973, sponsored by the Council for European Studies and the Giovanni Agnelli Foundation.*

SWERDLOW (IRVING) The public administration of economic development. New York, 1975. pp. 407.

ZAHN (FRANK) Macroeconomic theory and policy. Englewood Cliffs, [1975]. pp. 320. *bibliogs.*

BIERMANN (HERBERT) Ansatzpunkte einer allgemeinen Strukturpolitik: Destabilisierung von Managementgremien und/oder Organisationen als Voraussetzung für Wettbewerb und Demokratie. Berlin, [1976]. pp. 160. *bibliog.*

CURWEN (PETER J.) and FOWLER (A. H.) Economic policy. London, 1976. pp. 266. *bibliogs*

FRISCH (RAGNAR) Economic planning studies: a collection of essays;...selected, introduced and edited by Frank Long. Dordrecht, [1976]. pp. 198.

GROSSESCHMIDT (BRITA) Kritik der postkeynesianischen Stabilitätspolitik: ein Beitrag zur Phillips-Kurven-Diskussion. Berlin, [1976]. pp. 222. *bibliog.*

MEADE (JAMES EDWARD) The just economy:...being volume four of Principles of political economy. London, 1976. pp. 247.

MEIER (GERALD MARVIN) Leading issues in economic development. 3rd ed. New York, 1976. pp. 862.

NOVICK (DAVID) A world of scarcities: critical issues in public policy;...with Kurt Bleicken [and others]. London, 1976. pp. 194.

NUTTER (GILBERT WARREN) Central economic planning: the visible hand. Washington, D.C., 1976. pp. 23. *(American Enterprise Institute for Public Policy Research. Domestic Affairs Studies. 41)*

PEACOCK (ALAN TURNER) and SHAW (GRAHAM KEITH) The economic theory of fiscal policy. 2nd ed. London, 1976. pp. 192. *bibliogs.*

SPULBER (NICOLAS) and HOROWITZ (IRA) Quantitative economic policy and planning: theory and models of economic control. New York, [1976]. pp. 413.

VEREIN FÜR SOZIALPOLITIK. Schriften. Neue Folge. Band 86. Studien zum Marktsozialismus; von Gernot Gutmann [and others]; herausgegeben von Christian Watrin. Berlin, [1976]. pp. 118.

WIRTSCHAFTSPOLITIK: Wissenschaft und politische Aufgabe; Festschrift zum 65. Geburtstag von Karl Schiller; (Heiko Körner [and others], Herausgeber). Bern, [1976]. pp. 576. *bibliog.*

— Bibliography.

COMMONWEALTH BUREAU OF AGRICULTURAL ECONOMICS. Regional planning and rural development. [Farnham Royal, 1975]. pp. 32. *(Annotated Bibliographies. No. 35) Compiled from World Agricultural Economics and Rural Sociology Abstracts from 1974 to 1975.*

— Mathematical models.

SEVALDSON (PER) Data sources and user operations of MODIS, a macro-economic model for short term planning, etc. Oslo, 1971. pp. 31. *(Norway. Statistiske Centralbyrå. Artikler. Nr. 41)*

THENEVIN (PIERRE) Utilisation d'un modèle pour la planification régionale: application d'un modèle élaboré par la B.I.R.D. au Sud-Ouest de la Côte d'Ivoire. [Paris], 1973. pp. 94, 53. *(France. Secrétariat d'Etat aux Affaires Etrangères. Méthodologie de la Planification. 7)*

MILLER (PRESTON) and KAATZ (RONALD) Introduction to the use of econometric models in economic policy making. Minneapolis, 1974. pp. 23. *(Federal Reserve Bank of Minneapolis. Ninth District Economic Information Series)*

PESTON (MAURICE H.) Theory of macroeconomic policy. Deddington, Oxon., 1974. pp. 213. *bibliog.*

NYBERG (LARS) and VIOTTI (STAFFAN) A control systems approach to macroeconomic theory and policy in an open economy. Stockholm, 1975. 1 vol.(various pagings). *bibliog.*

MIKUS (RUDOLF) Die Theorie der indikativen Planung unter besonderer Berücksichtigung des Problems unvollkommener Information. Berlin, [1976]. pp. 147. *bibliog.*

ECONOMIC STABILIZATION.

KOCK (HEINZ) Stabilitätspolitik im föderalistischen System der Bundesrepublik Deutschland: Analyse und Reformvorschläge. Köln, [1975]. pp. 228. *bibliog.*

OBERHAUSER (ALOIS) Stabilitätspolitik bei steigender Staatsquote. Göttingen, [1975]. pp. 92. *(Kommission für Wirtschaftlichen und Sozialen Wandel. Schriften. 43)*

RALL (WILHELM) Zur Wirksamkeit der Einkommenspolitik. Tübingen, 1975. pp. 273. *bibliog. (Tübingen. Universität. Fachbereich Wirtschaftswissenschaft. Tübinger Wirtschaftswissenschaftliche Abhandlungen. Band 20)*

TAIT (ALAN A.) The economics of devolution: a knife edge problem. Edinburgh, [1975]. pp. 12. *bibliog. (Glasgow. University of Strathclyde. Fraser of Allander Institute. Speculative Papers. No.2)*

VEREIN FÜR SOZIALPOLITIK. Schriften. Neue Folge. Band 85. Stabilisierungspolitik in der Marktwirtschaft: (Verhandlungen auf der Tagung...in Zürich vom 2.-5. September 1974; herausgegeben von Hans K. Schneider [and others]). Berlin, [1975]. 2 vols.

GROSSESCHMIDT (BRITA) Kritik der postkeynesianischen Stabilitätspolitik: ein Beitrag zur Phillips-Kurven-Diskussion. Berlin, [1976]. pp. 222. *bibliog.*

— Mathematical models.

ANDERSSON (ROLF) and MEIDNER (RUDOLF) Arbetsmarknadspolitik och stabilisering. [Stockholm, 1973]. pp. 88. *(Institutet för Social Forskning. Skrifter. 4)*

FRIEDMAN (BENJAMIN M.) Economic stabilization policy: methods in optimization. Amsterdam, 1975. pp. 375. *bibliog.*

KAMINOW (IRA) Economic stabilization under fixed and flexible exchange rates. [London, 1975]. pp. 25,5. *bibliog.*

ECONOMIC ZONING

— Germany.

THELEN (PETER) and LUEHRS (GEORG) Abgrenzung von Fördergebieten: die Messung der Wirtschaftskraft und der strukturellen Gefährdung von Regionen. Hannover, [1971]. pp. 112. *bibliog. (Friedrich-Ebert-Stiftung. Forschungsinstitut. Schriftenreihe. Band 91)*

— Norway.

NORWAY. Statistiske Centralbyrå. 1974. Markedstall: folke- og boligtelling, 1970, etc. Oslo, 1974. pp. 139. *(Norges Offisielle Statistikk. Rekke A.659) In Norwegian and English.*

RIDENG (ARNE KJELL) Klassifering av kommunene i Norge, 1974...: classification of the municipalities of Norway, 1974. Oslo, 1974. pp. 56. *bibliog. (Norway. Statistiske Centralbyrå. Artikler. Nr. 67) With English summary. Map in end pocket.*

— Poland.

PISKOZUB (ANDRZEJ) Kształty polskiej przestrzeni. Warszawa, 1970. pp. 256.

— Russia.

KOZLOVSKAIA (LIUDMILA VASIL'EVNA) Territorial'naia kontsentratsiia promyshlennosti: ekonomicheskie i sotsial'nye aspekty. Minsk, 1975. pp. 160.

NEDESHEV (ALEKSEI ALEKSANDROVICH) Oblastnoi ekonomicheskii raion: issledovanie funktsii, struktury i protsessov razvitiia na primere Chitinskoi oblasti; otvetstvennyi redaktor...V.V. Vorob'ev. Novosibirsk, 1975. pp. 162. *bibliog.*

— — **Mathematical models.**

SHALABIN (GERAL'D VASIL'EVICH) Optimizatsiia dolgosrochnogo plana gruppy vzaimosviazannykh otraslei ekonomicheskogo raiona. Leningrad, 1975. pp. 128.

ECONOMICS.

MARSHALL (ALFRED) [Letters to Francis Ysidro Edgeworth. 1880-96]. 22 letters, 1 postcard. *Manuscript.*

L'HUILLIER (JACQUES A.) Réalité économique et science économique;...leçon inaugurale prononcée à l'Aula de l'Université de Genève, le 27 octobre 1948. Genève, 1948. pp. 22. *(Geneva. Université. Faculté des Sciences Economiques et Sociales. Publications. vol. 10)*

HEILBRONER (ROBERT LOUIS) Between capitalism and socialism: essays in political economics. New York, [1970]. pp. 294.

BENETTI (CARLO) and others. Economie classique: économie vulgaire; essais critiques. Grenoble, 1975. pp. 137.

DOPFER (KURT) ed. Economics in the future. London, 1976. pp. 123.

SMELSER (NEIL JOSEPH) The sociology of economic life. 2nd ed. Englewood Cliffs, [1976]. pp. 177. *bibliog.*

— **Bibliography.**

HARVARD UNIVERSITY. Graduate School of Business Administration. Baker Library. Author-title catalogue of the Baker Library, etc. Boston, Mass., 1971 in progress.

SIVOLGIN (VLADIMIR EPIFANOVICH) compiler. Politicheskaia ekonomika; Istoriia ekonomicheskoi mysli: annotirovannyi ukazatel' otechestvennykh bibliograficheskikh posobii, izdannykh v 1812-1972gg. Moskva, 1974. pp. 71.

OTTO (FRIEDA) compiler. Bibliographie wirtschafts- und sozialwissenschaftlicher Bibliographien: Zugänge der Bibliothek des Instituts für Weltwirtschaft, Kiel, in den Jahren 1968 bis 1973. Kiel, 1975. pp. 83. *(Kiel. Universität. Institut für Weltwirtschaft. Bibliothek. Kieler Schrifttumskunden zu Wirtschaft und Gesellschaft. 20)*

— **Dictionaries and encyclopaedias.**

MOROZENKO (V.V.) compiler. Anglo-russkii ekonomiko-statisticheskii slovar'...; pod redaktsiei R.M. Entova. Moskva, 1974. pp. 222.

LAMBERT (DENIS CLAIR) Dictionnaire français-anglais de l'économie monétaire: initiation économique. 2nd ed. Paris, [1975]. pp. 261.

MURUGIAH (R. THARMALINGAM) ed. Concise economic dictionary and encyclopaedia of socialist economics: German-English; by Manfred Engert [and others] . Berlin, [1975]. pp. 283.

RECKTENWALD (HORST CLAUS) Wörterbuch der Wirtschaft. 7th ed. Stuttgart, [1975]. pp. 555. *bibliog.*

MOFFAT (DONALD W.) Economics dictionary. New York, [1976]. pp. 301.

SELDON (ARTHUR) and PENNANCE (FRED G.) compilers. Everyman's dictionary of economics: an alphabetical exposition of economic concepts and their application. 2nd ed. London, 1976. pp. 360.

— **History.**

MARX (KARL) Theories of surplus-value: (volume IV of Capital): (translated by Emile Burns). Moscow, 1963 repr. 1969 in progress. pp. 506.

BURZHUAZNYE i melkoburzhuaznye ekonomicheskie kontseptsii sotsializma: kriticheskie ocherki, 1848-1917 gg. Moskva, 1974. pp. 341.

GROVES (HAROLD MARTIN) Tax philosophers: two hundred years of thought in Great Britain and the United States; edited by Donald J. Curran. Madison, Wis., 1974. pp. 158.

BURZHUAZNYE i melkoburzhuaznye ekonomicheskie teorii sotsializma: kriticheskie ocherki, 1917-1945 gg. Moskva, 1975. pp. 327.

CHEUNG (MICHAEL TOW) A study of the Clower-Leijonhufvud re-interpretation of the Keynesian model. 1975. fo.196. *bibliog. Typescript. Ph.D. (London) thesis: unpublished. This thesis is the property of London University and may not be removed from the Library.*

EKELUND (ROBERT B.) and HEBERT (ROBERT F.) A history of economic theory and method. New York, [1975]. pp. 508. *bibliogs.*

OSER (JACOB) and BLANCHFIELD (WILLIAM C.) The evolution of economic thought. 3rd ed. New York, [1975]. pp. 512. *bibliogs.*

PROJEKTGRUPPE ENTWICKLUNG DES MARXSCHEN SYSTEMS. Der 4. Band des "Kapital"?: Kommentar zu den "Theorien über den Mehrwert"; ([by] Helmut Asche [and others]). Westberlin, [1975]. pp. 677.

MINSKY (HYMAN P.) John Maynard Keynes. London, 1976. pp. 181. *bibliog.*

ROBBINS (LIONEL CHARLES) Baron Robbins. Political economy: past and present; a review of leading theories of economic policy. London, 1976. pp. 203.

— — **Bibliography.**

SIVOLGIN (VLADIMIR EPIFANOVICH) compiler. Politicheskaia ekonomika; Istoriia ekonomicheskoi mysli: annotirovannyi ukazatel' otechestvennykh bibliograficheskikh posobii, izdannykh v 1812-1972gg. Moskva, 1974. pp. 71.

— — **Bulgaria.**

ISTORIIA na ikonomicheskata misul v Bulgariia. Sofiia, 1971 in progress.

— — **Russia.**

BAZYLEV (NIKOLAI IVANOVICH) Stanovlenie ekonomicheskoi teorii sotsializma v SSSR. Minsk, 1975. pp. 175.

— — **Sweden.**

HERLITZ (LARS) Fysiokratismen i svensk tappning, 1767-1770. Göteborg, 1974. pp. 201. *bibliog. (Göteborgs Universitet. Ekonomisk-Historiska Institutionen. Meddelanden. 35)*

— — **United States.**

LODGE (GEORGE CABOT) The new American ideology: how the ideological basis of legitimate authority in America is being radically transformed, etc. New York, 1976. pp. 350,xv.

— **Methodology.**

McCLELLAND (PETER D.) Causal explanation and model building in history, economics and the new economic history. Ithaca, 1975. pp. 290. *bibliog.*

— **Philosophy.**

MILLAN-PUELLES (ANTONIO) Economia y libertad. Madrid, [1974]. pp. 448.

— **Psychological aspects.**

KATONA (GEORGE) Psychological economics. New York, [1975]. pp. 438. *bibliog.*

— **Study and teaching — Russia — Baltic States.**

PROBLEMY sovershenstvovaniia metodiki prepodavaniia politicheskoi ekonomii v vuzakh: mezhvuzovskii sbornik nauchno-metodicheskikh statei. Riga, 1974. pp. 199.

— **Terminology.**

DUNCKER (HERMANN) Volkswirtschaftliche Grundbegriffe, mit besonderer Berücksichtigung der ökonomischen Grundlehren von Karl Marx: als Leitfaden für Unterrichtskurse. Stuttgart, 1908. pp. 60.

LAMBERT (DENIS CLAIR) Dictionnaire français-anglais de l'économie monétaire: initiation économique. 2nd ed. Paris, [1975]. pp. 261.

— **1776-1876.**

ELDER (WILLIAM) M.D. Questions of the day: economic and social. Philadelphia, 1871. pp. 367.

HODGSON (WILLIAM BALLANTYNE) Inaugural address [in the University of Edinburgh];...3rd November, 1871. 2nd ed. Edinburgh, 1878. pp. 53.

MARX (KARL) Theories of surplus-value: (volume IV of Capital): (translated by Emile Burns). Moscow, 1963 repr. 1969 in progress. pp. 506.

KRITIK der bürgerlichen Ökonomie: neues Manuskript von Marx; und Rede von Engels über F. List. Berlin, [1972]. pp. 86.

MARSHALL (ALFRED) The early economic writings of Alfred Marshall, 1867-1890; edited and introduced by J.K. Whitaker. London, 1975 in progress.

MARX (KARL) and ENGELS (FRIEDRICH) Gesamtausgabe (MEGA)...; (Redaktionskommission der Gesamtausgabe: Günter Heyden und Anatoli Jegorow, Leiter). Berlin, 1975 in progress. *bibliogs. Each volume consists of 2 separate parts: Text and Apparat.*

MARX (KARL) Capital: a critique of political economy;...introduced by Ernest Mandel; translated by Ben Fowkes. Harmondsworth, 1976 in progress. *bibliog.*

SMITH (ADAM) LL.D., F.R.S. An inquiry into the nature and causes of the wealth of nations; general editors, R.H. Campbell and A.S. Skinner; textual editor, W.B. Todd. Oxford, 1976. 2 vols. *bibliog. (Glasgow. University. Glasgow Edition of the Works and Correspondence of Adam Smith)*

— **1876-1976.**

GREGORY (Sir THEODOR EMANUEL GUGENHEIM) [Unpublished economic and personal papers. 1910-34]. 6 pieces. *Manuscript, typescript, etc.*

HOBSON (JOHN ATKINSON) Confessions of an economic heretic: the autobiography of J.A. Hobson; edited...by Michael Freeden; [reprint, with a new introduction, of the work first published in 1938]. Hassocks, Sussex, 1976. pp. 217.

BAUMOL (WILLIAM JACK) Economic theory and operations analysis. 3rd ed. Englewood Cliffs, [1972]. pp. 626.

STAGER (DAVID) Economic analysis and Canadian policy. Toronto, [1973]. pp. 482. *bibliogs.*

VESVU-KONGRES, VRIJE UNIVERSITEIT AMSTERDAM, 1973. Krisis in de ekonomiese theorie: lezingen en diskussies van het VESVU-Kongres, etc. [Nijmegen, 1973]. pp. 117.

SELLEKAERTS (WILLY) ed. Econometrics and economic theory: essays in honour of Jan Tinbergen. London, 1974. pp. 298. *bibliogs.*

STUDI inediti in memoria di Gustavo Del Vecchio; ([by] G. Busino [and others]). Milano, 1974. pp. 251.

MARSHALL (ALFRED) The early economic writings of Alfred Marshall, 1867-1890; edited and introduced by J.K. Whitaker. London, 1975 in progress.

ATTALI (JACQUES) La parole et l'outil. [Paris, 1975]. pp. 243. *bibliog.*

DEWEY (DONALD) Microeconomics: the analysis of prices and markets. New York, 1975. pp. 338. *bibliogs.*

FEIWEL (GEORGE R.) The intellectual capital of Michał Kalecki: a study in economic theory and policy. Knoxville, [1975]. pp. 583. *bibliog.*

ECONOMICS.(Cont.)

HERENDEEN (JAMES B.) The economics of the corporate economy. New York, [1975]. pp. 262. *bibliogs.*

JONES (HYWEL G.) An introduction to modern theories of economic growth. London, 1975. pp. 253. *bibliogs.*

KOSHIMURA (SHINZABURO) Theory of capital reproduction and accumulation, translated by Toshihiro Ataka; edited by Jesse G. Schwartz. Kitchener, Ont., [1975]. pp. 161.

KOUTSOGIANNES (A.) Modern microeconomics. London, 1975. pp. 462. *bibliog.*

KREGEL (J.A.) The reconstruction of political economy: an introduction to post-Keynesian economics. 2nd ed. London, 1975. pp. 228. *bibliog.*

LIBER amicorum Professor Dr. Gaston Eyskens: economische opstellen aangeboden...ter gelegenheid van zijn emeritaatsviering op 4 oktober 1975. Leuven, 1975. pp. 521. *bibliogs.*

LIPPITT (VERNON GARVEY) The national economic environment. New York, [1975]. pp. 551.

MARSHALL (B.V.) Comprehensive economics: institutional, analytical and applied. 2nd ed. London, 1975. pp. 1163, li. *bibliogs.*

OTT (DAVID J.) and others. Macroeconomic theory. [New York, 1975]. pp. 401. *bibliogs.*

SHEIN (ALEKSANDR IVANOVICH) Kritika ekonomicheskikh teorii pravykh leiboristov Anglii. Moskva, 1975. pp. 200.

SHONE (ROBERT) Microeconomics: a modern treatment. London, 1975. pp. 330. *bibliog.*

SILK (LEONARD SOLOMON) Contemporary economics: principles and issues. 2nd ed. New York, [1975]. pp. 591. *bibliog.*

SYMPOSIUM ON ADAPTIVE ECONOMICS, MADISON, 1974. Adaptive economic models: (proceedings...); edited by Richard H. Day [and] Theodore Groves. New York, 1975. pp. 581. *bibliogs.* (*Wisconsin University, Madison. Mathematics Research Center, United States Army. Publications. No. 34*)

ZAHN (FRANK) Macroeconomic theory and policy. Englewood Cliffs, [1975]. pp. 320. *bibliogs.*

HARBURY (COLIN DESMOND) Descriptive economics. 5th ed. London, 1976. pp. 306.

HEWITT (GORDON) Economics of the market. Glasgow, 1976. pp. 343. *bibliog.*

MINSKY (HYMAN P.) John Maynard Keynes. London, 1976. pp. 181. *bibliog.*

— 1976— .

ASSOCIATION OF UNIVERSITY TEACHERS OF ECONOMICS. Annual Conference, 1975. Essays in economic analysis...; edited by M.J. Artis [and] A.R. Nobay. Cambridge, 1976. pp. 282. *bibliogs.*

AWH (ROBERT Y.) Microeconomics: theory and applications. Santa Barbara, [1976]. pp. 492.

BARRO (ROBERT J.) and GROSSMAN (HERSCHEL I.) Money, employment and inflation. Cambridge, 1976. pp. 264. *bibliog.*

BOSWELL (JONATHAN S.) Social and business enterprises: an introduction to organisational economics. London, 1976. pp. 216.

EVANS (DOUGLAS) and BODY (RICHARD) eds. Freedom and stability in the world economy. London, 1976. pp. 117.

FRONTIERS in social thought: essays in honor of Kenneth E. Boulding; edited by Martin Pfaff. Amsterdam, 1976. pp. 386. *bibliog.*

GWARTNEY (JAMES D.) Economics: private and public choice. New York, [1976]. pp. 656. *bibliog.*

HEATHFIELD (DAVID F.) ed. Topics in applied macroeconomics. London, 1976. pp. 230. *bibliogs.*

JOHNSON (DUDLEY W.) Macroeconomics: money, prices and income. Santa Barbara, [1976]. pp. 490.

KING (DUNCAN T.) and HAMILTON (G. DON) Economics in society: a basic course. London, 1976. pp. 261. *bibliog.*

KOJIMA (OSAMU) ed. Studies in the industrial economics; edited on behalf of Institute of Industrial Research, Kwansei Gakuin University. Kyoto, 1976. pp. 134.

LEIBENSTEIN (HARVEY) Beyond economic man: a new foundation for microeconomics. Cambridge, Mass., 1976. pp. 297.

LEVAČIĆ (ROSALIND) Macroeconomics: the static and dynamic analysis of a monetary economy. London, 1976. pp. 374. *bibliogs.*

LINDAUER (JOHN) Macroeconomics. 3rd ed. Santa Barbara, [1976]. pp. 425. *bibliogs.*

MEADE (JAMES EDWARD) The just economy:...being volume four of Principles of political economy. London, 1976. pp. 247.

RICHARDS (HAMISH) ed. Population, factor movements and economic development: studies presented to Brinley Thomas. Cardiff, 1976. pp. 288. *bibliog.*

STAFFORD (LEONARD W.T.) The modern economy: a theoretical debate and its practical implications. London, 1976. pp. 124. *bibliog.*

WYKOFF (FRANK C.) Macroeconomics: theory, evidence, and policy. Englewood Cliffs, [1976]. pp. 471. *bibliogs.*

ECONOMICS, COMPARATIVE.

FLOREK (HENRYK) and SZEFLER (STANISŁAW) Dywersja w ekonomice. Warszawa, 1970. pp. 176.

KRAWCZEWSKI (ANDRZEJ) Rewizjonizm a współczesna bur'zuazyjna ekonomia polityczna. Warszawa, 1970. pp. 114. *bibliog.* With English and Russian summaries.

ECONOMIC planning, east and west; edited and with an introduction by Morris Bornstein. Cambridge, Mass., [1975]. pp. 329. Revised papers from a conference conducted by the Comparative Economics Program at the University of Michigan in Bellagio, Italy, in 1973.

NAUCHNO-tekhnicheskaia revoliutsiia i preimushchestva sotsializma. Moskva, 1975. pp. 261.

YUGOSLAVIA. Savezni Zavod za Statistiku. Studije, Analize i Prikazi. 74. Uporedjenje jugoslovenske i madjarske industrije: produktivnost rada i struktura industrije, 1960-1970; Comparison between the Yugoslav and Hungarian industry: labour productivity and structure of industry, 1960-1970. Beograd, 1975. pp. 68. With English summary.

CASSEL (DIETER) and THIEME (H. JOERG) eds. Einkommensverteilung im Systemvergleich;...mit Beiträgen von Dieter Cassel [and others]. Stuttgart, 1976. pp. 213.

— Bibliography.

GERMANY (BUNDESREPUBLIK). Deutscher Bundestag. Wissenschaftliche Dienste. 1975. Konvergenztheorie: Angleichung der ökonomischen, sozialen und politischen Systeme von Ost und West; Auswahlbibliographie; [compiled by Gerhard Hahn]. Bonn, 1975. pp. 10. (*Bibliographien. 26. Nachtrag*)

ECONOMICS, MATHEMATICAL.

PAWŁOWSKI (ZBIGNIEW) Ekonometria. Warszawa, 1966. pp. 417. *bibliog.* With English and Russian summaries.

ANNALES DE L'INSÉÉ; [pd. by] Institut National de la Statistique et des Études Économiques [France]. 3 a yr., My 1969 (no.1)- Paris.

BAUMOL (WILLIAM JACK) Economic theory and operations analysis. 3rd ed. Englewood Cliffs, [1972]. pp. 626.

KUZNETS (SIMON SMITH) Data for quantitative economic analysis: problems of supply and demand. Stockholm, [1972]. pp. 27. (*Sveriges Industriförbund. [Nobel Prize] Lectures. 1971*)

MATEMATICHESKIE metody v ekonomike i mezhdunarodnykh otnosheniiakh. Moskva, 1972. pp. 299. *bibliog.* (*Akademiia Nauk SSSR. Institut Mirovoi Ekonomiki i Mezhdunarodnykh Otnoshenii. Nauchno-Metodicheskii Sovet po Primeneniiu Matematicheskikh Metodov. Problemy Ekonometricheskogo Modelirovaniia*)

STEINMETZ (VOLKER) Zur Existenz von Wachstumsgleichgewichten in Wachstumsmodellen vom von Neumannschen Typ. Meisenheim am Glan, [1972]. pp. 100. *bibliog.*

MAKAROV (VALERII LEONIDOVICH) and RUBINOV (ALEKSANDR MOISEEVICH) Matematicheskaia teoriia ekonomicheskoi dinamiki i ravnovesiia. Moskva, 1973. pp. 335. *bibliog.*

FAIR (RAY C.) A model of macroeconomic activity. Cambridge, Mass., [1974 in progress]. *bibliog.*

MATEMATICHESKOE programmirovanie i proizvodstvennye zadachi. Erevan, 1974. pp. 142. *bibliog.*

SELLEKAERTS (WILLY) ed. Econometrics and economic theory: essays in honour of Jan Tinbergen. London, 1974. pp. 298. *bibliogs.*

BARRAS (R.) and BROADBENT (T.A.) An activity-commodity formalism for socio-economic systems. London, 1975. pp. 41. *bibliog.* (*Centre for Environmental Studies. Research Papers. 18*)

The BROOKINGS model: perspective and recent developments; edited by Gary Fromm [and] Lawrence R. Klein; [papers of a conference held at Brookings Institution in February 1972]. Amsterdam, 1975. pp. 679.

CHEREMNYKH (IURII NIKOLAEVICH) Kachestvennoe issledovanie optimal'nykh traektorii dinamicheskikh modelei ekonomiki: voprosy magistral'noi teorii. Moskva, 1975. pp. 183. *bibliog.*

DOBROVOL'SKII (VLADIMIR KONSTANTINOVICH) Ekonomiko-matematicheskoe modelirovanie: voprosy metodologii. Kiev, 1975. pp. 183. *bibliog.*

DOORN (JOOST VAN) Disequilibrium economics. London, 1975. pp. 96. *bibliog.*

MAAREK (GERARD) Introduction au Capital de Karl Marx: un essai de formalisation. [Paris, 1975]. pp. 312. *bibliog.*

OTT (DAVID J.) and others. Macroeconomic theory. [New York, 1975]. pp. 401. *bibliogs.*

PAELINCK (JEAN H.P.) and NIJKAMP (PETER) Operational theory and method in regional economics. Farnborough, Hants, [1975?]. pp. 471. *bibliogs.*

PEACOCK (ALAN TURNER) The oil crisis and the professional economist. York, [1975]. pp. 19. (*York. University. Sir Ellis Hunter Memorial Lectures. 7*)

PERROUX (FRANÇOIS) Unités actives et mathématiques nouvelles: révision de la théorie de l'équilibre économique général. Paris, [1975]. pp. 274.

STATISTIKA i elektronno-vychislitel'naia tekhnika v ekonomike: sbornik statei. vyp.8. Moskva, 1975. pp. 231.

SYMPOSIUM ON ADAPTIVE ECONOMICS, MADISON, 1974. Adaptive economic models: (proceedings...); edited by Richard H. Day [and] Theodore Groves. New York, 1975. pp. 581. *bibliogs.* (*Wisconsin University, Madison. Mathematics Research Center, United States Army. Publications. No. 34*)

TREZZA (BRUNO) Economia e moneta: una riformulazione integrale della macroeconomia. Bologna, [1975]. pp. 237.

DESAI (MEGHNAD J.) Applied econometrics. Deddington, Oxon., 1976. pp. 277. *bibliogs.*

DIXIT (AVINASH K.) Optimization in economic theory. London, 1976. pp. 134. *bibliogs.*

HEATHFIELD (DAVID F.) ed. Topics in applied macroeconomics. London, 1976. pp. 230. *bibliogs.*

KOOYMAN (M.A.) Dummy variables in econometrics. Tilburg, 1976. pp. 197. *(Tilburg. Katholieke Hogeschool. Tilburg Institute of Economics. Tilburg Studies on Economics. 14)*

MADANSKY (ALBERT) Foundations of econometrics. Amsterdam, 1976. pp. 266. *bibliogs.*

MORGENSTERN (OSKAR) and THOMPSON (GERALD LUTHER) Mathematical theory of expanding and contracting economies. Lexington, Mass., [1976]. pp. 275. *bibliog.*

NEAL (FRANK) and SHONE (ROBERT) Economic model building. London, 1976. pp. 172. *bibliog.*

PINDYCK (ROBERT S.) and RUBINFELD (DANIEL L.) Econometric models and economic forecasts. New York, [1976]. pp. 576.

STEWART (JON) Understanding econometrics. London, 1976. pp. 243.

WYMER (CLIFFORD RONALD) Continuous time models in macro-economics: specification and estimation. [London], 1976. pp. 37, iv. *bibliog.*

ZAUBERMAN (ALFRED) Mathematical theory in Soviet planning: concepts, methods, techniques. London, 1976. pp. 464.

ECONOMICS, PRIMITIVE.

MEILLASSOUX (CLAUDE) Femmes, greniers et capitaux. Paris, 1975. pp. 254. *bibliog.*

ECONOMIES OF SCALE.

TUCKER (KENNETH ARTHUR) Economies of scale in retailing: an empirical study of plant size and cost structure. Farnborough, Hants, [1975]. pp. 234. *bibliog.*

ECONOMISTS.

A COLLECTION of photographs of portraits of economists and political philosophers. n.d. 1 vol. (unpaged).

JOHNSON (HARRY GORDON) Scholars as public adversaries: the case of economics. [Chicago], 1973. fo. 20.

— Biography.

MAI (LUDWIG HUBERT) Men and ideas in economics: a dictionary of world economists past and present. Totowa, N.J., 1975. pp. 270. *bibliog.*

— Italy.

NUCCIO (OSCAR) Economisti italiani del XVIII secolo: Ferdinando Galiani, Antonio Genovesi, Pietro Verri, Francesco Mengotti. Roma, 1974. pp. 286.

— Russia.

BELIANOVA (ANTONINA MIKHAILOVNA) O tempakh ekonomicheskogo razvitiia SSSR: po materialam diskussii 20-kh godov. Moskva, 1974. pp. 174.

ECUADOR

— Race question.

VILLAVICENCIO RIVADENEIRA (GLADYS) Relaciones interetnicas en Otavalo: una nacionalidad india en formacion?. Mexico, 1973. pp. 317. *bibliog. (Inter-American Indian Institute. Ediciones Especiales, 65)*

EDEN (ROBERT ANTHONY) 1st Earl of Avon.

REES-MOGG (WILLIAM) Sir Anthony Eden. London, 1956. pp. 116.

TRUKHANOVSKII (VLADIMIR GRIGOR'EVICH) Antoni Iden: stranitsy angliiskoi diplomatii, 30-50-e gody. Moskva, 1974. pp. 422.

EDEN (ROBERT ANTHONY) 1st Earl of Avon. Another world, 1897-1917. London, 1976. pp. 156.

EDGEWORTH (FRANCIS YSIDRO).

MARSHALL (ALFRED) [Letters to Francis Ysidro Edgeworth. 1880-96]. 22 letters, 1 postcard. *Manuscript.*

STEPHEN (Sir LESLIE) [Correspondence about Alfred Marshall's theory of consumers' rent. 1891]. 4 letters, 3 pages of notes. *Manuscript.*

HILDENBRAND (WERNER) and KIRMAN (A.P.) Introduction to equilibrium analysis: variations on themes by Edgeworth and Walras. Amsterdam, 1976. pp. 216. *bibliog.*

EDINBURGH

— Social history.

GRAY (ROBERT Q.) The labour aristocracy in Victorian Edinburgh. Oxford, 1976. pp. 220. *bibliog.*

EDUCATION.

COUNCIL OF EUROPE. Documentation Centre for Education in Europe. Information bulletin. 3 a yr., 1970 (1)- Strasbourg.

EASTHOPE (GARY) Community, hierarchy and open education. London, 1975. pp. 137. *bibliog.*

EDUCATION and population: mutual impacts; edited by Helmut V. Muhsam. Dolhain, Belgium, [1975]. pp. 337. *bibliogs.*

VAIZEY (JOHN ERNEST) Baron Vaizey. Education in the modern world. new ed. London, 1975. pp. 176. *bibliog.*

— Aims and objectives.

BERGGREN (CAROL) and BERGGREN (LARS) The literacy process: a practice in domestication or liberation. London, [1975]. pp. 47. *bibliog.*

FREIRE (PAULO) Education: the practice of freedom. London, 1976. pp. 162.

— Classification.

ORGANISATION FOR ECONOMIC CO-OPERATION AND DEVELOPMENT. Directorate for Scientific Affairs. 1975. Summary volume. Paris, 1975. pp. 49. *(Classification of Educational Systems in OECD Member Countries).*

— Curricula.

MACLURE (JOHN STUART) reporter. Styles of curriculum development: [report of a] conference held at...Monticello, Illinois...19-23 September, 1971; organised jointly by the Centre for Educational Research and Innovation...and the University of Illinois, etc. [Paris], Organisation or Economic Co-operation and Development, 1972. pp. 69.

The NATURE of the curriculum for the eighties and onwards: report on a workshop held at the Reinhardswaldschule, Kassel, Germany from 9th June to 4th July, 1970. [Paris], Organisation for Economic Co-operation and Development, 1972. pp. 90.

— Economic aspects.

HALLAK (JACQUES) À qui profite l'école?. [Paris], 1974. pp. 261.

McKENZIE (RICHARD B.) and STAAF (ROBERT J.) An economic theory of learning: student sovereignty and academic freedom. Blacksburg, [1974]. pp. 105. *bibliog. (Virginia Polytechnic Institute and State University. Center for the Study of Public Choice. Public Choice Society Book and Monograph Series)*

EDUCATION.

— — Nigeria.

IJEWERE (GABRIEL OYALETOR) Problems of educational planning for economic development in Nigeria. 1975. fo. 439. *bibliog. Typescript. Ph.D.(London) thesis: unpublished. This thesis is the property of London University and may not be removed from the Library.*

— — United States.

DAVIS (RUSSELL G.) and LEWIS (GARY M.) Education and employment: a future perspective of needs, policies, and programs. Lexington, Mass., [1975]. pp. 166. *bibliog.*

— Philosophy.

COLLIER (GERALD) and others, eds. Values and moral development in higher education. London, 1974. pp. 225.

BARROW (ROBIN) Moral philosophy for education. London, 1975. pp. 214. *bibliogs.*

The PHILOSOPHY of open education; edited and with an introduction by David Nyberg. London, 1975. pp. 213. "A number of the essays...were presented in a conference at the State University of New York at Buffalo, March 1974".

WORK, technology and education: dissenting essays in the intellectual foundations of American education; edited by Walter Feinberg and Henry Rosemont. Urbana, [1975]. pp. 220.

CONRAD (DAVID R.) Education for transformation: implications in Lewis Mumford's ecohumanism. Palm Springs, Calif., 1976. pp. 230. *bibliog.*

FLEW (ANTONY GARRARD NEWTON) Sociology, equality and education: philosophical essays in defence of a variety of differences. London, 1976. pp. 143. *bibliog.*

— America, Latin.

EDUCATIONAL alternatives in Latin America: social change and social stratification; edited by Thomas J. La Belle. Los Angeles, 1975. pp. 490. *bibliogs. (California University. Latin American Center. Latin American Studies. vol. 30)*

— Australia — Classification.

ORGANISATION FOR ECONOMIC CO-OPERATION AND DEVELOPMENT. Directorate for Scientific Affairs. 1975. Australia; Luxembourg; Switzerland. Paris, 1975. pp. 104. *bibliog. (Classification of Educational Systems in OECD Member Countries).*

— — Finance.

AUSTRALIA. Commonwealth Bureau of Census and Statistics. Expenditure on education. a., 1973/74- Canberra.

— Bangladesh.

ISLAM (TAHERUL) Social justice and the education system of Bangladesh. Dacca, [1975]. pp. 120. *bibliog.*

— Botswana — Statistics.

BOTSWANA. Education Statistics Unit. Education statistics. a., 1975(8th)- Gaborone.

— Brazil.

FREIRE (PAULO) Education: the practice of freedom. London, 1976. pp. 162.

— Canada — Finance.

CANADA. Statistics Canada. Financial statistics of education. a., 1971-72/1973-74- Ottawa. *[in English and French].*

— — New Brunswick.

NEW BRUNSWICK. Committee on Educational Planning. 1973. Education tomorrow: (report); [G.E. Malcolm Macleod and A.A. Pinet, co-chairmen]. Fredericton, 1973. fo. 106, vi, 105, vi. *In English and French.*

EDUCATION.(Cont.)

— — Ontario — Finance.

ONTARIO. Ministerial Commission on the Organization and Financing of the Public and Secondary School Systems in Metropolitan Toronto. 1974. Report; [Barry Lowes, chairman]. [Toronto, 1974]. pp. 311. *bibliog.*

— China.

PRICE (R.F.) Education in communist China. rev. ed. London, 1975. pp. 318. *bibliog.*

— Denmark.

ØRUM (BENTE) Uddannelsernes restgruppe: om dem, der ikke får uddanelse efter folkeskolen. København, 1975. fo. 26. *(Socialforskningsinstituttet. Meddelelser. 13)*

— Europe.

COUNCIL OF EUROPE. Documentation Centre for Education in Europe. Information bulletin. 3 a yr., 1970 (1)- Strasbourg.

EDUCATION without frontiers: a study of the future of education from the European Cultural Foundation's 'Plan Europe 2000'; edited by Gabriel Fragnière. London, 1976. pp. 207.

— Europe, Eastern.

INTERNATIONAL SLAVIC CONFERENCE, 1ST, BANFF, ALBERTA, 1974. Education and the mass media in the Soviet Union and Eastern Europe; [selected papers from the conference]; edited by Bohdan Harasymiw. New York, 1976. pp. 131.

— France.

HABY (RENE JEAN) Propositions pour une modernisation du système éducatif, 1975. Paris, 1975. p. 52 *(Cahiers Français, Les. Numéros Spéciaux Hors Série)*

FRANCE. Commission de l'Education et de la Formation. 1976. Rapport...: préparation du 7e Plan. Paris, 1976. pp. 212.

FRANCE. French Embassy, London. Service de Presse et d'Information. 1976. Education in France. London, 1976. pp. 54. *(France: facts, figures. A/113/4/76)*

— — Finance.

Les COÛTS par élève dans l'enseignement français en 1970: étude par filière et par payeur; sous la direction de Jean Claude Eicher. Paris, 1974. pp. 114. *(Centre National de la Recherche Scientifique. Actions Thématiques Programmées. No. 2)*

— Germany.

BUERGERLICHE Wissenschaftstheorie und ideologischer Klassenkampf: eine Auseinandersetzung mit bürgerlichen Wissenschaftsauffassungen; ([by] G. Domin [and others]). Berlin, 1973. pp. 266. *(Akademie der Wissenschaften der DDR. Institut für Wissenschaftstheorie und -organisation. Wissenschaft und Gesellschaft. Band 2)*

HEARNDEN (ARTHUR) Education, culture and politics in West Germany. Oxford, 1976. pp. 164. *bibliog.*

— Gilbert and Ellice Islands.

GILBERT AND ELLICE ISLANDS COLONY. Education Department. 1970. Education policy. Tarawa, 1970. pp. 27.

— Guatemala.

MOORE (ALEXANDER) Life cycles in Atchalán: the diverse careers of certain Guatemalans. New York, [1973]. pp. 220. *bibliog.*

— Iceland — Classification.

ORGANISATION FOR ECONOMIC CO-OPERATION AND DEVELOPMENT. Directorate for Scientific Affairs. 1975. Iceland; New Zealand; Portugal. Paris, 1975. pp. 79. *bibliog. (Classification of Educational Systems in OECD Member Countries).*

— Ireland (Republic).

AKENSON (DONALD HARMAN) A mirror to Kathleen's face: education in independent Ireland, 1922-1960. Montreal, [1975]. pp. 224. *bibliog.*

— — Finance.

NATIONAL ECONOMIC AND SOCIAL COUNCIL [EIRE]. Educational expenditure in Ireland; (report prepared by John Sheehan). Dublin, Stationery Office, [1975]. pp. 96. *([Reports]. No. 12)*

— Kenya.

OMINDE (SIMEON HONGO) The Harambee movement in educational development. Vienna, 1974. pp. 28. *(Wiener Institut für Entwicklungsfragen. Occasional Papers. 74/4)*

— Luxembourg — Classification.

ORGANISATION FOR ECONOMIC CO-OPERATION AND DEVELOPMENT. Directorate for Scientific Affairs. 1975. Australia; Luxembourg; Switzerland. Paris, 1975. pp. 104. *bibliog. (Classification of Educational Systems in OECD Member Countries).*

— Malaysia — Economic aspects.

McMEEKIN (ROBERT W.) Educational planning and expenditure decisions in developing countries: with a Malaysian case study. New York, 1975. pp. 195. *bibliog.*

— New Zealand — Classification.

ORGANISATION FOR ECONOMIC CO-OPERATION AND DEVELOPMENT. Directorate for Scientific Affairs. 1975. Iceland; New Zealand; Portugal. Paris, 1975. pp. 79. *bibliog. (Classification of Educational Systems in OECD Member Countries).*

— Nigeria — Statistics.

NIGERIA (WESTERN STATE). Ministry of Economic Planning and Reconstruction. Statistics Division. 1970. Report of a survey of manpower shortages and surpluses in the Western State and of the capacity utilisation of educational and training institutions. Ibadan, [1970]. pp. 82.

— Norway.

MØGLESTUE (IDAR ODDVAR) Befolkningens utdanningsbakgrunn: en analyse av tall fra folketelling 1970...: educational background of the population: an analysis of data from population census 1970. Oslo, 1975. pp. 88. *(Norway. Statistiske Centralbyrå. Artikler. 79)* With English summary.

— Poland — History.

STASIERSKI (KAZIMIERZ) Szkolnictwo polskie na Węgrzech w czasie drugiej wojny światowej. Poznań, 1969. pp. 230,[vi]. *(Poznań. Uniwersytet. Wydział Filozoficzno-Historyczny. Prace: Seria Historia. Nr.29)*

MROZOWSKA (KAMILLA) Józef Maciej Brodowicz: z dziejów organizacji nauki i nauczania w Wolnym Mieście Krakowie. Wrocław, 1971. pp. 352. *bibliog. (Polska Akademia Nauk. Zakład Historii Nauki i Techniki. Monografie z Dziejów Nauki i Techniki. t.73)* With Russian and English summaries.

— Portugal — Classification.

ORGANISATION FOR ECONOMIC CO-OPERATION AND DEVELOPMENT. Directorate for Scientific Affairs. 1975. Iceland; New Zealand; Portugal. Paris, 1975. pp. 79. *bibliog. (Classification of Educational Systems in OECD Member Countries).*

— Russia.

RUSSIA (USSR). Ministerstvo Vysshego i Srednego Spetsial'nogo Obrazovaniia. Nauchno-Tekhnicheskii Sovet. Sektsiia Narodonaseleniia. Narodonaselenie. 9. Obrazovatel'naia i sotsial'no-professional'naia struktura naseleniia SSSR. Moskva, 1975. pp. 103. *With English table of contents.*

INTERNATIONAL SLAVIC CONFERENCE, 1ST, BANFF, ALBERTA, 1974. Education and the mass media in the Soviet Union and Eastern Europe; [selected papers from the conference]; edited by Bohdan Harasymiw. New York, 1976. pp. 131.

— — Economic aspects.

TURCHENKO (VLADIMIR NIKOLAEVICH) and others, eds. Sotsiologicheskie i ekonomicheskie problemy obrazovaniia. Novosibirsk, 1969. pp. 436.

— — Ukraine — History.

KOSHARNYI (IVAN IAKOVLEVYCH) U suzir"ï sotsialistychnoï kul'tury: kul'turne budivnytstvo u vozz"iednanykh oblastiakh Ukraïns'koï RSR, 1939-1958 rr. L'viv, 1975. pp. 239.

— Sierra Leone — Economic aspects.

KETKAR (SUHAS L.) Economics of education in Sierra Leone. Ann Arbor, 1975. pp. 37. *bibliog. (Michigan University. Center for Research on Economic Development. Discussion Papers. No. 47)*

— Singapore.

SINGAPORE. Ministry of Education. 1972. Education in Singapore. 2nd ed. Singapore, 1972. pp. 99.

— South Africa.

TROUP (FREDA) Forbidden pastures: education under apartheid. London, 1976. pp. 72.

— — Statistics.

SOUTH AFRICA. Census, 1970. Population census, 1970: nature of education. [Pretoria, 1975]. pp. 316. *(Bureau of Statistics. Reports. No. 02-05-02) In English and Afrikaans.*

SOUTH AFRICA. Census, 1970. Population census, 1970: level of education. [Pretoria, 1976]. pp. 396. *(Bureau of Statistics. Reports. No.02-05-07) In English and Afrikaans.*

— — Transkei.

TRANSKEI. Commission of Inquiry into the Standard of Education in the Transkei. 1973. Report. [Umtata, 1973]. pp. 134.

— Spain — History.

JIMENEZ-LANDI MARTINEZ (ANTONIO) La Institucion Libre de Enseñanza y su ambiente. Madrid, [1973 in progress]. *bibliog.*

— Switzerland — Classification.

ORGANISATION FOR ECONOMIC CO-OPERATION AND DEVELOPMENT. Directorate for Scientific Affairs. 1975. Australia; Luxembourg; Switzerland. Paris, 1975. pp. 104. *bibliog. (Classification of Educational Systems in OECD Member Countries).*

— Tanzania.

MORRISON (DAVID R.) Education and politics in Africa: the Tanzanian case. London, [1976]. pp. 352. *bibliog.*

— Underdeveloped areas.

See UNDERDEVELOPED AREAS — Education.

— United Kingdom.

BOYSON (RHODES) The crisis in education. London, 1975. pp. 160.

EASTHOPE (GARY) Community, hierarchy and open education. London, 1975. pp. 137. *bibliog.*

LIBERAL PARTY. Advisory Panel for Education. Focus on education. London, 1976. pp. 16. *(Liberal Publication Department. Study Papers. No. 1)*

ROBINSON (PHILIP) Education and poverty. London, 1976. pp. 126. *bibliog.*

— — Curricula.

BROWNE (E.W.) and others. The school curriculum: a survey on the opinions of young men about the education they have had and the education they would like to have had. [Calcutta?], South East Asia Command, 1946. pp. 40.

— — Economic aspects.

ALLEN (GEORGE CYRIL) The British disease: a short essay on the nature and causes of the nation's lagging wealth. London, 1976. pp. 79. bibliog. (Institute of Economic Affairs. Hobart Papers. 67)

— — History.

DONY (JOHN GEORGE) A history of education in Luton. Luton, County Borough of Luton Museum and Art Gallery, 1970. p. 61. bibliog.

SILVER (PAMELA) and SILVER (HAROLD) The education of the poor: the history of a National school 1824- 1974. London, 1974. pp. 197. bibliog.

MIDDLETON (NIGEL GORDON) and WEITZMAN (SOPHIA) A place for everyone: a history of state education from the end of the 18th century to the 1970s. London, 1976. pp. 506. bibliog.

ROTHBLATT (SHELDON) Tradition and change in English liberal education: an essay in history and culture. London, 1976. pp. 216.

— — Statistics.

EDUCATION STATISTICS FOR THE UNITED KINGDOM; (prepared by the Department of Education and Science [U.K.] in collaboration with the Scottish Education Department, the Northern Ireland Ministry of Education, and the University Grants Committee). a., 1967 (1st)- London.

PICKETT (KATHLEEN GORDON) Sources of official data. London, 1974. pp. 150.

— — Devonshire.

EDUCATION and labour in the South-west; [papers presented at a seminar held at Dartington Hall in March 1974]; edited by Jeffrey Porter. Exeter, 1975. pp. 77. (Exeter. University. Department of Economic History. Exeter Papers in Economic History. No. 10)

— — Horncastle — History.

CLARK (J. NORMAN) Education in a market town: Horncastle, 1329-1970. London, 1976. pp. 183. bibliog.

— — Lincolnshire.

LINDSEY. County Council. Education Committee. End of a chapter: a report on education in Lindsey for the years from January 1970 to March 1974. [Lincoln, 1974]. pp. 119. bibliog.

— — Scarborough.

SCARBOROUGH FABIAN SOCIETY. Fabian agreed monograph on Scarborough education. Scarborough, [1976?]. pp. 21.

— — Commonwealth.

COMMONWEALTH EDUCATION LIAISON COMMITTEE. News-letter. irreg., My 1966 (v.1, no.1)- London.

EDUCATION IN THE DEVELOPING COUNTRIES OF THE COMMONWEALTH: abstracts of current research; [pd. by] Commonwealth Secretariat. bien., 1969 [1st bien. issue]- London.

— United States.

HYMAN (HERBERT HIRAM) and others. The enduring effects of education. Chicago, [1975]. pp. 313.

NAYLOR (THOMAS H.) and CLOTFELTER (JAMES) Strategies for change in the South. Chapel Hill, [1975]. pp. 316.

WORK, technology and education: dissenting essays in the intellectual foundations of American education; edited by Walter Feinberg and Henry Rosemont. Urbana, [1975]. pp. 220.

— — Economic aspects.

GINZBERG (ELI) The manpower connection: education and work. Cambridge, Mass., 1975. pp. 258.

EDUCATION, COOPERATIVE

— United States.

NATIONAL CONVENTION ON WORK AND THE COLLEGE STUDENT, 1ST., CARBONDALE, 1975. Work and the college student: proceedings of the...convention...; edited by Roland Keene [and others]. Carbondale, Ill., [1976]. pp. 466. bibliog.

EDUCATION, ELEMENTARY

— Germany.

ERLER (OTTO) Die Volksschule im Lichte des demokratischen Staates und des Sozialismus; für Laien, besonders für die Eltern geschrieben. Leipzig, 1919. pp. 48.

— Sudan.

GRIFFITHS (VINCENT LLEWELLYN) Teacher-centred: quality in Sudan primary education, 1930 to 1970. London. 1975. pp. 146.

EDUCATION, HIGHER.

INSTITUTIONAL management in higher education: report of a conference...[held in Paris, 2-5 November, 1971]. [Paris], Organisation for Economic Co-operation and Development, 1972. pp. 67. (Centre for Educational Research and Innovation. [Studies in Institutional Management in Higher Education])

COLLIER (GERALD) and others, eds. Values and moral development in higher education. London, 1974. pp. 225.

MEASUREMENT of human resources: (based on papers presented to a symposium held in Lisbon, June 1973, and sponsored by N.A.T.O); edited by W.T. Singleton and P. Spurgeon. London, 1975. pp. 370. bibliogs.

BEARD (RUTH M.) Teaching and learning in higher education. 3rd ed. Harmondsworth, 1976. pp. 251. bibliog.

— Bibliography.

ALTBACH (PHILIP G.) ed. Comparative higher education abroad: bibliography and analysis. New York, 1976. pp. 274. bibliogs.

— Denmark — Finance.

JENSEN (ARNE) and others. University of Copenhagen: decision, planning and budgeting. [Paris], Organisation for Economic Co-operation and Development, 1972. pp. 207. (Centre for Educational Research and Innovation. Studies in Institutional Management in Higher Education)

— Iran.

SHAHEEN (A. SH.) A preliminary study on economics of employment and higher education in Iran; (prepared for the Seminar on Planning and Development of Manpower in Iran). [Tehran], Bureau of Statistics, [1969]. pp. 34.

— Poland — Economic aspects.

GMYTRASIEWICZ (MICHAŁ) Ekonomiczne uwarunkowania szkolnictwa wy'zszego. Warszawa, 1975. pp. 287. bibliog. (Instytut Polityki Naukowej i Szkolnictwa Wy'zszego. Monografie i Studia) With Russian and English summaries.

— United Kingdom.

JACKS (DIGBY) Student politics and higher education. London, 1975. pp. 176.

COMMUNITY RELATIONS COMMISSION. A second chance: further education in multi-racial areas. London, 1976. pp. 134.

— — Finance.

BOTTOMLEY (J.A.) and others. University of Bradford: costs and potential economies. [Paris], Organisation for Economic Co-operation and Development, 1972. pp. 440. (Centre for Educational Research and Innovation. Studies in Institutional Management in Higher Education)

— United States.

RIESMAN (DAVID) and others. Academic values and mass education. New York, 1970, repr. 1975. pp. 331. bibliog.

CARNEGIE COUNCIL ON POLICY STUDIES IN HIGHER EDUCATION. Making affirmative action work in higher education: an analysis of institutional and federal policies with recommendations. San Francisco, 1975. pp. 272. bibliog.

CARNEGIE FOUNDATION FOR THE ADVANCEMENT OF TEACHING. More than survival: prospects for higher education in a period of uncertainty: a commentary with recommendations, etc. San Francisco, 1975. pp. 166. bibliog.

HENRY (DAVID D.) Challenges past, challenges present: an analysis of American higher education since 1930. San Francisco, 1975. pp. 173. bibliog.

SANDEEN (ARTHUR) Undergraduate education: conflict and change. Lexington, Mass., [1976]. pp. 143. bibliogs.

SCHOOLING and achievement in American society; edited by William Hamilton Sewell and others. New York, [1976]. pp. 535. bibliog. Papers originally presented at meetings of an American College Testing Research Institute seminar between Oct. 1971 and May 1973.

— — Economic aspects.

ADKINS (DOUGLAS L.) The great American degree machine: an economic analysis of the human resource output of higher education...; a technical report sponsored by the Carnegie Commission on Higher Education. Berkeley, Ca., [1975]. pp. 663. bibliog.

RADNER (ROY) and MILLER (LEONARD S.) Demand and supply in U.S. higher education; (a report prepared for the Carnegie Commission on Higher Education)...with the collaboration of Douglas L. Adkins and Frederick E. Balderston. New York, [1975]. pp. 468. bibliog.

EDUCATION, HUMANISTIC

— United Kingdom.

ROTHBLATT (SHELDON) Tradition and change in English liberal education: an essay in history and culture. London, 1976. pp. 216.

EDUCATION, PRESCHOOL

— Australia.

AUSTRALIA. Pre-Schools Committee. Care and education of young children. a., 1973- Canberra.

— Denmark.

NORD-LARSEN (MOGENS) Hvem bruger børnehaveklasserne?. København, 1975. pp. 66. (Socialforskningsinstituttet. Meddelelser. 9)

— United States.

LEVITAN (SAR A.) and ALDERMAN (KAREN CLEARY) Child care and ABC's too. Baltimore, [1975]. pp. 125.

EDUCATION, SECONDARY

— Curricula.

SEMINAR ON COMPUTER SCIENCES IN SECONDARY EDUCATION, SÈVRES, 1970. Seminar on computer sciences in secondary education organised by the O.E.C.D.,...at...Sèvres, France, March 9th-14th, 1970. [Paris], Organisation for Economic Co-operation and Development, 1971. pp. 240.

EDUCATION, SECONDARY (Cont.)

— Africa — Statistics.

FRANCE. Secrétariat d'Etat aux Affaires Etrangères. 1973. Statistiques de l'enseignement du second degré dans quatorzes états africains et malgache, 1961-1972. Paris, 1973. pp. 139.

— Europe.

KING (EDMUND JAMES) and others. Post compulsory education: a new analysis in western Europe. London, [1974-5]. 2 vols.

— France.

FRANCE. French Embassy, London. Service de Presse et d'Information. 1974. The reform of secondary education. London, 1974. pp. 11. *(France: facts, figures. A/96/3/74)*

— Hong Kong.

HONG KONG. Working Party on Pre-vocational Education. 1972. Report; [H.R. Knight, chairman]. Hong Kong, 1970 [or rather 1972]. pp. 12.

— Norway.

NORWAY. Statistiske Centralbyrå. Utdanningsstatistikk: videregående skoler: Educational statistics: upper secondary schools. a., 1973/74- Oslo. *[in Norwegian and English]. Supersedes NORWAY. Statistiske Centralbyrå. Utdanningsstatistikk: fag- og yrkesskoler og høgskoler and NORWAY. Statistiske Centralbyrå. Utdanningsstatistikk: folkehøgskolar, realskolar og gymnas.*

— United Kingdom.

FENWICK (I.G.K.) The comprehensive school, 1944-1970: the politics of secondary school reorganization. London, 1976. pp. 187. *bibliog.*

EDUCATION AND STATE

— Canada.

HURTUBISE (RENÉ) and ROWAT (DONALD CAMERON) L'université, la société et le gouvernement: rapport de la Commission d'étude sur les relations entre les universités et les gouvernements; commissaires, René Hurtubise, Donald C. Rowat. Ottawa, 1970. pp. 268. *bibliog.*

— — Ontario.

ONTARIO. Economic Council. 1976. Education: issues and alternatives, 1976. [Toronto], 1976. pp. 41.

— Nigeria.

NIGERIA. Federal Ministry of Education. 1971. A new policy on education in Nigeria; by A.Y. Eke, Federal Commissioner for Education. [Lagos, 1971?]. pp. 15.

— Pakistan.

PAKISTAN. Ministry of Education. 1972. The education policy, 1972-1980. Islamabad, 1972. pp. 45.

— Somali Republic.

SOMALI REPUBLIC. Ministry of Information and National Guidance. 1974. Our revolutionary education: its strategy and objectives. Mogadishu, 1974. pp. 67.

— Spain.

ALVAREZ DE MORALES (ANTONIO) Genesis de la universidad española contemporanea. Madrid, 1972. pp. 765. *bibliog. (Instituto de Estudios Administrativos. Estudios de Historia de la Administracion.[8])*

— Tanzania.

NYERERE (JULIUS KAMBARAGE) Education for self-reliance. Dar es Salaam, Information Services Division, Ministry of Information and Tourism, [1967]. pp. 28.

— United Kingdom.

KOGAN (MAURICE) Educational policy-making: a study of interest groups and Parliament. London, 1975. pp. 262. *bibliog.*

MIDDLETON (NIGEL GORDON) and WEITZMAN (SOPHIA) A place for everyone: a history of state education from the end of the 18th century to the 1970s. London, 1976. pp. 506. *bibliog.*

— United States.

CARNEGIE COUNCIL ON POLICY STUDIES IN HIGHER EDUCATION. Making affirmative action work in higher education: an analysis of institutional and federal policies with recommendations. San Francisco, 1975. pp. 272. *bibliog.*

WIRT (FREDERICK M.) ed. The polity of the school: new research in educational politics. Lexington, [1975]. pp. 333.

WILLIAMS (WALTER) Dr., and ELMORE (RICHARD F.) eds. Social program implementation. New York, [1976]. pp. 299. *bibliog.*

EDUCATION OF ADULTS

— Australia — Bibliography.

CREW (VERNON) compiler. A bibliography of Australian adult education, 1835-1965. Canberra, National Library of Australia in association with the Australian Association of Adult Education, 1968. pp. 107.

— Nigeria.

NIGERIA. Federal Ministry of Education. 1972. Eradication of illiteracy; by A.Y. Eke, Federal Commissioner for Education. Lagos, 1972. pp. 16.

— United Kingdom.

OPEN UNIVERSITY. Russell and after: a response to the Russell report Adult education: a plan for development. Milton Keynes, 1975. pp. 23.

EDUCATION OF THE AGED

— United Kingdom.

BUTTLE (BERNARD) Preparation for retirement. London, 1974. pp. 11. *bibliog. (Age Concern England. Manifesto Series. No. 20)*

CHARNLEY (ALAN H.) Education in retirement. London, 1974. pp. 15. *bibliog. (Age Concern England. Manifesto Series. No. 15)*

EDUCATION OF WOMEN.

SARAN (MARY) For community service: the Mount Carmel experiment. Oxford, [1974]. pp. 144.

EDUCATIONAL ASSISTANCE.

PARKINSON (Dame NANCY) Educational aid and national development: an international comparison of the past and recommendations for the future. London, 1976. pp. 411.

PHILLIPS (HERBERT MOORE) Educational cooperation between developed and developing countries; with a chapter by Francis J. Method. New York, 1976. pp. 331. *bibliog.*

EDUCATIONAL EQUALIZATION.

HUSÉN (TORSTEN) Social background and educational career: research perspectives on equality of educational opportunity. [Paris], Organisation for Economic Co-operation and Development, 1972. pp. 182. *bibliog.*

FLEW (ANTONY GARRARD NEWTON) Sociology, equality and education: philosophical essays in defence of a variety of differences. London, 1976. pp. 143. *bibliog.*

— United Kingdom.

EDUCATION and deprivation; edited by James Rushton [and] John D. Turner. Manchester, [1975]. pp. 105. *bibliog. A series of public lectures delivered in the School of Education at the University of Manchester in 1973.*

— United States.

LITTLE (ALAN) and SMITH (GEORGE K.) Strategies of compensation: a review of educational projects for the disadvantaged in the United States. [Paris], Organisation for Economic Co-operation and Development, 1971. pp. 151. *bibliog.*

BOWLES (SAMUEL) Economist, and GINTIS (HERBERT) Schooling in capitalist America: educational reform and the contradictions of economic life. London, 1976. pp. 340. *bibliogs.*

EDUCATIONAL EXCHANGES.

PHILLIPS (HERBERT MOORE) Educational cooperation between developed and developing countries; with a chapter by Francis J. Method. New York, 1976. pp. 331. *bibliog.*

EDUCATIONAL INNOVATIONS.

WORKSHOP ON THE MANAGEMENT OF INNOVATION IN EDUCATION, CAMBRIDGE, 1969. The management of innovation in education: report on a workshop held at St. John's College, Cambridge, June 29th to July 5th, 1969. [Paris], Organisation for Economic Co-operation and Development, [1971]. pp. 67.

— Tanzania.

LEMA (ANZA A.) Alternatives in education: Tanzania: education for self-reliance Vienna, 1974. pp. 47. *(Wiener Institut für Entwicklungsfragen. Occasional Papers. 74/5)*

— United States.

BOWLES (SAMUEL) Economist, and GINTIS (HERBERT) Schooling in capitalist America: educational reform and the contradictions of economic life. London, 1976. pp. 340. *bibliogs.*

EDUCATIONAL LAW AND LEGISLATION

— United Kingdom.

ANDREWS (LAWRENCE) The Education Act, 1918. London, 1976. pp. 107. *bibliog.*

TAYLOR (GEORGE) and SAUNDERS (JOHN BEECROFT) The law of education. 8th ed. London, 1976. pp. 570.

EDUCATIONAL PLANNING.

WORKSHOP ON THE MANAGEMENT OF INNOVATION IN EDUCATION, CAMBRIDGE, 1969. The management of innovation in education: report on a workshop held at St. John's College, Cambridge, June 29th to July 5th, 1969. [Paris], Organisation for Economic Co-operation and Development, [1971]. pp. 67.

McMEEKIN (ROBERT W.) Educational planning and expenditure decisions in developing countries: with a Malaysian case study. New York, 1975. pp. 195. *bibliog.*

— Mathematical models.

REDFERN (PERCY) Statistician. Input-output analysis and its application to education and manpower planning. 2nd ed. London, H.M.S.O., 1976. pp. 21. *bibliog. (Civil Service College [U.K.]. Occasional Papers. No. 5)*

— Argentine Republic.

ARGENTINE REPUBLIC. Ministerio de Cultura y Educacion. 1971. La reforma educativa: primer informe. Buenos Aires, 1971. fo. 105

— Europe.

EMMERIJ (LOUIS) and others. Alternative educational futures in the United States and in Europe: methods, issues and policy relevance; [prepared as Background Report No.12 for the Conference on Policies for Educational Growth, Paris, 1970]. [Paris], Organisation for Economic Co-operation and Development, 1972. pp. 214. *bibliog.*

EDUCATION without frontiers: a study of the future of education from the European Cultural Foundation's 'Plan Europe 2000'; edited by Gabriel Fragnière. London, 1976. pp. 207.

— Germany.

BAUER (HARTMUT) Räumliche Bestimmungsgründe der Situation im Bildungswesen als Grundlage regionaler Bildungsplanung: eine Untersuchung über Ostwestfalen und Südwestniedersachsen. Bonn-Bad Godesberg, 1973. pp. 87. bibliog. (Germany (Bundesrepublik). Institut für Raumordnung. Mitteilungen. Heft 80)

— Ghana.

TAYLOR (ERNEST) An organizational approach to the analysis of problems affecting education and manpower planning in Ghana. Bonn, [1974]. pp. 184. (Friedrich-Ebert-Stiftung. Forschungsinstitut. Schriftenreihe. Band 107)

— India.

INDIA. Ministry of Education and Social Welfare. 1975. Main schemes of non-formal education in the fifth five year plan. [Delhi], 1975. pp. 18. (Publications. No. 1027)

— Ireland (Republic).

NATIONAL ECONOMIC AND SOCIAL COUNCIL [EIRE]. Population projections 1971-86: the implications for education. Dublin, Stationery Office, [1976]. pp. 44. ([Reports]. No.18)

— Malawi.

MALAWI. Ministry of Education. 1973. Education plan of Malawi 1973-1980: primary education, primary teacher training, secondary education, Institute of Education; prepared by Cephas K. Reyes. [Zomba], 1973. pp. 198.

— Malaysia.

McMEEKIN (ROBERT W.) Educational planning and expenditure decisions in developing countries: with a Malaysian case study. New York, 1975. pp. 195. bibliog.

— New Zealand.

EDUCATIONAL planning in New Zealand: papers from a seminar [held at Victoria University of Wellington from 14 to 19 May 1972]; edited by W.L. Renwick and L.J. Ingham. Wellington, Government Printer, 1974. pp. 431.

ADVISORY COUNCIL ON EDUCATIONAL PLANNING [NEW ZEALAND]. Directions for educational development; a report. Wellington, Government Printer, 1975. pp. 142.

— Nigeria.

IJEWERE (GABRIEL OYALETOR) Problems of educational planning for economic development in Nigeria. 1975. fo. 439. bibliog. Typescript. Ph.D.(London) thesis: unpublished. This thesis is the property of London University and may not be removed from the Library.

— Underdeveloped areas.

See UNDERDEVELOPED AREAS — Educational planning.

— United Kingdom.

FENWICK (I.G.K.) The comprehensive school, 1944-1970: the politics of secondary school reorganization. London, 1976. pp. 187. bibliog.

— United States.

EMMERIJ (LOUIS) and others. Alternative educational futures in the United States and in Europe: methods, issues and policy relevance; [prepared as Background Report No.12 for the Conference on Policies for Educational Growth, Paris, 1970]. [Paris], Organisation for Economic Co-operation and Development, 1972. pp. 214. bibliog.

EDUCATIONAL PSYCHOLOGY.

LINDGREN (HENRY CLAY) Educational psychology in the classroom. 4th ed. New York, [1972]. pp. 516. bibliogs.

EDUCATIONAL RESEARCH

— United States.

LITTLE (ALAN) and SMITH (GEORGE K.) Strategies of compensation: a review of educational projects for the disadvantaged in the United States. [Paris], Organisation for Economic Co-operation and Development, 1971. pp. 151. bibliog.

EDUCATIONAL SOCIOLOGY.

TURCHENKO (VLADIMIR NIKOLAEVICH) and others, eds. Sotsiologicheskie i ekonomicheskie problemy obrazovaniia. Novosibirsk, 1969. pp. 436.

HUSÉN (TORSTEN) Social background and educational career: research perspectives on equality of educational opportunity. [Paris], Organisation for Economic Co-operation and Development, 1972. pp. 182. bibliog.

BERGGREN (CAROL) and BERGGREN (LARS) The literacy process: a practice in domestication or liberation. London, [1975]. pp. 47. bibliog.

EDUCATION and population: mutual impacts; edited by Helmut V. Muhsam. Dolhain, Belgium, [1975]. pp. 337. bibliogs.

FEATHER (NORMAN T.) Values in education and society. New York, [1975]. pp. 350. bibliog.

KLEY (PETER VAN DER) and WESSELINGH (ANTON) eds. Onderwijs en maatschappelijke ongelijkheid: terugblik en perspectief. Rotterdam, 1975. pp. 136. bibliog. (Mens en Maatschappij. Boekafleveringen. 1975)

NORD-LARSEN (MOGENS) Hvem bruger børnehaveklasserne?. København, 1975. pp. 66. (Socialforskningsinstituttet. Meddelelser. 9)

ØRUM (BENTE) Uddannelsernes restgruppe: om dem, der ikke får uddanelse efter folkeskolen. København, 1975. fo. 26. (Socialforskningsinstituttet. Meddelelser. 13)

BANKS (OLIVE LUCY) The sociology of education. 3rd ed. London, 1976. pp. 294. bibliog.

FLEW (ANTONY GARRARD NEWTON) Sociology, equality and education: philosophical essays in defence of a variety of differences. London, 1976. pp. 143. bibliog.

ROBINSON (PHILIP) Education and poverty. London, 1976. pp. 126. bibliog.

— Africa.

MURPHREE (MARSHALL WARNE) Education, development and change in Africa. [Johannesburg], 1976. pp. 25. (South African Institute of Race Relations. Hoernlé Memorial Lectures. 1976)

— Chile.

SILVERT (KALMAN HIRSCH) and REISSMAN (LEONARD) Education, class and nation: the experiences of Chile and Venezuela. New York, 1976. pp. 242.

— Sweden.

SWEDNER (HARALD) School segregation in Malmö. Chicago, [1971]. pp. 51. bibliog.

— United Kingdom.

ROSE (GORDON) and MARSHALL (TONY F.) Counselling and school social work: an experimental study...; with the assistance of R.F. Adamson and Pauline Avery. London, [1974]. pp. 347. bibliog.

— United States.

LITTLE (ALAN) and SMITH (GEORGE K.) Strategies of compensation: a review of educational projects for the disadvantaged in the United States. [Paris], Organisation for Economic Co-operation and Development, 1971. pp. 151. bibliog.

HAUSER (ROBERT MASON) Socioeconomic background and educational performance. Washington, [1973]. pp. 166. bibliog. (American Sociological Association. Arnold and Caroline Rose Monograph Series in Sociology)

SHIMAHARA (NOBUO KENNETH) and SCRUPSKI (ADAM) Social forces and schooling: an anthropological and sociological perspective. New York, [1975]. pp. 368.

BOWLES (SAMUEL) Economist, and GINTIS (HERBERT) Schooling in capitalist America: educational reform and the contradictions of economic life. London, 1976. pp. 340. bibliogs.

— Venezuela.

SILVERT (KALMAN HIRSCH) and REISSMAN (LEONARD) Education, class and nation: the experiences of Chile and Venezuela. New York, 1976. pp. 242.

EDUCATIONAL TECHNOLOGY.

EDUCATIONAL technology: the design and implementation of learning systems;...report...based on the work of CERI in the field of educational technology and on the results of a workshop on educational technology: strategies for implementation... organised by CERI [and others]...at Leiden, Netherlands,... April, 1970. [Paris], Organisation for Economic Co-operation and Development, 1971. pp. 86.

EDUCATIONAL TESTS AND MEASUREMENTS.

HALL (WILLIAM S.) and FREEDLE (ROY O.) Culture and language: the black American experience. New York, [1975]. pp. 191. bibliog.

EFFICIENCY, INDUSTRIAL.

KONSTANTINOVA (LIDIIA MIKHAILOVNA) and SOKOLINSKII (ZALMAN VENIAMINOVICH) Ekonomicheskaia effektivnost' obshchestvennogo proizvodstva: analiz statisticheskikh pokazatelei. Moskva, 1974. pp. 160.

PETRESCU (ION) Căi de creştere a eficienţei economice în industria chimică. Bucureşti, 1974. pp. 224.

NORTHERN REGION STRATEGY TEAM. Change and efficiency in manufacturing industry in the northern region, 1948-1973. Newcastle upon Tyne, 1975. 1 vol. (various pagings). (Technical Reports. No. 3)

EGYPT

— Commerce.

EGYPT. Central Agency for Public Mobilisation and Statistics. A.R.E. foreign trade according to the standard international trade classification, revised. a., 1973- [Cairo].

— Commercial policy.

HANSEN (BENT) and NASHASHIBI (KARIM A.) Foreign trade regimes and economic development: Egypt. New York, 1975. pp. 358. (National Bureau of Economic Research. Special Conference Series on Foreign Trade Regimes and Economic Development. vol. 4)

— Economic history.

MABRO (ROBERT) and RADWAN (SAMIR) The industrialization of Egypt, 1939-1973: policy and performance. Oxford, 1976. pp. 279. bibliog.

— Economic policy.

HANSEN (BENT) and NASHASHIBI (KARIM A.) Foreign trade regimes and economic development: Egypt. New York, 1975. pp. 358. (National Bureau of Economic Research. Special Conference Series on Foreign Trade Regimes and Economic Development. vol. 4)

MABRO (ROBERT) and RADWAN (SAMIR) The industrialization of Egypt, 1939-1973: policy and performance. Oxford, 1976. pp. 279. bibliog.

— Foreign relations — Arab countries.

DAWISHA (ADHID ISAM) Egypt in the Arab world: the elements of foreign policy. London, 1976. pp. 234. bibliog

— Industries.

MABRO (ROBERT) and RADWAN (SAMIR) The industrialization of Egypt, 1939-1973: policy and performance. Oxford, 1976. pp. 279. bibliog.

EGYPT(Cont.)

— Politics and government.

REJWAN (NISSIM) Nasserist ideology: its exponents and critics. New York, [1974]. pp. 271.

— Rural conditions.

ABDEL-FADIL (MAHMOUD) Development, income distribution and social change in rural Egypt, 1952-1970: a study in the political economy of agrarian transition. Cambridge, 1975. pp. 157. *bibliog. (Cambridge. University. Department of Applied Economics. Occasional Papers. 45)*

— Statistics.

EGYPT. Central Agency for Public Mobilisation and Statistics. Statistical yearbook. a., 1952/73- Cairo.

EIGHT HOUR MOVEMENT.

MILHAUD (EDGARD) La journée de huit heures et ses résultats d'après l'enquête sur la production. Genève, 1927. pp. 145. *(Reprinted from Revue Internationale du Travail 1925-26)*

EINAUDI (LUIGI).

VALITUTTI (SALVATORE) Ritratto di Einaudi. Roma, [1975]. pp. 67.

EISENHEIM.

See OBERHAUSEN

EISENHOWER (DWIGHT DAVID) President of the United States.

OTTO, Archduke of Austria. Dwight David Eisenhower. Lausanne, 1975. pp. 31. *(Lausanne. Université. Centre de Recherches Européennes. Publications. 4. L'Europe et les Pays Tiers)*

REICHARD (GARY W.) The reaffirmation of Republicanism: Eisenhower and the eighty-third Congress. Knoxville, Tenn., [1975]. pp. 303. *bibliog.*

ELBERFELD-BARMEN.

See WUPPERTAL.

ELBEUF.

FRANCE. Direction de la Documentation. La Documentation Française. Notes et Etudes Documentaires. Nos. 4,130 - 4, 131 - 4,132. Les villes françaises: l'agglomération Rouen-Elbeuf; [par François J. Gay]. Paris, 1974. pp. 92. *bibliog.*

ELECTION LAW

— Germany.

SCHREIBER (WOLFGANG) Handbuch des Wahlrechts zum Deutschen Bundestag. Köln, 1976 in progress.

— India.

INDIA. Statutes, etc. 1860-1971. Manual of election law...; a compilation of the statutory provisions governing elections to parliament and the state legislatures. 7th ed. [Delhi, 1972]. pp. 462.

— South Africa.

SOUTH AFRICA. Parliament. House of Assembly. Select Committee on the Electoral Consolidation Act. 1976. Report (with Proceedings and Minutes of evidence) (S.C.7-1976). in SOUTH AFRICA. Parliament. House of Assembly. Select Committee reports.

— United Kingdom.

SCHOFIELD (ALFRED NORMAN) Local government elections: seventh edition...by A.J. Little. London, 1976. pp. 604.

ELECTIONS.

EULAU (HEINZ) and CZUDNOWSKI (MOSHE M.) eds. Elite recruitment in democratic polities: comparative studies across nations. New York, [1976]. pp. 299.

— Algeria.

DUPOUY (BERNARD) Essai sur le problème electoral. Alger, 1958. pp. 35.

— Botswana.

BOTSWANA. Supervisor of Elections. 1974. Report to the Minister of State on the general elections, 1974. Gaborone, 1974. pp. 30.

— Finland.

FINLAND. Tilastokeskus. 1974. Kunnallisvaalit..., 1972. Helsinki, 1974. pp. 58. *(Finland. Suomen Virallinen Tilasto. Finlands Officiella Statistik. 29.B.4)* In Finnish and Swedish, with English summary.

— Germany.

GERMANY (BUNDESREPUBLIK). Deutscher Bundestag. Wissenschaftliche Dienste. 1975. Materialien zu den Landtags- und Kommunalwahlen im Jahre 1975: (with Nachtrag); [edited by Inge Schlieper and Edith Dalades]. Bonn, 1975. 2 parts. *(Materialien. 38)*

— — Bibliography.

GERMANY (BUNDESREPUBLIK). Deutscher Bundestag. Wissenschaftliche Dienste. 1976. Wahl zum Deutschen Bundestag: Wahlrecht, Wahlkampf, Wahlanalyse: Auswahlbibliographie mit Annotationen; [compiled by Inge Schlieper]. Bonn, 1976. pp. 30. *(Bibliographien. 45)*

SCHUMACHER (MARTIN) compiler. Wahlen und Abstimmungen, 1918-1933: eine Bibliographie zur Statistik und Analyse der politischen Wahlen in der Weimarer Republik. Düsseldorf, [1976]. pp. 155.

— — Hamburg.

TROITZSCH (KLAUS G.) Sozialstruktur und Wählerverhalten:...dargestellt am Beispiel der Wahlen in Hamburg von 1949 bis 1974. Meisenheim am Glan, 1976. pp. 142. *bibliog.*

— India.

INDIA. Election Commission. 1973. Bye-elections brochure 1972: an analysis: House of the People and Legislative Assemblies, Council of States and Legislative Councils, 1-1-1971 to 31-12-1972. [Delhi], 1973. pp. 111.

INDIA. Election Commission. 1974. Bye-elections brochure 1973: an analysis: House of the People and Legislative Assemblies, Council of States and Legislative Councils, 1-1-1973 to 31-12-1973. [Delhi], 1974. pp. 76.

ELKINS (DAVID J.) Electoral participation in a South Indian context. Durham, N.C., [1975]. pp. 251. *bibliog.*

— Ireland (Republic).

NEWLAND (ROBERT A.) Recent elections in the United Kingdom and Ireland. London, 1975. pp. 8.

— Japan.

SAKAGAMI (NOBUO) The Japanese electoral system. [Colchester], 1976. fo. 164. *bibliog.*

— Malaysia.

FEDERATION OF MALAYSIA. Election Commission. 1972. ...Report on the Parliamentary, Dewan Ra'ayat, and State Legislative Assembly general elections 1969 of the states of Malaya, Sabah and Sarawak. Kuala Lumpur, 1972. pp. 164. *In Malay and English.*

— Norway.

NORWAY. Statistiske Centralbyrå. 1976. Fylkestingsvalget, 1975, etc. Oslo, 1976. pp. 113. *(Norges Offisielle Statistikk. Rekke A. 770)*

— Pakistan.

PAKISTAN. Election Commission. 1972-75. Report on general elections, Pakistan, 1970-71. [Karachi, 1972-75]. 2 vols. (in 1).

— Spain.

TUSELL GOMEZ (JAVIER) Sociologia electoral de Madrid, (1903-1931). Madrid, 1969. pp. 219.

CILLAN APALATEGUI (ANTONIO) Sociologia electoral de Guipuzcoa, 1900-36. San Sebastian, 1975. pp. 749. *bibliog.*

Les ELECCIONS municipals a Barcelona del 16 d'octubre 1973: assaig de sociologia electoral; [by Ramon M. Canals and other members of the] Facultat de Dret, Universitat Autonoma de Barcelona; estudi i edició patrocinats per la Fundació Jaume Bofill. Barcelona, 1975. pp. 283. *With abstracts in Spanish and English.*

— Sweden.

GUSTAFSSON (GÖRAN) Partistyrka och partistyrkeförskjutningar: förändringar i svenskt väljarbeteende under 1960-talet belysta genom data på kommunnivå. Lund, 1974. pp. 308. *bibliog. With English summary.*

— United Kingdom.

NEWLAND (ROBRT A.) Recent elections in the United Kingdom and Ireland. London, 1975. pp. 8.

— United States.

WRIGHT (GERALD C.) Electoral choice in America: image, party, and incumbency in state and national elections. Chapel Hill, 1974. pp. 192. *bibliog.*

JENSEN (MERRILL MONROE) and BECKER (ROBERT A.) eds. The documentary history of the first federal elections, 1788-1790. Madison, 1976 in progress.

BLACK (EARL) Southern governors and civil rights: racial segregation as a campaign issue in the Second Reconstruction. Cambridge, Mass., 1976. pp. 408.

NIE (NORMAN H.) and others. The changing American voter. Cambridge, Mass., 1976. pp. 399.

— — Campaign funds.

ADAMANY (DAVID W.) and AGREE (GEORGE E.) Political money: a strategy for campaign financing in America. Baltimore, [1975]. pp. 242.

CADDY (DOUGLAS) How they rig our elections: the coming dictatorship of big labor and the radicals. New Rochelle, [1975]. pp. 280.

— Vietnam.

ELECTORAL politics in South Vietnam: [papers of a conference held by the Southeast Asia Development Advisory Group of the Asia Society in New York in 1971]; edited by John C. Donnell [and] Charles A. Joiner. Lexington, Mass., [1974]. pp. 198.

ELECTRIC ALARMS.

SOCIAL SERVICES RESEARCH AND INTELLIGENCE UNIT [PORTSMOUTH]. Information Sheets. No. 23. Alarm systems for the elderly and disabled people. Portsmouth, 1975. fo. 6.

ELECTRIC CONTRACTING

— Ireland (Republic).

O'SULLIVAN (DEREK) Profile of an industry: a sociologist's view of the electrical contracting business in Dublin. Dublin, Irish Productivity Centre, [1973]. pp. 121. *bibliog. (Human Sciences in Industry. Studies. No.9)*

ELECTRIC INDUSTRIES

— Germany.

KOCKA (JUERGEN) Unternehmensverwaltung und Angestelltenschaft am Beispiel Siemens, 1847-1914: zum Verhältnis von Kapitalismus und Bürokratie in der deutschen Industrialisierung. Stuttgart,[1969]. pp. 639. *bibliog. (Arbeitskreis für Moderne Sozialgeschichte. Industrielle Welt. Band 11)*

DELIUS (FRIEDRICH C.) Unsere Siemens-Welt: eine Festschrift zum 125jährigen Bestehen des Hauses S. Berlin, 1972 repr. 1975. pp. 110.

— — North Rhine—Westphalia.

NORTH RHINE-WESTPHALIA. Landesamt für Datenverarbeitung und Statistik. Beiträge zur Statistik des Landes Nordrhein- Westfalen. Heft 349. Die Elektroindustrie in Nordrhein-Westfalen, 1968 bis 1974. Düsseldorf, 1976. pp. 87.

— Malaysia.

POWER: staff magazine of the National Electricity Board of the States of Malaya. irreg., D 1975 (v.3, no.1)- [Kuala Lumpur].

— Switzerland.

VEREIN FÜR WIRTSCHAFTSHISTORISCHE STUDIEN. Schweizer Pioniere der Wirtschaft und Technik. 28. Alfred Zellweger, Uster, 1855-1916; Hans Blumer-Ris, Freiburg, 1902-1953; von Hans Rudolf Schmid. Zürich, 1975. pp. 113. *bibliog.*

ELECTRIC INDUSTRY WORKERS

— Hong Kong.

HONG KONG. Electrical Apparatus and Appliances Industrial Committee. 1971. Report...on the manpower survey of the electrical apparatus and appliances industry, 10th - 18th December, 1968. Hong Kong, 1969 [or rather 1971]. pp. 102. *In English and Chinese.*

HONG KONG. Electrical Apparatus and Appliances Industrial Committee. 1972. Minimum job standards and specifications for the principal jobs in the electrical apparatus and appliances industry. Hong Kong, 1971[or rather 1972]. pp. 69. *In English and Chinese.*

HONG KONG. Electrical Apparatus and Appliances Industrial Committee. 1975. Report...on the second manpower survey of the electrical apparatus and appliances industry, conducted from 3rd to 22nd July 1972. Hong Kong, 1974 [or rather 1975]. pp. 166. *In English and Chinese.*

— Malaysia.

POWER: staff magazine of the National Electricity Board of the States of Malaya. irreg., D 1975 (v.3, no.1)- [Kuala Lumpur].

ELECTRIC POWER-PLANTS.

— Environmental aspects — United States — Montana.

TOOLE (KENNETH ROSS) The rape of the Great Plains: northwest America, cattle and coal. Boston, [1976]. pp. 271. *bibliog.*

ELECTRICITY SUPPLY

— Australia — Victoria.

VICTORIA. State Electricity Commission. 1962. Serving Victoria: (electricity, brown coal, briquettes; published to mark the sixth plenary meeting of the World Power Conference). Melbourne, [1962]. pp. (30).

— New Zealand.

NEW ZEALAND. Department of Statistics. 1973. Report on the survey of household electricity consumption, 1971-72. Wellington, 1973. pp. 97.

— Russia.

LENINS'KYI plan elektryfikatsiï v diï. Kyïv, 1969. pp. 267.

NEKRASOVA (IDLENA MAKSIMOVNA) Razvitie elektrifikatsii SSSR, 40-60-e gody. Moskva, 1974. pp. 248.

— — Armenia.

VERMISHEV (KONSTANTIN KHRISTOFOROVICH) Preumnozhennye sily: (elektrifikatsiia Armenii v XX veke). Erevan, 1974. pp. 150.

— — Georgia.

CHARKVIANI (KA NIDI) Istoriia elektroenergetiki Sovetskoi Gruzii. Tbilisi, 1975. pp. 494.

— United Kingdom.

OXFORD. Electricity Committee. [Correspondence and papers. 1882-1946]. 20 vols. *Manuscript, typescript, etc.*

LONDON ELECTRICITY CONSULTATIVE COUNCIL. Annual report. a., 1974/1975- London. *Formerly included in LONDON ELECTRICITY BOARD. Annual report and accounts.*

U.K. Electricity Council. Intelligence Section. 1975. Electricity supply in Great Britain: organisation and development, 31 March 1975. London, 1975. pp. 48.

— — Rates.

REVIEW of payment and collection methods for gas and electricity bills; report of an informal inquiry; [Gordon Oakes, chairman] . London, Department of Energy, 1976. pp. 33.

— United States.

BERLIN (EDWARD) and others. Perspective on power: a study of the regulation and pricing of electric power. Cambridge, Mass., [1974]. pp. 174. *bibliog.*

GORDON (RICHARD L.) U.S. coal and the electric power industry. [Baltimore], [1975]. pp. 213. *bibliog.*

URI (NOEL D.) Towards an efficient allocation of electrical energy: an essay in applied welfare economics. Lexington, Mass., [1975]. pp. 159. *bibliog.*

— Yugoslavia.

BENDEKOVIĆ (JADRANKO) Politika cijena električne energije u cilju optimalizacije kapaciteta elektroenergetskog sistema. Zagreb, 1975. pp. 232,70. *bibliog.*

— Zambia.

ZAMBIA ELECTRICITY SUPPLY CORPORATION LIMITED. Annual report. a., 1972/73- Lusaka.

ELECTRONIC DATA PROCESSING.

DEARDEN (JOHN) Professor of Business Administration. Computers in business management. Homewood, Ill., 1966 repr. 1969. pp. 300.

PARKHILL (DOUGLAS F.) The challenge of the computer utility. Reading, Mass., [1966]. pp. 207. *bibliog.*

ACM 70, NEW YORK, 1970. Computers and crisis: how computers are shaping our future; [proceedings of ACM 70, a conference of the Association fpr Computing Machinery; edited by] R. W. Bemer [and] Susan Brewer. [New York, 1971]. pp. 503.

BENTON (WILLIAM KING) The use of the computer in planning. Reading, Mass., [1971]. pp. 160.

COMPUTER-aided information systems analysis and design; [papers presented at] the first Scandinavian workshop, [Aarhus, 1971]; (Janis Bubenko [and others] eds.). Stockholm, [1971]. pp. 206. *Organised by the Scandinavian Information Processing Project of Nordforsk.*

STEWART (ROSEMARY GORDON) How computers affect management. London, 1971. pp. 244.

OPERATING systems techniques: proceedings of a seminar held at Queen's University, Belfast, 1971; edited by C.A.R. Hoare [and] R.H. Perrott. London, 1972. pp. 390. *(Automatic Programming Information Centre. Studies in Data Processing. No. 9)*

PETROCELLI (ORLANDO R.) ed. The best computer papers of 1971. Princeton, [1972]. pp. 296. *bibliogs.*

READ (RONALD C.) ed. Graph theory and computing. New York, 1972. pp. 329. *bibliogs.*

SYMPOSIUM ON THE COMPLEXITY OF COMPUTER COMPUTATIONS, YORKTOWN HEIGHTS, N.Y., 1972. Complexity of computer computations: proceedings of a symposium... ; editors Raymond E. Miller [and] James W. Thatcher. New York, 1972. pp. 225. *bibliog. (International Business Machines Corporation. IBM Research Symposia Series)*

MARTIN (JAMES THOMAS). Security, accuracy, and privacy in computer systems. Englewood Cliffs, N.J., [1973]. pp. 626.

HOWARD (K.) and others. The scope for computer based systems to aid corporate decision- making in the short and medium term in the reorganised local authorities: a feasibility study. Peterlee, 1975. pp. 40. *bibliog. (IBM United Kingdom Limited. UK Scientific Centre. [Technical Reports]. 0074)*

ACM-SIGMOD INTERNATIONAL CONFERENCE ON MANAGEMENT OF DATA, SAN JOSE, 1975. [Proceedings]; edited by W.F.King. [New York, 1976?]. pp. 245. *bibliogs. Organized by Association for Computing Machinery and SIGMOD.*

ACM SIGMOD WORKSHOP ON DATA DESCRIPTION, ACCESS AND CONTROL, ANN ARBOR, 1974. [Papers of the workshop, excluding the debate]; edited by Randall Rustin. New York, [1976]. pp. 494. *bibliogs.*

LUCAS (HENRY C.) The analysis, design, and implementation of information systems. New York, [1976]. pp. 255. *bibliogs.*

— Bibliography.

PRITCHARD (ALAN) A guide to computer literature: an introductory survey of the sources of information. 2nd ed. London, 1972. pp. 194.

— Directories.

THOMAS (ANGELA) ed. LUCIS guide to computer-based information services. [London], 1975. 1 vol. (looseleaf). *Prepared for the Central Information Services of the Interim Library Resources Co-ordinating Committee of London University.*

— Library science.

HAYES (ROBERT MAYO) and BECKER (JOSEPH) Handbook of data processing for libraries. 2nd ed. Los Angeles, [1974]. pp. 688.

— Psycholinguistics.

SCHANK (ROGER C.) and COLBY (KENNETH MARK) eds. Computer models of thought and language. San Francisco, [1973]. pp. 454. *bibliog.*

ELECTRONIC DATA PROCESSING DEPARTMENTS.

BRANDON (DICK H.) and GRAY (MAX) Project control standards. New York, 1970. pp. 204. *bibliogs.*

LUCAS (HENRY C.) The analysis, design, and implementation of information systems. New York, [1976]. pp. 255. *bibliogs.*

— Security measures.

FARR (MICHAEL AUSTIN LINES) and others. Security for computer systems. [Newton Abbot], 1972 repr. 1974. pp. 172. *bibliog.*

MARTIN (JAMES THOMAS). Security, accuracy, and privacy in computer systems. Englewood Cliffs, N.J., [1973]. pp. 626.

ELECTRONIC DATA PROCESSING IN VOCATIONAL GUIDANCE.

WATTS (A.G.) The IBM/Cheshire interactive careers guidance project: an independent review. Peterlee, 1975. pp. 39. *bibliog. (IBM United Kingdom Limited. UK Scientific Centre. [Technical Reports]. 0072)*

ELECTRONIC DATA PROCESSING PERSONNEL.

MUMFORD (ENID) and WARD (THOMAS B.) Computers: planning for people. London, 1968. pp. 176. *bibliog.*

CHANDOR (ANTHONY) Choosing and keeping computer staff: recruitment, selection and development of computer personnel. London, 1976. pp. 203.

ELECTRONIC DIGITAL COMPUTERS.

OPERATING systems techniques: proceedings of a seminar held at Queen's University, Belfast, 1971; edited by C.A.R. Hoare [and] R.H. Perrott. London, 1972. pp. 390. *(Automatic Programming Information Centre. Studies in Data Processing. No. 9)*

PETROCELLI (ORLANDO R.) ed. The best computer papers of 1971. Princeton, [1972]. pp. 296. *bibliogs.*

LONDON. University. London School of Economics and Political Science. Graduate School of Geography. Discussion Papers. No. 55. Three-dimensional generation of erosion potentials using a digital computer; [by] Roger F. Moore. London, 1975. pp. 18.

— Bibliography.

PRITCHARD (ALAN) A guide to computer literature: an introductory survey of the sources of information. 2nd ed. London, 1972. pp. 194.

— Evaluation.

EUROPEAN COMPUTING CONFERENCE ON COMPUTER PERFORMANCE EVALUATION, LONDON, 1976. Computer performance evaluation. Uxbridge, Middx., [1976]. pp. 587. *bibliogs.* Papers presented at the Conference, with a number of additional papers. This conference was part of the European Computing Congress, 1976.

— Programming.

See PROGRAMMING (ELECTRONIC COMPUTERS).

ELECTRONIC INDUSTRIES

— Germany.

SCHEDL (HANS) Untersuchung zur Konzentrationsentwicklung in verschiedenen Untersektoren der elektrotechnischen Industrie in Deutschland: Rundfunk-, Fernseh- und Phonogeräte... Elektrohaushaltsgeräte, etc. [Brussels, European Communities, Directorate-General for Competition, 1973]. 1 vol. (various pagings).

ELECTRONIC INDUSTRY WORKERS

— Hong Kong.

HONG KONG. Electronics Industrial Committee. 1971. Report...on the second manpower survey of the electronics industry, conducted during 16th -21st March, 1970. Hong Kong, 1970 [or rather 1971]. pp. 61. *In English and Chinese.*

HONG KONG. Electronics Industrial Committee. 1972. Minimum job standards and specifications for the principal jobs in the electronics industry. Hong Kong, 1971 [or rather 1972]. pp. 33. *In English and Chinese.*

ELITE.

MAGEE (BRYAN EDGAR) and others. Are elites necessary?: [transcript of a discussion with Anthony Quinton [and] Raymond Williams;...transmitted 19 July 1973. London, [1973]. fo. 40. *(Thames Television. Something to Say)*

AUSTIN (LEWIS) Saints and samurai: the political culture of the American and Japanese elites. New Haven, 1975. pp. 197. *(Yale University. Yale Studies in Political Science. 27)*

EULAU (HEINZ) and CZUDNOWSKI (MOSHE M.) eds. Elite recruitment in democratic polities: comparative studies across nations. New York, [1976]. pp. 299.

PUTNAM (ROBERT D.) The comparative study of political elites. Englewood Cliffs, [1976]. pp. 246. *bibliog.*

— Arab countries.

HAZEN (WILLIAM EDWARD) and MUGHISUDDIN (MOHAMMED) Middle Eastern subcultures: a regional approach; [with contributions by] George N. Atiyeh [and others]. Lexington, [1975]. pp. 215. *bibliog.*

— Belgium.

MAERTINS (RENATE) Wertorientierungen und wirtschaftliches Erfolgsstreben mittelalterlicher Grosskaufleute: das Beispiel Gent im 13. Jahrhundert. Köln, 1976. pp. 356. *bibliog.*

— Canada.

CLEMENT (WALLACE) The Canadian corporate elite: an analysis of economic power. Toronto, [1975]. pp. 479. *bibliog. (Carleton University. Institute of Canadian Studies. The Carleton Library. No. 89)*

— China.

LIU (ALAN P.L.) Political culture and group conflict in communist China. Santa Barbara, [1976]. pp. 205. *bibliog.*

— Denmark.

DICH (JØRGEN S.) Den herskende klasse: en kritisk analyse af social udbytning og midlerne imod den. 4th ed. [Copenhagen, 1974]. pp. 260.

— East (Near East).

LENCZOWSKI (GEORGE) ed. Political elites in the Middle East. Washington, 1975. pp. 227. *(American Enterprise Institute for Public Policy Research. Foreign Affairs Studies. 19)*

TACHAU (FRANK) ed. Political elites and political development in the Middle East. New York, [1975]. pp. 310. *bibliogs.*

— Egypt.

DEKMEJIAN (RICHARD HRAIR) Patterns of political leadership: Egypt, Israel, Lebanon. Albany, N.Y., 1975. pp. 323. *bibliog.*

— Germany.

HENKELS (WALTER) Bonner Köpfe. 7th ed. Düsseldorf, 1970. pp. 379.

SCHOESSLER (DIETMAR) Der Primat des Zivilen: Konflikt und Konsens der Militärelite im politischen System der Bundesrepublik. Meisenheim am Glan, [1973]. pp. 163. *bibliog.*

HERZOG (DIETRICH) Politische Karrieren: Selektion und Professionalisierung politischer Führungsgruppen. Opladen, [1975]. pp. 249. *bibliog. (Berlin. Freie Universität. Zentralinstitut für Sozialwissenschaftliche Forschung. Schriften. Band 25)*

SPECHTER (OLAF) Die Osnabrücker Oberschicht im 17. und 18. Jahrhundert: eine sozial- und verfassungsgeschichtliche Untersuchung. Osnabrück, 1975. pp. 189. *bibliog. (Verein für Geschichte und Landeskunde von Osnabrück. Osnabrücker Geschichtsquellen und Forschungen. 20)*

— India.

BHATIA (BAL MOKAND) History and social development. Delhi, [1974 in progress]. *bibliog.*

ROY (S.K.) Corporate image in India: a study of elite attitudes towards private and public industry. New Delhi, [1974]. pp. 343.

— Indonesia.

EMMERSON (DONALD K.) Indonesia's elite: political culture and cultural politics. Ithaca, 1976. pp. 303. *bibliog.*

— Israel.

DEKMEJIAN (RICHARD HRAIR) Patterns of political leadership: Egypt, Israel, Lebanon. Albany, N.Y., 1975. pp. 323. *bibliog.*

— Lebanon.

DEKMEJIAN (RICHARD HRAIR) Patterns of political leadership: Egypt, Israel, Lebanon. Albany, N.Y., 1975. pp. 323. *bibliog.*

— Norway.

HIGLEY (JOHN) and others. Elite structure and ideology: a theory with applications to Norway. Oslo, [1976]. pp. 367. *bibliog.*

— Switzerland.

KLOETI (ULRICH) Die Chefbeamten der schweizerischen Bundesverwaltung: soziologische Querschnitte in den Jahren 1938, 1955 und 1969. Bern, [1972]. pp. 216. *bibliog. (Bern. Universität. Forschungszentrum für Schweizerische Politik. Helvetia Politica. Series B. vol. 8)*

— United Kingdom.

TAPPER (TED) Political education and stability: elite responses to political conflict. London, [1976]. pp. 265.

— United States.

DONOVAN (JOHN C.) The cold warriors: a policy-making elite. Lexington, Mass., [1974]. pp. 294.

MARGER (MARTIN) The force of ethnicity: a study of urban elites. Detroit, [1974]. pp. 110. *bibliog. (Journal of University Studies. vol. 10, no.5)*

DOMHOFF (G. WILLIAM) ed. New directions in power structure research. Eugene, Ore., 1975. pp. 264. *(Insurgent Sociologist, The. vol. 5, no.3)*

DYE (THOMAS R.) Who's running America?: institutional leadership in the United States. Englewood Cliffs, [1976]. pp. 222.

TAPPER (TED) Political education and stability: elite responses to political conflict. London, [1976]. pp. 265.

ELLIS ISLAND

— History.

PITKIN (THOMAS M.) Keepers of the gate: a history of Ellis Island. New York, 1975. pp. 226. *bibliog.*

EMERGENCY MEDICAL SERVICES

— Canada.

CANADA. Emergency Health Services Division. 1970. Emergency blood services. Ottawa, 1970. pp. 48.

EMIGRATION AND IMMIGRATION.

CONFERENCE ON MIGRATION AND ETHNICITY, OSHKOSH, WIS., 1973. Migration and development: implications for ethnic identity and political conflict: [selected papers from the conference held in conjunction with the 9th International Congress of Anthropological and Ethnological Sciences]; editors Helen I. Safa [and] Brian M. Du Toit. The Hague, [1975]. pp. 336. *bibliogs.*

CONFERENCE ON MIGRATION AND ETHNICITY, OSHKOSH, WIS., 1973. Migration and urbanization: models and adaptive strategies: [selected papers of the conference held in conjunction with the 9th International Congress of Anthropological and Ethnological Sciences]; editors Brian M. Du Toit [and] Helen I. Safa. The Hague, [1975]. pp. 305. *bibliogs.*

EMIGRATION AND IMMIGRATION LAW

— Botswana.

WILL (D.D.) The citizenship, immigration, and allied laws of Botswana. [Gaborone, Government of Botswana, 1972]. pp. 19.

EMPLOYEES' REPRESENTATION IN MANAGEMENT.

— United Kingdom.

CITIZENSHIP in Britain 1974:...conference deal[ing] especially with Pakistanis and...organised by the (Birmingham) Community Development Project. [Birmingham, Birmingham Community Development Project, 1974]. pp. 28. *Photocopy.*

EMIGRES.

DIESBACH (GHISLAIN DE) Histoire de l'émigration, 1789-1814. Paris, [1975]. pp. 581. *bibliog.*

EMINENT DOMAIN

— America, Latin.

KNUDSEN (HARALD) Expropriation of foreign private investments in Latin America. Bergen, [1974]. pp. 356. *bibliog.*

— United Kingdom.

U.K. Department of the Environment. 1973-74. Land compensation: your rights explained. Booklets 1-5. [London, 1973-74]. 5 pts.

COMPENSATION for compulsory purchase: papers from a conference organised by the Law Society, the Bar Council, and the Royal Institution of Chartered Surveyors [in 1974]. London, 1975. pp. 53. *(Journal of Planning and Environmental Law. Occasional Papers)*

NEWMAN (PHYLLIS E.) Town and country planning casebook. London, 1975. pp. 382. *bibliog.*

ENCYCLOPEDIA of planning law and practice: land development series; [edited by] Desmond Heap [and others]. London, 1976 in progress. *Loose leaf.*

CORFIELD (Sir FREDERICK VERNON) A guide to the Community Land Act. London, 1976. pp. 191[19].

MOORE (VICTOR) Community land: the new Act; a guide to the Community Land Act, 1975. London, 1976. pp. 145.

U.K. Department of the Environment. 1976. Community Land Act, 1975. [London], 1976. pp. (14).

U.K. Department of the Environment. 1976. The community land scheme. (Booklet) 1. An introduction. [London, 1976]. pp. 7.

— — Wales.

U.K. Welsh Office. 1975. Community ownership of development land in Wales: summary consultation document. [Cardiff?], 1975. 1 pamphlet (various pagings).

EMOTION.

MANDLER (GEORGE) Mind and emotion. New York, [1975]. pp. 280. *bibliog.*

EMPLOYEE-MANAGEMENT RELATIONS IN GOVERNMENT.

— United States.

CONFERENCE ON LABOR IN NONPROFIT INDUSTRY AND GOVERNMENT, PRINCETON UNIVERSITY, 1973. Labor in the public and nonprofit sectors: [papers of the conference, sponsored by the Industrial Relations Section of Princeton University and the Manpower Administration of the U.S. Department of Labor]; edited by Daniel S. Hamermesh. Princeton, [1975]. pp. 272. *bibliog.*

EMPLOYEE TRAINING DIRECTORS

— United Kingdom.

RODGER (ALEC) and others. The industrial training officer: his background and his work. London, 1971. pp. 57. *bibliog.*

EMPLOYEES, DISMISSAL OF

— Europe.

HARRISON (ROGER A.) Redundancy in Western Europe. London, [1975]. pp. 136. *bibliog. (Institute of Personnel Management. Information Reports. New Series. 20)*

— United Kingdom.

MUMFORD (PETER) Redundancy and security-of-employment. [Epping, Essex, 1975?]. pp. 166. *bibliog.*

JACKSON (DUDLEY A.S.) The law of unfair dismissal, job security and personal management. Cambridge, 1976. pp. 12. *(Cambridge. University. Department of Applied Economics. Reprint Series. No. 428) (Reprinted from Business Economist, vol. 7, no. 1)*

McGLYNE (JOHN E.) Unfair dismissal cases. London, 1976. pp. 279.

EMPLOYEES, TRAINING OF.

HAMBLIN (ANTHONY CRANDELL) Evaluation and control of training. London, [1974]. pp. 208. *bibliog.*

— Canada.

CANADA. Statistics Canada. Student Information Section. 1973. Training in industry...1969-70. Ottawa, 1973. pp. 75. *In English and French.*

— Hong Kong.

HONG KONG. Industrial Training Advisory Committee. 1971. The final report. Hong Kong, 1971. pp. 95.

— United Kingdom.

PAPER AND PAPER PRODUCTS INDUSTRY TRAINING BOARD [U.K.]. Annual report and statement of accounts. a., 1975 (7th)- London. *Formerly included in the file of British Parliamentary Papers.*

U.K. Department of Employment. 1976. Training for vital skills: a consultative document. London, 1976. pp. 33.

CONSTRUCTION BOARD NEWS: information from the Construction Industry Training Board [U.K.]. irreg. London. *Current issues only kept.*

EMPLOYEES' REPRESENTATION IN MANAGEMENT.

INSTITUT ZA DRUŠTVENO UPRAVLJANJE. Anthology of works, 1960-1970, on the occasion of the twentieth anniversary of selfmanagement and the second Congress of Selfmanagers of Yugoslavia. Zagreb, 1972. pp. 760.

NIKOLIĆ (MILOS) Razvoj ideje radničkog samoupravljanja. Subotica, 1973. pp. 173.

GRAETZ (WOLFHARD) Demokratisierung der Wirtschaft durch Mitbestimmung: Möglichkeiten und Grenzen eine Postulates in der Unternehmung. Diessenhofen/Schweiz, [1974]. pp. 297. *bibliog. St.Galler Dissertation.*

OP weg naar arbeiderszelfbestuur. Deventer, 1974. pp. 122. *(Wiardi Beckman Stichting. WBS-Cahiers. Studieproject Gelijkheid. Deel 9)*

REVOLUTIONARY WORKERS' PARTY (TROTSKYIST) The need for workers control in the mining industry. [Doncaster, 1974]. pp. 20.

SUPEK (RUDI) Participacija, radnička kontrola i samoupravljanje: prilog povijesnom kontinuitetu jedne ideje. Zagreb, 1974. pp. 204. *bibliog.*

EUROPEAN COMMUNITIES. Commission. 1975. Employee participation and company structure in the European Community. [Brussels], 1975. pp. 107. *(Bulletin of the European Communities. Supplements. [1975/8]).*

SELF-MANAGEMENT: new dimensions to democracy: [based on a week- long discussion held in October 1971 at the Center for the Study of Democratic Institutions in Santa Barbara]; edited by Ichak Adizes [and] Elisabeth Mann Borgese. Santa Barbara, [1975]. pp. 162. *bibliog.*

VANEK (JAROSLAV) ed. Self-management: economic liberation of man; selected readings. Harmondsworth, 1975. pp. 478. *bibliogs.*

EMPLOYEE participation and company reform: a report on the participating members and young leaders meetings [held in London and Paris in 1975]; edited by Fabio Basagni and François Sauzey with a commentary by Benjamin C. Roberts. Paris, [1976]. pp. 77. *(Atlantic Institute. Atlantic Papers. 1975.4)*

The WORKER directors: a sociology of participation; [by] Peter Brannen [and others]. London, 1976. pp. 278.

— Algeria.

NELLIS (JOHN R.) Workers' participation in Algeria's nationalized industries: la gestion socialiste des entreprises. Ottawa, 1976. pp. 33. *(Carleton University. Norman Paterson School of International Affairs. Occasional Papers. No. 30)*

— Chile.

ZIMBALIST (ANDREW) and PETRAS (JAMES FRANK) Workers' control in Allende's Chile. Nottingham, [1975?]. pp. 8. *(Institute for Workers' Control. Pamphlet Series. No.47*

— Denmark.

BETAENKNING afgivet af det under 15. oktober 1968 nedsatte udvalg til revision af samarbejdsudvalgsvirksomheden inden for statens styrelser m.v. [København], 1971. pp. 53. *(Denmark. Betaenkninger. Nr. 602)*

— France.

CONFEDERATION GENERALE DU TRAVAIL: FORCE OUVRIERE. Les délégués du personnel. [Paris, 195-]. pp. 96.

— Germany.

MITBESTIMMUNG im öffentlichen Dienst: ([by] Thomas Ellwein [and others]). Bad Godesberg, 1969. pp. 88.

RAEHLMANN (IRENE) Der Interessenstreit zwischen dem Deutschen Gewerkschaftsbund und der Bundesvereinigung der Deutschen Arbeitgeberverbände um die Ausweitung der qualifizierten Mitbestimmung: eine ideologiekritische Untersuchung. Köln, 1975. pp. 254. *bibliog. (Stiftung Mitbestimmung, and Hans-Böckler-Gesellschaft. Schriftenreihe. 6)*

— — Bibliography.

GERMANY (BUNDESREPUBLIK). Deutscher Bundestag. Wissenschaftliche Dienste. 1975. Mitbestimmung auf Unternehmensebene, 1969-1974: Auswahlbibliographie; [compiled by Vera Negwer, Hans Rainer Franzen and Alfred Drescher]. Bonn, 1975. pp. 117. *(Bibliographien. 41)*

— Japan.

ODAKA (KUNIO) Toward industrial democracy: management and workers in modern Japan. Cambridge, Mass., 1975. pp. 226. *bibliog. (Harvard University. East Asian Research Center. Harvard East Asian Series. 80)*

— Sweden.

JONES (H.G.) Planning and productivity in Sweden. London, 1976. pp. 212. *bibliog.*

— Switzerland.

SPIELER (WILLY) Kirche und Mitbestimmung: der Beitrag der katholischen Soziallehre...in der Schweiz. [Bern, 1976]. pp. 203. *bibliog.*

— United Kingdom.

EATON (JOHN) The new society: planning and workers' control. Nottingham, [1972]. pp. 16. *(Institute for Workers' Control. Pamphlet Series. No. 33)*

NATIONAL CONFERENCE ON WORKERS' CONTROL [AND INDUSTRIAL DEMOCRACY], 9TH, NOTTINGHAM, 1973. Workers' control: how far can the structure meet our demands?; [discussion at the conference by] Tony Benn, Walt Greendale and others. Nottingham, [1973]. pp. 15. *(Institute for Workers' Control. Pamphlet Series. No. 36)*

EMPLOYEES' REPRESENTATION IN MANAGEMENT.(Cont.)

BRITISH INSTITUTE OF MANAGEMENT. Employee participation: a management view; report of a...working party [Bernard Cotton, chairman]. London, [1975]. pp. 46. *bibliog.*

CITY COMPANY LAW COMMITTEE. First report: employee participation. [London, 1975]. pp. (13).

INDUSTRIAL democracy: Tony Benn at the IWC debate; an account of the Institute for Workers' Control meeting at the Labour Party conference, November 1974. Nottingham, [1975]. pp. 22. *(Institute for Workers' Control. Pamphlet Series. No. 45)*

ABEL (STEPHEN) and PICK (JOHN) Liberal. Democracy at work. London, 1976. pp. 25. *(Liberal Publication Department. Liberal Focus. No. 8)*

BATE (STUART PAUL) Workers' participation in industrial rule-making processes: a theoretical analysis and empirical investigation of a sample of employees in the Port of London. 1976. fo. 430. *bibliog. Typescript. Ph.D. (London) thesis: unpublished. This thesis is the property of London University and may not be removed from the Library.*

FABIAN SOCIETY. Fabian Tracts. [No.] 441. Workers in the boardroom; [produced by a] Fabian [working party on industrial democracy as] evidence to the Bullock committee on industrial democracy. London, 1976. pp. 19.

JAY (PETER) A general hypothesis of employment, inflation and politics; sixth Wincott Memorial Lecture...1975. London, 1976. pp. 34. *(Institute of Economic Affairs. Occasional Papers. 46)*

MARTIN-KAYE (NIEL) Democratic enterprise. London, [1976]. pp. 38. *(Liberal Party. Strategy 2,000. 1st Series. No. 8)*

The NEW worker co-operatives; edited by Ken Coates with contributions by Tony Benn [and others]. [Nottingham], 1976. pp. 227. *bibliog.*

ONE NATION GROUP. One nation at work. London, 1976. pp. 23. *(Conservative Political Centre. [Publications]. No. 585)*

EMPLOYERS' ASSOCIATIONS

— Germany.

RAEHLMANN (IRENE) Der Interessenstreit zwischen dem Deutschen Gewerkschaftsbund und der Bundesvereinigung der Deutschen Arbeitgeberverbände um die Ausweitung der qualifizierten Mitbestimmung: eine ideologiekritische Untersuchung. Köln, 1975. pp. 254. *bibliog. (Stiftung Mitbestimmung, and Hans-Böckler-Gesellschaft. Schriftenreihe. 6)*

— Italy.

SPERONI (DONATO) Il romanzo della Confindustria. Milano, [1975]. pp. 209. *bibliog.*

— Mexico.

ALCAZAR (MARCO ANTONIO) Las agrupaciones patronales en Mexico. Mexico, 1970. pp. 130. *(Mexico City. Colegio de Mexico. Jornadas. 66)*

— Spain.

IGLESIAS SELGAS (CARLOS) El sindicalismo español. Madrid, 1974. pp. 394. *bibliog.*

— United Kingdom.

EMPLOYERS' PARLIAMENTARY ASSOCIATION. [Correspondence with Sir R.A. Cooper. 1916]. 1 piece. *Typescript.*

DERBYSHIRE (JOHN DENIS) The Royal Commission on Trade Unions and Employers' Associations, 1965-1968: an analysis of a royal commission as an instrument for public policy making. 1976. fo. 325. *bibliog. Typescript. Ph.D. (London) thesis: unpublished. This thesis is the property of London University and may not be removed from the Library.*

EMPLOYMENT (ECONOMIC THEORY).

PINHEIRO (MARIA MADALENA PACHECO) Metodos de avaliação de projectos de investimento: a posição do emprego. Lisboa, 1974. pp. 41. *(Portugal. Ministerio do Trabalho. Gabinete de Planeamento. Serie Estudos. 22)* With abstracts in English, French and German.

LYDALL (HAROLD FRENCH) Trade and employment: a study of the effects of trade expansion on employment in developing and developed countries. Geneva, International Labour Office, 1975. pp. 140.

SABOLO (YVES) and others. The service industries. Geneva, International Labour Office, 1975. pp. 238. *bibliog.*

SCHNEIDER (MICHAEL) Das Arbeitsbeschaffungsprogramm des ADGB: zur gewerkschaftlichen Politik in der Endphase der Weimarer Republik; mit einer Einführung von George Garvy. Bonn-Bad Godesberg, [1975]. pp. 271. *bibliog. (Friedrich-Ebert-Stiftung. Forschungsinstitut. Schriftenreihe. Band 120)* With English introduction.

BARRO (ROBERT J.) and GROSSMAN (HERSCHEL I.) Money, employment and inflation. Cambridge, 1976. pp. 264. *bibliog.*

— Mathematical models.

BRISCOE (GEOFFREY) and PEEL (D.A.) The value of inter-related factor demand models for explaining short-term employment behaviour in the U.K. manufacturing sector. Coventry, 1974. 1 pamphlet (various pagings). *(University of Warwick. Centre for Industrial, Economic and Business Research. [Warwick Research in Industrial and Business Studies]. No.52]*

KRUG (WALTER) Quantifizierung des systematischen Fehlers in wirtschafts- und sozialstatistischen Daten: dargestellt an der Statistik der Erwerbstätigkeit. Berlin, [1976]. pp. 109. *bibliog.*

MUSSA (MICHAEL) Output and employment in a dynamic model of aggregate supply. rev. ed. [London], 1976. pp. 46. *bibliog.*

EMPLOYMENT AGENCIES

— Germany.

NEUMANN (FRITZ STEPHAN) Streikpolitik und Organisation der gemeinnützigen paritätischen Arbeitsnachweise in Deutschland. Jena, 1906. pp. 73. *bibliog.*

— Switzerland.

DALCHER (PAUL) Die Arbeitsvermittlung in der Schweiz. Pratteln, [imprint], 1920. pp. 263, iv. *bibliog.*

— United Kingdom.

FEDERATION OF PERSONNEL SERVICES OF GREAT BRITAIN. The private employment agencies: a survey of services to permanent and temporary office workers. London, [1975]. pp. 32.

— United States.

MARTINEZ (TOMÁS) The human marketplace: an examination of private employment agencies. New Brunswick, N.J., [1976]. pp. 159. *bibliog.*

EMPLOYMENT FORECASTING

— United Kingdom.

U.K. Economic Advisory Council. Sub-Committee on the Trend of Unemployment. Report; [H.D. Henderson, chairman]. London, 1935. pp. 43.

EMPLOYMENT MANAGEMENT.

ECONOMIC DEVELOPMENT COMMITTEE FOR THE DISTRIBUTIVE TRADES. Finding the better way: a wholesaler's guide to improved labour utilisation. London, H.M.S.O., 1973. pp. 121.

PIGORS (PAUL JOHN WILLIAM) and others, eds. Management of human resources: readings in personnel administration. 3rd ed. New York, [1973]. pp. 589.

ENCYCLOPAEDIAS AND DICTIONARIES

— Bibliography.

BREWER (ANNIE M.) ed. Dictionaries, encyclopedias, and other word-related books, 1966- 1974. Detroit, [1975]. pp. 591.

ENDOWMENTS

— United States.

FOUNDATION CENTER. The foundation directory;...Marianna O. Lewis, editor. 5th ed. New York, 1975. pp. 516.

FOUNDATION CENTER. The foundation grants index, 1975: a cumulative listing of foundation grants;...Lee Noe, grants editor. New York, 1976. pp. 355.

ENERGY CONSERVATION.

VAN TASSEL (ALFRED J.) ed. The environmental price of energy. Lexington, Mass., [1975]. pp. 326. *bibliogs.*

— United Kingdom.

U.K. Department of Energy. 1975. Energy conservation. [London], 1975. 1 pamphlet (unpaged). *(Circulars. 75/1)*

— United States — New York (State).

DARMSTADTER (JOEL) Conserving energy: prospects and opportunities in the New York region. Baltimore, [1975]. pp. 108. *bibliog.*

ENERGY CONSUMPTION.

MAKHIJANI (ARJUN) Energy and agriculture in the third world: (a report to the Energy Policy Project of the Ford Foundation). Cambridge, Mass., 1975. pp. 168. *bibliog.*

— Canada — Ontario.

CONSUMPTION OF FUEL AND ELECTRICITY BY ONTARIO MANUFACTURING INDUSTRIES; [pd. by] Statistical Centre, Ontario. a., 1972(2nd)- [Toronto].

— Dominican Republic.

ANTONINI (GUSTAVO A.) and others. Population and energy: a systems analysis of resource utilization in the Dominican Republic. Gainesville, Fla., 1975. pp. 166. *bibliog. (Florida University. School of Inter-American Studies. Latin American Monographs. 2nd Series. No.14)* With 8 maps in separate case.

— Russia.

TENDENTSII energopotrebleniia i ekonomicheskii rost. Moskva, 1974. pp. 248. *bibliog.*

— United Kingdom.

LEACH (GERALD) Energy and food production. Guildford, [1976]. pp. 137. *bibliog.*

ENERGY POLICY.

ENERGY: the policy issues; edited by Gary Eppen. Chicago, 1975. pp. 121. *A series of lectures delivered at the University of Chicago in 1974 and sponsored by the Graduate School of Business.*

PRIMAKOV (EVGENII MAKSIMOVICH) and others, eds. Energeticheskii krizis v kapitalisticheskom mire. Moskva, 1975. pp. 478.

WILLRICH (MASON) and others. Energy and world politics. New York, ?1975!. PP. 234 *BIBLIOG.*

EVANS (DOUGLAS) The politics of energy: the emergence of the superstate. London, 1976. pp. 155.

FOLEY (GERALD) The energy question. Harmondsworth, 1976. pp. 344. *bibliog.*

HAGEL (JOHN) Alternative energy strategies: constraints and opportunities. New York, [1976]. pp. 186. *bibliog.*

RYBCZYNSKI (TADEUSZ MIECZYSLAW) ed. The economics of the oil crisis. London, 1976. pp. 202. *bibliog.*

— **Congresses.**

La CRISI energetica: atti del convegno promosso da Politica ed Economia e dal Centro Documentazione e Ricerche per la Lombardia, Milano, 10 dicembre 1973. [Roma, 1974]. pp. 128. (*Politica ed Economia. Quaderni. 11*)

— **Mathematical models.**

WORKSHOP ON MODELING AND SIMULATION FOR ENERGY POLICY EVALUATION, SAN DIEGO, 1973. Energy policy evaluation: modeling and simulation approaches: [papers from the workshop held at the 44th National Meeting of the Operations Research Society of America]; edited by Dilip R. Limaye. Lexington, Mass., [1974]. pp. 215. *bibliog.*

— **Simulation methods.**

WORKSHOP ON MODELING AND SIMULATION FOR ENERGY POLICY EVALUATION, SAN DIEGO, 1973. Energy policy evaluation: modeling and simulation approaches: [papers from the workshop held at the 44th National Meeting of the Operations Research Society of America]; edited by Dilip R. Limaye. Lexington, Mass., [1974]. pp. 215. *bibliog.*

— **European Economic Community countries.**

INTERNATIONAL COLLOQUIUM ON ENERGY POLICY PLANNING IN THE EUROPEAN COMMUNITIES, TILBURG, 1974. Energy in the European Communities : [papers from the colloquium]; edited by Frans A.M. Alting von Geusau, with contributions from M.A. Adelman [and others]. Leyden, 1975. pp. 213. (*John F. Kennedy Institute. Center for International Studies. Publications. Nr. 9*)

— **Ireland (Republic).**

EIRE. Department of the Public Service. 1974. Restructuring the Department of Transport and Power: the separation of policy and execution. Dublin, 1974. pp. 78.

— **United States.**

DAVIS (DAVID HOWARD) Energy politics. London, [1974]. pp. 211.

The ENERGY crisis: (an AEI round table held on 25, 26 and 27 September 1973); Paul W. McCracken, moderator, etc. Washington, D.C., [1974]. pp. 110. (*American Enterprise Institute for Public Policy Research. Round Tables*)

FORD FOUNDATION. Energy Policy Project. A time to choose: America's energy future; final report. Cambridge, Mass., [1974]. pp. 511.

NATIONAL ACADEMY OF SCIENCES. Academy Forum, 2nd, 1974. Energy: future alternatives and risks. Cambridge, Mass., [1974]. pp. 227.

TILTON (JOHN E.) U.S. energy R and D policy: the role of economics. Washington, 1974. pp. 134. (*Resources for the Future, Inc. Working Papers. EN-4*)

WORKSHOP ON MODELING AND SIMULATION FOR ENERGY POLICY EVALUATION, SAN DIEGO, 1973. Energy policy evaluation: modeling and simulation approaches: [papers from the workshop held at the 44th National Meeting of the Operations Research Society of America]; edited by Dilip R. Limaye. Lexington, Mass., [1974]. pp. 215. *bibliog.*

BOHI (DOUGLAS R.) and RUSSELL (MILTON) U.S. energy policy: alternatives for security. Baltimore, [1975]. pp. 131.

BRUBAKER (STERLING) In command of tomorrow: resource and environmental strategies for Americans. Baltimore, [1975]. pp. 177.

ENERGY: the policy issues; edited by Gary Eppen. Chicago, 1975. pp. 121. *A series of lectures delivered at the University of Chicago in 1974 and sponsored by the Graduate School of Business.*

GRAY (JOHN E.) Energy policy: industry perspectives; (a report to the Energy Policy Project of the Ford Foundation). Cambridge, Mass., 1975. pp. 133.

KRUEGER (ROBERT B.) The United States and international oil: a report for the Federal Energy Administration on U.S. firms and government policy. New York, 1975. pp. 366.

LOVINS (AMORY BLOCH) and PRICE (JOHN H.) Non-nuclear futures: the case for an ethical energy strategy. San Francisco, [1975]. pp. 223.

RICHARDSON (HARRY WARD) Economic aspects of the energy crisis. Lexington, [1975]. pp. 233. *bibliog.*

RUEDISILI (LON C.) and FIREBAUGH (MORRIS W.) eds. Perspectives on energy: issues, ideas and environmental dilemmas. New York, 1975. pp. 527. *bibliogs.*

HAGEL (JOHN) Alternative energy strategies: constraints and opportunities. New York, [1976]. pp. 186. *bibliog.*

TIETENBERG (THOMAS HARRY) Energy planning and policy: the political economy of project independence. Lexington, [1976]. pp. 168.

WILDTHORN (SORREL) and others. How to save gasoline: public policy alternatives for the automobile. Cambridge, Mass., [1976]. pp. 324.

— — **Mathematical models.**

JORGENSON (DALE W.) ed. Econometric studies of U.S. energy policy. Amsterdam, 1976. pp. 251. *bibliog.*

ENGELS (FRIEDRICH).

GLASSER (M.) Über die Arbeitsmethoden der Klassiker des Marxismus- Leninismus. Berlin, [1948]. pp. 103.

MEUSEL (ALFRED) Die deutsche Revolution von 1848; mit einem Beitrag von Felix Albin: Marx und Engels und die Revolution von 1848. Berlin, [1948]. pp. 40.

EX libris Karl Marx und Friedrich Engels: Schicksal und Verzeichnis einer Bibliothek; Einleitung und Redaktion: Bruno Kaiser; Katalog und wissenschaftlicher Apparat: Inge Werchan. Berlin, 1967. pp. 229.

HUNT (RICHARD NORMAN) The political ideas of Marx and Engels. London, 1975 in progress. *bibliog.*

MARX (KARL) and ENGELS (FRIEDRICH) Gesamtausgabe (MEGA)...; (Redaktionskommission der Gesamtausgabe: Günter Heyden und Anatoli Jegorow, Leiter). Berlin, 1975 in progress. *bibliogs. Each volume consists of 2 separate parts: Text and Apparat.*

HAGER (KURT) Engels' "Dialektik der Natur" und die Gegenwart: Vortrag. ..gehalten am 3.12.1975. Berlin, 1975. pp. 63.

KOMMISSION DER HISTORIKER DER DDR UND DER UdSSR. Konferenz, 21., 1973. 125 Jahre Kommunistisches Manifest und bürgerlich- demokratische Revolution 1848/49: Referate und Diskussionsbeiträge; wissenschaftliche Redaktion: Gunther Hildebrandt und Walter Wittwer. Glashütten im Taunus, 1975. pp. 312.

LESSNER (FRIEDRICH) Ich brachte das "Kommunistische Manifest" zum Drucker; (zusammengestellt und eingeleitet von Ursula Herrmann und Gerhard Winkler). Berlin, 1975. pp. 392. *bibliog.*

LEVINE (NORMAN) The tragic deception: Marx contra Engels. Oxford, [1975]. pp. 259.

PELGER (HANS) and KNIERIEM (MICHAEL) Friedrich Engels als Bremer Korrespondent des Stuttgarter "Morgenblatts für gebildete Leser" und der Augsburger "Allgemeinen Zeitung". Trier, [1975]. pp. 64. (*Karl-Marx-Haus. Schriften. 15*)

TIMPANARO (SEBASTIANO) On materialism. London, 1975. pp. 260.

HENDERSON (WILLIAM OTTO) The life of Friedrich Engels. London, 1976. 2 vols. *bibliog. With selected documents.*

— **Bibliography.**

PRIZHIZNENNYE izdaniia i publikatsii proizvedenii K. Marksa i F. Engel'sa: bibliograficheskii ukazatel'. Moskva, 1974 in progress.

ENGINEERING

— **History.**

SPENDER (JOHN ALFRED) Weetman Pearson, first Viscount Cowdray, 1856-1927. London, 1930. pp. 316.

— **Ireland (Republic).**

KIERAN (JOHN) of the Science Policy Research Centre, University College, Dublin. Technology transfer: a study with reference to the Irish engineering industry; a report to the National Science Council. Dublin, Stationery Office, [1976]. pp. 28.

ENGINEERING AS A PROFESSION.

WATSON (HAMISH BROCKETT) Organizational bases of professional status: a comparative study of the engineering profession. 1975 [or rather 1976]. fo. 364. Typescript. Ph.D.(London) thesis: unpublished. This thesis is the property of London University and may not be removed from the Library.

ENGINEERS

— **Australia.**

SHERIDAN (THOMAS) B.A., Ph.D. Mindful militants: the Amalgamated Engineering Union in Australia, 1920-1972. Cambridge, 1975. pp. 329. *bibliog.*

— **Sweden.**

TORSTENDAHL (ROLF) Dispersion of engineers in a transitional society: Swedish technicians, 1860-1940. Uppsala, 1975. pp. 313. *bibliog.* (*Uppsala. Universitet. Historiska Institutionen. Studia Historica Upsaliensia. 73*)

— **United Kingdom.**

NATIONAL ECONOMIC DEVELOPMENT OFFICE. Shortages of qualified engineers: a report on factors affecting their supply and demand. London, 1975. pp. 22.

U.K. Department of Industry. 1976. Persons with qualifications in engineering, technology and science, census of population 1971, Great Britain;...compiled for the Department of Industry by the Office of Population Censuses and Surveys from the returns made in the 1971 census of population. London, 1976. pp. 207. (*Studies in Technological Manpower. No.5*)

WATSON (HAMISH BROCKETT) Organizational bases of professional status: a comparative study of the engineering profession. 1975 [or rather 1976]. fo. 364. Typescript. Ph.D.(London) thesis: unpublished. This thesis is the property of London University and may not be removed from the Library.

ENGLISH

— **Caricatures and cartoons.**

HEADS of the people; or, Portraits of the English; drawn by Kenny Meadows, with original essays by distinguished writers. London, [1840]. pp. 400.

ENGLISH LANGUAGE

— **Dictionaries.**

BERNSTEIN (THEODORE M.) Bernstein's reverse dictionary;...with the collaboration of Jane Wagner. London, 1976. pp. 276.

— — **Greek.**

PENGUIN-Hellenews agglo-ellenikon lexikon: basismeno eis ten ekdosin The Penguin English dictionary, by G.N. Garmonsway. Athens, 1975. pp. 926.

— — **Russian.**

MOROZENKO (V.V.) compiler. Anglo-russkii ekonomiko-statisticheskii slovar'...; pod redaktsiei R.M. Entova. Moskva, 1974. pp. 222.

— **Grammar, Generative.**

AKMAJIAN (ADRIAN) and HENY (FRANK) An introduction to the principles of transformational syntax. Cambridge, Mass., [1975] repr. 1976. pp. 419. *bibliogs.*

ENGLISH LANGUAGE (Cont.)

CHOMSKY (NOAM) The logical structure of linguistic theory. New York, [1975]. pp. 573. *bibliog.*

CULICOVER (PETER W.) Syntax. New York, [1976]. pp. 316. *bibliogs.*

EMONDS (JOSEPH E.) A transformational approach to English syntax: root, structure- preserving, and local transformations. New York, [1976]. pp. 266. *bibliog.*

— Prepositions.

BENNETT (DAVID C.) Spatial and temporal uses of English prepositions: an essay in stratificational semantics. London, 1975. pp. 235. *bibliog.*

— Slang — Dictionaries.

PARTRIDGE (ERIC HONEYWOOD) Smaller slang dictionary. 2nd ed. London, 1964 repr. 1976. pp. 204.

— Style.

STRUNK (WILLIAM) The elements of style;...with revisions, an introduction, and a chapter on writing by E.B. White. 2nd ed. New York, [1972]. pp. 78.

— Syntax.

AKMAJIAN (ADRIAN) and HENY (FRANK) An introduction to the principles of transformational syntax. Cambridge, Mass., [1975] repr. 1976. pp. 419. *bibliogs.*

CULICOVER (PETER W.) Syntax. New York, [1976]. pp. 316. *bibliogs.*

EMONDS (JOSEPH E.) A transformational approach to English syntax: root, structure- preserving, and local transformations. New York, [1976]. pp. 266. *bibliog.*

ENGLISH LANGUAGE IN AFRICA.

MAZRUI (ALI A.) The political sociology of the English language: an African perspective. The Hague, [1975]. pp. 231. *bibliog.*

ENGLISH LANGUAGE IN THE UNITED STATES

— Dialects.

DILLARD (JOEY LEE) ed. Perspectives in black English. The Hague, [1975]. pp. 391. *bibliogs.*

HALL (WILLIAM S.) and FREEDLE (ROY O.) Culture and language: the black American experience. New York, [1975]. pp. 191. *bibliog.*

ENGLISH LITERATURE

— Bibliography.

GUNN (DREWEY WAYNE) compiler. Mexico in American and British letters: a bibliography of fiction and travel books, citing original editions. Metuchen, N.J., 1974. pp. 150.

— History and criticism.

TOMLINSON (T.B.) The English middle-class novel. London, 1976. pp. 207.

ENGLISH NEWSPAPERS.

The INTERPRETATION by the Birmingham press of the housing finance issue; [by] David Alexander [and others]. Birmingham, 1973. pp. 26. *bibliog. (Birmingham. University. Centre for Urban and Regional Studies. Working Papers. No. 18)*

CRONJÉ (GILLIAN) Middle class opinion and the 1889 dock strike: a critique of Outcast London. London, 1975. pp. 24. *(Communist Party of Great Britain. History Group. Our History. No. 61)*

HAMILTON (Sir CHARLES DENIS) Who is to own the British press?. London, 1976. pp. 20. *(London. University. Birkbeck College. Haldane Memorial Lectures. 39)*

ENLIGHTENMENT.

HAY (JOSEPH) Staat, Volk und Weltbürgertum in der Berlinischen Monatsschrift von Friedrich Gedike und Johann Erich Biester, 1783-96. Berlin, 1913. pp. 83. *bibliog.*

KRIEGER (LEONARD) An essay on the theory of enlightened despotism. Chicago, 1975. pp. 115. *bibliog.*

MAY (HENRY FARNHAM) The enlightenment in America. New York, 1976. pp. 419.

PAYNE (HARRY C.) The philosophes and the people. New Haven, 1976. pp. 214. *bibliog.*

REDWOOD (JOHN) Reason, ridicule and religion: the age of enlightenment in England, 1660-1750. London, [1976]. pp. 287. *bibliog.*

ENTREPRENEUR.

ENTERPRISE and entrepreneurs in nineteenth- and twentieth-century France; [essays given as lectures in a series sponsored by the Catholic University of America and Johns Hopkins University in 1973]; edited...by Edward C. Carter [and others]. Baltimore, [1976]. pp. 207.

ENVIRONMENTAL ENGINEERING.

SCIENCE, technology and environmental management: [based on a symposium on 'Applied Environmental Science' held at the 1974 Annual Conference of the Institute of British Geographers]; edited by Richard D. Hey and Trevor D. Davies. Farnborough, Hants., [1975]. pp. 295. *bibliogs.*

TECHNOLOGICAL change: economics, management and environment: [studies derived from projects of the Research Program in Industrial Economics of Case Western Reserve University]; edited by Bela Gold. Oxford, 1975. pp. 175. *bibliogs.*

ENVIRONMENTAL HEALTH.

INSEL (PAUL M.) and MOOS (RUDOLF H.) eds. Health and the social environment. Lexington, Mass., [1974]. pp. 460. *bibliogs.*

ENVIRONMENTAL LAW.

BRITISH INSTITUTE OF INTERNATIONAL AND COMPARATIVE LAW. Selected documents on international environmental law; selected and arranged...from International protection of the environment: treaties and related documents, completed by Bernd Rüster and Bruno Simma, etc. Dobbs Ferry, N.Y., [1975]. pp. 197.

STEIN (ROBERT E.) ed. Critical environmental issues on the law of the sea; by Patricia W. Birnie [and others]. [Washington, D.C., 1975]. pp. 57. *(International Institute for Environment and Development. Reports)*

CONFERENCE ON INTERNATIONAL ENVIRONMENTAL LAW, LONDON, 1975. Environmental law: international and comparative aspects; a symposium; edited by Jolanta Nowak. London, 1976. pp. 193. *Conference sponsored by the British Institute of International and Comparative Law.*

— Belgium.

DIDIER (J.M.) AND ASSOCIATES. The law and practice relating to pollution control in Belgium and Luxembourg. London, European Communities, 1976. pp. 496. *bibliog.*

— Canada.

McGEE (GARY) Mining and environmental law. Ottawa, 1973. pp. 185. *(Canada. Mineral Resources Division. Mineral [Information] Bulletins. 138)*

— Denmark.

HAAGEN JENSEN (CLAUS) The law and practice relating to pollution control in Denmark. London, European Communities, 1976. pp. 208. *bibliog.*

— European Economic Community countries.

McLOUGHLIN (JAMES) The law and practice relating to pollution control in the member states of the European Communities: a comparative survey. London, European Communities, 1976. pp. 545.

— France.

COLLIARD (CLAUDE ALBERT) The law and practice relating to pollution control in France. London, European Communities, 1976. pp. 190. *bibliog.*

— Germany.

STEIGER (HEINHARD) and KIMMINICH (OTTO) The law and practice relating to pollution control in the Federal Republic of Germany. London, European Communities, 1976. pp. 420. *bibliog.*

— Ireland (Republic).

SCANNELL (YVONNE) The law and practice relating to pollution control in Ireland. London, European Communities, 1976. pp. 223.

— Italy.

ANNO (PAOLO DELL') The law and practice relating to pollution control in Italy. London, European Communities, 1976. pp. 342. *bibliog.*

— Luxembourg.

DIDIER (J.M.) AND ASSOCIATES. The law and practice relating to pollution control in Belgium and Luxembourg. London, European Communities, 1976. pp. 496. *bibliog.*

— Netherlands.

GRAEFF (J.J.DE) and POLACK (J.M.) The law and practice relating to pollution control in the Netherlands. London, European Communities, 1976. pp. 184.

— United Kingdom.

McLOUGHLIN (JAMES) The law and practice relating to pollution control in the United Kingdom. London, European Communities, 1976. pp. 386.

— United States.

ECONOMICS and decision-making for environmental quality; [papers based on seminars sponsored by the Food and Resource Economics Department, University of Florida in 1971]; edited by J. Richard Conner [and] Edna Loehman. [Gainesville, Fla.], 1974. pp. 299. *bibliogs.*

BARAM (MICHAEL S.) and others. Environmental law and the siting of facilities: issues in land use and coastal zone management. Cambridge, Mass., [1976]. pp. 255.

HEALY (ROBERT G.) Land use and the states. [Baltimore, 1976]. pp. 233.

LIROFF (RICHARD A.) A national policy for the environment: NEPA and its aftermath. Bloomington, Ind., [1976]. pp. 273. *bibliog.*

ENVIRONMENTAL POLICY.

CANADA. Department of the Environment. 1972. Conference on the Human Environment: (a report on Canada's preparations for and participation in the United Nations Conference on the Human Environment, Stockholm, 1972). Ottawa, 1972. pp. 71.

PESKIN (HENRY M.) National accounting and the environment, etc. Oslo, 1972. pp. 57. *bibliog. (Norway. Statistiske Centralbyrå. Artikler. Nr. 50)*

MEYER (JOHN ROBERT) and SMITH (EDWARD K.) Setting environmental standards: an economist's view: [and] Growth: meeting the challenge. New York, 1973. pp. 9. *(National Bureau of Economic Research. Reports. 12. Supplement)*

SOCIETY FOR SOCIAL RESPONSIBILITY IN SCIENCE. Annual Conference, 1971. Against pollution and hunger: [papers of the conference]; (Alice Mary Hilton, ed.). Oslo, [1974]. pp. 307.

ENVIRONMENTAL PROTECTION.

UNEP NEWS; [pd. by] United Nations Environment Programme. m., Je 1975 (v.1, no.7)- , with gaps. *Nairobi.*

CLARKE (ROBIN) ed. Notes for the future: an alternative history of the past decade. London, [1975]. pp. 230.

DEWEES (DONALD N.) and others. Economic analysis of environmental policies. Toronto, [1975]. pp. 175. *bibliog. (Ontario. Economic Council. Research Studies. 1)*

UNIVERSITIES-NATIONAL BUREAU COMMITTEE FOR ECONOMIC RESEARCH. Conference, 1972. Economic analysis of environmental problems: [proceedings of the conference sponsored jointly with Resources for the Future, Inc.]; edited by Edwin S. Mills. New York, 1975. pp. 472. *bibliogs. (National Bureau of Economic Research. Universities-National Bureau Conference Series. 26)*

UNITERRA; pd. by United Nations Environment Programme. m., Ag 1976 (v.1, no.1)- Nairobi. *Supersedes UNEP NEWS.*

ECKHOLM (ERIK P.) Losing ground: environmental stress and world food prospects. New York, [1976]. pp. 223. *bibliog.*

FOIN (THEODORE C.) Ecological systems and the environment. Boston, [Mass., 1976]. pp. 591. *bibliogs.*

GOODIN (ROBERT E.) The politics of rational man. London, [1976]. pp. 210. *bibliog.*

NATIONAL SYMPOSIUM ON CORPORATE SOCIAL POLICY, 2ND, CHICAGO, 1974. Environmental management: economic and social dimensions...; edited by George F. Rohrlich. Cambridge, Mass., [1976]. pp. 316. *Based on papers prepared for the symposium convened by the National Affiliation of Concerned Business Students.*

PEARCE (DAVID WILLIAM) Environmental economics. London, 1976. pp. 202. *bibliog.*

STRETTON (HUGH) Capitalism, socialism and the environment. Cambridge, 1976. pp. 332.

SYMPOSIUM ON INTERNATIONAL ECONOMIC DIMENSIONS OF ENVIRONMENTAL MANAGEMENT, NEW YORK, 1975. Studies in international environmental economics; edited by Ingo Walter. New York, [1976]. pp. 364. *bibliog.*

WARD (BARBARA) Baroness Jackson. The home of man. London, 1976. pp. 297.

— **Bibliography.**

MATTHEWS (WILLIAM HENRY) and others. Resource materials for environmental management and education. Cambridge, Mass., [1976]. pp. 259. *bibliogs.*

— **Mathematical models.**

COUPE (BERNARD EDDY MARIE GHISLAIN) Economics and environment: some models. [Rotterdam], 1976. fo. 236. *bibliog. Proefschrift (doctor)-Erasmus Universiteit Rotterdam.*

INTERNATIONAL CONFERENCE ON REGIONAL SCIENCE, ENERGY AND ENVIRONMENT, LOUVAIN, 1975. Environment, regional science and interregional modeling: proceedings of the...Conference...[vol.] 2...; edited by M. Chatterji and P. Van Rompuy. Berlin, 1976. pp. 211. *bibliogs.*

— **Study and teaching.**

MATTHEWS (WILLIAM HENRY) and others. Resource materials for environmental management and education. Cambridge, Mass., [1976]. pp. 259. *bibliogs.*

— **Africa.**

RICHARDS (PAUL WESTMACOTT) African environment: problems and perspectives. London, [1975]. pp. 117. *bibliog. (International African Institute and Environment Training Programme. African Environment Special Reports. 1)*

— **Canada.**

CANADA. Department of the Environment. 1972. Conference on the Human Environment: (a report on Canada's preparations for and participation in the United Nations Conference on the Human Environment, Stockholm, 1972). Ottawa, 1972. pp. 71.

CANADIAN ENVIRONMENTAL ADVISORY COUNCIL. Annual review. a., 1973/1974- Ottawa. *[In English and French].*

BUNGE (WILLIAM WHEELER) and BORDESSA (RON) The Canadian alternative: survival, expeditions and urban change. Toronto, 1975. pp. 432. *bibliog. (York University (Toronto). Department of Geography. Geographical Monographs. No.2)*

— — **Ontario.**

ONTARIO. Task Force on the Human Environment. 1974. Toward an environmental action plan; in response to the Conference on the Human Environment, Stockholm, 1972; [W.A. Steggles, chairman]. [Toronto], 1974. pp. 151.

SMITHIES (W.R.) The protection and use of natural resources in Ontario. [Toronto], Ontario Economic Council, 1974. pp. 89. *bibliog. (Evolution of Policy in Contemporary Ontario, The. 2)*

— **Europe.**

COUNCIL OF EUROPE. Directorate of Information. 1968. Europe Day, 5th May. Strasbourg, [1968]. pp. 8.

EUROPEAN CONSERVATION CONFERENCE, STRASBOURG, 1970. The management of the environment in tomorrow's Europe: (proceedings of the...Conference [held in] Strasbourg, 9-12 February, 1970). Strasbourg, Council of Europe, 1971. pp. 255. *bibliog.*

— **France.**

FRANCE. Groupe Interministériel d'Evaluation de l'Environnement. Rapport annuel. a., Jl 1974- Paris.

POUJADE (ROBERT) Le ministère de l'impossible. [Paris, 1975]. pp. 278.

FRANCE. Comité de l'Habitat. 1976. Rapport...: préparation du 7e Plan. Paris, 1976. pp. 204.

— **Germany.**

BALTES (HELMUT) and NOWAK (WERNER) Environmental statistics: an instrument of environmental planning. Stuttgart, 1975. pp. 17. *(Germany (Bundesrepublik). Statistisches Bundesamt. Studies on Statistics. No.31) Originally published in German in Wirtschaft und Statistik, vol. 4, April 1974.*

— **Russia.**

INTERNATIONAL SLAVIC CONFERENCE, 1ST, BANFF, ALBERTA, 1974. Environmental misuse in the Soviet Union: [selected papers from the conference]; edited by Fred Singleton. New York, 1976. pp. 100.

— **Singapore.**

WAN (FOOK KEE) Population growth and ecology with reference to Singapore: a country paper prepared for the Regional Seminar on Ecological Implications of Rural and Urban Population Growth, E[conomic] C[ommission for] A[sia and the] F[ar E[ast], Bangkok, 25 August to 3 September, 1971. Singapore, Family Planning and Population Board, [1971]. fo. 7. *(FPPB Papers. No. 11)*

— **Spain.**

NI desarrollo regional, ni ordenacion del territorio: el caso valenciano; informe dirigido por Mario Gaviria. Madrid, [1974]. pp. 445.

— **Sweden.**

MÄNNISKA och miljö: studier av samspelet mellan människans aktiviteter och utformningen av den regionala och lokala miljön; redaktion: Lennart Andersson och Ragnar Olsson. Göteborg, 1975. pp. 135. *bibliogs. (Göteborgs Universitet. Geografiska Institutioner. Meddelanden. Ser. B. Nr. 45) With English summary.*

— **United Kingdom.**

LONDON. Greater London Council. Environmental Group. London's environment: Environmental Group and Pollution Control Group: first report. [London, 1972?]. pp. 19.

U.K. Central Unit on Environmental Pollution. 1975. Controlling pollution: a review of government action related to recommendations by the Royal Commission on Environmental Pollution. London, 1975. pp. 31. *(Pollution Papers. No.4)*

— — **Wales.**

U.K. Welsh Office. 1972. Pollution: the challenge to Wales. [Cardiff, 1972]. pp. 16.

— **United States.**

ECONOMICS and decision-making for environmental quality; [papers based on seminars sponsored by the Food and Resource Economics Department, University of Florida in 1971]; edited by J. Richard Conner [and] Edna Loehman. [Gainesville, Fla.], 1974. pp. 299. *bibliogs.*

BRUBAKER (STERLING) In command of tomorrow: resource and environmental strategies for Americans. Baltimore, [1975]. pp. 177.

JONES (CHARLES OSCAR) Clean air: the policies and politics of pollution control. Pittsburgh, [1975]. pp. 372. *bibliog.*

LIROFF (RICHARD A.) A national policy for the environment: NEPA and its aftermath. Bloomington, Ind., [1976]. pp. 273. *bibliog.*

WATSON (JAMES WREFORD) and O'RIORDAN (TIMOTHY) eds. The American environment: perceptions and policies. London, [1976]. pp. 340. *bibliogs.*

ENVIRONMENTAL POLICY RESEARCH

— **France.**

FRANCE. Groupe Interministériel d'Evaluation de l'Environnement. Rapport annuel. a., Jl 1974- Paris.

ENVIRONMENTAL PROTECTION.

UNEP NEWS; [pd. by] United Nations Environment Programme. m., Je 1975 (v.1, no.7)- , with gaps. *Nairobi.*

DASMANN (RAYMOND FREDERICK) The conservation alternative. New York, [1975]. pp. 164. *bibliogs.*

UNITERRA; pd. by United Nations Environment Programme. m., Ag 1976 (v.1, no.1)- Nairobi. *Supersedes UNEP NEWS.*

GORMLEY (W. PAUL) Human rights and environment: the need for international co-operation. Leyden, 1976. pp. 255. *bibliog.*

— **Australia.**

AUSTRALIA. Department of Urban and Regional Development. 1973. The national estate: principles and policies; submission to the task force. Canberra, 1973. pp. 35.

AUSTRALIA. National Capital Development Commission. 1973. Submission to the inquiry into the national estate. Canberra, 1973. fo. 14. *Photocopy.*

AUSTRALIA. Interim Committee on the National Estate. 1974. Report; [David Yencken, chairman]. [Canberra], 1975. pp. 48.

CONACHER (A.J.) Environment-industry conflict: the Manjimup woodchip industry proposal, southwestern Australia. Nedlands, 1975. pp. 43. *(Western Australia, University of. Department of Geography. Geowest. No. 4)*

— **Canada.**

CANADIAN ENVIRONMENTAL ADVISORY COUNCIL. Annual review. a., 1973/1974- Ottawa. *[In English and French].*

ENVIRONMENTAL PROTECTION.(Cont.)

— Israel.

LUCKHURST (COLIN) Environmental conservation in Israel. London, 1975. pp. 20. *(Anglo-Israel Association. Pamphlets. No. 52)*

— South Africa.

SOUTH AFRICA. Department of Planning and the Environment. 1973. Environmental conservation. [Pretoria, 1973]. pp. 27.

— United Kingdom.

U.K. Department of the Environment. Miscellaneous local government and planning statistics. a., 1973- London.

SCIENCE, technology and environmental management: [based on a symposium on 'Applied Environmental Science' held at the 1974 Annual Conference of the Institute of British Geographers]; edited by Richard D. Hey and Trevor D. Davies. Farnborough, Hants., [1975]. pp. 295. *bibliogs.*

WOOD (CHRISTOPHER) Town planning and pollution control. Manchester, [1976]. pp. 239. *bibliogs.*

— — Citizen participation.

CHILTERN SOCIETY. Sixty-five [to] seventy-five: the Chiltern Society's first ten years. High Wycombe, [1975]. pp. 28.

— — Wales — Citizen participation.

HALL (IRENE M.) Community action versus pollution: a study of a residents' group in a Welsh urban area. Cardiff, 1976. pp. 130. *(Wales. University. Board of Celtic Studies. Social Science Monographs. No. 2)*

— United States.

TOOLE (KENNETH ROSS) The rape of the Great Plains: northwest America, cattle and coal. Boston, [1976]. pp. 271. *bibliog.*

— — Alaska.

MANNING (HARVEY) Cry crisis!: rehearsal in Alaska: with chapters by Kenneth Brower; ...edited by Hugh Nash. San Francisco, [1974], pp 313. *bibliog.*

ENVIRONMENTAL PSYCHOLOGY.

FREEDMAN (JONATHAN L.) Crowding and behavior. San Francisco, [1975]. pp. 177. *bibliog.*

MERCER (CHARLES) Living in cities: psychology and the urban environment. Harmondsworth, 1975. pp. 240. *bibliog.*

EPICURUS.

NICHOLS (JAMES H.) Epicurean political philosophy: the De rerum natura of Lucretius. Ithaca, N.Y., 1976. pp. 214.

EQUAL PAY FOR EQUAL WORK.

BUDINER (MELITTA) Le droit de la femme à l'égalité de salaire, et la convention No. 100 de l'Organisation Internationale du Travail. Paris, 1975. pp. 266. *bibliog.*

PETTMAN (B. O.) ed. Equal pay for women: progress and problems in seven countries. Bradford, [1975]. pp. 173.

— New Zealand.

NEW ZEALAND. Department of Labour. 1974. Equal pay. [Wellington, 1974]. pp. 6.

— United Kingdom.

INSTITUTE OF SCIENTIFIC BUSINESS. Report and Survey Series. No.9. Equal pay and low pay; by John Fyfe and Barrie O. Pettman. Bradford, 1974. pp. 39. *bibliog.*

HEWITT (PATRICIA) Rights for women: a guide to the Sex Discrimination Act, the Equal Pay Act, paid maternity leave, pension schemes and unfair dismissal. London, [1975]. pp. 98.

EQUALITY.

SVERIGES SOCIALDEMOKRATISKA ARBETAREPARTI and LANDSORGANISATIONEN I SVERIGE. Arbetsgrupp för Jämlikhetsfrågor. Jämlikhet: allas deltagande i arbetsliv och politik; (andra rapporten; [Alva Myrdal, chairman]). [Stockholm, 1972]. pp. 122.

NYERERE (JULIUS KAMBARAGE) Man and development. Dar es Salaam, 1974. pp. 125.

RAINWATER (LEE) What money buys: inequality and the social meanings of income. New York, [1974]. pp. 242.

DOEL (JOHANNES VAN DEN) and HOOGERWERF (A.) eds. Gelijkheid en ongelijkheid in Nederland: analyse en beleid. Alphen aan den Rijn, 1975. pp. 312. *bibliogs.*

HYMAN (RICHARD) and BROUGH (IAN) Social values and industrial relations: a study of fairness and equality. Oxford, [1975]. pp. 277. *bibliog. (Warwick Studies in Industrial Relations)*

THUROW (LESTER C.) Generating inequality. London, [1975]. pp. 258.

BRITISH ASSOCIATION FOR THE ADVANCEMENT OF SCIENCE. Section F. Meeting, 1975. Economics and equality: (papers...); edited by Rt. Hon. Aubrey Jones. Deddington, Oxford, 1976. pp. 164. *bibliogs.*

FABIAN SOCIETY. Fabian Tracts. [No.] 443. In pursuit of equality; [by] Barbara Wootton. London, 1976. pp. 12. *(Blanche Colebrook Memorial Lectures. 1975)*

MEADE (JAMES EDWARD) The just economy:...being volume four of Principles of political economy. London, 1976. pp. 247.

EQUILIBRIUM (ECONOMICS).

KORNAI (JÁNOS) Anti-equilibrium: on economic systems theory and the tasks of research. Amsterdam, 1971 repr. 1975. pp. 402. *bibliog.*

MAKAROV (VALERII LEONIDOVICH) and RUBINOV (ALEKSANDR MOISEEVICH) Matematicheskaia teoriia ekonomicheskoi dinamiki i ravnovesiia. Moskva, 1973. pp. 335. *bibliog.*

TARANTELLI (EZIO) Studi di economia del lavoro. Milano, 1974. pp. 257.

DOORN (JOOST VAN) Disequilibrium economics. London, 1975. pp. 96. *bibliog.*

NIKAIDO (HUKUKANE) Monopolistic competition and effective demand. Princeton, 1975. pp. 150. *bibliog.*

PERROUX (FRANÇOIS) Unités actives et mathématiques nouvelles: révision de la théorie de l'équilibre économique général. Paris, [1975]. pp. 274.

SIMPSON (DAVID) Economist. General equilibrium analysis: an introduction. Oxford, [1975]. pp. 164. *bibliog.*

HILDENBRAND (WERNER) and KIRMAN (A.P.) Introduction to equilibrium analysis: variations on themes by Edgeworth and Walras. Amsterdam, 1976. pp. 216. *bibliog.*

— Mathematical models.

JONSON (PETER DAVID) An investigation of the U.K. balance of payments with particular emphasis on the role of monetary factors and disequilibrium dynamics, 1882-1970. 1975. fo. 167. *bibliogs. Typescript. Ph.D.(London) thesis: unpublished. This thesis is the property of London University and may not be removed from the Library.*

MUSSA (MICHAEL) Sticky prices and disequilibrium adjustment in a rational model of the inflationary process. [London], 1976. pp. 28. *bibliog.*

EQUITY

— Australia.

HEYDON (JOHN DYSON) and others. Cases and materials on equity. Sydney, 1975. pp. 398.

MEAGHER (RODERICK PITT) and others. Equity: doctrines and remedies. Sydney, 1975. pp. 750.

— United Kingdom.

SELDEN SOCIETY. Publications. Vol.91. St. German's Doctor and student; edited...by...T. F.T. Plucknett and J.L. Barton. London, 1974. pp. 346. *In Latin and English.*

BRYSON (WILLIAM HAMILTON) The equity side of the Exchequer: its jurisdiction, administration, procedures and records. London, 1975. pp. 217. *bibliog. (Cambridge. University. Yorke Prize Essays. 1973)*

HANBURY (HAROLD GREVILLE) and MAUDSLEY (RONALD HARLING) Modern equity; tenth edition by R.H. Maudsley. London, 1976. pp. 705.

KEETON (GEORGE WILLIAMS) and SHERIDAN (LIONEL ASTOR) Equity. 2nd ed. Milton, Oxon, 1976. pp. 443.

ERICKSEN (EPHRAIM EDWARD).

ERICKSEN (EPHRAIM EDWARD) The psychological and ethical aspects of Mormon group life; [and] The religious thought of E.E. Ericksen; introductory essay by Sterling M. McMurrin. Salt Lake City, [1975]. pp. 101. *The main work was originally published in 1922.*

ERLANDER (TAGE).

ERLANDER (TAGE) 1901-1939. Stockholm, [1972]. pp. 320.

ERLANDER (TAGE) 1940-1949. Stockholm, [1973]. pp. 406.

ERLANDER (TAGE) 1949-1954. Stockholm, [1974]. pp. 392.

ERLER (FRITZ).

SOELL (HARTMUT) Fritz Erler: eine politische Biographie. Berlin, [1976]. 2 vols. *bibliog.*

EROSION

— Mathematical models.

LONDON. University. London School of Economics and Political Science. Graduate School of Geography. Discussion Papers. No. 55. Three-dimensional generation of erosion potentials using a digital computer; [by] Roger F. Moore. London, 1975. pp. 18.

ERSKINE (Hon. HENRY).

[HAMILTON (GEORGE) Minister of Gladsmuir] The telegraph: a consolatory epistle from Thomas Muir, Esq., of Botany Bay, to the Hon. Henry Erskine, late Dean of Faculty. [Edinburgh[!, 1796. pp. 11. *In verse.*

ESKIMOS

— Canada.

THOMAS (D.K.) and THOMPSON (CHARLES THOMAS) Eskimo housing as planned culture change; (with Northern rental housing program, Northwest Territories, 1966 to 1972). Ottawa, 1972. pp. 27; fo. (6). *bibliog. (Canada. Northern Science Research Group. Social Science Notes. 4)*

ESSEX

— Economic history.

LEWIS (FRANK) Essex and sugar: historic and other connections. London, 1976. pp. 132.

— Economic policy.

ESSEX. County Planning Department. North and central Essex structure plan: first report. [Chelmsford], 1975. pp. 158.

— History — Sources.

ESSEX. Quarter Sessions of the Peace. Essex Quarter Sessions Order Book, 1652-1661; [edited] by D.H. Allen. Chelmsford, 1974. pp. 236. *(Essex. Records Committee. Essex Record Office Publications. No. 65)*

— Politics and government.

EAST SUFFOLK. Reorganisation Committee. Local government in England: government proposals for reorganisation 1971: report. Ipswich, 1971. pp. 17.

— Social policy.

ESSEX. County Planning Department. North and central Essex structure plan: first report. [Chelmsford], 1975. pp. 158.

ESTIMATION THEORY.

HALL (ANTHONY DAVID) The relative efficiency of estimators of seemingly unrelated regressions. 1976. fo. 182. *bibliog. Typescript. Ph.D.(London) tesis: unpublished. This thesis is the property of London University and may not be removed from the Library.*

ESTONIA

— History.

ISTORIIA Estonskoi SSR. Tallin, 1961-74. 3 vols.

ESTUARIES.

BLACK (WILLIAM ALEXANDER) The view from Water Street. Ottawa, 1973. pp. 43. *bibliog. (Canada. Inland Waters Directorate. Social Science Series. No. 2)*

ETANG DE BERRE.

FRANCE. Direction de la Documentation. La Documentation Française. Notes et Etudes Documentaires. Nos. 4,164-4, 165-4,166. L'aménagement de la région Fos-Etang de Berre; par Didier Cultiaux. Paris, 1975. pp. 132.

ETHICS.

NELSON (LEONARD) Critique of practical reason;...translated by Norbert Guterman. [Scarsdale, N.Y., 1957]. pp. 565,xviii. *(Lectures on the foundations of ethics. vol. 1) Facsimile reproduction of typescript with translator's manuscript additions and corrections.*

BARROW (ROBIN) Moral philosophy for education. London, 1975. pp. 214. *bibliogs.*

SYMPOSIUM ON MORAL DEVELOPMENT, LOYOLA UNIVERSITY OF CHICAGO, 1973. Moral development: current theory and research; [papers] edited by David J. DePalma [and] Jeanne M. Foley. Hillsdale, 1975. pp. 206. *bibliogs.*

EMLER (NICHOLAS PETER) The development of moral reasoning in children: a theoretical and empirical study. [1976]. fo. 385. *bibliog. Typescript. Ph.D. (London) thesis: unpublished. This thesis is the property of London University and may not be removed from the Library.*

SMITH (ADAM) LL.D., F.R.S. The theory of moral sentiments; edited by D.D. Raphael and A.L. Macfie. Oxford, 1976. pp. 412. *bibliog.*

ETHIOPIA

— Constitutional law.

SCHOLLER (HEINRICH J.) and BRIETZKE (PAUL) Ethiopia: revolution, law and politics. München, 1976. pp. 216. *bibliog. (IFO-Institut für Wirtschaftsforschung. Afrika-Studien. 92)*

— Economic conditions.

ETHIOPIA. Ministry of Information. Department of Press. 1970. Ethiopia: forty years of reign, forty years of progress, 1930-70. Addis Ababa, 1970. pp. 141.

— Economic policy.

ETHIOPIA. 1975. Objectives of the development through cooperation, enlightenment and work campaign. [Addis Ababa, 1975]. fo. 20.

— History.

ETHIOPIA. Ministry of Information. Department of Press. 1970. Ethiopia: forty years of reign, forty years of progress, 1930-70. Addis Ababa, 1970. pp. 141.

LEGUM (COLIN) Ethiopia: the fall of Haile Selassie's empire. London, 1975. pp. 87.

— — Sources.

HAILE SELASSIE I., Emperor of Ethiopia. The autobiography of Emperor Haile Sellassie I: 'My life and Ethiopia's progress', 1892-1937; translated and annotated by Edward Ullendorff. London, 1976. pp. 337. *bibliog.*

— Occupations.

ETHIOPIA. Manpower Research and Statistics Section. 1971. A survey of the occupational pattern of employment in Ethiopia, 1962 E.C. [i.e. 1970 G.C.]. Addis Ababa, 1971. pp. 120.

— Politics and government.

LEGUM (COLIN) Ethiopia: the fall of Haile Selassie's empire. London, 1975. pp. 87.

THOMSON (BLAIR) Ethiopia: the country that cut off its head: a diary of the revolution. London, 1975. pp. 159. *bibliog.*

HAILE SELASSIE I., Emperor of Ethiopia. The autobiography of Emperor Haile Sellassie I: 'My life and Ethiopia's progress', 1892-1937; translated and annotated by Edward Ullendorff. London, 1976. pp. 337. *bibliog.*

SCHOLLER (HEINRICH J.) and BRIETZKE (PAUL) Ethiopia: revolution, law and politics. München, 1976. pp. 216. *bibliog. (IFO-Institut für Wirtschaftsforschung. Afrika-Studien. 92)*

— Social conditions.

ETHIOPIA. Ministry of Information. Department of Press. 1970. Ethiopia: forty years of reign, forty years of progress, 1930-70. Addis Ababa, 1970. pp. 141.

— Social policy.

ETHIOPIA. 1975. Objectives of the development through cooperation, enlightenment and work campaign. [Addis Ababa, 1975]. fo. 20.

ETHNIC ATTITUDES.

ROSE (PETER ISAAC) and others, eds. Through different eyes: black and white perspectives on American race relations. New York, 1973. pp. 453. *bibliog.*

MORSE (STANLEY J.) and ORPEN (CHRISTOPHER) eds. Contemporary South Africa: social psychological perspectives. Cape Town, 1975. pp. 294. *bibliogs.*

SCHNALL (DAVID J.) Ethnicity and suburban local politics. New York, 1975. pp. 168. *bibliog.*

— Bibliography.

OBUDHO (CONSTANCE E.) Black-white racial attitudes: an annotated bibliography. Westport, Conn., 1976. pp. 180.

ETHNIC GROUPS.

INTERNATIONAL CONGRESS OF ANTHROPOLOGICAL AND ETHNOLOGICAL SCIENCES. 9th Congress, 1973. Ethnicity and resource competition in plural societies: [papers from the Congress]; editor Leo A. Despres. The Hague, [1975]. pp. 221. *bibliogs.*

BOWKER (GORDON) and CARRIER (JOHN WOOLFE) eds. Race and ethnic relations: sociological readings; ...[with an] introductory essay by Percy Cohen. London, 1976. pp. 400. *bibliog.*

FRANCIS (EMERICH K.) Interethnic relations: an essay in sociological theory. New York, [1976]. pp. 432. *bibliog.*

NEUMAN (STEPHANIE GLICKSBERG) ed. Small states and segmented societies: national political integration in a global environment. New York, 1976. pp. 238.

ETHNICITY.

MARGER (MARTIN) The force of ethnicity: a study of urban elites. Detroit, [1974]. pp. 110. *bibliog. (Journal of University Studies. vol. 10, no.5)*

ETHNOLOGY.

TESELLE (SALLIE) ed. The rediscovery of ethnicity. New York, 1974. pp. 138.

CONFERENCE ON MIGRATION AND ETHNICITY, OSHKOSH, WIS., 1973. Migration and development: implications for ethnic identity and political conflict: [selected papers from the conference held in conjunction with the 9th International Congress of Anthropological and Ethnological Sciences]; editors Helen I. Safa [and] Brian M. Du Toit. The Hague, [1975]. pp. 336. *bibliogs.*

CONFERENCE ON MIGRATION AND ETHNICITY, OSHKOSH, WIS., 1973. Migration and urbanization: models and adaptive strategies: [selected papers of the conference held in conjunction with the 9th International Congress of Anthropological and Ethnological Sciences]; editors Brian M. Du Toit [and] Helen I. Safa. The Hague, [1975]. pp. 305. *bibliogs.*

ISAACS (HAROLD ROBERT) Idols of the tribe: group identity and political change. New York, [1975]. pp. 242.

ETHNOLOGY.

RETHINKING modernization: anthropological perspectives; edited by John J. Poggie, Jr., and Robert N. Lynch. Westport, Conn., 1974. pp. 405. *bibliog. Papers presented at a symposium held at the University of Rhode Island in 1971.*

WHITE (LESLIE ALVIN) The concept of cultural systems: a key to understanding tribes and nations. New York, 1975. pp. 192. *bibliog.*

— Africa.

ONWUEJEOGWU (M. ANGULU) The social anthropology of Africa: an introduction. London, 1975. pp. 296. *bibliogs.*

— Africa, Subsaharan.

STUDIES in African social anthropology; edited by Meyer Fortes and Sheila Patterson. London, 1975. pp. 267. *bibliogs. Essays presented to Professor Isaac Schapera.*

— America — Bibliography.

GUYOT (MIREILLE) compiler. Bibliographie américaniste: archéologie et préhistoire: anthropologie et ethnohistoire. Paris, 1972. fo. 234.

— America, Latin.

OLIEN (MICHAEL D.) Latin Americans: contemporary peoples and their cultural traditions. New York, [1973]. pp. 408. *bibliogs.*

— Asia.

ETNICHESKAIA istoriia narodov Azii. Moskva, 1972. pp. 295.

— India.

INDIA. Gazetteers Unit. 1965. The gazetteer of India: Indian union. Vol. 1. Country and people. [New Delhi], 1965 repr. 1973. pp. 652. *bibliogs. 2 maps in end pocket.*

— Nepal.

FUERER-HAIMENDORF (CHRISTOPH VON) Freiherr. Himalayan traders: life in highland Nepal. London, [1975]. pp. 316. *bibliog.*

— Russia.

KATZ (ZEV) and others, eds. Handbook of major Soviet nationalities. New York, [1975]. pp. 481. *bibliogs.*

SOVREMENNYE etnicheskie protsessy v SSSR. Moskva, 1975. pp. 543.

— — Kazakstan.

KHOZIAISTVENNO-kul'turnye traditsii narodov Srednei Azii i Kazakhstana. Moskva, 1975. pp. 231.

— — Soviet Central Asia.

KHOZIAISTVENNO-kul'turnye traditsii narodov Srednei Azii i Kazakhstana. Moskva, 1975. pp. 231.

ETHNOLOGY.(Cont.)

— — Yakutia.

IVANOV (VASILII FEDOTOVICH) Istoriko-etnograficheskoe izuchenie Iakutii XVII-XVIII vv. Moskva, 1974. pp. 287. *bibliog.*

— Taiwan.

COHEN (MYRON L.) House united, house divided: the Chinese family in Taiwan. New York, 1976. pp. 267. *bibliog.*

— Tanzania.

CAPLAN (ANN PATRICIA) Choice and constraint in a Swahili community: property, hierarchy and cognatic descent on the east African coast. London, 1975. pp. 162. *bibliog.*

HARTWIG (GERALD W.) The art of survival in East Africa: the Kerebe and long-distance trade. 1800-1895. New York, 1976. pp 253. *bibliog.*

— Yap.

LINGENFELTER (SHERWOOD GALEN) Yap: political leadership and culture change in an island society. Honolulu, [1975]. pp. 270. *bibliog.*

EUGENICS.

HILLEL (MARC) and HENRY (CLARISSA) Lebensborn e.V.: im Namen der Rasse; (berechtigte Übersetzung [from the French] von Annette Lallemand). Wien, [1975]. pp. 352. *bibliog.*

EUROBOND MARKET.

DONNERSTAG (HANS CHRISTIAN) The Eurobond market;...edited by Philip Thorn. London, [1975]. pp. 188. *bibliog.*

EURODOLLAR MARKET.

OWENS (JEFFREY P.) The growth of the euro-dollar market: an appraisal of its domestic and international implications. Bangor, 1974. pp. 167. *bibliog. (Wales. University. University College of North Wales. Bangor Occasional Papers in Economics. No.4)*

HEWSON (JOHN R.) Liquidity creation and distribution in the eurocurrency markets. Lexington, Mass., [1975]. pp. 172. *bibliog.*

McKENZIE (GEORGE W.) The economics of the Euro-currency system. London, 1976. pp. 141. *bibliogs.*

EUROPE

— Civilization.

COUNCIL OF EUROPE. Directorate of Information. 1968. Europe Day, 5th May. Strasbourg, [1968]. pp. 8.

KOCH (THILÔ) ed. Europa persönlich: Erlebnisse und Betrachtungen deutscher P. E.N.-Autoren; (siebzehn Schriftsteller fragen, schildern und bekennen). Tübingen, [1973]. pp. 306.

ESPACE, idéologie et société au XVIe siècle; [by] José Luis Alonso Hernandez [and others]. Grenoble, 1975. pp. 153. *(Paris. Université de Paris VIII (Paris-Vincennes). Equipe de Recherche "Culture et Société au XVIe Siècle". Documents et Travaux. tome 2)*

PACHTER (HENRY MAXIMILIAN) The fall and rise of Europe: a political, social and cultural history of the twentieth century. London, [1975]. pp. 481. *bibliog.*

PIOVENE (GUIDO) In search of Europe: portraits of the non-communist West...; translated by John Shepley. London, [1975]. pp. 342.

RABB (THEODORE K.) The struggle for stability in early modern Europe. New York, 1975. pp. 171. *bibliog.*

— Commerce.

UNITED NATIONS. Economic Commission for Europe. Annual bulletin of exports of chemical products. a., 1973 (v.1)- Geneva. *In English with summaries in French and Russian.*

HAGER (WOLFGANG) Europe's economic security: non-energy issues in the internationa political economy. Paris, 1975. pp. 78. *(Atlantic Institute. Atlantic Papers. 175.3)*

— Economic conditions.

BOUCKE (OSWALD FRED) Europe and the American tariff. New York, [1933]. pp. 163. *bibliog.*

CLOUT (HUGH DONALD) ed. Regional development in western Europe. London, [1975]. pp. 328. *bibliogs.*

HAGER (WOLFGANG) Europe's economic security: non-energy issues in the internationa political economy. Paris, 1975. pp. 78. *(Atlantic Institute. Atlantic Papers. 175.3)*

— Economic history.

CIPOLLA (CARLO MARIA) Before the industrial revolution: European society and economy, 1000-1700. London, 1976. pp. 326. *bibliog.*

KELLENBENZ (HERMANN) The rise of the European economy: an economic history of continental Europe from the fifteenth to the eighteenth century; (revised and edited by Gerhard Benecke). London, [1976]. pp. 354. *bibliog.*

— Economic integration.

HABERLER (GOTTFRIED VON) Probleme der wirtschaftlichen Integration Europas; [and] Fritz Machlup: Integrationshemmende Integrationspolitik; (erweiterte Fassung der Festvorlesungen...am 16 Juni 1974). Kiel, 1974. pp. 60. *(Kiel. Universität. Institut für Weltwirtschaft. Bernhard-Harms-Vorlesungen. 5/6)*

EUROPEAN integration; edited...by F. Roy Willis. New York, 1975. pp. 201. *bibliog.*

KROK-PASZKOWSKI (JAN) Między Brukselą a Moskwą: procesy integracyjne w Europie. London, 1975. pp. 159. *bibliog.*

BRACEWELL-MILNES (JOHN BARRY) Economic integration in East and West. London, 1976. pp. 218.

MENNIS (BERNARD) and SAUVANT (KARL P.) Emerging forms of transnational community: transnational business enterprises and regional integration. Lexington, Mass., [1976]. pp. 240. *bibliog.*

— Economic policy.

HANSEN (NILES M.) Public policy and regional economic development: the experience of nine western countries. Cambridge, Mass., [1974]. pp. 351. *bibliog.*

HAGER (WOLFGANG) Europe's economic security: non-energy issues in the internationa political economy. Paris, 1975. pp. 78. *(Atlantic Institute. Atlantic Papers. 175.3)*

— Emigration and immigration.

ABADAN-UNAT (NERMIN) ed. Turkish workers in Europe, 1960-1975: a socio-economic reappraisal. Leiden, 1976. pp. 424. *bibliog.*

ERICKSON (CHARLOTTE JOANNE) ed. Emigration from Europe, 1815-1914: select documents. London, 1976. pp. 320. *bibliog.*

JONES (MALDWYN ALLEN) Destination America. London, [1976]. pp. 256. *bibliog.*

— Foreign economic relations.

The POLITICAL implications of North Sea oil and gas: [papers presented to a conference at Tønsberg in February 1975, sponsored by the Norwegian Institute of International Affairs and the Royal Institute of International Affairs]; edited by Martin Saeter and Ian Smart. Oslo, [1975]. pp. 168.

— — Russia.

PIPES (RICHARD EDGAR) ed. Soviet strategy in Europe. London, 1976. pp. 316.

— Foreign relations.

KASSYANOWICZ (HENRYK) Odrodzenie Wehrmachtu czy bezpieczeństwo europejskie?. Warszawa, 1954. pp. 104.

LEE (DWIGHT ERWIN) Europe's crucial years: the diplomatic background of World War I, 1902-1914. Hanover, N.H., 1974. pp. 482. *bibliog.*

RAKHMANINOV (IURII NIKOLAEVICH) and URANOV (GENNADII VASIL'EVICH) Evropa: bezopasnost' i sotrudnichestvo. Moskva, 1974. pp. 208.

ALTING VON GEUSAU (FRANS ALPHONS MARIA) European perspectives on world order. Leyden, 1975. pp. 341. *(John F. Kennedy Institute. Center for International Studies. Publications. Nr. 10)*

HOLDSWORTH (RICHARD JULIAN) Lord Byron's Childe Harold's Pilgrimage as a liberal commentary on European relations around the close of the Napoleonic era. London, 1975. fo. 20. *(London. University. London School of Economics and Political Science. Gladstone Memorial Trust Prize Essays. 1975)* Typescript.

The POLITICAL implications of North Sea oil and gas: [papers presented to a conference at Tønsberg in February 1975, sponsored by the Norwegian Institute of International Affairs and the Royal Institute of International Affairs]; edited by Martin Saeter and Ian Smart. Oslo, [1975]. pp. 168.

BETTS (RAYMOND FREDERICK) The false dawn: European imperialism in the nineteenth century. Minneapolis, 1976. pp. 270. *bibliog.*

MARKS (SALLY JEAN) The illusion of peace: international relations in Europe, 1918- 1933. London, [1976]. pp. 184. *bibliog.*

— — America, Latin.

RODRIGUEZ O. (JAIME E.) The emergence of Spanish America: Vicente Rocafuerte and Spanish Americanism, 1808-1832. Berkeley, [1975]. pp. 311. *bibliog.*

— — America, North.

GOODMAN (ELLIOT RAYMOND) The fate of the Atlantic Community. New York, 1975. pp. 583.

— — France.

HATTON (RAGNHILD) ed. Louis XIV and Europe. London, 1976. pp. 311.

— — Germany.

EISNER (ERICH) Das europäische Konzept von Franz Josef Strauss: die gesamteuropäischen Ordnungsvorstellungen der CSU. Meisenheim am Glan, 1975. pp. 143. *bibliog.*

— — Russia.

DÉTENTE: (edited versions of interviews originally broadcast, in 1973-75, over Radio Free Europe); edited by G.R. Urban. London, 1976. pp. 368.

PIPES (RICHARD EDGAR) ed. Soviet strategy in Europe. London, 1976. pp. 316.

— — United Kingdom.

NEWMAN (FRANCIS WILLIAM) The place and duty of England in Europe: a lecture delivered at the third conversazione of the Friends of Italy on...April 28th, 1852;...to which is added an address...by M. Mazzini. London, 1852. pp. 23. *(Society of the Friends of Italy. Tracts. No. 5)*

CALDER (KENNETH JOHN) Britain and the origins of the new Europe, 1914-1918. Cambridge, 1976. pp. 268. *bibliog. (London. University. London School of Economics and Political Science. Centre for International Studies. International Studies)*

— — **Bibliography.**

BOETTCHER (WINFRIED) and others, compilers. Das britische Parlament und Europa, 1940-1972: eine Fachbibliographie. Baden-Baden, [1975]. pp. 186. *Contents, preface and list of subjects in various languages.*

— — **United States.**

ADAMS (DAVID KEITH) F[ranklin] D[elano] R[oosevelt], the New Deal and Europe; an inaugural lecture...given in the University of Keele, 23rd October 1973. Keele, [1974]. pp. 22.

MELANDRI (PIERRE) Les Etats-Unis et le "défi" européen, 1955-1958. Paris, [1975]. pp. 220. *bibliog. (Paris. Université de Paris I (Panthéon- Sorbonne). Publications. Nouvelle Série. Recherches. 19)*

CONFERENCE ON AMERICAN FOREIGN POLICY AND THE NEW EUROPE, BLACKSBURG, 1974. Changes in European relations: (proceedings of the conference); edited by James A. Kuhlman and Louis J. Mensonides. Leyden, 1976. pp. 214. *(East-West Foundation. East-West Perspectives. 1)*

LANGLEY (LESTER D.) Struggle for the American Mediterranean: United States- European rivalry in the Gulf-Caribbean, 1776-1904. Athens, Ga., [1976]. pp. 226. *bibliog.*

— **History.**

HAYES (CARLTON JOSEPH HUNTLEY) A political and cultural history of modern Europe. rev. ed. New York, 1932-39. 2 vols. *bibliog. "Based, but only in part, on the Political and social history of modern Europe". vol. 2 is of the shorter rev. ed.*

— — **Bibliography.**

HARVARD UNIVERSITY. Library. Widener Library Shelflists. [No.] 32. General European and world history. Cambridge, Mass., 1970. pp. 959.

— — **476-1492.**

HOLMES (GEORGE ANDREW) Europe: hierarchy and revolt, 1320-1450. Hassocks, Nr. Brighton, [1975]. pp. 352. *bibliog.*

— — **1592-1648.**

RABB (THEODORE K.) The struggle for stability in early modern Europe. New York, 1975. pp. 171. *bibliog.*

WILSON (CHARLES HENRY) The transformation of Europe, 1558-1648. Berkeley, [1976]. pp. 301. *bibliog.*

— — **1517-1648.**

MARCU (VALERIU) The birth of the nations, from the unity of faith to the democracy of money;...translated by Eden and Cedar Paul. London, 1932. pp. 287.

— — **1600-1699.**

RABB (THEODORE K.) The struggle for stability in early modern Europe. New York, 1975. pp. 171. *bibliog.*

— — **1900.**

PACHTER (HENRY MAXIMILIAN) The fall and rise of Europe: a political, social and cultural history of the twentieth century. London, [1975]. pp. 481. *bibliog.*

— **History, Military.**

HOWARD (MICHAEL ELIOT) War in European history. London, 1976. pp. 165. *bibliog.*

— **Industries.**

SYSTEME D'ETUDES DU SCHEMA GENERAL D'AMENAGEMENT DE LA FRANCE. Schéma général d'aménagement de la France: industries en Europe. Paris, 1974. pp. 311. *(France. Délégation à l'Aménagement du Territoire et à l'Action Régionale. Travaux et Recherches de Prospective. 46)*

— **Intellectual life.**

FIELD (FRANK) Three writers and the Great War: studies in the rise of communism and fascism. Cambridge, 1975. pp. 212. *bibliog.*

— **Nationalism.**

HROCH (MIROSLAV) Die Vorkämpfer der nationalen Bewegung bei den kleinen Völkern Europas: eine vergleichende Analyse zur gesellschaftlichen Schichtung der patriotischen Gruppen. Praha, [1968]. pp. 171. *(Karlova Universita. Acta Universitatis Carolinae. Philosophica et Historica. Monographia. 24)*

CALDER (KENNETH JOHN) Britain and the origins of the new Europe, 1914-1918. Cambridge, 1976. pp. 268. *bibliog. (London. University. London School of Economics and Political Science. Centre for International Studies. International Studies)*

— **Politics and government.**

HAYES (CARLTON JOSEPH HUNTLEY) A political and cultural history of modern Europe. rev. ed. New York, 1932-39. 2 vols. *bibliog. "Based, but only in part, on the Political and social history of modern Europe". vol. 2 is of the shorter rev. ed.*

MARCU (VALERIU) The birth of the nations, from the unity of faith to the democracy of money;...translated by Eden and Cedar Paul. London, 1932. pp. 287.

CASSELS (ALAN) Fascism. New York, [1975]. pp. 401. *bibliog.*

CROZIER (MICHEL) and others. The crisis of democracy...; report on the governability of democracies to the Trilateral Commission. [New York], 1975. pp. 211.

KOLINSKY (A. MARTIN) and PATERSON (WILLIAM EDGAR) eds. Social and political movements in western Europe. London, 1976. pp. 360.

— **Population.**

LAW and fertility in Europe: a study of legislation directly or indirectly affecting fertility in Europe; edited by Maurice Kirk [and others]. Dolhain, [1975]. 2 vols. *Essays and country reports of the Joint Working Group for the Study of Legislation directly or indirectly influencing Fertility in Europe, set up by the European Centre for Co-ordination of Research...in the Social Sciences and the International Union for the Scientific Study of Population.*

— **Social history.**

ESPACE, idéologie et société au XVIe siècle; [by] José Luis Alonso Hernandez [and others]. Grenoble, 1975. pp. 153. *(Paris. Université de Paris VIII (Paris-Vincennes). Equipe de Recherche "Culture et Société au XVIe Siècle". Documents et Travaux. tome 2)*

KNAPP (VINCENT J.) Europe in the era of social transformation, 1700-present. Englewood Cliffs, N.J., [1976]. pp. 253. *bibliog.*

— — **Sources.**

YOUNG (ARTHUR) F.R.S. Arthur Young and his times; edited by G.E. Mingay. London, 1975. pp. 264. *bibliog. Selections with introduction and commentary.*

— **Social policy.**

SHANKS (MICHAEL) Social priorities in Europe. London, [1975?]. pp. 14. *Paper delivered at the annual meeting of the London Council of Social Service, London, 1973.*

ESDP NEWS; (pd. by) United Nations European Social Development Programme. q., Jl 1976 (no.1)- Geneva.

HEIDENHEIMER (ARNOLD JOSEPH) and others. Comparative public policy: the politics of social choice in Europe and America. London, 1976. pp. 296.

— **Statistics — Bibliography.**

HARVEY (JOAN M.) Statistics Europe: sources for market research. 2nd ed. Beckenham, Kent, 1972. pp. 255.

HARVEY (JOAN M.) Statistics Europe: sources for social, economic and market research. 3rd ed. Beckenham, Kent, 1976. pp. 467.

EUROPE, EASTERN

— **Commerce.**

QUANTITATIVE and analytical studies in East-West economic relations; edited by Josef C. Brada. Bloomington, Ind., [1976]. pp. 133. *bibliogs. (Indiana University. International Development Research Center. Studies in East European and Soviet Planning, Development and Trade. No. 24) "Papers originally presented at a joint Romanian-American Seminar in Bucharest during June of 1974".*

— **Economic conditions.**

INTERNATIONAL SLAVIC CONFERENCE, 1ST, BANFF, ALBERTA, 1974. Economic development in the Soviet Union and Eastern Europe. ..; edited by Zbigniew M. Fallenbuchl. New York, 1975-76. 2 vols.

MIECZKOWSKI (BOGDAN) Personal and social consumption in eastern Europe: Poland, Czechoslovakia, Hungary, and East Germany. New York, [1975]. pp. 342. *bibliog.*

— **Economic policy.**

BRYSON (PHILLIP J.) Scarcity and control in socialism: essays on East European planning. Lexington, Mass., [1976]. pp. 202.

— **Foreign economic relations.**

INTERNATIONAL CONGRESS ON THE PROBLEMS OF EASTERN EUROPE, 6TH, 1971. Reformen und Dogmen in Osteuropa; [papers] herausgegeben von Alfred Domes; Beiträge von Gyula Borbándi [and others]. Köln, [1971]. pp. 269.

— — **France.**

FRANCE. Direction de la Documentation. La Documentation Française. Notes et Etudes Documentaires. Nos. 4,116-4, 117. Les échanges et la coopération économique avec les pays de l'Europe de l'Est; [par Alain Capian]. Paris, 1974. pp. 56. *bibliog.*

— **Foreign relations.**

CONFERENCE ON AMERICAN FOREIGN POLICY AND THE NEW EUROPE, BLACKSBURG, 1974. Changes in European relations: (proceedings of the conference); edited by James A. Kuhlman and Louis J. Mensonides. Leyden, 1976. pp. 214. *(East-West Foundation. East-West Perspectives. 1)*

— — **Germany.**

HACKE (CHRISTIAN) Die Ost- und Deutschlandpolitik der CDU/CSU: Wege und Irrwege der Opposition seit 1969. Köln, [1975]. pp. 151. *bibliog.*

SOWDEN (JOHN KENNETH) The German question, 1945-1973: continuity in change. London, 1975. pp. 404. *bibliog.*

ROTH (REINHOLD) Aussenpolitische Innovation und politische Herrschaftssicherung: eine Analyse...am Beispiel der sozialliberalen Koalition, 1969 bis 1973. Meisenheim am Glan, 1976. pp. 380. *bibliog.*

GERMANY (BUNDESREPUBLIK). Deutscher Bundestag. Wissenschaftliche Dienste. 1974. Die Ost- und Deutschlandpolitik der Bundesrepublik Deutschland, 1969-1973: Auswahlbibliographie mit Annotationen; [compiled by Hannelore Reiche-Juhr]. Bonn, 1974. pp. 167. *(Bibliographien. 40)*

— — **United Kingdom.**

BARKER (ELISABETH) British policy in south-east Europe in the Second World War. London, 1976. pp. 320. *bibliog.*

EUROPE, EASTERN(Cont.)

— — **United States.**

LUNDESTAD (GEIR) The American non-policy towards Eastern Europe, 1943-1947: universalism in an area not of essential interest to the United States. Tromsö, [1975]. pp. 654. *bibliog.*

— — **Yugoslavia.**

GASTEYGER (CURT) ed. Die feindlichen Brüder: Jugoslawiens neuer Konflikt mit dem Ostblock, 1958; ein Dokumentenband, etc. Bern, 1960. pp. 315. *bibliog. (Schweizerisches Ost-Institut. Schriftenreihe. Reihe Dokumente. Heft 2)*

— **Intellectual life.**

TRADITION et innovation dans la culture des pays du Sud-Est européen: colloque tenu...1967 à Bucarest à l'occasion de la IXe Assemblée Générale du CIPSH. Bucarest, 1969. pp. 149.

INTERNATIONAL CONGRESS ON THE PROBLEMS OF EASTERN EUROPE, 6TH, 197 Reformen und Dogmen in Osteuropa; [papers] herausgegeben von Alfred Domes; Beiträge von Gyula Borbándi [and others]. Köln, [1971]. pp. 269.

— **Politics and government.**

INTERNATIONAL CONGRESS ON THE PROBLEMS OF EASTERN EUROPE, 6TH, 197 Reformen und Dogmen in Osteuropa; [papers] herausgegeben von Alfred Domes; Beiträge von Gyula Borbándi [and others]. Köln, [1971]. pp. 269.

RADIO FREE EUROPE. Audience and Public Opinion Research Department. Attitudes toward communism and party preferences in East Europe. [Munich?], 1973. fo. 32.

TRISKA (JAN F.) and JOHNSON (PAUL M.) Political development and political change in eastern Europe: a comparative study. Colorado, [1975]. pp. 74. *(Denver. University. Social Science Foundation and Graduate School of International Studies. Monograph Series in World Affairs. vol. 13. No.2)*

INTERNATIONAL SLAVIC CONFERENCE, 1ST, BANFF, ALBERTA, 1974. Change and adaptation in Soviet and East European politics; edited by Jane P. Shapiro [and] Peter J. Potichnyj). New York, 1976. pp. 236.

— **Religion.**

INTERNATIONAL SLAVIC CONFERENCE, 1ST, BANFF, ALBERTA, 1974. Marxism and religion in Eastern Europe; papers presented at the...conference...; edited by Richard T. De George and James P. Scanlan. Dordrecht, [1976]. pp. 181. *(Freiburg (Switzerland). Universität. Ost-Europa Institut. Sovietica. vol. 36)*

— **Rural conditions — Bibliography.**

SANDERS (IRWIN TAYLOR) and others, compilers. East European peasantries: social relations: an annotated bibliography of periodical articles. Boston, [1976]. pp. 179. *bibliog. A bibliography of a collection of periodical articles at the Mugar Library, Boston University.*

— **Social conditions.**

MATEJKO (ALEXANDER) Social change and stratification in Eastern Europe: an interpretive analysis of Poland and her neighbors. New York, 1974. pp. 272. *bibliog.*

MIECZKOWSKI (BOGDAN) Personal and social consumption in eastern Europe: Poland, Czechoslovakia, Hungary, and East Germany. New York, [1975]. pp. 342. *bibliog.*

FABER (BERNARD LEWIS) ed. The social structure of eastern Europe: transition and process in Czechoslovakia, Hungary, Poland, Romania and Yugoslavia. New York, 1976. pp. 419.

EUROPEAN COMMISSION OF HUMAN RIGHTS.

EUROPEAN COMMISSION OF HUMAN RIGHTS. 1972. Bringing an application before the European Commission of Human Rights: (procedure and practice of the Commission). Strasbourg, 1972. pp. 41. *(Case-Law Topics. 3).*

EUROPEAN COMMISSION OF HUMAN RIGHTS. 1973. Human rights and their limitations. Strasbourg, 1973. pp. 58. *(Case-Law Topics. 4).*

EUROPEAN COMMITTEE ON LEGAL CO-OPERATION.

COUNCIL OF EUROPE. 1973. European Committee on Legal Co-operation 1963-1973. [Strasbourg], [1973]. pp. 105.

EUROPEAN COMMUNITIES.

COMMUNITY REPORT: bulletin pd. by the Dublin Office of the European Communities. m. Dublin. *Current issues only kept.*

Les REGIONS frontalières à l'heure du Marché Commun: colloque organisé les 27 et 28 novembre 1969 par l'Institut d'Etudes Européennes. Bruxelles, 1970. pp. 422. *bibliog. (Brussels. Université Libre. Institut d'Etudes Européennes. Colloques Européens)*

EIRE. Oireachtas. Joint Committee on the Secondary Legislation of the European Communities. 1974- . Reports; [Charles J. Haughey, chairman]. Dublin, [1974 in progress]. *In English and Irish.*

La COMMISSION des Communautés Européennes et l'élargissement de l'Europe: colloque organisé les 23-25 novembre 1972 par l'Institut d'Etudes européennes. Bruxelles, 1974. pp. 335. *(Brussels. Université Libre. Institut d'Etudes Européennes. Colloques Européens)*

PEDINI (MARIO) Une chance pour l'Europe: difficultés et progrès vers l'intégration; [translated by Onello Onelli]. Bruxelles, [1974]. pp. 198.

EUROPEAN PARLIAMENT. Directorate General for Research and Documentation. 1975. L'Europe aujourd'hui. [Luxembourg], 1975 in progress.

AUDRETSCH (H.A.H.) Communautaire controle: het toezicht in de Europese Gemeenschappen op de naleving van de verdragsverplichtingen door de Lid-Staten. Deventer, 1975. pp. 228. *bibliog. With French summary and English and French annexes.*

COLLINS (DOREEN) The European Communities: the social policy of the first phase. London, 1975. 2 vols. *bibliogs.*

Les COMMUNAUTES européennes et les finances publiques françaises: actes des journées d'études des 11 et 12 octobre 1974. Paris, 1975. pp. 834. *(Strasbourg. Université. Faculté de Droit et des Sciences Politiques. Annales. 27)*

EUROPEAN COMMUNITIES. Commission. 1975. Reports on European union: European Parliament, Court of Justice, Economic and Social Committee. [Brussels], 1975. pp. 34. *(Bulletin of the European Communities. Supplements. [1975/9])*

IONESCU (GHITA) Centripetal politics: government and the new centres of power. London, [1975]. pp. 231.

PAPISCA (ANTONIO) Europa '80, dalla comunità all'unione europea. Roma, [1975]. pp. 285.

DEUTSCHES INSTITUT FÜR WIRTSCHAFTSFORSCHUNG. Sonderhefte. [Neue Folge]. 112. Alternative Entscheidungsstrukturen in einer Wirtschafts- und Währungsunion; ([by] Fritz Franzmeyer). Berlin, 1976. pp. 69.

EUROPEAN COMMUNITIES. Commission. Spokesman's Group. Information memo. irreg. Brussels. *Current issues only kept.*

— **Officials and employees.**

HERZOG (HORST) Doppelte Loyalität: ein Problem für die zur Europäischen Gemeinschaft entsandten Beamten der Mitgliedstaaten. Berlin, [1975]. pp. 102. *bibliog.*

— **France.**

La FRANCE et les Communautés Européennes; sous la direction de Joël Rideau [and others]. Paris, [1975]. pp. 1071.

GREILSAMMER (ALAIN) Les mouvements fédéralistes en France de 1945 à 1974. Paris, [1975]. pp. 220. *bibliog.*

— **Germany.**

EINFLUESSE der Europäischen Gemeinschaft auf die Regionalpolitik in der Bundesrepublik Deutschland; von Fritz Franzmeyer [and others]. Göttingen, [1975]. 1 vol. (various pagings). *(Kommission für Wirtschaftlichen und Sozialen Wandel. Schriften. 46)*

— **Ireland (Republic).**

EIRE. Oireachtas. Joint Committee on the Secondary Legislation of the European Communities. 1974- . Reports; [Charles J. Haughey, chairman]. Dublin, [1974 in progress]. *In English and Irish.*

COMMUNITY REPORT: bulletin pd. by the Dublin Office of the European Communities. m. Dublin. *Current issues only kept.*

EUROPEAN CONVENTION ON HUMAN RIGHTS.

EUROPEAN COMMISSION OF HUMAN RIGHTS. 1975. European Convention on Human Rights: national aspects. Strasbourg, [Council of Europe], 1975. pp. 65. *bibliog. In English and French.*

EUROPEAN ECONOMIC COMMUNITY.

FRANCE. Ministère des Affaires Etrangères. Service d'Information et de Presse. 1972. La Communauté européenne après le sommet de Paris. Paris, 1972. pp. 15. *(Le Point sur...)*

ELSNER (WOLFRAM) Die EWG: Herausforderung und Antwort der Gewerkschaften. Köln, [1974]. pp. 208. *bibliog.*

HABERLER (GOTTFRIED VON) Probleme der wirtschaftlichen Integration Europas; [and] Fritz Machlup: Integrationshemmende Integrationspolitik; (erweiterte Fassung von Festvorlesungen...am 16 Juni 1974). Kiel, 1974. pp. 60. *(Kiel. Universität. Institut für Weltwirtschaft. Bernhard-Harms-Vorlesungen. 5/6)*

DANKERT (JOCHEN) and others. Politik in Westeuropa;... Integrationsprozesse vom Ende des zweiten Weltkrieges bis zur Gegenwart. Berlin, 1975. pp. 481.

MAILLET (PIERRE) La construction européenne: résultats et perspectives. [Paris, 1975]. pp. 243. *bibliog.*

U.K. EEC Information Unit. 1975. your questions answered. London, [1974 or rather 1975]. pp. 87. *bibliog.*

COFFEY (PETER) Economist. The external economic relations of the EEC. London, 1976. pp. 118.

EUROPEAN COMMUNITIES. Commission. 1976. European union: report by Mr. Leo Tindemans, Prime Minister of Belgium, to the European Council. [Brussels], 1976. pp. 36. *(Bulletin of the European Communities. Supplements. [1976/1])*

PAXTON (JOHN) The developing Common Market. London, 1976. pp. 240.

— **Africa.**

COSGROVE (CAROL ANN) The European Economic Community and the African associates. [1976]. fo. 366. *bibliog. Typescript. Ph.D. (London) thesis: unpublished. This thesis is the property of London University and may not be removed from the Library.*

EUROPEAN ECONOMIC COMMUNITY COUNTRIES.

— Denmark.

DENMARK. Markedssekretariatet. 1971-72. Faellesmarkedet og Danmark, etc. [Copenhagen, 1971-72]. 12 parts (in 1 vol.). bibliog. *(Informationsserie)*

— Greece.

DELIBANES (DEMETRIOS) Problèmes spéciaux découlant de l'association avec la Communauté économique européenne. Thessaloniki, 1965. pp. 213-219. *(Reprinted from the proceedings of the Congress of Thessaloniki, November 1964, entitled The integration of Europe and Greece)*

YANNOPOULOS (GEORGE NICOLAS) Greece and the European Communities: the first decade of a troubled association. Beverly Hills, [1975]. pp. 34.

EUROPEAN ECONOMIC COMMUNITY. Treaties. 1961-. Association between the European Economic Community and Greece: collected acts, [regulations, decisions, recommendations, etc.]. [Brussels, 1976 in progress]. 2 vols. (looseleaf).

— Mediterranean.

The EEC and the Mediterranean countries; (editors, Avi Shlaim and G.N. Yannopoulos). Cambridge, 1976. pp. 352.

— Norway.

NORWAY. Statistiske Centralbyrå. 1974. Folkerøystinga om EF: aktivitet blant veljarane, etc. Oslo, 1974. pp. 63. *(Statistiske Analyser. 11) With English summary.*

— Scandinavia.

HUMMEN (WILHELM) Die Auswirkungen der Erweiterung der EG auf Aussenhandel und Produktion der metallverarbeitenden Industrie in Schweden, Dänemark und Norwegen. Tübingen, 1976. pp. 263. bibliog.

— Sweden.

ENGMAN (HANS) Sverige och Europa: om internationellt handelspolitik och fackligt samarbete. [Stockholm, 1973]. pp. 124.

— Tunisia.

EUROPEAN ECONOMIC COMMUNITY. Treaties. 1969- Association between the European Economic Community and the Tunisian Republic: collected acts, [regulations, decisions, etc.]. [Brussels, 1975 in progress]. 1 vol. (looseleaf).

— Turkey.

EUROPEAN ECONOMIC COMMUNITY. Treaties. 1963- Association between the European Economic Community and Turkey; collected acts, [regulations, decisions, recommendations, etc.]. [Brussels, 1975 in progress]. 1 vol. (looseleaf).

— United Kingdom.

SOLDATOS (PANAYOTIS) Les données fondamentales de la politique britannique à l'égard de la Communauté économique européenne, 1955-1970 recherche effectuée sur la base des comptes rendus des débats de l'Assemblée consultative du Conseil de l'Europe. Bruxelles, 1973. pp. 190. bibliog. *(Brussels. Université Libre. Institut d'Etudes Européennes. Thèses et Travaux Politiques)*

EUROPEAN PARLIAMENT. Directorate General for Research and Documentation. 1974. The effects, in 1973, on the United Kingdom of membership of the European Communities. [Luxembourg], 1974. 1 vol. (various pagings).

CONFEDERATION OF BRITISH INDUSTRY. Europe Committee. British industry and Europe. London, 1975. pp. 63.

EUROPEAN PARLIAMENT. Directorate General for Research and Documentation. 1975. The effects on the United Kingdom of membership of the European Communities. [Luxembourg], 1975. 1 vol. (various pagings).

FEDERAL TRUST FOR EDUCATION AND RESEARCH. The CAP and the British consumer; a Federal Trust Study group report; [Tim Josling, chairman]. London,1975]. pp. 28,xv. *With technical annex.*

BRITAIN into Europe: public opinion and the EEC 1961-75; edited by Roger Jowell and Gerald Hoinville. London, 1976. pp. 128. bibliog.

BUTLER (DAVID HENRY EDGEWORTH) and KITZINGER (UWE WEBSTER) The 1975 referendum. London, 1976. pp. 315.

CONSERVATIVE POLITICAL CENTRE. [Publications]. No. 583. Our voice in Europe: a discussion document on direct elections to the European Parliament [based on a report of a policy group chaired by Anthony Royle]. London, 1976. pp. 16.

GOODHART (PHILIP) Full-hearted consent: the story of the referendum campaign - and the campaign for the referendum. London, 1976. pp. 264.

SMEDLEY (OLIVER) What is happening to the British economy? Saffron Walden, 1976. pp. 204. bibliog.

BOETTCHER (WINFRIED) and others, compilers. Das britische Parlament und Europa, 1940-1972: eine Fachbibliographie. Baden-Baden, [1975]. pp. 186. *Contents, preface and list of subjects in various languages.*

EUROPEAN ECONOMIC COMMUNITY ASSOCIATED COUNTRIES.

COSGROVE (CAROL ANN) The European Economic Community and the African associates. [1976]. fo. 366. bibliog. Typescript. Ph.D. (London) thesis: unpublished. *This thesis is the property of London University and may not be removed from the Library.*

EUROPEAN ECONOMIC COMMUNITY COUNTRIES.

EUROPEAN COMMUNITIES. European documentation. irreg., 1975 (no.1)- Luxembourg.

— Commerce — Africa.

EUROPEAN COMMUNITIES. Statistical Office. ACP: yearbook of foreign trade statistics; statistical abstract. a., 1968/1973- Luxembourg. *[In English and French]*

— — Asia.

TULLOCH (PETER) The seven outside: Commonwealth Asia's trade with the enlarged EEC. London, [1973]. pp. 67. bibliog.

— — Caribbean area.

EUROPEAN COMMUNITIES. Statistical Office. ACP: yearbook of foreign trade statistics; statistical abstract. a., 1968/1973- Luxembourg. *[In English and French]*

— — Pacific, The.

EUROPEAN COMMUNITIES. Statistical Office. ACP: yearbook of foreign trade statistics; statistical abstract. a., 1968/1973- Luxembourg. *[In English and French]*

— Commercial policy.

SLOT (PIETER J.) Technical and administrative obstacles to trade in the EEC. Leyden, 1975. pp. 294. bibliog.

— Economic conditions.

DOCUMENTATION EUROPEENNE: série agricole; ([pd. by] Presse et Information, Communautés Européennes). irreg. Bruxelles. *Current issues only kept.*

DOCUMENTATION EUROPEENNE: série syndicale et ouvrière; ([pd. by] Presse et Information, Communautés Européennes). irreg. Bruxelles. *Current issues only kept.*

— Economic policy.

GIUSSO (LUIGI) ed. Teoria delle unioni monetarie e integrazione europea: [an anthology]. Napoli, [1974]. pp. 402.

ROSENTHAL (GLENDA GOLDSTONE) The men behind the decisions: cases in European policy-making. Lexington, Mass., [1975]. pp. 166. bibliog.

WARNECKE (STEVEN JOSHUA) and SULEIMAN (EZRA N.) eds. Industrial policies in western Europe. New York, 1975. pp. 249.

EUROPEAN COMMUNITIES. Commission. 1976. European union: report by Mr. Leo Tindemans, Prime Minister of Belgium, to the European Council. [Brussels], 1976. pp. 36. *(Bulletin of the European Communities. Supplements. [1976/1])*

— Foreign economic relations.

COFFEY (PETER) Economist. The external economic relations of the EEC. London, 1976. pp. 118.

TUGENDHAT (CHRISTOPHER) Britain, Europe and the Third World. London, 1976. pp. 31. *(Conservative Political Centre. [Publications]. No. 587)*

TWITCHETT (KENNETH J.) ed. Europe and the world: the external relations of the Common Market. London, [1976]. pp. 210. bibliog.

— — Arab countries.

LIEBER (ROBERT J.) Oil and the Middle East war: Europe in the energy crisis. Cambridge, Mass., [1976]. pp. 75. *(Harvard University. Center for International Affairs. Harvard Studies in International Affairs. No. 35)*

— Foreign relations.

WISSENSCHAFTLICHE GESELLSCHAFT FÜR EUROPARECHT. Wissenschaftliches Kolloquium, Bad Ems, 1974. Die Aussenbeziehungen der Europäischen Gemeinschaft. Köln, [1975]. pp. 150. *(Cologne. Universität. Institut für das Recht der Europäischen Gemeinschaften. Kölner Schriften zum Europarecht. Band 25)*

TWITCHETT (KENNETH J.) ed. Europe and the world: the external relations of the Common Market. London, [1976]. pp. 210. bibliog.

— Industries.

MAILLET (PIERRE) L'évolution des structures de production au cours des quinze premières années du Marché commun européen. Lausanne, 1975. pp. 79. *(Lausanne. Université. Centre de Recherches Européennes. Publications. 6. Etudes Sectorielles)*

EUROPEAN COMMUNITIES. Statistical Office. Quarterly bulletin of industrial production. q., 1976 (no.1)- Luxembourg. *[In Community languages].*

— Population.

EUROPEAN COMMUNITIES. Statistical Office. Regional statistics: population, employment, living standards. a., 1973/74 [1st]- Luxembourg. *[In Community languages]. Formerly included in EUROPEAN COMMUNITIES. Statistical Office. Regional statistics.*

— Social conditions.

EUROPEAN COMMUNITIES. Commission. Report on the development of the social situation in the Communities (formerly Exposé sur l'évolution de la situation sociale dans la Communauté); published in conjunction with General report on the activities of the European Communities. a., 1967 (1st)- Brussels.

— Social policy.

EUROPEAN COMMUNITIES. Commission. Report on the development of the social situation in the Communities (formerly Exposé sur l'évolution de la situation sociale dans la Communauté); published in conjunction with General report on the activities of the European Communities. a., 1967 (1st)- Brussels.

— Statistical services.

EUROSTAT NEWS; [pd. by] Statistical Office of the European Communities. irreg., 1976 (no.1)- Luxembourg.

EUROPEAN ECONOMIC COMMUNITY COUNTRIES.(Cont.)

— Statistics — Bibliography.

EUROSTAT NEWS; [pd. by] Statistical Office of the European Communities. irreg., 1976 (no.1)- Luxembourg.

— Treaties.

PUISSOCHET (J.P.) The enlargement of the European Communities: a commentary on the treaty and the acts concerning the accession of Denmark, Ireland and the United Kingdom. Leyden, 1975. pp. 454. bibliog.

EUROPEAN FEDERATION.

DANKERT (JOCHEN) and others. Politik in Westeuropa;... Integrationsprozesse vom Ende des zweiten Weltkrieges bis zur Gegenwart. Berlin, 1975. pp. 481.

EISNER (ERICH) Das europäische Konzept von Franz Josef Strauss: die gesamteuropäischen Ordnungsvorstellungen der CSU. Meisenheim am Glan, 1975. pp. 143. bibliog.

EUROPEAN integration; edited...by F. Roy Willis. New York, 1975. pp. 201. bibliog.

GREILSAMMER (ALAIN) Les mouvements fédéralistes en France de 1945 à 1974. Paris, [1975]. pp. 220. bibliog.

L'IDEA dell'unificazione europea dalla prima alla seconda guerra mondiale: relazioni tenute al convegno di studi svoltosi presso la Fondazione Luigi Einaudi, Torino...1974; contributi di Arduino Agnelli [and others]; a cura di Sergio Pistone. Torino, 1975. pp. 243. (Fondazione Luigi Einaudi. Studi. 21)

PAPISCA (ANTONIO) Europa '80, dalla comunità all'unione europea. Roma, [1975]. pp. 285.

RIEBEN (HENRI) Le rendez-vous avec l'histoire: [concluding report to the XVIIes Journées du Mont Pèlerin, 1975]. Lausanne, 1975. pp. 68. (Lausanne. Université. Centre de Recherches Européennes. Publications. 2. Le Processus d'Union de l'Europe)

EUROPEAN COMMUNITIES. Commission. 1976. European union: report by Mr. Leo Tindemans, Prime Minister of Belgium, to the European Council. [Brussels], 1976. pp. 36. (Bulletin of the European Communities. Supplements. [1976/1])

TINDEMANS (LEO) European union: report...to the European Council. Brussels, Ministry of Foreign Affairs, External Trade and Cooperation in Development, 1976. pp. 122. (Memo from Belgium. No. 171)

EUROPEAN FREE TRADE ASSOCIATION.

EUROPEAN FREE TRADE ASSOCIATION. 1976. The European Free Trade Association: structure, rules and operation. Geneva, 1976. pp. 146. bibliog.

EUROPEAN PARLIAMENT.

EUROPEAN COMMUNITIES. Commission. 1975. Reports on European union: European Parliament, Court of Justice, Economic and Social Committee. [Brussels], 1975. pp. 34. (Bulletin of the European Communities. Supplements. [1975/9])

— Elections.

EUROPEAN PARLIAMENT. 1975. Elections to the European Parliament by direct universal suffrage: draft convention with explanatory statement. [Luxembourg?], 1975. pp. 63.

CONSERVATIVE POLITICAL CENTRE. [Publications]. No. 583. Our voice in Europe: a discussion document on direct elections to the European Parliament [based on a report of a policy group chaired by Anthony Royle]. London, 1976. pp. 16.

EUROPEAN WAR, 1914-1918.

U.K. War Cabinet. Eastern report; (with Appreciation). w., Je 28 1917 - Mr 21 1918(nos. 22-60). [London].

U.K. War Cabinet. Western and general report; (with Appreciation). w., Je 27[1917]- Mr 20 1918 (nos. 22-60). [London].

ISTORIIA pervoi mirovoi voiny, 1914-1918. Moskva, 1975. 2 vols. bibliog.

— Campaigns.

STROKOV (ALEKSANDR ALEKSANDROVICH) Vooruzhennye sily i voennoe iskusstvo v pervoi mirovoi voine. Moskva, 1974. pp. 616.

— — Eastern.

RUTHERFORD (WARD) The Russian army in World War I. London, 1975. pp. 303. bibliog.

— Causes.

ALLEN (JOHN WILLIAM) Germany and Europe. London, 1914. pp. 133.

McCABE (JOSEPH) Treitschke and the Great War. London, 1914. pp. 287.

VIVIANI (RENE) As we see it: France and the truth about the war;...English translation by Thomas R. Ybarra. London, [1923]. pp. 269.

HELLER (JOSEPH) Ph.D. British policy towards the Ottoman Empire, 1908-1914. 1970 [or rather 1971]. fo.510. bibliog. Typescript. Ph.D. (London) thesis: unpublished. This thesis is the property of London University and may not be removed from the Library.

LEE (DWIGHT ERWIN) Europe's crucial years: the diplomatic background of World War I, 1902-1914. Hanover, N.H., 1974. pp. 482. bibliog.

CHOUCRI (NAZLI) and NORTH (ROBERT CARVER) Nations in conflict: national growth and international violence. San Francisco, [1975]. pp. 356. bibliog.

HOELZLE (ERWIN) Die Selbstentmachtung Europas: das Experiment des Friedens vor und im Ersten Weltkrieg, etc. Göttingen, [1975]. pp. 601.

MOSES (JOHN A.) The politics of illusion: the Fischer controversy in German historiography. London, 1975. pp. 148. bibliog.

WUERTHLE (FRIEDRICH) Die Spur führt nach Belgrad: die Hintergründe des Dramas von Sarajevo, 1914. Wien, [1975]. pp. 352.

HAMILTON (KEITH ALEXANDER) The embassy of Sir Francis Bertie in Paris during the period 1905-1914. 1975 [or rather 1976]. fo. 447. bibliog. Typescript. Ph.D.(London) thesis: unpublished. This thesis is the property of London University and may not be removed from the Library.

— Church of England.

MARRIN (ALBERT) The last crusade: the Church of England in the First World War. Durham, N.C., 1974. pp. 303. bibliog.

— Diplomatic history.

UNITED STATES. Department of State. 1918-19. The Inquiry handbooks. Wilmington, 1974. 20 vols. bibliogs. Reprint of documents originally published in Washington, 1918-19.

GERMANY. Auswärtiges Amt. 1919. Die deutschen Dokumente zum Kriegsausbruch. Berlin, 1919-20. 5 vols. (in 3).

VIVIANI (RENE) As we see it: France and the truth about the war;...English translation by Thomas R. Ybarra. London, [1923]. pp. 269.

BLEY (HELMUT) Bebel und die Strategie der Kriegsverhütung, 1904-1913: eine Studie über Bebels Geheimkontakte mit der britischen Regierung, etc. Göttingen, 1975. pp. 254.

CUFF (ROBERT D.) and GRANATSTEIN (JACK LAWRENCE) Canadian-American relations in wartime: from the Great War to the cold war. Toronto, 1975. pp. 205.

— Economic aspects.

VECCHIO (EDOARDO DEL) La cooperazione economica e finanziaria nella politica di guerra dell'intesa. Napoli, [1974]. pp. 551.

— — Germany.

ZUNKEL (FRIEDRICH) Industrie und Staatssozialismus: der Kampf um die Wirtschaftsordnung in Deutschland, 1914-1918. Düsseldorf, [1974]. pp. 227. bibliog. (Tübingen. Universität. Seminar für Zeitgeschichte. Tübinger Schriften zur Sozial- und Zeitgeschichte. 3)

— Finance.

VECCHIO (EDOARDO DEL) La cooperazione economica e finanziaria nella politica di guerra dell'intesa. Napoli, [1974]. pp. 551.

— Historiography.

MOSES (JOHN A.) The politics of illusion: the Fischer controversy in German historiography. London, 1975. pp. 148. bibliog.

— Literature and the war.

FUSSELL (PAUL) The Great War and modern memory. New York, 1975. pp. 363.

— Peace.

FERRERO (GUGLIELMO) Die Tragödie des Friedens: von Versailles zur Ruhr; (berechtigte Übersetzung aus dem Italienischen von B. Pritchard). Jena, 1923. pp. 207. Collection of essays and articles, mainly from the journal "Secolo", 1918-23, and some unpublished material.

GEORGE (DAVID LLOYD) 1st Earl Lloyd George. Is it peace?. London, [1923]. pp. 291. Articles and addresses on the European situation.

HOELZLE (ERWIN) Die Selbstentmachtung Europas: das Experiment des Friedens vor und im Ersten Weltkrieg, etc. Göttingen, [1975]. pp. 601.

— Personal narratives, British.

GARRATT (VERO W.) A man in the street. London, 1939. pp. 317.

— Personal narratives, Serbian.

KORDA (JOVAN STEV.) Odesa, Arhangelsk, Solun: iz života ratnih dobrovoljaca. [Osijek?, 1929?]. pp. 299.

— Reparations.

GEORGE (DAVID LLOYD) 1st Earl Lloyd George. Is it peace?. London, [1923]. pp. 291. Articles and addresses on the European situation.

— Sources.

GERMANY. Auswärtiges Amt. 1919. Die deutschen Dokumente zum Kriegsausbruch. Berlin, 1919-20. 5 vols. (in 3).

— Territorial questions.

See also UPPER SILESIAN QUESTION.

— — Poland.

BUREAU POLONAIS DE PUBLICATIONS POLITIQUES. Mémoire sur les frontières nord et sud-est de la Pologne restaurée. Paris, 1919. pp. 16.

— Czechoslovakia.

ŽIPEK (ALOIS) Válka národů 1914-1918, a účast českého národa v boji za svobodu. Praha, 1921-22. 5 vols.

— France.

VIVIANI (RENE) As we see it: France and the truth about the war;...English translation by Thomas R. Ybarra. London, [1923]. pp. 269.

— Germany.

LIEBMANN (HERMANN) Die Politik der Generalkommission: ein Sündenregister der Zentralvorstände der freien Gewerkschaften Deutschlands und ein Wegweiser für die Zukunft. Leipzig, 1919. pp. 72.

SIGEL (ROBERT) Die Lensch-Cunow-Haenisch-Gruppe: eine Studie zum rechten Flügel der SPD im Ersten Weltkrieg. Berlin, [1976]. pp. 177. bibliog. (Munich. Universität. Institut für bayrische Geschichte. Beiträge zu einer Historischen Strukturanalyse Bayerns im Industriezeitalter. Band 14)

ULLRICH (VOLKER) Die Hamburger Arbeiterbewegung vom Vorabend des ersten Weltkrieges bis zur Revolution 1918/19. Hamburg, [1976]. 2 vols. bibliog. Band 2 contains notes and the bibliography.

— Russia.

RUTHERFORD (WARD) The Russian army in World War I. London, 1975. pp. 303. bibliog.

— — Bibliography.

RUTMAN (AISA EFIMOVNA) compiler. Rossiia period pervoi mirovoi voiny i fevral'skoi burzhuano-demokraticheskoi revoliutsii, iiul' 1914 - fevral' 1917 g.: bibliograficheskii ukzatel' sovetskoi literatury, izdannoi v 1953- 1968 gg.; pod redaktsiei...Iu.I. Kir'ianova. Leningrad, 1975. pp. 614.

— Switzerland.

EHRBAR (HANS RUDOLF) Schweizerische Militärpolitik im Ersten Weltkrieg: die militärischen Beziehungen zu Frankreich vor dem Hintergrund der schweizerischen Aussen- und Wirtschaftspolitik, 1914-1918. Bern, 1976. pp. 380. bibliog.

— Tasmania.

LAKE (MARILYN LEE) A divided society: Tasmania during World War I. Carlton, Vic., 1975. pp. 213. bibliog.

— United States.

LARSON (SIMEON) Labor and foreign policy: Gompers, the A[merican] F[ederation of] L[abor], and the first World War, 1914- 1918. Rutherford, N.J., [1975]. pp. 176. bibliog.

RYLEY (THOMAS W.) A little group of willful men: a study of congressional- presidential authority. Port Washington, N.Y., 1975. pp. 198. bibliog.

EVALUATION RESEARCH (SOCIAL ACTION PROGRAMMES).

HAMILTON-SMITH (ELERY) Evaluation of social development programmes: a handbook for evaluation with special reference to youth work; (prepared for the Commonwealth Secretariat). London, Commonwealth Secretariat, [1974]. pp. 75. bibliog.

DORNBUSCH (SANFORD MAURICE) and SCOTT (WILLIAM RICHARD) Evaluation and the exercise of authority. San Francisco, 1975. pp. 382. bibliog.

STRUENING (ELMER L.) and GUTTENTAG (MARCIA) eds. Handbook of evaluation research. Beverly Hills, [1975]. 2 vols. bibliogs.

THOMPSON (MARK S.) Evaluation for decision in social programmes. Farnborough, Hants, [1975]. pp. 196. bibliog.

— United States.

EVALUATION and experiment: some critical issues in assessing social programs; edited by Carl A. Bennett and Arthur A. Lumsdaine. New York, 1975. pp. 553. bibliogs. "This volume is an outgrowth of a symposium held at the Battelle Seattle Research Center in July, 1973".

ROBERTO (EDUARDO L.) Strategic decision-making in a social program: the case of family- planning diffusion. Lexington, Mass., [1975]. pp. 182.

SEIDLER (LEE J.) and SEIDLER (LYNN L.) eds. Social accounting: theory, issues, and cases. Los Angeles, [1975]. pp. 547. bibliogs.

WILLIAMS (WALTER) Dr., and ELMORE (RICHARD F.) eds. Social program implementation. New York, [1976]. pp. 299. bibliog.

EVANGELICAL REVIVAL.

BOLES (JOHN B.) The great revival, 1787-1805: (the origin of the southern evangelical mind). Lexington, Ky., [1972]. pp. 236. bibliog.

EVAPORATION (METEOROLOGY).

MORTON (F.I.) Evaporation and climate: a study in cause and effect. Ottawa, 1968 [or rather 1969]. pp. 32. (Canada. Inland Waters Branch. Scientific Series. No. 4)

EVIDENCE, CRIMINAL

— United Kingdom.

RELEASE. Lawyers Group. Guilty until proved innocent?: (an assessment of the Criminal Law Revision Committee's Eleventh Report; evidence, general); editor: Michael King. London, 1973. pp. 67.

ARCHBOLD (JOHN FREDERICK) Pleading, evidence and practice in criminal cases: thirty-ninth edition [by] Stephen Mitchell [and others]. London, 1976. pp. 1823. With cumulative supplement.

EVIDENCE, DOCUMENTARY.

SMITH (A.D.) Microfilm: some legal implications. [London, 1975]. fo. 8,viii.

EVOLUTION.

INTERNATIONAL CONGRESS OF ANTHROPOLOGICAL AND ETHNOLOGICAL SCIENCES. 9th Congress, 1973. Population, ecology and social evolution: [papers from the Congress]; editor Steven Polgar. The Hague, [1975]. pp. 354. bibliog.

BENNETT (JOHN WILLIAM) The ecological transition: cultural anthropology and human adaptation. New York, [1976]. pp. 378. bibliog.

EXAMINATIONS

— Nigeria.

NIGERIA. Tribunal appointed to inquire into Leakages of Examination Questions of the First School Leaving Certificate and the West African School Certificate Examinations in 1967. 1969. Report; [D.A.R. Alexander, chairman]. Lagos, [1969]. pp. 301. Bound with the Government's comments on the report.

NIGERIA. 1970. Comments of the Federal Military Government on the report of the Tribunal of Inquiry into Leakages of Examination Questions. Lagos, 1970. pp. 23. Bound with the report.

EXCHANGE OF PERSONS PROGRAMMES.

AMERICAN ACADEMY OF POLITICAL AND SOCIAL SCIENCE. Annals. vol. 424. International exchange of persons: a reassessment; special editor of this volume Kenneth Holland. Philadelphia, 1976. pp. 179. bibliog.

EXECUTIONS (LAW)

— Russia.

GRIN'KO (IURII IVANOVICH) Ispolnenie sudebnykh reshenii. Kazan', 1969. pp. 72.

EXECUTIVE ADVISORY BODIES

— Canada.

CANADIAN ENVIRONMENTAL ADVISORY COUNCIL. Annual review. a., 1973/1974- Ottawa. [In English and French].

— United Kingdom.

HAGUE (DOUGLAS CHALMERS) and others. Public policy and private interests: the institutions of compromise. London, 1975. pp. 433.

— United States.

SOCIOLOGY and public policy: the case of Presidential Commissions: [based on two plenary sessions of the Annual Meeting of the American Sociological Association in 1973]; edited by Mirra Komarovsky. New York, [1975]. pp. 183.

WOLANIN (THOMAS R.) Presidential advisory commissions: Truman to Nixon. Madison, Wis., 1975. pp. 298.

— — Directories.

ENCYCLOPEDIA of governmental advisory organizations: a reference guide to Presidential Advisory Committees, Public Advisory Committees, interagency committees and other government-related boards, panels, task forces, commissions, conferences...; editors: Linda E. Sullivan, Anthony T. Kruzas. 2nd ed. Detroit, [1975]. pp. 668.

EXECUTIVE POWER.

KLIEMAN (AARON S.) Emergency politics: the growth of crisis government. London, 1976. pp. 19. (Institute for the Study of Conflict. Conflict Studies. No. 70)

HARGROVE (ERWIN C.) The power of the modern presidency. New York, [1974]. pp. 353. bibliog.

EXECUTIVE PRIVILEGE (GOVERNMENT INFORMATION)

— United Kingdom.

YOUNG (HUGO) The Crossman affair. London, 1976. pp. 224.

EXECUTIVES

— Germany.

HOFFKNECHT (ADALBERT CHRISTIAN) Die leitenden Angestellten im Koalitions- und Arbeitskampfrecht. Berlin, [1975]. pp. 148. bibliog.

— United Kingdom.

CROSS (PETER) The British business creed: changing ideologies and self images of business elites and management in Britain. [1975]. fo. 488. bibliog. Typescript. Ph.D. (London) thesis: unpublished. This thesis is the property of London University and may not be removed from the Library.

GRANICK (DAVID) Equality of promotional opportunities in British industry. London, [1975]. pp. 13.

— United States.

FERNANDEZ (JOHN P.) Black managers in white corporations. New York, [1975]. pp. 308. bibliog.

EXILES.

EUROPEAN COURT OF HUMAN RIGHTS. Publications. Series A: Judgments ad Decisions. A 4. ..."De Becker" case; judgment of 27th March 1962. Strasbourg, Council of Europe, 1962. pp. 33[bis]. In English and French.

EXISTENTIALISM.

POSTER (MARK) Existential Marxism in postwar France: from Sartre to Althusser. Princeton, [1975]. pp. 415. bibliog.

ARCHARD (DAVID WILLIAM) Existentialism and Marxism: a critical study of the political philosophy of Jean-Paul Sartre and Maurice Merleau-Ponty. 1976. fo. 333. bibliog. Typescript. Ph.D.(London) thesis: unpublished. This thesis is the property of London University and may not be removed from the Library.

CRAIB (IAN) Existentialism and sociology: a study of Jean-Paul Sartre. Cambridge, [1976]. pp. 242. bibliog.

EXPENDITURES, PUBLIC.

BRETON (ALBERT) The economic theory of representative government. London, 1974. pp. 228.

EXPENDITURES, PUBLIC.(Cont.)

MACIARIELLO (JOSEPH A.) Dynamic cost-benefit analysis: evaluation of public policy in a dynamic urban model. Lexington, Mass., [1975]. pp. 184. *bibliog.*

VEREIN FÜR SOZIALPOLITIK. Schriften. Neue Folge. Band 75/IV. Öffentliche Finanzwirtschaft und Verteilung, IV; von Clemens-August Andreae [and others]; herausgegeben von Wilhelmine Dreissig. Berlin, [1976]. pp. 150. *With summaries and table of contents in English.*

EXPERIMENTAL DESIGN.

LINDMAN (HAROLD R.) Analysis of variance in complex experimental designs. San Francisco, [1974]. pp. 352. *bibliog.*

EXPLORERS

— Russia.

KOMISSAROV (BORIS NIKOLAEVICH) Grigorii Ivanovich Langsdorf, 1774-1852. Leningrad, 1975. pp. 124.

EXPORT CREDIT

— Germany.

POHL (MANFRED) Die Finanzierung der Russengeschäfte zwischen den beiden Weltkriegen: die Entwicklung der 12 grossen Russlandkonsortien. Frankfurt am Main, [1975]. pp. 48. *(Tradition: Zeitschrift für Firmengeschichte und Unternehmerbiographie. Beihefte. 9)*

EXSERVICEMEN

— Medical care — United States.

LINDSAY (COTTON M.) Veterans Administration hospitals: an economic analysis of government enterprise. Washington, D.C., [1975]. pp. 88. *(American Enterprise Institute for Public Policy Research. Evaluative Studies. 23)*

— United Kingdom.

SOCIAL SERVICES RESEARCH AND INTELLIGENCE UNIT [PORTSMOUTH]. Problems of rehousing exservice families in Gosport. Portsmouth, [1976?]. fo. 16.

EXTERNALITIES (ECONOMICS).

JAŠIĆ (ZORAN) Eksterni efekti i ekonomska politika. Zagreb, 1974. pp. 58. *bibliog.*

EXTERNALITIES in the transformation of agriculture: distribution of benefits and costs from development; edited by Earl O. Heady [and] Larry R. Whiting. Ames, 1975. pp. 341. *bibliogs.*

— Mathematical models.

DICK (DANIEL T.) Pollution, congestion and nuisance: the economics of nonmarket interdependence. Lexington, Mass., [1974]. pp. 177. *bibliog.*

KOHN (ROBERT E.) Air pollution control: welfare economic interpretation. Lexington, [1975]. pp. 155. *bibliog.*

EXTORTION

— United Kingdom.

HEPWORTH (MIKE) Blackmail: publicity and secrecy in everyday life. London, 1975. pp. 127.

EXTRADITION

— Europe.

EUROPEAN COMMITTEE ON CRIME PROBLEMS. 1970. Legal aspects of extradition among European states. Strasbourg, Council of Europe, 1970. pp. 91.

EUROPEAN COMMITTEE ON CRIME PROBLEMS. 1971. Problems arising from the practical application of the European Convention on Mutual Assistance in Criminal Matters. Strasbourg, Council of Europe, 1971. pp. 111.

FABIAN SOCIETY.

FABIAN SOCIETY. Minute books. [Brighton, 1975 in progress]. *Microfiches of manuscript, typescript and printed documents.*

GREAVES (HAROLD RICHARD GORING) [Unpublished political and personal papers. 1932-53]. 13 pieces. *Manuscript, typescript, etc.*

FABRI (FRIEDRICH).

BADE (KLAUS J.) Friedrich Fabri und der Imperialismus in der Bismarckzeit: Revolution, Depression, Expansion. Freiburg i. Br., [1975]. pp. 579. *bibliog.*

FACTORY LAWS AND LEGISLATION

— India — Bombay.

BOMBAY (STATE). Industrial Conditions Enquiry Committee. Final report...together with suggestions for a labour code, Bombay State; [Purushottam Kanji, chairman]. [Bombay, 1950]. pp. 133.

FACTORY SYSTEM

— United States.

NELSON (DANIEL) Managers and workers: origins of the new factory system in the United States, 1880-1920. Madison, 1975. pp. 234. *bibliog.*

FAIRNESS.

HYMAN (RICHARD) and BROUGH (IAN) Social values and industrial relations: a study of fairness and equality. Oxford, [1975]. pp. 277. *bibliog. (Warwick Studies in Industrial Relations)*

FALKLAND ISLANDS

— Economic conditions.

FALKLAND ISLANDS SURVEY TEAM. Economic survey of the Falkland Islands; chairman: Lord Shackleton;...presented to the Secretary of State for Foreign and Commonwealth Affairs; prepared by The Economist Intelligence Unit. [London], 1976. 2 vols. (in 1). *bibliog.*

FAMILY.

ACKERMAN (NATHAN W.) The psychodynamics of family life: diagnosis and treatment of family relationships. New York, [1958]. pp. 379. *bibliog.*

RABB (THEODORE K.) and ROTBERG (ROBERT IRWIN) eds. The family in history: interdisciplinary essays. New York, 1973. pp. 240. *bibliog. (Reprinted from the Journal of Interdisciplinary History)*

CONFIGURATIONS: biological and cultural factors in sexuality and family life; edited by Raymond Prince [and] Dorothy Barrier. Lexington, Mass., [1974]. pp. 193. *bibliogs. Papers of a conference held in Montreal, 1972, and sponsored by the Mental Hygiene Institute.*

CLAYTON (RICHARD R.) The family, marriage, and social change. Lexington, Mass., [1975]. pp. 579. *bibliog.*

MANOCCHIO (TONY) and PETITT (WILLIAM) Families under stress: a psychological interpretation. London, 1975. pp. 208. *bibliog.*

LESLIE (GERALD RONNELL) The family in social context. 3rd ed. New York, 1976. pp. 815. *bibliogs.*

SHORTER (EDWARD) The making of the modern family. London, 1976. pp. 369. *bibliog.*

ZARETSKY (ELI) Capitalism, the family and personal life. London, 1976. pp. 156.

— Australia.

The FAMILY in Australia: social, demographic and psychological aspects; edited by Jerzy Krupinski [and] Alan Stoller. Rushcutter Bay, N.S.W., 1974. pp. 273. *bibliog.*

— Europe.

FAMILY and inheritance: rural society in western Europe, 1200- 1800; edited by Jack Goody [and others]. Cambridge, 1976. pp. 421. *(Past and Present. Past and Present Publications) Revised versions of papers delivered at the annual conference of the Past and Present Society.*

— France.

TABARD (NICOLE) and others. Besoins et aspirations des familles et des jeunes. [Paris], 1974. pp. 512. *(Caisse Nationale des Allocations Familiales. Etudes. [16])*

— Germany.

SOZIALDEMOKRATISCHE PARTEI DEUTSCHLANDS. Vorstand. Familienpolitik...: Entwurf; (Materialien zum Parteitag vom 10.4.-14.4.1973, Hannover). Bonn, [1972]. pp. 44.

NEIDHARDT (FRIEDHELM) Die Familie in Deutschland: gesellschaftliche Stellung, Struktur und Funktion. 4th ed. Opladen, [1975]. pp. 101. *bibliog. (Hochschule für Wirtschaft und Politik, Hamburg. Beiträge zur Sozialkunde. Reihe B. Struktur und Wandel der Gesellschaft. 5)*

— India.

POFFENBERGER (THOMAS) Fertility and family life in an Indian village. Ann Arbor, 1975. pp. 114. *(Michigan University. Center for South and Southeast Asian Studies. Michigan Papers on South and Southeast Asia. No. 10)*

— Mediterranean.

MEDITERRANEAN family structures; edited by J.G. Peristiany. Cambridge, 1976. pp. 414. *bibliogs. Papers of a seminar convened by the Social Research Centre of Cyprus in 1970.*

— Nigeria.

BARRETT (STANLEY R.) Two villages on stilts: economic and family change in Nigeria. New York, [1974]. pp. 112. *bibliog.*

— Norway.

NORWAY. Statistiske Centralbyrå. 1975. Familiestatistikk, 1974, etc. Oslo, 1975. pp. 71. *(Norges Offisielle Statistikk. Rekke A. 738) In Norwegian and English.*

— Poland.

ADAMSKI (FRANCISZEK) Rodzina nowego miasta: kierunki przemian w strukturze społeczno- moralnej rodziny nowohuckiej. Warszawa, 1970. pp. 170.

DODZIUK-LITYŃSKA (ANNA) and MARKOWSKA (DANUTA) Współczesna rodzina w Polsce. Warszawa, 1975. pp. 259.

KOCZERSKA (MARIA) Rodzina szlachecka w Polsce późnego średniowiecza. Warszawa, 1975. pp. 197. *bibliog. With French summary.*

— Puerto Rico.

BUITRAGO ORTIZ (CARLOS) Esperanza: an ethnographic study of a peasant community in Puerto Rico. Tucson, [1973]. pp. 217. *bibliog. (Wenner-Gren Foundation for Anthropological Research. Viking Fund Publications in Anthropology. No. 50)*

— Taiwan.

COHEN (MYRON L.) House united, house divided: the Chinese family in Taiwan. New York, 1976. pp. 267. *bibliog.*

— United Kingdom.

COUSINS (CHRISTINE RUTH) The military family: a study of three communities in the British armed forces. 1975. fo. 130. *bibliog. Typescript. M.Phil.(London) thesis: unpublished. This thesis is the property of London University and may not be removed from the Library.*

RAPOPORT (RHONA) and RAPOPORT (ROBERT NORMAN) Leisure and the family life cycle;...with the collaboration of Ziona Strelitz. London, 1975. pp. 386. *bibliog.*

GITTUS (ELIZABETH) Flats, families and the under-fives. London, 1976. pp. 269. *bibliog.*

MARONEY (ROBERT M.) The family and the state: considerations for social policy. London, 1976. pp. 142.

RAPOPORT (RHONA) and RAPOPORT (ROBERT NORMAN) Dual-career families re-examined: new integrations of work and family. [2nd ed.] London, 1976. pp. 382. *bibliog. Title of first edition: Dual-career families.*

— United States.

KLATZKY (SHEILA R.) Patterns of contact with relatives. Washington, [1971]. pp. 117. *bibliog. (American Sociological Association. Arnold and Caroline Rose Monograph Series in Sociology)*

FAMILY socialization and the adolescent: determinants of self- concept, conformity, religiosity, and counterculture values; [by] Darwin L. Thomas [and others]. Lexington, Mass., [1974]. pp. 181. *bibliog.*

POWER in families; edited by Ronald E. Cromwell and David H. Olson. New York, [1975]. pp. 264. *bibliog. Based on a symposium held in June 1973 at the University of Missouri, Kansas City and sponsored by its Family Study Center.*

MINDEL (CHARLES H.) and HABENSTEIN (ROBERT WESLEY) eds. Ethnic families in America: patterns and variations. New York, [1976]. pp. 429. *bibliogs.*

FAMILY ALLOWANCES

— Canada.

CANADA. Statutes, etc. 1952-67. Family Allowances Act, R.S.C. 1952, c. 109, as amended by 1957, c. 14, 1966-67, c. 96; and Family Allowances Regulations, P.C. 1954-1508, as amended by P.C. 1975-456, [etc.]: (office consolidation). Ottawa, 1968. pp. 21.

— — Quebec.

QUEBEC (PROVINCE). Pension Board. Annual report [on the] Québec Family Allowances Plan. a., 1973/74- Quebec.

— European Economic Community countries.

LISEIN-NORMAN (MARGARETHA) Les prestations familiales dans l'Europe des Six. Bruxelles, 1974. pp. 419. *(Brussels. Université Libre. Institut d'Etudes Européennes. Thèses et Travaux Economiques)*

— Netherlands.

RAAD VOOR HET MIDDEN- EN KLEINBEDRIJF. Advies inzake bedrijfsbeëindiging en A[lgemene Bijstandswet] en kinderbijslag eerste en tweede kind. [The Hague, 1971]. pp. 14.

— United Kingdom.

HEATING ACTION GROUP. A guide to allowances for families and old people. London, [1974?]. pp. 22.

LISTER (RUTH) and EMMETT (TONY) Under the safety net. London, 1976. pp. 39. *(Child Poverty Action Group. Poverty Pamphlets. 25)*

FAMILY LIFE EDUCATION.

MARRIAGES and families: enrichment through communication; edited by Sherod Miller. London, 1975. pp. 125. *bibliog. Reprint of special issue of Small Group Behavior, Vol. 6, No. 1, February 1975.*

FAMILY PSYCHOTHERAPY.

ACKERMAN (NATHAN W.) The psychodynamics of family life: diagnosis and treatment of family relationships. New York, [1958]. pp. 379. *bibliog.*

FAMILY SIZE.

MOSTERT (W.P.) The family-building process among Afrikaans-speaking couples, phase II: three years after marriage. Pretoria, 1974. pp. 162. *bibliog. (Human Sciences Research Council [South Africa] . Institute for Sociological, Demographic and Criminological Research. Reports. No. S-21)*

BELOVA (VALENTINA ANDREEVNA) Chislo detei v sem'e. Moskva, 1975. pp. 175. *bibliog.*

RUPRECHT (THEODORE K.) and JEWETT (FRANK I.) The micro-economics of demographic change: family planning and economic well-being. New York, 1975. pp. 153.

TURCHI (BOONE A.) The demand for children: the economics of fertility in the United States. Cambridge, Mass., [1975]. pp. 238. *bibliog.*

FAMILY SOCIAL WORK

— France.

MARQUART (FRANÇOIS) and others. L'action sociale et l'économie sociale familiale. [Paris], 1974. pp. 302. *bibliog. (Caisse Nationale des Allocations Familiales. Etudes. [17])*

— United Kingdom.

LONDON. London Council of Social Service. Family Services Committee. Family groups: a report...on work with disadvantaged parents and their children. London, 1975. pp. 19.

FAMINES.

SOROKIN (PITIRIM ALEXANDROVITCH) Hunger as a factor in human affairs;...translated with a prologue by Elena P. Sorokin; edited and with an introduction by T. Lynn Smith. Gainesville, Flo., [1975]. pp. 319.

FAR EASTERN REPUBLIC

— Constitutional history.

SHERESHEVSKII (BORIS MIKHAILOVICH) V bitvakh za Dal'nii Vostok, 1920-1922 gg.: otvetstvennyi redaktor...V.A. Demidov. Novosibirsk, 1974. pp. 187.

FARM BUILDINGS

— France.

FRANCE. Ministère de l'Agriculture. Statistique agricole. Supplément. Série Etudes. No. 135. Enquête sur les bâtiments d'habitation et d'exploitation agricoles, 1965-1966. [Paris], 1975. 2 vols.

FARM INCOME

— Germany.

PETERS (WILHELM) Agronomist. Ausmass und Bestimmungsgründe der interregionalen Einkommensverteilung in der Landwirtschaft der Bundesrepublik Deutschland. Hannover, 1975. pp. 217. *bibliog. (Agrarwirtschaft. Sonderhefte. 62)*

FARM LIFE

— Germany.

GOLDE (GUENTER) Catholics and Protestants: agricultural modernization in two German villages. New York, [1975]. pp. 198. *bibliog.*

FARM MANAGEMENT.

EGAN (R.J.) Optimum combination of enterprises using linear programming. [Brisbane], 1968. fo. 40. *(Queensland. Department of Primary Industries. Economic Services Branch. Technical Bulletins. No. 4)*

WHITLAM (G.B.) and others. Methods of evaluation of farm development projects. [Brisbane], 1970. pp. 65. *bibliog. (Queensland. Department of Primary Industries. Economic Services Branch. Technical Bulletins. No. 7)*

INDIA. Ministry of Agriculture. Directorate of Economics and Statistics. 1973. Studies in the economics of farm management in Kerala: Alleppey and Quilon: combined report for the years 1962-63-- 1964-65. [Delhi], 1973. pp. 118.

ADHVARYU (J.H.) and PARIKH (GOKUL O.) Studies in the economics of farm management in Surat and Bulsar districts, Gujarat: report for the year 1966-67. [Delhi, Controller of Publications], 1974. pp. 370.

GOSWAMI (PRABHAS CHANDRA) and BORA (C.K.) Studies in the economics of farm management in Nowgong district, Assam: report[s] for the year[s] 1968-69 [and] 1969-70. [Delhi, Controller of Publications, 1974]. 2 vols. (in 1).

KAHLON (A.S.) and MIGLANI (SURJIT SINGH) Studies in the economics of farm management in Ferozepur district, Punjab: three-year consolidated report, 1967-68 to 1969-70. [Delhi, Controller of Publications, 1974]. pp. 274.

LAVANIA (GAURI SHANKAR) Studies in economics of farm management in Deoria, Uttar Pradesh: combined report, 1966-69. [Delhi, Controller of Publications, 1974]. pp. 294.

NARAYANA (D.L.) Studies in the economics of farm management in Cuddapah district, Andhra Pradesh: combined report for the period 1967-68 to 1969- 70. [Delhi, Manager of Publications, 1974]. pp. 160.

SHANMUGASUNDARAM (VEDAGIRI) Studies in economics of farm management in Thanjavur district, Tamil Nadu: combined report 1967-68 to 1969-70. [Delhi, Controller of Publications, 1974]. pp. 66.

SHANMUGASUNDARAM (VEDAGIRI) Studies in the economics of farm management in Thanjavur district, Tamil Nadu: report[s] for the year[s] 1967-68, 1968-69, 1969-70. [Delhi, Controller of Publications], 1974. 3 vols. (in 1).

SINGH (ROSHAN) and SINGH (RANBIR) Studies in the economics of farm management in Muzaffarnagar district, Uttar Pradesh: report for the year 1968-69. [Delhi, Controller of Publications], 1974. pp. 577.

ABERDEEN. University of Aberdeen. North of Scotland College of Agriculture. Bulletins. [New Series]. No. 10. Budgetary control in farm management. [Aberdeen], 1975. pp. 31.

KHARA (M. P.) Studies in the economics of farm management in Ahmednagar district, Maharashtra State: report for the year 1967-68. [Delhi, Controller of Publications], 1975. pp. 484.

MISRA (B.) Studies in the economics of farm management in Cuttack district, Orissa: combined report 1967-70. [Delhi, Controller of Publications, 1975]. pp. 64.

SINGH (ROSHAN) and SINGH (RANBIR) Studies in the economics of farm management in Muzaffarnagar district, U.P.: combined report for the years 1966-67 to 1968-69. [Delhi, Controller of Publications, 1975]. pp. 266.

ADHVARYU (J.H.) and PARIKH (GOKUL O.) Studies in the economics of farm management in the I[ntensive] A[gricultural] D[istrict] P[rogramme] region of Surat and Bulsar, Gujarat State: report for the year 1968-69. [Delhi, Controller of Publications], 1976. 2 vols.

FARM MECHANIZATION

— France.

FRANCE. Ministère de l'Agriculture. Statistique agricole. Supplément. Série Etudes. No. 108. L'équipement des exploitations agricoles françaises en machines et installations en 1967; [par Mlle. Cismigiu et M. Casemajor]. Paris, 1974. pp. 312.

— India — Goa, Daman and Diu.

GOA, DAMAN AND DIU. Bureau of Economics, Statistics and Evaluation. 1974. An evaluation of the scheme of utilization of agricultural machinery and implements in Goa. Panaji, 1974. pp. 85. *(Evaluation Reports. No. 9)*

— Underdeveloped areas.

See UNDERDEVELOPED AREAS — Farm mechanization.

FARM PRODUCE.

CHRYSOMILIDES (G.S.) Productivity standards of export crops in Cyprus, other major Mediterranean producers and the U.S.A.: suggestions for revising agricultural policies in Cyprus. Beirut, 1974. pp. 24. *bibliog. (Reprinted from Anaptyxis, vol. 3-4, June 1974)*

FARM PRODUCE.(Cont.)

— India — Marketing.

INDIA. Ministry of Agriculture. Directorate of Economics and Statistics. 1972- . Market intelligence in India. [Delhi, 1972 in progress].

— Malawi — Marketing.

MALAWI. Agro-Economic Survey. 1975. Agro-economic survey: report no. 16: marketing of smallholder agricultural produce in Malawi. Vol. 1. The origin, marketing and transport pattern of main agricultural products; prepared by K. Quinten. Lilongwe, 1975. fo. 89.

— Poland — Marketing.

KRAMER (TEODOR) Rynek wiejski a proces industrializacji. Warszawa, 1963. pp. 208. *bibliog.*

— Russia — Marketing.

KOVAL'CHENKO (IVAN DMITRIEVICH) and MILOV (LEONID VASIL'EVICH) Vserossiiskii agrarnyi rynok, XVIII - nachalo XX veka: opyt kolichestvennogo analiza. Moskva, 1974. pp. 412.

— United States.

SCHNEIDER (WILLIAM) Can we avert economic warfare in raw materials?: U.S. agriculture as a blue chip. New York, [1974]. pp. 43. *(National Strategy Information Center. Agenda Papers. No. 1)*

— — Marketing.

BREIMYER (HAROLD FREDERICK) Economics of the product markets of agriculture. Ames, Iowa, 1976. pp. 208.

FARMERS

— France.

FRANCE. Ministère de l'Agriculture. Statistique Agricole. Supplément. Série Etudes. No. 131. Projections 1980 de la population agricole familiale;...étude... rédigée par Solange Rattin. [Paris], 1975. pp. 60. *Cover title reads: Projection pour 1980 de la population agricole familiale.*

— Ghana.

BECKMAN (BJÖRN) Organising the farmers: cocoa politics and national development in Ghana. Uppsala, 1976. pp. 299. *bibliog.*

— United States.

McMATH (ROBERT C.) Populist vanguard: a history of the southern Farmers' Alliance. Chapel Hill, N.C., [1975].pp. 221. *bibliog.*

FARMS

— Japan.

JAPAN. Ministry of Agriculture and Forestry. 1972. Report of the 1970 world census of agriculture and forestry in Japan. [Tokyo, 1972]. pp. 77.

— New Zealand — Valuation.

REAL ESTATE MARKET IN NEW ZEALAND, THE; [pd. by] Valuation Department. a., 1975- Wellington. *Supersedes RURAL REAL ESTATE IN NEW ZEALAND and URBAN REAL ESTATE IN NEW ZEALAND.*

FARMS, COLLECTIVE

— Romania — Laws and legislation.

ROMANIA. Statutes, etc. 1965. Statutul uniunii naționale, uniunilor regionale și uniunilor raionale ale cooperativelor agricole de producție din Republica Socialistă România: proiect. București, 1965. pp. 30.

— Russia.

MEDVEDEV (N.A.) ed. Metodika perspektivnogo ekonomiko-sotsial'noo planirovaniia na sele. Leningrad, 1970. pp. 339.

OSOFSKY (STEPHEN) Soviet agricultural policy: toward the abolition of collective farms. New York, 1974. pp. 300. *bibliog.*

PANKRATOV (IVAN FERISANOVICH) Kolkhoznaia demokratiia na sovremennom etape. Moskva, 1974. pp. 190.

— — Law and legislation.

PODOPRIGORA (ZINAIDA ANDREEVNA) Grazhdanskopravovye problemy mezhkolkhoznogo sotrudnichestva. Moskva, 1972. pp. 144.

SOVETSKOE pravo i kolkhozy. Moskva, 1973. pp. 286.

STOROZHEV (NIKOLAI VASIL'EVICH) Pravovoe polozhenie kolkhoza na sovremennom etape: vnutrikhoziaistvennye aspekty. Minsk, 1975. pp. 247.

FASCISM.

MAN (HENRI DE) Sozialismus und Nationalfascismus. Potsdam, 1931. pp. 61.

BABICI (ION) Boevaia antifashistskaia solidarnost', 1933-1939 gg.; (perevod s rumynskogo Natalii i Konstantina Unguru). Bukharest, 1974. pp. 244. *(Academia de Științe Sociale și Politice a Republicii Socialiste România. Bibliotheca Historica Romaniae. Studies. 49)*

CASSELS (ALAN) Fascism. New York, [1975]. pp. 401. *bibliog.*

FELICE (RENZO DE) Intervista sul fascismo; a cura di Michael A. Ledeen. Roma, 1975. pp. 127.

REAPPRAISALS of fascism; edited...by Henry A. Turner. New York, 1975. pp. 238. *bibliog.*

SCHMITT-EGNER (PETER) Kolonialismus und Faschismus: eine Studie zur historischen und begrifflichen Genesis faschistischer Bewusstseinsformen am deutschen Beispiel. Giessen/Lollar, 1975. pp. 224. *bibliog.*

KITCHEN (MARTIN) Fascism. London, 1976. pp. 106. *bibliog.*

SIDENIUS (NIELS CHRISTIAN) Kommunistisk Internationale, 1928-1935: en analyse og kritik... specielt i forhold til fascismen og udviklingen i Tyskland. Århus, 1976. pp. 283. *bibliog.*

VAJDA (MIHALY) Fascism as a mass movement. London, [1976]. pp. 132.

WIPPERMANN (WOLFGANG) Faschismustheorien: zum Stand der gegenwärtigen Diskussion. Darmstadt, 1976. pp. 183. *bibliog.*

— Belgium.

DANNAU (WIM) Ainsi parla Léon Degrelle;...interviews au magnétophone et conversations avec...Léon Degrelle...recueillies par Wim Dannau de 1965 à 1972, les commentaires de l'auteur, etc. [Strombeek, 1973 in progress].

— Canada.

BETCHERMAN (LITA-ROSE) The swastika and the maple leaf: fascist movements in Canada in the thirties. Toronto, [1975]. pp. 167.

— France.

FIELD (FRANK) Three writers and the Great War: studies in the rise of communism and fascism. Cambridge, 1975. pp. 212. *bibliog.*

GUCHET (YVES) Georges Valois: l'Action Française, le Faisceau, la République Syndicale. Paris, [1975]. pp. 249. *bibliog.*

TUCKER (WILLIAM RAYBURN) The fascist ego: a political biography of Robert Brasillach. Berkeley, 1975. pp. 331. *bibliog.*

— Italy.

RASCHHOFER (HERMANN) Der politische Volksbegriff im modernen Italien. Berlin, 1936. pp. 207.

BORDONI (CARLO) Cultura e propaganda nell'Italia fascista: un saggio introduttivo con i confronti antologici da G. Gentile [and others]. Messina, 1974. pp. 192. *bibliog.*

FELICE (RENZO DE) Mussolini e Hitler: i rapporti segreti, 1922-1933; con documenti inediti. Firenze, [1975]. pp. 315.

GENTILE (EMILIO) Le origini dell'ideologia fascista, 1918-1925. Roma, [1975]. pp. 476. *(Rome. Università. Istituto di Storia Moderna. Ricerca su "Partito, Stato e Società Civile nell'Italia Fascista, 1922-1945". 9)*

GRIFONE (PIETRO) Capitalismo di Stato e imperialismo fascista; con i contributi di Giorgio Amendola e Camilla Ravera. Milano, [1975]. pp. 155.

PAPA (EMILIO RAFFAELE) Fascismo e cultura. Venezia, 1974 repr. 1975. pp. 291.

PISTILLO (MICHELE) Giuseppe Di Vittorio, 1924-1944: la lotta contro il fascismo e per l'unità sindacale. Roma, 1975. pp. 479.

ROSSI (ERNESTO) Un democratico ribelle: cospirazione antifascista, carcere, confino; scritti e testimonianze a cura di Giuseppe Armani. Parma, 1975. pp. 414.

SAPELLI (GIULIO) Fascismo grande industria e sindacato: il caso di Torino, 1929/1935. Milano, 1975. pp. 260.

TRENTIN (SILVIO) Dieci anni di fascismo totalitario in Italia: dall'istituzione del Tribunale speciale alla proclamazione dell'Impero; (traduzione di Antonio Capitanio); prefazione di Enzo Santarelli. Roma, 1975. pp. 267. *bibliog.*

SPINDLER (KATHARINA) Die Schweiz und der italienische Faschismus, 1922-1930: der Verlauf der diplomatischen Beziehungen durch das Bürgertum. Basel, 1976. pp. 304. *bibliog. Dissertation vorgelegt der Philosophisch-Historischen Fakultät der Universität Basel.*

— Romania.

CODREANU (CORNELIU ZELEA) Pentru legionari. v.1. Sibiu, 1936; [Munich, 1968]. pp. 482. *(Colecția "Omul nou")*

— Spain.

MARTINEZ VAL (JOSE MARIA) Por que no fue posible la Falange?. Barcelona, 1975. pp. 215.

— Switzerland.

SYFRIG (MAX) and DEFAYE (CHRISTIAN) L'extrême-droit en Suisse. Lausanne, [1967]. pp. 42. *Articles reprinted from the August and September 1967 issues of Tribune de Lausanne.*

FATHER SEPARATED CHILDREN.

GREEN (MAUREEN) Goodbye father. London, 1976. pp. 169. *bibliog.*

FATHERS.

GREEN (MAUREEN) Goodbye father. London, 1976. pp. 169. *bibliog.*

FECUNDITY.

See FERTILITY, HUMAN.

FEDERAL AID TO HIGHER EDUCATION

— United States.

GLADIEUX (LAWRENCE E.) and WOLANIN (THOMAS R.) Congress and the colleges: the national politics of higher education. Lexington, Mass., [1976]. pp. 273.

FEDERAL-CITY RELATIONS.

— United States.

BINGHAM (RICHARD D.) Public housing and urban renewal: an analysis of federal-local relations. New York, 1975. pp. 255. *bibliog.*

FRIEDEN (BERNARD J.) and KAPLAN (MARSHALL) The politics of neglect: urban aid from model cities to revenue sharing. Cambridge, Mass., [1975]. pp. 281. *(Massachusetts Institute of Technology and Harvard University. Joint Center for Urban Studies. Publications)*

GELFAND (MARK I.) A nation of cities: the federal government and urban America, 1933-1965. New York, 1975. pp. 476. *bibliog.*

PRESSMAN (JEFFREY L.) Federal programs and city politics: the dynamics of aid process in Oakland. Berkeley, [1975]. pp. 162. *bibliog.*

FEDERAL GOVERNMENT.

WEY (S.O.) Decision making in federal regimes. Lagos, Federal Ministry of Information, 1971. 1 vol. (various pagings).

BELLONI (GIULIO ANDREA) Carlo Cattaneo e la sua idea federale; a cura di Giuseppe Armani. Pisa, 1974. pp. 157. *(Domus Mazziniana. Collana Scientifica. 14)*

DIKSHIT (RAMESH DUTTA) The political geography of federalism: an inquiry into origins and stability. London, 1975. pp. 273. *bibliog.*

— Africa, East.

SOUTHALL (ROGER) Federalism and higher education in East Africa. Nairobi, 1974. pp. 160. *bibliog.*

— Austria—Hungary.

GORDON (HAROLD JACKSON) and GORDON (NANCY M.) eds. The Austrian Empire: abortive federation? Lexington, [1974]. pp. 159. *bibliog.*

— Cameroun.

NDONGKO (WILFRED AWUNG) Planning for economic development in a federal state: the case of Cameroon, 1960-1971. München, [1975]. pp. 203. *bibliog. (Ifo-Institut für Wirtschaftsforschung. Afrika- Studien. 85)*

— Canada.

MARTIN (JOE) Management Consultant. The role and place of Ontario in the Canadian confederation. [Toronto], Ontario Economic Council, 1974. pp. 68. *(Evolution of Policy in Contemporary Ontario, The. 4)*

BLACK (EDWIN R.) Divided loyalties: Canadian concepts of federalism. Montreal, 1975. pp. 272.

— Germany.

EHNI (HANS PETER) Bollwerk Preussen?: Preussen-Regierung, Reich-Länder- Problem und Sozialdemokratie, 1928-1932. Bonn-Bad Godesberg, [1975]. pp. 304. *bibliog. (Friedrich-Ebert-Stiftung. Forschungsinstitut. Schriftenreihe. Band 111)*

— Nigeria.

NIGERIA. Administrative Adviser's Office. 1968. Constitutional powers and functions in a federal system: from the administrative point of view. Lagos, 1968. fo. 36, 1 map.

WEY (S.O.) Decision making in federal regimes. Lagos, Federal Ministry of Information, 1971. 1 vol. (various pagings).

— Russia.

KIS (THEOFIL I.) Le fédéralisme soviétique: ses particularités typologiques. Ottawa, 1973. pp. 191. *bibliog. (Ottawa. Université. Faculté des Sciences Sociales. Collection des Sciences Sociales. No. 2)*

ZHELEZNOV (BORIS LEONIDOVICH) Kompetentsiia RSFSR i ee sub"ektov. Kazan', 1974. pp. 128.

— Switzerland.

NEIDHART (LEONHARD) Reform des Bundesstaates [Switzerland]: Analysen und Thesen. Bern, [1970]. pp. 135. *bibliog.*

NEIDHART (LEONHARD) Föderalismus in der Schweiz: zusammenfassender Bericht über die Föderalismus-Hearings der Stiftung für eidgenössische Zusammenarbeit in Solothurn. Zürich, [1975]. pp. 128.

— United States.

HAIDER (DONALD H.) When governments come to Washington: governors, mayors, and intergovernmental lobbying. New York, [1974]. pp. 336. *bibliog.*

HOLMES (MICHAEL S.) The New Deal in Georgia: an administrative history. Westport, Conn., [1975]. pp. 364. *bibliog.*

LIEBER (HARVEY) and ROSINOFF (BRUCE) Federalism and clean waters: the 1972 Water Pollution Control Act. Lexington, Mass., [1975]. pp. 288.

FEDERAL PARTY.

KOHN (RICHARD H.) Eagle and sword: the Federalists and the creation of the military establishment in America, 1783-1802. New York, [1975]. pp. 443. *bibliog.*

FÉDÉRATION NATIONALE DES RÉPUBLICAINS INDÉPENDENTS.

STEED (MICHAEL) The French threat. Wells, 1976. pp. 24.

FEDOROV (IVAN).

PERSHODRUKAR Ivan Fedorov ta ioho poslidovnyky na Ukraïni, XVI - persha polovyna XVII st.: zbirnyk dokumentiv. Kyïv, 1975. pp. 343. *bibliog. With Russian and English summaries.*

FEES, PROFESSIONAL

— United Kingdom.

COMMITTEE ON INVISIBLE EXPORTS. Overseas earnings of the British professions. London, 1972. fo. 55.

FEMINISM.

YATES (GAYLE GRAHAM) What women want: the ideas of the movement. Cambridge, Mass., 1975. pp. 230. *bibliog.*

EDMOND (WENDY) and FLEMING (SUZIE) eds. All work and no pay: women, housework, and the wages due. Bristol, 1975. pp. 128.

FREEMAN (JO) The politics of women's liberation: a case study of an emerging social movement and its relation to the policy process. New York, [1975]. pp. 268. *bibliog.*

FENIANS.

NEIDHARDT (W.S.) Fenianism in North America. University Park, Pa., [1975]. pp. 164. *bibliog.*

FERMAT (PIERRE DE).

RÉNYI (ALFRÉD) Letters on probability;...translated by László Vekerdi. Detroit, 1972. pp. 86. *bibliog.*

FERRIES

— Hong Kong.

HONG KONG. Transport Department. Research and Development Section. 1975. North Point - Kwun Tong: vehicular ferry service. [Hong Kong], 1975. pp. 18. *(Studies Reports. No. 75/3)*

HONG KONG. Transport Department. Research and Development Section. 1976. Survey on four HYF ferry Sunday routes, etc.; by Li Yuen- ting. [Hong Kong], 1976. pp. 27. *(Studies Reports. No. 76/3)*

FERTILITY, HUMAN.
In earlier supplements of this Bibliography similar works have been entered under FECUNDITY.

PALESTINE. Office of Statistics. Special Bulletins. No.3. The fertility of marriage in Palestine. Jerusalem, 1939. pp. 16.

PALESTINE. Central Bureau for Medical Statistics. 1945. Statistical tables on the mortality amongst the various sections of the population of Palestine. Jerusalem, 1945. 1 vol. (unpaged). *(Pamphlets. No.3) In English and Hebrew.*

MOSTERT (W.P.) The family-building process among Afrikaans-speaking couples, phase II: three years after marriage. Pretoria, 1974. pp. 162. *bibliog. (Human Sciences Research Council [South Africa]. Institute for Sociological, Demographic and Criminological Research. Reports. No. S-21)*

RUSSIA (USSR). Ministerstvo Vysshego i Srednego Spetsial'nogo Obrazovaniia. Nauchno-Tekhnicheskii Sovet. Sektsiia Narodonaseleniia. Narodonaselenie. 5. Demograficheskii analiz rozhdaemosti. Moskva, 1974. pp. 112. *With English table of contents.*

BALAKRISHNAN (T.R.) and others. Fertility and family planning in a Canadian metropolis. Montreal, 1975. pp. 217. *bibliog.*

BOUVIER (LEON F.) and RAO (SETHURAMAIAH LAKSHMINARAYANA) Socioreligious factors in fertility decline. Cambridge, Mass., [1975]. pp. 204. *bibliog.*

INTERNATIONAL CONGRESS OF ANTHROPOLOGICAL AND ETHNOLOGICAL SCIENCES. 9th Congress, 1973. Population and social organization: [papers from the Congress]; editor Moni Nag. The Hague, [1975]. pp. 367. *bibliogs.*

KUHN (DIETMAR) Der Geburtenrückgang in Österreich, etc. Wien, 1975. pp. 103.

LAW and fertility in Europe: a study of legislation directly or indirectly affecting fertility in Europe; edited by Maurice Kirk [and others]. Dolhain, [1975]. 2 vols. *Essays and country reports of the Joint Working Group for the Study of Legislation directly or indirectly influencing Fertility in Europe, set up by the European Centre for Co-ordination of Research...in the Social Sciences and the International Union for the Scientific Study of Population.*

POFFENBERGER (THOMAS) Fertility and family life in an Indian village. Ann Arbor, 1975. pp. 114. *(Michigan University. Center for South and Southeast Asian Studies. Michigan Papers on South and Southeast Asia. No. 10)*

SPILLANE (WILLIAM H.) and RYSER (PAUL E.) Male fertility survey: fertility knowledge, attitudes, and practices of married men. Cambridge, Mass., [1975]. pp. 191. *bibliog.*

TURCHI (BOONE A.) The demand for children: the economics of fertility in the United States. Cambridge, Mass., [1975]. pp. 238. *bibliog.*

— Mathematical models.

CHANDRASEKARAN (C.) and HERMALIN (ALBERT I.) eds. Measuring the effect of family planning programs on fertility. Dolhain, Belgium. [1975]. pp. 570. *bibliogs.*

FERTILIZER INDUSTRY

— Germany.

RUHR-STICKSTOFF AG. D[eutsche] A[mmoniak-]Vereinigung: Geschichte eines Unternehmens und Aspekte seiner Zeit. Bochum, [1974]. pp. 80.

FERTILIZERS AND MANURES.

BAADE (FRITZ) Hundred years of increasing crops thanks to the use of commercial fertilizers: a retrospective view at the year 1900 and an outlook on the year 2000. [Rome], 1973. pp. 29.

— Economic aspects — Tanzania.

RAIKES (PHILIP L.) Fertilizer projections for Tanzania up to 1974 and 1980. Dar es Salaam, 1974. pp. 51. *(Dar es Salaam. University. Economic Research Bureau. ERB Papers. 74.2)*

FETUS, DEATH OF THE.

NORWAY. Statistiske Centralbyrå. 1975. Dødeligheten omkring fødselen og i første leveår 1969-1972, etc. Oslo, 1975. pp. 107. *(Statistiske Analyser. 15) With English summary.*

FEUDALISM.

FEUDALISM.

FRANK (ANDRE GUNDER) On capitalist underdevelopment. Bombay, 1975. pp. 113. *bibliog.*

KULA (WITOLD) An economic theory of the feudal system: towards a model of the Polish economy, 1500-1800. London, 1976. pp. 191.

— **America, Latin.**

CARMAGNANI (MARCELLO) L'America Latina dal '500 a oggi: nascita, espansione e crisi di un sistema feudale. Milano, 1975. pp. 220. *bibliog.*

— **Denmark.**

SCOCOZZA (BENITO) Klassekampen i Danmarks historie: feudalismen; med et indledende afsnit om den historiske materialisme. [Copenhagen, 1976]. pp. 308. *bibliog.*

— **Germany.**

MĚTŠK (FRIDO) Die Stellung der Sorben in de territorialen Verwaltungsgliederung des deutschen Feudalismus: ein Beitrag zur Rechts- und Verfassungsgeschichte des deutschen Feudalismus im Sorbenland. Bautzen, 1968. pp. 171. *(Deutsche Akademie der Wissenschaften zu Berlin. Institut für Sorbische Volksforschung in Bautzen. Schriftenreihe. 43)*

— **Moldavia.**

DRAGNEV (DEMIR MIRONOVICH) Sel'skoe khoziaistvo feodal'noi Moldavii, konets XVII - nachalo XIX v. Kishinev, 1975. pp. 286.

— **Russia.**

TIKHONOV (IURII ALEKSANDROVICH) Pomeshchich'i krest'iane v Rossii: feodal'naia renta v XVII - nachale XVIII v. Moskva, 1974. pp. 335.

OBSHCHESTVO i gosudarstvo feodal'noi Rossii: sbornik statei, posviashchennyi 70-letiiu akademika L'va Vladimirovicha Cherepnina. Moskva, 1975. pp. 351.

— — **Crimea.**

FEODAL'NAIA Tavrika: materialy po istorii i arkheologii Kryma. Kiev, 1974. pp. 216.

FIBRES.

GRILLI (ENZO R.) The future for hard fibers and competition from synthetics. [Washington], International Bank for Reconstruction and Development, 1975. pp. 108. *bibliog. (World Bank Staff Occasional Papers. No. 19)*

FIBRES, SYNTHETIC.

GRILLI (ENZO R.) The future for hard fibers and competition from synthetics. [Washington], International Bank for Reconstruction and Development, 1975. pp. 108. *bibliog. (World Bank Staff Occasional Papers. No. 19)*

FIELD CROPS

— **Canada.**

CANADA. Department of Agriculture. Economics Branch. Market commentary: horticulture and special crops. s-a., D 1975- Ottawa.

— **Sweden.**

JORDBRUKETS UTREDNINGSINSTITUT. Meddelanden. 1974. Nr. 4. Energibalans för växtodlingen i svenskt jordbruk. Stockholm, 1974. pp. 65. *With English summary.*

FIJI ISLANDS

— **Economic policy.**

FIJI. Central Planning Office. 1966. Fiji development plan, 1966-1970: development planning review. in FIJI. Legislative Council. Journal. Sessions of 1966.

FIJI. Central Planning Office. 1966. Fiji development plan, 1966-1970: outline and public expenditure. in FIJI. Legislative Council. Journal. Sessions of 1966.

CASTLE (L.V.) Economic policy in an independent state. Suva, Fiji, [1973?]. pp. 39. *(University of the South Pacific. Raymond W. Parkinson Memorial Lectures. 1970)*

— **Legislative Council — Salaries, allowances, etc.**

FIJI. Legislative Council. Select Committee on the Emoluments and/or Other Allowances of Members of Legislative Council. 1966. Report; [H.P. Ritchie, chairman]. in FIJI. Legislative Council. Journal. Sessions of 1966.

— **Politics and government.**

FIJI. Parliament. Senate. Parliamentary debates (Hansard). sess., N/D 1972- Suva.

— **Social policy.**

FIJI. Central Planning Office. 1966. Fiji development plan, 1966-1970: development planning review. in FIJI. Legislative Council. Journal. Sessions of 1966.

FIJI. Central Planning Office. 1966. Fiji development plan, 1966-1970: outline and public expenditure. in FIJI. Legislative Council. Journal. Sessions of 1966.

FILE ORGANIZATION (COMPUTER SCIENCE).

LEFKOVITZ (DAVID) File structures for on-line systems. Rochelle Park, N.Y., [1969]. pp. 215. *bibliog. Based on lectures sponsored by the Professional Development Seminars of the Association for Computing Machinery in 1967 and 1968.*

WATERS (SAMUEL JOSEPH) Introduction to computer systems design: planning files and programs. Manchester, [1974] repr. 1976. pp. 198.

FINANCE.

GAUDEMET (PAUL MARIE) Finances publiques. Paris 1974 in progress. *bibliog.*

EUROPEAN FINANCE ASSOCIATION. 1st Meeting, 1974. Proceedings [of] meetings held in Jouy-en-Josas, October 31st - November 2nd, 1974; edited by Bertrand Jacquillat. Amsterdam, 1975. pp. 402. *bibliogs.*

HARRISON (THOMAS RUSSELL) A challenge to the presidency: Canada and inflation: cause, course, cost, correction, consolidation. Hicksville, N.Y., [1976]. pp. 151.

MONETARISM; edited by Jerome L. Stein. Amsterdam, 1976. pp. 342. *bibliogs. Based on a conference sponsored by the National Science Foundation.*

THIRLWALL (ANTHONY PHILIP) Financing economic development. London, 1976. pp. 95. *bibliog.*

VEREIN FÜR SOZIALPOLITIK. Schriften. Neue Folge. Band 75/IV. Öffentliche Finanzwirtschaft und Verteilung, IV; von Clemens-August Andreae [and others]; herausgegeben von Wilhelmine Dreissig. Berlin, [1976]. pp. 150. *With summaries and table of contents in English.*

— **Bibliography.**

COHEN (JACOB) Economist, compiler. Special bibliography in monetary economics and finance. New York, [1976]. pp. 200.

— **Law.**

PÉNZÜGYI bűntettek és szabálysértések: a pénzügyi kriminalitás kérdései az elméletben és gyakorlatban. Budapest, 1970. pp. 424. *With Russian and French tables of contents.*

— **Mathematical models.**

HANNA (R.S.) Composite lag distributions in the financial sector: multivariate time- and frequency-domain analyses. Lexington, Mass., [1975]. pp. 179. *bibliog.*

PEACOCK (ALAN TURNER) and SHAW (GRAHAM KEITH) The economic theory of fiscal policy. 2nd ed. London, 1976. pp. 192. *bibliogs.*

— **Statistics.**

OECD FINANCIAL STATISTICS: ([pd. by] Organisation for Economic Co-operation and Development. [in English and French]. 2 a yr., with bi-m. suppls., 1970 (1)- , with gap (1973, 8). Paris. *File includes Interest rates, 1960-1974.*

— **Africa, Subsaharan — Accounting.**

NDONGKO (WILFRED AWUNG) The treatment of subsistence ecnomic activity in the national accounts of African countries. Vienna, 1974. pp. 21. *bibliog. (Wiener Institut für Entwicklungsfragen. Occasional Papers. 74/3)*

— **Algeria.**

ALGERIA. Direction des Statistiques et de la Comptabilité Nationale. Statistiques financières. a., 1973(9th)- Alger. *[in French and Arabic].*

— **Australia — New South Wales.**

NEW SOUTH WALES. Commonwealth Bureau of Census and Statistics. New South Wales Office. Banking, insurance and other private finance. a., 1972-73/1973-74- Sydney.

NEW SOUTH WALES. Commonwealth Bureau of Census and Statistics. New South Wales Office. Public finance. a., 1972-73/1973-74- Sydney.

— **Bahrain.**

HAZLETON (JARED E.) Public finance prospects and policies for Bahrain, 1975-1985. Beirut, 1975. pp. 123. *bibliog.*

— **Canada.**

CANADA. Statutes, etc. 1952-69. Office consolidation of the Financial Administration Act, R. S., 1952, c. 116, as amended by 1955, c. 3, etc. Ottawa, 1969. pp. 51.

HARRISON (THOMAS RUSSELL) A challenge to the presidency: Canada and inflation: cause, course, cost, correction, consolidation. Hicksville, N.Y., [1976]. pp. 151.

— — **Toronto.**

TORONTO. Commissioner of Finance. Metropolitan Toronto estimates. a., 1975- [Toronto].

— **Communist countries.**

DEN'GI, kredit i finansy v sotsialisticheskom obshchestve. Moskva, 1975. pp. 263.

— **Confederate States of America.**

LESTER (RICHARD I.) Confederate finance and purchasing in Great Britain. Charlottesville, Va., 1975. pp. 267. *bibliog.*

— **Egypt.**

VAN OENEN (J.D.) Cairo as a financial centre and some of its implications. Cairo, 1975. pp. 21. *(National Bank of Egypt. Diamond Jubilee Lectures)*

— **European Economic Community countries.**

FRANCE. Direction de la Documentation. La Documentation Française. Notes et Etudes Documentaires. Nos. 4,088-4, 089-4,090. Les aspects financiers de la régionalisation en Europe: [études réalisées sous la direction de Paul Marie Gaudemet]. [Paris, 1974]. pp. 100. *bibliog.*

— **Fiji Islands.**

MATHEWS (RUSSELL LLOYD) Review of fiscal policy in Fiji: report to the Minister of Finance, etc. Suva, Government Printer, 1969. pp. 96.

— **France.**

Les COMMUNAUTES européennes et les finances publiques françaises: actes des journées d'études des 11 et 12 octobre 1974. Paris, 1975. pp. 834. *(Strasbourg. Université. Faculté de Droit et des Sciences Politiques. Annales. 27)*

FINANCIAL STATEMENTS.

— — Marseilles.

COURDURIE (MARCEL) La dette des collectivités publiques de Marseille au XVIIIe siècle: du débat sur le prêt à intérêt au financement par l'emprunt. [Marseilles, 1974]. pp. 375. *bibliog.*

— Germany.

OBERHAUSER (ALOIS) Stabilitätspolitik bei steigender Staatsquote. Göttingen, [1975]. pp. 92. *(Kommission für Wirtschaftlichen und Sozialen Wandel. Schriften. 43)*

— India.

INDIA. Department of Economic Affairs. 1975. India and international monetary reform. [Delhi, 1975]. pp. 215.

SESHADRI (S.) Parliamentary control over finance: a study of the public accounts committee of parliament. Bombay, 1975. pp. 295.

— — Goa, Daman and Diu.

GOA, DAMAN AND DIU. Bureau of Economics, Statistics and Evaluation. 1974. An abstract of public finance, 1964-65 to 1973-74. [Panaji, 1974]. pp. 49.

— Italy — Accounting.

FAUCCI (RICCARDO) Finanza, amministrazione e pensiero economico: il caso della contabiità di Stato da Cavour al Fascismo. Torino, 1975. pp. 209. *(Fondazione Luigi Einaudi. Studi. 20)*

— — Mathematical models.

BOSI (PAOLO) and CAVAZZUTI (FILIPPO) Gli strumenti fiscali nell'economia italiana: valutazioni di politiche alternative con un modello econometrico. Bologna, [1974]. pp. 172. *(Bologna. Università. Istituto di Scienze Economiche. Gruppo di Lavoro del Modello Econometrico. Contributi. 2)*

— — Milan.

CAPRARA (UGO) Previsioni e programmazioni finanziarie nell'economia di un grande comune, 1946-1975. Milano, 1975. pp. 708.

— Malaysia.

KANAPATHY (V.) Kuala Lumpur as a centre of international finance; (expanded version of an article...in The Times...on 31st May 1975). [Kuala Lumpur, 1975]. pp. 9.

— Poland.

CZERWIŃSKA (EL'ZBIETA) Samodzielność finansowa przedsiębiorstwa państwowego. Poznań, 1963. pp. 172. *bibliog. (Poznań. Poznańskie Towarzystwo Przyjaciół Nauk. Wydział Historii i Nauk Społecznych. Komisja Nauk Społecznych. Prace. t.11, z.1)* With English summary.

BOGUSZEWSKI (JAN) System finansowy przedsiębiorstw i zjednoczeń. 2nd ed. Warszawa, 1966. pp. 45.

GDAŃSK. Uniwersytet. Wydział Ekonomiki Produkcji. Zeszyty Naukowe. 6. Zagadnienia z finansów i statystyki. Gdańsk, 1975. pp. 179. *bibliog.* With English and Russian summaries.

— Portugal.

PORTUGAL. Instituto Nacional de Estatistica. Serviços Centrais. Boletim trimestral das estatisticas monetarias e financeiras: continente e ilhas adjacentes. q., 1975 (no.1/4)- Lisboa. *[In Portuguese and French].*

— Russia.

AKADEMIIA NAUK GRUZINSKOI SSR. Institut Ekonomiki i Prava. Ekonomika. t. 3. [Sbornik statei]. Tbilisi, 1971. pp. 417. *Articles are in Georgian or Russian.*

ECONOMIC aspects of life in the USSR: main findings of colloquium held 29th-31st January, 1975, in Brussels. Brussels, North Atlantic Treaty Organization, [1975]. pp. 284. *bibliogs. In English and French.*

— — White Russia.

OCHERKI razvitiia finansov i kredita v Belorussii. Minsk, 1970. pp. 208.

— Switzerland.

SWITZERLAND. Département Fédéral des Finances et des Douanes. 1968. Rapport et avant-projet concernant des dispositions constitutionnelles sur l'adaptation du régime des finances fédérales à l'accroissement des besoins. [Berne?], 1968. pp. 33.

— — Statistics.

SWITZERLAND. Bureau Fédéral de Statistique. 1974. Die Finanzen von Bund, Kantonen und Gemeinden...1938-1971; bearbeitet von der Eidgenössischen Steuerverwaltung, etc. Bern, 1974. pp. 121. *(Statistiques de la Suisse. 538e fasc.) In German and French.*

— Tasmania.

TASMANIA. Commonwealth Bureau of Census and Statistics. Tasmanian Office. Finance. a., 1969/70-1970/71. Hobart.

TASMANIA. Commonwealth Bureau of Census and Statistics. Tasmanian Office. Private finance. a., 1971/72- Hobart.

— Underdeveloped areas.

See UNDERDEVELOPED AREAS — Finance.

— United Kingdom.

ALEXANDER (MICHAEL VAN CLEAVE) Charles I's Lord Treasurer: Sir Richard Weston, Earl of Portland, 1577-1635. London, 1975. pp. 261.

U.K. National Health Service. Treasurers' Joint Accounting Committee. 1975. Problems of budgetary control in the reorganised National Health Service. rev. ed. Sheffield, 1975. fo. 13.

WADE (ARTHUR MAURICE) ed. Financial reality: must we return to the 1930's?; a study of Lord Melchett's solution taken from his book Modern money. Weston-Super-Mare, [1975]. pp. 30.

KING (DAVID N.) The fiscal implications of devolution. London, [1976]. 1 pamphlet (unpaged). *(Institute for Fiscal Studies. Lecture Series. No. 5)*

LABOUR PARTY. National Executive Committee. Banking and finance; a statement...[to be] presented to the Labour Party annual conference, Blackpool 1976. London, [1976]. pp. 24.

— — Liverpool.

WILSON (HUGH) AND WOMERSLEY (LEWIS) Firm, and TYM (ROGER) AND ASSOCIATES. Inner area study: Liverpool: area resource analysis: district D tables, 1973-74. [London], Department of the Environment, [1976]. pp. 125.

— — London.

LONDON. Greater London Council. Memorandum of evidence to the Committee of Inquiry into Local Government Finance under the chairmanship of Mr. F. Layfield Q.C. London, [1975]. pp. 27.

— United States.

HARRISS (CLEMENT LOWELL) Property taxation in government finance. New York, [1974]. pp. 61. *(Tax Foundation. Research Publications. New Series. No. 31)*

CONFERENCE ON FINANCIAL INNOVATION, NEW YORK UNIVERSITY, 1975. Financial innovation: [papers of the conference]; edited by William L. Silber. Lexington, Mass., [1975]. pp. 208. *Sponsored by Salomon Brothers Center for the Study of Financial Institutions, New York University.*

STORA (JEAN CLAUDE) Le marché financier américain. [Paris, 1975]. pp. 141. *bibliog.*

— — New York (City).

OTT (ATTIAT F.) and YOO (JANG H.) New York City's financial crisis: can the trend be reversed?. Washington, 1975. pp. 44. *(American Enterprise Institute for Public Policy Research. Domestic Affairs Studies. 40)*

— — Virginia.

FISCAL prospects and alternatives; by John L. Knapp [and others]; (a staff report to the Revenue Resources and Economic Study Commission). Richmond, Va., Division of State Planning and Community Affairs, 1971. pp. 375.

FINANCE, PERSONAL.

MANDELL (LEWIS) Economics from the consumer's perspective. Chicago, [1975]. pp. 279. *bibliogs.*

FINANCIAL INSTITUTIONS

— Government ownership — United Kingdom.

LABOUR PARTY. National Executive Committee. Banking and finance; a statement...[to be] presented to the Labour Party annual conference, Blackpool 1976. London, [1976]. pp. 24.

— United Kingdom.

NATIONAL CONFERENCE ON STRATEGIC PLANNING FOR FINANCIAL INSTITUTIONS, 1972. Strategic planning for financial institutions; edited by Bernard Taylor and Guy de Moubray. London, 1974. pp. 339. *Presentations to the conference organised by the Bank of England and the University of Bradford, with other articles and presentations.*

— United States.

CONFERENCE ON FINANCIAL INNOVATION, NEW YORK UNIVERSITY, 1975. Financial innovation: [papers of the conference]; edited by William L. Silber. Lexington, Mass., [1975]. pp. 208. *Sponsored by Salomon Brothers Center for the Study of Financial Institutions, New York University.*

FINANCIAL INSTITUTIONS, INTERNATIONAL.

WALLACE (DON) International regulation of multinational corporations. New York, 1976. pp. 233.

FINANCIAL STATEMENTS.

MACDONALD (GRAEME) and others. Statements of objectives and standard practice in financial reporting. [London, 197-]. 1 pamphlet (unpaged).

MOONITZ (MAURICE) Changing prices and financial reporting. Champaign, Ill., [1974]. pp. 59. *(Lancaster. University. International Centre for Research in Accounting. [ICRA Occasional Papers. No. 3])*

— Bibliography.

GRAY (S.J.) compiler. Financial reporting in the E.E.C. and the international economy: a selected bibliography. Lancaster, [1974]. pp. 56. *(Lancaster. University. International Centre for Research in Accounting. ICRA Occasional Papers. No.4)*

— European Economic Community countries.

GRAY (S.J.) Corporate reporting and investor decisions in the EEC: the comparability problem. Lancaster, [1973]. pp. 28. *(Lancaster. University. International Centre for Research in Accounting. ICRA Occasional Papers. No.2)*

— — Bibliography.

GRAY (S.J.) compiler. Financial reporting in the E.E.C. and the international economy: a selected bibliography. Lancaster, [1974]. pp. 56. *(Lancaster. University. International Centre for Research in Accounting. ICRA Occasional Papers. No.4)*

FINANCIAL STATEMENTS.(Cont.)

— United Kingdom.

MORRIS (RICHARD C.) Funds statement practices in the United Kingdom. Lancaster, [1974]. pp. 85. *bibliog. (Lancaster. University. International Centre for Research in Accounting. ICRA Occasional Papers. No. 6)*

FINLAND

— Biography.

VEM och vad?: biografisk handbok 1975; huvudredaktör: Henrik Ekberg. Helsingfors, [1974]. pp. 764.

— Commerce.

OKSANEN (HEIKKI) and PIHKALA (ERKKI) Suomen ulkomaankauppa, 1917-1949: (Finland's foreign trade, 1917-1949). Helsinki, [1975]. pp. 129. *(Suomen Pankki. Taloustieteelinen Tutkimuslaitos. Julkaisuja. Kasvututkimuksia. 6)*

— Economic history.

NORDISK HISTORIKERMØDE, 1974. Kriser och krispolitik i Norden under mellankrigstiden: Nordiska historikermötet i Uppsala 1974; mötesrapport. [Uppsala, 1974]. pp. 315. *In various Scandinavian languages.*

— Foreign relations.

FINLAND 1917-1967: an assessment of independence; [by] L.A. Puntila [and others]; editorial board, Jouko Hulkko [and others]. Helsinki, [1967]. pp. 172.

KORHONEN (KEIJO) ed. Urho Kekkonen: a statesman for peace; (English translation supervised by William R. Copeland and David Miller). London, 1975. pp. 186.

MAUDE (GEORGE) The Finnish dilemma: neutrality in the shadow of power. London, 1976. pp. 153. *bibliog.*

— — Russia.

KHOLODKOVSKII (VIKTOR MIKHAILOVICH) Finliandiia i Sovetskaia Rossiia, 1918-1920. Moskva, 1975. pp. 266. *bibliog.*

KIRBY (D.G.) ed. Finland and Russia, 1808-1920: from autonomy to independence: a selection of documents. London, 1975. pp. 265. *bibliog. (London. University. School of Slavonic and East European Studies. Studies in Russian and East European History)*

POKHLEBKIN (VIL'IAM VASIL'EVICH) SSSR - Finliandiia: 260 let otnoshenii, 1713-1973. Moskva, 1975. pp. 408.

— — Sweden.

JOHANSSON (ALF) Finlands sak: svensk politik och opinion under vinterkriget, 1939- 1940. Stockholm, 1973. pp. 402. *bibliog. With English summary.*

— Government publications — Bibliography.

FINLAND. Tilastokeskus. Suomen Virallinen Tilaston ja Tilastokeskuksen julkaisut: Publications in the Official Statistics of Finland and of the Central Statistical Office. a., 1975- Helsinki. *[In Finnish with notes and table headings in Swedish and English]*

— History.

FINLAND 1917-1967: an assessment of independence; [by] L.A. Puntila [and others]; editorial board, Jouko Hulkko [and others]. Helsinki, [1967]. pp. 172.

— — Sources.

KIRBY (D.G.) ed. Finland and Russia, 1808-1920: from autonomy to independence: a selection of documents. London, 1975. pp. 265. *bibliog. (London. University. School of Slavonic and East European Studies. Studies in Russian and East European History)*

— Industries.

FINLAND. Tilastokeskus. Lopetettujen liikevaihtoverovelvollisten yritysten ennakkotiedot...: Förhandsuppgifter om omsättningsskatteskyldiga företag vilkas verksamhet... a., 1972/73- Helsinki.

— — Accounting.

FINLAND. Tilastokeskus. Teollisuuden tasetilasto...: Statistics of profit and loss and balance sheet accounts of industry. a., 1973- Helsinki. *In Finnish with English summary and table headings.*

— Nationalism.

WILSON (WILLIAM ALBERT) Folklore and nationalism in modern Finland. Bloomington, Ind., [1976]. pp. 272. *bibliog.*

— Neutrality.

MAUDE (GEORGE) The Finnish dilemma: neutrality in the shadow of power. London, 1976. pp. 153. *bibliog.*

— Politics and government.

FINLAND 1917-1967: an assessment of independence; [by] L.A. Puntila [and others]; editorial board, Jouko Hulkko [and others]. Helsinki, [1967]. pp. 172.

NORDISK HISTORIKERMØDE, 1974. Kriser och krispolitik i Norden under mellankrigstiden: Nordiska historikermötet i Uppsala 1974; mötesrapport. [Uppsala, 1974]. pp. 315. *In various Scandinavian languages.*

— Population.

FINLAND. Tilastokeskus. 1974. Väestöennusteet, 1973-2000...:(koko maan väestöennusteet ja alueellisten laskelmien vertailu), etc. Helsinki, 1974. pp. 69. *bibliog. (Tilastollisia Tiedonantoja. 52) In Finnish and Swedish, with English summary.*

FINLAND. Tilastokeskus. 1975. Katsaus Suomen väestönkehitykseen. Helsinki, 1975. pp. 105. *bibliog. (Tilastollisia Tiedonantoja. 54)*

FINLAND. Tilastokeskus. 1975. The population of Finland: a World Population Year Monograph. [Helsinki], 1975. pp. 81. *(Committee for International Coordination of National Research in Demography. C.I.C.R.E.D. Series)*

IMHOF (ARTHUR ERWIN) Aspekte der Bevölkerungsentwicklung in den nordischen Ländern, 1720-1750. Bern, [1976]. 2 vols. *bibliog.*

— Relations (general) with Sweden.

CARLQUIST (ERIK) Solidaritet på prov: Finlandshjälp under vinterkriget. Stockholm, 1971. pp. 343. *bibliog. With English summary.*

— Social life and customs.

SARMELA (MATTI) Reciprocity systems of the rural society in the Finnish-Karelian culture area, with special reference to social intercourse of the youth. Helsinki, 1969. pp. 347. *bibliog. (Academia Scientiarum Fennica. FF Communications. No. 207)*

— Statistics — Bibliography.

FINLAND. Tilastokeskus. Suomen Virallinen Tilaston ja Tilastokeskuksen julkaisut: Publications in the Official Statistics of Finland and of the Central Statistical Office. a., 1975- Helsinki. *[In Finnish with notes and table headings in Swedish and English]*

— Statistics, Vital.

KOLARI (RISTO) Kuolleisuus...: kuolleisuuden alueellinen jakaantuminen Suomessa, 1961-1972, etc. Helsinki, 1975. pp. 85. *(Finland. Tilastokeskus. Tutkimuksia. 33) Tables in Finnish, Swedish and English, with summaries in English and Swedish.*

FINNISH LANGUAGE

— Phonology.

SKOUSEN (ROYAL) Substantive evidence in phonology: the evidence from Finnish and French. The Hague, 1975. pp. 135. *bibliog.*

FINNISH NEWSPAPERS.

VEHMAS (RAINO) Foreign news in the Finnish morning papers: a quantitative analysis. Turku, 1964. pp. 24. *(Åbo. Turun Yliopisto. Institute of Sociology. Publications. No.13) (Reprinted summary from Sanomalehtiemme Ulkomaanaineisto).*

FINNS IN THE UNITED STATES.

CONFERENCE ON THE FINNISH EXPERIENCE IN THE WESTERN GREAT LAKES REGION, UNIVERSITY OF MINNESOTA, 1974. The Finnish experience in the western Great Lakes region: new perspectives: [papers of the conference organized by the Immigration History Research Center, University of Minnesota]; edited by Michael G. Karni [and others]. Vammala, 1975. pp. 232. *(Åbo. Turun Yliopisto. Institute for Migration. Migration Studies. C 3)*

FINSTERWOLDE

— Politics and government.

BRAUN (MARIANNE) De regeringskommissaris in Finsterwolde: een bijdrage tot de geschiedschrijving van de koude oorlog in Nederland. Amsterdam, 1975. pp. 92. *bibliog.*

FIRE—DEPARTMENTS

— Ireland (Republic).

EIRE. Working Party on the Fire Service. 1975. Report to the Minister for Local Government. Dublin, 1975. pp. 120.

— United States.

CZAMANSKI (DANIEL Z.) The cost of preventive services: the case of fire departments. Lexington, Mass., [1975]. pp. 108. *bibliog.*

FIRMS.

URBAN (SABINE) Economie de marché et développement des entreprises. [Strasbourg, 1974]. pp. 287. *bibliog. (Strasbourg. Université de Strasbourg III. Institut d'Etudes Politiques. Cahiers. Nouvelle Série. 2)*

COHEN (KALMAN J.) and CYERT (RICHARD MICHAEL) Theory of the firm: resource allocation in a market economy. 2nd ed. Englewood Cliffs, N.J., [1975]. pp. 524. *bibliogs.*

CURWEN (PETER J.) The theory of the firm. London, 1976. pp. 189. *bibliog.*

VEREIN FÜR SOZIALPOLITIK. Schriften. Neue Folge. Band 88. Die Bedeutung gesellschaftlicher Veränderungen für die Willensbildung im Unternehmen: (Verhandlungen auf der Arbeitstagung...in Aachen vom 25.-27. September 1975; herausgegeben von Horst Albach und Dieter Sadowski). Berlin, [1976]. pp. 939. *bibliog. In German or English.*

— History — Burma.

BRAUND (HAROLD ERNEST WILTON) Calling to mind: being some account of the first hundred years, 1870 to 1970, of Steel Brothers and Company Limited. Oxford, 1975. pp. 151. *bibliog.*

— — France.

BEAUD (MICHEL) and others. Une multinationale française: Pechiney Ugine Kuhlmann. Paris, [1975]. pp. 288.

— — Germany.

KOCKA (JUERGEN) Unternehmensverwaltung und Angestelltenschaft am Beispiel Siemens, 1847-1914: zum Verhältnis von Kapitalismus und Bürokratie in der deutschen Industrialisierung. Stuttgart, [1969]. pp. 639. *bibliog. (Arbeitskreis für Moderne Sozialgeschichte. Industrielle Welt. Band 11)*

DELIUS (FRIEDRICH C.) Unsere Siemens-Welt: eine Festschrift zum 125jährigen Bestehen des Hauses S. Berlin, 1972 repr. 1975. pp. 110.

RUHR-STICKSTOFF AG. D[eutsche] A[mmoniak-]Vereinigung: Geschichte eines Unternehmens und Aspekte seiner Zeit. Bochum, [1974]. pp. 80.

— — Russia.

100 let Moskovskomu zavodu tekhnicheskikh izdelii. Moskva, 1969. pp. 85.

DARMANIAN (PETR EMMANUILOVICH) Zarevo nad martenami: ocherk. Volgograd, 1969. pp. 151. bibliog.

NOVIKOV (L.I.) and KHARIN (IURII ANDREEVICH) Zavod v puti. Volgograd, 1970. pp. 116.

— — — Estonia.

KARMA (O.) and SKOROKHOD (A.) Trudnaia sud'ba: kratkaia istoriia Russko-Baltiiskogo sudostroitel'nogo zavoda. Tallin, 1971. pp. 62.

— — — Kabardino—Balkarian Republic.

IAKOVLEV (PETR PAVLOVICH) Prokhladnenskii ordena Lenina krasnoznamennyi. Nal'chik, 1968. pp. 127.

— — — Karelia.

LEVIDOVA (SOF'IA MIKHAILOVNA) Istoriia Onezhskogo (byvsh. Aleksandrovskogo) zavoda. vyp.1. Zavod v krepostnuiu epokhu. Petrozavodsk, 1938. pp. 136. bibliog.

— — — Russia (RSFSR).

IMENI Voitovicha. Moskva, 1969. pp. 312.

PARKHOMENKO (V.) and CHARKIN (P.) 90 let zavodu imeni D.I. Mendeleeva. Iaroslavl', 1969. pp. 76.

PILEVSKII (GRIGORII LAZAR'EVICH) "Krasnyi gigant": ocherk istorii Klintsovskogo kozhevennogo zavoda. Briansk, 1969. pp. 210.

IVANOV (A.IA.) Vtoroi avtoremontnyi: ocherk istorii zavoda. Leningrad, 1970. pp. 128.

— — — Soviet Far East.

AMURSKIE arsenal'tsy: istoriia zavoda "Dal'dizel'". Khabarovsk, 1974. pp. 351.

— — — Ukraine.

PODOV (VLADIMIR IVANOVICH) Donsoda: ocherk iz istorii Donetskogo ordena Lenina sodovogo zavoda im. V.I. Lenina. Donetsk, 1969. pp. 135.

EVSELEVSKII (L.I.) and others. Kremenchugskii zavod dorozhnykh mashin: ocherki. Khar'kov, 1970. pp. 187.

MIKULENKO (V.V.) and others. Ordena Lenina Rubezhanskii khimicheskii kombinat: ocherk. Donetsk, 1973. pp. 181.

BAKALO (RUSLAN ALEKSANDROVICH) and SOKOLOV (VIACHESLAV NIKOLAEVICH) Arsenal zemledel'tsev. Odessa, 1974. pp. 99.

— — Switzerland.

ALUMINIUM-INDUSTRIE-AKTIEN-GESELLSCHAFT. Geschichte der Aluminium-Industrie-Aktien-Gesellschaft Neuhausen, 1888-1938; [by Walther Meier and others]. [Chippis?], 1942-43. 2 vols.

USTERI (EMIL) Die Webereien der Familie Näf von Kappel und Zürich, 1846-1946: (Festschrift zur Hundertjahr-Feier der Seidenstoffwebereien vormals Gebrüder Näf A.G.und der Seidenwarenfabrik vormals Edwin Naef A.G.). [Zurich], 1946. pp. 323. bibliogs. Table in end pocket.

FISCHER (GEORG) AKTIENGESELLSCHAFT. Hundertfünfzig Jahre Georg Fischer Werke, 1802/1952. Schaffhausen, [1952]. pp. 192.

VEREIN FÜR WIRTSCHAFTSHISTORISCHE STUDIEN. Schweizer Pioniere der Wirtschaft und Technik. 28. Alfred Zellweger, Uster, 1855-1916; Hans Blumer-Ris, Freiburg, 1902-1953; von Hans Rudolf Schmid. Zürich, 1975. pp. 113. bibliog.

— — United Kingdom.

SPENDER (JOHN ALFRED) Weetman Pearson, first Viscount Cowdray, 1856-1927. London, 1930. pp. 316.

MILLIGAN (JOHN) The resilient pioneers: a history of the Elastic Rail Spike Company and its associates. Aberdeen, 1975. pp. 143. bibliog.

PERKINS (EDWIN J.) Financing Anglo-American trade: the House of Brown, 1800- 1880. Cambridge, Mass., 1975. pp. 323. bibliog. (Harvard University. Harvard Studies in Business History. 28)

PIGOTT (STANLEY C.) O[gilvy] B[enson] M[ather]: a celebration: one hundred and twenty-five years in advertising. London, 1975. pp. 84. bibliog.

THORNE (VIC) Acrow: the success story of achievement through team spirit. [London, 1975]. pp. 108.

WRIGHT (LOUISE) The road from Aston Cross: an industrial history, 1875-1975. Leamington Spa, Warwicks., 1975. pp. 79.

BEAVER (PATRICK) Yes! We have some: the story of Fyffes. Stevenage, 1976. pp. 133.

MERRIAM (JOHN) Pioneering in plastics. Ipswich, 1976. pp. 118.

READER (WILLIAM JOSEPH) Metal Box: a history;...research by Judy Slinn. London, 1976. pp. 256. bibliog.

— — — Scotland.

VAMPLEN (WRAY) Salvesen of Leith. Edinburgh, 1975. pp. 311.

HOUSE (JACK) Pride of Perth: the story of Arthur Bell and Sons Ltd., Scotch Whisky distillers. London, 1976. pp. 135.

— — — United States.

ZILG (GERARD COLBY) Du Pont: behind the nylon curtain. Englewood Cliffs, [1974]. pp. 623.

PERKINS (EDWIN J.) Financing Anglo-American trade: the House of Brown, 1800- 1880. Cambridge, Mass., 1975. pp. 323. bibliog. (Harvard University. Harvard Studies in Business History. 28)

LEWIS (DAVID LANIER) The public image of Henry Ford: an American folk hero and his company. Detroit, 1976. pp. 598.

WILSON (WILLIAM L.) Full faith and credit: the story of C.I.T. Financial Corporation, 1908-1975. New York, [1976]. pp. 376.

— — — Bibliography.

DALLAS. Public Library. Business and Technology Division. Business history collection: a checklist. Dallas, 1974. pp. 236.

— France.

LAGRANGE (FRANÇOIS) The Sudreau report on company reform: a review, etc. London, 1975. pp. 20. (France. French Embassy, London. Service de Presse et d'Information. France: facts, figures. A/111/12/75)

— Jamaica.

JAMAICA PUBLIC SERVICE COMPANY. Jamaica Public Service Company. Kingston, Jamaica, [1958]. 1 vol. (various pagings).

— Romania.

STĂNESCU (VASILE) and CONSTANTINESCU (MIHAI) Unitatea economică socialistă: raportul dintre gestiunea economică, capacitatea juridică și subiectul de drept. București, 1974. pp. 207. bibliog. With English summary.

FISHERIES.

— United Kingdom.

COUNTER INFORMATION SERVICES and TRANSNATIONAL INSTITUTE. Where is Lucas going?. London, [1975?]. pp. 47. bibliog. (Counter Information Services. Anti-Reports. No. 12)

CLIFTON DATA RESEARCH SERVICES. Survey of British oil companies, 1976. St. Albans, 1976. 152 columns.

FISCHER (FRITZ).

MOSES (JOHN A.) The politics of illusion: the Fischer controversy in German historiography. London, 1975. pp. 148. bibliog.

FISH MEAL.

MITCHELL (C.L.) and McEACHERN (D.B.) Developments in the Atlantic coast herring fishery and fish meal industry, 1964-1968. Ottawa, Information Canada, 1970. pp. 26. bibliog. (Canadian Fisheries Reports. No. 16)

FISHER (Sir NORMAN FENWICK WARREN).

FISHER (Sir NORMAN FENWICK WARREN) [Unpublished political and defence papers. 1926-39]. 2 pieces. Typescript.

FISHERIES.

CUSHING (DAVID) Fisheries resources of the sea and their management. London, 1975. pp. 87. bibliog.

— Asia, Southeast.

MARR (JOHN C.) Fishery and resource management in southeast Asia. Washington, 1976. pp. 62. bibliog. (Resources for the Future, Inc. Program of International Studies of Fishery Arrangements. Papers. No 7)

— Canada.

NEWFOUNDLAND. 1963. National fisheries development: a presentation to the government of Canada by the government of Newfoundland. [St. John's], 1963. pp. 61.

— — British Columbia.

FORESTER (JOSEPH E.) and FORESTER (ANNE D.) Fishing: British Columbia's commercial fishing history. Saanichton, B.C., [1975]. pp. 224. bibliog.

— — Newfoundland.

NEWFOUNDLAND. Department of Fisheries. Annual report. a., 1973/74- St. John's.

— Indonesia.

INDONESIA. Direktorat Jenderal Perikanan. Fisheries statistics of Indonesia. a., 1972- Jakarta.

— Ireland (Republic).

EIRE. Inland Fisheries Commission. 1975. Report. Dublin, 1975. pp. 192.

— Peru.

SMETHERMAN (BOBBIE BRALY) and SMETHERMAN (ROBERT M.) Territorial seas and inter-American relations, with case studies of the Peruvian and U.S. fishing industries. New York, 1974. pp. 121.

— Portugal — Statistics.

PORTUGAL. Instituto Nacional de Estatistica. Serviços Centrais. Boletim mensal das estatisticas da agricultura e da pesca: continente e ilhas adjacentes (formerly Boletim trimestral das estatisticas da agricultura e da pesca: continente e ilhas adjacentes). m. (formerly q.) Ja/Mr 1975 (ano 1, no.1)- Lisboa. [In Portuguese and French].

— United States.

SMETHERMAN (BOBBIE BRALY) and SMETHERMAN (ROBERT M.) Territorial seas and inter-American relations, with case studies of the Peruvian and U.S. fishing industries. New York, 1974. pp. 121.

FISHERMEN

FISHERMEN
— Norway.

NORWAY. Statistiske Centralbyrå. 1976. Fiskerstatistikk, 1975, etc. Oslo, 1976. pp. 36. *(Norges Offisielle Statistikk. Rekke A. 805)*

— United States.

GERSUNY (CARL) and others. Some effects of technological change on New England fishermen. Kingston, Rhode Island, 1975. pp. 40. *bibliog. (Rhode Island. University. Department of Sociology and Anthropology. Marine Technical Reports. No. 42)*

FISHERY LAW AND LEGISLATION
— North Atlantic Ocean.

FISHERIES conflicts in the North Atlantic: problems of management and jurisdiction; edited by Giulio Pontecorvo. Cambridge, Mass., 1974. pp. 203. *A Law of the Sea Institute workshop, held in Hamilton, Bermuda, January 1974.*

FISHERY MANAGEMENT
— North Atlantic Ocean.

FISHERIES conflicts in the North Atlantic: problems of management and jurisdiction; edited by Giulio Pontecorvo. Cambridge, Mass., 1974. pp. 203. *A Law of the Sea Institute workshop, held in Hamilton, Bermuda, January 1974.*

FISHING BOATS
— Canada.

MITCHELL (C.L.) and FRICK (HAROLD C.) Government programs of assistance for fishing craft construction in Canada: an economic appraisal. Ottawa, Information Canada, 1970. pp. 59. *bibliog. (Canadian Fisheries Reports. No. 14)*

FIXED POINT THEOREMS (TOPOLOGY).

SMART (D.R.) Fixed point theorems. London, 1974. pp. 93. *bibliog.*

FJAERLAND, NORWAY
— Economic conditions.

BIVAND (ROGER S.) The economic geography of regional differentiation: studies in Sogn og Fjordane, Norway; [Ph.D. (London) thesis]. 1975. fo. 417. *bibliog. Typescript: unpublished. This thesis is the property of London University and may not be removed from the Library.*

FLEMISH MOVEMENT.

WILLEMSEN (A.W.) De Vlaamse Beweging. Hasselt, [1974 in progress]. *(Twintig eeuwen Vlaanderen. Deel 4, etc.)*

VROEDE (MAURITS DE) The Flemish movement in Belgium. Antwerp, 1975. pp. 96.

FLENSBURG
— Politics and government.

PUST (DIETER) Politische Sozialgeschichte der Stadt Flensburg: Untersuchungen zur politischen Führungsschicht Flensburgs im 18. und 19. Jahrhundert. [Flensburg, 1975]. pp. 365. *bibliog. (Flensburg. Gesellschaft für Flensburger Stadtgeschichte. Schriften. Nr.23)*

— Social history.

PUST (DIETER) Politische Sozialgeschichte der Stadt Flensburg: Untersuchungen zur politischen Führungsschicht Flensburgs im 18. und 19. Jahrhundert. [Flensburg, 1975]. pp. 365. *bibliog. (Flensburg. Gesellschaft für Flensburger Stadtgeschichte. Schriften. Nr.23)*

FLETCHER (CALVIN).

FLETCHER (CALVIN) The diary of Calvin Fletcher, vol. 3, 1844-1847, including letter to and from Calvin Fletcher; edited by Gayle Thornbrough and Dorothy L. Riker. Indianapolis, 1974. pp. 475.

FLORENCE
— History.

BARBIERI (ORAZIO) Ponti sull'Arno: la Resistenza a Firenze. 3rd ed. Roma, 1975. pp. 307.

FLORENCOURT FAMILY.

MONZ (HEINZ) and others. Zur Persönlichkeit von Marx' Schwiegervater Johann Ludwig von Westphalen. Trier, [1973]. pp. 166. *(Karl-Marx-Haus. Schriften. 9)*

FLORIDA
— Officials and employees.

FLORIDA. Legislature. House of Representatives. Committee on Labor and Industry. 1970. Collective bargaining in public employment; a study report. Tallahassee, 1970. pp. 84.

— Politics and government.

SHOFNER (JERRELL H.) Nor is it over yet: Florida in the era of reconstruction, 1863- 1877. Gainesville, Fla., 1974. pp. 412. *bibliog.*

FLOW OF FUNDS
— Pakistan.

FAROOQ (DANIAL M.) The flow of investment funds in Pakistan: specialized institutions. [Islamabad], 1975. fo. 21. *bibliog.*

— United Kingdom.

ECONOMIST INTELLIGENCE UNIT. Q[uarterly] E[conomic] R[eview] Specials. No. 25. OPEC funds and the UK; by Roger Middleton. London, 1975. pp. 86.

FOLK LORE
— Finland.

WILSON (WILLIAM ALBERT) Folklore and nationalism in modern Finland. Bloomington, Ind., [1976]. pp. 272. *bibliog.*

— Russia.

FOL'KLOR krest'ianskoi voiny 1773-1775 godov: k 200-letiiu pugachevskogo vosstaniia; sbornik nauchnykh statei. Leningrad, 1973. pp. 104.

BAZANOV (VASILII GRIGOR'EVICH) Russkie revoliutsionnye demokraty i narodoznanie. Leningrad, 1974. pp. 558.

— South Africa.

SCHEUB (HAROLD) The Xhosa ntsomi. Oxford, 1975. pp. 446. *bibliog.*

FOLK MUSIC, AFRICAN
— Argentine Republic.

ORTIZ ODERIGO (NESTOR) Aspectos de la cultura africana en el Rio de la Plata. [Buenos Aires, 1974]. pp. 200. *bibliog.*

— Uruguay.

ORTIZ ODERIGO (NESTOR) Aspectos de la cultura africana en el Rio de la Plata. [Buenos Aires, 1974]. pp. 200. *bibliog.*

FOLKPARTIET.

See LIBERAL PARTY — Sweden.

FOOD.

SCHMAUDERER (EBERHARD) Studien zur Geschichte der Lebensmittelwissenschaft. Wiesbaden, 1975. pp. 314. *bibliogs. (Vierteljahrschrift für Sozial- und Wirtschaftsgeschichte. Beihefte. Nr.62)*

FOOD CONSUMPTION
— Germany.

GERMANY (BUNDESREPUBLIK). Statistisches Bundesamt. 1976. Aufwendungen privater Haushalte für Nahrungs- und Genussmittel, Mahlzeiten ausser Haus, 1973. Wiesbaden, 1976. pp. 228. *(Preise, Löhne, Wirtschaftsrechnungen. Reihe 18. Einkommens- und Verbrauchsstichproben. 3)*

FOOD HABITS
— Germany.

HERRIG (GERTRUD) Ländliche Nahrung im Strukturwandel des 20. Jahrhunderts: Untersuchungen im Westeifeler Reliktgebiet am Beispiel der Gemeinde Wolsfeld. Meisenheim am Glan, 1974. pp. 239. *bibliog.*

FOOD INDUSTRY AND TRADE
— Canada.

CANADA. Statistics Canada. Merchandising and Services Division. 1973. Franchising in Canada's food serving industry...1971. Ottawa, 1973. 1 vol. (various pagings). *In English and French.*

MITCHELL (DON) The politics of food. Toronto, 1975. pp. 235. *bibliog.*

— France.

FRANCE. Ministère de l'Agriculture. Statistique agricole. Supplément. Série Etudes. No.139. Bilans alimentaires (et autres bilans) retrospectifs, 1959- 1974; [by Paulette Ferran]. Paris, 1975. pp. 194.

— Netherlands.

ECONOMISCH INSTITUUT VOOR HET MIDDEN- EN KLEINBEDRIJF. Algemeen- Economische en Statistische Publikaties. De structurele ontwikkeling van de detailhandel in voedings- en genotmiddelen. 's-Gravenhage, 1969. p. 131.

— Russia.

SEMIN (SERGEI IVANOVICH) Ekonomicheskie osnovy agrarno-promyshlennykh kompleksov. Moskva, 1973. pp. 104.

SIVACHENKO (IGOR' IUR'EVICH) Agrokompleks sotsialisticheskogo narodnogo khoziaistva: zakonomernosti formirovaniia i razvitiia. Moskva, 1973. pp. 94.

BYCHKOVA (TSETSILIIA VOLODYMYRIVNA) Pravovi pytannia ahrarno-promyslovoho kooperuvannia. Kyïv, 1974. pp. 120. *With Russian summary.*

NEGRU-VODE (ALEKSANDR STEPANOVICH) Agrarno-promyshlennoe kooperirovanie v SSSR. Moskva, 1975. pp. 184.

— — Bibliography.

GORBATOV (A.L.) compiler. Agrarno-promyshlennye kompleksy i ob"edineniia: bibliograficheskii ukazatel' otechestvennoi literatury za 1960- 1973 gg. v kolichestve 837 nazvanii i inostrannoi - za 1962-1973 gg. v kolichestve 215 nazvanii. 2nd ed. Moskva, 1973. pp. 190.

— — Daghestan.

SULEIMANOV (SADULLA MAGOMEDOVICH) Pishchevaia promyshlennost' v khoziaistvennom komplekse Dagestana. Makhachkala, 1969. pp. 44.

— **United Kingdom.**

BOND (MARIAN ELIZABETH) A structural approach to the demand for imported foods in the United Kingdom, 1950-1969. 1975. fo. 203. *bibliog.* Typescript. Ph. D.(London) thesis: unpublished. This thesis is the property of London University and may not be removed from the Library.

WRIGHT (LOUISE) The road from Aston Cross: an industrial history, 1875-1975. Leamington Spa, Warwicks., 1975. pp. 79.

— **United States.**

CROSS (JENNIFER) The supermarket trap: the consumer and the food industry. rev. ed. Bloomington, Ind., [1976]. pp. 306. *bibliog.*

FOOD LAW AND LEGISLATION

— **Canada.**

CANADA. Department of National Health and Welfare. Food and Drug Directorate. Educational Services. 1970. Health protection and food laws. [Ottawa, 1970]. pp. 45. *bibliogs.*

FOOD PRICES

— **Canada.**

CANADA. Department of Agriculture. 1971. Your food dollar. rev. ed. [Ottawa], 1971. pp. 18. *(Publications. 1354)*

FOOD RELIEF.

FOOD aid and international economic growth; ([by] Uma K. Srivastava [and others]). Ames, Iowa, 1975. pp. 160. *bibliog.*

— **United States.**

CLARKSON (KENNETH W.) Food stamps and nutrition. Washington, 1975. pp. 85. *(American Enterprise Institute for Public Policy Research. Evaluative Studies. 18)*

FOOD RESEARCH

— **United Kingdom.**

JOINT CONSULTATIVE ORGANISATION FOR RESEARCH AND DEVELOPMENT IN AGRICULTURE AND FOOD [U.K.]. Second reports of the boards of the...Organisation, etc. London, H.M.S.O., 1975. pp. 135.

FOOD SUPPLY.

ZIMMERMANN (WERNER) Economist, ed. Die Nahrungsquellen der Welt: Handbuch über Erzeugung und Handel der wichtigsten Agrarprodukte...; Verfasser:... Werner Zimmermann [and others]. Berlin, 1941. pp. 883. *bibliogs.*

CERES: FAO review; (pd. bi-m. by the Food and Agriculture Organization). bi-m., 1968 (v.1)- Rome. v.1, no.1 entitled FAO review.

ROGERS (PAUL) Food in our time: but not just yet; a report on the World Food Conference. London, [1974]. pp. 20.

SOCIETY FOR SOCIAL RESPONSIBILITY IN SCIENCE. Annual Conference, 1971. Against pollution and hunger: [papers of the conference]; (Alice Mary Hilton, ed.). Oslo, [1974]. pp. 307.

TRADE negotiations and world food problems; papers for a conference in London on 5 December 1974 [by]...Wilhelm Henrichsmeyer [and others]. London, [1974]. 1 vol. (various foliations). *(Trade Policy Research Centre. Conference Papers)*

BARRONS (KEITH CONVERSE) The food in your future: steps to abundance. New York, 1975. pp. 180. *bibliog.*

BROWN (LESTER RUSSELL) The politics and responsibility of the North American breadbasket. Washington, 1975. pp. 43. *(Worldwatch Institute. Worldwatch Papers. No.2)*

GREEN (DANIEL) The politics of food. London, [1975]. pp. 220. *bibliog.*

LAIDLAW (KEN) The party's over: grain: for the rich world's animals or the poor world's people?: an examination of how Britain supports famine. London, [1975]. pp. 34.

PAPADAKIS (JUAN) The world food problem: another low cost technology is needed: the failure of conventional agronomy. Buenos Aires, 1975. pp. 31. *bibliog.*

WORLD DEVELOPMENT MOVEMENT. Food for all. London, [1975?]. pp. 16.

ECKHOLM (ERIK P.) Losing ground: environmental stress and world food prospects. New York, [1976]. pp. 223. *bibliog.*

GEORGE (SUSAN) How the other half dies: the real reasons for world hunger. Harmondsworth, 1976. pp. 349. *bibliog.*

POWER (JONATHAN) and HOLENSTEIN (ANNE-MARIE) World of hunger: a strategy for survival. London, 1976. pp. 202.

SCHNEIDER (STEPHEN HENRY) The genesis strategy: climate and global survival. New York, [1976]. pp. 419.

SINHA (RADHARAMAN PRASAD) Food and poverty: the political economy of confrontation. London, 1976. pp. 196. *bibliog.*

WAGSTAFF (HOWARD) World food: a political task. London, 1976. pp. 23. *(Fabian Society. Research Series. [No.] 326)*

— **Congresses.**

WEISS (THOMAS GEORGE) and JORDAN (ROBERT S.) The World Food Conference and global problem solving; published in cooperation with the United Nations Institute for Training and Research (UNITAR). New York, 1976. pp. 170.

— **America, Latin.**

SMITH (THOMAS LYNN) The race between population and food supply in Latin America. Albuquerque, N.M., [1976]. pp. 194.

— **European Economic Community countries.**

U.K. Ministry of Agriculture, Fisheries and Food. Economics Division. 1974. E.E.C. agricultural and food statistics. [London], 1974. pp. 105.

— **Gambia.**

HASWELL (MARGARET ROSARY) The nature of poverty: a case-history of the first quarter-century after World War II. London, 1975. pp. 234. *bibliog.*

— **Germany.**

SCHMAUDERER (EBERHARD) Studien zur Geschichte der Lebensmittelwissenschaft. Wiesbaden, 1975. pp. 314. *bibliogs. (Vierteljahrschrift für Sozial- und Wirtschaftsgeschichte. Beihefte. Nr.62)*

— **Nigeria.**

SMITH (VICTOR EARLE) Efficient resource use for tropical nutrition: Nigeria. East Lansing, Mich., 1975. pp. 375. *bibliog. (Michigan State University. Institute for International Business and Economic Development Studies. MSU International Business and Economic Studies)*

— **Senegal.**

N'DONGO (SALLY) Voyage forcé: itinéraire d'un militant. Paris, 1975. pp. 224.

— **Underdeveloped areas.**

See UNDERDEVELOPED AREAS — Food supply.

— **United Kingdom.**

PAGE (WILF) Farming to feed Britain: a policy for farmers, farm workers and consumers. London, [1973?]. pp. 28. *(Communist Party of Great Britain. Communist Party Pamphlets)*

MELLANBY (KENNETH) Can Britain feed itself?. London, 1975. pp. 61.

LEACH (GERALD) Energy and food production. Guildford, [1976]. pp. 137. *bibliog.*

— **United States.**

BARRONS (KEITH CONVERSE) The food in your future: steps to abundance. New York, 1975. pp. 180. *bibliog.*

FOOTBALL

— **Social aspects.**

DERRICK (ED) and McRORY (JUDY) Cup in hand: Sunderland's self-image after the cup. Birmingham, 1973. pp. 20. *bibliog. (Birmingham. University. Centre for Urban and Regional Studies. Working Papers. No. 8)*

FOOTBRIDGES

— **United Kingdom.**

WILSON (HUGH) AND WOMERSLEY (LEWIS) Firm, and others. Report of the Urban Motorways Project Team to the Urban Motorways Committee: techniques used in the case studies. Technical paper no. 3. Pedestrian trip analysis. [London], Department of the Environment, 1974 [or rather 1975]. pp. 117.

FORD (GERALD RUDOLPH) President of the United States.

REEVES (RICHARD) A Ford, not a Lincoln: the decline of American political leadership. London, 1976. pp. 191.

FORD (HENRY).

WALCHER (JAKOB) Ford oder Marx: die praktische Lösung der sozialen Frage. Berlin, [1925]. pp. 158.

LEWIS (DAVID LANIER) The public image of Henry Ford: an American folk hero and his company. Detroit, 1976. pp. 598.

FORECASTING.

KOTHARI (RAJNI) Footsteps into the future: diagnosis of the present world and a design for an alternative. Amsterdam, [1974]. pp. 173. *(Institute for World Order. Preferred Worlds for the 1990's)*

CROSS (DONALD) Forecasting in urban and regional planning: a report to the Planning Committee of the S[ocial] S[cience] R[esearch] C[ouncil];...with the assistance of Malcolm Longair and Stephen Grigson. London, Social Science Research Council, [1975]. pp. 94. *bibliog.*

IKONNIKOVA (GENRIETTA IVANOVNA) Teoriia "postindustrial'nogo obshchestva": budushchee chelovechestva i ego burzhuaznye tolkovateli; kriticheskii analiz. Moskva, 1975. pp. 221. *(Akademiia Obshchestvennykh Nauk. Protiv Burzhuaznoi Ideologii)*

MILES (IAN) The poverty of prediction. Farnborough, Hants., [1975]. pp. 227. *bibliog.*

— **Congresses.**

INTERNATIONAL ECONOMIC ASSOCIATION. Conference, [1974?], Moscow. Methods of long-term planning and forecasting: proceedings of a conference...; edited by T.S. Khachaturov. London, 1976. pp. 461. *bibliogs.*

— **Research.**

SWEDEN. Utrikesdepartementet. 1974. To choose a future: a basis for discussion and deliberations on future studies in Sweden. Stockholm, 1974. pp. 162. *bibliog.*

FOREIGN EXCHANGE.

FOREIGN EXCHANGE.

FURNISS (EDGAR STEPHENSON) 1890- . Foreign exchange: the financing mechanism of international commerce. Boston, [Mass., 1922]. pp. 409.

ECKES (ALFRED E.) A search for solvency: Bretton Woods and the international monetary system, 1941-1971. Austin, [1975]. pp. 355. *bibliog.*

ETHIER (WILFRED) and BLOOMFIELD (ARTHUR I.) Managing the managed float. Princeton, 1975. pp. 23. *bibliog.* (*Princeton University. Department of Economics and Sociology. International Finance Section. Essays in International Finance. No. 112*)

AGGARWAL (RAJ) Financial policies for the multinational company: the management of foreign exchange. New York, 1976. pp. 161. *bibliog.*

FLOATING exchange rates: the lessons of recent experience; [proceedings of a colloquium organized by the Société Universitaire Européenne de Recherches Financières in Venice, 1974]; edited by H. Fournier and J.E. Wadsworth. Leyden, 1976. pp. 229. *In English and French.*

PRINDL (ANDREAS ROBERT) Foreign exchange risk. London, [1976]. pp. 169. *bibliog.*

YEAGER (LELAND BENNETT) International monetary relations: theory, history, and policy. 2nd ed. New York, [1976]. pp. 667.

— Law — Egypt.

HANSEN (BENT) and NASHASHIBI (KARIM A.) Foreign trade regimes and economic development: Egypt. New York, 1975. pp. 358. (*National Bureau of Economic Research. Special Conference Series on Foreign Trade Regimes and Economic Development. vol. 4*)

— — India.

BHAGWATI (JAGDISH NATWARLAL) and SRINIVASAN (T.N.) Foreign trade regimes and economic development: India. New York, 1975. pp. 261. (*National Bureau of Economic Research. Special Conference Series on Foreign Trade Regimes and Economic Development. vol. 6*)

— — Korea.

FRANK (CHARLES R.) and others. Foreign trade regimes and economic development: South Korea. New York, 1975. pp. 264. *bibliog.* (*National Bureau of Economic Research. Special Conference Series on Foreign Trade Regimes and Economic Development. vol. 7*)

— Mathematical models.

RUMM (ULRICH) Wirtschaftliches Wachstum, Aussenhandel und Preisniveau. Meisenheim am Glan, [1973]. pp. 135, xi. *bibliog.*

BOYER (RUSSELL S.) Fixed rates, flexible rates, and the international transmission of inflation. [London], 1975. 1 pamphlet (various pagings). *bibliog.*

KAMINOW (IRA) Economic stabilization under fixed and flexible exchange rates. [London, 1975]. pp. 25,5. *bibliog.*

ROTH (JUERGEN) Der internationale Konjunkturzusammenhang bei flexiblen Wechselkursen: eine modelltheoretische Analyse. Tübingen, 1975. pp. 264. *bibliog.* (*Kiel. Universität. Institut für Weltwirtschaft Kieler Studien. 135*)

MUSSA (MICHAEL) Real and monetary factors in a dynamic theory of foreign exchange. rev. ed. [London], 1976. pp. 28. *bibliog.*

— Underdeveloped areas.

See UNDERDEVELOPED AREAS — Foreign exchange.

— United Kingdom — Mathematical models.

CORDEN (WARNER MAX) and others. Import controls versus devaluation and Britain's economic prospects. London, [1975]. fo. 21. (*Trade Policy Research Centre. Guest Papers. No. 2*)

FOREIGN NEWS.

VEHMAS (RAINO) Foreign news in the Finnish morning papers: a quantitative analysis. Turku, 1964. pp. 24. (*Åbo. Turun Yliopisto. Institute of Sociology. Publications. No.13*) (*Reprinted summary from Sanomalehtiemme Ulkomaanaineisto*).

FOREIGN TRADE PROMOTION

— Ghana.

GHANA EXPORT PROMOTION COUNCIL. Export for prosperity. [Accra], 1975. pp. 83.

— United States.

KAUFMAN (BURTON IRA) Efficiency and expansion: foreign trade organization in the Wilson administration, 1913-1921. Westport, Conn., 1974. pp. 300. *bibliog.*

FOREIGN TRADE REGULATION.

ATLANTIC COUNCIL OF THE UNITED STATES. Trade Committee. Special Advisory Panel. GATT plus: a proposal for trade reform, with the text of the General Agreement; report. New York, 1975. pp. 194.

LORTIE (PIERRE) Economic integration and the law of GATT. New York, [1975]. pp. 177.

— European Economic Community countries.

SLOT (PIETER J.) Technical and administrative obstacles to trade in the EEC. Leyden, 1975. pp. 294. *bibliog.*

— Germany, Eastern.

KEMPER (MANFRED) and MASKOW (DIETRICH) Aussenwirtschaftsrecht der DDR. Berlin, 1975. pp. 368.

— United States.

FRANK (RICHARD ANTHONY) Enforcing the public's right to openness in the foreign affairs decision making process. New York, [1973]. pp. 31. (*New York (City). University. Center for International Studies. Policy Papers. vol. 5, no.4*)

FOREST (EVA).

FOREST (EVA) From a Spanish jail; translated [from the French] by Rosemary Sheed. Harmondsworth, 1975. pp. 191.

FOREST PRODUCTS

— Canada.

MANNING (GLENN H.) and GRINNELL (H. RAE) Forest resources and utilization in Canada to the year 2000. Ottawa, 1971. pp. 80. *bibliog.* (*Canada. Forestry Service. Publications. No. 1304*)

— Swaziland.

SWAZILAND. Central Statistical Office. Census of commercial timber plantations and wood and wood products. a., 1973 [4th]- Mbabane.

FORESTRY LAW AND LEGISLATION

— United Kingdom.

THOMPSON (EDWARD PALMER) Whigs and hunters: the origin of the Black Act. London, 1975. pp. 313.

FORESTRY RESEARCH

— Canada.

CANADA. Forestry Branch. 1968. Federal research in the forests: Alberta and territories. Ottawa, 1968. pp. 32.

FORESTS AND FORESTRY.

EARL (D.E.) Forest energy and economic development. Oxford, 1975. pp. 128. *bibliog.*

— Bibliography.

FOOD AND AGRICULTURE ORGANIZATION. Documentation Center. 1974. Forestry: annotated bibliography, (author and subject index), 1967-1973. (DC/Sp.28). [Rome, 1974]. 2 vols. (in 1).

— Economic aspects.

MANNING (GLENN H.) Linear programming, resource allocation and non-market benefits. Ottawa, 1971. pp. 18. *bibliog.* (*Canada. Forestry Service. Publications. No. 1298*)

— — Canada.

FOREST ECONOMICS RESEARCH INSTITUTE [CANADA]. Report, 1967-72. [Ottawa, 1972]. pp. 36.

— Canada.

CAYFORD (J.H.) and BICKERSTAFF (A.) Man-made forests in Canada. Ottawa, 1968. pp. 68. *bibliogs.* (*Canada. Forestry Branch. Publications. No. 1240*)

NAYSMITH (JOHN K.) The future value of Canada's northern forests. Ottawa, Information Canada, 1971. pp.21. *bibliog.*

ROWE (J.S.) Forest regions of Canada. [rev. ed.] Ottawa, 1972. pp. 172. *bibliog.* (*Canada. Forestry Service. Publications. No.1300*) Map in end pocket.

— New Zealand.

NEW ZEALAND. New Zealand Forest Service. 1974. Forestry development plan for north Canterbury planning district. Wellington, 1974. pp. 71.

NEW ZEALAND. New Zealand Forest Service. 1974. Forestry development plan for Otago planning district. Wellington, 1974. pp. 129.

NEW ZEALAND. New Zealand Forest Service. 1975. Forestry encouragement loans for local authorities. Wellington, 1975. pp. 11. (*Information Series. No. 71*)

— Norway.

FORVENTNINGER til rekreasjonsmiljøet i Oslomarka: analyse av fotografier, tegninger og litteratur med motiver fra skog generelt og Oslomarka spesielt: (delrapport fra prosjektet Friluftsliv i skog); [by] Joh[anne]s Oraug [and others]. Oslo, 1974. pp. 96. (*Norsk Institutt for By- og Regionforskning. Arbeidsrapporter. 10/74*)

FRILUFTSLIV i Oslomarka: analyse av en intervjuundersøkelse om publikums bruk av og krav til Oslomarka: (delrapport fra prosjektet Flerbruksplan for Oslomarka [and] Friluftsliv i skog); [by] Terje Lind [and others]. Oslo, 1974. pp. 96. (*Norsk Institutt for By- og Regionforskning. Arbeidsrapporter. 8/74*)

— South Africa.

FORESTRY COUNCIL [SOUTH AFRICA]. 1973/75 (1st)- Pretoria. *[In English and Afrikaans]. Included in the file of SOUTH AFRICA. Parliament. House of Assembly. Votes and proceedings (with Printed annexures).*

— Swaziland.

SWAZILAND. Central Statistical Office. Census of commercial timber plantations and wood and wood products. a., 1973 [4th]- Mbabane.

— Sweden.

HOLMSTRÖM (SVEN J.R.) Kombinerade skogs- och jordbruksföretag. Stockholm, 1974. pp. 34. (*Jordbrukets Utredningsinstitut. Meddelanden. 1974. Nr. 2*) *With English summary.*

JORDBRUKETS UTREDNINGSINSTITUT. Meddelanden. 1974. Nr. 6. Avverkning, skogsvård, sysselsättning hos enskilda skogsägare i södra Sverige. Stockholm, 1974. pp. 39. *With English summary.*

SKOLIG planering: en lägesrapport, etc. Stockholm, 1974. pp. 142. *bibliog. (Jordbrukets Utredningsinstitut. Meddelanden. 1974. Nr. 5) With English summary.*

— United Kingdom.

GOODALL (BRIAN) National forests and recreational opportunities. Reading, 1975. pp. 57. *bibliog. (Reading. University. Department of Geography. Reading Geographical Papers. No.39)*

— — Wales.

YOUTH HOSTELS ASSOCIATION (ENGLAND AND WALES). Landscape and forestry in Mid-Wales: a land-use survey. [London], 1974. pp. 9.

— United States.

ROBINSON (GLEN O.) The Forest Service: (a study in public land management). Baltimore, [1975]. pp. 337.

FOS.

FRANCE. Direction de la Documentation. La Documentation Française. Notes et Etudes Documentaires. Nos. 4,164-4, 165-4,166. L'aménagement de la région Fos-Etang de Berre; par Didier Cultiaux. Paris, 1975. pp. 132.

FOSTER HOME CARE

— United Kingdom.

SHEARER (ANN) Fostering mentally handicapped children: is it feasible?. London, 1974. pp. 31. *(Campaign for the Mentally Handicapped. Enquiry Papers. No. 3)*

— United States.

JENKINS (SHIRLEY) and NORMAN (ELAINE) Beyond placement: mothers view foster care. New York, 1975. pp. 149. *(Columbia University. School of Social Work. Social Work and Social Issues. [vol.4])*

SHAPIRO (DEBORAH) Agencies and foster children. New York, 1976. pp. 216. *(Columbia University. School of Social Work. Social Work and Social Issues. [vol. 5].)*

FOUNDLINGS

— Italy.

GORNI (MARIAGRAZIA) and PELLEGRINI (LAURA) Un problema di storia sociale: l'infanzia abbandonata in Italia nel secolo XIX. Firenze, 1974. pp. 241. *(Milan. Università. Facoltà di Lettere e Filosofia. Pubblicazioni. 74)*

FOURIER (FRANÇOIS CHARLES MARIE).

BRUCKNER (PASCAL) Fourier. [Paris, 1975]. pp. 192. *bibliog.*

FOXWELL (HERBERT SOMERTON).

GREGORY (Sir THEODOR EMANUEL GUGENHEIM) [Unpublished economic and personal papers. 1910-34]. 6 pieces. *Manuscript, typescript, etc.*

FRAGA IRIBARNE (MANUEL).

MILIAN MESTRE (MANUEL) Fraga Iribarne: retrato en tres tiempos. Barcelona, 1975. pp. 451.

FRANCE

— Army.

[MARTIN DE SALINS (C.C.)] Nécessité et moyens d'établir une loi agraire, d'assurer la subsistance des pauvres, de réformer le clergé et la constitution militaire; par C.C.M. de S...ns. n.p. 1789; repr. Paris, 1966. pp. 49. *Facsimile reprint.*

BAUDOIN (RÉMY) and others. Armée/nation: le rendez-vous manqué. [Paris, 1975]. pp. 382.

REMY (BERNARD) L'homme des casernes: "change-lutte", collectifs de soutien. Paris, 1975. pp. 280.

— Civilization.

DOLLOT (LOUIS) La France dans le monde actuel. 4th ed. Paris, 1975. pp. 128.

— Colonies — Administration.

ASIWAJU (ANTHONY IJAOLA) Western Yorubaland under European rule, 1889-1945: a comparative analysis of French and British colonialism. London, 1976. pp. 303. *bibliog.*

— — Economic conditions.

CAHIERS O.R.S.T.O.M.: série sciences humaines; ([pd. by] l'Office de la Recherche Scientifique et Technique Outre- Mer [France]). 4 a yr., 1963 (v.1)- Paris.

— — Social conditions.

CAHIERS O.R.S.T.O.M.: série sciences humaines; ([pd. by] l'Office de la Recherche Scientifique et Technique Outre- Mer [France]). 4 a yr., 1963 (v.1)- Paris.

— Commerce.

CARTER (WILLIAM) Clothier. The usurpations of France upon the trade of the woollen manufacture of England briefly hinted at; being the effects of thirty years observations...; or, A caution to England to improve a season now put into her hand, to secure herself. London, printed for R. Baldwin, 1695. pp. 30. *p.l bled. Wing 678.*

FRANCE. Direction des Ports Maritimes et des Voies Navigables. Service Central. L'activité des ports maritimes français de commerce (title varies). a., 1969- Paris.

FRANCE. Comité des Echanges Extérieurs. 1971. Préparation du VIe Plan...: rapport. Paris, 1971. pp. 231.

FRANCE. Direction des Ports Maritimes et des Voies Navigables. Rapport d'activité. a., 1973- Paris.

FRANCE. Direction du Commerce Intérieur. 1974. Population active du commerce et des services à caractère commercial: dossier statistique. [Paris], Direction du Commerce Intérieur, 1974. fo. 339.

FRANCE. Institut National de la Statistique et des Etudes Economiques. 1974. Les entreprises et établissements industriels et commerciaux en France en 1971. [Paris], 1974. 3 vols. (in 1).

DAYAN (ARMAND) La distribution des biens de consommation. [Paris], 1975. pp. 127. *bibliog.*

FRANCE. Ministère de l'Economie et des Finances. 1975. Nomenclature d'activités et de produits, 1973: édition avec notes explicatives, 1974. Paris, 1975. pp. 439.

FRANCE. Commission du Commerce, des Services et de l'Artisanat. 1976. Rapport...: préparation du 7e Plan. Paris, 1976. pp. 156.

— — Brazil.

SCHNEIDER (JUERGEN) Handel und Unternehmer im französischen Brasiliengeschäft, 1815-1848: Versuch einer quantitativen Strukturanalyse. Köln, 1975. pp. 649. *bibliog. With table of contents and summaries in various languages.*

— — United Kingdom.

NICOLLE (HILARY ANN) Anglo-French trade, 1540-1640. 1976. fo. 336. *bibliog. Typescript. Ph.D.(London) thesis: unpublished. This thesis is the property of London University and may not be removed from the Library.*

— Commercial policy.

ASSOCIATION POUR LA LIBERTE DES ECHANGES. Programme de réforme douanière proposé par l'Association pour la Liberté des Echanges. Paris, [1847]. pp. 29. *Signed by the President of the Association and by the general secretary, F. Bastiat. Issued with a covering circular from the secretary.*

— Constitution.

DEMICHEL (ANDRE) and others. Institutions et pouvoir en France: une traduction institutionnelle du capitalisme monopoliste d'état. Paris, [1975]. pp. 224.

— Constitutional history.

COURTIER (PAUL) La Quatrième République. Paris, 1975. pp. 128. *bibliog.*

— Defences.

FRANCE. French Embassy, London. Service de Presse et d'Information. 1974. French national defence. London, 1974. pp. 16. *(France: facts, figures. A/99/6/74)*

— Diplomatic and consular service.

LAUREN (PAUL GORDON) Diplomats and bureaucrats: the first institutional responses to twentieth-century diplomacy in France and Germany. Stanford, 1976. pp. 294. *bibliog. (Stanford University. Hoover Institution on War, Revolution and Peace. Hoover Institution Publications. 153)*

— Economic conditions.

CHAVAROCHE (J.) L'économie et la lutte politique en France. Paris, [1929]. pp. 125.

ECONOMIE ET STATISTIQUE: revue mensuelle; [pd. by] Institut National de la Statistique et des Etudes Economiques (République Française). m., My 1969 (1)- , with gap (S-Oc 1969: 4,5). Paris. *Supersedes Etudes et conjoncture (Jl 1953-Ap 1969).*

FRANCE. Délgation à l'Aménagement du Territoire et à l'Action Régionale. 1974. Le développement régional dans les domaines industriel et tertiaire: (dossier). [Paris, 1974]. pp. 50.

FRANCE. Délégation à l'Aménagement du Territoire et à l'Action Régionale. 1974. Investissements étrangers et aménagement du territoire: livre blanc. Paris, 1974. pp. 141. *Map in end pocket.*

MAILLET (PIERRE) La structure économique de la France. 6th ed. Paris, [1975]. pp. 128. *bibliog.*

CARRE (JEAN JACQUES) and others. French economic growth;...translated from the French by John P. Hatfield. Stanford, 1976. pp. 581.

— — Statistics.

ANNALES DE L'INSÉÉ; [pd. by] Institut National de la Statistique et des Études Économiques [France]. 3 a yr., My 1969 (no.1)- Paris.

— Economic history.

EQUIPE DE RECHERCHES DE GEOGRAPHIE INDUSTRIELLE. Recherches de géographie industrielle. Paris, 1974. pp. 298. *bibliog. (Service de Documentation et de Cartographie Géographiques. Mémoires et Documents. Nouvelle Série. vol. 14)*

SAVA (SORICA) Corelații macroeconomice în economia postbelică a Franței. București, 1974. pp. 260. *(Academia de Științe Sociale și Politice a Republicii Socialiste România. Institutul de Cercetări Economice. Bibliotheca Oeconomica. 28) With French, English, German and Russian tables of contents.*

— — Mathematical models.

SHEEN (JEFFREY R.) and SASSANPOUR (CYRUS) A comparison of money and economic activity in France and West Germany: 1959-1973. [London, 1976]. pp. 54. *bibliog.*

— Economic policy.

CHAVAROCHE (J.) L'économie et la lutte politique en France. Paris, [1929]. pp. 125.

BETTELHEIM (CHARLES) Le "plan Marshall" et ses conséquences pour l'économie française. [Paris, 1952]. pp. 27-42. *(Extracted from Cahiers Internationaux, 4e année, no. 40)*

FRANCE(Cont.)

ECONOMIE ET STATISTIQUE: revue mensuelle; [pd. by] Institut National de la Statistique et des Etudes Economiques (République Française). m., My 1969 (1)- , with gap (S-Oc 1969: 4,5). Paris. *Supersedes Etudes et conjuncture (Jl 1953-Ap 1969).*

PASCALLON (PIERRE) La planification de l'économie française. Paris, 1974. pp. 155.

QUERCIA (ROGER) Eléments pour une politique des quartiers généraux d'entreprises multinationales en France. [Paris], Documentation Française, 1974. pp. 202.

SYSTEME D'ETUDES DU SCHEMA GENERAL D'AMENAGEMENT DE LA FRANCE. Schéma général d'aménagement de la France: Sésame année 5. Paris, 1974. pp. 71. *(France. Délégation à l'Aménagement du Territoire et à l'Action Régionale. Travaux et Recherches de Prospective. 50)*

AUJAC (HENRI) Comparaison des potentiels de développement de la République fédérale d'Allemagne et de la France. Lausanne, 1975. pp. 43. *(Lausanne. Université. Centre de Recherches Européennes. Publications. 2. Le Processus d'Union de l'Europe)*

ULLMO (YVES) La planification en France. Paris, 1974 [or rather 1975]. pp. 625. *(Fondation Nationale des Sciences Politiques. Etudes Politiques, Economiques et Sociales)*

FRANCE. Comité de la Consommation. 1976. Rapport...: préparation du 7e Plan. Paris, 1976. pp. 86.

FRANCE. Commission du Développement. 1976. Rapport...: préparation du 7e Plan. Paris, 1976. pp. 155.

— Emigration and immigration.

CENTRE D'ETUDES ANTI-IMPERIALISTES. Les immigrés: contribution à l'histoire politique de l'immigration en France. [Paris, 1975]. pp. 384. *bibliog.*

TAPINOS (GEORGES PHOTIOS) L'immigration étrangère en France, 1946-1973. [Paris], 1975. pp. 151. *bibliog. (France. Institut National d'Etudes Démographiques. Travaux et Documents. Cahiers. No. 71)*

VIEUGUET (ANDRE) Français et immigrés: le combat du Parti communiste français. Paris, [1975]. pp. 223.

— Executive departments.

FRANCE. French Embassy, London. Service de Presse et d'Information. 1974. Area development and regional planning in France: the DATAR. London, 1974. pp. 20. *(France: facts, figures. A/102/9/74)*

HISTOIRE de l'administration française depuis 1800: problèmes et méthodes; actes du colloque organisé le 4 mars 1972 par l'Institut Français des Sciences Administratives et la IVe section de l'Ecole Pratique des Hautes Etudes. Genève, 1975. pp. 119. *bibliog. (Paris. Ecole Pratique des Hautes Etudes. Section des Sciences Historiques et Philologiques. Centre de Recherches d'Histoire et de Philologie. Hautes Etudes Médiévales et Modernes. 23)*

POUJADE (ROBERT) Le ministère de l'impossible. [Paris], 1975. pp. 278.

LAUREN (PAUL GORDON) Diplomats and bureaucrats: the first institutional responses to twentieth-century diplomacy in France and Germany. Stanford, 1976. pp. 294. *bibliog. (Stanford University. Hoover Institution on War, Revolution and Peace. Hoover Institution Publications. 153)*

— Foreign economic relations.

FRANCE. Commission des Relations Economiques et Financières avec l'Extérieur. 1976. Rapport...: préparation du 7e Plan. Paris, 1976. pp. 138.

— — Europe, Eastern.

FRANCE. Direction de la Documentation. La Documentation Française. Notes et Etudes Documentaires. Nos. 4,116-4, 117. Les échanges et la coopération économique avec les pays de l'Europe de l'Est; [par Alain Capian]. Paris, 1974. pp. 56. *bibliog.*

— — United Kingdom.

BOYCE (ROBERT WILLIAM DEWAR) Search for recovery: the influence of the United States and France on British plans for economic recovery, 1929-31. 1975. fo. 384. *bibliog.* Typescript. Ph.D. (London) thesis: unpublished. *This thesis is the property of London University and may not be removed from the Library.*

— — United States.

HOWELL (WILLIAMSON S.) ed. The United States and France: correspondence dealing with economic relations, 1811-1930; [with] Index. [Paris, 1931]. 18 vols. Microfilm: 7 reels. Index on reel 1. *Cover documents held at the U.S. Embassy in Paris.*

— Foreign population.

CENTRE D'ETUDES ANTI-IMPERIALISTES. Les immigrés: contribution à l'histoire politique de l'immigration en France. [Paris, 1975]. pp. 384. *bibliog.*

— Foreign relations.

PARTI COMMUNISTE FRANCAIS. Vous avez des soucis! pourquoi?: comment en sortir. Paris, [1952]. pp. 16.

GARAUDY (ROGER) La vérité sur Suez: intervention à l'Assemblée Nationale, le 16 octobre 1956, etc. Paris, [1956?]. pp. 23.

DULL (JONATHAN R.) The French navy and American independence: a study of arms and diplomacy, 1774-1787. Princeton, [1975]. pp. 437. *bibliog.*

PIKE (DAVID WINGEATE) Les Français et la guerre d'Espagne. Paris, 1975. pp. 467. *bibliog. (Paris. Université de Paris I (Panthéon- Sorbonne). Publications. Nouvelle Série. Recherches. 7)*

WINBERG (ALAN RONALD) Decision-making theory and the characteristics of crisis; with particular reference to the French reaction to the remilitarization of the Rhineland in 1936. [1976]. fo. 448. *bibliog.* Typescript. M.Phil.(London) thesis: unpublished. *This thesis is the property of London University and may not be removed from the Library.*

See also EUROPEAN COMMUNITIES — France.

— — Europe.

HATTON (RAGNHILD) ed. Louis XIV and Europe. London, 1976. pp. 311.

— — Germany.

BINOCHE (JACQUES) L'Allemagne et le Général de Gaulle, 1924-1970. [Paris, 1975]. pp. 229.

GRUBE (JOCHEN) Bismarks Politik in Europa und Übersee: seine "Annäherung" an Frankreich im Urteil der Pariser Presse, 1883-1885. Bern, 1975, pp 277. *bibliog.*

SEYDOUX (FRANÇOIS) Mémoires d'outre-Rhin. Paris, [1975]. pp. 309.

— — Lebanon.

SHORROCK (WILLIAM I.) French imperialism in the Middle East: the failure of policy in Syria and Lebanon, 1900-1914. Wisconsin, 1976. pp. 214. *bibliog.*

— — Russia.

MANFRED (AL'BERT ZAKHAROVICH) Obrazovanie russko-frantsuzskogo soiuza. Moskva, 1975. pp. 376. *bibliog.* With French table of contents.

— — Syria.

SHORROCK (WILLIAM I.) French imperialism in the Middle East: the failure of policy in Syria and Lebanon, 1900-1914. Wisconsin, 1976. pp. 214. *bibliog.*

— — United Kingdom.

Les RELATIONS Franco-Britanniques de 1935 à 1939: communications présentées aux colloques franco-britanniques tenus à Londres...1971, Paris...1972. Paris, 1975. pp. 440. *In English or French, with summaries in the alternative language.*

HAMILTON (KEITH ALEXANDER) The embassy of Sir Francis Bertie in Paris during the period 1905-1914. 1975 [or rather 1976]. fo. 447. *bibliog.* Typescript. Ph.D.(London) thesis: unpublished. *This thesis is the property of London University and may not be removed from the Library.*

HASWELL (JOCK) The battle for empire: a century of Anglo-French conflict. London, 1976. pp. 310. *bibliog.*

— — United States.

ZAHNISER (MARVIN R.) Uncertain friendship: American-French diplomatic relations through the cold war. New York, [1975]. pp. 314. *bibliog.*

— — Yugoslavia — Serbia.

ALEKSIĆ-PEJKOVIĆ (LJILJANA) Odnosi Srbije sa Francuskom i Engleskom, 1903-1914; urednik Jorjo Tadić...; Les relations entre la Serbie, la France et l'Angleterre, 1903-1914. Beograd, 1965. pp. 961. *(Istorijski Institut. Jugoslovenske Zemlje u XX Veku. knj. 3)* In Cyrillic.

— Government publications.

FRANCE. Commission de Coordination de la Documentation Administrative. 1975. La coordination documentaire: l'accès du public aux documents administratifs; deuxième rapport au Premier Ministre, Nov. 1974; documents annexes. Paris, 1975. pp. 91. *(Administration et Documentation)*

—History — 1500-1599.

SALMON (JOHN HEARSEY McMILLAN) Society in crisis: France in the sixteenth century. London, 1975. pp. 383. *bibliog.*

— — 1589-1789, Bourbons.

HATTON (RAGNHILD) ed. Louis XIV and absolutism. London, 1976. pp. 306.

— — 1789-1799, Revolution.

CARON (PIERRE) La première terreur, 1792. 1. Les missions du Conseil exécutif provisoire et de la Commune de Paris. Paris, 1950. pp. 222.

RUDÉ (GEORGE E.) Robespierre: portrait of a revolutionary democrat. London, 1975. pp. 254. *bibliog.*

— — — Influence.

SCHEEL (HEINRICH) Die Mainzer Republik, etc. Berlin, 1975 in progress. *bibliog. (Akademie der Wissenschaften der DDR. Zentralinstitut für Geschichte. Schriften. Bände 42, etc.)*

— — 1830, July Revolution.

MERRIMAN (JOHN M.) ed. 1830 in France. New York, 1975. pp. 232. *bibliogs.*

— — 1848, February Revolution.

PRICE (ROGER D.) ed. Revolution and reaction: 1848 and the second French Republic. London, 1975. pp. 333.

— — 1848-1852, Second Republic.

PRICE (ROGER D.) ed. Revolution and reaction: 1848 and the second French Republic. London, 1975. pp. 333.

— — 1851, Coup d'état.

DURRIEU (XAVIER) Le coup d'état de Louis Bonaparte: histoire de la persécution de décembre; événements, prisons, casemates et pontons. Bruxelles, Briard, 1852. pp. 217.

FRANCE(Cont.)

— — 1870-1940, Third Republic.

MANTOUX (ÉTIENNE) [Letters to Frank Hardie. 1933-35]. 6 letters, 2 postcards. *Manuscript.*

— — 1940-1945, German occupation.

AZEMA (JEAN PIERRE) La collaboration, 1940-1944. [Paris, 1975]. pp. 152. *bibliog.*

— Industries.

EQUIPE DE RECHERCHES DE GEOGRAPHIE INDUSTRIELLE. Recherches de géographie industrielle. Paris, 1974. pp. 298. *bibliog. (Service de Documentation et de Cartographie Géographiques. Mémoires et Documents. Nouvelle Série. vol. 14)*

FRANCE. Délgation à l'Aménagement du Territoire et à l'Action Régionale. 1974. Le développement régional dans les domaines industriel et tertiaire: (dossier). [Paris, 1974]. pp. 50.

FRANCE. Institut National de la Statistique et des Etudes Economiques. 1974. Les entreprises et établissements industriels et commerciaux en France en 1971. [Paris], 1974. 3 vols. (in 1).

FRANCE. Ministère de l'Economie et des Finances. 1975. Nomenclature d'activités et de produits, 1973: édition avec notes explicatives, 1974. Paris, 1975. pp. 439.

INSTITUT DE RECHERCHES EN ECONOMIE DE LA PRODUCTION. Analyse comparative des structures industrielles: la norme d'efficacité intersectorielle; (redigé par J. de Bandt). Paris, 1975. pp. 216. *(France. Ministère de l'Industrie et de la Recherche. Etudes de Politique Industrielle. 5)*

— Intellectual life.

FRANCE. Direction de la Documentation. La Documentation Française. Notes et Etudes Documentaires. Nos. 4,205-4, 206. Le projet suédois de démocratie culturelle; essai de comparaison avec la situation française; par Claude Fabrizio. Paris, 1975. pp. 72. *bibliog.*

FRANCE. French Embassy, London. Service de Presse et d'Information. 1975. France's foreign relations in the cultural scientific and technical fields. London, 1975. pp. 18. *(France: facts, figures. A/106/2/75)*

REARDON (BERNARD MORRIS GARVIN) Liberalism and tradition: aspects of Catholic thought in nineteenth-century France. Cambridge, 1975. pp. 308.

— Maps.

ATLAS de l'Est. [Strasbourg?, c. 1970 in progress]. *Loose leaf. New edition of ASSOCIATION POUR L'ATLAS DE LA FRANCE DE L'EST. Atlas de la France de l'Est.*

— Navy — History.

Les MUTINERIES de la Mer Noire, 1919-1969. Paris, [1969?]. pp. 40. *(Cahiers de Mai. Suppléments. 13)*

— Occupations.

FRANCE. Direction du Commerce Intérieur. 1974. Population active du commerce et des services à caractère commercial: dossier statistique. [Paris], Direction du Commerce Intérieur, 1974. fo. 339.

FRANCE. Institut National de la Statistique et des Etudes Economiques. 1975. Code des métiers: (code no.64 du recensement de la population de 1975). [Paris?], 1975. 2 vols. (in 1).

— Parliament — Assemblée Nationale.

BULLETIN DE L'ASSEMBLEE NATIONALE; [pd. by] Secrétariat Générale de l'Assemblée Nationale [France]. w., N 28 1972 (no.1)- Paris. *File includes Statistiques, 1975-*

— — Elections.

KENT (SHERMAN) The election of 1827 in France. Cambridge, Mass., 1975. pp. 225. *bibliog. (Harvard University. Harvard Historical Studies. vol. 91)*

— Politics and government.

BOURDOIS (JEAN PATRICK) La réforme administrative dans la "Revue générale d'administration", 1878-1928. Paris, [1975]. pp. 98. *(Paris. Université de Paris II. Travaux et Recherches. Série Science Administrative. 9)*

HISTOIRE de l'administration française depuis 1800: problèmes et méthodes; actes du colloque organisé le 4 mars 1972 par l'Institut Français des Sciences Administratives et la IVe section de l'Ecole Pratique des Hautes Etudes. Genève, 1975. pp. 119. *bibliog. (Paris. Ecole Pratique des Hautes Etudes. Section des Sciences Historiques et Philologiques. Centre de Recherches d'Histoire et de Philologie. Hautes Etudes Médiévales et Modernes. 23)*

— — 1589-1789.

HATTON (RAGNHILD) ed. Louis XIV and absolutism. London, 1976. pp. 306.

— — 1870-1940.

LACHAUD (GEORGES) Que vont devenir les bonapartistes?. Paris, 1879. pp. 71.

ELWITT (SANFORD) The making of the Third Republic: class and politics in France, 1868-1884. Baton Rouge, [1975]. pp. 329. *bibliog.*

NAVILLE (PIERRE) L'entre-deux guerres: la lutte des classes en France, 1927-1929 [or rather 1939]. Paris, [1975]. pp. 624. *bibliog. Cover title includes the dates 1926-1939.*

— — 1900— .

SOULIE (MICHEL) Le Cartel des gauches. Paris, [1974]. pp. 335. *bibliog.*

— — 1940-1945.

CREMIEUX-BRILHAC (JEAN LOUIS) ed. Les voix de la liberté: ici Londres, 1940-1944;...; avant-propos de Jean Marin. [Paris], Documentation Française, 1975-76. 5 vols.

— — 1945— .

PARTI COMMUNISTE FRANCAIS. Comment sortir de l'abîme?: programme d'indépendance nationale de progrès social de démocratie et de paix du Parti Communiste Français. Paris, [1951]. pp. 29.

PARTI COMMUNISTE FRANCAIS. Vous avez des soucis! pourquoi?: comment en sortir. Paris, [1952]. pp. 16.

BASTIEN-THIRY (JEAN MARIE) Déclaration du colonel Bastien-Thiry, 2 février 1963. [Paris], [1963]. pp. 54.

BLONDEL (JEAN) 1929- . Contemporary France: politics, society and institutions; revised, expanded and reprinted from France: a companion to French studies, edited by D.G. Charlton. London, 1974. pp. 91. *bibliog.*

CHABAN-DELMAS (JACQUES) L'ardeur. [Paris, 1975]. pp. 454.

COURTIER (PAUL) La Quatrième République. Paris, 1975. pp. 128. *bibliog.*

PLANTEY (ALAIN) Prospective de l'état. Paris, 1975. pp. 306.

POPEREN (JEAN) L'unité de la Gauche, 1965-1973. [Paris, 1975]. pp. 474. *bibliog.*

Des TRACTS en mai 68: mesures de vocabulaire et de contenu; ([by] Michel Demonet [and others]). Paris, [1975]. pp. 491. *bibliog. (Fondation Nationale des Sciences Politiques. Travaux et Recherches de Science Politique. 31)*

SCHONFELD (WILLIAM R.) Obedience and revolt: French behavior towards authority. Beverly Hills, [1976]. pp. 256.

— Population.

ORGANISATION D'ETUDES D'AMENAGEMENT DE L'AIRE METROPOLITAINE NANTES-SAINT-NAZAIRE. Schéma d'aménagement [de l'aire métropolitaine Nantes- Saint-Nazaire]: (annexe); démographie, emploi. Nantes, 1971. pp. 61.

ARMENGAUD (ANDRE) Les Français et Malthus. [Paris, 1975]. pp. 142. *bibliog.*

COLLOQUE NATIONAL DE DEMOGRAPHIE, IVième, 1973. Migrations intérieures: méthodes d'observation et d'analyse...: actes ([and] Atlas); [edited by P. Clerc]. Paris, 1975. pp. 564, and map case. *(Centre National de la Recherche Scientifique. Colloques Nationaux. No. 933)*

— Presidents — Election.

FRANCE. Direction de la Documentation. La Documentation Française. Notes et Etudes Documentaires. Nos. 4,201-4, 202-4,203. Textes et documents relatifs à l'élection présidentielle des 5 et 19 mai 1974. Paris, 1975. pp. 144.

PENNIMAN (HOWARD RAE) ed. France at the polls: the presidential election of 1974. Washington, 1975. pp. 324. *(American Enterprise Institute for Public Policy Research. Foreign Affairs Studies. 22)*

— Public works.

FRANCE. Direction du Bâtiment et des Travaux Publics et de la Conjoncture. Service des Statistiques et des Etudes Economiques. Sous-Direction des Etudes Economiques. 1974. La main-d'oeuvre dans le bâtiment et les travaux publics. Paris, 1974. pp. 61. *(France. Ministère de l'Equipement. Statistiques de la construction. Suppléments. No. 11)*

FRANCE. Comité du Bâtiment et des Travaux Publics. 1976. Rapport...: préparation du 7e Plan. Paris, 1976. pp. 234.

— Relations (general) with other countries.

FRANCE. French Embassy, London. Service de Presse et d'Information. 1975. France's foreign relations in the cultural scientific and technical fields. London, 1975. pp. 18. *(France: facts, figures. A/106/2/75)*

— Relations (general) with Poland.

ŚLADKOWSKI (WIESŁAW) Opinia publiczna we Francji wobec sprawy polskiej w latach 1914- 1918. Wrocław, 1976. pp. 311. *bibliog. (Lubelskie Towarzystwo Naukowe. Wydział Humanistyczny. Prace. Monografie. t.5) With French summary.*

— Relations (military) with Switzerland.

EHRBAR (HANS RUDOLF) Schweizerische Militärpolitik im Ersten Weltkrieg: die militärischen Beziehungen zu Frankreich vor dem Hintergrund der schweizerischen Aussen- und Wirtschaftspolitik, 1914-1918. Bern, 1976. pp. 380. *bibliog.*

— Rural conditions.

FRANCE. Ministère de l'Agriculture. Statistique agricole. Supplément . Série Etudes. No. 115. Enquête communale de 1969-1970; [par Pierre Greiner, puis par Eliane Hénon]. Paris, 1974. 2 vols.

FARCY (HENRI DE) L'espace rural. Paris, 1975. pp. 127. *bibliog.*

— Social conditions.

COLLIGNON (CLAUDE BONIFACE) L'avant-coureur du changement du monde entier par l'aisance, la bonne éducation et la prospérité générale de tous les hommes; ou, Prospectus d'un mémoire patriotique sur les causes de la grande misère qui existe par-tout, et sur les moyens de l'extirper radicalement. Londres, 1786; Milan, 1966. pp. 60. *Facsimile reprint.*

UNION DES FEMMES FRANCAIS. Conférence Nationale, 1946, Issy-les-Moulineaux. Par notre travail et notre union assurons le bonheur et la sécurité de nos foyers dans une France grande et démocratique: rapport présenté par Yvonne Dumont à la conference etc. Paris, 1946. pp. 32.

CAMILLERI (CARMEL) and TAPIA (CLAUDE) Jeunesse française et groupes sociaux après Mai 1968: enquêtes auprès des populations universitaires et scolaires de Paris et de province. Paris, 1974. pp. 183. *(Centre National de la Recherche Scientifique. Monographies Françaises de Psychologie. 27)*

FRANCE(Cont.)

OBSERVATOIRE ECONOMIQUE DE L'OUEST. 66 indicateurs sociaux par régions et départements: pour une réflexion sur les conditions de vie dans l'Ouest; recueil de données chiffrées...rassemblées et présentées...sous la direction de Patrick Mareschal. Nantes, 1974. pp. 159.

TABARD (NICOLE) and others. Besoins et aspirations des familles et des jeunes. [Paris], 1974. pp. 512. *(Caisse Nationale des Allocations Familiales. Etudes. [16])*

— — Statistics.

FRANCE. Institut National de la Statistique et des Etudes Economiques. 1974. Données sociales, etc. 2nd ed. Paris, 1974. pp. 244.

— Social history.

DUBY (GEORGES) and WALLON (ARMAND) eds. Histoire de la France rurale. [Paris, 1975 in progress]. *bibliogs.*

— Social policy.

DELION (ANDRE G.) Institutions sociales et aménagement du territoire: rapport au gouvernement; (Communication au Comité interministériel pour l'aménagement du territoire). [Paris], Documentation Française, 1974. pp. 76.

SYSTEME D'ETUDES DU SCHEMA GENERAL D'AMENAGEMENT DE LA FRANCE. Schéma général d'aménagement de la France: Sésame année 5. Paris, 1974. pp. 71. *(France. Délégation à l'Aménagement du Territoire et à l'Action Régionale. Travaux et Recherches de Prospective. 50)*

GREFFE (XAVIER) La politique sociale: étude critique. [Paris, 1975]. pp. 254. *bibliog.*

ULLMO (YVES) La planification en France. Paris, 1974 [or rather 1975]. pp. 625. *(Fondation Nationale des Sciences Politiques. Etudes Politiques, Economiques et Sociales)*

FRANCE. Comité des Revenus et des Transferts. 1976. Rapport...: préparation du 7e Plan. Paris, 1976. pp. 184.

FRANCE. Commission de la Vie Sociale. 1976. Rapport...: préparation du 7e Plan. Paris, 1976. pp. 134.

FRANCE. Commission du Développement. 1976. Rapport...: préparation du 7e Plan. Paris, 1976. pp. 155.

— Statistics, Medical.

INSTITUT NATIONAL DE LA SANTE ET DE LA RECHERCHE MEDICALE [FRANCE]. Statistique des causes médicales de décès. a., 1968- , with gaps (1968, tome 1, 1969, tome 1, 1970, tome 1). Paris. *In two volumes; Tome 1, Résultats France; Tome 2, Résultats par région.*

— Statistics, Vital.

INSTITUT NATIONAL DE LA SANTE ET DE LA RECHERCHE MEDICALE [FRANCE]. Statistique des causes médicales de décès. a., 1968- , with gaps (1968, tome 1, 1969, tome 1, 1970, tome 1). Paris. *In two volumes; Tome 1, Résultats France; Tome 2, Résultats par région.*

— — Bibliography.

MEUNIER (MARIE THERESE) and VALLIN (JACQUES) compilers. Bibliographie des tables de mortalité françaises. Paris, Institut National d'Etudes Démographiques, 1974. pp. 35.

— Territories and possessions.

FRANCE. French Embassy, London. Service de Presse et d'Information. 1975. France's overseas departments and territories. London, 1975. pp. 19. *bibliog. (France: facts, figures. A/110/10/75)*

— — Economic conditions.

FRANCE. Secrétariat Général pour l'Administration des Départements d'Outre-Mer. Service des Affaires Economiques et des Investissements. 1975. L'économie des DOM en 1974. [Paris], 1975. pp. 101.

— — Economic policy.

FRANCE. Commission Centrale des Départements d'Outre-Mer. 1972. Préparation du VIe Plan: rapport. Paris, 1972. pp. 508.

FRANCHISES (RETAIL TRADE)
— Canada.

CANADA. Statistics Canada. Merchandising and Services Division. 1973. Franchising in Canada's food serving industry...1971. Ottawa, 1973. 1 vol. (various pagings). *In English and French.*

— France.

GUYÉNOT (JEAN) The French law of agency and distributorship agreements. London, 1976. pp. 283.

FRANCIS FERDINAND, Archduke of Austria.

WUERTHLE (FRIEDRICH) Die Spur führt nach Belgrad: die Hintergründe des Dramas von Sarajevo, 1914. Wien, [1975]. pp. 352.

FRANCO BAHAMONDE (FRANCISCO).

HOTTINGER (ARNOLD) Spain in transition: Franco's regime. Beverly Hills, [1974]. pp. 62. *(Georgetown University. Center for Strategic and International Studies. Washington Papers. vol. 2/18)*

BLAYE (EDOUARD DE) Franco and the politics of Spain;...translated by Brian Pearce; postscript to part II by Richard Gott. Harmondsworth, 1976. pp. 576. *bibliog.*

FRANK (HANS).

POLAND (TERRITORY UNDER GERMAN OCCUPATION, 1939–1945). Generalgouverneur, 1975. Das Diensttagebuch des deutschen Generalgouverneurs in Polen, 1939-1945; herausgegeben von Werner Präg und Wolfgang Jacobmeyer. Stuttgart, 1975. pp. 1027. *(Institut für Zeitgeschichte. Quellen und Darstellungen zur Zeitgeschichte. Band 20)*

FREDERICK II, King of Prussia.

HUBATSCH (WALTHER) Frederick the Great of Prussia: absolutism and administration. London, [1975]. pp. 303. *bibliog.*

FREE LOVE.

ARMAND (EMILE) pseud. [i.e. Ernest Lucien JUIN] Entretien sur la liberté de l'amour. Orléans, Editions de L'En Dehors, [193-?]. pp. 16.

FREE TRADE AND PROTECTION.

ASSOCIATION POUR LA LIBERTE DES ECHANGES. Programme de réforme douanière proposé par l'Association pour la Liberté des Echanges. Paris, [1847]. pp. 29. *Signed by the President of the Association and by the general secretary, F. Bastiat. Issued with a covering circular from the secretary.*

BOUCKE (OSWALD FRED) Europe and the American tariff. New York, [1933]. pp. 163. *bibliog.*

HENTSCHEL (VOLKER) Die deutschen Freihändler und der volkswirtschaftliche Kongress, 1858 bis 1885. Stuttgart, [1975]. pp. 308. *bibliog. (Arbeitskreis für Moderne Sozialgeschichte. Industrielle Welt. Band 16)*

FREEDMEN IN THE UNITED STATES.

GERTEIS (LOUIS S.) From contraband to freedman: federal policy toward Southern blacks, 1861-1865. Westport, Conn., 1973. pp. 255. *bibliog.*

OSTHAUS (CARL R.) Freedmen, philanthropy, and fraud: a history of the Freedman's Savings Bank. Urbana, [1976]. pp. 257. *bibliog.*

FREEDOM OF ASSOCIATION
— Germany.

GERMANY. Reichstag. 1899. Die Zuchthausvorlage vor dem Reichstage: nach dem offiziellen stenographischen Bericht über die Verhandlungen des Deutschen Reichstages am 19., 20., 21. und 22. Juni 1899. Berlin, 1899. pp. 192.

FREEDOM OF INFORMATION
— France.

FRANCE. Commission de Coordination de la Documentation Administrative. 1975. La coordination documentaire: l'accès du public aux documents administratifs; deuxième rapport au Premier Ministre, Nov. 1974; documents annexes. Paris, 1975. pp. 91. *(Administration et Documentation)*

— Germany.

LASSALLE (FERDINAND JOHANN GOTTLIEB) Die Wissenschaft und die Arbeiter: eine Verteidigungs-Rede vor dem Berliner Kriminalgericht gegen die Anklage, die besitzlosen Klassen zum Hass und zur Verachtung gegen die Besitzenden öffentlich angereizt zu haben;...neue Ausgabe... von Eduard Bernstein. Berlin, 1908. pp. 55.

— United Kingdom.

YOUNG (HUGO) The Crossman affair. London, 1976. pp. 224.

— United States.

SHAPIRO (ANDREW O.) Media access: your rights to express your views on radio and television. Boston, [Mass., 1976]. pp. 297.

FREEMASONS
— United States.

MURASKIN (WILLIAM A.) Middle-class blacks in a white society: Prince Hall Freemasonry in America. Berkeley, [1975]. pp. 318. *bibliog.*

FREIE DEMOKRATISCHE PARTEI.

KAACK (HEINO) Zur Geschichte und Programmatik der Freien Demokratischen Partei: Grundriss und Materialien. Meisenheim am Glan, 1976. pp. 254. *bibliog.*

FREIGHT AND FREIGHTAGE
— Australia.

AUSTRALIA. Bureau of Transport Economics. 1973. Freight transport to north west Australia, 1975 to 1990. Canberra, 1973 repr. 1975. 1 vol. (various pagings).

— India — Mysore.

NATIONAL COUNCIL OF APPLIED ECONOMIC RESEARCH. Traffic survey of Mangalore and Malpe ports. Bangalore, Mysore Public Works Department, 1961. pp. 125.

— United Kingdom.

LONDON FREIGHT CONFERENCE, 1975. Freight in London: full review paper. [London], Greater London Council, 1975. pp. 145. *bibliog.*

LONDON FREIGHT CONFERENCE, 1975. Freight in London: short review paper, conference programme. [London], Greater London Council, 1975. pp. 20.

NATIONAL FREIGHT CORPORATION. Transport policy: the...Corporation's response to the consultation document. London, [1976]. pp. 66.

PAYNE (WILLIAM) Barrister-at-Law, and IVAMY (EDWARD RICHARD HARDY) Carriage of goods by sea; tenth edition by E.R. Hardy Ivamy. London, 1976. pp. 312.

FREISINNIG-DEMOKRATISCHE PARTEI.

For related heading see FREISINNIG-DEMOKRATISCHE PARTEI DES KANTONS SOLOTHURN.

FREISINNIG-DEMOKRATISCHE PARTEI DES KANTONS SOLOTHURN.

BUECHI (HERMANN) Hundert Jahre Solothurner Freisinn, 1830-1930. Solothurn, imprint, 1930. pp. 331.

FRENCH CANADIAN PERIODICALS.

JONES (RICHARD) 1943- . L'idéologie de L'Action Catholique, 1917-1939. Québec, 1974. pp. 359. *bibliog.*

FRENCH CANADIANS.

CLARK (ANDREW HILL) Acadia: the geography of early Nova Scotia to 1760. Madison, 1968. pp. 450. *bibliog.*

HUMPHREYS (JOHN) Historian. Plaisance: problems of settlement at this Newfoundland outpost of New France, 1660-1690. Ottawa, National Museums of Canada, 1970. pp. 24. *(National Museum of Man [Canada]. Publications in History. No. 3)*

JACKSON (JOHN D.) Community and conflict: (a study of French-English relations in Ontario). Toronto, [1975]. pp. 181. *bibliog.*

TROFIMENKOFF (SUSAN MANN) Action Française: French Canadian nationalism in the twenties. Toronto, [1975]. pp. 157. *bibliog.*

— **Bibliography.**

ALEXANDRIN (BARBARA) and BOTHWELL (ROBERT) compilers. Bibliography of the material culture of New France. Ottawa, National Museums of Canada, 1970. pp. 32. *(National Museum of Man [Canada]. Publications in History. No.4)*

FRENCH IN ALGERIA.

RIBS (JACQUES) Plaidoyer pour un million de victimes. Paris, [1975]. pp. 294.

FRENCH IN BOSNIA.

ŠAMIĆ (MIDHAT) Francuski putnici u Bosni na pragu XIX stoljeća i njihovi utisci o njoj; [translated from the French]. Sarajevo, 1966. pp. 312. *bibliog. With German summary.*

FRENCH IN BRAZIL.

SCHNEIDER (JUERGEN) Handel und Unternehmer im französischen Brasiliengeschäft, 1815-1848: Versuch einer quantitativen Strukturanalyse. Köln, 1975. pp. 649. *bibliog. With table of contents and summaries in various languages.*

FRENCH LANGUAGE

— **Dictionaries.**

LEXIS: dictionnaire de la langue française; (rédaction: Jean-Pierre Mével [and others]). Paris, [1975]. pp. 1950.

— — **English.**

LAMBERT (DENIS CLAIR) Dictionnaire français-anglais de l'économie monétaire: initiation économique. 2nd ed. Paris, [1975]. pp. 261.

— **Grammar.**

RUWET (NICOLAS) Théorie syntaxique et syntaxe du français. Paris, [1972]. pp. 299. *bibliog.*

— **Grammar, Generative.**

RUWET (NICOLAS) Problems in French syntax: transformational-generative studies; ...translated by Sheila M. Robins. London, 1976. pp. 307. *bibliog.*

— **Phonology.**

SKOUSEN (ROYAL) Substantive evidence in phonology: the evidence from Finnish and French. The Hague, 1975. pp. 135. *bibliog.*

— **Syntax.**

RUWET (NICOLAS) Théorie syntaxique et syntaxe du français. Paris, [1972]. pp. 299. *bibliog.*

KAYNE (RICHARD S.) French syntax: the transformational cycle. Cambridge, Mass., [1975]. pp. 473. *bibliog.*

RUWET (NICOLAS) Problems in French syntax: transformational-generative studies; ...translated by Sheila M. Robins. London, 1976. pp. 307. *bibliog.*

— **Vocabulary.**

Des TRACTS en mai 68: mesures de vocabulaire et de contenu; ([by] Michel Demonet [and others]). Paris, [1975]. pp. 491. *bibliog. (Fondation Nationale des Sciences Politiques. Travaux et Recherches de Science Politique. 31)*

FRENCH PERIODICALS.

BOURDOIS (JEAN PATRICK) La réforme administrative dans la "Revue générale d'administration", 1878-1928. Paris, [1975]. pp. 98. *(Paris. Université de Paris II. Travaux et Recherches. Série Science Administrative. 9)*

WINOCK (MICHEL) Histoire politique de la revue Esprit, 1930-1950. Paris, [1975]. pp. 447. *bibliog.*

FRENTE PORTUGAL LIVRE.

FRENTE PORTUGAL LIVRE. Declaracão, programa e estatutos da Frente Portugal Livre: liberdade, justiça, paz, revoluçao. [Paris, 1970]. pp. 11.

FRENTE PORTUGAL LIVRE. Déclaration, programme du Front Portugal Libre: liberté, justice, paix, révolution, etc. Paris, [1970?]. 1 pamphlet (unpaged).

FRESNEL (AUGUSTIN JEAN).

WORRALL (JOHN) The 19th century revolution in optics: a case study in the interaction between philosophy of science and history and sociology of science. 1975 [or rather 1976]. fo. 277. *bibliog. Typescript. Ph.D. (London) thesis: unpublished. This thesis is the property of London University and may not be removed from the Library.*

FREUD (SIGMUND).

LEE (SIDNEY GILMORE McKENZIE) and HERBERT (MARTIN) Freud and psychology: selected readings. Harmondsworth, 1970. pp. 398. *bibliogs.*

HOLMES (ROGER) Legitimacy and the politics of the knowable. London, 1976. pp. 191. *A collection of essays reprinted from various periodicals.*

FRIENDLY SOCIETIES.

ZORN (LEOPOLD) Die Entwicklung der Hilfskassen. Leipzig, 1912. pp. 82.

FRIENDS, SOCIETY OF.

DARTON (LAWRENCE) An account of the work of the Friends Committee for Refugees and Aliens, first known as the Germany Emergency Committee of the Society of Friends, 1933-1950. n.p., 1954. fo. 170.

SOCIETY OF FRIENDS. Friends' Peace and International Relations Committee. The abolition of torture folder. London, [1976?]. 1 folder.

FRIENDSHIP.

The COMPACT: selected dimensions of friendship; [including papers presented at a colloquium held in 1969 at St. John's, Newfoundland]; Elliott Leyton, editor. [St. John's, 1974]. pp. 162. *bibliog. (St. John's. Memorial University of Newfoundland. Institute of Social and Economic Research. Newfoundland Social and Economic Papers. No. 3)*

FRIULI

— **Social history.**

JACUMIN (RENATO) Le lotte contadine nel Friuli Orientale, 1891-1923. Udine, [1974]. pp. 525. *bibliog.*

FRONTIER AND PIONEER LIFE

— **United States.**

BRUCE (DICKSON D.) And they all sang hallelujah: plain-folk camp-meeting religion, 1800-1845. Knoxville, Tenn., [1974]. pp. 155. *bibliog.*

— — **New York (State).**

CONKLIN (HENRY) 1832-1915. Through "Poverty's Vale": a hardscrabble boyhood in upstate New York, 1832-1862;...edited with an introduction by Wendell Tripp. Syracuse, N.Y., 1974. pp. 264.

FRUIT JUICES.

VEREIN FÜR WIRTSCHAFTSHISTORISCHE STUDIEN. Schweizer Pioniere der Wirtschaft und Technik. 29. Herman Müller-Thurgau, 1850-1927...und weitere Pioniere der Qualitätsverbesserung des Weins und der unvergorenen Trauben- und Obstsäfte; von Robert Fritzsche [and others]. Zürich, 1974. pp. 131. *bibliog.*

FUEL

— **Prices — Bibliography.**

U.K. Electricity Council. Intelligence Section. Bibliographies. B 115. Social aspects of energy costs: select list of references, 1974- 1976: 31 references. London, 1976. pp. 8.

— **Sweden.**

OLSSON (SVEN OLOF) German coal and Swedish fuel, 1939-1945. Göteborg, 1975. pp. 348. *bibliog. (Göteborgs Universitet. Ekonomisk-Historiska Institutionen. Meddelanden. 36)*

— **United Kingdom — Prices.**

JOHNSON (MARIGOLD) and ROWLAND (MARK) Fuel debts and the poor. London, 1976. pp. 36. *(Child Poverty Action Group. Poverty Pamphlets. 24)*

U.K. Interdepartmental Working Group on Energy Tariffs. 1976. Energy tariffs and the poor. London, 1976. pp. 31.

FUEL TRADE

— **Netherlands.**

ECONOMISCH INSTITUUT VOOR HET MIDDEN- EN KLEINBEDRIJF. Bedrijfseconomische Publikaties. De bedrijfsstructuur en de bedrijfsuitkomsten van een aantal grotere detailhandelsbedrijven in vaste brandstof in de periode 1963/'64 tot en met 1966/'67. 's-Gravenhage, 1968. pp. 65.

FUENTERRABIA, SPAIN

— **Social conditions.**

GREENWOOD (DAVYDD J.) Unrewarding wealth: the commercialization and collapse of agriculture in a Spanish Basque town. Cambridge, 1976. pp. 223. *bibliog.*

FULL EMPLOYMENT POLICIES — Underdeveloped areas.

See UNDERDEVELOPED AREAS — Full employment policies.

FUNCTIONAL ANALYSIS.

HILLE (EINAR) and PHILLIPS (RALPH S.) Functional analysis and semi-groups. rev. ed. Providence, R.I., 1957 repr. 1974. pp. 808. *bibliog. (American Mathematical Society. Colloquium Publications. vol. 31)*

FUNCTIONAL ANALYSIS (SOCIAL SCIENCES).

ALBIN (PETER S.) The analysis of complex socioeconomic systems. Lexington, [1975]. pp. 150. *bibliog.*

FUND RAISING.

DAVIS (KING E.) Fund raising in the black community: history, feasibility, and conflict. Metuchen, N.J., 1975. pp. 169. *bibliog.*

FUR TRADE

— Canada.

CANADA. Department of Agriculture. Fur Section. 1971. The Canadian fur industry. rev. ed. [Ottawa], 1971. pp. 14. *(Department of Agriculture. Publications. 1201)*

— United States.

KERSEY (HARRY A.) Pelts, plumes and hides: white traders among the Seminole Indians, 1870-1930. Gainesville, Flo., 1975. pp. 158. *bibliog.*

FURNITURE INDUSTRY AND TRADE

— France.

FRANCE. Comité des Industries du Bois et de l'Ameublement. 1971. Préparation du VIe Plan...: rapport. [Paris], 1971. pp. 103.

GAJ (LJUDEVIT).

HORVAT (JOSIP) Ljudevit Gaj: njegov život, njegovo doba. Zagreb, 1975. pp. 399.

GALBRAITH (JOHN KENNETH).

DEUTSCH (JAN G.) compiler. Selling the people's Cadillac: the Edsel and corporate responsibility. New Haven, 1976. pp. 261.

GALIANI (FERDINANDO).

GALIANI (FERDINANDO) Nuovi saggi inediti di economia; a cura di Achille Agnati e introduzione di Giovanni Demaria. Padova, 1974. pp. 98.

NUCCIO (OSCAR) Economisti italiani del XVIII secolo: Ferdinando Galiani, Antonio Genovesi, Pietro Verri, Francesco Mengotti. Roma, 1974. pp. 286.

GALICIA (EASTERN EUROPE)

— History.

GRODZISKI (STANISŁAW) Historia ustroju społeczno politycznego Galicji, 1772-1848. Wrocław, 1971. pp. 301. *bibliog. (Polska Akademia Nauk. Oddział w Krakowie. Komisja Nauk Historycznych. Prace. Nr.28)* With German summary.

GLASSL (HORST) Das österreichische Einrichtungswerk in Galizien, 1772-1790. Wiesbaden, 1975. pp. 275. *bibliog. (Osteuropa-Institut, München. Veröffentlichungen. Reihe: Geschichte. Band 41)*

— — Sources.

OLSZAŃSKI (KAZIMIERZ) Prasa galicyjska wobec powstania styczniowego. Wrocław, 1975. pp. 254. *(Polska Akademia Nauk. Oddział w Krakowie. Komisja Nauk Historycznych. Prace. Nr.35)* With Russian and English summaries.

— Politics and government.

DZIKOWSKA (IRENA HOMOLA) Mikołaj Zyblikiewicz, 1823-1887. Wrocław, 1964. pp. 193. *(Polska Akademia Nauk. Oddział w Krakowie. Komisja Nauk Historycznych. Prace. Nr.10)*

— Population.

KOPCHAK (STEPAN IVANOVYCH) Naselennia Ukraïns'koho Prykarpattia: istoryko- demohrafichnyi narys: dokapitalistychnyi period. L'viv, 1974. pp. 186. *bibliog.*

GALICIA (SPAIN)

— Economic conditions.

CAMBRE MARIÑO (JESUS) Galicia ante el desequilibrio regional de España. Vigo, Galaxia, [1968]. pp. 61.

— Economic policy.

CAMBRE MARIÑO (JESUS) Galicia ante el desequilibrio regional de España. Vigo, Galaxia, [1968]. pp. 61.

GALLAGHER (JOHN).

LOUIS (WILLIAM ROGER) ed. Imperialism: the Robinson and Gallagher controversy. New York, 1976. pp. 252. *bibliog.*

GALWAY

— Civic improvement.

BUCHANAN (COLIN) AND PARTNERS. Galway city plan; a planning study commissioned by the United Nations on behalf of the government of Ireland. London, 1969 repr. 1970. pp. 127.

GAMBIA

— Census.

GAMBIA. Census, 1973. Population census 1973: statistics for settlements and enumeration areas. Banjul, 1974. 2 vols.

GAMBIA. Census, 1973. Population census, 1973: transcripts of recorded sample interviews. Banjul, 1974. fo.376.

— History.

ROBINSON (DAVID) Ph. D. Chiefs and clerics: Abdul Bokar Kan and Futa oro, 1853-1891. Oxford, 1975. pp. 239. *bibliog.*

— Politics and government.

HASWELL (MARGARET ROSARY) The nature of poverty: a case-history of the first quarter-century after World War II. London, 1975. pp. 234. *bibliog.*

— Social conditions.

HASWELL (MARGARET ROSARY) The nature of poverty: a case-history of the first quarter-century after World War II. London, 1975. pp. 234. *bibliog.*

GAMBLING.

ORE (OYSTEIN) Cardano: the gambling scholar;...with a translation from the Latin of Cardano's Book on games of chance, by Sydney Henry Gould: [reprint of the work originally published at Princeton, 1953]. New York, 1965. pp. 249. *bibliog.*

— United Kingdom.

GAMBLING, work and leisure: a study across three areas; [by] D.M. Downes [and others]. London, 1976. pp. 260.

GAMES, THEORY OF.

RAPOPORT (ANATOL) Two-person game theory: the essential ideas. Ann Arbor, [1966]. pp. 229. *bibliog.*

AUMANN (ROBERT J.) and SHAPLEY (L.S.) Values of non-atomic games. Princeton, N.J., [1974]. pp. 333. *bibliog. (Rand Corporation. Research Studies)*

SHUBIK (MARTIN) The uses and methods of gaming. New York, [1975]. pp. 208. *bibliog.*

GAMPER (MICHAEL).

EULER (ALOIS) Michael Gamper: Hirte und Herold von Südtirol; eine Dokumentation...; herausgegeben von Robert H. Drechsler. Wien, 1976. pp. 265.

GANDHI (MOHANDAS KARAMCHAND).

GOPALASWAMI (K.) Gandhi and Bombay. Bombay, 1969. pp. 566. *bibliog.*

GARAGES

— South Africa.

SOUTH AFRICA. Bureau of Statistics. 1976. Census of motor trade and repair services, 1970. [Pretoria, 1976]. pp. 148. *(Reports. No. 04-16-02)* In English and Afrikaans.

GARAUDY (ROGER).

GARAUDY (ROGER) Parole d'homme. Paris, [1975]. pp. 265.

GARDEN CITIES

— United Kingdom.

DARLEY (GILLIAN) Villages of vision. London, 1975. pp. 152. *bibliog.*

GARDINER DAM.

CANADA. Department of Regional Economic Expansion. 1970. South Saskatchewan river project, 1958-1967. [Ottawa, 1970]. 1 pamphlet (unpaged).

GARRATT (VERO W.)

GARRATT (VERO W.) A man in the street. London, 1939. pp. 317.

GARVEY (MARCUS).

CRONON (EDMUND DAVID) ed. Marcus Garvey. Englewood Cliffs, N.J., [1973]. pp. 176. *bibliog.*

GAS, NATURAL.

UNITED STATES. Central Intelligence Agency. 1976. Major oil and gas fields of the free world. [Washington], 1976. pp. 30. *(Research Aids. No.ER 76-10001)* Microfilm: 1 reel.

— Law and legislation — Canada.

CANADA. Statutes, etc. 1952-68. Office consolidation of the Canada Oil and Gas Land Regulations, oil and gas land orders, Public Lands Grants Act, Territorial Lands Act. [Ottawa], 1968. pp. 73.

— Europe.

The POLITICAL implications of North Sea oil and gas: [papers presented to a conference at Tønsberg in February 1975, sponsored by the Norwegian Institute of International Affairs and the Royal Institute of International Affairs]; edited by Martin Saeter and Ian Smart. Oslo, [1975]. pp. 168.

— Russia.

ECONOMIST INTELLIGENCE UNIT. Q[uarterly] E[conomic] R[eview] Specials. No. 24. Soviet natural gas to 1985. London, 1975. pp. 49.

KOSNIK (JOSEPH T.) Natural gas imports from the Soviet Union: financing the North Star Joint Venture Project. New York, 1975. pp. 214. *bibliog.*

— United Kingdom — Rates.

REVIEW of payment and collection methods for gas and electricity bills; report of an informal inquiry; [Gordon Oakes, chairman] . London, Department of Energy, 1976. pp. 33.

— United States.

EPPLE (DENNIS N.) Petroleum discoveries and government policy: an econometric study of supply. Cambridge, Mass., [1975]. pp. 139. *bibliog.*

KOSNIK (JOSEPH T.) Natural gas imports from the Soviet Union: financing the North Star Joint Venture Project. New York, 1975. pp. 214. *bibliog.*

GAS, NATURAL, IN SUBMERGED LANDS

— United Kingdom — Equipment and supplies.

U.K. Offshore Supplies Office. 1974. Offshore supplies interest relief grants: a guide for industry. 2nd ed. Glasgow, 1974. pp. 16.

U.K. Offshore Supplies Office. 1975. OSO: (background information which will help a company decide whether it can supply goods or a service needed offshore and how it could go about preparing its own market strategy). Glasgow, [1975]. pp. 144. *bibliog. In end pocket: Incentives for industry in the areas for expansion.*

GAS INDUSTRY

— Russia.

SYR'EVAIA baza gazovoi promyshlennosti SSSR deviatoi piatiletki: tematicheskii nauchno-tekhnicheskii obzor. Moskva, 1972. pp. 56. *bibliog.*

— — Ukraine.

PERSPEKTIVY obespecheniia gazovoi promyshlennosti USSR resursami prirodnogo gaza. Moskva, 1972. pp. 255.

GAULLE (CHARLES DE).

BINOCHE (JACQUES) L'Allemagne et le Général de Gaulle, 1924-1970. [Paris, 1975]. pp. 229.

COINTET (JEAN PAUL) La France Libre. [Paris], 1975. pp. 135. *bibliog.*

GÄVLE

— Politics and government.

ÅBERG (INGRID) Förening och politik: folkrörelsernas politiska aktivitet i Gävle under 1880-talet. Uppsala, 1975. pp. 163. *bibliog. (Uppsala. Universitet. Historiska Institutionen. Studia Historica Upsaliensia. 69) With English summary.*

GAY LIBERATION MOVEMENT.

LAURITSEN (JOHN) and THORSTAD (DAVID) The early homosexual rights movement, 1864-1935. New York, [1974]. pp. 93. *bibliog.*

GAZE

— Psychological aspects.

ARGYLE (MICHAEL) and COOK (MARK) Gaze and mutual gaze. Cambridge, 1976. pp. 210. *bibliog.*

GDANSK

— Politics and government.

DZIALACZE polscy i przedstawiciele RP w Wolnym Mieście Gdańsku. Gdańsk, 1974. pp. 261. *bibliog. (Gdańsk. Gdańskie Towarzystwo Naukowe. Wydział I Nauk Społecznych i Humanistycznych. Seria Popularnonaukowa Pomorze Gdańskie. Nr. 9)*

GENERAL AGREEMENT ON TARIFFS AND TRADE.

ATLANTIC COUNCIL OF THE UNITED STATES. Trade Committee. Special Advisory Panel. GATT plus: a proposal for trade reform, with the text of the General Agreement; report. New York, 1975. pp. 194.

LORTIE (PIERRE) Economic integration and the law of GATT. New York, [1975]. pp. 177.

GENERAL STRIKE, UNITED KINGDOM, 1926.

TRORY (ERNIE) Brighton and the General Strike. Brighton, 1975. pp. 32.

NOEL (GERARD EYRE) The great lock-out of 1926. London, 1976. pp. 239. *bibliog.*

PHILLIPS (GORDON A.) The General Strike: the politics of industrial conflict. London, [1976]. pp. 388. *bibliog.*

SKELLEY (JEFFREY) ed. The General Strike, 1926. London, 1976. pp. 412.

GENERALS.

SOLDIERS as statesmen; [based on papers presented at a symposium held at the Royal Military College of Canada, Kingston, Ontario in 1975]; edited by Peter Dennis and Adrian Preston. London, 1976. pp. 184. *bibliogs.*

GENERATIVE GRAMMAR.

GENERATIVE studies in historical linguistics: [papers presented at a colloquium at the University of North Carolina, 1969]; edited by Maria Tsiapera. Edmonton, [1971]. pp. 87. *bibliogs.*

CHOMSKY (NOAM) The logical structure of linguistic theory. New York, [1975]. pp. 573. *bibliog.*

BRAME (MICHAEL K.) Conjectures and refutations in syntax and semantics. New York, [1976]. pp. 160. *bibliog.*

CULICOVER (PETER W.) Syntax. New York, [1976]. pp. 316. *bibliogs.*

GENETICS

— Mathematical models.

THOMPSON (E.A.) Fellow of King's College, Cambridge. Human evolutionary trees. Cambridge, 1975. pp. 158. *bibliog.*

GENEVA (CANTON)

— Politics and government.

GROUNAUER (MARIE MADELEINE) La Genève rouge de Léon Nicole, 1933-1936. [Geneva, 1975]. pp. 236. *bibliog.*

GENEVA CONVENTIONS.

ZAORSKI (REMIGIUSZ) Konwencje genewskie o prawie morza. Gdynia, 1962. pp. 275. *bibliog. With Russian and English summaries.*

GENOVESI (ANTONIO).

NUCCIO (OSCAR) Economisti italiani del XVIII secolo: Ferdinando Galiani, Antonio Genovesi, Pietro Verri, Francesco Mengotti. Roma, 1974. pp. 286.

GENTILE (GIOVANNI).

LALLA (MANLIO DI) Vita di Giovanni Gentile. Firenze, [1975]. pp. 546.

GEOGRAPHERS.

DICKINSON (ROBERT ERIC) Regional concept: the Anglo-American leaders. London, 1976. pp. 408.

GEOGRAPHERS, MOHAMMEDAN.

MIQUEL (ANDRE) La géographie humaine du monde musulman jusqu'au milieu du 11e siècle. Paris, 1967-75. 2 vols. *bibliogs. (Paris. Ecole Pratique des Hautes Etudes. Section des Sciences Economiques et Sociales. Centre de Recherches Historiques. Civilisations et Sociétés. 7, 37)*

GEOGRAPHICAL DISTRIBUTION OF ANIMALS AND PLANTS.

BIOGEOGRAPHY and ecology in South America; edited by E.J. Fittkau [and others]. The Hague, 1968-9. 2 vols. *bibliogs. In various languages.*

GEOGRAPHICAL PERCEPTION.

POCOCK (DOUGLAS CHARLES DAVID) Durham: images of a cathedral city. Durham, 1975. pp. 80. *bibliog. (Durham. University. Department of Geography. Occasional Publications (New Series). No.6)*

SHANKLAND-COX PARTNERSHIP and INSTITUTE OF COMMUNITY STUDIES. Inner area study: Lambeth: schools project. [London], Department of the Environment, [1976]. pp. 28. (22).

WATSON (JAMES WREFORD) and O'RIORDAN (TIMOTHY) eds. The American environment: perceptions and policies. London, [1976]. pp. 340. *bibliogs.*

GEOGRAPHY

— Bibliography.

LESZCZYCKI (STANISŁAW) and WINID (BOGODAR) compilers. Bibliografia geografii polskiej, 1945-1951. Warszawa, 1956. pp. 218. *With Russian and English summaries.*

HARRIS (CHAUNCY DENNISON) compiler. Bibliography of geography. Chicago, 1976 in progress. *(Chicago. University. Department of Geography. Research Papers. No. 179)*

— History.

MIQUEL (ANDRE) La géographie humaine du monde musulman jusqu'au milieu du 11e siècle. Paris, 1967-75. 2 vols. *bibliogs. (Paris. Ecole Pratique des Hautes Etudes. Section des Sciences Economiques et Sociales. Centre de Recherches Historiques. Civilisations et Sociétés. 7, 37)*

— Methodology.

CHISHOLM (MICHAEL) Human geography: evolution or revolution?. Harmondsworth, 1975. pp. 207. *bibliog.*

— Periodicals — Indexes.

POLSKA AKADEMIA NAUK. Instytut Geografii. Geographia Polonica. Index to Geographia Polonica, volumes 1-32; compiled by Halina Tuszyńska-Rękawek [and others]. [Warsaw, 1976?]. pp. 34.

— Study and teaching.

INTERNATIONAL GEOGRAPHICAL UNION. Regional Conference [in New Zealand], 1974. Proceedings of the International Geographical Union Regional Conference and eighth New Zealand Geography Conference, Palmerston North, December 1974; edited by William Brockie [and others]. [Christchurch], 1975. pp. 380. *bibliogs. (New Zealand Geographical Society. Conference Series. No. 8)*

— — United Kingdom.

DICKINSON (ROBERT ERIC) Regional concept: the Anglo-American leaders. London, 1976. pp. 408.

— — United States.

DICKINSON (ROBERT ERIC) Regional concept: the Anglo-American leaders. London, 1976. pp. 408.

GEOGRAPHY, ECONOMIC.

QUAINI (MASSIMO) Marxismo e geografia. Firenze, 1974. pp. 162. *bibliog.*

CHISHOLM (GEORGE GOUDIE) Handbook of commercial geography; entirely rewritten by Sir Dudley Stamp; nineteenth edition revised by G. Noel Blake and Audrey N. Clark. London, 1975. pp. 984.

BERRY (BRIAN JOE LOBLEY) and others. The geography of economic systems. Englewood Cliffs, N.J., [1976]. pp. 529. *bibliogs.*

CONKLING (EDGAR C.) and YEATES (MAURICE H.) Man's economic environment. New York, [1976]. pp. 308. *bibliog.*

GEOGRAPHY, POLITICAL.

JACKSON (WILLIAM ARTHUR DOUGLAS) and BERGMAN (EDWARD F.) A geography of politics. Dubuque, Iowa, [1973]. pp. 92.

COX (KEVIN R.) and others, eds. Locational approaches to power and conflict. New York, [1974]. pp. 339. *bibliogs.*

BUSTEED (M.A.) Geography and voting behaviour. London, 1975. pp. 60. *bibliog.*

DIKSHIT (RAMESH DUTTA) The political geography of federalism: an inquiry into origins and stability. London, 1975. pp. 273. *bibliog.*

GEOLOGY

GEOLOGY

— Africa — Surveys.

U.K. Institute of Geological Sciences. 1973. 50th anniversary Geological Survey and Mines Department, Uganda. London, 1973. pp. 183. *bibliogs.* (*Overseas Geology and Mineral Resources. [New Series]. No.41*)

— Solomon Islands.

ALLUM (J.A.E.) Regional photogeological interpretation of the British Solomon Islands; report;...aerial geophysical surveys project UNSF- BSIP 1965-1968. Honiara, 1967. pp. 78. *bibliog. 10 maps in end pocket.*

— Somali Republic — Bibliography.

PURI (R.K.) compiler. Bibliography relating to geology, mineral resources, palaentology [sic] etc., of Somali Republic. [Hargeisa?], 1961. fo. 13. (*Somali Republic. Geological Survey. Reports. RKP/1*)

— Uganda — Surveys.

U.K. Institute of Geological Sciences. 1973. 50th anniversary Geological Survey and Mines Department, Uganda. London, 1973. pp. 183. *bibliogs.* (*Overseas Geology and Mineral Resources. [New Series]. No.41*)

— United Kingdom — Surveys.

BULLETIN OF THE GEOLOGICAL SURVEY OF GREAT BRITAIN (Institute of Geological Sciences [U.K.]). irreg., 1939 (no.1)- London.

— — Scotland.

SCOTLAND. Geological Survey. Memoirs. The geology of western Shetland; explanation of one-inch geological sheet western Shetland; comprising sheet 127 and parts of 125, 126 and 128; by W. Mykura and J. Phemister, with a contribution by P.A. Sabine. Edinburgh, 1976. pp. 304. *bibliogs.*

GEOMETRY, ALGEBRAIC.

GROTHENDIECK (A.) and DIEUDONNE (JEAN A.) Eléments de géométrie algébrique: I. Berlin, 1971. pp. 466. *bibliog.*

GEOMETRY, DIFFERENTIAL.

SPIVAK (MICHAEL) A comprehensive introduction to differential geometry. Boston, Mass., [1970-1975]. 5 vols. *bibliog.*

GEOMORPHOLOGY, CLIMATIC.

See CLIMATIC GEOMORPHOLOGY.

GEOPOLITICS.

MODZHORIAN (LIDIIA ARTEM'EVNA) Geopolitika na sluzhbe voennykh avantiur. Moskva, 1974. pp. 192.

PATRICK (RICHARD ARTHUR) Political geography and the Cyprus conflict, 1963-1971;...edited by James H. Bater and Richard Preston. Waterloo, Ont., [1976]. pp. 481. *bibliogs.* (*University of Waterloo, [Ontario]. Department of Geography. Publication Series. No.4*) *A collection of major published and unpublished works.*

GEORGE VI, King of Great Britain and Ireland.

TOWNSEND (PETER) 1914- . The last emperor: decline and fall of the British Empire. London, [1975]. pp. 287. *bibliog.*

GEORGE (DAVID LLOYD) 1st Earl Lloyd George.

ROWLAND (PETER) Lloyd George. London, 1975. pp. 872. *bibliog.*

SCALLY (ROBERT JAMES) The origins of the Lloyd George coalition: the politics of social-imperialism, 1900-1918. Princeton, [1975]. pp. 416. *bibliog.*

WRIGLEY (CHRIS) David Lloyd George and the British labour movement: peace and war. Hassocks, Sussex, 1976. pp. 298. *bibliog.*

GEORGIA

— Description and travel.

MESKHI (IIA SEMENOVNA) and TUNKEL' (ISAAK ROMANOVICH) Gruzinskie tetradi. Tbilisi, 1970. 4 vols. *Illustrated.*

— Economic conditions.

NATMELADZE (MAKVALA VASIL'EVNA) and STURUA (NIKOLAI IVANOVICH) Rabochii klass Gruzii v stroitel'stve material'no- tekhnicheskoi bazy sotsializma i kommunizma v SSSR. Tbilisi, 1975. pp. 97.

— History.

MESKHIA (SHOTA AMBAKOVICH) Didgorskaia bitva. Tbilisi, 1974. pp. 124. *Russian colophon gives author's patronymic as 'Ambrosovich'.*

— — Sources.

MATERIALY po istorii russko-gruzinskikh otnoshenii, 80-90-e gody XVII veka. Tbilisi, 1974 in progress.

— Industries.

KOBAKHIDZE (E.D.) Promyshlennyi kompleks Gruzinskoi SSR: ekonomiko-geograficheskoe issledovanie. Tbilisi, 1974. pp. 142.

— Politics and government.

PIRADOV (B.) Na rubezhe: M. Gor'kii v Gruzii nakanune revoliutsii 1905 goda. Tbilisi, 1975. pp. 211.

GEORGIA (UNITED STATES)

— Economic history.

HOLMES (MICHAEL S.) The New Deal in Georgia: an administrative history. Westport, Conn., [1975]. pp. 364. *bibliog.*

— Politics and government.

ANDERSON (WILLIAM) b. 1941. The wild man from Sugar Creek: the political career of Eugene Talmadge. Baton Rouge, 1975. pp. 268. *bibliog.*

GEORGIAN PERIODICALS.

ASATIANI (VLADIMIR ANTIMOZOVICH) Periodicheskaia pechat' Gruzii v bor'be za kollektivizatsiiu sel'skogo khoziaistva i likvidatsiiu kulachestva. Tbilisi, 1974. pp. 92.

GERHARDSEN (EINAR).

HELLE (EGIL) Einar Gerhardsen. [Oslo, 1975]. pp. 48.

GERMAN LANGUAGE

— Dictionaries — English.

MURUGIAH (R. THARMALINGAM) ed. Concise economic dictionary and encyclopaedia of socialist economics: German-English; by Manfred Engert [and others] . Berlin, [1975]. pp. 283.

GERMAN LITERATURE

— History and criticism.

ZETKIN (CLARA) Über Literatur und Kunst: [selected articles, originally published in "Die Gleichheit", 1906-1911]; zusammengestellt und herausgegeben von Emilia Zetkin-Milowidowa. Berlin, 1955. pp. 115.

GERMAN NAVAL MUTINY.

See KIEL MUTINY.

GERMAN NEWSPAPERS.

FISCHER (HEINZ DIETRICH) ed. Pressekonzentration und Zensurpraxis im Ersten Weltkrieg: Texte und Quellen. Berlin, 1973. pp. 301. *bibliogs.*

LIEBKNECHT (WILHELM PHILIPP MARTIN CHRISTIAN LUDWIG) Leitartikel und Beiträge in der Osnabrücker Zeitung, 1864- 1866; herausgegeben von Georg Eckert. Hildesheim, 1975. pp. 794. (*Historische Kommission für Niedersachsen und Bremen. Veröffentlichungen. 35*)

PELGER (HANS) and KNIERIEM (MICHAEL) Friedrich Engels als Bremer Korrespondent des Stuttgarter "Morgenblatts für gebildete Leser" und der Augsburger "Allgemeinen Zeitung". Trier, [1975]. pp. 64. (*Karl-Marx-Haus. Schriften. 15*)

TREUDE (BURKHARD) Konservative Presse und Nationalsozialismus: Inhaltsanalyse der 'Neuen Preussischen (Kreuz-) Zeitung' am Ende der Weimarer Republik. Bochum, 1975. pp. 195. *bibliog.*

BOSCH (MICHAEL) Liberale Presse in der Krise: die Innenpolitik der Jahre 1930 bis 1933 im Spiegel des "Berliner Tageblatts", der "Frankfurter Zeitung" und der "Vossischen Zeitung". Bern, 1976. pp. 343. *bibliog.*

TOELCKE (CARL WILHELM) Presseberichte zur Entwicklung der deutschen Sozialdemokratie, 1848-1893: Quellen zur Geschichte der deutschen Arbeiterbewegung; bearbeitet von Arno Herzig. München, 1976. pp. 278. *bibliog.* (*Institut für Zeitungsforschung der Stadt Dortmund. Dortmunder Beiträge zur Zeitungsforschung. Band 22*)

GERMAN PERIODICALS.

HAY (JOSEPH) Staat, Volk und Weltbürgertum in der Berlinischen Monatsschrift von Friedrich Gedike und Johann Erich Biester, 1783-96. Berlin, 1913. pp. 83. *bibliog.*

SCHOENBAUM (DAVID) Ein Abgrund von Landesverrat: die Affäre um den "Spiegel"; (aus dem Englischen übertragen von Armin Sellheim). Wien, 1968. pp. 254.

FUHRMANN (RAINER) Die Orientalische Frage, das "panslawistisch-chauvinistische Lager" und das Zuwarten auf Krieg und Revolution: die Osteuropaberichterstattung und -vorstellungen der "Deutschen Rundschau", 1874-1918. Bern, 1975. pp. 200. *bibliog. With English summary.*

SCHMOLLINGER (HORST W.) and STOESS (RICHARD) Die Parteien und die Presse der Parteien und Gewerkschaften in der Bundesrepublik Deutschland, 1945-1974: Materialien zur Parteien- und Gewerkschaftsforschung. München, 1975. pp. 480. *bibliogs.* (*Berlin. Freie Universität. Zentralinstitut für Sozialwissenschaftliche Forschung. Berichte und Materialien. Band 2*)

— Indexes.

HEINTZ (GEORG) compiler. Index des "Freien/Neuen Deutschland", Mexico, 1941-1946. [Worms, 1975]. pp. 110.

GERMAN REUNIFICATION QUESTION (1949—).

GERMANY (BUNDESREPUBLIK). Forschungsbeirat für Fragen der Wiedervereinigung Deutschlands. 1967. Preparing Germany's unity: excerpts from the fourth progress report, 1961-1965. Bonn, 1967. pp. 170. *Maps in end pocket.*

SCHLUETER (HILMAR WERNER) Die Wiedervereinigung Deutschlands: ein zeitgeschichtlicher Leitfaden. 6th ed. Bad Godesberg, 1967. pp. 184. *bibliog.*

ADAM (ALFRED) Pressesprecher. Das Bundesministerium für innerdeutsche Beziehungen. Bonn, [1971]. pp. 104. *bibliog.*

SOWDEN (JOHN KENNETH) The German question, 1945-1973: continuity in change. London, 1975. pp. 404. *bibliog.*

GERMANY

— Bibliography.

GERMANY (BUNDESREPUBLIK). Bundesministerium für Gesamtdeutsche Fragen. 1966. Literatur zur deutschen Frage: bibliographische Hinweise auf neuere Veröffentlichungen aus dem In- und Auslande; (bearbeitet...von Günter Fischbach). 4th ed. Bonn, [1966]. pp. 323.

GERMANI (GINO).

KAHL (JOSEPH ALAN) Modernization, exploitation and dependency in Latin America: Germani, González Casanova and Cardoso. New Brunswick, [1976]. pp. 215. *bibliogs.*

GERMANS IN BRAZIL.

ALBERSHEIM (URSULA) Uma comunidade teuto-brasileira: Jarim. Rio de Janeiro, Centro Brasileiro de Pesquisas Educacionais, 1962. pp. 236. *bibliog.* (*Publicações. Serie VI. Sociedade e Educação. Coleção O Brasil Provinciano. Vol.2*)

GERMANS IN CANADA.

MOELLMANN (ALBERT) Das Deutschtum in Montreal. Jena, 1937. pp. 124. *bibliog.* (*Marburg. Universität. Institut für Grenz- und Auslanddeutschtum. Schriften. Heft 11*)

GERMANS IN CZECHOSLOVAKIA.

CAMPBELL (F. GREGORY) Confrontation in Central Europe: Weimar Germany and Czechoslovakia. Chicago, 1975. pp. 383. *bibliog.*

PAUL (ERNST) Oswald Hillebrand: ein Lebensbild nach archivalischen Unterlagen, etc. Stuttgart, 1976. pp. 78.

ZESSNER (KLAUS) Josef Seliger und die nationale Frage in Böhmen: eine Untersuchung über die nationale Politik der deutschböhmischen Sozialdemokratie, 1899-1920. Stuttgart, [1976]. pp. 257. *bibliog.*

GERMANS IN DENMARK.

NOACK (JOHAN PETER) Det tyske mindretal i Nordslesvig under besaettelsen. [Copenhagen, 1975]. pp. 213. *bibliog.* (*Dansk Udenrigspolitisk Institut. Skrifter. 6*)

GERMANS IN EASTERN EUROPE.

HACKER (WERNER) Auswanderungen aus dem nördlichen Bodenseeraum im 17. und 18. Jahrhundert; archivalisch dokumentiert. Singen, 1975. pp. 400. *bibliog.* (*Verein für Geschichte des Hegaus. Hegau- Bibliothek. Band 29*)

GERMANS IN ESTONIA.

GARLEFF (MICHAEL) Deutschbaltische Politik zwischen den Weltkriegen: die parlamentarische Tätigkeit der deutschbaltischen Parteien in Lettland und Estland. Bonn-Bad Godesberg, [1976]. pp. 224. *bibliog.* (*Baltische Historische Kommission. Quellen und Studien zur Baltischen Geschichte. Band 2*)

GERMANS IN LATVIA.

GARLEFF (MICHAEL) Deutschbaltische Politik zwischen den Weltkriegen: die parlamentarische Tätigkeit der deutschbaltischen Parteien in Lettland und Estland. Bonn-Bad Godesberg, [1976]. pp. 224. *bibliog.* (*Baltische Historische Kommission. Quellen und Studien zur Baltischen Geschichte. Band 2*)

GERMANS IN MEXICO

— Periodicals — Indexes.

HEINTZ (GEORG) compiler. Index des "Freien/Neuen Deutschland", Mexico, 1941-1946. [Worms, 1975]. pp. 110.

GERMANS IN POLAND.

PARADOWSKA (MARIA) Bambrzy: mieszkańcy dawnych wsi miasta Poznania. Warszawa, 1975. pp. 177. (*Poznań. Urząd Miasta. Wydział Kultury. Biblioteka Kroniki Miasta Poznania*)

GERMANS IN SILESIA.

BIAŁY (FRANCISZEK) Niemieckie ochotnicze formacje Śląsku, 1918-1923. Katowice, 1976. pp. 210. *bibliog.*

GERMANS IN SUBSAHARAN AFRICA.

WEINBERGER (GERDA) An den Quellen der Apartheid: Studien über koloniale Ausbeutungs- und Herrschaftsmethoden in Südafrika, etc. Berlin, 1975. pp. 217. *bibliog.*

GERMANS IN THE BALTIC STATES.

LATVIISKII GOSUDARSTVENNYI UNIVERSITET. Uchenye Zapiski. t.219. Germaniia i Pribaltika. 3. Riga, 1974. pp. 107.

GERMANS IN THE UKRAINE.

ARNDT (NIKOLAUS) Die Shitomirer Arndts: eine Familienchronik auf dem Hintergrund hundertfünfzigjähriger Geschichte der westlichen Ukraine. Würzburg, [1970]. pp. 151. *bibliog.*

GERMANS IN THE UNITED STATES.

MOLTMANN (GUENTER) ed. Deutsche Amerikaauswanderung im 19. Jahrhundert: sozialgeschichtliche Beiträge;...von Harald Focke [and others]. Stuttgart, [1976]. pp. 218. *bibliog.* (*Deutsche Gesellschaft für Amerikastudien. Amerikastudien. Band 44*)

GERMANY

— Air force.

SCHAETZ (LUDWIG) Schüler-Soldaten: die Geschichte der Luftwaffenhelfer im zweiten Weltkrieg. 2nd ed. Darmstadt, 1974. pp. 160. *bibliog.*

— Armed forces.

HORNUNG (KLAUS) Staat und Armee: Studien zur Befehls- und Kommandogewalt und zum politisch-militärischen Verhältnis in der Bundesrepublik Deutschland. Mainz, [1975]. pp. 448. *bibliog.*

MILITAERGESCHICHTLICHES FORSCHUNGSAMT. Verteidigung im Bündnis: Planung, Aufbau und Bewährung der Bundeswehr, 1950-1972. München, [1975]. pp. 502. *bibliog.*

— Army — History.

ENGEL (GERHARD) Heeresadjutant bei Hitler, 1938-1943: Aufzeichnungen des Majors Engel; herausgegeben und kommentiert von Hildegard von Kotze. Stuttgart, [1974]. pp. 158. *bibliog.* (*Vierteljahrshefte für Zeitgeschichte. Schriftenreihe. Nr. 29*)

— Biography.

WER ist wer?: das deutsche Who's who, (1974/75)...; herausgegeben von Walter Habel; XVIII. Ausgabe von Degeners Wer ist's?: Bundesrepublik Deutschland und West-Berlin. Frankfurt am Main, [1975]. pp. 1222.

— — Bibliography.

INSTITUT FÜR ZEITGESCHICHTE. Bibliothek. Biographischer Katalog. Boston, Mass., 1967. pp. 764.

INSTITUT FÜR ZEITGESCHICHTE. Bibliothek. Erster Nachtragsband: Biographischer Katalog; Länderkatalog. Boston, Mass., 1973. pp. 588.

— Boundaries.

DOMINICZAK (HENRYK) Granica polsko-niemiecka 1919-1939: z dziejów formacji granicznych. Warszawa, 1975. pp. 292. *bibliog.*

SKUBISZEWSKI (KRZYSZTOF) Zachodnia granica Polski w świetle traktatów. Poznań, 1975. pp. 369. *bibliog.* (*Poznań. Instytut Zachodni. Studia Niemcoznawcze. Nr.26*) *With English summary.*

— — Denmark.

SVALASTOGA (KAARE) Where Europeans meet: a SOCIOLOGICAL INVESTIGATION OF A BORDER TOWN. Copenhagen, 1960. fo. 144. *Lacking section 7. Documents.*

— Bundesrat.

RAUSCH (HEINZ) Bundestag und Bundesregierung: eine Institutionenkunde. 4th ed. München, 1976. pp. 356. *bibliog.*

— Bundestag.

DOBIEY (BURKHARD) Die politische Planung als verfassungsrechtliches Problem zwischen Bundesregierung und Bundestag. Berlin, [1975]. pp. 170. *bibliog.*

GERMANY (BUNDESREPUBLIK). Deutscher Bundestag. Wissenschaftliche Dienste. 1975. Mitgliederstruktur des Deutschen Bundestages, I.- VII. Wahlperiode: Materialzusammenstellung und Auswahlbibliographie; [edited by Edith Dalades]. Bonn, 1975. pp. 314. *bibliog.* (*Materialen. 40*)

GERMANY (BUNDESREPUBLIK). Deutscher Bundestag. Wissenschaftliche Dienste. 1975. Die Wissenschaftlichen Dienste des Deutschen Bundestages. Bonn, 1975. pp. 18. (*Materialen. 41.*)

KISSLER (LEO) Die Öffentlichkeitsfunktion des Deutschen Bundestages: Theorie, Empirie, Reform. Berlin, [1976]. pp. 661. *bibliog.*

RAUSCH (HEINZ) Bundestag und Bundesregierung: eine Institutionenkunde. 4th ed. München, 1976. pp. 356. *bibliog.*

— — Committees.

PATZ (GUENTHER) Parlamentarische Kontrolle der Aussenpolitik: Fallstudien zur politischen Bedeutung des Auswärtigen Ausschusses des Deutschen Bundestages. Meisenheim am Glan, 1976. pp. 190. *bibliog.*

— — Elections.

SOZIALDEMOKRATISCHE PARTEI DEUTSCHLANDS. Vorstand. Bundestagswahlkampf 1972: ein Bericht...; herausgegeben von Holger Börner. Bonn, [1973]. pp. 63.

GERMANY (BUNDESREPUBLIK). Deutscher Bundestag. Wissenschaftliche Dienste. 1976. Wahl zum Deutschen Bundestag: Wahlrecht, Wahlkampf, Wahlanalyse: Auswahlbibliographie mit Annotationen; [compiled by Inge Schlieper]. Bonn, 1976. pp. 30. (*Bibliographien. 45*)

— — Resolutions.

GRUPP (CORNELIUS) Die parlamentarische Kontrolle der auswärtigen Gewalt in Form von Entschliessungen. Augsburg, 1975. pp. 194. *bibliog. Dissertation zur Erlangung des Grades eines Doktors der Rechte (Universität Augsburg).*

— — Rules and practice.

RUMMEL (ALOIS) Der Bundestagspräsident: Amt, Funktionen, Personen. Stuttgart, [1974]. pp. 162. *bibliog.*

— Census.

GERMANY. Statistisches Reichsamt. Statistik des Deutschen Reichs. Neue Folge. Band 32. Die Volkszählung im Deutschen Reich am 1. Dezember 1885. Osnabrück, 1974. pp. 96,245. *Photographic reprint of 1888 ed. originally published in Berlin. Map in end pocket.*

GERMANY. Statistisches Reichsamt. Statistik des Deutschen Reichs. Neue Folge. Band 68. Die Volkszählung am 1 Dezember 1890 im Deutschen Reich: Tabellen mit Erläuterungen und graphischen Darstellungen. Osnabrück, 1975. pp. 91,201. *Photographic reprint of 1894 ed. originally published in Berlin.*

— Civilization.

HEINEMANN (GUSTAV WALTER) Reden und Schriften. Frankfurt am Main, 1975 in progress.

GERMANY (Cont.)

— Colonies.

BADE (KLAUS J.) Friedrich Fabri und der Imperialismus in der Bismarckzeit: Revolution, Depression, Expansion. Freiburg i. Br., [1975]. pp. 579. *bibliog.*

GRUBE (JOCHEN) Bismarcks Politik in Europa und Übersee: seine "Annäherung" an Frankreich im Urteil der Pariser Presse, 1883-1885. Bern, 1975. pp. 277. *bibliog.*

SCHMITT-EGNER (PETER) Kolonialismus und Faschismus: eine Studie zur historischen und begrifflichen Genesis faschistischer Bewusstseinsformen am deutschen Beispiel. Giessen/Lollar, 1975. pp. 224. *bibliog.*

— Commerce.

ROSTIN (WERNER) Indices of foreign trade prices on base 1970. Stuttgart, 1974. pp. 13. *(Germany (Bundesrepublik). Statistisches Bundesamt. Studies on Statistics. No. 30) Originally published in German in Wirtschaft und Statistik, vol. 6, June 1974.*

GERMANY (BUNDESREPUBLIK). Statistisches Bundesamt. 1975. Aussenhandelsvolumen und Aussenhandelsindizes auf Basis 1970: Ergebnisse von 1952 bis 1974. Stuttgart, 1975. pp. 136. *(Aussenhandel. Reihe 7. Sonderbeiträge)*

— — Mathematical models.

DANCKWERTS (RUDOLF FERDINAND) and others. Konjunktur und Import: kurzfristige Bestimmungsgründe der Einfuhr von Waren und Dienstleistungen in der Bundesrepublik Deutschland. Hamburg, 1975. pp. 378. *bibliog. (Hamburg. Hamburgisches Welt-Wirtschafts-Archiv. Veröffentlichungen)*

— — America, Latin.

BROCKSTEDT (JUERGEN) Die Schiffahrts- und Handelsbeziehungen Schleswig-Holsteins nach Lateinamerika, 1815-1848. Köln, 1975. pp. 575. *bibliog.* With summaries in English and French.

— — Germany, Eastern.

WENIG (FRITZ HARALD) Rechtsprobleme des innerdeutschen Handels: eine Untersuchung über die Wirtschaftsbeziehungen der Bundesrepublik Deutschland und der Deutschen Demokratischen Republik aus verwaltungs-, staats- und völkerrechtlicher Sicht. Bern, 1975. pp. 272.

— — Russia.

POHL (MANFRED) Die Finanzierung der Russengeschäfte zwischen den beiden Weltkriegen: die Entwicklung der 12 grossen Russlandkonsortien. Frankfurt am Main, [1975]. pp. 48. *(Tradition: Zeitschrift für Firmengeschichte und Unternehmerbiographie. Beihefte. 9)*

— Commercial policy.

WERNICKE (JOHANNES) System der nationalen Schutzpolitik nach aussen, etc. Jena, 1896. pp. 332.

PUBLIC assistance to industry: protection and subsidies in Britain and Germany; edited by W.M. Corden and Gerhard Fels. London, 1976. pp. 233.

— Constitution.

GRADNAUER (GEORG) Verfassungswesen und Verfassungskämpfe in Deutschland. Berlin, 1909. pp. 158.

DOLLINGER (KARL) Politik, Staat und Verfassung in der Bundesrepublik Deutschland. 2nd ed. Köln, [1975]. pp. 184. *bibliog.*

HERRMANN (GUENTER) Fernsehen und Hörfunk in der Verfassung der Bundesrepublik Deutschland: zugleich ein Beitrag zu weiteren allgemeinen verfassungsrechtlichen und kommunikationsrechtlichen Fragen. Tübingen, 1975. pp. 422. *bibliog.*

KLOSS (GUENTHER) West Germany: an introduction. London, 1976. pp. 180. *bibliog.*

— Constitutional history.

INSTITUT FÜR ZEITGESCHICHTE. Westdeutschlands Weg zur Bundesrepublik, 1945-1949: Beiträge von Mitarbeitern, etc. München, [1976]. pp. 203. *bibliog.*

MARTINY (MARTIN) Integration oder Konfrontation?: Studien zur Geschichte der sozialdemokratischen Rechts- und Verfassungspolitik. Bonn-Bad Godesberg, [1976]. pp. 248. *bibliog. (Friedrich-Ebert-Stiftung. Forschungsinstitut. Schriftenreihe. Band 122)*

— Constitutional law.

LANKENAU (EHRFRIED) Die freiheitliche demokratische Grundordnung im Sinne des Grundgesetzes und ihre rechtliche Wirksamkeit. Essen, 1974. pp. 27. *bibliog.*

DOBIEY (BURKHARD) Die politische Planung als verfassungsrechtliches Problem zwischen Bundesregierung und Bundestag. Berlin, [1975]. pp. 170. *bibliog.*

LIPPHARDT (HANNS RUDOLF) Die Gleichheit der politischen Parteien vor der öffentlichen Gewalt: kritische Studie zur Wahl- und Parteienrechtsjudikatur des Bundesverfassungsgerichts. Berlin, [1975]. pp. 740. *bibliog.*

SEIFERT (KARL HEINZ) Die politischen Parteien im Recht der Bundesrepublik Deutschland. Köln, 1975. pp. 527. *bibliog.*

HENNIG (OTTFRIED) Die Bundespräsenz in West-Berlin: Entwicklung und Rechtscharakter. Köln, [1976]. pp. 367. *bibliog.*

WILKE (KAY MICHAEL) Bundesrepublik Deutschland und Deutsche Demokratische Republik: Grundlagen und ausgewählte Probleme des gegenseitigen Verhältnisses der beiden deutschen Staaten. Berlin, [1976]. pp. 351. *bibliog.* With summaries in English and French.

— Defences.

HAHN (WALTER F.) Between Westpolitik and Ostpolitik: changing West German security views. Beverly Hills, [1975]. pp. 89. *(Foreign Policy Research Institute. Foreign Policy Papers. vol. 1/3)*

KELLEHER (CATHERINE McARDLE) Germany and the politics of nuclear weapons. New York, 1975. pp. 372. *bibliog.*

SCHMIDT (MANFRED G.) Staatsapparat und Rüstungspolitik in der Bundesrepublik Deutschland, 1966-1973: Schranken und Folgeprobleme der Staatsinterventionspolitik im Militär- und Rüstungssektor. Giessen/Lollar, 1975. pp. 247. *bibliog.*

LOEWKE (UDO F.) Die SPD und die Wehrfrage, 1949 bis 1955. Bonn-Bad Godesberg, [1976]. pp. 185. *bibliog.*

— Description and travel.

BRODZKI (STANISŁAW) Księga wielu dzungli. Warszawa, 1953. pp. 232.

— Diplomatic and consular service.

HAAS (WILHELM) Beitrag zur Geschichte der Entstehung des Auswärtigen Dienstes der Bundesrepublik Deutschland. [Bremen, 1969]. pp. 531.

LAUREN (PAUL GORDON) Diplomats and bureaucrats: the first institutional responses to twentieth-century diplomacy in France and Germany. Stanford, 1976. pp. 294. *bibliog. (Stanford University. Hoover Institution on War, Revolution and Peace. Hoover Institution Publications. 153)*

— Economic conditions.

HESSE (ALBERT HERMANN) Die Wirkungen des Friedens von Versailles auf die Wirtschaft des deutschen Ostens. Jena, 1930. pp. 62.

WERNER (KURT) Die deutschen Wirtschaftsgebiete in der Krise: statistische Studie zur regional vergleichenden Konjunkturbetrachtung. Jena, 1932. pp. 71.

ARBEITSGEMEINSCHAFT DEUTSCHER WIRTSCHAFTSWISSENSCHAFTLICHER FORSCHUNGSINSTITUTE. The economic situation in the world and in Western Germany in spring 1972. Hamburg, 1972. pp. 16.

KLOSS (GUENTHER) West Germany: an introduction. London, 1976. pp. 180. *bibliog.*

— — Mathematical models.

KRELLE (WILHELM) Erfahrungen mit einem ökonometrischen Prognosemodell für die Bundesrepublik Deutschland. Meisenheim am Glan, [1974]. pp. 182.

FRERICHS (W.) Ein disaggregiertes Prognosesystem für die BRD. Meisenheim am Glan, 1975 in progress. *bibliog.*

— — Statistics.

CHRISTLICH-DEMOKRATISCHE UNION DEUTSCHLANDS. Wirtschaftsrat. Politik in Zahlen: Daten und Fakten zur Wirtschafts- und Gesellschaftspolitik. [Bonn, 1972]. pp. 106. *(Schriften)*

— Economic history.

CONRAD (KLAUS) of the University of Tübingen, and JORGENSON (DALE W.) Measuring performance in the private economy of the Federal Republic of Germany, 1950-1973. Tübingen, 1975. pp. 198. *bibliog. (Tübingen. Universität. Fachbereich Wirtschaftswissenschaft. Tübinger Wirtschaftswissenschaftliche Abhandlungen. Band 19)*

HENDERSON (WILLIAM OTTO) The rise of German industrial power, 1834-1914. London, 1975. pp. 264. *bibliog.*

SCHNEIDER (MICHAEL) Unternehmer und Demokratie: die freien Gewerkschaften in der unternehmerischen Ideologie der Jahre 1918 bis 1933. Bonn-Bad Godesberg, [1975]. pp. 219. *bibliog. (Friedrich-Ebert-Stiftung. Forschungsinstitut. Schriftenreihe. Band 116)*

— — Mathematical models.

SHEEN (JEFFREY R.) and SASSANPOUR (CYRUS) A comparison of money and economic activity in France and West Germany: 1959-1973. [London, 1976]. pp. 54. *bibliog.*

— Economic policy.

WERNICKE (JOHANNES) System der nationalen Schutzpolitik nach aussen, etc. Jena, 1896. pp. 332.

LIEFMANN (ROBERT) Arbeitslöhne und Unternehmergewinne nach dem Kriege. Stuttgart, 1919. pp. 24.

ROCKER (RUDOLF) Die Rationalisierung der Wirtschaft und die Arbeiterklasse. Berlin, 1927. pp. 84.

PAHL (WALTHER) and MENDELSOHN (KURT) eds. Handbuch der öffentlichen Wirtschaft; herausgegeben vom Vorstand des Gesamtverbandes der Arbeitnehmer der öffentlichen Betriebe und des Personen- und Warenverkehrs. Berlin, [1930]. pp. 696. *bibliog.*

MUELLER (JOHANNES) Die Industrialisierung der deutschen Mittelgebirge: eine wirtschaftskundliche Frage der Vergangenheit, ein wirtschaftspolitisches Problem der Gegenwart. Jena, 1938. pp. 241. *bibliog.*

GROTE-MISMAHL (ULRICH) Neubau deutscher Wirtschaft durch konstruktiven Sozialismus. n.p., 1951. pp. 498.

GRUNDLAGEN und Formen der Herrschaft des Finanzkapitals; Autorenkollektiv: Peter Hess [and others]. Frankfurt am Main, 1974. pp. 144.

HALLGARTEN (GEORGE WOLFGANG FELIX) and RADKAU (JOACHIM) Deutsche Industrie und Politik von Bismarck bis heute. Frankfurt am Main, [1974]. pp. 574. *bibliog.*

ZUNKEL (FRIEDRICH) Industrie und Staatssozialismus: der Kampf um die Wirtschaftsordnung in Deutschland, 1914-1918. Düsseldorf, [1974]. pp. 227. *bibliog. (Tübingen. Universität. Seminar für Zeitgeschichte. Tübinger Schriften zur Sozial- und Zeitgeschichte. 3)*

GERMANY(Cont.)

AUJAC (HENRI) Comparaison des potentiels de développement de la République fédérale d'Allemagne et de la France. Lausanne, 1975. pp. 43. *(Lausanne. Université. Centre de Recherches Européennes. Publications. 2. Le Processus d'Union de l'Europe)*

HENTSCHEL (VOLKER) Die deutschen Freihändler und der volkswirtschaftliche Kongress, 1858 bis 1885. Stuttgart, [1975]. pp. 308. *bibliog. (Arbeitskreis für Moderne Sozialgeschichte. Industrielle Welt. Band 16)*

HOEPFNER (KLAUS) Ökonomische Alternativen zur Ausländerbeschäftigung.. Göttingen, [1975]. pp. 210. *bibliog. (Kommission für Wirtschaftlichen und Sozialen Wandel. Schriften. 105)*

KOCK (HEINZ) Stabilitätspolitik im föderalistischen System der Bundesrepublik Deutschland: Analyse und Reformvorschläge. Köln, [1975]. pp. 228. *bibliog.*

OERTZEN (PETER VON) and others, eds. Thema: Wirtschaftspolitik; Materialien zum Orientierungsrahmen 1985 (der SPD). 2nd ed. Bonn-Bad Godesberg, 1975. pp. 249.

SCHNEIDER (MICHAEL) Das Arbeitsbeschaffungsprogramm des ADGB: zur gewerkschaftlichen Politik in der Endphase der Weimarer Republik; mit einer Einführung von George Garvy. Bonn-Bad Godesberg, [1975]. pp. 271. *bibliog. (Friedrich-Ebert-Stiftung. Forschungsinstitut. Schriftenreihe. Band 120)* With English introduction.

GUTERMUTH (ROLF) Ausbeutung in der BRD: zur Entwicklung der kapitalistischen Ausbeutung nach dem zweiten Weltkrieg. Berlin, 1976. pp. 256.

LAMPERT (HEINZ) Die Wirtschafts- und Sozialordnung der Bundesrepublik Deutschland. 5th ed. München, [1976]. pp. 319. *bibliogs.*

VEREIN FÜR SOZIALPOLITIK. Schriften. Neue Folge. Band 89. Probleme der nationalsozialistischen Wirtschaftspolitik; von Fritz Blaich [and others]; herausgegeben von Friedrich- Wilhelm Henning. Berlin, [1976]. pp. 174.

ZUMPE (LOTTE) ed. Wirtschaft und Staat im Imperialismus: Beiträge zur Entwicklungsgeschichte des staatsmonopolistischen Kapitalismus in Deutschland. Berlin, 1976. pp. 313.

— — **Bibliography.**

GERMANY (BUNDESREPUBLIK). Deutscher Bundestag. Wissenschaftliche Dienste. 1976. Wirtschaftsordnungsdebatte in der Bundesrepublik Deutschland; [compiled by Gerhard Hahn]. Bonn, 1976. pp. 134. *(Bibliographien. 46)*

— — **Mathematical models.**

CONRAD (KLAUS) of the University of Tübingen. Simulation und Optimierung mit einem nichtlinearen ökonometrischen Makromodell für die Bundesrepublik Deutschland. Meisenheim am Glan, 1975. pp. 398. *bibliog.*

— **Emigration and immigration.**

MERGEN (JOSEF) Die Auswanderungen aus den ehemals preussischen Teilen des Saarlandes im 19. Jahrhundert. Saarbrücken, 1973 in progress. *bibliog. (Institut für Landeskunde des Saarlandes. Veröffentlichungen. 20, etc.)*

HACKER (WERNER) Auswanderungen aus dem nördlichen Bodenseeraum im 17. und 18. Jahrhundert; archivalisch dokumentiert. Singen, 1975. pp. 400. *bibliog. (Verein für Geschichte des Hegaus. Hegau- Bibliothek. Band 29)*

— **Executive departments.**

GERMANY (BUNDESREPUBLIK). Auswärtiges Amt. Politisches Archiv. 1970. 100 Jahre Auswärtiges Amt, 1870-1970; zusammengestellt... unter der Leitung von...Heinz Günther Sasse in Verbindung mit...Ekkehard Eickhoff. Bonn, 1970. pp. 215.

ADAM (ALFRED) Pressesprecher. Das Bundesministerium für innerdeutsche Beziehungen. Bonn, [1971]. pp. 104. *bibliog.*

MORSBACH (JOSEF) Das Bundesministerium für Verkehr. Bonn, [1971]. pp. 123. *bibliog.*

SCHMID (GUENTHER) and TREIBER (HUBERT) Bürokratie und Politik: zur Struktur und Funktion der Ministerialbürokratie in der Bundesrepublik Deutschland. München, [1975]. pp. 317. *bibliog.*

SEEMANN (KLAUS) Entzaubertes Bundeskanzleramt: Denkwürdigkeiten eines Personalratsvorsitzenden. Landshut, [1975]. pp. 216.

LAUREN (PAUL GORDON) Diplomats and bureaucrats: the first institutional responses to twentieth-century diplomacy in France and Germany. Stanford, 1976. pp. 294. *bibliog. (Stanford University. Hoover Institution on War, Revolution and Peace. Hoover Institution Publications. 153)*

— **Foreign economic relations.**

ZUM Verhältnis von Aussenwirtschafts- und Entwicklungspolitik; [by] Axel Borrmann [and others]. Hamburg, 1975. pp. 409. *bibliog. (Hamburg. Hamburgisches Welt-Wirtschafts-Archiv. Veröffentlichungen)*

— — **GHANA.**

LANGER (PETER) Die Aussen- und Entwicklungspolitik der Bundesrepublik gegenüber Ghana: eine Fallstudie zur Überprüfung der neueren Imperialismus-Theorien. Meisenheim am Glan, 1975. pp. 201 *bibliog.*

— **Foreign opinion.**

GRUBE (JOCHEN) Bismarks Politik in Europa und Übersee: seine "Annäherung" an Frankreich im Urteil der Pariser Presse, 1883-1885. Bern, 1975, pp 277. *bibliog.*

— **Foreign population.**

GERMANY (BUNDESREPUBLIK). Statistisches Bundesamt. Ausländer. a., 1974- Wiesbaden. *(Bevölkerung und Kultur. Reihe 1.6)* Supersedes in part GERMANY (BUNDESREPUBLIK). Statistisches Bundesamt. Bevölkerungsstand und -entwicklung.

— **Foreign relations.**

STIER-SOMLO (FRITZ) Grund- und Zukunftsfragen deutscher Politik. Bonn, 1917. pp. 392.

REIMANN (MAX) Der deutsche Imperialismus, die Hauptgefahr für den Frieden in Europa. Rheinhausen, [1969]. pp. 32.

GERMANY (BUNDESREPUBLIK). Auswärtiges Amt. Politisches Archiv. 1970. 100 Jahre Auswärtiges Amt, 1870-1970; zusammengestellt... unter der Leitung von...Heinz Günther Sasse in Verbindung mit...Ekkehard Eickhoff. Bonn, 1970. pp. 215.

ADENAUER (KONRAD) Reden, 1917-1967: eine Auswahl; herausgegeben von Hans- Peter Schwarz. Stuttgart, [1975]. pp. 496.

GRUPP (CORNELIUS) Die parlamentarische Kontrolle der auswärtigen Gewalt in Form von Entschliessungen. Augsburg, 1975. p. 194. *bibliog. Dissertation zur Erlangung des Grades eines Doktors der Rechte (Universität Augsburg).*

HAHN (WALTER F.) Between Westpolitik and Ostpolitik: changing West German security views. Beverly Hills, [1975]. pp. 89. *(Foreign Policy Research Institute. Foreign Policy Papers. vol. 1/3)*

LIBERALISMUS und imperialistischer Staat: der Imperialismus als Problem liberaler Parteien in Deutschland, 1890-1914; mit Beiträgen von Lothar Albertin [and others]; herausgegeben von Karl Holl und Günther List. Göttingen, [1975]. pp. 176.

MOSES (JOHN A.) The politics of illusion: the Fischer controversy in German historiography. London, 1975. pp. 148. *bibliog.*

SCHMIDT (HELMUT) Dipl. rer. pol. Kontinuität und Konzentration: [speeches, articles, etc.]. Bonn-Bad Godesberg, [1975]. pp. 292.

SCHWARZ (HANS PETER) ed. Handbuch der deutschen Aussenpolitik. München, [1975]. pp. 849. *bibliogs.*

ZIEBURA (GILBERT) ed. Grundfragen der deutschen Aussenpolitik seit 1871. Darmstadt, 1975. pp. 503. *bibliog.*

BRANDT (WILLY) Begegnungen und Einsichten: die Jahre 1960-1975. Hamburg, 1976. pp. 655.

DAHRENDORF (RALF) Die Staatsräson der Bundesrepublik Deutschland. Konstanz, 1976. pp. 32. *(Constance. Universität. Waldemar-Besson-Gedächtnis-Vorlesungen. 1975)*

GEISS (IMANUEL) German foreign policy, 1871-1914. London, 1976. pp. 259. *bibliog.*

GERDES (DIRK) Abschreckung und Entspannung: legitimatorische Folgeprobleme bundesrepublikanischer Entspannungspolitik. Meisenheim am Glan, 1976. pp. 182. *bibliog.*

PATZ (GUENTHER) Parlamentarische Kontrolle der Aussenpolitik: Fallstudien zur politischen Bedeutung des Auswärtigen Ausschusses des Deutschen Bundestages. Meisenheim am Glan, 1976. pp. 190. *bibliog.*

See also EUROPEAN COMMUNITIES — Germany; NORTH ATLANTIC TREATY ORGANIZATION — Germany; UNITED NATIONS — Germany.

— — **Treaties.**

GLEICH (JOHANN GEORG) Die Anerkennung der DDR durch die Bundesrepublik: eine völkerrechtliche Untersuchung, etc. Bern, 1975. pp. 254. *bibliog.*

SCHRAMM (THEODOR) Das Verhältnis der Bundesrepublik Deutschland zur DDR nach dem Grundvertrag: eine Einführung in die staats- und völkerrechtlichen Problembereiche mit Dokumentensammlung. 2nd ed. Köln, 1975. pp. 275. *bibliog.*

WEIGAND (MATTHIAS) Der Vertrag über die gegenseitigen Beziehungen zwischen der Bundesrepublik Deutschland und der Tschechoslowakischen Sozialistischen Republik vom 11. Dezember 1973: eine völkerrechtliche Analyse. Bern, 1975. pp. 127. *bibliog.*

— — **Austria.**

LUZA (RADOMÍR) Austro-German relations in the Anschluss era. Princeton, [1975]. pp. 438. *bibliog.*

KATZENSTEIN (PETER J.) Disjoined partners: Austria and Germany since 1815. Berkeley, Calif., [1976]. pp. 263.

— — **Catholic Church.**

KLEIN (CHARLES) Pie XII face aux Nazis. Paris, [1975]. pp. 250.

— — **Czechoslovakia.**

CAMPBELL (F. GREGORY) Confrontation in Central Europe: Weimar Germany and Czechoslovakia. Chicago, 1975. pp. 383. *bibliog.*

WEIGAND (MATTHIAS) Der Vertrag über die gegenseitigen Beziehungen zwischen der Bundesrepublik Deutschland und der Tschechoslowakischen Sozialistischen Republik vom 11. Dezember 1973: eine völkerrechtliche Analyse. Bern, 1975. pp. 127. *bibliog.*

— — **Europe.**

EISNER (ERICH) Das europäische Konzept von Franz Josef Strauss: die gesamteuropäischen Ordnungsvorstellungen der CSU. Meisenheim am Glan, 1975. pp. 143. *bibliog.*

— — **Europe, Eastern.**

HACKE (CHRISTIAN) Die Ost- und Deutschlandpolitik der CDU/CSU: Wege und Irrwege der Opposition seit 1969. Köln, [1975]. pp. 151. *bibliog.*

SOWDEN (JOHN KENNETH) The German question, 1945-1973: continuity in change. London, 1975. pp. 404. *bibliog.*

GERMANY(Cont.)

ROTH (REINHOLD) Aussenpolitische Innovation und politische Herrschaftssicherung: eine Analyse...am Beispiel der sozialliberalen Koalition, 1969 bis 1973. Meisenheim am Glan, 1976. pp. 380. *bibliog.*

— — Bibliography.

GERMANY (BUNDESREPUBLIK). Deutscher Bundestag. Wissenschaftliche Dienste. 1974. Die Ost- und Deutschlandpolitik der Bundesrepublik Deutschland, 1969-1973: Auswahlbibliographie mit Annotationen; [compiled by Hannelore Reiche-Juhr]. Bonn, 1974. pp. 167. *(Bibliographien. 40)*

— — France.

BINOCHE (JACQUES) L'Allemagne et le Général de Gaulle, 1924-1970. [Paris, 1975]. pp. 229.

GRUBE (JOCHEN) Bismarks Politik in Europa und Übersee: seine "Annäherung" an frankreich im Urteil der Pariser Presse, 1883-1885. Bern, 1975, pp 277. *bibliog.*

SEYDOUX (FRANÇOIS) Mémoires d'outre-Rhin. Paris, [1975]. pp. 309.

— — Germany, Eastern.

ADAM (ALFRED) Pressesprecher. Das Bundesministerium für innerdeutsche Beziehungen. Bonn, [1971]. pp. 104. *bibliog.*

GLEICH (JOHANN GEORG) Die Anerkennung der DDR durch die Bundesrepublik: eine völkerrechtliche Untersuchung, etc. Bern, 1975. pp. 254. *bibliog.*

SCHRAMM (THEODOR) Das Verhältnis der Bundesrepublik Deutschland zur DDR nach dem Grundvertrag: eine Einführung in die staats- und völkerrechtlichen Problembereiche mit Dokumentensammlung. 2nd ed. Köln, 1975. pp. 275. *bibliog.*

GERMANY (BUNDESREPUBLIK). Deutscher Bundestag. Wissenschaftliche Dienste. 1974. Die Ost- und Deutschlandpolitik der Bundesrepublik Deutschland, 1969-1973: Auswahlbibliographie mit Annotationen; [compiled by Hannelore Reiche-Juhr]. Bonn, 1974. pp. 167. *(Bibliographien. 40)*

— — Poland.

PAJEWSKI (JANUSZ) ed. Problem polsko-niemiecki w Traktacie Wersalskim; praca zbiorowa pod redakcja J. Pajewskiego, etc. Poznań, 1963. pp. 652. *bibliog. (Poznań. Instytut Zachodni. Dzieje Polskiej Granicy Zachodniej. 3)*

KUBIAK (STANISŁAW) Niemcy a Wielkopolska, 1918-1919. Poznań, 1969. pp. 303. *bibliog. (Poznań. Instytut Zachodni. Dzieje Polskiej Granicy Zachodniej. 4)* With German summary.

SKIBIŃSKI (JERZY) Polska - RFN: problemy normalizacji stosunków; posłowie Ryszard Wojna. Warszawa, 1974. pp. 220.

ORTMAYER (LOUIS L.) Conflict, compromise, and conciliation: West German-Polish normalization, 1966-1976. Denver, [1975]. pp. 162. *(Denver. University. Social Science Foundation and Graduate School of International Studies. Monograph Series in World Affairs. vol. 13, no. 3)*

RAINA (PETER) Stosunki polsko-niemieckie 1937-1939: prawdziwy charakter polityki zagranicznej Józefa Becka. Londyn, 1975. pp. 172.

SCHWEITZER (CARL CHRISTOPH) and FEGER (HUBERT) eds. Das deutsch-polnische Konfliktverhältnis seit dem Zweiten Weltkrieg: multidisziplinäre Studien über konfliktfördernde und konfliktmindernde Faktoren in den internationalen Beziehungen. Boppard am Rhein, [1975]. pp. 596. *bibliogs. (Deutsche Gesellschaft für Friedens- und Konfliktforschung. Beiträge zur Konfliktforschung)*

KULSKI (WŁADYSŁAW WSZEBOR) Germany and Poland: from war to peaceful relations. Syracuse, N.Y., 1976. pp. 336. *bibliog.*

— — Russia.

AKHTAMZIAN (ABDULKHAN ABDURAKHMANOVICH) Rapall'skaia politika: sovetsko-germanskie diplomaticheskie otnosheniia v 1922-1932 godakh. Moskva, 1974. pp. 303.

ALLARDT (HELMUT) Moskauer Tagebuch: Beobachtungen, Notizen, Erlebnisse. 3rd ed. Düsseldorf, 1974. pp. 424. *bibliog.*

SKAZKIN (SERGEI DANILOVICH) Konets avstro-russko-germanskogo soiuza: issledovanie po istorii russko-germanskikh i russko-avstriiskikh otnoshenii v sviazi s vostochnym voprosom v 80-e gody XIX stoletiia. 2nd ed. Moskva, 1974. pp. 272. *Reproduces the text of the 1st ed. of 1928 with some omissions.*

ERICKSON (JOHN) The road to Stalingrad. London, [1975]. pp. 594. *bibliog. (Stalin's war with Germany. vol.1)*

MEISSNER (BORIS) ed. Moskau, Bonn: die Beziehungen zwischen der Sowjetunion und der Bundesrepublik Deutschland, 1955-1973; Dokumentation. KÖLN [1975]. 2 vols. *bibliog.*

PETERSON (GORDON LEROY) The rapprochement between the Federal Republic of Germany and the Soviet Union, and the policy of international linkage in east- west relations, 1965-1971; [Ph. D.(London) thesis]. [1975]. fo. 305. *bibliog. Typescript: unpublished. This thesis is the property of London University and may not be removed from the Library.*

— — South Africa.

RODE (REINHARD) Die Südafrikapolitik der Bundesrepublik Deutschland, 1968- 1972. München, [1975]. pp. 371. *bibliog. (Katholischer Arbeitskreis Entwicklung und Frieden. Wissenschaftliche Kommission. Wissenschaftliche Reihe. 7)* With summaries in French and English.

— — Spain.

RUHL (KLAUS JOERG) Spanien im Zweiten Weltkrieg: Franco, die Falange und das "Dritte Reich". Hamburg, 1975. pp. 414. *bibliog.* With English summary.

— — Sweden.

UHLIN (ÅKE) Februarikrisen 1942: svensk säkerhetspolitik och militär planering, 1941-1942. Stockholm, 1972. pp. 265. *bibliog.* With English summary.

— — United Kingdom.

BLEY (HELMUT) Bebel und die Strategie der Kriegsverhütung, 1904-1913: eine Studie über Bebels Geheimkontakte mit der britischen Regierung, etc. Göttingen, 1975. pp. 254.

— — United States.

POETTERING (HANS GERT) Adenauers Sicherheitspolitik, 1955-1963: ein Beitrag zum deutsch-amerikanischen Verhältnis. Düsseldorf, [1975]. pp. 240. *bibliog. (Bonn. Universität. Seminar für Politische Wissenschaft. Bonner Schriften zur Politik und Zeitgeschichte. 10)*

— Government publications — Bibliography.

STAATSBIBLIOTHEK PREUSSISCHER KULTURBESITZ. Abteilung Amtsdruckschriften. Deutsche Parlamentaria: ein Bestandsverzeichnis der bis 1945 erschienen Druckschriften. Berlin, 1970. pp. 140.

— Historiography.

GUTSCHE (WILLIBALD) Zur Imperialismus-Apologie in der BRD: "neue" Imperialismusdeutungen in der BRD-Historiographie zur deutschen Geschichte, 1898 bis 1917. Frankfurt/Main, 1975. pp. 83.

MOSES (JOHN A.) The politics of illusion: the Fischer controversy in German historiography. London, 1975. pp. 148. *bibliog.*

— History.

MEUSEL (ALFRED) Kampf um die nationale Einheit in Deutschland. [Berlin], 1947. pp. 32.

HEINEMANN (GUSTAV WALTER) Reden und Schriften. Frankfurt am Main, 1975 in progress.

— — Philosophy.

ZOEPFL (HEINRICH) Die Demokratie in Deutschland: ein Beitrag zur wissenschaftlichen Würdigung von: G.G. Gervinus, Einleitung in die Geschichte des neunzehnten Jahrhunderts. Stuttgart, 1853. pp. 106.

— — 1517-1871.

MEHRING (FRANZ) Absolutism and revolution in Germany, 1525-1848. London, [1975]. pp. 288.

— — 1848-1849, Revolution.

[REVOLUTION of 1848 in Germany: collection of appeals, petitions, manifestoes, proclamations, and similar material in the form of leaflets, posters, etc., including some manuscript letters; published in Prussia between 1848 and 1862]. v.p., 1848-62. 1 vol. (unpaged).

PAYER (FRIEDRICH) "Anno 48". Frankfurt am Main, 1923. pp. 54.

MEUSEL (ALFRED) Die deutsche Revolution von 1848; mit einem Beitrag von Felix Albin: Marx und Engels und die Revolution von 1848. Berlin, [1948]. pp. 40.

KOMMISSION DER HISTORIKER DER DDR UND DER UdSSR. Konferenz, 21., 1973. 125 Jahre Kommunistisches Manifest und bürgerlich- demokratische Revolution 1848/49: Referate und Diskussionsbeiträge; wissenschaftliche Redaktion: Gunther Hildebrandt und Walter Wittwer. Glashütten im Taunus, 1975. pp. 312.

SIEMANN (WOLFRAM) Die Frankfurter Nationalversammlung 1848/49 zwischen demokratischem Liberalismus und konservativer Reform: die Bedeutung der Juristendominanz in den Verfassungsverhandlungen des Paulskirchenparlaments. Bern, 1976. pp. 532. *bibliog.*

— — 1871-1918.

SHEEHAN (JAMES J.) ed. Imperial Germany. New York, 1976. pp. 282. *bibliog.*

— — 1900, Bibliography.

INSTITUT FÜR ZEITGESCHICHTE. Bibliothek. Alphabetischer Katalog; ([with] Erster Nachtragsband). Boston, Mass., 1967-73. 6 vols.

INSTITUT FÜR ZEITGESCHICHTE. Bibliothek. Sachkatalog; ([with] Erster Nachtragsband). Boston, Mass., 1967-73. 8 vols.

INSTITUT FÜR ZEITGESCHICHTE. Bibliothek. Biographischer Katalog. Boston, Mass., 1967. pp. 764.

INSTITUT FÜR ZEITGESCHICHTE. Bibliothek. Erster Nachtragsband: Biographischer Katalog; Länderkatalog. Boston, Mass., 1973. pp. 588.

— — 1918-1919, Revolution.

GROTEWOHL (OTTO) Dreissig Jahre später: die Novemberrevolution und die Lehren der Geschichte der deutschen Arbeiterbewegung. Berlin, [1948]. pp. 171.

INSTITUT FÜR MARXISMUS-LENINISMUS (BERLIN). Illustrierte Geschichte der Novemberrevolution in Deutschland; ...(Autorenkollektiv Günther Hortzschansky [and others]). Berlin, 1968. pp. 391.

DAEHN (HORST) Rätedemokratische Modelle: Studien zur Rätediskussion in Deutschland, 1918-1919. Meisenheim am Glan, 1975. pp. 584. *bibliog.*

— — 1945-1955, Allied occupation.

BADSTUEBNER (ROLF) and THOMAS (SIEGFRIED) Restauration und Spaltung: Entstehung und Entwicklung der BRD, 1945-1955. Köln, [1975]. pp. 512. *bibliog.*

— History, Military.

KITCHEN (MARTIN) A military history of Germany from the eighteenth century to the present day. Bloomington, [1975]. pp. 384. *bibliog.*

GERMANY (Cont.)

— Industries.

GERMANY. Statistisches Reichsamt. Statistik des Deutschen Reichs. Neue Folge. Bände 6-7. Gewerbestatistik nach der allgemeinen Berufszählung vom 5. Juni 1882. Berlin, 1885-86. 4 vols. (in 2). *Band 6 reprinted Osnabrück, 1974.*

MUELLER (JOHANNES) Der mitteldeutsche Industriebezirk. Jena, 1927. pp. 87. *bibliog.*

MUELLER (JOHANNES) Die Industrialisierung der deutschen Mittelgebirge: eine wirtschaftskundliche Frage der Vergangenheit, ein wirtschaftspolitisches Problem der Gegenwart. Jena, 1938. pp. 241. *bibliog.*

BAGEL-BOHLAN (ANJA E.) Hitlers industrielle Kriegsvorbereitung, 1936 bis 1939. Koblenz, [1975]. pp. 143. *bibliog. (Arbeitskreis für Wehrforschung. Beiträge zur Wehrforschung. Band 24)*

BOGUSZEWSKI (JAN) and WAGENER (HANS JUERGEN) Zur Industriestatistik der BRD, Österreichs, Polens und Ungarns. Wien, 1975. pp. 58. *(Wiener Institut für Internationale Wirtschaftsvergleiche. Forschungsberichte. Nr.24)*

HENDERSON (WILLIAM OTTO) The rise of German industrial power, 1834-1914. London, 1975. pp. 264. *bibliog.*

PANIĆ (M.) ed. The UK and West German manufacturing industry 1954-72: a comparison of structure and performance. London, National Economic Development Office, 1976. pp. 151. *(NEDO Monographs. 5)*

— Military policy.

KASSYANOWICZ (HENRYK) Odrodzenie Wehrmachtu czy bezpieczeństwo europejskie?. Warszawa, 1954. pp. 104.

STEPANIAN (STEPAN SMBATOVICH) Armeniia v politike imperialisticheskoi Germanii, konets XIX - nachalo XX veka. Erevan, 1975. pp. 243. *bibliog.*

LOEWKE (UDO F.) Die SPD und die Wehrfrage, 1949 bis 1955. Bonn-Bad Godesberg, [1976]. pp. 185. *bibliog.*

— Nationalism.

HAY (JOSEPH) Staat, Volk und Weltbürgertum in der Berlinischen Monatsschrift von Friedrich Gedike und Johann Erich Biester, 1783-96. Berlin, 1913. pp. 83. *bibliog.*

MEUSEL (ALFRED) Kampf um die nationale Einheit in Deutschland. [Berlin], 1947. pp. 32.

MOSSE (GEORGE L.) The nationalization of the masses: political symbolism and mass movements in Germany from the Napoleonic wars through the Third Reich. New York, 1975. pp. 252.

GABBE (JOERG) Parteien und Nation: zur Rolle des Nationalbewusstseins für die politischen Grundorientierungen der Parteien in der Anfangsphase der Bundesrepublik. Meisenheim am Glan, 1976. pp. 347. *bibliog.*

— Nationalversammlung.

PAYER (FRIEDRICH) "Anno 48". Frankfurt am Main, 1923. pp. 54.

PETZET (WOLFGANG) and SUTTER (OTTO ERNST) eds. Der Geist der Paulskirche: aus den Reden der Nationalversammlung, 1848-1849. Frankfurt a.M., 1923. pp. 375.

BLOS (WILHELM) Der Untergang des Frankfurter Parlaments. Frankfurt am Main, 1924. pp. 141.

SIEMANN (WOLFRAM) Die Frankfurter Nationalversammlung 1848/49 zwischen demokratischem Liberalismus und konservativer Reform: die Bedeutung der Juristendominanz in den Verfassungsverhandlungen des Paulskirchenparlaments. Bern, 1976. pp. 532. *bibliog.*

— Navy.

GEMZELL (CARL AXEL) Organization, conflict, and innovation: a study of German naval strategic planning, 1888-1940. Stockholm, [1973]. pp. 448. *bibliog. (Lund. Universitet. Historiska Institutionen. Lund Studies in International History. [No]. 4)*

— — History.

MEIER-DOERNBERG (WILHELM) Die Ölversorgung der Kriegsmarine, 1935 bis 1945. Freiburg, 1973. pp. 111. *bibliog. (Militärgeschichtliches Forschungsamt. Einzelschriften zur Militärischen Geschichte des Zweiten Weltkrieges. 11)*

— Neutrality.

DOHSE (RAINER) Der dritte Weg: Neutralitätsbestrebungen in Westdeutschland zwischen 1945 und 1955. Hamburg, 1974. pp. 239. *bibliog.*

— Nobility.

KUCZYNSKI (JUERGEN) Monopolisten und Junker: Todfeinde des deutschen Volkes. Berlin, [1946?]. pp. 46.

— Occupations.

GERMANY. Statistisches Reichsamt. Statistik des Deutschen Reichs. Neue Folge. Bände 2-4. Berufsstatistik nach der allgemeinen Berufszählung vom 5. Juni 1882. Berlin, 1884. 3 vols. (in 5). *Bände 3-4 reprinted Osnabrück, 1973-74.*

WIEK (KLAUS D.) Regionale Schwerpunkte und Schwächezonen in der Bevölkerungs-, Erwerbs- und Infrastruktur Deutschlands: Bemerkungen zu ihrer Erfassung. Bad Godesberg, 1967. pp. 64. *bibliogs. (Zentralausschuss für Deutsche Landeskunde and Germany (Bundesrepublik). Institut für Landeskunde. Forschungen zur Deutschen Landeskunde. Band 169)*

KNAUDT (NORBERT) Berufswahl und Berufsmobilität der Erwerbstätigen in zehn ehemals kleinbäuerlichen Dörfern der Bundesrepublik Deutschland, 1952 und 1972. Bonn, 1976. pp. 204. *bibliog. (Forschungsgesellschaft für Agrarpolitik und Agrarsoziologie. [Publications]. 231)*

— Officials and employees.

KRAUSE (ALFRED) of the Deutscher Beamtenbund. Staat und Staatsdienst heute. Bad Godesberg, 1968. pp. 87. *Revised versions of four lectures.*

MITBESTIMMUNG im öffentlichen Dienst: ([by] Thomas Ellwein [and others]). Bad Godesberg, 1969. pp. 88.

SCHMID (GUENTHER) and TREIBER (HUBERT) Bürokratie und Politik: zur Struktur und Funktion der Ministerialbürokratie in der Bundesrepublik Deutschland. München, [1975]. pp. 317. *bibliog.*

— Politics and government — 1789-1900.

ZOEPFL (HEINRICH) Die Demokratie in Deutschland: ein Beitrag zur wissenschaftlichen Würdigung von: G.G. Gervinus, Einleitung in die Geschichte des neunzehnten Jahrhunderts. Stuttgart, 1853. pp. 106.

HENTSCHEL (VOLKER) Die deutschen Freihändler und der volkswirtschaftliche Kongress, 1858 bis 1885. Stuttgart, [1975]. pp. 308. *bibliog. (Arbeitskreis für Moderne Sozialgeschichte. Industrielle Welt. Band 16)*

KOSZYK (KURT) and OBERMANN (KARL) eds. Zeitgenossen von Marx und Engels: ausgewählte Briefe aus den Jahren 1844 bis 1852. Assen, 1975. pp. 459. *(International Institute of Social History. Quellen und Untersuchungen zur Geschichte der Deutschen und Österreichischen Arbeiterbewegung. Neue Folge. 6)*

LIEBKNECHT (WILHELM PHILIPP MARTIN CHRISTIAN LUDWIG) Leitartikel und Beiträge in der Osnabrücker Zeitung, 1864- 1866; herausgegeben von Georg Eckert. Hildesheim, 1975. pp. 794. *(Historische Kommission für Niedersachsen und Bremen. Veröffentlichungen. 35)*

MOSSE (GEORGE L.) The nationalization of the masses: political symbolism and mass movements in Germany from the Napoleonic wars through the Third Reich. New York, 1975. pp. 252.

PLESSEN (MARIE LOUISE) Die Wirksamkeit des Vereins für Socialpolitik von 1872-1890: Studien zum Katheder- und Staatssozialismus. Berlin, [1975]. pp. 134. *bibliog.*

ZUCKER (STANLEY) Ludwig Bamberger: German liberal politician and social critic, 1823-1899. Pittsburgh, [1975]. pp. 343. *bibliog.*

— — 1871—1918.

SCHIPPEL (MAX) Sozialdemokratisches Reichstags-Handbuch: ein Führer durch die Zeit- und Streitfragen der Reichsgesetzgebung. Berlin, [1902]. pp. 1174.

STIER-SOMLO (FRITZ) Grund- und Zukunftsfragen deutscher Politik. Bonn, 1917. pp. 392.

CHICKERING (ROGER) Imperial Germany and a world without war: the peace movement and German society, 1892-1914. Princeton, [1975]. pp. 487. *bibliog.*

LIBERALISMUS und imperialistischer Staat: der Imperialismus als Problem liberaler Parteien in Deutschland, 1890-1914; mit Beiträgen von Lothar Albertin [and others]; herausgegeben von Karl Holl und Günther List. Göttingen, [1975]. pp. 176.

WHITE (DAN S.) The splintered party: National Liberalism in Hessen and the Reich, 1867-1918. Cambridge, Mass., 1976. pp. 303. *bibliog.*

— — 1900.

MOSSE (GEORGE L.) The nationalization of the masses: political symbolism and mass movements in Germany from the Napoleonic wars through the Third Reich. New York, 1975. pp. 252.

— — 1918-1945.

THAELMANN (ERNST) Kampfreden und Aufsätze. Berlin, 1932. pp. 96.

PRATT (JAMES ALEXANDER) The social basis of Nazism and communism in urban Germany. 1948. pp. 277. *bibliog. M.A.(Michigan State College of Agriculture and Applied Science) thesis: unpublished. Microfilm of typescript: 1 reel.*

MAMMACH (KLAUS) Der Kampf der deutschen Arbeiterklasse im August 1930 gegen Imperialismus, Militarismus und Krieg; mit einem Dokumentenanhang. Berlin, 1956. pp. 51. *(Institut für Marxismus-Leninismus (Berlin). Beiträge zur Geschichte und Theorie der Arbeiterbewegung. Heft 7)*

ADENAUER (KONRAD) Reden, 1917-1967: eine Auswahl; herausgegeben von Hans- Peter Schwarz. Stuttgart, [1975]. pp. 496.

DUPEUX (LOUIS) Stratégie communiste et dynamique conservatrice: essai sur les différents sens de l'expression "National-Bolchevisme" en Allemagne, sous la république de Weimar, 1919-1933. Paris, 1976. pp. 627. *bibliog. Thèse-Université de Paris I.*

SIDENIUS (NIELS CHRISTIAN) Kommunistisk Internationale, 1928-1935: en analyse og kritik... speciel i forhold til fascismen og udviklingen i Tyskland. Århus, 1976. pp. 283. *bibliog.*

— — 1918-1933.

KREBS (ALBERT) The infancy of Nazism: the memoirs of ex-Gauleiter Albert Krebs, 1923-1933; edited and translated by William Sheridan Allen. New York, 1976. pp. 328. *bibliog.*

— — 1945— .

WELTY (EBERHARD) Die Entscheidung in die Zukunft: Grundsätze und Hinweise zur Neuordnung im deutschen Lebensraum. Köln, [1946]. pp. 431.

GROTEWOHL (OTTO) Zur politischen Lage Deutschlands: ([Report to the] Parteivorstand der Sozialistischen Einheitspartei Deutschlands...am 22. Januar 1947). Berlin, [1947]. pp. 48.

GERMANY (Cont.)

ROCKER (RUDOLF) Zur Betrachtung der Lage in Deutschland: die Möglichkeiten einer freiheitlichen Bewegung; [edited by Helmut Rüdiger]. New York, 1947. pp. 36.

SCHOENBAUM (DAVID) Ein Abgrund von Landesverrat: die Affäre um den "Spiegel"; (aus dem Englischen übertragen von Armin Sellheim). Wien, 1968. pp. 254.

KESSELTREIBEN gegen wen?: die Legende einer Kampagne gegen Jochen Steffen; eine Dokumentation; herausgegeben von der Axel Springer Verlag AG, Abteilung Information. Berlin, [1971]. pp. 47.

BOELL (HEINRICH) Neue politische und literarische Schriften [1967-1972]. Köln, 1973. pp. 285. *bibliog.*

LATVIISKII GOSUDARSTVENNYI UNIVERSITET. Uchenye Zapiski. t.200. Voprosy kritiki burzhuaznoi politiki i ideologii. Riga, 1974. pp. 135. *bibliog.*

LOEWENTHAL (RICHARD) Sozialismus und aktive Demokratie: Essays zu ihren Voraussetzungen in Deutschland. Frankfurt am Main, [1974]. pp. 176.

HEINEMANN (GUSTAV WALTER) Reden und Schriften. Frankfurt am Main, 1975 in progress.

ADENAUER (KONRAD) Reden, 1917-1967: eine Auswahl; herausgegeben von Hans-Peter Schwarz. Stuttgart, [1975]. pp. 496.

DOBIEY (BURKHARD) Die politische Planung als verfassungsrechtliches Problem zwischen Bundesregierung und Bundestag. Berlin, [1975]. pp. 170. *bibliog.*

HORCHEM (HANS JOSEF) Right-wing extremism in Western Germany. London, 1975. pp. 11. *bibliog. (Institute for the Study of Conflict. Conflict Studies. No. 65)*

SCHMID (GUENTHER) and TREIBER (HUBERT) Bürokratie und Politik: zur Struktur und Funktion der Ministerialbürokratie in der Bundesrepublik Deutschland. München, [1975]. pp. 317. *bibliog.*

SCHMIDT (HELMUT) Dipl. rer. pol. Kontinuität und Konzentration: [speeches, articles, etc.]. Bonn-Bad Godesberg, [1975]. pp. 292.

SEEMANN (KLAUS) Entzaubertes Bundeskanzleramt: Denkwürdigkeiten eines Personalratsvorsitzenden. Landshut, [1975]. pp. 216.

BRANDT (WILLY) Begegnungen und Einsichten: die Jahre 1960-1975. Hamburg, 1976. pp. 655.

BRANDT (WILLY) and SCHMIDT (HELMUT) Federal German Chancellor. Deutschland 1976: zwei Sozialdemokraten im Gespräch; Gesprächsführung Jürgen Kellermeier. Reinbek bei Hamburg, 1976. pp. 172.

DAHRENDORF (RALF) Die Staatsräson der Bundesrepublik Deutschland. Konstanz, 1976. pp. 32. *(Constance. Universität. Waldemar-Besson-Gedächtnis-Vorlesungen. 1975)*

FRANK (DIETRICH) Politische Planung im Spannungsverhältnis zwischen Regierung und Parlament. Meisenheim am Glan, 1976. pp. 359. *bibliog.*

GIESECKE (HERMANN) and others. Gesellschaft und Politik in der Bundesrepublik: eine sozialkunde. Frankfurt am Main, 1976. pp. 335.

INSTITUT FÜR ZEITGESCHICHTE. Westdeutschlands Weg zur Bundesrepublik, 1945-1949: Beiträge von Mitarbeitern, etc. München, [1976]. pp. 203. *bibliog.*

KLOSS (GUENTHER) West Germany: an introduction. London, 1976. pp. 180. *bibliog.*

RAUSCH (HEINZ) Bundestag und Bundesregierung: eine Institutionenkunde. 4th ed. München, 1976. pp. 356. *bibliog.*

— Population.

WIEK (KLAUS D.) Regionale Schwerpunkte und Schwächezonen in der Bevölkerungs-, Erwerbs- und Infrastruktur Deutschlands: Bemerkungen zu ihrer Erfassung. Bad Godesberg, 1967. pp. 64. *bibliogs. (Zentralausschuss für Deutsche Landeskunde and Germany (Bundesrepublik). Institut für Landeskunde. Forschungen zur Deutschen Landeskunde. Band 169)*

GERMANY (BUNDESREPUBLIK). Statistisches Bundesamt. Alter und Familienstand der Bevölkerung. a., 1970- Wiesbaden. *(Bevölkerung und Kultur. Reihe 1.2) Supersedes in part the earlier series of GERMANY (BUNDESREPUBLIK). Statistisches Bundesamt. Bevölkerungsstand und -entwicklung.*

GERMANY (BUNDESREPUBLIK). Statistisches Bundesamt. Bevölkerungsstand und -entwicklung. a., 1970- Wiesbaden. *(Bevölkerung und Kultur. Reihe 1.1) Supersedes in part earlier publication of the same title.*

GERMANY (BUNDESREPUBLIK). Statistisches Bundesamt. Staatsangehörigkeit. a., 1970- Wiesbaden. *(Bevölkerung und Kultur. Reihe 1.5) Supersedes in part GERMANY (BUNDESREPUBLIK). Statistisches Bundesamt. Bevölkerungsstand und -entwicklung.*

GERMANY (BUNDESREPUBLIK). Statistisches Bundesamt. Bevölkerung der kreisfreien Städte und Landkreise. a., 1971- Wiesbaden. *(Bevölkerung und Kultur. Reihe 1.3) Supersedes in part GERMANY (BUNDESREPUBLIK). Statistisches Bundesamt. Bevölkerungsstand und -entwicklung.*

GERMANY (BUNDESREPUBLIK). Statistisches Bundesamt. Bevölkerung der Gemeinden. a., 1974- Wiesbaden. *(Bevölkerung und Kultur. Reihe 1.4) Supersedes in part GERMANY (BUNDESREPUBLIK). Statistisches Bundesamt. Bevölkerungsstand und -entwicklung.*

GERMANY (BUNDESREPUBLIK). Bundesinstitut für Bevölkerungsforschung. 1974. The population of the Federal Republic of Germany: a World Population Year monograph. Wiesbaden, [1974]. pp. 108. *bibliog. (Committee for International Coordination of National Research in Demography. C.I.C.R.E.D. Series)*

GATZWEILER (HANS PETER) Zur Selektivität interregionaler Wanderungen: ein theoretisch-empirischer Beitrag zur Analyse und Prognose altersspezifischer interregionaler Wanderungen. [Bad Godesberg], 1975. pp. 175. *bibliog. (Germany (Bundesrepublik). Bundesforschungsanstalt für Landeskunde und Raumordnung. Forschungen zur Raumentwicklung. 1)*

GERMANY (BUNDESREPUBLIK). Statistisches Bundesamt. 1975. Berufliche und soziale Umschichtung der Bevölkerung: Ergebnisse des Mikrozensus, April 1971. Stuttgart, 1975. pp. 72. *(Bevölkerung und Kultur. Reihe 6. Erwerbstätigkeit. Sonderbeiträge)*

— Population policy.

GLASS (DAVID VICTOR) [Materials for a study of national-socialist population policy and abortion law. 1912, 1931-38). 1 piece. *Manuscript, typescript, etc.*

— Presidents.

PIKART (EBERHARD) Theodor Heuss und Konrad Adenauer: die Rolle des Bundespräsidenten in der Kanzlerdemokratie. Zürich, [1976]. pp. 176. *bibliog.*

— Race question.

HILLEL (MARC) and HENRY (CLARISSA) Lebensborn e.V.: im Namen der Rasse; (berechtigte Übersetzung [from the French] von Annette Lallemand). Wien, [1975]. pp. 352. *bibliog.*

— Relations (general) with Eastern Germany.

WILKE (KAY MICHAEL) Bundesrepublik Deutschland und Deutsche Demokratische Republik: Grundlagen und ausgewählte Probleme des gegenseitigen Verhältnisses der beiden deutschen Staaten. Berlin, [1976]. pp. 351. *bibliog. With summaries in English and French.*

— Relations (general) with Russia.

FUHRMANN (RAINER) Die Orientalische Frage, das "panslawistisch-chauvinistische Lager" und das Zuwarten auf Krieg und Revolution: die Osteuropaberichterstattung und -vorstellungen der "Deutschen Rundschau", 1874-1918. Bern, 1975. pp. 200. *bibliog. With English summary.*

— Relations (military) with China.

MEHNER (KARL HEINZ LOUIS) Die Rolle deutscher Militärberater als Interessenvertreter des deutschen Imperialismus und Militarismus in China, 1928-1936. [Leipzig?, 1961]. pp. 226, lxix. *bibliog. Microfilm: 1 reel.*

— Rural conditions.

LEBENSVERHAELTNISSE in kleinbäuerlichen Dörfern, 1952 und 1972; im Auftrage des Bundesministeriums für Ernährung, Landwirtschaft und Forsten herausgegeben von B. van Deenen [and others]. Münster-Hiltrup, [1974]. pp. 402. *(Forschungsgesellschaft für Agrarpolitik und Agrarsoziologie. [Publications]. 230) With English summary.*

— Social conditions.

BITTMANN (KARL) Ausgewählte kleinere Schriften, etc. Jena, 1920. pp. 167.

GERMANY (BUNDESREPUBLIK). Statistisches Bundesamt. 1975. Berufliche und soziale Umschichtung der Bevölkerung: Ergebnisse des Mikrozensus, April 1971. Stuttgart, 1975. pp. 72. *(Bevölkerung und Kultur. Reihe 6. Erwerbstätigkeit. Sonderbeiträge)*

PANKOKE (ECKART) and others. Neue Formen gesellschaftlicher Selbststeuerung in der Bundesrepublik Deutschland: Diskussion an Beispielen aus den Bereichen Bildung, soziale Sicherung und kommunale Selbstverwaltung. Göttingen, [1975]. pp. 310. *bibliog. (Kommission für Wirtschaftlichen und Sozialen Wandel. Schriften. 86)*

BISCHOFF (JOACHIM) ed. Die Klassenstruktur der Bundesrepublik Deutschland: ein Handbuch zum sozialen System der BRD. Westberlin, [1976]. pp. 173. *bibliogs.*

GIESECKE (HERMANN) and others. Gesellschaft und Politik in der Bundesrepublik: eine sozialkunde. Frankfurt am Main, 1976. pp. 335.

KLOSS (GUENTHER) West Germany: an introduction. London, 1976. pp. 180. *bibliog.*

KREJČÍ (JAROSLAV) Social structure in divided Germany. London, 1976. pp. 272. *bibliog.*

— — Statistics.

CHRISTLICH-DEMOKRATISCHE UNION DEUTSCHLANDS. Wirtschaftsrat. Politik in Zahlen: Daten und Fakten zur Wirtschafts- und Gesellschaftspolitik. [Bonn, 1972]. pp. 106. (Schriften)

SOZIOLOGISCHER Almanach: Handbuch gesellschaftspolitischer Daten und Indikatoren für die Bundesrepublik Deutschland; von Eike Ballerstedt [and others]. Frankfurt, [1975]. pp. 531. *bibliog. (Frankfurt am Main. Universität, and Mannheim. Universität. Sozialpolitische Forschergruppe. SPES- Projekt. Schriftenreihe. Band 5)*

— Social history.

KAMPFFMEYER (PAUL) Geschichte der Gesellschaftsklassen in Deutschland. 2nd ed. Berlin, 1910. pp. 230.

SCHAEFERS (BERNHARD) Sozialstruktur und Wandel der Bundesrepublik Deutschland: ein Studienbuch zu ihrer Soziologie und Sozialgeschichte. Stuttgart, 1976. pp. 337. *bibliogs.*

— Social policy.

BRAUER (THEODOR) Sozialpolitik und Sozialreform. Jena, 1931. pp. 116.

BRUECK (GERHARD WILHELM) and EICHNER (HARALD) Perspektiven der Sozialpolitik: Synopse der sozialpolitischen Vorstellungen der Bundesregierung, SPD, FDP, CDU, CSU, DAG, des DGB und der Bundesvereinigung der Deutschen Arbeitgeberverbände. Göttingen, [1974]. pp. 312. *bibliog.* (*Kommission für Wirtschaftlichen und Sozialen Wandel. Schriften. 41*)

MASON (TIMOTHY W.) ed. Arbeiterklasse und Volksgemeinschaft: Dokumente und Materialien zur deutschen Arbeiterpolitik, 1936-1939. Opladen, [1975]. pp. 1299. *bibliog.* (*Institut für Politische Wissenschaft. Schriften. Band 22*)

PLESSEN (MARIE LOUISE) Die Wirksamkeit des Vereins für Socialpolitik von 1872-1890: Studien zum Katheder- und Staatssozialismus. Berlin, [1975]. pp. 134. *bibliog.*

SCHMITT (GUENTHER) and WITZKE (HARALD VON) Ziel- und Mittelkonflikte sektorspezifischer Systeme sozialer Sicherung: das Beispiel der landwirtschaftlichen Sozialpolitik in der Bundesrepublik Deutschland. Berlin, [1975]. pp. 86. *bibliog.*

LAMPERT (HEINZ) Die Wirtschafts- und Sozialordnung der Bundesrepublik Deutschland. 5th ed. München, [1976]. pp. 319. *bibliogs.*

MOLITOR (BRUNO) Sozialpolitik auf dem Prüfstand. Hamburg, 1976. pp. 356. *bibliog.* (*Hamburg. Hamburgisches Welt-Wirtschafts-Archiv. Veröffentlichungen*)

— **Statistics.**

BARTELS (HILDEGARD) Further development of regional statistics. Stuttgart, 1974. pp. 11. (*Germany. (Bundesrepublik). Statistisches Bundesamt. Studies on Statistics. No.29*) *Originally published in German in Wirtschaft und Statistik, vol.8, August 1971.*

BALTES (HELMUT) and NOWAK (WERNER) Environmental statistics: an instrument of environmental planning. Stuttgart, 1975. pp. 17. (*Germany (Bundesrepublik). Statistisches Bundesamt. Studies on Statistics. No.31*) *Originally published in German in Wirtschaft und Statistik, vol. 4, April 1974.*

HESSEN UNTER DEN LÄNDERN DER BUNDESREPUBLIK; (pd. by) Statistisches Landesamt, Hesse. s-a., 1976 (no.1)- Wiesbaden.

DEUTSCHE BUNDESBANK. Deutsches Geld- und Bankwesen in Zahlen, 1876-1975. Frankfurt am Main, [1976]. pp. 364. *bibliog.*

GERMANY, EASTERN.

GERMANY (BUNDESREPUBLIK). Bundesministerium für Innerdeutsche Beziehungen. 1975. DDR Handbuch; wissenschaftliche Leitung, Peter Christian Ludz, unter Mitwirkung von Johannes Kuppe. Köln, 1975. pp. 992.

THOMAS (RUEDIGER) Modell DDR: die kalkulierte Emanzipation. 5th ed. München, 1975. pp. 291. *bibliog.*

— **Commerce.**

HOFMANN (OTTO) and SCHARSCHMIDT (GERHARD) DDR: Aussenhandel gestern und heute. Berlin, [1975]. pp. 144.

— — **Germany.**

WENIG (FRITZ HARALD) Rechtsprobleme des innerdeutschen Handels: eine Untersuchung über die Wirtschaftsbeziehungen der Bundesrepublik Deutschland und der Deutschen Demokratischen Republik aus verwaltungs-, staats- und völkerrechtlicher Sicht. Bern, 1975. pp. 272.

— — **United Kingdom.**

CONFEDERATION OF BRITISH INDUSTRY. German Democratic Republic: major steps forward on trading relationships; the report of a C.B.I. mission led by Lord Layton, etc. London, 1975. pp. 18.

— **Commercial policy.**

DIETSCH (ULRICH) Aussenwirtschaftliche Aktivitäten der DDR. Hamburg, 1976. pp. 267. *bibliog.* (*Hamburg. Hamburgisches Welt-Wirtschafts-Archiv. Veröffentlichungen*)

— **Constitution.**

SIEVEKING (KLAUS) Die Entwicklung des sozialistischen Rechtsstaatsbegriffs in der DDR: eine Studie zur Auseinandersetzung mit dem Rechtsstaat in der SBZ-DDR zwischen 1945 und 1968. Berlin, 1975. pp. 144. *bibliog.* (*Berlin. Freie Universität. Osteuropa-Institut. Rechtswissenschaftliche Veröffentlichungen. Band 3*)

— **Economic conditions.**

GERMANY (BUNDESREPUBLIK). Forschungsbeirat für Fragen der Wiedervereinigung Deutschlands. 1967. Preparing Germany's unity: excerpts from the fourth progress report, 1961-1965. Bonn, 1967. pp. 170. *Maps in end pocket.*

Die DDR nach 25 Jahren; von Bruno Gleitze [and others] . Berlin, 1975. pp. 146. (*Germany (Bundesrepublik). Forschungsbeirat für Fragen der Wiedervereinigung Deutschlands. Wirtschaft und Gesellschaft in Mitteldeutschland. Band 10*)

— **Economic history.**

BEITRAEGE zu Problemen der historischen Geographie und der geographischen Wirtschaftsgeschichte in der Deutschen Demokratischen Republik; herausgegeben von Bruno Benthien und Wilfried Strenz. Gotha, 1970. pp. 152. *bibliogs.* (*Geographische Gesellschaft der Deutschen Demokratischen Republik. Wissenschaftliche Abhandlungen. Band 8*) *Revised versions of papers presented at a conference in Berlin in 1967.*

— **Economic policy.**

LEMMNITZ (ALFRED) Unser Plan zur Wiederherstellung und Entwicklung der Friedenswirtschaft in der sowjetischen Besatzungszone; nach einem Vortrag, etc. Berlin, [1949]. pp. 55.

ARNOLD (HANS) and LANGE (ALFRED) Die sozialistische Rekonstruktion der Industrie in der Deutschen Demokratischen Republik. Berlin, 1959. pp. 104.

POLITISCHE Ökonomie des Sozialismus und ihre Anwendung in der DDR: (Tafelwerk; Autorenkollektiv: M. Herold [and others]). Berlin, 1971. 1 vol. (various foliations).

SCHULZ (HANS DIETER) Die "dritte" DDR: ihre ökonomische Basis beim Start in das internationale Leben; aus Kommentaren des Deutschlandfunks [broadcast in 1972]. Köln, 1973. pp. 54. (*Deutschlandfunk. Hefte. 15*)

WAGNER (UWE) Vom Kollektiv zur Konkurrenz: Partei und Massenbewegung in der DDR. Berlin, 1974. pp. 232. *bibliog.*

KIERA (HANS GEORG) Partei und Staat im Planungssystem der DDR: die Planung in der Ära Ulbricht. Düsseldorf, [1975]. pp. 230. *bibliog.*

SOZIALISTISCHER Staat und staatliche Leitung: aktuelle Probleme der Tätigkeit der Staatsmacht in der DDR; (Autorenkollektiv: Walter Assmann und others]; Gesamtredaktion: Michael Benjamin [and others]). Berlin, 1976. pp. 439.

VERNER (PAUL) Für das Wohl der Arbeiterklasse und des ganzen Volkes: ausgewählte Reden und Aufsätze. Berlin, 1976. pp. 507.

— — **Mathematical models.**

KLEIN (WERNER) Prozesspolitische Hauptinstrumente der Wirtschaftspolitik in der DDR: eine betriebliche Wirkungsanalyse. Stuttgart, 1975. pp. 164. *bibliog.*

— **Foreign economic relations.**

DIETSCH (ULRICH) Aussenwirtschaftliche Aktivitäten der DDR. Hamburg, 1976. pp. 267. *bibliog.* (*Hamburg. Hamburgisches Welt-Wirtschafts-Archiv. Veröffentlichungen*)

LAMM (HANS SIEGFRIED) and KUPPER (SIEGFRIED) DDR und Dritte Welt. München, 1976. pp. 328. (*Deutsche Gesellschaft für Auswärtige Politik. Forschungsinstitut. Schriften. Band 39*)

— **Foreign relations.**

WIEWIÓRA (BOLESŁAW) Niemiecka Republika Demokratyczna jako podmiot prawa międzynarodowego. Poznań, 1961. pp. 178. *bibliog. With German summary.*

AXEN (HERMANN) Sozialismus und revolutionärer Weltprozess: ausgewählte Reden und Aufsätze. Berlin, 1976. pp. 614.

— — **Treaties.**

GLEICH (JOHANN GEORG) Die Anerkennung der DDR durch die Bundesrepublik: eine völkerrechtliche Untersuchung, etc. Bern, 1975. pp. 254. *bibliog.*

— — **Germany.**

ADAM (ALFRED) Pressesprecher. Das Bundesministerium für innerdeutsche Beziehungen. Bonn, [1971]. pp. 104. *bibliog.*

GLEICH (JOHANN GEORG) Die Anerkennung der DDR durch die Bundesrepublik: eine völkerrechtliche Untersuchung, etc. Bern, 1975. pp. 254. *bibliog.*

SCHRAMM (THEODOR) Das Verhältnis der Bundesrepublik Deutschland zur DDR nach dem Grundvertrag: eine Einführung in die staats- und völkerrechtlichen Problembereiche mit Dokumentensammlung. 2nd ed. Köln, 1975. pp. 275. *bibliog.*

GERMANY (BUNDESREPUBLIK). Deutscher Bundestag. Wissenschaftliche Dienste. 1974. Die Ost- und Deutschlandpolitik der Bundesrepublik Deutschland, 1969-1973: Auswahlbibliographie mit Annotationen; [compiled by Hannelore Reiche-Juhr]. Bonn, 1974. pp. 167. (*Bibliographien. 40*)

— — **Portugal.**

SOLIDARITY with Portugal! : end imperialist interference!. [Berlin, 1975]. pp. 15.

— **Historical geography.**

BEITRAEGE zu Problemen der historischen Geographie und der geographischen Wirtschaftsgeschichte in der Deutschen Demokratischen Republik; herausgegeben von Bruno Benthien und Wilfried Strenz. Gotha, 1970. pp. 152. *bibliogs.* (*Geographische Gesellschaft der Deutschen Demokratischen Republik. Wissenschaftliche Abhandlungen. Band 8*) *Revised versions of papers presented at a conference in Berlin in 1967.*

— **Politics and government.**

Die DDR nach 25 Jahren; von Bruno Gleitze [and others] . Berlin, 1975. pp. 146. (*Germany (Bundesrepublik). Forschungsbeirat für Fragen der Wiedervereinigung Deutschlands. Wirtschaft und Gesellschaft in Mitteldeutschland. Band 10*)

KIERA (HANS GEORG) Partei und Staat im Planungssystem der DDR: die Planung in der Ära Ulbricht. Düsseldorf, [1975]. pp. 230. *bibliog.*

STARRELS (JOHN M.) and DASBACH MALLINCKRODT (ANITA) Politics in the German Democratic Republic. New York, 1975. pp. 396.

SOZIALISTISCHER Staat und staatliche Leitung: aktuelle Probleme der Tätigkeit der Staatsmacht in der DDR; (Autorenkollektiv: Walter Assmann [and others]; Gesamtredaktion: Michael Benjamin [and others]). Berlin, 1976. pp. 439.

— **Relations (general) with Germany.**

WILKE (KAY MICHAEL) Bundesrepublik Deutschland und Deutsche Demokratische Republik: Grundlagen und ausgewählte Probleme der gegenseitigen Verhältnisses der beiden deutschen Staaten. Berlin, [1976]. pp. 351. *bibliog. With summaries in English and French.*

GERMANY, EASTERN.(Cont.)

— Social conditions.

GERMANY (BUNDESREPUBLIK). Forschungsbeirat für Fragen der Wiedervereinigung Deutschlands. 1967. Preparing Germany's unity: excerpts from the fourth progress report, 1961-1965. Bonn, 1967. pp. 170. *Maps in end pocket.*

Die DDR nach 25 Jahren; von Bruno Gleitze [and others] . Berlin, 1975. pp. 146. *(Germany (Bundesrepublik). Forschungsbeirat für Fragen der Wiedervereinigung Deutschlands. Wirtschaft und Gesellschaft in Mitteldeutschland. Band 10)*

KREJČÍ (JAROSLAV) Social structure in divided Germany. London, 1976. pp. 272. *bibliog.*

— Volkskammer.

GERMANY (DEUTSCHE DEMOKRATISCHE REPUBLIK). Statutes, etc. 1963-75. Aufgaben, Rechte und Pflichten der Abgeordneten: Rechtsvorschriften mit Anmerkungen und Sachregister. Berlin, 1975. pp. 215.

LAPP (PETER JOACHIM) Die Volkskammer der DDR. Opladen, [1975]. pp. 318. *bibliog.*

GERVINUS (GEORG GOTTFRIED).

ZOEPFL (HEINRICH) Die Demokratie in Deutschland: ein Beitrag zur wissenschaftlichen Würdigung von: G.G. Gervinus, Einleitung in die Geschichte des neunzehnten Jahrhunderts. Stuttgart, 1853. pp. 106.

GESELL (SILVIO)

— Bibliography.

HESS (WILLY) compiler. Die Werke von Silvio Gesell: Versuch eines vollständigen Verzeichnisses aller seiner Bücher, Broschüren, Flugblätter und Artikel. Bern, 1975. pp. 94.

GHANA.

GHANA. Information Services Department. 1976. Ghana: an official handbook. [Accra], 1976. pp. 472.

— Armed forces — Political activity.

POLITICIANS and soldiers in Ghana 1966-1972; edited by Dennis Austin and Robin Luckham. London, 1975. pp. 318. *bibliog.*

— Census.

GHANA. Census, 1970. 1970 population census of Ghana. Accra, 1971 in progress.

— Commerce.

GHANA. 1969. Ghana's economy and aid requirements, January 1969-June 1970. [Accra, 1969]. pp. 49.

— Economic conditions.

GHANA. Commissioner for Economic Affairs. 1967. The state of Ghana's economy today; an address by E.N. Omaboe...at the fifth annual "Bu Bere" School, Kumasi, 29th August, 1967. [Accra, 1967]. pp. 16.

GHANA. 1969. Ghana's economy and aid requirements, January 1969-June 1970. [Accra, 1969]. pp. 49.

GHANA. Capital Investments Board. 1969. Investors' manual. [2nd ed.] Accra, [1969?]. pp. 47.

— Economic history.

HALPERN (JAN) Nigeria i Ghana: z historii rozwoju gospodarczego. Warszawa, 1964. pp. 374. *With English and Russian summaries and tables of contents.*

GHANA. Commissioner for Economic Affairs. 1969. Developments in the Ghanaian economy between 1960 and 1968; statement by E.N. Omaboe, Commissioner. [Accra, 1969]. pp. 27.

— Economic policy.

NKRUMAH (KWAME) Building a socialist state: an address...to the C[onvention] P[eople's] P[arty] study group, April 22, 1961. [Accra, Ministry of Information and Broadcasting, 1962]. pp. 12.

GHANA. 1968. Two-year development plan: from stabilisation to development: a plan for the period mid-1968 to mid-1970. [Accra], 1968. pp. 112.

GHANA. Ministry of Information. 1968. Two years after liberation: a review of the second year of liberation. [Accra, 1968]. pp. 38.

GHANA. Information Services Department. 1969. Three years after liberation: a review of the third year of liberation. [Accra, 1969]. pp. 27.

GHANA. 1970. One-year development plan, July 1970 to June 1971. [Accra, 1970]. pp. 185.

TAYLOR (ERNEST) An organizational approach to the analysis of problems affecting education and manpower planning in Ghana. Bonn, [1974]. pp. 184. *(Friedrich-Ebert-Stiftung. Forschungsinstitut. Schriftenreihe. Band 107)*

— Executive departments.

GHANA. Information Services Department. 1976. Ghana: an official handbook. [Accra], 1976. pp. 472.

— Foreign economic relations — Germany.

LANGER (PETER) Die Aussen- und Entwicklungspolitik der Bundesrepublik gegenüber Ghana: eine Fallstudie zur Überprüfung der neueren Imperialismus-Theorien. Meisenheim am Glan, 1975. pp. 201 *bibliog.*

— Foreign relations.

LINDQVIST (STELLAN) Linkages between domestic and foreign policy: the record of Ghana, 1957-1966. Lund, 1974. pp. 155. *bibliog.*

— — Nigeria.

ALUKO (IYIOLA OLAJIDE) Ghana and Nigeria 1957-70: a study in inter-African discord. London, 1976. pp. 275. *bibliog.*

— — United Kingdom.

DANQUAH (JOSEPH BOAKYE) Journey to independence and after: J.B. Danquah's letters, 1947-1965;...compiled by H.K. Akyeampong. Accra, 1970 in progress.

— Maps.

GHANA NATIONAL ATLAS PROJECT. Ghana national atlas. [Accra, 1976 in progress].

— Nationalism.

NKRUMAH (KWAME) What I mean by positive action. [Accra, Ministry of Information and Broadcasting, 1962]. pp. 5.

— Officials and employees.

PRICE (ROBERT M.) Society and bureaucracy in contemporary Ghana. Berkeley, [1975]. pp. 261. *bibliog.*

— Politics and government.

NKRUMAH (KWAME) The People's Party: text of a speech by President Nkrumah at a rally held in the National Assembly in Accra on June 12th, 1965, to mark the 16th anniversary of the Convention People's Party. [London, Ghana High Commission], 1965. pp. (9). *(Ghana Today. Supplements)*

GHANA. Ministry of Information. 1968. Two years after liberation: a review of the second year of liberation. [Accra, 1968]. pp. 38.

GHANA. Information Services Department. 1969. Three years after liberation: a review of the third year of liberation. [Accra, 1969]. pp. 27.

DANQUAH (JOSEPH BOAKYE) Journey to independence and after: J.B. Danquah's letters, 1947-1965;...compiled by H.K. Akyeampong. Accra, 1970 in progress.

GHANA. National Redemption Council. 1974. The charter of the National Redemption Council: unity and self-reliance. [Accra, 1974]. pp. 19.

GHANA. National Redemption Council. 1974. A guide to the study of the charter of redemption: specially prepared for committees of the revolution. [Accra, 1974]. pp. 43.

LINDQVIST (STELLAN) Linkages between domestic and foreign policy: the record of Ghana, 1957-1966. Lund, 1974. pp. 155. *bibliog.*

AKYEM Abuakwa and the politics of the inter-war period in Ghana: [papers from two seminars held at the University of Ghana at Legon]; with contributions from R. Addo-Fening [and others . Basel, 1975. pp. 166. *bibliogs. (Basler Afrika Bibliographien. Mitteilungen. 12)*

POLITICIANS and soldiers in Ghana 1966-1972; edited by Dennis Austin and Robin Luckham. London, 1975. pp. 318. *bibliog.*

SMOCK (DAVID R.) and SMOCK (AUDREY C.) The politics of pluralism: a comparative study of Lebanon and Ghana. New York, [1975]. pp. 369. *bibliog.*

AUSTIN (DENNIS) Ghana observed: essays on the politics of a West African republic. Manchester, [1976]. pp. 199.

JONES (TREVOR) Ghana's first republic, 1960-1966: the pursuit of the political kingdom. London, 1976. pp. 366.

— Population.

TURKSON (RICHARD B.) Law and population growth in Ghana. Medford, Mass., 1975. pp. 55. *(Tufts University. Fletcher School of Law and Diplomacy. Law and Population Monograph Series. No. 33)*

GAISIE (SAMUEL KWESI) and DE GRAFT-JOHNSON (K.T.) The population of Ghana. [Legon?], 1976. pp. 139. *bibliog. (Committee for International Coordination of National Research in Demography. C.I.C.R.E.D. Series)*

— Social conditions.

CHANGING social structure in Ghana: essays in the comparative sociology of a new state and an old tradition; edited with an introduction by Jack Goody. London, 1975. pp. 285. *bibliog.*

PRICE (ROBERT M.) Society and bureaucracy in contemporary Ghana. Berkeley, [1975]. pp. 261. *bibliog.*

SMOCK (DAVID R.) and SMOCK (AUDREY C.) The politics of pluralism: a comparative study of Lebanon and Ghana. New York, [1975]. pp. 369. *bibliog.*

— Social history.

BUESE (JUERGEN E.) Gewerkschaften im Prozess des sozialen Wandels in Entwicklungsländern: Versuch einer...Analyse der Rolle der Gewerkschaften in Ghana. Bonn-Bad Godesberg, [1974]. pp. 315. *bibliog. (Friedrich-Ebert-Stiftung. Forschungsinstitut. Schriftenreihe. Band 112)*

— Social policy.

NKRUMAH (KWAME) Building a socialist state: an address...to the C[onvention] P[eople's] P[arty] study group, April 22, 1961. [Accra, Ministry of Information and Broadcasting, 1962]. pp. 12.

GHANA. 1968. Two-year development plan: from stabilisation to development: a plan for the period mid-1968 to mid-1970. [Accra], 1968. pp. 112.

GHANA. Information Services Department. 1969. Three years after liberation: a review of the third year of liberation. [Accra, 1969]. pp. 27.

GHANA. 1970. One-year development plan, July 1970 to June 1971. [Accra, 1970]. pp. 185.

GHENT

— Commerce.

MAERTINS (RENATE) Wertorientierungen und wirtschaftliches Erfolgsstreben mittelalterlicher Grosskaufleute: das Beispiel Gent im 13. Jahrhundert. Köln, 1976. pp. 356. *bibliog.*

GIBRALTAR

— Economic conditions.

MAXWELL STAMP ASSOCIATES and IBERPLAN. Gibraltar, British or Spanish?: the economic prospects; a research study. London, 1976. 1 vol. (various pagings).

— Foreign economic relations — Spain.

MAXWELL STAMP ASSOCIATES and IBERPLAN. Gibraltar, British or Spanish?: the economic prospects; a research study. London, 1976. 1 vol. (various pagings).

— Foreign relations — Spain.

MAXWELL STAMP ASSOCIATES and IBERPLAN. Gibraltar, British or Spanish?: the economic prospects; a research study. London, 1976. 1 vol. (various pagings).

— Politics and government.

MAXWELL STAMP ASSOCIATES and IBERPLAN. Gibraltar, British or Spanish?: the economic prospects; a research study. London, 1976. 1 vol. (various pagings).

GIFTS, SPIRITUAL.

WILSON (BRYAN RONALD) The noble savages: the primitive origins of charisma and its contemporary survival. Berkeley, [1975]. pp. 131.

GILBERT AND ELLICE ISLANDS COLONY

— Commerce.

GILBERT AND ELLICE ISLANDS COLONY. Statistical Unit. Half yearly trade statistics report (formerly Trade). s-a. (formerly a.) 1973 (2nd)- Tarawa.

GIPSIES

— Europe.

PUXON (GRATTAN) Rom: Europe's gypsies. London, [1973]. pp. 24. *bibliog. (Minority Rights Group. Reports. No.14)*

— United Kingdom.

ACTON (THOMAS ALAN) Gypsy politics and social change: the development of ethnic ideology and pressure politics among British gypsies from Victorian reformism to Romany nationalism. London, 1974. pp. 310. *bibliog.*

GIRLS.

KONOPKA (GISELA) Young girls: a portrait of adolescence. Englewood Cliffs, [1976]. pp. 176. *bibliogs.*

GLACIAL EPOCH

— Canada.

PREST (V.K.) and GRANT (D.R.) Retreat of the last ice sheet from the maritime provinces - Gulf of St. Lawrence region. Ottawa, 1969. pp. 15. *bibliog. (Canada. Geological Survey. Papers. 1969. 33)*

GLASGOW

— Commerce.

DEVINE (T.M.) The tobacco lords: a study of the tobacco merchants of Glasgow and their trading activities c. 1740-90. Edinburgh, [1975]. pp. 209. *bibliog.*

GLASS INDUSTRY AND TRADE

— Germany.

KUEHNERT (HERBERT) ed. Urkundenbuch zur thüringischen Glashüttengeschichte; [reprint of work originally published in 1934]; und Aufsätze zur thüringischen Glashüttengeschichte. Wiesbaden, 1973. pp. 467. *bibliog.*

— United Kingdom.

GODFREY (ELEANOR S.) The development of English glassmaking, 1560-1640. Oxford, 1975. pp. 288. *bibliog.*

GLUCOSE INDUSTRY

— Nigeria.

DINA (J.A.) and AKINRELE (I.A.) An economic feasibility study for the establishment of a glucose industry in Nigeria. Lagos, Federal Ministry of Industries, 1970. pp. 29. *(Federal Institute of Industrial Research [Nigeria]. Technical Memoranda. No. 25)*

GOA, DAMAN AND DIU

— Industries.

GOA, DAMAN AND DIU. Bureau of Economics, Statistics and Evaluation. Report on annual survey of industries. a., 1969/71- Panaji.

GOD.

ROBERTSON (JOHN MACKINNON) Godism. Bradford, [1896]. pp. 7. *(Papers for the People. No. 3)*

GODOLPHIN (SIDNEY) 1st Earl of Godolphin.

CHURCHILL (JOHN) 1st Duke of Marlborough, and GODOLPHIN (SIDNEY) 1st Earl of Godolphin. The Marlborough-Godolphin correspondence; edited by Henry L. Snyder. Oxford, 1975. 3 vols.

GODWIN (MARY).

GODWIN (MARY) Letters written during a short residence in Sweden, Norway, and Denmark; edited with an introduction by Carol H. Poston. Lincoln, Nebraska, [1976]. pp. 200. *bibliog.*

GOITRE

— Tanzania.

GOTTLIEB (MANUEL) The problem of goiter in Tanzania: a programme for prevention by salt iodization and a programme for improved salt marketing in Tanzania. Dar es Salaam, 1973. pp. 42. *bibliog. (Dar es Salaam. University. Economic Research Bureau. ERB Papers. 73.6)*

GOLD CLAUSE.

GOLD, money and the law; edited by Henry G. Manne [and] Roger LeRoy Miller. Chicago, 1975. pp. 220. *Papers and edited discussion of the inaugural conference of the Center for Studies in Law and Economics of University of Miami held in 1974.*

ZEHETNER (FRANZ) Geldwertklauseln im grenzüberschreitenden Wirtschaftsverkehr. Tübingen, 1976. pp. 161. *bibliog. (Max-Planck-Institut für Ausländisches und Internationales Privatrecht, Tübingen. Beiträge zum Ausländischen und Internationalen Privatrecht. 41)*

GOLD MINERS

— Ghana.

GHANA. Commission of Enquiry into Obuasi disturbances. 1970. Report; [Kwame Ata-Bedu, chairman]. [Accra], 1969 [or rather 1970]. fo. 65. *Bound with White Paper on the report.*

GHANA. 1971. White Paper on the report of the Commission appointed to enquire into the causes of the recent disturbances at Obuasi. [Accra], 1971. pp. 5. *(W[hite] P[apers]. 1971. No. 3) Bound with the report.*

— Rhodesia.

VAN ONSELEN (CHARLES) Chibaro: African mine labour in Southern Rhodesia, 1900-1933. London, 1976. pp. 326. *bibliog.*

GOLD MINES AND MINING

— Rhodesia.

VAN ONSELEN (CHARLES) Chibaro: African mine labour in Southern Rhodesia, 1900-1933. London, 1976. pp. 326. *bibliog.*

— South Africa.

JOHNSTONE (FREDERICK A.) Class, race and gold: a study of class relations and racial discrimination in South Africa. London, 1976. pp. 298. *bibliog.*

GOLD STANDARD.

MORGAN (EDWARD VICTOR) and MORGAN (ANN D.) Gold or paper?: an essay on governments' attempts to manage the post-war monetary system, and the case for and against restoring a link with gold. London, 1976. pp. 58. *bibliog. (Institute of Economic Affairs. Hobart Papers. 69)*

GOLDER (SIDNEY ELMER).

EUROPEAN COURT OF HUMAN RIGHTS. Publications. Series A: Judgments and Decisions. [A] 18. ...Golder case. 1. Decision of 7 May 1974. 2. Judgment of 21 February 1975. Strasbourg, Council of Europe, 1975. pp. 63 [bis]. *In English and French.*

EUROPEAN COURT OF HUMAN RIGHTS. Publications. Series B: Pleadings, Oral Arguments and Documents. [B16]. "Golder" case, (1973-1975). Strasbourg, Council of Europe, 1975. pp. 264bis, 265-310. *In English and French.*

GOLDMAN (EMMA).

GOLDMAN (EMMA) and BERKMAN (ALEXANDER) Nowhere at home: letters from exile of Emma Goldman and Alexander Berkman; edited by Richard and Anna Maria Drinnon. New York, [1975]. pp. 282.

GOLDMAN (PIERRE).

DEBRAY (REGIS) Les rendez-vous manqués: pour Pierre Goldman. Paris, [1975]. pp. 157.

GOLDSMITHERY

— United Kingdom.

REDDAWAY (THOMAS FIDDIAN) The early history of the Goldsmith's Company, 1327-1509;... prepared for publication with additional material including...The book of ordinances, 1478-83, by Lorna E.M. Walker. London, 1975. pp. 378. *bibliog.*

GOLODNAIA STEP'.

RUSSIA (EMPIRE). Glavnoe Upravlenie Zemleustroistva i Zemledeliia. Otdel Zemel'nykh Uluchshenii. Materialy i Issledovaniia k Proektu Orosheniia Golodnoi i Dal'verzinskoi Stepei. vyp.1. Golodnaia step' v ee proshlom i nastoiashchem: statistiko- ekonomicheskii ocherk po issledovaniiu 1914 g.; sostavil V.F. Karavaev. Petrograd, 1914. 1 vol.(various pagings).

KHODZHIEV (E.KH.) Istoriia orosheniia i osvoeniia Golodnoi stepi, 1917-1970 gg. Tashkent, 1975. pp. 187. *bibliog.*

GOLTHO, LINCOLNSHIRE

— Antiquities.

BERESFORD (GUY) The medieval clay-land village: excavations at Goltho and Barton Blount. London, 1975. pp. 113. *(Society for Medieval Archaeology. Monograph Series. No. 6)*

GOMBE EMIRATE

— Economic history.

TIFFEN (MARY GLADYS) Economic development in Gombe emirate, North Eastern State, Nigeria, 1900-1966. 1974. fo. 301. *Typescript. 2 offprints and 1 pamphlet included. Ph.D. (London) thesis: unpublished. This thesis is the property of London University and may not be removed from the library.*

GOMPERS (SAMUEL).

LARSON (SIMEON) Labor and foreign policy: Gompers, the A[merican] F[ederation of] L[abor], and the first World War, 1914- 1918. Rutherford, N.J., [1975]. pp. 176. *bibliog.*

GONZALEZ CASANOVA (PABLO).

KAHL (JOSEPH ALAN) Modernization, exploitation and dependency in Latin America: Germani, González Casanova and Cardoso. New Brunswick, [1976]. pp. 215. *bibliogs.*

GORBACHEVSKII (IVAN IVANOVICH).

SHATROVA (GALINA PETROVNA) Dekabrist I.I. Gorbachevskii. Krasnoiarsk, 1973. pp. 198.

GOR'KII (MAKSIM) pseud.

M. Gor'kii v epokhu revoliutsii 1905-1907 godov: materialy, vospominaniia, issledovaniia. Moskva, 1957. pp. 410.

BYKOVTSEVA (LIDIIA PETROVNA) Gor'kii v Italii: monografiia. Moskva, 1975. pp. 384.

PIRADOV (B.) Na rubezhe: M. Gor'kii v Gruzii nakanune revoliutsii 1905 goda. Tbilisi, 1975. pp. 211.

GOR'KII (OBLAST')

— History.

VOPROSY istorii sotsialisticheskoi revoliutsii i sotsialisticheskogo stroitel'stva. Gor'kii, 1973. pp. 100. *(Gor'kii. Universitet. Uchenye Zapiski. vyp.156. Seriia Istoricheskaia)*

GOSNAT (VENISE).

CHAUMEIL (JEAN) Venise Gosnat: (un militant exemplaire du mouvement ouvrier français). Paris, [1975]. pp. 237.

GOSUDARSTVENNYI BANK SSSR.

KORNEEVA (RAISA VASIL'EVNA) Kreditnye vzaimootnosheniia promyshlennosti s Gosbankom. Moskva, 1975. pp. 223.

GOTHENBURG

— Commerce.

ROCKBERGER (NICOLAUS) Göteborgstrafiken: svensk lejdtrafik under andra världskriget. Stockholm, 1973. pp. 332. *bibliog. With English summary.*

KJELLBERG (SVEN T.) De svenska ostindiska compagnierna, 1731-1813: kryddor, te, porslin, siden. 2nd ed. Malmö, [1975]. pp. 325. *bibliog. With English summary.*

— Social history.

FÄLLSTRÖM (ANNE-MARIE) Konjunktur och kriminalitet: studier i Göteborgs sociala historia, 1800-1840. Göteborg, [1974]. pp. 168. *bibliog. (Göteborgs Universitet. Historiska Institutionen. Meddelanden. Nr. 8) With English summary.*

GOULD (Sir RONALD).

GOULD (Sir RONALD) Chalk up the memory: an autobiography. Birmingham, 1976. pp. 176.

GOVERNMENT, COMPARATIVE.

ALMOND (GABRIEL ABRAHAM) ed. Comparative politics today: a world view. Boston, [1974]. pp. 477. *bibliog.*

COMPARATIVE community politics: [selected papers from three conferences organized by the Committee for Community Research of the International Sociological Association]; edited by Terry Nichols Clark. New York, [1974]. pp. 415. *bibliogs.*

KESSELMAN (MARK) and ROSENTHAL (DONALD B.) Local power and comparative politics. Beverly Hills, [1974]. pp. 53. *bibliog.*

VIG (NORMAN J.) and STIEFBOLD (RODNEY P.) eds. Politics in advanced nations: modernization, development, and contemporary change. Englewood Cliffs, [1974]. pp. 608.

McLENNAN (BARBARA N.) Comparative political systems: political processes in developed and developing states. North Scituate, Mass., [1975]. pp. 307. *bibliog.*

SMITH (T. ALEXANDER) The comparative policy process. Santa Barbara, [1975]. pp. 184.

CLAPHAM (CHRISTOPHER) Liberia and Sierra Leone: an essay in comparative politics. Cambridge, 1976. pp. 156. *bibliog. (Cambridge. University. African Studies Centre. African Studies Series. 20)*

CLAUDE (RICHARD P.) ed. Comparative human rights. Baltimore, [1976]. pp. 410.

EULAU (HEINZ) and CZUDNOWSKI (MOSHE M.) eds. Elite recruitment in democratic polities: comparative studies across nations. New York, [1976]. pp. 299.

LEEMANS (ARNE F.) ed. The management of change in government. The Hague, 1976. pp. 361. *(Hague. Institute of Social Studies. Series on the Development of Societies. vol.1)*

PIRAGES (DENNIS CLARK) Managing political conflict. New York, 1976. pp. 148. *bibliog.*

GOVERNMENT ADVERTISING

— Canada.

CANADA. Road Safety Branch. 1973. The Edmonton study: a pilot project to measure the effectiveness of community public information programs in changing knowledge, attitude and behaviour in relation to driving and the use of beverage alcohols. Ottawa, 1973. pp. 60.

GOVERNMENT AND THE PRESS

— Germany.

MEDIENPOLITIK, wozu?: die Gefährdung der praktischen Zeitungsarbeit durch Patentrezepte im empfindlichen Bereich des Pressewesens; (herausgegeben von der Axel Springer Verlag AG, Abteilung Information). Berlin, 1974. pp. 172. *bibliog. (Springer (Axel) Verlag. Nachrichten. Sonderausgaben. 1974)*

WETZEL (HANS WOLFGANG) Presseinnenpolitik im Bismarckreich, 1874-1890: das Problem der Repression oppositioneller Zeitungen. Bern, 1975. pp. 365. *bibliog.*

GOVERNMENT BUSINESS ENTERPRISES.

REES (RAY) Public enterprise economics. London, [1976]. pp. 196. *bibliog. (London. University. London School of Economics and Political Science. LSE Handbooks in Economic Analysis)*

SHEPHERD (WILLIAM G.) and others. Public enterprise: economic analysis of theory and practice. Lexington, Mass., [1976]. pp. 238.

— Law and legislation.

FRIEDMANN (WOLFGANG GASTON) ed. Public and private enterprise in mixed economies. London, 1974. pp. 410.

— Algeria.

NELLIS (JOHN R.) Workers' participation in Algeria's nationalized industries: la gestion socialiste des entreprises. Ottawa, 1976. pp. 33. *(Carleton University. Norman Paterson School of International Affairs. Occasional Papers. No. 30)*

— Ghana.

GHANA. 1971. White Paper on the report of the Committee of Enquiry on the erstwhile Football Pools Authority. [Accra], 1971. pp. 5. *(W[hite] P[apers]. 1971. No.1) Bound with the report.*

GHANA. Commission of Enquiry into the Diamond Mining Corporation. 1971. Report; [chairman Charles Sterling Acolatse, subsequently Saki Scheck]. Accra, [1971]. fo. 136.

GHANA. Committee of Enquiry on the erstwhile Football Pools Authority. 1971. Report; [P.V. Osei-Hwere, chairman]. [Accra, 1971]. fo. 218. *Bound with White Paper on the report.*

— Italy.

ALZONA (GIANLUIGI) L'EFIM: profilo di un ente a partecipazione statale. Milano, [1975]. pp. 178. *(Centro Studi di Politica Economica. Collana. 4)*

— Sri Lanka.

SRI LANKA. Development Division. 1961. State industrial projects. Colombo, [1961]. pp. 174. *(Bulletins. 1. Series 2 (State Industries))*

— Tanzania.

UNITED REPUBLIC OF TANZANIA. Bureau of Statistics. Analysis of accounts of parastatals. a., 1966/1973- Dar es Salaam.

— Underdeveloped areas.

See UNDERDEVELOPED AREAS — Government business enterprises.

GOVERNMENT CONSULTANTS

— United States.

GUTTMAN (DANIEL) and WILLNER (BARRY) The shadow government: the government's multi-billion-dollar giveaway of its decision-making powers to private management consultants, "experts" and think tanks. New York, [1976]. pp. 354.

GOVERNMENT EXECUTIVES

— Europe.

The MANDARINS of western Europe: the political role of top civil servants; edited by Mattei Dogan. New York, [1975]. pp. 314.

GOVERNMENT INFORMATION

— France.

FRANCE. Commission de Coordination de la Documentation Administrative. 1975. La coordination documentaire: l'accès du public aux documents administratifs; deuxième rapport au Premier Ministre, Nov. 1974; documents annexes. Paris, 1975. pp. 91. *(Administration et Documentation)*

GOVERNMENT LENDING

— Canada.

CANADA. Statutes, etc. 1968. Office consolidation of the General Adjustment Assistance Regulations; established by P.C. 1968-651, amended by P.C. 1968-853: (regulations pertaining to a general adjustment assistance program relating to the Kennedy Round agreements). Ottawa, 1968. pp. 8.

— New Zealand.

NEW ZEALAND. New Zealand Forest Service. 1975. Forestry encouragement loans for local authorities. Wellington, 1975. pp. 11. *(Information Series. No. 71)*

GOVERNMENT MONOPOLIES.

CLAUDE (HENRI) Le capitalisme monopoliste d'état: éléments pour une explication théorique;...textes de Lénine. Paris, 1971. fo. 38. *(Centre d'Etudes et de Recherches Marxistes. Cahiers. No. 91)*

GOVERNMENT OWNERSHIP

See also AGRICULTURE AND STATE; INDUSTRY AND STATE.

— Austria.

WEISSEL (ERWIN) Die Ohnmacht des Sieges: Arbeiterschaft und Sozialisierung nach dem Ersten Weltkrieg in Österreich. Wien, [1976]. pp. 465. *bibliog.* (*Ludwig-Boltzmann-Institut für Geschichte der Arbeiterbewegung. Veröffentlichungen*)

— Germany.

PAHL (WALTHER) and MENDELSOHN (KURT) eds. Handbuch der öffentlichen Wirtschaft; herausgegeben vom Vorstand des Gesamtverbandes der Arbeitnehmer der öffentlichen Betriebe und des Personen- und Warenverkehrs. Berlin, [1930]. pp. 696. *bibliog.*

WEISSEL (ERWIN) Die Ohnmacht des Sieges: Arbeiterschaft und Sozialisierung nach dem Ersten Weltkrieg in Österreich. Wien, [1976]. pp. 465. *bibliog.* (*Ludwig-Boltzmann-Institut für Geschichte der Arbeiterbewegung. Veröffentlichungen*)

— Romania.

CURTEANU (MARIA) Sectorul de stat în România anilor 1944-1947. București, 1974. pp. 192. *bibliog.* With French table of contents.

— Russia.

DROBIZHEV (VLADIMIR ZINOV'EVICH) ed. Rabochii kontrol' i natsionalizatsiia promyshlennosti Novgorodskoi gubernii v 1917-1921 gg.: sbornik dokumentov i materialov. Leningrad, 1974. pp. 136.

KOSSOI (AVRAM IOSIFOVICH) Gosudarstvennyi kapitalizm v usloviiakh stroitel'stva sotsializma. Moskva, 1975. pp. 307. (*Akademiia Nauk SSSR. Institut Ekonomiki. Problemy Sovetskoi Ekonomiki*)

ZYBKOVETS (VLADIMIR FILATOVICH) Natsionalizatsiia monastyrskikh imushchestv v Sovetskoi Rossii, 1917-1921 gg. Moskva, 1975. pp. 205.

— United Kingdom.

AIMS OF INDUSTRY. State capitalism: some reflections on the National Enterprise Board in the mirror of Italy's I[stituto per la] R[icostruzione] I[ndustriale]. London, [1974?]. pp. 9.

AIMS FOR FREEDOM AND ENTERPRISE. Let's back the workers on nationalization, and the Labour voter, too. London, [1975]. pp. 4.

U.K. Department of Industry. 1976. The National Enterprise Board: draft guidelines. London, 1976. pp. 14.

GOVERNMENT PUBLICATIONS

— Bibliography.

GOVERNMENT PUBLICATIONS GUIDE. a., 1974. Boston, Mass.

GOVERNMENT PUBLICITY

— Germany.

OEFFENTLICHKEITSARBEIT für Raumordnung und Landesplanung: Chancen, Möglichkeiten, Techniken; Tagungsbericht über das Kontaktseminar für Landes- und Regionalplanung veranstaltet vom Institut für Raumordnung am 14. und 15. Dezember 1972. Bonn-Bad Godesberg, 1973. pp. 129. (*Germany (Bundesrepublik). Institut für Raumordnung. Mitteilungen. Heft 78*)

— United Kingdom.

AIMS FOR FREEDOM AND ENTERPRISE. The image of Britain abroad: an investigation of attitudes by foreign correspondents to British industry. London, [1975]. pp. 11.

LECTURES ON RELATIONS BETWEEN THE CIVIL SERVICE AND THE PUBLIC. [London], Civil Service College, 1975.

GOVERNMENT PURCHASING

— Russia.

KOROTKOV (VASILII FEDOROVICH) Oplata truda rabotnikov organizatsii snabzheniia i zagotovok. Moskva, 1969. pp. 72.

— United Kingdom.

NATIONAL ECONOMIC DEVELOPMENT OFFICE. Investment by nationalised industries: relations with suppliers. London, 1975. pp. 41.

GOVERNMENTAL INVESTIGATIONS

— New Zealand.

NEW ZEALAND. 1974. Royal commissions and commissions of inquiry. Wellington, 1974. pp. 92.

— United Kingdom.

DERBYSHIRE (JOHN DENIS) The Royal Commission on Trade Unions and Employers' Associations, 1965-1968: an analysis of a royal commission as an instrument for public policy making. 1976. fo. 325. *bibliog.* Typescript. Ph.D. (London) thesis: unpublished. This thesis is the property of London University and may not be removed from the Library.

— United States.

HAMILTON (JAMES) 1938- . The power to probe: a study of congressional investigations. New York, [1976]. pp. 333.

GRADUATES

— Italy.

CENTORRINO (MARIO) and PICCONE STELLA (SIMONETTA) Laurea e sottosviluppo: il mercato del lavoro intellettuale nel Mezzogiorno. Bari, [1974]. pp. 229.

— Sri Lanka.

SRIVASTAVA (R.K.) and SELVARATNAM (S.) A note on graduate unemployment. Colombo, Ministry of Planning and Economic Affairs, [1968?]. fo. 9.

— United Kingdom.

INTER-UNIVERSITY COUNCIL FOR HIGHER EDUCATION OVERSEAS. The overseas postgraduate; report of a working party. London, 1972. pp. 15.

WESTOBY (ADAM) and others. Social scientists at work. Guildford, 1976. pp. 145. *bibliog.* (*Society for Research into Higher Education. Research into Higher Education Monographs. 25*)

— United States.

ADKINS (DOUGLAS L.) The great American degree machine: an economic analysis of the human resource output of higher education...; a technical report sponsored by the Carnegie Commission on Higher Education. Berkeley, Ca., [1975]. pp. 663. *bibliog.*

FREEMAN (RICHARD BARRY) The overeducated American. New York, [1976]. pp. 218.

SOLMON (LEWIS C.) Male and female graduate students: the question of equal opportunity. New York, 1976. pp. 146. *bibliog.*

GRAESTED, DENMARK.

SONDER (RIC) Graested: reflections on a Danish station-town; based on an investigation...by students of the Royal Academy of Fine Arts and the Polytechnic Institute, Copenhagen. New York, [1955?]. fo. 29.

GRAIN AS FEEDING STUFF.

LAIDLAW (KEN) The party's over: grain: for the rich world's animals or the poor world's people?: an examination of how Britain supports famine. London, [1975]. pp. 34.

GRAIN TRADE.

CANADA. Department of Agriculture. Economics Branch. Market commentary: grains and oilseeds. s-a., D 1975- Ottawa.

HOME-GROWN CEREALS AUTHORITY. Cereals statistics. a., 1975 (1st)- London.

LAIDLAW (KEN) The party's over: grain: for the rich world's animals or the poor world's people?: an examination of how Britain supports famine. London, [1975]. pp. 34.

— Canada.

CANADA. Department of Agriculture. Economics Branch. Market commentary: grains and oilseeds. s-a., D 1975- Ottawa.

— France.

TSOLAKIS (CHRISTINE) Evolution du commerce extérieur de l'orge et du maïs de 1965 à 1970. [Paris], Ministère de l'Agriculture, 1971. fo.23.

— United Kingdom.

HOME-GROWN CEREALS AUTHORITY. Cereals statistics. a., 1975 (1st)- London.

GRAMMAR, COMPARATIVE AND GENERAL.

CHOMSKY (NOAM) The logical structure of linguistic theory. New York, [1975]. pp. 573. *bibliog.*

— Clauses.

CHICAGO LINGUISTIC SOCIETY. Regional Meeting, 8th, 1972. Relative Clause Festival. The Chicago which hunt: papers from the...festival...: a paravolume to Papers from the eighth regional meeting; edited by Paul M. Peranteau [and others]. Chicago, [1972]. pp. 261. *bibliogs.*

— Phonology.

GENERATIVE studies in historical linguistics: [papers presented at a colloquium at the University of North Carolina, 1969]; edited by Maria Tsiapera. Edmonton, [1971]. pp. 87. *bibliogs.*

SKOUSEN (ROYAL) Substantive evidence in phonology: the evidence from Finnish and French. The Hague, 1975. pp. 135. *bibliog.*

— Syntax.

BACH (EMMON) Syntactic theory. New York, [1974]. pp. 298. *bibliog.*

MONTAGUE (RICHARD) Formal philosophy: selected papers of Richard Montague; edited and with an introduction by Richmond H. Thomason. New Haven, 1974. pp. 369. *bibliogs.*

AKMAJIAN (ADRIAN) and HENY (FRANK) An introduction to the principles of transformational syntax. Cambridge, Mass., [1975] repr. 1976. pp. 419. *bibliogs.*

TREMAINE (RUTH V.) Syntax and Piagetian operational thought: a developmental study of bilingual children. Washington, [1975]. pp. 131. *bibliog.*

BRAME (MICHAEL K.) Conjectures and refutations in syntax and semantics. New York, [1976]. pp. 160. *bibliog.*

CULICOVER (PETER W.) Syntax. New York, [1976]. pp. 316. *bibliogs.*

— Topic and comment.

SYMPOSIUM ON SUBJECT AND TOPIC, UNIVERSITY OF CALIFORNIA, SANTA BARBARA, 1975. Subject and topic; edited by Charles N. Li. New York, [1976]. pp. 594. *bibliog.*

GRAMSCI (ANTONIO).

AUCIELLO (NICOLA) Socialismo ed egemonia in Gramsci e Togliatti. Bari, [1974]. pp. 207.

GRAMSCI (ANTONIO).(Cont.)

PERLINI (TITO) Gramsci e il gramscismo. Milano, [1974]. pp. 197. *bibliog.*

BUCI-GLUCKSMANN (CHRISTINE) Gramsci et l'état: pour une théorie matérialiste de la philosophie. [Paris, 1975]. pp. 454.

GRISONI (DOMINIQUE) and MAGGIORI (ROBERT) Guida a Gramsci...; traduzione di Maria Grazia Meriggi con un glossario dei più importanti termini e concetti gramsciani. Milano, 1975. pp. 271. *bibliog.*

JOCTEAU (GIAN CARLO) Leggere Gramsci: una guida alle interpretazioni. Milano, 1975. pp. 169. *bibliog.*

ORMEA (FERDINANDO) Gramsci e il futuro dell'uomo. Roma, 1975. pp. 368.

BOGGS (CARL) Gramsci's marxism. London, 1976. pp. 145.

GRANDSTANDS

— Hong Kong.

COLLAPSE of spectator stand at Sek Kong on 9th November 1968; [W.K. Thomson, chairman]. Hong Kong, Government Printer, 1969. pp. 58.

GRANT (STAN).

GRANT (STAN) The call of mother Africa. Kingston, Jamaica, 1973. pp. 361.

GRAPH THEORY.

READ (RONALD C.) ed. Graph theory and computing. New York, 1972. pp. 329. *bibliogs.*

GRAUBUENDEN

— Economic history.

CAPAUL (DURI) Graubündner Kantonalbank, 1930-1970: 40 Jahre im Dienste der Bündner Volkswirtschaft. Chur, 1974. pp. 252.

GREAT LAKES.

UNITED STATES-CANADIAN JOINT WORKING GROUP ON GREAT LAKES POLLUTION. Joint U.S.-Canadian oil and hazardous materials pollution contingency plan for Great Lakes Region. Ottawa, Information Canada, 1971. 1 vol. (various pagings). *In English and French.*

GREAT PLAINS

— Economic conditions.

TOOLE (KENNETH ROSS) The rape of the Great Plains: northwest America, cattle and coal. Boston, [1976]. pp. 271. *bibliog.*

— History.

TOBIN (GREGORY M.) The making of a history: Walter Prescott Webb and the Great Plains. Austin, Tx., [1976]. pp. 184. *bibliog.*

GREAVES (HAROLD RICHARD GORING).

GREAVES (HAROLD RICHARD GORING) [Unpublished political and personal papers. 1932-53]. 13 pieces. *Manuscript, typescript, etc.*

GREECE

— Economic conditions.

TSORIS (NICHOLAS D.) The Greek economy: the two decades, 1950-1970. Athens, 1975. pp. 77. *bibliog.*

ZOLOTAS (XENOPHON) Developments and prospects of the Greek economy: an address. Athens, 1975. pp. 29. *(Bank of Greece. Papers and Lectures. 30)*

— Economic policy.

LASOS (VAIOS) Die staatliche Entwicklungspolitik in Griechenland zwischen 1942 und 1972: Erfolge und Fehlentwicklungen, etc. Berlin, 1975. pp. 209. *bibliog. Inaugural-Dissertation zur Erlangung des Grades eines Doktors der Wirtschaftswissenschaften der Freien Universität Berlin.*

— Emigration and immigration.

DIMITRAS (ELIE) Enquêtes sociologiques sur les émigrants grecs: deuxième enquête: lors du séjour en Europe occidentale. Athènes, Centre National de Recherches Sociales, 1971. pp. 219.

DIMITRAS (ELIE) Enquêtes sociologiques sur les émigrants grecs: première enquête: avant le départ de Grèce. Athènes, Centre National de Recherches Sociales, 1971. pp. 115.

DIMITRAS (ELIE) and VLACHOS (EVANGELOS C.) Sociological surveys on Greek emigrants: third survey: upon the return to Greece. Athens, National Centre of Social Research, 1971. pp. 131.

— Foreign relations.

FLEMING (DAVID C.) John Capodistrias and the Conference of London, 1828-1831. Thessaloniki, 1970. pp. 398. *bibliog. (Hidryma Meleton Chersonesou Tou Haimou. [Publications]. 124)*

See also EUROPEAN ECONOMIC COMMUNITY — Greece; UNITED NATIONS — Greece.

— History.

ZAKYTHINOS (D.A.) The making of modern Greece: from Byzantium to independence; translated with an introduction by K.R. Johnstone. Oxford, 1976. pp. 235. *bibliog. Based on a series of lectures given to the School of Political Sciences in the University of Athens, together with much unpublished material.*

— — Sources.

FLEMING (DAVID C.) John Capodistrias and the Conference of London, 1828-1831. Thessaloniki, 1970. pp. 398. *bibliog. (Hidryma Meleton Chersonesou Tou Haimou. [Publications]. 124)*

— — 1821— .

FLEMING (DAVID C.) John Capodistrias and the Conference of London, 1828-1831. Thessaloniki, 1970. pp. 398. *bibliog. (Hidryma Meleton Chersonesou Tou Haimou. [Publications]. 124)*

— — 1941-1944, Occupation.

OLSHAUSEN (KLAUS) Zwischenspiel auf dem Balkan: die deutsche Politik gegenüber Jugoslawien und Griechenland von März bis Juli 1941. Stuttgart, 1973. pp. 375. *bibliog. (Militärgeschichtliches Forschungsamt. Beiträge zur Militär- und Kriegsgeschichte. Band 14)* 7 *maps in end pocket.*

WOODHOUSE (CHRISTOPHER MONTAGUE) The struggle for Greece, 1941-1949. London, 1976. pp. 324. *bibliog.*

— — 1944-1949.

PEJOV (NAUM) Makedoncite i graganskata vojna vo Grcija. Skopje, 1968. pp. 212. *bibliog.*

WOODHOUSE (CHRISTOPHER MONTAGUE) The struggle for Greece, 1941-1949. London, 1976. pp. 324. *bibliog.*

— Industries.

ZOLOTAS (XENOPHON) Guidelines for industrial development in Greece: an address. Athens, 1976. pp. 20. *(Bank of Greece. Papers and Lectures. 31)*

— Relations (general) with Macedonia.

POPLAZAROV (RISTO) Grčkata politika sprema Makedonija vo vtorata polovina na XIX i početokot na XX vek: vooruženi, propagandni, diplomatski i drugi antimakedonski akcii i borbata protiv niv na terenot. Skopje, 1973. pp. 324. *bibliog. With Russian and English summaries.*

GREECE, ANCIENT

— Politics and government.

STROHM (GUSTAV) Demos und Monarch: Untersuchungen über die Auflösung der Demokratie. Stuttgart, 1922. pp. 221.

VLACHOS (GEORGES C.) Les sociétés politiques homériques. Paris, 1974. pp. 399.

GREEK LANGUAGE

— Dictionaries — English.

ARCHONTAKES (ELEUTHERIOS I.) Mega elleno-agglikon lexikon genikon kai emporikon-oikonomikon- technikon-allilografias. Athenai, [1974]. 2 vols. *Paged continuously.*

GREEKS IN AUSTRALIA.

PRICE (CHARLES ARCHIBALD) ed. Greeks in Australia. Canberra, 1975. pp. 228. *(Academy of the Social Sciences in Australia. Immigrants in Australia.5)*

GREEKS IN EUROPE.

DIMITRAS (ELIE) Enquêtes sociologiques sur les émigrants grecs: deuxième enquête: lors du séjour en Europe occidentale. Athènes, Centre National de Recherches Sociales, 1971. pp. 219.

DIMITRAS (ELIE) and VLACHOS (EVANGELOS C.) Sociological surveys on Greek emigrants: third survey: upon the return to Greece. Athens, National Centre of Social Research, 1971. pp. 131.

GREEKS IN THE UNITED STATES.

KOURVETARIS (GEORGE A.) First and second generation Greeks in Chicago: an inquiry into their stratification and mobility patterns. Athens, National Centre of Social Research, 1971. pp. 111. *bibliog.*

GREEN BELTS

— France.

FRANCE. Mission d'Etude d'Aménagement Rural. La trame verte de la Région Parisienne: localisation, différenciation, fonctions des espaces non construits; propositions pour une politique d'aménagement. [Paris], 1975. pp. 217. *Maps in end pocket.*

GREENLAND

— Social conditions.

SOCIALE problemer i Gronland: levevilkår og sociale problemer i Vestgrønland...; [by] (Anders From) [and others]. København, 1975. pp. 398. *bibliog. (Socialforskningsinstituttet. Publikationer. 64) With English summaries.*

GREGORY (Sir THEODOR EMANUEL GUGENHEIM).

GREGORY (Sir THEODOR EMANUEL GUGENHEIM) [Unpublished economic and personal papers. 1910-34]. 6 pieces. *Manuscript, typescript, etc.*

GRIEVANCE PROCEDURES

— United Kingdom.

THOMSON (ANDREW W.J.) and MURRAY (VICTOR V.) Grievance procedures. Farnborough, Hants, [1976]. pp. 192.

GRIGORENKO (PETR GRIGOR'EVICH).

GRIGORENKO (PETR GRIGOR'EVICH) The Grigorenko papers: writings by General P.G. Grigorenko and documents on his case. London, [1976]. pp. 187.

GROCERY TRADE

— Netherlands.

ECONOMISCH INSTITUUT VOOR HET MIDDEN- EN KLEINBEDRIJF. Bedrijfseconomische Publikaties. De commerciele samenwerking in de kruidenierswarenbranche ontwikkeling in de jaren zestig en zeventig. 's-Gravenhage, 1970. pp. 59.

ECONOMISCH INSTITUUT VOOR HET MIDDEN- EN KLEINBEDRIJF. Bedrijfseconomische Publikaties. Bedrijfsgegevens over 1969 en de geraamde uitkomsten over 1970 en 1971 voor het kruideniersbedrijf, XXX. 's-Gravenhage, 1971. pp. 83.

GROSS DOMESTIC PRODUCT

— Australia.

AUSTRALIAN NATIONAL ACCOUNTS: gross product by industry at current and constant prices; (pd. by) Commonwealth Bureau of Census and Statistics. a., 1962-63/1973-74- Canberra.

— Canada.

CANADA. Statistics Canada. Real domestic product by industry. a., 1971/74 (1st)- Ottawa.

— Hong Kong.

HONG KONG. Census and Statistics Department. 1975. Estimates of gross domestic product, 1961-73. Hong Kong, 1975. pp. 35.

— Nigeria.

NIGERIA. Federal Office of Statistics. 1972. Gross domestic product of Nigeria, 1958-59 to 1969-70. Lagos, 1972. pp. 30.

— United States.

NIEMI (ALBERT W.) Gross state product and productivity in the southeast. Chapel Hill, N.C., [1975]. pp. 119. bibliog.

GROSS NATIONAL PRODUCT.

LEVY (EMANUEL) M.A., Dr. rer.pol. Per capita product and the level of economic development. Basel, 1972. pp. 284. bibliog.

A SYSTEM of international comparisons of gross product and purchasing power: (United Nations International Comparison Project: phase one);...published for the World Bank. Baltimore, [1975]. pp. 294.

— Germany.

CONRAD (KLAUS) of the University of Tübingen, and JORGENSON (DALE W.) Measuring performance in the private economy of the Federal Republic of Germany, 1950-1973. Tübingen, 1975. pp. 198. bibliog. (Tübingen. Universität. Fachbereich Wirtschaftswissenschaft. Tübinger Wirtschaftswissenschaftliche Abhandlungen. Band 19)

GROSSRAMING

— History.

OFNER (JOSEF) Grossraming: Geschichte einer Bergbauerngemeinde im Ennstal; aus dem Nachlass herausgegeben von Manfred Brandl. Grossraming, 1975. pp. 250. bibliog.

GROUND—EFFECT MACHINES.

JOHNSON (PETER STEWART) The economics of invention and innovation: with a case study of the development of the hovercraft. London, 1975. pp. 329.

GROUP PSYCHOTHERAPY.

SHARP (VICTOR) Social control in the therapeutic community. Farnborough, Hants., [1975]. pp. 221. bibliog.

GROUP RELATIONS TRAINING.

COOPER (CARY LYNN) ed. Theories of group processes. London, [1975]. pp. 277.

GROUP WORK IN EDUCATION.

ZINBERG (NORMAN E.) and others. Teaching social change: a group approach. Baltimore, Ma., [1976]. pp. 252. bibliog.

GRUEN (KARL).

STRASSMAIER (JAMES) Karl Grün und die Kommunistische Partei, 1845-1848; [translated from the English by Franz Gebert and Gertrud Romaniuk]. Trier, [1973]. pp. 30. (Karl-Marx-Haus. Schriften. 10)

GSCHWIND (STEFAN).

ROSENFELD (LOTTE) Stefan Gschwind: ein Genossenschaftspionier. Basel, 1968. pp. 154. bibliog.

GUADELOUPE.

FRANCE. Direction de la Documentation. La Documentation Française. Notes et Etudes Documentaires. Nos. 4,135 - 4, 136 - 4,137. Les départements d'outre-mer: la Guadeloupe; [by Guy Lasserre and others]. Paris, 1974. pp. 83. bibliog.

GUAJIRO INDIANS.

WATSON (LAWRENCE CRAIG) Guajiro personality and urbanization. Los Angeles, 1968. pp. 209. bibliog. (California University. Latin American Center. Latin American Studies. vol. 10)

GUARANI INDIANS.

CLASTRES (HELENE) La terre sans mal: le prophétisme Tupi-Guarani. Paris, [1975]. pp. 157.

— Religion and mythology.

CLASTRES (PIERRE) Le grand parler: mythes et chants sacrés des Indiens Guarani. Paris, [1974]. pp. 143. bibliog.

GUARANTEED ANNUAL INCOME

— Canada.

CANADA. Department of National Health and Welfare. 1972. How to get your 1972 guaranteed income supplement. Ottawa, 1972. pp. 16, 16. In English and French.

— United States.

INTEGRATING income maintenance programs; edited by Irene Lurie. New York, [1975]. pp. 383. (Wisconsin University, Madison. Institute for Research on Poverty. Monograph Series). Papers presented at a conference held in Madison, 1972.

GUATEMALA

— Commerce.

GUATEMALA. Consejo Nacional de Planificacion Economica. Secretaria General. 1967. Investigacion de trafico, tarifas y costos en puertos de Guatemala; (bajo la direccion del Dr. Earle W. Orr). [Guatemala], 1967. 2 vols. (in 1).

— Economic conditions.

INTER-AMERICAN COMMITTEE FOR AGRICULTURAL DEVELOPMENT. 1971. Tenencia de la tierra y desarrollo socio-economico del sector agricola en Guatemala. Guatemala, 1971. pp. 395. bibliog.

— Economic policy.

ORGANIZATION OF AMERICAN STATES. Inter-American Economic and Social Council. Committee of Nine. 1966. Evaluation of Guatemala's 1965-1969 economic and social development plan; report presented to the Guatemalan government by the Ad Hoc Committee. Washington, 1966. pp. 274.

GUATEMALA. Consejo Nacional de Planificacion Economica. Secretaria General. 1970. Plan de desarrollo, 1971-1975. Tomo[s] I - II [and] Anexo III. Guatemala, 1970. 3 vols.

— Native races.

SOLANO Y PEREZ-LILA (FRANCISCO DE) Los Mayas del siglo XVIII: pervivencia y transformacion de la sociedad indigena guatemalteca durante la administracion borbonica. Madrid, 1974. pp. 483. bibliog.

— Social conditions.

INTER-AMERICAN COMMITTEE FOR AGRICULTURAL DEVELOPMENT. 1971. Tenencia de la tierra y desarrollo socio-economico del sector agricola en Guatemala. Guatemala, 1971. pp. 395. bibliog.

— Social life and customs.

MOORE (ALEXANDER) Life cycles in Atchalán: the diverse careers of certain Guatemalans. New York, [1973]. pp. 220. bibliog.

— Social policy.

ORGANIZATION OF AMERICAN STATES. Inter-American Economic and Social Council. Committee of Nine. 1966. Evaluation of Guatemala's 1965-1969 economic and social development plan; report presented to the Guatemalan government by the Ad Hoc Committee. Washington, 1966. pp. 274.

GUATEMALA. Consejo Nacional de Planificacion Economica. Secretaria General. 1970. Plan de desarrollo, 1971-1975. Tomo[s] I - II [and] Anexo III. Guatemala, 1970. 3 vols.

GUAYAQUI INDIANS

— Religion and mythology.

CLASTRES (PIERRE) Chronique des Indiens Guayaki: ce que savent les Aché, chasseurs nomades du Paraguay. [Paris, 1974]. pp. 357.

GUAYAQUIL (PROVINCE)

— Economic history.

HAMERLY (MICHAEL T.) Historia social y economica de la antigua provincia de Guayaquil, 1973-1842. Guayaquil, 1973. pp. 212. bibliog. (Archivo Historico del Guayas. Coleccion Monografica. Publicaciones. No.3)

— Social history.

HAMERLY (MICHAEL T.) Historia social y economica de la antigua provincia de Guayaquil, 1973-1842. Guayaquil, 1973. pp. 212. bibliog. (Archivo Historico del Guayas. Coleccion Monografica. Publicaciones. No.3)

GUERNICA

— Bombardment, 1937.

SOUTHWORTH (HERBERT RUTLEDGE) La destruction de Guernica: journalisme, diplomatie, propagande et histoire. Paris, [1975]. pp. 535. bibliog.

THOMAS (GORDON) and MORGAN-WITTS (MAX) The day Guernica died. London, [1975]. pp. 319. bibliog.

GUERNSEY

— Emigration and immigration.

GUERNSEY. States Insurance Authority. 1936. Memorandum on the problems of our greater adult population and the additional burden of new arrivals into the island at adult ages. [St. Peter Port], 1936. pp. 11.

— Politics and government.

GUERNSEY. 1958. States Committees as at 29th May, 1958. [St. Peter Port], 1958. pp. 67.

GUERNSEY(Cont.)

— Population.

GUERNSEY. States Insurance Authority. 1936. Memorandum on the problems of our greater adult population and the additional burden of new arrivals into the island at adult ages. [St. Peter Port], 1936. pp. 11.

GUERRILLA WARFARE.

MARTIĆ (MILOŠ) Insurrection: five schools of revolutionary thought. New York, [1975]. pp. 342. *bibliog.*

SARKESIAN (SAM CHARLES) ed. Revolutionary guerrilla warfare. Chicago, [1975]. pp. 623. *bibliog.*

GUERRILLAS

— Bolivia.

MOLINA CESPEDES (TOMAS) La ultima trinchera del "Che". Cochabamba, 1969. pp. 45.

— Brazil.

PARTIDO COMUNISTA DO BRASIL. Comite Central. La guerra popular en el Brasil. Montevideo, 1970. pp. 57.

— East (Near East).

EL-RAYYES (RIAD) and NAHAS (DUNIA HABIB) Guerrillas for Palestine. London, 1976. pp. 155.

— Guinea—Bissau.

CABRAL (AMILCAR) Unité et lutte. Paris, 1975. 2 vols. (in 1). *bibliog.*

GUEVARA (ERNESTO).

FRONTINI (NORBERTO A.) Criticas al libro "Mi amigo el Che". [Buenos Aires?, 1968]. pp. 64.

MOLINA CESPEDES (TOMAS) La ultima trinchera del "Che". Cochabamba, 1969. pp. 45.

GUILT.

MORRIS (HERBERT) On guilt and innocence: essays in legal philosophy and moral psychology. Berkeley, Calif., [1976]. pp. 161.

GUIMARÃES ROSA (JOÃO)

See ROSA (JOÃO GUIMARÃES).

GUINEA

— Economic policy.

ADAMOLEKUN ('LADIPO) Sékou Touré's Guinea: an experiment in nation building. London, 1976. pp. 250. *bibliog.*

— Politics and government.

ADAMOLEKUN ('LADIPO) Sékou Touré's Guinea: an experiment in nation building. London, 1976. pp. 250. *bibliog.*

— Social policy.

ADAMOLEKUN ('LADIPO) Sékou Touré's Guinea: an experiment in nation building. London, 1976. pp. 250. *bibliog.*

GUINEA-BISSAU.

— Nationalism.

CABRAL (AMILCAR) La conscience nouvelle que la lutte a forgée chez les hommes et les femmes de notre pays est l'arme la plus puissante de notre peuple contre les criminels colonialistes portugais; message...à l'occasion du XV anniversaire de la fondation du Parti. [Conakry], 1971. fo. 6.

CABRAL (AMILCAR) Les patriotes de Bissao et d'autres villes doivent chaque jour mieux s'organiser et agir avec intelligence et sûreté; message...à l'occasion du 3 août. [Conakry], 1971. fo. 6.

CABRAL (AMILCAR) Rapport bref sur la situation de la lutte, janvier-août 1971. [Conakry], 1971. fo. 32.

PARTIDO AFRICANO DA INDEPENDENCIA DA GUINE E CABO VERDE. Guinea-Bissau toward final victory!: selected speeches and documents from PAIC. Richmond, B. C., [1974]. pp. 96.

CABRAL (AMILCAR) Unité et lutte. Paris, 1975. 2 vols. (in 1). *bibliog.*

— Politics and government.

CABRAL (AMILCAR) La conscience nouvelle que la lutte a forgée chez les hommes et les femmes de notre pays est l'arme la plus puissante de notre peuple contre les criminels colonialistes portugais; message...à l'occasion du XV anniversaire de la fondation du Parti. [Conakry], 1971. fo. 6.

CABRAL (AMILCAR) Les patriotes de Bissao et d'autres villes doivent chaque jour mieux s'organiser et agir avec intelligence et sûreté; message...à l'occasion du 3 août. [Conakry], 1971. fo. 6.

CABRAL (AMILCAR) Rapport bref sur la situation de la lutte, janvier-août 1971. [Conakry], 1971. fo. 32.

CABRAL (AMILCAR) Unité et lutte. Paris, 1975. 2 vols. (in 1). *bibliog.*

PARTIDO AFRICANO DA INDEPENDÊNCIA DA GUINE E CABO VERDE. Conselho Superior da Luta. Declaração do Conselho Superior da Luta de 25 de junho de 1975. Bissau, Imprensa Nacional, 1975. pp. 11.

GUIPUZCOA

— Politics and government.

CILLAN APALATEGUI (ANTONIO) Sociologia electoral de Guipuzcoa, 1900-36. San Sebastian, 1975. pp. 749. *bibliog.*

GUJARAT

— Economic policy.

GUJARAT. General Administration Department (Planning). 1962. Development programme, 1961-62, Gujarat state. Baroda, 1962. pp. 126.

GUJARAT. General Administration Department (Planning). 1971. Development programme 1971-72. [Gandhinagar], 1971. pp. 222. *9b(Budget Publications. No. 10)*

— Social policy.

GUJARAT. General Administration Department (Planning). 1962. Development programme, 1961-62, Gujarat state. Baroda, 1962. pp. 126.

GUJARAT. General Administration Department (Planning). 1971. Development programme 1971-72. [Gandhinagar], 1971. pp. 222. *9b(Budget Publications. No. 10)*

GULF OF MEXICO

— History.

LANGLEY (LESTER D.) Struggle for the American Mediterranean: United States- European rivalry in the Gulf-Caribbean, 1776-1904. Athens, Ga., [1976]. pp. 226. *bibliog.*

GURUNGS.

MACFARLANE (ALAN DONALD JAMES) Resources and population: a study of the Gurungs of Nepal. Cambridge, 1976. pp. 364. *bibliog.*

GUYANA

— Appropriations and expenditures.

ODLE (MAURICE A.) The evolution of public expenditure: the case of a structurally dependent economy: Guyana. Kingston, Jamaica, 1976. pp. 271. *bibliog.*

— History.

NATH (DWARKA) A history of Guyana. London, [1975]. 3 vols. (in 2).

GUZMAN BLANCO (ANTONIO).

GOSLINGA (CORNELIS CH.) Curaçao and Guzmán Blanco: a case study of small power politics in the Caribbean. 's-Gravenhage, 1975. pp. 143. *bibliog. (Instituut voor Taal-, Land- en Volkenkunde. Verhandelingen. [Deel] 76)*

GWIAZDOWICZ (MICHAL).

GWIAZDOWICZ (MICHAŁ) Wspomnienia; do druku przygotował, poprzedził biografią, zebrał relacje o autorze i jego rodzinie Zygmunt Hemmerling. Warszawa, 1974. pp. 331.

GYPSUM

— Somali Republic.

SOMALILAND PROTECTORATE. Geological Survey. Mineral Resources Pamphlets. No. 1. Gypsum, anhydrite. Hargeisa, [1954]. fo. 4.

HABEAS CORPUS

— United Kingdom.

SHARPE (ROBERT J.) The law of Habeas Corpus. Oxford, 1976. pp. 254.

HABERMAS (JUERGEN).

SIMON-SCHAEFER (ROLAND) and ZIMMERLI (WALTHER CH.) Theorie zwischen Kritik und Praxis: Jürgen Habermas und die Frankfurter Schule. Stuttgart-Bad Cannstatt, [1975]. pp. 186. *bibliog. With English summary.*

HACKNEY

— Social conditions.

BARNES (RON) A licence to live:...scenes from a post-war working life in Hackney. London, [1974] repr. 1976. pp. 76.

HAEMOPHILIA.

MASSIE (ROBERT K.) and MASSIE (SUZANNE) Journey. London, 1975. pp. 417.

HAGUE

— International Court of Justice.

ROSENNE (SHABTAI) The world court: what it is and how it works. 3rd ed. Leiden, 1973. pp. 252.

GAMBLE (JOHN KING) and FISCHER (DANA D.) The International Court of Justice: an analysis of a failure. Lexington, Mass., [1976]. pp. 157.

GROSS (LEO) ed. The future of the International Court of Justice. Dobbs Ferry, N.Y., 1976. 2 vols.

HAILE SELASSIE I, Emperor of Ethiopia.

ULLENDORFF (EDWARD) The autobiography of Emperor Haile Sellassie of Ethiopia: conferenza tenuta nella seduta del 10 aprile 1974. Roma, 1974. pp. 14. *(Accademia Nazionale dei Lincei. Problemi Attuali di Scienza e di Cultura. Quaderni. N.197)*

HAILE SELASSIE I., Emperor of Ethiopia. The autobiography of Emperor Haile Sellassie I: 'My life and Ethiopia's progress', 1892-1937; translated and annotated by Edward Ullendorff. London, 1976. pp. 337. *bibliog.*

HAITI

— Commerce.

HAITI. Secrétairerie d'Etat du Commerce et de l'Industrie. Bulletin trimestriel; (formerly Bulletin mensuel). q., (formerly m.) Jl 1974 (no.2)- ; with gap (Ag 1974, no.3). Port-au-Prince.

— Economic conditions — Statistics.

HAITI. Département des Finances et des Affaires Economiques Bulletin. irreg., Ag 1972 - Jl 1974 (nos. 3-5); ceased pbln. [Port-au Prince].

— **Foreign relations — United States.**

HEALY (DAVID F.) Gunboat diplomacy in the Wilson era: the U.S. Navy in Haiti, 1915-1916. Madison, Wis., 1976. pp. 268. *bibliog.*

— **History — 1915—1934, American occupation.**

BELLEGARDE (LOUIS DANTES) L'occupation américaine d'Haiti: ses conséquences morales et économiques. Port-au-Prince, 1929. pp. 44.

— **Industries.**

HAITI. Secrétairerie d'Etat du Commerce et de l'Industrie. Bulletin trimestriel; (formerly Bulletin mensuel). q., (formerly m.). Jl 1974 (no.2)- ; with gap (Ag 1974, no.3). Port-au-Prince.

HALDANE (ELIZABETH SANDERSON).

HALDANE (ELIZABETH SANDERSON) From one century to another: the reminiscences of Elizabeth S. Haldane. London, 1937. pp. 322.

HALFWAY HOUSES.

EVALUATING community treatment programs: tools, techniques, and a case study; edited by Mercedese M. Miller. Lexington, Mass., [1975]. pp. 124. *bibliog.*

HALLE

— **Population.**

ALLENDORF (HANS) Der Zuzug in die Städte:...mit besonderer Berücksichtigung der Zuzugsverhältnisse der Stadt Halle a. S. im Jahre 1899. Jena, 1901. pp. 80. *bibliog. (Halle. Universität. Staatswissenschaftliches Seminar. Sammlung Nationalökonomischer und Statistischer Abhandlungen. 30. Band)*

HALLS OF RESIDENCE.

RUSSELL-GEBBETT (JEAN P.) Students in residence: a study of the background and attitudes of students in halls of residence and of their contemporaries electing to live in off-campus accommodation. Nottingham, 1975. pp. 57. *bibliog.*

HALMSTAD

— **Population.**

KRONBORG (BO) and NILSSON (THOMAS) Stadsflyttare: industrialisering, migration och social mobilitet med utgångspunkt från Halmstad, 1870-1910. Uppsala, 1975. pp. 298. *bibliog. (Uppsala. Universitet. Historiska Institutionen. Studia Historica Upsaliensia. 65)* With English summary.

HAMBURG

— **Commerce.**

BENEKE (ALFRED) Ein Hamburger auf Kuba: Briefe und Notizen des Kaufmanns... , 1842-1844; ausgewählt und erläutert von Renate Hauschild- Thiessen. Hamburg, 1971. pp. 120.

REISSMANN (MARTIN) Die hamburgische Kaufmannschaft des 17. Jahrhunderts in sozialgeschichtlicher Sicht. Hamburg, 1975. pp. 447. *bibliog. (Verein für Hamburgische Geschichte. Beiträge zur Geschichte Hamburgs. Band 4)*

— **Harbour.**

WIGET (AXEL) Entwicklungstendenzen des Seehafenwettbewerbs zwischen Hamburg, Kopenhagen und dänischen Provinzhäfen. Göttingen, [1975]. pp. 220. *bibliog. (Hamburg. Hansische Universität. Institut für Verkehrswissenschaft. Verkehrswissenschaftliche Studien. 27)*

— **History.**

LUETH (ERICH) Gabriel Riesser, 1806-1863: ein grosser Jude, Hamburger und deutscher Patriot. Hamburg, 1963. pp. 55.

HOCHMUTH (URSEL) ed. Candidates of humanity: Dokumentation zur Hamburger Weissen Rose anlässlich des 50. Geburtstages von Hans Leipelt. Hamburg, 1971. pp. 74. *bibliog. (Vereinigung der Antifaschisten und Verfolgten des Naziregimes, Land Hamburg. VAN-Dokumentationen. 2)*

VEREINIGUNG DER ANTIFASCHISTEN UND VERFOLGTEN DES NAZIREGIMES, LAND HAMBURG. Jacob und Schrübbers: heute wie damals; Dokumentation zum Berufsverbotsbeschluss und zum Fall Ilse Jacob, etc. 2nd ed. Hamburg, 1972. pp. 94. *(VAN-Documentationen. 4)*

— **Officials and employees.**

CRINIUS (WOLFGANG) and SCHAFT (WOLFGANG) Teilzeitbeschäftigung im öffentlichen Dienst: eine Untersuchung in den Behörden der Freien und Hansestadt Hamburg. Hamburg, 1976. pp. 263. *bibliog. (Hamburg. Hamburgisches Welt-Wirtschafts-Archiv. Veröffentlichungen)*

— **Politics and government.**

TROITZSCH (KLAUS G.) Sozialstruktur und Wählerverhalten:...dargestellt am Beispiel der Wahlen in Hamburg von 1949 bis 1974. Meisenheim am Glan, 1976. pp. 142. *bibliog.*

ULLRICH (VOLKER) Die Hamburger Arbeiterbewegung vom Vorabend des ersten Weltkrieges bis zur Revolution 1918/19. Hamburg, [1976]. 2 vols. *bibliog.* Band 2 contains notes and the bibliography.

— **Social conditions.**

[HAMBURG. Senat. 1971] Bericht über die wirtschaftliche und soziale Lage der ausländischen Arbeitnehmer in Hamburg. [Hamburg, imprint, 1971?]. pp. 86.

— **Social history.**

REISSMANN (MARTIN) Die hamburgische Kaufmannschaft des 17. Jahrhunderts in sozialgeschichtlicher Sicht. Hamburg, 1975. pp. 447. *bibliog. (Verein für Hamburgische Geschichte. Beiträge zur Geschichte Hamburgs. Band 4)*

ULLRICH (VOLKER) Die Hamburger Arbeiterbewegung vom Vorabend des ersten Weltkrieges bis zur Revolution 1918/19. Hamburg, [1976]. 2 vols. *bibliog.* Band 2 contains notes and the bibliography.

HAMILTON (ALEXANDER).

MITCHELL (BROADUS) Alexander Hamilton: a concise biography. New York, 1976. pp. 395. *bibliog.*

HAMILTON, ONTARIO

— **Social history.**

KATZ (MICHAEL B.) The people of Hamilton, Canada West: family and class in a mid-nineteenth-century city. Cambridge, Mass., 1975. pp. 381.

HAMMARSKJÖLD (DAG).

DAYAL (RAJESHWAR) Mission for Hammarskjold: the Congo crisis. London, 1976. pp. 335. *bibliog.*

HAMPSHIRE

— **Industries.**

KIRKBRIDE (DAVID) Factors affecting the future location of employment in South Hampshire. [Winchester], 1969. pp. 18. *bibliog. (South Hampshire Plan Technical Unit. Working Papers. 4)*

— **Politics and government.**

HAMPSHIRE REORGANISED; [pd.by] Hampshire County Council. a., 1975(1st)- Winchester.

— **Population.**

FRANCIS (KEITH) The natural increase of the private household population in South Hampshire 1966-2001: model, assumptions, projections. rev. ed. [Winchester], 1970. pp. 81. *bibliog. (South Hampshire Plan Technical Unit. Working Papers. 1)*

— **Social conditions.**

PRIESTNALL (DAVID J.) Implications of social area analysis in South Hampshire. [Winchester], 1972. 1 vol. (unpaged). *(South Hampshire Plan Technical Unit. Working Papers. 17)*

— **Transit systems.**

FRANCIS (KEITH) Commuting to and from South Hampshire: the present situation and likely trends to 2001. [Winchester], 1969. fo. 14. *(South Hampshire Plan Technical Unit. Working Papers. 2)*

HANDICAPPED

— **Australia.**

AUSTRALIA. Commonwealth Bureau of Census and Statistics. 1970. Chronic illnesses, injuries and impairments, May 1968. [Canberra, 1970]. pp. 43.

— **United Kingdom.**

BOLDERSON (HELENA MARGIT) Compensation, maintenance and rehabilitation: the conflict in British policies for the disabled, 1914-1946. [1976]. fo. 288. Typescript. Ph.D. (London) thesis: unpublished. This thesis is the property of London University and may not be removed from the Library.

MARONEY (ROBERT M.) The family and the state: considerations for social policy. London, 1976. pp. 142.

— **United States.**

MARTIN (ROLLAND A.) Occupational disability: causes, prediction, prevention. Springfield, Ill., [1975]. pp. 206. *bibliog.*

HANDICAPPED CHILDREN

— **Education.**

INTEGRATION of handicapped children in society: [papers presented to an international study group sponsored by the International Cerebral Palsy Society and the Spastics Society]; edited by James Loring and Graham Burn. London, 1975. pp. 217.

— **Rehabilitation.**

INTEGRATION of handicapped children in society: [papers presented to an international study group sponsored by the International Cerebral Palsy Society and the Spastics Society]; edited by James Loring and Graham Burn. London, 1975. pp. 217.

— **United Kingdom.**

COUNCIL FOR CHILDREN'S WELFARE. Occasional Papers on Child Welfare. No. 3. No childhood: the handicapped child at home and in hospital in the 1970's. London, 1975. pp. 24.

HANSA TOWNS.

FRITZE (KONRAD) and others, eds. Hansische Studien III: Bürgertum, Handelskapital, Städtebünde. Weimar, 1975. pp. 282. *(Historiker-Gesellschaft der Deutschen Demokratischen Republik. Hansische Arbeitsgemeinschaft. Abhandlungen zur Handels- und Sozialgeschichte. Band 15)*

HANSEATIC LEAGUE.

ZOELLNER (KLAUS PETER) Vom Strelasund zum Oslofjord: Untersuchungen zur Geschichte der Hanse und der Stadt Stralsund in der zweiten Hälfte des 16. Jahrhunderts. Weimar, 1974. pp. 200. *bibliog. (Historiker-Gesellschaft der Deutschen Demokratischen Republik. Hansische Arbeitsgemeinschaft. Abhandlungen zur Handels- und Sozialgeschichte. Band 14)*

KAZAKOVA (NATAL'IA ALEKSANDROVNA) Russko-livonskie i russko-ganzeiskie otnosheniia, konets XIV - nachalo XVI v. Leningrad, 1975. pp. 359.

HARBOURS

HARBOURS
— Denmark.

WIGET (AXEL) Entwicklungstendenzen des Seehafenwettbewerbs zwischen Hamburg, Kopenhagen und dänischen Provinzhäfen. Göttingen, [1975]. pp. 220. *bibliog*. (Hamburg. Hansische Universität. Institut für Verkehrswissenschaft. Verkehrswissenschaftliche Studien. 27)

— East (Far East).

GRUENFELD (ERNST) Hafenkolonien und kolonieähnliche Verhältnisse in China, Japan und Korea: eine kolonialpolitische Studie. Jena, 1913. pp. 239. *bibliog*.

— France.

FRANCE. Direction des Ports Maritimes et des Voies Navigables. Service Central. L'activité des ports maritimes français de commerce (title varies). a., 1969- Paris.

FRANCE. Direction des Ports Maritimes et des Voies Navigables. Rapport d'activité. a., 1973- Paris.

— Germany — Schleswig-Holstein.

FLENSBURG. Industrie- und Handelskammer. Schiffahrt und Häfen im Bereich der Industrie- und Handelskammer zu Flensburg; herausgegeben anlässlich ihres 100jährigen Jubiläums...; (Autoren: Gerd Andresen [and others]). Flensburg, [1971]. pp. 358. *bibliog*.

— Guatemala.

GUATEMALA. Consejo Nacional de Planificacion Economica. Secretaria General. 1967. Investigacion de trafico, tarifas y costos en puertos de Guatemala; (bajo la direccion del Dr. Earle W. Orr). [Guatemala], 1967. 2 vols. (in 1).

— United Kingdom — Finance.

NATIONAL PORTS COUNCIL. Finance Division. Financial objectives for the port industry. London, 1975. pp. 15.

HARRIMAN (WILLIAM AVERELL).

HARRIMAN (WILLIAM AVERELL) and ABEL (ELIE) Special envoy to Churchill and Stalin, 1941-1946. New York, [1975]. pp. 595.

HARRINGTON (JAMES).

SAPRYKIN (IURII MIKHAILOVICH) Politicheskoe uchenie Garringtona: iz istorii ideino- politicheskoi bor'by v gody angliiskoi burzhuaznoi revoliutsii XVII veka. Moskva, 1975. pp. 205.

HARRISON (THOMAS RUSSELL).

HARRISON (THOMAS RUSSELL) A challenge to the presidency: Canada and inflation: cause, course, cost, correction, consolidation. Hicksville, N.Y., [1976]. pp. 151.

HARROW SCHOOL.

HARROW SCHOOL. Orders, statutes, and rules, to be observed and kept by the governors of the Free Grammar School at Harrow-on-the-Hill, etc. London, printed by Mills, Howett, and Mills, 1833. pp. 43.

HART (Sir ROBERT).

HART (Sir ROBERT) The I.G. in Peking: letters of Robert Hart, Chinese Maritime Customs, 1868-1907...; edited by John King Fairbank [and others]. Cambridge, Mass., 1975. 2 vols. *Letters to his London agent, James Duncan Campbell.*

HARVARD UNIVERSITY.

LIPSET (SEYMOUR MARTIN) and RIESMAN (DAVID) Education and politics at Harvard;...two essays prepared for the Carnegie Commission on Higher Education. New York, [1975]. pp. 440. *bibliogs*.

HAWAIIAN ISLANDS
— Economic conditions — Mathematical models.

GHALI (MOHEB) and RENAUD (BERTRAND M.) The structure and dynamic properties of a regional economy: an econometric model for Hawaii. Lexington, [1975]. pp. 158. *bibliog*.

HAY
— Sweden.

JORDBRUKETS UTREDNINGSINSTITUT. Meddelanden. 1974. Nr. 3. Olika sätt att bereda vallfoder: en ekonomisk studie. Stockholm, 1974. pp. 47. *With English summary.*

HAYA (AFRICAN TRIBE).

RALD (JØRGEN) and RALD (KAREN) Rural organization in Bukoba district, Tanzania. Uppsala, 1975. pp. 122. *bibliog*.

HAYEK (FRIEDRICH AUGUST).

ESSAYS on Hayek; [by] William F. Buckley [and others]; (edited by Fritz Machlup; foreword by Milton Friedman). New York, 1976. pp. 182. *bibliog. Essays in honour of F.A. Hayek presented at a special regional meeting of the Mont Pelerin Society in 1975.*

HEALTH ATTITUDES.

MECHANIC (DAVID) The growth of bureaucratic medicine: an inquiry into the dynamics of patient behavior and the organization of medical care. New York, [1976]. pp. 345.

WORLD HEALTH ORGANIZATION/INTERNATIONAL COLLABORATIVE STUDY OF MEDICAL CARE UTILIZATION. 1976. Health care: an international study;...edited by Robert Kohn and Kerr L. White; with a foreword by Robert T. Bridgman. London, 1976. pp. 557. *bibliog*.

HEALTH CARE TEAMS
— United Kingdom.

MARSH (GEOFFREY) and KAIM-CAUDLE (P.R.) Team care in general practice. London, 1976. pp. 185.

HEALTH EDUCATION.

SAUBER (S. RICHARD) Preventive educational intervention for mental health. Cambridge, Mass., [1973]. pp. 182. *bibliogs*.

HEALTH SERVICES ADMINISTRATION
— United Kingdom — Bibliography.

U.K. Department of Health and Social Security. [Notices]: H.N. [Health Services Management]. irreg., Jl 1976 (no.127)- London.

— United States.

WEAVER (JERRY L.) Conflict and control in health care administration. Beverly Hills, [1975]. pp. 196. *bibliog*.

HEALTH SURVEYS.

WORLD HEALTH ORGANIZATION/INTERNATIONAL COLLABORATIVE STUDY OF MEDICAL CARE UTILIZATION. 1976. Health care: an international study;...edited by Robert Kohn and Kerr L. White; with a foreword by Robert T. Bridgman. London, 1976. pp. 557. *bibliog*.

HEATH ECOLOGY.

GIMINGHAM (CHARLES HENRY) An introduction to heathland ecology. Edinburgh, [1975]. pp. 124. *bibliog*.

HEBRANG (ANDRIJA).

MILATOVIĆ (MILE) Slučaj Andrije Hebranga. Beograd, 1952. pp. 267.

HECHT (ROBERT).

HUEMER (PETER) Sektionschef Robert Hecht und die Zerstörung der Demokratie in Österreich: eine historisch-politische Studie. Wien, 1975. pp. 372.

HEFNER (HUGH MARSTON).

BRADY (FRANK ROBERT) Hefner. London, 1975. pp. 224.

HEGEL (GEORG WILHELM FRIEDRICH).

GEGEL' i filosofiia v Rossii, 30-e gody XIX v. - 20-e gody XX v. Moskva, 1974. pp. 264. *bibliog*.

WILKINS (BURLEIGH TAYLOR) Hegel's philosophy of history. Ithaca, 1974. pp. 196. *bibliog*.

LUKÁCS (GEORG) Marxist. The young Hegel: studies in the relations between dialectics and economics. London, 1975. pp. 576.

SHKLAR (JUDITH N.) Freedom and independence: a study of the political ideas of Hegel's Phenomenology of mind. Cambridge, 1976. pp. 216.

HEILBRONN
— Politics and government.

GROSSHANS (ALBERT) ed. 100 Jahre SPD Heilbronn, 1874-1974. Heilbronn, 1974. pp. 200. *bibliog*.

HEINE (HEINRICH).

LEFEBVRE (JEAN PIERRE) Marx und Heine. Trier, [1972]. pp. 51. (Karl-Marx-Haus. Schriften. 7) *Xerox copy.*

HEMPEL (CARL GUSTAV).

HOWELLS (PETER GRAEME ALLISON) Economic theory in historical explanation: the Hempel explanation schema in economic history. 1976. fo. 239. *bibliog. Typescript. Ph.D. (London) thesis: unpublished. This thesis is the property of London University and may not be removed from the Library.*

HERDER (JOHANN GOTTFRIED VON).

BERLIN (Sir ISAIAH) Vico and Herder: two studies in the history of ideas. London, 1976. pp. 228.

HERMENEUTICS.

ESSAYS on explanation and understanding: studies in the foundations of humanities and social sciences; edited by Juha Manninen and Raimo Tuomela. Dordrecht, [1976]. pp. 440. *bibliogs. Includes papers from the International Colloquium on Explanation and Understanding, Helsinki, 1974.*

HEROES IN LITERATURE.

MATHEWSON (RUFUS WELLINGTON) The positive hero in Russian literature. 2nd ed. Stanford, 1975. pp. 369.

HEROIN.

BRILL (LEON) The de-addiction process: studies in the de-addiction of confirmed heroin addicts. Springfield, Ill., [1972]. pp. 166.

HEROIN HABIT.

LEVIN (GILBERT) and others. The persistent poppy: a computer-aided search for heroin policy. Cambridge, Mass., [1975]. pp. 229.

PLATT (JEROME J.) and LABATE (CHRISTINA) Heroin addiction: theory, research, and treatment. New York, [1976]. pp. 417. *bibliog*.

HERRING—FISHERIES
— Canada.

MITCHELL (C.L.) and McEACHERN (D.B.) Developments in the Atlantic coast herring fishery and fish meal industry, 1964-1968. Ottawa, Information Canada, 1970. pp. 26. *bibliog. (Canadian Fisheries Reports. No. 16)*

HERTZOG (JAMES BARRY MUNNIK).

SCHOLTZ (GERT DANIEL) Hertzog en Smuts en die Britse Ryk. Kaapstad, 1975. pp. 158. *bibliog.*

HERWEGH (GEORG).

MUSCHG (ADOLF) Von Herwegh bis Kaiseraugst: wie halten wir es als Demokraten mit unserer Freiheit?; mit ausgewählten politischen Gedichten von Georg Herwegh. Zürich, [1975]. pp. 61.

HESSE

— **Economic conditions.**

HESSE. Statistisches Landesamt. Beiträge zur Statistik Hessens. Neue Folge. Nr. 68. Die hessischen Landkreise und kreisfreien Städte nach Abschluss der Gebietsreform am 1. Januar 1977. Wiesbaden, 1975. 1 vol. (various pagings).

— **Landtag — Elections.**

HESSE. Statistisches Landesamt. Beiträge zur Statistik Hessens. Neue Folge. Nr. 69. Die Wahl zum Hessischen Landtag am 27. Oktober 1974. Wiesbaden, 1975. pp. 83.

— **Politics and government.**

WHITE (DAN S.) The splintered party: National Liberalism in Hessen and the Reich, 1867-1918. Cambridge, Mass., 1976. pp. 303. *bibliog.*

HEUSS (THEODOR).

PIKART (EBERHARD) Theodor Heuss und Konrad Adenauer: die Rolle des Bundespräsidenten in der Kanzlerdemokratie. Zürich, [1976]. pp. 176. *bibliog.*

HIDES AND SKINS.

KERSEY (HARRY A.) Pelts, plumes and hides: white traders among the Seminole Indians, 1870-1930. Gainesville, Flo., 1975. pp. 158. *bibliog.*

HIGH-RISE APARTMENT BUILDINGS.

— **United Kingdom.**

ADAMS (BARBARA) and CONWAY (JEAN) The social effects of living off the ground. London, Department of the Environment, [1975]. pp. 9. *(HDD Occasional Papers. 75/1)*

GITTUS (ELIZABETH) Flats, families and the under-fives. London, 1976. pp. 269. *bibliog.*

HIGH SCHOOLS

— **United States.**

TILLERY (DALE) and KILDEGAARD (THEODORE C.) Educational goals, attitudes and behaviors: a comparative study of high school seniors. Cambridge, Mass., [1973]. pp. 251. *bibliog.*

HIGHER EDUCATION AND STATE

— **Africa, East.**

SOUTHALL (ROGER) Federalism and higher education in East Africa. Nairobi, 1974. pp. 160. *bibliog.*

HILBERT SPACE.

AKHIEZER (NAUM IL'ICH) and GLAZMAN (I.M.) Theory of linear operators in Hilbert space...; translated from the Russian by Merlynd Nestell. New York, [1961-63] repr.1966. 2 vols.

HILL FARMING

— **Italy.**

LECHI (FRANCESCO) and RICCI (GIUSEPPE) L'agricoltura nella pianificazione delle comunità montane: il caso della Valle Sabbia. Milano, 1974. pp. 122.

HILLEBRAND (OSWALD).

PAUL (ERNST) Oswald Hillebrand: ein Lebensbild nach archivalischen Unterlagen, etc. Stuttgart, 1976. pp. 78.

HISTORIANS

— **Germany.**

MOSES (JOHN A.) The politics of illusion: the Fischer controversy in German historiography. London, 1975. pp. 148. *bibliog.*

— **Poland.**

MATERNICKI (JERZY) Idee i postawy: historia i historycy polscy, 1914-1918: studium historiograficzne. Warszawa, 1975. pp. 546. *bibliog.*

— — **Bibliography.**

KLARNER (IZABELA) and others, compilers. Bibliografia publikacji pracowników Instytutu Historycznego. z.1. 1945-1966. Warszawa, 1969. pp. 183.

— **Russia.**

RAZVITIE sovetskoi istoricheskoi nauki, 1970-1974. Moskva, 1975. pp. 479. *With English table of contents.*

— — **Ukraine.**

KOMARENKO (NAÏNA VASYLIVNA) Ustanovy istorychnoï nauky v Ukraïns'kii RSR, 1917-1937 rr. Kyïv, 1973. pp. 171. *With Russian summary.*

HISTORICAL FILMS.

SMITH (PAUL) 1937- , ed. The historian and film. Cambridge, [1976]. pp. 208. *bibliog.*

HISTORICAL RESEARCH.

CONFERENCE ON EARLY AMERICAN HISTORY, 27TH, 1970. Of mother country and plantations: proceedings of the... conference...; edited by Virginia Bever Platt and David Curtis Skaggs. Bowling Green, Ohio, 1971. pp. 127. *bibliog.*

HISTORICAL SOCIOLOGY.

FLORA (PETER) Modernisierungsforschung zur empirischen Analyse der gesellschaftlichen Entwicklung. Opladen, [1974]. pp. 203. *bibliog.*

FLORA (PETER) Indikatoren der Modernisierung: ein historisches Datenhandbuch. Opladen, [1975]. pp. 194. *bibliog.*

HISTORIOGRAPHY.

SCHAFF (ADAM) History and truth. Oxford, 1976. pp. 272. *bibliog.*

HISTORY

— **Bibliography.**

HARVARD UNIVERSITY. Library. Widener Library Shelflists. [No.] 32. General European and world history. Cambridge, Mass., 1970. pp. 959.

— **Congresses.**

INTERNATIONAL CONGRESS OF HISTORICAL STUDIES. 13th Congress, 1970. Doklady kongressa. t.1. Moskva, 1973-74. 1 vol.(in 7). *Papers are in the original Russian, English, French or German.*

— **Methodology.**

McCLELLAND (PETER D.) Causal explanation and model building in history, economics and the new economic history. Ithaca, 1975. pp. 290. *bibliog.*

— **Philosophy.**

KUYPERS (K.) and others. Sociologie en geschiedenis. Assen, 1961. pp. 46.

WILKINS (BURLEIGH TAYLOR) Hegel's philosophy of history. Ithaca, 1974. pp. 196. *bibliog.*

SKAGESTAD (PETER) Making sense of history: the philosophies of Popper and Collingwood. Oslo, [1975]. pp. 118. *bibliog. (Norges Almenvitenskapelige Forskningsråd. Gruppe: Språk og Historie) Based on lectures given at Brandeis University, Spring, 1973.*

BURGER (THOMAS) Max Weber's theory of concept formation: history, laws, and ide types. Durham, N.C., 1976. pp. 231. *bibliog.*

SCHAFF (ADAM) History and truth. Oxford, 1976. pp. 272. *bibliog.*

SCHULZE (HANS) Strategie der Gegenprophetie: zur Kritik der gegenwärtigen bürgerlichen Geschichtsphilosophie. Berlin, 1976. pp. 113.

SHAW (WILLIAM HARRY) Productive forces and relations of production: a study of the dynamics of Marx's theory of historical change. [1976]. fo. 509. *bibliog. Typescript. Ph.D.(London) thesis: unpublished. This thesis is the property of London University and may not be removed from the Library.*

SMITH (BROOKE WILLIAMS) Jacques Maritain: antimodern or ultramodern?: an historical analysis of his critics, his thought, and his life. New York, 1976. pp. 194. *bibliog.*

— **Statistical methods.**

SWIERENGA (ROBERT P.) ed. Quantification in American history: theory and research. New York, 1970. pp. 417. *bibliog.*

— **Study and teaching — Audio—visual aids.**

SMITH (PAUL) 1937- , ed. The historian and film. Cambridge, [1976]. pp. 208. *bibliog.*

— — **Belgium.**

MAES (LOUIS THEO) Prejudice and its impact on the teaching of history: an important Belgian initiative. Brussels, Ministry of Foreign Affairs, External Trade and Cooperation in Development, 1974. pp. 44. *bibliog. (Memo from Belgium. No. 165)*

HISTORY, MODERN

— **1700-1799.**

ROBERTS (JOHN MORRIS) Revolution and improvement: the Western world, 1775-1847. London, [1976]. pp. 290.

— **1800-1899.**

ROBERTS (JOHN MORRIS) Revolution and improvement: the Western world, 1775-1847. London, [1976]. pp. 290.

HISTORY, UNIVERSAL.

CAMERON (KENNETH NEILL) Humanity and society: a world history. Bloomington, ind., [1973]. pp. 470. *bibliog.*

HITLER (ADOLF).

RAUSCHNING (HERMANN) Gespräche mit Hitler. New York, [1940]. pp. 272.

ENGEL (GERHARD) Heeresadjutant bei Hitler, 1938-1943: Aufzeichnungen des Majors Engel; herausgegeben und kommentiert von Hildegard von Kotze. Stuttgart, [1974]. pp. 158. *bibliog. (Vierteljahrshefte für Zeitgeschichte. Schriftenreihe. Nr. 29)*

FELICE (RENZO DE) Mussolini e Hitler: i rapporti segreti, 1922-1933; con documenti inediti. Firenze, [1975]. pp. 315.

HOBBES (THOMAS).

MINOGUE (KENNETH ROBERT) Parts and wholes: twentieth century interpretation of Thomas Hobbes. Granada, 1974. pp. 31. *(Reprinted from Anales de la Catédra Francisco Suarez of the Universidad de Granada, no. 14, 1974)*

OAKESHOTT (MICHAEL JOSEPH) Hobbes on civil association. Oxford, [1975]. pp. 154.

TOENNIES (FERDINAND) Studien zur Philosophie und Gesellschaftslehre im 17. Jahrhundert; herausgegeben von E.G. Jacoby. Stuttgart-Bad Cannstatt, [1975]. pp. 384. *bibliog.*

HOBSON (JOHN ATKINSON).

HOBSON (JOHN ATKINSON) Confessions of an economic heretic: the autobiography of J.A. Hobson; edited...by Michael Freeden; [reprint, with a new introduction, of the work first published in 1938]. Hassocks, Sussex, 1976. pp. 217.

HOHOFF (WILHELM).

KREPPEL (KLAUS) Entscheidung für den Sozialismus: die politische Biographie Pastor Wilhelm Hohoffs, 1848-1923. Bonn-Bad Godesberg, [1974]. pp. 196. bibliog. (Friedrich-Ebert-Stiftung. Forschungsinstitut. Schriftenreihe. Band 114)

HOLIDAYS

— Norway.

NORWAY. Statistiske Centralbyrå. 1975. Ferieundersøkelsen, 1974, etc. Oslo, 1975. pp. 131. (Norges Offisielle Statistikk. Rekke A. 732) In Norwegian and English.

— United Kingdom.

SOCIAL TOURISM STUDY GROUP. Holidays: the social need; [D.O. Gladwin, chairman]. London, English Tourist Board, [1976]. pp. 74.

HOLSTEBRO

— Civic improvement.

HOLSTEBRO. Byplanudvalget. Dispositionsplan for Holstebro kommune. [Holstebro, 1962]. pp. 91.

HOLTROP (MARIUS WILHELM).

KESSLER (GELDOLPH A.) Monetary analysis and monetary policy. Amsterdam, [1973?]. pp. 25-46. (Nederlandsche Bank. Reprints. No. 1) (This article appeared in M.W. Holtrop, Money in an open economy, 1972)

HOLY ROMAN EMPIRE

— Constitutional history.

VANN (JAMES ALLEN) The Swabian Kreis: institutional growth in the Holy Roman Empire, 1648-1715. Bruxelles, 1975. pp. 338. bibliog. (International Commission for the History of Representative and Parliamentary Institutions. Studies. 53)

— Foreign relations — Russia.

PAMIATNIKI diplomaticheskikh snoshenii drevnei Rossii s derzhavami inostrannymi. t.7. Pamiatniki diplomaticheskikh snoshenii s Rimskoi imperiei. Sanktpeterburg, 1864. 1514 columns.

HOLYOAKE (GEORGE JACOB).

GRUGEL (LEE E.) George Jacob Holyoake: a study in the evolution of a Victorian radical. Philadelphia, 1976. pp. 189. bibliog.

HOME ACCIDENTS

— United Kingdom.

U.K. Department of Prices and Consumer Protection. 1976. Collection of information on accidents in the home: proposals for an accident surveillance system; (by Janet Thompson and Louise Hesketh). London, 1976. pp. 24.

HOME LABOUR

— Germany.

GAEBEL (KAETHE) Die Heimarbeit: das jüngste Problem des Arbeiterschutzes. Jena, 1913. pp. 246. bibliog.

ARNDT (PAUL) Professor in the University of Frankfort. Heimarbeiterelend in Deutschland. Jena, 1927. pp. 68.

— Italy.

CRESPI (FRANCO) and others. Il lavoro a domicilio: il caso dell'Umbria. Bari, [1975]. pp. 158.

HOME OWNERSHIP.

HOUSING RESEARCH FOUNDATION. Home ownership for lower income families. London, 1974. pp. 16.

ASHMORE (GRAHAM) The owner-occupied housing market. Birmingham, 1975. pp. 44. (Birmingham. University. Centre for Urban and Regional Studies. Research Memoranda No. 41)

DE VANE (RICHARD) Second home ownership: a case study. Cardiff, 1975. pp. 108. bibliogs. (Wales. University. University College of North Wales. Bangor Occasional Papers in Economics. No. 6)

KRAPOHL (PETER) Eigentumswohnungen in der Bundesrepublik Deutschland: Entwicklung und Beurteilung ihrer Marktfähigkeit. Bonn, [1975]. pp. 475. bibliog. (Cologne. Universität. Institut für Wohnungsrecht und Wohnungswirtschaft. Schriften. Band 43)

— United States.

STRUYK (RAYMOND J.) and MARSHALL (SUE A.) Urban homeownership: the economic determinants. Lexington, Mass., [1976]. pp. 198.

HOME RULE

— Ireland.

ROBERTSON (JOHN MACKINNON) Home rule and rule of thumb. Bradford, [1896]. pp. 7. (Papers for the People. No. 6)

IRELAND and the Union: a short sketch of the political history of Ireland and of her economic and social condition under the Union. Dublin, [1914?]. fo. 127,pp.ix.

LARKIN (EMMET) The Roman Catholic church and the creation of the modern Irish state, 1878-1886. Philadelphia, 1975. pp. 412.

O'BRIEN (JOSEPH V.) William O'Brien and the course of Irish politics, 1881-1918. Berkeley, [1976]. pp. 273. bibliog.

— Scotland.

HEALD (DAVID) Making devolution work. London, 1976. pp. 56. (Young Fabian Group. Young Fabian Pamphlets. 43)

SCOTLAND. Scottish Law Commission. 1976. Comments on White Paper: Our changing democracy: devolution to Scotland and Wales. [Edinburgh, 1976]. pp. 97. (Memoranda. No. 32) White Paper published as Cmnd. 6348, British Parliamentary Papers, Session 1975-76.

HOMER.

VLACHOS (GEORGES C.) Les sociétés politiques homériques. Paris, 1974. pp. 399.

HOMOSEXUALITY.

ALTMAN (DENNIS) Homosexual: oppression and liberation. rev. ed. London, 1974. pp. 252. bibliog. Rev. ed. first published in Australia in 1973.

— France.

FRONT HOMOSEXUEL D'ACTION REVOLUTIONNAIRE. Faggots and the revolution; [including articles from Tout]. London, [1973?]. pp. 16.

— Germany.

DANNECKER (MARTIN) and REICHE (REIMUT) Der gewöhnliche Homosexuelle: eine soziologische Untersuchung über männliche Homosexuelle in der Bundesrepublik. Frankfurt am Main, [1974]. pp. 393,36. bibliog.

— United Kingdom.

MILLIGAN (DON) The politics of homosexuality. London, 1973. pp. 19.

NATIONAL COUNCIL FOR CIVIL LIBERTIES. Reports. No. 8. Homosexuality and the teaching profession: results of a survey on the attitudes of local education authorities to the employment of homosexual women and men as teachers. London, 1975. pp. 21.

HONDURAS

— Economic policy.

ORGANIZATION OF AMERICAN STATES. Inter-American Economic and Social Council. Committee of Nine. 1966. Evaluation of Honduras' 1965-1969 national economic and social development plan; report submitted to the Honduran government by the Ad Hoc Committee. Washington, 1966. pp. 348.

HONDURAS. Consejo Superior de Planificacion Economica. Secretaria Tecnica. 1969. Plan de accion, 1969-1971. Parte II, Vol. 1, Partes III, IV. Tegucigalpa, 1969. 3 vols.

— Social policy.

ORGANIZATION OF AMERICAN STATES. Inter-American Economic and Social Council. Committee of Nine. 1966. Evaluation of Honduras' 1965-1969 national economic and social development plan; report submitted to the Honduran government by the Ad Hoc Committee. Washington, 1966. pp. 348.

HONG KONG.

HUGHES (RICHARD) Journalist. Borrowed place, borrowed time: Hong Kong and its many faces. London, 1976. pp. 191.

— Bibliography.

IP (DAVID FU-KEUNG) and others, compilers. Hong Kong: a social sciences bibliography:...[compiled] with the assistance of Tse-fun Chan. Hong Kong, 1974. pp. 355. (Hong Kong. University. Centre of Asian Studies. Bibliographies and Research Guides. No. 7)

— Census.

HONG KONG. Census, 1971. Hong Kong population and housing census 1971: main report. [Hong Kong, 1972]. pp. 248.

HONG KONG. Census, 1971. Population and housing census, 1971: transport characteristics. Hong Kong, [1974]. pp. 60.

— Constitution.

MINERS (NORMAN) The government and politics of Hong Kong. Hong Kong, 1975. pp. 300. bibliog.

— Economic conditions.

GRAVEREAU (JACQUES) Hong-Kong: analyse d'un boom. Paris, 1974. pp. 446. bibliog. (Centre d'Etudes des Techniques Economiques Modernes. TEM Analyse. 1)

HSIA (RONALD) and others. The structure and growth of the Hong Kong economy. Wiesbaden, [1975]. pp. 142. (Hamburg. Institut für Asienkunde. Schriften. Band 40)

— — Statistics.

HONG KONG SOCIAL AND ECONOMIC TRENDS; (pd. by) Census and Statistics Department. irreg., 1968/72 (1st)- Hong Kong.

— Emigration and immigration.

WATSON (JAMES L.) Emigration and the Chinese lineage: the Mans in Hong Kong and London. Berkeley, [1975]. pp. 242. bibliog.

— Executive departments.

MINERS (NORMAN) The government and politics of Hong Kong. Hong Kong, 1975. pp. 300. bibliog.

— Industries.

HONG KONG. Census and Statistics Department. 1972. 1971 census of manufacturing establishments. Hong Kong, [1972]. pp. 533.

HOUSING.

— Languages.

HONG KONG. Chinese Language Committee. 1971. The first report (with Second and third reports); [Sir] Kenneth Ping-fan Fung, chairman]. Hong Kong, 1971. 3 pt.

— Officials and employees — Salaries, allowances, etc.

HONG KONG. Standing Committee on Superscale/Upperscale Salaries. 1974. Fifth report; [G.R. Ross, chairman]. Hong Kong, 1974. pp. 13.

— Politics and government.

HONG KONG. Secretariat for Chinese Affairs. 1969. The City District Officer scheme; report by the Secretary for Chinese Affairs. Hong Kong, 1969. pp. 38.

MINERS (NORMAN) The government and politics of Hong Kong. Hong Kong, 1975. pp. 300. *bibliog.*

ENGLAND (JOE W.) Hong Kong: Britain's responsibility. London, 1976. pp. 31. *bibliog. (Fabian Society. Research Series. [No.] 324)*

— Population.

HONG KONG. Census and Statistics Department. 1973. Hong Kong population projections, 1971-1991. Hong Kong, [1973]. pp. 43.

FAN (SHUH CHING) The population of Hong Kong. [Hong Kong?, 1974]. pp. 50. *(Committee for International Coordination of National Research in Demography. C.I.C.R.E.D. Series)*

— Social conditions — Statistics.

HONG KONG SOCIAL AND ECONOMIC TRENDS; (pd. by) Census and Statistics Department. irreg., 1968/72 (1st)- Hong Kong.

— Statistics.

HONG KONG SOCIAL AND ECONOMIC TRENDS; (pd. by) Census and Statistics Department. irreg., 1968/72 (1st)- Hong Kong.

GERMANY (BUNDESREPUBLIK). Statistisches Bundesamt. Länderkurzberichte: Hong Kong. a., 1976- Wiesbaden.

— Statistics, Vital.

HONG KONG. Census and Statistics Department. 1973. Hong Kong life tables, 1971-1991. Hong Kong, [1973]. pp. 19.

HOOVER (HERBERT CLARK) President of the United States.

HERBERT Hoover and the crisis of American capitalism; contributors: Ellis W. Hawley [and others]. Cambridge, Mass., [1973]. pp. 138.

BEST (GARY DEAN) The politics of American individualism: Herbert Hoover in transition, 1918-1921. Westport, Conn., 1975. pp. 202. *bibliog.*

WILSON (JOAN HOFF) Herbert Hoover: forgotten progressive. Boston, Mass., [1975]. pp. 307. *bibliog.*

HOPPE (JAN).

HOPPE (JAN) Wspomnienia, przyczynki, refleksje. Londyn, 1972. pp. 395.

HORA (JOSEF).

HORA (JOSEF) Dny a lidé: [výbor z fejetonistiky]. Praha, 1961. pp. 286. *(Dílo Josefa Hory. sv. 16)*

HORNCASTLE

— Social history.

CLARK (J. NORMAN) Education in a market town: Horncastle, 1329-1970. London, 1976. pp. 183. *bibliog.*

HORTHY (MIKLÓS) Regent of Hungary.

SCHMIDT-PAULI (EDGAR VON) Nikolaus von Horthy: Admiral, Volksheld und Reichsverweser. 2nd ed. Hamburg, [1944?]. pp. 344.

HORTICULTURAL PRODUCTS

— United Kingdom.

ADVISORY COUNCIL FOR AGRICULTURE AND HORTICULTURE IN ENGLAND AND WALES. Report on supply/demand relationships in horticultural products. [London], 1975. pp. 38.

HORTICULTURE

— Canada.

CANADA. Department of Agriculture. Economics Branch. Market commentary: horticulture and special crops. s-a., D 1975- Ottawa.

— Germany — Saarland.

SAARGEBIET. Statistisches Amt. Einzelschriften zur Statistik des Saarlandes. Nr. 52. Strukturverhältnisse im Garten- und Obstbau: Ergebnisse der Gartenbauerhebung 1972/73. Saarbrücken, 1976. pp. 72.

HOSIERY WORKERS

— United Kingdom.

GURNHAM (RICHARD) A history of the trade union movement in the hosiery and knitwear industry, 1776-1976: the history of the National Union of Hosiery and Knitwear Workers, its evolution and its predecessors. Leicester, 1976. pp. 197. *bibliog.*

HOSPITALS.

THOMPSON (JOHN D.) and GOLDIN (GRACE) The hospital: a social and architectural history. New Haven, 1975. pp. 349. *bibliog.*

— Australia.

AUSTRALIA. Department of Health. Research Section. 1973. Hospitals in Australia, 1967-68 to 1970-71. Canberra, 1973. fo. 19.

— France — Finance.

FRANCE. Direction de la Comptabilité Publique. Le secteur public local: statistiques des comptes des établissements d'hospitalisation publics et des organismes d'habitations a loyer modéré. a., 1973- Paris.

— — Law and legislation.

FORGES (JEAN MICHEL DE) L'hospitalisé. Paris, 1975. pp. 316.

— New Zealand.

NEW ZEALAND. Department of Health. National Health Statistics Centre. Health statistics report: Hospital and selected morbidity data. a., 1971- . Wellington. *Formerly included in NEW ZEALAND. Department of Health. National Health Statistics Centre. Health statistics report.*

— United Kingdom.

U.K. Department of Health and Social Security. 1974. Community hospitals: their role and development in the National Health Service. [London, 1974]. pp. 13.

— — Wales — Personnel management.

WELSH HOSPITAL BOARD. Report of a working party on industrial relations; [J.O. Morris, chairman]. [Cardiff], 1972. fo. 25.

HOTELS, TAVERNS, ETC.

— United Kingdom — Employees.

SHAMIR (BOAS) A study of working environments and attitudes to work of employees in a number of British hotels. 1975. fo.304. *bibliog.* Typescript. Ph.D. (London) thesis: unpublished. *This thesis is the property of London University and may not be removed from the Library.*

— — Ireland, Northern.

NORTHERN IRELAND TOURIST BOARD. Research and Planning Department. Survey of accommodation. a., 1974- [Belfast].

— United States.

LEMASTERS (E.E.) Blue-collar aristocrats: life-styles at a working-class tavern. Madison, Wis., 1975. pp. 218.

HOURS OF LABOUR.

FRIEDRICH (ROBERT) Zur Methodologie des Arbeitszeitproblems. Jena, 1926. pp. 93. *(Gesellschaft für Soziale Reform. Schriften. Heft 78)*

— Bibliography.

GREENBERG (A. MORLEY) and WRIGHT (DAVID M.) compilers. The variable work week: a selected bibliography, 1967-1974. [Toronto], Ministry of Transportation and Communications, 1974. pp. 25.

— United Kingdom.

CENTRAL SHORT TIME COMMITTEE. A selection of facts and arguments in favour of the Ten Hours' Bill, as regards its probable effects on commerce and wages if universally adopted. Manchester, printed by Grant and Co., 1845. pp. 56.

The FALLACIES of the opponents to Lord Ashley's Ten Hours' Factory Bill completely exposed; by a tradesman. Manchester, printed by Grant and Co., 1845. pp. 8.

FERGUSSON (WILLIAM) Lecture on the evils of protracted hours of labour; published...at the request...of the Labour League Committee. Edinburgh, J. Hogg, 1847. pp. 24.

HOUSEHOLD APPLIANCES.

FRANCE. Institut National de la Statistique et des Etudes Economiques. L'équipement des ménages. a., 1973- Paris.

HOUSING.

TRUEDINGER (OTTO) Die Arbeiterwohnungsfrage und die Bestrebungen zur Lösung derselben. Jena, 1888. pp. 233.

WORLD HOUSING SURVEY: an overview of the state of housing, building and planning within human settlements; [pd. by] Department of Economic and Social Affairs, United Nations. a., 1974(1st)- New York.

OBSOLESCENCE in housing: theory and applications; [by] Bev Nutt [and others]. Farnborough, Hants., [1976]. pp. 194. *bibliog.*

WARD (BARBARA) Baroness Jackson. The home of man. London, 1976. pp. 297.

— Finance.

WORLD HOUSING SURVEY: an overview of the state of housing, building and planning within human settlements; [pd. by] Department of Economic and Social Affairs, United Nations. a., 1974(1st)- New York.

JØRGENSEN (NIELS OVE) Housing finance for low income groups, with special reference to developing countries. Rotterdam, 1975. pp. 247. *bibliog.*

SWEET (MORRIS L.) and WALTERS (SHERWOOD GEORGE) Mandatory housing finance programs: a comparative international analysis. New York, 1975. pp. 253. *bibliog.*

— Information services — United Kingdom.

CONNOLLY (KATHLEEN) compiler. Sources of information in housing. London, 1975. pp. 30. *(U.K. Department of the Environment. Library. Information Series)*

PLANT (J.J.) A survey of housing aid centre enquiries. London, [1975]. pp. 76. *(London. Greater London Council. Research Memoranda. 473)*

HOUSING.(Cont.)

— Statistics.

INTERNATIONAL INSTITUTE OF STATISTICS. International Statistics of Large Towns. Statistique du logement dans les grandes villes, 1928-1934. La Haye, 1940. pp. 170.

— Australia — New South Wales.

NEW SOUTH WALES. State Planning Authority. 1972. Planning control of residential development. [Sydney], 1972. pp. 47. *bibliog.*

— Austria — Vienna.

BOTZ (GERHARD) Wohnungspolitik und Judendeportation in Wien, 1938 bis 1945: zur Funktion des Antisemitismus als Ersatz nationalsozialistischer Sozialpolitik. Wien, 1975. pp. 200. *bibliog. (Salzburg. Universität. Historisches Institut. Veröffentlichungen. 13)*

— Canada.

THOMAS (D.K.) and THOMPSON (CHARLES THOMAS) Eskimo housing as planned culture change; (with Northern rental housing program, Northwest Territories, 1966 to 1972). Ottawa, 1972. pp. 27; fo. (6). *bibliog. (Canada. Northern Science Research Group. Social Science Notes. 4)*

— — Ontario.

ONTARIO. Economic Council. 1976. Housing: issues and alternatives, 1976. [Toronto], 1976. pp. 60.

— Denmark — Statistics.

DENMARK. Census, 1970. Folke- og boligtaellingen, 9.november 1970. København, 1972 in progress. *(Denmark. Danmarks Statistik. Statistisk Tabelvaerk. 1972. 3, etc.)*

— — Copenhagen.

COPENHAGEN. Boligkommission. Aarsberetning. a., 1945-1954. København.

— France.

MASSU (CLAUDE) Droit au logement: mythe ou réalité?. Paris, [1975]. pp. 142.

FRANCE. Comité de l'Habitat. 1976. Rapport...: préparation du 7e Plan. Paris, 1976. pp. 204.

— — Statistics.

FRANCE. Direction du Bâtiment et des Travaux Publics et de la Conjoncture. Service des Statistiques et des Etudes Economiques. Sous-Direction des Statistiques. 1974. Statistiques des permis de construire: résultats annuels, 1969- 1970-1971. Paris, 1974. 2 parts. *(France. Ministère de l'Equipement. Statistiques de la construction. Suppléments. Nos. 10,16)*

— Germany.

TRUEDINGER (OTTO) Die Arbeiterwohnungsfrage und die Bestrebungen zur Lösung derselben. Jena, 1888. pp. 233.

BLUMENROTH (ULRICH) Deutsche Wohnungspolitik seit der Reichsgründung: Darstellung und kritische Würdigung. Münster, Westf., 1975. pp. 410,xli. *bibliog. (Münster in Westfalen. Westfälische Wilhelms- Universität. Institut für Siedlungs- und Wohnungswesen, and Zentralinstitut für Raumplanung. Beiträge zum Siedlungs- und Wohnungswesen und zur Raumplanung. Band 25)*

KRAPOHL (PETER) Eigentumswohnungen in der Bundesrepublik Deutschland: Entwicklung und Beurteilung ihrer Marktfähigkeit. Bonn, [1975]. pp. 475. *bibliog. (Cologne. Universität. Institut für Wohnungsrecht und Wohnungswirtschaft. Schriften. Band 43)*

— — East Prussia.

POHLE (MARTIN) Wohnungsnot und Wohnungsbau in Ostpreussen. Jena, 1919. pp. 250. *(Kaliningrad. Universität. Institut für Ostdeutsche Wirtschaft. Schriften. 7. Heft)*

— — Frankfurt am Main.

HAEUSERRAT FRANKFURT. Wohnungskampf in Frankfurt. München, 1974. pp. 245. *bibliog.*

— — Hamburg.

NOERNBERG (HANS JUERGEN) and SCHUBERT (DIRK) Massenwohnungsbau in Hamburg: Materialien zur Entstehung und Veränderung Hamburger Arbeiterwohnungen und -siedlungen, 1800- 1967. Westberlin, [1975]. pp. 304. *bibliog.*

— — Westphalia.

TREMOEHLEN (ERNST) Wohnungsfürsorge für Industriearbeiter in der Provinz Westfalen, unter besonderer Berücksichtigung des Kleinwohnungsbaues. Jena, 1911. pp. 101. *bibliog. (Jena. Universität. Staatswissenschaftliches Seminar. Abhandlungen. 11. Band, 1 Heft)*

— Hong Kong.

DRAKAKIS-SMITH (D.W.) Housing provision in metropolitan Hong Kong. Hong Kong, 1973. pp. 187. *(Hong Kong. University. Centre of Asian Studies. Occasional Papers and Monographs. No. 16)*

— — Statistics.

HONG KONG. Census, 1971. Hong Kong population and housing census 1971: main report. [Hong Kong, 1972]. pp. 248.

— Ireland (Republic).

NATIONAL ECONOMIC AND SOCIAL COUNCIL [EIRE]. Population projections, 1971-1986: the implications for social planning: dwelling needs. Dublin, Stationery Office, [1976]. pp. 48. *bibliog. ([Reports]. No. 14)*

— Italy.

EDILI senza lavoro, operai senza casa; a cura di Riccardo Roscelli;...scritti di Riccardo Bedrone [and others]. Torino, [1975]. pp. 251.

— Kenya.

NATIONAL HOUSING CORPORATION OF KENYA. Annual accounts. a., 1974- Nairobi.

— Liberia.

LIBERIAN DEVELOPMENT CORPORATION. Annual report. a., 1974- Monrovia.

— Netherlands.

RIJKSUNIVERSITEIT TE UTRECHT. Instituut voor Staats- en Administratiefrecht. Werkgroep Bestuurskunde. De regeringspolitiek ten aanzien van de volkshuisvesting in het algemeen en de Utrechtse huisvestingsproblematiek in het bijzonder: rapport van de werkgroep...cursusjaar 1970-1971. IJmulden, [1972]. pp. 125. *bibliog.*

SAAL (C.D.) ed. Woonnood [equals] welzijnsnood. Alphen aan den Rijn, 1975. pp. 154. *bibliogs.*

— Norway — Statistics.

NORWAY. Statistiske Centralbyrå. 1974. Boforholdsundersøkelsen, 1973, etc. Oslo, 1974. pp. 175. *(Norges Offisielle Statistikk. Rekke A. 673) In Norwegian and English.*

NORWAY. Statistiske Centralbyrå. 1974. Markedstall: folke- og boligtelling, 1970, etc. Oslo, 1974. pp. 139. *(Norges Offisielle Statistikk. Rekke A.659) In Norwegian and English.*

— Poland — Law.

BUSZYŃSKI (MARIAN) and others. Prawo lokalowe, komentarz: przepisy wykonawcze i przepisy związkowe. Warszawa, 1961. pp. 286.

— Portugal — Statistics.

PORTUGAL. Instituto Nacional de Estatistica. Serviços Centrais. 1975. I recenseamento da habitação, 1970: continente e ilhas adjacentes; estimativa a 20 [per cent]. [Lisbon, 1975]. pp. 320.

— Russia — Law.

MASLOV (VASILII FILIPPOVICH) Zashchita zhilishchnykh prav grazhdan. Khar'kov, 1970. pp. 208.

— Sudan — Statistics.

SUDAN. Department of Statistics. 1967- . Population and housing survey, 1964-65(-66). Khartoum, 1967 in progress.

— Sweden — Finance.

BOSTAD och kapital: en studie av svensk bostadspolitik; ([by] Kenneth Boberg [and others]). [Stockholm, 1974]. pp. 162. *bibliog.*

— Switzerland — Finance.

NEEF (JOERG) Moderne Formen der Wohnbaufinanzierung aus bankwirtschaftlicher Sicht. Bern, 1976. pp. 192. *bibliog.* Dissertation der Universität Zürich zur Erlangung der Würde eines Doktors der Wirtschaftswissenschaft.

— Tanzania.

STREN (RICHARD E.) Urban inequality and housing policy in Tanzania: the problem of squatting. Berkeley, [1975]. pp. 112. *bibliog. (California University. Institute of International Studies. Research Series. No. 24)*

— Turkey — Ankara.

DRAKAKIS-SMITH (D.W.) and FISHER (WILLIAM BAYNE) Housing problems in Ankara. [Durham], 1975. pp. 93. *bibliog. (Durham. University. Deartment of Geography. Occasional Publications (New Series). No. 7)*

— Underdeveloped areas.

See UNDERDEVELOPED AREAS — Housing.

— United Kingdom.

ASHMORE (GRAHAM) The owner-occupied housing market. Birmingham, 1975. pp. 44. *(Birmingham. University. Centre for Urban and Regional Studies. Research Memoranda No. 41)*

HADJIMATHEOU (GEORGE G.) Housing and mortgage markets in the U.K. 1955-1972. [1975]. fo. 226. *bibliog.* Typescript. Ph.D. (London) thesis: unpublished. *This thesis is the property of London University and may not be removed from the Library.*

SHELTER. Shelter's submission to the Department of the Environment review of homelessness. London, 1975. pp. 23.

U.K. Department of the Environment. 1975. Homelessness: a consultation paper. [London], 1975. pp. 12.

U.K. Department of the Environment. 1975. The use of indicators for area action; Housing Act, 1974. London, [1975]. pp. 40. *bibliog. (Area Improvement Notes. 10)*

WOLMAN (HAROLD L.) Housing and housing policy in the U.S. and the U.K. Lexington, Mass., [1975]. pp. 125.

GITTUS (ELIZABETH) Flats, families and the under-fives. London, 1976. pp. 269. *bibliog.*

MURIE (ALAN S.) and others. Housing policy and the housing system. London, 1976. pp. 282. *(Birmingham. University. Centre for Urban and Regional Studies. Urban and Regional Studies. No.7)*

OBSOLESCENCE in housing: theory and applications; [by] Bev Nutt [and others]. Farnborough, Hants., [1976]. pp. 194. *bibliog.*

HOUSING.(Cont.)

U.K. Housing Development Directorate. 1976. Monitoring provision for small households: interim report of a study of 8 private sector schemes. [London], 1976. 1 vol. (various pagings).

WARD (COLIN) Housing: an anarchist approach. London, 1976. pp. 182.

— — Bibliography.

THOMPSON (MEG) compiler. Housing: a select list. London, 1975. pp. 115. (U.K. Department of the Environment. Library. Bibliographies. No.132).

— — Finance.

The INTERPRETATION by the Birmingham press of the housing finance issue; [by] David Alexander [and others]. Birmingham, 1973. pp. 26. bibliog. (Birmingham. University. Centre for Urban and Regional Studies. Working Papers. No. 18)

HOUSING finance: papers and proceedings of a conference held on 29th April, 1975 [under the auspices of the Institute for Fiscal Studies]. London, 1975. pp. 164. (Institute for Fiscal Studies. Publications. No. 12)

REVELL (JACK) Flexibility in housing finance. Bangor, [1975?]. pp. 59. bibliog. (Wales. University. University College of North Wales. Economic Research Papers. FIN 6)

— — Law.

LEGAL ACTION GROUP. Social Law and Practice Guides. No. 1. Law in a housing crisis: a guide to the law and practice on security, rent, repairs and rights to housing on marriage breakdown. London, [1975]. pp. 64.

SMITH (A. CHRISTOPHER D.) and HOATH (DAVID CHARLES) Law and the underprivileged. London, 1975. pp. 247.

— — Statistics.

U.K. Department of the Environment. Miscellaneous local government and planning statistics. a., 1973- London.

— — Birmingham.

LLEWELYN-DAVIES WEEKS [AND PARTNERS]. Inner area study: Birmingham: Little Green: a case study in urban renewal. [London], Department of the Environment, [1975]. pp. 200. bibliog.

SOCIAL AND COMMUNITY PLANNING RESEARCH. Inner area study: Birmingham: Small Heath, Birmingham: a social survey; report...for the consultants, Llewelyn-Davies Weeks Forestier-Walker and Bor; (by Jean Morton-Williams and Richard Stowell). [London], Department of the Environment, [1975]. pp. 167.

— — — Finance.

BIRMINGHAM COMMUNITY DEVELOPMENT PROJECT. Birmingham Council and the building societies: a social contract in six months? Birmingham, 1976. pp. 4.

— — Copeland.

CUMBRIA COMMUNITY DEVELOPMENT PROJECT. Housing in Copeland 1973-75: policies and practice as revealed by an examination of Council minutes and contemporary press cuttings. [Cleator Moor], 1976. pp. 27.

— — Cumbria.

CUMBRIA COMMUNITY DEVELOPMENT PROJECT. Report of a housing study of the Cleator Moor and Arlecdon/Frizington parishes; [by] John Pearce [and others]. Cleator Moor, [1974]. pp. 110.

— — Gosport.

SOCIAL SERVICES RESEARCH AND INTELLIGENCE UNIT [PORTSMOUTH]. Problems of rehousing exservice families in Gosport. Portsmouth, [1976?]. fo. 16.

— — Hampshire.

CAULFIELD (IAN) The classification and projection of socio-economic groups of households in South Hampshire. [Winchester], 1969. 1 vol. (unpaged). (South Hampshire Plan Technical Unit. Working Papers. 11)

CAULFIELD (IAN) An alternative method of projecting the number and size of households. [Winchester], 1970. pp. 10. (South Hampshire Plan Technical Unit. Working Papers. 12)

CAULFIELD (IAN) The development of house condition models. [Winchester], 1970. pp. 15. (South Hampshire Plan Technical Unit. Working Papers. 10)

CAULFIELD (IAN) Urban renewal, densities, infilling and the location of future housing capacity in South Hampshire. [Winchester], 1970. pp. 19. (South Hampshire Plan Technical Unit. Working Papers. 7)

CAULFIELD (IAN) and HALL (BRYAN D.) Housing improvement and renewal in South Hampshire: principal conclusions of the South Hampshire house condition survey, 1970. [Winchester], 1972. pp. 33. (South Hampshire Plan Technical Unit. Working Papers. 15)

HALL (BRYAN D.) Organisation, response, tabulations and statistical analysis of the South Hampshire house condition survey. 1970. [Winchester], 1972. 1 vol. (unpaged). (South Hampshire Plan Technical Unit. Working Papers. 16)

— — Leicester.

PRITCHARD (ROGER MARTIN) Housing and the spatial structure of the city: residential mobility and the housing market in an English city since the industrial revolution. Cambridge, [1976]. pp. 234. bibliog.

— — London.

EALING COMMUNITY RELATIONS COUNCIL. Housing Sub-Committee. A report on the pilot housing survey carried out in two parts of the London borough of Ealing, September-December 1969. London, [1970?]. pp. 23, 14.

BRACEWELL (IRENA B.) Report on the housing demolition survey. London, [1975]. pp. 55. (London. Greater London Council. Research Memoranda. 458)

DOCKLANDS JOINT COMMITTEE. Docklands Development Team. Housing. London, 1975. pp. 41. (Working Papers for Consultation. 4)

GRAYSON (LESLEY) The single homeless. rev. ed. [London], Greater London Council, 1975. pp. 13. bibliog. (London Topics. No. 2)

MURIE (ALAN S.) and others. A housing monitoring system: a report to the London borough of Islington. Birmingham, 1975. pp. 86. (Birmingham. University. Centre for Urban and Regional Studies. Research Memoranda. No. 50)

ROBERTS (TED) Housing and ministry: an experiment in the use of church land. London, [1975]. pp. 60.

SHANKLAND-COX PARTNERSHIP and INSTITUTE OF COMMUNITY STUDIES. Inner area study: Lambeth: housing and population projections. [London], Department of the Environment, [1975]. pp. 8.

SHANKLAND-COX PARTNERSHIP and INSTITUTE OF COMMUNITY STUDIES. Inner area study: Lambeth: housing stress. [London], Department of the Environment, [1975]. pp. 54.

WORKING PARTY ON THE PROVISION OF ACCOMMODATION FOR SINGLE PEOPLE. Interim report; [S. Woolf, chairman]. [London], Greater London Council, 1975. pp. 23. bibliog.

SHANKLAND-COX PARTNERSHIP and INSTITUTE OF COMMUNITY STUDIES. Inner area study: Lambeth: the implications of social ownership. [London], Department of the Environment, [1976]. pp. 69.

— — Manchester.

PONS (VALDO GUSTAVE) Housing conditions and residential patterns in Manchester of the 1830s and 1840s. 1975. fo. 94. bibliog. Typescript: unpublished.

— — Newcastle-upon-Tyne.

BENWELL COMMUNITY DEVELOPMENT PROJECT. Benwell's hidden property companies. Newcastle-upon-Tyne, 1976. pp. 60. (Working Papers. No.1)

— — Oxfordshire.

OXFORDSHIRE HOUSING STATISTICS; [pd. by] Oxfordshire County Council. a., 1975- Oxford.

— — West Bromwich.

The BEECHES road area study: a potential housing action area; [by] Pat Niner [and others]. Birmingham, 1975. pp. 136, 22. (Birmingham. University. Centre for Urban and Regional Studies. Research Memoranda. No. 49)

— — Ireland, Northern.

IRELAND, NORTHERN. Department of Housing, Local Government and Planning. Report. a., 1972/73 Belfast. 1965/66 [1st]- 1971/72 included as Report of the Ministry of Development in IRELAND, NORTHERN. Parliament. [Command papers]

NORTHERN IRELAND HOUSING EXECUTIVE. Corporate Planning Department. Housing condition survey, 1974: principal characteristics of the Northern Ireland dwelling stock by district. Belfast, [1974]. pp. 43.

— — — Statistics.

IRELAND, NORTHERN. Census, 1971. Census of population, 1971: housing and household composition tables. Belfast, 1975. pp. 188.

— — Scotland.

HARVEY (COLIN) Ha'penny help: a record of social improvement in Victorian Scotland. Glasgow, 1976. pp. 197.

— — Wales.

DE VANE (RICHARD) Second home ownership: a case study. Cardiff, 1975. pp. 108. bibliogs. (Wales. University. University College of North Wales. Bangor Occasional Papers in Economics. No. 6)

— United States.

HAAR (CHARLES MONROE) and IATRIDES (DEMETRIOS S.) Housing the poor in suburbia: public policy at the grass roots. Cambridge, Mass., [1974]. pp. 430. bibliogs.

HUGHES (JAMES W.) and BLEAKLY (KENNETH D.) Urban homesteading. New Brunswick, N.J., [1975]. pp. 276. bibliog.

WEXLER (HARRY J.) and PECK (RICHARD) Housing and local government: a research guide for policy makers and planners. Lexington, Mass., 1975. pp. 310. bibliog.

WOLMAN (HAROLD L.) Housing and housing policy in the U.S. and the U.K. Lexington, Mass., [1975]. pp. 125.

HOUSING costs and housing needs; edited by Alexander Greendale and Stanley F. Knock. New York, 1976. pp. 180. Papers of a conference held by the Interreligious Coalition for Housing in Washington, D.C., in 1975.

The POLITICS of housing in older urban areas; edited by Robert E. Mendelson [and] Michael A. Quinn. New York, 1976. pp. 261. Consists of revised versions of essays originally prepared for a seminar on "The Politics of Housing in Older Urban Areas" held in June 1974 at Southern Illinois University.

RICHARDSON (DAN K.) The cost of environmental protection: regulating housing development in the coastal zone. New Brunswick, N.J., [1976]. pp. 219. bibliog.

HOUSING.(Cont.)

STOKES (CHARLES J.) and FISHER (ERNEST McKINLEY) Housing market performance in the United States. New York, 1976. pp. 158.

— — Missouri.

KAIN (JOHN FORREST) and QUIGLEY (JOHN M.) Housing markets and racial discrimination: a microeconomic analysis. New York, 1975. pp. 393. *bibliog. (National Bureau of Economic Research. Urban and Regional Studies. 3)*

— — New York (State).

SANDS (GARY) and BOWER (LEWIS L.) Vacancy chains in the local housing market: an investigation of the public policy implications of housing turnover: a final report to the New York State Urban Development Corporation and the Ford Foundation. Ithaca, N.Y., 1974. pp. 283. *bibliog.*

— — Pittsburgh — Finance.

AHLBRANDT (ROGER S.) and BROPHY (PAUL C.) Neighborhood revitalization: theory and practice. Lexingon, [1975]. pp. 188. *bibliog.*

— Venezuela — Statistics.

VENEZUELA. Census, 1971. X censo de poblacion y vivienda: resumen nacional; caracteristicas generales de las viviendas. Caracas, 1974. pp. 43.

VENEZUELA. Census, 1971. X censo de poblacion y vivienda: resumen nacional; caracteristicas de las viviendas. Caracas, 1975. pp. 66.

VENEZUELA. Direccion General de Estadistica. 1975. XIX encuesta nacional de hogares por muestreo [1974]: datos generales de la poblacion y de las viviendas. Caracas, 1975. pp. 292.

HOUSING, COOPERATIVE

— France.

CENTRE DE RECHERCHES ET DE DOCUMENTATION SUR LA CONSOMMATION. Contribution sociologique en vue d'une nouvelle législation sur la copropriété dan les grands ensembles immobiliers, etc. Paris, 1975. 2 vols.

— United Kingdom.

A BETTER place: the story of the Holloway Tenant Co-operative compiled from records, letters and minutes of the members. London, 1974. pp. 62.

HOUSING, RURAL

— India — Goa, Daman and Diu.

GOA, DAMAN AND DIU. Bureau of Economics, Statistics and Evaluation. 1974. An evaluation of the housing scheme for backward classes, 1971-1972. Panaji, 1974. pp. 44. *(Evaluation Reports. No. 7)*

HOUSING FOR PHYSICALLY HANDICAPPED

— United Kingdom.

TESTER (SUSAN) Housing for disabled people in Greater London; interim report of a pilot study prepared for the Greater London Association for the Disabled. London, 1975. pp. 37. *bibliog.*

HOUSING MANAGEMENT.

U.K. Department of the Environment. 1975. Bill for the Transfer in New Towns of Housing and Related Assets: (consultation paper). [London, 1975]. pp. 10.

— Citizen participation.

SCOTT (GAY) Tenant participation. [London], Greater London Council, 1975. pp. 9. *bibliog. (London Topics. No. 8)*

HOUSING SUBSIDIES

— United Kingdom.

RICHARDSON (P.W.) A comparative analysis of housing subsidies received by owner-occupiers and local authority tenants. [London], 1973. fo. 29. *(U.K. Department of the Environment. Economic and Statistical Notes. No. 19)*

HOXTON

— Social conditions.

JASPER (ALBERT STANLEY) A Hoxton childhood;...[with] line drawings by James Boswell. London, [1969] repr. 1975. pp. 128.

HRVATSKA SELJACKA STRANKA.

BOBAN (LJUBO) Maček i politika Hrvatske seljačke stranke 1928-1941: iz povijesti hrvatskog pitanja. Zagreb, 1974. 2 vols.

HUA KOK, THAILAND

— Social life and customs.

KEMP (JEREMY HUGH) Social organization of a hamlet in Phitsanulok Province, north-central Thailand. 1976. fo. 358. *bibliog.* Typescript. Ph.D. (London) thesis: unpublished. This thesis is the property of London University and may not be removed from the Library.

HUEYAPAN

— History.

FRIEDLANDER (JUDITH) Being Indian in Hueyapan: a study of forced identity in contemporary Mexico. London, [1975]. pp. 205. *bibliog.*

— Social conditions.

FRIEDLANDER (JUDITH) Being Indian in Hueyapan: a study of forced identity in contemporary Mexico. London, [1975]. pp. 205. *bibliog.*

— Social life and customs.

FRIEDLANDER (JUDITH) Being Indian in Hueyapan: a study of forced identity in contemporary Mexico. London, [1975]. pp. 205. *bibliog.*

HULL

— Commerce.

JACKSON (GORDON) The trade and shipping of eighteenth century Hull. York, 1975. pp. 64. *bibliog. (East Yorkshire Local History Society. East Yorkshire Local History Series. No. 31)*

— Economic history.

JACKSON (GORDON) The trade and shipping of eighteenth century Hull. York, 1975. pp. 64. *bibliog. (East Yorkshire Local History Society. East Yorkshire Local History Series. No. 31)*

HUMAN BEHAVIOUR.

GASSON (RUTH M.) and others. Attitudes and facilitation in the attainment of status. Washington, [1973?]. pp. 37. *bibliog. (American Sociological Association. Arnold and Caroline Rose Monograph Series in Sociology)*

GOFFMAN (ERVING) Frame analysis: an essay on the organization of experience. Cambridge, Mass., 1974. pp. 586.

LISKA (ALLEN E.) ed. The consistency controversy: readings on the impact of attitude on behavior. New York, [1975]. pp. 277. *bibliog.*

THORBECKE (WILLIAM JOHAN RUDOLF) Mankind at the crossroads: an enquiry into the causes of the global predicaments and the means to overcome them. Leyden, 1975. pp. 217.

WARBURTON (DAVID M.) Brain, behaviour and drugs: introduction to the neurochemistry of behaviour. London, [1975]. pp. 280. *bibliog.*

ESSAYS on explanation and understanding: studies in the foundations of humanities and social sciences; edited by Juha Manninen and Raimo Tuomela. Dordrecht, [1976]. pp. 440. *bibliogs.* Includes papers from the International Colloquium on Explanation and Understanding, Helsinki, 1974.

MOOS (RUDOLF H.) The human context: environmental determinants of behavior. New York, [1976]. pp. 444.

HUMAN CAPITAL

See also LABOUR SUPPLY.

— Communist countries.

MIKUL'SKII (KONSTANTIN IVANOVICH) ed. Trudovye resursy i nauchno-tekhnicheskaia revoliutsiia: ispol'zovanie trudovykh resursov stran SEV v usloviiakh nauchno-tekhnicheskoi revoliutsii i sovershenstvovaniia metodov sotsialisticheskogo khoziaistvovaniia. Moskva, 1974. pp. 246.

— Russia.

KORCHAGIN (VIKTOR PAVLOVICH) Trudovye resursy v usloviiakh nauchno-tekhnicheskoi revoliutsii. Moskva, 1974. pp. 167.

KASIMOVSKII (EVGENII VASIL'EVICH) ed. Trudovye resursy: formirovanie i ispol'zovanie. Moskva, 1975. pp. 254.

MINTS (LEV EFIMOVICH) Trudovye resursy SSSR. Moskva, 1975. pp. 323.

— United States.

LEVITAN (SAR A.) and others. Human resources and labor markets: (labor and manpower in the American economy). 2nd ed. New York, [1976]. pp. 631. *bibliog.*

— Yugoslavia.

BREKIĆ (JOVO) and JURINA (MILAN) eds. Analiza i srednjeročna projekcija razvoja kadrova SRH 1967-1980 Zagreb, 1975. pp. 178. *bibliog.*

HUMAN ECOLOGY.

DANSEREAU (PIERRE) The hope of human ecology. [Ottawa], Canadian Commission for Unesco, 1969. pp. 14,9. *bibliog.* In English and French.

BLACK (WILLIAM ALEXANDER) The view from Water Street. Ottawa, 1973. pp. 43. *bibliog. (Canada. Inland Waters Directorate. Social Science Series. No. 2)*

LAIHONEN (AARNO) The framework of an information system of environmental statistics. [Helsinki], 1973. fo. 37. *bibliog. (Finland. Tilastokeskus. Tutkimuksia. 23)*

The HOSTILE environment of man: report of a symposium held on 1 May 1971 at the University of Leeds. [Edinburgh], 1974. pp. 46. *(Journal of the Royal College of General Practitioners. vol. 24. Supplement No. 1)*

MEREDITH MEMORIAL LECTURES. 1974. Our community and its environment. Bundoora, Victoria, 1974. 5 pts.

BOUGHEY (ARTHUR S.) Man and the environment: an introduction to human ecology and evolution. 2nd ed. New York, [1975]. pp. 576. *bibliogs.*

DASMANN (RAYMOND FREDERICK) The conservation alternative. New York, [1975]. pp. 164. *bibliogs.*

INTERNATIONAL CONGRESS OF ANTHROPOLOGICAL AND ETHNOLOGICAL SCIENCES. 9th Congress, 1973. Population, ecology and social evolution: [papers from the Congress]; editor Steven Polgar. The Hague, [1975]. pp. 354. *bibliog.*

INTERNATIONAL GEOGRAPHICAL UNION. Regional Conference [in New Zealand], 1974. Proceedings of the International Geographical Union Regional Conference and eighth New Zealand Geography Conference, Palmerston North, December 1974; edited by William Brockie [and others]. [Christchurch], 1975. pp. 380. *bibliogs. (New Zealand Geographical Society. Conference Series. No. 8)*

LEVI (LENNART) and ANDERSSON (LARS) Psychosocial stress: population, environment and quality of life. New York, [1975]. pp. 142. *bibliog. Prepared for the United Nations' World Population Conference in 1974.*

NATIONAL PLANNING ASSOCIATION. Reports. No. 143. The environment and man. Washington, [1975]. pp. 16.

BENNETT (JOHN WILLIAM) The ecological transition: cultural anthropology and human adaptation. New York, [1976]. pp. 378. *bibliog.*

GORMLEY (W. PAUL) Human rights and environment: the need for international co- operation. Leyden, 1976. pp. 255. *bibliog.*

GREENBIE (BARRIE B.) Design for diversity: planning for natural man in the neo-technic environment: an ethological approach. Amsterdam, 1976. pp. 209. *bibliog.*

MOOS (RUDOLF H.) The human context: environmental determinants of behavior. New York, [1976]. pp. 444.

RADICAL technology; edited by Peter Harper, Godfrey Boyle and the editors of Undercurrents. New York, [1976]. pp. 304. *bibliog.*

STONIER (TOM TED) The natural history of humanity: past, present and future. [Bradford, 1976]. pp. 48.

— Moral and religious aspects.

TAYLOR (JOHN VERNON) Enough is enough. London, 1975 repr. 1976. pp. 120. *bibliog.*

— Study and teaching.

GUNN (ANGUS M.) Man on the earth: teacher resource book for: population pressure in Indonesia: problems of industrialization in Eurasia: power blocs in Eurasia. Toronto, 1974. pp. 51.

— — United Kingdom.

SHANKLAND-COX PARTNERSHIP and INSTITUTE OF COMMUNITY STUDIES. Inner area study: Lambeth: schools project. [London], Department of the Environment, [1976]. pp. 28, (22).

— India.

WEINSTEIN (JAY A.) Madras: an analysis of urban ecological structure in India. Beverly Hills, Calif., [1974]. pp. 76. *bibliog.*

— United States — Public opinion.

WHISENHUNT (DONALD W.) The environment and the American experience: a historian looks at the ecological crisis. Port Washington, N.Y., 1974. pp. 136.

HUMAN ENGINEERING.

ETHNIC variables in human factors engineering: based on papers presented at a symposium...held in Oosterbeek, the Netherlands, 19-23 June 1972, under the auspices of...North Atlantic Treaty Organization; edited by Alphonse Chapanis. Baltimore, [1975]. pp. 290. *bibliogs.*

STOCKBRIDGE (HUGH C.W.) Behaviour and the physical environment: case studies in psychology and ergonomics. London, 1975. pp. 191. *bibliog.*

HUMAN EVOLUTION.

BOUGHEY (ARTHUR S.) Man and the environment: an introduction to human ecology and evolution. 2nd ed. New York, [1975]. pp. 576. *bibliogs.*

THORBECKE (WILLIAM JOHAN RUDOLF) Mankind at the crossroads: an enquiry into the causes of the global predicaments and the means to overcome them. Leyden, 1975. pp. 217.

HUMAN EXPERIMENTATION IN MEDICINE.

PHARMACOLOGICAL testing in a correctional institution: volunteer characteristics and motivations; by Stephen H. Wells [and others]. Springfield, Ill., [1975]. pp. 66. *bibliog.*

— Economic aspects — United States.

MEYER (PETER B.) Drug experiments on prisoners: ethical, economic, or exploitative? Lexington, Mass., [1976]. pp. 129.

HUMAN INFORMATION PROCESSING.

KEELE (STEVEN W.) Attention and human performance. Pacific Palisades, Cal., [1973]. pp. 184. *bibliog.*

MANDLER (GEORGE) Mind and emotion. New York, [1975]. pp. 280. *bibliog.*

MASSARO (DOMINIC W.) Experimental psychology and information processing. Chicago, [1975]. pp. 651. *bibliog.*

MASSARO (DOMINIC W.) ed. Understanding language: an information-processing analysis of speech perception, reading, and psycholinguistics. New York, [1975]. pp. 439. *bibliogs.*

HUMANITIES

— Bibliography.

BILBOUL (ROGER R.) ed. Retrospective index to theses of Great Britain and Ireland, 1716-1950. vol.1. Social sciences and humanities. Santa Barbara, [1975]. pp. 393.

— Research.

FRANCE. Délégation Générale à la Recherche Scientifique et Technique. 1974. Répertoire général de la recherche. Tome 3. Sciences sociales et humaines. Documentation arrêtée fin 1973. Paris, 1974. pp. 300. *(Répertoire National des Laboratoires)*

HUMBERSIDE

— Economic conditions.

U.K. Department of Industry. Yorkshire and Humberside Regional Office. 1975. Yorkshire and Humberside: centre of Britain. [Leeds, 1975]. pp. 12.

— Economic policy.

HUMBERSIDE. County Council. Planning Department. Structure plan report; pts. 1-6, 7a, 8a, 9a. [Beverley], 1975. 9 pts. (in 1 vol.).

— Social policy.

HUMBERSIDE. County Council. Planning Department. Structure plan report; pts. 1-6, 7a, 8a, 9a. [Beverley], 1975. 9 pts. (in 1 vol.).

HUME (DAVID).

FORBES (DUNCAN) M.A. Clare College, Cambridge. Hume's philosophical politics. Cambridge, 1975. pp. 338. *bibliog.*

HUNGARIAN LANGUAGE IN THE UNITED STATES.

FISHMAN (JOSHUA AARON) Hungarian language maintenance in the United States. Bloomington, Ind., [1966]. pp. 58. *bibliog. (Indiana University. Graduate School. Publications. Uralic and Altaic Series. vol. 62)*

HUNGARY

— Economic conditions.

HUNGARY. Központi Statisztikai Hivatal. 1971. Report...on the development of social and economic life and the fulfilment of the national economic plan during the period of the third five year plan, 1966-1970. [Budapest, 1971]. pp. 29.

ENYEDI (GYÖRGY) Hungary: an economic geography; English translation by Elek Helvei; translation revised and edited by Mary Völgyes. bOULDER, cOL., 1976. PP. 289. BIBLIOG.

— — Mathematical models.

HUNGARY. Központi Statisztikai Hivatal. 1975. Ágazati kapcsolatok mérlege, 1972. Budapest, 1975. pp. 581. *With Russian, German, English and French tables of contents.*

— Foreign relations — Czechoslovakia.

KRÁL (VÁCLAV) Intervenční válka československé buržoasie proti Maďarské sovětské republice v roce 1919. Praha, 1954. pp. 290,32.

— History — Sources.

BAYERLE (GUSTAV) Ottoman diplomacy in Hungary: letters from the Pashas of Buda, 1590-1593. Bloomington, Ind [1972]. pp 204. *bibliog. (Indiana University Graduate School. Publications. Uralic and Altaic Series. vol. 101.)*

— — 1848-1849, Uprising of.

CHOWNITZ (JULIAN FEODOR JOSEPH) Geschichte der ungarischen Revolution in den Jahren 1848 und 1849, mit Rückblicken auf die Bewegung in den österreichischen Erbländern; in zwei Bänden. Stuttgart, Rieger, 1849. 2 vols. (in 1).

SPIRA (GYÖRGY) A Hungarian count in the revolution of 1848. Budapest, 1974. pp. 346.

— — 1918-1919, Revolution.

KRÁL (VÁCLAV) Intervenční válka československé buržoasie proti Maďarské sovětské republice v roce 1919. Praha, 1954. pp. 290,32.

— — 1956, Uprising of.

LOMAX (BILL) Hungary 1956. London, 1976. pp. 222. *bibliog.*

— Industries.

HUNGARY. Központi Statisztikai Hivatal. 1964. A magyar népgazdaság ágazati kapcsolatainak mérlege 1961. évben; (Interindustry relations of the Hungarian national economy in 1961: input-output tables). Budapest, 1964. pp. 208,15. *With English summary.*

BOGUSZEWSKI (JAN) and WAGENER (HANS JUERGEN) Zur Industriestatistik der BRD, Österreichs, Polens und Ungarns. Wien, 1975. pp. 58. *(Wiener Institut für Internationale Wirtschaftsvergleiche. Forschungsberichte. Nr.24)*

YUGOSLAVIA. Savezni Zavod za Statistiku. Studije, Analize i Prikazi. 74. Uporedjenje jugoslovenske i madjarske industrije: produktivnost rada i struktura industrije, 1960-1970; Comparison between the Yugoslav and Hungarian industry: labour productivity and structure of industry, 1960-1970. Beograd, 1975. pp. 68. *With English summary.*

— Intellectual life.

HUNGARY. Központi Statisztikai Hivatal. 1962. A családok kulturális kiadásai. Budapest, 1962. pp. 93.

— Politics and government.

BONIS (JACQUES DE) En direct avec un dirigeant hongrois: György Aczél. Paris, [1975]. pp. 185.

HRANCHAK (IVAN MYKHAILOVYCH) and LEBOVICH (MARTIN FARKASHEVICH) Bela Kun - vydaiushchiisia deiatel' vengerskogo i mezhdunarodnogo revoliutsionnogo dvizheniia. Moskva, 1975. pp. 165.

KÁDÁR (JÁNOS) Izbrannye stat'i i rechi, fevral' 1970 g. dekabr' 1975 g.; [perevod s vengerskogo]. Moskva, 1976. pp. 534.

— Rural conditions.

HOLÁCS (IBOLYA) Change of the way of living in six transdanubian co-operative villages. Keszthely, 1974. pp. 91. *bibliog. (Keszthelyi Agrártudományi Egyetem. Studies.5)*

— Social conditions.

HUNGARY. Központi Statisztikai Hivatal. 1971. Report...on the development of social and economic life and the fulfilment of the national economic plan during the period of the third five year plan, 1966-1970. [Budapest, 1971]. pp. 29.

HUNGARY(Cont.)

— Statistics — Bibliography.

HUNGARY. Központi Statisztikai Hivatal. Könyvtár és Dokumentációs Szolgálat. 1975. Statisztikai adatforrások, 1945-1974: bibliográfia. Budapest, 1975. pp. 209.

HUNTING, PRIMITIVE

— Canada.

RICHARDSON (BOYCE) Strangers devour the land: a chronicle of the assault upon the last coherent hunting culture in North America, the Cree Indians of northern Quebec, and their vast primeval homelands. New York, 1976. pp. 342,xiii.

HUSBAND AND WIFE

— Canada — Manitoba.

MANITOBA. Law Reform Commission. 1975. Working paper on family law. Part 1. The support obligation. Part 2. Property disposition. Winnipeg, 1975. pp. 63.

— South Africa.

HAHLO (HERMAN ROBERT) The South African law of husband and wife, with an appendix on Jurisdiction and conflict of laws by Ellison Kahn. 4th ed. Cape Town, 1975. pp. 754.

SOUTH AFRICAN LAW COMMISSION. Report in regard to the right of recourse of a spouse married out of community of property in respect of contributions for necessaries for the joint household in terms of section 3 of the Matrimonial Affairs Act, 1953 (Act 37 of 1953) (R.P. 79/1975). in SOUTH AFRICA. Parliament. House of Assembly. Votes and proceedings; (with Printed annexures).

— United Kingdom.

JACKSON (JOSEPH) Matrimonial finance and taxation; second edition by J. Jackson and D.T.A. Davies. London, 1975. pp. 397.

HUYSMANS (CAMILLE).

WEERDT (DENISE DE) and GELDOLF (WIM) Camille Huysmans en Belgie tijdens Wereldoorlog I. Antwerpen, [1975]. pp. 137. *bibliog. (Camille Huysmans geschriften en documenten. 2)*

HYDROLOGY.

RODDA (JOHN C.) ed. Facets of hydrology. London, [1976]. pp. 368. *bibliogs.*

— Simulation methods.

FLEMING (GEORGE) Computer simulation techniques in hydrology. New York, [1975]. pp. 333. *bibliogs.*

— Italy — Mathematical models.

VENEZIA e i problemi dell'ambiente: studio e impiego de modelli matematici; [research papers produced in collaboration by the Centro di Ricerca of IBM Italia and the Laboratorio per lo Studio della Dinamica delle Grandi Masse de Consiglio Nazionale delle Ricerche]. Bologna, [1975]. pp. 360.

HYGIENE.

The HOSTILE environment of man: report of a symposium held on 1 May 1971 at the University of Leeds. [Edinburgh], 1974. pp. 46. *(Journal of the Royal College of General Practitioners. vol. 24. Supplement No. 1)*

WILSON (MICHAEL) Health is for people. London, 1975. pp. 134.

HYGIENE, PUBLIC.

ITALY. Servizio Studi, Legislazione e Inchieste Parlamentari. 1975. Modelli italiani e stranieri di assistenza sanitaria. [Rome], 1975. 2 vols. *(Quaderni di Studi e Legislazione. 18-19)*

SUONOJA (KYÖSTI) and others. Terveydenhuollon tavoitteet ja painopisteet: eräiden maiden terveyspoliittisten suunitelmien tarkastelua, etc. Helsinki, 1975. pp. 163. *bibliog. (Finland. Suomen Virallinen Tilasto. Finlands Officiella Statistik. 32. Sosiaalisia Erikoistutkimuksia. 43)* With English summary.

— International cooperation.

GORMLEY (W. PAUL) Human rights and environment: the need for international co-operation. Leyden, 1976. pp. 255. *bibliog.*

— America.

BOLETIN DE LA OFICINA SANITARIA PANAMERICANA: English ed: selections [of the articles, reports, and news items pd. in the m. Boletin by] Pan American Sanitary Bureau. a., 1966 [1st English ed.]- Washington, D.C.

— Canada — New Brunswick.

NEW BRUNSWICK. Health Education Division. 1968. Health services in New Brunswick: a quick reference to organization and services. [Fredericton, 1968?]. pp. 4,4. *Reprinted from Public Health News, December 1967. In English and French.*

— France.

ECONOMIE ET SANTE: supplément au Bulletin des statistiques de santé et de sécurité sociale; [pd. by] Ministère de la Santé Publique et de la Sécurité Sociale [France]. irreg., Mr 1972 (1)- Paris.

— Germany, Eastern — Law and legislation.

HARMSEN (HANS) ed. Gesundheitsvorsorge und Betriebsgesundheitswesen in der DDR: ein Beitrag zur Sozialrechtsgestaltung. Hamburg, 1975. pp. 116. *(Akademie für Staatsmedizin in Hamburg. Zur Entwicklung und Organisation des Gesundheitswesens in Sowjetrussland, in Osteuropäischen Volksdemokratien und in der DDR. Band 72)*

— Ghana.

GHANA. Ministry of Health. 1967. The health services in Ghana. [Accra, 1967]. pp. 47.

— India.

KARAN SINGH, Maharaja. Population, poverty and the future of India. [New Delhi, National Institute of Family Planning, 1975] . pp. 142,iii.

— Italy.

ITALY. Servizio Studi, Legislazione e Inchieste Parlamentari. 1975. Modelli italiani e stranieri di assistenza sanitaria. [Rome], 1975. 2 vols. *(Quaderni di Studi e Legislazione. 18-19)*

— Poland.

W walce o zdrowie wsi Polskiej: referaty wygłoszone na Konferencji, poświęconej opiece lekarskiej na wsi, zwołanej przez Instytut Spraw Społecznych w Warszawie w dniach 31.1.- 1. i 2. II. 1937: Campaign for the health of the rural population in Poland; reports held at the Conference of Medical Service for Rural Population organised by the Institute for Social Problems on the 31.1.-1. and 2.II. 1937. Warszawa, 1937. pp. 320. *(Instytut Spraw Społecznych. Sprawy Zdrowia Publicznego. Nr.2)* With English summary.

— Russia.

GOLOVTEEV (VIKTOR VASIL'EVICH) and others. Osnovy ekonomiki sovetskogo zdravookhraneniia. Moskva, 1974. pp. 199.

— — Finance.

SOBOLEVSKII (GENNADII NIKOLAEVICH) and others. Osnovy finansirovaniia uchrezhdenii zdravookhraneniia. Moskva, 1974. pp. 144. *bibliog.*

— — Russia (RSFSR).

ISAKOV (ANDREI VASIL'EVICH) Razvitie zdravookhraneniia v Amurskoi oblasti. Khabarov, 1967. pp. 86.

ZABEZHINSKII (LEV MOISEEVICH) Zdravookhranenie Penzenskoi oblasti za 50 let Sovetskoi vlasti: materialy k istorii. Saratov, 1968. pp. 128.

— Sweden.

EKMAN (SVEN) 100 år för hälsan: Göteborgs Hälsovårdsnämnd, 1875-1975. [Gothenburg, 1975]. pp. 87. *With English summary.*

— United Kingdom.

JONES (KATHLEEN) Health and social service merry go-round. London, 1973. pp. 15. *(National Association for Mental Health. Occasional Papers. No.1)*

BIRMINGHAM. University. Health Services Research Centre. Probes for health; [by] J. Selwyn Crawford [and others]; edited by Gordon McLachlan. London, 1975. pp. 180. *bibliogs.*

U.K. Department of Health and Social Security. [Circulars] H.C. [Health]. irreg., Ja 1976 (no.1)- London.

— — Ireland, Northern.

IRELAND, NORTHERN. Eastern Health and Social Services Board. Annual report. a., 1973/74(1st)- Belfast.

— United States.

TAYLOR (LLOYD C.) The medical profession and social reform, 1885-1945. New York, [1974]. pp. 168.

— Yugoslavia — Croatia.

ANTIĆ (LAZO) Samoupravni i programirani razvoj zdravstvenih institucija u gradu Zagrebu. Zagreb, 1974. pp. 27.

IBADAN UNIVERSITY.

NIGERIA. University of Ibadan Commission of Inquiry into Disturbances on the Campus on 1st February, 1971. Report; [B.O. Kazeem, sole commissioner]. [Lagos, 1971]. pp. 187. *Bound with Comments of the federal military government on the report.*

IBM 370 (computers).

KATZAN (HARRY) Computer organization and the system/370. New York, [1971]. pp. 308.

IBOS.

NJAKA (MAZI ELECHUKWU NNADIBUAGHA) Igbo political culture. Evanston, 1974. pp. 173. *bibliog.*

UKAEGBU (ALFRED ONYEOHUHU) Marriage and fertility in east central Nigeria: a case study of Ngwa Igbo women. 1975. fo. 367. *bibliog.* Typescript. *Ph.D.(London) thesis: unpublished. This thesis is the property of London University and may not be removed from the Library.*

ISICHEI (ELIZABETH ALLO) A history of the Igbo people. London, 1976. pp. 303. *bibliog.*

ICELAND

— Census.

HANSEN (HANS OLUF) Manntal, 1729, i pbremur sýslum, etc. Reykjavík, 1975. pp. 40. *(Iceland. Hagstofa. Hagskýrslur Íslands. 2[Series]. 59) With English summary.*

IDEALISM.

VEL'TSMAN (VLADIMIR NIKOLAEVICH) V.I. Lenin o klassovykh i gnoseologicheskikh korniakh idealizma. Khar'kov, 1974. pp. 200. *bibliog.*

IDENTIFICATION

— **Russia.**

GAPANOVICH (NIKOLAI NIKOLAEVICH) Opoznanie v sudoproizvodstve: protsessual'nye i psikhologicheskie problemy. Minsk, 1975. pp. 175.

IDEOLOGY.

MATTELART (ARMAND) and others. La ideologia de la dominacion en una sociedad dependiente: la respuesta ideologica de la clase dominante chilena al reformismo. Buenos Aires, 1970. pp. 319. *bibliog.*

THOMAS (JOHN CLAYTON) The decline of ideology in Western political parties: a study of changing policy orientations. London, [1975]. pp. 68. *bibliog.*

GEORGE (VICTOR N.) and WILDING (PAUL) Ideology and social welfare. London, 1976. pp. 162. *bibliog.*

GOULDNER (ALVIN WARD) The dialectic of ideology and technology: the origins, grammar, and future of ideology. London, 1976. pp. 304.

LODGE (GEORGE CABOT) The new American ideology: how the ideological basis of legitimate authority in America is being radically transformed, etc. New York, 1976. pp. 350,xv.

LUDZ (PETER CHRISTIAN) Ideologiebegriff und marxistische Theorie: Ansätze zu einer immanenten Kritik. Opladen, [1976]. pp. 337. *bibliog. Collection of essays.*

SELIGER (MARTIN) Ideology and politics. London, 1976. pp. 352. *bibliog.*

IDOMAS.

MAGID (ALVIN) Men in the middle: leadership and role conflict in a Nigerian society. Manchester, [1976]. pp. 292. *bibliog.*

ILLEGITIMACY.

HARTLEY (SHIRLEY FOSTER) Illegitimacy. Berkeley, Cal., [1975]. pp. 288. *bibliog.*

ILLITERACY.

BERGGREN (CAROL) and BERGGREN (LARS) The literacy process: a practice in domestication or liberation. London, [1975]. pp. 47. *bibliog.*

— **India.**

INDIA. Ministry of Education and Social Welfare. 1975. Main schemes of non-formal education in the fifth five year plan. [Delhi], 1975. pp. 18. *(Publications. No. 1027)*

— **Nigeria.**

NIGERIA. Federal Ministry of Education. 1972. Eradication of illiteracy; by A.Y.Eke, Federal Commissioner for Education. Lagos, 1972. pp. 16.

— **United States.**

LOCKRIDGE (KENNETH A.) Literacy in colonial New England: an enquiry into the social contexts of literacy in the early modern West. New York, [1974]. pp. 164. *bibliog.*

IMLAY (GILBERT).

GODWIN (MARY) Letters written during a short residence in Sweden, Norway, and Denmark; edited with an introduction by Carol H. Poston. Lincoln, Nebraska, [1976]. pp. 200. *bibliog.*

IMPERIALISM.

INTERNATIONAL SOCIALIST CONGRESS, 1921. L'impérialisme et la révolution sociale: résolution votée à la Conférence internationale socialiste de Vienne, 22-27 février 1921. [Paris, 192-?]. pp. 7. *(Femme Socialiste, La. Publications)*

IMPERIALIZM i bor'ba rabochego klassa: sbornik statei pamiati akademika Fedora Aronovicha Rotshteina. Moskva, 1960. pp. 507.

CORAL (JUAN CARLOS) Indoamerica frente al imperialismo. Buenos Aires, 1966. pp. 76.

SANTOS (THEOTONIO DOS) Imperialismo y empresas multinacionales. Buenos Aires, 1973. pp. 142.

ORGANIZZAZIONE COMUNISTA (MARXISTA-LENINISTA). Congresso Nazionale, 1, 1974. Crisi, revisionismo e partito: tesi. Milano, 1974. pp. 115.

WEHLER (HANS ULRICH) Der Aufstieg des amerikanischen Imperialismus: Studien zur Entwicklung des Imperium Americanum, 1865-1900. Göttingen, 1974. pp. 426. *bibliog.*

FRANK (ANDRE GUNDER) On capitalist underdevelopment. Bombay, 1975. pp. 113. *bibliog.*

GRIFONE (PIETRO) Capitalismo di Stato e imperialismo fascista; con i contributi di Giorgio Amendola e Camilla Ravera. Milano, [1975]. pp. 155.

GUTSCHE (WILLIBALD) Zur Imperialismus-Apologie in der BRD: "neue" Imperialismusdeutungen in der BRD-Historiographie zur deutschen Geschichte, 1898 bis 1917. Frankfurt/Main, 1975. pp. 83.

LIBERALISMUS und imperialistischer Staat: der Imperialismus als Problem liberaler Parteien in Deutschland, 1890-1914; mit Beiträgen von Lothar Albertin [and others]; herausgegeben von Karl Holl und Günther List. Göttingen, [1975]. pp. 176.

MACINTYRE (STUART) Imperialism and the British labour movement in the 1920's: an examination of Marxist theory. London, 1975. pp. 24. *(Communist Party of Great Britain. History Group. Our History. No. 64)*

SCHMITT-EGNER (PETER) Kolonialismus und Faschismus: eine Studie zur historischen und begrifflichen Genesis faschistischer Bewusstseinsformen am deutschen Beispiel. Giessen/Lollar, 1975. pp. 224. *bibliog.*

SINE (BABAKAR) Impérialisme et théories sociologiques du développement; présentation par Samir Amin. Paris, [1975]. pp. 396. *bibliog.*

BETTS (RAYMOND FREDERICK) The false dawn: European imperialism in the nineteenth century. Minneapolis, 1976. pp. 270. *bibliog.*

HAMPE (PETER) Die "ökonomische Imperialismustheorie": kritische Untersuchungen. München, [1976]. pp. 399. *bibliog. (Munich. Universität. Geschwister-Scholl- Institut für Politische Wissenschaft. Münchener Studien zur Politik. 24.Band)*

LOUIS (WILLIAM ROGER) ed. Imperialism: the Robinson and Gallagher controversy. New York, 1976. pp. 252. *bibliog.*

ROZENTAL' (MARK MOISEEVICH) Dialektika leninskogo issledovaniia imperializma i revoliutsii. Moskva, 1976. pp. 520.

IMPORT QUOTAS

— **United Kingdom — Mathematical models.**

CORDEN (WARNER MAX) and others. Import controls versus devaluation and Britain's economic prospects. London, [1975]. fo. 21. *(Trade Policy Research Centre. Guest Papers. No. 2)*

IMRO.

See **VŬTRESHNA MAKEDONSKA REVOLIUTSIONNA ORGANIZATSIIA.**

INCAS.

WACHTEL (NATHAN) Sociedad e ideologia: ensayos de historia y antropologia andinas. Lima, 1973. pp. 239. *bibliog. (Instituto de Estudios Peruanos. Historia Andina. 1)*

INCENTIVES IN INDUSTRY.

RADAEV (VALERII VIKTOROVICH) Ekonomicheskie interesy pri sotsializme. Moskva, 1971. pp. 336.

UCHENYE ZAPISKI KAFEDR OBSHCHESTVENNYKH NAUK VUZOV LENINGRADA. Politicheskaia ekonomiia. vyp. 12. Ekonomicheskie interesy pri sotsializme i formy ikh realizatsii. Leningrad, 1971. pp. 191.

INTERESY v sisteme ekonomicheskikh otnoshenii sotsializma. Kiev 1974. pp. 240.

VYSHNEVETS'KYI (IOSIF ANTONOVYCH) Ekonomichni interesy sotsialistychnoho suspil'stva. Kyïv, 1975. pp. 102.

— **Germany.**

LUTZ (BURKART) Krise des Lohnanreizes: ein empirisch-historischer Beitrag zum Wandel der Formen betrieblicher Herrschaft am Beispiel der deutschen Stahlindustrie. Frankfurt, 1975. pp. 363. *(Institut für Sozialwissenschaftliche Forschung, München. Arbeiten)*

INCOME.

MALAKHINOVA (ROZA PAVLOVNA) Chistyi dokhod obshchestva: teoreticheskii ocherk. Moskva, 1974. pp. 135.

A SYSTEM of international comparisons of gross product and purchasing power: (United Nations International Comparison Project: phase one);...published for the World Bank. Baltimore, [1975]. pp. 294.

KING (JOHN E.) and REGAN (PHILIP) Relative income shares. London, 1976. pp. 87. *bibliog.*

— **Canada.**

COURCHENE (THOMAS J.) Migration, income and employment: Canada, 1965-68. [Montreal, 1974]. pp. 155. *(Howe (C.D.) Research Institute. Special Studies.1.)*

— **Communist countries.**

SITNIN (VSEVOLOD VLADIMIROVICH) Chistyi dokhod. Moskva, 1974. pp. 199.

— **France.**

FRANCE. Centre d'Etude des Revenus et des Coûts. 1973. Les connaissances et opinions de Français dans le domaine des revenus: analyse des résultats d'une enquête. Paris, 1973. pp. 210. *(Documents. Nos. 19-20)*

FRANCE. Comité des Revenus et des Transferts. 1976. Rapport...: préparation du 7e Plan. Paris, 1976. pp. 184.

— **Japan.**

JAPAN. Bureau of Statistics. 1976- . 1974 national survey of family income and expenditures. [Tokyo, 1976 in progress]. *In English and Japanese.*

— **Netherlands.**

RAAD VOOR HET MIDDEN- EN KLEINBEDRIJF. Documentatie inkomenspositie en -ontwikkeling van werknemers en zelfstandigen in het midden- en kleinbedrijf. 's-Gravenhage, 1971. PP. 25. *([Publikaties]. 1971, no. 1)*

— **Norway — Mathematical models.**

RINGSTAD (VIDAR) PRIM II: en revidert versjon av pris- og intektsmodellen...: PRIM II: a revised version of the price and income model. Oslo, 1972. pp. 43. *(Norway. Statistiske Centralbyrå. Artikler. Nr.44)*

— **Poland.**

RUTKOWSKI (TADEUSZ) Wyznaczanie czynnik0w określających dochody ludności: zastosowanie metod statystyczno-matematycznych. Warszawa, 1975. pp. 110. *bibliog. (Polska Akademia Nauk. Komitet Przestrzennego Zagospodarowania Kraju. Studia. t.52) With Russian and English summaries.*

— **Russia.**

MALAKHINOVA (ROZA PAVLOVNA) Chistyi dokhod obshchestva: teoreticheskii ocherk. Moskva, 1974. pp. 135.

ANDREEV (ALEKSEI KUZ'MIN) Balans denezhnykh dokhodov i raskhodov naseleniia: na primere Kazakhskoi SSR. Moskva, 1975. pp. 111.

INCOME.(Cont.)

— **South Africa.**

SOUTH AFRICA. Census, 1970. Population census, 1970: income and work status by district and economic region. [Pretoria, 1975]. pp. 384. *(Bureau of Statistics. Reports. No. 02-01-07) In English and Afrikaans.*

SOUTH AFRICA. Census, 1970. Population census, 1970: occupations: income, industry and identity. [Pretoria, 1975]. pp. 360. *(Bureau of Statistics. Reports. No. 02-05-04) In English and Afrikaans.*

SOUTH AFRICA. Census, 1970. Population census, 1970: personal income. [Pretoria, 1975]. pp. 311. *(Bureau of Statistics. Reports. No. 02-01-08) In English and Afrikaans.*

— **Sweden.**

JULANDER (CLAES-ROBERT) Sparande och effekter av ökad kunskap om inkomstens användning: en beteendevetenskaplig studie av individers inkomstanvändning. Stockholm, 1975. pp. 343. *bibliog. With English summary.*

— **Trinidad and Tobago.**

TRINIDAD AND TOBAGO. Central Statistical Office. 1974. Income; industry; based on 1970 population census. Port of Spain, 1974. pp. 222. *(Manpower Reports. vol. 1. no. 4)*

TRINIDAD AND TOBAGO. Central Statistical Office. Continuous Sample Survey of Population. Income: earnings of individuals, (provisional). [Port-of-Spain, 1972]. pp. 11. *(Bulletins. Vol. 1. No. 12)*

— **Underdeveloped areas.**

See UNDERDEVELOPED AREAS — Income.

— **United Kingdom.**

NORTHERN REGION STRATEGY TEAM. Personal incomes in the northern region. Newcastle upon Tyne, 1975. 1 vol. (various pagings). *(Technical Reports. No. 5)*

— **United States.**

RAINWATER (LEE) What money buys: inequality and the social meanings of income. New York, [1974]. pp. 242.

INCOME DISTRIBUTION.

LOONEY (ROBERT E.) Income distribution policies and economic growth in semiindustrialized countries: a comparative study of Iran, Mexico, Brazil, and South Korea. New York, 1975. pp. 194. *bibliog.*

The PERSONAL distribution of incomes; edited by A.B. Atkinson for the...Society. London, 1976. pp. 352. *bibliogs. Papers presented at a conference organised by the Royal Economic Society in Lancaster in 1974.*

RUNGE (HARRY) Der Einfluss der personellen Einkommensverteilung auf den Wert des Volkseinkommens. Berlin, [1976]. pp. 139. *bibliog.*

SAWYER (MALCOLM C.) and WASSERMAN (MARK) Income distribution in OECD countries; [and] Public sector budget balances; by Mark Wasserman. [Paris], Organisation for Economic Co-operation and Development, 1976. pp. 51. *(OECD Economic Outlook. Occasional Studies)*

VEREIN FÜR SOZIALPOLITIK. Schriften. Neue Folge. Band 75/IV. Öffentliche Finanzwirtschaft und Verteilung, IV; von Clemens-August Andreae [and others]; herausgegeben von Wilhelmine Dreissig. Berlin, [1976]. pp. 150. *With summaries and table of contents in English.*

— **Mathematical models.**

NIKAIDO (HUKUKANE) Monopolistic competition and effective demand. Princeton, 1975. pp. 150. *bibliog.*

— **America, Latin.**

INCOME distribution in Latin America; edited by Alejandro Foxley. Cambridge, 1976. pp. 244. *Papers of a conference sponsored by the Center for National Planning Studies of the Catholic University of Chile in 1973.*

— **Asia.**

INCOME distribution, employment and economic development in Southeast and East Asia: papers and proceedings of the seminar sponsored jointly by the Japan Economic Research Center and the Council for Asian Manpower Studies...1974; with contribution from the ILO World Employment Programme. Tokyo, 1975. pp. 791.

— **Belgium.**

BELLINGEN (P. VAN) Meerwaarde en inkomensherverdeling in België. Antwerpen, [1974]. pp. 156. *bibliog.*

— **Chile.**

BIENESTAR y pobreza; edicion preparada por CEPLAN; (edicion a cargo de Raul Gutierrez). Santiago, Chile, 1974. pp. 315. *Includes papers presented to the Seminario Internacional de Distribucion del Ingreso y Desarrollo, 1973, organized by the Centro de Estudios de Planificacion Nacional.*

— **Colombia.**

BERRY (ALBERT) and URRUTIA (MIGUEL) Income distribution in Colombia. New Haven, 1976. pp. 281.

— **Egypt.**

ABDEL-FADIL (MAHMOUD) Development, income distribution and social change in rural Egypt, 1952-1970: a study in the political economy of agrarian transition. Cambridge, 1975. pp. 157. *bibliog. (Cambridge. University. Department of Applied Economics. Occasional Papers. 45)*

— **Europe, Eastern.**

CASSEL (DIETER) and THIEME (H. JOERG) eds. Einkommensverteilung im Systemvergleich;...mit Beiträgen von Dieter Cassel [and others]. Stuttgart, 1976. pp. 213.

— **Germany.**

EHRENBERG (HERBERT) and STREICHAN (PETER) eds. Dokumente zur Vermögenspolitik. Bonn-Bad Godesberg, [1974]. pp. 127. *bibliog.*

FREY (HANS DIETER) Auswirkungen von Preissteigerungen auf die Verteilung des Einkommens und des Vermögens. Tübingen, 1975. pp. 428. *bibliog. (Tübingen. Institut für Angewandte Wirtschaftsforschung. Schriftenreihe. Band 28)*

MUECKL (WOLFGANG J.) Vermögenspolitische Konzepte in der Bundesrepublik Deutschland: Analyse der Ziele, Mittel und Wirkungen. Göttingen, [1975]. pp. 112. *bibliog. (Kommission für Wirtschaftlichen und Sozialen Wandel. Schriften. 34)*

WICKE (LUTZ) Vermögensverteilung und schleichende Inflation: eine Analyse. ..in der Bundesrepublik Deutschland. Meisenheim am Glan, 1975. pp. 273. *bibliog.*

CASSEL (DIETER) and THIEME (H. JOERG) eds. Einkommensverteilung im Systemvergleich;...mit Beiträgen von Dieter Cassel [and others]. Stuttgart, 1976. pp. 213.

SCHILLERT (ULLRICH) Gewinne als Quelle der Vermögenspolitik?: die Belastbarkeit der Unternehmensgewinne durch vermögenspolitische Massnahmen. Berlin, [1976]. pp. 270. *bibliog.*

— **India.**

NATIONAL COUNCIL OF APPLIED ECONOMIC RESEARCH. Changes in rural income in India, 1968-69, 1969-70, 1970-71. New Delhi, [1975]. pp. 155.

— **Ireland (Republic).**

NATIONAL ECONOMIC AND SOCIAL COUNCIL [EIRE]. Income distribution: a preliminary report. Dublin, Stationery Office, [1975]. pp. 58. *([Reports]. No.11)*

— **Netherlands.**

DOEL (JOHANNES VAN DEN) and HOOGERWERF (A.) eds. Gelijkheid en ongelijkheid in Nederland: analyse en beleid. Alphen aan den Rijn, 1975. pp. 312. *bibliogs.*

— **Norway.**

AUKRUST (ODD) and BORGENVIK (HALLVARD) Inntektsfordelingsvirkninger av skattereformen av 1969.... income distribution effects of the taxation reform of 1969. Oslo, 1969. pp. 29. *(Norway. Statistiske Centralbyrå. Artikler. Nr. 33)*

— **Sweden.**

SPÅNT (ROLAND) Den svenska inkomstfördelningens utveckling. Uppsala, 1976. pp. 239. *bibliog. (Uppsala Universitet. Acta Universitatis Upsaliensis. Studia Oeconomica Upsaliensia. 4) With English summary.*

— **Tunisia.**

KLEVE (JACOB GEERT) and STOLPER (WOLFGANG FRIEDRICH) Changes in income distribution, 1961-1971. [Ann Arbor, 1975?]. pp. 30.

— **United States.**

BROWNING (EDGAR K.) Redistribution and the welfare system. Washington, 1975. pp. 131. *(American Enterprise Institute for Public Policy Research. Evaluative Studies. 22).*

TAUBMAN (PAUL J.) Sources of inequality in earnings: personal skills, random events, preferences towards risk and other occupational characteristics. Amsterdam, 1975. pp. 273. *bibliog.*

THUROW (LESTER C.) Generating inequality. London, [1975]. pp. 258.

LEBERGOTT (STANLEY) The American economy: income, wealth and want. Princeton, N.J., [1976]. pp. 382.

INCOME MAINTENANCE PROGRAMMES

— **Australia.**

SALMON (JAN) Resources for poor families: an experimental income supplement scheme. Canberra, Australian Government Publishing Service, 1974. pp. 96.

— **United Kingdom.**

STEIN (BRUNO) Work and welfare in Britain and the U.S.A. London, 1976. pp. 112.

— **United States.**

STEIN (BRUNO) Work and welfare in Britain and the U.S.A. London, 1976. pp. 112.

INCOME TAX.

U.K. Board of Inland Revenue. 1976- . Income taxes outside the United Kingdom: [booklets]. London, 1976 in progress. 5 vols. (loose-leaf).

— **Botswana.**

BOTSWANA. Department of Taxes. Annual report. a., 1972/73- Gaborone.

— **Germany — Hesse.**

HESSE. Statistisches Landesamt. Beiträge zur Statistik Hessens. Neue Folge. Nr. 72. Der Bruttolohn und seine Besteuerung, 1971: Ergebnisse der Lohnsteuerstatistik, 1971. Wiesbaden, 1975. pp. 34.

— — **North Rhine-Westphalia.**

NORTH RHINE-WESTPHALIA. Landesamt für Datenverarbeitung und Statistik. Beiträge zur Statistik des Landes Nordrhein- Westfalen. Heft 348. Steuern vom Einkommen in Nordrhein-Westfalen, 1971. Düsseldorf, 1976. pp. 183.

— **India.**

INDIA. Committee on Taxation of Agricultural Wealth and Income. 1972. Report; [K.N. Raj, chairman]. [Delhi?], 1972. pp. 169.

— **New Zealand — Law.**

MOLLOY (ANTHONY PATRICK) On income tax. Wellington, 1976. pp. 724.

— Poland.

BIAŁOBRZESKI (JANUSZ) Opodatkowanie rzemiosła i innej działalności zarobkowej: przepisy i komentarz; według stanu prawnego na dzień 1 marca 1974 r. Warszawa, 1974. pp. 323.

— Rhodesia.

RHODESIA. Department of Taxes. 1974. Income tax in Rhodesia: information pamphlet setting out the main features of direct taxation in Rhodesia. Salisbury, 1974. pp. 10.

— United Kingdom.

MACDONALD (GRAEME) Taxation and the family unit. London, [1976]. pp. 12. *(Institute for Fiscal Studies. Lecture Series. No.6)*

— — Law.

WHITEMAN (PETER GEORGE) and WHEATCROFT (GEORGE SHORROCK ASHCROFT) On income tax; second edition by P.G. Whiteman and David C. Milne. London, 1976. pp. 1088.

— United States.

GOODE (RICHARD B.) The individual income tax. rev. ed. Washington, [1976]. pp. 346. *(Brookings Institution. Studies of Government Finance)*

INDEPENDENT REGULATORY COMMISSIONS

— United Kingdom.

HAGUE (DOUGLAS CHALMERS) and others. Public policy and private interests: the institutions of compromise. London, 1975. pp. 433.

INDEPENDENT SOCIAL DEMOCRATIC PARTY (GERMANY).

See UNABHAENGIGE SOZIALDEMOKRATISCHE PARTEI DEUTSCHLANDS.

INDEX NUMBERS (ECONOMICS).

ITALY. Istituto Centrale di Statistica. 1967. Numeri indici della produzione industriale, base 1966 [equals] 100. Roma, 1967. pp. 91. *(Metodi e Norme. Serie A. N.7)*

LIBYA. Census and Statistical Department. 1968. External trade indices, 1962-1966. Tripoli, [1968]. fo. (30). *In English and Arabic.*

BRENNA (SVEIN FREDRIK) Revisjon av indeksene for utenrikshandelen...: revision of indices for foreign trade. Oslo, 1973. pp. 47. *(Norway. Statistiske Centralbyrå. Artikler. Nr.57) With tables in Norwegian and English.*

ALLEN (Sir ROY GEORGE DOUGLAS) Index numbers in theory and practice. London, 1975. pp. 278. *bibliog.*

GERMANY (BUNDESREPUBLIK). Statistisches Bundesamt. 1975. Aussenhandelsvolumen und Aussenhandelsindizes auf Basis 1970: Ergebnisse von 1952 bis 1974. Stuttgart, 1975. pp. 136. *(Aussenhandel. Reihe 7. Sonderbeiträge)*

U. K. Welsh Office. 1976. The index of industrial production for Wales. Cardiff, 1976. pp. 29. *(Occasional Papers. No. 3)*

INDEXATION (ECONOMICS).

CUDDY (J.D.A.) International price indexation. Farnborough, Hants., [1976]. pp. 144.

MORGAN (DAVID RAYMOND) Indexation of personal income taxation. 1976. fo. 376. *bibliog. Typescript. Ph.D. (London) thesis: unpublished. This thesis is the property of London University and may not be removed from the Library.*

INDIA

— Census.

INDIA. Census, 1971. Census of India, 1971. Series [vols.]. [Delhi, 1972 in progress].

— Commerce.

ECONOMIC AND COMMERCIAL NEWS; [issued...by...Ministry of Foreign Trade, India]. w., Je 5 1971 (v.1, no.1)- , with gap (Je 26 1971: v. 1, no. 4). New Delhi.

— Commercial policy.

BHAGWATI (JAGDISH NATWARLAL) and SRINIVASAN (T.N.) Foreign trade regimes and economic development: India. New York, 1975. pp. 261. *(National Bureau of Economic Research. Special Conference Series on Foreign Trade Regimes and Economic Development. vol. 6)*

— Commercial treaties.

INDIA. Directorate of Exhibitions and Commercial Publicity. 1973. India's trade agreements with other countries as in force on January 1, 1973. New Delhi, [1973]. pp. 546.

— Constitution.

INDIA. Constituent Assembly. Drafting Committee. 1948. Draft constitution of India. New Delhi, 1948. pp. 214.

INDIA. Constitution. 1949. The constitution of India. Delhi, 1949. pp. 251.

— Constitutional history.

INDIA. Parliament. Lok Sabha. Secretariat. 1975. Constitution amendment in India. 4th ed. New Delhi, 1974 [or rather 1975]. pp. 334.

— Defences.

INTERNATIONAL INSTITUTE FOR STRATEGIC STUDIES. Adelphi Papers. No. 125. India's security in the 1980s; by G.S. Bhargava. London, 1976. pp. 30.

— Economic conditions.

ECONOMIC AND COMMERCIAL NEWS; [issued...by...Ministry of Foreign Trade, India]. w., Je 5 1971 (v.1, no.1)- , with gap (Je 26 1971: v. 1, no. 4). New Delhi.

DAS (NABAGOPAL) The Indian economy under planning. Calcutta, 1972. pp. 140. *bibliog.*

INDUSTRIAL DEVELOPMENT BANK OF INDIA. Annual report. a., 1973/74- Bombay.

ECONOMIC and social aspects of Indian development; an A.B.O.C. S. symposium; editor, Peter Meyer-Dohm. Tübingen, [1975]. pp. 293. *bibliog. (Bochum. Ruhr-Universität. Institut für Entwicklungsforschung und Entwicklungspolitik. Bochumer Schriften zur Entwicklungsforschung und Entwicklungspolitik. Band 19)*

FONSECA (ALOYSIUS JOSEPH) Wage issues in a developing economy: the Indian experience. Bombay, 1975. pp. 264.

RESPONSES to population growth in India: changes in social, political, and economic behavior; edited by Marcus F. Franda. New York, 1975. pp. 275. *Papers of a conference organized by the India Council of the Asia Society, Racine, Wisconsin, 1974.*

— Economic history.

DAVEY (BRIAN) The economic development of India: a Marxist analysis. Nottingham, 1975. pp. 232. *bibliog.*

INDIA. Gazetteers Unit. 1975. The gazetteer of India: Indian union. Vol. 3. Economic structure and activities. [New Delhi], 1975. pp. 1278.

— Economic policy.

SEN (KHAGENDRA NATH) Economic reconstruction of India: a study in economic planning; with a foreword by Pandit Jawaharlal Nehru. Calcutta, 1939. pp. 500.

INDIA. Planning Commission. 1953. First five year plan; (people's edition). Delhi, 1953. pp. 263.

INDIA. Administrative Reforms Commission. 1968. Report: economic administration. [New Delhi], 1968. pp. 96.

INDIA. Planning Commission. 1969. Annual plan progress report, 1967-68. [Delhi, 1969]. pp. 168.

SOCIAL sciences and planning in India; edited by Radhakamal Mukerjee. London, [1970]. pp. 208. *Papers of a seminar held at Bakshi-Ka-Talab in 1965 under the joint auspices of the Social Science Department of the University of Lucknow and the Orientation and Study Centre, Bakshi-Ka-Talab under the Ministry of Community Development and Cooperation.*

DAS (NABAGOPAL) The Indian economy under planning. Calcutta, 1972. pp. 140. *bibliog.*

INDUSTRIAL DEVELOPMENT BANK OF INDIA. Annual report. a., 1973/74- Bombay.

INDIA. Planning Commission. 1973-74. Draft fifth five year plan, 1974-79. [Delhi, 1973-74]. 2 vols. (in 1).

GHOSH (SANTIKUMAR) Development performance and stagflation. Calcutta, 1974. pp. 60. *bibliog.*

BHAGWATI (JAGDISH NATWARLAL) and SRINIVASAN (T.N.) Foreign trade regimes and economic development: India. New York, 1975. pp. 261. *(National Bureau of Economic Research. Special Conference Series on Foreign Trade Regimes and Economic Development. vol. 6)*

BHULESHKAR (ASHOK VASANTRAO) ed. Growth of Indian economy in socialism. Bombay, 1975. pp. 607. *(Jawaharlal Nehru Memorial Institute of Development Studies. Jawaharlal Nehru Memorial Series. 3)*

ECONOMIC and social aspects of Indian development; an A.B.O.C. S. symposium; editor, Peter Meyer-Dohm. Tübingen, [1975]. pp. 293. *bibliog. (Bochum. Ruhr-Universität. Institut für Entwicklungsforschung und Entwicklungspolitik. Bochumer Schriften zur Entwicklungsforschung und Entwicklungspolitik. Band 19)*

GANDHI (INDIRA) The years of endeavour: selected speeches...August 1969-August 1972. [New Delhi], Publications Division, Ministry of Information and Broadcasting, 1975. pp. 827.

INDIA. Ministry of Information and Broadcasting. Directorate of Advertising and Visual Publicity. 1975. A hundred new gains. [Delhi, 1975?]. pp. 32.

INDIA. Ministry of Information and Broadcasting. Publications Division. 1975. Timely steps. New Delhi, [1975]. pp. 77.

INDIA. Planning Commission. 1975. The planning process. [Delhi, 1975]. pp. 84.

MELLOR (JOHN WILLIAMS) The new economics of growth: a strategy for India and the developing world. Ithaca, N.Y., 1976. pp. 335.

— — Mathematical models.

INDIA. Planning Commission. Perspective Planning Division. 1973. A technical note on the approach to the fifth plan of India, 1974- 79. New Delhi, 1973. pp. 91.

— Executive departments.

INDIA. Administrative Reforms Commission. 1968. Report: economic administration. [New Delhi], 1968. pp. 96.

INDIA. Institute of Secretariat Training and Management. 1975. Organisational set-up and functions of the ministries/departments of the government of India. 5th ed. New Delhi, [1975]. pp. 425.

INDIA(Cont.)

— Foreign relations.

MENON (KUMARA PADMANABHA SIVASANKARA) The Indo-Soviet treaty: setting and sequel. 2nd ed. Delhi, 1972. pp. 156.

CHOPRA (PRAN) India's second liberation. Cambridge, Mass., 1974. pp. 270.

HUSAIN (ZAKIR) President of the Indian Republic. President Zakir Husain's speeches. New Delhi, Publications Division, Ministry of Information and Broadcasting, 1974. pp. 386.

GANDHI (INDIRA) Indira Gandhi speaks on democracy, socialism and third world nonalignment; edited and with an introduction by Henry M. Christman. New York, 1975. pp. 157.

GANDHI (INDIRA) The years of endeavour: selected speeches...August 1969-August 1972. [New Delhi], Publications Division, Ministry of Information and Broadcasting, 1975. pp. 827.

NASENKO (IURII PETROVICH) Dzhavakharlal Neru i vneshniaia politika Indii. Moskva, 1975. pp. 383. *bibliog.*

INDIAN foreign policy: the Nehru years: [a series of lectures delivered in the Nehru Memorial Museum and Library in 1973-74]; edited by B.R. Nanda. Delhi, [1976]. pp. 279.

KAPUR (ASHOK) India's nuclear option: atomic diplomacy and decision making. New York, 1976. pp. 295. *bibliog.*

— — Russia.

REMNEK (RICHARD B.) Soviet scholars and Soviet foreign policy: a case study in Soviet policy towards India. Durham, N.C., 1975. pp. 343. *bibliog.*

— — United Kingdom.

LIPTON (MICHAEL) and FIRN (JOHN) The erosion of a relationship: India and Britain since 1960. London, 1975. pp. 427. *Published for the Royal Institute of International Affairs.*

— — — Commonwealth.

TINKER (HUGH) Separate and unequal: India and the Indians in the British Commonwealth, 1920-1950. London, [1976]. pp. 460. *bibliog.*

— History — 1700-1799.

LAWFORD (JAMES PHILIP) Clive, proconsul of India: a biography. London, 1976. pp. 432. *bibliog.*

— — 1765-1947, British occupation.

GRIFFITHS (Sir PERCIVAL) The British in India. London, 1946. pp. 222.

— Industries.

SHIROKOV (GLERII KUZ'MICH) Industrializatsiia Indii. Moskva, 1971. pp. 390. *bibliog.*

PRASAD (KEDARNATH) The strategy of industrial dispersal and decentralized development: a case study. New Delhi, 1975. pp. 516. *bibliog.*

— Maps.

INDIA. Ministry of Information and Broadcasting. Publications Division. 1950. India in maps. [Delhi?], 1950. pp. 55.

— Nationalism.

D'IAKOV (ALEKSEI MIKHAILOVICH) Natsional'nyi vopros v sovremennoi Indii. Moskva, 1963. pp. 196.

CORR (GERARD H.) The war of the springing tigers. London, 1975. pp. 200. *bibliog.*

NARAYAN (JAYAPRAKASH) Nation building in India;...edited by Brahmanand. Varanasi, [1975]. pp. 430.

TORRI (MICHELGUGLIELMO) Dalla collaborazione alla rivoluzione non violenta: il nazionalismo indiano da movimento di élite a movimento di massa. Torino, [1975]. pp. 364.

— Parliament — Committees.

SESHADRI (S.) Parliamentary control over finance: a study of the public accounts committee of parliament. Bombay, 1975. pp. 295.

— Politics and government.

KNIGHTON (WILLIAM) LL.D. The policy of the future in India: a letter to the Right Hon. Lord Cranborne, Secretary of State for India, etc., etc. London, 1867. pp. 28.

— — 1919-1947.

NARAYAN (JAYAPRAKASH) Nation building in India;...edited by Brahmanand. Varanasi, [1975]. pp. 430.

— — 1947— .

SINGH (BALJIT) b. 1929, and VAJPEYI (DHIRENDRA K.) Political stability and continuity in the Indian states during the Nehru era, 1947-1964: a statistical analysis. [East Lansing], 1973. pp. 54. *(Michigan State University. Asian Studies Center. South Asia Series. Occasional Papers. No. 19)*

HUSAIN (ZAKIR) President of the Indian Republic. President Zakir Husain's speeches. New Delhi, Publications Division, Ministry of Information and Broadcasting, 1974. pp. 386.

DUTT (VIDYA PRAKASH) Emergency in India: the background. New Delhi, [1975]. pp. 20.

GAJENDRAGADKAR (PRAHLAD BALACHARYA) Indian democracy: its major imperatives. Bombay, [1975]. pp. 112. *bibliog. (Mohan Kumaramangalam Memorial Lectures. 1974)*

GANDHI (INDIRA) Indira Gandhi speaks on democracy, socialism and third world nonalignment; edited and with an introduction by Henry M. Christman. New York, 1975. pp. 157.

GANDHI (INDIRA) The years of endeavour: selected speeches...August 1969-August 1972. [New Delhi], Publications Division, Ministry of Information and Broadcasting, 1975. pp. 827.

INDIA. Ministry of Home Affairs. 1975. Why emergency?. [Delhi], 1975. pp. 59.

INDIA. Ministry of Information and Broadcasting. Publications Division. 1975. Timely steps. New Delhi, [1975]. pp. 77.

INDIA. Office of the High Commissioner for India. 1975. Recent events in India; [by] B.K. Nehru. [London, 1975]. pp. 8.

INDIA. Office of the High Commissioner for India. Information Service. 1975. Democracy preserved: facts about the emergency in India. [London, 1975]. pp. 33.

NARAYAN (JAYAPRAKASH) Nation building in India;...edited by Brahmanand. Varanasi, [1975]. pp. 430.

HIRO (DILIP) Inside India today. London, 1976. pp. 331. *bibliog.*

KAPUR (ASHOK) India's nuclear option: atomic diplomacy and decision making. New York, 1976. pp. 295. *bibliog.*

KLIEMAN (AARON S.) Emergency politics: the growth of crisis government. London, 1976. pp. 19. *(Institute for the Study of Conflict. Conflict Studies. No. 70)*

RAI (E.N. MANGAT) Patterns of administrative development in independent India. London, 1976. pp. 167. *(London. University. Institute of Commonwealth Studies. Commonwealth Papers. 19)*

— Population.

INDIA. Office of the Registrar General. Vital Statistics Division. 1972. Sex composition in India. New Delhi, 1972. pp. 42. *bibliog. (Sample Registration System Analytical Series. No. 4)*

RESPONSES to population growth in India: changes in social, political, and economic behavior; edited by Marcus F. Franda. New York, 1975. pp. 275. *Papers of a conference organized by the India Council of the Asia Society, Racine, Wisconsin, 1974.*

— Population policy.

SONI (VEENA) A demographic analysis of the sterilisation programme in the Indian states, 1957-73. 1975. fo 248. *bibliog.* Typescript. Ph.D.(London) thesis: unpublished. This thesis is the property of London University and may not be removed from the Library.

— Religion.

THURSBY (G.R.) Hindu-Muslim relations in British India: a study of controversy, conflict, and communal movements in northern India, 1923-1928. Leiden, 1975. pp. 194. *bibliog. (Numen. Supplements: Studies in the History of Religions. 35)*

— Rural conditions.

NATIONAL COUNCIL OF APPLIED ECONOMIC RESEARCH. Changes in rural income in India, 1968-69, 1969-70, 1970-71. New Delhi, [1975]. pp. 155.

— Social conditions.

INDIA. Gazetteers Unit. 1965. The gazetteer of India: Indian union. Vol. 1. Country and people. [New Delhi], 1965 repr. 1973. pp. 652. *bibliogs.* 2 maps in end pocket.

HUSAIN (ZAKIR) President of the Indian Republic. President Zakir Husain's speeches. New Delhi, Publications Division, Ministry of Information and Broadcasting, 1974. pp. 386.

ECONOMIC and social aspects of Indian development; an A.B.O.C.S. symposium; editor, Peter Meyer-Dohm. Tübingen, [1975]. pp. 293. *bibliog. (Bochum. Ruhr-Universität. Institut für Entwicklungsforschung und Entwicklungspolitik. Bochumer Schriften zur Entwicklungsforschung und Entwicklungspolitik. Band 19)*

RESPONSES to population growth in India: changes in social, political, and economic behavior; edited by Marcus F. Franda. New York, 1975. pp. 275. *Papers of a conference organized by the India Council of the Asia Society, Racine, Wisconsin, 1974.*

— Social history.

BHATIA (BAL MOKAND) History and social development. Delhi, [1974 in progress]. *bibliog.*

— Social life and customs.

WIEBE (PAUL D.) Social life in an Indian slum. Delhi, [1975]. pp. 179. *bibliog.*

— Social policy.

INDIA. Planning Commission. 1953. First five year plan; (people's edition). Delhi, 1953. pp. 263.

INDIA. Planning Commission. 1969. Annual plan progress report, 1967-68. [Delhi, 1969]. pp. 168.

SOCIAL sciences and planning in India; edited by Radhakamal Mukerjee. London, [1970]. pp. 208. *Papers of a seminar held at Bakshi-Ka-Talab in 1965 under the joint auspices of the Social Science Department of the University of Lucknow and the Orientation and Study Centre, Bakshi-Ka-Talab under the Ministry of Community Development and Cooperation.*

INDIA. Planning Commission. 1973-74. Draft fifth five year plan, 1974-79. [Delhi, 1973-74]. 2 vols. (in 1).

ECONOMIC and social aspects of Indian development; an A.B.O.C. S. symposium; editor, Peter Meyer-Dohm. Tübingen, [1975]. pp. 293. *bibliog.* *(Bochum. Ruhr-Universität. Institut für Entwicklungsforschung und Entwicklungspolitik. Bochumer Schriften zur Entwicklungsforschung und Entwicklungspolitik. Band 19)*

GANDHI (INDIRA) The years of endeavour: selected speeches...August 1969-August 1972. [New Delhi], Publications Division, Ministry of Information and Broadcasting, 1975. pp. 827.

INDIA. Planning Commission. 1975. The planning process. [Delhi, 1975]. pp. 84.

SOCIAL welfare: legend and legacy: silver jubilee commemoration volume of the Indian Council of Social Welfare; edited by S.D. Gokhale. Bombay, 1975. pp. 432.

— Statistical services.

INDIA. Central Statistical Organisation. 1958. Statistical system in India, 1955. New Delhi, [1958]. pp. 129.

INDIA. Central Statistical Organisation. 1958. Statistical system in India, 1957. New Delhi, [1958]. pp. 158.

INDIA—PAKISTAN CONFLICT, 1971.

CHOPRA (PRAN) India's second liberation. Cambridge, Mass., 1974. pp. 270.

JACKSON (ROBERT VICTOR) South Asian crisis: India, Pakistan and Bangla Desh: a political and historical analysis of the 1971 war. New York, 1975. pp. 240. *bibliog.*

INDIAN NATIONAL ARMY.

CORR (GERARD H.) The war of the springing tigers. London, 1975. pp. 200. *bibliog.*

INDIAN NATIONAL CONGRESS.

GHOSE (SANKAR) Indian National Congress: its history and heritage. New Delhi, 1975. pp. 390.

INDIAN OCEAN REGION.

The INDIAN Ocean and the threat to the West: four studies in global strategy; [by] Anthony Harrigan [and others]; edited by Patrick Wall. London, 1975. pp. 198.

— Defences.

INDIAN Ocean power rivalry; edited by T.T. Poulose. New Delhi, 1974. pp. 317. *"Papers presented at a national seminar on Indian Ocean, organized by the Disarmament Studies Division of the School of International Studies [Jawaharlal Nehru University] on 18 and 19 February 1974".*

— Foreign relations.

INDIAN Ocean power rivalry; edited by T.T. Poulose. New Delhi, 1974. pp. 317. *"Papers presented at a national seminar on Indian Ocean, organized by the Disarmament Studies Division of the School of International Studies [Jawaharlal Nehru University] on 18 and 19 February 1974".*

INTERNATIONAL CONFERENCE ON THE PERSIAN GULF AND INDIAN OCEAN, TEHRAN, 1975. The Persian Gulf and Indian Ocean in international politics: edited by Abbas Amirie. Tehran, 1975. pp. 417. *Papers from the conference held under the auspices of the Institute for International Political and Economic Studies.*

— Military policy.

INDIAN Ocean power rivalry; edited by T.T. Poulose. New Delhi, 1974. pp. 317. *"Papers presented at a national seminar on Indian Ocean, organized by the Disarmament Studies Division of the School of International Studies [Jawaharlal Nehru University] on 18 and 19 February 1974".*

INDIANAPOLIS

— Social history — Sources.

FLETCHER (CALVIN) The diary of Calvin Fletcher, vol. 3, 1844-1847, including letter to and from Calvin Fletcher; edited by Gayle Thornbrough and Dorothy L. Riker. Indianapolis, 1974. pp. 475.

INDIANS

— Antiquities.

PREHISTORIC man in the new world; edited by Jesse D. Jennings [and] Edward Norbeck. Chicago, 1964, repr. 1974. pp. 633. *bibliogs. Papers based on a symposium entitled "Prehistoric Man in the New World", forming part of the fifteenth anniversary festivities of Rice University in 1962.*

INDIANS, TREATMENT OF.

HANKE (LEWIS ULYSSES) All mankind is one: a study of the disputation between Bartolomé de Las Casas and Juan Ginés de Sepúlveda in 1550 on the intellectual and religious capacity of the American Indians. Dekalb, Illinois, [1974]. pp. 205. *bibliog.*

— Canada.

CHAMBERLIN (J.E.) The harrowing of Eden: white attitudes toward North American natives. Toronto, [1975]. pp. 248.

— United States.

CHAMBERLIN (J.E.) The harrowing of Eden: white attitudes toward North American natives. Toronto, [1975]. pp. 248.

INDIANS OF CENTRAL AMERICA

— Guatemala.

MOORE (ALEXANDER) Life cycles in Atchalán: the diverse careers of certain Guatemalans. New York, [1973]. pp. 220. *bibliog.*

INDIANS OF MEXICO.

FRIEDLANDER (JUDITH) Being Indian in Hueyapan: a study of forced identity in contemporary Mexico. London, [1975]. pp. 205. *bibliog.*

INDIANS OF NORTH AMERICA

— Government relations.

HILL (EDWARD E.) The Office of Indian Affairs, 1824-1880: historical sketches. New York, [1974]. pp. 246.

LEVITAN (SAR A.) and JOHNSTON (WILLIAM B.) Indian giving: federal programs for native Americans. Baltimore, [1975]. pp. 83.

ROGIN (MICHAEL PAUL) Fathers and children: Andrew Jackson and the subjugation of the American Indian. New York, 1975. pp. 373, xii.

SATZ (RONALD N.) American Indian policy in the Jacksonian era. Lincoln, Neb., [1975]. pp. 343. *bibliog.*

TRENNERT (ROBERT A.) Alternative to extinction: federal Indian policy and the beginnings of the reservation system, 1846-51. Philadelphia, 1975. pp. 263. *bibliog.*

— History.

TRENNERT (ROBERT A.) Alternative to extinction: federal Indian policy and the beginnings of the reservation system, 1846-51. Philadelphia, 1975. pp. 263. *bibliog.*

— Land transfers.

ROGIN (MICHAEL PAUL) Fathers and children: Andrew Jackson and the subjugation of the American Indian. New York, 1975. pp. 373, xii.

SATZ (RONALD N.) American Indian policy in the Jacksonian era. Lincoln, Neb., [1975]. pp. 343. *bibliog.*

— Mixed bloods.

HOWARD (JOSEPH KINSEY) Strange empire: Louis Riel and the Métis people. Toronto, 1974. pp. 601. *bibliog. Originally published in 1952 in New York.*

— Urban residence.

STANBURY (WILLIAM T.) Success and failure: Indians in urban society;...assisted by Jay H. Siegel. [Vancouver, 1975]. pp. 415. *bibliog.*

— California.

COOK (SHERBURNE FRIEND) The conflict between the Californian Indian and white civilization. Berkeley, Calif., [1976]. pp. 522. *(Reprinted from Ibero-Americana, vols. 17-24, 1940-43)*

COOK (SHERBURNE FRIEND) The population of the California Indians, 1769-1970. Berkeley, Calif., [1976]. pp. 222. *bibliog.*

— Canada.

BRAROE (NIELS WINTHER) Indian and white: self-image and interaction in a Canadian plains community. Stanford, 1975. pp. 205. *bibliog.*

— — Government relations.

CANADA. Department of Indian Affairs and Northern Development. 1969. Statement by the Honourable Jean Chretien, Minister of Indian Affairs and Northern Development, based on a speech delivered in Regina, October 2, 1969. Ottawa, 1969. pp. 7,7. *In English and French.*

CANADA. Department of Indian Affairs and Northern Development. 1971. Indian Economic Development Fund: a source of financing for Canadian Indian businessmen. [Ottawa], 1971. pp. 8,8. *In English and French.*

FERRARI (LEO C.) Human rights and the Canadian Indian. Fredericton, New Brunswick Human Rights Commission, [1973]. fo. 37, 3.

JOINT VENTURES : the Indian Economic Development Fund annual review. a., 1974/75- Ottawa. *In English and French.*

— — Legal status, laws, etc.

CANADA. Indian Affairs Branch. 1971. Discussion notes on the Indian Act. [Ottawa, 1971]. pp. 15,17. *In English and French.*

— — Transportation.

MAIN (J.R.K.) Early transportation in Canada. Ottawa, Queen's Printer, 1969. pp. 7,7. *In English and French.*

— — British Columbia.

STANBURY (WILLIAM T.) Success and failure: Indians in urban society;...assisted by Jay H. Siegel. [Vancouver, 1975]. pp. 415. *bibliog.*

— — — Government relations.

FIELDS (DONALD B.) and STANBURY (WILLIAM T.) The economic impact of the public sector upon the Indians of British Columbia: an examination of the incidence of taxation and expenditure of three levels of government: a report submitted to the Department of Indian Affairs and Northern Development. Vancouver, 1973. pp. 284.

— United States.

WILSON (JAMES) b. 1948. The original Americans: U.S. Indians. London, 1976. pp. 28. *bibliog. (Minority Rights Group. Reports. No. 31)*

INDIANS OF SOUTH AMERICA.

WASSÉN (S. HENRY) The use of some specific kinds of South American Indian snuff and related paraphernalia. Göteborg, 1965. pp. 132. *bibliog. (Gothenburg. Etnografiska Museet. Etnologiska Studier. 28)*

INDIANS OF SOUTH AMERICA.(Cont.)

— **Bolivia.**

GOSLING (CECIL) [Foreign Office papers. 1910-21]. 1 piece. *Typescript and printed matter.*

— **Brazil.**

MURPHY (ROBERT FRANCIS) and QUAIN (BUELL) The Trumaí Indians of central Brazil. Seattle, 1955 repr. 1966. pp. 108. *bibliog. (American Ethnological Society. Monographs. 24)*

— **Ecuador.**

VILLAVICENCIO RIVADENEIRA (GLADYS) Relaciones interetnicas en Otavalo: una nacionalidad india en formacion?. Mexico, 1973. pp. 317. *bibliog. (Inter-American Indian Institute. Ediciones Especiales, 65)*

— **Venezuela.**

WILBERT (JOHANNES) Survivors of Eldorado: four Indian cultures of South America. New York, 1972. pp. 212. *bibliogs.*

INDIVIDUALISM.

CHATTOPADHYAY(DEBIPRASAD) Individuals and societies: a methodological inquiry. 2nd ed. Calcutta, 1975. pp. 281. *bibliog.*

ABRAMS (PHILIP) and McCULLOCH (ANDREW) Communes, sociology and society. Cambridge, 1976. pp. 239. *bibliog.*

ZARETSKY (ELI) Capitalism, the family and personal life. London, 1976. pp. 156.

INDONESIA

— **Census.**

INDONESIA. Census, 1971. 1971 population census...: preliminary figures. Djakarta, [1972]. 3pts. (in 1 vol.) *(Series B. Nos. 1-3) In English and Bahasa Indonesia.*

INDONESIA. Census, 1971. 1971 population census...: population of Indonesia. Jakarta, 1975. pp. 255. *(Series D) In English and Bahasa Indonesia.*

— **Economic conditions.**

UNITED STATES. Embassy (Indonesia). Indonesia: economic trends report. a., 1975- Jakarta.

— **Economic history.**

FURNIVALL (JOHN SYDENHAM) Netherlands India: a study of plural economy. Amsterdam, 1976. pp. 502. *bibliogs. Reprint of the edition first published in Cambridge, 1944.*

— **Foreign relations — China.**

MOZINGO (DAVID) Chinese policy towards Indonesia, 1949 1967. Ithaca, N.Y., 1976. pp. 303. *bibliog.*

— — **United States.**

CALDWELL (MALCOLM) ed. Ten years' military terror in Indonesia. Nottingham, 1975. pp. 295.

— **History — Sources.**

KWANTES (R.C.) ed. De ontwikkeling van de nationalistische beweging in Nederlandsch- Indië: bronnenpublikatie; Development of the nationalist movement in the Netherlands-Indies: with introduction and survey of the selected documents in English. Groningen, 1975 in progress. *(Nederlands Historisch Genootschap. Commissie voor Bronnenpublicatie betreffende de Geschiedenis van Nederlandsch-Indië 1900-1942. Uitgaven. 8, etc.)*

— — **1945-1949, Revolution.**

LOCKWOOD (RUPERT) Black armada. Sydney, 1975. pp. 352.

— **Nationalism.**

KWANTES (R.C.) ed. De ontwikkeling van de nationalistische beweging in Nederlandsch- Indië: bronnenpublikatie; Development of the nationalist movement in the Netherlands-Indies: with introduction and survey of the selected documents in English. Groningen, 1975 in progress. *(Nederlands Historisch Genootschap. Commissie voor Bronnenpublicatie betreffende de Geschiedenis van Nederlandsch-Indië 1900-1942. Uitgaven. 8, etc.)*

SOEKARNO (ACHMED) Indonesia accuses!: Soekarno's defence oration in the political trial of 1930; edited, translated, annotated and introduced by Roger K. Paget. Kuala Lumpur, 1975. pp. 153.

— **Politics and government.**

FURNIVALL (JOHN SYDENHAM) Netherlands India: a study of plural economy. Amsterdam, 1976. pp. 502. *bibliogs. Reprint of the edition first published in Cambridge, 1944.*

CALDWELL (MALCOLM) ed. Ten years' military terror in Indonesia. Nottingham, 1975. pp. 295.

EMMERSON (DONALD K.) Indonesia's elite: political culture and cultural politics. Ithaca, 1976. pp. 303. *bibliog.*

— **Population — Study and teaching.**

GUNN (ANGUS M.) Man on the earth: teacher resource book for: population pressure in Indonesia: problems of industrialization in Eurasia: power blocs in Eurasia. Toronto, 1974. pp. 51.

— **Social conditions.**

EMMERSON (DONALD K.) Indonesia's elite: political culture and cultural politics. Ithaca, 1976. pp. 303. *bibliog.*

— **Social history.**

FURNIVALL (JOHN SYDENHAM) Netherlands India: a study of plural economy. Amsterdam, 1976. pp. 502. *bibliogs. Reprint of the edition first published in Cambridge, 1944.*

INDOSOVIET TREATY OF PEACE, FRIENDSHIP AND COOPERATION, 1971.

MENON (KUMARA PADMANABHA SIVASANKARA) The Indo-Soviet treaty: setting and sequel. 2nd ed. Delhi, 1972. pp. 156.

INDUSTRIAL ACCIDENTS

— **Finland.**

LÄHTEINEN (MARTTI) and others. Työtapaturmat, työntekijäin ominaisuudet ja tapaturmien sattumisajankohta, etc. Helsinki, 1974. pp. 177. *bibliog. (Finland. Suomen Virallinen Tilasto. Finlands Officiella Statistik. 32. Sosiaalisia Erikoistutkimuksia. 38)*

ÄIKÄS (TIMO) Kuolemantapaukset työ- ja matkatapaturmissa vuonna 1972, etc. Helsinki, 1975. pp. 117. *bibliog. (Finland. Suomen Virallinen Tilasto. Finlands Officiella Statistik. 32. Sosiaalisia Erikoistutkimuksia. 42) With English summary.*

INDUSTRIAL BUILDINGS

— **Landscape architecture.**

TANDY (CLIFF) Landscape of industry;...with a section on hydrology by Peter Nelson. London, 1975. pp. 314. *bibliogs.*

INDUSTRIAL CONCENTRATION.

STOJANOVIĆ (SRBOLJUB) Informacioni pristup mjerenju koncentracije i mjerenju sličnosti struktura. Zagreb, 1974. pp. 135.

FEUERSTACK (RAINER) Unternehmenskonzentration: theoretische Grundbegriffe und empirische Ergebnisse für die Bundesrepublik Deutschland, 1960-1970. Neuwied, [1975]. pp. 234. *bibliog.*

— **Germany.**

FISCHER (HEINZ DIETRICH) ed. Pressekonzentration und Zensurpraxis im Ersten Weltkrieg: Texte und Quellen. Berlin, 1973. pp. 301. *bibliogs.*

BAUM (CLEMENS) and MOELLER (HANS HERMANN) Die Messung der Unternehmenskonzentration und ihre statistischen Voraussetzungen in der Bundesrepublik Deutschland. Meisenheim am Glan, 1976. pp. 89. *bibliog.*

— — **Bibliography.**

GERMANY (BUNDESREPUBLIK). Deutscher Bundestag. Wissenschaftliche Dienste. 1975. Wettbewerb und Konzentration: zur Wettbewerbs- und Konzentrationspolitik in der Bundesrepublik Deutschland: Auswahlbibliographie mit Annotationen; [compiled by Bernhard Georg Scheibler]. Bonn, 1975. pp. 109. *(Bibliographien. 42)*

— **United Kingdom.**

AIMS OF INDUSTRY. Economic Arguments. Industrial concentration and public policy. London, [1973?]. pp. 6.

HANNAH (LESLIE) The rise of the corporate economy. London, 1976. pp. 243. *bibliog.*

— **United States.**

VERTICAL integration in the oil industry; edited by Edward J. Mitchell. Washington, 1976. pp. 214. *(American Enterprise Institute for Public Policy Research. National Energy Studies. 11)*

INDUSTRIAL DISTRICTS

— **India.**

SOMASEKHARA (N.) The efficacy of industrial estates in India with particular reference to Mysore. Delhi, [1975]. pp. 157. *bibliog.*

— — **Mysore.**

SOMASEKHARA (N.) The efficacy of industrial estates in India with particular reference to Mysore. Delhi, [1975]. pp. 157. *bibliog.*

— **Poland.**

DUMAŁA (KRZYSZTOF) Przemiany przestrzenne miast i rozwój osiedli przemysłowych w Królestwie Polskim w latach 1831-1869. Wrocław, 1974. pp. 411. *bibliog. With French summary.*

INDUSTRIAL EQUIPMENT

— **United Kingdom.**

NATIONAL ECONOMIC DEVELOPMENT OFFICE. Investment by nationalised industries: relations with suppliers. London, 1975. pp. 41.

U.K. Offshore Supplies Office. 1975. OSO: (background information which will help a company decide whether it can supply goods or a service needed offshore and how it could go about preparing its own market strategy). Glasgow, [1975]. pp. 144. *bibliog. In end pocket: Incentives for industry in the areas for expansion.*

INDUSTRIAL HOUSING

— **Finance.**

SWEET (MORRIS L.) and WALTERS (SHERWOOD GEORGE) Mandatory housing finance programs: a comparative international analysis. New York, 1975. pp. 253. *bibliog.*

INDUSTRIAL HYGIENE

— **Germany, Eastern — Law and legislation.**

HARMSEN (HANS) ed. Gesundheitsvorsorge und Betriebsgesundheitswesen in der DDR: ein Beitrag zur Sozialrechtsgestaltung. Hamburg, 1975. pp. 116. *(Akademie für Staatsmedizin in Hamburg. Zur Entwicklung und Organisation des Gesundheitswesens in Sowjetrussland, in Osteuropäischen Volksdemokratien und in der DDR. Band 72)*

— South Africa.

SOUTH AFRICA. Commission of Enquiry on Occupational Health. 1976. Report (R.P. 55/1976). in SOUTH AFRICA. Parliament. House of Assembly. Votes and proceedings; (with Printed annexures).

— United Kingdom.

BRIGGS (JOE H.) and MURRAY (ROBERT) Dr. Responsibilities of industry in the field of health. London, [1975]. fo. 16. *(Foundation for Business Responsibilities. Foundation Dialogues)*

GREGORY (DENIS) and McCARTY (JOE) The shop steward's guide to workplace health and safety: a critical analysis of industry's health and safety problems and the Health and Safety at Work Act 1974: implications and suggestions for trade union action. Nottingham, 1975. pp. 69.

LABOUR RESEARCH DEPARTMENT. LRD guide to the Health and Safety at Work Act. London, 1975. pp. 20. *bibliog.*

— United States.

ASHFORD (NICHOLAS ASKOUNES) Crisis in the workplace: occupational disease and injury: a report to the Ford Foundation. Cambridge, Mass., [1976]. pp. 589. *bibliog.*

INDUSTRIAL LAWS AND LEGISLATION

— Nepal.

NEPAL. Statutes, etc. 1961-68. Industrial Enterprise Act, 2018(1961);...incorporating the amendments of November 16, 1961, April 12,1963, Oct. 10,1966 and Oct. 25, 1968. Kathmandu, [1970]. pp. 18.

NEPAL INDUSTRIAL DEVELOPMENT CORPORATION. Investment Promotion and Publicity Division. Investing in Nepal: a resume of Nepal laws and regulations governing the establishment and operation of an industrial enterprise. Kathmandu, 1970 [or rather 1971]. pp. 149.

— Russia.

IAKOVLEVA (VALENTINA FEDOROVNA) Spetsializatsiia i kooperirovanie promyshlennosti: pravovye voprosy. Moskva, 1974. pp. 232.

— United Kingdom.

ROBERTSON (DAVID) 1943- . A guide to the Industry Bill. London, 1975. pp. 24.

INDUSTRIAL MANAGEMENT.

The ECONOMICS of multi-plant operation: an international comparisons study; [by] F.M. Scherer [and others]. Cambridge, Mass., 1975. pp. 448. *(Harvard University. Harvard Economic Studies. vol. 145)*

— Study and teaching — United Kingdom.

NATIONAL ECONOMIC DEVELOPMENT COUNCIL. Management Education, Training and Development Committee. Management training in industrial relations. London, National Economic Development Office, 1975. pp. 40. *bibliog.*

— Brazil.

ECONOMIST INTELLIGENCE UNIT. Q[uarterly] E[conomic] R[eview] Specials. No. 22. Management under inflation;...by Harry Simonsen and... Richard Morris. London, [1975]. pp. 73. *bibliog.*

— Communist countries.

GVISHIANI (DZHERMEN MIKHAILOVICH) and others, eds. Osnovy organizatsii upravleniia promyshlennym ob"edineniem i predpriiatiem. vyp.4. Moskva, 1973. pp. 214.

— Europe, Eastern.

GRANICK (DAVID) Enterprise guidance in eastern Europe: a comparison of four socialist economies. Princeton, N.J., [1975]. pp. 505.

— Germany.

KOCKA (JUERGEN) Unternehmensverwaltung und Angestelltenschaft am Beispiel Siemens, 1847-1914: zum Verhältnis von Kapitalismus und Bürokratie in der deutschen Industrialisierung. Stuttgart,[1969]. pp. 639. *bibliog. (Arbeitskreis für Moderne Sozialgeschichte. Industrielle Welt. Band 11)*

— Germany, Eastern.

WEIDAUER (RUDI) and WETZEL (ALBERT) Sozialistische Leitung im Betrieb und Kombinat. Berlin, 1972. pp. 336.

LEHMANN (GUENTER) and SCHULZ (HANS JOACHIM) Ordnung und Sicherheit im sozialistischen Wettbewerb. Berlin, 1975. pp. 96.

— Japan.

MARSH (ROBERT MORTIMER) and MANNARI (HIROSHI) Modernization and the Japanese factory. Princeton, N.J., [1976]. pp. 437. *bibliog.*

— Netherlands.

OP weg naar arbeiderszelfbestuur. Deventer, 1974. pp. 122. *(Wiardi Beckman Stichting. WBS-Cahiers. Studieproject Gelijkheid. Deel 9)*

— Russia.

MIKHNEVICH (IURII MAKSIMOVICH) Ekonomicheskie problemy upravleniia nauchno-tekhnicheskim progressom. Leningrad, 1974. pp. 151.

RYAVEC (KARL W.) Implementation of Soviet economic reforms: political, organizational, and social processes. New York, 1975. pp. 360. *bibliog.*

ANDRLE (VLADIMIR) Managerial power in the Soviet Union. Farnborough, Hants, [1976]. pp. 176. *bibliog.*

— United Kingdom.

McLENNAN (ROY) Cases in organisational behaviour. London, 1975. pp. 282. *bibliogs.*

— United States.

ACKERMAN (ROBERT W.) The social challenge to business. Cambridge, Mass., 1975. pp. 345.

INDUSTRIAL MANAGEMENT AND INFLATION.

ECONOMIST INTELLIGENCE UNIT. Q[uarterly] E[conomic] R[eview] Specials. No. 22. Management under inflation;...by Harry Simonsen and... Richard Morris. London, [1975]. pp. 73. *bibliog.*

HUSSEY (DAVID E.) Inflation and business policy. London, 1976. pp. 150. *bibliogs.*

INDUSTRIAL ORGANIZATION.

The ECONOMICS of multi-plant operation: an international comparisons study; [by] F.M. Scherer [and others]. Cambridge, Mass., 1975. pp. 448. *(Harvard University. Harvard Economic Studies. vol. 145)*

MICHIGAN UNIVERSITY. Michigan Business Studies. [New Series]. vol. 1 no. 2. Industrial market structure and performance, 1960-1968; [by] Daryl N. Winn. Ann Arbor, [1975]. pp. 226. *bibliog.*

The QUALITY of working life...; [edited by] Louis E. Davis [and] Albert B. Cherns and associates. New York, [1975]. 2 vols. *Papers based on the International Conference on the Quality of Working Life, Harriman, New York, 1972.*

WILLIAMSON (OLIVER E.) Markets and hierarchies: analysis and antitrust implications: a study in the economics of internal organization. New York, [1975]. pp. 286. *bibliog.*

MARKETS, corporate behaviour and the state: international aspects of industrial organization; editors, A.P. Jacquemin and H.W. de Jong. The Hague, 1976. pp. 353. *bibliogs. (Instituut voor Bedrijfskunde. Nijenrode Studies in Economics. vol. 1) Based on a conference held at the Instituut voor Bedrijfskunde, Nijenrode, in 1974.*

— China.

BRUGGER (WILLIAM C.) Democracy and organisation in the Chinese industrial enterprise, 1948-1953. Cambridge, 1976. pp. 374. *bibliog. (London. University. School of Oriental and African Studies. Contemporary China Institute. Publications)*

— Communist countries.

OS'MOVA (MARKIANA NIKOLAEVNA) Formirovanie struktur v promyshlennom proizvodstve v usloviiakh sotsialisticheskoi integratsii. Moskva, 1975. pp. 158.

— Germany, Eastern.

ARNOLD (HANS) and LANGE (ALFRED) Die sozialistische Rekonstruktion der Industrie in der Deutschen Demokratischen Republik. Berlin, 1959. pp. 104.

INITIATIVE und ihre Leitung in der Wirtschaft. Berlin, 1975. pp. 205. *(Zentralinstitut für Sozialistische Wirtschaftsführung. Schriften zur Sozialistischen Wirtschaftsführung)*

Die INTENSIVIERUNG der sozialistischen Industrieproduktion und die wachsende Rolle der Arbeiterklasse; (Autoren: Karl Hartmann [and others]). Berlin, 1975. pp. 332.

FIEDLER (HELENE) and others, eds. 30 Jahre volkseigene Betriebe: Dokumente und Materialien zum 30. Jahrestag des Volksentscheids in Sachsen. Berlin, 1976. pp. 255.

FITZE (WERNER) and others. Wissenschaftlich-technischer Fortschritt, sozialistische Arbeit, Persönlichkeit. Berlin, 1976. pp. 166.

— Japan.

CAVES (RICHARD E.) and UEKUSA (MASU) Industrial organization in Japan. Washington, D.C., [1976]. pp. 169.

— Poland.

KORTAN (JERZY) Planowanie w przedsiębiorstwie przemysłowym. 2nd ed. Warszawa, 1958. pp. 68.

ZBICHORSKI (ZYGMUNT) Zasady organizacji przedsiębiorstwa przemysłowego. 2nd ed. Warszawa, 1958. pp. 86.

CZERWIŃSKA (EL'ZBIETA) Samodzielność finansowa przedsiębiorstwa państwowego. Poznań, 1963. pp. 172. *bibliog. (Poznań. Poznańskie Towarzystwo Przyjaciół Nauk. Wydział Historii i Nauk Społecznych. Komisja Nauk Społecznych. Prace. t.11, z.1) With English summary.*

BOGUSZEWSKI (JAN) System finansowy przedsiębiorstw i zjednoczeń. 2nd ed. Warszawa, 1966. pp. 45.

— Russia.

KAMENITSER (SOLOMON EFREMOVICH) ed. Spravochnik ekonomista promyshlennogo predpriiatiia. Moskva, 1974. pp. 663. *bibliog.*

MARKIN (A.A.) ed. Effektivnost' khoziaistvennykh ob"edinenii. Leningrad, 1974. pp. 191.

SEMENOV (VISSARION FEDOROVICH) Kontsentratsiia sotsialisticheskogo proizvodstva. Kazan', 1974. pp. 216.

— — Kazakstan.

DOSYMBEKOV (SULTAN NAZAROVICH) Problemy gosudarstvennogo upravleniia promyshlennost'iu v soiuznoi respublike. Moskva, 1974. pp. 464.

— — Uzbekistan.

EFFEKTIVNOST' ob"edinenii promyshlennosti Uzbekistana. Tashkent, 1975. pp. 170.

INDUSTRIAL ORGANIZATION.(Cont.)

— Sweden.

EDGREN (JAN) With varying success: a Swedish experiment in wage systems and shop floor organization. Stockholm, [1974]. pp. 100.

— United Kingdom.

HUGHES (JOHN DENNIS) Industrial restructuring: some manpower aspects. London, National Economic Development Office, 1976. pp. 62. *(Discussion Papers. 4)*

SHAW (R.W.) and SUTTON (C.J.) Industry and competition: industrial case studies. London, 1976. pp. 210. *bibliogs.*

— United States.

CONFERENCE ON LABOR MARKET SEGMENTATION, HARVARD UNIVERSITY, 1973. Labor market segmentation: [papers presented at the conference]; edited by Richard C. Edwards [and others]. Lexington, Mass., [1975]. pp. 297. *bibliogs.*

— Yugoslavia.

GORUPIĆ (DRAGO) Osnovna i složena organizacija udruženog rada u privredi. Zagreb, 1975. pp. iii,136.

INDUSTRIAL ORGANIZATION (ECONOMIC THEORY).

SHAW (R.W.) and SUTTON (C.J.) Industry and competition: industrial case studies. London, 1976. pp. 210. *bibliogs.*

INDUSTRIAL PROJECT MANAGEMENT.

INDIA. Committee on Plan Projects. Management Group. 1966. Feasibility studies for public sector projects. [New Delhi], 1966. pp. 186. *bibliog.*

BRANDON (DICK H.) and GRAY (MAX) Project control standards. New York, 1970. pp. 204. *bibliogs.*

INDUSTRIAL PROMOTION

— Nepal.

NEPAL INDUSTRIAL DEVELOPMENT CORPORATION. Investment Promotion and Publicity Division. Nepal Industrial Development Corporation: an introduction. [Kathmandu, 1971]. pp. 16.

— United Kingdom.

NORTHERN REGION STRATEGY TEAM. Evaluation of the impact of regional policy on manufacturing industry in the northern region. Newcastle upon Tyne, 1975. 1 vol. (various pagings). *(Technical Reports. No. 2)*

INDUSTRIAL PUBLICITY.

AIMS FOR FREEDOM AND ENTERPRISE. The image of Britain abroad: an investigation of attitudes by foreign correspondents to British industry. London, [1975]. pp. 11.

INDUSTRIAL RELATIONS.

ESTUDIOS LABORALES; [pd. by] Instituto de Estudios Laborales y de Seguridad Social, Ministerio de Trabajo. irreg., My 1975(no.1)- Madrid.

HYMAN (RICHARD) and BROUGH (IAN) Social values and industrial relations: a study of fairness and equality. Oxford, [1975]. pp. 277. *bibliog. (Warwick Studies in Industrial Relations)*

KUJAWA (DUANE) ed. International labor and the multinational enterprise. New York, 1975. pp. 213.

WORKER militancy and its consequences, 1965-75: new directions in Western industrial relations; edited by Solomon Barkin. New York, 1975. pp. 408.

— Congresses.

DUKE OF EDINBURGH'S STUDY CONFERENCES. 4th Conference, 1974. Industry in society: a record of...[the] fourth Commonwealth study conference held in the United Kingdom, 5-20 July 1974. London, 1975. pp. 112.

— Australia.

NILAND (JOHN R.) and ISAAC (JOSEPH EZRA) eds. Australian labour economics: readings. [2nd ed.] Melbourne, 1975. pp. 676. *bibliogs.*

— Canada.

CANADA. Labour Relations Board. Annual report. a., 1973/75 (1st)- Ottawa. *[In English and French].*

CANADA. Department of Labour. 1973. Information on the new Union-Management Services Branch. Ottawa, 1973. 1 pamphlet (unpaged) *In English and French.*

CANADIAN LABOUR CONGRESS. Submission...to the special joint committee on employer-employee relations in the public service. Ottawa, 1975. fo. 32.

HAMEED (SYED M. A.) ed. Canadian industrial relations: (a book of readings). Toronto, [1975]. pp. 378. *bibliog.*

JAIN (HEM. C.) ed. Canadian labour and industrial relations: public and private sectors; text and readings. Toronto, [1975]. pp. 328. *bibliog.*

— Europe, Eastern.

LOWIT (THOMAS) and others. Le système des relations professionnelles dans l'entreprise industrielle des pays de l'Est européen. Paris, 1974. fo. 344.

— European Economic Community countries.

STEWART (MARGARET) Employment conditions in Europe. 2nd ed. Epping, Essex, 1976. pp. 249. *bibliog.*

— Germany.

DAHRENDORF (RALF) Conflict and contract: industrial relations and the political community in times of crisis. Liverpool, 1975. pp. 18. *(Leverhulme Memorial Lectures. [New Series]. 1975)*

SCHNEIDER (MICHAEL) Unternehmer und Demokratie: die freien Gewerkschaften in der unternehmerischen Ideologie der Jahre 1918 bis 1933. Bonn-Bad Godesberg, [1975]. pp. 219. *bibliog. (Friedrich-Ebert-Stiftung. Forschungsinstitut. Schriftenreihe. Band 116)*

Die INTERESSENVERTRETUNG der Arbeitnehmer im Betrieb; ([by] Adolf Brock [and others]). new ed. [Cologne], 1976. pp. 118. *bibliog.*

— Hong Kong.

ENGLAND (JOE W.) and REAR (JOHN) Chinese labour under British rule: a critical study of labour relations and law in Hong Kong. Hong Kong, 1975. pp. 379.

— India.

TATA (NAVAL H.) In pursuit of industrial harmony: an employer's perspective. Bombay, [1976]. pp. 267.

— Italy.

MASI (DOMENICO DE) and FEVOLA (GIUSEPPE) eds. I lavoratori nell'industria italiana. Milano, [1974]. 2 vols. (in 4). *(Istituto per gli Studi sullo Sviluppo Economico e il Progresso Tecnico. Collana Isvet. n.28-29) With summaries in various languages.*

SAPELLI (GIULIO) Fascismo grande industria e sindacato: il caso di Torino, 1929/1935. Milano, 1975. pp. 260.

— Japan.

CONFERENCE ON JAPANESE ORGANIZATION AND DECISION-MAKING, HAWAII, 1973. Modern Japanese organization and decision-making; edited by Ezra F. Vogel. Berkeley, [1975]. pp. 340. *Proceedings of a conference sponsored by the Joint Committee on Japanese Studies of the American Council of Learned Societies and the Social Science Research Council.*

— Sweden.

JONES (H.G.) Planning and productivity in Sweden. London, 1976. pp. 212. *bibliog.*

— United Kingdom.

A PROGRAMME for working together; winning papers [in a competition organized by the Working Together Campaign; by] J.A. Fletcher [and others]. London, [1973]. pp. 23.

BRYDER (TOM) Power and responsibility: contending approaches to industrial relations and decision-making in Britain 1963-1971. Lund, [1975]. pp. 212. *bibliog. Ph.D. avhandling - Universitet i Lund.*

BURGESS (KEITH) The origins of British industrial relations: the nineteenth century experience. London, [1975]. pp. 331. *bibliog.*

CLEGG (STEWART) Power, rule and domination: a critical and empirical understanding of power in sociological theory and organizational life. London, 1975. pp. 208. *bibliog.*

DAHRENDORF (RALF) Conflict and contract: industrial relations and the political community in times of crisis. Liverpool, 1975. pp. 18. *(Leverhulme Memorial Lectures. [New Series]. 1975)*

ELLIOTT (RUTH HELEN) A case study of management and worker attitudes to managerial authority and prerogatives. 1975. fo. 366. *Typescript. Ph.D. (London) thesis: unpublished. This thesis is the property of London University and may not be removed from the Library.*

HYMAN (RICHARD) and BROUGH (IAN) Social values and industrial relations: a study of fairness and equality. Oxford, [1975]. pp. 277. *bibliog. (Warwick Studies in Industrial Relations)*

ROBERTSON (DAVID) 1943- . A guide to the Industry Bill. London, 1975. pp. 24.

SISSON (KEITH) Industrial relations in Fleet Street: a study in pay structure. Oxford, [1975]. pp. 185. *(Warwick Studies in Industrial Relations)*

STUTTARD (GEOFFREY) Learning from industrial relations. London, 1975. pp. 147.

BOWEN (PETER) Social control in industrial organisations: industrial relations and industrial sociology: a strategic and occupational study of British steelmaking. London, 1976. pp. 270. *bibliog.*

DERBYSHIRE (JOHN DENIS) The Royal Commission on Trade Unions and Employers' Associations, 1965-1968: an analysis of a royal commission as an instrument for public policy making. 1976. fo. 325. *bibliog. Typescript. Ph.D. (London) thesis: unpublished. This thesis is the property of London University and may not be removed from the Library.*

HAWKINS (KEVIN H.) British industrial relations, 1945-1975. London, 1976. pp. 223.

— — Study and teaching.

NATIONAL ECONOMIC DEVELOPMENT COUNCIL. Management Education, Training and Development Committee. Management training in industrial relations. London, National Economic Development Office, 1975. pp. 40. *bibliog.*

— — Wales.

WELSH HOSPITAL BOARD. Report of a working party on industrial relations; [J.O. Morris, chairman]. [Cardiff], 1972. fo. 25.

— United States.

McCULLOCH (FRANK W.) and BORNSTEIN (TIM) The National Labor Relations Board. New York, 1974. pp. 200. *bibliog.*

KILGOUR (JOHN G.) The U.S. merchant marine: national maritime policy and industrial relations. New York, 1975. pp. 231. *bibliog.*

NELSON (DANIEL) Managers and workers: origins of the new factory system in the United States, 1880-1920. Madison, 1975. pp. 234. *bibliog.*

PUBLIC SECTOR LABOR RELATIONS CONFERENCE BOARD. Annual Conference, 3rd, University of Maryland, 1973. Challenges in public sector labor relations; editor, Paul A. Weinstein. College Park, Md., [1975]. pp. 121. *(Public Sector Labor Relations Conference Board. Publications. No. 2)*

BRANDES (STUART D.) American welfare capitalism, 1880-1940. Chicago, 1976. pp. 210. *bibliog.*

GUTMAN (HERBERT GEORGE) Work, culture and society in industrializing America: essays in American working-class and social history. New York, 1976. pp. 343, xvi. *Reprinted from various sources.*

McDOWELL (DOUGLAS S.) and HUHN (KENNETH C.) N[ational] L[abor] R[elations] B[oard] remedies for unfair labor practices. Philadelphia, [1976]. pp. 304. *(Pennsylvania University. Wharton School of Finance and Commerce. Industrial Research Unit. Labor Relations and Public Policy Series. Reports. No. 12.)*

— — **Bibliography.**

MORRIS (JAMES OLIVER) compiler. Bibliography of industrial relations in the railroad industry. Ithaca, N.Y., [1975]. pp. 153. *(Cornell University. New York State School of Industrial and Labor Relations. Bibliography Series. No. 12)*

— — **California.**

CALIFORNIA INDUSTRIAL RELATIONS REPORTS; [pd. by] California Department of Industrial Relations, Division of Labor Statistics and Research. irreg., Ag 1953 (no.3)- , with gaps (nos.6-14,19,26,28-33). San Francisco.

INDUSTRIAL SAFETY

— **United Kingdom.**

CHICKEN (JOHN C.) Hazard control policy in Britain. Oxford, 1975. pp. 193.

GREGORY (DENIS) and McCARTY (JOE) The shop steward's guide to workplace health and safety: a critical analysis of industry's health and safety problems and the Health and Safety at Work Act 1974: implications and suggestions for trade union action. Nottingham, 1975. pp. 69.

LABOUR RESEARCH DEPARTMENT. LRD guide to the Health and Safety at Work Act. London, 1975. pp. 20. *bibliog.*

— **United States.**

ASHFORD (NICHOLAS ASKOUNES) Crisis in the workplace: occupational disease and injury: a report to the Ford Foundation. Cambridge, Mass., [1976]. pp. 589. *bibliog.*

INDUSTRIAL SOCIOLOGY.

SARAPATA (ADAM) and DOKTÓR (KAZIMIERZ) Elementy socjologii przemysłu. Warszawa, 1962. pp. 300. *bibliog.*

AKTUAL'NYE problemy sotsiologii truda. Moskva, 1975. pp. 243.

CRUTCHLEY (JOHN FREDERICK) Work situation and social imagery: factors affecting the social and political outlooks of industrial workers. 1975. fo. 355. *bibliog. Typescript. Ph.D. (London) thesis: unpublished. This thesis is the property of London University and may not be removed from the Library.*

The QUALITY of working life...; [edited by] Louis E. Davis [and] Albert B. Cherns and associates. New York, [1975]. 2 vols. *Papers based on the International Conference on the Quality of Working Life, Harriman, New York, 1972.*

FORM (WILLIAM HUMBERT) Blue-collar stratification: autoworkers in four countries. Princeton, 1976. pp. 335. *bibliog.*

NICHOLS (THEO) and ARMSTRONG (PETER) Workers divided. [London], 1976. pp. 221. *bibliog.*

— **Ireland (Republic).**

O'SULLIVAN (DEREK) Profile of an industry: a sociologist's view of the electrical contracting business in Dublin. Dublin, Irish Productivity Centre, [1973]. pp. 121. *bibliog. (Human Sciences in Industry. Studies. No.9)*

— **Japan.**

MARSH (ROBERT MORTIMER) and MANNARI (HIROSHI) Modernization and the Japanese factory. Princeton, N.J., [1976]. pp. 437. *bibliog.*

— **Russia.**

KAIDALOV (DMITRII PETROVICH) and SUIMENKO (EVGENII IVANOVICH) Aktual'nye problemy sotsiologii truda. Moskva, 1974. pp. 238.

— **United Kingdom.**

SHAMIR (BOAS) A study of working environments and attitudes to work of employees in a number of British hotels. 1975. fo.304. *bibliog. Typescript. Ph.D. (London) thesis: unpublished. This thesis is the property of London University and may not be removed from the Library.*

BOWEN (PETER) Social control in industrial organisations: industrial relations and industrial sociology: a strategic and occupational study of British steelmaking. London, 1976. pp. 270. *bibliog.*

— **United States.**

CONFERENCE ON LABOR MARKET SEGMENTATION, HARVARD UNIVERSITY, 1973. Labor market segmentation: [papers presented at the conference]; edited by Richard C. Edwards [and others]. Lexington, Mass., [1975]. pp. 297. *bibliogs.*

INDUSTRIALIZATION.

HUNKER (HENRY L.) Industrial development: concepts and principles. Lexington, Mass., [1974]. pp. 322. *bibliog.*

— **Study and teaching.**

GUNN (ANGUS M.) Man on the earth: teacher resource book for: population pressure in Indonesia: problems of industrialization in Eurasia: power blocs in Eurasia. Toronto, 1974. pp. 51.

INDUSTRIES, LOCATION OF.

KIRKBRIDE (DAVID) Factors affecting the future location of employment in South Hampshire. [Winchester], 1969. pp. 18. *bibliog. (South Hampshire Plan Technical Unit. Working Papers. 4)*

HUNKER (HENRY L.) Industrial development: concepts and principles. Lexington, Mass., [1974]. pp. 322. *bibliog.*

CASTELLS (MANUEL) Sociologie de l'espace industriel. Paris, [1975]. pp. 221.

MILLS (EDWIN S.) and OATES (WALLACE E.) eds. Fiscal zoning and land use controls: the economic issues. Lexington, Mass., [1975]. pp. 205. *bibliogs.*

PARRY (THOMAS GREGORY) The international location of production: studies in the trade and non-trade servicing of international markets by multinational manufacturing enterprise; [Ph.D. (London) thesis]. 1975. fo. 299. *2 offprints in end pocket. Typescript: unpublished. This thesis is the property of London University and may not be removed from the Library.*

— **Bibliography.**

GOMERSALL (ALAN) compiler. Industrial relocation. London, 1975. pp. 21. *(London. Greater London Council. Research Library. Research Bibliographies. No. 61)*

— **Mathematical models.**

COOPER (MALCOLM J.M.) The industrial location decision making process. Birmingham, 1975. pp. 108. *bibliog. (Birmingham. University. Centre for Urban and Regional Studies. Occasional Papers. No. 34)*

INDUSTRIES, LOCATION OF.

— **Austria.**

BOBEK (HANS) and STEINBACH (JOSEF) Die Regionalstruktur der Industrie Österreichs. Wien, 1975. pp. 80. *(Österreichische Akademie der Wissenschaften. Kommission für Raumforschung. Beiträge zur Regionalforschung. Band 1) 4 maps in end pocket.*

— **Canada.**

TODD (DANIEL) Polarization in a peripheral regional economy: a spatial analysis of manufacturing industry, with reference to Nova Scotia, Canada; [Ph.D. (London) thesis]. 1975. fo. 360. *bibliog. Typescript: unpublished. This thesis is the property of London University and may not be removed from the Library.*

— **France.**

EQUIPE DE RECHERCHES DE GEOGRAPHIE INDUSTRIELLE. Recherches de géographie industrielle. Paris, 1974. pp. 298. *bibliog. (Service de Documentation et de Cartographie Géographiques. Mémoires et Documents. Nouvelle Série. vol. 14)*

— **India.**

MEHTA (MADHAVA MAL) Structure of cotton-mill industry of India: a study in the size and location of industrial units in the cotton-mill industry of India. Allahabad, 1949. pp. 328. *bibliog. Ph.D. thesis, University of Allahabad.*

PRASAD (KEDARNATH) The strategy of industrial dispersal and decentralized development: a case study. New Delhi, 1975. pp. 516. *bibliog.*

— **Russia.**

ADAMESKU (ALEKO ALEKSANDROVICH) and AKIN'SHIN (NIKOLAI NIKIFOROVICH) Problemy razvitiia i razmeshcheniia proizvoditel'nykh sil Volgo-Viatskogo raiona. Moskva, 1974. pp. 264. *bibliog.*

KOZLOVSKAIA (LIUDMILA VASIL'EVNA) Territorial'naia kontsentratsiia promyshlennosti: ekonomicheskie i sotsial'nye aspekty. Minsk, 1975. pp. 160.

— **South Africa.**

SOUTH AFRICA. Department of Planning and the Environment. 1974. Decentralisation-growth points...1974. Johannesburg, [1974?]. pp. 440. *In English and Afrikaans.*

— **United Kingdom.**

LEMON (ANTHONY) Postwar industrial growth in East Anglian small towns: a study of migrant firms, 1945-1970. Oxford, 1975. pp. 40. *bibliog. (Oxford. University. School of Geography. Research Papers. No. 12)*

SANT (MORGAN EUGENE CYRIL) Industrial movement and regional development: the British case. Oxford, 1975. pp. 253. *bibliog.*

NORTHERN REGION STRATEGY TEAM. Movement of manufacturing industry: the northern region, 1961-1973. Newcastle-upon-Tyne, 1976. 1 vol. (various pagings). *(Technical Reports. No.10)*

— **United States.**

COHEN (YEHOSHUA S.) and BERRY (BRIAN JOE LOBLEY) Spatial components of manufacturing change, 1950-1960. Chicago, 1975. pp. 262. *bibliog. (Chicago. University. Department of Geography. Research Papers. No.172)*

CONROY (MICHAEL E.) Regional economic growth: diversification and control. New York, 1975. pp. 163. *bibliog.*

MANDELL (LEWIS) Industrial location decisions: Detroit compared with Atlanta and Chicago. New York, 1975. pp. 120.

STRUYK (RAYMOND J.) and JAMES (FRANKLIN J.) Intrametropolitan industrial location: the pattern and process of change. Lexington, Mass., [1975]. pp. 190.

INDUSTRIES, LOCATION OF.(Cont.)

INDUSTRIAL invasion of nonmetropolitan America: a quarter century of experience; ([by] Gene F. Summers [and others]). New York, 1976. pp. 231. *bibliogs.*

— Yugoslavia.

ZDUNIĆ (STJEPAN) Kriteriji i metode regionalnog razmještaja industrije u planiranju gospodarskog razvitka. Zagreb, 1975. pp. 168. *bibliog.*

INDUSTRIES, SIZE OF.

MEHTA (MADHAVA MAL) Structure of cotton-mill industry of India: a study in the size and location of industrial units in the cotton-mill industry of India. Allahabad, 1949. pp. 328. *bibliog.* Ph.D. thesis, University of Allahabad.

AMSTERDAM. Universiteit. Stichting voor Economisch Onderzoek. Studie betreffende de ontwikkeling van de concentratie in de rijwiel- en bromfietsenindustrie in Nederland, etc; [by H.W. de Jong and A.H. Smolders]. [Brussels, European Communities, Directorate-General for Competition, 1973]. pp. 12.

AMSTERDAM. Universiteit. Stichting voor Economisch Onderzoek. Studie betreffende de ontwikkeling van de concentratie in enkele bedrijfstakken in de chemische industrie in Nederland: farmaceutische industrie...fotochemische industrie... onderhoudsmiddelen, etc; [by H.W. de Jong and A.H. Smolders] . [Brussels, European Communities, Directorate-General for Competition, 1973]. 1 vol. (various pagings).

ATOR CONSULENZA AZIENDALE. Analisi generale della concentrazione industriale in Italia dalla costituzione del Mercato Comune, 1959-1968: gli indici di concentrazione impiegati nella ricerca. [Brussels, European Communities, Directorate-General for Competition, 1973]. pp. 34.

ATOR CONSULENZA AZIENDALE. Studio sull'evoluzione della concentrazione in alcuni settori dell'industria chimica in Italia: farmaceutico...; fotografico...; prodotti di manutenzione, etc. [Brussels, European Communities, Directorate-General for Competition, 1973]. 1 vol. (various pagings).

ATOR CONSULENZA AZIENDALE. Studio sull'evoluzione della concentrazione nell'industria di cicli, motocicli e ciclomotori in Italia. [Brussels, European Communities, Directorate-General for Competition, 1973]. 1 vol. (various pagings).

MUELLER (JAN) Untersuchung zur Konzentrationsentwicklung in verschiedenen Untersektoren der Maschinenbauindustrie in Deutschland, etc. [Brussels, European Communities, Directorate-General for Competition, 1973]. 1 vol. (various pagings).

SCHEDL (HANS) Untersuchung zur Konzentrationsentwicklung in verschiedenen Untersektoren der elektrotechnischen Industrie in Deutschland: Rundfunk-, Fernseh- und Phonogeräte... Elektrohaushaltsgeräte, etc. [Brussels, European Communities, Directorate-General for Competition, 1973]. 1 vol. (various pagings).

SOCIETÀ RICERCHE E STUDI. Evoluzione della concentrazione dal 1962 al 1969 in alcuni settori dell'industria italiana: metodologia; [by Piera Balliano and others]. [Brussels, European Communities, Directorate-General for Competition, 1973]. pp. 23.

SOCIETÀ RICERCHE E STUDI. Studio sull'evoluzione della concentrazione in Italia dell'industria della carta e della sua trasformazione: carta,... cartotecnica, etc; [by Piera Balliano and others]. [Brussels, European Communities, Directorate General for Competition, 1973]. 1 vol.(various pagings)

ATOR CONSULENZA AZIENDALE. Studio sull'evoluzione della concentrazione nell'industria di cicli, motocicli e ciclomotori in Italia 1970-1972. [Brussels, European Communities, Directorate-General for Competition], 1975. pp. 87.

INDUSTRY.

INSTITUT DE RECHERCHES EN ECONOMIE DE LA PRODUCTION. Analyse comparative des structures industrielles: la norme d'efficacité intersectorielle; (redigé par J. de Bandt). Paris, 1975. pp. 216. *(France. Ministère de l'Industrie et de la Recherche. Etudes de Politique Industrielle. 5)*

— Mathematical models.

ANDREWS (PHILIP WALTER SAWFORD) and BRUNNER (ELIZABETH) Studies in pricing. London, 1975. pp. 176.

— Social aspects.

CASTELLS (MANUEL) Sociologie de l'espace industriel. Paris, [1975]. pp. 221.

HEILBRONER (ROBERT LOUIS) Business civilization in decline. New York, [1976]. pp. 127.

JOBS and the environment; contributions to a conference [held in 1975 by the Southeast London branches of the Socialist Environment and Resources Association and the Institute for Workers' Control] by Pat Kinnersly [and] Mike Cooley; edited by Jeremy Dale and Tony Emerson. Leeds, [1976]. pp. 15.

MEAKIN (DAVID) Man and work: literature and culture in industrial society. London, 1976. pp. 215. *bibliog.*

— — Congresses.

DUKE OF EDINBURGH'S STUDY CONFERENCES. 4th Conference, 1974. Industry in society: a record of...[the] fourth Commonwealth study conference held in the United Kingdom, 5-20 July 1974. London, 1975. pp. 112.

— — Australia.

CONACHER (A.J.) Environment-industry conflict: the Manjimup woodchip industry proposal, southwestern Australia. Nedlands, 1975. pp. 43. *(Western Australia, University of. Department of Geography. Geowest. No. 4)*

— — United Kingdom.

HARGREAVES (B.J.A.) Policy for responsibility. London, [1975]. pp. 4. *(Foundation for Business Responsibilities. Seminar Papers)*

JOSEPH (Sir KEITH SINJOHN) Business and the climate of opinion. London, 1975. pp. 8. *(Foundation for Business Responsibilities. Seminar Papers)*

U.K. Social Science Research Council. Panel on the Social Responsibilities of Industry. 1976. The social responsibilities of business; a report to the... Council; [Charles F. Carter, chairman]. London, [1976]. pp. (32),4.

— — United States.

CORSON (JOHN JAY) and others. Measuring business's social performance: the corporate social audit. New York, [1974]. pp. 75. *(Committee for Economic Development. Supplementary Papers. No. 39)*

ACKERMAN (ROBERT W.) The social challenge to business. Cambridge, Mass., 1975. pp. 345.

GALAMBOS (LOUIS) The public image of big business in America, 1880-1940: a quantitative study in social change;...with the assistance of Barbara Barrow Spence. Baltimore, [1975]. pp. 324.

EWEN (STUART) Captains of consciousness: advertising and the social roots of the consumer culture. New York, [1976]. pp. 261. *bibliog.*

INDUSTRY AND EDUCATION.

NATIONAL CONVENTION ON WORK AND THE COLLEGE STUDENT, 1ST., CARBONDALE, 1975. Work and the college student: proceedings of the...convention...; edited by Roland Keene [and others]. Carbondale, Ill., [1976]. pp. 466. *bibliog.*

— United Kingdom — Scotland.

WORKING PARTY FOR SCHOOLS AND INDUSTRY LIAISON IN THE HIGHLANDS AND ISLANDS. Schools/industry liaison in the highlands and islands; an independent working party report. Inverness, [Highlands and Islands Development Board], 1975. pp. 55.

INDUSTRY AND STATE.

SZEWORSKI (ADAM) Cykl koniunkturalny a interwencja państwa. Warszawa, 1965. pp. 255. *bibliog.*

McGREGOR (IAN) Businessman. The critical point. London, [1975]. pp. 13. *(Foundation for Business Responsibilities. Sir George Earle Memorial Lectures. 1975)*

MULTINATIONAL corporations and governments: business-government relations in an international context; edited by Patrick M. Boarman [and] Hans Schollhammer. New York, 1975. pp. 229. *Papers of a conference held jointly by the Center for International Business, Pepperdine University, and the Graduate School of Management of the University of California at Los Angeles in 1973.*

TREILLE (J.M.) Pour définir une stratégie industrielle: rapport de recherche sur des instruments et une méthode de définition et de programmation d'objectifs de recherche, de développemeni et de stratégie industrielle. Paris, 1975. pp. 116. *(France. Ministère de l'Industrie et de la Recherche. Etudes de Politique Industrielle. 7)*

HOLLAND (STUART) The regional problem. London, 1976. pp. 179.

WALLACE (DON) International regulation of multinational corporations. New York, 1976. pp. 233.

— Australia — Congresses.

AUSTRALIAN INSTITUTE OF POLITICAL SCIENCE. 40th Summer School, Canberra, 1974. Industrial Australia, 1975-2000: preparing for change; [papers read...by Stephen Hill and others]; edited by Gordon McCarthy. Sydney, [1974]. pp. 182. *bibliogs.*

— Canada.

CANADA. Department of Indian Affairs and Northern Development. 1971. Indian Economic Development Fund: a source of financing for Canadian Indian businessmen. [Ottawa], 1971. pp. 8,8. *In English and French.*

— European Economic Community countries.

WARNECKE (STEVEN JOSHUA) and SULEIMAN (EZRA N.) eds. Industrial policies in western Europe. New York, 1975. pp. 249.

— Germany.

PAHL (WALTHER) and MENDELSOHN (KURT) eds. Handbuch der öffentlichen Wirtschaft; herausgegeben vom Vorstand des Gesamtverbandes der Arbeitnehmer der öffentlichen Betriebe und des Personen- und Warenverkehrs. Berlin, [1930]. pp. 696 *bibliog.*

HALLGARTEN (GEORGE WOLFGANG FELIX) and RADKAU (JOACHIM) Deutsche Industrie und Politik von Bismarck bis heute. Frankfurt am Main, [1974]. pp. 574. *bibliog.*

ZUNKEL (FRIEDRICH) Industrie und Staatssozialismus: der Kampf um die Wirtschaftsordnung in Deutschland, 1914-1918. Düsseldorf, [1974]. pp. 227. *bibliog. (Tübingen. Universität. Seminar für Zeitgeschichte. Tübinger Schriften zur Sozial- und Zeitgeschichte. 3)*

PUBLIC assistance to industry: protection and subsidies in Britain and Germany; edited by W.M. Corden and Gerhard Fels. London, 1976. pp. 233.

— India.

INDIA. Committee on Plan Projects. Management Group. 1966. Feasibility studies for public sector projects. [New Delhi], 1966. pp. 186. *bibliog.*

— Italy.

SCALFARI (EUGENIO) and TURANI (GIUSEPPE) Razza padrona: storia della borghesia di stato. Milano, 1974 repr. 1975. pp. 478.

— **Nigeria.**

NIGERIA. [Federal Ministry of Information]. 1971. Building the new Nigeria: industry. [Lagos, 1971]. pp. 41.

NIGERIA. 1972. Government role in the Nigerian oil industry. [Lagos, 1972]. pp. 19.

— **South Africa.**

SOUTH AFRICA. Department of Planning and the Environment. 1974. Decentralisation-growth points...1974. Johannesburg, [1974?]. pp. 440. *In English and Afrikaans.*

— **Sri Lanka.**

SRI LANKA. Development Division. 1961. Investors' guide. Colombo, 1961. pp. 41. *(Bulletins. 1. Series 1 (Industrial Development))*

SRI LANKA. Development Division. 1961. State industrial projects. Colombo, [1961]. pp. 174. *(Bulletins. 1. Series 2 (State Industries))*

— **United Kingdom.**

AIMS OF INDUSTRY. Economic Arguments. Industrial concentration and public policy. London, [1973?]. pp. 6.

LAZAR (HARVEY) Politics, public policy formation and the Lancashire textile industry, 1954-70; [Ph. D. (London) thesis]. 1975. fo. 423. *bibliog. Typescript: unpublished. This thesis is the property of London University and may not be removed from the Library.*

SENDALL (WILFRED) Government, parliament and industry. London, 1975. pp. 4.

ALLEN (GEORGE CYRIL) The British disease: a short essay on the nature and causes of the nation's lagging wealth. London, 1976. pp. 79. *bibliog. (Institute of Economic Affairs. Hobart Papers. 67)*

PUBLIC assistance to industry: protection and subsidies in Britain and Germany; edited by W.M. Corden and Gerhard Fels. London, 1976. pp. 233.

THOMAS (RAYMOND ELLIOTT) The government of business. Deddington, Oxford, 1976. pp. 216. *bibliog.*

U.K. Department of Industry. 1976. The National Enterprise Board: draft guidelines. London, 1976. pp. 14.

— **United States.**

MEDVIN (NORMAN) and others. The energy cartel: big oil vs. the public interest; prepared... by...[members of the firm] of Ruttenberg, Friedman, Kilgallon, Gutchess and Associates. Washington, 1975. pp. 439.

KINSLEY (MICHAEL E.) Outer space and inner sanctums: government, business, and satellite communication. New York, [1976]. pp. 280.

INFANTICIDE.

SMITH (SELWYN M.) The battered child syndrome. London, 1975. pp. 292. *bibliog.*

INFANTS

— **Mortality.**

INDIA. Office of the Registrar General. Vital Statistics Division. 1971. Infant mortality in India. New Delhi, 1971. pp. 34. *bibliog. (Sample Registration System Analytical Series. No. 1)*

CERIT (SEVIL) Factors affecting the level and trend of infant mortality in Turkey since World War II; [Ph. D. (London) thesis]. 1975. fo. 188. *bibliog. Typescript: unpublished. This thesis is the property of London University and may not be removed from the Library.*

NORWAY. Statistiske Centralbyrå. 1975. Dødeligheten omkring fødselen og i første leveår 1969-1972, etc. Oslo, 1975. pp. 107. *(Statistiske Analyser. 15) With English summary.*

INFANTS (NEW-BORN).

— **Norway.**

BACKER (JULIE E.) Variasjoner i utviklingen hos nyfødte barn...: variations in the maturity level of new born infants. Oslo, 1970. pp. 36. *(Norway. Statistiske Centralbyrå. Artikler. Nr. 39) With English summary.*

INFLATION (FINANCE).

BOUEY (GERALD K.) Remarks...to the Men's Canadian Club of Winnipeg, November 26, 1974. [Ottawa, 1974]. fo. 13.

BANNOCK (GRAHAM) How to survive the slump: a guide to the economic crisis. Harmondsworth, 1975. pp. 170. *bibliog.*

CENTRO STUDI E RICERCHE SUI PROBLEMI ECONOMICO-SOCIALI. Seminario Internazionale, 10, 1974. Anti-inflationary policies: East-West; [Proceedings]. Milano, [1975]. pp. 382.

ECONOMIST INTELLIGENCE UNIT. Q[uarterly] E[conomic] R[eview] Specials. No. 22. Management under inflation;...by Harry Simonsen and... Richard Morris. London, [1975]. pp. 73. *bibliog.*

ELLIOTT (CHARLES) Inflation and the compromised Church. Belfast, 1975. pp. 148. *bibliogs.*

GENBERG (HANS) World inflation and the small open economy. [Stockholm, 1975]. pp. 97.

HARRISS (CLEMENT LOWELL) ed. Inflation: long-term problems. New York, 1975. pp. 214.

HARTLAND-THUNBERG (PENELOPE) ed. Commissioned papers on inflation/recession, energy and the international financial structure. Washington, [1975]. pp. 62.

JACKSON (DUDLEY A.S.) and others. Do trade unions cause inflation?: two studies, with a theoretical introduction and policy conclusion. 2nd ed. Cambridge, 1975. pp. 126. *(Cambridge. University. Department of Applied Economics. Papers in Industrial Relations and Labour. 2)*

MEISTER (ALBERT) L'inflation créatrice: essai sur les fonctions socio-politiques de l'inflation. [Paris, 1975]. pp. 310.

TOFFLER (ALVIN) The eco-spasm report. New York, 1975. pp. 116. *bibliog.*

BARRO (ROBERT J.) and GROSSMAN (HERSCHEL I.) Money, employment and inflation. Cambridge, 1976. pp. 264. *bibliog.*

CONFERENCE ON INFLATION IN THE WORLD ECONOMY, UNIVERSITY OF MANCHESTER, 1974. Inflation in the world economy: [proceedings];...edited by Michael Parkin and George Zis. Manchester, 1976. pp. 334. *bibliogs.*

CURWEN (PETER J.) Inflation. London, 1976. pp. 180. *bibliog.*

FLEMMING (JOHN STANTON) Inflation. London, 1976. pp. 136. *bibliogs.*

GAMBLE (ANDREW) and WALTON (PAUL) Capitalism in crisis: inflation and the state. London, 1976. pp. 218.

GRIFFITHS (BRIAN) Inflation: the price of prosperity. London, [1976]. pp. 300. *bibliog.*

HARRISON (THOMAS RUSSELL) A challenge to the presidency: Canada and inflation: cause, course, cost, correction, consolidation. Hicksville, N.Y., [1976]. pp. 151.

HAYEK (FRIEDRICH AUGUST) Choice in currency: a way to stop inflation...with commentaries by Ivor F. Pearce [and others]. London, 1976. pp. 46. *(Institute of Economic Affairs. Occasional Papers. 46)*

HUSSEY (DAVID E.) Inflation and business policy. London, 1976. pp. 150. *bibliogs.*

The ILLUSION of wage and price control: essays on inflation, its causes and its cures; contributors...David Laidler [and others]; Michael Walker, editor. Vancouver, 1976. pp. 236.

INFLATION, trade and taxes: essays in honor of Alice Bourneuf; edited by David A. Belsley [and others]. Columbus, Ohio, [1976]. pp. 252. *bibliogs.*

MAYNARD (GEOFFREY) and VAN RYCKEGHEM (WILLY) A world of inflation. London, 1976. pp. 272.

The 'NEW inflation' and monetary policy; proceedings of a conference organised by the Banca Commerciale Italiana and the Department of Economics of Università Bocconi in Milan, 1974; edited by Mario Monti. London, 1976. pp. 307.

— **Mathematical models.**

BOYER (RUSSELL S.) Fixed rates, flexible rates, and the international transmission of inflation. [London], 1975. 1 pamphlet (various pagings). *bibliog.*

BOYER (RUSSELL S.) Monetary experiments in a neoclassical model. [London], 1975. 1 pamphlet (various foliations). *bibliog.*

FLANDERS (M. JUNE) The Scandinavian model and the balance of payments. [London], 1975. pp. (24). *bibliog.*

ROTH (JUERGEN) Der internationale Konjunkturzusammenhang bei flexiblen Wechselkursen: eine modelltheoretische Analyse. Tübingen, 1975. pp. 264. *bibliog. (Kiel. Universität. Institut für Weltwirtschaft Kieler Studien. 135)*

INFLATION in small countries; proceedings of an international conference held at the Institute for Advanced Studies, Vienna, November 1974. Berlin, 1976. pp. 356. *bibliogs.*

MUSSA (MICHAEL) Sticky prices and disequilibrium adjustment in a rational model of the inflationary process. [London], 1976. pp. 28. *bibliog.*

— **Brazil.**

BELTRÃO (HELIO) Retomada do desenvolvimento e contrôle da inflação. [Rio de Janeiro], Departamento de Imprensa Nacional, 1967. pp. 75.

BOERGEL (HANNELORE) Abhängige Entwicklung und Inflation in Brasilien. Berlin, 1974. pp. 271. *bibliog.*

ECONOMIST INTELLIGENCE UNIT. Q[uarterly] E[conomic] R[eview] Specials. No. 22. Management under inflation;...by Harry Simonsen and... Richard Morris. London, [1975]. pp. 73. *bibliog.*

— **Fiji Islands.**

FIJI. Prices and Incomes Board. 1975. Fighting inflation in Fiji: an account of the work of the Prices and Incomes Board during the year ended 30th June, 1974. Suva, 1975. pp. 70.

FIJI. Prices and Incomes Board. 1975. Inflation in Fiji: a further account of the work of the Prices and Incomes Board. Suva, [1975]. pp. 46.

FIJI. Prices and Incomes Board. 1975. A report covering the three months ended 30th June, 1975. [Suva, 1975]. pp. 4.

— **Germany.**

WICKE (LUTZ) Vermögensverteilung und schleichende Inflation: eine Analyse. ..in der Bundesrepublik Deutschland. Meisenheim am Glan, 1975. pp. 273. *bibliog.*

— **India.**

DAS (NABAGOPAL) The runaway rupee: a study of inflation in India. Calcutta, 1975. pp. 81. *bibliog.*

— **Indonesia — Mathematical models.**

AGHEVLI (BIJAN B.) and KHAN (MOHSIN SAID) Inflationary finance and the dynamics of inflation: Indonesia 1954- 1972. [London, 1975]. pp. (25). *bibliog.*

INFLATION (FINANCE).(Cont.)

— **Ireland (Republic).**

MORGAN (EDWARD VICTOR) Causes and effects of inflation in Ireland. Dublin, Stationery Office, [1975]. pp. 222. *(National Economic and Social Council [Eire]. [Reports]. No.10)*

— **Pakistan.**

UZAIR (MOHAMMAD) Economic growth and rise in prices. [Islamabad, Information and Broadcasting Division, 1975]. pp. 19.

— **Portugal.**

RAMALHO (MARIA MADALENA) Algumas causas de inflação. Lisboa, 1974. pp. 71. *(Portugal. Ministerio do Trabalho. Gabinete de Planeamento. Serie Estudos. 16) With abstracts in English, French and German.*

— **South Africa.**

SOUTH AFRICA. Ministry of Economic Affairs. 1973. Inflation and our welfare. Pretoria, [1973]. pp. 32.

— **Switzerland.**

KLEINEWEFERS (HENNER) Inflation und Inflationsbekämpfung in der Schweiz. Frauenfeld, [1976]. pp. 345.

— **United Kingdom.**

MAHONEY (DENNIS MICHAEL) Inflation expectations in the United Kingdom, 1964-1974: an empirical study of their determinants and role; [Ph.D. (London) thesis]. 1975. fo. 225. *bibliog. Typescript: unpublished. This thesis is the property of London University and may not be removed from the Library.*

NATIONAL ECONOMIC DEVELOPMENT OFFICE. Financial performance and inflation. London, [1975]. pp. 83.

JAY (PETER) A general hypothesis of employment, inflation and politics; sixth Wincott Memorial Lecture...1975. London, 1976. pp. 34. *(Institute of Economic Affairs. Occasional Papers. 46)*

— — **Mathematical models.**

ESPASA (ANTONI) A wages-earnings-prices inflation model for United Kingdom 1950- 1970: its specification and estimation by classical and spectral methods; [Ph. D. (London) thesis]. 1975. fo. 327. *bibliog. Typescript: unpublished. This thesis is the property of London University and may not be removed from the Library.*

— **United States.**

CONFERENCE ON THE ANALYSIS OF INFLATION, GEORGETOWN UNIVERSITY, WASHINGTON, D.C., 1974. Analysis of inflation: [papers from the Conference]; edited by Paul H. Earl. Lexington, [1974]. pp. 232. *bibliogs.*

KOSTERS (MARVIN H.) Controls and inflation: the economic stabilization program in retrospect. Washington, 1975. pp. 135. *(American Enterprise Institute for Public Policy Research. Domestic Affairs Studies. 37)*

INFORMATION SCIENCE.

ANNUAL REVIEW OF INFORMATION SCIENCE AND TECHNOLOGY; (pd. by American Society for Information Science). a. 1972 (v.7) Washington, D.C.

JONES (KAREN SPARCK) and KAY (MARTIN) Linguistics and information science. New York, 1973. pp. 244. *bibliog. (International Federation for Documentation. Publications. No.492)*

FLOWERDEW (A.D.J.) and WHITEHEAD (CHRISTINE MARGARET ELIZABETH) Cost-effectiveness and cost-benefit analysis in information science. London, 1974. pp. 71.

BATTEN (WILLIAM EDWARD) ed. Handbook of special librarianship and information work. 4th ed. London, 1975. pp. 430. *bibliogs.*

U.K. Department of Education and Science. 1975. Census of staff in librarianship and information work in the United Kingdom, 1972. [London, 1975]. pp. 31.

INFORMATION SERVICES

— **Directories.**

INTERNATIONAL CO-OPERATIVE ALLIANCE. Directory of co-operative libraries and documentation services etc. London, 1974. pp. 69. *In English, French and German.*

INVENTORY of information resources in the social sciences; prepared by the University of Bath for the Organisation for Economic Co-operation and Development; edited by J.M. Brittain and S.A. Roberts. Farnborough, [1975]. pp. 239.

— **Economic aspects.**

PRATT (GORDON E.C.) and HARVEY (SUSAN) compilers. Information economics: costs and prices of machine-readable information in Europe; edited by Gordon Pratt. London, [1976]. pp. 115. *(Association of Special Libraries and Information Bureaux and European Association of Scientific Information Dissemination Centres. European User Series. 2)*

— **Handbooks, manuals, etc.**

BATTEN (WILLIAM EDWARD) ed. Handbook of special librarianship and information work. 4th ed. London, 1975. pp. 430. *bibliogs.*

— **Canada.**

PUBLIC POLICY CONCERN. Community information centres: a proposal for Canada in the 70's; a study prepared for the government of Canada. Ottawa, Information Canada, 1971 repr. 1972. pp. 68. *bibliog.*

— **Germany.**

GERMANY (BUNDESREPUBLIK). Deutscher Bundestag. Wissenschaftliche Dienste. 1975. Die Wissenschaftlichen Dienste des Deutschen Bundestages. Bonn, 1975. pp. 18. *(Materialen. 41.)*

— **United Kingdom.**

CUMBRIA COMMUNITY DEVELOPMENT PROJECT. Working papers of the C[ommunity] I[nformation and] A[ction] C[entre], 1973/74. Cleator Moor, [1974]. pp. 35.

CUMBRIA COMMUNITY DEVELOPMENT PROJECT. Community information and action centre; report, assessment and recommendations from a community development project in west Cumbria. [York, 1975]. pp. 105. *(Papers in Community Studies. No. 1)*

INFORMATION STORAGE AND RETRIEVAL SYSTEMS.

FAIRTHORNE (ROBERT ARTHUR) Towards information retrieval. Hamden, Conn., 1968. pp. 211. *Reprint of the work originally published in London, 1961.*

EMERY (JAMES C.) Organizational planning and control systems: theory and technology. New York, [1969]. pp. 166. *bibliog.*

VICKERY (BRIAN CAMPBELL) Techniques of information retrieval. London, 1970 repr. 1971. pp. 262. *bibliog.*

WHISENAND (PAUL M.) and TAMARU (TUG T.) Automated police information systems. New York, [1970]. pp. 338. *bibliogs.*

COMPUTER-aided information systems analysis and design; [papers presented at] the first Scandinavian workshop, [Aarhus, 1971]; (Janis Bubenko [and others] eds. Stockholm, [1971]. pp. 206. *Organised by the Scandinavian Information Processing Project of Nordforsk.*

HENLEY (JOHN PATRICK) Computer-based library and information systems. 2nd ed. london, 1972. pp. 106. *bibliog.*

LUCAS (HENRY C.) The analysis, design, and implementation of information systems. New York, [1976]. pp. 255. *bibliogs.*

— **Historical research 1971.**

CONFERENCE ON EARLY AMERICAN HISTORY, 27TH, 1970. Of mother country and plantations: proceedings of the... conference...; edited by Virginia Bever Platt and David Curtis Skaggs. Bowling Green, Ohio, 1971. pp. 127. *bibliog.*

— **Law enforcement.**

NEW ZEALAND. Government Caucus Committee on the Proposed Law Enforcement Information System. 1973. Report; [R.P.B. Drayton, chairman]. Wellington, 1973. pp. 58.

— **Retail trade.**

COLLIN (W.G.) Computers in distribution. Manchester, [1975]. pp. 117.

— **Social sciences.**

NORDBOTTEN (SVEIN MARTINIUS) Personmodeller, personregnskapssystemet og persondataarkiver...: population models, population accounting systems and individual data banks. Oslo, 1970. pp. 28. *(Norway. Statistiske Centralbyrå. Artikler. Nr. 38) With English summary.*

— **Theatre.**

SCHNEIDER (BEN ROSS) Travels in computerland; or, Incompatibilities and interfaces: a full and true account of the implementation of the London Stage Information Bank. Reading, Mass., [1974]. pp. 244.

— **Wholesale trade.**

COLLIN (W.G.) Computers in distribution. Manchester, [1975]. pp. 117.

INFORMATION THEORY.

BRILLOUIN (LEON) Science and information theory. 2nd ed. New York, [1962]. pp. 351. *bibliog.*

YOUNG (JOHN F.) Information theory. London, 1971. pp. 168. *bibliog.*

ALBARDA (JOAN DIEDERIK) Structures and relations in information. Rotterdam, 1974. pp. 65. *bibliog. With Dutch summary.*

INFORMATION THEORY IN ECONOMICS.

ARROW (KENNETH JOSEPH) Information and economic behavior. Stockholm, [1973]. pp. 28. *bibliog. (Sveriges Industriförbund. [Nobel Prize] Lectures. 1973)*

EKONOMICHESKAIA informatsiia: metodologicheskie problemy. Moskva, 1974. pp. 239. *bibliog.*

STOJANOVIĆ (SRBOLJUB) Informacioni pristup mjerenju koncentracije i mjerenju sličnosti struktura. Zagreb, 1974. pp. 135.

INHERITANCE AND SUCCESSION.

RUBANOV (AVGUST AFANAS'EVICH) Zagranichnye nasledstva: otnosheniia mezhdu sotsialisticheskimi i kapitalisticheskimi stranami. Moskva, 1975. pp. 276.

— **Communist countries.**

RUBANOV (AVGUST AFANAS'EVICH) Zagranichnye nasledstva: otnosheniia mezhdu sotsialisticheskimi i kapitalisticheskimi stranami. Moskva, 1975. pp. 276.

— **Europe.**

FAMILY and inheritance: rural society in western Europe, 1200- 1800; edited by Jack Goody [and others]. Cambridge, 1976. pp. 421. *(Past and Present. Past and Present Publications) Revised versions of papers delivered at the annual conference of the Past and Present Society.*

INSURANCE, SOCIAL.

— New Zealand.

NEW ZEALAND. Property Law and Equity Reform Committee. 1974. Report...on the effect of divorce on testate succession; [C.P. Hutchinson, chairman]. [Wellington, 1974]. pp. 11,2.

INHERITANCE AND TRANSFER TAX

— United Kingdom.

HAYTON (DAVID J.) and TILEY (JOHN) Elements of capital transfer tax. London, 1975. pp. 243.

HEPKER (MICHAEL Z.) and WHITEHOUSE (CHRISTOPHER J.) Capital transfer tax. London, 1975. pp. 167.

INLAND NAVIGATION.

INTERNATIONAL navigable waterways: financial and legal aspects of their improvement and maintenance; report on the symposium held at Buenos Aires from 30 November to 4 December, 1970; based on the discussions...and the working papers prepared by Richard Baxter [and others]. New York, United Nations Institute for Training and Research, 1975. pp. 253. *(UNITAR Studies. No.6.)*

— European Economic Community countries.

INLAND WATERWAYS ASSOCIATION. Inland Shipping Group. Report on continental waterways: a contemporary study. London, [1975]. pp. 77.

— United Kingdom.

INLAND WATERWAYS AMENITY ADVISORY COUNCIL [U.K.]. Water shortages on British Waterways Board system: a report to the Secretary of State for the Environment. [London], 1974. fo. 6.

INLAND WATERWAYS AMENITY ADVISORY COUNCIL [U.K.]. Observations on the Review of the water industry in England and Wales: the government consultative document. London, [1976]. pp. (39).

INSANE, CRIMINAL AND DANGEROUS

— United States.

STEADMAN (HENRY J.) and COCOZZA (JOSEPH J.) Careers of the criminally insane: excessive social control of deviance. Lexington, Mass., [1974]. pp. 206. *bibliog.*

INSTALMENT PLAN

— Europe.

INTERNATIONAL INSTITUTE FOR THE UNIFICATION OF PRIVATE LAW. 1970. Sales of movables by instalment and on credit in the member states of the Council of Europe: study in comparative law. Strasbourg, Council of Europe, 1970. pp. 253.

INSTITUCION LIBRE DE ENSEÑANZA.

JIMENEZ-LANDI MARTINEZ (ANTONIO) La Institucion Libre de Enseñanza y su ambiente. Madrid, [1973 in progress]. *bibliog.*

INSTITUTE OF BANKERS.

INSTITUTE OF BANKERS. The first fifty years of the Institute of Bankers, 1879-1929: published under the authority of the Council of the Institute. London, 1929. pp. 69.

INSTITUTIONAL CARE

— United Kingdom.

U.K. Department of Health and Social Security. 1975. The census of residential accommodation, 1970. [London, 1975]. 2 pts.

INSURANCE.

KROMMENACKER (RAYMOND J.) Les Nations Unies et l'assurance-réassurance: l'assurance-réassurance de droit privé dans les relations entre pays développés et pays en voie de développement et l'action des organisations internationales. Paris, 1975. pp. 215. *bibliog.*

— Australia — New South Wales.

NEW SOUTH WALES. Commonwealth Bureau of Census and Statistics. New South Wales Office. Banking, insurance and other private finance. a., 1972-73/1973-74- Sydney.

— United Kingdom — History — Sources.

COCKERELL (HUGH ANTHONY LEWIS) and GREEN (EDWIN) The British insurance business, 1547-1970: an introduction and guide to historical records in the United Kingdom. London, 1976. pp. 142. *bibliog.*

INSURANCE, ACCIDENT.

GHOSH (DEBAPRIYA) and others. The economics of personal injury. Farnborough, Hants, [1976]. pp. 137. *bibliog.*

— Poland.

SZYMAŃSKI (ZDZISŁAW) Ubezpieczenie od nieszczęśliwych wypadków. Warszawa, 1960. pp. 239.

— Switzerland.

KRUMBIEGEL (KURT) Die schweizerische Sozialversicherung,...verglichen mit der entsprechenden deutschen Gesetzgebung. Jena, 1913. pp. 106. *bibliog. (Jena. Universität. Staatswissenschaftliches Seminar. Abhandlungen. 13. Band, 2. Heft)*

INSURANCE, AGRICULTURAL

— Crops — Mauritius.

MAURITIUS. Cyclone and Drought Insurance Board. 1971. Assurance récolte à l'Ile Maurice, 1946-1971. [Port Louis, 1971]. pp. 45. *Cover title.*

INSURANCE, AUTOMOBILE

— Ireland (Republic) — Rates and premiums.

EIRE. Motor Premiums Advisory Committee. 1975. Report on applications for increases in motor insurance premiums, with an extract from a report of the National Prices Commission. Dublin, [1975]. pp. 27.

INSURANCE, CREDIT

— Canada.

CANADA. Statutes, etc. 1968. Office consolidation of the General Adjustment Assistance Regulations; established by P.C. 1968-651, amended by P.C. 1968-853: (regulations pertaining to a general adjustment assistance program relating to the Kennedy Round agreements). Ottawa, 1968. pp. 8.

INSURANCE, HEALTH

— Canada.

SUN VALLEY FORUM ON NATIONAL HEALTH. Symposium, 4th, 1974. National health insurance: can we learn from Canada?: (a volume on current health care issues from the Sun Valley Forum) ; edited by Spyros Andreopoulos. New York, [1975]. pp. 273.

— European Economic Community countries.

LANGENDONCK (JOZEF VAN) Prelude to harmony on a community theme: health care insurance policies in the Six and Britain;...introduced and edited by Gordon Forsyth. London, 1975. pp. 303.

— France.

FRANCE. Direction de la Documentation. La Documentation Française. Notes et Etudes Documentaires. Nos. 4,195-4, 196. Le médicament et l'assurance-maladie; [by] (J.-C. Sournia et Mme. Arsac). Paris, 1975. pp. 88. *bibliog.*

— Switzerland.

KRUMBIEGEL (KURT) Die schweizerische Sozialversicherung,...verglichen mit der entsprechenden deutschen Gesetzgebung. Jena, 1913. pp. 106. *bibliog. (Jena. Universität. Staatswissenschaftliches Seminar. Abhandlungen. 13. Band, 2. Heft)*

KOCHER (GERHARD) Verbandseinfluss auf die Gesetzgebung: Aerzteverbindung, Krankenkassenverbände und die Teilrevision 1964 des Kranken- und Unfallversicherungsgesetzes. 2nd ed. Bern, 1972. pp. 268. *bibliog. (Bern. Universität. Forschungszentrum für Schweizerische Politik. Helvetia Politica. Series B. vol. 1)*

SWITZERLAND. Commission Fédérale d'Experts Chargée d'Examiner un Nouveau Régime d'Assurance-Maladie. 1972. Rapport...du 11 février 1972. Berne, 1972. pp. 104.

— United Kingdom.

U.K. PRIVATE MEDICAL CARE: provident schemes statistics; report for the Department of Health and Social Security. a., 1972 [2nd]- London.

— United States.

BLAIR (ROGER D.) and VOGEL (RONALD J.) The cost of health insurance administration: an economic analysis. Lexington, Mass., 1975. pp. 177. *bibliog.*

HETHERINGTON (ROBERT W.) and others. Health insurance plans: promise and performance. New York, [1975]. pp. 341. *bibliogs.*

HOLAHAN (JOHN) Financing health care for the poor: the Medicaid experience. Lexington, Mass., [1975]. pp. 152. *bibliog.*

INSURANCE, LIFE.

BORIE (VICTOR) Le patrimoine universel. 12th ed. Paris, 1882. pp. 47.

— France.

CHEYSSON (EMILE) L'assurance sur la vie et les habitations à bon marché: application de l'article 7 de la loi du 30 novembre 1894: rapport au Congrès des Habitations à Bon Marché tenu... 1895. 2nd ed. Paris, 1896. pp. 40.

INSURANCE, MARINE

— United Kingdom.

CHALMERS (Sir MACKENZIE DALZELL EDWIN STEWART) Marine Insurance Act, 1906...; eighth edition by E.R. Hardy Ivamy. London, 1976. pp. 256.

INSURANCE, MATERNITY

— Germany.

FUERTH (HENRIETTE) Die Mutterschaftsversicherung. Jena, 1911. pp. 220. *bibliog.*

INSURANCE, SOCIAL.

FERREIRA (MARIA MARGARIDA PONTE) Segurança social e emprego: incidências de curto prazo. Lisboa, 1974. pp. 59. *(Portugal. Ministerio do Trabalho. Gabinete de Planeamento. Serie Estudos. 18) With abstracts in English, French and German.*

— Australia.

AUSTRALIA. Department of Social Security. 1974. Interim handbook. [Canberra], 1974. pp. 95.

AUSTRALIA. Commission of Inquiry into Poverty. 1975. Poverty in Australia: first main report; [Ronald F. Henderson, chairman]. Canberra, 1975. 2 vols. (in 1).

LEWIS (MARGARET T.) Values in Australian income security policies. Canberra, Australian Government Publishing Service, 1975. pp. 37.

— Austria.

ZADEK (J.) Die Arbeiterversicherung: eine social-hygienische Kritik. Jena, 1895. pp. 66. *bibliog. Based on a paper to the 8th International Congress of Hygiene and Demography.*

INSURANCE, SOCIAL.(Cont.)

— Bolivia.

BOLIVIA. Comision Especial del Seguro Social Campesino. 1972. [Report]. La Paz, 1972. 5 vols.(in 3).

— Canada.

CANADA. Immigration Division. 1968. Canadian opportunities: social benefits. [Ottawa, 1968]. pp. 22.

CANADA. Unemployment Insurance Commission. 1969. The story of the S[ocial] I[nsurance] N[umber]. Ottawa, 1969. 1 pamphlet (unpaged). *In English and French.*

— — Ontario.

ONTARIO. Economic Council. 1976. Social security: issues and alternatives, 1976. [Toronto], 1976. pp. 50.

— Europe.

VILLARS (CHARLES) La Convention européenne de sécurité sociale et la Suisse. Genève, 1975. pp. 289. *(Institut für Europäisches und Internationales Wirtschafts- und Sozialrecht, and Centre d'Etudes Juridiques Européennes. Schweizerische Beiträge zum Europarecht. Band 17)*

— European Economic Community countries.

FRANCE. Direction de la Documentation. La Documentation Française. Notes et Etudes Documentaires. No. 4,129. Les règlements de sécurité sociale de l'Europe des Neuf; [par René Bonnet]. Paris, 1974. pp. 43. *bibliog.*

MILAN. Università Commerciale Luigi Bocconi. Centro per lo Studio dei Problemi dell'Economia del Lavoro. [Publications]. 2. I sistemi di sicurezza sociale nei principali paesi Comunità europee. [Milan, 1975]. pp. 264.

STEWART (MARGARET) Employment conditions in Europe. 2nd ed. Epping, Essex, 1976. pp. 249. *bibliog.*

— Germany.

ZADEK (J.) Die Arbeiterversicherung: eine social-hygienische Kritik. Jena, 1895. pp. 66. *bibliog. Based on a paper to the 8th International Congress of Hygiene and Demography.*

EGGER (ALOIS) Die Belastung der deutschen Wirtschaft durch die Sozialversicherung. Jena, 1929. pp. 290. *bibliog.*

KNOCH (WALTER) Reich und Länder in der Organisation der Sozialversicherung. Leipzig, 1932. pp. 51. *bibliog.*

GERMANY (BUNDESREPUBLIK). Statistisches Bundesamt. 1974. Laufende Leistungen der Hilfe zum Lebensunterhalt, Juni 1972. Wiesbaden, 1974. pp. 63. *(Germany (Bundesrepublik). Statistisches Bundesamt. Öffentliche Sozialleistungen. Reihe 1. Sozialhilfe, Kriegsopferfürsorge. Sonderbeiträge)*

RUSS (DIETER) Die Sozialversicherung im Spannungsfeld umfassender sozialer Sicherheit und volkswirtschaftlicher Leistungsfähigkeit. Berlin, 1975. pp. 200. *bibliog. Inaugural-Dissertation zur Erlangung des Grades eines Doktors der Wirtschaftswissenschaften der Freien Universität Berlin.*

— Germany, Eastern.

BUNZEL (ERWIN) Die Beschwerdekommissionen für Sozialversicherung. Berlin, 1975. pp. 72.

— Italy.

ITALY. Istituto Nazionale delle Assicurazioni. 1964. Uomini prevendi, popolo civile. Roma, 1964. pp. 62.

— Korea.

PARK (CHONG KEE) Social security in Korea: an approach to socio-economic development. Seoul, 1975. pp. 197. *bibliog.*

— Luxembourg.

LUXEMBOURG. Inspection Générale de la Sécurité Sociale. Rapport général sur la sécurité sociale au Grand-Duché de Luxembourg. a., 1974 (1st)- Luxembourg.

— Netherlands.

VERENIGING VOOR DE STAATHUISHOUDKUNDE. Praeadviezen. 1974. Sociale zekerheid: enige kwantitatieve, economisch-theoretische en beleidsmatige beschouwingen over de toekomstige ontwikkeling van de sociale zekerheid; preadviezen van A.F. Bakhoven [and others]. 's-Gravenhage, 1974. pp. 78. *bibliog.*

— New Zealand.

NEW ZEALAND. Department of Social Welfare. 1975. Survey of persons aged 65 years and over: report of results relating to social security benefit rates. Wellington, 1975. pp. 57.

— Russia.

ZABOTA partii i pravitel'stva o blage naroda: sbornik dokumentov, oktiabr' 1964-1973. Moskva, 1974. pp. 847.

— Switzerland.

KRUMBIEGEL (KURT) Die schweizerische Sozialversicherung,...verglichen mit der entsprechenden deutschen Gesetzgebung. Jena, 1913. pp. 106. *bibliog. (Jena. Universität. Staatswissenschaftliches Seminar. Abhandlungen. 13. Band, 2. Heft)*

HESS (WALTER) Ökonomische Aspekte der Sozialen Sicherung: eine Untersuchung...unter besonderer Berücksichtigung der schweizerischen Verhältnisse. Bern, [1975]. pp. 192. *bibliog.*

VILLARS (CHARLES) La Convention européenne de sécurité sociale et la Suisse. Genève, 1975. pp. 289. *(Institut für Europäisches und Internationales Wirtschafts- und Sozialrecht, and Centre d'Etudes Juridiques Européennes. Schweizerische Beiträge zum Europarecht. Band 17)*

— United Kingdom.

ISLINGTON FABIAN SOCIETY. About our welfare benefits. London, [1969]. fo. 22.

BURGESS (PAUL) Selected or neglected?: welfare rights and the elderly. London, 1974. pp. 13. *bibliog. (Age Concern England. Manifesto Series. No. 16)*

JUSTICE, discretion and poverty: supplementary benefit appeal tribunals in Britain; edited by Michael Adler and Anthony Bradley. London, 1975. pp. 229. *Papers of a conference held at Edinburgh University on 13th and 14th December 1974, sponsored by the Socio-Legal Studies Committee of the University.*

KINCAID (J.C.) Poverty and equality in Britain: a study of social security and taxation. rev. ed. Harmondsworth, 1975. pp. 245.

SMITH (A. CHRISTOPHER D.) and HOATH (DAVID CHARLES) Law and the underprivileged. London, 1975. pp. 247.

ADVICE services in welfare rights; editor, Rosalind Brooke; [by] Paul Burgess [and others]. London, 1976. pp. 36. *(Fabian Society. Research Series. [No.] 329)*

HOWELL (RALPH FREDERIC) Why work?: a challenge to the Chancellor. London, 1976. pp. 39. *(Conservative Political Centre. [Publications]. No. 582)*

JOHNSON (MARIGOLD) and ROWLAND (MARK) Fuel debts and the poor. London, 1976. pp. 36. *(Child Poverty Action Group. Poverty Pamphlets. 24)*

LISTER (RUTH) and EMMETT (TONY) Under the safety net. London, 1976. pp. 39. *(Child Poverty Action Group. Poverty Pamphlets. 25)*

LISTER (RUTH) and WILSON (LEO) The unequal breadwinner: a new perspective on women and social security. London, [1976]. pp. 24.

MICKLETHWAIT (Sir ROBERT) The National Insurance Commissioners. London, 1976. pp. 151. *(Hamlyn Lectures. 28th Series)*

TUNNARD (JO) No father, no home?: a study of 30 fatherless families in mortgaged homes. London, 1976. pp. 43. *(Child Poverty Action Group. Poverty Pamphlets. 28)*

U.K. Supplementary Benefits Commission. 1976. Living together as husband and wife; report...to the Secretary of State for Social Services. London, 1976. pp. 31. *(Supplementary Benefits Administration Papers. 5)*

— — Ireland, Northern.

IRELAND, NORTHERN. Ministry of Health and Social Services. 1973. Everybody's guide to social security in Northern Ireland. [rev. ed.] [Belfast], 1973. pp. 74.

IRELAND, NORTHERN. Department of Health and Social Services 1975. Family benefits and pensions in Northern Ireland. 2nd ed. [Belfast], 1975. pp. 44.

IRELAND, NORTHERN. Supplementary Benefits Commission. 1975. Supplementary benefits handbook. 3rd ed. Belfast, 1975. pp. 70.

INSURANCE, UNEMPLOYMENT.

MITTELSTAEDT (AXEL) and others. Unemployment benefits and related payments in seven major countries; Surpluses and deficits in the balance of payments... [by] Erwin Veil; [and] Comparability of consumer prices indices in OECD countries [by] Charlotte Vannereau. [Paris], Organisation for Economic Cooperation and Development, 1975. pp. 56. *(OECD Economic Outlook. Occasional Studies)*

— Canada.

CANADA. Unemployment Insurance Commission. 1970. Questions and answers on unemployment insurance in the 70's. [Ottawa, 1970?]. pp. 14, 14. *In English and French.*

— Germany.

IMLE (FANNY) Kritisches und Positives zur Frage der Arbeitslosenfürsorge. Jena, 1907. pp. 71.

— Netherlands.

RAAD VOOR HET MIDDEN- EN KLEINBEDRIJF. Advies inzake bedrijfsbeëindiging en A[lgemene Bijstandswet] en kinderbijslag eerste en tweede kind. [The Hague, 1971]. pp. 14.

RAAD VOOR HET MIDDEN- EN KLEINBEDRIJF. Nota inzake de grondslag van de premieheffing voor loondervingsverzekeringen. [The Hague, 1971]. pp. 12.

— South Africa.

SOUTH AFRICA. Department of Labour. Report of the Unemployment Insurance Fund. a., 1974- Pretoria. *[In English and Afrikaans].*

— Sweden.

DAHLBERG (ANITA) Arbetslöshetsstöd: arbetslöshetsförsäkringen och det kontanta arbetsmarknadsstödet. Stockholm, [1974]. pp. 217. *bibliog.*

— United States — Nebraska.

NEBRASKA. Division of Employment Security. 1954. Financing unemployment insurance in Nebraska: complete report and digest. Lincoln, 1954. pp. 199.

INSURANCE COMPANIES

— Ireland (Republic).

EIRE. Committee of Inquiry into the Insurance Industry. 1976. Final report; [M.O'Donoghue, chairman]. Dublin, 1976. pp. 261. *bibliog.*

— United Kingdom.

COUNTER INFORMATION SERVICES. Your money and your life: insurance companies and pension funds. London, [1973]. pp. 33. *bibliog. (Anti-Reports. No.7)*

— United States.

BLAIR (ROGER D.) and VOGEL (RONALD J.) The cost of health insurance administration: an economic analysis. Lexington, Mass., 1975. pp. 177. *bibliog.*

INSURANCE LAW.

ETUDES offertes à...André Besson. Paris, 1976. pp. 342.

— New Zealand.

NEW ZEALAND. Contracts and Commercial Law Reform Committee. 1975. Aspects of insurance law; report; [C.I. Patterson, chairman]. [Wellington, 1975]. 1 pamphlet (various pagings).

— United Kingdom.

MACGILLIVRAY (EVAN JAMES) and PARKINGTON (MICHAEL) Insurance law, relating to all risks other than marine; sixth edition [by] M. Parkington [and others]. London, 1975. pp. 1187.

INSURGENCY

— America, Latin.

DIEZ años de insurreccion en America Latina; ([by] Vania Bambirra [and others]). Santiago, Chile, [1971]. 2 vols. (in 1).

INTEGER PROGRAMMING.

MILIOTIS (PANAYOTIS) Combining cutting-plane and branch-and-bound methods to solve integer programming problems: applications to the travelling salesman problem and the l-matching problem; [Ph.D.(London) thesis]. 1975. fo. 234. *bibliog. Typescript: unpublished. This thesis is the property of London University and may not be removed from the Library.*

INTEGRALS, STOCHASTIC.

McSHANE (EDWARD JAMES) Stochastic calculus and stochastic models. New York, 1974. pp. 239. *bibliog.*

INTELLECT.

INTELLIGENCE and aphasia; [edited by] Yvan Lebrun and Richard Hoops. Amsterdam, 1974. pp. 139. *bibliog. Based on an international conference held in Brussels in 1973, sponsored by the Contact Group Neurolinguistics of the Belgian Foundation for Medical Scientific Research and others.*

INTELLECTUAL PROPERTY

— United States.

MILLER (RICHARD IRWIN) Legal aspects of technology utilization. Lexington, Mass., [1974]. pp. 164.

INTELLECTUALS

— China.

MARKOVA (SVETLANA DANILOVNA) Maoizm i intelligentsiia: problemy i sobytiia, 1956-1973 gg. Moskva, 1975. pp. 245. *bibliog.*

— France.

NAVILLE (PIERRE) La révolution et les intellectuels. new ed. [Paris, 1975]. pp. 214. *Articles originally published separately in 1926, 1927 and 1956.*

— Germany.

SONTHEIMER (KURT) Das Elend unserer Intellektuellen: linke Theorie in der Bundesrepublik Deutschland. Hamburg, 1976. pp. 303.

— Russia.

GLAZOV (IURII) Tesnye vrata: vozrozhdenie russkoi intelligentsii; Narrow gates: revival of the Russian intelligentsia. London, 1973. pp. 263.

REMNEK (RICHARD B.) Soviet scholars and Soviet foreign policy: a case study in Soviet policy towards India. Durham, N.C., 1975. pp. 343. *bibliog.*

— United Kingdom.

HALL (JOHN ANTHONY) The crisis of the Edwardian intelligentsia, 1900-1920: a thesis in sociology. 1976. fo. 626. *bibliog. Typescript. Ph.D. (London) thesis: unpublished. This thesis is the property of London University and may not be removed from the Library.*

— Yugoslavia.

MARKOVIĆ (MIHAILO) and COHEN (ROBERT SONNE). Yugoslavia: the rise and fall of socialist humanism: a history of the Praxis Group. Nottingham, 1975. pp. 93.

INTELLIGENCE SERVICE

— South Africa.

INTERNATIONAL DEFENCE AND AID FUND. B[ureau] o[f] S[tate] S[ecurity]: the first 5 years. London, 1975. pp. 40.

— United States.

PERKUS (CATHY) ed. Cointelpro: the FBI's secret war on political freedom: [based on material originally prepared for the Militant]. New York, 1975. pp. 190.

AYERS (BRADLEY EARL) The war that never was: an insider's account of C.I.A. covert operations against Cuba. Indianapolis, [1976]. pp. 235.

INTERACTIVE COMPUTER SYSTEMS.

MEADOW (CHARLES TROUB) Man-machine communication. New York, [1970]. pp. 422.

HURRION (ROBERT DONALD) The design, use and required facilities of an interactive visual computer simulation language to explore production planning problems. 1976. pp. 232. *bibliog. Typescript. Ph.D. (London) thesis: unpublished. This thesis is the property of London University and may not be removed from the Library.*

INTERCULTURAL COMMUNICATION.

OSGOOD (CHARLES EGERTON) and others. Cross-cultural universals of affective meaning. Urbana, [1975]. pp. 486. *bibliog.*

INTERDISCIPLINARY APPROACH IN EDUCATION.

INTERDISCIPLINARITY: problems of teaching and research in universities; this report is based on the results of a seminar on interdisciplinarity in universities...[held at] the University of Nice,...September 7th-12th, 1970; (organised by CERI...with the French Ministry of Education]. [Paris], Organisation for Economic Co-operation and Development, 1972. pp. 321. *bibliogs.*

INTERGOVERNMENTAL FISCAL RELATIONS

— Germany.

KOCK (HEINZ) Stabilitätspolitik im föderalistischen System der Bundesrepublik Deutschland: Analyse und Reformvorschläge. Köln, [1975]. pp. 228. *bibliog.*

— Underdeveloped areas.

See UNDERDEVELOPED AREAS — Intergovernmental fiscal relations.

— United States.

COLE (RICHARD L.) and CAPUTO (DAVID A.) Urban politics and decentralization: the case of general revenue sharing. Lexington, Mass., [1974]. pp. 180.

BAHL (ROY W.) and VOGT (WALTER) Fiscal centralization and tax burdens: state and regional financing of city services. Cambridge, Mass., [1975]. pp. 173. *bibliog.*

FINANCING the new federalism: revenue sharing, conditional grants and taxation; papers by Robert P. Inman [and others]. Baltimore, [1975]. pp. 160. *(Resources for the Future, Inc. Governance of Metropolitan Regions. No.5)*

MIRENGOFF (WILLIAM) and RINDLER (LESTER) The Comprehensive Employment and Training Act: impact on people, places, programs: an interim report...prepared for the Committee on Evaluation of Employment and Training Programs, Assembly of Behavioral and Social Sciences, National Research Council. Washington, 1976. pp. 175. *bibliog.*

INTERGOVERNMENTAL TAX RELATIONS

— United States.

BAHL (ROY W.) and VOGT (WALTER) Fiscal centralization and tax burdens: state and regional financing of city services. Cambridge, Mass., [1975]. pp. 173. *bibliog.*

INTERINDUSTRY ECONOMICS.

HUNGARY. Központi Statisztikai Hivatal. 1964. A magyar népgazdaság ágazati kapcsolatainak mérlege 1961. évben; (Interindustry relations of the Hungarian national economy in 1961: input-output tables). Budapest, 1964. pp. 208,15. *With English summary.*

MATON (J.G.) De input-output tabel als instrument van sociaal-economische analyse in een dualistische huishouding, met een proeve van toepassing op de economie van Ituri. Gent, [c. 1965]. fo. 233. *bibliog.*

ISRAEL. Central Bureau of Statistics. Special Series. No. 352. Transport in Israel: input and output and physical data, 1970. Jerusalem, 1971. pp. 82. *In Hebrew with English preface. Cover title reads: Transport in Israel: input and output - operational data, 1970.*

ACCARDO (GIANFRANCO) Quantitative Fragen aus der Marxschen Wertlehre. Berlin, 1973. pp. 152. *bibliog.*

MERKWITZ (JUERGEN) Stationäre Güterverteilungen. Meisenheim am Glan, [1973]. pp. 85. *bibliog.*

MEZHOTRASLEVYE issledovaniia: sbornik statei. Moskva, 1974. pp. 144. *bibliog.*

SHNIPER (RUVIN ISAKOVICH) and DENISOVA (LILIIA PETROVNA) eds. Mezhotraslevye sviazi i narodnokhoziaistvennye proportsii Vostochnoi Sibiri i Dal'nego Vostoka. Novosibirsk, 1974. pp. 315.

FRERICHS (W.) Ein disaggregiertes Prognosesystem für die BRD. Meisenheim am Glan, 1975 in progress. *bibliog.*

GERSHENZON (MIKHAIL ABRAMOVICH) Analiz uproshchennykh dinamicheskikh modelei mezhotraslevogo balansa; otvetstvennye redaktory...N.F. Shatilov, ...B.G. Mirkin. Novosibirsk, 1975. pp. 219.

NEW ZEALAND. Department of Statistics. 1975. Inter-industry study of the New Zealand economy 1965-66. [Wellington, 1975]. 2 vols. (in 1).

REDFERN (PERCY) Statistician. Input-output analysis and its application to education and manpower planning. 2nd ed. London, H.M.S.O., 1976. pp. 21. *bibliog. (Civil Service College [U.K.]. Occasional Papers. No. 5)*

— Bibliography.

TREML (VLADIMIR G.) Input-output analysis and the Soviet economy: an annotated bibliography. New York, 1975. pp. 180.

— Mathematical models.

INTERNATIONAL CONFERENCE ON INPUT-OUTPUT TECHNIQUES, 6TH, VIENNA, 1974. Advances in input-output analysis; edited by Karen R. Polenske [and] Jiri V. Skolka. Cambridge, Mass., [1976]. pp. 602. *bibliogs.*

INTERLIBRARY LOANS

— United Kingdom.

BLL REVIEW; [pd. by] British Library Lending Division. q., Jl 1973 (v.1, no.1)- London. *Supersedes NLL review (Ja 1971 - Ap 1973).*

BRITISH LIBRARY. Lending Division. News Sheet. irreg. Boston Spa. *Current issues only kept.*

INTERNAL REVENUE LAW

INTERNAL MACEDONIAN REVOLUTIONARY ORGANIZATION.
See VŬTRESHNA MAKEDONSKA REVOLIUTSIONNA ORGANIZATSIIA.

INTERNAL REVENUE LAW

— United Kingdom.

A LETTER from a Member of Parliament on the plate-tax. London, J. Scott, 1756. pp. 31.

PINSON (BARRY) Revenue law: comprising income tax, capital gains tax, corporation tax, capital transfer tax, stamp duties, tax planning; ninth edition by B. Pinson and John Gardiner. London, 1975. pp. 640.

PINSON (BARRY) On revenue law: comprising income tax; capital gains tax; development land tax; corporation tax; capital transfer tax; value added tax, etc. 10th ed. London, 1976. pp. 666.

INTERNAL SECURITY

— Japan.

MITCHELL (RICHARD HANKS) Thought control in prewar Japan. Ithaca, 1976. pp. 226. *bibliog.*

INTERNATIONAL, THE.

AGOSTI (ALDO) La Terza Internazionale: storia documentaria. Roma, 1974 in progress.

BAKUNIN (MIKHAIL ALEKSANDROVICH) Michel Bakounine et ses relations slaves, 1870-1875; textes établis et annotés par Arthur Lehning. Leiden, 1974. pp. 586. *(International Institute of Social History. Archives Bakounine. 5)*

GOMEZ CASAS (JUAN) La Primera Internacional en España: estudio y documentos. Bilbao, 1974. pp. 159. *bibliog.*

GRUBER (HELMUT) Soviet Russia masters the Comintern: international communism in the era of Stalin's ascendancy. Garden City, N.Y., 1974. pp. 544. *bibliogs. With documents.*

LEIBZON (BORIS MOISEEVICH) and SHIRINIA (KIRILL KIRILLOVICH) Povorot v politike Kominterna: istoricheskoe znachenie VII kongressa Kominterna. 2nd ed. Moskva, 1975. pp. 420. *1st ed. had sub-title: k 30-letiiu VII kongressa.*

PETRY (LOTHAR) Die Erste Internationale in der Berliner Arbeiterbewegung. Erlangen, 1975. pp. 381. *bibliog.*

WHEELER (ROBERT F.) USPD und Internationale: sozialistischer Internationalismus in der Zeit der Revolution; (Übersetzung aus dem Amerikanischen von Agnes Bländsdorf). Frankfurt/M, [1975]. pp. 384. *bibliog.*

SIDENIUS (NIELS CHRISTIAN) Kommunistisk Internationale, 1928-1935: en analyse og kritik... specielt i forhold til fascismen og udviklingen i Tyskland. Århus, 1976. pp. 283. *bibliog.*

— Bibliography.

BAKH (I.A.) and KAMENETSKII (B.A.) eds. I Internatsional i Parizhskaia Kommuna: ukazatel' literatury, vyshedshei v SSSR 1917-1970, etc. Moskva, 1971. pp. 127.

— Congresses.

COMMUNIST INTERNATIONAL. World Congress, 2nd, 1920. Vtoroi kongress Kominterna, iiul' - avgust 1920 g.; pod redaktsiei O. Piatnitskogo [and others]. Moskva, 1934. pp. 754. *(Institut Marksa-Engel'sa-Lenina. Protokoly Kongressov Kommunisticheskogo Internatsionala)*

VII kongress Kommunisticheskogo Internatsionala i bor'ba protiv fashizma i voiny: sbornik dokumentov. Moskva, 1975. pp. 527.

TRETII kongress Kominterna: razvitie kongressom politicheskoi linii kommunisticheskogo dvizheniia. Kommunisty i massy. Moskva, 1975. pp. 632. *(Institut Marksizma-Leninizma. Osnovnye Etapy Istorii Mezhdunarodnogo Kommunisticheskogo Dvizheniia)*

INTERNATIONAL AGENCIES.

UNION OF INTERNATIONAL ASSOCIATIONS. The open society of the future: report of a seminar to reflect on the network of international associations. Brussels, Ministry of Foreign Affairs, External Trade and Cooperation in Development, 1973. pp. 148. *(Memo from Belgium. No. 161)*

SENTI (RICHARD) ed. Die Schweiz und die internationalen Wirtschaftsorganisationen; [by] Arthur Dunkel [and others]. Zürich, [1975]. pp. 189. *bibliog.*

WEISS (THOMAS GEORGE) International bureaucracy: an analysis of the operation of functional and global international secretariats. Lexington, Mass., [1975]. pp. 187. *bibliog.*

INTERNATIONAL organisations in world politics: yearbook, 1975; edited by Avi Shlaim. London, 1976. pp. 226.

— Bibliography.

GOVERNMENT PUBLICATIONS GUIDE. a., 1974. Boston, Mass.

— Directories.

UNION OF INTERNATIONAL ASSOCIATIONS and MANKIND 2000. Year-book of world problems and human potential: a framework for representation of perceptions of interlinked networks of world problems, etc. Brussels, 1976. pp. 1136. *bibliogs.*

— Law and legislation.

SCHWARZENBERGER (GEORG) International law as applied by international courts and tribunals. vol. 3. International constitutional law. London, 1976. pp. 680. *bibliog.*

— Officials and employees.

BEIGBEDER (YVES) La représentation du personnel à l'Organisation Mondiale de la Santé, et dans les principales institutions spécialisées des Nations Unies ayant leur siège en Europe. Paris, 1975. pp. 289. *bibliog.*

INTERNATIONAL AGENCIES IN AFRICA

— Directories.

UNITED NATIONS. Economic Commission for Africa. 1976. Directory of intergovernmental cooperation organizations in Africa. (E/CN.14/CEC/1/Rev.2). [Addis Ababa], 1976. pp. 170.

INTERNATIONAL AGENCIES IN EASTERN EUROPE.

SZAWLOWSKI (RICHARD) The system of the international organizations of the communist countries. Leyden, 1976. pp. 322. *bibliog.*

INTERNATIONAL AGENCIES IN EUROPE.

INTERNATIONAL organizations in Europe and the changing European system; [proceedings of a conference sponsored by the European Centre of the Carnegie Endowment for International Peace, held at Geneva in 1970; working paper and report by Klaus Törnudd]. Geneva, [1970]. pp. 56.

INTERNATIONAL AGENCIES IN SWITZERLAND.

Les ORGANISATIONS non gouvernementales en Suisse: colloque des 8 et 9 juin 1972. Genève, 1973. pp. 152. *(Geneva. Graduate Institute of International Studies. Etudes et Travaux. No. 14)*

INTERNATIONAL AND MUNICIPAL LAW

— Europe.

COUNCIL OF EUROPE. 1975. The practical guide to the recognition and enforcement of foreign judicial decisions in civil and commercial law. Strasbourg, 1975. pp. 500.

EUROPEAN COMMISSION OF HUMAN RIGHTS. 1975. European Convention on Human Rights: national aspects. Strasbourg, [Council of Europe], 1975. pp. 65. *bibliog. In English and French.*

— United Kingdom — Commonwealth.

PARRY (CLIVE) and HOPKINS (JOHN ALAN) eds. Commonwealth international law cases; collected and edited under the auspices of the International Law Fund. Dobbs Ferry, N.Y., 1974 in progress.

INTERNATIONAL BANK FOR RECONSTRUCTION AND DEVELOPMENT.

OLIVER (ROBERT W.) International economic co-operation and the World Bank. London, 1975. pp. 421. *bibliog.*

INTERNATIONAL BROADCASTING.

LISANN (MAURY) Broadcasting to the Soviet Union: international politics and radio. New York, 1975. pp. 199. *bibliog.*

INTERNATIONAL BUSINESS ENTERPRISES.

KAPOOR (ASHOK) and GRUB (PHILLIP D.) eds. The multinational enterprise in transition: selected readings and essays. Princeton, [1972] repr. 1973. pp. 505.

MODELSKI (JERZY ALEKSANDER) ed. Multinational corporations and world order. Beverly Hills, [1973]. pp. 160. *bibliogs.*

SANTOS (THEOTONIO DOS) Imperialismo y empresas multinacionales. Buenos Aires, 1973. pp. 142.

BEHRMAN (JACK N.) Conflicting constraints on the multinational enterprise: potential for resolution. New York, 1974. pp. 109.

FRANCE. Délégation à l'Aménagement du Territoire et à l'Action Régionale. 1974. Investissements étrangers et aménagement du territoire: livre blanc. Paris, 1974. pp. 141. *Map in end pocket.*

GRANELL TRIAS (FRANCISCO) Las empresas multinacionales y el desarrollo. Barcelona, [1974]. pp. 271. *bibliog.*

MAZZOLINI (RENATO) European transnational concentrations: top management's perspective on the obstacles to corporate unions in the EEC. London, [1974]. pp. 243. *bibliog.*

QUERCIA (ROGER) Eléments pour une politique des quartiers généraux d'entreprises multinationales en France. [Paris], Documentation Française, 1974. pp. 202.

AMERICAN ASSEMBLY. 47th Assembly, December, 1974. Global companies: the political economy of world business; [edited by George W. Ball]. Englewood Cliffs, [1975]. pp. 179.

BEAUD (MICHEL) and others. Une multinationale française: Pechiney Ugine Kuhlmann. Paris, [1975]. pp. 288.

DEVERELL (JOHN) and others. Falconbridge: portrait of a Canadian mining multinational; [by] John Deverell and the Latin American Working Group. Toronto, 1975. pp. 184.

The FUTURE of the United States multinational corporation: [proceedings of a symposium organized by the John Bassett Moore Society in 1974]; edited by Lee D. Unterman and Christine W. Swent. Charlottesville, 1975. pp. 161.

GILPIN (ROBERT) U.S. power and the multinational corporation: the political economy of foreign direct investment. New York, [1975]. pp. 291.

GRUENAERML (FROHMUND) Multinationale Unternehmen und staatliche Wirtschaftspolitik. Göttingen, [1975]. pp. 212. *bibliog. (Kommission für Wirtschaftlichen und Sozialen Wandel. Schriften. 101)*

HUMBLE (JOHN WILLIAM) The responsible multinational enterprise. London, [1975]. pp. 76. *bibliog.*

INTERNATIONAL ECONOMIC RELATIONS.

KUJAWA (DUANE) ed. International labor and the multinational enterprise. New York, 1975. pp. 213.

LABORATOIRE DE CONJONCTURE ET PROSPECTIVE. Schéma général d'aménagement de la France: firmes multinationales et division internationale du travail. Paris, 1975. pp. 90. *(France. Délégation à l'Aménagement du Territoire et à l'Action Régionale. Travaux et Recherches de Prospective. 55)*

LIEBHABERG (BRUNO) Stratégies et tactiques syndicales face aux entreprises multinationales. Bruxelles, [1975]. fo. 162. *bibliog. Mémoire (ingénieur commercial)-Université Libre de Bruxelles.*

MALIK (REX) And tomorrow...the world?: inside IBM. London, 1975. pp. 496. *bibliog.*

MULTINATIONAL corporations and governments: business-government relations in an international context; edited by Patrick M. Boarman [and] Hans Schollhammer. New York, 1975. pp. 229. *Papers of a conference held jointly by the Center for International Business, Pepperdine University, and the Graduate School of Management of the University of California at Los Angeles in 1973.*

MURRAY (ROBIN) Multinational companies and nation states: two essays. Nottingham, 1975. pp. 108.

The NATION-state and transnational corporations in conflict: with special reference to Latin America; edited by Jon P. Gunnemann. New York, 1975. pp. 242. *Papers of the consultation organized by the Council on Religion and International Affairs at Aspen Institute, Colorado, in 1973.*

NEGANDHI (ANANT R.) and PRASAD (S. BENJAMIN) The frightening angels: a study of U.S. multinationals in developing nations. Kent, Ohio, [1975]. pp. 249. *bibliog.*

PALLOIX (CHRISTIAN) L'économie mondiale capitaliste et les firmes multinationales. Paris, 1975. 2 vols.(in 1).

PARRY (THOMAS GREGORY) The international location of production: studies in the trade and non-trade servicing of international markets by multinational manufacturing enterprise; [Ph.D. (London) thesis]. 1975. fo. 299. *2 offprints in end pocket. Typescript: unpublished. This thesis is the property of London University and may not be removed from the Library.*

SKLAR (RICHARD L.) Corporate power in an African state: the political impact of multinational mining companies in Zambia. Berkeley, 1975. pp. 245. *bibliog.*

STRATEGIES des firmes chimiques: perspectives de développement; (par Michel Hors [and others]). Paris, 1975. pp. 173. *(France. Ministère de l'Industrie et de la Recherche. Etudes de Politique Industrielle. 3)*

TORNEDEN (ROGER L.) Foreign disinvestment by U.S. multinational corporations; with eight case studies. New York, 1975. pp. 156. *bibliog.*

BUCKLEY (PETER J.) and CASSON (MARK C.) The future of the multinational enterprise. London, 1976. pp. 116.

EELLS (RICHARD) Global corporations: the emerging system of world economic power. rev. ed. New York, [1976]. pp. 262.

FRANKO (LAWRENCE G.) The European multinationals: a renewed challenge to American and British big business. London, [1976]. pp. 276. *bibliog.*

MENNIS (BERNARD) and SAUVANT (KARL P.) Emerging forms of transnational community: transnational business enterprises and regional integration. Lexington, Mass., [1976]. pp. 240. *bibliog.*

NIECKELS (LARS) Transfer pricing in multinational firms: a heuristic programming approach and a case study. Stockholm, 1976. pp. 190. *bibliog.*

PRATTEN (CLIFFORD FREDERICK) Labour productivity differentials within international companies. Cambridge, 1976. pp. 118. *(Cambridge. University. Department of Applied Economics. Occasional Papers. 50)*

WALLACE (DON) International regulation of multinational corporations. New York, 1976. pp. 233.

WIECHMANN (ULRICH E.) Marketing management in multinational firms: the consumer packaged goods industry. New York, 1976. pp. 103. *bibliog.*

WILCZYNSKI (JOZEF) The multinationals and East-West relations: towards transideological collaboration. London, 1976. pp. 235. *bibliog.*

— Finance.

AGGARWAL (RAJ) Financial policies for the multinational company: the management of foreign exchange. New York, 1976. pp. 161. *bibliog.*

INTERNATIONAL COOPERATION.

COOPERATIVE approaches to world energy problems: a tripartite report by...Guy de Carmoy [and others]. Washington, [1974]. pp. 51.

INDEPENDANCE et interdépendances au Maghreb; par W.K. Ruf [and others]. Paris, 1974. pp. 359. *(Centre de Recherches et d'Etudes sur les Sociétés Méditerranéennes. Collection)*

INTERNATIONAL ECONOMIC INTEGRATION.

SOŁDACZUK (JÓZEF) Integracja gospodarcza we współczesnym kapitalizmie. Warszawa, 1963. pp. 175.

MARKUSHINA (VERA IVANOVNA) Mezhdunarodnye nauchno-tekhnicheskie sviazi v sisteme sovremennogo kapitalizma. Moskva, 1972. pp. 271. *(Akademiia Nauk SSSR. Institut Mirovoi Ekonomiki i Mezhdunarodnykh Otnoshenii. Mezhdunarodnye Monopolii i Imperialisticheskaia Integratsiia)*

HABERLER (GOTTFRIED VON) Probleme der wirtschaftlichen Integration Europas; [and] Fritz Machlup: Integrationshemmende Integrationspolitik; (erweiterte Fassung der Festvorlesungen...am 16 Juni 1974). Kiel, 1974. pp. 60. *(Kiel. Universität. Institut für Weltwirtschaft. Bernhard-Harms-Vorlesungen. 5/6)*

GEIGER (THEODORE) and others. North American integration and economic blocs. London, 1975. pp. 54. *(Trade Policy Research Centre. Thames Essays. No. 7)*

HAAS (ERNST BERNARD) The obsolescence of regional integration theory. Berkeley, [1975]. pp. 123. *bibliog. (California University. Institute of International Studies. Research Series. No. 25)*

INTERNATIONAL ECONOMIC ASSOCIATION. Congress, 4th, Budapest, 1974. Ökonomische Integration: Beiträge der DDR-Teilnehmer zum IV. Weltkongress der Ökonomen; herausgegeben von Fred Oelssner. Berlin, 1975. pp. 202.

JOHNSON (HARRY GORDON) Technology and economic interdependence. London, 1975. pp. 187. *bibliog. (Trade Policy Research Centre. World Economic Issues)*

LORTIE (PIERRE) Economic integration and the law of GATT. New York, [1975]. pp. 177.

BESCHAEFTIGUNGSWIRKUNGEN einer verstärkten Arbeitsteilung zwischen der Bundesrepublik und den Entwicklungsländern; ([by] Hugo Dicke [and others]). Tübingen, 1976. pp. 225. *bibliog. (Kiel. Universität. Institut für Weltwirtschaft. Kieler Studien. 137)*

BRACEWELL-MILNES (JOHN BARRY) Economic integration in East and West. London, 1976. pp. 218.

INTERNATIONAL ECONOMIC RELATIONS.

KÁLLAI (PÁL) Nemzetközi ipari kooperáció. Budapest, 1971. pp. 313. *bibliog. With Russian, German and English summaries.*

ARBEITSGEMEINSCHAFT DEUTSCHER WIRTSCHAFTSWISSENSCHAFTLICHER FORSCHUNGSINSTITUTE. The economic situation in the world and in Western Germany in spring 1972. Hamburg, 1972. pp. 16.

CORBET (HUGH) Agriculture's place in commercial diplomacy; essays on a conference at Ditchley Park,...1973. Enstone, [1974]. pp. 42. *(Ditchley Foundation. Ditchley Papers. No. 48)*

MONTBRIAL (THIERRY DE) Le désordre économique mondial: essai d'interprétation monétaire. [Paris, 1974]. pp. 187.

SCHNEIDER (WILLIAM) Can we avert economic warfare in raw materials?: U.S. agriculture as a blue chip. New York, [1974]. pp. 43. *(National Strategy Information Center. Agenda Papers. No. 1)*

TRADE negotiations and world food problems; papers for a conference in London on 5 December 1974 [by]...Wilhelm Henrichsmeyer [and others]. London, [1974]. 1 vol. (various foliations). *(Trade Policy Research Centre. Conference Papers)*

URI (PIERRE) Développement sans dépendance. [Paris, 1974]. pp. 261.

ASHBY (ERIC) Baron Ashby. A second look at doom. Southampton, 1975. pp. 18. *(Southampton. University. Fawley Foundation. Lectures. 21*

Un DEBAT sur l'échange inégal: salaires, sous-développement, impérialisme; [by] Arghiri Emmanuel [and others]; traduit de l'italien par M.C. Paoletti et A. Benaneti. Paris, 1975. pp. 160.

DOCKES (PIERRE) L'internationale du capital. [Paris], 1975. pp. 287. *bibliog.*

GISCARD D'ESTAING (VALERY) A new world economic order: (a talk...at the Ecole Polytechnique on 28 October 1975). London, French Embassy, Service de Presse et d'Information, 1975. pp. 20. *(Speeches and statements)*

HANSEN (ROGER D.) A new international economic order?; an outline for a constructive U.S. response. Washington, 1975. pp. 34. *(Overseas Development Council. Development Papers. 19)*

HILTON (STANLEY E.) Brazil and the great powers, 1930-1939: the politics of trade rivalry. Austin, [1975]. pp. 304. *bibliog. (Texas University. Institute of Latin American Studies. Latin American Monographs. No.38)*

The INTERACTION of economics and foreign policy; edited by Robert A. Bauer. Charlottesville, Va., 1975. pp. 154. *Essays first presented at a Kenyon Public Affairs Forum Conference in April 1974.*

ISOLATION or interdependence?: today's choices for tomorrow's world; (papers...prepared for a conference at the University of Chicago...1974); edited by Morton A. Kaplan. New York, [1975]. pp. 254. *bibliog.*

MATIÈRES premières minérales et relations internationales; ([by] P. Bourrelier [and others]). Lausanne, 1975. pp. 62. *(Lausanne. Université. Centre de Recherches Européennes. Publications: 4. L'Europe et les Pays Tiers)*

MYRDAL (GUNNAR) The equality issue in world development. [Stockholm?], 1975. fo. 21.

A NEW world order?; [by] Cyril E. Black [and others]; [papers presented at the first of a series of Princeton University conferences held in 1974]. Princeton, 1975. pp. 87. *(Princeton University. Center of International Studies. World Order Studies Program. Occasional Papers. No. 1)*

OLIVER (ROBERT W.) International economic co-operation and the World Bank. London, 1975. pp. 421. *bibliog.*

PALLOIX (CHRISTIAN) L'économie mondiale capitaliste et les firmes multinationales. Paris, 1975. 2 vols.(in 1).

POPESCU (MARIA D.) Imperativele noii ordini economice internaționale: rațiunea și strategia cooperării. București, 1975. pp. 210. *bibliog. With English summary and English, French and Russian tables of contents.*

ROGERS (PAUL) and DICKSON (BOB) Producer power: the third world hits back. London, [1975]. pp. 50.

La SITUAZIONE economica internazionale e le prospettive italiane: interventi di Nino Andreatta [and others]. Bologna, [1975]. pp. 111.

TAYLOR (JOHN VERNON) Enough is enough. London, 1975 repr. 1976. pp. 120. *bibliog.*

INTERNATIONAL ECONOMIC RELATIONS.(Cont.)

THIRD WORLD FORUM. Special Task Force, Mexico, 1975. Proposals for a new international economic order. Mexico City, 1975. pp. 16.

ZUM Verhältnis von Aussenwirtschafts- und Entwicklungspolitik; [by] Axel Borrmann [and others]. Hamburg, 1975. pp. 409. *bibliog.* (*Hamburg. Hamburgisches Welt-Wirtschafts-Archiv. Veröffentlichungen*)

BLAKE (DAVID H.) and WALTERS (ROBERT S.) The politics of global economic relations. Englewood Cliffs, [1976]. pp. 240.

CHOUCRI (NAZLI) and FERRARO (VINCENT) International politics of energy interdependence: the case of petroleum. Lexington, Mass., [1976]. pp. 250. *bibliog.*

EVANS (DOUGLAS) and BODY (RICHARD) eds. Freedom and stability in the world economy. London, 1976. pp. 117.

GEORGE (SUSAN) How the other half dies: the real reasons for world hunger. Harmondsworth, 1976. pp. 349. *bibliog.*

GOULET (DENIS) World interdependence: verbal smokescreen or new ethic?. Washington, 1976. pp. 32. (*Overseas Development Council. Development Papers. 21*)

INTERNATIONAL economic relations of the Western world, 1959-1971; edited by Andrew Shonfield assisted by Hermia Oliver. London, 1976. 2 vols.

MACBEAN (ALASDAIR I.) and BALASUBRAMANYAM (V.N.) Meeting the Third World challenge. London, 1976. pp. 272. *bibliog.*

MIKDASHI (ZUHAYR) The international politics of natural resources. Ithaca, 1976. pp. 214.

NOVICK (DAVID) A world of scarcities: critical issues in public policy;...with Kurt Bleicken [and others]. London, 1976. pp. 194.

RYBCZYNSKI (TADEUSZ MIECZYSLAW) ed. The economics of the oil crisis. London, 1976. pp. 202. *bibliog.*

SYMPOSIUM ON INTERNATIONAL ECONOMIC DIMENSIONS OF ENVIRONMENTAL MANAGEMENT, NEW YORK, 1975. Studies in international environmental economics; edited by Ingo Walter. New York, [1976]. pp. 364. *bibliog.*

TANNER (JOHN) A new deal for the poor: what a new economic order would mean for Britain and the third world. London, 1976. pp. 24. *bibliog.*

TOWARDS a new international economic order; a further report by a Commonwealth Experts' Group; [Alister McIntyre, chairman]. London, Commonwealth Secretariat, [1976]. pp. 35.

UNION OF INTERNATIONAL ASSOCIATIONS and MANKIND 2000. Year-book of world problems and human potential: a framework for representation of perceptions of interlinked networks of world problems, etc. Brussels, 1976. pp. 1136. *bibliogs.*

URI (PIERRE) Development without dependence. New York, 1976. pp. 166.

WALLACE (DON) International regulation of multinational corporations. New York, 1976. pp. 233.

WESTLAKE (MELVYN) World poverty. London, 1976. pp. 32. (*Young Fabian Group. Young Fabian Pamphlets. 44*)

— **Mathematical models.**

ROTH (JUERGEN) Der internationale Konjunkturzusammenhang bei flexiblen Wechselkursen: eine modelltheoretische Analyse. Tübingen, 1975. pp. 264. *bibliog.* (*Kiel. Universität. Institut für Weltwirtschaft Kieler Studien. 135*)

INTERNATIONAL FINANCE.

UNITED NATIONS. Conference on Trade and Development. 1966. Payments arrangements among the developing countries for trade expansion: report of the group of experts. (TD/B/80/Rev.1) (TD/B/C.3/24/Rev.1). Geneva, 1966. pp. 32.

EHRLICH (BENJAMIN) The world bank of issue; projected by Benjamin Ehrlich. Lisbon, 1972. pp. 275. *bibliog.*

INTERNATIONAL BANK FOR RECONSTRUCTION AND DEVELOPMENT. Borrowing in international capital markets: foreign and international bond issues: publicized Eurocurrency credits. q., 1974 (3rd quarter)- [Washington D.C.].

ALIBER (ROBERT Z.) Policies toward the O[rganization of] P[etroleum] E[xporting] C[ountries'] oil and wealth. Tübingen, 1975. pp. 14. (*Kiel. Universität. Institut für Weltwirtschaft. Kieler Vorträge. Neue Folge. 80*)

ECKES (ALFRED E.) A search for solvency: Bretton Woods and the international monetary system, 1941-1971. Austin, [1975]. pp. 355. *bibliog.*

HARTLAND-THUNBERG (PENELOPE) ed. Commissioned papers on inflation/recession, energy and the international financial structure. Washington, [1975]. pp. 62.

HIGHER oil prices: worldwide financial implications; [consisting of] a policy statement by the British-North American Committee [and] a research report by Sperry Lea. [Washington], 1975. pp. x, 31.

INDIA. Department of Economic Affairs. 1975. India and international monetary reform. [Delhi, 1975]. pp. 215.

INTERNATIONAL capital markets; edited by Edwin J. Elton [and] Martin J. Gruber. Amsterdam, 1975. pp. 387. *bibliogs.*

INTERNATIONAL trade and finance: frontiers for research; edited by Peter B. Kenen. Cambridge, [1975]. pp. 539. *bibliogs. The nine papers in this volume were written for a conference held at Princeton University in March 1973.*

KANAPATHY (V.) Kuala Lumpur as a centre of international finance; (expanded version of an article...in The Times...on 31st May 1975). [Kuala Lumpur, 1975]. pp. 9.

MORSE (Sir CHRISTOPHER JEREMY) The international monetary kaleidoscope. Reading, [1975]. pp. 20. (*Reading. University. Mercantile Credit Lectures. 1975*)

PALLOIX (CHRISTIAN) L'internationalisation du capital: éléments critiques. Paris, 1975. pp. 203. *bibliog.*

VAN OENEN (J.D.) Cairo as a financial centre and some of its implications. Cairo, 1975. pp. 21. (*National Bank of Egypt. Diamond Jubilee Lectures*)

WILLETT (THOMAS D.) The oil-transfer problem and international economic stability. Princeton, 1975. pp. 34. *bibliog.* (*Princeton University. Department of Economics and Sociology. International Finance Section. Essays in International Finance. No. 113*)

ZWASS (ADAM) Monetary cooperation between East and West. White Plains, N.Y., [1975]. pp. 265. *bibliog.*

ALIBER (ROBERT Z.) The international money game. 2nd ed. New York, [1976]. pp. 312.

COOMBS (CHARLES A.) The arena of international finance. New York, [1976]. pp. 243.

HELLEINER (GERALD KARL) ed. A world divided: the less developed countries in the international economy. Cambridge, 1976. pp. 299. *bibliogs.* (*McGill University. Centre for Developing Area Studies. Perspectives on Development. 5*)

INTERNATIONAL economic relations of the Western world, 1959-1971; edited by Andrew Shonfield assisted by Hermia Oliver. London, 1976. 2 vols.

PARK (YOON S.) Oil money and the world economy. Boulder, Colorado, 1976. pp. 205. *bibliog.*

YEAGER (LELAND BENNETT) International monetary relations: theory, history, and policy. 2nd ed. New York, [1976]. pp. 667.

— **Mathematical models.**

BOYER (RUSSELL S.) Devaluation and portfolio balance. [London], 1975. 1 pamphlet (various foliations). *bibliog.*

KNIGHT (MALCOLM DONALD) and WYMER (CLIFFORD RONALD) A monetary model of an open economy with particular reference to the United Kingdom. [London, 1975]. pp. 24, iii. *bibliog.*

— **Europe.**

GRAUWE (PAUL DE) Monetary interdependence and international monetary reform: a European case study. Farnborough, Hants., [1976]. pp. 118. *bibliog.*

INTERNATIONAL LAW.

UNITED STATES. Department of State. 1918-19. The Inquiry handbooks. Wilmington, 1974. 20 vols. *bibliogs. Reprint of documents originally published in Washington, 1918-19.*

ANTONOWICZ (LECH) Likwidacja kolonializmu ze stanowiska prawa międzynarodowego. Warszawa, 1964. pp. 190. *bibliog.*

NAHLIK (STANISŁAW EDWARD) Wstęp do nauki prawa międzynarodowego. Warszawa, 1967. pp. 432. *With French table of contents.*

McNAIR (ARNOLD DUNCAN) 1st Baron McNair. Selected papers and bibliography. Leiden, 1974. pp. 395. *bibliog.*

ASBECK (FREDERIK MARI VAN) Baron. International society in search of a transnational legal order: selected writings and bibliography; edited by H.F. van Panhuys and Mrs. M. van Leeuwen Boomkamp. Leyden, 1976. pp. 604. *bibliog. In English or French.*

ESSAYS on international law in honour of Krishna Rao; edited by M.K. Nawaz. Leyden, 1976. pp. 361.

GREIG (D.W.) International law. 2nd ed. London, 1976. pp. 944.

MERRILLS (J.G.) Anatomy of international law: a study of the role of international law in the contemporary world. London, 1976. pp. 106. *bibliog.*

SCHWARZENBERGER (GEORG) The dynamics of international law. Milton, 1976. pp. 139. *bibliog.*

SCHWARZENBERGER (GEORG) and BROWN (E.D.) A manual of international law. 6th ed. Abingdon, 1976. pp. 612. *bibliog.*

— **Bibliography.**

DOIMI DI DELUPIS (INGRID) Bibliography of international law. London, [1975]. pp. 670.

— **Cases.**

PARRY (CLIVE) and HOPKINS (JOHN ALAN) eds. Commonwealth international law cases; collected and edited under the auspices of the International Law Fund. Dobbs Ferry, N.Y., 1974 in progress.

— **Codification.**

ROSENNE (SHABTAI) ed. League of Nations Conference for the Codification of International Law, 1930: [reports and official records of proceedings]. Dobbs Ferry, N.Y., 1975. 4 vols.

— **History — Africa.**

MENSAH-BROWN (A.K., ed. African international legal history. New York, United Nations Institute for Training and Research, 1975. pp. 234. *bibliog.* (*UNITAR Studies. No.9*)

— — **Malaya.**

RUBIN (ALFRED P.) The international personality of the Malay Peninsula: a study of the international law of imperialism. Kuala Lumpur, 1974. pp. 327. *bibliog.*

—— Russia.

CHARVIN (ROBERT) Aperçu de la conception soviétique du droit international public général. Paris, 1971. fo. 26. (Centre d'Etudes et de Recherches Marxistes. Cahiers. No. 90)

— Philosophy.

SAUER (ERNST FRIEDRICH) Pragmatik: bessere Politik durch besseres Völkerrecht. Bonn, 1974. pp. 170. bibliog.

INTERNATIONAL LAW, PRIVATE

— Executions.

WESER (MARTHA) Convention communautaire sur la compétence judiciaire et l'exécution des décisions, complété par l'étude des droits internes et des traités bilatéraux des Etats contractants. Bruxelles, 1975. pp. 773. bibliogs. (Centre Interuniversitaire de Droit Comparé. [Publications]. 19)

— Husband and wife — South Africa.

HAHLO (HERMAN ROBERT) The South African law of husband and wife, with an appendix on Jurisdiction and conflict of laws by Ellison Kahn. 4th ed. Cape Town, 1975. pp. 754.

— Jurisdiction.

JACKSON (DAVID C.) The "conflicts" process: jurisdiction and choice in private international law. Dobbs Ferry, N.Y., 1975. pp. 408.

— Sales.

INTERNATIONAL INSTITUTE FOR THE UNIFICATION OF PRIVATE LAW. 1970. Sales of movables by instalment and on credit in the member states of the Council of Europe: study in comparative law. Strasbourg, Council of Europe, 1970. pp. 253.

— Australia.

SYKES (EDWARD I.) and PRYLES (MICHAEL CHARLES) International and interstate conflict of laws: cases and materials. Sydney, 1975. pp. 914.

— Austria.

SCHWIND (FRITZ) Handbuch des österreichischen internationalen Privatrechts. Wien, 1975. pp. 418. bibliog.

— Canada.

CASTEL (JEAN GABRIEL) Conflict of laws: cases, notes and materials. 3rd ed. Toronto, 1974. pp. 836.

INTERNATIONAL MONETARY FUND.

CANADA. Statutes, etc. 1969. An act to amend the Bretton Woods Agreement Act and the Currency, Mint and Exchange Fund Act, 1969. [Ottawa, 1969]. pp. 44. In English and French.

UNITED NATIONS. Conference on Trade and Development. 1969. International monetary system: issues relating to development financing and trade of developing countries, etc. (TD/B/198/Rev. 1). New York, 1969. pp. 33.

UNITED NATIONS. Conference on Trade and Development. Expert Group on International Monetary Issues. 1969. International monetary reform and co-operation for development: report, with bibliog. (TD/B/285/Rev.1). New York, 1969. pp. 26.

UNIVERSITY OF KENT AT CANTERBURY. Keynes Seminar, 2nd, 1974. Keynes and international monetary relations...; edited by A.P. Thirlwall. London, 1976. pp. 126.

YEAGER (LELAND BENNETT) International monetary relations: theory, history, and policy. 2nd ed. New York, [1976]. pp. 667.

INTERNATIONAL OFFICIALS AND EMPLOYEES.

WEISS (THOMAS GEORGE) International bureaucracy: an analysis of the operation of functional and global international secretariats. Lexington, Mass., [1975]. pp. 187. bibliog.

INTERNATIONAL ORGANIZATION.

VELEZ GOMEZ (CARLOS) Integration and development. Manizales, 1974. pp. 170.

GOODMAN (ELLIOT RAYMOND) The fate of the Atlantic Community. New York, 1975. pp. 583.

ON the creation of a just world order: preferred worlds for the 1990s; edited by Saul H. Mendlovitz. New York, [1975]. pp. 302. A program of the World Order Models Project.

PLANNING alternative world futures: values, methods, and models; edited by Louis René Beres, Harry R. Targ. New York, 1975. pp. 307.

AKINDELE (R.A.) The organization and promotion of world peace: a study of universal-regional relationships. Toronto, [1976]. pp. 204. bibliog.

BIBÒ (ISTVÀN) The paralysis of international institutions and the remedies: a study of self-determination, concord among the major powers, and political arbitration. New York, [1976]. pp. 152.

PADELFORD (NORMAN JUDSON) and others. The dynamics of international politics. 3rd ed. New York, [1976]. pp. 603. bibliogs.

INTERNATIONAL RELATIONS.

VÄYRYNEN (RAIMO) Militarization, conflict behavior and interaction: three ways of analyzing the Cold War. Tampere, [1973]. pp. 230. bibliog. (Tampere Peace Research Institute. Research Reports. No.3)

PFISTER (JAMES W.) The compulsion to war: a quantitative exploration of remote international relations. Beverly Hills, [1974]. pp. 82. bibliog.

STRAUSZ-HUPÉ (ROBERT) Strategy and values: selected writings...; edited by William R. Kintner and Robert L. Pfaltzgraff. Lexington, Mass., [1974]. pp. 127.

ALTING VON GEUSAU (FRANS ALPHONS MARIA) European perspectives on world order. Leyden, 1975. pp. 341. (John F. Kennedy Institute. Center for International Studies. Publications. Nr. 10)

CHATTERJEE (PARTHA) Arms, alliances and stability: the development of the structure of international politics. New York, 1975. pp. 292. bibliog.

CLINE (RAY S.) World power assessment: a calculus of strategic drift. Boulder, Col., [1975]. pp. 173.

COPLIN (WILLIAM D.) and KEGLEY (CHARLES WILLIAM) eds. Analyzing international relations: a multimethod introduction. New York, 1975. pp. 381. bibliog.

The INTERACTION of economics and foreign policy; edited by Robert A. Bauer. Charlottesville, Va., 1975. pp. 154. Essays first presented at a Kenyon Public Affairs Forum Conference in April 1974.

INTERNATIONAL SCHOOL ON DISARMAMENT AND RESEARCH ON CONFLICTS, 5TH, URBINO, 1974. International terrorism and world security: [proceedings of the fifth course]; edited by David Carlton and Carlo Schaerf. London, 1975. pp. 332.

L'IPOTESI del tripolarismo: Stati Uniti, URSS e Cina; a cura di Franco Soglian. Bari, [1975]. pp. 428. (Milan. Istituto per gli Studi di Politica Internazionale. Saggi di Storia Contemporanea. 1)

KARDELJ (EDVARD) Nacija i medjunarodni odnosi: [a collection of articles]. Beograd, 1975. pp. 249.

MERRITT (RICHARD LAWRENCE) ed. Foreign policy analysis. Lexington, Mass., [1975]. pp. 159. bibliogs.

MIDLARSKY (MANUS I.) On war: political violence in the international system. New York, [1975]. pp. 229.

SJAASTAD (ANDERS C.) and SKOGAN (JOHN KRISTEN) Politikk og sikkerhet i Norskehavsområdet: om de enkelte land og våre felles problemer. Oslo, 1975. pp. 301. (Norsk Utenrikspolitisk Institutt. Utenrikspolitiske Studier. Nr. 18)

SOTSIALIZM i mezhdunarodnye otnosheniia. Moskva, 1975. pp. 424.

ASBECK (FREDERIK MARI VAN) Baron. International society in search of a transnational legal order: selected writings and bibliography; edited by H.F. van Panhuys and Mrs. M. van Leeuwen Boomkamp. Leyden, 1976. pp. 604. bibliog. In English or French.

MANSBACH (RICHARD W.) and others. The web of world politics: nonstate actors in the global system. Englewood Cliffs, [1976]. pp. 326.

MORSE (EDWARD L.) Modernization and the transformation of international relations. New York, [1976]. pp. 203.

NEUMAN (STEPHANIE GLICKSBERG) ed. Small states and segmented societies: national political integration in a global environment. New York, 1976. pp. 238.

NORTHEDGE (FREDERICK SAMUEL) The international political system. London, 1976. pp. 336. bibliog.

PADELFORD (NORMAN JUDSON) and others. The dynamics of international politics. 3rd ed. New York, [1976]. pp. 603. bibliogs.

WINBERG (ALAN RONALD) Decision-making theory and the characteristics of crisis; with particular reference to the French reaction to the remilitarization of the Rhineland in 1936. [1976]. fo. 448. bibliog. Typescript. M.Phil.(London) thesis: unpublished. This thesis is the property of London University and may not be removed from the Library.

WORLD politics: an introduction; [edited by] James Rosenau [and others]. New York, [1976]. pp. 754.

— Methodology.

POWER, balance of power, and status in nineteenth century international relations; [by] Richard Rosecrance [and others]. Beverly Hills, [1974]. pp. 63. bibliog.

CHOUCRI (NAZLI) and NORTH (ROBERT CARVER) Nations in conflict: national growth and international violence. San Francisco, [1975]. pp. 356. bibliog.

— Moral and religious aspects.

MIDGLEY (ERNEST BRIAN FRANCIS) The natural law tradition and the theory of international relations. London, 1975. pp. 587. bibliog.

— Research.

HAAS (MICHAEL) International conflict. Indianapolis, [1974]. pp. 681.

PLANNING alternative world futures: values, methods, and models; edited by Louis René Beres, Harry R. Targ. New York, 1975. pp. 307.

—— United States.

CONFERENCE ON THE NATIONAL ARCHIVES AND FOREIGN RELATIONS RESEARCH, WASHINGTON, 1969. The National Archives and foreign relations research: (papers and proceedings of the Conference...sponsored by the National Archives and Records Service); edited by Milton O. Gustafson. Athens, Ohio, [1974]. pp. 292. (United States. National Archives. National Archives Conferences. vol. 4)

INTERNATIONAL RELIEF.

CIVIL wars and the politics of international relief: Africa, South Asia, and the Caribbean; edited by Morris Davis. New York, 1975. pp. 109.

INTERNATIONAL RELIEF.(Cont.)

— **Lesotho.**

LINDEN (EUGENE) The alms race: the impact of American voluntary aid abroad. New York, [1976]. pp. 275.

INTERNATIONAL SOCIALISTS.

PURDY (DAVID) The Soviet Union: state capitalist or socialist?: a Marxist critique of the International Socialists. London, [1976]. pp. 46. *bibliog.*

INTERNATIONAL TELECOMMUNICATION SATELLITE ORGANIZATION.

SNOW (MARCELLUS S.) International commercial satellite communications: economic and political issues of the first decade of INTELSAT. New York, 1976. pp. 170. *bibliog.*

INTERNATIONAL TRAINING CENTRE FOR COMMUNITY SERVICES.

See MOUNT CARMEL CENTRE.

INTERNATIONAL UNION OF REVOLUTIONARY WRITERS.

IZ istorii Mezhdunarodnogo ob"edineniia revoliutsionnykh pisatelei (MORP). Moskva, 1969. pp. 680. *(Akademiia Nauk SSSR. Institut Mirovoi Literatury. Literaturnoe Nasledstvo. t.81)* Documents in original languages.

INTERNATIONALISM.

SALIEV (A.) ed. Natsional'noe i internatsional'noe v iskusstve. Frunze, 1973. pp. 253.

BRATSTVO narodov i internatsional'noe vospitanie: [materialy respublikanskoi nauchno-teoreticheskoi konferentsii "Torzhestvo leninskikh idei bratstva narodov i internatsional'noe vospitanie trudiashchikhsia"]. Tashkent, 1974. pp. 266.

INTERNATSIONALIZM i problemy sotsialisticheskoi ekonomicheskoi integratsii. Moskva, 1974. pp. 311.

SOTSIALISTICHESKII internatsionalizm v deistvii. Moskva, 1974. pp. 254.

TORZHESTVO leninskikh idei proletarskogo internatsionalizma: na materialakh respublik Srednei Azii i Kazakhstana, 1917-1972 gg. Moskva, 1974. pp. 531.

VOPLOSHCHENIE sotsialisticheskogo internatsionalizma. Baku, 1974. pp. 227.

ANOSHKIN (IVAN FEDOROVICH) Internatsionalizm vnutrennei politiki KPSS: iz teoreticheskogo naslediia V.I. Lenina. Moskva, 1975. pp. 191.

DOBROTIN (EVGENII VLADIMIROVICH) Proletarskii internatsionalizm i edinstvo mirovogo kommunisticheskogo dvizheniia. Moskva, 1975. pp. 63.

INTERNATSIONAL'NYI printsip v stroitel'stve i deiatel'nosti KPSS. Moskva, 1975. pp. 296.

MATIUSHKIN (NIKOLAI IVANOVICH) Patriotizm i internatsionalizm sovetskogo naroda: istoricheskii opyt i sovremennaia deiatel'nost' KPSS. Moskva, 1975. pp. 416.

OSUSHCHESTVLENIE printsipov internatsionalizma v natsional'noi politike KPSS. Moskva, 1975. pp. 342.

SHEVELEV (ALEKSEI GEORGIEVICH) Sovremennaia epokha i proletarskii internatsionalizm. Leningrad, 1975. pp. 136.

INTERPERSONAL RELATIONS.

ALLEN (DONALD E.) and GUY (REBECCA F.) Conversation analysis: the sociology of talk. The Hague, 1974. pp. 284. *bibliog.*

KJØLLER (METTE) Interaktionen mellem interviewer og respondent, etc. København, 1975. pp. 241. *bibliog. (Socialforskningsinstituttet. Studier. 32)* With English summaries.

MARWELL (GERALD) and SCHMITT (DAVID R.) Cooperation: an experimental analysis. New York, 1975. pp. 209. *bibliog.*

WILMOT (WILLIAM W.) Dyadic communication: a transactional perspective. Reading, Mass., [1975]. pp. 196. *bibliog.*

— **Mathematical models.**

PANIOTTO (VLADIMIR IL'ICH) Struktura mezhlichnostnykh otnoshenii: metodika i matematicheskie metody issledovaniia. Kiev, 1975. pp. 127. *bibliog.* With English summary.

INTERVENTION (INTERNATIONAL LAW).

BENNOUNA (MOHAMED) Le consentement à l'ingérence militaire dans les conflits internes. Paris, 1974. pp. 235. *bibliog.*

LITTLE (RICHARD) Intervention: external involvement in civil wars. London, 1975. p. 236.

INTERVIEWING.

CONVERSE (JEAN M.) and SCHUMAN (HOWARD) Conversations at random: survey research as interviewers see it. New York, [1974]. pp. 111.

GORDEN (RAYMOND L.) Interviewing: strategy, techniques, and tactics. rev.ed. Homewood, Ill., 1975. pp. 587. *bibliog.*

KAHN (ROBERT LOUIS) and CANNELL (CHARLES F.) The dynamics of interviewing: theory, technique and cases. New York, [1957]. pp. 368. *bibliog.*

KJØLLER (METTE) Interaktionen mellem interviewer og respondent, etc. København, 1975. pp. 241. *bibliog. (Socialforskningsinstituttet. Studier. 32)* With English summaries.

INTERVIEWING IN MARKETING RESEARCH.

BELSON (WILLIAM A.) Tape recording: its effect on accuracy of response in survey interviews. London, [1967]. pp. 12. *bibliog. (London. University. London School of Economics and Political Science. Survey Research Centre. Reprint Series. 38)* (Reprinted from Journal of Marketing Research vol. 4, 1967)

INVENTIONS.

JOHNSON (PETER STEWART) The economics of invention and innovation: with a case study of the development of the hovercraft. London, 1975. pp. 329.

INVENTORIES

— **Canada — Mathematical models.**

MONTMARQUETTE (CLAUDE) A model of inventory holdings with empirical application to Canadian manufacturing industries. Montreal, 1974. fo. 63. *bibliog. (Montreal. Université. Département des Sciences Economiques. Cahiers. [No.] 7407)*

INVESTMENT BANKING

— **Ghana.**

NATIONAL INVESTMENT BANK [GHANA]. The National Investment Bank: objectives and functions. Accra, [1970?]. pp. 13.

INVESTMENT OF PUBLIC FUNDS

— **European Economic Community countries.**

EUROPEAN COMMUNITIES. Statistical Office. Regional statistics: the Communty's financial participation in investments. a., 1973- Luxembourg. *In Community languages.* Supplementary to the relevant section of EUROPEAN COMMUNITIES. Statistical Office. Regional statistics: yearbook.

— **United States — Montana.**

MONTANA. Legislative Council. 1964. The investment of public funds; a report to the thirty-ninth Legislative Assembly. [Helena], 1964. pp. 59. *(Reports. No. 14)*

INVESTMENTS.

PEASNELL (KEN V.) The usefulness of accounting information to investors. Lancaster, [1973]. pp. 29. *(Lancaster. University. International Centre for Research in Accounting. ICRA Occasional Papers. No. 1)*

FOSTER (EARL M.) Common stock investment. Lexington, Mass., [1974]. pp. 178.

BRANCH (BEN) Fundamentals of investing. Santa Barbara, [1976]. pp. 301. *bibliogs.*

— **Mathematical models.**

STEHLING (FRANK) Optimale Konsum- und Investitionsquoten. Meisenheim am Glan, [1972]. pp. 124. *bibliog.*

BALESTRIERI (GIOVANNI) Considerazioni sugli aspetti dinamici del modello neo-classico di investimento. Milano, 1973. pp. 19. *(Naples. Università. Centro di Specializzazione e Ricerche Economico-Agrarie per il Mezzogiorno. Estratti. 134)* (Reprinted from Annali della Facoltà di Scienze Politiche, Università di Pisa, 1973)

HELLWIG (KLAUS) Die Lösung ganzzahliger investitionstheoretischer Totalmodelle durch Partialmodelle. Meisenheim am Glan, [1973]. pp. 77. *bibliog.*

BOYER (RUSSELL S.) Devaluation and portfolio balance. [London], 1975. 1 pamphlet (various foliations). *bibliog.*

SPINNEWYN (FRANS) Dynamic portfolio selection: a class of models with application to financial institutions; [Ph.D. (London) thesis]. 1975. fo. 245. *bibliog.* Typescript: unpublished. This thesis is the property o London University and may not be removed from the Library.

HELLIWELL (JOHN F.) ed. Aggregate investment: selected readings. Harmondsworth, 1976. pp. 344. *bibliogs.*

— **Mathematics.**

LESZCZYŃSKI (KAZIMIERZ) Methods for selection of investment projects. Warsaw, 1974. pp. 60. *(Instytut Gospodarki Krajów Rozwijajacych Się. Teaching Papers: Advanced Course in National Economic Planning. vol. 19)*

— **Taxation — European Economic Community countries.**

SNOY (BERNARD) Taxes on direct investment income in the EEC: a legal and economic analysis. New York, 1975. pp. 349. *bibliog.*

— **Australia — New South Wales.**

NEW SOUTH WALES. Department of Decentralisation and Development. 1972. New South Wales: a handbook for investors. rev. ed. Sydney, 1972. pp. 191. *bibliog.*

— **East (Near East).**

KAPOOR (ASHOK) Foreign investments and the new Middle East: a survey of prospects, problems, and planning strategies. Princeton, [1975]. fo. 118. *bibliog.*

— **European Economic Community countries.**

GRAY (S.J.) Corporate reporting and investor decisions in the EEC: the comparability problem. Lancaster, [1973]. pp. 28. *(Lancaster. University. International Centre for Research in Accounting. ICRA Occasional Papers. No.2)*

PLASMANS (J.E.J.) Production investment behaviour: application to six EEC countries. Tilburg, 1975. pp. 333. *bibliog. (Tilburg. Katholieke Hogeschool. Tilburg Institute of Economics. Tilburg Studies on Economics. 11)*

— **Germany.**

VOIGTLAENDER (HUBERT) Investitionslenkung oder Marktsteuerung?: ein Beitrag zur politischen Ökonomie des Godesberger Programms. Bonn-Bad Godesberg, [1975]. pp. 100. *bibliog.*

— Nepal.

NEPAL INDUSTRIAL DEVELOPMENT CORPORATION. Investment Promotion and Publicity Division. Investing in Nepal: a resume of Nepal laws and regulations governing the establishment and operation of an industrial enterprise. Kathmandu, 1970 [or rather 1971]. pp. 149.

— Pakistan.

FAROOQ (DANIAL M.) The flow of investment funds in Pakistan: specialized institutions. [Islamabad], 1975. fo. 21. bibliog.

— Papua New Guinea.

AUSTRALIA. Department of External Territories. 1971. Investment pulse Papua and New Guinea. Canberra, 1971. pp. 54.

— Sri Lanka.

SRI LANKA. Development Division. 1961. Investors' guide. Colombo, 1961. pp. 41. (Bulletins. 1. Series 1 (Industrial Development))

— United States.

MARCUS (BRUCE W.) Competing for capital: a financial relations approach. New York, [1975]. pp. 265. bibliogs.

INVESTMENTS, AMERICAN.

WILKINS (MIRA) The maturing of multinational enterprise: American business abroad from 1914 to 1970. Cambridge, Mass., 1974. pp. 590. bibliog. (Harvard University. Harvard Studies in Business History. 27)

MIKESELL (RAYMOND FRECH) Nonfuel minerals: U.S. investment policies abroad. Beverly Hills, [1975]. pp. 97. bibliog. (Georgetown University. Center for Strategic and International Studies. Washington Papers. vol. 3/23)

TORNEDEN (ROGER L.) Foreign disinvestment by U.S. multinational corporations; with eight case studies. New York, 1975. pp. 156. bibliog.

— Taxation.

U.S. taxation of American business abroad: an exchange of views; [by] G.C. Hufbauer [and others]. Washington, 1975. pp. 101. (American Enterprise Institute for Public Policy Research and Stanford University. Hoover Institution on War, Revolution and Peace. AEI-Hoover Policy Studies. 16)

— America, Latin.

SWANSBROUGH (ROBERT H.) The embattled colossus: economic nationalism and United States investors in Latin America. Gainesville, Florida, 1976. pp. 261. bibliog. (Florida University. School of Inter-American Studies. Latin American Monographs. 2nd Series. 16)

— Brazil.

PEREIRA (OSNY DUARTE) A Transamazônica: pros e contras. Rio de Janeiro, 1971. pp. 368. bibliog.

— South Africa.

McHENRY (DONALD) United States firms in South Africa. Bloomington, 1975. pp. 74.

— Spain.

VAZQUEZ MONTALBAN (MANUEL) La penetracion americana en España. Madrid, [1974]. pp. 439.

— United Kingdom.

ECONOMIST INTELLIGENCE UNIT. Q[uarterly] E[conomic] R[eview] Specials. No. 23. U.S. direct investment in the U.K.: has the optimism been justified?; by Robert A. Lincoln. London, 1975. pp. 69.

INVESTMENTS, ARAB

— Africa.

CHIBWE (E.C.) Arab dollars for Africa. London, 1976. pp. 147.

INVESTMENTS, BRITISH.

COTTRELL (P.L.) British overseas investment in the nineteenth century. London, 1975. pp. 79. bibliog. (Economic History Society. Studies in Economic and Social History)

— Romania.

CONFEDERATION OF BRITISH INDUSTRY. Romania: an opportunity for joint investment; a report on a visit made by a CBI industrial delegation to Romania, October 1973, leader, Mr. Ralph Bateman. London, 1974. pp. 34.

INVESTMENTS, DUTCH

— Indonesia.

TIJDSCHRIFT VOOR ANTI-IMPERIALISME SCHOLING. Jaargang 9, nr. 1. Nederlandse investeringen in Indonesië. [Amsterdam], 1974. pp. 56.

INVESTMENTS, FOREIGN.

EDWARDS (GEORGE WILLIAM) Investing in foreign securities. New York, [1926]. pp. 373. bibliog.

INTERNATIONAL capital markets; edited by Edwin J. Elton [and] Martin J. Gruber. Amsterdam, 1975. pp. 387. bibliogs.

— Law and legislation.

INTERNATIONAL CENTRE FOR SETTLEMENT OF INVESTMENT DISPUTES. 1968-70. Convention on the Settlement of Investment Disputes between States and Nationals of Other States:...analysis of documents concerning the origin and the formulation of the Convention. Washington, 1968-70. 3 vols. In various languages.

— — Canada.

CANADA. Foreign Investment Review Agency. Annual report. a., 1974/75 (1st)- Ottawa. [In English and French].

— — Spain.

GARCÉS BRUSÉS (VENTURA) Legal aspects of foreign investments in Spain; translated by Kenneth Lyons. Barcelona, [1976]. pp. 440.

— Africa.

THOMAS (D. BABATUNDE) Importing technology into Africa: foreign investment and the supply of technological innovations. New York, 1976. pp. 202. bibliog.

— Africa, West.

NDOMA-EGBA (BASSEY) Foreign investment and economic transformation in West Africa 1870-1930, with emphasis on Nigeria. Lund, 1974. pp. 164. bibliog. (Lund. Ekonomisk-Historiska Föreningen. Skrifter. vol. 15) Ph.D. dissertation - University of Lund.

— America, Latin.

KNUDSEN (HARALD) Expropriation of foreign private investments in Latin America. Bergen, [1974]. pp. 356. bibliog.

— Argentine Republic.

ACUMULACION y centralizacion del capital en la industria argentina; [by] Elsa Cimillo [and others]. Buenos Aires, [1973]. pp. 191.

MATO (DANIEL) and COLMAN (MARTA) Caracteristicas y analisis historico de las inversiones extranjeras en la Argentina, 1930-1973. Buenos Aires, [1974]. pp. 135.

— Australia.

AUSTRALIA. Commonwealth Bureau of Census and Statistics. 1968. Overseas participation in Australian mining industry, 1963 to 1965 Canberra, [1968]. pp. 31.

— Canada.

FAYERWEATHER (JOHN) Foreign investment in Canada: prospects for national policy. White Plains, N.Y, [1973]. pp. 200.

— East (Near East).

KAPOOR (ASHOK) Foreign investments and the new Middle East: a survey of prospects, problems, and planning strategies. Princeton, [1975]. fo. 118. bibliog.

— France.

FRANCE. Délégation à l'Aménagement du Territoire et à l'Action Régionale. 1974. Investissements étrangers et aménagement du territoire: livre blanc. Paris, 1974. pp. 141. Map in end pocket.

— Ghana.

GHANA. Capital Investments Board. 1969. Investors' manual. [2nd ed.] Accra, [1969?]. pp. 47.

— Japan — Statistics.

BANK OF TOKYO. Trade and Investment Information Service Office. Revised statistical data as supplement to Setting up enterprises in Japan and...The overseas investment guidebook. Tokyo, [1975]. pp. 108.

— New Zealand.

DEANE (RODERICK S.) An economic policy dilemma: the case of foreign investment in New Zealand. Wellington, 1975. pp. 23. (Reserve Bank of New Zealand. Research Papers. No. 18)

— Nigeria.

NDOMA-EGBA (BASSEY) Foreign investment and economic transformation in West Africa 1870-1930, with emphasis on Nigeria. Lund, 1974. pp. 164. bibliog. (Lund. Ekonomisk-Historiska Föreningen. Skrifter. vol. 15) Ph.D. dissertation - University of Lund.

— Papua New Guinea.

MIKESELL (RAYMOND FRECH) Foreign investment in copper mining: case studies of mines in Peru and Papua New Guinea. Baltimore, [1975]. pp. 143.

— Peru.

MIKESELL (RAYMOND FRECH) Foreign investment in copper mining: case studies of mines in Peru and Papua New Guinea. Baltimore, [1975]. pp. 143.

— South Africa.

FOREIGN investment in South Africa: the policy debate...; [by] Charles Harvey [and others]. [London], 1975. pp. 247. (Study Project on External Investment in South Africa and Namibia (S.W. Africa). Study Project Papers. [vol. 5])

SUCKLING (JOHN) and others. Foreign investment in South Africa: the economic factor. [London], 1975. pp. 195. (Study Project on External Investment in South Africa and Namibia (S.W. Africa). Study Project Papers. [vol. 2])

— South West Africa.

The ROLE of foreign firms in Namibia: studies on external investment and black workers' conditions in Namibia; [by] Roger Murray [and others]. Uppsala, 1974. pp. 220. bibliogs. (Study Project on External Investment in South Africa and Namibia (S.W. Africa). Study Project Papers. [vol. 3])

FOREIGN investment in South Africa: the policy debate...; [by] Charles Harvey [and others]. [London], 1975. pp. 247. (Study Project on External Investment in South Africa and Namibia (S.W. Africa). Study Project Papers. [vol. 5])

— Spain.

GRANELL TRIAS (FRANCISCO) Las empresas multinacionales y el desarrollo. Barcelona, [1974]. pp. 271. bibliog.

INVESTMENTS, FOREIGN.(Cont.)

— Underdeveloped areas.

See UNDERDEVELOPED AREAS — Investments, Foreign.

— United Kingdom.

CAIRNCROSS (Sir ALEXANDER KIRKLAND) Home and foreign investment, 1870-1913: studies in capital accumulation. Hassocks, 1975. pp. 251. *Originally published in 1953.*

INVESTMENTS, SCOTTISH

— United States.

KERR (W.G.) Scottish capital on the American credit frontier. Austin, [1976]. pp. 246. *bibliog.*

— — Texas.

KERR (W.G.) Scottish capital on the American credit frontier. Austin, [1976]. pp. 246. *bibliog.*

IRAN

— Economic conditions.

BELGIUM. Office Belge du Commerce Extérieur. 1974. Iran. Bruxelles, 1974. pp. 80. *(Un Marché. 32)*

FRANCE. Direction de la Documentation. La Documentation Française. Notes et Etudes Documentaires. Nos. 4,188-4, 189. L'Iran et les pétrodollars; (Étude...due à J. Regard). Paris, 1975. pp. 78.

FESHARAKI (FEREIDUN) Development of the Iranian oil industry: international and domestic aspects. New York, 1976. pp. 315. *bibliog.*

— Economic policy.

INTERNATIONAL LABOUR OFFICE. World Employment Programme. 1973. Employment and income policies for Iran. Geneva, 1973. pp. 100.

FRANCE. Direction de la Documentation. La Documentation Française. Notes et Etudes Documentaires. Nos. 4,188-4, 189. L'Iran et les pétrodollars; (Étude...due à J. Regard). Paris, 1975. pp. 78.

— Foreign relations.

RAMAZANI (ROUHOLLAH KAREGAR) Iran's foreign policy, 1941-1973: a study of foreign policy in modernizing nations. Charlottesville, Va., 1975. pp. 507. *bibliog.*

— History.

WILBER (DONALD NEWTON) Riza Shah Pahlavi: the resurrection and reconstruction of Iran. Hicksville, N.Y., [1975]. pp. 301. *bibliog.*

— Politics and government.

WILBER (DONALD NEWTON) Riza Shah Pahlavi: the resurrection and reconstruction of Iran. Hicksville, N.Y., [1975]. pp. 301. *bibliog.*

— Population.

IRAN. Population and Manpower Bureau. Planning Division. 1973. Iran's population: past, present and future. Tehran, 1973. pp. 75. *bibliog.*

SANEY (PARVIZ) Law and population growth in Iran. Medford, Mass., 1974. pp. 33. *(Tufts University. Fletcher School of Law and Diplomacy. Law and Population Monograph Series. No.21)*

— Social conditions.

PRIGMORE (CHARLES S.) Social work in Iran since the White Revolution. University, Ala., [1976]. pp. 194. *bibliog.*

— Social policy.

FRANCE. Direction de la Documentation. La Documentation Française. Notes et Etudes Documentaires. Nos. 4,188-4, 189. L'Iran et les pétrodollars; (Étude...due à J. Regard). Paris, 1975. pp. 78.

IRAQ

— Economic policy.

IRAQ. Directorate General of Information. 1970. The 17th July revolution in two years. [Baghdad], 1970. pp. 19.

IRAQ. Directorate General of Information. 1971. The revolution in its third year. [Baghdad, 1971]. pp. 154.

IRAQ. Directorate General of Information. 1973. The revolution in its fourth year. [Baghdad], 1973. pp. 91.

— History.

KEDOURIE (ELIE) Continuity and change in modern Iraqi history. London, [1975]. pp. 6.

— Politics and government.

IRAQ. Directorate General of Information. 1970. The 17th July revolution in two years. [Baghdad], 1970. pp. 19.

IRAQ. Directorate General of Information. 1973. The revolution in its fourth year. [Baghdad], 1973. pp. 91.

BAATH ARAB SOCIALIST PARTY. Revolutionary Iraq, 1968-1973: [political report delivered to the 8th Regional Congress] by...Ahmad Hassan Al-Bakr. n.p., [1974]. pp. 263.

— Social policy.

IRAQ. Directorate General of Information. 1970. The 17th July revolution in two years. [Baghdad], 1970. pp. 19.

IRAQ. Directorate General of Information. 1971. The revolution in its third year. [Baghdad, 1971]. pp. 154.

IRAQ. Directorate General of Information. 1973. The revolution in its fourth year. [Baghdad], 1973. pp. 91.

IRELAND

— History.

WORKERS ASSOCIATION FOR THE DEMOCRATIC SETTLEMENT OF THE NATIONAL CONFLICT IN IRELAND. The myth of the "historic Irish nation". [Belfast, 1972?]. pp. 4.

A NEW history of Ireland; edited by T.W. Moody [and others] . Oxford, 1976 in progress. *bibliogs.*

HULL (ROGER H.) The Irish triangle: conflict in Northern Ireland. Princeton, [1976]. pp. 312. *bibliog.*

Ó BROIN (LEON) Revolutionary underground: the story of the Irish Republican Brotherhood, 1858-1924. Dublin, 1976. pp. 245. *bibliog.*

— — 1558-1603.

CANNY (NICHOLAS P.) The Elizabethan conquest of Ireland: a pattern established, 1565-76. Hassocks, Sussex, 1976. pp. 205. *bibliog.*

— — 1800-1899.

LEE (JOSEPH J.) The modernisation of Irish society, 1848-1918. Dublin, [1973]. pp. 180. *bibliog.*

— — 1900-1999.

LEE (JOSEPH J.) The modernisation of Irish society, 1848-1918. Dublin, [1973]. pp. 180. *bibliog.*

— — 1910-1921.

TOWNSHEND (CHARLES JEREMY NIGEL) The British campaign in Ireland, 1919-1921: the development of political and military policies. London, 1975. pp. 242. *bibliog.*

— Nationalism.

WORKERS ASSOCIATION FOR THE DEMOCRATIC SETTLEMENT OF THE NATIONAL CONFLICT IN IRELAND. The myth of the "historic Irish nation". [Belfast, 1972?]. pp. 4.

Ó BROIN (LEON) Revolutionary underground: the story of the Irish Republican Brotherhood, 1858-1924. Dublin, 1976. pp. 245. *bibliog.*

— Politics and government.

O'SULLIVAN (JAMES L.) Systems of local government and administration in Ireland. [191-]. pp. (124). *bibliog. Typescript.*

IRELAND and the Union: a short sketch of the political history of Ireland and of her economic and social condition under the Union. Dublin, [1914?]. fo. 127,pp.ix.

ROBINSON (Sir HENRY AUGUSTUS) Memories: wise and otherwise. London, 1923 repr. 1924. pp. 348.

O'BRIEN (JOSEPH V.) William O'Brien and the course of Irish politics, 1881-1918. Berkeley, [1976]. pp. 273. *bibliog.*

— Social history.

LEE (JOSEPH J.) The modernisation of Irish society, 1848-1918. Dublin, [1973]. pp. 180. *bibliog.*

IRELAND (REPUBLIC)

— Appropriations and expenditures.

NATIONAL ECONOMIC AND SOCIAL COUNCIL [EIRE]. Report on public expenditure. Dublin, Stationery Office, [1976]. pp. 80. *([Reports]. No. 21)*

WISEMAN (JACK) and STAFFORD (BERNARD) The future of public expenditures in Ireland. Dublin, Stationery Office, [1976]. pp. 90. *(National Economic and Social Council [Eire]. [Reports]. No.20)*

— Directories.

INSTITUTE OF PUBLIC ADMINISTRATION, DUBLIN. Ireland: a directory and yearbook, 1976. Dublin, [1976]. pp. 317.

— Economic policy.

OFFICE location and regional development; proceedings of a conference organised by An Foras Forbartha...Dublin, March 1973. Dublin, An Foras Forbartha, 1973. pp. 76.

— Executive departments.

EIRE. Department of the Public Service. 1974. Restructuring the Department of Transport and Power: the separation of policy and execution. Dublin, 1974. pp. 78.

— Foreign relations.

See also EUROPEAN COMMUNITIES — Ireland (Republic).

— Industries.

O'FARRELL (PATRICK N.) Regional industrial development trends in Ireland, 1960-1973. Dublin, Industrial Development Authority, 1975. pp. 66. *bibliog. (Publication Series. Paper 1)*

— Oireachtas — Privileges and immunities.

EIRE. Dail Eireann. Committee on Procedure and Privileges. 1975. Report...arising from allegations made by two members against the Minister for Local Government in the Dail. Dublin, 1975. pp. (11). *In English and Irish.*

— — Rules and practice.

EIRE. Seanad Eireann. Committee on Procedure and Privileges. 1975. Report...on amendment to standing order providing for attendance of Attorney General. Dublin, 1975. pp. 3. *In English and Irish.*

— Statistics, Vital.

EIRE. Central Statistics Office. Quarterly report on births, deaths and marriages and on certain infectious diseases. q., Oc 1875 / Mr. 1876 - Jl/D 1895 (nos. 56-128), with gaps; 1910- , with gaps. *Dublin. 1864-1921 were pd. as IRELAND. Q. return of the marriages, births and deaths registered, etc.*

— **Year-books.**

INSTITUTE OF PUBLIC ADMINISTRATION, DUBLIN. Ireland: a directory and yearbook, 1976. Dublin, [1976]. pp. 317.

IRELAND, NORTHERN
— **Census.**

IRELAND, NORTHERN. Census, 1971. Census of population, 1971: housing and household composition tables. Belfast, 1975. pp. 188.

IRELAND, NORTHERN. Census, 1971. Census of population, 1971: religion tables, Northern Ireland. Belfast, 1975. pp. 56.

IRELAND, NORTHERN. Census, 1971. Census of population, 1971: workplace and transport to work tables. Belfast, 1975. pp. 42.

IRELAND, NORTHERN. Census, 1971. Census of population, 1971: migration tables. Belfast, 1976. pp. 49.

— **Constitution.**

IRELAND, NORTHERN. Northern Ireland Convention. Report of debates. irreg., My 8 1975 (plenary session 1)- Belfast.

KNIGHT (JAMES S.) Northern Ireland: the election of the constitutional convention, May 1975. London, [1975]. pp. 63.

PICKVANCE (T.J.) Peace through equity: proposals for a permanent settlement of the Northern Ireland conflict. Birmingham, [1975]. pp. 33.

— **Convention.**

KNIGHT (JAMES S.) Northern Ireland: the election of the constitutional convention, May 1975. London, [1975]. pp. 63.

— **Economic policy.**

IRELAND, NORTHERN. Department of Housing, Local Government and Planning. Report. a., 1972/73- Belfast. *1965/66 [1st]- 1971/72 included as Report of the Ministry of Development in IRELAND, NORTHERN. Parliament. [Command papers]*

IRELAND, NORTHERN. Department of Housing, Local Government and Planning. 1975. Regional physical development strategy, 1975-95; (Northern Ireland discussion paper). Belfast, 1975. pp. 39, 1 map.

— **Historic houses, etc.**

HISTORIC BUILDINGS COUNCIL FOR NORTHERN IRELAND. Annual report. a., 1974/75(1st)- Belfast.

— **History.**

MAWHINNEY (BRIAN) and WELLS (RONALD) Conflict and Christianity in Northern Ireland. Berkhamsted, 1975. pp. 127. *bibliog.*

— **Politics and government.**

LATVIISKII GOSUDARSTVENNYI UNIVERSITET. Uchenye Zapiski. t.200. Voprosy kritiki burzhuaznoi politiki i ideologii. Riga, 1974. pp. 135. *bibliog.*

POLOZHENIE i bor'ba britanskogo rabochego klassa. Moskva, 1974. pp. 352.

IRELAND, NORTHERN. Northern Ireland Convention. Report of debates. irreg., My 8 1975 (plenary session 1)- Belfast.

BRENNAN (IRENE) Northern Ireland: a programme for action. London, [1975]. pp. 28. *(Communist Party of Great Britain. Communist Party Pamphlets)*

FISK (ROBERT) 1946- . The point of no return: the strike which broke the British in Ulster. London, 1975. pp. 264.

PICKVANCE (T.J.) Peace through equity: proposals for a permanent settlement of the Northern Ireland conflict. Birmingham, [1975]. pp. 33.

DARBY (JOHN P.) Conflict in Northern Ireland: the development of a polarised community. Dublin, 1976. pp. 268. *bibliog.*

FARRELL (MICHAEL) Northern Ireland: the orange state. London, 1976. pp. 406. *bibliog.*

HULL (ROGER H.) The Irish triangle: conflict in Northern Ireland. Princeton, [1976]. pp. 312. *bibliog.*

ROSE (RICHARD) Northern Ireland: a time of choice. London, 1976. pp. 175. *bibliog.*

— **Religion.**

IRELAND, NORTHERN. Census, 1971. Census of population, 1971: religion tables, Northern Ireland. Belfast, 1975. pp. 56.

MAWHINNEY (BRIAN) and WELLS (RONALD) Conflict and Christianity in Northern Ireland. Berkhamsted, 1975. pp. 127. *bibliog.*

— **Social conditions.**

DARBY (JOHN P.) Conflict in Northern Ireland: the development of a polarised community. Dublin, 1976. pp. 268. *bibliog.*

IRISH.

O'HANLON (THOMAS J.) The Irish: portrait of a people. London, 1976. pp. 316. *bibliog.*

IRISH IN NEW ZEALAND.

DAVIS (RICHARD P.) Irish issues in New Zealand politics, 1868-1922. Dunedin, N.Z., 1974. pp. 248. *bibliog.*

IRISH IN THE UNITED STATES.

GREELEY (ANDREW M.) That most distressful nation: the taming of the American Irish. Chicago, 1972. pp. 281.

CLARK (DENNIS) The Irish in Philadelphia: ten generations of urban experience. Philadelphia, 1973 repr. 1974. pp. 246. *bibliog.*

McCAFFREY (LAWRENCE JOHN) The Irish diaspora in America. Bloomington, Ind., [1976]. pp. 214. *bibliog.*

IRISH QUESTION.

ARMOUR (WILLIAM STAVELEY) Facing the Irish question. London, 1935. pp. 271. *bibliog.*

BRENNAN (IRENE) Northern Ireland: a programme for action. London, [1975]. pp. 28. *(Communist Party of Great Britain. Communist Party Pamphlets)*

PICKVANCE (T.J.) Peace through equity: proposals for a permanent settlement of the Northern Ireland conflict. Birmingham, [1975]. pp. 33.

LEBOW (RICHARD NED) White Britain and black Ireland: the influence of stereotypes on colonial policy. Philadelphia, [1976]. pp. 152. *bibliog.*

IRON AGE.

HARDING (DEREK WILLIAM) The iron age in lowland Britain. London, 1974. pp. 260. *bibliog.*

IRON AND STEEL WORKERS
— **Belgium.**

GOFFIN (L.) Les sidérurgistes belges de la province de Luxembourg: étude sociographique. Arlon, 1974. pp. 105. *(Fondation Universitaire Luxembourgeoise. Série "Documents")*

— **Germany.**

HOEHNE (GERD) Wir gehn nach vorn!: eRFAHRUNGSBERICHT ÜBER DIE aRBEITSKAMPFE BEI mANNESMANN. bERLIN, ?1974!. PP. 96.

SCHNEIDER (MICHAEL) ed. Auf dem Weg in die Krise: Thesen und Materialien zum Ruhreisenstreit 1928/29. Wentorf bei Hamburg, 1974. pp. 91.

— **Hong Kong.**

HONG KONG. Machine Shop and Metal Working Industrial Committee. 1972. Minimum job standards and specifications for the principal jobs in the machine shop and metal working trades. Hong Kong, 1971 [or rather 1972]. pp. 100. *In English and Chinese.*

HONG KONG. Machine Shop and Metal Working Industrial Committee. 1974. Report...on the second manpower survey of the machine shop and metal working industry, 8th November - 4th December 1971. Hong Kong, 1973 [or rather 1974] pp. 110. *In English and Chinese.*

— **United Kingdom.**

BRANDT (GERHARD) Gewerkschaftliche Interessenvertretung und sozialer Wandel: eine soziologische Untersuchung...in der britischen Eisen- und Stahlindustrie, 1886-1917. Frankfurt, [1975]. pp. 467. *bibliog. (Frankfurt am Main. Universität. Institut für Sozialforschung. Studienreihe. Band 3)*

IRON INDUSTRY AND TRADE
— **Russia.**

GOLUBTSOV (VADIM SERGEEVICH) Chernaia metallurgiia Urala v pervye gody Sovetskoi vlasti, 1917-1923 gg. Moskva, 1975. pp. 230.

— — **Karelia.**

LEVIDOVA (SOF'IA MIKHAILOVNA) Istoriia Onezhskogo (byvsh. Aleksandrovskogo) zavoda. vyp.1. Zavod v krepostnuiu epokhu. Petrozavodsk, 1938. pp. 136. *bibliog.*

— — **Siberia.**

KAPUSTIN (MIKHAIL IVANOVICH) Deiatel'nost' KPSS po sozdaniiu tret'ei metallurgicheskoi bazy strany: rukovodstvo partii razvitiem chernoi metallurgii Sibiri i Dal'nego Vostoka v period mezhdu XX i XXIII s"ezdami KPSS. Irkutsk, 1974. pp. 639.

— — **Soviet Far East.**

KAPUSTIN (MIKHAIL IVANOVICH) Deiatel'nost' KPSS po sozdaniiu tret'ei metallurgicheskoi bazy strany: rukovodstvo partii razvitiem chernoi metallurgii Sibiri i Dal'nego Vostoka v period mezhdu XX i XXIII s"ezdami KPSS. Irkutsk, 1974. pp. 639.

— — **Ukraine.**

ORLOVS'KYI (BORYS MYKHAILOVYCH) Zalizorudna promyslovist' Ukraïny v dorevoliutsiinyi period: istoryko-ekonomichnyi narys. Kyïv, 1974. pp. 183. *bibliog. With Russian summary and table of contents.*

IRRIGATION
— **Canada — Saskatchewan.**

CANADA. Department of Regional Economic Expansion. 1970. P[rairie] F[arm] R[ehabilitation] A[ct]: irrigation in southwest Saskatchewan. [Ottawa, 1970]. 1 pamphlet (unpaged).

— **Malaysia.**

EDWARDS (ROBERT HOWARD) Public agricultural finance and technological change: a Malaysian case study; [Ph. D. (London) thesis]. 1975. fo. 188. *Typescript: unpublished. This thesis is the property of London University and may not be removed from the Library.*

— **Russia — Uzbekistan.**

IRRIGATSIIA Uzbekistana. Tashkent, 1975 in progress.

KHODZHIEV (E.KH.) Istoriia orosheniia i osvoeniia Golodnoi stepi, 1917-1970 gg. Tashkent, 1975. pp. 187. *bibliog.*

— **South Africa.**

SOUTH AFRICA. Parliament. House of Assembly. Select Committe on Irrigation Matters. 1976. First and second reports (with Proceedings) (S.C.8-1976). in SOUTH AFRICA. Parliament. House of Assembly. Select Committee reports.

ISLANDS.

PLURALISM and development in island communities; report of the commonwealth seminar held in Mauritius, January 1975. [London], Commonwealth Secretariat, [1975]. pp. 94. *bibliog.*

ISLE OF MAN

— History.

KINVIG (ROBERT HENRY) The Isle of Man: a social, cultural, and political history. 3rd ed. Liverpool, 1975. pp. 198. *bibliog.*

ISLE OF WIGHT

— Economic conditions.

ISLE OF WIGHT. County Council. County structure plan: report of survey. Newport, I.W., 1976. 1 vol. (unpaged).

— Economic policy.

ISLE OF WIGHT. County Council. County structure plan: written statement. Newport, I.W., 1976. 1 vol. (unpaged).

— Social conditions.

ISLE OF WIGHT. County Council. County structure plan: report of survey. Newport, I.W., 1976. 1 vol. (unpaged).

— Social policy.

ISLE OF WIGHT. County Council. County structure plan: written statement. Newport, I.W., 1976. 1 vol. (unpaged).

ISRAEL

— Army.

LUTTWAK (EDWARD) and HOROWITZ (DAN) 1928- The Israeli army. London, 1975. pp. 461.

— Economic policy.

LERNER (ABBA PTACHYA) and BEN-SHAHAR (HAIM) The economics of efficiency and growth: lessons from Israel and the West Bank. Cambridge, Mass., [1975]. pp. 187.

— Emigration and immigration.

SAMUEL (EDWIN) 2nd Viscount Samuel. Israel's immigration cycle. London, 1976. pp. 19. *bibliog.* (Anglo-Israel Association. Pamphlets. No.54)

— Foreign opinion.

RADIO FREE EUROPE. Audience and Public Opinion Research Department. East European sympathies in the Arab-Israeli conflict. [Munich?], 1974. fo. 21.

— Foreign relations — Arab countries.

DMITRIEV (E.) and LADEIKIN (VLADIMIR PETROVICH) Put' k miru na Blizhnem Vostoke. Moskva, 1974. pp. 248.

— — United States.

GOLAN (MATTI) The secret conversations of Henry Kissinger: step-by-step diplomacy in the Middle East;...translated by Ruth Geyra Stern and Sol Stern. New York, [1976]. pp. 280.

— Government publications — Bibliography.

ISRAEL. State Archives. 1972. Israel government publications, 1948-1964. [Jerusalem], 1972. 3 pts. and Index. *In English and Hebrew.*

— Knesset.

ISRAEL. Knesset. Secretariat. 1958. The Knesset: its origin, form and procedure. Jerusalem, [1958]. pp. 24. *bibliog.*

— Military policy.

TAMARIN (GEORGES R.) The Israeli dilemma: essays on a warfare state;...edited by Johan Niezing. Rotterdam, 1973. pp. 190. *(Vrije Universiteit Brussel. Polemological Centre. Publications. 2)*

— Politics and government.

TAMARIN (GEORGES R.) The Israeli dilemma: essays on a warfare state;...edited by Johan Niezing. Rotterdam, 1973. pp. 190. *(Vrije Universiteit Brussel. Polemological Centre. Publications. 2)*

COSGRAVE (PATRICK) Impressions of Israel. London, 1975. pp. 13. *(Anglo-Israel Association. Pamphlets No. 53)*

ISAAC (RAEL JEAN) Israel divided: ideological politics in the Jewish state. Baltimore, [1976]. pp. 227. *bibliog.*

— Social conditions.

TAMARIN (GEORGES R.) The Israeli dilemma: essays on a warfare state;...edited by Johan Niezing. Rotterdam, 1973. pp. 190. *(Vrije Universiteit Brussel. Polemological Centre. Publications. 2)*

COSGRAVE (PATRICK) Impressions of Israel. London, 1975. pp. 13. *(Anglo-Israel Association. Pamphlets No. 53)*

ISRAEL and the Palestinians; [papers delivered at a conference organized by the Richardson Institute in London in 1974]; edited by Uri Davis [and others]. London, 1975. pp. 409.

ISRAEL—ARAB CONFLICT, 1948—

GADHAFI (MOAMMAR) The battle of destiny: speeches and interviews. London, 1976. pp. 137.

LORCH (NETANEL) One long war: Arab versus Jew since 1920. Jerusalem, [1976]. pp. 254. *bibliog.*

ISRAEL-ARAB WAR, 1967.

BULL (ODD) War and peace in the Middle East: the experiences and views of a U.N. observer. London, 1976. pp. 205.

— Occupied territories.

ISRAEL INFORMATION CENTRE. Information Briefings. 28. Facts about the administered areas. Jerusalem, [1973?]. pp. 168. *bibliog.*

ISRAEL-ARAB WAR, 1973.

HERZOG (CHAIM) The war of atonement. London, [1975]. pp. 300.

GOLAN (MATTI) The secret conversations of Henry Kissinger: step-by-step diplomacy in the Middle East;...translated by Ruth Geyra Stern and Sol Stern. New York, [1976]. pp. 280.

LIEBER (ROBERT J.) Oil and the Middle East war: Europe in the energy crisis. Cambridge, Mass., [1976]. pp. 75. *(Harvard University. Center for International Affairs. Harvard Studies in International Affairs. No. 35)*

ITALIAN PERIODICALS.

LEDDA (ISABELLA) and ZANELLA (GABRIELLA) I periodici di Padova, 1866-1926, liberali, radicali, socialisti. Padova, 1973. pp. 252. *(Centro per la Storia del Movimento Operaio nel Veneto, and Padua. Università. Istituto di Storia Medioevale e Moderna. Movimenti Politici e Sociali dell'Età Contemporanea nel Veneto. Collana.4)*

ITALIANS IN AUSTRALIA

— Bibliography.

AUSTRALIA. Department of Immigration. Library. 1968. Italian immigrants in Australia: a select reading list. [Canberra, 1968?]. 1 pamphlet (unfoliated).

ITALIANS IN BRAZIL.

AZEVEDO (THALES DE) Italianos e gauchos: os anos pioneiros da colonização italiana no Rio Grande do Sul. Porto Alegre, 1975. pp. 310. *bibliog.*

LORENZONI (JULIO) Memorias de um imigrante italiano; traduçao de Armida Lorenzoni Parreira. Porto Alegre, [1975]. pp. 264.

ITALIANS IN POLAND.

QUIRINI-POPŁAWSKA (DANUTA) Działalność włochów w Polsce w I połowie XVI wieku na dworze królewskim, w dyplomacji i hierarchii kościelnej. Wrocław, 1973. pp. 140. *(Polska Akademia Nauk. Oddział w Krakowie. Komisja Nauk Historycznych. Prace. Nr.32) With Italian summary.*

ITALIANS IN THE UNITED STATES.

GALLO (PATRICK J.) Ethnic alienation: the Italian-Americans. Rutherford, N.J., [1974]. pp. 254. *bibliog.*

GIOVANNETTI (ALBERTO) L'America degli italiani. [Modena, 1975]. pp. 341. *bibliog.*

ITALO-ETHIOPIAN WAR, 1935-1936.

WALEY (DANIEL) British public opinion and the Abyssinian War, 1935-6. London, 1975. pp. 176.

ITALY

— Armed forces.

CERQUETTI (ENEA) Le forze armate italiane dal 1945 al 1975: strutture e dottrine. Milano, 1975. pp. 424.

— Army.

BOLDRINI (ARRIGO) and ALESSIO (ALDO D') Esercito e politica in Italia. Roma, 1974. pp. 352.

— Biography.

ANDREUCCI (FRANCO) and DETTI (TOMMASO) Il movimento operaio italiano: dizionario biografico, 1853-1943. Roma, 1975 in progress. *bibliogs.*

— Constitution.

PESTALOZZA (LUIGI) La costituzione e lo stato: manuale di educazione civica; con la collaborazione di Franco Brumana. Roma, 1975. pp. 349.

RESCIGNO (UGO) Costituzione italiana e stato borghese. Roma, 1975. pp. 168.

— Defences.

AMMINISTRAZIONE DELLA DIFESA, L': pubblicazione trimestrale edita dal Servizio Pubblica Informazione del Ministero della Difesa [Italy]. q., Mr 1968 (1)- , with gap (Ja 1971). Roma.

— Economic conditions.

PUNTA (VENIERO DEL) I malanni dell'economia italiana: la crisi economica era prevedibile. Firenze, [1974]. pp. 304.

TAGLIACARNE (GUGLIELMO) Livello di vita e tendenze di sviluppo delle aree socio-economiche del Mezzogiorno. [Milano], 1974. pp. 66. *(Associazione per lo Sviluppo dell' Industria nel Mezzogiorno. Centro per gli Studi sullo Sviluppo Economico. Collana di Monografie)*

CIRAVEGNA (DANIELE) Dinamica dei principali settori produttivi in Italia. Torino, 1975. pp. 274. *(Fondazione Giovanni Agnelli. Progetto Politica Industriale. Quaderni di Ricerca. n.3)*

FRATIANNI (MICHELE) and others. L'economia italiana, 1974-75; con la collaborazione di Roberto Coppola e Laura Montana. Milano, [1975]. pp. 109. *(Centro Studi di Politica Economica. Collana. 3)*

La SITUAZIONE economica internazionale e le prospettive italiane: interventi di Nino Andreatta [and others]. Bologna, [1975]. pp. 111.

— Economic history.

SERENI (EMILIO) Capitalismo e mercato nazionale in Italia. 2nd ed. Roma, 1974. pp. 461.

ITALY

CIANO (CESARE) Stato ed economia in Italia tra le due guerre mondiali. [Pisa, 1975]. pp. 242. *(Pisa. Università. Istituto di Storia. Collana di Studi e Testi. 4)*

CONFLITTI sociali e accumulazione capitalistica da Giolitti alla guerra fascista: (lezioni tenute presso l'Istituto Romano per la Storia d'Italia dal Fascismo alla Resistenza). Roma, [1975]. pp. 158. *bibliog. (Istituto Romano per la Storia d'Italia dal Fascismo alla Resistenza. Testi per le 150 Ore. n.1)*

FAUCCI (RICCARDO) Finanza, amministrazione e pensiero economico: il caso della contabiità di Stato da Cavour al Fascismo. Torino, 1975. pp. 209. *(Fondazione Luigi Einaudi. Studi. 20)*

PORISINI (GIORGIO) Il capitalismo italiano nella prima guerra mondiale: [an anthology]. Firenze, 1975. pp. 179. *bibliog.*

VILLARI (LUCIO) ed. Il capitalismo italiano del Novecento: [an anthology]. 2nd ed. Roma, 1975. 2 vols. *Paged continuously.*

WEBSTER (RICHARD A.) Industrial imperialism in Italy, 1908-1915. Berkeley, 1975. pp. 392.

— Economic policy.

ITALY. Cassa per Opere Straordinarie di Pubblico Interesse nell'Italia Meridionale. 1956. Cassa per il Mezzogiorno: scopi e realizzazioni in atto. [Rome?, 1956?]. pp. 18.

MEZZOGIORNO e classe operaia; ([by] Enrico Pugliese [and others]); [proceedings of a conference held by the Centro Operaio in November 1972]. Roma, 1973 repr. 1974. pp. 136. *(Centro Operaio. Quaderni. N. 2)*

LA MALFA (UGO) La Caporetto economica. Milano, 1974. pp. 260. *Articles, letters, speeches, etc., 1968-1974.*

LANDOLFI (ANTONIO) Lo stato, la Cassa, il Mezzogiorno: la crisi dell'intervento pubblico nel Sud. Roma, [1974]. pp. 119.

LOMBARDINI (SIRO) L'economia italiana al bivio: cronache di un'alternativa mancata: [articles]. Bologna, [1974]. pp. 373. *Articles originally published 1972-1974 in Giorno.*

MEZZOGIORNO e sinistra di classe: atti del convegno sul Mezzogiorno dell'8-9 dicembre 1973, organizzato dal Centro del Manifesto e dalla Federazione del PdUP di Palermo. Palermo, [1974]. pp. 183.

PUNTA (VENIERO DEL) I malanni dell'economia italiana: la crisi economica era prevedibile. Firenze, [1974]. pp. 304.

CATALANO (FRANCO) Politica economica e classe dirigente. Milano, [1975 in progress].

BACHELET (VITTORIO) Legge e attività amministrativa nella programmazione economica. Milano, 1975. pp. 224.

BARCA (LUCIANO) and others, eds. I comunisti e l'economia italiana, 1944-1974: antologia di scritti e documenti. Bari, [1975]. pp. 447.

CACACE (NICOLA) Mezzogiorno, occupazione e sviluppo; con interventi di Pierre Carniti e Alfredo Reichlin. Venezia, 1975. pp. 125.

FRATIANNI (MICHELE) and others. L'economia italiana, 1974-75; con la collaborazione di Roberto Coppola e Laura Montana. Milano, [1975]. pp. 109. *(Centro Studi di Politica Economica. Collana. 3)*

PARETO (VILFREDO) Battaglie liberiste: raccolta di articoli e saggi comparsi sulla stampa italiana; introduzione e note di Lucio Avagliano. [Salerno, 1975]. pp. 763.

PER un progetto economico in Italia: atti del convegno di Spoleto, Chiostro di S. Nicolò, 10-12 luglio 1974; ([contributions by] Carlo M. Santoro [and others]). Venezia, [1975]. pp. 189. *bibliog. Conference sponsored by the city of Spoleto and the Regione dell'Umbria.*

SOCIETÀ ITALIANA DEGLI ECONOMISTI. Riunione Scientifica, 13a, Roma, 1972. Politiche e strumenti per l'espansione economica italiana. Milano, 1975. pp. 159.

— Emigration and immigration.

AZEVEDO (THALES DE) Italianos e gauchos: os anos pioneiros da colonização italiana no Rio Grande do Sul. Porto Alegre, 1975. pp. 310. *bibliog.*

— Foreign opinion.

SPINDLER (KATHARINA) Die Schweiz und der italienische Faschismus, 1922-1930: der Verlauf der diplomatischen Beziehungen und die Beurteilung durch das Bürgertum. Basel, 1976. pp. 304. *bibliog. Dissertation vorgelegt der Philosophisch-Historischen Fakultät der Universität Basel.*

— Foreign relations.

DECLEVA (ENRICO) L'Italia e la politica internazionale dal 1870 al 1914: l'ultima fra le grandi potenze. Milano, [1974]. pp. 194. *bibliog.*

— — Austria.

TOSCANO (MARIO) Alto Adige-South Tyrol: Italy's frontier with the German world;...edited by George A. Carbone. Baltimore, [1975]. pp. 283.

— — Russia.

KONFERENTSIIA SOVETSKIKH I ITAL'IANSKIKH ISTORIKOV, 4-aia, RIM, 1969. Rossiia i Italia: materialy IV Konferentsii sovetskikh i ital'ianskikh istorikov, Rim, 1969; Russkii i ital'ianski srednevekovyi gorod; Russko-ital'ianskie otnosheniia v 1900- 1914 gg. Moskva, 1972. pp. 477.

SERRA (ENRICO) Nitti e la Russia. Bari, [1975]. pp. 212. *(Milan. Istituto per gli Studi di Politica Internazionale. Saggi di Storia Contemporanea. 2)*

— — Switzerland.

SPINDLER (KATHARINA) Die Schweiz und der italienische Faschismus, 1922-1930: der Verlauf der diplomatischen Beziehungen und die Beurteilung durch das Bürgertum. Basel, 1976. pp. 304. *Dissertation vorgelegt der Philosophisch-Historischen Fakultät der Universität Basel.*

— — Yugoslavia.

SUCCESSFUL negotiation: Trieste 1954; an appraisal by the five participants; edited by John C. Campbell. Princeton, [1976]. pp. 181.

— Historiography.

SECHI (SALVATORE) Movimento operaio e storiografia marxista: rassegne e note critiche. Bari, [1974]. pp. 327.

VALIANI (LEO) Questioni di storia del socialismo. [2nd ed.] Torino, [1975]. pp. 427. *bibliog.*

— History.

STORIA d'Italia; coordinatori dell'opera Ruggiero Romano e Corrado Vivanti). Torino, [1972 in progress]. *bibliog.*

— — 1870— .

COLOMBO (ARTURO) Teorie politiche e dialettica democratica: saggi di storia e politica. Milano, [1974]. pp. 183. *bibliog.*

— — 1914-1945.

VALERI (NINO) Dalla "belle époque" al fascismo: momenti e personaggi. Roma, 1975. pp. 138.

MACK SMITH (DENIS) Mussolini's Roman empire. New York, 1976. pp. 322. *bibliog.*

— Industries.

ITALY. Istituto Centrale di Statistica. 1967. Numeri indici della produzione industriale, base 1966 [equals] 100. Roma, 1967. pp. 91. *(Metodi e Norme. Serie A. N.7)*

ATOR CONSULENZA AZIENDALE. Analisi generale della concentrazione industriale in Italia dalla costituzione del Mercato Comune, 1959-1968: gli indici di concentrazione impiegati nella ricerca. [Brussels, European Communities, Directorate-General for Competition, 1973]. pp. 34.

SOCIETÀ RICERCHE E STUDI. Evoluzione della concentrazione dal 1962 al 1969 in alcuni settori dell'industria italiana: metodologia; [by Piera Balliano and others]. [Brussels, European Communities, Directorate-General for Competition, 1973]. pp. 23.

BATTISTINI (ROBERTO DE) 10 grandi dell'economia italiana. Torino, 1975. pp. 95. *bibliog. (Fondazione Giovanni Agnelli. Progetto Politica Industriale. Quaderni di Ricerca. n.2)*

CONFEDERAZIONE GENERALE DELL'INDUSTRIA ITALIANA. Servizio Studi e Rilevazioni. Collana di Studi e Documentazione. 36. Aspetti quantitativi dello sviluppo industriale, 1951- 1972; (ricerca...svolta da Giuseppe Rosa). Roma, [1975]. pp. 209. *bibliog.*

CREMONESE (MASSIMO) Radiografia della media industria italiana. Torino, 1975. pp. 222.

MONOTTI (CARLO) ed. I gruppi industriali in Italia. Torino, 1975. pp. 381.

La PICCOLA e media industria nella crisi dell'economia italiana: atti del convegno tenuto a Milano 4-5-6 novembre 1974; a cura di Carlo Catena. Roma, 1975. 2 vols. *(Istituto Gramsci. Atti)*

SCARAFFIA (LUCETTA) and TESTA (DANIELA) Le industrie nel Sud. Milano, [1975]. pp. 274.

SPERONI (DONATO) Il romanzo della Confidustria. Milano, [1975]. pp. 209. *bibliog.*

WEBSTER (RICHARD A.) Industrial imperialism in Italy, 1908-1915. Berkeley, 1975. pp. 392.

— Intellectual life.

BORDONI (CARLO) Cultura e propaganda nell'Italia fascista: un saggio introduttivo con i confronti antologici da G. Gentile [and others]. Messina, 1974. pp. 192. *bibliog.*

PAPA (EMILIO RAFFAELE) Fascismo e cultura. Venezia, 1974 repr. 1975. pp. 291.

— Military policy.

BOLDRINI (ARRIGO) and ALESSIO (ALDO D') Esercito e politica in Italia. Roma, 1974. pp. 352.

— Officials and employees.

ITALY. Statutes, etc. 1961-1969. Raccolta di giurisprudenza sull'E[nte] N[azionale di] P[revidenza ed] A[ssistenza per i] Dipendenti] S[tatali], 1961-1969: aggiornamento alla raccolta 1942-1961; a cura di Raffaele Bernardo e Francesco di Rocco. Roma, 1970. pp. 207.

— Parliament.

CHIMENTI (CARLO) Il controllo parlamentare nell'ordinamento italiano. Milano, 1974. pp. 309. *(Giurisprudenza Costituzionale. Quaderni. Nuova Serie. 2)*

— — Elections.

BILANCIO delle elezioni: atti della tavola rotonda svoltasi a Roma il 23 maggio 1972. Roma, [1972?]. pp. 47. *(Movimento Gaetano Salvemini. Quaderni del Salvemini. 7)*

CACIAGLI (MARIO) and SPREAFICO (ALBERTO) eds. Un sistema politico alla prova: studi sulle elezioni politiche italiane del 1972. Bologna, [1975]. pp. 383.

— — History.

CAZZOLA (FRANCO) Governo e opposizione nel Parlamento italiano: dal centrismo al centro-sinistra; il sistema della crisi. Milano, 1974. pp. 140.

— — Rules and practice.

CIOLO (VITTORIO DI) Le fonti del diritto parlamentare: introduzione, testi normativi, note di commento, nota bibliografica. 2nd ed. Milano, 1975. pp. 537.

ITALY(Cont.)

— Politics and government.

CABOARA (LORENZO) La partitocrazia cancrena dello stato. Roma, 1975. pp. 205.

TARANTINI (DOMENICO) La maniera forte: elogio della polizia; storia del potere politico in Italia, 1860-1975. Verona, [1975]. pp. 382.

ACQUAVIVA (SABINO SAMELE) and SANTUCCIO (MARIO) Social structure in Italy: crisis of a system;...translated from the Italian by Colin Hamer. London, 1976. pp. 236. *bibliog.*

— — Caricatures and cartoons.

ISTITUTO DI STORIA MODERNA E CONTEMPORANEA. Biblioteca. Caricatura e satira politica in Italia dal 1848 all'unità: [catalogue of an exhibition], Roma, Palazzo Antici Mattei.. .1975. Roma, 1975. pp. 79, 8 plates. *With summaries in various languages.*

— — 1900— .

COLOMBO (ARTURO) Teorie politiche e dialettica democratica: saggi di storia e politica. Milano, [1974]. pp. 183. *bibliog.*

— — 1914-1945.

GRONCHI (GIOVANNI) Per una democrazia cristiana e popolare, 1919-1926; a cura di Gianfranco Merli. Roma, [1975]. pp. 358.

— — 1922-1945.

MERLI (STEFANO) Fronte antifascista e politica di classe: socialisti e comunisti in Italia, 1923-1939. Bari, [1975]. pp. 355.

— — 1945— .

ORGANIZZAZIONE COMUNISTA AVANGUARDIA OPERAIA. Conferenza Nazionale, 2a, 1972. Documenti. Milano, 1973. 2 vols. *(Quaderni. 7)*

TAMBURRANO (GIUSEPPE) Dal centrosinistra al neocentrismo, 1962-1972: i difficili rapporti tra cattolici e socialisti. Firenze, [1973]. pp. 156. *bibliog.*

CAZZOLA (FRANCO) Governo e opposizione nel Parlamento italiano: dal centrismo al centro-sinistra; il sistema della crisi. Milano, 1974. pp. 140.

ASSEMBLEA NAZIONALE CORPORATIVA, 1A, 1974. Atti. Roma, [1975]. pp. 356.

BACHELET (VITTORIO) Legge e attività amministrativa nella programmazione economica. Milano, 1975. pp. 224.

BERLINGUER (ENRICO) Unità del popolo per salvare l'Italia: (il testo integrale del rapporto tenuto al XIV Congresso nazionale del Partito comunista italiano). Roma, [1975]. pp. 111.

CAPANNA (MARIO) Monopoli, DC, compromesso storico. Milano, [1975]. pp. 286.

COLLOQUIO PER L'ALTERNATIVA, 1, 1975. Per l'alternativa, dal partito del mutamento al progetto socialista; (a cura di) Massimo Teodori. Milano, 1975. pp. 248. *Proceedings of the first conference organised by Azione e Ricerca per l'Alternativa.*

LEONE (GIOVANNI) La società italiana e le sue istituzioni: messaggi e discorsi 1971-1975; [edited by] Nino Valentino [and others]). [Vicenza, 1975]. pp. 229.

LONGO (LUIGI) Chi ha tradito la Resistenza? Roma, 1975. pp. 373.

RUFFOLO (GIORGIO) Riforme e controriforme. Roma, 1975. pp. 133.

— Relations (general) with Poland.

QUIRINI-POPŁAWSKA (DANUTA) Działalność włochów w Polsce w I połowie XVI wieku na dworze królewskim, w dyplomacji i hierarchii kościelnej. Wrocław, 1973. pp. 140. *(Polska Akademia Nauk. Oddział w Krakowie. Komisja Nauk Historycznych. Prace. Nr.32) With Italian summary.*

— Social conditions.

SERENI (EMILIO) La questione agraria nella rinascita nazionale italiana. 2nd ed. Torino, [1975]. pp. 450.

ACQUAVIVA (SABINO SAMELE) and SANTUCCIO (MARIO) Social structure in Italy: crisis of a system;...translated from the Italian by Colin Hamer. London, 1976. pp. 236. *bibliog.*

BARBERIS (CORRADO) La società italiana: classi e caste nello sviluppo economico. Milano, [1976]. pp. 355.

— Social history.

CHERUBINI (GIOVANNI) Signori, contadini, borghesi: ricerche sulla società italiana del basso Medioevo. Firenze, 1974. pp. 596.

— Social policy.

PARETO (VILFREDO) Battaglie liberiste: raccolta di articoli e saggi comparsi sulla stampa italiana; introduzione e note di Lucio Avagliano. [Salerno, 1975]. pp. 763.

RUFFOLO (GIORGIO) Riforme e controriforme. Roma, 1975. pp. 133.

ACCATTATIS (VINCENZO) Istituzioni e lotte di classe: dalla crisi dello stato di diritto al sorgere dello stato assistenziale. Milano, 1976. pp. 149.

IVANO-FRANKOVSK (OBLAST').

— Statistics.

IVANO-FRANKOVSK (OBLAST'). Statystychne Upravlinnia. Narodne hospodarstvo Ivano-Frankivs'koï oblasti v 1968 rotsi: statystychnyi zbirnyk. L'viv, 1970. pp. 182.

IVORY COAST

— Economic conditions.

EDIAFRIC-SERVICE. L'économie ivoirienne. 4th ed. Paris, 1975. pp. 253. *(Bulletin de l'Afrique Noire. Numéro Spécial)*

— Economic policy.

THENEVIN (PIERRE) Utilisation d'un modèle pour la planification régionale: application d'un modèle élaboré par la B.I.R.D. au Sud- Ouest de la Côte d'Ivoire. [Paris], 1973. pp. 94, 53. *(France. Secrétariat d'Etat aux Affaires Etrangères. Méthodologie de la Planification. 7)*

FYOT (JEAN LOUIS) L'expérience de la Côte d'Ivoire. 3rd ed. Paris, 1974. pp. 82. *(France. Secrétariat d'Etat aux Affaires Etrangères. Méthodologie de la Planification.2)*

JACKSON (ANDREW) President of the United States.

CRENSON (MATTHEW A.) The federal machine: beginnings of bureaucracy in Jacksonian America. Baltimore, [1975]. pp. 186. *bibliog.*

ROGIN (MICHAEL PAUL) Fathers and children: Andrew Jackson and the subjugation of the American Indian. New York, 1975. pp. 373, xii.

CURTIS (JAMES C.) Andrew Jackson and the search for vindication. Boston, Mass., [1976]. pp. 194. *bibliog.*

JACKSON (GEORGE LESTER).

DURDEN-SMITH (JO) Who killed George Jackson?. New York, 1976. pp. 292, xii.

JACOB (ILSE).

VEREINIGUNG DER ANTIFASCHISTEN UND VERFOLGTEN DES NAZIREGIMES, LAND HAMBURG. Jacob und Schrübbers: heute wie damals; Dokumentation zum Berufsverbotsbeschluss und zum Fall Ilse Jacob, etc. 2nd ed. Hamburg, 1972. pp. 94. *(VAN-Documentationen. 4)*

JACOBINS.

SCHEEL (HEINRICH) Die Mainzer Republik, etc. Berlin, 1975 in progress. *bibliog. (Akademie der Wissenschaften der DDR. Zentralinstitut für Geschichte. Schriften. Bände 42, etc.)*

JACOBITES.

BENNETT (GARETH VAUGHAN) The Tory crisis in church and state, 1688-1730: the career of Francis Atterbury, Bishop of Rochester. Oxford, 1975. pp. 335. *bibliog.*

FRITZ (PAUL SAMUEL) The English ministers and Jacobitism between the rebellions of 1715 and 1745. Toronto, [1975]. pp. 180. *bibliog.*

JACOBY (JOHANN).

SILBERNER (EDMUND) Johann Jacoby: Politiker und Mensch. Bonn-Bad Godesberg, [1976]. pp. 647. *bibliog. (Institut für Sozialgeschichte Braunschweig. Veröffentlichungen)*

JALE (PAPUAN PEOPLE).

KOCH (KLAUS FRIEDRICH) War and peace in Jalémó: the management of conflict in highland New Guinea. Cambridge, Mass., 1974. pp. 265. *bibliog.*

JALON (CESAR).

JALON (CESAR) Memorias politicas: periodista, ministro, presidiario. Madrid, [1973]. pp. 430.

JALUIT-GESELLSCHAFT.

TREUE (WOLFGANG) Die Jaluit-Gesellschaft auf den Marshall-Inseln, 1887-1914: ein Beitrag zur Kolonial- und Verwaltungsgeschichte in der Epoche des deutschen Kaiserreichs. Berlin, [1976]. pp. 197. *bibliog.*

JAMAICA

— Economic conditions.

KUPER (ADAM) Changing Jamaica. London, 1976. pp. 163. *bibliog.*

— Industries.

JAMAICA. Department of Statistics. Production statistics. a., 1974- Kingston. *1973 catalogued and shelved separately.*

— Politics and government.

KUPER (ADAM) Changing Jamaica. London, 1976. pp. 163. *bibliog.*

— Population.

JAMAICA. Department of Statistics. Demographic statistics. a.(formerly q.). 1971- Kingston.

KUPER (ADAM) Changing Jamaica. London, 1976. pp. 163. *bibliog.*

— Social conditions.

KUPER (ADAM) Changing Jamaica. London, 1976. pp. 163. *bibliog.*

— Statistics.

JAMAICA. Department of Statistics. Statistical abstract. q., Ja/Mr 1975 (1st)- Kingston.

JAPAN.

SOVREMENNAIA Iaponiia: [spravochnoe izdanie]. 2nd ed. Moskva, 1973. pp. 853.

— Armed forces.

BUCK (JAMES H.) ed. The modern Japanese military system. Beverly Hills, [1975]. pp. 249. *bibliog.*

— Civilization.

GIBNEY (FRANK) Japan: the fragile superpower. New York, [1975]. pp. 347.

JAPANESE.

The MODERNIZATION of Japan and Russia: a comparative study; [by] Cyril E. Black [and others]. New York, [1975]. pp. 386. *bibliog.*

— **Defences.**

BUCK (JAMES H.) ed. The modern Japanese military system. Beverly Hills, [1975]. pp. 249. *bibliog.*

ENDICOTT (JOHN E.) Japan's nuclear option: political, technical, and strategic factors. New York, 1975. pp. 289. *bibliog.*

JAPAN. Defense Agency. 1976. Defense of Japan. [Tokyo], 1976. pp. 167.

— **Economic conditions.**

BANK OF JAPAN. Economic Research Department. Special Papers. No. 56. The Japanese economy in 1974. Tokyo, 1975. pp. 35.

BOLTHO (ANDREA) Japan: an economic survey, 1953-1973. London, 1975. pp. 204. *bibliog.*

SOCIAL structures and economic dynamics in Japan up to 1980; [papers presented at a symposium held in Milan in 1974]; edited by Gianni Fodella. Milan, [1975]. pp. 322. *bibliogs. (Milan. Università Commerciale Luigi Bocconi. Institute of Economic and Social Studies for East Asia. Series on East Asian Economy and Society. vol.1)*

DENISON (EDWARD FULTON) and CHUNG (WILLIAM K.) How Japan's economy grew so fast: the sources of postwar expansion. Washington, D.C., [1976]. pp. 267.

PATRICK (HUGH TALBOT) and ROSOVSKY (HENRY) eds. Asia's new giant: how the Japanese economy works; [by] Hugh Patrick [and others]. Washington, D.C., [1976]. pp. 943.

SEMINAR ON THE FUTURE OF JAPAN, YALE UNIVERSITY, 1973. Japan: the paradox of progress; edited by Lewis Austin. New Haven, 1976. pp. 338.

— — **Statistics.**

BANK OF TOKYO. Trade and Investment Information Service Office. Revised statistical data as supplement to Setting up enterprises in Japan and...The overseas investment guidebook. Tokyo, [1975]. pp. 108.

— **Economic history.**

BOLTHO (ANDREA) Japan: an economic survey, 1953-1973. London, 1975. pp. 204. *bibliog.*

The MODERNIZATION of Japan and Russia: a comparative study; [by] Cyril E. Black [and others]. New York, [1975]. pp. 386. *bibliog.*

OKITA (SABURO) Japan in the world economy. Tokyo, 1975. pp. 235.

DENISON (EDWARD FULTON) and CHUNG (WILLIAM K.) How Japan's economy grew so fast: the sources of postwar expansion. Washington, D.C., [1976]. pp. 267.

— **Economic policy.**

KITAMURA (HIROSHI) Choices for the Japanese economy. London, [1976]. pp. 211. *bibliog.*

KOJIMA (OSAMU) ed. Studies in the industrial economics; edited on behalf of Institute of Industrial Research, Kwansei Gakuin University. Kyoto, 1976. pp. 134.

PATRICK (HUGH TALBOT) and ROSOVSKY (HENRY) eds. Asia's new giant: how the Japanese economy works; [by] Hugh Patrick [and others]. Washington, D.C., [1976]. pp. 943.

— **Foreign economic relations.**

BRYANT (WILLIAM E.) Japanese private economic diplomacy: an analysis of business- government linkages. New York, 1975. pp. 138. *bibliog.*

OKITA (SABURO) Japan in the world economy. Tokyo, 1975. pp. 235.

— — **United States.**

JAPAN-U.S. ASSEMBLY, 1974. The Japan-U.S. Assembly: proceedings of a conference on Japan-U.S. economic policy; (sponsored by the Conference Board on U.S.-Japan Economic Policy). Washington, [1975]. pp. 154.

ROEMER (JOHN E.) U.S.-Japanese competition in international markets: a study of the trade-investment cycle in modern capitalism. Berkeley, [1975]. pp. 242. *bibliog. (California University. Institute of International Studies. Research Series. No. 22)*

— **Foreign opinion, American.**

MUTUAL images: essays in American-Japanese relations [given at a conference held on Kauai, Hawaii in 1972] (by Priscilla A. Clapp [and others]); edited by Akira Iriye. Cambridge, Mass., 1975. pp. 304. *(Harvard University. Harvard Studies in American-East Asian Relations. 7)*

— **Foreign relations.**

ENDICOTT (JOHN E.) Japan's nuclear option: political, technical, and strategic factors. New York, 1975. pp. 289. *bibliog.*

MUELLER (PETER G.) and ROSS (DOUGLAS A.) China and Japan: emerging global powers. New York, 1975. pp. 218. *bibliog.*

— — **Asia.**

LEBRA (JOYCE CHAPMAN) ed. Japan's Greater East Asia Co-Prosperity Sphere in World War II: selected readings and documents. Kuala Lumpur, 1975. pp. 212. *bibliog.*

— — **China.**

CHOW (JEN HWA) China and Japan: the history of Chinese diplomatic missions in Japan 1877-1911. Singapore, 1975. pp. 317. *bibliog.*

SLADKOVSKII (MIKHAIL IOSIFOVICH) China and Japan, past and present; edited and translated by Robert F. Price. Gulf Breeze, Fla., 1975. pp. 286.

— — **Peru.**

GARDINER (CLINTON HARVEY) The Japanese and Peru, 1873-1973. Albuquerque, [1975]. pp. 202. *bibliog.*

— — **Russia.**

KIM (YOUNG C.) Japanese-Soviet relations: interaction of politics, economics and national security. Beverly Hills, [1974]. pp. 88. *bibliog. (Georgetown University. Center for Strategic and International Studies. Washington Papers. vol. 2/21)*

— **History — 1900— .**

OCHERKI noveishei istorii Iaponii. Moskva, 1957. pp. 367.

— — **1945— .**

GIBNEY (FRANK) Japan: the fragile superpower. New York, [1975]. pp. 347.

— — **1945-1952, Allied occupation.**

OPPLER (ALFRED CHRISTIAN) Legal reform in occupied Japan: a participant looks back. Princeton, [1976]. pp. 345.

— **Industries.**

CAVES (RICHARD E.) and UEKUSA (MASU) Industrial organization in Japan. Washington, D.C., [1976]. pp. 169.

— **Military policy.**

ENDICOTT (JOHN E.) Japan's nuclear option: political, technical, and strategic factors. New York, 1975. pp. 289. *bibliog.*

— **Officials and employees.**

AUSTIN (LEWIS) Saints and samurai: the political culture of the American and Japanese elites. New Haven, 1975. pp. 197. *(Yale University. Yale Studies in Political Science. 27)*

— **Politics and government.**

CONFERENCE ON JAPANESE ORGANIZATION AND DECISION-MAKING, HAWAII, 1973. Modern Japanese organization and decision-making; edited by Ezra F. Vogel. Berkeley, [1975]. pp. 340. *Proceedings of a conference sponsored by the Joint Committee on Japanese Studies of the American Council of Learned Societies and the Social Science Research Council.*

CROZIER (MICHEL) and others. The crisis of democracy...; report on the governability of democracies to the Trilateral Commission. [New York], 1975. pp. 211.

The MODERNIZATION of Japan and Russia: a comparative study; [by] Cyril E. Black [and others]. New York, [1975]. pp. 386. *bibliog.*

MASSEY (JOSEPH A.) Youth and politics in Japan. Lexington, Mass., [1976]. pp. 233. *bibliog.*

MITCHELL (RICHARD HANKS) Thought control in prewar Japan. Ithaca, 1976. pp. 226. *bibliog.*

SEMINAR ON THE FUTURE OF JAPAN, YALE UNIVERSITY, 1973. Japan: the paradox of progress; edited by Lewis Austin. New Haven, 1976. pp. 338.

— **Population.**

JAPAN. Institute of Population Problems. English Pamphlet Series. Tokyo, 1972 in progress.

JAPAN. Institute of Population Problems. Research Series. [Tokyo], 1974 in progress. *In English and Japanese.*

— **Relations (general) with China.**

POSPELOV (BORIS VASIL'EVICH) Iaponskaia obshchestvenno-politicheskaia mysl' i maoizm: kritika antimarksistskikh kontseptsii sushchnosti maoizma. Moskva, 1975. pp. 224. *bibliog.*

— **Relations (general) with the United States.**

JOHNSON (SHEILA K.) American attitudes toward Japan, 1941-1975. Washington, 1975. pp. 114. *(American Enterprise Institute for Public Policy Research and Stanford University. Hoover Institution on War, Revolution and Peace. AEI-Hoover Policy Studies. 15)*

MUTUAL images: essays in American-Japanese relations [given at a conference held on Kauai, Hawaii in 1972] (by Priscilla A. Clapp [and others]); edited by Akira Iriye. Cambridge, Mass., 1975. pp. 304. *(Harvard University. Harvard Studies in American-East Asian Relations. 7)*

— **Social conditions.**

FUSÉ (TOYOMASA) ed. Modernization and stress in Japan. Leiden, 1975. pp. 94. *bibliogs.*

PLATH (DAVID WILLIAM) ed. Adult episodes in Japan. Leiden, 1975. pp. 90. *bibliogs.*

SOCIAL structures and economic dynamics in Japan up to 1980; [papers presented at a symposium held in Milan in 1974]; edited by Gianni Fodella. Milan, [1975]. pp. 322. *bibliogs. (Milan. Università Commerciale Luigi Bocconi. Institute of Economic and Social Studies for East Asia. Series on East Asian Economy and Society. vol.1)*

PATRICK (HUGH TALBOT) and ROSOVSKY (HENRY) eds. Asia's new giant: how the Japanese economy works; [by] Hugh Patrick [and others]. Washington, D.C., [1976]. pp. 943.

SEMINAR ON THE FUTURE OF JAPAN, YALE UNIVERSITY, 1973. Japan: the paradox of progress; edited by Lewis Austin. New Haven, 1976. pp. 338.

JAPANESE.

PLATH (DAVID WILLIAM) ed. Adult episodes in Japan. Leiden, 1975. pp. 90. *bibliogs.*

JAPANESE IN CHINA.

LI (LINCOLN) The Japanese army in North China, 1937-1941: problems of political and economic control. Tokyo, 1975. pp. 278. *bibliog.*

JAPANESE IN THE UNITED STATES.

KITANO (HARRY HARUS LEE) Japanese Americans: the evolution of a subculture. 2nd ed. Englewood Cliffs, N.J., [1976]. pp. 231. *bibliog.*

JASPER (ALBERT STANLEY).

JASPER (ALBERT STANLEY) A Hoxton childhood;...[with] line drawings by James Boswell. London, [1969] repr. 1975. pp. 128.

JAURES (JEAN).

CHALLAYE (FELICIEN) Jaurès. Paris, [1936]. pp. 319.

JEHOVAH'S WITNESSES.

HODGES (TONY) Jehovah's Witnesses in Central Africa. London, 1976. pp. 16. *bibliog. (Minority Rights Group. Reports. No.29)*

JEWISH-ARAB RELATIONS.

CONGRES POPULAIRE PALESTINIEN, CAIRO, 1972. Le programme politique de la révolution palestinienne. Damas, 1972. fo. 15.

CONGRES POPULAIRE PALESTINIEN, CAIRO, 1972. Projet d'unification des fractions de la résistance palestinienne. Damas, 1972. fo. 21.

HARKABI (YEHOSHAFAT) Palestinians and Israel. New York, [1974]. pp. 285.

LIEBMAN (SEYMOUR B.) The Middle East: a return to facts. [New York, 1974]. pp. 148.

BEN-MEIR (ALON) The Middle East: imperatives and choices. Mount Vernon, N.Y., [1975]. pp. 221.

DOBSON (CHRISTOPHER) Black September: its short, violent history. London, [1975]. pp. 192.

The ELUSIVE peace in the Middle East; edited by Malcolm H. Kerr. Albany, 1975. pp. 347.

FRIEDLAENDER (SAUL) and HUSSEIN (MAHMOUD) pseud. [i.e. Bahgat EL NADI and Adel RIFAAT] Arabs and Israelis: a dialogue;...moderated by Jean Lacouture; translated by Paul Auster and Lydia Davis. New York, 1975. pp. 223. *Translation of Arabes et Israéliens in which the authors' names appeared in reverse order.*

GLASSMAN (JON D.) Arms for the Arabs: the Soviet Union and war in the Middle East. Baltimore, [1975]. pp. 243. *bibliog.*

BULL (ODD) War and peace in the Middle East: the experiences and views of a U.N. observer. London, 1976. pp. 205.

ISAAC (RAEL JEAN) Israel divided: ideological politics in the Jewish state. Baltimore, [1976]. pp. 227. *bibliog.*

LORCH (NETANEL) One long war: Arab versus Jew since 1920. Jerusalem, [1976]. pp. 254. *bibliog.*

JEWS.

SANDMEL (SAMUEL) After the ghetto: Jews in western culture, art and intellect. Syracuse, N.Y., 1974. pp. 20. *(Syracuse University. B.G. Rudolph Lectures in Judaic Studies. 1974)*

HEBREW UNIVERSITY. Institute of Contemporary Jewry, and INSTITUTE OF JEWISH AFFAIRS. Studies in Jewish demography: survey for 1969-1971; edited by U.O. Schmelz [and others]. Jerusalem, 1975. pp. 353.

— History.

BEN-SASSON (HAIM HILLEL) ed. A history of the Jewish people. London, [1976]. pp. 1170. *bibliog.*

— Persecutions.

[ZIONIST ORGANISATION]. Die Judenpogrome in Russland; herausgegeben im Auftrag des Zionistischen Hilfsfonds in London von der zur Erforschung der Pogrome eingesetzten Kommission; [by A. Linden and others]. Köln, 1910. 2 vols.

DAWIDOWICZ (LUCY S.) The war against the Jews, 1933-1945. London, [1975]. pp. 460. *bibliog.*

— Political and social conditions.

VLAVIANOS (BASIL JOHN) and GROSS (FELIKS) eds. Struggle for tomorrow: modern political ideologies of the Jewish people; ([by] Gregory Aronson [and others]). New York, [1954]. pp. 303. *bibliogs.*

— Restoration.

VLAVIANOS (BASIL JOHN) and GROSS (FELIKS) eds. Struggle for tomorrow: modern political ideologies of the Jewish people; ([by] Gregory Aronson [and others]). New York, [1954]. pp. 303. *bibliogs.*

ISRAEL and the Palestinians; [papers delivered at a conference organized by the Richardson Institute in London in 1974]; edited by Uri Davis [and others]. London, 1975. pp. 409.

REINHARZ (JEHUDA) Fatherland or promised land: the dilemma of the German Jew, 1893-1914. Ann Arbor, [1975]. pp. 328. *bibliog.*

VITAL (DAVID) The origins of Zionism. Oxford, 1975. pp. 396. *bibliog.*

JEWS IN AUSTRIA.

BOTZ (GERHARD) Wohnungspolitik und Judendeportation in Wien, 1938 bis 1945: zur Funktion des Antisemitismus als Ersatz nationalsozialistischer Sozialpolitik. Wien, 1975. pp. 200. *bibliog. (Salzburg. Universität. Historisches Institut. Veröffentlichungen. 13)*

JEWS IN EUROPE.

DAWIDOWICZ (LUCY S.) The war against the Jews, 1933-1945. London, [1975]. pp. 460. *bibliog.*

JEWS IN GERMANY.

LUETH (ERICH) Gabriel Riesser, 1806-1863: ein grosser Jude, Hamburger und deutscher Patriot. Hamburg, 1963. pp. 55.

BOLKOSKY (SIDNEY M.) The distorted image: German Jewish perceptions of Germans and Germany, 1918-1935. New York, [1975]. pp. 247. *bibliog.*

LAUFNER (RICHARD) and RAUCH (ALBERT) Die Familie Marx und die Trierer Judenschaft. Trier, [1975]. pp. 40. *(Karl-Marx-Haus. Schriften. 14)*

REINHARZ (JEHUDA) Fatherland or promised land: the dilemma of the German Jew, 1893-1914. Ann Arbor, [1975]. pp. 328. *bibliog.*

JEWS IN ITALY.

CIRIACONO (SALVATORE) Olio ed ebrei nella Repubblica veneta del Settecento. Venezia, 1975. pp. 208. *(Deputazione di Storia Patria per le Venezie. Miscellanea di Studi e Memorie. vol. 16)*

JEWS IN POLAND.

LANDAU (SAUL RAPHAEL) Unter jüdischen Proletariern: Reiseschilderungen aus Ostgalizien und Russland. Wien, 1898. pp. 87.

SAKOWSKA (RUTA) Ludzie z dzielnicy zamkniętej: 'zydzi w Warszawie w okresie hitlerowskiej okupacji październik 1939 - marzec 1943. Warszawa, 1975. pp. 399. *bibliog. With English and Russian tables of contents.*

EISENBACH (ARTUR) Wielka Emigracja wobec kwestii 'zydowskiej, 1831-1849. Warszawa, 1976. pp. 475.

JEWS IN RUSSIA.

LANDAU (SAUL RAPHAEL) Unter jüdischen Proletariern: Reiseschilderungen aus Ostgalizien und Russland. Wien, 1898. pp. 87.

[ZIONIST ORGANISATION]. Die Judenpogrome in Russland; herausgegeben im Auftrag des Zionistischen Hilfsfonds in London von der zur Erforschung der Pogrome eingesetzten Kommission; [by A. Linden and others]. Köln, 1910. 2 vols.

FLEGON (ALEC) and NAUMOV (IU.) compilers. Russkii antisemitizm i evrei: sbornik. London, [1968]. pp. 224.

KLEJNER (ISRAEL) Anekdotychna trahediia. Miunkhen, 1974. pp. 156.

JEWS IN THE UNITED KINGDOM.

KOSMIN (BARRY A.) and GRIZZARD (NIGEL) Jews in an inner London borough: a study of the Jewish population of the London borough of Hackney based on the 1971 census. London, [1975]. pp. 39.

WILLIAMS (BILL) The making of Manchester Jewry, 1740-1875. Manchester, [1976]. pp. 454. *bibliog.*

JEWS IN THE UNITED STATES.

FEINGOLD (HENRY L.) Zion in America: the Jewish experience from colonial times to the present. New York, [1974]. pp. 357. *bibliog.*

LEVINE (NAOMI) and HOCHBAUM (MARTIN) eds. Poor Jews: an American awakening. New Brunswick, [1974]. pp. 206.

GINSBERG (YONA) Jews in a changing neighborhood: the study of Mattapan. New York, [1975]. pp. 214. *bibliog.*

HEITZMANN (WILLIAM RAY) American Jewish voting behavior: a history and analysis. San Francisco, 1975. pp. 121. *bibliog.*

JOB ANALYSIS.

MEASUREMENT of human resources: (based on papers presented to a symposium held in Lisbon, June 1973, and sponsored by N.A.T.O); edited by W.T. Singleton and P. Spurgeon. London, 1975. pp. 370. *bibliogs.*

JOB EVALUATION.

NIGERIA. Public Service Review Commission. 1974. Report on grading and pay. vol.3. 1972-74. Lagos, 1974. pp. 446.

HUSBAND (TOM M.) Work analysis and pay structure. London, [1976]. pp. 233. *bibliog.*

JOB SATISFACTION.

DENMARK. Arbejdsmiljøgruppen. Rapporter. København, 1973 in progress.

LAWLER (EDWARD E.) Motivation in work organizations. Monterey, [1973]. pp. 224. *bibliog.*

The QUALITY of working life...; [edited by] Louis E. Davis [and] Albert B. Cherns and associates. New York, [1975]. 2 vols. *Papers based on the International Conference on the Quality of Working Life, Harriman, New York, 1972.*

SCHEER (LORE) Zufriedenheit am Arbeitsplatz. [Vienna, 1975]. pp. 56. *bibliog. (Arbeitsgemeinschaft für Lebensniveauvergleiche. Was Heisst Gut Leben? 5) With English summary.*

SHAMIR (BOAS) A study of working environments and attitudes to work of employees in a number of British hotels. 1975. fo.304. *bibliog. Typescript. Ph.D. (London) thesis: unpublished. This thesis is the property of London University and may not be removed from the Library.*

GLASER (EDWARD M.) Productivity gains through worklife improvements. New York, [1976]. pp. 342. *bibliog.*

JOGJAKARTA

— Economic conditions.

UNITED NATIONS. Centre for Regional Development, Nagoya. 1975. Regional development of Yogyakarta: a comprehensive planning report. Jakarta, Directorate General of Housing, Building, Planning and Urban Development, [1975]. 4 vols. (in 8 pts.). *Vol.1 Book 4 is out of print.*

— Economic policy.

UNITED NATIONS. Centre for Regional Development, Nagoya. 1975. Regional development of Yogyakarta: a comprehensive planning report. Jakarta, Directorate General of Housing, Building, Planning and Urban Development, [1975]. 4 vols. (in 8 pts.). *Vol.1 Book 4 is out of print.*

— Social conditions.

UNITED NATIONS. Centre for Regional Development, Nagoya. 1975. Regional development of Yogyakarta: a comprehensive planning report. Jakarta, Directorate General of Housing, Building, Planning and Urban Development, [1975]. 4 vols. (in 8 pts.). *Vol.1 Book 4 is out of print.*

— Social policy.

UNITED NATIONS. Centre for Regional Development, Nagoya. 1975. Regional development of Yogyakarta: a comprehensive planning report. Jakarta, Directorate General of Housing, Building, Planning and Urban Development, [1975]. 4 vols. (in 8 pts.). *Vol.1 Book 4 is out of print.*

JOHANSEN (HANS).

RINGNES (HAAGEN) Hans i Halvorstua: arbeiderveteranen Hans Johansen forteller. [Oslo], 1975. pp. 163.

JOHNSON (LYNDON BAINES) President of the United States.

KEARNS (DORIS) Lyndon Johnson and the American dream. New York, [1976]. pp. 432.

JOHORE

— History.

ANDAYA (LEONARD Y.) The kingdom of Johor, 1641-1728. Kuala Lumpur, 1975. pp. 394. *bibliog.*

JOINT ADVENTURES

— Russia.

KOSNIK (JOSEPH T.) Natural gas imports from the Soviet Union: financing the North Star Joint Venture Project. New York, 1975. pp. 214. *bibliog.*

— Yugoslavia.

LAMERS (E.A.A.M.) Joint ventures between Yugoslav and foreign enterprises. Tilburg, 1976. pp. 256. *bibliog. (Tilburg. Katholieke Hogeschool. Tilburg Institute of Economics. Tilburg Studies on Economics. 16)*

JOLIOT—CURIE (JEAN FRÉDÉRIC).

GOLDSMITH (MAURICE) Frédéric Joliot-Curie: a biography. London, 1976. pp. 260. *bibliog.*

JONES (MARY HARRIS).

FETHERLING (DALE) Mother Jones the miners' angel: a portrait. Carbondale, [1974]. pp. 263. *bibliog.*

JORDAN

— Economic policy.

JORDAN. National Planning Council. 1976. Five year plan for economic and social development. 1976-1980. [Amman? 1976?]. pp. 785.

— Foreign relations.

FADDAH (MOHAMMAD IBRAHIM) The Middle East in transition: a study of Jordan's foreign policy. London, [1974]. pp. 339. *bibliog.*

— — United Kingdom.

KIRKBRIDE (Sir ALEC) From the wings: Amman memoirs 1947-1951. London, 1976. pp. 159.

— History — Sources.

KIRKBRIDE (Sir ALEC) From the wings: Amman memoirs 1947-1951. London, 1976. pp. 159.

— Social policy.

JORDAN. National Planning Council. 1976. Five year plan for economic and social development. 1976-1980. [Amman? 1976?]. pp. 785.

JORDAN VALLEY.

HAZELTON (JARED E.) The impact of the East Ghor canal project on land consolidation, distribution and tenure. Amman, 1974. fo. 49. *(Royal Scientific Society [Jordan]. Economic Research Department. Jordan Economic Studies. 04-06)*

JOURNALISM

— Political aspects.

STEWART (DONALD HENDERSON) The opposition press of the Federalist period. Albany, [1969]. pp. 957. *bibliog.*

— Bulgaria.

BULGARSKATA zhurnalistika po leninski put. Sofiia, 1970. pp. 271.

— France.

BORIS (CLAUDE) Les tigres de papier: crise de la presse et autocritique du journalisme. Paris, [1975]. pp. 315.

— Russia.

BEREZINA (VALENTINA GRIGOR'EVNA) Belinskii i voprosy istorii russkoi zhurnalistiki. Leningrad, 1973. pp. 144.

JOURNALISM, COMMERCIAL

— France.

PIGASSE (JEAN PAUL) La difficulté d'informer: vérités sur la presse économique. Paris, [1975]. pp. 334. *bibliog.*

JUCHEN (TRIBE).

LEN'KOV (VITALII DMITRIEVICH) Metallurgiia i metalloobrabotka u chzhurchzhenei v XII veke: po materialam issledovanii Shaiginskogo gorodishcha; otvetstvennyi redaktor... E.V. Shavkunov. Novosibirsk, 1974. pp. 172,[xiii].

JUDAISM AND SOCIAL PROBLEMS.

ASPEN INTERRELIGIOUS CONSULTATION, ASPEN, 1974. Global justice and development: report of the...consultation...; sponsored by the Overseas Development Council with the support of the Aspen Institute for Humanistic Studies and the Johnson Foundation. Washington, [1975]. pp. 175.

JUDGES

— Czechoslovakia.

ULČ (OTTO) Malá doznání okresního soudce. Toronto, 1974. pp. 321.

— Europe.

JUSTICE et politique: actes du colloque tenu à l'I.E.P. de Strasbourg les 6, 7 et 8 avril 1973 sous la direction de Gérard Duprat. [Strasbourg, 1974]. pp. 262. *(Strasbourg. Université de Strasbourg III. Institut d'Etudes Politiques. Cahiers. Nouvelle Série. 3)*

— United Kingdom.

SHETREET (SHIMON) Judges on trial: a study of the appointment and accountability of the English judiciary: edited by Gordon J. Borrie. Amsterdam, 1976. pp. 432.

JUDGMENT.

HUMAN judgment and decision processes; edited by Martin F. Kaplan and Steven Schwartz. New York, 1975. pp. 325. *bibliogs.* Expanded versions of papers delivered at a conference held at Northern Illinois University in October 1974.

JUDGMENT (ETHICS).

LEICHMAN (GLENN ALAN) The effect of age and educational environment on the development of achievement evaluations and moral judgements. [1976]. fo. 243. *bibliog. Typescript.* Ph.D. (London) thesis: unpublished. This thesis is the property of London University and may not be removed from the Library.

JUDGMENTS, DECLARATORY.

YOUNG (P.W.) Declaratory orders. Sydney, 1975. pp. 205.

JUDGMENTS, FOREIGN

— Europe.

COUNCIL OF EUROPE. 1975. The practical guide to the recognition and enforcement of foreign judicial decisions in civil and commercial law. Strasbourg, 1975. pp. 500.

— European Economic Community countries.

WESER (MARTHA) Convention communautaire sur la compétence judiciaire et l'exécution des décisions, complété par l'étude des droits internes et des traités bilatéraux des Etats contractants. Bruxelles, 1975. pp. 773. *bibliogs. (Centre Interuniversitaire de Droit Comparé. [Publications]. 19)*

JUDICIAL ASSISTANCE

— Europe.

EUROPEAN COMMITTEE ON CRIME PROBLEMS. 1971. Problems arising from the practical application of the European Convention on Mutual Assistance in Criminal Matters. Strasbourg, Council of Europe, 1971. pp. 111.

— Germany.

ROGGEMANN (HERWIG) Strafrechtsanwendung und Rechtshilfe zwischen beiden deutschen Staaten: Grundlagen, Entwicklung und rechtspolitische Aspekte einer Neuordnung des Strafrechtsverkehrs zwischen Bundesrepublik und DDR. Berlin, 1975. pp. 124. *(Berlin. Freie Universität. Osteuropa-Institut. Rechtswissenschaftliche Veröffentlichungen. Band 5)*

JUDICIAL DISCRETION

— Europe.

DAVIS (KENNETH CULP) and others. Discretionary justice in Europe and America, [by] K.C. Davis and European associates. Urbana, [1976]. pp. 203.

— United States.

DAVIS (KENNETH CULP) and others. Discretionary justice in Europe and America, [by] K.C. Davis and European associates. Urbana, [1976]. pp. 203.

JUDICIAL REVIEW

— Poland.

PALIWODA (JÓZEF) Nadzór ogólny prokuratury, według stanu prawnego na 31.XII. 1960. Warszawa, 1961. pp. 211. *bibliog.*

— Russia.

PROKURORSKII nadzor po grazhdanskim delam. 2nd ed. Moskva, 1975. pp. 352.

SAVITSKII (VALERII MIKHAILOVICH) Ocherk teorii prokurorskogo nadzora v ugolovnom sudoproizvodstve. Moskva, 1975. pp. 383.

JUDICIAL STATISTICS

JUDICIAL STATISTICS

— Methodology.

BATALINA (TAT'IANA SERGEEVNA) Nekotorye metodologicheskie voprosy sudebnoi statistiki. Leningrad, 1975. pp. 56. *bibliog.*

JURA

— Nationalism.

HUGUELET (FRANCIS) Pourquoi je suis autonomiste: un jeune Jurassien à ses compatriotes... 2nd ed., [Delémont, imprint], 1967. pp. 61. *bibliog.*

BEGUELIN (ROLAND) and SCHAFFTER (ROGER) L'autodisposition du peuple jurassien et ses conséquences. [Delémont], 1974. pp. 106.

THUERER (DANIEL) Das Selbstbestimmungsrecht der Völker, mit einem Exkurs zur Jurafrage. Bern, 1976. pp. 256. *bibliog.*

JURISDICTION (INTERNATIONAL LAW).

SCIENCE, technology and sovereignty in the Polar regions: [revised papers of a colloquium held in Washington, 1973]; edited by Gerald S. Schatz. Lexington, Mass., [1974]. pp. 215.

CIOBANU (DAN) Preliminary objections related to the jurisdiction of the United Nations political organs. The Hague, 1975. pp. 230.

WESER (MARTHA) Convention communautaire sur la compétence judiciaire et l'exécution des décisions, complété par l'étude des droits internes et des traités bilatéraux des Etats contractants. Bruxelles, 1975. pp. 773. *bibliogs. (Centre Interuniversitaire de Droit Comparé. [Publications]. 19)*

JURISPRUDENCE.

OPAŁEK (KAZIMIERZ) Problemy metodologiczne nauki prawa. Warszawa, 1962. pp. 366. *With Russian and English summaries.*

DIAS (REGINALD WALTER MICHAEL) Jurisprudence. 4th ed. London, 1976. pp. 709. *bibliogs.*

JURISTIC PERSONS

— France.

DELCROS (BERTRAND) L'unité de la personnalité juridique de l'état: étude sur les services non personnalisés de l'état. Paris, 1976. pp. 322. *bibliog.*

— Romania.

STĂNESCU (VASILE) and CONSTANTINESCU (MIHAI) Unitatea economică socialistă: raportul dintre gestiunea economică, capacitatea juridică şi subiectul de drept. Bucureşti, 1974. pp. 207. *bibliog. With English summary.*

JUST WAR DOCTRINE.

See WAR.

JUSTICE.

MITCHISON (NAOMI MARGARET) Sittlichkeit. London, [1975]. pp. 19. *(London. University. Birkbeck College. Haldane Memorial Lectures. 38)*

ROSEN (FREDERICK) The political context of Aristotle's categories of justice. [Assen], 1975. pp. 12. *(Reprint from , Phronesis, vol. 20, no. 3, 1975)*

JUSTICE, ADMINISTRATION OF.

ABRAHAM (HENRY JULIAN) The judicial process: an introductory analysis of the courts of the United States, England and France. 3rd ed. New York, 1975. pp. 543. *bibliog.*

— Canada — Quebec.

QUEBEC (PROVINCE). Department of Justice. 1975. La justice contemporaine. [Quebec, 1975]. pp. 360.

— Czechoslovakia.

ULČ (OTTO) Malá doznání okresního soudce. Toronto, 1974. pp. 321.

— Europe.

COUNCIL OF EUROPE. 1975. Judicial organisation in Europe. Strasbourg, 1975. pp. 159.

— Finland.

UOTILA (JAAKKO) ed. The Finnish legal system. Helsinki, 1966. pp. 263. *bibliogs. (Suomalainen Lakimiesyhdistys. Julkaisuja. [D- Sarja: Ius Finlandiae]. No. 26)*

— Germany.

BOBERACH (HEINZ) ed. Richterbriefe: Dokumente zur Beeinflussung der deutschen Rechtsprechung, 1942-1944;...mit Beiträgen von Robert M.W. Kempner und Theo Rasehorn. Boppard am Rhein, 1975. pp. 515. *(Germany (Bundesrepublik). Bundesarchiv. Schriften. 21)*

— Russia.

FARFEL' (ARON SAMOILOVICH) Bor'ba narodnykh mass protiv kontrrevoliutsionnoi iustitsii Vremennogo pravitel'stva. Minsk, 1969. pp. 119. *bibliog.*

— Tasmania.

TASMANIA. Commonwealth Bureau of Census and Statistics. Tasmanian Office. Public justice. a., 1973/74 (1st)- Hobart. *Formerly included in TASMANIA. Commonwealth Bureau of Census and Statistics. Tasmanian Office. Social.*

TASMANIA. Crown Advocate. Annual report. a., 1973/74 [1st]- Hobart. *Included in TASMANIA. Parliament. Journals and printed papers.*

— United Kingdom.

DENNING (ALFRED THOMPSON) Baron Denning. Let justice be done: an oration delivered at Birkbeck College, London, 3rd December 1974, by the President of the College in celebration of the 151st anniversary of its foundation. [London, 1974]. pp. 16. *(London. University. Birkbeck College. Foundation Orations. 1974)*

DREWRY (GAVIN) Law, justice and politics. London, 1975. pp. 173. *bibliog. (Politics Association. Political Realities)*

WALKER (RONALD JACK) and WALKER (MICHAEL GEORGE) The English legal system. 4th ed. London, 1976. pp. 616.

ZANDER (MICHAEL) Cases and materials on the English legal system. 2nd ed. London, 1976. pp. 492.

— United States.

VANDERBILT (ARTHUR T.) ed. Minimum standards of judicial administration: a survey of the extent to which the standards of the American Bar Association for improving the administration of justice have been accepted throughout the country. New York, 1949. pp. 752.

VANDERBILT (ARTHUR T.) Cases and other materials on modern procedure and judicial administration. New York, 1952. pp. 1390.

GRILLIOT (HAROLD J.) Introduction to law and the legal system. Boston, [1975]. pp. 506.

STUMPF (HARRY P.) Community politics and legal services: the other side of the law. Beverly Hills, [1975]. pp. 309. *bibliog.*

AUERBACH (JEROLD S.) Unequal justice: lawyers and social change in modern America. New York, 1976. pp. 395. *bibliog.*

JUSTICE AND POLITICS

— Europe.

JUSTICE et politique: actes du colloque tenu à l'I.E.P. de Strasbourg les 6, 7 et 8 avril 1973 sous la direction de Gérard Duprat. [Strasbourg, 1974]. pp. 262. *(Strasbourg, Université de Strasbourg III. Institut d'Etudes Politiques. Cahiers. Nouvelle Série. 3)*

JUSTICES OF THE PEACE

— United Kingdom.

HARRIS (BRIAN) The criminal jurisdiction of magistrates. 4th ed. London, 1974. pp. 466.

JUTE

— India.

INDIA. Tariff Commission. Jute. Report on the price structure of different varieties of jute goods. Delhi, 1973. pp. 237.

— Kenya.

COOPER (CHARLES) and KAPLINSKY (RAPHAEL) Second-hand equipment in a developing country: a study of jute- processing in Kenya. Geneva, International Labour Office, 1974. pp. 145.

JUTE INDUSTRY WORKERS

— India.

INDIA. Labour Bureau. 1975. Report on survey of labour conditions in jute factories in India, 1971. [Delhi, 1975]. pp. 79.

JUVENILE COURTS

— United Kingdom.

FORD (DONALD) Children, courts and caring: a study of the Children and Young Persons Act, 1969. London, 1975. pp. 199. *bibliog.*

TOMLINSON (PENELOPE JANE) Process and conflict in the juvenile court; [Ph.D. (London) thesis]. 1975. fo. 241. *bibliog. Typescript: unpublished. This thesis is the property of London University and may not be removed from the Library.*

— United States.

EXPERIMENT in a juvenile court: a study of a program of volunteers working with juvenile probationers; by Robert J. Berger [and others]. Ann Arbor, 1975. 1 vol. (various pagings). *bibliog.*

KLEIN (MALCOLM W.) ed. The juvenile justice system. Beverly Hills, [1976]. pp. 287. *bibliogs.*

JUVENILE DELINQUENCY.

HARDY (RICHARD E.) and CULL (JOHN G.) eds. Problems of adolescents: social and psychological approaches. Springfield, Ill., [1974]. pp. 278. *bibliogs.*

— Research — United Kingdom.

BELSON (WILLIAM A.) Juvenile theft: the causal factors: a report of an investigation of the tenability of various causal hypotheses about the development of stealing by London boys, etc. London, 1975. pp. 411.

— Ireland (Republic).

EIRE. Interdepartmental Committee on Mentally Ill and Maladjusted Persons. 1975. First interim report...: assessment services for the courts in respect of juveniles. Dublin, [1975]. pp. 8.

EIRE. Interdepartmental Committee on Mentally Ill and Maladjusted Persons. 1975. Second interim report...: the provision of treatment for juvenile offenders and potential juvenile offenders. Dublin, [1975]. pp. 12.

— **New Zealand.**

O'CONNELL (BERNADETTE MARY) The home situations of juvenile offenders. [Wellington], 1975. pp. 21. *bibliog.* (*New Zealand. Department of Social Welfare. Research Section. General Research Reports. No. 2*)

— **Puerto Rico.**

FERRACUTI (FRANCO) and others. Delinquents and nondelinquents in the Puerto Rican slum culture. Columbus, Oh., [1975]. pp. 249. *bibliog.*

— **United Kingdom.**

COLTON (MARY) Care without control. London, [1975]. pp. 10.

FORD (DONALD) Children, courts and caring: a study of the Children and Young Persons Act, 1969. London, 1975. pp. 199. *bibliog.*

NATIONAL ASSOCIATION FOR MENTAL HEALTH. Mind Reports. 14. The Act on trial: the non-implementation of the Children and Young Persons' Act 1969. London, 1975. pp. 23.

— **United States.**

KLEIN (MALCOLM W.) ed. The juvenile justice system. Beverly Hills, [1976]. pp. 287. *bibliogs.*

— — **Kansas.**

JUVENILE delinquency prevention and control planning in Kansas: programmatic dimensions of the planning task; the final report of the first phase of comprehensive planning, etc.; (project sponsored by the Division of Institutional Management, State Department of Social Welfare, in cooperation with the Governor's Committee on Criminal Administration). Topeka, [1970]. pp. 318.

A COMPREHENSIVE plan for the prevention and control of juvenile delinquency in Kansas; (project sponsored by the Division of Institutional Management, State Department of Social Welfare, in cooperation with the Governor's Committee on Criminal Administration). [Topeka], 1972. 4 vols. *bibliogs.*

K—THEORY.

MILNOR (JOHN) Introduction to algebraic K-theory. Princeton, N.J., 1971. pp. 184. (*Annals of Mathematics. Studies. No.72*)

KABYLIA

— **Economic policy.**

ALGERIA. Direction de la Documentation et des Publications. 1969. La Grande Kabylie: réalités et développement. [Algiers, 1969]. pp. 85.

— **Social policy.**

ALGERIA. Direction de la Documentation et des Publications. 1969. La Grande Kabylie: réalités et développement. [Algiers, 1969]. pp. 85.

KÁDÁR (JÁNOS).

KÁDÁR (JÁNOS) Izbrannye stat'i i rechi, fevral' 1970 g. - dekabr' 1975 g.; [perevod s vengerskogo]. Moskva, 1976. pp. 534.

KAINGANGUE INDIANS.

HENRY (JULES) Jungle people: a Kaingáng tribe of the highlands of Brazil. New York, [1964]. pp. 215. *First published in New York in 1941.*

KALECKI (MICHAL).

FEIWEL (GEORGE R.) The intellectual capital of Michał Kalecki: a study in economic theory and policy. Knoxville, [1975]. pp. 583. *bibliog.*

KALININ (MIKHAIL IVANOVICH).

KALININ (MIKHAIL IVANOVICH) Izbrannye proizvedeniia; (sostaviteli F.G. Vashchenko [and others]). Moskva, 1975. pp. 448.

KALININGRAD

— **Population.**

GRAMBERG (ANNELIESE) Die Bevölkerung der Stadt Königsberg. Jena, 1926. pp. 116. *bibliog.* (*Kaliningrad. Universität. Institut für Ostdeutsche Wirtschaft. Schriften. 14. Heft*)

KALININGRAD (OBLAST')

— **Economic conditions.**

BERENBEIM (D.IA.) and others. Kaliningradskaia oblast': ocherki prirody. Kaliningrad, 1969. pp. 206.

KALLER (MAXIMILIAN).

REIFFERSCHEID (GERHARD) Das Bistum Ermland und das Dritte Reich. Köln, 1975. pp. 351. *bibliog.*

KALMYK REPUBLIC

— **Economic conditions.**

RUSSIA (EMPIRE). Ministerstvo Gosudarstvennykh Imushchestv. 1868. Kalmytskaia step' Astrakhanskoi gubernii po issledovaniiam Kumo-Manychskoi ekspeditsii. S.-Peterburg, 1868. 3 pts (in 1).

KAMBAS.

MUNRO (J. FORBES) Colonial rule and the Kamba: social change in the Kenya Highlands 1889-1939. Oxford, 1975. pp. 276. *bibliog.*

TIGNOR (ROBERT L.) The colonial transformation of Kenya: the Kamba, Kikuyu, and Maasai from 1900 to 1939. Princeton, [1976]. p. 372. *bibliog.*

KANT (IMMANUEL).

KRITICHESKIE ocherki po filosofii Kanta. Kiev, 1975. pp. 367. *bibliog.*

MARXISMO ed etica: testi sul dibattito intorno al "socialismo neokantiano", 1896-1911, con un saggio introduttivo di Hans Jörg Sandkühler; edizione italiana a cura di Emilio Agazzi. Milano, 1975. pp. 317. *bibliog.*

KARAGWE KINGDOM

— **History.**

KATOKE (ISRAEL K.) The Karagwe kingdom: a history of the Abanyambo of north western Tanzania, c1400-1915. Nairobi, 1975. pp. 183. *bibliog.*

KARAKALPAK REPUBLIC

— **History.**

BOR'BA trudiashchikhsia Karakalpakii protiv sotsial'nogo i kolonial'nogo gneta, 1873 - fevral' 1917 g. Tashkent, 1971. pp. 155.

ISTORIIA Karakalpakskoi ASSR. Tashkent, 1974. 2 vols.

— **Religion.**

BAZARBAEV (ZHUMANAZAR) Sekuliarizatsiia naseleniia sotsialisticheskoi Karakalpakii. Nukus, 1973. pp. 181.

KARAMZIN (NIKOLAI MIKHAILOVICH).

BLACK (JOSEPH LAURENCE) Nicholas Karamzin and Russian society in the nineteenth century: a study in Russian political and historical thought. Toronto, [1975]. pp. 264. *bibliog.*

KARELIA

— **Politics and government.**

OCHERKI istorii Karel'skoi organizatsii KPSS. Petrozavodsk, 1974. pp. 590.

— **Statistics.**

KARELIA. Statisticheskoe Upravlenie. 1972. Narodnoe khoziaistvo Karel'skoi ASSR: statisticheskii sbornik k 50-letiiu obrazovaniia SSSR. Petrozavodsk, 1972. pp. 150.

KARIYA

— **Economic history.**

ALLINSON (GARY D.) Japanese urbanism: industry and politics in Kariya, 1872-1972. Berkeley, [1975]. pp. 276. *bibliog.*

— **Politics and government.**

ALLINSON (GARY D.) Japanese urbanism: industry and politics in Kariya, 1872-1972. Berkeley, [1975]. pp. 276. *bibliog.*

— **Social history.**

ALLINSON (GARY D.) Japanese urbanism: industry and politics in Kariya, 1872-1972. Berkeley, [1975]. pp. 276. *bibliog.*

KASHINAUA INDIANS.

The CASHINAHUA of eastern Peru; by Kenneth M. Kensinger [and others]; edited by Jane Powell Dwyer. [Providence, R.I., 1975]. pp. 237. *bibliog.* (*Brown University. Haffenreffer Museum of Anthropology. Studies in Anthropology and Material Culture. vol. 1*)

KASTAMONU

— **Economic policy.**

KADIOGLU (KAMIL) Regionalplanung in der Türkei am Beispiel der Provinz Kastamonu. Hamburg, 1975. pp. 234. *bibliog.* (*Deutsches Orient-Institut and Deutsches Übersee-Institut. Mitteilungen. Nr.7*)

KAUNDA (KENNETH DAVID).

HATCH (JOHN CHARLES) Two African statesmen: Kaunda of Zambia and Nyerere of Tanzania. London, 1976. pp. 268.

KAZAKSTAN

— **Constitutional history — Sources.**

SOVETY i revkomy v Kazakhstane, oktiabr' 1917-1920 gg.: dokumenty i materialy. Alma-Ata, 1971. pp. 224.

— **Economic conditions.**

GEOGRAFIIA prirodnykh resursov Kazakhstana. Alma-Ata, 1974. pp. 200. *bibliog.* (*Akademiia Nauk Kazakhskoi SSR. Sektor Geografii. Voprosy Geografii Kazakhstana. vyp.16*)

KUZEMBAEV (NURDAVLET KUZEMBAEVICH) Razmeshchenie proizvoditel'nykh sil i narodnokhoziaistvennye proportsii v Kazakhstane. Alma-Ata, 1975. pp. 295. *bibliog.*

— **Economic history.**

KHOZIAISTVENNO-kul'turnye traditsii narodov Srednei Azii i Kazakhstana. Moskva, 1975. pp. 231.

— **History — 1917-1921, Revolution — Chronology.**

GRAZHDANSKAIA voina v Kazakhstane: letopis' sobytii. Alma-Ata, 1974. pp. 391. *bibliog.*

— **Industries.**

DOSYMBEKOV (SULTAN NAZAROVICH) Problemy gosudarstvennogo upravleniia promyshlennost'iu v soiuznoi respublike. Moskva, 1974. pp. 464.

PROMYSHLENNYI kompleks raiona i puti povysheniia ego effektivnosti. Alma-Ata, 1975. pp. 150. *bibliog.*

— **Nationalism.**

ZIMANOV (SALYK ZIMANOVICH) and others. Kazakhskii otdel Narodnogo komissariata po delam natsional'nostei RSFSR. Alma-Ata, 1975. pp. 222,(xviii).

— **Politics and government.**

TORZHESTVO leninskikh idei proletarskogo internatsionalizma: na materialakh respublik Srednei Azii i Kazakhstana, 1917-1972 gg. Moskva, 1974. pp. 531.

KAZAKSTAN(Cont.)

— Population.

SUZHIKOV (MARAT MUKHAMBETKALIEVICH) and DEMAKOV (GEORGII ALEKSEEVICH) Vliianie podvizhnosti naseleniia na sblizhenie natsii. Alma-Ata, 1974. pp. 200.

NASELENIE Kazakhstana v 1959-1970 gg.: strukturnye sdvigi i ikh otsenka. Alma-Ata, 1975. pp. 159.

— Statistics.

KAZAKSTAN. Tsentral'noe Statisticheskoe Upravlenie. 1972. Narodnoe khoziaistvo Kazakhstana v 1971 g.: statisticheskii sbornik. Alma-Ata, 1972. pp. 432.

KAZAN'

— Politics and government.

ENIKEEV (ERIK AKHMETOVICH) Deiatel'nost' kazanskikh bol'shevikov po revoliutsionnomu vospitaniiu studencheskoi molodezhi, 1905 - fevral' 1917 gg. Kazan', 1973. pp. 205.

KECHUA INDIANS.

GIFFORD (DOUGLAS F.) and HOGGARTH (PAULINE F.) Carnival and coca leaf: some traditions of the Peruvian Quechua Ayllu. Edinburgh, 1976. pp. 111. *bibliog. In Quechua, Spanish and English.*

KECHUA LANGUAGE.

GIFFORD (DOUGLAS F.) and HOGGARTH (PAULINE F.) Carnival and coca leaf: some traditions of the Peruvian Quechua Ayllu. Edinburgh, 1976. pp. 111. *bibliog. In Quechua, Spanish and English.*

KEKKONEN (URHO KALEVA).

KORHONEN (KEIJO) ed. Urho Kekkonen: a statesman for peace; (English translation supervised by William R. Copeland and David Miller). London, 1975. pp. 186.

KELANTAN

— Politics and government.

BEAGLEHOLE (JOHN HOLT) The district: a study in decentralization in West Malaysia. London, 1976. pp. 122. *bibliog. (Hull. University. Centre for South-East Asian Studies. Monographs on South-East Asia. No. 6)*

KENNEDY (JOHN FITZGERALD) President of the United States.

IAKOVLEV (NIKOLAI NIKOLAEVICH) Prestupivshie gran'. Moskva, 1970. pp. 352.

MEUNIER (ROBERT F.) Shadows of doubt: the Warren Commission cover-up. Hicksville, N.Y., [1976]. pp. 165. *bibliog.*

KENNEDY (ROBERT FRANCIS).

IAKOVLEV (NIKOLAI NIKOLAEVICH) Prestupivshie gran'. Moskva, 1970. pp. 352.

KENT

— Economic policy.

KENT. Planning Department. Towards a structure plan for Kent: the main issues; a report for discussion purposes on the studies and progress so far made. Maidstone, 1975. pp. 147.

— Historical geography.

WITNEY (K.P.) The Jutish forest: a study of the Weald of Kent from 450 to 1380 A.D. London, 1976. pp. 339. *bibliog.*

— Social policy.

KENT. Planning Department. Towards a structure plan for Kent: the main issues; a report for discussion purposes on the studies and progress so far made. Maidstone, 1975. pp. 147.

KENYA

— Description and travel.

PERHAM (Dame MARGERY FREDA) East African journey: Kenya and Tanganyika, 1929-30. London, 1976. pp. 246.

— Economic conditions.

BURROWS (JOHN R.) Kenya: into the second decade; report of a mission sent to Kenya by the World Bank. Baltimore, International Bank for Reconstruction and Development, 1975. pp. 533. *bibliog. (Country Economic Reports)*

— Economic history.

VAN ZWANENBERG (R.M.A.) and KING (ANNE) An economic history of Kenya and Uganda, 1800-1970. London, 1975. pp. 326. *bibliog.*

— Economic policy.

KENYA. Town Planning Department. 1971. North Eastern Province regional physical development plan. [Nairobi], 1971. fo. 36.

CONFERENCE ON COMPARATIVE ADMINISTRATION IN EAST AFRICA, ARUSHA, 1971. Rural administration in Kenya: a critical appraisal: [papers from the conference]; edited by David K. Leonard. Nairobi, 1973. pp. 165. *bibliogs.*

OMINDE (SIMEON HONGO) The Harambee movement in educational development. Vienna, 1974. pp. 28. *(Wiener Institut für Entwicklungsfragen. Occasional Papers. 74/4)*

BURROWS (JOHN R.) Kenya: into the second decade; report of a mission sent to Kenya by the World Bank. Baltimore, International Bank for Reconstruction and Development, 1975. pp. 533. *bibliog. (Country Economic Reports)*

NYANGIRA (NICHOLAS) Relative modernization and public resource allocation in Kenya: comparative analysis. Kampala, 1975. pp. 169. *bibliog.*

— History.

TIGNOR (ROBERT L.) The colonial transformation of Kenya: the Kamba, Kikuyu, and Maasai from 1900 to 1939. Princeton, [1976]. p. 372. *bibliog.*

— Industries — Directories.

KENYA. Central Bureau of Statistics. 1974. Directory of industries, 1974. [Nairobi?], 1974. pp. 238.

— Politics and government.

MUNRO (J. FORBES) Colonial rule and the Kamba: social change in the Kenya Highlands 1889-1939. Oxford, 1975. pp. 276. *bibliog.*

PERHAM (Dame MARGERY FREDA) East African journey: Kenya and Tanganyika, 1929-30. London, 1976. pp. 246.

— Population.

UCHE (U.U.) Law and population growth in Kenya. Medford, Mass., 1974. pp. 40. *(Tufts University. Fletcher School of Law and Diplomacy. Law and Population Monograph Series. No.22)*

OMINDE (SIMEON HONGO) The population of Kenya-Uganda-Tanzania. [Nairobi?], 1975. pp. 124. *(Committee for International Coordination of National Research in Demography. C.I.C.R.E.D. Series)*

— Rural conditions.

MBITHI (PHILIP M.) Rural sociology and rural development: its application in Kenya. Kampala, 1974. pp. 229. *bibliogs.*

— Social conditions.

SOCIAL PERSPECTIVES; (pd. by) Central Bureau of Statistics, Ministry of Finance and Planning, Kenya. irreg., Je 1976 (v.1, no. 1)- Nairobi.

— Social policy.

OMINDE (SIMEON HONGO) The Harambee movement in educational development. Vienna, 1974. pp. 28. *(Wiener Institut für Entwicklungsfragen. Occasional Papers. 74/4)*

SOCIAL PERSPECTIVES; (pd. by) Central Bureau of Statistics, Ministry of Finance and Planning, Kenya. irreg., Je 1976 (v.1, no. 1)- Nairobi.

KERALA

— Economic conditions.

KERALA. State Planning Board. 1971. Economic review, Kerala, 1970. Trivandrum, 1971. pp. 123.

— Economic policy.

KERALA. 1965. Preliminary memorandum on the fourth five year plan, Kerala. Trivandrum, 1965. pp. 63.

KERALA. State Planning Board. 1970. Fourth five year plan, 1969-74. Trivandrum, [1970]. pp. 203.

— Population.

INDIA. Census, 1971. Series 9. Kerala: a portrait of population; [by] K. Narayanan. [Delhi, 1974]. pp. 197.

— Social policy.

KERALA. 1965. Preliminary memorandum on the fourth five year plan, Kerala. Trivandrum, 1965. pp. 63.

KERALA. State Planning Board. 1970. Fourth five year plan, 1969-74. Trivandrum, [1970]. pp. 203.

KEREBE (BANTU PEOPLE).

HARTWIG (GERALD W.) The art of survival in East Africa: the Kerebe and long-distance trade, 1800-1895. New York, 1976. pp. 253. *bibliog.*

KERGARADEC

— Economic conditions.

MICHON (HENRI) Une zone d'activités: Brest-Kergaradec. [Paris, La Documentation Française, 1974]. pp. 50.

KEYNES (JOHN MAYNARD) 1st Baron Keynes.

CHEUNG (MICHAEL TOW) A study of the Clower-Leijonhufvud re-interpretation of the Keynesian model. 1975. fo.196. *bibliog.* Typescript. Ph.D. (London) thesis: unpublished. This thesis is the property of London University and may not be removed from the Library.

MINSKY (HYMAN P.) John Maynard Keynes. London, 1976. pp. 181. *bibliog.*

MOGGRIDGE (DONALD EDWARD) Keynes. London, 1976. pp. 189. *bibliog.*

PATINKIN (DON) Keynes' monetary thought: a study of its development. Durham, N.C., 1976. pp. 163. *bibliog.*

UNIVERSITY OF KENT AT CANTERBURY. Keynes Seminar, 2nd, 1974. Keynes and international monetary relations...; edited by A.P. Thirlwall. London, 1976. pp. 126.

KHARKOV (OBLAST')

— Politics and government.

NARYSY istoriï Kharkivs'koï oblasnoï partiinoï orhanizatsiï. Kharkiv, 1970. pp. 803.

KHIVA KHANATE.

See also SOVIET CENTRAL ASIA.

KHMEL'NITSKII (OBLAST')

— Statistics.

KHMEL'NITSKII (OBLAST'). Statystychne Upravlinnia. Narodne hospodarstvo Khmel'nyts'koï oblasti: statystychnyi zbirnyk. Kyïv, 1972. pp. 202.

KHRUSHCHEV (NIKITA SERGEEVICH).

McNEAL (ROBERT HATCH) The Bolshevik tradition: Lenin, Stalin, Khrushchev, Brezhnev. 2nd ed. Englewood Cliffs, [1975]. pp. 210. *bibliog*.

KIDNEYS

— Diseases.

CANADA. Statistics Canada. Health and Welfare Division. Vital Statistics Section. 1973. Cardiovascular-renal mortality...1950-1968. Ottawa, 1973. pp. 96. *In English and French*.

KIELCE (PROVINCE)

— Politics and government.

NAUMIUK (JAN) Polska Partia Robotnicza na Kielecczyźnie. Warszawa, 1976. pp. 567. *bibliog*.

— Population.

'ZUREK (AGNIESZKA) Struktura przestrzenna przepływów ludności miast województwa kieleckiego. Wrocław, 1975. pp. 112. *bibliog*. (*Polska Akademia Nauk. Instytut Geografii i Przestrzennego Zagospodarowania. Prace Geograficzne. Nr. 113*) With Russian and English summaries.

KIKUYUS.

BULLOCK (R.A.) Ndeiya, Kikuyu frontier: the Kenya land problem in microcosm. Waterloo, Ont., [1975]. pp. 144. (*University of Waterloo, [Ontario]. Department of Geography. Publication Series. No. 6*)

TIGNOR (ROBERT L.) The colonial transformation of Kenya: the Kamba, Kikuyu, and Maasai from 1900 to 1939. Princeton, [1976]. p. 372. *bibliog*.

KIM (IL-SUNG).

COMRADE Kim Il Sung: an ingenious thinker and theoretician. Pyongyang, 1975. pp. 160.

KING (WILLIAM LYON MACKENZIE).

GRANATSTEIN (J.L.) Canada's war: the politics of the Mackenzie King government, 1939-1945. Toronto, 1975. pp. 436.

KINGSTON, JAMAICA

— Growth.

CLARKE (COLIN G.) Kingston, Jamaica: urban development and social change, 1692- 1962. Berkeley, 1975. pp. 270. *bibliog*. (*American Geographical Society. Research Series. No. 27*)

— Social history.

CLARKE (COLIN G.) Kingston, Jamaica: urban development and social change, 1692- 1962. Berkeley, 1975. pp. 270. *bibliog*. (*American Geographical Society. Research Series. No. 27*)

KINGSTON, NEW YORK

— Economic history.

BLUMIN (STUART M.) The urban threshold: growth and change in a nineteenth-century American community. Chicago, 1976. pp. 298. *bibliog*.

— Social history.

BLUMIN (STUART M.) The urban threshold: growth and change in a nineteenth-century American community. Chicago, 1976. pp. 298. *bibliog*.

KINGSTON PENITENTIARY.

CANADA. Commission of Inquiry into Certain Disturbances at Kingston Penitentiary during April, 1971. 1973. Report; J.W. Swackhamer, chairman. Ottawa, 1973. pp. 63.

KINSHIP.

MAYER (ADRIAN CURTIS) Caste and kinship in central India: a village and its region. Berkeley, [1960] repr. 1966. pp. 295. *bibliog*.

CLAUSEN (MARION TANDIWE WHEELER) An anthropological and psychological investigation of use and understanding of kin terms by English children: implications for kinship theory. [1975]. 1 vol. (various foliations). *bibliog. Typescript. M.Phil.(London) thesis: unpublished. This thesis is the property of London University and may not be removed from the library*.

GUDEMAN (STEPHAN) Relationships, residence and the individual: a rural Panamanian community. London, 1976. pp. 274. *bibliog*.

MEDITERRANEAN family structures; edited by J.G. Peristiany. Cambridge, 1976. pp. 414. *bibliogs. Papers of a seminar convened by the Social Research Centre of Cyprus in 1970*.

— Terminology.

DYEN (ISIDORE) and ABERLE (DAVID F.) Lexical reconstruction: the case of the proto-Athapaskan kinship system. London, 1974. pp. 498. *bibliog*.

— Hong Kong.

WATSON (JAMES L.) Emigration and the Chinese lineage: the Mans in Hong Kong and London. Berkeley, [1975]. pp. 242. *bibliog*.

— United States.

WITHERSPOON (GARY) Navajo kinship and marriage. Chicago, 1975. pp. 137. *bibliog*.

KIPPEL

— Social life and customs.

FRIEDL (JOHN) Kippel: a changing village in the Alps. New York, [1974]. pp. 129. *bibliog*.

KIRGHIZIA

— Economic history.

OROZALIEV (KERIMKUL KENZHEVICH) Istoricheskii opyt perekhoda kirgizskogo naroda k sotsializmu, minuia kapitalizm. Frunze, 1974. pp. 377. *bibliog*.

— History — Sources.

KPSS i Sovetskoe pravitel'stvo o Sovetskom Kirgizstane: (sbornik dokumentov, 1924-1974). Frunze, 1974. pp. 380.

— Learned institutions and societies.

KARAKEEV (KURMAN-GALI KARAKEEVICH) Akademiia nauk Kirgizskoi SSR. Frunze, 1974. pp. 229.

— Politics and government.

KPSS i Sovetskoe pravitel'stvo o Sovetskom Kirgizstane: (sbornik dokumentov, 1924-1974). Frunze, 1974. pp. 380.

— Religion.

RELIGIIA, svobodomyslie, ateizm. Frunze, 1967. pp. 96.

KIRKBRIDE (Sir ALEC).

KIRKBRIDE (Sir ALEC) From the wings: Amman memoirs 1947-1951. London, 1976. pp. 159.

KIRKLEES

— Population — Maps.

BARROWCLOUGH (RON) A social atlas of Kirklees: patterns of social differentiation in a new metropolitan district based on evidence from the 1971 census. Batley, [1975]. pp. 60. (*Huddersfield Polytechnic. Department of Geography and Geology. Occasional Papers. No. 3*)

— Social conditions — Maps.

BARROWCLOUGH (RON) A social atlas of Kirklees: patterns of social differentiation in a new metropolitan district based on evidence from the 1971 census. Batley, [1975]. pp. 60. (*Huddersfield Polytechnic. Department of Geography and Geology. Occasional Papers. No. 3*)

KIROV (OBLAST')

— Statistics.

KIROV (OBLAST'). Statisticheskoe Upravlenie. Narodnoe khoziaistvo Kirovskoi oblasti: statisticheskii sbornik. Gor'kii, 1971. pp. 183.

KISELEV (PAVEL DMITRIEVICH).

KONIUKHOVA (TAT'IANA ALEKSANDROVNA) Gosudarstvennaia derevnia Litvy i reforma P.D. Kiseleva, 1840- 1857 gg.: Vilenskaia i Kovenskaia gubernii. Moskva, 1975. pp. 251.

KISSINGER (HENRY ALFRED).

ALROY (GIL CARL) The Kissinger experience: American policy in the Middle East. New York, [1975]. pp. 189.

LISKA (GEORGE) Beyond Kissinger: ways of conservative statecraft. Baltimore, [1975]. pp. 159. *bibliog*. (*Johns Hopkins University. Washington Center of Foreign Policy Research. Studies in International Affairs. No. 26*)

NUTTER (GILBERT WARREN) Kissinger's grand design. Washington, 1975. pp. 111. *bibliog*. (*American Enterprise Institute for Public Policy Research. Foreign Affairs Studies. 27*)

GOLAN (MATTI) The secret conversations of Henry Kissinger: step-by-step diplomacy in the Middle East;...translated by Ruth Geyra Stern and Sol Stern. New York, [1976]. pp. 280.

KLEINER (IZRAÏL' ABRAMOVYCH).

See Klejner (Israel).

KLEJNER (ISRAEL).

KLEJNER (ISRAEL) Anekdotychna trahediia. Miunkhen, 1974. pp. 156.

KLIUCHEVSKII (VASILII OSIPOVICH).

ISSLEDOVANIIA po istorii Mordovskoi ASSR. Saransk, 1974. pp. 124. (*Nauchno-Issledovatel'skii Institut Iazyka, Literatury, Istorii i Ekonomiki Mordovskoi ASSR. Trudy. vyp. 47*)

KLOTZ (GEORG).

DRECHSLER (ROBERT H.) Georg Klotz: der Schicksalsweg des Südtiroler Schützenmajors, 1919-1976; Dokumentation. Wien, 1976. pp. 299.

KNIES (CARL GUSTAV ADOLF).

WEBER (MAX) Roscher and Knies: the logical problems of historical economics translated with an introduction by Guy Oakes. New York, [1975]. pp. 294. *bibliog*.

KNIGHT (WILLIAM).

CARVER (MARCELLA M.) A positivist life: a personal memoir of my father, William Knight, 1845-1901. London, 1976. pp. 78.

KNOWLEDGE, SOCIOLOGY OF.

BLOOR (DAVID) Knowledge and social imagery. London, 1976. pp. 156. *bibliog*.

KNOWLEDGE, THEORY OF.

KNOWLEDGE, THEORY OF.

NEKOTORYE problemy dialektiki i metodologii poznaniia. Tashkent, 1973. pp. 188. *(Tashkent. Universitet. Nauchnye Trudy. vyp.452)*

SCHEIPERMEIER (GUENTER) Erfahrung und Methode:...Theorie der Erfahrungswissenschaft im Hinblick auf die Sozialwissenschaften, insbesondere die Nationalökonomie. Berlin, [1975]. pp. 275. *bibliog.*

UNGER (ROBERTO MANGABEIRA) Knowledge and politics. New York, [1975]. pp. 336.

HOLMES (ROGER) Legitimacy and the politics of the knowable. London, 1976. pp. 191. *A collection of essays reprinted from various periodicals.*

MACH (ERNST) Knowledge and error: sketches on the psychology of enquiry; (translation from the 5th edition, 1926). Dordrecht, [1976]. pp. 393. *bibliogs.*

STERNBERG (ELAINE) The logical conditions of public experience, examined with special reference to rationalism, empiricism and pragmatism. [1976]. fo. 214. *bibliog. Typescript. Ph.D. (London) thesis: unpublished. This thesis is the property of London University and may not be removed from the Library.*

KOCHANOWICZ (TADEUSZ).

KOCHANOWICZ (TADEUSZ) Na wojennej emigracji: wspomnienia z lat 1942-1944. Warszawa, 1975. pp. 303.

KOEPLINGER (RUDOLF).

EUROPEAN COMMISSION OF HUMAN RIGHTS. 1969. The Köplinger case: (Application No. 1850/63 by Rudolf Köplinger against Austria). Strasbourg, Council of Europe, 1969. pp. 215.

KOKAND KHANATE.

See also SOVIET CENTRAL ASIA.

KOLLONTAI (ALEKSANDRA MIKHAILOVNA).

BRESLAV (EVA IVANOVNA) Aleksandra Mikhailovna Kollontai. Moskva, 1974. pp. 110. *bibliog. (Kommunisticheskaia Partiia Sovetskogo Soiuza. Tsentral'nyi Komitet. Vysshaia Partiinaia Shkola. Kafedra Zhurnalistiki. Partiinye Publitsisty)*

KONARSKI (SZYMON).

KONARSKI (SZYMON) Dziennik z lat 1831-1834; przygotowali do druku Bolesław Łopuszański i Anatol Smirnow. Wrocław, 1973. pp. 361. *(Polska Akademia Nauk. Oddział w Krakowie. Komisja Nauk Historycznych. Materiały. Nr.23) With Russian and French summaries.*

KONKUNAD

— Social life and customs.

OUDEN (J.H.B. DEN) De onaanraakbaren van Konkunad: een onderzoek naar de positieverandering van de scheduled castes in een dorp van het district Coimbatore, India. Wageningen, 1975 in progress. *(Wageningen. Landbouwhogeschool. Mededelingen. 75-11) With English summary.*

KÖPLINGER.

See KOEPLINGER.

KORANYI (KAROL)

— Bibliography.

MISCELLANEA iuridica zlo'zone w darze Karolowi Koranyiemu w czterdziestolecie pracy naukowej. Warszawa, 1961. pp. 196. *bibliog. With French table of contents.*

KOREA.

— Commerce.

INTERNATIONAL SYMPOSIUM ON TRADE AND DEVELOPMENT IN KOREA, 3RD., 1974. Trade and development in Korea: proceedings of [the] conference (sponsored jointly by the Korea Development Institute and the Harvard International Institute of Development); Wontack Hong and Anne O. Krueger, editors. Seoul, 1975. pp. 253. *bibliogs.*

HONG (WONTACK) Factor supply and factor intensity of trade in Korea. Seoul, 1976. pp. 236. *bibliog.*

— Commercial policy.

FRANK (CHARLES R.) and others. Foreign trade regimes and economic development: South Korea. New York, 1975. pp. 264. *bibliog. (National Bureau of Economic Research. Special Conference Series on Foreign Trade Regimes and Economic Development. vol. 7)*

STECHER (BERND) Erfolgsbedingungen der Importsubstitution und der Exportdiversifizierung im Industrialisierungsprozess: die Erfahrungen in Chile, Mexiko und Südkorea. Tübingen, 1976. pp. 207. *bibliog. (Kiel. Universität. Institut für Weltwirtschaft. Kieler Studien. 136)*

— Constitution.

KIM (IL-SUNG) On the socialist constitution of the Democratic People's Republic of Korea;[translation of the texts edited by Fukushima Masao]. Pyongyang, 1975. pp. 329.

— Defences.

CLOUGH (RALPH N.) Deterrence and defense in Korea: the role of U.S. forces. Washington, [1976]. pp. 61. *(Brookings Institution. Studies in Defense Policy)*

— Economic conditions.

INTERNATIONAL SYMPOSIUM ON TRADE AND DEVELOPMENT IN KOREA, 3RD., 1974. Trade and development in Korea: proceedings of [the] conference (sponsored jointly by the Korea Development Institute and the Harvard International Institute of Development); Wontack Hong and Anne O. Krueger, editors. Seoul, 1975. pp. 253. *bibliogs.*

— Economic policy.

FRANK (CHARLES R.) and others. Foreign trade regimes and economic development: South Korea. New York, 1975. pp. 264. *bibliog. (National Bureau of Economic Research. Special Conference Series on Foreign Trade Regimes and Economic Development. vol. 7)*

INTERNATIONAL SYMPOSIUM ON TRADE AND DEVELOPMENT IN KOREA, 3RD., 1974. Trade and development in Korea: proceedings of [the] conference (sponsored jointly by the Korea Development Institute and the Harvard International Institute of Development); Wontack Hong and Anne O. Krueger, editors. Seoul, 1975. pp. 253. *bibliogs.*

PALAIS (JAMES B.) Politics and policy in traditional Korea. Cambridge, 1975. pp. 390. *bibliog. (Harvard University. East Asian Research Center. Harvard East Asian Series. 82)*

— Foreign relations.

KIM (IL-SUNG) For the independent, peaceful reunification of the country. Pyongyang, 1976. pp. 331.

— — United States.

BALDWIN (FRANK) ed. Without parallel: the American-Korean relationship since 1945. New York, [1974]. pp. 376.

NOBLE (HAROLD JOYCE) Embassy at war;...edited with an introduction by Frank Baldwin. Seattle, [1975]. pp. 328. *(Columbia University. East Asian Institute. Studies)*

— Politics and government.

KIM (ILPYONG J.) Communist politics in North Korea. New York, 1975. pp. 121.

PALAIS (JAMES B.) Politics and policy in traditional Korea. Cambridge, 1975. pp. 390. *bibliog. (Harvard University. East Asian Research Center. Harvard East Asian Series. 82)*

RESISTANCE continues: reports from South Korea; by T.K. Pyongyang, 1975. pp. 176.

WRIGHT (EDWARD REYNOLDS) ed. Korean politics in transition;...contributors, Suk-choon Cho [and others]. Seattle, 1975. pp. 399. *bibliog.*

KIM (IL-SUNG) For the independent, peaceful reunification of the country. Pyongyang, 1976. pp. 331.

REES (DAVID) North Korea: undermining the truce. London, 1976. pp. 14. *(Institute for the Study of Conflict. Conflict Studies. No. 69)*

— Population.

The POPULATION of Korea; by Tai Hwan Kwon [and others]. Seoul, 1975. pp. 154. *bibliog. (Committee for International Coordination of National Research in Demography. C.I.C.R.E.D. Series)*

KOREAN REUNIFICATION QUESTION (1945—).

REES (DAVID) North Korea: undermining the truce. London, 1976. pp. 14. *(Institute for the Study of Conflict. Conflict Studies. No. 69)*

KOREAN WAR, 1950-1953.

MUSZKAT (MARIAN) Konflikt koreański: zagadnienia prawno-międzynarodowe wojny i likwidacji jej skutków. Warszawa, 1956. pp. 368.

— Armistices.

BALICKI (JAN) Rozejm koreański w teorii i praktyce: wybrane problemy prawne. Warszawa, 1956. pp. 425. *bibliog. With Russian and English summaries.*

— United States.

NOBLE (HAROLD JOYCE) Embassy at war;...edited with an introduction by Frank Baldwin. Seattle, [1975]. pp. 328. *(Columbia University. East Asian Institute. Studies)*

KOSOVO

— Constitution.

USTAV Socijalističke Republike Srbije; Ustav Socijalističke Autonomne Pokrajine Vojvodine; Ustav Socijalističke Autonomne Pokrajine Kosova; sa ustavnim zakonima i registrima pojmova. Beograd, 1974. pp. 750. *In Cyrillic.*

KREBS (ALBERT).

KREBS (ALBERT) The infancy of Nazism: the memoirs of ex-Gauleiter Albert Krebs, 1923-1933; edited and translated by William Sheridan Allen. New York, 1976. pp. 328. *bibliog.*

KROPOTKIN (PETR ALEKSEEVICH) Prince.

MILLER (MARTIN ALAN) Kropotkin. Chicago, 1976. pp. 342. *bibliog.*

KRUGER (STEPHANUS JOHANNES PAULUS).

JUTA (MARJORIE) The pace of the ox: a life of Paul Kruger; [the edition of 1937 reprinted with corrections and a new foreword]. Cape Town, 1975. pp. 228. *bibliog.*

KUALA LUMPUR

— Commerce.

KANAPATHY (V.) Kuala Lumpur as a centre of international finance; (expanded version of an article...in The Times...on 31st May 1975). [Kuala Lumpur, 1975]. pp. 9.

KUEHLMANN (MIRA VON).

KUEHLMANN (MIRA VON) Frieden ohne Widerruf: Erinnerungen aus meinem Leben. Berlin, [1975]. pp. 160.

KÜHLMANN.

See KUEHLMANN.

KUIBYSHEV

— Politics and government.

PERVYE samarskie lenintsy: ocherki o chlenakh marksistskogo kruzhka, sozdannogo V.I. Leninym v Samare. Kuibyshev, 1969. pp. 192.

KUIBYSHEV (OBLAST')

— History.

VELIKII Oktiabr' i kommunisticheskoe stroitel'stvo na Srednei Volge: materialy Kuibyshevskoi oblastnoi teoreticheskoi konferentsii, posviashchennoi 50-letiiu Velikoi Oktiabr'skoi sotsialisticheskoi revoliutsii. Kuibyshev, 1969. pp. 495.

KUMAON

— Rural conditions.

SANWAL (RAM DATT) Social stratification in rural Kumaon. Delhi, 1976. pp. 213.

KUN (BÉLA).

HRANCHAK (IVAN MYKHAILOVYCH) and LEBOVICH (MARTIN FARKASHEVICH) Bela Kun - vydaiushchiisia deiatel' vengerskogo i mezhdunarodnogo revoliutsionnogo dvizheniia. Moskva, 1975. pp. 165.

KURPIE

— Social conditions.

PAPROCKA (WANDA) Współczesne przemiany wsi kurpiowskiej. Wrocław, 1975. pp. 176. (Polska Akademia Nauk. Instytut Historii Kultury Materialnej. Biblioteka Etnografii Polskiej. Nr.31) With English summary.

KUWAIT

— Census.

KUWAIT. Census, 1970. Population census, 1970. Kuwait, Central Statistical Office, 1972. pp. 111, fo.3.

KUZNETSOV (EDUARD SAMUILOVICH).

KUZNETSOV (EDUARD SAMUILOVICH) Dnevniki. Paris, 1973. pp. 374.

LABOUR AND LABOURING CLASSES.

MEANS (DAVID MACGREGOR) Industrial freedom. New York, 1897. pp. 248.

MOGILEVSKII (SOLOMON ABRAMOVICH) Noveishaia istoriia mezhdunarodnogo kommunisticheskogo i rabochego dvizheniia, 1917-1970 gg. Leningrad, 1971. pp. 160. bibliog.

DEBOLINI (MARINO) Lavoro e danaro nell'ordine economico-sociale. Roma, [1974]. pp. 103.

SILVERMAN (BERTRAM) and YANOWITCH (MURRAY) eds. The worker in "post-industrial" capitalism: liberal and radical responses. New York, [1974]. pp. 473.

ESTUDIOS LABORALES; [pd. by] Instituto de Estudios Laborales y de Seguridad Social, Ministerio de Trabajo. irreg., My 1975(no.1)- Madrid.

GRUNDMANN (SIEGFRIED) Arbeiterklasse: Gegenwart und Zukunft; weltanschauliche und soziologische Probleme der Voraussage und Gestaltung sozialer Prozesse. Berlin, 1975. pp. 203.

RABOCHII klass v mirovom revoliutsionnom protsesse. Moskva, 1975. pp. 362.

ARBEITERKLASSE im Kapitalismus: Klassenkampf und Klassenstruktur; ([by] Hellmuth Kolbe [and others]). Berlin, 1976. pp. 256.

— Statistics.

INTERNATIONAL LABOUR OFFICE. 1976. Technical guide: descriptions of series published in the Bulletin of Labour Statistics (and the Year Book of Labour Statistics). 5th ed. Geneva, 1976. 2 vols. (in 1)

— — Methodology.

SIVERTSEV (M.A.) Problemy tipologii v mezhdunarodnoi statistike zaniatosti. Moskva, 1975. pp. 208. bibliog. (Akademiia Nauk SSSR. Institut Mezhdunarodnogo Rabochego Dvizheniia. Problemy Sovetskoi Ekonomiki)

— Africa.

BRAGINSKII (MOISEI ISAAKOVICH) Formirovanie afrikanskogo proletariata. Moskva, 1974. pp. 303. bibliog.

The DEVELOPMENT of an African working class: studies in class formation and action: [based on a conference held at the University of Toronto in 1973, sponsored by the University's International Studies Programme]; edited by Richard Sandbrook and Robin Cohen. London, [1975]. pp. 330. bibliog.

— Australia.

GOLLAN (ROBIN) Revolutionaries and reformists: communism and the Australian labour movement, 1920-1955. Richmond, Surrey, 1975. pp. 330. bibliog.

RICHARDS (GRAHAM MARTIN) Labour's share in the value added of Australian manufacturing industry: the post-war experience; [Ph.D.(London) thesis]. 1975. fo. 362. bibliog. Typescript: unpublished. This thesis is the property of London University and may not be removed from the Library.

RICKARD (JOHN DAVID) Class and politics: New South Wales, Victoria and the early Commonwealth, 1890-1910. Canberra, 1976. pp. 371. bibliog.

— Bulgaria.

DIMITROV (GEORGI) Selected works. Sofia, 1972. 3 vols.

— Canada.

CANADA. Department of Labour. 1968. Vital partner of workers and employers: Canada Department of Labour. [Ottawa, 1968]. 1 pamphlet (unpaged).

McEWEN (TOM) The forge glows red: from blacksmith to revolutionary. Toronto, 1974. pp. 260.

— — New Brunswick.

NEW BRUNSWICK LABOUR FORCE REPORT; pd. by Labour Market Services Branch, Department of Labour and Manpower. m., My 1976 [1st]- Fredericton. Supersedes LABOUR FORCE REVIEW.

— China.

KHOLODKOVSKAIA (ADELIIA VLADIMIROVNA) Rabochii klass Kitaia v period "uregulirovaniia", 1961-1965. Moskva, 1975. pp. 157. bibliog.

— Communist countries.

STELTNER (GUENTER) and others. Die Arbeiterklasse der sozialistischen Gemeinschaft in den siebziger Jahren: die Politik der Bruderparteien, etc. Berlin, 1976. pp. 163.

— Curaçao.

ANDERSON (WILLIAM AVERETTE) and DYNES (RUSSELL ROWE) Social movements, violence and change: the May Movement in Curaçao. Columbus, Ohio, [1975]. pp. 175. bibliog.

— Czechoslovakia.

PURŠ (JAROSLAV) Dělnické hnutí v českých zemích, 1849-1867. [Praha], 1961. pp. 148. bibliog. (Československá Akademie Věd. Rozpravy: Řada Společenských Věd. Ročník, sešit 6) With Russian summary.

— Denmark.

DENMARK. Arbejdsmiljøgruppen. Rapporter. København, 1973 in progress.

KARLSSON (HENRY) ed. Dansk arbejderbevaegelse, 1871-1939. Copenhagen, [1975]. pp. 144. bibliog. Selected documents.

— — Education.

SKOVMAND (ROAR) Lys over landet: traek af arbejderoplysningens historie i Danmark. København, 1949. pp. 256. bibliog.

— Egypt, Ancient.

MONICA (MADELINE DELLA) La classe ouvrière sous les Pharaons: étude du village de Deir el Medineh. Paris, [1975]. pp. 199. bibliog.

— Finland.

LÄHTEINEN (MARTTI) Ikä ongelmana työelämässä: eri-ikäisten teollisuuden työntekijäin ongelmia kartoittava tutkimus, etc. Helsinki, 1975. pp. 126. bibliog. (Finland. Suomen Virallinen Tilasto. Finlands Officiella Statistik. 32. Sosiaalisia Erikoistutkimuksia. 44) With English summary.

— France.

KAPLOW (JEFFRY) The names of kings: the Parisian laboring poor in the eighteenth century. New York, [1972]. pp. 222.

FREYSSENET (MICHEL) Schéma général d'aménagement de la France: tendances et mise en question. Paris, 1975. pp. 195. bibliog. (France. Délégation à l'Aménagement du Territoire et à l'Action Régionale. Travaux et Recherches de Prospective. 57)

MALLET (SERGE) The new working class; translated by Andrée and Bob Shepherd. Nottingham, 1975. pp. 210.

— Germany.

BITTMANN (KARL) Ausgewählte kleinere Schriften, etc. Jena, 1920. pp. 167.

ARBEITERKAMPF in Deutschland: Klassenzusammensetzung und Kampfformen der Arbeiter seit dem Nationalsozialismus. München, 1973. pp. 175.

NICK (FRANZ R.) and EHREISER (HANS JOERG) Unterschiede zwischen Arbeitern und Angestellten im Betrieb: eine empirische Untersuchung zur Selbsterkennung und Selbsteinschätzung;...Forschungsbericht. Mannheim, 1974. pp. 65, xxvi. bibliog.

BROCKHAUS (ECKHARD) Zusammensetzung und Neustrukturierung der Arbeiterklasse vor dem Ersten Weltkrieg: zur Krise der professionellen Arbeiterbewegung. München, 1975. pp. 155. bibliog.

MASON (TIMOTHY W.) ed. Arbeiterklasse und Volksgemeinschaft: Dokumente und Materialien zur deutschen Arbeiterpolitik, 1936-1939. Opladen, [1975]. pp. 1299. bibliog. (Institut für Politische Wissenschaft. Schriften. Band 22)

GROSS (JOHANNA) Profit kontra humane Arbeitswelt. Frankfurt am Main, 1976. pp. 130.

— — Bibliography.

DOWE (DIETER) compiler. Bibliographie zur Geschichte der deutschen Arbeiterbewegung, sozialistischen und kommunistischen Bewegung von den Anfängen bis 1863, etc. Bonn-Bad Godesberg, 1976. pp. 303. bibliog. (Archiv für Sozialgeschichte. Beihefte. 5)

— — Biography.

EMMERICH (WOLFGANG) ed. Proletarische Lebensläufe: autobiographische Dokumente zur Entstehung der Zweiten Kultur in Deutschland. Reinbek bei Hamburg, 1974-75. 2 vols. bibliogs.

LABOUR AND LABOURING CLASSES.(Cont.)

— — Dwellings.

EISENHEIM 1844-1972: (rettet Eisenheim); gegen die Zerstörung der ältesten Arbeitersiedlung des Ruhrgebietes; [by] Projektgruppe Eisenheim, Design Grundlagen, Fachhochschule Bielefeld. 2nd ed. Westberlin, 1973. pp. 180. bibliog.

— — Ruhr.

KROMBACH (UWE) Zur Lage der arbeitenden Bevölkerung im Ruhrgebiet. Frankfurt, [1974 in progress]. bibliog.

— — Saarland.

SAARGEBIET. Statistisches Amt. Einzelschriften zur Statistik des Saarlandes. Nr. 43. Nichtlandwirtschaftliche Arbeitsstätten im Saarland am 27. Mai 1970. Saarbrücken, 1973. pp. 276.

— Greece.

BURGEL (GUY) La condition industrielle à Athènes: étude socio- géographique. Athènes, Centre National de Recherches Sociales, 1970-72. 2 vols. *35 map sheets with each volume, boxed separately.*

— Hong Kong.

ENGLAND (JOE W.) and REAR (JOHN) Chinese labour under British rule: a critical study of labour relations and law in Hong Kong. Hong Kong, 1975. pp. 379.

— Hungary.

VASS (HENRIK) ed. Studies on the history of the Hungarian working-class movement, 1867-1966. Budapest, 1975. pp. 429. bibliog.

— Italy.

MEZZOGIORNO e classe operaia; ([by] Enrico Pugliese [and others]); [proceedings of a conference held by the Centro Operaio in November 1972]. Roma, 1973 repr. 1974. pp. 136. *(Centro Operaio. Quaderni. N. 2)*

BARONE(ANTONIO) Piazza Spartaco: il movimento operaio e socialista a Castellammare di Stabia, 1900-1922. Roma, 1974. pp 237.

CRESPI (PIETRO) Esperienze operaie: contributo alla sociologia delle classi subalterne. Milano, [1974]. pp. 394. bibliog.

MASI (DOMENICO DE) and FEVOLA (GIUSEPPE) eds. I lavoratori nell'industria italiana. Milano, [1974]. 2 vols. (in 4). *(Istituto per gli Studi sullo Sviluppo Economico e il Progresso Tecnico. Collana Isvet. n.28-29) With summaries in various languages.*

SECHI (SALVATORE) Movimento operaio e storiografia marxista: rassegne e note critiche. Bari, [1974]. pp. 327.

ANDREUCCI (FRANCO) and DETTI (TOMMASO) Il movimento operaio italiano: dizionario biografico, 1853-1943. Roma, 1975 in progress. bibliogs.

BIANCHI (ANTONIO) Storia del movimento operaio di La Spezia e Lunigiana, 1861- 1945. Roma, 1975. pp. 403.

GUERRAZZI (VINCENZO) ed. L'altra cultura: inchiesta operaia. Venezia, 1975. pp. 375.

MAIONE (GIUSEPPE) Il biennio rosso: autonomia e spontaneità operaia nel 1919-1920. Bologna, [1975]. pp. 398.

— Japan.

ODAKA (KUNIO) Toward industrial democracy: management and workers in modern Japan. Cambridge, Mass., 1975. pp. 226. bibliog. *(Harvard University. East Asian Research Center. Harvard East Asian Series. 80)*

— Kenya.

VAN ZWANENBERG (R.M.A.) Colonial capitalism and labour in Kenya, 1919-1939. Kampala, 1975. pp. 314. bibliog.

— Mexico.

ANDERSON (RODNEY D.) Outcasts in their own land: Mexican industrial workers, 1906-1911. DeKalb, Ill., 1976. pp. 407. bibliog.

RUIZ (RAMON EDUARDO) Labor and the ambivalent revolutionaries: Mexico, 1911-1923. Baltimore, [1976]. pp. 145. bibliog.

— Morocco.

MOROCCO. Ministère du Travail et des Affaires Sociales. 1968. Le Maroc au travail. [Mohammedia, imprint], 1968. pp. 137.

— Netherlands — Education.

BERG (HARRY VAN DEN) and VEER (CEES VAN DER) Vormingswerk in de vakbeweging. [Nijmegen], 1973. pp. 113. bibliog.

— New Zealand.

SEIDMAN (JOEL ISAAC) Attitudes of New Zealand workers. Wellington, 1975. pp. 114. *(Victoria University of Wellington. Industrial Relations Centre. Industrial Relations Research Monographs. No.1)*

— Poland.

MORTIMER-SZYMCZAK (HALINA) ed. Problemy demografii i zatrudnienia na terenie miasta Łodzi: praca zbiorowa. Łódź, 1967. pp. 168. *(Łódź. Łódzkie Towarzystwo Naukowe. Wydział 2 Nauk Historycznych i Społecznych. Prace. Nr.68) With English and Russian summaries.*

ARCHIWUM ruchu robotniczego. Warszawa, 1973 in progress.

POLSKA klasa robotnicza: zarys dziejów. Warszawa, 1974 in progress.

CHŁOPOROBOTNICY o sobie: studium autobiografii; wstęp Dyzma Gałaj. Warszawa, 1974. pp. 296.

BRZEZIŃSKI (BOGDAN) Klasa robotnicza Warszawy, 1944-1949. Warszawa, 1975. pp. 279.

FAL'KOVICH (SVETLANA MIKHAILOVNA) Proletariat Rossii i Pol'shi v sovmestnoi revoliutsionnoi bor'be, 1907-1912. Moskva, 1975. pp. 379.

— — Silesia.

HAWRANEK (FRANCISZEK) Ruch robotniczy na Śląsku Opolskim w latach 1918-1944. Chorzów, 1974. pp. 136. bibliog.

— Russia.

RUSSIA (U.S.S.R.). Sovet Ministrov. Gosudarstvennyi Komitet po Voprosam Truda i Zarabotnoi Platy. Biulleten'. m., 1962- , with gap (1967: 3). Moskva.

NEKOTORYE voprosy sotsialisticheskogo stroitel'stva i formirovaniia rabochego klassa SSSR v predvoennye gody. Murmansk, 1971. pp. 250. *(Leningrad. Leningradskii Gosudarstvennyi Pedagogicheskii Institut. Uchenye Zapiski. t.329)*

BAEVSKII (DAVID ANATOL'EVICH) Rabochii klass v pervye gody Sovetskoi vlasti, 1917-1921 gg. Moskva, 1974. pp. 336.

EZHOV (VIKTOR ANATOL'EVICH) and OVSIANKIN (V.A.) eds. Rabochii klass SSSR na sovremennom etape. vyp.3. Leningrad, 1974. pp. 196.

GANIN (NIKOLAI IVANOVICH) Zakonomernosti sotsialisticheskoi revoliutsii i istoricheskii opyt KPSS. Moskva, 1974. pp. 255.

KAIDALOV (DMITRII PETROVICH) and SUIMENKO (EVGENII IVANOVICH) Aktual'nye problemy sotsiologii truda. Moskva, 1974. pp. 238.

NOSKOV (ALEKSANDR PETROVICH) and IANOVSKII (RUDOL'F GRIGOR'EVICH) Dva urovnia soznaniia i politicheskie ubezhdeniia; otvetstvennyi redaktor...V.A. Rebrin. Novosibirsk, 1974. pp. 94.

VOENNYE organizatsii rossiiskogo proletariata i opyt ego vooruzhennoi bor'by, 1903-1917. Moskva, 1974. pp. 418. bibliog.

AKTUAL'NYE problemy sotsiologii truda. Moskva, 1975. pp. 243.

ARUTIUNOV (GEORGII ANASTASOVICH) Rabochee dvizhenie v Rossii v period novogo revoliutsionnogo pod"ema 1910-1914 gg. Moskva, 1975. pp. 408.

BORISOV (IURII STEPANOVICH) and others, eds. Sovetskii rabochii klass: kratkii istoricheskii ocherk, 1917-1973. Moskva, 1975. pp. 576.

BREZHNEV (LEONID IL'ICH) O kommunisticheskom vospitanii trudiashchikhsia: rechi i stat'i. 2nd ed. Moskva, 1975. pp. 639.

DROBIZHEV (VLADIMIR ZINOV'EVICH) and others. Rabochii klass Sovetskoi Rossii v pervyi god proletarskoi diktatury: opyt strukturnogo analiza po materialam professional'noi perepisi 1918 g. Moskva, 1975. pp. 224.

FAL'KOVICH (SVETLANA MIKHAILOVNA) Proletariat Rossii i Pol'shi v sovmestnoi revoliutsionnoi bor'be, 1907-1912. Moskva, 1975. pp. 379.

GEGEMONIIA proletariata v trekh russkikh revoliutsiiakh. Moskva, 1975. pp. 352.

PETROCHENKO (PETR FEDOROVICH) Vliianie nauchno-tekhnicheskogo progressa na soderzhanie i organizatsiiu truda. Moskva, 1975. pp. 230.

PETROVA (NINA KONSTANTINOVNA) Mezhdunarodnye proizvodstvennye sviazi rabochego klassa SSSR, 1959- 1970 gg. Moskva, 1975. pp. 304.

RABOCHEE dvizhenie v Rossii v 1901-1904 gg.: sbornik dokumentov Leningrad, 1975. pp. 591. bibliog.

RABOCHII klass i industrial'noe razvitie SSSR. Moskva, 1975. pp. 486.

SABUROV (NIKOLAI NIKOLAEVICH) Bor'ba partii za ustanovlenie ekonomicheskoi smychki rabochego klassa s trudiashchimsia krest'ianstvom, 1921-1925 gg.; pod redaktsiei...V.A. Smyshliaeva. Leningrad, 1975. pp. 119.

SARALIEVA (ZARETKHAN KHADZHI-MURZAEVNA) "Kapital" K. Marksa i rabochee dvizhenie Rossii, 1895-1917 gg. : rasprostranenie i propaganda. Moskva, 1975. pp. 211. bibliog.

TRUKAN (GERMAN ANTONOVICH) Rabochii klass v bor'be za pobedu i uprochenie Sovetskoi vlasti. Moskva, 1975. pp. 303.

VOROZHEIKIN (IVAN EGOROVICH) Ocherk istoriografii rabochego klassa SSSR. Moskva, 1975. pp. 288. bibliog.

ZLOBINA (VERA MAKSIMOVNA) Bor'ba partii bol'shevikov protiv melkoburzhuaznogo vliianiia na rabochii klass v pervye gody nepa, 1921-1925 gg. Moskva, 1975. pp. 168.

VOLKOV (A.P.) and others, eds. Arbeit und Arbeitslohn in der UdSSR. Berlin, [1976]. pp. 495.

— — Azerbaijan.

OCHERKI istorii rabochego klassa Azerbaidzhanskoi SSR. Baku, 1974 in progress.

VOPLOSHCHENIE sotsialisticheskogo internatsionalizma. Baku, 1974. pp. 227.

— — Georgia.

NATMELADZE (MAKVALA VASIL'EVNA) and STURUA (NIKOLAI IVANOVICH) Rabochii klass Gruzii v stroitel'stve material'no- tekhnicheskoi bazy sotsializma i kommunizma v SSSR. Tbilisi, 1975. pp. 97.

— — Lithuania.

MERKYS (V.) Razvitie promyshlennosti i formirovanie proletariata Litvy v XIX v. Vil'nius, 1969. pp. 447. bibliog.

— — **Moldavian Republic.**

SOTSIALISTICHESKAIA industrializatsiia i razvitie rabochego klassa Sovetskoi Moldavii, 1926-1958 gg.: sbornik dokumentov i materialov; redaktsionnaia kollegiia N.K. Bibileishvili [and others]. Kishinev, 1970. pp. 595.

— — **Siberia.**

RABOCHII klass i krest'ianstvo natsional'nykh raionov Sibiri. Novosibirsk, 1974. pp. 174.

— — **Ukraine.**

SUSPIL'NO-polytychne zhyttia trudiashchykh Ukraïns'kï RSR. Kyïv, 1973-4. 2 vols.

LOBURETS' (VASYL' IEHOROVYCH) Formuvannia kadriv radians'koho robitnychoho klasu Ukraïny, 1921-1932 rr. Kharkiv, 1974. pp. 158. *bibliog.*

HRYTSENKO (ADELINA PAVLIVNA) Robitnychyi klas Ukraïny u Zhovtnevii revoliutsiï, berezen' 1917 - sichen' 1918 rr. Kyïv, 1975. pp. 239.

KUL'CHYTS'KYI (STANYSLAV VLADYSLAVOVYCH) Uchast' robitnykiv Ukraïny u stvorenni fondu sotsialistychnoï industrializatsiï. Kyïv, 1975. pp. 175.

SYDORENKO (VALENTYNA PAVLIVNA) Presa iak dzherelo z istoriï robitnychoho klasu Ukraïny v period sotsialistychnoho budivnytstva, 1921-1941 rr. Kyïv, 1975. pp. 107.

— — **Uzbekistan.**

MUMINOV (I.M.) ed. Istoriia rabochego klassa Sovetskogo Uzbekistana. Tashkent, 1974. pp. 357.

SHISTER (GRIGORII ARONOVICH) Promyshlennye rabochie Uzbekistana: izmeneniia v chislennosti i sostave, 1959-1970 gody. Tashkent, 1975. pp. 290.

— **Sardinia.**

SOTGIU (GIROLAMO) Lotte sociali e politiche nella Sardegna contemporanea, 1848-1922. Cagliari, [1974]. pp. 439.

SOTGIU (GIROLAMO) ed. Il movimento operaio in Sardegna, 1890-1915: testi di A. Battelli [and others]. Cagliari, [1974]. pp. 575.

— **Somali Republic.**

SOMALI REPUBLIC. Ministry of Information and National Guidance. 1974. The revolutionary generation of tomorrow: youth, sports and manpower. Mogadishu, 1974. pp. 72.

— **South Africa.**

LANDSORGANISATIONEN I SVERIGE and TJÄNSTEM ÄNNENS CENTRALORGANISATION. South Africa: black labour - Swedish capital; a report by the LO/TCO study delegation to South Africa 1975; English translation: Jaak Talvend. [Stockholm], 1975. pp. 193. *bibliog.*

— **Spain.**

COMISION DE REFORMAS SOCIALES. Burgueses y proletarios: clase obrera y reforma social en la Restauracion, 1884-1889; ([edited by] Maria del Carmen Iglesias [and] Antonio Elorza); [with] edicion critica del informe de la Agrupacion Socialista Madrileña (Informe Vera) por Tomas Jimenez Araya. Barcelona, 1973. pp. 465.

DIAZ-NOSTY (BERNARDO) La comuna asturiana: revolucion de octubre de 1934. Bilbao, 1974 repr. 1975. pp. 400. *bibliog.*

GOMEZ CASAS (JUAN) La Primera Internacional en España: estudio y documentos. Bilbao, 1974. pp. 159. *bibliog.*

— **Sweden.**

SCASE (RICHARD) ed. Readings in the Swedish class structure. Oxford, 1976. pp. 314.

— **Switzerland.**

BRUNNER (JOHANN CASPAR) Soziale Gedanken eines schweizerischen Arbeitgebers vor 40 Jahren; [edited by Ferdinand Buomberger]. Zürich, 1913. pp. 95. *Selected chapters from several pamphlets and passages from "Konkordia", 1871-74.*

ARBEITSGRUPPE FÜR GESCHICHTE DER ARBEITERBEWEGUNG ZÜRICH. Schweizerische Arbeiterbewegung: Dokumente zu Lage, Organisation und Kämpfen der Arbeiter von der Frühindustrialisierung bis zur Gegenwart. Zürich, [1975]. pp. 411. *bibliog.* (Studienbibliothek zur Geschichte der Arbeiterbewegung, Zürich. Schriftenreihe. Band 2)

— **Tasmania.**

TASMANIA. Commonwealth Bureau of Statistics. Tasmanian Office. Labour, wages and prices. a., 1973/74- Hobart.

— **United Kingdom.**

ROBERTSON (JOHN MACKINNON) The people and their leaders. bradford, [1896]. pp. 12. *(Papers for the People. No. 2)*

JASPER (ALBERT STANLEY) A Hoxton childhood;...[with] line drawings by James Boswell. London, [1969] repr. 1975. pp. 128.

BIRIUKOV (IGOR' DMITRIEVICH) Pod sen'iu monopolii: burzhuaznaia ideologiia - vrag rabochego klassa Britanii. Moskva, 1972. pp. 287.

BARNES (RON) A licence to live:...scenes from a post-war working life in Hackney. London, [1974] repr. 1976. pp. 76.

POLOZHENIE i bor'ba britanskogo rabochego klassa. Moskva, 1974. pp. 352.

CONFERENCE ON THE OCCUPATIONAL COMMUNITY OF THE TRADITIONAL WORKER, DURHAM, 1972. Working-class images of society: [papers presented to the conference]; edited by Martin Bulmer. London, 1975. pp. 278. *bibliog.*

CRUTCHLEY (JOHN FREDERICK) Work situation and social imagery: factors affecting the social and political outlooks of industrial workers. 1975. fo. 355. *bibliog. Typescript. Ph.D. (London) thesis: unpublished. This thesis is the property of London University and may not be removed from the Library.*

EDUCATION and labour in the South-west; [papers presented at a seminar held at Dartington Hall in March 1974]; edited by Jeffrey Porter. Exeter, 1975. pp. 77. *(Exeter. University. Department of Economic History. Exeter Papers in Economic History. No. 10)*

PIEPE (ANTHONY) and others. Television and the working class. Farnborough, Hants., [1975]. pp. 170. *bibliogs.*

TUC YOUTH CONFERENCE, LONDON, 1975. Trade union youth in conference; report of the...conference. London, [1975]. pp. 55.

FORESTER (TOM) Journalist. The Labour Party and the working class. London, 1976. pp. 166. *bibliog.*

KYNASTON (DAVID) King labour: the British working class, 1850-1914. London, 1976. pp. 184. *bibliog.*

NICHOLS (THEO) and ARMSTRONG (PETER) Workers divided. [London], 1976. pp. 221. *bibliog.*

SHERGOLD (PETER ROGER) The standard of life of manual workers in the first decade of the twentieth-century: a comparative study of Birmingham, U.K., and Pittsburgh, U.S.A. 1976. fo. 691. *bibliog. Typescript. Ph.D. (London) thesis: unpublished. This thesis is the property of London University and may not be removed from the Library.*

— — **Scotland.**

GRAY (ROBERT Q.) The labour aristocracy in Victorian Edinburgh. Oxford, 1976. pp. 220. *bibliog.*

— **United States.**

SAMSON (LEON) Toward a united front: a philosophy for American workers. New York, [1933]. pp. 276.

ROUSSOPOULOS (DIMITRIOS J.) ed. The political economy of the state: Québec, Canada, U.S.A. Montréal, 1973. pp. 195.

ARONOWITZ (STANLEY) False promises: the shaping of American working class consciousness. New York, 1974. pp. 465. *bibliog.*

FETHERLING (DALE) Mother Jones the miners' angel: a portrait. Carbondale, [1974]. pp. 263. *bibliog.*

LEMASTERS (E.E.) Blue-collar aristocrats: life-styles at a working-class tavern. Madison, Wis., 1975. pp. 218.

ROOT AND BRANCH. Root and Branch: the rise of the workers' movements. Greenwich, Conn., 1975. pp. 544.

GUTMAN (HERBERT GEORGE) Work, culture and society in industrializing America: essays in American working-class and social history. New York, 1976. pp. 343, xvi. *Reprinted from various sources.*

KRICKUS (RICHARD) Pursuing the American dream: white ethnics and the new populism. Bloomington, 1976. pp. 424.

SHERGOLD (PETER ROGER) The standard of life of manual workers in the first decade of the twentieth-century: a comparative study of Birmingham, U.K., and Pittsburgh, U.S.A. 1976. fo. 691. *bibliog. Typescript. Ph.D. (London) thesis: unpublished. This thesis is the property of London University and may not be removed from the Library.*

SOMBART (WERNER) Why is there no socialism in the United States?;...translated by Patricia M. Hocking and C.T. Husbands; edited and with an introductory essay by C.T. Husbands, etc. London, 1976. pp. 187. *bibliog.*

LABOUR CONTRACT

— **Germany.**

FLUEHMANN (ADRIAN W.) Die Auswirkung von Arbeitskämpfen im Arbeitsvertragsrecht. Bern, 1976. pp. 85. *bibliog.*

— **Netherlands.**

ZONDERLAND (PIETER) De arbeidsovereenkomst. Groningen, 1975. pp. 286.

— **Switzerland.**

FLUEHMANN (ADRIAN W.) Die Auswirkung von Arbeitskämpfen im Arbeitsvertragsrecht. Bern, 1976. pp. 85. *bibliog.*

— **United Kingdom.**

FREEDLAND (MARK ROBERT) The contract of employment. Oxford, 1976. pp. 398. *bibliog.*

LABOUR COSTS

— **Canada.**

CANADA. Statistics Canada. Labour costs in Canada: education, libraries and museums. a., 1974- Ottawa.

LABOUR DISCIPLINE

— **France.**

COURTIEU (GUY) L'entreprise, société féodale. Paris, [1975]. pp. 204.

— **United Kingdom.**

ADVISORY CONCILIATION AND ARBITRATION SERVICE [U.K.]. Draft code of practice: disciplinary practice and procedures. [London, 1976]. pp. 7.

LABOUR DISPUTES

LABOUR DISPUTES
— Canada.

COLLECTIVE bargaining in the essential and public service sectors: proceedings of a conference held...1975, organized...through the Centre for Industrial Relations, University of Toronto; (Morley Gunderson, editor). Toronto, [1975]. pp. 159.

— Germany.

FLUEHMANN (ADRIAN W.) Die Auswirkung von Arbeitskämpfen im Arbeitsvertragsrecht. Bern, 1976. pp. 85. *bibliog.*

— Switzerland.

FLUEHMANN (ADRIAN W.) Die Auswirkung von Arbeitskämpfen im Arbeitsvertragsrecht. Bern, 1976. pp. 85. *bibliog.*

LABOUR ECONOMICS.

TARANTELLI (EZIO) Studi di economia del lavoro. Milano, 1974. pp. 257.

NILAND (JOHN R.) and ISAAC (JOSEPH EZRA) eds. Australian labour economics: readings. [2nd ed.] Melbourne, 1975. pp. 676. *bibliogs.*

GINZBERG (ELI) The human economy. New York, [1976]. pp. 274. *bibliog.*

LABOUR LAWS AND LEGISLATION.

ESTUDIOS LABORALES; [pd. by] Instituto de Estudios Laborales y de Seguridad Social, Ministerio de Trabajo. irreg., My 1975(no.1)- Madrid.

— Canada — New Brunswick.

NEW BRUNSWICK. Department of Labour. 1972. A layman's handbook to the Industrial Relations Act. [Fredericton], 1972. pp. 82.

— Denmark.

DAHL PEDERSEN (VAGN) Danmark og de internationale arbejdskonventioner. [Albertslund, 1974]. pp. 332. *bibliog.* *With English summary.*

— Europe, Eastern.

TRÓCSÁNYI (LÁSZLO) Le droit de procédure en matière de conflits du travail dans les pays socialistes européens; (traduit par Béla Végh). Budapest, 1974. pp. 147.

— European Economic Community countries.

EUROPEAN COMMUNITIES. Directorate-General for the Internal Market. 1972. Régime juridique concernant l'accès aux activités non salariées de l'industrie, de l'artisanat, du commerce et des entreprises de services et l'exercice de celles-ci dans les etats membres des Communautés européennes: situation au 31. 12.1970. [Luxembourg, 1972]. pp. 807.

— France.

CONFEDERATION GENERALE DU TRAVAIL: FORCE OUVRIERE. Les délégués du personnel. [Paris, 195-]. pp. 96.

COLLECTIF D'ALPHABÉTISATION and GROUPE D'INFORMATION ET DE SOUTIEN DES TRAVAILLEURS IMMIGRÉS. Le petit livre juridique des travailleurs immigrés. 2nd ed. Paris, 1975. pp. 128.

— Germany.

KLEEMANN (KURT) Die Sozialpolitik der Reichs-Post- und Telegraphenverwaltung gegenüber ihren Beamten, Unterbeamten und Arbeitern. Jena, 1914. pp. 253. *bibliog.* *(Jena. Universität. Staatswissenschaftliches Seminar. Abhandlungen. 14. Band, 1. Heft)*

HOFFKNECHT (ADALBERT CHRISTIAN) Die leitenden Angestellten im Koalitions- und Arbeitskampfrecht. Berlin, [1975]. pp. 148. *bibliog.*

PREMSSLER (MANFRED) Arbeiterrechte in der BRD: Sozialdemagogie und Wirklichkeit. Berlin, 1975. pp. 222.

— Germany, Eastern.

GERMANY (DEUTSCHE DEMOKRATISCHE REPUBLIK). Statutes, etc. 1961-1974 Gesetzbuch der Arbeit und weitere arbeitsrechtliche Vorschriften: Textausgabe mit Anmerkungen und Sachregister; herausgegeben vom Staatssekretariat für Arbeit und Löhne; (zusammengestellt und bearbeitet von Volker Dähne und Harald Widlak). Berlin, 1975. pp. 188.

— Guatemala.

BAUER PAIZ (ALFONSO) Catalogacion de leyes y disposiciones de trabajo de Guatemala del periodo 1872 a 1930. Guatemala, 1965. fo. 222.

— Indonesia.

INDONESIA. Department of Manpower, Transmigration and Cooperatives. Bureau of Legal Affairs. 1974. Indonesian labour legislation. 2nd ed. [Djakarta], 1974. pp. 297.

— Russia.

RUSSIA (USSR). Statutes, etc. 1974. Sbornik zakonodatel'nykh aktov o trude. Moskva, 1974. pp. 1070.

TAITS (IL'IA ARKAD'EVICH) Kodeksy zakonov o trude soiuznykh respublik: sopostavitel'nye tablitsy. Moskva, 1975. pp. 431.

— — Georgia.

GEORGIA (RUSSIA). Statutes, etc. 1973. Kodeks zakonov o trude Gruzinskoi SSR. Tbilisi, 1974. pp. 148.

— — Russia (RSFSR).

RUSSIA (RSFSR). Statutes, etc. 1971. Kodeks zakonov o trude RSFSR: ofitsial'nyi tekst. Moskva, 1974. pp. 80.

— Spain.

PESO Y CALVO (CARLOS DEL) Legislacion laboral basica, etc. 8th ed. Madrid, 1966. pp. 371.

— Sweden.

ADLERCREUTZ (AXEL) Svensk arbetsrätt. 5th ed. Stockholm, 1975. pp. 166. *bibliog.*

— Trinidad and Tobago.

OKPALUBA (CHUKS) Statutory regulation of collective bargaining, with special reference to the Industrial Stabilisation Act of Trinidad and Tobago. Mona, 1975. pp. 183. *bibliog.* *(West Indies, University of the. Institute of Social and Economic Research. Law and Society in the Caribbean. No. 5)*

— United Kingdom.

ELSNER (WOLFGANG) Die Bedeutung des Industrial Relations Act 1971 für das britische Arbeitsrecht bis zu seiner Abschaffung im Jahre 1974. Mannheim, 1975. pp. 129. *bibliog.*

FRANK (WILLIAM FRANCIS) and ROYALL (DAVID V.E.) The legal aspects of industry and commerce. 7th ed. London, 1975. pp. 289. *bibliog.*

HARRIES (JOHN V.) Employment protection - the 1975 Act explained. London, 1975. pp. 194.

ANDERMAN (STEVEN D.) Employment protection: a new legal framework. London, 1976. pp. 310.

RIDEOUT (ROGER W.) Principles of labour law. 2nd ed. London, 1976. pp. 457.

SELWYN (NORMAN M.) Law of employment. London, 1976. pp. 236.

— United States.

WOOD (CLEMENT) and COLEMAN (McALISTER) Don't tread on me: a study of aggressive legal tactics for labor;...in collaboration with Arthur Garfield Hays. New York, 1928. pp. 135.

LABOUR LAWS AND LEGISLATION, INTERNATIONAL.

DAHL PEDERSEN (VAGN) Danmark og de internationale arbejdskonventioner. [Albertslund, 1974]. pp. 332. *bibliog.* *With English summary.*

BUDINER (MELITTA) Le droit de la femme à l'égalité de salaire, et la convention No. 100 de l'Organisation Internationale du Travail. Paris, 1975. pp. 266. *bibliog.*

LABOUR MOBILITY

— Mathematical models.

JONES (DONALD W.) 1948- . Migration and urban unemployment in dualistic economic development. Chicago, 1975. pp. 174. *bibliog.* *(Chicago. University. Department of Geography. Research Papers. No. 165)*

PULLUM (THOMAS W.) Measuring occupational inheritance. Amsterdam, 1975. pp. 184. *bibliog.*

— Austria.

BACH (HANS) Berufliche Mobilität und Anpassungshilfen im Agrarbereich. Linz, 1972. pp. 85. *bibliog.* *(Österreichisches Institut für Arbeitsmarktpolitik. Arbeitsmarktpolitik. Heft 12)*

— Denmark.

SOCIALFORSKNINGSINSTITUTTET. Arbejdskraftens mobilitet, etc. København, 1974 in progress. (Studier. Nr. 30. etc.)

— European Economic Community countries.

EUROPEAN COMMUNITIES. Directorate-General for the Internal Market. 1972. Régime juridique concernant l'accès aux activités non salariées de l'industrie, de l'artisanat, du commerce et des entreprises de services et l'exercice de celles-ci dans les etats membres des Communautés européennes: situation au 31. 12.1970. [Luxembourg, 1972]. pp. 807.

— France.

DESTEFANIS (MICHEL) and VASSEUR (ANNE MARIE) Le fonctionnement d'un marché du travail local: le bassin de main-d'oeuvre d'Annecy. [Paris], 1974. pp. 281. *bibliog.* *(France. Centre d'Etudes de l'Emploi. Cahiers. 5) With summaries in English and German.*

— Italy.

ARINGA (CARLO DELL') La mobilità del lavoro nell'industria italiana: struttura e dinamica emporale; con un'appendice di Francesco Spinelli. Milano, 1974. pp. 105.

— United Kingdom — Ireland, Northern.

SOME aspects of labour mobility in Northern Ireland; by W.D. Birrell [and others]. [Coleraine, 1975]. pp. 81. *(New University of Ulster. Priorities: Occasional Papers in Social Administration)*

LABOUR PARTY

— Israel.

SHAPIRO (YONATHAN) The formative years of the Israeli Labour Party: the organisation of power, 1919-1930. London, [1976]. pp. 282. *bibliog.*

— New Zealand.

EDWARDS (BRIAN) Author of The public eye, ed. Right out: Labour victory '72: the inside story. Wellington, N.Z., 1973. pp. 262.

GUSTAFSON (BARRY) Social change and party organization: the New Zealand Labour Party since 1945. Beverly Hills, [1976]. pp. 59. *bibliog.*

— United Kingdom.

INDEPENDENT LABOUR PARTY. [Minute books of the National Administrative Council and branch minute books. 1893-1931]. 14 vols. *Manuscript, typescript, etc.*

SOUTH PADDINGTON DIVISIONAL LABOUR PARTY. [Minute book. 1929-31]. 1 vol. *Manuscript.*

LABOUR SUPPLY.

BRITISH AND IRISH COMMUNIST ORGANISATION. What is the British Labour Party?. Belfast, 1974. pp. 24.

DURR (ANDY) ed. A history of Brighton Trades Council and Labour Movement, 1890-1970. Brighton, 1974. pp. 80. *(Brighton Hove and District Trades Council. History Sub-Committee. Pamphlets)*

POLOZHENIE i bor'ba britanskogo rabochego klassa. Moskva, 1974. pp. 352.

AIMS FOR FREEDOM AND ENTERPRISE. Labour and industry: the last steps. London, [1975]. pp. 10.

HOLLAND (STUART) Strategy for socialism: the challenge of Labour's programme. Nottingham, 1975. pp. 95.

LABOUR PARTY. A pictorial history of the Labour Party, 1900-1975, to celebrate the seventy-fifth anniversary of its birth. London, 1975. pp. 64.

MACINTYRE (STUART) Imperialism and the British labour movement in the 1920's: an examination of Marxist theory. London, 1975. pp. 24. *(Communist Party of Great Britain. History Group. Our History. No. 64)*

POLIANSKII (FEDOR IAKOVLEVICH) Kritika reformistskikh kontseptsii sovremennogo kapitalizma. Moskva, 1975. pp. 264.

SHEIN (ALEKSANDR IVANOVICH) Kritika ekonomicheskikh teorii pravykh leiboristov Anglii. Moskva, 1975. pp. 200.

BURRIDGE (TREVOR D.) British Labour and Hitler's war. London, 1976. pp. 206. *bibliog.*

FORESTER (TOM) Journalist. The Labour Party and the working class. London, 1976. pp. 166. *bibliog.*

HOWELL (DAVID) 1937- . British social democracy: a study in development and decay. London, [1976]. pp. 320. *bibliog.*

LABOUR PARTY. Labour against racism. London, [1976]. pp. 7.

LABOUR PARTY. National Executive Committee. Banking and finance; a statement...[to be] presented to the Labour Party annual conference, Blackpool 1976. London, [1976]. pp. 24.

LABOUR PARTY. National Executive Committee. Labour's programme for Britain: annual conference, 1976. London, 1976. pp. 147.

LABOUR'S social priorities;...[by] Andrew Creese [and others];...[edited by] Howard Glennerster. London, 1976. pp. 36. *(Fabian Society. Research Series. [No.] 327)*

PANITCH (LEO VICTOR) Social democracy and industrial militancy: the Labour Party, the trade unions and incomes policy, 1945-1974. Cambridge, 1976. pp. 318.

PELLING (HENRY MATHISON) A short history of the Labour Party. 5th ed. London, 1976. pp. 180.

TRADES UNION CONGRESS and LABOUR PARTY. Liaison Committee. The next three years and the problem of priorities. London, 1976. pp. 15.

— — Scotland.

HEALD (DAVID) Making devolution work. London, 1976. pp. 56. *(Young Fabian Group. Young Fabian Pamphlets. 43)*

LABOUR POLICY

— European Economic Community countries.

COLLINS (DOREEN) The European Communities: the social policy of the first phase. London, 1975. 2 vols. *bibliogs.*

— Mexico.

RUIZ (RAMON EDUARDO) Labor and the ambivalent revolutionaries: Mexico, 1911-1923. Baltimore, [1976]. pp. 145. *bibliog.*

— Rhodesia.

VAN ONSELEN (CHARLES) Chibaro: African mine labour in Southern Rhodesia, 1900-1933. London, 1976. pp. 326. *bibliog.*

— Russia.

SCHNEIDERMAN (JEREMIAH) Sergei Zubatov and revolutionary marxism: the struggle for the working class in tsarist Russia. Ithaca, N.Y., 1976. pp. 401. *bibliog.*

— Sweden.

JONES (H.G.) Planning and productivity in Sweden. London, 1976. pp. 212. *bibliog.*

— United Kingdom.

DAHRENDORF (RALF) Conflict and contract: industrial relations and the political community in times of crisis. Liverpool, 1975. pp. 18. *(Leverhulme Memorial Lectures. [New Series]. 1975)*

WIGHAM (ERIC LEONARD) Strikes and the government, 1893-1974. London, 1976. pp. 206. *bibliog.*

— United States.

MILLS (DANIEL QUINN) Government, labor, and inflation: wage stabilization in the United States. Chicago, [1975]. pp. 331.

LABOUR SUPPLY.

BUCHEGGER (REINER) Bestimmungsgründe der Erwerbsquoten und Prognose des Arbeitskräftepotentials: eine Übersicht, etc. Linz, 1972. pp. 94. *bibliog. (Österreichisches Institut für Arbeitsmarktpolitik. Arbeitsmarktpolitik. Heft 11)*

TARANTELLI (EZIO) Studi di economia del lavoro. Milano, 1974. pp. 257.

VOORDEN (WILLEM VAN) Institutionalisering en arbeidsmarktbeleid. Alphen aan den Rijn, 1975. pp. 270. *bibliog. With English summary.*

See also HUMAN CAPITAL.

— Bibliography.

[ROBERTSON (JOHN HENRY)] compiler. Labour utilization: an annotated bibliography of village studies; compiled by John Connell [pseud.]...; prepared for the International Labour Office within the framework of the World Employment Programme. [Brighton], University of Sussex, Institute of Development Studies, 1975. pp. 305.

— Mathematical models.

LAURSEN (KARSTEN) Development of the labour surplus economy: essays in theory and case studies of Colombia. Århus, 1972 repr. 1975. 1 vol. (various pagings). *bibliog. (Aarhus. Universitet. Økonomiske Institut. Memos. 1975.2.)*

WABE (J. STUART) and others. Problems in manpower forecasting. Farnborough, Hants, [1974]. pp. 287. *bibliogs.*

CARNEGIE-ROCHESTER CONFERENCE ON PUBLIC POLICY. 1973, April Conference. The Phillips curve and labor markets: [papers and discussions from the conference]; editors Karl Brunner [and] Allan H. Meltzer. Amsterdam, 1976. pp. 164. *bibliogs. (Journal of Monetary Economics. Carnegie- Rochester Conference Series on Public Policy. vol.1)*

LENDERINK (R.S.G.) and SIEBRAND (J.C.) A disequilibrium analysis of the labour market. Rotterdam, 1976. pp. 117.

— Africa, Central.

UNION DOUANIERE ET ECONOMIQUE DE L'AFRIQUE CENTRALE. Département des Statistiques. 1971. Situation de l'emploi en U.D.E.A.C. Brazzaville, 1971. fo. 64. *(Etudes Statistiques. No. 20)*

— Asia.

UNITED NATIONS. Economic and Social Commission for Asia and the Pacific. Asian Population Studies Series. New York, 1966 in progress.

— Australia.

NILAND (JOHN R.) and ISAAC (JOSEPH EZRA) eds. Australian labour economics: readings. [2nd ed.] Melbourne, 1975. pp. 676. *bibliogs.*

— Azores.

RAMOS (ANTONIO BRITO) Demografia e emprego nas ilhas adjacentes. Lisboa, 1974. pp. 191. *(Portugal. Ministerio do Trabalho. Gabinete de Planeamento. Serie Estudos. 20) With abstracts in English, French and German.*

— Botswana.

BOTSWANA. Central Statistics Office. Employment survey. a., 1973 (4th)- Gaborone.

— Canada.

CANADA MANPOWER AND IMMIGRATION REVIEW (formerly Canada manpower review); [pd. by] Government of Canada Department of Manpower and Immigration. [in English and French]. q., 1970 (v.3)- Ottawa.

COURCHENE (THOMAS J.) Migration, income and employment: Canada, 1965-68. [Montreal, 1974]. pp. 155. *(Howe (C.D.) Research Institute. Special Studies.1.)*

PEITCHINIS (STEPHEN GABRIEL) The Canadian labour market. Toronto, 1975. pp. 367. *bibliogs.*

— — Manitoba.

ECONOMIC DEVELOPMENT ADVISORY BOARD OF MANITOBA. Manpower issues in Manitoba. [Winnipeg], 1975. pp. 276. *bibliog.*

MANITOBA. Department of Industry and Commerce. 1975. A guide to employment and value of production data for industries in Manitoba. [Winnipeg, 1975]. pp. 169.

— — New Brunswick.

LABOUR FORCE REVIEW: a bi-m. pbln. of the Research and Planning Branch of the N[ew] B[runswick] Department of Labour. bi-m., 1973-1975 (v.1-v.3,no.3)., ceased pbln. Fredericton. *Superseded by NEW BRUNSWICK LABOUR FORCE REPORT.*

— Colombia — Mathematical models.

LAURSEN (KARSTEN) Development of the labour surplus economy: essays in theory and case studies of Colombia. Århus, 1972 repr. 1975. 1 vol. (various pagings). *bibliog. (Aarhus. Universitet. Økonomiske Institut. Memos. 1975.2.)*

— European Economic Community countries.

EUROPEAN COMMUNITIES. Statistical Office. Regional statistics: population, employment, living standards. a., 1973/74 [1st]- Luxembourg. *[In Community languages]. Formerly included in EUROPEAN COMMUNITIES. Statistical Office. Regional statistics.*

STEWART (MARGARET) Employment conditions in Europe. 2nd ed. Epping, Essex, 1976. pp. 249. *bibliog.*

— Fiji.

FIJI. Bureau of Statistics. Quarterly survey of employment. q., My 1975- Suva.

— France.

FRANCE. Institut National de la Statistique et des Etudes Economiques. Emploi salarié par région. a., 1967/70- Paris.

ORGANISATION D'ETUDES D'AMENAGEMENT DE L'AIRE METROPOLITAINE NANTES- SAINT-NAZAIRE. Schéma d'aménagement [de l'aire métropolitaine Nantes- Saint-Nazaire]: (annexe); démographie, emploi. Nantes, 1971. pp. 61.

LABOUR SUPPLY.(Cont.)

DESTEFANIS (MICHEL) and VASSEUR (ANNE MARIE) Le fonctionnement d'un marché du travail local: le bassin de main-d'oeuvre d'Annecy. [Paris], 1974. pp. 281. bibliog. *(France. Centre d'Etudes de l'Emploi. Cahiers. 5) With summaries in English and German.*

FRANCE. Direction de la Documentation. La Documentation Française. Notes et Etudes Documentaires. Nos. 4,093-4, 094. Les instruments de la politique de l'emploi; [par Aude Bénoit]. Paris, 1974. pp. 88. *bibliog.*

— Germany.

SOGEMEIER (MARTIN) Die Entwicklung und Regelung des Arbeitsmarktes im rheinisch- westfälischen Industriegebiet im Kriege und in der Nachkriegszeit: ein Beitrag zur Weiterentwicklung des Arbeitsnachweiswesens. Jena, 1922. pp. 123. *(Volkswirtschaftliche Vereinigung im Rheinisch- Westfälischen Industriegebiet. Schriften. Heft 2)*

BESCHAEFTIGUNGSWIRKUNGEN einer verstärkten Arbeitsteilung zwischen der Bundesrepublik und den Entwicklungsländern; ([by] Hugo Dicke [and others]). Tübingen, 1976. pp. 225. bibliog. *(Kiel. Universität. Institut für Weltwirtschaft. Kieler Studien. 137)*

KOERNER (HELLMUT) Der Zustrom von Arbeitskräften in die Bundesrepublik Deutschland, 1950-1972: Auswirkungen auf die Funktionsweise des Arbeitsmarktes. Bern, 1976. pp. 353. bibliog. *(Hamburg. Hansische Universität. Sozialökonomisches Seminar. Schriftenreihe. Band 3)*

— Ghana.

GHANA. Manpower Division. 1972. High level and skilled manpower survey in Ghana, 1968, and assessment of manpower situation, 1971. Accra, 1971 [or rather 1972]. pp. 64.

— India — Mysore.

MYSORE. Directorate of Evaluation and Manpower. 1968. Fact book on manpower. [Bangalore, 1968]. pp. 83.

— Iran.

SHAHEEN (A. SH.) A preliminary study on economics of employment and higher education in Iran; (prepared for the Seminar on Planning and Development of Manpower in Iran). [Tehran], Bureau of Statistics, [1969]. pp. 34.

INTERNATIONAL LABOUR OFFICE. World Employment Programme. 1973. Employment and income policies for Iran. Geneva, 1973. pp. 100.

IRVIN (G.W.) and others. Roads and redistribution: social costs and benefits of labour- intensive road construction in Iran. Geneva, International Labour Office, 1975. pp. 162.

— Jamaica.

JAMAICA. Department of Statistics. The labour force. a., 1973- Kingston.

— Kenya.

VAN ZWANENBERG (R.M.A.) Colonial capitalism and labour in Kenya, 1919-1939. Kampala, 1975. pp. 314. *bibliog.*

— Korea.

HONG (WONTACK) Factor supply and factor intensity of trade in Korea. Seoul, 1976. pp. 236. *bibliog.*

— Madeira.

RAMOS (ANTONIO BRITO) Demografia e emprego nas ilhas adjacentes. Lisboa, 1974. pp. 191. *(Portugal. Ministerio do Trabalho. Gabinete de Planeamento. Serie Estudos. 20) With abstracts in English, French and German.*

— Malaysia.

SAW (SWEE HOCK) Population and labour force projections for West Malaysia, 1962- 1987. Hong Kong, 1970. pp. 27. *(Hong Kong. University. Centre of Asian Studies. Occasional Papers and Monographs. No. 1)*

SAW (SWEE HOCK) Estimates of population and labour force by age group for West Malaysia and Singapore, 1958-1967. Hong Kong, 1971. pp. 38. *(Hong Kong. University. Centre of Asian Studies. Occasional Papers and Monographs. No. 6)*

— Netherlands.

VOORDEN (WILLEM VAN) Institutionalisering en arbeidsmarktbeleid. Alphen aan den Rijn, 1975. pp. 270. bibliog. *With English summary.*

— — Mathematical models.

LENDERINK (R.S.G.) and SIEBRAND (J.C.) A disequilibrium analysis of the labour market. Rotterdam, 1976. pp. 117.

— New Zealand.

NEW ZEALAND. Department of Labour. Research and Planning Division. Reports Series. Wellington, 1972 in progress.

— — Mathematical models.

GALLACHER (JOHN) Estimation of aggregate employment and production functions for New Zealand. Wellington, 1975. pp. 47. *(Reserve Bank of New Zealand. Research Papers. No. 16)*

— Nigeria.

NIGERIA (WESTERN STATE). Ministry of Economic Planning and Reconstruction. Statistics Division. 1970. Report of a survey of manpower shortages and surpluses in the Western State and of the capacity utilisation of educational and training institutions. Ibadan, [1970]. pp. 82.

— Norway.

RASMUSSEN (TOR FR.) Yrkesbefolkningen i Norge...: the economically active population in Norway. Oslo, 1975. pp. 95. *(Norway. Statistiske Centralbyrå. Artikler. Nr.76) With English summary.*

— Poland.

KSZTALTOWANIE się załóg w regionach uprzemysławianych. Warszawa, 1974. pp. 316. *(Szkoła Główna Planowania i Statystyki. Monografie i Opracowania. 34)*

— Portugal.

PORTUGAL. Ministerio do Trabalho. Gabinete de Estudos, Planeamento e Organização. Relatorio de conjuntura. q., 1974 (no.4)- Lisboa.

RAMOS (ANTONIO BRITO) O emprego no sector terciario metropolitano: tentatiras de localização do crescimento. Lisboa, 1974. pp. 103. *(Portugal. Ministerio do Trabalho. Gabinete de Planeamento. Serie Estudos. 24) With abstracts in English, French and German.*

RODRIGUES (ELIA MARIA) População potencialmente activa: situação passada, presente e futura. Lisboa, 1974. pp. 37. *(Portugal, Ministerio do Trabalho. Gabinete de Planeamento. Serie Estudos. 28) With abstracts in English, French and German.*

VITAL (MARIA ODETE) O emprego nos planos de fomento portugueses. Lisboa, 1974. pp. 65. *(Portugal. Ministerio do Trabalho. Gabinete de Planeamento. Serie Estudos. 25) With abstracts in English, French and German.*

VITAL (MARIA ODETE) and FIALHO (JOSE ANTONIO SOUSA) Aspectos globais do problema do emprego em Portugal continental. Lisboa, 1974. pp. 28. *(Portugal. Ministerio do Trabalho. Gabinete de Planeamento. Serie Estudos. 17) With abstracts in English, French and German.*

— Russia.

RUSSIA (USSR). Ministerstvo Vysshego i Srednego Spetsial'nogo Obrazovaniia. Nauchno-Tekhnicheskii Sovet. Sektsiia Narodonaseleniia. Narodonaselenie. 3. Naselenie i trudovye resursy. Moskva, 1973. pp. 79. *With English table of contents.*

RUSSIA (USSR). Ministerstvo Vysshego i Srednego Spetsial'nogo Obrazovaniia. Nauchno-Tekhnicheskii Sovet. Sektsiia Narodonaseleniia. Narodonaselenie. 4. Prikladnaia demografiia. Moskva, 1973. pp. 136. *With English table of contents.*

BREEV (BORIS DMITRIEVICH) and KRIUKOV (V.P.) Mezhotraslevoi balans dvizheniia naseleniia i trudovykh resursov: metodologicheskie voprosy. Moskva, 1974. pp. 183. *bibliog.*

KASIMOVSKII (EVGENII VASIL'EVICH) ed. Trudovye resursy: formirovanie i ispol'zovanie. Moskva, 1975. pp. 254.

RUZAVINA (EKATERINA IVANOVNA) Zaniatost' v usloviiakh intensifikatsii proizvodstva. Moskva, 1975. pp. 124.

— Singapore.

SAW (SWEE HOCK) Estimates of population and labour force by age group for West Malaysia and Singapore, 1958-1967. Hong Kong, 1971. pp. 38. *(Hong Kong. University. Centre of Asian Studies. Occasional Papers and Monographs. No. 6)*

REPORT ON THE LABOUR FORCE SURVEY OF SINGAPORE, [pd. by] Ministry of Labour. 1975 (2nd)- Singapore.

— South Africa.

SOUTH AFRICA. Census, 1970. Population census, 1970: occupations: income, industry and identity. [Pretoria, 1975]. pp. 360. *(Bureau of Statistics. Reports. No. 02-05-04) In English and Afrikaans.*

ORPEN (CHRISTOPHER) Productivity and black workers in South Africa. Cape Town, [1976]. pp. 283. *bibliog.*

SOUTH AFRICA. Census, 1970. Population census, 1970: occupation and industry by district and economic region. [Pretoria, 1976]. pp. 230. *(Bureau of Statistics. Reports. No. 02-05-06) In English and Afrikaans.*

— Sri Lanka.

SRIVASTAVA (R.K.) and others. Manpower matrix, (Ceylon), 1966; draft. Colombo, Ministry of Planning and Economic Affairs, 1968. 1 pamphlet (various foliations).

WILSON (PITIYAGE) Economic implications of population growth: Sri Lanka labour force, 1946-81. Canberra, 1975. pp. 240. *bibliog.*

— Swaziland.

SWAZILAND. Central Statistical Office. Employment and wages. a., 1970/71(3rd)- [Mbabane].

— Sweden.

SWEDEN. Statistiska Centralbyrån. Arbetsmarknadsstatistisk årsbok. a., 1973 (1st)- Stockholm. *In Swedish, with notes and headings in English.*

ANDERSSON (ROLF) and MEIDNER (RUDOLF) Arbetsmarknadspolitik och stabilisering. [Stockholm, 1973]. pp. 88. *(Institutet för Social Forskning. Skrifter. 4)*

— Trinidad and Tobago.

CHERNICK (SIDNEY E.) and others. Employment in Trinidad and Tobago. [Washington], International Bank for Reconstruction and Development, 1973. 2 vols. *(Country Economic Reports)*

— Turkey.

HIÇ (MÜKERREM) Employment and wages in the automotive and other assembly industries in Turkey. Istanbul, 1974. pp. 58. *(Istanbul. Üniversitesi. Iktisat Fakültesi. Institute of Economic Development. Yayinlari. No. 23)*

— Uganda.

UGANDA. Manpower Planning Division. 1970. High level manpower survey, 1967 and analyses of requirements, 1967- 1981. [Entebbe, 1970]. pp. 53.

— Underdeveloped areas.

See UNDERDEVELOPED AREAS — Labour supply.

— United Kingdom.

FRANCIS (KEITH) The working population of South Hampshire: the present situation and likely trends to 2001. [Winchester], 1969. pp. 14. *(South Hampshire Plan Technical Unit. Working Papers. 3)*

SMITH (BARBARA M.D.) Regional unemployment differentials and regional policy: a review of events. Birmingham, 1973. fo. 22. *bibliog. (Birmingham. University. Centre for Urban and Regional Studies. Working Papers. No. 11)*

CUMBRIA COMMUNITY DEVELOPMENT PROJECT. Reports on employment, unemployment and population trends in Cleator Moor and Frizington. [Cleator Moor], 1974. pp. 29.

NATIONAL ECONOMIC DEVELOPMENT OFFICE. A study of two local labour markets: short summary of report on research carried out in Manchester and Liverpool by Michael Woodhead. London, 1975. pp. 16.

PETTMAN (B. O.) ed. Labour turnover and retention. Epping, Essex, 1975. pp. 204. *bibliog.*

U.K. Department of Employment. 1975. Monitoring of the west midlands regional strategy: employment trends in the region. [London, 1975]. pp. 12. *Photocopy.*

U.K. Department of Employment. Unit for Manpower Studies. 1975. The changing structure of the labour force; project report. London, [1975]. pp. 41.

HUGHES (JOHN DENNIS) Industrial restructuring: some manpower aspects. London, National Economic Development Office, 1976. pp. 62. *(Discussion Papers. 4)*

LONDON. University. London School of Economics and Political Science. Department of Geography. British cities: urban population and employment trends 1951-71; (Part 1 of the final report of a study of Urban change in Britain, 1951-71, undertaken...on behalf of the Urban Affairs and Commercial Property Directorate of the Department of the Environment). [London, 1976]. pp. 69. *(U.K. Department of the Environment. Research Reports. 10)*

NORTHERN REGION STRATEGY TEAM. Economic activity rates in the northern region. Newcastle upon Tyne, 1976. 1 vol. (various pagings). *(Technical Reports. No. 7)*

SMITH (JOHN W.) Labour supply and employment duration in London Transport. London, 1976. pp. 65. *(London. University. London School of Economics and Political Science. Greater London Group. Greater London Papers. No.15)*

U.K. Census, 1971. Census, 1971: England and Wales: economic activity sub- regional tables; 10 per cent sample. London, 1976. pp. 411.

U.K. Census, 1971. Census, 1971: England and Wales: new towns: economic activity, workplace and transport to work tables; 10 per cent sample. London, 1976. pp. 107.

U.K. Census, 1971. Census, 1971: Great Britain: qualified manpower tables; 10 per cent sample. London, 1976. pp. 138.

U.K. Central Statistical Office. 1976. Qualified manpower in Great Britain, 1971 census of population. London, 1976. pp. 32. *(Studies in Official Statistics. No. 29)*

— — Mathematical models.

WABE (J. STUART) and others. Problems in manpower forecasting. Farnborough, Hants, [1974]. pp. 287. *bibliogs.*

— — Scotland.

CARSTAIRS (ANDREW McLAREN) The Tayside industrial population: the changing character and distribution of the industrial population in the Tayside area, 1911- 1951. Dundee, 1974. pp. 115. *(Abertay Historical Society. Publications. No. 17)*

SCOTLAND. Census, 1971. Census, 1971: Scotland: economic activity: county tables, 10 per cent sample. Edinburgh, 1975. 4 pts. (in 1 vol.).

— United States.

CONFERENCE ON LABOR IN NONPROFIT INDUSTRY AND GOVERNMENT, PRINCETON UNIVERSITY, 1973. Labor in the public and nonprofit sectors: [papers of the conference, sponsored by the Industrial Relations Section of Princeton University and the Manpower Administration of the U.S. Department of Labor]; edited by Daniel S. Hamermesh. Princeton, [1975]. pp. 272. *bibliog.*

CONFERENCE ON LABOR MARKET SEGMENTATION, HARVARD UNIVERSITY, 1973. Labor market segmentation: [papers presented at the conference]; edited by Richard C. Edwards [and others]. Lexington, Mass., [1975]. pp. 297. *bibliogs.*

KREPS (JUANITA MORRIS) and CLARK (ROBERT) Sex, age, and work: the changing composition of the labor force. Baltimore, [1975]. pp. 95. *bibliog.*

FREEMAN (RICHARD BARRY) The overeducated American. New York, [1976]. pp. 218.

HANSEN (NILES M.) Improving access to economic opportunity: nonmetropolitan labor markets in an urban society. Cambridge, Mass., [1976]. pp. 192.

LEVITAN (SAR A.) and others. Human resources and labor markets: (labor and manpower in the American economy). 2nd ed. New York, [1976]. pp. 631. *bibliog.*

ORNSTEIN (MICHAEL D.) Entry into the American labor force. New York, [1976]. pp. 220. *bibliog.*

— — California.

CALIFORNIA COMMUNITY LABOR MARKET SURVEYS; [pd. by] Department of Human Resources Development (California). bien., 1969/1970- San Francisco.

— Yugoslavia.

YUGOSLAVIA. Savezni Zavod za Statistiku. Studije, Analize i Prikazi. 68. Raspored opština u Jugoslaviji prema veličini udela zaposlenih društvenog sektora u primarnim, sekundarnim i tercijarnim delatnostima 31. marta 1971.; Distribution des communes en Yougoslavie selon la part de la main-d'oeuvre du secteur social dans les activités primaires, secondaires et tertiaires au 31 mars 1971; [by] Božidar Stevanović. Beograd, 1974. pp. 75. *With French summary. Cover gives author's name as Stefanović.*

LABOUR TURNOVER

— United Kingdom.

SMITH (JOHN W.) Labour supply and employment duration in London Transport. London, 1976. pp. 65. *(London. University. London School of Economics and Political Science. Greater London Group. Greater London Papers. No.15)*

LABRADOR

— Economic conditions.

NEWFOUNDLAND. Royal Commission on Labrador, 1974. Summary of the report; (with Recommendations). [St. John's], 1974. 2 vols.

— Social conditions.

NEWFOUNDLAND. Royal Commission on Labrador, 1974. Summary of the report; (with Recommendations). [St. John's], 1974. 2 vols.

LABRIOLA (ANTONIO).

LABRIOLA (ANTONIO) Lettere a Benedetto Croce, 1885-1904. Napoli, 1975. pp. 423.

PANE (LUIGI DAL) Antonio Labriola nella politica e nella cultura italiana. Torino, [1975]. pp. 509.

LA FOLLETTE (ROBERT MARION) the Elder.

THELEN (DAVID P.) Robert M. La Follette and the insurgent spirit. Boston, Mass., [1976]. pp. 211. *bibliog.*

LA HAYE (LOUIS MARIE DE) Vicomte de Cormenin.

MIRECOURT (EUGENE DE) pseud. [i.e. Charles Jean Baptiste JACQUOT] Cormenin. Paris, Chez l'Auteur, 1858. pp. 89. *(Les Contemporains)*

LAM (JAN).

LAM (JAN) Wybór kronik; (opracował Stanisław Frybes). Warszawa, 1954. pp. 386. *Articles first published in Gazeta narodowa and Dziennik polski, 1868-85.*

LAMB (WILLIAM) 2nd Viscount Melbourne.

MARSHALL (DOROTHY) Lord Melbourne. London, [1975?]. pp. 173. *bibliog.*

LAMBETH

— Civic improvement.

SHANKLAND-COX PARTNERSHIP and INSTITUTE OF COMMUNITY STUDIES. Inner area study: Lambeth: policies and structure. [London], Department of the Environment, [1975]. pp. 70.

SHANKLAND-COX PARTNERSHIP and INSTITUTE OF COMMUNITY STUDIES. Inner area study: Lambeth: London's inner area: problems and possibilities. [London], Department of the Environment, [1976]. pp. 53.

— Politics and government.

SHANKLAND-COX PARTNERSHIP and INSTITUTE OF COMMUNITY STUDIES. Inner area study: Lambeth: local services: consumers sample. [London], Department of the Environment, [1975]. pp. 13.

— Poor.

SHANKLAND-COX PARTNERSHIP and INSTITUTE OF COMMUNITY STUDIES. Inner area study: Lambeth: poverty and multiple deprivation. [London], Department of the Environment, [1975]. pp. 30.

— Social conditions.

SHANKLAND-COX PARTNERSHIP and INSTITUTE OF COMMUNITY STUDIES. Inner area study: Lambeth: schools project. [London], Department of the Environment, [1976]. pp. 28, (22).

— Social policy.

SHANKLAND-COX PARTNERSHIP and INSTITUTE OF COMMUNITY STUDIES. Inner area study: Lambeth: London's inner area: problems and possibilities. [London], Department of the Environment, [1976]. pp. 53.

LAMPSON (MILES WEDDERBURN) 1st Baron Killearn.

KANE (HAROLD EDWIN) Sir Miles Lampson at the Peking legation, 1926-1933. 1975. fo. 192. *bibliog. Typescript. Ph.D.(London) thesis: unpublished. This thesis is the property of London University and may not be removed from the Library.*

LANCASHIRE

— Economic history.

HUTCHINS (ELIZABETH LEIGH) [Correspondence about women's employment in Lancashire. 1914]. 12 letters. *Manuscript.*

LANCASTER UNIVERSITY.

SIMPSON (M.G.) and others. University of Lancaster: planning university development. [Paris], Organisation for Economic Co-opération and Development, 1972. pp. 134. *(Centre for Educational Research and Innovation. Studies in Institutional Management in Higher Education)*

LAND.

LAND.

DENMAN (DONALD ROBERT) Land economy: an education and a career. Berkhamsted, [1975]. pp. 32. *bibliog.*

STABLER (M.J.) Agricultural economics and rural land-use. London, 1975. pp. 95. *bibliog.*

VASHANOV (VIACHESLAV ALEKSEEVICH) and LOIKO (PETR FEDOROVICH) Zemlia i liudi: ispol'zovanie zemel'nykh resursov v usloviiakh nauchno-tekhnicheskoi revoliutsii. Moskva, 1975. pp. 199.

CONKLING (EDGAR C.) and YEATES (MAURICE H.) Man's economic environment. New York, [1976]. pp. 308. *bibliog.*

— Taxation.

SKOURAS (ATHANASSIOS S.) An examination of some theoretical aspects of land taxation with a concluding reference to certain practical problems; [Ph.D. (London) thesis]. 1975. fo. 214. *bibliog. Typescript: unpublished. This thesis is the property of London University and may not be removed from the Library.*

— Africa.

LAND ADMINISTRATION AND THE DEVELOPMENT OF AFRICAN RESOURCES SEMINAR, IBADAN, 1972. Report of proceedings [of the]...Seminar [held at the] University of Ibadan, Nigeria, (27 November - 2 December) 1972. [Addis Ababa], United Nations Economic Commission for Africa, 1972. 1 vol. (various pagings)

— Australia — Queensland.

AUSTRALIA. Bureau of Agricultural Economics. 1968. The economics of land development in the Belyando-Suttor rivers region, Queensland. Canberra, 1968. pp. 64. *bibliog. Map in end pocket.*

— — Victoria.

NEWELL (J.W.) Soils and land use in the Ovens and Buffalo river valleys, Victoria. Melbourne, 1970. pp. 51,18 maps. *bibliog. (Victoria. Department of Agriculture. Technical Bulletins. No. 21)*

SKENE (J.K.M.) Soils and land use in the mid-Loddon valley, Victoria, etc. Melbourne, 1971. pp. 57,42 maps. *bibliog. (Victoria. Department of Agriculture. Technical Bulletins. No. 22) Map in end pocket.*

— Canada.

PIERCE (JOHN TISDALE) Urban growth in Canada: a study of land conversion, 1966-1971. 1976. fo. 332. *bibliog. Typescript. Ph.D. (London) thesis: unpublished. This thesis is the property of London University and may not be removed from the Library.*

— — Ontario.

MAHANEY (WILLIAM C.) and ERMUTH (FREDERICK) The effects of agriculture and urbanization on the natural environment: a study of human impact in southern Ontario. Toronto, 1974. pp. 152. *bibliog. (York University (Toronto). Department of Geography. Geographical Monographs. No. 7)*

— — — Classification.

ONTARIO. Ministry of Treasury, Economics and Intergovernmental Affairs. Local Planning Policy Branch. 1974. Ontario land use classification: activity and structure. [Toronto], 1974. fo. 93. *bibliog.*

— Ethiopia.

DEVELOPMENT prospects in the southern Rift Valley, Ethiopia; [by] M.J. Makin [and others]. Tolworth, 1975. pp. 266. *bibliog. (U.K. Ministry of Overseas Development. Land Resources Division. Land Resource Studies. 21) Map sheet in end pocket.*

— Nigeria.

GODDARD (A.D.) Population movements and land shortages in the Sokoto close-settled zone, Nigeria. Zaria, 1973. pp. 18. *bibliog. (Ahmadu Bello University. Institute for Agricultural Research. Samaru Research Bulletins. [No]. 201)*

— Poland — Law.

MIZERA (STEFAN) and POCZOBUTT-ODLANICKI (ANDRZEJ) Ceny i opłaty za grunty w miastach i na wsi: problematyka prawna; stan prawny na dzień 15 marca 1974 r. Wrocław, 1974. pp. 282. *bibliog.*

— Switzerland.

SWITZERLAND. Bureau Fédéral de Statistique. 1972. Arealstatistik der Schweiz...1972. Bern, 1972. pp. 121 and 19 maps. *(Statistiques de la Suisse. 488e fasc.) In German and French.*

— Underdeveloped areas.

See UNDERDEVELOPED AREAS — Land.

— United Kingdom.

CROSBIE (GEORGE VERTUE) Observations on the emancipation of industry. London, 1892. pp. 138.

ROYAL INSTITUTION OF CHARTERED SURVEYORS. The land problem: a fresh approach. London, [1974]. pp. 43.

DOUGLAS (ROY) Land, people and politics: a history of the land question in the United Kingdom, 1878-1952. London, [1976]. pp. 239. *bibliog.*

— — Classification.

U.K. Study Group on Agricultural Land Classification. 1966. Agricultural land classification; first progress report; [D.J. Griffiths, chairman]. [London], 1966 [repr. 1974]. pp. 27. *bibliog. (U.K. Ministry of Agriculture, Fisheries and Food. Agricultural Land Service. Technical Reports. No. 11)*

— — Prices.

AGRICULTURAL LAND PRICES IN ENGLAND AND WALES; [pd. by] Ministry of Agriculture, Fisheries and Food, (Economic and Statistics Group and Agricultural Land Service), [U.K.]. a., 1970 (no.3)- London.

NEUBURGER (H.L.I.) and NICHOL (B.M.) The recent course of land and property prices and the factors underlying it. [London, 1976]. pp. 61. *(U.K. Department of the Environment. Research Reports. 4)*

— United States.

BARAM (MICHAEL S.) and others. Environmental law and the siting of facilities: issues in land use and coastal zone management. Cambridge, Mass., [1976]. pp. 255.

PROPERTY taxation, land use and public policy; edited by Arthur D. Lynn, Jr. Madison, Wis., 1976. pp. 252. *(Committee on Taxation, Resources and Economic Development. Publications.8) Proceedings of a symposium held at the University of Wisconsin-Madison, 1973.*

SIEGAN (BERNARD H.) Other people's property. Lexington, Mass., [1976]. pp. 147.

WATSON (JAMES WREFORD) and O'RIORDAN (TIMOTHY) eds. The American environment: perceptions and policies. London, [1976]. pp. 340. *bibliogs.*

— — Pennsylvania.

STRONG (ANN LOUISE) Private property and the public interest: the Brandywine experience. Baltimore, [1975]. pp. 206. *(Johns Hopkins University. Center for Metropolitan Planning and Research. Johns Hopkins Studies in Urban Affairs)*

— Zambia.

LAND resources of the Northern and Luapula provinces, Zambia: a reconnaissance assessment; [by] J.E. Mansfield [and others]. Tolworth, 1975-76. 6 vols. *bibliogs. (U.K. Ministry of Overseas Development. Land Resources Division. Land Resource Studies. 19)*

LAND, NATIONALIZATION OF

— United Kingdom.

LAWRENCE (MICHAEL) Your home in their hands: the future under the Community Land Act. London, 1976. pp. 13.

U.K. Department of the Environment. 1976. Community Land Act, 1975. [London], 1976. pp. (14).

U.K. Department of the Environment. 1976. The community land scheme. (Booklet) 1. An introduction. [London, 1976]. pp. 7.

U.K. Department of the Environment. 1976. The community land scheme. (Booklet) 2. Planning applications and permissions for relevant development. [London, 1976]. pp. 14.

— — Wales.

U.K. Welsh Office. 1975. Community ownership of development land in Wales: summary consultation document. [Cardiff?], 1975. 1 pamphlet (various pagings).

LAND REFORM

— Africa.

LAND ADMINISTRATION AND THE DEVELOPMENT OF AFRICAN RESOURCES SEMINAR, IBADAN, 1972. Report of proceedings [of the]...Seminar [held at the] University of Ibadan, Nigeria, (27 November - 2 December) 1972. [Addis Ababa], United Nations Economic Commission for Africa, 1972. 1 vol. (various pagings)

— America, Latin.

FALS BORDA (ORLANDO) El reformismo por dentro en America Latina. Mexico, 1972. pp. 211.

SMITH (CLIFFORD THORPE) ed. Studies in Latin-American agrarian reform. Liverpool, 1974. pp. 84. *(Liverpool. University. Centre for Latin American Studies. Monograph Series. No. 5)*

— — Bibliography.

WISCONSIN UNIVERSITY, MADISON. Land Tenure Center. Library. Agrarian reform in Latin America: an annotated bibliography; compiled by the staff of the Land Tenure Center Library. Madison, 1974. 2 vols. (in 1). *(Land Economics. Monograph Series. No. 5)*

— Bolivia.

BEYOND the revolution: Bolivia since 1952; James M. Malloy and Richard S. Thorn, editors. Pittsburgh, [1971]. pp. 402. *Based on an interdisciplinary seminar held at the University of Pittsburgh, sponsored by the University's Center for International Studies and Center for Latin American Studies.*

— Chile.

SAAVEDRA (ALEJANDRO) Capitalismo y lucha de clases en el campo: Chile 1970-72. Madrid, 1975. pp. 291.

LOVEMAN (BRIAN) Struggle in the countryside: politics and rural labor in Chile, 1919-1973. Bloomington, Ind., [1976]. pp. 439. *bibliog. (Indiana University. International Development Research Center. Studies in Development. No. 10)*

— Dominican Republic.

CLAUSNER (MARLIN D.) Rural Santo Domingo: settled, unsettled, and resettled. Philadelphia, 1973. pp. 323. *bibliog.*

— **Finland.**

SCHROWE (YRJÖ JOHANNES VON) Die finnischen Gemeinheitsteilungen im 18. Jahrhundert: Beitrag zur Agrargeschichte Finnlands. Berlin, 1928. pp. 153. *bibliog. (Sozialwissenschaftliche Arbeitsgemeinschaft. Sozialwissenschaftliche Forschungen. Abteilung 2, Heft 4) 5 maps in end pocket.*

— **Germany.**

TRITTEL (GUENTER J.) Die Bodenreform in der britischen Zone, 1945-1949. Stuttgart, [1975]. pp. 185. *bibliog. (Vierteljahrshefte für Zeitgeschichte. Schriftenreihe. Nr.31)*

— **India — Goa, Daman and Diu.**

GOA, DAMAN AND DIU. Land Reforms Committee. 1971. Report; [Anthony J. D'Souza, chairman]. [Panaji, 1971]. pp. 58.

— **Jordan.**

HAZELTON (JARED E.) The impact of the East Ghor canal project on land consolidation, distribution and tenure. Amman, 1974. fo. 49. *(Royal Scientific Society [Jordan]. Economic Research Department. Jordan Economic Studies. 04-06)*

— **Philippine Islands.**

ESTRELLA (CONRADO F.) The meaning of land reform. Manila, 1974. pp. 78.

— **Russia.**

KOSTRIKIN (VASILII IVANOVICH) Zemel'nye komitety v 1917 godu. Moskva, 1975. pp. 336.

ZYBKOVETS (VLADIMIR FILATOVICH) Natsionalizatsiia monastyrskikh imushchestv v Sovetskoi Rossii, 1917-1921 gg. Moskva, 1975. pp. 205.

— **Underdeveloped areas.**

See UNDERDEVELOPED AREAS — Land reform.

LAND SETTLEMENT

— **Dominican Republic.**

CLAUSNER (MARLIN D.) Rural Santo Domingo: settled, unsettled, and resettled. Philadelphia, 1973. pp. 323. *bibliog.*

— **Kenya.**

BULLOCK (R.A.) Ndeiya, Kikuyu frontier: the Kenya land problem in microcosm. Waterloo, Ont., [1975]. pp. 144. *(University of Waterloo, [Ontario]. Department of Geography. Publication Series. No. 6)*

— **Peru.**

COLLIER (DAVID) Squatters and oligarchs: authoritarian rule and policy change in Peru. Baltimore, [1976]. pp. 187. *bibliog.*

— **Rhodesia.**

CATHOLIC COMMISSION FOR JUSTICE AND PEACE IN RHODESIA. The man in the middle: torture, resettlement and eviction. London, [1975]. pp. 22.

— **Romania.**

RELATIONS between the autochthonous population and the migratory populations on the territory of Romania: a collection of studies; editors Miron Constantinescu [and others]. Bucuresti, 1975. pp. 323. *(Academia Republicii Socialiste Romania. Sectia de Stiinte Istorice, Filozofice si Economico-Juridice. Bibliotheca Historica Romaniae. Monographies. 16)*

— **Saint Lucia.**

FOREMAN (R. ASTON) Land settlement scheme for Saint Lucia, based on a survey of the agricultural and social conditions of the island. Castries, 1958. pp. 54.

— **Sweden.**

ENEQUIST (GERD) Geographical changes of rural settlement in northwestern Sweden since 1523. Uppsala, [1959]. pp. 44. *bibliog. (Uppsala. Universitet. Årsskrifter. 1959.8)*

— **United Kingdom — Kent.**

WITNEY (K.P.) The Jutish forest: a study of the Weald of Kent from 450 to 1380 A.D. London, 1976. pp. 339. *bibliog.*

LAND TENURE.

[GOSSELIN (CHARLES ROBERT)] Réflexions d'un citoyen adressées aux notables sur la question proposée par un grand roi: "En quoi consiste le bonheur des peuples et quels sont les moyens de le procurer?"; ou sur cette autre: "D'où vient la misère des peuples, et quels sont les moyens d'y rémédier?". [Paris], 1787; repr. Paris, 1966. pp. vi, 76. *Facsimile reprint.*

UNITED NATIONS. Department of Economic and Social Affairs. 1973-75. Urban land policies and land-use control measures. New York, 1973-75. 7 vols. (in 1).

— **Law.**

SIMPSON (STANHOPE ROWTON) Land law and registration. Cambridge, 1976. pp. 726. *bibliog. This work is intended to replace E. Dowson and V.L.O. Sheppard's Land Registration.*

— **America, Latin.**

SHAW (R. PAUL) Land tenure and the rural exodus in Chile, Colombia, Costa Rica, and Peru. Gainesville, Fla., 1976. pp. 180. *bibliog. (Florida University. School of Inter-American Studies. Latin American Monographs. 2nd Series. [No]. 19)*

— **Belgium — Law.**

DELNOY (PAUL) Politique agricole des structures et régimes juridiques d'exploitation du facteur terre. Liège, 1975. pp. 546. *bibliog. (Liège. Université. Faculté de Droit. Collection Scientifique. 38)*

— **Chile.**

LOVEMAN (BRIAN) Struggle in the countryside: politics and rural labor in Chile, 1919-1973. Bloomington, Ind., [1976]. pp. 439. *bibliog. (Indiana University. International Development Research Center. Studies in Development. No. 10)*

— **Cyprus.**

KAROUZIS (GEORGE) Proposals for a solution to the Cyprus problem. Nicosia, 1976. pp. 208. *bibliog.*

— **Denmark.**

MOGENSEN (MARGIT) Faestebønderne i Odsherred: studier over sociale og økonomiske forhold ca. 1750-1800. København, 1974. pp. 212. *bibliog. (Københavns Universitet. Lokalhistorisk Afdeling. Skrifter. Nr. 4)*

— **Ethiopia.**

COHEN (JOHN M.) and WEINTRAUB (DOV) Land and peasants in imperial Ethiopia: the social background to a revolution. Assen, 1975. pp. 115.

— **Europe.**

EUROPEAN peasants and their markets: essays in agrarian economic history; edited by William N. Parker and Eric L. Jones. Princeton, [1975]. pp. 366.

FAMILY and inheritance: rural society in western Europe, 1200- 1800; edited by Jack Goody [and others]. Cambridge, 1976. pp. 421. *(Past and Present. Past and Present Publications) Revised versions of papers delivered at the annual conference of the Past and Present Society.*

— **France.**

[MARTIN DE SALINS (C.C.)] Nécessité et moyens d'établir une loi agraire, d'assurer la subsistance des pauvres, de réformer le clergé et la constitution militaire; par C.C.M. de S...ns. n.p. 1789; repr. Paris, 1966. pp. 49. *Facsimile reprint.*

— **Guatemala.**

INTER-AMERICAN COMMITTEE FOR AGRICULTURAL DEVELOPMENT. 1971. Tenencia de la tierra y desarrollo socio-economico del sector agricola en Guatemala. Guatemala, 1971. pp. 395. *bibliog.*

— **Ireland (Republic) — Law.**

WYLIE (J.C.W.) Irish land law. London, 1975. pp. 914.

— **Italy.**

SERENI (EMILIO) La questione agraria nella rinascita nazionale italiana. 2nd ed. Torino, [1975]. pp. 450.

— **Kenya.**

MBITHI (PHILIP M.) and BARNES (CAROLYN) The spontaneous settlement problem in Kenya. Kampala, 1975. pp. 192.

— **Mexico.**

FIGUEROA (FERNANDO) Las comunidades agrarias. Mexico, 1970. pp. 229. *bibliog.*

— **New Guinea, German — Law.**

GERMAN NEW GUINEA. Statutes, etc. 1885-1914. The land law of German New Guinea: a collection of documents; [edited by] Peter and Bridget Sack. Canberra, 1975. pp. 120. *bibliog.*

— **New Zealand.**

NEW ZEALAND. Commission of Inquiry into Maori Reserved Land. 1975. Report; [Bartholomew Sheehan, chairman]. Wellington, 1975. pp. 498.

— **Peru.**

PIEL (JEAN) Capitalisme agraire au Pérou. Paris, 1975 in progress. *(Institute Ffrançais d'Etudes Andines. Travaux)*

— **Poland.**

STELMACHOWSKI (ANDRZEJ) ed. Przemiany własności ziemi w rolnictwie polskim. Wrocław, 1974. pp. 189.

WAWRZYŃCZYK (ALINA) Studia nad wydajnością produkcji rolnej dóbr królewskich w drugiej połowie XVI wieku. Wrocław, 1974. pp. 230. *With French summary.*

— **Russia.**

PORITSKII (VLADIMIR ANDREEVICH) Leninskii dekret o zemle i ego burzhuaznye kritiki. Moskva, 1975. pp. 126. *bibliog.*

— — **Law.**

KOLOTINSKAIA (ELENA NIKOLAEVNA) Pravovye osnovy sovetskogo zemel'nogo kadastra. Moskva, 1974 in progress.

SYRODOEV (NIKOLAI ALEKSEEVICH) Zemlepol'zovanie sotsialisticheskikh organizatsii i grazhdan. Moskva, 1975. pp. 255.

— **Sicily.**

CANCILA (ORAZIO) Gabelloti e contadini in un comune rurale, secc. XVIII-XIX. Caltanissetta, 1974. pp. 219. *(Unione delle Camere di Commercio, Industria, Artigianato ed Agricoltura della Regione Siciliana. Storia Economica di Sicilia. Testi e Ricerche. 21-22)*

— **Tanzania.**

PIPPING (KNUT) Land holding in the Usangu plain: a survey of two villages in the Southern highlands of Tanzania. Uppsala, 1976. pp. 122. *bibliog. (Nordiska Afrikainstitutet. Research Reports. No. 33)*

LAND TENURE.(Cont.)

— Underdeveloped areas.

See UNDERDEVELOPED AREAS — Land tenure.

— United Kingdom — Law.

DALTON (PATRICK J.) Land law. 2nd ed. London, 1975. pp. 332.

SIMPSON (STANHOPE ROWTON) Land law and registration. Cambridge, 1976. pp. 726. *bibliog.* This work is intended to replace E. Dowson and V.L.O. Sheppard's *Land Registration.*

— — Ireland.

O'BRIEN (JOSEPH V.) William O'Brien and the course of Irish politics, 1881-1918. Berkeley, [1976]. pp. 273. *bibliog.*

— — Ireland, Northern — Law.

WYLIE (J.C.W.) Irish land law. London, 1975. pp. 914.

LAND TITLES

— Registration and transfer.

SIMPSON (STANHOPE ROWTON) Land law and registration. Cambridge, 1976. pp. 726. *bibliog.* This work is intended to replace E. Dowson and V.L.O. Sheppard's *Land Registration.*

— — United Kingdom.

SIMPSON (STANHOPE ROWTON) Land law and registration. Cambridge, 1976. pp. 726. *bibliog.* This work is intended to replace E. Dowson and V.L.O. Sheppard's *Land Registration.*

LANDLORD AND TENANT

— Canada — Ontario.

ONTARIO. Law Reform Commission. 1976. Report on landlord and tenant law. [Toronto], 1976. pp. 364.

— Fiji Islands.

FIJI. Commercial Rents Committee. 1966. Report; [R.M. Major, chairman]. in FIJI. Legislative Council. Journal. Sessions of 1966.

— Poland.

RADWAŃSKI (ZBIGNIEW) Najem mieszkań w świetle publicznej gospodarki lokalami. Warszawa, 1961. pp. 238.

— United Kingdom.

SHELTER. Tenants' guide to the new Rent Act. London, 1974. pp. (4).

LEGAL ACTION GROUP. Social Law and Practice Guides. No. 1. Law in a housing crisis: a guide to the law and practice on security, rent, repairs and rights to housing on marriage breakdown. London, [1975]. pp. 64.

U.K. Department of the Environment. 1975. Regulated tenancies: your rents, rights and responsibilities: a guide for private landlords and tenants. [London], 1975. pp. 44.

HILL (HAROLD ARTHUR) and REDMAN (JOSEPH HAWORTH) Law of landlord and tenant; sixteenth edition by Michael Barnes [and others]. London, 1976. pp. 2141.

LANDSCAPE.

WESTMACOTT (RICHARD) and WORTHINGTON (TOM) New agricultural landscapes: report of a study undertaken on behalf of the Countryside Commission...during 1972. Cheltenham, Countryside Commission, 1974. pp. 98. *bibliog.*

APPLETON (JAY) The experience of landscape. London, [1975]. pp. 293. *bibliog.*

TAYLOR (CHRISTOPHER) 1935- . Fields in the English landscape. London, 1975. pp. 174. *bibliog.*

LANDSCAPE ARCHITECTURE.

ROPER (LAURA WOOD) A biography of Frederick Law Olmsted. Baltimore, [1973]. pp. 555.

LANDSCAPE PROTECTION.

TANDY (CLIFF) Landscape of industry;...with a section on hydrology by Peter Nelson. London, 1975. pp. 314. *bibliogs.*

— United Kingdom.

COUNCIL FOR THE PROTECTION OF RURAL ENGLAND. Development control: package buildings. London, [1974]. pp. 34.

MACEWEN (MALCOLM) ed. Future landscapes. London, 1976. pp. 224.

— — Wales.

YOUTH HOSTELS ASSOCIATION (ENGLAND AND WALES). Landscape and forestry in Mid-Wales: a land-use survey. [London], 1974. pp. 9.

LANGE (FRIEDRICH ALBERT).

KNOLL (JOACHIM H.) and SCHOEPS (JULIUS H.) eds. Friedrich Albert Lange: Leben und Werk. Duisburg, 1975. pp. 287. *bibliog.* (*Duisburg. Stadtarchiv. Duisburger Forschungen. Band 21*)

LANGSDORF (GRIGORII IVANOVICH).

KOMISSAROV (BORIS NIKOLAEVICH) Grigorii Ivanovich Langsdorf, 1774-1852. Leningrad, 1975. pp. 124.

LANGUAGE AND LANGUAGES.

CHOMSKY (NOAM) Reflections on language. New York, [1975]. pp. 269. *bibliog.*

— Handbooks, manuals, etc.

ALLEN (CHARLES GEOFFRY) A manual of European languages for librarians. London, [1975]. pp. 803.

LANGUAGES

— Philosophy.

MORAVCSIK (J.M.E.) ed. Logic and philosophy for linguists: a book of readings. The Hague, [1974]. pp. 347. *bibliogs.*

MIND and language...; edited by Samuel Guttenplan. Oxford, 1975. pp. 158. (*Oxford. University. Wolfson College. Wolfson College Lectures. 1974*)

PUTNAM (HILARY) Philosophical papers. Cambridge, 1975. 2 vols. *bibliogs.*

— Political aspects.

BLOCH (MAURICE E.F.) ed. Political language and oratory in traditional society. London, 1975. pp. 240. *bibliog.*

Les ETATS multilingues: problèmes et solutions...; présentation: Jean Guy Savard [and] Richard Vigneault. Québec, 1975. pp. 591. *bibliogs.* (*Quebec. Université Laval. Centre International de Recherche sur le Bilinguisme. Travaux. A. 9*) Papers of a Round Table of the International Political Science Association, Quebec, 1972. *In English or French.*

MAZRUI (ALI A.) The political sociology of the English language: an African perspective. The Hague, [1975]. pp. 231. *bibliog.*

LA SPEZIA (PROVINCE)

— Politics and government.

BIANCHI (ANTONIO) Storia del movimento operaio di La Spezia e Lunigiana, 1861- 1945. Roma, 1975. pp. 403.

LATIN AMERICAN FREE TRADE ASSOCIATION.

GONZALEZ LAPEYRE (EDISON) Inmunidades y privilegios de A.L.A.L.C. Montevideo, 1968. pp. 80.

LATIN AMERICANS IN THE UNITED STATES.

ZISMAN (PAUL M.) Education and economic success of urban Spanish-speaking immigrants. San Francisco, 1975. pp. 166. *bibliog.*

LATTICE THEORY.

BIRKHOFF (GARRETT) Lattice theory. 3rd ed. Providence, R.I., [1967] repr. 1973. pp. 418. *bibliog.* (*American Mathematical Society. Colloquium Publications. vol. 25*)

LATVIA

— Commerce.

PUTINTSEV (A.I.) Razvitie kooperativnoi torgovli Latvii. Riga, 1974. pp. 125.

— Statistics.

LATVIA. Tsentral'noe Statisticheskoe Upravlenie. 1973. Latviiskaia SSR v tsifrakh v 1972 godu: kratkii statisticheskii sbornik. Riga, 1973. pp. 416.

LATVIANS IN FOREIGN COUNTRIES.

LATVIISKII GOSUDARSTVENNYI UNIVERSITET. Uchenye Zapiski. t.200. Voprosy kritiki burzhuaznoi politiki i ideologii. Riga, 1974. pp. 135. *bibliog.*

LATYMER SCHOOL, EDMONTON.

MORRIS (JOSEPH ACTON) A history of the Latymer School at Edmonton. Edmonton, 1975. pp. 314.

LAUGHTER.

CHAPMAN (ANTHONY J.) and FOOT (HUGH C.) eds. Humour and laughter: theory, research and applications. London, [1976]. pp. 348. *bibliogs.*

LAVROV (PETR LAVROVICH).

SAPIR (BORIS) ed. Lavrov - gody emigratsii: arkhivnye materialy v dvukh tomakh; Lavrov - years of emigration: letters and documents in two volumes. Dordrecht, [1974]. 2 vols. (*International Institute of Social History. Russian Series on Social History*)

LAW (JOHN).

LE COUTEUX (BERNARD) Law et le commerce colonial. Paris, 1921. pp. 100. *bibliog.* Thèse (doctorat) - Faculté de Droit de l'Université de Paris.

LAW.

WEERAMANTRY (CHRISTOPHER GREGORY) The law in crisis: bridges of understanding. London, 1975. pp. 303.

— Bibliography.

SZLADITS (CHARLES) the Younger, compiler. A bibliography on foreign and comparative law: books and articles in English, 1966-1971. Dobbs Ferry, N.Y., 1975. 2 vols. (*Columbia University. Parker School of Foreign and Comparative Law. Studies in Foreign and Comparative Law*)

— Codification — Translations — Bibliography.

COUNCIL OF EUROPE. 1975. Bibliography of translations of codes and other laws of private law. Strasbourg, 1975. pp. 314.

— History and criticism.

ULLMAN (WALTER) Law and politics in the Middle Ages: an introduction to the sources of medieval political ideas. Ithaca, N.Y., 1975. pp. 320. *bibliog.*

— Philosophy.

GUASTINI (RICCARDO) Marx: dalla filosofia del diritto alla scienza della società; il lessico giuridico marxiano, 1842-1851. Bologna, [1974]. pp. 542.

LAW, COMPARATIVE.

— Study and teaching — Communist countries.

VYSOKÁ ŠKOLA EKONOMICKÁ V BRATISLAVE. Medzinárodný vedecký seminár o problematike výuky práva na vysokých školách ekonomických v socialistických krajinách. Bratislava, 1972. pp. 350. bibliog. *With Russian and German introductions and Russian summaries.*

— — Germany.

SIEMANN (WOLFRAM) Die Frankfurter Nationalversammlung 1848/49 zwischen demokratischem Liberalismus und konservativer Reform: die Bedeutung der Juristendominanz in den Verfassungsverhandlungen des Paulskirchenparlaments. Bern, 1976. pp. 532. bibliog.

— Translations — Bibliography.

COUNCIL OF EUROPE. 1975. Bibliography of translations of codes and other laws of private law. Strasbourg, 1975. pp. 314.

— Africa.

GONIDEC (PIERRE FRANÇOIS) Les droits africains: évolution et sources. 2nd ed. Paris, 1976. pp. 290. bibliog.

— America, Latin.

KARST (KENNETH L.) and ROSENN (KEITH S.) Law and development in Latin America: a case book. Berkeley, [1975]. pp. 738. *(California University. Latin American Center. Latin American Studies. vol. 28)*

— Canada.

CORRY (JAMES ALEXANDER) The power of the law. Toronto, [1971]. pp. 63. *(Canadian Broadcasting Corporation. Massey Lectures. 11th series)*

— Communist countries — Codification.

LEIDEN. Rijks Universiteit. Documentation Office for East European Law. Law in Eastern Europe. No. 19. Codification in the communist world: symposium in memory of Zsolt Szirmai, 1903-1973; organised by Donald D. Barry [and others]. Leiden, 1975. pp. 353.

— European Economic Community countries.

COMMUNITY LAW: extract from the...General report on the activities of the European Communities. a., 1965/66- Luxembourg.

PUISSOCHET (J.P.) The enlargement of the European Communities: a commentary on the treaty and the acts concerning the accession of Denmark, Ireland and the United Kingdom. Leyden, 1975. pp. 454. bibliog.

CONGRES INTERNATIONAL DE DROIT EUROPEEN, 6ME, 1973. La jurisprudence européenne après vingt ans d'expérience communautaire. Köln, [1976]. pp. 1121. *(Cologne. Universität. Institut für das Recht der Europäischen Gemeinschaften. Kölner Schriften zum Europarecht. Band 24) In French or German.*

LASOK (DOMINIK) and BRIDGE (J.W.) An introduction to the law and institutions of the European Communities. 2nd ed. London, 1976. pp. 370. bibliog.

— Finland.

UOTILA (JAAKKO) ed. The Finnish legal system. Helsinki, 1966. pp. 263. bibliogs. *(Suomalainen Lakimiesyhdistys. Julkaisuja. [D- Sarja: Ius Finlandiae]. No. 26)*

— Germany.

SCHIPPEL (MAX) Sozialdemokratisches Reichstags-Handbuch: ein Führer durch die Zeit- und Streitfragen der Reichsgesetzgebung. Berlin, [1902]. pp. 1174.

— Italy.

INTERNATIONAL ASSOCIATION OF LAW LIBRARIES. Courses in Law Librarianship, 4th, 1972. The unification of private law and law and legal literature in Italy. Marburg, 1974. pp. 120. bibliog.

— Poland.

OPAŁEK (KAZIMIERZ) Problemy metodologiczne nauki prawa. Warszawa, 1962. pp. 366. *With Russian and English summaries.*

— — History and criticism.

MISCELLANEA iuridica zlo'zone w darze Karolowi Koranyiemu w czterdziestolecie pracy naukowej. Warszawa, 1961. pp. 196. bibliog. *With French table of contents.*

BUCZEK (KAROL) Targi i miasta na prawie polskim: okres wczesnośredniowieczny. Wrocław, 1964. pp. 140. *(Polska Akademia Nauk. Oddział w Krakowie. Komisja Nauk Historycznych. Prace. Nr.11) With Russian and French tables of contents.*

— Romania.

Le DROIT et la croissance de la population en Roumanie: (ouvrage élaboré sous les auspices du Conseil législatif et de la Commission Nationale de Démographie de la République Socialiste de Roumanie); [by] Ioan Ceterchi [and others]. Bucarest, 1974. pp. 334. *(Le Droit et la Population]*

ROMANIA. Statutes, etc. 1965-75. Législation roumaine. Bucarest, 1975. pp. 208.

ROMANIA. Statutes, etc. 1969-74. Digest of general laws of Romania. [Bucharest, 1975]. pp. 234.

— Russia.

PROBLEMY sravnitel'nogo issledovaniia zakonodatel'stva soiuznykh respublik. Tashkent, 1974. pp. 236.

ALEKSEEV (SERGEI SERGEEVICH) Struktura sovetskogo prava. Moskva, 1975. pp. 263.

LESAGE (MICHEL) Le droit soviétique. Paris, [1975]. pp. 127.

RUSSIA (RSFSR). Statutes, etc. 1919-1920. Dekrety Sovetskoi vlasti. t.7. 10 dekabria 1919 g. - 31 marta 1920 g. Moskva, 1975. pp. 676.

— — Interpretation and construction.

BRATUS' (SERGEI NIKITICH) ed. Sudebnaia praktika v sovetskoi pravovoi sisteme, etc. Moskva, 1975. pp. 328.

— — Uzbekistan.

GOSUDARSTVENNOE stroitel'stvo i pravo v Uzbekskoi SSR. Tashkent, 1974. pp. 366.

— South Africa.

SOUTH AFRICAN LAW COMMISSION. Annual report. a., 1974 [1st]- Pretoria. *[in English and Afrikaans]. Included in the file of SOUTH AFRICA. Parliament. House of Assembly. Votes and proceedings; (with Printed annexures).*

— — Interpretation and construction.

COCKRAM (GAIL MARYSE) The interpretation of statutes. Cape Town, 1975. pp. 88.

— Spain — History and criticism.

HILLERS DE LUQUE (SIGFREDO) España: una revolucion pendiente. Madrid, [1975]. pp. 487. bibliog.

— United Kingdom.

BLACKSTONE (Sir WILLIAM) One of the Justices of the Court of Common Pleas. The sovereignty of the law: selections from Blackstone's Commentaries on the laws of England; edited with an introduction by Gareth Jones. London, 1973. pp. 254.

FRANK (WILLIAM FRANCIS) The general principles of English law. 6th ed. London, [1975]. pp. 242.

JAMES (Sir ARTHUR EVAN) Law in our time. Birmingham, 1976. pp. 19. *(Birmingham. University. Holdsworth Club. Presidential Addresses. 1976)*

JAMES (PHILIP SEAFORTH) Introduction to English law: chapter on Revenue law by G.N. Glover. 9th ed. London, 1976. pp. 498.

WALKER (RONALD JACK) and WALKER (MICHAEL GEORGE) The English legal system. 4th ed. London, 1976. pp. 616.

— — Bibliography.

PARTINGTON (MARTIN) and others, compilers. Welfare rights: a bibliography on law and the poor, 1970-1975. London, 1976. pp. 167.

— — Dictionaries and encyclopedias.

OSBORN (PERCY GEORGE) Concise law dictionary; sixth edition by John Burke. London, 1976. pp. 396.

— — History and criticism.

LEGAL HISTORY CONFERENCE, 1972. Legal history studies, 1972: papers presented to the Legal History Conference, Aberystwyth, 18-21 July 1972; edited by Dafydd Jenkins. Cardiff, 1975. pp. 155.

— — Interpretation and construction.

CROSS (Sir RUPERT) Statutory interpretation. London, 1976. pp. 180.

— — Scotland.

SCOTLAND. Scottish Law Commission. Memoranda. [Edinburgh, 1968 in progress].

SCOTLAND. Scottish Law Commission. 1976. Comments on White Paper: Our changing democracy: devolution to Scotland and Wales. [Edinburgh, 1976]. pp. 97. *(Memoranda. No. 32) White Paper published as Cmnd. 6348, British Parliamentary Papers, Session 1975-76.*

— — Commonwealth.

COMMONWEALTH LAW BULLETIN; ([pd. by] the Commonwealth Secretariat). irreg., Ja 1975 (no.2)- London.

— United States.

HAY (PETER) An introduction to United States law. Amsterdam, 1976. pp. 232.

— Venezuela.

KARST (KENNETH L.) and others. The evolution of law in the barrios of Caracas. Los Angeles, 1973. pp. 125. *(California University. Latin American Center. Latin American Studies. vol. 20)*

— Yugoslavia.

CONGRES INTERNATIONAL DE DROIT COMPARE, 1974. 9e Congrès. Rapports nationaux yougoslaves au IXe Congrès International de Droit Comparé, Teheran, 1974: Yugoslav reports for the ninth International Congress of Comparative Law, Tehran, 1974. Beograd, 1974. pp. 250. *In English or French.*

LAW, COMPARATIVE.

CONGRES INTERNATIONAL DE DROIT COMPARE, 1974. 9e Congrès. Rapports nationaux yougoslaves au IXe Congrès International de Droit Comparé, Teheran, 1974: Yugoslav reports for the ninth International Congress of Comparative Law, Tehran, 1974. Beograd, 1974. pp. 250. *In English or French.*

PROBLEMY sravnitel'nogo issledovaniia zakonodatel'stva soiuznykh respublik. Tashkent, 1974. pp. 236.

HOOKER (M.B.) Legal pluralism: an introduction to colonial and neo-colonial laws. Oxford, 1975. pp. 601. bibliog.

PAPACHRISTOS (A.C.) La réception des droits privés étrangers comme phénomène de sociologie juridique. Paris, 1975. pp. 154. bibliog.

LAW, COMPARATIVE.(Cont.)

— Bibliography.

SZLADITS (CHARLES) the Younger, compiler. A bibliography on foreign and comparative law: books and articles in English, 1966-1971. Dobbs Ferry, N.Y., 1975. 2 vols. *(Columbia University. Parker School of Foreign and Comparative Law. Studies in Foreign and Comparative Law)*

LAW, MOHAMMEDAN.

ANDERSON (Sir JAMES NORMAN DALRYMPLE) Law reform in the Muslim world. London, 1976. pp. 235. *(London. University. Institute of Advanced Legal Studies. University of London Legal Series. 11)*

LAW AND ETHICS.

SAWICKI (JERZY) Tajniki dyscypliny. Warszawa, 1965. pp. 391.

BLOM-COOPER (LOUIS JACQUES) and DREWRY (GAVIN) eds. Law and morality: (a reader). London, 1976. pp. 265.

LAW AND POLITICS.

DREWRY (GAVIN) Law, justice and politics. London, 1975. pp. 173. *bibliog. (Politics Association. Political Realities)*

YOUNG (HUGO) The Crossman affair. London, 1976. pp. 224.

LAW AND SOCIALISM.

STOYANOVITCH (KONSTANTIN) La pensée marxiste et le droit. [Paris], 1974. pp. 196.

DALLIGNY (SUZANNE) Essai sur les principes d'un droit civil socialiste. Paris, 1976. pp. 428.

MARTINY (MARTIN) Integration oder Konfrontation?: Studien zur Geschichte der sozialdemokratischen Rechts- und Verfassungspolitik. Bonn-Bad Godesberg, [1976]. pp. 248. *bibliog. (Friedrich-Ebert-Stiftung. Forschungsinstitut. Schriftenreihe. Band 122)*

LAW ENFORCEMENT.

GREGORY (FRANK E.C.) Protest and violence: the police response: a comparative analysis of democratic methods. London, 1976. pp. 15. *(Institute for the Study of Conflict. Conflict Studies. No. 75)*

McDONALD (LYNN) The sociology of law and order. London, 1976. pp. 340. *bibliog.*

— Italy.

TARANTINI (DOMENICO) La maniera forte: elogio della polizia; storia del potere politico in Italia, 1860-1975. Verona, [1975]. pp. 382.

— New Zealand.

NEW ZEALAND. Government Caucus Committee on the Proposed Law Enforcement Information System. 1973. Report; [R.P.B. Drayton, chairman]. Wellington, 1973. pp. 58.

— United Kingdom.

NAUNTON (BERYL) compiler. A tree of law and order. Chichester, [1970]. pp. 206.

— United States.

DOLBEARE (KENNETH M.) ed. Public policy evaluation;...with a section on crime control evaluation edited by John A. Gardiner. Beverly Hills, [1975]. pp. 286.

SEYMOUR (WHITNEY NORTH) United States attorney: an inside view of "justice" in America under the Nixon administration. New York, 1975. pp. 248.

LAW REFORM.

REPPY (ALISON) ed. David Dudley Field: centenary essays, celebrating one hundred years of legal reform. New York, 1949. pp. 400. *bibliog.*

ANDERSON (Sir JAMES NORMAN DALRYMPLE) Law reform in the Muslim world. London, 1976. pp. 235. *(London. University. Institute of Advanced Legal Studies. University of London Legal Series. 11)*

— Japan.

OPPLER (ALFRED CHRISTIAN) Legal reform in occupied Japan: a participant looks back. Princeton, [1976]. pp. 345.

— United Kingdom — Scotland.

SCOTLAND. Scottish Law Commission. Memoranda. [Edinburgh, 1968 in progress].

LAW REPORTS, DIGESTS, ETC.

— Russia — Russia (RSFSR).

RUSSIA (RSFSR). Statutes, etc. 1964-1972. Sbornik postanovlenii Prezidiuma i opredelenii Sudebnoi kollegii po ugolovnym delam Verkhovnogo Suda RSFSR, 1964-1972 gg.; otvetstvennyi redaktor...A.K. Orlov. Moskva, 1974. pp. 646.

— United Kingdom.

LONDON. London Record Society. Publications. vol. 12. The London Eyre of 1276; edited by Martin Weinbaum. London, 1976. pp. 188.

LAWLESS (GERARD RICHARD).

EUROPEAN COURT OF HUMAN RIGHTS. Publications. Series A: Judgments and Decisions. [A1]. ..."Lawless" case; preliminary objections and questions of procedure, judgment of 14th November 1960. Strasbourg, Council of Europe, 1961. pp. 20 [bis]. *In English and French.*

EUROPEAN COURT OF HUMAN RIGHTS. Publications. Series A: Judgments and Decisions. [A2]. ..."Lawless" case: judgment of 7th April 1961. Stasbourg, Council of Europe, 1961. pp. 23-24 [bis]. *In English and French.*

EUROPEAN COURT OF HUMAN RIGHTS. Publications. Series A: Judgments and Decisions. [A3]. ..."Lawless" case; merits; judgment of 1st July 1961. Strasbourg, Council of Europe, 1961. pp. 27-67 [bis]. *In English and French.*

LAWRENCE (THOMAS EDWARD).

MEYERS (JEFFREY) A fever at the core: the idealist in politics. London, 1976. pp. 172. *bibliog.*

LAWYERS

— Canada.

BELLEAU (HENRI-GEORGES) The lawyer in eastern Canada: a sociological study of the notary public in Quebec. 1975. fo. 551. *bibliog.* Typescript. M.Phil. (London) thesis: unpublished. This thesis is the property of London University and may not be removed from the Library.

— Russia.

RECHI sovetskikh advokatov po ugolovnym delam. Moskva, 1975. pp. 214.

— United Kingdom.

BOULTON (Sir WILLIAM WHYTEHEAD) A guide to conduct and etiquette at the Bar of England and Wales. 6th ed. London, 1975. pp. 118.

WICKENDEN (C.D.) The modern family solicitor: guidelines for practice today and tomorrow. London, 1975. pp. 237.

— — Scotland.

STAIR SOCIETY. [Publications]. 29. The minute book of the Faculty of Advocates, vol.1, 1661- 1712; edited by John Macpherson Pinkerton. Edinburgh, 1976. pp. 306.

— United States.

STUMPF (HARRY P.) Community politics and legal services: the other side of the law. Beverly Hills, [1975]. pp. 309. *bibliog.*

AUERBACH (JEROLD S.) Unequal justice: lawyers and social change in modern America. New York, 1976. pp. 395. *bibliog.*

LAZO (SERGEI GEORGIEVICH).

SERGEI Lazo: vospominaniia i dokumenty. Moskva, 1974. pp. 239.

LEAD MINES AND MINING

— United Kingdom.

TURNBULL (LES) The history of lead mining in the north east of England. Newcastle, 1975. pp. 80.

LEADERSHIP.

BARTOL (KATHRYN M.) Male and female leaders in small work groups: an empirical study of satisfaction, performance and perceptions of leader behavior. East Lansing, 1973. pp. 154. *bibliog. (Michigan State University. MSU Business Studies)*

HERZOG (JUERGEN) Traditionelle Institutionen und nationale Befreiungsrevolution in Tansania: zum Problem der revolutionären Überwindung vorkapitalistischer gesellschaftlicher Verhältnisse im heutigen Afrika. Berlin, 1975. pp. 314. *(Zentraler Rat für Asien-, Afrika- und Lateinamerika- Wissenschaften in der DDR. Studien über Asien, Afrika und Lateinamerika. Band 18)*

WILSON (BRYAN RONALD) The noble savages: the primitive origins of charisma and its contemporary survival. Berkeley, [1975]. pp. 131.

MAGID (ALVIN) Men in the middle: leadership and role conflict in a Nigerian society. Manchester, [1976]. pp. 292. *bibliog.*

LEAFLETS DROPPED FROM AIRCRAFT.

KIRCHNER (KLAUS) Flugblattpropaganda im 2. Weltkrieg: Europa. München, [1972]. pp. 37. *bibliog.* With English summary.

LEAGUE OF ARAB STATES.

SOMALI REPUBLIC. Ministry of Information and National Guidance. 1974. Somalia and the Arab League: a wider role in Afro-Arab affairs. Mogadishu, 1974. pp. 45.

HASSOUNA (HUSSEIN A.) The League of Arab States and regional disputes: a study of middle east conflicts. Dobbs Ferry, N.Y., 1975. pp. 512. *bibliog.*

LEAGUE OF NATIONS.

RAFFO (PETER) The League of Nations. London, 1974. pp. 29. *bibliog. (Historical Association. Appreciations in History. No. 3)*

AKINDELE (R.A.) The organization and promotion of world peace: a study of universal-regional relationships. Toronto, [1976]. pp. 204. *bibliog.*

— Canada.

VEATCH (RICHARD) Canada and the League of Nations. Toronto, [1975]. pp. 224. *bibliog.*

LEARNING, PSYCHOLOGY OF.

INHELDER (BÄRBEL) and others. Learning and the development of cognition;...translated by Susan Wedgwood. London, 1974. pp. 308. *bibliog.*

REILLY (MARY) ed. Play as exploratory learning: studies of curiosity behavior. Beverly Hills, [1974]. pp. 317. *bibliogs.*

HANDBOOK of learning and cognitive processes; edited by W.K. Estes. Hillsdale, N.J., 1975 in progress. *bibliogs.*

RESTLE (FRANK JOSEPH) Learning: animal behavior and human cognition. New York, [1975]. pp. 330. *bibliog.*

BEARD (RUTH M.) Teaching and learning in higher education. 3rd ed. Harmondsworth, 1976. pp. 251. *bibliog.*

LEARNING AND SCHOLARSHIP.

HYMAN (HERBERT HIRAM) and others. The enduring effects of education. Chicago, [1975]. pp. 313.

LEASES

— Hong Kong.

HONG KONG. Advisory Comittee on Private Recreational Leases. 1968. Report; [Sir Albert Rodrigues, chairman]. Hong Kong, 1968. pp. 23, 24. *In English and Chinese.*

LEATHER INDUSTRY AND TRADE

— Russia — Russia (RSFSR).

PILEVSKII (GRIGORII LAZAR'EVICH) "Krasnyi gigant": ocherk istorii Klintsovskogo kozhevennogo zavoda. Briansk, 1969. pp. 210.

LEBANESE IN SIERRA LEONE.

LAAN (H.L. VAN DER) The Lebanese traders in Sierra Leone. The Hague, [1975]. pp. 385. *bibliog.* *(Afrika-Studiecentrum. Change and Continuity in Africa)*

LEBANON

— Foreign relations — France.

SHORROCK (WILLIAM I.) French imperialism in the Middle East: the failure of policy in Syria and Lebanon, 1900-1914. Wisconsin, 1976. pp. 214. *bibliog.*

— History — 1958, Intervention.

BULL (ODD) War and peace in the Middle East: the experiences and views of a U.N. observer. London, 1976. pp. 205.

— Industries.

INOTAI (ANDRÁS) Az iparfejlesztés szerepe és lehetőségei a libanoni gazdaságpolitikában. Budapest, 1969. pp. 24. *(Magyar Tudományos Akadémia. Afro-Ázsiai Kutató Központ. Studies on Developing Countries. No.28)*

— Politics and government.

SMOCK (DAVID R.) and SMOCK (AUDREY C.) The politics of pluralism: a comparative study of Lebanon and Ghana. New York, [1975]. pp. 369. *bibliog.*

KELIDAR (ABBAS) and BURRELL (MICHAEL) Lebanon: the collapse of a state: regional dimensions of the struggle. London, 1976. pp. 19. *bibliog. (Institute for the Study of Conflict. Conflict Studies. No.74)*

— Social conditions.

SMOCK (DAVID R.) and SMOCK (AUDREY C.) The politics of pluralism: a comparative study of Lebanon and Ghana. New York, [1975]. pp. 369. *bibliog.*

LECTURES AND LECTURING.

DAMASCHKE (ADOLF) Volkstümliche Redekunst: Erfahrungen und Ratschläge. Jena, 1919. pp. 96.

LEFT AND RIGHT (POLITICAL SCIENCE).

ORGANIZZAZIONE COMUNISTA (MARXISTA-LENINISTA). Congresso Nazionale, 1, 1974. Crisi, revisionismo e partito: tesi. Milano, 1974. pp. 115.

LEGAL AID.

CAPPELLETTI (MAURO) and others. Towards equal justice: a comparative study of legal aid in modern societies, text and materials; with original contributions by P.O. Bolding [and others]. milano, 1975. pp. 756. *bibliog. (Florence. Università degli Studi di Firenze, Istituto di Diritto Comparato. 13)*

— Australia.

SACKVILLE (RONALD) Legal aid in Australia. Canberra, 1975. pp. 209. *(Australia. Commission of Inquiry into Poverty. Law and Poverty Series)*

— Norway.

EIDESEN (ARILD) and others, eds. Rettshjelp og samfunnsstruktur. Oslo, [1975]. pp. 213.

— United Kingdom.

VAUXHALL COMMUNITY LAW CENTRE. Annual report, 1st June 1973 to 1st June 1974; (by John L. Linden). [Liverpool, 1974]. fo.9.

BENWELL COMMUNITY LAW PROJECT. Annual report, June 1975. [Newcastle-upon-Tyne], 1975. pp. 22.

— United States.

STUMPF (HARRY P.) Community politics and legal services: the other side of the law. Beverly Hills, [1975]. pp. 309. *bibliog.*

LEGAL COMPOSITION.

PIESSE (EDMUND LEONLIN) The elements of drafting;...fifth edition by J.K. Aitken. Sydney, 1976. pp. 170. *bibliog.*

LEGAL ETHICS

— United Kingdom.

BOULTON (Sir WILLIAM WHYTEHEAD) A guide to conduct and etiquette at the Bar of England and Wales. 6th ed. London, 1975. pp. 118.

LEGISLATION.

HERMAN (VALENTINE) and MENDEL (FRANÇOISE) Parliaments of the world: a reference compendium; ([edited by] Inter-parliamentary Union). London, 1976. pp. 985. *bibliog.*

— Russia.

MITSKEVICH (ALEKSEI VALENTINOVICH) ed. Pravotvorchestvo v SSSR. Moskva, 1974. pp. 319.

NIKOLAEVA (MARINA NIKOLAEVNA) Normativnye akty ministerstv i vedomstv SSSR. Moskva, 1975. pp. 143.

LEGISLATIVE BODIES.

HERMAN (VALENTINE) and MENDEL (FRANÇOISE) Parliaments of the world: a reference compendium; ([edited by] Inter-parliamentary Union). London, 1976. pp. 985. *bibliog.*

— Officials and employees.

LEGISLATIVE staffing: a comparative perspective; edited by James J. Heaphey and Alan P. Balutis. New York, [1975]. pp. 244.

— Germany.

WASSER (HARTMUT) Parlamentarismuskritik vom Kaiserreich zur Bundesrepublik: Analyse und Dokumentation. Stuttgart-Bad Cannstatt, [1974]. pp. 197. *bibliog.*

FRIEDRICH (MANFRED) Landesparlamente in der Bundesrepublik: [five articles]. Opladen, [1975]. pp. 165.

— — Bibliography.

STAATSBIBLIOTHEK PREUSSISCHER KULTURBESITZ. Abteilung Amtsdruckschriften. Deutsche Parlamentaria: ein Bestandsverzeichnis der bis 1945 erschienen Druckschriften. Berlin, 1970. pp. 140.

— Russia.

FILIPPOV (ALEKSANDR NIKITICH) Istoriia Senata v pravlenie Verkhovnogo tainogo soveta i Kabineta. ch.1. Senat v pravlenie Verkhovnogo tainogo soveta. Iur'ev, 1895. pp. xii,486. *Offprint from Uchenye zapiski Imp. Iur'evskogo universiteta. No more published.*

KORENEVSKAIA (ELENA IGNAT'EVNA) Stanovlenie vysshikh organov sovetskogo gosudarstvennogo upravleniia: pravovye osnovy organizatsii i deiatel'nosti Sovetskogo pravitel'stva v 1917-1922 gg. Moskva, 1975. pp. 159.

MUKHAMEDSHIN (KASHIF DZHIGANSHIEVICH) Deiatel'nost' Prezidiuma Verkhovnogo Soveta soiuznoi respubliki po ukrepleniiu zakonnosti. Moskva, 1975. pp. 128.

— United States.

PATTERSON (SAMUEL C.) and others. Representatives and represented: bases of public support for the American legislatures. New York, [1975]. pp. 212.

— — Officials and employees.

BALUTIS (ALAN P.) and HEAPHEY (JAMES J.) Public administration and the legislative process. Beverly Hills, [1974]. pp. 58. *bibliog.*

LEGISLATIVE staffing: a comparative perspective; edited by James J. Heaphey and Alan P. Balutis. New York, [1975]. pp. 244.

LEGISLATIVE POWER

— Thailand.

ENGEL (DAVID M.) Law and kingship in Thailand during the reign of King Chulalongkorn. Ann Arbor, 1975. pp. 131. *bibliog. (Michigan University. Center for South and Southeast Asian Studies. Michigan Papers on South and Southeast Asia. No. 9)*

LEGISLATORS.

BELL (CHARLES G.) and PRICE (CHARLES M.) The first term: a study of legislative socialization. Beverly Hills, [1975]. pp. 213.

— Canada.

JACKSON (ROBERT J.) and ATKINSON (MICHAEL M.) The Canadian legislative system: politicians and policy-making. [Toronto], 1974. pp. 196.

— Germany.

HENKELS (WALTER) Bonner Köpfe. 7th ed. Düsseldorf, 1970. pp. 379.

GERMANY (BUNDESREPUBLIK). Deutscher Bundestag. Wissenschaftliche Dienste. 1975. Mitgliederstruktur des Deutschen Bundestages, I.- VII. Wahlperiode: Materialzusammenstellung und Auswahlbibliographie; [edited by Edith Dalades]. Bonn, 1975. pp. 314. *bibliog. (Materialen. 40)*

HERZOG (DIETRICH) Politische Karrieren: Selektion und Professionalisierung politischer Führungsgruppen. Opladen, [1975]. pp. 249. *bibliog. (Berlin. Freie Universität. Zentralinstitut für Sozialwissenschaftliche Forschung. Schriften. Band 25)*

GERMANY (BUNDESREPUBLIK). Deutscher Bundestag. Wissenschaftliche Dienste. 1976. Parlamentarierinnen in deutschen Parlamenten, 1919-1976; [edited by Edith Dalades]. Bonn, 1976. pp. 274. *(Materialien. 42)*

SIEMANN (WOLFRAM) Die Frankfurter Nationalversammlung 1848/49 zwischen demokratischem Liberalismus und konservativer Reform: die Bedeutung der Juristendominanz in den Verfassungsverhandlungen des Paulskirchenparlaments. Bern, 1976. pp. 532. *bibliog.*

— South Africa.

STULTZ (NEWELL M.) Who goes to parliament?. Grahamstown, S.A., 1975. pp. 106. *bibliog. (Rhodes University. Institute of Social and Economic Research. Occasional Papers. No. 19)*

— United Kingdom.

MACKINTOSH (Sir ALEXANDER) From Gladstone to Lloyd George: Parliament in peace and war. London, [1921]. pp. 333.

LEGISLATORS.(Cont.)

ROTH (ANDREW) The business background of members of Parliament: [1963 edition]. London, [1963]. pp. 240. *(Parliamentary Profile Services. Parliamentary Profiles)*

STANCER (JOHN DAVID) A study of back bench members of Parliament between 1945 and 1965. 1973. fo. 477. bibliog. Typescript. Ph.D.(London) thesis: unpublished. This thesis is the property of London University and may not be removed from the Library.

ROTH (ANDREW) The business background of M.Ps: 1975-76 edition;...with Janice Kerbey and Judy Tench. London, 1975. pp. 282. *(Parliamentary Profile Services. Parliamentary Profiles)*

— United States.

BEARD (EDMUND) and HORN (STEPHEN) Congressional ethics: the view from the House. Washington, D.C., [1975]. pp. 87.

WHO's who in American politics: fifth edition 1975-1976;... consulting editors Edmund L. Henshaw [and] Paul A. Theis. New York, [1975]. pp. 1090.

COLE (LEONARD A.) Blacks in power: a comparative study of black and white elected officials. Princeton, [1976]. pp. 267.

LEGITIMACY OF GOVERNMENTS.

ROGOWSKI (RONALD) Rational legitimacy: a theory of political support. Princeton, [1974]. pp. 313. bibliog.

LEHMAN (HERBERT HENRY).

INGALLS (ROBERT P.) Herbert H. Lehman and New York's Little New Deal. New York, 1975. pp. 287. bibliog.

LEICESTER

— Social history.

PRITCHARD (ROGER MARTIN) Housing and the spatial structure of the city: residential mobility and the housing market in an English city since the industrial revolution. Cambridge, [1976]. pp. 234. bibliog.

LEIJONHUFVUD (AXEL).

CHEUNG (MICHAEL TOW) A study of the Clower-Leijonhufvud re-interpretation of the Keynesian model. 1975. fo.196. bibliog. Typescript. Ph.D. (London) thesis: unpublished. This thesis is the property of London University and may not be removed from the Library.

LEISURE.

KAPLAN (MAX) Leisure: theory and policy. New York, [1975]. pp. 444.

SYMPOSIUM ON LEISURE TIME NEEDS OF THE RETARDED, LONDON, 1973. A philosophy of leisure in relation to the retarded; [inaugural address by Kenneth Solly and conclusions of the symposium organized by the National Society for Mentally Handicapped Children]. London, [1975?]. 1 pamphlet (unpaged).

MACCANNELL (DEAN) The tourist: a new theory of the leisure class. London, 1976. pp. 214.

PARKER (STANLEY ROBERT) The sociology of leisure. New York, 1976. pp. 157.

— Bibliography.

COMMONWEALTH BUREAU OF AGRICULTURAL ECONOMICS. Tourism and the leisure industry: (international problems and prospects). rev. ed. [Farnham Royal, 1975]. pp. 56. *(Annotated Bibliographies. No. 32)*

— Bangladesh.

FAROUK (A.) and ALI (MUHAMMAD) The hardworking poor: a survey on how people use their time in Bangladesh. Dacca, 1975. 1 vol. (various pagings).

— Israel.

KATZ (ELIHU) and GUREVITCH (MICHAEL) The secularization of leisure: culture and communication in Israel. London, 1976. pp. 288.

— Russia.

UCHENYE ZAPISKI KAFEDR OBSHCHESTVENNYKH NAUK VUZOV LENINGRADA. Istoriia KPSS. vyp.9. Istoriia KPSS. Leningrad, 1969. pp. 158.

NETSENKO (ALEKSANDR VASIL'EVICH) Sotsial'no-ekonomicheskie problemy svobodnogo vremeni pri sotsializme. Leningrad, 1975. pp. 167.

— United Kingdom.

RAPOPORT (RHONA) and RAPOPORT (ROBERT NORMAN) Leisure and the family life cycle;...with the collaboration of Ziona Strelitz. London, 1975. pp. 386. bibliog.

LELEWEL (JOACHIM).

POPKOV (BORIS SERGEEVICH) Pol'skii uchenyi i revoliutsioner Ioakhim Lelevel': russkaia problematika i kontakty. Moskva, 1974. pp. 211.

LENIN (VLADIMIR IL'ICH).

GLASSER (M.) Über die Arbeitsmethoden der Klassiker des Marxismus- Leninismus. Berlin, [1948]. pp. 103.

BUKHARIN (NIKOLAI IVANOVICH) Lénine marxiste. Paris, [1966]. pp. 36. *(Partisans. Dossiers Partisans)* With preface by Joh. Knief and illustrations.

SCHAELIKE (LUISE) ed. Genosse Lenin: Erinnerungen von Zeitgenossen. Berlin, 1967. pp. 283.

PERVYE samarskie lenintsy: ocherki o chlenakh marksistskogo kruzhka, sozdannogo V.I. Leninym v Samare. Kuibyshev, 1969. pp. 192.

TEREKHOV (IVAN SEMENOVICH) V.I. Lenin i stroitel'stvo partii v period ot Fevralia k Oktiabriu, 1917 g. Saratov, 1969. pp. 259.

V.I. Lenin i revoliutsiinyi rukh na zakhidnoukraïns'kykh zemliakh. L'viv, 1969. pp. 167.

BULGARSKATA zhurnalistika po leninski put. Sofiia, 1970. pp. 271.

LENINSKAIA "Iskra" o Sibiri, dekabr' 1900 - oktiabr' 1903 gg.: sbornik dokumental'nykh materialov. Novosibirsk, 1970. pp. 174.

NARIMANOV (NARIMAN NADZHAF-OGLY) Lenin i Vostok: [sbornik statei, 1924-25; pod redaktsiei Dzh. B. Gulieva]. Baku, 1970. pp. 47.

RADZHABOV (SOLEKH ASHUROVICH) V.I. Lenin i sovetskaia natsional'naia gosudarstvennost'. Dushanbe, 1970. pp. 47.

UCHENYE ZAPISKI KAFEDR OBSHCHESTVENNYKH NAUK VUZOV LENINGRADA. Istoriia KPSS. vyp.10. Po leninskomu puti. Leningrad, 1970. pp. 141.

VALENTINOV (NIKOLAI VLADISLAVOVICH) pseud. [i.e. Nikolai Vladislavovich VOL'SKII] Maloznakomyi Lenin. Paris, 1972. pp. 197.

PEREPISKA V.I. Lenina i rukovodimykh im uchrezhdenii RSDRP s partiinymi organizatsiiami, 1903-1905 gg. Moskva, 1974 in progress.

BULATOV (MIKHAIL ALEKSANDROVICH) Leninskii analiz nemetskoi klassicheskoi filosofii: logiko-dialekticheskie i istoriko-filosofskie problemy. Kiev, 1974. pp. 271. bibliog.

GORBUNOV (VLADIMIR VLADIMIROVICH) V.I. Lenin i Proletkul't. Moskva, 1974. pp. 239.

KOSICHEV (ANATOLII DANILOVICH) Teoreticheskoe obobshchenie V.I. Leninym opyta Oktiabr'skoi revoliutsii i stroitel'stva sotsializma v SSSR. Moskva, 1974. pp. 314.

NAIAKSHIN (KUZ'MA IAKOVLEVICH) Krest'ianskii vopros v trudakh V.I. Lenina. Kuibyshev, 1974. pp. 239.

TERLETS'KYI (VALENTYN MYKHAILOVICH) Leninskoe ideinoe nasledie i problemy sovetskogo stroitel'stva. Kiev, 1974. pp. 263. bibliog.

VEL'TSMAN (VLADIMIR NIKOLAEVICH) V.I. Lenin o klassovykh i gnoseologicheskikh korniakh idealizma. Khar'kov, 1974. pp. 200. bibliog.

ANOSHKIN (IVAN FEDOROVICH) Internatsionalizm vnutrennei politiki KPSS: iz teoreticheskogo naslediia V.I. Lenina. Moskva, 1975. pp. 191.

LENIN (VLADIMIR IL'ICH) On the Soviet state apparatus: articles and speeches. rev. ed. Moscow, 1975. pp. 445.

McNEAL (ROBERT HATCH) The Bolshevik tradition: Lenin, Stalin, Khrushchev, Brezhnev. 2nd ed. Englewood Cliffs, [1975]. pp. 210. bibliog.

MUKHINA (GALINA ZOTIKOVNA) Sotsialisticheskaia revoliutsiia i gosudarstvo: razrabotka V.I. Leninym voprosa o gosudarstve diktatury proletariata v period bor'by za Oktiabr' i uprochenie ego zavoevanii, mart 1917 - mart 1918. Moskva, 1975. pp. 277.

PORITSKII (VLADIMIR ANDREEVICH) Leninskii dekret o zemle i ego burzhuaznye kritiki. Moskva, 1975. pp. 126. bibliog.

RADJAVI (KAZEM) La dictature du prolétariat et le dépérissement de l'Etat de Marx à Lénine. Paris, [1975]. pp. 438. bibliog.

SAVITSKAIA (RAISA MALAKHOVNA) Deiatel'nost' V.I. Lenina v oblasti ekonomicheskogo stroitel'stva, oktiabr' 1917 - iiul' 1918 g.: istoriograficheskii ocherk. Moskva, 1975. pp. 276.

SOLZHENITSYN (ALEKSANDR ISAEVICH) Lenin v Tsiurikhe: glavy. Paris, 1975. pp. 241.

VOLKOV (VLADIMIR AKIMOVICH) V.I. Lenin i razvitie khimicheskoi promyshlennosti SSSR. Moskva, 1975. pp. 285. bibliog.

ZETKIN (CLARA) Erinnerungen an Lenin; mit einem Anhang: Aus dem Briefwechsel Clara Zetkins mit W.I. Lenin und N.K. Krupskaja. 3rd ed. Berlin, 1975. pp. 112.

ROZENTAL' (MARK MOISEEVICH) Dialektika leninskogo issledovaniia imperializma i revoliutsii. Moskva, 1976. pp. 520.

— Bibliography.

KEL'DIEV (IMOMNAZAR) Izdanie i rasprostranenie proizvedenii klassikov marksizma-leninizma v Tadzhikistane. Dushanbe, 1973. pp. 190.

RAVNOPOLETS (LIUDMILA SILOVNA) Iz istorii izdaniia i rasprostraneniia proizvedenii V.I. Lenina v Belorussii. Moskva, 1974. pp. 159.

LENINGRAD

— Economic history.

EZHOV (VIKTOR ANATOL'EVICH) and OVSIANKIN (V.A.) eds. Rabochii klass SSSR na sovremennom etape. vyp.3. Leningrad, 1974. pp. 196.

BATER (JAMES H.) St. Petersburg: industrialization and change. London, 1976. pp. 174. bibliog.

— History.

PRINTSEVA (GALINA ALEKSANDROVNA) and BASTAREVA (LIUDMILA IVANOVNA) Dekabristy v Peterburge. Leningrad, 1975. pp. 279. bibliog.

— Politics and government.

KUZNETSOVA (LIDIIA SERGEEVNA) Leningradskaia partiinaia organizatsiia v predvoennye gody, 1938 g. - iiun' 1941 g. Leningrad, 1974. pp. 254.

OL'KHOVSKII (EVGENII ROMANOVICH) Leninskaia "Iskra" v Peterburge. Leningrad, 1975. pp. 359.

— Siege, 1941—1944.

SHUMILOV (NIKOLAI DMITRIEVICH) V dni blokady. Moskva, 1974. pp. 252.

LIBERALISM.

LENINGRAD (OBLAST')

— Economic conditions.

DARINSKII (ANATOLII VIKTOROVICH) Leningradskaia oblast'. 2nd ed. Leningrad, 1975. pp. 384. *bibliog.*

— Politics and government.

KOMMUNISTICHESKAIA PARTIIA SOVETSKOGO SOIUZA. Leningradskii oblastnoi Komitet. Institut Istorii Partii. Leningradskaia organizatsiia KPSS v tsifrakh, 1917-1973. Leningrad, 1974. pp. 144.

LESOTHO

— Industries.

SELWYN (PERCY) Industries in the southern African periphery: a study of industrial development in Botswana, Lesotho and Swaziland. London, 1975. pp. 156. *bibliog.*

LESSNER (FRIEDRICH).

LESSNER (FRIEDRICH) Ich brachte das "Kommunistische Manifest" zum Drucker; (zusammengestellt und eingeleitet von Ursula Herrmann und Gerhard Winkler). Berlin, 1975. pp. 392. *bibliog.*

LETTERS OF CREDIT

— United Kingdom.

GUTTERIDGE (HAROLD COOKE) and MEGRAH (MAURICE HENRY) The law of bankers' commercial credits. 5th ed. London, 1976. pp. 298. *bibliog.*

LEVELLERS.

MORTON (ARTHUR LESLIE) ed. Freedom in arms: a selection of Leveller writings. London, 1975. pp. 354.

LEVER (WILLIAM HESKETH) 1st Viscount Leverhulme.

JOLLY (WILLIAM PERCY) Lord Leverhulme: a biography. London, 1976. pp. 246.

LEVI—STRAUSS (CLAUDE).

POUILLON (JEAN) and MARANDA (PIERRE) eds. Echanges et communications: mélanges offerts à Claude Lévi-Strauss à l'occasion de son 60ème anniversaire. Paris, 1970. 2 vols. *bibliogs.*

BADCOCK (CHRISTOPHER ROBERT) Lévi-Strauss, structuralism and sociological theory. London, 1975. pp. 125. *bibliog.*

LEVSKI (VASIL).

LEVSKI (VASIL) Sviata i chista republika: pisma i dokumenti; sustaviteli Ivan Undzhiev, Nikola Kondarev. [Sofiia], 1971. pp. 222,[xvi].

KARAKOSTOV (STEFAN) ed. Levski v spomenite na suvremennitsite si. Sofiia, 1973. pp. 568.

LIBEL AND SLANDER

— United Kingdom.

O'MALLEY (PATRICK TERENCE) The politics of defamation: the state, press interests and English libel law. [1976]. fo. 346. *bibliog. Typescript. Ph.D. (London) thesis: unpublished. This thesis is the property of London University and may not be removed from the Library.*

LIBELT (KAROL).

KAROL Libelt, 1807-1875. Poznań, 1976. pp. 361. *bibliog. In Polish.*

LIBERAL PARTY

— Australia.

AITCHISON (RAY) ed. Looking at the Liberals. Melbourne, 1974. pp. 258.

— Canada.

SMITH (DAVID E.) 1936- . Prairie liberalism: the Liberal Party in Saskatchewan, 1905- 71. Toronto, [1975]. pp. 352. *bibliog.*

— — Quebec.

PARTI LIBÉRAL DU QUEBEC. A new plan for action. [Montreal, 1973]. pp. 75.

— Denmark.

VENSTRE i 100 år, 1870-(1970); [by] Hans Lund [and others]. København, 1970. 3 vols. *bibliog.*

— Italy.

BIGNARDI (AGOSTINO) Politica di centro. Firenze, [1974]. pp. 101.

— Sweden.

ZETTERBERG (KENT) Liberalism i kris: (Folkpartiet, 1939-1945). Stockholm, 1975. pp. 428. *bibliog. With English summary.*

— United Kingdom.

ROBERTSON (JOHN MACKINNON) The people and their leaders. bradford, [1896]. pp. 12. *(Papers for the People. No. 2)*

COOK (CHRISTOPHER PIERS) A short history of the Liberal Party, 1900-1976. London, 1976. pp. 179. *bibliog.*

MARTIN-KAYE (NIEL) Democratic enterprise. London, [1976]. pp. 38. *(Liberal Party. Strategy 2,000. 1st Series. No. 8)*

MAYHEW (CHRISTOPHER PAGET) Blueprint for a breakthrough. London, [1976]. pp. 14.

LIBERAL UNIONIST PARTY.

DAVIS (PETER GEORGE) The role of the Liberal Unionist Party in British politics 1886-1895. 1974. fo. 335. *bibliog. Typescript. Ph.D.(London) thesis: unpublished. This thesis is the property of London University and may not be removed from the Library.*

LIBERALISM.

FLACH (KARL HERMANN) Noch eine Chance für die Liberalen; oder, Die Zukunft der Freiheit: eine Streitschrift. Frankfurt am Main, [1971]. pp. 96.

UNGER (ROBERTO MANGABEIRA) Knowledge and politics. New York, [1975]. pp. 336.

ABBOTT (PHILIP) The shotgun behind the door: liberalism and the problem of political obligation. Athens, Ga., [1976]. pp. 208.

SMITH (N.A.) The new Enlightenment: an essay in political and social realism. London, 1976. pp. 256.

— America, Latin.

RODRIGUEZ O. (JAIME E.) The emergence of Spanish America: Vicente Rocafuerte and Spanish Americanism, 1808-1832. Berkeley, [1975]. pp. 311. *bibliog.*

— Argentine Republic.

CARRETERO (ANDRES M.) Liberalismo y dependencia. Buenos Aires, 1975. pp. 381. *bibliogs.*

— Europe.

HOLDSWORTH (RICHARD JULIAN) Lord Byron's Childe Harold's Pilgrimage as a liberal commentary on European relations around the close of the Napoleonic era. London, 1975. fo. 20. *(London. University. London School of Economics and Political Science. Gladstone Memorial Trust Prize Essays. 1975) Typescript.*

STEED (MICHAEL) The French threat. Wells, 1976. pp. 24.

— France.

SEMAINE DE LA PENSEE LIBERALE, 6e, 1973. Le libéralisme: un projet de société...; texte intégral des débats. Paris, [1974]. pp. 203.

— Germany.

LIBERALISMUS und imperialistischer Staat: der Imperialismus als Problem liberaler Parteien in Deutschland, 1890-1914; mit Beiträgen von Lothar Albertin [and others]; herausgegeben von Karl Holl und Günther List. Göttingen, [1975]. pp. 176.

BOSCH (MICHAEL) Liberale Presse in der Krise: die Innenpolitik der Jahre 1930 bis 1933 im Spiegel des "Berliner Tageblatts", der "Frankfurter Zeitung" und der "Vossischen Zeitung". Bern, 1976. pp. 343. *bibliog.*

— — Prussia.

GUGEL (MICHAEL) Industrieller Aufstieg und bürgerliche Herrschaft: sozioökonomische Interessen und politische Ziele des liberalen Bürgertums in Preussen zur Zeit des Verfassungskonflikts, 1857-1867. Köln, [1975]. pp. 304. *bibliog.*

— Hungary.

SPIRA (GYÖRGY) A Hungarian count in the revolution of 1848. Budapest, 1974. pp. 346.

— Italy — Periodicals.

LEDDA (ISABELLA) and ZANELLA (GABRIELLA) I periodici di Padova, 1866-1926, liberali, radicali, socialisti. Padova, 1973. pp. 252. *(Centro per la Storia del Movimento Operaio nel Veneto, and Padua. Università. Istituto di Storia Medioevale e Moderna. Movimenti Politici e Sociali dell'Età Contemporanea nel Veneto. Collana.4)*

— Mexico.

CORDOVA (ARNALDO) La ideologia de la Revolucion Mexicana: la formacion del nuevo regimen. Mexico, 1973 repr. 1974. pp. 508.

— Russia.

ZOR'KIN (VALERII DMITRIEVICH) Iz istorii burzhuazno-liberal'noi politicheskoi mysli Rossii vtoroi poloviny XIX - nachala XX v.: B.N. Chicherin. Moskva, 1975. pp. 173.

— — Ukraine.

VOLOSHCHENKO (AZA KYRYLIVNA) Narysy z istoriï suspil'no-politychnoho rukhu na Ukraïni v 70-kh - na pochatku 80-kh rokiv XIX st. Kyïv, 1974. pp. 222.

— Spain.

ALVAREZ DE MORALES (ANTONIO) Genesis de la universidad española contemporanea. Madrid, 1972. pp. 765. *bibliog. (Instituto de Estudios Administrativos. Estudios de Historia de la Administracion.[8])*

GARRORENA MORALES (ANGEL) El Ateneo de Madrid y la teoria de la monarquia liberal, 1836- 1847. Madrid, 1974. pp. 876.

KERN (ROBERT W.) Liberals, reformers and caciques in Restoration Spain, 1875-1909. Albuquerque, [1974]. pp. 153. *bibliog.*

— Sweden.

TORSTENDAHL (ROLF) Mellan nykonservatism och liberalism: idébrytningar inom högern och bondepartierna, 1918-1934. Stockholm, [1969]. pp. 230. *bibliog. (Uppsala. Universitet. Historiska Institutionen. Studia Historica Upsaliensia. 29) With English summary.*

— United Kingdom — Scotland.

McCRACKEN (ELIZABETH C.) Memoirs. n.p., [1920]. pp. 172.

— United States.

BUCHANAN (PATRICK J.) Conservative votes, liberal victories: why the right has failed. New York, [1975]. pp. 184.

LIBERIA

LIBERIA

— Commerce.

NEAL (D. FRANKLIN) Liberia's foreign trade pattern, 1940-1968. Monrovia, Department of Planning and Economic Affairs, [1969?]. fo. 29. *(Conference on Development Objectives and Strategy, Monrovia, 1969. Documents. 1) Xerox copy.*

— Commercial treaties — Sierra Leone.

LIBERIA. Treaties. 1973-74. Mano River Declaration, signed in Malema, 3 October, 1973; and protocols to the Declaration, signed in Bo, 3 October, 1974. [Monrovia, 1975]. fo. 14. *Xerox copy.*

— Economic conditions.

MORRIS (RICHARD M.) Characteristic features of the over-all economic growth in recent years. Monrovia, Department of Planning and Economic Affairs, [1969?]. fo. 49. *(Conference on Development Objectives and Strategy, Monrovia, 1969. Documents. 2) Xerox copy.*

— Economic history.

MORRIS (RICHARD M.) Characteristic features of the over-all economic growth in recent years. Monrovia, Department of Planning and Economic Affairs, [1969?]. fo. 49. *(Conference on Development Objectives and Strategy, Monrovia, 1969. Documents. 2) Xerox copy.*

— Economic policy.

NATIONAL CONFERENCE ON DEVELOPMENT OBJECTIVES AND STRATEGY, 3rd, MONROVIA, 1973. Highlights of the conference. Monrovia, Ministry of Planning and Economic Affairs, 1973. pp. 13. *(Report Documents. DC/3-RD(1)[i])*

NATIONAL CONFERENCE ON DEVELOPMENT OBJECTIVES AND STRATEGY, 3rd, MONROVIA, 1973. Summary report of the conference. [Monrovia], Ministry of Planning and Economic Affairs, 1973. fo. 48. *(Report Documents. DC/3-RD (1) [ii])*

LIBERIA. Ministry of Action for Development and Progress. Annual report. a., 1974- Monrovia.

LIBERIA. Ministry of Planning and Economic Affairs. Activity report...: achievements, non-achievements and problems. a., 1974- Monrovia.

LIBERIAN DEVELOPMENT CORPORATION. Annual report. a., 1974- Monrovia.

— Politics and government.

GRANT (STAN) The call of mother Africa. Kingston, Jamaica, 1973. pp. 361.

LIBERIA. Ministry of Information, Cultural Affairs and Tourism. 1975. Inspired to lead: a short biography of President William R. Tolbert, Jr. [Monrovia, 1975]. fo. 178. *Photocopy.*

CLAPHAM (CHRISTOPHER) Liberia and Sierra Leone: an essay in comparative politics. Cambridge, 1976. pp. 156. *bibliog. (Cambridge. University. African Studies Centre. African Studies Series. 20)*

LOWENKOPF (MARTIN) Politics in Liberia: the conservative road to development. Stanford, 1976. pp. 237. *bibliog. (Stanford University. Hoover Institution on War, Revolution and Peace. Hoover Institution Publications. 151)*

— Social policy.

NATIONAL CONFERENCE ON DEVELOPMENT OBJECTIVES AND STRATEGY, 3rd, MONROVIA, 1973. Highlights of the conference. Monrovia, Ministry of Planning and Economic Affairs, 1973. pp. 13. *(Report Documents. DC/3-RD(1)[i])*

NATIONAL CONFERENCE ON DEVELOPMENT OBJECTIVES AND STRATEGY, 3rd, MONROVIA, 1973. Summary report of the conference. [Monrovia], Ministry of Planning and Economic Affairs, 1973. fo. 48. *(Report Documents. DC/3-RD (1) [ii])*

LIBERIA. Ministry of Action for Development and Progress. Annual report. a., 1974- Monrovia.

LIBERIA. Ministry of Planning and Economic Affairs. Activity report...: achievements, non-achievements and problems. a., 1974- Monrovia.

LIBERTY.

RUTT (JOHN TOWILL) The sympathy of priests; addressed to Thomas Fysche Palmer, Port-Jackson; to which are added, odes, written in 1792. Cambridge, B. Flower, 1795. pp. 28.

JOAD (CYRIL EDWIN MITCHINSON) Liberty today. rev. ed. London, 1938. pp. 221.

DAHRENDORF (RALF) Gesellschaft und Freiheit: zur soziologischen Analyse der Gegenwart. München, 1961 repr. 1963. pp. 454. *bibliog. (Hochschule für Wirtschaft und Politik, Hamburg. Veröffentlichungen). Essays and lectures, 1954-1960; some not previously published.*

FREIHEIT und Gesellschaft: die Freiheitsauffassung im Marxismus-Leninismus; (Autorenkollektiv: Gottfried Stiehler [and others]. Berlin, 1973. pp. 331.

MEREDITH MEMORIAL LECTURES. 1973. Our freedom and its responsibilities. Bundoora, Victoria, 1973. 4 pts.

NIKOLAEVA (LIDIIA VASIL'EVNA) Ob"ektivnye i sub"ektivnye faktory sotsial'nogo progressa i svobody. Moskva, 1974. pp. 259.

DUNAYEVSKAYA (RAYA) Marxism and freedom from 1776 until today. 4th ed. London, 1975. pp. 378. *bibliog.*

SOZIALDEMOKRATISCHE PARTEI DEUTSCHLANDS. Rechtspolitischer Kongress, 4., 1975. Freiheit in der sozialen Demokratie... Dokumentation; herausgegeben von Diether Posser [and others]. Karlsruhe, 1975. pp. 338.

ARENS (UWE) Die andere Freiheit: die Freiheit in Theorie und Praxis der Sozialistischen Einheitspartei Deutschlands. München, 1976. pp. 291. *bibliog.*

ELLUL (JACQUES) The ethics of freedom;...translated and edited by Geoffrey W. Bromiley. London, 1976. pp. 517.

JORDAN (WILLIAM) Freedom and the welfare state. London, 1976. pp. 224.

McKERCHER (WILLIAM RUSSELL) English libertarian thought in the late nineteenth century. 1976. fo. 438. *bibliog. Typescript. Ph.D.(London) thesis: unpublished. This thesis is the property of London University and may not be removed from the Library.*

MILL (JOHN STUART) John Stuart Mill on politics and society; selected and edited by Geraint L. Williams. London, 1976. pp. 412. *bibliog.*

SHKLAR (JUDITH N.) Freedom and independence: a study of the political ideas of Hegel's Phenomenology of mind. Cambridge, 1976. pp. 216.

LIBERTY OF INFORMATION

— Russia.

MEDVEDEV (ZHORES ALEKSANDROVICH) Secrecy of correspondence is guaranteed by law. Nottingham, [1975]. pp. 180. *(Medvedev Papers. vol. 2)*

LIBERTY OF SPEECH

— France.

KING (JEROME B.) Law v. order: legal process and free speech in contemporary France. Hamden, Conn., 1975. pp. 206. *bibliog.*

— Switzerland.

ZELLWEGER (IVO) Die strafrechtlichen Beschränkungen der politischen Meinungsäusserungsfreiheit: Propagandaverbote. Zürich, [1975]. pp. 192. *bibliog. (Zürich. Universität. Rechts- und Staatswissenschaftliche Fakultät. Zürcher Beiträge zur Rechtswissenschaft. Neue Folge. Heft 481)*

— United States.

OWEN (BRUCE M.) Economics and freedom of expression: media structure and the first amendment. Cambridge, Mass., [1975]. pp. 202. *bibliog.*

LIBERTY OF THE PRESS.

MURPHY (DAVID) The silent watchdog: the press in local politics. London, 1976. pp. 186. *bibliog.*

— Bibliography.

GERMANY (BUNDESREPUBLIK). Deutscher Bundestag. Wissenschaftliche Dienste. 1974. Medienfreiheit, Pressekonzentration, Presserechtsrahmengesetz: Auswahlbibliographie mit Annotationen; [compiled by Claus- Peter Gerber]. Bonn, 1974. pp. 107. *(Bibliographien. 38)*

— Germany.

SCHOENBAUM (DAVID) Ein Abgrund von Landesverrat: die Affäre um den "Spiegel"; (aus dem Englischen übertragen von Armin Sellheim). Wien, 1968. pp. 254.

FISCHER (HEINZ DIETRICH) ed. Pressekonzentration und Zensurpraxis im Ersten Weltkrieg: Texte und Quellen. Berlin, 1973. pp. 301. *bibliogs.*

WETZEL (HANS WOLFGANG) Presseinnenpolitik im Bismarckreich, 1874-1890: das Problem der Repression oppositioneller Zeitungen. Bern, 1975. pp. 365. *bibliog.*

— Rhodesia.

WASON (EUGENE) Banned: the story of the African Daily News, Southern Rhodesia, 1964. London, 1976. pp. 161.

— Sweden.

LENHAMMAR (HARRY) Religion och tryckfrihet i Sverige, 1809-1840: Religion and free dom of the press in Sweden, 1809-1840. Uppsala, 1974. pp. 300. *bibliog. (Uppsala. Universitet. Acta Universitatis Upsaliensis. Studia Historico-Ecclesiastica Upsaliensia. 26) In Swedish, with English summary.*

— United States.

SCHMIDT (BENNO C.) Freedom of the press vs. public access. New York, [1976]. pp. 296.

LIBRARIANS

— United Kingdom.

U.K. Department of Education and Science. 1975. Census of staff in librarianship and information work in the United Kingdom, 1972. [London, 1975]. pp. 31.

LIBRARIES

— Automation.

HENLEY (JOHN PATRICK) Computer-based library and information systems. 2nd ed. london, 1972. pp. 106. *bibliog.*

HAYES (ROBERT MAYO) and BECKER (JOSEPH) Handbook of data processing for libraries. 2nd ed. Los Angeles, [1974]. pp. 688.

— Germany.

BUSSE (GISELA VON) and ERNESTUS (HORST) Das Bibliothekswesen der Bundesrepublik Deutschland: eine Einführung. Wiesbaden, 1968. pp. 302.

— Nigeria.

NATIONAL LIBRARY OF NIGERIA. A catalogue of selected publications of selected libraries, the Nigerian Library Association, and library related institutions in Nigeria; exhibited at the IFLA general council meeting, Washington, 1974. Lagos, 1974. pp. 8.

— Russia.

BIBLIOTEKI SSSR: spravochnik. Moskva, 1973-4. 2 vols.

— Singapore.

BYRD (CECIL K.) Books in Singapore: a survey of publishing, printing, bookselling and library activity in the Republic of Singapore. Singapore, 1970. pp. 161.

— United Kingdom — Censorship.

THOMPSON (ANTHONY HUGH) Censorship in public libraries in the United Kingdom during the twentieth century. Epping, Essex, 1975. pp. 236.

— United States — Special collections.

DALLAS. Public Library. Business and Technology Division. Business history collection: a checklist. Dallas, 1974. pp. 236.

LIBRARIES, NATIONAL

— United Kingdom.

BLL REVIEW; [pd. by] British Library Lending Division. q., Jl 1973 (v.1, no.1)- London. *Supersedes NLL review (Ja 1971 - Ap 1973).*

BRITISH LIBRARY. Lending Division. News Sheet. irreg. Boston Spa. *Current issues only kept.*

LIBRARIES, PRIVATE

— Germany.

EX libris Karl Marx und Friedrich Engels: Schicksal und Verzeichnis einer Bibliothek; Einleitung und Redaktion: Bruno Kaiser; Katalog und wissenschaftlicher Apparat: Inge Werchan. Berlin, 1967. pp. 229.

LIBRARIES, SPECIAL

— Directories.

INTERNATIONAL CO-OPERATIVE ALLIANCE. Directory of co-operative libraries and documentation services etc. London, 1974. pp. 69. *In English, French and German.*

— Handbooks, manuals, etc.

BATTEN (WILLIAM EDWARD) ed. Handbook of special librarianship and information work. 4th ed. London, 1975. pp. 430. *bibliogs.*

LIBRARY ADMINISTRATION.

THOMAS (PAULINE ANN) and WARD (VALERIE A.) An analysis of managerial activities in libraries. London, [1974]. pp. 68. *bibliog. (Association of Special Libraries and Information Bureaux. Aslib Occasional Publications. No. 14)*

PLANNING, programming, budgeting systems in libraries: a symposium [organized by the East Midlands Branch of the Library Association in 1971]. [Etwall, Derbyshire], 1975. pp. 55.

BROPHY (PETER) and others, eds. Reader in operations research for libraries. Englewood, Colorado, 1976. pp. 392. *bibliogs.*

LIBRARY FINANCE.

PLANNING, programming, budgeting systems in libraries: a symposium [organized by the East Midlands Branch of the Library Association in 1971]. [Etwall, Derbyshire], 1975. pp. 55

LIBRARY LEGISLATION

— United Kingdom.

HEWITT (ARTHUR R.) Public library law and the law as to museums and art galleries in England and Wales, Scotland and Northern Ireland. 5th ed. London, 1975. pp. 109.

LIBRARY PLANNING.

PLANNING, programming, budgeting systems in libraries: a symposium [organized by the East Midlands Branch of the Library Association in 1971]. [Etwall, Derbyshire], 1975. pp. 55.

LIBRARY SCIENCE

— Abbreviations.

MONTGOMERY (A.C.) compiler. Acronyms and abbreviations in library and information work: a reference handbook of British usage. London, [1975]. pp. 97.

— Bibliography.

NATIONAL LIBRARY OF NIGERIA. A catalogue of selected publications of selected libraries, the Nigerian Library Association, and library related institutions in Nigeria; exhibited at the IFLA general council meeting, Washington, 1974. Lagos, 1974. pp. 8.

LIBYA.

La LIBYE nouvelle: rupture et continuité; par G. Albergoni [and others]. Paris, 1975. pp. 303. *bibliog. (Centre de Recherches et d'Etudes sur les Sociétés Méditerranéennes. Collection)*

— Commerce.

LIBYA. Census and Statistical Department. 1968. External trade indices, 1962-1966. Tripoli, [1968]. fo. (30). *In English and Arabic.*

— Economic conditions.

BELGIUM. Office Belge du Commerce Extérieur. 1973. Libye. Bruxelles, 1973. pp. 47. *(Un Marché. 20)*

— Economic policy.

LIBYA. Ministry of Planning and Development. 1964. Five-year economic and social development plan, 1963-1968. [Tripoli, 1964?]. pp. 153.

— Foreign relations.

GADHAFI (MOAMMAR) The battle of destiny: speeches and interviews. London, 1976. pp. 137.

— Industries.

LIBYA. Census and Statistical Department. 1965. Report of the industrial census, 1964. Tripoli, [1965]. fo. 110.

— Social policy.

LIBYA. Ministry of Planning and Development. 1964. Five-year economic and social development plan, 1963-1968. [Tripoli, 1964?]. pp. 153.

LICENCES

— France.

LIVET (PIERRE) L'autorisation administrative préalable et les libertés publiques. Paris, 1974. pp. 334. *bibliog.*

LIEBKNECHT (KARL).

KARL Liebknechts Vermächtnis für die deutsche Nation: Protokoll des wissenschaftlichen Seminars des Instituts für Marxismus-Leninismus beim ZK der SED am 4.August 1961 in Berlin. Berlin, 1962. pp. 152.

LIEBKNECHT (WILHELM PHILIPP MARTIN CHRISTIAN LUDWIG).

LIEBKNECHT (WILHELM PHILIPP MARTIN CHRISTIAN LUDWIG) Erinnerungen eines Soldaten der Revolution; (zusammengestellt und eingeleitet von Heinrich Gemkow). Berlin, 1976. pp. 450. *bibliog.*

LIECHTENSTEIN.

KRANZ (WALTHER) ed. The principality of Liechtenstein: a documentary handbook; translated from the German by G.D.C. Martin. 2nd ed. [Vaduz], Press and Information Office of the Government of Liechtenstein, 1969. pp. 205. *bibliog.*

FRANCE. Direction de la Documentation. La Documentation Française. Notes et Etudes Documentaires. No. 4,210. Les micro-états européens: Monaco - Saint-Marin - Liechtenstein; par Jean-Jacques L. Tur. Paris, 1975. pp. 41. *bibliog.*

— Statistics.

GERMANY (BUNDESREPUBLIK). Statistisches Bundesamt. Länderkurzberichte: Liechtenstein. a., 1975- Wiesbaden.

LIFE EXPECTANCY.

NEWSHOLME (Sir ARTHUR) The Brighton life table: based on the mortality of the ten years, 1881-90. Brighton, 1893. pp. 39.

JONES-LEE (M.W.) The value of life: an economic analysis. London, 1976. pp. 162. *bibliogs.*

LIGHTHOUSES.

HAGUE (DOUGLAS B.) and CHRISTIE (ROSEMARY) Lighthouses: their architecture, history and archaeology. [Llandysul], 1975. pp. 307. *bibliog.*

LIGNITE

— Australia — Victoria.

VICTORIA. State Electricity Commission. 1962. Serving Victoria: (electricity, brown coal, briquettes; published to mark the sixth plenary meeting of the World Power Conference). Melbourne, [1962]. pp. (30).

LIGURIA

— History.

ASSERETO (GIOVANNI) La Repubblica Ligure: lotte politiche e problemi finanziari, 1797-1799. Torino, 1975. pp. 285. *(Fondazione Luigi Einaudi. Studi. 18)*

LILONGWE

— Markets.

MALAWI. National Statistical Office. 1973. Lilongwe town market survey, 1971-1972. Zomba, 1973. pp. 82.

LIMA

— History — Sources.

MUGABURU (JOSEPHE DE) and MUGABURU (FRANCISCO DE) Chronicle of colonial Lima: the diary of Josephe and Francisco Mugaburu, 1640-1697; translated and edited by Robert Ryal Miller. Norman, Ok., [1975]. pp. 342.

— Social conditions.

COLLIER (DAVID) Squatters and oligarchs: authoritarian rule and policy change in Peru. Baltimore, [1976]. pp. 187. *bibliog.*

LINDSAY (MICHAEL FRANCIS MORRIS) 2nd Baron Lindsay.

LINDSAY (MICHAEL FRANCIS MORRIS) 2nd Baron Lindsay. The unknown war: north China 1937-1945. London, 1975. 1 vol. (unpaged) *bibliog.*

LINEAR OPERATORS.

AKHIEZER (NAUM IL'ICH) and GLAZMAN (I.M.) Theory of linear operators in Hilbert space...; translated from the Russian by Merlynd Nestell. New York, [1961-63] repr.1966. 2 vols.

LINEAR PROGRAMMING.

EGAN (R.J.) Optimum combination of enterprises using linear programming. [Brisbane], 1968. fo. 40. *(Queensland. Department of Primary Industries. Economic Services Branch. Technical Bulletins. No. 4)*

MANNING (GLENN H.) Linear programming, resource allocation and non-market benefits. Ottawa, 1971. pp. 18. *bibliog. (Canada. Forestry Service. Publications. No. 1298)*

PIMENTEL (RUDERICO FERRAZ) Application of several different linear programming techniques to the generalized transportation problem. 1976. fo. 250. *bibliog. Typescript. Ph.D. (London) thesis: unpublished. This thesis is the property of London University and may not be removed from the Library.*

LINEAR TOPOLOGICAL SPACES.

LINEAR TOPOLOGICAL SPACES.

SCHAEFER (HELMUT H.) Topological vector spaces. New York, [1966] repr. 1971. pp. 294. *bibliog.*

LINEN

— **United Kingdom.**

BENJAMIN (FREDERICK A.) The Ruskin linen industry of Keswick. Beckermet, Cumbria, 1974. pp. 43.

LINGUISTIC ANALYSIS (LINGUISTICS).

NORMAN (DONALD A.) and RUMELHART (DAVID E.) Explorations in cognition. San Francisco, [1975]. pp. 430. *bibliog.*

LINGUISTICS.

CHICAGO LINGUISTIC SOCIETY. Regional Meeting, 6th, 1970. Papers, etc. Chicago, [1970]. pp. 588. *bibliogs.*

CHICAGO LINGUISTIC SOCIETY. Regional Meeting, 7th, 1971. Papers, etc. Chicago, [1971]. pp. 568. *bibliogs.*

JONES (KAREN SPARCK) and KAY (MARTIN) Linguistics and information science. New York, 1973. pp. 244. *bibliog. (International Federation for Documentation. Publications. No.492)*

CHICAGO LINGUISTIC SOCIETY. Regional Meeting, 10th, 1974. Papers from the...meeting...; edited by Michael W. La Galy [and others]. Chicago, [1974]. pp. 801. *bibligs.*

HARMAN (GILBERT) ed. On Noam Chomsky: critical essays. Garden City, N.Y., 1974. pp. 345. *bibliogs.*

PARRET (HERMAN) Discussing language: dialogues with Wallace L. Chafe [and others]. tHE hAGUE, 1974. PP. 428. BIBLIOG.

BARTSCH (RENATE) and VENNEMANN (THEO) eds. Linguistics and neighboring disciplines. Amsterdam, 1975. pp. 247. *bibliogs.*

ROBINSON (IAN) Lecturer in English language in the University College of Swansea. The new grammarians' funeral: a critique of Noam Chomsky's linguistics. Cambridge, 1975. pp. 189.

LIQUIDITY (ECONOMICS).

BOIKOV (SERGEI IVANOVICH) Ekonomicheskie funktsii i formy dvizheniia sredstv razvitogo sotsialisticheskogo obshchestva. Leningrad, 1975. pp. 126.

ECONOMIC DEVELOPMENT COMMITTEE FOR THE DISTRIBUTIVE TRADES. Profitability and liquidity in the distributive trades: an examination of financial data in selected sectors; based on a report prepared for the Distributive Trades EDC by Whitefield Associates and Company. London, National Economic Development Office, 1975. pp. 123.

HEWSON (JOHN R.) Liquidity creation and distribution in the eurocurrency markets. Lexington, Mass., [1975]. pp. 172. *bibliog.*

LIQUOR HABIT

— **United Kingdom.**

SOCIAL MORALITY COUNCIL. Study Group on Education and Drug Dependence. Education and drug dependence. London, 1975. pp. 78.

LIQUOR PROBLEM.

BRUUN (KETTIL) and others. The gentlemen's club: international control of drugs and alcohol. Chicago, 1975. pp. 338. *bibliog.*

— **United Kingdom.**

SOCIAL MORALITY COUNCIL. Study Group on Education and Drug Dependence. Education and drug dependence. London, 1975. pp. 78.

BRAKE (GEORGE THOMPSON) Alcohol: its consumption and control: objective facts about a widespread habit: the personal and social problems involved in its abuse: and efforts to control it by legislation in England and Wales and in other European countries. London, 1976. pp. 42.

ROBINSON (DAVID) 1941- . From drinking to alcoholism: a sociological commentary. London, [1976]. pp. 211.

— **United States.**

CAHALAN (DON) and others. American drinking practices: a national study of drinking behavior and attitudes. New Brunswick, N.J., [1969]. pp. 260. *bibliog. (Rutgers University. Rutgers Center of Alcohol Studies. Monographs. No.6)*

LIST (GEORG FRIEDRICH).

KRITIK der bürgerlichen Ökonomie: neues Manuskript von Marx; und Rede von Engels über F. List. Berlin, [1972]. pp. 86.

LIST PROCESSING (ELECTRONIC COMPUTERS).

FOSTER (JOHN MICHAEL) List processing. London, 1967 repr. 1970. pp. 54. *bibliog.*

LITERATURE

— **Bibliography.**

ROSS (DONALD ARMSTRONG) ed. The reader's guide to Everyman's Library. 4th ed. London, 1976. pp. 596.

LITERATURE, IMMORAL.

ZURCHER (LOUIS A.) and KIRKPATRICK (ROBERT GEORGE) Citizens for decency: antipornography crusades as status defense. Austin, [1976]. pp. 412. *bibliog.*

LITERATURE, MODERN

— **1700—1799.**

DAWSON (ROBERT L.) Baculard d'Arnaud: life and prose fiction. Banbury, 1976. 2 vols. *bibliog. (Studies on Voltaire and the Eighteenth Century. vols. 141-142)*

LITERATURE AND REVOLUTIONS.

SWINGEWOOD (ALAN WILLIAM) The novel and revolution. London, 1975. pp. 288.

LITERATURE AND SOCIETY.

ZETKIN (CLARA) Über Literatur und Kunst: [selected articles, originally published in "Die Gleichheit", 1906-1911]; zusammengestellt und herausgegeben von Emilia Zetkin-Milowidowa. Berlin, 1955. pp. 115.

BOELL (HEINRICH) Neue politische und literarische Schriften [1967-1972]. Köln, 1973. pp. 285. *bibliog.*

SWINGEWOOD (ALAN WILLIAM) The novel and revolution. London, 1975. pp. 288.

MEAKIN (DAVID) Man and work: literature and culture in industrial society. London, 1976. pp. 215. *bibliog.*

LITERATURE AND STATE.

DUNHAM (VERA SANDOMIRSKY) In Stalin's time: middleclass values in Soviet fiction. Cambridge, 1976. pp. 283. *bibliog.*

LITHUANIA

— **History.**

DAUMANTAS (JUOZAS) pseud. [i.e. Juozas LUKŠA]. Fighters for freedom: Lithuanian partisans versus the U.S.S.R., 1944-1947. New York, [1975]. pp. 254.

— **Industries.**

MERKYS (V.) Razvitie promyshlennosti i formirovanie proletariata Litvy v XIX v. Vil'nius, 1969. pp. 447. *bibliog.*

— **Nationalism.**

DAUMANTAS (JUOZAS) pseud. [i.e. Juozas LUKŠA]. Fighters for freedom: Lithuanian partisans versus the U.S.S.R., 1944-1947. New York, [1975]. pp. 254.

LIU (SHAO-CH'I).

LI (TIEN-MIN) Liu Shao-ch'i: Mao's first heir-apparent. Taipei, 1975. pp. 223. *bibliog.*

LIVERPOOL

— **Civic improvement.**

WILSON (HUGH) AND WOMERSLEY (LEWIS) Firm, and others. Inner area study: Liverpool: third study review. [London], Department of the Environment, [1975]. pp. 23.

WILSON (HUGH) AND WOMERSLEY (LEWIS) Firm, and others. Inner area study: Liverpool: work programme, 1975-76. [London], Department of the Environment, [1975]. pp. 17.

WILSON (HUGH) AND WOMERSLEY (LEWIS) Firm, and TYM (ROGER) AND ASSOCIATES. Inner area study: Liverpool: vacant land. [London], Department of the Environment, [1976]. pp. 32.

— **Politics and government.**

COOPER (ROBERT) Ph.D. Managing inner city renewal: Liverpool Corporation and the Vauxhall Community Development Project. [Liverpool, Vauxhall Community Development Project], 1972. fo. 21.

WILSON (HUGH) AND WOMERSLEY (LEWIS) Firm, and TYM (ROGER) AND ASSOCIATES. Inner area study: Liverpool: area management progress report. [London], Department of the Environment, [1975]. pp. 25.

WILSON (HUGH) AND WOMERSLEY (LEWIS) Firm, and TYM (ROGER) AND ASSOCIATES. Inner area study: Liverpool: area resource analysis: district D tables, 1973-74. [London], Department of the Environment, [1976]. pp. 125.

— **Social conditions.**

VAUXHALL COMMUNITY DEVELOPMENT PROJECT. Interim report of Project Director to David Lane, Minister of State for Home Office. [Liverpool], 1972. fo. 49.

VAUXHALL COMMUNITY DEVELOPMENT PROJECT. Report of the Project Director to the Home Secretary. [Liverpool], 1973. fo. 33.

WEBBER (RICHARD J.) Liverpool social area study: 1971 data: final report. London, 1975. pp. 142. *(Planning Research Applications Group. PRAG Technical Papers. TP 14)*

WILSON (HUGH) AND WOMERSLEY (LEWIS) Firm, and others. Inner area study: Liverpool: third study review. [London], Department of the Environment, [1975]. pp. 23.

— **Social policy.**

WILSON (HUGH) AND WOMERSLEY (LEWIS) Firm, and others. Inner area study: Liverpool: third study review. [London], Department of the Environment, [1975]. pp. 23.

WILSON (HUGH) AND WOMERSLEY (LEWIS) Firm, and others. Inner area study: Liverpool: work programme, 1975-76. [London], Department of the Environment, [1975]. pp. 17.

LIVONIA

— **Foreign economic relations — Russia.**

KAZAKOVA (NATAL'IA ALEKSANDROVNA) Russko-livonskie i russko-ganzeiskie otnosheniia, konets XIV - nachalo XVI v. Leningrad, 1975. pp. 359.

LOANS, BRITISH

— Argentine Republic.

CHIAPELLA (ARMANDO O.) El destino del emprestito Baring Brothers, 1824-1826. Buenos Aires, 1975. pp. 141.

LOANS, FOREIGN.

UNITED NATIONS. Conference on Trade and Development. 1972. Debt problems of developing countries: report by the UNCTAD Secretariat. (TD/118/Supp.G/Rev.1). New York, 1972. pp. 31.

INTERNATIONAL BANK FOR RECONSTRUCTION AND DEVELOPMENT. Borrowing in international capital markets: foreign and international bond issues: publicized Eurocurrency credits. q., 1974 (3rd quarter)- [Washington D.C.].

UNITED NATIONS. Conference on Trade and Development. 1974. Debt problems in the context of development: report by the UNCTAD Secretariat. (TD/B/C.3/109/Rev.1). New York, 1974. pp. 35.

— Bulgaria.

TODOROVA (TSVETANA) Diplomaticheska istoriia na vunshnite zaemi na Bulgariia, 1888- 1912. Sofiia, 1971. pp. 497. *With English summary and table of contents.*

LOBBYISTS

— United States.

HAIDER (DONALD H.) When governments come to Washington: governors, mayors, and intergovernmental lobbying. New York, [1974]. pp. 336. *bibliog.*

LOCAL BUDGETS

— Germany, Eastern.

ROHDE (ERWIN) and SIEBENHAAR (HEINZ) Haushalts- und Finanzwirtschaft der Städte und Gemeinden. 2nd ed. Berlin, 1975. pp. 192. *bibliog.*

LOCAL FINANCE.

MILLS (EDWIN S.) and OATES (WALLACE E.) eds. Fiscal zoning and land use controls: the economic issues. Lexington, Mass., [1975]. pp. 205. *bibliogs.*

STEISS (ALAN WALTER) Local government finance: capital facilities planning and debt administration. Lexington, Mass., [1975]. pp. 300.

— Argentine Republic.

ARGENTINE REPUBLIC. Direccion Nacional de Programacion e Investigacion. 1975. Presupuestos provinciales y presupuesto nacional: distribuidos por provincias; ejercicio 1971 y 1972. Buenos Aires, 1975. pp. 234.

— Canada — Ontario.

ONTARIO. Economic Council. Annual report. a., 1975/76 (2nd)- Toronto.

— Finland.

VUODEN 1974 kuntien kalleustutkimus; [by Tuula] (Lind) [and others]. Helsinki, 1975. 1 vol. (various pagings). *(Finland. Tilastokeskus. Tutkimuksia. 31)*

— France.

FRANCE. Direction de la Comptabilité Publique. Le secteur public local: statistiques des comptes des communes, de la ville de Paris, des départements et de leurs établissements publics. a., 1973- Paris. *In two volumes: Fascicule 1. Synthèse nationale analyse financière et études régionales; Fascicule 2: Tableaux comptables.*

FRANCE. Direction de la Comptabilité Publique. Le secteur public local: statistiques des comptes des communes de moins de 10, 000 habitants de la métropole. a., 1973- Paris. *In two volumes Fascicule 1, Analyse financière synthèse nationale, études régionales; Fascicule 2, Tableaux comptables nationaux et régionalisés.*

— Germany, Eastern.

ROHDE (ERWIN) and SIEBENHAAR (HEINZ) Haushalts- und Finanzwirtschaft der Städte und Gemeinden. 2nd ed. Berlin, 1975. pp. 192. *bibliog.*

— Israel — Accounting.

ISRAEL. Central Bureau of Statistics. Special Series. No. 151. Receipts and expenditure of the local authorities: economic analysis for the national accounts of Israel, 1959/60-1961/62. Jerusalem, 1964. pp. 79. *In English and Hebrew.*

— New Zealand.

NEW ZEALAND. Local Authority Finance Committee. 1973. Local authority finance in New Zealand: report; [P.J. O'Dea, chairman]. Wellington, 1973. pp. 99. *bibliog.*

— Poland.

ZAWADZKI (ALEKSANDER WŁADYSŁAW) Finanse samorządu terytorialnego w latach 1918-1939. Warszawa, 1971. pp. 291. *bibliog.*

— Russia.

DEMCHENKOV (VIKTOR SEMENOVICH) and UZHVENKO (MIKHAIL FEDOROVICH) Regulirovanie mestnykh biudzhetov: raspredelenie dokhodov mezhdu biudzhetami. Moskva, 1975. pp. 88.

— Tasmania.

TASMANIA. Commonwealth Bureau of Census and Statistics. Tasmanian Office. Local government finance. a., 1972/73(2nd)- Hobart.

— United Kingdom.

NORTH WEST ECONOMIC PLANNING COUNCIL. The Committee of Inquiry into Local Government Finance: a submission of evidence. [Manchester], 1974. pp. 58.

ASSOCIATION OF METROPOLITAN AUTHORITIES. Evidence to the committee of inquiry into local government finance (the Layfield committee). London, 1975. pp. 24.

COMMUNITY DEVELOPMENT PROJECT. Rates of decline: an unacceptable base of public finance; a submission to the Layfield Committee on Local Government Finance. [London, 1975] repr. 1976. pp. 51. *bibliog.*

NORTH WEST ECONOMIC PLANNING COUNCIL. The Committee of Inquiry into Local Government Finance: supplementary evidence. [Manchester], 1975. pp. 21.

U.K. Price Commission. 1975. Local authorities and the price code. [London, 1975]. 1 pamphlet (unfoliated).

HEPWORTH (NOEL PEERS) The finance of local government. 3rd ed. London, 1976. pp. 304. *bibliog.*

U.K. Committee of Inquiry into Local Government Finance. 1976. Local government finance: appendi[ces] 1-9 to the report of the committee of inquiry under the chairmanship of Frank Layfield. London, 1976. 9 pts. (in 6 vols.) *Report itself published as British Parliamentary Paper Cmnd. 6453, Session 1975-76.*

[U.K. Department of the Environment. 1972]. Local government audit: code of practice. [London, 1972]. fo. 9, 4.

— — Law.

RATING law and practice; by H.J. Wright [and others]. London, 1974. pp. 336.

RYDE (WALTER CRANLEY) On rating: the law and practice; thirteenth edition by David Widdicombe [and others]. London, 1976. pp. 1454, 84.

— United States — Massachusetts.

SLAVET (JOSEPH S.) and others. Financing state-local services: a new strategy for greater equity. Lexington, Mass., [1975]. pp. 147.

LOCAL GOVERNMENT.

JONES (GILBERT) Local authority offices: areas and costs. [London], Department of the Environment, Local Government and Development, [1971]. pp. 62.

COMPARATIVE community politics: [selected papers from three conferences organized by the Committee for Community Research of the International Sociological Association]; edited by Terry Nichols Clark. New York, [1974]. pp. 415. *bibliogs.*

— Study and teaching — United Kingdom.

LOCAL GOVERNMENT TRAINING BOARD. Policy statement, 1975-6. [London, 1974]. pp. 5.

— Belgium.

FAIDER (CHARLES) Coup-d'oeil historique sur les institutions provinciales et communales en Belgique, suivi de quelques mots sur les principes d'organisation. Bruxelles, 1834. pp. 117.

— Canada — Manitoba.

MANITOBA. Local Government Boundaries Commission. 1970. Provisional plan for the boundaries and structure of local government units within the Metropolitan Winnipeg area and its additional zone; [R.G. Smellie, chairman]. [Winnipeg], 1970. pp. 347.

— — Newfoundland and Labrador.

NEWFOUNDLAND. Royal Commission on Municipal Government in Newfoundland and Labrador, 1972. Report; [H.J. Whalen, chairman]. [St. John's, 1974]. pp. 711.

— — Ontario.

FELDMAN (LIONEL D.) Ontario 1945-1973: the municipal dynamic. [Toronto], Ontario Economic Council, 1974. pp. 47. *bibliog. (Evolution of Policy in Contemporary Ontario, The. 5)*

— China.

CONFLICT and control in late imperial China; edited by Frederic Wakeman and Carolyn Grant. Berkeley, California, [1975]. pp. 328. *Papers from a conference sponsored by the Center for Chinese Studies, University of California, and the Committee on Studies of Chinese Civilization of the American Council of Learned Societies.*

— Europe.

MUNTZKE (HANS) Maintien et renforcement des communes, fondement de l'état; documents d'étude conçus et rassemblés pour les VIIIes Etats Généraux des Communes d'Europe...Berlin 7-11 juin 1967. [Paris, 1967]. pp. 79.

— Italy.

DEMOCRAZIA CRISTIANA. Regioni, enti locali per lo sviluppo nella libertà: [selections from the proceedings of several meetings held in 1974]. [Rome], 1975. pp. 255.

— Malaysia.

FEDERATION OF MALAYSIA. Royal Commission of Enquiry to investigate into the Workings of Local Authorities in West Malaysia, 1965. Report; [Dato' Athi Nahappan, chairman]. Kuala Lumpur, 1970. pp. 347.

BEAGLEHOLE (JOHN HOLT) The district: a study in decentralization in West Malaysia. London, 1976. pp. 122. *bibliog. (Hull. University. Centre for South-East Asian Studies. Monographs on South-East Asia. No. 6)*

— New Zealand.

NEW ZEALAND. Local Government Commission. 1975. Northland region: provisional scheme and explanatory statement. [Wellington], 1975. 1 vol. (various pagings). 3 maps in end pocket.

LOCAL GOVERNMENT.(Cont.)

— **Philippine Islands.**

POLITICAL change in the Philippines: studies of local politics preceding martial law; edited by Benedict J. Kerkvliet. [Honolulu], 1974. pp. 258. *(Hawaii University. Asian Studies Program. Asian Studies of Hawaii. 14) Based on essays presented at the Association of Asian Studies meeting in New York in 1972 and at a regional meeting of AAS in 1972.*

LEICHTER (HOWARD M.) Political regime and public policy in the Philippines : a comparison of Bacolod and Iloilo Cities. [DeKalb, Ill.], 1975. pp. 163. *bibliog. (Northern Illinois University. Center for Southeast Asian Studies. Special Reports. No. 11)*

— **Poland.**

LEOŃSKI (ZBIGNIEW) Ewolucja Rad Narodowych w Polsce Ludowej. Poznań, 1974. pp. 83.

DAWIDOWICZ (WACŁAW) Zarys ustroju organów administracji terytorialnej w Polsce. Warszawa, 1976. pp. 265.

— **Russia.**

KLIUSHNICHENKO (ANATOLII PETROVICH) and SHERGIN (ANATOLII PAVLOVICH) Administrativnye komissii. Moskva, 1975. pp. 111.

MOSKALEV (ALEKSANDR VASIL'EVICH) Sessionnaia deiatel'nost' mestnykh Sovetov. Moskva, 1975. pp. 143.

— **Sierra Leone.**

BARROWS (WALTER L.) Grassroots politics in an African state: integration and development in Sierra Leone. New York, 1976. pp. 265.

— **South Africa — Transkeian Territories.**

HAMMOND-TOOKE (W.D.) Command or consensus: the development of Transkeian local government. Cape Town, 1975. pp. 240. *bibliog.*

— **Switzerland.**

MEYLAN (JEAN PIERRE) Evolution de l'autonomie communale en Suisse. Lausanne, 1968. fo. 25.

— **United Kingdom.**

HADFIELD (ELLIS CHARLES RAYMOND) and MACCOLL (JAMES E.) British local government. London, [1950]. pp. 172.

EAST SUFFOLK. Reorganisation Committee. Local government in England: government proposals for reorganisation 1971: report. Ipswich, 1971. pp. 17.

NATIONAL BUILDING AGENCY. Control of capital works programmes; [prepared by W.P. Ridgeway] . London, 1972. pp. 16. *(National Building Agency. Local Government Re- organisation: Management Guides. No. 1)*

NATIONAL BUILDING AGENCY. Merging direct labour building organisations; [prepared by W.P. Ridgeway]. London, 1972. pp. 15. *(National Building Agency. Local Government Re- organisation: Management Guides. No. 2)*

U.K. Department of the Environment. Miscellaneous local government and planning statistics. a., 1973- London.

BAKER (JOHN) of the Association for Neighbourhood Councils and YOUNG (MICHAEL DUNLOP) The Hornsey plan: a role for neighbourhood councils in the new local government. 4th ed. Halstead, Essex, 1973. pp. 20.

ELEY (A.W.) The passing of rural independence: the story of a rural district council. Milton Keynes, 1973. 1 pamphlet(unpaged). *(Bradwell Abbey Field Centre for the Study of Archaeology, Natural History and Environmental Studies. Occasional Papers. No. 1)*

LANSLEY (JOHN) Community organisations and local government reform; first interim report [for the Community Councils Development Group]. Liverpool, 1973. pp. 36.

U.K. Department of the Environment. 1974. Area management. [London, 1974]. fo. 5.

ARNOLD-BAKER (CHARLES) Local council administration in English parishes and Welsh communities. [London], 1975. pp. 736.

ILERSIC (ALFRED ROMAN) Local government at the crossroads. London, [1975]. pp. 13.

RICHARDS (PETER GODFREY) The Local Government Act, 1972: problems of implementation. London, 1975. pp. 207.

RICHARDS (PETER GODFREY) The reformed local government system. 2nd ed. london, 1975. pp. 192. *bibliog.*

U.K. Department of the Environment. 1975. Bill for the Transfer in New Towns of Housing and Related Assets: (consultation paper). [London, 1975]. pp. 10.

BENINGTON (JOHN) Local government becomes big business. 2nd ed. London, Community Development Project, 1976. pp. 28.

MURPHY (DAVID) The silent watchdog: the press in local politics. London, 1976. pp. 186. *bibliog.*

— — **Information services — Bibliography.**

SCOTT (GAY) compiler. Information for members. London, 1975. pp. 6. *(London. Greater London Council. Research Library. [Research Bibliographies]. No. 64)*

— — **Ireland.**

O'SULLIVAN (JAMES L.) Systems of local government and administration in Ireland. [191-]. pp. (124). *bibliog. Typescript.*

ROBINSON (Sir HENRY AUGUSTUS) Memories: wise and otherwise. London, 1923 repr. 1924. pp. 348.

— — **Ireland, Northern.**

IRELAND, NORTHERN. Department of Housing, Local Government and Planning. Report. a., 1972/73- Belfast. *1965/66 [1st]- 1971/72 included as Report of the Ministry of Development in IRELAND, NORTHERN. Parliament. [Command papers]*

— — **Scotland.**

SCOTLAND. Commissioner for Local Administration in Scotland. Report. pd. by Commission for Local Authority Accounts in Scotland. a., 1975/76(1st)- Edinburgh.

— — **United States.**

POLITICAL science and state and local government: [papers presented at a conference held in Biloxi, Mississippi in October 1972, organized by the American Political Science Association]. Washington, [1973]. pp. 141. *bibliogs.*

LAMB (CURT) Political power in poor neighborhoods. New York, [1975]. pp. 315. *bibliog.*

SCHNALL (DAVID J.) Ethnicity and suburban local politics. New York, 1975. pp. 168. *bibliog.*

BINGHAM (RICHARD D.) The adoption of innovation by local government;...with the assistance of Thomas P. McNaught. Lexington, [1976]. pp. 271. *bibliog.*

LOCAL GOVERNMENT OFFICIALS AND EMPLOYEES

— **India — Bombay — Salaries, pensions, etc.**

REPORT of the Committee under the Minimum Wages Act, 1948, in respect of employment under local authorities; [Champaklal G. Modi, chairman]. Bombay, Government Central Press, 1955. pp. 24.

— **Nigeria.**

MAGID (ALVIN) Men in the middle: leadership and role conflict in a Nigerian society. Manchester, [1976]. pp. 292. *bibliog.*

— **United Kingdom — Salaries, pensions, etc.**

LOCAL GOVERNMENT TRAINING BOARD. Salary gradings, age and sex distribution. [London, 1973]. pp. 11. *(Local Government Training Board. Manpower Survey. Reports. 3)*

— **United States.**

COLE (LEONARD A.) Blacks in power: a comparative study of black and white elected officials. Princeton, [1976]. pp. 267.

COOK (EDWARD M.) The fathers of the towns: leadership and community structure in eighteenth-century New England. Baltimore, [1976]. pp. 273. *bibliog. (Johns Hopkins University. Studies in Historical and Political Science. Series 94. No.2)*

GUSTELY (RICHARD D.) Municipal public employment and public expenditure. Lexington, Mass., [1974]. pp. 111. *bibliog.*

TILOVE (ROBERT) Public employee pension funds: a Twentieth Century Fund report. New York, 1976. pp. 370.

LOCAL TAXATION

— **United States.**

SCHROEDER (LARRY D.) and SJOQUIST (DAVID L.) The property tax and alternative local taxes: an economic analysis. New York, 1975. pp. 114. *bibliog.*

LOCAL TRANSIT

— **Costs.**

SMITH (EDWARD) B.S. An economic comparison of urban railways and express buses. [London], Greater London Council, 1972. 1 pamphlet (unfoliated). *Photocopy.*

— **Fares.**

BAACK (RAINER) Preisintegrierung und Preisharmonisierung bei Betrieben des öffentlichen Personennahverkehrs. Berlin, 1973. pp. 226. *bibliog.*

— **Australia.**

AUSTRALIA. Commonwealth Bureau of Census and Statistics. 1972. Journey to work and journey to school, May 1970. [Canberra, 1972]. pp. 22.

— **Hong Kong.**

MILLER (PETER) Public transport in Tsuen Wan new town. [Hong Kong], 1974. 1 vol. (various pagings). *(Hong Kong. Transport Department. Research and Development Section. Studies Reports. No. 74/8)*

HONG KONG. Transport Department. Research and Development Section. 1975. Public transport in Fanling and Sheung Shui. [Hong Kong], 1975. pp. (54). *(Studies Reports. No. 75/5)*

HONG KONG. Transport Department. Research and Development Section. 1976. Public transport facilities in Kwun Tong. [Hong Kong], 1976. pp. 18. *(Studies Reports. No. 76/2)*

HONG KONG. Transport Department. Research and Development Section. 1976. Public transport in Choi Hung and Ping Shek estates. [Hong Kong], 1976. pp. 61. *(Studies Reports. No. 76/4)*

— **United Kingdom.**

SUGDEN (ROBERT) Unskilled and unemployed in west Cumbria: a study of unemployment in relation to economic planning and public transportation policies. [York, 1975]. pp. 51. *bibliog. (Papers in Community Studies. No. 3)*

— — **Rates.**

GREY (ALEXANDER) Urban fares policy. Farnborough, Hants., [1975]. pp. 160.

— — **United States.**

HAMER (ANDREW MARSHALL) The selling of rail rapid transit: a critical look at urban transportation planning. Lexington, Mass., [1976]. pp. 336. *bibliog.*

LOCKE (JOHN).

LOCKE (JOHN) the Philosopher. The correspondence of John Locke; edited by E.S. de Beer. Oxford, 1976 in progress. *bibliog.*

LÓDZ

— History.

PRÓCHNIK (ADAM) Bunt łódzki w roku 1892: studium historyczne. Warszawa, 1950. pp. 156. *Reprint of 1st ed. of 1932 with some omissions.*

— Population.

MORTIMER-SZYMCZAK (HALINA) ed. Problemy demografii i zatrudnienia na terenie miasta Łodzi: praca zbiorowa. Łódź, 1967. pp. 168. *(Łódź. Łódzkie Towarzystwo Naukowe. Wydział 2 Nauk Historycznych i Społecznych. Prace. Nr.68) With English and Russian summaries.*

LÓDZ (PROVINCE)

— Economic conditions.

'ZYCIE społeczno-gospodarcze Łodzi i województwa łódzkiego. Łódź, 1964. pp. 317.

— Social conditions.

'ZYCIE społeczno-gospodarcze Łodzi i województwa łódzkiego. Łódź, 1964. pp. 317.

LOFA COUNTY, LIBERIA

— History.

CORDOR (S. HENRY) Zubaryea Akoi Tellewoyan of Liberia: the man and his work: a portrait of a great African tribal ruler: an introduction to the history of Lofa County, Liberia's largest region, through the lives of great history-makers, with emphasis on Zubaryea Akoi Tellewoyan and a study of the folkways of the Lorma people in Liberia. Voinjama, Liberia, [1967]. fo. 101.

LOGIC.

LATVIISKII GOSUDARSTVENNYI UNIVERSITET. Uchenye Zapiski. t.198. Voprosy logiki i metodologii poznaniia. Riga, 1973. pp. 100. *bibliog.*

HAACK (SUSAN) Deviant logic: some philosophical issues. London, 1974. pp. 191. *bibliog.*

MORAVCSIK (J.M.E.) ed. Logic and philosophy for linguists: a book of readings. The Hague, [1974]. pp. 347. *bibliogs.*

ARISTOTLE. Posterior analytics; translated with notes by Jonathan Barnes. Oxford, 1975. pp. 277. *bibliog.*

LOGIC, SYMBOLIC AND MATHEMATICAL.

WHAT is mathematical logic?; ([by] J.N. Crossley [and others]). London, 1972. pp. 82. *bibliog. Based on lectures delivered at Monash University and the University of Melbourne in 1971.*

MONTAGUE (RICHARD) Formal philosophy: selected papers of Richard Montague; edited and with an introduction by Richmond H. Thomason. New Haven, 1974. pp. 369. *bibliogs.*

LAKATOS (IMRE) Proofs and refutations: the logic of mathematical discovery; edited by John Worrall and Elie Zahar. Cambridge, 1976. pp. 174. *bibliog.*

LOGICAL POSITIVISM.

BOESELAGER (WOLFHARD F.) The Soviet critique of neopositivism: the history and structure of the critique of logical positivism and related doctrines by Soviet philosophers in the years 1947-1967. Dordrecht, [1975]. pp. 157. *bibliog. (Freiburg (Switzerland). Universität. Ost-Europa Institut. Sovietica. vol. 35)*

HINTIKKA (KAARLO JAAKKO JUHANI) ed. Rudolf Carnap, logical empiricist: materials and perspectives. Dordrecht, [1975]. pp. 400. *bibliogs. Includes Rudolf Carnap's Observation language and theoretical language, and his Notes on probability and induction.*

The POSITIVIST dispute in German sociology; [by] Theodor W. Adorno [and others]; translated by Glyn Adey and David Frisby. London, [1976]. pp. 307. *bibliog.*

LOHRENZ (WILHELM).

LOHRENZ (WILHELM) Hinter den Kulissen der SPD-Führung: Tatsachenbericht übe die Spionagetätigkeit des SPD-Vorstandes. Berlin, [1949]. pp. 31.

LOIRE (DEPARTMENT).

FRANCE. Direction de la Documentation. La Documentation Française. Notes et Etudes Documentaires. Nos. 4,104 - 4, 105. Les départements français. 42. Loire, Rhône-Alpes; [par Michel Désarmaux]. Paris, 1974. pp. 56. *bibliog.*

LOM'ZA

— Politics and government.

KOWALCZYK (JÓZEF) Komunistyczna Partia Polski w okręgu łom'zyńskim, 1919- 1938. Warszawa, 1975. pp. 312. *bibliog. (Białystok. Ośrodek Badań Naukowych. Seria Rozprawy i Monografie. Nr.4)*

LONDON

— Bibliography.

SCOTT (ANDREW J.C.) compiler. London borough departmental publications, 1965-1972. London, 1973. fo. 162. *(London. Greater London Council. Research Library. [Research] Bibliographies. No. 50)*

SKINNER (IAN) compiler. Thamesmead. London, 1975. pp. 20. *(London. Greater London Council. Research Library. Research Bibliographies. No. 62)*

— Churches.

ROBERTS (TED) Housing and ministry: an experiment in the use of church land. London, [1975]. pp. 60.

— Civic improvement.

LONDON. Greater London Council. Environmental Group. London's environment: Environmental Group and Pollution Control Group: first report. [London, 1972?]. pp. 19.

DOCKLANDS JOINT COMMITTEE. Docklands Development Team. Conservation and the role of the river. London, 1975. pp. 48. *(Working Papers for Consultation. 8)*

HART (DOUGLAS ALLEN) Strategic road planning and the concept of urban order: an analysis of policy making in Greater London, 1943-1973; [Ph.D. (London) thesis]. 1975. fo. 308. *bibliog. Typescript: unpublished. This thesis is the property of London University and may not be removed from the Library.*

LONDON. Greater London Council. Modified Greater London development plan: explanatory memorandum from the Department of the Environment; draft written statement, draft roads map, draft key diagram, draft urban landscape diagram; reasoned statement of the modifications proposed by the Secretary of State for the Environment. London, [1975]. pp. 164. *3 maps in end pocket.*

LONDON. Greater London Council. South Bank Comprehensive Development Area Inter-departmental Working Party. The future of the South Bank: a report on planning principles and the scope for the provision of housing; [A. Matthews, chairman] . London, 1975. pp. 40.

DOCKLANDS JOINT COMMITTEE. London docklands: a strategic plan; a draft published...for public consultation. London, 1976. pp. 115.

LONDON. Greater London Council. Greater London development plan; approved by the Secretary of State for the Environment on 9 July 1976: notice of approval, written statement, roads map, key diagram, urban landscape diagram. London, [1976]. pp. 132. *3 maps in end pocket.*

— Description.

LONDON. Greater London Council. Survey of London. vol. 38. The museums area of South Kensington and Westminster. London, 1975. pp. 465, 118.

— Directories.

LONDON BOROUGHS ASSOCIATION. London Boroughs Association handbook. London, [1976 in progress]. *Current issue only kept.*

— Docks.

DOCKLANDS JOINT COMMITTEE. Docklands Development Team. Conservation and the role of the river. London, 1975. pp. 48. *(Working Papers for Consultation. 8)*

DOCKLANDS JOINT COMMITTEE. London docklands: a strategic plan; a draft published...for public consultation. London, 1976. pp. 115.

— — Bibliography.

SKINNER (IAN) compiler. Docklands. London, 1976. pp. 39. *(London. Greater London Council. Research Library. Research Bibliographies. No. 73)*

— Foreign population.

DENCH (GEOFFREY HERBERT) The London Maltese: collective responsibility and community structure; [Ph. D. (London) thesis]. 1972. fo. 322. *bibliog. Typescript: unpublished. This thesis is the property of London University and may not be removed from the Library.*

— Gilds — Cutlers' Company.

GIRTIN (TOM) The mark of the sword: a narrative history of the Cutlers' Company, 1189-1975. London, 1975. pp. 448. *bibliog.*

— — Goldsmiths' Company.

REDDAWAY (THOMAS FIDDIAN) The early history of the Goldsmith's Company, 1327-1509;... prepared for publication with additional material including...The book of ordinances, 1478-83, by Lorna E.M. Walker. London, 1975. pp. 378. *bibliog.*

— — Grocers' Company.

LONDON. Worshipful Company of Grocers. The case of the Company of Grocers stated; and their condition...truly represented....to which is added a short account of their charter and confirmation...and their by-laws and ordinances. .; ([signed] W. Ravenhill, Clerk of the Company of Grocers). London, printed for the Company of Grocers, 1686. pp. 34. *Wing 324.*

— History.

LONDON. Greater London Council. Survey of London. vol. 38. The museums area of South Kensington and Westminster. London, 1975. pp. 465, 118.

— — Sources.

LONDON. London Record Society. Publications. vol. 12. The London Eyre of 1276; edited by Martin Weinbaum. London, 1976. pp. 188.

— Hospitals.

U.K. Department of Health and Social Security. 1975. Rationalisation of services: a revised hospital plan for inner London. [London], 1975. pp. 24.

— Industries.

LONDON. Greater London Council. Industrial policy and employment in London. [London, 1976]. pp. 16.

— Markets.

LONDON. Court of Common Council. A copy of the report of the Committee of Common Council, appointed to consider of the abuses committed by the farmers of the City markets, "c., London, May 29. 1696. [London], 1696. s. sh. *Not in Wing.*

LONDON(Cont.)

— Officials and employees.

LONDON. Greater London Council. Public Information Branch. Make London's future your future. [London, 1974]. pp. 22.

— — Salaries, allowances, etc.

LONDON. London County Council. London County Council (Superannuation) Scheme, 1958. London, [1958]. pp. 68.

— Parks.

CARRINGTON (RON C.) Alexandra Park and Palace: a history. London, Greater London Council, [1975]. pp. 215.

— Politics and government.

KENNINGTON CONSERVATIVE ASSOCIATION. Executive Committee. [Minute books. 1924-62]. 3 vols. *Manuscript.*

SOUTH PADDINGTON DIVISIONAL LABOUR PARTY. [Minute book. 1929-31]. 1 vol. *Manuscript.*

YOUNG (KENNETH GEORGE) Local politics and the rise of party: the London Municipal Society and the Conservative intervention in local elections, 1894-1963. Leicester, 1975. pp. 255. *bibliog.*

LONDON BOROUGHS ASSOCIATION. London Boroughs Association handbook. London, [1976 in progress]. *Current issue only kept.*

— Population.

DUGMORE (KEITH) Social characteristics of the tenants of seventy-two GLC housing estates. London, [1975]. pp. 38. *bibliog. (London. Greater London Council. Research Memoranda. 474)*

GILJE (EIVIND K.) Migration patterns in and around London. London, [1975]. pp. 30. *bibliog. (London. Greater London Council. Research Memoranda. 470)*

GILJE (EIVIND K.) and HOLLIS (JOHN) Writer on Population. Demographic projections for Greater London and the London boroughs, 1974. London, [1975]. pp. 254. *bibliog. (London. Greater London Council. Research Memoranda. 455)*

SHANKLAND-COX PARTNERSHIP and INSTITUTE OF COMMUNITY STUDIES. Inner area study: Lambeth: housing and population projections. [London], Department of the Environment, [1975]. pp. 8.

THOMPSON (RICHARD) of the Greater London Council and PLANK (DAVID) Demographic projections for Greater London and the London boroughs, 1974: a brief commentary for London borough social services departments. London, [1975]. pp. 30. *(London. Greater London Council. Research Memoranda. 463)*

WILLMOTT (PETER) Whatever's happening to London?; an analysis of changes in population structure and their effects on community life. London, 1975. pp. 14. *bibliog. Paper delivered at the meeting of the London Council of Social Service in London in 1974.*

— Port.

BATE (STUART PAUL) Workers' participation in industrial rule-making processes: a theoretical analysis and empirical investigation of a sample of employees in the Port of London. 1976. fo. 430. *bibliog. Typescript. Ph.D. (London) thesis: unpublished. This thesis is the property of London University and may not be removed from the Library.*

— Recreational activities.

LONDON. Greater London Council. Greater London recreation study. London, [1975-76]. 3 pts. (in 1 vol.) *(Research Reports. No. 19)*

NICHOLLS (M.) Recreationally disadvantaged areas in Greater London: report of an analysis of provision for sports and active recreation. London, [1975]. pp. 25. *(London. Greater London Council. Research Memoranda. 467)*

— — Bibliography.

SCOTT (ANDREW J.C.) compiler. Indoor recreation. London, 1975. pp. 13. *(London. Greater London Council. Research Library. Research Bibliographies. No. 70)*

— Schools.

WEST LONDON SCHOOLS CAMPAIGN. A golden opportunity: an alternative to the I[nner] L[ondon] E[ducation] A[uthority]'s green paper. London, [1973?]. pp. 18.

SILVER (PAMELA) and SILVER (HAROLD) The education of the poor: the history of a National school 1824- 1974. London, 1974. pp. 197. *bibliog.*

— Social conditions.

DOCKLANDS JOINT COMMITTEE. Docklands Development Team. Education, health, welfare and recreation. London, 1975. pp. 40. *(Working Papers for Consultation. 7)*

DOCKLANDS JOINT COMMITTEE. Docklands Development Team. Report on the response to Docks 73: education, health, welfare and recreation. [London], 1975. pp. 36.

RICHARDSON (CHARLES JAMES) Aspects of contemporary social mobility in the London region. 1975 [or rather 1976]. fo. 392. *bibliog. Typescript. Ph.D. (London) thesis: unpublished. This thesis is the property of London University and may not be removed from the Library.*

WILLMOTT (PETER) Whatever's happening to London?; an analysis of changes in population structure and their effects on community life. London, 1975. pp. 14. *bibliog. Paper delivered at the meeting of the London Council of Social Service in London in 1974.*

— Social policy.

DOCKLANDS JOINT COMMITTEE. Docklands Development Team. Education, health, welfare and recreation. London, 1975. pp. 40. *(Working Papers for Consultation. 7)*

DOCKLANDS JOINT COMMITTEE. Docklands Development Team. Report on the response to Docks 73: education, health, welfare and recreation. [London], 1975. pp. 36.

— Stores, shopping centres, etc.

DOCKLANDS JOINT COMMITTEE. Docklands Development Team. Shopping. London, 1975. pp. 24. *(Working Papers for Consultation. 5)*

— Transit systems.

TALBOT (M.F.) Warehouse traffic generation study: pilot survey. London, [1974]. pp. 101. *(London. Greater London Council. Department of Planning and Transportation. Research Memoranda. 400)*

DOCKLANDS JOINT COMMITTEE. Docklands Development Team. The docklands spine: tube, bus or tram?. London, 1975. pp. 30. *(Working Papers for Consultation. 3)*

DOCKLANDS JOINT COMMITTEE. Docklands Development Team. Transport. London, 1975. pp. 55. *(Working Papers for Consultation. 6)*

FAIRHURST (M.H.) and MORRIS (P.J.) Variations in the demand for bus and rail travel (in London) up to 1974. [London], London Transport Executive, 1975. 1 vol. (various pagings). *(Economic and Operational Research Office. Economic Research Reports. 210)*

GREATER London transportation survey. [London, Greater London Council, 1975]. 9 vols. (in 2).

LONDON. Greater London Council. Transport: a programme for action, 1976-77. [London, 1975]. pp. 19.

SMITH (PAUL PRESTWOOD) and SMITH (J.E.R.) Greater London transportation survey: initial results. rev. ed. London, 1975. pp. 24. *bibliog. (London. Greater London Council. Intelligence Unit. Greater London Research. Research Reports. No. 18)*

SMITH (JOHN W.) Labour supply and employment duration in London Transport. London, 1976. pp. 65. *(London. University. London School of Economics and Political Science. Greater London Group. Greater London Papers. No.15)*

— — Mathematical models.

FAIRHURST (M.H.) Modelling London Transport's demand and supply markets. [London], London Transport Executive, 1975. pp. 25. *(Economic and Operational Research Office. Technical Notes. 90) Xerox copy*

LONDON, TREATY OF, 1915.

MARJANOVIĆ (MILAN) Londonski ugovor iz godine 1915: prilog povijesti borbe za Jadran, 1914-1917. Zagreb, 1960. pp. 469. *bibliog.*

LONDON MUNICIPAL SOCIETY.

YOUNG (KENNETH GEORGE) Local politics and the rise of party: the London Municipal Society and the Conservative intervention in local elections, 1894-1963. Leicester, 1975. pp. 255. *bibliog.*

LONDON UNIVERSITY

— Bedford College.

LONDON. University. University College, and London School of Economics and Political Science. Joint Unit for Planning Research. Networks of urban activities: internal and external linkages in an urban university. [London], 1971. 2 vols. (in 1). *bibliog.*

— London School of Economics and Political Science.

CLARK (Sir GEORGE NORMAN) [Correspondence about the publication of Agenda: a quarterly journal of reconstruction. 1941-43]. 1 folder. *Manuscript, typescript, etc.*

LONDONDERRY

— Civic improvement.

IRELAND, NORTHERN. Department of Housing, Local Government and Planning. 1975. Londonderry area plan: further statement by Department of Housing, Local Government and Planning. Belfast, 1975. pp. 25.

IRELAND, NORTHERN. Town and Country Planning Service. 1975. Londonderry area plan. [Belfast], [1975]. 3 maps.

MITCHELL (WALTER F.) Londonderry area plan public inquiry; report; ...and recommendations by the Planning Appeals Commission to the Department of Housing. Local Government and Planning. [Belfast, H.M.S.O., 1975]. pp. 185.

— Maps.

IRELAND, NORTHERN. Town and Country Planning Service. 1975. Londonderry area plan. [Belfast], [1975]. 3 maps.

LONSDALE (JOHN) 1737-1807.

SURTEES SOCIETY. Publications. vol.188. Lonsdale documents; edited by Elizabeth Playne and G. de Boer. Gateshead, 1976. pp. 158.

LORENZONI (JULIO).

LORENZONI (JULIO) Memorias de um imigrante italiano; tradução de Armida Lorenzoni Parreira. Porto Alegre, [1975]. pp. 264.

LORRAINE

— Economic conditions.

DOSSIERS DE L'ECONOMIE LORRAINE, LES: revue mensuelle; ([pd. by] Institut National de la Statistique et des Etudes Economiques,...Direction Régionale de Nancy [France]). m., 1972- Nancy.

— Industries.

MORAND (JEAN CLAUDE) Les créations d'établissements industriels en Lorraine, 1958- 1972. Nancy, 1975. pp. 147. *(Observatoire Economique de l'Est. Rapports de l'I.N.S.E.E. - Lorraine) Maps in end pocket.*

LOS ANGELES

— Politics and government.

AMBRECHT (BILIANA C.S.) Politicizing the poor: the legacy of the war on poverty in a Mexican-American community. New York, 1976. pp. 223. *bibliog.*

LOTTERIES

— Law and legislation — United Kingdom.

[U.K. Home Office. 1976]. Lotteries Act 1975: regulations under the act; consultative document. [London, 1976]. fo. 7, 2.

LOUIS XIV, King of France.

HATTON (RAGNHILD) ed. Louis XIV and absolutism. London, 1976. pp. 306.

HATTON (RAGNHILD) ed. Louis XIV and Europe. London, 1976. pp. 311.

LOVEA, CAMBODIA.

MARTEL (GABRIELLE) Lovea, village des environs d'Angkor: aspects démographiques, économiques et sociologiques du monde rural cambodgien dans la province de Siem-Réap. Paris, 1975. pp. 359. *(Ecole Française d'Extrême-Orient. Publications. vol. 98)*

LOWE (ROBERT) 1st Viscount Sherbrooke.

WINTER (JAMES) 1925- . Robert Lowe. Toronto, [1976]. pp. 368. *bibliog.*

LOWER SAXONY

— Politics and government.

SOZIALDEMOKRATISCHE PARTEI DEUTSCHLANDS. Landesausschuss Niedersachsen. Die Politik der SPD für Niedersachsen in den nächsten vier Jahren. [Hanover, 1974?]. pp. 77.

LOYALTY-SECURITY PROGRAM, 1947— .

THEOHARIS (ATHAN G.) Seeds of repression: Harry S.Truman and the origins of McCarthyism. Chicago, 1971. pp. 238.

GOLDSTON (ROBERT) The American nightmare: Senator Joseph McCarthy and the politics of hate. Indianapolis, [1973]. pp. 202. *bibliog.*

FRIED (RICHARD M.) Men against McCarthy. New York, 1976. pp. 428. *bibliog.*

LUCRETIUS CARUS (TITUS).

NICHOLS (JAMES H.) Epicurean political philosophy: the De rerum natura of Lucretius. Ithaca, N.Y., 1976. pp. 214.

LUD POLSKI (1835-1846).

SIKORA (ADAM) Gromady Ludu Polskiego. Warszawa, 1974. pp. 284.

LUDDITES.

RADCLIFFE (Sir JOSEPH) [Luddite papers; consisting mainly of letters to Sir Joseph Radcliffe, or to the Huddersfield magistrates, together with drafts or copies of his replies, February 1812 to February 1813] . [1812-13]. *Manuscript, with typescript list of contents. Microfilm: 1 reel.*

LUEBECK

— Constitutional history.

ENDE (BERNHARD AM) Studien zur Verfassungsgeschichte Lübecks im 12. und 13. Jahrhundert. Lübeck, 1975. pp. 239. *bibliog. (Lübeck. Archiv. Veröffentlichungen zur Geschichte der Hansestadt Lübeck. Reihe B. Band 2)*

LUKÀCS (GEORG).

GEORG Lukàcs [sic]: Verdinglichung und Klassenbewusstsein; (Mitglieder des Autorenkollektivs: Manon Baukhage [and others]). Westberlin, 1975. pp. 201.

LUMLEY (E. K.).

LUMLEY (E.K.) Forgotten mandate: a British district officer in Tanganyika. London, [1976]. pp. 178.

LUNDA (BANTU TRIBE).

BUSTIN (EDOUARD) Lunda under Belgium rule: the politics of ethnicity. Cambridge, Mass., 1975. pp. 303. *bibliog.*

LUNGS

— Cancer.

NEW ZEALAND. Department of Health. National Health Statistics Centre. 1973. Cancer of the lung in New Zealand;...by J. Borrie [and others]. Wellington, 1973. pp. 67. *(Department of Health. Special Report Series. No. 42)*

LUNIN (MIKHAIL SERGEEVICH).

BARRATT (GLYNN R.V.) M.S. Lunin, Catholic Decembrist. The Hague, 1976. pp. 137. *bibliog.*

LUNN (Sir HENRY SIMPSON).

LUNN (Sir HENRY SIMPSON) Nearing harbour: the log of Sir Henry S. Lunn. London, 1934. pp. 328.

LUSTY (Sir ROBERT FRITH).

LUSTY (Sir ROBERT FRITH) Bound to be read. London, 1975. pp. 314.

LUTHERAN CHURCH IN SWEDEN.

LENHAMMAR (HARRY) Religion och tryckfrihet i Sverige, 1809-1840: Religion and free dom of the press in Sweden, 1809-1840. Uppsala, 1974. pp. 300. *bibliog. (Uppsala. Universitet. Acta Universitatis Upsaliensis. Studia Historico-Ecclesiastica Upsaliensia. 26) In Swedish, with English summary.*

LUTHERANS IN GERMANY.

WAGNER (OSKAR) Pfarrer. Der Evangelische Handwerker-Verein von 1848 e.V., München, 1848 bis 1973: ein Beitrag zur Geschichte der evangelischen Gemeinde und der evangelischen Sozialarbeit in München. München, [1973]. pp. 91. *(Evangelischer Handwerker-Verein von 1848, and Bayerischer Handwerkstag. Kirche und Handwerk. Heft 2)*

LUTHERANS IN THE ARGENTINE REPUBLIC.

FLODELL (SVEN ARNE) Tierra nueva: svensk grupputvandring till Latinamerika; integration och församlingsbildning: Swedish emigration to Latin America; integration and church growth. [Stockholm], [1974]. pp. 217. *bibliog. In Swedish, with English summary.*

LUTON

— Schools.

DONY (JOHN GEORGE) A history of education in Luton. Luton, County Borough of Luton Museum and Art Gallery, 1970. p. 61. *bibliog.*

LUXEMBOURG

— Economic history.

WEBER (PAUL) Secrétaire Général de la Chambre de Commerce, Luxembourg. Histoire de l'économie luxembourgeoise; publiée à l'occasion du centenaire de la Chambre de Commerce. Luxembourg, 1950. pp. 431.

— Population.

ALS (GEORGES) La population du Grand-Duché de Luxembourg...: (1974, Année Mondiale de la Population). Luxembourg, 1975. pp. 197. *(Committee for International Coordination of National Research in Demography. C.I.C.R.E.D. Series)*

LUXEMBURG (ROSA).

EVZEROV (ROBERT IAKOVLEVICH) and IAZHBOROVSKAIA (INESSA SERGEEVNA) Roza Liuksemburg: biograficheskii ocherk. Moskva, 1974. pp. 327.

BADIA (GILBERT) Rosa Luxemburg: journaliste, polémiste, révolutionnaire. Paris, [1975]. pp. 930. *bibliog.*

BASSO (LELIO) Rosa Luxemburg: a reappraisal;...translated by Douglas Parmée. London, 1975. pp. 183.

FAGGI (VICO) and SQUARZINA (LUIGI) Rosa Luxemburg: dramma in nove quadri. Roma, 1975. pp. 220. *Also contains letters and articles by Rosa Luxemburg.*

HENTZE (JUERGEN) Nationalismus und Internationalismus bei Rosa Luxemburg. Bern, 1975. pp. 217. *bibliog.*

GERAS (NORMAN) The legacy of Rosa Luxemburg. London, 1976. pp. 210. *bibliog.*

LYONS.

FRANCE. Direction de la Documentation. La Documentation Française. Notes et Etudes Documentaires. Nos. 4,207-4, 208-4,209. Les villes françaises: Lyon et son agglomération; (par Jacques Bonnet). Paris, 1975. pp. 132. *bibliog.*

— Social history.

LEON (PIERRE) Géographie de la fortune et structures sociales à Lyon au XIXe siècle, 1815-1914;...avec la collaboration de Simone Gellibert [and others]. Lyon, [1974]. pp. 440. *bibliog. (Lyons. Université de Lyon II. Centre d'Histoire Economique et Sociale de la Région Lyonnaise. [Publications]. 4)*

McADOO (WILLIAM GIBBS).

BROESAMLE (JOHN J.) William Gibbs McAdoo: a passion for change, 1863-1917. Port Washington, N.Y., 1973. pp. 304. *bibliog.*

MACARTHUR (DOUGLAS).

JAMES (DORRIS CLAYTON) The years of MacArthur. Boston, 1975 in progress. *bibliog.*

McCARTHY (JOSEPH RAYMOND).

THEOHARIS (ATHAN G.) Seeds of repression: Harry S.Truman and the origins of McCarthyism. Chicago, 1971. pp. 238.

GOLDSTON (ROBERT) The American nightmare: Senator Joseph McCarthy and the politics of hate. Indianapolis, [1973]. pp. 202. *bibliog.*

FRIED (RICHARD M.) Men against McCarthy. New York, 1976. pp. 428. *bibliog.*

OSHINSKY (DAVID M.) Senator Joseph McCarthy and the American labor movement. Columbia, Mo., 1976. pp. 206. *bibliog.*

MACCHIAVELLI (NICCOLÒ).

LEFORT (CLAUDE) Le travail de l'oeuvre Machiavel. [Paris, 1972]. pp. 778.

MACCHIAVELLI (NICCOLÒ).(Cont.)

CADONI (GIORGIO) Machiavelli: regno di Francia e "principato civile", etc. Roma, [1974]. pp. 221.

BRUSCAGLI (RICCARDO) Niccolò Machiavelli. Firenze, 1975. pp. 163. *bibliog.*

McCRACKEN (ELIZABETH C.).

McCRACKEN (ELIZABETH C.) Memoirs. n.p., [1920]. pp. 172.

MACEDONIA

— Historiography.

INSTITUT ZA NACIONALNA ISTORIJA. The foreign and Yugoslav historiography of Macedonia and the Macedonian people. Skopje, 1970. pp. 204. *bibliogs.*

— History — Bibliography.

INSTITUT ZA NACIONALNA ISTORIJA. Historiographie de Macédoine, 1945-1970. Skopje, 1970 in progress.

— — Sources.

LAPE (LJUBEN) ed. Izveštai od 1903 godina na srpskite konsuli, mitropoliti i učilišni inspektori vo Makedonija. Skopje, 1954. pp. 395. *(Institut za Nacionalna Istorija. Materijali za Istorijata na Makedonija. kn.1) Documents in the original Serbo-Croat in Cyrillic. With German summary.*

— Politics and government.

DELČEV (GOCE) Pisma i drugi materiali: izdiril i podgotvil za pečat Dino K'osev. Sofiia, 1967. pp. 348.

— Relations (general) with Greece.

POPLAZAROV (RISTO) Grčkata politika sprema Makedonija vo vtorata polovina na XIX i početokot na XX vek: vooruženi, propagandni, diplomatski i drugi antimakedonski akcii i borbata protiv niv na terenot. Skopje, 1973. pp. 324. *bibliog. With Russian and English summaries.*

MACEDONIAN QUESTION.

RAZVITOK na državnosta na makedonskiot narod: materijali od Simpoziumot po povod 20-godišninata od Prvoto zasedanie na ASNOM održan na 23 i 24 oktomvri 1964 godina. Skopje, 1966. pp. 558. *With Russian and English summaries.*

ANDONOV-POLJANSKI (HRISTO) Velika Britanija i makedonskoto prašanje na Pariskata mirovna konferencija vo 1919 godina, so izbor od dokumentacijata; Great Britain and the Macedonian Question at the Paris Peace Conference 1919, with a selection of records. Skopje, 1973. pp. 167. *bibliog. With English summary.*

POPLAZAROV (RISTO) Grčkata politika sprema Makedonija vo vtorata polovina na XIX i početokot na XX vek: vooruženi, propagandni, diplomatski i drugi antimakedonski akcii i borbata protiv niv na terenot. Skopje, 1973. pp. 324. *bibliog. With Russian and English summaries.*

ZOGRAFSKI (TODOR G.) and ZOGRAFSKI (DIMČE A.) KPJ i VMRO (Obedineta) vo Vardarska Makedonija vo periodot 1920-1930. Skopje, 1974. pp. 292.

MACEDONIAN REPUBLIC

— History.

RAZVOJOT i karakteristikite na Narodnoosloboditelnata vojna i na Revolucijata vo Makedonija: simpozium, Skopje, 9-10 dekemvri 1971 godina. Skopje, 1973. pp. 857. *bibliog.*

MACEDONIANS IN GREECE.

MOJSOV (LAZO) Okolu prašanjeto na makedonskoto nacionalno malcinstvo vo Grcija: eden pogled vrz opsežnata dokumentacija. Skopje, 1954. pp. 392. *bibliog. With French summary and table of contents.*

PEJOV (NAUM) Makedoncite i graganskata vojna vo Grcija. Skopje, 1968. pp. 212. *bibliog.*

MACEK (VLADKO).

BOBAN (LJUBO) Maček i politika Hrvatske seljačke stranke 1928-1941: iz povijesti hrvatskog pitanja. Zagreb, 1974. 2 vols.

McEWAN (TOM).

McEWEN (TOM) The forge glows red: from blacksmith to revolutionary. Toronto, 1974. pp. 260.

MACHINE PARTS.

COUNTER INFORMATION SERVICES and TRANSNATIONAL INSTITUTE. Where is Lucas going?. London, [1975?]. pp. 47. *bibliog. (Counter Information Services. Anti-Reports. No. 12)*

MACHINE-READABLE BIBLIOGRAPHIC DATA.

PRATT (GORDON E.C.) and HARVEY (SUSAN) compilers. Information economics: costs and prices of machine-readable information in Europe; edited by Gordon Pratt. London, [1976]. pp. 115. *(Association of Special Libraries and Information Bureaux and European Association of Scientific Information Dissemination Centres. European User Series. 2)*

MACHINERY

— Prices.

UNITED STATES. Central Intelligence Agency. 1975. Prices of machinery and equipment in the People's Republic of China. [Washington], 1975. pp. 23. *(Research Aids. No.A(ER)75-64) Microfilm: 1 reel.*

— Trade and manufacture — China.

UNITED STATES. Central Intelligence Agency. 1974. People's Republic of China: foreign trade in machinery and equipment since 1952. [Washington], 1974. pp. 33. *(Research Aids. No.A(ER)75-60)Microfilm: 1 reel.*

UNITED STATES. Central Intelligence Agency. 1975. Prices of machinery and equipment in the People's Republic of China. [Washington], 1975. pp. 23. *(Research Aids. No.A(ER)75-64) Microfilm: 1 reel.*

UNITED STATES. Central Intelligence Agency. 1975. Production of machinery and equipment in the People's Republic of China. [Washington], 1975. pp. 31. *(Research Aids. No.A(ER)75-63) Microfilm: 1 reel.*

— — Germany.

MUELLER (JAN) Untersuchung zur Konzentrationsentwicklung in verschiedenen Untersektoren der Maschinenbauindustrie in Deutschland, etc. [Brussels, European Communities, Directorate-General for Competition, 1973]. 1 vol. (various pagings).

— — Russia.

100 let Moskovskomu zavodu tekhnicheskikh izdelii Moskva, 1969. pp. 85.

— — Georgia.

AKADEMIIA NAUK GRUZINSKOI SSR. Institut Ekonomiki i Prava. Ekonomika. t. 3. [Sbornik statei]. Tbilisi, 1971. pp. 417. *Articles are in Georgian or Russian.*

— — Switzerland.

FISCHER (GEORG) AKTIENGESELLSCHAFT. Hundertfünfzig Jahre Georg Fischer Werke, 1802/1952. Schaffhausen, [1952]. pp. 192.

— — Turkey.

HIÇ (MÜKERREM) Employment and wages in the automotive and other assembly industries in Turkey. Istanbul, 1974. pp. 58. *(Istanbul. Üniversitesi. Iktisat Fakültesi. Institute of Economic Development. Yayinlari. No. 23)*

MACHINERY IN INDUSTRY.

MARSH (ROBERT MORTIMER) and MANNARI (HIROSHI) Modernization and the Japanese factory. Princeton, N.J., [1976]. pp. 437. *bibliog.*

MACKINDER (Sir HALFORD JOHN).

MACKINDER (Sir HALFORD JOHN) [Correspondence concerning the foundation of a national theatre in London. 1913]. 1 piece. *Manuscript.*

BLOUET (BRIAN) Sir Halford Mackinder, 1861-1947: some new perspectives. Oxford, 1975. pp. 49. *bibliog. (Oxford. University. School of Geography. Research Papers. No.13)*

MACRO PROCESSORS.

CAMPBELL-KELLY (M.) An introduction to macros. London, [1973] repr. 1974. pp. 122. *bibliog.*

BROWN (PETER J.) Macro processors and techniques for portable software. London, [1974]. pp. 244. *bibliog.*

MADAGASCAR

— Economic conditions.

BELGIUM. Office Belge du Commerce Extérieur. 1972. Madagascar. Bruxelles, 1972. pp. 45. *(Un Marché. 13)*

— Foreign relations.

MUTIBWA (PHARES M.) The Malagasy and the Europeans: Madagas[c]ar's foreign relations, 1861-1895. London, 1974. pp. 411. *bibliog.*

— Politics and government.

OSTHEIMER (JOHN M.) ed. The politics of the western Indian Ocean islands. New York, 1975. pp. 260. *bibliog.*

MADEIRA

— Population.

RAMOS (ANTONIO BRITO) Demografia e emprego nas ilhas adjacentes. Lisboa, 1974. pp. 191. *(Portugal. Ministerio do Trabalho. Gabinete de Planeamento. Serie Estudos. 20) With abstracts in English, French and German.*

MADHYA PRADESH

— Economic policy.

MADHYA PRADESH. Planning and Development Department. 1961-62. Third five year plan, 1961-1966. Bhopal, 1961-62. 2 vols. (in 1).

— Social policy.

MADHYA PRADESH. Planning and Development Department. 1961-62. Third five year plan, 1961-1966. Bhopal, 1961-62. 2 vols. (in 1).

MADRAS

— Economic conditions.

MADRAS. Finance Department. 1971. Tamil Nadu: an economic appraisal, 1971-72. Madras, [1971]. pp. 326.

DJURFELDT (GÖRAN) and LINDBERG (STAFFAN) Behind poverty: the social formation in a Tamil village. Lund, 1975. pp. 340. *bibliog. (Scandinavian Institute of Asian Studies. Monograph Series. No. 22)*

— Economic policy.

MADRAS. Post-War Reconstruction Committee. 1945. Post-war reconstruction and development schemes of the government of Madras. Madras, 1945. pp. 198.

MADRAS. Finance Department. 1967. Fourth five-year plan Madras State: review of progress during 1966-67 and programme for 1967-68. Madras, 1967. pp. 323.

MADRAS. State Planning Commission. 1974. The perspective plan for Tamil Nadu, 1974-84; (with Summary). Madras, 1974. 2 pts. (in 1 vol.).

— Social conditions.

DJURFELDT (GÖRAN) and LINDBERG (STAFFAN) Behind poverty: the social formation in a Tamil village. Lund, 1975. pp. 340. *bibliog.* (Scandinavian Institute of Asian Studies. Monograph Series. No. 22)

DJURFELDT (GÖRAN) and LINDBERG (STAFFAN) Pills against poverty: a study of the introduction of western medicine in a Tamil village. Lund, 1975. pp. 232. *bibliog.* (Scandinavian Institute of Asian Studies. Monograph Series. No. 23)

— Social policy.

MADRAS. Post-War Reconstruction Committee. 1945. Post-war reconstruction and development schemes of the government of Madras. Madras, 1945. pp. 198.

MADRAS. Finance Department. 1967. Fourth five-year plan Madras State: review of progress during 1966-67 and programme for 1967-68. Madras, 1967.pp. 323.

MADRAS. State Planning Commission. 1974. The perspective plan for Tamil Nadu, 1974-84; (with Summary). Madras, 1974. 2 pts. (in 1 vol.).

MADRAS (CITY)

— Social conditions.

WEINSTEIN (JAY A.) Madras: an analysis of urban ecological structure in India. Beverly Hills, Calif., [1974]. pp. 76. *bibliog.*

MADRAS PRESIDENCY

— Politics and government.

BAKER (CHRISTOPHER JOHN) The politics of south India, 1920-1937. Cambridge, 1976. pp. 363. *bibliog.* (Cambridge. University. Centre of South Asian Studies. Cambridge South Asian Studies. No.17)

MADRID

— Economic conditions.

SANZ GARCIA (JOSE MARIA) Madrid: capital del capital español?; contribucion a la geografia urbana y a las funciones geoeconomicas de la villa y corte. Madrid, 1975 in progress.

— Learned institutions and societies.

GARRORENA MORALES (ANGEL) El Ateneo de Madrid y la teoria de la monarquia liberal, 1836- 1847. Madrid, 1974. pp. 876.

— Politics and government.

TUSELL GOMEZ (JAVIER) Sociologia electoral de Madrid, (1903-1931). Madrid, 1969. pp. 219.

MAGNETIC RECORDERS AND RECORDING.

BELSON (WILLIAM A.) Tape recording: its effect on accuracy of response in survey interviews. London, [1967]. pp. 12. *bibliog.* (London. University. London School of Economics and Political Science. Survey Research Centre. Reprint Series. 38) (Reprinted from Journal of Marketing Research vol. 4, 1967)

MAHARASHTRA

— Statistics, Vital.

INDIA. Office of the Registrar General. Vital Statistics Division. 1973. Seasonality in vital events and rates. New Delhi, 1973. pp. 25. *bibliog.* (Sample Registration System Analytical Series. No. 5)

MAIN, RIVER

— Navigation — Laws and regulations.

ZEMANEK (KARL) Die Schiffahrtsfreiheit auf der Donau und das Künftige Regime der Rhein-Main-Donau-Grosschiffahrtsstrasse: eine völkerrechtliche Untersuchung. Wien, [1976]. pp. 73. (Österreichische Zeitschrift für öffentliches Recht. Supplementa.4)

MAINE

— Population.

MAINE. State Planning Office. 1972. Maine population trends, 1960-1970. [Augusta], 1972. pp. 30.

MAINZ

— History.

SCHEEL (HEINRICH) Die Mainzer Republik, etc. Berlin, 1975 in progress. *bibliog.* (Akademie der Wissenschaften der DDR. Zentralinstitut für Geschichte. Schriften. Bände 42, etc.)

MAIZE

— Malawi.

MALAWI. Agro-Economic Survey. 1975. Agro-economic survey: report no. 17: marketing of smallholder agricultural produce in Malawi. Vol. 2. The production, consumption and marketing of maize; prepared by K. Quinten and J. Sterkenburg. Lilongwe, 1975. fo. 107. *bibliog.*

MAKHNO (NESTOR).

MALET (MICHAEL IAN GRENVILLE) Nestor Makchno [sic] in the Russian civil war 1917-21. 1975. fo. 326. *bibliog.* Typescript. Ph.D.(London) thesis: unpublished. *This thesis is the property of London University and may not be removed from the library.*

MALAWI

— Economic conditions.

MALAWI. Department of Information. 1974. Building the nation: Malawi 1964-1974. [Blantyre, 1974]. pp. 36.

— Population.

MALAWI. National Statistical Office. 1973. Malawi population change survey, February 1970-January 1972. Zomba, 1973. pp. 83.

— Social conditions.

MALAWI. Department of Information. 1974. Building the nation: Malawi 1964-1974. [Blantyre, 1974]. pp. 36.

MALAYA

— Foreign relations.

RUBIN (ALFRED P.) The international personality of the Malay Peninsula: a study of the international law of imperialism. Kuala Lumpur, 1974. pp. 327. *bibliog.*

MALAYSIA

— Commerce — New Zealand.

NEW ZEALAND. Department of Trade and Industry. 1975. Malaysia and Brunei: handbook. [Wellington], 1975. pp. 87. *bibliog.*

— Economic conditions.

LIM (DAVID) ed. Readings on Malaysian economic development. Kuala Lumpur, 1975. pp. 421. *bibliogs.*

— — Mathematical models.

LOPE (RAJA) An exploratory macroeconomic model of the Malaysian economy, 1961- 1972; [Ph. D. (London) thesis]. 1975. fo. 170. *bibliog.* Typescript: unpublished. *This thesis is the property of London University and may not be removed from the Library.*

— Economic policy.

LIM (DAVID) ed. Readings on Malaysian economic development. Kuala Lumpur, 1975. pp. 421. *bibliogs.*

— Politics and government.

CARLSON (SEVINC) Malaysia: search for national unity and economic growth. Beverly Hills, [1975]. pp. 80. *bibliog.* (Georgetown University. Center for Strategic and International Studies. Washington Papers. vol. 3/25)

MEANS (GORDON P.) Malaysian politics. 2nd ed. London, 1976. pp. 483. *bibliog.*

— Population.

SAW (SWEE HOCK) Population and labour force projections for West Malaysia, 1962- 1987. Hong Kong, 1970. pp. 27. (Hong Kong. University. Centre of Asian Studies. Occasional Papers and Monographs. No. 1)

SAW (SWEE HOCK) Estimates of population and labour force by age group for West Malaysia and Singapore, 1958-1967. Hong Kong, 1971. pp. 38. (Hong Kong. University. Centre of Asian Studies. Occasional Papers and Monographs. No. 6)

FERNANDEZ (DOROTHY Z.) and others. The population of Malaysia...edited by R. Chandler. [Kuala Lumpur?], 1975. pp. 106. (Committee for International Coordination of National Research in Demography. C.I.C.R.E.D. Series)

— Statistics, Vital.

FEDERATION OF MALAYSIA. Registrar-General of Births and Deaths. Report...on population, births, deaths, marriages and adoptions. a., 1968- Kuala Lumpur.

MALDIVE ISLANDS

— Politics and government.

OSTHEIMER (JOHN M.) ed. The politics of the western Indian Ocean islands. New York, 1975. pp. 260. *bibliog.*

MALI (REPUBLIC).

FRANCE. Direction de la Documentation. La Documentation Française. Notes et Etudes Documentaires. Nos. 4,081-4, 082-4,083. Le Mali; (par Gérard Brasseur). Paris, 1974. pp. 113. *bibliog.*

— Economic policy.

MALI. Commission Nationale de Planification de l'Economie Rurale. 1974. Rapport final...pour l'élaboration du Plan Quinquennal 1974- 78, etc. [Bamako, 1974?]. 2 vols. (in 1).

— Rural conditions.

MALI. Commission Nationale de Planification de l'Economie Rurale. 1974. Rapport final...pour l'élaboration du Plan Quinquennal 1974- 78, etc. [Bamako, 1974?]. 2 vols. (in 1).

— Social policy.

MALI. Commission Nationale de Planification de l'Economie Rurale. 1974. Rapport final...pour l'élaboration du Plan Quinquennal 1974- 78, etc. [Bamako, 1974?]. 2 vols. (in 1).

MALMÖ

— Population.

OHLSSON (ROLF) Invandrarna på arbetsmarknaden: en undersökning av invandrare i Malmö under perioden 1945-1967. Lund, [1975]. pp. 155. *bibliog.* (Lund. Ekonomisk-Historiska Föreningen. Skrifter. vol. 16) With English summary.

MALNUTRITION.

GEORGE (SUSAN) How the other half dies: the real reasons for world hunger. Harmondsworth, 1976. pp. 349. *bibliog.*

MALPE

— Harbour.

NATIONAL COUNCIL OF APPLIED ECONOMIC RESEARCH. Traffic survey of Mangalore and Malpe ports. Bangalore, Mysore Public Works Department, 1961. pp. 125.

MALRAUX (ANDRE).

MEYERS (JEFFREY) A fever at the core: the idealist in politics. London, 1976. pp. 172. *bibliog.*

MALTA

MALTA

— Government publications.

SCIBERRAS (LILLIAN) Malta: official statistical publications in the reference department of the Royal University of Malta Library. Msida, 1975. pp. 31.

— Statistics.

SCIBERRAS (LILLIAN) Malta: official statistical publications in the reference department of the Royal University of Malta Library. Msida, 1975. pp. 31.

MALTESE IN THE UNITED KINGDOM.

DENCH (GEOFFREY HERBERT) The London Maltese: collective responsibility and community structure; [Ph. D. (London) thesis]. 1972. fo. 322. bibliog. Typescript: unpublished. This thesis is the property of London University and may not be removed from the Library.

MALTHUSIANISM.

ARMENGAUD (ANDRE) Les Français et Malthus. [Paris, 1975]. pp. 142. bibliog.

MAN.

UCHENYE ZAPISKI KAFEDR OBSHCHESTVENNYKH NAUK VUZOV LENINGRADA. Filosofiia. vyp.8. Filosofskie i sotsiologicheskie issledovaniia. Leningrad, 1967. pp. 239.

STONIER (TOM TED) The natural history of humanity: past, present and future. [Bradford, 1976]. pp. 48.

TOYNBEE (ARNOLD JOSEPH) and IKEDA (DAISEKU) The Toynbee-Ikeda dialogue: man himself must choose. Tokyo, 1976. pp. 348.

UNION OF INTERNATIONAL ASSOCIATIONS and MANKIND 2000. Year-book of world problems and human potential: a framework for representation of perceptions of interlinked networks of world problems, etc. Brussels, 1976. pp. 1136. bibliogs.

— Influence on nature.

MAHANEY (WILLIAM C.) and ERMUTH (FREDERICK) The effects of agriculture and urbanization on the natural environment: a study of human impact in southern Ontario. Toronto, 1974. pp. 152. bibliog. (York University (Toronto). Department of Geography. Geographical Monographs. No. 7)

INTERNATIONAL GEOGRAPHICAL UNION. Regional Conference [in New Zealand], 1974. Proceedings of the International Geographical Union Regional Conference and eighth New Zealand Geography Conference, Palmerston North, December 1974; edited by William Brockie [and others]. [Christchurch], 1975. pp. 380. bibliogs. (New Zealand Geographical Society. Conference Series. No. 8)

RIVERS (PATRICK) The survivalists. London, 1975. pp. 224. bibliog.

SCHNEIDER (STEPHEN HENRY) The genesis strategy: climate and global survival. New York, [1976]. pp. 419.

— Origin.

ARDREY (ROBERT) The hunting hypothesis: a personal conclusion concerning the evolutionary nature of man. London, 1976. pp. 242. bibliog.

MAN, PREHISTORIC

— America.

PREHISTORIC man in the new world; edited by Jesse D. Jennings [and] Edward Norbeck. Chicago, 1964, repr. 1974. pp. 633. bibliogs. Papers based on a symposium entitled "Prehistoric Man in the New World", forming part of the fifteenth anniversary festivities of Rice University in 1962.

MAN, PRIMITIVE.

MEEK (RONALD LINDLEY) Social science and the ignoble savage. Cambridge, 1976. pp. 249.

MANAGEMENT.

DEARDEN (JOHN) Professor of Business Administration. Computers in business management. Homewood, Ill., 1966 repr. 1969. pp. 300.

STEWART (ROSEMARY GORDON) How computers affect management. London, 1971. pp. 244.

AMEY (LLOYD RONALD) ed. Readings in management decision; edited on behalf of the Association of University Teachers of Accounting in the United Kingdom, etc. London, 1973. pp. 272. bibliogs.

AMEY (LLOYD RONALD) and EGGINTON (DON A.) Management accounting: a conceptual approach. London, 1973, repr. 1975. pp. 684. bibliogs.

KELLY (JOE) Organizational behaviour: an existential-systems approach. rev. ed. Homewood, Ill., 1974. pp. 770. bibliog.

BECKER (SELWYN W.) and NEUHAUSER (DUNCAN) The efficient organization. New York, [1975]. pp. 237. bibliog.

CROSS (PETER) The British business creed: changing ideologies and self images of business elites and management in Britain. [1975]. fo. 488. bibliog. Typescript. Ph.D. (London) thesis: unpublished. This thesis is the property of London University and may not be removed from the Library.

ELLIOTT (RUTH HELEN) A case study of management and worker attitudes to managerial authority and prerogatives. 1975. fo. 366. Typescript. Ph.D. (London) thesis: unpublished. This thesis is the property of London University and may not be removed from the Library.

KLINGEN (JOHANNES SEBASTIANUS) Company strategy: a managerial approach. Farnborough, Hants, [1975]. pp. 205. bibliog.

MUMFORD (ENID) and PETTIGREW (ANDREW M.) Implementing strategic decisions. London, 1975. pp. 241. bibliog.

U.K. Department of Health and Social Security. 1975. Guide to planning in the National Health Service; (draft) . London, 1975. fo. 66.

WHITE (MICHAEL J.) Management science in federal agencies: the adoption and diffusion of a socio-technical innovation. Lexington, Mass., [1975]. pp. 111.

U.K. Department of Health and Social Security. 1976. The N[ational] H[ealth] S[ervice] planning system. [London], 1976. pp. 54.

— Bibliography.

VERNON (K.D.C.) ed. Use of management and business literature. London, 1975. pp. 327. bibliogs.

— Information services.

VERNON (K.D.C.) ed. Use of management and business literature. London, 1975. pp. 327. bibliogs.

— Study and teaching — Europe.

MOSSON (THOMAS MICHAEL) Management education in five European countries. London, 1965. pp. 234. bibliog.

— — United Kingdom.

HILTON (KENNETH) Control systems for social and economic management; an inaugural lecture [delivered at the University of Southampton in 1975]. Southampton, 1975. pp. 24.

MANAGEMENT GAMES.

FOSTER (JOHN L.) and others. National policy game: a simulation of the American political process. New York, [1975]. pp. 108.

MANAGEMENT INFORMATION SYSTEMS.

HARTMAN (W.) and others. Information systems handbook: analysis, requirements determination, design and development, implementation and evaluation. Apeldoorn, [1968 repr. 1972]. 1 vol. (various pagings). bibliog.

LI (DAVID HSIANG-FU) Design and management of information systems. Chicago, [1972]. pp. 312.

COUGER (J. DANIEL) and KNAPP (ROBERT W.) eds. System analysis techniques. New York, [1974]. pp. 509. bibliogs.

DAVIS (GORDON B.) Management information systems: conceptual foundations, structure, and development. New York, [1974]. pp. 482. bibliogs.

MANAGERIAL ECONOMICS.

HERENDEEN (JAMES B.) The economics of the corporate economy. New York, [1975]. pp. 262. bibliogs.

LOASBY (BRIAN J.) Choice, complexity and ignorance: an enquiry into economic theory and the practice of decision-making. Cambridge, 1976. pp. 242. bibliog.

NEWBOULD (GERALD D.) Academic salaries: a personal application of managerial economics. Bradford, [1975]. pp. 14. (University of Bradford. Inaugural Lectures. 1975)

MANCHESTER

— Civic improvement.

ROBERTSON (IAN) Community self-surveys in urban renewal. [Manchester, 1976]. pp. 140. bibliog. (Manchester. University. Department of Adult Education. Manchester Monographs. 4)

— Economic conditions.

GREATER MANCHESTER COUNCIL. County structure plan: report of survey. [Manchester], 1975. 8 parts (in 1 vol.).

— History.

WILLIAMS (BILL) The making of Manchester Jewry, 1740-1875. Manchester, [1976]. pp. 454. bibliog.

— Social conditions.

GREATER MANCHESTER COUNCIL. County structure plan: report of survey. [Manchester], 1975. 8 parts (in 1 vol.).

MANCHESTER MASSACRE, 1819.

A FULL report of the speeches and proceedings of the Westminster general meeting, held...on Thursday, September 2, 1819, to take into consideration the propriety of addressing the Prince Regent and the nation, on the subject of the late barbarous transactions at Manchester!...the address...the resolutions...; by an eminent short-hand writer. London, printed...for Thomas Dolby, 1819. pp. 19.

MANCHESTER UNIVERSITY.

MANCHESTER. University. Report on student participation in academic affairs; [by a] (working party [set up] to consider the academic implications of the joint statement issued by the Committee of Vice- Chancellors and Principals and the National Union of Students on October 7th 1968). Manchester, [1969]. pp. 11.

MANDATES

— South West Africa.

COCKRAM (GAIL MARYSE) South West African mandate. Cape Town, 1976. pp. 531. bibliog.

MANDEVILLE (BERNARD DE).

PRIMER (IRWIN) ed. Mandeville studies: new explorations in the art and thought of Dr. Bernard Mandeville, 1670-1733. The Hague, 1975. pp. 223. bibliog.

MANETTI (CESARE).

CAMPINOTI (RENATO) Cesare Manetti: un quadro operaio del comunismo italiano, 1901- 1945. Roma, 1974. pp. 175.

MANGALORE

— Harbour.

NATIONAL COUNCIL OF APPLIED ECONOMIC RESEARCH. Traffic survey of Mangalore and Malpe ports. Bangalore, Mysore Public Works Department, 1961. pp. 125.

MANITOBA

— Economic conditions.

MANITOBA. Department of Industry and Commerce. The economy of the province of Manitoba. a., 1973- [Winnipeg].

— History.

CANADA. Public Archives. 1970. The birth of Manitoba. Ottawa, 1970. pp. 25, 26. *In English and French.*

— Industries.

MANITOBA. Department of Industry and Commerce. 1975. A guide to employment and value of production data for industries in Manitoba. [Winnipeg, 1975]. pp. 169.

— Politics and government.

CRUNICAN (PAUL) Priests and politicians: Manitoba schools and the election of 1896 Toronto, [1974]. pp. 369. *bibliog.*

— Population policy.

MANITOBA 2000: population size and distribution; edited by K.B. Richmond and J.J. Keleher. [Winnipeg], Manitoba Environmental Council, 1975. 1 vol. (various pagings). *(Manitoba Environmental Council. Studies. No. 5)*

MANNHEIM UNIVERSITY.

Die UNIVERSITAET Mannheim in Vergangenheit und Gegenwart; Herausgeber: Eduard Gaugler [and others]. Mannheim, 1976. pp. 348. *bibliog.*

MANORIAL COURTS

— United Kingdom.

EMMISON (FREDERICK GEORGE) Elizabethan life: home, work and land; from Essex wills and sessions and manorial records. Chelmsford, 1976. pp. 364. *(Essex. Records Committee. Essex Record Office Publications. No. 69)*

MANORIAL EXTENTS.

RAFTIS (J. AMBROSE) Assart data and land values: two studies in the East Midlands, 1200-1350. Toronto, 1974. pp. 169. *(Pontifical Institute of Mediaeval Studies. Subsidia Mediaevalia. 3)*

MANPOWER POLICY.

SEMINAR ON MANPOWER PLANNING IN THE SOUTH PACIFIC, FIJI, 1970. Seminar on Manpower Planning in the South Pacific; address by Walter Elkan...at opening of regional seminar [organised by the University of the South Pacific; and summary report]. [London, 1971]. pp. 18. *(Commonwealth Foundation. Occasional Papers. No. 11)*

MEASUREMENT of human resources: (based on papers presented to a symposium held in Lisbon, June 1973, and sponsored by N.A.T.O.; edited by W.T. Singleton and P. Spurgeon. London, 1975. pp. 370. *bibliogs.*

GINZBERG (ELI) The human economy. New York, [1976]. pp. 274. *bibliog.*

— Mathematical models.

U.K. Civil Service Department. Statistics Division. Manplan Project Team. 1975. A management guide to manpower planning models. London, 1975. pp. 49.

REDFERN (PERCY) Statistician. Input-output analysis and its application to education and manpower planning. 2nd ed. London, H.M.S.O., 1976. pp. 21. *bibliog. (Civil Service College [U.K.]. Occasional Papers. No. 5)*

— Australia.

NILAND (JOHN R.) and ISAAC (JOSEPH EZRA) eds. Australian labour economics: readings. [2nd ed.] Melbourne, 1975. pp. 676. *bibliogs.*

— Canada — Manitoba.

ECONOMIC DEVELOPMENT ADVISORY BOARD OF MANITOBA. Manpower issues in Manitoba. [Winnipeg], 1975. pp. 276. *bibliog.*

— Ghana.

TAYLOR (ERNEST) An organizational approach to the analysis of problems affecting education and manpower planning in Ghana. Bonn, [1974]. pp. 184. *(Friedrich-Ebert-Stiftung. Forschungsinstitut. Schriftenreihe. Band 107)*

— United Kingdom.

THAKUR (MANAB) Manpower planning in action. London, 1975. pp. 113. *bibliog. (Institute of Personnel Management. Information Reports. New Series. 19)*

STEIN (BRUNO) Work and welfare in Britain and the U.S.A. London, 1976. pp. 112.

— United States.

ABOUD (GRACE) Hiring and training the disadvantaged for public employment. Ithaca, N.Y., 1973. pp. 45. *bibliog. (Cornell University. New York State School of Industrial and Labor Relations. Key Issue Series. No. 11)*

DAVIS (RUSSELL G.) and LEWIS (GARY M.) Education and employment: a future perspective of needs, policies, and programs. Lexington, Mass., [1975]. pp. 166. *bibliog.*

GINZBERG (ELI) The manpower connection: education and work. Cambridge, Mass., 1975. pp. 258.

NATIONAL RESEARCH COUNCIL. Assembly of Behavioral and Social Sciences. Committee on Department of Labor Manpower Research and Development. Knowledge and policy in manpower: a study of the manpower research and development program in the Department of Labor. Washington, D.C.1975. pp. 171. *bibliog.*

SEIDMAN (LAURENCE S.) The design of federal employment programs. Lexington, Mass., [1975]. pp. 202. *bibliog.*

THOMPSON (FRANK J.) Personnel policy in the city: the politics of jobs in Oakland. Berkeley, [1975]. pp. 209. *bibliog.*

HANSEN (NILES M.) Improving access to economic opportunity: nonmetropolitan labor markets in an urban society. Cambridge, Mass., [1976]. pp. 192.

LEVITAN (SAR A.) and others. Human resources and labor markets: (labor and manpower in the American economy). 2nd ed. New York, [1976]. pp. 631. *bibliog.*

MIRENGOFF (WILLIAM) and RINDLER (LESTER) The Comprehensive Employment and Training Act: impact on people, places, programs: an interim report...prepared for the Committee on Evaluation of Employment and Training Programs, Assembly of Behavioral and Social Sciences, National Research Council. Washington, 1976. pp. 175. *bibliog.*

STEIN (BRUNO) Work and welfare in Britain and the U.S.A. London, 1976. pp. 112.

MANTARO VALLEY

— Rural conditions.

ALBERTI (GIORGIO) and SANCHEZ (RODRIGO) Poder y conflicto social en el valle del Mantaro, 1900-1974. Lima, 1974. pp. 220. *bibliog. (Instituto de Estudios Peruanos. Peru Problema. 10)*

MANTOUX (ETIENNE).

MANTOUX (ÉTIENNE) [Letters to Frank Hardie. 1933-35]. 6 letters, 2 postcards. *Manuscript.*

MANUSCRIPTS

— United Kingdom — Bibliography.

BATTS (JOHN STUART) British manuscript diaries of the nineteenth century: an annotated listing. Totowa, 1976. pp. 345.

MAO (TSE—TUNG).

IURKOV (S.G.) and PETROV (G.P.) eds. Vneshnepoliticheskie kontseptsii maoizma: pravovye aspekty. Moskva, 1975. pp. 256.

MARKOVA (SVETLANA DANILOVNA) Maoizm i intelligentsiia: problemy i sobytiia, 1956-1973 gg. Moskva, 1975. pp. 245. *bibliog.*

POSPELOV (BORIS VASIL'EVICH) Iaponskaia obshchestvenno-politicheskaia mysl' i maoizm: kritika antimarksistskikh kontseptsii sushchnosti maoizma. Moskva, 1975. pp. 224. *bibliog.*

UHALLEY (STEPHEN) Mao Tse-tung: a critical biography. New York, 1975. pp. 233. *bibliog.*

WANG (MING) Polveka KPK i predatel'stvo Mao Tsze-duna. Moskva, 1975. pp. 311.

HAN (SUYIN) pseud. [i.e. Elizabeth COMBER] Wind in the tower: Mao Tsetung and the Chinese revolution, 1949-1975. London, 1976. pp. 404.

OSNOVNYE aspekty kitaiskoi problemy, 1965-1975. Moskva, 1976. pp. 279.

MAORIS.

MACRAE (JOHN TAIT) A study in the application of economic analysis to social issues: the Maori and the New Zealand economy. 1975. fo. 416. *bibliog. Typescript. Ph.D. (London) thesis: unpublished. This thesis is the property of London University and may not be removed from the Library.*

NEW ZEALAND. Commission of Inquiry into Maori Reserved Land. 1975. Report; [Bartholomew Sheehan, chairman]. Wellington, 1975. pp. 498.

METGE (ALICE JOAN) The Maoris of New Zealand: Rautahi. rev. ed. London, 1976. pp. 382. *bibliog.*

MAPS.

McAREVEY (MARY) compiler. A guide to definitive maps of public paths: a guide to the preparation of draft, provisional and definitive maps of public paths, revised maps and details of public rights of representation and objection. 3rd ed. London, 1974. pp. 37.

MAR DEL PLATA

— History.

SEBRELI (JUAN JOSE) Mar del Plata: el ocio represivo. Buenos Aires, [1970]. pp. 141. *bibliog.*

MARC SYSTEM

— United Kingdom.

UK MARC manual; first standard edition. London, British Library, Bibliographic Services Division, 1975. pp. 117.

MARCHLEWSKI (JULIAN BALTAZAR).

KRZYWOBŁOCKA (BO'ZENA) ed. Julian Marchlewski. Warszawa, 1975. pp. 129. *With brief Russian, English and German summaries.*

MARCHLEWSKI (JULIAN BALTAZAR) Listy do 'zony i córki; słowo wią'zące Zofia Marchlewska, opracowała Bo'zena Wróblewska, wstęp Janusz Durko. Warszawa, 1975. pp. 395.

MARCUSE (HERBERT).

GABRIEL (OSCAR W.) Herbert Marcuses Thesen zur Universalität der Herrschaft in der industriellen Gesellschaft: Anmerkungen zu einer Schlüsselkategorie der Gesellschaftsanalyse Herbert Marcuses. Hamburg, 1975. pp. 609. *bibliog.*

MARGAI (Sir MILTON AUGUSTUS STRIEBY).

SIERRA LEONE. Ministry of Information and Broadcasting. 1963. Meet Sir Milton. [Freetown, 1963?]. pp. 23.

MARI LITERATURE.

See CHEREMISSIAN LITERATURE.

MARIANSKA (ANIELA).

MARIAŃSKA (ANIELA) Wiklinowe kosz. Warszawa, 1959. pp. 311.

MARIHUANA.

AMERICAN CIVIL LIBERTIES UNION. Marijuana. New York, [1973?]. pp. 15.

MARINE RESOURCES

— Law and legislation.

SREENIVASA RAO (PEMMARAJU) The public order of ocean resources: a critique of the contemporary law of the sea. Cambridge, Mass., [1975]. pp. 313. *bibliog.*

JOHNSTON (DOUGLAS M.) ed. Marine policy and the coastal community: the impact of the law of the sea. London, [1976]. pp. 336.

MARITAIN (JACQUES).

SMITH (BROOKE WILLIAMS) Jacques Maritain: antimodern or ultramodern?: an historical analysis of his critics, his thought, and his life. New York, 1976. pp. 194. *bibliog.*

MARITIME LAW.

ZAORSKI (REMIGIUSZ) Konwencje genewskie o prawie morza. Gdynia, 1962. pp. 275. *biblog. With Russian and English summaries.*

SREENIVASA RAO (PEMMARAJU) The public order of ocean resources: a critique of the contemporary law of the sea. Cambridge, Mass., [1975]. pp. 313. *bibliog.*

STEIN (ROBERT E.) ed. Critical environmental issues on the law of the sea; by Patricia W. Birnie [and others]. [Washington, D.C., 1975]. pp. 57. *(International Institute for Environment and Development. Reports)*

JOHNSTON (DOUGLAS M.) ed. Marine policy and the coastal community: the impact of the law of the sea. London, [1976]. pp. 336.

— Congresses.

UNIVERSITY OF RHODE ISLAND. Law of the Sea Institute. Annual Conference, 4th, 1969. The law of the sea: national policy recommendations; proceedings...; edited by Lewis M. Alexander. Kingston, R.I., 1970. pp. 533.

— America, Latin.

URUGUAY. Presidencia. Secretaria. 1971. America Latina y la extension del mar territorial: regimen juridico. Montevideo, 1971. pp. 440. *bibliog.*

— United Kingdom.

[TEMPERLEY (ROBERT)] The Merchant Shipping Acts; seventh edition by Michael Thomas and David Steel. London, 1976. pp. 1001.

— United States.

The LAW of the sea: U.S. interests and alternatives; [proceedings of] a conference sponsored by the American Enterprise Institute for Public Policy Research and the U. S. Department of the Treasury; edited by Ryan C. Amacher and Richard James Sweeney. Washington, [1976]. pp. 196.

MARKET SURVEYS

— Canada.

CANADA. Statistics Canada. Market research handbook. a., 1975- Ottawa. *In English and French.*

MARKETING.

DAYAN (ARMAND) La distribution des biens de consommation. [Paris], 1975. pp. 127. *bibliog.*

DOUGLAS (EDNA) Economics and marketing. New York, [1975]. pp. 728.

GREENHUT (MELVIN LEONARD) and OHTA (HIROSHI) Theory of spatial pricing and market areas. Durham, N.C., 1975. pp. 262.

LEVY (SIDNEY J.) and ZALTMAN (GERALD) Marketing, society, and conflict. Englewood Cliffs, [1975]. pp. 134.

BAKER (MICHAEL J.) ed. Marketing in adversity. London, 1976. pp. 110.

LIVINGSTONE (JAMES MACCARDLE) International marketing management. London, 1976. pp. 170. *bibliog.*

— Mathematical models.

PARSONS (LEONARD J.) and SCHULTZ (RANDALL L.) Marketing models and econometric research. New York, [1976]. pp. 300. *bibliog.*

— Social aspects.

FERRELL (O.C.) and LAGARCE (RAYMOND) eds. Public policy issues in marketing. Lexington, Mass., [1975]. pp. 192.

LEVY (SIDNEY J.) and ZALTMAN (GERALD) Marketing, society, and conflict. Englewood Cliffs, [1975]. pp. 134.

— Japan.

YOSHINO (MICHAEL Y.) Marketing in Japan: a management guide. New York, 1975. pp. 156.

MARKETING MANAGEMENT.

WIECHMANN (ULRICH E.) Marketing management in multinational firms: the consumer packaged goods industry. New York, 1976. pp. 103. *bibliog.*

MARKETING RESEARCH

— Mathematical models.

PARSONS (LEONARD J.) and SCHULTZ (RANDALL L.) Marketing models and econometric research. New York, [1976]. pp. 300. *bibliog.*

MARKETS

— France.

FRANCE. Direction Générale du Commerce Intérieur et des Prix. Service du Commerce. Les centres commerciaux de gros:...document d'orientation...à la suite du colloque organisé...par la Chambre de Commerce et d'Industrie de Nantes, au mois de décembre 1970. Paris, 1971. pp. 73.

— Mexico.

MARKETS in Oaxaca: [papers from a symposium held in Tucson, 1971, sponsored by the Southwestern Anthropological Association]; edited by Scott Cook and Martin Diskin. Austin, Texas, [1976]. pp. 329. *bibliog. (Texas University. Institute of Latin American Studies. Special Publications)*

— Netherlands.

ECONOMISCH INSTITUUT VOOR HET MIDDEN- EN KLEIN BEDRIJF. Sociaal- Economische Publikaties. De warenmarkten in Nederland. 'sGravenhage, 1974. pp. 91.

— Poland.

BUCZEK (KAROL) Targi i miasta na prawie polskim: okres wczesnośredniowieczny. Wrocław, 1964. pp. 140. *(Polska Akademia Nauk. Oddział w Krakowie. Komisja Nauk Historycznych. Prace. Nr.11) With Russian and French tables of contents.*

MARKOVIC (SVETOZAR).

PISAREK (HENRIK) Filozofija Svetozara Markovića, 1846-1875. Novi Sad, 1974. pp. 170. *(Matica Srpska. Odeljenje za Društvene Nauke. Studije i Gradja o Ujedinjenoj Omladini Srpskoj) With Russian summary. In Cyrillic.*

MARQUART (FRANK).

MARQUART (FRANK) An auto worker's journal: the UAW from crusade to one-party union. University Park, Pa., [1975]. pp. 162. *bibliog.*

MARRIAGE.

CONFIGURATIONS: biological and cultural factors in sexuality and family life; edited by Raymond Prince [and] Dorothy Barrier. Lexington, Mass., [1974]. pp. 193. *bibliogs. Papers of a conference held in Montreal, 1972, and sponsored by the Mental Hygiene Institute.*

CLAYTON (RICHARD R.) The family, marriage, and social change. Lexington, Mass., [1975]. pp. 579. *bibliog.*

— Denmark.

KOCH-NIELSEN (INGER) Aegteskabet og loven. etc. København, 1975. pp. 143. *bibliog. (Socialforskningsinstituttet. Publikationer. 66) With English summaries.*

— France.

GIRARD (ALAIN) Le choix du conjoint: une enquête psycho-sociologique en France; nouvelle édition augmentée d'une préface. [Paris], 1974. pp. 201. *(France. Institut National d'Etudes Démographiques. Travaux et Documents. Cahiers. No.70)*

— India — Bengal.

INDEN (RONALD B.) Marriage and rank in Bengali culture: a history of caste and clan in middle period Bengal. Berkeley, Calif., [1976]. pp. 161. *bibliog.*

— Nigeria.

UKAEGBU (ALFRED ONYEOHUHU) Marriage and fertility in east central Nigeria: a case study of Ngwa Igbo women. 1975. fo. 367. *bibliog. Typescript. Ph.D.(London) thesis. unpublished. This thesis is the property of London University and may not be removed from the Library.*

— Spain.

FERRANDIZ (ALEJANDRA) and VERDU (VICENTE) Noviazgo y matrimonio en la burguesia española. Madrid, 1974 repr. 1975. pp. 283.

— United Kingdom.

HART (NICKY) When marriage ends: a study in status passage. London, 1976. pp. 277. *bibliog.*

— United States.

CARTER (HUGH SEIVER) and GLICK (PAUL CHARLES) Marriage and divorce: a social and economic study. rev. ed. Cambridge, Mass., 1976. pp. 508. *(American Public Health Association. Vital and Health Statistics Monographs)*

MARRIAGE, MIXED.

INTERNATIONAL CONSULTATION ON MIXED MARRIAGE, DUBLIN, 1974. Beyond tolerance: the challenge of mixed marriage; a record of the...consultation...; edited...by Michael Hurley. London, [1975]. pp. 1913.

MARRIAGE LAW

— Denmark.

KOCH-NIELSEN (INGER) Aegteskabet og loven, etc. København, 1975. pp. 143. *bibliog.* *(Socialforskningsinstituttet. Publikationer. 66) With English summaries.*

MARSEILLES

— Commerce.

CARRIERE (CHARLES) Négociants marseillais au XVIIIe siècle: contribution à l'étude des économies maritimes. [Marseilles, 1973]. 2 vols.

— Economic history.

COURDURIE (MARCEL) La dette des collectivités publiques de Marseille au XVIIIe siècle: du débat sur le prêt à intérêt au financement par l'emprunt. [Marseilles, 1974]. pp. 375. *bibliog.*

MARSHALL (ALFRED).

MARSHALL (ALFRED) [Letters to Francis Ysidro Edgeworth. 1880-96]. 22 letters, 1 postcard. *Manuscript.*

STEPHEN (Sir LESLIE) [Correspondence about Alfred Marshall's theory of consumers' rent. 1891]. 4 letters, 3 pages of notes. *Manuscript.*

MARSHALL ISLANDS

— History.

TREUE (WOLFGANG) Die Jaluit-Gesellschaft auf den Marshall-Inseln, 1887-1914: ein Beitrag zur Kolonial- und Verwaltungsgeschichte in der Epoche des deutschen Kaiserreichs. Berlin, [1976]. pp. 197. *bibliog.*

MARTI (JOSE).

MIRANDA VALERA (AURELIO) Martí político: a la luz actual. La Habana, 1969. pp. 156.

MARTIN GARCIA ISLAND.

FITTE (ERNESTO J.) Martín García: historia de una isla argentina. Buenos Aires, [1971]. pp. 209.

MARX (JENNY).

REETZ (JUERGEN) Vier Briefe von Jenny Marx aus den Jahren 1856-1860. Trier, [1970]. pp. 16. *(Karl-Marx-Haus. Schriften. 3)*

MONZ (HEINZ) and others. Zur Persönlichkeit von Marx' Schwiegervater Johann Ludwig von Westphalen. Trier, [1973]. pp. 166. *(Karl-Marx-Haus. Schriften. 9)*

SCHWERIN VON KROSIGK (LUTZ) Graf. Jenny Marx: Liebe und Leid im Schatten von Karl Marx; eine Biographie nach Briefen, Tagebüchern und anderen Dokumenten. Wuppertal, [1975]. pp. 264. *bibliog.*

MARX (KARL).

KARL Marx: eine Sammlung von Erinnerungen und Aufsätzen. Berlin, [1947]. pp. 203.

GLASSER (M.) Über die Arbeitsmethoden der Klassiker des Marxismus-Leninismus. Berlin, [1948]. pp. 103.

MEUSEL (ALFRED) Die deutsche Revolution von 1848; mit einem Beitrag von Felix Albin: Marx und Engels und die Revolution von 1848. Berlin, [1948]. pp. 40.

KATZ (HENRYK) Karol Marks i jego epoka. Warszawa, 1965. pp. 371.

EX libris Karl Marx und Friedrich Engels: Schicksal und Verzeichnis einer Bibliothek; Einleitung und Redaktion: Bruno Kaiser; Katalog und wissenschaftlicher Apparat: Inge Werchan. Berlin, 1967. pp. 229.

MASSICZEK (ALBERT) Der menschliche Mensch: Karl Marx' jüdischer Humanismus. Wien, [1968]. pp. 654. *bibliog.*

RUBIN (ISAAK IL'ICH) Essays on Marx's theory of value; translated by Miloš Samardźya and Fredy Perlman from the third edition...1928. Montréal, [1968]. pp. 275.

RUBEL (MAXIMILIEN) Russland und die russische Revolution im Denken von Karl Marx. Trier, [1969]. pp. 36. *(Karl-Marx-Haus. Schriften. 2)*

COMYN (MARIAN) Meine Erinnerungen an Karl Marx: [an article from The Nineteenth Century, 1922, vol. 91, nr. 539]; übersetzt und annotiert von Frank T. Walker. Trier, [1970]. pp. 23. *(Karl-Marx-Haus. Schriften. 5) Xerox copy.*

LEFEBVRE (JEAN PIERRE) Marx und Heine. Trier, [1972]. pp. 51. *(Karl-Marx-Haus. Schriften. 7) Xerox copy.*

ESTABLET (ROGER) and MACHEREY (PIERRE) Lire Le capital IV. Paris, 1973. pp. 119.

RANCIERE (JACQUES) Lire Le capital III. Paris, 1973. pp. 127.

HAUG (WOLFGANG FRITZ) Vorlesungen zur Einführung ins Kapital. Köln, [1974]. pp. 196.

HUNT (RICHARD NORMAN) The political ideas of Marx and Engels. London, 1975 in progress. *bibliog.*

MARX (KARL) and ENGELS (FRIEDRICH) Gesamtausgabe (MEGA)...; (Redaktionskommission der Gesamtausgabe: Günter Heyden und Anatoli Jegorow, Leiter). Berlin, 1975 in progress. *bibliogs. Each volume consists of 2 separate parts: Text and Apparat.*

HOWARD (MICHAEL C.) and KING (JOHN E.) The political economy of Marx. Harlow, Essex, 1975. pp. 279. *bibliog.*

KOMMISSION DER HISTORIKER DER DDR UND DER UdSSR. Konferenz, 21., 1973. 125 Jahre Kommunistisches Manifest und bürgerlich-demokratische Revolution 1848/49: Referate und Diskussionsbeiträge; wissenschaftliche Redaktion: Gunther Hildebrandt und Walter Wittwer. Glashütten im Taunus, 1975. pp. 312.

KONIUSHAIA (RAISA PAVLOVNA) Karl Marks i revoliutsionnaia Rossiia. Moskva, 1975. pp. 440.

KRADER (LAWRENCE) The Asiatic mode of production: sources, development and critique in the writings of Karl Marx. Assen, 1975. pp. 454. *bibliog. Including excerpts taken by Marx from the work of M.M. Kovalevskii, with Marx's notes thereon.*

LESSNER (FRIEDRICH) Ich brachte das "Kommunistische Manifest" zum Drucker; (zusammengestellt und eingeleitet von Ursula Herrmann und Gerhard Winkler). Berlin, 1975. pp. 392. *bibliog.*

LEVINE (NORMAN) The tragic deception: Marx contra Engels. Oxford, [1975]. pp. 259.

MAAREK (GERARD) Introduction au Capital de Karl Marx: un essai de formalisation. [Paris, 1975]. pp. 312. *bibliog.*

MAGNIS (FRANZ VON) Normative Voraussetzungen im Denken des jungen Marx, 1843-1848. Freiburg, [1975]. pp. 429. *bibliog.*

PLAMENATZ (JOHN PETROV) Karl Marx's philosophy of man. Oxford, 1975. pp. 484.

PROJEKTGRUPPE ENTWICKLUNG DES MARXSCHEN SYSTEMS. Der 4. Band des "Kapital"?: Kommentar zu den "Theorien über den Mehrwert"; ([by] Helmut Asche [and others]). Westberlin, [1975]. pp. 677.

BORTKEVICH (VLADISLAV IOSIFOVICH) Wertrechnung und Preisrechnung im Marxschen System. Lollar/Giessen, [1976]. pp. 213. *bibliog. Collection of articles originally published between 1906 and 1921.*

HANSEN (DONALD ANDREW) An invitation to critical sociology: involvement, criticism, exploration. New York, [1976]. pp. 258. *bibliog.*

HENRY (MICHEL) Marx. [Paris, 1976]. 2 vols.

SHAW (WILLIAM HARRY) Productive forces and relations of production: a study of the dynamics of Marx's theory of historical change. [1976]. fo. 509. *bibliog. Typescript. Ph.D.(London) thesis: unpublished. This thesis is the property of London University and may not be removed from the Library.*

ULLRICH (HORST) Zur Reaktion der bürgerlichen Ideologie auf die Entstehung des Marxismus. Frankfurt/Main, 1976. pp. 99.

VYGODSKII (VITALII SOLOMONOVICH) Wie"Das Kapital" entstand; aus dem Russischen; (Übersetzer: Günter Wermusch). Berlin, [1976]. pp. 219.

— Bibliography.

PRIZHIZNENNYE izdaniia i publikatsii proizvedenii K. Marksa i F. Engel'sa: bibliograficheskii ukazatel'. Moskva, 1974 in progress.

MARX FAMILY.

REETZ (JUERGEN) Vier Briefe von Jenny Marx aus den Jahren 1856-1860. Trier, [1970]. pp. 16. *(Karl-Marx-Haus. Schriften. 3)*

LAUFNER (RICHARD) and RAUCH (ALBERT) Die Familie Marx und die Trierer Judenschaft. Trier, [1975]. pp. 40. *(Karl-Marx-Haus. Schriften. 14)*

MARXIAN ECONOMICS.

DUNCKER (HERMANN) Volkswirtschaftliche Grundbegriffe, mit besonderer Berücksichtigung der ökonomischen Grundlehren von Karl Marx: als Leitfaden für Unterrichtskurse. Stuttgart, 1908. pp. 60.

FLOREK (HENRYK) and SZEFLER (STANISŁAW) Dywersja w ekonomice. Warszawa, 1970. pp. 176.

HEILBRONER (ROBERT LOUIS) Between capitalism and socialism: essays in political economics. New York, [1970]. pp. 294.

KRAWCZEWSKI (ANDRZEJ) Rewizjonizm a współczesna bur'zuazyjna ekonomia polityczna. Warszawa, 1970. pp. 114. *bibliog. With English and Russian summaries.*

CLAUDE (HENRI) Le capitalisme monopoliste d'état: éléments pour une explication théorique;...textes de Lénine. Paris, 1971. fo. 38. *(Centre d'Etudes et de Recherches Marxistes. Cahiers. No. 91)*

RADAEV (VALERII VIKTOROVICH) Ekonomicheskie interesy pri sotsializme. Moskva, 1971. pp. 336.

UCHENYE ZAPISKI KAFEDR OBSHCHESTVENNYKH NAUK VUZOV LENINGRADA. Politicheskaia ekonomiia. vyp. 12. Ekonomicheskie interesy pri sotsializme i formy ikh realizatsii. Leningrad, 1971. pp. 191.

ACCARDO (GIANFRANCO) Quantitative Fragen aus der Marxschen Wertlehre. Berlin, 1973. pp. 152. *bibliog.*

AKTUAL'NYE problemy ekonomicheskoi teorii. Moskva, 1973. pp. 319.

ÉRDEKVISZONYOK a szocializmusban. Budapest, 1973. pp. 211.

ANDERS (HANS DIETER) and others. Zum Bewertungsproblem im Sozialismus. Berlin, 1974. pp. 120. *(Akademie der Wissenschaften der DDR. Zentralinstitut für Wirtschaftswissenschaften. Forschungsberichte. Nr.12)*

BELIANOVA (ANTONINA MIKHAILOVNA) O tempakh ekonomicheskogo razvitiia SSSR: po materialam diskussii 20-kh godov. Moskva, 1974. pp. 174.

CHAO (TZU-YUAN) Neue Arbeitswerttheorie: der Weg nach Utopia;...aus dem Chinesischen übertragen von Christian Gries in Zusammenarbeit mit dem Autor. Hamburg, [1974]. pp. 173. *With English summary.*

MARXIAN ECONOMICS.(Cont.)

DESAI (MEGHNAD J.) Marxian economic theory. London, 1974. pp. 157. *bibliog.*

GRUNDLAGEN und Formen der Herrschaft des Finanzkapitals; Autorenkollektiv: Peter Hess [and others]. Frankfurt am Main, 1974. pp. 144.

INTERESY v sisteme ekonomicheskikh otnoshenii sotsializma. Kiev 1974. pp. 240.

KHARBEDIIA (RAFAEL' PARNAOZOVICH) Sistema ekonomicheskikh zakonov sotsializma i kommunizma i ee ispol'zovanie: voprosy teorii i metodologii. Tbilisi, 1974. pp. 118.

KRITIKA burzhuaznykh kontseptsii ekonomiki sotsializma. Moskva, 1974. pp. 159.

KUZ'MINOV (IVAN IVANOVICH) Ocherki politicheskoi ekonomii sotsializma: protsess sotsialisticheskogo proizvodstva. Moskva, 1974. pp. 284.

PREDMET i metod politicheskoi ekonomii sotsializma; (predislovie A.I. Pashkova). Saratov, 1974. pp. 482.

UCHENYE ZAPISKI KAFEDR OBSHCHESTVENNYKH NAUK VUZOV LENINGRADA. Politicheskaia Ekonomiia. vyp.15. Osnovnoi ekonomicheskii zakon sotsializma. Leningrad, 1974. pp. 223.

VARGA (JENO) Izbrannye proizvedeniia. Moskva, 1974. 3 vols.

AGAFONOV (ALEKSANDR KONSTANTINOVICH) Tovarnoe proizvodstvo i zakon stoimosti pri sotsializme. Kiev, 1975. pp. 240. *bibliog.*

BAZYLEV (NIKOLAI IVANOVICH) Stanovlenie ekonomicheskoi teorii sotsializma v SSSR. Minsk, 1975. pp. 175.

CSIKÓS-NAGY (BÉLA) Socialist price theory and price policy; (translated by Elek Helvey...and István Véges). Budapest, 1975. pp. 371.

DAVEY (BRIAN) The economic development of India: a Marxist analysis. Nottingham, 1975. pp. 232. *bibliog.*

HOWARD (MICHAEL C.) and KING (JOHN E.) The political economy of Marx. Harlow, Essex, 1975. pp. 279. *bibliog.*

KRADER (LAWRENCE) The Asiatic mode of production: sources, development and critique in the writings of Karl Marx. Assen, 1975. pp. 454. *bibliog. Including excerpts taken by Marx from the work of M.M. Kovalevskii, with Marx's notes thereon.*

KUCZYNSKI (JUERGEN) Vier Revolutionen der Produktivkräfte: Theorie und Vergleiche; mit kritischen Bemerkungen und Ergänzungen von Wolfgang Jonas. Berlin, 1975. pp. 194.

KUZ'MINOV (IVAN IVANOVICH) and ROGACHEV (SERGEI VLADIMIROVICH) eds. Politicheskaia ekonomiia sotsializma - nauchnaia osnova rukovodstva narodnym khoziaistvom. Moskva, 1975. pp. 255.

LATOUCHE (SERGE) Le projet marxiste: analyse économique et matérialisme historique. [Paris, 1975]. pp. 208.

OSAD'KO (MIKHAIL PETROVICH) Teoreticheskie osnovy raspredeleniia chistogo produkta sotsialisticheskogo predpriiatiia. Moskva, 1975. pp. 311.

OSAD'KO (MIKHAIL PETROVICH) ed. Protsess sotsialisticheskogo nakopleniia. Moskva, 1975. pp. 140.

PURTON (JOHN ANTHONY) Political economy: a Communist Party study course. London, [1975]. pp. 26. *bibliog.*

SOTSIALISTICHESKII produkt i ego formy. Moskva, 1975. pp. 183.

SOTSIALIZM: dialektika razvitiia proizvoditel'nykh sil i proizvodstvennykh otnoshenii. Moskva, 1975. pp. 333.

VYSHNEVETS'KYI (IOSIF ANTONOVYCH) Ekonomichni interesy sotsialistychnoho suspil'stva. Kyïv, 1975. pp. 102.

POLITISCHE Ökonomie...; ([by] A.M. Alexejewa [and others; edited by] I.D. Schirinski [and others]; Übersetzung: Leon Nebenzahl). Berlin, 1976 in progress.

BAISCH (HELMUT) Wert, Preis und Allokation: eine Verallgemeinerung des Marxschen Reproduktionsmodells. Meisenheim am Glan, 1976. pp. 318. *bibliog. With English summary.*

BETTELHEIM (CHARLES) Economic calculation and forms of property. London, 1976. pp. 151. *bibliogs.*

BORTKEVICH (VLADISLAV IOSIFOVICH) Wertrechnung und Preisrechnung im Marxschen System. Lollar/Giessen, [1976]. pp. 213. *bibliog. Collection of articles originally published between 1906 and 1921.*

ECONOMIC analysis of the Soviet-type system; [edited by] Judith Thornton. Cambridge, 1976. pp. 372. *bibliogs.*

HEINRICHS (WOLFGANG) and MAIER (HARRY) eds. Gesetzmässigkeiten der intensiv erweiterten Reproduktion bei der weiteren Gestaltung der entwickelten sozialistischen Gesellschaft. Berlin, 1976. 2 vols. *(Akademie der Wissenschaften der DDR. Zentralinstitut der Wirtschaftswissenschaften. Schriften. Nr. 13)*

HELLER (AGNES) The theory of need in Marx. London, [1976]. pp. 135.

HOWARD (MICHAEL C.) and KING (JOHN E.) eds. The economics of Marx: selected readings of exposition and criticism. Harmondsworth, 1976. pp. 278. *bibliogs.*

MAERZ (EDUARD) Einführung in die Marxsche Theorie der wirtschaftlichen Entwicklung: Frühkapitalismus und Kapitalismus der freien Konkurrenz, etc. Wien, [1976]. pp. 356.

MAIZENBERG (LEV IL'ICH) Problemy tsenoobrazovaniia v razvitom sotsialisticheskom obshchestve. Moskva, 1976. pp. 192.

OEKONOMISCHE Probleme der wissenschaftlich-technischen Revolution im Sozialismus...; (Redaktionskollegium: L.M. Gatowski [and others]). Berlin, 1976. pp. 252.

SHAW (WILLIAM HARRY) Productive forces and relations of production: a study of the dynamics of Marx's theory of historical change. [1976]. fo. 509. *bibliog.* Typescript. Ph.D.(London) thesis: unpublished. *This thesis is the property of London University and may not be removed from the Library.*

SIVOLGIN (VLADIMIR EPIFANOVICH) compiler. Politicheskaia ekonomika; Istoriia ekonomicheskoi mysli: annotirovannyi ukazatel' otechestvennykh bibliograficheskikh posobii, izdannykh v 1812-1972gg. Moskva, 1974. pp. 71.

MARXISM.

WALCHER (JAKOB) Ford oder Marx: die praktische Lösung der sozialen Frage. Berlin, [1925]. pp. 158.

NEURATH (OTTO) Lebensgestaltung und Klassenkampf. Berlin, 1928. pp. 152.

GROTEWOHL (OTTO) Die geistige Situation der Gegenwart und der Marxismus: (Rede auf dem ersten Kulturtag der Sozialistischen Einheitspartei Deutschlands am 5. Mai 1948). Berlin, [1948]. pp. 48.

LEDUC (VICTOR) Ist der Marxismus überholt?; (ins Deutsche übertragen von Erich Winguth). Berlin, [1949]. pp. 138.

Der DIALEKTISCHE Materialismus und der Aufbau des Sozialismus: Konferenz des Instituts für Gesellschaftswissenschaften beim ZK der SED...5. und 6. Mai in Berlin: Diskussionsbeiträge. bERLIN, 1958. PP. 19:.

SMISAO i perspektive socijalizma: zbornik (radova drugog zasjedanja Korčulanske ljetne škole, Korčula, 1964). Zagreb, 1965. pp. 358.

ERNESTAN, pseud. [i.e. Ernest TANREZ] Pages choisies: Valeur de la liberté, Le socialisme contre l'autorité, Socialisme et humanisme. Paris, [1966]. pp. 191.

UCHENYE ZAPISKI KAFEDR OBSHCHESTVENNYKH NAUK VUZOV LENINGRADA. Filosofiia. vyp. 9. Filosofskie i sotsiologicheskie issledovaniia. Leningrad, 1968. pp. 189.

PROBLEMY istorii i teorii nauchnogo kommunizma: materialy nauchno- teoreticheskoi konferentsii. Moskva, 1969. pp. 267.

NAMIOTKIEWICZ (WALERY) Myśl polityczna marksizmu a rewizjonizm. 2nd ed. Warszawa, 1970. pp. 295.

JAEGLE (PIERRE) Essai sur l'espace et le temps du point de vue du matérialisme dialectique. Paris, 1971. fo. 27. *(Centre d'Etudes et de Recherches Marxistes. Cahiers. No. 97)*

LEHNING (ARTHUR) Marxismus und Anarchismus in der russischen Revolution; [and] rEVOLUTIONÄR-SYNDIKALISTISCHE bEWEGUNG IN rUSSLAND; ?BY g. p.! mAXIMOFF. 2ND ED. bERLIN, 1971. PP. 146.

BUERGERLICHE Wissenschaftstheorie und ideologischer Klassenkampf: eine Auseinandersetzung mit bürgerlichen Wissenschaftsauffassungen; ([by] G. Domin [and others]). Berlin, 1973. pp. 266. *(Akademie der Wissenschaften der DDR. Institut für Wissenschaftstheorie und -organisation. Wissenschaft und Gesellschaft. Band 2)*

FREIHEIT und Gesellschaft: die Freiheitsauffassung im Marxismus-Leninismus; (Autorenkollektiv: Gottfried Stiehler [and others]). Berlin, 1973. pp. 331.

NEKOTORYE problemy dialektiki i metodologii poznaniia. Tashkent, 1973. pp. 188. *(Tashkent. Universitet. Nauchnye Trudy. vyp.452)*

TASHKENT. Universitet. Nauchnye Trudy. vyp.453. Filosofiia. Tashkent, 1973. pp. 264.

ALTHUSSER (LOUIS) Éléments d'autocritique. [Paris, 1974]. pp. 127.

BORODAI (IURII MEFOD'EVICH) and others. Nasledie K. Marksa i problemy teorii obshchestvenno-ekonomicheskoi formatsii. Moskva, 1974. pp. 309.

FOR Dirk Struik: scientific, historical and political essays in honor of Dirk J. Struik; edited by R.S. Cohen [and others] . Dordrecht, [1974]. pp. 652. *bibliogs. (Boston Colloquium for the Philosophy of Science. Boston Studies in the Philosophy of Science. vol.15)*

GUASTINI (RICCARDO) Marx: dalla filosofia del diritto alla scienza della società; il lessico giuridico marxiano, 1842-1851. Bologna, [1974]. pp. 542.

HOLZ (HANS HEINZ) and others. Conversations with Lukács;... edited by Theo Pinkus; (translated by David Fernbach). London, [1974]. pp. 155.

NIKOLAEVA (LIDIIA VASIL'EVNA) Ob"ektivnye i sub"ektivnye faktory sotsial'nogo progressa i svobody. Moskva, 1974. pp. 259.

PISAREK (HENRIK) Filozofija Svetozara Markovića, 1846-1875. Novi Sad, 1974. pp. 170. *(Matica Srpska. Odeljenje za Društvene Nauke. Studije i Gradja o Ujedinjenoj Omladini Srpskoj) With Russian summary. In Cyrillic.*

QUAINI (MASSIMO) Marxismo e geografia. Firenze, 1974. pp. 162. *bibliog.*

RANCIÈRE (JACQUES) La leçon d'Althusser. [Paris, 1974]. pp. 277.

SALERNO (MICHELE) Contro la ragion pigra: pagine di critica marxista. Roma, [1974]. pp. 195.

SORG (RICHARD) Marxismus und Protestantismus in Deutschland: eine religionssoziologisch-sozialgeschichtliche Studie zur Marxismus- Rezeption in der evangelischen Kirche, 1848-1948. Köln, [1974]. pp. 237. *bibliog.*

STOYANOVITCH (KONSTANTIN) La pensée marxiste et le droit. [Paris], 1974. pp. 196.

VEL'TSMAN (VLADIMIR NIKOLAEVICH) V.I. Lenin o klassovykh i gnoseologicheskikh korniakh idealizma. Khar'kov, 1974. pp. 200. *bibliog.*

MARX (KARL) and ENGELS (FRIEDRICH) Gesamtausgabe (MEGA)...; (Redaktionskommission der Gesamtausgabe: Günter Heyden und Anatoli Jegorow, Leiter). Berlin, 1975 in progress. *bibliogs. Each volume consists of 2 separate parts: Text and Apparat.*

ALLEN (VICTOR LEONARD) Social analysis: a Marxist critique and alternative. London, 1975. pp. 316.

BLAKELEY (THOMAS J.) ed. Themes in Soviet Marxist philosophy: selected articles from the Filosofskaja enciklopedija. Dordrecht, [1975]. pp. 224. *(Freiburg (Switzerland). Universität. Ost-Europa Institut. Sovietica. vol.37)*

BOTTOMORE (THOMAS BURTON) Marxist sociology. London, 1975. pp. 78. *bibliog.*

CARLO (ANTONIO) Crisi economica e dialettica storica: saggi di teoria marxista. Roma, [1975]. pp. 234. *bibliog.*

CURI (UMBERTO) Sulla "scientificità" del marxismo: filosofia e critica dell'economia politica nel marxismo italiano degli anni Sessanta. Milano, 1975. pp. 75.

DUNAYEVSKAYA (RAYA) Marxism and freedom from 1776 until today. 4th ed. London, 1975. pp. 378. *bibliog.*

EICHHORN (WOLFGANG) and others, eds. Die Gesetzmässigkeit der sozialen Entwicklung: ausgewählte Beiträge. Berlin, 1975. pp. 194.

ERDMANN (HANS) and others. Ökonomie und Moral im Sozialismus: zur Dialektik von materiellen Verhältnissen und Moral beim Aufbau der sozialistischen Gesellschaft. Berlin, 1975. pp. 292.

FINGER (OTTO) Philosophie der Revolution: Studie zur Herausbildung der marxistisch-leninistischen Theorie der Revolution, etc. Berlin, 1975. pp. 470.

GEORG Lukàcs [sic]: Verdinglichung und Klassenbewusstsein; (Mitglieder des Autorenkollektivs: Manon Baukhage [and others]). Westberlin, 1975. pp. 201.

GRUNDMANN (SIEGFRIED) Arbeiterklasse: Gegenwart und Zukunft; weltanschauliche und soziologische Probleme der Voraussage und Gestaltung sozialer Prozesse. Berlin, 1975. pp. 203.

GULIEV (VLADIMIR EVGEN'EVICH) and KUZ'MIN (EDUARD LEONIDOVICH) Gosudarstvo i demokratiia: kritika antimarksistskikh teorii. Moskva, 1975. pp. 215.

HODGSON (GEOFF) Trotsky and fatalistic Marxism. Nottingham, 1975. pp. 88.

HOFFMAN (JOHN) Marxism and the theory of praxis: a critique of some new versions of old fallacies. London, [1975]. pp. 239.

HOOK (SIDNEY) Revolution, reform and social justice: studies in the theory and practice of marxism. New York, 1975. pp. 307.

IAKUSHEVSKII (IGOR' TITOVICH) Dialektika i "sovetologiia": kriticheskii analiz "sovetologicheskikh" interpretatsii materialisticheskoi dialektiki. Leningrad, 1975. pp. 207.

KOELSCH (HANS) Theorie und Taktik im Kampf der Arbeiterklasse. Berlin, 1975. pp. 161.

KRITISCHER Rationalismus und Sozialdemokratie: herausgegeben von Georg Lührs [and others]; mit einem Vorwort von Helmut Schmidt. Berlin, 1975. pp. 482.

LENIN (VLADIMIR IL'ICH) On the Soviet state apparatus: articles and speeches. rev. ed. Moscow, 1975. pp. 445.

LEVINE (NORMAN) The tragic deception: Marx contra Engels. Oxford, [1975]. pp. 259.

LINDENBERG (DANIEL) Le marxisme introuvable. [Paris, 1975]. pp. 250. *bibliog.*

MACINTYRE (STUART) Imperialism and the British labour movement in the 1920's: an examination of Marxist theory. London, 1975. pp. 24. *(Communist Party of Great Britain. History Group. Our History. No. 64)*

MARKOVIĆ (MIHAILO) and COHEN (ROBERT SONNE). Yugoslavia: the rise and fall of socialist humanism: a history of the Praxis Group. Nottingham, 1975. pp. 93.

MARKSISTSKO-leninskoe uchenie o sotsializme i sovremennost'. Moskva, 1975. pp. 487.

MARXISMO ed etica: testi sul dibattito intorno al "socialismo neokantiano", 1896-1911, con un saggio introduttivo di Hans Jörg Sandkühler; edizione italiana a cura di Emilio Agazzi. Milano, 1975. pp. 317. *bibliog.*

PLAMENATZ (JOHN PETROV) Karl Marx's philosophy of man. Oxford, 1975. pp. 484.

PLEBE (ARMANDO) La civiltà del postcomunismo. Roma, [1975]. pp. 646. *Part 1 consists of the proceedings of the international congress organised by the Associazione Internazionale per la Cultura Occidentale in Rome in March 1975.*

PLEKHANOV (GEORGII VALENTINOVICH) Kunst und gesellschaftliches Leben; herausgegeben von Alexander Uschakow und Pjotr Nikolajew. Berlin, 1975. pp. 463. *bibliog.*

POSTER (MARK) Existential Marxism in postwar France: from Sartre to Althusser. Princeton, [1975]. pp. 415. *bibliog.*

RADJAVI (KAZEM) La dictature du prolétariat et le dépérissement de l'Etat de Marx à Lénine. Paris, [1975]. pp. 438. *bibliog.*

ROEMER (JOACHIM) Ethos und Schöpfertum der Arbeiterklasse im Sozialismus, etc. Berlin, 1975. pp. 168.

SETTEMBRINI (DOMENICO) Il labirinto marxista: antologia ragionata. Milano, 1975. pp. 447. *bibliog.*

SLAUGHTER (CLIFF) Marxism and the class struggle. London, [1975]. pp. 166. *bibliog.*

SWINGEWOOD (ALAN WILLIAM) Marx and modern social theory. London, 175. pp. 248. *bibliog.*

TIMPANARO (SEBASTIANO) On materialism. London, 1975. pp. 260.

UCHENYE ZAPISKI KAFEDR OBSHCHESTVENNYKH NAUK VUZOV LENINGRADA. Filosofiia. vyp.16. Filosofskie i sotsiologicheskie issledovaniia. Leningrad, 1975. pp. 207.

VODOLAZOV (GRIGORII GRIGOR'EVICH) Dialektika i revoliutsiia: metodologicheskie problemy sotsial'noi revoliutsii. Moskva, 1975. pp. 230.

ARCHARD (DAVID WILLIAM) Existentialism and Marxism: a critical study of the political philosophy of Jean-Paul Sartre and Maurice Merleau-Ponty. 1976. fo. 333. *bibliog. Typescript. Ph.D.(London) thesis: unpublished. This thesis is the property of London University and may not be removed from the Library.*

BOGGS (CARL) Gramsci's marxism. London, 1976. pp. 145.

CALLINICOS (ALEX) Althusser's Marxism. London, 1976. pp. 133. *bibliog.*

EAGLETON (TERRY) Marxism and literary criticism. London, 1976. pp. 88. *bibliog.*

GARAUDY (ROGER) The alternative future: a vision of Christian Marxism;... translated by Leonard Mayhew. Harmondsworth, 1976. pp. 221.

HALFMANN (JOST) and REXROTH (TILLMAN) Marxismus als Erkenntniskritik: Sohn-Rethels Revision der Werttheorie und die produktiven Folgen eines Missverständnisses. München, [1976]. pp. 169. *bibliog.*

HARRINGTON (MICHAEL) b. 1928. The twilight of capitalism. New York, [1976]. pp. 446. *bibliog.*

INTERNATIONAL SLAVIC CONFERENCE, 1ST, BANFF, ALBERTA, 1974. Marxism and religion in Eastern Europe; papers presented at the...conference...; edited by Richard T. De George and James P. Scanlan. Dordrecht, [1976]. pp. 181. *(Freiburg (Switzerland). Universität. Ost-Europa Institut. Sovietica. vol. 36)*

MASARYK (THOMAS GARRIGUE).

JAKUBOWSKI (FRANZ) Ideology and superstructure in historical materialism. London, 1976. pp. 132.

KOSING (ALFRED) Nation in Geschichte und Gegenwart: Studie zur historisch- materialistischen Theorie der Nation. Berlin, 1976. pp. 310.

LUDZ (PETER CHRISTIAN) Ideologiebegriff und marxistische Theorie: Ansätze zu einer immanenten Kritik. Opladen, [1976]. pp. 337. *bibliog. Collection of essays.*

MÍGUEZ BONINO (JOSÉ) Christians and Marxists: the mutual challenge to revolution. London, [1976]. pp. 158. *(London Lectures in Contemporary Christianity. 1974)*

PEARCE (FRANK) Crimes of the powerful: Marxism, crime and deviance. London, 1976. pp. 172.

PURDY (DAVID) The Soviet Union: state capitalist or socialist?: a Marxist critique of the International Socialists. London, [1976]. pp. 46. *bibliog.*

SARTRE (JEAN PAUL) Critique of dialectical reason. 1. Theory of practical ensembles; translated by Alan Sheridan-Smith; edited by Jonathan Ree. London, 1976. pp. 836. *"The projected second volume, of which two chapters were completed...has not been published".*

SMART (BARRY) Sociology, phenomenology and marxian analysis: a critical discussion of the theory and practice of a science of society. London, 1976. pp. 206. *bibliog.*

STUDIENTEXTE zur marxistisch-leninistischen Ethik; [edited by Günter Junghänel and Sigrid Tackmann]. Berlin, 1976. pp. 356.

THERBORN (G:RAN) Science, class and society: on the formation of sociology and historical materialism. London, [1976]. pp. 461. *bibliog.*

WESSON (ROBERT GALE) Why Marxism?: the continuing success of a failed theory. New York, [1976]. pp. 281.

KEL'DIEV (IMOMNAZAR) Izdanie i rasprostranenie proizvedenii klassikov marksizma-leninizma v Tadzhikistane. Dushanbe, 1973. pp. 190.

SARALIEVA (ZARETKHAN KHADZHI-MURZAEVNA) "Kapital" K. Marksa i rabochee dvizhenie Rossii, 1895-1917 gg. : rasprostranenie i propaganda. Moskva, 1975. pp. 211. *bibliog.*

MARYLAND

— Constitutional history.

YAZAWA (MELVIN) ed. Representative government and the revolution: the Maryland constitutional crisis of 1787. Baltimore, [1975]. pp. 187. *(Maryland Bicentennial Commission. Maryland Bicentennial Studies)*

— Population.

MARYLAND. Department of State Planning. Division of Research Programs. 1971. Maryland population, 1930-1970, by election districts, cities and towns. Baltimore, 1971. pp. 102. *(Department of State Planning. Publications. No. 171)*

MASAI.

TIGNOR (ROBERT L.) The colonial transformation of Kenya: the Kamba, Kikuyu, and Maasai from 1900 to 1939. Princeton, [1976]. pp. 372. *bibliog.*

MASARYK (JAN).

ZEMAN (ZBYNĚK ANTHONY BOHUSLAV) The Masaryks: the making of Czechoslovakia. London, [1976]. pp. 230.

MASARYK (THOMAS GARRIGUE).

MASARYK (THOMAS GARRIGUE) Masaryk erzählt sein Leben: Gespräche mit Karel Čapek; (aus dem Tschechischen übersetzt von Camill Hoffmann). Zürich, [1936?]. pp. 340.

BELD (ANTONIE VAN DEN) Humanity: the political and social philosophy of Thomas G. Masaryk. The Hague, [1975]. pp. 162. *bibliog.*

MASARYK (THOMAS GARRIGUE).(Cont.)

ZEMAN (ZBYNĚK ANTHONY BOHUSLAV) The Masaryks: the making of Czechoslovakia. London, [1976]. pp. 230.

MASIUTKO (MYKHAILO SAVOVYCH).

UKRAÏNS'KA inteligentsiia pid sudom KGB: materiialy z protsesiv V. Chornovola, M. Masiutka, M. Ozernoho ta in.; Ukrainian intellectuals tried by the KGB. [Miunkhen], 1970. pp. 243.

MASS MEDIA

— Political aspects.

SCHATZ-BERGFELD (MARIANNE) Massenkommunikation und Herrschaft: zur Rolle von Massenkommunikation als Steuerungselement moderner demokratischer Gesellschaften. Meisenheim am Glan, [1974]. pp. 276. *bibliog.*

CHAFFEE (STEVEN H.) ed. Political communication: issues and strategies for research. Beverly Hills, [1975]. pp. 319. *bibliogs.*

— — Bibliography.

GERMANY (BUNDESREPUBLIK). Deutscher Bundestag. Wissenschaftliche Dienste. 1974. Medienfreiheit, Pressekonzentration, Presserechtsrahmengesetz: Auswahlbibliographie mit Annotationen; [compiled by Claus- Peter Gerber]. Bonn, 1974. pp. 107. *(Bibliographien. 38)*

— — Germany.

SCHATZ-BERGFELD (MARIANNE) Massenkommunikation und Herrschaft: zur Rolle von Massenkommunikation als Steuerungselement moderner demokratischer Gesellschaften. Meisenheim am Glan, [1974]. pp. 276. *bibliog.*

— Psychological aspects.

CHAFFEE (STEVEN H.) and PETRICK (MICHAEL J.) Using the mass media: communication problems in American society. New York, [1975]. pp. 264. *bibliogs.*

— Social aspects.

DAVIS (ROBERT EDWARD) Response to innovation: a study of popular argument about new mass media. New York, 1976. pp. 725. *bibliog. Dissertation (Ph.D.) - University of Iowa, 1965.*

— — India.

MISHRA (VISHWA MOHAN) Communication and modernization in urban slums. New York, [1972]. pp. 128. *bibliog.*

— — United States.

CHAFFEE (STEVEN H.) and PETRICK (MICHAEL J.) Using the mass media: communication problems in American society. New York, [1975]. pp. 264. *bibliogs.*

— Australia.

AUSTRALIA. Department of the Media. Planning and Research Section. 1974. A study of interlocking patterns of ownership and control in Australian media industries: initial progress report. [Canberra], 1974. fo. (38).

— Belgium.

BOL (JEAN MARIE VAN) Social communications media in Belgium. Brussels, Ministry of Foreign Affairs, External Trade and Cooperation in Development, 1975. pp. 119. *bibliog. (Memo from Belgium. No. 169)*

— Europe, Eastern.

INTERNATIONAL SLAVIC CONFERENCE, 1ST, BANFF, ALBERTA, 1974. Education and the mass media in the Soviet Union and Eastern Europe; [selected papers from the conference]; edited by Bohdan Harasymiw. New York, 1976. pp. 131.

— Norway.

BERG (MIE) ed. Massemedier i Norge: en artikkelsamling...; bidrag av Svennik Høyer [and others]. Oslo, 1975. pp. 361. *bibliog.*

— Russia.

INTERNATIONAL SLAVIC CONFERENCE, 1ST, BANFF, ALBERTA, 1974. Education and the mass media in the Soviet Union and Eastern Europe; [selected papers from the conference]; edited by Bohdan Harasymiw. New York, 1976. pp. 131.

— United Kingdom.

NATIONAL UNION OF STUDENTS. Student unions and the media: an N.U.S. guide to the relationship between student representatives and the communications media. London, [1975]. pp. 18.

— United States.

CONCENTRATION of mass media ownership: assessing the state of current knowledge...; [by] Walter S. Baer [and others]. Santa Monica, 1974. pp. 202. *bibliog. (Rand Corporation. [Rand Reports]. 1584)*

OWEN (BRUCE M.) Economics and freedom of expression: media structure and the first amendment. Cambridge, Mass., [1975]. pp. 202. *bibliog.*

MASS MEDIA AND RACE PROBLEMS

— United Kingdom.

HUSBAND (CHARLES H.) ed. White media and black Britain: a critical look at the role of the media in race relations today. London, 1975. pp. 222. *bibliogs.*

MASS SOCIETY.

MOSSE (GEORGE L.) The nationalization of the masses: political symbolism and mass movements in Germany from the Napoleonic wars through the Third Reich. New York, 1975. pp. 252.

GINER (SALVADOR) Mass society. London, [1976]. pp. 288. *bibliog.*

MASSACHUSETTS

— Politics and government.

ZEMSKY (ROBERT) Merchants, farmers, and river gods: an essay on eighteenth-century American politics. Boston. 1971. pp. 361. *bibliog.*

MASSIE (ROBERT) the Younger.

MASSIE (ROBERT K.) and MASSIE (SUZANNE) Journey. London, 1975. pp. 417.

MASSIE (ROBERT K.).

MASSIE (ROBERT K.) and MASSIE (SUZANNE) Journey. London, 1975. pp. 417.

MASSIE (SUZANNE).

MASSIE (ROBERT K.) and MASSIE (SUZANNE) Journey. London, 1975. pp. 417.

MASTER AND SERVANT

— United Kingdom.

The LAW of master and servant. London, [1909]. pp. 15.

MATABELE.

BECKER (PETER) of Johannesburg. Path of blood: the rise and conquests of Mzilikazi, founder of the Matabele tribe of Southern Africa. London, 1962 repr. 1976. pp. 289. *bibliog.*

MATERA (PROVINCE)

— Economic conditions.

CONVEGNO SULLE PROSPETTIVE DI SVILUPPO ECONOMICO DELLA PROVINCIA DI MATERA NEL QUADRO DELLA PROGRAMMAZIONE ECONOMICA, MATERA, 1967. Convegno sulle prospettive di sviluppo economico...: [proceedings]. [Matera, 1967]. pp. 200.

MATERIALISM.

TIMPANARO (SEBASTIANO) On materialism. London, 1975. pp. 260.

MATERNAL AND INFANT WELFARE

— Denmark.

WAGNER (MARSDEN) and WAGNER (MARY) The Danish national child-care system: a successful system as model for the reconstruction of American child care. Boulder, Co., 1976. pp. 183.

— Sweden.

WALLACE (HELEN M.) ed. Health care of mothers and children in national health services: implication[s] for the United States. Cambridge, Mass., [1975]. pp. 325. *bibliogs.*

— United Kingdom.

WALLACE (HELEN M.) ed. Health care of mothers and children in national health services: implication[s] for the United States. Cambridge, Mass., [1975]. pp. 325. *bibliogs.*

MATERNITY LEAVE

— Canada.

CANADA. Women's Bureau. 1969. Maternity leave policies: a survey. Ottawa, 1969. pp. 137. *In English and French.*

MATHEMATICAL ANALYSIS.

ROYDEN (H.L.) Real analysis. 2nd ed. New York, [1968]. pp. 349. *bibliog.*

CHOQUET (GUSTAVE) Lectures on analysis;...edited by J. Marsden [and others]. Reading, Mass., 1969, repr. 1976. 3 vols. *bibliog.*

MATHEMATICAL MODELS.

CHANGE (CHEN CHUNG) and KEISLER (H. JEROME) Model theory. Amsterdam, 1973. pp. 550. *bibliog.*

MATHEMATICAL OPTIMIZATION.

BOL (GEORG) Stetigkeit und Effizienz bei mengenwertigen Produktionsfunktionen. Meisenheim am Glan, [1973]. pp. 73. *bibliog.*

SPREMANN (KLAUS) and GESSNER (PETER) Konstruktive Optimierung dynamischer und stochastischer Prozesse. Meisenheim am Glan, [1973]. pp. 120. *bibliog.*

CONRAD (KLAUS) of the University of Tübingen. Simulation und Optimierung mit einem nichtlinearen ökonometrischen Makromodell für die Bundesrepublik Deutschland. Meisenheim am Glan, 1975. pp. 398. *bibliog.*

SYLWESTROWICZ (JERZY DOWOYNA) Numerical optimization of non-linear functions of several variables using random search techniques; [Ph.D.(London) thesis]. 1975. fo. 185. *bibliog. Typescript: unpublished. This thesis is the property of London University and may not be removed from the Library.*

DIXIT (AVINASH K.) Optimization in economic theory. London, 1976. pp. 134. *bibliogs.*

MATHEMATICS.

HOLDEN (K.) and PEARSON (A.W.) Mathematics for economists. Newton Abbot, [1975]. pp. 338. *bibliog.*

— Philosophy.

FOR Dirk Struik: scientific, historical and political essays in honor of Dirk J. Struik; edited by R.S. Cohen [and others] . Dordrecht, [1974]. pp. 652. bibliogs. (Boston Colloquium for the Philosophy of Science. Boston Studies in the Philosophy of Science. vol.15)

PUTNAM (HILARY) Philosophical papers. Cambridge, 1975. 2 vols. bibliogs.

LAKATOS (IMRE) Proofs and refutations: the logic of mathematical discovery; edited by John Worrall and Elie Zahar. Cambridge, 1976. pp. 174. bibliog.

WITTGENSTEIN (LUDWIG) Lectures on the foundations of mathematics, Cambridge, 1939, from the notes of R.G. Bosanquet [and others]; edited by Cora Diamond. Ithaca, N.Y., 1976. pp. 300.

MATRICES.

HILTON (GORDON) Intermediate politometrics. New York, 1976. pp. 282. bibliogs.

MATRIMONIAL ACTIONS

— United Kingdom.

JACKSON (JOSEPH) Matrimonial finance and taxation; second edition by J. Jackson and D.T.A. Davies. London, 1975. pp. 397.

MATRIX INVERSION.

BOULLION (THOMAS L.) and ODELL (PATRICK L.) Generalized inverse matrices. New York, [1971]. pp. 103. bibliog.

RAO (CALYAMPUDI RADHAKRISHNA) and MITRA (SUJIT KUMAR) Generalized inverse of matrices and its applications. New York, [1971]. pp. 240. bibliog.

BEN-ISRAEL (ADI) and GREVILLE (THOMAS NALL EDEN) Generalized inverses: theory and applications. New York, [1974]. pp. 395. bibliogs.

MATZNETTER (OTTO).

EUROPEAN COURT OF HUMAN RIGHTS. Publications. Series A: Judgments and Decisions. [A10]. ..."Matznetter" case; judgment of 10th November 1969. Strasbourg, Council of Europe, 1969. pp. 50 [bis]. In English and French.

EUROPEAN COURT OF HUMAN RIGHTS. Publications. Series B: Pleadings. Oral Arguments and Documents. [B8]. "Matznetter" case, (1967-1969). Strasbourg, Council of Europe, 1970. pp. 255 [bis], 257-291. In English and French.

MAURIN (JOAQUIN).

MAURIN (JOAQUIN) En las prisiones de Franco. Mexico, [1974]. pp. 213.

MAURITIUS.

PERSPECTIVE: reflet de l'actualité mauricienne: [pd. by Ministry of Information and Broadcasting]. m., current issue only [Port Louis].

— Economic conditions.

MAURITIUS. Ministry of Economic Planning and Development. 1973. Mauritius economic survey, 1970-72. [Port Louis], 1973. pp. 108.

DURAND (JEAN PIERRE) and DURAND (JOYCE) L'Ile Maurice, quelle indépendance?: la reproduction des rapports de production capitalistes dans une formation sociale dominée. Paris, [1975]. pp. 254.

— Economic policy.

MAURITIUS. Ministry of Economic Planning and Development. 1973. Mauritius economic survey, 1970-72. [Port Louis], 1973. pp. 108.

— Nationalism.

DURAND (JEAN PIERRE) and DURAND (JOYCE) L'Ile Maurice, quelle indépendance?: la reproduction des rapports de production capitalistes dans une formation sociale dominée. Paris, [1975]. pp. 254.

— Officials and employees — Salaries, allowances, etc.

MAURITIUS. Salaries Commission. 1973. Report; [P.C.M. Sedgwick, commissioner]. Port Louis, 1973. pp. 350.

MAURITIUS. Para-Statal Salaries Commission. 1974. Report; [Donald Chesworth, chairman]. Port Louis, 1974. pp. 165.

— Social conditions.

DURAND (JEAN PIERRE) and DURAND (JOYCE) L'Ile Maurice, quelle indépendance?: la reproduction des rapports de production capitalistes dans une formation sociale dominée. Paris, [1975]. pp. 254.

MAYAS.

SOLANO Y PEREZ-LILA (FRANCISCO DE) Los Mayas del siglo XVIII: pervivencia y transformacion de la sociedad indigena guatemalteca durante la administracion borbonica. Madrid, 1974. pp. 483. bibliog.

MAYORS

— United States.

KOTTER (JOHN P.) and LAWRENCE (PAUL ROGER) Mayors in action: five approaches to urban governance. New York, [1974]. pp. 287. bibliog.

COLE (LEONARD A.) Blacks in power: a comparative study of black and white elected officials. Princeton, [1976]. pp. 267.

MAZAHUA INDIANS.

ARIZPE-SCHLOSSER (LOURDES) Migration and ethnicity: the Mazahua Indians of Mexico. 1975. fo. 386. bibliog. Typescript. Ph.D.(London) thesis: unpublished. This thesis is the property of London University and may not be removed from the Library.

MAZZINI (GIUSEPPE).

ACCADEMIA NAZIONALE DEI LINCEI. Problemi Attuali di Scienza e di Cultura. Quaderni. N.201. Atti del Convegno sul tema: Mazzini e l'Europa, Roma, 9-10 novembre 1972. Roma, 1974. pp. 127.

SANTONASTASO (GIUSEPPE) and RALLI (MARCELLO) eds. Il pensiero e l'opera politica di G. Mazzini: testi antologici da A. Comba [and others]. Messina, 1975. pp. 401. bibliog.

MBUNDU (AFRICAN PEOPLE).

MILLER (JOSEPH C.) Kings and kinsmen: early Mbundu states in Angola. Oxford, 1976. pp. 312. bibliog.

MEAD (GEORGE HERBERT).

HANSEN (DONALD ANDREW) An invitation to critical sociology: involvement, criticism, exploration. New York, [1976]. pp. 258. bibliog.

MEANING.

MORAVCSIK (J.M.E.) ed. Logic and philosophy for linguists: a book of readings. The Hague, [1974]. pp. 347. bibliogs.

CAMBRIDGE COLLOQUIUM ON FORMAL SEMANTICS OF NATURAL LANGUAGE, 1973. Formal semantics of natural language: papers from [the] colloquium sponsored by the King's College Research Centre, Cambridge; edited by Edward L. Keenan. Cambridge, 1975. pp. 475. bibliogs.

OSGOOD (CHARLES EGERTON) and others. Cross-cultural universals of affective meaning. Urbana, [1975]. pp. 486. bibliog.

MEANING (PHILOSOPHY).

POLANYI (MICHAEL) and PROSCH (HARRY) Meaning. Chicago, 1975. pp. 246. bibliog.

MEAT

— Prices — Australia.

AUSTRALIA. Parliament. Joint Committee on Prices. 1973. Stabilisation of meat prices; report; [C.J. Hurford, chairman]. Canberra, 1973. fo.(49).

MEAT INDUSTRY AND TRADE

— Australia.

AUSTRALIA. Bureau of Agricultural Economics. 1970. Household meat consumption in Melbourne. Canberra, 1970. pp. 105. (Beef Research Reports. No. 8)

AUSTRALIA. Bureau of Agricultural Economics. 1973. Statistical handbook of the meat industry. Canberra, 1973. pp. 112.

AUSTRALIA. Bureau of Agricultural Economics. 1975. Statistical handbook of the meat industry. 2nd ed. Canberra, 1975. pp. (152).

MECHLIN

— History.

MAES (LOUIS THEO) The Parliament and Great Council of Malines, 1473-1796, an institution of a European dimension. Brussels, Ministry of Foreign Affairs, External Trade and Cooperation in Development, 1973. pp. 32. (Memo from Belgium. No. 160)

MEDIATION, INTERNATIONAL.

RAMAN (K. VENKATA) The ways of the peacemaker: a study of United Nations intermediary assistance in the peaceful settlement of disputes. New York, United Nations Institute for Training and Research, 1975. pp. 142. bibliog. (Peaceful Settlement Series. No. 8)

MEDIATION AND CONCILIATION, INDUSTRIAL

— Australia.

AUSTRALIA. Department of Labour and National Service. 1971. Conciliation and Arbitration Act: ministerial statement by the Minister for Labour and National Service. [Canberra], 1971. fo. 31.

AUSTRALIA. Committee of Inquiry on Co-ordinated Industrial Organisations. 1974. Report; [John Bernard Sweeney, chairman]. Canberra, 1974. pp. 59.

— United Kingdom.

WIGHAM (ERIC LEONARD) Strikes and the government, 1893-1974. London, 1976. pp. 206. bibliog.

MEDICAL CARE.

HUMANIZING health care: [including papers presented at a symposium in San Francisco, 1972; edited by] Jan Howard [and] Anselm Strauss. New York, [1975]. pp. 326.

INTERNATIONAL CONGRESS OF ANTHROPOLOGICAL AND ETHNOLOGICAL SCIENCES. 9th Congress, 1973. Topias and utopias in health: policy studies: [papers from the Congress]; editor[s] Stanley R. Ingman, Anthony E. Thomas. The Hague, [1975]. pp. 548. bibliogs.

MILIO (NANCY) The care of health in communities: access for outcasts. New York, [1976]. pp. 402.

SUONOJA (KYÖSTI) and others. Terveydenhuollon tavoitteet ja painopisteet: eräiden maiden terveyspoliittisten suunitelmien tarkastelua, etc. Helsinki, 1975. pp. 163. bibliog. (Finland. Suomen Virallinen Tilasto. Finlands Officiella Statistik. 32. Sosiaalisia Erikoistutkimuksia. 43) With English summary.

WILSON (MICHAEL) Health is for people. London, 1975. pp. 134.

MEDICAL CARE.(Cont.)

ABEL-SMITH (BRIAN) Value for money in health services: a comparative study. London, 1976. pp. 230.

DONABEDIAN (AVEDIS) Benefits in medical care programs. Cambridge, Mass., 1976. pp. 436.

MECHANIC (DAVID) The growth of bureaucratic medicine: an inquiry into the dynamics of patient behavior and the organization of medical care. New York, [1976]. pp. 345.

WORLD HEALTH ORGANIZATION/INTERNATIONAL COLLABORATIVE STUDY OF MEDICAL CARE UTILIZATION. 1976. Health care: an international study;...edited by Robert Kohn and Kerr L. White; with a foreword by Robert T. Bridgman. London, 1976. pp. 557. bibliog.

— Canada — Ontario.

ONTARIO. Economic Council. 1976. Health: issues and alternatives, 1976. [Toronto], 1976. pp. 54.

— China.

HEALTH care in China: an introduction; the report of a [Christian Medical Commission] study group in Hongkong; E. H. Paterson, chairman. Geneva, 1974. pp. 140. bibliog.

— Europe.

BLANPAIN (JAN) and DELESIE (LUK) Community health investment: health services research in Belgium, France, Federal German Republic and the Netherlands;... edited by Gordon McLachlan. Oxford, 1976. pp. 474. bibliogs.

— Germany.

LAEPPLE (FRIEDEL) Profit durch Krankheit?: das Gesundheitswesen aus Arbeitnehmersicht. Bonn-Bad Godesberg, [1975]. pp. 262. bibliog.

— Germany, Eastern.

HARMSEN (HANS) ed. Gesundheitspolitische Probleme und Lösungen in der DDR und UdSSR. Hamburg, 1976. pp. 98.

— Ghana.

GHANA. Ministry of Health. 1971. Ghana medical facilities. [Accra, 1971]. pp. 28.

— Ireland (Republic).

A REVIEW of Irish health services; seminar proceedings; held in Waterford 15th-17th May, 1975. [Dublin], Department of Health, 1975. pp. 86.

— Russia.

HARMSEN (HANS) ed. Gesundheitspolitische Probleme und Lösungen in der DDR und UdSSR. Hamburg, 1976. pp. 98.

— Switzerland.

GYGI (PIERRE) and HENNY (HEINER) Das schweizerische Gesundheitswesen: Aufwand, Struktur und Preisbildung im Pflegebereich: (Le secteur sanitaire suisse, etc.). Bern, [1976]. pp. 96,96. In German and French.

— Underdeveloped areas.

See UNDERDEVELOPED AREAS — Medical care.

— United States.

ACTON (JAN PAUL) Evaluating public programs to save lives: the case of heart attacks. Santa Monica, 1973. pp. 136. bibliog. (Rand Corporation. [Rand Reports]. 950)

NATIONAL HEALTH FORUM, 1973. The changing role of the public and private sectors in health care: report of the...forum of the National Health Council; editors Neil Hollander [and] Robert G. Joyce. New York, [1973]. pp. 150.

SHENKIN (BUDD N.) Health care for migrant workers: policies and politics. Cambridge, Mass., [1974]. pp. 270.

WAITZKIN (HOWARD B.) and WATERMAN (BARBARA) The exploitation of illness in capitalist society. Indianapolis, [1974 repr. 1976]. pp. 133. bibliog.

CARLSON (RICK J.) The end of medicine. New York, [1975]. pp. 290. bibliog.

LEHMAN (EDWARD W.) Coordinating health care: explorations in interorganizational relations. Beverly Hills, [1975]. pp. 251. bibliogs. (Center for Policy Research, Inc. Policy Research Series)

RUSHMER (ROBERT FRAZER) Humanizing health care: alternative futures for medicine. Cambridge, Mass., [1975]. pp. 210. bibliogs.

DONABEDIAN (AVEDIS) Benefits in medical care programs. Cambridge, Mass., 1976. pp. 436.

GREENE (RICHARD) Assuring quality in medical care: the state of the art. Cambridge, Mass., [1976]. pp. 293.

MECHANIC (DAVID) The growth of bureaucratic medicine: an inquiry into the dynamics of patient behavior and the organization of medical care. New York, [1976]. pp. 345.

— — Utilization.

The HEALTH gap: medical services and the poor; edited by Robert L. Kane [and others]. New York, [1976]. pp. 321. bibliog.

— Vietnam.

McMICHAEL (JOAN KATHERINE) ed. Health in the third world: studies from Vietnam. Nottingham, [1976]. pp. 341.

MEDICAL CARE, COST OF.

The HEALTH care cost explosion: which way now?; edited by David Alan Ehrlich; based on a symposium in Geneva organized by the Henry Dunant Institute. Bern, [1975]. pp. 250.

— Canada — Ontario.

FRASER (RODERICK DOUGLAS) A research agenda in health care economics. Toronto, Ontario Economic Council, 1975. 1 vol. (various pagings). (Ontario. Economic Council. Working Papers. 1975. No. 3)

— France.

ECONOMIE ET SANTE: supplément au Bulletin des statistiques de santé et de sécurité sociale; [pd. by] Ministère de la Santé Publique et de la Sécurité Sociale [France]. irreg., Mr 1972 (1)- Paris.

— Russia.

GOLOVTEEV (VIKTOR VASIL'EVICH) and others. Osnovy ekonomiki sovetskogo zdravookhraneniia. Moskva, 1974. pp. 199.

MEDICAL CENTRES

— United Kingdom.

SOCIALIST MEDICAL ASSOCIATION. Health centres: the next step. Birmingham, [1975?]. pp. 20. bibliog.

MEDICAL COOPERATION.

LEHMAN (EDWARD W.) Coordinating health care: explorations in interorganizational relations. Beverly Hills, [1975]. pp. 251. bibliogs. (Center for Policy Research, Inc. Policy Research Series)

MEDICAL ECONOMICS.

SORKIN (ALAN L.) Health economics: an introduction. Lexington, Mass., [1975]. pp. 205.

WARD (RICHARD ALEXANDER) The economics of health resources. Reading, Mass., [1975]. pp. 150.

— Canada.

SUN VALLEY FORUM ON NATIONAL HEALTH. Symposium, 4th, 1974. National health insurance: can we learn from Canada?: (a volume on current health care issues from the Sun Valley Forum) ; edited by Spyros Andreopoulos. New York, [1975]. pp. 273.

— Switzerland.

GYGI (PIERRE) and HENNY (HEINER) Das schweizerische Gesundheitswesen: Aufwand, Struktur und Preisbildung im Pflegebereich: (Le secteur sanitaire suisse, etc.). Bern, [1976]. pp. 96,96. In German and French.

— United States.

REINHARDT (UWE E.) Physician productivity and the demand for health manpower. Cambridge, Mass., [1975]. pp. 311. bibliog.

SORKIN (ALAN L.) Health economics: an introduction. Lexington, Mass., [1975]. pp. 205.

DONABEDIAN (AVEDIS) Benefits in medical care programs. Cambridge, Mass., 1976. pp. 436.

MEDICAL FEES

— Canada.

CANADA. Department of National Health and Welfare. Health Economics and Statistics Directorate. Health Care Series. [Memoranda]. No. 29. Earnings of physicians in Canada, 1960-1970. [Ottawa, 1971]. pp. 45.

MEDICAL INNOVATIONS

— United States.

The DIFFUSION of medical technology: policy and research planning perspectives; edited by Gerald Gordon [and] G. Lawrence Fisher. Cambridge, Mass., [1975]. pp. 210. bibliog. Based on a conference held at Cornell University in September 1972, and sponsored by the National Institutes of Health.

MEDICAL PERSONNEL

— United States.

REINHARDT (UWE E.) Physician productivity and the demand for health manpower. Cambridge, Mass., [1975]. pp. 311. bibliog.

MEDICAL POLICY

— United States.

The DIFFUSION of medical technology: policy and research planning perspectives; edited by Gerald Gordon [and] G. Lawrence Fisher. Cambridge, Mass., [1975]. pp. 210. bibliog. Based on a conference held at Cornell University in September 1972, and sponsored by the National Institutes of Health.

MEDICAL RESEARCH

— United States.

The DIFFUSION of medical technology: policy and research planning perspectives; edited by Gerald Gordon [and] G. Lawrence Fisher. Cambridge, Mass., [1975]. pp. 210. bibliog. Based on a conference held at Cornell University in September 1972, and sponsored by the National Institutes of Health.

MEDICINE.

CARLSON (RICK J.) The end of medicine. New York, [1975]. pp. 290. bibliog.

— History.

IMHOF (ARTHUR ERWIN) and LARSEN (ØIVIND) Sozialgeschichte und Medizin: Probleme der quantifizierenden Quellenbearbeitung in der Sozial- und Medizingeschichte. Oslo, 1975. pp. 322. bibliog.

— **Information services.**

INTERNATIONAL SYMPOSIUM ON COMPUTERS IN MEDICINE, 2ND, BLACKBURN, 1971. Computers in medicine: proceedings...; edited by J. Rose. [Bristol], 1972. pp. 166. *bibliogs.*

— **Specialities and specialists — United States.**

RUSHING (WILLIAM A.) Community, physicians and inequality: a sociological study of the maldistribution of physicians. Lexington, Mass., [1975]. pp. 255. *bibliog.*

— **Study and teaching — Poland.**

MROZOWSKA (KAMILLA) Józef Maciej Brodowicz: z dziejów organizacji nauki i nauczania w Wolnym Mieście Krakowie. Wrocław, 1971. pp. 352. *bibliog.* (Polska Akademia Nauk. Zakład Historii Nauki i Techniki. *Monografie z Dziejów Nauki i Techniki. t.73*) With Russian and English summaries.

— **United Kingdom.**

PARRY (NOEL) and PARRY (JOSÉ) The rise of the medical profession: a study of collective social mobility. London, [1976]. pp. 282. *bibliog.*

MEDICINE, PREVENTIVE.

GOTTLIEB (MANUEL) The problem of goiter in Tanzania: a programme for prevention by salt iodization and a programme for improved salt marketing in Tanzania. Dar es Salaam, 1973. pp. 42. *bibliog.* (Dar es Salaam. University. Economic Research Bureau. *ERB Papers. 73.6*)

MEDICINE, PSYCHOSOMATIC.

INSEL (PAUL M.) and MOOS (RUDOLF H.) eds. Health and the social environment. Lexington, Mass., [1974]. pp. 460. *bibliogs.*

MEDICINE, RURAL

— **India.**

DJURFELDT (GÖRAN) and LINDBERG (STAFFAN) Pills against poverty: a study of the introduction of western medicine in a Tamil village. Lund, 1975. pp. 232. *bibliog.* (Scandinavian Institute of Asian Studies. *Monograph Series. No. 23*)

— **Tanzania.**

ETTEN (GEERT M. VAN) Rural health development in Tanzania: a case-study of medical sociology in a developing country. Assen, 1976. pp. 181. *bibliog.*

MEDICINE, STATE

— **France.**

FRANCE. Commission de la Santé et l'Assurance Maladie. 1976. Rapport...: préparation du 7e Plan. Paris, 1976. pp. 239.

— **Russia.**

GOLOVTEEV (VIKTOR VASIL'EVICH) and others. Osnovy ekonomiki sovetskogo zdravookhraneniia. Moskva, 1974. pp. 199.

— **Sweden.**

WALLACE (HELEN M.) ed. Health care of mothers and children in national health services: implication[s] for the United States. Cambridge, Mass., [1975]. pp. 325. *bibliogs.*

— **Tanzania.**

GISH (OSCAR) Planning the health sector: the Tanzanian experience. London, 1975. pp. 209.

— **United Kingdom.**

COMMUNIST PARTY OF GREAT BRITAIN. The N[ational] H[ealth] S[ervice] Co. Ltd.; notes on the health service reorganisation. [London, 1972?]. pp. 16.

HEALTH services in new towns; report of Working Group II: planning health services in new communities: the technical problems; [P.A. Draper, chairman]. [London, Department of Health and Social Security, 1972?]. pp. 47. *bibliog.*

BROWN (MALCOLM J.) and BURNETT (MARGARET E.) The health and personal social services: problems of working together. Birmingham, [1974]. pp. 8.

HULL. University. Institute for Health Studies. Humberside Reorganisation Project. [Interim Reports. 4] New bottles: old wine?; [by] R.G.S. Brown [and others]. Hull, 1975. pp. 125.

NHS reorganisation: issues and prospects: [a series of lectures given by staff of the Nuffield Centre for Health Services Studies at the University of Leeds], Donald Macmillan [and others]; edited...by Keith Barnard and Kenneth Lee. Leeds, [1975]. pp. 143.

U.K. Department of Health and Social Security. 1975. Guide to planning in the National Health Service; (draft). London, 1975. fo. 66.

U.K. National Health Service. Treasurers' Joint Accounting Committee. 1975. Problems of budgetary control in the reorganised National Health Service. rev. ed. Sheffield, 1975. fo. 13.

U.K. Resource Allocation Working Party. 1975. First interim report...: allocations to regions in 1976/77; [J.C. C. Smith, chairman]. [London], 1975. pp. 26.

WEST MIDLANDS REGIONAL HEALTH AUTHORITY. Strategy for health, 1976-1986: a consultative document. Birmingham, 1975. pp. 12.

U.K. Department of Health and Social Security. (Circulars): H.C. (F.P.) [Family Practitioner Services]. irreg., Ag 1976 (no.3)- London.

U.K. Department of Health and Social Security. [Circulars] H.C. [Health]. irreg., Ja 1976 (no.1)- London.

CULYER (ANTHONY J.) Need and the National Health Service: economics and social change. London, 1976. pp. 163. *bibliogs.*

FABIAN SOCIETY. Fabian Tracts. [No.] 440. N[ational] H[ealth] S[ervice] revisited; [by] Barbara Castle. London, 1976. pp. 12. (Nye Bevan Memorial Lectures. *1975*)

LEVITT (RUTH) The reorganised National Health Service. London, 1976. pp. 251.

SOCIOLOGICAL REVIEW, THE; [published by] University of Keele. Monographs. [No.] 22. The sociology of the National Health Service; issue editor, Margaret Stacey. Keele, 1976. pp. 200. *bibliogs.*

U.K. Department of Health and Social Security. 1976. Financial allocations to regional health authorities, 1976/77. London, 1976. fo. 5.

U.K. Department of Health and Social Security. 1976. The N[ational] H[ealth] S[ervice] planning system. [London], 1976. pp. 54.

U.K. Department of Health and Social Security. 1976. Priorities for health and personal social services in England: a consultative document. London, H.M.S.O., 1976. pp. 83.

WALLACE (HELEN M.) ed. Health care of mothers and children in national health services: implication[s] for the United States. Cambridge, Mass., [1975]. pp. 325. *bibliogs.*

— — **Ireland, Northern.**

IRELAND, NORTHERN. Department of Health and Social Services 1975. Strategy for the development of health and personal social services in Northern Ireland. Belfast, 1975. pp. 43.

— — **Scotland.**

SCOTTISH HEALTH SERVICE PLANNING COUNCIL. Report. a, 1974 (1st)- Edinburgh.

— — **Wales.**

HEALTH SERVICES WALES...: report of the Chief Medical Officer; (pd. by) Welsh Office. a., 1974(1st)- Cardiff.

U.K. Welsh Office. Health and Social Work Department. 1975. Health service planning: a short guide. [Cardiff, 1975]. pp. 19.

— **United States.**

HOLAHAN (JOHN) Financing health care for the poor: the Medicaid experience. Lexington, Mass., [1975]. pp. 152. *bibliog.*

DONABEDIAN (AVEDIS) Benefits in medical care programs. Cambridge, Mass., 1976. pp. 436.

MEDICINE AS A PROFESSION.

BERLANT (JEFFREY LIONEL) Profession and monopoly: a study of medicine in the United States and Great Britain. Berkeley, [1975]. pp. 337. *bibliog.*

MEDITERRANEAN

— **Commerce.**

SCHÉMA général d'aménagement de la France: regard prospectif sur le Bassin Méditerranéen; [report of a working group]. Paris, 1973. pp. 138. (France. Délégation à l'Aménagement du Territoire et à l'Action Régionale. *Travaux et Recherches de Prospective. 41*)

— **Economic conditions.**

SCHÉMA général d'aménagement de la France: regard prospectif sur le Bassin Méditerranéen; [report of a working group]. Paris, 1973. pp. 138. (France. Délégation à l'Aménagement du Territoire et à l'Action Régionale. *Travaux et Recherches de Prospective. 41*)

— **Foreign relations — United Kingdom.**

PRATT (LAWRENCE R.) East of Malta, west of Suez: Britain's Mediterranean crisis, 1936-1939. Cambridge, 1975. pp. 215. *bibliog.*

MEDVEDEV (ZHORES ALEKSANDROVICH).

MEDVEDEV (ZHORES ALEKSANDROVICH) Secrecy of correspondence is guaranteed by law. Nottingham, [1975]. pp. 180. (Medvedev Papers. *vol. 2*)

MELONS.

KING (PATRICIA) The market for melons in selected western European countries. London, Tropical Products Institute, 1976. pp. 63. *bibliog.* ([Reports]. *G104*)

MEMORY.

BADDELEY (ALAN D.) The psychology of memory. New York, [1976]. pp. 430. *bibliog.*

MENDÈS-FRANCE (PIERRE).

MENDÈS-FRANCE (PIERRE) Face to face with Asia; translated from the French by Susan Danon. New York, [1974]. pp. 255.

MENGOTTI (FRANCESCO) Conte.

NUCCIO (OSCAR) Economisti italiani del XVIII secolo: Ferdinando Galiani, Antonio Genovesi, Pietro Verri, Francesco Mengotti. Roma, 1974. pp. 286.

MENNONITES IN CANADA.

EPP (FRANK H.) Mennonites in Canada, 1786-1920: the history of a separate people. Toronto, [1974] repr. 1975. pp. 480. *bibliog.*

MENNONITES IN KANSAS.

JUHNKE (JAMES C.) A people of two kingdoms: the political acculturation of the Kansas Mennonites. Newton, Kan., [1975]. pp. 215. *bibliog.*

MENSURATION.

MENSURATION.

CONFERENCE ON THE HISTORY OF QUANTIFICATION IN THE SCIENCES, NEW YORK, 1959. Quantification: a history of the meaning of measurement in the natural and social sciences; edited by Harry Woolf. Indianapolis, [1961]. pp. 222. *Papers from the conference organized by the Joint Committee on the History of Science of the Social Science Research Council and the National Research Council.*

MENTAL HEALTH LAWS

— United Kingdom.

GOSTIN (LARRY O.) A human condition: the Mental Health Act from 1959 to 1975: observations, analysis and proposals for reform...; edited by Anne Ross. [London, 1976 in progress]. *(National Association for Mental Health. Mind Special Reports)*

MENTAL HEALTH SERVICES

— Evaluation.

PROGRAM evaluation: alcohol, drug abuse, and mental health services; edited by Jack Zusman [and] Cecil R. Wurster. Lexington, Mass., [1975]. pp. 278. *Based on papers presented at a Conference sponsored by the Alcohol, Drug Abuse and Mental Health Administration held in Washington in 1974.*

NEW ENGLAND CONFERENCE ON EVALUATION OF MENTAL HEALTH SERVICES, 1ST, BOSTON, MASS., 1975. Trends in mental health evaluation: [papers from the conference; edited by] Elizabeth Warren Markson [and] David Franklyn Allen. Lexington, Mass., [1976]. pp. 150. *bibliogs.*

MENTAL HYGIENE.

SAUBER (S. RICHARD) Preventive educational intervention for mental health. Cambridge, Mass., [1973]. pp. 182. *bibliogs.*

— Canada.

CANADA'S MENTAL HEALTH: q. jl. of the Department of National Health and Welfare, (Mental Health Division). Q. oTTAWA. cURRENT ISSUES ONLY KEPT.

— New Zealand.

NEW ZEALAND. Department of Health. National Health Statistics Centre. Health statistics report: Mental health data. a., 1971- . Wellington. *Formerly included in NEW ZEALAND. Department of Health. National Health Statistics Centre. Health statistics report.*

— United States.

FELICETTI (DANIEL A.) Mental health and retardation politics: the mind lobbies in Congress. New York, 1975. pp. 199. *bibliog.*

MENTAL ILLNESS.

COLLINEAU ( ) Sécretaire général de la Société médico-pratique de Paris. Les commotions politiques dans leurs rapports avec l'aliénation;...mémoire lu à la société médico- pratique, séance du 26 juin 1872. Paris, [imprint], 1873. pp. 16.

— United Kingdom.

CLARKE (BASIL) Mental disorder in earlier Britain: exploratory studies. Cardiff, 1975. pp. 335. *bibliog.*

COMMUNITY RELATIONS COMMISSION. Mental health among minority ethnic groups: research summaries and bibliography. London, [1975]. 1 pamphlet(various pagings).

MENTALLY HANDICAPPED

— Employment — United Kingdom.

NATIONAL ASSOCIATION FOR MENTAL HEALTH. Mind Reports. No.8. Jobs: but not for the disabledc'. IONDON, 1972. FO. 8.

— Rehabilitation.

AMMINISTRAZIONE PER LE ATTIVITA ASSISTENZIALI ITALIANE E INTERNAZIONALI. Il laboratorio protetto. Roma, 1971. pp. 200. *bibliogs. (Sussidi Tecnici per i Servizi Sociali. 19)*

— Denmark.

KÖRMENDI (ESZTER) Psykisk handicappede: intelligenshaemmedes og udskrevne psykiatriske patienters sociale forhold, etc. København, 1975. pp. 256. *(Socialforskningsinstituttet. Publikationer.67) With English summaries.*

— United Kingdom.

NATIONAL ASSOCIATION FOR MENTAL HEALTH. Mind Reports. No. 11. Community care provisions for mentally ill and mentally handicapped men and women. London, 1973. fo. 9.

A WORKSHOP on participation; [organized by the Campaign for the Mentally Handicapped at Wallingford in 1973]. London, [1974]. pp. 29.

CAMPAIGN FOR THE MENTALLY HANDICAPPED and others. Hospital land: a resource for the future?. Bristol, 1975. pp. 10,4.

PEMBRIDGE INFORMATION EXCHANGE SESSIONS. 1st Series, London, 1973-74. New prospects for retarded citizens;...reports [of sessions].. .; editor, E.R. Tudor-Davies. London, [1975]. pp. 153. *bibliogs.*

U.K. Department of Health and Social Security. 1975. Mental handicap policy; text of Secretary of State's speech to the National Society for Mentally Handicapped Children's conference on mental handicap, deployment of resources on 26 February 1975. [London, 1975]. pp. 5.

— United States.

FELICETTI (DANIEL A.) Mental health and retardation politics: the mind lobbies in Congress. New York, 1975. pp. 199. *bibliog.*

The MENTALLY retarded and society: a social science perspective; edited by Michael J. Begab and Stephen A. Richardson. Baltimore, [1975]. pp. 492. *bibliogs. Proceedings of a conference held in Niles, Michigan, in 1974 and sponsored by the National Institute of Child Health and Human Development and the Rose F. Kennedy Center at Albert Einstein College of Medicine.*

MENTALLY HANDICAPPED CHILDREN

— Care and treatment — United Kingdom.

WOODS (GRACE E.) The handicapped child: assessment and management. Oxford, 1975. pp. 341. *bibliogs.*

— United Kingdom.

SHEARER (ANN) Fostering mentally handicapped children: is it feasible?. London, 1974. pp. 31. *(Campaign for the Mentally Handicapped. Enquiry Papers. No. 3)*

HANNAM (CHARLES) Parents and mentally handicapped children. Harmondsworth, 1975. pp. 128. *bibliog.*

SYMPOSIUM ON LEISURE TIME NEEDS OF THE RETARDED, LONDON, 1973. A philosophy of leisure in relation to the retarded; [inaugural address by Kenneth Solly and conclusions of the symposium organized by the National Society for Mentally Handicapped Children]. London, [1975?]. 1 pamphlet (unpaged).

— United States.

DEMPSEY (JOHN J.) ed. Community services for retarded children: the consumer provider relationship. Baltimore, [1975]. pp. 311. *bibliog.*

MENTALLY ILL

— Care and treatment — United Kingdom.

NATIONAL ASSOCIATION FOR MENTAL HEALTH. Mind Reports. No. 10. Patients' rights: the mentally disordered in hospital. London, [1973]. pp. 14.

NATIONAL ASSOCIATION FOR MENTAL HEALTH. Mind Reports. No. 11. Community care provisions for mentally ill and mentally handicapped men and women. London, 1973. fo. 9.

SHARP (VICTOR) Social control in the therapeutic community. Farnborough, Hants., [1975]. pp. 221. *bibliog.*

— Employment — United Kingdom.

NATIONAL ASSOCIATION FOR MENTAL HEALTH. Mind Reports. No.8. Jobs: but not for the disabledā'. lONDON, 1972. FO. 8.

— Rehabilitation.

BAUMAN (GERALD) and GRUNES (RUTH) Psychiatric rehabilitation in the ghetto: an educational approach. Lexington, Mass., [1974]. pp. 177. *bibliog.*

— — United Kingdom.

MENTAL illness in Kensington and Chelsea and Hammersmith 1970: an examination of the geographical distribution of psychiatric patients discharged to the Royal Borough of Kensington and Chelsea and the London Borough of Hammersmith; [by] Gerald Woolfson [and others]. London, 1973. pp. 37. *bibliog.*

— Denmark.

KÖRMENDI (ESZTER) Psykisk handicappede: intelligenshaemmedes og udskrevne psykiatriske patienters sociale forhold, etc. København, 1975. pp. 256. *(Socialforskningsinstituttet. Publikationer.67) With English summaries.*

MERCHANT MARINE

— France.

FRANCE. French Embassy, London. Service de Presse et d'Information. 1974. The French merchant navy. London, 1974. pp. 12. *(France: facts, figures. A/104/11/74)*

— Germany.

BROCKSTEDT (JUERGEN) Die Schiffahrts- und Handelsbeziehungen Schleswig-Holsteins nach Lateinamerika, 1815-1848. Köln, 1975. pp. 575. *bibliog. With summaries in English and French.*

— Italy.

NIEPHAUS (HEINZ THEO) Genuas Seehandel von 1746-1848: die Entwicklung der Handelsbeziehungen zur Iberischen Halbinsel, zu West- und Nordeuropa sowie den Überseegebieten. Köln, 1975. pp. 486. *bibliog. With summaries and tables of contents in Italian and English.*

— United States.

KILGOUR (JOHN G.) The U.S. merchant marine: national maritime policy and industrial relations. New York, 1975. pp. 231. *bibliog.*

MERCHANTS, BELGIAN.

MAERTINS (RENATE) Wertorientierungen und wirtschaftliches Erfolgsstreben mittelalterlicher Grosskaufleute: das Beispiel Gent im 13. Jahrhundert. Köln, 1976. pp. 356. *bibliog.*

MERCHANTS, BRITISH.

BRAUND (HAROLD ERNEST WILTON) Calling to mind: being some account of the first hundred years, 1870 to 1970, of Steel Brothers and Company Limited. Oxford, 1975. pp. 151. *bibliog.*

MERCHANTS, EUROPEAN.

LE GOFF (JACQUES) Marchands et banquiers du Moyen Âge. 5th ed. Paris, 1972. pp. 128. *bibliog.*

MERCHANTS, FRENCH.

CARRIERE (CHARLES) Négociants marseillais au XVIIIe siècle: contribution à l'étude des économies maritimes. [Marseilles, 1973]. 2 vols.

SCHNEIDER (JUERGEN) Handel und Unternehmer im französischen Brasiliengeschäft, 1815-1848: Versuch einer quantitativen Strukturanalyse. Köln, 1975. pp. 649. *bibliog.* *With table of contents and summaries in various languages.*

MERCHANTS, GERMAN.

PUST (DIETER) Politische Sozialgeschichte der Stadt Flensburg: Untersuchungen zur politischen Führungsschicht Flensburgs im 18. und 19. Jahrhundert. [Flensburg, 1975]. pp. 365. *bibliog.* (Flensburg. Gesellschaft für Flensburger Stadtgeschichte. Schriften. Nr.23)

REISSMANN (MARTIN) Die hamburgische Kaufmannschaft des 17. Jahrhunderts in sozialgeschichtlicher Sicht. Hamburg, 1975. pp. 447. *bibliog.* (Verein für Hamburgische Geschichte. Beiträge zur Geschichte Hamburgs. Band 4)

MERCHANTS, SCOTTISH.

DEVINE (T.M.) The tobacco lords: a study of the tobacco merchants of Glasgow and their trading activities c. 1740-90. Edinburgh, [1975]. pp. 209. *bibliog.*

MERLEAU-PONTY (MAURICE).

ARCHARD (DAVID WILLIAM) Existentialism and Marxism: a critical study of the political philosophy of Jean-Paul Sartre and Maurice Merleau-Ponty. 1976. fo. 333. *bibliog.* Typescript. Ph.D.(London) thesis: unpublished. *This thesis is the property of London University and may not be removed from the Library.*

MERSEYSIDE

— Transit systems.

U.K. Department of the Environment. 1975. Merseyside interchange experiments: passenger transport interchanges on Merseyside: demonstration programme results and conclusions;...summary of a report prepared by Peat Marwick Mitchell and Co for the Merseyside Passenger Transport Executive and the Department of the Environment. [London, 1975]. pp. 31.

MERTON (ROBERT KING).

COSER (LEWIS ALFRED) ed. The idea of social structure: papers in honor of Robert K. Merton. New York, [1975]. pp. 547. *bibliog.*

METAL TRADE

— Russia.

DARMANIAN (PETR EMMANUILOVICH) Zarevo nad martenami: ocherk. Volgograd, 1969. pp. 151. *bibliog.*

— Scandinavia.

HUMMEN (WILHELM) Die Auswirkungen der Erweiterung der EG auf Aussenhandel und Produktion der metallverarbeitenden Industrie in Schweden, Dänemark und Norwegen. Tübingen, 1976. pp. 263. *bibliog.*

METAL WORK

— United Kingdom.

READER (WILLIAM JOSEPH) Metal Box: a history;...research by Judy Slinn. London, 1976. pp. 256. *bibliog.*

METAL WORKERS

— Hong Kong.

HONG KONG. Machine Shop and Metal Working Industrial Committee. 1972. Minimum job standards and specifications for the principal jobs in the machine shop and metal working trades. Hong Kong, 1971 [or rather 1972]. pp. 100. *In English and Chinese.*

HONG KONG. Machine Shop and Metal Working Industrial Committee. 1974. Report...on the second manpower survey of the machine shop and metal working industry, 8th November - 4th December 1971. Hong Kong, 1973 [or rather 1974] pp. 110. *In English and Chinese.*

— Italy.

GHEZA (FRANCO) Cattolici e sindacato: un esperienza di base; la FIM-CISL di Brescia. Roma, 1975. pp. 266.

— Poland.

NAUMIUK (JAN) Klasowy ruch zawodowy metalowców w Zagłębiu Staropolskim w latach 1918-1939. Łódź, 1975. pp. 171. *bibliog.*

— Russia.

KUL'TURA i byt gorniakov i metallurgov Nizhnego Tagila, 1917- 1970. Moskva, 1974. 7p. 319.

— — Georgia.

KINKADZE (TAT'IANA VLADIMIROVNA) Konkretno-sotsiologicheskoe izuchenie protsessa professional'nykh izmenenii v sostave rabochikh kadrov Rustavskogo metallurgicheskogo zavoda. Tbilisi, 1973. pp. 126. *bibliog.*

— Sweden.

JOHANNESSON (CONNY) De centrala avtalsförhandlingarna och den fackliga demokratin: studier över Svenska metallindustriarbetareförbundets förhandlingsorganisation vid förbundsförhandlingar, med samordning. Lund, 1975. pp. 437. *bibliog.* Akademisk avhandling, Universitetet i Lund; with English summary.

METALLURGY

— Russia — Soviet Far East.

LEN'KOV (VITALII DMITRIEVICH) Metallurgiia i metalloobrabotka u chzhurchzhenei v XII veke: po materialam issledovanii Shaiginskogo gorodishcha; otvetstvennyi redaktor... E.V. Shavkunov. Novosibirsk, 1974. pp. 172,[xiii].

METAPHYSICS.

KANT (IMMANUEL) Metaphysical foundations of natural science; translated, with introduction and essay, by James Ellington. Indianapolis, [1970]. pp. 230.

METEOROLOGY, AGRICULTURAL

— South Africa.

THERON (MARGRIET J.) and others. The economic importance of the weather and weather services to the South African agricultural sector: a Delphi survey. Pretoria, 1973. fo. 134. (South Africa. Council for Scientific and Industrial Research. CSIR Research Reports. 321)

METHODOLOGY.

HOLLINGER (DAVID A.) Morris R. Cohen and the scientific ideal. Cambridge, Mass., [1975]. pp. 262.

METIS PEOPLE.

See INDIANS OF NORTH AMERICA — Mixed bloods.

METROPOLITAN AREAS

— France.

FRANCE. Direction de la Documentation. La Documentation Française. Notes et Etudes Documentaires. No. 3,633. Aménagement du territoire. (1). Métropoles d'équilibre et aires métropolitaines: introduction; par Michel Colot. Paris, 1969. pp. 14.

FRANCE. Direction de la Documentation. La Documentation Française. Notes et Etudes Documentaires. No. 3,634. Aménagement du territoire. (2). Organisation d'études d'aménagement de l'aire métropolitaine Lyon-Saint- Etienne: objectifs et principes généraux d'aménagement, octobre 1967. Paris, 1969. pp. 35.

FRANCE. Direction de la Documentation. La Documentation Française. Notes et Etudes Documentaires. Nos. 3,635-3, 636. Aménagement du territoire. (3). Organisation d'études d'aménagement de l'aire métropolitaine du Nord: pour une politique d'aménagement régional, février 1968. Paris, 1969. pp. 48.

FRANCE. Direction de la Documentation. La Documentation Française. Notes et Etudes Documentaires. Nos. 3,637-3, 638-3,639. Aménagement du territoire. (4). Organisation d'études d'aménagement de l'aire métropolitaine Metz-Nancy-Thionville: données et orientations pour l'aménagement d'une métropole lorraine, septembre 1968. Paris, 1969. pp. 78.

FRANCE. Direction de la Documentation. La Documentation Française. Notes et Etudes Documentaires. Nos. 3,640-3, 641-3,642. Aménagement du territoire. (5). Organisation d'études d'aménagement de l'aire métropolitaine marseillaise, décembre 1967. Paris, 1969. pp. 93.

FRANCE. Direction de la Documentation. La Documentation Française. Notes et Etudes Documentaires. Nos. 3,643-3, 644. Aménagement du territoire. (6). Organisation d'études d'aménagement de l'aire métropolitaine Nantes-Saint- Nazaire: bilan et perspectives, décembre 1968, etc. Paris, 1969. pp. 73.

FRANCE. Ministère de l'Equipement et du Logement. Direction Départementale de l'Equipement du Nord. Groupe d'Etudes et de Programmation. 1970. Douai: livre blanc; une politique de conversion. [Douai, 1970]. fo. 101.

ORGANISATION D'ETUDES D'AMENAGEMENT DE L'AIRE METROPOLITAINE NANTES-SAINT-NAZAIRE. Schéma d'aménagement [de l'aire métropolitaine Nantes- Saint-Nazaire]: (annexe); démographie, emploi. Nantes, 1971. pp. 61.

ORGANISATION D'ETUDES D'AMENAGEMENT DE L'AIRE METROPOLITAINE NANTES-SAINT-NAZAIRE. Schéma d'aménagement de l'aire métropolitaine [Nantes- Saint-Nazaire]: (annexe); développement tertiaire. Nantes, 1973. pp. 131. *bibliog.*

ORGANISATION D'ETUDES D'AMENAGEMENT DE L'AIRE METROPOLITAINE NANTES-SAINT-NAZAIRE. Schéma d'aménagement de l'aire métropolitaine [Nantes- Saint-Nazaire]: (annexe); programmation. Nantes, 1973. pp. 126. *bibliog.*

FRANCE. Direction de la Documentation. La Documentation Française. Notes et Etudes Documentaires. Nos. 4,142-4, 143. Place, vocation et avenir de Paris et de sa région; rapport présenté par Jacqueline Beaujeu-Garnier au Comité consultatif économique et social de la Région Parisienne. Paris, 1974. pp. 64.

— United States.

EDMONSTON (BARRY) Population distribution in American cities. Lexington, Mass., [1975]. pp. 156. *bibliog.*

LAMB (RICHARD) 1943- . Metropolitan impacts of rural America. Chicago, 1975. pp. 196. *bibliog.* (Chicago. University. Department of Geography. Research Papers. No. 162)

METROPOLITAN America in contemporary perspective; edited by Amos H. Hawley and Vincent P. Rock; prepared for the Social Science Panel on the Significance of Community in the Metropolitan Environment of the...[National Research Council]. New York, [1975]. pp. 504. *bibliog.*

PUBLIC needs and private behavior in metropolitan areas; edited by John E. Jackson. Cambridge, Mass., [1975]. pp. 228. *Papers presented to a meeting of the Metropolitan Governance Research Committee, sponsored by Resources for the Future and the Academy for Contemporary Problems, October, 1973.*

RUST (EDGAR) No growth: impacts on metropolitan areas. Lexington, Mass., [1975]. pp. 241. *bibliog.*

STERNLIEB (GEORGE S.) and HUGHES (JAMES W.) eds. Post-industrial America: metropolitan decline and inter- regional job shifts. New Brunswick, [1975]. pp. 267.

STRUYK (RAYMOND J.) and JAMES (FRANKLIN J.) Intrametropolitan industrial location: the pattern and process of change. Lexington, Mass., [1975]. pp. 190.

METROPOLITAN GOVERNMENT

METROPOLITAN GOVERNMENT
— United States.

PUBLIC needs and private behavior in metropolitan areas; edited by John E. Jackson. Cambridge, Mass., [1975]. pp. 228. *Papers presented to a meeting of the Metropolitan Governance Research Committee, sponsored by Resources for the Future and the Academy for Contemporary Problems, October, 1973.*

METTERNICH-WINNEBURG (CLEMENS WENZESLAUS NEPOMUK LOTHAR VON) Prince.

CRISIS and controversy: essays in honour of A.J.P. Taylor; edited by Alan Sked and Chris Cook. London, 1976. pp. 198.

MEXICANS IN THE UNITED STATES.

MEXICAN-Americans tomorrow: educational and economic perspectives; Gus Tyler, editor. Albuquerque, N.M., [1975]. pp. 208. *Papers of a conference held at the Aspen Institute for Humanistic Studies, Colorado, in 1972, sponsored by the Weatherhead Foundation.*

ZISMAN (PAUL M.) Education and economic success of urban Spanish-speaking immigrants. San Francisco, 1975. pp. 166. *bibliog.*

AMBRECHT (BILIANA C.S.) Politicizing the poor: the legacy of the war on poverty in a Mexican-American community. New York, 1976. pp. 223. *bibliog.*

MEXICO
— Commerce — History — Sources.

El COMERCIO exterior y la expulsion de los españoles. Mexico, 1966. pp. 326. *(Banco Nacional de Comercio Exterior. Coleccion de Documentos para la Historia del Comercio Exterior de Mexico. 2a Serie. 2)*

— Commercial policy.

STECHER (BERND) Erfolgsbedingungen der Importsubstitution und der Exportdiversifizierung im Industrialisierungsprozess: die Erfahrungen in Chile, Mexiko und Südkorea. Tübingen, 1976. pp. 207. *bibliog. (Kiel. Universität. Institut für Weltwirtschaft. Kieler Studien. 136)*

— Constitutional history.

NIEMEYER (EBERHARDT VICTOR) Revolution at Queretaro: the Mexican Constitutional Convention of 1916-1917. Austin, [1974]. pp. 297. *bibliog. (Texas University. Institute of Latin American Studies. Latin American Monographs. No. 33)*

— Description and travel — Bibliography.

GUNN (DREWEY WAYNE) compiler. Mexico in American and British letters: a bibliography of fiction and travel books, citing original editions. Metuchen, N.J., 1974. pp. 150.

— Economic conditions.

RAMOS GIRAULT (MARIO) Problemas y posibilidades economicas de Mexico, 1971-1980. Mexico, 1969 repr. 1970. pp. 223.

SOLIS M. (LEOPOLDO) Controversias sobre el crecimiento y la distribucion: las opiniones de economistas mexicanos acerca de la politica economica. Mexico, 1972. pp. 230. *bibliog.*

El MILAGRO mexicano; [by] Fernando Carmona [and others]. 3rd ed. Mexico, 1973 repr. 1976. pp. 403.

— Economic policy.

MEXICO. Secretaria de Gobernacion. 1946. Seis años de actividad nacional. Mexico, 1946. pp. 797.

RAMOS GIRAULT (MARIO) Problemas y posibilidades economicas de Mexico, 1971-1980. Mexico, 1969 repr. 1970. pp. 223.

SOLIS M. (LEOPOLDO) Controversias sobre el crecimiento y la distribucion: las opiniones de economistas mexicanos acerca de la politica economica. Mexico, 1972. pp. 230. *bibliog.*

— Executive departments.

GARCIA Y GARCIA (J. JESUS) Guia de archivos: contiene material de interes para el estudio del desarrollo socioeconomico de Mexico. Mexico, 1972. pp. 187. *bibliog.*

— Foreign relations — United States.

BRACK (GENE M.) Mexico views manifest destiny, 1821-1846: an essay on the origins of the Mexican war. Albuquerque, N.M., [1975]. pp. 194. *bibliog.*

— Government publications.

COSTELOE (MICHAEL P.) Mexico state papers, 1744-1843: a descriptive catalogue of the G. R.G. Conway Collection in the Institute of Historical Research, University of London. London, 1976. pp. 153. *(London. University. Institute of Latin American Studies. Monographs. 6)*

— History.

RODRIGUEZ OCHOA (AGUSTIN) Mexico contemporaneo, 1867-1940: Cardenas en su historia. 2nd ed. Mexico, 1974. pp. 318. *bibliog.*

— — Bibliography.

COSIO VILLEGAS (DANIEL) Ultima bibliografia politica de la historia moderna de Mexico. Mexico, 1972. pp. 41-222. *(Sobretiro de la Memoria del Colegio Nacional, tomo 7, num. 1, año de 1970)*

— — Sources.

COSTELOE (MICHAEL P.) Mexico state papers, 1744-1843: a descriptive catalogue of the G. R.G. Conway Collection in the Institute of Historical Research, University of London. London, 1976. pp. 153. *(London. University. Institute of Latin American Studies. Monographs. 6)*

— — 1867—1910.

HANNAY (DAVID) Diaz. London, 1917. pp. 319. *bibliog.*

— — 1910—1929, Revolution.

CORDOVA (ARNALDO) La ideologia de la Revolucion Mexicana: la formacion del nuevo regimen. Mexico, 1973 repr. 1974. pp. 508.

— Nationalism.

SOLIS M. (LEOPOLDO) Controversias sobre el crecimiento y la distribucion: las opiniones de economistas mexicanos acerca de la politica economica. Mexico, 1972. pp. 230. *bibliog.*

— Native races.

La POLITICA indigenista en Mexico: metodos y resultados; [by] Alfonso Caso [and others]. 2nd ed. Mexico, Instituto Nacional Indigenista, 1954 repr. 1973. 2 vols. *bibliogs.*

— Politics and government.

MEXICO. Secretaria de Gobernacion. 1946. Seis años de actividad nacional. Mexico, 1946. pp. 797.

UNZUETA (GERARDO) Sobre el problema estudiantil-popular: cartas desde la prison. Mexico, 1969. pp. 63.

El MILAGRO mexicano; [by] Fernando Carmona [and others]. 3rd ed. Mexico, 1973 repr. 1976. pp. 403.

PURCELL (SUSAN KAUFMAN) The Mexican profit-sharing decision: politics in an authoritarian regime. Berkeley, [1975]. pp. 216. *bibliog.*

PADGETT (L. VINCENT) The Mexican political system. 2nd ed. Boston, [1976]. pp. 332. *bibliog.*

RUIZ (RAMON EDUARDO) Labor and the ambivalent revolutionaries: Mexico, 1911-1923. Baltimore, [1976]. pp. 145. *bibliog.*

— — Bibliography.

COSIO VILLEGAS (DANIEL) Ultima bibliografia politica de la historia moderna de Mexico. Mexico, 1972. pp. 41-222. *(Sobretiro de la Memoria del Colegio Nacional, tomo 7, num. 1, año de 1970)*

— Population.

GONZALEZ NAVARRO (MOISES) Poblacion y sociedad en Mexico, 1900-1970. Mexico, 1974. 2 vols. (in 1). *bibliog.*

— Social conditions.

El MILAGRO mexicano; [by] Fernando Carmona [and others]. 3rd ed. Mexico, 1973 repr. 1976. pp. 403.

— Social history.

GONZALEZ NAVARRO (MOISES) Poblacion y sociedad en Mexico, 1900-1970. Mexico, 1974. 2 vols. (in 1). *bibliog.*

— Social policy.

MEXICO. Secretaria de Gobernacion. 1946. Seis años de actividad nacional. Mexico, 1946. pp. 797.

MEXICO CITY
— Poor.

CORNELIUS (WAYNE A.) Politics and the migrant poor in Mexico City. Stanford, 1975. pp. 319. *bibliog.*

MEXICO IN LITERATURE
— Bibliography.

GUNN (DREWEY WAYNE) compiler. Mexico in American and British letters: a bibliography of fiction and travel books, citing original editions. Metuchen, N.J., 1974. pp. 150.

MIAO PEOPLE.

GEDDES (WILLIAM ROBERT) Migrants of the mountains: the cultural ecology of the Blue Miao (Hmong Njua) of Thailand. Oxford, 1976. pp. 274. *bibliog.*

MICHAEL III, Voyvode of Wallachia.

OLTEANU (ŞTEFAN) Les pays roumains à l'époque de Michel le Brave, l'union de 1600. București, 1975. pp. 159. *(Academia Republicii Socialiste România. Secţia de Ştiinţe Istorice, Filozofice şi Economico-Juridice. Bibliotheca Historica Romaniae. Monographies. 14)*

MICHELSEN (CHRISTIAN).

WYLLER (THOMAS CHRISTIAN) Christian Michelsen, politikeren. Oslo, [1975]. pp. 250. *bibliog.*

MICHIGAN
— Politics and government.

SHIPSTEAD (PATRICK E.) New perspectives on American politics: a report from Michigan on the busing issue. Princeton, [1973]. pp. 69. *(Princeton University. Woodrow Wilson School of Public and International Affairs. Woodrow Wilson Association Monograph Series in Public Affairs. No. 5)*

MICKIEWICZ (ADAM)
— Bibliography.

ŚLIWIŃSKA (IRMINA) and others, compilers. Adam Mickiewicz: zarys bibliograficzny. [Warszawa], 1957. pp. 354.

MICROFILMS.

SMITH (A.D.) Microfilm: some legal implications. [London, 1975]. fo. 8,viii.

MINERAL INDUSTRIES.

MICRONESIA

— Foreign relations — United States.

McHENRY (DONALD F.) Micronesia: trust betrayed: altruism vs. self interest in American foreign policy. New York, [1975]. pp. 260. *bibliog.*

MIDDLE CLASSES

— Brazil.

FERNANDES (FLORESTAN) A revolução burguesa no Brasil: ensaio de interpretação sociologica. Rio de Janeiro, 1975. pp. 413. *bibliog.*

— Germany.

FUERTH (HENRIETTE) Der Haushalt vor und nach dem Krieg: dargestellt an Hand eines mittelbürgerlichen Budgets. Jena, 1922. pp. 65.

— — Prussia.

GUGEL (MICHAEL) Industrieller Aufstieg und bürgerliche Herrschaft: sozioökonomische Interessen und politische Ziele des liberalen Bürgertums in Preussen zur Zeit des Verfassungskonflikts, 1857-1867. Köln, [1975]. pp. 304. *bibliog.*

— Russia.

LAVERYCHEV (VLADIMIR IAKOVLEVICH) Krupnaia burzhuaziia v poreformennoi Rossii, 1861-1900. Moskva, 1974. pp. 252.

STEPIN (ANATOLII PETROVICH) Sotsialisticheskoe preobrazovanie obshchestvennykh otnoshenii gorodskikh srednikh sloev. Moskva, 1975. pp. 235.

DUNHAM (VERA SANDOMIRSKY) In Stalin's time: middleclass values in Soviet fiction. Cambridge, 1976. pp. 283. *bibliog.*

— United Kingdom.

HUTBER (PATRICK) The decline and fall of the middle class - and how it can fight back. London, 1976. pp. 184.

TOMLINSON (T.B.) The English middle-class novel. London, 1976. pp. 207.

— United States.

WARREN (DONALD I.) The radical center: middle Americans and the politics of alienation. Notre Dame, Ind., [1976]. pp. 260. *bibliog.*

MIDHURST GRAMMAR SCHOOL.

LUCAS (NORMAN BERNARD CHARLES) An experience of teaching. London, [1975]. pp. 196.

MIGRANT AGRICULTURAL LABOURERS

— United States.

DUNBAR (ANTHONY) and KRAVITZ (LINDA) Hard traveling: migrant farm workers in America. Cambridge, Mass., [1976]. pp. 158.

— — California.

LEVY (JACQUES E.) Cesar Chavez: autobiography of La Causa. New York, [1975]. pp. 546.

TAYLOR (RONALD B.) Chavez and the farm workers. Boston, [1975]. pp. 342. *bibliog.*

YINGER (WINTHROP) Cesar Chavez: the rhetoric of nonviolence. Hicksville, N.Y., [1975]. pp. 143. *bibliog.*

MIGRANT LABOUR.

YUGOSLAVIA. Savezni Zavod za Statistiku. Studije, Analize i Prikazi. 67. Porast stanovništva u periodu 1961-1971, odnosno, odlazak na privremeni rad u inostranstvo i neki indikatori ekonomske razvijenosti opština; Increase of population in the period 1961- 1971 and our workers on temporary work abroad and some indicators of economic development of communes; [by] Nikola Marković. Beograd, 1974. pp. 94. *bibliog. With English summary.*

— Europe.

BAPTISTA (JOSÉ) Pour un mouvement autonome des travailleurs étrangers, pour une sociologie politique des migrations internationales en Europe. Vienna, 1974. pp. 13. *(Wiener Institut für Entwicklungsfragen. Occasional Papers. 74/2)*

— United Kingdom.

FABIAN SOCIETY. Fabian Tracts. [No.] 444. Britain's migrant workers; [by] Sue Ashtiany. London, 1976. pp. 24.

— United States.

SHENKIN (BUDD N.) Health care for migrant workers: policies and politics. Cambridge, Mass., [1974]. pp. 270.

MILITARISM

— Europe.

WAR, economy and the military mind; edited by Geoffrey Best and Andrew Wheatcroft. London, 1976. pp. 136.

— France.

REMY (BERNARD) L'homme des casernes: "change-lutte", collectifs de soutien. Paris, 1975. pp. 280.

— Germany.

MAMMACH (KLAUS) Der Kampf der deutschen Arbeiterklasse im August 1930 gegen Imperialismus, Militarismus und Krieg; mit einem Dokumentenanhang. Berlin, 1956. pp. 51. *(Institut für Marxismus-Leninismus (Berlin). Beiträge zur Geschichte und Theorie der Arbeiterbewegung. Heft 7)*

REIMANN (MAX) Der deutsche Imperialismus, die Hauptgefahr für den Frieden in Europa. Rheinhausen, [1969]. pp. 32.

MESSERSCHMIDT (MANFRED) Militär und Politik in der Bismarckzeit und im Wilhelminischen Deutschland. Darmstadt, 1975. pp. 163. *bibliog.*

— United States.

KOHN (RICHARD H.) Eagle and sword: the Federalists and the creation of the military establishment in America, 1783-1802. New York, [1975]. pp. 443. *bibliog.*

MILITARY ART AND SCIENCE.

STROKOV (ALEKSANDR ALEKSANDROVICH) Vooruzhennye sily i voennoe iskusstvo v pervoi mirovoi voine. Moskva, 1974. pp. 616.

MILITARY EDUCATION

— Russia.

KOVALEV (IVAN IAKOVLEVICH) Komsomol i oborona Rodiny, 1921-1941 gg.: na materialakh Ukrainy. Kiev, 1975. pp. 207.

MILITARY LAW

— France.

MOUVEMENT D'ACTION JUDICIAIRE. Les droits du soldat: statut, discipline et justice militaire; [by] G. Braun [and others]. Paris, 1975. pp. 131.

MILITARY OFFENCES

— Germany.

ROHDE (ACHIM) Kriminalität in der Bundeswehr: Verstösse gegen das WStG. Bonn, 1967. pp. 254. *bibliog.*

MILITARY POLICY.

VÄYRYNEN (RAIMO) Militarization, conflict behavior and interaction: three ways of analyzing the Cold War. Tampere, [1973]. pp. 230. *bibliog. (Tampere Peace Research Institute. Research Reports. No.3)*

MILITARY SERVICE, COMPULSORY

— Bibliography.

ANDERSON (MARTIN) Ph.D. and BLOOM (VALERIE) compilers. Conscription: a select and annotated bibliography. Stanford, Calif., 1976. pp. 453.

MILITARY SERVICE AS A PROFESSION.

SARKESIAN (SAM CHARLES) The professional army officer in a changing society. Chicago, [1975]. pp. 268. *bibliog.*

MILK SUPPLY.

BIOLOGISCH-technische Fortschritte in der Milchproduktion und Proteingewinnung: Dokumentation des Forschungsvorhabens, etc. Hamburg, 1975. 3 vols. *bibliogs. (Germany (Bundesrepublik). Bundesministerium für Ernährung, Landwirtschaft und Forsten. Berichte über Landwirtschaft. Neue Folge. Sonderhefte. 190,191,192)*

— United Kingdom — Scotland.

SCOTLAND. Scottish Milk Marketing Board. Marketing Services Department. 1975. The structure of Scottish milk production at 1975. [Paisley, 1975]. pp. 92. *Summarises the main findings of the 1975 Scottish dairy farm census.*

MILK TRADE

— United Kingdom.

CONSUMERS' COMMITTEE FOR ENGLAND AND WALES. Report on the effect of the milk marketing scheme on consumers; [A. M. Ward-Jackson, chairman]. [London], Ministry of Agriculture, Fisheries and Food, 1974. pp. 34. *bibliog.*

MILL (JOHN STUART).

McKERCHER (WILLIAM RUSSELL) English libertarian thought in the late nineteenth century. 1976. fo. 438. *bibliog. Typescript. Ph.D.(London) thesis: unpublished. This thesis is the property of London University and may not be removed from the Library.*

MILNER (ALFRED) 1st Viscount Milner.

MARLOWE (JOHN) pseud. Milner, apostle of empire: a life of Alfred George the Right Honourable Viscount Milner of St. James's and Cape Town, KG, GCB, GCMG, 1854-1925. London, 1976. pp. 394. *bibliog.*

MILWAUKEE

— Politics and government.

EISINGER (PETER K.) Patterns of interracial politics: conflict and cooperation in the city. New York, [1976]. pp. 202. *(Wisconsin University, Madison. Institute for Research on Poverty. Monograph Series)*

— Social conditions.

TAMNEY (JOSEPH B.) Solidarity in a slum. New York, [1975]. pp. 182. *bibliog.*

MINE SAFETY

— Law and legislation — United Kingdom.

BRYAN (Sir ANDREW MEIKLE) The evolution of health and safety in mines. [London, 1975] pp. 192.

MINERAL INDUSTRIES.

REEVES (J.E.) Factors of particular significance to the economics of industrial minerals. Ottawa, 1968. pp. 16. *bibliog. (Canada. Mines Branch. Information Circulars. 202)*

HERFINDAHL (ORRIS CLEMENS) Resource economics; selected works...edited by David B. Brooks. Baltimore, [1974]. pp. 316. *bibliog.*

— Classification.

MALHOTRA (SAT PAL) Correlation of commodity-industry classifications in the mineral industry. Ottawa, 1971. pp. 23. *(Canada. Mineral Resources Division. Mineral [Information] Bulletins. 116)*

MINERAL INDUSTRIES.(Cont.)

— Environmental aspects — Canada.

McGEE (GARY) Mining and environmental law. Ottawa, 1973. pp. 185. *(Canada. Mineral Resources Division. Mineral [Information] Bulletins. 138)*

— Australia — Northern Territory.

AUSTRALIA. Department of the Northern Territory. 1973. Northern Territory mineral industry. Canberra, 1973. pp. 23.

— South Africa — Mathematical models.

VAN RENSBURG (W.C.J.) "Reserves" as a leading indicator to future mineral production. Braamfontein, 1975. pp. 34.

— United Kingdom.

U.K. Business Statistics Office. Minerals. a., 1974/1975- London.

MINERS.

REVOLUTIONARY WORKERS' PARTY (TROTSKYIST) The need for workers control in the mining industry. [Doncaster, 1974]. pp. 20.

— Bolivia.

BROWN (JACK) and others. Informe Cornell: el minero boliviano de Colquiri. La Paz, 1968. pp. 89. *(La Paz. Universidad Mayor de San Andres. Facultad de Derecho y Ciencias Politicas. Cuadernos de Sociologia. No. 29)*

— Russia.

KUL'TURA i byt gorniakov i metallurgov Nizhnego Tagila, 1917- 1970. Moskva, 1974. 7p. 319.

— United States.

FINLEY (JOSEPH E.) The corrupt kingdom: the rise and fall of the United Mine Workers. New York, [1972]. pp. 315. *bibliog.*

MINES AND MINERAL RESOURCES.

MATIÈRES premières minérales et relations internationales; ([by] P. Bourrelier [and others]). Lausanne, 1975. pp. 62. *(Lausanne. Université. Centre de Recherches Européennes. Publications. 4. L'Europe et les Pays Tiers)*

MIKESELL (RAYMOND FRECH) Nonfuel minerals: U.S. investment policies abroad. Beverly Hills, [1975]. pp. 97. *bibliog. (Georgetown University. Center for Strategic and International Studies. Washington Papers. vol. 3/23)*

— Africa.

U.K. Institute of Geological Sciences. 1973. 50th anniversary Geological Survey and Mines Department, Uganda. London, 1973. pp. 183. *bibliogs. (Overseas Geology and Mineral Resources. [New Series]. No.41)*

— Canada — Northwest Territories.

McGLYNN (J.C.) Metallic mineral industry, District of Mackenzie, Northwest Territories. Ottawa, 1971. pp. 194. *bibliog. (Canada. Geological Survey. Papers. 1970.17)* 2 maps and table in end pocket.

— France.

FRANCE. Bureau Statistique de l'Energie. Combustibles minéraux solides: statistique mensuelle. m., Ja 1973- Paris.

— Germany.

KRAATZ (HANS J.) Die Versorgung der Bundesrepublik Deutschland mit ausgewählten Erzen und Metallen und ihre künftige Sicherung. Berlin, 1975. pp. 235. *bibliog. Inaugural-Dissertation zur Erlangung des Grades eines Doktors der Wirtschaftswissenschaften der Freien Universität Berlin.*

— Somali Republic — Bibliography.

PURI (R.K.) compiler. Bibliography relating to geology, mineral resources, palaeontology [sic] etc., of Somali Republic. [Hargeisa?], 1961. fo. 13. *(Somali Republic. Geological Survey. Reports. RKP/1)*

— Uganda.

U.K. Institute of Geological Sciences. 1973. 50th anniversary Geological Survey and Mines Department, Uganda. London, 1973. pp. 183. *bibliogs. (Overseas Geology and Mineral Resources. [New Series]. No.41)*

— United Kingdom.

BRYAN (Sir ANDREW MEIKLE) Planning permission and the place of the public inquiry in the development of mineral resources in Britain: problems of potash extraction in Yorkshire. [London], 1971. pp. 63-72,129-138. *(Reprinted from Transactions of the Institute of Mining and Metallurgy. Section A, vol.80,1971)*

BROWN (IVOR J.) The mines of Shropshire. [Stafford, 1976]. pp. 112. *bibliog.*

— Zambia.

ZAMBIA. Mines Development Department. Annual report. a., 1972- Lusaka.

ZAMBIA. Mines Safety Department. Annual report. a., 1972- Lusaka.

MINING CORPORATIONS.

SKLAR (RICHARD L.) Corporate power in an African state: the political impact of multinational mining companies in Zambia. Berkeley, 1975. pp. 245. *bibliog.*

— Australia.

AUSTRALIA. Commonwealth Bureau of Census and Statistics. 1968. Overseas participation in Australian mining industry, 1963 to 1965 Canberra, [1968]. pp. 31.

MINING INDUSTRY AND FINANCE

— Canada.

CANADA. Department of Indian Affairs and Northern Development. Oil and Mineral Division. 1969. Northern mineral exploration assistance program: Yukon and Northwest Territories. Ottawa, 1969. pp. (4), 14.

— — Newfoundland.

NEWFOUNDLAND. Royal Commission on Mineral Revenue, 1973. Report. St. John's, 1974. 1 vol. (various pagings).

MINISTERIAL RESPONSIBILITY

— Papua New Guinea.

AUSTRALIA. Prime Minister. 1970. Steps towards self-government in Papua and New Guinea: speech by the Prime Minister, the Rt Hon. John Gorton, M. P., at Papua Hotel, Port Moresby, 6 July 1970; [and] Increased responsibility for ministerial members and assistant ministerial members: statement by the Minister for External Territories, the Hon. C.E. Barnes, M.P., Port Moresby, 6 July 1970. Canberra, 1970. pp. 31.

MINKOV (SVETOSLAV).

DIMITUR Talev, Svetoslav Minkov, Dimitur Dimov v spomenite na suvremennitsite si. Sofiia, 1973. pp. 755.

MINORITIES.

ISAACS (HAROLD ROBERT) Idols of the tribe: group identity and political change. New York, [1975]. pp. 242.

PEACH (GUTHLAC CERI KLAUS) ed. Urban social segregation. London, 1975. pp. 444. *bibliogs.*

YETMAN (NORMAN R.) and STEELE (C. HOY) eds. Majority and minority: the dynamics of racial and ethnic relations. 2nd ed. Boston, Mass., 1975. pp. 640. *bibliogs.*

— Employment — United Kingdom.

ETHNIC MINORITIES AND EMPLOYMENT; [pd. by] Employment Section, Community Relations Commission. q., D 1975 (no.1)- London.

— — United States.

CARNEGIE COUNCIL ON POLICY STUDIES IN HIGHER EDUCATION. Making affirmative action work in higher education: an analysis of institutional and federal policies with recommendations. San Francisco, 1975. pp. 272. *bibliog.*

KRANZ (HARRY) The participatory bureaucracy: women and minorities in a more representative public service. Lexington, Mass., [1976]. pp. 244.

— Housing — United Kingdom.

WORKING PARTY OF HOUSING DIRECTORS [U.K.]. Housing in multi-racial areas; [Harry Simpson, chairman]. [London, Community Relations Commission], 1976. pp. 56.

— — — London.

LONDON. Greater London Council. Housing Management Committee. Race and council housing: preliminary report of the GLC housing lettings survey; (report by Director of Housing Management and Maintenance). [London], 1976. pp. 15.

— Austria.

EINSPIELER (VALENTIN) Verhandlungen über die der slowenischen Minderheit angebotene Kulturautonomie, 1925-1930. Klagenfurt, 1976. pp. 171. *bibliog.*

— Germany, Eastern.

CYŻ (BENO) Die DDR und die Sorben: eine Dokumentation zur Nationalitätenpolitik in der DDR. Bautzen, [1969]. pp. 543. *bibliog.*

— India.

WADHWA (KAMLESH KUMAR) Minority safeguards in India: constitutional provisions and their implementation. Delhi, 1975. pp. 273. *bibliog.*

— Netherlands.

DOEL (JOHANNES VAN DEN) and HOOGERWERF (A.) eds. Gelijkheid en ongelijkheid in Nederland: analyse en beleid. Alphen aan den Rijn, 1975. pp. 312. *bibliogs.*

— Russia.

AKTUAL'NYE problemy razvitiia natsional'nykh otnoshenii v SSSR. Makhachkala, 1973. pp. 266. *With English and German tables of contents.*

SUZHIKOV (MARAT MUKHAMBETKALIEVICH) and DEMAKOV (GEORGII ALEKSEEVICH) Vliianie podvizhnosti naseleniia na sblizhenie natsii. Alma-Ata, 1974. pp. 200.

KOZLOV (VIKTOR IVANOVICH) Natsional'nosti SSSR: etnodemograficheskii obzor. Moskva, 1975. pp. 263. *With English table of contents.*

SHPILIUK (VLADIMIR ARONOVICH) Mezhrespublikanskaia migratsiia i sblizhenie natsii v SSSR. L'vov, 1975. pp. 167.

— — Ukraine.

NAULKO (VSEVOLOD IVANOVICH) Razvitie mezhetnicheskikh sviazei na Ukraine: istoriko-etnograficheskii ocherk. Kiev, 1975. pp. 276.

— United Kingdom.

PYKE-LEES (CELIA) and GARDINER (SUE) Elderly ethnic minorities. London, 1974. pp. 17. *bibliog. (Age Concern England. Manifesto Series. No. 18)*

HECHTER (MICHAEL) Internal colonialism: the Celtic fringe in British national development, 1536-1966. London, 1975. pp. 361.

STEPHEN (DAVID) Minority rights and minority morale in the U.S.A.: how relevant to Britain is U.S. experience?;...a memorandum submitted to the House of Commons Select Committee on Race Relations and Immigration, May 1975. London, 1975. fo. 12.

— United States.

TESELLE (SALLIE) ed. The rediscovery of ethnicity. New York, 1974. pp. 138.

HELMER (JOHN) Drugs and minority oppression. New York, [1975]. pp. 192.

STEPHEN (DAVID) Minority rights and minority morale in the U.S.A.: how relevant to Britain is U.S. experience?;...a memorandum submitted to the House of Commons Select Committee on Race Relations and Immigration, May 1975. London, 1975. fo. 12.

SYMPOSIUM ON THE STATE OF THE BLACK ECONOMY, 3rd and 4th, 1973 and 1974. Minorities at the crossroads: selected proceedings of the third and fourth...symposiums...edited by Gerald F. Whittaker. [Chicago], 1975. pp. 177. *bibliog.*

YETMAN (NORMAN R.) and STEELE (C. HOY) eds. Majority and minority: the dynamics of racial and ethnic relations. 2nd ed. Boston, Mass., 1975. pp. 640. *bibliogs.*

KRICKUS (RICHARD) Pursuing the American dream: white ethnics and the new populism. Bloomington, 1976. pp. 424.

MINDEL (CHARLES H.) and HABENSTEIN (ROBERT WESLEY) eds. Ethnic families in America: patterns and variations. New York, [1976]. pp. 429. *bibliogs.*

MINORITY BUSINESS ENTERPRISES

— United States.

DOMINGUEZ (JOHN R.) Capital flows in minority areas. Lexington, Mass., [1976]. pp. 164. *bibliog.*

MINTS (ISAAK IZRAILEVICH).

ISTORICHESKII opyt Velikogo Oktiabria: k 80-letiiu laureata Leninskoi premii akademika I.I. Mintsa. Moskva, 1975. pp. 423.

MISCONDUCT IN OFFICE

— Sierra Leone.

SIERRA LEONE. Wales Commission of Inquiry into the Conduct of the Immigration Quota Committee from 1st January, 1961 to 23rd March, 1967. 1969. Report...amd government statement thereon; [J.G. Wales, commissioner]. [Freetown, 1969?]. pp. 52.

SIERRA LEONE. Faulkner Commission of Inquiry into the Finance and Administration of the Transport and General Workers' Union. 1971. Report...and government statement thereon; [M.C. d'Alves Faulkner, commissioner]. [Freetown, 1971]. pp. 102.

SIERRA LEONE. Commission appointed to inquire into the Activities of the Posts and Telecommunications Department from 1st January, 1961. 1972. Report...and the government statement thereon; [Percy R. Davies, Commissioner]. [Freetown?, 1972]. pp. 85.

SIERRA LEONE. Commission of Inquiry on the Sierra Leone Co- operative Marketing Federation of Sierra Leone. 1972. Report; [D.E.M. Williams, chairman]. [Freetown, 1972]. pp. 38.

MISSIONS

— Colombia.

FRIEDE (JUAN) La explotacion indigena en Colombia bajo el gobierno de las misiones: el caso de los aruacos de la Sierra Nevada de Santa Marta. 2nd ed. Bogota, [1973]. pp. 184. *bibliog.*

— Peru.

DUVIOLS (PIERRE) La lutte contre les religions autochtones dans le Pérou colonial: "l'extirpation de l'idolâtrie" entre 1532 et 1660. Lima, [1972]. pp. 428. *bibliog. (Institut Français d'Etudes Andines. Travaux. 13)*

— Rhodesia.

VAMBE (LAWRENCE) From Rhodesia to Zimbabwe. Pittsburgh, 1976. pp. 290.

— South Africa.

CALLAWAY (GODFREY) South Africa from within: made known in the letters of a magistrate. London, 1930. pp. 158.

— Vietnam.

LÊ (NICOLE DOMINIQUE) Les missions-étrangères et la pénétration française au Viêt-Nam. Paris, [1975]. pp. 228. *bibliog. (Nice. Université. Faculté des Lettres et Sciences Humaines. Institut d'Etudes et de Recherches Interethniques et Interculturelles. Publications. 5)*

MISSIONS, CANADIAN.

OGELSBY (J.C.M.) Gringos from the far North: essays in the history of Canadian- Latin American relations, 1866-1968. Toronto, [1976]. pp. 346. *bibliog.*

MISSIONS, FRENCH.

LÊ (NICOLE DOMINIQUE) Les missions-étrangères et la pénétration française au Viêt-Nam. Paris, [1975]. pp. 228. *bibliog. (Nice. Université. Faculté des Lettres et Sciences Humaines. Institut d'Etudes et de Recherches Interethniques et Interculturelles. Publications. 5)*

MISSISSIPPI VALLEY

— History.

TOBIN (GREGORY M.) The making of a history: Walter Prescott Webb and the Great Plains. Austin, Tx., [1976]. pp. 184. *bibliog.*

MITTERRAND (FRANÇOIS).

CAMPBELL (IAN R.) The end of the Mitterrand experiment? Coventry, 1975. pp. 57. *(University of Warwick. Department of Politics. Working Papers. No. 5)*

MNIKÓW.

KUTRZEBA-POJNAROWA (ANNA) Tradycyjna społeczność wiejska w procesie przemian współczesnych: studium wsi Mników powiatu krakowskiego. Wrocław, 1968. pp. 80. *(Polska Akademia Nauk. Oddział w Krakowie. Komisja Socjologiczna. Prace. Nr.13)* With Russian and French summaries.

MODENA (PROVINCE)

— History.

CANOVA (F.) and others. Lotta di liberazione nella Bassa Modenese. Modena, [1974]. pp. 419. *bibliog.*

MODERNISM

— Catholic Church.

BEDESCHI (LORENZO) Interpretazioni e sviluppo del modernismo cattolico. Milano, [1975]. pp. 206. *bibliog.*

MOHAMMEDANISM.

TURNER (BRYAN S.) Weber and Islam: a critical study. London, 1974. pp. 212.

GADHAFI (MOAMMAR) The battle of destiny: speeches and interviews. London, 1976. pp. 137.

MOHAMMEDANS IN BOSNIA.

HADŽIJAHIĆ (MUHAMED) Od tradicije do identiteta: geneza nacionalnog pitanja bosanskih Muslimana. Sarajevo, 1974. pp. 263.

MOHAMMEDANS IN INDIA.

ZAIDI (A. MOIN) ed. Evolution of Muslim political thought in India. New Delhi, 1975 in progress.

MOHAMMEDANS IN KIRGHIZIA.

RELIGIIA, svobodomyslie, ateizm. Frunze, 1967. pp. 96.

MOLDAVIA

— Social life and customs.

POPOVICH (IURII VASIL'EVICH) Moldavskie novogodnie prazdniki, XIX - nachalo XX v. Kishinev, 1974. pp. 183. *bibliog.*

MOLDAVIAN REPUBLIC

— Constitutional history.

REPIDA (AFANASII VASIL'EVICH) Obrazovanie Moldavskoi ASSR. Kishinev, 1974. pp. 183. *bibliog.*

— History.

LAZAREV (ARTEM MARKOVICH) Moldavskaia Sovetskaia gosudarstvennost' i bessarabskii vopros. Kishinev, 1974. pp. 910. *bibliog.*

— Industries.

SOTSIALISTICHESKAIA industrializatsiia i razvitie rabochego klassa Sovetskoi Moldavii, 1926-1958 gg.: sbornik dokumentov i materialov; redaktsionnaia kollegiia N.K. Bibileishvili [and others]. Kishinev, 1970. pp. 595.

TSARANOV (VLADIMIR IVANOVICH) Po puti industrializatsii: osushchevstlenie sotsialisticheskoi industrializatsii i dal'neishee razvitie promyshlennosti Moldavskoi SSR; pod redaktsiei...M.P. Kima. Kishinev, 1975. pp. 328.

— Statistics.

MOLDAVIAN REPUBLIC. Tsentral'noe Statisticheskoe Upravlenie. 1975. Narodnoe khoziaistvo Moldavskoi SSR, 1924-1974: iubileinyi statisticheskii sbornik. Kishinev, 1975. pp. 286.

MOLUCCANS IN THE NETHERLANDS.

RINSAMPESSY (ELIAS P.) De mogelijke gronden van agressie onder Molukse jongeren geplaatst in het kader van de integratieproblematiek. Utrecht, 1975. pp. 76. *bibliog.*

WAT moeten ze hier?: Zuidmolukkers op weg naar vrijheid; [by Gerhard Knot and others]. Groningen, [1975]. pp. 96. *bibliog.*

MONACO.

FRANCE. Direction de la Documentation. La Documentation Française. Notes et Etudes Documentaires. No. 4,210. Les micro-états européens: Monaco - Saint-Marin - Liechtenstein; par Jean-Jacques L. Tur. Paris, 1975. pp. 41. *bibliog.*

MONARCHY, BRITISH.

ROBERTSON (JOHN MACKINNON) Why preserve the monarchy?. Bradford, [1897]. pp. 7. *(Papers for the People. No. 12)*

MONASTERIES

— Russia.

ZYBKOVETS (VLADIMIR FILATOVICH) Natsionalizatsiia monastyrskikh imushchestv v Sovetskoi Rossii, 1917-1921 gg. Moskva, 1975. pp. 205.

— United Kingdom.

CAMDEN SOCIETY. [Publications]. 4th Series. vol. 16. The account-book of Beaulieu Abbey; edited...by S.F. Hockey. London, 1975. pp. 348. *bibliog.*

MONETARY UNIONS.

GIUSSO (LUIGI) ed. Teoria delle unioni monetarie e integrazione europea: [an anthology]. Napoli, [1974]. pp. 402.

MONEY.

UNITED NATIONS. Conference on Trade and Development. 1969. International monetary system: issues relating to development financing and trade of developing countries, etc. (TD/B/198/Rev. 1). New York, 1969. pp. 33.

MONEY.(Cont.)

UNITED NATIONS. Conference on Trade and Development. Expert Group on International Monetary Issues. 1969. International monetary reform and co-operation for development: report, etc. (TD/B/285/Rev.1). New York, 1969. pp. 26.

KESSLER (GELDOLPH A.) Monetary analysis and monetary policy. Amsterdam, [1973?]. pp. 25-46. *(Nederlandsche Bank. Reprints. No. 1)* (This article appeared in M.W. Holtrop, Money in an open economy, 1972)

BOUEY (GERALD K.) Remarks...to the Men's Canadian Club of Winnipeg, November 26, 1974. [Ottawa, 1974]. fo. 13.

DEBOLINI (MARINO) Lavoro e danaro nell'ordine economico-sociale. Roma, [1974]. pp. 103.

MODY (R.J.) New dimensions of monetary management. Delhi, [1974]. pp. 124. *bibliog.*

MONTBRIAL (THIERRY DE) Le désordre économique mondial: essai d'interprétation monétaire. [Paris, 1974]. pp. 187.

BANK OF JAPAN. Economic Research Department. Special Papers. No. 55. Future monetary policy actions: stronger efforts required for stable prices while keeping the tight money stance. Tokyo, 1975. pp. 4.

BOLOGNA-CLAREMONT CONFERENCE ON INTERNATIONAL MONETARY PROBLEMS, 4th, 1973. Key issues in international monetary reform: [proceedings of the conference held at Claremont]; edited by Randall Hinshaw. New York, [1975]. pp. 163.

ESSAIS en l'honneur de Jean Marchal; [edited by] Jacques Lecaillon ([and] Paul Coulbois). Paris, [1975]. 2 vols.

GALBRAITH (JOHN KENNETH) Money: whence it came, where it went. London, 1975. pp. 324.

MASERA (FRANCESCO) ed. Bilancia dei pagamenti e sistema monetario internazionale: saggi raccolti. Milano, 1975. pp. 171. *(Rome. Università Internazionale degli Studi Sociali. Pubblicazioni. Studi Economici. 2)*

SHAPIRO (EDWARD) Understanding money. New York, [1975]. pp. 438.

TREZZA (BRUNO) Economia e moneta: una riformulazione integrale della macroeconomia. Bologna, [1975]. pp. 237.

YASSUKOVICH (STANISLAS M.) Oil and money flows: the problems of recycling. London, [1975]. pp. 95.

FISHER (DOUGLAS) Monetary policy. London, 1976. pp. 91. *bibliog.*

FRENKEL (JACOB A.) and JOHNSON (HARRY GORDON) eds. The monetary approach to the balance of payments. London, 1976. pp. 388. *bibliogs.*

HAYEK (FRIEDRICH AUGUST) Choice in currency: a way to stop inflation...with commentaries by Ivor F. Pearce [and others]. London, 1976. pp. 46. *(Institute of Economic Affairs. Occasional Papers. 46)*

HAYEK (FRIEDRICH AUGUST) Denationalisation of money: an analysis of the theory and practice of concurrent currencies. London, 1976. pp. 107. *bibliog. (Institute of Economic Affairs. Hobart Papers. 70)*

JOHNSON (DUDLEY W.) Macroeconomics: money, prices and income. Santa Barbara, [1976]. pp. 490.

MONETARISM; edited by Jerome L. Stein. Amsterdam, 1976. pp. 342. *bibliogs. Based on a conference sponsored by the National Science Foundation.*

The 'NEW inflation' and monetary policy; proceedings of a conference organised by the Banca Commerciale Italiana and the Department of Economics of Università Bocconi in Milan, 1974; edited by Mario Monti. London, 1976. pp. 307.

PAQUIN (LLOYD TURNER) Problems in the foundations of monetary theory. 1976. fo. 187. *bibliog.* Typescript. Ph. D. (London) thesis : unpublished. This thesis is the property of London University and may not be removed from the Library.

PATINKIN (DON) Keynes' monetary thought: a study of its development. Durham, N.C., 1976. pp. 163. *bibliog.*

SIMPSON (THOMAS D.) Money, banking, and economic analysis. Englewood Cliffs, [1976]. pp. 493. *bibliogs.*

UNIVERSITY OF KENT AT CANTERBURY. Keynes Seminar, 2nd, 1974. Keynes and international monetary relations...; edited by A.P. Thirlwall. London, 1976. pp. 126.

WORLD monetary disorder: national policies vs. international imperatives; (edited by Patrick M. Boarman [and] David G. Tuerck). New York, 1976. pp. 264. *Papers presented at a conference held in May 1974 at Malibu, California, under the sponsorship of the Center for International Business, Pepperdine University.*

WRIGHTSMAN (DWAYNE) An introduction to monetary theory and policy. 2nd ed. New York, [1976]. pp. 338. *bibliogs.*

— **Bibliography.**

COHEN (JACOB) Economist, compiler. Special bibliography in monetary economics and finance. New York, [1976]. pp. 200.

— **Congresses.**

SOCIETÀ ITALIANA DEGLI ECONOMISTI. Riunione Scientifica, 12a, Roma, 1971. Politica monetaria e sviluppo economico. Milano, 1975. pp. 151.

— **Dictionaries and encyclopaedias.**

LAMBERT (DENIS CLAIR) Dictionnaire français-anglais de l'économie monétaire: initiation économique. 2nd ed. Paris, [1975]. pp. 261.

— **History.**

VILAR (PIERRE) A history of gold and money, 1450-1920; translated by Judith White. London, 1976. pp. 360.

— **Mathematical models.**

BOYER (RUSSELL S.) Devaluation and portfolio balance. [London], 1975. 1 pamphlet (various foliations). *bibliog.*

BOYER (RUSSELL S.) Monetary experiments in a neoclassical model. [London], 1975. 1 pamphlet (various foliations). *bibliog.*

HANNA (R.S.) Composite lag distributions in the financial sector: multivariate time- and frequency-domain analyses. Lexington, Mass., [1975]. pp. 179. *bibliog.*

KNIGHT (MALCOLM DONALD) and WYMER (CLIFFORD RONALD) A monetary model of an open economy with particular reference to the United Kingdom. [London, 1975]. pp. 24, iii. *bibliog.*

WOOD (JOHN HAROLD) Commercial bank loan and investment behaviour. London, [1975]. pp. 153. *bibliog.*

MUSSA (MICHAEL) Real and monetary factors in a dynamic theory of foreign exchange. rev. ed. [London], 1976. pp. 28. *bibliog.*

— **Terminology.**

LAMBERT (DENIS CLAIR) Dictionnaire français-anglais de l'économie monétaire: initiation économique. 2nd ed. Paris, [1975]. pp. 261.

— **Africa.**

FURNESS (ERIC L.) Money and credit in developing Africa. London, 1975. pp. 308. *bibliogs.*

— **Argentine Republic.**

AISENSTEIN (SALVADOR) El Banco Central de la Republica Argentina y su funcion reguladora de la moneda y del credito. 2nd ed. Buenos Aires, 1942. pp. 280. *bibliog.*

— **Australia.**

STANDEN (BRUCE JAMES) Some economic implications of monetary and credit policies on rural industries in Australia. 1976. fo. 263. *bibliogs.* Typescript. *Ph.D.(London) thesis: unpublished. This thesis is the property of London University and may not be removed from he Library.*

— **Belgium.**

BELGIUM. Ministère des Affaires Etrangères, du Commerce Extérieur et de la Coopération au Développement. 1975. The Belgian monetary system. Brussels, 1975. pp. 64. *(Memo from Belgium. No. 168)*

— **Communist countries.**

DEN'GI, kredit i finansy v sotsialisticheskom obshchestve. Moskva, 1975. pp. 263.

— **Europe — Mathematical models.**

GRAUWE (PAUL DE) Monetary interdependence and international monetary reform: a European case study. Farnborough, Hants., [1976]. pp. 118. *bibliog.*

— **Europe, Eastern.**

BANKING, money and credit in Eastern Europe: main findings of colloquium held 24th-26th January, 1973, in Brussels; [edited by] Yves Laulan. [Brussels], North Atlantic Treaty Organization, [1973?] . pp. 166. *In English and French.*

— **European Economic Community countries.**

ANSIAUX (HUBERT JACQUES NICOLAS) Baron, and DESSART (MICHEL) Dossier pour l'histoire de l'Europe monétaire, 1958-1973. Bruxelles, [1975]. pp. 173.

FRANCE. Direction de la Documentation. La Documentation Française. Notes et Etudes Documentaires. Nos. 4,214-4, 215. La politique monétaire des pays de la Communauté européenne; [by] Georges Chevallier [and others]. Paris, 1975. pp. 71.

KATHOLIEKE UNIVERSITEIT TE LEUVEN. Instituut voor Economisch, Sociaal en Politiek Onderzoek. Centrum voor Economische Studiën. Monetaire Integratie Werkgroep. A new move to launch the European Monetary Union?;[by]... P. de Grauwe, D. Heremans, and E. van Rompuy. Brussels, Ministry of Foreign Affairs, External Trade and Cooperation in Development, 1975. pp. 49. *(Memo from Belgium. No. 170)*

— **France — Mathematical models.**

SHEEN (JEFFREY R.) and SASSANPOUR (CYRUS) A comparison of money and economic activity in France and West Germany: 1959-1973. [London, 1976]. pp. 54. *bibliog.*

— **Germany.**

SPRANDEL (ROLF) Das mittelalterliche Zahlungssystem, nach hansisch-nordischen Quellen des 13.-15. Jahrhunderts. Stuttgart, 1975. pp. 226. *bibliog.*

DEUTSCHE BUNDESBANK. Deutsches Geld- und Bankwesen in Zahlen, 1876-1975. Frankfurt am Main, [1976]. pp. 364. *bibliog.*

— — **Mathematical models.**

SHEEN (JEFFREY R.) and SASSANPOUR (CYRUS) A comparison of money and economic activity in France and West Germany: 1959-1973. [London, 1976]. pp. 54. *bibliog.*

— **India.**

MODY (R.J.) New dimensions of monetary management. Delhi, [1974]. pp. 124. *bibliog.*

— — **Mathematical models.**

BHATTACHARYA (B. B.) Short-term income determination. Delhi, 1975. pp. 172. *bibliog.*

— Netherlands.

DUNNEN (EMILE DEN) Monetary policy in the Netherlands. Amsterdam, [1974?]. pp. 282-328. *bibliog.* (Nederlandse Bank. Reprints. No.5) (This article appeared in K. Holbik (ed.) Monetary policy in twelve industrial countries, 1973)

NIEUWKERK (MARIUS VAN) The money stock in the Netherlands, 1900-1945. Amsterdam, [1975?]. pp. 17. (Nederlandse Bank. Reprints. No. 10) (Reprinted from Quarterly Statistics of De Nederlandsche Bank, no. 3, 1974

— Scandinavia.

SPRANDEL (ROLF) Das mittelalterliche Zahlungssystem, nach hansisch-nordischen Quellen des 13.-15. Jahrhunderts. Stuttgart, 1975. pp. 226. *bibliog.*

TEIGEN (RONALD L.) Financial development and stabilization policy: a study of the Scandinavian economies. Stockholm, 1976. pp. 71. *bibliog.*

— Singapore.

SINGAPORE. Board of Commissioners of Currency. Annual report and accounts. a., 1967(1st)- Singapore.

— Spain.

SARDA DEXEUS (JUAN) La intervencion monetaria y el comercio de divisas en España. Barcelona, 1936; 1975. pp. 282. Reprint of the 1936 ed. in book form of articles originally published between 1935 and 1936 in the periodical España Bancaria.

— Sweden — Mathematical models.

LYBECK (JOHAN A.) A disequilibrium model of the Swedish financial sector. Stockholm, 1975. pp. 403. *bibliogs.*

— Switzerland.

ROTH (JEAN PIERRE) La politique monétaire suisse: son efficacité en changes fixes et flottants. Berne, 1975. pp. 315. *bibliog.*

— United Kingdom.

HOWSON (SUSAN) Domestic monetary management in Britain, 1919-38. Cambridge, 1975. pp. 213. *bibliog.* (Cambridge. University. Department of Applied Economics. Occasional Papers. 48)

PEPPER (GORDON T.) and WOOD (G.E.) M.A. Too much money...?: an analysis of the machinery of monetary expansion and its control. London, 1976. pp. 58. *bibliog.* (Institute of Economic Affairs. Hobart Papers. 68)

— — Mathematical models.

JONSON (PETER DAVID) An investigation of the U.K. balance of payments with particular emphasis on the role of monetary factors and disequilibrium dynamics, 1882-1970. 1975. fo. 167. *bibliogs.* Typescript. Ph.D.(London) thesis: unpublished. This thesis is the property of London University and may not be removed from the Library.

JONSON (PETER DAVID) Money and economic activity in the open economy: the U.K., 1880- 1970. [London], 1975. pp. 90. *bibliog.*

— United States.

MYERS (C.V.) The coming deflation: its dangers and opportunities. New Rochelle, N.Y., [1976]. pp. 218.

TEIGEN (RONALD L.) Financial development and stabilization policy: a study of the Scandinavian economies. Stockholm, 1976. pp. 71. *bibliog.*

TEMIN (PETER) Did monetary forces cause the Great Depression? New York, [1976]. pp. 201. *bibliog.*

— Venezuela.

MACHADO GOMEZ (ALFREDO) Crisis y recuperacion: la economia monetaria venezolana entre 1961- 1968. Caracas, 1972. pp. 469. (Banco Central de Venezuela. Coleccion XXX Aniversario)

— Yugoslavia.

PERIŠIN (IVO) Transformacija monetarnog i bankarsko-kreditnog sistema Jugoslavije; (monetarni sistem i ustavna reforma). Zagreb, 1975. pp. 59. (Zagreb. Ekonomski Institut. Ekonomska Biblioteka: Aktuelni Problemi. 1/75)

ŠOKMAN (ANTUN) Kvantitativni i kvalitativni efekti monetizacije. Zagreb, 1975. pp. 17.

STRANJAK (ASIM) Stvaranje i emisija novca u socijalističkoj samoupravnoj privredi. Zagreb, 1975. pp. 108. *bibliog.* (Zagreb. Ekonomski Institut. Ekonomska Biblioteka: Aktuelni Problemi. 2/75)

MONGOLIA.

BAVRIN (E.P.) and others, eds. Mongol'skaia Narodnaia Respublika. Moskva, 1974. pp. 144. (Akademiia Nauk SSSR. Institut Ekonomiki Mirovoi Sotsialisticheskoi Sistemy. Ekonomika i Politika Zarubezhnykh Stran Sotsializma)

— History.

LEGRAND (JACQUES) Le choix mongol de la féodalité au socialisme. Paris, [1975]. pp. 287. *bibliog.*

MONOPOLIES.

KUEHNE (KARL) Commonweal enterprise a regulative factor in competition: suggestions for a further development of the theory of imperfect competition; with a terminological epilogue by Karl Kühne. Francfort, [1973]. pp. 61. (Bank für Gemeinwirtschaft Aktiengesellschaft. Series Commonweal Economy. No. 6)

— Germany.

KUCZYNSKI (JUERGEN) Monopolisten und Junker: Todfeinde des deutschen Volkes. Berlin, [1946?]. pp. 46.

— United Kingdom.

KORAH (VALENTINE) Competition law of Britain and the Common Market. London, 1975. pp. 311. *bibliog.*

— United States.

KUDLIŃSKI (ROMUALD) Strukturalne podstawy monopolu w przemyśle USA. Warszawa, 1963. pp. 232. *bibliog.*

CONCENTRATION of mass media ownership: assessing the state of current knowledge...; [by] Walter S. Baer [and others]. Santa Monica, 1974. pp. 202. *bibliog.* (Rand Corporation. [Rand Reports]. 1584)

MONROE DOCTRINE.

MAY (ERNEST RICHARD) The making of the Monroe doctrine. Cambridge, Mass., 1975. pp. 306. *bibliog.*

MONTANA

— Politics and government.

SPENCE (CLARK C.) Territorial politics and government in Montana, 1864-89. Urbana, Ill., [1975]. pp. 327. *bibliog.*

MONTECASTELLO DI VIBIO

— Social life and customs.

SILVERMAN (SYDEL) Three bells of civilization: the life of an Italian hill town. New York, 1975. pp. 263. *bibliog.*

MONTICELLI

— History.

CANCILA (ORAZIO) Gabelloti e contadini in un comune rurale, secc. XVIII-XIX. Caltanissetta, 1974. pp. 219. (Unione delle Camere di Commercio, Industria, Artigianato ed Agricoltura della Regione Siciliana. Storia Economica di Sicilia. Testi e Ricerche. 21-22)

MOROCCO

MONTREAL

— Social history.

MOELLMANN (ALBERT) Das Deutschtum in Montreal. Jena, 1937. pp. 124. *bibliog.* (Marburg. Universität. Institut für Grenz- und Auslanddeutschtum. Schriften. Heft 11)

MONUMENTS

— United Kingdom — Preservation.

PLANNING and the historic environment: papers presented to a conference in Oxford, 1975; edited by Trevor Rowley and Mike Breakell. Oxford, 1975. pp. 127.

MORAL EDUCATION.

COLLIER (GERALD) and others, eds. Values and moral development in higher education. London, 1974. pp. 225.

MORDVINIAN REPUBLIC

— Economic conditions.

GORTSEV (VASILII IVANOVICH) Geografiia Mordovskoi ASSR. Saransk, 1968. pp. 128.

— Economic history.

TIUGAEV (NIKOLAI FEDOROVICH) Krepostnaia derevnia Mordovii v kontse XVIII - pervoi polovine XIX veka. Saransk, 1975. pp. 256.

— History.

ISSLEDOVANIIA po istorii Mordovskoi ASSR. Saransk, 1974. pp. 124. (Nauchno-Issledovatel'skii Institut Iazyka, Literatury, Istorii i Ekonomiki Mordovskoi ASSR. Trudy. vyp. 47)

MORGAN (ARTHUR ERNEST).

MORGAN (ARTHUR ERNEST) The making of the TVA. Buffalo, 1974. pp. 205.

MORGAN (LEWIS HENRY).

COLSON (ELIZABETH) Tradition and contract: the problem of order. London, 1975. pp. 140. *bibliog.* (Rochester, N.Y. University. Lewis Henry Morgan Lectures. 1973)

MORMONS AND MORMONISM.

ERICKSEN (EPHRAIM EDWARD) The psychological and ethical aspects of Mormon group life; [and] The religious thought of E.E. Ericksen; introductory essay by Sterling M. McMurrin. Salt Lake City, [1975]. pp. 101. *The main work was originally published in 1922.*

MOROCCO

— Bibliography.

BIBLIOGRAPHIE NATIONALE MAROCAINE: [index of periodical articles on Morocco]; [pd. by] Bibliothèque Générale et Archives du Maroc. [in French and Arabic]. m., Ja 1969 (n.s., no.73)- Rabat.

— Civilization.

RABINOW (PAUL) Symbolic domination: cultural form and historical change in Morocco. Chicago, 1975. pp. 107.

— Constitution.

MOROCCO. Constitution. 1970. Kingdom of Morocco: constitution. [Rabat], 1970. pp. 38.

— Economic conditions.

SEDDON (JOHN DAVID) Modern economic and political change in northeast Morocco. 1975 [or rather 1976]. fo. 433. *bibliog.* Typescript. Ph.D. (London) thesis: unpublished. This thesis is the property of London University and may not be removed from the Library.

— Foreign relations.

PARSONS (FREDERICK V.) The origins of the Morocco question, 1800-1900. London, 1976. pp. 663. *bibliog.*

MOROCCO (Cont.)

— History — 1800-1899.

PARSONS (FREDERICK V:) The origins of the Morocco question, 1800-1900. London, 1976. pp. 663. *bibliog.*

— Politics and government.

SEDDON (JOHN DAVID) Modern economic and political change in northeast Morocco. 1975 [or rather 1976]. fo. 433. *bibliog.* Typescript. Ph.D. (London) thesis: unpublished. *This thesis is the property of London University and may not be removed from the Library.*

— Religion.

RABINOW (PAUL) Symbolic domination: cultural form and historical change in Morocco. Chicago, 1975. pp. 107.

— Social conditions.

SEDDON (JOHN DAVID) Modern economic and political change in northeast Morocco. 1975 [or rather 1976]. fo. 433. *bibliog.* Typescript. Ph.D. (London) thesis: unpublished. *This thesis is the property of London University and may not be removed from the Library.*

MOROZ (VALENTYN IAKOVYCH).

MOROZ (VALENTYN IAKOVYCH) Eseï, lysty i dokumenty; essays, letters and documents. Miunkhen, 1975. pp. 288. *bibliog.*

MORRIS (ROBERT).

MORRIS (ROBERT) 1734-1806. The papers of Robert Morris 1781-1784; E. James Ferguson, editor. [Pittsburgh, 1973 in progress].

MORTALITY.

CLARKSON (LESLIE A.) Death, disease and famine in pre-industrial England. Dublin, 1975. pp. 188. *bibliog.*

IMHOF (ARTHUR ERWIN) and LARSEN (ØIVIND) Sozialgeschichte und Medizin: Probleme der quantifizierenden Quellenbearbeitung in der Sozial- und Medizingeschichte. Oslo, 1975. pp. 322. *bibliog.*

RETHERFORD (ROBERT D.) The changing sex differential in mortality. Westport, Conn., 1975. pp. 139. *bibliog.* (California University. International Population and Urban Research. Studies in Population and Urban Demography. No. 1)

— Tables.

NEWSHOLME (Sir ARTHUR) The Brighton life table: based on the mortality of the ten years, 1881-90. Brighton, 1893. pp. 39.

CANADA. Dominion Bureau of Statistics. Health and Welfare Division. Vital Statistics Section. 1971. Life tables, Canada and provinces...1965-1967. Ottawa, 1971. pp. 55. *In English and French.*

HONG KONG. Census and Statistics Department. 1973. Hong Kong life tables, 1971-1991. Hong Kong, [1973]. pp. 19.

MEUNIER (MARIE THERESE) compiler. Bibliographie des tables de mortalité: Europe et pays anglo-saxons d'outre-mer, 1960-1973;...sous la direction de Jacques Vallin. Paris, Institut National d'Etudes Démographiques, 1974. pp. 53, 4.

MEUNIER (MARIE THERESE) and VALLIN (JACQUES) compilers. Bibliographie des tables de mortalité françaises. Paris, Institut National d'Etudes Démographiques, 1974. pp. 35.

NORWAY. Statistiske Centralbyrå. 1974. Dødelighetsutvikling og dødsårsaksmønster, 1951-1970, etc. Oslo, 1974. pp. 208. (Statistiske Analyser. 9) *With English summary.*

NORWAY. Statistiske Centralbyrå. 1974. Regional dødelighet, 1969-1972, etc. Oslo, 1974. pp. 89. (Norges Offisielle Statistikk. Rekke A. 672) *In Norwegian and English.*

KOLARI (RISTO) Kuolleisuus...: kuolleisuuden alueellinen jakaantuminen Suomessa, 1961-1972, etc. Helsinki, 1975. pp. 85. (Finland. Tilastokeskus. Tutkimuksia. 33) *Tables in Finnish, Swedish and English, with summaries in English and Swedish.*

SWITZERLAND. Bureau Fédéral de Statistique. 1975. Schweizerische Sterbetafel...1968-1973: Grundzahlen und Nettowerte, etc. Bern, 1975. pp. 89. (Statistiques de la Suisse. 559e fasc.) *In German and French.*

VAN TONDER (JAN LOUIS) and VAN EEDEN (IZAK JOHANNES) Abridged life tables for all the population groups in the Republic of South Africa (1921-70). Pretoria, 1975. pp. 89. *bibliog.* (Human Sciences Research Council [South Africa]. Institute for Sociological, Demographic and Criminological Research. Reports. No. S-34)

MORTGAGE LOANS

— Ireland (Republic).

NATIONAL ECONOMIC AND SOCIAL COUNCIL [EIRE]. Some aspects of finance for owner-occupied housing. Dublin, Stationery Office, [1976]. pp. 64. *bibliog.* ([Reports]. No.16)

— United States.

KERR (W.G.) Scottish capital on the American credit frontier. Austin, [1976]. pp. 246. *bibliog.*

MORTGAGES

— United Kingdom.

SHELTER HOUSING AID CENTRE, [LONDON]. Pamphlets. 2. Mortgages in London. 2nd ed. London, 1973. 1 pamphlet (unpaged).

BIRMINGHAM COMMUNITY DEVELOPMENT PROJECT. Instalment mortgages in Saltley: a report to the Director of Fair Trading under the 1974 Consumer Credit Act and to the Secretary of State for the Environment. [Birmingham], 1975. pp. 19.

HADJIMATHEOU (GEORGE G.) Housing and mortgage markets in the U.K. 1955-1972. [1975]. fo. 226. *bibliog.* Typescript. Ph.D. (London) thesis: unpublished. *This thesis is the property of London University and may not be removed from the Library.*

TUNNARD (JO) No father, no home?: a study of 30 fatherless families in mortgaged homes. London, 1976. pp. 43. (Child Poverty Action Group. Poverty Pamphlets. 28)

MORTMAIN

— Canada — Ontario.

ONTARIO. Law Reform Commission. 1976. Report on mortmain, charitable uses and religious institutions. [Toronto], 1976. pp. 75.

MOSCOW

— Civic improvement.

HAMILTON (FREDERICK EDWIN IAN) The Moscow city region. London, 1976. pp. 48. *bibliog.*

— Description.

MIACHIN (IVAN KIRILLOVICH) Moskva: putevoditel'. 6th ed. Moskva, 1973. pp. 647.

— Economic conditions.

HAMILTON (FREDERICK EDWIN IAN) The Moscow city region. London, 1976. pp. 48. *bibliog.*

— Economic history.

PROFSOIUZY Moskvy: ocherki istorii. Moskva, 1975. pp. 415.

— Economic policy.

HAMILTON (FREDERICK EDWIN IAN) The Moscow city region. London, 1976. pp. 48. *bibliog.*

— Growth.

HAMILTON (FREDERICK EDWIN IAN) The Moscow city region. London, 1976. pp. 48. *bibliog.*

— History.

IGNAT'EV (GENNADII SEMENOVICH) Moskva v pervyi god proletarskoi diktatury. Moskva, 1975. pp. 379.

MOSCOW, BATTLE OF, 1941-1942.

REINHARDT (KLAUS) Die Wende vor Moskau: das Scheitern der Strategie Hitlers im Winter 1941/42. Stuttgart, 1972. pp. 355. *bibliog.* (Militärgeschichtliches Forschungsamt. Beiträge zur Militär- und Kriegsgeschichte. Band 13) *7 maps in end pocket.*

MOSCOW TRIALS, 1936-1937.

HUMBLES, LES: revue littéraire des primaires. Cahiers. Nos. 9-10. Après le 30 juin de Staline: dossier des fusilleurs; pour une commission d'enquête!. Paris, 1936. pp. 96.

CARMICHAEL (JOEL) Stalin's masterpiece: the show trials and purges of the thirties: the consolidation of the Bolshevik dictatorship. London, [1976]. pp. 238. *bibliog.*

MOTHERS

— Employment.

COOK (ALICE HANSON) The working mother: a survey of problems and programs in nine countries. Ithaca, N.Y., 1975. pp. 71. *bibliog.*

MOTIVATION (PSYCHOLOGY).

THEORIES of cognitive consistency: a sourcebook; edited by Robert P. Abelson [and others]. Chicago, [1968]. pp. 901. *bibliog.*

LAWLER (EDWARD E.) Motivation in work organizations. Monterey, [1973]. pp. 224. *bibliog.*

DECI (EDWARD L.) Intrinsic motivation. New York, [1975]. pp. 324. *bibliog.*

MOTOR BUS LINES

— Finland.

FINLAND. Tilastokeskus. Linja- autoliikenteen tasetilasto...: Statistics of profit and loss and balance sheet accounts of bus traffic. a., 1972?5th]- Helsinki. *[In Finnish with English summary and table headings]*

— Hong Kong.

HONG KONG. Transport Department. Research and Development Section. 1975. Bus services in TSZ Wan Shan: a study of the level of service provided by KMB routes 2F, etc. [Hong Kong], 1975. 1 vol (various pagings). (Studies Reports. No. 75/2)

HONG KONG. Transport Department. Research and Development Section. 1975. Public light bus routes and fare structure: 1973, August, 1974, September, and 1975, October. [Hong Kong], 1975. 1 pamphlet (various foliations). (Studies Reports. No. 75/6)

— United Kingdom.

ANDREWS (R.D.) A survey of bus crew scheduling practices. Crowthorne, 1973. pp. 39. *bibliog.* (U.K. Transport and Road Research Laboratory. Reports. LR 576)

— — Cost of operation.

SYMPOSIUM ON THE COSTING OF BUS OPERATIONS, CROWTHORNE, 1975. Symposium on the costing of bus operations; the proceedings, etc. Crowthorne, 1975. pp. 118. (U.K. Transport and Road Research Laboratory. Supplementary Reports. 180 UC)

MOTOR CYCLES

— Trade and manufacture — Italy.

ATOR CONSULENZA AZIENDALE. Studio sull'evoluzione della concentrazione nell'industria di cicli, motocicli e ciclomotori in Italia. [Brussels, European Communities, Directorate-General for Competition, 1973]. 1 vol. (various pagings).

ATOR CONSULENZA AZIENDALE. Studio sull'evoluzione della concentrazione nell'industria di cicli, motocicli e ciclomotori in Italia 1970-1972. [Brussels, European Communities, Directorate-General for Competition], 1975. pp. 87.

— — Netherlands.

AMSTERDAM. Universiteit. Stichting voor Economisch Onderzoek. Studie betreffende de ontwikkeling van de concentratie in de rijwiel- en bromfietsenindustrie in Nederland, etc; [by H.W. de Jong and A.H. Smolders]. [Brussels, European Communities, Directorate-General for Competition, 1973]. pp. 12.

MOTOR TRUCK DRIVERS.

WYCKOFF (D. DARYL) and MAISTER (DAVID H.) The owner-operator: independent trucker. Lexington, Mass., [1975]. pp. 166. *bibliog.*

MOTOR TRUCKS

— Law and legislation — United Kingdom.

U.K. Road Freight Division. 1975. Foreign lorries in Great Britain: conditions of entry into Great Britain for vehicles used for the transport of goods by road. London, 1975. pp. 25.

MOTOR VEHICLES

— Maintenance and repair.

IAKOVLEV (PETR PAVLOVICH) Prokhladnenskii ordena Lenina krasnoznamennyi. Nal'chik, 1968. pp. 127.

IVANOV (A.IA.) Vtoroi avtoremontnyi: ocherk istorii zavoda. Leningrad, 1970. pp. 128.

MOUNT CARMEL CENTRE.

SARAN (MARY) For community service: the Mount Carmel experiment. Oxford, [1974]. pp. 144.

MOUNTAINS

— Germany.

MUELLER (JOHANNES) Die Industrialisierung der deutschen Mittelgebirge: eine wirtschaftskundliche Frage der Vergangenheit, ein wirtschaftspolitisches Problem der Gegenwart. Jena, 1938. pp. 241. *bibliog.*

MOUVEMENT NATIONAL DES QUEBECOIS.

HAMEL (JACQUES) La culture politique du Mouvement National des Québécois. Québec, 1973. fo. 207.

MOVIMENTO DAS FORÇAS ARMADAS.

FIELDS (RONA M.) The Portuguese revolution and the Armed Forces Movement. New York, [1976]. pp. 288.

MOVIMIENTO DE LA IZQUIERDA REVOLUCIONARIA.

MOVIMIENTO DE LA IZQUIERDA REVOLUCIONARIA. Chile: news from the resistance. [London?, 1974?]. pp. 52. *(Bulletin of the Movement of the Revolutionary Left in the Exterior. Nos. 3-4)*

MOVIMIENTO NACIONALISTA REVOLUCIONARIO.

HOLTEY (JOSEPH) The Movimiento Nacionalista Revolucionario: Bolivia's National Revolutionary Party. Tempe, 1973. fo. 32. *bibliog. (Arizona State University. Center for Latin American Studies. Special Studies. No. 12)*

MOVING PICTURE INDUSTRY

— France.

FRANCE. Centre National de la Cinématographie. Service de la Documentation. 1974- . Textes du cinéma français. Paris, [1974 in progress]. 2 vols.(loose-leaf).

— Germany — Finance.

DEUTSCHES INSTITUT FÜR WIRTSCHAFTSFORSCHUNG. Sonderhefte. [Neue Folge]. 111. Filmförderung in der Bundesrepublik Deutschland: Versuch einer Erfolgskontrolle der Subventionspolitik; ([by] Burkhard Dreher). Berlin, 1976. pp. 267. *bibliog.*

— Hong Kong.

HONG KONG. Television and Films Authority. Annual departmental report by the Commissioner for Television and Films. a., 1974/75- Hong Kong.

— Japan.

FRANCE. Direction de la Documentation. La Documentation Française. Notes et Etudes Documentaires. Nos. 4,158-4, 159. Le cinéma japonais; par Pierre de Castillon. Paris, 1975. pp. 56.

MOVING PICTURES

— Censorship — Italy.

ARGENTIERI (MINO) La censura nel cinema italiano. Roma, 1974. pp. 250.

— Social aspects.

MONACO (PAUL) Cinema and society: France and Germany during the twenties. New York, [1976]. pp. 194. *bibliog.*

— France.

MONACO (PAUL) Cinema and society: France and Germany during the twenties. New York, [1976]. pp. 194. *bibliog.*

— Germany.

MONACO (PAUL) Cinema and society: France and Germany during the twenties. New York, [1976]. pp. 194. *bibliog.*

— Russia.

GRASSO (ALDO) ed. L'irrealismo socialista. Roma, 1973. pp. 157. *(Bianco e Nero. Studi Monografici. 3) (Estratto da Bianco e Nero, fascicolo 1/2, 1973)*

MOVING PICTURES IN HISTORIOGRAPHY.

SMITH (PAUL) 1937- , ed. The historian and film. Cambridge, [1976]. pp. 208. *bibliog.*

MOZAMBIQUE

— Census.

MOZAMBIQUE. Census, 1970. IV recenseamento geral da população, 1970. [Lourenço Marques, 1974]. 9 vols.

— History.

MARTINS (ELISIO) Colonialism and imperialism in Mozambique: the beginning of the end. [Copenhagen, 1974]. pp. 206.

— Nationalism.

MARTINS (ELISIO) Colonialism and imperialism in Mozambique: the beginning of the end. [Copenhagen, 1974]. pp. 206.

— Politics and government.

MARTINS (ELISIO) Colonialism and imperialism in Mozambique: the beginning of the end. [Copenhagen, 1974]. pp. 206.

— Social conditions.

MARTINS (ELISIO) Colonialism and imperialism in Mozambique: the beginning of the end. [Copenhagen, 1974]. pp. 206.

— Statistics.

GERMANY(BUNDESREPUBLIK). Statistisches Bundesamt. Länderkurzberichte: Mosambik. a., 1975- Wiesbaden.

MUELLER (JOSEF).

MUELLER (JOSEF) of the Christlich-Soziale Union. Bis zur letzten Konsequenz: ein Leben für Frieden und Freiheit. München, [1975]. pp. 384. *bibliog.*

MUELLER-THURGAU (HERMANN).

VEREIN FÜR WIRTSCHAFTSHISTORISCHE STUDIEN. Schweizer Pioniere der Wirtschaft und Technik. 29. Herman Müller-Thurgau, 1850-1927...und weitere Pioniere der Qualitätsverbesserung des Weins und der unvergorenen Trauben- und Obstsäfte; von Robert Fritzsche [and others]. Zürich, 1974. pp. 131. *bibliog.*

MUGGING

— United Kingdom.

PAUL, JIMMY AND MUSTAFA SUPPORT COMMITTEE. 20 years. Birmingham, [1973]. pp. 63.

— United States.

HUNT (MORTON M.) The mugging; [first published in the United States in 1972]. Harmondsworth, 1975. pp. 413. *bibliog.*

MUIR (THOMAS).

[HAMILTON (GEORGE) Minister of Gladsmuir] The telegraph: a consolatory epistle from Thomas Muir, Esq., of Botany Bay, to the Hon. Henry Erskine, late Dean of Faculty. [Edinburgh[!, 1796. pp. 11. *In verse.*

MULTIVARIATE ANALYSIS.

BISHOP (YVONNE M.M.) and others. Discrete multivariate analysis: theory and practice. Cambridge, Mass., [1975]. pp. 557. *bibliog.*

HILTON (GORDON) Intermediate politometrics. New York, 1976. pp. 282. *bibliogs.*

MUMFORD (LEWIS).

CONRAD (DAVID R.) Education for transformation: implications in Lewis Mumford's ecohumanism. Palm Springs, Calif., 1976. pp. 230. *bibliog.*

MUNDURUCU INDIANS.

MURPHY (YOLANDA) and MURPHY (ROBERT FRANCIS) Women of the forest. New York, 1974. pp. 236. *bibliog.*

MUNICH

— Statistics.

STATISTISCHES HANDBUCH DER LANDESHAUPTSTADT MÜNCHEN. [No.5] 1875-1975: 100 Jahre Städtestatistik in München . München, [1974]. pp. 603. *bibliog.*

MUNICH FOUR POWER AGREEMENT, 1938.

BENEŠ (EDVARD) Mnichovské dny: paměti; [with an appendix of documents]. [Praha], 1968. pp. 555.

MUNICIPAL BUDGETS

— United States — Michigan.

FRIEDMAN (LEWIS B.) Budgeting municipal expenditures: a study in comparative policy making. New York, 1975. pp. 249.

MUNICIPAL FINANCE

MUNICIPAL FINANCE

— Canada — Newfoundland.

NEWFOUNDLAND. Department of Municipal Affairs and Housing. Annual report of municipal statistics. a., 1971- St. John's.

— Finland — Accounting.

FINLAND. Tilastokeskus. Kuntainliittojen talous. a., 1973- Helsinki. *[In Finnish and Swedish]*

— United States.

COLE (RICHARD L.) and CAPUTO (DAVID A.) Urban politics and decentralization: the case of general revenue sharing. Lexington, Mass., [1974]. pp. 180.

GUSTELY (RICHARD D.) Municipal public employment and public expenditure. Lexington, Mass., [1974]. pp. 111. *bibliog.*

BAHL (ROY W.) and VOGT (WALTER) Fiscal centralization and tax burdens: state and regional financing of city services. Cambridge, Mass., [1975]. pp. 173. *bibliog.*

— — Michigan.

FRIEDMAN (LEWIS B.) Budgeting municipal expenditures: a study in comparative policy making. New York, 1975. pp. 249.

MUNICIPAL GOVERNMENT

— Canada.

CANADIAN FEDERATION OF MAYORS AND MUNICIPALITIES. Annual Conference, 36th, 1973. Proceedings...: Compte rendu, etc. [Ottawa, 1973]. pp. 135. *In English or French.*

— France.

DUPUY (FERNAND) Etre maire communiste. [Paris, 1975]. pp. 254.

— United Kingdom.

COX (W. HARVEY) Cities: the public dimension. Harmondsworth, 1976. pp. 244.

FRASER (DEREK) Urban politics in Victorian England: the structure of politics in Victorian cities. Leicester, 1976. pp. 324.

— United States.

LEACH (RICHARD HEALD) and O'ROURKE (TIMOTHY G.) compilers. Dimensions of state and urban policy making. New York, [1975]. pp. 418. *bibliogs.*

STAVE (BRUCE M.) ed. Socialism and the cities. Port Washington, N.Y., 1975. pp. 210. *bibliog.*

STEGGERT (FRANK X.) Community action groups and city governments: perspectives from ten American cities. Cambridge, Mass., [1975]. pp. 105. *bibliog.*

TEAFORD (JON C.) The municipal revolution in America: origins of modern urban government 1650-1825. Chicago, 1975. pp. 152. *bibliog.*

YIN (ROBERT K.) and YATES (DOUGLAS) Street-level governments: assessing decentralization and urban services. Lexington, Mass., [1975]. pp. 272. *bibliogs.*

AWERBUCH (SHIMON) and WALLACE (WILLIAM A.) Policy evaluation for community development: decision tools for local government. New York, 1976. pp. 286. *bibliog.*

COOK (EDWARD M.) The fathers of the towns: leadership and community structure in eighteenth-century New England. Baltimore, [1976]. pp. 273. *bibliog. (Johns Hopkins University. Studies in Historical and Political Science. Series 94. No.2)*

EISINGER (PETER K.) Patterns of interracial politics: conflict and cooperation in the city. New York, [1976]. pp. 202. *(Wisconsin University, Madison. Institute for Research on Poverty. Monograph Series)*

LIEBERT (ROLAND J.) Disintegration and political action: the changing functions of city governments in America. New York, [1976]. pp. 223. *bibliog.*

The NEW urban politics; edited by Louis H. Masotti and Robert L. Lineberry. Cambridge, Mass., [1976]. pp. 264.

MUNICIPAL OWNERSHIP

— United Kingdom.

FABIAN SOCIETY. Fabian Tracts. [No.] 445. Changing prospects for direct labour; [by] John Tilley. London, 1976. pp. 15. *(Fabian Society. Initiatives in Local Government. 3)*

SHANKLAND-COX PARTNERSHIP and INSTITUTE OF COMMUNITY STUDIES. Inner area study: Lambeth: the implications of social ownership. [London], Department of the Environment, [1976]. pp. 69.

SHERMAN (ALFRED V.) Waste in Wandsworth: how direct labour squanders ratepayers' money and the nation's resources. London, [1976?]. pp. 14.

STUDY GROUP ON PROGRAMMES OF SOCIAL OWNERSHIP AND RENOVATION OF COUNCIL DWELLINGS. First report; [Reg Freeson, chairman]. [London, Department of the Environment, 1976]. 1 pamphlet (various pagings).

MUNICIPAL POWERS AND SERVICES BEYOND CORPORATE LIMITS

— United States.

SLAVET (JOSEPH S.) and others. Financing state-local services: a new strategy for greater equity. Lexington, Mass., [1975]. pp. 147.

MUNICIPAL RESEARCH.

The CITY in comparative perspective: cross-national research and new directions in theory; edited by John Walton and Louis H. Masotti. New York, [1976]. pp. 313. *bibliogs.*

MUNICIPAL SERVICES

— Canada — Newfoundland.

NEWFOUNDLAND. Department of Municipal Affairs and Housing. Annual report of municipal statistics. a., 1971- St. John's.

— United States.

PUBLIC needs and private behavior in metropolitan areas; edited by John E. Jackson. Cambridge, Mass., [1975]. pp. 228. *Papers presented to a meeting of the Metropolitan Governance Research Committee, sponsored by Resources for the Future and the Academy for Contemporary Problems, October, 1973.*

— — Boston.

SLAVET (JOSEPH S.) and others. Financing state-local services: a new strategy for greater equity. Lexington, Mass., [1975]. pp. 147.

MUNITIONS.

The OTHER arms race: new technologies and non-nuclear conflict; edited by Geoffrey Kemp [and others]. Lexington, Mass., [1975]. pp. 218. *Revised papers of a conference held in 1974 by the International Security Studies Program of the Fletcher School of Law and Diplomacy.*

INTERNATIONAL INSTITUTE FOR STRATEGIC STUDIES. Adelphi Papers. No. 126. New weapons technologies: debate and directions; by Richard Burt. London, 1976. pp. 32.

— Trade and manufacture — Canada.

REGEHR (ERNIE) Making a killing: Canada's arms industry. Toronto, [1975]. pp. 135.

— — Germany.

ROCKER (RUDOLF) Die Waffen niederc' Die Hämmer nieder: Rede... gehalten auf der Reichs-Konferenz der Rüstungsarbeiter Deutschlands, abgehalten vom 18. bis 22. März 1919 in Erfurt. Berlin, [1919]. pp. 16. *Also published in Erfurt under the title Keine Kriegswaffen mehrt'*

— Europe.

WAR, economy and the military mind; edited by Geoffrey Best and Andrew Wheatcroft. London, 1976. pp. 136.

MURDER

— Australia — Victoria — Statistics.

VICTORIA. Social Welfare Department. Research and Statistics Division. 1973. People imprisoned in Victoria for murder and manslaughter, 1962- 1971; by Joseph Martin. Melbourne, 1973. fo.82.

— Canada — Statistics.

CANADA. Statistics Canada. Judicial Division. 1973. Murder statistics...1961-1970. Ottawa, 1973. pp. 67. *In English and French.*

MUSEUMS

— Canada.

CANADA. Statistics Canada. Cultural Information Section. 1972. Museums, art galleries and related institutions...1970. Ottawa, 1972. pp. 70. *In English and French.*

— South Africa.

SOUTH AFRICA. Commission of Inquiry into the Co-ordination of Museums on a National Level. 1975. Report (R.P.113/1975). in SOUTH AFRICA. Parliament. House of Assembly. Votes and proceedings; (with Printed annexures).

— United Kingdom — Law and legislation.

HEWITT (ARTHUR R.) Public library law and the law as to museums and art galleries in England and Wales, Scotland and Northern Ireland. 5th ed. London, 1975. pp. 109.

MUSIC AND SOCIETY.

KRIZIS burzhuaznoi kul'tury i muzyka: sbornik statei. vyp.2. Moskva, 1973. pp. 245.

MUSSOLINI (BENITO).

BRISSAUD (ANDRE) Mussolini. [Paris, 1975 in progress].

FELICE (RENZO DE) Mussolini e Hitler: i rapporti segreti, 1922-1933; con documenti inediti. Firenze, [1975]. pp. 315.

MACK SMITH (DENIS) Mussolini's Roman empire. New York, 1976. pp. 322. *bibliog.*

MUTINY

— France.

Les MUTINERIES de la Mer Noire, 1919-1969. Paris, [1969?]. pp. 40. *(Cahiers de Mai. Suppléments. 13)*

— United Kingdom.

PREBBLE (JOHN) Mutiny: Highland regiments in revolt, 1743-1804. London, 1975. pp. 542. *bibliog.*

MYRDAL (GUNNAR)

— Bibliography.

BOHRN (HARALD) compiler. Gunnar Myrdal: a bibliography, 1919-1976. Stockholm, 1976. pp. 186. *(Stockholm. Kungliga Biblioteket. Acta Bibliothecae Regiae Stockholmiensis. 27)*

MYSORE

— Appropriations and expenditures.

MYSORE. Finance Department. 1972. Statistics of Mysore State finances: a compendium of statistics of Mysore State finances, 1961-62 to 1970-71. 2nd ed. Bangalore, 1972. pp. 126.

— Economic policy.

MYSORE. 1968. Fourth five year plan, 1969-74: a draft outline. Bangalore, [1968]. pp. 297.

MYSORE. Finance Department. 1968. Review of the working of government departments with special reference to development, 1968. Bangalore, 1968. pp. 165.

— Officials and employees.

MYSORE. 1969. Mysore after integration: a survey of development of different regions. [Bangalore, 1969?]. pp. 53.

— Social policy.

MYSORE. 1968. Fourth five year plan, 1969-74: a draft outline. Bangalore, [1968]. pp. 297.

MYSORE. Finance Department. 1968. Review of the working of government departments with special reference to development, 1968. Bangalore, 1968. pp. 165.

— Statistics.

MYSORE. 1969. Mysore after integration: a survey of development of different regions. [Bangalore, 1969?]. pp. 53.

MYTHOLOGY, GREEK.

FRONTISI-DUCROUX (FRANÇOISE) Dédale: mythologie de l'artisan en Grèce ancienne. Paris, 1975. pp. 227.

MZILIKAZI, King of the Matabele.

BECKER (PETER) of Johannesburg. Path of blood: the rise and conquests of Mzilikazi, founder of the Matabele tribe of Southern Africa. London, 1962 repr. 1976. pp. 289. *bibliog.*

NABOKOV (VLADIMIR DMITRIEVICH).

NABOKOV (VLADIMIR DMITRIEVICH) V.D. Nabokov and the Russian provisional government, 1917; edited by Virgil D. Medlin and Steven L. Parsons. New Haven, 1976. pp. 188.

NADER (RALPH).

DE TOLEDANO (RALPH) Hit and run: the rise-and fall?- of Ralph Nader. New Rochelle, N.Y., [1975]. pp. 160.

NAIROBI

— Politics and government.

ROSS (MARC HOWARD) Grass roots in an African city: political behavior in Nairobi. Cambridge, Mass., [1975]. pp. 169.

— Social conditions.

ROSS (MARC HOWARD) Grass roots in an African city: political behavior in Nairobi. Cambridge, Mass., [1975]. pp. 169.

NAIRS.

JEFFREY (ROBIN) The decline of Nayar dominance: society and politics in Travancore, 1847-1908. London, 1976. pp. 376. *bibliog.*

NAMES, GEOGRAPHICAL

— Canada — Prince Edward Island.

RAYBURN (ALAN) Geographical names of Prince Edward Island. Ottawa, 1973. pp. 135. *bibliog. (Canada. Canadian Permanent Committee on Geographical Names. Toponymy Studies. 1)* Map in end pocket.

NAPLES

— Economic conditions.

GALIANI (FERDINANDO) Nuovi saggi inediti di economia; a cura di Achille Agnati e introduzione di Giovanni Demaria. Padova, 1974. pp. 98.

— Economic history.

ALIBERTI (GIOVANNI) Economia e società a Napoli dal Settecento al Novecento. [Reggio Calabria, 1974]. pp. 428. *bibliog.*

— History.

PORCARO (GIUSEPPE) Chiesa e stato a Napoli dopo l'unità: congiure e processi politici. [Naples, 1974]. pp. 327. *bibliog.*

— Politics and government.

ALOSCO (ANTONIO) Il Partito d'Azione a Napoli. Napoli, [1975]. pp. 189. *bibliog.*

— Social history.

ALIBERTI (GIOVANNI) Economia e società a Napoli dal Settecento al Novecento. [Reggio Calabria, 1974]. pp. 428. *bibliog.*

NAPOLEON I, Emperor of the French.

PARIS. Bibliothèque Nationale. Département des Imprimés. Catalogue des ouvrages de Napoléon Ier et Napoléon III conservés au Département des Imprimés; (rédigé par Mme Duprat-Odend'hal). Paris, 1933. pp. 131. *(Extrait du tome CXXII du Catalogue général des livres imprimés)*

NAPOLEON III, Emperor of the French.

PARIS. Bibliothèque Nationale. Département des Imprimés. Catalogue des ouvrages de Napoléon Ier et Napoléon III conservés au Département des Imprimés; (rédigé par Mme Duprat-Odend'hal). Paris, 1933. pp. 131. *(Extrait du tome CXXII du Catalogue général des livres imprimés)*

NARCOTIC ADDICTS

— Rehabilitation.

SELLS (SAUL B.) ed. Studies of the effectiveness of treatments for drug abuse. Cambridge, Mass., [1974]. 2 vols. *Cover title: The effectiveness of drug abuse treatment.*

PLATT (JEROME J.) and LABATE (CHRISTINA) Heroin addiction: theory, research, and treatment. New York, [1976]. pp. 417. *bibliog.*

— — Germany.

EBERLE (GUDRUN) Die Rehabilitation von Drogenabhängigen in der Bundesrepublik Deutschland, etc. [Erlangen, 1975]. pp. 457,xl. *bibliog. Inaugural-Dissertation zur Erlangung des akademischen Grades eines Doktors der Wirtschafts- und Sozialwissenschaften der Friedrich-Alexander-Universität Erlangen-Nürnberg.*

— — United States.

BRILL (LEON) The de-addiction process: studies in the de-addiction of confirmed heroin addicts. Springfield, Ill., [1972]. pp. 166.

— United States.

BROWN (JAMES W.) and others. Narcotics knowledge and nonsense: program disaster versus a scientific model. Cambridge, Mass., [1974]. pp. 109. *bibliog.*

NARCOTIC HABIT.

BULLETIN ON NARCOTICS; ([pd. by] Division of Narcotic Drugs), United Nations. q., 1973 (v.25)- [New York].

— United Kingdom.

SOCIAL MORALITY COUNCIL. Study Group on Education and Drug Dependence. Education and drug dependence. London, 1975. pp. 78.

NARCOTICS.

UNITED NATIONS. Conference to Consider Amendments to the Single Convention on Narcotic Drugs, 1961, Geneva, 1972. United Nations conference...[held at] Geneva, 6-24 March, 1972: official records. (E/CONF.63/10 and Add.1). New York, 1973-74. 2 vols.

SCHLEIFFER (HEDWIG) ed. Sacred narcotic plants of the New World Indians: an anthology of texts from the sixteenth century to date. New York, [1973]. pp. 156.

NARCOTICS, CONTROL OF.

BULLETIN ON NARCOTICS; ([pd. by] Division of Narcotic Drugs), United Nations. q., 1973 (v.25)- [New York].

UNITED NATIONS. Secretary-General. 1973. Commentary on the Single Convention on Narcotic Drugs, 1961; prepared...in accordance with paragraph 1 of Economic and Social Council resolution 914D (XXXIV) of 3 August 1962. New York, 1973. pp. 489.

BRUUN (KETTIL) and others. The gentlemen's club: international control of drugs and alcohol. Chicago, 1975. pp. 338. *bibliog.*

— Europe.

EUROPEAN COMMITTEE ON CRIME PROBLEMS. 1974. Penal aspects of drug abuse. Strasbourg, Council of Europe, 1974. pp. 264.

— United States.

BROWN (JAMES W.) and others. Narcotics knowledge and nonsense: program disaster versus a scientific model. Cambridge, Mass., [1974]. pp. 109. *bibliog.*

LEVIN (GILBERT) and others. The persistent poppy: a computer-aided search for heroin policy. Cambridge, Mass., [1975]. pp. 229.

RACHIN (RICHARD L.) and CZAJKOSKI (EUGENE H.) eds. Drug abuse control: administration and politics. Lexington, [1975]. pp. 181. *bibliog.*

NARODOWA PARTIA ROBOTNICZA.

PAŹDZIORA (MAREK) Górnośląska Narodowa Partia Robotnicza po zamachu majowym, 1926-1937. Katowice, 1975. pp. 264. *bibliog.*

NASSER (GAMAL ABDEL).

REJWAN (NISSIM) Nasserist ideology: its exponents and critics. New York, [1974]. pp. 271.

NATANSON (MARK ANDREEVICH).

OWEN (RICHARD CHARLES) The revolutionary career of M.A. Natanson, 1868-1906. 1975. fo. 361. *bibliog. Typescript. Ph.D.(London) thesis: unpublished. This thesis is the property of London University and may not be removed from the Library.*

NATIONAL CHARACTERISTICS, AMERICAN.

NOVAK (MICHAEL) Choosing our king: powerful symbols in presidential politics. New York, [1974]. pp. 324. *bibliog.*

BERCOVITCH (SACVAN) The Puritan origins of the American self. New Haven, 1975. pp. 250.

BOORSTIN (DANIEL JOSEPH) The exploring spirit: America and the world experience. London, 1976. pp. 102. *(British Broadcasting Corporation. Reith Lectures. 1975)*

FAIRLIE (HENRY) The spoiled child of the Western world: the miscarriage of the American idea in our time. New York, 1976. pp. 350.

NATIONAL CHARACTERISTICS, EUROPEAN.

NATIONAL CHARACTERISTICS, EUROPEAN.

PIOVENE (GUIDO) In search of Europe: portraits of the non-communist West...; translated by John Shepley. London, [1975]. pp. 342.

NATIONAL CHARACTERISTICS, GERMAN.

MOSSE (GEORGE L.) The nationalization of the masses:political symbolism and mass movements in Germany from the Napoleonic wars through the Third Reich. New York, 1975. pp. 252.

NATIONAL CHARACTERISTICS, IRISH.

O'HANLON (THOMAS J.) The Irish: portrait of a people. London, 1976. pp. 316. bibliog.

NATIONAL CHARACTERISTICS, JAPANESE.

GIBNEY (FRANK) Japan: the fragile superpower. New York, [1975]. pp. 347.

NATIONAL CHARACTERISTICS, PORTUGUESE.

PESCATELLO (ANN M.) Power and pawn: the female in Iberian families, societies, and cultures. Westport, Conn., 1976. pp. 281. bibliog. (Council on Intercultural and Comparative Studies. Contributions in Intercultural and Comparative Studies. No. 1)

NATIONAL CHARACTERISTICS, SPANISH.

PESCATELLO (ANN M.) Power and pawn: the female in Iberian families, societies, and cultures. Westport, Conn., 1976. pp. 281. bibliog. (Council on Intercultural and Comparative Studies. Contributions in Intercultural and Comparative Studies. No. 1)

NATIONAL INCOME.

ESSAIS en l'honneur de Jean Marchal; [edited by] Jacques Lecaillon ([and] Paul Coulbois). Paris, [1975]. 2 vols.

RUNGE (HARRY) Der Einfluss der personellen Einkommensverteilung auf den Wert des Volkseinkommens. Berlin, [1976]. pp. 139. bibliog.

— Accounting.

STONE (JOHN RICHARD NICHOLAS) Social accounts at the regional level: a survey. Cambridge, 1961. pp. 31. bibliog. (Cambridge. University. Department of Applied Economics. Reprint Series. No. 177)

PESKIN (HENRY M.) National accounting and the environment, etc. Oslo, 1972. pp. 57. bibliog. (Norway. Statistiske Centralbyrå. Artikler. Nr. 50)

BEIER (JOACHIM) Zeitraumanalyse: Bindeglied einzel- und gesamtwirtschaftlicher Unternehmensstatistik. Berlin, [1975]. pp. 337. bibliog.

NASJONALREGNSKAP, modeller og analyse; en artikkelsamling til Odd Aukrusts 60-årsdag: national accounts, models and analysis; to Odd Aukrust in honour of his sixtieth birthday. Oslo, 1975. pp. 321. (Norway. Statistiske Centralbyrå. Samfunnsokonomiske Studier. 26)

— Cameroun — Accounting.

COMPTES NATIONAUX DU CAMEROUN: (PRINCIPAUX TABLEAUX); (pd. by) Direction de la Statistique et de la Comptabilité Nationale. a., 1971/72- [Yaoundé].

— Chile — Accounting.

CUENTAS NACIONALES DE CHILE. a., 1965/72- [Santiago].

— Communist countries.

POLSKA AKADEMIA NAUK. Komitet Przestrzennego Zagospodarowania Kraju. Studia. t.51. Metodologiia izucheniia natsional'nogo dokhoda i gorodskikh aglomeratsii v sotsialisticheskikh stranakh: materialy III Soveshchaniia predstavitelei nauchnykh uchrezhdenii sotsialisticheskikh stran-chlenov SEV po voprosam metodologii regional'nykh issledovanii, Varshava, 4-8 dekabria 1974 g. Varshava, 1975. pp. 270.

— Dutch Guiana — Accounting.

DUTCH GUIANA. Algemeen Bureau voor de Statistiek. Nationale rekeningen: (Consolidated accounts for the nation). a., 1974 [3rd]- Paramaribo.

— European Economic Community countries.

EUROPEAN COMMUNITIES. Statistical Office. National accounts: aggregates. irreg., 1951/1972- Luxembourg. In Community languages.

— Fiji Islands — Accounting.

WARD (MICHAEL) The national income and balance of payments accounts of Fiji. [Suva], Bureau of Statistics, [1970]. pp. 105.

— Finland — Accounting.

FINLAND. Tilastokeskus. Kansantalouden tilinpito: National accounting. irreg., 1964/75 (no.1/2)- Helsinki. [In Finnish with English and Swedish summary and table headings]

FINLAND. Tilastokeskus. 1974. Kansantalouden tilinpito..., 1964-1974/I-II. Helsinki, 1974. pp. 104. (Tilastotiedotus. KT. 1974.4)

FINLAND. Tilastokeskus. 1975. Aluetilinpito...: tuotanto, työllisyys ja kiinteän pääoman bruttomuodostus lääneittäin vuosina 1960 ja 1970, etc. Helsinki, 1975. pp. 170. (Tilastollisia Tiedonantoja, 53) In Finnish and Swedish, with English summary.

— French Territory of the Afars and the Issas — Accounting.

FRANCE. Institut National de la Statistique et des Etudes Economiques. 1971. Comptes économiques du Territoire Français des Afars et des Issas, 1969-1970. Paris, [1971?]. pp. 35.

— Germany — Accounting.

CONRAD (KLAUS) of the University of Tübingen, and JORGENSON (DALE W.) Measuring performance in the private economy of the Federal Republic of Germany, 1950-1973. Tübingen, 1975. pp. 198. bibliog. (Tübingen. Universität. Fachbereich Wirtschaftswissenschaft. Tübinger Wirtschaftswissenschaftliche Abhandlungen. Band 19)

— — Saxony.

FUHRMANN (ERICH) Das Volksvermögen und Volkseinkommen des Königreichs Sachsen. Leipzig, 1914. pp. 60. bibliog.

— India — Accounting.

INDIA. Committee on Regional Accounts. 1974. First report; [M. Mukherjee, chairman]. [Delhi], 1974. pp. 86.

— — Mathematical models.

BHATTACHARYA (B. B.) Short-term income determination. Delhi, 1975. pp. 172. bibliog.

— Italy.

TAGLIACARNE (GUGLIELMO) Il reddito prodotto nelle province italiane nel 1973 e confronti con gli anni 1951, 1971 e 1972: indici di alcuni consumi e del risparmio assicurativo. Milano, [1975]. pp. 133. (Unione Italiana delle Camere di Commercio, Industria e Agricoltura. Quaderni di Sintesi Economica. 4)

— Liberia — Accounting.

LIBERIA. Department of Planning and Economic Affairs. 1968. National income of Liberia, 1966. Monrovia, 1968. fo. 160. Photocopy.

— Mauritania — Accounting.

COMPTES ECONOMIQUES DE LA MAURITANIE; (pd.by) Direction de la Statistique, Ministère de Planification et du Développement Industriel. a., 1973- Nouakchott.

— Morocco — Accounting.

MOROCCO. Division de la Comptabilité Nationale et des Synthèses. Comptes de la nation. a., 1964/1974- [Rabat].

— Norway — Accounting.

BJERKE (JUUL) Estimering av konsumfunksjoner på grunnlag av nasjonalregnskapsdata, 1865-1968...: consumption functions from national accounts data, 1865-1968. Oslo, 1972. pp. 60. (Norway. Statistiske Centralbyrå. Artikler. Nr. 53) With English summary.

SEVALDSON (PER) Om oppstilling og bruk av regionalt nasjonalregnskap...: construction and use of regional national accounts. Oslo, 1973. pp. 74. (Norway. Statistiske Centralbyrå. Artikler. Nr. 60)

RINGSTAD (VIDAR) Prisutvikling og prisatferd i 1960-årene: en presentasjon og analyse av nasjonalregnskapets prisdata, 1961-1969: the development and behaviour of prices in the 1960's: presentation and analysis of the price-data of the Norwegian national accounts, 1961-1969. Oslo, 1974. pp. 478. bibliog. (Norway. Statistiske Centralbyrå. Samfunnsøkonomiske Studier. 23) With English summary.

NASJONALREGNSKAP, modeller og analyse; en artikkelsamling til Odd Aukrusts 60-årsdag: national accounts, models and analysis; to Odd Aukrust in honour of his sixtieth birthday. Oslo, 1975. pp. 321. (Norway. Statistiske Centralbyrå. Samfunnsokonomiske Studier. 26)

NORWAY. Statistiske Centralbyrå. 1975. Revidert nasjonalregnskap. Oslo, 1975. pp. 63. (Statistiske Analyser. 14)

— Papua New Guinea — Accounting.

PAPUA NEW GUINEA. Bureau of Statistics. Statistical bulletin: national accounts statistics: consolidated accounts for the nation. a., 1974/75(no.1)- Port Moresby.

— South Africa — Accounting.

SOUTH AFRICA. Bureau of Statistics. National accounts of the Bantu homelands. a., 1969-70/1973-74 (1st)- Pretoria. [in English and Afrikaans].

— Swaziland — Accounting.

SWAZILAND. Central Statistical Office. National accounts. a., 1968/69, 1972- Mbabane.

— Togo — Accounting.

TOGO REPUBLIC. Direction de la Statistique. Comptes nationaux. a., 1969- Lomé.

— United Kingdom.

NASIŁOWSKI (MIECZYSŁAW) Udział płac w dochodzie narodowym USA i Anglii. Warszawa, 1962. pp. 235. bibliog. With English and Russian summaries.

— United States.

NASIŁOWSKI (MIECZYSŁAW) Udział płac w dochodzie narodowym USA i Anglii. Warszawa, 1962. pp. 235. bibliog. With English and Russian summaries.

— — Accounting.

SEIDLER (LEE J.) and SEIDLER (LYNN L.) eds. Social accounting: theory, issues, and cases. Los Angeles, [1975]. pp. 547. bibliogs.

— Yugoslavia — Accounting.

YUGOSLAVIA. Savezni Zavod za Statistiku. Studije, Analize i Prikazi. 73. Privredni bilansi Jugoslavije, 1973; Economic balances of Yugoslavia, 1973; Balansy narodnogo khoziaistva Iugoslavii, 1973. Beograd, 1975. pp. 191. With English and Russian summaries.

NATIONAL LIBERAL PARTY (GERMANY).

WHITE (DAN S.) The splintered party: National Liberalism in Hessen and the Reich, 1867-1918. Cambridge, Mass., 1976. pp. 303. *bibliog.*

NATIONAL PARTY (SOUTH AFRICA).

GEYSER (O.) and MARAIS (A.H.) eds. Die Nasionale Party. Pretoria, 1975 in progress.

NATIONAL SOCIALISM.

GLASS (DAVID VICTOR) [Materials for a study of national-socialist population policy and abortion law. 1912, 1931-38]. 1 piece. *Manuscript, typescript, etc.*

ASSOCIATION DES ECRIVAINS ET ARTISTES REVOLUTIONNAIRES. Ceux qui ont choisi...:contre le fascisme en Allemagne, contre l'impérialisme français; ([by] Henri Barbusse [and others]). Paris, [1933?]. pp. 24.

DICKS (HENRY VICTOR) German political attitudes: an analysis and forecast of likely reactions confronting the Allies in occupied Germany. London, 1944. pp. 13. *(U.K. War Office. Directorate of Army Psychiatry. Research Memoranda. No.45/03/11)*

PRATT (JAMES ALEXANDER) The social basis of Nazism and communism in urban Germany. 1948. pp. 277. *bibliog. M.A.(Michigan State College of Agriculture and Applied Science) thesis: unpublished. Microfilm of typescript: 1 reel.*

WAR ich ein Nazi?: Politik, Anfechtung des Gewissens; mit Beiträgen von Joachim Günther [and others]; und mit einer Anleitung für den Leser von Ludwig Marcuse. München, [1968]. pp. 167.

MITSCHERLICH (ALEXANDER) and MITSCHERLICH (MARGARETE) Eine deutsche Art zu lieben. München, [1970]. pp. 119. *Revised version of the first chapter of their Die Unfähigkeit zu trauern.*

HALLGARTEN (GEORGE WOLFGANG FELIX) and RADKAU (JOACHIM) Deutsche Industrie und Politik von Bismarck bis heute. Frankfurt am Main, [1974]. pp. 574. *bibliog.*

WAGNER (WALTER) Der Volksgerichtshof im nationalsozialistischen Staat. Stuttgart, 1974. pp. 992. *(Institut für Zeitgeschichte. Quellen und Darstellungen zur Zeitgeschichte. Band 16/3)*

BOTZ (GERHARD) Wohnungspolitik und Judendeportation in Wien, 1938 bis 1945: zur Funktion des Antisemitismus als Ersatz nationalsozialistischer Sozialpolitik. Wien, 1975. pp. 200. *bibliog. (Salzburg. Universität. Historisches Institut. Veröffentlichungen. 13)*

FELICE (RENZO DE) Mussolini e Hitler: i rapporti segreti, 1922-1933; con documenti inediti. Firenze, [1975]. pp. 315.

FRENZEL (MAX) and others. Gesprengte Fesseln: ein Bericht über den antifaschistischen Widerstand und die Geschichte der illegalen Parteiorganisation der KPD im Zuchthaus Brandenburg-Goerden von 1933 bis 1945. Berlin, [1975]. pp. 347.

HILLEL (MARC) and HENRY (CLARISSA) Lebensborn e.V.: im Namen der Rasse; (berechtigte Übersetzung [from the French] von Annette Lallemand). Wien, [1975]. pp. 352. *bibliog.*

Das JAHR 1934: 25.Juli; Protokoll des Symposiums in Wien am 8.Oktober 1974; (herausgegeben von Ludwig Jedlicka und Rudolf Neck). Wien, 1975. pp. 154. *(Theodor-Körner-Stiftungsfonds, and Leopold-Kunschak-Preis. Wissenschaftliche Kommission zur Erforschung der Österreichischen Geschichte der Jahre 1927 bis 1938. Veröffentlichungen. Band 3)*

KUEHNL (REINHARD) ed. Der deutsche Faschismus in Quellen und Dokumenten. Köln, [1975]. pp. 512. *bibliog.*

LUZA (RADOMÍR) Austro-German relations in the Anschluss era. Princeton, [1975]. pp. 438. *bibliog.*

MASON (TIMOTHY W.) ed. Arbeiterklasse und Volksgemeinschaft: Dokumente und Materialien zur deutschen Arbeiterpolitik, 1936-1939. Opladen, [1975]. pp. 1299. *bibliog. (Institut für Politische Wissenschaft. Schriften. Band 22)*

POLAND (TERRITORY UNDER GERMAN OCCUPATION, 1939—1945). Generalgouverneur, 1975. Das Diensttagebuch des deutschen Generalgouverneurs in Polen, 1939-1945; herausgegeben von Werner Präg und Wolfgang Jacobmeyer. Stuttgart, 1975. pp. 1027. *(Institut für Zeitgeschichte. Quellen und Darstellungen zur Zeitgeschichte. Band 20)*

SAUER (PAUL) Württemberg in der Zeit des Nationalsozialismus. Ulm, 1975. pp. 519. *bibliog.*

SCHELLENBERGER (BARBARA) Katholische Jugend und Drittes Reich: eine Geschichte des Katholischen Jungmännerverbandes, 1933-1939, etc. Mainz, [1975]. pp. 202. *bibliog. (Kommission für Zeitgeschichte. Veröffentlichungen. Reihe B: Forschungen. Band 17)*

STACHURA (PETER D.) Nazi youth in the Weimar Republic. Santa Barbara, [1975]. pp. 301. *bibliog.*

STEPHENSON (JILL) Women in Nazi society. London, 1975. pp. 223. *bibliog.*

TILTON (TIMOTHY ALAN) Nazism, neo-Nazism, and the peasantry. Bloomington, [1975]. pp. 186. *bibliog. (Indiana University. Publications. Social Science Series. No. 31)*

TREUDE (BURKHARD) Konservative Presse und Nationalsozialismus: Inhaltsanalyse der 'Neuen Preussischen (Kreuz-) Zeitung' am Ende der Weimarer Republik. Bochum, 1975. pp. 195. *bibliog.*

JAGSCHITZ (GERHARD) Der Putsch: die Nationalsozialisten 1934 in Österreich. Graz, [1976]. pp. 260. *bibliog.*

KREBS (ALBERT) The infancy of Nazism: the memoirs of ex-Gauleiter Albert Krebs, 1923-1933; edited and translated by William Sheridan Allen. New York, 1976. pp. 328. *bibliog.*

SYWOTTEK (JUTTA) Mobilmachung für den totalen Krieg: die propagandistische Vorbereitung der deutschen Bevölkerung auf den Zweiten Weltkrieg. Opladen, [1976]. pp. 398. *bibliog. (Hamburg. Hansische Universität. Studien zur Modernen Geschichte. Band 18)*

VEREIN FÜR SOZIALPOLITIK. Schriften. Neue Folge. Band 89. Probleme der nationalsozialistischen Wirtschaftspolitik; von Fritz Blaich [and others]; herausgegeben von Friedrich-Wilhelm Henning. Berlin, [1976]. pp. 174.

— Bibliography.

INSTITUT FÜR ZEITGESCHICHTE. Bibliothek. Alphabetischer Katalog; ([with] Erster Nachtragsband). Boston, Mass., 1967-73. 6 vols.

INSTITUT FÜR ZEITGESCHICHTE. Bibliothek. Sachkatalog; ([with] Erster Nachtragsband). Boston, Mass., 1967-73. 8 vols.

INSTITUT FÜR ZEITGESCHICHTE. Bibliothek. Biographischer Katalog. Boston, Mass., 1967. pp. 764.

INSTITUT FÜR ZEITGESCHICHTE. Bibliothek. Erster Nachtragsband: Biographischer Katalog; Länderkatalog. Boston, Mass., 1973. pp. 588.

NATIONAL SONGS, CANADIAN.

CANADA. Parliament. Special Joint Committee of the Senate and House of Commons on the National and Royal Anthems. 1967-68. Minutes of proceedings (including evidence and reports); joint chairmen: Maurice Bourget and S. Perry Ryan. Ottwa, 1967-68. 3 pts.

NATIONALISM.

FELS (JOSEF) Begriff und Wesen der Nation: eine soziologische Untersuchung und Kritik. Münster in Westfalen, 1927. pp. 147. *bibliog.*

FRANCIS (EMERICH K.) Interethnic relations: an essay in sociological theory. New York, [1976]. pp. 432. *bibliog.*

NATURAL RESOURCES.

NATIONALIST movements; edited by Anthony D. Smith. London, 1976. pp. 185.

ZWERIN (MICHAEL) A case for the balkanization of practically everyone: the new nationalism. London, 1976. pp. 190. *bibliog.*

— Asia.

CHAVAN (R.S.) Nationalism in Asia. New Delhi, 1973. pp. 595. *bibliog.*

NATIONALISM AND SOCIALISM.

DICKMANN (ADOLFO) El socialismo y el principio de nacionalidad. Buenos Aires, 1916. pp. 62.

MAN (HENRI DE) Sozialismus und Nationalfascismus. Potsdam, 1931. pp. 61.

MOMMSEN (HANS) Nationalitätenfrage und Arbeiterbewegung. Trier, [1971]. pp. 46. *(Karl-Marx-Haus. Schriften. 6) Xerox copy.*

HENTZE (JUERGEN) Nationalismus und Internationalismus bei Rosa Luxemburg. Bern, 1975. pp. 217. *bibliog.*

KARDELJ (EDVARD) Nacija i medjunarodni odnosi: [a collection of articles]. Beograd, 1975. pp. 249.

OSUSHCHESTVLENIE printsipov internatsionalizma v natsional'noi politike KPSS. Moskva, 1975. pp. 342.

KONRAD (HELMUT) Nationalismus und Internationalismus: die österreichische Arbeiterbewegung vor dem Ersten Weltkrieg. Wien, 1976. pp. 214. *bibliog. (Ludwig-Boltzmann-Institut für Geschichte der Arbeiterbewegung. Materialien zur Arbeiterbewegung. Nr.4)*

KOSING (ALFRED) Nation in Geschichte und Gegenwart: Studie zur historisch-materialistischen Theorie der Nation. Berlin, 1976. pp. 310.

NATURAL LAW.

MIDGLEY (ERNEST BRIAN FRANCIS) The natural law tradition and the theory of international relations. London, 1975. pp. 587. *bibliog.*

NATURAL RESOURCES.

The ECONOMICS of natural resource depletion: (papers...given at a conference...organised jointly by the...Environmental Economics Study Group...and the Institute of Environmental Sciences); edited by D.W. Pearce assisted by J. Rose. London, 1975. pp. 220. *Includes additional essay by Ivor Pearce.*

MIKDASHI (ZUHAYR) The international politics of natural resources. Ithaca, 1976. pp. 214.

NOVICK (DAVID) A world of scarcities: critical issues in public policy;...with Kurt Bleicken [and others]. London, 1976. pp. 194.

STRETTON (HUGH) Capitalism, socialism and the environment. Cambridge, 1976. pp. 332.

— Canada.

CANADA. Department of Energy, Mines and Resources. 1968. Highlights '67. Ottawa, 1968. pp. 20.

ROTSTEIN (ABRAHAM) ed. Beyond industrial growth. Toronto, 1976. pp. 131. *Lectures given at Massey College, University of Toronto, 1974-1975.*

— Dominican Republic.

ANTONINI (GUSTAVO A.) and others. Population and energy: a systems analysis of resource utilization in the Dominican Republic. Gainesville, Fla., 1975. pp. 166. *bibliog. (Florida University. School of Inter-American Studies. Latin American Monographs. 2nd Series. No.14) With 8 maps in separate case.*

— Norway.

NORWAY. Statistiske Centralbyrå. 1976. Miljøstatistikk, 1976: naturressurser og forurensninger, etc. Oslo, 1976. pp. 228. *(Statistiske Analyser. 22) With English summary.*

NATURAL RESOURCES.(Cont.)

— Russia.

KOMAR (IGOR' VALERIANOVICH) Ratsional'noe ispol'zovanie prirodnykh resursov i resursnye tsikly. Moskva, 1975. pp. 212. *bibliog. (Akademiia Nauk SSSR. Institut Geografii. Problemy Konstruktivnoi Geografii)*

— — Kazakstan.

GEOGRAFIIA prirodnykh resursov Kazakhstana. Alma-Ata, 1974. pp. 200. *bibliog. (Akademiia Nauk Kazakhskoi SSR. Sektor Geografii. Voprosy Geografii Kazakhstana. vyp.16)*

NAVAHO INDIANS.

WITHERSPOON (GARY) Navajo kinship and marriage. Chicago, 1975. pp. 137. *bibliog.*

— Government relations.

PARMAN (DONALD L.) The Navajos and the New Deal. New Haven, 1976. pp. 316. *bibliog.*

NAVAL ART AND SCIENCE.

ROHWER (JUERGEN) Superpower confrontation on the seas: naval development and strategy since 1945; [translated from the German by Walter F. Hahn]. Beverly Hills, [1975]. pp. 89. *bibliog. (Georgetown University. Center for Strategic and International Studies. Washington Papers. vol. 3/26)*

NAVIES.

CONFERENCE ON PROBLEMS OF NAVAL ARMAMENTS, ITHACA, 1972. Sea power in the 1970s; George H. Quester, editor. New York, [1975]. pp. 248. *Papers of the conference sponsored by the Cornell University Program on Peace Studies.*

N'DONGO (SALLY).

N'DONGO (SALLY) Voyage forcé: itinéraire d'un militant. Paris, 1975. pp. 224.

NEBRASKA

— Rural conditions.

NEBRASKA. Legislative Council. Committee on the Problems of Local Communities. 1964. Report. [Lincoln], 1964. fo. 13. *(Legislative Council. Committee Reports. No. 137)*

NECHAEV (SERGEI GENNADIEVICH).

AVRICH (PAUL HENRY) Bakunin and Nechaev. London, 1974. pp. 32. *bibliog.*

NEGLIGENCE

— United Kingdom.

TEFF (HARVEY) and MUNRO (COLIN R.) Thalidomide: the legal aftermath. Farnborough, [1976]. pp. 154.

NEGOTIABLE INSTRUMENTS

— United Kingdom.

RICHARDSON (DUDLEY) Guide to negotiable instruments and the Bills of Exchange Acts. 5th ed. London, 1976. pp. 188.

NEGOTIATION.

JÖNSSON (CHRISTER) The Soviet Union and the test ban: a study in Soviet negotiating behavior. Lund, 1975. pp. 221. *bibliog.*

RUBIN (JEFFREY Z.) and BROWN (BERT R.) The social psychology of bargaining and negotiation. New York, 1975. pp. 359. *bibliog.*

MARTIN (WILFRED B.W.) The negotiated order of the school. [Toronto, 1976]. pp. 191. *bibliog.*

NEGRO CHURCHES.

WILLIAMS (MELVIN D.) Community in a black pentecostal church: an anthropological study. Pittsburgh, [1974]. pp. 202. *bibliog.*

NELSEN (HART M.) and NELSEN (ANNE KUSENER) Black church in the sixties. [Lexington, Ky., 1975]. pp. 172.

NEGRO ENGLISH DIALECTS.

DILLARD (JOEY LEE) ed. Perspectives in black English. The Hague, [1975]. pp. 391. *bibliogs.*

NEGRO EXECUTIVES.

FERNANDEZ (JOHN P.) Black managers in white corporations. New York, [1975]. pp. 308. *bibliog.*

NEGRO FAMILIES.

STACK (CAROL B.) All our kin: strategies for survival in a black community. New York, [1974]. pp. 175. *bibliog.*

NEGRO RACE

— Race identity.

GURIN (PATRICIA) and EPPS (EDGAR G.) Black consciousness, identity and achievement: a study of students in historically black colleges. New York, [1975]. pp. 545. *bibliog.*

NEGRO STUDENTS.

GURIN (PATRICIA) and EPPS (EDGAR G.) Black consciousness, identity and achievement: a study of students in historically black colleges. New York, [1975]. pp. 545. *bibliog.*

— Political activity.

ORUM (ANTHONY M.) Black students in protest: a study of the origins of the black student movement. Washington, [1974]. pp. 89. *bibliog. (American Sociological Association. Arnold and Caroline Rose Monograph Series in Sociology)*

NEGRO YOUTH

— Employment — Rhodesia.

MURPHREE (MARSHALL WARNE) ed. Education, race and employment in Rhodesia. Salisbury, Rhodesia, 1975. pp. 478. *bibliog.*

— — United Kingdom.

FIGUEROA (PETER EUGENE) West Indian school-leavers in London: a sociological study in ten schools in a London borough, 1966-1967; [Ph.D. (London) thesis]. 1974 (or rather 1975). fo. 541. *bibliog. Typescript: unpublished. This thesis is the property of London University and may not be removed from the Library.*

NEGROES.

MYRDAL (GUNNAR) An American dilemma revisited: main assumptions for a new book. [Stockholm?], 1974. fo. 46.

WINTERSMITH (ROBERT F.) Police and the black community. Lexington, Mass., [1974]. pp. 149. *bibliog.*

DAVIS (GEORGE A.) and DONALDSON (O. FRED) Blacks in the United States: a geographic perspective. Boston, [1975]. pp. 270. *bibliogs.*

— Charities.

DAVIS (KING E.) Fund raising in the black community: history, feasibility, and conflict. Metuchen, N.J., 1975. pp. 169. *bibliog.*

— Civil rights.

BROOKS (THOMAS R.) Walls come tumbling down: a history of the civil rights movement, 1940-1970. Englewood Cliffs, [1974]. pp. 309. *bibliog.*

McPHERSON (JAMES M.) The abolitionist legacy: from reconstruction to the N.A.A.C.P. Princeton, 1975. pp. 438. *bibliog.*

NELSEN (HART M.) and NELSEN (ANNE KUSENER) Black church in the sixties. [Lexington, Ky., 1975]. pp. 172.

TURNER (ROBERT PHILLIP) Up to the front of the line: blacks in the American political system. Port Washington, N.Y., 1975. pp. 225. *bibliog.*

BLACK (EARL) Southern governors and civil rights: racial segregation as a campaign issue in the Second Reconstruction. Cambridge, Mass., 1976. pp. 408.

RUSTIN (BAYARD) Strategies for freedom: the changing patterns of black protest. New York, 1976. pp. 82. *(Columbia University. William Radner Lectures. [1974?])*

WYNN (NEIL A.) The Afro-American and the second world war. London, 1976. pp. 183. *bibliog.*

— Colonization.

DICK (ROBERT C.) Black protest: issues and tactics. Westport, Conn., 1974. pp. 338. *bibliog.*

— — Canada.

WALKER (JAMES W. ST. G.) The black loyalists: the search for a promised land in Nova Scotia and Sierra Leone, 1783-1870. London, 1976. pp. 438. *bibliog.*

— — Sierra Leone.

WALKER (JAMES W. ST. G.) The black loyalists: the search for a promised land in Nova Scotia and Sierra Leone, 1783-1870. London, 1976. pp. 438. *bibliog.*

— Economic conditions.

RACISM and inequality: the policy alternatives; edited by Harrell R. Rodgers. San Francisco, [1975]. pp. 220.

— Education.

WILLIAMS (ROBERT L.) Educational alternatives for colonized people: models for liberation...; edited by Anne M. St. Pierre. New York, [1974]. pp. 130. *bibliog.*

— Employment.

FLETCHER (ARTHUR) The silent sell-out: government betrayal of blacks to the craft unions. New York, [1973]. pp. 121.

CULL (JOHN G.) and HARDY (RICHARD E.) eds. Career guidance for black adolescents: a guide to selected professional occupations. Springfield, Ill., [1975]. pp. 148. *bibliogs.*

FERNANDEZ (JOHN P.) Black managers in white corporations. New York, [1975]. pp. 308. *bibliog.*

— History.

DICK (ROBERT C.) Black protest: issues and tactics. Westport, Conn., 1974. pp. 338. *bibliog.*

FRANKLIN (JOHN HOPE) From slavery to freedom: a history of Negro Americans. 4th ed. New York, 1974. pp. 548,xlii. *bibliog.*

SEAGRAVE (CHARLES EDWIN) The southern negro agricultural worker, 1850-1870. New York, 1975. pp. 119. *bibliog. Ph. D. dissertation-Stanford University, 1971.*

RUSTIN (BAYARD) Strategies for freedom: the changing patterns of black protest. New York, 1976. pp. 82. *(Columbia University. William Radner Lectures. [1974?])*

— Housing.

RACISM and inequality: the policy alternatives; edited by Harrell R. Rodgers. San Francisco, [1975]. pp. 220.

— Language.

HALL (WILLIAM S.) and FREEDLE (ROY O.) Culture and language: the black American experience. New York, [1975]. pp. 191. *bibliog.*

— Politics and suffrage.

DICK (ROBERT C.) Black protest: issues and tactics. Westport, Conn., 1974. pp. 338. *bibliog.*

GILLIAM (REGINALD EARL) Black political development: an advocacy analysis. Port Washington, N.Y., [1975]. pp. 334. *bibliog.*

MORRIS (MILTON D.) The politics of black America. New York, [1975]. pp. 319. *bibliogs.*

TURNER (ROBERT PHILLIP) Up to the front of the line: blacks in the American political system. Port Washington, N.Y., 1975. pp. 225. *bibliog.*

WALTON (HANES) Black Republicans: the politics of the black and tans. Metuchen, N.J., 1975. pp. 199. *bibliog.*

COLE (LEONARD A.) Blacks in power: a comparative study of black and white elected officials. Princeton, [1976]. pp. 267.

GROSSMAN (LAWRENCE) The Democratic Party and the negro: northern and national politics, 1868-92. Urbana, [1976]. pp. 212. *bibliog.*

— Race identity — Bibliography.

OBUDHO (CONSTANCE E.) Black-white racial attitudes: an annotated bibliography. Westport, Conn., 1976. pp. 180.

— Segregation.

FOREMAN (THOMAS ELTON) Discrimination against the Negro in American athletics: a thesis. San Francisco, 1957 repr. 1975. pp. 72. *bibliog.* Thesis (M.A.)-Fresno State College.

FISCHER (ROGER A.) The segregation struggle in Louisiana, 1862-77. Urbana, Ill., [1974]. pp. 168. *bibliog.*

BLACK (EARL) Southern governors and civil rights: racial segregation as a campaign issue in the Second Reconstruction. Cambridge, Mass., 1976. pp. 408.

— Social conditions.

PETERSON (JAMES) Escape from poverty: occupational and economic mobility among urban blacks. Chicago, [1974]. pp. 176. *bibliog. (Chicago. University. Community and Family Study Center. Community and Family Monographs)*

STACK (CAROL B.) All our kin: strategies for survival in a black community. New York, [1974]. pp. 175. *bibliog.*

MURASKIN (WILLIAM A.) Middle-class blacks in a white society: Prince Hall Freemasonry in America. Berkeley, [1975]. pp. 318. *bibliog.*

RACISM and inequality: the policy alternatives; edited by Harrell R. Rodgers. San Francisco, [1975]. pp. 220.

WYNN (NEIL A.) The Afro-American and the second world war. London, 1976. pp. 183. *bibliog.*

— Social life and customs.

JOHNSON (CHARLES SPURGEON) Shadow of the plantation. Chicago, 1934 repr. 1969. pp. 215.

ASCHENBRENNER (JOYCE) Lifelines: black families in Chicago. New York, [1975]. pp. 146. *bibliog.*

— Chicago.

ASCHENBRENNER (JOYCE) Lifelines: black families in Chicago. New York, [1975]. pp. 146. *bibliog.*

— Cleveland.

KUSMER (KENNETH L.) A ghetto takes shape: black Cleveland, 1870-1930. Urbana, Ill., [1976]. pp. 305. *bibliog.*

— Louisiana.

FISCHER (ROGER A.) The segregation struggle in Louisiana, 1862-77. Urbana, Ill., [1974]. pp. 168. *bibliog.*

NEGROES AS CONSUMERS.

ANDREASEN (ALAN R.) The disadvantaged consumer. New York, [1975]. pp. 366.

NEGROES IN COLOMBIA.

WHITTEN (NORMAN E.) Black frontiersmen: a South American case. New York, [1974]. pp. 221. *bibliog.*

NEGROES IN CUBA.

KIPLE (KENNETH F.) Blacks in colonial Cuba, 1774-1899. Gainesville, Fla., 1976. pp. 115. *bibliog. (Florida University. School of Inter-American Studies. Latin American Monographs. 2nd Series. No. 17)*

NEGROES IN ECUADOR.

WHITTEN (NORMAN E.) Black frontiersmen: a South American case. New York, [1974]. pp. 221. *bibliog.*

NEGROES IN LATIN AMERICA.

KNIGHT (FRANKLIN W.) The African dimension in Latin American societies. New York, 1974. pp. 148. *bibliog.*

MELLAFE (ROLANDO) Negro slavery in Latin America;...translated by J.W.S. Judge. Berkeley, [1975]. pp. 172. *bibliog.*

NEGROES IN RHODESIA.

CATHOLIC COMMISSION FOR JUSTICE AND PEACE IN RHODESIA. The man in the middle: torture, resettlement and eviction. London, [1975]. pp. 22.

VAN ONSELEN (CHARLES) Chibaro: African mine labour in Southern Rhodesia, 1900-1933. London, 1976. pp. 326. *bibliog.*

NEGROES IN SOUTH AFRICA.

FOREIGN investment in South Africa: the conditions of the black worker; [by] W.H. Thomas [and others]. [London], 1975. pp. 295. *(Study Project on External Investment in South Africa and Namibia (S.W. Africa). Study Project Papers. [vol. 4])*

NATTRASS (JILL) and DUNCAN (IAN G.) A study of employers' attitudes towards African worker representation. Durban, 1975. pp. 36. *(Natal University. Department of Economics. Black/White Income Gap Project. Interim Research Project. No.1)*

THOMPSON (RICHARD) Writer on race relations. Retreat from apartheid: New Zealand's sporting contacts with South Africa. Wellington, 1975. pp. 102.

ORPEN (CHRISTOPHER) Productivity and black workers in South Africa. Cape Town, [1976]. pp. 283. *bibliog.*

NEGROES IN SOUTH WEST AFRICA.

The ROLE of foreign firms in Namibia: studies on external investment and black workers' conditions in Namibia; [by] Roger Murray [and others]. Uppsala, 1974. pp. 220. *bibliogs. (Study Project on External Investment in South Africa and Namibia (S.W. Africa). Study Project Papers. [vol. 3])*

NEGROES IN THE ARGENTINE REPUBLIC.

ORTIZ ODERIGO (NESTOR) Aspectos de la cultura africana en el Rio de la Plata. [Buenos Aires, 1974]. pp. 200. *bibliog.*

NEGROES IN URUGUAY.

ORTIZ ODERIGO (NESTOR) Aspectos de la cultura africana en el Rio de la Plata. [Buenos Aires, 1974]. pp. 200. *bibliog.*

NEHRU (JAWAHARLAL).

RAU (M. CHALAPATHI) Jawaharlal Nehru. New Delhi, 1973. pp. 428. *(Builders of Modern India)*

GOPAL (SARVEPALLI) Jawaharlal Nehru: a biography. London, 1975 in progress. *bibliog.*

NASENKO (IURII PETROVICH) Dzhavakharlal Neru i vneshniaia politika Indii. Moskva, 1975. pp. 383. *bibliog.*

INDIAN foreign policy: the Nehru years: [a series of lectures delivered in the Nehru Memorial Museum and Library in 1973- 74]; edited by B.R. Nanda. Delhi, [1976]. pp. 279.

PANDEY (BISHWA NATH) Nehru. London, 1976. pp. 499. *bibliog.*

NEIGHBOURHOOD.

BATLEY (RICHARD) The neighbourhood scheme: cases of central government intervention in local deprivation. London, 1975. pp. 112. *bibliog. (Centre for Environmental Studies. Research Papers. 19)*

NEIGHBOURLINESS.

AGE CONCERN ENGLAND. Good neighbours. London, [1972]. pp. 6. *bibliog.*

NEPAL

— Economic policy.

NEPAL. National Planning Commission. 1972. Fourth plan, 1970-1975. Kathmandu, 1972. pp. 291, 1 map.

NEPAL. National Planning Commission. 1974. Policy guidelines for the fifth plan, 1975-1980. [Kathmandu], 1974. pp. 132.

VIKAS: a journal of development; [pd. by] Secretariat, National Planning Commission, Nepal. s-a., N 1975(v.1, no.2)- Kathmandu.

NEPAL. National Planning Commission. 1975. The fifth plan, 1975-80, in brief. [Kathmandu], 1975. pp. 54.

— Nationalism.

GAIGE (FREDERICK H.) Regionalism and national unity in Nepal. Berkeley, [1975]. pp. 234. *bibliog.*

— Population.

MACFARLANE (ALAN DONALD JAMES) Resources and population: a study of the Gurungs of Nepal. Cambridge, 1976. pp. 364. *bibliog.*

— Social policy.

NEPAL. National Planning Commission. 1972. Fourth plan, 1970-1975. Kathmandu, 1972. pp. 291, 1 map.

NEPAL. National Planning Commission. 1974. Policy guidelines for the fifth plan, 1975-1980. [Kathmandu], 1974. pp. 132.

VIKAS: a journal of development; [pd. by] Secretariat, National Planning Commission, Nepal. s-a., N 1975(v.1, no.2)- Kathmandu.

NEPAL. National Planning Commission. 1975. The fifth plan, 1975-80, in brief. [Kathmandu], 1975. pp. 54.

— Statistics.

ECONOMIC DATA PAPERS - NEPAL; [pd. by] Economic Planning Section, Program Office, USAID/Nepal. a., My 1968 [covering 1967]-1973 (v.10-14); ceased pbln. [Kathmandu].

NESSELRODE (KARL ROBERT VON) Graf.

INGLE (HAROLD N.) Nesselrode and the Russian rapprochement with Britain, 1836-1844. Berkeley, [1976]. pp. 196. *bibliog.*

NETHERLANDS

— Civilization.

HALEY (KENNETH HAROLD DOBSON) The Dutch in the seventeenth century. London, [1972]. pp. 216. *bibliog.*

— Economic conditions.

TUSSENTIJDS BESTEK, AMSTERDAM, 1975. Nederland en de grenzen aan de groei: [proceedings of the symposium]. Utrecht, 1975. pp. 174.

— Economic policy.

TUSSENTIJDS BESTEK, AMSTERDAM, 1975. Nederland en de grenzen aan de groei: [proceedings of the symposium]. Utrecht, 1975. pp. 174.

NETHERLANDS(Cont.)

— Famines.

FAMINE and human development: the Dutch hunger winter of 1944- 1945; [by] Zena Stein [and others]. New York, 1975. pp. 284. *bibliog.*

— Foreign population.

DUIJN (JAN VAN) Ordnung muss sein: vervreemdeling in Nederland;... diskussiedokumentatie voor het Studium Generale Vervreemding in Nederland...1972 van de Rijksuniversiteit te Utrecht. 2nd ed. Amsterdam, 1973. 1 vol. (various pagings).

— Foreign relations — Australia.

LOCKWOOD (RUPERT) Black armada. Sydney, 1975. pp. 352.

— History.

ANGLO-DUTCH HISTORICAL CONFERENCE, 5TH, 1973. Britain and the Netherlands...: some political mythologies; papers delivered to the...conference; edited by J.S. Bromley and E.H. Kossmann. The Hague, 1975. pp. 212.

— — 1556-1648, Wars of Independence.

HALEY (KENNETH HAROLD DOBSON) The Dutch in the seventeenth century. London, [1972]. pp. 216. *bibliog.*

— — 1648—1714.

HALEY (KENNETH HAROLD DOBSON) The Dutch in the seventeenth century. London, [1972]. pp. 216. *bibliog.*

— Industries.

PINDER (DAVID) The Netherlands. Folkestone, Kent, 1976. pp. 194. *bibliog.*

— Intellectual life.

PRICE (JOHN LESLIE) Culture and society in the Dutch Republic during the 17th century. London, 1974. pp. 260. *bibliog.*

— Parliament.

DREES (WILLEM) Het Nederlandse Parlement: vroeger en nu. Naarden, 1975. pp. 319.

— Politics and government.

MAES (LOUIS THEO) The Parliament and Great Council of Malines, 1473-1796, an institution of a European dimension. Brussels, Ministry of Foreign Affairs, External Trade and Cooperation in Development, 1973. pp. 32. *(Memo from Belgium. No. 160)*

LIJPHART (AREND) The politics of accommodation: pluralism and democracy in the Netherlands. 2nd ed. Berkeley, Calif., 1975. pp. 231.

— Population.

GLASBERGEN (P.) and ZANDANEL (R.) Bevolkingsgroei en welvaartsstaat: een sociologische interpretatie van veranderend fertiliteitsgedrag in Nederland. Assen, 1976. pp. 129. *bibliog.*

— Race question.

RINSAMPESSY (ELIAS P.) De mogelijke gronden van agressie onder Molukse jongeren geplaatst in het kader van de integratieproblematiek. Utrecht, 1975. pp. 76. *bibliog.*

— Social conditions.

DOEL (JOHANNES VAN DEN) and HOOGERWERF (A.) eds. Gelijkheid en ongelijkheid in Nederland: analyse en beleid. Alphen aan den Rijn, 1975. pp. 312. *bibliogs.*

— Social history.

PRICE (JOHN LESLIE) Culture and society in the Dutch Republic during the 17th century. London, 1974. pp. 260. *bibliog.*

— Social policy.

BOND VOOR WETENSCHAPPELIJKE ARBEIDERS. Werkgroep Welzijnszorg. Naar een politieke analyse van het welzijnswerkbestel. Nijmegen, [1974]. pp. 47.

SOARES (MARIA CÂNDIDA MEDEIROS) and others. Aspectos do desenvolvimento social na Holanda. Lisboa, 1975. pp. 115. *(Portugal. Ministerio do Trabalho. Gabinete de Planeamento. Serie Estudos. 31)* With abstracts in English, French and German.

WELZIJNSWERK en welzijnspolitiek; [by] Max van den Berg [and others]. Amsterdam, 1975. pp. 144.

NETHERLANDS ANTILLES

— Economic conditions.

ECONOMISCHE NOTITIES; van het Departement van Economische Zaken, Nederlands Antillen. irreg., 1972 (1)- Willemstad.

NEUMEISTER (FRITZ).

EUROPEAN COURT OF HUMAN RIGHTS. Publications. Series A: Judgments and Decisions. [A8]. ..."Neumeister" case; judgment of 27th June 1968. Strasbourg, Council of Europe, 1968. 48 [bis]. *In English and French.*

EUROPEAN COURT OF HUMAN RIGHTS. Publications. Series B: Pleadings, Oral Arguments and Documents. [B6]. "Neumeister" case (1966-1969). Strasbourg, Council of Europe, 1969. pp. 307[bis], 309-338. *In English and French.*

EUROPEAN COURT OF HUMAN RIGHTS. Publications. Series A: Judgments and Decisions. [A] 17. ...Neumeister case: judgment of 7 May 1974; question of the application of Article 50 of the Convention. Strasbourg, Council of Europe, 1974. pp. 21 [bis]. *In English and French.*

EUROPEAN COURT OF HUMAN RIGHTS. Publications. Series B: Pleadings, Oral Arguments and Documents. [B15]. "Neumeister" case: question of the application of Article 50 of the Convention, (1971-1974). Strasbourg, Council of Europe, 1974. pp. 142 [bis], 143-170. *In English and French.*

NEUROCHEMISTRY.

WARBURTON (DAVID M.) Brain, behaviour and drugs: introduction to the neurochemistry of behaviour. London, [1975]. pp. 280. *bibliog.*

NEUROPSYCHOLOGY.

MARUSZEWSKI (MARIUSZ) Language communication and the brain: a neuropsychological study. The Hague, 1975. pp. 217. *bibliog.*

NEUTRALITY.

RADOVANOVIĆ (LJUBOMIR) Nesvrstanost: osnovi jedne doktrine medjunarodne politike. Beograd, 1973. pp. 252. *bibliog.*

SIMON (SHELDON W.) Asian neutralism and U.S. policy. Washington, 1975. pp. 111. *(American Enterprise Institute for Public Policy Research. Foreign Affairs Studies. 21)*

NEW ENGLAND

— Church history.

HOLIFIELD (E. BROOKS) The covenant sealed: the development of Puritan sacramental theology in old and New England, 1570-1720. New Haven, 1974. pp. 248. *bibliog.*

— Description and travel.

PEIRCE (NEAL R.) The New England states: people, politics and power in the six New England states. New York, [1976]. pp. 447. *bibliog.*

— History.

HAFFENDEN (PHILIP S.) New England in the English nation, 1689-1713. Oxford, 1974. pp. 326. *bibliog.*

COOK (EDWARD M.) The fathers of the towns: leadership and community structure in eighteenth-century New England. Baltimore, [1976]. pp. 273. *bibliog. (Johns Hopkins University. Studies in Historical and Political Science. Series 94. No.2)*

— Intellectual life.

BERCOVITCH (SACVAN) The Puritan origins of the American self. New Haven, 1975. pp. 250.

— Politics and government.

PEIRCE (NEAL R.) The New England states: people, politics and power in the six New England states. New York, [1976]. pp. 447. *bibliog.*

NEW HAMPSHIRE

— History.

VAN DEVENTER (DAVID E.) The emergence of provincial New Hampshire, 1623-1741. Baltimore, [1976]. pp. 302. *bibliog.*

NEW JERSEY

— Politics and government.

POLITICS in New Jersey; edited by Alan Rosenthal and John Blydenburgh. New Brunswick, N.J., [1975]. pp. 290.

NEW PRODUCTS.

KALISIAK (JERZY) Planowanie nowego produktu. Warszawa, 1974. pp. 183. *bibliog. (Szkoła Główna Planowania i Statystyki. Monografie i Opracowania. 35)*

NEW SOUTH WALES

— Economic conditions.

NEW SOUTH WALES. Department of Decentralisation and Development. 1972. New South Wales: a handbook for investors. rev. ed. Sydney, 1972. pp. 191. *bibliog.*

NEW SOUTH WALES. State Planning Authority. 1972. Hunter region: growth and change: prelude to a plan. Sydney, 1972. pp. 112.

— Emigration and immigration.

AUSTRALIA. Migrant Task Force Committee, New South Wales. 1973. First report...into the immediate problems of migrants and recommendations for their resolution; [R.E. Klugman, chairman]. [Sydney, 1973]. 1 pamphlet (various foliations).

— Rural conditions.

UNIVERSITY OF NEW ENGLAND, ARMIDALE. Department of Sociology. Rural poverty in northern New South Wales. Canberra, Australian Government Publishing Service, 1974. pp. 169.

NEW SPAIN (VICEROYALTY)

— Intellectual life.

TRABULSE (ELIAS) Ciencia y religion en el siglo XVII. Mexico, [1974]. pp. 286. *bibliog. (Mexico City. Colegio de Mexico. Centro de Estudios Historicos. Nueva Serie. 18)*

NEW TOWNS.

APGAR (MAHLON) ed. New perspectives on community development. London, [1976]. pp. 363.

— Australia.

ROBINSON (ALBERT JOHN) Economics and new towns: a comparative study of the United States, the United Kingdom, and Australia. New York, 1975. pp. 142.

— United Kingdom.

ROBINSON (ALBERT JOHN) Economics and new towns: a comparative study of the United States, the United Kingdom, and Australia. New York, 1975. pp. 142.

WIRZ (HANS M.) Social aspects of planning in new towns. Farnborough, Hants., [1975]. pp. 237. *bibliog.*

LEVIN (PETER H.) Government and the planning process: an analysis and appraisal of government decision-making processes with special reference to the launching of new towns and town development schemes. London, 1976. pp. 337.

— United States.

ROBINSON (ALBERT JOHN) Economics and new towns: a comparative study of the United States, the United Kingdom, and Australia. New York, 1975. pp. 142.

WATTERSON (WAYT T.) and WATTERSON (ROBERTA S.) The politics of new communities: a case study of San Antonio Ranch. New York, 1975. pp. 142. bibliog.

BURBY (RAYMOND J.) and WEISS (SHIRLEY FRIEDLANDER) New communities: U.S.A. Lexington, Mass., [1976]. pp. 593. bibliog.

NEW WINDSOR

— History — Sources.

NEW WINDSOR. The second hall book of the Borough of New Windsor, 1726-1783; edited, with an introduction, by Jane Langton. Windsor, 1973. pp. 182. (New Windsor. Windsor Borough Historical Records Publications. vol. 2)

— Politics and government.

NEW WINDSOR. The second hall book of the Borough of New Windsor, 1726-1783; edited, with an introduction, by Jane Langton. Windsor, 1973. pp. 182. (New Windsor. Windsor Borough Historical Records Publications. vol. 2)

NEW YEAR.

POPOVICH (IURII VASIL'EVICH) Moldavskie novogodnie prazdniki, XIX - nachalo XX v. Kishinev, 1974. pp. 183. bibliog.

NEW YORK (CITY)

— Charters.

STATE CHARTER REVISION COMMISSION FOR NEW YORK CITY. Final report of the...Commission, etc.; [Roy M. Goodman, chairman]. New York, [1975]. pp. 35.

STATE CHARTER REVISION COMMISSION FOR NEW YORK CITY. Preliminary recommendations of the...Commission, etc.; [Roy M. Goodman, chairman]. New York, 1975. pp. 243.

STATE CHARTER REVISION COMMISSION FOR NEW YORK CITY. Proposed amendments to the charter for the City of New York; [Roy M. Goodman, chairman]. New York, 1975. 1 vol. (various pagings).

— Description — Guide—books.

The 1866 guide to New York City: New York as it is; or, Stranger's guide-book to the cities of New York, Brooklyn and adjacent places, etc. New York, 1975. 1 vol. (various pagings). Reprint of the work originally published in 1866.

— Foreign population.

DOLAN (JAY P.) The immigrant church: New York's Irish and German Catholics, 1815-1865. Baltimore, [1975]. pp. 221.

— Poor.

OSTOW (MIRIAM) and DUTKA (ANNA B.) Work and welfare in New York City. Baltimore, [1975]. pp. 93. Prepared for the Manpower Administration, U.S. Department of Labor.

— Religion.

DOLAN (JAY P.) The immigrant church: New York's Irish and German Catholics, 1815-1865. Baltimore, [1975]. pp. 221.

NEW YORK (STATE)

— Legislature — Officials and employees.

BALUTIS (ALAN P.) and HEAPHEY (JAMES J.) Public administration and the legislative process. Beverly Hills, [1974]. pp. 58. bibliog.

— Politics and government.

INGALLS (ROBERT P.) Herbert H. Lehman and New York's Little New Deal. New York, 1975. pp. 287. bibliog.

NEW ZEALAND

— Commerce — Brunei.

NEW ZEALAND. Department of Trade and Industry. 1975. Malaysia and Brunei: handbook. [Wellington], 1975. pp. 87. bibliog.

— — China.

NEW ZEALAND. Department of Trade and Industry. 1975. The People's Republic of China: handbook. [Wellington], 1975. pp. 70. bibliog.

— — Malaysia.

NEW ZEALAND. Department of Trade and Industry. 1975. Malaysia and Brunei: handbook. [Wellington], 1975. pp. 87. bibliog.

— Economic conditions.

NATIONAL DEVELOPMENT COUNCIL [NEW ZEALAND]. Targets Advisory Group. New Zealand in the 70's: growth for better living. [Wellington, Government Printer, 1972]. pp. 32.

MACRAE (JOHN TAIT) A study in the application of economic analysis to social issues: the Maori and the New Zealand economy. 1975. fo. 416. bibliog. Typescript. Ph.D. (London) thesis: unpublished. This thesis is the property of London University and may not be removed from the Library.

— Economic policy.

NATIONAL DEVELOPMENT COUNCIL [NEW ZEALAND]. Secretariat. A guide to the national development councils. rev. ed. [Wellington], 1972. pp. 67. (National Development Conference, Wellington. [Reports]. N.D.C. 21 Rev. 3)

NATIONAL DEVELOPMENT COUNCIL [NEW ZEALAND]. Targets Advisory Group. New Zealand in the 70's: growth for better living. [Wellington, Government Printer, 1972]. pp. 32.

— Emigration and immigration.

NATIONAL DEVELOPMENT COUNCIL [NEW ZEALAND]. Targets Advisory Group. Report...on population and migration. [Wellington, Government Printer], 1973. pp. 64.

— Industries.

NEW ZEALAND. Department of Statistics. 1975. Inter-industry study of the New Zealand economy 1965-66. [Wellington, 1975]. 2 vols. (in 1).

— Maps.

NEW Zealand atlas; edited by Ian Wards. Wellington, Government Printer, 1976. pp. 292.

— Parliament — Elections.

EDWARDS (BRIAN) Author of The public eye, ed. Right out: Labour victory '72: the inside story. Wellington, N.Z., 1973. pp. 262.

— — Rules and practice.

NEW ZEALAND. [General Assembly]. House of Representatives. Standing Orders Committee. 1967. Report;...[R.E. Jack, chairman]. Wellington, 1967. pp. 16.

— Politics and government.

DAVIS (RICHARD P.) Irish issues in New Zealand politics, 1868-1922. Dunedin, N.Z., 1974. pp. 248. bibliog.

BASSETT (JUDITH) Sir Harry Atkinson, 1831-1892. Auckland, 1975. pp. 196. bibliog.

MAY (PHILIP ROSS) ed. Miners and militants: politics in Westland, 1865-1918: six essays. Christchurch, N.Z., 1975. pp. 174. (Christchurch, New Zealand. University of Canterbury. Publications. No.21)

— Population.

NATIONAL DEVELOPMENT COUNCIL [NEW ZEALAND]. Targets Advisory Group. Report...on population and migration. [Wellington, Government Printer], 1973. pp. 64.

— Relations (general) with South Africa.

THOMPSON (RICHARD) Writer on race relations. Retreat from apartheid: New Zealand's sporting contacts with South Africa. Wellington, 1975. pp. 102.

— Social policy.

NATIONAL DEVELOPMENT COUNCIL [NEW ZEALAND]. Secretariat. A guide to the national development councils. rev. ed. [Wellington], 1972. pp. 67. (National Development Conference, Wellington. [Reports]. N.D.C. 21 Rev. 3)

— Statistics, Medical.

NEW ZEALAND. Department of Health. National Health Statistics Centre. Health statistics report: Hospital and selected morbidity data. a., 1971- . Wellington. Formerly included in NEW ZEALAND. Department of Health. National Health Statistics Centre. Health statistics report.

NEW ZEALAND. Department of Health. National Health Statistics Centre. Health statistics report: Mortality and demographic data. a., 1971- . Wellington. Formerly included in NEW ZEALAND. Department of Health. National Health Statistics Centre. Health statistics report.

— Statistics, Vital.

NEW ZEALAND. Department of Health. National Health Statistics Centre. Health statistics report: Mortality and demographic data. a., 1971- . Wellington. Formerly included in NEW ZEALAND. Department of Health. National Health Statistics Centre. Health statistics report.

NEWCASTLE—UPON—TYNE

— Description and travel.

BENWELL COMMUNITY DEVELOPMENT PROJECT. Benwell town trail; (by Tessa Hunkin). [Newcastle-upon-Tyne, 1976]. pp. 16. bibliog.

— Economic history.

BENWELL COMMUNITY DEVELOPMENT PROJECT. West Newcastle in growth and decline. [Newcastle-upon-Tyne], 1976. pp. 10.

— Foreign population.

TAYLOR (JOHN HENRY) The half-way generation: a study of Asian youths in Newcastle upon Tyne. Windsor, Berks., 1976. pp. 267. bibliog.

— Politics and government.

CADOGAN (PETER) Early radical Newcastle. Consett, [1975]. pp. 153. bibliog.

NEWFOUNDLAND

— History.

HUMPHREYS (JOHN) Historian. Plaisance: problems of settlement at this Newfoundland outpost of New France, 1660-1690. Ottawa, National Museums of Canada, 1970. pp. 24. (National Museum of Man [Canada]. Publications in History. No. 3)

NEWFOUNDLAND AND LABRADOR

— Statistics.

NEWFOUNDLAND. Central Statistical Services. Chartbook of selected statistics for Newfoundland and Labrador. s-a., N 1974- [St. John's].

NEWSPAPER PUBLISHING.

HØYER (SVENNIK) and others. The politics and economics of the press: a developmental perspective. London, [1975]. pp. 42. *bibliog.*

— United Kingdom.

SISSON (KEITH) Industrial relations in Fleet Street: a study in pay structure. Oxford, [1975]. pp. 185. *(Warwick Studies in Industrial Relations)*

NEWSPAPERS

— Bibliography.

BRITISH LIBRARY. Catalogue of the Newspaper Library, Colindale. London, 1975. 8 vols.

NICARAGUA

— Economic policy.

ORGANIZATION OF AMERICAN STATES. Inter-American Economic and Social Council. Committee of Nine. 1966. Evaluation of national economic and social development plan of Nicaragua; report presented to the government of Nicaragua by the Ad Hoc Committee. Washington, 1966. pp. 312.

— Social policy.

ORGANIZATION OF AMERICAN STATES. Inter-American Economic and Social Council. Committee of Nine. 1966. Evaluation of national economic and social development plan of Nicaragua; report presented to the government of Nicaragua by the Ad Hoc Committee. Washington, 1966. pp. 312.

NICHOLSON (JOHN).

ARBUCKLE (ROBERT D.) Pennsylvania speculator and patriot: the entrepreneurial John Nicholson, 1757-1800. University Park, Pa., [1975]. pp. 266. *bibliog.*

NICKEL INDUSTRY

— Canada.

DEVERELL (JOHN) and others. Falconbridge: portrait of a Canadian mining multinational; [by] John Deverell and the Latin American Working Group. Toronto, 1975. pp. 184.

NICOLE (LEON).

GROUNAUER (MARIE MADELEINE) La Genève rouge de Léon Nicole, 1933-1936. [Geneva, 1975]. pp. 236. *bibliog.*

NIEBUHR (REINHOLD).

MERKLEY (PAUL) Reinhold Niebuhr: a political account. Montreal, 1975. pp. 289. *bibliog.*

NIETZSCHE (FRIEDRICH WILHELM).

STRONG (TRACY B.) Friedrich Nietzsche and the politics of transfiguration. Berkeley, [1975]. pp. 357. *bibliog.*

NIGER

— Economic policy.

NEMO (J.) and BATHANY (J.) L'expérience nigérienne de planification permanente. Paris, 1974. pp. 193. *(France. Secrétariat d'Etat aux Affaires Etrangères. Méthodologie de la Planification. 6)*

NIGERIA

— Commerce.

OLATUNBOSUN ('DUPE) Nigeria's neglected rural majority. Ibadan, 1975. pp. 175. *bibliog.*

— Constitution.

CONFERENCE ON INSTITUTIONAL AND ADMINISTRATIVE PERSPECTIVES FOR NATIONAL DEVELOPMENT, ZARIA, 1972. Nigeria in search of a viable polity: [papers of the conference; edited by Mahmud Tukur and Tunji Olagunju]. Zaria, [1973?]. pp. 343. *Revised papers of the conference organized by the Institute of Administration, Ahmadu Bello University.*

IGIEHON (NOSER) To build a Nigerian nation. Ilfracombe, Devon, 1975. pp. 352.

— Economic conditions.

NIGERIA. Federal Ministry of Economic Development and Reconstruction. 1972. Foundation for sound development; by A. Adedeji, Federal Commissioner for Economic Development and Reconstruction. [Lagos, 1972]. pp. 16.

NIGERIA. Federal Ministry of Economic Development and Reconstruction. 1973. Nigeria's economic position today: text of a broadcast on national network of Radio Nigeria by Adebayo Adedeji...on the occasion of the 13th independence anniversary of Nigeria. [Lagos, 1973?]. pp. 9.

NIGERIA. Federal Ministry of Information. Information Division. 1974. Great leap forward in North-Western State: (Head of State's tour of developments). Lagos, [1974]. pp. 40.

— Economic history.

HALPERN (JAN) Nigeria i Ghana: z historii rozwoju gospodarczego. Warszawa, 1964. pp. 374. *With English and Russian summaries and tables of contents.*

NDOMA-EGBA (BASSEY) Foreign investment and economic transformation in West Africa 1870-1930, with emphasis on Nigeria. Lund, 1974. pp. 164. *bibliog. (Lund. Ekonomisk-Historiska Föreningen. Skrifter. vol. 15) Ph.D. dissertation - University of Lund.*

— Economic policy.

GOWON (YAKUBU) Nigeria's forward march: broadcast...on the occasion of the launching of Nigeria's second development plan, 1970-74; and Highlights of the plan. [Lagos, 1970?]. pp. 30.

NIGERIA (RIVERS STATE). Ministry of Economic Development and Reconstruction. 1970. First development plan, 1970-74. Port Harcourt, [1970]. pp. 124.

LAGOS STATE DEVELOPMENT AND PROPERTY CORPORATION. Annual report. a., 1972/73 (1st)- Lagos.

NIGERIA. Central Planning Office. 1972. Second national development plan, 1970-74: first progress report. Lagos, [1972?]. pp. 327.

NIGERIAN INSTITUTE OF MANAGEMENT. Conference, 10th, Ibadan, 1972. Indigenisation and economic development;...proceedings of the... conference. Ibadan, 1972. pp. 39.

GOWON (YAKUBU) With peace and plenty: fourteenth independence anniversal broadcast...1st October, 1974. Lagos, Federal Ministry of Information, [1974]. pp. 30.

NIGERIA. Central Planning Office. 1974. Second national development plan, 1970-74: second progress report. Lagos, [1974]. pp. 342.

BERGER (MANFRED) Industrialisation policies in Nigeria. München, [1975]. pp. 333. *bibliog. (Ifo-Institut für Wirtschaftsforschung. Afrika- Studien. 88)*

NIGERIA. Central Planning Office. 1975. Third national development plan, 1975-80. Lagos, 1975. 2 vols. (in 1).

OLATUNBOSUN ('DUPE) Nigeria's neglected rural majority. Ibadan, 1975. pp. 175. *bibliog.*

— Foreign relations.

ADEYEMI (SYLVESTER OLABODE) Nigeria and Africa: a study of federal government policies, 1966- 1973; [Ph. D. (London) thesis]. 1975. fo . 363. *bibliog. Typescript: unpublished. This thesis is the property of London University and may not be removed from the Library.*

OGUNBADEJO (FREDERICK OYE) Civil strife in international relations: a case study of the Nigerian Civil War, 1967-1970; [Ph.D. (London) thesis]. 1974 [or rather 1975]. fo. 393. *bibliog. Typescript: unpublished. This thesis is the property of London University and may not be removed from the Library.*

— — Ghana.

ALUKO (IYIOLA OLAJIDE) Ghana and Nigeria 1957-70: a study in inter-African discord. London, 1976. pp. 275. *bibliog.*

— History.

ASIWAJU (ANTHONY IJAOLA) Western Yorubaland under European rule, 1889-1945: a comparative analysis of French and British colonialism. London, 1976. pp. 303. *bibliog.*

ISICHEI (ELIZABETH ALLO) A history of the Igbo people. London, 1976. pp. 303. *bibliog.*

— — 1967—1970, Civil War.

OGUNBADEJO (FREDERICK OYE) Civil strife in international relations: a case study of the Nigerian Civil War, 1967-1970; [Ph.D. (London) thesis]. 1974 [or rather 1975]. fo. 393. *bibliog. Typescript: unpublished. This thesis is the property of London University and may not be removed from the Library.*

— — — Personal narratives.

OYEWOLE (FOLA) Reluctant rebel. London, 1975. pp. 210.

— Industries.

BERGER (MANFRED) Industrialisation policies in Nigeria. München, [1975]. pp. 333. *bibliog. (Ifo-Institut für Wirtschaftsforschung. Afrika- Studien. 88)*

THOMAS (D. BABATUNDE) Capital accumulation and technology transfer: a comparative analysis of Nigerian manufacturing industries. New York, 1975. pp. 152. *bibliog.*

— Officials and employees.

NIGERIA. Public Service Review Commission. 1974. Report on grading and pay. vol.3. 1972-74. Lagos, 1974. pp. 446.

— Politics and government.

CONFERENCE ON INSTITUTIONAL AND ADMINISTRATIVE PERSPECTIVES FOR NATIONAL DEVELOPMENT, ZARIA, 1972. Nigeria in search of a viable polity: [papers of the conference; edited by Mahmud Tukur and Tunji Olagunju]. Zaria, [1973?]. pp. 343. *Revised papers of the conference organized by the Institute of Administration, Ahmadu Bello University.*

GOWON (YAKUBU) With peace and plenty: fourteenth independence anniversal broadcast...1st October, 1974. Lagos, Federal Ministry of Information, [1974]. pp. 30.

ADEYEMI (SYLVESTER OLABODE) Nigeria and Africa: a study of federal government policies, 1966- 1973; [Ph. D. (London) thesis]. 1975. fo . 363. *bibliog. Typescript: unpublished. This thesis is the property of London University and may not be removed from the Library.*

CAMPBELL (IAN R.) Nigeria: prologue to a coup. Coventry, 1975. pp. 86. *(University of Warwick. Department of Politics. Working Papers. No. 7)*

IGIEHON (NOSER) To build a Nigerian nation. Ilfracombe, Devon, 1975. pp. 352.

PEIL (MARGARET) Nigerian politics: the people's view. London, 1976. pp. 209. *bibliog.*

— **Population.**

GODDARD (A.D.) Population movements and land shortages in the Sokoto close-settled zone, Nigeria. Zaria, 1973. pp. 18. *bibliog.* (*Ahmadu Bello University. Institute for Agricultural Research. Samaru Research Bulletins.* [No]. 201)

UKAEGBU (ALFRED ONYEOHUHU) Marriage and fertility in east central Nigeria: a case study of Ngwa Igbo women. 1975. fo. 367. *bibliog. Typescript. Ph.D.(London) thesis: unpublished. This thesis is the property of London University and may not be removed from the Library.*

AJAEGBU (H.I.) Urban and rural development in Nigeria. London, 1976. pp. 112. *bibliogs.*

— **Public works.**

LAGOS STATE DEVELOPMENT AND PROPERTY CORPORATION. Annual report. a., 1972/73 (1st)- Lagos.

— **Rural conditions.**

OLATUNBOSUN ('DUPE) Nigeria's neglected rural majority. Ibadan, 1975. pp. 175. *bibliog.*

AJAEGBU (H.I.) Urban and rural development in Nigeria. London, 1976. pp. 112. *bibliogs.*

— **Social conditions.**

NIGERIA. Federal Ministry of Information. Information Division. 1974. Great leap forward in North-Western State: (Head of State's tour of developments). Lagos, [1974]. pp. 40.

— **Social policy.**

GOWON (YAKUBU) Nigeria's forward march: broadcast...on the occasion of the launching of Nigeria's second development plan, 1970-74; and Highlights of the plan. [Lagos, 1970?]. pp. 30.

NIGERIA (RIVERS STATE). Ministry of Economic Development and Reconstruction. 1970. First development plan, 1970-74. Port Harcourt, [1970]. pp. 124.

NIGERIA. [Federal Ministry of Information]. 1971. Building the new Nigeria: social services. [Lagos, 1971]. pp. 27.

NIGERIA. Central Planning Office. 1972. Second national development plan, 1970-74: first progress report. Lagos, [1972?]. pp. 327.

GOWON (YAKUBU) With peace and plenty: fourteenth independence annivarsal broadcast...1st October, 1974. Lagos, Federal Ministry of Information, [1974]. pp. 30.

NIGERIA. Central Planning Office. 1974. Second national development plan, 1970-74: second progress report. Lagos, [1974]. pp. 342.

NIGERIA. Central Planning Office. 1975. Third national development plan, 1975-80. Lagos, 1975. 2 vols. (in 1).

— **Statistics.**

NIGERIA (SOUTH EASTERN STATE). Ministry of Economic Development and Reconstruction. Statistics Branch. Statistical digest. a., 1970 (2nd)- Calabar.

KANO STATE STATISTICAL YEAR BOOK; (pd. by) Economic Planning Division. a., 1972(2nd)- Kano.

NIKA (BANTU TRIBE).

KNIGHT (C. GREGORY) Ecology and change: rural modernization in an African community. New York, [1974]. pp. 300. *bibliog.*

NIS

— **Economic history.**

ANDREJEVIĆ (SEVDELIN) Ekonomski razvoj Niša od 1830. do 1946 godine. Niš, 1970. pp. 247. *bibliog. In Cyrillic.*

NITTI (FRANCESCO SAVERIO).

SERRA (ENRICO) Nitti e la Russia. Bari, [1975]. pp. 212. (*Milan. Istituto per gli Studi di Politica Internazionale. Saggi di Storia Contemporanea. 2*)

NIXON (RICHARD MILHOUS) President of the United States.

FANNING (LOUIS A.) Betrayal in Vietnam. New Rochelle, N.Y., [1976]. pp. 256. *bibliog.*

WOODWARD (BOB) and BERNSTEIN (CARL) The final days. London, 1976. pp. 476.

NOBLE (HAROLD JOYCE).

NOBLE (HAROLD JOYCE) Embassy at war;...edited with an introduction by Frank Baldwin. Seattle, [1975]. pp. 328. (*Columbia University. East Asian Institute. Studies*)

NOMADS

— **Africa.**

INTERNATIONAL AFRICAN SEMINAR. 13th Seminar, Niamey, 1972. Pastoralism in tropical Africa: studies presented and discussed at the...seminar...; edited with an introduction by Théodore Monod. London, 1975. pp. 502. *bibliogs. In English or French.*

— **Saudi Arabia.**

COLE (DONALD POWELL) Nomads of the nomads: the Al Murrah Bedouin of the Empty Quarter. Chicago, 1975. pp. 179. *bibliog.*

— **Yugoslavia.**

VUCINICH (WAYNE S.) A study in social survival: katun in the Bileća Rudine. Denver, [1975]. pp. 194. (*Denver. University. Social Science Foundation and Graduate School of International Studies. Monograph Series in World Affairs. vol. 13, no. 1*)

NONALIGNMENT.

See NEUTRALITY.

NONVERBAL COMMUNICATION.

WEITZ (SHIRLEY) ed. Nonverbal communication: readings with commentary. New York, 1974. pp. 351. *bibliogs.*

SYMPOSIUM ON COMMUNICATION AND AFFECT, 4TH, ERINDALE COLLEGE, 1974. Nonverbal communication of aggression: (proceedings); edited by Patricia Pliner [and others]. New York, [1975]. pp. 196. *bibliogs.*

NONVIOLENCE.

PELTON (LEROY H.) The psychology of nonviolence. New York, [1974]. pp. 291. *bibliog.*

YINGER (WINTHROP) Cesar Chavez: the rhetoric of nonviolence. Hicksville, N.Y., [1975]. pp. 143. *bibliog.*

NORDIC COUNCIL.

See NORDISK RÅD.

NORDISK RÅD.

WALLENSTEEN (PETER) and others. The Nordic system: structure and change, 1920-1970. Tampere, [1973]. pp. 126. *bibliog.* (*Tampere Peace Research Institute. Research Reports. No. 6*)

NORDISK RÅD. Plenary session: (summary of the various matters to be considered by the plenary assembly). sess., F 28/Mr 4 1976 (24th session)- Copenhagen.

NORMANDY

— **Population.**

CAEN. Université. Département de Géographie. Migrations et croissances démographiques: dossier. Caen, 1972. pp. 113. *bibliog.* (*Centre Régional de Recherche et de Documentation Pédagogiques de Caen. Annales*)

NORRIS (WILLIAM).

McKERCHER (WILLIAM RUSSELL) English libertarian thought in the late nineteenth century. 1976. fo. 438. *bibliog. Typescript. Ph.D.(London) thesis: unpublished. This thesis is the property of London University and may not be removed from the Library.*

NORRKÖPING

— **Economic history.**

GODLUND (SVEN) Näringsliv och styrcentra, produktutveckling och trygghet: The economy and control centres, product development and security. Göteborg, [1972]. pp. 85-118, fo.20. *bibliog.* (*Göteborgs Universitet. Geografiska Institutioner. Meddelanden. Ser.B. Nr.25*) (*Särtryck ur "Regioner att leva i", Uddevalla, 1972*) In Swedish, with abridged English version.

NORTH (Sir DUDLEY BURTON NAPIER).

MARDER (ARTHUR JACOB) Operation 'Menace': the Dakar expedition and the Dudley North affair. London, 1976. pp. 289.

NORTH (FREDERICK) 2nd Earl of Guilford.

THOMAS (PETER DAVID GARNER) Lord North. London, 1976. pp. 176. *bibliog.*

NORTH ATLANTIC TREATY ORGANIZATION.

LUNS (JOSEPH MARIE ANTOINE HUBERT) Présent et avenir des relations atlantiques. Lausanne, 1975. pp. 23. (*Lausanne. Université. Centre de Recherches Européennes. Publications. 4. L'Europe et les Pays Tiers*)

INTERNATIONAL INSTITUTE FOR STRATEGIC STUDIES. Adelphi Papers. No. 120. The alliance and Europe: part V: nuclear weapons and east-west negotiation; by Uwe Nerlich. London, 1976. pp. 35.

NORTH ATLANTIC TREATY ORGANIZATION. Information Service. 1976. NATO: facts and figures. Brussels, 1976. pp. 379.

— **Germany.**

KELLEHER (CATHERINE McARDLE) Germany and the politics of nuclear weapons. New York, 1975. pp. 372. *bibliog.*

— **United Kingdom.**

IS Britain's contribution to NATO adequate?: should other NATO countries do more?; report of a seminar held at the Royal United Services Institute for Defence Studies on Wednesday 13 November 1974. London, 1975. pp. 13.

NORTH EASTERN RAILWAY.

IRVING (ROBERT JAMES) The North Eastern Railway Company, 1870-1914: an economic history. Leicester, 1976. pp. 320. *bibliog.*

NORTH RHINE-WESTPHALIA.

— **Census.**

NORTH RHINE-WESTPHALIA. Statistisches Landesamt. Beiträge zur Statistik des Landes Nordrhein-Westfalen. Sonderreihe Volkszählung 1970. Heft 16. Ausgewählte Gemeindeergebnisse: Gebietsstand 1.1.1975; Ergebnisse der Volkszählung 1970. Düsseldorf, 1976. pp. 165.

— **Commerce.**

NORTH RHINE-WESTPHALIA. Landesamt für Datenverarbeitung und Statistik. Beiträge zur Statistik des Landes Nordrhein- Westfalen. Heft 354. Der Aussenhandel Nordrhein-Westfalens, 1949 bis 1975. Düsseldorf, 1976. pp. 53.

— **Economic conditions.**

HELLEN (JOHN A.) North Rhine-Westphalia. London, 1974. pp. 48. *bibliog.*

NORTH RHINE-WESTPHALIA(Cont.)

— Economic policy.

HELLEN (JOHN A.) North Rhine-Westphalia. London, 1974. pp. 48. *bibliog.*

NORTH SEA.

SJAASTAD (ANDERS C.) and SKOGAN (JOHN KRISTEN) Politikk og sikkerhet i Norskehavsområdet: om de enkelte land og våre felles problemer. Oslo, 1975. pp. 301. *(Norsk Utenrikspolitisk Institutt. Utenrikspolitiske Studier. Nr. 18)*

NORTH—WEST TERRITORIES

— Appropriations and expenditures.

CANADA. Advisory Committee on Northern Development. Annual Northern expenditure plan. a., 1975/76 (1st)- Ottawa.

NORTHUMBERLAND

— Biography.

HUNT (CHRISTOPHER JOHN) The book trade in Northumberland and Durham to 1860: a biographical dictionary of printers, engravers, lithographers, booksellers, stationers, publishers, mapsellers, printsellers, musicsellers, bookbinders, newsagents and owners of circulating libraries. Newcastle, 1975. pp. 116.

NORWAY

— Biography.

HVEM er hvem?, utgitt av Bjorn Steenstrup. [11th ed.] Oslo, 1973. pp. 632.

— Economic conditions.

LINDSTAD (ODD) Nord-Norge: makroøkonomiske oversiktsregnskaper for 1972: beskrivelse av den økonomiske virksomhet i Nordland, Troms og Finnmark med tilbakeblikk. [Oslo], Transportøkonomisk Institutt, 1974. pp. 48,32.

— Economic history.

HODNE (FRITZ) An economic history of Norway, 1815-1970. Preliminary ed. [Trondheim], 1975. pp. 549. *bibliog.*

— Economic policy.

SEVALDSON (PER) Data sources and user operations of MODIS, a macro-economic model for short term planning, etc. Oslo, 1971. pp. 31. *(Norway. Statistiske Centralbyrå. Artikler. Nr. 41)*

LONDON. University. London School of Economics and Political Science. Graduate School of Geography. Discussion Papers. No. 56. Norway's regional policy dilemma; [by] Roger Bivand. London, 1975. pp. 27. *bibliog.*

— Emigration and immigration.

SVALESTUEN (ANDRES A.) Tinns emigrasjonshistorie, 1837-1907: en undersøkelse med saerlig vekt på den demografiske, økonomiske og sosiale bakgrunn for Amerikafarten, etc. Oslo, [1972]. pp. 337. *bibliog.*

— Foreign relations.

SKAGESTAD (ODD GUNNAR) Norsk polarpolitikk: hovedtrekk og'utviklingslinjer, 1905-1974. Oslo, 1975. pp. 303. *bibliog. (Fridtjof Nansen Stiftelsen på Polhøgda. New Territories in International Politics. No.4) With English summary.*

See also EUROPEAN ECONOMIC COMMUNITY — Norway.

— History — 1905— .

DAHL (HANS FREDRIK) Norge mellom krigene: det norske samfunn i krise og konflikt, 1918- 1940. 3rd ed. Oslo, 1975. pp. 125. *bibliog.*

— Industries.

TO artikler om norsk industri:...Industrial development in an open economy: the case of Norway; [by] (Bela Belassa): [and]...Industriens plass i det okonomiske totalbilde; [by] (Odd Aukrust): two articles on Norwegian manufacturing industries, etc. Oslo, 1969. pp. 38. *(Norway. Statistiske Centralbyrå. Artikler. Nr. 30)*

NORWAY. Statistiske Centralbyrå. 1974. Regnskapsanalyse: industri og engroshandel, etc. Oslo, 1974. pp. 131. *(Statistiske Analyser. 12) With summary in English.*

NORWAY. Statistiske Centralbyrå. 1976- . Bedriftstelling, 1974. Oslo, 1976 in progress. *bibliog. (Norges Offisielle Statistikk. Rekke A. 771, etc.)*

— Maps.

BYFUGLIEN (JAN) Bosettingskart over Norge, 1970: grunnlag, innhold og bruk...: map of the population distribution of Norway, 1970: basis, contents and use. Oslo, 1974. pp. 43. *bibliog. (Norway. Statistiske Centralbyrå. Artikler. Nr. 65) With English summary.*

— Politics and government.

BULL (TRYGVE) Aerlig talt. new ed. Oslo, [1974]. pp. 200. *bibliog.* Collection of articles and speeches.

— Population.

BRUNBORG (HELGE) Framskriving av folkemengden i Norge, 1973-2100: et analytisk eksperiment...: population projections for Norway, 1973-2100: an analytic experiment. Oslo, 1974. pp. 100. *bibliog. (Norway. Statistiske Centralbyrå. Artikler. Nr. 69) With English summary.*

BYFUGLIEN (JAN) Bosettingskart over Norge, 1970: grunnlag, innhold og bruk...: map of the population distribution of Norway, 1970: basis, contents and use. Oslo, 1974. pp. 43. *bibliog. (Norway. Statistiske Centralbyrå. Artikler. Nr. 65) With English summary.*

NORWAY. Statistiske Centralbyrå. 1974. Markedstall: folke- og boligtelling, 1970, etc. Oslo, 1974. pp. 139. *(Norges Offisielle Statistikk. Rekke A.659) In Norwegian and English.*

RIDENG (ARNE KJELL) and TØNNESEN (BJØRN LIED) Statistisk Sentralbyrås regionale befolkningsframskrivninger: nåvaerend opplegg og atviklingsplaner, 1974...: the regional population projections of the Central Bureau of Statistics of Norway: current procedure and plans for the future, 1974. Oslo, 1974. pp. 25. *bibliog. (Norway. Statistiske Centralbyrå. Artikler. Nr. 62)*

NORWAY. Statistiske Centralbyrå. 1975. Familiestatistikk, 1974, etc. Oslo, 1975. pp. 71. *(Norges Offisielle Statistikk. Rekke A. 738) In Norwegian and English.*

NORWAY. Statistiske Centralbyrå. 1975. Flyttingene i Norge 1971 og 1949-1973: rapport nr. 3 fra flyttemotivundersøkelsen 1972, etc. Oslo, 1975. pp. 63. *bibliog. (Statistiske Analyser. 13) With summary in English.*

ØSTBY (LARS) Hvem flytter i Norge?: tendenser i flyttegruppenes sammensetning etter 1950...: the migrants in Norway: trends in the composition of the migrant group after 1950. Oslo, 1975. pp. 375-392. *(Norway. Statistiske Centralbyrå. Artikler. Nr. 73) Reprinted from the anniversary book of the Norges Almenvitenskapelige Forskningsråd "I forskningers lys".*

NORWAY. Statistiske Centralbyrå. 1976. Framskriving av folkemengden, 1975-2000: regionale tall, etc. Oslo, 1976. pp. 185. *bibliog. (Norges Offisielle Statistikk. Rekke A. 762)*

— Rural conditions.

ANDERSEN (BO LILLEDAL) and others, eds. Trassige folk: sjølvhjelp og lokaldemokrati i norske småsamfunn. Oslo, 1975. pp. 166.

— Social conditions.

NORWAY. Statistiske Centralbyrå. 1974. Sosialt utsyn, 1974, etc. Oslo, 1974. pp. 267. *(Statistiske Analyser. 10) With English summary.*

— Statistics.

KARLSEN (KARI) and SKAUG (HELGE) Statistisk Sentralbyrås sentrale registre...:registers in the Central Bureau of Statistics. Oslo, 1968. pp. 24. *(Norway. Statistiske Centralbyrå. Artikler. Nr. 22)*

RIDENG (ARNE KJELL) Klassifering av kommunene i Norge, 1974...: classification of the municipalities of Norway, 1974. Oslo, 1974. pp. 56. *bibliog. (Norway. Statistiske Centralbyrå. Artikler. Nr. 67) With English summary. Map in end pocket.*

— — Bibliography.

NORWAY. Statistiske Centralbyrå. 1976. Veiviser i norsk statistikk, etc. [3rd ed]. Oslo, 1976. pp. 92. *In Norwegian and English.*

— Statistics, Vital.

BACKER (JULIE E.) Variasjoner i utviklingen hos nyfødte barn...: variations in the maturity level of new born infants. Oslo, 1970. pp. 36. *(Norway. Statistiske Centralbyrå. Artikler. Nr. 39) With English summary.*

NORWAY. Statistiske Centralbyrå. 1974. Dødelighetsutvikling og dødsårsaksmønster, 1951-1970, etc. Oslo, 1974. pp. 208. *(Statistiske Analyser. 9) With English summary.*

NORWAY. Statistiske Centralbyrå. 1974. Regional dødelighet, 1969-1972, etc. Oslo, 1974. pp. 89. *(Norges Offisielle Statistikk. Rekke A. 672) In Norwegian and English.*

NORWAY. Statistiske Centralbyrå. 1975. Dødeligheten omkring fødselen og i første leveår 1969-1972, etc. Oslo, 1975. pp. 107. *(Statistiske Analyser. 15) With English summary.*

NORWAY. Statistiske Centralbyrå. 1976. Yrke og dødelighet, 1970-1973, etc. Oslo, 1976. pp. 105. *bibliog. (Statistiske Analyser. 21) With English summary.*

NORWEGIAN LITERATURE

— History and criticism.

ZETKIN (CLARA) Über Literatur und Kunst: [selected articles, originally published in "Die Gleichheit", 1906-1911]; zusammengestellt und herausgegeben von Emilia Zetkin-Milowidowa. Berlin, 1955. pp. 115.

NOTARIES

— Italy.

AMELOTTI (MARIO) and COSTAMAGNA (GIORGIO) Alle origini del notariato italiano. Roma, 1975. pp. 346. *(Consiglio Nazionale del Notariato. Studi Storici sul Notariato Italiano. 2)*

NOTTINGHAM

— Transit systems.

NOTTINGHAM. Transport Steering Group. People and traffic - now: report...on possible short term solutions (to the traffic problems inside the central core of the city). Nottingham, 1971. fo. 49.

NOVA SCOTIA

— Economic conditions.

ECONOMIC PROFILE; [pd. by] Department of Development, Planning and Economics Branch...Nova Scotia. irreg., 1959 (v.1)- Halifax, N.S.

— Historical geography.

CLARK (ANDREW HILL) Acadia: the geography of early Nova Scotia to 1760. Madison, 1968. pp. 450. *bibliog.*

— Industries.

TODD (DANIEL) Polarization in a peripheral regional economy: a spatial analysis of manufacturing industry, with reference to Nova Scotia, Canada; [Ph.D. (London) thesis]. 1975. fo. 360. *bibliog. Typescript: unpublished. This thesis is the property of London University and may not be removed from the Library.*

NOVELISTS, FRENCH.

FIELD (FRANK) Three writers and the Great War: studies in the rise of communism and fascism. Cambridge, 1975. pp. 212. *bibliog.*

NOVGOROD (OBLAST')

— Industries.

DROBIZHEV (VLADIMIR ZINOV'EVICH) ed. Rabochii kontrol' i natsionalizatsiia promyshlennosti Novgorodskoi gubernii v 1917-1921 gg.: sbornik dokumentov i materialov. Leningrad, 1974. pp. 136.

NOVOSEL'SKII (ALEKSEI ANDREEVICH).

DVORIANSTVO i krepostnoi stroi Rossii XVI-XVIII vv.: sbornik statei, posviashchennyi pamiati Alekseia Andreevicha Novosel'skogo. Moskva, 1975. pp. 345.

NOVOTNY (ANTONÍN).

NOVOTNÝ (ANTONÍN) Projevy a stati, 1954-(1964). Praha, 1964. 3 vols.

NOWA HUTA

— Social conditions.

ADAMSKI (FRANCISZEK) Rodzina nowego miasta: kierunki przemian w strukturze społeczno-moralnej rodziny nowohuckiej. Warszawa, 1970. pp. 170.

NOWOTKO (MARCELI).

MALINOWSKI (MARIAN) Marceli Nowotko. Warszawa, 1976. pp. 86.

NOZHIN (NIKOLAI DMITRIEVICH).

RUDNITSKAIA (EVGENIIA L'VOVNA) Shestidesiatnik Nikolai Nozhin. Moskva, 1975. pp. 230.

NUMERICAL ANALYSIS.

U.K. National Physical Laboratory. Engineering Sciences Group. 1972-75. Engineering Sciences Group research, 1971(-1972-4). Vol. 1. Computer science, numerical analysis and computing. London, 1972-75. 2 pts. *bibliogs.*

NUREMBERG

— Social history.

SCHOENLANK (BRUNO) Sociale Kämpfe vor dreihundert Jahren: altenürnbergische Studien. Leipzig, 1907. pp. 212.

NURSES AND NURSING

— Ireland (Republic).

SURVEY of workload of public health nurses; report of Working Group appointed by Minister for Health; [Valentine Barry, chairman]. Dublin, Stationery Office, [1975]. pp. 104.

— United States.

DELOUGHERY (GRACE L.) and GEBBIE (KRISTINE M.) Political dynamics: impact on nurses and nursing. Saint Louis, 1975. pp. 236. *bibliogs.*

NUTRITION.

SOUTH AFRICA. Department of Information. 1971. Nutrition and the Bantu. [Pretoria, 1971]. pp. 24.

NUTRITION POLICY

— India — Goa, Daman and Diu.

GOA, DAMAN AND DIU. Bureau of Economics, Statistics and Evaluation. 1975. Reports on: an evaluation of applied nutrition programme; an evaluation of special nutrition programme; an evaluation of mid-day meals scheme. Panaji, 1975. pp. 141. *(Evaluation Reports. Nos. 10-12)*

— United States.

CLARKSON (KENNETH W.) Food stamps and nutrition. Washington, 1975. pp. 85. *(American Enterprise Institute for Public Policy Research. Evaluative Studies. 18)*

NUTRITION SURVEYS

— United Kingdom — Commonwealth.

U.K. Economic Advisory Council. Committee on Nutrition in the Colonial Empire. 1939. First report. Part 2. Summary of information regarding nutrition in the colonial empire, with special reference to the replies received to the circular despatch from the Secretary of State for the Colonies, dated 18th April, 1936. London, 1939. pp. 136.

NYERERE (JULIUS KAMBARAGE).

HATCH (JOHN CHARLES) Two African statesmen: Kaunda of Zambia and Nyerere of Tanzania. London, 1976. pp. 268.

PRATT (CRANFORD) The critical phase in Tanzania, 1945-1968: Nyerere and the emergence of a socialist strategy. Cambridge, 1976. pp. 309. *bibliog.*

NYERI

— Social conditions.

DUTTO (CARL A.) Nyeri townsmen, Kenya. Kampala, 1975. pp. 265. *bibliog.*

— Social life and customs.

DUTTO (CARL A.) Nyeri townsmen, Kenya. Kampala, 1975. pp. 265. *bibliog.*

OAKLAND, CALIFORNIA

— Officials and employees.

THOMPSON (FRANK J.) Personnel policy in the city: the politics of jobs in Oakland. Berkeley, [1975]. pp. 209. *bibliog.*

— Politics and government.

PRESSMAN (JEFFREY L.) Federal programs and city politics: the dynamics of aid process in Oakland. Berkeley, [1975]. pp. 162. *bibliog.*

THOMPSON (FRANK J.) Personnel policy in the city: the politics of jobs in Oakland. Berkeley, [1975]. pp. 209. *bibliog.*

OAKLAND UNIVERSITY.

RIESMAN (DAVID) and others. Academic values and mass education. New York, 1970, repr. 1975. pp. 331. *bibliog.*

OAXACA VALLEY

— Economic conditions.

MARKETS in Oaxaca: [papers from a symposium held in Tucson, 1971, sponsored by the Southwestern Anthropological Association]; edited by Scott Cook and Martin Diskin. Austin, Texas, [1976]. pp. 329. *bibliog. (Texas University. Institute of Latin American Studies. Special Publications)*

OBERHAUSEN

— Social history.

EISENHEIM 1844-1972: (rettet Eisenheim); gegen die Zerstörung der ältesten Arbeitersiedlung des Ruhrgebietes; [by] Projektgruppe Eisenheim, Design Grundlagen, Fachhochschule Bielefeld. 2nd ed. Westberlin, 1973. pp. 180. *bibliog.*

OBITUARIES

— United Kingdom.

ROBERTS (FRANK C.) compiler. Obituaries from the Times, 1961-1970 including an index to all obituaries and tributes appearing in the Times during the years 1961-1970. Reading, [1975]. pp. 952.

OBLIGATIONS (LAW)

— Germany.

ESSER (JOSEF) Professor at Mainz University. Schuldrecht. Karlsruhe, 1971 in progress. Band 1 revised by Eike Schmidt.

— Russia.

IOFFE (OLIMPIAD SOLOMONOVICH) Obiazatel'stvennoe pravo. Moskva, 1975. pp. 880.

OBÓZ ZJEDNOCZENIA NARODOWEGO.

WYNOT (EDWARD D.) Polish politics in transition: the Camp of National Unity and the struggle for power, 1935-1939. Athens, Ga., [1974]. pp. 294. *bibliog.*

O'BRIEN (WILLIAM).

O'BRIEN (JOSEPH V.) William O'Brien and the course of Irish politics, 1881-1918. Berkeley, [1976]. pp. 273. *bibliog.*

OCCUPATIONAL MOBILITY.

CURIE (JACQUES) Le devenir des travailleurs d'origine agricole: contribution à l'étude de la transformation des conduites de travail. Paris, 1975. pp. 529. *bibliog. Thèse présentée devant l'Université de Toulouse-le-Mirail.*

— Mathematical models.

PULLUM (THOMAS W.) Measuring occupational inheritance. Amsterdam, 1975. pp. 184. *bibliog.*

— Germany.

KNAUDT (NORBERT) Berufswahl und Berufsmobilität der Erwerbstätigen in zehn ehemals kleinbäuerlichen Dörfern der Bundesrepublik Deutschland, 1952 und 1972. Bonn, 1976. pp. 204. *bibliog. (Forschungsgesellschaft für Agrarpolitik und Agrarsoziologie. [Publications]. 231)*

— United States.

ORNSTEIN (MICHAEL D.) Entry into the American labor force. New York, [1976]. pp. 220. *bibliog.*

OCCUPATIONAL MORTALITY

— Finland.

ÄIKÄS (TIMO) Kuolemantapaukset työ- ja matkatapaturmissa vuonna 1972, etc. Helsinki, 1975. pp. 117. *bibliog. (Finland. Suomen Virallinen Tilasto. Finlands Officiella Statistik. 32. Sosiaalisia Erikoistutkimuksia. 42) With English summary.*

— Norway.

NORWAY. Statistiske Centralbyrå. 1976. Yrke og dødelighet, 1970-1973, etc. Oslo, 1976. pp. 105. *bibliog. (Statistiske Analyser. 21) With English summary.*

OCCUPATIONAL TRAINING

— Germany.

GERMANY (BUNDESREPUBLIK). Bundesanstalt für Arbeit. Förderung der beruflichen Bildung: Ergebnisse der Teilnähmerstatistik über berufliche Fortbildung, Umschulung und Einarbeitung. a., 1972/1973- Nürnberg.

GERMANY (BUNDESREPUBLIK). Deutscher Bundestag. Wissenschaftliche Dienste. 1975. Zur Reform der beruflichen Bildung; [edited by Hans-Joachim Stelzl]. Bonn, 1975. pp. 61. *(Materialien. 39)*

— United States.

LEVITAN (SAR A.) and JOHNSTON (BENJAMIN H.) The Job Corps: a social experiment that works. Baltimore, [1975]. pp. 118.

OCCUPATIONS.

DUNKERLEY (DAVID) Occupations and society. London, 1975. pp. 87. *bibliog.*

OCCUPATIONS.(Cont.)

UNION OF INTERNATIONAL ASSOCIATIONS and MANKIND 2000. Year-book of world problems and human potential: a framework for representation of perceptions of interlinked networks of world problems, etc. Brussels, 1976. pp. 1136. *bibliogs.*

— Classification.

FRANCE. Institut National de la Statistique et des Etudes Economiques. 1975. Code des métiers: (code no.64 du recensement de la population de 1975). [Paris?], 1975. 2 vols. (in 1).

SIVERTSEV (M.A.) Problemy tipologii v mezhdunarodnoi statistike zaniatosti. Moskva, 1975. pp. 208. *bibliog.* (Akademiia Nauk SSSR. Institut Mezhdunarodnogo Rabochego Dvizheniia. Problemy Sovetskoi Ekonomiki)

OCCUPATIONS AND RACE.

CULL (JOHN G.) and HARDY (RICHARD E.) eds. Career guidance for black adolescents: a guide to selected professional occupations. Springfield, Ill., [1975]. pp. 148. *bibliogs.*

OCEAN BOTTOM.

SOLLIE (FINN) and others. The challenge of new territories. Oslo, [1974]. pp. 172. *(Fridtjof Nansen Stiftelsen på Polhøgda. New Territories in International Politics. No. 1)*

OGLEY (RODERICK) Whose common heritage: creating a law for the seabed. London, 1975. pp. 48.

OESTERREICHISCHE VOLKSPARTEI.

REICHHOLD (LUDWIG) ed. Die Programmdiskussion in der ÖVP in [sic] Spiegel der "Österreichischen Monatshefte", [1971- 1972]. Wien, [1972]. pp. 124.

REICHHOLD (LUDWIG) Geschichte der ÖVP. Graz, [1975]. pp. 503.

VODOPIVEC (ALEXANDER) Taus Busek: Persönlichkeit, Konzept und Stil des neuen Führungsteams der ÖVP. Wien, [1975]. pp. 120.

OFFICE BUILDINGS.

JONES (GILBERT) Local authority offices: areas and costs. [London], Department of the Environment, Local Government and Development, [1971]. pp. 62.

OFFICES.

NORTHERN REGION STRATEGY TEAM. Office activity in the northern region. Newcastle-upon-Tyne, 1976. 1 vol. (various pagings). *(Technical Reports. No.8)*

— Location.

OFFICE location and regional development; proceedings of a conference organised by An Foras Forbartha...Dublin, March 1973. Dublin, An Foras Forbartha, 1973. pp. 76.

— — Ireland (Republic).

OFFICE location and regional development; proceedings of a conference organised by An Foras Forbartha...Dublin, March 1973. Dublin, An Foras Forbartha, 1973. pp. 76.

— — United Kingdom.

SIDWELL (ELIZABETH MARY) Office decentralisation: a case study of the social and environmental effects of a migration from London to Bristol. [1976]. fo. 417. *bibliog. Typescript. Ph.D.(London) thesis: unpublished. This thesis is the property of London University and may not be removed from the Library.*

U.K. Urban Affairs and Commercial Property Directorate. 1976. The office location review. [London], 1976. 1 vol. (unpaged). *bibliog.*

OGAREV (NIKOLAI PLATONOVICH).

STEPANISHCHEV (SERGEI SEMENOVICH) Razvitie obshchestvennoi mysli v trudakh russkikh revoliutsionerov-demokratov: analiz sotsial'no-politicheskikh, ateisticheskikh i eticheskikh idei A.N. Radishcheva, V.G. Belinskogo, N.P. Ogareva. Minsk, 1975. pp. 478.

OIL AND GAS LEASES

— Kuwait.

CHISHOLM (ARCHIBALD HUGH TENNANT) The first Kuwait oil concession agreement: a record of the negotiations, 1911-1934. London, 1975. pp. 254. *bibliog. Includes documents.*

OIL POLLUTION OF RIVERS, HARBOURS, ETC.

U.K. Department of Trade. Marine Division. 1976. The battle against oil pollution at sea. London, 1976. pp. 12.

OIL SPILLS

— Canada.

MARINE OPERATIONS. Interim federal contingency plan for combatting oil and toxic material spills. [Ottawa, Ministry of Transport, 1971?]. fo. 26.

— Great Lakes.

UNITED STATES-CANADIAN JOINT WORKING GROUP ON GREAT LAKES POLLUTION. Joint U.S.-Canadian oil and hazardous materials pollution contingency plan for Great Lakes Region. Ottawa, Information Canada, 1971. 1 vol. (various pagings). *In English and French.*

— United Kingdom.

ACCIDENTAL oil pollution of the sea: a report by officials on oil spills and clean-up measures; [G.D. Crane, chairman]. London, H.M.S.O., 1976. pp. 169. *bibliog. (Pollution Papers. No.8)*

U.K. Department of Trade. 1976. Report...on the action taken to deal with the oil spilled as a result of the collision in the Dover Strait on 12 November 1975 between the M/T Olympic Alliance and HMS Achilles. London, 1976. pp. 21.

OILSEEDS.

CANADA. Department of Agriculture. Economics Branch. Market commentary: grains and oilseeds. s-a., D 1975- Ottawa.

OLD AGE

— Care and hygiene.

BROCKLEHURST (JOHN CHARLES) ed. Geriatric care in advanced societies. Baltimore, 1975. pp. 160. *bibliogs.*

HAZELL (KENNETH) Social and medical problems of the elderly. 4th ed. London, 1976. pp. 328.

See also COMMUNITY HEALTH SERVICES FOR THE AGED.

— Dwellings.

GUBRIUM (JABER F.) ed. Late life: communities and environmental policy. Springfield, Ill., [1974]. pp. 285. *bibliogs.*

— Education.

See EDUCATION OF THE AGED.

— Research.

FORBES (LINDA) A review of research on the relocation of the elderly. [Coventry], Coventry Community Development Project, 1973. pp. 17. *bibliog. (CDP Occasional Papers. No.9)*

— Transportation — United States.

FALCOCCHIO (JOHN C.) and CANTILLI (EDMUND J.) Transportation and the disadvantaged: the poor, the young, the elderly, the handicapped. Lexington, [1974]. pp. 189.

— Australia.

SACH (SUSAN) The aged. 1. Accommodation for the aged in Melbourne; [with] 2. Income and poverty among retired Presbyterian ministers; [by] Jennifer Brown. Canberra, Australian Government Publishing Service, 1975. pp. 76.

— — Dwellings.

AUSTRALIA. Committee of Enquiry into Aged Persons' Housing. 1973. Aged persons' housing: interim report; [K.D. Seaman, chairman]. [Canberra, 1973]. fo. 18.

SACH (SUSAN) The aged. 1. Accommodation for the aged in Melbourne; [with] 2. Income and poverty among retired Presbyterian ministers; [by] Jennifer Brown. Canberra, Australian Government Publishing Service, 1975. pp. 76.

— Canada.

CANADA. Department of National Health and Welfare. Research and Statistics Directorate. 1968. New dimensions in aging. Ottawa, 1968. pp. 71.

— Denmark.

RAO (JONATHAN) The European Community and the elderly: the care and welfare of the elderly in the European Economic Community with special reference to Denmark, the Federal Republic of Germany and the Netherlands.. London, 1975. pp. 15. *bibliog. (Age Concern England. Manifesto Series. No. 29)*

— European Economic Community countries.

RAO (JONATHAN) The European Community and the elderly: the care and welfare of the elderly in the European Economic Community with special reference to Denmark, the Federal Republic of Germany and the Netherlands.. London, 1975. pp. 15. *bibliog. (Age Concern England. Manifesto Series. No. 29)*

— Finland.

SINTONEN (HARRI) Vanhusten huoltokustannuksiin vaikuttavista tekijöistä, etc. Helsinki, 1974. pp. 127. *bibliog. (Finland. Suomen Virallinen Tilasto. Finlands Officiella Statistik. 32. Sosiaalisia Erikoistutkimuksia. 40) With English summary.*

— France.

FRANCE. Comité National d'Information des Personnes Agées. 1975. Pour mieux informer les personnes agées. 2nd ed. Paris, 1975. pp. 313.

— Germany.

RAO (JONATHAN) The European Community and the elderly: the care and welfare of the elderly in the European Economic Community with special reference to Denmark, the Federal Republic of Germany and the Netherlands.. London, 1975. pp. 15. *bibliog. (Age Concern England. Manifesto Series. No. 29)*

— Japan.

PALMORE (ERDMAN B.) The honorable elders: a cross-cultural analysis of aging in Japan. Durham, N.C., 1975. pp. 148. *bibliog.*

— Netherlands.

RAO (JONATHAN) The European Community and the elderly: the care and welfare of the elderly in the European Economic Community with special reference to Denmark, the Federal Republic of Germany and the Netherlands.. London, 1975. pp. 15. *bibliog. (Age Concern England. Manifesto Series. No. 29)*

— New Zealand.

NEW ZEALAND. Department of Social Welfare. 1975. Survey of persons aged 65 years and over: report of results relating to social security benefit rates. Wellington, 1975. pp. 57.

— Norway.

ELDEN (TOR) Gammel i utkant-Norge: en sosiologisk undersøkelse av de eldres service- og miljøsituasjon. Oslo, 1974. pp. 182. *bibliog. (Norsk Institutt for By- og Regionforskning. Arbeidsrapporter. 7/74)*

— South Africa.

RIP (COLIN M.) and others. Socio-economic position of aged Indians in Natal. Pretoria, 1974. pp. 32. *bibliog. (Human Sciences Research Council [South Africa]. Institute for Sociological, Demographic and Criminological Research. Research Findings. No. S-N-45)*

— United Kingdom.

HEALY (PAT) Social and community support for the retired and the elderly. London, 1973. pp. 14. *bibliog. (Age Concern England. Manifesto Series. No. 2)*

PYKE-LEES (CELIA) and GARDINER (SUE) Elderly ethnic minorities. London, 1974. pp. 17. *bibliog. (Age Concern England. Manifesto Series. No. 18)*

U.K. Department of Health and Social Security. Reports on Health and Social Subjects. The care of the elderly; proceedings of a conference organised jointly by the Department of Health and Social Security and the British Geriatrics Society on 23 November 1973. [London, 1974?]. pp. 57. *Published by the Department and not in the numbered H.M.S.O. series.*

AGE CONCERN ENGLAND. Manifesto Series. No. 33. The place of the retired and the elderly in modern society: views of Manifesto discussion groups. London, [1975]. pp. 72.

SOCIAL SERVICES RESEARCH AND INTELLIGENCE UNIT [PORTSMOUTH]. Information Sheets. No. 23. Alarm carried systems for the elderly and disabled people. Portsmouth, 1975. fo. 6.

REES (ANTHONY M.) Old people and the social services: a study in Sunderland. [Southampton, 1976]. pp. 211.

— — Care and hygiene.

AGE CONCERN ENGLAND. Good neighbours. London, [1972]. pp. 6. *bibliog.*

LEWIS (SHIRLEY) Health of the retired and the elderly. London, 1973. pp. 16. *bibliog. (Age Concern England. Manifesto Series. No. 6)*

GARDEN (JACKIE) Mobility and the elderly. London, 1974. pp. 12. *bibliog. (Age Concern England. Manifesto Series. No. 21)*

HADLEY (ROGER DENHAM) and WEBB (ADRIAN L.) Loneliness, social isolation and old people: some implications for social policy. London, 1974. pp. 22. *(Age Concern England. Manifesto Series. No. 25)*

— — Dwellings.

BRITTON (RACHEL) Housing and finance: survey of older people's housing circumstances and related benefits. London, 1974. pp. 45. *(Age Concern England. Manifesto Series. No. 31)*

— — Recreation.

BARR (PAT) Occupation and leisure of the retired and the elderly. London, 1973. pp. 16. *bibliog. (Age Concern England. Manifesto Series. No. 5)*

AGE CONCERN ENGLAND. Age Concern on occupation: views of retired people on how and why they spend their time in paid and unpaid work. London, 1975. pp. 24.

— — Rehabilitation.

STEWART (MONNICA CHARLOTTE) Social rehabilitation of the elderly. London, 1974. pp. 11. *bibliog. (Age Concern England. Manifesto Series. No. 24)*

— — Scotland.

GRIFFIN (Rev. JOHN M.) All day clubs for the elderly. Edinburgh, [1974?]. pp. 17. *bibliog.*

ISAACS (BERNARD) and NEVILLE (YVONNE) The measurement of need in old people;...[prepared] with the collaboration of Agnes Kennie [and others]. [Edinburgh, Scottish Home and Health Department, 1975]. pp. 166. *bibliog. (Scottish Health Service Studies. No. 34)*

— — Wales.

THOMASON (GEORGE F.) Rural depopulation in Wales. London, 1974. pp. 9. *bibliog. (Age Concern England. Manifesto Series. No. 23)*

WELSH COUNCIL. Services for the elderly in Wales. [Cardiff], 1976. pp. 68.

— United States.

BARSBY (STEVE L.) and COX (DENNIS R.) Interstate migration of the elderly: an economic analysis. Lexington, Mass., [1975]. pp. 149. *bibliog.*

STEPHENS (JOYCE) Loners, losers, and lovers: elderly tenants in a slum hotel. Seattle, [1976]. pp. 118. *bibliog.*

— — Care and hygiene.

HARDY (RICHARD E.) and CULL (JOHN G.) eds. Organization and administration of service programs for the older American. Springfield, Ill., [1975]. pp. 240.

— — Dwellings.

STEPHENS (JOYCE) Loners, losers, and lovers: elderly tenants in a slum hotel. Seattle, [1976]. pp. 118. *bibliog.*

— — Alaska.

ALASKA. Department of Health and Social Services. 1972. Alaska comprehensive study on aging; final report; (surveys and research carried out by the staff of) the Seattle Consortium (comprised of Human Resources Planning Institute and the Institute of Urban Affairs of Seattle University). [Juneau?], 1972. 1 vol. (various pagings). *bibliog.*

— — Maine.

MAINE. Governor's Committee on Aging. 1970. Steps for Maine's elderly: report. [Augusta], 1970. pp. 262. *bibliog.*

OLD AGE AND CONSUMPTION.

See AGED AS CONSUMERS.

OLD AGE ASSISTANCE

— United Kingdom.

AGE CONCERN ENGLAND. Voluntary organisations and the retired and the elderly. London, 1973. pp. 13. *bibliog. (Age Concern England. Manifesto Series. No. 4)*

BRITTON (RACHEL) Housing and finance: survey of older people's housing circumstances and related benefits. London, 1974. pp. 45. *(Age Concern England. Manifesto Series. No. 31)*

BURGESS (PAUL) Selected or neglected?: welfare rights and the elderly. London, 1974. pp. 13. *bibliog. (Age Concern England. Manifesto Series. No. 16)*

HEATING ACTION GROUP. A guide to allowances for families and old people. London, [1974?]. pp. 22.

OLD AGE HOMES

— United States.

MANARD (BARBARA BOLLING) and others. Old-age institutions. Lexington, Mass., [1975]. pp. 157.

STEPHENS (JOYCE) Loners, losers, and lovers: elderly tenants in a slum hotel. Seattle, [1976]. pp. 118. *bibliog.*

OLD AGE PENSIONS.

RAMALHO (MARIA MADALENA) As normas na segurança social: prestações de velhice. Lisboa, 1973. pp. 89. *(Portugal. Ministerio das Corporações e Previdencia Social. Gabinete de Planeamento. Serie Estudos. 12) With abstracts in English, French and German.*

— Canada.

CANADA. Department of National Health and Welfare. 1972. How to get your 1972 guaranteed income supplement. Ottawa, 1972. pp. 16, 16. *In English and French.*

BRYDEN (KENNETH) Old age pensions and policy-making in Canada. Montreal, 1974. pp. 264. *(Institute of Public Administration of Canada. Canadian Public Administration Series)*

— United Kingdom.

AGE CONCERN ENGLAND. Public opinion on pensions. London, 1974. pp. 14. *(Age Concern England. Manifesto Series. No. 30)*

HEWITT (PATRICIA) Age Concern England on pensioner incomes: a report...on the financial position and prospects of the retired. rev. ed. London, 1974. pp. 24.

CLARKE (KENNETH) and MOCKLER (CHRISTOPHER) An end to the earnings rule?. London, 1976. pp. 22. *(Conservative Political Centre. [Publications]. No. 589)*

OLIGARCHY.

[SHARPE (GREGORY)] A short dissertation upon that species of misgovernment, called an oligarchy. London, printed for J. Freeman, 1748. pp. 58.

OLIGOPOLIES.

LAMBIN (JEAN JACQUES) Advertising, competition and market conduct in oligopoly over time: an econometric investigation in western European countries. Amsterdam, 1976. pp. 312. *bibliog.*

OLIVE INDUSTRY AND TRADE

— Italy.

CIRIACONO (SALVATORE) Olio ed ebrei nella Repubblica veneta del Settecento. Venezia, 1975. pp. 208. *(Deputazione di Storia Patria per le Venezie. Miscellanea di Studi e Memorie. vol. 16)*

OLMSTED (FREDERICK LAW).

ROPER (LAURA WOOD) A biography of Frederick Law Olmsted. Baltimore, [1973]. pp. 555.

OMAN

— Politics and government.

OMAN: a class analysis: [translated and] published by the Gulf Committee. London, [1974]. pp. 20. *(Gulf Committee. 9th June Studies)*

The OMAN war, 1957-1959: a critical history; [translated and published by the Gulf Committee. London, [1974]. pp. 24. *(Gulf Committee. 9th June Studies)*

— Social conditions.

OMAN: a class analysis: [translated and] published by the Gulf Committee. London, [1974]. pp. 20. *(Gulf Committee. 9th June Studies)*

OMBUDSMAN.

CONFERENCE OF AUSTRALASIAN AND PACIFIC OMBUDSMEN, WELLINGTON, NEW ZEALAND, 1974. Official record of proceedings. Wellington, Office of Ombudsman, [1975]. pp. 214.

— United Kingdom.

NATIONAL COUNCIL FOR CIVIL LIBERTIES. Reports. The children's ombudsman. London, 1975. pp. 10.

— — Scotland.

SCOTLAND. Commissioner for Local Administration in Scotland. Report, pd. by Commission for Local Authority Accounts in Scotland. a., 1975/76(1st)- Edinburgh.

— Zambia.

ZAMBIA. Commission for Investigations. Annual report. a., 1974- Lusaka.

ONTARIO

ONTARIO

— Economic conditions — Maps.

DEAN (WILLIAM G.) ed. Economic atlas of Ontario;...G.J. Matthews, cartographer;... published for the government of Ontario. [Toronto], 1969. 113 plates. *In English and French.*

— Economic policy.

RICHMOND (D.R.) The economic transformation of Ontario, [1945-1973]. [Toronto], Ontario Economic Council, 1974. pp. 56. *(Evolution of Policy in Contemporary Ontario, The. 1)*

ONTARIO. Economic Council. Annual report. a., 1975/76 (2nd)- Toronto.

ONTARIO. Economic Council. 1976. Northern Ontario development: issues and alternatives, 1976. [Toronto], 1976. pp. 40.

— History — Bibliography.

ONTARIO HISTORICAL STUDIES SERIES. Ontario since 1867: a bibliography. [Toronto?], 1973. pp. 330.

— Industries.

CONSUMPTION OF FUEL AND ELECTRICITY BY ONTARIO MANUFACTURING INDUSTRIES; [pd. by] Statistical Centre, Ontario. a., 1972(2nd)- [Toronto].

— Legislative Assembly.

ONTARIO. Commission on the Legislature. 1973-75. Report; [Dalton Kingsley Camp, chairman]. Toronto, 1973-75. 5 vols. (in 1).

— Politics and government.

MANTHORPE (JONATHAN) The power and the Tories: Ontario politics, 1943 to the present. Toronto, [1974]. pp. 305.

MARTIN (JOE) Management Consultant. The role and place of Ontario in the Canadian confederation. [Toronto], Ontario Economic Council, 1974. pp. 68. *(Evolution of Policy in Contemporary Ontario, The. 4)*

MACDONALD (DONALD C.) ed. Government and politics of Ontario. [Toronto, 1975]. pp. 367. *bibliogs.*

— Social policy.

LANG (VERNON) The service state emerges in Ontario 1945-1973. [Toroto], Ontario Economic Council, 1974. pp. 83. *bibliog. Evolution of Policy in Contemporary Ontario, The. 3)*

ONTARIO. Economic Council. Annual report. a., 1975/76 (2nd)- Toronto.

ONTOLOGY.

GALE (RICHARD M.) Negation and non-being. Oxford, 1976. pp. 117. *(American Philosophical Quarterly. Monograph Series. No. 10)*

OOMS (FRANZ).

EUROPEAN COURT OF HUMAN RIGHTS. Publications. Series A: Judgments and Decisions. [A12]. ...De Wilde, Ooms and Versyp cases; "vagrancy" cases. 1. Decision of 28th May 1970. 2. Judgment of 18th November 1970; question of procedure. 3. Judgment of 18th June 1971. Strasbourg, Council of Europe, 1971. pp. 75 [bis].

EUROPEAN COURT OF HUMAN RIGHTS. Publications. Series B: Pleadings, Oral Arguments and Documents.[B10]. "De Wilde, Ooms and Versyp" cases: "vagrancy" cases, 1969-1971. Strasbourg, Council of Europe, 1971. pp. 405 [bis], 407-474. *In English and French.*

EUROPEAN COURT OF HUMAN RIGHTS. Publications. Series A: Judgments and Decisions. [A] 14. ...De Wilde, Ooms and Versyp cases: "vagrancy" cases; judgment of 10 March 1972; question of the application of Article 50 of the Convention. Strasbourg, Council of Europe, 1972. pp. 22 [bis]. *In English and French.*

EUROPEAN COURT OF HUMAN RIGHTS. Publications. Series B: Pleadings, Oral Arguments and Documents. [B12]. "De Wilde, Ooms and Versyp" cases: "vagrancy" cases; question of the application of Article 50 of the Convention, (1971-1972). Strasbourg, Council of Europe, 1973. pp. 97 [bis], 99-126. *In English and French.*

OPEN-CAST MINING

— Environmental aspects — United States — Montana.

TOOLE (KENNETH ROSS) The rape of the Great Plains: northwest America, cattle and coal. Boston, [1976]. pp. 271. *bibliog.*

OPEN UNIVERSITY.

BRITISH BROADCASTING CORPORATION. The BBC and the Open University: an educational partnership. London, [1975]. pp. 12.

OPERATIONS RESEARCH.

BROWN (ARTHUR ROBERT) Optimum packing and depletion: the computer in space- and resource- usage problems. London, [1971]. pp. 107. *bibliog.*

TAHA (HAMDY A.) Operations research: an introduction. New York, [1971]. pp. 703. *bibliogs.*

BAUMOL (WILLIAM JACK) Economic theory and operations analysis. 3rd ed. Englewood Cliffs, [1972]. pp. 626.

BYRD (JACK) Operations research models for public administration. Lexington, Mass., [1975]. pp. 276. *bibliog.*

BROPHY (PETER) and others, eds. Reader in operations research for libraries. Englewood, Colorado, 1976. pp. 392. *bibliogs.*

OPPENHEIMER (JULIUS ROBERT).

YORK (HERBERT FRANK) The advisors: Oppenheimer, Teller, and the superbomb. San Francisco, [1976]. pp. 175.

OPPOSITION (POLITICAL SCIENCE).

FISHEL (JEFF) Party and opposition: congressional challengers in American politics. New York, [1973]. pp. 254. *bibliog.*

HACKE (CHRISTIAN) Die Ost- und Deutschlandpolitik der CDU/CSU: Wege und Irrwege der Opposition seit 1969. Köln, [1975]. pp. 151. *bibliog.*

OBERREUTER (HEINRICH) ed. Parlamentarische Opposition: ein internationaler Vergleich. Hamburg, 1975. pp. 293.

OPTICAL CHARACTER RECOGNITION.

See OPTICAL PATTERN RECOGNITION.

OPTICAL PATTERN RECOGNITION.

ULLMANN (J.R.) Pattern recognition techniques. London, 1973. pp. 412. *bibliog.*

OPTICS.

WORRALL (JOHN) The 19th century revolution in optics: a case study in the interaction between philosophy of science and history and sociology of science. 1975 [or rather 1976]. fo. 277. *bibliog. Typescript. Ph.D. (London) thesis: unpublished. This thesis is the property of London University and may not be removed from the Library.*

OPUS DEI.

ESCRIVA DE BALAGUER Y ALBAS (JOSEMARIA) The way. Chicago, 1964. pp. 278.

ORATORY.

BLOCH (MAURICE E.F.) ed. Political language and oratory in traditional society. London, 1975. pp. 240. *bibliog.*

ÖREBRO LÄN

— Population.

NORMAN (HANS) Från Bergslagen till Nordamerika: studier i migrationsmönster, social rörlighet och demografisk struktur med utgångspunkt från Örebro Län, 1851-1915. Uppsala, 1974. pp. 372. *bibliog. (Uppsala. Universitet. Historiska Institutionen. Studia Historica Upsaliensia. 62) With English summary.*

OREL (OBLAST')

— Statistics.

OREL (OBLAST'). Statisticheskoe Upravlenie. Narodnoe khoziaistvo Orlovskoi oblasti: statisticheskii sbornik. Orel, 1972. pp. 230.

ORGANISATION DE LIBERATION PALESTINIENNE.

See PALESTINE LIBERATION ORGANIZATION.

ORGANISATION FOR ECONOMIC COOPERATION AND DEVELOPMENT.

CAMPS (MIRIAM) "First world" relationships: the role of the OECD. Paris, [1975]. pp. 56. *(Atlantic Institute. Atlantic Papers. 1975/2)*

ORGANIZATION.

EMERY (JAMES C.) Organizational planning and control systems: theory and technology. New York, [1969]. pp. 166. *bibliog.*

HALL (RICHARD H.) ed. The formal organization. New York, [1972]. pp. 290. *bibliogs. (American Sociological Association. Issues and Trends in Sociology)*

ORGANIZED social complexity: challenge to politics and policy; edited by Todd R. La Porte. Princeton, [1975]. pp. 373. *bibliog.*

BECKER (SELWYN W.) and NEUHAUSER (DUNCAN) The efficient organization. New York, [1975]. pp. 237. *bibliog.*

CONFERENCE ON JAPANESE ORGANIZATION AND DECISION-MAKING, HAWAII, 1973. Modern Japanese organization and decision-making; edited by Ezra F. Vogel. Berkeley, [1975]. pp. 340. *Proceedings of a conference sponsored by the Joint Committee on Japanese Studies of the American Council of Learned Societies and the Social Science Research Council.*

DORNBUSCH (SANFORD MAURICE) and SCOTT (WILLIAM RICHARD) Evaluation and the exercise of authority. San Francisco, 1975. pp. 382. *bibliog.*

ETZIONI (AMITAI) A comparative analysis of complex organizations: on power, involvement, and their correlates. rev. ed. New York, [1975]. pp. 584. *bibliog.*

MICHELSEN TERRY (CARLOS JOSE) A theoretical and empirical study of perceptions of relative power among the staff of some Mexican industrial organizations; [Ph.D. (London) thesis]. 1975. 1 vol. (various foliations). *Typescript: unpublished. This thesis is the property of London University and may not be removed from the Library.*

MOUZELIS (NICOLAS P.) Organisation and bureaucracy: an analysis of modern theories; [reprint with a new introduction of the edition of 1967]. London, 1975. pp. 234.

WEXLEY (KENNET N.) and YUKL (GARY A.) eds. Organizational behavior and industrial psychology: readings with comentary. New York, 1975. pp. 641. *bibliog.*

BOSWELL (JONATHAN S.) Social and business enterprises: an introduction to organisational economics. London, 1976. pp. 216.

HANDY (CHARLES B.) Understanding organizations. Harmondsworth, 1976. pp. 447. *bibliogs.*

PUGH (DEREK SALMAN) and HICKSON (DAVID J.) Organizational structure in its context: the Aston programme 1. Farnborough, Hants, [1976]. pp. 231. *bibliog.*

ORGANIZATION OF AFRICAN UNITY.

OAU REVIEW; (pd. by Information Division, OAU General Secretariat). q., n.s. Ja/Mr 1975 (no.2)- Addis Ababa.

EL-AYOUTY (YASSIN) ed. The Organization of African Unity after ten years: comparative perspectives. New York, 1975. pp. 262.

ANDEMICAEL (BERHANYKUN) The OAU and the UN: relations between the Organization of African Unity and the United Nations. New York, 1976. pp. 331. *bibliog. (United Nations Institute for Training and Research. Regional Studies. No.2)*

WOLFERS (MICHAEL) Politics in the Organization of African Unity. London, 1976. pp. 229. *bibliog.*

ORGANIZATION OF AMERICAN STATES.

LEVIN (AIDA LUISA) The Organization of American States and the United Nations: relations in the peace and security field. New York, United Nations Institute for Training and Research, 1974. pp. 114. *bibliog. (Peaceful Settlement [Series] No. 7)*

ORGANIZATION OF THE PETROLEUM EXPORTING COUNTRIES.

FRANCE. Direction de la Documentation. La Documentation Française. Notes et Etudes Documentaires. Nos. 4,133 - 4, 134. L'Organisation des pays exportateurs de pétrole; [par Mahmoud Montazer-Zohour]. Paris, 1974. pp. 46. *bibliog.*

ALIBER (ROBERT Z.) Policies toward the O[rganization of] P[etroleum] E[xporting] C[ountries'] oil and wealth. Tübingen, 1975. pp. 14. *(Kiel. Universität. Institut für Weltwirtschaft. Kieler Vorträge. Neue Folge. 80)*

ECONOMIST INTELLIGENCE UNIT. Q[uarterly] E[conomic] R[eview] Specials. No. 25. OPEC funds and the UK; by Roger Middleton. London, 1975. pp. 86.

ROBINSON (COLIN) Energy depletion and the economics of OPEC. London, 1975. pp. 32. *(Henley Centre for Forecasting. Occasional Papers. No.1)*

ORGANIZED CRIME

— United States.

PEARCE (FRANK) Crimes of the powerful: Marxism, crime and deviance. London, 1976. pp. 172.

ORIENTAL STUDIES

— Russia.

BAZIIANTS (ASHOT PATVAKANOVICH) Lazarevskii institut v istorii otechestvennogo vostokovedeniia. Moskva, 1973. pp. 224. *bibliog.*

ORIGIN AND DESTINATION TRAFFIC SURVEYS

— Mathematical models.

HOTT (SHARON KAY) Combining the trip distribution and traffic assignment stages in modelling a transportation system; [M. Phil. (London) thesis]. 1975. fo.124. *bibliog. Typescript: unpublished. This thesis is the property of London University and may not be removed from the Library.*

ORISSA

— Economic history.

ORISSA. Bureau of Statistics and Economics. 1972. The economic base of Orissa for the fifth plan. [Cuttack, 1972]. pp. 78.

— Industries.

ROSEN (DAVID F.) A report on industrial planning, with special reference to the province of Orissa. Cuttack, Orissa Government Press, 1949. pp. 23.

— Population.

INDIA. Census, 1971. Series 16. A portrait of population: Orissa; [by] B. Tripathi. Delhi, [1973]. pp. 374.

ORLEANS.

FRANCE. Direction de la Documentation. La Documentation Française. Notes et Etudes Documentaires. Nos. 4,153-4, 154-4,155. Les villes françaises: Orleéans et son agglomération; [par Serge Vassal]. Paris, 1975. pp. 116. *bibliog.*

ORTEGA Y GASSET (JOSE).

FERNANDEZ LALCONA (JAVIER) El idealismo politico de Ortega y Gasset: un analisis sintetico de la evolucion de su filosofia politica. Madrid, 1974. pp. 372.

ORTHODOX EASTERN CHURCH, RUSSIAN.

NOSOVA (GALINA ALEKSEEVNA) Iazychestvo v pravoslavii. Moskva, 1975. pp. 152. *bibliog.*

RELIGIIA i tserkov' v istorii Rossii: sovetskie istoriki o pravoslavnoi tserkvi v Rossii. Moskva, 1975. pp. 255.

OSLO

— Civic improvement.

OSLO. Byplankontoret. Oslo, planlegging og utvikling: Planning and development...; (utarbeidelse: Magne Helvig [and] Kenneth J. Jones). Oslo, 1960. pp. 91. *In Norwegian and English.*

— Social conditions.

BEFRING (EDVARD) Ungdom i et bysamfunn: en socialpedagogisk studie av Oslo-ungdom. Oslo, 1973 repr. 1975. pp. 413. *bibliog.*

OSNABRUECK

— Politics and government.

SPECHTER (OLAF) Die Osnabrücker Oberschicht im 17. und 18. Jahrhundert: eine sozial- und verfassungsgeschichtliche Untersuchung. Osnabrück, 1975. pp. 189. *bibliog. (Verein für Geschichte und Landeskunde von Osnabrück. Osnabrücker Geschichtsquellen und Forschungen. 20)*

— Social history.

SPECHTER (OLAF) Die Osnabrücker Oberschicht im 17. und 18. Jahrhundert: eine sozial- und verfassungsgeschichtliche Untersuchung. Osnabrück, 1975. pp. 189. *bibliog. (Verein für Geschichte und Landeskunde von Osnabrück. Osnabrücker Geschichtsquellen und Forschungen. 20)*

OSSETIANS.

KALOEV (BORIS ALEKSANDROVICH) Material'naia kul'tura i prikladnoe iskusstvo osetin: al'bom. Moskva, 173. pp. 147.

OSTOJA-ZAGORSKI (WLODZIMIERZ).

See ZAGORSKI-OSTOJA (WLODZIMIERZ).

OSVOBOZHDENIE TRUDA.

ZHUIKOV (GENNADII SEMENOVICH) Peterburgskie marksisty i gruppa "Osvobozhdeniia truda". Leningrad, 1975. pp. 328.

OTAVALO VALLEY.

VILLAVICENCIO RIVADENEIRA (GLADYS) Relaciones interetnicas en Otavalo: una nacionalidad india en formacion?. Mexico, 1973. pp. 317. *bibliog. (Inter-American Indian Institute. Ediciones Especiales, 65)*

OTTAWA

— Politics and government.

ROWAT (DONALD CAMERON) ed. Urban politics in Ottawa-Carleton: research essays. Ottawa, [1974] repr. 1975. pp. 132.

OUTDOOR RECREATION.

CICCHETTI (CHARLES J.) and SMITH (VINCENT KERRY) The costs of congestion: an econometric analysis of wilderness recreation. Cambridge, Mass., [1976]. pp. 112. *bibliog.*

— Norway.

FRILUFTSLIV i Oslomarka: analyse av en intervjuundersokelse om publikums bruk av og krav til Oslomarka: (delrapport fra prosjektene Flerbruksplan for Oslomarka [and] Friluftsliv i skog); [by] Terje Lind [and others]. Oslo, 1974. pp. 96. *(Norsk Institutt for By- og Regionforskning. Arbeidsrapporter. 8/74)*

NORWAY. Statistiske Centralbyrå. 1975. Friluftslivundersøkelse, 1974, etc. Oslo, 1975. pp. 133. *(Norges Offisielle Statistikk. Rekke A. 725) In Norwegian and English.*

— United Kingdom.

GREAVES (JOAN) National parks and access to the countryside and coast: trends in research, 1964-1968; paper prepared for the Town Planning Institute Calendar of Planning Research, 3rd edition. [London], Countryside Commission, 1968. fo. 7. *bibliog.*

DARTINGTON AMENITY RESEARCH TRUST. Public transport for countryside recreation; a report to the Countryside Commission. [London, Countryside Commission], 1976. pp. 52. *bibliog. (Publications. No. 21)*

— — Directories.

U.K. Countryside Commission. 1973. Countryside information directory. [London, 1973]. *Loose leaf binder.*

OWAMBO

— Politics and government.

OWAMBO. Legislative Council. Proceedings. sess., My 1974 (2nd session)- Ongwediva. *In Afrikaans and English. File includes Special sessions.*

OYEWOLE (FOLA).

OYEWOLE (FOLA) Reluctant rebel. London, 1975. pp. 210.

OZERNYI (MYKHAILO DMYTROVYCH).

UKRAÏNS'KA inteligentsiia pid sudom KGB: materiialy z protsesiv V. Chornovola, M. Masiutka, M. Ozernoho ta in.; Ukrainian intellectuals tried by the KGB. [Miunkhen], 1970. pp. 243.

PACIFIC, THE

— Commerce.

NEW ZEALAND. Ministry of Foreign Affairs. 1973. South Pacific trade, 1972: a study of trade and economic development in the five island members of the South Pacific Forum, the Cook Islands, Fiji, Nauru, Tonga, Western Samoa. Wellington, 1973. pp. 128.

— — European Economic Community countries.

EUROPEAN COMMUNITIES. Statistical Office. ACP: yearbook of foreign trade statistics; statistical abstract. a., 1968/1973- Luxembourg. *[In English and French]*

— Economic conditions.

The NEW political economy of the Pacific; [papers presented at a conference at the New England Center for Continuing Education in 1973]; edited by Bernard K. Gordon [and] Kenneth J. Rothwell. Cambridge, Mass., [1975]. pp. 177. *bibliogs.*

— Economic policy.

SOUTH PACIFIC CONFERENCE. Report [title varies]. a., (formerly trien.), 1950 (1st)- v.p. *[in English and French]. 4th-6th reports published under title Pacific forum. Reports 7-13 also contain Proceedings of the South Pacific Commission.*

PACIFIC, THE (Cont.)

— Foreign economic relations.

The NEW political economy of the Pacific; [papers presented at a conference at the New England Center for Continuing Education in 1973]; edited by Bernard K. Gordon [and] Kenneth J. Rothwell. Cambridge, Mass., [1975]. pp. 177. *bibliogs.*

PACIFIC TRADE AND DEVELOPMENT CONFERENCE, 7TH, AUCKLAND, 1975. Co-operation and development in the Asia/Pacific region: relations between large and small countries: papers and proceedings of the...Conference...sponsored by the New Zealand Association of Economists; edited by Leslie V. Castle and Sir Frank Holmes. Tokyo, [1976]. pp. 310.

— Foreign relations.

The NEW political economy of the Pacific; [papers presented at a conference at the New England Center for Continuing Education in 1973]; edited by Bernard K. Gordon [and] Kenneth J. Rothwell. Cambridge, Mass., [1975]. pp. 177. *bibliogs.*

— — Canada.

LOWER (J. ARTHUR) Canada on the Pacific rim. Toronto, [1975]. pp. 230. *bibliog.*

— — United States.

WU (YUAN-LI) U.S. policy and strategic interests in the western Pacific. New York, [1975]. pp. 214.

— Social policy.

SOUTH PACIFIC CONFERENCE. Report [title varies]. a., (formerly trien.), 1950 (1st)- v.p. *[in English and French]. 4th-6th reports published under title Pacific forum. Reports 7-13 also contain Proceedings of the South Pacific Commission.*

PACIFIC SETTLEMENT OF INTERNATIONAL DISPUTES.

LEVIN (AIDA LUISA) The Organization of American States and the United Nations: relations in the peace and security field. New York, United Nations Institute for Training and Research, 1974. pp. 114. *bibliog. (Peaceful Settlement [Series] No. 7)*

BIBO (ISTVÀN) The paralysis of international institutions and the remedies: a study of self-determination, concord among the major powers, and political arbitration. New York, [1976]. pp. 152.

PACIFISM.

FELLOWSHIP OF RECONCILIATION. [Minute books and papers. 1915-62]. 43 pieces. *Manuscript, typescript, etc.*

LAKEY (GEORGE) Draft manifesto for nonviolent revolution; [to be presented to] (War Resisters' International 14th Triennial Conference, Sheffield...1972). [London?], 1972. pp. 31. *With a separate pamphlet of comments attached.*

PACKAGE TOURS

— Germany.

YACOUMIS (JOHN) Air inclusive tour marketing: the retail distribution channels in the U.K. and West Germany. London, 1975. pp. 71. *(International Tourism Quarterly. ITQ Special [Publications]. No. 2)*

— United Kingdom.

YACOUMIS (JOHN) Air inclusive tour marketing: the retail distribution channels in the U.K. and West Germany. London, 1975. pp. 71. *(International Tourism Quarterly. ITQ Special [Publications]. No. 2)*

PADUA (PROVINCE)

— Economic history.

MONTELEONE (GIULIO) Industria e agricoltura nel Padovano durante l'età giolittiana. Venezia, 1973. pp. 150. *(Deputazione di Storia Patria per le Venezie. Biblioteca dell' "Archivio Veneto". vol.5)*

PAGANISM.

NOSOVA (GALINA ALEKSEEVNA) Iazychestvo v pravoslavii. Moskva, 1975. pp. 152. *bibliog.*

PAHLAVI (RIZA SHAH) Shah of Iran.

See RIZA SHAH PAHLAVI, Shah of Iran.

PAKISTAN

— Economic conditions.

PAKISTAN BASIC FACTS; (pd. by) Economic Adviser's Wing, Ministry of Finance, Planning and Development. a., 1965/66(5th), 1967/68(7th)- Islamabad.

Die WIRTSCHAFTLICHE Situation Pakistans nach der Sezession Bangladeshs; von Winfried von Urff [and others]. Wiesbaden, 1974. pp. 453. *bibliog. (Heidelberg. Universität. Südasien-Institut. Beiträge zur Südasienforschung. Band 6)*

— Economic policy.

SADEQUE (ABDUS) Pakistan's first five year plan in theory and operation. Dacca, Provincial Statistical Board and Bureau of Commercial and Industrial Intelligence, [1957]. pp. 334, xli.

PAKISTAN. Planning Commission. 1968. Third plan in perspective. [Karachi, 1968?]. pp. 46.

UZAIR (MOHAMMAD) Economic growth and rise in prices. [Islamabad, Information and Broadcasting Division, 1975]. pp. 19.

— Politics and government.

BHUTTO (ZULFIKAR ALI) Political situation in Pakistan. Karachi, [1968?]. pp. 59. *(Pakistan People's Party. Political Series. No. 1)*

PAKISTAN. Senate. Debates: official report. sess., Ag 6 1973 (v.1, no.1)- ; with gap Ap - Je 1974 (v.2, nos. 3-16). Karachi. *[In English and Urdu].*

JUNAID (M.M.) The resurgence of Pakistan. n.p. [1975]. pp. 187.

WILLIAMS (LAURENCE FREDERIC RUSHBROOK) Pakistan under challenge. London, 1975. pp. 233.

BHUTTO (ZULFIKAR ALI) Address to the nation, December 20, 1975. [Islamabad, Information and Broadcasting Division, 1976?]. pp. 32.

BHUTTO (ZULFIKAR ALI) Interview to Asia Observer, London; Larkana, December 24, 1975. [Islamabad, Information and Broadcasting Division, 1976?]. pp. 20.

— Rural conditions.

RESEARCH WORKSHOP ON RURAL DEVELOPMENT IN PAKISTAN, MICHIGAN STATE UNIVERSITY, 1971. Rural development in Bangladesh and Pakistan; edited by Robert D. Stevens [and others]. Honolulu, [1976]. pp. 399. *bibliogs. Revised versions of papers presented at the workshop.*

— Social conditions.

PAKISTAN BASIC FACTS; (pd. by) Economic Adviser's Wing, Ministry of Finance, Planning and Development. a., 1965/66(5th), 1967/68(7th)- Islamabad.

— Social policy.

SADEQUE (ABDUS) Pakistan's first five year plan in theory and operation. Dacca, Provincial Statistical Board and Bureau of Commercial and Industrial Intelligence, [1957]. pp. 334, xli.

PAKISTAN. Planning Commission. 1968. Third plan in perspective. [Karachi, 1968?]. pp. 46.

PAKISTANIS IN THE UNITED KINGDOM.

CITIZENSHIP in Britain 1974:...conference deal[ing] especially with Pakistanis and...organised by the (Birmingham) Community Development Project. [Birmingham, Birmingham Community Development Project, 1974]. pp. 28. *Photocopy.*

JORDANHILL COLLEGE OF EDUCATION. The immigrant school learner: a study of Pakistani pupils in Glasgow; [by] L. Dickinson [and others for the! Jordanhill College of Education. Windsor, 1975. pp. 200. *bibliog.*

JEFFERY (PATRICIA) Migrants and refugees: Muslim and Christian Pakistani families in Bristol. Cambridge, 1976. pp. 221. *bibliog.*

PALAEONTOLOGY

— Somali Republic — Bibliography.

PURI (R.K.) compiler. Bibliography relating to geology, mineral resources, palaentology [sic] etc., of Somali Republic. [Hargeisa?], 1961. fo. 13. *(Somali Republic. Geological Survey. Reports. RKP/1)*

PALESTINE

— Statistics, Vital.

PALESTINE. Office of Statistics. Special Bulletins. No.3. The fertility of marriage in Palestine. Jerusalem, 1939. pp. 16.

PALESTINE. Central Bureau for Medical Statistics. 1945. Statistical tables on the mortality amongst the various sections of the population of Palestine. Jerusalem, 1945. 1 vol. (unpaged). *(Pamphlets. No.3) In English and Hebrew.*

PALESTINE LIBERATION ARMY.

EL-RAYYES (RIAD) and NAHAS (DUNIA HABIB) Guerrillas for Palestine. London, 1976. pp. 155.

PALESTINE LIBERATION ORGANIZATION.

CONGRES POPULAIRE PALESTINIEN, CAIRO, 1972. Le programme politique de la révolution palestinienne. Damas, 1972. fo. 15.

CONGRES POPULAIRE PALESTINIEN, CAIRO, 1972. Projet d'unification des fractions de la résistance palestinienne. Damas, 1972. fo. 21.

PRICE (D.L.) Jordan and Palestinians: the P[alestine] L[iberation O[rganisation]'s prospects. London, 1975. pp. 15. *(Institute for the Study of Conflict. Conflict Studies. No. 66)*

EL-RAYYES (RIAD) and NAHAS (DUNIA HABIB) Guerrillas for Palestine. London, 1976. pp. 155.

PALESTINIAN ARABS

— Israel.

ISRAEL and the Palestinians; [papers delivered at a conference organized by the Richardson Institute in London in 1974]; edited by Uri Davis [and others]. London, 1975. pp. 409.

— Jordan.

PRICE (D.L.) Jordan and Palestinians: the P[alestine] L[iberation O[rganisation]'s prospects. London, 1975. pp. 15. *(Institute for the Study of Conflict. Conflict Studies. No. 66)*

PALMER (THOMAS FYSCHE).

RUTT (JOHN TOWILL) The sympathy of priests; addressed to Thomas Fysche Palmer, Port-Jackson; to which are added, odes, written in 1792. Cambridge, B. Flower, 1795. pp. 28.

PAMIR

— Description and travel.

LUKNITSKII (PAVEL NIKOLAEVICH) Puteshestviia po Pamiru. Moskva, 1955. pp. 502.

— **Native races.**

LITVINSKII (BORIS ANATOL'EVICH) Drevnie kochevniki "Kryshi mira". Moskva, 1972. pp. 269. *bibliog.*

PAMPHLETS.

WOŹNOWSKI (WACŁAW) Pamflet obyczajowy w czasach Stanisława Augusta. Wrocław, 1973. pp. 179. *(Polska Akademia Nauk. Oddział w Krakowie. Komisja Historycznoliteracka. Prace. Nr.30) With French summary.*

TKACHEV (PAVEL IVANOVICH) Idu na "vy": zametki o pamflete. Minsk, 1975. pp. 254.

PANAFRICANISM.

PAN-AFRICAN CULTURAL FESTIVAL, 1ST, ALGIERS, 1969. News bulletin 1. [Algiers], 1969. pp. 31.

GRANT (STAN) The call of mother Africa. Kingston, Jamaica, 1973. pp. 361.

MINOGUE (MARTIN) and MOLLOY (JUDITH) eds. African aims and attitudes: selected documents. London, 1974. pp. 400. *bibliog.*

PANAMA

— **Rural conditions.**

GUDEMAN (STEPHAN) Relationships, residence and the individual: a rural Panamanian community. London, 1976. pp. 274. *bibliog.*

— **Social life and customs.**

GUDEMAN (STEPHAN) Relationships, residence and the individual: a rural Panamanian community. London, 1976. pp. 274. *bibliog.*

PANGERMANISM.

WHITESIDE (ANDREW GLADDING) The socialism of fools: Georg Ritter von Schönerer and Austrian Pan-Germanism. Berkeley, 1975. pp. 404. *bibliog.*

PANIN (DIMITRII MIKHAILOVICH).

PANIN (DIMITRII MIKHAILOVICH) The notebooks of Sologdin; translated by John Moore. New York, [1976 in progress].

PANIN (NIKITA IVANOVICH).

RANSEL (DAVID L.) The politics of Catherinian Russia: the Panin party. New Haven, 1975. pp. 327. *bibliog.*

PANPACIFIC RELATIONS.

PACIFIC TRADE AND DEVELOPMENT CONFERENCE, 7TH, AUCKLAND, 1975. Co-operation and development in the Asia/Pacific region: relations between large and small countries: papers and proceedings of the...Conference...sponsored by the New Zealand Association of Economists; edited by Leslie V. Castle and Sir Frank Holmes. Tokyo, [1976]. pp. 310.

PAPAIN.

FLYNN (G.) The market potential for papain. London, Tropical Products Institute, 1975. pp. 58. *bibliog.* *([Reports]. G99)*

PAPER INDUSTRY WORKERS

— **United Kingdom.**

PAPER AND PAPER PRODUCTS INDUSTRY TRAINING BOARD [U.K.]. Report... on the manpower survey. a., 1974- Potters Bar.

PAPER MAKING AND TRADE

— **Canada — New Brunswick.**

NEW BRUNSWICK. 1972. Provincial position on matters relating to the report of the Industrial Inquiry Commission on the Pulp and Paper Industry in New Brunswick. [Fredericton, 1972]. fo. 11.

— **Italy.**

SOCIETÀ RICERCHE E STUDI. Studio sull'evoluzione della concentrazione in Italia dell'industria della carta e della sua trasformazione: carta,... cartotecnica, etc; [by Piera Balliano and others]. [Brussels, European Communities, Directorate General for Competition, 1973]. 1 vol.(various pagings)

— **Underdeveloped areas.**

See UNDERDEVELOPED AREAS — Paper making and trade.

— **United Kingdom.**

PAPER AND PAPER PRODUCTS INDUSTRY TRAINING BOARD [U.K.]. Annual report and statement of accounts. a., 1975 (7th)- London. *Formerly included in the file of British Parliamentary Papers.*

PAPUA NEW GUINEA

— **Appropriations and expenditures.**

PAPUA NEW GUINEA. Financial statements. a., 1971/72, 1974/75- Port Moresby.

— **Census.**

PAPUA NEW GUINEA. Bureau of Statistics. 1970. Census pretest, 1970: urban Goroka. Konedobu, 1970. pp. 9. *(Statistical Bulletins)*

PAPUA NEW GUINEA. Census, 1971. Population census, 1971: summary of population estimates, pre- release: population distribution. Konedobu, 1973. pp. 7.

— **Commerce.**

PAPUA NEW GUINEA. Bureau of Statistics. International trade statistics. a., 1972/73- Port Moresby.

— **Economic conditions.**

AUSTRALIA. Department of External Territories. 1971. Investment pulse Papua and New Guinea. Canberra, 1971. pp. 54.

— **Economic policy.**

AUSTRALIA. Department of External Territories. 1968. Papua and New Guinea: a guide to growth. [Canberra, 1968]. 1 pamphlet (unpaged).

AUSTRALIA. Department of External Territories. 1971. Papua New Guinea: a guide to growth. [rev. ed.] Canberra, 1971. 1 pamphlet (unpaged).

— **Foreign relations — Australia.**

HUDSON (W.J.) ed. Australia's New Guinea question. Melbourne, 1975. pp. 163.

— **Politics and government.**

AUSTRALIA. Prime Minister. 1970. Steps towards self-government in Papua and New Guinea: speech by the Prime Minister, the Rt Hon. John Gorton, M. P., at Papua Hotel, Port Moresby, 6 July 1970; [and] Increased responsibility for ministerial members and assistant ministerial members: statement by the Minister for External Territories, the Hon. C.E. Barnes, M.P., Port Moresby, 6 July 1970. Canberra, 1970. pp. 31.

ADMINISTRATION FOR DEVELOPMENT: jl. of the Administrative College of Papua New Guinea. s-a., Ja 1974 (no.1)- Boroko.

HUDSON (W.J.) ed. Australia's New Guinea question. Melbourne, 1975. pp. 163.

— **Social policy.**

AUSTRALIA. Department of External Territories. 1968. Papua and New Guinea: a guide to growth. [Canberra, 1968]. 1 pamphlet (unpaged).

AUSTRALIA. Department of External Territories. 1971. Papua New Guinea: a guide to growth. [rev. ed.] Canberra, 1971. 1 pamphlet (unpaged).

PARIS.

— **Statistics.**

GERMANY (BUNDESREPUBLIK). Statistisches Bundesamt. Länderkurzberichte: Papua-Neuguinea. a., 1975- Wiesbaden.

PARAGUAY

— **Economic policy.**

CONGRESO DE ENTIDADES ECONOMICAS PRIVADAS DEL PARAGUAY, 2o, ASUNCION, 1965. II Congreso de Entidades Economicas Privadas, 27 de septiembre a 1o de octubre. [Asuncion], 1965 [or rather 1966]. pp. 230. *Resolutions and recommendations made by the 2nd conference organised by the Federacion de la Produccion, la Industria y el Comercio.*

PARENT AND CHILD.

NEWSON (JOHN) and NEWSON (ELIZABETH) Seven years old in the home environment. London, 1976. pp. 436. *bibliog.*

PARIS.

FRANCE. Direction de la Documentation. La Documentation Française. Notes et Etudes Documentaires. Nos. 4,142-4, 143. Place, vocation et avenir de Paris et de sa région; rapport présenté par Jacqueline Beaujeu-Garnier au Comité consultatif économique et social de la Région Parisienne. Paris, 1974. pp. 64.

— **Civic improvement.**

BASTIE (JEAN) and others. 20 ans de transformations de Paris, 1954-1974: (étude réalisée sous la direction du Professeur Jean Bastié). Paris, [1975?]. 1 vol. (unpaged).

— **Economic conditions.**

GRANELLE (JEAN JACQUES) La valeur du sol urbain et la propriété foncière: le marché des terrains à Paris. Paris, [1975]. pp. 240. *bibliog.*

— **Growth.**

BASTIE (JEAN) and others. 20 ans de transformations de Paris, 1954-1974: (étude réalisée sous la direction du Professeur Jean Bastié). Paris, [1975?]. 1 vol. (unpaged).

ESPACES ET SOCIETES. N. 13-14. Paris: urbanisme, classes, pouvoir. Paris, 1974. pp. 212.

— **History — 1799-1815, Consulate and Empire.**

ROUSSIER (MICHEL) Le Conseil général de la Seine sous le Consulat. Paris, 1960. pp. 73.

— — **1871, Commune — Bibliography.**

BAKH (I.A.) and KAMENETSKII (B.A.) eds. I Internatsional i Parizhskaia Kommuna: ukazatel' literatury, vyshedshei v SSSR 1917-1970, etc. Moskva, 1971. pp. 127.

— **Maps.**

BASTIE (JEAN) and others. 20 ans de transformations de Paris, 1954-1974: (étude réalisée sous la direction du Professeur Jean Bastié). Paris, [1975?]. 1 vol. (unpaged).

— **Police.**

ANDRIEUX (LOUIS) Souvenirs d'un préfet de police. Paris, 1885. 2 vols.

— **Politics and government.**

ETIENNE (MARCEL) Le Statut de Paris. Paris, 1975. pp. 181.

— **Poor.**

KAPLOW (JEFFRY) The names of kings: the Parisian laboring poor in the eighteenth century. New York, [1972]. pp. 222.

— **Social conditions.**

ESPACES ET SOCIETES. N. 13-14. Paris: urbanisme, classes, pouvoir. Paris, 1974. pp. 212.

PARIS.(Cont.)

— Social history.

KAPLOW (JEFFRY) The names of kings: the Parisian laboring poor in the eighteenth century. New York, [1972]. pp. 222.

PARIS (REGION)

— Economic policy.

FRANCE. French Embassy, London. Service de Presse et d'Information. 1974. The Paris region: planning and development. London, 1974. pp. 24. *(France: facts, figures. A/103/9/74)*

— Social policy.

FRANCE. French Embassy, London. Service de Presse et d'Information. 1974. The Paris region: planning and development. London, 1974. pp. 24. *(France: facts, figures. A/103/9/74)*

— Statistics.

ASPECTS STATISTIQUES DE LA REGION PARISIENNE: revue mensuelle; ([pd. by] Institut National de la Statistique et des Etudes Economiques,...Direction Régionale de Paris [France]). 11 a yr., Jl 1971 (no.1)- Paris.

— Transit systems.

ORSELLI (JEAN) Transports individuels et collectifs en région parisienne. Paris, 1975. pp. 208. *bibliog.*

PARMA AND PIACENZA (DUCHY)

— Economic history.

ROMANI (MARZIO ACHILLE) Nella spirale di una crisi: popolazione, mercato e prezzi a Parma tra Cinque e Seicento. Milano, 1975. pp. 338. *(Parma. Università. Istituto di Storia Economica e Sociale "Gino Luzzatto". Saggi. 5)*

PAROLE

— Tasmania.

TASMANIA. Probation and Parole Service. Report. a., 1972/73 (1st)- Hobart. *Included in TASMANIA. Parliament. Journals and printed papers.*

— United Kingdom.

MORRIS (PAULINE J.) and BEVERLY (FARIDA) On licence: a study of parole. London, [1975]. pp. 178.

— United States.

STANLEY (DAVID T.) Prisoners among us: the problem of parole. Washington, D.C. [1976]. pp. 205. *bibliog.*

PART—TIME EMPLOYMENT

— Germany.

CRINIUS (WOLFGANG) and SCHAFT (WOLFGANG) Teilzeitbeschäftigung im öffentlichen Dienst: eine Untersuchung in den Behörden der Freien und Hansestadt Hamburg. Hamburg, 1976. pp. 263. *bibliog. (Hamburg. Hamburgisches Welt-Wirtschafts-Archiv. Veröffentlichungen)*

PART—TIME FARMING

— France.

FRANCE. Ministère de l'Agriculture. Statistique agricole. Supplément. Série Etudes. No. 119. Les agricultures à temps partiel dans l'agriculture française. II. Evolution 1963-1967: quelques enseignements; (étude... rédigée par André Brun [and others]). Paris, 1974. pp. 144.

PARTI CONGOLAIS DU TRAVAIL.

NGOUABI (MARIEN) Vers la construction d'une société socialiste en Afrique: écrits et discours du Président du Comité Central du Parti Congolais du Travail, Président de la République Populaire du Congo. Paris, [1975]. pp. 727.

PARTI SOCIALISTE UNIFIE.

DEPREUX (EDOUARD) Servitude et grandeur du P.S.U. Paris, [1974]. pp. 297.

PARTIDO ACCION NACIONAL.

VON SAUER (FRANZ A.) The alienated "loyal" opposition: Mexico's Partido Accion Nacional. Albuquerque, [1974]. pp. 197. *bibliog.*

PARTIDO AFRICANO DA INDEPENDENCIA DA GUINE E CABOVERDE.

PARTIDO AFRICANO DA INDEPENDENCIA DA GUINE E CABO VERDE. Guinea-Bissau toward final victory!: selected speeches and documents from PAIC. Richmond, B. C., [1974]. pp. 96.

PARTIDO COMUNISTA PERUANO.

See COMMUNIST PARTY — Peru.

PARTIDO NACIONALISTA (PUERTO RICO).

ALBIZU CAMPOS (PEDRO) La conciencia nacional puertorriqueña...; seleccion, introduccion y notas de Manuel Maldonado-Denis. Mexico, 1972. pp. 218.

PARTIIA NARODNOGO PRAVA.

SHIROKOVA (VARVARA VASIL'EVNA) Partiia "Narodnogo prava": iz istorii osvoboditel'nogo dvizheniia 90-kh godov XIX veka. Saratov, 1972. pp. 206.

PARTITIONS (MATHEMATICS).

BUSSAB (WILTON DE OLIVEIRA) Hierarchical dichotomous partitions in cluster analysis. 1976. fo. 236. *bibliog.* Typescript. Ph.D. (London) thesis: unpublished. *This thesis is the property of London University and may not be removed from the Library.*

PARTITO D'AZIONE.

ALOSCO (ANTONIO) Il Partito d'Azione a Napoli. Napoli, [1975]. pp. 189. *bibliog.*

PARTITO DI UNITÀ PROLETARIA PER IL COMUNISMO.

PARTITO DI UNITÀ PROLETARIA PER IL COMUNISMO. Federazione Fiorentina. Discussione sul partito in un partito in costruzione: seminario... marzo 1975. Roma, [1975]. pp. 103.

PARTITO POPOLARE ITALIANO.

CAMERINI (IVO ULISSE) Il Partito Popolare Italiano dall'Aventino alla discesa nelle catacombe, 1924-1926. Roma, [1975]. pp. 135. *bibliog.*

GRONCHI (GIOVANNI) Per una democrazia cristiana e popolare, 1919-1926; a cura di Gianfranco Merli. Roma, [1975]. pp. 358.

PARTNERSHIP

— United Kingdom.

UNDERHILL (Sir ARTHUR) Principles of the law of partnership; tenth edition by E.R. Hardy Ivamy. London, 1975. pp. 211.

— — Taxation.

LAWTON (PHILIP) and others. The law of partnership taxation. London, 1976. pp. 265.

PARTY AFFILIATION.

WORKSHOP ON PARTICIPATION, VOTING, AND PARTY COMPETITION, STRASBOURG, 1974. Party identification and beyond: representations of voting and party competition; edited by Ian Budge [and others]. London, [1976]. pp. 393. *bibliogs.*

PASCAL (BLAISE).

RÉNYI (ALFRÉD) Letters on probability;...translated by László Vekerdi. Detroit, 1972. pp. 86. *bibliog.*

DAVIDSON (HUGH M.) and DUBE (PIERRE H.) eds. A concordance to Pascal's Pensées. Ithaca, N.Y., 1975. pp. 1476.

PASSPORTS.

JUSTICE (BRITISH SECTION OF THE INTERNATIONAL COMMISSION OF JURISTS) Going abroad: a report on passports; chairman of committee, Cedric Thornberry. Chichester, [1974]. pp. 32.

PASTURES

— Economic aspects — Australia — New South Wales.

AUSTRALIA. Bureau of Agricultural Economics. 1974. Economic aspects of pasture improvement: a case study in the New England region of New South Wales; (by J. M. Malecky and M.G. Cook). Canberra, 1974. pp. 103. *(Wool Economic Research Reports. No. 25)*

— — — Queensland.

VAN HAERINGEN (J.) and BAMFORD (E.J.) Dairy pasture subsidy scheme: report on the first year of its operation. [Brisbane], 1971. pp. 36. *(Queensland. Department of Primary Industries. Economic Services Branch. Research Bulletins. No. 21)*

PATENT LAWS AND LEGISLATION

— Russia.

BALZ (MANFRED WILHELM) Invention and innovation under Soviet law: a comparative analysis. Lexington, Mass., [1975]. pp. 187.

GARIBIAN (AMIK MKRTYCHEVICH) Avtorskoe pravo na proizvedeniia nauki. Erevan, 1975. pp. 194.

— United States.

MILLER (RICHARD IRWIN) Legal aspects of technology utilization. Lexington, Mass., [1974]. pp. 164.

PATENTS

— Statistics.

WORLD INTELLECTUAL PROPERTY ORGANIZATION. International Bureau. Industrial property: statistics. a., 1973- Geneva. *[In English and French].*

PATENTS (INTERNATIONAL LAW).

EMPEL (M. VAN) The granting of European patents: introduction to the Convention on the Grant of European Patents, Munich, October 5, 1973. Leyden, 1975. pp. 435. *bibliog. (Council of Europe. European Aspects. Series E: Law. No. 16)*

PATERNITY

— France.

FRANCE. Direction de la Documentation. La Documentation Française. Notes et Etudes Documentaires. No. 4,204. La réforme du droit de la filiation, loi du 3 janvier 1972. Paris, 1975. pp. 47. *bibliog. Contains text of the law.*

PATHANS.

AHMED (AKBAR S.) Millennium and charisma among Pathans: a critical essay in social anthropology. London, 1976. pp. 173. *bibliog.*

PATRIOTISM

— Russia.

MATIUSHKIN (NIKOLAI IVANOVICH) Patriotizm i internatsionalizm sovetskogo naroda: istoricheskii opyt i sovremennaia deiatel'nost' KPSS. Moskva, 1975. pp. 416.

PAUL (Sir GEORGE ONESIPHORUS).

WHITING (J.R.S.) Prison reform in Gloucestershire 1776-1820: a study of the work of Sir George Onesiphorus Paul, Bart. London, 1975. pp. 287. *bibliog.*

PAYS DE LA LOIRE

— Economic conditions.

FRANCE. Direction de la Documentation. La Documentation Française. Notes et Etudes Documentaires. Nos. 4,095-4, 096-4,097. Les économies régionales: l'économie de la région des Pays de la Loire; (réalisé...par un comité de rédaction animé par [Jean] de la Mardière). Paris, 1974. pp. 104. *bibliog.*

PEACE.

BRANDT (WILLY) Peace: writings and speeches of the Nobel Peace Prize winner, 1971. Bonn-Bad Godesberg, 1971. pp. 165.

ANDREEVA (ISKRA STEPANOVNA) Problema mira v zapadnoevropeiskoi filosofii. Moskva, 1975. pp. 223. *bibliog.*

CHICKERING (ROGER) Imperial Germany and a world without war: the peace movement and German society, 1892-1914. Princeton, [1975]. pp. 487. *bibliog.*

ON the creation of a just world order: preferred worlds for the 1990s; edited by Saul H. Mendlovitz. New York, [1975]. pp. 302. *A program of the World Order Models Project.*

SOMERVILLE (JOHN) 1905- . The peace revolution: ethos and social process. Westport, Conn., 1975. pp. 236.

CHAMBERS (JOHN WHITECLAY) ed. The eagle and the dove: the American peace movement and United States foreign policy, 1900-1922. New York, 1976. pp. 575. *bibliog.*

PATTERSON (DAVID S.) Toward a warless world: the travail of the American peace movement, 1887-1914. Bloomington, Ind., [1976]. pp. 339.

— Congresses.

INTERNATIONAL CONFERENCE OF WOMEN WORKERS TO PROMOTE PERMANENT PEACE, SAN FRANCISCO, 1915. Women, world war and permanent peace; [edited] by May Wright Sewall. San Francisco, 1915; Westport, Conn., 1976. pp. 206.

WORLD PACIFIST MEETING, INDIA, 1949. The task of peace-making: reports of the World Pacifist Meeting, Santiniketan and Sevagram, 1949. Calcutta, 1951. pp. 181.

— Research.

[CARNEGIE ENDOWMENT FOR INTERNATIONAL PEACE]. Carnegie Endowment for International Peace. New York, [1974]. pp. 60.

PEACE IN LITERATURE.

MEYER (HENRY) Voltaire on war and peace. Banbury, 1976. pp. 202. *bibliog. (Studies on Voltaire and the Eighteenth Century.* vol. 144)

PEACE RIVER

— Delta.

PEACE-ATHABASCA DELTA PROJECT GROUP. The Peace-Athabasca delta: a Canadian resource:...a report on low water levels in Lake Athabasca and their effects on the Peace-Athabasca delta: (summary report, 1972). [Ottawa, Information Canada, 1972]. pp. 144.

PEACE SOCIETIES.

CAMARA (HELDER) Archbishop of Olinda and Recife. Espiral de violencia; (tradujo Alejandro Sierra sobre el original francés). Salamanca, 1970. pp. 81.

[CARNEGIE ENDOWMENT FOR INTERNATIONAL PEACE]. Carnegie Endowment for International Peace. New York, [1974]. pp. 60.

PEAK NATIONAL PARK.

VOLUNTARY JOINT COMMITTEE FOR THE PEAK DISTRICT NATIONAL PARK. A motorway [from] Sheffield to Manchester through Longdendale in the Peak District National Park: a calculated prediction of the dangers threatening the...park,...and an appeal for help to avert it. Sheffield, [1974?]. pp. 16.

PEANUTS.

WILSON (ROGER J.) The market for edible groundnuts. London, Tropical Products Institute, 1975. pp. 119. *bibliog.* ([Reports). G 96) With summaries in French and Spanish.

PEARSON (LESTER BOWLES).

PEARSON (LESTER BOWLES) Mike: the memoirs...volume 3, 1957-1968; edited by John A. Munro and Alex I. Inglis. London, 1975. pp. 338.

PEARSON (WEETMAN DICKINSON) 1st Viscount Cowdray.

SPENDER (JOHN ALFRED) Weetman Pearson, first Viscount Cowdray, 1856-1927. London, 1930. pp. 316.

PEASANT UPRISINGS.

ALAVI (HAMZA) Theorie der Bauernrevolution. Offenbach, 1972. pp. 66.

PAIGE (JEFFERY M.) Agrarian revolution: social movements and export agriculture in the underdeveloped world. New York, [1975]. pp. 435. *bibliog.*

— Europe.

REVOLTE und Revolution in Europa: Referate und Protokolle des Internationalen Symposiums zur Erinnerung an den Bauernkrieg 1525, Memmingen, 24.-27. März 1975; herausgegeben von Peter Blickle. München, 1975. pp. 334. (*Historische Zeitschrift. Beihefte. Neue Folge.* 4)

— Philippine Islands.

STURTEVANT (DAVID R.) Popular uprisings in the Philippines, 1840-1940. Ithaca, 1976. pp. 317. *bibliog.*

— Russia.

BENSIDOUN (SYLVAIN) L'agitation paysanne en Russie de 1881 à 1902: étude comparative entre le Černozem central et la Nouvelle Russie. Paris, [1975]. pp. 483. *bibliog. (Fondation Nationale des Sciences Politiques. Cahiers.* 198)

RADKEY (OLIVER HENRY) The unknown civil war in Soviet Russia: a study of the Green movement in the Tambov region, 1920-1921. Stanford, [1976]. pp. 457. *bibliog. (Stanford University. Hoover Institution on War, Revolution and Peace. Hoover Institution Publications.* 155)

PEASANTRY.

STAVENHAGEN (RODOLFO) Social classes in agrarian societies. New York, 1975. pp. 266.

— America, Latin.

PEARSE (ANDREW) The Latin American peasant. London, 1975. pp. 289. *bibliog.*

— Brazil.

FORMAN (SHEPARD) The Brazilian peasantry. New York, 1975. pp. 319. *bibliog.*

— Bukovina.

BOTUSHANS'KYI (VASYL'MEFODIIOVYCH) Stanovyshche i klasova borot'ba selianstva Pivnichnoï Bukovyny v period imperializmu, 1900-1914 rr. Kyïv, 1975. pp. 175.

— Caribbean Area.

MINTZ (SIDNEY WILFRED) Caribbean transformations. Chicago, 1974. pp. 355. *bibliog.*

— China.

ALAVI (HAMZA) Theorie der Bauernrevolution. Offenbach, 1972. pp. 66.

— Denmark.

MOGENSEN (MARGIT) Faestebønderne i Odsherred: studier over sociale og økonomiske forhold ca. 1750-1800. København, 1974. pp. 212. *bibliog. (Københavns Universitet. Lokalhistorisk Afdeling. Skrifter.* Nr. 4)

— Ethiopia.

COHEN (JOHN M.) and WEINTRAUB (DOV) Land and peasants in imperial Ethiopia: the social background to a revolution. Assen, 1975. pp. 115.

— Europe.

EUROPEAN peasants and their markets: essays in agrarian economic history; edited by William N. Parker and Eric L. Jones. Princeton, [1975]. pp. 366.

FAMILY and inheritance: rural society in western Europe, 1200- 1800; edited by Jack Goody [and others]. Cambridge, 1976. pp. 421. (*Past and Present. Past and Present Publications*) Revised versions of papers delivered at the annual conference of the Past and Present Society.

— Europe, Eastern — Bibliography.

SANDERS (IRWIN TAYLOR) and others, compilers. East European peasantries: social relations: an annotated bibliography of periodical articles. Boston, [1976]. pp. 179. *bibliog.* A bibliography of a collection of periodical articles at the Mugar Library, Boston University.

— Fiji Islands.

ANDERSON (A.G.) Indo-Fijian smallfarming: profiles of a peasantry. Auckland, N.Z., [1974]. pp. 199. *bibliog.*

— France.

DUBY (GEORGES) and WALLON (ARMAND) eds. Histoire de la France rurale. [Paris, 1975 in progress]. *bibliogs.*

— Germany.

BAUER, was nun?: Beiträge zur Agrarfrage in der BRD. Offenbach, 1972. pp. 80.

— — Schleswig—Holstein.

TILTON (TIMOTHY ALAN) Nazism, neo-Nazism, and the peasantry. Bloomington, [1975]. pp. 186. *bibliog.* (*Indiana University. Publications. Social Science Series.* No. 31)

— Germany, Eastern.

REUTTER (RUDOLF) Grossgrundbesitzerland wird wieder Bauernland. Weimar, [1946]. pp. 31.

REUTTER (RUDOLF) Die Bauernpolitik der SED. Berlin, [1947]. pp. 32.

— India.

ALAVI (HAMZA) Theorie der Bauernrevolution. Offenbach, 1972. pp. 66.

— Italy.

JACUMIN (RENATO) Le lotte contadine nel Friuli Orientale, 1891-1923. Udine, [1974]. pp. 525. *bibliog.*

— Peru.

MACDONALD (A.L.) Agricultural technology in developing countries: social factors related to the use of modern techniques in two rural areas in Peru. Rotterdam, 1976. pp. 236. *bibliog.*

— Poland.

KRASIŃSKI (ADAM) Hrabia. Geschichtliche Darstellung der Bauern-Verhältnisse in Polen und der wirthschaftlich-rechtlichen Reformen im ersten Decennium der Regierung Stanislaus Augustus, 1764-1774. Krakau, 1898. 2 vols (in 1).

PEASANTRY.(Cont.)

CHŁOPOROBOTNICY o sobie: studium autobiografii; wstęp Dyzma Gałaj. Warszawa, 1974. pp. 296.

RUCH ludowy na Mazowszu, Kurpiach i Podlasiu: materiały sesji popularnonaukowej zorganizowanej przez Zakład Historii Ruchu Ludowego przy NK ZSL i Komisję Historyczną WK ZSL w Warszawie w dniu 20 I 1973. Warszawa, 1975. pp. 485.

— Russia.

SEMENOV-TIAN-SHANSKII (PETR PETROVICH) Epokha osvobozhdeniia krest'ian v Rossii, 1857-1861 gg., v vospominaiiakh P.P. Semenova-Tian-Shanskogo. t.1. S.-Peterburg, 1911. pp. xv,440.

ALAVI (HAMZA) Theorie der Bauernrevolution. Offenbach, 1972. pp. 66.

NAIAKSHIN (KUZ'MA IAKOVLEVICH) Krest'ianskii vopros v trudakh V.I. Lenina. Kuibyshev, 1974. pp. 239.

TIKHONOV (IURII ALEKSANDROVICH) Pomeshchich'i krest'iane v Rossii: feodal'naia renta v XVII - nachale XVIII v. Moskva, 1974. pp. 335.

DUBROVSKII (SERGEI MITROFANOVICH) Sel'skoe khoziaistvo i krest'ianstvo Rossii v period imperializma; [redaktiroval knigu...A.F. Smirnov]. Moskva, 1975. pp. 398.

GILL (GRAEME JOSEPH) The role of the peasants in revolution in European Russia between March and November 1917. 1975. fo. 354. *bibliog. Typescript. Ph. D. (London) thesis: unpublished. This thesis is the property of London University and may not be removed from the Library.*

POGUDIN (VASILII IVANOVICH) Put' sovetskogo krest'ianstva k sotsializmu: istoriograficheskii ocherk. Moskva, 1975. pp. 276.

SABUROV (NIKOLAI NIKOLAEVICH) Bor'ba partii za ustanovlenie ekonomicheskoi smychki rabochego klassa s trudiashchimsia krest'ianstvom, 1921-1925 gg.; pod redaktsiei...V.A. Smyshliaeva. Leningrad, 1975. pp. 119.

IZ istorii ekonomicheskoi i obshchestvennoi zhizni Rossii: sbornik statei k 90-letiiu akademika Nikolaia Mikhailovicha Druzhinina. Moskva, 1976. pp. 288.

SMIRNOV (ALEKSANDR SERGEEVICH) Bol'sheviki i krest'ianstvo v Oktiabr'skoi revoliutsii. Moskva, 1976. pp. 232.

— — Georgia.

ANTELAVA (IRAKLII GEORGIEVICH) Gosudarstvennye krest'iane Gruzii v XIX veke. Sukhumi, 1955-62. 2 vols. *Vol.1 has title: Gosudarstvennye krest'iane Gruzii v pervoi polovine XIX veka, do krest'ianskoi reformy 1864 goda.*

— — Latvia.

LATVIISKII GOSUDARSTVENNYI UNIVERSITET. Uchenye Zapiski. t.219. Germaniia i Pribaltika. 3. Riga, 1974. pp. 107.

— — Lithuania.

KONIUKHOVA (TAT'IANA ALEKSANDROVNA) Gosudarstvennaia derevnia Litvy i reforma P.D. Kiseleva, 1840- 1857 gg.: Vilenskaia i Kovenskaia gubernii. Moskva, 1975. pp. 251.

— — Mordvinian Republic.

KLEIANKIN (ALEKSEI VASIL'EVICH) Khoziaistvo pomeshchich'ikh i udel'nykh krest'ian Simbirskoi gubernii v pervoi polovine XIX veka: sotsial'no-ekonomicheskii ocherk. Saransk, 1974. pp. 186.

— — Siberia.

RABOCHII klass i krest'ianstvo natsional'nykh raionov Sibiri. Novosibirsk, 1974. pp. 174.

GROMYKO (MARINA MIKHAILOVNA) Trudovye traditsii russkikh krest'ian Sibiri, XVIII - pervaia polovina XIX v. Novosibirsk, 1975. pp. 351.

GUSHCHIN (NIKOLAI IAKOVLEVICH) and others. Krest'ianstvo Zapadnoi Sibiri v dovoennye gody, 1935-1941; otvetstvennyi redaktor...R.S. Rusakov. Novosibirsk, 1975. pp. 287.

KREST'IANSTVO Sibiri XVIII - nachala XX v.: klassovaia bor'ba, obshchestvennoe soznanie i kul'tura. Novosibirsk, 1975. pp. 219.

— — Uzbekistan.

ALIMOV (IBRAGIM ABDUGAPPAROVICH) Uzbekskoe dekhkanstvo na puti k sotsializmu: sotsial'no-ekonomicheskie preobrazovaniia v uzbekskom kishlake v 1921-1925 gg. Tashkent, 1974. pp. 239. *bibliog.*

— — White Russia.

LIPINSKII (LEONID PAVLOVICH) Krest'ianskoe dvizhenie v Belorussii v 1914-1917 gg. Minsk, 1975. pp. 184. *bibliog.*

— Sweden.

ALEXANDERSSON (ERLAND) Bondeståndet i riksdagen, 1760-1772. [Lund, 1975]. pp. 253. *bibliog. Akademisk avhandling, Universitetet i Lund; with English summary.*

— Tanzania.

AWITI (ADHU) The development of ujamaa villages and the peasant question in Iringa district: a study outline. Dar es Salaam, 1973. pp. 48. *bibliog. (Dar es Salaam. University. Economic Research Bureau. ERB Papers. 73.4)*

— Underdeveloped areas.

See UNDERDEVELOPED AREAS — Peasantry.

— Yugoslavia.

VUCINICH (WAYNE S.) A study in social survival: katun in the Bileća Rudine. Denver, [1975]. pp. 194. *(Denver. University. Social Science Foundation and Graduate School of International Studies. Monograph Series in World Affairs. vol. 13, no. 1)*

PEASANTS' WAR, 1524-1525.

REVOLTE und Revolution in Europa: Referate und Protokolle des Internationalen Symposiums zur Erinnerung an den Bauernkrieg 1525, Memmingen, 24.-27. März 1975; herausgegeben von Peter Blickle. München, 1975. pp. 334. *(Historische Zeitschrift. Beihefte. Neue Folge. 4)*

PEDESTRIAN CROSSINGS.

LALANI (N.) Safety investigation of pelican crossing sites. London, [1975]. pp. 105. *(London. Greater London Council. Research Memoranda. 469)*

PEDESTRIANS

— United Kingdom.

MYERSCOUGH (CYRIL) ed. Feet first: a pedestrian survival handbook;...published on behalf of the Pedestrians' Association for Road Safety. London, 1975. pp. 125.

WILSON (HUGH) AND WOMERSLEY (LEWIS) Firm, and others. Report of the Urban Motorways Project Team to the Urban Motorways Committee: techniques used in the case studies. Technical paper no. 3. Pedestrian trip analysis. [London], Department of the Environment, 1974 [or rather 1975]. pp. 117.

— United States.

PUSHKAREV (BORIS SERGEEVICH) and ZUPAN (JEFFREY MICHAEL) Urban space for pedestrians: a report of the Regional Plan Association. Cambridge, Mass., [1975]. pp. 212. *bibliog.*

PEEKSKILL, NEW YORK

— Riots, 1949.

FAST (HOWARD MELVIN) Peekskill: USA; a personal experience. Moscow, 1954. pp. 110

PEFFER (WILLIAM ALFRED).

ARGERSINGER (PETER H.) Populism and politics: William Alfred Peffer and the People's Party. Lexington, Ky., [1974]. pp. 337.

PENAL INSTITUTIONS

— United Kingdom.

BOARDS of visitors of penal institutions; report of a committee set up by Justice, the Howard League for Penal Reform [and] the National Association for the Care and Resettlement of Offenders; chairman...[Lord] Jellicoe. Chichester, [1975]. pp. 96.

PENSIONS

— Germany.

RIEDLBAUER (ERICH) Die betriebliche Altersversorgung: ihre Eingliederung in ein Gesamtversorgungssystem in der BRD. Karlsruhe, 1975. pp. 112. *bibliog.*

— Netherlands.

RAAD VOOR HET MIDDEN- EN KLEINBEDRIJF. Advies oudedagsreserve/beroepspensioenfondsen. 's-Gravenhage, 1975. pp. 54. *([Publikaties]. 1975, no. 1).*

— Romania.

ROMANIA. Statutes, etc. 1967. Lege privind pensiile de asigurări sociale de stat şi pensia suplimentară. Bucureşti, 1967. pp. 45.

— Russia.

ZAIKIN (ALEKSEI DANILOVICH) Pravootnosheniia po pensionnomu obespecheniiu; pod redaktsiei...N. G. Aleksandrova. Moskva, 1974. pp. 191.

— United Kingdom.

COUNTER INFORMATION SERVICES. Your money and your life: insurance companies and pension funds. London, [1973]. pp. 33. *bibliog. (Anti-Reports. No.7)*

METROPOLITAN PENSIONS ASSOCIATION. The Castle scheme and its effect on the design of occupational pension schemes. London, 1975. pp. 52.

TRADES UNION CONGRESS. Occupational pension schemes. London, 1976. pp. 103. *bibliog.*

— United States.

DRUCKER (PETER FERDINAND) The unseen revolution: how pension fund socialism came to America. London, 1976. pp. 214.

PENSIONS, MILITARY

— Canada.

CANADA. Department of Veterans Affairs. 1971. Pensions for disability and death related to military service. Ottawa, 1971. pp. 27,29. *In English and French.*

PENTECOSTAL CHURCHES

— South Africa.

DUBB (ALLIE A.) Community of the saved: an African revivalist church in the east Cape. Johannesburg, 1976. pp. 175. *bibliog.*

— United States.

WILLIAMS (MELVIN D.) Community in a black pentecostal church: an anthropological study. Pittsburgh, [1974]. pp. 202. *bibliog.*

PENZA (OBLAST')

— Politics and government.

OCHERKI istorii Penzenskoi organizatsii KPSS. Penza, 1974. pp. 527.

— Social history.

ZABEZHINSKII (LEV MOISEEVICH) Zdravookhranenie Penzenskoi oblasti za 50 let Sovetskoi vlasti: materialy k istorii. Saratov, 1968. pp. 128.

PEOPLE (CONSTITUTIONAL LAW)

— Italy.

RASCHHOFER (HERMANN) Der politische Volksbegriff im modernen Italien. Berlin, 1936. pp. 207.

PEOPLE'S DEMOCRACIES.

DOKOV (DOKO) Durzhavata na natsionalnata demokratsiia; L'état de démocratie nationale. Sofiia, 1969. pp. 466. bibliog. With Russian and French summaries.

PERCEPTION.

INFANT perception: from sensation to cognition; edited by Leslie B. Cohen and Philip Salapatek. New York, [1975]. 2 vols. bibliogs.

PEREZ JIMENEZ (MARCOS).

PEREZ JIMENEZ (MARCOS) defendant. Proceso a un ex-dictador...: juicio al general (r) Marcos Perez Jimenez; [edited by] Jose Agustin Catala. Caracas, 1968-69 [or rather 1969]. 2 vols. (in 1).

PERHAM (Dame MARGERY FREDA).

PERHAM (Dame MARGERY FREDA) East African journey: Kenya and Tanganyika, 1929-30. London, 1976. pp. 246.

PERIODICALS

— Bibliography.

BRITISH LIBRARY. Catalogue of the Newspaper Library, Colindale. London, 1975. 8 vols.

BRITISH LIBRARY. Lending Division. Current serials received, September 1975. Boston Spa, [1975]. pp. 416.

ULRICH (CAROLYN FARQUHAR) ed. International periodicals directory: (a classified guide to current periodicals, foreign and domestic). 16th ed. New York, [1975]. pp. 2289.

IRREGULAR serials and annuals: an international directory. 4th ed. New York, 1976. pp. 1068. bibliog.

UNION OF INTERNATIONAL ASSOCIATIONS and MANKIND 2000. Year-book of world problems and human potential: a framework for representation of perceptions of interlinked networks of world problems, etc. Brussels, 1976. pp. 1136. bibliogs.

PERM' (OBLAST')

— Politics and government.

PERMSKAIA oblastnaia organizatsiia KPSS v tsifrakh, 1917-1973: statisticheskii sbornik. Perm', 1974. pp. 191.

— Rural conditions.

PERMSKAIA OBLASTNAIA KONFERENTSIIA KOLKHOZNIKOV. 1969. Permskaia oblastnaia konferentsiia kolkhoznikov, 17 oktiabria 1969 goda: stenograficheskii otchet. Perm', 1970. pp. 107.

PERMUTATIONS.

LAPORTE (GILBERT) Permutation programming: problems, methods and application; [Ph. D. (London) thesis]. 1975. fo. 358. bibliog. Typescript: unpublished. This thesis is the property of London University and may not be removed from the Library.

PERON (JUAN DOMINGO).

PERELMAN (ANGEL) Como hicimos el 17 de octubre. Buenos Aires, 1961. pp. 80.

PAVON PEREYRA (ENRIQUE) Peron tal como es. [Buenos Aires], 1973. pp. 341.

PERON (JUAN DOMINGO) Seleccion de sus escritos, conferencias y discursos. Buenos Aires, [1973]. pp. 301.

ALBERTI (BLAS MANUEL) Peronismo, burocracia y burguesia nacional; apendice documental con texto de Marx y Le Duan. [Buenos Aires, 1974]. pp. 248. Articles originally published in the periodicals Lucha Obrera and Izquierda Nacional.

PERP (COMPUTER PROGRAM).

ROYAL INSTITUTE OF PUBLIC ADMINISTRATION. Local Government Operational Research Unit. Development plan evaluation and robustness: application of an analytical program and a review of measures of performance; report prepared for the Secretary of State for the Environment. London, [1976]. pp. 111. bibliog. (U.K. Department of the Environment. Research Reports. 5)

PERSECUTION.

DUVIOLS (PIERRE) La lutte contre les religions autochtones dans le Pérou colonial: "l'extirpation de l'idolâtrie" entre 1532 et 1660. Lima, [1972]. pp. 428. bibliog. (Institut Français d'Etudes Andines. Travaux. 13)

PERSIAN GULF

— Foreign economic relations.

PRICE (D.L.) Stability in the gulf: the oil revolution. London, 1976. pp. 14. bibliog. (Institute for the Study of Conflict. Conflict Studies. No. 71)

— Foreign relations.

INTERNATIONAL CONFERENCE ON THE PERSIAN GULF AND INDIAN OCEAN, TEHRAN, 1975. The Persian Gulf and Indian Ocean in international politics: edited by Abbas Amirie. Tehran, 1975. pp. 417. Papers from the conference held under the auspicies of the Institute for International Political and Economic Studies.

PRICE (D.L.) Stability in the gulf: the oil revolution. London, 1976. pp. 14. bibliog. (Institute for the Study of Conflict. Conflict Studies. No. 71)

— — United States.

NAKHLEH (EMILE A.) Arab-American relations in the Persian Gulf. Washington, [1975]. pp. 82. (American Enterprise Institute for Public Policy Research. Foreign Affairs Studies. No. 17)

— Politics and government.

PRICE (D.L.) Stability in the gulf: the oil revolution. London, 1976. pp. 14. bibliog. (Institute for the Study of Conflict. Conflict Studies. No. 71)

PERSONAL INJURIES

— Ireland (Republic).

ADVISORY COMMITTEE ON LAW REFORM [EIRE]. Report:...reform of law of occupiers' liability in Ireland, incorporating a study entitled: Occupiers' liability in Ireland: survey and proposals for reform; by Bryan M. E. McMahon. Dublin, Stationery Office, [1975]. pp. 87.

PERSONAL PROPERTY

— Russia.

KHALFINA (RAISA OSIPOVNA) Das persönliche Eigentumsrecht in der UdSSR; (übersetzt von E. Brosig). Moskau, 1976. pp. 213.

PERSONALITY.

WARR (PETER B.) ed. Thought and personality: selected readings. Harmondsworth, 1970. pp. 447. bibliogs.

LUNDBERG (MARGARET J.) The incomplete adult: social class constraints on personality development. Westport, Conn., [1974]. pp. 245. bibliog.

PERSONALITY TESTS.

JACKSON (THOMAS WILLIAM KEVIN) The effects of the experimenter's profession on experimental results. [1974]. fo. 217. bibliog. Typescript. Ph. D.(London) thesis: unpublished. This thesis is the property of London University and may not be removed from the Library.

PERSONNEL SERVICE IN EDUCATION

— United Kingdom.

ROSE (GORDON) and MARSHALL (TONY F.) Counselling and school social work: an experimental study...; with the assistance of R.F. Adamson and Pauline Avery. London, [1974]. pp. 347. bibliog.

— United States.

WILLIAMSON (EDMUND GRIFFITH) and BIGGS (DONALD A.) Student personnel work: a program of development relationships. New York, [1975]. pp. 390. bibliogs.

PERSONS (INTERNATIONAL LAW).

FEL'DMAN (DAVID ISAAKOVICH) and KURDIUKOV (GENNADII IRINARKHOVICH) Osnovnye tendentsii razvitiia mezhdunarodnoi pravosub"ektnosti. Kazan', 1974. pp. 131.

PERU

— Armed forces — Political activity.

VILLANUEVA (VICTOR) Golpe en el Peru. Montevideo, 1969. pp. 95.

MONTEFORTE TOLEDO (MARIO) La solucion militar a la peruana, 1968-1970. Mexico, 1973. pp. 184. bibliog.

MIDDLEBROOK (KEVIN J.) and PALMER (DAVID SCOTT) Military government and political development: lessons from Peru. London, [1975]. pp. 60. bibliog.

CHAPLIN (DAVID) ed. Peruvian nationalism: a corporatist revolution. New Brunswick, [1976]. pp. 494. bibliog.

— Description and travel.

SMIRNOV (SERGEI SERGEEVICH) Mesiats v Peru. [2nd ed.] Moskva, 1975. pp. 256.

— Economic conditions.

The PERUVIAN experiment: continuity and change under military rule; edited by Abraham F. Lowenthal. Princeton, [1975]. pp. 479. bibliog. Also contains revised versions of papers presented at the Seminar on Continuity and Change in Contemporary Peru held at and sponsored by the Center for Inter-American Relations in New York, 1973.

FITZGERALD (E.V.K.) The state and economic development: Peru since 1968. Cambridge, [1976]. pp. 127. bibliog. (Cambridge. University. Department of Applied Economics. Occasional Papers. 49)

— Economic history.

PIEL (JEAN) Capitalisme agraire au Pérou. Paris, 1975 in progress. (Institute Ffrançais d'Etudes Andines. Travaux)

— Economic policy.

ALIANZA NACIONAL. El problema economico del Peru: consideraciones esenciales para la elaboracion del programa economico de la Alianza Nacional. [Lima, 1949?]. pp. 95.

The PERUVIAN experiment: continuity and change under military rule; edited by Abraham F. Lowenthal. Princeton, [1975]. pp. 479. bibliog. Also contains revised versions of papers presented at the Seminar on Continuity and Change in Contemporary Peru held at and sponsored by the Center for Inter-American Relations in New York, 1973.

FITZGERALD (E.V.K.) The state and economic development: Peru since 1968. Cambridge, [1976]. pp. 127. bibliog. (Cambridge. University. Department of Applied Economics. Occasional Papers. 49)

PERU(Cont.)

— Foreign relations — Japan.

GARDINER (CLINTON HARVEY) The Japanese and Peru, 1873-1973. Albuquerque, [1975]. pp. 202. *bibliog.*

— History.

WACHTEL (NATHAN) Sociedad e ideologia: ensayos de historia y antropologia andinas. Lima, 1973. pp. 239. *bibliog. (Instituto de Estudios Peruanos. Historia Andina. 1)*

— — Sources.

MUGABURU (JOSEPHE DE) and MUGABURU (FRANCISCO DE) Chronicle of colonial Lima: the diary of Josephe and Francisco Mugaburu, 1640-1697; translated and edited by Robert Ryal Miller. Norman, Ok., [1975]. pp. 342.

— — 1548-1820.

DUVIOLS (PIERRE) La lutte contre les religions autochtones dans le Pérou colonial: "l'extirpation de l'idolâtrie" entre 1532 et 1660. Lima, [1972]. pp. 428. *bibliog. (Institut Français d'Etudes Andines. Travaux. 13)*

— Politics and government.

VILLANUEVA (VICTOR) Golpe en el Peru. Montevideo, 1969. pp. 95.

MONTEFORTE TOLEDO (MARIO) La solucion militar a la peruana, 1968-1970. Mexico, 1973. pp. 184. *bibliog.*

ZIMMERMANN ZAVALA (AUGUSTO) El plan Inca: objectivo revolucion peruana. [Lima, 1974]. pp. 242.

MIDDLEBROOK (KEVIN J.) and PALMER (DAVID SCOTT) Military government and political development: lessons from Peru. London, [1975]. pp. 60. *bibliog.*

The PERUVIAN experiment: continuity and change under military rule; edited by Abraham F. Lowenthal. Princeton, [1975]. pp. 479. *bibliog. Also contains revised versions of papers presented at the Seminar on Continuity and Change in Contemporary Peru held at and sponsored by the Center for Inter-American Relations in New York, 1973.*

CHAPLIN (DAVID) ed. Peruvian nationalism: a corporatist revolution. New Brunswick, [1976]. pp. 494. *bibliog.*

— Rural conditions.

ALBERTI (GIORGIO) and MAYER (ENRIQUE) eds. Reciprocidad e intercambio en los Andes peruanos. Lima, 1974. pp. 360. *bibliog. (Instituto de Estudios Peruanos. Peru Problema. 12)*

— Social conditions.

The PERUVIAN experiment: continuity and change under military rule; edited by Abraham F. Lowenthal. Princeton, [1975]. pp. 479. *bibliog. Also contains revised versions of papers presented at the Seminar on Continuity and Change in Contemporary Peru held at and sponsored by the Center for Inter-American Relations in New York, 1973.*

CHAPLIN (DAVID) ed. Peruvian nationalism: a corporatist revolution. New Brunswick, [1976]. pp. 494. *bibliog.*

— Social policy.

CHAPLIN (DAVID) ed. Peruvian nationalism: a corporatist revolution. New Brunswick, [1976]. pp. 494. *bibliog.*

PERUGIA (PROVINCE)

— Economic history.

CHIACCHELLA (RITA) Economia e amministrazione a Perugia nel Seicento. Reggio Calabria, 1974. pp. 259. *bibliog.*

PET INDUSTRY

— United States.

BENNING (LEE EDWARDS) The pet profiteers: the exploitation of pet owners and pets in America. New York, [1976]. pp. 211.

PÉTAIN (HENRI PHILIPPE BÉNONI OMER JOSEPH).

ISORNI (JACQUES) Lettre anxieuse au Président de la République Française au sujet de Philippe Pétain. Paris, [1975]. pp. 121.

PETRAZHITSKII (LEV IOSIFOVICH).

See PETRAZYCKI (LEON).

PETRAZYCKI (LEON).

LESZCZYNA (HENRYK) Petrazycki. Warszawa, 1974. pp. 188.

GORECKI (JAN) ed. Sociology and jurisprudence of Leon Petrazycki. Urbana, Ill., [1975]. pp. 144. *bibliog.*

PETROL.

EIRE. Restrictive Practices Commission. 1975. Report of special review of the operation of Article 3 of the Restrictive Trade Practices Motor Spirit Order, 1972. Dublin, [1975]. pp. 18.

— Prices — Canada.

CANADA. Restrictive Trade Practices Commission. [Reports]. RTPC No.48. Prices of gasoline, Sudbury: report in the matter of an inquiry relating to the distribution and sale of gasoline and related products in the Sudbury area. Ottawa, 1969. pp. 42.

PETROLEUM.

TIRATSOO (E.N.) Oilfields of the world. 2nd ed. Beaconsfield, Bucks, 1976. pp. 384.

UNITED STATES. Central Intelligence Agency. 1976. Major oil and gas fields of the free world. [Washington], 1976. pp. 30. *(Research Aids. No.ER 76-10001) Microfilm: 1 reel.*

— United States — Alaska — Pipe lines.

MANNING (HARVEY) Cry Crisis!: rehearsal in Alaska; with chapters by Kenneth Brower: ...edited by Hugh Nash, San Francisco. [1974]. pp. 313. *bibliog.*

PETROLEUM CHEMICALS INDUSTRY

— Europe, Eastern.

RAJANA (CECIL) The chemical and petro-chemical industries of Russia and Eastern Europe, 1960-1980. London, 1975. 1 vol. (various pagings). *Includes appendix of 534 tables.*

— Russia.

RAJANA (CECIL) The chemical and petro-chemical industries of Russia and Eastern Europe, 1960-1980. London, 1975. 1 vol. (various pagings). *Includes appendix of 534 tables.*

— — Russia (RSFSR).

PARKHOMENKO (V.) and CHARKIN (P.) 90 let zavodu imeni D.I. Mendeleeva. Iaroslavl', 1969. pp. 76.

PETROLEUM ENGINEERING.

OFFSHORE EUROPE 75 CONFERENCE, ABERDEEN, 1975. Conference papers. Kingston-upon-Thames, 1975. 1 vol.(looseleaf). *bibliogs.*

PETROLEUM IN SUBMERGED LANDS.

SCOTTISH COUNCIL (DEVELOPMENT AND INDUSTRY). North East Office. World offshore oil and gas: a review of offshore activity and an assessment of worldwide market prospects for offshore exploration/production equipment and materials. Aberdeen, 1975. pp. 211.

— Atlantic Ocean.

OFFSHORE EUROPE 75 CONFERENCE, ABERDEEN, 1975. Conference papers. Kingston-upon-Thames, 1975. 1 vol.(looseleaf). *bibliogs.*

— North Sea.

OFFSHORE EUROPE 75 CONFERENCE, ABERDEEN, 1975. Conference papers. Kingston-upon-Thames, 1975. 1 vol.(looseleaf). *bibliogs.*

The POLITICAL implications of North Sea oil and gas: [papers presented to a conference at Tønsberg in February 1975, sponsored by the Norwegian Institute of International Affairs and the Royal Institute of International Affairs]; edited by Martin Saeter and Ian Smart. Oslo, [1975]. pp. 168.

COOPER (BRYAN) and GASKELL (T.F.) The adventure of North Sea oil. London, 1976. pp. 293.

McRAE (THOMAS WATSON) North Sea oil: mecca or mirage?. [Bradford, 1976]. pp. 37. *bibliog.*

— United Kingdom.

CELTIC SEA OIL WORKING PARTY. The implications of off-shore oil and gas for the South West; report of a Joint Working Party. [Bristol], South West Economic Planning Council, [1975]. pp. 72.

— — Equipment and supplies.

U.K. Offshore Supplies Office. 1974. Offshore supplies interest relief grants: a guide for industry. 2nd ed. Glasgow, 1974. pp. 16.

U.K. Offshore Supplies Office. 1975. OSO: (background information which will help a company decide whether it can supply goods or a service needed offshore and how it could go about preparing its own market strategy). Glasgow, [1975]. pp. 144. *bibliog. In end pocket: Incentives for industry in the areas for expansion.*

— — Scotland.

U.K. Scial Science Research Council. North Sea Oil Panel. Bulletin. q., current issues only. Glasgow.

PETROLEUM INDUSTRY AND TRADE.

FRIED (EDWARD R.) and SCHULTZE (CHARLES L.) eds. Higher oil prices and the world economy: the adjustment problem; [by] Edward R. Fried [and others]. Washington, [1975]. pp. 284.

KRUEGER (ROBERT B.) The United States and international oil: a report for the Federal Energy Administration on U.S. firms and government policy. New York, 1975. pp. 366.

RIFAÏ (TAKI) The pricing of crude oil: economic and strategic guidelines for an international,energy policy. [rev. ed]. New York, 1975. pp. 400. *bibliog.*

SCOTTISH COUNCIL (DEVELOPMENT AND INDUSTRY). North East Office. World offshore oil and gas: a review of offshore activity and an assessment of worldwide market prospects for offshore exploration/production equipment and materials. Aberdeen, 1975. pp. 211.

WILLETT (THOMAS D.) The oil-transfer problem and international economic stability. Princeton, 1975. pp. 34. *bibliog. (Princeton University. Department of Economics and Sociology. International Finance Section. Essays in International Finance. No. 113)*

WILLRICH (MASON) and others. Energy and world politics. New York, ?1975!. PP. 234 *BIBLIOG.*

YASSUKOVICH (STANISLAS M.) Oil and money flows: the problems of recycling. London, [1975]. pp. 95.

PETROLEUM INDUSTRY AND TRADE.

ORGANIZATION OF THE PETROLEUM EXPORTING COUNTRIES. Information Department. Weekly bulletin: review of the press. w., F 9 1976 (v.7, no 5)- Vienna.

CHOUCRI (NAZLI) and FERRARO (VINCENT) International politics of energy interdependence: the case of petroleum. Lexington, Mass., [1976]. pp. 250. *bibliog.*

PARK (YOON S.) Oil money and the world economy. Boulder, Colorado, 1976. pp. 205. *bibliog.*

— Congresses.

La CRISI energetica: atti del convegno promosso da Politica ed Economia e dal Centro Documentazione e Ricerche per la Lombardia, Milano, 10 dicembre 1973. [Roma, 1974]. pp. 128. *(Politica ed Economia. Quaderni. 11)*

— Environmental aspects — United Kingdom — Shetland Islands.

SULLOM VOE ENVIRONMENTAL ADVISORY GROUP. Oil terminal at Sullom Voe: environmental impact assessment. Sandwick, Shetland, 1976. pp. 133. *bibliog.*

— Finance.

FALLON (NICHOLAS R.) Middle East oil money and its future expenditure. London, 1975. pp. 240. *bibliog.*

— Statistics.

ORGANIZATION OF THE PETROLEUM EXPORTING COUNTRIES. Statistical Unit. Annual statistical bulletin. a., 1974- Vienna. *1966/73 is available on microfilm.*

— Algeria.

MAZRI (HAMID) Les hydrocarbures dans l'économie algérienne. Alger, [1975]. pp. 263. *bibliog.*

— Arab countries.

ORGANIZATION OF ARAB PETROLEUM EXPORTING COUNTRIES. Information Department. News bulletin. m., N 1975 (v.1, no.1)- Kuwait.

CASADIO (GIAN PAOLO) The economic challenge of the Arabs. Farnborough, Hants., [1976]. pp. 216. *bibliog.*

ORGANIZATION OF ARAB PETROLEUM EXPORTING COUNTRIES. General Secretariat. Oil and Arab cooperation. q., current issues only. Kuwait. *[In English and Arabic].*

— Bolivia.

CANEDO M. (OSCAR JUSTINIANO) Tesis de nacionalizacion de los bienes de la empresa Bolivian Gulf Oil Co.: Bolivia sera libre y soberana por la voluntad del pueblo. 2nd ed. La Paz, 1969. pp. 104.

— Brazil.

COTTA (PERY) O petroleo e nosso?. Rio de Janeiro, 1975. pp. 343.

— China.

CHENG (CHU-YUAN) China's petroleum industry: output growth and export potential. New York, 1976. pp. 244. *bibliog.*

— East (Near East).

FALLON (NICHOLAS R.) Middle East oil money and its future expenditure. London, 1975. pp. 240. *bibliog.*

The MIDDLE East: oil, politics, and development; edited by John Duke Anthony. Washington, [1975]. pp. 109. *Proceedings of a conference held at the University of Toronto in 1974, sponsored by the Middle East Studies Committee of the International Studies Programme, University of Toronto, and the Canadian Institute of International Affairs.*

PEACOCK (ALAN TURNER) The oil crisis and the professional economist. York, [1975]. pp. 19. *(York. University. Sir Ellis Hunter Memorial Lectures. 7)*

RAND (CHRISTOPHER T.) Making democracy safe for oil: oilmen and the Islamic east. Boston, Mass., [1975]. pp. 422. *bibliog.*

STORK (JOE) Middle East oil and the energy crisis. New York, [1975]. pp. 326.

KENT (MARIAN) Oil and empire: British policy and Mesopotamian oil 1900-1920. London, 1976. pp. 273. *bibliog.*

LIEBER (ROBERT J.) Oil and the Middle East war: Europe in the energy crisis. Cambridge, Mass., [1976]. pp. 75. *(Harvard University. Center for International Affairs. Harvard Studies in International Affairs. No. 35)*

SHERBINY (NAIEM A.) and TESSLER (MARK A.) eds. Arab oil: impact on the Arab countries and global implications. New York, 1976. pp. 327.

— Europe.

The POLITICAL implications of North Sea oil and gas: [papers presented to a conference at Tønsberg in February 1975, sponsored by the Norwegian Institute of International Affairs and the Royal Institute of International Affairs]; edited by Martin Saeter and Ian Smart. Oslo, [1975]. pp. 168.

— — Bibliography.

CENTRE D'ETUDES INDUSTRIELLES. The petroleum industry in western Europe: a guide to information sources;...Lawrence G. Franko, general editor. London, 1975. pp. 170. *bibliogs.*

— — Information services.

CENTRE D'ETUDES INDUSTRIELLES. The petroleum industry in western Europe: a guide to information sources;...Lawrence G. Franko, general editor. London, 1975. pp. 170. *bibliogs.*

— European Economic Community countries.

KRAEMER (HANS R.) Die Europäische Gemeinschaft und die Ölkrise. Baden-Baden, [1974]. pp. 226.

— France.

ACTIVITE DE L'INDUSTRIE PETROLIERE; [pd. by] Ministère du Développement Industriel et Scientifique, Direction des Carburants [France]. a., 1970- Paris.

MENDERSHAUSEN (HORST) Coping with the oil crisis: French and German experiences. Baltimore, [1976]. pp. 110.

— Germany.

MEIER-DOERNBERG (WILHELM) Die Ölversorgung der Kriegsmarine, 1935 bis 1945. Freiburg, 1973. pp. 111. *bibliog. (Militärgeschichtliches Forschungsamt. Einzelschriften zur Militärischen Geschichte des Zweiten Weltkrieges. 11)*

MENDERSHAUSEN (HORST) Coping with the oil crisis: French and German experiences. Baltimore, [1976]. pp. 110.

— Iran.

FRANCE. Direction de la Documentation. La Documentation Française. Notes et Etudes Documentaires. Nos. 4,188-4, 189. L'Iran et les pétrodollars; (Étude...due à J. Regard). Paris, 1975. pp. 78.

FESHARAKI (FEREIDUN) Development of the Iranian oil industry: international and domestic aspects. New York, 1976. pp. 315. *bibliog.*

— Iraq.

IRAQ NATIONAL OIL COMPANY. Annual review. a., 1972- Baghdad.

— Italy.

BIANCHINI (GIOVANNI) Politica di piano e concorrenza nell'industria petrolifera italiana. Milano, [1974]. pp. 110. *bibliog. (Milan. Università Commerciale Luigi Bocconi. Istituto di Economia delle Fonti di Energia. Pubblicazioni. N.10)*

— Mediterranean.

MADELIN (HENRI) Oil and politics;...translated from the French by Margaret Totman. Farnborough, Hants., [1975]. pp. 241. *bibliog.*

— Mexico.

BORACRÈS (PAUL) El petroleo mexicano...es "cosa robada"?; traduccion del folleto editado por "Les éditions internationales". [Mexico!, 1939?]. pp. 71.

— Nigeria.

NIGERIA. Federal Ministry of Mines and Power. 1971. The future of the petroleum industry in Nigeria: a paper presented by Philip C. Asiodu...at the Economic Development Plan Seminar held in March, 1971 in Lagos. [Lagos, 1971]. pp. 10.

NIGERIA. 1972. Government role in the Nigerian oil industry. [Lagos, 1972]. pp. 19.

— Norway.

BROTNOV (JAN H.) ed. Oljen i samfunnsmaskineriet: de norske oljemilliardenes innvirkning bl. a. på samfunnsøkonomien, naeringsliv...; av Bodil Bjartnes [and others]. Oslo, [1975]. pp. 93. *bibliog.*

WYLLER (KARI BRUUN) and WYLLER (THOMAS CHRISTIAN) eds. Norsk oljepolitikk; bidrag av: Jon Naustdalslid [and others]. Oslo, [1975]. pp. 199.

— Russia — Russia (RSFSR).

KURASHEV (ARTEM VASIL'EVICH) Kuibyshevskaia neft': iz istorii razvitiia neftianoi promyshlennosti oblasti. Kuibyshev, 1969. pp. 239.

— South Africa.

MEINTJES (JOHANNES) Sasol 1950-1975. Cape Town, 1975. pp. 174. *bibliog.*

— Spain.

BANCO URQUIJO. Servicio de Estudios en Barcelona. El petroleo en Cataluña: analisis economico. Barcelona, 1969. 2 vols. (in 1). *bibliog.*

— United Kingdom.

CLIFTON DATA RESEARCH SERVICES. Survey of British oil companies, 1976. St. Albans, 1976. 152 columns.

COOPER (BRYAN) and GASKELL (T.F.) The adventure of North Sea oil. London, 1976. pp. 293.

KENT (MARIAN) Oil and empire: British policy and Mesopotamian oil 1900-1920. London, 1976. pp. 273. *bibliog.*

McRAE (THOMAS WATSON) North Sea oil: mecca or mirage?. [Bradford, 1976]. pp. 37. *bibliog.*

— — Scotland.

HUTCHESON (ALEXANDER MACGREGOR) and HOGG (ALEXANDER) eds. Scotland and oil. 2nd ed. Edinburgh, [1975]. pp. 127. *bibliog.*

MACKAY (DONALD IAIN) North Sea oil through speculative glasses. Glasgow, [1975]. pp. 17. *(Glasgow. University of Strathclyde. Fraser of Allander Institute. Speculative Papers. No. 4)*

U.K. Advisory Group on Research into the Social Impact of North Sea Oil Developments in Scotland. 1975. Research into the social impact of North Sea oil developments in Scotland; report; [W.G. Runciman, chairman]. London, [1975]. 1 vol. (various pagings).

— — — Shetland Islands.

NICOLSON (JAMES R.) Shetland and oil. London, [1975]. pp. 208. *bibliog.*

— United States.

EPPLE (DENNIS N.) Petroleum discoveries and government policy: an econometric study of supply. Cambridge, Mass., [1975]. pp. 139. *bibliog.*

PETROLEUM INDUSTRY AND TRADE.(Cont.)

KRUEGER (ROBERT B.) The United States and international oil: a report for the Federal Energy Administration on U.S. firms and government policy. New York, 1975. pp. 366.

MEDVIN (NORMAN) and others. The energy cartel: big oil vs. the public interest; prepared... by...[members of the firm] of Ruttenberg, Friedman, Kilgallon, Gutchess and Associates. Washington, 1975. pp. 439.

NEWLON (DANIEL H.) and BRECKNER (NORMAN V.) The oil security system: an import strategy for achieving oil security and reducing oil prices. Lexington, Mass., [1975]. pp. 112. bibliog.

RAND (CHRISTOPHER T.) Making democracy safe for oil: oilmen and the Islamic east. Boston, Mass., [1975]. pp. 422. bibliog.

VERTICAL integration in the oil industry; edited by Edward J. Mitchell. Washington, 1976. pp. 214. (American Enterprise Institute for Public Policy Research. National Energy Studies. 11)

PETROLEUM LAW AND LEGISLATION

— Canada.

CANADA. Statutes, etc. 1952-68. Office consolidation of the Canada Oil and Gas Land Regulations, oil and gas land orders, Public Lands Grants Act, Territorial Lands Act. [Ottawa], 1968. pp. 73.

PETROLEUM PRODUCTS

— Prices.

FRIED (EDWARD R.) and SCHULTZE (CHARLES L.) eds. Higher oil prices and the world economy: the adjustment problem; [by] Edward R. Fried [and others]. Washington, [1975]. pp. 284.

HIGHER oil prices: worldwide financial implications; [consisting of] a policy statement by the British-North American Committee [and] a research report by Sperry Lea..[Washington], 1975. pp. x, 31.

PEACOCK (ALAN TURNER) The oil crisis and the professional economist. York, [1975]. pp. 19. (York. University. Sir Ellis Hunter Memorial Lectures. 7)

RIFAÏ (TAKI) The pricing of crude oil: economic and strategic guidelines for an international energy policy. [rev. ed]. New York, 1975. pp. 400. bibliog.

WILLETT (THOMAS D.) The oil-transfer problem and international economic stability. Princeton, 1975. pp. 34. bibliog. (Princeton University. Department of Economics and Sociology. International Finance Section. Essays in International Finance. No. 113)

RYBCZYNSKI (TADEUSZ MIECZYSLAW) ed. The economics of the oil crisis. London, 1976. pp. 202. bibliog.

— — Italy.

BIANCHINI (GIOVANNI) Politica di piano e concorrenza nell'industria petrolifera italiana. Milano, [1974]. pp. 110. bibliog. (Milan. Università Commerciale Luigi Bocconi. Istituto di Economia delle Fonti di Energia. Pubblicazioni. N.10)

PETROLEUM REFINERIES.

UNITED STATES. Central Intelligence Agency. 1974. World oil refineries. [Washington], 1974. pp. 46. (Research Aids. No.A(ER)74-61) Microfilm: 1 reel.

UNITED STATES. Central Intelligence Agency. 1975. Export refining centers of the world. [Washington], 1975. pp. 31. (Intelligence Handbooks No.A(ER)75-66) Microfilm: 1 reel.

UNITED STATES. Central Intelligence Agency. 1975. Free world oil refineries. [Washington], 1975. pp. 59. (Research Aids. No.A(ER)75-67) Microfilm: 1 reel.

PETROLEUM SHIPPING TERMINALS

— United States.

The CHALLENGE of deepwater terminals; by Louis K. Bragaw [and others]. Lexington, Mass., [1975]. pp. 162. bibliog.

PETROLEUM WORKERS

— Libya.

LIBYA. Census and Statistical Department. 1966. Employment in the petroleum mining industry in Libya, 1964. Tripoli, [1966?]. fo. 17.

PHARMACEUTICAL RESEARCH.

PHARMACOLOGICAL testing in a correctional institution: volunteer characteristics and motivations: social, psychological and attitudinal implications; by Stephen H. Wells [and others] . Springfield, Ill., [1975]. pp. 66. bibliog.

PHENOMENOLOGY.

BOGDAN (ROBERT) and TAYLOR (STEVEN J.) Introduction to qualitative research methods: a phenomenological approach to the social sciences. New York, [1975]. pp. 266. bibliog.

PHILADELPHIA

— History.

CLARK (DENNIS) The Irish in Philadelphia: ten generations of urban experience. Philadelphia, 1973 repr. 1974. pp. 246. bibliog.

— Politics and government.

MILLER (RICHARD G.) Philadelphia - the Federalist city: a study of urban politics, 1789-1801. Port Washington, N.Y., 1976. pp. 192. bibliog.

PHILIP II, King of Spain.

PIERSON (PETER) Philip II of Spain. London, [1975]. pp. 240. bibliog.

PHILIPPINE ISLANDS

— Commerce.

PHILIPPINE ISLANDS. Department of Trade. Trade journal. m., Jl 1975 (no.6)- Quezon City.

— Foreign relations — United States.

POMEROY (WILLIAM J.) An American made tragedy: neo-colonialism and dictatorship in the Philippines. New York, 1974. pp. 190. bibliog.

THOMPSON (W. SCOTT) Unequal partners: Philippine and Thai relations with the United States 1965-75. Lexington, [1975]. pp. 183.

— History.

FURNIVALL (JOHN SYDENHAM) Experiment in independence: the Philippines;...edited posthumously by Frank N. Trager. Detroit, 1974. pp. 103.

STURTEVANT (DAVID R.) Popular uprisings in the Philippines, 1840-1940. Ithaca, 1976. pp. 317. bibliog.

— — 1898-1946.

COMPADRE colonialism: studies on the Philippines under American rule; edited by Norman G. Owen. Ann Arbor, 1971. pp. 252. bibliog. (Michigan University. Center for South and Southeast Asian Studies. Michigan Papers on South and Southeast Asia. No. 3)

— Industries.

PHILIPPINE ISLANDS. Department of Trade. Trade journal. m., Jl 1975 (no.6)- Quezon City.

— Politics and government.

COMPADRE colonialism: studies on the Philippines under American rule; edited by Norman G. Owen. Ann Arbor, 1971. pp. 252. bibliog. (Michigan University. Center for South and Southeast Asian Studies. Michigan Papers on South and Southeast Asia. No. 3)

FURNIVALL (JOHN SYDENHAM) Experiment in independence: the Philippines;...edited posthumously by Frank N. Trager. Detroit, 1974. pp. 103.

POLITICAL change in the Philippines: studies of local politics preceding martial law; edited by Benedict J. Kerkvliet. [Honolulu], 1974. pp. 258. (Hawaii University. Asian Studies Program. Asian Studies of Hawaii. 14) Based on essays presented at the Association of Asian Studies meeting in New York in 1972 and at a regional meeting of AAS in 1972.

KLIEMAN (AARON S.) Emergency politics: the growth of crisis government. London, 1976. pp. 19. (Institute for the Study of Conflict. Conflict Studies. No. 70)

MANGLAPUS (RAUL S.) Philippines: the silenced democracy. Maryknoll, N.Y., [1976]. pp. 205. bibliog.

— Social conditions.

JOCANO (F. LANDA) Slum as a way of life: a study of coping behavior in an urban environment. Quezon City, 1975. pp. 203.

PHILOSOPHERS

— Directories.

INTERNATIONL directory of philosophy and philosophers, 1974-75; third edition edited by Ramona Cormier [and others]. Bowling Green, Ohio, [1974]. pp. 557.

PHILOSOPHICAL ANTHROPOLOGY.

RICOEUR (PAUL) Political and social essays; collected and edited by David Stewart and Joseph Bien. Athens, Ohio, [1974]. pp. 293.

PLAMENATZ (JOHN PETROV) Karl Marx's philosophy of man. Oxford, 1975. pp. 484.

PHILOSOPHY.

UCHENYE ZAPISKI KAFEDR OBSHCHESTVENNYKH NAUK VUZOV LENINGRADA. Filosofiia. vyp.8. Filosofskie i sotsiologicheskie issledovaniia. Leningrad, 1967. pp. 239.

— Directories.

INTERNATIONL directory of philosophy and philosophers, 1974-75; third edition edited by Ramona Cormier [and others]. Bowling Green, Ohio, [1974]. pp. 557.

PHILOSOPHY, AMERICAN.

HOFSTADTER (RICHARD) Social Darwinism in American thought. rev. ed. New York, 1959 repr. 1969. pp. 248. bibliog.

PHILOSOPHY, ANCIENT.

ARISTOTLE. Posterior analytics; translated with notes by Jonathan Barnes. Oxford, 1975. pp. 277. bibliog.

PHILOSOPHY, ARMENIAN.

AREVSHATIAN (SEN SURENOVICH) Formirovanie filosofskoi nauki v drevnei Armenii, V-VI vv. Erevan, 1973. pp. 350. bibliog.

PHILOSOPHY, BULGARIAN.

KRATKA istoriia na bulgarskata filosofska misul. Sofiia, 1973. pp. 592. bibliog.

PHILOSOPHY, FRENCH.

POSTER (MARK) Existential Marxism in postwar France: from Sartre to Althusser. Princeton, [1975]. pp. 415. bibliog.

MEEK (RONALD LINDLEY) Social science and the ignoble savage. Cambridge, 1976. pp. 249.

PARKER (MAXWELL NOEL LEWIS) Rousseau and the contradictions of rationalism: a critical study of Rousseau's social and political theory in the context of eighteenth-century social and philosophical developments. [1976]. fo. 264. *bibliog. Typescript. Ph.D. (London) thesis: unpublished. This thesis is the property of London University and may not be removed from the Library.*

PAYNE (HARRY C.) The philosophes and the people. New Haven, 1976. pp. 214. *bibliog.*

PHILOSOPHY, GERMAN.

BULATOV (MIKHAIL ALEKSANDROVICH) Leninskii analiz nemetskoi klassicheskoi filosofii: logiko-dialekticheskie i istoriko-filosofskie problemy. Kiev, 1974. pp. 271. *bibliog.*

PHILOSOPHY, MODERN.

ZSCHIMMER (EBERHARD) Philosophische Briefe an einen Arbeiter...1. Teil. Briefe über Logik und Philosophie der Natur, mit Anmerkungen. 2nd ed. Jena, 1920. pp. 139.

GILL (JERRY H.) ed. Philosophy today: [a collection of recent articles]. New York, 1968 in progress.

UCHENYE ZAPISKI KAFEDR OBSHCHESTVENNYKH NAUK VUZOV LENINGRADA. Filosofiia. vyp. 9. Filosofskie i sotsiologicheskie issledovaniia. Leningrad, 1968. pp. 189.

RODO (JOSE ENRIQUE) Motivos de Proteo; [and] Nuevos motivos de Proteo. Mexico, 1969. pp. 245.

LENINGRAD. Universitet. Voprosy Filosofii i Sotsiologii. vyp. 5. Problemy materialisticheskoi dialektiki i logiki; pod redaktsiei. ..A.M. Plotnikova. Leningrad, 1973. pp. 128.

NEKOTORYE problemy dialektiki i metodologii poznaniia. Tashkent, 1973. pp. 188. *(Tashkent. Universitet. Nauchnye Trudy. vyp.452.)*

HOLZ (HANS HEINZ) and others. Conversations with Lukács;... edited by Theo Pinkus; (translated by David Fernbach). London, 1974. pp. 155.

ANDREEVA (ISKRA STEPANOVNA) Problema mira v zapadnoevropeiskoi filosofii. Moskva, 1975. pp. 223. *bibliog.*

PUTNAM (HILARY) Philosophical papers. Cambridge, 1975. 2 vols. *bibliogs.*

SIMON-SCHAEFER (ROLAND) and ZIMMERLI (WALTHER CH.) Theorie zwischen Kritik und Praxis: Jürgen Habermas und die Frankfurter Schule. Stuttgart-Bad Cannstatt, [1975]. pp. 186. *bibliog. With English summary.*

TOENNIES (FERDINAND) Studien zur Philosophie und Gesellschaftslehre im 17. Jahrhundert; herausgegeben von E.G. Jacoby. Stuttgart-Bad Cannstatt, [1975]. pp. 384. *bibliog.*

GRENE (MARJORIE GLICKSMAN) Philosophy in and out of Europe. Berkeley, 1976. pp. 169.

INTERNATIONAL SLAVIC CONFERENCE, 1ST, BANFF, ALBERTA, 1974. Marxism and religion in Eastern Europe; papers presented at the...conference...; edited by Richard T. De George and James P. Scanlan. Dordrecht, [1976]. pp. 181. *(Freiburg (Switzerland). Universität. Ost-Europa Institut. Sovietica. vol. 36)*

NORDHOFEN (ECKHARD) Das Bereichsdenken im Kritischen Rationalismus: zur finitistischen Tradition der Popperschule. München, [1976]. pp. 214. *bibliog.*

SOCIAL ends and political means; edited by Ted Honderich. London, 1976. pp. 177.

SOREL (GEORGES) From Georges Sorel: essays in socialism and philosophy; edited with an introduction by John L. Stanley and translated by John and Charlotte Stanley. New York, 1976. pp. 388. *bibliog.*

PHILOSOPHY, RUSSIAN.

UCHENYE ZAPISKI KAFEDR OBSHCHESTVENNYKH NAUK VUZOV LENINGRADA. Filosofiia. vyp. 9. Filosofskie i sotsiologicheskie issledovaniia. Leningrad, 1968. pp. 189.

UCHENYE ZAPISKI KAFEDR OBSHCHESTVENNYKH NAUK VUZOV LENINGRADA. Filosofiia. vyp.10. Filosofskie i sotsiologicheskie issledovaniia. Leningrad, 1969. pp. 231.

TASHKENT. Universitet. Nauchnye Trudy. vyp.453. Filosofiia. Tashkent, 1973. pp. 264.

GEGEL' i filosofiia v Rossii, 30-e gody XIX v. - 20-e gody XX v. Moskva, 1974. pp. 264. *bibliog.*

ADELMANN (FREDERICK J.) ed. Philosophical investigations in the U.S.S.R. Chestnut Hill, 1975. pp. 128. *bibliog. (Boston College. Studies in Philosophy. vol. 4)*

BLAKELEY (THOMAS J.) ed. Themes in Soviet Marxist philosophy: selected articles from the Filosofskaja enciklopedija. Dordrecht, [1975]. pp. 224. *(Freiburg (Switzerland). Universität. Ost-Europa Institut. Sovietica. vol.37)*

BOESELAGER (WOLFHARD F.) The Soviet critique of neopositivism: the history and structure of the critique of logical positivism and related doctrines by Soviet philosophers in the years 1947-1967. Dordrecht, [1975]. pp. 157. *bibliog. (Freiburg (Switzerland). Universität. Ost-Europa Institut. Sovietica. vol. 35)*

UCHENYE ZAPISKI KAFEDR OBSHCHESTVENNYKH NAUK VUZOV LENINGRADA. Filosofiia. vyp. 16. Filosofskie i sotsiologicheskie issledovaniia. Leningrad, 1975. pp. 207.

PHILOSOPHY, SCOTTISH.

MEEK (RONALD LINDLEY) Social science and the ignoble savage. Cambridge, 1976. pp. 249.

PHILOSOPHY, SPANISH.

NUÑEZ RUIZ (DIEGO) La mentalidad positiva en España: desarrollo y crisis. Madrid, [1975]. pp. 278.

PHILOSOPHY, YUGOSLAV.

SMISAO i perspektive socijalizma: zbornik (radova drugog zasjedanja Korčulanske ljetne škole, Korčula, 1964). Zagreb, 1965. pp. 358.

PHOSPHATE INDUSTRY

— **Russia — Ukraine.**

BAKALO (RUSLAN ALEKSANDROVICH) and SOKOLOV (VIACHESLAV NIKOLAEVICH) Arsenal zemledel'tsev. Odessa, 1974. pp. 99.

— **United Kingdom.**

GROVE (RICHARD) The Cambridgeshire coprolite mining rush. Cambridge, [1976]. pp. 51. *bibliog.*

PHOSPHATIC FERTILIZERS.

WELLS (FREDERICK J.) The long-run availability of phosphorus: a case study in mineral resource analysis. Baltimore, [1975]. pp. 121. *bibliog.*

PHOSPHORUS.

WELLS (FREDERICK J.) The long-run availability of phosphorus: a case study in mineral resource analysis. Baltimore, [1975]. pp. 121. *bibliog.*

PHOTOGRAPHIC INDUSTRY

— **United States.**

JENKINS (REESE V.) Images and enterprise: technology and the American photographic industry, 1839 to 1925. Baltimore, [1975]. pp. 371. *bibliog.*

PHOTOGRAPHY, AERIAL.

PHOTOGRAPHIE aérienne et urbanisme. [Paris, 1969]. pp. 244. *bibliog.*

PHYSICAL EDUCATION AND TRAINING.

SOCIAL problems in athletics: essays in the sociology of sport; edited by Daniel M. Landers. Urbana, [1976]. pp. 251. *bibliogs. Essays based on a conference on "Sport and Social Deviance" which was held at State University College, Brockport, New York*

PHYSICAL GEOGRAPHY

— **America, North.**

PATERSON (JOHN HARRIS) North America: a geography of Canada and the United States. 5th ed. New York, 1975. pp. 368. *bibliog.*

— **Greece.**

RECHERCHES sur la Grèce rurale. Paris, 1972 [or rather 1973]. pp. 138. *(Service de Documentation et de Cartographie Géographiques. Mémoires et Documents. Nouvelle Série. vol. 13)*

— **India.**

INDIA. Gazetteers Unit. 1965. The gazetteer of India: Indian union. Vol. 1. Country and people. [New Delhi], 1965 repr. 1973. pp. 652. *bibliogs. 2 maps in end pocket.*

— **Poland.**

POLSKA ACADEMIA NAUK. Instytut Geografii. Geographia Polonica. 33. The 23rd International Geographical Congress, Moscow, 1976: [proceedings]. Warszawa, 1976. 2 vols. *bibliogs.*

— — **Bibliography.**

LESZCZYCKI (STANISŁAW) and WINID (BOGODAR) compilers. Bibliografia geografii polskiej, 1945-1951. Warszawa, 1956. pp. 218. *With Russian and English summaries.*

— **Russia.**

PARKER (WILLIAM HENRY) The Soviet Union. Chicago, 1969. pp. 188. *bibliog.*

LYDOLPH (PAUL E.) Geography of the U.S.S.R. 2nd ed. New York, [1970]. pp. 683. *bibliogs.*

— — **Mordvinian Republic.**

GORTSEV (VASILII IVANOVICH) Geografiia Mordovskoi ASSR. Saransk, 1968. pp. 128.

— — **Russia (RSFSR).**

BERENBEIM (D.IA.) and others. Kaliningradskaia oblast': ocherki prirody. Kaliningrad, 1969. pp. 206.

PHYSICAL THERAPISTS

— **Canada.**

CANADA. Statistics Canada. Health manpower: physiotherapists. a., 1973 (1st)- Ottawa. *[In English and French].*

PHYSICALLY HANDICAPPED

— **Bibliography.**

MURRAY (NICK) compiler. Outdoor mobility for the disabled. London, 1975. pp. 7. *(London. Greater London Council. Research Library. [Research] Bibliographies. No. 65)*

— **Rehabilitation — United Kingdom — Wales.**

REHABILITATION services in industrial south Wales; report of a Working Party appointed by the Secretary of State for Wales; [R.T. Bevan, chairman]. [Cardiff?, Welsh Office], 1975. pp. 92.

— — **United States.**

The SOCIOLOGY of physical disability and rehabilitation; Gary L. Albrecht, editor. Pittsburgh, [1976]. pp. 303. *bibliogs.*

PHYSICALLY HANDICAPPED(Cont.)

— United Kingdom.

GREAVES (MARY) Increasing physical disablement in retirement. London, 1974. pp. 10. bibliog. (Age Concern England. Manifesto Series. No. 11)

SOCIAL SERVICES RESEARCH AND INTELLIGENCE UNIT [PORTSMOUTH]. Information Sheets. No. 23. Alarm systems for the elderly and disabled people. Portsmouth, 1975. fo. 6.

— United States.

The SOCIOLOGY of physical disability and rehabilitation; Gary L. Albrecht, editor. Pittsburgh, [1976]. pp. 303. bibliogs.

PHYSICALLY HANDICAPPED CHILDREN

— Care and treatment — United Kingdom.

WOODS (GRACE E.) The handicapped child: assessment and management. Oxford, 1975. pp. 341. bibliogs.

PHYSICIANS

— Norway.

NORWAY. Statistiske Centralbyrå. Legestatistikk: Statistics on physicians. a., 1974- Oslo. In Norwegian and English.

— Switzerland.

KOCHER (GERHARD) Verbandseinfluss auf die Gesetzgebung: Aerzteverbindung, Krankenkassenverbände und die Teilrevision 1964 des Kranken- und Unfallversicherungsgesetzes. 2nd ed. Bern, 1972. pp. 268. bibliog. (Bern. Universität. Forschungszentrum für Schweizerische Politik. Helvetia Politica. Series B. vol. 1)

— United Kingdom.

BERLANT (JEFFREY LIONEL) Profession and monopoly: a study of medicine in the United States and Great Britain. Berkeley, [1975]. pp. 337. bibliog.

PARRY (NOEL) and PARRY (JOSÉ) The rise of the medical profession: a study of collective social mobility. London, [1976]. pp. 282. bibliog.

— United States.

TAYLOR (LLOYD C.) The medical profession and social reform, 1885-1945. New York, [1974]. pp. 168.

BERLANT (JEFFREY LIONEL) Profession and monopoly: a study of medicine in the United States and Great Britain. Berkeley, [1975]. pp. 337. bibliog.

FREIDSON (ELIOT) Doctoring together: a study of professional social control. New York, [1975]. pp. 298. bibliog.

REINHARDT (UWE E.) Physician productivity and the demand for health manpower. Cambridge, Mass., [1975]. pp. 311. bibliog.

— — Supply and demand.

RUSHING (WILLIAM A.) Community, physicians and inequality: a sociological study of the maldistribution of physicians. Lexington, Mass., [1975]. pp. 255. bibliog.

PHYSICIANS (GENERAL PRACTICE)

— United Kingdom.

U.K. Department of Health and Social Security. [Circulars]: H.C. (F.P.) [Family Practitioner Services]. irreg., Ag 1976 (no.3)- London.

MARSH (GEOFFREY) and KAIM-CAUDLE (P.R.) Team care in general practice. London, 1976. pp. 185.

— — Salaries, pensions, etc.

HEANEY (CHARLES THOMAS) The payment of general practitioners in Great Britain, 1834- 1974; [Ph. D. (London) thesis]. 1975. fo. 322. bibliog. Typescript: unpublished. This thesis is the property of London University and may not be removed from the Library.

PHYSICIANS, FOREIGN

— United Kingdom.

COMMUNITY RELATIONS COMMISSION. Doctors from overseas: a case for consultation. London, 1976. pp. 32.

PHYSIOCRATS.

HERLITZ (LARS) Fysiokratismen i svensk tappning, 1767-1770. Göteborg, 1974. pp. 201. bibliog. (Göteborgs Universitet. Ekonomisk-Historiska Institutionen. Meddelanden. 35)

FOX-GENOVESE (ELIZABETH) The origins of physiocracy: economic revolution and social order in eighteenth-century France. Ithaca, N.Y., 1976. pp. 325. bibliog.

PHYSIOLOGY

— Early works to 1800.

DESCARTES (RENE) Treatise of man; French text with translation and commentary by Thomas Steele Hall. Cambridge, Mass., 1972. pp. 232. bibliog.

PIAGET (JEAN).

BEARD (RUTH M.) An outline of Piaget's developmental psychology for students and teachers. London, 1969 repr. 1974. pp. 128. bibliog.

TREMAINE (RUTH V.) Syntax and Piagetian operational thought: a developmental study of bilingual children. Washington, [1975]. pp. 131. bibliog.

HOLMES (ROGER) Legitimacy and the politics of the knowable. London, 1976. pp. 191. A collection of essays reprinted from various periodicals.

PIAROA INDIANS.

KAPLAN (JOANNA OVERING) The Piaroa: a people of the Orinoco basin: a study in kinship and marriage. Oxford, 1975. pp. 236. bibliog.

PICKERSGILL (JOHN WHITNEY).

PICKERSGILL (JOHN WHITNEY) My years with Louis St Laurent: a political memoir. Toronto, [1975]. pp. 334.

PIECK (WILHELM).

VOSSKE (HEINZ) ed. Wilhelm Pieck, 1876-1960: Bilder und Dokumente aus seinem Leben. Berlin, [1975]. pp. 329.

VOSSKE (HEINZ) and NITZSCHE (GERHARD) Wilhelm Pieck: bigraphischer Abriss. Berlin, 1975. pp. 406. bibliog.

ZIMMERLING (ZENO) Wilhelm Pieck: Geschichte und Geschichten eines grossen Lebens. Berlin, [1976]. pp. 191.

PIL'NIAK (BORIS ANDREEVICH).

RECK (VERA T.) Boris Pil'niak: a Soviet writer in conflict with the state. Montreal, 1975. pp. 243. bibliog.

PISA

— History.

SHIMIZU (KOICHIRO) L'amministrazione del contado pisano nel Trecento attraverso un manuale notarile. [Pisa, 1975]. pp. 143. bibliog. (Bollettino Storico Pisano. Biblioteca. Collana Storica. 13)

PITT (WILLIAM) Earl of Chatham.

AYLING (STANLEY EDWARD) The elder Pitt, Earl of Chatham. London, 1976. pp. 478. bibliog.

PITTSBURGH

— Civic improvement.

AHLBRANDT (ROGER S.) and BROPHY (PAUL C.) Neighborhood revitalization: theory and practice. Lexingon, [1975]. pp. 188. bibliog.

— Politics and government.

STAVE (BRUCE M.) The New Deal and the last hurrah: Pittsburgh machine politics. Pittsburgh, [1970]. pp. 262. bibliog.

— Social history.

SHERGOLD (PETER ROGER) The standard of life of manual workers in the first decade of the twentieth-century: a comparative study of Birmingham, U.K., and Pittsburgh, U.S.A. 1976. fo. 691. bibliog. Typescript. Ph.D. (London) thesis: unpublished. This thesis is the property of London University and may not be removed from the Library.

PIUS XII, Pope.

KLEIN (CHARLES) Pie XII face aux Nazis. Paris, [1975]. pp. 250.

PLAN EVALUATION AND ROBUSTNESS PROGRAM (COMPUTER PROGRAM).

See PERP (COMPUTER PROGRAM).

PLANNING.

ACKOFF (RUSSELL LINCOLN) A concept of corporate planning. New York, [1970]. pp. 158. bibliog.

BENTON (WILLIAM KING) The use of the computer in planning. Reading, Mass., [1971]. pp. 160.

RONNEBERGER (FRANZ) and others. Entwicklung von Strategien zur Einbeziehung der Öffentlichkeit in den Planungsprozess für Standortprogramme. Essen, 1972. fo. 105. bibliog.

CATANESE (ANTHONY JAMES) Planners and local politics: impossible dreams. Beverly Hills, [1974]. pp. 188. bibliog.

FORWARD planning in the service sectors: [proceedings of a Science Policy Foundation symposium held in London in 1973]; edited by Maurice Goldsmith. London, 1975. pp. 165.

LICHFIELD (NATHANIEL) and others. Evaluation in the planning process. Oxford, 1975. pp. 325. bibliog.

NOVE (ALEXANDER) Planning: what, how and why. Edinburgh, [1975]. pp. 23. (Glasgow. University of Strathclyde. Fraser of Allander Institute. Speculative Papers. No. 1)

QAYUM (ABDUL) Techniques of national economic planning. Bloomington, [1975]. pp. 240. (Indiana University. International Development Research Center. Studies in Development. 9)

GUNSTEREN (HERMAN R. VAN) The quest for control: a critique of the rational-central-rule approach in public affairs. London, [1976]. pp. 162. bibliogs.

— Congresses.

INTERNATIONAL ECONOMIC ASSOCIATION. Conference, [1974?], Moscow. Methods of long-term planning and forecasting: proceedings of a conference...; edited by T.S. Khachaturov. London, 1976. pp. 461. bibliogs.

PLANTATION LIFE.

TEA: the colonial legacy; [written for the Cambridge World Development Action Group by John Hamilton and others]. Cambridge, [1974]. pp. 22,iv. bibliog.

— United States.

JOHNSON (CHARLES SPURGEON) Shadow of the plantation. Chicago, 1934 repr. 1969. pp. 215.

PLASTICS IN PACKAGING.

ECONOMIC DEVELOPMENT COMMITTEE FOR CHEMICALS. Plastics Steering Committee. Prospects for the plastics packaging industry: a report based on a study of past performance, future investment requirements and constraints to profitable growth. London, National Economic Development Office, 1976. pp. 54.

PLASTICS INDUSTRY AND TRADE

— **United Kingdom.**

MERRIAM (JOHN) Pioneering in plastics. Ipswich, 1976. pp. 118.

PLASTICS WORKERS

— **Hong Kong.**

HONG KONG. Plastics Industrial Committee. 1972. Minumum job standards and specifications for the principal jobs in the plastics industry. Hong Kong, 1971[or rather 1972]. pp. 72. *In English and Chinese.*

PLATE

— **United Kingdom.**

A LETTER from a Member of Parliament on the plate-tax. London, J. Scott, 1756. pp. 31.

PLAY.

REILLY (MARY) ed. Play as exploratory learning: studies of curiosity behavior. Beverly Hills, [1974]. pp. 317. *bibliogs.*

PLAY SCHOOLS.

VAUXHALL COMMUNITY DEVELOPMENT PROJECT. Report of the preschool survey, July 1972; (by Keith Pulham) . [Liverpool, 1972]. pp. 2.

PLAYGROUNDS

— **United Kingdom.**

CUMBRIA COMMUNITY DEVELOPMENT PROJECT. Only playtime: the Area Play Organiser report to the agencies supporting the experiment: Community Development Project, Education Committee, Social Services Committee. [Cleator Moor, 1974]. pp. 34.

PLEADING

— **United Kingdom.**

BULLEN (EDWARD) and others. Precedents of pleadings in the Queen's Bench Division of the High Court of Justice; twelfth edition by I.H. Jacob. London, 1975. pp. 1457.

PLEBISCITE

— **France.**

DENQUIN (JEAN MARIE) Référendum et plébiscite: essai de théorie générale. Paris, 1976. pp. 353. *bibliog.*

PLEKHANOV (GEORGII VALENTINOVICH).

ZHUIKOV (GENNADII SEMENOVICH) Peterburgskie marksisty i gruppa "Osvobozhdeniia truda". Leningrad, 1975. pp. 328.

PLIMSOLL (SAMUEL).

PETERS (Rev. GEORGE H.) The Plimsoll line: the story of Samuel Plimsoll, Member of Parliament for Derby from 1868-1880. Chichester, [1975]. pp. 203. *bibliog.*

PLISCHKE (OSKAR).

EUROPEAN COMMISSION OF HUMAN RIGHTS. 1965. The Plischke case:...[application No. 1446/62 by Oskar Plischke against Austria]. Strasbourg, Council of Europe, 1965. pp. 36.

PLIUSCH (LEONID IVANOVICH).

The CASE of Leonid Plyushch; translated from the Russian by Marite Sapiets, Peter Reddaway and Caryl Emerson; editor of the Russian edition, Tatyana Khodorovich, etc. London, [1976]. pp. 152. *Includes a selection of his letters.*

PLOZEVET

— **Rural conditions.**

BURGUIÈRE (ANDRE) Bretons de Plozévet. [Paris, 1975]. pp. 383. *bibliog.*

PLURALISM (SOCIAL SCIENCES).

GALTUNG (JOHAN) Pluralism and the future of human society. Antwerpen, 1971. pp. 87. *(National Hoger Instituut voor Bouwkunst en Stedebouw [Antwerp]. Sociale Verandering en Revolutie.* i) With summaries in Dutch and French.

HOOKER (M.B.) Legal pluralism: an introduction to colonial and neo-colonial laws. Oxford, 1975. pp. 601. *bibliog.*

INTERNATIONAL CONGRESS OF ANTHROPOLOGICAL AND ETHNOLOGICAL SCIENCES. 9th Congress, 1973. Ethnicity and resource competition in plural societies: [papers from the Congress]; editor Leo A. Despres. The Hague, [1975]. pp. 221. *bibliogs.*

PLURALISM and development in island communities; report of the commonwealth seminar held in Mauritius, January 1975. [London], Commonwealth Secretariat, [1975]. pp. 94. *bibliog.*

SMOCK (DAVID R.) and SMOCK (AUDREY C.) The politics of pluralism: a comparative study of Lebanon and Ghana. New York, [1975]. pp. 369. *bibliog.*

YOUNG (CRAWFORD) The politics of cultural pluralism. Madison, Wisconsin, 1976. pp. 560.

POLAND.

POLSKA: obrazy i opisy. Lwów, 1906-09. 2 vols (in 4). *(Macierza Polska. Wydawnictwa. Nr.83 [being also] Fundacja imienia Tadeusza Kościuszki. [Publications]. Nr.4)*

POLSKA 75. Warszawa, 1976. pp. 767.

— **Army — History.**

POLSKI SZTAB GŁÓWNY W LONDYNIE. Komisja Historyczna. Polskie Siły Zbrojne w drugiej wojnie światowej. t.3. Armia Krajowa. Londyn, 1950. pp. 972.

— **Boundaries.**

WRZESIŃSKI (WOJCIECH) Ruch polski na Warmii, Mazurach i Powślu w latach 1920-1939. Poznań, 1963. pp. 436. *bibliog. (Poznań. Instytut Zachodni. Prace. Nr.34)* With German summary.

PRUS-WIŚNIEWSKI (JÓZEF) Dawne granice Polski i organizacja Kościoła Rzymsko- Katolickiego w Polsce po 1945 roku. [Londyn, 1973]. pp. 88.

DOMINICZAK (HENRYK) Granica polsko-niemiecka 1919-1939: z dziejów formacji granicznych. Warszawa, 1975. pp. 292. *bibliog.*

SKUBISZEWSKI (KRZYSZTOF) Zachodnia granica Polski w świetle traktatów. Poznań, 1975. pp. 369. *bibliog. (Poznań. Instytut Zachodni. Studia Niemcoznawcze. Nr.26)* With English summary.

— **Census.**

POLAND. Census, 1960. Spis powszechny z dnia 6 grudnia 1960 r.: wyniki ostateczne; ludność, gospodarstwa domowe. Warszawa, 1964-65. 23 pts. (in 6 vols.). *(Statystyka Polski. Seria L)* Some parts incomplete.

POLAND. Census, 1960. Spis powszechny z dnia 6 grudnia 1960 r.: wyniki ostateczne; mieszkania, budynki mieszkalne. z. 2-12, 14-23. Warszawa, 1965-66. 21 pts. (in 2 vols.). *(Statystyka Polski. Seria M.)*

— **Civilization.**

HENSEL (WITOLD) Początki państwa polskiego i jego kultury. Wrocław, 1971. pp. 196. *bibliog.*

— **Climate.**

POLSKA AKADEMIA NAUK. Instytut Geografii. Geographia Polonica. 31. Warszawa, 1975. pp. 235. *bibliogs. No title: papers mainly concerned with Poland.*

POLSKA AKADEMIA NAUK. Instytut Geografii. Geographia Polonica. 33. The 23rd International Geographical Congress, Moscow, 1976: [proceedings]. Warszawa, 1976. 2 vols. *bibliogs.*

— **Commerce.**

WOJCIECHOWSKI (BRONISŁAW) Foreign trade of Poland: its growth, structure and economic system. Warsaw, 1974. pp. 59. *bibliog.*

TEICHMANOWA (EUFEMIA) Koszt transportu w handlu międzynarodowym: ze szczególnym uwzględnieniem handlu zagranicznego Polski. Warszawa, 1975. pp. 182. *bibliog. (Szkoła Główna Planowania i Statystyki. Monografie i Opracowania. 31)*

— **Constitution.**

POLAND. Constitution. 1935. Konstytucja Rzeczypospolitej Polskiej. [Jerusalem?, 1944]. pp. 71.

— **Constitutional history.**

KRASIŃSKI (ADAM) Hrabia. Geschichtliche Darstellung der Bauern-Verhältnisse in Polen und der wirthschaftlich-rechtlichen Reformen im ersten Decennium der Regierung Stanislaus Augustus, 1764-1774. Krakau, 1898. 2 vols (in 1).

— **Constitutional law — Terminology.**

KIELAR (BARBARA Z.) Angielskie ekwiwalenty polskich terminów prawno-ustrojowych. Warszawa, 1973. pp. 115. *bibliog.* With brief English summary.

— **Description and travel.**

POLSKA AKADEMIA NAUK. Instytut Geografii. Geographia Polonica. 33. The 23rd International Geographical Congress, Moscow, 1976: [proceedings]. Warszawa, 1976. 2 vols. *bibliogs.*

— **Diplomatic and consular service.**

LIBERA (KAZIMIERZ) Opieka konsularna. Warszawa, 1958. pp. 92.

— **Economic conditions.**

RAKOWSKI (MIECZYSŁAW F.) Nasza gospodarka i jej perspektywy. Warszawa, 1958. pp. 72.

SZELIGA (ZYGMUNT) Dwa dwudziestolecia. Warszawa, 1965. pp. 430.

FLOREK (HENRYK) and SZEFLER (STANISŁAW) Dywersja w ekonomice. Warszawa, 1970. pp. 176.

KARPIŃSKI (ANDRZEJ) Gospodarcza pozycja Polski w świecie. Warszawa, 1973. pp. 429. *bibliog.*

FUNKCJONOWANIE i rozwój gospodarki PRL: materiały I Sesji Naukowej młodych pracowników Wydziału Ekonomiki Produkcji, listopad 1973. Warszawa, 1975. pp. 219. *(Szkoła Główna Planowania i Statystyki. Monografie i Opracowania. 43)*

POLSKA AKADEMIA NAUK. Instytut Geografii. Geographia Polonica. 31. Warszawa, 1975. pp. 235. *bibliogs. No title: papers mainly concerned with Poland.*

POLSKA AKADEMIA NAUK. Instytut Geografii. Geographia Polonica. 33. The 23rd International Geographical Congress, Moscow, 1976: [proceedings]. Warszawa, 1976. 2 vols. *bibliogs.*

— **Economic history.**

KALIŃSKI (JANUSZ) and LANDAU (ZBIGNIEW) eds. Gospodarka Polski Ludowej, 1944-1955. Warszawa, 1974 in progress.

KUBICZEK (FRANCISZEK) Społeczno-gospodarczy rozw0j Polski w latach 1971-1975. Warszawa, 1975. pp. 336.

POLAND.(Cont.)

— Economic policy.

BRZEZINSKI (WACŁAW) Le rôle des organes de l'état dans la planification de la République Populaire de Pologne. [Warsaw?, 1966?]. pp. 50-63. *Ms. note: "Rapport au 7e Congrès Intern. de droit comparé, 1966".*

BRABANT (JOZEF M.P. VAN) Reflections on Poland's economic policies in the 1960s. Berlin, 1973. pp. 46. *(Berlin. Freie Universität. Osteuropa-Institut. Berichte: Reihe Wirtschaft und Recht. Heft 99)*

— — Bibliography.

SZKOŁA GŁÓWNA PLANOWANIA I STATYSTYKI. Planowanie gospodarki narodowej w Polsce Ludowej: materiały do bibliografii. zeszyt 3. okres 1956-1965. Warszawa, 1975. pp. 310.

— Emigration and immigration.

BOBIŃSKA (CELINA) and PILCH (ANDRZEJ) eds. Employment-seeking emigrations of the Poles world-wide, XIX and XXC. [Cracow], 1975. pp. 194. *(Zeszyty Naukowe Uniwersytetu Jagiellońskiego. Prace Polonijne, z. 1) 3 maps in end pocket.*

KLARNER (IZABELA) Emigracja z Królestwa Polskiego do Brazylii, 1890-1914. Warszawa, 1975. pp. 169. *bibliog.*

— Foreign economic relations — Cuba.

LEGOMSKA-DWORNIAK (EWA) Polska - Kuba: gospodarka współpraca. Warszawa, 1975. pp. 280. *bibliog.*

— — Prussia.

WILDER (JAN ANTONI) Traktat handlowy polsko-pruski z roku 1775: gospodarcze znaczenie utraty dostępu do morza; Polish-Prussian commercial treaty of 1775: Poland's loss of access to the sea, its economic consequences. Warszawa, 1937. pp. 357. *bibliog. (Towarzystwo Naukowe Warszawskie. Rozprawy Historyczne. t.20, z.2) With English summary.*

— — United States.

STASHEVSKYI (DMYTRO MYKOLAIOVYCH) Interwencja pod pozorem pomocy: działalność misji 'żywnościowych Stanów Zjednoczonych w Polsce; [translation from Russian]. Kraków, 1964. pp. 119.

— Foreign opinion.

SCHWEITZER (CARL CHRISTOPH) and FEGER (HUBERT) eds. Das deutsch-polnische Konfliktverhältnis seit dem Zweiten Weltkrieg: multidisziplinäre Studien über konfliktfördernde und konfliktmindernde Faktoren in den internationalen Beziehungen. Boppard am Rhein, [1975]. pp. 596. *bibliogs. (Deutsche Gesellschaft für Friedens- und Konfliktforschung. Beiträge zur Konfliktforschung)*

— Foreign opinion, French.

ŚLADKOWSKI (WIESŁAW) Opinia publiczna we Francji wobec sprawy polskiej w latach 1914- 1918. Wrocław, 1976. pp. 311. *bibliog. (Lubelskie Towarzystwo Naukowe. Wydział Humanistyczny. Prace. Monografie. t.5) With French summary.*

— Foreign opinion, German.

ROSENTHAL (HARRY KENNETH) German and Pole: national conflict and modern myth. Gainesville, Fla., [1976]. pp. 175. *bibliog.*

— Foreign relations.

GAJDA (EUGENIUSZ) Polska polityka zagraniczna 1944-1974: podstawowe problemy. Warszawa, 1974. pp. 353.

RAKOWSKI (MIECZYSŁAW F.) Polityka zagraniczna PRL: szkice z historii trzydziestolecia. Warszawa, 1974. pp. 207.

— — Czechoslovakia — Bibliography.

NOWAK (C.M.) compiler. Czechoslovak-Polish relations 1918-1939: a selected and annotated bibliography. Stanford, Ca., 1976. pp. 219. *(Stanford University. Hoover Institution on War, Revolution and Peace. Bibliographical Series. 55)*

— — Germany.

PAJEWSKI (JANUSZ) ed. Problem polsko-niemiecki w Traktacie Wersalskim; praca zbiorowa pod redakcja J. Pajewskiego, etc. Poznań, 1963. pp. 652. *bibliog. (Poznań. Instytut Zachodni. Dzieje Polskiej Granicy Zachodniej. 3)*

KUBIAK (STANISŁAW) Niemcy a Wielkopolska, 1918-1919. Poznań, 1969. pp. 303. *bibliog. (Poznań. Instytut Zachodni. Dzieje Polskiej Granicy Zachodniej. 4) With German summary.*

SKIBIŃSKI (JERZY) Polska - RFN: problemy normalizacji stosunków; posłowie Ryszard Wojna. Warszawa, 1974. pp. 220.

ORTMAYER (LOUIS L.) Conflict, compromise, and conciliation: West German-Polish normalization, 1966-1976. Denver, [1975]. pp. 162. *(Denver. University. Social Science Foundation and Graduate School of International Studies. Monograph Series in World Affairs. vol. 13, no. 3)*

RAINA (PETER) Stosunki polsko-niemieckie 1937-1939: prawdziwy charakter polityki zagranicznej Józefa Becka. Londyn, 1975. pp. 172.

SCHWEITZER (CARL CHRISTOPH) and FEGER (HUBERT) eds. Das deutsch-polnische Konfliktverhältnis seit dem Zweiten Weltkrieg: multidisziplinäre Studien über konfliktfördernde und konfliktmindernde Faktoren in den internationalen Beziehungen. Boppard am Rhein, [1975]. pp. 596. *bibliogs. (Deutsche Gesellschaft für Friedens- und Konfliktforschung. Beiträge zur Konfliktforschung)*

KULSKI (WŁADYSŁAW WSZEBOR) Germany and Poland: from war to peaceful relations. Syracuse, N.Y., 1976. pp. 336. *bibliog.*

— — United Kingdom.

NOWAK-KIEŁBIKOWA (MARIA) Polska-Wielka Brytania w latach 1918-1923: kształtowanie się stosunków politycznych. Warszawa, 1975. pp. 447. *bibliog.*

PISZCZKOWSKI (TADEUSZ) Anglia a Polska, 1914-1939: w świetle dokumentów brytyjskich. Londyn, 1975. pp. 456.

NEWMAN (SIMON) March 1939: the British guarantee to Poland: a study in the continuity of British foreign policy. Oxford, 1976. pp. 253. *bibliog.*

— Historiography.

MATERNICKI (JERZY) Idee i postawy: historia i historycy polscy, 1914-1918: studium historiograficzne. Warszawa, 1975. pp. 546. *bibliog.*

— History.

HENSEL (WITOLD) Początki państwa polskiego i jego kultury. Wrocław, 1971. pp. 196. *bibliog.*

XXX rocznica powstania Polskiej Rzeczypospolitej Ludowej: materiały sesji naukowej Polskiej Akademii Nauk, 24 VI 1974. Wrocław, 1974. pp. 152.

— — Bibliography.

KLARNER (IZABELA) and others, compilers. Bibliografia publikacji pracowników Instytutu Historycznego. z.1. 1945-1966. Warszawa, 1969. pp. 183.

— — Sources.

ŁUCZAK (CZESŁAW) compiler. Poło'zenie polskich robotników przymusowych w Rzeszy, 1939- 1945: wybór źródeł, etc. Poznań, 1975. pp. cvi, 358. *(Poznań. Instytut Zachodni. Documenta Occupationis. 9) Documents in the original German, with Polish, Russian, English and German introductions.*

— — 1863-1864, Revolution. .

OLSZAŃSKI (KAZIMIERZ) Prasa galicyjska wobec powstania styczniowego. Wrocław, 1975. pp. 254. *(Polska Akademia Nauk. Oddział w Krakowie. Komisja Nauk Historycznych. Prace. Nr.35) With Russian and English summaries.*

— — 1900— .

ROSE (WILLIAM JOHN) The Polish memoirs of William John Rose; edited by Daniel Stone. Toronto, [1975]. pp. 248.

— — 1939-1945, Occupation.

BRZESKA (MARIA) Through a woman's eyes: life in Poland under the German occupation. London, [1944?]. pp. 92.

DURACZYŃSKI (EUGENIUSZ) Wojna i okupacja, wrzesień 1939- kwiecień 1943. Warszawa, 1974. pp. 492. *bibliog.*

POLAND (TERRITORY UNDER GERMAN OCCUPATION, 1939-1945). Generalgouverneur, 1975. Das Diensttagebuch des deutschen Generalgouverneurs in Polen, 1939-1945; herausgegeben von Werner Präg und Wolfgang Jacobmeyer. Stuttgart, 1975. pp. 1027. *(Institut für Zeitgeschichte, Quellen und Darstellungen zur Zeitgeschichte. Band 20)*

— — 1970, Uprising.

ROTE Fahnen über Polen: seit wann schiesst die Arbeiterklasse auf sich selbst?; der Kampf der polnischen Arbeiter gegen einen falschen Sozialismus; (Übersetzung aus dem Polnischen). München, 1972 repr. 1973. pp. 146.

— Industries.

KRAMER (TEODOR) Rynek wiejski a proces industrializacji. Warszawa, 1963. pp. 208. *bibliog.*

LATUCH (MIKOŁAJ) Migracje wewnętrzne w Polsce na tle industrializacji, 1950-1960. Warszawa, 1970. pp. 243. *bibliog.*

BOGUSZEWSKI (JAN) and WAGENER (HANS JUERGEN) Zur Industriestatistik der BRD, Österreichs, Polens und Ungarns. Wien, 1975. pp. 58. *(Wiener Institut für Internationale Wirtschaftsvergleiche. Forschungsberichte. Nr.24)*

STELMACHOWSKI (ANDRZEJ) ed. Kształtowanie rozwoju społeczno-ekonomicznego rejonów uprzemysławianych: wybór studiów. Warszawa, 1975. pp. 274. *bibliog. (Polska Akademia Nauk. Komitet Badań Rejonów Uprzemysławianych. Problemy Rejonów Uprzemysławianych)*

— Intellectual life.

SOKORSKI (WŁODZIMIERZ) Kultura i polityka: szkice i artykuły. Warszawa, 1970. pp. 132.

WERBLAN (ANDRZEJ) Szkice i polemiki; [collected articles, 1958-1969]. Warszawa, 1970. pp. 301.

— Kings and rulers.

WAWRZYŃCZYK (ALINA) Studia nad wydajnością produkcji rolnej dóbr królewskich w drugiej połowie XVI wieku. Wrocław, 1974. pp. 230. *With French summary.*

— Learned institutions and societies.

TRZYNADLOWSKI (JAN) Zakład Narodowy imienia Ossolińskich, 1817-1967: zarys dziejów. Wrocław, 1967. pp. 165. *bibliog. (Wrocław. Zakład Narodowy Imienia Ossolińskich. Wydawnictwa Jubileuszowe)*

— Military history.

KUKIEL (MARJAN) Zarys historji wojskowości w Polsce. 3rd ed. Kraków, 1929. pp. 356. *bibliog.*

— Nobility.

KOCZERSKA (MARIA) Rodzina szlachecka w Polsce późnego średniowiecza. Warszawa, 1975. pp. 197. *bibliog. With French summary.*

— Politics and government.

LAM (JAN) Wybór kronik; (opracował Stanisław Frybes). Warszawa, 1954. pp. 386. *Articles first published in Gazeta narodowa and Dziennik polski, 1868-85.*

MARIAŃSKA (ANIELA) Wiklinowe kosz. Warszawa, 1959. pp. 311.

RAWICZ (JERZY) Generał Zagórski zaginął...: z tajemnic lat międzywojennych. [Warszawa, 1963]. pp. 376.

HOPPE (JAN) Wspomnienia, przyczynki, refleksje. Londyn, 1972. pp. 395.

KONARSKI (SZYMON) Dziennik z lat 1831-1834; przygotowali do druku Bolesław Łopuszański i Anatol Smirnow. Wrocław, 1973. pp. 361. *(Polska Akademia Nauk. Oddział w Krakowie. Komisja Nauk Historycznych. Materiały. Nr.23) With Russian and French summaries.*

GWIAZDOWICZ (MICHAŁ) Wspomnienia; do druku przygotował, poprzedził biografią, zebrał relacje o autorze i jego rodzinie Zygmunt Hemmerling. Warszawa, 1974. pp. 331.

WYNOT (EDWARD D.) Polish politics in transition: the Camp of National Unity and the struggle for power, 1935-1939. Athens, Ga., [1974]. pp. 294. *bibliog.*

POLSKA myśl polityczna XIX i XX wieku. Wrocław, 1975 in progress.

BENDER (RYSZARD) Chrześcijanie w polskich ruchach demokratycznych XIX stulecia. Warszawa, 1975. pp. 361. *bibliog.*

MARCHLEWSKI (JULIAN BALTAZAR) Listy do 'zony i córki; słowo wią'zące Zofia Marchlewska, opracowała Bo'zena Wróblewska, wstęp Janusz Durko. Warszawa, 1975. pp. 395.

PRAGIER (ADAM) Czas teraźniejszy. Londyn, 1975. pp. 240.

RUCH ludowy na Mazowszu, Kurpiach i Podlasiu: materiały sesji popularnonaukowej zorganizowanej przez Zakład Historii Ruchu Ludowego przy NK ZSL i Komisję Historyczną WK ZSL w Warszawie w dniu 20 I 1973. Warszawa, 1975. pp. 485.

NARKIEWICZ (OLGA A.) The green flag: Polish populist politics, 1867-1970. London, 1976. pp. 314. *bibliog.*

— Politics and government.

LAMMICH (SIEGFRIED) Regierung und Verwaltung in Polen. Köln, [1975]. pp. 347. *bibliog. (Cologne. Universität. Institut für Ostrecht, and others. Dokumente zum Ostrecht. Band 8)*

— Population.

POLAND. Główny Urząd Statystyczny. Biblioteka Wiadomości Statystycznych. tom 4. Problemy demograficzne Polski Ludowej: Sympozjum 5-7.X.1967. Warszawa, 1967. pp. 380. *With Russian, French and English summaries.*

POLAND. Główny Urząd Statystyczny. Biblioteka Wiadomości Statystycznych. t.24. Aktualne problemy demograficzne kraju: Konferencja naukowa, Warszawa 17-18 IV 1974 r. Warszawa, 1974. pp. 344.

POLSKA AKADEMIA NAUK. Komitet Nauk Demograficznych. Sekcja Demografii Historycznej. Przesztos demograficzna Polski Materiàty i studia. 6. Warszawa, 1974. pp. 15. *bibliog. With English table of contents.*

POLSKA AKADEMIA NAUK. Committee for Demographic Studies. The population of Poland. Warszawa, 1975. pp. 143. *(Committee for International Coordination of National Research in Demography. C.I.C.R.E.D. Series)*

ROSSET (EDWARD) Demografia Polski. Warszawa, 1975. 2 vols. *bibliog.*

— Relations (general) with France.

ŚLADKOWSKI (WIESŁAW) Opinia publiczna we Francji wobec sprawy polskiej w latach 1914- 1918. Wrocław, 1976. pp. 311. *bibliog. (Lubelskie Towarzystwo Naukowe. Wydział Humanistyczny. Prace. Monografie. t.5) With French summary.*

— Relations (general) with Italy.

QUIRINI-POPŁAWSKA (DANUTA) Działalność włochów w Polsce w I połowie XVI wieku na dworze królewskim, w dyplomacji i hierarchii kościelnej. Wrocław, 1973. pp. 140. *(Polska Akademia Nauk. Oddział w Krakowie. Komisja Nauk Historycznych. Prace. Nr.32) With Italian summary.*

— Relations (general) with Russia.

ŚLIWOWSKA (WIKTORIA) Związki rewolucjonistów polskich i rosyjskich w XIX wieku, materiały sesji naukowej Poznań, 12-14 listopada 1970. Wrocław, 1972. pp. 268. *Some articles in Russian.*

— Religion.

PIEKARSKI (ADAM) Szkice o kościele w Polsce: fakty, liczby, informacje. Warszawa, 1974. pp. 224. *bibliog.*

MYSŁEK (WIESŁAW) and STASZEWSKI (MICHAŁ T.) eds. Polityka wyznaniowa: tło, warunki, realizacja. Warszawa, 1975. pp. 475. *With Russian and English tables of contents.*

— Rural conditions.

W walce o zdrowie wsi Polskiej: referaty wygłoszone na Konferencji, poświęconej opiece lekarskiej na wsi, zwołanej przez Instytut Spraw Społecznych w Warszawie w dniach 31.1.- 1. i 2. II. 1937: Campaign for the health of the rural population in Poland; reports held at the Conference of Medical Service for Rural Population organised by the Institute for Social Problems on the 31.1.-1. and 2.II. 1937. Warszawa, 1937. pp. 320. *(Instytut Spraw Społecznych. Sprawy Zdrowia Publicznego. Nr.2) With English summary.*

IGNAR (STEFAN) and JUSZKIEWICZ (ALEKSANDER) Wieś polska wobec zadań czwartego roku naszej sześciolatki. Warszawa, 1953. pp. 112.

KUTRZEBA-POJNAROWA (ANNA) Tradycyjna społeczność wiejska w procesie przemian współczesnych: studium wsi Mników powiatu krakowskiego. Wrocław, 1968. pp. 80. *(Polska Akademia Nauk. Oddział w Krakowie. Komisja Socjologiczna. Prace. Nr.13) With Russian and French summaries.*

BIERNACKA (MARIA) Kształtowanie się nowej społeczności wiejskiej w Bieszczadach. Wrocław, 1974. pp. 211. *(Polska Akademia Nauk. Instytut Historii Kultury Materialnej. Biblioteka Etnografii Polskiej. Nr.29) With English summary.*

PAPROCKA (WANDA) Współczesne przemiany wsi kurpiowskiej. Wrocław, 1975. pp. 176. *(Polska Akademia Nauk. Instytut Historii Kultury Materialnej. Biblioteka Etnografii Polskiej. Nr.31) With English summary.*

— Sejm.

AJNENKIEL (ANDRZEJ) Parlamentaryzm II Rzeczypospolitej. Warszawa, 1975. pp. 412. *bibliog.*

— Social conditions.

WIDERSZPIL (STANISŁAW) Przeobra'zenia struktury społecznej w Polsce Ludowej. Warszawa, 1973. pp. 288.

MATEJKO (ALEXANDER) Social change and stratification in Eastern Europe: an interpretive analysis of Poland and her neighbors. New York, 1974. pp. 272. *bibliog.*

— Social history.

WASYLEWSKI (STANISŁAW) 'Zycie polskie w XIX wieku; opracował, przedmową i przypisami opatrzył Zbigniew Jabłoński. Kraków, 1962. pp. 683.

WOŹNOWSKI (WACŁAW) Pamflet obyczajowy w czasach Stanisława Augusta. Wrocław, 1973. pp. 179. *(Polska Akademia Nauk. Oddział w Krakowie. Komisja Historycznoliteracka. Prace. Nr.30) With French summary.*

POLAR REGIONS.

SOLLIE (FINN) and others. The challenge of new territories. Oslo, [1974]. pp. 172. *(Fridtjof Nansen Stiftelsen på Polhøgda. New Territories in International Politics. No. 1)*

POLES IN THE UNITED STATES.

SKAGESTAD (ODD GUNNAR) Norsk polarpolitikk: hovedtrekk og utviklingslinjer, 1905-1974. Oslo, 1975. pp. 303. *bibliog. (Fridtjof Nansen Stiftelsen på Polhøgda. New Territories in International Politics. No.4) With English summary.*

— International status.

SCIENCE, technology and sovereignty in the Polar regions: [revised papers of a colloquium held in Washington, 1973]; edited by Gerald S. Schatz. Lexington, Mass., [1974]. pp. 215.

POLES IN BRAZIL.

KLARNER (IZABELA) Emigracja z Królestwa Polskiego do Brazylii, 1890-1914. Warszawa, 1975. pp. 169. *bibliog.*

POLES IN FOREIGN COUNTRIES.

DWORKIN (EUZEBIUSZ) Od Manzanares do Oki: wspomnienia dąbrowszczaka. Warszawa, 1974. pp. 119.

SIKORA (ADAM) Gromady Ludu Polskiego. Warszawa, 1974. pp. 284.

KATELBACH (TADEUSZ) O zjednoczenie i legalizm: ostatni akt 'zycia publicznego Kazimierza Sosnkowskiego. New York, 1975. pp. 328.

PRAGIER (ADAM) Czas teraźniejszy. Londyn, 1975. pp. 240.

EISENBACH (ARTUR) Wielka Emigracja wobec kwestii 'zydowskiej, 1831-1849. Warszawa, 1976. pp. 475.

POLES IN GERMANY.

ŁUCZAK (CZESŁAW) compiler. Poło'zenie polskich robotników przymusowych w Rzeszy, 1939- 1945: wybór źródeł, etc. Poznań, 1975. pp. cvi, 358. *(Poznań. Instytut Zachodni. Documenta Occupationis. 9) Documents in the original German, with Polish, Russian, English and German introductions.*

POLES IN HUNGARY.

STASIERSKI (KAZIMIERZ) Szkolnictwo polskie na Węgrzech w czasie drugiej wojny światowej. Poznań, 1969. pp. 230,[vi]. *(Poznań. Uniwersytet. Wydział Filozoficzno-Historyczny. Prace: Seria Historia. Nr.29)*

POLES IN NEW ZEALAND.

SKWARKO (KRYSTYNA) The invited...: the story of 733 Polish children who grew up in New Zealand. Wellington, N.Z., [1974]. 1 vol. (unpaged).

POLES IN RUSSIA.

STĘPIEŃ (MARIAN) Zagadnienia literackie w publicystyce Polonii radzieckiej, 1918- 1939. Wrocław, 1968. pp. 191. *(Polska Akademia Nauk. Oddział w Krakowie. Komisja Historycznoliteracka. Prace. Nr.19) With Russian and French summaries.*

FEDOSOVA (TAMARA FEDOROVNA) Pol'skie revoliutsionnye organizatsii v Moskve, 60-e gody XIX veka. Moskva, 1974. pp. 204.

SKOK (HENRYK) Polacy nad Bajkałem, 1863-1883. Warszawa, 1974. pp. 336.

POLES IN THE UNITED KINGDOM.

RZADKOWSKA (HELENA) Działalność Centralizacji londyńskiej Towarzystwa Demokratycznego Polskiego, 1850-1862. Wrocław, 1971. pp. 163. *(Polska Akademia Nauk. Oddział w Krakowie. Komisja Nauk Historycznych. Prace. Nr.29) With Russian and English summaries.*

KOCHANOWICZ (TADEUSZ) Na wojennej emigracji: wspomnienia z lat 1942-1944. Warszawa, 1975. pp. 303.

POLES IN THE UNITED STATES.

BUCZEK (DANIEL STEPHEN) Immigrant pastor: the life of the Right Reverend Monsignor Lucyan Bójnowski of New Britain, Connecticut. Waterbury, Conn., 1974. pp. 184. *bibliog.*

GRZELOŃSKI (BOGDAN) ed. Ameryka w pamiętnikach Polaków: antologia. Warszawa, 1975. pp. 307. *bibliog.*

POLES IN THE UNITED STATES.(Cont.)

DROHOJOWSKI (JAN) Polacy w Ameryce. Warszawa, 1976. pp. 172.

LOPATA (HELENA ZNANIECKI) Polish Americans: status competition in an ethnic community. Englewood Cliffs, [1976]. pp. 174. *bibliog.*

POLICE.

GREGORY (FRANK E.C.) Protest and violence: the police response: a comparative analysis of democratic methods. London, 1976. pp. 15. *(Institute for the Study of Conflict. Conflict Studies. No. 75)*

— Information services.

WHISENAND (PAUL M.) and TAMARU (TUG T.) Automated police information systems. New York, [1970]. pp. 338. *bibliogs.*

— Belgium.

EUROPEAN COURT OF HUMAN RIGHTS. Publications. Series A. Judgments and Decisions. [A 19]. ...National Union of Belgian Police case - 1. Decision of 12 April 1975. 2. Judgment of 27 October 1975. Strasbourg, Council of Europe, 1975. pp. 44 [bis]. *In English and French.*

— Canada — Quebec.

QUEBEC (PROVINCE). Department of Justice, 1971. The police and public security. [Quebec, 1971]. pp. 176.

— Italy.

TARANTINI (DOMENICO) La maniera forte: elogio della polizia; storia del potere politico in Italia, 1860-1975. Verona, [1975]. pp. 382.

— Japan.

BAYLEY (DAVID HUME) Forces of order: police behavior in Japan and the United States. Berkeley, Calif., [1976]. pp. 201.

— Nigeria.

NIGERIA. Police Service Commission. Annual report. a., 1972(1st)- [Lagos].

— Sierra Leone.

SIERRA LEONE. Ministry of Information and Broadcasting. 1965. Sierra Leone today: unity, freedom, justice. Freetown, 1965. pp. 30.

— United Kingdom.

NATIONAL COUNCIL FOR CIVIL LIBERTIES. Submissions to the public enquiry...to review the events at Red Lion Square on the 15th June 1974: the Scarman enquiry. London, 1974. pp. 19.

The POLICE and the community; edited by John Brown and Graham Howes. Farnborough, Hants, [1975]. pp. 106. *Papers from a conference organised by the Language and Social Studies Department of the Cranfield Institute of Technology in September 1974.*

BOWDEN (TOM) Men in the middle: the U.K. police. London, 1976. pp. 19. *bibliog. (Institute for the Study of Conflict. Conflict Studies. No. 68)*

— — Ireland, Northern.

NATIONAL COUNCIL FOR CIVIL LIBERTIES. Reports. The Royal Ulster Constabulary: a report on the complaints procedure. London, 1975. pp. 14.

— United States.

HALPERN (STEPHEN C.) Police-association and department leaders: the politics of co- optation. Lexington, Mass., [1974]. pp. 127.

WINTERSMITH (ROBERT F.) Police and the black community. Lexington, Mass., [1974]. pp. 149. *bibliog.*

CARTE (GENE E.) and CARTE (ELAINE H.) Police reform in the United States: the era of August Vollmer, 1905-1932. Berkeley, [1975]. pp. 137. *bibliog.*

BAYLEY (DAVID HUME) Forces of order: police behavior in Japan and the United States. Berkeley, Calif., [1976]. pp. 201.

POLICE, POLITICAL AND SECRET

— Germany — Pomerania.

THEVOZ (ROBERT) and others. Pommern 1934/35 im Spiegel von Gestapo-Lageberichten und Sachaktens: (die Geheime Staatspolizei in den preussischen Ostprovinzen, 1934—1936), Köln, 1974. 2 vols. *bibliog. (Veröffentlichungen aus den Archiven Preussischer Kulturbesitz. Band 11-12)*

— Russia.

VASIL'EV (ALEKSEI TIKHONOVICH) The Ochrana: the Russian secret police;...edited and with an introduction by René Fülöp-Miller. London, 1930. pp. 320.

— United Kingdom.

BUNYAN (TONY) The history and practice of the political police in Britain. London, 1976. pp. 320. *bibliog.*

POLICY SCIENCES.

CATANESE (ANTHONY JAMES) Planners and local politics: impossible dreams. Beverly Hills, [1974]. pp. 188. *bibliog.*

ORGANIZED social complexity: challenge to politics and policy; edited by Todd R. La Porte. Princeton, [1975]. pp. 373. *bibliog.*

DOLBEARE (KENNETH M.) ed. Public policy evaluation;...with a section on crime control evaluation edited by John A. Gardiner. Beverly Hills, [1975]. pp. 286.

HOROWITZ (IRVING LOUIS) and KATZ (JAMES EVERETT) Social science and public policy in the United States. New York, 1975. pp. 187. *bibliogs.*

LAZARSFELD (PAUL FELIX) and REITZ (JEFFREY G.) An introduction to applied sociology. New York, [1975]. pp. 196.

POLICY sciences and population; edited by Warren F. Ilchman [and others]. Lexington, Mass., [1975]. pp. 305.

POLICY studies and the social sciences; edited by Stuart S. Nagel. Lexington, Mass., [1975]. pp. 307. *"Based on symposia coordinated by the Policy Studies Organization".*

POLICY studies in America and elsewhere: (based on symposia coordinated by the Policy Studies Organization); edited by Stuart S. Nagel. Lexington, [1975]. pp. 229. *bibliogs.*

The POLICY vacuum: toward a more professional political science; [by] Robert N. Spadaro [and others]. Lexington, [1975]. pp. 215. *bibliogs.*

QUADE (EDWARD S.) Analysis for public decisions. New York, [1975]. pp. 322. *bibliogs.*

RODWIN (LLOYD) The educational perspective of regional science and urban studies. Reading, 1975. pp. 18. *(Reading. University. Department of Geography. Reading Geographical Papers. No.38)*

ROUX (JEAN) La rationalisation des choix politiques. Paris, 1975. pp. 227. *bibliog.*

SMITH (T. ALEXANDER) The comparative policy process. Santa Barbara, [1975]. pp. 184.

WHITE (MICHAEL J.) and others, eds. Management and policy science in American government: problems and prospects. Lexington, Mass., [1975]. pp. 319.

The DYNAMICS of public policy: a comparative analysis; edited by Richard Rose. London, [1976]. pp. 268. *bibliogs. Papers based on a conference of the Comparative Public Policy work group of the Committee on Political Sociology, at Cumberland Lodge, Windsor Great Park, May 6-10, 1974.*

MELTSNER (ARNOLD J.) Policy analysts in the bureaucracy. Berkeley, Calif., [1976]. pp. 310.

PROBLEMS of theory in policy analysis; edited by Phillip M. Gregg. Lexington, Mass., [1976]. pp. 186. *Essays arising from research at the Workshop in Political Theory and Policy Analysis of Indiana University.*

SMITH (BRIAN CLIVE) Policy-making in British government: an analysis of power and rationality. London, 1976. pp. 210.

STRATEGIC perspectives on social policy; editors: John E. Tropman [and others]. New York, [1976]. pp. 367. *bibliogs.*

— Methodology.

SCIOLI (FRANK P.) and COOK (THOMAS J.) eds. Methodologies for analyzing public policies. Lexington, Mass., [1975]. pp. 168.

POLISH LITERATURE.

GRYNBERG (HENRYK) 'Zycie ideologiczne. Londyn, 1975. pp. 112.

— History and criticism.

STĘPIEŃ (MARIAN) Zagadnienia literackie w publicystyce Polonii radzieckiej, 1918- 1939. Wrocław, 1968. pp. 191. *(Polska Akademia Nauk. Oddział w Krakowie. Komisja Historycznoliteracka. Prace. Nr.19) With Russian and French summaries.*

WOŹNOWSKI (WACŁAW) Pamflet obyczajowy w czasach Stanisława Augusta. Wrocław, 1973. pp. 179. *(Polska Akademia Nauk. Oddział w Krakowie. Komisja Historycznoliteracka. Prace. Nr.30) With French summary.*

POLISH PERIODICALS.

MAREK (FRANCISZEK ANTONI) Najdawniejsze czasopisma polskie na Śląsku, 1789-1854. Wrocław, 1972. pp. 319. *With English, French, German and Russian summaries.*

POLISH QUESTION.

POLONSKY (ANTONY) ed. The great powers and the Polish question, 1941-45: a documentary study in cold war origins. London, 1976. pp. 282.

ŚLADKOWSKI (WIESŁAW) Opinia publiczna we Francji wobec sprawy polskiej w latach 1914- 1918. Wrocław, 1976. pp. 311. *bibliog. (Lubelskie Towarzystwo Naukowe. Wydział Humanistyczny. Prace. Monografie. t.5) With French summary.*

POLITICAL BALLADS AND SONGS, SWEDISH.

STREJK!: en bok om strejker och strejkvisor...; samlad, redigerad och kommenterad av Visgruppen inom Arkivet för folkets historia: Catrin Andersson [and others]. Stockholm, [1974]. pp. 174. *bibliog.*

POLITICAL CONVENTIONS.

MAILER (NORMAN) Some honorable men: political conventions 1960-1972. Boston, 1976. pp. 499.

POLITICAL CRIMES AND OFFENCES

— Chile.

IDOC-NORTH AMERICA. Chile: under military rule; a dossier of documents and analyses compiled by the staff of IDOC/International Documentation with the special assistance of guest editor Gary MacEoin. New York, [1974]. pp. 164. *bibliog. (Idoc/International Documentation. Nos. 62 and 64)*

SILVA (RAUL) and others. Evidence on the terror in Chile...; translated by Brian McBeth. London, [1974]. pp. 139.

— Japan.

MITCHELL (RICHARD HANKS) Thought control in prewar Japan. Ithaca, 1976. pp. 226. *bibliog.*

POLITICAL PARTIES.

— **Russia.**

UKRAINIAN INFORMATION SERVICE. The Shelepin file: planned and executed murders of Ukrainian political leaders. London, 1975. pp. 64.

— **South Africa.**

SOUTH AFRICAN LAW COMMISSION. Report on the codification of the common law relating to crimes against the state (R.P. 17/1976). in SOUTH AFRICA. Parliament. House of Assembly. Votes and proceedings; (with Printed annexures).

POLITICAL ETHICS.

BEARD (EDMUND) and HORN (STEPHEN) Congressional ethics: the view from the House. Washington, D.C., [1975]. pp. 87.

BICKEL (ALEXANDER MORDECAI) The morality of consent. New Haven, 1975. pp. 156. *bibliog. (Yale University. William C. DeVane Lectures. 1973)*

BERGER (PETER L.) Pyramids of sacrifice: political ethics and social change. London, 1976. pp. 272.

GOODIN (ROBERT E.) The politics of rational man. London, [1976]. pp. 210. *bibliog.*

POLITICAL PARTICIPATION.

PENNOCK (JAMES ROLAND) and CHAPMAN (JOHN WILLIAM) eds. Participation in politics. New York, 1975. pp. 300. *(American Society for Political and Legal Philosophy. Nomos. 16)*

BIOLOGY and politics: recent explorations; [proceedings of a conference held in Paris, 1975; edited by] Albert Somit. Paris, [1976]. pp. 330. *bibliog. (International Social Science Council. Publications. 19)*

HUNTINGTON (SAMUEL PHILLIPS) and NELSON (JOAN M.) No easy choice: political participation in developing countries. Cambridge, Mass., 1976. pp. 195.

— **Africa.**

KASFIR (NELSON) The shrinking political arena: participation and ethnicity in African politics, with a case study of Uganda. Berkeley, Calif., [1976]. pp. 323. *bibliog.*

— **Belgium.**

SOCIÉTÉ D'ÉTUDES POLITIQUES ET SOCIALES. Cahiers. No. 5. La participation politique en Belgique. Louvain, 1966. pp. 57.

— **China.**

LIU (ALAN P.L.) Political culture and group conflict in communist China. Santa Barbara, [1976]. pp. 205. *bibliog.*

— **Germany.**

ARMBRUSTER (BERNT) and LEISNER (RAINER) Bürgerbeteiligung in der Bundesrepublik: zur Freizeitaktivität verschiedener Bevölkerungsgruppen in ausgewählten Beteiligungsfeldern, etc. Göttingen, [1975]. pp. 291. *bibliog. (Kommission für Wirtschaftlichen und Sozialen Wandel. Schriften. 54)*

ELLWEIN (THOMAS) and others. Politische Beteiligung in der Bundesrepublik Deutschland. Göttingen, [1975]. pp. 199. *bibliog. (Kommission für Wirtschaftlichen und Sozialen Wandel. Schriften. 89)*

LAMMERT (NORBERT) Lokale Organisationsstrukturen innerparteilicher Willensbildung: Fallstudie am Beispiel eines CDU-Kreisverbandes im Ruhrgebiet. Bonn, [1976]. pp. 224. *bibliog. (Institut für Kommunalwissenschaften [Bonn]. Schriftenreihe. Band 5)*

— **India.**

ELKINS (DAVID J.) Electoral participation in a South Indian context. Durham, N.C., [1975]. pp. 251. *bibliog.*

GOEL (MADAN LAL) Political participation in a developing nation: India. New York, [1975]. pp. 234. *bibliog.*

— **Kenya.**

ROSS (MARC HOWARD) Grass roots in an African city: political behavior in Nairobi. Cambridge, Mass., [1975]. pp. 169.

— **Mexico.**

CORNELIUS (WAYNE A.) Politics and the migrant poor in Mexico City. Stanford, 1975. pp. 319. *bibliog.*

— **Netherlands.**

MAESEN (CONSTANCE E. VAN DER) Participatie en democratie: onderzoek naar houding en mening van Amsterdammers met betrekking tot de plaatselijke politieke structuur. Amsterdam, 1975. pp. 264. *bibliog.* With English summary. *Proefschrift - Universiteit van Amsterdam.*

— **Norway.**

ANDERSEN (BO LILLEDAL) and others, eds. Trassige folk: sjølvhjelp og lokaldemokrati i norske småsamfunn. Oslo, 1975. pp. 166.

— **Turkey.**

POLITICAL participation in Turkey: historical background and present problems; [papers presented at a colloquium held at Princeton University in 1972]; edited by Engin D. Akarli.. [and] Gabriel Ben-Dor. Istanbul, 1975. pp. 192. *bibliog. (Boğaziçi Üniversitesi. Publications)*

— **United Kingdom.**

FRASER (DEREK) Urban politics in Victorian England: the structure of politics in Victorian cities. Leicester, 1976. pp. 324.

LUCAS (JOHN RANDOLPH) Democracy and participation. Harmondsworth, 1976. pp. 290.

MARSH (ALAN JOHN) The social psychology of political protest: a U.K. national survey of political attitudes and behaviour. 1976. fo. 478. *bibliog.* Typescript. Ph.D. (London) thesis: unpublished. This thesis is the property of London University and may not be removed from the Library. Includes two offprints from periodicals.

TAPPER (TED) Political education and stability: elite responses to political conflict. London, [1976]. pp. 265.

— **United States.**

FIORINA (MORRIS P.) Representatives, roll calls, and constituencies. Lexington, Mass., [1974]. pp. 143. *bibliog.*

DELOUGHERY (GRACE L.) and GEBBIE (KRISTINE M.) Political dynamics: impact on nurses and nursing. Saint Louis, 1975. pp. 236. *bibliogs.*

GILMOUR (ROBERT S.) and LAMB (ROBERT B.) Political alienation in contemporary America. New York, [1975]. pp. 198.

STEGGERT (FRANK X.) Community action groups and city governments: perspectives from ten American cities. Cambridge, Mass., [1975]. pp. 105. *bibliog.*

YIN (ROBERT K.) and YATES (DOUGLAS) Street-level governments: assessing decentralization and urban services. Lexington, Mass., [1975]. pp. 272. *bibliogs.*

AMBRECHT (BILIANA C.S.) Politicizing the poor: the legacy of the war on poverty in a Mexican-American community. New York, 1976. pp. 223. *bibliog.*

CHENG (CHARLES W.) Altering collective bargaining: citizen participation in educational decision making. New York, 1976. pp. 179. *bibliog.*

EISINGER (PETER K.) Patterns of interracial politics: conflict and cooperation in the city. New York, [1976]. pp. 202. *(Wisconsin University, Madison. Institute for Research on Poverty. Monograph Series)*

IPPOLITO (DENNIS S.) and others. Public opinion and responsible democracy. Englewood Cliffs, N.J., [1976]. pp. 330. *bibliog.*

JANOWITZ (MORRIS) Social control of the welfare state. New York, [1976]. pp. 170. *bibliog.*

TAPPER (TED) Political education and stability: elite responses to political conflict. London, [1976]. pp. 265.

WARREN (DONALD I.) The radical center: middle Americans and the politics of alienation. Notre Dame, Ind., [1976]. pp. 260. *bibliog.*

POLITICAL PARTIES.

MAISEL (LOUIS) and SACKS (PAUL M.) eds. The future of political parties. Beverly Hills, [1975]. pp. 277. *bibliogs.*

THOMAS (JOHN CLAYTON) The decline of ideology in Western political parties: a study of changing policy orientations. London, [1975]. pp. 68. *bibliog.*

SARTORI (GIOVANNI) Parties and party systems: a framework for analysis. Cambridge, 1976 in progress.

ROBERTSON (DAVID BRUCE) A theory of party competition. London, [1976]. pp. 210. *bibliog.*

— **Canada.**

ENGELMANN (FREDERICK C.) and SCHWARTZ (MILDRED A.) Canadian political parties: origin, character, impact. Scarborough, Ontario, [1975]. pp. 358. *bibliog.*

— **Caribbean area.**

AMERINGER (CHARLES D.) The democratic left in exile: the antidictatorial struggle in the Caribbean, 1945-1959. Coral Gables, [1974]. pp. 352. *bibliog.*

— **Europe.**

KOLINSKY (A. MARTIN) and PATERSON (WILLIAM EDGAR) eds. Social and political movements in western Europe. London, 1976. pp. 360.

— **France.**

LACHAUD (GEORGES) Que vont devenir les bonapartistes?. Paris, 1879. pp. 71.

SOULIE (MICHEL) Le Cartel des gauches. Paris, [1974]. pp. 335. *bibliog.*

POPEREN (JEAN) L'unité de la Gauche, 1965-1973. [Paris, 1975]. pp. 474. *bibliog.*

— **Germany.**

FLECHTHEIM (OSSIP KURT) ed. Die Parteien in der Bundesrepublik Deutschland. Hamburg, 1973. pp. 597.

HERGT (SIEGFRIED) ed. Ergänzungsband Parteiprogramme: Orientierungsrahmen der SPD Mannheimer Erklärung der CDU, Parteienfinanzierung 1974. Leverkusen-Opladen, [1975]. pp. 154.

LIPPHARDT (HANNS RUDOLF) Die Gleichheit der politischen Parteien vor der öffentlichen Gewalt: kritische Studie zur Wahl- und Parteienrechtsjudikatur des Bundesverfassungsgerichts. Berlin, [1975]. pp. 740. *bibliog.*

SCHMOLLINGER (HORST W.) and STOESS (RICHARD) Die Parteien und die Presse der Parteien und Gewerkschaften in der Bundesrepublik Deutschland, 1945-1974: Materialien zur Parteien- und Gewerkschaftsforschung. München, 1975. pp. 480. *bibliogs. (Berlin. Freie Universität. Zentralinstitut für Sozialwissenschaftliche Forschung. Berichte und Materialien. Band 2)*

SEIFERT (KARL HEINZ) Die politischen Parteien im Recht der Bundesrepublik Deutschland. Köln, 1975. pp. 527. *bibliog.*

TRAUTMANN (HELMUT) Innerparteiliche Demokratie im Parteienstaat. Berlin, [1975]. pp. 323. *bibliog.*

GABBE (JOERG) Parteien und Nation: zur Rolle des Nationalbewusstseins für die politischen Grundorientierungen der Parteien in der Anfangsphase der Bundesrepublik. Meisenheim am Glan, 1976. pp. 347. *bibliog.*

LIESE (HANS J.) Zielvorstellungen der Parteien. München, [1976]. pp. 182. *bibliog.*

POLITICAL PARTIES.(Cont.)

PULTE (PETER) ed. Politische Jugendorganisationen: Programmatik, Beschlüsse, Forderungen und Thesen von Jungsozialisten, Junger Union, Jungdemokraten. 2nd ed. Leverkusen, [1976]. pp. 356. *bibliog.*

STARITZ (DIETRICH) ed. Das Parteiensystem der Bundesrepublik: Geschichte, Entstehung, Entwicklung. Opladen, 1976. pp. 255. *bibliogs.*

— India.

BUENO DE MESQUITA (BRUCE) Strategy, risk and personality in coalition politics: the case of India. Cambridge, 1975. pp. 198. *bibliog.*

— Italy.

ORGANIZZAZIONE COMUNISTA AVANGUARDIA OPERAIA. Conferenza Nazionale, 2a, 1972. Documenti. Milano, 1973. 2 vols. *(Quaderni. 7)*

TAMBURRANO (GIUSEPPE) Dal centrosinistra al neocentrismo, 1962-1972: i difficili rapporti tra cattolici e socialisti. Firenze, [1973]. pp. 156. *bibliog.*

CABOARA (LORENZO) La partitocrazia cancrena dello stato. Roma, 1975. pp. 205.

GALLI (GIORGIO) Dal bipartitismo imperfetto alla possibile alternativa. Bologna, [1975]. pp. 223.

RADI (LUCIANO) Partiti e classi in Italia. Torino, 1975. pp. 167.

— Poland.

KOZIK (ZENOBIUSZ) Partie i stronnictwa polityczne w Krakowskiem, 1945-1947. Kraków, 1975. pp. 471. *bibliog.*

— Sierra Leone.

SIERRA LEONE. 1966. Government white paper on the proposed introduction of a democratic one party system in Sierra Leone. [Freetown, 1966]. pp. (2).

— Sweden.

TORSTENDAHL (ROLF) Mellan nykonservatism och liberalism: idébrytningar inom högern och bondepartierna, 1918-1934. Stockholm, [1969]. pp. 230. *bibliog. (Uppsala. Universitet. Historiska Institutionen. Studia Historica Upsaliensia. 29)* With English summary.

— Switzerland.

JOOS (EDUARD) Parteien und Presse im Kanton Schaffhausen. Schaffhausen, 1975. pp. 623. *bibliog.* 3 tables in end pocket.

— Turkey.

ONULDURAN (ERSIN) Political development and political parties in Turkey. Ankara, 1974. pp. 116. *bibliog. (Ankara. Üniversitesi. Siyasal Bilgiler Fakültesi. Yayinlari. No. 370)*

— United Kingdom.

HARRISON (STEPHEN JOHN) The British general election of 1924. 1971. pp. 561. *bibliog. Ph.D.(Catholic University of America) thesis: unpublished. Microfilm of typescript: 1 reel.*

BRYDER (TOM) Power and responsibility: contending approaches to industrial relations and decision-making in Britain 1963-1971. Lund, [1975]. pp. 212. *bibliog. Ph.D avhandling - Universitet i Lund.*

U.K. Central Office of Information. Reference Division. 1975. Organisation of political parties in Britain. rev. ed. London, 1975. pp. 15. *bibliog.*

BREWER (JOHN) Ph.D. Party ideology and popular politics at the accession of George III. Cambridge, 1976. pp. 382. *bibliog.*

HILL (BRIAN WILLIAM) The growth of parliamentary parties, 1689-1742. London, 1976. pp. 265. *bibliog.*

— — Ireland, Northern.

LAVER (MICHAEL) The theory and practice of party competition: Ulster 1973-75. London, [1976]. pp. 47. *bibliog.*

— United States.

WESTERFIELD (HOLT BRADFORD) Foreign policy and party politics: Pearl Harbor to Korea. New York, 1972. pp. 448. *bibliog. First published in 1955 by Yale University Press.*

KARP (WALTER) Indispensable enemies: the politics of misrule in America. Baltimore, 1974. pp. 324.

CONFERENCE ON AMERICAN POLITICAL PARTY DEVELOPMENT, ST LOUIS, 1966. The American party systems: stages of political development; edited by William Nisbet Chambers and Walter Dean Burnham; contributors, Frank J. Sorauf [and others]. 2nd ed. New York, 1975. pp. 374. *Papers of the conference sponsored by the Department of History and of Political Science of Washington University.*

GRAHAM (HUGH DAVIS) ed. American politics and government: party, ideology, and reform in American history. New York, [1975]. pp. 351. *bibliog.*

LADD (EVERETT CARLL) and HADLEY (CHARLES D.) Transformations of the American party system: political coalitions from the New Deal to the 1970s. New York, [1975]. pp. 371.

MAISEL (LOUIS) and SACKS (PAUL M.) eds. The future of political parties. Beverly Hills, [1975]. pp. 277. *bibliogs.*

RANNEY (AUSTIN) Curing the mischiefs of faction: party reform in America: [expanded version of the Jefferson Memorial Lectures given at the University of California, Berkeley 1973]. Berkeley, [1975]. pp. 218.

SCHLESINGER (STEPHEN C.) The new reformers: forces for change in American politics. Boston, Mass., 1975. pp. 238.

SHAPIRO (H.R.) The bureaucratic state: party bureaucracy and the decline of democracy in America. New York, [1975]. pp. 366. *bibliogs.*

MAILER (NORMAN) Some honorable men: political conventions 1960-1972. Boston, 1976. pp. 499.

— — Pennsylvania.

MILLER (RICHARD G.) Philadelphia - the Federalist city: a study of urban politics, 1789-1801. Port Washington, N.Y., 1976. pp. 192. *bibliog.*

— — Tennessee.

HART (ROGER L.) Redeemers, Bourbons and Populists: Tennessee, 1870-1896. Baton Rouge, La., [1975]. pp. 290. *bibliog.*

POLITICAL POETRY, ENGLISH.

ASHRAF (MARY) ed. Political verse and song from Britain and Ireland. London, 1975. pp. 440. *bibliog.*

POLITICAL POETRY, IRISH.

ASHRAF (MARY) ed. Political verse and song from Britain and Ireland. London, 1975. pp. 440. *bibliog.*

POLITICAL PRISONERS

— Czechoslovakia.

The STRUGGLE for socialist democracy: political prisoners in Czechoslovakia and the U.S.S.R.; [by] Tamara Deutscher [and others]. Nottingham, [1975?]. pp. 19. *(Spokesman, The. Pamphlets. No. 45)*

— Germany, Eastern.

STERN (JOACHIM R.) Und der Westen schweigt: Erlebnisse, Berichte, Dokumente über Mitteldeutschland, 1945-1975. Preussisch Oldendorf, 1976. pp. 332. *bibliog.*

— India.

AMNESTY INTERNATIONAL. Research Department. Short report on detention conditions in West Bengal jails prepared...on the basis of newspaper reports and individual statements made to Amnesty International. London, 1974. pp. 5,2,4.

— Indonesia.

TAPOL (BRITISH CAMPAIGN FOR THE RELEASE OF INDONESIAN POLITICAL PRISONERS). Indonesia: the prison state. London, 1975. pp. 16. *bibliog. (Tapol Background and Information Series. No. 1)*

— Russia.

SOLZHENITSYN (ALEKSANDR ISAEVICH) Arkhipelag GULag, 1918-1956: opyt khudozhestvennogo issledovaniia. Paris, 1973-75. 7 vols.(in 3).

SKOK (HENRYK) Polacy nad Bajkałem, 1863-1883. Warszawa, 1974. pp. 336.

AMNESTY INTERNATIONAL. Prisoners of conscience in the U.S.S.R.: their treatment and conditions. London, 1975. pp. 154.

SSYLKA i katorga v Sibiri, XVIII - nachalo XX v. Novosibirsk, 1975. pp. 304.

The STRUGGLE for socialist democracy: political prisoners in Czechoslovakia and the U.S.S.R.; [by] Tamara Deutscher [and others]. Nottingham, [1975?]. pp. 19. *(Spokesman, The. Pamphlets. No. 45)*

BUCA (EDWARD) Vorkuta;...translated from the Polish by Michal Lisinski and Kennedy Wells. London, 1976. pp. 352.

The CASE of Leonid Plyushch; translated from the Russian by Marite Sapiets, Peter Reddaway and Caryl Emerson; editor of the Russian edition, Tatyana Khodorovich, etc. London, [1976]. pp. 152. *Includes a selection of his letters.*

— — Personal narratives.

SUKLOVA (MARIIA) The life story of a Russian exile: the remarkable experience of a young girl: being an account of her peasant childhood in prison, her exile to Siberia and escape from there;...translated by Gregory Yarros. London, 1915. pp. 251.

PANIN (DIMITRII MIKHAILOVICH) The notebooks of Sologdin; translated by John Moore. New York, [1976 in progress].

— — Ukraine.

MOROZ (VALENTYN IAKOVYCH) Eseï, lysty i dokumenty; essays, letters and documents. Miunkhen, 1975. pp. 288. *bibliog.*

— Spain.

MAURIN (JOAQUIN) En las prisiones de Franco. Mexico, [1974]. pp. 213.

— — Personal narratives.

FOREST (EVA) From a Spanish jail; translated [from the French] by Rosemary Sheed. Harmondsworth, 1975. pp. 191.

POLITICAL PSYCHOLOGY.

MITSCHERLICH (ALEXANDER) and MITSCHERLICH (MARGARETE) Eine deutsche Art zu lieben. München, [1970]. pp. 119. *Revised version of the first chapter of their Die Unfähigkeit zu trauern.*

HAMSHER (J. HERBERT) and SIGALL (HAROLD) eds. Psychology and social issues. New York, [1973]. pp. 550. *bibliogs.*

FREEDMAN (ANNE E.) and FREEDMAN (P.E.) The psychology of political control: comprising dialogues between a modern prince and his tutor on the application of basic psychological principles to the realm of politics. New York, [1975]. pp. 276. *bibliog.*

POLITICAL SCIENCE.

ROSENBAUM (WALTER A.) Political culture. New York, 1975. pp. 181. *bibliog.*

BIOLOGY and politics: recent explorations; [proceedings of a conference held in Paris, 1975; edited by] Albert Somit. Paris, [1976]. pp. 330. *bibliog. (International Social Science Council. Publications. 19)*

ELCOCK (HOWARD JAMES) Political behaviour. London, 1976. pp. 339. *bibliog.*

MARSH (ALAN JOHN) The social psychology of political protest: a U.K. national survey of political attitudes and behaviour. 1976. fo. 478. *bibliog. Typescript. Ph.D. (London) thesis: unpublished. This thesis is the property of London University and may not be removed from the Library. Includes two offprints from periodicals.*

POLITICAL QUESTIONS AND JUDICIAL POWER

— Germany.

KOMMERS (DONALD P.) Judicial politics in west Germany: a study of the Federal Constitutional Court. Beverly Hills, Cal., [1976]. pp. 312.

POLITICAL SATIRE, AMERICAN.

LEVINE (DAVID) 1926- . No known survivors: David Levine's political plank; introduced and selected by John Kenneth Galbraith. Boston, 1970. pp. 196.

POLITICAL SCIENCE.

GREAVES (HAROLD RICHARD GORING) [Unpublished political and personal papers. 1932-53]. 13 pieces. *Manuscript, typescript, etc.*

ABDEL-MALEK (ANOUAR) ed. La pensée politique arabe contemporaine: [readings]. 2nd ed. Paris, [1970!. pp. 384. *bibliog.*

CRISIS, choice and change: historical studies of political development; edited by Gabriel A. Almond [and others]. Boston, [1973]. pp. 717. *bibliogs.*

ORTEGA Y GASSET (JOSE) Rectificacion de la Republica: escritos politicos, III, 1929/1933. Madrid, [1973]. pp. 273.

ORTEGA Y GASSET (JOSE) La redencion de las provincias: escritos politicos, II, 1918/1928. Madrid, [1973]. pp. 299.

ORTEGA Y GASSET (JOSE) Vieja y nueva politica: escritos politicos, I, 1908/1918. Madrid, [1973]. pp. 312.

IZ-POD glyb: sbornik statei...Moskva, 1974. Paris, [1974]. pp. 281.

LAWRENCE (REGINALD JAMES) Politics and political science: an inaugural lecture. Belfast, [1974]. pp. 20. *(Belfast. Queen's University. Lectures. New Series. No. 86)*

MANOV (GRIGORII NAUMOVICH) Gosudarstvo i politicheskaia organizatsiia obshchestva. Moskva, 1974. pp. 320. *bibliog.*

PALMER (MONTE) and others. The interdisciplinary study of politics. New York, [1974]. pp. 177.

RICOEUR (PAUL) Political and social essays; collected and edited by David Stewart and Joseph Bien. Athens, Ohio, [1974]. pp. 293.

VIG (NORMAN J.) and STIEFBOLD (RODNEY P.) eds. Politics in advanced nations: modernization, development, and contemporary change. Englewood Cliffs, [1974]. pp. 608.

BIRNBAUM (PIERRE) Le pouvoir politique: (textes et commentaires). Paris, [1975]. pp. 241.

BURKE (EDMUND) Edmund Burke on government, politics and society; selected and edited by B.W. Hill. Hassocks, Sussex, 1975. pp. 382. *bibliog.*

DODGE (DOROTHY RAE) and BAIRD (DUNCAN H.) eds. Continuities and discontinuities in political thought. New York, [1975]. pp. 314.

DOLLINGER (KARL) Politik, Staat und Verfassung in der Bundesrepublik Deutschland. 2nd ed. Köln, [1975]. pp. 184. *bibliog.*

FRAGA IRIBARNE (MANUEL) Legitimidad y representacion. Barcelona, [1975]. pp. 384.

The POLICY vacuum: toward a more professional political science; [by] Robert N. Spadaro [and others]. Lexington, [1975]. pp. 215. *bibliogs.*

RANNEY (AUSTIN) The governing of men. 4th ed. Hinsdale, Ill., 1975. pp. 708. *bibliog.*

RIDLEY (FREDERICK FERNAND) ed. Studies in politics: essays to mark the 25th anniversary of the Political Studies Association. Oxford, 1975. pp. 408.

UNGER (ROBERTO MANGABEIRA) Knowledge and politics. New York, [1975]. pp. 336.

BLONDEL (JEAN) 1929- . Thinking politically. London, 1976. pp. 165. *bibliog.*

The DYNAMICS of public policy: a comparative analysis; edited by Richard Rose. London, [1976]. pp. 268. *bibliogs. Papers based on a conference of the Comparative Public Policy work group of the Committee on Political Sociology, at Cumberland Lodge, Windsor Great Park, May 6-10, 1974.*

GOODIN (ROBERT E.) The politics of rational man. London, [1976]. pp. 210. *bibliog.*

GRIFFITH (JOHN ANEURIN GREY) ed. From policy to administration: essays in honour of William A. Robson. London, 1976. pp. 216.

HARRIS (PETER B.) Foundations of political science. London, 1976. pp. 352. *bibliog.*

SELIGER (MARTIN) Ideology and politics. London, 1976. pp. 352. *bibliog.*

SOCIAL ends and political means; edited by Ted Honderich. London, 1976. pp. 177.

STANKIEWICZ (WLADYSLAW JOZEF) Aspects of political theory: classical concepts in an age of relativism. London, 1976. pp. 175.

— Bibliography.

HARVARD UNIVERSITY. Library. Widener Library Shelflists. [No.] 22. Government. Cambridge, Mass., 1969. pp. 263.

INTER-UNIVERSITY CONSORTIUM FOR POLITICAL AND SOCIAL RESEARCH. Guide to resources and services, 1976-1977. [Ann Arbor, 1976]. pp. 386. *bibliogs.*

— History.

HEATER (DEREK BENJAMIN) Contemporary political ideas. London, 1974. pp. 130. *bibliog. (Politics Association. Political Realities)*

KRIEGER (LEONARD) An essay on the theory of enlightened despotism. Chicago, 1975. pp. 115. *bibliog.*

ULLMAN (WALTER) Law and politics in the Middle Ages: an introduction to the sources of medieval political ideas. Ithaca, N.Y., 1975. pp. 320. *bibliog.*

— — Byzantine Empire.

AHRWEILER (HELENE) L'idéologie politique de l'Empire byzantin. [Paris, 1975]. pp. 158. *bibliog.*

— — France.

BAUMGARTNER (FREDERIC J.) Radical reactionaries: the political thought of the French Catholic League. Genève, 1975 [or rather 1976]. pp. 317. *bibliog.*

SAINT-SIMON (CLAUDE HENRI DE) Comte. The political thought of Saint-Simon; edited by Ghița Ionescu. London, 1976. pp. 245. *bibliog.*

— — Germany.

WENDE (PETER) Radikalismus im Vormärz: Untersuchungen zur politischen Theorie der frühen deutschen Demokratie. Wiesbaden, 1975. pp. 228. *bibliog.*

— — Greece, Ancient.

VLACHOS (GEORGES C.) Les sociétés politiques homériques. Paris, 1974. pp. 399.

— — India.

ZAIDI (A. MOIN) ed. Evolution of Muslim political thought in India. New Delhi, 1975 in progress.

— — Italy.

RASCHHOFER (HERMANN) Der politische Volksbegriff im modernen Italien. Berlin, 1936. pp. 207.

GALASSO (GIUSEPPE) Da Mazzini a Salvemini: il pensiero democratico nell'Italia moderna. Firenze, 1974. pp. 343. *bibliogs.*

TITONE (VIRGILIO) Il pensiero politico italiano nell'età barocca, con un'appendice sulla storia del ceto medio. Caltanissetta, [1974]. pp. 333.

— — Mexico.

CORDOVA (ARNALDO) La ideologia de la Revolucion Mexicana: la formacion del nuevo regimen. Mexico, 1973 repr. 1974. pp. 508.

— — Russia.

BLACK (JOSEPH LAURENCE) Nicholas Karamzin and Russian society in the nineteenth century: a study in Russian political and historical thought. Toronto, [1975]. pp. 264. *bibliog.*

— — Spain.

MARAVALL (JOSE ANTONIO) Estudios de historia del pensamiento español: serie primera: Edad Media. 2nd ed. Madrid, 1973. pp. 507.

GARRORENA MORALES (ANGEL) El Ateneo de Madrid y la teoria de la monarquia liberal, 1836- 1847. Madrid, 1974. pp. 876.

— — United Kingdom.

McKERCHER (WILLIAM RUSSELL) English libertarian thought in the late nineteenth century. 1976. fo. 438. *bibliog. Typescript. Ph.D.(London) thesis: unpublished. This thesis is the property of London University and may not be removed from the Library.*

— — United States.

GRAHAM (HUGH DAVIS) ed. American politics and government: party, ideology, and reform in American history. New York, [1975]. pp. 351. *bibliog.*

LODGE (GEORGE CABOT) The new American ideology: how the ideological basis of legitimate authority in America is being radically transformed, etc. New York, 1976. pp. 350,xv.

— Information services.

INTER-UNIVERSITY CONSORTIUM FOR POLITICAL AND SOCIAL RESEARCH. A guide to resources and services of the...Consortium...1971-72. [Ann Arbor, 1972]. pp. 108. *bibliogs.*

INTER-UNIVERSITY CONSORTIUM FOR POLITICAL AND SOCIAL RESEARCH. Guide to resources and services, 1976-1977. [Ann Arbor, 1976]. pp. 386. *bibliogs.*

— Mathematical models.

COLEMAN (STEPHEN) Measurement and analysis of political systems: a science of social behavior. New York, [1975]. pp. 219. *bibliog.*

— Methodology.

EISENSTADT (SHMUEL N.) and ROKKAN (STEIN) eds. Building states and nations. Beverly Hills, [1973]. 2 vols. *bibliogs.*

POLITICAL SCIENCE.(Cont.)

HILTON (GORDON) Intermediate politometrics. New York, 1976. pp. 282. *bibliogs.*

TULLOCK (GORDON) The vote motive: an essay in the economics of politics with applications to the British economy...with a British commentary by Morris Perlman. London, 1976. pp. 88. *bibliogs. (Institute of Economic Affairs. Hobart Paperbacks. 9.)*

— Periodicals.

CLARK (Sir GEORGE NORMAN) [Correspondence about the publication of Agenda: a quarterly journal of reconstruction. 1941-43]. 1 folder. *Manuscript, typescript, etc.*

LEDDA (ISABELLA) and ZANELLA (GABRIELLA) I periodici di Padova, 1866-1926, liberali, radicali, socialisti. Padova, 1973. pp. 252. *(Centro per la Storia del Movimento Operaio nel Veneto, and Padua. Università. Istituto di Storia Medioevale e Moderna. Movimenti Politici e Sociali dell'Età Contemporanea nel Veneto. Collana.4)*

WINOCK (MICHEL) Histoire politique de la revue Esprit, 1930-1950. Paris, [1975]. pp. 447. *bibliog.*

— Simulation methods.

FOSTER (JOHN L.) and others. National policy game: a simulation of the American political process. New York, [1975]. pp. 108.

— Study and teaching — Africa, East.

PREWITT (KENNETH) ed. Education and political values: an East African case study. Nairobi, 1971. pp. 249.

— Terminology.

Des TRACTS en mai 68: mesures de vocabulaire et de contenu; ([by] Michel Demonet [and others]). Paris, [1975]. pp. 491. *bibliog. (Fondation Nationale des Sciences Politiques. Travaux et Recherches de Science Politique. 31)*

FETSCHER (IRING) and RICHTER (HORST EBERHARD) eds. Worte machen keine Politik: Beiträge zu einem Kampf um politische Begriffe. Reinbek bei Hamburg, 1976. pp. 152. *bibliog.*

POLITICAL SCIENCE IN LITERATURE.

MATHEWSON (RUFUS WELLINGTON) The positive hero in Russian literature. 2nd ed. Stanford, 1975. pp. 369.

POLITICAL SCIENTISTS.

A COLLECTION of photographs of portraits of economists and political philosophers. n.d. 1 vol. (unpaged).

POLITICAL SOCIALIZATION.

PREWITT (KENNETH) ed. Education and political values: an East African case study. Nairobi, 1971. pp. 249.

BELL (CHARLES G.) and PRICE (CHARLES M.) The first term: a study of legislative socialization. Beverly Hills, [1975]. pp. 213.

PATTERSON (SAMUEL C.) and others. Representatives and represented: bases of public support for the American legislatures. New York, [1975]. pp. 212.

IPPOLITO (DENNIS S.) and others. Public opinion and responsible democracy. Englewood Cliffs, N.J., [1976]. pp. 330. *bibliog.*

MASSEY (JOSEPH A.) Youth and politics in Japan. Lexington, Mass., [1976]. pp. 233. *bibliog.*

TAPPER (TED) Political education and stability: elite responses to political conflict. London, [1976]. pp. 265.

POLITICAL SOCIOLOGY.

BIRNBAUM (PIERRE) La fin du politique. Paris, [1975]. pp. 285. *bibliog.*

HAMILTON (RICHARD F.) Restraining myths: critical studies of U.S. social structure and politics. New York, [1975]. pp. 296.

MOORE (SALLY FALK) and MYERHOFF (BARBARA G.) eds. Symbol and politics in communal ideology: cases and questions. Ithaca, 1975. pp. 245. *bibliogs.*

ROSENBAUM (WALTER A.) Political culture. New York, 1975. pp. 181. *bibliog.*

ELCOCK (HOWARD JAMES) Political behaviour. London, 1976. pp. 339. *bibliog.*

HIGLEY (JOHN) and others. Elite structure and ideology: a theory with applications to Norway. Oslo, [1976]. pp. 367. *bibliog.*

PIRAGES (DENNIS CLARK) Managing political conflict. New York, 1976. pp. 148. *bibliog.*

WRIGHT (JAMES D.) The dissent of the governed: alienation and democracy in America. New York, 1976. pp. 329. *bibliog.*

— Mathematical models.

COLEMAN (STEPHEN) Measurement and analysis of political systems: a science of social behavior. New York, [1975]. pp. 219. *bibliog.*

POLITICS, PRACTICAL.

LAMMERT (NORBERT) Lokale Organisationsstrukturen innerparteilicher Willensbildung: Fallstudie am Beispiel eines CDU-Kreisverbandes im Ruhrgebiet. Bonn, [1976]. pp. 224. *bibliog. (Institut für Kommunalwissenschaften [Bonn]. Schriftenreihe. Band 5)*

POLITICS IN LITERATURE.

NICHOLS (JAMES H.) Epicurean political philosophy: the De rerum natura of Lucretius. Ithaca, N.Y., 1976. pp. 214.

POLLITT (HARRY).

MAHON (JOHN A.) Harry Pollitt: a biography. London, 1976. pp. 567. *bibliog.*

POLLUTION.

PROFESSIONAL INSTITUTIONS COUNCIL FOR CONSERVATION. Environmental pollution; [report of a working party; edited by J.T. Williams]. [London, 1974]. pp. 47.

SOCIETY FOR SOCIAL RESPONSIBILITY IN SCIENCE. Annual Conference, 1971. Against pollution and hunger: [papers of the conference]; (Alice Mary Hilton, ed.). Oslo, [1974]. pp. 307.

VAN TASSEL (ALFRED J.) ed. The environmental price of energy. Lexington, Mass., [1975]. pp. 326. *bibliogs.*

SAUNDERS (P.J.W.) The estimation of pollution damage. Manchester, [1976]. pp. 126. *bibliog.*

— Economic aspects.

DEWEES (DONALD N.) and others. Economic analysis of environmental policies. Toronto, [1975]. pp. 175. *bibliog. (Ontario. Economic Council. Research Studies. 1)*

UNIVERSITIES-NATIONAL BUREAU COMMITTEE FOR ECONOMIC RESEARCH. Conference, 1972. Economic analysis of environmental problems: [proceedings of the conference sponsored jointly with Resources for the Future, Inc.]; edited by Edwin S. Mills. New York, 1975. pp. 472. *bibliogs. (National Bureau of Economic Research. Universities-National Bureau Conference Series. 26)*

WALTER (INGO) International economics of pollution. London, 1975. pp. 208. *bibliogs.*

COUPE (BERNARD EDDY MARIE GHISLAIN) Economics and environment: some models. [Rotterdam], 1976. fo. 236. *bibliog. Proefschrift (doctor)-Erasmus Universiteit Rotterdam.*

PEARCE (DAVID WILLIAM) Environmental economics. London, 1976. pp. 202. *bibliog.*

SYMPOSIUM ON INTERNATIONAL ECONOMIC DIMENSIONS OF ENVIRONMENTAL MANAGEMENT, NEW YORK, 1975. Studies in international environmental economics; edited by Ingo Walter. New York, [1976]. pp. 364. *bibliog.*

— — Germany.

JARRE (JAN) Umweltbelastungen und ihre Verteilung auf soziale Schichten. Göttingen, [1975]. pp. 112. *bibliog. (Kommission für Wirtschaftlichen und Sozialen Wandel. Schriften. 32)*

— — United Kingdom.

BECKERMAN (WILFRED) Pricing for pollution: an analysis of market pricing and government regulation in environment consumption and policy. London, 1975. pp. 72. *bibliog. (Institute of Economic Affairs. Hobart Papers. 66)*

— — United States.

ECONOMICS and decision-making for environmental quality; [papers based on seminars sponsored by the Food and Resource Economics Department, University of Florida in 1971]; edited by J. Richard Conner [and] Edna Loehman. [Gainesville, Fla.], 1974. pp. 299. *bibliogs.*

— International cooperation.

WALTER (INGO) International economics of pollution. London, 1975. pp. 208. *bibliogs.*

— Belgium.

DIDIER (J.M.) AND ASSOCIATES. The law and practice relating to pollution control in Belgium and Luxembourg. London, European Communities, 1976. pp. 496. *bibliog.*

— Denmark.

HAAGEN JENSEN (CLAUS) The law and practice relating to pollution control in Denmark. London, European Communities, 1976. pp. 208. *bibliog.*

— European Economic Community countries.

McLOUGHLIN (JAMES) The law and practice relating to pollution control in the member states of the European Communities: a comparative survey. London, European Communities, 1976. pp. 545.

— France.

COLLIARD (CLAUDE ALBERT) The law and practice relating to pollution control in France. London, European Communities, 1976. pp. 190. *bibliog.*

— Germany.

STEIGER (HEINHARD) and KIMMINICH (OTTO) The law and practice relating to pollution control in the Federal Republic of Germany. London, European Communities, 1976. pp. 420. *bibliog.*

— Ireland (Republic).

SCANNELL (YVONNE) The law and practice relating to pollution control in Ireland. London, European Communities, 1976. pp. 223.

— Italy.

ANNO (PAOLO DELL') The law and practice relating to pollution control in Italy. London, European Communities, 1976. pp. 342. *bibliog.*

— Luxembourg.

DIDIER (J.M.) AND ASSOCIATES. The law and practice relating to pollution control in Belgium and Luxembourg. London, European Communities, 1976. pp. 496. *bibliog.*

— Netherlands.

GRAEFF (J.J.DE) and POLACK (J.M.) The law and practice relating to pollution control in the Netherlands. London, European Communities, 1976. pp. 184.

— **Norway.**

NORWAY. Statistiske Centralbyrå. 1976. Miljøstatistikk, 1976: naturressurser og forurensninger, etc. Oslo, 1976. pp. 228. *(Statistiske Analyser. 22) With English summary.*

— **Russia.**

INTERNATIONAL SLAVIC CONFERENCE, 1ST, BANFF, ALBERTA, 1974. Environmental misuse in the Soviet Union: [selected papers from the conference]; edited by Fred Singleton. New York, 1976. pp. 100.

— **United Kingdom.**

SCIENCE, technology and environmental management: [based on a symposium on 'Applied Environmental Science' held at the 1974 Annual Conference of the Institute of British Geographers]; edited by Richard D. Hey and Trevor D. Davies. Farnborough, Hants., [1975]. pp. 295. *bibliogs.*

U.K. Central Unit on Environmental Pollution. 1975. Controlling pollution: a review of government action related to recommendations by the Royal Commission on Environmental Pollution. London, 1975. pp. 31. *(Pollution Papers. No.4)*

McLOUGHLIN (JAMES) The law and practice relating to pollution control in the United Kingdom. London, European Communities, 1976. pp. 386.

— — **Wales.**

U.K. Welsh Office. 1972. Pollution: the challenge to Wales. [Cardiff, 1972]. pp. 16.

HALL (IRENE M.) Community action versus pollution: a study of a residents' group in a Welsh urban area. Cardiff, 1976. pp. 130. *(Wales. University. Board of Celtic Studies. Social Science Monographs. No. 2)*

— **United States.**

BRUBAKER (STERLING) In command of tomorrow: resource and environmental strategies for Americans. Baltimore, [1975]. pp. 177.

POLSKA PARTIA ROBOTNICZA.

See COMMUNIST PARTY — Poland.

POLSKIE STRONNICTWO LUDOWE.

BOBEK (PAWEŁ) Wspomnienia i zapiski; przygotował do druku i biografią poprzedził Franciszek Serafin. Warszawa, 1974. pp. 143.

— **Congresses.**

POLSKIE STRONNICTWO LUDOWE. Kongres, 5-y, Londyn, 1975. Piąty Kongres Polskiego Stronnictwa Ludowego, Londyn 3- 4. V. 1975: referaty, przemówienia, uchwały, władze naczelne. Londyn, 1975. pp. 69.

POLTAVA (OBLAST')

— **Politics and government.**

NARYSY istoriï Poltavs'koï oblasnoï partiĭnoï orhanizatsiï. Kharkiv, 1970. pp. 452.

POOR

— **Medical care — United States.**

KOSA (JOHN) and ZOLA (IRVING KENNETH) eds. Poverty and health: a sociological analysis. [2nd ed.] Cambridge, Mass., 1975. pp. 456.

The HEALTH gap: medical services and the poor; edited by Robert L. Kane [and others]. New York, [1976]. pp. 321. *bibliog.*

— **America, Latin.**

PORTES (ALEJANDRO) and WALTON (JOHN) Urban Latin America: the political condition from above and below. Austin, Texas, [1976]. pp. 217. *bibliog.*

— **Australia.**

SALMON (JAN) Resources for poor families: an experimental income supplement scheme. Canberra, Australian Government Publishing Service, 1974. pp. 96.

AUSTRALIA. Commission of Inquiry into Poverty. 1975. Poverty in Australia: first main report; [Ronald F. Henderson, chairman]. Canberra, 1975. 2 vols. (in 1).

— **France.**

[MARTIN DE SALINS (C.C.)] Nécessité et moyens d'établir une loi agraire, d'assurer la subsistance des pauvres, de réformer le clergé et la constitution militaire; par C.C.M. de S...ns. n.p. 1789; repr. Paris, 1966. pp. 49. *Facsimile reprint.*

— **India — Madras.**

DJURFELDT (GÖRAN) and LINDBERG (STAFFAN) Behind poverty: the social formation in a Tamil village. Lund, 1975. pp. 340. *bibliog. (Scandinavian Institute of Asian Studies. Monograph Series. No. 22)*

DJURFELDT (GÖRAN) and LINDBERG (STAFFAN) Pills against poverty: a study of the introduction of western medicine in a Tamil village. Lund, 1975. pp. 232. *bibliog. (Scandinavian Institute of Asian Studies. Monograph Series. No. 23)*

— **Philippine Islands.**

JOCANO (F. LANDA) Slum as a way of life: a study of coping behavior in an urban environment. Quezon City, 1975. pp. 203.

— **South Africa.**

POTGIETER (J.F.) The household subsistence level in the major urban centres of the Republic of South Africa: October, 1975. Port Elizabeth, 1975. pp. 80. *bibliog. (University of Port Elizabeth. Institute for Planning Research. Research Reports. No. 15)*

— **Sweden.**

LUNDSJÖ (OLLE) Fattigdomen på den svenska landsbygden under 1800-talet. [Stockholm, 1975]. pp. 208. *bibliog. (Stockholms Universitet. Ekonomisk-Historiska Institutionen. Stockholm Studies in Economic History. 1) With English summary.*

— **Switzerland.**

MEYER (JUERG) Journalist. Armut in der Schweiz. Zürich, [1974]. pp. 141.

— **Underdeveloped areas.**

See UNDERDEVELOPED AREAS — Poor.

— **United Kingdom.**

BUTTERWORTH (ERIC) and HOLMAN (ROBERT) eds. Social welfare in modern Britain: [a reader]. [London], 1975. pp. 443. *bibliog.*

FIELD (FRANK) 1942- . Back to the thirties for the poor?. London, [1975]. pp. 4. *(Child Poverty Action Group. Reports on the Living Standards of the Poor in 1975. No. 1)*

FIELD (FRANK) 1942- . Poverty: the facts. London, 1975. pp. 46. *(Child Poverty Action Group. Poverty Pamphlets. 21)*

FIELD (FRANK) 1942- . The new corporate interest. London, 1976. pp. 27. *(Child Poverty Action Group. Poverty Pamphlets. 23)*

KEATING (PETER J.) ed. Into unknown England, 1866-1913; selections from the social explorers. Manchester, 1976. pp. 320. *bibliog.*

ROBINSON (PHILIP) Education and poverty. London, 1976. pp. 126. *bibliog.*

— — **Bibliography.**

PARTINGTON (MARTIN) and others, compilers. Welfare rights: a bibliography on law and the poor, 1970-1975. London, 1976. pp. 167.

— — **Ireland, Northern.**

EVASON (EILEEN) Poverty: the facts in Northern Ireland. London, 1976. ppp. 48. *(Child Poverty Action Group. Poverty Pamphlets. 27)*

— **United States.**

HAMILTON (DAVID BOYCE) A primer on the economics of poverty. New York, [1968]. pp. xvii, 133. *bibliog.*

CONFERENCE ON PUBLIC POLICY FOR URBAN MINORITIES AND THE POOR IN THE 1970S, NASHVILLE, 1972. The urban scene in the seventies: (proceedings...); edited by James F. Blumstein and Eddie J. Martin. Nashville, 1974. pp. 256. *bibliogs. Proceedings of a conference sponsored by the Urban Affairs Institute of Fisk University and the Urban and Regional Development Center of Vanderbilt University.*

HAAR (CHARLES MONROE) and IATRIDES (DEMETRIOS S.) Housing the poor in suburbia: public policy at the grass roots. Cambridge, Mass., [1974]. pp. 430. *bibliogs.*

HAMPDEN-TURNER (CHARLES) From poverty to dignity: a strategy for poor Americans. Garden City, N.Y., 1974. pp. 300. *bibliog.*

LEVINE (NAOMI) and HOCHBAUM (MARTIN) eds. Poor Jews: an American awakening. New Brunswick, [1974]. pp. 206.

PETERSON (JAMES) Escape from poverty: occupational and economic mobility among urban blacks. Chicago, [1974]. pp. 176. *bibliog. (Chicago. University. Community and Family Study Center. Community and Family Monographs)*

SMITH (THOMAS LYNN) Studies of the great rural tap roots of urban poverty in the United States. New York, [1974]. pp. 144.

STACK (CAROL B.) All our kin: strategies for survival in a black community. New York, [1974]. pp. 175. *bibliog.*

FEAGIN (JOE R.) Subordinating the poor: welfare and American beliefs. Englewood Cliffs, N.J., [1975]. pp. 180.

LAMB (CURT) Political power in poor neighborhoods. New York, [1975]. pp. 315. *bibliog.*

O'BRIEN (DAVID J.) Neighborhood organization and interest-group processes. Princeton, [1975]. pp. 263. *bibliog.*

TUSSING (A. DALE) Poverty in a dual economy. New York, [1975]. pp. 229. *bibliogs.*

WILBER (GEORGE LEWIN) ed. Poverty: a new perspective. Lexington, Ky., [1975]. pp. 197. *bibliog.*

LEBERGOTT (STANLEY) The American economy: income, wealth and want. Princeton, N.J., [1976]. pp. 382.

— — **California.**

AMBRECHT (BILIANA C.S.) Politicizing the poor: the legacy of the war on poverty in a Mexican-American community. New York, 1976. pp. 223. *bibliog.*

— — **Massachusetts.**

BAILIS (LAWRENCE NEIL) Bread or justice: grassroots organizing in the welfare rights movement. Lexington, Mass., [1974]. pp. 175.

POOR, RURAL.

See RURAL POOR.

POOR AS CONSUMERS

— **United Kingdom.**

JOHNSON (MARIGOLD) and ROWLAND (MARK) Fuel debts and the poor. London, 1976. pp. 36. *(Child Poverty Action Group. Poverty Pamphlets. 24)*

U.K. Interdepartmental Working Group on Energy Tariffs. 1976. Energy tariffs and the poor. London, 1976. pp. 31.

POOR AS CONSUMERS(Cont.)

— United States.

ANDREASEN (ALAN R.) The disadvantaged consumer. New York, [1975]. pp. 366.

POOR LAWS

— United Kingdom.

MOSLEY (JOHN VERNON) Poor law administration in England and Wales, 1834 to 1850 with special reference to the problem of able-bodied pauperism. 1975. fo. 335. bibliog. Typescript. Ph.D.(London) thesis: unpublished. *This thesis is the property of London University and may not be removed from the Library.*

FRASER (DEREK) ed. The new poor law in the nineteenth century. London, 1976. pp. 218. *bibliog.*

— — Scotland.

LINDSAY (JEAN) The Scottish Poor Law: its operation in the north-east from 1745 to 1845. Ilfracombe, 1975. pp. 265. *bibliog.*

POPPER (IULIU).

See POPPER (JULIO).

POPPER (JULIO).

LEWIN (BOLESLAO) Popper: un conquistador patagonico; sus hazañas, sus escritos. Buenos Aires, [1967]. pp. 233.

POPPER (Sir KARL RAIMUND).

SKAGESTAD (PETER) Making sense of history: the philosophies of Popper and Collingwood. Oslo, [1975]. pp. 118. bibliog. *(Norges Almenvitenskapelige Forskningsråd. Gruppe: Språk og Historie) Based on lectures given at Brandeis University, Spring, 1973.*

NORDHOFEN (ECKHARD) Das Bereichsdenken im Kritischen Rationalismus: zur finitistischen Tradition der Popperschule. München, [1976]. pp. 214. *bibliog.*

POPULAR FRONTS.

BABICI (ION) Boevaia antifashistskaia solidarnost', 1933-1939 gg.; (perevod s rumynskogo Natalii i Konstantina Unguru). Bukharest, 1974. pp. 244. *(Academia de Ştiinţe Sociale şi Politice a Republicii Socialiste România. Bibliotheca Historica Romaniae. Studies. 49)*

PRZYGOŃSKI (ANTONI) Z zagadnień strategii frontu narodowego PPR, 1942-1945. Warszawa, 1976. pp. 400. *bibliog.*

POPULATION.

ROBERTSON (JOHN MACKINNON) The population question. Bradford, [1897]. pp. 7. *(Papers for the People. No. 10)*

VIELROSE (EGON) Elementy ruchu naturalnego ludności. Warszawa, 1961. pp. 365.

INTERNATIONAL COUNCIL OF VOLUNTARY AGENCIES. Documents. No. 18. Population questions: a contribution to World Population Year. Geneva, 1974. pp. 88.

RUSSIA (USSR). Ministerstvo Vysshego i Srednego Spetsial'nogo Obrazovaniia. Nauchno-Tekhnicheskii Sovet. Sektsiia Narodonaseleniia. Narodonaselenie. 6. Narodonaselenie zarubezhnykh stran. Moskva, 1974. pp. 93. *With English table of contents.*

AMERICAN ASSOCIATION FOR THE ADVANCEMENT OF SCIENCE. Population: dynamics, ethics and policy;...edited by Priscilla Reining and Irene Tinker. Washington, D.C., [1975]. pp. 184. *(Articles reprinted from Science, 1966-1975).*

EDUCATION and population: mutual impacts; edited by Helmut V. Muhsam. Dolhain, Belgium, [1975]. pp. 337. *bibliogs.*

FRANCE. Direction de la Documentation. La Documentation Française. Notes et Etudes Documentaires. Nos. 4,218-4, 219-4,220. La population du monde et la Conférence de Bucarest; par Yves Charbit. Paris, 1975. pp. 112.

GOLDSTEIN (SIDNEY) and SLY (DAVID F.) eds. The measurement of urbanization and projection of urban population. Dolhain, [1975]. pp. 224. *bibliogs. (International Union for the Scientific Study of Population. Committee on Urbanization and Population Redistribution. Working Papers. 2)*

INTERNATIONAL CONGRESS OF ANTHROPOLOGICAL AND ETHNOLOGICAL SCIENCES. 9th Congress, 1973. Population, ecology and social evolution: [papers from the Congress]; editor Steven Polgar. The Hague, [1975]. pp. 354. *bibliog.*

KELLOGG (EDMUND H.) and others. The world's laws and practices on population and sexuality education. Medford, Mass., 1975. pp. 127. *(Tufts University. Fletcher School of Law and Diplomacy. Law and Population Monograph Series. No. 25)*

LEVI (LENNART) and ANDERSSON (LARS) Psychosocial stress: population, environment and quality of life. New York, [1975]. pp. 142. bibliog. *Prepared for the United Nations' World Population Conference in 1974.*

PETERSEN (WILLIAM) 1912- . Population. 3rd ed. New York, [1975]. pp. 784. *bibliogs.*

SAUVY (ALFRED) Zero growth?; (translator, A. Maguire). Oxford, 1975. pp. 266.

BOWEN (IAN) Economics and demography. London, 1976. pp. 168. *bibliog.*

INTERNATIONAL ECONOMIC ASSOCIATION. Conference, 1973, Valescure. Eonomic factor in population growth: proceedings...; edited by Ansley J. Coale. London, 1976. pp. 600. *bibliogs.*

MACFARLANE (ALAN DONALD JAMES) Resources and population: a study of the Gurungs of Nepal. Cambridge, 1976. pp. 364. *bibliog.*

McKEOWN (THOMAS) The modern rise of population. London, 1976. pp. 168.

RICHARDS (HAMISH) ed. Population, factor movements and economic development: studies presented to Brinley Thomas. Cardiff, 1976. pp. 288. *bibliog.*

WORLD CONGRESS OF SOCIOLOGY, 8TH, 1974. Internal migration: the New World and the Third World; edited by Anthony H. Richmond and Daniel Kubat. London, [1976]. pp. 315. *bibliogs. Based on a selection of papers presented in the sessions of the International Sociological Association's Research Committee on Migration at the Congress.*

— Bibliography.

UNITED STATES. Smithsonian Institution. Interdisciplinary Communication Program. International Program for Population Analysis. Annotated bibliography. s-a., 1973 (v.1, no.1)- Washington.

— Congresses.

WORLD POPULATION CONFERENCE, 2ND, BELGRADE, 1965. [A collection of working and background papers prepared for the Conference; mimeographed documents issued to participants. (E/CONF 41)]. [New York], United Nations, [1965]. 209 parts.

SYMPOSIUM ON LAW AND POPULATION, TUNIS, 1974. Text of recommendations. Medford, Mass., 1974. pp. 49. *(Tufts University. Fletcher School of Law and Diplomacy. Law and Population Monograph Series. No. 20)*

— Mathematical models.

NORDBOTTEN (SVEIN MARTINIUS) Personmodeller, personregnskapssystemet og persondataarkiver...: population models, population accounting systems and individual data banks. Oslo, 1970. pp. 28. *(Norway. Statistisk Centralbyrå. Artikler. Nr. 38) With English summary.*

— Statistics.

INTERNATIONAL INSTITUTE OF STATISTICS. International Statistics of Large Towns. Territoire et population des grandes villes, 1928-1934. La Haye, 1939. pp. 300.

POPULATION FORECASTING.

HOEM (JAN M.) Levels of error in population forecasts...: usikkerhetsnivåer ved befolkningsprognoser; with an appendix by Leo Törnqvist. Oslo, 1973. pp. 46. bibliog. *(Norway. Statistiske Centralbyrå. Artikler. Nr. 61) Condensed English version of Usikkerhet med befolkningsprognoser. (Artikler. Nr. 54)*

PITTENGER (DONALD B.) Projecting state and local populations. Cambridge, Mass., [1976]. pp. 246. *bibliog.*

— Canada — Manitoba.

MANITOBA 2000: population size and distribution; edited by K.B. Richmond and J.J. Keleher. [Winnipeg], Manitoba Environmental Council, 1975. 1 vol. (various pagings). *(Manitoba Environmental Council. Studies. No. 5)*

— Finland.

FINLAND. Tilastokeskus. 1974. Väestöennusteet, 1973-2000...:(koko maan väestöennusteet ja alueellisten laskelmien vertailu), etc. Helsinki, 1974. pp. 69. bibliog. *(Tilastollisia Tiedonantoja. 52) In Finnish and Swedish, with English summary.*

— Germany — Berlin.

DEUTSCHES INSTITUT FÜR WIRTSCHAFTSFORSCHUNG. Sonderhefte. [Neue Folge]. 110. Modelle der Bevölkerungsentwicklung in Berlin, West, bis zum Jahre 1990; ([by] Peter Ring und Ingo Pfeiffer). Berlin, 1975. pp. 115. *bibliog.*

— Hong Kong.

HONG KONG. Census and Statistics Department. 1973. Hong Kong life tables, 1971-1991. Hong Kong, [1973]. pp. 19.

HONG KONG. Census and Statistics Department. 1973. Hong Kong population projections, 1971-1991. Hong Kong, [1973]. pp. 43.

— Ireland (Republic).

NATIONAL ECONOMIC AND SOCIAL COUNCIL [EIRE]. Population projections 1971-86: the implications for education. Dublin, Stationery Office, [1976]. pp. 44. *([Reports]. No.18)*

NATIONAL ECONOMIC AND SOCIAL COUNCIL [EIRE]. Population projections, 1971-1986: the implications for social planning: dwelling needs. Dublin, Stationery Office, [1976]. pp. 48. bibliog. *([Reports]. No. 14)*

— Israel.

ISRAEL. Central Bureau of Statistics. Special Series. No. 242. Projection of the population in Israel up to 1985, based on the population at the end of 1965. Jerusalem, 1968. pp. 27. *In English and Hebrew.*

— Norway.

HOEM (JAN M.) and RIDENG (ARNE KJELL) Kommentarer til Statistisk Sentralbyrås framskriving av folkemengden i kommunene, 1972-2000...: comments to the regional population projections for Norway, 1972-2000. Oslo, 1972. pp. 29. *(Norway. Statistiske Centralbyrå. Artikler. Nr. 52)*

BRUNBORG (HELGE) Framskriving av folkemengden i Norge, 1973-2100: et analytisk eksperiment...: population projections for Norway, 1973-2100: an analytic experiment. Oslo, 1974. pp. 100. bibliog. *(Norway. Statistiske Centralbyrå. Artikler. Nr. 69) With English summary.*

RIDENG (ARNE KJELL) and TØNNESEN (BJØRN LIED) Statistisk Sentralbyrås regionale befolkningsframskrivinger: nåvaerend opplegg og atviklingsplaner, 1974...: the regional population projections of the Central Bureau of Statistics of Norway: current procedure and plans for the future, 1974. Oslo, 1974. pp. 25. bibliog. (Norway. Statistiske Centralbyrå. Artikler. Nr. 62)

SØRENSEN (KNUT Ø.) Statistisk Sentralbyrås befolkningsprognosemodell ved de regionale framskrivinger, 1975...: the population projection model of the Central Bureau of Statistics of Norway in the regional projections, 1975. Oslo, 1975. pp. 48. (Norway. Statistiske Centralbyrå. Artikler. 80)

NORWAY. Statistiske Centralbyrå. 1976. Framskriving av folkemengden, 1975-2000: regionale tall, etc. Oslo, 1976. pp. 185. bibliog. (Norges Offisielle Statistikk. Rekke A. 762)

— Singapore.

SAW (SWEE HOCK) Population projections for Singapore, 1970-2070. Singapore, National Statistical Commission, 1974. fo. 15.

— United Kingdom.

U.K. Office of Population Censuses and Surveys. Population estimates: the Registrar General's estimates of the population of regions and local government areas of England and Wales by sex and age. a., 1974/1975- London.

U.K. Office of Population Censuses and Surveys. Variant population projections: population projections by sex and age, with varying fertility assumptions, for Great Britain. a., 1974/2011- London.

GILJE (EIVIND K.) and HOLLIS (JOHN) Writer on Population. Demographic projections for Greater London and the London boroughs, 1974. London, [1975]. pp. 254. bibliog. (London. Greater London Council. Research Memoranda. 455)

THOMPSON (RICHARD) of the Greater London Council and PLANK (DAVID) Demographic projections for Greater London and the London boroughs, 1974: a brief commentary for London borough social services departments. London, [1975]. pp. 30. (London. Greater London Council. Research Memoranda. 463)

HOLLIS (JOHN) Writer on Population. Demographic projections for the counties of south east England, 1975. London, 1976. pp. 165. bibliog. (London. Greater London Council. Research Memoranda. 482)

— United States.

PITTENGER (DONALD B.) Projecting state and local populations. Cambridge, Mass., [1976]. pp. 246. bibliog.

POPULATION GENETICS.

EUGENICS SOCIETY. Annual Symposium, 10th, 1973. Population and the new biology: proceedings...; edited by Bernard Benjamin [and others]. London, 1974. pp. 187. bibliogs.

POPULATION POLICY.

IN search of population policy: views from the developing world: a report on five regional seminars conducted in 1973 by Office of the Foreign Secretary, Commission on International Relations, National Academy of Sciences-National Research Council and cosponsoring institutions in developing countries. Washington, D.C., 1974. pp. 109.

COMPARATIVE policy analysis: the study of population policy determinants in developing countries; [papers of a workshop sponsored by Battelle Population Study Center]; edited by R. Kenneth Godwin. Lexington, Mass., [1975]. pp. 333. bibliog.

INTERNATIONAL CONGRESS OF ANTHROPOLOGICAL AND ETHNOLOGICAL SCIENCES. 9th Congress, 1973. Population and social organization: [papers from the Congress]; editor Moni Nag. The Hague, [1975]. pp. 367. bibliogs.

LEE (LUKE TSUNG-CHOU) Legal implications of the world population plan of action. Medford, Mass., 1975. pp. 375-417. (Tufts University. Fletcher School of Law and Diplomacy. Law and Population Monograph Series. No. 28) (Reprinted from Journal of International Law and Economics, vol. 9, no. 3)

POLICY sciences and population; edited by Warren F. Ilchman [and others]. Lexington, Mass., [1975]. pp. 305.

ROBINSON (WARREN C.) ed. Population and development planning. New York, [1975]. pp. 263.

— Mathematical models.

POPULATION, public policy, and economic development; edited by Michael C. Keeley. New York, 1976. pp. 259. bibliog.

POPULATION RESEARCH.

UNITED NATIONS. Economic and Social Commission for Asia and the Pacific. Asian Population Studies Series. New York, 1966 in progress.

POPULATION TRANSFERS.

— Germans.

MERKER (PAUL) Die nächsten Schritte zur Lösung des Umsiedlerproblems; herausgegeben vom Zentralsekretariat der Sozialistischen Einheitspartei Deutschlands. Berlin, [1947]. pp. 32.

POPULISM IN BRAZIL.

IANNI (OCTAVIO) Crisis in Brazil; translated by Phyllis B. Eveleth. New York, 1970. pp. 244. bibliog.

POPULISM IN LATIN AMERICA.

IANNI (OCTAVIO) La formacion del Estado populista en America Latina. Mexico, 1975. pp. 177.

POPULISM IN MEXICO.

CORDOVA (ARNALDO) La ideologia de la Revolucion Mexicana: la formacion del nuevo regimen. Mexico, 1973 repr. 1974. pp. 508.

POPULISM IN POLAND.

NARKIEWICZ (OLGA A.) The green flag: Polish populist politics, 1867-1970. London, 1976. pp. 314. bibliog.

POPULISM IN RUSSIA.

BAZANOV (VASILII GRIGOR'EVICH) Russkie revoliutsionnye demokraty i narodoznanie. Leningrad, 1974. pp. 558.

REVOLIUTSIONNO-osvoboditel'noe dvizhenie v XIX-XX vv. v Povolzh'e i Priural'e. Kazan', 1974. pp. 115.

OWEN (RICHARD CHARLES) The revolutionary career of M.A. Natanson, 1868-1906. 1975. fo. 361. bibliog. Typescript. Ph.D.(London) thesis: unpublished. This thesis is the property of London University and may not be removed from the Library.

POPULISM IN THE ARGENTINE REPUBLIC.

El POPULISMO en la Argentina; (Jose Isaacson, coordinator). Buenos Aires, [1974]. pp. 213.

POPULISM IN THE UKRAINE.

VOLOSHCHENKO (AZA KYRYLIVNA) Narysy z istoriï suspil'no-politychnoho rukhu na Ukraïni v 70-kh - na pochatku 80-kh rokiv XIX st. Kyïv, 1974. pp. 222.

POPULISM IN THE UNITED STATES.

ARGERSINGER (PETER H.) Populism and politics: William Alfred Peffer and the People's Party. Lexington, Ky., [1974]. pp. 337.

HART (ROGER L.) Redeemers, Bourbons and Populists: Tennessee, 1870-1896. Baton Rouge, La., [1975]. pp. 290. bibliog.

McMATH (ROBERT C.) Populist vanguard: a history of the southern Farmers' Alliance. Chapel Hill, N.C., [1975].pp. 221. bibliog.

YOUNGDALE (JAMES M.) Populism: a psychohistorical perspective. Port Washington, N.Y., 1975. pp. 220. bibliog.

PORT ANTONIO, JAMAICA

— Social conditions.

SOCIAL problems in a small Jamaican town, [by] Curtis C. Roseman [and others]. Urbana, 1973. pp. 82. bibliog. (Illinois University. Department of Geography. Occasional Publications. No. 6)

PORT MORESBY

— Social conditions.

REW (ALAN) Social images and process in urban New Guinea: a study of Port Moresby. St. Paul, [1974]. pp. 262. bibliog. (American Ethnological Society. Monographs. 57)

PORTSMOUTH

— Maps.

PORTSMOUTH POLYTECHNIC. Department of Geography. Atlas of Portsmouth. Portsmouth, [1975]. 1 vol. (unpaged).

— Social policy.

HALL (DEREK) Residents' concern for community problems. Portsmouth, 1975. fo. 10. (Social Services Research and Intelligence Unit [Portsmouth]. Information Sheets. No 24)

PORTSMOUTH, TREATY OF, 1905.

TRANI (EUGENE P.) The Treaty of Portsmouth: an adventure in American diplomacy. Lexington, Ky., [1969]. pp. 194. bibliog.

PORTUGAL

— Armed forces — Political activity.

ALVES (MARCIO MOREIRA) Les soldats socialistes du Portugal. [Paris, 1975]. pp. 239. bibliog.

— Colonies.

ALMEIDA (ANIBAL) ed. Sobre o ultramar: fascismo e guerra colonial; documento publicado em 1969, "ja a boca das urnas", por intermedio da Comissão Democratica Eleitoral de Coimbra. Coimbra, 1974. pp. 139.

— Foreign relations — Asia, Southeast.

PFISTER (JAMES W.) The compulsion to war: a quantitative exploration of remote international relations. Beverly Hills, [1974]. pp. 82. bibliog.

— — Germany, Eastern.

SOLIDARITY with Portugal! : end imperialist interference!. [Berlin, 1975]. pp. 15.

— History — 1974, Revolution.

FIELDS (RONA M.) The Portuguese revolution and the Armed Forces Movement. New York, [1976]. pp. 288.

— Industries.

ALMEIDA (MARIA HENRIQUETA DE) Factores determinantes das diferenciações salariais inter- industrias. Lisboa, 1974. pp. 77. (Portugal. Ministerio do Trabalho. Gabinete de Planeamento. Serie Estudos. 21) With abstracts in English, French and German.

PORTUGAL. Instituto Nacional de Estadistica. Serviços Centrais. Boletim mensal das estatisticas industriais: continente e ilhas adjacentes. m., 1976 (ano.1, no. 1/2)- Lisboa. [In Portuguese and French].

PORTUGAL(Cont.)

— Politics and government.

FRENTE PORTUGAL LIVRE. Declaracão, programa e estatutos da Frente Portugal Livre: liberdade, justiça, paz, revoluçao. [Paris, 1970]. pp. 11.

FRENTE PORTUGAL LIVRE. Déclaration, programme du Front Portugal Libre: liberté, justice, paix, révolution, etc. Paris, [1970?]. 1 pamphlet (unpaged).

RIO (MANUEL) pseud. [i.e. Manuel Coelho da SILVA] Message du Portugal: récit sur quarante-trois ans de fascisme et de colonialisme portugais, etc. [Paris], 1971. pp. 63.

ALVES (MARCIO MOREIRA) Les soldats socialistes du Portugal. [Paris, 1975]. pp. 239. *bibliog.*

HARSGOR (MIKHAËL) Naissance d'un nouveau Portugal. Paris, 1975. pp. 237. *bibliog.*

OSORIO (JOSE EDUARDO SANCHES) El engaño del 25 de abril en Portugal. Madrid, 1975. pp. 175.

SOLIDARITY with Portugal! : end imperialist interference!. [Berlin, 1975]. pp. 15.

SUNDAY TIMES. Insight Team. Insight on Portugal: the year of the captains. London, 1975. pp. 273.

WISE (AUDREY) Eyewitness in revolutionary Portugal. Nottingham, 1975. pp. 72.

FIELDS (RONA M.) The Portuguese revolution and the Armed Forces Movement. New York, [1976]. pp. 288.

POSITIVISM.

COMTE (ISIDORE AUGUSTE MARIE FRANÇOIS XAVIER) Philosophie première: cours de philosophie positive, leçons 1 à 45; présentation et notes par Michel Serres [and others]. Paris, [1975]. pp. 882. *Originally published 1830-1835.*

COMTE (ISIDORE AUGUSTE MARIE FRANÇOIS XAVIER) Physique sociale: cours de philosophie positive, leçons 46 à 60; présentation et notes par Jean-Paul Enthoven. Paris, 1975. pp. 803. *Originally published 1839-1842.*

LAFFITTE (PIERRE) Cours de philosophie première. Paris, 1889-94. 2 vols.

COMTE (ISIDORE AUGUSTE MARIE FRANÇOIS XAVIER) Auguste Comte and positivism: the essential writings; edited and with an introduction by Gertrud Lenzer. New York, 1975. pp. 505. *bibliog.*

NUÑEZ RUIZ (DIEGO) La mentalidad positiva en España: desarrollo y crisis. Madrid, [1975]. pp. 278.

CARVER (MARCELLA M.) A positivist life: a personal memoir of my father, William Knight, 1845-1901. London, 1976. pp. 78.

POSTAL SERVICE

— France.

FRANCE. Commission des Transmissions. 1971. Préparation du VIe Plan: rapport. Paris, 1971. pp. 195.

— Germany — Employees.

KLEEMANN (KURT) Die Sozialpolitik der Reichs-Post- und Telegraphenverwaltung gegenüber ihren Beamten, Unterbeamten und Arbeitern. Jena, 1914. pp. 253. *bibliog.* *(Jena. Universität. Staatswissenschaftliches Seminar. Abhandlungen. 14. Band, 1. Heft)*

— Russia.

MEDVEDEV (ZHORES ALEKSANDROVICH) Secrecy of correspondence is guaranteed by law. Nottingham, [1975]. pp. 180. *(Medvedev Papers. vol. 2)*

— Sierra Leone.

SIERRA LEONE. Commission appointed to inquire into the Activities of the Posts and Telecommunications Department from 1st January, 1961. 1972. Report...and the government statement thereon; [Percy R. Davies, Commissioner]. [Freetown?, 1972]. pp. 85.

— United Kingdom.

ASHURST (WILLIAM HENRY) of New Bridge Street, Blackfriars. Facts and reasons in support of Mr. Rowland Hill's plan for a universal penny postage. London, Hooper, 1838. pp. viii, 95.

— — Rates.

POST OFFICE USERS' NATIONAL COUNCIL. Report...on the Post Office's proposed increased postal tariffs. London, 1970. pp. 35.

POST OFFICE USERS' NATIONAL COUNCIL. Report...on the Post Office proposals for increased postal, telecommunications and Giro and remittance service charges. London, 1975. pp. 64. *(Reports. No. 12)*

POST OFFICE USERS' NATIONAL COUNCIL. Report on Post Office proposals for increased postal charges. London, 1976. pp. 31. *(Reports. No. 13)*

— United States.

MYERS (ROBERT JOHN) The coming collapse of the Post Office. Englewood Cliffs, [1975]. pp. 182.

POTASH INDUSTRY AND TRADE

— United Kingdom.

BRYAN (Sir ANDREW MEIKLE) Planning permission and the place of the public inquiry in the development of mineral resources in Britain: problems of potash extraction in Yorkshire. [London], 1971. pp. 63-72,129-138. *(Reprinted from Transactions of the Institute of Mining and Metallurgy. Section A, vol.80,1971)*

POTATOES

— France.

FRANCE. Ministère de l'Agriculture. Statistique agricole. Supplément. Série Etudes. No. 12. Enquête sur la production de pommes de terre de conservation en 1965; [rédigée par Philippe Fournier]. Paris, 1966. pp. 28.

POTTERS

— Denmark.

THYGESEN (ERIK) ed. Erfaringer fra en arbejdskamp: plattekonflikten på den kgl. Porcelainsfabrik, 1972-73. København, [1974]. pp. 102. *bibliog.*

— India.

INDIA. Labour Bureau. 1975. Report on survey of labour conditions in manufacture of pottery, china and earthenware factories in India, 1971. [Delhi, 1975]. pp. 98.

POUGET (EMILE).

VILLARD (RENE) Le syndicalisme révolutionnaire; biographie d'Emile Pouget, par Renée Lamberet. Toulouse, [1967]. pp. 48. *bibliog. (Association Internationale des Travailleurs [Syndicalist]. Des Faits, des Idées, des Hommes)*

POULTRY

— Australia.

AUSTRALIA. Chicken Meat Research Committee. Annual report. a., 1969/70 (1st)- Canberra.

POULTRY RESEARCH

— United States.

PETERSON (WILLIS L.) Returns to poultry research in the United States. 1966. pp. 88. *bibliog.* *Ph.D.(Chicago) thesis: unpublished. Microfilm of typescript: 1 reel (1st item on it).*

POUND (EZRA).

HEYMANN (C. DAVID) Ezra Pound: the last rower: a political profile. London, 1976. pp. 372.

POUND, BRITISH.

SIEVEKING (KARL) Geschichte des Pfund Sterlings. n.d. (142 sheets). *Microfilm of manuscript: 1 reel. No part of the contents may be published without the consent of the Staatsarchiv Hamburg.*

POUND STERLING.

See POUND, BRITISH.

POVERTY.

HAMILTON (DAVID BOYCE) A primer on the economics of poverty. New York, [1968]. pp. xvii, 133. *bibliog.*

CAPITANI (OVIDIO) ed. La concezione della povertà nel Medioevo: antologia di scritti. Bologna, [1974]. pp. 355.

ELLIOTT (CHARLES) and MORSIER (FRANÇOISE DE) Patterns of poverty in the Third World: a study of social and economic stratification. New York, 1975. pp. 416.

INTERNATIONAL BANK FOR RECONSTRUCTION AND DEVELOPMENT. 1975. The assault on world poverty: problems of rural development, education and health; with a preface by Robert S. McNamara. Baltimore, [1975]. pp. 425.

WILBER (GEORGE LEWIN) ed. Poverty: a new perspective. Lexington, Ky., [1975]. pp. 197. *bibliog.*

COLE (JOHN) Journalist. The poor of the earth. London, 1976. pp. 144.

— Psychological aspects.

BAUMAN (GERALD) and GRUNES (RUTH) Psychiatric rehabilitation in the ghetto: an educational approach. Lexington, Mass., [1974]. pp. 177. *bibliog.*

POWER (SOCIAL SCIENCES).

COHEN (ABNER) Two-dimensional man: an essay on the anthropology of power and symbolism in complex society. London, 1974. pp. 156. *bibliog.*

COX (KEVIN R.) and others, eds. Locational approaches to power and conflict. New York, [1974]. pp. 339. *bibliogs.*

WIRT (FREDERICK M.) Power in the city: decision making in San Francisco. Berkeley, [1974]. pp. 417.

BILLY (JACQUES) Les technocrates. 3rd ed. Paris, 1975. pp. 128. *bibliog.*

BIRNBAUM (PIERRE) La fin du politique. Paris, [1975]. pp. 285. *bibliog.*

BIRNBAUM (PIERRE) Le pouvoir politique: (textes et commentaires). Paris, [1975]. pp. 241.

CLEGG (STEWART) Power, rule and domination: a critical and empirical understanding of power in sociological theory and organizational life. London, 1975. pp. 208. *bibliog.*

CZARTORYSKI (ANDREW) Education for power. London, 1975. pp. 198.

DOMHOFF (G. WILLIAM) ed. New directions in power structure research. Eugene, Ore., 1975. pp. 264. *(Insurgent Sociologist, The. vol. 5, no.3)*

ELLIOTT (RUTH HELEN) A case study of management and worker attitudes to managerial authority and prerogatives. 1975. fo. 366. *Typescript. Ph.D. (London) thesis: unpublished. This thesis is the property of London University and may not be removed from the Library.*

MICHELSEN TERRY (CARLOS JOSE) A theoretical and empirical study of perceptions of relative power among the staff of some Mexican industrial organizations; [Ph.D. (London) thesis]. 1975. 1 vol. (various foliations). *Typescript: unpublished. This thesis is the property of London University and may not be removed from the Library.*

POWER in families; edited by Ronald E. Cromwell and David H. Olson. New York, [1975]. pp. 264. *bibliog. Based on a symposium held in June 1973 at the University of Missouri, Kansas City and sponsored by its Family Study Center.*

ACQUAVIVA (SABINO SAMELE) and SANTUCCIO (MARIO) Social structure in Italy: crisis of a system;...translated from the Italian by Colin Hamer. London, 1976. pp. 236. *bibliog.*

PORTES (ALEJANDRO) and WALTON (JOHN) Urban Latin America: the political condition from above and below. Austin, Texas, [1976]. pp. 217. *bibliog.*

POWER and political theory: some European perspectives; edited by Brian Barry. London, [1976]. pp. 296. *bibliog. Includes papers from a workshop sponsored by the European Consortium for Political Research, and held at the University of Strasbourg, 1974.*

PUTNAM (ROBERT D.) The comparative study of political elites. Englewood Cliffs, [1976]. pp. 246. *bibliog.*

POWER RESOURCES.

LOWITSCH (ALFRED) Energie, Planwirtschaft und Sozialismus. Jena, [1929]. pp. 77. *(Urania: kulturpolitische Monatshefte über Natur und Gesellschaft. Jahrgang 1928/29. Buchbeigaben. 4)*

COAL AND ENERGY QUARTERLY; ([pd. by] NCB [National Coal Board, U.K.). q., summer 1974 (no.1)- London.

COOPERATIVE approaches to world energy problems: a tripartite report by...Guy de Carmoy [and others]. Washington, [1974]. pp. 51.

MADDOX (JOHN) Beyond the energy crisis. London, 1975. pp. 208. *bibliog.*

ROBINSON (COLIN) Energy depletion and the economics of OPEC. London, 1975. pp. 32. *(Henley Centre for Forecasting. Occasional Papers. No.1)*

RUEDISILI (LON C.) and FIREBAUGH (MORRIS W.) eds. Perspectives on energy: issues, ideas and environmental dilemmas. New York, 1975. pp. 527. *bibliogs.*

VAN TASSEL (ALFRED J.) ed. The environmental price of energy. Lexington, Mass., [1975]. pp. 326. *bibliogs.*

WILLRICH (MASON) and others. Energy and world politics. New York, ?1975!. PP. 234 BIBLIOG.

WORLD SYMPOSIUM ON ENERGY AND RAW MATERIALS, 1ST., PARIS, 1974. Summary of the proceedings. New York, [1975]. pp. 116.

CHOUCRI (NAZLI) and FERRARO (VINCENT) International politics of energy interdependence: the case of petroleum. Lexington, Mass., [1976]. pp. 250. *bibliog.*

HAGEL (JOHN) Alternative energy strategies: constraints and opportunities. New York, [1976]. pp. 186. *bibliog.*

INTERNATIONAL CONFERENCE ON REGIONAL SCIENCE, ENERGY AND ENVIRONMENT, LOUVAIN, 1975. Energy, regional science and public policy: proceedings of the... Conference...[vol.] 1...; edited by M. Chatterji and P. Van Rompuy. Berlin, 1976. pp. 316. *bibliogs.*

McMULLAN (JOHN T.) and others. Energy resources and supply. London, [1976]. pp. 508. *bibliogs.*

— Congresses.

La CRISI energetica: atti del convegno promosso da Politica ed Economia e dal Centro Documentazione e Ricerche per la Lombardia, Milano, 10 dicembre 1973. [Roma, 1974]. pp. 128. *(Politica ed Economia. Quaderni. 11)*

— Research — New Zealand.

NEW ZEALAND. Department of Scientific and Industrial Research. 1974. The role of research and development in New Zealand's energy economy. [Wellington?], 1974. pp. 78.

— Europe, Eastern.

DEUTSCHES INSTITUT FÜR WIRTSCHAFTSFORSCHUNG. Sonderhefte. [Neue Folge]. 104. Bedeutung und Möglichkeiten des Ost-West-Handels mit Energierohstoffen; ([by] Jochen Bethkenhagen). Berlin, 1975. pp. 302. *bibliog.*

— European Economic Community countries.

EUROPEAN COMMUNITIES. Commission. 1974. Energy for Europe: research and development; communication of the Commission transmitted to the Council on 5 April, 1974. [Brussels], 1974. pp. 16. *Bulletin of the European Communities. Supplements. ?1974/5!)*

INTERNATIONAL COLLOQUIUM ON ENERGY POLICY PLANNING IN THE EUROPEAN COMMUNITIES, TILBURG, 1974. Energy in the European Communities : [papers from the colloquium]; edited by Frans A.M. Alting von Geusau, with contributions from M.A. Adelman [and others]. Leyden, 1975. pp. 213. *(John F. Kennedy Institute. Center for International Studies. Publications. Nr. 9)*

LIEBER (ROBERT J.) Oil and the Middle East war: Europe in the energy crisis. Cambridge, Mass., [1976]. pp. 75. *(Harvard University. Center for International Affairs. Harvard Studies in International Affairs. No. 35)*

— France.

FRANCE. Commission de l'Energie. 1976. Rapport...: préparation du 7e Plan. Paris, 1976. pp. 79.

— Germany.

DEUTSCHES INSTITUT FÜR WIRTSCHAFTSFORSCHUNG. Sonderhefte. [Neue Folge]. 113. Sicherheits-, Preis- und Umweltaspekte der Energieversorgung; ([by] Urs Dolinski und Hans-Joachim Ziesing). Berlin, 1976. pp. 303.

— India.

HENDERSON (PATRICK DAVID) India: the energy sector. Delhi, International Bank for Reconstruction and Development, 1975. pp. 191.

— Poland.

WYBRANE problemy rozwoju energetyki w Polsce do roku 2000. Warszawa, 1975. pp. 80. *(Polska Akademia Nauk. Komitet Przestrzennego Zagospodarowania Kraju. Studia. t.53) With Russian and English summaries.*

— Russia.

RUSSELL (JEREMY) Energy as a factor in Soviet foreign policy. Farnborough, Hants., [1976]. pp. 241. *bibliog.*

— United Kingdom.

COAL AND ENERGY QUARTERLY; ([pd. by] NCB [National Coal Board, U.K.). q., summer 1974 (no.1)- London.

U.K. Department of Energy. 1975- . Fact sheets. [London, 1975 in progress].

CHAPMAN (PETER) Fuel's paradise; energy options for Britain. Harmondsworth, 1975. pp. 236. *bibliog.*

CONFEDERATION OF BRITISH INDUSTRY. A statistical survey of industrial fuel and energy use. London, 1975. pp. 36.

ENERGY options in the United Kingdom: a symposium [held in London in 1975]; edited by Simon Caradoc Evans. London, 1975. pp. 128.

— — Statistics.

DIGEST OF UNITED KINGDOM ENERGY STATISTICS; ([pd. by] Department of Energy [U.K.]). [title varies]. 1948/1949; a., 1950- London. *Previous issues are included in the file of British Parliamentary Papers.*

ENERGY TRENDS: a statistical bulletin;...prepared by the Economics and Statistics Division of the Department of Energy [U.K.]. m., Ag 1974 [no.1]- London.

— United States.

NATIONAL ACADEMY OF SCIENCES. Academy Forum, 2nd, 1974. Energy: future alternatives and risks. Cambridge, Mass., [1974]. pp. 227.

CORNELL AGRICULTURAL WASTE MANAGEMENT CONFERENCE, 1975. Energy, agriculture and waste management...; edited by William J. Jewell. Ann Arbor, [1975]. pp. 540. *Proceedings of the conference sponsored by Cornell University, New York State College of Agriculture and Life Sciences and the National Science Foundation.*

GORDON (RICHARD L.) U.S. coal and the electric power industry. [Baltimore], [1975]. pp. 213. *bibliog.*

GRAY (JOHN E.) Energy policy: industry perspectives; (a report to the Energy Policy Project of the Ford Foundation). Cambridge, Mass., 1975. pp. 133.

RICHARDSON (HARRY WARD) Economic aspects of the energy crisis. Lexington, [1975]. pp. 233. *bibliog.*

RUEDISILI (LON C.) and FIREBAUGH (MORRIS W.) eds. Perspectives on energy: issues, ideas and environmental dilemmas. New York, 1975. pp. 527. *bibliogs.*

HAGEL (JOHN) Alternative energy strategies: constraints and opportunities. New York, [1976]. pp. 186. *bibliog.*

POZNAN

— History.

DZIESIĘĆ wieków Poznania. Poznań, 1956. 3 vols.

— Social history.

PARADOWSKA (MARIA) Bambrzy: mieszkańcy dawnych wsi miasta Poznania. Warszawa, 1975. pp. 177. *(Poznań. Urząd Miasta. Wydział Kultury. Biblioteka Kroniki Miasta Poznania)*

POZNAN (PROVINCE)

— History.

PAPROCKI (FRANCISZEK) Wielkie Księstwo Poznańskie w okresie rządów Flottwella, 1830-1841. Poznań, 1970. pp. 473. *bibliog (Poznań. Uniwersytet. Wydział Filozoficzno-Historyczny. Seria Historia. Nr.33) With German summary.*

PRAGIER (ADAM).

PRAGIER (ADAM) Czas teraźniejszy. Londyn, 1975. pp. 240.

PRAGMATICS.

SAUER (ERNST FRIEDRICH) Pragmatik: bessere Politik durch besseres Völkerrecht. Bonn, 1974. pp. 170. *bibliog.*

PRAIRIES.

LONGLEY (RICHMOND W.) The climate of the prairie provinces. Ottawa, Information Canada, 1972. pp. 79. *bibliog. (Climatological Studies. No. 13)*

PREGNANCY.

LEE (LUKE TSUNG-CHOU) and PAXMAN (JOHN M.) Pregnancy and abortion in adolescence: a comparative legal survey and proposals for reform. Medford, Mass., 1975. pp. 48. *(Tufts University. Fletcher School of Law and Diplomacy. Law and Population Monograph Series. No. 26) Reprinted from Columbia Human Rights Law Review, vol. 6, no. 2.*

— Nutritional aspects.

FAMINE and human development: the Dutch hunger winter of 1944- 1945; [by] Zena Stein [and others]. New York, 1975. pp. 284. *bibliog.*

PRENATAL INFLUENCES.

PREJUDICES AND ANTIPATHIES.
See ANTIPATHIES AND PREJUDICES.
PRENATAL INFLUENCES.

FAMINE and human development: the Dutch hunger winter of 1944- 1945; [by] Zena Stein [and others]. New York, 1975. pp. 284. *bibliog.*

PRESS
— America, Latin — Bibliography.

GARDNER (MARY A.) The press of Latin America: a tentative and selected bibliography in Spanish and Portuguese. Austin, 1973. pp. 34. *(Texas University. Institute of Latin American Studies. Guides and Bibliographies Series. No. 4)*

— Bulgaria — Statistics.

BULGARIA. Tsentralno Statistichesko Upravlenie. 1964. Knigoizdavane i pechat v Narodna Republika Bulgariia: statisticheski sbornik, 1962-1963. Sofiia, 1964. pp. 65,[xxxvi]. *With Russian and French captions.*

— Chile.

MATTELART (ARMAND) and others. La ideologia de la dominacion en una sociedad dependiente: la respuesta ideologica de la clase dominante chilena al reformismo. Buenos Aires, 1970. pp. 319. *bibliog.*

— France.

BORIS (CLAUDE) Les tigres de papier: crise de la presse et autocritique du journalisme. Paris, [1975]. pp. 315.

CABANIS (ANDRE) La presse sous le Consulat et l'Empire, 1799-1814. Paris, 1975. pp. 354. *bibliog. (Société des Etudes Robespierristes. Bibliothèque d'Histoire Révolutionnaire. 3e Série. No. 16)*

FRANCE. French Embassy, London. Service de Presse et d'Information. 1975. The French press. London, 1975. pp. 16. *bibliog. (France: facts, figures. A/109/7/75)*

GRUBE (JOCHEN) Bismarcks Politik in Europa und Ubersee: seine "Annäherung" an Frankreich im Urteil der Pariser Presse, 1883-1885. Bern, 1975. pp. 277. *bibliog.*

— Ghana.

JONES-QUARTEY (K.A.B.) A summary history of the Ghana press, 1822-1960. [Accra, Ghana Information Services Department, 1974]. pp. 68. *bibliog.*

— Poland.

CIEŚLAK (TADEUSZ) Z dziejów prasy polskiej na Pomorzu Gdańskim w okresie zaboru pruskiego. Gdańsk, 1964. pp. 185. *bibliog. (Gdańsk. Gdańskie Towarzystwo Naukowe. Wydział 1 Nauk Społecznych i Humanistycznych. Seria Monografii. Nr.19) With Russian and English summaries.*

OLSZAŃSKI (KAZIMIERZ) Prasa galicyjska wobec powstania styczniowego. Wrocław, 1975. pp. 254. *(Polska Akademia Nauk. Oddział w Krakowie. Komisja Nauk Historycznych. Prace. Nr.35) With Russian and English summaries.*

— Russia — Kirghizia.

SORONBAEV (KERIM) Pechat' Sovetskogo Kirgizstana. Frunze, 1970. pp. 36.

— — Tajikistan — Statistics.

TAJIKISTAN. Knizhnaia Palata. 1971. Pechat' Tadzhikskoi SSR, 1964-1968: statisticheskie materialy. Dushanbe, 1971. pp. 87.

— — Ukraine.

SYDORENKO (VALENTYNA PAVLIVNA) Presa iak dzherelo z istoriï robitnychoho klasu Ukraïny v period sotsialistychnoho budivnytstva, 1921-1941 rr. Kyïv, 1975. pp. 107.

— — — Statistics.

UKRAINE. Knizhnaia Palata. 1974. Presa Ukraïns'koï RSR, 1918-1973: naukovo-statystychnyi dovidnyk. Kharkiv, 1974. pp. 215.

— — White Russia — Statistics.

WHITE RUSSIA. Knizhnaia Palata. 1972. Druk Belaruskai SSR, 1966-1970: statystychnyia materyialy; skladal'nik Rabushka L.P. Minsk, 1972. pp. 128.

— Spain.

HERAS FEBRERO (JESUS DE LAS) and VILLARIN GARCIA (JUAN) eds. El año Arias: diario politico español 1974. Madrid, 1975. pp. 893.

PRESS, CATHOLIC
— Spain.

SAEZ ALBA (A.) La otra "Cosa Nostra": la Asociacion Catolica Nacional de Propagandistas y el caso de 'El Correo' de Andalucia. Paris, [1974]. pp. 325.

PRESS, LABOUR
— Germany.

SCHMOLLINGER (HORST W.) and STOESS (RICHARD) Die Parteien und die Presse der Parteien und Gewerkschaften in der Bundesrepublik Deutschland, 1945-1974: Materialien zur Parteien- und Gewerkschaftsforschung. München, 1975. pp. 480. *bibliogs. (Berlin. Freie Universität. Zentralinstitut für Sozialwissenschaftliche Forschung. Berichte und Materialien. Band 2)*

PRESS AND POLITICS
— Germany.

KESSELTREIBEN gegen wen?: die Legende einer Kampagne gegen Jochen Steffen; eine Dokumentation; herausgegeben von der Axel Springer Verlag AG, Abteilung Information. Berlin, [1971]. pp. 47.

SCHMOLLINGER (HORST W.) and STOESS (RICHARD) Die Parteien und die Presse der Parteien und Gewerkschaften in der Bundesrepublik Deutschland, 1945-1974: Materialien zur Parteien- und Gewerkschaftsforschung. München, 1975. pp. 480. *bibliogs. (Berlin. Freie Universität. Zentralinstitut für Sozialwissenschaftliche Forschung. Berichte und Materialien. Band 2)*

BOSCH (MICHAEL) Liberale Presse in der Krise: die Innenpolitik der Jahre 1930 bis 1933 im Spiegel des "Berliner Tageblatts", der "Frankfurter Zeitung" und der "Vossischen Zeitung". Bern, 1976. pp. 343. *bibliog.*

— — Berlin.

ADOMATIS (HANS JOACHIM) Von Berlin aus gesehen: die Springer-Partei. Wuppertal, 1975. pp. 102.

— Switzerland.

JOOS (EDUARD) Parteien und Presse im Kanton Schaffhausen. Schaffhausen, 1975. pp. 623. *bibliog. 3 tables in end pocket.*

— United Kingdom.

BREWER (JOHN) Ph.D. Party ideology and popular politics at the accession of George III. Cambridge, 1976. pp. 382. *bibliog.*

MURPHY (DAVID) The silent watchdog: the press in local politics. London, 1976. pp. 186. *bibliog.*

PRESS LAW.

STĘPIŃSKA (KRYSTYNA) Sprostowanie prasowe w świetle prawa. Warszawa, 1964. pp. 114. *bibliog.*

— France.

KING (JEROME B.) Law v. order: legal process and free speech in contemporary France. Hamden, Conn., 1975. pp. 206. *bibliog.*

— United Kingdom.

O'MALLEY (PATRICK TERENCE) The politics of defamation: the state, press interests and English libel law. [1976]. fo. 346. *bibliog.* Typescript. *Ph.D. (London) thesis: unpublished. This thesis is the property of London University and may not be removed from the Library.*

PRESSURE GROUPS
— Canada.

PRESSURE group behaviour in Canadian politics; edited by A. Paul Pross. [Scarborough, Ont., 1975]. pp. 196. *bibliog.*

— Norway.

KVAVIK (ROBERT B.) Interest groups in Norwegian politics. Oslo, [1976]. pp. 206. *bibliog.*

— Switzerland.

KOCHER (GERHARD) Verbandseinfluss auf die Gesetzgebung: Aerzteverbindung, Krankenkassenverbände und die Teilrevision 1964 des Kranken- und Unfallversicherungsgesetzes. 2nd ed. Bern, 1972. pp. 268. *bibliog. (Bern. Universität. Forschungszentrum für Schweizerische Politik. Helvetia Politica. Series B. vol. 1)*

— United Kingdom.

ALLAN (GORDON FRANCIS) Pressure groups and the British political process: a case study: the 'Save the Argylls' campaign; [Ph.D. (London) thesis] . 1974. fo. 598. *bibliog.* Typescript: *unpublished. This thesis is the property of London University and may not be removed from the Library.*

COMMUNITY politics; edited by Peter Hain. London, 1976. pp. 226.

— — Directories.

SHIPLEY (PETER) ed. The Guardian directory of pressure groups and representative associations; research by Chris Bazlinton and Anne Cowen, etc. London, 1976. pp. 265.

— — Wales.

HALL (IRENE M.) Community action versus pollution: a study of a residents' group in a Welsh urban area. Cardiff, 1976. pp. 130. *(Wales. University. Board of Celtic Studies. Social Science Monographs. No. 2)*

— United States.

FIORINA (MORRIS P.) Representatives, roll calls, and constituencies. Lexington, Mass., [1974]. pp. 143. *bibliog.*

FELICETTI (DANIEL A.) Mental health and retardation politics: the mind lobbies in Congress. New York, 1975. pp. 199. *bibliog.*

McMATH (ROBERT C.) Populist vanguard: a history of the southern Farmers' Alliance. Chapel Hill, N.C., [1975].pp. 221. *bibliog.*

ZURCHER (LOUIS A.) and KIRKPATRICK (ROBERT GEORGE) Citizens for decency: antipornography crusades as status defense. Austin, [1976]. pp. 412. *bibliog.*

PRESTES (LUIS CARLOS).

MACAULAY (NEILL) The Prestes column: revolution in Brazil. New York, 1974. pp. 281.

PRESTIGE.

LUBECKI (PAUL) Interaktion und Berufsprestige: eine empirische Untersuchung zur Bewertung von Berufen. [Erlangen-Nürnberg, 1976]. 1 vol.(various pagings). *bibliog. Inaugural-Dissertation zur Erlangung des akademischen Grades eines Doktors der Wirtschafts- und Sozialwissenschaften der Friedrich-Alexander-Universität Erlangen-Nürnberg.*

PRESTON

— Antiquities.

GEORGE (ANTHONY DAVID) The industrial archaeology of Preston. [Manchester, 1974]. pp. 8.

PRICE INDEXES.

MITTELSTAEDT (AXEL) and others. Unemployment benefits and related payments in seven major countries; Surpluses and deficits in the balance of payments... [by] Erwin Veil; [and] Comparability of consumer prices indices in OECD countries [by] Charlotte Vannereau. [Paris], Organisation for Economic Cooperation and Development, 1975. pp. 56. *(OECD Economic Outlook. Occasional Studies)*

— Mathematical models.

GENBFRG (HANS) World inflation and the small open economy. [Stockholm, 1975]. pp. 97.

— Africa, Central.

UNION DOUANIERE ET ECONOMIQUE DE L'AFRIQUE CENTRALE. Département des Statistiques. 1976. Indices du commerce exterieur des états de l'U.D.E.A.C. sauf le Cameroun, de 1963 à 1971. [Brazzaville], 1976. pp. 108. *(Etudes Statistiques. No. 23)*

— Germany.

ROSTIN (WERNER) Indices of foreign trade prices on base 1970. Stuttgart, 1974. pp. 13. *(Germany (Bundesrepublik). Statistisches Bundesamt. Studies on Statistics. No. 30) Originally published in German in Wirtschaft und Statistik, vol. 6, June 1974.*

— Norway.

BRENNA (SVEIN FREDRIK) Revisjon av indeksene for utenrikshandelen...: revision of indices for foreign trade. Oslo, 1973. pp. 47. *(Norway. Statistiske Centralbyrå. Artikler. Nr.57)* With tables in Norwegian and English.

— Tanzania.

UNITED REPUBLIC OF TANZANIA. Bureau of Statistics. 1974. National consumer price index 1969-1973: basic material, computations and results. Dar es Salaam, 1974. fo. 62.

— United Kingdom.

PRICE INDEX NUMBERS FOR CURRENT COST ACCOUNTING. irreg., Ap 1976 (no.1)- London.

PRICE MAINTENANCE

— Australia.

NIEUWENHUYSEN (JOHN PETER) and OAKLEY (E.E.) Competition in Australian bookselling: resale price maintenance and after. Melbourne, 1975. pp. 82. *bibliog.*

PRICE REGULATION.

ECONOMIST INTELLIGENCE UNIT. Q[uarterly] E[conomic] R[eview] Specials. No. 27. The potential for new commodity cartels: copying OPEC, or improved international agreements?; by Anthony Edwards. London, 1975. pp. 96.

— Communist countries.

ABDEL-FADIL (MAHMOUD) La planification des prix en économie socialiste: essai méthodologique. Paris, 1975. pp. 296. *bibliog. (Paris. Université de Paris I (Panthéon-Sorbonne). Publications. Série Sciences Economiques. 3)*

— Tanzania.

UNITED REPUBLIC OF TANZANIA. Statutes, etc. 1973. The Regulation of Prices Act, 1973. Dar es Salaam, 1973. pp. (22).

— United Kingdom.

U.K. Price Commission. Reports. London, 1974 in progress.

U.K. Department of Prices and Consumer Protection. 1975. Consultative document on amendments to the Price Code. [London, 1975]. pp. (5).

U.K. Price Commission. 1975. Local authorities and the price code. [London, 1975]. 1 pamphlet (unfoliated).

— United States.

KRAFT (JOHN) and ROBERTS (BLAINE) eds. Wage and price controls: the U.S. experiment. New York, 1975. pp. 149.

PRICES.

FRANCE. Centre d'Etude des Revenus et des Coûts. 1973. L'évolution des prix à la consommation en France et à l'étranger de 1955 à fin de 1972. Paris, 1973. pp. 29. *(Documents. No.17)*

MOONITZ (MAURICE) Changing prices and financial reporting. Champaign, Ill., [1974]. pp. 59. *(Lancaster. University. International Centre for Research in Accounting. [ICRA Occasional Papers. No. 3])*

ANDREWS (PHILIP WALTER SAWFORD) and BRUNNER (ELIZABETH) Studies in pricing. London, 1975. pp. 176.

CSIKÓS-NAGY (BÉLA) Socialist price theory and price policy; (translated by Elek Helvey...and István Véges). Budapest, 1975. pp. 371.

GREENHUT (MELVIN LEONARD) and OHTA (HIROSHI) Theory of spatial pricing and market areas. Durham, N.C., 1975. pp. 262.

RONCAGLIA (ALESSANDRO) Sraffa e la teoria dei prezzi. Roma, 1975. pp. 200. *bibliog.*

HIRSHLEIFER (JACK) Price theory and applications. Englewood Cliffs, [1976]. pp. 506.

LIVESEY (F.) Pricing. London, 1976. pp. 170. *bibliogs.*

MARGLIN (STEPHEN ALAN) Value and price in the labour-surplus economy. Oxford, 1976. pp. 252. *bibliog.*

WEBB (MICHAEL G.) Pricing policies for public enterprises. London, 1976. pp. 96. *bibliog.*

— Mathematical models.

EICHHORN (WOLFGANG) Modelle der vertikalen Preisbildung. Meisenheim am Glan, [1973]. pp. 67. *bibliog.*

RUMM (ULRICH) Wirtschaftliches Wachstum, Aussenhandel und Preisniveau. Meisenheim am Glan, [1973]. pp. 135, xi. *bibliog.*

ANDREWS (PHILIP WALTER SAWFORD) and BRUNNER (ELIZABETH) Studies in pricing. London, 1975. pp. 176.

NIKAIDO (HUKUKANE) Monopolistic competition and effective demand. Princeton, 1975. pp. 150. *bibliog.*

BAISCH (HELMUT) Wert, Preis und Allokation: eine Verallgemeinerung des Marxschen Reproduktionsmodells. Meisenheim am Glan, 1976. pp. 318. *bibliog. With English summary.*

MUSSA (MICHAEL) Sticky prices and disequilibrium adjustment in a rational model of the inflationary process. [London], 1976. pp. 28. *bibliog.*

SCHAIK (A.B.T.M. VAN) Reproduction and fixed capital. Tilburg, 1976. pp. 306. *bibliog. (Tilburg. Katholieke Hogeschool. Tilburg Institute of Economics. Tilburg Studies on Economics. 13)*

— Statistics.

INTERNATIONAL LABOUR OFFICE. 1976. Technical guide: descriptions of series published in the Bulletin of Labour Statistics (and the Year Book of Labour Statistics). 5th ed. Geneva, 1976. 2 vols. (in 1)

— Australia.

NIEUWENHUYSEN (JOHN PETER) and NORMAN (NEVILLE R.) Australian competition and prices policy: trade practices, tariffs and prices justification. London, [1976]. pp. 173. *bibliog.*

— Austria.

MARON (ÁDÁM) Consumer prices in Austria and Hungary, 1945-1972: some aspects of price formation, price development and price patterns. [Vienna], 1974. pp. 174. *(Wiener Institut für Internationale Wirtschaftsvergleiche. Forschungsberichte. Nr. 22)*

— Canada.

CANADA. Statistics Canada. Consumer price indexes for regional cities. m., Ag 1975 (1st)- Ottawa. *In English and French.*

CANADA. Statistics Canada. Consumer prices and price indexes. q., Oc/D 1975(1st)- Ottawa. *[In English and French]. File includes Year-end supplemen 1975- .*

— Europe, Eastern — Bibliography.

ROMAN (VIOREL S.) compiler. Auswahlbibliographie zur Preisbildung in der sozialistischen Planwirtschaft. Bremen, [1976]. fo.41.

— France.

FRANCE. Centre d'Etude des Revenus et des Coûts. 1973. L'évolution des prix à la consommation en France et à l'étranger de 1955 à fin de 1972. Paris, 1973. pp. 29. *(Documents. No.17)*

— Germany.

GERMANY (BUNDESREPUBLIK). Statistisches Bundesamt. Umsätze und Beschäftige (Messzahlen). a., 1975- Wiesbaden. *(Gross- und Einzelhandel, Gastgewerbe, Reiseverkehr. Reihe 3.1).*

FREY (HANS DIETER) Auswirkungen von Preissteigerungen auf die Verteilung des Einkommens und des Vermögens. Tübingen, 1975. pp. 428. *bibliog. (Tübingen. Institut für Angewandte Wirtschaftsforschung. Schriftenreihe. Band 28)*

— Hungary.

MARTON (ÁDÁM) Consumer prices in Austria and Hungary, 1945-1972: some aspects of price formation, price development and price patterns. [Vienna], 1974. pp. 174. *(Wiener Institut für Internationale Wirtschaftsvergleiche. Forschungsberichte. Nr. 22)*

— Japan.

JAPAN. Bureau of Statistics. 1974. 1971 national survey of prices. Vols. 10-11. Summary and analysis of retail (and wholesale) price survey(s). [Tokyo, 1974?]. 2 pts. *In Japanese.*

— Korea.

KOREA (REPUBLIC). Bureau of Statistics. Annual report on the price survey. a., 1974(10th)- Seoul.

— Norway.

RINGSTAD (VIDAR) Prisutvikling og prisatferd i 1960-årene: en presentasjon og analyse av nasjonalregnskapets prisdata, 1961-1969: the development and behaviour of prices in the 1960's: presentation and analysis of the price-data of the Norwegian national accounts, 1961-1969. Oslo, 1974. pp. 478. *bibliog. (Norway. Statistiske Centralbyrå. Samfunnsøkonomiske Studier. 23) With English summary.*

— — Mathematical models.

RINGSTAD (VIDAR) PRIM II: en revidert versjon av pris- og intektsmodellen...: PRIM II: a revised version of the price and income model. Oslo, 1972. pp. 43. *(Norway. Statistiske Centralbyrå. Artikler. Nr.44)*

PRICES.(Cont.)

— Russia.

D'IACHENKO (VASILII PETROVICH) Problemy planovogo tsenoobrazovaniia; (raboty, napisannye v 1961-1970 gg.; redaktsionnaia kollegiia P.S. Mstislavskii [and others]). Moskva, 1974. pp. 488. *bibliog.*

ROZHNEVA (LIUDMILA STEPANOVNA) Osobennosti tsenoobrazovaniia na produktsiiu prikladnykh issledovanii i razrabotok. Leningrad, 1974. pp. 120.

BOROZDIN (IURII VLADIMIROVICH) Tsenoobrazovanie i potrebitel'naia stoimost' produktsii. Moskva, 1975. pp. 144.

MALAFEEV (ALEKSEI NIKOLAEVICH) and others, eds. Tsena i khoziaistvennyi raschet v sisteme upravleniia sotsialisticheskoi ekonomikoi. Leningrad, 1975. pp. 200.

MAIZENBERG (LEV IL'ICH) Problemy tsenoobrazovaniia v razvitom sotsialisticheskom obshchestve. Moskva, 1976. pp. 192.

— Sweden.

NYSTRÖM (LENNART) Löner och priser. [Stockholm, 1973]. pp. 64.

— Tasmania.

TASMANIA. Commonwealth Bureau of Statistics. Tasmanian Office. Labour, wages and prices. a., 1973/74- Hobart.

— Underdeveloped areas.

See UNDERDEVELOPED AREAS — Prices.

— United Kingdom.

U.K. Price Commission. Reports. London, 1974 in progress.

— United States — Mathematical models.

CONFERENCE ON THE ANALYSIS OF INFLATION, GEORGETOWN UNIVERSITY, WASHINGTON, D.C., 1974. Analysis of inflation: [papers from the Conference]; edited by Paul H. Earl. Lexington, [1974]. pp. 232. *bibliogs.*

— Yugoslavia.

DAŠIĆ (DAVID) Sistem i politika cena u uslovima socijalističkog samoupravljanja. Beograd, 1974. pp. 209. *bibliog.*

BENDEKOVIĆ (JADRANKO) Politika cijena električne energije u cilju optimalizacije kapaciteta elektroenergetskog sistema. Zagreb, 1975. pp. 232,70. *bibliog.*

PRIME MINISTERS

— Denmark.

KAMPMANN (VIGGO) Seks socialdemokratiske statsministre, skildre af den syvende. [Copenhagen, 1973]. pp. 94.

— Germany.

SEEMANN (KLAUS) Entzaubertes Bundeskanzleramt: Denkwürdigkeiten eines Personalratsvorsitzenden. Landshut, [1975]. pp. 216.

— United Kingdom.

BLAKE (ROBERT NORMAN WILLIAM) Baron Blake. The office of Prime Minister. London, 1975. pp. 74. *(British Academy. Thank-Offering to Britain Fund Lectures. 1974)*

PRINTERS

— Canada.

CANADA. Treasury Board. 1968. Agreement between the Treasury Board and the Council of Graphic Arts Unions of the Public Service of Canada, Printing Operations Group, non-supervisory. [Ottawa, 1968]. pp. 101. *In English and French.*

PRINTING

— History — Germany.

SCHMIDT UND KLAUNIG, BUCHDRUCKEREI UND VERLAG. 100 Jahre, 1869-1969, Buchdruckerei und Verlag Schmidt Klaunig, Kiel. Kiel, [1969]. 1 vol. (unpaged).

— — Poland.

BURBIANKA (MARTA) Produkcja typograficzna Scharffenbergów we Wrocławiu. Wrocław, 1968. pp. 296,[xxx]. *(Wrocław. Wrocławskie Towarzystwo Naukowe. Śląskie Prace Bibliograficzne i Bibliotekoznawcze. t.12) With French summary.*

— — Russia — Ukraine.

PERSHODRUKAR Ivan Fedorov ta ioho poslidovnyky na Ukraïni, XVI - persha polovyna XVII st.: zbirnyk dokumentiv. Kyïv, 1975. pp. 343. *bibliog. With Russian and English summaries.*

— — United Kingdom.

UNWIN (PHILIP) The printing Unwins: a short history of Unwin Brothers: the Gresham Press. 1826-1976. London, 1976. pp. 159. *bibliog.*

PRINTING, PUBLIC

— United Kingdom.

TESTER (H.O.) Her Majesty's Stationery Office and parliamentary printing: a general survey of the principal items of parliamentary printing undertaken by H.M.S.O. [London, H.M.S.O, 1975]. pp. 26.

PRISON PSYCHOLOGY.

PHARMACOLOGICAL testing in a correctional institution: volunteer characteristics and motivations: social, psychological and attitudinal implications; by Stephen H. Wells [and others]. Springfield, Ill., [1975]. pp. 66. *bibliog.*

BARTOLLAS (CLEMENS) and others. Juvenile victimization: the institutional paradox. New York, [1976]. pp. 324. *bibliog.*

PRISON RIOTS

— Canada — Ontario.

CANADA. Commission of Inquiry into Certain Disturbances at Kingston Penitentiary during April, 1971. 1973. Report; J.W. Swackhamer, chairman. Ottawa, 1973. pp. 63.

PRISONERS

— Legal status, laws, etc.

EUROPEAN COMMISSION OF HUMAN RIGHTS. 1971. Human rights in prison. Strasbourg, 1971. pp. 46. *(Case-Law Topics. 1).*

EUROPEAN COURT OF HUMAN RIGHTS. Publications. Series A: Judgments and Decisions. [A] 18. ...Golder case. 1. Decision of 7 May 1974. 2. Judgment of 21 February 1975. Strasbourg, Council of Europe, 1975. pp. 63 [bis]. *In English and French.*

EUROPEAN COURT OF HUMAN RIGHTS. Publications. Series B: Pleadings, Oral Arguments and Documents. [B16]. "Golder" case, (1973-1975). Strasbourg, Council of Europe, 1975. pp. 264[bis], 265-310. *In English and French.*

— Australia — Victoria.

VICTORIA. Social Welfare Department. Research and Statistics Division. 1973. People imprisoned in Victoria for murder and manslaughter, 1962- 1971; by Joseph Martin. Melbourne, 1973. fo.82.

— Germany.

EUROPEAN COMMISSION OF HUMAN RIGHTS. 1968. The Zeidler-Kornmann case: (Application No. 2686/65 by Heinz Zeidler-Kornmann against the Federal Republic of Germany). Strasbourg, Council of Europe, 1968. pp. 120.

— New Zealand.

NEW ZEALAND. Department of Justice. Research Section. 1975. Justice Department penal census, 1972. [Wellington], 1975. pp. 46.

— United Kingdom.

PROP (PRESERVATION OF THE RIGHTS OF PRISONERS). "Political prisoners" and prisoners' unions: conflict or cooperation?. London, 1973. pp. 24.

BANKS (CHARLOTTE) and FAIRHEAD (SUZAN) The petty short-term prisoner:...revised version of an address given to a Howard League Summer School. London, 1976. pp. 23. *bibliog.*

— United States.

MEYER (PETER B.) Drug experiments on prisoners: ethical, economic, or exploitative? Lexington, Mass., [1976]. pp. 129.

PRISONERS OF WAR.

MILLER (RICHARD IRWIN) ed. The law of war. Lexington, Mass., [1975]. pp. 329.

— United States.

UNITED STATES. Prisoner of War Operations Division. 1945-46. Historical monograph [on the] Prisoner of War Operations Division, Office of the Provost Marshal General; with appendices and supplement. [Washington, 1945-46]. 4 vols. *Microfilm: 2 reels. Deals with prisoner of war operations in the United States during World War II.*

PRISONS

— Europe.

EUROPEAN GROUP FOR THE STUDY OF DEVIANCE AND SOCIAL CONTROL. Conference, 1st, Impruneta, 1973. Deviance and control in Europe: papers...; edited by Herman Bianchi [and others]. London, [1975]. pp. 209.

— — Laws and regulations.

EUROPEAN COMMITTEE ON CRIME PROBLEMS. 1973. Standard minimum rules for the treatment of prisoners. Strasbourg, Council of Europe, 1973. pp. 28.

— Russia.

KUZNETSOV (EDUARD SAMUILOVICH) Dnevniki. Paris, 1973. pp. 374.

— Spain.

MAURIN (JOAQUIN) En las prisiones de Franco. Mexico, [1974]. pp. 213.

— United Kingdom.

McCONVILLE (SEAN) ed. The use of imprisonment: essays in the changing state of English penal policy. London, 1975. pp. 128. *bibliog.*

KING (ROY DAVID) and MORGAN (RODNEY) A taste of prison: custodial conditions for trial and remand prisoners. London, 1976. pp. 100. *bibliog.*

— — Gloucestershire.

WHITING (J.R.S.) Prison reform in Gloucestershire 1776-1820: a study of the work of Sir George Onesiphorus Paul, Bart. London, 1975. pp. 287. *bibliog.*

— United States.

ORLAND (LEONARD) Prisons: houses of darkness. New York, [1975]. pp. 224. *bibliog.*

DURDEN-SMITH (JO) Who killed George Jackson?. New York, 1976. pp. 292, xii.

HAWKINS (GORDON J.) The prison: policy and practice. Chicago, 1976. pp. 217. bibliog.

SOMMER (ROBERT) The end of imprisonment. New York, 1976. pp. 211. bibliog.

— — California.

MITFORD (JESSICA) Kind and usual punishment in California. Boston, Mass., [1971]. pp. 8.

PRIVACY, RIGHT OF.

DWORKIN (GERALD) The common law protection of privacy. [Hobart, 1967]. pp. 418-445. (Reprinted from vol.2 of the University of Tasmania Law Review)

MARTIN (JAMES THOMAS). Security, accuracy, and privacy in computer systems. Englewood Cliffs, N.J., [1973]. pp. 626.

— Europe.

HONDIUS (FRITS WILLEM) Emerging data protection in Europe. Amsterdam, 1975. pp. 282. bibliog.

— New Zealand.

NEW ZEALAND. Government Caucus Committee on the Proposed Law Enforcement Information System. 1973. Report; [R.P.B. Drayton, chairman]. Wellington, 1973. pp. 58.

— United Kingdom.

SIEGHART (PAUL) Privacy and computers. London, 1976. pp. 228. bibliog.

PRIVATE LANGUAGE PROBLEM.

FODOR (JERRY ALAN) The language of thought. New York, [1975]. pp. 214. bibliog.

PROBABILITIES.

BILLINGSLEY (PATRICK) Convergence of probability measures. New York, Wiley, [1968]. pp. xiii, 253. bibliog.

RÉNYI (ALFRÉD) Foundations of probability. San Francisco, [1970]. pp. 366.

RÉNYI (ALFRÉD) Letters on probability;...translated by László Vekerdi. Detroit, 1972. pp. 86. bibliog.

MAISTROV (LEONID EFIMOVICH) Probability theory: a historical sketch;...translated and edited by Samuel Kotz. New York, 1974. pp. 281. bibliog.

HACKING (IAN) The emergence of probability: a philosophical study of early ideas about probability, induction and statistical inference. London, 1975. pp. 209. bibliog.

RESEARCH CONFERENCE ON SUBJECTIVE PROBABILITY, UTILITY AND DECISION MAKING, 4TH, ROME, 1973. Utility, probability, and human decision making: selected proceedings...; edited by Dirk Wendt and Charles Vlek. Dordrecht, [1975]. pp. 418. bibliogs.

PROBATION

— Tasmania.

TASMANIA. Probation and Parole Service. Report. a., 1972/73 (1st)- Hobart. Included in TASMANIA. Parliament. Journals and printed papers.

— United States.

EXPERIMENT in a juvenile court: a study of a program of volunteers working with juvenile probationers; by Robert J. Berger [and others]. Ann Arbor, 1975. 1 vol. (various pagings). bibliog.

PROBATION SYSTEM

— Europe.

EUROPEAN COMMITTEE ON CRIME PROBLEMS. 1970. Practical organisation of measures for the supervision and after-care of conditionally sentenced or conditionally released offenders: report, etc. Strasbourg, Council of Europe, 1970. pp. 286. bibliog.

PROBLEM CHILDREN

— United Kingdom.

DOUGLAS (JAMES WILLIAM BRUCE) Early hospital admissions and later disturbances of behaviour and learning. [London], 1975. pp. 25. bibliog. (Reprinted from Developmental Medicine and Child Neurology, vol. 17 no. 4, August 1975)

LUCAS (NORMAN BERNARD CHARLES) An experience of teaching. London, [1975]. pp. 196.

NATIONAL ASSOCIATION FOR MENTAL HEALTH. Assessment of children and their families. London, 1975. pp. 41. bibliog.

SOCIAL SERVICES RESEARCH AND INTELLIGENCE UNIT [PORTSMOUTH]. First year at Fairfield Lodge: a children's observation and assessment centre in Hampshire. Portsmouth, 1976. pp. 142. bibliog.

PROBLEM FAMILY

— United Kingdom.

TONGE (W.L.) and others. Families without hope: a controlled study of 33 problem families. Ashford, 1975. pp. 156. bibliog. (British Journal of Psychiatry. Special Publications. No. 11)

PROCEDURE (LAW)

— United Kingdom.

WALKER (RONALD JACK) and WALKER (MICHAEL GEORGE) The English legal system. 4th ed. London, 1976. pp. 616.

— United States.

VANDERBILT (ARTHUR T.) Cases and other materials on modern procedure and judicial administration. New York, 1952. pp. 1390.

PRODUCE TRADE.

SORENSON (VERNON L.) International trade policy: agriculture and development. East Lansing, Mich., 1975. pp. 290. bibliog. (Michigan State University. MSU International Business and Economic Studies)

NAGLE (JACK C.) Agricultural trade policies. Farnborough, Hants., [1976]. pp. 170.

— Cyprus.

CHRYSSOMELIDIS (G.S.) The competitiveness of Cyprus in export crops. Thessaloniki, 1974. pp. 25. bibliog. (Reprinted from Hellenic Agricultural Economic Review, vol. 10, no. 1, January 1974)

— Sudan.

BESHAI (ADEL AMIN) Export performance and economic development in Sudan, 1900-1967. London, 1976. pp. 358. bibliog. (Oxford. University. St. Antony's College. Middle East Centre. St. Antony's Middle East Monographs. No. 3)

PRODUCTION (ECONOMIC THEORY)

— Mathematical models.

MUSSA (MICHAEL) Output and employment in a dynamic model of aggregate supply. rev. ed. [London], 1976. pp. 46. bibliog.

SCHAIK (A.B.T.M. VAN) Reproduction and fixed capital. Tilburg, 1976. pp. 306. bibliog. (Tilburg. Katholieke Hogeschool. Tilburg Institute of Economics. Tilburg Studies on Economics. 13)

UEBE (GOETZ) Produktionstheorie. Berlin, 1976. pp. 301. bibliog.

PRODUCTION FUNCTIONS (ECONOMIC THEORY).

BOL (GEORG) Stetigkeit und Effizienz bei mengenwertigen Produktionsfunktionen. Meisenheim am Glan, [1973]. pp. 73. bibliog.

GALLACHER (JOHN) Estimation of aggregate employment and production functions for New Zealand. Wellington, 1975. pp. 47. (Reserve Bank of New Zealand. Research Papers. No. 16)

BOSWORTH (DEREK L.) Production functions: a theoretical and empirical study. Farnborough, Hants., [1976]. pp. 158. bibliog.

HASENKAMP (GEORG) Specification and estimation of multiple-output production functions. Berlin, 1976. pp. 151. bibliog.

PRODUCTION MANAGEMENT.

BAKER (MICHAEL J.) and McTAVISH (RONALD) Product policy and management. London, 1976. pp. 182.

LOCKYER (KEITH GERALD) Production management: the unaccepted challenge. [Bradford, 1976?]. pp. 21.

PRODUCTION PLANNING.

STAUB (KURT E.) Die Unternehmungskooperation für Produktinnovationen. Bern, [1975]. pp. 233. bibliog.

BAKER (MICHAEL J.) and McTAVISH (RONALD) Product policy and management. London, 1976. pp. 182.

— Automation.

HURRION (ROBERT DONALD) The design, use and required facilities of an interactive visual computer simulation language to explore production planning problems. 1976. pp. 232. bibliog. Typescript. Ph.D. (London) thesis: unpublished. This thesis is the property of London University and may not be removed from the Library.

PRODUCTIVITY.

CHRYSOMILIDES (G.S.) Productivity standards of export crops in Cyprus, other major Mediterranean producers and the U.S.A.: suggestions for revising agricultural policies in Cyprus. Beirut, 1974. pp. 24. bibliog. (Reprinted from Anaptyxis, vol. 3-4, June 1974)

INDUSTRIAL RELATIONS RESEARCH ASSOCIATION. Collective bargaining and productivity; authors, Joseph Goldberg [and others]. Madison, Wis., [1975]. pp. 194.

GLASER (EDWARD M.) Productivity gains through worklife improvements. New York, [1976]. pp. 342. bibliog.

PRATTEN (CLIFFORD FREDERICK) Labour productivity differentials within international companies. Cambridge, 1976. pp. 118. (Cambridge. University. Department of Applied Economics. Occasional Papers. 50)

— Asia.

APO NEWS (formerly Asian productivity: m. bulletin); pd by Asian Productivity Organization. m., Ja 1969 - My 1971 (v.9, no.1 - v.11, no.5); Je 1971 ([n. s.] v.1, no.1)- with gap (Oc - D 1971; [n.s.] v.1, nos.5- 7). Tokyo.

— Australia.

AUSTRALIA. Commonwealth Bureau of Census and Statistics. 1969. Indexes of factory production, 1949-50 to 1966-67. Canberra, [1969]. pp. 20.

— Germany.

PANIĆ (M.) ed. The UK and West German manufacturing industry 1954-72: a comparison of structure and performance. London, National Economic Development Office, 1976. pp. 151. (NEDO Monographs. 5)

PRODUCTIVITY.(Cont.)

— Germany, Eastern.

Die INTENSIVIERUNG der sozialistischen Industrieproduktion und die wachsende Rolle der Arbeiterklasse; (Autoren: Karl Hartmann [and others]). Berlin, 1975. pp. 332.

— Russia.

EKONOMICHESKII zakon neuklonnogo rosta proizvoditel'nosti truda: sushchnost', deistvie i ispol'zovanie. Moskva, 1974. pp. 263.

— — Mathematical models.

METODOLOGICHESKIE voprosy prognozirovaniia proizvoditel'nosti truda. Kiev, 1975. pp. 216. *bibliog.*

— — Ukraine.

REZERVY rosta proizvoditel'nosti truda v narodnom khoziaistve Ukrainskoi SSR. Kiev, 1975. pp. 200.

— Sweden.

JONES (H.G.) Planning and productivity in Sweden. London, 1976. pp. 212. *bibliog.*

— United Kingdom.

ECONOMIC DEVELOPMENT COMMITTEE FOR THE CLOTHING INDUSTRY. Unlocking productivity potential: the experience of seven firms in the clothing industry. London, National Economic Development Office, 1975. pp. 58.

PANIĆ (M.) ed. The UK and West German manufacturing industry 1954-72: a comparison of structure and performance. London, National Economic Development Office, 1976. pp. 151. *(NEDO Monographs. 5)*

PRODUCTIVITY (ECONOMIC THEORY).

KRADER (LAWRENCE) The Asiatic mode of production: sources, development and critique in the writings of Karl Marx. Assen, 1975. pp. 454. *bibliog. Including excerpts taken by Marx from the work of M.M. Kovalevskii, with Marx's notes thereon.*

PROFESSIONAL EDUCATION

— Germany.

WARLITZER (VOLKER) Ermittlung des Bestandes und Bedarfes an Planstellen in den Bereichen Raumordnung, Landes- und Regionalplanung im höheren Dienst und in vergleichbaren Vergütungsgruppen. Bonn-Bad Godesberg, 1972. 1 vol. (various pagings). *(Germany (Bundesrepublik). Institut für Raumordnung. Mitteilungen. Heft 77)*

— Prussia.

LUNDGREEN (PETER) Techniker in Preussen während der frühen Industrialisierung: Ausbildung und Berufsfeld einer entstehenden sozialen Gruppe. Berlin, 1975. pp. 307. *bibliog. (Historische Kommission zu Berlin. Einzelveröffentlichungen. Band 16)*

— Romania.

PERȚ (STELIANA) Cu privire la contribuția formării profesionale a forței de muncă la creșterea economică. București, 1974. pp. 265. *bibliog. (Academia de Științe Sociale și Politice a Republicii Socialiste România. Institutul de Cercetări Economice. Bibliotheca Oeconomica. 30) With English summary and English and French tables of contents.*

— United Kingdom.

TURNER (JOHN DERFEL) and RUSHTON (JAMES) eds. Education for the professions. Manchester, [1976]. pp. 119. *bibliog.*

— Yugoslavia.

BREKIĆ (JOVO) ed. Samoupravna koncepcija razvitka kadrova: kadrološki apekti usklađivanja obrazovanja, zapošljavanja i profesionalnog razvoja kadrova, etc. Zagreb, 1975. pp. 262. *bibliog. With English summary.*

PROFESSIONAL STANDARDS REVIEW ORGANIZATIONS (MEDICINE)

— Law and legislation — United States.

GOSFIELD (ALICE) PSROs: the law and the health consumer. Cambridge, Mass., [1975]. pp. 264.

PROFESSIONS

— Finland.

HELENIUS (RALF) Akademikernas fackliga organisationsberedskap. Helsingfors, 1975. pp. 229. *bibliog. (Svenska Handelshögskolan. Ekonomi och Samhälle. Nr. 24)*

— Russia.

RUSSIA (USSR). Ministerstvo Vysshego i Srednego Spetsial'nogo Obrazovaniia. Nauchno-Tekhnicheskii Sovet. Sektsiia Narodonaseleniia. Narodonaselenie. 9. Obrazovatel'naia i sotsial'no-professional'naia struktura naseleniia SSSR. Moskva, 1975. pp. 103. *With English table of contents.*

STEPIN (ANATOLII PETROVICH) Sotsialisticheskoe preobrazovanie obshchestvennykh otnoshenii gorodskikh srednikh sloev. Moskva, 1975. pp. 235.

— Scandinavia.

HELENIUS (RALF) Akademikernas fackliga organisationsberedskap. Helsingfors, 1975. pp. 229. *bibliog. (Svenska Handelshögskolan. Ekonomi och Samhälle. Nr. 24)*

— United Kingdom.

LAYDER (DEREK ROY) Occupational careers in contemporary Britain: with special reference to the acting profession. 1976. fo. 376. *bibliog. Typescript. Ph.D. (London) thesis: unpublished. This thesis is the property of London University and may not be removed from the Library.*

— United States.

CULL (JOHN G.) and HARDY (RICHARD E.) eds. Career guidance for black adolescents: a guide to selected professional occupations. Springfield, Ill., [1975]. pp. 148. *bibliogs.*

WOMEN in the professions; edited by Laurily Keir Epstein. Farnborough, Hants, [1975]. pp. 142. *Papers from a conference held at Washington University, St. Louis, Apr. 1975; sponsored by Monticello College Foundation and Washington University.*

PROFIT.

SADZIKOWSKI (WIESŁAW) Współczesne burżuazyjne teorie zysku. Warszawa, 1963. pp. 226. *bibliog. With English and Russian summaries.*

WOOD (ADRIAN) A theory of profits. Cambridge, 1975. pp. 184. *bibliog.*

— United Kingdom.

ECONOMIC DEVELOPMENT COMMITTEE FOR THE DISTRIBUTIVE TRADES. Profitability and liquidity in the distributive trades: an examination of financial data in selected sectors; based on a report prepared for the Distributive Trades EDC by Whitefield Associates and Company. London, National Economic Development Office, 1975. pp. 123.

PROFIT SHARING

— France.

FRANCE. Centre d'Etude des Revenus et des Coûts. 1971. La participation des salariés aux fruits de l'expansion: l'ordonnance du 17 août 1967 et les accords dérogatoires. Paris, 1971. pp. 170. *(Documents. No. 10)*

— Germany.

ARMBRUSTER (BERNT) Transformationsprobleme im Spätkapitalismus: zur Dialektik spätkapitalistischer Reformpolitik am Beispiel der "Vermögensbildung in Arbeitnehmerhand". Heidelberg, 1975. pp. 278. *bibliog. Inauguraldissertation, Wirtschafts- und Sozialwissenschaftliche Fakultät, Universität Heidelberg.*

SCHILLERT (ULLRICH) Gewinne als Quelle der Vermögenspolitik?: die Belastbarkeit der Unternehmensgewinne durch vermögenspolitische Massnahmen. Berlin, [1976]. pp. 270. *bibliog.*

— Mexico.

PURCELL (SUSAN KAUFMAN) The Mexican profit-sharing decision: politics in an authoritarian regime. Berkeley, [1975]. pp. 216. *bibliog.*

PROGRAMME BUDGETING

— New Zealand.

NEW ZEALAND. Treasury. 1973. The planning and control of government expenditures: planning, programming and budgeting system. Wellington, 1973. pp. 77.

PROGRAMMING (ELECTRONIC COMPUTERS).

WEGNER (PETER) Programming languages, information structures and machine organization. New York, [1968]. pp. 401. *bibliogs.*

CUTTLE (GEOFFREY) and ROBINSON (PHILIP B.) eds. Executive programs and operating systems. London, 1970. pp. 116. *bibliog.*

SOFTWARE engineering techniques: report on a conference sponsored by the NATO Science Committee, Rome, Italy, 27th to 31st October 1969;...[edited by] J.N. Buxton and B. Randell. [Brussels], North Atlantic Treaty Organization, 1970. pp. 164. *bibliogs.*

BARRON (DAVID WILLIAM) Computer operating systems. London, 1971 repr. 1975. pp. 135.

COLIN (ANDREW JOHN THEODORE) Introduction to operating systems. London, [1971]. pp. 120. *bibliog.*

KATZAN (HARRY) Computer organization and the system/370. New York, [1971]. pp. 308.

WEINBERG (GERALD M.) The psychology of computer programming. New York, [1971]. pp. 288. *bibliogs.*

DAHL (OLE-JOHAN) and others. Structured programming. London, 1972 repr. 1975. pp. 220. *bibliogs. (Automatic Programming Information Centre. Studies in Data Processing. No. 8)*

DONOVAN (JOHN J.) Systems programming. New York, [1972]. pp. 488. *bibliog.*

SYMPOSIUM ON THE COMPLEXITY OF COMPUTER COMPUTATIONS, YORKTOWN HEIGHTS, N.Y., 1972. Complexity of computer computations: proceedings of a symposium... ; editors Raymond E. Miller [and] James W. Thatcher. New York, 1972. pp. 225. *bibliog. (International Business Machines Corporation. IBM Research Symposia Series)*

HUMBY (EDWARD) Programs from decision tables. London, [1973]. pp. 91. *bibliog.*

PAGE (E.S.) and WILSON (L.B.) Information representation and manipulation in a computer. Cambridge, 1973 repr. 1976. pp. 244. *bibliogs.*

ARON (JOEL D.) The program development process. Reading, Mass., [1974] in progress.

KERNIGHAN (BRIAN W.) and PLAUGER (P.J.) The elements of programming style. New York, [1974]. pp. 147. *bibliog.*

MADNICK (STUART E.) and DONOVAN (JOHN J.) Operating systems. New York, [1974]. pp. 640. *bibliog.*

WATERS (SAMUEL JOSEPH) Introduction to computer systems design: planning files and programs. Manchester, [1974] repr. 1976. pp. 198.

BOCK (WOLFGANG ANDREAS) A string-oriental technique for the analysis of medium-sized computer programs to recognize and expose sections which could be performed in parallel; [Ph.D.(London) thesis]. 1975. fo. 175. bibliog. Typescript: unpublished. This thesis is the property of London University and may not be removed from the Library.

BROOKS (FREDERICK PHILLIPS) The mythical man-month: essays on software engineering. Reading, Mass., [1975]. pp. 195.

BURGE (WILLIAM H.) Recursive programming techniques. Reading, Mass., [1975]. pp. 277. bibliogs.

EUROPEAN COMPUTING CONFERENCE ON INTERACTIVE SYSTEMS, LONDON, 1975. Interactive systems. Uxbridge, [1975]. pp. 556. bibliogs. Papers presented at the Conference. This conference was part of the European Computing Congress, 1975.

FORMAL aspects of computing science: proceedings of the Joint IBM University of Newcastle upon Tyne Seminar held in the University Computing Laboratory, 3rd-6th September 1974; edited by B. Shaw. Newcastle upon Tyne, 1975. pp. 213.

MYERS (GLENFORD J.) Reliable software through composite design. New York, 1975. pp. 159. bibliog.

YOURDON (EDWARD) Technique of program structure and design. Englewood Cliffs, [1975]. pp. 364. bibliogs.

CHAKRAVARTY (AMIYA KUMAR) Optional segmentation and scheduling of computer programs in a multiprogramming environment. 1976. fo. 202. bibliog. Typescript. Ph.D. (London) thesis: unpublished. This thesis is the property of London University and may not be removed from the Library.

EUROPEAN COMPUTING CONFERENCE ON SOFTWARE SYSTEMS ENGINEERING, LONDON, 1976. Software systems engineering. Uxbridge, Middx., [1976]. pp. 543. bibliogs. Papers presented at the Conference, with a number of additional papers. This conference was part of the European Computing Congress, 1976.

WEIZENBAUM (JOSEPH) Computer power and human reason: from judgment to calculation. San Francisco, [1976]. pp. 300.

WIRTH (NIKLAUS) Algorithms [plus] data structures [equal] programs. Englewood Cliffs, N.J., [1976]. pp. 366. bibliogs.

PROGRAMMING (MATHEMATICS).

BROWN (ARTHUR ROBERT) Optimum packing and depletion: the computer in space- and resource- usage problems. London, [1971]. pp. 107. bibliog.

MATEMATICHESKOE programmirovanie i proizvodstvennye zadachi. Erevan, 1974. pp. 142. bibliog.

LAPORTE (GILBERT) Permutation programming: problems, methods and application; [Ph. D. (London) thesis]. 1975. fo. 358. bibliog. Typescript: unpublished. This thesis is the property of London University and may not be removed from the Library.

PROGRAMMING LANGUAGES (ELECTRONIC COMPUTERS).

HIGMAN (BRYAN) A comparative study of programming languages. London, 1967 repr. 1973. pp. 164. bibliog.

NATO ADVANCED STUDY INSTITUTE, VILLARD-DE-LANS, 1966. Programming languages: N.A.T.O. advanced study institute; edited by F. Genuys. London, 1968. pp. 395.

LEE (JOHN A.N.) Computer semantics: studies of algorithms, processors and languages. New York, [1972]. pp. 397. bibliog.

IFIP TC-2 SPECIAL WORKING CONFERENCE ON DATA BASE DESCRIPTION, WEPION, BELGIUM, 1975. Data base description: proceedings of the...conference...; edited by B.C.M. Douqué and G.M. Nijssen. Amsterdam, 1975. pp. 382. bibliogs.

NICHOLLS (JOHN E.) The structure and design of programming languages. Reading, Mass., [1975]. pp. 572. bibliog.

HURRION (ROBERT DONALD) The design, use and required facilities of an interactive visual computer simulation language to explore production planning problems. 1976. pp. 232. bibliog. Typescript. Ph.D. (London) thesis: unpublished. This thesis is the property of London University and may not be removed from the Library.

MILNE (ROBERT E.) and STRACHEY (CHRISTOPHER) A theory of programming language semantics. London, 1976. 2 vols.

PROGRESS.

BARBÉ (CARLOS) Progresso e sviluppo: la formazione della teoria dello sviluppo e lo sviluppo come ideologia; Auguste Comte, Herbert Spencer. Torino, 1974. pp. 241. (Turin. Università. Istituto di Scienze Politiche. Pubblicazioni. vol. 32)

NIKOLAEVA (LIDIIA VASIL'EVNA) Ob"ektivnye i sub"ektivnye faktory sotsial'nogo progressa i svobody. Moskva, 1974. pp. 259.

MEEK (RONALD LINDLEY) Social science and the ignoble savage. Cambridge, 1976. pp. 249.

PROGRESSIVE PARTY (SOUTH AFRICA).

STRANGWAYES-BOOTH (JOANNA) A cricket in the thorn tree: Helen Suzman and the Progressive Party of South Africa. London, 1976. pp. 320. bibliog.

PROGRESSIVISM (U.S. POLITICS).

EKIRCH (ARTHUR ALPHONSE) Progressivism in America: a study of the era from Theodore Roosevelt to Woodrow Wilson. New York, 1974. pp. 308. bibliog.

GOULD (LEWIS L.) ed. The progressive era. Syracuse, N.Y., 1974. pp. 238.

FILLER (LOUIS) Appointment at Armageddon: muckraking and progressivism in the American tradition. Westport, Conn., 1976. pp. 476. bibliog.

PROMOTIONS.

GRANICK (DAVID) Equality of promotional opportunities in British industry. London, [1975]. pp. 13.

PROPAGANDA, AMERICAN.

BOGART (LEO) Premises for propaganda: the United States Information Agency's operating assumptions in the Cold War;...abridged by Agnes Bogart. New York, [1976]. pp. 250. bibliog.

PROPAGANDA, COMMUNIST.

AKADEMIIA OBSHCHESTVENNYKH NAUK. Kafedra Teorii i Metodov Ideologicheskoi Raboty. Voprosy Teorii i Metodov Ideologicheskoi Raboty. vyp.2. [Sbornik statei]. Moskva, 1973. pp. 325.

NAUCHNYE osnovy partiinoi propagandy. Gor'kii, 1973. pp. 161. (Gor'kii. Universitet. Uchenye Zapiski. vyp.165. Seriia Istoricheskaia)

UCHENOVA (VIKTORIIA VASIL'EVNA) Publitsistika i politika. Moskva, 1973. pp. 232.

BRESLAV (EVA IVANOVNA) Aleksandra Mikhailovna Kollontai. Moskva, 1974. pp. 110. bibliog. (Kommunisticheskaia Partiia Sovetskogo Soiuza. Tsentral'nyi Komitet. Vysshaia Partiinaia Shkola. Kafedra Zhurnalistiki. Partiinye Publitsisty)

NOSKOV (ALEKSANDR PETROVICH) and IANOVSKII (RUDOL'F GRIGOR'EVICH) Dva urovnia soznaniia i politicheskie ubezhdeniia; otvetstvennyi redaktor...V.A. Rebrin. Novosibirsk, 1974. pp. 94.

PROPERTY TAX.

AKADEMIIA OBSHCHESTVENNYKH NAUK. Kafedra Teorii i Metodov Ideologicheskoi Raboty. Voprosy Teorii i Metodov Ideologicheskoi Raboty. vyp.4. Problemy effektivnosti ideino-vospitatel'noi deiatel'nosti. Moskva, 1975. pp. 333.

PROPAGANDA, GERMAN.

SYWOTTEK (JUTTA) Mobilmachung für den totalen Krieg: die propagandistische Vorbereitung der deutschen Bevölkerung auf den Zweiten Weltkrieg. Opladen, [1976]. pp. 398. bibliog. (Hamburg. Hansische Universität. Studien zur Modernen Geschichte. Band 18)

PROPAGANDA, INTERNATIONAL.

LISANN (MAURY) Broadcasting to the Soviet Union: international politics and radio. New York, 1975. pp. 199. bibliog.

PROPAGANDA, ITALIAN.

BORDONI (CARLO) Cultura e propaganda nell'Italia fascista: un saggio introduttivo con i confronti antologici da G. Gentile [and others]. Messina, 1974. pp. 192. bibliog.

PROPAGANDA, RUSSIAN.

POWELL (DAVID E.) Antireligious propaganda in the Soviet Union: a study of mass persuasion. Cambridge, [1975]. pp. 206. bibliog.

PROPERTY.

BECHERAND (J.) L'antiproudhonisme: de la propriété et de son droit; ou, De la légitimité et de l'inviolabilité du respect dû à la propriété;...en réponse à l'article du 16 août 1848 pour jour le Représentant du Peuple, etc. Paris, Desloges, 1848. pp. 16.

KING (JOHN E.) and REGAN (PHILIP) Relative income shares. London, 1976. pp. 87. bibliog.

— Poland.

JABŁOŃSKI (ZBIGNIEW) Organizacja sklepów a ochrona mienia społecznego. Warszawa, 1954. pp. 154. bibliog.

SZER (SEWERYN) Własność spółdzielcza: z wyjątkiem własności spółdzielni produkcyjnych w rolnictwie. Warszawa, 1960. pp. 219. bibliog. With French and Russian summaries.

— Russia.

SOTSIALISTICHESKAIA sobstvennost' i sovershenstvovanie form obshchestvennoi organizatsii proizvodstva. Kazan', 1974. pp. 286.

SEMENOV (VISSARION FEDOROVICH) Razvitie sotsialisticheskoi sobstvennosti v usloviiakh kommunisticheskogo stroitel'stva. Kazan', 1975. pp. 205.

PROPERTY TAX.

MILLS (EDWIN S.) and OATES (WALLACE E.) eds. Fiscal zoning and land use controls: the economic issues. Lexington, Mass., [1975]. pp. 205. bibliogs.

PAUL (DIANE B.) The politics of the property tax. Lexington, Mass., [1975]. pp. 158.

— Germany.

SCHWARZE (ELISABETH) Soziale Struktur und Besitzverhältnisse der ländlichen Bevölkerung Ostthüringens im 16. Jahrhundert;...mit einer Einführung: Die Land- und Türkensteuerregister...; von Hans Eberhardt. Weimar, 1975. pp. 216. bibliog.

— United Kingdom.

LAWTON (PHILIP) The taxation of property. London, [1975]. 1 pamphlet (unpaged). (Institute for Fiscal Studies. Lecture Series. No.3)

— United States.

HARRISS (CLEMENT LOWELL) Property taxation in government finance. New York, [1974]. pp. 61. (Tax Foundation. Research Publications. New Series. No. 31)

PROPERTY TAX.(Cont.)

PAUL (DIANE B.) The politics of the property tax. Lexington, Mass., [1975]. pp. 158.

SCHROEDER (LARRY D.) and SJOQUIST (DAVID L.) The property tax and alternative local taxes: an economic analysis. New York, 1975. pp. 114. *bibliog.*

PROPORTIONAL REPRESENTATION

— United Kingdom.

ADVERSARY politics and electoral reform; edited by S.E. Finer. [London, 1975]. pp. 374.

EASY as A.B.C.: electoral reform; by Tom Benyon [and others]. London, 1976. pp. 14.

ELECTORAL REFORM SOCIETY. Evidence to the Hansard Society Commission on Electoral Reform, 1976. London, 1976. pp. 12. *bibliog.*

MAYHEW (CHRISTOPHER PAGET) Blueprint for a breakthrough. London, [1976]. pp. 14.

MAYHEW (CHRISTOPHER PAGET) The disillusioned voter's guide to electoral reform. London, 1976. pp. 63.

NEWLAND (ROBERT A.) Electing the United Kingdom Parliament. London, 1976. pp. 16. *bibliog.*

— — Scotland.

GILMOUR (JAMES) Ph.D. Participation by representation: the case for STV in Scotland. London, 1974. pp. 8.

GILMOUR (JAMES) Ph.D. and WOODWARD-NUTT (JAMES) Electing the Scottish Assembly. London, 1975. pp. 36. *bibliog.*

PROSTITUTION

— Denmark.

HAUGAARD JENSEN (JENS) and others. Sociale studier: kriminalitet, prostitution og fattigdom i Århus, ca. 1870-1906. Aarhus, 1975. pp. 483. *bibliogs.*

PROTESTANTS IN CHILE.

LALIVE D'ÉPINAY (CHRISTIAN) Religion, dynamique sociale et dépendance: les mouvements protestants en Argentine et au Chili. Paris, [1975]. pp. 367. *bibliog.*

PROTESTANTS IN FRANCE.

DAVIE (GRACE RIESTRA CLAIRE) Right wing politics among French Protestants, 1900-1944, with special reference to the Association Sully. 1975. fo.323. *bibliog.* Typescript. Ph.D.(London) thesis: unpublished. *This thesis is the property of London University and may not be removed from the Library.*

PROTESTANTS IN NORTHERN IRELAND.

GIBBON (PETER) The origins of Ulster Unionism: the formation of popular Protestant politics and ideology in nineteenth-century Ireland. Manchester, [1975]. pp. 163. *bibliog.*

BELL (GEOFFREY) of Belfast. The Protestants of Ulster. London, 1976. pp. 159.

PROTESTANTS IN THE ARGENTINE REPUBLIC.

LALIVE D'ÉPINAY (CHRISTIAN) Religion, dynamique sociale et dépendance: les mouvements protestants en Argentine et au Chili. Paris, [1975]. pp. 367. *bibliog.*

PROUDHON (PIERRE JOSEPH).

BECHERAND (J.) L'antiproudhonisme: de la propriété et de son droit; ou, De la légitimité et de l'inviolabilité du respect dû à la propriété;...en réponse à l'article du 16 août 1848 du journal le Représentant du Peuple, etc. Paris, Desloges, 1848. pp. 16.

PROVENCE

— History.

PILLORGET (RENE) Les mouvements insurrectionnels de Provence entre 1596 et 1715. Paris, 1975. pp. 1044. *bibliog.*

PROVENCE – CÔTE D'AZUR

— Economic conditions.

REGARDS sur l'espace rural: Provence Côte-d'Azur. Paris, 1974. pp. 525. *(Regards sur la France. Février, 1974)*

PRUSSIA

— Constitutional history.

GUGEL (MICHAEL) Industrieller Aufstieg und bürgerliche Herrschaft: sozioökonomische Interessen und politische Ziele des liberalen Bürgertums in Preussen zur Zeit des Verfassungskonflikts, 1857-1867. Köln, [1975]. pp. 304. *bibliog.*

— — Sources.

[REVOLUTION of 1848 in Germany: collection of appeals, petitions, manifestoes, proclamations, and similar material in the form of leaflets, posters, etc., including some manuscript letters; published in Prussia between 1848 and 1862). v.p., 1848-62. 1 vol. (unpaged).

— Economic history.

LUNDGREEN (PETER) Techniker in Preussen während der frühen Industrialisierung: Ausbildung und Berufsfeld einer entstehenden sozialen Gruppe. Berlin, 1975. pp. 307. *bibliog.* (*Historische Kommission zu Berlin. Einzelveröffentlichungen. Band 16*)

— Foreign economic relations — Poland.

WILDER (JAN ANTONI) Traktat handlowy polsko-pruski z roku 1775: gospodarcze znaczenie utraty dostępu do morza; Polish-Prussian commercial treaty of 1775: Poland's loss of access to the sea, its economic consequences. Warszawa, 1937. pp. 357. *bibliog.* (*Towarzystwo Naukowe Warszawskie. Rozprawy Historyczne. t.20, z.2*) With English summary.

— History — 1848-1849, Revolution.

[REVOLUTION of 1848 in Germany: collection of appeals, petitions, manifestoes, proclamations, and similar material in the form of leaflets, posters, etc., including some manuscript letters; published in Prussia between 1848 and 1862). v.p., 1848-62. 1 vol. (unpaged).

— Nationalism.

HAY (JOSEPH) Staat, Volk und Weltbürgertum in der Berlinischen Monatsschrift von Friedrich Gedike und Johann Erich Biester, 1783-96. Berlin, 1913. pp. 83. *bibliog.*

— Nationalversammlung.

[REVOLUTION of 1848 in Germany: collection of appeals, petitions, manifestoes, proclamations, and similar material in the form of leaflets, posters, etc., including some manuscript letters; published in Prussia between 1848 and 1862). v.p., 1848-62. 1 vol. (unpaged).

— Politics and government .

[REVOLUTION of 1848 in Germany: collection of appeals, petitions, manifestoes, proclamations, and similar material in the form of leaflets, posters, etc., including some manuscript letters; published in Prussia between 1848 and 1862). v.p., 1848-62. 1 vol. (unpaged).

EHNI (HANS PETER) Bollwerk Preussen?: Preussen-Regierung, Reich-Länder- Problem und Sozialdemokratie, 1928-1932. Bonn-Bad Godesberg, [1975]. pp. 304. *bibliog.* (*Friedrich-Ebert-Stiftung. Forschungsinstitut. Schriftenreihe. Band 111*)

PSYCHIATRIC HOSPITALS

— United Kingdom.

NATIONAL ASSOCIATION FOR MENTAL HEALTH. Mind Reports. No. 10. Patients' rights: the mentally disordered in hospital. London, [1973]. pp. 14.

NATIONAL ASSOCIATION FOR MENTAL HEALTH. Mind Reports. No.13. Co-ordination or chaos?: the run-down of psychiatric hospitals. London, 1974. pp. 30.

— — Design and construction.

U.K. Department of Health and Social Security. 1973. Hospital building for the mentally handicapped; a background to design. [London, 1973?]. 1 vol. (unpaged). (*Design Bulletins. No. 1*).

— United States.

The FUTURE role of the state hospital; edited by Jack Zusman [and] Elmer F. Bertsch. Lexington, Mass., [1975]. pp. 410. *Includes papers presented at a conference organized by the Division of Community Psychiatry of the State University of New York at Buffalo, 1973.*

REYNOLDS (DAVID K.) and FARBEROW (NORMAN LOUIS) Suicide inside and out. Berkeley, 1976. pp. 226. *bibliog.*

PSYCHIATRIC SOCIAL WORK

— United Kingdom.

PROCEEDINGS of a conference held jointly by the Royal College of Psychiatrists, the Royal College of General Practitioners, the Association of Directors of Social Services and the Department of Health and Social Security on 3 October 1975. [London, Department of Health and Social Security, 1975?]. pp. 39.

PSYCHIATRY.

CLARE (ANTHONY) Psychiatry in dissent: controversial issues in thought and practice. London, 1976. pp. 438. *bibliogs.*

— Canada — Study and teaching.

CAMERON (PAUL M.) and GREBEN (STANLEY E.) Comprehensive training in psychiatry. [Ottawa], Department of National Health and Welfare, [1972]. pp. 10. (*Canada's Mental Health. Supplements. 72*)

PSYCHOANALYSIS.

LEE (SIDNEY GILMORE McKENZIE) and HERBERT (MARTIN) Freud and psychology: selected readings. Harmondsworth, 1970. pp. 398. *bibliogs.*

MILLER (JEAN BAKER) ed. Psychoanalysis and women. Harmondsworth, 1973, repr. 1974. pp. 415. *bibliog.*

PSYCHOLINGUISTICS.

FODOR (JERRY ALAN) The language of thought. New York, [1975]. pp. 214. *bibliog.*

FOUNDATIONS of language development: a multidisciplinary approach; edited by Eric H. Lenneberg [and] Elizabeth Lenneberg. Paris, Unesco Press, 1975. 2 vols. *bibliogs.*

MARUSZEWSKI (MARIUSZ) Language communication and the brain: a neuropsychological study. The Hague, 1975. pp. 217. *bibliog.*

MASSARO (DOMINIC W.) ed. Understanding language: an information-processing analysis of speech perception, reading, and psycholinguistics. New York, [1975]. pp. 439. *bibliogs.*

NORMAN (DONALD A.) and RUMELHART (DAVID E.) Explorations in cognition. San Francisco, [1975]. pp. 430. *bibliog.*

OSGOOD (CHARLES EGERTON) and others. Cross-cultural universals of affective meaning. Urbana, [1975]. pp. 486. *bibliog.*

SEMINAR ON LANGUAGE AND LEARNING, 1ST, 1973. Problems of language and learning: [papers of a seminar organised by the Scottish Council for Research in Education and sponsored by the Educational Research Board of the Social Science Research Council]; edited by Alan Davies. London, 1975. pp. 154. *bibliog.*

RODGON (MARIS MONITZ) Single-word usage, cognitive development and the beginnings of combinatorial speech: a study of ten English-speaking children. Cambridge, 1976. pp. 163. *bibliog.*

— Mathematical models.

SCHANK (ROGER C.) and COLBY (KENNETH MARK) eds. Computer models of thought and language. San Francisco, [1973]. pp. 454. *bibliog.*

PSYCHOLOGICAL RESEARCH.

MEYERS (LAWRENCE S.) and GROSSEN (NEAL E.) Behavioral research: theory, procedure and design. San Francisco, [1974]. pp. 355. *bibliog.*

PSYCHOLOGY.

HAMSHER (J. HERBERT) and SIGALL (HAROLD) eds. Psychology and social issues. New York, [1973]. pp. 550. *bibliogs.*

RAT, myth and magic: a political critique of psychology; [by Nigel Armistead and others]. n.p., [1973?]. pp. 63. *bibliogs.*

BROWN (ROGER W.) and HERRNSTEIN (RICHARD JULIUS) Psychology. London, 1975. pp. 762. *bibliog.*

INTERNATIONAL ASSOCIATION FOR CROSS-CULTURAL PSYCHOLOGY. International Conference, 2nd, Kingston, Ont., 1974. Applied cross-cultural psychology: selected papers from the... conference...; edited by J.W. Berry and W.J. Lonner. Amsterdam, 1975. pp. 338. *bibliogs.*

— Methodology.

ROSENTHAL (ROBERT) and ROSNOW (RALPH L.) Primer of methods for the behavioral sciences. New York, [1975]. pp. 117. *bibliog.*

PSYCHOLOGY, EXPERIMENTAL.

CALFEE (ROBERT C.) Human experimental psychology. New York, [1975]. pp. 532. *bibliogs.*

PSYCHOLOGY, FORENSIC.

MONAHAN (JOHN) ed. Community mental health and the criminal justice system. New York, [1976]. pp. 332. *bibliogs.*

PSYCHOLOGY, INDUSTRIAL.

STANSFIELD (RONALD G.) Flux in the factory. London, 1967. pp. 8. *(Hollenden Lectures. No. 15. 1967) (Reprinted from the Clothing Institute Journal, vol. 15, no. 3, 1967)*

LAWLER (EDWARD E.) Motivation in work organizations. Monterey, [1973]. pp. 224. *bibliog.*

KELLY (JOE) Organizational behaviour: an existential-systems approach. rev. ed. Homewood, Ill., 1974. pp. 770. *bibliog.*

The QUALITY of working life...; [edited by] Louis E. Davis [and] Albert B. Cherns and associates. New York, [1975]. 2 vols. *Papers based on the International Conference on the Quality of Working Life, Harriman, New York, 1972.*

WEXLEY (KENNET N.) and YUKL (GARY A.) eds. Organizational behavior and industrial psychology: readings with comentary. New York, 1975. pp. 641. *bibliog.*

PSYCHOLOGY, PHYSIOLOGICAL.

JACKSON (THOMAS WILLIAM KEVIN) The effects of the experimenter's profession on experimental results. [1974]. fo. 217. *bibliog.* Typescript. *Ph. D.(London) thesis: unpublished. This thesis is the property of London University and may not be removed from the Library.*

MASSARO (DOMINIC W.) Experimental psychology and information processing. Chicago, [1975]. pp. 651. *bibliog.*

PSYCHOSES.

FREEMAN (THOMAS) M.D. Psychopathology of the psychoses. New York, [1969]. pp. 215. *bibliog.*

PSYCHOTHERAPY.

ROGERS (CARL RANSOM) On becoming a person: a therapist's view of psychotherapy. London, 1967 repr. 1974. pp. 420. *bibliogs.*

BANNISTER (DONALD) ed. Issues and approaches in the psychological therapies. London, [1975]. pp. 286. *bibliogs.*

PSYCHOTROPIC DRUGS.

UNITED NATIONS. Conference for the Adoption of a Protocol on Psychotropic Substances, Vienna, 1971. United Nations conference...[held at] Vienna, 11 January- 19 February 1971: official records. (E/CONF.58/7 and Add.1). New York, 1973. 2 vols.

OFFICE OF HEALTH ECONOMICS. [Studies in Current Health Problems]. No. 54. Medicines which affect the mind. London, [1975]. pp. 44.

PUBLIC HEALTH RESEARCH.

BLANPAIN (JAN) and DELESIE (LUK) Community health investment: health services research in Belgium, France, Federal German Republic and the Netherlands;... edited by Gordon McLachlan. Oxford, 1976. pp. 474. *bibliogs.*

PUBLIC HOUSING

— France — Finance.

FRANCE. Direction de la Comptabilité Publique. Le secteur public local: statistiques des comptes des établissements d'hospitalisation publics et des organismes d'habitations a loyer modéré. a., 1973- Paris.

— Singapore.

YEH (STEPHEN H.K.) ed. Public housing in Singapore: a multi-disciplinary study; published...for Housing and Development Board. Singapore, 1975. pp. 439. *bibliog.*

— United Kingdom.

GRAYSON (LESLEY) Vandalism on housing estates. [London], Greater London Council, 1975. pp. 8. *bibliog. (London Topics. No. 7)*

HOLE (WINIFRED VERE) and BLACK (F.W.) The use of existing records for the assessment by local authorities of current housing needs and policies. Watford, [1975]. pp. 19. *(Building Research Establishment [U.K.]. Current Papers. 75/5)*

MURIE (ALAN S.) The sale of council houses: a study in social policy. [Birmingham], 1975. pp. 166. *(Birmingham. University. Centre for Urban and Regional Studies. Occasional Papers. No. 35)*

U.K. Department of the Environment. 1975. Bill for the Transfer in New Towns of Housing and Related Assets: (consultation paper). [London, 1975]. pp. 10.

COMMUNITY DEVELOPMENT PROJECT. Whatever happened to council housing?. London, 1976. pp. 93.

STUDY GROUP ON PROGRAMMES OF SOCIAL OWNERSHIP AND RENOVATION OF COUNCIL DWELLINGS. First report; [Reg Freeson, chairman]. [London, Department of the Environment, 1976]. 1 pamphlet (various pagings).

— — Liverpool.

VAUXHALL COMMUNITY DEVELOPMENT PROJECT. Woodstock Gardens survey, June 1973: initial report; (by) P. R. Topping. [Liverpool], 1973. 2 pts.

WILSON (HUGH) AND WOMERSLEY (LEWIS) Firm. Inner area study: Liverpool: housing maintenance project. [London], Department of the Environment, [1976]. pp. 32.

— — London.

DUGMORE (KEITH) Social characteristics of the tenants of seventy-two GLC housing estates. London, [1975]. pp. 38. *bibliog. (London. Greater London Council. Research Memoranda. 474)*

LONDON. Greater London Council. South Bank Comprehensive Development Area Inter-departmental Working Party. The future of the South Bank: a report on planning principles and the scope for the provision of housing; [A. Matthews, chairman] . London, 1975. pp. 40.

RUNNYMEDE TRUST. Race and council housing in London: census returns examined by the Runnymede Trust research staff. London, 1975. fo.11. *bibliog.*

SOUTHWARK COMMUNITY DEVELOPMENT PROJECT. Report on local authority housing in Newington; prepared by C[ommunity] D[evelopment] P[roject] Research Director. [London, 1975]. pp. 64.

WILLMOTT (PETER) Whatever's happening to London?; an analysis of changes in population structure and their effects on community life. London, [1975]. pp. 14. *bibliog. Paper delivered at the meeting of the London Council of Social Service in London in 1974.*

ACTION GROUP ON LONDON HOUSING. The public sector housing pipeline in London; fifth report to the Minister for Housing and Construction; [Ernest Armstrong, chairman]. [London], Department of the Environment, 1976. pp. 82.

LONDON. Greater London Council. Housing Management Committee. Race and council housing: preliminary report of the GLC housing lettings survey; (report by Director of Housing Management and Maintenance). [London], 1976. pp. 15.

— — Newcastle-upon-Tyne.

BENWELL COMMUNITY DEVELOPMENT PROJECT. Noble Street and Norwich Place report. [Newcastle-upon-Tyne], 1974 repr. 1975. fo. 59.

BENWELL: news and views from Benwell Community Project. Special issue (summer 1976) on council housing. [Newcastle-upon-Tyne, Benwell Community Development Project], 1976. pp. 12.

— — Scotland — Glasgow.

JACOBS (SIDNEY) The right to a decent house. London, 1976. pp. 161.

— United States.

BINGHAM (RICHARD D.) Public housing and urban renewal: an analysis of federal-local relations. New York, 1975. pp. 255. *bibliog.*

PUBLIC INTEREST.

FERRELL (O.C.) and LAGARCE (RAYMOND) eds. Public policy issues in marketing. Lexington, Mass., [1975]. pp. 192.

MEYER (WILLIAM J.) Public good and political authority: a pragmatic proposal. Port Washington, 1975. pp. 147. *bibliog.*

MARTIN-KAYE (NIEL) Democratic enterprise. London, [1976]. pp. 38. *(Liberal Party. Strategy 2,000. 1st Series. No. 8)*

SHAPIRO (ANDREW O.) Media access: your rights to express your views on radio and television. Boston, [Mass., 1976]. pp. 297.

PUBLIC OFFICERS.

KAYE (SEYMOUR P.) and MARSH (ARTHUR IVOR) eds. International manual on collective bargaining for public employees. New York, 1973. pp. 389.

PUBLIC OPINION

PUBLIC OPINION
— Czechoslovakia.

RADIO FREE EUROPE. Audience and Public Opinion Research Department. Economic expectations in Czechoslovakia; comparison of an internal poll and RFE/APOR findings. [Munich?], 1973. fo. 9.

— Europe, Eastern.

RADIO FREE EUROPE. Audience and Public Opinion Research Department. Attitudes toward communism and party preferences in East Europe. [Munich?], 1973. fo. 32.

RADIO FREE EUROPE. Audience and Public Opinion Research Department. East European expectations, wishes and fears concerning domestic developments in the 1970s. [Munich?], 1974. fo. 32.

RADIO FREE EUROPE. Audience and Public Opinion Research Department. East European sympathies in the Arab-Israeli conflict. [Munich?], 1974. fo. 21.

— France.

FRANCE. Centre d'Etude des Revenus et des Coûts. 1973. Les connaissances et opinions de Français dans le domaine des revenus: analyse des résultats d'une enquête. Paris, 1973. pp. 210. *(Documents. Nos. 19-20)*

PIKE (DAVID WINGEATE) Les Français et la guerre d'Espagne. Paris, 1975. pp. 467. *bibliog. (Paris. Université de Paris I (Panthéon- Sorbonne). Publications. Nouvelle Série. Recherches. 7)*

ŚLADKOWSKI (WIESŁAW) Opinia publiczna we Francji wobec sprawy polskiej w latach 1914- 1918. Wrocław, 1976. pp. 311. *bibliog. (Lubelskie Towarzystwo Naukowe. Wydział Humanistyczny. Prace. Monografie. t.5)* With French summary.

— New Zealand.

SEIDMAN (JOEL ISAAC) Attitudes of New Zealand workers. Wellington, 1975. pp. 114. *(Victoria University of Wellington. Industrial Relations Centre. Industrial Relations Research Monographs. No.1)*

— Nigeria.

PEIL (MARGARET) Nigerian politics: the people's view. London, 1976. pp. 209. *bibliog.*

— Sweden.

ÅMARK (KLAS) Makt eller moral: svensk offentlig debatt om internationell politik och svensk utrikes- och försvarspolitik 1938-1939. Stockholm, 1973. pp. 324. *bibliog.* With English summary.

— Switzerland.

Les SUISSES et la politique: enquête sur les attitudes d'électeurs suisses, 1972; par Dusan Sidjanski [and others]. Berne, 1975. pp. 216. *bibliog.*

— United Kingdom.

SOCIAL SURVEYS (GALLUP POLL) LIMITED. Crime and the police: a gallup poll conducted for the Daily Telegraph. London, 1961. pp. 15.

AGE CONCERN ENGLAND. Public opinion on pensions. London, 1974. pp. 14. *(Age Concern England. Manifesto Series. No. 30)*

AIMS FOR FREEDOM AND ENTERPRISE. The public want sacrifices: results of a national opinion poll survey. London, 1974. pp. 3.

AIMS FOR FREEDOM AND ENTERPRISE. Let's back the workers on nationalization, and the Labour voter, too. London, [1975]. pp. 4.

CRONJÉ (GILLIAN) Middle class opinion and the 1889 dock strike: a critique of Outcast London. London, 1975. pp. 24. *(Communist Party of Great Britain. History Group. Our History. No. 61)*

HALL (DEREK) Residents' concern for community problems: Portsmouth. Portsmouth, 1975. fo. 10. *(Social Services Research and Intelligence Unit [Portsmouth]. Information Sheets. No. 24)*

JOSEPH (Sir KEITH SINJOHN) Business and the climate of opinion. London, 1975. pp. 8. *(Foundation for Business Responsibilities. Seminar Papers)*

WALEY (DANIEL) British public opinion and the Abyssinian War, 1935-6. London, 1975. pp. 176.

BRITAIN into Europe: public opinion and the EEC 1961-75; edited by Roger Jowell and Gerald Hoinville. London, 1976. pp. 128. *bibliog.*

— United States.

COMMITTEE FOR ECONOMIC DEVELOPMENT. Research and Policy Committee. Program Committee. Restoring confidence in the political process. New York, [1974]. pp. 20. *(Committee for Economic Development. Research and Policy Committee. Statements on National Policy)*

REED (JOHN SHELTON) The enduring South: subcultural persistence in mass society. Chapel Hill, [1974]. pp. 135. *bibliog.*

BLUMENTHAL (MONICA D.) and others. More about justifying violence: methodological studies of attitudes and behavior. Ann Arbor, 1975. pp. 401. *bibliog.*

IPPOLITO (DENNIS S.) and others. Public opinion and responsible democracy. Englewood Cliffs, N.J., [1976]. pp. 330. *bibliog.*

NIE (NORMAN H.) and others. The changing American voter. Cambridge, Mass., 1976. pp. 399.

WHEELER (MICHAEL) Lies, damn lies, and statistics: the manipulation of public opinion in America. New York, [1976]. pp. 300. *bibliog.*

PUBLIC OPINION POLLS.

WHEELER (MICHAEL) Lies, damn lies, and statistics: the manipulation of public opinion in America. New York, [1976]. pp. 300. *bibliog.*

PUBLIC PROSECUTORS
— Poland.

DASZKIEWICZ (WIESŁAW) Proces adhezyjny na tle prawa polskiego. Warszawa, 1961. pp. 172.

PUBLIC RELATIONS.

MARCUS (BRUCE W.) Competing for capital: a financial relations approach. New York, [1975]. pp. 265. *bibliogs.*

— Police.

SOCIAL SURVEYS (GALLUP POLL) LIMITED. Crime and the police: a gallup poll conducted for the Daily Telegraph. London, 1961. pp. 15.

WINTERSMITH (ROBERT F.) Police and the black community. Lexington, Mass., [1974]. pp. 149. *bibliog.*

— America, North.

CRISPO (JOHN H.G.) ed. The public right to know: accountability in the secretive society. Toronto, [1975]. pp. 395. *Includes extensive quotations from books and articles.*

PUBLIC UTILITIES.

MILLS (EDWIN S.) and OATES (WALLACE E.) eds. Fiscal zoning and land use controls: the economic issues. Lexington, Mass., [1975]. pp. 205. *bibliogs.*

— Statistics.

INTERNATIONAL INSTITUTE OF STATISTICS. International Statistics of Large Towns. Statistique de l'électricité, du gaz et de l'eau dans les grandes villes, 1934. La Haye, 1939. pp. 97.

— Germany.

MANNHEIM. Stadtwerke, and ENERGIE- UND WASSERWERKE RHEIN- NECKAR AG. Mannheimer Energien: 100 Jahre Versorgungswirtschaft seit Übernahme des Gaswerkes Mannheim in städtische Regie, 1873-1973. [Mannheim, 1973]. pp. 171. *bibliog.*

— Sweden.

WEISSGLAS (GÖSTA) Studies on service problems in the sparsely populated areas in Northern Sweden. Umeå, 1975. pp. 220. *bibliog. (Universitetet i Umeå. Department of Geography. Geographical Reports. 5) Akademisk avhandling, filosofie doctorsexamen - Umeå Universitet.*

— United States.

PUBLIC utility regulation: change and scope; edited by Werner Sichel and Thomas G. Gies. Lexington, Mass., [1975]. pp. 99. *Essays prepared for presentation at a two-day seminar held at Western Michigan University in 1974.*

PUBLISHERS AND PUBLISHING.

AMERICAN ACADEMY OF POLITICAL AND SOCIAL SCIENCE. Annals. vol. 421. Perspectives on publishing; special editors of this volume, Philip G. Altbach [and] Sheila McVey. Philadelphia, 1975. pp. 215.

PERSPECTIVES on publishing; edited by Philip G. Altbach [and] Sheila McVey. Lexington, Mass., [1976]. pp. 283.

— Bulgaria — Statistics.

BULGARIA. Tsentralno Statistichesko Upravlenie. 1964. Knigoizdavane i pechat v Narodna Republika Bulgariia: statisticheski sbornik, 1962-1963. Sofiia, 1964. pp. 65,[xxxvi]. *With Russian and French captions.*

— Germany.

SCHMIDT UND KLAUNIG, BUCHDRUCKEREI UND VERLAG. 100 Jahre, 1869-1969, Buchdruckerei und Verlag Schmidt Klaunig, Kiel. Kiel, [1969]. 1 vol. (unpaged).

SCHEFFLER (HEINRICH) Wölffische Lehrjahre: Marginalien zum Ausklang des Kurt Wolff Verlages, 1932-1934. [Frankfurt am Main, 1975]. pp. 61.

— Ireland (Republic) — Directories.

CASSELL'S directory of publishing 1976-1977, in Great Britain, the Commonwealth, Ireland, South Africa and Pakistan. 8th ed. London, 1976. pp. 581.

— Italy.

PER una editoria democratica: atti del convegno di Rimini, 7-9 giugno 1974; a cura di Giorgio Giovagnoli [and others]. Rimini, [1975]. pp. 255. *bibliog. A conference sponsored by a group of publishers, Einaudi, Feltrinelli, Guaraldi, etc.*

— Pakistan — Directories.

CASSELL'S directory of publishing 1976-1977, in Great Britain, the Commonwealth, Ireland, South Africa and Pakistan. 8th ed. London, 1976. pp. 581.

— Russia — Tatar Republic.

KARIMULLIN (ABRAR GIBADULLOVICH) Tatarskaia kniga nachala XX veka. Kazan', 1974. pp. 319. *bibliog.*

— South Africa — Directories.

CASSELL'S directory of publishing 1976-1977, in Great Britain, the Commonwealth, Ireland, South Africa and Pakistan. 8th ed. London, 1976. pp. 581.

— United Kingdom.

ATTENBOROUGH (JOHN) A living memory: Hodder and Stoughton, publishers 1868-1975. London, [1975]. pp. 287.

LUSTY (Sir ROBERT FRITH) Bound to be read. London, 1975. pp. 314.

CASSELL'S directory of publishing 1976-1977, in Great Britain, the Commonwealth, Ireland, South Africa and Pakistan. 8th ed. London, 1976. pp. 581.

— — Commonwealth — Directories.

CASSELL'S directory of publishing 1976-1977, in Great Britain, the Commonwealth, Ireland, South Africa and Pakistan. 8th ed. London, 1976. pp. 581.

— United States.

TEBBEL (JOHN WILLIAM) A history of book publishing in the United States. New York, 1972 in progress.

VANIER (DINOO JAL) Market structure and the business of book publishing. New York, [1973]. pp. 213. *bibliog.*

PUERTO RICANS IN THE UNITED STATES.

WAGENHEIM (KAL) A survey of Puerto Ricans on the U.S. mainland in the 1970s. New York, 1975. pp. 133.

PUERTO RICO

— Economic conditions.

CLARK (TRUMAN R.) Puerto Rico and the United States, 1917-1933. [Pittsburgh, 1975]. pp. 238. *bibliog.*

QUESADA (CARLOS) Excedente economico y subdesarrollo: el caso de Puerto Rico. Barcelona, [1975]. pp. 247.

— Foreign relations — United States.

ALBIZU CAMPOS (PEDRO) La conciencia nacional puertorriqueña...; seleccion, introduccion y notas de Manuel Maldonado-Denis. Mexico, 1972. pp. 218.

— Politics and government.

CLARK (TRUMAN R.) Puerto Rico and the United States, 1917-1933. [Pittsburgh, 1975]. pp. 238. *bibliog.*

— Relations (general) with the United States.

CLARK (TRUMAN R.) Puerto Rico and the United States, 1917-1933. [Pittsburgh, 1975]. pp. 238. *bibliog.*

— Rural conditions.

BUITRAGO ORTIZ (CARLOS) Esperanza: an ethnographic study of a peasant community in Puerto Rico. Tucson, [1973]. pp. 217. *bibliog. (Wenner-Gren Foundation for Anthropological Research. Viking Fund Publications in Anthropology. No. 50)*

PUNISHMENT.

GIBBS (JACK P.) Crime, punishment, and deterrence. New York, [1975]. pp. 259. *bibliog.*

MORRIS (HERBERT) On guilt and innocence: essays in legal philosophy and moral psychology. Berkeley, Calif., [1976]. pp. 161.

— Russia.

BAGRII-SHAKHMATOV (LEONID VASIL'EVICH) Ugolovnaia otvetstvennost' i nakazanie. Minsk, 1976. pp. 383.

— United Kingdom.

MAYS (JOHN BARRON) Crime and its treatment. 2nd ed. London, 1975. pp. 173. *bibliog.*

PURCHASING POWER.

A SYSTEM of international comparisons of gross product and purchasing power: (United Nations International Comparison Project: phase one);...published for the World Bank. Baltimore, [1975]. pp. 294.

PURITANS.

BERCOVITCH (SACVAN) The Puritan origins of the American self. New Haven, 1975. pp. 250.

PUTNEY

— Poor.

A CHARGE on the parish: the treatment of poverty in Putney 1620-1834; [by] L. Attwood and others]. London, [1974]. pp. 77. *(Wandsworth Historical Society. Wandsworth Papers. No.1)*

QATAR

— Politics and government.

The UNITED Arab Amirates and Qatar: pro-imperialist oil producers in the gulf; translated and edited by the Gulf Committee. London, 1974. pp. 36. *(Gulf Committee. 9th June Studies)*

QUALITY CONTROL.

DROGI podniesienia jakości zaopatrzenia towarowego: materiały konferencji naukowej Katedr Handlu i Towaroznawstwa, Zakopane 16.VI. - 30.VI. 1955. Warszawa, 1956. pp. 164.

SHELESTOV (VLADIMIR STEPANOVICH) Dogovor postavki i kachestvo produktsii. Moskva, 1974. pp. 176.

QUARTZ

— Zambia.

KLINCK (B.A.) Vein-quartz at Naluama. Lusaka, 1973. pp. 6. *(Zambia. Geological Survey Department. Economic Reports. No. 41) 4 maps in end pocket.*

QUEBEC (PROVINCE)

— Economic conditions.

ECONOMIC SITUATION [IN] QUEBEC, THE; [pd. by] Department of Industry and Commerce [Quebec]. a., 1970 [10th]- Quebec. *File includes French ed., La Situation économique au Québec, 1971-*

— Economic policy.

BENJAMIN (JACQUES) Planification et politique au Québec. Montréal, 1974. pp. 142. *bibliog.*

— History.

CONFERENCE ON EARLY AMERICAN HISTORY, 27TH, 1970. Of mother country and plantations: proceedings of the... conference...; edited by Virginia Bever Platt and David Curtis Skaggs. Bowling Green, Ohio, 1971. pp. 127. *bibliog.*

— Nationalism.

HAMEL (JACQUES) La culture politique du Mouvement National des Québécois. Québec, 1973. fo. 207.

MILNER (HENRY) and MILNER (SHEILAGH HODGINS) The decolonization of Quebec: an analysis of left-wing nationalism. Toronto, [1973]. pp. 257. *bibliog.*

CAMERON (DAVID ROBERTSON) Nationalism, self-determination and the Quebec question. [Toronto], 1974. pp. 177. *bibliog.*

TROFIMENKOFF (SUSAN MANN) Action Française: French Canadian nationalism in the twenties. Toronto, [1975]. pp. 157. *bibliog.*

— Politics and government.

BERGERON (GERARD) Du Duplessisme à Trudeau et Bourassa, 1956-1971. 2nd ed. Ottawa, [1971]. pp. 631.

ROUSSOPOULOS (DIMITRIOS J.) ed. The political economy of the state: Québec, Canada, U.S.A. Montréal, 1973. pp. 195.

TROFIMENKOFF (SUSAN MANN) Action Française: French Canadian nationalism in the twenties. Toronto, [1975]. pp. 157. *bibliog.*

— Social policy.

BENJAMIN (JACQUES) Planification et politique au Québec. Montréal, 1974. pp. 142. *bibliog.*

QUECHUA INDIANS.

See KECHUA INDIANS.

QUECHUA LANGUAGE.

See KECHUA LANGUAGE.

QUEENSLAND

— Economic conditions.

QUEENSLAND. Department of Industrial Development. 1967. Progress with Queensland. [Brisbane, 1967]. pp. 31.

— Emigration and immigration.

AUSTRALIA. Migrant Task Force Committee, Queensland. 1974. Report to the Minister for Immigration; chairman: Manfred Cross. [Brisbane, 1974]. fo. 19.

— Legislative Assembly — Elections.

QUEENSLAND. Legislative Assembly. 1975. Details of polling at general election held on December 7, 1974. (A.3-1975). Brisbane, 1975. pp. 53.

QUESNAY (FRANÇOIS).

FOX-GENOVESE (ELIZABETH) The origins of physiocracy: economic revolution and social order in eighteenth-century France. Ithaca, N.Y., 1976. pp. 325. *bibliog.*

QUEUEING THEORY.

NEWELL (GORDON F.) Applications of queueing theory. London, 1971. pp. 148.

QUINE (WILLARD VAN ORMAN).

HARDING (SANDRA G.) ed. Can theories be refuted?: essays on the Duhem-Quine thesis. Dordrecht, [1976]. pp. 318. *bibliogs. Reprinted from various sources.*

RACE.

BOWKER (GORDON) and CARRIER (JOHN WOOLFE) eds. Race and ethnic relations: sociological readings; ...[with an] introductory essay by Percy Cohen. London, 1976. pp. 400. *bibliog.*

RACE DISCRIMINATION.

YETMAN (NORMAN R.) and STEELE (C. HOY) eds. Majority and minority: the dynamics of racial and ethnic relations. 2nd ed. Boston, Mass., 1975. pp. 640. *bibliogs.*

BARCLAY (WILLIAM) 1944- , and others, eds. Racial conflict, discrimination, and power: historical and contemporary studies. New York, [1976]. pp. 437. *bibliogs.*

ZINBERG (NORMAN E.) and others. Teaching social change: a group approach. Baltimore, Ma., [1976]. pp. 252. *bibliog.*

— Law and legislation — Africa, East.

DON NANJIRA (DANIEL D.C.) The status of aliens in East Africa: Asians and Europeans in Tanzania, Uganda, and Kenya. New York, 1976. pp. 230.

— — United Kingdom.

COMMUNITY RELATIONS COMMISSION. Digest of views on review of race relations legislation. London, [1975]. pp. 25.

MADGE (NIC) Racial discrimination:...comments on the white paper. London, 1975. pp. 17. *(National Council for Civil Liberties. Reports. No 10)*

U.K. Race Relations Board. 1975. Comments of the Race Relations Board on the White Paper: racial discrimination. [London, 1975]. fo. 11. *White Paper itself published as Cmnd. 6234 in British Parliamentary Papers, Session 1975-76.*

RACE DISCRIMINATION.(Cont.)

COMMUNITY RELATIONS COMMISSION. Liaison Division. The Race Relations Bill and ethnic minority participation; a report on five regional conferences on the Race Relations Bill. London, 1976. 1 pamphlet (various pagings).

— South Africa.

BUIS (ROBERT) Religious beliefs and white prejudice. Johannesburg, 1975. pp. 71. *bibliog.*

— United Kingdom.

HIRO (DILIP) Black British, white British. rev. ed. New York, [1973]. pp. 346. *bibliog.*

U.K. Department of Employment. 1973. Complaints of racial discrimination. London, 1973. pp. 2. *(Circulars. 32/2)*

LABOUR PARTY. Labour against racism. London, [1976]. pp. 7.

RACE PROBLEMS.

BAKER (DONALD G.) ed. Politics of race: comparative studies. Farnborough, Hants, [1975]. pp. 312. *bibliog.*

BETTELHEIM (BRUNO) and JANOWITZ (MORRIS) Social change and prejudice: including Dynamics of prejudice. New York, 1964 repr. 1975. pp. xxxviii, 337. *Dynamics of prejudice first published in 1950. The 1975 reprint contains a new prologue by the authors.*

KUPER (LEO) ed. Race, science and society. Paris, Unesco Press, 1975. pp. 370.

BARCLAY (WILLIAM) 1944- , and others, eds. Racial conflict, discrimination, and power: historical and contemporary studies. New York, [1976]. pp. 437. *bibliogs.*

BOWKER (GORDON) and CARRIER (JOHN WOOLFE) eds. Race and ethnic relations: sociological readings; ...[with an] introductory essay by Percy Cohen. London, 1976. pp. 400. *bibliog.*

FRANCIS (EMERICH K.) Interethnic relations: an essay in sociological theory. New York, [1976]. pp. 432. *bibliog.*

— Research.

U.K. Social Science Research Council. Research Unit on Ethnic Relations. 1975. Ethnic relations: the work of the...Unit...at the University of Bristol, 1970-74. [London, 1975]. pp. 23. *bibliog.*

RACETRACKS (HORSE-RACING).

— Hong Kong.

HONG KONG. Race Courses Committee. 1968. Report; [G.C. Hamilton, chairman]. Hong Kong, [1968]. pp. 19.

RADCHENKO (STEPAN IVANOVICH).

MEL'NIKOV (A.B.) Khranitel' partiinykh tain: [ocherk zhizni i deiatel'nosti S. I. Radchenko]. Moskva, 1975. pp. 168. *bibliog.*

RADCLIFFE (Sir JOSEPH).

RADCLIFFE (Sir JOSEPH) [Luddite papers; consisting mainly of letters to Sir Joseph Radcliffe, or to the Huddersfield magistrates, together with drafts or copies of his replies, February 1812 to February 1813]. [1812-13]. *Manuscript, with typescript list of contents. Microfilm: 1 reel.*

RADEV (SIMEON).

RADEV (SIMEON) Stroitelite na suvremenna Bulgariia; predgovor i obshta redaktsiia...Pantelei Zarev [of works first published 1911-12]. Sofiia, 1973. 2 vols.

RADICALISM IN FRANCE.

LOUBÈRE (LEO A.) Radicalism in Mediterranean France: its rise and decline, 1848- 1914. Albany, N.Y., 1974. pp. 258. *bibliog.*

BAUMGARTNER (FREDERIC J.) Radical reactionaries: the political thought of the French Catholic League. Genève, 1975 [or rather 1976]. pp. 317. *bibliog.*

RADICALISM IN GERMANY.

HANNS-SEIDEL-STIFTUNG. Angriff auf unsere Demokratie; (verantwortlich: Willibald Fink). 3rd ed. München, 1974. pp. 159.

PROKOP (SIEGFRIED) Studenten im Aufbruch: zur studentischen Opposition in der BRD. Dortmund, [1974]. pp. 184. *bibliog.*

WENDE (PETER) Radikalismus im Vormärz: Untersuchungen zur politischen Theorie der frühen deutschen Demokratie. Wiesbaden, 1975. pp. 228. *bibliog.*

BOCK (HANS MANFRED) Geschichte des "linken Radikalismus" in Deutschland: ein Versuch. Frankfurt am Main, 1976. pp. 370. *bibliog.*

SONTHEIMER (KURT) Das Elend unserer Intellektuellen: linke Theorie in der Bundesrepublik Deutschland. Hamburg, 1976. pp. 303.

RADICALISM IN ITALY

— Periodicals.

LEDDA (ISABELLA) and ZANELLA (GABRIELLA) I periodici di Padova, 1866-1926, liberali, radicali, socialisti. Padova, 1973. pp. 252. *(Centro per la Storia del Movimento Operaio nel Veneto, and Padua. Università. Istituto di Storia Medioevale e Moderna. Movimenti Politici e Sociali dell'Età Contemporanea nel Veneto. Collana.4)*

RADICALISM IN POLAND.

BENDER (RYSZARD) Chrześcijanie w polskich ruchach demokratycznych XIX stulecia. Warszawa, 1975. pp. 361. *bibliog.*

RADICALISM IN RUSSIA.

SHIROKOVA (VARVARA VASIL'EVNA) Partiia "Narodnogo prava": iz istorii osvoboditel'nogo dvizheniia 90-kh godov XIX veka. Saratov, 1972. pp. 206.

GERTSEN (ALEKSANDR IVANOVICH) and OGAREV (NIKOLAI PLATONOVICH) Golosa iz Rossii: sborniki A.I. Gertsena i N.P. Ogareva. Moskva, 1974 in progress.

BAZANOV (VASILII GRIGOR'EVICH) Russkie revoliutsionnye demokraty i narodoznanie. Leningrad, 1974. pp. 558.

FEDOSOVA (TAMARA FEDOROVNA) Pol'skie revoliutsionnye organizatsii v Moskve, 60-e gody XIX veka. Moskva, 1974. pp. 204.

ILLERITSKII (VLADIMIR EVGEN'EVICH) Revoliutsionnaia istoricheskaia mysl' v Rossii: domarksistskii period. Moskva, 1974. pp. 350.

REVOLIUTSIONNO-osvoboditel'noe dvizhenie v XIX-XX vv. v Povolzh'e i Priural'e. Kazan', 1974. pp. 115.

TKACHEV (PETR NIKITICH) Sochineniia v dvukh tomakh. Moskva, 1975 in progress.

RUDNITSKAIA (EVGENIIA L'VOVNA) Shestidesiatnik Nikolai Nozhin. Moskva, 1975. pp. 230.

SHABLIOVSKII (EVGENII STEPANOVICH) T.G. Shevchenko i russkie revoliutsionnye demokraty. 2nd ed. Kiev, 1975. pp. 391. *1st Ukrainian ed. dates from 1935. This ed. is a revision of 1st Russian ed. of 1962.*

STEPANISHCHEV (SERGEI SEMENOVICH) Razvitie obshchestvennoi mysli v trudakh russkikh revoliutsionerov-demokratov: analiz sotsial'no-politicheskikh, ateisticheskikh i eticheskikh idei A.N. Radishcheva, V.G. Belinskogo, N.P. Ogareva. Minsk, 1975. pp. 478.

RADICALISM IN THE UNITED KINGDOM.

CADOGAN (PETER) Early radical Newcastle. Consett, [1975]. pp. 153. *bibliog.*

BREWER (JOHN) Ph.D. Party ideology and popular politics at the accession of George III. Cambridge, 1976. pp. 382. *bibliog.*

WIDGERY (DAVID) ed. The Left in Britain 1956-68. Harmondsworth, 1976. pp. 549. *bibliog.*

RADICALISM IN THE UNITED STATES.

COSER (LEWIS ALFRED) and HOWE (IRVING) eds. The new conservatives: a critique from the left. New York, [1974]. pp. 343.

DEWITT (HOWARD A.) Images of ethnic and radical violence in California politics, 1917- 1930: a survey. San Francisco, 1975. pp. 136. *bibliog.*

KRUEGER (MARLIS) and SILVERT (FRIEDA) Dissent denied: the technocratic response to protest. New York, [1975]. pp. 194.

McNALL (SCOTT G.) Career of a radical rightist: a study in failure. Port Washington, N.Y., 1975. pp. 202.

WEINSTEIN (JAMES) Ambiguous legacy: the Left in American politics. New York, 1975. pp. 179.

The AMERICAN Revolution: explorations in the history of American radicalism; edited by Alfred F. Young. DeKalb, Ill., 1976. pp. 481.

WARREN (DONALD I.) The radical center: middle Americans and the politics of alienation. Notre Dame, Ind., [1976]. pp. 260. *bibliog.*

RADIO

— Germany — Laws and regulations.

HERRMANN (GUENTER) Fernsehen und Hörfunk in der Verfassung der Bundesrepublik Deutschland: ein Beitrag zu weiteren allgemeinen verfassungsrechtlichen und kommunikationsrechtlichen Fragen. Tübingen, 1975. pp. 422. *bibliog.*

— United States — Laws and regulations.

SCHMIDT (BENNO C.) Freedom of the press vs. public access. New York, [1976]. pp. 296.

RADIO ADVERTISING

— United Kingdom.

INDEPENDENT BROADCASTING AUTHORITY. The IBA code of advertising standards and practice. [rev. ed.] London, 1975. pp. 20.

RADIO AUDIENCES

— Israel.

ISRAEL. Central Bureau of Statistics. Special Series. No. 321. Radio listening and television watching, January 1969. Pt.2. Jerusalem, 1970. pp. 18. *In English and Hebrew.*

RADIO AUSTRALIA.

AUSTRALIA. Australian Broadcasting Commission. Press and Public Information Department. 1969. The constant voice: Radio Australia 30th anniversary, 1939- 1969. [2nd ed.] [Melbourne?, 1969]. pp. 48.

RADIO BROADCASTING

— France.

CHEVALLIER (JACQUES) La Radio Télévision Française entre deux réformes. Paris, 1975. pp. 342. *bibliog.*

THOMAS (RUTH) B.A. Broadcasting and democracy in France. Bradford, 1976. pp. 211. *bibliog.*

— Germany.

WILLIAMS (ARTHUR) M.A. Broadcasting and democracy in West Germany. Bradford, 1976. pp. 198. *bibliog.*

— Sierra Leone.

SIERRA LEONE. Committee of Broadcasting Consultants on the Sierra Leone Radio and Sierra Leone Television Services. 1969. Report...and the Government statement thereon; [Hugh Palmer, chairman]. [Freetown, 1969]. pp. 25.

— United Kingdom.

COMMUNITY RELATIONS COMMISSION. The future of broadcasting: Community Relations Commission evidence to the Annan Committee. [London, 1975]. fo. 8.

SWANN (Sir MICHAEL MEREDITH) Freedom and restraint in broadcasting: the British experience. London, [1975]. pp. 31. (Queen's Lectures. 1975) With German translation.

— United States.

SHAPIRO (ANDREW O.) Media access: your rights to express your views on radio and television. Boston, [Mass., 1976]. pp. 297.

RADIO IN POLITICS

— France.

THOMAS (RUTH) B.A. Broadcasting and democracy in France. Bradford, 1976. pp. 211. bibliog.

— Germany.

WILLIAMS (ARTHUR) M.A. Broadcasting and democracy in West Germany. Bradford, 1976. pp. 198. bibliog.

— Switzerland.

Die WAHLSENDUNGEN zu den Nationalratswahlen vom Herbst 1971: eine Aussagen-Analyse der deutschsprachien Sendungen des Radios der deutschen und rätoromanischen Schweiz; [by] Florian H. Fleck [and others]. Freiburg/Schweiz, 1974. pp. 120. bibliog. (Freiburg (Switzerland). Universität. Institut für Journalistik. Öffentliche Soziale Kommunikationen. Werkpapiere. 3)

RADIO IN PROPAGANDA.

LISANN (MAURY) Broadcasting to the Soviet Union: international politics and radio. New York, 1975. pp. 199. bibliog.

RADIO JOURNALISM.

SCHLESINGER (PHILIP RONALD) The social organisation of news production: a case study of BBC radio and television news; [Ph.D. (London) thesis]. [1975]. fo. 393. Typescript: unpublished. This thesis is the property of London University and may not be removed from the Library.

RADIOACTIVE POLLUTION.

UNION OF CONCERNED SCIENTISTS. The nuclear fuel cycle: a survey of the public health, environmental, and national security effects of nuclear power. rev.ed. Cambridge, Mass., [1975]. pp. 291. bibliogs.

RADISHCHEV (ALEKSANDR NIKOLAEVICH).

ASHESHOV (NIKOLAI) A.N. Radishchev: pervyi russkii respublikanets. Petrograd, 1919. pp. 54.

LANG (DAVID MARSHALL) The first Russian radical: Alexander Radishchev, 1749-1802. London, 1959. pp. 298. bibliog.

STEPANISHCHEV (SERGEI SEMENOVICH) Razvitie obshchestvennoi mysli v trudakh russkikh revoliutsionerov-demokratov: analiz sotsial'no-politicheskikh, ateisticheskikh i etichestkikh idei A.N. Radishcheva, V.G. Belinskogo, N.P. Ogareva. Minsk, 1975. pp. 478.

RAILWAYS

— Environmental aspects — Denmark.

SONDER (RIC) Graested: reflections on a Danish station-town; based on an investigation...by students of the Royal Academy of Fine Arts and the Polytechnic Institute, Copenhagen. New York, [1955?]. fo. 29.

— Africa, East — Employees.

GRILLO (R.D.) Race, class, and militancy: an African trade union, 1939-1965. New York, [1974]. pp. 151. bibliog.

— Canada — History.

CANADA. Public Archives. 1972. Towards C[anadian] N[ational]: from portage railway to a national system: an exhibition prepared by the Public Archives of Canada to celebrate the 50th anniversary of the incorporation of the Canadian National Railway Company. Ottawa, 1972. pp. 58,58. In English and French.

— China — History.

SCHMIDT (VERA) Die deutsche Eisenbahnpolitik in Shantung, 1898-1914: ein Beitrag zur Geschichte des deutschen Imperialismus in China. Wiesbaden, 1976. pp. 240. bibliog. (Bochum. Ruhr-Universität. Ostasien-Institut. Veröffentlichungen. Band 16)

— France.

FRANCE. Direction de la Documentation. La Documentation Française. Notes et Etudes Documentaires. Nos. 4,121-4, 122. Le chemin de fer en France; par René Parès. Paris, 1974. pp. 84.

FRANCE. French Embassy, London. Service de Presse et d'Information. 1975. French railways: an investment programme for energy conservation. London, 1975. pp. 11. (France: facts, figures. A/105/1/75)

— Germany — History.

KREIDLER (EUGEN) Die Eisenbahnen im Machtbereich der Achsenmächte während des Zweiten Weltkrieges: Einsatz und Leistung für die Wehrmacht und Kriegswirtschaft. Göttingen, [1975]. pp. 440. bibliog. (Arbeitskreis für Wehrforschung. Studien und Dokumente zur Geschichte des Zweiten Weltkrieges. Band 15)

— Italy.

CAGLIOZZI (ROBERTO) L'ammodernamento delle ferrovie ed il ruolo del trasporto ferroviario nel Mezzogiorno. Milano, 1975. pp. 173. (Associazione per lo Sviluppo dell'Industria nel Mezzogiorno. Centro per gli Studi sullo Sviluppo Economico. Collana di Monografie)

— Russia — Employees.

METEL'KOV (PETR FEDOROVICH) Zheleznodorozhniki v revoliutsii, fevral' 1917 - iiun' 1918. Leningrad, 1970. pp. 359.

UCHENYE ZAPISKI KAFEDR OBSHCHESTVENNYKH NAUK VUZOV LENINGRADA. Istoriia KPSS. vyp.10. Po leninskomu puti. Leningrad, 1970. pp. 141.

PUSHKAREVA (IRINA MIKHAILOVNA) Zheleznodorozhniki Rossii v burzhuazno-demokraticheskikh revoliutsiiakh. Moskva, 1975. pp. 390.

— — History.

SAJDL (JOSEF) Českoslovenští železničáři v sibiřské anabasi. [Praha], 1924. pp. 108,[x].

— — Passenger traffic.

BELEN'KII (MARK NAUMOVICH) Ekonomika passazhirskikh perevozok. Moskva, 1974. pp. 272. bibliog.

— — Estonia — History.

GUSAROVA (VERA GRIGOR'EVNA) and others. 100 let zheleznykh dorog Estonii. Tallin, 1970. pp. 243.

— — Russia (RSFSR) — Rolling-stock.

IMENI Voitovicha. Moskva, 1969. pp. 312.

— South Africa.

SOUTH AFRICA. South African Railways and Harbours. 1976. Report...relative to the construction of new lines of railway from: 1. Thabazimbi station to a terminal point on the farm Naauw Ontkomen; and 2. Nseleni station to a terminal point on the farm known as K44 No.13587 (R.P.49-1976). in SOUTH AFRICA. Parliament. House of Assembly. Votes and proceedings; (with Printed annexures).

— Sweden — Employees.

EUROPEAN COURT OF HUMAN RIGHTS. Publications. Series A: Judgments and Decisions. [A 20]. ...Swedish Engine Drivers' Union case; judgment of 6 February, 1976. Strasbourg, Council of Europe, 1976. pp. 18[bis]. In English and French.

— Tanzania.

BAILEY (MARTIN DAWSON) Freedom railway: China and the Tanzania-Zambia link. London, 1976. pp. 168. bibliog.

— United Kingdom.

PRYKE (RICHARD W.S.) and DODGSON (JOHN S.) The rail problem. London, 1975. pp. 294.

HALL (PETER GEOFFREY) and SMITH (EDWARD) Civil engineer. Better use of rail ways. Reading, 1976. pp. 130. bibliog. (Reading. University. Department of Geography. Reading Geographical Papers. No. 43)

U.K. British Railways Board. 1976. Transport policy: an opportunity for change: comments by British Railways Board on the government consultation document; (with Summary). [London, 1976]. 2 pts.

— — Electrification.

U.K. British Railways. London Midland Region. 1960. Change at Crewe; commemorating the completion of stage one, Manchester-Crewe, of the Manchester-Liverpool-Euston electrification scheme. [London], 1960. 1 pamphlet (unpaged).

— — Equipment and supplies.

MILLIGAN (JOHN) The resilient pioneers: a history of the Elastic Rail Spike Company and its associates. Aberdeen, 1975. pp. 143. bibliog.

— United States.

HAMER (ANDREW MARSHALL) The selling of rail rapid transit: a critical look at urban transportation planning. Lexington, Mass., [1976]. pp. 336. bibliog.

— — Accounts, bookkeeping, etc.

WHITTEN (HERBERT O.) Utilization and capacity costing and rate of return measurement: a report and proposal for a cost accounting and analysis system to be used by railroads and other forms of transport. Shaker Heights, [1960]. pp. 49.

— — Employees — Bibliography.

MORRIS (JAMES OLIVER) compiler. Bibliography of industrial relations in the railroad industry. Ithaca, N.Y., [1975]. pp. 153. (Cornell University. New York State School of Industrial and Labor Relations. Bibliography Series. No. 12)

— — California — History.

McAFEE (WARD) California's railroad era 1850-1911. San Marino, California, [1973]. pp. 256. bibliog.

— Zambia.

BAILEY (MARTIN DAWSON) Freedom railway: China and the Tanzania-Zambia link. London, 1976. pp. 168. bibliog.

RAILWAYS, LOCAL AND LIGHT

— Europe.

CENTRO STUDI SUI SISTEMI DI TRASPORTO. Le ferrovie urbane: realizzazione per fasi; a cura di Giuseppe Sciarrone. Roma, 1975. pp. 198. bibliog. (Quaderni . N. 10)

RAILWAYS AND STATE

— United Kingdom.

ROBERTSON (JOHN MACKINNON) Railway nationalisation. Bradford, [1897]. pp. 7. (Papers for the People. No. 11)

RAILWAYS AND STATE(Cont.)

— United States.

GODFREY (AARON AUSTIN) Government operation of the railroads: its necessity, success, and consequences, 1918-1920. Austin, Texas, 1974. pp. 190. *bibliog.*

RAKOVSKII (KHRISTIAN GEORGIEVICH).

CONTE (FRANCIS) Christian Rakovski, 1873-1941: essai de biographie politique. Paris, 1975. 2 vols. (in 1). *bibliog. Thèse présentée devant l'Université de Bordeaux III.*

RAMAPO MOUNTAIN PEOPLE.

COHEN (DAVID STEVEN) The Ramapo Mountain people. New Brunswick, N.J., [1974]. pp. 285. *bibliog.*

RAMING.

See GROSSRAMING.

RAPALLO, TREATY OF, 1922.

AKHTAMZIAN (ABDULKHAN ABDURAKHMANOVICH) Rapall'skaia politika: sovetsko-germanskie diplomaticheskie otnosheniia v 1922-1932 godakh. Moskva, 1974. pp. 303.

RAPESEED.

BELL (JESS MARY K.) The market for rapeseed and its products in western Europe with particular reference to the UK. London, Tropical Products Institute, 1975. pp. 105. *bibliog. ([Reports]. G 100)*

RATIONALISM.

KRITISCHER Rationalismus und Sozialdemokratie: herausgegeben von Georg Lührs [and others]; mit einem Vorwort von Helmut Schmidt. Berlin, 1975. pp. 482.

ALBERT (HANS) Aufklärung und Steuerung: Aufsätze zur Sozialphilosophie und zur Wissenschaftslehre der Sozialwissenschaften. Hamburg, [1976]. pp. 196. *bibliog.*

PARKER (MAXWELL NOEL LEWIS) Rousseau and the contradictions of rationalism: a critical study of Rousseau's social and political theory in the context of eighteenth-century social and philosophical developments. [1976]. fo. 264. *bibliog. Typescript. Ph.D. (London) thesis: unpublished. This thesis is the property of London University and may not be removed from the Library.*

RAW MATERIALS.

SCHNEIDER (WILLIAM) Can we avert economic warfare in raw materials?: U.S. agriculture as a blue chip. New York, [1974]. pp. 43. *(National Strategy Information Center. Agenda Papers. No. 1)*

WORLD SYMPOSIUM ON ENERGY AND RAW MATERIALS, 1ST., PARIS, 1974. Summary of the proceedings. New York, [1975]. pp. 116.

RAWLS (JOHN).

DANIELS (NORMAN) ed. Reading Rawls: critical studies on Rawls' "A theory of justice". Oxford, [1975]. pp. 352. *bibliog.*

RAZGON (IZRAIL' MENDELEEVICH).

PROBLEMY istorii Oktiabr'skoi revoliutsii i grazhdanskoi voiny v SSSR; (sbornik, posviashchennyi 70-letiiu professora I.M. Razgona). Tomsk, 1975. pp. 401.

READING.

— Religion.

YEO (STEPHEN) Religion and voluntary organisations in crisis. London, 1976. pp. 426.

— Social history.

YEO (STEPHEN) Religion and voluntary organisations in crisis. London, 1976. pp. 426.

READING.

MASSARO (DOMINIC W.) ed. Understanding language: an information-processing analysis of speech perception, reading, and psycholinguistics. New York, [1975]. pp. 439. *bibliogs.*

READING UNIVERSITY.

GILES (A.K.) University of Reading, agricultural economics, 1923-73: published on the occasion of the 50th anniversary of the department. Reading, 1973. pp. 92. *bibliog.*

REAL COVENANTS

— United Kingdom.

PRESTON (CECIL HERBERT SANSOME) and NEWSOM (GEORGE HAROLD) Restrictive covenants affecting freehold land; sixth edition by G. H. Newsom assisted by G.L. Newsom. London, 1976. pp. 366.

REAL ESTATE AGENTS

— South Africa.

SOUTH AFRICA. Parliament. House of Assembly. Select Committee on the Estate Agents Bill. 1976. Report (with Proceedings and Minutes of evidence) (S.C.5- 1976). in SOUTH AFRICA. Parliament. House of Assembly. Select Committee reports.

REAL ESTATE BUSINESS

— France.

DHUYS (JEAN FRANÇOIS) Les promoteurs. Paris, [1975]. pp. 205. *bibliog.*

— New Zealand.

REAL ESTATE MARKET IN NEW ZEALAND, THE; [pd. by] Valuation Department. a., 1975- Wellington. *Supersedes RURAL REAL ESTATE IN NEW ZEALAND and URBAN REAL ESTATE IN NEW ZEALAND.*

— South Africa.

SOUTH AFRICA. Parliament. Senate. Select Committee on Allegation by Senator. 1975. Report; (with Proceedings and minutes of evidence) (S.C. 1/1975). in SOUTH AFRICA. Parliament. Senate. Reports from the Sessional and Select Committees.

— United Kingdom.

U.K. Department of Prices and Consumer Protection. 1975. The regulation of estate agency: a consultative document. London, 1975. pp. 24.

REAL ESTATE INVESTMENT

— United Kingdom.

AMBROSE (PETER JOHN) and COLENUTT (ROBERT J.) The property machine. Harmondsworth, 1975. pp. 192. *bibliog.*

BENWELL COMMUNITY DEVELOPMENT PROJECT. Benwell's hidden property companies. Newcastle-upon-Tyne, 1976. pp. 60. *(Working Papers. No.1)*

REAL PROPERTY

— France — Prices.

GRANELLE (JEAN JACQUES) La valeur du sol urbain et la propriété foncière: le marché des terrains à Paris. Paris, [1975]. pp. 240. *bibliog.*

— Germany — North Rhine—Westphalia.

NORTH RHINE-WESTPHALIA. Landesamt für Datenverarbeitung und Statistik. Beiträge zur Statistik des Landes Nordrhein- Westfalen. Heft 339. Einheitswerte des Grundbesitzes in Nordrhein-Westfalen, 1964. Düsseldorf, 1975 in progress.

— Ireland (Republic).

WYLIE (J.C.W.) Irish land law. London, 1975. pp. 914.

— New Guinea, German.

GERMAN NEW GUINEA. Statutes, etc. 1885-1914. The land law of German New Guinea: a collection of documents; [edited by] Peter and Bridget Sack. Canberra, 1975. pp. 120. *bibliog.*

— Poland.

LUSTRACJA województwa ruskiego, 1661-1665. Wrocław, 1970-74. 2 vols.(in 1). *(Polska Akademia Nauk. Instytut Historii. Lustracje Dóbr Królewskich XVI-XVIII Wieku)*

— Switzerland.

SWITZERLAND. Bureau Fédéral de Statistique. 1972. Arealstatistik der Schweiz...1972. Bern, 1972. pp. 121 and 19 maps. *(Statistiques de la Suisse. 488e fasc.) In German and French.*

— United Kingdom.

DALTON (PATRICK J.) Land law. 2nd ed. London, 1975. pp. 332.

MEGARRY (Sir ROBERT EDGAR) A manual of the law of real property; fifth edition by P.V. Baker. London, 1975. pp. 610.

CHESHIRE (GEOFFREY CHEVALIER) Modern law of real property; twelfth edition by E.H. Burn. London, 1976. pp. 1039.

— — Prices.

NEUBURGER (H.L.I.) and NICHOL (B.M.) The recent course of land and property prices and the factors underlying it. [London, 1976]. pp. 61. *(U.K. Department of the Environment. Research Reports. 4)*

— — Ireland, Northern.

WYLIE (J.C.W.) Irish land law. London, 1975. pp. 914.

— United States.

McDOUGAL (MYRES SMITH) and HABER (DAVID) Property, wealth, land: allocation, planning and development; selected cases and other materials on the law of real property; an introduction. Charlottesville, Va., 1948. pp. 1213.

— — Valuation.

BEDNARZ (ROBERT S.) The effect of air pollution on property value in Chicago. Chicago, 1975. pp. 111. *bibliog. (Chicago. University. Department of Geography. Research Papers. No. 166)*

REAL PROPERTY TAX

— United Kingdom.

RATING law and practice; by H.J. Wright [and others]. London, 1974. pp. 336.

RYDE (WALTER CRANLEY) On rating: the law and practice; thirteenth edition by David Widdicombe [and others]. London, 1976. pp. 1454, 84.

U.K. Board of Inland Revenue. 1976. Development Land Tax Bill: explanatory notes. [London], 1976. pp. 95.

— United States.

PROPERTY taxation, land use and public policy; edited by Arthur D. Lynn, Jr. Madison, Wis., 1976. pp. 252. *(Committee on Taxation, Resources and Economic Development. Publications.8) Proceedings of a symposium held at the University of Wisconsin-Madison, 1973.*

REAL-TIME DATA PROCESSING.

ROTHSTEIN (MICHAEL F.) Guide to the design of real-time systems. New York, [1970]. pp. 243.

REASON.

NELSON (LEONARD) Critique of practical reason;...translated by Norbert Guterman. [Scarsdale, N.Y., 1957]. pp. 565,xviii. *(Lectures on the foundations of ethics. vol. 1) Facsimile reproduction of typescript with translator's manuscript additions and corrections.*

RATIONALITY and the social sciences: contributions to the philosophy and methodology of the social sciences; edited by S.I. Benn and G.W.Mortimore. London, 1976. pp. 416. *bibliogs. Includes papers from a seminar sponsored by the Philosophy Department of the Research School of Social Sciences, Australian National University, in 1971.*

REASONING.

REASONING: representation and process in children and adults; edited by Rachel Joffe Falmagne. Hillsdale, N.J., 1975. pp. 275. *bibliogs. Expansion of material from a symposium held at the annual meeting of the Eastern Psychological Association, 1973.*

RECIDIVISTS

— United Kingdom.

CHRISTIAN ECONOMIC AND SOCIAL RESEARCH FOUNDATION. Occasional Papers. Series C, No.1. Recidivism among drunken motorists, England and Wales, 1964 to 1973. London, 1975. pp. 29.

RECLAMATION OF LAND.

TANDY (CLIFF) Landscape of industry;...with a section on hydrology by Peter Nelson. London, 1975. pp. 314. *bibliogs.*

— Russia — Uzbekistan.

KHODZHIEV (E.KH.) Istoriia orosheniia i osvoeniia Golodnoi stepi, 1917-1970 gg. Tashkent, 1975. pp. 187. *bibliog.*

RECOGNITION (INTERNATIONAL LAW).

GLEICH (JOHANN GEORG) Die Anerkennung der DDR durch die Bundesrepublik: eine völkerrechtliche Untersuchung, etc. Bern, 1975. pp. 254. *bibliog.*

VERHOEVEN (JOE) La reconnaissance internationale dans la pratique contemporaine: les relations publiques internationales. Paris, 1975. pp. 861. *bibliog. (Revue Générale de Droit International Public. Publications. Nouvelle Série. No. 24)*

RECOGNITION (PSYCHOLOGY).

BROWN (JOHN) 1925- , ed. Recall and recognition. London, [1976]. pp. 275. *bibliog.*

RECOLLECTION (PSYCHOLOGY).

BROWN (JOHN) 1925- , ed. Recall and recognition. London, [1976]. pp. 275. *bibliog.*

RECONSTRUCTION (1939-1951).

CLARK (Sir GEORGE NORMAN) [Correspondence about the publication of Agenda: a quarterly journal of reconstruction. 1941-43]. 1 folder. *Manuscript, typescript, etc.*

RECONSTRUCTION (UNITED STATES).

BENEDICT (MICHAEL LES) A compromise of principle: Congressional Republicans and reconstruction, 1863-1869. New York, [1974]. pp. 493. *bibliog.*

SHOFNER (JERRELL H.) Nor is it over yet: Florida in the era of reconstruction, 1863- 1877. Gainesville, Fla., 1974. pp. 412. *bibliog.*

RADICAL republicans in the North: state politics during reconstruction; edited by James C. Mohr. Baltimore, [1976]. pp. 200. *bibliog.*

RECREATION.

PARKER (STANLEY ROBERT) The sociology of leisure. New York, 1976. pp. 157.

— Norway.

TEIGLAND (JON) Friluftsliv, idrett og mosjon...: outdoor recreation, sport and exercise. Oslo, 1975. pp. 112. *bibliog. (Norway. Statistiske Centralbyrå. Samfunnsøkonomiske Studier. 25) With English summary.*

— United Kingdom.

COPPOCK (JOHN TERENCE) and DUFFIELD (BRIAN SNOWDEN) Recreation in the countryside: a spatial analysis. London, 1975. pp. 262. *bibliog.*

VICKERMAN (ROGER W.) The economics of leisure and recreation. London, 1975. pp. 229. *bibliog.*

WESTMINSTER. Department of Architecture and Planning. Westminster Development Plan Publications. Topic Papers. T 4. Recreation and leisure. [London], 1975. pp. 104.

— United States — Administration.

BANNON (JOSEPH J.) Leisure resources: its comprehensive planning. Englewood Cliffs, [1976]. pp. 454. *bibliogs.*

RECREATION AREAS

— Finland.

VUORISTO (KAI VEIKKO) Talviulkoilualueet, niiden edellytykset ja käyttöö erityisesti etelä-Suomen olosuheissa: talousmaantieteellinen selvity; summary Winter recreation areas, condition for and use of them especially in southern Finland: a geographical survey. Helsinki, 1971. pp. 101. *bibliog. (Helsinki. Kauppakorkeakoulu. Julkaisuja. Sarja C. II:10)*

— United Kingdom.

YOUNG (DAVID) of the South Hampshire Plan Technical Unit. Factors affecting the future location of major recreational areas in South Hampshire. [Winchester], 1970. pp. 10. *(South Hampshire Plan Technical Unit. Working Papers. 9)*

RECREATIONAL land management in the South West: papers presented at a conference organised by the Department of Surveying, Bristol Polytechnic, 16 and 17 May 1974; edited by R.C.D. Netting, T.B. Stapleton). Bristol, [1974]. fo. 91.

GOODALL (BRIAN) National forests and recreational opportunities. Reading, 1975. pp. 57. *bibliog. (Reading. University. Department of Geography. Reading Geographical Papers. No.39)*

— — Wales.

YOUTH HOSTELS ASSOCIATION (ENGLAND AND WALES). Landscape and forestry in Mid-Wales: a land-use survey. [London], 1974. pp. 9.

RECREATION RESEARCH.

GREAVES (JOAN) National parks and access to the countryside and coast: trends in research, 1964-1968; paper prepared for the Town Planning Institute Calendar of Planning Research, 3rd edition. [London], Countryside Commission, 1968. fo. 7. *bibliog.*

RECURSIVE PROGRAMMING.

BURGE (WILLIAM H.) Recursive programming techniques. Reading, Mass., [1975]. pp. 277. *bibliogs.*

RED RIVER REBELLION, 1869-1870.

HOWARD (JOSEPH KINSEY) Strange empire: Louis Riel and the Métis people. Toronto, 1974. pp. 601. *bibliog. Originally published in 1952 in New York.*

REFERENDUM

— France.

DENQUIN (JEAN MARIE) Référendum et plébiscite: essai de théorie générale. Paris, 1976. pp. 353. *bibliog.*

— Norway.

NORWAY. Statistiske Centralbyrå. 1974. Folkerøystinga om EF: aktivitet blant veljarane, etc. Oslo, 1974. pp. 63. *(Statistiske Analyser. 11) With English summary.*

— United Kingdom.

ALDERSON (STANLEY) Yea nor nay?: referenda in the United Kingdom. London, 1975. pp. 136. *bibliog.*

GRIMOND (JOSEPH) and NEVE (BRIAN) The referendum. London, 1975. pp. 128. *bibliog.*

BRITAIN into Europe: public opinion and the EEC 1961-75; edited by Roger Jowell and Gerald Hoinville. London, 1976. pp. 128. *bibliog.*

BUTLER (DAVID HENRY EDGEWORTH) and KITZINGER (UWE WEBSTER) The 1975 referendum. London, 1976. pp. 315.

GOODHART (PHILIP) Full-hearted consent: the story of the referendum campaign - and the campaign for the referendum. London, 1976. pp. 264.

REFORMATION.

MARCU (VALERIU) The birth of the nations, from the unity of faith to the democracy of money;...translated by Eden and Cedar Paul. London, 1932. pp. 287.

— Germany.

HANNEMANN (MANFRED) The diffusion of the Reformation in southwestern Germany, 1518- 1534. Chicago, 1975. pp. 235. *bibliog. (Chicago. University. Department of Geography. Research Papers. No.167)*

OZMENT (STEVEN E.) The Reformation in the cities: the appeal of Protestantism to sixteenth-century Germany and Switzerland. New Haven, 1975. pp. 237.

— Switzerland.

OZMENT (STEVEN E.) The Reformation in the cities: the appeal of Protestantism to sixteenth-century Germany and Switzerland. New Haven, 1975. pp. 237.

REFORMATORIES

— Europe.

EUROPEAN COMMITTEE ON CRIME PROBLEMS. 1967. Short-term methods of treatment for young offenders: report, etc. Strasbourg, Council of Europe, 1967. pp. 88. *bibliog.*

— Ireland (Republic).

OSBOROUGH (NIAL) Borstal in Ireland: custodial provision for the young adult offender, 1906-1974. Dublin, [1975]. pp. 184. *bibliog.*

— United Kingdom — Ireland, Northern.

OSBOROUGH (NIAL) Borstal in Ireland: custodial provision for the young adult offender, 1906-1974. Dublin, [1975]. pp. 184. *bibliog.*

— United States.

McARTHUR (A. VERNE) Coming out cold: community reentry from a state reformatory. Lexington, Mass., [1974]. pp. 131. *bibliog.*

REFUGEES.

HOLBORN (LOUISE W.) and others. Refugees: a problem of our time: the work of the United Nations High Commissioner for Refugees, 1951-1972. Metuchen, N.J., 1975. 2 vols. *bibliog.*

REFUGEES, AUSTRIAN.

MAIMANN (HELENE) Politik im Wartesaal: österreichische Exilpolitik in Grossbritannien, 1938-1945. Wien, 1975. pp. 355. *bibliog. (Kommission für Neuere Geschichte Österreichs. Veröffentlichungen. 62)*

REFUGEES, GERMAN.

GARFINKELS (BETTY) Belgique, terre d'accueil: problème du réfugié, 1933-1940. Bruxelles, 1974. pp. 240. *bibliog.*

— Periodicals — Indexes.

HEINTZ (GEORG) compiler. Index des "Freien/Neuen Deutschland", Mexico, 1941-1946. [Worms, 1975]. pp. 110.

REFUGEES, POLITICAL.

REFUGEES, POLITICAL.

MISGELD (KLAUS) Die "Internationale Gruppe demokratischer Sozialisten" in Stockholm, 1942-1945: zur sozialistischen Friedensdiskussion während des Zweiten Weltkrieges. Uppsala, 1976. pp. 212. bibliog. *(Uppsala. Universitet. Historiska Institutionen. Studia Historica Upsaliensia. 79)*

REFUGEES, SPANISH.

BERRUEZO (JOSE) Contribucion a la historia de la C.N.T. de España en el exilio. Mexico, 1967. pp. 303.

GARFINKELS (BETTY) Belgique, terre d'accueil: problème du réfugié, 1933-1940. Bruxelles, 1974. pp. 240. bibliog.

ROS (ANTONIO) Diario de un refugiado republicano. Barcelona, [1975 repr. 1976]. pp. 426.

REFUGEES IN BELGIUM.

GARFINKELS (BETTY) Belgique, terre d'accueil: problème du réfugié, 1933-1940. Bruxelles, 1974. pp. 240. bibliog.

REFUGEES IN EASTERN GERMANY.

MERKER (PAUL) Die nächsten Schritte zur Lösung des Umsiedlerproblems; herausgegeben vom Zentralsekretariat der Sozialistischen Einheitspartei Deutschlands. Berlin, [1947]. pp. 32.

REFUGEES IN EUROPE.

DARTON (LAWRENCE) An account of the work of the Friends Committee for Refugees and Aliens, first known as the Germany Emergency Committee of the Society of Friends, 1933-1950. n.p., 1954. fo. 170.

REFUGEES IN FRANCE.

PECH (KARLHEINZ) An der Seite der Résistance: zum Kampf der Bewegung "Freies Deutschland" für den Westen in Frankreich, 1943- 1945. Berlin, 1974. pp. 387. bibliog.

RIBS (JACQUES) Plaidoyer pour un million de victimes. Paris, [1975]. pp. 294.

ROS (ANTONIO) Diario de un refugiado republicano. Barcelona, [1975 repr. 1976]. pp. 426.

REFUGEES IN GERMANY.

MERKER (PAUL) Die nächsten Schritte zur Lösung des Umsiedlerproblems; herausgegeben vom Zentralsekretariat der Sozialistischen Einheitspartei Deutschlands. Berlin, [1947]. pp. 32.

REFUGEES IN MEXICO

— Periodicals — Indexes.

HEINTZ (GEORG) compiler. Index des "Freien/Neuen Deutschland", Mexico, 1941-1946. [Worms, 1975]. pp. 110.

REFUGEES IN SWEDEN.

MISGELD (KLAUS) Die "Internationale Gruppe demokratischer Sozialisten" in Stockholm, 1942-1945: zur sozialistischen Friedensdiskussion während des Zweiten Weltkrieges. Uppsala, 1976. pp. 212. bibliog. *(Uppsala. Universitet. Historiska Institutionen. Studia Historica Upsaliensia. 79)*

REFUGEES IN THE UNITED KINGDOM.

MAIMANN (HELENE) Politik im Wartesaal: österreichische Exilpolitik in Grossbritannien, 1938-1945. Wien, 1975. pp. 355. bibliog. *(Kommission für Neuere Geschichte Österreichs. Veröffentlichungen. 62)*

REFUSE AND REFUSE DISPOSAL.

GODDARD (HAYNES C.) Managing solid wastes: economics, technology, and institutions. New York, 1975. pp. 368. bibliog.

— Belgium.

ECONOMISCHE RAAD VOOR OOST-VLAANDEREN. Huisvuilverwijdering en -verwerking in Oost-Vlaanderen. [Ghent], 1971. fo. 127.

— United States.

BROWN (F. LEE) and LEBECK (A.O.) Cars, cans and dumps: solutions for rural residuals. Baltimore, [1976]. pp. 206. bibliog.

KEMPER (PETER) and QUIGLEY (JOHN M.) The economics of refuse collection. Cambridge, Mass., [1976]. pp. 181. bibliog.

REGION CENTRE

— Economic policy.

REGION CENTRE. Préparation du VIe plan: élaboration de l'esquisse de programme régional. [Paris], 1970. 1 vol. (various pagings).

REGION CENTRE. Préparation du VIe plan: élaboration de l'esquisse de programme régional; documents de travail, etc. [Paris], 1970. 1 vol. (various pagings).

— Social policy.

REGION CENTRE. Préparation du VIe plan: élaboration de l'esquisse de programme régional. [Paris], 1970. 1 vol. (various pagings).

REGION CENTRE. Préparation du VIe plan: élaboration de l'esquisse de programme régional; documents de travail, etc. [Paris], 1970. 1 vol. (various pagings).

REGION PARISIENNE.

See PARIS (REGION).

REGIONAL ECONOMICS.

THELEN (PETER) and LUEHRS (GEORG) Abgrenzung von Fördergebieten: die Messung der Wirtschaftskraft und der strukturellen Gefährdung von Regionen. Hannover, [1971]. pp. 112. bibliog. *(Friedrich-Ebert-Stiftung. Forschungsinstitut. Schriftenreihe. Band 91)*

HOLLAND (STUART) Capital versus the regions. London, 1976. pp. 328.

HOLLAND (STUART) The regional problem. London, 1976. pp. 179.

INTERNATIONAL CONFERENCE ON REGIONAL SCIENCE, ENERGY AND ENVIRONMENT, LOUVAIN, 1975. Energy, regional science and public policy: proceedings of the... Conference...[vol.] 1...; edited by M. Chatterji and P. Van Rompuy. Berlin, 1976. pp. 316. bibliogs.

REGIONAL analysis...; edited by Carol A. Smith. New York, [1976]. 2 vols. bibliogs. *Papers prepared for a conference held in Santa Fe, New Mexico, in 1973.*

UNIVERSITY SYMPOSIUM ON REGIONAL SCIENCE, BINGHAMTON, NEW YORK, 1974 Space, location and regional development; (editor, M. Chatterji). London, [1976]. pp. 239. bibliogs.

— Mathematical models.

INTERNATIONAL CONFERENCE ON REGIONAL SCIENCE, ENERGY AND ENVIRONMENT, LOUVAIN, 1975. Environment, regional science and interregional modeling: proceedings of the...Conference...[vol.] 2...; edited by M. Chatterji and P. Van Rompuy. Berlin, 1976. pp. 211. bibliogs.

REGIONAL PLANNING.

ONTARIO PLANNING SEMINAR, TORONTO, 1970. Ontario planning seminar, 1970, for senior municipal planners: process, model, data; papers and proceedings. Toronto, Queen's Printer, [1971]. 1 vol. (various pagings).

HAY (ALAN M.) and others. Government intervention. Milton Keynes, 1974. pp. 110. bibliogs. *(Open University. Social Sciences: a third level course. Regional analysis and development 4: Units 14-16)*

PERRIN (JEAN CLAUDE) Le développement régional. [Paris], 1974. pp. 208.

SOARES (MARIA CÂNDIDA MEDEIROS) Aspectos do desenvolvimento regional socio economico. Lisboa, 1974. pp. 65. *(Portugal. Ministerio do Trabalho. Gabinete de Planeamento. Serie Estudos. 26) With abstracts in English, French and German.*

ACTION-oriented approaches to regional development planning; edited by Avrom Bendavid-Val [and] Peter P. Waller. New York, 1975. pp. 132.

CROSS (DONALD) Forecasting in urban and regional planning; a report to the Planning Committee of the S[ocial] S[cience] R[esearch] C[ouncil];...with the assistance of Malcolm Longair and Stephen Grigson. London, Social Science Research Council, [1975]. pp. 94. bibliog.

GILLINGWATER (DAVID) Regional planning and social change: a responsive approach. Farnborough, Hants., [1975]. pp. 272. bibliog.

APGAR (MAHLON) ed. New perspectives on community development. London, [1976]. pp. 363.

INTERNATIONAL CONFERENCE ON REGIONAL SCIENCE, ENERGY AND ENVIRONMENT, LOUVAIN, 1975. Energy, regional science and public policy: proceedings of the... Conference...[vol.] 1...; edited by M. Chatterji and P. Van Rompuy. Berlin, 1976. pp. 316. bibliogs.

UNIVERSITY SYMPOSIUM ON REGIONAL SCIENCE, BINGHAMTON, NEW YORK, 1974 Space, location and regional development; (editor, M. Chatterji). London, [1976]. pp. 239. bibliogs.

— Bibliography.

AASE (MONICA) compiler. Regional ökonomi og regional planlegging: en bibliografi. Bergen, 1974. fo. 105,viii.

COMMONWEALTH BUREAU OF AGRICULTURAL ECONOMICS. Regional planning and rural development. [Farnham Royal, 1975]. pp. 32. *(Annotated Bibliographies. No. 35) Compiled from World Agricultural Economics and Rural Sociology Abstracts from 1974 to 1975.*

— Evaluation — Computer programs.

See also PERP (COMPUTER PROGRAM).

— Law and legislation — United States.

HEALY (ROBERT G.) Land use and the states. [Baltimore, 1976]. pp. 233.

— Africa.

TOURNIER (MAURICE) L'échelon régional et la planification nationale. Paris, 1975. pp. 111. bibliog. *(France. Secrétariat d'Etat aux Affaires Etrangères. Méthodologie de la Planification. 3) Refonte complète de "Le travail du planificateur au niveau régional pour l'exécution d'un plan national" publié en 1970.*

— America, North.

HANSEN (NILES M.) Public policy and regional economic development: the experience of nine western countries. Cambridge, Mass., [1974]. pp. 351. bibliog.

— Australia.

STILWELL (FRANK J.B.) Australian urban and regional development. Sydney, [1974]. pp. 206.

— — New South Wales.

NEW SOUTH WALES. State Planning Authority. 1972. Hunter region: growth and change: prelude to a plan. Sydney, 1972. pp. 112.

REGIONAL PLANNING.

— **Austria.**

FUERSTENBERG (FRIEDRICH) and others. Arbeitnehmerinteressen in der Raumplanung. [Linz, 1974]. pp. 98. *bibliog. (Linz. Hochschule für Sozial- und Wirtschaftswissenschaften. Institut für Kommunalwissenschaften, and others. Kommunale Forschung in Österreich. 15)*

— **Belgium.**

DESCHAMPS (CLAUDE) Planification et decentralisation économique en Belgique. Bruxelles, 1973. 1 vol. (loose-leaf).

— **Canada.**

CONFERENCE ON REGIONAL ECONOMIC DEVELOPMENT, OTTAWA, 1972. Regional economic development: [revised papers from the conference held in Ottawa, March 2-4, 1972, organized by the University of Ottawa]; edited by O.J. Firestone. Ottawa, 1974. pp. 274. *(Ottawa. Université. Cahiers des Sciences Sociales. No. 9) In English or French, with summaries in the alternative language.*

McMASTER UNIVERSITY. Interdepartmental Committee on Communist and East European Affairs. Annual Conference, 7th, 1973. Development regions in the Soviet Union, eastern Europe, and Canada; (edited by Andrew F. Burghardt). New York, 1975. pp. 192. *(McMaster University. McMaster University Studies on Soviet and East European Affairs)*

— — **Nova Scotia.**

TODD (DANIEL) Polarization in a peripheral regional economy: a spatial analysis of manufacturing industry, with reference to Nova Scotia, Canada; [Ph.D. (London) thesis]. 1975. fo. 360. *bibliog. Typescript: unpublished. This thesis is the property of London University and may not be removed from the Library.*

— — **Ontario.**

ONTARIO PLANNING SEMINAR, TORONTO, 1970. Ontario planning seminar, 1970, for senior municipal planners: process, model, data; papers and proceedings. Toronto, Queen's Printer, [1971]. 1 vol. (various pagings).

— **Communist countries.**

POLSKA AKADEMIA NAUK. Komitet Przestrzennego Zagospodarowania Kraju. Studia. t.51. Metodologiia izucheniia natsional'nogo dokhoda i gorodskikh aglomeratsii v sotsialisticheskikh stranakh: materialy III Soveshchaniia predstavitelei nauchnykh uchrezhdenii sotsialisticheskikh stran-chlenov SEV po voprosam metodologii regional'nykh issledovanii, Varshava, 4-8 dekabria 1974 g. Varshava, 1975. pp. 270.

— **Denmark.**

COPENHAGEN. Egnsplanrådet. Planlaegningsafdeling. Strukturplan 1972 for hovedstadsregionen. København, 1973. pp. 88.

COPENHAGEN. Egnsplanrådet. Planlaegningsafdeling. Regionplan 1973 for hovedstadsregionen: hovedstruktur og byvaekst. København, 1974. pp. 72. *Map in end pocket.*

— **Europe.**

HANSEN (NILES M.) Public policy and regional economic development: the experience of nine western countries. Cambridge, Mass., [1974]. pp. 351. *bibliog.*

CLOUT (HUGH DONALD) ed. Regional development in western Europe. London, [1975]. pp. 328. *bibliogs.*

KONJUNKTURPOLITIK: Zeitschrift für angewandte Konjunkturforschung. Beihefte. Heft 22. Regionalpolitik und Agrarpolitik in Europa: Bericht über den wissenschaftlichen Teil der 38. Mitgliederversammlung der Arbeitsgemeinschaft deutscher wirtschaftswissenschaftlicher Forschungsinstitute...1975. Berlin, [1975]. pp. 135. *bibliog. In German or English.*

— **France.**

REGION CENTRE. Préparation du VIe plan: élaboration de l'esquisse de programme régional. [Paris], 1970. 1 vol. (various pagings).

REGION CENTRE. Préparation du VIe plan: élaboration de l'esquisse de programme régional; documents de travail, etc. [Paris], 1970. 1 vol. (various pagings).

FRANCE. Commissariat Général du Plan. Service Régional et Urbain. 1973. Les programmes régionaux de développement et d'équipement du VIe Plan. Paris, 1973. pp. 298.

FRANCE. French Embassy, London. Service de Presse et d'Information. 1974. Area development and regional planning in France: the DATAR. London, 1974. pp. 20. *(France: facts, figures. A/102/9/74)*

FRANCE. French Embassy, London. Service de Presse et d'Information. 1974. The Paris region: planning and development. London, 1974. pp. 24. *(France: facts, figures. A/103/9/74)*

FRANCE. Direction de la Documentation. La Documentation Française. Notes et Etudes Documentaires. Nos. 4,164-4, 165-4,166. L'aménagement de la région Fos-Etang de Berre; par Didier Cultiaux. Paris, 1975. pp. 132.

SOCIETE D'ETUDES PROSPECTIVE ET AMENAGEMENT. Schéma général d'aménagement de la France: dynamique urbaine et projet régional: un exemple: la région Alsace; (réalisée sous la direction d'Augustin Antunes. Paris, 1975. pp. 141. *(France. Délégation à l'Aménagement du Territoire et à l'Action Régionale. Travaux et Recherches de Prospective. 56)*

ULLMO (YVES) La planification en France. Paris, 1974 [or rather 1975]. pp. 625. *(Fondation Nationale des Sciences Politiques. Etudes Politiques, Economiques et Sociales)*

— **Germany.**

GERMANY (BUNDESREPUBLIK). Institut für Raumordnung. 1972. Zielsetzungen in den Entwicklungsprogrammen und -plänen der Länder, etc. Bonn-Bad Godesberg, 1972. pp. 211. *(Mitteilungen. Heft 73)*

GRUNDFRAGEN einer zusammenfassenden Darstellung raumbedeutsamer Planungen und Massnahmen gemäss [para.] 4 Abs. 1 des Raumordnungsgesetzes vom 8. April 1965; von Reimut Jochimsen [and others], etc. Bonn-Bad Godesberg, 1972. pp. 186. *bibliog. (Germany (Bundesrepublik). Institut für Raumordnung. Mitteilungen. Heft 76)*

RAUMORDNUNG in den Ländern II: Baden-Württemberg, Bayern, Hessen, Rheinland-Pfalz, Saarland: Tagungsbericht über das Fortbildungsseminar des Instituts für Raumordnung vom 4. bis 6. Mai, 1971. Bonn-Bad Godesberg, 1972. pp. 123. *(Germany (Bundesrepublik). Institut für Raumordnung. Mitteilungen. Heft 72)*

WARLITZER (VOLKER) Ermittlung des Bestandes und Bedarfes an Planstellen in den Bereichen Raumordnung, Landes- und Regionalplanung im höheren Dienst und in vergleichbaren Vergütungsgruppen. Bonn-Bad Godesberg, 1972. 1 vol. (various pagings). *(Germany (Bundesrepublik). Institut für Raumordnung. Mitteilungen. Heft 77)*

BAUER (HARTMUT) Räumliche Bestimmungsgründe der Situation im Bildungswesen als Grundlage regionaler Bildungsplanung: eine Untersuchung über Ostwestfalen und Südwestniedersachsens. Bonn-Bad Godesberg, 1973. pp. 87. *bibliog. (Germany (Bundesrepublik). Institut für Raumordnung. Mitteilungen. Heft 80)*

OEFFENTLICHKEITSARBEIT für Raumordnung und Landesplanung: Chancen, Möglichkeiten, Techniken; Tagungsbericht über das Kontaktseminar für Landes- und Regionalplanung veranstaltet vom Institut für Raumordnung am 14. und 15. Dezember 1972. Bonn-Bad Godesberg, 1973. pp. 129. *(Germany (Bundesrepublik). Institut für Raumordnung. Mitteilungen. Heft 78)*

EINFLUESSE der Europäischen Gemeinschaft auf die Regionalpolitik in der Bundesrepublik Deutschland; von Fritz Franzmeyer [and others]. Göttingen, [1975]. 1 vol. (various pagings). *(Kommission für Wirtschaftlichen und Sozialen Wandel. Schriften. 46)*

— **Hungary.**

McMASTER UNIVERSITY. Interdepartmental Committee on Communist and East European Affairs. Annual Conference, 7th, 1973. Development regions in the Soviet Union, eastern Europe, and Canada; (edited by Andrew F. Burghardt). New York, 1975. pp. 192. *(McMaster University. McMaster University Studies on Soviet and East European Affairs)*

— **Kenya.**

KENYA. Town Planning Department. 1971. North Eastern Province regional physical development plan. [Nairobi], 1971. fo. 36.

— **Netherlands.**

MEURS (P.K. VAN) Bestuurlijke kanten van de ruimtelijke ordening in Nederland. 's-Gravenhage, 1965 repr. 1975. pp. 220. *bibliog.*

— **Norway.**

BIVAND (ROGER S.) The economic geography of regional differentiation: studies in Sogn og Fjordane, Norway; [Ph.D. (London) thesis]. 1975. fo. 417. *bibliog. Typescript: unpublished. This thesis is the property of London University and may not be removed from the Library.*

LONDON. University. London School of Economics and Political Science. Graduate School of Geography. Discussion Papers. No. 56. Norway's regional policy dilemma; [by] Roger Bivand. London, 1975. pp. 27. *bibliog.*

— **Poland.**

McMASTER UNIVERSITY. Interdepartmental Committee on Communist and East European Affairs. Annual Conference, 7th, 1973. Development regions in the Soviet Union, eastern Europe, and Canada; (edited by Andrew F. Burghardt). New York, 1975. pp. 192. *(McMaster University. McMaster University Studies on Soviet and East European Affairs)*

WZORCE planów regionalnych. Warszawa, 1976. pp. 144. *(Polska Akademia Nauk. Komitet Przestrzennego Zagospodarowania Kraju. Studia. t.54) With Russian and English summaries.*

— **Russia.**

ZENCHENKO (N.S.) ed. Planirovanie kompleksnogo razvitiia khoziaistva oblasti, kraia, ASSR. Moskva, 1974. pp. 189. *bibliog.*

McMASTER UNIVERSITY. Interdepartmental Committee on Communist and East European Affairs. Annual Conference, 7th, 1973. Development regions in the Soviet Union, eastern Europe, and Canada; (edited by Andrew F. Burghardt). New York, 1975. pp. 192. *(McMaster University. McMaster University Studies on Soviet and East European Affairs)*

WAGENER (HANS JUERGEN) Regionalentwicklung und Regionalpolitik in der Sowjetunion. Wien, 1975. fo.30. *bibliog. (Wiener Institut für Internationale Wirtschaftsvergleiche. Forschungsberichte. Nr.25)*

— **South Africa.**

SOUTH AFRICA. Department of Planning and the Environment. 1974. Proposals for a guide plan for the P[retoria] W[itwatersrand] V[ereeniging]. [Pretoria], 1974. pp. 86, 1 map.

SOUTH AFRICA. Department of Planning and the Environment. 1975. National physical development plan. [Pretoria], 1975. pp. 54, 1 map.

— — **Natal.**

NATAL. Town and Regional Planning Commission. Natal Town and Regional Planning Reports. Vol. 24. Pietermaritzburg-Durban region: regional guide plan. Pietermaritzburg, 1973. pp. 114.

NATAL. Town and Regonal Planning Commission. Natal Town and Regional Planning Reports. vol. 29. Draft regional plan for the south coast. Pietermaritzburg, 1974. pp. 141. *bibliog.*

REGIONAL PLANNING.(Cont.)

— Spain.

REGIONALIZACION de la economía española; ([by] Rafael Martinez Cortiña [and others]). Madrid, [1975]. pp. 611. *(Confederacion Española de Cajas de Ahorros. Fondo para la Investigacion Economica y Social. Publicaciones. 66)*

RICHARDSON (HARRY WARD) Regional development policy and planning in Spain. Farnborough, Hants., [1975]. pp. 250. *bibliog.*

— Sweden.

WEISSGLAS (GÖSTA) Studies on service problems in the sparsely populated areas in Northern Sweden. Umeå, 1975. pp. 220. *bibliog. (Universitetet i Umeå. Department of Geography. Geographical Reports. 5) Akademisk avhandling, filosofie doctorsexamen - Umeå Universitet.*

— Switzerland.

SWITZERLAND. Commission Fédérale d'Experts pour l'Etude de l'Aménagement du Territoire. 1967. Rapport...du 6 octobre 1966. [Berne, 1967]. pp. 131. *bibliog.*

— Turkey.

KADIOGLU (KAMIL) Regionalplanung in der Türkei am Beispiel der Provinz Kastamonu. Hamburg, 1975. pp. 234. *bibliog. (Deutsches Orient-Institut and Deutsches Übersee-Institut. Mitteilungen. Nr.7)*

— Underdeveloped areas.

See UNDERDEVELOPED AREAS — Regional planning.

— United Kingdom.

BRYAN (Sir ANDREW MEIKLE) Planning permission and the place of the public inquiry in the development of mineral resources in Britain: problems of potash extraction in Yorkshire. [London], 1971. pp. 63-72,129-138. *(Reprinted from Transactions of the Institute of Mining and Metallurgy. Section A, vol.80,1971)*

HERTFORDSHIRE. County Planning Officer. Hertfordshire structure plan: project report. Hertford, 1972. fo. 13.

YOUNG (DAVID)of the South Hampshire Plan Technical Unit. Evaluation of alternative strategies. [Winchester], 1972. 1 vol. (unpaged). *(South Hampshire Plan Technical Unit. Working Papers. 18)*

SOUTH YORKSHIRE. County Council. Doncaster district structure plan: report of survey. [Doncaster, afterwards Barnsley], 1973-5. 9 parts (in 2 vols.).

SMITH (BARBARA M.D.) Regional unemployment differentials and regional policy: a review of events. Birmingham, 1973. fo. 22. *bibliog. (Birmingham. University. Centre for Urban and Regional Studies. Working Papers. No. 11)*

ECONOMIC AND SOCIAL TRENDS; [pd. by] North West Economic Planning Council [U.K.]. a., 1974 [2nd ed.]- Manchester.

REVIEW OF DEVELOPMENTS IN THE NORTHERN REGION; [pd. by] Northern Economic Planning Council. s-a., F 1974 (no. 1)- Newcastle upon Tyne.

NORTH WEST JOINT PLANNING TEAM. Strategic plan for the north west, 1973. Technical papers. Nos. 1-12, 14, 16-17. [Manchester], 1973 [or rather 1974-76). 18 pts. (in 3 vols) *Nos. 13 and 15 not allocated.*

COUNCIL FOR THE PROTECTION OF RURAL ENGLAND. Development control: package buildings. London, [1974]. pp. 34.

DENMAN (DONALD ROBERT) Prospects of cooperative planning. Berkhamsted, [1974]. pp. 27. *(Warburton Lectures. 1973)*

LANGLEY (P.E.) Methods of defining and assessing the importance of structure plan objectives. London, Department of the Environment, 1974. fo. 18. *bibliog. (Planning Techniques Papers. 74/2)*

NORTH WEST INDUSTRIAL DEVELOPMENT ASSOCIATION. Strategic plan for the North West: comments of the... association. Manchester, 1974. pp. 9.

WEST MIDLANDS JOINT MONITORING STEERING GROUP. Annual report. a., 1975(1st)- London.

WEST YORKSHIRE. Metropolitan County Council. West Yorkshire structure plan. Annual statement. a., 1975(1st)- Wakefield.

EAST SUSSEX. Planning Department. County structure plan 1975; [and] Report of survey 1975. Lewes, 1975. 2 vols (in 1).

ESSEX. County Planning Department. North and central Essex structure plan: first report. [Chelmsford], 1975. pp. 158.

GREATER MANCHESTER COUNCIL. County structure plan: report of survey. [Manchester], 1975. 8 parts (in 1 vol.).

HUMBERSIDE. County Council. Planning Department. Structure plan report; pts. 1-6, 7a, 8a, 9a. [Beverley], 1975. 9 pts. (in 1 vol.).

KENT. Planning Department. Towards a structure plan for Kent: the main issues; a report for discussion purposes on the studies and progress so far made. Maidstone, 1975. pp. 147.

LICHFIELD (NATHANIEL) and others. Evaluation in the planning process. Oxford, 1975. pp. 325. *bibliog.*

SANT (MORGAN EUGENE CYRIL) Industrial movement and regional development: the British case. Oxford, 1975. pp. 253. *bibliog.*

U.K. Department of the Environment. 1975. Regional strategy for the North West: government response to the strategic plan. [London], 1975. pp. 15.

ASPECTS of structure planning in Britain; [by] Madeline Drake [and others]. London, 1976. pp. 214. *bibliog. (Centre for Environmental Studies. Research Papers. 20)*

BUCKINGHAMSHIRE. County Planning Department. Buckinghamshire County structure plan 1976: written statement; draft for consultation. Aylesbury, 1976. pp. 96.

DEVELOPMENT of the strategic plan for the South East: interim report. London, Department of the Environment, 1976. pp. 78.

ISLE OF WIGHT. County Council. County structure plan: written statement. Newport, I.W., 1976. 1 vol. (unpaged).

NORTHERN REGION STRATEGY TEAM. Second interim report: strategic choices. Newcastle-upon-Tyne, 1976. pp. 58.

U.K. Department of the Environment. 1976. East Anglia regional strategy: government response to Strategic choice for East Anglia. [London], 1976. pp. 14.

— — Citizen participation.

SHEFFIELD. University. Department of Extramural Studies. Linked research project into public participation in structure planning: interim papers. Sheffield, 1974-75. 8 vols. (in 1).

PUBLIC participation in structure planning: the Teesside experience; a study initiated by Community Advancement Project [by Peter Ferres and others]. London, 1976. pp. 87. *bibliog. (Centre for Environmental Studies. Research Papers. 14)*

— — Mathematical models.

MENCZER (P.F.) and FRANCIS (M.K.) The South Hampshire activities allocation model. [Winchester], 1972. 1 vol. (unpaged). *(South Hampshire Plan Technical Unit. Working Papers. 6)*

BARRAS (R.) and others. The use of models in structure planning: applications in Cleveland. London, 1975. pp. 32. *bibliog. (Planning Research Applications Group. PRAG Technical Papers. TPIO)*

— — Ireland, Northern.

IRELAND, NORTHERN. Department of Housing, Local Government and Planning. 1975. North Down area plan: statement by Department of Housing, Local Government and Planning. Belfast, [1975]. pp. 25.

IRELAND, NORTHERN. Department of Housing, Local Government and Planning. 1975. Regional physical development strategy, 1975-95; (Northern Ireland discussion paper). Belfast, 1975. pp. 39, 1 map.

— — Scotland.

SCOTLAND. Scottish Development Department. Planning and development in Scotland. a., 1973/74- Edinburgh.

PLANNING EXCHANGE CONFERENCE ON THE WEST CENTRAL SCOTLAND PLAN, GLASGOW, 1974. Proceedings of the conference, etc. Glasgow, 1975. pp. 102.

— United States.

LINOWES (R. ROBERT) and ALLENSWORTH (DONALD TRUDEAU) The states and land-use control. New York, 1975. pp. 243.

PRESCOTT (JAMES RUSSELL) and LEWIS (W. CRIS) Urban-regional economic growth and policy. Ann Arbor, [1975]. pp. 220. *bibliogs.*

HANSEN (NILES M.) Improving access to economic opportunity: nonmetropolitan labor markets in an urban society. Cambridge, Mass., [1976]. pp. 192.

— — Citizen participation.

STRONG (ANN LOUISE) Private property and the public interest: the Brandywine experience. Baltimore, [1975]. pp. 206. *(Johns Hopkins University. Center for Metropolitan Planning and Research. Johns Hopkins Studies in Urban Affairs)*

— — California.

BUHR (WALTER) Die Rolle der materiellen infrastruktur im regionalen Wirtschaftswachstum: Studien über die Infrastruktur eines städtischen Gebietes; der Fall Santa Clara County, California. Berlin, [1975]. pp. 309. *bibliog.*

— — New York (State).

KOPPELMAN (LEE E.) and others. A methodology to achieve the integration of coastal zone science and regional planning: detailed work program. New York, 1974. pp. 116. *bibliog.*

— — Pennsylvania.

STRONG (ANN LOUISE) Private property and the public interest: the Brandywine experience. Baltimore, [1975]. pp. 206. *(Johns Hopkins University. Center for Metropolitan Planning and Research. Johns Hopkins Studies in Urban Affairs)*

— Zambia.

ZEHENDER (WOLFGANG) Regionalpolitische Auswahlkriterien für Entwicklungsländer: Untersuchung am Beispiel Zambias. Berlin, [1976]. pp. 161. *bibliog. (Deutsches Institut für Entwicklungspolitik. Schriften. Band 35)*

REGIONALISM.

KOTHARI (RAJNI) Footsteps into the future: diagnosis of the present world and a design for an alternative. Amsterdam, [1974]. pp. 173. *(Institute for World Order. Preferred Worlds for the 1990's)*

LONG (NORTON ENNEKING) and others. Regionalism toward the year 2000. [St. Louis, 1974]. fo. 50. *bibliog.*

RODWIN (LLOYD) The educational perspective of regional science and urban studies. Reading, 1975. pp. 18. *(Reading. University. Department of Geography. Reading Geographical Papers. No.38)*

ROSE (RICHARD) and URWIN (DEREK W.) Regional differentiation and political unity in Western nations. London, [1975]. pp. 53. *bibliog.*

DICKINSON (ROBERT ERIC) Regional concept: the Anglo-American leaders. London, 1976. pp. 408.

— **Belgium.**

FROGNIER (ANDRE PAUL) and others. Vote, clivages socio-politiques et développement régional en Belgique. Louvain, [1974]. pp. 149.

— **European Economic Community countries.**

Les REGIONS frontalières à l'heure du Marché Commun: colloque organisé les 27 et 28 novembre 1969 par l'Institut d'Etudes Européennes. Bruxelles, 1970. pp. 422. *bibliog. (Brussels. Université Libre. Institut d'Etudes Européennes. Colloques Européens)*

FRANCE. Direction de la Documentation. La Documentation Française. Notes et Etudes Documentaires. Nos. 4,088-4, 089-4,090. Les aspects financiers de la régionalisation en Europe: [études réalisées sous la direction de Paul Marie Gaudemet]. [Paris, 1974.] pp. 100. *bibliog.*

MASSART-PIERARD (FRANÇOISE) Pour une doctrine de la région en Europe: régionalisation et régionalisme. Bruxelles, 1974. pp. 160. *bibliog.*

— **France.**

BOUCHER (MARGUERITE) La région...; (with Notices 1-8). Paris, 1973. 9 parts. *bibliog. (Cahiers Français, Les. No. 158-159)*

BOURDOIS (JEAN PATRICK) La réforme administrative dans la "Revue générale d'administration", 1878-1928. Paris, [1975]. pp. 98. *(Paris. Université de Paris II. Travaux et Recherches. Série Science Administrative. 9)*

— **Italy.**

SANTARELLI (ENZO) Il regionalismo nell'Italia unita: storia dell'idea regionalista fino alla Repubblica. Firenze, [1973]. pp. 194.

DEMOCRAZIA CRISTIANA. Regioni, enti locali per lo sviluppo nella libertà: [selections from the proceedings of several meetings held in 1974]. [Rome], 1975. pp. 255.

PARTITO LIBERALE ITALIANO. Segreteria Regionale d'Emilia- Romagna. Dare un senso liberale alla regione: 1970/1975; cinque anni di lotte per una regione dei cittadini contro una regione dei partiti. Firenze, 1975. pp. 284.

— **Nepal.**

GAIGE (FREDERICK H.) Regionalism and national unity in Nepal. Berkeley, [1975]. pp. 234. *bibliog.*

— **United Kingdom.**

BULPITT (JIM G.) The problem of "the north parts": territorial integration in Tudor and Stuart England. Coventry, 1975. pp. 45. *(University of Warwick. Department of Politics. Working Papers. No. 6)*

REGIONAL devolution and social policy: [based on a two-day seminar held at the Centre for Studies in Social Policy in September 1974]; edited by Edward Craven. London, 1975. pp. 207.

TAIT (ALAN A.) The economics of devolution: a knife edge problem. Edinburgh, [1975]. pp. 12. *bibliog. (Glasgow. University of Strathclyde. Fraser of Allander Institute. Speculative Papers. No.2)*

— — **Bibliography.**

JOHNSTONE (PAMELA) compiler. Devolution in the United Kingdom: a select list of references. London, 1975. pp. 13. *(U.K. Department of the Environment. Library. Bibliographies. No. 193).*

— **United States.**

GASTIL (RAYMOND D.) Cultural regions of the United States. Seattle, [1975]. pp. 366. *bibliog.*

REGIONALISM (INTERNATIONAL ORGANIZATION).

LEVIN (AIDA LUISA) The Organization of American States and the United Nations: relations in the peace and security field. New York, United Nations Institute for Training and Research, 1974. pp. 114. *bibliog. (Peaceful Settlement [Series] No. 7)*

AKINDELE (R.A.) The organization and promotion of world peace: a study of universal-regional relationships. Toronto, [1976]. pp. 204. *bibliog.*

REGISTERS OF BIRTH, ETC.

— **Sri Lanka.**

SRI LANKA. Department of Census and Statistics. 1971. A study of the extent of under-registration of births and deaths in Ceylon. Colombo, 1970 [or rather 1971]. pp. 29. *In English and Sinhala.*

REGNI.

CUNLIFFE (BARRINGTON WINDSOR) The Regni. London, 1973. pp. 153. *bibliog.*

REGRESSION ANALYSIS.

HILTON (GORDON) Intermediate politometrics. New York, 1976. pp. 282. *bibliogs.*

REHABILITATION.

An EVALUATION of policy-related rehabilitation research; [by] Monroe Berkowitz [and others]. New York, 1975. pp. 221. *bibliogs.*

REHABILITATION, RURAL

— **Bibliography.**

COMMONWEALTH BUREAU OF AGRICULTURAL ECONOMICS. Regional planning and rural development. [Farnham Royal, 1975]. pp. 32. *(Annotated Bibliographies. No. 35) Compiled from World Agricultural Economics and Rural Sociology Abstracts from 1974 to 1975.*

— **Australia.**

AUSTRALIA. Bureau of Agricultural Economics. 1973. The rural reconstruction scheme: a review of progress. Canberra, 1973. pp. 42.

AUSTRALIA. Bureau of Agricultural Economics. 1974. The rural reconstruction scheme: a review of progress; second report. Canberra, 1974. pp. 62.

— **Liberia.**

YAIDOO (H.W.) Rural development in Liberia. Monrovia, Department of Planning and Economic Affairs, [1969?]. fo. 51. *(Conference on Development Objectives and Strategy, Monrovia, 1969. Documents. 9) Xerox copy.*

— **Russia.**

MEDVEDEV (N.A.) ed. Metodika perspektivnogo ekonomiko-sotsial'noo planirovaniia na sele. Leningrad, 1970. pp. 339.

REHABILITATION COUNSELLING.

HOSFORD (RAY E.) and MOSS (C. SCOTT) eds. The crumbling walls: treatment and counseling of prisoners. Urbana, [1975]. pp. 257. *bibliogs.*

REHABILITATION OF CRIMINALS.

La CHARITE et les détenus libérés; (traduit de l'allemand). n.p., [18--?]. pp. 40.

EVALUATING community treatment programs: tools, techniques, and a case study; edited by Mercedese M. Miller. Lexington, Mass., [1975]. pp. 124. *bibliog.*

— **Europe.**

EUROPEAN COMMITTEE ON CRIME PROBLEMS. 1970. Practical organisation of measures for the supervision and after- care of conditionally sentenced or conditionally released offenders: report, etc. Strasbourg, Council of Europe, 1970. pp. 286. *bibliog.*

— **United Kingdom.**

BEAN (PHILIP T.) Rehabilitation and deviance. London, 1976. pp. 168. *bibliog.*

— **United States — California.**

HOSFORD (RAY E.) and MOSS (C. SCOTT) eds. The crumbling walls: treatment and counseling of prisoners. Urbana, [1975]. pp. 257. *bibliogs.*

REHABILITATION OF JUVENILE DELINQUENTS

— **Europe.**

EUROPEAN COMMITTEE ON CRIME PROBLEMS. 1967. Short-term methods of treatment for young offenders: report, etc. Strasbourg, Council of Europe, 1967. pp. 88. *bibliog.*

— **United States.**

McARTHUR (A. VERNE) Coming out cold: community reentry from a state reformatory. Lexington, Mass., [1974]. pp. 131. *bibliog.*

BARTOLLAS (CLEMENS) and others. Juvenile victimization: the institutional paradox. New York, [1976]. pp. 324. *bibliog.*

— **Yugoslavia.**

VODOPIVEC (KATJA) ed. Maladjusted youth: an experiment in rehabilitation;...in collaboration with Milica Bergant [and others]. Farnborough, Hants., [1974]. pp. 275. *bibliogs.*

REHABILITATION RESEARCH.

An EVALUATION of policy-related rehabilitation research; [by] Monroe Berkowitz [and others]. New York, 1975. pp. 221. *bibliogs.*

REINSURANCE.

KROMMENACKER (RAYMOND J.) Les Nations Unies et l'assurance-réassurance: l'assurance-réassurance de droit privé dans les relations entre pays développés et pays en voie de développement et l'action des organisations internationales. Paris, 1975. pp. 215. *bibliog.*

RELIGION.

NEEDHAM (JOSEPH) Moulds of understanding: a pattern of natural philosophy: [selected essays]; edited and introduced by Gary Werskey. London, 1976. pp. 320. *bibliog.*

TOYNBEE (ARNOLD JOSEPH) and IKEDA (DAISEKU) The Toynbee-Ikeda dialogue: man himself must choose. Tokyo, 1976. pp. 348.

WILSON (BRYAN RONALD) Contemporary transformations of religion. London, 1976. pp. 116. *(Newcastle-upon-Tyne. University. Riddell Memorial Lectures. 45th series)*

RELIGION AND SCIENCE.

TRABULSE (ELIAS) Ciencia y religion en el siglo XVII. Mexico, [1974]. pp. 286. *bibliog. (Mexico City. Colegio de Mexico. Centro de Estudios Historicos. Nueva Serie. 18)*

RELIGION AND SOCIOLOGY.

MOL (JOHANNIS JACOB) ed. Western religion: a country by country sociological inquiry. The Hague, [1972]. pp. 642. *bibliogs.*

BOURGUIGNON (ERIKA) ed. Religion, altered states of consciousness, and social change. Columbus, Ohio, 1973. pp. 389.

DENIEL (RAYMOND) Religions dans la ville: croyances et changements sociaux à Abidjan. Abidjan, [1975]. pp. 208.

RELIGION AND SOCIOLOGY.(Cont.)

JONES (SUZANNE ALICE CAMPBELL) Stability and change in religious communities: a sociological study of two congregations of Roman Catholic sisters. [1976]. fo. 348. Typescript. Ph.D. (London) thesis: unpublished. This thesis is the property of London University and may not be removed from the Library.

WILSON (BRYAN RONALD) Contemporary transformations of religion. London, 1976. pp. 116. (Newcastle-upon-Tyne. University. Riddell Memorial Lectures. 45th series)

YEO (STEPHEN) Religion and voluntary organisations in crisis. London, 1976. pp. 426.

RELIGIONS.

WERBLOWSKY (RAPHAEL JEHUDA ZWI) Beyond tradition and modernity: changing religions in a changing world. London, 1976. pp. 146. bibliog. (London. University. School of Oriental and African Studies. Jordan Lectures in Comparative Religion. 11)

RELIGIOUS EDUCATION

— United Kingdom.

ROBERTSON (JOHN MACKINNON) The priest and the child. Bradford, [1896]. pp. 8. (Papers for the People. No. 1)

RELIGIOUS LIBERTY

— Argentine Republic.

DICKMANN (ENRIQUE) Contra el odio de razas y la persecucion religiosa. Buenos Aires, 1943. pp. 61.

RELOCATION (HOUSING)

— United States.

SCHORR (PHILIP) Planned relocation. Lexington, Mass., [1975]. pp. 227. bibliog.

REMAND HOMES

— United Kingdom.

KING (ROY DAVID) and MORGAN (RODNEY) A taste of prison: custodial conditions for trial and remand prisoners. London, 1976. pp. 100. bibliog.

REMY (BERNARD).

REMY (BERNARD) L'homme des casernes: "change-lutte", collectifs de soutien. Paris, 1975. pp. 280.

RENAISSANCE.

VOET (LEON) De gouden eeuw van Antwerpen: bloei en uitstraling van de metropool in de zestiende eeuw. Antwerpen, 1974. pp. 487. bibliog. Maps in end pockets.

RENT

— Germany.

HAEUSERRAT FRANKFURT. Wohnungskampf in Frankfurt. München, 1974. pp. 245. bibliog.

— Poland.

MIZERA (STEFAN) and POCZOBUTT-ODLANICKI (ANDRZEJ) Ceny i opłaty za grunty w miastach i na wsi: problematyka prawna; stan prawny na dzień 15 marca 1974 r. Wrocław, 1974. pp. 282. bibliog.

— South Africa.

ANDERSON (W.W.) and MASON (J.) Rental survey: Springfield. Durban, 1972. fo. 15,6. (Chatsworth Community and Research Centre. Research Reports. No. 1)

— Switzerland.

LOERTSCHER (RUDOLF) Eine empirische Untersuchung über die Entwicklung der Mietpreise in der Agglomeration Zürich. [Zürich?, 1975]. pp. 225. bibliog. Dissertation der Universität Zürich zur Erlangung der Würde eines Doktors der Wirtschaftswissenschaft.

— United Kingdom.

CROSBIE (GEORGE VERTUE) Observations on the emancipation of industry. London, 1892. pp. 138.

RENT (ECONOMIC THEORY).

MIESZCZANKOWSKI (MIECZYSŁAW) Teoria renty absolutnej. Warszawa, 1964. pp. 490. With English and Russian summaries.

RENT CONTROL

— Fiji Islands.

FIJI. Commercial Rents Committee. 1966. Report; [R.M. Major, chairman]. in FIJI. Legislative Council. Journal. Sessions of 1966.

— United Kingdom.

U.K. Department of the Environment. 1973. Rents of regulated tenancies: a guide for private landlords and tenants. rev. ed. [London], 1973. pp. 16.

SHELTER. Tenants' guide to the new Rent Act. London, 1974. pp. (4).

HEDDLE (JOHN) and LINACRE (VIVIAN) A new lease of life: a solution to rent control. London, 1975. pp. 28. (Conservative Political Centre. [Publications]. No. 579)

U.K. Department of the Environment. 1975. Regulated tenancies: your rents, rights and responsibilities: a guide for private landlords and tenants. [London], 1975. pp. 44.

— — Ireland, Northern.

IRELAND, NORTHERN. Committee on Rent Restriction Law. 1975. Rent restriction law of Northern Ireland; report of the committee under the chairmanship of Sir Robert Porter. Belfast, 1975. pp. 96.

REPARATION

— Ireland (Republic).

CRIMINAL INJURIES COMPENSATION TRIBUNAL [EIRE]. Annual report. a., [1974/75(1st)]- Dublin.

— Poland.

DASZKIEWICZ (WIESŁAW) Proces adhezyjny na tle prawa polskiego. Warszawa, 1961. pp. 172.

REPEAL OF LEGISLATION

— Germany.

GERMANY (BUNDESREPUBLIK). Deutscher Bundestag. Wissenschaftliche Dienste. 1974. Verzeichnis der ganz oder teilweise für nichtig erklärten Bundesgesetze: Stand: 31.Dezember 1973; [edited by Bernd Rader]. Bonn, 1974. pp. 8. (Materialien. 37)

REPLACEMENT OF INDUSTRIAL EQUIPMENT.

POLTORYGIN (VIKTOR KUZ'MICH) Effektivnost' tekhnicheskogo perevooruzheniia sotsialisticheskogo proizvodstva: voprosy teorii, metodologii i praktiki. Moskva, 1975. pp. 328.

REPRESENTATIVE GOVERNMENT AND REPRESENTATION.

BRETON (ALBERT) The economic theory of representative government. London, 1974. pp. 228.

FIORINA (MORRIS P.) Representatives, roll calls, and constituencies. Lexington, Mass., [1974]. pp. 143. bibliog.

FLACHOWSKY (GERT) Demokratie als Entscheidungsprozess: eine ideologiekritische und organisationssoziologische Studie zum Problem der parlamentarischen Demokratie. Mannheim, 1975. fo.128. bibliog.

PULZER (PETER GEORGE JULIUS) Political representation and elections in Britain. 3rd ed. London, 1975. pp. 176. bibliog.

— Germany.

WASSER (HARTMUT) Parlamentarismuskritik vom Kaiserreich zur Bundesrepublik: Analyse und Dokumentation. Stuttgart-Bad Cannstatt, [1974]. pp. 197. bibliog.

FRANK (DIETRICH) Politische Planung im Spannungsverhältnis zwischen Regierung und Parlament. Meisenheim am Glan, 1976. pp. 359. bibliog.

— Papua New Guinea.

AUSTRALIA. Prime Minister. 1970. Steps towards self-government in Papua and New Guinea: speech by the Prime Minister, the Rt Hon. John Gorton, M.P., at Papua Hotel, Port Moresby, 6 July 1970; [and] Increased responsibility for ministerial members and assistant ministerial members: statement by the Minister for External Territories, the Hon. C.E. Barnes, M.P., Port Moresby, 6 July 1970. Canberra, 1970. pp. 31.

— Sweden.

ALEXANDERSSON (ERLAND) Bondeståndet i riksdagen, 1760-1772. [Lund, 1975]. pp. 253. bibliog. Akademisk avhandling, Universitetet i Lund; with English summary.

FÖRHAMMAR (STAFFAN) Reformvilja eller riksdagstaktik?: junkrarna och representationsfrågan, 1847-54. Stockholm, [1975]. pp. 128. bibliog. (Stockholms Universitet. Acta Universitatis Stockholmiensis. Stockholm Studies in History. 22) With English summary.

REPUBLICAN PARTY (UNITED STATES).

BENEDICT (MICHAEL LES) A compromise of principle: Congressional Republicans and reconstruction, 1863-1869. New York, [1974]. pp. 493. bibliog.

REICHARD (GARY W.) The reaffirmation of Republicanism: Eisenhower and the eighty- third Congress. Knoxville, Tenn., [1975]. pp. 303. bibliog.

WALTON (HANES) Black Republicans: the politics of the black and tans. Metuchen, N.J., 1975. pp. 199. bibliog.

RADICAL republicans in the North: state politics during reconstruction; edited by James C. Mohr. Baltimore, [1976]. pp. 200. bibliog.

REQUISITIONS, MILITARY

— United Kingdom.

U.K. Emergency Compensation Committee. 1930. Report; [Sir W.F.K. Taylor, chairman]. London, 1930. pp. 33.

RESEARCH

— Management.

WIRT (JOHN G.) and others. R and D management: methods used by federal agencies. Santa Monica, 1974. pp. 261. (Rand Corporation. [Rand Reports]. 1156)

— Canada — Bibliography.

NATIONAL SCIENCE LIBRARY [CANADA]. Scientific policy, research and development in Canada...: a bibliography...; revised to June 1970; (with Supplement covering period June 1970-June 1972). Ottawa, 1970-72. 2 pts. In English and French.

— Communist countries.

KLOSE (GERHARD) and others. Sozialistische Forschungskooperation: Grundfragen. Berlin, [1973]. pp. 118. bibliog.

— Germany.

DEUTSCHE FORSCHUNGSGEMEINSCHAFT. Aufgaben und Finanzierung, V : 1976-1978. Boppard, [1976]. pp. 365.

— Germany, Eastern.

KLOSE (GERHARD) and others. Sozialistische Forschungskooperation: Grundfragen. Berlin, [1973]. pp. 118. bibliog.

— Norway.

HOVLAND (EDGAR) ed. The Norwegian Research Council for Science and the Humanities, 1949-1974. Oslo 1974. pp. 57.

— Russia.

ORGANIZATSIIA sovetskoi nauki v 1926-1932 gg.: sbornik dokumentov. Leningrad, 1974. pp. 408.

ROZHNEVA (LIUDMILA STEPANOVNA) Osobennosti tsenoobrazovaniia na produktsiiu prikladnykh issledovanii i razrabotok. Leningrad, 1974. pp. 120.

RESEARCH, INDUSTRIAL.

TREILLE (J.M.) Pour définir une stratégie industrielle: rapport de recherche sur des instruments et une méthode de définition et de programmation d'objectifs de recherche, de développement et de stratégie industrielle. Paris, 1975. pp. 116. *(France. Ministère de l'Industrie et de la Recherche. Etudes de Politique Industrielle. 7)*

— United Kingdom.

The UNIVERSITIES and applied research: their relevance to social and industrial needs; [proceedings of a symposium of the Research and Development Society held in London in 1974]. London, [1974]. pp. 90.

RESEARCH AND DEVELOPMENT CONTRACTS

— United States.

NATIONAL RESEARCH COUNCIL. Assembly of Behavioral and Social Sciences. Committee on Department of Labor Manpower Research and Development. Knowledge and policy in manpower: a study of the manpower research and development program in the Department of Labor. Washington, D.C.1975. pp. 171. *bibliog.*

RESIDENTIAL MOBILITY

— United Kingdom.

PONS (VALDO GUSTAVE) Housing conditions and residential patterns in Manchester of the 1830s and 1840s. 1975. fo. 94. *bibliog. Typescript: unpublished.*

PRITCHARD (ROGER MARTIN) Housing and the spatial structure of the city: residential mobility and the housing market in an English city since the industrial revolution. Cambridge, [1976]. pp. 234. *bibliog.*

— United States.

SPEARE (ALDEN) and others. Residential mobility, migration, and metropolitan change. Cambridge, Mass., [1975]. pp. 313. *bibliog.*

RESPONDEAT SUPERIOR.

GREEN (LESLIE CLAUDE) Superior orders in national and international law. Leyden, 1976. pp. 374.

RESPONSIBILITY.

MORRIS (HERBERT) On guilt and innocence: essays in legal philosophy and moral psychology. Berkeley, Calif., [1976]. pp. 161.

RESPONSIBILITY, LEGAL

— Russia.

KHOMENKO (VASILII NIKOLAEVICH) Otvetstvennost' v khoziaistvennom prave. Kiev, 1975. pp. 171.

RESTRAINT OF TRADE

— Canada.

CANADA. Restrictive Trade Practices Commission. [Reports]. RTPC No.48. Prices of gasoline, Sudbury: report in the matter of an inquiry relating to the distribution and sale of gasoline and related products in the Sudbury area. Ottawa, 1969. pp. 42.

CANADA. Restrictive Trade Practices Commission. [Reports]. RTPC No. 49. Road paving in Ontario: report in the matter of an inquiry relating to the supply and transportation of asphalt paving materials in the province of Ontario. Ottawa, 1970. pp. 37.

— Ireland (Republic).

EIRE. Restrictive Practices Commission. 1975. Report of special review of the operation of Article 3 of the Restrictive Trade Practices Motor Spirit Order, 1972. Dublin, [1975]. pp. 18.

RETAIL TRADE.

TUCKER (KENNETH ARTHUR) Economies of scale in retailing: an empirical study of plant size and cost structure. Farnborough, Hants, [1975]. pp. 234. *bibliog.*

— Information storage and retrieval systems.

See INFORMATION STORAGE AND RETRIEVAL SYSTEMS — Retail trade.

— Finland.

FINLAND. Tilastokeskus. Tukku- ja vähittäiskaupan tasetilasto. ..: Statistics of profit and loss and balance sheet accounts of wholesale and retail trade. a., 1972- Helsinki. *In Finnish with notes and headings in Swedish and English.*

FINLAND. Tilastokeskus. Vähittäiskauppa: Detaljhandeln. a., 1972- Helsinki.

— France.

NATIONAL CHAMBER OF TRADE. Distributive development in France; a report of a study tour by representatives of the National Chamber of Trade. Henley, 1973. pp. 56.

— Germany.

GERMANY (BUNDESREPUBLIK). Statistisches Bundesamt. Umsätze und Beschäftige (Messzahlen). a., 1975- Wiesbaden. *(Gross- und Einzelhandel, Gastgewerbe, Reiseverkehr. Reihe 3.1).*

— — Saarland.

SAARGEBIET. Statistisches Amt. Einzelschriften zur Statistik des Saarlandes. Nr. 47. Einzelhandel im Saarland. Saarbrücken, 1972. pp. 76.

— India — Goa, Daman and Diu.

GOA, DAMAN AND DIU. Bureau of Economics, Statistics and Evaluation. 1974. A pilot survey of distributive trade. Panaji, [1974]. pp. 107.

— Iran.

IRAN. Bureau of Statistics. 1971. Internal retail trade statistics, Iran urban areas, 1967. Tehran, [1971]. pp. 141.

— Ireland (Republic).

EIRE. Central Statistics Office. 1975. Summary results for retail and wholesale trade, census of distribution, 1971. Dublin, 1975. pp. 48.

— Netherlands.

ECONOMISCH INSTITUUT VOOR HET MIDDEN- EN KLEINBEDRIJF. Algemeen- Economische en Statistische Publikaties. De structurele ontwikkeling van de detailhandel in voedings- en genotmiddelen. 's-Gravenhage, 1969. pp. 131.

ECONOMISCH INSTITUUT VOOR HET MIDDEN- EN KLEINBEDRIJF. Bedrijfseconomische Publikaties. De omzetten per M2 bedrijfsruimte resp. verkoopruimte in een aantal branches van het midden- en kleinbedrijf in 1968. 's-Gravenhage, 1969. pp. 8.

— New Zealand.

NEW ZEALAND. Department of Statistics. 1975- . Census of distribution, 1972-73: (statistical bulletins). Wellington, 1975 in progress.

— Papua New Guinea.

PAPUA NEW GUINEA. Bureau of Statistics. Statistical bulletin: survey of retail sales and selected services. a., 1967-68/1972-73- Port Moresby.

— Poland.

KAWALEC (R.) and SACKIEWICZ (D.) Planowanie nakładów handlowych w wielosklepowym przedsiębiorstwie handlu detalicznego. Warszawa, 1954. pp. 184. *bibliog.*

— Portugal.

RAMOS (ANTONIO BRITO) O emprego no sector terciario metropolitano: tentativas de localização do crescimento. Lisboa, 1974. pp. 103. *(Portugal. Ministerio do Trabalho. Gabinete de Planeamento. Serie Estudos. 24) With abstracts in English, French and German.*

— South Africa.

SOUTH AFRICA. Bureau of Statistics. 1976- . Census of wholesale and retail trade, 1970-71. [Pretoria, 1976 in progress]. *(Reports. No. 04-11-02, etc.) In English and Afrikaans.*

— United Kingdom.

ECONOMIC DEVELOPMENT COMMITTEE FOR THE DISTRIBUTIVE TRADES. Profitability and liquidity in the distributive trades: an examination of financial data in selected sectors; based on a report prepared for the Distributive Trades EDC by Whitefield Associates and Company. London, National Economic Development Office, 1975. pp. 123.

ECONOMIC DEVELOPMENT COMMITTEE FOR THE DISTRIBUTIVE TRADES. Industrial Strategies Working Party. Industrial strategies in the distributive trades: report from the. ..Working Party...under the chairmanship of W.T. Welch. [London, National Economic Development Office], 1976. pp. 50.

ROBINSON (OLIVE) and WALLACE (JOHN) Pay and employment in retailing. Farnborough, Hants, [1976]. pp. 177.

WILLAN (THOMAS STUART) The inland trade: studies in English internal trade in the sixteenth and seventeenth centuries. Manchester, [1976]. pp. 154.

— — Mathematical models.

SIBLEY (DAVID) The small shop in the city. Hull, [1975]. pp. 52. *bibliog. (Hull. University. Department of Geography. Occasional Papers in Geography. No. 22)*

RETHEL (ALFRED SOHN-).

See SOHN-RETHEL (ALFRED).

RETIREMENT.

BUTTLE (BERNARD) Preparation for retirement. London, 1974. pp. 11. *bibliog. (Age Concern England. Manifesto Series. No. 20)*

GREAVES (MARY) Increasing physical disablement in retirement. London, 1974. pp. 10. *bibliog. (Age Concern England. Manifesto Series. No. 11)*

KARN (VALERIE A.) Retiring to the seaside. London, [1974]. pp. 12. *bibliog. (Age Concern England. Manifesto Series. No. 9)*

GORDON (IAN R.) The retirement industry in the South West; a survey of its size, distribution and economic aspects. [Bristol, South West Economic Planning Council, 1975]. pp. 78.

ATCHLEY (ROBERT C.) The sociology of retirement. Cambridge, Mass., [1976]. pp. 158. *bibliog.*

RETIREMENT, PLACES OF

— United States.

JACOBS (JERRY) Older persons and retirement communities: case studies in social gerontology. Springfield, Ill., [1975]. pp. 129. *bibliog.*

RETIREMENT INCOME

— United Kingdom.

AGE CONCERN ENGLAND. Age Concern on occupation: views of retired people on how and why they spend their time in paid and unpaid work. London, 1975. pp. 24.

— United States.

PROVIDING adequate retirement income: pension reform in the United States and abroad; by James Schulz [and others]. Hanover, N.H., 1974. pp. 330. *bibliog.*

REUNION ISLAND

— Economic policy.

DEBRÉ (MICHEL) Une politique pour la Réunion. Paris, 1974]. pp. 222.

— Politics and government.

OSTHEIMER (JOHN M.) ed. The politics of the western Indian Ocean islands. New York, 1975. pp. 260. *bibliog.*

— Social policy.

DEBRÉ (MICHEL) Une politique pour la Réunion. Paris, 1974]. pp. 222.

REVOLUTIONISTS.

MAZLISH (BRUCE) The revolutionary ascetic: evolution of a political type. New York, [1976]. pp. 261.

— Bibliography.

BLACKEY (ROBERT) Modern revolutions and revolutionists: a bibliography. Santa Barbara, [1976]. pp. 257.

REVOLUTIONISTS, BRITISH.

SHIPLEY (PETER) Revolutionaries in modern Britain. London, 1976. pp. 256. *bibliog.*

REVOLUTIONISTS, INDIAN.

GHOSH (SANKAR) The Naxalite movement: a Maoist experiment. Calcutta, 1974. pp. 183.

REVOLUTIONISTS, JEWISH.

WISTRICH (ROBERT S.) Revolutionary Jews from Marx to Trotsky. London, 1976. pp. 254. *bibliog.*

REVOLUTIONISTS, LATIN AMERICAN.

DIEZ años de insurreccion en America Latina; ([by] Vania Bambirra [and others]). Santiago, Chile, [1971]. 2 vols. (in 1).

REVOLUTIONISTS, POLISH.

KONARSKI (SZYMON) Dziennik z lat 1831-1834; przygotowali do druku Bolesław Łopuszański i Anatol Smirnow. Wrocław, 1973. pp. 361. *(Polska Akademia Nauk. Oddział w Krakowie. Komisja Nauk Historycznych. Materiały. Nr.23) With Russian and French summaries.*

REVOLUTIONISTS, RUSSIAN.

RUBEL (MAXIMILIEN) Russland und die russische Revolution im Denken von Karl Marx. Trier, [1969]. pp. 36. *(Karl-Marx-Haus. Schriften. 2)*

REVOLUTIONS.

BURNS (CECIL DELISLE) The principles of revolution: a study in ideals. London, 1920. pp. 155.

PROUDHON (PIERRE JOSEPH) General idea of the revolution in the nineteenth century;... translated from the French by John Beverley Robinson. London, 1923. pp. 302.

LAKEY (GEORGE) Draft manifesto for nonviolent revolution; [to be presented to] (War Resisters' International 14th Triennial Conference, Sheffield...1972). [London?], 1972. pp. 31. *With a separate pamphlet of comments attached.*

SETTEMBRINI (DOMENICO) Socialismo e rivoluzione dopo Marx. Napoli, [1974]. pp. 701.

STUDIEN zur vergleichenden Revolutionsgeschichte, 1500-1917; herausgegeben von Manfred Kossok. Berlin, 1974. pp. 216.

BAECHLER (JEAN) Revolution. Oxford, [1975]. pp. 208. *bibliog.*

FINGER (OTTO) Philosophie der Revolution: Studie zur Herausbildung der marxistisch-leninistischen Theorie der Revolution, etc. Berlin, 1975. pp. 470.

MARTIĆ (MILOŠ) Insurrection: five schools of revolutionary thought. New York, [1975]. pp. 342. *bibliog.*

SARKESIAN (SAM CHARLES) ed. Revolutionary guerrilla warfare. Chicago, [1975]. pp. 623. *bibliog.*

VODOLAZOV (GRIGORII GRIGOR'EVICH) Dialektika i revoliutsiia: metodologicheskie problemy sotsial'noi revoliutsii. Moskva, 1975. pp. 230.

— Bibliography.

BLACKEY (ROBERT) Modern revolutions and revolutionists: a bibliography. Santa Barbara, [1976]. pp. 257.

— Africa, Subsaharan.

STOCKHOLM INTERNATIONAL PEACE RESEARCH INSTITUTE. Southern Africa: the escalation of a conflict: a politico-military study. New York, [1976]. pp. 235. *bibliog.*

— America, Latin.

BLASIER (COLE) The hovering giant: U.S. responses to revolutionary change in Latin America. Pittsburgh, [1976]. pp. 315.

— Bolivia.

BEYOND the revolution: Bolivia since 1952; James M. Malloy and Richard S. Thorn, editors. Pittsburgh, [1971]. pp. 402. *Based on an interdisciplinary seminar held at the University of Pittsburgh, sponsored by the University's Center for International Studies and Center for Latin American Studies.*

— Cuba.

CASTRO RUZ (FIDEL) La historia me absolvera. Havana, 1969. pp. 107.

— France.

PILLORGET (RENE) Les mouvements insurrectionnels de Provence entre 1596 et 1715. Paris, 1975. pp. 1044. *bibliog.*

— Russia.

GEGEMONIIA proletariata v trekh russkikh revoliutsiiakh. Moskva, 1975. pp. 352.

IZ istorii ekonomicheskoi i obshchestvennoi zhizni Rossii: sbornik statei k 90-letiiu akademika Nikolaia Mikhailovicha Druzhinina. Moskva, 1976. pp. 288.

PORTER (CATHY) Fathers and daughters: Russian women in revolution. London, 1976. pp. 309. *bibliog.*

REZA SHAH PAHLAVI, Shah of Iran.

See RIZA SHAH PAHLAVI, Shah of Iran.

RHINE

— Navigation — Laws and regulations.

ZEMANEK (KARL) Die Schiffahrtsfreiheit auf der Donau und das Künftige Regime der Rhein-Main-Donau-Grossschiffahrtsstrasse: eine völkerrechtliche Untersuchung. Wien, [1976]. pp. 73. *(Österreichische Zeitschrift für öffentliches Recht. Supplementa. 4)*

RHINE PROVINCE

— Politics and government.

WINBERG (ALAN RONALD) Decision-making theory and the characteristics of crisis; with particular reference to the French reaction to the remilitarization of the Rhineland in 1936. [1976]. fo. 448. *bibliog. Typescript. M.Phil.(London) thesis: unpublished. This thesis is the property of London University and may not be removed from the Library.*

RHODE ISLAND

— Constitutional history.

DENNISON (GEORGE M.) The Dorr War: Republicanism on trial, 1831-1861. Lexington, Ky., [1967]. pp. 250. *bibliog.*

— History.

BRIDENBAUGH (CARL) Fat mutton and liberty of conscience: society in Rhode Island, 1636-1690. Providence, R.I., [1974]. pp. 157.

— Population.

BOUVIER (LEON F.) and RAO (SETHURAMAIAH LAKSHMINARAYANA) Socioreligious factors in fertility decline. Cambridge, Mass., [1975]. pp. 204. *bibliog.*

SPEARE (ALDEN) and others. Residential mobility, migration, and metropolitan change. Cambridge, Mass., [1975]. pp. 313. *bibliog.*

RHODESIA.

FOCUS ON RHODESIA; (pd. by the Rhodesian Ministry of Information, Immigration and Tourism). m., Mr 1976 (v.1, no.1)- [Salisbury]. *Supersedes RHODESIAN COMMENTARY.*

— Constitution.

JACOBS (WALTER DARNELL) A constitution for Rhodesia: an analysis submitted to the American-African Affairs Association. New York, [1969?]. pp. 33.

— Foreign relations.

See also UNITED NATIONS — Rhodesia.

— History.

VAMBE (LAWRENCE) From Rhodesia to Zimbabwe. Pittsburgh, 1976. pp. 290.

— Native races.

RHODESIA. Central Statistical Office. Agricultural production in African purchase areas: national and provincial totals. a., 1973(5th)- Salisbury.

— Politics and government.

CENTRE PARTY (RHODESIA). Blueprint for Rhodesia. Salisbury, 1970. fo. 4. *Photocopy.*

INTERNATIONAL DEFENCE AND AID FUND. Zimbabwe quiz: basic facts and figures about Rhodesia. London, 1975. pp. 42. *bibliog.*

INTERNATIONAL COMMISSION OF JURISTS. Racial discrimination and repression in Southern Rhodesia: a legal study. London, [1976]. pp. 119.

— Race question.

MURPHREE (MARSHALL WARNE) ed. Education, race and employment in Rhodesia. Salisbury, Rhodesia, 1975. pp. 478. *bibliog.*

INTERNATIONAL COMMISSION OF JURISTS. Racial discrimination and repression in Southern Rhodesia: a legal study. London, [1976]. pp. 119.

VAMBE (LAWRENCE) From Rhodesia to Zimbabwe. Pittsburgh, 1976. pp. 290.

RHODESIAN NEWSPAPERS.

WASON (EUGENE) Banned: the story of the African Daily News, Southern Rhodesia, 1964. London, 1976. pp. 161.

RHÔNE (DEPARTMENT).

FRANCE. Direction de la Documentation. La Documentation Française. Notes et Etudes Documentaires. Nos. 4,160-4, 161-4,162-4,163. Les départements français. 69. Rhône, Rhône-Alpes; [par Jeanne Filloux]. Paris, 1975. pp. 164.

RICE

— Marketing.

OKOSO-AMAA (KWEKU) Rice marketing in Ghana: an analysis of government intervention in business. Uppsala, 1975. pp. 102. *bibliog. Avhandling (doktor) - Uppsala Universitet.*

— Ghana.

OKOSO-AMAA (KWEKU) Rice marketing in Ghana: an analysis of government intervention in business. Uppsala, 1975. pp. 102. *bibliog. Avhandling (doktor) - Uppsala Universitet.*

— India.

BULLETIN ON RICE STATISTICS IN INDIA (DISTRICT-WISE); [pd. by] Directorate of Economics and Statistics, Ministry of Agriculture, [New Delhi]. a., 1974 (1st)- New Delhi.

— — Goa, Daman and Diu.

GOA, DAMAN AND DIU. Bureau of Economics, Statistics and Evaluation. 1975. An evaluation of the high yielding varieties programme, Kharif, 1974-75. Panaji, 1975. pp. 85. *(Evaluation Reports. No. 14)*

— Liberia.

LIBERIA. Ministry of Agriculture. National rice production estimates. a., 1974(1st)- Monrovia.

— Malaysia.

EDWARDS (ROBERT HOWARD) Public agricultural finance and technological change: a Malaysian case study; [Ph. D. (London) thesis]. 1975. fo. 188. *Typescript: unpublished. This thesis is the property of London University and may not be removed from the Library.*

— Pakistan.

KHAN (MAHMOOD HASAN) The economics of the green revolution in Pakistan. New York, 1975. pp. 226.

— Philippine Islands.

ROUMASSET (JAMES A.) Rice and risk: decision making among low-income farmers. Amsterdam, 1976. pp. 251. *bibliog.*

RICKERT (HEINRICH).

BURGER (THOMAS) Max Weber's theory of concept formation: history, laws, and ideal types. Durham, N.C., 1976. pp. 231. *bibliog.*

RIEL (LOUIS DAVID).

HOWARD (JOSEPH KINSEY) Strange empire: Louis Riel and the Métis people. Toronto, 1974. pp. 601. *bibliog. Originally published in 1952 in New York.*

CHARLEBOIS (PETER) The life of Louis Riel. Toronto, [1975]. pp. 255. *bibliog.*

RIEL REBELLION, 1885.

HOWARD (JOSEPH KINSEY) Strange empire: Louis Riel and the Métis people. Toronto, 1974. pp. 601. *bibliog. Originally published in 1952 in New York.*

RIESSER (GABRIEL).

LUETH (ERICH) Gabriel Riesser, 1806-1863: ein grosser Jude, Hamburger und deutscher Patriot. Hamburg, 1963. pp. 55.

RIGHT AND LEFT (POLITICAL SCIENCE).

ORGANIZZAZIONE COMUNISTA AVANGUARDIA OPERAIA. Conferenza Nazionale, 2a, 1972. Documenti. Milano, 1973. 2 vols. *(Quaderni. 7)*

AMERINGER (CHARLES D.) The democratic left in exile: the antidictatorial struggle in the Caribbean, 1945-1959. Coral Gables, [1974]. pp. 352. *bibliog.*

BRITISH AND IRISH COMMUNIST ORGANISATION. The Tories and the left. Belfast, 1974. pp. 11.

MEZZOGIORNO e sinistra di classe: atti del convegno sul Mezzogiorno dell'8-9 dicembre 1973, organizzato dal Centro del Manifesto e dalla Federazione del PdUP di Palermo. Palermo, [1974]. pp. 183.

SOULIE (MICHEL) Le Cartel des gauches. Paris, [1974]. pp. 335. *bibliog.*

CAMPBELL (IAN R.) The end of the Mitterrand experiment? Coventry, 1975. pp. 57. *(University of Warwick. Department of Politics. Working Papers. No. 5)*

COHN-BENDIT (DANIEL) Le grand bazar: entretiens avec Michel Lévy, Jean-Marc Salmon, Maren Sell. Paris, [1975]. pp. 192.

DAVIE (GRACE RIESTRA CLAIRE) Right wing politics among French Protestants, 1900-1944, with special reference to the Association Sully. 1975. fo.323. *bibliog. Typescript. Ph.D.(London) thesis: unpublished. This thesis is the property of London University and may not be removed from the Library.*

HORCHEM (HANS JOSEF) Right-wing extremism in Western Germany. London, 1975. pp. 11. *bibliog. (Institute for the Study of Conflict. Conflict Studies. No. 65)*

McNALL (SCOTT G.) Career of a radical rightist: a study in failure. Port Washington, N.Y., 1975. pp. 202.

POPEREN (JEAN) L'unité de la Gauche, 1965-1973. [Paris, 1975]. pp. 474. *bibliog.*

RIGHT OF REPLY

— United States.

SHAPIRO (ANDREW O.) Media access: your rights to express your views on radio and television. Boston, [Mass., 1976]. pp. 297.

RIGHT TO LABOUR.

DUFAURE (JULES ARMAND STANISLAS) Discours prononcé à l'Assemblée nationale sur le droit au travail. Paris, M. Lévy, 1848. pp. 35.

RINGEISEN (MICHAEL).

EUROPEAN COURT OF HUMAN RIGHTS. Publications. Series A: Judgments and Decisions. [A 13]. ...Ringeisen case; judgment of 16th July 1971. Strasbourg, Council of Europe, 1971. pp. 56 [bis]. *In English and French.*

EUROPEAN COURT OF HUMAN RIGHTS. Publications. Series A: Judgments and Decisions. [A] 15. ...Ringeisen case: judgment of 22 June /([; QUESTION OF THE APPLICATION OF aRTICLE 5: OF THE cONVENTION. sTRASBOURG, cOUNCIL OF eUROPE, 1972. PP. 12 ?BIS!. iN eNGLISH AND fRENCH.

EUROPEAN COURT OF HUMAN RIGHTS. Publications. Series B: Pleadings, Oral Arguments and Documents. [B11]. "Ringeisen" case, (1970-1971). Strasbourg, Council of Europe, 1972. pp. 299 [bis], 301-371. *In English and French.*

EUROPEAN COURT OF HUMAN RIGHTS. Publications. Series A: Judgments and Decisions. [A] 16. ...Ringeisen case: interpretation of the judgment of 22 June 1972; judgment of 23 June 1973. Strasbourg, Council of Europe, 1973. pp. 13 [bis]. *In English and French.*

EUROPEAN COURT OF HUMAN RIGHTS. Publications. Series B: Pleadings, Oral Arguments and Documents. [B13]. "Ringeisen" case: question of the application of Article 50 of the Convention, (1971-1972). Strasbourg, Council of Europe, 1973. pp. 89 [bis], 91-119. *In English and French.*

EUROPEAN COURT OF HUMAN RIGHTS. Publications. Series B: Pleadings, Oral Arguments and Documents. [B14]. "Ringeisen" case: interpretation of the judgment of 22nd June 1972, (1972-1973). Strasbourg, Council of Europe, 1973. pp. 42 [bis], 43-58. *In English and French.*

RIO DE JANEIRO

— Politics and government.

PERLMAN (JANICE E.) The myth of marginality: urban poverty and politics in Rio de Janeiro. Berkeley, [1976]. pp. 341. *bibliog.*

— Poor.

PERLMAN (JANICE E.) The myth of marginality: urban poverty and politics in Rio de Janeiro. Berkeley, [1976]. pp. 341. *bibliog.*

RIO GRANDE DO SUL

— Bibliography.

BRAZIL. Superintendência do Desenvolvimento da Região Sul. 1976. Listagem bibliografica dos documentos constantes no acervo da Divisão de Documentação: Rio Grande do Sul. Porto Alegre, 1976. fo. 139.

— Emigration and immigration.

AZEVEDO (THALES DE) Italianos e gauchos: os anos pioneiros da colonização italiana no Rio Grande do Sul. Porto Alegre, 1975. pp. 310. *bibliog.*

RIOTS

— Ghana.

GHANA. Commission of Enquiry into Obuasi disturbances. 1970. Report; [Kwame Ata-Bedu, chairman]. [Accra], 1969 [or rather 1970]. fo. 65. *Bound with White Paper on the report.*

GHANA. 1971. White Paper on the report of the Commission appointed to enquire into the causes of the recent disturbances at Obuasi. [Accra], 1971. pp. 5. *(W[hite] P[apers]. 1971. No. 3) Bound with the report.*

— South Africa.

WORLD PEACE COUNCIL and AFRICAN NATIONAL CONGRESS (SOUTH AFRICA). Spotlight on Soweto. Helsinki, [1976]. pp. 23.

— United States.

KNOPF (TERRY ANN) Rumors, race and riots. New Brunswick, [1975]. pp. 398.

RIPON

— Civic improvement.

U.K. Department of the Environment. Yorkshire and Humberside Regional Office. 1975. Ripon: an environmental study. [Leeds], 1974 [or rather 1975]. pp. 138. *bibliog. Cover title: A study of the environment in Ripon.*

RIQUETTI (VICTOR) Marquis de Mirabeau.

FOX-GENOVESE (ELIZABETH) The origins of physiocracy: economic revolution and social order in eighteenth-century France. Ithaca, N.Y., 1976. pp. 325. *bibliog.*

RIS (HANS BLUMER-).

See BLUMER-RIS (HANS).

RISK.

RISK.

PRINDL (ANDREAS ROBERT) Foreign exchange risk. London, [1976]. pp. 169. *bibliog.*

— Mathematical models.

ROUMASSET (JAMES A.) Rice and risk: decision making among low-income farmers. Amsterdam, 1976. pp. 251. *bibliog.*

RITES AND CEREMONIES.

NIEBURG (HAROLD L.) Culture storm: politics and the ritual order. London, [1973]. pp. 262. *bibliog.*

RIZA SHAH PAHLAVI, Shah of Iran.

WILBER (DONALD NEWTON) Riza Shah Pahlavi: the resurrection and reconstruction of Iran. Hicksville, N.Y., [1975]. pp. 301. *bibliog.*

ROAD ACCIDENTS

— Kenya.

JACOBS (G.D.) and SAYER (I.A.) An analysis of road accidents in Kenya in 1972. Crowthorne, 1976. pp. 26. *(U.K. Transport and Road Research Laboratory. Supplementary Reports. 227 UC.)*

— Switzerland.

BALLMER (ROGER) Economist. Versuch einer Erfassung der Strassenverkehrsunfallfolgekosten für die Schweiz, 1972. Berne, 1975. pp. 224. *bibliog. (Geneva. Université. Faculté des Sciences Economiques et Sociales. Collection des Thèses. No.235)*

— United Kingdom.

JOHNSON (H.D.) Motorway accidents in fog and darkness. Crowthorne, 1973. pp. 14. *(U.K. Transport and Road Research Laboratory. Reports. LR 573)*

FAULKNER (C.R.) Distribution of accidents in urban areas of Great Britain. Crowthorne, 1975. pp. 37. *(U.K. Transport and Road Research Laboratory. Supplementary Reports. 159 UC)*

ROAD CONSTRUCTION

— Canada.

CANADA. Restrictive Trade Practices Commission. [Reports]. RTPC No. 49. Road paving in Ontario: report in the matter of an inquiry relating to the supply and transportation of asphalt paving materials in the province of Ontario. Ottawa, 1970. pp. 37.

— Iran.

IRVIN (G.W.) and others. Roads and redistribution: social costs and benefits of labour-intensive road construction in Iran. Geneva, International Labour Office, 1975. pp. 162.

— Nigeria.

NIGERIA. 1971. Comments of the Federal Military Government on the report of the Tribunal of Inquiry into the affairs of the Apapa Road Project. Lagos, 1971. pp. 34.

— United Kingdom.

U.K. Department of the Environment. 1971. Motorway across the Pennines: the Lancashire-Yorkshire motorway M62 and the Scammonden Dam. [London, 1971]. pp. 50.

ROAD MACHINERY.

EVSELEVSKII (L.I.) and others. Kremenchugskii zavod dorozhnykh mashin: ocherki. Khar'kov, 1970. pp. 187.

ROAD SAFETY

— Nigeria.

NIGERIA. Advisory Committee on Road Safety. 1970. Report...November 1968; [J.O. Shojobi, chairman]. Lagos, 1970. pp. 96.

ROADS

— Economic aspects — United Kingdom — Computer programs.

TINDALL (J.I.) RUCL: a road user cost program for London. London, [1975]. pp. 46. *(London. Greater London Council Research Memoranda. 475)*

— Environmental aspects — United Kingdom.

DAWSON (R.F.F) Environmental effects of Alton by-pass. Crowthorne, 1973. pp. 29. *(U.K. Transport and Road Research Laboratory. Reports. LR 589)*

VOLUNTARY JOINT COMMITTEE FOR THE PEAK DISTRICT NATIONAL PARK. A motorway [from] Sheffield to Manchester through Longdendale in the Peak District National Park: a calculated prediction of the dangers threatening the...park,...and an appeal for help to avert it. Sheffield, [1974?]. pp. 16.

LLEWELYN-DAVIES WEEKS [AND PARTNERS] and MORGAN (R. TRAVERS) AND PARTNERS. Report of the Urban Motorways Project Team to the Urban Motorways Committee: techniques used in the case studies. Technical paper no. 2. Social surveys;...advised by Social and Community Planning Research. [London], Department of the Environment, 1974 [or rather 1975]. pp. 156.

MORGAN (R. TRAVERS) AND PARTNERS. Report of the Urban Motorways Project Team to the Urban Motorways Committee: techniques used in the case studies. Technical paper no. 1. Environmental evaluation: the cost-benefit approach. [London], Department of the Environment, 1974 [or rather 1975]. pp. 64.

— — — Evaluation.

LASSIERE (A.) The environmental evaluation of transport plans. [London, 1976]. pp. 265. *bibliog. (U.K. Department of the Environment. Research Reports. 8)*

— Germany.

LAERMER (KARL) Autobahnbau in Deutschland, 1933 bis 1945: zu den Hintergründen. Berlin, 1975. pp. 163. *bibliog.*

— Mauritius.

MAURITIUS. Ministry of Works. 1973. Development of roads and road traffic in Mauritius. Port Louis, 1973. pp. 21.

— Tropics — Bibliography.

U.K. Transport and Road Research Laboratory. 1975. Reports on roads and transport planning in tropical and sub-tropical countries: [bibliography]. Crowthorne, 1975. pp. 75. *(Supplementary Reports. 162 UC).*

— United Kingdom — Design.

U.K. Department of the Environment. 1971. Motorway across the Pennines: the Lancashire-Yorkshire motorway M62 and the Scammonden Dam. [London, 1971]. pp. 50.

— — Estimates and costs.

NATIONAL FREIGHT CORPORATION. Infrastructure costs and road user taxation; an annexe to the NFC's main response to the consultation document on transport policy. London, 1976. pp. 11.

— — London.

HART (DOUGLAS ALLEN) Strategic road planning and the concept of urban order: an analysis of policy making in Greater London, 1943-1973; [Ph.D. (London) thesis]. 1975. fo. 308. *bibliog. Typescript: unpublished. This thesis is the property of London University and may not be removed from the Library.*

HART (DOUGLAS ALLEN) Strategic planning in London: the rise and fall of the primary road network. Oxford, 1976. pp. 237. *bibliog.*

— United States — Economic aspects.

HARRIS (CURTIS C.) Regional economic effects of alternative highway systems. Cambridge, Mass., [1974]. pp. 344.

— Yugoslavia.

PADJEN (JURAJ) and NIKIĆ (GORAZD) An evaluation of the economic efficiency of alternative routes for the Rijeka-Trieste highway; (translated by Roger Cowan). Zagreb, 1970. pp. 63. *bibliog.*

ROADS, ROMAN

— United Kingdom.

MARGARY (IVAN DONALD) Roman roads in Britain. 3rd ed. London, 1973. pp. 550.

ROBESPIERRE (FRANÇOIS MAXIMILIEN JOSEPH ISIDORE).

PARIS. Bibliothèque Nationale. Département des Imprimés. Catalogue des ouvrages de Robespierre conservés au Département des Imprimés; (notices...établies et coordonnées par Gérard Walter). Paris, 1941. pp. 23. *(Extrait du tome CLIII du Catalogue général des livres imprimés)*

HAMPSON (NORMAN) The life and opinions of Maximilien Robespierre. London, 1974. pp. 313. *bibliog.*

RUDÉ (GEORGE E.) Robespierre: portrait of a revolutionary democrat. London, 1975. pp. 254. *bibliog.*

ROBINSON (Sir HENRY AUGUSTUS).

ROBINSON (Sir HENRY AUGUSTUS) Memories: wise and otherwise. London, 1923 repr. 1924. pp. 348.

ROBINSON (RONALD EDWARD).

LOUIS (WILLIAM ROGER) ed. Imperialism: the Robinson and Gallagher controversy. New York, 1976. pp. 252. *bibliog.*

ROCAFUERTE (VICENTE).

RODRIGUEZ O. (JAIME E.) The emergence of Spanish America: Vicente Rocafuerte and Spanish Americanism, 1808-1832. Berkeley, [1975]. pp. 311. *bibliog.*

RODO (JOSE ENRIQUE).

RODO (JOSE ENRIQUE) Motivos de Proteo; [and] Nuevos motivos de Proteo. Mexico, 1969. pp. 245.

ROEPKE (WILHELM).

ROEPKE (WILHELM) Wilhelm Röpke, Briefe 1934-1966: der innere Kompass; herausgegeben von Eva Röpke. Erlenbach-Zürich, [1976]. pp. 215.

ROLE CONFLICT.

MAGID (ALVIN) Men in the middle: leadership and role conflict in a Nigerian society. Manchester, [1976]. pp. 292. *bibliog.*

ROMANIA

— Annexation — Transylvania.

CONSTANTINESCU (MIRON) and PASCU (ŞTEFAN) eds. Desăvîrşirea unificării statului naţional român: unirea Transilvaniei cu vechea Românie. Bucureşti, 1968. pp. 512. *(Academia Republicii Socialiste România. Secţia de Ştiinţe Istorice, Filozofice şi Economico-Juridice. Bibliotheca Historica Romaniae. Monographies. 5)*

— Antiquities.

RELATIONS between the autochthonous population and the migratory populations on the territory of Romania: a collection of studies; editors Miron Constantinescu [and others]. Bucuresti, 1975. pp. 323. *(Academia Republicii Socialiste Romania. Sectia de Ştiinte Istorice, Filozofice şi Economico-Juridice. Bibliotheca Historica Romaniae. Monographies. 16)*

— Army — History.

PAGES from the history of the Romanian army. Bucureşti, 1975. pp. 242. *(Academia Republicii Socialiste Romania. Sectia de Ştiinţe Istorice, Filozofice şi Economico-Juridice. Bibliotheca Historica Romaniae. Monographies. 15)*

— Civilization.

ARMBRUSTER (ADOLF) Romanitatea românilor: istoria unei idei. Bucureşti, 1972. pp. 282. *bibliog. (Academia de Ştiinţe Sociale şi Politice a Republicii Socialiste România. Biblioteca Istorică. 35) With German summary and table of contents.*

— Commerce — Austria-Hungary.

BINDREITER (UTA) Die diplomatischen und wirtschaftlichen Beziehungen zwischen Österreich-Ungarn und Rumänien in den Jahren 1875-1888. Wien, 1976. pp. 322. *bibliog. (Kommission für Neuere Geschichte Österreichs. Veröffentlichungen. 63)*

— — Balkan States.

RELAŢIILE comerciale ale Ţării Româneşti cu Peninsula Balcanică, 1829-1858. Bucureşti, 1970. pp. 308. *(Academia Republicii Socialiste România. Institutul de Studii Sud-Est Europene. Biblioteca Istorică. 22) With French summary.*

— Constitution.

ROMANIA. Statutes, etc. 1965-75. Législation roumaine. Bucarest, 1975. pp. 208.

— Economic conditions.

GILBERG (TROND) Modernization in Romania since World War II. New York, 1975. pp. 261. *bibliog.*

— Economic history.

CURTEANU (MARIA) Sectorul de stat în România anilor 1944-1947. Bucureşti, 1974. pp. 192. *bibliog. With French table of contents.*

— Foreign economic relations.

POPESCU (MARIA D.) Imperativele noii ordini economice internaţionale: raţiunea şi strategia cooperării. Bucureşti, 1975. pp. 210. *bibliog. With English summary and English, French and Russian tables of contents.*

— — United Kingdom.

CONFEDERATION OF BRITISH INDUSTRY. Romania: an opportunity for joint investment; a report on a visit made by a CBI industrial delegation to Romania, October 1973, leader, Mr. Ralph Bateman. London, 1974. pp. 34.

— Foreign relations — Austria-Hungary.

BINDREITER (UTA) Die diplomatischen und wirtschaftlichen Beziehungen zwischen Österreich-Ungarn und Rumänien in den Jahren 1875-1888. Wien, 1976. pp. 322. *bibliog. (Kommission für Neuere Geschichte Österreichs. Veröffentlichungen. 63)*

— — Russia.

ZALYSHKIN (MIKHAIL MIKHAILOVICH) Vneshniaia politika Rumynii i rumyno-russkie otnosheniia, 1875- 1878. Moskva, 1974. pp. 291. *bibliog.*

— — United Kingdom.

DEMÉNY (LUDOVIC) and CERNOVODEANU (PAUL) Relaţiile politice ale Angliei cu Moldova, Ţara Românească şi Transilvania în secolele XVI-XVIII. Bucureşti, 1974. pp. 287. *(Academia de Ştiinţe Sociale şi Politice a Republicii Socialiste România. Biblioteca Istorică. 42) With English summary and table of contents.*

— History.

CHRONOLOGICAL history of Romania; [by] Horia C. Matei [and others]...under the guidance of Constantin C. Giurescu 2nd ed. Bucharest, 1974. pp. 608. *bibliog.*

OLTEANU (ŞTEFAN) Les pays roumains à l'époque de Michel le Brave, l'union de 1600. Bucureşti, 1975. pp. 159. *(Academia Republicii Socialiste România. Secţia de Ştiinţe Istorice, Filozofiçe Economico-Juridice. Bibliotheca Historica Romaniae. Monographies. 14)*

RELATIONS between the autochthonous population and the migratory populations on the territory of Romania: a collection of studies; editors Miron Constantinescu [and others]. Bucuresti, 1975. pp. 323. *(Academia Republicii Socialiste Romania. Sectia de Stiinte Istorice, Filozofice şi Economico-Juridice. Bibliotheca Historica Romaniae. Monographies. 16)*

— — Bibliography.

CRĂCIUN (IOACHIM) and others, compilers. Bibliografia istorică a României: bibliografie selectivă. Bucureşti, 1970 in progress.

— — Chronology.

IZ khroniki istoricheskikh dnei, 1 maia 1944 - 6 marta 1945 gg.; (perevod s rumynskogo Ally Lazia). Bukharest, 1974. pp. 251. *(Academia de Ştiinţe Sociale şi Politice a Republicii Socialiste România. Bibliotheca Historica Romaniae. Studies. 48)*

— History, Military.

PAGES from the history of the Romanian army. Bucureşti, 1975. pp. 242. *(Academia Republicii Socialiste Romania. Sectia de Ştiinţe Istorice, Filozofice şi Economico-Juridice. Bibliotheca Historica Romaniae. Monographies. 15)*

— — Sources.

BERINDEI (DAN) and others, eds. Războiul pentru independenţă naţională, 1877-1878: documente militare; volum realizat de...Dan Berindei,... Leonida Loghin,...Gheorghe Stoean. Bucureşti, 1971. pp. lii,660.

— Nationalism.

ARMBRUSTER (ADOLF) Romanitatea românilor: istoria unei idei. Bucureşti, 1972. pp. 282. *bibliog. (Academia de Ştiinţe Sociale şi Politice a Republicii Socialiste România. Biblioteca Istorică. 35) With German summary and table of contents.*

— Politics and government.

CODREANU (CORNELIU ZELEA) Pentru legionari. v.1. Sibiu, 1936; [Munich, 1968]. pp. 482. *(Colecţia "Omul nou")*

GILBERG (TROND) Modernization in Romania since World War II. New York, 1975. pp. 261. *bibliog.*

— Population.

Le DROIT et la croissance de la population en Roumanie: (ouvrage élaboré sous les auspices du Conseil législatif et de la Commission Nationale de Démographie de la République Socialiste de Roumanie); [by] Ioan Ceterchi [and others]. Bucarest, 1974. pp. 334. *(Le Droit et la Population]*

ROMANIA. Comisia Naţională pentru Demografie. 1974. La population de la Roumanie. Bucarest, 1974. pp. 125. *bibliog. (Committee for International Coordination of National Research in Demography. C.I.C.R.E.D. Series)*

RELATIONS between the autochthonous population and the migratory populations on the territory of Romania: a collection of studies; editors Miron Constantinescu [and others]. Bucuresti, 1975. pp. 323. *(Academia Republicii Socialiste Romania. Sectia de Stiinte Istorice, Filozofice şi Economico-Juridice. Bibliotheca Historica Romaniae. Monographies. 16)*

— Relations (general) with China.

TRADI ŢII ale poporului român de solidaritate şi prietenie cu poporul chinez. Bucureşti, 1973. pp. 478.

— Social conditions.

GILBERG (TROND) Modernization in Romania since World War II. New York, 1975. pp. 261. *bibliog.*

ROME, ANCIENT

— Religion.

SCHEID (JOHN) Les Frères Arvales: recrutement et origine sociale sous les empereurs julio-claudiens. Paris, 1975. pp. 431. *bibliog. (Paris. Ecole Pratique des Hautes Etudes. Bibliothèque: Section des Sciences Réligieuses. vol. 77)*

ROOSEVELT (FRANKLIN DELANO) President of the United States.

ADAMS (DAVID KEITH) F[ranklin] D[elano] R[oosevelt], the New Deal and Europe; an inaugural lecture...given in the University of Keele, 23rd October 1973. Keele, [1974]. pp. 22.

SUTTON (ANTONY C.) Wall Street and FDR. New Rochelle, [1975]. pp. 200. *bibliog.*

FLYNN (GEORGE Q.) Roosevelt and Romanism: Catholics and American diplomacy, 1937- 1945. Westport, 1976. pp. 268. *bibliog.*

ROOSEVELT (THEODORE) President of the United States.

BURTON (DAVID H.) Theodore Roosevelt and his English correspondents: a special relationship of friends. Philadelphia, 1973. pp. 70. *bibliog. (American Philosophical Society. Transactions. New Series. vol. 63, part 2)*

RÖPKE.

See ROEPKE.

ROSA (JOAO GUIMARÃES).

MARTINS (WILSON) Structural perspectivism in Guimarães Rosa. New York, 1973. pp. 23. *(New York (City). University. Ibero-American Language and Area Center. Occasional Papers. No.3)*

ROSAS (JUAN MANUEL DE).

ASTESANO (EDUARDO B.) Rosas: bases del nacionalismo popular. Buenos Aires, 1960. pp. 78.

ROSCHER (WILHELM).

WEBER (MAX) Roscher and Knies: the logical problems of historical economics translated with an introduction by Guy Oakes. New York, [1975]. pp. 294. *bibliog.*

ROSE (WILLIAM JOHN).

ROSE (WILLIAM JOHN) The Polish memoirs of William John Rose; edited by Daniel Stone. Toronto, [1975]. pp. 248.

ROSSI (ERNESTO).

ROSSI (ERNESTO) Un democratico ribelle: cospirazione antifascista, carcere, confino; scritti e testimonianze a cura di Giuseppe Armani. Parma, 1975. pp. 414.

ROTSHTEIN (FEDOR ARONOVICH).

IMPERIALIZM i bor'ba rabochego klassa: sbornik statei pamiati akademika Fedora Aronovicha Rotshteina. Moskva, 1960. pp. 507.

ROUEN.

FRANCE. Direction de la Documentation. La Documentation Française. Notes et Etudes Documentaires. Nos. 4,130 - 4, 131 - 4,132. Les villes françaises: l'agglomération Rouen-Elbeuf; [par François J. Gay]. Paris, 1974. pp. 92. *bibliog.*

ROUSSEAU (JEAN JACQUES).

ELLENBURG (STEPHEN) Rousseau's political philosophy: an interpretation from within. Ithaca, N.Y., 1976. pp. 335.

HUIZINGA (JACOB HERMAN) The making of a saint: the tragi-comedy of Jean-Jacques Rousseau. London, 1976. pp. 284. *bibliog.*

ROUSSEAU (JEAN JACQUES).(Cont.)

PARKER (MAXWELL NOEL LEWIS) Rousseau and the contradictions of rationalism: a critical study of Rousseau's social and political theory in the context of eighteenth-century social and philosophical developments. [1976]. fo. 264. *bibliog. Typescript. Ph.D. (London) thesis: unpublished. This thesis is the property of London University and may not be removed from the Library.*

ROVNO (OBLAST')

— History — 1917-1921, Revolution.

HOLOVAN' (VASYL' PETROVYCH) and MYKHAILIUTA (TROKHYM IVANOVYCH) Borot'ba bil'shovykiv Rovenshchyny za vladu Rad. L'viv, 1968. pp. 70.

— Statistics.

ROVNO(OBLAST'). Statystychne Upravlinnia. Narodne hospodarstvo Rovens'koï oblasti: statystychnyi zbirnyk. L'viv, 1970. pp. 167.

ROWELL (NEWTON WESLEY).

PRANG (MARGARET) N.W. Rowell: Ontario nationalist. Toronto, [1975]. pp. 553.

ROYER (JEAN).

JOUET (MICHEL) and MARTIN (JEAN JACQUES) Jean Royer: un réformisme autoritaire. Paris, [1975]. pp. 128.

ROZEN (ANDREI EVGEN'EVICH) Baron.

BARRATT (GLYNN R.V.) The rebel on the bridge: a life of the Decembrist Baron Andrey Rozen, 1800-84. London, 1975. pp. 310. *bibliog.*

RUBBER INDUSTRY AND TRADE

— Bolivia.

GOSLING (CECIL) [Foreign Office papers. 1910-21]. 1 piece. *Typescript and printed matter.*

— Germany.

PEFFGEN (ELFRIED) Die gummi- und asbestverarbeitende Industrie aus der Sicht der siebziger Jahre. Berlin, [1976]. pp. 98. *(Ifo-Institut für Wirtschaftsforschung. Struktur und Wachstum. Reihe Industrie. Heft 27)*

RUHR

— Economic conditions.

KROMBACH (UWE) Zur Lage der arbeitenden Bevölkerung im Ruhrgebiet. Frankfurt, [1974 in progress]. *bibliog.*

LOEBBE (KLAUS) and KRUCK (ROSWITHA) Wirtschaftsstrukturelle Bestandsaufnahme für das Ruhrgebiet. Berlin, [1976]. pp. 196. *bibliog. (Rheinisch-Westfälisches Institut für Wirtschaftsforschung, Essen. Schriftenreihe. Neue Folge. 37)*

— Economic policy.

RHEINISCH-WESTFÄLISCHES INSTITUT FÜR WIRTSCHAFTSFORSCHUNG, ESSEN and NEDERLANDS ECONOMISCH INSTITUUT. Wirtschaftliche Entwicklung im Ruhrgebiet. Essen, 1974. pp. 136. *(Siedlungsverband Ruhrkohlenbezirk. Schriftenreihe. Nr.46)*

RULE OF LAW

— Russia.

MUKHAMEDSHIN (KASHIF DZHIGANSHIEVICH) Deiatel'nost' Prezidiuma Verkhovnogo Soveta soiuznoi respubliki po ukrepleniiu zakonnosti. Moskva, 1975. pp. 128.

RUMOUR.

KNOPF (TERRY ANN) Rumors, race and riots. New Brunswick, [1975]. pp. 398.

RUPPRECHT (ADOLF).

RUPPRECHT (ADOLF) Wie die Nazis das Eigentum der SPD raubten und zerstörten: aus den Aufzeichnungen eines ehemaligen leitenden sozialdemokratischen Funktionärs. Berlin, 1960. pp. 56.

RURAL HEALTH SERVICES

— United States.

NORTH CENTRAL REGIONAL CENTER FOR RURAL DEVELOPMENT. Rural health services: organization, delivery, and use; [edited by Edward W. Hassinger and Larry R. Whiting]. Ames, Iowa, 1976. pp. 308.

RURAL POOR

— Australia — New South Wales.

UNIVERSITY OF NEW ENGLAND, ARMIDALE. Department of Sociology. Rural poverty in northern New South Wales. Canberra, Australian Government Publishing Service, 1974. pp. 169.

RURAL—URBAN MIGRATION.

CONFERENCE ON MIGRATION AND ETHNICITY, OSHKOSH, WIS., 1973. Migration and urbanization: models and adaptive strategies: [selected papers of the conference held in conjunction with the 9th International Congress of Anthropological and Ethnological Sciences]; editors Brian M. Du Toit [and] Helen I. Safa. The Hague, [1975]. pp. 305. *bibliogs.*

CURIE (JACQUES) Le devenir des travailleurs d'origine agricole: contribution à l'étude de la transformation des conduites de travail. Paris, 1975. pp. 529. *bibliog. Thèse présentée devant l'Université de Toulouse-le-Mirail.*

— Mathematical models.

JONES (DONALD W.) 1948- . Migration and urban unemployment in dualistic economic development. Chicago, 1975. pp. 174. *bibliog. (Chicago. University. Department of Geography. Research Papers. No. 165)*

— Africa, Subsaharan.

INTERNATIONAL AFRICAN SEMINAR. 12th Seminar, University of Zambia, Lusaka, 1972. Town and country in central and eastern Africa: studies presented and discussed at the...seminar...; edited with an introduction by David Parkin. London, 1975. pp. 362. *bibliog.*

— America, Latin.

SHAW (R. PAUL) Land tenure and the rural exodus in Chile, Colombia, Costa Rica, and Peru. Gainesville, Fla., 1976. pp. 180. *bibliog. (Florida University. School of Inter-American Studies. Latin American Monographs. 2nd Series. [No]. 19)*

— Brazil.

COSTA (MANOEL AUGUSTO) Urbanization and migration in Brazil, with particular reference to trends since 1940; [Ph.D. (London) thesis]. 1975. pp. 298. *bibliog. Typescript: unpublished. This thesis is the property of London University and may not be removed from the Library.*

— Germany.

ALLENDORF (HANS) Der Zuzug in die Städte:...mit besonderer Berücksichtigung der Zuzugsverhältnisse der Stadt Halle a. S. im Jahre 1899. Jena, 1901. pp. 80. *bibliog. (Halle. Universität. Staatswissenschaftliches Seminar. Sammlung Nationalökonomischer und Statistischer Abhandlungen. 30. Band)*

— Greece.

KAYSER (BERNARD) and others. Exode rural et attraction urbaine en Grèce: matériaux pour étude géographique des mouvements de population dans la Grèce contemporaine. Athènes, 1971. pp. 263. *bibliog. With map in end-pocket.*

— Mexico.

ARIZPE-SCHLOSSER (LOURDES) Migration and ethnicity: the Mazahua Indians of Mexico. 1975. fo. 386. *bibliog. Typescript. Ph.D.(London) thesis: unpublished. This thesis is the property of London University and may not be removed from the Library.*

CORNELIUS (WAYNE A.) Politics and the migrant poor in Mexico City. Stanford, 1975. pp. 319. *bibliog.*

— Poland.

LATUCH (MIKOŁAJ) Migracje wewnętrzne w Polsce na tle industrializacji, 1950-1960. Warszawa, 1970. pp. 243. *bibliog.*

HERER (WIKTOR) and SADOWSKI (WŁADYSŁAW) Migracja z rolnictwa: efekty i koszty. Warszawa, 1975. pp. 382. *With Russian and English summaries.*

I'ZYK (WANDA) Ruchy migracyjne w rejonie uprzemysławianym. Warszawa, 1975. pp. 142. *bibliog. (Polska Akademia Nauk. Komitet i Zakład Badań Rejonów Uprzemysławianych. Problemy Rejonów Uprzemysławianych) With Russian and English summaries.*

'ZUREK (AGNIESZKA) Struktura przestrzenna przepływów ludności miast województwa kieleckiego. Wrocław, 1975. pp. 112. *bibliog. (Polska Akademia Nauk. Instytut Geografii i Przestrzennego Zagospodarowania. Prace Geograficzne. Nr. 113) With Russian and English summaries.*

— Spain.

ACEVES (JOSEPH BUENAVENTURA) and DOUGLASS (WILLIAM A.) eds. The changing faces of rural Spain. New York, [1976]. pp. 205. *bibliog.*

— Underdeveloped areas.

See UNDERDEVELOPED AREAS — Rural—urban migration.

— United Kingdom — Wales.

THOMASON (GEORGE F.) Rural depopulation in Wales. London, 1974. pp. 9. *bibliog. (Age Concern England. Manifesto Series. No. 23)*

— United States.

SMITH (THOMAS LYNN) Studies of the great rural tap roots of urban poverty in the United States. New York, [1974]. pp. 144.

RURAL YOUTH

— Finland.

SARMELA (MATTI) Reciprocity systems of the rural society in the Finnish-Karelian culture area, with special reference to social intercourse of the youth. Helsinki, 1969. pp. 347. *bibliog. (Academia Scientiarum Fennica. FF Communications. No. 207)*

RUSSIA

— Annexation — Bessarabia.

KOPANSKII (IAKOV MIKHAILOVICH) Internatsional'naia solidarnost' s bor'boi trudiashchikhsia Bessarabii za vossoedinenie s Sovetskoi Rodinoi, 1918-1940; otvetstvennyi redaktor...A.M. Lazarev. Kishinev, 1975. pp. 337.

— — Ukraine, Western.

RUDNYTS'KA (MILENA) ed. Zakhidnia Ukraïna pid bol'shevykamy, IX.1939 - VI.1941: zbirnyk; Western Ukraine under the Bolsheviks, IX.1939 - VI.1941. N'iu-Iork, 1958. pp. 494.

— Armed forces.

GRECHKO (ANDREI ANTONOVICH) Vooruzhennye Sily Sovetskogo gosudarstva. Moskva, 1974. pp. 406.

GRECHKO (ANDREI ANTONOVICH) Vooruzhennye Sily Sovetskogo gosudarstva. 2nd ed. Moskva, 1975. pp. 438.

RUSSIA

— **Army.**

RUTHERFORD (WARD) The Russian army in World War I. London, 1975. pp. 303. *bibliog.*

— **Census.**

LEVIT (M.E.) ed. Mekhanizirovannaia razrabotka materialov vsesoiuznoi perepisi naseleniia 1970 g. na EVM "Minsk-32". Moskva, 1974. pp. 207.

DROBIZHEV (VLADIMIR ZINOV'EVICH) and others. Rabochii klass Sovetskoi Rossii v pervyi god proletarskoi diktatury: opyt strukturnogo analiza po materialam professional'noi perepisi 1918 g. Moskva, 1975. pp. 224.

— **Civil defence.**

GOURE (LEON) War survival in Soviet strategy: USSR civil defense. Miami, 1976. pp. 218. *(Miami (Florida). University. Center for Advanced International Studies. Monographs in International Affairs)*

— **Civilization.**

KATZ (ZEV) and others, eds. Handbook of major Soviet nationalities. New York, [1975]. pp. 481. *bibliogs.*

The MODERNIZATION of Japan and Russia: a comparative study; [by] Cyril E. Black [and others]. New York, [1975]. pp. 386. *bibliog.*

— — **Baltic influences.**

The INFLUENCE of east Europe and the Soviet west on the USSR; edited by Roman Szporluk. New York, 1975. pp. 258. *Based on revised and updated papers presented at a conference sponsored by the Center for Russian and East European Studies, University of Michigan, May, 1970.*

— — **East European influences.**

The INFLUENCE of east Europe and the Soviet west on the USSR; edited by Roman Szporluk. New York, 1975. pp. 258. *Based on revised and updated papers presented at a conference sponsored by the Center for Russian and East European Studies, University of Michigan, May, 1970.*

— **Commerce.**

EKONOMIKA i planirovanie sovetskoi torgovli, etc. Moskva, 1966. pp. 344.

KAPELINSKII (IURII NAUMOVICH) Na vzaimovygodnoi osnove: torgovlia SSSR s razvitymi kapitalisticheskimi stranami. Moskva, 1975. pp. 224.

PETROV (DMITRII GRIGOR'EVICH) Effektivnost' kapital'nykh vlozhenii v sfere tovarnogo obrashcheniia: voprosy teorii i praktiki. Kiev, 1975. pp. 288.

— — **Germany.**

POHL (MANFRED) Die Finanzierung der Russengeschäfte zwischen den beiden Weltkriegen: die Entwicklung der 12 grossen Russlandkonsortien. Frankfurt am Main, [1975]. pp. 48. *(Tradition: Zeitschrift für Firmengeschichte und Unternehmerbiographie. Beihefte. 9)*

— — **United States.**

WILSON (JOAN HOFF) Ideology and economics: U.S. relations with the Soviet Union, 1918-1933. Columbia, Mo., 1974. pp. 192. *bibliog.*

KIRCHNER (WALTHER) Studies in Russian-American commerce, 1820-1860. Leiden, 1975. pp. 265. *bibliog.*

STOWELL (CHRISTOPHER E.) Soviet industrial import priorities, with marketing considerations for exporting to the USSR. New York, 1975. pp. 505. *bibliog.*

GIBSON (JAMES R.) Imperial Russia in frontier America: the changing geography of supply of Russian America, 1784-1867. New York, 1976. pp. 257. *bibliogs.*

— **Constitution.**

POLITICHESKAIA organizatsiia i upravlenie obshchestvom pri sotsializme. Moskva, 1975. pp. 159.

— **Constitutional history.**

RADZHABOV (SOLEKH ASHUROVICH) V.I. Lenin i sovetskaia natsional'naia gosudarstvennost'. Dushanbe, 1970. pp. 687.

TERLETS'KYI (VALENTYN MYKHAILOVICH) Leninskoe ideinoe nasledie i problemy sovetskogo stroitel'stva. Kiev, 1974. pp. 263. *bibliog.*

KHESIN (SAMUIL SEMENOVICH) Stanovlenie proletarskoi diktatury v Rossii: voprosy ustanovleniia Sovetskoi vlasti i skladyvaniia proletarskoi gosudarstvennoi sistemy, noiabr' 1917 - mart 1918 g. Moskva, 1975. pp. 471.

KORENEVSKAIA (ELENA IGNAT'EVNA) Stanovlenie vysshikh organov sovetskogo gosudarstvennogo upravleniia: pravovye osnovy organizatsii i deiatel'nosti Sovetskogo pravitel'stva v 1917-1922 gg. Moskva, 1975. pp. 159.

— — **Sources.**

VORONKOVA (SVETLANA VLADIMIROVNA) Materialy osobogo soveshchaniia po oborone gosudarstva: istochnikovedcheskoe issledovanie. Moskva, 1975. pp. 189.

— **Constitutional law — Bibliography.**

SOVETSKOE gosudarstvennoe konstitutsionnoe pravo: bibliografiia 1957-1970. Irkutsk, 1972. pp. 557.

— **Defences.**

HOLZMAN (FRANKLYN DUNN) Financial checks on Soviet defense expenditures. Lexington, Mass., [1975]. pp. 103. *bibliog.*

KOVALEV (IVAN IAKOVLEVICH) Komsomol i oborona Rodiny, 1921-1941 gg.: na materialakh Ukrainy. Kiev, 1975. pp. 207.

KUBLANOV (ARKADII L'VOVICH) Sovet Rabochei i Krest'ianskoi Oborony, noiabr' 1918 - mart 1920 g. Leningrad, 1975. pp. 256.

VORONKOVA (SVETLANA VLADIMIROVNA) Materialy osobogo soveshchaniia po oborone gosudarstva: istochnikovedcheskoe issledovanie. Moskva, 1975. pp. 189.

GRAY (COLIN S.) The Soviet-American arms race. Farnborough, Hants, [1976]. pp. 196.

PIPES (RICHARD EDGAR) ed. Soviet strategy in Europe. London, 1976. pp. 316.

— **Description and travel.**

KOBER (AUGUST HEINRICH) Unter der Gewalt des Hungers: vom neuen Werden in Russland. Jena, 1922. pp. 110.

PARKER (WILLIAM HENRY) The Soviet Union. Chicago, 1969. pp. 188. *bibliog.*

DAVIDOW (MIKE) Cities without crisis. New York, [1976]. pp. 240.

— **Economic conditions.**

OKTIABR'SKAIA revoliutsiia i formirovanie novykh obshchestvennykh otnoshenii: k 50-letiiu Velikoi Oktiabr'skoi sotsialisticheskoi revoliutsii. Orel, 1967. pp. 221. *(Orlovskii Gosudarstvennyi Pedagogicheskii Institut. Uchenye Zapiski. t.37)*

PARKER (WILLIAM HENRY) The Soviet Union. Chicago, 1969. pp. 188. *bibliog.*

LYDOLPH (PAUL E.) Geography of the U.S.S.R. 2nd ed. New York, [1970]. pp. 683. *bibliogs.*

BELOUSOV (REM ALEKSANDROVICH) Rost ekonomicheskogo potentsiala. Moskva, 1971. pp. 55.

UCHENYE ZAPISKI KAFEDR OBSHCHESTVENNYKH NAUK VUZOV LENINGRADA. Politicheskaia ekonomiia. vyp. 12. Ekonomicheskie interesy pri sotsializme i formy ikh realizatsii. Leningrad, 1971. pp. 191.

GREGORY (PAUL R.) and STUART (ROBERT C.) Soviet economic structure and performance. New York, 1974. pp. 478. *bibliogs.*

KLIMIN (N.V.) and DEVIATKIN (L.M.) eds. Proizvoditel'nye sily sotsializma v usloviiakh nauchno-tekhnicheskoi revoliutsii. Leningrad, 1974. pp. 232.

KUZ'MINOV (IVAN IVANOVICH) Ocherki politicheskoi ekonomii sotsializma: protsess sotsialisticheskogo proizvodstva. Moskva, 1974. pp. 284.

SEMENOV (VISSARION FEDOROVICH) Kontsentratsiia sotsialisticheskogo proizvodstva. Kazan', 1974. pp. 216.

INTERNATIONAL SLAVIC CONFERENCE, 1ST, BANFF, ALBERTA, 1974. Economic development in the Soviet Union and Eastern Europe. ..; edited by Zbigniew M. Fallenbuchl. New York, 1975-76. 2 vols.

ECONOMIC aspects of life in the USSR: main findings of colloquium held 29th-31st January, 1975, in Brussels. Brussels, North Atlantic Treaty Organization, [1975]. pp. 284. *bibliogs. In English and French.*

EGANIAN (MIKHAIL NIKOLAEVICH) Rasshirennoe vosproizvodstvo natsional'nogo bogatstva SSSR. Erevan, 1975. pp. 277.

KHACHATUROV (TIGRAN SERGEEVICH) Sovetskaia ekonomika na sovremennom etape. Moskva, 1975. pp. 367.

MATHIESON (RAYMOND SUCCESS) The Soviet Union: an economic geography. London, 1975. pp. 342. *bibliog.*

NESTERENKO (ALEKSEI ALEKSEEVICH) Zakonomernosti sotsial'no-ekonomicheskogo razvitiia goroda i derevni. Kiev, 1975. pp. 311.

SOTSIALIZM: dialektika razvitiia proizvoditel'nykh sil i proizvodstvennykh otnoshenii. Moskva, 1975. pp. 333.

ZAKUMBAEV (ABDRAKHMAN KYZDARBEKOVICH) Metody otsenki urovnia ekonomicheskogo razvitiia soiuznykh respublik i raionov. Alma-Ata, 1975. pp. 151.

DYKER (DAVID A.) The Soviet economy. London, 1976. pp. 173.

TREML (VLADIMIR G.) Input-output analysis and the Soviet economy: an annotated bibliography. New York, 1975. pp. 180.

— — **Mathematical models.**

DADAIAN (VLADISLAV SURENOVICH) Ökonomische Gesetze des Sozialismus und optimale Entscheidungen; (ins Deutsche übersetzt [from the Russian] von Klaus-Dieter Goll). Berlin, 1973. pp. 328.

CHETYRKIN (EVGENII MIKHAILOVICH) Statisticheskie metody prognozirovaniia. Moskva, 1975. pp. 184.

— **Economic history.**

CARR (EDWARD HALLETT) and DAVIES (ROBERT WILLIAM) Foundations of a planned economy, 1926-1929. London, 1969 in progress. *(A history of Soviet Russia) vol.1 is the Penguin Books reprint of 1974.*

BELIANOVA (ANTONINA MIKHAILOVNA) O tempakh ekonomicheskogo razvitiia SSSR: po materialam diskussii 20-kh godov. Moskva, 1974. pp. 174.

LAVERYCHEV (VLADIMIR IAKOVLEVICH) Krupnaia burzhuaziia v poreformennoi Rossii, 1861-1900. Moskva, 1974. pp. 252.

NOVAIA ekonomicheskaia politika: voprosy teorii i istorii. Moskva, 1974. pp. 360. *bibliog.*

The MODERNIZATION of Japan and Russia: a comparative study; [by] Cyril E. Black [and others]. New York, [1975]. pp. 386. *bibliog.*

SABUROV (NIKOLAI NIKOLAEVICH) Bor'ba partii za ustanovlenie ekonomicheskoi smychki rabochego klassa s trudiashchimisia krest'ianstvom, 1921-1925 gg.; pod redaktsiei...V.A. Smyshliaeva. Leningrad, 1975. pp. 119.

RUSSIA(Cont.)

ZLOBINA (VERA MAKSIMOVNA) Bor'ba partii bol'shevikov protiv melkoburzhuaznogo vliianiia na rabochii klass v pervye gody nepa, 1921-1925 gg. Moskva, 1975. pp. 168.

CRISP (OLGA) Studies in the Russian economy before 1914. London, 1976. pp. 278. *bibliog.*

FUNKEN (KLAUS) Die ökonomischen Voraussetzungen der Oktoberrevolution: zur Entwicklung des Kapitalismus in Russland. Zürich, 1976. pp. 372. *bibliog.*

IZ istorii ekonomicheskoi i obshchestvennoi zhizni Rossii: sbornik statei k 90-letiiu akademika Nikolaia Mikhailovicha Druzhinina. Moskva, 1976. pp. 288.

— — Bibliography.

GENKINA (ESFIR' BORISOVNA) ed. Sovetskaia strana v period vosstanovleniia narodnogo khoziaistva, 1921-1925 gg.: bibliograficheskii ukazatel' dokumental'nykh publikatsii. Moskva, 1975. pp. 692.

— — Historiography.

LEL'CHUK (VITALII SEMENOVICH) Sotsialisticheskaia industrializatsiia SSSR i ee osveshchenie v sovetskoi istoriografii. Moskva, 1975. pp. 312.

SAVITSKAIA (RAISA MALAKHOVNA) Deiatel'nost' V.I. Lenina v oblasti ekonomicheskogo stroitel'stva, oktiabr' 1917 - iiul' 1918 g.: istoriograficheskii ocherk. Moskva, 1975. pp. 276.

VOROZHEIKIN (IVAN EGOROVICH) Ocherk istoriografii rabochego klassa SSSR. Moskva, 1975. pp. 288. *bibliog.*

— — Sources.

RABOCHEE dvizhenie v Rossii v 1901-1904 gg.: sbornik dokumentov Leningrad, 1975. pp. 591. *bibliog.*

— Economic policy.

ALESSANDRI (PIERRE) Le socialisme vainqueur: U.R.S.S. Paris, [1936]. pp. 63. *Not to be consulted without the permission of the Superintendent of Readers' Services.*

VALENTINOV (NIKOLAI VLADISLAVOVICH) pseud. [i.e. Nikolai Vladislavovich VOL'SKII] Novaia ekonomicheskaia politika i krizis partii posle smerti Lenina: gody raboty v VSNKh vo vremia NEP: vospominaniia....; The new economic policy and the Party crisis after the death of Lenin: reminiscences of my work at the VSNKh during the NEP; edited by J. Bunyan and V. Butenko, etc. Stanford, 1971. pp. 256.

PROSPECTS for Soviet economic growth in the 1970s: main findings of symposium held 14-16th April, 1971 in Brussels; [edited by] Yves Laulan. [Brussels]. North Atlantic Treaty Organization, [1972?]. pp. 156. *In English and French.*

The PLATFORM of the joint opposition, 1927. London, 1973. pp. 117.

BELIANOVA (ANTONINA MIKHAILOVNA) O tempakh ekonomicheskogo razvitiia SSSR: po materialam diskussii 20-kh godov. Moskva, 1974. pp. 174.

GREGORY (PAUL R.) and STUART (ROBERT C.) Soviet economic structure and performance. New York, 1974. pp. 478. *bibliogs.*

KOTOV (FEDOR IVANOVICH) Organizatsiia planirovaniia narodnogo khoziaistva SSSR. Moskva, 1974. pp. 224.

MUSHKETIK (LEONID MIKHAILOVICH) Kompleksnyi territorial'nyi plan v usloviiakh otraslevogo upravleniia. Kiev, 1974. pp. 192. *bibliog.*

PLANIROVANIE khoziaistvennogo i kul'turnogo stroitel'stva. Moskva, 1974. pp. 463.

PROBLEMY ekonomiki razvitogo sotsializma v SSSR. Alma-Ata, 1974. pp. 200.

TARNAPOL'SKII (RUSTEM IL'IASOVICH) Pravovye voprosy upravleniia narodnym khoziaistvom v avtonomnoi respublike: vzaimootnosheniia Soveta Ministrov ASSR s nepodvedomstvennymi organizatsiiami. Kazan', 1974. pp. 120.

ZENCHENKO (N.S.) ed. Planirovanie kompleksnogo razvitiia khoziaistva oblasti, kraia, ASSR. Moskva, 1974. pp. 189. *bibliog.*

BREZHNEV (LEONID IL'ICH) Ob osnovnykh voprosakh ekonomicheskoi politiki KPSS na sovremennom etape: rechi i doklady. Moskva, 1975. 2 vols.

BYKOV (ANATOLII GRIGOR'EVICH) Plan i khoziaistvennyi dogovor. Moskva, 1975. pp. 158.

CACCIARI (MASSIMO) and PERULLI (PAOLO) Piano economico e composizione di classe: il dibattito sull'industrializzazione e lo scontro politico durante la NEP. Milano, 1975. pp. 201.

GOKHBERG (MARK IAKOVLEVICH) and SOLOV'EV (NIKOLAI ALEKSANDROVICH) Problemy razvitiia i razmeshcheniia proizvoditel'nykh sil Tsentral'nogo raiona. Moskva, 1975. pp. 238. *bibliog.*

KUZ'MINOV (IVAN IVANOVICH) and ROGACHEV (SERGEI VLADIMIROVICH) eds. Politicheskaia ekonomiia sotsializma - nauchnaia osnova rukovodstva narodnym khoziaistvom. Moskva, 1975. pp. 255.

MALAFEEV (ALEKSEI NIKOLAEVICH) and others, eds. Tsena i khoziaistvennyi raschet v sisteme upravleniia sotsialisticheskoi ekonomikoi. Leningrad, 1975. pp. 200.

OZNOBIN (NIKOLAI MAKAROVICH) and PAVLOV (ALEKSEI SERGEEVICH) Kompleksnoe planirovanie nauchno-tekhnicheskogo progressa. Moskva, 1975. pp. 263. *bibliog.*

RYAVEC (KARL W.) Implementation of Soviet economic reforms: political, organizational, and social processes. New York, 1975. pp. 360. *bibliog.*

SABUROV (NIKOLAI NIKOLAEVICH) Bor'ba partii za ustanovlenie ekonomicheskoi smychki rabochego klassa s trudiashchimsia krest'ianstvom, 1921-1925 gg.; pod redaktsiei...V.A. Smyshliaeva. Leningrad, 1975. pp. 119.

SHLIKHTER (OLEKSANDR HRYHOROVYCH) Agrarnyi vopros i prodovol'stvennaia politika v pervye gody Sovetskoi vlasti; [selected works edited by A.M. Rumiantsev and others]. Moskva, 1975. pp. 448.

STOWELL (CHRISTOPHER E.) Soviet industrial import priorities, with marketing considerations for exporting to the USSR. New York, 1975. pp. 505. *bibliog.*

DYKER (DAVID A.) The Soviet economy. London, 1976. pp. 173.

FUNKEN (KLAUS) Die ökonomischen Voraussetzungen der Oktoberrevolution: zur Entwicklung des Kapitalismus in Russland. Zürich, 1976. pp. 372. *bibliog.*

— — Mathematical models.

ARUTIUNIAN (ARTASHES GALUSTOVICH) and others. Primenenie matematicheskikh metodov i EVM v narodnom khoziaistve. Erevan, 1974. pp. 327. *bibliog.*

FEL'ZENBAUM (VADIM GRIGOR'EVICH) Ekonomicheskaia effektivnost' vzaimozameniaemykh sredstv proizvodstva: metodologiia izmereniia. Moskva, 1974. pp. 198.

MEZHOTRASLEVYE issledovaniia: sbornik statei. Moskva, 1974. pp. 144. *bibliog.*

POMERANTSEV (VLADIMIR VLADIMIROVICH) Analiz vremennykh riadov v planirovanii. Moskva, 1974. pp. 223.

SHATILOV (NIKOLAI FILIPPOVICH) Analiz zavisimostei sotsialisticheskogo rasshirennogo vosproizvodstva i opyt ego modelirovaniia; otvetstvennyi redaktor... V.K. Ozerov. Novosibirsk, 1974. pp. 250.

VAL'TUKH (KONSTANTIN KURTOVICH) ed. Narodnokhoziaistvennye modeli: tendentsii razvitiia ekonomiki SSSR. Novosibirsk, 1974. pp. 346. *(Akademiia Nauk SSSR. Sibirskoe Otdelenie. Institut Ekonomiki i Organizatsii Promyshlennogo Proizvodstva. Problemy Narodnokhoziaistvennogo Optimuma. [vyp. 3])*

AGANBEGIAN (ABEL GEZEVICH) and VAL'TUKH (KONSTANTIN KURTOVICH) eds. Ispol'zovanie narodnokhoziaistvennykh modelei v planirovanii. Moskva, 1975. pp. 231. *bibliog.*

CHEREMNYKH (IURII NIKOLAEVICH) Kachestvennoe issledovanie optimal'nykh traektorii dinamicheskikh modelei ekonomiki: voprosy magistral'noi teorii. Moskva, 1975. pp. 183. *bibliog.*

DANILOV-DANIL'IAN (V.I.) and ZAVEL'SKII (MIKHAIL GRIGOR'EVICH) Sistema optimal'nogo perspektivnogo planirovaniia narodnogo khoziaistva: problemy teorii i metodologii. Moskva, 1975. pp. 320. *bibliog.*

DOBROVOL'SKII (VLADIMIR KONSTANTINOVICH) Ekonomiko-matematicheskoe modelirovanie: voprosy metodologii. Kiev, 1975. pp. 183. *bibliog.*

GERSHENZON (MIKHAIL ABRAMOVICH) Analiz uproshchennykh dinamicheskikh modelei mezhotraslevogo balansa; otvetstvennye redaktory...N.F. Shatilov, ...B.G. Mirkin. Novosibirsk, 1975. pp. 219.

RAIZBERG (BORIS ABRAMOVICH) and others. Sistemnyi podkhod v perspektivnom planirovanii. Moskva, 1975. pp. 271. *bibliog.*

SHALABIN (GERAL'D VASIL'EVICH) Optimizatsiia dolgosrochnogo plana gruppy vzaimosviazannykh otraslei ekonomicheskogo raiona. Leningrad, 1975. pp. 128.

STATISTICHESKIE modeli v optimal'nom otraslevom planirovanii. Moskva, 1975. pp. 191. *bibliog.*

ZAUBERMAN (ALFRED) Mathematical theory in Soviet planning: concepts, methods, techniques. London, 1976. pp. 464.

— — Executive departments.

FILIPPOV (ALEKSANDR NIKITICH) Istoriia Senata v pravlenie Verkhovnogo tainogo soveta i Kabineta. ch.1. Senat v pravlenie Verkhovnogo tainogo soveta. Iur'ev, 1895. pp. xii,486. Offprint from Uchenye zapiski Imp. Iur'evskogo universiteta. *No more published.*

KORENEVSKAIA (ELENA IGNAT'EVNA) Stanovlenie vysshikh organov sovetskogo gosudarstvennogo upravleniia: pravovye osnovy organizatsii i deiatel'nosti Sovetskogo pravitel'stva v 1917-1922 gg. Moskva, 1975. pp. 159.

KUBLANOV (ARKADII L'VOVICH) Sovet Rabochei i Krest'ianskoi Oborony, noiabr' 1918 - mart 1920 g. Leningrad, 1975. pp. 256.

MAKAROV (BORIS MIKHAILOVICH) Narodnyi kontrol': organy i pravovye formy deiatel'nosti; otvetstvennyi redaktor V.I. Turovtsev. Moskva, 1975. pp. 151.

NIKOLAEVA (MARINA NIKOLAEVNA) Normativnye akty ministerstv i vedomstv SSSR. Moskva, 1975. pp. 143.

VORONKOVA (SVETLANA VLADIMIROVNA) Materialy osobogo soveshchaniia po oborone gosudarstva: istochnikovedcheskoe issledovanie. Moskva, 1975. pp. 189.

— Famines.

KOBER (AUGUST HEINRICH) Unter der Gewalt des Hungers: vom neuen Werden in Russland. Jena, 1922. pp. 110.

— Foreign economic relations.

INTERNATIONAL SLAVIC CONFERENCE, 1ST, BANFF, ALBERTA, 1974. Soviet economic and political relations with the developing world; edited by Roger E. Kanet [and] Donna Bahry. New York, 1975. pp. 237.

KAZAKOVA (NATAL'IA ALEKSANDROVNA) Russko-livonskie i russko-ganzeiskie otnosheniia, konets XIV - nachalo XVI v. Leningrad, 1975. pp. 359.

RUSSIA(Cont.)

ZAKHAROV (STANISLAV NIKOLAEVICH) Raschety effektivnosti vneshneekonomicheskikh sviazei: voprosy metodologii i metodika raschetov. Moskva, 1975. pp. 223.

RUSSELL (JEREMY) Energy as a factor in Soviet foreign policy. Farnborough, Hants., [1976]. pp. 241. bibliog.

— — Communist countries.

LAVROVA (LARISA FEDOROVNA) Internatsionalizm sovetskogo naroda: sotsial'naia aktivnost' narodnykh mass v sfere mezhdunarodnogo sotsialisticheskogo sotrudnichestva. Kiev, 1975. pp. 143.

PETROVA (NINA KONSTANTINOVNA) Mezhdunarodnye proizvodstvennye sviazi rabochego klassa SSSR, 1959- 1970 gg. Moskva, 1975. pp. 304.

RYBAKOV (OLEG KONSTANTINOVICH) Ekonomicheskaia effektivnost' sotrudnichestva SSSR s sotsialisticheskimi stranami: teoreticheskie i metodologicheskie problemy. Moskva, 1975. pp. 272.

— — Europe.

PIPES (RICHARD EDGAR) ed. Soviet strategy in Europe. London, 1976. pp. 316.

— — Livonia.

KAZAKOVA (NATAL'IA ALEKSANDROVNA) Russko-livonskie i russko-ganzeiskie otnosheniia, konets XIV - nachalo XVI v. Leningrad, 1975. pp. 359.

— — United Kingdom.

SEMENOV (LEONID SERGEEVICH) Rossiia i Angliia: ekonomicheskie otnosheniia v seredine XIX veka; pod red. ...S.B. Okunia. Leningrad, 1975. pp. 165.

— Foreign opinion.

OPYT sotsialisticheskikh preobrazovanii v SSSR i ego mezhdunarodnoe znachenie: Mezhdunarodnaia nauchnaia konferentsiia v Tashkente, 16-19 oktiabria 1972 g. Moskva, 1974. pp. 336.

FUHRMANN (RAINER) Die Orientalische Frage, das "panslawistisch-chauvinistische Lager" und das Zuwarten auf Krieg und Revolution: die Osteuropaberichterstattung und -vorstellungen der "Deutschen Rundschau", 1874-1918. Bern, 1975. pp. 200. bibliog. With English summary.

MAN'KOV (ARKADII GEORGIEVICH) ed. Inostrannye izvestiia o vosstanii Stepana Razina: materialy i issledovaniia. Leningrad, 1975. pp. 191.

ORLIK (OL'GA VASIL'EVNA) Dekabristy i evropeiskoe osvoboditel'noe dvizhenie. Moskva, 1975. pp. 191. bibliog.

— Foreign relations.

CARR (EDWARD HALLETT) and DAVIES (ROBERT WILLIAM) Foundations of a planned economy, 1926-1929. London, 1969 in progress. (A history of Soviet Russia) vol.1 is the Penguin Books reprint of 1974.

BOBROV (ROMAN L'VOVICH) Shag, produktovannyi istoriei: mezhdunarodno-pravovoe priznanie Sovetskogo gosudarstva. Moskva, 1974. pp. 183.

GRUBER (HELMUT) Soviet Russia masters the Comintern: international communism in the era of Stalin's ascendancy. Garden City, N.Y., 1974. pp. 544. bibliogs. With documents.

JACOBSEN (CARL G.) Soviet strategy - Soviet foreign policy: military considerations affecting Soviet policy-making. 2nd ed. Glasgow, 1974. pp. 269.

LONDON (KURT) ed. The Soviet impact on world politics. New York, [1974]. pp. 312.

SIPOLS (VILNIS IANOVICH) Sovetskii Soiuz v bor'be za mir i bezopasnost', 1933-1939. Moskva, 1974. pp. 428.

BREZHNEV (LEONID IL'ICH) O vneshnei politike KPSS i Sovetskogo gosudarstva: rechi i stat'i. 2nd ed. Moskva, 1975. pp. 879.

EISSENSTAT (BERNARD W.) ed. The Soviet Union: the seventies and beyond. Lexington, Mass., [1975]. pp. 352. Includes papers presented at the twelfth annual meeting of the Central Slavic Conference, Department of History, Oklahoma State University.

GINTHER (KONRAD) Neutralität und Neutralitätspolitik: die österreichische Neutralität zwischen Schweizer Muster und sowjetischer Koexistenzdoktrin. Wien, 1975. pp. 168. bibliog.

INTERNATIONAL SLAVIC CONFERENCE, 1ST, BANFF, ALBERTA, 1974. Soviet economic and political relations with the developing world; edited by Roger E. Kanet [and] Donna Bahry. New York, 1975. pp. 237.

JÖNSSON (CHRISTER) The Soviet Union and the test ban: a study in Soviet negotiating behavior. Lund, 1975. pp. 221. bibliog.

OT Dekreta o mire do Programmy mira, 1917-1975: letopis' sovetskoi vneshnei politiki. Moskva, 1975. pp. 287.

SCALAPINO (ROBERT A.) Asia and the road ahead: issues for the major powers. Berkeley, [1975]. pp. 337. bibliog.

VOSHCHENKOV (KONSTANTIN PAVLOVICH) SSSR v bor'be za mir: mezhdunarodnye konferentsii, 1944-1974 gg.; obshchaia redaktsiia i predislovie...B.G. Trukhanovskogo. Moskva, 1975. pp. 255.

ISTORIIA vneshnei politiki SSSR, 1917-1975; pod redaktsiei A.A. Gromyko, B.N. Ponomareva. 2nd ed. Moskva, 1976. 2 vols. bibliog. 1st ed. had sub-title: 1917-1970.

ULAM (ADAM BRUNO) Ideologies and illusions: revolutionary thought from Herzen to Solzhenitsyn. Cambridge, Mass., 1976. pp. 335.

WOLYNSKI (ALEXANDER) Western economic aid to the USSR. London, 1976. pp. 12. (Institute for the Study of Conflict. Conflict Studies. No. 72)

— — Africa, Subsaharan.

STEVENS (CHRISTOPHER ANTHONY) The Soviet Union and black Africa. London, 1976. pp. 236. bibliog.

— — Austria.

WODAK (WALTER) Diplomatie zwischen Ost und West. Graz, [1976]. pp. 235. (Österreichische Gesellschaft für Aussenpolitik und Internationale Beziehungen. Österreichische Diplomaten) Collection of lectures and essays, in German or English. Includes correspondence with Karl Renner.

— — Austria—Hungary.

SKAZKIN (SERGEI DANILOVICH) Konets avstro-russko-germanskogo soiuza: issledovanie po istorii russko-germanskikh i russko-avstriiskikh otnoshenii v sviazi s vostochnym voprosom v 80-e gody XIX stoletiia. 2nd ed. Moskva, 1974. pp. 272. Reproduces the text of the 1st ed. of 1928 with some omissions.

— — Bulgaria.

BULGARIA. Ministerstvo na Vunshnite Raboti. 1974. Bulgaro-suvetski otnosheniia, 1948-1970: dokumenti i materiali. Sofiia, 1974. pp. 815.

MEL'TSER (DAVID BORISOVICH) Sovetsko-bolgarskie otnosheniia, 1917-1935 gg. Minsk, 1975. pp. 222.

— — Catholic Church.

WINTER (EDUARD J.) Die Sowjetunion und der Vatikan: Teil 3 der Trilogie Russland und das Papsttum. Berlin, 1972. pp. 338. bibliog. (Akademie der Wissenschaften der DDR. Zentralinstitut für Geschichte. Quellen und Studien zur Geschichte Osteuropas. Band 6, Teil 3)

— — Cuba.

DINERSTEIN (HERBERT SAMUEL) The making of a missile crisis: October 1962. Baltimore, [1976]. pp. 302.

— — Czechoslovakia.

RUSSIA (USSR). Ministerstvo Inotrannykh Del. 1975. Sovetsko-chekhoslovatskie otnosheniia, 1961-1971: dokumenty i materialy. Moskva, 1975. pp. 703.

SVEDECTVO dokumentov a faktov. [Bratislava, 1975]. pp. 455.

— — East (Near East).

CARRERE D'ENCAUSSE (HELENE) La politique soviétique au Moyen-Orient, 1955-1975. Paris, [1975]. pp. 328. (Fondation Nationale des Sciences Politiques. Cahiers. 200)

FREEDMAN (ROBERT OWEN) Soviet policy toward the Middle East since 1970. New York, 1975. pp. 198. bibliog.

GEORGIEV (VLADIMIR ANATOL'EVICH) Vneshniaia politika Rossii na Blizhnem Vostoke v kontse 30 - nachale 40-kh godov XIX v. Moskva, 1975. pp. 200. bibliog.

GLASSMAN (JON D.) Arms for the Arabs: the Soviet Union and war in the Middle East. Baltimore, [1975]. pp. 243. bibliog.

— — Europe.

DÉTENTE: (edited versions of interviews originally broadcast, in 1973-75, over Radio Free Europe); edited by G.R. Urban. London, 1976. pp. 368.

PIPES (RICHARD EDGAR) ed. Soviet strategy in Europe. London, 1976. pp. 316.

— — Finland.

KHOLODKOVSKII (VIKTOR MIKHAILOVICH) Finliandiia i Sovetskaia Rossiia, 1918-1920. Moskva, 1975. pp. 266. bibliog.

KIRBY (D.G.) ed. Finland and Russia, 1808-1920: from autonomy to independence: a selection of documents. London, 1975. pp. 265. bibliog. (London. University. School of Slavonic and East European Studies. Studies in Russian and East European History)

POKHLEBKIN (VIL'IAM VASIL'EVICH) SSSR - Finliandiia: 260 let otnoshenii, 1713-1973. Moskva, 1975. pp. 408.

— — France.

MANFRED (AL'BERT ZAKHAROVICH) Obrazovanie russko-frantsuzskogo soiuza. Moskva, 1975. pp. 376. bibliog. With French table of contents.

— — Germany.

AKHTAMZIAN (ABDULKHAN ABDURAKHMANOVICH) Rapall'skaia politika: sovetsko-germanskie diplomaticheskie otnosheniia v 1922-1932 godakh. Moskva, 1974. pp. 303.

ALLARDT (HELMUT) Moskauer Tagebuch: Beobachtungen, Notizen, Erlebnisse. 3rd ed. Düsseldorf, 1974. pp. 424. bibliog.

SKAZKIN (SERGEI DANILOVICH) Konets avstro-russko-germanskogo soiuza: issledovanie po istorii russko-germanskikh i russko-avstriiskikh otnoshenii v sviazi s vostochnym voprosom v 80-e gody XIX stoletiia. 2nd ed. Moskva, 1974. pp. 272. Reproduces the text of the 1st ed. of 1928 with some omissions.

ERICKSON (JOHN) The road to Stalingrad. London, [1975]. pp. 594. bibliog. (Stalin's war with Germany. vol.1)

MEISSNER (BORIS) ed. Moskau, Bonn: die Beziehungen zwischen der Sowjetunion und der Bundesrepublik Deutschland, 1955-1973; Dokumentation. KÖLN [1975]. 2 vols. bibliog.

PETERSON (GORDON LEROY) The rapprochement between the Federal Republic of Germany and the Soviet Union, and the policy of international linkage in east- west relations, 1965-1971; [Ph. D.(London) thesis]. [1975]. fo. 305. bibliog. Typescript: unpublished. This thesis is the property of London University and may not be removed from the Library.

RUSSIA(Cont.)

— — **Holy Roman Empire.**

PAMIATNIKI diplomaticheskikh snoshenii drevnei Rossii s derzhavami inostrannymi. t.7. Pamiatniki diplomaticheskikh snoshenii s Rimskoi imperiei. Sanktpeterburg, 1864. 1514 columns.

— — **India.**

REMNEK (RICHARD B.) Soviet scholars and Soviet foreign policy: a case study in Soviet policy towards India. Durham, N.C., 1975. pp. 343. *bibliog.*

— — **Italy.**

KONFERENTSIIA SOVETSKIKH I ITAL'IANSKIKH ISTORIKOV, 4-aia, RIM, 1969. Rossiia i Italiia: materialy IV Konferentsii sovetskikh i ital'ianskikh istorikov, Rim, 1969; Russkii i ital'ianskii srednevekovyi gorod; Russko-ital'ianskie otnosheniia v 1900- 1914 gg. Moskva, 1972. pp. 477.

SERRA (ENRICO) Nitti e la Russia. Bari, [1975]. pp. 212. *(Milan. Istituto per gli Studi di Politica Internazionale. Saggi di Storia Contemporanea. 2)*

— — **Japan.**

KIM (YOUNG C.) Japanese-Soviet relations: interaction of politics, economics and national security. Beverly Hills, [1974]. pp. 88. *bibliog.* *(Georgetown University. Center for Strategic and International Studies. Washington Papers. vol. 2/21)*

— — **Romania.**

ZALYSHKIN (MIKHAIL MIKHAILOVICH) Vneshniaia politika Rumynii i rumyno-russkie otnosheniia, 1875- 1878. Moskva, 1974. pp. 291. *bibliog.*

— — **Switzerland.**

BRINGOLF (WALTHER) Die Schweiz und die Sowjetunion: zur Krise unserer Aussenpolitik. [Schaffhausen, imprint, 1944]. pp. 23.

— — **United Kingdom.**

PANTEV (ANDREI LAZAROV) Angliia sreshtu Rusiia na Balkanite, 1879-1894. Sofiia, 1972. pp. 307. *bibliog. With Russian and English summaries.*

MAIER (LOTHAR AUGUST) Bündnispolitik und revolutionäre Krise: zu einigen Aspekten der britisch-russischen Beziehungen, 1917. Heidelberg, 1975. pp. 238. *bibliog. Inaugural-Dissertation zur Erlangung der Doktorwürde der Philosophisch-historischen Fakultät der Universität Heidelberg.*

INGLE (HAROLD N.) Nesselrode and the Russian rapprochement with Britain, 1836-1844. Berkeley, [1976]. pp. 196. *bibliog.*

— — **United States.**

WILSON (JOAN HOFF) Ideology and economics: U.S. relations with the Soviet Union, 1918-1933. Columbia, Mo., 1974. pp. 192. *bibliog.*

BOLKHOVITINOV (NIKOLAI NIKOLAEVICH) Russko-amerikanskie otnosheniia, 1815-1832; Russian-American relations. Moskva, 1975. pp. 626. *bibliog. With English table of contents.*

PETROV (VLADIMIR) U.S.-Soviet detente: past and future. Washington, 1975. pp. 60. *(American Enterprise Institute for Public Policy Research. Foreign Affairs Studies. 18)*

DÉTENTE: (edited versions of interviews originally broadcast, in 1973-75, over Radio Free Europe); edited by G.R. Urban. London, 1976. pp. 368.

GRAY (COLIN S.) The Soviet-American arms race. Farnborough, Hants, [1976]. pp. 196.

INTERNATIONAL SLAVIC CONFERENCE, 1ST, BANFF, ALBERTA, 1974. From the cold war to detente; [selected papers from the conference]; edited by Peter J. Potichnyj [and] Jane P. Shapiro. New York, 1976. pp. 223.

— — **Vietnam.**

ISAEV (MIKHAIL PETROVICH) and CHERNYSHEV (AL'BERT SERGEEVICH) Sovetsko-v'etnamskie otnosheniia. Moskva, 1975. pp. 327.

— — **Yugoslavia.**

O neistinitim i nepravednim optužbama protiv naše Partije i naše zemlje. Beograd, 1948. pp. 62. *Articles reprinted from "Borba", Oct. 2, 3 and 4, 1948. In Cyrillic.*

CLISSOLD (STEPHEN) ed. Yugoslavia and the Soviet Union, 1939-1973: a documentary survey. London, 1975. pp. 318.

ŠTRBAC (ČEDOMIR) Jugoslavija i odnosi izmedju socijalističkih zemalja: sukob KPJ i Informbiroa. Beograd, 1975. pp. 231. *bibliog. With English and Russian summaries.*

— **Gentry.**

DVORIANSTVO i krepostnoi stroi Rossii XVI-XVIII vv.: sbornik statei, posviashchennyi pamiati Alekseia Andreevicha Novosel'skogo. Moskva, 1975. pp. 345.

— **Government publications — Bibliography.**

MASHIKHIN (EVGENII ALEKSANDROVICH) and SIMCHERA (VASILII MIKHAILOVICH) compilers. Statisticheskie publikatsii v SSSR: bibliograficheskii ukazatel'. Moskva, 1975. pp. 280.

— — **Historiography.**

ILLERITSKII (VLADIMIR EVGEN'EVICH) Revoliutsionnaia istoricheskaia mysl' v Rossii: domarksistskii period. Moskva, 1974. pp. 350.

BLACK (JOSEPH LAURENCE) Nicholas Karamzin and Russian society in the nineteenth century: a study in Russian political and historical thought. Toronto, [1975]. pp. 264. *bibliog.*

RAZVITIE sovetskoi istoricheskoi nauki, 1970-1974. Moskva, 1975. pp. 479. *With English table of contents.*

— — **Bibliography.**

KOSYKH (G.T.) compiler. Protiv burzhuaznoi fal'sifikatsii istorii KPSS i sovetskogo obshchestva: ukazatel' literatury; pod redaktsiei...V.V. Privalova. Leningrad, 1974. pp. 118.

— **History.**

OBSHCHESTVO i gosudarstvo feodal'noi Rossii: sbornik statei, posviashchennyi 70-letiiu akademika L'va Vladimirovicha Cherepnina. Moskva, 1975. pp. 351.

AUTY (ROBERT) and OBOLENSKY (DIMITRI) Prince, eds. An introduction to Russian history: (Companion to Russian studies, 1). Cambridge, 1976. pp. 403. *bibliog.*

— — **Sources.**

REVOLIUTSIIA 1905-1907 godov: dokumenty i materialy. Moskva, 1975. pp. 406,[17]. *bibliog.*

— — **1606-1607, Bolotnikov Uprising.**

KORETSKII (VADIM IVANOVICH) Formirovanie krepostnogo prava i pervaia krest'ianskaia voina v Rossii. Moskva, 1975. pp. 391.

— — **1667-1671, Rebellion of Stenka Razin.**

MAN'KOV (ARKADII GEORGIEVICH) ed. Inostrannye izvestiia o vosstanii Stepana Razina: materialy i issledovaniia. Leningrad, 1975. pp. 191.

— — **1689-1800.**

RAEFF (MARC) ed. Catherine the Great: a profile. London, 1972. pp. 330. *bibliog.*

— — **1773-1775, Pugachev Uprising.**

FOL'KLOR krest'ianskoi voiny 1773-1775 godov: k 200-letiiu pugachevskogo vosstaniia; sbornik nauchnykh statei. Leningrad, 1973. pp. 104.

— — **1905, Revolution of.**

M. Gor'kii v epokhu revoliutsii 1905-1907 godov: materialy, vospominaniia, issledovaniia. Moskva, 1957. pp. 410.

RADZHABOV (ZARIF SHARIPOVICH) Turkestan na stranitsakh bol'shevistskikh gazet perioda pervoi russkoi revoliutsii, 1905-1907 gg.; otvet. redaktor G.E. Beliakov. Dushanbe, 1970. pp. 225.

BOL'SHEVISTSKAIA partiia v revoliutsii 1905-1907 gg. Moskva, 1975. pp. 142.

PERVAIA russkaia...: sbornik vospominanii aktivnykh uchastnikov revoliutsii, 1905-1907 gg. Moskva, 1975. pp. 304.

PERVAIA russkaia revoliutsiia i ee istoricheskoe znachenie: (sbornik dokumentov i materialov). Moskva, 1975. pp. 519.

PROBLEMY gegemonii proletariata v demokraticheskoi revoliutsii, 1905 - fevral' 1917 gg. Moskva, 1975. pp. 311.

PUSHKAREVA (IRINA MIKHAILOVNA) Zheleznodorozhniki Rossii v burzhuazno-demokraticheskikh revoliutsiiakh. Moskva, 1975. pp. 390.

REVOLIUTSIIA 1905-1907 godov: dokumenty i materialy. Moskva, 1975. pp. 406,[17]. *bibliog.*

REVOLIUTSIIA 1905-1907 godov v Rossii i profsoiuzy: k 70-letiiu pervoi russkoi burzhuazno-demokraticheskoi revoliutsii; sbornik statei. Moskva, 1975. pp. 160. *bibliog.*

SENCHAKOVA (LARISA TIMOFEEVNA) Boevaia rat' revoliutsii: ocherk o boevykh organizatsiiakh RSDRP i rabochikh druzhinakh 1905-1907 gg. Moskva, 1975. pp. 192.

— — **1917— .**

VELIKII Sovetskii narod. Kiev, 1976. pp. 502. *bibliog.*

— — **1917, February Revolution.**

FARFEL' (ARON SAMOILOVICH) Bor'ba narodnykh mass protiv kontrrevoliutsionnoi iustitsii Vremennogo pravitel'stva. Minsk, 1969. pp. 119. *bibliog.*

GILL (GRAEME JOSEPH) The role of the peasants in revolution in European Russia between March and November 1917. 1975. fo. 354. *bibliog. Typescript. Ph. D. (London) thesis: unpublished. This thesis is the property of London University and may not be removed from the Library.*

MAIER (LOTHAR AUGUST) Bündnispolitik und revolutionäre Krise: zu einigen Aspekten der britisch-russischen Beziehungen, 1917. Heidelberg, 1975. pp. 238. *bibliog. Inaugural-Dissertation zur Erlangung der Doktorwürde der Philosophisch-historischen Fakultät der Universität Heidelberg.*

PROBLEMY gegemonii proletariata v demokraticheskoi revoliutsii, 1905 - fevral' 1917 gg. Moskva, 1975. pp. 311.

PUSHKAREVA (IRINA MIKHAILOVNA) Zheleznodorozhniki Rossii v burzhuazno-demokraticheskikh revoliutsiiakh. Moskva, 1975. pp. 390.

— — **Bibliography.**

RUTMAN (AISA EFIMOVNA) compiler. Rossiia period pervoi mirovoi voiny i fevral'skoi burzhuano-demokraticheskoi revoliutsii, iiul' 1914 - fevral' 1917 g.: bibliograficheskii ukazatel' sovetskoi literatury, izdannoi v 1953- 1968 gg.; pod redaktsiei...Iu.I. Kir'ianova. Leningrad, 1975. pp. 614.

— — **1917-1921, Revolution.**

NAUMOV (I.K.) Les journées d'Octobre. Paris, [1924?]. pp. 111.

LUXEMBURG (ROSA) Die russische Revolution; eingeleitet und herausgegeben von Ossip K. Flechtheim. Frankfurt am Main, [1963]. pp. 88.

METEL'KOV (PETR FEDOROVICH) Zheleznodorozhniki v revoliutsii, fevral' 1917 - iiun' 1918. Leningrad, 1970. pp. 359.

RUSSIA(Cont.)

LEHNING (ARTHUR) Marxismus und Anarchismus in der russischen Revolution; [and] Revolutionär-syndikalistische Bewegung in Russland: [by G.P.] Maximoff. 2nd ed. Berlin, 1971. pp. 146.

BAEVSKII (DAVID ANATOL'EVICH) Rabochii klass v pervye gody Sovetskoi vlasti, 1917-1921 gg. Moskva, 1974. pp. 336.

KOSICHEV (ANATOLII DANILOVICH) Teoreticheskoe obobshchenie V.I. Leninym opyta Oktiabr'skoi revoliutsii i stroitel'stva sotsializma v SSSR. Moskva, 1974. pp. 314.

BRADLEY (JOHN F.N.) Civil war in Russia, 1917-1920. London, 1975. pp. 197. *bibliog.*

ISTORICHESKII opyt Velikogo Oktiabria: k 80-letiiu laureata Leninskoi premii akademika I.I. Mintsa. Moskva, 1975. pp. 423.

KHESIN (SAMUIL SEMENOVICH) Stanovlenie proletarskoi diktatury v Rossii: voprosy ustanovleniia Sovetskoi vlasti i skladyvaniia proletarskoi gosudarstvennoi sistemy, noiabr' 1917 - mart 1918 g. Moskva, 1975. pp. 471.

KITAEV (MIKHAIL ALEKSEEVICH) Partiinoe stroitel'stvo v gody grazhdanskoi voiny. Moskva, 1975. pp. 256.

MALET (MICHAEL IAN GRENVILLE) Nestor Makchno [sic] in the Russian civil war 1917-21. 1975. fo. 326. *bibliog.* Typescript. *Ph.D.(London) thesis: unpublished. This thesis is the property of London University and may not be removed from the library.*

MUKHINA (GALINA ZOTIKOVNA) Sotsialisticheskaia revoliutsiia i gosudarstvo: razrabotka V.I. Leninym voprosa o gosudarstve diktatury proletariata v period bor'by za Oktiabr' i uprochenie ego zavoevanii, mart 1917 - mart 1918. Moskva, 1975. pp. 277.

PROBLEMY istorii Oktiabr'skoi revoliutsii i grazhdanskoi voiny v SSSR; (sbornik, posviashchennyi 70-letiiu professora I.M. Razgona). Tomsk, 1975. pp. 401.

TRUKAN (GERMAN ANTONOVICH) Rabochii klass v bor'be za pobedu i uprochenie Sovetskoi vlasti. Moskva, 1975. pp. 303.

FUNKEN (KLAUS) Die ökonomischen Voraussetzungen der Oktoberrevolution: zur Entwicklung des Kapitalismus in Russland. Zürich, 1976. pp. 372. *bibliog.*

NABOKOV (VLADIMIR DMITRIEVICH) V.D. Nabokov and the Russian provisional government, 1917; edited by Virgil D. Medlin and Steven L. Parsons. New Haven, 1976. pp. 188.

SMIRNOV (ALEKSANDR SERGEEVICH) Bol'sheviki i krest'ianstvo v Oktiabr'skoi revoliutsii. Moskva, 1976. pp. 232.

— — — Campaigns.

VOENNYE organizatsii rossiiskogo proletariata i opyt ego vooruzhennoi bor'by, 1903-1917. Moskva, 1974. pp. 418. *bibliog.*

GEROICHESKOE podpol'e v tylu denikinskoi armii: vospominaniia. Moskva, 1975. pp. 416.

— — — Foreign participation, Czechoslovak.

SAJDL (JOSEF) Českoslovenští železničáři v sibiřské anabasi. [Praha], 1924. pp. 108,[x].

— — — Personal narratives.

GEROICHESKOE podpol'e v tylu denikinskoi armii: vospominaniia. Moskva, 1975. pp. 416.

— — — Sources.

BUCHANAN (MERIEL) The dissolution of an empire. London, 1932. pp. 312.

— — 1918-1920, Allied intervention.

MUKHACHEV (BORIS IVANOVICH) Stanovlenie Sovetskoi vlasti i bor'ba s inostrannoi ekspansiei na Severo-Vostoke SSSR, 1917-1920 gg.; otvetstvennyi redaktor. ..I.M. Razgon. Novosibirsk, 1975. pp. 201.

MACLAREN (ROY) Canadians in Russia, 1918-1919. Toronto, [1976]. pp. 301. *bibliog.*

— — 1953— .

EISSENSTAT (BERNARD W.) ed. The Soviet Union: the seventies and beyond. Lexington, Mass., [1975]. pp. 352. *Includes papers presented at the twelfth annual meeting of the Central Slavic Conference, Department of History, Oklahoma State University.*

— Industries.

ISTORIIA industrializatsii Zapadnogo raiona, 1926-1937 gg., etc. Briansk, 1972. pp. 615.

KAMENITSER (SOLOMON EFREMOVICH) ed. Spravochnik ekonomista promyshlennogo predpriiatiia. Moskva, 1974. pp. 663. *bibliog.*

PAVLOV (VALENTIN SERGEEVICH) Oborotnye sredstva promyshlennosti: formirovanie i ispol'zovanie. Moskva, 1974. pp. 142.

KORNEEVA (RAISA VASIL'EVNA) Kreditnye vzaimootnosheniia promyshlennosti s Gosbankom. Moskva, 1975. pp. 223.

LEL'CHUK (VITALII SEMENOVICH) Sotsialisticheskaia industrializatsiia SSSR i ee osveshchenie v sovetskoi istoriografii. Moskva, 1975. pp. 312.

OSAD'KO (MIKHAIL PETROVICH) Teoreticheskie osnovy raspredeleniia chistogo produkta sotsialisticheskogo predpriiatiia. Moskva, 1975. pp. 311.

RABOCHII klass i industrial'noe razvitie SSSR. Moskva, 1975. pp. 486.

STOWELL (CHRISTOPHER E.) Soviet industrial import priorities, with marketing considerations for exporting to the USSR. New York, 1975. pp. 505. *bibliog.*

DEWDNEY (JOHN CHRISTOPHER) The USSR. Folkestone, 1976. pp. 262. *bibliog.*

— — Mathematical models.

SMIRNITSKII (EVGENII KONSTANTINOVICH) Ekonomicheskie pokazateli promyshlennosti: spravochnik. Moskva, 1974. pp. 381. *bibliog.*

— Intellectual life.

GORBUNOV (VLADIMIR VLADIMIROVICH) V.I. Lenin i Proletkul't. Moskva, 1974. pp. 239.

KUL'TURNAIA zhizn' v SSSR: khronika. Moskva, 1975 in progress.

READ (CHRISTOPHER JOHN) Religion and revolution in the thought of the Russian intelligentsia from 1900 to 1912: the Vekhi debate and its intellectual background. [1975]. fo. 353. *bibliog.* Typescript. *Ph.D.(London) thesis: unpublished. This thesis is the property of London University and may not be removed from the Library.*

KEMP-WELCH (ANTHONY) The origins and formative years of the Writers' Union of the U.S.S.R., 1932-1936. 1975 [or rather 1976]. fo. 167. *bibliog.* Typescript. *Ph.D. (London) thesis: unpublished. This thesis is the property of London University and may not be removed from the Library.*

ULAM (ADAM BRUNO) Ideologies and illusions: revolutionary thought from Herzen to Solzhenitsyn. Cambridge, Mass., 1976. pp. 335.

— Kings and rulers.

DAVIDOVICH (ALEKSANDR MIKHAILOVICH) Samoderzhavie v epokhu imperializma: klassovaia sushchnost' i evoliutsiia absoliutizma v Rossii. Moskva, 1975. pp. 351.

— Learned institutions and societies.

BAZIIANTS (ASHOT PATVAKANOVICH) Lazarevskii institut v istorii otechestvennogo vostokovedeniia. Moskva, 1973. pp. 224. *bibliog.*

KOMKOV (GENNADII DANILOVICH) and others. Akademiia nauk SSSR: kratkii istoricheskii ocherk. Moskva, 1974. pp. 522.

— Military policy.

JACOBSEN (CARL G.) Soviet strategy - Soviet foreign policy: military considerations affecting Soviet policy-making. 2nd ed. Glasgow, 1974. pp. 269.

SOKOLOVSKII (VASILII DANILOVICH) Soviet military strategy (third edition); ...edited, with an analysis and commentary, by Harriet Fast Scott. London, [1975]. pp. 494. *bibliog.*

SOVIET naval policy: objectives and constraints; [deriving from a seminar held at Dalhousie University, Halifax, Nova Scotia in 1973]; edited by Michael MccGwire [and others]. New York, 1975. pp. 660.

SOLZHENITSYN (ALEKSANDR ISAEVICH) Warning to the Western world. London, 1976. pp. 45. *Consists of text of interview with Michael Charlton on BBC television's Panorama, 1 March 1976, and of a BBC radio broadcast, 24 March, 1976.*

WOLYNSKI (ALEXANDER) Western economic aid to the USSR. London, 1976. pp. 12. (Institute for the Study of Conflict. Conflict Studies. No. 72)

— Nationalism.

RADZHABOV (SOLEKH ASHUROVICH) V.I. Lenin i sovetskaia natsional'naia gosudarstvennost'. Dushanbe, 1970. pp. 687.

AKTUAL'NYE problemy razvitiia natsional'nykh otnoshenii v SSSR. Makhachkala, 1973. pp. 266. *With English and German tables of contents.*

SUZHIKOV (MARAT MUKHAMBETKALIEVICH) and DEMAKOV (GEORGII ALEKSEEVICH) Vliianie podvizhnosti naseleniia na sblizhenie natsii. Alma-Ata, 1974. pp. 200.

KATZ (ZEV) and others, eds. Handbook of major Soviet nationalities. New York, [1975]. pp. 481. *bibliogs.*

KOZLOV (VIKTOR IVANOVICH) Natsional'nosti SSSR: etnodemograficheskii obzor. Moskva, 1975. pp. 263. *With English table of contents.*

MATIUSHKIN (NIKOLAI IVANOVICH) Patriotizm i internatsionalizm sovetskogo naroda: istoricheskii opyt i sovremennaia deiatel'nost' KPSS. Moskva, 1975. pp. 416.

SHPILIUK (VLADIMIR ARONOVICH) Mezhrespublikanskaia migratsiia i sblizhenie natsii v SSSR. L'vov, 1975. pp. 167.

VELIKII Sovetskii narod. Kiev, 1976. pp. 502. *bibliog.*

— Native races.

RABOCHII klass i krest'ianstvo natsional'nykh raionov Sibiri. Novosibirsk, 1974. pp. 174.

KOZLOV (VIKTOR IVANOVICH) Natsional'nosti SSSR: etnodemograficheskii obzor. Moskva, 1975. pp. 263. *With English table of contents.*

— Navy.

SOVIET naval policy: objectives and constraints; [deriving from a seminar held at Dalhousie University, Halifax, Nova Scotia in 1973]; edited by Michael MccGwire [and others]. New York, 1975. pp. 660.

— Non-Russian territories — Bibliography.

ALLWORTH (EDWARD) compiler. Soviet Asia, bibliographies: a compilation of social science and humanities sources on the Iranian, Mongolian, and Turkic nationalities, with an essay on the Soviet-Asian controversy. New York, 1975. pp. 686.

— Politics and government.

GLAZOV (IURII) Tesnye vrata: vozrozhdenie russkoi intelligentsii; Narrow gates: revival of the Russian intelligentsia. London, 1973. pp. 263.

RUSSIA (Cont.)

BRATSTVO narodov i internatsional'noe vospitanie: [materialy respublikanskoi nauchno-teoreticheskoi konferentsii "Torzhestvo leninskikh idei bratstva narodov i internatsional'noe vospitanie trudiashchikhsia"]. Tashkent, 1974. pp. 266.

GANIN (NIKOLAI IVANOVICH) Zakonomernosti sotsialisticheskoi revoliutsii i istoricheskii opyt KPSS. Moskva, 1974. pp. 255.

IZ-POD glyb: sbornik statei...Moskva, 1974. Paris, [1974]. pp. 281.

NOSKOV (ALEKSANDR PETROVICH) and IANOVSKII (RUDOL'F GRIGOR'EVICH) Dva urovnia soznaniia i politicheskie ubezhdeniia; otvetstvennyi redaktor...V.A. Rebrin. Novosibirsk, 1974. pp. 94.

The MODERNIZATION of Japan and Russia: a comparative study; [by] Cyril E. Black [and others]. New York, [1975]. pp. 386. *bibliog.*

POLITIKA i obshchestvo: sotsial'no-politicheskie problemy razvitogo sotsializma. Leningrad, 1975. pp. 191.

SOVETSKII narod - novaia istoricheskaia obshchnost' liudei: stanovlenie i razvitie. Moskva, 1975. pp. 520. *bibliog.*

ULAM (ADAM BRUNO) Ideologies and illusions: revolutionary thought from Herzen to Solzhenitsyn. Cambridge, Mass., 1976. pp. 335.

— — Bibliography.

IVANOV (V.K.) ed. Sotsial'no-politicheskoe razvitie sovetskogo obshchestva na sovremennom etape: rekomendatel'nyi ukazatel' literatury, etc. Moskva, 1974. pp. 80. *bibliog.*

— — 1689-1800.

RANSEL (DAVID L.) The politics of Catherinian Russia: the Panin party. New Haven, 1975. pp. 327. *bibliog.*

— — 1800-1899.

SHIROKOVA (VARVARA VASIL'EVNA) Partiia "Narodnogo prava": iz istorii osvoboditel'nogo dvizheniia 90-kh godov XIX veka. Saratov, 1972. pp. 206.

— — 1894-1917.

BUCHANAN (MERIEL) The dissolution of an empire. London, 1932. pp. 312.

TEREKHOV (IVAN SEMENOVICH) V.I. Lenin i stroitel'stvo partii v period ot Fevralia k Oktiabriu, 1917 g. Saratov, 1969. pp. 259.

LISETSKII (ANATOLII MIKHAILOVICH) Bol'sheviki vo glave massovykh stachek, mart - oktiabr' 1917 g. Kishinev, 1974. pp. 423. *bibliog.*

USHAKOV (ANATOLII VASIL'EVICH) Bor'ba partii za gegemoniiu proletariata v revoliutsionno-demokraticheskom dvizhenii Rossii, 1895-1904. Moskva, 1974. pp. 224.

VOENNYE organizatsii rossiiskogo proletariata i opyt ego vooruzhennoi bor'by, 1903-1917. Moskva, 1974. pp. 418. *bibliog.*

DAVIDOVICH (ALEKSANDR MIKHAILOVICH) Samoderzhavie v epokhu imperializma: klassovaia sushchnost' i evoliutsiia absoliutizma v Rossii. Moskva, 1975. pp. 351.

FAL'KOVICH (SVETLANA MIKHAILOVNA) Proletariat Rossii i Pol'shi v sovmestnoi revoliutsionnoi bor'be, 1907-1912. Moskva, 1975. pp. 379.

NABOKOV (VLADIMIR DMITRIEVICH) V.D. Nabokov and the Russian provisional government, 1917; edited by Virgil D. Medlin and Steven L. Parsons. New Haven, 1976. pp. 188.

— — 1917— .

BERTSCH (GARY K.) Value change and political community: the multinational Czechoslovak, Soviet, and Yugoslav cases. Beverly Hills, [1974]. pp. 60. *bibliog.*

— — 1917-1953.

KALININ (MIKHAIL IVANOVICH) Izbrannye proizvedeniia; (sostaviteli F.G. Vashchenko [and others]). Moskva, 1975. pp. 448.

— — 1917-1936.

VALENTINOV (NIKOLAI VLADISLAVOVICH) pseud. [i.e. Nikolai Vladislavovich VOL'SKII] Novaia ekonomicheskaia politika i krizis partii posle smerti Lenina: gody raboty v VSNKh vo vremia NEP; vospominaniia....; The new economic policy and the Party crisis after the death of Lenin: reminiscences of my work at the VSNKh during the NEP; edited by J. Bunyan and V. Butenko, etc. Stanford, 1971. pp. 256.

KRASNOV (ALEKSANDR VASIL'EVICH) TsKK-RKI v bor'be za sotsializm: rol' TsKK-RKI v osushchestvlenii leninskogo plana postroeniia sotsializma v SSSR, 1923-1934 gg. Irkutsk, 1973. pp. 560. *bibliog.*

The PLATFORM of the joint opposition, 1927. London, 1973. pp. 117.

TITOV (ALEKSANDR GRIGOR'EVICH) and others. Bor'ba Kommunisticheskoi partii s antileninskimi gruppami i techeniiami v posleoktiabr'skii period, 1917-1934 gg. Moskva, 1974. pp. 359.

LENIN (VLADIMIR IL'ICH) On the Soviet state apparatus: articles and speeches. rev. ed. Moscow, 1975. pp. 445.

TRIFONOV (IVAN IAKOVLEVICH) Likvidatsiia ekspluatatorskikh klassov v SSSR. Moskva, 1975. pp. 406.

TRUKAN (GERMAN ANTONOVICH) Rabochii klass v bor'be za pobedu i uprochenie Sovetskoi vlasti. Moskva, 1975. pp. 303.

— — 1936-1953.

MEDVEDEV (ROI ALEKSANDROVICH) K sudu istorii: genezis i posledstviia stalinizma; Let history judge: the origins and consequences of Stalinism. 2nd ed. New York, 1974. pp. 1136.

— — 1953— .

KIRK (IRINA) Profiles in Russian resistance. New York, [1975]. pp. 299.

— — 1964— .

BREZHNEV (LEONID IL'ICH) O kommunisticheskom vospitanii trudiashchikhsia: rechi i stat'i. 2nd ed. Moskva, 1975. pp. 639.

— Population.

NASELENIE SSSR: chislennost', sostav i dvizhenie naseleniia...; statisticheskii sbornik; [pd. by] Tsentral'noe Statisticheskoe Upravlenie. a., 1973 (1st)- Moscow.

RUSSIA (USSR). Ministerstvo Vysshego i Srednego Spetsial'nogo Obrazovaniia. Nauchno-Tekhnicheskii Sovet. Sektsiia Narodonaseleniia. Narodonaselenie. 1. [Sbornik statei]. Moskva, 1973. pp. 79. *With English table of contents.*

RUSSIA (USSR). Ministerstvo Vysshego i Srednego Spetsial'nogo Obrazovaniia. Nauchno-Tekhnicheskii Sovet. Sektsiia Narodonaseleniia. Narodonaselenie. 2. Naselenie i ekonomika. Moskva, 1973. pp. 112. *With English table of contents.*

RUSSIA (USSR). Ministerstvo Vysshego i Srednego Spetsial'nogo Obrazovaniia. Nauchno-Tekhnicheskii Sovet. Sektsiia Narodonaseleniia. Narodonaselenie. 3. Naselenie i trudovye resursy. Moskva, 1973. pp. 79. *With English table of contents.*

RUSSIA (USSR). Ministerstvo Vysshego i Srednego Spetsial'nogo Obrazovaniia. Nauchno-Tekhnicheskii Sovet. Sektsiia Narodonaseleniia. Narodonaselenie. 4. Prikladnaia demografiia. Moskva, 1973. pp. 136. *With English table of contents.*

VODARSKII (IAROSLAV EVGEN'EVICH) Naselenie Rossii za 400 let, XVI - nachalo XX vv. Moskva, 1973. pp. 159. *bibliog.*

BREEV (BORIS DMITRIEVICH) and KRIUKOV (V.P.) Mezhotraslevoi balans dvizheniia naseleniia i trudovykh resursov: metodologicheskie voprosy. Moskva, 1974. pp. 183. *bibliog.*

RUSSIA (USSR). Ministerstvo Vysshego i Srednego Spetsial'nogo Obrazovaniia. Nauchno-Tekhnicheskii Sovet. Sektsiia Narodonaseleniia. Narodonaselenie. 5. Demograficheskii analiz rozhdaemosti. Moskva, 1974. pp. 112. *With English table of contents.*

RUSSIA (USSR). Ministerstvo Vysshego i Srednego Spetsial'nogo Obrazovaniia. Nauchno-Tekhnicheskii Sovet. Sektsiia Narodonaseleniia. Narodonaselenie. 7. Razvitie naseleniia. Moskva, 1974. pp. 94. *With English table of contents.*

RUSSIA (USSR). Ministerstvo Vysshego i Srednego Spetsial'nogo Obrazovaniia. Nauchno-Tekhnicheskii Sovet. Sektsiia Narodonaseleniia. Narodonaselenie. 8. Prodolzhitel'nost' zhizni. Moskva, 1974. pp. 120. *With English table of contents.*

SUZHIKOV (MARAT MUKHAMBETKALIEVICH) and DEMAKOV (GEORGII ALEKSEEVICH) Vliianie podvizhnosti naseleniia na sblizhenie natsii. Alma-Ata, 1974. pp. 200.

FEDOR (THOMAS STANLEY) Patterns of urban growth in the Russian Empire during the nineteenth century. Chicago, 1975. pp. 245. *bibliog.* (Chicago. University. Department of Geography. Research Papers. No. 163) *With Russian summary.*

KALINIUK (IRAIDA VLADIMIROVNA) Vozrastnaia struktura naseleniia SSSR; nauchnyi redaktor A.Ia. Kvasha. Moskva, 1975. pp. 112.

PEREVEDENTSEV (VIKTOR IVANOVICH) Metody izucheniia migratsii naseleniia. Moskva, 1975. pp. 231. *bibliog.*

SHPILIUK (VLADIMIR ARONOVICH) Mezhrespublikanskaia migratsiia i sblizhenie natsii v SSSR. L'vov, 1975. pp. 167.

— Population policy.

ARUTIUNIAN (LIUDMILA AKOPOVNA) Sotsialisticheskii zakon narodonaseleniia. Moskva, 1975. pp. 95.

— — Mathematical models.

MATLIN (IL'IA SEMENOVICH) Modelirovanie razmeshcheniia naseleniia. Moskva, 1975. pp. 167. *bibliog.* (Akademiia Nauk SSSR. Tsentral'nyi Ekonomiko-Matematicheskii Institut. Problemy Sovetskoi Ekonomiki)

— Relations (general) with Bulgaria.

SOTSIALISTICHESKII internatsionalizm v deistvii. Moskva, 1974. pp. 254.

— Relations (general) with Czechoslovakia.

TSELISHCHEV (NIKOLAI NIKOLAEVICH) and BRODSKII (IGOR' STEPANOVICH) Marshrutami druzhby. Sverdlovsk, 1969. pp. 115.

— Relations (general) with Germany.

FUHRMANN (RAINER) Die Orientalische Frage, das "panslawistisch-chauvinistische Lager" und das Zuwarten auf Krieg und Revolution: die Osteuropaberichterstattung und -vorstellungen der "Deutschen Rundschau", 1874-1918. Bern, 1975. pp. 200. *bibliog. With English summary.*

— Relations (general) with other countries.

OPYT sotsialisticheskikh preobrazovanii v SSSR i ego mezhdunarodnoe znachenie: Mezhdunarodnaia nauchnaia konferentsiia v Tashkente, 16-19 oktiabria 1972 g. Moskva, 1974. pp. 336.

IOFFE (ALEKSANDR EVSEEVICH) Mezhdunarodnye sviazi sovetskoi nauki, tekhniki i kul'tury, 1917- 1932. Moskva, 1975. pp. 429. *bibliog.*

L'VUNIN (IURII ALEKSANDROVICH) Bor'ba Kommunisticheskoi partii za ukreplenie internatsional'nykh sviazei rabochego klassa SSSR, 1924-1928 gg. Moskva, 1975. pp. 304.

MEDVEDEV (ZHORES ALEKSANDROVICH) National frontiers and international scientific co-operation. Nottingham, 1975. pp. 296. *(Medvedev Papers. vol. 1)*

— **Relations (general) with Poland.**

ŚLIWOWSKA (WIKTORIA) Związki rewolucjonistów polskich i rosyjskich w XIX wieku, materiały sesji naukowej Poznań, 12-14 listopada 1970. Wrocław, 1972. pp. 268. *Some articles in Russian.*

— **Relations (general) with the United Kingdom.**

NATIONAL CONGRESS OF PEACE AND FRIENDSHIP WITH THE U.S.S.R. 1st Congress, 1935. Britain and the Soviets: the Congress of Peace and Friendship with the U.S.S.R.; (verbatim report). London, 1936. pp. 197.

CALHOUN (DANIEL FAIRCHILD) The united front: the TUC and the Russians, 1923-1928. Cambridge, 1976. pp. 450. *bibliog.*

— **Religion.**

NOSOVA (GALINA ALEKSEEVNA) Iazychestvo v pravoslavii. Moskva, 1975. pp. 152. *bibliog.*

POWELL (DAVID E.) Antireligious propaganda in the Soviet Union: a study of mass persuasion. Cambridge, [1975]. pp. 206. *bibliog.*

RELIGIIA i tserkov' v istorii Rossii: sovetskie istoriki o pravoslavnoi tserkvi v Rossii. Moskva, 1975. pp. 255.

INTERNATIONAL SLAVIC CONFERENCE, 1ST, BANFF, ALBERTA, 1974. Marxism and religion in Eastern Europe; papers presented at the...conference...; edited by Richard T. De George and James P. Scanlan. Dordrecht, [1976]. pp. 181. *(Freiburg (Switzerland). Universität. Ost-Europa Institut. Sovietica. vol. 36)*

LANE (CHRISTEL OLGA) The impact of communist ideology and the Soviet order on Christian religion in the contemporary U.S.S.R., 1959-1974. 1976. fo. 489. *bibliog. Typescript. Ph.D. (London) thesis: unpublished. This thesis is the property of London University and may not be removed from the Library.*

— **Rural conditions.**

BUXTON (CHARLES RODEN) In a Russian village. London, 1922. pp. 96.

BODIUL (IVAN IVANOVICH) Sotsial'no-ekonomicheskie otnosheniia v derevne na stadii razvitogo sotsializma. Moskva, 1974. pp. 384.

NESTERENKO (ALEKSEI ALEKSEEVICH) Zakonomernosti sotsial'no-ekonomicheskogo razvitiia goroda i derevni. Kiev, 1975. pp. 311.

PROBLEMY istorii sovremennoi sovetskoi derevni, 1946-1973 gg. Moskva, 1975. pp. 508.

KRUT'KO (NIKOLAI GRIGOR'EVICH) and KVOCHKIN (M.P.) eds. Sblizhenie goroda i derevni v protsesse stroitel'stva sotsializma i kommunizma: tematicheskii sbornik. Minsk, 1976. pp. 176.

— — **Bibliography.**

STOL'NIKOVA (R.G.) and others, compilers. Istoriia sovetskoi derevni, 1917-1967: ukazatel' literatury, 1945-1967 gg. Moskva, 1975. 4 vols.(in 1).

— **Social conditions.**

GALIN (LEO) Sowjet-Russland in der Wirklichkeit. Stuttgart, 1920. pp. 72.

OKTIABR'SKAIA revoliutsiia i formirovanie novykh obshchestvennykh otnoshenii: k 50-letiiu Velikoi Oktiabr'skoi sotsialisticheskoi revoliutsii. Orel, 1967. pp. 221. *(Orlovskii Gosudarstvennyi Pedagogicheskii Institut. Uchenye Zapiski. t.37)*

AUSTIN (MICHAEL) 1941- . The great experiment: a study of Soviet society. London, 1975. pp. 218.

ECONOMIC aspects of life in the USSR: main findings of colloquium held 29th-31st January, 1975, in Brussels. Brussels, North Atlantic Treaty Organization, [1975]. pp. 284. *bibliogs. In English and French.*

DAVIDOW (MIKE) Cities without crisis. New York, [1976]. pp. 240.

— — **Bibliography.**

IVANOV (V.K.) ed. Sotsial'no-politicheskoe razvitie sovetskogo obshchestva na sovremennom etape: rekomendatel'nyi ukazatel' literatury, etc. Moskva, 1974. pp. 80. *bibliog.*

— **Social history.**

AUSTIN (MICHAEL) 1941- . The great experiment: a study of Soviet society. London, 1975. pp. 218.

BONGIOVANNI (BRUNO) ed. L'antistalinismo di sinistra e la natura sociale dell'URSS: [an anthology]. Milano, 1975. pp. 391. *bibliog.*

IZ istorii ekonomicheskoi i obshchestvennoi zhizni Rossii: sbornik statei k 90-letiiu akademika Nikolaia Mikhailovicha Druzhinina. Moskva, 1976. pp. 288.

— **Social life and customs.**

KHODAKOV (MIKHAIL SERGEEVICH) Kak ne nado sebia vesti. 2nd ed. Moskva, 1975. pp. 143.

— **Social policy.**

FORMIROVANIE novogo cheloveka - stroitelia kommunizma. Kishinev, 1973. pp. 127.

EL'MEEV (VASILII IAKOVLEVICH) Metodologicheskie osnovy planirovaniia sotsial'nogo razvitiia. Moskva, 1974. pp. 167.

ZABOTA partii i pravitel'stva o blage naroda: sbornik dokumentov, oktiabr' 1964-1973. Moskva, 1974. pp. 847.

— **Statistics.**

RUSSIA (U.S.S.R.) Tsentral'noe Statisticheskoe Upravlenie. U.S.S.R. in figures: statistical handbook. a., 1974- Moscow.

STATISTICHESKIE modeli v optimal'nom otraslevom planirovanii. Moskva, 1975. pp. 191. *bibliog.*

— — **Bibliography.**

MASHIKHIN (EVGENII ALEKSANDROVICH) and SIMCHERA (VASILII MIKHAILOVICH) compilers. Statisticheskie publikatsii v SSSR: bibliograficheskii ukazatel'. Moskva, 1975. pp. 280.

RUSSIA (RSFSR)

— **Constitution.**

ZHELEZNOV (BORIS LEONIDOVICH) Kompetentsiia RSFSR i ee sub"ektov. Kazan', 1974. pp. 128.

— **Economic conditions.**

ADAMESKU (ALEKO ALEKSANDROVICH) and AKIN'SHIN (NIKOLAI NIKIFOROVICH) Problemy razvitiia i razmeshcheniia proizvoditel'nykh sil Volgo-Viatskogo raiona. Moskva, 1974. pp. 264. *bibliog.*

— **Executive departments.**

ZIMANOV (SALYK ZIMANOVICH) and others. Kazakhskii otdel Narodnogo komissariata po delam natsional'nostei RSFSR. Alma-Ata, 1975. pp. 222,(xviii).

RUSSIAN FICTION

— **History and criticism.**

DUNHAM (VERA SANDOMIRSKY) In Stalin's time: middleclass values in Soviet fiction. Cambridge, 1976. pp. 283. *bibliog.*

RUSSIAN LITERATURE

— **History and criticism.**

ASADULLAEV (SEIFULLA) Stanovlenie sotsialisticheskogo realizma v rannei sovetskoi literature. Baku, 1974. pp. 295.

BAZANOV (VASILII GRIGOR'EVICH) and VATSURO (V.E.) eds. Literaturnoe nasledie dekabristov. Leningrad, 1975. pp. 400.

MATHEWSON (RUFUS WELLINGTON) The positive hero in Russian literature. 2nd ed. Stanford, 1975. pp. 369.

RUSSIAN NEWSPAPERS.

OL'KHOVSKII (EVGENII ROMANOVICH) Leninskaia "Iskra" v Peterburge. Leningrad, 1975. pp. 359.

RUSSIANS IN CHINA.

NA kitaiskoi zemle: vospominaniia sovetskikh dobrovol'tsev, 1925-1945. Moskva, 1974. pp. 372.

RUSSIANS IN NORTH AMERICA.

GIBSON (JAMES R.) Imperial Russia in frontier America: the changing geography of supply of Russian America, 1784-1867. New York, 1976. pp. 257. *bibliogs.*

RUSSIANS IN THE NEAR EAST.

ARENDARENKO (GEORGII ALEKSEEVICH) Bukhara i Afganistan v nachale 80-kh godov XIX veka: zhurnaly komandirovok G.A. Arendarenko; [redaktsionnaia kollegiia B.G. Gafurov (and others)]. Moskva, 1974. pp. 142.

RUSSIANS IN THE UKRAINE.

NAULKO (VSEVOLOD IVANOVICH) Razvitie mezhetnicheskikh sviazei na Ukraine: istoriko-etnograficheskii ocherk. Kiev, 1975. pp. 276.

RUSSO-FINNISH WAR, 1939-1940.

CARLQUIST (ERIK) Solidaritet på prov: Finlandshjälp under vinterkriget. Stockholm, 1971. pp. 343. *bibliog. With English summary.*

JOHANSSON (ALF) Finlands sak: svensk politik och opinion under vinterkriget, 1939- 1940. Stockholm, 1973. pp. 402. *bibliog. With English summary.*

RUSSO-TURKISH WAR, 1877-1878.

MEGRELIDZE (SHAMSHE VARFALOMEEVICH) Zakavkaz'e v russko-turetskoi voine, 1877-1878 gg. Tbilisi, 1972. pp. 303.

ZALYSHKIN (MIKHAIL MIKHAILOVICH) Vneshniaia politika Rumynii i rumyno-russkie otnosheniia, 1875- 1878. Moskva, 1974. pp. 291. *bibliog.*

RUTHENIA

— **Politics and government.**

VELYKYI Zhovten' i rozkvit vozz"iednanoho Zakarpattia: materialy naukovoï sesiï, prysviachenoï 50-richchiu Velykoï Zhovtnevoï sotsialistychnoï revoliutsiï, 29 chervnia - 2 lypnia 1967 r. Uzhhorod, 1970. pp. 605.

RWANDA

— **Biography.**

CODERE (HELEN) The biography of an African society: Rwanda, 1900-1960; based on forty-eight Rwandan autobiographies. Tervuren, 1973. pp. 399. *bibliog. (Tervueren. Musée Royal de l'Afrique Centrale. Annales. Série in -8. Sciences Humaines. No. 79)*

— **Social conditions.**

CODERE (HELEN) The biography of an African society: Rwanda, 1900-1960; based on forty-eight Rwandan autobiographies. Tervuren, 1973. pp. 399. *bibliog. (Tervueren. Musée Royal de l'Afrique Centrale. Annales. Série in -8. Sciences Humaines. No. 79)*

SAARLAND

SAARLAND

— Census.

SAARGEBIET. Census, 1970. Volks- und Berufszählung 1970. Saarbrücken, 1973-74. 3 vols. (in 2). *(Saargebiet. Statistisches Amt. Einzelschriften zur Statistik des Saarlandes. Nr. 40, 44, 45)*

— Emigration and immigration.

MERGEN (JOSEF) Die Auswanderungen aus den ehemals preussischen Teilen des Saarlandes im 19. Jahrhundert. Saarbrücken, 1973 in progress. *bibliog. (Institut für Landeskunde des Saarlandes. Veröffentlichungen. 20, etc.)*

— Occupations.

SAARGEBIET. Statistisches Amt. Einzelschriften zur Statistik des Saarlandes. Nr. 43. Nichtlandwirtschaftliche Arbeitsstätten im Saarland am 27. Mai 1970. Saarbrücken, 1973. pp. 276.

— Population.

SAARGEBIET. Statistisches Amt. Einzelschriften zur Statistik des Saarlandes. Nr. 50. Amtliches Gemeindeverzeichnis. 12. Auflage nach dem Stand am 1.1.1974, Neugliederungsgesetz, und am 31.12.1974 mit einer Verwaltungskarte. Saarbrücken, 1975. pp. 64.

— Statistics.

SAARGEBIET. Statistisches Amt. Einzelschriften zur Statistik des Saarlandes. Nr. 41. Gemeindestatistik 1970: weitere Strukturdaten. Saarbrücken, 1974. pp. 72.

— — Bibliography.

SAARGEBIET. Statistisches Amt. Einzelschriften zur Statistik des Saarlandes. Nr. 53. Quellennachweise zur Statistik des Saarlandes. Saarbrücken, 1976. pp. 302.

SABAH

— Politics and government — Bibliography.

NATIONAL LIBRARY OF AUSTRALIA. Sabah: a bibliography of the dispute between Malaysia and the Philippines. Canberra, 1969. pp. 30.

SAHEL

— Famines.

COPANS (JEAN) ed. Sécheresses et famines du Sahel...; par Yves Albouy [and others]. Paris, 1975. 2 vols (in 1). *(Paris. Ecole des Hautes Etudes en Sciences Sociales. Centre d'Etudes Africaines. Dossiers Africains)*

The POLITICS of natural disaster: the case of the Sahel drought; edited by Michael H. Glantz. New York, 1976. pp. 336. *bibliogs.*

ST. GALL (CANTON)

— Social conditions.

HABICHT (HANS MARTIN) Rickentunnel-Streik und Rorschacher Krawall: St.Gallische Fremdarbeiterprobleme vor dem Ersten Weltkrieg. St. Gallen, 1975. pp. 60. *bibliog. (Historischer Verein des Kantons St. Gallen. Neujahrsblatt. 115)*

ST. HELENA

— Economic policy.

ST. HELENA. 1946. Ten year plan of economic development and social welfare. [Jamestown, 1946]. pp. 17.

— Social policy.

ST. HELENA. 1946. Ten year plan of economic development and social welfare. [Jamestown, 1946]. pp. 17.

ST. KILDA

— History.

STEEL (TOM) The life and death of St. Kilda. [new ed.] London, 1975. pp. 255. *bibliog.*

ST. LAURENT (LOUIS STEPHEN).

PICKERSGILL (JOHN WHITNEY) My years with Louis St Laurent: a political memoir. Toronto, [1975]. pp. 334.

SAINT—LOUIS, SENEGAL

— Civic improvement.

REGION DU FLEUVE [SENEGAL]. Commission Régionale d'Urbanisme. 1974. Aperçu sur l'organisation et l'équipement de la commune de Saint-Louis. Saint-Louis, [1974?]. fo. 43. *Xerox copy.*

SAINT LUCIA

— Economic conditions.

BRITISH DEVELOPMENT DIVISION IN THE CARIBBEAN. St. Lucia: economic survey and projections. [Bridgetown?], 1970. fo. 28.

— Legislative Council — Elections.

SAINT LUCIA. Supervisor of Elections. 1954. Report on general election, 1954. Castries, 1954. pp. 20.

SAINT LUCIA. Supervisor of Elections. 1958. Report on Legislative Council general elections, 1957. Castries, 1958. pp. 22.

SAINT-SIMON (CLAUDE HENRI DE) Comte.

SAINT-SIMON (CLAUDE HENRI DE) Comte. The political thought of Saint-Simon; edited by Ghiţa Ionescu. London, 1976. pp. 245. *bibliog.*

ST. VINCENT

— House of Assembly — Elections.

ST. VINCENT. Supervisor of Elections. 1975. Report on the general election held on 9th December, 1974. Kingstown, 1975. fo. 9. *Photocopy.*

SALARIED EMPLOYEES

— Germany.

KOCKA (JUERGEN) Unternehmensverwaltung und Angestelltenschaft am Beispiel Siemens, 1847-1914: zum Verhältnis von Kapitalismus und Bürokratie in der deutschen Industrialisierung. Stuttgart,[1969]. pp. 639. *bibliog. (Arbeitskreis für Moderne Sozialgeschichte. Industrielle Welt. Band 11)*

NICK (FRANZ R.) and EHREISER (HANS JOERG) Unterschiede zwischen Arbeitern und Angestellten im Betrieb: eine empirische Untersuchung zur Selbsterkennung und Selbsteinschätzung;...Forschungsbericht. Mannheim, 1974. pp. 65, xxvi. *bibliog.*

KADRITZKE (ULF) Angestellte: die geduldigen Arbeiter; zur Soziologie und sozialen Bewegung der Angestellten. Frankfurt am Main, [1975]. pp. 411. *bibliog.*

SALE

— Social history.

BROWN (KENNETH L.) People of Salé: tradition and change in a Moroccan city, 1830-1930. Manchester, [1976]. pp. 265. *bibliog.*

SALT INDUSTRY AND TRADE

— Tanzania.

GOTTLIEB (MANUEL) The problem of goiter in Tanzania: a programme for prevention by salt iodization and a programme for improved salt marketing in Tanzania. Dar es Salaam, 1973. pp. 42. *bibliog. (Dar es Salaam. University. Economic Research Bureau. ERB Papers. 73.6)*

SALVADOR

— Economic policy.

ORGANIZATION OF AMERICAN STATES. Inter-American Economic and Social Council. Committee of Nine. 1966. Evaluation of the 1965-1969 economic and social development plan of El Salavador; report submitted to the Salavadorean government by the Ad Hoc Committee. Washington, 1966. pp. 362.

SALVADOR. Consejo Nacional de Planificacion y Coordinacion Economica. 1967. Plan de desarrollo economico y social, 1968-1972; parte general. [San Salvador, 1967?]. pp. 200.

SALVADOR. Consejo Nacional de Planificacion y Coordenacion Economica. 1972. Plan de desarrollo economico y social, 1973-1977. [San Salvador, 1972?]. pp. 244.

— Social policy.

ORGANIZATION OF AMERICAN STATES. Inter-American Economic and Social Council. Committee of Nine. 1966. Evaluation of the 1965-1969 economic and social development plan of El Salavador; report submitted to the Salavadorean government by the Ad Hoc Committee. Washington, 1966. pp. 362.

SALVADOR. Consejo Nacional de Planificacion y Coordinacion Economica. 1967. Plan de desarrollo economico y social, 1968-1972; parte general. [San Salvador, 1967?]. pp. 200.

SALVADOR. Consejo Nacional de Planificacion y Coordenacion Economica. 1972. Plan de desarrollo economico y social, 1973-1977. [San Salvador, 1972?]. pp. 244.

SALZBURG (STATE)

— Economic policy.

SOZIALISTISCHE PARTEI ÖSTERREICHS. [Landesparteiorganisation?] Salzburg. Der Salzburgplan: ein Programm der SPÖ für die gesunde Weiterentwicklung des Landes Salzburg. Salzburg, [1973]. pp. 214.

— Politics and government.

SOZIALISTISCHE PARTEI ÖSTERREICHS. [Landesparteiorganisation?] Salzburg. Der Salzburgplan: ein Programm der SPÖ für die gesunde Weiterentwicklung des Landes Salzburg. Salzburg, [1973]. pp. 214.

SAMPLING (STATISTICS).

TAMSFOSS (STEINAR) Om bruk av stikkprøver ved kontoret for intervjuundersøkelser, Statistik Sentralbyrå...: on the use of sampling surveys by the Central Bureau of Statistics, Norway. Oslo, 1970. pp. 46. *(Norway. Statistiske Centralbyrå. Artikler. Nr. 37) With English summary.*

KIAER (ANDERS NICOLAI) Den repraesentative undersøgelsesmethode; ny utgave med engelsk oversettelse ved Statistisk Sentralbyrås 100-års jubileum 1976: the representative method of statistical surveys; new edition with English translation at the centenary of the Central Bureau of Statistics, 1976. Oslo, 1976. pp. 64. *(Norway. Statistiske Centralbyrå. Samfunnsøkonomiske Studier. 27) Map in end pocket.*

KRUG (WALTER) Quantifizierung des systematischen Fehlers in wirtschafts- und sozialstatistischen Daten: dargestellt an der Statistik der Erwerbstätigkeit. Berlin, [1976]. pp. 109. *bibliog.*

SAN FRANCISCO

— Politics and government.

WIRT (FREDERICK M.) Power in the city: decision making in San Francisco. Berkeley, [1974]. pp. 417.

SAN MARINO.

FRANCE. Direction de la Documentation. La Documentation Française. Notes et Etudes Documentaires. No. 4,210. Les micro-états européens: Monaco - Saint-Marin - Liechtenstein; par Jean-Jacques L. Tur. Paris, 1975. pp. 41. *bibliog.*

SANCHEZ—ALBORNOZ (CLAUDIO).

SANCHEZ-ALBORNOZ (CLAUDIO) Mi testamento historico-politico. Barcelona, [1975]. pp. 256.

SANCTIONS (INTERNATIONAL LAW).

ZACKLIN (RALPH) The United Nations and Rhodesia: a study in international law. New York, 1974. pp. 188.

SANCTIS (GAETANO DE).

ACCAME (SILVIO) Gaetano De Sanctis fra cultura e politica: esperienze di militanti cattolici a Torino, 1919-1929. Firenze, 1975. pp. 545.

SANTA CLARA COUNTY
— Economic policy.

BUHR (WALTER) Die Rolle der materiellen infrastruktur im regionalen Wirtschaftswachstum: Studien über die Infrastruktur eines städtischen Gebietes; der Fall Santa Clara County, California. Berlin, [1975]. pp. 309. bibliog.

SARAN (MARY).

SARAN (MARY) Never give up: memoirs. London, 1976. pp. 145.

SARAWAK
— Officials and employees — Salaries, allowances, etc.

FEDERATION OF MALAYSIA. 1971. Revision of salaries and terms and conditions of service of officers in the public services in East Malaysia, Sarawak. Kuching, 1971. pp. 236.

— Politics and government.

LEIGH (MICHAEL BECKETT) The rising moon: political change in Sarawak. Sydney, 1974. pp. 232. bibliog.

SARDINIA
— History.

SOTGIU (GIROLAMO) Lotte sociali e politiche nella Sardegna contemporanea, 1848-1922. Cagliari, [1974]. pp. 439.

— — Sources.

SOTGIU (GIROLAMO) ed. Il movimento operaio in Sardegna, 1890-1915: testi di A. Battelli [and others]. Cagliari, [1974]. pp. 575.

— Rural conditions.

ANGIONI (GIULIO) Rapporti di produzione e cultura subalterna: contadini in Sardegna. Cagliari, [1974]. pp. 326. bibliog.

— Social conditions.

ANGIONI (GIULIO) Rapporti di produzione e cultura subalterna: contadini in Sardegna. Cagliari, [1974]. pp. 326. bibliog.

LELLI (MARCELLO) Proletariato e ceti medi in Sardegna: una società dipendente. Bari, [1975]. pp. 228.

SARTRE (JEAN PAUL).

POSTER (MARK) Existential Marxism in postwar France: from Sartre to Althusser. Princeton, [1975]. pp. 415. bibliog.

ARCHARD (DAVID WILLIAM) Existentialism and Marxism: a critical study of the political philosophy of Jean-Paul Sartre and Maurice Merleau-Ponty. 1976. fo. 333. bibliog. Typescript. Ph.D.(London) thesis: unpublished. This thesis is the property of London University and may not be removed from the Library.

CRAIB (IAN) Existentialism and sociology: a study of Jean-Paul Sartre. Cambridge, [1976]. pp. 242. bibliog.

— Bibliography.

WILCOCKS (ROBERT) compiler. Jean-Paul Sartre: a bibliography of international criticism. Edmonton, 1975. pp. 767.

SASKATCHEWAN
— Politics and government.

SMITH (DAVID E.) 1936- . Prairie liberalism: the Liberal Party in Saskatchewan, 1905- 71. Toronto, [1975]. pp. 352. bibliog.

SASOLBURG, ORANGE FREE STATE
— History.

MEINTJES (JOHANNES) Sasol 1950-1975. Cape Town, 1975. pp. 174. bibliog.

SATIRE, GERMAN.

DELIUS (FRIEDRICH C.) Unsere Siemens-Welt: eine Festschrift zum 125jährigen Bestehen des Hauses S. Berlin, 1972 repr. 1975. pp. 110.

SATIRE, POLISH.

LAM (JAN) Wybór kronik; (opracował Stanisław Frybes). Warszawa, 1954. pp. 386. Articles first published in Gazeta narodowa and Dziennik polski, 1868-85.

SATISFACTION.

ECONOMIC means for human needs: social indicators of well-being and discontent; edited by Burkhard Strumpel. Ann Arbor, 1976. pp. 303. bibliogs.

SAUD FAMILY.

TROELLER (GARY) The birth of Saudi Arabia: Britain and the rise of the House of Sa'ud. London, 1976. pp. 287. bibliog.

SAUDI ARABIA
— Commerce.

SAUDI ARABIA. Ministry of Information. 1966. Trade and industry. [Riyadh?, 1966?]. 1 pamphlet (unpaged). (Book 6)

— Economic conditions.

SAUDI ARABIA. Ministry of Information. 1967. Saudi Arabia in pictures and figures. Riyadh, 1967. pp. 96. In English, French and Arabic.

KNAUERHASE (RAMON) The Saudi Arabian economy. New York, 1975. pp. 359. bibliog.

— Foreign relations — United Kingdom.

TROELLER (GARY) The birth of Saudi Arabia: Britain and the rise of the House of Sa'ud. London, 1976. pp. 287. bibliog.

— — United States.

NAKHLEH (EMILE A.) The United States and Saudi Arabia: a policy analysis. Washington, 1975. pp. 69. (American Enterprise Institute for Public Policy Research. Foreign Affairs Studies. 26)

— History.

TROELLER (GARY) The birth of Saudi Arabia: Britain and the rise of the House of Sa'ud. London, 1976. pp. 287. bibliog.

— Industries.

SAUDI ARABIA. Ministry of Information. 1966. Trade and industry. [Riyadh?, 1966?]. 1 pamphlet (unpaged). (Book 6)

— Politics and government.

FAISAL, King of Saudi Arabia. Faisal speaks. [Riyadh, 1970?]. pp. 160. (Saudi Arabia. Ministry of Information. Book 12)

— Social conditions.

SAUDI ARABIA. Ministry of Information. 1967. Saudi Arabia in pictures and figures. Riyadh, 1967. pp. 96. In English, French and Arabic.

SAVING AND INVESTMENT.

ROBERTSON (JOHN MACKINNON) Saving and waste. Bradford, [1896]. pp. 7. (Papers for the People. No. 5)

— Denmark.

DENMARK. Økonomiske Råd. Formandskabet. 1972. Økonomisk demokrati i samfundsøkonomisk belysning. København, 1972. pp. 100.

— Europe.

REVELL (JACK) Savings flows in Europe: personal saving and borrowing. London, [1976]. pp. 191. bibliogs. (Wales. University. University College of North Wales. Institute of European Finance. Research Studies)

— Germany.

GERMANY (BUNDESREPUBLIK). Statistisches Bundesamt. 1975. Vermögensbestände und Schulden privater Haushalte, 1973. Wiesbaden, 1975. pp. 212. (Preise, Löhne, Wirtschaftsrechnungen. Reihe 18. Einkommens- und Verbrauchsstichproben. 2)

— India.

NATIONAL COUNCIL OF APPLIED ECONOMIC RESEARCH. Changes in rural income in India, 1968-69, 1969-70, 1970-71. New Delhi, [1975]. pp. 155.

— Italy.

VITALI (ORNELLO) La formazione del capitale in Italia. Milano, 1968. pp. 100. (Scuola Enrico Mattei di Studi Superiori sugli Idrocarburi. Pubblicazioni. N. 27)

ACCADEMIA NAZIONALE DEI LINCEI. Atti dei Convegni Lincei. 3. Tavola rotonda sul tema: Il risparmio in Italia oggi, Roma, 8 marzo 1974. Roma, 1975. pp. 93.

— Nigeria.

THOMAS (D. BABATUNDE) Capital accumulation and technology transfer: a comparative analysis of Nigerian manufacturing industries. New York, 1975. pp. 152. bibliog.

— Scandinavia — Mathematical models.

AMUNDSEN (ARNE) Konsumets og sparingens langsiktige utvikling…: consumption and saving in the process of long-term growth. Oslo, 1970. pp. 18. (Norway. Statistiske Centralbyrå. Artikler. Nr.36)

— Sudan.

SUDAN. Department of Statistics. 1961. Capital formation and increase in national income in Sudan in 1955-1959. Khartoum, 1961. pp. 135, 1 map. bibliog.

— Sweden.

JULANDER (CLAES-ROBERT) Sparande och effekter av ökad kunskap om inkomstens användning: en beteendevetenskaplig studie av individers inkomstanvändning. Stockholm, 1975. pp. 343. bibliog. With English summary.

— United Kingdom.

CAIRNCROSS (Sir ALEXANDER KIRKLAND) Home and foreign investment, 1870-1913: studies in capital accumulation. Hassocks, 1975. pp. 251. Originally published in 1953.

BANNOCK (GRAHAM) How to survive the slump: a guide to the economic crisis. Harmondsworth, 1975. pp. 170. bibliog.

JENKINS (D.T.) The West Riding wool textile industry 1770-1835: a study of fixed capital formation. Edington, 1975. pp. 336. bibliog. (Pasold Research Fund. Pasold Occasional Papers. vol. 4)

SAVINGS BANKS

— Denmark.

CHRISTENSEN (OLAV) Toftlund og Omegns Sparekasse, 1872-1972; med bidrag til Toftlund sogns historie, 1864-1920. [Toftlund, 1972]. pp. 144.

— Germany.

WYSOCKI (JOSEF) 75 Thaler sind schon ein Capital: Jubiläumsschrift zum 150jährigen Bestehen der Stadtsparkasse Osnabrück. Frankfurt am Main, [1975]. pp. 290. *bibliog.*

— United States.

OSTHAUS (CARL R.) Freedmen, philanthropy, and fraud: a history of the Freedman's Savings Bank. Urbana, [1976]. pp. 257. *bibliog.*

SAXONY

— Industries.

FIEDLER (HELENE) and others, eds. 30 Jahre volkseigene Betriebe: Dokumente und Materialien zum 30. Jahrestag des Volksentscheids in Sachsen. Berlin, 1976. pp. 255.

SCALE ANALYSIS (PSYCHOLOGY).

MARANELL (GARY M.) ed. Scaling: a sourcebook for behavioral scientists. Chicago, 1974. pp. 436. *bibliogs.*

SCANDINAVIA

— Description and travel.

GODWIN (MARY) Letters written during a short residence in Sweden, Norway, and Denmark; edited with an introduction by Carol H. Poston. Lincoln, Nebraska, [1976]. pp. 200. *bibliog.*

— Economic history.

NORDISK HISTORIKERMØDE, 1974. Kriser och krispolitik i Norden under mellankrigstiden: Nordiska historikermötet i Uppsala 1974; mötesrapport. [Uppsala, 1974]. pp. 315. *In various Scandinavian languages.*

— Foreign relations.

LUNTINEN (PERTTI) The Baltic question, 1903-1908. Helsinki, 1975. pp. 252. *bibliog. (Academia Scientiarum Fennica. Annales. Ser. B. Tom. 195)*

See also EUROPEAN ECONOMIC COMMUNITY — Scandinavia.

— Politics and government.

NORDISK HISTORIKERMØDE, 1974. Kriser och krispolitik i Norden under mellankrigstiden: Nordiska historikermötet i Uppsala 1974; mötesrapport. [Uppsala, 1974]. pp. 315. *In various Scandinavian languages.*

— Population.

IMHOF (ARTHUR ERWIN) Aspekte der Bevölkerungsentwicklung in den nordischen Ländern, 1720-1750. Bern, [1976]. 2 vols. *bibliog.*

— Statistics, Vital.

IMHOF (ARTHUR ERWIN) and LARSEN (ØIVIND) Sozialgeschichte und Medizin: Probleme der quantifizierenden Quellenbearbeitung in der Sozial- und Medizingeschichte. Oslo, 1975. pp. 322. *bibliog.*

SCANDINAVIANISM.

WALLENSTEEN (PETER) and others. The Nordic system: structure and change, 1920-1970. Tampere, [1973]. pp. 126. *bibliog. (Tampere Peace Research Institute. Research Reports. No. 6)*

SCEPTICISM.

STERNBERG (ELAINE) The logical conditions of public experience, examined with special reference to rationalism, empiricism and pragmatism. [1976]. fo. 214. *bibliog. Typescript. Ph.D. (London) thesis: unpublished. This thesis is the property of London University and may not be removed from the Library.*

SCHAFFERER (KARL).

SCHAFFERER (KARL) and EULER (ALOIS) Süd-Tirol erlebt, erlitten: eine Dokumentation;... eingeleitet und herausgegeben von Robert H. Drechsler. Wien, 1975. pp. 231.

SCHAFFHAUSEN (CANTON)

— Politics and government.

JOOS (EDUARD) Parteien und Presse im Kanton Schaffhausen. Schaffhausen, 1975. pp. 623. *bibliog. 3 tables in end pocket.*

SCHAPERA (ISAAC).

STUDIES in African social anthropology; edited by Meyer Fortes and Sheila Patterson. London, 1975. pp. 267. *bibliogs. Essays presented to Professor Isaac Schapera.*

SCHARFFENBERG FAMILY.

BURBIANKA (MARTA) Produkcja typograficzna Scharffenbergów we Wrocławiu. Wrocław, 1968. pp. 296,[xxx]. *(Wrocław. Wrocławskie Towarzystwo Naukowe. Śląskie Prace Bibliograficzne i Bibliotekoznawcze. t.12) With French summary.*

SCHEFFLER (HEINRICH).

SCHEFFLER (HEINRICH) Wölffische Lehrjahre: Marginalien zum Ausklang des Kurt Wolff Verlages, 1932-1934. [Frankfurt am Main, 1975]. pp. 61.

SCHLESWIG—HOLSTEIN

— Commerce.

BROCKSTEDT (JUERGEN) Die Schiffahrts- und Handelsbeziehungen Schleswig-Holsteins nach Lateinamerika, 1815-1848. Köln, 1975. pp. 575. *bibliog. With summaries in English and French.*

— Politics and government.

TILTON (TIMOTHY ALAN) Nazism, neo-Nazism, and the peasantry. Bloomington, [1975]. pp. 186. *bibliog. (Indiana University. Publications. Social Science Series. No. 31)*

SCHLESWIG-HOLSTEIN QUESTION.

CALLESEN (GERD) ed. Socialdemokratiet og internationalismen: kilder til belysning af det danske socialdemokratis syn på det slesvigske spørgsmål, 1906-24. København, [1973]. pp. 40. *bibliog.*

SANDIFORD (KEITH A.P.) Great Britain and the Schleswig-Holstein question, 1848-64: a study in diplomacy, politics, and public opinion. Toronto, [1975]. pp. 204. *bibliog.*

SCHLESWIG-HOLSTEIN WAR, 1864.

SANDIFORD (KEITH A.P.) Great Britain and the Schleswig-Holstein question, 1848-64: a study in diplomacy, politics, and public opinion. Toronto, [1975]. pp. 204. *bibliog.*

SCHMIDT (FOLKE).

EUROPEAN COURT OF HUMAN RIGHTS. Publications. Series A: Judgments and Decisions. [A 21]. ...Schmidt and Dahlström case; judgment of 6 February, 1976. Strasbourg, Council of Europe, 1976. pp. 18bis. *In English and French.*

SCHOENERER (GEORG VON).

WHITESIDE (ANDREW GLADDING) The socialism of fools: Georg Ritter von Schönerer and Austrian Pan-Germanism. Berkeley, 1975. pp. 404. *bibliog.*

SCHOLARS, AMERICAN.

BLAIR (CALVIN PATTON) and others. Responsibilities of the foreign scholar to the local scholarly community: studies of U.S. research in Guatemala, Chile and Paraguay;...edited and with an introduction by Richard N. Adams. [Austin, Texas], [1969]. pp. 112. *bibliogs.*

SCHOOL ATTENDANCE

— United Kingdom.

PEASE (THOMAS) [Unpublished material on school attendance, Westbury on Trym, Bristol. 1881-82]. 1 piece. *Manuscript, etc.*

— — Wales.

U.K. Department of Education and Science. 1975. Absenteeism in the schools of Wales. [London, 1975?]. fo. 25.

SCHOOL CHILDREN.

LEICHMAN (GLENN ALAN) The effect of age and educational environment on the development of achievement evaluations and moral judgements. [1976]. fo. 243. *bibliog. Typescript. Ph.D. (London) thesis: unpublished. This thesis is the property of London University and may not be removed from the Library.*

— Food.

FIELD (FRANK) 1942- . The stigma of free school meals. London, 1974. pp. 7.

— Transportation — United States.

SHIPSTEAD (PATRICK E.) New perspectives on American politics: a report from Michigan on the busing issue. Princeton, [1973]. pp. 69. *(Princeton University. Woodrow Wilson School of Public and International Affairs. Woodrow Wilson Association Monograph Series in Public Affairs. No. 5)*

SHAPIRO (H.R.) The bureaucratic state: party bureaucracy and the decline of democracy in America. New York, [1975]. pp. 366. *bibliogs.*

— United Kingdom.

FIELD (FRANK) 1942- . The stigma of free school meals. London, 1974. pp. 7.

LUCAS (NORMAN BERNARD CHARLES) An experience of teaching. London, [1975]. pp. 196.

— United States.

TILLERY (DALE) and KILDEGAARD (THEODORE C.) Educational goals, attitudes and behaviors: a comparative study of high school seniors. Cambridge, Mass., [1973]. pp. 251. *bibliog.*

SCHOOL DISTRICTS

— United States — Finance.

DAVID (MIRIAM E.) School rule: a case study of participation in budgeting in America. Cambridge, Mass., [1975]. pp. 152. *bibliog.*

SCHOOL ENVIRONMENT.

LEICHMAN (GLENN ALAN) The effect of age and educational environment on the development of achievement evaluations and moral judgements. [1976]. fo. 243. *bibliog. Typescript. Ph.D. (London) thesis: unpublished. This thesis is the property of London University and may not be removed from the Library.*

SCHOOL INTEGRATION

— United States.

RACISM and inequality: the policy alternatives; edited by Harrell R. Rodgers. San Francisco, [1975]. pp. 220.

SCHOOL MANAGEMENT AND ORGANIZATION.

MANAGEMENT in education: reader 1: the management of organizations and individuals; edited by Vincent Houghton [and others] for the Management in Education Course Team at the Open University. London, 1975. pp. 436. *bibliogs.*

MANAGEMENT in education: reader 2: some techniques and systems; edited by Lance Dobson [and others] for the Management in Education Course Team at the Open University. London, 1975. pp. 405. *bibliogs.*

— Canada — Ontario.

ONTARIO. Ministerial Commission on the Organization and Financing of the Public and Secondary School Systems in Metropolitan Toronto. 1974. Report; [Barry Lowes, chairman]. [Toronto, 1974]. pp. 311. *bibliog.*

— France.

SCHONFELD (WILLIAM R.) Obedience and revolt: French behavior towards authority. Beverly Hills, [1976]. pp. 256.

— Italy.

CHIARANTE (GIUSEPPE) and NAPOLITANO (GIORGIO) La democrazia nella scuola: (la posizione dei comunisti sui nuovi organi di governo negli istituti e nei distretti scolastici). Roma, [1974]. pp. 137.

— United Kingdom.

MIDWINTER (ERIC CLARE) Education and the community. London, 1975. pp. 163. *bibliog.*

AULD (ROBIN ERNEST) The William Tyndale Junior and Infants Schools: report of the public inquiry...into the teaching, organization and management of the William Tyndale Junior and Infants Schools, Islington, London, N.1. London, Inner London Education Authority, 1976. 1 vol. (various pagings).

CORBETT (ANNE) Whose schools?;...Fabian evidence to the Taylor committee. London, 1976. pp. 28. *(Fabian Society. Research Series. [No.] 328)*

RAISON (TIMOTHY) The act and the partnership: an essay on educational administration in England [based on a seminar held at the Centre for Studies in Social Policy in 1974 and 1975]. London, [1976]. pp. 80. *(Centre for Studies in Social Policy. Doughty Street Papers. No. 3)*

WILLIAM Tyndale: the teachers' story; [by] Terry Ellis [and others]. London, 1976. pp. 171.

— United States.

WIRT (FREDERICK M.) ed. The polity of the school: new research in educational politics. Lexington, [1975]. pp. 333.

SCHOOL SOCIAL WORK

— United Kingdom.

ROSE (GORDON) and MARSHALL (TONY F.) Counselling and school social work: an experimental study...; with the assistance of R.F. Adamson and Pauline Avery. London, [1974]. pp. 347. *bibliog.*

SCHOOLS

— Canada — Manitoba.

CRUNICAN (PAUL) Priests and politicians: Manitoba schools and the election of 1896 Toronto, [1974]. pp. 369. *bibliog.*

— United Kingdom.

FENWICK (I.G.K.) The comprehensive school, 1944-1970: the politics of secondary school reorganization. London, 1976. pp. 187. *bibliog.*

— United States.

SHIMAHARA (NOBUO KENNETH) and SCRUPSKI (ADAM) Social forces and schooling: an anthropological and sociological perspective. New York, [1975]. pp. 368.

BOWLES (SAMUEL) Economist, and GINTIS (HERBERT) Schooling in capitalist America: educational reform and the contradictions of economic life. London, 1976. pp. 340. *bibliogs.*

— — Accounting.

DAVID (MIRIAM E.) School rule: a case study of participation in budgeting in America. Cambridge, Mass., [1975]. pp. 152. *bibliog.*

SCHRÜBBERS.

See SCHRUEBBERS

SCHRUEBBERS (HUBERT).

VEREINIGUNG DER ANTIFASCHISTEN UND VERFOLGTEN DES NAZIREGIMES, LAND HAMBURG. Jacob und Schrübbers: heute wie damals; Dokumentation zum Berufsverbotsbeschluss und zum Fall Ilse Jacob, etc. 2nd ed. Hamburg, 1972. pp. 94. *(VAN-Documentationen. 4)*

SCHULZE (FIETE).

HOCHMUTH (URSEL) ed. Fiete Schulze; oder, Das dritte Urteil. Hamburg, 1971. pp. 117. *bibliog. (Vereinigung der Antifaschisten und Verfolgten des Naziregimes, Land Hamburg. VAN-Dokumentationen. 3)*

SCHWAB (CHARLES MICHAEL).

HESSEN (ROBERT) Ph.D. Steel titan: the life of Charles M. Schwab. New York, 1975. pp. 350.

SCIENCE

— History.

FOR Dirk Struik: scientific, historical and political essays in honor of Dirk J. Struik; edited by R.S. Cohen [and others]. Dordrecht, [1974]. pp. 652. *bibliogs. (Boston Colloquium for the Philosophy of Science. Boston Studies in the Philosophy of Science. vol.15)*

METHOD and appraisal in the physical sciences: the critical background to modern science, 1800-1905; edited by Colin Howson. Cambridge, 1976. pp. 344. *bibliogs.*

The PATRONAGE of science in the nineteenth century; by R. Fox [and others]; edited by G.L'E. Turner. Leyden, 1976. pp. 218.

WORRALL (JOHN) The 19th century revolution in optics: a case study in the interaction between philosophy of science and history and sociology of science. 1975 [or rather 1976]. fo. 277. *bibliog.* Ph.D. (London) thesis: unpublished. *This thesis is the property of London University and may not be removed from the Library.*

ZIMAN (JOHN MICHAEL) The force of knowledge: the scientific dimension of society. Cambridge, [1976]. pp. 374. *bibliog.*

— — Greece, Ancient.

SAMBURSKY (SHMUEL) The physical world of the Greeks; translated from the Hebrew by Merton Dagut. London, 1963. pp. 255. *bibliog.*

— — United States.

ROSENBERG (CHARLES E.) No other gods: on science and American social thought. Baltimore, [1976]. pp. 273. *bibliog.*

— International cooperation.

SCIENCE, technology and sovereignty in the Polar regions; [revised papers of a colloquium held in Washington, 1973]; edited by Gerald S. Schatz. Lexington, Mass., [1974]. pp. 215.

MEDVEDEV (ZHORES ALEKSANDROVICH) National frontiers and international scientific co-operation. Nottingham, 1975. pp. 296. *(Medvedev Papers. vol. 1)*

VIEWS of science, technology and development; edited by Eugene Rabinowitch and Victor Rabinowitch. Oxford, 1975. pp. 285. *Consists mainly of papers presented to recent Pugwash conferences.*

— Methodology.

CONFERENCE ON THE HISTORY OF QUANTIFICATION IN THE SCIENCES, NEW YORK, 1959. Quantification: a history of the meaning of measurement in the natural and social sciences; edited by Harry Woolf. Indianapolis, [1961]. pp. 222. *Papers from the conference organized by the Joint Committee on the History of Science of the Social Science Research Council and the National Research Council.*

MEDAWAR (Sir PETER BRIAN) Induction and intuition in scientific thought. London, 1969 repr. 1970. pp. 62. *(American Philosophical Society. Jayne Lectures. [8th Series]. 1968)*

TONDL (LADISLAV) Scientific procedures: a contribution concerning the methodological problems of scientific concepts and scientific explanation. Dordrecht, [1973]. pp. 268. *bibliog. (Boston Colloquium for the Philosophy of Science. Boston Studies in the Philosophy of Science. vol. 10)*

HARDING (SANDRA G.) ed. Can theories be refuted?: essays on the Duhem-Quine thesis. Dordrecht, [1976]. pp. 318. *bibliogs. Reprinted from various sources.*

MACH (ERNST) Knowledge and error: sketches on the psychology of enquiry; (translation from the 5th edition, 1926). Dordrecht, [1976]. pp. 393. *bibliogs.*

METHOD and appraisal in the physical sciences: the critical background to modern science, 1800-1905; edited by Colin Howson. Cambridge, 1976. pp. 344. *bibliogs.*

— Philosophy.

TARRIDA DEL MARMOL (FERNANDO) Problemas trascendentales: estudios de sociologia y ciencia moderna. Barcelona, 1930. pp. 202.

MEDAWAR (Sir PETER BRIAN) Induction and intuition in scientific thought. London, 1969 repr. 1970. pp. 62. *(American Philosophical Society. Jayne Lectures. [8th Series]. 1968)*

BUERGERLICHE Wissenschaftstheorie und ideologischer Klassenkampf: eine Auseinandersetzung mit bürgerlichen Wissenschaftsauffassungen; ([by] G. Domin [and others]). Berlin, 1973. pp. 266. *(Akademie der Wissenschaften der DDR. Institut für Wissenschaftstheorie und -organisation. Wissenschaft und Gesellschaft. Band 2)*

TONDL (LADISLAV) Scientific procedures: a contribution concerning the methodological problems of scientific concepts and scientific explanation. Dordrecht, [1973]. pp. 268. *bibliog. (Boston Colloquium for the Philosophy of Science. Boston Studies in the Philosophy of Science. vol. 10)*

AMERICAN ASSOCIATION FOR THE ADVANCEMENT OF SCIENCE. Section L. Annual Meeting, 1969. Philosophical foundations of science: proceedings...; edited by Raymond J. Seeger and Robert S. Cohen. Dordrecht, [1974]. pp. 545. *bibliogs. (Boston Colloquium for the Philosophy of Science. Boston Studies in the Philosophy of Science. vol.11)*

FOR Dirk Struik: scientific, historical and political essays in honor of Dirk J. Struik; edited by R.S. Cohen [and others]. Dordrecht, [1974]. pp. 652. *bibliogs. (Boston Colloquium for the Philosophy of Science. Boston Studies in the Philosophy of Science. vol.15)*

PHILOSOPHY OF SCIENCE ASSOCIATION. 3rd Biennial Meeting, 1972. PSA 1972: proceedings...; edited by Kenneth F. Schaffner and Robert S. Cohen. Dordrecht, [1974]. pp. 445. *bibliogs. (Boston Colloquium for the Philosophy of Science. Boston Studies in the Philosophy of Science. vol. 20)*

ARISTOTLE. Posterior analytics; translated with notes by Jonathan Barnes. Oxford, 1975. pp. 277. *bibliog.*

BLOOR (DAVID) Knowledge and social imagery. London, 1976. pp. 156. *bibliog.*

BURGER (THOMAS) Max Weber's theory of concept formation: history, laws, and ide types. Durham, N.C., 1976. pp. 231. *bibliog.*

SCIENCE (Cont.)

GIDDENS (ANTHONY) New rules of sociological method: a positive critique of interpretative sociologies. London, 1976. pp. 192. *bibliog.*

HARDING (SANDRA G.) ed. Can theories be refuted?: essays on the Duhem-Quine thesis. Dordrecht, [1976]. pp. 318. *bibliogs. Reprinted from various sources.*

MACH (ERNST) Knowledge and error: sketches on the psychology of enquiry; (translation from the 5th edition, 1926). Dordrecht, [1976]. pp. 393. *bibliogs.*

NEEDHAM (JOSEPH) Moulds of understanding: a pattern of natural philosophy: [selected essays]; edited and introduced by Gary Werskey. London, 1976. pp. 320. *bibliog.*

WORRALL (JOHN) The 19th century revolution in optics: a case study in the interaction between philosophy of science and history and sociology of science. 1975 [or rather 1976]. fo. 277. *bibliog. Typescript. Ph.D. (London) thesis: unpublished. This thesis is the property of London University and may not be removed from the Library.*

— Social aspects.

SEMENOV (NIKOLAI NIKOLAEVICH) Nauka i obshchestvo: stat'i i rechi, [1957-72 gg.]. Moskva, 1973. pp. 479.

KUCZYNSKI (JUERGEN) Wissenschaft und Gesellschaft: Studien und Essays über sechs Jahrtausende. Köln, 1974. pp. 240.

AMERICAN ASSOCIATION FOR THE ADVANCEMENT OF SCIENCE. Committee on Scientific Freedom and Responsibility. Scientific freedom and responsibility: a report... prepared... by John T. Edsall. Washington, 1975. pp. 50. *bibliog.*

KOELNER ZEITSCHRIFT FÜR SOZIOLOGIE UND SOZIALPSYCHOLOGIE. Sonderhefte. 18. Wissenschaftssoziologie: Studien und Materialien; herausgegeben von Nico Stehr und René König. Opladen, 1975. pp. 525. *bibliogs.*

SCIENCE and social responsibility: [a Science Policy Foundation symposium held in London in 1973]; edited by Maurice Goldsmith. London, 1975. pp. 169.

WISSENSCHAFT: Stellung, Funktion und Organisation in der entwickelten sozialistischen Gesellschaft; (Herausgeber: Günter Kröber, Hubert Laitko). Berlin, 1975. pp. 415.

NEEDHAM (JOSEPH) Moulds of understanding: a pattern of natural philosophy: [selected essays]; edited and introduced by Gary Werskey. London, 1976. pp. 320. *bibliog.*

SCIENCE and its public: the changing relationship; edited by Gerald Holton and William A. Blanpied. Dordrecht, [1976]. pp. 289. *(Boston Colloquium for the Philosophy of Science. Boston Studies in the Philosophy of Science. vol. 33) Conference held under the joint auspices of the Harvard Program on Public Conceptions of Science and Daedalus, journal of the American Academy of Arts and Sciences.*

ZIMAN (JOHN MICHAEL) The force of knowledge: the scientific dimension of society. Cambridge, [1976]. pp. 374. *bibliog.*

— — United States.

ROSENBERG (CHARLES E.) No other gods: on science and American social thought. Baltimore, [1976]. pp. 273. *bibliog.*

— Study and teaching — Finance.

The PATRONAGE of science in the nineteenth century; by R. Fox [and others]; edited by G.L'E. Turner. Leyden, 1976. pp. 218.

— Canada.

CANADA. Statistics Canada. Expenditures on scientific activities by private non-profit organizations. bien., 1973- Ottawa. *In English and French.*

— Russia.

SEMENOV (NIKOLAI NIKOLAEVICH) Nauka i obshchestvo: stat'i i rechi, [1957-72 gg.]. Moskva, 1973. pp. 479.

HUTCHINGS (RAYMOND FRANCIS DUDLEY) Soviet science, technology, design: interaction and convergence. London, 1976. pp. 320. *bibliog.*

— Underdeveloped areas.

See UNDERDEVELOPED AREAS — Science.

SCIENCE AND STATE.

LONG (THEODORE DIXON) and WRIGHT (CHRISTOPHER) eds. Science policies of industrial nations: case studies of the United States, Soviet Union, United Kingdom, France, Japan, and Sweden. New York, 1975. pp. 232. *bibliog.*

SCIENCE and its public: the changing relationship; edited by Gerald Holton and William A. Blanpied. Dordrecht, [1976]. pp. 289. *(Boston Colloquium for the Philosophy of Science. Boston Studies in the Philosophy of Science. vol. 33) Conference held under the joint auspices of the Harvard Program on Public Conceptions of Science and Daedalus, journal of the American Academy of Arts and Sciences.*

— Canada — Bibliography.

NATIONAL SCIENCE LIBRARY [CANADA]. Scientific policy, research and development in Canada...: a bibliography...; revised to June 1970; (with Supplement covering period June 1970-June 1972). Ottawa, 1970-72. 2 pts. *In English and French.*

— Communist countries.

WISSENSCHAFT: Stellung, Funktion und Organisation in der entwickelten sozialistischen Gesellschaft; (Herausgeber: Günter Kröber, Hubert Laitko). Berlin, 1975. pp. 415.

— Russia.

ORGANIZATSIIA sovetskoi nauki v 1926-1932 gg.: sbornik dokumentov. Leningrad, 1974. pp. 408.

— United States.

BOFFEY (PHILIP M.) The brain bank of America: an inquiry into the politics of science; (prepared with the cooperation of the Center for Study of Responsive Law). New York, [1975]. pp. 312.

JACHIM (ANTON G.) Science policy making in the United States and the Batavia accelerator. Carbondale, Ill., [1975]. pp. 208. *bibliog.*

LAMBRIGHT (W. HENRY) Governing science and technology. New York, 1976. pp. 218.

SCIENTISTS

— Russia.

ZAUZOLKOV (FEDOR NIKOLAEVICH) Kommunisticheskaia partiia - organizator sozdaniia nauchnoi i proizvodstvenno-tekhnicheskoi intelligentsii SSSR. Moskva, 1973. pp. 127.

KLIMENIUK (VALERII NIKOLAEVICH) Upravlenie razvitiem i ispol'zovaniem nauchnogo potentsiala. Kiev, 1974. pp. 207. *bibliog.*

— United Kingdom.

U.K. Department of Industry. 1976. Persons with qualifications in engineering, technology and science, census of population 1971, Great Britain;...compiled for the Department of Industry by the Office of Population Censuses and Surveys from the returns made in the 1971 census of population. London, 1976. pp. 207. *(Studies in Technological Manpower. No.5)*

SCIENTOLOGY.

CHURCH OF SCIENTOLOGY. Scientology: the other case; [a pamphlet submitted to Sir Keith Joseph, Secretary of State for the Social Services, in reply to the 1971 Foster report]. [East Grinstead, 1972]. pp. 23.

SCOTLAND

— Census.

SCOTLAND. Census, 1971. Census, 1971: Scotland: economic activity: county tables, 10 per cent sample. Edinburgh, 1975. 4 pts. (in 1 vol.).

SCOTLAND. Census, 1971. Census, 1971: Scotland: workplace and transport tables; 10 per cent sample. Edinburgh, 1975. pp. 142.

SCOTLAND. Census, 1971. 1971 Census statistics: new local government areas as constituted 16 May 1975. Edinburgh, 1976. pp. 75.

SCOTLAND. Census, 1971. Census, 1971: Scotland: report[s] for...region[s] as constituted on 16th May 1975. Edinburgh, 1976. 9 pts. (in 2 vols.).

— Economic conditions.

HUTCHESON (ALEXANDER MACGREGOR) and HOGG (ALEXANDER) eds. Scotland and oil. 2nd ed. Edinburgh, [1975]. pp. 127. *bibliog.*

The RED paper on Scotland; [edited by Gordon Brown]. Edinburgh, 1975. pp. 368.

U.K. Social Science Research Council. North Sea Oil Panel. Bulletin. q., current issues only. Glasgow.

— Economic history.

HUNTER (JAMES) Ph.D. The making of the crofting community. Edinburgh, [1976]. pp. 309. *bibliog.*

— Economic policy.

SCOTLAND. Scottish Development Department. Planning and development in Scotland. a., 1973/74- Edinburgh.

The RED paper on Scotland; [edited by Gordon Brown]. Edinburgh, 1975. pp. 368.

TAIT (ALAN A.) The economics of devolution: a knife edge problem. Edinburgh, [1975]. pp. 12. *bibliog. (Glasgow. University of Strathclyde. Fraser of Allander Institute. Speculative Papers. No.2)*

— Intellectual life.

MILLER (KARL) Cockburn's millennium. London, 1975. pp. 322.

— Maps.

SKINNER (DAVID N.) The coast of Scotland: some recently collected survey material; prepared for the Scottish Development Department. [Edinburgh], 1974 [or rather 1976 in progress]. 1 vol. (loose-leaf). *bibliog.*

— Politics and government.

MILLER (KARL) Cockburn's millennium. London, 1975. pp. 322.

The RED paper on Scotland; [edited by Gordon Brown]. Edinburgh, 1975. pp. 368.

TAIT (ALAN A.) The economics of devolution: a knife edge problem. Edinburgh, [1975]. pp. 12. *bibliog. (Glasgow. University of Strathclyde. Fraser of Allander Institute. Speculative Papers. No.2)*

HEALD (DAVID) Making devolution work. London, 1976. pp. 56. *(Young Fabian Group. Young Fabian Pamphlets. 43)*

LIBERAL PARTY. Machinery of Government Panel. Our declining democracy; ...evidence to the Privy Council on the government's White Paper: Our changing democracy. London, [1976]. pp. 14. *(Liberal Publication Department. Study Papers. No. 2) White Paper published as Cmnd. 6348, British Parliamentary Papers, Session 1975-76.*

SCOTLAND. Scottish Law Commission. 1976. Comments on White Paper: Our changing democracy: devolution to Scotland and Wales. [Edinburgh, 1976]. pp. 97. *(Memoranda. No. 32) White Paper published as Cmnd. 6348, British Parliamentary Papers, Session 1975-76.*

— **Rural conditions.**

FENTON (ALEXANDER) Scottish country life. Edinburgh, [1976]. pp. 255. *bibliog.*

— **Social conditions.**

U.K. Scial Science Research Council. North Sea Oil Panel. Bulletin. q., current issues only. Glasgow.

— **Social history.**

PREBBLE (JOHN) Mutiny: Highland regiments in revolt, 1743-1804. London, 1975. pp. 542. *bibliog.*

HARVEY (COLIN) Ha'penny help: a record of social improvement in Victorian Scotland. Glasgow, 1976. pp. 197.

HUNTER (JAMES) Ph.D. The making of the crofting community. Edinburgh, [1976]. pp. 309. *bibliog.*

SOCIAL class in Scotland: past and present; edited by A. Allan MacLaren. Edinburgh, [1976]. pp. 195.

SEA POWER.

CONFERENCE ON PROBLEMS OF NAVAL ARMAMENTS, ITHACA, 1972. Sea power in the 1970s; George H. Quester, editor. New York, [1975]. pp. 248. *Papers of the conference sponsored by the Cornell University Program on Peace Studies.*

INTERNATIONAL INSTITUTE FOR STRATEGIC STUDIES. Adelphi Papers. No. 122. Power at sea: 1: the new environment; papers presented...at the seventeenth annual conference of the IISS at Ronneby Brunn, Sweden, in September 1975. London, 1976. pp. 39.

INTERNATIONAL INSTITUTE FOR STRATEGIC STUDIES. Adelphi Papers. No. 123. Power at sea: 2: superpowers and navies; papers presented... at the seventeenth annual conference of the IISS at Ronneby Brunn, Sweden, in September 1975. London, 1976. pp. 32.

INTERNATIONAL INSTITUTE FOR STRATEGIC STUDIES. Adelphi Papers. No. 124. Power at sea: 3: competition and conflict; papers presented... at the seventeenth annual conference of the IISS at Ronneby Brunn, Sweden, in September 1975. London, 1976. pp. 36.

SEASIDE RESORTS.

KARN (VALERIE A.) Retiring to the seaside. London, [1974]. pp. 12. *bibliog. (Age Concern England. Manifesto Series. No. 9)*

SEASONAL LABOUR

— **Russia.**

SHINIK (D.N.) Pravovoe regulirovanie trudovykh otnoshenii sezonnykh rabochikh i sluzhashchikh; pod redaktsiei... V.N. Petrova. Kishinev, 1975. pp. 120. *bibliog.*

SECONDAT (CHARLES LOUIS DE) Baron de Montesquieu.

BAUM (JOHN ALAN) Montesquieu as sociologist: an analysis of his contribution to the development of sociological theory and method. 1975 [or rather 1976]. fo. 288. *bibliog. Typescript. Ph.D. (London) thesis: unpublished. This thesis is the property of London University and may not be removed from the Library.*

SECRET SOCIETIES

— **India.**

KISHORE (NAWAL) Anand Marg: the truth. [Delhi, Ministry of Information and Broadcasting, Directorate of Advertising and Visual Publicity, 1975]. pp. 16.

SECTIONALISM (UNITED STATES).

POTTER (DAVID MORRIS) The impending crisis, 1848-1861; completed and edited by Don E. Fehrenbacher. New York, [1976]. pp. 638. *bibliog.*

SECTS.

BOURGUIGNON (ERIKA) ed. Religion, altered states of consciousness, and social change. Columbus, Ohio, 1973. pp. 389.

SECULARISM.

HOLYOAKE (GEORGE JACOB) English secularism: a confession of belief. Chicago, 1896. pp. 146. *Originally appeared as a series of articles in The Open Court.*

— **Europe.**

CHADWICK (WILLIAM OWEN) The secularization of the European mind in the nineteenth century. Cambridge, 1975. pp. 286. *(Gifford Lectures. 1973-1974)*

SECURITY, INTERNATIONAL.

GOLDMAN (KJELL) Bipolarisering och spänning i internationella system: en teoretisk diskussion. Stockholm, 1971. pp. 44. *(Utrikespolitiska Institutet. Internationella Studier. 1971, Nr.8)*

BAILEY (SYDNEY D.) The procedure of the UN Security Council. Oxford, 1975. pp. 424. *bibliog.*

BERLIA (GEORGES) Problèmes de sécurité internationale et de défense. Paris, [1975]. pp. 272, vi.

HARTLAND-THUNBERG (PENELOPE) ed. Commissioned papers on inflation/recession, energy and the international financial structure. Washington, [1975]. pp. 62.

The INDIAN Ocean and the threat to the West: four studies in global strategy; [by] Anthony Harrigan [and others]; edited by Patrick Wall. London, 1975. pp. 198.

INTERNATIONAL SCHOOL ON DISARMAMENT AND RESEARCH ON CONFLICTS, 5TH, URBINO, 1974. International terrorism and world security: [proceedings of the fifth course]; edited by David Carlton and Carlo Schaerf. London, 1975. pp. 332.

POETTERING (HANS GERT) Adenauers Sicherheitspolitik, 1955-1963: ein Beitrag zum deutsch-amerikanischen Verhältnis. Düsseldorf, [1975]. pp. 240. *bibliog. (Bonn. Universität. Seminar für Politische Wissenschaft. Bonner Schriften zur Politik und Zeitgeschichte. 10)*

SJAASTAD (ANDERS C.) and SKOGAN (JOHN KRISTEN) Politikk og sikkerhet i Norskehavsområdet: om de enkelte land og våre felles problemer. Oslo, 1975. pp. 301. *(Norsk Utenrikspolitisk Institutt. Utenrikspolitiske Studier. Nr. 18)*

GERDES (DIRK) Abschreckung und Entspannung: legitimatorische Folgeprobleme bundesrepublikanischer Entspannungspolitik. Meisenheim am Glan, 1976. pp. 182. *bibliog.*

SEDITION

— **Switzerland.**

ZELLWEGER (IVO) Die strafrechtlichen Beschränkungen der politischen Meinungsäusserungsfreiheit: Propagandaverbote. Zürich, [1975]. pp. 192. *bibliog. (Zürich. Universität. Rechts- und Staatswissenschaftliche Fakultät. Zürcher Beiträge zur Rechtswissenschaft. Neue Folge. Heft 481)*

SEEMANN (KLAUS).

SEEMANN (KLAUS) Entzaubertes Bundeskanzleramt: Denkwürdigkeiten eines Personalratsvorsitzenden. Landshut, [1975]. pp. 216.

SEGREGATION IN EDUCATION

— **Sweden.**

SWEDNER (HARALD) School segregation in Malmö. Chicago, [1971]. pp. 51. *bibliog.*

SEGREGATION IN SPORTS.

FOREMAN (THOMAS ELTON) Discrimination against the Negro in American athletics: a thesis. San Francisco, 1957 repr. 1975. pp. 72. *bibliog. Thesis (M.A.)-Fresno State College.*

THOMPSON (RICHARD) Writer on race relations. Retreat from apartheid: New Zealand's sporting contacts with South Africa. Wellington, 1975. pp. 102.

SÉGUY (GEORGES).

SÉGUY (GEORGES) Lutter: conversations avec Philippe Dominique. [Paris, 1975]. pp. 366.

SEKONDI-TAKORADI.

— **Politics and government.**

GHANA. 1970. White Paper on the report of the Commission of Enquiry into the affairs of the Sekondi-Takoradi City Council. [Accra], 1970. pp. 11. *(W[hite] P[apers] 1970. No. 6) Bound with the Report.*

GHANA. Commission appointed...to enquire into the affairs of the Sekondi-Takoradi City Council. 1970. Report; [Edmund Brite Gaisie, chairman]. [Accra], 1970. pp. 113. *Bound with the White Paper on the Report.*

SELEBI-PIKWE.

— **Census.**

BOTSWANA. Central Statistics Office. 1975. Report of the census of Selebi-Pikwe. Gaborone, [1975?]. 1 vol. (various pagings).

SELF-DETERMINATION, NATIONAL.

BIBO (ISTVÀN) The paralysis of international institutions and the remedies: a study of self-determination, concord among the major powers, and political arbitration. New York, [1976]. pp. 152.

THUERER (DANIEL) Das Selbstbestimmungsrecht der Völker, mit einem Exkurs zur Jurafrage. Bern, 1976. pp. 256. *bibliog.*

SELF-EMPLOYED.

— **Pensions — Netherlands.**

RAAD VOOR HET MIDDEN- EN KLEINBEDRIJF. Nota inzake oudedagsvoorziening voor ondernemers in het midden- en kleinbedrijf. [The Hague, 1970?]. pp. 20.

RAAD VOOR HET MIDDEN- EN KLEINBEDRIJF. Advies inzake bedrijfsbeëindiging en A[lgemene Bijstandswet] en kinderbijslag eerste en tweede kind. [The Hague, 1971]. pp. 14.

— **Netherlands.**

RAAD VOOR HET MIDDEN- EN KLEINBEDRIJF. Documentatie inkomenspositie en -ontwikkeling van werknemers en zelfstandigen in het midden- en kleinbedrijf. 's-Gravenhage, 1971. PP. 25. *(?pUBLIKATIES!. 1971, NO. 1)*

RAAD VOOR HET MIDDEN- EN KLEINBEDRIJF. Advies gewaardeerd ondernemersloon. 's-Gravenhage, 1975. pp. 25. *([Publikaties]. 1975, no.2)*

SELF-EVALUATION.

NICK (FRANZ R.) and EHREISER (HANS JOERG) Unterschiede zwischen Arbeitern und Angestellten im Betrieb: eine empirische Untersuchung zur Selbsterkennung und Selbsteinschätzung;...Forschungsbericht. Mannheim, 1974. pp. 65, xxvi. *bibliog.*

CROSS (PETER) The British business creed: changing ideologies and self images of business elites and management in Britain. [1975]. fo. 488. *bibliog. Typescript. Ph.D. (London) thesis: unpublished. This thesis is the property of London University and may not be removed from the Library.*

WELLS (L. EDWARD) and MARWELL (GERALD) Self-esteem: its conceptualization and measurement. Beverly Hills, [1976]. pp. 290. *bibliog.*

SELF-HELP GROUPS.

SELF-HELP GROUPS.

KATZ (ALFRED HYMAN) and BENDER (EUGENE I.) eds. The strength in us: self-help groups in the modern world. New York, 1976. pp. 258.

SELF SERVICE STORES
— United States.

CROSS (JENNIFER) The supermarket trap: the consumer and the food industry. rev. ed. Bloomington, Ind., [1976]. pp. 306. *bibliog.*

SELIGER (JOSEF).

ZESSNER (KLAUS) Josef Seliger und die nationale Frage in Böhmen: eine Untersuchung über die nationale Politik der deutschböhmischen Sozialdemokratie, 1899-1920. Stuttgart, [1976]. pp. 257. *bibliog.*

SEMANTICS.

BRAME (MICHAEL K.) Conjectures and refutations in syntax and semantics. New York, [1976]. pp. 160. *bibliog.*

MARATSOS (MICHAEL P.) The use of definite and indefinite reference in young children: an experimental study of semantic acquisition. Cambridge, 1976. pp. 144. *bibliog.*

SEMIGROUPS.

HILLE (EINAR) and PHILLIPS (RALPH S.) Functional analysis and semi-groups. rev. ed. Providence, R.I., 1957 repr. 1974. pp. 808. *bibliog. (American Mathematical Society. Colloquium Publications. vol. 31)*

SEMINOLE INDIANS.

KERSEY (HARRY A.) Pelts, plumes and hides: white traders among the Seminole Indians, 1870-1930. Gainesville, Flo., 1975. pp. 158. *bibliog.*

SENEGAL
— Economic conditions.

BACHMANN (HEINZ B.) and others. Senegal: tradition, diversification and economic development: this report was prepared by the economic mission which visited Senegal in...1972, etc. Washington, International Bank for Reconstruction and Development, 1974. pp. 341. *(Country Economic Reports)*

REBOUL (CLAUDE) Causes économiques de la sécheresse au Sénégal: systèmes de culture et calamités naturelles;...document de travail. Paris, Institut National de la Recherche Agronomique, 1975. fo. 59. *bibliog.*

— Economic policy.

SENEGAL. Secrétariat d'Etat auprès du Premier Ministre chargé du Plan. 1969. Réajustement du troisième plan quadriennal de développement économique et social, 1969-1973. Tome 1. [Dakar, 1969?]. fo. 148. *Xerox copy.*

SENEGAL. Secrétariat d'Etat auprès du Premier Ministre chargé du Plan. 1972. Communication au Conseil Supérieur du Plan sur les grandes orientations et les objectifs généraux par secteur du IVe plan. Dakar, 1972. fo. 64. *Xerox copy.*

SENEGAL. Secrétariat d'Etat auprès du Premier Ministre chargé du Plan. 1972. Communication au Conseil Supérieur du Plan sur les travaux de préparation du IVe plan. Dakar, 1972. fo. 38. *Xerox copy.*

BACHMANN (HEINZ B.) and others. Senegal: tradition, diversification and economic development: this report was prepared by the economic mission which visited Senegal in...1972, etc. Washington, International Bank for Reconstruction and Development, 1974. pp. 341. *(Country Economic Reports)*

— History.

ROBINSON (DAVID) Ph. D. Chiefs and clerics: Abdul Bokar Kan and Futa oro, 1853-1891. Oxford, 1975. pp. 239. *bibliog.*

— Politics and government.

SCHUMACHER (EDWARD JAY) Politics, bureaucracy and rural development in Senegal. Berkeley, [1975]. pp. 279. *bibliog.*

— Rural conditions.

SCHUMACHER (EDWARD JAY) Politics, bureaucracy and rural development in Senegal. Berkeley, [1975]. pp. 279. *bibliog.*

— Social policy.

SENEGAL. Secrétariat d'Etat auprès du Premier Ministre chargé du Plan. 1969. Réajustement du troisième plan quadriennal de développement économique et social, 1969-1973. Tome 1. [Dakar, 1969?]. fo. 148. *Xerox copy.*

SENEGAL. Secrétariat d'Etat auprès du Premier Ministre chargé du Plan. 1972. Communication au Conseil Supérieur du Plan sur les grandes orientations et les objectifs généraux par secteur du IVe plan. Dakar, 1972. fo. 64. *Xerox copy.*

SENEGAL. Secrétariat d'Etat auprès du Premier Ministre chargé du Plan. 1972. Communication au Conseil Supérieur du Plan sur les travaux de préparation du IVe plan. Dakar, 1972. fo. 38. *Xerox copy.*

SENEGALESE IN FRANCE.

N'DONGO (SALLY) Voyage forcé: itinéraire d'un militant. Paris, 1975. pp. 224.

SENEGAMBIA
— Economic history.

CURTIN (PHILIP DEARMOND) Economic change in precolonial Africa: Senegambia in the era of the slave trade. Madison, Wis., 1975. pp. 363.

SEPARATION OF POWERS
— France.

ANCEL (FRÉDÉRIC) Les incompatibilités parlementaires sous la Ve République. Paris, [1975]. pp. 136. *bibliog. (Paris. Université de Paris II. Travaux et Recherches. Série Science Politique. 4)*

SEPÚLVEDA (JUAN GINÉS DE).

HANKE (LEWIS ULYSSES) All mankind is one: a study of the disputation between Bartolomé de Las Casas and Juan Ginés de Sepúlveda in 1550 on the intellectual and religious capacity of the American Indians. Dekalb, Illinois, [1974]. pp. 205. *bibliog.*

SERBIA
— Boundaries.

DJORDJEVIĆ (DIMITRIJE) Izlazak Srbije na Jadransko More i Konferencija ambasadora u Londonu, 1912. Beograd, 1956. pp. 160. *bibliog. In Cyrillic.*

— Constitution.

USTAV Socijalističke Republike Srbije; Ustav Socijalističke Autonomne Pokrajine Vojvodine; Ustav Socijalističke Autonomne Pokrajine Kosova; sa ustavnim zakonima i registrima pojmova. Beograd, 1974. pp. 750. *In Cyrillic.*

— Foreign relations — France.

ALEKSIĆ-PEJKOVIĆ (LJILJANA) Odnosi Srbije sa Francuskom i Engleskom, 1903-1914; urednik Jorjo Tadić...; Les relations entre la Serbie, la France et l'Angleterre, 1903-1914. Beograd, 1965. pp. 961. *(Istorijski Institut. Jugoslovenske Zemlje u XX Veku. knj. 3) In Cyrillic.*

— — United Kingdom.

ALEKSIĆ-PEJKOVIĆ (LJILJANA) Odnosi Srbije sa Francuskom i Engleskom, 1903-1914; urednik Jorjo Tadić...; Les relations entre la Serbie, la France et l'Angleterre, 1903-1914. Beograd, 1965. pp. 961. *(Istorijski Institut. Jugoslovenske Zemlje u XX Veku. knj. 3) In Cyrillic.*

— History.

GERŠIĆ (GIGA) Posle pedeset godina: uspomene i refleksije o srpskom pokretu g. 1848. Zemun, 1912. pp. 169.

ŽIVANOVIĆ (ŽIVAN) Politička istorija Srbije u drugoj polovini devetnaestog veka. knj.1. Od Sveto-Andrejske Skupštine do proglasa nezavisnosti Srbije, 1858-1878. Beograd, 1923. pp. 394. *In Cyrillic.*

— Statistics.

SERBIA. Republički Zavod za Statistiku. 1965. Socijalistička Republika Srbija, 1959-1964: statistički podaci. Beograd, 1965. pp. 147. *In Cyrillic.*

SERENTE INDIANS.

NIMUENDAJÚ (CURT) The Šerente;...translated from the manuscript by Robert H. Lowie. Los Angeles, 1942 repr. 1967. pp. 106. *bibliog. (Frederick Webb Hodge Anniversary Publication Fund. Publications. vol. 4)*

SERFDOM
— Russia.

SEMENOV-TIAN-SHANSKII (PETR PETROVICH) Epokha osvobozhdeniia krest'ian v Rossii, 1857-1861 gg., v vospominaiiakh P.P. Semenova-Tian-Shanskogo. t.1. S.-Peterburg, 1911. pp. xv,440.

DVORIANSTVO i krepostnoi stroi Rossii XVI-XVIII vv.: sbornik statei, posviashchennyi pamiati Alekseia Andreevicha Novosel'skogo. Moskva, 1975. pp. 345.

KORETSKII (VADIM IVANOVICH) Formirovanie krepostnogo prava i pervaia krest'ianskaia voina v Rossii. Moskva, 1975. pp. 391.

— — Mordvinian Republic.

TIUGAEV (NIKOLAI FEDOROVICH) Krepostnaia derevnia Mordovii v kontse XVIII - pervoi polovine XIX veka. Saransk, 1975. pp. 256.

SERICULTURE
— India.

RESERVE BANK OF INDIA. Agricultural Credit Department. Report on financing the crash programme for the development of sericulture in Karnataka; [by B. Venkata Rao]. Bombay, 1974. pp. 132.

SERMONS, ENGLISH.

HUNT (WILLIAM HENRY) ed. Churchmanship and labour: sermons on social subjects preached at S. Stephen's Church, Walbrook, by H. Scott Holland [and others]. London, 1906. pp. 272.

SERVANTS
— France.

McBRIDE (THERESA M.) The domestic revolution: the modernisation of household service in England and France, 1820-1920. New York, 1976. pp. 160. *bibliog.*

— United Kingdom.

McBRIDE (THERESA M.) The domestic revolution: the modernisation of household service in England and France, 1820-1920. New York, 1976. pp. 160. *bibliog.*

SERVICE INDUSTRIES.

De TERTIAIRE sector: studie over de invloed der ontwikkeling op de vermindering van de omvang der economische fluctuaties; [by] Paul Bairoch [and others]; onder leiding van H. Vander Eycken, P. Frantzen. Bruxelles, [1970]. pp. 185. *(Brussels. Université Libre. Institut de Sociologie. Etudes d'Economie Politique.)*

FORWARD planning in the service sectors: [proceedings of a Science Policy Foundation symposium held in London in 1973]; edited by Maurice Goldsmith. London, 1975. pp. 165.

SABOLO (YVES) and others. The service industries. Geneva, International Labour Office, 1975. pp. 238. *bibliog.*

— **France.**

ORGANISATION D'ETUDES D'AMENAGEMENT DE L'AIRE METROPOLITAINE NANTES-SAINT-NAZAIRE. Schéma d'aménagement de l'aire métropolitaine [Nantes- Saint-Nazaire]: (annexe); développement tertiaire. Nantes, 1973. pp. 131. *bibliog.*

FRANCE. Institut National de la Statistique et des Etudes Economiques. 1974. Les entreprises et établissements industriels et commerciaux en France en 1971. [Paris], 1974. 3 vols. (in 1).

FRANCE. Commission du Commerce, des Services et de l'Artisanat. 1976. Rapport...: préparation du 7e Plan. Paris, 1976. pp. 156.

— **New Zealand.**

NEW ZEALAND. Department of Statistics. 1975- . Census of distribution, 1972-73: (statistical bulletins). Wellington, 1975 in progress.

— **Papua New Guinea.**

PAPUA NEW GUINEA. Bureau of Statistics. Statistical bulletin; survey of retail sales and selected services. a., 1967-68/1972-73- Port Moresby.

— **Portugal.**

RAMOS (ANTONIO BRITO) O emprego no sector terciario metropolitano: tentatiras de localização do crescimento. Lisboa, 1974. pp. 103. *(Portugal. Ministerio do Trabalho. Gabinete de Planeamento. Serie Estudos. 24)* With abstracts in English, French and German.

— **Russia.**

MANOKHIN (VASILII MIKHAILOVICH) Khoziaistvennoe obsluzhivanie organizatsii i grazhdan: organizatsionno-pravovye voprosy. Moskva, 1975. pp. 222.

— — **Mathematical models.**

PLANIROVANIE otraslei bytovogo obsluzhivaniia naseleniia. Moskva, 1974. pp. 303.

SET THEORY.

DRAKE (FRANK R.) Set theory: an introduction to large cardinals. Amsterdam, 1974. pp. 351. *bibliog.*

KAUFMANN (ARNOLD) Introduction to the theory of fuzzy subsets. volume 1. Fundamental theoretical elements. New York, 1975. pp. 416. *bibliog.*

SEVILLE (PROVINCE)

— **Economic history.**

BERNAL (ANTONIO MIGUEL) and DRAIN (MICHEL) Les campagnes sevillanes aux XIXe-XXe siècles: renovation ou stagnation?. [Paris], 1975. pp. 133. *(Madrid. Casa de Velázquez. Publications. Série "Recherches en Sciences Sociales". Fasc. 2)*

SEWAGE DISPOSAL

— **Canada — Quebec — Costs.**

TATE (DONALD M.) Economic and financial aspects of wastewater treatment in the Yamaska river basin, Quebec. Ottawa, 1972 [or rather 1973]. pp. 20. *(Canada. Inland Waters Directorate. Social Science Series. No. 3)*

SEWARD (WILLIAM HENRY).

FERRIS (NORMAN B.) Desperate diplomacy: William H. Seward's foreign policy, 1861. Knoxville, [1976]. pp. 265. *bibliog.*

SEWERAGE, RURAL

— **United States.**

WARNER (DENNIS) and DAJANI (JARIR S.) Water and sewer development in rural America: a study of community impacts. Lexington, Mass., [1975]. pp. 128. *bibliog.*

SEX.

ZINBERG (NORMAN E.) and others. Teaching social change: a group approach. Baltimore, Ma., [1976]. pp. 252. *bibliog.*

— **Comic books, strips, etc.**

CURTIS (SARAH) Don't rush me!: the comic-strip, sex education and a multi- racial society. London, Community Relations Commission, 1975. pp. 52.

— **Statistics.**

RETHERFORD (ROBERT D.) The changing sex differential in mortality. Westport, Conn., 1975. pp. 139. *bibliog.* *(California University. International Population and Urban Research. Studies in Population and Urban Demography. No. 1)*

SEX AND LAW.

KELLOGG (EDMUND H.) and others. The world's laws and practices on population and sexuality education. Medford, Mass., 1975. pp. 127. *(Tufts University. Fletcher School of Law and Diplomacy. Law and Population Monograph Series. No. 25)*

— **United Kingdom.**

NATIONAL COUNCIL FOR CIVIL LIBERTIES. Reports. No. 13. Sexual offences: evidence to the Criminal Law Revision Committee. London, 1976. pp. 23. *bibliog.*

SEX CUSTOMS.

CONFIGURATIONS: biological and cultural factors in sexuality and family life; edited by Raymond Prince [and] Dorothy Barrier. Lexington, Mass., [1974]. pp. 193. *bibliogs.* Papers of a conference held in Montreal, 1972, and sponsored by the Mental Hygiene Institute.

SHORTER (EDWARD) The making of the modern family. London, 1976. pp. 369. *bibliog.*

SEX DIFFERENCES.

PERCEIVING women; edited by Shirley Ardener. London, 1975. pp. 167. *bibliog.*

SEX DISCRIMINATION

— **Law and legislation — United Kingdom.**

U.K. Equal Opportunities Commission. 1975. Equal opportunities: a short guide to the Sex Discrimination Act, 1975. [London, 1975]. pp. (6).

U.K. Equal Opportunities Commission. 1975. Equal opportunities: housing, goods, facilities and services; Sex Discrimination Act, 1975. [London, 1975]. pp. (5).

U.K. Home Office. 1975. Sex discrimination: a guide to the Sex Discrimination Act, 1975. [London, 1975]. pp. 54.

WALKER (D.J.) Sex discrimination: a simple guide to the provisions of the Sex Discrimination Act 1975. London, 1975 repr. 1976. pp. 293.

SEX DISCRIMINATION AGAINST WOMEN

— **Law and legislation — United Kingdom.**

HEWITT (PATRICIA) Rights for women: a guide to the Sex Discrimination Act, the Equal Pay Act, paid maternity leave, pension schemes and unfair dismissal. London, [1975]. pp. 98.

— **America, Latin.**

SEX and class in Latin America; edited by June Nash and Helen Icken Safa. New York, 1976. pp. 330. *bibliogs.* Papers from a conference sponsored by American Council of Learned Societies and Social Science Research Council. Joint Committee on Latin American Studies.

— **United Kingdom.**

LISTER (RUTH) and WILSON (LEO) The unequal breadwinner: a new perspective on women and social security. London, [1976]. pp. 24.

SEX DISCRIMINATION IN EDUCATION

— **Law and legislation — United Kingdom.**

U.K. Equal Opportunities Commission. 1975. Equal opportunities: education; Sex Discrimination Act, 1975. [London, 1975]. pp. (6).

SEX DISCRIMINATION IN EMPLOYMENT

— **Law and legislation — United Kingdom.**

U.K. Equal Opportunities Commission. 1975. Equal opportunities: a guide for employees; Sex Discrimination Act, 1975. [London, 1975]. pp. 12.

U.K. Equal Opportunities Commission. 1975. Equal opportunities: a guide for employers; Sex Discrimination Act, 1975. [London, 1975]. pp. 11.

— — **United States.**

WOMEN in academia: evolving policies toward equal opportunities; edited by Elga Wasserman [and others]. New York, 1975. pp. 169. *bibliog.* Based on a symposium held at the 138th annual meeting of the American Association for the Advancement of Science in Philadelphia on December 30, 1971.

— — **United Kingdom.**

CHIPLIN (BRIAN) and SLOANE (PETER J.) Sex discrimination in the labour market. London, 1976. pp. 161.

SEX INSTRUCTION.

KELLOGG (EDMUND H.) and others. The world's laws and practices on population and sexuality education. Medford, Mass., 1975. pp. 127. *(Tufts University. Fletcher School of Law and Diplomacy. Law and Population Monograph Series. No. 25)*

CURTIS (SARAH) Don't rush me!: the comic-strip, sex education and a multi- racial society. London, Community Relations Commission, 1975. pp. 52.

— **United States.**

HOTTOIS (JAMES) and MILNER (NEAL A.) The sex education controversy: a study of politics, education, and morality. Lexington, [1975]. pp. 136.

SEX ROLE.

ANGRIST (SHIRLEY S.) and ALMQUIST (ELIZABETH M.) Careers and contingencies: how college women juggle with gender. New York, [1975]. pp. 269. *bibliog.*

MEDNICK (MARTHA TAMARA SHUCH) and others, eds. Women and achievement: social and motivational analyses. Washington, [1975]. pp. 447. *bibliogs.*

ADAMS (CAROL) and LAURIKIETIS (RAE) The gender trap: a closer look at sex roles. London, 1976 in progress.

BRITISH SOCIOLOGICAL ASSOCIATION. Annual Conference, 1974. Sexual divisions and society: process and change; [papers presented at the conference]; edited by Diana Leonard Barker and Sheila Allen. London, 1976. pp. 286. *bibliogs.* *(British Sociological Association. Explorations in Sociology. 6)*

SEXUAL BEHAVIOUR IN ANIMALS.

CONFIGURATIONS: biological and cultural factors in sexuality and family life; edited by Raymond Prince [and] Dorothy Barrier. Lexington, Mass., [1974]. pp. 193. *bibliogs.* Papers of a conference held in Montreal, 1972, and sponsored by the Mental Hygiene Institute.

SEXUAL ETHICS

— **Congresses.**

SEXUAL REFORM CONGRESS, 3RD, LONDON, 1929. Proceedings...; edited by Norman Haire. London, 1930. pp. 670. In English, French and German.

SEYCHELLES

SEYCHELLES
— Politics and government.

OSTHEIMER (JOHN M.) ed. The politics of the western Indian Ocean islands. New York, 1975. pp. 260. *bibliog.*

LEE (CHRISTOPHER) Seychelles: political castaways. London, 1976. pp. 169.

SEYDOUX (FRANÇOIS).

SEYDOUX (FRANÇOIS) Mémoires d'outre-Rhin. Paris, [1975]. pp. 309.

SHABA
— Politics and government.

SHABA. 1962. Livre blanc du gouvernement katangais sur les événements de septembre et décembre 1961: The Katangese government's white paper on the events of September and December, 1961. [Elisabethville?, 1962]. pp. 111. *In French and English.*

BUSTIN (EDOUARD) Lunda under Belgium rule: the politics of ethnicity. Cambridge, Mass., 1975. pp. 303. *bibliog.*

SHAW (GEORGE BERNARD).

EVANS (THOMAS FRANCIS) ed. Shaw: the critical heritage. London, 1976. pp. 422. *bibliog. Consists of review articles, comments in the letters of contemporaries, and obituary notices.*

SHEEP
— Australia.

AUSTRALIA. Bureau of Agricultural Economics. 1971. A study of supply relationships in the Australian sheep and wool industry; (by J.M. Malecky). Canberra, 1971. pp. 98. *(Wool Economic Research Reports. No. 19)*

— Canada.

ALLEN (W.L.) Sheep raising in Canada. Ottawa, 1969. pp. 55. *(Canada. Department of Agriculture. Publications. 1401)*

— United Kingdom.

U.K. Ministry of Agriculture, Fisheries and Food. Fat sheep guarantee scheme. a., 1976/77 [1st]- London. *Supersedes U.K. Ministry of Agriculture, Fisheries and Food, and others. Fatstock guarantee scheme.*

WHETHAM (EDITH H.) Beef cattle and sheep, 1910-1940: a description of the production and marketing of beef cattle and sheep in Great Britain from the early 20th century to the Second World War. Cambridge, 1976. pp. 59. *bibliog. (Cambridge. University. Department of Land Economy. Occasional Papers. No.5)*

SHEEP RANCHES
— Australia.

AUSTRALIA. Bureau of Agricultural Economics. 1969. An economic survey of drought affected pastoral properties, New South Wales and Queensland, 1964-65 to 1965-66; (by E.S. Malikides and others). Canberra, 1969. pp. 51. *(Wool Economic Research Reports. No. 15)*

SHEFFIELD
— Social conditions.

BALDWIN (JOHN) Ph.D., and BOTTOMS (A.E.) The urban criminal: a study in Sheffield;...in collaboration with Monica A. Walker. London, 1976. pp. 262. *bibliog.*

SHETLAND ISLANDS
— Economic conditions.

NICOLSON (JAMES R.) Shetland and oil. London, [1975]. pp. 208. *bibliog.*

SHEVCHENKO (TARAS GRIGOR'EVICH).

CHERNYSHEVSKAIA (NINA MIKHAILOVNA) N.G. Chernyshevskii i T.G. Shevchenko: vospominaniia, zametki, materialy; (poslеslovie E.S. Shablinskogo). Kiev, 1974. pp. 136.

SHABLIOVSKII (EVGENII STEPANOVICH) T.G. Shevchenko i russkie revoliutsionnye demokraty. 2nd ed. Kiev, 1975. pp. 391. *1st Ukrainian ed. dates from 1935. This ed. is a revision of 1st Russian ed. of 1962.*

SHIPBUILDING
— Russia — Estonia.

KARMA (O.) and SKOROKHOD (A.) Trudnaia sud'ba: kratkaia istoriia Russko-Baltiiskogo sudostroitel'nogo zavoda. Tallin, 1971. pp. 62.

— United Kingdom — Ireland, Northern.

IRELAND, NORTHERN. Department of Commerce. 1975. Harland and Wolff Limited, Belfast: copy of an information document made available to members of both Houses of Parliament prior to debate on the Shipbuilding Industry, No. 2, Northern Ireland, Order 1975. Belfast, [1975]. pp. 15.

SHIPBUILDING WORKERS
— Hong Kong.

HONG KONG. Shipbuilding and Ship Repairs Industrial Committee. 1974. Minimum job standards and specifications for the principal jobs in the shipbuilding and ship repairs industry. Hong Kong, 1973 [or rather 1974]. pp. 88. *In English and Chinese.*

— United Kingdom.

DOUGAN (DAVID) The shipwrights: the history of the Shipconstructors' and Shipwrights' Association, 1882-1963. Newcastle upon Tyne, 1975. pp. 341. *bibliog.*

SHIPPING
— Finland.

FINLAND. Tilastokeskus. Kauppamerenkulum sekä huolinta- ja ahtaustoiminnan tasetilasto...3 statistics of profit ad loss and balance sheet accounts of sea transport, stevedoring and forwarding. a., 1971/72- Helsinki. *In Finnish with English summary and table headings.*

— France.

FRANCE. Département des a Statistiques des Transports. Enquête annuelle d'entreprise: auxiliaires des transports maritimes. a., 1973[1st]- Paris.

FRANCE. Direction des Ports Maritimes et des Voies Navigables. Rapport d'activité. a., 1973- Paris.

— Germany — Schleswig-Holstein.

FLENSBURG. Industrie- und Handelskammer. Schiffahrt und Häfen im Bereich der Industrie- und Handelskammer zu Flensburg; herausgegeben anlässlich ihres 100jährigen Jubiläums...; (Autoren: Gerd Andresen [and others]). Flensburg, [1971]. pp. 358. *bibliog.*

— Netherlands.

NETHERLANDS. Centraal Bureau voor de Statistiek. Statistiek van de koopvaardijvloot: (Statistics of the merchant marine). a., 1976- s'-Gravenhage.

— Tasmania.

TASMANIA. Commonwealth Bureau of Census and Statistics. Tasmanian Office. Trade and shipping. a., 1969/70- Hobart.

— United Kingdom.

GARDINER (DOROTHY M.) A calendar of early Chancery proceedings relating to West Country shipping, 1388-1493. [Exeter], 1976. pp. 131. *(Devon and Cornwall Record Society. [Publications]. New Series. vol. 21)*

— — Scotland.

VAMPLEN (WRAY) Salvesen of Leith. Edinburgh, 1975. pp. 311.

SHIPS
— Cargo.

INTER-GOVERNMENTAL MARITIME CONSULTATIVE ORGANIZATION. 1972- . International Maritime Dangerous Goods Code; (with Supplements). London, 1972 in progress. *List of old IMCO Code page numbers with corresponding new IMCO Code page numbers and UN numbers is bound with the original volume of this set.*

— Maintenance and repair.

HONG KONG. Shipbuilding and Ship Repairs Industrial Committee. 1974. Minimum job standards and specifications for the principal jobs in the shipbuilding and ship repairs industry. Hong Kong, 1973 [or rather 1974]. pp. 88. *In English and Chinese.*

— Safety regulations — United Kingdom.

PETERS (Rev. GEORGE H.) The Plimsoll line: the story of Samuel Plimsoll, Member of Parliament for Derby from 1868-1880. Chichester, [1975]. pp. 203. *bibliog.*

SHOP STEWARDS
— United Kingdom.

GREGORY (DENIS) and McCARTY (JOE) The shop steward's guide to workplace health and safety: a critical analysis of industry's health and safety problems and the Health and Safety at Work Act 1974: implications and suggestions for trade union action. Nottingham, 1975. pp. 69.

SHOPPING
— Bibliography.

MURRAY (NICK) compiler. Shopping in urban areas. London, 1975. pp. 29. *(London. Greater London Council. Research Library. [Research] Bibliographies. No. 71)*

SHOPPING CENTRES
— France.

BUREAU D'ETUDES TECHNIQUES DE L'URBANISME ET DE L'EQUIPEMENT. Grandes surfaces commerciales périphériques: éléments d'information pour les responsables de l'aménagement urbain, septembre 1974; [by A. Fournie and others]. Paris, 1975. pp. 139.

— United Kingdom.

HALL (BRYAN D.) Analysis of the results of a survey of shoppers in South Hampshire. [Winchester], 1969. 1 vol. (unpaged). *(South Hampshire Plan Technical Unit. Working Papers. 8)*

RHODES (TIM) Factors affecting the future location of new shopping developments in South Hampshire. [Winchester], 1972. pp. 15. *(South Hampshire Plan Technical Unit. Working Papers. 5)*

SHOPPING MALLS
— Bibliography.

GOMERSALL (ALAN) compiler. Pedestrianisation. London, 1975. pp. 15. *(London. Greater London Council. Research Library. [Research] Bibliographies. No. 66)*

— United Kingdom.

MYATT (PETER R.) Carnaby Street study. London, [1975]. pp. 57. *(London. Greater London Council. Research Memoranda. 466)*

SHROPSHIRE
— Economic history.

BROWN (IVOR J.) The mines of Shropshire. [Stafford, 1976]. pp. 112. *bibliog.*

SIBERIA

— Economic conditions.

SHNIPER (RUVIN ISAKOVICH) and DENISOVA (LILIIA PETROVNA) eds. Mezhotraslevye sviazi i narodnokhoziaistvennye proportsii Vostochnoi Sibiri i Dal'nego Vostoka. Novosibirsk, 1974. pp. 315.

— Economic history.

KOMOROWSKI (WŁADYSŁAW) Syberja jako czynnik gospodarstwa światowego. Warszawa, 1936. pp. 492. *bibliog.*

NEKOTORYE voprosy sotsialisticheskogo stroitel'stva i formirovaniia rabochego klassa SSSR v predvoennye gody. Murmansk, 1971. pp. 250. *(Leningrad. Leningradskii Gosudarstvennyi Pedagogicheskii Institut. Uchenye Zapiski. t.329)*

RABOCHII klass i krest'ianstvo natsional'nykh raionov Sibiri. Novosibirsk, 1974. pp. 174.

RABINOVICH (GRIGORII KHATSKEL'EVICH) Krupnaia burzhuaziia i monopolisticheskii kapital v ekonomike Sibiri kontsa XIX - nachala XX vv. Tomsk, 1975. pp. 328.

— Foreign economic relations.

KOMOROWSKI (WŁADYSŁAW) Syberja jako czynnik gospodarstwa światowego. Warszawa, 1936. pp. 492. *bibliog.*

— History.

SHUNKOV (VIKTOR IVANOVICH) Voprosy agrarnoi istorii Rossii; (redkollegiia A.P. Okladnikov [and others]). Moskva, 1974. pp. 376. *Selected works.*

— Industries.

MOSKOVSKII (ALEKSEI STEPANOVICH) Promyshlennoe osvoenie Sibiri v period stroitel'stva sotsializma, 1917-1937 gg.: istoriko-ekonomicheskii ocherk. Novosibirsk, 1975. pp. 263.

— Politics and government.

LENINSKAIA "Iskra" o Sibiri, dekabr' 1900 - oktiabr' 1903 gg.: sbornik dokumental'nykh materialov. Novosibirsk, 1970. pp. 174.

— Social life and customs.

GROMYKO (MARINA MIKHAILOVNA) Trudovye traditsii russkikh krest'ian Sibiri, XVIII - pervaia polovina XIX v. Novosibirsk, 1975. pp. 351.

SICILY

— Commerce.

BANCO DI SICILIA. Servizio Studi. 50 anni di commercio estero della Sicilia, 1924-1973. Palermo, [1976]. pp. 410.

— Economic conditions.

SCHNEIDER (JANE) and SCHNEIDER (PETER) of Fordham University, New York. Culture and political economy in western Sicily. New York, [1976]. pp. 256. *bibliog.*

— Economic history.

BAVIERA ALBANESE (ADELAIDE) In Sicilia nel sec.XVI: verso una rivoluzione industriale?. Caltanissetta, 1974. pp. 265. *(Unione delle Camere di Commercio, Industria, Artigianato ed Agricoltura della Regione Siciliana. Storia Economica di Sicilia. Testi e Ricerche. 19-20)*

CANCILA (ORAZIO) Gabelloti e contadini in un comune rurale, secc. XVIII-XIX. Caltanissetta, 1974. pp. 219. *(Unione delle Camere di Commercio, Industria, Artigianato ed Agricoltura della Regione Siciliana. Storia Economica di Sicilia. Testi e Ricerche. 21-22)*

— Industries.

BAVIERA ALBANESE (ADELAIDE) In Sicilia nel sec.XVI: verso una rivoluzione industriale?. Caltanissetta, 1974. pp. 265. *(Unione delle Camere di Commercio, Industria, Artigianato ed Agricoltura della Regione Siciliana. Storia Economica di Sicilia. Testi e Ricerche. 19-20)*

— Social conditions.

GIORDANO (CHRISTIAN) and HETTLAGE (ROBERT) Mobilisierung oder Scheinmobilisierung?: Genossenschaften und traditionelle Sozialstruktur am Beispiel Siziliens; mit einer Einführung von Paul Trappe: Aspekte der Massenmobilisierung. Basel, 1975. pp. 103. *bibliogs. (Basel. Universität. Soziologisches Seminar. Social Strategies. vol.1)*

SCHNEIDER (JANE) and SCHNEIDER (PETER) of Fordham University, New York. Culture and political economy in western Sicily. New York, [1976]. pp. 256. *bibliog.*

SICK.

FORGES (JEAN MICHEL DE) L'hospitalisé. Paris, 1975. pp. 316.

SIDI LAHCEN.

RABINOW (PAUL) Symbolic domination: cultural form and historical change in Morocco. Chicago, 1975. pp. 107.

SIERRA LEONE

— Armed forces — Political activity.

COX (THOMAS S.) Civil-military relations in Sierra Leone: a case study of African soldiers in politics. Cambridge, Mass., 1976. pp. 271. *bibliog.*

— Army.

SIERRA LEONE. Ministry of Information and Broadcasting. 1965. Sierra Leone today: unity, freedom, justice. Freetown, 1965. pp. 30.

— Commercial treaties — Liberia.

LIBERIA. Treaties. 1973-74. Mano River Declaration, signed in Malema, 3 October, 1973; and protocols to the Declaration, signed in Bo, 3 October, 1974. [Monrovia, 1975]. fo. 14. *Xerox copy.*

— Economic conditions.

SIERRA LEONE. Ministry of Development. 1963. The first year: a progress report on the ten-year plan. [Freetown, 1963]. pp. 14.

— Economic history.

LAAN (H.L. VAN DER) The Lebanese traders in Sierra Leone. The Hague, [1975]. pp. 385. *bibliog. (Afrika-Studiecentrum. Change and Continuity in Africa)*

— Economic policy.

SIERRA LEONE. National Reformation Council. 1968. The state of the nation: address delivered by the Chairman, National Reformation Council, Brigadier A.T. Juxon-Smith, on the occasion of the opening session of the Civilian Rule Committee..., 2st February, 1968. [Freetown, 1968]. pp. 10.

— Emigration and immigration.

SIERRA LEONE. Wales Commission of Inquiry into the Conduct of the Immigration Quota Committee from 1st January, 1961 to 23rd March, 1967. 1969. Report...amd government statement thereon; [J.G. Wales, commissioner]. [Freetown, 1969?]. pp. 52.

— Executive departments.

SIERRA LEONE. Commission appointed to inquire into the Activities of the Posts and Telecommunications Department from 1st January, 1961. 1972. Report...and the government statement thereon; [Percy R. Davies, Commissioner]. [Freetown?, 1972]. pp. 85.

— Politics and government.

SIERRA LEONE. 1966. Government white paper on the proposed introduction of a democratic one party system in Sierra Leone. [Freetown, 1966]. pp. (2).

SIERRA LEONE. National Reformation Council. 1968. The state of the nation: address delivered by the Chairman, National Reformation Council, Brigadier A.T. Juxon-Smith, on the occasion of the opening session of the Civilian Rule Committee..., 2st February, 1968. [Freetown, 1968]. pp. 10.

BARROWS (WALTER L.) Grassroots politics in an African state: integration and development in Sierra Leone. New York, 1976. pp. 265.

CLAPHAM (CHRISTOPHER) Liberia and Sierra Leone: an essay in comparative politics. Cambridge, 1976. pp. 156. *bibliog. (Cambridge. University. African Studies Centre. African Studies Series. 20)*

COX (THOMAS S.) Civil-military relations in Sierra Leone: a case study of African soldiers in politics. Cambridge, Mass., 1976. pp. 271. *bibliog.*

— Social conditions.

SIERRA LEONE. Ministry of Development. 1963. The first year: a progress report on the ten-year plan. [Freetown, 1963]. pp. 14.

SIGNS AND SYMBOLS

— Germany.

MOSSE (GEORGE L.) The nationalization of the masses: political symbolism and mass movements in Germany from the Napoleonic wars through the Third Reich. New York, 1975. pp. 252.

SILESIA

— Economic conditions.

RAUZIŃSKI (ROBERT) Czynnik ludzki w gospodarce Śląska Opolskiego w latach 1950- 1990. Wrocław, 1975. pp. 146. *bibliog. (Opole. Opolskie Towarzystwo Przyjaciół Nauk. Wydział Nauk Historyczno-Społecznych. Prace)*

— History — 1919-1922, Partition

COMITE REPRESENTANT LES PARTIS ALLEMANDS DU TERRITOIRE INDUSTRIEL DE LA MORAVIE ET SILESIE DE L'EST. Mémoire concernant la future organisation politique du territoire industriel de la Moravie et Silésie de l'Est. Teschen, [1919?]. pp. 27.

— Politics and government.

HAWRANEK (FRANCISZEK) Ruch robotniczy na Śląsku Opolskim w latach 1918-1944. Chorzów, 1974. pp. 136. *bibliog.*

PAŹDZIORA (MAREK) Górnośląska Narodowa Partia Robotnicza po zamachu majowym, 1926-1937. Katowice, 1975. pp. 264. *bibliog.*

BIAŁY (FRANCISZEK) Niemieckie ochotnicze formacje zbrojne na Śląsku, 1918-1923. Katowice, 1976. pp. 210. *bibliog.*

— Population.

RAUZIŃSKI (ROBERT) Czynnik ludzki w gospodarce Śląska Opolskiego w latach 1950- 1990. Wrocław, 1975. pp. 146. *bibliog. (Opole. Opolskie Towarzystwo Przyjaciół Nauk. Wydział Nauk Historyczno-Społecznych. Prace)*

SILESIAN PERIODICALS.

MAREK (FRANCISZEK ANTONI) Najdawniejsze czasopisma polskie na Śląsku, 1789-1854. Wrocław, 1972. pp. 319. *With English, French, German and Russian summaries.*

SILK MANUFACTURE AND TRADE

SILK MANUFACTURE AND TRADE
— Switzerland.

USTERI (EMIL) Die Webereien der Familie Näf von Kappel und Zürich, 1846-1946: (Festschrift zur Hundertjahr-Feier der Seidenstoffwebereien vormals Gebrüder Näf A.G.und der Seidenwarenfabrik vormals Edwin Naef A.G.). [Zurich], 1946. pp. 323. bibliogs. Table in end pocket.

SIMULATION METHODS.

CONRAD (KLAUS) of the University of Tübingen. Simulation und Optimierung mit einem nichtlinearen ökonometrischen Makromodell für die Bundesrepublik Deutschland. Meisenheim am Glan, 1975. pp. 398. bibliog.

BLOOM (PAUL N.) Advertising, competition, and public policy: a simulation study. Cambridge, Mass., [1976]. pp. 203.

HURRION (ROBERT DONALD) The design, use and required facilities of an interactive visual computer simulation language to explore production planning problems. 1976. pp. 232. bibliog. Typescript. Ph.D. (London) thesis: unpublished. This thesis is the property of London University and may not be removed from the Library.

SINGAPORE
— Civic improvement.

PLANNING in Singapore: selected aspects and issues; edited by Chua Peng Chye. Singapore, 1973. pp. 114. bibliogs. "Based on a series of public lectures organised by the Singapore Institute of Planners...during the months of September to December, 1972".

— Economic conditions.

SINGAPORE. Economic Development Board. Annual report. a., 1970- Singapore.

— Economic policy.

SINGAPORE. Ministry of Culture. Publicity Division. 1962. Year of fulfilment: June 1961-June 1962. Singapore, [1962]. pp. (47).

— Executive departments.

SINGAPORE. Economic Development Board. Annual report. a., 1970- Singapore.

— Government publications — Bibliography.

SINGAPORE. National Statistical Commission. An annotated bibliography of statistical publications. a., 1973- Singapore.

— Moral conditions.

SEMINAR ON NATIONAL VALUES OF SINGAPORE FOR PRE-UNIVERSITY STUDENTS, SINGAPORE, 1974. National values of Singapore. Singapore, Ministry of Education, 1974. pp. 84.

— Politics and government.

SINGAPORE. Ministry of Culture. Publicity Division. 1962. Year of fulfilment: June 1961-June 1962. Singapore, [1962]. pp. (47).

— Population.

SAW (SWEE HOCK) Estimates of population and labour force by age group for West Malaysia and Singapore, 1958-1967. Hong Kong, 1971. pp. 38. (Hong Kong. University. Centre of Asian Studies. Occasional Papers and Monographs. No. 6)

WAN (FOOK KEE) Population growth and ecology with reference to Singapore: a country paper prepared for the Regional Seminar on Ecological Implications of Rural and Urban Population Growth, E[conomic] C[ommission for] A[sia and the] F[ar E[ast], Bangkok, 25 August to 3 September, 1971. Singapore, Family Planning and Population Board, [1971]. fo. 7. (FPPB Papers. No. 11)

SAW (SWEE HOCK) Population projections for Singapore, 1970-2070. Singapore, National Statistical Commission, 1974. fo. 15.

— Social policy.

SINGAPORE. Ministry of Culture. Publicity Division. 1962. Year of fulfilment: June 1961-June 1962. Singapore, [1962]. pp. (47).

— Statistical services.

SINGAPORE. National Statistical Commission. Annual report. a., 1973 (2nd)- Singapore.

— Statistics — Bibliography.

SINGAPORE. National Statistical Commission. An annotated bibliography of statistical publications. a., 1973- Singapore.

SINGLE PARENT FAMILY.

FERRI (ELSA) Growing up in a one-parent family: a long-term study of child development. Windsor, Berks., 1976. pp. 196. bibliog.

— United Kingdom.

FERRI (ELSA) and ROBINSON (HILARY) Coping alone. London, 1976. pp. 80. (National Children's Bureau. Reports)

TUNNARD (JO) No father, no home?: a study of 30 fatherless families in mortgaged homes. London, 1976. pp. 43. (Child Poverty Action Group. Poverty Pamphlets. 28)

SINGLE PEOPLE
— Dwellings — United Kingdom.

WORKING PARTY ON THE PROVISION OF ACCOMMODATION FOR SINGLE PEOPLE. Interim report; [S. Woolf, chairman]. [London], Greater London Council, 1975. pp. 23. bibliog.

SINGLE TAX.

The FOUNDATIONS of freedom: the land and the people; a series of essays on the taxation of land values. Middleton, 1912. pp. 160.

SIQINIQMIUT (ESKIMO TRIBE).

RICHES (DAVID JOHN) A study of social change amongst the Killinirngmiut Eskimo of Canada's East Arctic; [Ph. D. (London) thesis]. 1975. fo. 410. bibliog. Typescript: unpublished. This thesis is the property of London University and may not be removed from the Library. Killinirngmiut spelt Killiniqmiut throughout the text.

SISTERHOODS.

JONES (SUZANNE ALICE CAMPBELL) Stability and change in religious communities: a sociological study of two congregations of Roman Catholic sisters. [1976]. fo. 348. Typescript. Ph.D. (London) thesis: unpublished. This thesis is the property of London University and may not be removed from the Library.

SIT DOWN STRIKES
— United Kingdom.

TRANSPORT AND GENERAL WORKERS' UNION. Why Imperial Typewriters must not close: the case for government aid to maintain production, and/or to establish a cooperative to assume ownership and management of the plant; a preliminary statement. Nottingham, [1975]. pp. 16. (Institute for Workers' Control. Pamphlet Series. No. 46)

SKILLED LABOUR
— France.

MOSS (BERNARD H.) The origins of the French labor movement, 1830-1914: the socialism of skilled workers. Berkeley, Calif., [1976]. pp. 217. bibliog.

— Romania.

PERȚ (STELIANA) Cu privire la contribuția formării profesionale a forței de muncă la creșterea economică. București, 1974. pp. 265. bibliog. (Academia de Științe Sociale și Politice a Republicii Socialiste România. Institutul de Cercetări Economice. Bibliotheca Oeconomica. 30) With English summary and English and French tables of contents.

— Russia — Georgia.

KINKADZE (TAT'IANA VLADIMIROVNA) Konkretno-sotsiologicheskoe izuchenie protsessa professional'nykh izmenenii v sostave rabochikh kadrov Rustavskogo metallurgicheskogo zavoda. Tbilisi, 1973. pp. 126. bibliog.

— — Ukraine.

LOBURETS' (VASYL' IEHOROVYCH) Formuvannia kadriv radians'koho robitnychoho klasu Ukraïny, 1921-1932 rr. Kharkiv, 1974. pp. 158. bibliog.

SKYE
— Economic conditions.

BROWNRIGG (MARK) and GREIG (MICHAEL A.) The economic impact of tourist spending in Skye. [Inverness, Highlands and Islands Development Board], 1974. pp. 62. (Special Reports. 13)

SLATE INDUSTRY
— United Kingdom.

ASTON (MICHAEL) Stonesfield slate. [Oxford], 1974. pp. 85. (Oxfordshire. Department of Museum Services. Publications. No.5)

GEDDES (R. STANLEY) Burlington blue-grey: a history of the slate quarries, Kirkby-in- Furness. Kirkby-in-Furness, Cumbria, 1975. pp. 320.

SLAVE TRADE.

RACE and slavery in the western hemisphere: quantitative studies; edited by Stanley L. Engerman and Eugene D. Genovese. Princeton, N.J., [1975]. pp. 556. (Mathematical Social Science Board. History Advisory Committee. Quantitative Studies in History). Papers of a conference sponsored by the History Advisory Committee and held at the University of Rochester in 1972.

— Africa.

MIERS (SUZANNE) Britain and the ending of the slave trade. London, 1975. pp. 405. bibliog.

— Africa, East.

BEACHEY (RAYMOND WENDELL) The slave trade of eastern Africa. London, 1976. pp. 324. bibliog.

BEACHEY (RAYMOND WENDELL) compiler. A collection of documents on the slave trade of eastern Africa. London, 1976. pp. 140.

SLAVERY
— Emancipation.

MIERS (SUZANNE) Britain and the ending of the slave trade. London, 1975. pp. 405. bibliog.

SLAVERY IN AMERICA.

RACE and slavery in the western hemisphere: quantitative studies; edited by Stanley L. Engerman and Eugene D. Genovese. Princeton, N.J., [1975]. pp. 556. (Mathematical Social Science Board. History Advisory Committee. Quantitative Studies in History). Papers of a conference sponsored by the History Advisory Committee and held at the University of Rochester in 1972.

SLAVERY IN CUBA.

KIPLE (KENNETH F.) Blacks in colonial Cuba, 1774-1899. Gainesville, Fla., 1976. pp. 115. bibliog. (Florida University. School of Inter-American Studies. Latin American Monographs. 2nd Series. No. 17)

SLAVERY IN LATIN AMERICA.

KNIGHT (FRANKLIN W.) The African dimension in Latin American societies. New York, 1974. pp. 148. *bibliog.*

MELLAFE (ROLANDO) Negro slavery in Latin America;...translated by J.W.S. Judge. Berkeley, [1975]. pp. 172. *bibliog.*

SLAVERY IN MEXICO.

PALMER (COLIN A.) Slaves of the White God: blacks in Mexico, 1570-1650. Cambridge, Mass., 1976. pp. 234. *bibliog.*

SLAVERY IN THE CARIBBEAN AREA.

MINTZ (SIDNEY WILFRED) Caribbean transformations. Chicago, 1974. pp. 355. *bibliog.*

SLAVERY IN THE UNITED KINGDOM

— Antislavery movements.

DAVIS (DAVID BRION) The problem of slavery in the age of revolution, 1770-1823. Ithaca, 1975. pp. 576.

SLAVERY IN THE UNITED STATES.

RAWICK (GEORGE P.) From sundown to sunup: the making of the black community. Westport, Conn., 1972 repr. 1973. pp. 208. *bibliog. (The American slave: a composite autobiography. vol. 1)*

McMANUS (EDGAR J.) Black bondage in the North. Syracuse, 1973. pp. 236. *bibliog.*

MILLER (ELINOR) and GENOVESE (EUGENE D.) eds. Plantation, town, and country: essays on the local history of American slave society. Urbana, Ill., [1974]. pp. 457.

GENOVESE (EUGENE D.) Roll, Jordan, roll: the world the slaves made. London, 1975. pp. 823.

SEAGRAVE (CHARLES EDWIN) The southern negro agricultural worker, 1850-1870. New York, 1975. pp. 119. *bibliog.* Ph. D. dissertation-Stanford University, 1971.

TURNER (ROBERT PHILLIP) Up to the front of the line: blacks in the American political system. Port Washington, N.Y., 1975. pp. 225. *bibliog.*

GOLDIN (CLAUDIA DALE) Urban slavery in the American south, 1820-1860: a quantitative history. Chicago, 1976. pp. 168. *bibliog.*

ROSE (WILLIE LEE) ed. A documentary history of slavery in North America. New York, 1976. pp. 537. *bibliog.* With commentary.

— Antislavery movements.

DICK (ROBERT C.) Black protest: issues and tactics. Westport, Conn., 1974. pp. 338. *bibliog.*

DAVIS (DAVID BRION) The problem of slavery in the age of revolution, 1770-1823. Ithaca, 1975. pp. 576.

DEGLER (CARL N.) The other South: southern dissenters in the nineteenth century. New York, 1975. pp. 392. *bibliog.*

— Emancipation.

GERTEIS (LOUIS S.) From contraband to freedman: federal policy toward Southern blacks, 1861-1865. Westport, Conn., 1973. pp. 255. *bibliog.*

SLAVERY IN THE WEST INDIES

— Emancipation.

GREEN (WILLIAM A.) British slave emancipation: the sugar colonies and the great experiment, 1830-1865. Oxford, 1976. pp. 449. *bibliog.*

SLAVOPHILISM.

WALICKI (ANDRZEJ) The Slavophile controversy: history of a conservative utopia in nineteenth-century Russian thought. London, 1975. pp. 609.

SLAVS.

ZARUBEZHNYE slaviane i Rossiia. Moskva, 1975 in progress.

SLOVAKIA

— History.

ZA nové Československo: materiály z celoštátnej vedeckej konferencie k 25. výročiu osłobodenia Československa, ktorú usporiadal Ústav marxizmu-leninizmu ÚV KSS v Bratislave, 27., 28. a 29. apríla 1970. Bratislava, 1972. pp. 270. *(Komunistická Strana Slovenska. Ústredný Výbor. Ústav Marxizmu-Leninizmu. roč. 12, č. 1)*

— Learned institutions and societies.

WINKLER (TOMÁŠ) Matica slovenská v rokoch 1919-1945: z problémov a dokumentov ústredia MS. Martin, 1971. pp. 396.

— Politics and government.

ZA nové Československo: materiály z celoštátnej vedeckej konferencie k 25. výročiu osłobodenia Československa, ktorú usporiadal Ústav marxizmu-leninizmu ÚV KSS v Bratislave, 27., 28. a 29. apríla 1970. Bratislava, 1972. pp. 270. *(Komunistická Strana Slovenska. Ústredný Výbor. Ústav Marxizmu-Leninizmu. roč. 12, č. 1)*

SLOVENES IN CARINTHIA.

EINSPIELER (VALENTIN) Verhandlungen über die der slowenischen Minderheit angebotene Kulturautonomie, 1925-1930. Klagenfurt, 1976. pp. 171. *bibliog.*

SLUMS

— Brazil — Rio de Janeiro.

PERLMAN (JANICE E.) The myth of marginality: urban poverty and politics in Rio de Janeiro. Berkeley, [1976]. pp. 341. *bibliog.*

— Denmark — Copenhagen.

PLOVSING (JAN) Sanering på Nørrebro, etc. København, 1975. pp. 286. *bibliog. (Socialforskningsinstituttet. Publikationer. 65)* With English summaries.

— India.

MISHRA (VISHWA MOHAN) Communication and modernization in urban slums. New York, [1972]. pp. 128. *bibliog.*

— — Madras (City).

WIEBE (PAUL D.) Social life in an Indian slum. Delhi, [1975]. pp. 179. *bibliog.*

— Philippine Islands.

JOCANO (F. LANDA) Slum as a way of life: a study of coping behavior in an urban environment. Quezon City, 1975. pp. 203.

— Puerto Rico — San Juan.

FERRACUTI (FRANCO) and others. Delinquents and nondelinquents in the Puerto Rican slum culture. Columbus, Oh., [1975]. pp. 249. *bibliog.*

— United Kingdom.

CONQUEST (JOAN) The naked truth: shocking revelations about the slums; by an ex- nursing sister. London, 1933. pp. 158.

— United States — Wisconsin.

TAMNEY (JOSEPH B.) Solidarity in a slum. New York, [1975]. pp. 182. *bibliog.*

SMALL BUSINESS

— Finance.

BATES (JAMES A.) The financing of small business. 2nd ed. London, 1971. pp. 193.

— France.

PARTI COMMUNISTE FRANÇAIS. Artisans, commerçants: comment se defendre. Paris, [1954]. pp. 31.

CHATAIN (JEAN) and GAUDON (ROGER) Petites et moyennes entreprises: l'heure du choix. Paris, [1975]. pp. 157. *bibliog.*

— Italy.

FEDERAZIONE LAVORATORI METALMECCANICI. [Segreteria Provinciale di Bergamo]. Sindacato e piccola impresa: strategia del capitale e azione sindacale nel decentramento produttivo. Bari, [1975]. pp. 237.

La PICCOLA e media industria nella crisi dell'economia italiana: atti del convegno tenuto a Milano 4-5-6 novembre 1974; a cura di Carlo Catena. Roma, 1975. 2 vols. *(Istituto Gramsci. Atti)*

— Netherlands.

RAAD VOOR HET MIDDEN- EN KLEINBEDRIJF. Documentatie inkomenspositie en -ontwikkeling van werknemers en zelfstandigen in het midden- en kleinbedrijf. 's-Gravenhage, 1971. PP. 25. *(?pUBLIKATIES!. 1971, NO. 1)*

RAAD VOOR HET MIDDEN- EN KLEINBEDRIJF. Interimrapport: de gevolgen van stadsvernieuwing voor het midden- en kleinbedrijf: een overzicht van zich voordoende knelpunten. 's-Gravenhage, 1974. pp. 40. *([Publikaties]. 1974, no. 1)*

RAAD VOOR HET MIDDEN- EN KLEINBEDRIJF. Enige korte adviezen en notities II. 's-Gravenhage, 1975. pp. 70. *([Publikaties]. 1975, no. 2)*

RAAD VOOR HET MIDDEN- EN KLEINBEDRIJF. Rapport: de participatie van het midden- en kleinbedrijf in het stadsvernieuwingsproces. 's-Gravenhage, 1976. pp. 26. *bibliog. ([Publikaties]. 1976, no.1)*

— — Finance.

RAAD VOOR HET MIDDEN- EN KLEINBEDRIJF. Rapport bedrijfseconomische normen inzake de continuïtet van ondernemingen. 's-Gravenhage, 1973. pp. 39. *([Publikaties]. 1973, no. 1)*

RAAD VOOR HET MIDDEN- EN KLEINBEDRIJF. Advies inzake het rapport garantiekredietverlening aan het midden- en kleinbedrijf. 's-Gravenhage, 1974. pp. 18. *([Publikaties]. 1974, no. 3)*

— — Information services.

NETHERLANDS. Commissie Bedrijfsvoorlichting. 1971. Individuele bedrijfsvoorlichting midden- en kleinbedrijf. [The Hague, 1971]. pp. 24.

NETHERLANDS. Commissie Bedrijfsvoorlichting. 1972. Rapport-Kreiken: bedrijfsvoorlichting. [The Hague, 1972]. pp. 24.

— Nigeria.

ALUKO (AMUEL ADEPOJU) and others, eds. Small-scale industries: Mid-Western State, Kwara State and Lagos State of Nigeria. [Ile-Ife, 1973]. pp. 276.

— United Kingdom.

SMALL businesses: strategy for survival; [by] Rosemary Brown [and others]. London, 1976. pp. 68. *(Conservative Political Centre. [Publications]. No. 592)*

SMALL GROUPS.

CAVALLARO (RENATO) La sociologia dei gruppi primari: formazione e dinamica dei raggruppamenti sociali di base; con uno studio sulle associazioni volontarie nel Molise. Napoli, 1975. pp. 382. *bibliog.*

SMALL HOLDINGS

— Russia.

BASHMAKOV (GEORGII STEPANOVICH) Priusadebnoe zemlepol'zovanie. Moskva, 1975. pp. 72.

SMITH (ADAM).

SKINNER (ANDREW S.) and WILSON (THOMAS) Ph.D., eds. Essays on Adam Smith. Oxford, 1975. pp. 647.

RECKTENWALD (HORST CLAUS) Adam Smith: sein Leben und sein Werk. München, [1976]. pp. 312.

REISMAN (DAVID ALEXANDER) Adam Smith's sociological economics. London, 1976. pp. 274. *bibliog.*

SMITH (ADAM) LL.D., F.R.S. The theory of moral sentiments; edited by D.D. Raphael and A.L. Macfie. Oxford, 1976. pp. 412. *bibliog.*

SMITH (FREDERICK EDWIN) 1st Earl of Birkenhead.

BULMER-THOMAS (IVOR) Our Lord Birkenhead: an Oxford appreciation. London, 1930. pp. 208.

SMITH (WILLIAM ALEXANDER) afterwards Amor DE COSMOS.

See DE COSMOS (AMOR).

SMOKE PREVENTION.

NORTH WEST ECONOMIC PLANNING COUNCIL. Smoke control. [Manchester, 1970]. fo. 16.

SMOKING.

TOBACCO RESEARCH COUNCIL. Review of activities, 1970-74. London, 1975. pp. 113. *bibliogs.*

TODD (GEORGE FREDERICK) Changes in smoking patterns in the U.K. London, 1975. pp. 68. *(Tobacco Research Council. Occasional Papers. 1)*

SMOLENSK (OBLAST')

— Politics and government.

OCHERKI istorii Smolenskoi organizatsii KPSS. Moskva, 1970. pp. 574.

SMUTS (JAN CHRISTIAAN).

SCHOLTZ (GERT DANIEL) Hertzog en Smuts en die Britse Ryk. Kaapstad, 1975. pp. 158. *bibliog.*

SNOWDONIA

— Economic conditions.

SNOWDONIA NATIONAL PARK PLAN TEAM. Snowdonia national park plan...: working paper no.3...: living and working; (by G.F. Broom [and others]). Penrhyndeudraeth, 1976. pp. 48bis, (2). *In English and Welsh.*

— Social conditions.

SNOWDONIA NATIONAL PARK PLAN TEAM. Snowdonia national park plan...: working paper no.3...: living and working; (by G.F. Broom [and others]). Penrhyndeudraeth, 1976. pp. 48bis, (2). *In English and Welsh.*

SNUFF.

WASSÉN (S. HENRY) The use of some specific kinds of South American Indian snuff and related paraphernalia. Göteborg, 1965. pp. 132. *bibliog.* (Gothenburg. Etnografiska Museet. Etnologiska Studier. 28)

SOCCER

— Ghana.

GHANA. 1971. White Paper on the report of the Committee of Enquiry on the erstwhile Football Pools Authority. [Accra], 1971. pp. 5. (W[hite] P[apers]. 1971. No.1) *Bound with the report.*

GHANA. Committee of Enquiry on the erstwhile Football Pools Authority. 1971. Report; [P.V. Osei-Hwere, chairman]. [Accra, 1971]. fo. 218. *Bound with White Paper on the report.*

SOCIAL ACTION.

VOLUNTARY action research, 1973; edited by David Horton Smith. Lexington, Mass., [1973]. pp. 406. *bibliogs.*

BRITISH ASSOCIATION OF SOCIAL WORKERS. Working Party on Social Action. Social action and social work: report of the working party. Birmingham, [1974?]. pp. 10. *(British Association of Social Workers. Publications. 6)*

VOLUNTARY action research, 1974: the nature of voluntary action around the world; edited by David Horton Smith. Lexington, Mass., [1974]. pp. 323. *bibliogs.*

BRUNET-JAILLY (JOSEPH) and DALOZ (JEAN PIERRE). Decision-making method in the social action field. Strasbourg, Council of Europe, 1976. pp. 63. *bibliog.*

WILLIAMS (WALTER) Dr., and ELMORE (RICHARD F.) eds. Social program implementation. New York, [1976]. pp. 299. *bibliog.*

SOCIAL CASE WORK.

BLOOM (MARTIN) The paradox of helping: introduction to the philosophy of scientific practice. New York, [1975]. pp. 283. *bibliog.*

RAPOPORT (LYDIA) Creativity in social work: selected writings of Lydia Rapoport; edited by Sanford N. Katz. Philadelphia, 1975. pp. 228.

SCHWARTZ (ARTHUR) and GOLDIAMOND (ISRAEL) Social casework: a behavioral approach. New York, 1975. pp. 315. *bibliog.*

SOCIAL CHANGE.

THOMAS (D.K.) and THOMPSON (CHARLES THOMAS) Eskimo housing as planned culture change; (with Northern rental housing program, Northwest Territories, 1966 to 1972). Ottawa, 1972. pp. 27; fo. (6). *bibliog. (Canada. Northern Science Research Group. Social Science Notes. 4)*

WESTHUES (KENNETH) Society's shadow: studies in the sociology of countercultures. Toronto, [1972]. pp. 223. *bibliog.*

BOURGUIGNON (ERIKA) ed. Religion, altered states of consciousness, and social change. Columbus, Ohio, 1973. pp. 389.

BARBÉ (CARLOS) Progresso e sviluppo: la formazione della teoria dello sviluppo e lo sviluppo come ideologia; Auguste Comte, Herbert Spencer. Torino, 1974. pp. 241. *(Turin. Università. Istituto di Scienze Politiche. Pubblicazioni. vol. 32)*

BEE (ROBERT L.) Patterns and processes: an introduction to anthropological strategies for the study of sociocultural change. New York, [1974]. pp. 260. *bibliog.*

DEBOLINI (MARINO) Lavoro e danaro nell'ordine economico-sociale. Roma, [1974]. pp. 103.

KNIGHT (C. GREGORY) Ecology and change: rural modernization in an African community. New York, [1974]. pp. 300. *bibliog.*

RETHINKING modernization: anthropological perspectives; edited by John J. Poggie, Jr., and Robert N. Lynch. Westport, Conn., 1974. pp. 405. *bibliog. Papers presented at a symposium held at the University of Rhode Island in 1971.*

BETTELHEIM (BRUNO) and JANOWITZ (MORRIS) Social change and prejudice: including Dynamics of prejudice. New York, 1964 repr. 1975. pp. xxxviii, 337. *Dynamics of prejudice first published in 1950. The 1975 reprint contains a new prologue by the authors.*

CLAYTON (RICHARD R.) The family, marriage, and social change. Lexington, Mass., [1975]. pp. 579. *bibliog.*

DYNAMIC change and the urban ghetto; [by] Alan Walter Steiss [and others]. Lexington, Mass., [1975]. pp. 124. *bibliog.*

EICHHORN (WOLFGANG) and others, eds. Die Gesetzmässigkeit der sozialen Entwicklung: ausgewählte Beiträge. Berlin, 1975. pp. 194.

FRAGA IRIBARNE (MANUEL) Legitimidad y representacion. Barcelona, [1975]. pp. 384.

GILLINGWATER (DAVID) Regional planning and social change: a responsive approach. Farnborough, Hants., [1975]. pp. 272. *bibliog.*

GOLDTHORPE (JOHN ERNEST) The sociology of the Third World: disparity and involvement. Cambridge, 1975. pp. 325. *bibliogs.*

INCIARDI (JAMES A.) and SIEGAL (HARVEY A.) compilers. Emerging social issues: a sociological perspective. New York, 1975. pp. 204. *bibliogs.*

LEVY (SIDNEY J.) and ZALTMAN (GERALD) Marketing, society, and conflict. Englewood Cliffs, [1975]. pp. 134.

RIVERS (PATRICK) The survivalists. London, 1975. pp. 224. *bibliog.*

BELL (DANIEL) The cultural contradictions of capitalism. London, 1976. pp. 301.

BERGER (PETER L.) Pyramids of sacrifice: political ethics and social change. London, 1976. pp. 272.

BLACK (CYRIL EDWIN) ed. Comparative modernization: a reader. New York, [1976]. pp. 441.

CHIROT (DANIEL) Social change in a peripheral society: the creation of a Balkan colony. New York, [1976]. pp. 179. *bibliog.*

GARAUDY (ROGER) The alternative future: a vision of Christian Marxism;... translated by Leonard Mayhew. Harmondsworth, 1976. pp. 221.

NISBET (ROBERT ALEXANDER) Twilight of authority. London, 1976. pp. 287.

PURDIE (WILLIAM K.) and TAYLOR (BERNARD) eds. Business strategies for survival: planning for social and political change. London, 1976. pp. 231.

SOCIAL change: explorations, diagnoses, and conjectures; edited by George K. Zollschan and Walter Hirsch. New York, [1976]. pp. 985. *bibliogs.*

VEREIN FÜR SOZIALPOLITIK. Schriften. Neue Folge. Band 88. Die Bedeutung gesellschaftlicher Veränderungen für die Willensbildung im Unternehmen: (Verhandlungen auf der Arbeitstagung...in Aachen vom 25.-27. September 1975; herausgegeben von Horst Albach und Dieter Sadowski). Berlin, [1976]. pp. 939. *bibliog. In German or English.*

SOCIAL CLASSES.

LUNDBERG (MARGARET J.) The incomplete adult: social class constraints on personality development. Westport, Conn., [1974]. pp. 245. *bibliog.*

SLAUGHTER (CLIFF) Marxism and the class struggle. London, [1975]. pp. 166. *bibliog.*

STAVENHAGEN (RODOLFO) Social classes in agrarian societies. New York, 1975. pp. 266.

ABRAHAMSON (MARK) and others. Stratification and mobility. New York, [1976]. pp. 388.

KRAUSS (IRVING) Stratification, class, and conflict. New York, [1976]. pp. 502.

THERBORN (G:RAN) Science, class and society: on the formation of sociology and historical materialism. London, [1976]. pp. 461. *bibliog.*

— America, Latin.

MASSES in Latin America; edited by Irving Louis Horowitz. New York, 1970. pp. 608.

Las CLASES sociales en America Latina: problemas de conceptualizacion; seminario de Merida, Yuc.;...coordinado por Raul Benitez Zenteno. Mexico, 1973. pp. 453.

PIKE (FREDRICK BRAUN) Spanish America, 1900-1970: tradition and social innovation. New York, 1973. pp. 180. *bibliog.*

SOCIAL CONFLICT.

CASTELLS (MANUEL) ed. Estructura de clases y politica urbana en America Latina. Buenos Aires, 1974. pp. 286.

EDUCATIONAL alternatives in Latin America: social change and social stratification; edited by Thomas J. La Belle. Los Angeles, 1975. pp. 490. *bibliogs. (California University. Latin American Center. Latin American Studies. vol. 30)*

SEX and class in Latin America; edited by June Nash and Helen Icken Safa. New York, 1976. pp. 330. *bibliogs. Papers from a conference sponsored by American Council of Learned Societies and Social Science Research Council. Joint Committee on Latin American Studies.*

— **Argentine Republic.**

ESTUDIOS sobre los origenes del peronismo; [by] Miguel Murmis [and others]. Buenos Aires, 1971-73. 2 vols. (in 1). *Vol. 1 reprinted in 1972.*

— **Australia.**

RICKARD (JOHN DAVID) Class and politics: New South Wales, Victoria and the early Commonwealth, 1890-1910. Canberra, 1976. pp. 371. *bibliog.*

— **Chile.**

MATTELART (ARMAND) and others. La ideologia de la dominacion en una sociedad dependiente: la respuesta ideologica de la clase dominante chilena al reformismo. Buenos Aires, 1970. pp. 319. *bibliog.*

FLORES OLEA (VICTOR) ed. El golpe de estado en Chile. Mexico, 1975. pp. 324.

— **Europe, Eastern.**

MATEJKO (ALEXANDER) Social change and stratification in Eastern Europe: an interpretive analysis of Poland and her neighbors. New York, 1974. pp. 272. *bibliog.*

— **France.**

ELWITT (SANFORD) The making of the Third Republic: class and politics in France, 1868-1884. Baton Rouge, [1975]. pp. 329. *bibliog.*

— **Germany.**

KAMPFFMEYER (PAUL) Geschichte der Gesellschaftsklassen in Deutschland. 2nd ed. Berlin, 1910. pp. 230.

PRATT (JAMES ALEXANDER) The social basis of Nazism and communism in urban Germany. 1948. pp. 277. *bibliog. M.A.(Michigan State College of Agriculture and Applied Science) thesis: unpublished. Microfilm of typescript: 1 reel.*

BISCHOFF (JOACHIM) ed. Die Klassenstruktur der Bundesrepublik Deutschland: ein Handbuch zum sozialen System der BRD. Westberlin, [1976]. pp. 173. *bibliogs.*

— **India.**

MILLER (D.B.) From hierarchy to stratification: changing patterns of social inequality in a north Indian village. Delhi, 1975. pp. 229. *bibliog.*

SANWAL (RAM DATT) Social stratification in rural Kumaon. Delhi, 1976. pp. 213.

— **Italy.**

PICHIERRI (ANGELO) ed. Le classi sociali in Italia, 1870-1970: [an anthology]. Torino, 1974. pp. 480. *bibliog.*

CATALANO (FRANCO) Politica economica e classe dirigente. Milano, [1975 in progress].

RADI (LUCIANO) Partiti e classi in Italia. Torino, 1975. pp. 167.

BARBERIS (CORRADO) La società italiana: classi e caste nello sviluppo economico. Milano, [1976]. pp. 355.

— **Norway.**

ASSUM (TERJE YNGVAR) Hvem har nytte av forbrukerservice?...: to whose benefit is the consumer service?. Oslo, 1974. pp. 22. *(Norway. Statistiske Centralbyrå. Artikler. Nr.64) With English summary.*

— **Poland.**

MATEJKO (ALEXANDER) Social change and stratification in Eastern Europe: an interpretive analysis of Poland and her neighbors. New York, 1974. pp. 272. *bibliog.*

— **Russia.**

CACCIARI (MASSIMO) and PERULLI (PAOLO) Piano economico e composizione di classe: il dibattito sull'industrializzazione e lo scontro politico durante la NEP. Milano, 1975. pp. 201.

— **Sardinia.**

LELLI (MARCELLO) Proletariato e ceti medi in Sardegna: una società dipendente. Bari, [1975]. pp. 228.

— **South Africa.**

JOHNSTONE (FREDERICK A.) Class, race and gold: a study of class relations and racial discrimination in South Africa. London, 1976. pp. 298. *bibliog.*

— **Sweden.**

SWEDNER (HARALD) School segregation in Malmö. Chicago, [1971]. pp. 51. *bibliog.*

SCASE (RICHARD) ed. Readings in the Swedish class structure. Oxford, 1976. pp. 314.

— **Uganda.**

MAMDANI (MAHMOOD) Politics and class formation in Uganda. New York, [1976]. pp. 339. *bibliog.*

— **United Kingdom.**

CAULFIELD (IAN) The classification and projection of socio-economic groups of households in South Hampshire. [Winchester], 1969. 1 vol. (unpaged). *(South Hampshire Plan Technical Unit. Working Papers. 11)*

CONFERENCE ON THE OCCUPATIONAL COMMUNITY OF THE TRADITIONAL WORKER, DURHAM, 1972. Working-class images of society: [papers presented to the conference]; edited by Martin Bulmer. London, 1975. pp. 278. *bibliog.*

CRUTCHLEY (JOHN FREDERICK) Work situation and social imagery: factors affecting the social and political outlooks of industrial workers. 1975. fo. 355. *bibliog. Typescript. Ph.D. (London) thesis: unpublished. This thesis is the property of London University and may not be removed from the Library.*

— — **Scotland.**

SOCIAL class in Scotland: past and present; edited by A. Allan MacLaren. Edinburgh, [1976]. pp. 195.

— **United States.**

KOURVETARIS (GEORGE A.) First and second generation Greeks in Chicago: an inquiry into their stratification and mobility patterns. Athens, National Centre of Social Research, 1971. pp. 111. *bibliog.*

HAMILTON (RICHARD F.) Restraining myths: critical studies of U.S. social structure and politics. New York, [1975]. pp. 296.

ABRAHAMSON (MARK) and others. Stratification and mobility. New York, [1976]. pp. 388.

KRAUSS (IRVING) Stratification, class, and conflict. New York, [1976]. pp. 502.

SOCIAL CONFLICT.

NEURATH (OTTO) Lebensgestaltung und Klassenkampf. Berlin, 1928. pp. 152.

COX (KEVIN R.) and others, eds. Locational approaches to power and conflict. New York, [1974]. pp. 339. *bibliogs.*

AHO (JAMES ALFRED) German realpolitik and American sociology: an inquiry into the sources and political significance of the sociology of conflict. Lewisburg, [1975]. pp. 346. *bibliog.*

A DOCUMENTATION of class struggle in 1974; (produced by people in and close to Big Flame). [Birmingham, 1975]. 1 vol. (various pagings).

MAGALINE (A.D.) Lutte de classes et dévalorisation du capital: contribution à la critique du révisionnisme. Paris, 1975. pp. 198. *bibliog.*

SCHULMAN (MICHAEL DAVID) Value consensus and the social cohesion of liberal democracy. 1975. pp. 366. *bibliog. Photocopy of typescript. Ph.D. thesis - Wisconsin University.*

THORBECKE (WILLIAM JOHAN RUDOLF) Mankind at the crossroads: an enquiry into the causes of the global predicaments and the means to overcome them. Leyden, 1975. pp. 217.

ARBEITERKLASSE im Kapitalismus: Klassenkampf und Klassenstruktur; ([by] Hellmuth Kolbe [and others]). Berlin, 1976. pp. 256.

GORZ (ANDRE) ed. The division of labour: the labour process and class-struggle in modern capitalism. Hassocks, Sussex, 1976. pp. 189.

KRAUSS (IRVING) Stratification, class, and conflict. New York, [1976]. pp. 502.

PIRAGES (DENNIS CLARK) Managing political conflict. New York, 1976. pp. 148. *bibliog.*

— **Mathematical models.**

WILKINSON (DAVID) 1943-1971. Cohesion and conflict: lessons from the study of three-party interaction. London, 1976. pp. 274.

— **Asia.**

SMITH (BARDWELL L.) ed. Religion and social conflict in south Asia. Leiden, 1976. pp. 115.

— **Bolivia.**

ZAVALETA MERCADO (RENE). El poder dual en America Latina: (estudio de los casos de Bolivia y Chile). Mexico, 1974. pp. 270.

— **Chile.**

CASANUEVA VALENCIA (FERNANDO) and FERNANDEZ CANQUE (MANUEL) El Partido Socialista y la lucha de clases en Chile. Santiago de Chile, 1973. pp. 342. *bibliog.*

BIG FLAME. Brixton Group. Chile si!: the continuing class war. [London, 1974]. pp. 52.

TARIQ ALI and HEDLEY (GERRY) Chile: lessons of the coup; which way to workers power?. London, [1974?]. pp. 48. *(International Marxist Group. Red Pamphlets. No. 7)*

ZAVALETA MERCADO (RENE). El poder dual en America Latina: (estudio de los casos de Bolivia y Chile). Mexico, 1974. pp. 270.

SAAVEDRA (ALEJANDRO) Capitalismo y lucha de clases en el campo: Chile 1970-72. Madrid, 1975. pp. 291.

— **Denmark.**

SCOCOZZA (BENITO) Klassekampen i Danmarks historie: feudalismen; med et indledende afsnit om den historiske materialisme. [Copenhagen, 1976]. pp. 308. *bibliog.*

— **France.**

NAVILLE (PIERRE) L'entre-deux guerres: la lutte des classes en France, 1927-1929 [or rather 1939]. Paris, [1975]. pp. 624. *bibliog. Cover title includes the dates 1926-1939.*

SOCIAL CONFLICT.(Cont.)

— Germany.

ARBEITERKAMPF in Deutschland: Klassenzusammensetzung und Kampfformen der Arbeiter seit dem Nationalsozialismus. München, 1973. pp. 175.

— Italy.

ACCATTATIS (VINCENZO) Istituzioni e lotte di classe: dalla crisi dello stato di diritto al sorgere dello stato assistenziale. Milano, 1976. pp. 149.

— Mexico.

GESSNER (VOLKMAR) Recht und Konflikt: eine soziologische Untersuchung privatrechtlicher Konflikte in Mexiko. Tübingen, 1976. pp. 290. *bibliog.* (*Max-Planck-Institut für Ausländisches und Internationales Privatrecht Tübingen. Beiträge zum Ausländischen und Internationalen Privatrecht. 40*)

— Russia.

TRIFONOV (IVAN IAKOVLEVICH) Likvidatsiia ekspluatatorskikh klassov v SSSR. Moskva, 1975. pp. 406.

— Sardinia.

SOTGIU (GIROLAMO) Lotte sociali e politiche nella Sardegna contemporanea, 1848-1922. Cagliari, [1974]. pp. 439.

— Tanzania.

SHIVJI (ISSA G.) Class struggles in Tanzania. London, 1976. pp. 182.

SOCIAL CONTROL.

COLSON (ELIZABETH) Tradition and contract: the problem of order. London, 1975. pp. 140. *bibliog.* (*Rochester, N.Y. University. Lewis Henry Morgan Lectures. 1973*)

EUROPEAN GROUP FOR THE STUDY OF DEVIANCE AND SOCIAL CONTROL. Conference, 1st, Impruneta, 1973. Deviance and control in Europe: papers...; edited by Herman Bianchi [and others]. London, [1975]. pp. 209.

SOCIAL CREDIT.

BARR (JOHN J.) The dynasty: the rise and fall of Social Credit in Alberta. Toronto, [1974]. pp. 256.

SOCIAL DEMOCRATIC PARTY (DENMARK).

CALLESEN (GERD) ed. Socialdemokratiet og internationalismen: kilder til belysning af det danske socialdemokratis syn på det slesvigske spørgsmål, 1906-24. København, [1973]. pp. 40. *bibliog.*

NIELSEN (MOGENS) ed. Enhed i arbejderbevaegelsen: kilder til belysning af forhandlingerne mellem Danmarks kommunistiske Parti og Socialdemokratiet, 1945. København, [1973]. pp. 47. *bibliog.*

OLSEN (JØRGEN) and SCHOUBYE (BJARNE) eds. Reformpolitik eller revolution: kilder til belysning af brydninger i dansk arbejderbevaegelse, 1908-22. København, [1973]. pp. 101. *bibliog.*

NIELSEN (VAGN OLUF) ed. Danmarks første arbejderflertal: kilder til belysning af det parlamentariske samarbejde mellem Socialdemokratiet og Socialistisk Folkeparti, 1966-1967. København, [1974]. pp. 80. *bibliog.*

PETERSEN (EGGERT) Har Socialdemokratiet en fremtid?: randbemaerkninger til et parti i krise. [Copenhagen, 1974]. pp. 111.

SALOMONSSON (PER) Socialismen og socialdemokratiet: indføring i dansk arbejderbevaegelses teoridannelse, 1871-84. [Copenhagen, 1974]. pp. 128. *bibliog.* (*Selskabet til Forskning i Arbejderbevaegelsens Historie. Publikationer. 1*)

SONNE (HARDING) Stauning eller kaos: Socialdemokratiet og krisen i trediverne. København, 1974. pp. 142. *bibliog.*

KARLSSON (HENRY) ed. Dansk arbejderbevaegelse, 1871-1939. Copenhagen, [1975]. pp. 144. *bibliog. Selected documents.*

BORDING (KRISTEN MORTENSEN) Dagbog over Danmarks første socialdemokratiske ministerium, 1924-26; ved Karen Marie Olsen og Hans Sode-Madsen. Aarhus, 1976. pp. 131. *bibliog.*

SOCIAL DEMOCRATIC PARTY (GERMANY).

HEINEMANN (HUGO) Die sozialistischen Errungenschaften der Kriegszeit. Chemnitz, [1914]. pp. 16.

SOZIALISTISCHE EINHEITSPARTEI DEUTSCHLANDS. Landesvorstand Gross-Berlin. Die Krise der SPD und die Politik der SED. Gross-Berlin, [1947]. pp. 102. (*Material für die Funktionäre der SED*)

LOHRENZ (WILHELM) Hinter den Kulissen der SPD-Führung: Tatsachenbericht übe die Spionagetätigkeit des SPD-Vorstandes. Berlin, [1949]. pp. 31.

BEHR (WOLFGANG) Sozialdemokratie und Konservatismus: ein empirischer und theoretischer Beitrag zur regionalen Parteianalyse am Beispiel der Geschichte und Nachkriegsentwicklung Bayerns. Hannover, [1969]. pp. 298. *bibliog.* (*Friedrich-Ebert-Stiftung. Forschungsinstitut. Schriftenreihe. Band 72*)

SCHMIDT (RUDI) and others, eds. Das Blockwahlsystem in der SPD: zur Herrschaftstechnik des Parteiapparates. Hamburg, [1970]. pp. 112.

SCHUMACHER (KURT) 1895-1952, and others. Der Auftrag des demokratischen Sozialismus. Bonn-Bad Godesberg, [1972]. pp. 96.

SOZIALDEMOKRATISCHE PARTEI DEUTSCHLANDS. Vorstand. Familienpolitik...: Entwurf; (Materialien zum Parteitag vom 10.4.-14.4.1973, Hannover). Bonn, [1972]. pp. 44.

FLOHR (HEINER) and others, eds. Freiheitlicher Sozialismus: Beiträge zu seinem heutigen Selbstverständnis; (Gerhard Weisser zum 75. Geburtstag). Bonn-Bad Godesberg, 1973. pp. 256. *bibliog.* (*Friedrich-Ebert-Stiftung. Forschungsinstitut. Schriftenreihe. Band 95*)

SOZIALDEMOKRATISCHE PARTEI DEUTSCHLANDS. Vorstand. Bundestagswahlkampf 1972: ein Bericht...; herausgegeben von Holger Börner. Bonn, [1973]. pp. 63.

GROSSHANS (ALBERT) ed. 100 Jahre SPD Heilbronn, 1874-1974. Heilbronn, 1974. pp. 200. *bibliog.*

KLUEBER (FRANZ) Katholische Soziallehre und demokratischer Sozialismus. Bonn-Bad Godesberg, [1974]. pp. 156.

SEELIGER (ROLF) ed. SPD offensiv: Beiträge zur Auseinandersetzung mit der CDU/CSU. München, 1974. pp. 107.

SOZIALDEMOKRATISCHE PARTEI DEUTSCHLANDS. Landesausschuss Niedersachsen. Die Politik der SPD für Niedersachsen in den nächsten vier Jahren. [Hanover, 1974?]. pp. 77.

AREND (PETER) Die innerparteiliche Entwicklung der SPD, 1966-1975. Bonn, [1975]. pp. 209. *bibliog.* (*Sozialwissenschaftliches Forschungsinstitut. Sozialwissenschaftliche Studien zur Politik. Band 7*)

BEYER (MARGA) and WINKLER (GERHARD) Revolutionäre Arbeitereinheit: Eisenach, Gotha, Erfurt. Berlin, 1975. pp. 128.

BLEY (HELMUT) Bebel und die Strategie der Kriegsverhütung, 1904-1913: eine Studie über Bebels Geheimkontakte mit der britischen Regierung, etc. Göttingen, 1975. pp. 254.

BRANDIS (KURT) pseud. [i.e. Karl Friedrich BROCKSCHMIDT] Der Anfang vom Ende der Sozialdemokratie: die SPD bis zum Fall des Sozialistengesetzes, etc. new ed. Berlin, [1975]. pp. 111.

BUSE (DIETER K.) ed. Parteiagitation und Wahlkreisvertretung: eine Dokumentation über Friedrich Ebert und seinen Reichstagswahlkreis Elberfeld-Barmen, 1910-1918. Bonn-Bad Godesberg, [1975]. pp. 135. (*Archiv für Sozialgeschichte. Beihefte. 3*)

BUTTERWEGGE (CHRISTOPH) Jungsozialisten und SPD, etc. Hamburg, [1975]. pp. 157.

CHRIST (KARL) Sozialdemokratie und Volkserziehung: die Bedeutung des Mannheimer Parteitags der SPD im Jahre 1906 für die Entwicklung der Bildungspolitik...vor dem Ersten Weltkrieg. Bern, 1975. pp. 298. *bibliog. Inaugural-Dissertation der Philosophischen Fakultät der Friedrich-Alexander-Universität zu Erlangen-Nürnberg.*

ECKERT (RAINER) Das ist "demokratischer Sozialismus": eine Antwort auf Johano Strassers Frage: "Was ist demokratischer Sozialismus?". Frankfurt am Main, [1975]. pp. 72.

EHNI (HANS PETER) Bollwerk Preussen?: Preussen-Regierung, Reich-Länder-Problem und Sozialdemokratie, 1928-1932. Bonn-Bad Godesberg, [1975]. pp. 304. *bibliog.* (*Friedrich-Ebert-Stiftung. Forschungsinstitut. Schriftenreihe. Band 111*)

ETTELT (WERNER) and KRAUSE (HANS DIETER) Der Kampf um eine marxistische Gewerkschaftspolitik in der deutschen Arbeiterbewegung, 1868 bis 1878. Berlin, 1975. pp. 640.

GESCHICHTE der deutschen Sozialdemokratie, 1863-1975; [by] Jutta von Freyberg [and others]; mit einem Vorwort von Wolfgang Abendroth. Köln, [1975]. pp. 457. *bibliog.*

GODESBERG und die Gegenwart: ein Beitrag zur innerparteilichen Diskussion über Inhalte und Methoden sozialdemokratischer Politik; [by Hermann Buschfort and others]. Bonn-Bad Godesberg, [1975]. pp. 93.

HEIMANN (HORST) Theoriediskussion in der SPD: Ergebnisse und Perspektiven. Frankfurt am Main, [1975]. pp. 308.

HOFSCHEN (HEINZ GERD) and others. SPD im Widerspruch: zur Entwicklung und Perspektive der Sozialdemokratie im System der BRD. Köln, [1975]. pp. 182. *bibliog.*

INSTITUT FÜR MARXISTISCHE STUDIEN UND FORSCHUNGEN. Der SPD Orientierungsrahmen '85: Analyse und Kommentar zum zweiten Entwurf des SPD-Parteivorstandes eines ökonomisch-politischen Orientierungsrahmens für die Jahre 1975-1985, OR 85. Frankfurt/Main, 1975]. pp. 165. *bibliog.* (*Informationsberichte. Nr.17*)

KLOENNE (ARNO) ed. Machte Wehner die SPD kaputt?: eine Dokumentation über den Identitätsverlust der bundesdeutschen Sozialdemokratie. Landshut, 1975. pp. 276.

MUELLER (DIRK H.) Idealismus und Revolution: zur Opposition der Jungen gegen den sozialdemokratischen Parteivorstand, 1890 bis 1894. Berlin, 1975. pp. 186. *bibliog.* (*IWK: internationale wissenschaftliche Korrespondenz zur Geschichte der deutschen Arbeiterbewegung. Beihefte. 3*)

OERTZEN (PETER VON) and others, eds. Thema: Wirtschaftspolitik; Materialien zum Orientierungsrahmen 1985 (der SPD). 2nd ed. Bonn-Bad Godesberg, 1975. pp. 249.

PETRY (LOTHAR) Die Erste Internationale in der Berliner Arbeiterbewegung. Erlangen, 1975. pp. 381. *bibliog.*

ROEDER (KARL HEINZ) Die Formel von der "sozialen Demokratie": Staat und Demokratie in der Ideologie des Sozialreformismus. Frankfurt/Main, 1975. pp. 101.

SCHMIDT (HELMUT) Dipl. rer. pol. Kontinuität und Konzentration: [speeches, articles, etc.]. Bonn-Bad Godesberg, [1975]. pp. 292.

SCHROEDER (WOLFGANG) Partei und Gewerkschaften: die Gewerkschaftsbewegung in der Konzeption der revolutionären Sozialdemokratie, 1868/69 bis 1893. Berlin, 1975. pp. 488.

SEELIGER (ROLF) ed. Was alles auf dem Spiel steht: SPD, Bilanz und Ausblick. München, 1975. pp. 138.

VOIGTLAENDER (HUBERT) Investitionslenkung oder Marktsteuerung?: ein Beitrag zur politischen Ökonomie des Godesberger Programms. Bonn-Bad Godesberg, [1975]. pp. 100. *bibliog.*

BARTH (DIETER) Orientierungsrahmen '85 der SPD. 2nd ed. Köln, [1976]. pp. 64. *(Institut der Deutschen Wirtschaft. Beiträge zur Gesellschafts- und Bildungspolitik. 1)*

BRANDT (WILLY) and SCHMIDT (HELMUT) Federal German Chancellor. Deutschland 1976: zwei Sozialdemokraten im Gespräch; Gesprächsführung Jürgen Kellermeier. Reinbek bei Hamburg, 1976. pp. 172.

LOEWKE (UDO F.) Die SPD und die Wehrfrage, 1949 bis 1955. Bonn-Bad Godesberg, [1976]. pp. 185. *bibliog.*

MARTINY (MARTIN) Integration oder Konfrontation?: Studien zur Geschichte der sozialdemokratischen Rechts- und Verfassungspolitik. Bonn-Bad Godesberg, [1976]. pp. 248. *bibliog. (Friedrich-Ebert-Stiftung. Forschungsinstitut. Schriftenreihe. Band 122)*

NARR (WOLF DIETER) and others. SPD: Staatspartei oder Reformpartei?. München, [1976]. pp. 237.

SCHLEI (MARIE) and WAGNER (JOACHIM) Freiheit, Gerechtigkeit, Solidarität: Grundwerte und praktische Politik; mit einem Vorwort von Helmut Schmidt. Bonn-Bad Godesberg, [1976]. pp. 165.

SIGEL (ROBERT) Die Lensch-Cunow-Haenisch-Gruppe: eine Studie zum rechten Flügel der SPD im Ersten Weltkrieg. Berlin, [1976]. pp. 177. *bibliog. (Munich. Universität. Institut für Bayerische Geschichte. Beiträge zu einer Historischen Strukturanalyse Bayerns im Industriezeitalter. Band 14)*

SOZIALDEMOKRATISCHE PARTEI DEUTSCHLANDS. Parteitag, 1975. Orientierungsrahmen '85: Text und Diskussion; ([edited by] Peter von Oertzen [and others]); bearbeitet von Heiner Lindner. Bonn-Bad Godesberg, [1976]. pp. 441. *bibliog.*

SPD in der Krise: die deutsche Sozialdemokratie seit 1945; ([by] Hans Jochen Brauns [and others]). Frankfurt am Main, 1976. pp. 406. *bibliog.*

STEHLING (JUTTA) Weimarer Koalition und SPD in Baden: ein Beitrag zur Geschichte der Partei- und Kulturpolitik in der Weimarer Republik. Frankfurt/Main, [1976]. pp. 347. *bibliog.* Zur Erlangung des akademischen Grades eines Doktors der Philosophie von der Universität Karlsruhe genehmigte Dissertation.

TOELCKE (CARL WILHELM) Presseberichte zur Entwicklung der deutschen Sozialdemokratie, 1848-1893: Quellen zur Geschichte der deutschen Arbeiterbewegung; bearbeitet von Arno Herzig. München, 1976. pp. 278. *bibliog. (Institut für Zeitungsforschung der Stadt Dortmund. Dortmunder Beiträge zur Zeitungsforschung. Band 22)*

— Bibliography.

GUENTHER (KLAUS) and SCHMITZ (KURT THOMAS) compilers. SPD, KPD/DKP, DGB in den Westzonen und in der Bundesrepublik Deutschland, 1945-1973: eine Bibliographie. Bonn-Bad Godesberg, 1976. pp. 176. *(Archiv für Sozialgeschichte. Beihefte. 6)*

SOCIAL DEMOCRATIC PARTY (POLAND).

FAL'KOVICH (SVETLANA MIKHAILOVNA) Proletariat Rossii i Pol'shi v sovmestnoi revoliutsionnoi bor'be, 1907-1912. Moskva, 1975. pp. 379.

SOCIAL DEMOCRATIC PARTY (RUSSIA).

HOLOVAN' (VASYL' PETROVYCH) and MYKHAILIUTA (TROKHYM IVANOVYCH) Borot'ba bil'shovykiv Rovenshchyny za vladu Rad. L'viv, 1968. pp. 70.

TEREKHOV (IVAN SEMENOVICH) V.I. Lenin i stroitel'stvo partii v period ot Fevralia k Oktiabriu, 1917 g. Saratov, 1969. pp. 259.

NARYSY istoriï Poltavs'koï oblasnoï partiinoï orhanizatsiï. Kharkiv, 1970. pp. 452.

ENIKEEV (ERIK AKHMETOVICH) Deiatel'nost' kazanskikh bol'shevikov po revoliutsionnomu vospitaniiu studencheskoi molodezhi, 1905 - fevral' 1917 gg. Kazan', 1973. pp. 205.

PEREPISKA V.I. Lenina i rukovodimykh im uchrezhdenii RSDRP s partiinymi organizatsiiami, 1903-1905 gg. Moskva, 1974 in progress.

ANIKEEV (VLADIMIR VSEVOLODOVICH) Deiatel'nost' TsK RSDRP(b)-RKP(b) v 1917-1918 godakh: khronika sobytii: oktiabr' 1917... oktiabr' 1918. Moskva, 1974. pp.557.

ESENOV (RAKHIM MAKHTUMOVICH) Bol'shevistskoe podpol'e Zakaspiia. Moskva, 1974. pp. 215. *bibliog.*

LISETSKII (ANATOLII MIKHAILOVICH) Bol'sheviki vo glave massovykh stachek, mart - oktiabr' 1917 g. Kishinev, 1974. pp. 423. *bibliog.*

UCHENYE ZAPISKI KAFEDR OBSHCHESTVENNYKH NAUK VUZOV LENINGRADA. Istoriia KPSS. vyp.14. Iz istorii sozdaniia i deiatel'nosti partii. Leningrad, 1974. pp. 197.

USHAKOV (ANATOLII VASIL'EVICH) Bor'ba partii za gegemoniiu proletariata v revoliutsionno-demokraticheskom dvizhenii Rossii, 1895-1904. Moskva, 1974. pp. 224.

VOENNYE organizatsii rossiiskogo proletariata i opyt ego vooruzhennoi bor'by, 1903-1917. Moskva, 1974. pp. 418. *bibliog.*

ARUTIUNOV (GEORGII ANASTASOVICH) Rabochee dvizhenie v Rossii v period novogo revoliutsionnogo pod"ema 1910-1914 gg. Moskva, 1975. pp. 408.

BOL'SHEVISTSKAIA partiia v revoliutsii 1905-1907 gg. Moskva, 1975. pp. 142.

FAL'KOVICH (SVETLANA MIKHAILOVNA) Proletariat Rossii i Pol'shi v sovmestnoi revoliutsionnoi bor'be, 1907-1912. Moskva, 1975. pp. 379.

KITAEV (MIKHAIL ALEKSEEVICH) Partiinoe stroitel'stvo v gody grazhdanskoi voiny. Moskva, 1975. pp. 256.

KUVSHINOV (VLADIMIR ALEKSANDROVICH) Partiia bol'shevikov posle sverzheniia samoderzhaviia, mart - nachalo aprelia 1917 goda. Moskva, 1975. pp. 248.

SENCHAKOVA (LARISA TIMOFEEVNA) Boevaia rat' revoliutsii: ocherk o boevykh organizatsiiakh RSDRP i rabochikh druzhinakh 1905-1907 gg. Moskva, 1975. pp. 192.

SMIRNOV (ALEKSANDR SERGEEVICH) Bol'sheviki i krest'ianstvo v Oktiabr'skoi revoliutsii. Moskva, 1976. pp. 232.

— Periodicals.

LENINSKAIA "Iskra" o Sibiri, dekabr' 1900 - oktiabr' 1903 gg.: sbornik dokumental'nykh materialov. Novosibirsk, 1970. pp. 174.

RADZHABOV (ZARIF SHARIPOVICH) Turkestan na stranitsakh bol'shevistskikh gazet perioda pervoi russkoi revoliutsii, 1905-1907 gg.; otvet. redaktor G.E. Beliakov. Dushanbe, 1970. pp. 225.

GAIDASHENKO (KONSTANTIN PORFIR'EVICH) Pervaia gazeta simbirskikh bol'shevikov. Ul'ianovsk, 1973. pp. 59.

KOSTIN (ALEKSANDR FEDOROVICH) Boevoi organ revoliutsii: k 70-letiiu gazety "Vpered". Moskva, 1975. pp. 224,[xiii].

OL'KHOVSKII (EVGENII ROMANOVICH) Leninskaia "Iskra" v Peterburge. Leningrad, 1975. pp. 359.

SOCIAL DEMOCRATIC PARTY (RUSSIA) (MENSHEVIKS)

— Periodicals.

[MENSHEVIK NEWSPAPERS AND PERIODICALS]; (published by Rossiiskaia Sotsial-Demokraticheskaia Rabochaia Partiia [Mensheviki]). irreg., 1896-1940. Petrograd, etc. Microfilm : 49 reels.

SOCIAL DEMOCRATIC PARTY (SWEDEN).

ERLANDER (TAGE) 1901-1939. Stockholm, [1972]. pp. 320.

ERLANDER (TAGE) 1940-1949. Stockholm, [1973]. pp. 406.

ERLANDER (TAGE) 1949-1954. Stockholm, [1974]. pp. 392.

LEION (ANDERS) Den svenska modellen: hur ska det gå med socialdemokratin, ekonomin och den offentliga sektorn?. Stockholm, 1974. pp. 180.

SOCIAL DEMOCRATIC PARTY (YUGOSLAVIA).

STRUGAR (VLADO) Jugoslavenske socijaldemokratske stranke, 1914-1918. Zagreb, 1963. pp. 322. *bibliog. (Jugoslavenska Akademija Znanosti i Umjetnosti. Prilozi Novijoj Jugoslavenskoj Historiji. knj.4)*

SOCIAL EXCHANGE.

CHADWICK-JONES (JOHN K.) Social exchange theory: its structure and influence in social psychology. London, 1976. pp. 431. *bibliog. (European Association of Experimental Social Psychology. European Monographs in Social Psychology. 8)*

HEATH (ANTHONY) Rational choice and social exchange: a critique of exchange theory. Cambridge, 1976. pp. 194. *bibliog.*

SOCIAL GROUP WORK.

PHILLIPS (HELEN UPSON) Essentials of social group work skill: [reprint of the work originally published in 1957]. Philadelphia, 1975. pp. 180. *bibliog.*

FELDMAN (RONALD A.) and WODARSKI (JOHN S.) Contemporary approaches to group treatment. San Francisco, 1975. pp. 248. *bibliog.*

SOCIAL GROUPS.

HAZEN (WILLIAM EDWARD) and MUGHISUDDIN (MOHAMMED) Middle Eastern subcultures: a regional approach; [with contributions by] George N. Atiyeh [and others]. Lexington, [1975]. pp. 215. *bibliog.*

KIDDER (LOUISE H.) and STEWART (V. MARY) The psychology of intergroup relations: conflict and consciousness. New York, [1975]. pp. 128. *bibliog.*

BILLIG (MICHAEL) Social psychology and intergroup relations. London, 1976. pp. 428. *bibliog. (European Association of Experimental Social Psychology. European Monographs in Social Psychology.9)*

— Mathematical models.

WILKINSON (DAVID) 1943-1971. Cohesion and conflict: lessons from the study of three-party interaction. London, 1976. pp. 274.

SOCIAL HISTORY.

BLACK (CYRIL EDWIN) ed. Comparative modernization: a reader. New York, [1976]. pp. 441.

— Historiography.

IMHOF (ARTHUR ERWIN) and LARSEN (ØIVIND) Sozialgeschichte und Medizin: Probleme der quantifizierenden Quellenbearbeitung in der Sozial- und Medizingeschichte. Oslo, 1975. pp. 322. *bibliog.*

SOCIAL INDICATORS.

KNIGHT (T.E.) A conceptual background to the use of social indicators for the identification of areas of urban deprivation. [London], 1974. fo. 11. *(U.K. Department of the Environment. Economic and Statistical Notes. No. 21)*

DE NEUFVILLE (JUDITH INNES) Social indicators and public policy: interactive processes of design and application. Amsterdam, 1975. pp. 311. *bibliog.*

SOCIAL INDICATORS.(Cont.)

— Mathematical models.

SOCIAL indicator models; edited by Kenneth C. Land and Seymour Spilerman. New York, [1975]. pp. 411. *bibliogs.*

— European Economic Community countries.

The FUTURES of Europe; edited...by Wayland Kennet, Director of the Europe Plus Thirty Project; based on a report to the Commission of the European Communities. Cambridge, 1976. pp. 242.

— France.

OBSERVATOIRE ECONOMIQUE DE L'OUEST. 66 indicateurs sociaux par régions et départements: pour une réflexion sur les conditions de vie dans l'Ouest; recueil de données chiffrées...rassemblées et présentées...sous la direction de Patrick Mareschal. Nantes, 1974. pp. 159.

— Germany.

SOZIOLOGISCHER Almanach: Handbuch gesellschaftspolitischer Daten und Indikatoren für die Bundesrepublik Deutschland; von Eike Ballerstedt [and others]. Frankfurt, [1975]. pp. 531. *bibliog. (Frankfurt am Main. Universität, and Mannheim. Universität. Sozialpolitische Forschergruppe. SPES- Projekt. Schriftenreihe. Band 5)*

— India.

ECONOMIC AND SOCIAL INDICATORS: INDIA; [pd. by] United States Agency for International Development, New Delhi, India. a., 1972- New Delhi.

— Trinidad and Tobago.

TRINIDAD AND TOBAGO. Central Statistical Office. 1975. Social indicators. [Port of Spain, 1975]. pp. 106.

— Turkey.

ECONOMIC AND SOCIAL INDICATORS: TURKEY; [pd. by] United States Agency for International Development, Ankara, Turkey. a., Jl 1970- Ankara.

— United Kingdom.

U.K. Department of the Environment. 1975. The use of indicators for area action; Housing Act, 1974. London, [1975]. pp. 40. *bibliog. (Area Improvement Notes. 10)*

— United States.

ECONOMIC means for human needs: social indicators of well-being and discontent; edited by Burkhard Strumpel. Ann Arbor, 1976. pp. 303. *bibliogs.*

LIU (BEN-CHIEH) Quality of life indicators in U.S. metropolitan areas: a statistical analysis. New York, 1976. pp. 315. *bibliog.*

SOCIAL INTERACTION.

MOSS (GORDON ERVIN) Illness, immunity, and social interaction: the dynamics of biosocial resonation. New York, [1973]. pp. 281. *bibliog.*

PERFIL'EV (MARAT NIKOLAEVICH) Obshchestvennye otnosheniia: metodologicheskie i sotsiologicheskie problemy. Leningrad, 1974. pp. 237.

MARTIN (WILFRED B.W.) The negotiated order of the school. [Toronto, 1976]. pp. 191. *bibliog.*

SOCIAL ISOLATION.

HADLEY (ROGER DENHAM) and WEBB (ADRIAN L.) Loneliness, social isolation and old people: some implications for social policy. London, 1974. pp. 22. *(Age Concern England. Manifesto Series. No. 25)*

PEACH (GUTHLAC CERI KLAUS) ed. Urban social segregation. London, 1975. pp. 444. *bibliogs.*

SOCIAL JUSTICE.

DANIELS (NORMAN) ed. Reading Rawls: critical studies on Rawls' "A theory of justice". Oxford, [1975]. pp. 352. *bibliog.*

MILLER (DAVID) D. Phil. Social justice. Oxford, 1976. pp. 367. *bibliog.*

SOCIAL LEGISLATION

— Austria.

EBERT (KURT) Die Anfänge der modernen Sozialpolitik in Österreich: die Taaffesche Sozialgesetzgebung für die Arbeiter im Rahmen der Gewerbeordnungsreform, 1879-1885. Wien, 1975. pp. 320. *bibliog. (Österreichische Akademie der Wissenschaften. Kommission für die Geschichte der Österreichisch- Ungarischen Monarchie, 1848-1918. Studien zur Geschichte der Österreichisch-Ungarischen Monarchie. Band 15)*

— Spain.

HILLERS DE LUQUE (SIGFREDO) España: una revolucion pendiente. Madrid, [1975]. pp. 487. *bibliog.*

— United Kingdom.

HODDER (EDWIN) The seventh Earl of Shaftesbury, K.G., as social reformer. London, 1897. pp. 195.

McCLEAN (J.D.) The legal context of social work. London, 1975. pp. 171.

SOCIAL MEDICINE.

MOSS (GORDON ERVIN) Illness, immunity, and social interaction: the dynamics of biosocial resonation. New York, [1973]. pp. 281. *bibliog.*

WAITZKIN (HOWARD B.) and WATERMAN (BARBARA) The exploitation of illness in capitalist society. Indianapolis, [1974 repr. 1976]. pp. 133. *bibliog.*

CARLSON (RICK J.) The end of medicine. New York, [1975]. pp. 290. *bibliog.*

COX (CAROLINE) and MEAD (ADRIANNE) eds. A sociology of medical practice. London, [1975]. pp. 318. *bibliogs.*

HUMANIZING health care: [including papers presented at a symposium in San Francisco, 1972; edited by] Jan Howard [and] Anselm Strauss. New York, [1975]. pp. 326.

INTERNATIONAL CONGRESS OF ANTHROPOLOGICAL AND ETHNOLOGICAL SCIENCES. 9th Congress, 1973. Topias and utopias in health: policy studies: [papers from the Congress; editor[s] Stanley R. Ingman, Anthony E. Thomas. The Hague, [1975]. pp. 548. *bibliogs.*

SOCIOLOGICAL REVIEW, THE; [published by] University of Keele. Monographs. [No.] 22. The sociology of the National Health Service; issue editor, Margaret Stacey. Keele, 1976. pp. 200. *bibliogs.*

TUCKETT (DAVID) ed. An introduction to medical sociology. London, 1976. pp. 412. *bibliogs.*

SOCIAL MOBILITY.

ABRAHAMSON (MARK) and others. Stratification and mobility. New York, [1976]. pp. 388.

— Europe, Eastern.

FABER (BERNARD LEWIS) ed. The social structure of eastern Europe: transition and process in Czechoslovakia, Hungary, Poland, Romania and Yugoslavia. New York, 1976. pp. 419.

— United Kingdom.

RICHARDSON (CHARLES JAMES) Aspects of contemporary social mobility in the London region. 1975 [or rather 1976]. fo. 392. *bibliog.* Typescript. Ph.D. (London) thesis: unpublished. This thesis is the property of London University and may not be removed from the Library.

PARRY (NOEL) and PARRY (JOSÉ) The rise of the medical profession: a study of collective social mobility. London, [1976]. pp. 282. *bibliog.*

— United States.

KOURVETARIS (GEORGE A.) First and second generation Greeks in Chicago: an inquiry into their stratification and mobility patterns. Athens, National Centre of Social Research, 1971. pp. 111. *bibliog.*

PETERSON (JAMES) Escape from poverty: occupational and economic mobility among urban blacks. Chicago, [1974]. pp. 176. *bibliog. (Chicago. University. Community and Family Study Center. Community and Family Monographs)*

ESSLINGER (DEAN R.) Immigrants and the city: ethnicity and mobility in a nineteenth- century midwestern community. Port Washington, N.Y., 1975. pp. 156. *bibliog.*

ABRAHAMSON (MARK) and others. Stratification and mobility. New York, [1976]. pp. 388.

WEBER (MICHAEL P.) Social change in an industrial town: patterns of progress in Warren, Pennsylvania, from Civil War to World War I. University Park, Pa., [1976]. pp. 185.

SOCIAL MOVEMENTS.

ALLEN (ROBERT L.) 1942- , and ALLEN (PAMELA PARKER) Reluctant reformers: racism and social reform movements in the United States. Washington, D.C., 1974. pp. 324.

— Canada.

CLARK (SAMUEL DELBERT) and others, eds. Prophecy and protest: social movements in twentieth-century Canada. Toronto, [1975]. pp. 437.

SOCIAL PARTICIPATION.

ARMBRUSTER (BERNT) and LEISNER (RAINER) Bürgerbeteiligung in der Bundesrepublik: zur Freizeitaktivität verschiedener Bevölkerungsgruppen in ausgewählten Beteiligungsfeldern, etc. Göttingen, [1975]. pp. 291. *bibliog. (Kommission für Wirtschaftlichen und Sozialen Wandel. Schriften. 54)*

PANKOKE (ECKART) and others. Neue Formen gesellschaftlicher Selbststeuerung in der Bundesrepublik Deutschland: Diskussion an Beispielen aus den Bereichen Bildung, soziale Sicherung und kommunale Selbstverwaltung. Göttingen, [1975]. pp. 310. *bibliog. (Kommission für Wirtschaftlichen und Sozialen Wandel. Schriften. 86)*

SOCIAL PERCEPTION.

KIDDER (LOUISE H.) and STEWART (V. MARY) The psychology of intergroup relations: conflict and consciousness. New York, [1975]. pp. 128. *bibliog.*

SOCIAL POLICY.

KOTHARI (RAJNI) Footsteps into the future: diagnosis of the present world and a design for an alternative. Amsterdam, [1974]. pp. 173. *(Institute for World Order. Preferred Worlds for the 1990's)*

SYSTEME D'ETUDES DU SCHEMA GENERAL D'AMENAGEMENT DE LA FRANCE. Schéma général d'aménagement de la France: Sésame année 5. Paris, 1974. pp. 71. *(France. Délégation à l'Aménagement du Territoire et à l'Action Régionale. Travaux et Recherches de Prospective. 50)*

AMERICAN ASSOCIATION FOR THE ADVANCEMENT OF SCIENCE. Population: dynamics, ethics and policy;...edited by Priscilla Reining and Irene Tinker. Washington, D.C., [1975]. pp. 184. *(Articles reprinted from Science, 1966-1975).*

DE NEUFVILLE (JUDITH INNES) Social indicators and public policy: interactive processes of design and application. Amsterdam, 1975. pp. 311. *bibliog.*

GILLINGWATER (DAVID) Regional planning and social change: a responsive approach. Farnborough, Hants., [1975]. pp. 272. *bibliog.*

GREFFE (XAVIER) La politique sociale: étude critique. [Paris, 1975]. pp. 254. *bibliog.*

SOCIAL SCIENCES.

ROUX (JEAN) La rationalisation des choix politiques. Paris, 1975. pp. 227. *bibliog.*

WILENSKY (HAROLD L.) The welfare state and equality: structural and ideological roots of public expenditures. Berkeley, [1975]. pp. 151. *bibliog.*

BELSHAW (CYRIL SHIRLEY) The sorcerer's apprentice: an anthropology of public policy. New York, 1976. pp. 342.

GEORGE (VICTOR N.) and WILDING (PAUL) Ideology and social welfare. London, 1976. pp. 162. *bibliog.*

INTERNATIONAL SOCIOLOGICAL ASSOCIATION. Research Committee on Sociotechnics. 1st Meeting, Loughborough, 1973. Sociotechnics: [selected papers from the meeting]; edited by Albert Cherns. London, 1976. pp. 310. *bibliogs.*

MOLITOR (BRUNO) Sozialpolitik auf dem Prüfstand. Hamburg, 1976. pp. 356. *bibliog. (Hamburg. Hamburgisches Welt-Wirtschafts-Archiv. Veröffentlichungen)*

SOCIAL ends and political means; edited by Ted Honderich. London, 1976. pp. 177.

STRATEGIC perspectives on social policy; editors: John E. Tropman [and others]. New York, [1976]. pp. 367. *bibligs.*

— Research — United States.

ETHICAL and legal issues of social experimentation: [based on a conference convened by the Brookings Panel on Social Experimentation in 1973]; contributors, Alice M. Rivlin [and others]; [editors Alice M. Rivlin [and] P. Michael Timpane). Washington, [1975]. pp. 188. *(Brookings Institution. Brookings Studies in Social Experimentation)*

SOCIAL PREDICTION.

PROGRESS and problems in social forecasting: disciplinary contributions to an interdisciplinary task; editors: Christopher Freeman, Marie Jahoda and Ian Miles; (papers presented to the Social Science Research Council seminars). [London, Social Science Research Council, 1976]. pp. 85. *bibligs.*

SOCIAL PROBLEMS.

COLLIGNON (CLAUDE BONIFACE) L'avant-coureur du changement du monde entier par l'aisance, la bonne éducation et la prospérité générale de tous les hommes; ou, Prospectus d'un mémoire patriotique sur les causes de la grande misère qui existe par-tout, et sur les moyens de l'extirper radicalement. Londres, 1786; Milan, 1966. pp. 60. *Facsimile reprint.*

DEAN (GEORGE ALFRED) Fallacies and tendencies of the age. London, 1871. pp. 251. *Essays on social and political problems written by way of narrative and dialogue.*

ALDEN (Sir PERCY) Democratic England. New York, 1912. pp. 271. *"The greater part of this book has already appeared in the shape of a series of articles written for the Chautauquan Magazine".*

JACOBS (GLENN) ed. The participant observer. New York, [1970]. pp. 302.

HAMSHER (J. HERBERT) and SIGALL (HAROLD) eds. Psychology and social issues. New York, [1973]. pp. 550. *bibligs.*

HOULT (THOMAS FORD) ed. Social justice and its enemies. New York, [1975]. pp. 584. *bibliog.*

INCIARDI (JAMES A.) and SIEGAL (HARVEY A.) compilers. Emerging social issues: a sociological perspective. New York, 1975. pp. 204. *bibligs.*

MERTON (ROBERT KING) and NISBET (ROBERT ALEXANDER) eds. Contemporary social problems. 4th ed. New York, [1976]. pp. 782. *bibligs.*

SOCIAL PSYCHIATRY.

MAZER (MILTON) People and predicaments. Cambridge, Mass., 1976. pp. 279. *bibliog.*

SOCIAL PSYCHOLOGY.

GINSBERG (MORRIS) The psychology of society. London, 1921. pp. 174. *bibliog.*

MITSCHERLICH (ALEXANDER) and MITSCHERLICH (MARGARETE) Eine deutsche Art zu lieben. München, [1970]. pp. 119. *Revised version of the first chapter of their Die Unfähigkeit zu trauern.*

MANIS (JEROME G.) and MELTZER (BERNARD N.) eds. Symbolic interaction: a reader in social psychology. 2nd ed. Boston, [1972] repr. 1975. pp. 593. *bibligs.*

HAMSHER (J. HERBERT) and SIGALL (HAROLD) eds. Psychology and social issues. New York, [1973]. pp. 550. *bibliog.*

APPLYING social psychology: implications for research, practice, and training; edited by Morton Deutsch [and] Harvey A. Hornstein. Hillsdale, N.J., 1975. pp. 287. *bibligs. Papers of a conference sponsored by the Committee on Transnational Social Psychology of the Social Science Research Council.*

MORSE (STANLEY J.) and ORPEN (CHRISTOPHER) eds. Contemporary South Africa: social psychological perspectives. Cape Town, 1975. pp. 294. *bibligs.*

BILLIG (MICHAEL) Social psychology and intergroup relations. London, 1976. pp. 428. *bibliog. (European Association of Experimental Social Psychology. European Monographs in Social Psychology.9)*

CHADWICK-JONES (JOHN K.) Social exchange theory: its structure and influence in social psychology. London, 1976. pp. 431. *bibliog. (European Association of Experimental Social Psychology. European Monographs in Social Psychology. 8)*

HANSEN (DONALD ANDREW) An invitation to critical sociology: involvement, criticism, exploration. New York, [1976]. pp. 258. *bibliog.*

HOLMES (ROGER) Legitimacy and the politics of the knowable. London, 1976. pp. 191. *A collection of essays reprinted from various periodicals.*

TEDESCHI (JAMES T.) and LINDSKOLD (SVENN) Social psychology: interdependence, interaction, and influence. New York, [1976]. pp. 705. *bibliog.*

SOCIAL REFORMERS

— United States.

SCHLESINGER (STEPHEN C.) The new reformers: forces for change in American politics. Boston, Mass., 1975. pp. 238.

SOCIAL SCIENCE RESEARCH.

HABENSTEIN (ROBERT W.) ed. Pathways to data: field methods for studying ongoing social organizations. Chicago, 1970. pp. 276. *bibliog.*

FRANKLIN (BILLY J.) and OSBORNE (HAROLD W.) eds. Research methods: issues and insights. Belmont, Cal., [1971]. pp. 472. *bibligs.*

STEISS (ALAN WALTER) Urban systems dynamics. Lexington, Mass., [1974]. pp. 323.

FERMAN (GERALD S.) and LEVIN (JACK) Statistician. Social science research: a handbook for students. New York, [1975]. pp. 138. *bibliog.*

WARWICK (DONALD P.) and LININGER (CHARLES ANDREW) The sample survey: theory and practice. New York, [1975]. pp. 344. *bibliog.*

BLACK (JAMES A.) and CHAMPION (DEAN J.) Methods and issues in social research. New York, [1976]. pp. 445. *bibliog.*

PHILLIPS (BERNARD S.) Social research: strategy and tactics. 3rd ed. New York, [1976]. pp. 365.

—'Bibliography.

INTER-UNIVERSITY CONSORTIUM FOR POLITICAL AND SOCIAL RESEARCH. Guide to resources and services, 1976-1977. [Ann Arbor, 1976]. pp. 386. *bibligs.*

— Information services.

INTER-UNIVERSITY CONSORTIUM FOR POLITICAL AND SOCIAL RESEARCH. Guide to resources and services, 1976-1977. [Ann Arbor, 1976]. pp. 386. *bibligs.*

— America, Latin.

BLAIR (CALVIN PATTON) and others. Responsibilities of the foreign scholar to the local scholarly community: studies of U.S. research in Guatemala, Chile and Paraguay;...edited and with an introduction by Richard N. Adams. [Austin, Texas], [1969]. pp. 112. *bibligs.*

— Europe.

DEMANDS for social knowledge: the role of research organisations; edited by Elisabeth Crawford and Norman Perry. London, [1976]. pp. 274. *bibligs. Essays arising from a seminar held at Trinity College, Cambridge, 1974, to review progress on the European Survey of Social Science Research Organisation.*

— France — Directories.

FRANCE. Délégation Générale à la Recherche Scientifique et Technique. 1974. Répertoire général de la recherche. Tome 3. Sciences sociales et humaines. Documentation arrêtée fin 1973. Paris, 1974. pp. 300. *(Répertoire National des Laboratoires)*

— India.

SOCIAL sciences and planning in India; edited by Radhakamal Mukerjee. London, [1970]. pp. 208. *Papers of a seminar held at Bakshi-Ka-Talab in 1965 under the joint auspices of the Social Science Department of the University of Lucknow and the Orientation and Study Centre, Bakshi-Ka-Talab under the Ministry of Community Development and Cooperation.*

— Ireland (Republic).

ECONOMIC AND SOCIAL RESEARCH INSTITUTE. Register of research projects in the social sciences in progress in Ireland, November 1975; compiled by Maria Maher. Dublin, [1975]. pp. 30.

— United Kingdom.

CULLEN (MICHAEL J.) The statistical movement in early Victorian Britain: the foundations of empirical social research. Hassocks, Sussex, 1975. pp. 205. *bibliog.*

LEES (RAY) Research strategies for social welfare. London, 1975. pp. 105. *bibliog.*

U.K. Advisory Group on Research into the Social Impact of North Sea Oil Developments in Scotland. 1975. Research into the social impact of North Sea oil developments in Scotland; report; [W.G. Runciman, chairman]. London, [1975]. 1 vol. (various pagings).

— United States.

HOROWITZ (IRVING LOUIS) ed. The rise and fall of Project Camelot: studies in the relationship between social science and practical politics. rev. ed. Cambridge, Mass., [1974]. pp. 409.

GOODWIN (LEONARD) Can social science help resolve national problems?: welfare, a case in point. New York, [1975]. pp. 214.

JOHNSON (JOHN M.) Doing field research. New York, [1975]. pp. 225.

LAZARSFELD (PAUL FELIX) and REITZ (JEFFREY G.) An introduction to applied sociology. New York, [1975]. pp. 196.

SOCIAL SCIENCES.

HOBSON (JOHN ATKINSON) Confessions of an economic heretic: the autobiography of J.A. Hobson; edited...by Michael Freeden; [reprint, with a new introduction, of the work first published in 1938]. Hassocks, Sussex, 1976. pp. 217.

PALMER (MONTE) and others. The interdisciplinary study of politics. New York, [1974]. pp. 177.

SOCIAL SCIENCES.(Cont.)

BRUNO (ANTONINO) Croce e le scienze politico-sociali. Firenze, 1975. pp. 139.

GOMBRICH (Sir ERNST HANS) Art history and the social sciences. Oxford, 1975. pp. 60. *(Oxford. University. Romanes Lectures. 1973)*

HOROWITZ (IRVING LOUIS) and KATZ (JAMES EVERETT) Social science and public policy in the United States. New York, 1975. pp. 187. *bibliogs.*

KARAVAEV (G.G.) ed. Problema zakona i zakonomernostei v obshchestvoznanii. Leningrad, 1975. pp. 99.

MYRDAL (GUNNAR) The unity of the social sciences. [Stockholm?], 1975. fo. 16.

POLICY studies and the social sciences; edited by Stuart S. Nagel. Lexington, Mass., [1975]. pp. 307. *"Based on symposia coordinated by the Policy Studies Organization".*

ALBERT (HANS) Aufklärung und Steuerung: Aufsätze zur Sozialphilosophie und zur Wissenschaftslehre der Sozialwissenschaften. Hamburg, [1976]. pp. 196. *bibliog.*

BERGNER (DIETER) and MOCEK (REINHARD) Bürgerliche Gesellschaftstheorien: Studien zu den weltanschaulichen Grundlagen und ideologischen Funktionen bürgerlicher Gesellschaftsauffassungen. Berlin, 1976. pp. 295.

FRONTIERS in social thought: essays in honor of Kenneth E. Boulding; edited by Martin Pfaff. Amsterdam, 1976. pp. 386. *bibliog.*

— Abstracting and indexing.

UNIVERSITY OF BATH. Library. Design of Information Systems in the Social Sciences. Research Reports. Series A. No. 5. The planning of indexing and abstracting services in the social sciences: coverage, overlap and content. Bath, 1976. 1 vol. (various pagings). *bibliog.*

— Bibliography.

BILBOUL (ROGER R.) ed. Retrospective index to theses of Great Britain and Ireland, 1716-1950. vol.1. Social sciences and humanities. Santa Barbara, [1975]. pp. 393.

LU (JOSEPH K.) compiler. U.S. government publications relating to the social sciences: a selected annotated guide. Beverly Hills, [1975]. pp. 260.

OTTO (FRIEDA) compiler. Bibliographie wirtschafts- und sozialwissenschaftlicher Bibliographien: Zugänge der Bibliothek des Instituts für Weltwirtschaft, Kiel, in den Jahren 1968 bis 1973. Kiel, 1975. pp. 83. *(Kiel. Universität. Institut für Weltwirtschaft. Bibliothek. Kieler Schrifttumskunden zu Wirtschaft und Gesellschaft. 20)*

BOHRN (HARALD) compiler. Gunnar Myrdal: a bibliography, 1919-1976. Stockholm, 1976. pp. 186. *(Stockholm. Kungliga Biblioteket. Acta Bibliothecae Regiae Stockholmiensis. 27)*

— Information services.

BURRINGTON (GILLIAN A.) How to find out about the social sciences. Oxford, 1975. pp. 144. *bibliog.*

INVENTORY of information resources in the social sciences; prepared by the University of Bath for the Organisation for Economic Co-operation and Development; edited by J.M. Brittain and S.A. Roberts. Farnborough, [1975]. pp. 239.

UNIVERSITY OF BATH. Library. Design of Information Systems in the Social Sciences. Research Reports. Series A. No. 5. The planning of indexing and abstracting services in the social sciences: coverage, overlap and content. Bath, 1976. 1 vol. (various pagings). *bibliog.*

— Mathematical models.

EDINBURGH SEMINAR IN THE SOCIAL SCIENCES, 10TH, 1972. The use of models in the social sciences: [papers of the seminar] ; edited by Lyndhurst Collins. London, 1976. pp. 238. *bibliogs.*

— Methodology.

CONFERENCE ON THE HISTORY OF QUANTIFICATION IN THE SCIENCES, NEW YORK, 1959. Quantification: a history of the meaning of measurement in the natural and social sciences; edited by Harry Woolf. Indianapolis, [1961]. pp. 222. *Papers from the conference organized by the Joint Committee on the History of Science of the Social Science Research Council and the National Research Council.*

ANNALES DE L'INSÉÉ; [pd. by] Institut National de la Statistique et des Études Économiques [France]. 3 a yr., My 1969 (no.1)- Paris.

HABENSTEIN (ROBERT W.) ed. Pathways to data: field methods for studying ongoing social organizations. Chicago, 1970. pp. 276. *bibliog.*

KRAUSZ (ERNEST) and MILLER (STEPHEN H.) Social research design. London, 1974. pp. 118.

ALBIN (PETER S.) The analysis of complex socioeconomic systems. Lexington, [1975]. pp. 150. *bibliog.*

BABBIE (EARL R.) The practice of social research. Belmont, [1975]. pp. 511. *bibliogs.*

ROSENTHAL (ROBERT) and ROSNOW (RALPH L.) Primer of methods for the behavioral sciences. New York, [1975]. pp. 117. *bibliog.*

WEBER (MAX) Roscher and Knies: the logical problems of historical economics translated with an introduction by Guy Oakes. New York, [1975]. pp. 294. *bibliog.*

BLACK (JAMES A.) and CHAMPION (DEAN J.) Methods and issues in social research. New York, [1976]. pp. 445. *bibliog.*

EDINBURGH SEMINAR IN THE SOCIAL SCIENCES, 10TH, 1972. The use of models in the social sciences: [papers of the seminar] ; edited by Lyndhurst Collins. London, 1976. pp. 238. *bibliogs.*

McGAW (DICKINSON) and WATSON (GEORGE) 1943- . Political and social inquiry. New York, [1976]. pp. 496.

RATIONALITY and the social sciences: contributions to the philosophy and methodology of the social sciences; edited by S.I. Benn and G.W.Mortimore. London, 1976. pp. 416. *bibliogs. Includes papers from a seminar sponsored by the Philosophy Department of the Research School of Social Sciences, Australian National University, in 1971.*

— Philosophy.

SCHEIPERMEIER (GUENTER) Erfahrung und Methode:...Theorie der Erfahrungswissenschaft im Hinblick auf die Sozialwissenschaften, insbesondere die Nationalökonomie. Berlin, [1975]. pp. 275. *bibliog.*

RATIONALITY and the social sciences: contributions to the philosophy and methodology of the social sciences; edited by S.I. Benn and G.W.Mortimore. London, 1976. pp. 416. *bibliogs. Includes papers from a seminar sponsored by the Philosophy Department of the Research School of Social Sciences, Australian National University, in 1971.*

— Societies.

PLESSEN (MARIE LOUISE) Die Wirksamkeit des Vereins für Socialpolitik von 1872-1890: Studien zum Katheder- und Staatssozialismus. Berlin, [1975]. pp. 134. *bibliog.*

— Statistical methods.

TUFTE (EDWARD R.) Data analysis for politics and policy. Englewood Cliffs, [1974]. pp. 179.

HEISE (DAVID R.) Causal analysis. New York, [1975]. pp. 301. *bibliogs.*

— Terminology.

UNITED NATIONS INDUSTRIAL DEVELOPMENT ORGANIZATION. 1971- . Thesaurus of industrial development terms. (UNIDO/LIB/SER.C/1-). New York, United Nations, 1971 in progress.

FERRAÙ (ALESSANDRO) Prontuario dei termini politici, economici, sociali in uso in Italia. Roma, [1974]. pp. 151. *bibliog.*

INTERNATIONAL LABOUR OFFICE. Library. 1976. Thesaurus of descriptors used for information processing in the ILO Library. Geneva, 1976. pp. 198. *In English, French and Spanish.*

WILLIAMS (RAYMOND) Keywords: a vocabulary of culture and society. London, [1976]. pp. 286. *bibliog.*

SOCIAL SCIENCES AND ETHICS.

MACRAE (DUNCAN) The social function of social science. New Haven, 1976. pp. 352. *bibliog.*

SOCIAL SCIENCES AND STATE

— United States.

SOCIOLOGY and public policy: the case of Presidential Commissions: [based on two plenary sessions of the Annual Meeting of the American Sociological Association in 1973]; edited by Mirra Komarovsky. New York, [1975]. pp. 183.

SOCIAL SCIENTISTS

— United Kingdom.

WESTOBY (ADAM) and others. Social scientists at work. Guildford, 1976. pp. 145. *bibliog. (Society for Research into Higher Education. Research into Higher Education Monographs. 25)*

— United States.

AMERICAN men and women of science:...a biographical directory...: the social and behavioral sciences. 12th ed. New York, 1973. 2 vols.

HOROWITZ (IRVING LOUIS) and KATZ (JAMES EVERETT) Social science and public policy in the United States. New York, 1975. pp. 187. *bibliogs.*

SOCIAL SERVICE.

ALGIE (JIMMY) Social values, objectives and action. London, 1975. pp. 491. *bibliog.*

FISCHER (JOEL) and GOCHROS (HARVEY L.) Planned behavior change: behavior modification in social work. New York, [1975]. pp. 525. *bibliog.*

RAPOPORT (LYDIA) Creativity in social work: selected writings of Lydia Rapoport; edited by Sanford N.Katz. Philadelphia, 1975. pp. 228.

SIPORIN (MAX) Introduction to social work practice. New York, [1975]. pp. 468.

— Methodology.

BLOOM (MARTIN) The paradox of helping: introduction to the philosophy of scientific practice. New York, [1975]. pp. 283. *bibliog.*

— Research.

PHILIP (ALISTAIR E.) and others. Social work research and the analysis of social data. Oxford, 1975. pp. 234. *bibliogs.*

— Australia.

AUSTRALIA. Department of Social Security. 1974. Interim handbook. [Canberra], 1974. pp. 95.

AUSTRALIA. Social Welfare Commission. Annual report. a., 1975(1st)- Canberra.

SOCIAL SERVICE.

— — South Australia.

AUSTRALIA. Migrant Task Force, South Australia. 1973. First report to the Minister for Immigration; [R.T. Gun, chairman]. Adelaide, 1973. fo. 44.

— — Victoria.

AUSTRALIA. Migrant Task Force Committee, Victoria. 1973. Recommendations to the Minister for Immigration, 30th June 1973; chairman: H.J. Garrick. [Melbourne, 1973]. fo. 77. *Photocopy.*

— Canada.

ARMITAGE (ANDREW) Social welfare in Canada: ideals and realities. Toronto, [1975]. pp. 234. *bibliog.*

— — British Columbia.

BRITISH COLUMBIA. Department of Human Resources. Services for people: annual report... a., 1975 (with fiscal addendum for 1974/75)- Victoria.

— Finland — Finance.

SINTONEN (HARRI) Vanhusten huoltokustannuksiin vaikuttavista tekijöistä, etc. Helsinki, 1974. pp. 127. *bibliog. (Finland. Suomen Virallinen Tilasto. Finlands Officiella Statistik. 32. Sosiaalisia Erikoistutkimuksia. 40) With English summary.*

— France.

DELION (ANDRE G.) Institutions sociales et aménagement du territoire: rapport au gouvernement; (Communication au Comité interministériel pour l'aménagement du territoire). [Paris], Documentation Française, 1974. pp. 76.

— — Societies, etc.

PARIS. Musée Social. Le Musée Social, société reconnue d'utilité publique par décret en date du 31 août 1894: statuts, organisation, services. Paris, 1897. pp. 96.

— Germany.

GERMANY (BUNDESREPUBLIK). Statistisches Bundesamt. 1974. Laufende Leistungen der Hilfe zum Lebensunterhalt, Juni 1972. Wiesbaden, 1974. pp. 63. *(Germany (Bundesrepublik). Statistisches Bundesamt. Öffentliche Sozialleistungen. Reihe 1. Sozialhilfe, Kriegsopferfürsorge. Sonderbeiträge)*

— India.

SOCIAL welfare: legend and legacy: silver jubilee commemoration volume of the Indian Council of Social Welfare; edited by S.D. Gokhale. Bombay, 1975. pp. 432.

— Iran.

PRIGMORE (CHARLES S.) Social work in Iran since the White Revolution. University, Ala., [1976]. pp. 194. *bibliog.*

— Israel.

ISRAEL. Israel Office of Information, [Switzerland]. 1962. Soziale Wohlfahrt in Israel. Zürich, [1962]. pp. 31. *(Schriftenreihe Israel. [7]).*

— Italy.

ITALY. Statutes, etc. 1961-1969. Raccolta di giurisprudenza sull'E[nte] N[azionale di] P[revidenza ed] A[ssistenza per i Dipendenti] S[tatali], 1961-1969: aggiornamento alla raccolta 1942-1961; a cura di Raffaele Bernardo e Francesco di Rocco. Roma, 1970. pp. 207.

ASSISTENZA, emarginazione e lotta di classe ieri e oggi; ([by] G. Alasia [and others]). Milano, 1975. pp. 206.

— Netherlands.

NETHERLANDS. Ministerie van Cultuur, Recreatie en Maatschappelijk Werk. Directie Bijstandszaken. 1971. Korte samenvatting van de algemeene bijstandswet en de rijksgroepsregelingen. 's-Gravenhage, 1971. pp. 45.

BOND VOOR WETENSCHAPPELIJKE ARBEIDERS. Werkgroep Welzijnszorg. Naar een politieke analyse van het welzijnswerkbestel. Nijmegen, [1974]. pp. 47.

WELZIJNSWERK en welzijnspolitiek; [by] Max van den Berg [and others]. Amsterdam, 1975. pp. 144.

— Nigeria.

NIGERIA (LAGOS STATE). Social Welfare Division. Annual report. a., 1970/1972- Yaba.

— South Africa.

SOUTH AFRICA. Department of Social Welfare and Pensions. 1975. Memorandum on social relief. Pretoria, 1975. 1 vol. (various pagings). *In English and Afrikaans.*

— Tasmania.

AUSTRALIA. Migrant Task Force Committee, Tasmania. 1973. Report to the Minister for Immigration; chairman: Ray Sherry. [Hobart, 1973]. fo. 40.

— United Kingdom.

ISLINGTON FABIAN SOCIETY. Social welfare agencies. London, [1967?]. fo. 22.

ISLINGTON FABIAN SOCIETY. About our welfare benefits. London, [1969]. fo. 22.

PRIESTNALL (DAVID J.) The provision of social services in South Hampshire. [Winchester], 1970. pp. 36. *(South Hampshire Plan Technical Unit. Working Papers. 13)*

ISLINGTON FABIAN SOCIETY. How are we doing?: a statistical comparison of Inner London boroughs' welfare services. London, [1971?]. 1 pamphlet (unpaged).

U.K. Social Work Service. Social work service. 3 a yr., Mr 1973 (no.1)- London.

JONES (KATHLEEN) Health and social service merry go-round. London, 1973. pp. 15. *(National Association for Mental Health. Occasional Papers. No.1)*

BROWN (MALCOLM J.) and BURNETT (MARGARET E.) The health and personal social services: problems of working together. Birmingham, [1974]. pp. 8.

BAILEY (ROY V.) and BRAKE (MIKE) eds. Radical social work. London, 1975. pp. 170. *bibliog.*

BUTTERWORTH (ERIC) and HOLMAN (ROBERT) eds. Social welfare in modern Britain: [a reader]. [London], 1975. pp. 443. *bibliog.*

HALL (DEREK) Residents' concern for community problems. Portsmouth, 1975. fo. 10. *(Social Services Research and Intelligence Unit [Portsmouth]. Information Sheets. No. 24)*

LEES (RAY) Research strategies for social welfare. London, 1975. pp. 105. *bibliog.*

WINSTANLEY (MICHAEL) and DUNKLEY (RUTH) Know your rights. London, [1975]. pp. 123. *bibliogs.*

ADVICE services in welfare rights; editor, Rosalind Brooke; [by] Paul Burgess [and others]. London, 1976. pp. 36. *(Fabian Society. Research Series. [No.] 329)*

BROWN (MURIEL) Introduction to social administration in Britain. 3rd ed. London, 1976. pp. 239. *bibliogs.*

GEORGE (VICTOR N.) and WILDING (PAUL) Ideology and social welfare. London, 1976. pp. 162. *bibliog.*

MARONEY (ROBERT M.) The family and the state: considerations for social policy. London, 1976. pp. 142.

MINORS (MICHAEL) and KENNY (DOREEN) Personal social services: estimated net revenue expenditure on client groups in the London boroughs, 1973-74. London, [1976]. pp. 6. *(London. Greater London Council. Research Memoranda. 484)*

ROBSON (WILLIAM ALEXANDER) Welfare state and welfare society: illusion and reality. London, 1976. pp. 184.

TRADITIONS of social policy: essays in honour of Violet Butler; edited by A.H. Halsey. Oxford, [1976]. pp. 285.

U.K. Department of Health and Social Security. 1976. Priorities for health and personal social services in England: a consultative document. London, H.M.S.O., 1976. pp. 83.

— — Bibliography.

BLACKSTONE (TESSA ANN VOSPER) Social policy and administration in Britain: a bibliography;... with the assistance of Peter Vines. London, 1975. pp. 130.

PARTINGTON (MARTIN) and others, compilers. Welfare rights: a bibliography on law and the poor, 1970-1975. London, 1976. pp. 167.

— — Directories.

NATIONAL COUNCIL OF SOCIAL SERVICE. Voluntary social services: directory of organisations and handbook of information. rev.ed. London, 1975. pp. 152.

— — Research.

VOLUNTEER CENTRE. Current research involving the community in meeting social need. Berkhamsted, [1975]. pp. 13.

— — Ireland, Northern.

IRELAND, NORTHERN. Eastern Health and Social Services Board. Annual report. a., 1973/74(1st)- Belfast.

IRELAND, NORTHERN. Department of Health and Social Services 1975. Strategy for the development of health and personal social services in Northern Ireland. Belfast, 1975. pp. 43.

— — Scotland — Statistics.

ADVISORY COUNCIL ON SOCIAL WORK [SCOTLAND]. Committee on Social Work Statistics. Final report; (with Annex: The case return system: evaluation of alternative forms); [F.M. Martin, chairman]. [Edinburgh], Scottish Education Department, Social Work Services Group, [1975]. 3 pts.

— United States.

BROWNING (EDGAR K.) Redistribution and the welfare system. Washington, 1975. pp. 131. *(American Enterprise Institute for Public Policy Research. Evaluative Studies. 22).*

COORDINATING human services; [by Michael Aiken and others]. San Francisco, 1975. pp. 206. *bibliog.*

FEAGIN (JOE R.) Subordinating the poor: welfare and American beliefs. Englewood Cliffs, N.J., [1975]. pp. 180.

GALPER (JEFFRY H.) The politics of social services. Englewood Cliffs, N.J., [1975]. pp. 237.

GANS (SHELDON P.) and HORTON (GERALD T.) Integration of human services: the state and municipal levels. New York, 1975. pp. 345.

GOODWIN (LEONARD) Can social science help resolve national problems?: welfare, a case in point. New York, [1975]. pp. 214.

MANDELL (BETTY REID) ed. Welfare in America: controlling the "dangerous classes". Englewood Cliffs, N.J., [1975]. pp. 185.

PERLMAN (ROBERT) Consumers and social services. New York, [1975]. pp. 126.

TROLANDER (JUDITH ANN) Settlement houses and the great depression. Detroit, 1975. pp. 216. *bibliog.*

TUSSING (A. DALE) Poverty in a dual economy. New York, [1975]. pp. 229. *bibliogs.*

— — Massachusetts.

BAILIS (LAWRENCE NEIL) Bread or justice: grassroots organizing in the welfare rights movement. Lexington, Mass., [1974]. pp. 175.

SOCIAL SERVICE.(Cont.)

— — New York (City).

OSTOW (MIRIAM) and DUTKA (ANNA B.) Work and welfare in New York City. Baltimore, [1975]. pp. 93. *Prepared for the Manpower Administration, U.S. Department of Labor.*

SOCIAL SETTLEMENTS.

TROLANDER (JUDITH ANN) Settlement houses and the great depression. Detroit, 1975. pp. 216. *bibliog.*

SOCIAL STABILITY.

ASHBY (ERIC) Baron Ashby. A second look at doom. Southampton, 1975. pp. 18. *(Southampton. University. Fawley Foundation. Lectures. 21*

SOCIAL STATUS.

GASSON (RUTH M.) and others. Attitudes and facilitation in the attainment of status. Washington, [1973?]. pp. 37. *bibliog. (American Sociological Association. Arnold and Caroline Rose Monograph Series in Sociology)*

LUBECKI (PAUL) Interaktion und Berufsprestige: eine empirische Untersuchung zur Bewertung von Berufen. [Erlangen-Nürnberg, 1976]. 1 vol.(various pagings). *bibliog. Inaugural-Dissertation zur Erlangung des akademischen Grades eines Doktors der Wirtschafts- und Sozialwissenschaften der Friedrich-Alexander-Universität Erlangen-Nürnberg.*

SMITH (BARDWELL L.) ed. Religion and social conflict in south Asia. Leiden, 1976. pp. 115.

SOCIAL SURVEYS.

DAVIS (JAMES ALLAN) Elementary survey analysis. Englewood Cliffs, [1971]. pp. 195.

BABBIE (EARL R.) Survey research methods. Belmont, Cal., [1973]. pp. 384. *bibliogs.*

CONVERSE (JEAN M.) and SCHUMAN (HOWARD) Conversations at random: survey research as interviewers see it. New York, [1974]. pp. 111.

SUDMAN (SEYMOUR) and BRADBURN (NORMAN M.) Response effects in surveys: a review and synthesis. Chicago, 1974. pp. 257. *bibliog. (National Opinion Research Center. Monographs in Social Research. 16)*

ESSER (HARTMUT) Soziale Regelmässigkeiten des Befragtenverhaltens. Meisenheim am Glan, 1975. pp. 409. *bibliog.*

WARWICK (DONALD P.) and LININGER (CHARLES ANDREW) The sample survey: theory and practice. New York, [1975]. pp. 344. *bibliog.*

— Africa, West.

PEIL (MARGARET) and LUCAS (DAVID) Survey research methods for West Africa: a student handbook. Lagos, [1972?]. pp. 80. *bibliog. (Lagos. University. Human Resources Research Unit. Monographs. No. 1)*

— Botswana.

BOTSWANA. Central Statistics Office. 1974. A social and economic survey in three peri-urban areas in Botswana, 1974. Gaborone, 1974. pp. 110.

— Germany.

GERMANY (BUNDESREPUBLIK). Statistisches Bundesamt. 1974. Aufgabe, Methode und Durchführung der Einkommens- und Verbrauchsstichprobe, 1969. Wiesbaden, 1974. pp. 113. *(Preise, Löhne, Wirtschaftsrechnungen. Reihe 18. Einkommens- und Verbrauchsstichproben. 6)*

LAUMANN (EDWARD O.) and PAPPI (FRANZ URBAN) Networks of collective action: a perspective on community influence systems. New York, [1976]. pp. 329. *bibliog.*

— United Kingdom.

SOUTH HAMPSHIRE PLAN TECHNICAL UNIT. Technical Memoranda. A survey of shoppers in South Hampshire: design and response to the survey. 1969. 1 pamphlet (unfoliated). *Xerographic copy.*

U.K. Social Survey. The general household survey. a., 1971- London.

MARSH (ALAN JOHN) The social psychology of political protest: a U.K. national survey of political attitudes and behaviour. 1976. fo. 478. *bibliog. Typescript. Ph.D. (London) thesis: unpublished. This thesis is the property of London University and may not be removed from the Library. Includes two offprints from periodicals.*

— United States.

REED (JOHN SHELTON) The enduring South: subcultural persistence in mass society. Chapel Hill, [1974]. pp. 135. *bibliog.*

SOCIAL SYSTEMS.

ORGANIZED social complexity: challenge to politics and policy; edited by Todd R. La Porte. Princeton, [1975]. pp. 373. *bibliog.*

BATES (FREDERICK L.) and HARVEY (CLYDE C.) The structure of social systems. New York, [1975]. pp. 419.

PROBLEMY sotsial'no-ekonomicheskikh formatsii: istoriko- tipologicheskie issledovaniia. Moskva, 1975. pp. 296.

REGIONAL analysis...; edited by Carol A. Smith. New York, [1976]. 2 vols. *bibliogs. Papers prepared for a conference held in Santa Fe, New Mexico, in 1973.*

SOCIAL VALUES.

SEMINAR ON NATIONAL VALUES OF SINGAPORE FOR PRE-UNIVERSITY STUDENTS, SINGAPORE, 1974. National values of Singapore. Singapore, Ministry of Education, 1974. pp. 84.

ALGIE (JIMMY) Social values, objectives and action. London, 1975. pp. 491. *bibliog.*

FEATHER (NORMAN T.) Values in education and society. New York, [1975]. pp. 350. *bibliog.*

HYMAN (RICHARD) and BROUGH (IAN) Social values and industrial relations: a study of fairness and equality. Oxford, [1975]. pp. 277. *bibliog. (Warwick Studies in Industrial Relations)*

LEWIS (MARGARET T.) Values in Australian income security policies. Canberra, Australian Government Publishing Service, 1975. pp. 37.

SCHULMAN (MICHAEL DAVID) Value consensus and the social cohesion of liberal democracy. 1975. pp. 366. *bibliog. Photocopy of typescript. Ph.D. thesis — Wisconsin University.*

SOCIAL WORK AS A PROFESSION.

BRITISH ASSOCIATION OF SOCIAL WORKERS. Working Party on Social Action. Social action and social work: report of the working party. Birmingham, [1974?]. pp. 10. *(British Association of Social Workers. Publications. 6)*

BAILEY (ROY V.) and BRAKE (MIKE) eds. Radical social work. London, 1975. pp. 170. *bibliog.*

BRAWLEY (EDWARD ALLAN) The new human service worker: community college education and the social services. New York, 1975. pp. 178. *bibliog.*

SOCIAL WORK EDUCATION.

BRAWLEY (EDWARD ALLAN) The new human service worker: community college education and the social services. New York, 1975. pp. 178. *bibliog.*

— Asia.

ASIAN social problems: new strategies for social work education; proceedings of the third Asian regional seminar, "Development of teaching resources and interdisciplinary communication", held August 25-30, 1975, in Hong Kong; [edited by] Mary B. Garcia and Andrij Witiuk. New York, 1976. pp. 168. *Sponsored by the International Association of Schools of Social Work.*

— Iran.

PRIGMORE (CHARLES S.) Social work in Iran since the White Revolution. University, Ala., [1976]. pp. 194. *bibliog.*

— United Kingdom.

CENTRAL COUNCIL FOR EDUCATION AND TRAINING IN SOCIAL WORK [U.K.]. Education and training for social work; (a working group discussion paper). London, 1975. pp. 56. *bibliog. (Papers. 10)*

CENTRAL COUNCIL FOR EDUCATION AND TRAINING IN SOCIAL WORK [U.K.]. Social work education, 1973-74: (a year of consolidation and progress). *[London, 1975]. pp. 48. (REPORTS. 2)*

DAY services: an action plan for training; report of the working party on training for employment in day centres providing care, education and occupational opportunities; [T. White, chairman]. London, Central Council for Education and Training in Social Work, 1975. pp. 86. *bibliog. (Papers. 12)*

TRADITIONS of social policy: essays in honour of Violet Butler; edited by A.H. Halsey. Oxford, [1976]. pp. 285.

SOCIAL WORK WITH CHILDREN

— United Kingdom.

WARDLE (MICHAEL) The Lordsville project: experimental group work in a deprived area. [Welwyn], 1970. pp. 6. *(Reprinted from Case Conference, vol. 16, no.11, March 1970)*

SOCIAL WORK WITH DELINQUENTS AND CRIMINALS

— Italy.

AMMINISTRAZIONE PER LE ATTIVITÀ ASSISTENZIALI ITALIANE E INTERNAZIONALI. Il servizio sociale per minorenni con manifestazioni antisociali. Roma, 1972. pp. 119. *(Sussidi Tecnici per i Servizi Sociali. 21)*

— South Africa.

MIDGLEY (JAMES) and others eds. Crime and punishment in South Africa. Johannesburg, [1975]. pp. 261. *bibliogs.*

SOCIAL WORK WITH THE HOMELESS

— Ireland (Republic).

HART (IAN) and McMAHON (DERMOT) A group approach to socially deprived people. [Dublin, 1975]. pp. 61. *bibliog.*

SOCIAL WORK WITH YOUTH

— United States.

HARDY (RICHARD E.) and CULL (JOHN G.) eds. Problems of adolescents: social and psychological approaches. Springfield, Ill., [1974]. pp. 278. *bibliogs.*

SOCIAL WORKERS

— United Kingdom.

VAUXHALL COMMUNITY DEVELOPMENT PROJECT. Neighbourhood community workers: proposal to create two new posts; report of Project Director. [Liverpool, 1972]. pp. 4.

McCLEAN (J.D.) The legal context of social work. London, 1975. pp. 171.

THOMAS (DAVID NICHOLAS) Organising for social change: a study in the theory and practice of community work. London, 1976. pp. 199. *(National Institute for Social Work Training. National Institute Social Services Library. No. 30)*

SOCIALISM.

THOMPSON (THOMAS PHILLIPS) The politics of labor;...with an introduction by Jay Atherton. Toronto, 1975. pp. 264. *Reprint of the 1887 edition published in New York, with new introduction and appendices.*

CHURCH OF ENGLAND. Church Congress, Swansea, 1909. The official report of the Church Congress, held at Swansea,.. .1909; edited by the Rev. C. Dunkley. London, 1909. pp. 575. *Contains the debate on "Socialism from the standpoint of Christianity".*

PFLUEGER (PAUL) Einführung in die soziale Frage. Zürich, 1910. pp. 200.

KAMPFFMEYER (PAUL) Arbeiterbewegung und Sozialdemokratie. Berlin, 1919. pp. 300.

PROUDHON (PIERRE JOSEPH) General idea of the revolution in the nineteenth century;... translated from the French by John Beverley Robinson. London, 1923. pp. 302.

LOWITSCH (ALFRED) Energie, Planwirtschaft und Sozialismus. Jena, [1929]. pp. 77. *(Urania: kulturpolitische Monatshefte über Natur und Gesellschaft. Jahrgang 1928/29. Buchbeigaben. 4)*

MAN (HENRI DE) Die sozialistische Idee. Jena, [1933]. pp. 343.

ISTORIJA medjunarodnog radničkog i socijalističkog pokreta; po predavanjima održanim na Višoj partijskoj školi "Djuro Djaković" u 1950/51 godini. Beograd, 1952. pp. 636.

SMISAO i perspektive socijalizma: zbornik (radova drugog zasjedanja Korčulanske ljetne škole, Korčula, 1964). Zagreb, 1965. pp. 358.

ERNESTAN, pseud. [i.e. Ernest TANREZ] Pages choisies: Valeur de la liberté, Le socialisme contre l'autorité, Socialisme et humanisme. Paris, [1966]. pp. 191.

WARD (BENJAMIN N.) The socialist economy: a study of organizational alternatives. New York, [1967]. pp. 272.

ROSEWELL (ROGER) The struggle for workers' power. London, [1972?]. pp. 40.

LUEHRS (GEORG) ed. Beiträge zur Theoriediskussion. Berlin, [1973-74]. 2 vols.

FLOHR (HEINER) and others, eds. Freiheitlicher Sozialismus: Beiträge zu seinem heutigen Selbstverständnis; (Gerhard Weisser zum 75. Geburtstag). Bonn-Bad Godesberg, 1973. pp. 256. *bibliog. (Friedrich-Ebert-Stiftung. Forschungsinstitut. Schriftenreihe. Band 95)*

BURZHUAZNYE i melkoburzhuaznye ekonomicheskie kontseptsii sotsializma: kriticheskie ocherki, 1848-1917 gg. Moskva, 1974. pp. 341.

SETTEMBRINI (DOMENICO) Socialismo e rivoluzione dopo Marx. Napoli, [1974]. pp. 701.

UCHENYE ZAPISKI KAFEDR OBSHCHESTVENNYKH NAUK VUZOV LENINGRADA. Problemy Nauchnogo Kommunizma. vyp.8. Kritika osnovnykh napravlenii sovremennogo antikommunizma; pod red.... A.K. Belykh i .... V.P. Gulina. Leningrad, 1974. pp. 184.

BAUER (OTTO) Werkausgabe;...(Redaktion: Hugo Pepper). Wien, [1975 in progress]. *bibliogs.*

MARX (KARL) and ENGELS (FRIEDRICH) Gesamtausgabe (MEGA)...; (Redaktionskommission der Gesamtausgabe: Günter Heyden und Anatoli Jegorow, Leiter). Berlin, 1975 in progress. *bibliogs. Each volume consists of 2 separate parts: Text and Apparat.*

BARNSBY (GEORGE) 1945: year of victory. London, 1975. pp. 37. *bibliog. (Communist Party of Great Britain. History Group. Our History. No. 62)*

BRANDT (WILLY) and others. Briefe und Gespräche, 1972 bis 1975. Frankfurt, [1975]. pp. 133.

BURZHUAZNYE i melkoburzhuaznye ekonomicheskie teorii sotsializma: kriticheskie ocherki, 1917-1945 gg. Moskva, 1975. pp. 327.

CHITARIN (ATTILIO) Sulla transizione: saggi di sociologia economica e politica. Roma, [1975]. pp. 247.

IVERSEN (HERBERT UTZON) Socialistiske essays; udvalg og inledning ved Carl Erik Bay. [Risskov], 1975. 2 vols.(in 1).

KRITISCHER Rationalismus und Sozialdemokratie: herausgegeben von Georg Lührs [and others]; mit einem Vorwort von Helmut Schmidt. Berlin, 1975. pp. 482.

MARKSISTSKO-leninskoe uchenie o sotsializme i sovremennost'. Moskva, 1975. pp. 309.

NIEUWENHUIS (FERDINAND DOMELA) Le socialisme en danger; édition établie par Jean-Yves Bériou. Paris, 1975. pp. 281. *bibliog.*

POLIANSKII (FEDOR IAKOVLEVICH) Kritika reformistskikh kontseptsii sovremennogo kapitalizma. Moskva, 1975. pp. 264.

ROEDER (KARL HEINZ) Die Formel von der "sozialen Demokratie": Staat und Demokratie in der Ideologie des Sozialreformismus. Frankfurt/Main, 1975. pp. 101.

ROEMER (JOACHIM) Ethos und Schöpfertum der Arbeiterklasse im Sozialismus, etc. Berlin, 1975. pp. 168.

SOTSIALIZM: dialektika razvitiia proizvoditel'nykh sil i proizvodstvennykh otnoshenii. Moskva, 1975. pp. 333.

BAUMAN (ZYGMUNT) Socialism: the active utopia. London, 1976. pp. 150.

LANE (DAVID) The socialist industrial state: towards a political sociology of state socialism. London, 1976. pp. 230. *bibliog.*

MILL (JOHN STUART) John Stuart Mill on politics and society; selected and edited by Geraint L. Williams. London, 1976. pp. 412. *bibliog.*

SHAW (GEORGE BERNARD) Practical politics: twentieth-century views on politics and economics; edited by Lloyd J. Hubenka. Lincoln, Neb., [1976]. pp. 266.

SOREL (GEORGES) From Georges Sorel: essays in socialism and philosophy; edited with an introduction by John L. Stanley and translated by John and Charlotte Stanley. New York, 1976. pp. 388. *bibliog.*

STRETTON (HUGH) Capitalism, socialism and the environment. Cambridge, 1976. pp. 332.

VEREIN FÜR SOZIALPOLITIK. Schriften. Neue Folge. Band 86. Studien zum Marktsozialismus; von Gernot Gutmann [and others]; herausgegeben von Christian Watrin. Berlin, [1976]. pp. 118.

— **History.**

KATZ (HENRYK) Karol Marks i jego epoka. Warszawa, 1965. pp. 371.

MOGILEVSKII (SOLOMON ABRAMOVICH) Noveishaia istoriia mezhdunarodnogo kommunisticheskogo i rabochego dvizheniia, 1917-1970 gg. Leningrad, 1971. pp. 160. *bibliog.*

KOSZYK (KURT) and OBERMANN (KARL) eds. Zeitgenossen von Marx und Engels: ausgewählte Briefe aus den Jahren 1844 bis 1852. Assen, 1975. pp. 459. *(International Institute of Social History. Quellen und Untersuchungen zur Geschichte der Deutschen und Österreichischen Arbeiterbewegung. Neue Folge. 6)*

VALIANI (LEO) Questioni di storia del socialismo. [2nd ed.] Torino, [1975]. pp. 427. *bibliog.*

— **Study and teaching.**

BRITISH EMPIRE UNION. Research Department. Danger ahead : socialist and proletarian Sunday schools. London, [1922]. pp. 14.

SOCIALISM, CHRISTIAN.

POUJOL (PIERRE) Socialistes et chrétiens, 1848-1924. Paris, [1956]. pp. 79.

SORG (RICHARD) Marxismus und Protestantismus in Deutschland: eine religionssoziologisch-sozialgeschichtliche Studie zur Marxismus- Rezeption in der evangelischen Kirche, 1848-1948. Köln, [1974]. pp. 237. *bibliog.*

UHL (BERND) Die Idee des Christlichen Sozialismus in Deutschland, 1945- 1947. Mainz, [1975]. pp. 185. *bibliog. (Institut für Begabtenförderung. Beiträge zu Wissenschaft und Politik. Band 11)*

SOCIALISM AND CATHOLIC CHURCH.

KLUEBER (FRANZ) Katholische Soziallehre und demokratischer Sozialismus. Bonn-Bad Godesberg, [1974]. pp. 156.

KREPPEL (KLAUS) Entscheidung für den Sozialismus: die politische Biographie Pastor Wilhelm Hohoffs, 1848-1923. Bonn-Bad Godesberg, [1974]. pp. 196. *bibliog. (Friedrich-Ebert-Stiftung. Forschungsinstitut. Schriftenreihe. Band 114)*

UHL (BERND) Die Idee des Christlichen Sozialismus in Deutschland, 1945- 1947. Mainz, [1975]. pp. 185. *bibliog. (Institut für Begabtenförderung. Beiträge zu Wissenschaft und Politik. Band 11)*

SOCIALISM AND EDUCATION.

ERLER (OTTO) Die Volksschule im Lichte des demokratischen Staates und des Sozialismus; für Laien, besonders für die Eltern geschrieben. Leipzig, 1919. pp. 48.

CHRIST (KARL) Sozialdemokratie und Volkserziehung: die Bedeutung des Mannheimer Parteitags der SPD im Jahre 1906 für die Entwicklung der Bildungspolitik...vor dem Ersten Weltkrieg. Bern, 1975. pp. 298. *bibliog. Inaugural-Dissertation der Philosophischen Fakultät der Friedrich-Alexander-Universität zu Erlangen-Nürnberg.*

SOCIALISM AND ETHICS.

ERDMANN (HANS) and others. Ökonomie und Moral im Sozialismus: zur Dialektik von materiellen Verhältnissen und Moral beim Aufbau der sozialistischen Gesellschaft. Berlin, 1975. pp. 292.

SOCIALISM AND RELIGION.

SORG (RICHARD) Marxismus und Protestantismus in Deutschland: eine religionssoziologisch-sozialgeschichtliche Studie zur Marxismus- Rezeption in der evangelischen Kirche, 1848-1948. Köln, [1974]. pp. 237. *bibliog.*

NEEDHAM (JOSEPH) Moulds of understanding: a pattern of natural philosophy: [selected essays]; edited and introduced by Gary Werskey. London, 1976. pp. 320. *bibliog.*

SOCIALISM AND YOUTH.

GROTEWOHL (OTTO) Jugend und Partei: (aus einer Rede...des Parteivorstandes der SED, 20 und 21. Juli 1949). Berlin, [1949]. pp. 23.

VARIN (JACQUES) Jeunes comme J.C.: sur la Jeunesse communiste. Paris, 1975 in progress.

BUTTERWEGGE (CHRISTOPH) Jungsozialisten und SPD, etc. Hamburg, [1975]. pp. 157.

MUELLER (DIRK H.) Idealismus und Revolution: zur Opposition der Jungen gegen den sozialdemokratischen Parteivorstand, 1890 bis 1894. Berlin, 1975. pp. 186. *bibliog. (IWK: internationale wissenschaftliche Korrespondenz zur Geschichte der deutschen Arbeiterbewegung. Beihefte. 3)*

SOCIALISM IN AFRICA.

NYERERE (JULIUS KAMBARAGE) Man and development. Dar es Salaam, 1974. pp. 125.

SOCIALISM IN AUSTRIA.

BAUER (OTTO) Werkausgabe;...(Redaktion: Hugo Pepper). Wien, [1975 in progress]. *bibliogs.*

SOCIALISM IN AUSTRIA-HUNGARY.

SOCIALISM IN AUSTRIA-HUNGARY

STUDIEN zur Geschichte der Österreichisch-Ungarischen Monarchie: [papers of a conference held in Budapest in 1958]; redigiert von V. Sándor und P. Hanák. Budapest, 1961. pp. 524. *(Magyar Tudományos Akadémia. Studia Historica. 51)*

SOCIALISM IN BELGIUM.

DELVO (EDGARD) Sociale collaboratie: pleidooi voor een volksnationale sociale politiek. Antwerpen, [1975]. pp. 266.

SOCIALISM IN CHILE.

SWEEZY (PAUL MARLOR) and MAGDOFF (HARRY) eds. Revolution and counter-revolution in Chile. New York, [1974]. pp. 169. *Articles from Monthly Review, 1971-1973.*

The LESSONS of Chile: the Chilean coup and the future of socialism; (a selection of papers and discussion from the proceedings of a conference held in Amsterdam on 22-24 February, 1974...organised by the Transnational Institute); edited by John Gittings. Nottingham, 1975. pp. 91.

SOCIALISM IN CHINA.

MAO (TSE-TUNG) Mao Tsé-toung et la construction du socialisme: modèle soviétique ou voie chinoise; textes inédits traduits et présentés par Hu Chi-Hsi. Paris, [1975]. pp. 192.

BERNAL (MARTIN) Chinese socialism to 1907. Ithaca, N.Y., 1976. pp. 259. *bibliog.*

SOCIALISM IN CUBA.

El DEBATE cubano sobre el funcionamiento de la ley del valor en el socialismo; ([by] Ernesto "Che" Guevara [and others]) Barcelona, 1974. pp. 357.

SOCIALISM IN CZECHOSLOVAKIA.

PURŠ (JAROSLAV) Dělnické hnutí v českých zemích, 1849-1867. [Praha], 1961. pp. 148. *bibliog. (Československá Akademie Věd. Rozpravy: Řada Společenských Věd. Ročník, sešit 6) With Russian summary.*

PAUL (ERNST) Oswald Hillebrand: ein Lebensbild nach archivalischen Unterlagen, etc. Stuttgart, 1976. pp. 78.

PELIKÁN (JIRÍ) Socialist opposition in Eastern Europe: the Czechoslovak example; translated by Marian Sling and V. and R. Tosek. London, 1976. pp. 221.

ZESSNER (KLAUS) Josef Seliger und die nationale Frage in Böhmen: eine Untersuchung über die nationale Politik der deutschböhmischen Sozialdemokratie, 1899-1920. Stuttgart, [1976]. pp. 257. *bibliog.*

SOCIALISM IN DENMARK.

SALOMONSSON (PER) Socialismen og socialdemokratiet: indføring i dansk arbejderbevaegelses teoridannelse, 1871-84. [Copenhagen, 1974]. pp. 128. *bibliog. (Selskabet til Forskning i Arbejderbevaegelsens Historie. Publikationer. 1)*

SOCIALISM IN ETHIOPIA.

ETHIOPIA. 1975. Objectives of the development through cooperation, enlightenment and work campaign. [Addis Ababa, 1975]. fo. 20.

SOCIALISM IN EUROPE.

FABIAN SOCIETY. Fabian Tracts. [No]. 438. Social democracy in Europe; [by] Anthony Crosland. London, 1975. pp. 14.

LESSNER (FRIEDRICH) Ich brachte das "Kommunistische Manifest" zum Drucker; (zusammengestellt und eingeleitet von Ursula Herrmann und Gerhard Winkler). Berlin, 1975. pp. 392. *bibliog.*

The LESSONS of Chile: the Chilean coup and the future of socialism; (a selection of papers and discussion from the proceedings of a conference held in Amsterdam on 22-24 February, 1974...organised by the Transnational Institute); edited by John Gittings. Nottingham, 1975. pp. 91.

SZENDE (STEFAN) Zwischen Gewalt und Toleranz: Zeugnisse und Reflexionen eines Sozialisten; mit einem Vorwort von Willy Brandt. Frankfurt am Main, [1975]. pp. 332.

WISTRICH (ROBERT S.) Revolutionary Jews from Marx to Trotsky. London, 1976. pp. 254. *bibliog.*

SOCIALISM IN FRANCE.

BLUM (LEON) Pour la vieille maison: intervention au Congrès de Tours, 1920. Paris, 1934. pp. 43.

LUKIN (NIKOLAI MIKHAILOVICH) ed. Sotsialisticheskoe dvizhenie vo Frantsii. Moskva, 1934. pp. 376.

ASSISES DU SOCIALISME, 1974. Pour le socialisme: [report and proceedings of a meeting held in Paris, October 1974]. [Paris, 1974]. pp. 199.

CHARZAT (MICHEL) and OUTAIN (GHISLAINE) Le C.E.R.E.S.: un combat pour le socialisme. [Paris, 1975]. pp. 279. *bibliog.*

MOSS (BERNARD H.) The origins of the French labor movement, 1830-1914: the socialism of skilled workers. Berkeley, Calif., [1976]. pp. 217. *bibliog.*

SOCIALISM IN GERMANY.

LASSALLE (FERDINAND JOHANN GOTTLIEB) Die Wissenschaft und die Arbeiter: eine Verteidigungs-Rede vor dem Berliner Kriminalgericht gegen die Anklage, die besitzlosen Klassen zum Hass und zur Verachtung gegen die Besitzenden öffentlich angereizt zu haben;...neue Ausgabe... von Eduard Bernstein. Berlin, 1908. pp. 55.

KAMPFFMEYER (PAUL) Arbeiterbewegung und Sozialdemokratie. Berlin, 1919. pp. 300.

LIEFMANN (ROBERT) Arbeitslöhne und Unternehmergewinne nach dem Kriege. Stuttgart, 1919. pp. 24.

ROCKER (RUDOLF) Zur Betrachtung der Lage in Deutschland: die Möglichkeiten einer freiheitlichen Bewegung; [edited by Helmut Rüdiger]. New York, 1947. pp. 36.

GROTE-MISMAHL (ULRICH) Neubau deutscher Wirtschaft durch konstruktiven Sozialismus. n.p., [1951]. pp. 498.

KRITIK der bürgerlichen Ökonomie: neues Manuskript von Marx; und Rede von Engels über F. List. Berlin, [1972]. pp. 86.

LUEHRS (GEORG) ed. Beiträge zur Theoriediskussion. Berlin, [1973-74]. 2 vols.

FLOHR (HEINER) and others, eds. Freiheitlicher Sozialismus: Beiträge zu seinem heutigen Selbstverständnis; (Gerhard Weisser zum 75. Geburtstag). Bonn-Bad Godesberg, 1973. pp. 256. *bibliog. (Friedrich-Ebert-Stiftung. Forschungsinstitut. Schriftenreihe. Band 95)*

EHRENBURG (HERBERT) and STREICHAN (PETER) eds. Dokumente zur Vermögenspolitik. Bonn-Bad Godesberg, [1974]. pp. 127. *bibliog.*

LOEWENTHAL (RICHARD) Sozialismus und aktive Demokratie: Essays zu ihren Voraussetzungen in Deutschland. Frankfurt am Main, [1974]. pp. 176.

ECKERT (RAINER) Das ist "demokratischer Sozialismus": eine Antwort auf Johano Strassers Frage: "Was ist demokratischer Sozialismus?". Frankfurt am Main, [1975]. pp. 72.

LIEBKNECHT (WILHELM PHILIPP MARTIN CHRISTIAN LUDWIG) Leitartikel und Beiträge in der Osnabrücker Zeitung, 1864- 1866; herausgegeben von Georg Eckert. Hildesheim, 1975. pp. 794. *(Historische Kommission für Niedersachsen und Bremen. Veröffentlichungen. 35)*

BOCK (HANS MANFRED) Geschichte des "linken Radikalismus" in Deutschland: ein Versuch. Frankfurt am Main, 1976. pp. 370. *bibliog.*

SCHLEI (MARIE) and WAGNER (JOACHIM) Freiheit, Gerechtigkeit, Solidarität: Grundwerte und praktische Politik; mit einem Vorwort von Helmut Schmidt. Bonn-Bad Godesberg, [1976]. pp. 165.

ULLRICH (VOLKER) Die Hamburger Arbeiterbewegung vom Vorabend des ersten Weltkrieges bis zur Revolution 1918/19. Hamburg, [1976]. 2 vols. *bibliog. Band 2 contains notes and the bibliography.*

— **Bibliography.**

DOWE (DIETER) compiler. Bibliographie zur Geschichte der deutschen Arbeiterbewegung, sozialistischen und kommunistischen Bewegung von den Anfängen bis 1863, etc. Bonn-Bad Godesberg, 1976. pp. 303. *bibliog. (Archiv für Sozialgeschichte. Beihefte. 5)*

SOCIALISM IN GHANA.

NKRUMAH (KWAME) Building a socialist state: an address...to the C[onvention] P[eople's] P[arty] study group, April 22, 1961. [Accra, Ministry of Information and Broadcasting, 1962]. pp. 12.

SOCIALISM IN INDIA.

BHULESHKAR (ASHOK VASANTRAO) ed. Growth of Indian economy in socialism. Bombay, 1975. pp. 607. *(Jawaharlal Nehru Memorial Institute of Development Studies. Jawaharlal Nehru Memorial Series. 3)*

SOCIALISM IN ITALY.

BARONE (ANTONIO) Piazza Spartaco: il movimento operaio e socialista a Castellammare di Stabia, 1900-1922. Roma, 1974. pp 237.

VALIANI (LEO) Questioni di storia del socialismo. [2nd ed.] Torino, [1975]. pp. 427. *bibliog.*

— **Periodicals.**

LEDDA (ISABELLA) and ZANELLA (GABRIELLA) I periodici di Padova, 1866-1926, liberali, radicali, socialisti. Padova, 1973. pp. 252. *(Centro per la Storia del Movimento Operaio nel Veneto, and Padua. Università. Istituto di Storia Medioevale e Moderna. Movimenti Politici e Sociali dell'Età Contemporanea nel Veneto. Collana.4)*

SOCIALISM IN KOREA.

KIM (IL-SUNG) On the socialist constitution of the Democratic People's Republic of Korea;[translation of the texts edited by Fukushima Masao]. Pyongyang, 1975. pp. 329.

SOCIALISM IN LATIN AMERICA.

HERRERA OROPEZA (JOSE) America Latina: proceso hacia el socialismo. Caracas, 1972. pp. 224. *bibliog.*

SOCIALISM IN POLAND.

PRÓCHNIK (ADAM) Bunt łódzki w roku 1892: studium historyczne. Warszawa, 1950. pp. 156. *Reprint of 1st ed. of 1932 with some omissions.*

ARCHIWUM ruchu robotniczego. Warszawa, 1973 in progress.

MARCHLEWSKI (JULIAN BALTAZAR) Listy do 'zony i córki; słowo wią'zące Zofia Marchlewska, opracowała Bo'zena Wróblewska, wstęp Janusz Durko. Warszawa, 1975. pp. 395.

TYCH (FELIKS) ed. Polskie programy socjalistyczne, 1878-1918, etc. Warszawa, 1975. pp. 575.

SOCIALISM IN PORTUGAL.

ALVES (MARCIO MOREIRA) Les soldats socialistes du Portugal. [Paris, 1975]. pp. 239. *bibliog.*

SOCIALISM IN RUSSIA.

PERVYE samarskie lenintsy: ocherki o chlenakh marksistskogo kruzhka, sozdannogo V.I. Leninym v Samare. Kuibyshev, 1969. pp. 192.

RUBEL (MAXIMILIEN) Russland und die russische Revolution im Denken von Karl Marx. Trier, [1969]. pp. 36. *(Karl-Marx-Haus. Schriften. 2)*

REVOLIUTSIONNO-osvoboditel'noe dvizhenie v XIX-XX vv. v Povolzh'e i Priural'e. Kazan', 1974. pp. 115.

GEGEMONIIA proletariata v trekh russkikh revoliutsiiakh. Moskva, 1975. pp. 352.

KONIUSHAIA (RAISA PAVLOVNA) Karl Marks i revoliutsionnaia Rossiia. Moskva, 1975. pp. 440.

MAO (TSE-TUNG) Mao Tsé-toung et la construction du socialisme: modèle soviétique ou voie chinoise; textes inédits traduits et présentés par Hu Chi-Hsi. Paris, [1975]. pp. 192.

RABOCHEE dvizhenie v Rossii v 1901-1904 gg.: sbornik dokumentov Leningrad, 1975. pp. 591. bibliog.

SARALIEVA (ZARETKHAN KHADZHI-MURZAEVNA) "Kapital" K. Marksa i rabochee dvizhenie Rossii, 1895-1917 gg. : rasprostranenie i propaganda. Moskva, 1975. pp. 211. bibliog.

ZHUIKOV (GENNADII SEMENOVICH) Peterburgskie marksisty i gruppa "Osvobozhdeniia truda". Leningrad, 1975. pp. 328.

SOCIALISM IN SCOTLAND.

The RED paper on Scotland; [edited by Gordon Brown]. Edinburgh, 1975. pp. 368.

SOCIALISM IN SERBIA.

LAPČEVIĆ (DRAGIŠA) Istorija socijalizma u Srbiji. Beograd, 1922. pp. 180. *In Cyrillic.*

SOCIALISM IN SILESIA.

HAWRANEK (FRANCISZEK) Ruch robotniczy na Śląsku Opolskim w latach 1918-1944. Chorzów, 1974. pp. 136. bibliog.

SOCIALISM IN SPAIN.

SABORIT (ANDRES) Joaquin Costa y el socialismo. Madrid, 1970. pp. 178.

BESTEIRO FERNANDEZ (JULIAN) Historia parlamentaria del socialismo: Julian Besteiro...; edicion, guia historica y notas de Fermin Solana. Madrid, [1975 in progress].

AISA (JAVIER) and ARBELOA MURU (VICTOR MANUEL) Historia de la Union General de Trabajadores. Bilbao, 1975. pp. 285.

SOCIALISM IN SWEDEN.

MISGELD (KLAUS) Die "Internationale Gruppe demokratischer Sozialisten" in Stockholm, 1942-1945: zur sozialistischen Friedensdiskussion während des Zweiten Weltkrieges. Uppsala, 1976. pp. 212. bibliog. (Uppsala. Universitet. Historiska Institutionen. Studia Historica Upsaliensia. 79)

SOCIALISM IN SWITZERLAND.

PFLUEGER (PAUL) Einführung in die soziale Frage. Zürich, 1910. pp. 200.

ARBEITSGRUPPE FÜR GESCHICHTE DER ARBEITERBEWEGUNG ZÜRICH. Schweizerische Arbeiterbewegung: Dokumente zu Lage, Organisation und Kämpfen der Arbeiter von der Frühindustrialisierung bis zur Gegenwart. Zürich, [1975]. pp. 411. bibliog. (Studienbibliothek zur Geschichte der Arbeiterbewegung, Zürich. Schriftenreihe. Band 2)

LANG (KARL MAX) Kritiker, Ketzer, Kämpfer: das Leben des Arbeiterarztes Fritz Brupbacher. Zürich, [1975]. pp. 361. bibliog. (Studienbibliothek zur Geschichte der Arbeiterbewegung, Zürich. Schriftenreihe. Band 3)

SOCIALISM IN TANZANIA.

NYERERE (JULIUS KAMBARAGE) Socialism and rural development. [Dar es Salaam, Government Printer, 1967]. pp. 31.

AWITI (ADHU) The development of ujamaa villages and the peasant question in Iringa district: a study outline. Dar es Salaam, 1973. pp. 48. bibliog. (Dar es Salaam. University. Economic Research Bureau. ERB Papers. 73.4)

RAIKES (PHILIP L.) Economic evaluation criteria for ujamaa villages. Dar es Salaam, 1973. pp. 36. bibliog. (Dar es Salaam. University. Economic Research Bureau. ERB Papers. 73. 3)

PRATT (CRANFORD) The critical phase in Tanzania, 1945-1968: Nyerere and the emergence of a socialist strategy. Cambridge, 1976. pp. 309. bibliog.

SOCIALISM IN THE ARGENTINE REPUBLIC.

DICKMANN (ADOLFO) El socialismo y el principio de nacionalidad. Buenos Aires, 1916. pp. 62.

SOCIALISM IN THE CONGO (BRAZZAVILLE).

NGOUABI (MARIEN) Vers la construction d'une société socialiste en Afrique: écrits et discours du Président du Comité Central du Parti Congolais du Travail, Président de la République Populaire du Congo. Paris, [1975]. pp. 727.

SOCIALISM IN THE NETHERLANDS.

HARMSEN (GER) Historisch overzicht van socialisme en arbeidersbeweging in Nederland. [Nijmegen, c. 1973 in progress].

SOCIALISM IN THE UKRAINE.

VOLOSHCHENKO (AZA KYRYLIVNA) Narysy z istoriï suspil'no-politychnoho rukhu na Ukraïni v 70-kh - na pochatku 80-kh rokiv XIX st. Kyïv, 1974. pp. 222.

SOCIALISM IN THE UNDERDEVELOPED AREAS.
See UNDERDEVELOPED AREAS — Socialism.

SOCIALISM IN THE UNITED KINGDOM.

ANTI-SOCIALIST UNION OF GREAT BRITAIN. Statement of objects, policy, and work. London, 1908. pp. 12.

HOLLAND (STUART) Strategy for socialism: the challenge of Labour's programme. Nottingham, 1975. pp. 95.

HOWELL (DAVID) 1937- . British social democracy: a study in development and decay. London, [1976]. pp. 320. bibliog.

SHIPLEY (PETER) Revolutionaries in modern Britain. London, 1976. pp. 256. bibliog.

WIDGERY (DAVID) ed. The Left in Britain 1956-68. Harmondsworth, 1976. pp. 549. bibliog.

SOCIALISM IN THE UNITED STATES.

SOCIALIST LABOR PARTY OF AMERICA and SOCIALIST TRADE AND LABOR ALLIANCE OF THE UNITED STATES AND CANADA. Report on the labor movement in the United States of America to the International Socialist and Trade-Union Congress, London, July 27th, 1896. n.p., [1896?]. pp. 4.

SAMSON (LEON) Toward a united front: a philosophy for American workers. New York, [1933]. pp. 276.

CANNON (JAMES PATRICK) America's road to socialism. 2nd ed. New York, 1975. pp. 124.

STAVE (BRUCE M.) ed. Socialism and the cities. Port Washington, N.Y., 1975. pp. 210. bibliog.

WEINSTEIN (JAMES) Ambiguous legacy: the Left in American politics. New York, 1975. pp. 179.

BARNES (JACK) American socialist, and WATERS (MARY-ALICE) eds. Prospects for socialism in America; [by] Jack Barnes [and others]. New York, 1976. pp. 265.

SOMBART (WERNER) Why is there no socialism in the United States?;...translated by Patricia M. Hocking and C.T. Husbands; edited and with an introductory essay by C.T. Husbands, etc. London, 1976. pp. 187. bibliog.

SOCIALISM IN WHITE RUSSIA.

RAVNOPOLETS (LIUDMILA SILOVNA) Iz istorii izdaniia i rasprostraneniia proizvedenii V.I. Lenina v Belorussii. Moskva, 1974. pp. 159.

SOCIALISM IN YUGOSLAVIA.

MARKOVIĆ (MIHAILO) and COHEN (ROBERT SONNE). Yugoslavia: the rise and fall of socialist humanism: a history of the Praxis Group. Nottingham, 1975. pp. 93.

SOCIALIST COMPETITION.

SALIEV (SULTANMURAD) Novyi etap sotsialisticheskogo sorevnovaniia: deiatel'nost' Kompartii Uzbekistana po organizatsii i rukovodstvu dvizheniem za kommunisticheskoe otnoshenie k trudu, v promyshlennosti respubliki, 1959-1965 gg. Tashkent, 1975. pp. 184.

SOCIALIST ETHICS.

MARXISMO ed etica: testi sul dibattito intorno al "socialismo neokantiano", 1896-1911, con un saggio introduttivo di Hans Jörg Sandkühler; edizione italiana a cura di Emilio Agazzi. Milano, 1975. pp. 317. bibliog.

SOCIALIST PARTY (ARGENTINE REPUBLIC).

DICKMANN (ENRIQUE) Democracia y socialismo. Buenos Aires, 1917. pp. 203.

SOCIALIST PARTY (AUSTRIA).

KREISKY (BRUNO) Politik für Österreichs Zukunft.... Regierungserklärung vom 5.11.1971. [Vienna, 1971]. pp. 63.

SOZIALISTISCHE PARTEI ÖSTERREICHS. Programm und Statut. [Vienna, 1972?]. 1 vol. (looseleaf).

SOZIALISTISCHE PARTEI ÖSTERREICHS. [Landesparteiorganisation?] Salzburg. Der Salzburgplan: ein Programm der SPÖ für die gesunde Weiterentwicklung des Landes Salzburg. Salzburg, [1973]. pp. 214.

BAUER (OTTO) Werkausgabe;...(Redaktion: Hugo Pepper). Wien, [1975 in progress]. bibliogs.

DUCZYNSKA (ILONA) Der demokratische Bolschewik: zur Theorie und Praxis der Gewalt; mit einem Vorwort von Friedrich Heer. München, [1975]. pp. 383.

KONRAD (HELMUT) Nationalismus und Internationalismus: die österreichische Arbeiterbewegung vor dem Ersten Weltkrieg. Wien, 1975. pp. 214. bibliog. (Ludwig-Boltzmann-Institut für Geschichte der Arbeiterbewegung. Materialien zur Arbeiterbewegung. Nr.4)

KYKAL (INEZ) and STADLER (KARL RUDOLF) Richard Bernaschek: Odyssee eines Rebellen. Wien, [1976]. pp. 317. bibliog. (Ludwig-Boltzmann-Institut für Geschichte der Arbeiterbewegung. Veröffentlichungen)

SOCIALIST PARTY (CHILE).

CASANUEVA VALENCIA (FERNANDO) and FERNANDEZ CANQUE (MANUEL) El Partido Socialista y la lucha de clases en Chile. Santiago de Chile, 1973. pp. 342. bibliog.

SOCIALIST PARTY (FRANCE).

CAMPBELL (IAN R.) The end of the Mitterrand experiment? Coventry, 1975. pp. 57. (University of Warwick. Department of Politics. Working Papers. No. 5)

SOCIALIST PARTY (ITALY).

CRISI della DC e alternativa socialista: per una trasformazione democratica del paese; ([by] Riccardo Lombardi [and others]). Venezia, 1975. pp. 146. *Proceedings of a conference held by the Partito Socialista Italiano in Trento in 1974.*

MERLI (STEFANO) Fronte antifascista e politica di classe: socialisti e comunisti in Italia, 1923-1939. Bari, [1975]. pp. 355.

SOCIALIST PARTY (POLAND).

SYZDEK (BRONISŁAW) Polska Partia Socjalistyczna w latach 1944-1948. Warszawa, 1974. pp. 495. *bibliog.*

SOCIALIST PARTY (SWITZERLAND).

GROUNAUER (MARIE MADELEINE) La Genève rouge de Léon Nicole, 1933-1936. [Geneva, 1975]. pp. 236. *bibliog.*

SOCIALIST PARTY (UNITED KINGDOM).

BARLTROP (ROBERT) The monument: the story of the Socialist Party of Great Britain. London, 1975. pp. 200.

SOCIALIST-REVOLUTIONARY PARTY (RUSSIA).

GUSEV (KIRILL VLADIMIROVICH) Partiia eserov: ot melkoburzhuaznogo revoliutsionarizma k kontrrevoliutsii: istoricheskii ocherk. Moskva, 1975. pp. 383.

OWEN (RICHARD CHARLES) The revolutionary career of M.A. Natanson, 1868-1906. 1975. fo. 361. *bibliog. Typescript. Ph.D.(London) thesis: unpublished. This thesis is the property of London University and may not be removed from the Library.*

SOCIALIST WORKERS PARTY (UNITED STATES).

CANNON (JAMES PATRICK) The Socialist Workers Party in World War II: (writings and speeches, 1940-43); (edited by Les Evans). New York, 1975. pp. 446.

BARNES (JACK) American socialist, and WATERS (MARY-ALICE) eds. Prospects for socialism in America; [by] Jack Barnes [and others]. New York, 1976. pp. 265.

SOCIALISTS

— Denmark.

KAMPMANN (VIGGO) Seks socialdemokratiske statsministre, skildre af den syvende. [Copenhagen, 1973]. pp. 94.

— Germany.

KOSZYK (KURT) and OBERMANN (KARL) eds. Zeitgenossen von Marx und Engels: ausgewählte Briefe aus den Jahren 1844 bis 1852. Assen, 1975. pp. 459. *(International Institute of Social History. Quellen und Untersuchungen zur Geschichte der Deutschen und Österreichischen Arbeiterbewegung. Neue Folge. 6)*

— Italy.

ANDREUCCI (FRANCO) and DETTI (TOMMASO) Il movimento operaio italiano: dizionario biografico, 1853-1943. Roma, 1975 in progress. *bibliogs.*

— Russia.

SAPIR (BORIS) ed. Lavrov - gody emigratsii: arkhivnye materialy v dvukh tomakh; Lavrov - years of emigration: letters and documents in two volumes. Dordrecht, [1974]. 2 vols. *(International Institute of Social History. Russian Series on Social History)*

SOCIALIZATION.

WATSON (LAWRENCE CRAIG) Guajiro personality and urbanization. Los Angeles, 1968. pp. 209. *bibliog. (California University. Latin American Center. Latin American Studies. vol. 10)*

FAMILY socialization and the adolescent: determinants of self- concept, conformity, religiosity, and counterculture values; [by] Darwin L. Thomas [and others]. Lexington, Mass., [1974]. pp. 181. *bibliog.*

FREEDMAN (ANNE E.) and FREEDMAN (P.E.) The psychology of political control: comprising dialogues between a modern prince and his tutor on the application of basic psychological principles to the realm of politics. New York, [1975]. pp. 276. *bibliog.*

SOCIALIZATION and values in Canadian society; edited by Elia Zureik and Robert M. Pike. Toronto, 1975. 2 vols. *bibliogs.*

SCHONFELD (WILLIAM R.) Obedience and revolt: French behavior towards authority. Beverly Hills, [1976]. pp. 256.

SOCIALLY HANDICAPPED.

KNIGHT (T.E.) A conceptual background to the use of social indicators for the identification of areas of urban deprivation. [London], 1974. fo. 11. *(U.K. Department of the Environment. Economic and Statistical Notes. No. 21)*

— United Kingdom.

LIVERPOOL. Corporation. Vauxhall Community Development Project Interdepartmental Working Party. The concept of need and the formulation of standards for the provision of services. [Liverpool, 1972]. fo. 4.

COMMUNITY DEVELOPMENT PROJECT. Rates of decline: an unacceptable base of public finance; a submission to the Layfield Committee on Local Government Finance. [London, 1975] repr. 1976. pp. 51. *bibliog.*

SMITH (A. CHRISTOPHER D.) and HOATH (DAVID CHARLES) Law and the underprivileged. London, 1975. pp. 247.

SOCIAL TOURISM STUDY GROUP. Holidays: the social need; [D.O. Gladwin, chairman]. London, English Tourist Board, [1976]. pp. 74.

— — Research.

U.K. Joint Working Party on Transmitted Deprivation. 1975. Second report; [R.C.O. Matthews, chairman]. London, [1975]. fo. 6,iii.

SOCIALLY HANDICAPPED CHILDREN

— Education — United Kingdom.

EDUCATION and deprivation; edited by James Rushton [and] John D. Turner. Manchester, [1975]. pp. 105. *bibliog. A series of public lectures delivered in the School of Education at the University of Manchester in 1973.*

NATIONAL CONFERENCE ON EDUCATIONAL DISADVANTAGE, LONDON, 1975. Educational disadvantage: perspectives and policies; the report of a conference convened by the Secretary of State for Education and Science on 16 April 1975. London, 1975. pp. 23. *(U.K. Department of Education and Science. Education Information)*

SOCIALLY HANDICAPPED YOUTH

— Colombia.

WALTER (JOHN P.) and others. Deprived urban youth: an economic and cross-cultural analysis of the United States, Colombia, and Peru. New York, 1975. pp. 147.

— Peru.

WALTER (JOHN P.) and others. Deprived urban youth: an economic and cross-cultural analysis of the United States, Colombia, and Peru. New York, 1975. pp. 147.

— United States.

WALTER (JOHN P.) and others. Deprived urban youth: an economic and cross-cultural analysis of the United States, Colombia, and Peru. New York, 1975. pp. 147.

SOCIETY FOR THE DIFFUSION OF USEFUL KNOWLEDGE.

SMITH (HAROLD) Librarian. The Society for the Diffusion of Useful Knowledge, 1826- 1846: a social nd bibliographical evaluation. London, 1974. pp. 100. *bibliog. (Dalhousie University. Libraries and School of Library Service. Occasional Papers. No. 8)*

SOCIJALISTICKI SAVEZ RADNOG NARODA SRBIJE

— Congresses.

SOCIJALISTIČKI SAVEZ RADNOG NARODA SRBIJE. Kongres, 6-i, 1966. Šesti kongres SSRN Srbije, 22,23,24, februar, 1966, Beograd. Beograd, 1966. pp. 286. *In Cyrillic.*

SOCIOLINGUISTICS.

ALLEN (DONALD E.) and GUY (REBECCA F.) Conversation analysis: the sociology of talk. The Hague, 1974. pp. 284. *bibliog.*

GILES (HOWARD) and POWESLAND (PETER F.) Speech style and social evaluation. London, 1975. pp. 218. *bibliog. (European Association of Experimental Social Psychology. European Monographs in Social Psychology. 7)*

HALL (WILLIAM S.) and FREEDLE (ROY O.) Culture and language: the black American experience. New York, [1975]. pp. 191. *bibliog.*

PLATT (JOHN T.) and PLATT (HEIDI K.) The social significance of speech: an introduction to and workbook in sociolinguistics. Amsterdam, 1975. pp. 194. *bibliogs.*

SEMINAR ON LANGUAGE AND LEARNING, 1ST, 1973. Problems of language and learning: [papers of a seminar organised by the Scottish Council for Research in Education and sponsored bythe Educational Research Board of the Social Science Research Council]; edited by Alan Davies. London, 1975. pp. 154. *bibliog.*

WOOTTON (ANTHONY) Dilemmas of discourse: controversies about the sociological interpretation of language. London, 1975. pp. 125. *bibliog.*

WILLIAMS (RAYMOND) Keywords: a vocabulary of culture and society. London, [1976]. pp. 286. *bibliog.*

SOCIOLOGICAL JURISPRUDENCE.

TIMASHEV (NIKOLAI SERGEEVICH) An introduction to the sociology of law [originally published 1939, Cambridge, Mass.]. Westport, Conn., 1974. pp. 418. *bibliog. (Harvard University. Harvard Sociological Studies. vol. 3)*

FRIEDMAN (LAWRENCE MEIR) The legal system: a social science perspective. New York, [1975]. pp. 338. *bibliog.*

PAPACHRISTOS (A.C.) La réception des droits privés étrangers comme phénomène de sociologie juridique. Paris, 1975. pp. 154. *bibliog.*

GESSNER (VOLKMAR) Recht und Konflikt: eine soziologische Untersuchung privatrechtlicher Konflikte in Mexiko. Tübingen, 1976. pp. 290. *bibliog. (Max-Planck-Institut für Ausländisches und Internationales Privatrecht Tübingen. Beiträge zum Ausländischen und Internationalen Privatrecht. 40)*

PEPINSKY (HAROLD E.) Crime and conflict: a study of law and society. London, 1976. pp. 159. *bibliogs.*

RENNER (KARL) The institutions of private law and their social functions; edited with an introduction and notes, by O. Kahn-Freund; translated by Agnes Schwarzschild. London, 1949 repr. 1976. pp. 307.

UNGER (ROBERTO MANGABEIRA) Law in modern society: toward a criticism of social theory. New York, [1976]. pp. 309.

SOCIOLOGICAL RESEARCH.

WINTON (CHESTER ALLEN) Theory and measurement in sociology. New York, [1974]. pp. 124.

BOGDAN (ROBERT) and TAYLOR (STEVEN J.) Introduction to qualitative research methods: a phenomenological approach to the social sciences. New York, [1975]. pp. 266. *bibliog.*

MAYNTZ (RENATE) and others. Introduction to empirical sociology; translated by A. Hammond [and others]. Harmondsworth, 1976. pp. 240. *bibliog.*

WORLD CONGRESS OF SOCIOLOGY, 8TH, 1974. Sociological praxis: current roles and settings: [some papers from the congress]; edited by Elisabeth Crawford and Stei Rokkan. London, [1976]. pp. 175.

— Australia.

BALDOCK (CORA VELLEKOOP) and LALLY (JIM) Sociology in Australia and New Zealand: theory and methods. Westport, Conn., 1974. pp. 328. *bibliog.*

SOCIOLOGY.

— Germany, Eastern.

KOCH (URSULA) Bürgerliche und sozialistische Forschungsmethoden?: zur Rezeption empirischer Sozialforschung in der DDR. Frankfurt, [1976]. pp. 162. bibliog.

— New Zealand.

BALDOCK (CORA VELLEKOOP) and LALLY (JIM) Sociology in Australia and New Zealand: theory and methods. Westport, Conn., 1974. pp. 328. bibliog.

— Russia.

PROBLEMY istorii i teorii nauchnogo kommunizma: materialy nauchno- teoreticheskoi konferentsii. Moskva, 1969. pp. 267.

BOKAREV (NIKOLAI NIKOLAEVICH) Voprosy sotsiologii v partiinoi rabote. Moskva, 1974. pp. 168. bibliog.

SLEPENKOV (IVAN MARKELOVICH) Metodologicheskie printsipy i metodika konkretno-sotsiologicheskogo issledovaniia v nauchnom kommunizme. Moskva, 1974. pp. 128. bibliog.

UCHENYE ZAPISKI KAFEDR OBSHCHESTVENNYKH NAUK VUZOV LENINGRADA. Filosofiia. vyp.16. Filosofskie i sotsiologicheskie issledovaniia. Leningrad, 1975. pp. 207.

— United Kingdom.

PLATT (JENNIFER) Realities of social research: an empirical study of British sociologists. London, 1976. pp. 223.

— United States.

CAREY (JAMES T.) Sociology and public affairs: the Chicago School. Beverly Hills, [1975]. pp. 204. bibliog.

LAZARSFELD (PAUL FELIX) and REITZ (JEFFREY G.) An introduction to applied sociology. New York, [1975]. pp. 196.

SOCIOLOGISTS.

SYMPOSIUM ON SOCIOLOGY AND SOCIAL DEVELOPMENT IN ASIA, TOKYO, 1973. Sociology and social development in Asia: proceedings of the symposium [organized by the Japan Sociological Society in collaboration with the Japanese National Commission for Unesco]; edited by Tadashi Fukutake [and] Kiyomi Morioka. Tokyo, [1974]. pp. 447.

BRYANT (CHRISTOPHER G.A.) Sociology in action; a critique of selected conceptions of the social role of the sociologist. London, 1976. pp. 378. bibliog.

— Germany.

AHO (JAMES ALFRED) German realpolitik and American sociology: an inquiry into the sources and political significance of the sociology of conflict. Lewisburg, [1975]. pp. 346. bibliog.

The POSITIVIST dispute in German sociology; [by] Theodor W. Adorno [and others]; translated by Glyn Adey and David Frisby. London, [1976]. pp. 307. bibliog.

— United Kingdom.

PLATT (JENNIFER) Realities of social research: an empirical study of British sociologists. London, 1976. pp. 223.

— United States.

AHO (JAMES ALFRED) German realpolitik and American sociology: an inquiry into the sources and political significance of the sociology of conflict. Lewisburg, [1975]. pp. 346. bibliog.

CAREY (JAMES T.) Sociology and public affairs: the Chicago School. Beverly Hills, [1975]. pp. 204. bibliog.

SOCIOLOGY.

GENTILE (GIOVANNI) Genesi e struttura della società: saggio di filosofia pratica. Firenze, 1975. pp. 191. Originally published in 1945 in Opere complete di Giovanni Gentile.

DAHRENDORF (RALF) Gesellschaft und Freiheit: zur soziologischen Analyse der Gegenwart. München, 1961 repr. 1963. pp. 454. bibliog. (Hochschule für Wirtschaft und Politik, Hamburg. Veröffentlichungen). Essays and lectures, 1954-1960; some not previously published.

UCHENYE ZAPISKI KAFEDR OBSHCHESTVENNYKH NAUK VUZOV LENINGRADA. Filosofiia. vyp.8. Filosofskie i sotsiologicheskie issledovaniia. Leningrad, 1967. pp. 239.

ALLEN (VICTOR LEONARD) Social analysis: a Marxist critique and alternative. London, 1975. pp. 316.

BADCOCK (CHRISTOPHER ROBERT) Lévi-Strauss, structuralism and sociological theory. London, 1975. pp. 125. bibliog.

BOTTOMORE (THOMAS BURTON) Marxist sociology. London, 1975. pp. 78. bibliog.

COSER (LEWIS ALFRED) ed. The idea of social structure: papers in honor of Robert K. Merton. New York, [1975]. pp. 547. bibliog.

FORCESE (DENNIS P.) and RICHER (STEPHEN) eds. Issues in Canadian society: an introduction to sociology. Scarborough, Ont., [1975]. pp. 517. bibliogs.

GOLDTHORPE (JOHN ERNEST) The sociology of the Third World: disparity and involvement. Cambridge, 1975. pp. 325. bibliogs.

KLAGES (HELMUT) Die unruhige Gesellschaft: Untersuchungen über Grenzen und Probleme sozialer Stabilität. München, [1975]. pp. 198.

SIMON-SCHAEFER (ROLAND) and ZIMMERLI (WALTHER CH.) Theorie zwischen Kritik und Praxis: Jürgen Habermas und die Frankfurter Schule. Stuttgart-Bad Cannstatt, [1975]. pp. 186. bibliog. With English summary.

SITES (PAUL) Control and constraint: an introduction to sociology. New York, [1975]. pp. 470.

SKIDMORE (WILLIAM L.) Sociology's models of man: the relationships of models of man to sociological explanation in three sociological theories. New York, [1975]. pp. 203. bibliog.

The STRUCTURE of human society; [by] Philip E. Hammond [and others]. Lexington, Mass., [1975]. pp. 718. bibliogs.

SWINGEWOOD (ALAN WILLIAM) Marx and modern social theory. London, 1975. pp. 248. bibliog.

ULEDOV (ALEKSANDR KONSTANTINOVICH) Sotsiologicheskie zakony. Moskva, 1975. pp. 296.

VAN DEN BERGHE (PIERRE LOUIS) Man in society: a biosocial view. New York, [1975]. pp. 300. bibliog.

WORLD CONGRESS OF SOCIOLOGY, 8TH, 1974. Crisis and contention in sociology: [revised papers from a round table meeting at the congress]; edited by Tom Bottomore. London, [1975]. pp. 215. bibliog.

BAUMAN (ZYGMUNT) Towards a critical sociology: an essay on commonsense and emancipation. London, 1976. pp. 115.

BERGER (PETER L.) and BERGER (BRIGITTE) Sociology: a biographical approach. rev. ed. Harmondsworth, 1976. pp. 411. bibliogs.

BERGNER (DIETER) and MOCEK (REINHARD) Bürgerliche Gesellschaftstheorien: Studien zu den weltanschaulichen Grundlagen und ideologischen Funktionen bürgerlicher Gesellschaftsauffassungen. Berlin, 1976. pp. 295.

BRYANT (CHRISTOPHER G.A.) Sociology in action; a critique of selected conceptions of the social role of the sociologist. London, 1976. pp. 378. bibliog.

COMTE (ISIDORE AUGUSTE MARIE FRANÇOIS XAVIER) Auguste Comte: the foundation of sociology; [extracts from his works, including correspondence with Mill; edited by] Kenneth Thompson. London, 1976. pp. 220. bibliog.

CRAIB (IAN) Existentialism and sociology: a study of Jean-Paul Sartre. Cambridge, [1976]. pp. 242. bibliog.

HANSEN (DONALD ANDREW) An invitation to critical sociology: involvement, criticism, exploration. New York, [1976]. pp. 258. bibliog.

KLOSS (ROBERT MARSH) and others. Sociology with a human face: sociology as if people mattered. Saint Louis, 1976. pp. 311.

NEW directions in sociology; edited by David C. Thorns. Newton Abbot, 1976. pp. 192. bibliog.

SMART (BARRY) Sociology, phenomenology and marxian analysis: a critical discussion of the theory and practice of a science of society. London, 1976. pp. 206. bibliog.

SMELSER (NEIL JOSEPH) The sociology of economic life. 2nd ed. Englewood Cliffs, [1976]. pp. 177. bibliog.

THERBORN (G:RAN) Science, class and society: on the formation of sociology and historical materialism. London, [1976]. pp. 461. bibliog.

— Dictionaries and encyclopaedias.

ENCYCLOPEDIA of sociology; [editor, Peter J. O'Connell]. Guildford, Conn., [1974]. pp. 328. bibliog.

— History.

AHO (JAMES ALFRED) German realpolitik and American sociology: an inquiry into the sources and political significance of the sociology of conflict. Lewisburg, [1975]. pp. 346. bibliog.

TOENNIES (FERDINAND) Studien zur Philosophie und Gesellschaftslehre im 17. Jahrhundert; herausgegeben von E.G. Jacoby. Stuttgart-Bad Cannstatt, [1975]. pp. 384. bibliog.

STRASSER (HERMANN) The normative structure of sociology: conservative and emancipatory themes in social thought. London, 1976. pp. 275. bibliog.

— — America, Latin.

KAHL (JOSEPH ALAN) Modernization, exploitation and dependency in Latin America: Germani, González Casanova and Cardoso. New Brunswick, [1976]. pp. 215. bibliogs.

— — Germany.

The POSITIVIST dispute in German sociology; [by] Theodor W. Adorno [and others]; translated by Glyn Adey and David Frisby. London, [1976]. pp. 307. bibliog.

— — Russia.

VUCINICH (ALEXANDER) Social thought in Tsarist Russia: the quest for a general science of society, 1861-1917. Chicago, 1976. pp. 294. bibliog.

— — United States — Bibliography.

MARK (CHARLES) and MARK (PAULA F.) Sociology of America: a guide to information sources. Detroit, [1976]. pp. 454.

— Mathematical models.

BLALOCK (HUBERT M.) and others, eds. Quantitative sociology: international perspectives on mathematical and statistical modeling. New York, 1975. pp. 643. bibliogs.

— Methodology.

UCHENYE ZAPISKI KAFEDR OBSHCHESTVENNYKH NAUK VUZOV LENINGRADA. Filosofiia. vyp. 9. Filosofskie i sotsiologicheskie issledovaniia. Leningrad, 1968. pp. 189.

WAX (ROSALIE H.) Doing fieldwork: warnings and advice. Chicago, 1971. pp. 395. bibliog.

SOCIOLOGY.(Cont.)

BABBIE (EARL R.) Survey research methods. Belmont, Cal., [1973]. pp. 384. *bibliogs.*

DEUTSCHER (IRWIN) What we say, what we do: sentiments and acts. Glenview, Ill., [1973]. pp. 370. *bibliogs.*

WINTON (CHESTER ALLEN) Theory and measurement in sociology. New York, [1974]. pp. 124.

BOGDAN (ROBERT) and TAYLOR (STEVEN J.) Introduction to qualitative research methods: a phenomenological approach to the social sciences. New York, [1975]. pp. 266. *bibliog.*

CHATTOPADHYAY(DEBIPRASAD) Individuals and societies: a methodological inquiry. 2nd ed. Calcutta, 1975. pp. 281. *bibliog.*

DYNAMIC change and the urban ghetto; [by] Alan Walter Steiss [and others]. Lexington, Mass., [1975]. pp. 124. *bibliog.*

BURGER (THOMAS) Max Weber's theory of concept formation: history, laws, and ide types. Durham, N.C., 1976. pp. 231. *bibliog.*

GIDDENS (ANTHONY) New rules of sociological method: a positive critique of interpretative sociologies. London, 1976. pp. 192. *bibliog.*

MAYNTZ (RENATE) and others. Introduction to empirical sociology; translated by A. Hammond [and others]. Harmondsworth, 1976. pp. 240. *bibliog.*

NEW directions in sociology; edited by David C. Thorns. Newton Abbot, 1976. pp. 192. *bibliog.*

— Philosophy.

TARRIDA DEL MARMOL (FERNANDO) Problemas trascendentales: estudios de sociologia y ciencia moderna. Barcelona, 1930. pp. 202.

KUYPERS (K.) and others. Sociologie en geschiedenis. Assen, 1961. pp. 46.

LEWIS (JOHN) B.Sc., Ph.D. Max Weber and value-free sociology: a Marxist critique. London, 1975. pp. 192. *bibliog.*

PROBLEMS of reflexivity and dialectics in sociological inquiry: language theorizing difference; [by] Barry Sandywell [and others]. London, 1975. pp. 196. *bibliogs.*

BURGER (THOMAS) Max Weber's theory of concept formation: history, laws, and ide types. Durham, N.C., 1976. pp. 231. *bibliog.*

STRASSER (HERMANN) The normative structure of sociology: conservative and emancipatory themes in social thought. London, 1976. pp. 275. *bibliog.*

— Statistics.

SERGEANT (GRAHAM A.V.) A statistical source-book for sociologists. 2nd ed. London, 1973. pp. 160. *bibliogs.*

— Study and teaching — America, Latin.

IANNI (OCTAVIO) Sociologia y dependencia en America Latina; [three essays edited and translated from the Portuguese by] Centro Paraguayo de Estudios Sociologicos. Asuncion, 1972. pp. 85.

— — Asia.

SYMPOSIUM ON SOCIOLOGY AND SOCIAL DEVELOPMENT IN ASIA, TOKYO, 1973. Sociology and social development in Asia: proceedings of the symposium [organized by the Japan Sociological Society in collaboration with the Japanese National Commission for Unesco]; edited by Tadashi Fukutake [and] Kiyomi Morioka. Tokyo, [1974]. pp. 447.

— — Italy.

BALBO (LAURA) and others. L'inferma scienza: tre saggi sulla istituzionalizzazione della sociologia in Italia. Bologna, [1975]. pp. 314.

SOCIOLOGY, CHRISTIAN.

REES (D. BEN) Chapels in the valley: a study in the sociology of Welsh nonconformity. Upton, Wirral, [1975]. pp. 222. *bibliog.*

GILBERT (ALAN D.) Religion and society in industrial England: church, chapel and social change, 1740-1914. London, 1976. pp. 251. *bibliog.*

WILSON (BRYAN RONALD) Contemporary transformations of religion. London, 1976. pp. 116. (*Newcastle-upon-Tyne. University. Riddell Memorial Lectures. 45th series*)

— Catholic.

KLUEBER (FRANZ) Katholische Soziallehre und demokratischer Sozialismus. Bonn-Bad Godesberg, [1974]. pp. 156.

SOCIOLOGY, INDUSTRIAL.

See INDUSTRIAL SOCIOLOGY.

SOCIOLOGY, MILITARY.

COUSINS (CHRISTINE RUTH) The military family: a study of three communities in the British armed forces. 1975. fo. 130. *bibliog.* Typescript. M.Phil.(London) thesis: unpublished. This thesis is the property of London University and may not be removed from the Library.

DOORN (JACOBUS ADRIANUS ANTONIUS VAN) The soldier and social change: comparative studies in the history and sociology of the military. Beverly Hills, [1975]. pp. 189.

JANOWITZ (MORRIS) Military conflict: essays in the institutional analysis of war and peace. Beverly Hills, [1975]. pp. 319.

SARKESIAN (SAM CHARLES) The professional army officer in a changing society. Chicago, [1975]. pp. 268. *bibliog.*

WILLEQUET (JACQUES) The science of polemology at the University of Brussels. Brussels, Ministry of Foreign Affairs, External Trade and Cooperation in Development, 1975. pp. 44. (*Memo from Belgium. No. 167*)

LISSAK (MOSHE) Military roles in modernization: civil-military relations in Thailand and Burma. Beverly Hills, [1976]. pp. 255. (*Inter-University Seminar on Armed Forces and Society. [Publications]. vol.8*)

SOCIOLOGY, RURAL.

ANNALES D'ECONOMIE ET DE SOCIOLOGIE RURALES; [pd. by] Institut National de la Recherche Agronomique [France]. [with summaries in English]. s-a., 1972 (v.1)- Paris.

BOWERS (WILLIAM L.) The country life movement in America, 1900-1920. Port Washington, N.Y., 1974. pp. 189. *bibliog.*

LOOMIS (CHARLES PRICE) and BEEGLE (JOSEPH ALLAN) A strategy for rural change. New York, [1975]. pp. 525.

SOCIOLOGY, URBAN.

RYBICKI (PAWEŁ) Społeczeństwo miejskie. Warszawa, 1972. pp. 455. *bibliog.*

STEISS (ALAN WALTER) Urban systems dynamics. Lexington, Mass., [1974]. pp. 323.

WEINSTEIN (JAY A.) Madras: an analysis of urban ecological structure in India. Beverly Hills, Calif., [1974]. pp. 76. *bibliog.*

DYNAMIC change and the urban ghetto; [by] Alan Walter Steiss [and others]. Lexington, Mass., [1975]. pp. 124. *bibliog.*

MERCER (CHARLES) Living in cities: psychology and the urban environment. Harmondsworth, 1975. pp. 240. *bibliog.*

PEACH (GUTHLAC CERI KLAUS) ed. Urban social segregation. London, 1975. pp. 444. *bibliogs.*

PONS (VALDO GUSTAVE) Imagery and symbolism in urban society. Hull, 1975. pp. 25. (*Hull. University. Inaugural Lectures*)

ROBSON (BRIAN T.) Urban social areas. London, 1975. pp. 64. *bibliog.*

ABRAHAMSON (MARK) Urban sociology. Englewood Cliffs, N.J., [1976]. pp. 280.

BALDWIN (JOHN) Ph.D., and BOTTOMS (A.E.) The urban criminal: a study in Sheffield;...in collaboration with Monica A. Walker. London, 1976. pp. 262. *bibliog.*

The CITY in comparative perspective: cross-national research and new directions in theory; edited by John Walton and Louis H. Masotti. New York, [1976]. pp. 313. *bibliogs.*

GUIDICINI (PAOLO) Sociologia dei quartieri urbani: analisi dinamica di un'ipotesi. Milano, [1976]. pp. 183. *bibliog.*

SOCIOLOGY AS A PROFESSION.

WORLD CONGRESS OF SOCIOLOGY, 8TH, 1974. Sociological praxis: current roles and settings: [some papers from the congress]; edited by Elisabeth Crawford and Stei Rokkan. London, [1976]. pp. 175.

SODA INDUSTRY

— Russia — Ukraine.

PODOV (VLADIMIR IVANOVICH) Donsoda: ocherk iz istorii Donetskogo ordena Lenina sodovogo zavoda im. V.I. Lenina. Donetsk, 1969. pp. 135.

SOEKARNO (ACHMED).

SOEKARNO (ACHMED) Indonesia accuses!: Soekarno's defence oration in the political trial of 1930; edited, translated, annotated and introduced by Roger K. Paget. Kuala Lumpur, 1975. pp. 153.

SOFIA

— Politics and government.

REVOLIUTSIONNA Sofiia, 1891-1944: spomeni. [Sofiia], 1969. pp. 750.

SOFTWARE COMPATIBILITY.

BROWN (PETER J.) Macro processors and techniques for portable software. London, [1974]. pp. 244. *bibliog.*

SOGN OG FJORDANE, NORWAY

— Economic policy.

BIVAND (ROGER S.) The economic geography of regional differentiation: studies in Sogn og Fjordane, Norway; [Ph.D. (London) thesis]. 1975. fo. 417. *bibliog.* Typescript: unpublished. This thesis is the property of London University and may not be removed from the Library.

SOHN-RETHEL (ALFRED).

HALFMANN (JOST) and REXROTH (TILLMAN) Marxismus als Erkenntniskritik: Sohn-Rethels Revision der Werttheorie und die produktiven Folgen eines Missverständnisses. München, [1976]. pp. 169. *bibliog.*

SOIL EROSION

— Spain.

THORNES (JOHN B.) Semi-arid erosional systems: case studies from Spain. London, 1976. pp. 79. *bibliog.* (*London. University. London School of Economics and Political Science. Department of Geography. Geographical Papers. No. 7*)

SOIL SURVEYS

— Australia — Victoria.

NEWELL (J.W.) Soils and land use in the Ovens and Buffalo river valleys, Victoria. Melbourne, 1970. pp. 51,18 maps. *bibliog.* (*Victoria. Department of Agriculture. Technical Bulletins. No. 21*)

SKENE (J.K.M.) Soils and land use in the mid-Loddon valley, Victoria, etc. Melbourne, 1971. pp. 57,42 maps. *bibliog.* (Victoria. Department of Agriculture. Technical Bulletins. No. 22) Map in end pocket.

SOILS.

RICHARDS (BRYANT N.) Introduction to the soil ecosystem. London, 1974 repr. 1976. pp. 266. *bibliogs.*

— **Bibliography.**

ATKINSON (H.J.) compiler. A bibliography of Canadian soil science. [Ottawa], 1971. pp. 303. *(Canada. Department of Agriculture. Publications. 1452)*

— **Canada — Bibliography.**

ATKINSON (H.J.) compiler. A bibliography of Canadian soil science. [Ottawa], 1971. pp. 303. *(Canada. Department of Agriculture. Publications. 1452)*

— — **Ontario.**

MAHANEY (WILLIAM C.) and ERMUTH (FREDERICK) The effects of agriculture and urbanization on the natural environment: a study of human impact in southern Ontario. Toronto, 1974. pp. 152. *bibliog.* (York University (Toronto). Department of Geography. Geographical Monographs. No. 7)

— **Sabah.**

The SOILS of Sabah; [by] B.D. Acres [and others]. Tolworth, 1975. 5 vols. (in 2), 10 maps. *bibliog.* (U.K. Ministry of Overseas Development. Land Resources Division. Land Resource Studies. No. 20)

— **United Kingdom.**

COURTNEY (FRANK M.) and TRUDGILL (STEPHEN T.) The soil: an introduction to soil study in Britain. London, 1976. pp. 120. *bibliog.*

SOLDIERS

— **Family relationships.**

FAMILIES in the military system: edited by Hamilton I. McCubbin [and others]. Beverly Hills, [1976]. pp. 393. *bibliog.* (Inter-University Seminar on Armed Forces and Society. Sage Series on Armed Forces and Society. vol. 9)

— **France.**

MOUVEMENT D'ACTION JUDICIAIRE. Les droits du soldat: statut, discipline et justice militaire; [by] G. Braun [and others]. Paris, 1975. pp. 131.

— **United Kingdom.**

BROWNE (E.W.) and others. The school curriculum: a survey on the opinions of young men about the education they have had and the education they would like to have had. [Calcutta?], South East Asia Command, 1946. pp. 40.

BROWNE (E.W.) and others. The soldier and the army: opinions on some aspects of army life expressed by troops in S[outh] E[ast] A[sia] C[ommand] . [Calcutta?], South East Asia Command, 1946. pp. 40, x.

— — **Scotland.**

PREBBLE (JOHN) Mutiny: Highland regiments in revolt, 1743-1804. London, 1975. pp. 542. *bibliog.*

SOLIDARITY.

TAMNEY (JOSEPH B.) Solidarity in a slum. New York, [1975]. pp. 182. *bibliog.*

ABRAMS (PHILIP) and McCULLOCH (ANDREW) Communes, sociology and society. Cambridge, 1976. pp. 239. *bibliog.*

SOLINGEN

— **History.**

SBOSNY (INGE) and SCHABROD (KARL) Widerstand in Solingen: aus dem Leben antifaschistischer Kämpfer. Frankfurt/Main, [1975]. pp. 135.

SOLOTHURN

— **History.**

BUECHI (HERMANN) Hundert Jahre Solothurner Freisinn, 1830-1930. Solothurn, imprint, 1930. pp. 331.

SOLZHENITSYN (ALEKSANDR ISAEVICH).

SAKHAROV (ANDREI DMITRIEVICH) O pis'me Aleksandra Solzhenitsyna "Vozhdiam Sovetskogo Soiuza". N'iu-Iork, 1974. pp. 14.

RESHETOVSKAIA (NATAL'IA) V spore so vremenem. Moskva, 1975. pp. 207.

SOLZHENITSYN (ALEKSANDR ISAEVICH) Warning to the Western world. London, 1976. pp. 45. *Consists of text of interview with Michael Charlton on BBC television's Panorama, 1 March 1976, and of a BBC radio broadcast, 24 March, 1976.*

SOMALI REPUBLIC

— **Commerce.**

SOMALI REPUBLIC. Central Statistical Department. Foreign trade returns. a., 1968- Mogadiscio. *[In English and Italian]*

— **Economic conditions.**

ISTITUTO NAZIONALE PER IL COMMERCIO ESTERO. 1967. Somalia. Roma, 1967. pp. 198.

— **Economic policy.**

SOMALI REPUBLIC. Ministry of Information and National Guidance. 1974. Somalia: five years of revolutionary progress. [Mogadishu, 1974]. pp. 119.

— **Foreign relations.**

SOMALI REPUBLIC. Ministry of Information and National Guidance. 1974. Somalia: five years of revolutionary progress. [Mogadishu, 1974]. pp. 119.

— **Industries.**

SOMALI REPUBLIC. Central Statistical Department. Industrial production. a., 1969- Mogadiscio.

— **Legislative Council.**

SOMALILAND PROTECTORATE. Commission on Representational Reform. 1959. Report; [A.L. Scawin, chairman]. [Hargeisa, 1959]. fo. 55, 1 map.

— **Politics and government.**

SOMALI REPUBLIC. Ministry of Information and National Guidance. 1974. Somalia: five years of revolutionary progress. [Mogadishu, 1974]. pp. 119.

— **Relations (general) with Arab countries.**

SOMALI REPUBLIC. Ministry of Information and National Guidance. 1974. Somalia and the Arab League: a wider role in Afro-Arab affairs. Mogadishu, 1974. pp. 45.

— **Social policy.**

SOMALI REPUBLIC. Ministry of Information and National Guidance. 1974. Somalia: five years of revolutionary progress. [Mogadishu, 1974]. pp. 119.

SOMERS (JOHN) Baron Somers.

SACHSE (WILLIAM LEWIS) Lord Somers: a political portrait. Manchester, [1975]. pp. 336.

SOMERSET

— **History.**

UNDERDOWN (DAVID) Somerset in the Civil War and Interregnum. Newton Abbot, [1973]. pp. 229. *bibliog.*

SOREL (GEORGES).

SOREL (GEORGES) From Georges Sorel: essays in socialism and philosophy; edited with an introduction by John L. Stanley and translated by John and Charlotte Stanley. New York, 1976. pp. 388. *bibliog.*

SORTING (ELECTRONIC COMPUTERS).

LORIN (HAROLD) Sorting and sort systems. Reading, Mass., [1975]. 1 vol. (various pagings).

SOSNKOWSKI (KAZIMIERZ).

KATELBACH (TADEUSZ) O zjednoczenie i legalizm: ostatni akt 'zycia publicznego Kazimierza Sosnkowskiego. New York, 1975. pp. 328.

SOUFRIERE

— **Civic improvement.**

SAINT LUCIA. Central Housing and Planning Authority. 1956. The Soufrière regional scheme for the control of development of the area comprising the town of Soufrière and surrounding land. Castries, 1956. pp. 18.

SOUTH AFRICA

— **Census.**

SOUTH AFRICA. Census, 1970. Population census, 1970: nature of education. [Pretoria, 1975]. pp. 316. *(Bureau of Statistics. Reports. No. 02-05-02) In English and Afrikaans.*

SOUTH AFRICA. Census, 1970. Population census, 1970: occupations: income, industry and identity. [Pretoria, 1975]. pp. 360. *(Bureau of Statistics. Reports. No. 02-05-04) In English and Afrikaans.*

SOUTH AFRICA. Census, 1970. Population census, 1970: personal income. [Pretoria, 1975]. pp. 311. *(Bureau of Statistics. Reports. No. 02-01-08) In English and Afrikaans.*

SOUTH AFRICA. Census, 1970. Population census, 1970: religion. [Pretoria, 1975]. pp. 107. *(Bureau of Statistics. Reports. No. 02-05-03) In English and Afrikaans.*

SOUTH AFRICA. Census, 1970. Population census, 1970: age, marital status and type of dwelling by district and economic region. [Pretoria, 1976]. pp. 540. *(Bureau of Statistics. Reports. No.02-05-08)*

SOUTH AFRICA. Census, 1970. Population census, 1970: geographical distribution of the population. [Pretoria, 1976]. pp. 87. *(Bureau of Statistics. Reports No. 02-05-10) In English and Afrikaans.*

SOUTH AFRICA. Census, 1970. Population census, 1970: level of education. [Pretoria, 1976]. pp. 396. *(Bureau of Statistics. Reports. No.02-05-07) In English and Afrikaans.*

SOUTH AFRICA. Census, 1970. Population census, 1970: occupation and industry by district and economic region. [Pretoria, 1976]. pp. 230. *(Bureau of Statistics. Reports. No. 02-05-06) In English and Afrikaans.*

SOUTH AFRICA. Census, 1970. Single ages, 1941 to 1970. [Pretoria, 1976]. pp. 240. *(Bureau of Statistics. Reports. No. 02-05-05) In English and Afrikaans.*

— **Constitution.**

RAUNARD (A.V.) The alternative: an analysis of a possible new political future for South Africa. Windhoek, [1975]. pp. 133.

— **Constitutional law.**

COCKRAM (GAIL MARYSE) Constitutional law in the Republic of South Africa. Cape Town, 1975. pp. 86.

— **Defences.**

FINAN (JAMES STUART) Chemical and biological weapons: their potential for nations outside the principal alliances, with special reference to the possibilities open to the Republic of South Africa over the next ten years. 1975. fo. 308. *bibliog. Typescript. Ph.D. (London) thesis: unpublished. This thesis is the property of London University and may not be removed from the Library.*

SOUTH AFRICA (Cont.)

SPENCE (JOHN EDWARD) Foreign investment in South Africa:... the political and military framework. [London], 1975. pp. 111. *(Study Project on External Investment in South Africa and Namibia (S.W. Africa). Study Project Papers. [vol. 1])*

— Description and travel.

CALLAWAY (GODFREY) South Africa from within: made known in the letters of a magistrate. London, 1930. pp. 158.

— Economic conditions.

SOUTH AFRICA. Department of Information. 1969. South African quiz. [Pretoria], 1969. pp. 156.

HOMELANDS:...the role of the corporations in the republic of South Africa; (compiled under the editorial control of P. Smit [and others]). [rev. ed.]. Johannesburg, [1975]. pp. 181. *In English and Afrikaans.*

SUCKLING (JOHN) and others. Foreign investment in South Africa: the economic factor. [London], 1975. pp. 195. *(Study Project on External Investment in South Africa and Namibia (S.W. Africa). Study Project Papers. [vol. 2])*

LEMON (ANTHONY) Apartheid: a geography of separation. Farnborough, Hants., [1976]. pp. 261. *bibliog.*

— — Statistics.

SOUTH AFRICA. Statistical survey in connection with the budget speech. a., 1974/75- Pretoria. *[In English and Afrikaans].*

— Economic history.

HOUGHTON (DESMOND HOBART) The South African economy. 4th ed. Cape Town, 1976. pp. 310. *bibliog.*

— Economic policy.

BANTU INVESTMENT CORPORATION OF SOUTH AFRICA LIMITED. Annual report. a., 1969/70-1971/72 (11th-13th), 1974 (15th)- Pretoria. *[in English and Afrikaans].*

SOUTH AFRICA. Ministry of Economic Affairs. 1973. Inflation and our welfare. Pretoria, [1973]. pp. 32.

HOMELANDS:...the role of the corporations in the republic of South Africa; (compiled under the editorial control of P. Smit [and others]). [rev. ed.]. Johannesburg, [1975]. pp. 181. *In English and Afrikaans.*

SOUTH AFRICA. Bureau for Economic Research re Bantu Development. 1976. Black development in South Africa: the economic development of the Black peoples in the homelands of the Republic of South Africa. Pretoria, 1976. pp. 208, 1 map. *bibliog.*

— Foreign economic relations.

SUCKLING (JOHN) and others. Foreign investment in South Africa: the economic factor. [London], 1975. pp. 195. *(Study Project on External Investment in South Africa and Namibia (S.W. Africa). Study Project Papers. [vol. 2])*

— Foreign relations.

LEGUM (COLIN) Southern Africa: the secret diplomacy of detente; South Africa at the crossroads. London, 1975. pp. 91.

SPENCE (JOHN EDWARD) Foreign investment in South Africa:... the political and military framework. [London], 1975. pp. 111. *(Study Project on External Investment in South Africa and Namibia (S.W. Africa). Study Project Papers. [vol. 1])*

SPENCE (JOHN EDWARD) South African foreign policy in today's world. Braamfontein, 1975. pp. 16.

See also UNITED NATIONS — South Africa.

— — Africa, Subsaharan.

LEGUM (COLIN) Southern Africa: the secret diplomacy of detente; South Africa at the crossroads. London, 1975. pp. 91.

FRIEDMAN (BERNARD) M.B., Ch.B., D.L.O., R.C.P and S. From...isolation to detente. Johannesburg, 1976. pp. 18. *(South African Institute of Race Relations. Presidential Addresses. 1976)*

— — Germany.

RODE (REINHARD) Die Südafrikapolitik der Bundesrepublik Deutschland, 1968- 1972. München, [1975]. pp. 371. *bibliog. (Katholischer Arbeitskreis Entwicklung und Frieden. Wissenschaftliche Kommission. Wissenschaftliche Reihe. 7) With summaries in French and English.*

— — United Kingdom — Commonwealth.

SCHOLTZ (GERT DANIEL) Hertzog en Smuts en die Britse Ryk. Kaapstad, 1975. pp. 158. *bibliog.*

— History.

ENGLISH-speaking South Africa today: proceedings of the National Conference, July 1974; edited by André de Villiers. Cape Town, 1976. pp. 387. *Conference sponsored by the 1820 Settlers National Monument Foundation.*

LEMON (ANTHONY) Apartheid: a geography of separation. Farnborough, Hants., [1976]. pp. 261. *bibliog.*

— Industries.

SOUTH AFRICA. Bureau of Statistics. 1975- . Census of manufacturing, 1970. [Pretoria, 1975 in progress]. *(Reports. No. 10-21-26, etc.) In English and Afrikaans.*

SOUTH AFRICA. Census, 1970. Population census, 1970: occupation and industry by district and economic region. [Pretoria, 1976]. pp. 230. *(Bureau of Statistics. Reports. No. 02-05-06) In English and Afrikaans.*

— Languages.

ENGLISH-speaking South Africa today: proceedings of the National Conference, July 1974; edited by André de Villiers. Cape Town, 1976. pp. 387. *Conference sponsored by the 1820 Settlers National Monument Foundation.*

— Manufactures.

SOUTH AFRICA. Bureau of Statistics. 1975- . Census of manufacturing, 1970. [Pretoria, 1975 in progress]. *(Reports. No. 10-21-26, etc.) In English and Afrikaans.*

— Military policy.

FINAN (JAMES STUART) Chemical and biological weapons: their potential for nations outside the principal alliances, with special reference to the possibilities open to the Republic of South Africa over the next ten years. 1975. fo. 308. *bibliog. Typescript. Ph.D. (London) thesis: unpublished. This thesis is the property of London University and may not be removed from the Library.*

— Native races.

CALLAWAY (GODFREY) South Africa from within: made known in the letters of a magistrate. London, 1930. pp. 158.

BANTU INVESTMENT CORPORATION OF SOUTH AFRICA LIMITED. Annual report. a., 1969/70-1971/72 (11th-13th), 1974 (15th)- Pretoria. *[in English and Afrikaans].*

SOUTH AFRICA. Bureau of Statistics. Statistics of Bantu affairs administration boards. a., 1973/74 (1st)- Pretoria. *[In English and Afrikaans].*

SOUTH AFRICA . Department of Information. 1973. Progress through separate development: South Africa in peaceful transition. 4th ed. [Pretoria], 1973. pp. 128.

BALDWIN (ALAN) Uprooting a nation: the study of 3 million evictions in South Africa. London, 1974. pp. 36. *(Africa Publications Trust. Studies in the Mass Removal of Population in South Africa. No. 2)*

GREST (JEREMY) African wages in Grahamstown: a survey. Johannesburg, 1974. pp. 17.

HOMELANDS:...the role of the corporations in the republic of South Africa; (compiled under the editorial control of P. Smit [and others]). [rev. ed.]. Johannesburg, [1975]. pp. 181. *In English and Afrikaans.*

SOUTH AFRICA. Bureau for Economic Research re Bantu Development. 1976. Black development in South Africa: the economic development of the Black peoples in the homelands of the Republic of South Africa. Pretoria, 1976. pp. 208, 1 map. *bibliog.*

SOUTH AFRICA. Parliament. House of Assembly. Select Committee on Bantu Affairs. 1976. First and second reports (with Proceedings) (S.C.6-1976). in SOUTH AFRICA. Parliament. House of Assembly. Select Committee reports.

— Parliament.

STULTZ (NEWELL M.) Who goes to parliament?. Grahamstown, S.A., 1975. pp. 106. *bibliog. (Rhodes University. Institute of Social and Economic Research. Occasional Papers. No. 19)*

— — Rules and practice.

SOUTH AFRICA. Parliament. Senate. Committee on Standing Orders. 1976. Report (S.C.1/1976). in SOUTH AFRICA. Parliament. Senate. Reports from the Sessional and Select Committees.

— Politics and government.

RACE and politics in South Africa: a series of lectures given at the 1973 summer school, [University of Cape Town]. Cape Town, [1973?]. 1 vol. (various pagings).

CHANGE in contemporary South Africa; edited by Leonard Thompson and Jeffrey Butler. Berkeley, [1975]. pp. 447. *bibliog. Based on papers of a conference held at Seven Springs Farm Center, Mount Kisco, New York, in April 1974.*

LEGUM (COLIN) Southern Africa: the secret diplomacy of detente; South Africa at the crossroads. London, 1975. pp. 91.

LINT (GEORGE J. DE) The United Nations: the abhorrent misapplication of the Charter in respect of South Africa. Zwolle, [1976]. pp. 121.

TAYLOR (CATHERINE) If courage goes: my twenty years in South African politics. Johannesburg, 1976. pp. 316.

— Population.

MOSTERT (W.P.) The family-building process among Afrikaans-speaking couples, phase II: three years after marriage. Pretoria, 1974. pp. 162. *bibliog. (Human Sciences Research Council [South Africa] . Institute for Sociological, Demographic and Criminological Research. Reports. No. S-21)*

— Public lands.

SOUTH AFRICA. Parliament. House of Assembly. Select Committee on State-owned Land. 1976. Report (with Proceedings) (S.C.9-1976). in SOUTH AFRICA. Parliament. House of Assembly. Select Committee reports.

— Race question.

ADAMS (FARIED) and others, defendants. Summary of the preparatory examination of the treason trial; issued by the Treason Trials Defence Fund Committee. Johannesburg, 1957. fo. 5. *Privately issued.*

TREASON TRIALS DEFENCE FUND. Press Summaries. Nos. 1-58. [A week-by-week resumé of the proceedings of the treason trial of Regina vs. Faried Adams and others in the Special Criminal Court, Pretoria, August 1958 to March 1961]. Johannesburg, 1958-61. 58 pts. (in 2 vols.).

SOUTH AFRICA. Supreme Court. Special Criminal Court, Pretoria. 1961. In the case of Regina vs. Farid Adams and others: judgement as read out to Court by the presiding judge, Mr. Justice F.L.H. Rumpff, on Wednesday 29th March, 1961. [Johannesburg?, 1961]. fo. 12.

SOUTH AFRICA. Supreme Court. Special Criminal Court, Pretoria. 1961. In the matter of the application of Farrid Adams and 29 others and the Crown: reasons for judgment [Mr. Justice Rumpff]. [Johannesburg?, 1961]. fo. 11.

SOUTH AFRICA. Supreme Court. Special Criminal Court, Pretoria. 1961. In the matter of the application of Farrid Adams and 29 others, and the Crown; reasons for judgment [Mr. Justice Bekker]. [Johannesburg?, 1961]. fo. 8.

RACE and politics in South Africa: a series of lectures given at the 1973 summer school, [University of Cape Town]. Cape Town, [1973?]. 1 vol. (various pagings).

SOUTH AFRICA . Department of Information. 1973. Progress through separate development: South Africa in peaceful transition. 4th ed. [Pretoria], 1973. pp. 128.

BALDWIN (ALAN) Uprooting a nation: the study of 3 million evictions in South Africa. London, 1974. pp. 36. (Africa Publications Trust. Studies in the Mass Removal of Population in South Africa. No. 2)

CHANGE in contemporary South Africa; edited by Leonard Thompson and Jeffrey Butler. Berkeley, [1975]. pp. 447. bibliog. Based on papers of a conference held at Seven Springs Farm Center, Mount Kisco, New York, in April 1974.

LANDSORGANISATIONEN I SVERIGE and TJÄNSTEM ÄNNENS CENTRALORGANISATION. South Africa: black labour - Swedish capital; a report by the LO/TCO study delegation to South Africa 1975; English translation: Jaak Talvend. [Stockholm], 1975. pp. 193. bibliog.

MORSE (STANLEY J.) and ORPEN (CHRISTOPHER) eds. Contemporary South Africa: social psychological perspectives. Cape Town, 1975. pp. 294. bibliogs.

RAUNARD (A.V.) The alternative: an analysis of a possible new political future for South Africa. Windhoek, [1975]. pp. 133.

STAUB (HANS O.) Südafrikareport: Rassentrennung; Wunschtraum, Wahn und Wirklichkeit. Wien, [1975]. pp. 168. bibliog.

WEINBERGER (GERDA) An den Quellen der Apartheid: Studien über koloniale Ausbeutungs- und Herrschaftsmethoden in Südafrika, etc. Berlin, 1975. pp. 217. bibliog.

WILSON (MARY MONICA) So truth be in the field. Johannesburg, 1975. pp. 26. (South African Institute of Race Relations. Hoernlé Memorial Lectures. 1975)

ANDRIOLA (JOSEPH) The white South African: an endangered species. Cape Town, 1976. pp. 172.

BRICKHILL (JOAN) Race against race: South Africa's multi-national sport fraud. London, 1976. pp. 77.

JOHNSTONE (FREDERICK A.) Class, race and gold: a study of class relations and racial discrimination in South Africa. London, 1976. pp. 298. bibliog.

LEMON (ANTHONY) Apartheid: a geography of separation. Farnborough, Hants., [1976]. pp. 261. bibliog.

WORLD PEACE COUNCIL and AFRICAN NATIONAL CONGRESS (SOUTH AFRICA). Spotlight on Soweto. Helsinki, [1976]. pp. 23.

— Relations (general) with New Zealand.

THOMPSON (RICHARD) Writer on race relations. Retreat from apartheid: New Zealand's sporting contacts with South Africa. Wellington, 1975. pp. 102.

— Religion.

BUIS (ROBERT) Religious beliefs and white prejudice. Johannesburg, 1975. pp. 71. bibliog.

SOUTH AFRICA. Census, 1970. Population census, 1970: religion. [Pretoria, 1975]. pp. 107. (Bureau of Statistics. Reports. No. 02-05-03) In English and Afrikaans.

DUBB (ALLIE A.) Community of the saved: an African revivalist church in the east Cape. Johannesburg, 1976. pp. 175. bibliog.

— Social conditions.

SOUTH AFRICA. Department of Information. 1969. South African quiz. [Pretoria], 1969. pp. 156.

CHANGE in contemporary South Africa; edited by Leonard Thompson and Jeffrey Butler. Berkeley, [1975]. pp. 447. bibliog. Based on papers of a conference held at Seven Springs Farm Center, Mount Kisco, New York, in April 1974.

MORSE (STANLEY J.) and ORPEN (CHRISTOPHER) eds. Contemporary South Africa: social psychological perspectives. Cape Town, 1975. pp. 294. bibliogs.

— Statistics, Vital.

VAN TONDER (JAN LOUIS) and VAN EEDEN (IZAK JOHANNES) Abridged life tables for all the population groups in the Republic of South Africa (1921-70). Pretoria, 1975. pp. 89. bibliog. (Human Sciences Research Council [South Africa] . Institute for Sociological, Demographic and Criminological Research. Reports. No. S-34)

SOUTH AUSTRALIA

— Emigration and immigration.

AUSTRALIA. Migrant Task Force, South Australia. 1973. First report to the Minister for Immigration; [R.T. Gun, chairman]. Adelaide, 1973. fo. 44.

SOUTH BEND, INDIANA

— Foreign population.

ESSLINGER (DEAN R.) Immigrants and the city: ethnicity and mobility in a nineteenth- century midwestern community. Port Washington, N.Y., 1975. pp. 156. bibliog.

— Growth.

ESSLINGER (DEAN R.) Immigrants and the city: ethnicity and mobility in a nineteenth- century midwestern community. Port Washington, N.Y., 1975. pp. 156. bibliog.

SOUTH PACIFIC COMMISSION.

SOUTH PACIFIC CONFERENCE. Report [title varies]. a., (formerly trien.), 1950 (1st)- v.p. [in English and French]. 4th-6th reports published under title Pacific forum. Reports 7-13 also contain Proceedings of the South Pacific Commission.

SOUTH SASKATCHEWAN RIVER.

CANADA. Department of Regional Economic Expansion. 1970. South Saskatchewan river project, 1958-1967. [Ottawa, 1970]. 1 pamphlet (unpaged).

SOUTH WEST AFRICA

— Economic conditions.

HOMELANDS:...the role of the corporations in the republic of South Africa; (compiled under the editorial control of P. Smit [and others]). [rev. ed.]. Johannesburg, [1975]. pp. 181. In English and Afrikaans.

— Economic policy.

HOMELANDS:...the role of the corporations in the republic of South Africa; (compiled under the editorial control of P. Smit [and others]). [rev. ed.]. Johannesburg, [1975]. pp. 181. In English and Afrikaans.

— History.

COCKRAM (GAIL MARYSE) South West African mandate. Cape Town, 1976. pp. 531. bibliog.

— International status.

COCKRAM (GAIL MARYSE) South West African mandate. Cape Town, 1976. pp. 531. bibliog.

— Native races.

WAGNER (GUENTER) A study of Okahandja district, South West Africa;... revised and edited by O. Köhler. Pretoria, 1957. pp. 106. (South Africa. Department of Bantu Administration and Development. Ethnological Publications. No.38)

SUDHOLT (GERT) Die deutsche Eingeborenenpolitik in Südwestafrika, von den Anfängen bis 1904. Hildesheim, 1975. pp. 241. bibliog.

— Politics and government.

FRIENDS OF NAMIBIA COMMITTEE. The Namibia file. London, [1974]. pp. 67. bibliog.

CONSTITUTIONAL CONFERENCE OF SOUTH WEST AFRICA, WINDHOEK, 1975-76. [Report]. [Windhoek, 1976]. pp. 128.

— Social policy.

CONSTITUTIONAL CONFERENCE OF SOUTH WEST AFRICA, WINDHOEK, 1975-76. [Report]. [Windhoek, 1976]. pp. 128.

SOUTHAMPTON

— History — Sources.

SOUTHAMPTON. University. Southampton Records Series. Vols. 19 and 20. The cartulary of God's House, Southampton; edited by J.M. Kaye. Southampton, 1976. 2 vols.

SOUTHWARK

— Social policy.

THOMAS (DAVID NICHOLAS) Organising for social change: a study in the theory and practice of community work. London, 1976. pp. 199. (National Institute for Social Work Training. National Institute Social Services Library. No. 30)

SOVIET CENTRAL ASIA

— Economic history.

KHOZIAISTVENNO-kul'turnye traditsii narodov Srednei Azii i Kazakhstana. Moskva, 1975. pp. 231.

— History.

KHIDOIATOV (GOGA ABRAROVICH) and DMITRIEV (G.L.) eds. Materialy po istorii i arkheologii Uzbekistana. Tashkent, 1973. pp. 215. (Tashkent. Universitet. Nauchnye Trudy. vyp.441)

KHALFIN (NAFTULA ARONOVICH) Rossiia i khanstva Srednei Azii, pervaia polovina XIX veka. Moskva, 1974. pp. 406.

— Politics and government.

NARIMANOV (NARIMAN NADZHAF-OGLY) Lenin i Vostok: [sbornik statei, 1924-25; pod redaktsiei Dzh. B. Gulieva]. Baku, 1970. pp. 47.

RADZHABOV (SOLEKH ASHUROVICH) V.I. Lenin i sovetskaia natsional'naia gosudarstvennost'. Dushanbe, 1970. pp. 687.

TORZHESTVO leninskikh idei proletarskogo internatsionalizma: na materialakh respublik Srednei Azii i Kazakhstana, 1917-1972 gg. Moskva, 1974. pp. 531.

SOVIET FAR EAST

— Constitutional history — Sources.

REVKOMY Severo-Vostoka SSSR, 1922-1928 gg.: sbornik dokumentov i materialov. Magadan, 1973. pp. 240.

— Economic conditions.

SHNIPER (RUVIN ISAKOVICH) and DENISOVA (LILIIA PETROVNA) eds. Mezhotraslevye sviazi i narodnokhoziaistvennye proportsii Vostochnoi Sibiri i Dal'nego Vostoka. Novosibirsk, 1974. pp. 315.

SOVIET FAR EAST (Cont.)

— Executive departments.

REVKOMY Severo-Vostoka SSSR, 1922-1928 gg.: sbornik dokumentov i materialov. Magadan, 1973. pp. 240.

— History.

ISTORIIA i kul'tura narodov Dal'nego Vostoka: doklady i soobshcheniia, prochitannye na 2-i sessii Dal'nevostochnykh istoricheskikh chtenii v g. Iuzhno-Sakhalinske v dekabre 1971 g. Iuzhno-Sakhalinsk, 1973. pp. 311.

— — 1917—1921, Revolution.

SHERESHEVSKII (BORIS MIKHAILOVICH) V bitvakh za Dal'nii Vostok, 1920-1922 gg.: otvetstvennyi redaktor...V.A. Demidov. Novosibirsk, 1974. pp. 187.

SMITH (CANFIELD F.) Vladivostok under red and white rule: revolution and counterrevolution in the Russian Far East, 1920-1922. Seattle, [1975]. pp. 304. *bibliog. (Washington State University. Institute for Comparative and Foreign Area Studies. Publications on Russia and Eastern Europe. No.6)*

— — — Campaigns.

MUKHACHEV (BORIS IVANOVICH) Stanovlenie Sovetskoi vlasti i bor'ba s inostrannoi ekspansiei na Severo-Vostoke SSSR, 1917-1920 gg.; otvetstvennyi redaktor. ..I.M. Razgon. Novosibirsk, 1975. pp. 201.

SOVIET NORTH

— Economic history.

NEKOTORYE voprosy sotsialisticheskogo stroitel'stva i formirovaniia rabochego klassa SSSR v predvoennye gody. Murmansk, 1971. pp. 250. *(Leningrad. Leningradskii Gosudarstvennyi Pedagogicheskii Institut. Uchenye Zapiski. t.329)*

— Economic policy.

DOGAEV (IURII MIKHAILOVICH) Ekonomika nauchno-tekhnicheskogo progressa: regional'nye problemy. Moskva, 1975. pp. 286. *bibliog.*

POVYSHENIE effektivnosti proizvodstva Evropeiskogo Severo- Vostoka. Moskva, 1975. pp. 237.

SOVIETS

— Germany.

DAEHN (HORST) Rätedemokratische Modelle: Studien zur Rätediskussion in Deutschland, 1918-1919. Meisenheim am Glan, 1975. pp. 584. *bibliog.*

— Russia.

TERLETS'KYI (VALENTYN MYKHAILOVICH) Leninskoe ideinoe nasledie i problemy sovetskogo stroitel'stva. Kiev, 1974. pp. 263. *bibliog.*

— — Kazakstan.

SOVETY i revkomy v Kazakhstane, oktiabr' 1917-1920 gg.: dokumenty i materialy. Alma-Ata, 1971. pp. 224.

— — Russia (RSFSR).

SOVETY Vladimirskoi gubernii v period podgotovki i razvitiia Velikoi Oktiabr'skoi sotsialisticheskoi revoliutsii, 1917-1918 gg.: sbornik statei. Vladimir, 1969. pp. 71.

— — Ukraine.

HAMRETS'KYI (IURII MARKOVYCH) and others. Rady Ukraïny v 1917 r.: lypen' - hruden', 1917 r. Kyïv, 1974. pp. 343.

SPACE AND TIME.

JAEGLE (PIERRE) Essai sur l'espace et le temps du point de vue du matérialisme dialectique. Paris, 1971. fo. 27. *(Centre d'Etudes et de Recherches Marxistes. Cahiers. No. 97)*

SPACE IN ECONOMICS.

JUDGE (GEORGE G.) and TAKAYAMA (TAKASHI) eds. Studies in economic planning over space and time. Amsterdam, 1973. pp. 727. *bibliogs.*

BEIER (JOACHIM) Zeitraumanalyse: Bindeglied einzel- und gesamtwirtschaftlicher Unternehmensstatistik. Berlin, [1975]. pp. 337. *bibliog.*

COHEN (YEHOSHUA S.) and BERRY (BRIAN JOE LOBLEY) Spatial components of manufacturing change, 1950-1960. Chicago, 1975. pp. 262. *bibliog. (Chicago. University. Department of Geography. Research Papers. No.172)*

GREENHUT (MELVIN LEONARD) and OHTA (HIROSHI) Theory of spatial pricing and market areas. Durham, N.C., 1975. pp. 262.

PAELINCK (JEAN H.P.) and NIJKAMP (PETER) Operational theory and method in regional economics. Farnborough, Hants, [1975?]. pp. 471. *bibliogs.*

GILBERT (ALAN GRAHAM) ed. Development planning and spatial structure. London, [1976]. pp. 207. *bibliogs.*

SPAIN

— Civilization.

SANCHEZ-ALBORNOZ (CLAUDIO) Mi testamento historico-politico. Barcelona, [1975]. pp. 256.

— Commerce — United Kingdom.

The ADVANTAGES and disadvantages which will attend the prohibition of the merchandizes of Spain, impartially examined, and humbly offered to...Parliament; by a Sussex farmer. London, J. Roberts, [1740?]. pp. 34.

— Cortes.

BESTEIRO FERNANDEZ (JULIAN) Historia parlamentaria del socialismo: Julian Besteiro...; edicion, guia historica y notas de Fermin Solana. Madrid, [1975 in progress].

— Economic conditions.

SPAIN in crisis: the evolution and decline of the Franco régime; editor Paul Preston. Hassocks, 1976. pp. 341.

SPAIN in the 1970s: economics, social structure, foreign policy; [papers presented at a conference held in Washington in 1973]; edited by William T. Salisbury [and] James D. Theberge. New York, 1976. pp. 184. *(South Carolina University. Institute of International Studies. International Relations Series. No. 5)*

— Economic history.

CAPITALISMO español: de la autarquia a la estabilizacion, 1939- 1959; [by] Joan Clavera [and others]. Madrid, 1973. 2 vols. *bibliog.*

— Economic policy.

REGIONALIZACION de la economia española; ([by] Rafael Martinez Cortiña [and others]). Madrid, [1975]. pp. 611. *(Confederacion Española de Cajas de Ahorros. Fondo para la Investigacion Economica y Social. Publicaciones. 66)*

— Foreign economic relations — Gibraltar.

MAXWELL STAMP ASSOCIATES and IBERPLAN. Gibraltar, British or Spanish?: the economic prospects; a research study. London, 1976. 1 vol. (various pagings).

— Foreign relations.

BROUGHAM (HENRY PETER) 1st Baron Brougham and Vaux. Substance of Mr. Brougham's speech, in the House of Commons, February 4, 1823, upon the war with Spain. London, printed for J. Ridgway, [1823]. pp. 36.

SOUTHWORTH (HERBERT RUTLEDGE) La destruction de Guernica: journalisme, diplomatie, propagande et histoire. Paris, [1975]. pp. 535. *bibliog.*

SPAIN in the 1970s: economics, social structure, foreign policy; [papers presented at a conference held in Washington in 1973]; edited by William T. Salisbury [and] James D. Theberge. New York, 1976. pp. 184. *(South Carolina University. Institute of International Studies. International Relations Series. No. 5)*

— — Germany.

RUHL (KLAUS JOERG) Spanien im Zweiten Weltkrieg: Franco, die Falange und das "Dritte Reich". Hamburg, 1975. pp. 414. *bibliog. With English summary.*

— — Gibraltar.

MAXWELL STAMP ASSOCIATES and IBERPLAN. Gibraltar, British or Spanish?: the economic prospects; a research study. London, 1976. 1 vol. (various pagings).

— History.

HERR (RICHARD) An historical essay on modern Spain. Berkeley, 1974. pp. 308. *bibliog. Originally published in 1971 under the title Spain.*

PROBLEMY ispanskoi istorii. Moskva, 1975. pp. 264.

SANCHEZ-ALBORNOZ (CLAUDIO) Mi testamento historico-politico. Barcelona, [1975]. pp. 256.

— — Sources.

GARCIA-NIETO (MARIA CARMEN) and others, eds. Bases documentales de la España contemporanea. Madrid, [1971-75]. 11 vols. *bibliogs.*

CATALINAS CALLEJA (JOSE LUIS) and ECHENAGUSIA BELDA (JAVIER) eds. La Primera Republica: reformismo y revolucion social. [Madrid, 1973]. pp. 514. *bibliog.*

— — 711-1516.

MARAVALL (JOSE ANTONIO) Estudios de historia del pensamiento español: serie primera: Edad Media. 2nd ed. Madrid, 1973. pp. 507.

HILLGARTH (J.N.) The Spanish kingdoms 1250-1516. Oxford, 1976 in progress. *bibliog.*

— — 1516-1700, House of Austria.

ROWDON (MAURICE) The Spanish terror: Spanish imperialism in the sixteenth century. London, 1974. pp. 335. *bibliog.*

— — 1700-1799.

ANES ALVAREZ (GONZALO) El Antiguo Regimen: los Borbones. Madrid, [1975]. pp. 516. *bibliog.*

— — 1873-1875, Republic.

CATALINAS CALLEJA (JOSE LUIS) and ECHENAGUSIA BELDA (JAVIER) eds. La Primera Republica: reformismo y revolucion social. [Madrid, 1973]. pp. 514. *bibliog.*

— — 1900.

JALON (CESAR) Memorias politicas: periodista, ministro, presidiario. Madrid, [1973]. pp. 430.

— — 1931-1939, Republic.

CAMPS (MARGARITA) Spain under the Republican government. London, 1937. pp. 7. *(Reprinted from Pax International, February, 1937)*

GONZALEZ MUÑIZ (MIGUEL ANGEL) Problemas de la segunda republica. Madrid, 1974. pp. 411.

BLINKHORN (MARTIN) Carlism and crisis in Spain, 1931-1939. Cambridge, 1975. pp. 394. *bibliog.*

COSTA CLAVELL (XAVIER) Los ultimos dias de la Republica. Barcelona, 1975. pp. 192. *bibliog.*

— — 1936-1939, Civil War.

STALINISMUS und Anarchismus in der spanischen Revolution; oder, Bruno Frei und die Methode der Denunziation; ([by] Hans Peter Duerr, Augustin Souchy). Berlin, [1973]. pp. 56.

— — — Aerial operations.

THOMAS (GORDON) and MORGAN-WITTS (MAX) The day Guernica died. London, [1975]. pp. 319. bibliog.

— — — Foreign participation.

U.K. Delegation to the International Committee for the Application of the Agreement regarding Non-Intervention in Spain. 1936-39. [Papers of the Delegation, consisting mainly of the minutes and memoranda of the Committee and its various sub-committees]. (FO 849/1-41). London, 1936-39. Microfilm: 24 reels.

BELL (JOHN BOWYER) The Non-Intervention Committee and the Spanish Civil War, 1936-1939. 1958. pp. 371. bibliog. Ph.D.(Duke University) thesis: unpublished. Microfilm of typescript: 1 reel.

COVERDALE (JOHN F.) Italian intervention in the Spanish Civil War. Princeton, [1975]. pp. 455. bibliog.

USTVEDT (YNGVAR) Arbeidere under våpen: norske frivillige i den spanske borgerkrig. Oslo, [1975]. pp. 285. bibliog.

— — — Foreign public opinion.

PIKE (DAVID WINGEATE) Les Français et la guerre d'Espagne. Paris, 1975. pp. 467. bibliog. (Paris. Université de Paris I (Panthéon- Sorbonne). Publications. Nouvelle Série. Recherches. 7)

SOUTHWORTH (HERBERT RUTLEDGE) La destruction de Guernica: journalisme, diplomatie, propagande et histoire. Paris, [1975]. pp. 535. bibliog.

— — — Personal narratives.

ELOSEGI (JOSEBA) Quiero morir por algo. [Bordeaux?, 1971]. pp. 329.

GUZMAN (EDUARDO DE) La muerte de la esperanza. Madrid, [1973]. pp. 397.

GARCIA PRADAS (JOSE) Teniamos que perder! Madrid, [1974]. pp. 332.

THOMAS (GORDON) and MORGAN-WITTS (MAX) The day Guernica died. London, [1975]. pp. 319. bibliog.

CARRILLO (SANTIAGO) Dialogue on Spain; ...with Régis Debray and Max Gallo. London, 1976. pp. 222.

— — — Prisoners and prisons.

JALON (CESAR) Memorias politicas: periodista, ministro, presidiario. Madrid, [1973]. pp. 430.

GUZMAN (EDUARDO DE) El año de la victoria. Madrid, [1974]. pp. 376.

— — 1939— .

BLAYE (EDOUARD DE) Franco and the politics of Spain;...translated by Brian Pearce; postscript to part II by Richard Gott. Harmondsworth, 1976. pp. 576. bibliog.

— Industries.

SPAIN. Instituto Nacional de Industria. Resumen de actividades. a., 1973- [Madrid].

— Kings and rulers.

ESPAÑA, su monarquia y Europa: ciclo de conferencias sobre el tema "La evolucion politica, economica, cultural, social y religiosa de la monarquia española en relacion con Europa", [sponsored by Club Siglo XXI]. Madrid, 1974. pp. 309.

— Politics and government.

BROUGHAM (HENRY PETER) 1st Baron Brougham and Vaux. Substance of Mr. Brougham's speech, in the House of Commons, February 4, 1823, upon the war with Spain. London, printed for J. Ridgway, [1823]. pp. 36.

ORTEGA Y GASSET (JOSE) Rectificacion de la Republica: escritos politicos, III, 1929/1933. Madrid, [1973]. pp. 273.

ORTEGA Y GASSET (JOSE) La redencion de las provincias: escritos politicos, II, 1918/1928. Madrid, [1973]. pp. 299.

ORTEGA Y GASSET (JOSE) Vieja y nueva politica: escritos politicos, I, 1908/1918. Madrid, [1973]. pp. 312.

CARRILLO (SANTIAGO) Demain l'Espagne: entretiens avec Régis Debray et Max Gallo. Paris, [1974]. pp. 225.

ESPAÑA, su monarquia y Europa: ciclo de conferencias sobre el tema "La evolucion politica, economica, cultural, social y religiosa de la monarquia española en relacion con Europa", [sponsored by Club Siglo XXI]. Madrid, 1974. pp. 309.

HOTTINGER (ARNOLD) Spain in transition: Franco's regime. Beverly Hills, [1974]. pp. 62. (Georgetown University. Center for Strategic and International Studies. Washington Papers. vol. 2/18)

HOTTINGER (ARNOLD) Spain in transition: prospects and policies. Beverly Hills, [1974]. pp. 65. (Georgetown University. Center for Strategic and International Studies. Washington Papers. vol. 2/19)

FRAGA IRIBARNE (MANUEL) Legitimidad y representacion. Barcelona, [1975]. pp. 384.

FRANCO BAHAMONDE (FRANCISCO) Pensamiento politico de Franco: antologia;...sistematizacion de textos y preambulo de Agustin del Rio Cisneros. Madrid, 1975. 2 vols.

HERAS FEBRERO (JESUS DE LAS) and VILLARIN GARCIA (JUAN) eds. El año Arias: diario politico español 1974. Madrid, 1975. pp. 893.

PEREZ SADABA (VICENTE) Problemas politicos de la España actual. Madrid, [1975]. pp. 257.

SANCHEZ-ALBORNOZ (CLAUDIO) Mi testamento historico-politico. Barcelona, [1975]. pp. 256.

BLAYE (EDOUARD DE) Franco and the politics of Spain;...translated by Brian Pearce; postscript to part II by Richard Gott. Harmondsworth, 1976. pp. 576. bibliog.

CARRILLO (SANTIAGO) Dialogue on Spain; ...with Régis Debray and Max Gallo. London, 1976. pp. 222.

FARREL (J.M.) Spain after Franco: the workers' struggle. Leeds, [1976]. pp. 50.

SPAIN in crisis: the evolution and decline of the Franco régime; editor Paul Preston. Hassocks, 1976. pp. 341.

SPAIN in the 1970s: economics, social structure, foreign policy; [papers presented at a conference held in Washington in 1973]; edited by William T. Salisbury [and] James D. Theberge. New York, 1976. pp. 184. (South Carolina University. Institute of International Studies. International Relations Series. No. 5)

— Population.

REGIONALIZACION de la economia española; ([by] Rafael Martinez Cortiña [and others]). Madrid, [1975]. pp. 611. (Confederacion Española de Cajas de Ahorros. Fondo para la Investigacion Economica y Social. Publicaciones. 66)

— Relations (general) with the United States.

VAZQUEZ MONTALBAN (MANUEL) La penetracion americana en España. Madrid, [1974]. pp. 439.

— Rural conditions.

ACEVES (JOSEPH BUENAVENTURA) and DOUGLASS (WILLIAM A.) eds. The changing faces of rural Spain. New York, [1976]. pp. 205. bibliog.

— Social conditions.

ALVAREZ DE TOLEDO (ISABEL) Duquesa de Medina Sidonia. La huelga: novela. Buenos Aires, 1974 [or rather 1975]. pp. 285.

SPAIN in crisis: the evolution and decline of the Franco régime; editor Paul Preston. Hassocks, 1976. pp. 341.

SPAIN in the 1970s: economics, social structure, foreign policy; [papers presented at a conference held in Washington in 1973]; edited by William T. Salisbury [and] James D. Theberge. New York, 1976. pp. 184. (South Carolina University. Institute of International Studies. International Relations Series. No. 5)

SPANIARDS IN MEXICO.

El COMERCIO exterior y la expulsion de los españoles. Mexico, 1966. pp. 326. (Banco Nacional de Comercio Exterior. Coleccion de Documentos para la Historia del Comercio Exterior de Mexico. 2a Serie. 2)

SPANISH SAHARA.

MERCER (JOHN) Spanish Sahara. London, 1976. pp. 264. bibliog.

SPANISH SUCCESSION, WAR OF, 1701-1714.

CHURCHILL (JOHN) 1st Duke of Marlborough, and GODOLPHIN (SIDNEY) 1st Earl of Godolphin. The Marlborough-Godolphin correspondence; edited by Henry L. Snyder. Oxford, 1975. 3 vols.

SPASOWICZ (WLODZIMIERZ).

KULCZYCKA-SALONI (JANINA) Włodzimierz Spasowicz: zarys monograficzny. Wrocław, 1975. pp. 223. (Towarzystwo Literackie imienia Adama Mickiewicza. Biblioteka. t.9)

SPECIAL DISTRICTS

— United States — Illinois.

STETZER (DONALD FOSTER) Special districts in Cook County: toward a geography of local government. Chicago, 1975. pp. 177. bibliog. (Chicago. University. Department of Geography. Research Papers. No. 169)

SPECIAL DRAWING RIGHTS.

CLINE (WILLIAM R.) International monetary reform and the developing countries. Washington, D.C., [1976]. pp. 126.

SPECULATION.

TEWELES (RICHARD JACK) and others. The commodity futures game: who wins?, who loses?, why?. New York, [1974]. pp. 638. bibliog. Edition for 1969 published under title: The commodity futures trading guide.

SPEECH.

MARUSZEWSKI (MARIUSZ) Language communication and the brain: a neuropsychological study. The Hague, 1975. pp. 217. bibliog.

MASSARO (DOMINIC W.) ed. Understanding language: an information-processing analysis of speech perception, reading, and psycholinguistics. New York, [1975]. pp. 439. bibliogs.

SPEECH, DISORDERS OF.

FOUNDATIONS of language development: a multidisciplinary approach; edited by Eric H. Lenneberg [and] Elizabeth Lenneberg. Paris, Unesco Press, 1975. 2 vols. bibliogs.

SPEECH AND SOCIAL STATUS.

GILES (HOWARD) and POWESLAND (PETER F.) Speech style and social evaluation. London, 1975. pp. 218. bibliog. (European Association of Experimental Social Psychology. European Monographs in Social Psychology. 7)

SPENCER (HERBERT).

HOFSTADTER (RICHARD) Social Darwinism in American thought. rev. ed. New York, 1959 repr. 1969. pp. 248. *bibliog.*

BARBÉ (CARLOS) Progresso e sviluppo: la formazione della teoria dello sviluppo e lo sviluppo come ideologia; Auguste Comte, Herbert Spencer. Torino, 1974. pp. 241. *(Turin. Università. Istituto di Scienze Politiche. Pubblicazioni. vol. 32)*

SPINOZA (BENEDICTUS DE).

TOENNIES (FERDINAND) Studien zur Philosophie und Gesellschaftslehre im 17. Jahrhundert; herausgegeben von E.G. Jacoby. Stuttgart-Bad Cannstatt, [1975]. pp. 384. *bibliog.*

SPORTS

— Social aspects.

SOCIAL problems in athletics: essays in the sociology of sport; edited by Daniel M. Landers. Urbana, [1976]. pp. 251. *bibliogs. Essays based on a conference on "Sport and Social Deviance" which was held at State University College, Brockport, New York*

— Somali Republic.

SOMALI REPUBLIC. Ministry of Information and National Guidance. 1974. The revolutionary generation of tomorrow: youth, sports and manpower. Mogadishu, 1974. pp. 72.

— South Africa.

BRICKHILL (JOAN) Race against race: South Africa's multi-national sport fraud. London, 1976. pp. 77.

— United Kingdom.

NICHOLLS (M.) Recreationally disadvantaged areas in Greater London: report of an analysis of provision for sports and active recreation. London, [1975]. pp. 25. *(London. Greater London Council. Research Memoranda. 467)*

SPORTS BETTING.

GHANA. 1971. White Paper on the report of the Committee of Enquiry on the erstwhile Football Pools Authority. [Accra], 1971. pp. 5. *(W[hite] P[apers]. 1971. No.1) Bound with the report.*

GHANA. Committee of Enquiry on the erstwhile Football Pools Authority. 1971. Report; [P.V. Osei-Hwere, chairman]. [Accra, 1971]. fo. 218. *Bound with White Paper on the report.*

SPRINGER (AXEL).

ADOMATIS (HANS JOACHIM) Von Berlin aus gesehen: die Springer-Partei. Wuppertal, 1975. pp. 102.

SQUATTERS

— Kenya.

ROSS (MARC HOWARD) The political integration of urban squatters. Evanston, 1973. pp. 228. *bibliog.*

MBITHI (PHILIP M.) and BARNES (CAROLYN) The spontaneous settlement problem in Kenya. Kampala, 1975. pp. 192.

— Peru.

COLLIER (DAVID) Squatters and oligarchs: authoritarian rule and policy change in Peru. Baltimore, [1976]. pp. 187. *bibliog.*

— Tanzania.

STREN (RICHARD E.) Urban inequality and housing policy in Tanzania: the problem of squatting. Berkeley, [1975]. pp. 112. *bibliog. (California University. Institute of International Studies. Research Series. No. 24)*

— Underdeveloped areas.

See UNDERDEVELOPED AREAS — Squatters.

— United Kingdom.

EMPTY property: a guide for local groups; [by] C[ampaign for the] H[omeless] a[nd] R[ootless and others]. London, [1975]. pp. 38.

— Venezuela.

KARST (KENNETH L.) and others. The evolution of law in the barrios of Caracas. Los Angeles, 1973. pp. 125. *(California University. Latin American Center. Latin American Studies. vol. 20)*

SRAFFA (PIERO).

RONCAGLIA (ALESSANDRO) Sraffa e la teoria dei prezzi. Roma, 1975. pp. 200. *bibliog.*

SRI LANKA

— Commerce.

SRI LANKA. Department of Commerce. 1965. Department of Commerce, Colombo. [Colombo, 1965]. pp. 16.

— Economic conditions.

SRI LANKA. Department of Census and Statistics. 1969. The Ceylon economic atlas. [Colombo], 1969. pp. 69.

— Executive departments.

SRI LANKA. Department of Commerce. 1965. Department of Commerce, Colombo. [Colombo, 1965]. pp. 16.

— History.

WEERASOORIA (N.E.) Ceylon and her people. Colombo, 1970. pp. 359.

— Parliament — Elections.

WILSON (ALFRED JEYARATNAM) Electoral politics in an emergent state: the Ceylon general election of May 1970. London, 1975. pp. 240. *bibliog. (McGill University. Centre for Developing-Area Studies. Perspectives on Development. 3)*

— Population.

SRI LANKA. Department of Census and Statistics. 1974. The population of Sri Lanka. [Colombo, 1974]. pp. 128. *(Committee for International Coordination of National Research in Demography. C.I.C.R.E.D. Series)*

WILSON (PITIYAGE) Economic implications of population growth: Sri Lanka labour force, 1946-81. Canberra, 1975. pp. 240. *bibliog.*

— Social conditions.

JAYARAMAN (RAJA) Caste continuities in Ceylon: a study of the social structure of three tea plantations. Bombay, 1975. pp. 240. *bibliog.*

— Statistics, Vital.

SRI LANKA. Department of Census and Statistics. 1971. Life tables, Ceylon, 1962-1967. Colombo, 1970 [or rather 1971]. pp. 39. *In English and Sinhala.*

STAFFORDSHIRE

— Economic history.

DILWORTH (DOUGLAS A.) The Tame mills of Staffordshire. London, 1976. pp. 212. *bibliog.*

STALIN (IOSIF VISSARIONOVICH).

GLASSER (M.) Über die Arbeitsmethoden der Klassiker des Marxismus- Leninismus. Berlin, [1948]. pp. 103.

MEDVEDEV (ROI ALEKSANDROVICH) K sudu istorii: genezis i posledstviia stalinizma; Let history judge: the origins and consequences of Stalinism. 2nd ed. New York, 1974. pp. 1136.

McNEAL (ROBERT HATCH) The Bolshevik tradition: Lenin, Stalin, Khrushchev, Brezhnev. 2nd ed. Englewood Cliffs, [1975]. pp. 210. *bibliog.*

CARMICHAEL (JOEL) Stalin's masterpiece: the show trials and purges of the thirties: the consolidation of the Bolshevik dictatorship. London, [1976]. pp. 238. *bibliog.*

STANDARDIZATION

— Communist countries — Bibliography.

RUSSIA (USSR). Gosudarstvennyi Komitet Standartov. 1972. Ukazatel' rekomendatsii po standartizatsii Soveta Ekonomicheskoi Vzaimopomoshchi: bibliograficheskaia informatsiia. Moskva, 1972. pp. 196.

STATE, THE.

FELS (JOSEF) Begriff und Wesen der Nation: eine soziologische Untersuchung und Kritik. Münster in Westfalen, 1927. pp. 147. *bibliog.*

RASCHHOFER (HERMANN) Der politische Volksbegriff im modernen Italien. Berlin, 1936. pp. 207.

GENTILE (GIOVANNI) Genesi e struttura della società: saggio di filosofia pratica. Firenze, 1975. pp. 191. *Originally published in 1945 in Opere complete di Giovanni Gentile.*

EISENSTADT (SHMUEL N.) and ROKKAN (STEIN) eds. Building states and nations. Beverly Hills, [1973]. 2 vols. *bibliogs.*

MANOV (GRIGORII NAUMOVICH) Gosudarstvo i politicheskaia organizatsiia obshchestva. Moskva, 1974. pp. 320. *bibliog.*

BUCI-GLUCKSMANN (CHRISTINE) Gramsci et l'état: pour une théorie matérialiste de la philosophie. [Paris, 1975]. pp. 454.

GULIEV (VLADIMIR EVGEN'EVICH) and KUZ'MIN (EDUARD LEONIDOVICH) Gosudarstvo i demokratiia: kritika antimarksistskikh teorii. Moskva, 1975. pp. 215.

PLANTEY (ALAIN) Prospective de l'état. Paris, 1975. pp. 306.

ROUX (JEAN) La rationalisation des choix politiques. Paris, 1975. pp. 227. *bibliog.*

DAHRENDORF (RALF) Die Staatsräson der Bundesrepublik Deutschland. Konstanz, 1976. pp. 32. *(Constance. Universität. Waldemar-Besson-Gedächtnis-Vorlesungen. 1975)*

DELCROS (BERTRAND) L'unité de la personnalité juridique de l'état: étude sur les services non personnalisés de l'état. Paris, 1976. pp. 322. *bibliog.*

TAYLOR (MICHAEL) Anarchy and cooperation. London, [1976]. pp. 151. *bibliog.*

— Economic aspects.

TULLOCK (GORDON) The vote motive: an essay in the economics of politics with applications to the British economy...with a British commentary by Morris Perlman. London, 1976. pp. 88. *bibliogs. (Institute of Economic Affairs. Hobart Paperbacks. 9.)*

STATE ENCOURAGEMENT OF SCIENCE, LITERATURE AND ART

The PATRONAGE of science in the nineteenth century; by R. Fox [and others]; edited by G.L'E. Turner. Leyden, 1976. pp. 218.

— United Kingdom.

REDCLIFFE-MAUD (JOHN PRIMATT REDCLIFFE) Baron Redcliffe-Maud. Support for the arts in England and Wales: a report to the Calouste Gulbenkian Foundation. London, 1976. pp. 201.

STATE FARMS

— Russia.

MEDVEDEV (N.A.) ed. Metodika perspektivnogo ekonomiko-sotsial'noo planirovaniia na sele. Leningrad, 1970. pp. 339.

— — Kazakstan.

ARYSTANBEKOV (KHAIDAR ARYSTANBEKOVICH) and AUTOV (RAKHIMZHAN RAKHMEDINOVICH) Voprosy ekonomiki sovkhoznogo proizvodstva Kazakhstana. Alma-Ata, 1973. pp. 186.

— — Siberia.

LAVRUKHIN (BORIS PETROVICH) Povyshenie ekonomicheskoi effektivnosti sovkhozov; nauchnyi redaktor...V. Zolotarev. Novosibirsk, 1969. pp. 68.

— — Ukraine — Statistics.

UKRAINE. Tsentral'noe Statisticheskoe Upravlenie. 1973. Radhospy Ukraïns'koï RSR v tsyfrakh: statystychnyi zbirnyk. Kyïv, 1973. pp. 322.

STATE GOVERNMENTS

— United States.

POLITICAL science and state and local government: [papers presented at a conference held in Biloxi, Mississippi in October 1972, organized by the American Political Science Association]. Washington, [1973]. pp. 141. *bibliogs.*

LEACH (RICHARD HEALD) and O'ROURKE (TIMOTHY G.) compilers. Dimensions of state and urban policy making. New York, [1975]. pp. 418. *bibliogs.*

— — Mathematical models.

CHO (YONG HYO) and FREDERICKSON (H. GEORGE) Determinants of public policy in the American states: a model for synthesis. Beverly Hills, [1973]. pp. 55. *bibliog.*

STATE SUCCESSION.

BURLET (JACQUES DE) Nationalité des personnes physiques et décolonisation: essai de contribution à la théorie de la succession d'Etats. Bruxelles, 1975. pp. 223. *bibliog. (Louvain. Université. Faculté de Droit. Bibliothèque. 10)*

STATES, NEW.

BURLET (JACQUES DE) Nationalité des personnes physiques et décolonisation: essai de contribution à la théorie de la succession d'Etats. Bruxelles, 1975. pp. 223. *bibliog. (Louvain. Université. Faculté de Droit. Bibliothèque. 10)*

KILSON (MARTIN) ed. New states in the modern world. Cambridge, Mass., 1975. pp. 254. *bibliog.*

STATES, SMALL.

HROCH (MIROSLAV) Die Vorkämpfer der nationalen Bewegung bei den kleinen Völkern Europas: eine vergleichende Analyse zur gesellschaftlichen Schichtung der patriotischen Gruppen. Praha, [1968]. pp. 171. *(Karlova Universita. Acta Universitatis Carolinae. Philosophica et Historica. Monographia. 24)*

JOHNSTON (PETER) Appropriate technologies for small developing countries. Brighton, [1974]. pp. 38. *bibliog.*

NEUMAN (STEPHANIE GLICKSBERG) ed. Small states and segmented societies: national political integration in a global environment. New York, 1976. pp. 238.

ZWERIN (MICHAEL) A case for the balkanization of practically everyone: the new nationalism. London, 1976. pp. 190. *bibliog.*

STATESMEN.

SOLDIERS as statesmen; [based on papers presented at a symposium held at the Royal Military College of Canada, Kingston, Ontario in 1975]; edited by Peter Dennis and Adrian Preston. London, 1976. pp. 184. *bibliogs.*

— America, Latin.

LATIN American government leaders; second edition edited by David William Foster. Tempe, 1975. pp. 130.

— United States.

[PEARSON (DREW) and ALLEN (ROBERT SHARON)] Washington merry-go-round. New York, 1931. pp. 366.

WHO's who in American politics: fifth edition 1975-1976;... consulting editors Edmund L. Henshaw [and] Paul A. Theis. New York, [1975]. pp. 1090.

STATISTICS

— Bibliography.

U.K. Stationery Office. 1975- . Statistics: publications of UK government departments and international organisations. [London], 1975 in progress. *(Subject Catalogues. No. 1)* Current issue only kept.

LIBRARY ASSOCIATION and ROYAL STATISTICAL SOCIETY. Committee of Librarians and Statisticians. Recommended basic statistical sources: international. London, 1975. pp. 35.

— Dictionaries and encyclopaedias.

MOROZENKO (V.V.) compiler. Anglo-russkii ekonomiko-statisticheskii slovar'...; pod redaktsiei R.M. Entova. Moskva, 1974. pp. 222.

— History — United Kingdom.

CULLEN (MICHAEL J.) The statistical movement in early Victorian Britain: the foundations of empirical social research. Hassocks, Sussex, 1975. pp. 205. *bibliog.*

— Theory, methods, etc.

BIØRN (ERIK) Fordelingsvirkninger av indirekte skatter og subsidier...: distributive effects of indirect taxes and subsidies. Oslo, 1971. pp. 42. *(Norway. Statistiske Centralbyrå. Artikler. Nr. 42)* With English summary.

HOEM (JAN M.) On the statistical theory of analytic graduation, etc. Oslo, 1972. pp. 569-600. *bibliog. (Norway. Statistiske Centralbyrå. Artikler. Nr. 49)* Reprinted from Volume 1 of the Proceedings of the Sixth Berkeley Symposium on Mathematical Statistics and Probability.

HOEM (JAN M.) Two articles on the interpretation of vital rates, etc. Oslo, 1972. pp. 319-327,454-468. *bibliog. (Norway. Statistiske Centralbyrå. Artikler. Nr. 46)* Reprinted from Theoretical Population Biology, vol. 2, nos. 3 and 4.

SAVAGE (LEONARD JIMMIE) The foundations of statistics. 2nd ed. New York, 1972. pp. 310. *bibliog.*

DAGSVIK (JOHN) Etterhåndsstratifisering og estimering innen del-bestanden...: post-stratification and estimation within subpopulations. Oslo, 1974. pp. 49. *bibliog. (Norway. Statistiske Centralbyrå. Artikler. Nr. 66)*

TUFTE (EDWARD R.) Data analysis for politics and policy. Englewood Cliffs, [1974]. pp. 179.

AITCHISON (JOHN) and DUNSMORE (IAN ROBERT) Statistical prediction analysis. Cambridge, 1975. pp. 273. *bibliog.*

ANDERSON (THEODORE ROBERT) and ZELDITCH (MORRIS) A basic course in statistics with sociological applications. 3rd ed. New York, [1975]. pp. 372. *bibliog.*

BROWN (FOSTER LLOYD) and others. Statistical concepts: a basic program. 2nd ed. New York, [1975]. pp. 148. *bibliog.*

CHETYRKIN (EVGENII MIKHAILOVICH) Statisticheskie metody prognozirovaniia. Moskva, 1975. pp. 184.

EHRENBERG (ANDREW SAMUEL CHRISTOPHER) Data reduction: analysing and interpreting statistical data. London, [1975]. pp. 391. *bibliog.*

GOVINDARAJULU (Z.) Sequential statistical procedures. New York, 1975. pp. 565. *bibliog.*

HAMMERTON (M.) Statistics for the human sciences. London, 1975. pp. 182.

SUSLOV (IVAN PETROVICH) Teoriia statisticheskikh pokazatelei. Moskva, 1975. pp. 264. *bibliog.*

SVERDRUP (ERLING) Multiple comparisons by binary and multinary observations...: multiple sammenlikninger ved binaere og multinaere observasjoner. Oslo, 1975. pp. 33. *bibliog. (Norway. Statistiske Centralbyra. Artikler. Nr. 75)*

STAUNING (THORVALD AUGUST MARINUS).

SONNE (HARDING) Stauning eller kaos: Socialdemokratiet og krisen i trediverne. København, 1974. pp. 142. *bibliog.*

STEALING.

BELSON (WILLIAM A.) Juvenile theft: the causal factors: a report of an investigation of the tenability of various causal hypotheses about the development of stealing by London boys, etc. London, 1975. pp. 411.

STEAM ENGINES.

BUCHANAN (R.A.) and WATKINS (GEORGE) The industrial archaeology of the stationary steam engine. London, 1976. pp. 199. *bibliog.*

STEAMBOAT LINES

— Austria.

COONS (RONALD E.) Steamships, statesmen, and bureaucrats: Austrian policy towards the Steam Navigation Company of the Austrian Lloyd, 1836- 1848. Wiesbaden, 1975. pp. 209. *bibliog. (Institut für Europäische Geschichte. Veröffentlichungen. Band 74)*

STEEL INDUSTRY AND TRADE.

RUSSELL (CLIFFORD S.) and VAUGHAN (WILLIAM J.) Steel production: processes, products, and residuals. Baltimore, [1976]. pp. 328. *bibliog.*

— Germany.

LUTZ (BURKART) Krise des Lohnanreizes: ein empirisch-historischer Beitrag zum Wandel der Formen betrieblicher Herrschaft am Beispiel der deutschen Stahlindustrie. Frankfurt, 1975. pp. 363. *(Institut für Sozialwissenschaftliche Forschung, München. Arbeiten)*

— Switzerland.

FISCHER (GEORG) AKTIENGESELLSCHAFT. Hundertfünfzig Jahre Georg Fischer Werke, 1802/1952. Schaffhausen, [1952]. pp. 192.

— United Kingdom.

BRITISH STEEL: (a q. review pd. by the British Steel Corporation). q., Ap 1968 [no.1]- London. *Supersedes Steel review (Ap 1961 - Jl 1967)*

BOWEN (PETER) Social control in industrial organisations: industrial relations and industrial sociology: a strategic and occupational study of British steelmaking. London, 1976. pp. 270. *bibliog.*

— United States.

HESSEN (ROBERT) Ph.D. Steel titan: the life of Charles M. Schwab. New York, 1975. pp. 350.

STEEL-WORKS.

— Environmental aspects.

RUSSELL (CLIFFORD S.) and VAUGHAN (WILLIAM J.) Steel production: processes, products, and residuals. Baltimore, [1976]. pp. 328. *bibliog.*

— Waste disposal.

RUSSELL (CLIFFORD S.) and VAUGHAN (WILLIAM J.) Steel production: processes, products, and residuals. Baltimore, [1976]. pp. 328. *bibliog.*

STEEN (JOHANNES VILHELM).

STEEN (JOHANNES VILHELM).

SUNNANÅ (OLAV) Johannes Steen: statsminister og parlamentarisk førar. Oslo, 1967. pp. 384. *bibliog. With English summary.*

STEFFEN (JOCHEN).

KESSELTREIBEN gegen wen?: die Legende einer Kampagne gegen Jochen Steffen; eine Dokumentation; herausgegeben von der Axel Springer Verlag AG, Abteilung Information. Berlin, [1971]. pp. 47.

STEFFENS (JOSEPH LINCOLN).

HORTON (RUSSELL M.) Lincoln Steffens. New York, [1974]. pp. 169. *bibliog.*

STEPHEN (Sir LESLIE).

STEPHEN (Sir LESLIE) [Correspondence about Alfred Marshall's theory of consumers' rent. 1891]. 4 letters, 3 pages of notes. *Manuscript.*

STEPPES.

RUSSIA (EMPIRE). Ministerstvo Gosudarstvennykh Imushchestv. 1868. Kalmytskaia step' Astrakhanskoi gubernii po issledovaniiam Kumo-Manychskoi ekspeditsii. S.-Peterburg, 1868. 3 pts (in 1).

STERILIZATION (BIRTH CONTROL).

SONI (VEENA) A demographic analysis of the sterilisation programme in the Indian states, 1957-73. 1975. fo 248. *bibliog. Typescript. Ph.D.(London) thesis: unpublished. This thesis is the property of London University and may not be removed from the Library.*

STEVENSON (ADLAI EWING).

MARTIN (JOHN BARTLOW) Adlai Stevenson of Illinois: the life of Adlai E. Stevenson. New York, 1976. pp. 828. *bibliog.*

STEWART (HENRY ROBERT) Viscount Castlereagh, 2nd Marquess of Londonderry.

DERRY (JOHN WESLEY) Castlereagh. London, 1976. pp. 247. *bibliog.*

STOCHASTIC DIFFERENTIAL EQUATIONS.

McSHANE (EDWARD JAMES) Stochastic calculus and stochastic models. New York, 1974. pp. 239. *bibliog.*

STOCHASTIC PROCESSES.

IOSIFESCU (MARIUS) and TAUTU (PETRE) Stochastic processes and applications in biology and medicine. Bucureşti, 1973. 2 vols.

SYLWESTROWICZ (JERZY DOWOYNA) Numerical optimization of non-linear functions of several variables using random search techniques; [Ph.D.(London) thesis]. 1975. fo. 185. *bibliog. Typescript: unpublished. This thesis is the property of London University and may not be removed from the Library.*

STOCK AND STOCK BREEDING

— Africa.

INTERNATIONAL AFRICAN SEMINAR. 13th Seminar, Niamey, 1972. Pastoralism in tropical Africa: studies presented and discussed at the...seminar...; edited with an introduction by Théodore Monod. London, 1975. pp. 502. *bibliogs. In English or French.*

— Portugal.

PORTUGAL. Instituto Nacional de Estatistica. Serviços Centrais. 1975. Arrolamento geral do gado, 1972: continente e ilhas adjacentes. [Lisbon, 1975]. pp. 489.

— Switzerland.

SWITZERLAND. Bureau Fédéral de Statistique. 1974. Nutztierbestand der Schweiz...1973. Bern, 1974. pp. 367. *(Statistiques de la Suisse. 550e fasc.) In German and French.*

— Tanzania.

MACKENZIE (WILLIAM) B.Sc. (Glasgow). The livestock economy of Tanzania. Dar es Salaam, 1973. pp. 97. *bibliog. (Dar es Salaam. University. Economic Research Bureau. ERB Papers. 73.5)*

— Uruguay.

PLUSVALIA agropecuaria del Uruguay, 1930-1954; [by] Alfredo Echegaray [and others]. Montevideo, 1971. 2 vols. (in 1). *bibliog.*

STOCK EXCHANGE

— Germany — Law.

TILLY (WOLFGANG M.) Die amtliche Kursnotierung an den Wertpapierbörsen: eine Untersuchung zur Entwicklung des deutschen Börsenrechts. Baden-Baden, [1975]. pp. 196. *bibliog.*

— Luxembourg — Law.

LUXEMBOURG. Statutes, etc. 1873-1975. Recueil de la législation sur les banque et bourse: textes coordonnés et jurisprudence; [edited by] (Raymond Weydert). Luxembourg, 1975. pp. 264.

STOCK—RANGES.

CANADA. Department of Agriculture. 1971. Management of the western range; [by] Robert W. Lodge [and others]. [Ottawa], 1971. pp. 34. *bibliog. (Publications. 1425)*

STOCKHOLDERS

— Norway.

TANGEN (DAG) Makt og eiendom: hvem styrer norsk industri? Oslo, [1975]. pp. 131.

— Pakistan.

RANJHA (KHALID) Company law and the shareholder. Lahore, 1975. pp. 542. *bibliog.*

— United Kingdom.

MIDGLEY (KENNETH) The relationship between large British public companies and their voting shareholders; [Ph.D.(London) thesis]. 1975. fo. 278. *bibliog. Typescript: unpublished. This thesis is the property of London University and may not be removed from the Library.*

STOCKS.

FOSTER (EARL M.) Common stock investment. Lexington, Mass., [1974]. pp. 178.

— Prices — United Kingdom.

FIRTH (MICHAEL A.) Share prices and mergers: a study of stock market efficiency. Farnborough, Hants, [1976]. pp. 187. *bibliog.*

— Switzerland.

ZINGG (WALTER) Indizes, Kenn- und Messziffern für kotierte Schweizeraktien. Bern, 1976. pp. 220. *bibliog.*

— Venezuela.

GARCIA-VELUTINI (OSCAR) Dinamica del mercado de valores. Caracas, 1974. pp. 92. *bibliog.*

STOEGMUELLER (ERNST).

EUROPEAN COURT OF HUMAN RIGHTS. Publications. Series A: Judgments and Decisions. [A9]. ..."Stögmüller case; judgment of 10th November 1969. Strasbourg, Council of Europe, 1969. pp. 47 [bis]. *In English and French.*

EUROPEAN COURT OF HUMAN RIGHTS. Publications. Series B: Pleadings, Oral Arguments and Documents. [B7]. "Stögmüller" case, (1967-1969). Strasbourg, Council of Europe, 1970. pp. 228 [bis], 229-256. *In English and French.*

STOIANOV (ZAKHARII).

KHRISTOV (KHRISTO) Zakharii Stoianov: obshtestvena i politicheska deinost; Zachari Stoïanov: son activité sociale et politique. Sofiia, 1948. pp. 155. *(Sofia. Universitet. Istoriko-Filologicheski Fakultet. Godishnik. t.44, kn.2) With French summary.*

STORES, RETAIL.

JABŁOŃSKI (ZBIGNIEW) Organizacja sklepów a ochrona mienia społecznego. Warszawa, 1954. pp. 154. *bibliog.*

STRALSUND

— History.

ZOELLNER (KLAUS PETER) Vom Strelasund zum Oslofjord: Untersuchungen zur Geschichte der Hanse und der Stadt Stralsund in der zweiten Hälfte des 16. Jahrhunderts. Weimar, 1974. pp. 200. *bibliog. (Historiker-Gesellschaft der Deutschen Demokratischen Republik. Hansische Arbeitsgemeinschaft. Abhandlungen zur Handels- und Sozialgeschichte. Band 14)*

STRATEGY.

ASPLUND (GÖRAN) Strategy formulation: an intervention study of a complex group decision process. Stockholm, 1975. pp. 222. *bibliog. Avhandling (doktor) - Stockholm School of Economics.*

CONTEMPORARY strategy: theories and policies; [by] John Baylis [and others]. London, [1975]. pp. 324.

KAHAN (JEROME H.) Security in the nuclear age: developing U.S. strategic arms policy. Washington, D.C., [1975]. pp. 361.

STRAUSS (FRANZ JOSEF).

EISNER (ERICH) Das europäische Konzept von Franz Josef Strauss: die gesamteuropäischen Ordnungsvorstellungen der CSU. Meisenheim am Glan, 1975. pp. 143. *bibliog.*

STREAM MEASUREMENTS

— United Kingdom — Statistical methods.

BLOOMER (R.J.G.) and SEXTON (J.R.) The generation of synthetic river flow data. Reading, 1972. pp. 81. *bibliog. (U.K. Water Resources Board. Publications. No. 15)*

STRESS (PHYSIOLOGY).

MOSS (GORDON ERVIN) Illness, immunity, and social interaction: the dynamics of biosocial resonation. New York, [1973]. pp. 281. *bibliog.*

JOB demands and worker health: main effects and occupational differences; [by] Robert D. Caplan [and others]. [Washington, D.C.,] 1975. pp. 342. *bibliog. (United States. National Institute for Occupational Safety and Health. Research Reports)*

MANOCCHIO (TONY) and PETITT (WILLIAM) Families under stress: a psychological interpretation. London, 1975. pp. 208. *bibliog.*

SPIELBERGER (CHARLES DONALD) and SARASON (IRWIN GERALD) eds. Stress and anxiety. Washington, [1975]. 2 vols. *bibliogs.*

STRIKES AND LOCKOUTS

— Canada — Newfoundland.

NEWFOUNDLAND. Royal Commission on Illegal Work Stoppages, 1973. Report; [Edward A. Neary, commissioner]. [St. John's], 1973. pp. 82.

STUDENTS

— — **Quebec (Province).**

DUMAS (EVELYN) The bitter thirties in Québec;...translated from the French by Arnold Bennett. Montréal, 1975. pp. 145.

— **Denmark.**

ANDERSEN (DORRIT) ed. Storlockout og Septemberforlig: kilder til belysning af storkonflikten, 1899. København, [1974]. pp. 59. *bibliog.*

THYGESEN (ERIK) ed. Erfaringer fra en arbejdskamp: plattekonflikten på den kgl. Porcelainsfabrik, 1972-73. København, [1974]. pp. 102. *bibliog.*

— **Germany.**

GERMANY. Reichstag. 1899. Die Zuchthausvorlage vor dem Reichstage: nach dem offiziellen stenographischen Bericht über die Verhandlungen des Deutschen Reichstages am 19., 20., 21. und 22. Juni 1899. Berlin, 1899. pp. 192.

HOEHNE (GERD) Wir gehn nach vorn!: Erfahrungsbericht über die Arbeitskampfe bei Mannesmann. Berlin, [1974]. pp.96.

SCHNEIDER (MICHAEL) ed. Auf dem Weg in die Krise: Thesen und Materialien zum Ruhreisenstreit 1928/29. Wentorf bei Hamburg, 1974. pp. 91.

WERKKREIS LITERATUR DER ARBEITSWELT. Jury Streikberichte. Dieser Betrieb wird bestreikt: Berichte über die Arbeitskämpfe in der BRD; herausgegeben von...Jürgen Alberts [and others]. Frankfurt am Main, 1974. pp. 268. *bibliog.*

— **Mexico.**

PAVON FLORES (MARIO) El ABC de las huelgas. [Mexico], 1937. pp. 199.

ANDERSON (RODNEY D.) Outcasts in their own land: Mexican industrial workers, 1906-1911. DeKalb, Ill., 1976. pp. 407. *bibliog.*

— **Poland.**

ROTE Fahnen über Polen: seit wann schiesst die Arbeiterklasse auf sich selbst?; der Kampf der polnischen Arbeiter gegen einen falschen Sozialismus; (Übersetzung aus dem Polnischen). München, 1972 repr. 1973. pp. 146.

— **Russia.**

LISETSKII (ANATOLII MIKHAILOVICH) Bol'sheviki vo glave massovykh stachek, mart - oktiabr' 1917 g. Kishinev, 1974. pp. 423. *bibliog.*

— **South Africa.**

INSTITUTE FOR INDUSTRIAL EDUCATION. The Durban strikes 1973: human beings with souls. Durban, 1974. pp. 195. *bibliog.*

— **Spain.**

ALVAREZ DE TOLEDO (ISABEL) Duquesa de Medina Sidonia. La huelga: novela. Buenos Aires, 1974 [or rather 1975]. pp. 285.

— **Sweden.**

STREJK!: en bok om strejker och strejkvisor...; samlad, redigerad och kommenterad av Visgruppen inom Arkivet för folkets historia: Catrin Andersson [and others]. Stockholm, [1974]. pp. 174. *bibliog.*

— **United Kingdom.**

JENKINS (MICK) Time and motion strike, Manchester, 1934-7: the wiredrawers' struggle against the Bedoux system at Richard Johnson's. London, 1974. pp. 34. *(Communist Party of Great Britain. History Group. Our History. No. 60)*

CRONJÉ (GILLIAN) Middle class opinion and the 1889 dock strike: a critique of Outcast London. London, 1975. pp. 24. *(Communist Party of Great Britain. History Group. Our History. No. 61)*

PEARCE (CYRIL) The Manningham Mills strike, Bradford, December 1890-April 1891. Hull, 1975. pp. 85. *(Hull. University. Occasional Papers in Economic and Social History. No. 7)*

N.O.P. MARKET RESEARCH. Public's message: we back the constitution; results of a survey for Aims for Freedom and Enterprise. London, 1976. 1 folded leaf.

WIGHAM (ERIC LEONARD) Strikes and the government, 1893-1974. London, 1976. pp. 206. *bibliog.*

— — **Ireland, Northern.**

FISK (ROBERT) 1946- . The point of no return: the strike which broke the British in Ulster. London, 1975. pp. 264.

— **United States.**

MURPHY (PAUL L.) and others. The Passaic textile strike of 1926. Belmont, [1974]. pp. 185. *bibliog.*

— **Zanzibar.**

CLAYTON (ANTHONY) The 1948 Zanzibar general strike. Uppsala, 1976. pp. 66. *(Nordiska Afrikainstitutet. Research Reports. No. 32)*

STRONNICTWO LUDOWE.

BUCZEK (ROMAN) Stronnictwo Ludowe w latach 1939-1945: organizacja i polityka. Londyn, 1975. pp. 503. *bibliog.*

STRUCTURALISM.

POUILLON (JEAN) and MARANDA (PIERRE) eds. Echanges et communications: mélanges offerts à Claude Lévi-Strauss à l'occasion de son 60ème anniversaire. Paris, 1970. 2 vols. *bibliogs.*

LEFEBVRE (HENRI) L'idéologie structuraliste. [Paris, 1975]. pp. 253. *Consists of essays reprinted from "Au-delà du structuralisme", published in 1971.*

BADCOCK (CHRISTOPHER ROBERT) Lévi-Strauss, structuralism and sociological theory. London, 1975. pp. 125. *bibliog.*

STUDENT AID

— **Canada.**

WEST (E.G.) Student loans: a reappraisal...with special reference to Ontario's and Canada's changing needs in educational finance; ...assisted by Michael McKee. Toronto, Ontario Economic Council, 1975. 1 vol. (various pagings). *bibliog. (Ontario. Economic Council. Working Papers. 1975. No. 4)*

— **United Kingdom.**

FEDERATION OF CONSERVATIVE STUDENTS. Student grants: the reorganisation of undergraduate finance. London, 1974. 1 pamphlet (unpaged)

— **United States.**

MONEY, marbles or chalk: student financial support in higher education; edited by Roland Keene [and others]. Carbondale, [1975]. pp. 343. *bibliog.*

STUDENT ASPIRATIONS

— **United States.**

TILLERY (DALE) and KILDEGAARD (THEODORE C.) Educational goals, attitudes and behaviors: a comparative study of high school seniors. Cambridge, Mass., [1973]. pp. 251. *bibliog.*

STUDENT EVALUATION OF TEACHERS.

DOYLE (KENNETH O.) Student evaluation of instruction. Lexington, Mass., [1975]. pp. 144. *bibliog.*

STUDENT PARTICIPATION IN ADMINISTRATION

— **United Kingdom.**

MANCHESTER. University. Report on student participation in academic affairs; [by a] (working party [set up] to consider the academic implications of the joint statement issued by the Committee of Vice- Chancellors and Principals and the National Union of Students on October 7th 1968). Manchester, [1969]. pp. 11.

STUDENT UNIONS.

NATIONAL UNION OF STUDENTS. Student unions and the media: an N.U.S. guide to the relationship between student representatives and the communications media. London, [1975]. pp. 18.

STUDENTS

— **Attitudes.**

ZINBERG (NORMAN E.) and others. Teaching social change: a group approach. Baltimore, Ma., [1976]. pp. 252. *bibliog.*

— **Africa — Political activity.**

HANNA (WILLIAM JOHN) and others. University students and African politics. New York, 1975. pp. 296.

— **Africa, East — Political activity.**

PREWITT (KENNETH) ed. Education and political values: an East African case study. Nairobi, 1971. pp. 249.

— **Africa, Subsaharan — Political activity.**

BARKAN (JOEL D.) An African dilemma: university students, development and politics in Ghana, Tanzania and Uganda. Nairobi, 1975. pp. 259. *bibliog.*

— **America, Latin — Political activity.**

ANDER EGG (EZEQUIEL) Rebelion estudiantil y revolucion. Cordoba, 1970. pp. 96.

— **Brazil — Political activity.**

JARBAS CERQUEIRA (JOSE) Rebelion estudiantil brasileña. Montevideo, [1969?]. pp. 63.

— **China — Political activity.**

ISRAEL (JOHN) and KLEIN (DONALD WALKER) Rebels and bureaucrats: China's December 9ers. Berkeley, Calif., [1976]. pp. 303. *bibliog. (Columbia University. East Asian Institute. Studies)*

— **France.**

CAMILLERI (CARMEL) and TAPIA (CLAUDE) Jeunesse française et groupes sociaux après Mai 1968: enquêtes sur des populations universitaires et scolaires de Paris et de province. Paris, 1974. pp. 183. *(Centre National de la Recherche Scientifique. Monographies Françaises de Psychologie. 27)*

— **Germany — Political activity.**

SOZIALISTISCHER DEUTSCHER STUDENTENBUND. Die Strategiediskussion des SDS von 1963-66. [Berlin, 1971]. pp. 119.

PROKOP (SIEGFRIED) Studenten im Aufbruch: zur studentischen Opposition in der BRD. Dortmund, [1974]. pp. 184. *bibliog.*

BOCK (HANS MANFRED) Geschichte des "linken Radikalismus" in Deutschland: ein Versuch. Frankfurt am Main, 1976. pp. 370. *bibliog.*

SONTHEIMER (KURT) Das Elend unserer Intellektuellen: linke Theorie in der Bundesrepublik Deutschland. Hamburg, 1976. pp. 303.

— **Mexico — Political activity.**

UNZUETA (GERARDO) Sobre el problema estudiantil-popular: cartas desde la prision. Mexico, 1969. pp. 63.

STUDENTS(Cont.)

— Nigeria.

NIGERIA. University of Ibadan Commission of Inquiry into Disturbances on the Campus on 1st February, 1971. Report; [B.O. Kazeem, sole commissioner]. [Lagos, 1971]. pp. 187. *Bound with Comments of the federal military government on the report.*

— Norway.

NORWAY. Statistiske Centralbyrå. 1975. Forbruksundersøkelse for skoleungdom og studenter, 1973-1974, etc. Oslo, 1975. pp. 144. *(Norges Offisielle Statistikk. Rekke A. 717) In Norwegian and English.*

— Russia — Political activity.

ENIKEEV (ERIK AKHMETOVICH) Deiatel'nost' kazanskikh bol'shevikov po revoliutsionnomu vospitaniiu studencheskoi molodezhi, 1905 - fevral' 1917 gg. Kazan', 1973. pp. 205.

— Spain.

KAGAN (RICHARD L.) Students and society in early modern Spain. Baltimore, [1974]. pp. 278. *bibliog.*

— Switzerland.

PETERS (MATTHIAS U.) and ZEUGIN (PETER G.) Zur ökonomischen und sozialen Lage der Studenten an der Universität Zürich: Ergebnisse einer Representativumfrage vom Sommer 1975. Zürich, [1976]. pp. 250. *bibliog.*

— United Kingdom.

BATTY (WILLIAM) and WANKOWSKI (J.A.) Admission grades, selection and constancy of learning behaviour in transition from school to university: reflections on studies of random sample students and overall populations as compared with students in the department of chemistry in one university. Birmingham, [1974]. pp. 26. *bibliog.*

RUSSELL-GEBBETT (JEAN P.) Students in residence: a study of the background and attitudes of students in halls of residence and of their contemporaries electing to live in off-campus accommodation. Nottingham, 1975. pp. 57. *bibliog.*

CITRIN (JACK) and ELKINS (DAVID J.) Political disaffection among British university students: concepts, measurement, and causes. Berkeley, [1975]. pp. 69. *bibliog. (California University. Institute of International Studies. Research Series. No. 23)*

JACKS (DIGBY) Student politics and higher education. London, 1975. pp. 176.

— United States.

TILLERY (DALE) Distribution and differentiation of youth: a study of transition from school to college. Cambridge, Mass., [1973]. pp. 164. *bibliog.*

NATIONAL CONVENTION ON WORK AND THE COLLEGE STUDENT, 1ST., CARBONDALE, 1975. Work and the college student: proceedings of the...convention...; edited by Roland Keene [and others]. Carbondale, Ill., [1976]. pp. 466. *bibliog.*

SOLMON (LEWIS C.) Male and female graduate students: the question of equal opportunity. New York, 1976. pp. 146. *bibliog.*

— — Political activity.

ALBERTSON (DEAN) ed. Rebels or revolutionaries?: student movements of the 1960's. New York, [1975]. pp. 190. *bibliog.*

KRUEGER (MARLIS) and SILVERT (FRIEDA) Dissent denied: the technocratic response to protest. New York, 1975]. pp. 194.

LIPSET (SEYMOUR MARTIN) and RIESMAN (DAVID) Education and politics at Harvard;...two essays prepared for the Carnegie Commission on Higher Education. New York, [1975]. pp. 440. *bibliogs.*

The POWER of protest; [by] Alexander W. Astin [and others]. San Francisco, 1975. pp. 208. *bibliog.*

TAFT (JOHN) Mayday at Yale; a case study in student radicalism. Boulder, Co., 1976. pp. 224.

WESTBY (DAVID L.) The clouded vision: the student movement in the United States in the 1960s. Lewisburg, [1976]. pp. 291. *bibliog.*

STUDENTS, FOREIGN

— United Kingdom.

INTER-UNIVERSITY COUNCIL FOR HIGHER EDUCATION OVERSEAS. The overseas postgraduate; report of a working party. London, 1972. pp. 15.

— United States.

SPAULDING (SETH) and others. The world's students in the United States: a review and evaluation of research on foreign students. New York, 1976. pp. 520. *bibliog.*

— — Bibliography.

SPAULDING (SETH) and others. The world's students in the United States: a review and evaluation of research on foreign students. New York, 1976. pp. 520. *bibliog.*

STUDENTS, PART-TIME.

— United Kingdom.

NATIONAL CONFERENCE ON DEGREE SANDWICH COURSES, UNIVERSITY OF BATH, 1975. [Proceedings of the conference] organized by the Universities' Committee on Integrated Sandwich Courses...; edited by Garry Denbury. Bath, [1976]. pp. 85.

SMITHERS (ALAN G.) Sandwich courses: an integrated education?. Windsor, 1976. pp. 180. *bibliog.*

STUDENTS' SOCIETIES

— Germany.

SOZIALISTISCHER DEUTSCHER STUDENTENBUND. Die Strategiediskussion des SDS von 1963-66. [Berlin, 1971]. pp. 119.

STUDENTS' SOCIOECONOMIC STATUS

— United States.

SCHOOLING and achievement in American society; edited by William Hamilton Sewell and others. New York, [1976]. pp. 535. *bibliog. Papers originally presented at meetings of an American College Testing Research Institute seminar between Oct. 1971 and May 1973.*

SUBJECT HEADINGS

— Social sciences.

UNITED NATIONS INDUSTRIAL DEVELOPMENT ORGANIZATION. 1971- . Thesaurus of industrial development terms. (UNIDO/LIB/SER.C/1-). New York, United Nations, 1971 in progress.

INTERNATIONAL LABOUR OFFICE. Library. 1976. Thesaurus of descriptors used for information processing in the ILO Library. Geneva, 1976. pp. 198. *In English, French and Spanish.*

SUBSIDIES.

DENTON (GEOFFREY) and others. Trade effects of public subsidies to private enterprise. London, 1975. pp. 293. *bibliog.*

VEREIN FÜR SOZIALPOLITIK. Schriften. Neue Folge. Band 75/IV. Öffentliche Finanzwirtschaft und Verteilung, IV; von Clemens-August Andreae [and others]; herausgegeben von Wilhelmine Dreissig. Berlin, [1976]. pp. 150. *With summaries and table of contents in English.*

— Canada.

CANADA. Department of Indian Affairs and Northern Development. Oil and Mineral Division. 1969. Northern mineral exploration assistance program: Yukon and Northwest Territories. Ottawa, 1969. pp. (4), 14.

CANADA. Department of Industry. 1969. PAIT: program for advancement of industrial technology. Ottawa, [1969]. pp. 13.

MITCHELL (C.L.) and FRICK (HAROLD C.) Government programs of assistance for fishing craft construction in Canada: an economic appraisal. Ottawa, Information Canada, 1970. pp. 59. *bibliog. (Canadian Fisheries Reports. No. 14)*

— Germany.

TIEDEMANN (KLAUS) Subventionskriminalität in der Bundesrepublik: Erscheinungsformen, Ursachen, Folgerungen. Reinbek, 1974. pp. 382. *bibliog.*

DEUTSCHES INSTITUT FÜR WIRTSCHAFTSFORSCHUNG. Sonderhefte. [Neue Folge]. 111. Filmförderung in der Bundesrepublik Deutschland: Versuch einer Erfolgskontrolle der Subventionspolitik; ([by] Burkhard Dreher). Berlin, 1976. pp. 267. *bibliog.*

— United Kingdom.

U.K. Offshore Supplies Office. 1974. Offshore supplies interest relief grants: a guide for industry. 2nd ed. Glasgow, 1974. pp. 16.

NORTHERN REGION STRATEGY TEAM. Evaluation of the impact of regional policy on manufacturing industry in the northern region. Newcastle upon Tyne, 1975. 1 vol. (various pagings). *(Technical Reports. No. 2)*

U.K. Parliament. House of Commons. Library. Research Division. Background Papers. No. 48. Regional employment premium. [London, 1976]. pp. 7. *bibliog.*

SUBURBS

— United States.

HAAR (CHARLES MONROE) and IATRIDES (DEMETRIOS S.) Housing the poor in suburbia: public policy at the grass roots. Cambridge, Mass., [1974]. pp. 430. *bibliogs.*

UNITED STATES. President's Task Force on Suburban Problems. 1974. Final report: edited by Charles M. Haar. Cambridge, Mass., [1974]. pp. 213.

AMERICAN ACADEMY OF POLITICAL AND SOCIAL SCIENCE. Annals. vol. 422. The suburban seventies; special editor of this volume, Louis H. Masotti. Philadelphia, 1975. pp. 218.

SCHNALL (DAVID J.) Ethnicity and suburban local politics. New York, 1975. pp. 168. *bibliog.*

The CHANGING face of the suburbs; edited by Barry Schwartz. Chicago, 1976. pp. 355. *bibliogs.*

SUBVERSIVE ACTIVITIES.

MOSS (ROBERT) The collapse of democracy. London, 1975. pp. 300.

— Germany.

HANNS-SEIDEL-STIFTUNG. Angriff auf unsere Demokratie; (verantwortlich: Willibald Fink). 3rd ed. München, 1974. pp. 159.

— India.

KISHORE (NAWAL) Anand Marg: the truth. [Delhi, Ministry of Information and Broadcasting, Directorate of Advertising and Visual Publicity, 1975]. pp. 16.

SUDAN

— Commerce.

BESHAI (ADEL AMIN) Export performance and economic development in Sudan, 1900-1967. London, 1976. pp. 358. *bibliog. (Oxford. University. St. Antony's College. Middle East Centre. St. Antony's Middle East Monographs. No 3)*

— **Economic conditions.**

NIMEIRI (SAYED) Taxation and economic development: a case study of the Sudan. Khartoum, 1974. pp. 228. *bibliog.*

— **Population.**

SUDAN. Department of Statistics. 1967- . Population and housing survey, 1964-65(-66). Khartoum, 1967 in progress.

SUEZ CANAL.

GARAUDY (ROGER) La vérité sur Suez: intervention à l'Assemblée Nationale, le 16 octobre 1956, etc. Paris, [1956?]. pp. 23.

GEORGES-PICOT (JACQUES) La véritable crise de Suez: fin d'une grande oeuvre du XIXe siècle. Paris, [1975]. pp. 339.

SUFFRAGE

— **Somali Republic.**

SOMALILAND PROTECTORATE. Commission on Representational Reform. 1959. Report; [A.L. Scawin, chairman]. [Hargeisa, 1959]. fo. 55, 1 map.

SUGAR.

INTERNATIONAL SUGAR ORGANIZATION. National Sugar Economies and Policies. [London], 1976 in progress. *This series updates the original 2 volume work published in 1963 entitled The world sugar economy structure and policies.*

— **Manufacture and refining — India.**

INDIA. Sugar Industry Enquiry Commission. 1974. Report...volume 1 and 2; [Shri Deep Narain Sinha, then Shri V. Bhargava, chairman]. [New Delhi], 1974. 2 vols. (in 1).

— — **United Kingdom.**

VAUXHALL COMMUNITY DEVELOPMENT PROJECT. Tate and Lyle: the campaign to save jobs. [Liverpool, 1975]. pp. 24.

LEWIS (FRANK) Essex and sugar: historic and other connections. London, 1976. pp. 132.

SUGAR GROWING.

HAGELBERG (G.B.) Instability of world centrifugal sugar production. Berlin, 1975. pp. 61. *bibliog.* (Berlin. Technische Universität Berlin- Charlottenburg. Institut für Zuckerindustrie. Forschungsberichte. 2)

— **Bangladesh.**

BANGLADESH. Ministry of Information and Broadcasting. 1972. Sugar industry in Bangladesh. [Dacca, 1972]. pp. 49. *bibliog.*

— **India.**

INDIA. Sugar Industry Enquiry Commission. 1974. Report...volume 1 and 2; [Shri Deep Narain Sinha, then Shri V. Bhargava, chairman]. [New Delhi], 1974. 2 vols. (in 1).

— **Mauritius.**

MAURITIUS. Committee of Enquiry (Sugar Industry). 1973. [Report; K. Lutchmeenaraidoo, chairman]. Port Louis, 1973. pp. 97.

SUGAR TRADE.

INTERNATIONAL SUGAR ORGANIZATION. National Sugar Economies and Policies. [London], 1976 in progress. *This series updates the original 2 volume work published in 1963 entitled The world sugar economy structure and policies.*

— **Bangladesh.**

BANGLADESH. Ministry of Information and Broadcasting. 1972. Sugar industry in Bangladesh. [Dacca, 1972]. pp. 49. *bibliog.*

SUGAR WORKERS

— **Saint Lucia.**

REPORT of the Commission appointed by His Excellency the Governor to enquire into the stoppage of work at the sugar factories in St. Lucia in March, 1952 and into the adequacy of the existing wage-fixing machinery in that colony; Sir Clement Malone, chairman. [Castries, 1952]. pp. 81.

REPORT of the Commission appointed by His Excellency the Acting Governor to investigate the causes of the stoppage of work in the sugar industry during March and April, 1957, the wage structure, the terms and conditions of employment and other matters relating to all the foregoing in the industry in St. Lucia; Sir Donald Jackson, chairman. [Castries, 1957]. fo. (36).

— **United Kingdom.**

VAUXHALL COMMUNITY DEVELOPMENT PROJECT. Tate and Lyle: the campaign to save jobs. [Liverpool, 1975]. pp. 24.

SUICIDE.

STENGEL (ERWIN) Suicide and attempted suicide. [3rd ed.] Harmondsworth, 1973 repr. 1975. pp. 159. *bibliog. Reprint with revisions of the revised edition of 1970.*

POPE (WHITNEY) Durkheim's Suicide: a classic analyzed. Chicago, 1976. pp. 229. *bibliog.*

— **France.**

Le SUICIDE: [deux "journées"... organisées par le Ministère de la Santé, décembre 1972]. Paris, 1975. pp. 211. *(Pour une Politique de la Santé. 4)*

— **South Africa.**

MEER (FATIMA) Race and suicide in South Africa. London, 1976. pp. 319.

— **United States.**

REYNOLDS (DAVID K.) and FARBEROW (NORMAN LOUIS) Suicide inside and out. Berkeley, 1976. pp. 226. *bibliog.*

SUKLOVA (MARIIA).

SUKLOVA (MARIIA) The life story of a Russian exile: the remarkable experience of a young girl: being an account of her peasant childhood in prison, her exile to Siberia and escape from there;...translated by Gregory Yarros. London, 1915. pp. 251.

SUMMER HOMES

— **Norway.**

NORWAY. Statistiske Centralbyrå. 1976. Fritidshus, 1970, etc. Oslo, 1976. pp. 85. *bibliog. (Statistiske Analyser. 20) With English summary.*

SUMNER (WILLIAM GRAHAM).

HOFSTADTER (RICHARD) Social Darwinism in American thought. rev. ed. New York, 1959 repr. 1969. pp. 248. *bibliog.*

SUNDERLAND FOOTBALL CLUB.

DERRICK (ED) and McRORY (JUDY) Cup in hand: Sunderland's self-image after the cup. Birmingham, 1973. pp. 20. *bibliog. (Birmingham. University. Centre for Urban and Regional Studies. Working Papers. No. 8)*

SUNNMØRE

— **Economic history.**

KJØDE (LARS) and MÄSEIDVÅG (SVERRE) Industriundret på Sunnmøre?: eit verkeleg under?. Oslo, 1975. pp. 150. *bibliogs.*

SUPERMARKETS

— **United Kingdom — Bibliography.**

MURRAY (NICK) compiler. Hypermarkets. London, 1975. pp. 10. *(London. Greater London Council. Research Library. [Research] Bibliographies. No. 72)*

SUPERVISION OF SOCIAL WORKERS.

KADUSHIN (ALFRED) Supervision in social work. New York, 1976. pp. 486. *bibliog.*

SUPPLEMENTARY EMPLOYMENT

— **Poland.**

CHŁOPOROBOTNICY o sobie: studium autobiografii; wstęp Dyzma Gałaj. Warszawa, 1974. pp. 296.

SUPPLY AND DEMAND

— **Mathematical models.**

KUZNETS (SIMON SMITH) Data for quantitative economic analysis: problems of supply and demand. Stockholm, [1972]. pp. 27. *(Sveriges Industriförbund. [Nobel Prize] Lectures. 1971)*

BRISCOE (GEOFFREY) and PEEL (D.A.) The value of inter-related factor demand models for explaining short-term employment behaviour in the U.K. manufacturing sector. Coventry, 1974. 1 pamphlet (various pagings). *(University of Warwick. Centre for Industrial, Economic and Business Research. [Warwick Research in Industrial and Business Studies]. No.52)*

MUSSA (MICHAEL) Output and employment in a dynamic model of aggregate supply. rev. ed. [London], 1976. pp. 46. *bibliog.*

SUPPORT (DOMESTIC RELATIONS)

— **Canada.**

CANADA. Department of National Health and Welfare. Welfare Research Division. 1973. Deserted wives' and children's maintenance legislation in Canada. [Ottawa], 1973. pp. 107.

— — **Manitoba.**

MANITOBA. Law Reform Commission. 1975. Working paper on family law. Part 1. The support obligation. Part 2. Property disposition. Winnipeg, 1975. pp. 63.

SUSSEX

— **History.**

FLETCHER (ANTHONY) A county community in peace and war: Sussex, 1600-1660. London, 1975. pp. 445. *bibliog.*

SUZMAN (HELEN).

STRANGWAYES-BOOTH (JOANNA) A cricket in the thorn tree: Helen Suzman and the Progressive Party of South Africa. London, 1976. pp. 320. *bibliog.*

SVENSKA OSTINDISKA COMPAGNIET.

See SWEDISH EAST INDIA COMPANY.

SWABIA

— **Kreistag.**

VANN (JAMES ALLEN) The Swabian Kreis: institutional growth in the Holy Roman Empire, 1648-1715. Bruxelles, 1975. pp. 338. *(International Commission for the History of Representative and Parliamentary Institutions. Studies. 53)*

SWAZILAND

— **Appropriations and expenditures.**

SWAZILAND. Capital fund estimates. a., 1973/74- [Mbabane].

SWAZILAND(Cont.)

SWAZILAND. Recurrent estimates of public expenditure. a., 1973/74, 1975/76- [Mbabane].

SWAZILAND. Recurrent estimates of public revenue and statutory expenditure. a., 1973/74- [Mbabane].

— Economic conditions.

SWAZILAND. [Central Statistical Office]. Economic review. a., 1974 [covers 1970-1974]- [Mbabane].

— Government publications — Bibliography.

PRETORIA. State Library. Bibliographies. No. 18. Swaziland official publications, 1880-1972: a bibliography of the original and microfiche edition. Pretoria, 1975. pp. 190.

— Industries.

SWAZILAND. Central Statistical Office. Census of industrial production. a., 1970/71- Mbabane.

SELWYN (PERCY) Industries in the southern African periphery: a study of industrial development in Botswana, Lesotho and Swaziland. London, 1975. pp. 156. *bibliog.*

SWEDEN

— Constitutional history.

ALEXANDERSSON (ERLAND) Bondeståndet i riksdagen, 1760-1772. [Lund, 1975]. pp. 253. *bibliog. Akademisk avhandling, Universitetet i Lund; with English summary.*

FÖRHAMMAR (STAFFAN) Reformvilja eller riksdagstaktik?: junkrarna och representationsfrågan, 1847-54. Stockholm, [1975]. pp. 128. *bibliog. (Stockholms Universitet. Acta Universitatis Stockholmiensis. Stockholm Studies in History. 22) With English summary.*

— Defences.

UHLIN (ÅKE) Februarikrisen 1942: svensk säkerhetspolitik och militär planering, 1941-1942. Stockholm, 1972. pp. 265. *bibliog. With English summary.*

ÄMARK (KLAS) Makt eller moral: svensk offentlig debatt om internationell politik och svensk utrikes- och försvarspolitik 1938-1939. Stockholm, 1973. pp. 324. *bibliog. With English summary.*

MÅNSSON (OLLE) Industriell beredskap: om ekonomisk försvarsplanering inför andra världskriget. Stockholm, 1976. pp. 269. *bibliog. With English summary.*

ROBERTS (EDWARD ADAM) Nations in arms: the theory and practice of territorial defence. London, 1976. pp. 288.

— Economic conditions.

SCASE (RICHARD) ed. Readings in the Swedish class structure. Oxford, 1976. pp. 314.

— Economic policy.

GODLUND (SVEN) Näringsliv och styrcentra, produktutveckling och trygghet: The economy and control centres, product development and security. Göteborg, [1972]. pp. 85-118, fo.20. *bibliog. (Göteborgs Universitet. Geografiska Institutioner. Meddelanden. Ser.B. Nr.25) (Särtryck ur "Regioner att leva i", Uddevalla, 1972) In Swedish, with abridged English version.*

LINDBÄCK (ASSAR) Blandekonomi i omvandling: fyra föredrag om utvecklingstendenser i svensk ekonomi. Stockholm, 1973. pp. 156.

ARBETE, kapital och stat: politisk-ekonomiska studier i svensk kapitalism; [based on a symposium held at Gothenburg in 1973]; redigerade av Peter Dencik och Bengt-Åke Lundvall. [Stockholm, 1974]. pp. 284.

LEION (ANDERS) Den svenska modellen: hur ska det gå med socialdemokratin, ekonomin och den offentliga sektorn?. Stockholm, 1974. pp. 180.

SWEDEN. Utrikesdepartementet. 1974. To choose a future: a basis for discussion and deliberations on future studies in Sweden. Stockholm, 1974. pp. 162. *bibliog.*

— — Mathematical models.

ANDERSSON (ROLF) and MEIDNER (RUDOLF) Arbetsmarknadspolitik och stabilisering. [Stockholm, 1973]. pp. 88. *(Institutet för Social Forskning. Skrifter. 4)*

— Emigration and immigration.

KRONBORG (BO) and NILSSON (THOMAS) Stadsflyttare: industrialisering, migration och social mobilitet med utgångspunkt från Halmstad, 1870-1910. Uppsala, 1975. pp. 298. *bibliog. (Uppsala. Universitet. Historiska Institutionen. Studia Historica Upsaliensia. 65) With English summary.*

— Foreign relations.

ÄMARK (KLAS) Makt eller moral: svensk offentlig debatt om internationell politik och svensk utrikes- och försvarspolitik 1938-1939. Stockholm, 1973. pp. 324. *bibliog. With English summary.*

ERLANDER (TAGE) 1940-1949. Stockholm, [1973]. pp. 406.

ERLANDER (TAGE) 1949-1954. Stockholm, [1974]. pp. 392.

See also EUROPEAN ECONOMIC COMMUNITY — Sweden.

— — Treaties.

SWEDEN. Utrikesdepartementet. Register över Sveriges överenskommelser med främmande makter. bien., 1972- Stockholm.

— — Finland.

JOHANSSON (ALF) Finlands sak: svensk politik och opinion under vinterkriget, 1939- 1940. Stockholm, 1973. pp. 402. *bibliog. With English summary.*

— — Germany.

UHLIN (ÅKE) Februarikrisen 1942: svensk säkerhetspolitik och militär planering, 1941-1942. Stockholm, 1972. pp. 265. *bibliog. With English summary.*

— History.

KOBLIK (STEVEN) ed. Sweden's development from poverty to affluence, 1750-1970;... translated by Joanne Johnson, etc. Minneapolis, [1975]. pp. 380. *bibliog.*

— Industries.

BENTZEL (RAGNAR) and BECKEMAN (JAN) Framtidsperspektiv för svensk industri, 1965-1980. Stockholm, 1966. pp. 184.

— Intellectual life.

FRANCE. Direction de la Documentation. La Documentation Française. Notes et Etudes Documentaires. Nos. 4,205-4, 206. Le projet suédois de démocratie culturelle: essai de comparaison avec la situation française; par Claude Fabrizio. Paris, 1975. pp. 72. *bibliog.*

— Neutrality.

UHLIN (ÅKE) Februarikrisen 1942: svensk säkerhetspolitik och militär planering, 1941-1942. Stockholm, 1972. pp. 265. *bibliog. With English summary.*

— Officials and employees — Salaries, allowances, etc.

GUSTAFSSON (SIV) Lönebildning och lönestruktur inom den statliga sektorn. Stockholm, [1976]. pp. 260. *bibliog. With English summary.*

— Politics and government.

TORSTENDAHL (ROLF) Mellan nykonservatism och liberalism: idébrytningar inom högern och bondepartierna, 1918-1934. Stockholm, [1969]. pp. 230. *bibliog. (Uppsala. Universitet. Historiska Institutionen. Studia Historica Upsaliensia. 29) With English summary.*

ERLANDER (TAGE) 1901-1939. Stockholm, [1972]. pp. 320.

ERLANDER (TAGE) 1940-1949. Stockholm, [1973]. pp. 406.

ERLANDER (TAGE) 1949-1954. Stockholm, [1974]. pp. 392.

HERMANSSON (CARL HENRIK) För socialismen: (artiklar och tal, 1964-74). Stockholm, 1974. pp. 279.

HAGÅRD (BIRGER) Nils Wohlin: konservativ centerpolitiker. [Stockholm?, 1976]. pp. 467. *bibliog. Akademisk avhandling, filosofie doktorsgrad, Stockholms Universitet.*

— Population.

SWEDEN. Utrikesdepartementet. 1974. The biography of a people: past and future population changes in Sweden: conditions and consequences; (a contribution to the United Nations World Population Conference). Stockholm, [1974]. pp. 204.

— Population, Rural.

ENEQUIST (GERD) Geographical changes of rural settlement in northwestern Sweden since 1523. Uppsala, [1959]. pp. 44. *bibliog. (Uppsala. Universitet. Årsskrifter. 1959.8)*

— Relations (general) with Finland.

CARLQUIST (ERIK) Solidaritet på prov: Finlandshjälp under vinterkriget. Stockholm, 1971. pp. 343. *bibliog. With English summary.*

— Relations (military) with Denmark.

TORELL (ULF) Hjälp till Danmark: militära och politiska förbindelser, 1943-1945. Stockholm, 1973. pp. 385. *bibliog. With English summary.*

— Riksdag.

ALEXANDERSSON (ERLAND) Bondeståndet i riksdagen, 1760-1772. [Lund, 1975]. pp. 253. *bibliog. Akademisk avhandling, Universitetet i Lund; with English summary.*

FÖRHAMMAR (STAFFAN) Reformvilja eller riksdagstaktik?: junkrarna och representationsfrågan, 1847-54. Stockholm, [1975]. pp. 128. *bibliog. (Stockholms Universitet. Acta Universitatis Stockholmiensis. Stockholm Studies in History. 22) With English summary.*

— Rural conditions.

LUNDSJÖ (OLLE) Fattigdomen på den svenska landsbygden under 1800-talet. [Stockholm, 1975]. pp. 208. *bibliog. (Stockholms Universitet. Ekonomisk-Historiska Institutionen. Stockholm Studies in Economic History. 1) With English summary.*

— Social conditions.

SVERIGES SOCIALDEMOKRATISKA ARBETAREPARTI and LANDSORGANISATIONEN I SVERIGE. Arbetsgrupp för Jämlikhetsfrågor. Jämlikhet: allas deltagande i arbetsliv och politik; (andra rapporten); [Alva Myrdal, chairman]). [Stockholm, 1972]. pp. 122.

SCASE (RICHARD) ed. Readings in the Swedish class structure. Oxford, 1976. pp. 314.

— Social policy.

SWEDEN. Utrikesdepartementet. 1974. To choose a future: a basis for discussion and deliberations on future studies in Sweden. Stockholm, 1974. pp. 162. *bibliog.*

SWEDES IN BRAZIL.

FLODELL (SVEN ARNE) Tierra nueva: svensk grupputvandring till Latinamerika; integration och församlingsbildning: Swedish emigration to Latin America; integration and church growth. [Stockholm], [1974]. pp. 217. *bibliog. In Swedish, with English summary.*

SWEDES IN THE ARGENTINE REPUBLIC.

FLODELL (SVEN ARNE) Tierra nueva: svensk grupputvandring till Latinamerika; integration och församlingsbildning: Swedish emigration to Latin America; integration and church growth. [Stockholm], [1974]. pp. 217. bibliog. In Swedish, with English summary.

SWEDES IN THE UNITED STATES.

NORMAN (HANS) Från Bergslagen till Nordamerika: studier i migrationsmönster, social rörlighet och demografisk struktur med utgångspunkt från Örebro Län, 1851-1915. Uppsala, 1974. pp. 372. bibliog. (Uppsala. Universitet. Historiska Institutionen. Studia Historica Upsaliensia. 62) With English summary.

SWEDISH EAST INDIA COMPANY.

KJELLBERG (SVEN T.) De svenska ostindiska compagnierna, 1731-1813: kryddor, te, porslin, siden. 2nd ed. Malmö, [1975]. pp. 325. bibliog. With English summary.

SWINDON

— Civic improvement.

HARLOE (MICHAEL) Swindon: a town in transition: a study in urban development and overspill policy. London, 1975. pp. 290.

SWINE

— Economic aspects.

WILLIAMS (L.E.) and CLIFT (P.F.) Pig budgeting: a multivariable approach. [Brisbane], 1970. 1 vol. (unpaged). (Queensland. Department of Primary Industries. Economic Services Branch. Technical Bulletins. No. 6)

SWINE BREEDING

— India — Goa, Daman and Diu.

GOA, DAMAN AND DIU. Bureau of Economics, Statistics and Evaluation. 1975. An evaluation of the piggery development scheme in Goa. Panaji, 1975. pp. 42. (Evaluation Reports. No. 13)

SWITZERLAND.

HUGHES (CHRISTOPHER) Switzerland. London, 1975. pp. 303. bibliog.

— Constitution.

NEIDHART (LEONHARD) Reform des Bundesstaates Switzerland]: Analysen und Thesen. Bern, [1970]. pp. 135. bibliog.

GERMANN (RAIMUND E.) Politische Innovation und Verfassungsreform: ein Beitrag zur schweizerischen Diskussion über die Totalrevision der Bundesverfassung. Bern, [1975]. pp. 247. bibliog. (Hochschule St. Gallen für Wirtschafts- und Sozialwissenschaften. Forschungsstelle für Politikwissenschaft. St.Galler Studien zur Politikwissenschaft. Band 3)

— Economic history.

WEISZ (LEO) Studien zur Handels- und Industriegeschichte der Schweiz. [Zürich], 1938-40. 2 vols. (Sonderabdruck aus der Neuen Zürcher Zeitung)

— Foreign economic relations.

SENTI (RICHARD) ed. Die Schweiz und die internationalen Wirtschaftsorganisationen; [by] Arthur Dunkel [and others]. Zürich, [1975]. pp. 189. bibliog.

— Foreign relations — Italy.

SPINDLER (KATHARINA) Die Schweiz und der italienische Faschismus, 1922-1930: der Verlauf der diplomatischen Beziehungen und die Beurteilung durch das Bürgertum. Basel, 1976. pp. 304. bibliog. Dissertation vorgelegt der Philosophisch-Historischen Fakultät der Universität Basel.

— — Russia.

BRINGOLF (WALTHER) Die Schweiz und die Sowjetunion: zur Krise unserer Aussenpolitik. [Schaffhausen, imprint, 1944]. pp. 23.

— Industries.

WEISZ (LEO) Studien zur Handels- und Industriegeschichte der Schweiz. [Zürich], 1938-40. 2 vols. (Sonderabdruck aus der Neuen Zürcher Zeitung)

— Nationalrat — Elections.

Die WAHLSENDUNGEN zu den Nationalratswahlen vom Herbst 1971: eine Aussagen-Analyse der deutschsprachien Sendungen des Radios der deutschen und rätoromanischen Schweiz; [by] Florian H. Fleck [and others]. Freiburg/Schweiz, 1974. pp. 120. bibliog. (Freiburg (Switzerland). Universität. Institut für Journalistik. Öffentliche Soziale Kommunikationen. Werkpapiere. 3)

— Neutrality.

GINTHER (KONRAD) Neutralität und Neutralitätspolitik: die österreichische Neutralität zwischen Schweizer Muster und sowjetischer Koexistenzdoktrin. Wien, 1975. pp. 168. bibliog.

— Politics and government.

MUSCHG (ADOLF) Von Herwegh bis Kaiseraugst: wie halten wir es als Demokraten mit unserer Freiheit?; mit ausgewählten politischen Gedichten von Georg Herwegh. Zürich, [1975]. pp. 61.

Les SUISSES et la politique: enquête sur les attitudes d'électeurs suisses, 1972; par Dusan Sidjanski [and others]. Berne, 1975. pp. 216. bibliog.

TSCHAENI (HANS) Demokratie auf dem Holzweg: Bemerkungen zur helvetischen Dauerkrise. Zürich, [1975]. pp. 118. bibliog.

TSHUDI (HANS PETER) Soziale Demokratie: Reden und Aufsätze; herausgegeben und eingeleitet von Alfred A. Häsler. Basel. [1975]. pp. 200. bibliog.

— Population.

SWITZERLAND. Bureau Fédéral de Statistique. 1974. La population de la Suisse; [by] J. Cipriani [and others] . Berne, 1974. pp. 261. bibliog. (Committee for International Coordination of National Research in Demography. C.I.C.R.E.D. Series)

— Race question.

SYFRIG (MAX) and DEFAYE (CHRISTIAN) L'extrême-droit en Suisse. Lausanne, [1967]. pp. 42. Articles reprinted from the August and September 1967 issues of Tribune de Lausanne.

— Relations (military) with France.

EHRBAR (HANS RUDOLF) Schweizerische Militärpolitik im Ersten Weltkrieg: die militärischen Beziehungen zu Frankreich vor dem Hintergrund der schweizerischen Aussen- und Wirtschaftspolitik, 1914-1918. Bern, 1976. pp. 380. bibliog.

— Social policy.

HESS (WALTER) Ökonomische Aspekte der Sozialen Sicherung: eine Untersuchung...unter besonderer Berücksichtigung der schweizerischen Verhältnisse. Bern, 1975. pp. 192. bibliog.

TSHUDI (HANS PETER) Soziale Demokratie: Reden und Aufsätze; herausgegeben und eingeleitet von Alfred A. Häsler. Basel. [1975]. pp. 200. bibliog.

— Statistics.

SWITZERLAND. Bureau Fédéral de Statistique. 1972. Arealstatistik der Schweiz...1972. Bern, 1972. pp. 121 and 19 maps. (Statistiques de la Suisse. 488e fasc.) In German and French.

— Statistics, Vital.

SWITZERLAND. Bureau Fédéral de Statistique. 1975. Schweizerische Sterbetafel...1968-1973: Grundzahlen und Nettowerte, etc. Bern, 1975. pp. 89. (Statistiques de la Suisse. 559e fasc.) In German and French.

SYLT.

For related heading see WESTERLAND.

SYMBOLISM.

COHEN (ABNER) Two-dimensional man: an essay on the anthropology of power and symbolism in complex society. London, 1974. pp. 156. bibliog.

NOVAK (MICHAEL) Choosing our king: powerful symbols in presidential politics. New York, [1974]. pp. 324. bibliog.

CONFERENCE ON NEW DIRECTIONS IN SOCIAL ANTHROPOLOGY, OXFORD, 1973 The interpretation of symbolism: [papers of the session convened on 10 July]; edited by Roy Willis. London, 1975. pp. 181. bibliogs. (Association of Social Anthropologists of the Commonwealth. A.S.A. Studies. 3)

MOORE (SALLY FALK) and MYERHOFF (BARBARA G.) eds. Symbol and politics in communal ideology: cases and questions. Ithaca, 1975. pp. 245. bibliogs.

PEACOCK (JAMES L.) Consciousness and change: symbolic anthropology in evolutionary perspective. Oxford, [1975]. pp. 264. bibliog.

PONS (VALDO GUSTAVE) Imagery and symbolism in urban society. Hull, 1975. pp. 25. (Hull. University. Inaugural Lectures)

SPERBER (DAN) Rethinking symbolism;...translated by Alice L. Morton. Cambridge, 1975. pp. 153. bibliog.

SYMONDS (JOHN).

AMBROSOLI (MAURO) John Symonds: agricoltura e politica in Corsica e in Italia, 1765-1770. Torino, 1974. pp. 165. bibliog. (Fondazione Luigi Einaudi. Studi. 17)

SYNDICALISM.

VILLARD (RENE) Le syndicalisme révolutionnaire; biographie d'Emile Pouget, par Renée Lamberet. Toulouse, [1967]. pp. 48. bibliog. (Association Internationale des Travailleurs [Syndicalist]. Des Faits, des Idées, des Hommes)

— France.

CONFEDERATION GENERALE DU TRAVAIL SYNDICALISTE REVOLUTIONNAIRE. Brochures. No. 1. Le syndicalisme et la guerre. [Paris, imprint], [192-!]. pp. 14.

CONFEDERATION GENERALE DU TRAVAIL SYNDICALISTE REVOLUTIONNAIRE. Les buts et l'organisation du syndicalisme révolutionnaire. 2nd ed. Limoges, 1936. pp. 66.

SCHNEIDER (DIETER MARC) Revolutionärer Syndikalismus und Bolschewismus: der Prozess der ideologischen Auseinandersetzung französischer Syndikalisten mit den Bolschewiki, 1914-1922. Erlangen, 1974. pp. 353. bibliog.

— Russia.

UCHENYE ZAPISKI KAFEDR OBSHCHESTVENNYKH NAUK VUZOV LENINGRADA. Istoriia KPSS. vyp.10. Po leninskomu puti. Leningrad, 1970. pp. 141.

— Spain.

SOLANO (ERNESTO G.) El ocaso del sindicalismo?. Barcelona, [1922?]. pp. 143.

BERRUEZO (JOSE) Contribucion a la historia de la C.N.T. de España en el exilio. Mexico, 1967. pp. 303.

SYNDICATES (FINANCE)

— Germany.

POHL (MANFRED) Die Finanzierung der Russengeschäfte zwischen den beiden Weltkriegen: die Entwicklung der 12 grossen Russlandkonsortien. Frankfurt am Main, [1975]. pp. 48. (*Tradition: Zeitschrift für Firmengeschichte und Unternehmerbiographie. Beihefte. 9*)

SYRIA

— Economic conditions.

BELGIUM. Office Belge du Commerce Extérieur. 1972. Syrie. Bruxelles, 1972. pp. 39. (*Un Marché. 14*)

— Foreign relations — France.

SHORROCK (WILLIAM I.) French imperialism in the Middle East: the failure of policy in Syria and Lebanon, 1900-1914. Wisconsin, 1976. pp. 214. *bibliog.*

— Industries.

OFFICE ARABE DE PRESSE ET DE DOCUMENTATION. Série "Etudes". 151. Etude sur l'industrie syrienne, Septembre 1973. Damas, [1973]. fo. 58.

SYSTEM ANALYSIS.

DEMASI (RONALD J.) An introduction to business systems analysis. Reading, Mass., [1969]. pp. 206. *bibliog.*

COMPUTER-aided information systems analysis and design; [papers presented at] the first Scandinavian workshop, [Aarhus, 1971]; [Janis Bubenko [and others] eds.). Stockholm, [1971]. pp. 206. *Organised by the Scandinavian Information Processing Project of Nordforsk.*

COUGER (J. DANIEL) and KNAPP (ROBERT W.) eds. System analysis techniques. New York, [1974]. pp. 509. *bibliogs.*

NYBERG (LARS) and VIOTTI (STAFFAN) A control systems approach to macroeconomic theory and policy in an open economy. Stockholm, 1975. 1 vol.(various pagings). *bibliog.*

RAIZBERG (BORIS ABRAMOVICH) and others. Sistemnyi podkhod v perspektivnom planirovanii. Moskva, 1975. pp. 271. *bibliog.*

BYRNE (BRENDAN) and others. The art of systems analysis; edited by Brian Rothery. London, 1976. pp. 265.

SYSTEM THEORY.

KLIR (GEORGE J.) An approach to general systems theory. New York, [1969]. pp. 323. *bibliog.*

— Mathematical models.

BARRAS (R.) and BROADBENT (T.A.) An activity-commodity formalism for socio-economic systems. London, 1975. pp. 41. *bibliog.* (*Centre for Environmental Studies. Research Papers. 18*)

SYSTEMS ENGINEERING.

HARTMAN (W.) and others. Information systems handbook: analysis, requirements determination, design and development, implementation and evaluation. Apeldoorn, [1968 repr. 1972]. 1 vol. (various pagings). *bibliog.*

CUTTLE (GEOFFREY) and ROBINSON (PHILIP B.) eds. Executive programs and operating systems. London, 1970. pp. 116. *bibliog.*

ORGANICK (ELLIOTT I.) Computer system organization: the B5700/B6700 series. New York, 1973. pp. 132. *bibliog.* (*Association for Computing Machinery. ACM Monograph Series*)

WORKSHOP ON APPROACHES TO SYSTEMS DESIGN, ROYAL HOLLOWAY COLLEGE, 1972. Approaches to systems design: [proceedings of the workshop organized by the National Computing Centre]; edited by R. Boot. Manchester, [1973]. pp. 165. *bibliogs.* (*National Computing Centre. Computers and the Professional*)

WATERS (SAMUEL JOSEPH) Introduction to computer systems design: planning files and programs. Manchester, [1974] repr. 1976. pp. 198.

EUROPEAN COMPUTING CONFERENCE ON INTERACTIVE SYSTEMS, LONDON, 1975. Interactive systems. Uxbridge, [1975]. pp. 556. *bibliogs.* Papers presented at the Conference. This conference was part of the European Computing Congress, 1975.

GIBBONS (TERRY) Integrity and recovery in computer systems. Manchester, 1976. pp. 137. (*London. University. London School of Economics and Political Science and National Computing Centre. Information Systems Analysis and Design Series*)

SZÉCHENYI (ISTVÁN) Gróf.

SPIRA (GYÖRGY) A Hungarian count in the revolution of 1848. Budapest, 1974. pp. 346.

SZENDE (STEFAN).

SZENDE (STEFAN) Zwischen Gewalt und Toleranz: Zeugnisse und Reflexionen eines Sozialisten; mit einem Vorwort von Willy Brandt. Frankfurt am Main, [1975]. pp. 332.

TAIWAN

— Social life and customs.

COHEN (MYRON L.) House united, house divided: the Chinese family in Taiwan. New York, 1976. pp. 267. *bibliog.*

— Statistics.

MONTHLY BULLETIN OF STATISTICS [OF] THE REPUBLIC OF CHINA; [pd. by] Directorate-General of Budget, Accounting and Statistics [Formosa]. q., Jl 1975 (v.1,no. 1)- Taipei.

STATISTICAL YEARBOOK OF THE REPUBLIC OF CHINA; [pd. by] Directorate-General of Budget, Accounting and Statistics, Executive Yuan. a., 1975- Taipei.

TAJIKISTAN.

ASIMOV (M.S.) and others, eds. Tadzhikskaia Sovetskaia Sotsialisticheskaia Respublika. Dushanbe, 1974. pp. 406.

— History — 1917 - 1921, Revolution.

IRKAEV (MULLO IRKAEVICH) Istoriia grazhdanskoi voiny v Tadzhikistane. 2nd ed. Dushanbe, 1971. pp. 696.

— Politics and government.

KEL'DIEV (IMOMNAZAR) Izdanie i rasprostranenie proizvedenii klassikov marksizma-leninizma v Tadzhikistane. Dushanbe, 1973. pp. 190.

TALEV (DIMITUR).

DIMITUR Talev, Svetoslav Minkov, Dimitur Dimov v spomenite na suvremennitsite si. Sofiia, 1973. pp. 755.

TALL BUILDINGS.

ATKINSON (GEORGE A.) High buildings in Britain: some historical aspects. Watford, [1975]. pp. 9. (*Building Research Establishment [U.K.]. Current Papers. 75/24*)

TALLIN

— History.

PULLAT (RAIMO) ed. Istoriia Tallina s nachala 60-kh godov XIX stoletiia do 1970 goda; (perevod s estonskogo). Tallin, 1972. pp. 466. *bibliog.*

TALMADGE (EUGENE).

ANDERSON (WILLIAM) b. 1941. The wild man from Sugar Creek: the political career of Eugene Talmadge. Baton Rouge, 1975. pp. 268. *bibliog.*

TAMBOV (OBLAST')

— History — 1917—1921, Revolution.

RADKEY (OLIVER HENRY) The unknown civil war in Soviet Russia: a study of the Green movement in the Tambov region, 1920-1921. Stanford, [1976]. pp. 457. *bibliog.* (*Stanford University. Hoover Institution on War, Revolution and Peace. Hoover Institution Publications. 155*)

TANGANYIKA AFRICAN NATIONAL UNION.

TANGANYIKA AFRICAN NATIONAL UNION. Tanzania: party guidelines; [translated from Swahili by the Development Studies Department of the University of Dar-es-Salaam]. Richmond, B.C., 1973. pp. 12.

TANK—VESSELS

— Fires and fire prevention.

MAKHIJA (B.S.) Report on the explosion and fire involving S.S. 'Cerberus' and M.V. 'Coastal Sentry'. Vol. 1. (Main report of the inquiry) . Hong Kong, Government Printer, [1969]. pp. 42. *Vols. 2 and 3 not acquired by Library.*

TANZANIA

— Commerce.

HARTWIG (GERALD W.) The art of survival in East Africa: the Kerebe and long-distance trade, 1800-1895. New York, 1976. pp. 253. *bibliog.*

— Constitution.

UNITED REPUBLIC OF TANZANIA. Constitution. 1965-72. Interim constitution of Tanzania, 1965...[and] amendments up to 31st December, 1972. Dar es Salaam, 1973. pp. 61.

— Description and travel.

LUMLEY (E.K.) Forgotten mandate: a British district officer in Tanganyika. London, [1976]. pp. 178.

PERHAM (Dame MARGERY FREDA) East African journey: Kenya and Tanganyika, 1929-30. London, 1976. pp. 246.

— Economic conditions.

UNITED REPUBLIC OF TANZANIA. Annual plan. a., 1971/72 (2nd). [Dar es Salaam].

UNITED REPUBLIC OF TANZANIA. Economic survey, The. a., 1973/74- Dar es Salaam.

— Economic policy.

UNITED REPUBLIC OF TANZANIA. Ministry of Economic Affairs and Development Planning. 1965. First year progress report on the implementation of the five-year development plan, public sector, 1st July, 1964 to 30th June, 1965. Dar es Salaam, [1965?]. pp. 16.

UNITED REPUBLIC OF TANZANIA. Annual plan. a., 1971/72 (2nd). [Dar es Salaam].

NYERERE (JULIUS KAMBARAGE) President's report to the T[anganyika] A[frican] N[ational] U[nion] conference, September 1973. [Dar es Salaam, Government Printer, 1973]. pp. 22.

SZENTES (TAMÁS) Vtoroi piatiletnii plan Tanzanii, s 1-ogo iiulia 1969 g. do 30-ogo iiunia 1974 g. Budapesht, 1973. pp. 89. (*Magyar Tudományos Akadémia. Afro-Ázsiai Kutató Központ. Studies on Developing Countries. No. 46*)

— Executive departments.

UNITED REPUBLIC OF TANZANIA. Ministry of Economic Affairs and Development Planning. 1968. Plan for statistical development: a project memorandum. Dar es Salaam, 1968. fo. 85.

TAXATION.

— Foreign relations — China.

YU (GEORGE T.) China's African policy: a study of Tanzania. New York, 1975. pp. 200. *bibliog.*

— Politics and government.

TANGANYIKA. Tanganyika Information Services. 1961. Responsible government in Tanganyika; extracts from speeches by Ministers in the first meeting of the Tanganyika Legislative Council, 36th session, after the introduction of responsible government. Dar es Salaam, 1961]. pp. 9.

HERZOG (JUERGEN) Traditionelle Institutionen und nationale Befreiungsrevolution in Tansania: zum Problem der revolutionären Überwindung vorkapitalistischer gesellschaftlicher Verhältnisse im heutigen Afrika. Berlin, 1975. pp. 314. *(Zentraler Rat für Asien-, Afrika- und Lateinamerika- Wissenschaften in der DDR. Studien über Asien, Afrika und Lateinamerika. Band 18)*

MORRISON (DAVID R.) Education and politics in Africa: the Tanzanian case. London, [1976]. pp. 352. *bibliog.*

PERHAM (Dame MARGERY FREDA) East African journey: Kenya and Tanganyika, 1929-30. London, 1976. pp. 246.

PRATT (CRANFORD) The critical phase in Tanzania, 1945-1968: Nyerere and the emergence of a socialist strategy. Cambridge, 1976. pp. 309. *bibliog.*

— Population.

OMINDE (SIMEON HONGO) The population of Kenya-Uganda-Tanzania. [Nairobi?], 1975. pp. 124. *(Committee for International Coordination of National Research in Demography. C.I.C.R.E.D. Series)*

— Rural conditions.

KNIGHT (C. GREGORY) Ecology and change: rural modernization in an African community. New York, [1974]. pp. 300. *bibliog.*

— Social history.

HERZOG (JUERGEN) Traditionelle Institutionen und nationale Befreiungsrevolution in Tansania: zum Problem der revolutionären Überwindung vorkapitalistischer gesellschaftlicher Verhältnisse im heutigen Afrika. Berlin, 1975. pp. 314. *(Zentraler Rat für Asien-, Afrika- und Lateinamerika- Wissenschaften in der DDR. Studien über Asien, Afrika und Lateinamerika. Band 18)*

— Social policy.

UNITED REPUBLIC OF TANZANIA. Ministry of Economic Affairs and Development Planning. 1965. First year progress report on the implementation of the five-year development plan, public sector, 1st July, 1964 to 30th June, 1965. Dar es Salaam, [1965?]. pp. 16.

NYERERE (JULIUS KAMBARAGE) Socialism and rural development. [Dar es Salaam, Government Printer, 1967]. pp. 31.

UNITED REPUBLIC OF TANZANIA. Annual plan. a., 1971/72 (2nd). [Dar es Salaam].

NYERERE (JULIUS KAMBARAGE) President's report to the T[anganyika] A[frican] N[ational] U[nion] conference, September 1973. [Dar es Salaam, Government Printer, 1973]. pp. 22.

— Statistical services.

UNITED REPUBLIC OF TANZANIA. Central Statistical Bureau. 1968. A five-year plan for statistical development in Tanzania; revised. Dar es Salaam, 1968. fo. 119.

UNITED REPUBLIC OF TANZANIA. Ministry of Economic Affairs and Development Planning. 1968. Plan for statistical development: a project memorandum. Dar es Salaam, 1968. pp. 85.

TAPIRAPE INDIANS.

BALDUS (HERBERT) Tapirape: tribo tupi no Brasil central. São Paulo, 1970. pp. 511. *bibliog.*

TAQRAMIUT (ESKIMO TRIBE).

RICHES (DAVID JOHN) A study of social change amongst the Killinirngmiut Eskimo of Canada's East Arctic; [Ph. D. (London) thesis]. 1975. fo. 410. *bibliog. Typescript: unpublished. This thesis is the property of London University and may not be removed from the Library. Killinirngmiut spelt Killiniqmiut throughout the text.*

TARIFFS

— Australia.

NIEUWENHUYSEN (JOHN PETER) and NORMAN (NEVILLE R.) Australian competition and prices policy: trade practices, tariffs and prices justification. London, [1976]. pp. 173. *bibliog.*

— Brazil.

BRAZIL. Secretaria da Receita Federal. Centro de Informações Economico-Fiscais. Rendas aduaneiras...: arrecadação, regimes de tributação, preços de referência, panta de valor minimo. a., 1973 (v.1)- Brasilia.

— European Economic Community countries.

EUROPEAN COMMUNITIES. 1976. European Community customs valuation. [Luxembourg], 1976. 1 vol. (looseleaf).

— France.

ASSOCIATION POUR LA LIBERTE DES ECHANGES. Programme de réforme douanière proposé par l'Association pour la Liberté des Echanges. Paris, [1847]. pp. 29. *Signed by the President of the Association and by the general secretary, F. Bastiat. Issued with a covering circular from the secretary.*

— India.

INDIA. Tariff Revision Committee. 1968. Report on the central excise tariff. New Delhi, 1967 [or rather 1968]. pp. 111.

INDIA. Department of Commercial Intelligence and Statistics. 1969. Indian customs and central excise tariff: fifty-ninth issue, as in operation on the 15th May, 1969. Volume 1. Customs tariff only. Calcutta, 1969. pp. 310.

— Scandinavia.

HUMMEN (WILHELM) Die Auswirkungen der Erweiterung der EG auf Aussenhandel und Produktion der metallverarbeitenden Industrie in Schweden, Dänemark und Norwegen. Tübingen, 1976. pp. 263. *bibliog.*

— Underdeveloped areas.

See UNDERDEVELOPED AREAS — Tariffs.

— United Kingdom — Mathematical models.

CORDEN (WARNER MAX) and others. Import controls versus devaluation and Britain's economic prospects. London, [1975]. fo. 21. *(Trade Policy Research Centre. Guest Papers. No. 2)*

— United States.

BOUCKE (OSWALD FRED) Europe and the American tariff. New York, [1933]. pp. 163. *bibliog.*

CAHILL (HARRY A.) The China trade and U.S. tariffs. New York, 1973. pp. 161. *bibliog.*

TASMANIA

— Commerce.

TASMANIA. Commonwealth Bureau of Census and Statistics. Tasmanian Office. Trade and shipping. a., 1969/70- Hobart.

— Emigration and immigration.

AUSTRALIA. Migrant Task Force Committee, Tasmania. 1973. Report to the Minister for Immigration; chairman: Ray Sherry. [Hobart, 1973]. fo. 40.

— Industries.

TASMANIA. Commonwealth Bureau of Census and Statistics. Tasmanian Office. Primary industries (excluding mining), (formerly Primary industries). a., 1969/70, 1971/72- Hobart.

TASMANIA. Directorate of Industrial Development and Trade. Research Section. Survey of recent developments in the Tasmanian economy, A. s-a., Ja 1974- Hobart.

— Parliament — Salaries, pensions, etc.

TASMANIA. Parliamentary Superannuation Trust. Annual report. a., 1973/74 (1st)- Hobart. *Included in TASMANIA. Parliament. Journals and printed papers.*

— Politics and government.

TASMANIA. Commonwealth Bureau of Census and Statistics. Tasmanian Office. Social. a., 1970- Hobart.

— Population.

TASMANIA. Commonwealth Bureau of Census and Statistics. Tasmanian Office. Demography. a., 1970- Hobart.

— Social conditions — Statistics.

TASMANIA. Commonwealth Bureau of Census and Statistics. Tasmanian Office. Social. a., 1970- Hobart.

— Social history.

LAKE (MARILYN LEE) A divided society: Tasmania during World War I. Carlton, Vic., 1975. pp. 213. *bibliog.*

— Statistics.

TASMANIA. Commonwealth Bureau of Census and Statistics. Tasmanian Office. Statistical summary of Tasmania. a., 1971/72- Hobart.

— Statistics, Vital.

TASMANIA. Commonwealth Bureau of Census and Statistics. Tasmanian Office. Causes of death. a., 1974 (1st)- Hobart.

TAUS (JOSEF).

VODOPIVEC (ALEXANDER) Taus Busek: Persönlichkeit, Konzept und Stil des neuen Führungsteams der ÖVP. Wien, [1975]. pp. 120.

TAX ADMINISTRATION

— Canada.

CANADA. Department of National Revenue, Taxation. 1970. Thirty-two million dollars a day. [Ottawa, 1970]. pp. 70.

TAX EVASION.

ECONOMIST INTELLIGENCE UNIT. Q[uarterly] E[conomic] R[eview] Specials. No. 21. Tax havens and their uses; by Caroline Doggart. new ed. London, 1975. pp. 107.

TAX PLANNING

— Germany.

WARNEKE (PERYGRIN) Gewinnrealisierung durch Steuerentstrickung bei internationaler Geschäftstätigkeit deutscher Unternehmen. Hamburg, 1975. pp. 182. *bibliog.*

— United Kingdom.

TAX simplification and anti-avoidance legislation; (papers and summary of discussion of a conference) [arranged by the Institute for Fiscal Studies and held in London in 1974]. London, 1974. fo. 51.

LAWTON (PHILIP) and SUMPTION (ANTHONY) Tax planning. 7th ed. London, 1975. pp. 182.

TAXATION.

BRETON (ALBERT) The economic theory of representative government. London, 1974. pp. 228.

TAXATION.(Cont.)

INFLATION, trade and taxes: essays in honor of Alice Bourneuf; edited by David A. Belsley [and others]. Columbus, Ohio, [1976]. pp. 252. *bibliogs.*

MITSCHKE (JOACHIM) Über die Eignung von Einkommen, Konsum und Vermögen als Bemessungsgrundlagen der direkten Besteuerung: eine messtechnische Analyse. Berlin, [1976]. pp. 233. *bibliog.*

— Africa, Central.

EYENE (VICTOR EMILE) Etude sur les productions sous le régime de la taxe unique en UDEAC en 1973. [Brazzaville], 1975. pp. 19. *(Union Douanière et Economique de l'Afrique Centrale. Département des Statistiques. Etudes Statistiques. No. 22)*

— Africa, East.

HAMMOND (ROBERT C.) Fiscal harmonization in the East African Community. Amsterdam, 1975. pp. 134. *bibliog. (International Bureau of Fiscal Documentation. Series on International Fiscal Harmonization. No. 2)*

— Botswana.

BOTSWANA. Department of Taxes. Annual report. a., 1972/73- Gaborone.

— Canada.

CANADA. Department of National Revenue, Taxation. 1970. Thirty-two million dollars a day. [Ottawa, 1970]. pp. 70.

— China.

CONFLICT and control in late imperial China; edited by Frederic Wakeman and Carolyn Grant. Berkeley, California, [1975]. pp. 328. *Papers from a conference sponsored by the Center for Chinese Studies, University of California, and the Committee on Studies of Chinese Civilization of the American Council of Learned Societies.*

— European Economic Community countries.

EUROPEAN COMMUNITIES. Directorate of Taxation. Inventory of taxes. irreg., 1972- Brussels. *[1965 and 1967 separately catalogued and filed at R(O): EEC(107) and EEC(109) respectively].*

— Fiji Islands.

MATHEWS (RUSSELL LLOYD) Review of fiscal policy in Fiji: report to the Minister of Finance, etc. Suva, Government Printer, 1969. pp. 96.

— France.

FRANCE. Comité des Revenus et des Transferts. 1976. Rapport...: préparation du 7e Plan. Paris, 1976. pp. 184.

— Greece.

MOSCHOLIOS (NIKOLAOS M.) A critism of the Greek system of taxation. Athens, 1968. pp. 48. *bibliog.*

— Norway.

AUKRUST (ODD) and BORGENVIK (HALLVARD) Inntektsfordelingsvirkninger av skattereformen av 1969...: income distribution effects of the taxation reform of 1969. Oslo, 1969. pp. 29. *(Norway. Statistiske Centralbyrå. Artikler. Nr. 33)*

BORGENVIK (HALLVARD) and FLØ (HALLVARD) Virkninger av skattereformen av 1969...: effects of the taxation reform of 1969. Oslo, 1969. pp. 35. *(Norway. Statistiske Centralbyrå. Artikler. Nr.31)*

NORWAY. Statistiske Centralbyrå. Aktuelle kattetall: Current tax data. A. 1970- ; with gap (1971). Oslo *[In Norwegian with summary and table headings in English].*

NORWAY. Statistiske Centralbyrå. 1974- . Det norske skattesystemet...: the Norwegian system of taxation. Revised and extended ed. Oslo, 1974 in progress. *bibliog. (Samfunnsøkonomiske Studier. 24, etc.) With English summary.*

— — Mathematical models.

BIØRN (ERIK) Fordelingsvirkninger av indirekte skatter og subsidier...: distributive effects of indirect taxes and subsidies. Oslo, 1971. pp. 42. *(Norway. Statistiske Centralbyrå. Artikler. Nr. 42) With English summary.*

ENGREBRETSEN (JON DAHL) En modell for analyse av utviklingen i de direkte skatter: skattemodellen i MODIS IV...: a model for analysis of the development in direct taxes: tax model in MODIS IV. Oslo, 1974. pp. 65. bibliog. *(Norway. Statistiske Centralbyrå. Artikler. Nr. 72) With English summary.*

— Pakistan.

PAKISTAN. Taxation Enquiry Committee. 1961. Report. Volume 1; [Zahid Husain, subsequently Abdul Qadir, chairmen]. Karachi, 1961. pp. 396.

— Sudan.

NIMEIRI (SAYED) Taxation and economic development: a case study of the Sudan. Khartoum, 1974. pp. 228. *bibliog.*

— Switzerland.

SWITZERLAND. Bureau Fédéral de Statistique. 1974. Vierzig Jahre Steuern...; bearbeitet von der Eidgenössischen Steuerverwaltung, etc. Bern, 1974. pp. 242. *(Statistiques de la Suisse. 544e fasc.) In German and French.*

— Underdeveloped areas.

See UNDERDEVELOPED AREAS — Taxation.

— United Kingdom.

GROVES (HAROLD MARTIN) Tax philosophers: two hundred years of thought in Great Britain and the United States; edited by Donald J. Curran. Madison, Wis., 1974. pp. 158.

KINCAID (J.C.) Poverty and equality in Britain: a study of social security and taxation. rev. ed. Harmondsworth, 1975. pp. 245.

MESSERE (KEN) Recent and prospective trends in tax levels and tax structures. London, [1975]. 1 pamphlet (unpaged). *(Institute for Fiscal Studies. Lecture Series. No. 2)*

WARD (SUE) and POND (CHRIS) The £6 trap. London. 1975. fo. 6. *(Low Pay Unit. Low Pay Papers. No. 6)*

HOWELL (RALPH FREDERIC) Why work?: a challenge to the Chancellor. London, 1976. pp. 39. *(Conservative Political Centre. [Publications]. No. 582)*

MORGAN (DAVID RAYMOND) Indexation of personal income taxation. 1976. fo. 376. *bibliog. Typescript.* Ph.D. (London) thesis: unpublished. *This thesis is the property of London University and may not be removed from the Library.*

— — Law.

TAX simplification and anti-avoidance legislation; (papers and summary of discussion of a conference) [arranged by the Institute for Fiscal Studies and held in London in 1974]. London, 1974. fo. 51.

HEPKER (MICHAEL Z.) A modern approach to tax law. 2nd ed. London, 1975. pp. 427.

PARTINGTON (MARTIN) The brain drain tax proposal: a lawyer's view. [Oxford], 1975. pp. 717-749. *(Reprinted from World Development, 1975, vol. 3, no. 10)*

PINSON (BARRY) Revenue law: comprising income tax, capital gains tax, corporation tax, capital transfer tax, stamp duties, tax planning; ninth edition by B. Pinson and John Gardiner. London, 1975. pp. 640.

GROUT (VICTOR) Tolley's tax cases: (a summary of the official Reports of tax cases from 1875 to April 1976 applicable to current legislation). Croydon, [1976]. pp. 276.

PINSON (BARRY) On revenue law: comprising income tax; capital gains tax; development land tax; corporation tax; capital transfer tax; value added tax, etc. 10th ed. London, 1976. pp. 666.

— — Man, Isle of.

SOLLY (MARK) Anatomy of a tax haven: the Isle of Man. Douglas, I.O.M., 1975. pp. 132. *With interim supplement.*

— United States.

GROVES (HAROLD MARTIN) Tax philosophers: two hundred years of thought in Great Britain and the United States; edited by Donald J. Curran. Madison, Wis., 1974. pp. 158.

— — Law.

LEE (R. ALTON) A history of regulatory taxation. Lexington, [1973]. pp. 228.

TAXATION, DOUBLE

— Germany.

MUELHAUSEN (DIETER) Das Verständigungsverfahren im deutschen internationalen Steuerrecht. Berlin, [1976]. pp. 243. *bibliog.*

TAYLOR (CATHERINE).

TAYLOR (CATHERINE) If courage goes: my twenty years in South African politics. Johannesburg, 1976. pp. 316.

TAYSIDE

— Population.

CARSTAIRS (ANDREW McLAREN) The Tayside industrial population: the changing character and distribution of the industrial population in the Tayside area, 1911- 1951. Dundee, 1974. pp. 115. *(Abertay Historical Society. Publications. No. 17)*

TEA.

TEA: the colonial legacy; [written for the Cambridge World Development Action Group by John Hamilton and others]. Cambridge, [1974]. pp. 22,iv. *bibliog.*

— Bangladesh.

BANGLADESH. Ministry of Information and Broadcasting. 1972. Tea industry in Bangladesh. [Dacca, 1972]. pp. 50.

TEA TRADE.

TANNER (JOHN) A new deal for the poor: what a new economic order would mean for Britain and the third world. London, 1976. pp. 24. *bibliog.*

TEACHERS

— Supply and demand — United States.

CARTTER (ALLAN MURRAY) Ph.D.'s and the academic labor market. New York, [1976]. pp. 260. *bibliog. A report prepared for the Carnegie Commission on Higher Education.*

— Canada.

CANADA. Statistics Canada. Educational staff in public trade schools and similar institutions. a., 1971/72- Ottawa. *In English and French.*

CANADA. Statistics Canada. Qualifications and age of teachers in degree-awarding institutions. a., 1971/72(1st)- Ottawa. *[in English and French].*

— Germany — Political activity.

DOERING (HERBERT) Political historian. Der Weimarer Kreis: Studien zum politischen Bewusstsein verfassungstreuer Hochschullehrer in der Weimarer Republik. Meisenheim am Glan, 1975. pp. 336. *bibliog.*

— **Poland.**

WOJCIECHOWSKI (KAZIMIERZ) ed. Nauczyciele w walce o nową Polskę. Warszawa, 1970. pp. 451.

— **United Kingdom.**

OLLERENSHAW (Dame KATHLEEN) and FLUDE (CHRISTINE) Returning to teaching; research project sponsored by the Department of Education and Science in the Department of Educational Research, University of Lancaster, etc. Lancaster, 1974. 1 vol. (various pagings).

NATIONAL COUNCIL FOR CIVIL LIBERTIES. Reports. No. 8. Homosexuality and the teaching profession: results of a survey on the attitudes of local education authorities to the employment of homosexual women and men as teachers. London, 1975. pp. 21.

GOULD (Sir RONALD) Chalk up the memory: an autobiography. Birmingham, 1976. pp. 176.

— — **Salaries, pensions, etc.**

ASSOCIATION OF UNIVERSITY TEACHERS. Salary submission to the national board for prices and incomes. [London], 1969. pp. 24.

NEWBOULD (GERALD D.) Academic salaries: a personal application of managerial economics. Bradford, [1975]. pp. 14. (*University of Bradford. Inaugural Lectures. 1975*)

— — **Tenure.**

HIGGS (PETER) and SAVILLE (JOHN) Craigie College of Education: the findings of a commission of inquiry established by the Council for Academic Freedom and Democracy in February 1971. London, [1972?]. pp. 24.

— — **Ireland, Northern.**

A TEACHING Council for Northern Ireland; report of the Working Party appointed by the Minister of Education in 1970 [E.J. Kirkpatrick, chairman]. Belfast, H.M.S.O., 1975. pp. 54.

— — — **Salaries, pensions, etc.**

U.K. Government Actuary's Department. 1974. Report by the Government Actuary on the Teachers Superannuation Scheme, Northern Ireland, as at 31st March 1971. Belfast, [1974]. pp. 14.

— **United States.**

LEWIS (LIONEL STANLEY) Scaling the ivory tower: merit and its limits in academic careers. Baltimore, [1975]. pp. 238.

— — **Political activity.**

LADD (EVERETT CARLL) and LIPSET (SEYMOUR MARTIN) The divided academy: professors and politics. New York, [1975]. pp. 407. *bibliog.*

CHENG (CHARLES W.) Altering collective bargaining: citizen participation in educational decision making. New York, 1976. pp. 179. *bibliog.*

— — **Salaries, pensions, etc.**

WEITZMAN (JOAN) The scope of bargaining in public employment. New York, 1975. pp. 384. *bibliog.*

CHENG (CHARLES W.) Altering collective bargaining: citizen participation in educational decision making. New York, 1976. pp. 179. *bibliog.*

TEACHERS, TRAINING OF

— **United Kingdom.**

NIBLETT (WILLIAM ROY) and others. The university connection: (the antecedents, concept and development of institutes of education, 1922-1972). Windsor, Berks, 1975. pp. 300. *bibliog.*

TEACHERS' UNIONS

— **United States.**

ENCOUNTERING the unionized university; Jack H. Schuster, issue editor. San Francisco, 1974. pp. 106. *bibliogs.* (*New Directions for Higher Education. No. 5*) *Papers of a session at the 1973 annual meeting of the American Political Science Association.*

EATON (WILLIAM EDWARD) The American Federation of Teachers, 1916-1961: a history of the movement. Carbondale, Ill., [1975]. pp. 240. *bibliog.*

KEMERER (FRANK R.) and BALDRIDGE (J. VICTOR) Unions on campus. San Francisco, 1975. pp. 248. *bibliog.*

TEACHING.

BEARD (RUTH M.) Teaching and learning in higher education. 3rd ed. Harmondsworth, 1976. pp. 251. *bibliog.*

TEACHING, FREEDOM OF

— **Germany.**

VEREINIGUNG DER ANTIFASCHISTEN UND VERFOLGTEN DES NAZIREGIMES, LAND HAMBURG. Jacob und Schrübbers: heute wie damals; Dokumentation zum Berufsverbotsbeschluss und zum Fall Ilse Jacob, etc. 2nd ed. Hamburg, 1972. pp. 94. (*VAN-Documentationen. 4*)

WEBER (MAX) Max Weber on universities: the power of the state and the dignity of the academic calling in imperial Germany; translated, edited and with an introductory note by Edward Shils. Chicago, 1974. pp. 62. (*Reprinted from Minerva, vol. 11, no.4, October 1973*)

TECHNICAL ASSISTANCE.

VIEWS of science, technology and development; edited by Eugene Rabinowitch and Victor Rabinowitch. Oxford, 1975. pp. 285. *Consists mainly of papers presented to recent Pugwash conferences.*

TECHNICAL ASSISTANCE, AMERICAN.

SOMMER (JOHN G.) U[nited] S[tates] voluntary aid to the third world: what is its future?. Washington, 1975. pp. 65. (*Overseas Development Council. Development Papers. 20*)

— **India.**

JOHANSEN (ROBERT C.) United States foreign aid to India: a case study of the impact of U.S. foreign policy on the prospects for world order reform. Princeton, N.J., 1975. pp. 136. (*Princeton University. Center of International Studies. World Order Studies Program. Occasional Papers. No. 2*)

TECHNICAL ASSISTANCE, CHINESE

— **Africa, East.**

BAILEY (MARTIN DAWSON) Freedom railway: China and the Tanzania-Zambia link. London, 1976. pp. 168. *bibliog.*

TECHNICAL ASSISTANCE, JAPANESE.

HASEGAWA (SUKEHIRO) Japanese foreign aid: policy and practice. New York, 1975. pp. 172. *bibliog.*

TECHNICAL ASSISTANCE, RUSSIAN.

BYKOV (ALEKSANDR NAUMOVICH) and others. Soviet experience in transfer of technology to industrially less developed countries. New York, United Nations Institute for Training and Research, 1973. pp. 188. (*Research Reports. No. 15*)

PETROVA (NINA KONSTANTINOVNA) Mezhdunarodnye proizvodstvennye sviazi rabochego klassa SSSR, 1959- 1970 gg. Moskva, 1975. pp. 304.

TECHNICAL ASSISTANCE IN EAST AFRICA.

MAZZEO (DOMENICO) Foreign assistance and the East African Common Services, 1960-1970; with special reference to multilateral contributions. München, [1975]. pp. 235. *bibliog.* (*Ifo-Institut für Wirtschaftsforschung. Afrika- Studien. 89*)

TECHNICAL ASSISTANCE IN PAKISTAN.

NAQVI (SYED NAWAB HAIDER) The incubus of foreign aid. Karachi, [1971]. pp. 19. *bibliog.* (*Pakistan Institute of Development Economics. Essays in Development Economics. No.2*)

TECHNICAL EDUCATION

— **Colombia.**

SAFFORD (FRANK) 1935- . The ideal of the practical: Colombia's struggle to form a technical elite. Austin, [1976]. pp. 373. *bibliog.* (*Texas University. Institute of Latin American Studies. Latin American Monographs. No. 39*)

— **Hong Kong.**

HONG KONG. Industrial Training Advisory Committee. 1971. The final report. Hong Kong, 1971. pp. 95.

— — **Teacher training.**

HONG KONG. Ad Hoc Working Party on Instructor Training. 1970-71. Report on the survey of instructors; (with Supplement); [W.D.F. Williams, chairman]. Hong Kong, 1969-70 [or rather 1970-71]. 2 pts. *In English and Chinese.*

— **Sweden.**

TORSTENDAHL (ROLF) Teknologins nytta: motiveringar för det svenska tekniska utbildningsväsendets framväxt framförda av riksdagsmän och utbildningsadministratörer, 1810-1870. Uppsala, 1975. pp. 274. *bibliog.* (*Uppsala. Universitet. Historiska Institutionen. Studia Historica Upsaliensia.66*) *With English summary.*

— **United Kingdom.**

NATIONAL CONFERENCE ON DEGREE SANDWICH COURSES, UNIVERSITY OF BATH, 1975. [Proceedings of the conference] organized by the Universities' Committee on Integrated Sandwich Courses...; edited by Garry Denbury. Bath, [1976]. pp. 85.

SMITHERS (ALAN G.) Sandwich courses: an integrated education?. Windsor, 1976. pp. 180. *bibliog.*

TECHNICIANS IN INDUSTRY

— **Prussia.**

LUNDGREEN (PETER) Techniker in Preussen während der frühen Industrialisierung: Ausbildung und Berufsfeld einer entstehenden sozialen Gruppe. Berlin, 1975. pp. 307. *bibliog.* (*Historische Kommission zu Berlin. Einzelveröffentlichungen. Band 16*)

— **Russia.**

ZAUZOLKOV (FEDOR NIKOLAEVICH) Kommunisticheskaia partiia - organizator sozdaniia nauchnoi i proizvodstvenno-tekhnicheskoi intelligentsii SSSR. Moskva, 1973. pp. 127.

TECHNOCRACY.

BILLY (JACQUES) Les technocrates. 3rd ed. Paris, 1975. pp. 128. *bibliog.*

TECHNOLOGICAL FORECASTING.

CHACKO (GEORGE KUTTICKAL) Technological forecontrol: prospects, problems, and policy: managing today's technology for tomorrow's living. Amsterdam, 1975. pp. 457.

ZYKOV (IURII ANATOL'EVICH) Ekonomicheskoe prognozirovanie nauchno-tekhnicheskogo progressa: voprosy metodologii. Moskva, 1975. pp. 168.

TECHNOLOGICAL FORECASTING.(Cont.)

The FUTURES of Europe; edited...by Wayland Kennet, Director of the Europe Plus Thirty Project; based on a report to the Commission of the European Communities. Cambridge, 1976. pp. 242.

TECHNOLOGICAL INNOVATIONS.

VARSAVSKY (OSCAR A.) Estilos tecnologicos: propuestas para la seleccion de tecnologias bajo racionalidad socialista. Buenos Aires, [1974]. pp. 239. bibliog.

JOHNSON (PETER STEWART) The economics of invention and innovation: with a case study of the development of the hovercraft. London, 1975. pp. 329.

STAUB (KURT E.) Die Unternehmungskooperation für Produktinnovationen. Bern, [1975]. pp. 233. bibliog.

UCHENYE ZAPISKI KAFEDR OBSHCHESTVENNYKH NAUK VUZOV LENINGRADA. Filosofiia. vyp.16. Filosofskie i sotsiologicheskie issledovaniia. Leningrad, 1975. pp. 207.

OEKONOMISCHE Probleme der wissenschaftlich-technischen Revolution im Sozialismus...; (Redaktionskollegium: L.M. Gatowski [and others]). Berlin, 1976. pp. 252.

— Social aspects.

STANSFIELD (RONALD G.) Flux in the factory. London, 1967. pp. 8. (Hollenden Lectures. No. 15. 1967) (Reprinted from the Clothing Institute Journal, vol. 15, no. 3, 1967)

ROBBINS (LIONEL CHARLES) Baron Robbins. Technology and social welfare. Haifa, 1972. pp. 24. (Technion-Israel Institute of Technology. Joseph Wunsch Lectures. 1972) Photocopy.

NAUCHNO-tekhnicheskaia revoliutsiia i obshchestvo. Moskva, 1973. pp. 480.

AKHIEZER (ALEKSANDR SAMOILOVICH) Nauchno-tekhnicheskaia revoliutsiia i nekotorye sotsial'nye problemy proizvodstva i upravleniia. Moskva, 1974. pp. 310.

NAUCHNO-tekhnicheskaia revoliutsiia: lichnost', deiatel'nost', kollektiv; sotsial'no-psikhologicheskii aspekt. Kiev, 1975. pp. 344.

— Africa.

THOMAS (D. BABATUNDE) Importing technology into Africa: foreign investment and the supply of technological innovations. New York, 1976. pp. 202. bibliog.

— Canada.

CANADA. Department of Industry. 1969. PAIT: program for advancement of industrial technology. Ottawa, [1969]. pp. 13.

— Communist countries.

MIKUL'SKII (KONSTANTIN IVANOVICH) ed. Trudovye resursy i nauchno-tekhnicheskaia revoliutsiia: ispol'zovanie trudovykh resursov stran SEV v usloviiakh nauchno- tekhnicheskoi revoliutsii i sovershenstvovaniia metodov sotsialisticheskogo khoziaistvovaniia. Moskva, 1974. pp. 246.

NAUCHNO-tekhnicheskaia revoliutsiia i preimushchestva sotsializma. Moskva, 1975. pp. 261.

— Germany, Eastern.

INITIATIVE und ihre Leitung in der Wirtschaft. Berlin, 1975. pp. 205. (Zentralinstitut für Sozialistische Wirtschaftsführung. Schriften zur Sozialistischen Wirtschaftsführung)

FITZE (WERNER) and others. Wissenschaftlich-technischer Fortschritt, sozialistische Arbeit, Persönlichkeit. Berlin, 1976. pp. 166.

— Ireland (Republic).

O'DOHERTY (DERMOT P.) Innovation in Ireland: case studies; a report to the National Science Council. Dublin, Stationery Office, [1976]. pp. 62. bibliog.

— Russia.

ARTOBOLEVSKII (I.I.) and others, eds. Partiia i sovremennaia nauchno-tekhnicheskaia revoliutsiia v SSSR. Moskva, 1974. pp. 336. bibliog.

KLIMIN (N.V.) and DEVIATKIN (L.M.) eds. Proizvoditel'nye sily sotsializma v usloviiakh nauchno-tekhnicheskoi revoliutsii. Leningrad, 1974. pp. 232.

KORCHAGIN (VIKTOR PAVLOVICH) Trudovye resursy v usloviiakh nauchno-tekhnicheskoi revoliutsii. Moskva, 1974. pp. 167.

MIKHNEVICH (IURII MAKSIMOVICH) Ekonomicheskie problemy upravleniia nauchno-tekhnicheskim progressom. Leningrad, 1974. pp. 151.

BABAK (VASILII FEDOROVICH) Kredit i tekhnicheskii progress: dolgosrochnyi kredit i kapitalovlozheniia v usloviiakh nauchno-tekhnicheskoi revoliutsii. Moskva, 1975. pp. 168.

DOGAEV (IURII MIKHAILOVICH) Ekonomika nauchno-tekhnicheskogo progressa: regional'nye problemy. Moskva, 1975. pp. 286. bibliog.

OZNOBIN (NIKOLAI MAKAROVICH) and PAVLOV (ALEKSEI SERGEEVICH) Kompleksnoe planirovanie nauchno-tekhnicheskogo progressa. Moskva, 1975. pp. 263. bibliog.

PETROCHENKO (PETR FEDOROVICH) Vliianie nauchno-tekhnicheskogo progressa na soderzhanie i organizatsiiu truda. Moskva, 1975. pp. 230.

— — Udmurt Republic.

BELOSLUDTSEVA (ELIZAVETA IVANOVNA) Nauchno-tekhnicheskii progress i sovershenstvovanie promyshlennogo kompleksa Udmurtii. Izhevsk, 1974. pp. 151.

— United Kingdom.

PROGRAMMES ANALYSIS UNIT. A technological forecast for the United Kingdom textile industry, 1972-1990: summary report; (by A.G. Hamlin and others). Chilton, 1973. pp. 78. ([Publications]. P.A.U. R.73/5)

— United States.

GERSUNY (CARL) and others. Some effects of technological change on New England fishermen. Kingston, Rhode Island, 1975. pp. 40. bibliog. (Rhode Island. University. Department of Sociology and Anthropology. Marine Technical Reports. No. 42)

TECHNOLOGICAL change: economics, management and environment: [studies derived from projects of the Research Program in Industrial Economics of Case Western Reserve University]; edited by Bela Gold. Oxford, 1975. pp. 175. bibliogs.

TECHNOLOGISTS

— United Kingdom.

U.K. Department of Industry. 1976. Persons with qualifications in engineering, technology and science, census of population 1971, Great Britain;...compiled for the Department of Industry by the Office of Population Censuses and Surveys from the returns made in the 1971 census of population. London, 1976. pp. 207. (Studies in Technological Manpower. No.5)

TECHNOLOGY.

JOHNSON (HARRY GORDON) Technology and economic interdependence. London, 1975. pp. 187. bibliog. (Trade Policy Research Centre. World Economic Issues)

RADICAL technology; edited by Peter Harper, Godfrey Boyle and the editors of Undercurrents. New York, [1976]. pp. 304. bibliog.

— International cooperation.

VIEWS of science, technology and development; edited by Eugene Rabinowitch and Victor Rabinowitch. Oxford, 1975. pp. 285. Consists mainly of papers presented to recent Pugwash conferences.

— Social aspects.

KINTNER (WILLIAM ROSCOE) and SICHERMAN (HARVEY) Technology and international politics: the crisis of wishing. Lexington, [1975]. pp. 177. (Foreign Policy Research Institute. Book Series)

SCIENCE and social responsibility: [a Science Policy Foundation symposium held in London in 1973]; edited by Maurice Goldsmith. London, 1975. pp. 169.

— Nigeria.

THOMAS (D. BABATUNDE) Capital accumulation and technology transfer: a comparative analysis of Nigerian manufacturing industries. New York, 1975. pp. 152. bibliog.

— Russia.

HUTCHINGS (RAYMOND FRANCIS DUDLEY) Soviet science, technology, design: interaction and convergence. London, 1976. pp. 320. bibliog.

— Underdeveloped areas.

See UNDERDEVELOPED AREAS — Technology.

TECHNOLOGY AND CIVILIZATION.

BHALLA (A.S.) ed. Technology and employment in industry: a case study approach;... foreword by Amartya Sen. Geneva, International Labour Office, 1975. pp. 324.

TECHNOLOGY AND LAW.

OKOLIE (CHARLES CHUKWUMA) Legal aspects of the international transfer of technology to developing countries. New York, 1975. pp. 187.

TECHNOLOGY AND STATE.

LONG (THEODORE DIXON) and WRIGHT (CHRISTOPHER) eds. Science policies of industrial nations: case studies of the United States, Soviet Union, United Kingdom, France, Japan, and Sweden. New York, 1975. pp. 232. bibliog.

— United States.

LAMBRIGHT (W. HENRY) Governing science and technology. New York, 1976. pp. 218.

TECHNOLOGY TRANSFER.

ANNERSTEDT (JAN) and GUSTAVSSON (ROLF) Towards a new international economic division of labor?: patterns of dependence and conditions for liberation in the periphery of capitalism. [Roskilde], 1975. pp. 111.

KINTNER (WILLIAM ROSCOE) and SICHERMAN (HARVEY) Technology and international politics: the crisis of wishing. Lexington, [1975]. pp. 177. (Foreign Policy Research Institute. Book Series)

OKOLIE (CHARLES CHUKWUMA) Legal aspects of the international transfer of technology to developing countries. New York, 1975. pp. 187.

SOLO (ROBERT A.) Organizing science for technology transfer in economic development. [East Lansing], 1975. pp. 224.

THOMAS (D. BABATUNDE) Capital accumulation and technology transfer: a comparative analysis of Nigerian manufacturing industries. New York, 1975. pp. 152. bibliog.

HORVÁTH (JÁNOS) Chinese technology transfer to the third world: a grants economy analysis. New York, 1976. pp. 100. bibliog.

KIERAN (JOHN) of the Science Policy Research Centre, University College, Dublin. Technology transfer: a study with reference to the Irish engineering industry; a report to the National Science Council. Dublin, Stationery Office, [1976]. pp. 28.

THOMAS (D. BABATUNDE) Importing technology into Africa: foreign investment and the supply of technological innovations. New York, 1976. pp. 202. bibliog.

WOLYNSKI (ALEXANDER) Western economic aid to the USSR. London, 1976. pp. 12. *(Institute for the Study of Conflict. Conflict Studies. No. 72)*

— Underdeveloped areas.

See UNDERDEVELOPED AREAS — Technology transfer.

TECUMSEH, ONTARIO

— Social conditions.

JACKSON (JOHN D.) Community and conflict: (a study of French-English relations in Ontario). Toronto, [1975]. pp. 181. *bibliog.*

TEESSIDE

— Economic policy.

PUBLIC participation in structure planning: the Teesside experience; a study initiated by Community Advancement Project [by Peter Ferres and others]. London, 1976. pp. 87. *bibliog. (Centre for Environmental Studies. Research Papers. 14)*

— Social policy.

PUBLIC participation in structure planning: the Teesside experience; a study initiated by Community Advancement Project [by Peter Ferres and others]. London, 1976. pp. 87. *bibliog. (Centre for Environmental Studies. Research Papers. 14)*

TELECOMMUNICATION.

MARTIN (JAMES THOMAS) Telecommunications and the computer. Englewood Cliffs, [1969]. pp. 470.

— Canada.

CANADA. Department of Communications. 1973. Computer/communications policy: a position statement by the government of Canada. Ottawa, 1973. pp. 17,17. *In English and French.*

BABE (ROBERT E.) Cable television and telecommunication in Canada: an economic ana East Lansing, Mich., 1975. pp. 287. *bibliog. (Michigan State University. MSU International Business and Economic Studies.)*

— France.

FRANCE. Commission des Transmissions. 1971. Préparation du VIe Plan: rapport. Paris, 1971. pp. 195.

— Sierra Leone.

SIERRA LEONE. Commission appointed to inquire into the Activities of the Posts and Telecommunications Department from 1st January, 1961. 1972. Report...and the government statement thereon; [Percy R. Davies, Commissioner]. [Freetown?, 1972]. pp. 85.

— United Kingdom — Rates.

POST OFFICE USERS' NATIONAL COUNCIL. Report...on the Post Office proposals for increased postal, telecommunications and Giro and remittance service charges. London, 1975. pp. 64. *(Reports. No. 12)*

TELEGRAPH

— Germany — Employees.

KLEEMANN (KURT) Die Sozialpolitik der Reichs-Post- und Telegraphenverwaltung gegenüber ihren Beamten, Unterbeamten und Arbeitern. Jena, 1914. pp. 253. *bibliog. (Jena. Universität. Staatswissenschaftliches Seminar. Abhandlungen. 14. Band, 1. Heft)*

TELEPHONE

— Finland.

FINLAND. Tilastokeskus. Puhelinlaitosten tasetilasto...: Statistics of profit and loss and balance sheet accounts of telephone companies. a., 1973 [6th]- Helsinki. *[In Finnish with English summary and table headings].*

— Switzerland.

VEREIN FÜR WIRTSCHAFTSHISTORISCHE STUDIEN. Schweizer Pioniere der Wirtschaft und Technik. 28. Alfred Zellweger, Uster, 1855-1916; Hans Blumer-Ris, Freiburg, 1902-1953; von Hans Rudolf Schmid. Zürich, 1975. pp. 113. *bibliog.*

TELEVISION

— Germany — Laws and regulations.

HERRMANN (GUENTER) Fernsehen und Hörfunk in der Verfassung der Bundesrepublik Deutschland; zugleich ein Beitrag zu weiteren allgemeinen verfassungsrechtlichen und kommunikationsrechtlichen Fragen. Tübingen, 1975. pp. 422. *bibliog.*

— United States — Laws and regulations.

SCHMIDT (BENNO C.) Freedom of the press vs. public access. New York, [1976]. pp. 296.

TELEVISION AND CHILDREN.

CATER (DOUGLASS) and STRICKLAND (STEPHEN P.) TV violence and the child: the evolution and fate of the Surgeon General's report. New York, [1975]. pp. 167.

NOBLE (GRANT) Children in front of the small screen. London, 1975. pp. 256. *bibliog.*

TELEVISION AUDIENCES

— Israel.

ISRAEL. Central Bureau of Statistics. Special Series. No. 321. Radio listening and television watching, January 1969. Pt.2. Jerusalem, 1970. pp. 18. *In English and Hebrew.*

TELEVISION BROADCASTING

— Bibliography.

COMSTOCK (GEORGE A.) and FISHER (MARILYN) compilers. Television and human behavior: a guide to the pertinent scientific literature; prepared under a grant from the Edna McConnell Clark Foundation. Santa Monica, Calif., 1975. pp. 344. *(Rand Corporation. [Rand Reports]. 1746)*

COMSTOCK (GEORGE A.) and LINDSEY (GEORG) compilers. Television and human behavior: the research horizon, future and present; prepared under a grant from the Edna McConnell Clark Foundation...with the assistance of Marilyn Fisher. Santa Monica, Calif., 1975. pp. 120. *(Rand Corporation. [Rand Reports]. 1748)*

COMSTOCK (GEORGE A.) and others, compilers. Television and human behavior: the key studies; prepared under a grant from the Edna McConnell Clark Foundation. Santa Monica, Calif., [1975]. pp. 251. *(Rand Corporation. [Rand Reports]. 1747)*

— Social aspects.

WELLS (ALAN FRANK) Picture-tube imperialism?: the impact of U.S. television on Latin America. Maryknoll, [1972]. pp. 197. *bibliog.*

PIEPE (ANTHONY) and others. Television and the working class. Farnborough, Hants., [1975]. pp. 170. *bibliogs.*

— — Bibliography.

COMSTOCK (GEORGE A.) and FISHER (MARILYN) compilers. Television and human behavior: a guide to the pertinent scientific literature; prepared under a grant from the Edna McConnell Clark Foundation. Santa Monica, Calif., 1975. pp. 344. *(Rand Corporation. [Rand Reports]. 1746)*

COMSTOCK (GEORGE A.) and LINDSEY (GEORG) compilers. Television and human behavior: the research horizon, future and present; prepared under a grant from the Edna McConnell Clark Foundation...with the assistance of Marilyn Fisher. Santa Monica, Calif., 1975. pp. 120. *(Rand Corporation. [Rand Reports]. 1748)*

COMSTOCK (GEORGE A.) and others, compilers. Television and human behavior: the key studies; prepared under a grant from the Edna McConnell Clark Foundation. Santa Monica, Calif., [1975]. pp. 251. *(Rand Corporation. [Rand Reports]. 1747)*

— — United States.

ASPEN WORKSHOP CONFERENCE ON TELEVISION, 1974. Television as a social force: new approaches to TV criticism; [papers deriving from the conference];...Richard Adler, project editor, etc. New York, [1975]. pp. 171.

— America, Latin.

WELLS (ALAN FRANK) Picture-tube imperialism?: the impact of U.S. television on Latin America. Maryknoll, [1972]. pp. 197. *bibliog.*

— France.

CHEVALLIER (JACQUES) La Radio Télévision Française entre deux réformes. Paris, 1975. pp. 342. *bibliog.*

THOMAS (RUTH) B.A. Broadcasting and democracy in France. Bradford, 1976. pp. 211. *bibliog.*

— Germany.

WILLIAMS (ARTHUR) M.A. Broadcasting and democracy in West Germany. Bradford, 1976. pp. 198. *bibliog.*

— Hong Kong.

HONG KONG. Television and Films Authority. Annual departmental report by the Commissioner for Television and Films. a., 1974/75- Hong Kong.

— Sierra Leone.

SIERRA LEONE. Committee of Broadcasting Consultants on the Sierra Leone Radio and Sierra Leone Television Services. 1969. Report...and the Government statement thereon; [Hugh Palmer, chairman]. [Freetown, 1969]. pp. 25.

— United Kingdom.

COMMUNITY RELATIONS COMMISSION. The future of broadcasting: Community Relations Commission evidence to the Annan Committee. [London, 1975]. fo. 8.

PIEPE (ANTHONY) and others. Television and the working class. Farnborough, Hants., [1975]. pp. 170. *bibliogs.*

SWANN (Sir MICHAEL MEREDITH) Freedom and restraint in broadcasting: the British experience. London, [1975]. pp. 31. *(Queen's Lectures. 1975) With German translation.*

— United States.

BARNOUW (ERIK) Tube of plenty: the evolution of American television. New York, 1975. pp. 518. *bibliog. A condensation and updating of material previously published in his A history of broadcasting in the United States.*

CATER (DOUGLASS) and STRICKLAND (STEPHEN P.) TV violence and the child: the evolution and fate of the Surgeon General's report. New York, [1975]. pp. 167.

BUNCE (RICHARD) Television in the corporate interest. New York, 1976. pp. 150.

SHAPIRO (ANDREW O.) Media access: your rights to express your views on radio and television. Boston, [Mass., 1976]. pp. 297.

TELEVISION BROADCASTING OF NEWS

— United Kingdom.

SCHLESINGER (PHILIP RONALD) The social organisation of news production: a case study of BBC radio and television news; [Ph.D. (London) thesis]. [1975]. fo. 393. *Typescript: unpublished. This thesis is the property of London University and may not be removed from the Library.*

TELEVISION BROADCASTING OF NEWS(Cont.)

— United States.

DIAMOND (EDWIN) The tin kazoo: television, politics, and the news. Cambridge, Mass., [1975]. pp. 269.

GELFMAN (JUDITH S.) Women in television news. New York, 1976. pp. 186. *bibliog.*

TELEVISION CRITICISM.

ASPEN WORKSHOP CONFERENCE ON TELEVISION, 1974. Television as a social force: new approaches to TV criticism; [papers deriving from the conference];...Richard Adler, project editor, etc. New York, [1975]. pp. 171.

TELEVISION IN ADVERTISING.

INDEPENDENT BROADCASTING AUTHORITY. The IBA code of advertising standards and practice. [rev. ed.] London, 1975. pp. 20.

TELEVISION IN POLITICS

— France.

THOMAS (RUTH) B.A. Broadcasting and democracy in France. Bradford, 1976. pp. 211. *bibliog.*

— Germany.

WILLIAMS (ARTHUR) M.A. Broadcasting and democracy in West Germany. Bradford, 1976. pp. 198. *bibliog.*

TELEVISION PROGRAMMES, PUBLIC SERVICE.

GILLESPIE (GILBERT) Public access cable television in the United States and Canada; with an annotated bibliography. New York, 1975. pp. 157.

TELLER (EDWARD).

YORK (HERBERT FRANK) The advisors: Oppenheimer, Teller, and the superbomb. San Francisco, [1976]. pp. 175.

TELLEWOYAN (ZUBARYEA AKOI).

CORDOR (S. HENRY) Zubaryea Akoi Tellewoyan of Liberia: the man and his work: a portrait of a great African tribal ruler: an introduction to the history of Lofa County, Liberia's largest region, through the lives of great history-makers, with emphasis on Zubaryea Akoi Tellewoyan and a study of the folkways of the Lorma people in Liberia. Voinjama, Liberia, [1967]. fo. 101.

TEMPORARY EMPLOYMENT

— United Kingdom.

FEDERATION OF PERSONNEL SERVICES OF GREAT BRITAIN. The temporary: a national survey of attitudes, comments and regional statistics. London, [1975]. pp. 36, xii.

TENNESSEE

— Politics and government.

HART (ROGER L.) Redeemers, Bourbons and Populists: Tennessee, 1870-1896. Baton Rouge, La., [1975]. pp. 290. *bibliog.*

TENNESSEE VALLEY AUTHORITY.

MORGAN (ARTHUR ERNEST) The making of the TVA. Buffalo, 1974. pp. 205.

TEREK

— Constitutional history.

KONIEV (IU.I.) Natsional'no-gosudarstvennoe stroitel'stvo na Tereke. Ordzhonikidze, 1969. pp. 98.

TERRITORIAL WATERS.

JOHNSTON (DOUGLAS M.) ed. Marine policy and the coastal community: the impact of the law of the sea. London, [1976]. pp. 336.

— America, Latin.

URUGUAY. Presidencia. Secretaria. 1971. America Latina y la extension del mar territorial: regimen juridico. Montevideo, 1971. pp. 440. *bibliog.*

— Peru.

SMETHERMAN (BOBBIE BRALY) and SMETHERMAN (ROBERT M.) Territorial seas and inter-American relations, with case studies of the Peruvian and U.S. fishing industries. New York, 1974. pp. 121.

TERRORISM.

BELL (J. BOWYER) Transnational terror. Washington, 1975. pp. 91. *bibliog.* (*American Enterprise Institute for Public Policy Research and Stanford University. Hoover Institution on War, Revolution and Peace. AEI-Hoover Policy Studies. 17*)

BURTON (ANTHONY M.) Urban terrorism: theory, practice and response. London, 1975. pp. 259. *bibliog.*

INTERNATIONAL SCHOOL ON DISARMAMENT AND RESEARCH ON CONFLICTS, 5TH, URBINO, 1974. International terrorism and world security: [proceedings of the fifth course]; edited by David Carlton and Carlo Schaerf. London, 1975. pp. 332.

JENKINS (BRIAN MICHAEL) International terrorism: a new mode of conflict. Los Angeles, 1975. pp. 48. (*California Seminar on Arms Control and Foreign Policy. Research Papers. No. 48*)

PAINE (LAURAN) The terrorists. London, 1975. pp. 176.

INTERNATIONAL terrorism: national, regional, and global perspectives; edited by Yonah Alexander. New York, 1976. pp. 390. *bibliog.*

WILKINSON (PAUL) Terrorism versus liberal democracy: the problems of response. London, 1976. pp. 19. (*Institute for the Study of Conflict. Conflict Studies. No. 67*)

— Bibliography.

GERMANY (BUNDESREPUBLIK). Deutscher Bundestag. Wissenschaftliche Dienste. 1975. Terrorismus und Gewalt: Auswahlbibliographie mit Annotationen; [compiled by Günther Hoherz]. Bonn, 1975. pp. 86. (*Bibliographien. 43.*)

— East (Near East).

DOBSON (CHRISTOPHER) Black September: its short, violent history. London, [1975]. pp. 192.

— Yugoslavia.

VODINELIĆ (VLADIMIR) 10 verzija više jedna jednako istina: zapisi o Bonskom i Stockholmskom procesu ustaškim teroristima. Split, 1973. pp. 236.

TESCHEN.

See CIESZYN.

TEXAS

— History.

NACKMAN (MARK E.) A nation within a nation: the rise of Texas nationalism. Port Washington, N.Y., 1975. pp. 183. *bibliog.*

— Nationalism.

NACKMAN (MARK E.) A nation within a nation: the rise of Texas nationalism. Port Washington, N.Y., 1975. pp. 183. *bibliog.*

TEXTILE FIBRES, SYNTHETIC

— United States.

AUSTRALIA. Bureau of Agricultural Economics. 1970. End uses of fibres in the U.S.A.; (by J.L. Sault). Canberra, 1970. pp. 96. (*Wool Economic Research Reports. No. 18*)

TEXTILE INDUSTRY AND FABRICS

— Germany — North Rhine-Westphalia.

NORTH RHINE-WESTPHALIA. Landesamt für Datenverarbeitung und Statistik. Beiträge zur Statistik des Landes Nordrhein- Westfalen. Heft 350. Die Textilindustrie in Nordrhein-Westfalen, 1968 bis 1974. Düsseldorf, 1976. pp. 89.

— Italy.

SOCIETÀ RICERCHE E STUDI. Studio sull'evoluzione della concentrazione in alcuni settori dell'industria tessile in Italia: lana,...cotone,...magliera e calzetteria, etc; [by Piera Balliano and others]. [Brussels, European Communities, Directorate-General for Competition, 1973]. 1 vol. (various pagings).

— United Kingdom.

PROGRAMMES ANALYSIS UNIT. A technological forecast for the United Kingdom textile industry, 1972-1990: summary report; (by A.G. Hamlin and others). Chilton, 1973. pp. 78. (*[Publications]. P.A.U. R.73/5*)

COUNTER INFORMATION SERVICES and TRANSNATIONAL INSTITUTE. Courtaulds inside-out. London, [1975?]. pp. 42. *bibliog.* (*Counter Information Services. Anti-Reports. No. 10*)

LAZAR (HARVEY) Politics, public policy formation and the Lancashire textile industry, 1954-70; [Ph. D. (London) thesis]. 1975. fo. 423. *bibliog. Typescript: unpublished. This thesis is the property of London University and may not be removed from the Library.*

TEXTILE WORKERS

— Hong Kong.

HONG KONG. Textile Industrial Committee. 1970-72. Minimum job standards and specifications for the principal jobs in the textile industry. rev. ed. Hong Kong, 1970-71 [or rather - 72]. 6 pts. (in 1 vol.). *In English and Chinese.*

— India.

INDIA. Labour Bureau. 1975. Report on survey of labour conditions in woollen factories in India, 1971. [Delhi, 1975]. pp. 96.

— — Bombay.

BOMBAY (STATE). Industrial Conditions Enquiry Committee. Final report...together with suggestions for a labour code, Bombay State; [Purushottam Kanji, chairman]. [Bombay, 1950]. pp. 133.

— Switzerland.

MARTI (ERNST) 50 Jahre schweizerische Textil- und Fabrikarbeiter- Organisationen, 1903-1953. [Zürich, 1954]. pp. 275.

— United Kingdom.

PEARCE (CYRIL) The Manningham Mills strike, Bradford, December 1890-April 1891. Hull, 1975. pp. 85. (*Hull. University. Occasional Papers in Economic and Social History. No. 7*)

— United States.

MURPHY (PAUL L.) and others. The Passaic textile strike of 1926. Belmont, [1974]. pp. 185. *bibliog.*

THAILAND

— Armed forces — Political activity.

LISSAK (MOSHE) Military roles in modernization: civil-military relations in Thailand and Burma. Beverly Hills, [1976]. pp. 255. (*Inter-University Seminar on Armed Forces and Society. [Publications]. vol.8*)

— Economic conditions.

BELGIUM. Office Belge du Commerce Extérieur. 1972. Thaïlande. Bruxelles, 1972. pp. 69. (*Un Marché. 10*)

— Economic policy.

RUBIN (HERBERT J.) The dynamics of development in rural Thailand. [Dekalb, Ill.], 1974. fo. 156. *(Northern Illinois University. Center for Southeast Asian Studies. Special Reports. No. 8)*

— Foreign relations — United States.

THOMPSON (W. SCOTT) Unequal partners: Philippine and Thai relations with the United States 1965-75. Lexington, [1975]. pp. 183.

— Industries.

THAILAND. National Statistical Office. Quarterly and annual industrial production indexes. a., 1973 (2nd)- [Bangkok].

— Kings and rulers.

ENGEL (DAVID M.) Law and kingship in Thailand during the reign of King Chulalongkorn. Ann Arbor, 1975. pp. 131. *bibliog. (Michigan University. Center for South and Southeast Asian Studies. Michigan Papers on South and Southeast Asia. No. 9)*

— Politics and government.

LISSAK (MOSHE) Military roles in modernization: civil-military relations in Thailand and Burma. Beverly Hills, [1976]. pp. 255. *(Inter-University Seminar on Armed Forces and Society. [Publications]. vol.8)*

— Rural conditions.

RUBIN (HERBERT J.) The dynamics of development in rural Thailand. [Dekalb, Ill.], 1974. fo. 156. *(Northern Illinois University. Center for Southeast Asian Studies. Special Reports. No. 8)*

KEMP (JEREMY HUGH) Social organization of a hamlet in Phitsanulok Province, north- central Thailand. 1976. fo. 358. *bibliog.* Typescript. Ph.D. (London) thesis: unpublished. This thesis is the property of London University and may not be removed from the Library.

THALIDOMIDE.

TEFF (HARVEY) and MUNRO (COLIN R.) Thalidomide: the legal aftermath. Farnborough, [1976]. pp. 154.

THAMES, RIVER.

DOCKLANDS JOINT COMMITTEE. Docklands Development Team. Conservation and the role of the river. London, 1975. pp. 48. *(Working Papers for Consultation. 8)*

THEATRE

— Finance.

VEREIN FÜR SOZIALPOLITIK. Schriften. Neue Folge. Band 75/IV. Öffentliche Finanzwirtschaft und Verteilung, IV; von Clemens-August Andreae [and others]; herausgegeben von Wilhelmine Dreissig. Berlin, [1976]. pp. 150. *With summaries and table of contents in English.*

— Information storage and retrieval systems.

See INFORMATION STORAGE AND RETRIEVAL SYSTEMS — Theatre.

— United Kingdom.

MACKINDER (Sir HALFORD JOHN) [Correspondence concerning the foundation of a national theatre in London. 1913]. 1 piece. *Manuscript.*

THEOLOGY, PURITAN

— United States.

HOLIFIELD (E. BROOKS) The covenant sealed: the development of Puritan sacramental theology in old and New England, 1570-1720. New Haven, 1974. pp. 248. *bibliog.*

THIEL (ERNEST JACQUES).

FRITZ (MARTIN) Ernest Thiel: finansman i genombrottstid. Göteborg, 1974. pp. 51. *bibliog. (Göteborgs Universitet. Ekonomisk-Historiska Institutionen. Meddelanden. 33)*

THOMAS [BECKET], Saint, Archbishop of Canterbury.

GARNIER, de Pont Sainte Maxence. Garnier's Becket; translated from the 12th-century Vie Saint Thomas le Martyr de Cantorbire of Garnier of Pont- Sainte-Maxence by Janet Shirley. London, 1975. pp. 191.

THOREZ (MAURICE).

ROBRIEUX (PHILIPPE) Maurice Thorez: vie secrète et vie publique. [Paris, 1975]. pp. 661. *bibliog.*

THOUGHT AND THINKING.

WARR (PETER B.) ed. Thought and personality: selected readings. Harmondsworth, 1970. pp. 447. *bibliogs.*

DE BONO (EDWARD FRANCIS CHARLES PUBLIUS) Practical thinking: four ways to be right, five ways to be wrong, five ways to understand. London, 1971. pp. 198.

MIND and language...; edited by Samuel Guttenplan. Oxford, 1975. pp. 158. *(Oxford. University. Wolfson College. Wolfson College Lectures. 1974)*

MACH (ERNST) Knowledge and error: sketches on the psychology of enquiry; (translation from the 5th edition, 1926). Dordrecht, [1976]. pp. 393. *bibliogs.*

THUGUTT (STANISLAW).

THUGUTT (STANISŁAW) Wybór pism i autobiografia. Glasgow, 1943. pp. 218. *bibliog.*

THURINGIA

— Economic history.

SCHWARZE (ELISABETH) Soziale Struktur und Besitzverhältnisse der ländlichen Bevölkerung Ostthüringens im 16. Jahrhundert;...mit einer Einführung: Die Land- und Türkensteuerregister...; von Hans Eberhardt. Weimar, 1975. pp. 216. *bibliog.*

— Social history.

SCHWARZE (ELISABETH) Soziale Struktur und Besitzverhältnisse der ländlichen Bevölkerung Ostthüringens im 16. Jahrhundert;...mit einer Einführung: Die Land- und Türkensteuerregister...; von Hans Eberhardt. Weimar, 1975. pp. 216. *bibliog.*

TIERRA DEL FUEGO.

LEWIN (BOLESLAO) Popper: un conquistador patagonico; sus hazañas, sus escritos. Buenos Aires, [1967]. pp. 233.

TIMBER

— Canada.

MANNING (GLENN H.) and GRINNELL (H. RAE) Forest resources and utilization in Canada to the year 2000. Ottawa, 1971. pp. 80. *bibliog. (Canada. Forestry Service. Publications. No. 1304)*

TIME ALLOCATION.

SACKS (MICHAEL PAUL) Women's work in Soviet Russia: continuity in the midst of change. New York, [1976]. pp. 221. *bibliog.*

TIME ALLOCATION SURVEYS

— Norway.

NORWAY. 1975. Tidsnyttingsundersøkelsen, 1971-72, etc. Oslo, 1975. 2 vols. *(Norges Offisielle Statistikk. Rekke A. 692 and 662) In Norwegian and English.*

NORWAY. Statistiske Centralbyrå. 1975. Tid nyttet til egenarbeid, etc. Oslo, 1975. pp. 77. *(Statistiske Analyser. 19) With English summary.*

TIME AND ECONOMIC REACTIONS.

JUDGE (GEORGE G.) and TAKAYAMA (TAKASHI) eds. Studies in economic planning over space and time. Amsterdam, 1973. pp. 727. *bibliogs.*

BEIER (JOACHIM) Zeitraumanalyse: Bindeglied einzel- und gesamtwirtschaftlicher Unternehmensstatistik. Berlin, [1975]. pp. 337. *bibliog.*

HANNA (R.S.) Composite lag distributions in the financial sector: multivariate time- and frequency-domain analyses. Lexington, Mass., [1975]. pp. 179. *bibliog.*

WYMER (CLIFFORD RONALD) Continuous time models in macro-economics: specification and estimation. [London], 1976. pp. 37, iv. *bibliog.*

TIME SERIES ANALYSIS.

POMERANTSEV (VLADIMIR VLADIMIROVICH) Analiz vremennykh riadov v planirovanii. Moskva, 1974. pp. 223.

KAZINETS (LEV SEMENOVICH) Tempy rosta i absoliutnye prirosty: izmerenie i analiz. Moskva, 1975. pp. 191. *bibliog.*

OSBORN (DENISE RAE) Time series analysis and dynamic specification in econometric models, with an application to the Australian wool market. 1975. fo. 251. *bibliog.* Typescript. Ph.D. (London) thesis: unpublished. This thesis is the property of London University and may not be removed from the Library.

TIME-SHARING COMPUTER SYSTEMS.

SCHERR (ALLAN LEE) An analysis of time-shared computer systems. Cambridge, Mass., 1967. pp. 115. *bibliog.*

WILKES (MAURICE VINCENT) Time-sharing computer systems. 3rd ed. London, 1975. pp. 166. *bibliog.*

TIMOR

— Politics and government.

FRENEY (DENIS) Timor: freedom caught between the powers. Nottingham, 1975. pp. 68.

TIN

— Congresses.

UNITED NATIONS. Tin Conference, 1st, Geneva, 1950-53. Final documents in order of event; [1st Session, October- November, 1950]. [Geneva, 1950]. 1 vol. (various pagings).

UNITED NATIONS. Tin Conference, 1st, Geneva, 1950-53. All papers grouped by committees; [2nd Session, November- December, 1953]. [Geneva, 1953]. 1 vol. (various pagings).

UNITED NATIONS. Tin Conference, 2nd, New York, 1960. (Final papers). [New York, 1960]. 1 vol. (various pagings).

UNITED NATIONS. Tin Conference, 2nd, New York, 1960. [Papers and documents]. [New York], 1960. 1 vol. (various pagings).

UNITED NATIONS. Tin Conference, 3rd, New York, 1965. [Papers and documents]. [New York], 1965. 1 vol. (various pagings).

TECHNICAL CONFERENCE ON TIN, [1ST], LONDON, 1967. A technical conference on tin, London, 1967. London, International Tin Council, 1968. 2 vols. *bibliogs.*

TECHNICAL CONFERENCE ON TIN, 2ND, BANGKOK, 1969. A second technical conference on tin, Bangkok, 1969. London, International Tin Council, 1970. 3 vols.

— Statistics.

INTERNATIONAL TIN COUNCIL. 1960. Statistical papers: July 1958-June 1960. [London, 1960]. 1 vol. (various pagings).

TIN CONTAINERS.

READER (WILLIAM JOSEPH) Metal Box: a history;...research by Judy Slinn. London, 1976. pp. 256. *bibliog.*

TIN INDUSTRY

— Statistics.

INTERNATIONAL TIN COUNCIL. 1960. Statistical papers: July 1958-June 1960. [London, 1960]. 1 vol. (various pagings).

TIN MINES AND MINING.

TECHNICAL CONFERENCE ON TIN, [1ST], LONDON, 1967. A technical conference on tin, London, 1967. London, International Tin Council, 1968. 2 vols. *bibliogs.*

TECHNICAL CONFERENCE ON TIN, 2ND, BANGKOK, 1969. A second technical conference on tin, Bangkok, 1969. London, International Tin Council, 1970. 3 vols.

— Malaya.

YIP (YAT HOONG) The development of the tin mining industry of Malaya. Kuala Lumpur, 1969. pp. 446. *bibliog.*

— United Kingdom — Cornwall.

EDUCATION and labour in the South-west; [papers presented at a seminar held at Dartington Hall in March 1974]; edited by Jeffrey Porter. Exeter, 1975. pp. 77. *(Exeter. University. Department of Economic History. Exeter Papers in Economic History. No. 10)*

TINKERS

— Ireland (Republic).

GMELCH (SHARON BOHN) Tinkers and travellers. Dublin, 1975. pp. 144. *bibliog.*

TINN

— Population.

SVALESTUEN (ANDRES A.) Tinns emigrasjonshistorie, 1837-1907: en undersøokelse med saerlig vekt på den demografiske, økonomiske og sosiale bakgrunn for Amerikafarten, etc. Oslo, [1972]. pp. 337. *bibliog.*

TITHES

— United Kingdom.

EVANS (ERIC J.) The contentious tithe: the tithe problem and English agriculture, 1750-1850. London, 1976. pp. 185. *bibliog.*

TKACHEV (PETR NIKITICH).

TKACHEV (PETR NIKITICH) Sochineniia v dvukh tomakh. Moskva, 1975 in progress.

TOBACCO.

ECONOMIST INTELLIGENCE UNIT. Q[uarterly] E[conomic] R[eview] Specials. No. 29. Prospects for unmanufactured tobacco to 1984: by Andrew Shepherd. London, 1975. pp. 76.

TOBACCO HABIT.

SOCIAL MORALITY COUNCIL. Study Group on Education and Drug Dependence. Education and drug dependence. London, 1975. pp. 78.

ALCOHOL dependence and smoking behaviour; edited by Griffith Edwards [and others] on behalf of the Addiction Research Unit, Institute of Psychiatry, University of London. Farnborough, Hants., [1976]. pp. 268. *bibliog.*

TOBACCO MANUFACTURE AND TRADE

— France.

PRICE (JACOB MYRON) France and the Chesapeake: a history of the French tobacco monopoly, 1674-1791, and of its relationship to the British and American tobacco trades. Ann Arbor, [1973]. 2 vols. *bibliog.*

— United Kingdom.

PRICE (JACOB MYRON) France and the Chesapeake: a history of the French tobacco monopoly, 1674-1791, and of its relationship to the British and American tobacco trades. Ann Arbor, [1973]. 2 vols. *bibliog.*

— — Scotland.

DEVINE (T.M.) The tobacco lords: a study of the tobacco merchants of Glasgow and their trading activities c. 1740-90. Edinburgh, [1975]. pp. 209. *bibliog.*

— United States.

PRICE (JACOB MYRON) France and the Chesapeake: a history of the French tobacco monopoly, 1674-1791, and of its relationship to the British and American tobacco trades. Ann Arbor, [1973]. 2 vols. *bibliog.*

TODOROV (KOSTA).

TODOROV (KOSTA) Balkan firebrand: the autobiography of a rebel, soldier and statesman. Chicago, [1943]. pp. 340.

TOFTLUND

— History.

CHRISTENSEN (OLAV) Toftlund og Omegns Sparekasse, 1872-1972; med bidrag til Toftlund sogns historie, 1864-1920. [Toftlund, 1972]. pp. 144.

TOGLIATTI (PALMIRO).

AUCIELLO (NICOLA) Socialismo ed egemonia in Gramsci e Togliatti. Bari, [1974]. pp. 207.

TOGO

— Statistics.

ANNUAIRE STATISTIQUE DU TOGO; [pd. by] Direction de la Statistique [Togo Republic]. a., 1971- Lomé.

TOKYO.

FRANCE. Direction de la Documentation. La Documentation Française. Notes et Etudes Documentaires. Nos. 4,118-4, 119-4,120. Les grandes villes du monde: l'agglomération de Tokyo; [par Jacques Pezeu-Massabuau]. Paris, 1974. pp. 108. *bibliog.*

TOLBERT (WILLIAM RICHARD).

LIBERIA. Ministry of Information, Cultural Affairs and Tourism. 1975. Inspired to lead: a short biography of President William R. Tolbert, Jr. [Monrovia, 1975]. fo. 178. *Photocopy.*

TOLERATION.

KING (PRESTON THEODORE) Toleration. London, 1976. pp. 239. *bibliog.*

TINDER (GLENN ERIN) Tolerance: toward a new civility. Amherst, 1976. pp. 187.

TOLL ROADS

— United Kingdom.

PAWSON (ERIC) The turnpike trusts of the eighteenth century: a study of innovation and diffusion. Oxford, 1975. pp. 40. *bibliog. (Oxford. University. School of Geography. Research Papers. No. 14)*

TOMATOES

— United Kingdom — Guernsey.

FOLLEY (ROGER ROLAND WESTWELL) An island horticulture: economic aspects of tomato-growing in Guernsey;...commissioned by the States of Guernsey. [St. Peter Port, 1962]. pp. 44.

TOPOLOGICAL VECTOR SPACES.

See LINEAR TOPOLOGICAL SPACES.

TOPOLOGY.

MILNOR (JOHN W.) Topology from the differentiable viewpoint. [2nd ed.]. Charlottesville, 1969 repr. 1976. pp. 64. *(Virginia University. Page-Barbour Lectures. 1963)*

TORIES, ENGLISH.

BENNETT (GARETH VAUGHAN) The Tory crisis in church and state, 1688-1730: the career of Francis Atterbury, Bishop of Rochester. Oxford, 1975. pp. 335. *bibliog.*

TORONTO

— Population.

BALAKRISHNAN (T.R.) and others. Fertility and family planning in a Canadian metropolis. Montreal, 1975. pp. 217. *bibliog.*

TORTS

— United Kingdom.

ATIYAH (PATRICK SELIM) Accidents, compensation and the law. 2nd ed. London, 1975. pp. 646.

CLERK (JOHN FREDERIC) and LINDSELL (WILLIAM HARRY BARBER) On torts; fourteenth edition (by Arthur L. Armitage [and others]). London, 1975. pp. 1269.

STREET (HARRY) The law of torts. 6th ed. London, 1976. pp. 528.

WILLIAMS (GLANVILLE LLEWELLYN) and HEPPLE (BOB ALEXANDER) Foundations of the law of tort. London, 1976. pp. 182. *bibliog.*

TORTURE.

WORKSHOP ON HUMAN RIGHTS, LONDON, 1975. Report and recommendations [of the workshop organized by the Campaign for the Abolition of Torture]. London, [1975]. pp. 15.

SOCIETY OF FRIENDS. Friends' Peace and International Relations Committee. The abolition of torture folder. London, [1976?]. 1 folder.

— Chile.

SILVA (RAUL) and others. Evidence on the terror in Chile...; translated by Brian McBeth. London, [1974]. pp. 139.

— Israel.

EIDE (ASBJORN) and others. Report of an Amnesty International mission to Israel and the Syrian Arab Republic to investigate allegations of ill- treatment and torture, 10-24 October 1974. London, [1975]. pp. 34.

— Rhodesia.

CATHOLIC COMMISSION FOR JUSTICE AND PEACE IN RHODESIA. The man in the middle: torture, resettlement and eviction. London, [1975]. pp. 22.

— Spain.

AMNESTY INTERNATIONAL. Report of an Amnesty International mission to Spain. London, 1975. pp. 24.

— **Syria.**

EIDE (ASBJORN) and others. Report of an Amnesty International mission to Israel and the Syrian Arab Republic to investigate allegations of ill- treatment and torture, 10-24 October 1974. London, [1975]. pp. 34.

TOUCOULEURS.

ROBINSON (DAVID) Ph. D. Chiefs and clerics: Abdul Bokar Kan and Futa oro, 1853-1891. Oxford, 1975. pp. 239. *bibliog.*

TOURE (SEKOU).

ADAMOLEKUN ('LADIPO) Sékou Touré's Guinea: an experiment in nation building. London, 1976. pp. 250. *bibliog.*

TOURISTS.

OPÉRATIONS du tourisme international et transports aériens; par J. David [and others]; colloque dans le cadre du Centre de Transports Aériens. Paris, 1975. pp. 164.

GEARING (CHARLES E.) and others. Planning for tourism development: quantitative approaches. New York, 1976. pp. 217. *bibliogs.*

MACCANNELL (DEAN) The tourist: a new theory of the leisure class. London, 1976. pp. 214.

— **Bibliography.**

COMMONWEALTH BUREAU OF AGRICULTURAL ECONOMICS. Tourism and the leisure industry: (international problems and prospects). rev. ed. [Farnham Royal, 1975]. pp. 56. *(Annotated Bibliographies. No. 32)*

— **Statistics.**

INTERNATIONAL INSTITUTE OF STATISTICS. International Statistics of Large Towns. Statistique du tourisme dans les grandes villes, 1929-1934. La Haye, 1938. pp. 89.

— **Africa, East.**

OUMA (JOSEPH P.B.M.) Evolution of tourism in East Africa, 1900-2000. Nairobi, 1970. pp. 138. *bibliog.*

— **Bahamas.**

BAHAMAS. Ministry of Tourism. Annual report of tourism; (formerly Visitor statistics). a., 1969 (2nd rep.), 1973- [Nassau].

— **Botswana.**

BOTSWANA. Central Statistics Office. Tourist statistics. a., 1974 (1st)- Gaborone.

— **Fiji Islands.**

FIJI. Bureau of Statistics. 1973. A statistical report on tourism in Fiji 1963-72, incorporating statistics on visitor and other arrivals, statistics on the hotel industry in Fiji. Suva, 1973. 1 vol. (various pagings).

TOURISM development programme for Fiji;...prepared by Belt, Collins and Associates, Ltd., [and others]. [Suva?], 1973. pp. 232. *bibliog.*

— **Gambia.**

ESH (TINA) and ROSENBLUM (ILLITH) Tourism in developing countries: trick or treat?: a report from the Gambia. Uppsala, 1975. pp. 76. *(Nordiska Afrikainstitutet. Research Reports. No. 31)*

— **Germany.**

BIENERT (FRANK) Zur Bestimmung der ökonomischen Auswirkungen des Fremdenverkehrs...: eine empirische Fallstudie, dargestellt am Beispiel der Stadt Westerland auf Sylt. Berlin, 1974. pp. 287. *bibliog. Inaugural-Dissertation zur Erlangung des Grades eines Doktors der Wirtschaftswissenschaften der Freien Universität Berlin.*

— **India.**

NATIONAL COUNCIL OF APPLIED ECONOMIC RESEARCH. Cost-benefit study of tourism. New Delhi, [1975]. pp. 91.

— — **Goa, Daman and Diu.**

GOA, DAMAN AND DIU. Bureau of Economics, Statistics and Evaluation. 1972. Report on the survey of potentialities of tourism in Goa. Panaji, [1972]. pp. 197.

— **Ireland (Republic).**

EIRE. Department of the Public Service. 1974. Restructuring the Department of Transport and Power: the separation of policy and execution. Dublin, 1974. pp. 78.

— **Italy.**

ITALY. Ente Nazionale Italiano per il Turismo. Centro di Documentazione. 1968. Indagine turistica alle frontiere 1966-1967. Rome, 1968. pp. 142. *(Collana di Monografie Turistiche. 20)*

BERTOLINO (ALBERTO) Saggi di economia del turismo; con un saggio introduttivo di A. Gay. Firenze, [1974]. pp. 248. *bibliog. (Centro di Studi Turistici [Florence]. Collana)*

— **Singapore.**

SINGAPORE. Tourist Promotion Board. Annual statistical report on visitor arrivals. a., 1969- Singapore.

— **Tanzania.**

REPORT ON TOURISM STATISTICS IN TANZANIA; (pd. by) Bureau of Statistics, Ministry of Economic Affairs and Development Planning. a., 1969. Dar es Salaam.

— **Underdeveloped areas.**

See UNDERDEVELOPED AREAS — Tourists.

— **United Kingdom.**

BRITISH HOME TOURISM SURVEY; (pd. by English Tourist Board). a., 1972 (1st)- London.

RILEY (STUART) Tourism and the community; a report for Cumberland County Council Community Development Project. [York, 1973]. pp. 14.

P.A. MANAGEMENT CONSULTANTS LTD. Economic Studies and Market Research Division. The development and marketing of tourism in north west England; main report; [by] H.F.R. Perrin [and others]. [London, English Tourist Board], 1974. fo. 73.

BRITISH TOURIST AUTHORITY. Survey among visitors to London, summer 1974. [London, 1975]. pp. 28.

INBUCON/AIC MANAGEMENT CONSULTANTS LIMITED. A study of tourism in the east midlands: a report commissioned by the English Tourist Board for the East Midlands Tourist Board. [London], English Tourist Board, [1976]. 2 pts.

TOURISM in the south west region: methodological report; by S. L. Edwards [and others]. [Bristol], South West Economic Planning Council, [1976]. pp. (74). *bibliog.*

— — **Scotland.**

BROWNRIGG (MARK) and GREIG (MICHAEL A.) The economic impact of tourist spending in Skye. [Inverness, Highlands and Islands Development Board], 1974. pp. 62. *(Special Reports. 13)*

SCOTTISH TOURIST BOARD. Research and Planning Division. Planning for tourism in Scotland: a preliminary national strategy; main report. Edinburgh, 1975. fo. 66.

TOWARZYSTWO DEMOKRATYCZNE POLSKIE.

RZADKOWSKA (HELENA) Działalność Centralizacji londyńskiej Towarzystwa Demokratycznego Polskiego, 1850-1862. Wrocław, 1971. pp. 163. *(Polska Akademia Nauk. Oddział w Krakowie. Komisja Nauk Historycznych. Prace. Nr.29)With Russian and English summaries.*

TRADE AND PROFESSIONAL ASSOCIATIONS

— **Canada.**

FORBES (ELIZABETH LAMONT) With enthusiasm and faith: history of the Canadian Federation of Business and Professional Women's Clubs...1930-1972. [Ottawa], 1974. pp. 170.

— **European Economic Community countries.**

WARNECKE (STEVEN JOSHUA) and SULEIMAN (EZRA N.) eds. Industrial policies in western Europe. New York, 1975. pp. 249.

— **France.**

FRANCE. Direction de la Documentation. La Documentation Française. Notes et Etudes Documentaires. Nos. 4,199-4, 200. Les chambres de métiers; (par les services de l'Assemblée permanente des chambres de métiers). Paris, 1975. pp. 59.

— **Germany.**

WAGNER (OSKAR) Pfarrer. Der Evangelische Handwerker-Verein von 1848 e.V., München, 1848 bis 1973: ein Beitrag zur Geschichte der evangelischen Gemeinde und der evangelischen Sozialarbeit in München. München, [1973]. pp. 91. *(Evangelischer Handwerker-Verein von 1848, and Bayerischer Handwerkstag. Kirche und Handwerk. Heft 2)*

— **Nicaragua.**

STRACHAN (HARRY W.) Family and other business groups in economic development: the case of Nicaragua. New York, 1976. pp. 129.

— **Sweden.**

FREDRIKSSON (BERT) and GUNNMO (ALF) Våra fackliga organisationer. [Stockholm, 1974]. pp. 208.

— **United Kingdom — Commonwealth.**

TETT (NORMAN) and CHADWICK (GERALD WILLIAM ST. JOHN) eds. Professional organizations in the Commonwealth. 2nd ed. London, 1976. pp. 584.

— **United States.**

HIMMELBERG (ROBERT F.) The origins of the National Recovery Administration: business, government and the trade association issue, 1921-1933. New York, 1976. pp. 232. *bibliog.*

TRADE REGULATION

— **Australia.**

NIEUWENHUYSEN (JOHN PETER) and NORMAN (NEVILLE R.) Australian competition and prices policy: trade practices, tariffs and prices justification. London, [1976]. pp. 173. *bibliog.*

— **United Kingdom.**

U.K. Office of Fair Trading. 1976. The work of the Office of Fair Trading. [London, 1976]. pp. 24.

— **United States.**

ECONOMIC regulatory policies; edited by James E. Anderson. Lexington, Mass., [1976]. pp. 211.

TRADE UNIONS.

BOLZE (WALDEMAR) Der Weg der Gewerkschaften. [Bremen, 1971]. pp. 181.

SEMINAR ON SOME SELECTED TRENDS IN TRADE UNIONISM, PORT DICKSON, 1973. Some selected trends in trade unionism; report of a...seminar... [sponsored by the Friedrich-Naumann-Stiftung and Deutsche Angestellten Gewerkschaft and held in cooperation with the International Federation of Commercial, Clerical and Technical Employees-affiliates of the region]. Kuala Lumpur, 1973. pp. 66. *(Friedrich Naumann-Stiftung and Deutsche Angestellten-Gewerkschaft. [Seminar] Reports. No. 3)*

TRADE UNIONS.(Cont.)

ELSNER (WOLFRAM) Die EWG: Herausforderung und Antwort der Gewerkschaften. Köln, [1974]. pp. 208. *bibliog.*

JACKSON (DUDLEY A.S.) and others. Do trade unions cause inflation?: two studies, with a theoretical introduction and policy conclusion. 2nd ed. Cambridge, 1975. pp. 126. *(Cambridge. University. Department of Applied Economics. Papers in Industrial Relations and Labour. 2)*

LIEBHABERG (BRUNO) Stratégies et tactiques syndicales face aux entreprises multinationales. Bruxelles, [1975]. fo. 162. *bibliog. Mémoire (ingénieur commercial)- Université Libre de Bruxelles.*

WORKER militancy and its consequences, 1965-75: new directions in Western industrial relations; edited by Solomon Barkin. New York, 1975. pp. 408.

— Africa.

The DEVELOPMENT of an African working class: studies in class formation and action: [based on a conference held at the University of Toronto in 1973, sponsored by the University's International Studies Programme]; edited by Richard Sandbrook and Robin Cohen. London, [1975]. pp. 330. *bibliog.*

— Africa, East.

GRILLO (R.D.) Race, class, and militancy: an African trade union, 1939-1965. New York, [1974]. pp. 151. *bibliog.*

— Argentine Republic.

ZORRILLA (RUBEN H.) Estructura y dinamica del sindicalismo argentino. Buenos Aires, [1974]. pp. 221.

— Australia.

MARTIN (ROSS MURDOCH) Trade unions in Australia. Ringwood, Victoria, 1975. pp. 150.

SHERIDAN (THOMAS) B.A., Ph.D. Mindful militants: the Amalgamated Engineering Union in Australia, 1920-1972. Cambridge, 1975. pp. 329. *bibliog.*

— Austria.

HEMALA (FRANZ) Geschichte der Gewerkschaften. 2nd ed. Wien, 1930. pp. 327.

BENYA (ANTON) Gewerkschaften in der Gesellschaft von heute. Wien, [1975]. pp. 86. *(Österreichischer Gewerkschaftsbund. Theorie und Praxis der Gewerkschaften. 6)*

HINDELS (JOSEF) Österreichs Gewerkschaften im Widerstand, 1934-1945. Wien, [1976]. pp. 435. *bibliog.*

KONRAD (HELMUT) Nationalismus und Internationalismus: die österreichische Arbeiterbewegung vor dem Ersten Weltkrieg. Wien, 1976. pp. 214. *bibliog. (Ludwig-Boltzmann-Institut für Geschichte der Arbeiterbewegung. Materialien zur Arbeiterbewegung. Nr.4)*

— Belgium.

LAAR (ALBERT VAN) Geschiedenis van de arbeidersbeweging te Antwerpen en omliggende. Antwerpen, 1926; Antwerpen, 1974. pp. 582. *bibliog. Facsimile reprint.*

DELVO (EDGARD) Sociale collaboratie: pleidooi voor een volksnationale sociale politiek. Antwerpen, [1975]. pp. 266.

EUROPEAN COURT OF HUMAN RIGHTS. Publications. Series A. Judgments and Decisions. [A 19]. ...National Union of Belgian Police case - 1. Decision of 12 April 1975. 2. Judgment of 27 October 1975. Strasbourg, Council of Europe, 1975. pp. 44 [bis]. *In English and French.*

— Bulgaria.

ISTORIIA na profsuiuznoto dvizhenie v Bulgariia. 2nd ed. Sofiia, 1973. pp. 803. *bibliog.*

— Canada.

FINLEY (JOSEPH E.) White collar union: the story of the OPEIU and its people. New York, 1975. pp. 275.

— Chile.

CHILE SOLIDARITY CAMPAIGN. Chile: trade unions and the coup. [London, 1973?]. pp. 12.

— Denmark.

NIELSEN (SIGURD) Fagforeninger indenfor dansk mejeribrug i tiden 1907-1924. [Horsens, imprint], 1973. pp. 172.

OLSEN (JØRGEN) and SCHOUBYE (BJARNE) eds. Reformpolitik eller revolution: kilder til belysning af brydninger i dansk arbejderbevaegelse, 1908-22. København, [1973]. pp. 101. *bibliog.*

KARLSSON (HENRY) ed. Dansk arbejderbevaegelse, 1871-1939. Copenhagen, [1975]. pp. 144. *bibliog. Selected documents.*

PEDERSEN (SØREN RISHØJ) ed. Fagbevaegelsen og socialpolitikken. København, 1976. pp. 88. *(Socialpolitisk Forening. Småskrifter. Nr. 46)*

— Europe.

ENGMAN (HANS) Sverige och Europa: om internationellt handelspolitik och fackligt samarbete. [Stockholm, 1973]. pp. 124.

CAREW (ANTHONY) Democracy and government in European trade unions. London, 1976. pp. 244.

— European Economic Community countries.

DOCUMENTATION EUROPEENNE: série syndicale et ouvrière; ([pd. by] Presse et Information, Communautés Européennes). irreg. Bruxelles. *Current issues only kept.*

— Finland.

HELENIUS (RALF) Akademikernas fackliga organisationsberedskap. Helsingfors, 1975. pp. 229. *bibliog. (Svenska Handelshögskolan. Ekonomi och Samhälle. Nr. 24)*

— France.

BOTHEREAU (ROBERT) Le "drame" confédéral. [Paris], 1947. pp. 14. *(Confédération Générale du Travail: Force Ouvrière. Documents Syndicalistes)*

DECLERCQ (GILBERT) Syndicaliste en liberté: entretiens avec A. Besson et J. Julliard. Paris, [1974]. pp. 188.

SCHNEIDER (DIETER MARC) Revolutionärer Syndikalismus und Bolschewismus: der Prozess der ideologischen Auseinandersetzung französischer Syndikalisten mit den Bolschewiki, 1914-1922. Erlangen, 1974. pp. 353. *bibliog.*

BERGOUNIOUX (ALAIN) Force ouvrière. Paris, [1975]. pp. 254. *bibliog.*

FRANCE. Direction de la Documentation. La Documentation Française. Notes et Etudes Documentaires. Nos. 4,197-4, 198. Le syndicalisme dans la fonction publique; [by] Yves Saint-Jours. Paris, 1975. pp. 65. *bibliog.*

FRANCE. French Embassy, London. Service de Presse et d'Information. 1975. An outline of French trade unionism. London, 1975. pp. 19. *bibliog. (France: facts, figures. A/108/5/75)*

MAIRE (EDMOND) and JULLIARD (JACQUES) La C[onfédération] F[rançaise] D[émocratique des] T[ravailleurs] d'aujourd'hui. Paris, [1975]. pp. 206. *bibliog.*

SÉGUY (GEORGES) Lutter: conversations avec Philippe Dominique. [Paris, 1975]. pp. 366.

MOSS (BERNARD H.) The origins of the French labor movement, 1830-1914: the socialism of skilled workers. Berkeley, Calif., [1976]. pp. 217. *bibliog.*

— Germany.

LIEBMANN (HERMANN) Die Politik der Generalkommission: ein Sündenregister der Zentralvorstände der freien Gewerkschaften Deutschlands und ein Wegweiser für die Zukunft. Leipzig, 1919. pp. 72.

VORWERCK (KARL) Die wirtschaftsfriedliche Arbeitnehmerbewegung Deutschlands, etc. Jena, 1926. pp. 150. *bibliog.*

SEIDEL (RICHARD) Gewerkschaften und politische Parteien in Deutschland. Berlin, [1928]. pp. 71.

HEMALA (FRANZ) Geschichte der Gewerkschaften. 2nd ed. Wien, 1930. pp. 327.

BOLZE (WALDEMAR) Der Weg der Gewerkschaften. [Bremen, 1971]. pp. 181.

CHRISTLICH-DEMOKRATISCHE UNION DEUTSCHLANDS. Wirtschaftsrat. Gewerkschaften in Zahlen: Daten und Fakten; Gewerkschaften in der Bundesrepublik Deutschland. [Bonn, 1973]. pp. 78. *(Schriften)*

INDUSTRIEGEWERKSCHAFT DRUCK UND PAPIER. Hauptvorstand. Rolle und Aufgaben der Gewerkschaften im letzten Viertel des zwanzigsten Jahrhunderts, etc. Stuttgart, [1974]. pp. 104.

BERGMANN (JOACHIM E.) and others. Gewerkschaften in der Bundesrepublik: gewerkschaftliche Lohnpolitik zwischen Mitgliederinteressen und ökonomischen Systemzwängen. Frankfurt, [1975]. pp. 439. *bibliog. (Frankfurt am Main. Universität. Institut für Sozialforschung. Studienreihe. Band 1)*

ETTELT (WERNER) and KRAUSE (HANS DIETER) Der Kampf um eine marxistische Gewerkschaftspolitik in der deutschen Arbeiterbewegung, 1868 bis 1878. Berlin, 1975. pp. 640.

KADRITZKE (ULF) Angestellte: die geduldigen Arbeiter; zur Soziologie und sozialen Bewegung der Angestellten. Frankfurt am Main, [1975]. pp. 411. *bibliog.*

LEMINSKY (GERHARD) and OTTO (BERND) eds. Gewerkschaften und Entwicklungspolitik. Köln, [1975]. pp. 496.

LIESEGANG (HELMUTH C.F.) ed. Gewerkschaften in der Bundesrepublik Deutschland: Dokumente, etc. Berlin, 1975. pp. 222. *bibliog.*

RAEHLMANN (IRENE) Der Interessenstreit zwischen dem Deutschen Gewerkschaftsbund und der Bundesvereinigung der Deutschen Arbeitgeberverbände um die Ausweitung der qualifizierten Mitbestimmung: eine ideologiekritische Untersuchung. Köln, 1975. pp. 254. *bibliog. (Stiftung Mitbestimmung, and Hans-Böckler-Gesellschaft. Schriftenreihe. 6)*

SCHNEIDER (MICHAEL) Das Arbeitsbeschaffungsprogramm des ADGB: zur gewerkschaftlichen Politik in der Endphase der Weimarer Republik; mit einer Einführung von George Garvy. Bonn-Bad Godesberg, [1975]. pp. 271. *bibliog. (Friedrich-Ebert-Stiftung. Forschungsinstitut. Schriftenreihe. Band 120) With English introduction.*

SCHNEIDER (MICHAEL) Unternehmer und Demokratie: die freien Gewerkschaften in der unternehmerischen Ideologie der Jahre 1918 bis 1933. Bonn-Bad Godesberg, [1975]. pp. 219. *bibliog. (Friedrich-Ebert-Stiftung. Forschungsinstitut. Schriftenreihe. Band 116)*

SCHROEDER (WOLFGANG) Partei und Gewerkschaften: die Gewerkschaftsbewegung in der Konzeption der revolutionären Sozialdemokratie, 1868/69 bis 1893. Berlin, 1975. pp. 488.

VETTER (HEINZ OSKAR) ed. Vom Sozialistengesetz zur Mitbestimmung: zum 100. Geburtstag von Hans Böckler. Köln, [1975]. pp. 546. *bibliog.*

Die INTERESSENVERTRETUNG der Arbeitnehmer im Betrieb; ([by] Adolf Brock [and others]). new ed. [Cologne], 1976. pp. 118. *bibliog.*

TRADE UNIONS.(Cont.)

— — **Bibliography.**

GUENTHER (KLAUS) and SCHMITZ (KURT THOMAS) compilers. SPD, KPD/DKP, DGB in den Westzonen und in der Bundesrepublik Deutschland, 1945-1973: eine Bibliographie. Bonn-Bad Godesberg, 1976. pp. 176. *(Archiv für Sozialgeschichte. Beihefte. 6)*

— **Germany, Eastern.**

BEDNARECK (HORST) and others, eds. Gewerkschaftlicher Neubeginn: Dokumente zur Gründung des F[reien] D[eutschen] G[ewerkschafts]B[undes] und zu seiner Entwicklung von Juni 1945 bis Februar 1946. [Westberlin, 1975]. pp. 284.

— **Ghana.**

BUESE (JUERGEN E.) Gewerkschaften im Prozess des sozialen Wandels in Entwicklungsländern: Versuch einer...Analyse der Rolle der Gewerkschaften in Ghana. Bonn-Bad Godesberg, [1974]. pp. 315. *bibliog. (Friedrich-Ebert-Stiftung. Forschungsinstitut. Schriftenreihe. Band 112)*

— **India.**

MASANI (MINOCHEHER RUSTOM) Indian trade unions and society: B.P. Wadia's vision and the reality. Bangalore, 1974. pp. 26. *(Indian Institute of World Culture. Transactions. No. 45)*

— **Israel.**

MEIR (ZIONA) Die Gewerkschaftsbewegung in Israel. Zürich, [1962]. pp. 32. *(Israel. Israel Office of Information, [Switzerland]. Schriftenreihe Israel. [9])*

— **Italy.**

BONZANINI (ANGELO) Il movimento sindacale in Italia: temi e momenti. Roma, 1974. pp. 228.

BARTOCCI (ENZO) ed. Sindacato, classe, società: scritti di E. Bartocci [and others]. Padova, 1975. pp. 405.

BUOZZI (BRUNO) Scritti e discorsi; a cura di E. Guglielmo Epifani. Roma, 1975. pp. 351.

FEDERAZIONE LAVORATORI METALMECCANICI. [Segreteria Provinciale di Bergamo]. Sindacato e piccola impresa: strategia del capitale e azione sindacale nel decentramento produttivo. Bari, [1975]. pp. 237.

PISTILLO (MICHELE) Giuseppe Di Vittorio, 1924-1944: la lotta contro il fascismo e per l'unità sindacale. Roma, 1975. pp. 479.

— **Kenya.**

LUBEMBE (CLEMENT ANDREW KALANI) The inside of labour movement in Kenya. Nairobi, 1968. pp. 240. *bibliog.*

— **Mexico.**

DOMITRA (MICHAEL) Die Rolle der Gewerkschaften im mexikanischen Herrschaftssystem: ein Beitrag zur Theorie der Gewerkschaften in Entwicklungsländern. Bonn-Bad Godesberg, [1975]. pp. 312. *bibliog. (Friedrich-Ebert-Stiftung. Forschungsinstitut. Schriftenreihe. Band 121)*

— **Netherlands.**

HARMSEN (GER) Historisch overzicht van socialisme en arbeidersbeweging in Nederland. [Nijmegen, c. 1973 in progress].

BERG (HARRY VAN DEN) and VEER (CEES VAN DER) Vormingswerk in de vakbeweging. [Nijmegen], 1973. pp. 113. *bibliog.*

HARMSEN (GER) and REINALDA (BOB) Voor de bevrijding van de arbeid: beknopte geschiedenis van de Nederlandse vakbeweging. Nijmegen, [1975]. pp. 461. *bibliog.*

HUYBREGTS (SJEF) and HUIGE (JOHN) De geschiedenis van de arbeidersbeweging. Odijk, [1975?]. pp. 110. *bibliog.*

— **Norway.**

COLBJØRNSEN (TOM) and NORDHAUG (ODD) Norsk fagbevegelse: en organisasjonssosiologisk studie. Bergen, 1975. fo. 218. *bibliog. (Bergen. Universitet. Sosiologisk Institutt. Sosiale Indikatorer. Rapporter. 15)*

— **Pakistan.**

MAHMUD (KHALID) Trade unionism in Pakistan. Lahore, 1958. pp. 148. *bibliog. (Panjab University [Pakistan]. Department of Political Science. Studies in Political Science, Public Administration and International Affairs. No. 4)*

— **Poland.**

NAUMIUK (JAN) Klasowy ruch zawodowy metalowców w Zagłębiu Staropolskim w latach 1918-1939. Łódź, 1975. pp. 171. *bibliog.*

RATYŃSKI (WŁADYSŁAW) Lewica Związkowa w II Rzeczypospolitej. Warszawa, 1976. pp. 330. *bibliog.*

— **Russia.**

KOMMUNISTICHESKAIA PARTIIA SOVETSKOGO SOIUZA. KPSS o profsoiuzakh, [1899-1974]. Moskva, 1974. pp. 503.

PROFSOIUZY Moskvy: ocherki istorii. Moskva, 1975. pp. 415.

REVOLIUTSIIA 1905-1907 godov v Rossii i profsoiuzy: k 70-letiiu pervoi russkoi burzhuazno-demokraticheskoi revoliutsii; sbornik statei. Moskva, 1975. pp. 160. *bibliog.*

KEMP-WELCH (ANTHONY) The origins and formative years of the Writers' Union of the U.S.S.R., 1932-1936. 1975 [or rather 1976]. fo. 167. *bibliog.* Typescript. Ph.D. (London) thesis: unpublished. *This thesis is the property of London University and may not be removed from the Library.*

— — **Finance.**

CHUVPILO (LIDIIA VASIL'EVNA) and others. Finansovaia rabota profsoiuzov. 2nd ed. Moskva, 1975. pp. 255.

— — **Handbooks, manuals, etc.**

SPRAVOCHNIK profsoiuznogo rabotnika. Moskva, 1974. pp. 495.

SPRAVOCHNIK profsoiuznogo rabotnika. Moskva, 1975. pp. 480.

— **Scandinavia.**

HELENIUS (RALF) Akademikernas fackliga organisationsberedskap. Helsingfors, 1975. pp. 229. *bibliog. (Svenska Handelshögskolan. Ekonomi och Samhälle. Nr. 24)*

— **Sierra Leone.**

SIERRA LEONE. Faulkner Commission of Inquiry into the Finance and Administration of the Transport and General Workers' Union. 1971. Report...and government statement thereon; [M.C. d'Alves Faulkner, commissioner]. [Freetown, 1971]. pp. 102.

— **South Africa.**

FEIT (EDWARD) Workers without weapons: the South African Congress of Trade Unions and the Organization of the African Workers. Hamden, Conn., 1975. pp. 230. *bibliog.*

NATTRASS (JILL) and DUNCAN (IAN G.) A study of employers' attitudes towards African worker representation. Durban, 1975. pp. 36. *(Natal University. Department of Economics. Black/White Income Gap Project. Interim Research Project. No.1)*

— **Spain.**

ARRESE (JOSE LUIS DE) La revolucion social del nacional-sindicalismo; ([and] El estado totalitario en el pensamiento de Jose Antonio). Madrid, 1959. pp. 210. *Reissue of two works previously published separately, the first in 1935, the second in 1955.*

IGLESIAS SELGAS (CARLOS) Los sindicatos en España. [Madrid], 1965. pp. 473. *bibliog.*

SPAIN: the workers' commissions: basic documents 1966-71; translated by Vicente Romano, Peter Turton and Gloria Montero; edited by David Fulton. Toronto, [1973]. pp. 95.

IGLESIAS SELGAS (CARLOS) El sindicalismo español. Madrid, 1974. pp. 394. *bibliog.*

AISA (JAVIER) and ARBELOA MURU (VICTOR MANUEL) Historia de la Union General de Trabajadores. Bilbao, 1975. pp. 285.

— **Sweden.**

JOHANNESSON (CONNY) De centrala avtalsförhandlingarna och den fackliga demokratin: studier över Svenska metallindustriarbetareförbundets förhandlingsorganisation vid förbundsförhandlingar, med samordning. Lund, 1975. pp. 437. *bibliog. Akademisk avhandling, Universitetet i Lund; with English summary.*

EUROPEAN COURT OF HUMAN RIGHTS. Publications. Series A: Judgments and Decisions. [A 20]. ...Swedish Engine Drivers' Union case; judgment of 6 February, 1976. Strasbourg, Council of Europe, 1976. pp. 18bis. *In English and French.*

— — **Law.**

EUROPEAN COURT OF HUMAN RIGHTS. Publications. Series A: Judgments and Decisions. [A 21]. ...Schmidt and Dahlström case; judgment of 6 February, 1976. Strasbourg, Council of Europe, 1976. pp. 18bis. *In English and French.*

— — **Political activity.**

WHEELER (CHRISTOPHER) White-collar power: changing patterns of interest group behavior in Sweden. Urbana, [1975]. pp. 210.

— **Switzerland.**

JAEGER (J.H.) Geschichte der schweizerischen Zimmererbewegung. 1. Band. Basel, 1914. pp. 310. *bibliog.*

MARTI (ERNST) 50 Jahre schweizerische Textil- und Fabrikarbeiter- Organisationen, 1903-1953. [Zürich, 1954]. pp. 275.

ARBEITSGRUPPE FÜR GESCHICHTE DER ARBEITERBEWEGUNG ZÜRICH. Schweizerische Arbeiterbewegung: Dokumente zu Lage, Organisation und Kämpfen der Arbeiter von der Frühindustrialisierung bis zur Gegenwart. Zürich, [1975]. pp. 411. *bibliog. (Studienbibliothek zur Geschichte der Arbeiterbewegung, Zürich. Schriftenreihe. Band 2)*

Die GEWERKSCHAFTEN in der Schweiz; ([by Fritz Leuthy and others]; herausgegeben vom Schweizerischen Gewerkschaftsbund. [Bern?, 1975]. pp. 169. *(Schweizerischer Gewerkschaftsbund. Schriftenreihe)*

— **Turkey.**

ASPECTS of modern Turkey; edited by William M. Hale. London, 1976. pp. 129. *bibliog. (Durham. University. Centre for Middle Eastern and Islamic Studies. [Publications. New Series]. 1) Papers of a conference held in April 1973 at the University of Durham, under the auspices of the University's Centre for Middle Eastern and Islamic Studies.*

— **Underdeveloped areas.**

See **UNDERDEVELOPED AREAS — Trade unions.**

— **United Kingdom.**

ASSOCIATION OF PATTERN MAKERS AND ALLIED CRAFTSMEN. Birkenhead Branch. [Minute book. 1885-91]. 1 vol. Manuscript.

EMPLOYERS' PARLIAMENTARY ASSOCIATION. [Correspondence with Sir R.A. Cooper. 1916]. 1 piece. Typescript.

TRADE UNIONS.(Cont.)

DURR (ANDY) ed. A history of Brighton Trades Council and Labour Movement, 1890-1970. Brighton, 1974. pp. 80. *(Brighton Hove and District Trades Council. History Sub-Committee. Pamphlets)*

BRANDT (GERHARD) Gewerkschaftliche Interessenvertretung und sozialer Wandel: eine soziologische Untersuchung...in der britischen Eisen- und Stahlindustrie, 1886-1917. Frankfurt, [1975]. pp. 467. *bibliog. (Frankfurt am Main. Universität. Institut für Sozialforschung. Studienreihe. Band 3)*

BURKE (BARRY) Rebels with a cause: the history of Hackney Trades Council, 1900-1975. London, [1975]. pp. 87. *bibliog.*

DOUGAN (DAVID) The shipwrights: the history of the Shipconstructors' and Shipwrights' Association, 1882-1963. Newcastle upon Tyne, 1975. pp. 341. *bibliog.*

EDELSTEIN (J. DAVID) and WARNER (MALCOLM) Comparative union democracy: organisation and opposition in British and American unions. London, 1975. pp. 378. *bibliog.*

KIRBY (RAY G.) and MUSSON (ALBERT EDWARD) The voice of the people: John Doherty, 1798-1854, trade unionist, radical and factory reformer. Manchester, [1975]. pp. 474.

MACINTYRE (STUART) Imperialism and the British labour movement in the 1920's: an examination of Marxist theory. London, 1975. pp. 24. *(Communist Party of Great Britain. History Group. Our History. No. 64)*

TOPHAM (ANTHONY) The organized worker. London, 1975. pp. 96. *(Society of Industrial Tutors. Trade Union Industrial Studies)*

ADVISORY CONCILIATION AND ARBITRATION SERVICE [U.K.]. Draft code of practice: time off for trade union duties and activities. [London, 1976]. pp. (13).

COCKBURN (CLAUD) Union power: the growth and challenge in perspective. London, 1976. pp. 206.

DERBYSHIRE (JOHN DENIS) The Royal Commission on Trade Unions and Employers' Associations, 1965-1968: an analysis of a royal commission as an instrument for public policy making. 1976. fo. 325. *bibliog.* Typescript. *Ph.D. (London) thesis: unpublished. This thesis is the property of London University and may not be removed from the Library.*

GOULD (Sir RONALD) Chalk up the memory: an autobiography. Birmingham, 1976. pp. 176.

GURNHAM (RICHARD) A history of the trade union movement in the hosiery and knitwear industry, 1776-1976: the history of the National Union of Hosiery and Knitwear Workers, its evolution and its predecessors. Leicester, 1976. pp. 197. *bibliog.*

MILLIGAN (STEPHEN) The new barons: union power in the 1970s. London, 1976. pp. 254.

NICHOLS (THEO) and ARMSTRONG (PETER) Workers divided. [London], 1976. pp. 221. *bibliog.*

PANITCH (LEO VICTOR) Social democracy and industrial militancy: the Labour Party, the trade unions and incomes policy, 1945-1974. Cambridge, 1976. pp. 318.

PELLING (HENRY MATHISON) A history of British trade unionism. 3rd ed. London, 1976. pp. 326. *bibliog.*

WRIGLEY (CHRIS) David Lloyd George and the British labour movement: peace and war. Hassocks, Sussex, 1976. pp. 298. *bibliog.*

— — Elections.

ABBOTT (STEPHEN) How to bring democracy and participation to the trade unions. London, [1976]. pp. 12.

— — Information services.

BIRMINGHAM COMMUNITY DEVELOPMENT PROJECT. Proposals for a trade union research unit in east Birmingham. [Birmingham], 1975. pp. (9).

— — Political activity.

CALHOUN (DANIEL FAIRCHILD) The united front: the TUC and the Russians, 1923-1928. Cambridge, 1976. pp. 450. *bibliog.*

— — Wales.

ARNOT (ROBERT PAGE) South Wales miners: Glowyr de Cymru: a history of the South Wales Miners' Federation, 1914-1926. Cardiff, 1975. pp. 356.

— United States.

KROUSE (RUTH) The attitude of the American Federation of Labor towards immigration. [1931]. pp. 75. *bibliog. M.A.(Columbia University) thesis: unpublished. Microfilm of typescripts: 1 reel.*

FINLEY (JOSEPH E.) The corrupt kingdom: the rise and fall of the United Mine Workers. New York, [1972]. pp. 315. *bibliog.*

ARONOWITZ (STANLEY) False promises: the shaping of American working class consciousness. New York, 1974. pp. 465. *bibliog.*

HALPERN (STEPHEN C.) Police-association and department leaders: the politics of co-optation. Lexington, Mass., [1974]. pp. 127.

CONFERENCE ON LABOR IN NONPROFIT INDUSTRY AND GOVERNMENT, PRINCETON UNIVERSITY, 1973. Labor in the public and nonprofit sectors: [papers of the conference, sponsored by the Industrial Relations Section of Princeton University and the Manpower Administration of the U.S. Department of Labor]; edited by Daniel S. Hamermesh. Princeton, [1975]. pp. 272. *bibliog.*

DOBBS (FARRELL) Teamster politics. New York, 1975. pp. 256.

EDELSTEIN (J. DAVID) and WARNER (MALCOLM) Comparative union democracy: organisation and opposition in British and American unions. London, 1975. pp. 378. *bibliog.*

FINLEY (JOSEPH E.) White collar union: the story of the OPEIU and its people. New York, 1975. pp. 275.

LARSON (SIMEON) Labor and foreign policy: Gompers, the A[merican] F[ederation of] L[abor], and the first World War, 1914-1918. Rutherford, N.J., [1975]. pp. 176. *bibliog.*

MARQUART (FRANK) An auto worker's journal: the UAW from crusade to one-party union. University Park, Pa., [1975]. pp. 162. *bibliog.*

ROOT AND BRANCH. Root and Branch: the rise of the workers' movements. Greenwich, Conn., 1975. pp. 544.

OSHINSKY (DAVID M.) Senator Joseph McCarthy and the American labor movement. Columbia, Mo., 1976. pp. 206. *bibliog.*

WYNN (DAVID ROBERT) Trade unions and the 'new' immigration: a study of the United Mine Workers of America, 1890-1920. 1976. fo. 452. *bibliog.* Typescript. *Ph.D. (London) thesis: unpublished. This thesis is the property of London University and may not be removed from the Library.*

— — Political activity.

CADDY (DOUGLAS) How they rig our elections: the coming dictatorship of big labor and the radicals. New Rochelle, [1975]. pp. 280.

FOSTER (JAMES CALDWELL) The union politic: the CIO Political Action Committee. Columbia, Miss., 1975. pp. 247. *bibliog.*

— — California.

LEVY (JACQUES E.) Cesar Chavez: autobiography of La Causa. New York, [1975]. pp. 546.

TAYLOR (RONALD B.) Chavez and the farm workers. Boston, [1975]. pp. 342. *bibliog.*

TRADE UNIONS, CATHOLIC

— France.

CONFEDERATION FRANÇAISE DES TRAVAILLEURS CHRETIENS. Comment fonder un syndicat?. Paris, [19--]. pp. 14.

— Italy.

GHEZA (FRANCO) Cattolici e sindacato: un esperienza di base; la FIM-CISL di Brescia. Roma, 1975. pp. 266.

TRADE UNIONS AND COMMUNISM.

BOLZE (WALDEMAR) Der Weg der Gewerkschaften. [Bremen, 1971]. pp. 181.

— Germany.

LEHNDORFF (STEFFEN) Wie kam es zur R[evolutionären]G[ewerkschafts]O[pposition] ?: Probleme der Gewerkschaftsentwicklung in der Weimarer Republik von 1927 bis 1929. Frankfurt am Main, 1975. pp. 159.

— United Kingdom.

HINTON (JAMES) and HYMAN (RICHARD) Trade unions and revolution: the industrial politics of the early British Communist Party. London, 1975. pp. 78.

CALHOUN (DANIEL FAIRCHILD) The united front: the TUC and the Russians, 1923-1928. Cambridge, 1976. pp. 450. *bibliog.*

TRADE UNIONS AND FOREIGN POLICY

— United States.

GERSHMAN (CARL) The foreign policy of American labor. Beverly Hills, [1975]. pp. 82. *bibliog. (Georgetown University. Center for Strategic and International Studies. Washington Papers. vol. 3/29)*

TRAFFIC ASSIGNMENT

— Mathematical models.

HOTT (SHARON KAY) Combining the trip distribution and traffic assignment stages in modelling a transportation system; [M. Phil. (London) thesis]. 1975. fo.124. *bibliog.* Typescript: *unpublished. This thesis is the property of London University and may not be removed from the Library.*

VAN VLIET (DIRCK) A road assignment model. London, [1975]. pp. 41. *bibliog. (London. Greater London Council. Research Memoranda. 450)*

INTERNATIONAL SYMPOSIUM ON TRAFFIC EQUILIBRIUM METHODS, MONTREAL, 1974. Traffic equilibrium methods: proceedings of the...Symposium held at the Université de Montreal, November 21-23, 1974; edited by M.A. Florian. Berlin, 1976. pp. 432. *bibliogs.*

TRAFFIC ENGINEERING

— Mathematical models.

INTERNATIONAL SYMPOSIUM ON TRAFFIC EQUILIBRIUM METHODS, MONTREAL, 1974. Traffic equilibrium methods: proceedings of the...Symposium held at the Université de Montreal, November 21-23, 1974; edited by M.A. Florian. Berlin, 1976. pp. 432. *bibliogs.*

TRAFFIC ESTIMATION

— Mathematical models.

STOPHER (PETER R.) and MEYBURG (ARNIM H.) Urban transportation modeling and planning. Lexington, Mass., [1975]. pp. 345.

TRAFFIC NOISE

— Bibliography.

GOMERSALL (ALAN) compiler. Traffic noise. London, 1975. pp. 19. *(London. Greater London Council. Research Library. [Research] Bibliographies. No. 69)*

TRAFFIC REGULATIONS

— Poland.

URBAN (MARIAN) Prawo transportu drogowego: komentarz. Warszawa, 1958. pp. 340.

— United Kingdom.

SUPPLEMENTARY licensing; [shortened report]; (prepared by a group of officers from the Greater London Council, the Department of the Environment, the Metropolitan Police and the London Boroughs Association). London, Greater London Council, [1974]. pp. 27.

TRAFFIC SURVEYS

— United Kingdom — London.

TALBOT (M.F.) Warehouse traffic generation study: pilot survey. London, [1974]. pp. 101. *(London. Greater London Council. Department of Planning and Transportation. Research Memoranda. 400)*

TRAMPS

— Australia.

AUSTRALIA. Working Party on Homeless Men and Women. 1973. Report...to the Minister for Social Security; [J. Wall, chairman]. Canberra, 1973 repr. 1974. pp. 39. *bibliog.*

— South Africa.

NATIONAL INSTITUTE FOR CRIME PREVENTION AND REHABILITATION OF OFFENDERS [SOUTH AFRICA]. "Vagrancy": a limited study of "vagrants" in the metropolitan area of Cape Town; (with Annexure: a legal fact paper on vagrancy and related offences). [Cape Town, 1974]. fo. 14, 11.

— United Kingdom.

GRAYSON (LESLEY) The single homeless. rev. ed. [London], Greater London Council, 1975. pp. 13. *bibliog.* *(London Topics. No. 2)*

TRANSFER PRICING.

NIECKELS (LARS) Transfer pricing in multinational firms: a heuristic programming approach and a case study. Stockholm, 1976. pp. 190. *bibliog.*

TRANSKEI.

CAMPION (HARVEY) The new Transkei. Sandton, 1976. pp. 158.

TRANSPORT WORKERS

— United Kingdom.

SMITH (JOHN W.) Labour supply and employment duration in London Transport. London, 1976. pp. 65. *(London. University. London School of Economics and Political Science. Greater London Group. Greater London Papers. No.15)*

— United States.

DOBBS (FARRELL) Teamster politics. New York, 1975. pp. 256.

TRANSPORTATION.

INTERNATIONAL FEDERATION FOR HOUSING AND PLANNING. Standing Committee on Traffic Problems. Urban pattern and transportation system: report for the Tokyo Congress of the IFHP/1966, based on reports...by P.H. Bendtsen [and others]; prepared by S. Dziewulski [and] B. Ledworowski. [Warsaw], 1966. 1 vol. (various pagings).

TRANSPORT ECONOMICS AND OPERATIONAL ANALYSIS; [pd. by] Bureau of Transport Economics, Canberra. irreg., Mr 1975 (no.1)- Canberra.

KNEAFSEY (JAMES T.) Transportation economic analysis. Lexington, Mass., [1975]. pp. 418. *bibliogs.*

SCHEPPACH (RAYMOND C.) and WOEHLCKE (L. CARL) Transportation productivity: measurement and policy applications. Lexington, Mass., [1975]. pp. 124.

U.K. Science Research Council. 1975. Advanced ground transport: a review of research possibilities. London, 1975. pp. 73.

MOHRING (HERBERT DICK) Transportation economics. Cambridge, Mass., [1976]. pp. 174. *bibliog.*

NASH (CHRISTOPHER A.) Public versus private transport. London, 1976. pp. 96. *bibliog.*

— Cost of operation.

TEICHMANOWA (EUFEMIA) Koszt transportu w handlu międzynarodowym: ze szczególnym uwzględnieniem handlu zagranicznego Polski. Warszawa, 1975. pp. 182. *bibliog. (Szkoła Główna Planowania i Statystyki. Monografie i Opracowania. 31)*

— Costs.

McINTOSH (P.T.) and QUARMBY (D.A.) Generalised costs, and the estimation of movement costs and benefits in transport planning. [London], 1970. fo. 38. *(U.K. Department of the Environment. Mathematical Advisory Unit. MAU Notes. 179)*

— Environmental aspects — Bibliography.

STANLEY (JOHN K.) compiler. Environmental effects and transport. Southampton, [1974]. fo. 5. *bibliog.* *(Southampton. University. Environmental Economics Study Group. Bibliography Series. No. 12)*

— — United Kingdom.

ROYAL AUTOMOBILE CLUB. Traffic and the environment and Urban transport planning; memoranda of evidence...to the Greater London Council and to the Expenditure Committee...House of Commons. London, [1973]. pp. 13.

— Mathematical models.

PIMENTEL (RUDERICO FERRAZ) Application of several different linear programming techniques to the generalized transportation problem. 1976. fo. 250. *bibliog.* Typescript. Ph.D. (London) thesis: unpublished. *This thesis is the property of London University and may not be removed from the Library.*

— Passenger traffic.

HEGGIE (IAN G.) ed. Modal choice and the value of travel time. Oxford, 1976. pp. 190.

— — Mathematical models.

DALY (ANDREW JOHN) and GALE (H.S.) Elasticity of demand for public transport. [Crowthorne, 1974]. pp. 37. *bibliog. (U.K. Transport and Road Research Laboratory. Supplementary Reports. 68 UC).*

— Research — United Kingdom.

U.K. Science Research Council. 1975. Advanced ground transport: a review of research possibilities. London, 1975. pp. 73.

— America, Latin.

TRANSPORTATION CONSULTANTS INC., and others. Central American transportation study, 1964-1965: report prepared for the Central American Bank for Economic Integration. [San Jose, Central American Bank for Economic Integration, 1965]. 2 vols.

— Australia.

AUSTRALIA. Commonwealth Bureau of Census and Statistics. Rail, bus and air transport. a., 1973/74 (1st)- Canberra. *Supersedes in part AUSTRALIA. Commonwealth Bureau of Census and Statistics. Transport and communications bulletin.*

TRANSPORT ECONOMICS AND OPERATIONAL ANALYSIS; [pd. by] Bureau of Transport Economics, Canberra. irreg., Mr 1975 (no.1)- Canberra.

— Brazil — Passenger traffic.

FOURACRE (P.R.) The development of public transport in Curitiba, Brazil. Crowthorne, 1975. pp. 17. *bibliog. (U.K. Transport and Road Research Laboratory. Supplementary Reports. 197 UC).*

— Communist countries.

ROL' transporta v integratsii ekonomiki stran-chlenov SEV. Moskva, 1973. pp. 221. *bibliog. (Institut Kompleksnykh Transportnykh Problem. Trudy. vyp.37)*

— Ecuador — Statistics.

ECUADOR. Instituto Nacional de Estadistica. Anuario de estadisticas de transporte. a., 1972/1973- Quito.

— France.

FRANCE. Département des Statistiques des Transports. Enquête annuelle d'entreprise: auxiliaries des transports terrestres. a., 1973- Paris.

FRANCE. French Embassy, London. Service de Presse et d'Information. 1973. Transport in France. London, [1973]. pp. 42.

— — Passenger traffic.

FRANCE. Département des Statistiques des Transports. Enquête annuelle d'entreprise: les transports urbains et routiers de voyageurs. a., 1973- Paris.

— — Statistics.

FRANCE. Département des Statistiques des Transports. 1974-75. Enquête sur la structure des entreprises de transport routier en 1972. Paris, 1974-75. 8 fascicules (in 1 vol).

— Germany.

MORSBACH (JOSEF) Das Bundesministerium für Verkehr. Bonn, [1971]. pp. 123. *bibliog.*

— — Finance.

DEUTSCHES INSTITUT FÜR WIRTSCHAFTSFORSCHUNG. Sonderhefte. [Neue Folge]. 109. Verkehrswege und Ersatzbedarf; ([by] Bernd Bartholmai). Berlin, 1975. pp. 125.

— Hong Kong — Statistics.

HONG KONG. Census, 1971. Population and housing census, 1971: transport characteristics. Hong Kong, [1974]. pp. 60.

— India — Jammu and Kashmir.

NATIONAL COUNCIL OF APPLIED ECONOMIC RESEARCH. Regional transport survey of Jammu and Kashmir. New Delhi. [1975]. pp.22.

— Ireland (Republic).

EIRE. Department of the Public Service. 1974. Restructuring the Department of Transport and Power: the separation of policy and execution. Dublin, 1974. pp. 78.

— Israel — Statistics.

ISRAEL. Central Bureau of Statistics. Special Series. No. 352. Transport in Israel: input and output and physical data, 1970. Jerusalem, 1971. pp. 82. *In Hebrew with English preface. Cover title reads: Transport in Israel: input and output - operational data, 1970.*

— Jamaica.

ROOKE (C.E.) Report on transport in Jamaica. [London, Colonial Office], 1946. pp. (120).

— Mexico — Statistics.

MEXICO. Direccion General de Estadistica. Censo de Transportes, 1971. VII censo de transportes, 1971; datos de 1970. Mexico, 1974 [or rather 1975]. pp. 453.

TRANSPORTATION.(Cont.)

— Mozambique — Statistics.

MOZAMBIQUE. Direcção Provincial dos Serviços de Estatística. Estatísticas dos transportes: statistiques des transports. a., 1971 (1st)- Louvenco Marques. *[in Portuguese and French].*

— Nigeria.

WALKER (GILBERT JAMES) Nigerian transport in 1950, being a study of transport in an under- developed tropical territory. [London], Colonial Office, 1955. pp. 343.

— Norway — Cost of operation.

SAGER (TORE) Kostnader og lønnsomhet i transport: oversiktsregnskaper for innenlands transportvirksomhet i 1963, 1967 og 1970. [Oslo], Transportøkonomisk Institutt, 1973. 2 parts. *With English summary.*

— Poland — Cost of operation.

TEICHMANOWA (EUFEMIA) Koszt transportu w handlu międzynarodowym: ze szczególnym uwzględnieniem handlu zagranicznego Polski. Warszawa, 1975. pp. 182. *bibliog. (Szkoła Główna Planowania i Statystyki. Monografie i Opracowania. 31)*

— Russia — Buryat Republic.

KHABALOV (SERGEI MIKHAILOVICH) and RADNAEV (BAIR LUBSANOVICH) O roli transporta v razvitii i razmeshchenii proizvoditel'nykh sil Buriatskoi ASSR. Ulan-Ude, 1973. pp. 55. *bibliog.*

— — Karakalpak Republic.

KAMALOV (T.K.) and UMAROV (E.K.) Nekotorye problemy razvitiia transporta v Karakalpakii. Nukus, 1970. pp. 131.

— — Soviet North.

PROBLEMY razvitiia transporta Severo-Vostoka SSSR. Novosibirsk, 1974. pp. 143.

— — Uzbekistan.

MANGEL'DIN (DAN'IAR ISKANDEROVICH) Novye rubezhi transporta i sviazi Uzbekistana. Tashkent, 1970. pp. 155.

— South Africa — Statistics.

SOUTH AFRICA. Bureau of Statistics. 1975. Census of transport and allied services, 1970. [Pretoria, 1975]. pp. 37. *(Bureau of Statistics. Reports. No. 22-01-01) In English and Afrikaans.*

— Switzerland.

KASPAR (CLAUDE A.) Die schweizerische Verkehrspolitik im Rückblick. Bern, [1976]. pp. 130. *bibliog. (Hochschule St. Gallen für Wirtschafts- und Sozialwissenschaften. Institut für Fremdenverkehr und Verkehrswirtschaft. St. Galler Beiträge zum Fremdenverkehr und zur Verkehrswirtschaft. Reihe Verkehrswirtschaft. 6)*

— Tropics — Bibliography.

U.K. Transport and Road Research Laboratory. 1975. Reports on roads and transport planning in tropical and sub- tropical countries: [bibliography]. Crowthorne, 1975. pp. 75. *(Supplementary Reports. 162 UC).*

— United Kingdom.

CUMBRIA COMMUNITY DEVELOPMENT PROJECT. Rural transport exhibition and open meeting, October 1974: a report. Cleator Moor, [1974]. pp. (36).

TRADES UNION CONGRESS. Transport Industries Committee. T.U.C. statements on transport. 2nd ed. London, [1975]. pp. 51.

DARTINGTON AMENITY RESEARCH TRUST. Public transport for countryside recreation; a report to the Countryside Commission. [London, Countryside Commission], 1976. pp. 52. *bibliog. (Publications. No. 21)*

HALL (PETER GEOFFREY) and SMITH (EDWARD) Civil engineer. Better use of rail ways. Reading, 1976. pp. 130. *bibliog. (Reading. University. Department of Geography. Reading Geographical Papers. No. 43)*

NASH (CHRISTOPHER A.) Public versus private transport. London, 1976. pp. 96. *bibliog.*

— — Laws and regulations.

BUTTON (K.J.) The 1968 Transport Act and after. Loughborough, 1974. pp. 22. *bibliog. (Loughborough University of Technology. Department of Economics. Loughborough Papers on Recent Developments in Economic Policy and Thought. No. 6)*

— — Passenger traffic.

U.K. Department of the Environment. 1975. Long distance travel from the Lancashire and Yorkshire conurbations; report on the first of the postal survey series. [London, 1975]. pp. 61.

— — Rates.

GLAISTER (STEPHEN) Aspects of optimum transport pricing: theoretical and empirical investigations. [1976]. fo. 122. *bibliog. Typescript. Ph.D.(London) thesis: unpublished. This thesis is the property of London University and may not be removed from the Library.*

— — Societies, etc.

PUGH (HILARY A.) compiler. United Kingdom transport organisations: a select list. [London], Department of the Environment, 1975. 1 pamphlet (unpaged).

— — Statistics.

TRANSPORT STATISTICS GREAT BRITAIN; (pd. by) Department of the Environment. a., 1964/74 (1st)- London. *Supersedes PASSENGER TRANSPORT IN GREAT BRITAIN, and U.K. Department of the Environment. Highway statistics.*

— — Scotland.

HIGHLANDS AND ISLANDS DEVELOPMENT BOARD. Highlands and islands transport review, 1975. [Inverness, 1975]. pp. 93. *(Occasional Bulletins. No. 6)*

— — Wales.

GLAMORGAN-GLYNCORRWG COMMUNITY DEVELOPMENT PROJECT. Mobility. [Port Talbot], 1973. fo. 20. *Photocopy.*

— United States.

KNEAFSEY (JAMES T.) Transportation economic analysis. Lexington, Mass., [1975]. pp. 418. *bibliogs.*

WATSON (JAMES WREFORD) and O'RIORDAN (TIMOTHY) eds. The American environment: perceptions and policies. London, [1976]. pp. 340. *bibliogs.*

— — Finance.

WHITTEN (HERBERT O.) Utilization and capacity costing and rate of return measurement: a report and proposal for a cost accounting and analysis system to be used by railroads and other forms of transport. Shaker Heights, [1960]. pp. 49.

— — Passenger traffic.

FARRIS (MARTIN T.) and HARDING (FORREST E.) Passenger transportation. Englewood Cliffs, [1976]. pp. 290. *bibliogs.*

TRANSPORTATION, AUTOMOTIVE

— Taxation — United Kingdom.

NATIONAL FREIGHT CORPORATION. Infrastructure costs and road user taxation; an annexe to the NFC's main response to the consultation document on transport policy. London, 1976. pp. 11.

— Europe — Freight.

MOORE (THOMAS GALE) Trucking regulation: lessons from Europe. Washington, 1976. pp. 148. *(American Enterprise Institute for Public Policy Research and Stanford University. Hoover Institution on War, Revolution and Peace. AEI-Hoover Policy Studies. 18)*

— France.

FRANCE. Département des Statistiques des Transports. Enquête annuelle d'entreprise: les transports urbains et routiers de voyageurs. a., 1973- Paris.

— — Freight.

FRANCE. Départment des Statistiques des Transports. Enquête annuelle d'entreprise: transports routiers de marchandises. a., 1973[ist]-Paris.

— Kenya — Cost of operation.

The KENYA road transport cost study: research on vehicle operating costs; by H. Hide [and others]. Crowthorne, 1975. pp. 105. *(U.K. Transport and Road Research Laboratory. Reports. LR 672)*

— Mauritius.

MAURITIUS. Ministry of Works. 1973. Development of roads and road traffic in Mauritius. Port Louis, 1973. pp. 21.

— Norway — Freight.

NORWAY. Statistiske Centralbyrå. Lastebiltransport: utvalgsundersøkelse: Road goods transport: sample survey. quinquennial., 1963- Oslo.

— United Kingdom — Freight.

STANDING CONFERENCE ON LONDON AND SOUTH EAST REGIONAL PLANNING. Lorry routing: report by the working group. London, 1975. pp. 12.

U.K. Department of the Environment. Statistics Transport B Division. 1975. The transport of goods by road in Great Britain, 1973. London, 1975. pp. 18.

— — Laws and regulations.

U.K. Road Freight Division. 1975. Foreign lorries in Great Britain: conditions of entry into Great Britain for vehicles used for the transport of goods by road. London, 1975. pp. 25.

— United States — Freight.

WYCKOFF (D.DARYL) Organizational formality and performance in the motor-carrier industry. Lexington, Mass., [1974]. pp. 125. *bibliog.*

WYCKOFF (D. DARYL) and MAISTER (DAVID H.) The owner-operator: independent trucker. Lexington, Mass., [1975]. pp. 166. *bibliog.*

TRANSPORTATION, PRIMITIVE.

MAIN (J.R.K.) Early transportation in Canada. Ottawa, Queen's Printer, 1969. pp. 7,7. *In English and French.*

TRANSPORTATION AND STATE

— Canada.

CONFERENCE ON CANADIAN NATIONAL TRANSPORT POLICY, YORK UNIVERSITY, TORONTO, 1972. Issues in Canadian transport policy: (papers and discussions from the Conference...); edited and with an introduction by K.W. Studnicki-Gizhert. Toronto, [1974]. pp. 476.

— European Economic Community countries.

SANTORO (FRANCESCO) La politica dei trasporti della Communità Economica Europea. [Turin, 1974?]. pp. 444.

COATES (IRENE) and HAIGH (NIGEL) Comon transport policy; [report prepared on behalf of the Conservation Society]. Chertsey, 1975. pp. 19.

— United Kingdom — Scotland.

SCOTTISH ASSOCIATION FOR PUBLIC TRANSPORT. Scotland's transport tomorrow: a programme 1975-2000; [prepared for Transport 2000]. [Glasgow, 1975]. pp. 12.

SCOTTISH ASSOCIATION FOR PUBLIC TRANSPORT. Memoranda. 75/1. Submission to the Lothian region: transport policies and programme. Glasgow, 1975. fo. 7.

SCOTTISH ASSOCIATION FOR PUBLIC TRANSPORT. Memoranda. 75/2. Submission to the Tayside amd Fife regions' transport policies and programmes. Glasgow, 1975. pp. 5.

— United States.

OWEN (WILFRED) Transportation for cities: the role of federal policy. Washington, D.C., [1976]. pp. 70.

TRANSPORTATION PLANNING

— United Kingdom.

WHITE (PETER R.) Planning for public transport. London, 1976. pp. 224. *bibliogs.*

— — Evaluation.

LASSIERE (A.) The environmental evaluation of transport plans. [London, 1976]. pp. 265. *bibliog.* (U.K. Department of the Environment. Research Reports. 8)

— United States.

HAMER (ANDREW MARSHALL) The selling of rail rapid transit: a critical look at urban transportation planning. Lexington, Mass., [1976]. pp. 336. *bibliog.*

TRANSVAAL

— Economic conditions.

SOUTH AFRICA. Department of Planning and the Environment. 1974. Proposals for a guide plan for the P[retoria] W[itwatersrand] V[ereeniging]. [Pretoria], 1974. pp. 86, 1 map.

TRANSYLVANIA

— Annexation to Romania.

CONSTANTINESCU (MIRON) and PASCU (ŞTEFAN) eds. Desăvîrşirea unificării statului naţional român: unirea Transilvaniei cu vechea Românie. Bucureşti, 1968. pp. 512. (*Academia Republicii Socialiste România. Secţia de Ştiinţe Istorice, Filozofice şi Economico-Juridice. Bibliotheca Historica Romaniae. Monographies. 5*)

TRAVANCORE

— Politics and government.

JEFFREY (ROBIN) The decline of Nayar dominance: society and politics in Travancore, 1847-1908. London, 1976. pp. 376. *bibliog.*

— Social history.

JEFFREY (ROBIN) The decline of Nayar dominance: society and politics in Travancore, 1847-1908. London, 1976. pp. 376. *bibliog.*

TRAVEL.

REASON (JAMES) Man in motion: the psychology of travel. London, [1974]. pp. 246.

TREASON

— Poland.

WOJCIECHOWSKA (JANINA) Zdrada ojczyzny w polskim prawie karnym na tle porównawczym. Wrocław, 1975. pp. 180. *bibliog. With Russian and German summaries.*

TREATIES.

BLIX (HANS) and EMERSON (JIRINA H.) eds. The treaty maker's handbook. Dobbs Ferry, N.Y., 1973. pp. 355.

COUNCIL OF EUROPE. 1975. The practical guide to the recognition and enforcement of foreign judicial decisions in civil and commercial law. Strasbourg, 1975. pp. 500.

TREATY—MAKING POWER

— Canada.

JACOMY-MILLETTE (ANNE MARIE) Treaty law in Canada; (translated from the French by Thomas V. Helwig). rev. ed. Ottawa, 1975. pp. 431. *bibliog.* (*Ottawa. Université. Faculté de Droit. Collection des Travaux. Monographies Juridiques. No. 8*)

— Germany.

SATTLER (MARTIN J.) Der deutsch-französische Zusammenarbeitsvertrag: eine Untersuchung zur Vertragsmacht des Bundes und der Länder. Meisenheim am Glan, 1976. pp. 156. *bibliog.*

TREES

— Russia — Uzbekistan.

AKHUNOV (KH.M.) Opredelitel' derev'ev i kustarnikov Chirchik-Akhangaranskogo basseina: metodicheskoe posobie; otvetstvennyi redaktor...I.I. Granitov. Tashkent, 1974. pp. 90.

TREITSCHKE (HEINRICH VON).

McCABE (JOSEPH) Treitschke and the Great War. London, 1914. pp. 287.

TREVIRANUS (GOTTFRIED REINHOLD).

TREVIRANUS (GOTTFRIED REINHOLD) Für Deutschland im Exil; [edited by Kurt Pentzlin]. Düsseldorf, 1973. pp. 215.

TRIALS

— Austria.

EUROPEAN COMMISSION OF HUMAN RIGHTS. 1965. The Plischke case:...[application No. 1446/62 by Oskar Plischke against Austria]. Strasbourg, Council of Europe, 1965. pp. 36.

EUROPEAN COMMISSION OF HUMAN RIGHTS. 1969. The Köplinger case: (Application No. 1850/63 by Rudolf Köplinger against Austria). Strasbourg, Council of Europe, 1969. pp. 215.

— Russia.

RECHI sovetskikh advokatov po ugolovnym delam. Moskva, 1975. pp. 214.

TRIALS (MURDER)

— Germany.

UKRAINIAN INFORMATION SERVICE. The Shelepin file: planned and executed murders of Ukrainian political leaders. London, 1975. pp. 64.

— United States.

HUNT (MORTON M.) The mugging; [first published in the United States in 1972]. Harmondsworth, 1975. pp. 413. *bibliog.*

TRIALS (POLITICAL CRIMES AND OFFENCES)

— Indonesia.

SOEKARNO (ACHMED) Indonesia accuses!: Soekarno's defence oration in the political trial of 1930; edited, translated, annotated and introduced by Roger K. Paget. Kuala Lumpur, 1975. pp. 153.

— Tunisia.

BOURGUIBA (HABIB) defendant. 9 avril 1938: le "procès" Bourguiba; texte intéegral des interrogatoires et dépositions; articles de presse et correspondance de Bourguiba. Tunis, 1967. 2 vols,(in 1).

— Venezuela.

PEREZ JIMENEZ (MARCOS) defendant. Proceso a un ex-dictador...: juicio al general (r) Marcos Perez Jimenez; [edited by] Jose Agustin Catala. Caracas, 1968-69 [or rather 1969]. 2 vols. (in 1).

TRIALS (ROBBERY)

— United Kingdom.

PAUL, JIMMY AND MUSTAFA SUPPORT COMMITTEE. 20 years. Birmingham, [1973]. pp. 63.

TRIALS (TREASON)

— Russia.

KUZNETSOV (EDUARD SAMUILOVICH) Dnevniki. Paris, 1973. pp. 374.

— South Africa.

ADAMS (FARIED) and others, defendants. Summary of the preparatory examination of the treason trial; issued by the Treason Trials Defence Fund Committee. Johannesburg, 1957. fo. 5. *Privately issued.*

TREASON TRIALS DEFENCE FUND. Press Summaries. Nos. 1-58. [A week-by-week resumé of the proceedings of the treason trial of Regina vs. Faried Adams and others in the Special Criminal Court, Pretoria, August 1958 to March 1961]. Johannesburg, 1958-61. 58 pts. (in 2 vols.).

SOUTH AFRICA. Supreme Court. Special Criminal Court, Pretoria. 1961. In the case of Regina vs. Farid Adams and others: judgement as read out to Court by the presiding judge, Mr. Justice F.L.H. Rumpff, on Wednesday 29th March, 1961. [Johannesburg?, 1961]. fo. 12.

SOUTH AFRICA. Supreme Court. Special Criminal Court, Pretoria. 1961. In the matter of the application of Farrid Adams and 29 others, and the Crown; reasons for judgment [Mr. Justice Bekker]. [Johannesburg?, 1961]. fo. 8.

SOUTH AFRICA. Supreme Court. Special Criminal Court, Pretoria. 1961. In the matter of the application of Farrid Adams and 29 others and the Crown: reasons for judgment [Mr. Justice Rumpff]. [Johannesburg?, 1961]. fo. 11.

— Yugoslavia.

MILATOVIĆ (MILE) Slučaj Andrije Hebranga. Beograd, 1952. pp. 267.

TRIBES AND TRIBAL SYSTEM

— South Africa.

JACKSON (A.O.) The ethnic composition of the Ciskei and Transkei. Pretoria, 1975. pp. 81, 7 maps. *bibliog.* (*South Africa. Department of Bantu Administration and Development. Ethnological Publications. No. 53*)

TRIER

— Social history.

LAUFNER (RICHARD) and RAUCH (ALBERT) Die Familie Marx und die Trierer Judenschaft. Trier, [1975]. pp. 40. (*Karl-Marx-Haus. Schriften. 14*)

TRIESTE

— Politics and government.

SUCCESSFUL negotiation: Trieste 1954; an appraisal by the five participants; edited by John C. Campbell. Princeton, [1976]. pp. 181.

TRINIDAD AND TOBAGO

— Appropriations and expenditures.

TRINIDAD AND TOBAGO. Central Statistical Office. 1974. An analysis of government revenue and expenditure, 1966-1971. Port of Spain, 1974. pp. 23.

TRINIDAD AND TOBAGO(Cont.)

— Economic policy.

CHERNICK (SIDNEY E.) and others. Employment in Trinidad and Tobago. [Washington], International Bank for Reconstruction and Development, 1973. 1 vol. (various pagings) *(Country Economic Reports)*

— Population.

HAREWOOD (JACK) The population of Trinidad and Tobago. n.p., 1975. pp. 237. *bibliog. (Committee for International Coordination of National Research in Demography. C.I.C.R.E.D. Series)*

— Social conditions — Statistics.

TRINIDAD AND TOBAGO. Central Statistical Office. 1975. Social indicators. [Port of Spain, 1975]. pp. 106.

— Statistics.

CHERNIK (SIDNEY E.) and others. Employment in Trinidad and Tobago. [Washington], International Bank for Reconstruction and Development, 1973. 1 vol. (various pagings) *(Country Economic Reports)*

TROTSKII (LEV DAVYDOVICH).

UCHENYE ZAPISKI KAFEDR OBSHCHESTVENNYKH NAUK VUZOV LENINGRADA. Istoriia KPSS. vyp.9. Istoriia KPSS. Leningrad, 1969. pp. 158.

ABOSCH (HEINZ) Trotzki und der Bolschewismus. Basel, [1975]. pp. 199.

HODGSON (GEOFF) Trotsky and fatalistic Marxism. Nottingham, 1975. pp. 88.

SERGE (VICTOR) pseud. [i.e. Viktor L'vovich KIBAL'CHICH] and SEDOVA (NATAL'IA IVANOVNA) The life and death of Leon Trotsky;...translated by Arnold J. Pomerans. London, 1975. pp. 296. *French title: Vie et mort de Leon Trotsky.*

MAVRAKIS (KOSTAS) On Trotskyism: problems of theory and history. London, 1976. pp. 248. *bibliog.*

TRUMAÍ INDIANS.

MURPHY (ROBERT FRANCIS) and QUAIN (BUELL) The Trumaí Indians of central Brazil. Seattle, 1955 repr. 1966. pp. 108. *bibliog. (American Ethnological Society. Monographs. 24)*

TRUMAN (HARRY S.) President of the United States.

THEOHARIS (ATHAN G.) Seeds of repression: Harry S.Truman and the origins of McCarthyism. Chicago, 1971. pp. 238.

TRUMBIC (ANTE).

TRUMBIĆ (ANTE) Suton Austro-Ugarske i Riječka rezolucija. Zagreb, 1936. pp. 112.

TRUST TERRITORIES.

McNEILL (JOHN HENDERSON) The strategic trust territory in international law. Ann Arbor, Mich., 1974 repr. 1976 fo. 500. *bibliog.*

— Oceania.

McHENRY (DONALD F.) Micronesia: trust betrayed: altruism vs. self interest in American foreign policy. New York, [1975]. pp. 260. *bibliog.*

TRUSTS, INDUSTRIAL.

ECONOMIST INTELLIGENCE UNIT. Q[uarterly] E[conomic] R[eview] Specials. No. 27. The potential for new commodity cartels: copying OPEC, or improved international agreements?; by Anthony Edwards. London, 1975. pp. 96.

WILLIAMSON (OLIVER E.) Markets and hierarchies: analysis and antitrust implications: a study in the economics of internal organization. New York, [1975]. pp. 286. *bibliog.*

U.K. Department of Trade. 1976. Survey of international cartels and internal cartels, 1944, 1946. [London, 1976]. 2 vols. (in 1).

— Canada — Law.

CANADA. Statutes, etc. 1952-68. Combines Investigation Act, R.S.C., 1952, c. 314, as amended by 1953-54, c. 51 etc.: (office consolidation). Ottawa, 1968. pp. 23.

— Germany — Bibliography.

GERMANY (BUNDESREPUBLIK). Deutscher Bundestag. Wissenschaftliche Dienste. 1975. Wettbewerb und Konzentration: zur Wettbewerbs- und Konzentrationspolitik in der Bundesrepublik Deutschland: Auswahlbibliographie mit Annotationen; [compiled by Bernhard Georg Scheibler]. Bonn, 1975. pp. 109. *(Bibliographien. 42)*

— — Law.

ROBERT (RUEDIGER) Konzentrationspolitik in der Bundesrepublik: das Beispiel der Entstehung des Gesetzes gegen Wettbewerbsbeschränkungen. Berlin, [1976]. pp. 404. *bibliog.*

— Italy.

BATTISTINI (ROBERTO DE) 10 grandi dell'economia italiana. Torino, 1975. pp. 95. *bibliog. (Fondazione Giovanni Agnelli. Progetto Politica Industriale. Quaderni di Ricerca. n.2)*

MONOTTI (CARLO) ed. I gruppi industriali in Italia. Torino, 1975. pp. 381.

— United Kingdom.

U.K. Department of Trade. 1976. Survey of international cartels and internal cartels, 1944, 1946. [London, 1976]. 2 vols. (in 1).

— United States.

MEDVIN (NORMAN) and others. The energy cartel: big oil vs. the public interest; prepared... by...[members of the firm] of Ruttenberg, Friedman, Kilgallon, Gutchess and Associates. Washington, 1975. pp. 439.

MICHIGAN UNIVERSITY. Michigan Business Studies. [New Series]. vol. 1 no. 2. Industrial market structure and performance, 1960-1968; [by] Daryl N. Winn. Ann Arbor, [1975]. pp. 226. *bibliog.*

SHEPHERD (WILLIAM G.) The treatment of market power: antitrust, regulation and public enterprise. New York, 1975. pp. 326. *bibliog.*

— — Law.

HIMMELBERG (ROBERT F.) The origins of the National Recovery Administration: business, government and the trade association issue, 1921-1933. New York, 1976. pp. 232. *bibliog.*

TRUTH.

WILSON (MARY MONICA) So truth be in the field. Johannesburg, 1975. pp. 26. *(South African Institute of Race Relations. Hoernlé Memorial Lectures. 1975)*

TSAFENDAS (DEMITRIOS).

SCHOEMAN (B.M.) Die sluipmoord op Dr. Verwoerd. Pretoria, 1975. pp. 148.

TUBMAN (WILLIAM VACANARAT SHADRACH).

WREH (TUAN) The love of liberty...: the rule of President William V.S. Tubman, 1944-1971. London, [1976]. pp. 138.

TULA (OBLAST')

— Statistics.

TULA (OBLAST'). Statisticheskoe Upravlenie. Narodnoe khoziaistvo Tul'skoi oblasti: statisticheskii sbornik. Tula, 1973. pp. 304.

TUNDRAS.

KHANTIMER (ISMAIL SYDDYKOVICH) Sel'skokhoziaistvennoe osvoenie tundry; Agricultural development of tundra regions. Leningrad, 1974. pp. 226. *bibliog. With brief English summary.*

TUNISIA

— Commercial policy.

BLAKE (ROBERT) Economist. Import controls and production in Tunisia during the 1960's. [Ann Arbor, 1975?]. pp. 41. *bibliog.*

— Foreign relations.

For related heading see EUROPEAN ECONOMIC COMMUNITY — Tunisia.

TURIN

— Economic history.

SAPELLI (GIULIO) Fascismo grande industria e sindacato: il caso di Torino, 1929/1935. Milano, 1975. pp. 260.

— Intellectual life.

ACCAME (SILVIO) Gaetano De Sanctis fra cultura e politica: esperienze di militanti cattolici a Torino, 1919-1929. Firenze, 1975. pp. 545.

TURKESTAN

— Politics and government.

RADZHABOV (ZARIF SHARIPOVICH) Turkestan na stranitsakh bol'shevistskikh gazet perioda pervoi russkoi revoliutsii, 1905-1907 gg.; otvet. redaktor G.E. Beliakov. Dushanbe, 1970. pp. 225.

TURKEY

— Economic policy.

ASFOUR (EDMOND YOUSSEF) and others. Turkey: prospects and problems of an expanding economy; this report was prepared by the economic mission which visited Turkey during...1973, etc. Washington, International Bank for Reconstruction and Development, 1975. pp. 475. *(Country Economic Reports)*

ASPECTS of modern Turkey; edited by William M. Hale. London, 1976. pp. 129. *bibliog. (Durham. University. Centre for Middle Eastern and Islamic Studies. [Publications. New Series]. 1) Papers of a conference held in April 1973 at the University of Durham, under the auspices of the University's Centre for Middle Eastern and Islamic Studies.*

— Emigration and immigration.

ABADAN-UNAT (NERMIN) ed. Turkish workers in Europe, 1960-1975: a socio-economic reappraisal. Leiden, 1976. pp. 424. *bibliog.*

— Foreign relations.

KARPAT (KEMAL H.) and others. Turkey's foreign policy in transition, 1950-1974. Leiden, 1975. pp. 233. *bibliog.*

TURKISH FOREIGN POLICY REPORT; pd. by Policy Research Department, Directorate-General of Policy Research and Planning, [Turkey]. m., F 1976 (no.11)- Ankara.

See also EUROPEAN ECONOMIC COMMUNITY — Turkey.

— — Austria.

BAYERLE (GUSTAV) Ottoman diplomacy in Hungary: letters from the Pashas of Buda, 1590-1593. Bloominton Ind., [1972]. pp. 204. *bibliog. (Indiana University. Graduate School. Publications. Uralic and Altaic Series. vol. 101.)*

— — **United Kingdom.**

HELLER (JOSEPH) Ph.D. British policy towards the Ottoman Empire, 1908-1914. 1970 [or rather 1971]. fo.510. *bibliog. Typescript. Ph.D. (London) thesis: unpublished. This thesis is the property of London University and may not be removed from the Library.*

— **History — 1453—1683.**

KORTEPETER (CARL MAX) Ottoman imperialism during the Reformation: Europe and the Caucasus. New York, 1972. pp. 278. *bibliog. (New York (City). University. Studies in Near Eastern Civilization. No. 5)*

— **Politics and government.**

ONULDURAN (ERSIN) Political development and political parties in Turkey. Ankara, 1974. pp. 116. *bibliog. (Ankara. Üniversitesi. Siyasal Bilgiler Fakültesi. Yayinlari. No. 370)*

ASPECTS of modern Turkey; edited by William M. Hale. London, 1976. pp. 129. *bibliog. (Durham. University. Centre for Middle Eastern and Islamic Studies. [Publications. New Series]. 1) Papers of a conference held in April 1973 at the University of Durham, under the auspices of the University's Centre for Middle Eastern and Islamic Studies.*

— **Rural conditions.**

ASPECTS of modern Turkey; edited by William M. Hale. London, 1976. pp. 129. *bibliog. (Durham. University. Centre for Middle Eastern and Islamic Studies. [Publications. New Series]. 1) Papers of a conference held in April 1973 at the University of Durham, under the auspices of the University's Centre for Middle Eastern and Islamic Studies.*

— **Social policy.**

ASFOUR (EDMOND YOUSSEF) and others. Turkey: prospects and problems of an expanding economy; this report was prepared by the economic mission which visited Turkey during...1973, etc. Washington, International Bank for Reconstruction and Development, 1975. pp. 475. *(Country Economic Reports)*

— **Statistics, Vital.**

CERIT (SEVIL) Factors affecting the level and trend of infant mortality in Turkey since World War II; [Ph. D. (London) thesis]. 1975. fo. 188. *bibliog. Typescript: unpublished. This thesis is the property of London University and may not be removed from the Library.*

TURKMENISTAN

— **History — 1917-1921, Revolution.**

ESENOV (RAKHIM MAKHTUMOVICH) Bol'shevistskoe podpol'e Zakaspiia. Moskva, 1974. pp. 215. *bibliog.*

— **Industries.**

GEL'DYEV (BIASHIM) and others. Razvitie promyshlennosti Turkmenistana za 50 let. Ashkhabad, 1974. pp. 126.

TURKMENS IN IRAN.

ATAEV (KHOMMAT ATAEVICH) Osvoboditel'noe dvizhenie turkmen v Irane, 1917-1925 gg.; otvetstvennyi redaktor P.P. Bushev. Ashkhabad, 1970. pp. 127.

TURKS IN EUROPE.

ABADAN-UNAT (NERMIN) ed. Turkish workers in Europe, 1960-1975: a socio-economic reappraisal. Leiden, 1976. pp. 424. *bibliog.*

TURNOVER (BUSINESS)

— **Netherlands.**

ECONOMISCH INSTITUUT VOOR HET MIDDEN- EN KLEINBEDRIJF. Bedrijfseconomische Publikaties. De omzetten per M2 bedrijfsruimte resp. verkoopruimte in een aantal branches van het midden- en kleinbedrijf in 1968. 's-Gravenhage, 1969. pp. 8.

TURNOVER TAX

— **Finland.**

FINLAND. Tilastokeskus. Lopetettujen liikevaihtoverovelvollisten yritysten ennakkotiedot...: Förhandsuppgifter om omsättningsskatteskyldiga företag vilkas verksamhet... a., 1972/73- Helsinki.

TUVA

— **Constitution.**

KHOROSHII (NIKOLAI NIKOLAEVICH) Sotsialisticheskaia gosudarstvennost' tuvinskogo naroda. Kyzyl, 1974. pp. 138.

TUVERI (GIOVANNI BATTISTA).

CONTU (GIANFRANCO) G.B. Tuveri: vita e opere. Cagliari, [1973]. pp. 203. *bibliog.*

TWENTIETH CENTURY

— **Forecasts.**

ASHBY (ERIC) Baron Ashby. A second look at doom. Southampton, 1975. pp. 18. *(Southampton. University. Fawley Foundation. Lectures. 21*

HILSMAN (ROGER) The crouching future: international politics and U.S. foreign policy; a forecast. Garden City, N.Y. 1975. pp. 666.

TWENTY—FIRST CENTURY

— **Forecasts.**

HILSMAN (ROGER) The crouching future: international politics and U.S. foreign policy; a forecast. Garden City, N.Y. 1975. pp. 666.

STONIER (TOM TED) The natural history of humanity: past, present and future. [Bradford, 1976]. pp. 48.

TYNDALE JUNIOR AND INFANTS SCHOOLS.

See WILLIAM TYNDALE JUNIOR AND INFANTS SCHOOLS.

TYNEMOUTH

— **Social conditions.**

NORTH TYNESIDE COMMUNITY DEVELOPMENT PROJECT. Community profile. [North Shields], 1973. pp. 34.

TYPEWRITER INDUSTRY

— **United Kingdom.**

TRANSPORT AND GENERAL WORKERS' UNION. Why Imperial Typewriters must not close: the case for government aid to maintain production, and/or to establish a cooperative to assume ownership and management of the plant; a preliminary statement. Nottingham, [1975]. pp. 16. *(Institute for Workers' Control. Pamphlet Series. No. 46)*

TYPHOID FEVER

— **India — Bombay.**

BOMBAY (STATE). Typhoid Enquiry Committee. 1953. Report. Bombay, 1953. pp. 15.

TYRES

— **United Kingdom.**

ECONOMIST INTELLIGENCE UNIT. Q[uarterly] E[conomic] R[eview] Specials. No. 26. Rubber and the automotive industry in the UK and North America. London, 1976. pp. 54.

— **United States.**

ECONOMIST INTELLIGENCE UNIT. Q[uarterly] E[conomic] R[eview] Specials. No. 26. Rubber and the automotive industry in the UK and North America. London, 1976. pp. 54.

UDMURT REPUBLIC

— **Industries.**

BELOSLUDTSEVA (ELIZAVETA IVANOVNA) Nauchno-tekhnicheskii progress i sovershenstvovanie promyshlennogo kompleksa Udmurtii. Izhevsk, 1974. pp. 151.

UGANDA

— **Armed forces — Political activity.**

MAZRUI (ALI A.) Soldiers and kinsmen in Uganda: the making of a military ethnocracy. Beverly Hills, [1975]. pp. 325. *bibliog.*

— **Economic history.**

VAN ZWANENBERG (R.M.A.) and KING (ANNE) An economic history of Kenya and Uganda, 1800-1970. London, 1975. pp. 326. *bibliog.*

— **Economic policy.**

UGANDA. 1966. Work for progress: the second five-year plan 1966-1971. [Entebbe, 1966]. pp. 182.

AMIN DADA (IDI) Second anniversary presidential address, (January 25, 1973). Kampala, Ministry of Information and Broadcasting, [1973]. pp. 33.

— **Politics and government.**

UGANDA. 1972. Achievements of the government of Uganda during the first year of the Second Republic. [Entebbe, 1972]. pp. 102.

AMIN DADA (IDI) Second anniversary presidential address, (January 25, 1973). Kampala, Ministry of Information and Broadcasting, [1973]. pp. 33.

STRATE (JEFFREY T.) Post-military coup strategy in Uganda: Amin's early attempts to consolidate political support. Athens, Oh., 1973. pp. 58. *(Ohio University. Center for International Studies. Papers in International Studies. Africa Series. No. 18)*

MAZRUI (ALI A.) Soldiers and kinsmen in Uganda: the making of a military ethnocracy. Beverly Hills, [1975]. pp. 325. *bibliog.*

MITTELMAN (JAMES H.) Ideology and politics in Uganda: from Obote to Amin. Ithaca, 1975. pp. 302. *bibliog.*

KASFIR (NELSON) The shrinking political arena: participation and ethnicity in African politics, with a case study of Uganda. Berkeley, Calif., [1976]. pp. 323. *bibliog.*

MAMDANI (MAHMOOD) Politics and class formation in Uganda. New York, [1976]. pp. 339. *bibliog.*

— **Population.**

OMINDE (SIMEON HONGO) The population of Kenya-Uganda-Tanzania. [Nairobi?], 1975. pp. 124. *(Committee for International Coordination of National Research in Demography. C.I.C.R.E.D. Series)*

— **Social policy.**

UGANDA. 1966. Work for progress: the second five-year plan 1966-1971. [Entebbe, 1966]. pp. 182.

UGANDAN ASIANS.

See EAST INDIANS IN THE UNITED KINGDOM, [UGANDA, etc.].

UKRAINE

— **Bibliography.**

AKADEMIIA NAUK UKRAÏNS'KOÏ RSR. Tsentral'na Naukova Biblioteka. Vydannia Akademiï nauk URSR, 1919-1967 - suspil'ni nauky: bibliohrafichnyi pokazhchyk. Kyïv, 1969. pp. 650.

UKRAINE(Cont.)

— Constitutional history.

HAMRETS'KYI (IURII MARKOVYCH) and others. Rady Ukraïny v 1917 r.: lypen' - hruden', 1917 r. Kyïv, 1974. pp. 343.

— Description and travel.

AVROSHKO (AL'BERG IAKOVLEVICH) Chetyre puteshestviia po industrial'nomu Prikarpat'iu: Borislav, Stebnik, Novyi Rozdol, Novoiavorovskoe; Chotyry podorozhi po industrial'nomu Prykarpattiu, etc. L'viv, 1974. pp. 67. *In Russian and Ukrainian.*

— Economic conditions.

REZERVY rosta proizvoditel'nosti truda v narodnom khoziaistve Ukrainskoi SSR. Kiev, 1975. pp. 200.

— — Dictionaries and encyclopaedias.

ENTSYKLOPEDIIA narodnoho hospodarstva Ukraïns'koï RSR. Kyïv, 1969-72. 4 vols.

— Economic history.

EKONOMIKA Sovetskoi Ukrainy, 1945-1975 gg. Kiev, 1975. pp. 407.

— — Sources.

SYDORENKO (VALENTYNA PAVLIVNA) Presa iak dzherelo z istoriï robitnychoho klasu Ukraïny v period sotsialistychnoho budivnytstva, 1921-1941 rr. Kyïv, 1975. pp. 107.

— Economic policy.

McMASTER CONFERENCE ON CONTEMPORARY UKRAINE, HAMILTON, ONTARIO, 1974. Ukraine in the seventies;...papers and proceedings of the... Conference...; (edited by Peter J. Potichnyj). Oakville, Ont., [1975]. pp. 355.

— Foreign relations.

ZABIHAILO (KOSTIANTYN SEMENOVYCH) ed. V interesakh myru i druzhby mizh narodamy: mizhnarodnopravova diial'nist' Ukraïns'koï RSR, 1945-1972; dokumenty i komentari. Kyïv, 1974. pp. 335. *bibliog.*

See also UNITED NATIONS — Russia — Ukraine.

— — Czechoslovakia.

HODNETT (GREY) and POTICHNYJ (PETER J.) The Ukraine and the Czechoslovak crisis. Canberra, 1970. pp. 154. *(Australian National University. Research School of Social Sciences. Department of Political Science. Occasional Papers. No. 6)*

— Historiography.

KOMARENKO (NAÏNA VASYLIVNA) Ustanovy istorychnoï nauky v Ukraïns'kii RSR, 1917-1937 rr. Kyïv, 1973. pp. 171. *With Russian summary.*

— History — 1917-1921, Revolution.

HRYTSENKO (ADELINA PAVLIVNA) Robitnychyi klas Ukraïny u Zhovtnevii revoliutsiï, berezen' 1917 - sichen' 1918 rr. Kyïv, 1975. pp. 239.

— Industries.

AVROSHKO (AL'BERG IAKOVLEVICH) Chetyre puteshestviia po industrial'nomu Prikarpat'iu: Borislav, Stebnik, Novyi Rozdol, Novoiavorovskoe; Chotyry podorozhi po industrial'nomu Prykarpattiu, etc. L'viv, 1974. pp. 67. *In Russian and Ukrainian.*

DEREV"IANKIN (TYMOFII IVANOVYCH) Promyslovyi perevorot na Ukraïni: pytannia teoriï ta istoriï. Kyïv, 1975. pp. 279. *bibliog.*

KUL'CHYTS'KYI (STANYSLAV VLADYSLAVOVYCH) Uchast' robitnykiv Ukraïny u stvorenni fondu sotsialistychnoï industrializatsiï. Kyïv, 1975. pp. 175.

— Intellectual life.

UKRAÏNS'KA inteligentsiia pid sudom KGB: materiialy z protsesiv V. Chornovola, M. Masiutka, M. Ozernoho ta in.; Ukrainian intellectuals tried by the KGB. [Miunkhen], 1970. pp. 243.

— Nationalism.

UKRAINIAN CONGRESS COMMITTEE OF AMERICA. Ukrainian resistance: the story of the Ukrainian national liberation movement in modern times. New York, 1949. pp. 143. *bibliog.*

HAMOL'S'KYI (LEONID VOLODYMYROVYCH) Tryzub i "zirka" Davyda. Dnipropetrovs'k, 1975. pp. 191.

MALET (MICHAEL IAN GRENVILLE) Nestor Makchno [sic] in the Russian civil war 1917-21. 1975. fo. 326. *bibliog. Typescript. Ph.D.(London) thesis: unpublished. This thesis is the property of London University and may not be removed from the library.*

MOROZ (VALENTYN IAKOVYCH) Eseï, lysty i dokumenty; essays, letters and documents. Miunkhen, 1975. pp. 288. *bibliog.*

— Politics and government.

VOLOSHCHENKO (AZA KYRYLIVNA) Narysy z istoriï suspil'no-politychnoho rukhu na Ukraïni v 70-kh - na pochatku 80-kh rokiv XIX st. Kyïv, 1974. pp. 222.

McMASTER CONFERENCE ON CONTEMPORARY UKRAINE, HAMILTON, ONTARIO, 1974. Ukraine in the seventies;...papers and proceedings of the... Conference...; (edited by Peter J. Potichnyj). Oakville, Ont., [1975]. pp. 355.

— Population.

McMASTER CONFERENCE ON CONTEMPORARY UKRAINE, HAMILTON, ONTARIO, 1974. Ukraine in the seventies;...papers and proceedings of the... Conference...; (edited by Peter J. Potichnyj). Oakville, Ont., [1975]. pp. 355.

NAULKO (VSEVOLOD IVANOVICH) Razvitie mezhetnicheskikh sviazei na Ukraine: istoriko-etnograficheskii ocherk. Kiev, 1975. pp. 276.

— Social policy.

McMASTER CONFERENCE ON CONTEMPORARY UKRAINE, HAMILTON, ONTARIO, 1974. Ukraine in the seventies;...papers and proceedings of the... Conference...; (edited by Peter J. Potichnyj). Oakville, Ont., [1975]. pp. 355.

UKRAINE, WESTERN

— Annexation to Russia.

RUDNYTS'KA (MILENA) ed. Zakhidnia Ukraïna pid bol'shevykamy, IX.1939 - VI.1941: zbirnyk; Western Ukraine under the Bolsheviks, IX.1939 - VI.1941. N'iu-Iork, 1958. pp. 494.

— Intellectual life.

KOSHARNYI (IVAN IAKOVLEVYCH) U suzir"ï sotsialistychnoï kul'tury: kul'turne budivnytstvo u vozz"iednanykh oblastiakh Ukraïns'koï RSR, 1939-1958 rr. L'viv, 1975. pp. 239.

— Nationalism.

PRAVDU ne zdolaty: trudiashchi zakhidnykh oblastei URSR v borot'bi proty ukraïns'kykh burzhuaznykh natsionalistiv u roky sotsialistychnykh peretvoren'. L'viv, 1974. pp. 278.

— Politics and government.

V.I. Lenin i revoliutsiinyi rukh na zakhidnoukraïns'kykh zemliakh. L'viv, 1969. pp. 167.

— Population.

KOPCHAK (STEPAN IVANOVYCH) Naselennia Ukraïns'koho Prykarpattia: istoryko- demohrafichnyi narys: dokapitalistychnyi period. L'viv, 1974. pp. 186. *bibliog.*

UKRAINIAN STUDIES.

McMASTER CONFERENCE ON CONTEMPORARY UKRAINE, HAMILTON, ONTARIO, 1974. Ukraine in the seventies;...papers and proceedings of the... Conference...; (edited by Peter J. Potichnyj). Oakville, Ont., [1975]. pp. 355.

UKRAINIANS IN THE UNITED KINGDOM.

ASSOCIATION OF UKRAINIAN FORMER COMBATANTS IN GREAT BRITAIN. Al'manakh ObVU, 1949-1964: [iuvileine vydannia]. London, [1967]. pp. 152.

ULAD STUT (ARAB TRIBE).

SEDDON (JOHN DAVID) Modern economic and political change in northeast Morocco. 1975 [or rather 1976]. fo. 433. *bibliog. Typescript. Ph.D. (London) thesis: unpublished. This thesis is the property of London University and may not be removed from the Library.*

ULC (OTTO).

ULČ (OTTO) Malá doznání okresního soudce. Toronto, 1974. pp. 321.

ULSTER UNIONIST PARTY.

GIBBON (PETER) The origins of Ulster Unionism: the formation of popular Protestant politics and ideology in nineteenth-century Ireland. Manchester, [1975]. pp. 163. *bibliog.*

UMBRIA

— Social conditions.

CRESPI (FRANCO) and others. Il lavoro a domicilio: il caso dell'Umbria. Bari, [1975]. pp. 158.

UNABHAENGIGE SOZIALDEMOKRATISCHE PARTEI DEUTSCHLANDS.

KRAUSE (HARTFRID) USPD: zur Geschichte der Unabhängigen Sozialdemokratischen Partei Deutschlands. Frankfurt am Main, [1975]. pp. 397. *bibliog.*

MORGAN (DAVID W.) The socialist Left and the German revolution: a history of the German Independent Social Democratic Party, 1917-1922. Ithaca, [1975]. pp. 499. *bibliog.*

WHEELER (ROBERT F.) USPD und Internationale: sozialistischer Internationalismus in der Zeit der Revolution; (Übersetzung aus dem Amerikanischen von Agnes Blänsdorf). Frankfurt/M, [1975]. pp. 384. *bibliog.*

UNABHÄNGIGE SOZIALDEMOKRATISCHE PARTEI DEUTSCHLANDS.

See UNABHAENGIGE SOZIALDEMOKRATISCHE PARTEI DEUTSCHLANDS.

UNDERDEVELOPED AREAS.

KLEER (JERZY) Zapoczątkowanie rozwoju ekonomicznego we współczesnych krajach słabo rozwiniętych. Warszawa, 1962. pp. 218. *bibliog. With English and Russian summaries.*

NIEKTÓRE aspekty rozwoju krajów słabo rozwiniętych gospodarczo. Warszawa, 1966. pp. 275.

DEVELOPMENT FORUM; pd. by the U.N. Centre for Economic and Social Information. m., F 1973 (v.1, no.1)- Geneva.

ACTION-oriented approaches to regional development planning; edited by Avrom Bendavid-Val [and] Peter P. Waller. New York, 1975. pp. 132.

ERB (GUY F.) and KALLAB (VALERIANA) eds. Beyond dependency: the developing world speaks out. [Washington], 1975. pp. 238.

UNDERDEVELOPED AREAS.

FRANK (ANDRE GUNDER) On capitalist underdevelopment. Bombay, 1975. pp. 113. *bibliog.*

GOLDTHORPE (JOHN ERNEST) The sociology of the Third World: disparity and involvement. Cambridge, 1975. pp. 325. *bibliogs.*

MYRDAL (GUNNAR) The equality issue in world development. [Stockholm?], 1975. fo. 21.

SINGH (SATEESH KUMAR) Development economics: some findings. Lexington, Mass., [1975]. pp. 296. *bibliog.*

WESTLAKE (MELVYN) World poverty. London, 1976. pp. 32. *(Young Fabian Group. Young Fabian Pamphlets. 44)*

— Abstracts.

U.S. Agency for International Development. A.I.D. research and development abstracts. q., Jl 1973 (v.1,no.1)- Washington, D.C.

— Agricultural credit.

FAO/CARIPLO WORKING GROUP. Agricultural credit for development; [working document prepared for the] World Conference on Credit for Farmers in Developing Countries, Rome, 14-21 October 1975. Milan, 1975. pp. 160. *(Cassa di Risparmio delle Provincie Lombarde. Credit Markets of Africa. 13)*

INTERNATIONAL BANK FOR RECONSTRUCTION AND DEVELOPMENT. 1975. The assault on world poverty: problems of rural development, education and health; with a preface by Robert S. McNamara. Baltimore, [1975]. pp. 425.

— Agricultural education.

TRAINING FOR AGRICULTURE AND RURAL DEVELOPMENT; (formerly Training for agriculture); [pd. by] Food and Agriculture Organization. a., 1975- Rome.

— Agriculture.

JAMAICA. Ministry of Rural Land Development. Report. a., 1970/71 (2nd). Kingston.

AGRICULTURE in development theory: [papers presented at a conference held in Bellagio, Italy, in 1973, under the auspices of the Economic Growth Center, Yale University]; edited by Lloyd G. Reynolds. New Haven, 1975. pp. 510. *Yale University. Economic Growth Center. Publications)*

DUMETT (RAYMOND E.) and BRAINARD (LAWRENCE J.) eds. Problems of rural development: case studies and multi-disciplinary perspectives. Leiden, 1975. pp. 148. *bibliog.*

EXTERNALITIES in the transformation of agriculture: distribution of benefits and costs from development; edited by Earl O. Heady [and] Larry R. Whiting. Ames, 1975. pp. 341. *bibliogs.*

LIM (DAVID) Supply responses of primary producers. Kuala Lumpur, 1975. pp. 166. *bibliog.*

MAKHIJANI (ARJUN) Energy and agriculture in the third world: (a report to the Energy Policy Project of the Ford Foundation). Cambridge, Mass., 1975. pp. 168. *bibliog.*

PAIGE (JEFFERY M.) Agrarian revolution: social movements and export agriculture in the underdeveloped world. New York, [1975]. pp. 435. *bibliog.*

VIEWS of science, technology and development; edited by Eugene Rabinowitch and Victor Rabinowitch. Oxford, 1975. pp. 285. *Consists mainly of papers presented to recent Pugwash conferences.*

— — Bibliography.

COMMONWEALTH BUREAU OF AGRICULTURAL ECONOMICS. Land and population in agricultural development. [Farnham Royal, 1974]. pp. 24. *(Annotated Bibliographies. No. 33) Compiled from World Agricultural Economics and Rural Sociology Abstracts from 1964 to 1974.*

— Automation — Economic aspects.

ROUND-TABLE DISCUSSION ON THE MANPOWER PROBLEMS ASSOCIATED WITH THE INTRODUCTION OF AUTOMATION AND ADVANCED TECHNOLOGY IN DEVELOPING COUNTRIES, GENEVA, 1970. Automation in developing countries. Geneva, International Labour Office, 1972. pp. 246.

— Banks and banking, Cooperative.

HESSELBACH (WALTER) Commonweal banks in developing nations: a model study; with a terminological epilogue by Karl Kühne. Francfort, [1974]. pp. 27. *bibliog. (Bank für Gemeinwirtschaft Aktiengesellschaft. Series Commonweal Economy. No. 8)*

— Birth control.

CHANDRASEKARAN (C.) and HERMALIN (ALBERT I.) eds. Measuring the effect of family planning programs on fertility. Dolhain, Belgium. [1975]. pp. 570. *bibliogs.*

— Book industries and trade.

PROBLEMS of the bookworld and how they could be solved: (a digest of recommendations emerging from the seminars organised under the Unesco project on reading materials). Karachi, 1963. pp. 120.

— Budget.

HANGA (FRED) The development budget as an instrument of planning and budgetary policies. Monrovia, Department of Planning and Economic Affairs, [1969?]. fo. 15. *(Conference on Development Objectives and Strategy, Monrovia, 1969. Documents. 4) Xerox copy.*

— Child welfare.

ASSIGNMENT CHILDREN: (Les Carnets de l'enfance); [pd. by] United Nations Children's Fund. [articles in English or French, with abstracts in English or French, Spanish and German]. q. (formerly s-a., previously irreg.), [1965] (3)- Neuilly. *3-5 are in English only.*

— Cities and towns.

MANGIN (WILLIAM) ed. Peasants in cities: readings in the anthropology of urbanization. Boston, [Mass.], [1970]. pp. 207. *bibliog.*

RIVKIN (MALCOLM D.) Land use and the intermediate-size city in developing countries: with case studies of Turkey, Brazil, and Malaysia. New York, 1976. pp. 136.

— — Planning.

BAIROCH (PAUL) Urban unemployment in developing countries: the nature of the problem and proposals for its solution. Geneva, International Labour Office. 1973. pp.99.

— Commerce.

UNITED NATIONS. Conference on Trade and Development. 1966. Payments arrangements among the developing countries for trade expansion: report of the group of experts. (TD/B/80/Rev.1) (TD/B/C.3/24/Rev.1). Geneva, 1966. pp. 32.

UNITED NATIONS. Conference on Trade and Development. 1968. Towards a global strategy of development: report by the Secretary-General of the United Nations Conference on Trade and Development to the second session of the Conference. (TD/3/Rev.1). New York, 1968. pp. 76.

BARRETT (CHARLES ALEXANDER) Foreign enterprise and manufactured exports: case studies of five developing countries; [Ph.D. (London) thesis]. 1975. fo. 346 *Typescript: unpublished. This thesis is the property of London University and may not be removed from the Library.*

SORENSON (VERNON L.) International trade policy: agriculture and development. East Lansing, Mich., 1975. pp. 290. *bibliog. (Michigan State University. MSU International Business and Economic Studies)*

BESCHAEFTIGUNGSWIRKUNGEN einer verstärkten Arbeitsteilung zwischen der Bundesrepublik und den Entwicklungsländern; ([by] Hugo Dicke [and others]). Tübingen, 1976. pp. 225. *bibliog. (Kiel. Universität. Institut für Weltwirtschaft. Kieler Studien. 137)*

REGIONAL analysis...; edited by Carol A. Smith. New York, [1976]. 2 vols. *bibliogs. Papers prepared for a conference held in Santa Fe, New Mexico, in 1973.*

TANNER (JOHN) A new deal for the poor: what a new economic order would mean for Britain and the third world. London, 1976. pp. 24. *bibliog.*

— Commercial policy.

STECHER (BERND) Erfolgsbedingungen der Importsubstitution und der Exportdiversifizierung im Industrialisierungsprozess: die Erfahrungen in Chile, Mexiko und Südkorea. Tübingen, 1976. pp. 207. *bibliog. (Kiel. Universität. Institut für Weltwirtschaft. Kieler Studien. 136)*

— Commercial products.

PAYER (CHERYL) ed. Commodity trade of the third world. London, 1975. pp. 192. *bibliogs.*

— Corporations, Foreign.

The NATION-state and transnational corporations in conflict: with special reference to Latin America; edited by Jon P. Gunnemann. New York, 1975. pp. 242. *Papers of the consultation organized by the Council on Religion and International Affairs at Aspen Institute, Colorado, in 1973.*

NEGANDHI (ANANT R.) and PRASAD (S. BENJAMIN) The frightening angels: a study of U.S. multinationals in developing nations. Kent, Ohio, [1975]. pp. 249. *bibliog.*

— Debts, External.

UNITED NATIONS. Conference on Trade and Development. 1972. Debt problems of developing countries: report by the UNCTAD Secretariat. (TD/118/Supp.G/Rev.1). New York, 1972. pp. 31.

UNITED NATIONS. Conference on Trade and Development. 1974. Debt problems in the context of development: report by the UNCTAD Secretariat. (TD/B/C.3/109/Rev.1). New York, 1974. pp. 35.

INTERNATIONAL BANK FOR RECONSTRUCTION AND DEVELOPMENT. World debt tables: external public debt of L.D.Cs. a., 1975- [Washington D.C.]. *In two volumes.*

— Development banks.

KHERADJOU (A.G.) The development bank in a fast developing economy. New Delhi, 1975. pp. 63. *(Industrial Finance Corporation of India. Silver Jubilee Memorial Lectures.1975)*

— Economic conditions.

POPULATION growth and economic development in the Third World; edited by Léon Tabah. Dolhain, [1975]. 2 vols. *"The result of the work of the IUSSP Committee on Economics and Demography".*

COLE (JOHN) Journalist. The poor of the earth. London, 1976. pp. 144.

MACBEAN (ALASDAIR I.) and BALASUBRAMANYAM (V.N.) Meeting the Third World challenge. London, 1976. pp. 272. *bibliog.*

— — Bibliography.

JOINT BANK-FUND LIBRARY. 1976. The developing areas: a classed bibliography. Boston, Mass., 1976. 3 vols.

— Economic policy.

PROKHOROV (GRIGORII MIKHAILOVICH) Ekonomicheskoe sotrudnichestvo i razvitie. Budapesht, 1968. pp. 32. *bibliog. (Magyar Tudományos Akadémia. Afro-Ázsiai Kutató Központ. Studies on Developing Countries. No. 15)*

UNDERDEVELOPED AREAS.(Cont.)

HANGA (FRED) The development budget as an instrument of planning and budgetary policies. Monrovia, Department of Planning and Economic Affairs, [1969?]. fo. 15. *(Conference on Development Objectives and Strategy, Monrovia, 1969. Documents. 4) Xerox copy.*

INDUSTRIALISIERUNG in Entwicklungsländern: Bedingungen, Konzeptionen, Tendenzen; Autorenkollektiv unter Leitung von Horst Grienig [and others]. Berlin, 1975. pp. 680. *bibliog. (Zentraler Rat für Asien-, Afrika- und Lateinamerika-Wissenschaften in der DDR. Studien über Asien, Afrika und Lateinamerika. Band 7)*

JALAN (BIMAL) Essays in development policy. Delhi, 1975. pp. 156. *bibliog.*

LELE (UMA J.) The design of rural development: lessons from Africa; published for the World Bank. Baltimore, [1975]. pp. 246. *bibliog.*

MAKHIJANI (ARJUN) Energy and agriculture in the third world: (a report to the Energy Policy Project of the Ford Foundation). Cambridge, Mass., 1975. pp. 168. *bibliog.*

MORGAN (JOSEPH THEODORE) Economic development: concept and strategy. New York, [1975]. pp. 429.

REHOVOT CONFERENCE, 7TH, 1973. Economic growth in developing countries - material and human resources: proceedings...; edited by Yohanan Ramati. New York, 1975. pp. 501.

ALEXANDER (ROBERT JACKSON) A new development strategy. Maryknoll, N.Y., [1976]. pp. 169. *bibliog.*

BERGER (PETER L.) Pyramids of sacrifice: political ethics and social change. London, 1976. pp. 272.

GILBERT (ALAN GRAHAM) ed. Development planning and spatial structure. London, [1976]. pp. 207. *bibliogs.*

KALECKI (MICHAŁ) Essays on developing economies. Hassocks, Sussex, 1976. pp. 208.

MELLOR (JOHN WILLIAMS) The new economics of growth: a strategy for India and the developing world. Ithaca, N.Y., 1976. pp. 335.

SINHA (RADHARAMAN PRASAD) Food and poverty: the political economy of confrontation. London, 1976. pp. 196. *bibliog.*

STECHER (BERND) Erfolgsbedingungen der Importsubstitution und der Exportdiversifizierung im Industrialisierungsprozess: die Erfahrungen in Chile, Mexiko und Südkorea. Tübingen, 1976. pp. 207. *bibliog. (Kiel. Universität. Institut für Weltwirtschaft. Kieler Studien. 136)*

— — **Bibliography.**

JOINT BANK-FUND LIBRARY. 1976. The developing areas: a classed bibliography. Boston, Mass., 1976. 3 vols.

— — **Mathematical models.**

McINTOSH (JAMES PETRIE) Descriptive models for developing countries. 1976. fo. 108,2. *bibliog. Typescript. Ph.D. (London) thesis: unpublished. This thesis is the property of London University and may not be removed from the Library.*

— **Education.**

EDUCATION IN THE DEVELOPING COUNTRIES OF THE COMMONWEALTH: abstracts of current research; [pd. by] Commonwealth Secretariat. bien., 1969 [1st bien.' issue]- London.

SHPIRT (A.IU.) Problemy razvitiia obrazovaniia i nauki v natsional'nykh gosudarstvakh Azii i Afriki. Budapesht, 1970. pp. 47. *bibliog. (Magyar Tudományos Akadémia. Afro-Ázsiai Kutató Központ. Studies on Developing Countries. No. 52)*

EDUCATION and development reconsidered: the Bellagio conference papers: [papers from two meetings for heads of assistance agencies organized by the Rockefeller Foundation and the Ford Foundation in Bellagio, 1972 and 1973]; (edited by F. Champion Ward). New York, 1974. pp. 328. *bibliogs.*

BUCHANAN (KEITH McPHERSON) Reflections on education in the third world. Nottingham, 1975. pp. 80.

D'AETH (RICHARD) Education and development in the Third World. Farnborough, Hants., [1975]. pp. 126. *bibliog.*

EDUCATIONAL alternatives in Latin America: social change and social stratification; edited by Thomas J. La Belle. Los Angeles, 1975. pp. 490. *bibliogs. (California University. Latin American Center. Latin American Studies. vol. 30)*

PHILLIPS (HERBERT MOORE) Educational cooperation between developed and developing countries; with a chapter by Francis J. Method. New York, 1976. pp. 331. *bibliog.*

— **Education, Rural.**

COMMONWEALTH CONFERENCE ON EDUCATION IN RURAL AREAS, ACCRA, 1970. Education in rural areas; report of the...conference...held at the University of Ghana. London, Commonwealth Secretariat, [1970]. pp. 314.

— **Educational planning.**

JONES (GAVIN W.) Population growth and educational planning in developing nations. New York, [1975]. pp. 238.

— **Emigration and immigration.**

PARTINGTON (MARTIN) The brain drain tax proposal: a lawyer's view. [Oxford], 1975. pp. 717-749. *(Reprinted from World Development, 1975, vol. 3, no. 10)*

— **Farm mechanization.**

MARSDEN (KEITH) and others. Mechanisation and employment in agriculture; case studies from four continents. Geneva, International Labour Office, 1974. pp. 192.

— **Finance.**

KALECKI (MICHAŁ) and SACHS (IGNACY) Z zagadnień finanswania rozwoju krajóow o "gospodarce mieszanej": [trzy prace]. Warszawa, 1967. pp. 147.

UNITED NATIONS. Conference on Trade and Development. 1968. Towards a global strategy of development: report by the Secretary-General of the United Nations Conference on Trade and Development to the second session of the Conference. (TD/3/Rev.1). New York, 1968. pp. 76.

UNITED NATIONS. Conference on Trade and Development. 1969. International monetary system: issues relating to development financing and trade of developing countries, etc. (TD/B/198/Rev. 1). New York, 1969. pp. 33.

HICKS (URSULA KATHLEEN) Federal finance in a developing economy. New Delhi, 1971. pp. 14. *(Indian Institute of Public Administration. Financial Management Unit. Occasional Lectures. 2)*

MÁRQUEZ (JAVIER) A fejlodo országok és a nemzetközi valutarendszer: a hatalom megoszlása es ennek hatásai. Budapest, 1971. pp. 32. *(Magyar Tudományos Akadémia. Afro-Ázsiai Kutató Központ. Studies on Developing Countries. No.47)*

INTERNATIONAL LABOUR OFFICE. World Employment Programme. 1974. Fiscal measures for employment promotion in developing countries. Geneva, 1974. pp. 342.

— — **Bibliography.**

JOINT BANK-FUND LIBRARY. 1976. The developing areas: a classed bibliography. Boston, Mass., 1976. 3 vols.

— **Food supply.**

POWER (JONATHAN) and HOLENSTEIN (ANNE-MARIE) World of hunger: a strategy for survival. London, 1976. pp. 202.

— **Foreign economic relations.**

KODACHENKO (ALEKSANDR SERGEEVICH) A fejlodo országok kölcsönös együttmuködése és gazdasági függetlensége. Budapest, 1973. pp. 83. *(Magyar Tudományos Akadémia. Afro-Ázsiai Kutató Központ. Studies on Developing Countries. No.59)*

CANADA. Parliament. House of Commons. Standing Committee on External Affairs and National Defence. Sub-Committee on International Development. Minutes of proceedings and evidence. irreg., Jl 22 1975 (no.1)- . *In English and French.*

INTERNATIONAL SLAVIC CONFERENCE, 1ST, BANFF, ALBERTA, 1974. Soviet economic and political relations with the developing world; edited by Roger E. Kanet [and] Donna Bahry. New York, 1975. pp. 237.

HELLEINER (GERALD KARL) ed. A world divided: the less developed countries in the international economy. Cambridge, 1976. pp. 299. *bibliogs. (McGill University. Centre for Developing Area Studies. Perspectives on Development. 5)*

LAMM (HANS SIEGFRIED) and KUPPER (SIEGFRIED) DDR und Dritte Welt. München, 1976. pp. 328. *(Deutsche Gesellschaft für Auswärtige Politik. Forschungsinstitut. Schriften. Band 39)*

TOWARDS a new international economic order; a further report by a Commonwealth Experts' Group; [Alister McIntyre, chairman]. London, Commonwealth Secretariat, [1976]. pp. 35.

TUGENDHAT (CHRISTOPHER) Britain, Europe and the Third World. London, 1976. pp. 31. *(Conservative Political Centre. [Publications]. No. 587)*

— **Foreign exchange.**

CLINE (WILLIAM R.) International monetary reform and the developing countries. Washington, D.C., [1976]. pp. 126.

— **Foreign relations.**

GURTOV (MELVIN) The United States against the third world: antinationalism and intervention. New York, 1974. pp. 260. *bibliog.*

INTERNATIONAL SLAVIC CONFERENCE, 1ST, BANFF, ALBERTA, 1974. Soviet economic and political relations with the developing world; edited by Roger E. Kanet [and] Donna Bahry. New York, 1975. pp. 237.

KORANY (BAHGAT) Social change, charisma and international behaviour: toward a theory of foreign policy-making in the third world. Leiden, 1976. pp. 460. *bibliog. (Geneva. Graduate Institute of International Studies. Collection de Relations Internationales. 4)*

— **Full employment policies.**

ROUND-TABLE DISCUSSION ON THE MANPOWER PROBLEMS ASSOCIATED WITH THE INTRODUCTION OF AUTOMATION AND ADVANCED TECHNOLOGY IN DEVELOPING COUNTRIES, GENEVA, 1970. Automation in developing countries. Geneva, International Labour Office, 1972. pp. 246.

INTERNATIONAL LABOUR OFFICE. Employment Research Papers. Strategies for employment promotion: an evaluation of four inter- agency employment missions. Geneva, 1973. pp. 162.

INTERNATIONAL LABOUR OFFICE. World Employment Programme. 1974. Fiscal measures for employment promotion in developing countries. Geneva, 1974. pp. 342.

BHALLA (A.S.) ed. Technology and employment in industry: a case study approach;... foreword by Amartya Sen. Geneva, International Labour Office, 1975. pp. 324.

COMMONWEALTH YOUTH PROGRAMME. Employment: problems and strategies. London, Commonwealth Secretariat, [1976]. pp. 77. *bibliog. (Employment Series. Special Issues)*

UNDERDEVELOPED AREAS.(Cont.)

— Government business enterprises.

SACHS (IGNACY) Sektor państwowy a rozwój gospodarczy. Warszawa, 1961. pp. 203.

— Housing.

JØRGENSEN (NIELS OVE) Housing finance for low income groups, with special reference to developing countries. Rotterdam, 1975. pp. 247. *bibliog.*

— Income.

MAKHIJANI (ARJUN) Energy and agriculture in the third world: (a report to the Energy Policy Project of the Ford Foundation). Cambridge, Mass., 1975. pp. 168. *bibliog.*

CAIRNCROSS (Sir ALEXANDER KIRKLAND) and PURI (MOHINDER) eds. Employment, income distribution and development strategy: problems of the developing countries: essays in honour of H. W. Singer. London, 1976. pp. 264. *bibliog.*

— Industries.

MOUNTJOY (ALAN BERTRAM) Industrialization and developing countries. 4th ed. London, 1975. pp. 200. *bibliogs.*

— Intergovernmental fiscal relations.

HICKS (URSULA KATHLEEN) Federal finance in a developing economy. New Delhi, 1971. pp. 14. *(Indian Institute of Public Administration. Financial Management Unit. Occasional Lectures. 2)*

— Investments, Foreign.

BARRETT (CHARLES ALEXANDER) Foreign enterprise and manufactured exports: case studies of five developing countries; [Ph.D. (London) thesis]. 1975. fo. 346 *Typescript: unpublished. This thesis is the property of London University and may not be removed from the Library.*

— Investments, German.

JUETTNER (HEINRICH) Förderung und Schutz deutscher Direktinvestitionen in Entwicklungsländern, etc. Baden-Baden, 1975. pp. 417. *bibliog. (Rheinisch-Westfälische Technische Hochschule Aachen. Forschungsinstitut für Internationale Technisch-Wirtschaftliche Zusammenarbeit. Internationale Kooperation. 15)*

— Labour supply.

DURAND (JOHN DANA) The labor force in economic development: a comparison of international census data, 1946-1966. Princeton, 1975. pp. 259.

CAIRNCROSS (Sir ALEXANDER KIRKLAND) and PURI (MOHINDER) eds. Employment, income distribution and development strategy: problems of the developing countries: essays in honour of H. W. Singer. London, 1976. pp. 264. *bibliog.*

MARGLIN (STEPHEN ALAN) Value and price in the labour-surplus economy. Oxford, 1976. pp. 252. *bibliog.*

— Land.

JAMAICA. Ministry of Rural Land Development. Report. a., 1970/71 (2nd). Kingston.

U.K. Ministry of Overseas Development. Land Resources Division. Progress report. irreg., Ap 1971/Mr 1974- Surbiton, Surrey.

INTERNATIONAL GEOGRAPHICAL UNION. Regional Conference [in New Zealand], 1974. Proceedings of the International Geographical Union Regional Conference and eighth New Zealand Geography Conference, Palmerston North, December 1974; edited by William Brockie [and others]. [Christchurch], 1975. pp. 380. *bibliogs. (New Zealand Geographical Society. Conference Series. No. 8)*

COMMONWEALTH BUREAU OF AGRICULTURAL ECONOMICS. Land and population in agricultural development. [Farnham Royal, 1974]. pp. 24. *(Annotated Bibliographies. No. 33) Compiled from World Agricultural Economics and Rural Sociology Abstracts from 1964 to 1974.*

— Land reform.

INTERNATIONAL BANK FOR RECONSTRUCTION AND DEVELOPMENT. 1975. The assault on world poverty: problems of rural development, education and health; with a preface by Robert S. McNamara. Baltimore, [1975]. pp. 425.

— Machinery.

JAMES (DILMUS DELANO) The economic feasibility of employing used machinery in less developed countries. 1970. pp. 303. *bibliog. Ph.D. (Michigan State University) thesis: unpublished. Microfilm of typescript: 1 reel.*

— Medical care.

MILIO (NANCY) The care of health in communities: access for outcasts. New York, [1976]. pp. 402.

SORKIN (ALAN L.) Health economics: an introduction. Lexington, Mass., [1975]. pp. 205.

— Paper making and trade.

MEYER (K. RUDY) The transfer of technology to developing countries: the pulp and paper industry. New York, United Nations Institute for Training and Research, 1974. pp. 45. *(Research Reports. No. 19)*

— Peasantry.

MANGIN (WILLIAM) ed. Peasants in cities: readings in the anthropology of urbanization. Boston, [Mass.], [1970]. pp. 207. *bibliog.*

PAIGE (JEFFERY M.) Agrarian revolution: social movements and export agriculture in the underdeveloped world. New York, [1975]. pp. 435. *bibliog.*

— Politics.

HUNTINGTON (SAMUEL PHILLIPS) and NELSON (JOAN M.) No easy choice: political participation in developing countries. Cambridge, Mass., 1976. pp. 195.

YOUNG (CRAWFORD) The politics of cultural pluralism. Madison, Wisconsin, 1976. pp. 560.

— Population.

IN search of population policy: views from the developing world: a report on five regional seminars conducted in 1973 by Office of the Foreign Secretary, Commission on International Relations, National Academy of Sciences-National Research Council and cosponsoring institutions in developing countries. Washington, D.C., 1974. pp. 109.

COMPARATIVE policy analysis: the study of population policy determinants in developing countries; [papers of a workshop held by Battelle Population Study Center]; edited by R. Kenneth Godwin. Lexington, Mass., [1975]. pp. 333. *bibliog.*

JONES (GAVIN W.) Population growth and educational planning in developing nations. New York, [1975]. pp. 238.

POLICY sciences and population; edited by Warren F. Ilchman [and others]. Lexington, Mass., [1975]. pp. 305.

POPULATION growth and economic development in the Third World; edited by Léon Tabah. Dolhain, [1975]. 2 vols. *"The result of the work of the IUSSP Committee on Economics and Demography".*

— — Bibliography.

COMMONWEALTH BUREAU OF AGRICULTURAL ECONOMICS. Land and population in agricultural development. [Farnham Royal, 1974]. pp. 24. *(Annotated Bibliographies. No. 33) Compiled from World Agricultural Economics and Rural Sociology Abstracts from 1964 to 1974.*

— — Mathematical models.

McINTOSH (JAMES PETRIE) Descriptive models for developing countries. 1976. fo. 108,2. *bibliog. Typescript. Ph.D. (London) thesis: unpublished. This thesis is the property of London University and may not be removed from the Library.*

— Prices.

CUDDY (J.D.A.) International price indexation. Farnborough, Hants., [1976]. pp. 144.

— Regional planning.

ZEHENDER (WOLFGANG) Regionalpolitische Auswahlkriterien für Entwicklungsländer: Untersuchung am Beispiel Zambias. Berlin, [1976]. pp. 161. *bibliog. (Deutsches Institut für Entwicklungspolitik. Schriften. Band 35)*

— Rural conditions.

INTERNATIONAL BANK FOR RECONSTRUCTION AND DEVELOPMENT. 1975. The assault on world poverty: problems of rural development, education and health; with a preface by Robert S. McNamara. Baltimore, [1975]. pp. 425.

— Rural—urban migration.

MANGIN (WILLIAM) ed. Peasants in cities: readings in the anthropology of urbanization. Boston, [Mass.], [1970]. pp. 207. *bibliog.*

BAIROCH (PAUL) Urban unemployment in developing countries: the nature of the problem and proposals for its solution. Geneva, International Labour Office. 1973. pp.99.

— Science.

SHPIRT (A.IU.) Problemy razvitiia obrazovaniia i nauki v natsional'nykh gosudarstvakh Azii i Afriki. Budapesht, 1970. pp. 47. *bibliog. (Magyar Tudományos Akadémia. Afro-Ázsiai Kutató Központ. Studies on Developing Countries. No. 52)*

VIEWS of science, technology and development; edited by Eugene Rabinowitch and Victor Rabinowitch. Oxford, 1975. pp. 285. *Consists mainly of papers presented to recent Pugwash conferences.*

— Social conditions.

ELLIOTT (CHARLES) and MORSIER (FRANÇOISE DE) Patterns of poverty in the Third World: a study of social and economic stratification. New York, 1975. pp. 416.

LELE (UMA J.) The design of rural development: lessons from Africa; published for the World Bank. Baltimore, [1975]. pp. 246. *bibliog.*

POPULATION growth and economic development in the Third World; edited by Léon Tabah. Dolhain, [1975]. 2 vols. *"The result of the work of the IUSSP Committee on Economics and Demography".*

STAVENHAGEN (RODOLFO) Social classes in agrarian societies. New York, 1975. pp. 266.

BERGER (PETER L.) Pyramids of sacrifice: political ethics and social change. London, 1976. pp. 272.

HOOGVELT (ANKIE M.M.) The sociology of developing societies. London, 1976. pp. 202.

YOUNG (CRAWFORD) The politics of cultural pluralism. Madison, Wisconsin, 1976. pp. 560.

— — Bibliography.

JOINT BANK-FUND LIBRARY. 1976. The developing areas: a classed bibliography. Boston, Mass., 1976. 3 vols.

— Socialism.

DESFOSSES (HELEN) and LEVESQUE (JACQUES) eds. Socialism in the Third World. New York, 1975. pp. 321. *bibliogs.*

CARRIER (FRED J.) The third world revolution. Amsterdam, 1976. pp. 354.

— Squatters — Bibliography.

BUICK (BARBARA) compiler. Squatter settlements in developing countries: a bibliography. Canberra, 1975. pp. 158. *(Australian National University. Research School of Pacific Studies. Aids to Research Series. No.A/3)*

UNDERDEVELOPED AREAS.(Cont.)

— Tariffs.

FELDSIEPER (MANFRED) Zollpräferenzen für Entwicklungsländer. Tübingen, [1975]. pp. 114. *bibliog.* *(Bochum. Ruhr-Universität. Institut für Entwicklungsforschung und Entwicklungspolitik. Bochumer Schriften zur Entwicklungsforschung und Entwicklungspolitik. Band 20)*

— Taxation.

TAXATION and development; edited by N.T. Wang. New York, 1976. pp. 287.

— Technology.

JOHNSTON (PETER) Appropriate technologies for small developing countries. Brighton, [1974]. pp. 38. *bibliog.*

VIEWS of science, technology and development; edited by Eugene Rabinowitch and Victor Rabinowitch. Oxford, 1975. pp. 285. *Consists mainly of papers presented to recent Pugwash conferences.*

— Technology transfer.

BYKOV (ALEKSANDR NAUMOVICH) and others. Soviet experience in transfer of technology to industrially less developed countries. New York, United Nations Institute for Training and Research, 1973. pp. 188. *(Research Reports. No. 15)*

MEYER (K. RUDY) The transfer of technology to developing countries: the pulp and paper industry. New York, United Nations Institute for Training and Research, 1974. pp. 45. *(Research Reports. No. 19)*

— Tourists.

ESH (TINA) and ROSENBLUM (ILLITH) Tourism in developing countries: trick or treat?: a report from the Gambia. Uppsala, 1975. pp. 76. *(Nordiska Afrikainstitutet. Research Reports. No. 31)*

— Trade unions.

LEMINSKY (GERHARD) and OTTO (BERND) eds. Gewerkschaften und Entwicklungspolitik. Köln, [1975]. pp. 496.

— Unemployed.

BAIROCH (PAUL) Urban unemployment in developing countries: the nature of the problem and proposals for its solution. Geneva, International Labour Office. 1973. pp.99.

— Women.

SARAN (MARY) For community service: the Mount Carmel experiment. Oxford, [1974]. pp. 144.

— Youth.

WORKSHOP ON NATIONAL YOUTH PROGRAMMES AND NATIONAL SERVICE, ACCRA, 1975. Youth for development: an African perspective; report. London, Commonwealth Secretariat, [1975]. pp. 203.

— — Employment.

SINGER (HANS WOLFGANG) and REYNOLDS (LYN) Employment and youth. London, Commonwealth Secretariat, [1975]. pp. 82. *bibliog. (Commonwealth Youth Programme Occasional Papers)*

— — Employment policies.

COMMONWEALTH YOUTH PROGRAMME. Employment: problems and strategies. London, Commonwealth Secretariat, [1976]. pp. 77. *bibliog. (Employment Series. Special Issues)*

UNDERGROUND LITERATURE

— Netherlands.

SIMONI (ANNA ELIZABETH CHARLOTTE) compiler. Publish and be free: a catalogue of clandestine books printed in the Netherlands 1940-1945 in the British Library. The Hague, 1975. pp. 289.

— Russia.

IZ-POD glyb: sbornik statei...Moskva, 1974. Paris, [1974]. pp. 281.

DVE press-konferentsii: k sborniku "Iz-pod glyb"; press-konferentsiia v Moskve, 14 noiabria 1974 g.; press-konferentsiia v Tsiurikhe, 16 noiabria 1974 g. Paris, [1975]. pp. 87.

SARALIEVA (ZARETKHAN KHADZHI-MURZAEVNA) "Kapital" K. Marksa i rabochee dvizhenie Rossii, 1895-1917 gg. : rasprostranenie i propaganda. Moskva, 1975. pp. 211. *bibliog.*

— — Siberia.

PALIKOVA (ALLA KONSTANTINOVNA) Rukopisnye zhurnaly Sibiri 900-kh [sic] godov. Ulan-Ude, 1974. pp. 70.

UNEMPLOYED.

MEYERINCK (HANS VON) Praktische Massregeln zur Bekämpfung der Arbeitslosigkeit: eine kurze Darstellung der bisher angewandten Mittel und Reformvorschläge für Deutschland. Jena, 1896. pp. 127.

The CONCEPT and measurement of involuntary unemploymnent; edited by G.D.N. Worswick for the Royal Economic Society. Boulder, Col., 1976. pp. 327. *bibliog. Papers presented at a conference organised by the Society in Durham in 1974.*

— Mathematical models.

JONES (DONALD W.) 1948- . Migration and urban unemployment in dualistic economic development. Chicago, 1975. pp. 174. *bibliog. (Chicago. University. Department of Geography. Research Papers. No. 165)*

— Africa, Subsaharan.

SYMPOSIUM ON UNEMPLOYED YOUTH, DAR-ES-SALAAM, 1962. Symposium...[held] 25-29 September, 1962: reports and recommendations. Lagos, 1962. 1 vol.(looseleaf.) *In English and French.*

— Australia.

JORDAN (ALAN K.) Long term unemployed people under conditions of full employment. Canberra, Australian Government Publishing Service, 1975. pp. 56. *bibliog.*

— Caribbean Area.

CARIBBEAN SYMPOSIUM ON EMPLOYMENT STRATEGIES AND PROGRAMMES, BARBADOS, 1975. The young unemployed: a Caribbean development problem. London, Commonwealth Secretariat, [1976]. pp. 112. *bibliog.*

— France.

MICHON (FRANÇOIS) Chômeurs et chômage. Paris, [1975]. pp. 290. *bibliog. (Paris. Université de Paris I (Panthéon- Sorbonne). Publications. Série Sciences Économiques. 4)*

— Germany.

MEYERINCK (HANS VON) Praktische Massregeln zur Bekämpfung der Arbeitslosigkeit: eine kurze Darstellung der bisher angewandten Mittel und Reformvorschläge für Deutschland. Jena, 1896. pp. 127.

— India.

KRISHNA (RAJ) Unemployment in India. New York, 1974. pp. 14. *bibliog. (Agricultural Development Council. Teaching Forum)*

— Netherlands.

LANDELIJK WERKERS OVERLEG. Projekten Jongeren Zonder Werk. Afvaljeugd 15 tot 25 jaar: ons eigen werkboek om de politiek van regeringen en parlement mee door te lichten. 's-Hertogenbosch, 1974 repr. 1975. pp. 116.

LANDELIJK WERKERS OVERLEG. Projekten Jongeren Zonder Werk. Werklozenverzet het explosieve vervolg op Afvaljeugd, samengesteld door en voor werklozen. 's-Hertogenbosch, 1975. pp. 118-262.

— Nigeria.

LAGOS. University. Human Resources Research Unit. Research Project No. 2. Population, employment and living conditions in Lagos. Research Bulletins. [No. 3]. Characteristics of the unemployed in Lagos. Lagos, 1974. fo. 20.

— Portugal.

RAMALHO (MARIA MADALENA) A protecção no desemprego. Lisboa, 1974. pp. 81. *(Portugal. Ministerio do Trabalho. Gabinete de Planeamento. Serie Estudos. 19) With abstracts in English, French and German.*

— Sri Lanka.

SRIVASTAVA (R.K.) and SELVARATNAM (S.) A note on graduate unemployment. Colombo, Ministry of Planning and Economic Affairs, [1968?]. fo. 9.

— Sweden.

DAHLBERG (ANITA) Arbetslöshetsstöd: arbetslöshetsförsäkringen och det kontanta arbetsmarknadsstödet. Stockholm, [1974]. pp. 217. *bibliog.*

— Switzerland.

NEF (CLARA) Beten, schaffen, danken: eine Familie erlebt Not und Arbeitslosigkeit. Bern, [1974]. pp. 48.

— Underdeveloped areas.

See UNDERDEVELOPED AREAS — Unemployed.

— United Kingdom.

U.K. Economic Advisory Council. Sub-Committee on the Trend of Unemployment. Report; [H.D. Henderson, chairman]. London, 1935. pp. 43.

CUMBRIA COMMUNITY DEVELOPMENT PROJECT. Reports on employment, unemployment and population trends in Cleator Moor and Frizington. [Cleator Moor], 1974. pp. 29.

NATIONAL ECONOMIC DEVELOPMENT OFFICE. A study of two local labour markets: short summary of report on research carried out in Manchester and Liverpool by Michael Woodhead. London, 1975. pp. 16.

NORTHERN REGION STRATEGY TEAM. The characteristics of the.unemployed in the northern region, 1966- 1974. Newcastle upon Tyne, 1975. pp. 78. *(Technical Reports. No. 6)*

SUGDEN (ROBERT) Unskilled and unemployed in west Cumbria: a study of unemployment in relation to economic planning and public transportation policies. [York, 1975]. pp. 51. *bibliog. (Papers in Community Studies. No. 3)*

The CONCEPT and measurement of involuntary unemploymnent; edited by G.D.N. Worswick for the Royal Economic Society. Boulder, Col., 1976. pp. 327. *bibliog. Papers presented at a conference organised by the Society in Durham in 1974.*

NORTHERN REGION STRATEGY TEAM. Causes of the recent improvement in the rate of unemployment in the northern region relative to Great Britain. Newcastle-upon-Tyne, 1976. pp. 40. *(Technical Reports. No.11)*

— United States.

BELLUSH (BERNARD) The failure of the N[ational] R[ecovery] A[dministration] . New York, [1975]. pp. 197. *bibliog.*

STOKES (HOUSTON H.) and others. Unemployment and adjustment in the labor market: a comparison between the regional and national responses. Chicago, 1975. pp. 125. *bibliog. (Chicago. University. Department of Geography. Research Papers. No. 177)*

— — New York (City).

OSTOW (MIRIAM) and DUTKA (ANNA B.) Work and welfare in New York City. Baltimore, [1975]. pp. 93. *Prepared for the Manpower Administration, U.S. Department of Labor.*

UNEMPLOYMENT, TECHNOLOGICAL.

MARSDEN (KEITH) and others. Mechanisation and employment in agriculture; case studies from four continents. Geneva, International Labour Office, 1974. pp. 192.

UNIDAD POPULAR.

TOHA (JOSE) defendant. Revolucion, Congreso y constitucion: el caso Toha; [edited by] Joan E. Garces. Santiago de Chile, 1972. pp. 415.

ALGUNOS fundamentos de la intervencion militar en Chile, septiembre 1973. 2nd ed. Santiago de Chile, 1974. pp. 137.

TOER (MARIO) La 'via chilena': un balance necesario. Buenos Aires, [1974]. pp. 320.

SAAVEDRA (ALEJANDRO) Capitalismo y lucha de clases en el campo: Chile 1970-72. Madrid, 1975. pp. 291.

ALLENDE's Chile; edited by Philip O'Brien. New York, 1976. pp. 296. *bibliog.*

UNION LEAGUE OF PHILADELPHIA.

WHITEMAN (MAXWELL) Gentlemen in crisis: the first century of the Union League of Philadelphia, 1862-1962. Philadelphia, 1975. pp. 386.

UNITED ARAB EMIRATES

— Politics and government.

The UNITED Arab Amirates and Qatar: pro-imperialist oil producers in the gulf; translated and edited by the Gulf Committee. London, 1974. pp. 36. *(Gulf Committee. 9th June Studies)*

UNITED KINGDOM

— Antiquities.

HARDING (DEREK WILLIAM) The iron age in lowland Britain. London, 1974. pp. 260. *bibliog.*

BERESFORD (GUY) The medieval clay-land village: excavations at Goltho and Barton Blount. London, 1975. pp. 113. *(Society for Medieval Archaeology. Monograph Series. No. 6)*

PLANNING and the historic environment: papers presented to a conference in Oxford, 1975; edited by Trevor Rowley and Mike Breakell. Oxford, 1975. pp. 127.

— Antiquities, Roman.

CONFERENCE ON ROMANO-BRITISH CANTONAL CAPITALS, LEICESTER UNIVERSITY, 1963. The civitas capitals of Roman Britain: papers given at a conference [organised by the Department of Adult Education]...University of Leicester...; edited by J.S. Wacher. Leicester, 1975. pp. 128. *bibliog.*

— Appropriations and expenditures.

The DILEMMAS of government expenditure: essays in political economy by economists and parliamentarians: [based on a seminar; contributors] Robert Bacon [and others]. [London], 1976. pp. 109. *(Institute of Economic Affairs. Readings. 15)*

GALLOWAY (DAVID) The public prodigals: the growth of government spending and how to control it. London, 1976. pp. 256.

KLEIN (RUDOLF EWALD) and others. Constraints and choices: a commentary on the 1976 Public Expenditure White Paper. London, 1976. fo. 97. *bibliog. (Centre for Studies in Social Policy. Working Papers)*

— Armed forces.

COUSINS (CHRISTINE RUTH) The military family: a study of three communities in the British armed forces. 1975. fo. 130. *bibliog.* Typescript. *M.Phil.(London) thesis: unpublished. This thesis is the property of London University and may not be removed from the Library.*

— Army — Argyll and Sutherland Highlanders.

ALLAN (GORDON FRANCIS) Pressure groups and the British political process: a case study: the 'Save the Argylls' campaign; [Ph.D. (London) thesis] . 1974. fo. 598. *bibliog. Typescript: unpublished. This thesis is the property of London University and may not be removed from the Library.*

— — History.

CUNNINGHAM (HUGH) The volunteer force: a social and political history 1859-1908. London, 1975. pp. 168. *bibliog.*

PREBBLE (JOHN) Mutiny: Highland regiments in revolt, 1743-1804. London, 1975. pp. 542. *bibliog.*

— — Military life.

BROWNE (E.W.) and others. The soldier and the army: opinions on some aspects of army life expressed by troops in S[outh] E[ast] A[sia] C[ommand] . [Calcutta?], South East Asia Command, 1946. pp. 40, x.

— Biography.

SUFFRAGE ANNUAL AND WOMEN'S WHO'S WHO, THE; edited by A.J.R. a. 1913. London.

COMMUNITY ACTION. Investigators' handbook: a guide for tenants, workers and action groups on how to investigate companies, organisations and individuals. London, [1975]. pp. 55.

ROBERTS (FRANK C.) compiler. Obituaries from the Times, 1961-1970 including an index to all obituaries and tributes appearing in the Times during the years 1961-1970. Reading, [1975]. pp. 952.

— Census — 1851.

U.K. Census, 1851. Census of Great Britain, 1851: religious worship in England and Wales; abridged from the official report made by Horace Mann to...Registrar-General. London, 1854. pp. 142.

— — 1971.

LOMAS (GLENYS BARBARA GILLIAN) The coloured population of Great Britain: a comparative study of coloured households in four county boroughs, based on the 1971 census of population. London, 1975. pp. 91.

LOMAS (GLENYS BARBARA GILLIAN) and others. Census 1971: the coloured population of Great Britain: a comparative study of coloured households in 4 county boroughs (Bradford, Leicester, Manchester, Wolverhampton); [summarized by the Runnymede Trust]. London, [1975?]. fo. 12. *(Runnymede Trust. Briefing Papers)*

U.K. Census, 1971. Census, 1971: England and Wales: workplace and transport to work tables, 10 per cent sample. London, 1975. 2 pts. (in 1 vol.).

U.K. Census, 1971. Census, 1971: England and Wales: economic activity sub- regional tables; 10 per cent sample. London, 1976. pp. 411.

U.K. Census, 1971. Census, 1971: England and Wales: new towns: economic activity, workplace and transport to work tables; 10 per cent sample. London, 1976. pp. 107.

U.K. Census, 1971. Census, 1971: Great Britain: qualified manpower tables; 10 per cent sample. London, 1976. pp. 138.

U.K. Central Statistical Office. 1976. Qualified manpower in Great Britain, 1971 census of population. London, 1976. pp. 32. *(Studies in Official Statistics. No. 29)*

U.K. Department of Industry. 1976. Persons with qualifications in engineering, technology and science, census of population 1971, Great Britain;...compiled for the Department of Industry by the Office of Population Censuses and Surveys from the returns made in the 1971 census of population. London, 1976. pp. 207. *(Studies in Technological Manpower. No.5)*

— Church history.

WARD (WILLIAM REGINALD) Religion and society in England, 1790-1850. New York, 1973. pp. 339. *bibliog.*

— Civilization.

ROTHBLATT (SHELDON) Tradition and change in English liberal education: an essay in history and culture. London, 1976. pp. 216.

— — Bibliography.

HAVIGHURST (ALFRED FREEMAN) Modern England, 1901-1970. Cambridge, 1976. pp. 109. *(Conference on British Studies. Bibliographical Handbooks)*

— Commerce.

CARTER (WILLIAM) Clothier. The usurpations of France upon the trade of the woollen manufacture of England briefly hinted at; being the effects of thirty years observations...; or, A caution to England to improve a season now put into her hand, to secure herself. London, printed for R. Baldwin, 1695. pp. 30. *p.1 bled. Wing 678.*

COMMITTEE ON INVISIBLE EXPORTS. Overseas earnings of the British professions. London, 1972. fo. 55.

NATIONAL PORTS COUNCIL. Economics and Statistics Division. United Kingdom international trade, 1980-1985. London, 1976. pp. 173. *bibliog.*

WILLAN (THOMAS STUART) The inland trade: studies in English internal trade in the sixteenth and seventeenth centuries. Manchester, [1976]. pp. 154.

— — Mathematical models.

HUTTON (JOHN P.) and MINFORD (ANTHONY PATRICK LESLIE) A model of UK manufactured exports and export prices. London, H.M.S.O., 1975. pp. 41. *(Government Economic Service Occasional Papers. 11)*

— — France.

NICOLLE (HILARY ANN) Anglo-French trade, 1540-1640. 1976. fo. 336. *bibliog.* Typescript. *Ph.D.(London) thesis: unpublished. This thesis is the property of London University and may not be removed from the Library.*

— — Germany, Eastern.

CONFEDERATION OF BRITISH INDUSTRY. German Democratic Republic: major steps forward on trading relationships; the report of a C.B.I. mission led by Lord Layton, etc. London, 1975. pp. 18.

— — Spain.

The ADVANTAGES and disadvantages which will attend the prohibition of the merchandizes of Spain, impartially examined, and humbly offered to...Parliament; by a Sussex farmer. London, J. Roberts, [1740?]. pp. 34.

— — United States.

CONFERENCE ON EARLY AMERICAN HISTORY, 27TH, 1970. Of mother country and plantations: proceedings of the... conference...; edited by Virginia Bever Platt and David Curtis Skaggs. Bowling Green, Ohio, 1971. pp. 127. *bibliog.*

— Commercial policy.

The ADVANTAGES and disadvantages which will attend the prohibition of the merchandizes of Spain, impartially examined, and humbly offered to...Parliament; by a Sussex farmer. London, J. Roberts, [1740?]. pp. 34.

UNITED KINGDOM (Cont.)

BOYCE (ROBERT WILLIAM DEWAR) Search for recovery: the influence of the United States and France on British plans for economic recovery, 1929-31. 1975. fo. 384. bibliog. Typescript. Ph.D. (London) thesis: unpublished. This thesis is the property of London University and may not be removed from the Library.

TYNDALL (JOHN) Fascist. The case for economic nationalism. London, [1975]. pp. 14.

KENT (MARIAN) Oil and empire: British policy and Mesopotamian oil 1900-1920. London, 1976. pp. 273. bibliog.

PUBLIC assistance to industry: protection and subsidies in Britain and Germany; edited by W.M. Corden and Gerhard Fels. London, 1976. pp. 233.

— Constitution.

STACEY (FRANK ARTHUR) British government, 1966 to 1975: years of reform. London, 1975. pp. 243. bibliog.

KING (DAVID N.) The fiscal implications of devolution. London, [1976]. 1 pamphlet (unpaged). (Institute for Fiscal Studies. Lecture Series. No. 5)

— Constitutional history.

MACY (JESSE) The English constitution: a commentary on its nature and growth. New York, 1897. pp. 519.

SHAW (CHARLES JAMES DALRYMPLE) Baron Kilbrandon. A background to constitutional reform. Birmingham, 1975. pp. 20. (Birmingham. University. Holdsworth Club. Presidential Addresses. 1974)

— Defences.

ALLAUN (FRANK) The wasted £30,000,000,000 spent on false security. 4th ed. London, [1975]. pp. 39.

BOYD (LASLO V.) Britain's search for a role. Farnborough, Hants., [1975]. pp. 170.

U.K. Ministry of Defence. 1975. Our contribution to the price of peace: Britain's defence policy and expenditure. [London, 1975]. pp. 22.

The MANAGEMENT of defence: papers presented [at a residential seminar] at the National Defence College, Latimer, in September 1974; edited by Laurence Martin. London, 1976. pp. 137.

PATTIE (GEOFFREY) Towards a new defence policy. London, [1976]. pp. 28. (Conservative Political Centre. [Publications]. No. 591)

— Description and travel.

BRODZKI (STANISŁAW) Księga wielu dżungli. Warszawa, 1953. pp. 232.

— Economic conditions.

U.K. Economic Advisory Council. Committee on Economic Information. Report. irreg., Oc 1930-Jl 1939 (1st-27th). London.

ECONOMIC PROGRESS REPORT; prepared by the Information Division of the Treasury [U.K.]. m., Ja 1970 (no.1)- London. File includes suppl. Monthly economic assessment, Ja 1970- F 1974(no.48) not distributed and Mr 1974 not pd. Supersedes DEA PROGRESS REPORT (Ja 1965-S 1969; ceased pbln.)

NORTH WEST JOINT PLANNING TEAM. Strategic plan for the north west, 1973. Technical papers. Nos. 1-12, 14, 16-17. [Manchester], 1973 [or rather 1974-76]. 18 pts. (in 3 vols) Nos. 13 and 15 not allocated.

HUDSON INSTITUTE EUROPE. The United Kingdom in 1980: the Hudson report;...by James Bellini [and others]; (director of study: Edmund Stillman). London, 1974. pp. 126.

BANNOCK (GRAHAM) How to survive the slump: a guide to the economic crisis. Harmondsworth, 1975. pp. 170. bibliog.

ECONOMIST INTELLIGENCE UNIT. Q[uarterly] E[conomic] R[eview] Specials. No. 25. OPEC funds and the UK; by Roger Middleton. London, 1975. pp. 86.

MORRELL (JAMES) ed. Britain in the 1980's: a study jointly sponsored by the Henley Centre for Forecasting and the Berger Group. London, 1975. pp. 361.

NORTHERN REGION STRATEGY TEAM. First interim report. Newcastle upon Tyne, 1975. pp. 125.

SHEIN (ALEKSANDR IVANOVICH) Kritika ekonomicheskikh teorii pravykh leiboristov Anglii. Moskva, 1975. pp. 200.

ALLEN (GEORGE CYRIL) The British disease: a short essay on the nature and causes of the nation's lagging wealth. London, 1976. pp. 79. bibliog. (Institute of Economic Affairs. Hobart Papers. 67)

BACON (ROBERT WILLIAM) and ELTIS (WALTER ALFRED) Britain's economic problem: too few producers; [based on articles published in the Sunday Times]. London, 1976. pp. 194.

DONALDSON (PETER) Guide to the British economy. 4th ed. Harmondsworth, 1976. pp. 253. bibliog.

HARBURY (COLIN DESMOND) Descriptive economics. 5th ed. London, 1976. pp. 306.

SMEDLEY (OLIVER) What is happening to the British economy? Saffron Walden, 1976. pp. 204. bibliog.

— — Mathematical models.

U.K. Treasury. 1976. HM Treasury macroeconomic model: technical manual. London, 1976. 1 vol. (various pagings). Updated to describe model as at 1st October, 1975.

— Economic history.

COBDEN (RICHARD) [Letters to Thomas Thomasson. 1850-64]. 23 letters, 1 memorandum. Manuscript.

ASHTON (THOMAS SOUTHCLIFFE) [Unpublished historical papers and notes. 1927-62]. 20 pieces. Manuscript, typescript, etc.

CHURCH (ROY A.) The great Victorian boom, 1850-1873. London, 1975. pp. 95. bibliog. (Economic History Society. Studies in Economic and Social History)

COOK (CHRISTOPHER PIERS) and KEITH (BRENDAN) British historical facts, 1830-1900. London, 1975. pp. 279. bibliogs.

NORTHERN REGION STRATEGY TEAM. Cyclical fluctuations in economic activity in the northern region, 1958-1973. Newcastle upon Tyne, 1975. 1 pamphlet (various pagings). (Technical Reports. No. 1)

U.K. [Cabinet Office]. History of the Second World War: United Kingdom Civil Series. British war economy; by W.K. Hancock and M.M. Gowing. rev. ed. London, 1975. pp. 634. Confidential version with full source references.

ALLEN (GEORGE CYRIL) The British disease: a short essay on the nature and causes of the nation's lagging wealth. London, 1976. pp. 79. bibliog. (Institute of Economic Affairs. Hobart Papers. 67)

CHAMBERLIN (E.R.) The awakening giant: Britain in the Industrial Revolution. London, 1976. pp. 168. bibliog.

COLEMAN (DONALD CUTHBERT) and JOHN (ARTHUR HENRY) eds. Trade, government and economy in pre-industrial England: essays presented to F.J. Fisher. London, [1976]. pp. 302. bibliog.

GLYNN (SEAN) and OXBORROW (JOHN) Interwar Britain: a social and economic history. London, 1976. pp. 276.

HOLMES (GRAEME M.) Britain and America: a comparative economic history, 1850-1939. Newton Abbot, 1976. pp. 224. bibliog.

LITTLE (ANTHONY J.) Deceleration in the eighteenth-century British economy. London, 1976. pp. 111. bibliog.

NATIONAL ECONOMIC DEVELOPMENT OFFICE. Cyclical fluctuations in the United Kingdom economy. London, 1976. pp. 40. (Discussion Papers. 3)

NORTHERN REGION STRATEGY TEAM. Growth and structural change in the economy of the northern region since 1952. Newcastle upon Tyne, 1976. 1 vol. (various pagings). (Technical Reports. No. 4)

— — Bibliography.

CHALONER (WILLIAM HENRY) and RICHARDSON (R.C.) compilers. British economic and social history: a bibliographical guide. Manchester, [1976]. pp. 130.

— — Mathematical models.

JONSON (PETER DAVID) Money and economic activity in the open economy: the U.K., 1880- 1970. [London], 1975. pp. 90. bibliog.

— — Sources.

RAFTIS (J. AMBROSE) Assart data and land values: two studies in the East Midlands, 1200-1350. Toronto, 1974. pp. 169. (Pontifical Institute of Mediaeval Studies. Subsidia Mediaevalia. 3)

CAMDEN SOCIETY. [Publications]. 4th Series. vol. 16. The account-book of Beaulieu Abbey; edited...by S.F. Hockey. London, 1975. pp. 348. bibliog.

COCKERELL (HUGH ANTHONY LEWIS) and GREEN (EDWIN) The British insurance business, 1547-1970: an introduction and guide to historical records in the United Kingdom. London, 1976. pp. 142. bibliog.

— Economic policy.

SCHWARTZ (GEORGE) Bread and circuses, 1945-1958. [London, 1959]. pp. 220. Articles from the Sunday Times.

ECONOMIC AND SOCIAL TRENDS; [pd. by] North West Economic Planning Council [U.K.]. a., 1974 [2nd ed.]- Manchester.

REVIEW OF DEVELOPMENTS IN THE NORTHERN REGION; [pd. by] Northern Economic Planning Council. s-a., F 1974 (no. 1)- Newcastle upon Tyne.

NORTH WEST JOINT PLANNING TEAM. Strategic plan for the north west, 1973. Technical papers. Nos. 1-12, 14, 16-17. [Manchester], 1973 [or rather 1974-76]. 18 pts. (in 3 vols) Nos. 13 and 15 not allocated.

HUDSON INSTITUTE EUROPE. The United Kingdom in 1980: the Hudson report;...by James Bellini [and others]; (director of study: Edmund Stillman). London, 1974. pp. 126.

WEST MIDLANDS JOINT MONITORING STEERING GROUP. Annual report. a., 1975(1st)- London.

BELLERBY (JOHN ROTHERFORD) Britain in debt?. Oxford, 1975. pp. 32.

CENTRE FOR POLICY STUDIES. Why Britain needs a social market economy. London, 1975. pp. 16.

HOLLAND (STUART) Strategy for socialism: the challenge of Labour's programme. Nottingham, 1975. pp. 95.

JONES (JAMES LARKIN) A world to win. London, 1975. pp. 14. (London. University. Birkbeck College. Foundation Orations. 1975)

LERUEZ (JACQUES) Economic planning and politics in Britain;...translated by Martin Harrison. London, 1975. pp. 324. bibliog.

MATTHEWS (GEORGE) Communist. Britain's crisis, cause and cure: the £6 fraud exposed. London, [1975], pp. 30. (Communist Party of Great Britain. Communist Party Pamphlets)

NORTHERN REGION STRATEGY TEAM. First interim report. Newcastle upon Tyne, 1975. pp. 125.

SUGDEN (ROBERT) Unskilled and unemployed in west Cumbria: a study of unemployment in relation to economic planning and public transportation policies. [York, 1975]. pp. 51. bibliog. (Papers in Community Studies. No. 3)

TYNDALL (JOHN) Fascist. The case for economic nationalism. London, [1975]. pp. 14.

UNITED KINGDOM (Cont.)

ALLEN (GEORGE CYRIL) The British disease: a short essay on the nature and causes of the nation's lagging wealth. London, 1976. pp. 79. *bibliog.* (*Institute of Economic Affairs. Hobart Papers. 67*)

BACON (ROBERT WILLIAM) and ELTIS (WALTER ALFRED) Britain's economic problem: too few producers; [based on articles published in the Sunday Times]. London, 1976. pp. 194.

BOW GROUP. Economic Affairs Standing Committee. A chancellor's primer: ...proposals for radical cuts in public expenditure; by Andrew Dalton [and others]. London, 1976. pp. 20.

BRITISH ASSOCIATION FOR THE ADVANCEMENT OF SCIENCE. Section F. Meeting, 1975. Economics and equality: (papers...); edited by Rt. Hon. Aubrey Jones. Deddington, Oxford, 1976. pp. 164. *bibliogs.*

CATCH '76..?: 14 escapes from economic derangement; [by] John Flemming [and others]. London, 1976. pp. 123. (*Institute of Economic Affairs. Occasional Papers. 47*)

CURWEN (PETER J.) and FOWLER (A. H.) Economic policy. London, 1976. pp. 266. *bibliogs.*

JOSEPH (Sir KEITH SINJOHN) Monetarism is not enough. London, 1976. pp. 24. *One of the 1976 Stockton Lectures.*

KING (DAVID N.) The fiscal implications of devolution. London, [1976]. 1 pamphlet (unpaged). (*Institute for Fiscal Studies. Lecture Series. No. 5*)

LEWIS (W. RUSSELL) Neither freedom nor enterprise. London, [1976?]. pp. 17.

MARTIN-KAYE (NIEL) Democratic enterprise. London, [1976]. pp. 38. (*Liberal Party. Strategy 2,000. 1st Series. No. 8*)

NORTHERN REGION STRATEGY TEAM. Second interim report: strategic choices. Newcastle-upon-Tyne, 1976. pp. 58.

SMEDLEY (OLIVER) What is happening to the British economy? Saffron Walden, 1976. pp. 204. *bibliog.*

TRADES UNION CONGRESS and LABOUR PARTY. Liaison Committee. The next three years and the problem of priorities. London, 1976. pp. 15.

TULLOCK (GORDON) The vote motive: an essay in the economics of politics with applications to the British economy...with a British commentary by Morris Perlman. London, 1976. pp. 88. *bibliogs.* (*Institute of Economic Affairs. Hobart Paperbacks. 9.*)

— — Mathematical models.

CORDEN (WARNER MAX) and others. Import controls versus devaluation and Britain's economic prospects. London, [1975]. fo. 21. (*Trade Policy Research Centre. Guest Papers. No. 2*)

— Emigration and immigration.

MOORE (ROBERT) and WALLACE (TINA) Slamming the door: the administration of immigration control. London, 1975. pp. 126.

BIRMINGHAM COMMUNITY DEVELOPMENT PROJECT. The convenient scapegoat: facts and arguments against racialism. [Birmingham, 1976]. pp. 16.

— Executive departments.

U.K. Department of Industry. 1976. The National Enterprise Board: draft guidelines. London, 1976. pp. 14.

U.K. Property Services Agency. 1976. PSA: its work and its people. [London, 1976]. pp. 17.

— Foreign economic relations.

BOYD (LASLO V.) Britain's search for a role. Farnborough, Hants., [1975]. pp. 170.

See also EUROPEAN ECONOMIC COMMUNITY — United Kingdom.

— — Confederate States of America.

LESTER (RICHARD I.) Confederate finance and purchasing in Great Britain. Charlottesville, Va., 1975. pp. 267. *bibliog.*

— — France.

BOYCE (ROBERT WILLIAM DEWAR) Search for recovery: the influence of the United States and France on British plans for economic recovery, 1929-31. 1975. fo. 384. *bibliog.* Typescript. Ph.D. (London) thesis: unpublished. *This thesis is the property of London University and may not be removed from the Library.*

— — Romania.

CONFEDERATION OF BRITISH INDUSTRY. Romania: an opportunity for joint investment; a report on a visit made by a CBI industrial delegation to Romania, October 1973, leader, Mr. Ralph Bateman. London, 1974. pp. 34.

— — Russia.

SEMENOV (LEONID SERGEEVICH) Rossiia i Angliia: ekonomicheskie otnosheniia v seredine XIX veka; pod red. ...S.B. Okunia. Leningrad, 1975. pp. 165.

— — United States.

BOYCE (ROBERT WILLIAM DEWAR) Search for recovery: the influence of the United States and France on British plans for economic recovery, 1929-31. 1975. fo. 384. *bibliog.* Typescript. Ph.D. (London) thesis: unpublished. *This thesis is the property of London University and may not be removed from the Library.*

— Foreign opinion.

AIMS FOR FREEDOM AND ENTERPRISE. The image of Britain abroad: an investigation of attitudes by foreign correspondents to British industry. London, [1975]. pp. 11.

— Foreign population.

HIRO (DILIP) Black British, white British. rev. ed. New York, [1973]. pp. 346. *bibliog.*

COMMUNITY RELATIONS COMMISSION. Mental health among minority ethnic groups: research summaries and bibliography. London, [1975]. 1 pamphlet (various pagings).

KOHLER (DAVID F.) Ethnic minorities in Britain: statistical data. 5th ed. London, Community Relations Commission, 1975. pp. 21.

LOMAS (GLENYS BARBARA GILLIAN) The coloured population of Great Britain: a comparative study of coloured households in four county boroughs, based on the 1971 census of population. London, 1975. pp. 91.

LOMAS (GLENYS BARBARA GILLIAN) and others. Census 1971: the coloured population of Great Britain: a comparative study of coloured households in 4 county boroughs (Bradford, Leicester, Manchester, Wolverhampton); [summarized by the Runnymede Trust]. London, [1975?]. fo. 12. (*Runnymede Trust. Briefing Papers*)

KHAN (NASEEM) The arts Britain ignores: the arts of ethnic minorities in Britain;...sponsored by Arts Council of Great Britain, Calouste Gulbenkian Foundation and Community Relations Commission. [London, Community Relations Commission], 1976. pp. 175.

WORKING PARTY OF HOUSING DIRECTORS [U.K.]. Housing in multi-racial areas; [Harry Simpson, chairman]. [London, Community Relations Commission], 1976. pp. 56.

— — Societies, etc. — Directories.

COMMUNITY RELATIONS COMMISSION. Directory of ethnic minority organisations in the U.K. 2nd ed. London, 1976. pp. 67,ii.

— Foreign relations.

BROWNE (JOHN HUTTON BALFOUR) Essays, critical and political. vol. 2. Political. London, 1907. pp. 333. *Of the eleven essays nine are reprinted from the Westminster Review, 1876-1886 and one from the National Review, 1906.*

COLLIER (Sir LAURENCE) [Impressions of Sir Eyre Crowe: the roots of appeasement. 1960-70]. 1 piece. Typescript.

ARMS LIMITATION AND DISARMAMENT (formerly Arms control and disarmament): notes on current developments; issued by the Foreign and Commonwealth Office [U.K.]. irreg., Ap 1967 [no.1]- London.

TRUKHANOVSKII (VLADIMIR GRIGOR'EVICH) Antoni Iden: stranitsy angliiskoi diplomatii, 30-50-e gody. Moskva, 1974. pp. 422.

BARCLAY (Sir RODERICK EDWARD) Ernest Bevin and the Foreign Office, 1932-1969. London, 1975. pp. 166.

BOYD (LASLO V.) Britain's search for a role. Farnborough, Hants., [1975]. pp. 170.

CHERNIAK (EFIM BORISOVICH) Sekretnaia diplomatiia Velikobritanii: iz istorii tainoi voiny. Moskva, 1975. pp. 372.

FABIAN SOCIETY. Fabian Tracts. [No]. 439. Challenges and opportunities for British foreign policy; [by] Jim Callaghan. London, 1975. pp. 16.

MIERS (SUZANNE) Britain and the ending of the slave trade. London, 1975. pp. 405. *bibliog.*

PALLISER (Sir ARTHUR MICHAEL) Britain and British diplomacy in a world of change. London, [1975]. pp. 12. (*David Davies Memorial Institute of International Studies. Annual Memorial Lectures. 1975*)

PORTER (BERNARD) The lion's share: a short history of British imperialism, 1850-1970. London, 1975. pp. 408.

SANDIFORD (KEITH A.P.) Great Britain and the Schleswig-Holstein question, 1848-64: a study in diplomacy, politics, and public opinion. Toronto, [1975]. pp. 204. *bibliog.*

WALLACE (WILLIAM) Lecturer in government, University of Manchester. The foreign policy process in Britain. London, [1975]. pp. 320. *bibliog.*

CRISIS and controversy: essays in honour of A.J.P. Taylor; edited by Alan Sked and Chris Cook. london, 1976. pp. 198.

DIXON (PETER) Canning: politician and statesman. London, [1976]. pp. 355. *bibliog.*

KENT (MARIAN) Oil and empire: British policy and Mesopotamian oil 1900-1920. London, 1976. pp. 273. *bibliog.*

See also subdivision United Kingdom under EUROPEAN ECONOMIC COMMUNITY; NORTH ATLANTIC TREATY ORGANIZATION.

— — Asia, Southeast.

TARLING (NICHOLAS) Imperial Britain in South-east Asia; [articles]. Kuala Lumpur, 1975. pp. 273. *Revisions of articles previously published in various journals.*

— — Balkan States.

BARKER (ELISABETH) British policy in south-east Europe in the Second World War. London, 1976. pp. 320. *bibliog.*

— — Belgium.

WAUGH (MAUREEN CRAIGIE) British foreign policy and the security of Belgium's frontiers, 1934-1939. [1976]. fo. 257. *bibliog.* Typescript. Ph.D. (London) thesis: unpublished. *This thesis is the property of London University and may not be removed from the Library.*

— — Canada.

BRITAIN and Canada: survey of a changing relationship; edited by Peter Lyon. London, 1976. pp. 191. *Based on papers presented at a conference held at St. Catherine's Cumberland Lodge in 1971.*

UNITED KINGDOM(Cont.)

— — China.

KANE (HAROLD EDWIN) Sir Miles Lampson at the Peking legation, 1926-1933. 1975. fo. 192. *bibliog. Typescript. Ph.D.(London) thesis: unpublished. This thesis is the property of London University and may not be removed from the Library.*

BOARDMAN (ROBERT) Britain and the People's Republic of China 1949-74. London, 1976. pp. 210. *bibliog.*

— — East (Near East).

KEDOURIE (ELIE) Arabic political memoirs and other studies. London, 1974. pp. 327. *bibliog. This book continues the author's previously published work The Chatham House version and other Middle-Eastern studies.*

KEDOURIE (ELIE) In the Anglo-Arab labyrinth: the McMahon-Husayn correspondence and its interpretations, 1914-1939. Cambridge, 1976. pp. 330. *bibliog.*

— — Europe.

NEWMAN (FRANCIS WILLIAM) The place and duty of England in Europe: a lecture delivered at the third conversazione of the Friends of Italy on...April 28th, 1852;...to which is added an address...by M. Mazzini. London, 1852. pp. 23. *(Society of the Friends of Italy. Tracts. No. 5)*

CALDER (KENNETH JOHN) Britain and the origins of the new Europe, 1914-1918. Cambridge, 1976. pp. 268. *bibliog. (London. University. London School of Economics and Political Science. Centre for International Studies. International Studies)*

— — — Bibliography.

BOETTCHER (WINFRIED) and others, compilers. Das britische Parlament und Europa, 1940-1972: eine Fachbibliographie. Baden-Baden, [1975]. pp. 186. *Contents, preface and list of subjects in various languages.*

— — Europe, Eastern.

BARKER (ELISABETH) British policy in south-east Europe in the Second World War. London, 1976. pp. 320. *bibliog.*

— — France.

Les RELATIONS Franco-Britanniques de 1935 à 1939: communications présentées aux colloques franco-britanniques tenus à Londres...1971, Paris...1972. Paris, 1975. pp. 440. *In English or French, with summaries in the alternative language.*

HAMILTON (KEITH ALEXANDER) The embassy of Sir Francis Bertie in Paris during the period 1905-1914. 1975 [or rather 1976]. fo. 447. *bibliog. Ph.D.(London) thesis: unpublished. This thesis is the property of London University and may not be removed from the Library.*

HASWELL (JOCK) The battle for empire: a century of Anglo-French conflict. London, 1976. pp. 310. *bibliog.*

— — Germany.

BLEY (HELMUT) Bebel und die Strategie der Kriegsverhütung, 1904-1913: eine Studie über Bebels Geheimkontakte mit der britischen Regierung, etc. Göttingen, 1975. pp. 254.

— — Ghana.

DANQUAH (JOSEPH BOAKYE) Journey to independence and after: J.B. Danquah's letters, 1947-1965;...compiled by H.K. Akyeampong. Accra, 1970 in progress.

— — India.

LIPTON (MICHAEL) and FIRN (JOHN) The erosion of a relationship: India and Britain since 1960. London, 1975. pp. 427. *Published for the Royal Institute of International Affairs.*

— — Jordan.

KIRKBRIDE (Sir ALEC) From the wings: Amman memoirs 1947-1951. London, 1976. pp. 159.

— — Mediterranean.

PRATT (LAWRENCE R.) East of Malta, west of Suez: Britain's Mediterranean crisis, 1936-1939. Cambridge, 1975. pp. 215. *bibliog.*

— — Poland.

NOWAK-KIEŁBIKOWA (MARIA) Polska-Wielka Brytania w latach 1918-1923: kształtowanie się stosunków politycznych. Warszawa, 1975. pp. 447. *bibliog.*

PISZCZKOWSKI (TADEUSZ) Anglia a Polska, 1914-1939: w świetle dokumentów brytyjskich. Londyn, 1975. pp. 456.

NEWMAN (SIMON) March 1939: the British guarantee to Poland: a study in the continuity of British foreign policy. Oxford, 1976. pp. 253. *bibliog.*

— — Romania.

DEMÉNY (LUDOVIC) and CERNOVODEANU (PAUL) Relaţiile politice ale Angliei cu Moldova, Ţara Românească şi Transilvania în secolele XVI-XVIII. Bucureşti, 1974. pp. 287. *(Academia de Ştiinţe Sociale şi Politice a Republicii Socialiste România. Biblioteca Istorica. 42) With English summary and table of contents.*

— — Russia.

PANTEV (ANDREI LAZAROV) Angliia sreshtu Rusiia na Balkanite, 1879-1894. Sofiia, 1972. pp. 307. *bibliog. With Russian and English summaries.*

MAIER (LOTHAR AUGUST) Bündnispolitik und revolutionäre Krise: zu einigen Aspekten der britisch-russischen Beziehungen, 1917. Heidelberg, 1975. pp. 238. *bibliog. Inaugural-Dissertation zur Erlangung der Doktorwürde der Philosophisch-historischen Fakultät der Universität Heidelberg.*

INGLE (HAROLD N.) Nesselrode and the Russian rapprochement with Britain, 1836-1844. Berkeley, [1976]. pp. 196. *bibliog.*

— — Saudi Arabia.

TROELLER (GARY) The birth of Saudi Arabia: Britain and the rise of the House of Sa'ud. London, 1976. pp. 287. *bibliog.*

— — Turkey.

HELLER (JOSEPH) Ph.D. British policy towards the Ottoman Empire, 1908-1914. 1970 [or rather 1971]. fo.510. *bibliog. Typescript. Ph.D. (London) thesis: unpublished. This thesis is the property of London University and may not be removed from the Library.*

— — United States.

BURTON (DAVID H.) Theodore Roosevelt and his English correspondents: a special relationship of friends. Philadelphia, 1973. pp. 70. *bibliog. (American Philosophical Society. Transactions. New Series. vol. 63, part 2)*

JENKINS (BRIAN) Britain and the war for the Union. Montreal, 1974 in progress. *bibliog.*

KNEER (WARREN G.) Great Britain and the Caribbean, 1901-1913: a study in Anglo-American relations. Michigan, [1975]. pp. 242. *bibliog.*

A TUG of loyalties: Anglo-American relations, 1765-85; edited by Esmond Wright. London, 1975. pp. 92. *(London. University. Institute of United States Studies. Monographs. 2) Lectures delivered at a colloquium at the Institute of United States Studies, University of London, 1972.*

WRIGHT (JAMES LEITCH) Britain and the American frontier, 1783-1815. Athens, Ga., [1975]. pp. 251. *bibliog.*

CONTRAST and connection: bicentennial essays in Anglo-American history; edited by H.C. Allen and Roger Thompson. London, 1976. pp. 373.

FERRIS (NORMAN B.) Desperate diplomacy: William H. Seward's foreign policy, 1861. Knoxville, [1976]. pp. 265. *bibliog.*

— — Yugoslavia — Serbia.

ALEKSIĆ-PEJKOVIĆ (LJILJANA) Odnosi Srbije sa Francuskom i Engleskom, 1903-1914; urednik Jorjo Tadić...; Les relations entre la Serbie, la France et l'Angleterre, 1903-1914. Beograd, 1965. pp. 961. *(Istorijski Institut. Jugoslovenske Zemlje u XX Veku. knj. 3) In Cyrillic.*

— Foreign relations administration.

WALLACE (WILLIAM) Lecturer in government, University of Manchester. The foreign policy process in Britain. London, [1975]. pp. 320. *bibliog.*

— Full employment policies.

SMITH (BARBARA M.D.) Regional unemployment differentials and regional policy: a review of events. Birmingham, 1973. fo. 22. *bibliog. (Birmingham. University. Centre for Urban and Regional Studies. Working Papers. No. 11)*

JAY (PETER) A general hypothesis of employment, inflation and politics; sixth Wincott Memorial Lecture...1975. London, 1976. pp. 34. *(Institute of Economic Affairs. Occasional Papers. 46)*

— Government publications.

PICKETT (KATHLEEN GORDON) Sources of official data. London, 1974. pp. 150.

— — Bibliography.

U.K. Stationery Office. 1975- . Statistics: publications of UK government departments and international organisations. [London], 1975 in progress. *(Subject Catalogues. No. 1) Current issue only kept.*

— — Indexes.

U.K. Stationery Office. Consolidated index to government publications. quinquennial. 1936/1940 (1st)- London.

RICHARD (STEPHEN) compiler. British government publications: an index to chairmen and authors, 1900-1940. London, 1974. pp. 174.

— Historical geography.

PERRY (P.J.) A geography of 19th-century Britain. London, 1975. pp. 187. *bibliogs.*

TAYLOR (CHRISTOPHER) 1935- . Fields in the English landscape. London, 1975. pp. 174. *bibliog.*

WARREN (KENNETH) The geography of British heavy industry since 1800. London, 1976. pp. 60. *bibliog.*

— History — Bibliography.

GRAVES (EDGAR B.) ed. A bibliography of English history to 1485: based on The sources and literature of English history from the earliest times to about 1485, by Charles Gross. Oxford, 1975. pp. 1103.

HANHAM (HAROLD JOHN) compiler. Bibliography of British history, 1851-1914. London, 1976. pp. 1606.

HAVIGHURST (ALFRED FREEMAN) Modern England, 1901-1970. Cambridge, 1976. pp. 109. *(Conference on British Studies. Bibliographical Handbooks)*

— — Pictorial works.

SYMONS (JULIAN) The angry 30s. London, 1976. 1 vol. (unpaged).

— — Sources.

CHURCHILL (JOHN) 1st Duke of Marlborough, and GODOLPHIN (SIDNEY) 1st Earl of Godolphin. The Marlborough-Godolphin correspondence; edited by Henry L. Snyder. Oxford, 1975. 3 vols.

DERING (Sir EDWARD) The diaries and papers of Sir Edward Dering, Second Baronet, 1644 to 1684; edited by Maurice F. Bond. London, 1976. pp. 237. *(U.K. Parliament. House of Lords. Record Office. Occasional Publications. No.1) Genealogical table in end pocket.*

UNITED KINGDOM (Cont.)

—— 449-1066, Anglo-Saxon period.

HUMBLE (RICHARD) The fall of Saxon England. London [1975]. pp. 242. *bibliog.*

—— 1300-1399.

HOLMES (GEORGE ANDREW) The Good Parliament. Oxford, 1975. pp. 206.

—— 1399-1485, Lancaster and York.

DAVIES (CLIFFORD STEPHEN LLOYD) Peace, print and Protestantism, 1450-1558. London, 1976. pp. 365. *bibliog.*

—— 1485— .

ANGLO-DUTCH HISTORICAL CONFERENCE, 5TH, 1973. Britain and the Netherlands...: some political mythologies; papers delivered to the...conference; edited by J.S. Bromley and E.H. Kossmann. The Hague, 1975. pp. 212.

—— 1485-1603, Tudors.

BULPITT (JIM G.) The problem of "the north parts": territorial integration in Tudor and Stuart England. Coventry, 1975. pp. 45. *(University of Warwick. Department of Politics. Working Papers. No. 6)*

DAVIES (CLIFFORD STEPHEN LLOYD) Peace, print and Protestantism, 1450-1558. London, 1976. pp. 365. *bibliog.*

—— 1603-1714, Stuarts.

BULPITT (JIM G.) The problem of "the north parts": territorial integration in Tudor and Stuart England. Coventry, 1975. pp. 45. *(University of Warwick. Department of Politics. Working Papers. No. 6)*

—— 1603-1649, Early Stuarts.

MORRILL (J.S.) The revolt of the provinces: conservatives and radicals in the English Civil War, 1630-1650. London, 1976. pp. 234. *bibliog.*

—— 1642-1660, Puritan Revolution.

PAVLOVA (TAT'IANA ALEKSANDROVNA) Vtoraia angliiskaia respublika, 1659-1660. Moskva, 1974. pp. 224. *bibliog.*

—— 1642-1649, Civil War.

UNDERDOWN (DAVID) Somerset in the Civil War and Interregnum. Newton Abbot, [1973]. pp. 229. *bibliog.*

MORTON (ARTHUR LESLIE) ed. Freedom in arms: a selection of Leveller writings. London, 1975. pp. 354.

—— 1649-1660, Commonwealth and Protectorate.

UNDERDOWN (DAVID) Somerset in the Civil War and Interregnum. Newton Abbot, [1973]. pp. 229. *bibliog.*

—— 1800-1899.

COOK (CHRISTOPHER PIERS) and KEITH (BRENDAN) British historical facts, 1830-1900. London, 1975. pp. 279. *bibliogs.*

JONES (R. BEN) The Victorians: a century of achievement. St. Albans, [1975]. pp. 273. *bibliog.*

MOORE (DAVID CRESAP) The politics of deference: a study of the mid-nineteenth century English political system. Hassocks, Sussex, 1976. pp. 529. *bibliog.*

—— 1837— .

PORTER (BERNARD) The lion's share: a short history of British imperialism, 1850-1970. London, 1975. pp. 408.

—— 1900— .

FISHER (Sir NORMAN FENWICK WARREN) [Unpublished political and defence papers. 1926-39]. 2 pieces. *Typescript.*

SYMONS (JULIAN) The angry 30s. London, 1976. 1 vol. (unpaged).

— History, Naval.

BELCHER (Sir EDWARD) [Naval and literary correspondence. 1859-63]. 20 letters. *Manuscript.*

— Industries.

BRISCOE (GEOFFREY) and PEEL (D.A.) The value of inter-related factor demand models for explaining short-term employment behaviour in the U.K. manufacturing sector. Coventry, 1974. 1 pamphlet (various pagings). *(University of Warwick. Centre for Industrial, Economic and Business Research. [Warwick Research in Industrial and Business Studies]. No.52)*

AIMS FOR FREEDOM AND ENTERPRISE. Labour and industry: the last steps. London, [1975]. pp. 10.

COLEMAN (DONALD CUTHBERT) Industry in Tudor and Stuart England. London, 1975. pp. 63. *bibliog.*

CONFEDERATION OF BRITISH INDUSTRY. A statistical survey of industrial fuel and energy use. London, 1975. pp. 36.

CONFEDERATION OF BRITISH INDUSTRY. Europe Committee. British industry and Europe. London, 1975. pp. 63.

MARSHALL (B.V.) Comprehensive economics: institutional, analytical and applied. 2nd ed. London, 1975. pp. 1163, li. *bibliogs.*

NATIONAL ECONOMIC DEVELOPMENT OFFICE. Process Plant Working Party. Process industries investment forecasts: the tenth report by the.. .Working Party. London, 1975. pp. 27.

NORTHERN REGION STRATEGY TEAM. Change and efficiency in manufacturing industry in the northern region, 1948-1973. Newcastle upon Tyne, 1975. 1 vol. (various pagings). *(Technical Reports. No. 3)*

NORTHERN REGION STRATEGY TEAM. Evaluation of the impact of regional policy on manufacturing industry in the northern region. Newcastle upon Tyne, 1975. 1 vol. (various pagings). *(Technical Reports. No. 2)*

SANT (MORGAN EUGENE CYRIL) Industrial movement and regional development: the British case. Oxford, 1975. pp. 253. *bibliog.*

WEST MIDLANDS JOINT MONITORING STEERING GROUP. Joint Technical Working Group. West midlands industry. [London, Department of the Environment, 1975]. 1 vol. (various pagings). *Photocopy.*

PANIĆ (M.) ed. The UK and West German manufacturing industry 1954-72: a comparison of structure and performance. London, National Economic Development Office, 1976. pp. 151. *(NEDO Monographs. 5)*

SHAW (R.W.) and SUTTON (C.J.) Industry and competition: industrial case studies. London, 1976. pp. 210. *bibliogs.*

WARREN (KENNETH) The geography of British heavy industry since 1800. London, 1976. pp. 60. *bibliog.*

WATKINSON (HAROLD ARTHUR) 1st Viscount Watkinson. Blueprint for industrial survival: what has gone wrong in industrial Britain since the war?. London, 1976. pp. 154.

— Intellectual life.

REDWOOD (JOHN) Reason, ridicule and religion: the age of enlightenment in England, 1660-1750. London, [1976]. pp. 287. *bibliog.*

— Manufactures.

NORTHERN REGION STRATEGY TEAM. Change and efficiency in manufacturing industry in the northern region, 1948-1973. Newcastle upon Tyne, 1975. 1 vol. (various pagings). *(Technical Reports. No. 3)*

— Maps.

U.K. Department of the Environment. Northern Regional Housing and Planning Office. 1973- . Northern regional atlas. [Newcastle-upon-Tyne?, 1973 in progress]. 1 vol. (loose leaf).

— Military policy.

WAUGH (MAUREEN CRAIGIE) British foreign policy and the security of Belgium's frontiers, 1934-1939. [1976]. fo. 257. *bibliog. Typescript. Ph.D. (London) thesis: unpublished. This thesis is the property of London University and may not be removed from the Library.*

— Nationalism.

HECHTER (MICHAEL) Internal colonialism: the Celtic fringe in British national development, 1536-1966. London, 1975. pp. 361.

— Nobility.

LANDER (JACK ROBERT) Crown and nobility, 1450-1509. London, 1976. pp. 340.

— Officials and employees.

U.K. Civil Service Department. Statistics Division. A statistical review of the Economist Group. irreg., 1972/73- London.

U.K. Civil Service Department. Statistics Division. Manplan Project Team. 1975. A management guide to manpower planning models. London, 1975. pp. 49.

— Parliament — Biography.

MACKINTOSH (Sir ALEXANDER) From Gladstone to Lloyd George: Parliament in peace and war. London, [1921]. pp. 333.

—— Elections.

COSTER (THOMAS) A list of the free-holders and free-men, who voted at the election for members of parliament for the city and county of Bristol, begun Wednesday May 15, MDCCXXXIV...at which election the candidates were, John Scrope, Sir Abraham Elton, Thomas Coster; done from Mr. Coster's original poll-book. Bristol, Felix Farley, [1734?]. pp. 160. *Fly-leaf contains biographical information and list of Coster's agents. This copy was presented to his agent Henry Hart. Some ms. amendments in the text. Title on spine: Bristol poll book, 1734.*

The BRISTOL poll book, being a list of the freeholders and freemen who voted at the general election for members to serve in Parliament for the city and county of Bristol, which commenced at the Guildhall, on...October 6, 1812 and finished...the 16th, etc. Bristol, 1818. pp. 136. *Bound with The poll book of the electors of...Bristol...1832.*

The POLL book of the electors of the electoral district of the city of Bristol, who voted at the general election in December, 1832; with some introductory notes by T.J. Manchee, etc. Bristol, 1833. pp. 195. *Bound with The Bristol poll book...general election...1812.*

SIMPKINS (EDGAR) [Scrapbook containing election literature, newspaper cuttings and correspondence relating to the by-election campaign of W.E. Simpkins at Chichester, 1958 , and his general election campaign at Folkestone, 1959]. 1958-59. 2 vols.(in 1 slipcase).

HARRISON (STEPHEN JOHN) The British general election of 1924. 1971. pp. 561. *bibliog. Ph.D.(Catholic University of America) thesis: unpublished. Microfilm of typescript: 1 reel.*

CRAIG (FREDERICK WALTER SCOTT) ed. British general election manifestos, 1900-1974. London, 1975. pp. 484. *Revised and enlarged edition of British general election manifestos, 1918-1966.*

HIRST (DEREK) The representative of the people?: voters and voting in England under the early Stuarts. Cambridge, 1975. pp. 306. *bibliog.*

PULZER (PETER GEORGE JULIUS) Political representation and elections in Britain. 3rd ed. London, 1975. pp. 176. *bibliog.*

UNITED KINGDOM(Cont.)

FRASER (DEREK) Urban politics in Victorian England: the structure of politics in Victorian cities. Leicester, 1976. pp. 324.

NEWLAND (ROBERT A.) Electing the United Kingdom Parliament. London, 1976. pp. 16. *bibliog.*

ROGALY (JOE) Parliament for the people: a handbook of electoral reform. London, 1976. pp. 181. *bibliog.*

— — History.

HOLMES (GEORGE ANDREW) The Good Parliament. Oxford, 1975. pp. 206.

— — — Bibliography.

BOETTCHER (WINFRIED) and others, compilers. Das britische Parlament und Europa, 1940-1972: eine Fachbibliographie. Baden-Baden, [1975]. pp. 186. *Contents, preface and list of subjects in various languages.*

— — — Sources.

CARR-GOMM (HUBERT WILLIAM CULLING) [Recollections of Parliament and letters from Winston S. Churchill. 1903-29]. 1 piece. *Manuscript, typescript.*

— — House of Commons.

FIDLON (PAUL GEOFFREY) The House of Commons and the control of the executive, 1914-1918. 1972. fo. 491. *bibliog. Typescript. Ph.D.(London) thesis: unpublished. This thesis is the property of London University and may not be removed from the Library.*

STANCER (JOHN DAVID) A study of back bench members of Parliament between 1945 and 1965. 1973. fo. 477. *bibliog. Typescript. Ph.D.(London) thesis: unpublished. This thesis is the property of London University and may not be removed from the Library.*

NORTON (PHILIP) ed. Dissension in the House of Commons: intra-party dissent in the House of Commons' division lobbies 1945-1974. London, 1975. pp. 643. *bibliog.*

— — — Privileges and immunities.

MAY (THOMAS ERSKINE) Baron Farnborough. Treatise on the law, privileges, proceedings and usage of Parliament; nineteenth edition [by] David Lidderdale [and others]. London, 1976. pp. 1156.

— — — Rules and practice.

TESTER (H.O.) Her Majesty's Stationery Office and parliamentary printing: a general survey of the principal items of parliamentary printing undertaken by H.M.S.O. [London, H.M.S.O, 1975]. pp. 26.

U.K. Parliament. House of Commons. Library. Research Division. Background Papers. No. 44. Use of the guillotine since 1945. [London, 1975]. fo. 4.

MAY (THOMAS ERSKINE) Baron Farnborough. Treatise on the law, privileges, proceedings and usage of Parliament; nineteenth edition [by] David Lidderdale [and others]. London, 1976. pp. 1156.

U.K. Parliament. House of Lords. 1976. Companion to the standing orders and guide to the proceedings of the House of Lords. [13th ed.] [London], 1976. pp. 280.

— Politics and government.

DEAN (GEORGE ALFRED) Fallacies and tendencies of the age. London, 1871. pp. 251. *Essays on social and political problems written by way of narrative and dialogue.*

GRIFFITH (JOHN ANEURIN GREY) ed. From policy to administration: essays in honour of William A. Robson. London, 1976. pp. 216.

SMITH (BRIAN CLIVE) Policy-making in British government: an analysis of power and rationality. London, 1976. pp. 210.

— — Bibliography.

JOHNSTONE (PAMELA) compiler. Devolution in the United Kingdom: a select list of references. London, 1975. pp. 13. *(U.K. Department of the Environment. Library. Bibliographies. No. 193).*

— — To 1603.

LANDER (JACK ROBERT) Crown and nobility, 1450-1509. London, 1976. pp. 340.

— — 1603-1714.

ALEXANDER (MICHAEL VAN CLEAVE) Charles I's Lord Treasurer: Sir Richard Weston, Earl of Portland, 1577-1635. London, 1975. pp. 261.

— — 1660-1714.

BENNETT (GARETH VAUGHAN) The Tory crisis in church and state, 1688-1730: the career of Francis Atterbury, Bishop of Rochester. Oxford, 1975. pp. 335. *bibliog.*

CHURCHILL (JOHN) 1st Duke of Marlborough, and GODOLPHIN (SIDNEY) 1st Earl of Godolphin. The Marlborough-Godolphin correspondence; edited by Henry L. Snyder. Oxford, 1975. 3 vols.

— — 1700-1799.

ARISTOCRATIC government and society in eighteenth-century England: the foundations of stability; edited with an introduction by Daniel A. Baugh. New York, 1975. pp. 274. *bibliog.*

— — 1714-1756.

BENNETT (GARETH VAUGHAN) The Tory crisis in church and state, 1688-1730: the career of Francis Atterbury, Bishop of Rochester. Oxford, 1975. pp. 335. *bibliog.*

FRITZ (PAUL SAMUEL) The English ministers and Jacobitism between the rebellions of 1715 and 1745. Toronto, [1975]. pp. 180. *bibliog.*

— — 1756-1837.

BREWER (JOHN) Ph.D. Party ideology and popular politics at the accession of George III. Cambridge, 1976. pp. 382. *bibliog.*

DERRY (JOHN WESLEY) Castlereagh. London, 1976. pp. 247. *bibliog.*

DERRY (JOHN WESLEY) English politics and the American Revolution. London, 1976. pp. 215. *bibliog.*

DIXON (PETER) Canning: politician and statesman. London, [1976]. pp. 355. *bibliog.*

THOMAS (PETER DAVID GARNER) Lord North. London, 1976. pp. 176. *bibliog.*

— — 1800-1899.

COOK (CHRISTOPHER PIERS) and KEITH (BRENDAN) British historical facts, 1830-1900. London, 1975. pp. 279. *bibliogs.*

MOORE (DAVID CRESAP) The politics of deference: a study of the mid-nineteenth century English political system. Hassocks, Sussex, 1976. pp. 529. *bibliog.*

— — 1837-1901.

BRIGHT (JACOB) Speeches of Jacob Bright, M.P., 1869 to 1884; edited by Mrs. Jacob Bright. London, 1885. pp. 382.

ROBERTSON (JOHN MACKINNON) The people and their leaders. bradford, [1896]. pp. 12. *(Papers for the People. No. 2)*

BROWNE (JOHN HUTTON BALFOUR) Essays, critical and political. vol. 2. Political. London, 1907. pp. 333. *Of the eleven essays nine are reprinted from the Westminster Review, 1876-1886 and one from the National Review, 1906.*

O'CONNOR (THOMAS POWER) Sir Henry Campbell-Bannerman. London, 1908. pp. 167.

ELIAS (FRANK) The Right Hon.H.H. Asquith, M.P.: a biography and appreciation. London, 1909. pp. 248.

MACKINTOSH (Sir ALEXANDER) From Gladstone to Lloyd George: Parliament in peace and war. London, [1921]. pp. 333.

HENDERSON (WILLIAM OTTO) Charles Pelham Villiers and the repeal of the Corn Laws. [Manchester, 1975]. pp. 81.

JAMES (ROBERT RHODES) The British revolution: British politics, 1880-1939. London, 1976 in progress. *bibliog.*

FOOT (Sir DINGLE MACKINTOSH) British political crises. London, 1976. pp. 221. *bibliog.*

WINTER (JAMES) 1925- . Robert Lowe. Toronto, [1976]. pp. 368. *bibliog.*

— — 1900— .

ELLIS (R.J.) He walks alone...: the public and private life of Captain Cunningham-Reid, D.F.C., Member of Parliament 1922-45. London, [1945]. pp. 292.

BUTLER (DAVID HENRY EDGEWORTH) and SLOMAN (ANNE) British political facts, 1900-1975. 4th ed. London, 1975. pp. 432. *bibliog.*

CRAIG (FREDERICK WALTER SCOTT) ed. The most gracious speeches to Parliament, 1900-1974: statements of government policy and achievements. London, 1975. pp. 240.

— — 1901-1945.

MACKINTOSH (Sir ALEXANDER) From Gladstone to Lloyd George: Parliament in peace and war. London, [1921]. pp. 333.

HOBSON (JOHN ATKINSON) Confessions of an economic heretic: the autobiography of J.A. Hobson; edited...by Michael Freeden; [reprint, with a new introduction, of the work first published in 1938]. Hassocks, Sussex, 1976. pp. 217.

IMPERIALIZM i bor'ba rabochego klassa: sbornik statei pamiati akademika Fedora Aronovicha Rotshteina. Moskva, 1960. pp. 507.

ROWLAND (PETER) Lloyd George. London, 1975. pp. 872. *bibliog.*

JAMES (ROBERT RHODES) The British revolution: British politics, 1880-1939. London, 1976 in progress. *bibliog.*

CRISIS and controversy: essays in honour of A.J.P. Taylor; edited by Alan Sked and Chris Cook. london, 1976. pp. 198.

FOOT (Sir DINGLE MACKINTOSH) British political crises. London, 1976. pp. 221. *bibliog.*

— — 1901-1918.

O'CONNOR (THOMAS POWER) Sir Henry Campbell-Bannérman. London, 1908. pp. 167.

ELIAS (FRANK) The Right Hon.H.H. Asquith, M.P.: a biography and appreciation. London, 1909. pp. 248.

FIDLON (PAUL GEOFFREY) The House of Commons and the control of the executive, 1914-1918. 1972. fo. 491. *bibliog. Typescript. Ph.D.(London) thesis: unpublished. This thesis is the property of London University and may not be removed from the Library.*

SCALLY (ROBERT JAMES) The origins of the Lloyd George coalition: the politics of social-imperialism, 1900-1918. Princeton, [1975]. pp. 416. *bibliog.*

WRIGLEY (CHRIS) David Lloyd George and the British labour movement: peace and war. Hassocks, Sussex, 1976. pp. 298. *bibliog.*

— — 1918-1945.

CHAMBERLAIN (ARTHUR NEVILLE) The struggle for peace;...[edited by Arthur Bryant]. London, [1939]. pp. 434. *A reissue of In search of peace, with additional matter.*

— — 1936-1945.

ADDISON (PAUL) The road to 1945: British politics and the Second World War. London, 1975. pp. 334. *bibliog.*

UNITED KINGDOM (Cont.)

—— 1945—.

BIRIUKOV (IGOR' DMITRIEVICH) Pod sen'iu monopolii: burzhuaznaia ideologiia - vrag rabochego klassa Britanii. Moskva, 1972. pp. 287.

AIMS FOR FREEDOM AND ENTERPRISE. The public want sacrifices: results of a national opinion poll survey. London, 1974. pp. 3.

CROSSMAN (RICHARD HOWARD STAFFORD) The diaries of a cabinet minister. London, 1975 in progress.

AMERY (JULIAN) Towards a solution; [speeches]. London, [1975]. pp. 36.

BOYSON (RHODES) ed. 1985: an escape from Orwell's 1984: a Conservative path to freedom. Enfield, 1975. pp. 146.

BRYDER (TOM) Power and responsibility: contending approaches to industrial relations and decision-making in Britain 1963-1971. Lund, [1975]. pp. 212. *bibliog. Ph.D. avhandling - Universitet i Lund.*

HAYWARD (JACK ERNEST SHALOM) Political inertia. Hull, 1975. pp. 24. *(Hull. University. Inaugural Lectures)*

IONESCU (GHITA) Centripetal politics: government and the new centres of power. London, [1975]. pp. 231.

MOSS (ROBERT) The collapse of democracy. London, 1975. pp. 300.

STACEY (FRANK ARTHUR) British government, 1966 to 1975: years of reform. London, 1975. pp. 243. *bibliog.*

BIFFEN (JOHN) A nation in doubt. London, 1976. pp. 18. *(Conservative Political Centre. [Publications]. No. 594)*

BRUCE-GARDYNE (JOCK) and LAWSON (NIGEL) The power game: an examination of decision-making in government. London, 1976. pp. 204. *bibliog.*

COMMUNITY politics; edited by Peter Hain. London, 1976. pp. 226.

CONSERVATIVE CENTRAL OFFICE. The right approach: a statement of Conservative aims. London, 1976. pp. 71.

FALBER (REUBEN) Britain needs socialism. London, [1976]. pp. 28. *(Communist Party of Great Britain. Communist Party Pamphlets)*

GOODHART (PHILIP) Full-hearted consent: the story of the referendum campaign - and the campaign for the referendum. London, 1976. pp. 264.

HASELER (STEPHEN MICHAEL ALAN) The death of British democracy: a study of Britain's political present and future. London, 1976. pp. 262.

KELLNER (PETER) and HITCHENS (CHRISTOPHER) Callaghan: the road to Number Ten. London, 1976. pp. 187. *bibliog.*

LABOUR PARTY. National Executive Committee. Labour's programme for Britain: annual conference, 1976. London, 1976. pp. 147.

LEWIS (W. RUSSELL) Neither freedom nor enterprise. London, [1976?]. pp. 17.

LUCAS (JOHN RANDOLPH) Democracy and participation. Harmondsworth, 1976. pp. 290.

MARSH (ALAN JOHN) The social psychology of political protest: a U.K. national survey of political attitudes and behaviour. 1976. fo. 478. *bibliog. Typescript. Ph.D. (London) thesis: unpublished. This thesis is the property of London University and may not be removed from the Library. Includes two offprints from periodicals.*

STANKIEWICZ (WLADYSLAW JOZEF) ed. British government in an era of reform. London, 1976. pp. 355.

WHY is Britain becoming harder to govern?; based on the BBC 1 series Politics now; [by] Anthony King [and others]; edited by Anthony King. London, 1976. pp. 142.

— Population.

U.K. Regional Plans Directorate. National Framework Division. 1973. De facto urban areas in England and Wales, 1966. [London, 1973?] repr. 1974. 2 pts. *Map in end pocket.*

U.K. Office of Population Censuses and Surveys. Population estimates: the Registrar General's estimates of the population of regions and local government areas of England and Wales by sex and age. a., 1974 /1975- London.

PICKETT (KATHLEEN GORDON) Sources of official data. London, 1974. pp. 150.

CLARKSON (LESLIE A.) Death, disease and famine in pre-industrial England. Dublin, 1975. pp. 188. *bibliog.*

LONDON. University. London School of Economics and Political Science. Graduate School of Geography. Discussion Papers. No. 54. A classification of the components of intra urban and inter urban population change in England and Wales between 1961-1971; [by] Stephen Kennett. London, 1975. pp. 52. *bibliog.*

WEST MIDLANDS JOINT MONITORING STEERING GROUP. Joint Technical Working Group. General migration analysis. [London, Department of the Environment], 1975. 1 pamphlet (various foliations). *Photocopy.*

HOLLIS (JOHN) Writer on Population. Demographic projections for the counties of south east England, 1975. London, 1976. pp. 165. *bibliog. (London. Greater London Council. Research Memoranda. 482)*

LONDON. University. London School of Economics and Political Science. Department of Geography. British cities: urban population and employment trends 1951-71; (Part 1 of the final report of a study of Urban change in Britain, 1951-71, undertaken...on behalf of the Urban Affairs and Commercial Property Directorate of the Department of the Environment). [London, 1976]. pp. 69. *(U.K. Department of the Environment. Research Reports. 10)*

NORTHERN REGION STRATEGY TEAM. Population trends in the northern region. Newcastle upon Tyne, [1976]. 1 vol. (various pagings). *(Technical Reports. No. 9)*

— Public buildings.

U.K. Property Services Agency. 1976. PSA: its work and its people. [London, 1976]. pp. 17.

— Race question.

CRC JOURNAL; produced by Information Department, Community Relations Commission. m. (sometime bi-m.), Ap 1973 (v.2, no.2)- London.

HIRO (DILIP) Black British, white British. rev. ed. New York, [1973]. pp. 346. *bibliog.*

EQUALS; (prepared by the Race Relations Board and the Central Office of Information [U.K.]). bi-m., Ap/My 1975 (no.1)- London.

BARKER (ANTHONY) Strategy and style in local community relations;...submitted to the House of Commons Select Committee on Race Relations and Immigration, May 1975. London, 1975. pp. 57.

COMMUNITY RELATIONS COMMISSION. The future of broadcasting: Community Relations Commission evidence to the Annan Committee. [London, 1975]. fo. 8.

COMMUNITY RELATIONS COMMISSION. The government's role in race relations: Community Relations Commission additional evidence to the Select Committee on Race Relations and Immigration. [London, 1975]. pp. 4, v.

COMMUNITY RELATIONS COMMISSION. Organisation of race relations administration: Community Relations Commission evidence to the Select Committee on Race Relations and Immigration. [London, 1975]. pp. 15.

HUSBAND (CHARLES H.) ed. White media and black Britain: a critical look at the role of the media in race relations today. London, 1975. pp. 222. *bibliogs.*

LOMAS (GLENYS BARBARA GILLIAN) The coloured population of Great Britain: a comparative study of coloured households in four county boroughs, based on the 1971 census of population. London, 1975. pp. 91.

BIRMINGHAM COMMUNITY DEVELOPMENT PROJECT. The convenient scapegoat: facts and arguments against racialism. [Birmingham, 1976]. pp. 16.

MORRISON (LIONEL) As they see it: a race relations study of three areas from a black viewpoint. London, Community Relations Commission, 1976. pp. 127.

RUNNYMEDE TRUST. Race and the dangers of benign neglect;...report for 1975. London, [1976]. pp. 20.

TAYLOR (JOHN HENRY) The half-way generation: a study of Asian youths in Newcastle upon Tyne. Windsor, Berks., 1976. pp. 267. *bibliog.*

— Relations (general) with Russia.

NATIONAL CONGRESS OF PEACE AND FRIENDSHIP WITH THE U.S.S.R. 1st Congress, 1935. Britain and the Soviets: the Congress of Peace and Friendship with the U.S.S.R.; (verbatim report). London, 1936. pp. 197.

CALHOUN (DANIEL FAIRCHILD) The united front: the TUC and the Russians, 1923-1928. Cambridge, 1976. pp. 450. *bibliog.*

— Relations (general) with the United States.

CONTRAST and connection: bicentennial essays in Anglo-American history; edited by H.C. Allen and Roger Thompson. London, 1976. pp. 373.

— Religion.

U.K. Census, 1851. Census of Great Britain, 1851: religious worship in England and Wales; abridged from the official report made by Horace Mann to...Registrar-General. London, 1854. pp. 142.

GILBERT (ALAN D.) Religion and society in industrial England: church, chapel and social change, 1740-1914. London, 1976. pp. 251. *bibliog.*

REDWOOD (JOHN) Reason, ridicule and religion: the age of enlightenment in England, 1660-1750. London, [1976]. pp. 287. *bibliog.*

— Social conditions.

DEAN (GEORGE ALFRED) Fallacies and tendencies of the age. London, 1871. pp. 251. *Essays on social and political problems written by way of narrative and dialogue.*

ALDEN (Sir PERCY) Democratic England. New York, 1912. pp. 271. *"The greater part of this book has already appeared in the shape of a series of articles written for the Chautauquan Magazine".*

CONQUEST (JOAN) The naked truth: shocking revelations about the slums; by an ex- nursing sister. London, 1933. pp. 158.

NORTH WEST JOINT PLANNING TEAM. Strategic plan for the north west, 1973. Technical papers. Nos. 1-12, 14, 16-17. [Manchester], 1973 [or rather 1974-76]. 18 pts. (in 3 vols) *Nos. 13 and 15 not allocated.*

COMMUNITY ACTION. Investigators' handbook: a guide for tenants, workers and action groups on how to investigate companies, organisations and individuals. London, [1975]. pp. 55.

NORTHERN REGION STRATEGY TEAM. First interim report. Newcastle upon Tyne, 1975. pp. 125.

BROWN (MURIEL) Introduction to social administration in Britain. 3rd ed. London, 1976. pp. 239. *bibliogs.*

—— Statistics.

U.K. Social Survey. The general household survey. a., 1971- London.

UNITED KINGDOM (Cont.)

— Social history.

ASHTON (JOHN) Antiquary. Social England under the Regency. East Ardsley, Wakefield, 1975 in progress. *Reprint of 1st ed. of 1890.*

WARD (WILLIAM REGINALD) Religion and society in England, 1790-1850. New York, 1973. pp. 339. *bibliog.*

RAFTIS (J. AMBROSE) Warboys: two hundred years in the life of an English mediaeval village. Toronto, 1974. pp. 267. *bibliog. (Pontifical Institute of Mediaeval Studies. Studies and Texts. 29)*

ALBION'S fatal tree: crime and society in eighteenth-century England; [by] Douglas Hay [and others]. London, 1975. pp. 352.

ARISTOCRATIC government and society in eighteenth-century England: the foundations of stability; edited with an introduction by Daniel A. Baugh. New York, 1975. pp. 274. *bibliog.*

BRANSON (NOREEN) Britain in the nineteen twenties. London, [1975]. pp. 274. *bibliog.*

CLARKSON (LESLIE A.) Death, disease and famine in pre-industrial England. Dublin, 1975. pp. 188. *bibliog.*

COOK (CHRISTOPHER PIERS) and KEITH (BRENDAN) British historical facts, 1830-1900. London, 1975. pp. 279. *bibliogs.*

FINLAY (JOHN L.) Canada in the North Atlantic triangle: two centuries of social change. Toronto, 1975. pp. 343. *bibliog.*

THOMPSON (EDWARD PALMER) Whigs and hunters: the origin of the Black Act. London, 1975. pp. 313.

CHAMBERLIN (E.R.) The awakening giant: Britain in the Industrial Revolution. London, 1976. pp. 168. *bibliog.*

CRISIS and controversy: essays in honour of A.J.P. Taylor; edited by Alan Sked and Chris Cook. london, 1976. pp. 198.

EMMISON (FREDERICK GEORGE) Elizabethan life: home, work and land; from Essex wills and sessions and manorial records. Chelmsford, 1976. pp. 364. *(Essex. Records Committee. Essex Record Office Publications. No. 69)*

GLYNN (SEAN) and OXBORROW (JOHN) Interwar Britain: a social and economic history. London, 1976. pp. 276.

MELLER (HELEN E.) Leisure and the changing city, 1870-1914. London, 1976. pp. 308. *bibliog.*

— — Bibliography.

CHALONER (WILLIAM HENRY) and RICHARDSON (R.C.) compilers. British economic and social history: a bibliographical guide. Manchester, [1976]. pp. 130.

— — Sources.

BARKER (THEODORE CARDWELL) ed. The long march of everyman. London, 1975. pp. 301. *Based on part of a BBC Radio 4 series broadcast November 1971 - May 1972.*

COCKERELL (HUGH ANTHONY LEWIS) and GREEN (EDWIN) The British insurance business, 1547-1970: an introduction and guide to historical records in the United Kingdom. London, 1976. pp. 142. *bibliog.*

KEATING (PETER J.) ed. Into unknown England, 1866-1913; selections from the social explorers. Manchester, 1976. pp. 320. *bibliog.*

— Social life and customs.

HEADS of the people; or, Portraits of the English; drawn by Kenny Meadows, with original essays by distinguished writers. London, [1840]. pp. 400.

— Social policy.

NORTH WEST JOINT PLANNING TEAM. Strategic plan for the north west, 1973. Technical papers. Nos. 1-12, 14, 16-17. [Manchester], 1973 [or rather 1974-76]. 18 pts. (in 3 vols) *Nos. 13 and 15 not allocated.*

FIELD (FRANK) 1942- , and TOWNSEND (PETER BRERETON) A social contract for families: memorandum to the Chancellor of the Exchequer, November 1974. London, 1975. pp. 45. *(Child Poverty Action Group. Poverty Pamphlets. 19)*

JONES (JAMES LARKIN) A world to win. London, 1975. pp. 14. *(London. University. Birkbeck College. Foundation Orations. 1975)*

NORTHERN REGION STRATEGY TEAM. First interim report. Newcastle upon Tyne, 1975. pp. 125.

REGIONAL devolution and social policy: [based on a two-day seminar held at the Centre for Studies in Social Policy in September 1974]; edited by Edward Craven. London, 1975. pp. 207.

WIRZ (HANS M.) Social aspects of planning in new towns. Farnborough, Hants., [1975]. pp. 237. *bibliog.*

BROWN (MURIEL) Introduction to social administration in Britain. 3rd ed. London, 1976. pp. 239. *bibliogs.*

FABIAN SOCIETY. Fabian Tracts. [No.] 443. In pursuit of equality; [by] Barbara Wootton. London, 1976. pp. 12. *(Blanche Colebrook Memorial Lectures. 1975)*

KLEIN (RUDOLF EWALD) and others. Constraints and choices: a commentary on the 1976 Public Expenditure White Paper. London, 1976. fo. 97. *bibliog. (Centre for Studies in Social Policy. Working Papers)*

LABOUR'S social priorities;...[by] Andrew Creese [and others];...[edited by] Howard Glennerster. London, 1976. pp. 36. *(Fabian Society. Research Series. [No.] 327)*

MARONEY (ROBERT M.) The family and the state: considerations for social policy. London, 1976. pp. 142.

NORTHERN REGION STRATEGY TEAM. Second interim report: strategic choices. Newcastle-upon-Tyne, 1976. pp. 58.

ROBSON (WILLIAM ALEXANDER) Welfare state and welfare society: illusion and reality. London, 1976. pp. 184.

TRADES UNION CONGRESS and LABOUR PARTY. Liaison Committee. The next three years and the problem of priorities. London, 1976. pp. 15.

— — Bibliography.

BLACKSTONE (TESSA ANN VOSPER) Social policy and administration in Britain: a bibliography;... with the assistance of Peter Vines. London, 1975. pp. 130.

— Statistics.

U.K. [Cabinet Office]. History of the Second World War: United Kingdom Civil Series. Statistical digest of the war; prepared in the Central Statistical Office. London, 1951 repr. 1975. pp. 248.

SERGEANT (GRAHAM A.V.) A statistical source-book for sociologists. 2nd ed. London, 1973. pp. 160. *bibliogs.*

PICKETT (KATHLEEN GORDON) Sources of official data. London, 1974. pp. 150.

U.K. Central Statistical Office. 1974. Facts in focus. 2nd ed. Harmondsworth, 1974. pp. 245.

COOK (CHRISTOPHER PIERS) and KEITH (BRENDAN) British historical facts, 1830-1900. London, 1975. pp. 279. *bibliogs.*

U.K. Central Statistical Office. Guide to official statistics. a., 1976 (no.1)- London.

U.K. Stationery Office. 1975- . Statistics: publications of UK government departments and international organisations. [London], 1975 in progress. *(Subject Catalogues. No. 1) Current issue only kept.*

U.K. Central Statistical Office. Guide to official statistics. a., 1976 (no.1)- London.

U.K. Office of Population Censuses and Surveys. OPCS Monitor[s]. irreg., current issues only. London.

— Statistics, Medical.

U.K. Office of Population Censuses and Surveys. OPCS Monitor[s]. irreg., current issues only. London.

— Statistics, Vital.

U.K. Office of Population Censuses and Surveys. OPCS Monitor[s]. irreg., current issues only. London.

U.K. Office of Population Censuses and Surveys. Population estimates: the Registrar General's estimates of the population of regions and local government areas of England and Wales by sex and age. a., 1974/1975- London.

PERMANAND (R.) and FIELD (A. MIRYAM) Birth registration trends, 1965-1975. London, [1975]. pp. 24. *bibliog. (London. Greater London Council. Research Memoranda. 464)*

— Commonwealth.

BROWNE (JOHN HUTTON BALFOUR) Essays, critical and political. vol. 2. Political. London, 1907. pp. 333. *Of the eleven essays nine are reprinted from the Westminster Review, 1876-1886 and one from the National Review, 1906.*

FESTIVAL OF EMPIRE, 1911. [Minute book and descriptive volume. 1911]. 2 vols. *Typescript and printed matter.*

GRAF (GEORG ENGELBERT) England am Scheidewege. Berlin, 1927. pp. 48. *bibliog. (Reichsleitung der Jungsozialisten. Jungsozialistische Schriftenreihe)*

COMMONWEALTH RECORD OF RECENT EVENTS; [pd. by] Commonwealth Secretariat. q. London. *Current issues only kept.*

— — Commercial policy.

ANDERSON (MOSA) Opening the Empire door: a positive policy for peace. London, 1937. pp. 8. *bibliog.*

— — Emigration and immigration.

HUTTENBACK (ROBERT A.) Racism and empire: white settlers and colored immigrants in the British self-governing colonies, 1830-1910. Ithaca, N.Y., 1976. pp. 359. *bibliog.*

— — Foreign relations — India.

TINKER (HUGH) Separate and unequal: India and the Indians in the British Commonwealth, 1920-1950. London, [1976]. pp. 460. *bibliog.*

— — South Africa.

SCHOLTZ (GERT DANIEL) Hertzog en Smuts en die Britse Ryk. Kaapstad, 1975. pp. 158. *bibliog.*

— — History.

PORTER (BERNARD) The lion's share: a short history of British imperialism, 1850- 1970. London, 1975. pp. 408.

TOWNSEND (PETER) 1914- . The last emperor: decline and fall of the British Empire. London, [1975]. pp. 287. *bibliog.*

HYAM (RONALD) Britain's imperial century, 1815-1914: a study of empire and expansion. London, 1976. pp. 462.

— — Officials and employees.

LUMLEY (E.K.) Forgotten mandate; a British district officer in Tanganyika. London, [1976]. pp. 178.

— — Politics and government.

ASIWAJU (ANTHONY IJAOLA) Western Yorubaland under European rule, 1889-1945: a comparative analysis of French and British colonialism. London, 1976. pp. 303. *bibliog.*

WARD (JOHN MANNING) Colonial self-government: the British experience, 1759-1856. London, 1976. pp. 399. *bibliog.*

— — Race question.

HUTTENBACK (ROBERT A.) Racism and empire: white settlers and colored immigrants in the British self-governing colonies, 1830-1910. Ithaca, N.Y., 1976. pp. 359. *bibliog.*

UNITED NATIONS.

BRONIAREK (ZYGMUNT) Gorące dni Manhattanu. Warszawa, [1961]. pp. 83.

UNITED NATIONS. 1971-73. Repertory of practice of United Nations organs; (Supplement No. 3). New York, 1971-73. 4 vols(in 2). *For the original Repertory which this supplement continues see UN. V. 1955.2.*

The UNITED Nations: problems and prospects; [papers presented at a conference held at St. Louis in 1971]; Edwin H. Fedder, editor. St. Louis, 1971. pp. 191. *(Missouri University, St. Louis. Center for International Studies. Monographs. No. 3)*

The UNITED Nations in international politics; edited by Leon Gordenker. Princeton, 1971. pp. 241.

ANDEMICAEL (BERHANYKUN) and MURDOCH (ANTHONY J.) eds. International youth organizations and the United Nations;... contributions by Louis Simon [and others]. New York, United Nations Institute for Training and Research, 1973. pp. 95. *bibliog. (Research Reports. No. 17)*

HILL (WILLIAM MARTIN) Towards greater order, coherence and co-ordination in the United Nations system. New York, United Nations Institute for Training and Research, [1974]. pp. 115. *(Research Reports. No. 20)*

LEVIN (AIDA LUISA) The Organization of American States and the United Nations: relations in the peace and security field. New York, United Nations Institute for Training and Research, 1974. pp. 114. *bibliog. (Peaceful Settlement [Series] No. 7)*

ROWE (EDWARD THOMAS) Strengthening the United Nations: a study of the evolution of member state commitments. Beverly Hills, [1974]. pp. 88. *bibliog.*

BAILEY (SYDNEY D.) The procedure of the UN Security Council. Oxford, 1975. pp. 424. *bibliog.*

CIOBANU (DAN) Preliminary objections related to the jurisdiction of the United Nations political organs. The Hague, 1975. pp. 230.

HOLBORN (LOUISE W.) and others. Refugees: a problem of our time: the work of the United Nations High Commissioner for Refugees, 1951-1972. Metuchen, N.J., 1975. 2 vols. *bibliog.*

LARSEN (CHERYL BETH) The United Nations Convention on the Political Rights of Women, 1952: a political analysis of its origin, negotiation and effects. 1975. fo. 229. *bibliog. Typescript. Ph.D. (London) thesis: unpublished. This thesis is the property of London University and may not be removed from the Library.*

RAMAN (K. VENKATA) The ways of the peacemaker: a study of United Nations intermediary assistance in the peaceful settlement of disputes. New York, United Nations Institute for Training and Research, 1975. pp. 142. *bibliog. (Peaceful Settlement Series. No. 8)*

THEODOULOU (CHRISTOS A.) The United Nations from the inside and a note on the position and role of Greece and Cyprus. [New York, 1975]. pp. 30. *With Greek text.*

AKINDELE (R.A.) The organization and promotion of world peace: a study of universal-regional relationships. Toronto, [1976]. pp. 204. *bibliog.*

ANDEMICAEL (BERHANYKUN) The OAU and the UN: relations between the Organization of African Unity and the United Nations. New York, 1976. pp. 331. *bibliog. (United Nations Institute for Training and Research. Regional Studies. No.2)*

SALAS (RAFAEL M.) People: an international choice: the multilateral approach to population. Oxford, 1976. pp. 154.

SCHWARZENBERGER (GEORG) International law as applied by international courts and tribunals. vol. 3. International constitutional law. London, 1976. pp. 680. *bibliog.*

— Armed forces.

BULL (ODD) War and peace in the Middle East: the experiences and views of a U.N. observer. London, 1976. pp. 205.

DAYAL (RAJESHWAR) Mission for Hammarskjold: the Congo crisis. London, 1976. pp. 335. *bibliog.*

MOSKOS (CHARLES C.) Peace soldiers: the sociology of a United Nations military force. Chicago, 1976. pp. 171.

— Bibliography.

UNITED NATIONS. Monthly selection of new publications. m., current issues only. Geneva. *[In English and French].*

— Economic assistance.

UNITED NATIONS. Development Programme. Annual report. a., 1972- New York.

DEVELOPMENT FORUM; pd. by the U.N. Centre for Economic and Social Information. m., F 1973 (v.1, no.1)- Geneva.

ETUDES de doctrine et de droit international du développement; par Alain Colombeau [and others]. Paris, 1975. pp. 385. *bibliog. (Université d'Aix-Marseille. Faculté de Droit et de Science Politique. Travaux et Mémoires. No. 21)*

— Officials and employees.

SZALAI (SANDOR) The situation of women in the United Nations: a report based on the proceedings of the Colloquium of Senior United Nations Officials held on 4-6 July 1972 at Schloss Hernstein (Austria). [New York], United Nations Institute for Training and Research, 1973. pp. 49. *(Research Reports. No. 18)*

— Technical assistance.

UNITED NATIONS. Development Programme. Annual report. a., 1972- New York.

— Cyprus.

THEODOULOU (CHRISTOS A.) The United Nations from the inside and a note on the position and role of Greece and Cyprus. [New York, 1975]. pp. 30. *With Greek text.*

MOSKOS (CHARLES C.) Peace soldiers: the sociology of a United Nations military force. Chicago, 1976. pp. 171.

— Germany.

GERMANY (BUNDESREPUBLIK). Presse- und Informationsamt. 1974. The Federal Republic of Germany, member of the United Nations: a documentation. Bonn, [1974]. pp. 200.

— Greece.

THEODOULOU (CHRISTOS A.) The United Nations from the inside and a note on the position and role of Greece and Cyprus. [New York, 1975]. pp. 30. *With Greek text.*

— Rhodesia.

ZACKLIN (RALPH) The United Nations and Rhodesia: a study in international law. New York, 1974. pp. 188.

— Russia — Ukraine.

ZABIHAILO (KOSTIANTYN SEMENOVYCH) ed. V interesakh myru i druzhby mizh narodamy: mizhnarodnopravova diial'nist' Ukraïns'koï RSR, 1945-1972; dokumenty i komentari. Kyïv, 1974. pp. 335. *bibliog.*

— South Africa.

LINT (GEORGE J. DE) The United Nations: the abhorrent misapplication of the Charter in respect of South Africa. Zwolle, [1976]. pp. 121.

UNITED NATIONS CONFERENCE ON TRADE AND DEVELOPMENT.

KROMMENACKER (RAYMOND J.) Les Nations Unies et l'assurance-réassurance: l'action du droit privé dans les relations entre pays développés et pays en voie de développement et l'action des organisations internationales. Paris, 1975. pp. 215. *bibliog.*

UNITED NATIONS ECONOMIC COMMISSION FOR EUROPE.

UNITED NATIONS. Economic Commission for Europe. 1970- . Terms of reference and rules of procedure of the Economic Commission for Europe. (E/ECE/778 and Revs.). New York, 1970 in progress.

UNITED SOUTH AFRICAN NATIONAL PARTY.

TAYLOR (CATHERINE) If courage goes: my twenty years in South African politics. Johannesburg, 1976. pp. 316.

UNITED STATES

— Appropriations and expenditures.

GIST (JOHN R.) Mandatory expenditures and the defense sector: theory of budgetary incrementalism. Beverly Hills, [1974]. pp. 39. *bibliog.*

FISHER (LOUIS) Presidential spending power. Princeton, [1975]. pp. 345.

— Armed forces.

CENTER FOR DEFENSE INFORMATION. Current issues in U.S. defense policy; edited by David Thomas Johnson [and] Barry R. Schneider. New York, 1976. pp. 254.

— — Negroes.

FONER (JACK D.) Blacks and the military in American history: a new perspective. New York, 1974. pp. 278. *bibliog.*

— — Korea.

CLOUGH (RALPH N.) Deterrence and defense in Korea: the role of U.S. forces. Washington, [1976]. pp. 61. *(Brookings Institution. Studies in Defense Policy)*

— Army — History.

KOHN (RICHARD H.) Eagle and sword: the Federalists and the creation of the military establishment in America, 1783-1802. New York, [1975]. pp. 443. *bibliog.*

— Army officers.

SARKESIAN (SAM CHARLES) The professional army officer in a changing society. Chicago, [1975]. pp. 268. *bibliog.*

— Biography.

AMERICAN men and women of science:...a biographical directory... the social and behavioral sciences. 12th ed. New York, 1973. 2 vols.

WHO's who in American politics: fifth edition 1975-1976;... consulting editors Edmund L. Henshaw [and] Paul A. Theis. New York, [1975]. pp. 1090.

— Boundaries.

WRIGHT (JAMES LEITCH) Britain and the American frontier, 1783-1815. Athens, Ga., [1975]. pp. 251. *bibliog.*

— — Canada.

INTERNATIONAL JOINT COMMISSION, CANADA AND UNITED STATES. Rules of procedure and text of treaty. [Washington, 1968]. pp. 22.

UNITED STATES (Cont.)

— Civilization.

NELSON (KEITH L.) ed. The impact of war on American life: the twentieth-century experience. New York, [1971]. pp. 395. *bibliog.*

NIEBURG (HAROLD L.) Culture storm: politics and the ritual order. London, [1973]. pp. 262. *bibliog.*

WHISENHUNT (DONALD W.) The environment and the American experience: a historian looks at the ecological crisis. Port Washington, N.Y., 1974. pp. 136.

COONTZ (STEPHANIE) and FRANK (CARL) eds. Life in capitalist America: private profit and social decay; [by] Stephanie Coontz [and others]. New York, [1975]. pp. 285. *(Reprinted from International Socialist Review, 1971-74)*

The RISING South;...edited by Donald R. Noble and Joab L. Thomas. Alabama, [1976 in progress].

BOORSTIN (DANIEL JOSEPH) The exploring spirit: America and the world experience. London, 1976. pp. 102. *(British Broadcasting Corporation. Reith Lectures. 1975)*

CAMPBELL (ALBERT ANGUS) and others. The quality of American life: perceptions, evaluations and satisfactions. New York, [1976]. pp. 583. *bibliog.*

— Commerce.

COMMERCE AMERICA (formerly Commerce today); [pd. by] U.S. Department of Commerce. s-m. (formerly w.), Oc 19 1970 (v.1, no.1)- Washington.

SAMUELSON (PAUL ANTHONY) International trade for a rich country. Stockholm, 1972. pp. 27. *(Sveriges Industriförbund. [Nobel Prize] Lectures. 1972)*

KAUFMAN (BURTON IRA) Efficiency and expansion: foreign trade organization in the Wilson administration, 1913-1921. Westport, Conn., 1974. pp. 300. *bibliog.*

— — China.

CAHILL (HARRY A.) The China trade and U.S. tariffs. New York, 1973. pp. 161. *bibliog.*

— — Communist countries.

RYANS (JOHN K.) and others, eds. China, the U.S.S.R. and eastern Europe: a U.S. trade perspective. Kent, Ohio, [1974]. pp. 196. *bibliog.*

— — Russia.

WILSON (JOAN HOFF) Ideology and economics: U.S. relations with the Soviet Union, 1918-1933. Columbia, Mo., 1974. pp. 192. *bibliog.*

KIRCHNER (WALTHER) Studies in Russian-American commerce, 1820-1860. Leiden, 1975. pp. 265. *bibliog.*

STOWELL (CHRISTOPHER E.) Soviet industrial import priorities, with marketing considerations for exporting to the USSR. New York, 1975. pp. 505. *bibliog.*

GIBSON (JAMES R.) Imperial Russia in frontier America: the changing geography of supply of Russian America, 1784-1867. New York, 1976. pp. 257. *bibliogs.*

— — United Kingdom.

CONFERENCE ON EARLY AMERICAN HISTORY, 27TH, 1970. Of mother country and plantations: proceedings of the... conference...; edited by Virginia Bever Platt and David Curtis Skaggs. Bowling Green, Ohio, 1971. pp. 127. *bibliog.*

— Commercial policy.

KAUFMAN (BURTON IRA) Efficiency and expansion: foreign trade organization in the Wilson administration, 1913-1921. Westport, Conn., 1974. pp. 300. *bibliog.*

— Congress.

FISHEL (JEFF) Party and opposition: congressional challengers in American politics. New York, [1973]. pp. 254. *bibliog.*

BARBER (SOTIRIOS A.) The constitution and the delegation of Congressional power. Chicago, 1975. pp. 153.

CONGRESS against the president; (edited by Harvey C. Mansfield). New York, 1975. pp. 200. *Includes essays discussed at a conference sponsored by the Academy of Political Science at Columbia University in 1975.*

ORNSTEIN (NORMAN J.) ed. Congress in change: evolution and reform. New York, 1975. pp. 298. *bibliog.*

REICHARD (GARY W.) The reaffirmation of Republicanism: Eisenhower and the eighty-third Congress. Knoxville, Tenn., [1975]. pp. 303. *bibliog.*

— — Elections.

SHIPSTEAD (PATRICK E.) New perspectives on American politics: a report from Michigan on the busing issue. Princeton, [1973]. pp. 69. *(Princeton University. Woodrow Wilson School of Public and International Affairs. Woodrow Wilson Association Monograph Series in Public Affairs. No. 5)*

— — House of Representatives.

BEARD (EDMUND) and HORN (STEPHEN) Congressional ethics: the view from the House. Washington, D.C., [1975]. pp. 87.

— — Officials and employees.

LEGISLATIVE staffing: a comparative perspective; edited by James J. Heaphey and Alan P. Balutis. New York, [1975]. pp. 244.

— — Powers and duties.

HAMILTON (JAMES) 1938- . The power to probe: a study of congressional investigations. New York, [1976]. pp. 333.

— Constitution.

MITCHELL (BROADUS) and MITCHELL (LOUISE PEARSON) A biography of the constitution of the United States: its origin, formation, adoption, interpretation. 2nd ed. New York, 1975. pp. 401. *bibliog.*

AMERICAN ACADEMY OF POLITICAL AND SOCIAL SCIENCE. Annals. vol. 426. Bientennial conference on the constitution: a report to the Academy; special editor of this volume: Marvin E. Wolfgang. Philadelphia, 1976. pp. 281. *bibliog.*

ECKHARDT (ROBERT CHRISTIAN) and BLACK (CHARLES LUND) The tides of power: conversations on the American constitution. New Haven, 1976. pp. 225.

MILLER (ARTHUR SELWYN) The modern corporate state: private governments and the American constitution. Westport, Conn., 1976. pp. 269.

VILE (MAURICE JOHN CRAWLEY) Politics in the U.S.A. rev. ed. London, 1976. pp. 318. *bibliog.*

— Constitutional history.

MITCHELL (BROADUS) and MITCHELL (LOUISE PEARSON) A biography of the constitution of the United States: its origin, formation, adoption, interpretation. 2nd ed. New York, 1975. pp. 401. *bibliog.*

— Constitutional law.

CONANT (MICHAEL) The constitution and capitalism. St. Paul, Minn., 1974. pp. 306.

BARBER (SOTIRIOS A.) The constitution and the delegation of Congressional power. Chicago, 1975. pp. 153.

BICKEL (ALEXANDER MORDECAI) The morality of consent. New Haven, 1975. pp. 156. *bibliog. (Yale University. William C. DeVane Lectures. 1973)*

AMERICAN SOCIETY OF INTERNATIONAL LAW. Panel on the Constitution and the Conduct of Foreign Policy. The constitution and the conduct of foreign policy: an inquiry by a panel of the...Society...; edited by Francis O. Wilcox [and] Richard A. Frank. New York, [1976]. pp. 145.

CORWIN (EDWARD SAMUEL) Presidential power and the constitution: essays...; edited with an introduction by Richard Loss. Ithaca, 1976. pp. 185. *bibliog.*

— Defences.

SANDERS (RALPH) The politics of defense analysis. New York, [1973]. pp. 361.

GIST (JOHN R.) Mandatory expenditures and the defense sector: theory of budgetary incrementalism. Beverly Hills, [1974]. pp. 39. *bibliog.*

MUSKIE (EDMUND S.) and BROCK (BILL) What price defense?. Washington, [1974]. pp. 73. *(American Enterprise Institute for Public Policy Research. Rational Debate Seminars. [7th Series. 3])*

ALIANO (RICHARD A.) American defense policy from Eisenhower to Kennedy: the politics of changing military requirements, 1957-1961. Athens, Oh., [1975]. pp. 309. *bibliog.*

CENTER FOR DEFENSE INFORMATION. Current issues in U.S. defense policy; edited by David Thomas Johnson [and] Barry R. Schneider. New York, 1976. pp. 254.

GRAY (COLIN S.) The Soviet-American arms race. Farnborough, Hants, [1976]. pp. 196.

INTERNATIONAL INSTITUTE FOR STRATEGIC STUDIES. Adelphi Papers. No. 121. Limited nuclear options: deterrence and the new American doctrine; by Lynn Etheridge Davis. London, 1976. pp. 22.

The MANAGEMENT of defence: papers presented [at a residential seminar] at the National Defence College, Latimer, in September 1974; edited by Laurence Martin. London, 1976. pp. 137.

QUANBECK (ALTON H.) and WOOD (ARCHIE L.) Modernizing the strategic bomber force: why and how. Washington, [1976]. pp. 116. *(Brookings Institution. Studies in Defense Policy)*

— Description and travel.

FOX (GEORGE TOWNSEND) American journals...1831-1868; editor, Bernard Crick. London, [1961]. 4 vols. *(British Association for American Studies. British Records relating to America in Microform. Series B) Microfilm of manuscript: 1 reel. No part of the contents may be published without the consent of the Librarian, South Shields Public Library.*

GASTIL (RAYMOND D.) Cultural regions of the United States. Seattle, [1975]. pp. 366. *bibliog.*

— Economic conditions.

BJORK (GORDON C.) Private enterprise and public interest: the development of American capitalism. Englewood Cliffs, [1969]. pp. xi,243.

MANDELL (LEWIS) Economics from the consumer's perspective. Chicago, [1975]. pp. 279. *bibliogs.*

NAYLOR (THOMAS H.) and CLOTFELTER (JAMES) Strategies for change in the South. Chapel Hill, [1975]. pp. 316.

PEIRCE (NEAL R.) The Border South States: people, politics and power in the five Border South States. New York, [1975]. pp. 415. *bibliog.*

ROSEN (SUMNER M.) ed. Economic power failure: the current American crisis. New York, [1975]. pp. 295. *bibliog.*

SALE (KIRKPATRICK) Power shift: the rise of the southern rim and its challenge to the eastern establishment. New York, [1975]. pp. 362.

The RISING South;...edited by Donald R. Noble and Joab L. Thomas. Alabama, [1976 in progress].

ECONOMIC means for human needs: social indicators of well-being and discontent; edited by Burkhard Strumpel. Ann Arbor, 1976. pp. 303. *bibliogs.*

PARAMETERS and policies in the U.S. economy; editor Otto Eckstein. Amsterdam, 1976. pp. 389. *bibliogs.*

TYLER (GUS) Scarcity: a critique of the American economy. New York, [1976]. pp. 245.

UNITED STATES (Cont.)

— — Mathematical models.

The BROOKINGS model: perspective and recent developments; edited by Gary Fromm [and] Lawrence R. Klein; [papers of a conference held at Brookings Institution in February 1972]. Amsterdam, 1975. pp. 679.

HICKMAN (BERT G.) and COEN (ROBERT M.) An annual growth model of the U.S. economy. Amsterdam, 1976. pp. 287. *bibliog.*

PARAMETERS and policies in the U.S. economy; editor Otto Eckstein. Amsterdam, 1976. pp. 389. *bibliogs.*

— Economic history.

COCHRAN (THOMAS CHILDS) and MILLER (WILLIAM) 1912- . The age of enterprise: a social history of industrial America. rev. ed. New York, 1961. pp. 396. *bibliog.*

BJORK (GORDON C.) Private enterprise and public interest: the development of American capitalism. Englewood Cliffs, [1969]. pp. xi,243.

HERBERT Hoover and the crisis of American capitalism; contributors: Ellis W. Hawley [and others]. Cambridge, Mass., [1973]. pp. 138.

GHOSH (SANTIKUMAR) Development of the American economy. [Calcutta, United States Information Service, 1974?]. pp. 42.

ZILG (GERARD COLBY) Du Pont: behind the nylon curtain. Englewood Cliffs, [1974]. pp. 623.

GOODWIN (CRAUFURD D. W.) ed. Exhortation and controls: the search for a wage-price policy, 1945-1971. Washington, D.C., [1975]. pp. 432. *bibliog. (Brookings Institution. Studies in Wage-Price Policy)*

KLINGAMAN (DAVID C.) and VEDDER (RICHARD K.) eds. Essays in nineteenth century economic history: the old Northwest. Athens, Ohio, [1975]. pp. 356. *bibliogs.*

TEMIN (PETER) Causal factors in American economic growth in the nineteenth century. London, 1975. pp. 80. *bibliog. (Economic History Society. Studies in Economic and Social History)*

HIMMELBERG (ROBERT F.) The origins of the National Recovery Administration: business, government and the trade association issue, 1921-1933. New York, 1976. pp. 232. *bibliog.*

HOLMES (GRAEME M.) Britain and America: a comparative economic history, 1850-1939. Newton Abbot, 1976. pp. 224. *bibliog.*

HUGHES (JONATHAN ROBERTS TYSON) Social control in the colonial economy. Charlottesville, Va., 1976. pp. 178.

— Economic policy.

STAVE (BRUCE M.) The New Deal and the last hurrah: Pittsburgh machine politics. Pittsburgh, [1970]. pp. 262. *bibliog.*

HERBERT Hoover and the crisis of American capitalism; contributors: Ellis W. Hawley [and others]. Cambridge, Mass., [1973]. pp. 138.

CONFERENCE ON PUBLIC POLICY FOR URBAN MINORITIES AND THE POOR IN THE 1970S, NASHVILLE, 1972. The urban scene in the seventies: (proceedings...); edited by James F. Blumstein and Eddie J. Martin. Nashville, 1974. pp. 256. *bibliogs. Proceedings of a conference sponsored by the Urban Affairs Institute of Fisk University and the Urban and Regional Development Center of Vanderbilt University.*

BELLUSH (BERNARD) The failure of the N[ational] R[ecovery] A[dministration]. New York, [1975]. pp. 197. *bibliog.*

BRAEMAN (JOHN) and others, eds. The New Deal. Columbus, Ohio, 1975. 2 vols.

DOLBEARE (KENNETH M.) ed. Public policy evaluation;...with a section on crime control evaluation edited by John A. Gardiner. Beverly Hills, [1975]. pp. 286.

HOLMES (MICHAEL S.) The New Deal in Georgia: an administrative history. Westport, Conn., [1975]. pp. 364. *bibliog.*

INGALLS (ROBERT P.) Herbert H. Lehman and New York's Little New Deal. New York, 1975. pp. 287. *bibliog.*

ISOLATION or interdependence?: today's choices for tomorrow's world; (papers...prepared for a conference at the University of Chicago...1974); edited by Morton A. Kaplan. New York, [1975]. pp. 254. *bibliog.*

KOSTERS (MARVIN H.) Controls and inflation: the economic stabilization program in retrospect. Washington, 1975. pp. 135. *(American Enterprise Institute for Public Policy Research. Domestic Affairs Studies. 37)*

PRESCOTT (JAMES RUSSELL) and LEWIS (W. CRIS) Urban-regional economic growth and policy. Ann Arbor, [1975]. pp. 220. *bibliogs.*

ROSEN (SUMNER M.) ed. Economic power failure: the current American crisis. New York, [1975]. pp. 295. *bibliog.*

SHEPHERD (WILLIAM G.) The treatment of market power: antitrust, regulation and public enterprise. New York, 1975. pp. 326. *bibliog.*

STEIN (HERBERT) Economic planning and the improvement of economic policy. Washington, D.C., 1975. pp. 33. *(American Enterprise Institute for Public Policy Research. Domestic Affairs Studies. 38)*

STIGLER (GEORGE JOSEPH) The citizen and the state: essays on regulation. Chicago, 1975. pp. 209.

SUTTON (ANTONY C.) Wall Street and FDR. New Rochelle, [1975]. pp. 200. *bibliog.*

TWIGHT (CHARLOTTE) America's emerging fascist economy. New Rochelle, N.Y., [1975]. pp. 315.

ECONOMIC regulatory policies; edited by James E. Anderson. Lexington, Mass., [1976]. pp. 211.

GRAHAM (OTIS L.) Toward a planned society: from Roosevelt to Nixon. New York, 1976. pp. 357. *bibliog.*

HARRINGTON (MICHAEL) b. 1928. The twilight of capitalism. New York, [1976]. pp. 446. *bibliog.*

JANOWITZ (MORRIS) Social control of the welfare state. New York, [1976]. pp. 170. *bibliog.*

LAMBRO (DONALD) The conscience of a young conservative. New Rochelle, N.Y., [1976]. pp. 125.

LEVITAN (SAR A.) and TAGGART (ROBERT) The promise of greatness. Cambridge, Mass., 1976. pp. 316.

NUTTER (GILBERT WARREN) Central economic planning: the visible hand. Washington, D.C., 1976. pp. 23. *(American Enterprise Institute for Public Policy Research. Domestic Affairs Studies. 41)*

PARAMETERS and policies in the U.S. economy; editor Otto Eckstein. Amsterdam, 1976. pp. 389. *bibliogs.*

STEVENS (ROBERT WARREN) Vain hopes, grim realities: the economic consequences of the Vietnam war. New York, 1976. pp. 229.

— — Congresses.

CAPITALISM and freedom: problems and prospects: proceedings of a conference in honor of Milton Friedman [held at the University of Virginia in 1972]; edited by Richard T. Selden. Charlottesville, Va., 1975. pp. 331.

— — Mathematical models.

PARAMETERS and policies in the U.S. economy; editor Otto Eckstein. Amsterdam, 1976. pp. 389. *bibliogs.*

— Emigration and immigration.

KROUSE (RUTH) The attitude of the American Federation of Labor towards immigration. [1931]. pp. 75. *bibliog. M.A.(Columbia University) thesis: unpublished. Microfilm of typescripts: 1 reel.*

PITKIN (THOMAS M.) Keepers of the gate: a history of Ellis Island. New York, 1975. pp. 226. *bibliog.*

JONES (MALDWYN ALLEN) Destination America. London, [1976]. pp. 256. *bibliog.*

WYNN (DAVID ROBERT) Trade unions and the 'new' immigration: a study of the United Mine Workers of America, 1890-1920. 1976. fo. 452. *bibliog. Typescript. Ph.D. (London) thesis: unpublished. This thesis is the property of London University and may not be removed from the Library.*

— Executive departments.

McCULLOCH (FRANK W.) and BORNSTEIN (TIM) The National Labor Relations Board. New York, 1974. pp. 200. *bibliog.*

BELLUSH (BERNARD) The failure of the N[ational] R[ecovery] A[dministration]. New York, [1975]. pp. 197. *bibliog.*

CRENSON (MATTHEW A.) The federal machine: beginnings of bureaucracy in Jacksonian America. Baltimore, [1975]. pp. 186. *bibliog.*

HOLMES (MICHAEL S.) The New Deal in Georgia: an administrative history. Westport, Conn., [1975]. pp. 364. *bibliog.*

LEVINE (ARTHUR L.) The future of the U.S. space program. New York, 1975. pp. 198. *bibliog.*

ROBINSON (GLEN O.) The Forest Service: (a study in public land management). Baltimore, [1975]. pp. 337.

WHITE (MICHAEL J.) Management science in federal agencies: the adoption and diffusion of a socio-technical innovation. Lexington, Mass., [1975]. pp. 111.

GOLDWATER (BARRY MORRIS) The coming breakpoint. New York, [1976]. pp. 184.

KAUFMAN (HERBERT) Are government organizations immortal?. Washington, 1976. pp. 79.

McDOWELL (DOUGLAS S.) and HUHN (KENNETH C.) N[ational] L[abor] R[elations] B[oard] remedies for unfair labor practices. Philadelphia, [1976]. pp. 304. *(Pennsylvania University. Wharton School of Finance and Commerce. Industrial Research Unit. Labor Relations and Public Policy Series. Reports. No. 12.)*

— Foreign economic relations.

HOWELL (WILLIAMSON S.) ed. The United States and France: correspondence dealing with economic relations, 1811-1930; [with] Index. [Paris, 1931]. 18 vols. *Microfilm: 7 reels. Index on reel 1. Cover documents held at the U.S. Embassy in Paris.*

ECKES (ALFRED E.) A search for solvency: Bretton Woods and the international monetary system, 1941-1971. Austin, [1975]. pp. 355. *bibliog.*

GILPIN (ROBERT) U.S. power and the multinational corporation: the political economy of foreign direct investment. New York, [1975]. pp. 291.

HANSEN (ROGER D.) A new international economic order?; an outline for a constructive U.S. response. Washington, 1975. pp. 34. *(Overseas Development Council. Development Papers. 19)*

ISOLATION or interdependence?: today's choices for tomorrow's world; (papers...prepared for a conference at the University of Chicago...1974); edited by Morton A. Kaplan. New York, [1975]. pp. 254. *bibliog.*

MONROE (WILBUR F.) The new internationalism: strategy and intiatives for U.S. foreign economic policy. Lexington, Mass., [1976]. pp. 238.

— — America, Latin.

HANSEN (ROGER D.) U.S.-Latin American economic policy: bilateral, regional, or global? Washington, D.C., 1975. pp. 69. *(Overseas Development Council. Development Papers. 18)*

UNITED STATES(Cont.)

SWANSBROUGH (ROBERT H.) The embattled colossus: economic nationalism and United States investors in Latin America. Gainesville, Florida, 1976. pp. 261. *bibliog.* (Florida University. School of Inter-American Studies. Latin American Monographs. 2nd Series. 16)

—— Arab countries.

AL-HAMAD (ABDLATIF Y.) The Middle East's economic aspirations and the United States. [Kuwait], 1975. pp. 11.

—— Brazil.

SOARES (ORLANDO ESTEVÃO DA COSTA) Desenvolvimento econômico-social do Brasil y EUA. [Rio de Janeiro, 1975]. pp. 170. *bibliog.*

—— Canada.

GONICK (CY) Inflation or depression: the continuing crisis of the Canadian economy. Toronto, 1975. pp. 448. *bibliog.*

—— Chile.

PETRAS (JAMES FRANK) and MORLEY (MORRIS H.) The United States and Chile: imperialism and the overthrow of the Allende government. New York, [1975]. pp. 217.

—— France.

HOWELL (WILLIAMSON S.) ed. The United States and France: correspondence dealing with economic relations, 1811-1930; [with] Index. [Paris, 1931]. 18 vols. *Microfilm:* 7 reels. Index on reel 1. Cover documents held at the U.S. Embassy in Paris.

—— Japan.

JAPAN-U.S. ASSEMBLY, 1974. The Japan-U.S. Assembly: proceedings of a conference on Japan-U.S. economic policy; (sponsored by the Conference Board on U.S.-Japan Economic Policy). Washington, [1975]. pp. 154.

ROEMER (JOHN E.) U.S.-Japanese competition in international markets: a study of the trade-investment cycle in modern capitalism. Berkeley, [1975]. pp. 242. *bibliog.* (California University. Institute of International Studies. Research Series. No. 22)

—— Poland.

STASHEVSKYI (DMYTRO MYKOLAIOVYCH) Interwencja pod pozorem pomocy: działalność misji 'żywnościowych Stanów Zjednoczonych w Polsce; [translation from Russian]. Kraków, 1964. pp. 119.

—— United Kingdom.

BOYCE (ROBERT WILLIAM DEWAR) Search for recovery: the influence of the United States and France on British plans for economic recovery, 1929-31. 1975. fo. 384. *bibliog. Typescript. Ph.D. (London) thesis: unpublished. This thesis is the property of London University and may not be removed from the Library.*

— Foreign opinion, Japanese.

MUTUAL images: essays in American-Japanese relations [given at a conference held on Kauai, Hawaii in 1972] (by Priscilla A. Clapp [and others]); edited by Akira Iriye. Cambridge, Mass., 1975. pp. 304. (Harvard University. Harvard Studies in American-East Asian Relations. 7)

— Foreign relations.

WESTERFIELD (HOLT BRADFORD) Foreign policy and party politics: Pearl Harbor to Korea. New York, 1972. pp. 448. *bibliog. First published in 1955 by Yale University Press.*

RAKOWSKI (MIECZYSŁAW F.) Zachód szuka ideologii. Warszawa, 1961. pp. 113.

McCARTHY (EUGENE J.) The limits of power: America's role in the world. New York, [1967]. pp. 246.

TRANI (EUGENE P.) The Treaty of Portsmouth: an adventure in American diplomacy. Lexington, Ky., [1969]. pp. 194. *bibliog.*

BERNSTEIN (BARTON J.) and MATUSOW (ALLEN J.) eds. Twentieth century America: recent interpretations. 2nd ed. New York, [1972]. pp. 582. *bibliogs.*

[CARNEGIE ENDOWMENT FOR INTERNATIONAL PEACE]. Carnegie Endowment for International Peace. New York, [1974]. pp. 60.

CONFERENCE ON THE NATIONAL ARCHIVES AND FOREIGN RELATIONS RESEARCH, WASHINGTON, 1969. The National Archives and foreign relations research: (papers and proceedings of the Conference...sponsored by the National Archives and Records Service); edited by Milton O. Gustafson. Athens, Ohio, [1974]. pp. 292. (United States. National Archives. National Archives Conferences. vol. 4)

DONOVAN (JOHN C.) The cold warriors: a policy-making elite. Lexington, Mass., [1974]. pp. 294.

GURTOV (MELVIN) The United States against the third world: antinationalism and intervention. New York, 1974. pp. 260. *bibliog.*

WEHLER (HANS ULRICH) Der Aufstieg des amerikanischen Imperialismus: Studien zur Entwicklung des Imperium Americanum, 1865-1900. Göttingen, 1974. pp. 426. *bibliog.*

CHRISTIE (JEAN OGILVY) and DINNERSTEIN (LEONARD) eds. Decisions and revisions: interpretations of twentieth-century American history. New York, 1975. pp. 371. *bibliogs.*

CUNY CONFERENCE ON HISTORY AND POLITICS, 1ST, NEW YORK, 1974. Detente in historical perspective;...[proceedings of the] conference...; [edited by] George Schwab...[and] Henry Friedlander, etc. New York, [1975]. pp. 171.

ESTERLINE (JOHN H.) and BLACK (ROBERT B.) Inside foreign policy: the Department of State political system and its subsystems. Palo Alto, Calif., 1975. pp. 271. *bibliog.*

FALK (RICHARD A.) A global approach to national policy. Cambridge, Mass., 1975. pp. 320.

FERRELL (ROBERT H.) ed. America in a divided world, 1945-1972; [documents]. New York, [1975]. pp. 353. *bibliog.*

GILPIN (ROBERT) U.S. power and the multinational corporation: the political economy of foreign direct investment. New York, [1975]. pp. 291.

HARRIMAN (WILLIAM AVERELL) and ABEL (ELIE) Special envoy to Churchill and Stalin, 1941-1946. New York, [1975]. pp. 595.

HIGHAM (ROBIN) ed. Intervention or abstention: the dilemma of American foreign policy. Lexington, Ky., [1975]. pp. 221. *bibliogs.*

LARSON (SIMEON) Labor and foreign policy: Gompers, the A[merican] F[ederation of] L[abor], and the first World War, 1914- 1918. Rutherford, N.J., [1975]. pp. 176. *bibliog.*

LISKA (GEORGE) Beyond Kissinger: ways of conservative statecraft. Baltimore, [1975]. pp. 159. *bibliog.* (Johns Hopkins University. Washington Center of Foreign Policy Research. Studies in International Affairs. No. 26)

MARTÍ (JOSÉ) Inside the monster...; writings on the United States and American imperialism; translated by Elinor Randall...; edited, with an introduction and notes, by Philip S. Foner. New York, [1975]. pp. 386.

MAY (ERNEST RICHARD) The making of the Monroe doctrine. Cambridge, Mass., 1975. pp. 306. *bibliog.*

NUTTER (GILBERT WARREN) Kissinger's grand design. Washington, 1975. pp. 111. *bibliog.* (American Enterprise Institute for Public Policy Research. Foreign Affairs Studies. 27)

OFFNER (ARNOLD A.) The origins of the Second World War: American foreign policy and world politics, 1917-1941. New York, 1975. pp. 268. *bibliog.*

POOLE (PETER A.) America in world politics: foreign policy and policy-makers since 1898. New York, 1975. pp. 262. *bibliogs.*

RYLEY (THOMAS W.) A little group of willful men: a study of congressional- presidential authority. Port Washington, N.Y., 1975. pp. 198. *bibliog.*

SCALAPINO (ROBERT A.) Asia and the road ahead: issues for the major powers. Berkeley, [1975]. pp. 337. *bibliog.*

SHERWIN (MARTIN J.) A world destroyed: the atomic bomb and the grand alliance. New York, 1975. pp. 326. *bibliog.*

ZHURKIN (VITALII VLADIMIROVICH) SSHA i mezhdunarodno-politicheskie krizisy. Moskva, 1975. pp. 326. *bibliog.*

AMERICAN SOCIETY OF INTERNATIONAL LAW. Panel on the Constitution and the Conduct of Foreign Policy. The constitution and the conduct of foreign policy: an inquiry by a panel of the...Society...; edited by Francis O. Wilcox [and] Richard A. Frank. New York, [1976]. pp. 145.

BALL (GEORGE W.) Diplomacy for a crowded world: an American foreign policy. Boston, [Mass.], [1976]. pp. 356.

CHAMBERS (JOHN WHITECLAY) ed. The eagle and the dove: the American peace movement and United States foreign policy, 1900-1922. New York, 1976. pp. 575. *bibliog.*

CRABB (CECIL VAN METER) Policy-makers and critics: conflicting theories of American foreign policy. New York, 1976. p. 322. *bibliog.*

FERRIS (NORMAN B.) Desperate diplomacy: William H. Seward's foreign policy, 1861. Knoxville, [1976]. pp. 265. *bibliog.*

FLYNN (GEORGE Q.) Roosevelt and Romanism: Catholics and American diplomacy, 1937- 1945. Westport, 1976. pp. 268. *bibliog.*

GRANTHAM (DEWEY WESLEY) The United States since 1945: the ordeal of power. New York, [1976]. pp. 310. *bibliogs.*

LAKE (ANTHONY) ed. The Vietnam legacy: the war, American society and the future of American foreign policy. New York, 1976. pp. 440.

ROSECRANCE (RICHARD NEWTON) ed. America as an ordinary country: U.S. foreign policy and the future. Ithaca, N.Y., 1976. pp. 276.

WALKER (J. SAMUEL) Henry A. Wallace and American foreign policy. Westport, Conn., 1976. pp. 224.

—— Law and legislation.

FRANK (RICHARD ANTHONY) Enforcing the public's right to openness in the foreign affairs decision making process. New York, [1973]. pp. 31. (New York (City). University. Center for International Studies. Policy Papers. vol. 5, no.4)

—— Treaties.

KAVASS (IGOR IVAR) and SPRUDZS (ADOLF) compilers. UST cumulative index, 1950-1970: cumulative index to United States treaties and other international agreements...; 1 UST-21 UST, TIAS Nos. 2010-7034. Buffalo, N.Y., 1973. 4 vols.

KAVASS (IGOR IVAR) and MICHAEL (MARK A.) compilers. United States treaties and other international agreements: cumulative index, 1776-1949;...index to...treaties...as published in Statutes at Large, Malloy, Miller, Bevans and other relevant sources. Buffalo, N.Y., 1975. 4 vols.

—— Africa.

ARKHURST (FREDERICK S.) ed. U.S. policy toward Africa. New York, 1975. pp. 255.

UNITED STATES(Cont.)

— — **Africa, Subsaharan.**

UNITED STATES. National Security Council. Interdepartmental Groups for Africa. 1975. The Kissinger study on southern Africa. Nottingham, 1975. pp. 134.

— — **America, Latin.**

CORAL (JUAN CARLOS) Indoamerica frente al imperialismo. Buenos Aires, 1966. pp. 76.

SMETHERMAN (BOBBIE BRALY) and SMETHERMAN (ROBERT M.) Territorial seas and inter-American relations, with case studies of the Peruvian and U.S. fishing industries. New York, 1974. pp. 121.

HELLMAN (RONALD G.) and ROSENBAUM (H. JON) eds. Latin America: the search for a new international role. New York, [1975]. pp. 297. bibliogs. (Center for Inter-American Relations. Latin American International Affairs Series. vol. 1)

BLASIER (COLE) The hovering giant: U.S. responses to revolutionary change in Latin America. Pittsburgh, [1976]. pp. 315.

— — **Angola.**

HARSCH (ERNEST) and THOMAS (TONY) Angola: the hidden history of Washington's war;...edited with an introduction by Malik Miah. New York, 1976. pp. 157. bibliog.

— — **Arab countries.**

STOOKEY (ROBERT W.) America and the Arab states: an uneasy encounter. New York, [1975]. pp. 298. bibliog.

— — **Asia.**

SIMON (SHELDON W.) Asian neutralism and U.S. policy. Washington, 1975. pp. 111. (American Enterprise Institute for Public Policy Research. Foreign Affairs Studies. 21)

— — **Bolivia.**

BEYOND the revolution: Bolivia since 1952; James M. Malloy and Richard S. Thorn, editors. Pittsburgh, [1971]. pp. 402. Based on an interdisciplinary seminar held at the University of Pittsburgh, sponsored by the University's Center for International Studies and Center for Latin American Studies.

— — **Bulgaria.**

BULGARIA. Ministerstvo na Vunshnite Raboti. 1952. Documents on the hostile and aggressive policy of the government of the United States of America against the People's Republic of Bulgaria. Sofia, 1952. pp. 287.

— — **Canada.**

CUFF (ROBERT D.) and GRANATSTEIN (JACK LAWRENCE) Canadian-American relations in wartime: from the Great War to the cold war. Toronto, 1975. pp. 205.

DICKEY (JOHN SLOAN) Canada and the American presence: the United States interest in an independent Canada. New York, 1975. pp. 202.

SWANSON (ROGER FRANK) ed. Canadian-American summit diplomacy, 1923-1973: selected speeches and documents. Toronto, [1975]. pp. 314. (Carleton University. Institute of Canadian Studies. Carleton Library. No.81)

— — **Caribbean area.**

MUNRO (DANA GARDNER) The United States and the Caribbean republics, 1921-1933. Princeton, [1974]. pp. 394.

— — **Chile.**

PETRAS (JAMES FRANK) and MORLEY (MORRIS H.) The United States and Chile: imperialism and the overthrow of the Allende government. New York, [1975]. pp. 217.

— — **China.**

KALICKI (JAN HENRYK) The pattern of Sino-American crises in the 1950's: political- military interactions under stress. 1971. fo. 442. bibliog. Typescript. Ph.D. (London) thesis: unpublished. This thesis is the property of London University and may not be removed from the Library. End pocket contains two offprints from The World Today, April and September 1970.

SERGEICHUK (S.) Through Russian eyes: American-Chinese relations;... (translation by Elizabeth Cody-Rutter; edited by Philip A. Garon). Arlington, Va., 1975. pp. 220.

FAIRBANK (JOHN KING) China perceived: images and policies in Chinese-American relations. London, 1976. pp. 254.

— — **Crete.**

MARCOGLOU (EMMANUEL E.) The American interest in the Cretan revolution, 1866-69. Athens, National Centre of Social Research, 1971. pp. 149. bibliog.

— — **Cuba.**

BENDER (LYNN DARRELL) The politics of hostility: Castro's revolution and United States policy. Hato Rey, Puerto Rico, 1975. pp. 156. bibliog.

AYERS (BRADLEY EARL) The war that never was: an insider's account of C.I.A. covert operations against Cuba. Indianapolis, [1976]. pp. 235.

— — **East (Far East).**

BURNS (RICHARD DEAN) and BENNETT (EDWARD MOORE) eds. Diplomats in crisis: United States-Chinese-Japanese relations, 1919-1941. Santa Barbara, Ca., [1974]. pp. 346.

— — **East (Near East).**

COGRESSIONAL QUARTERLY INC. The Middle East: U.S. policy, Israel, oil and the Arabs. Washington, 1974. pp. 100. bibliog.

ALROY (GIL CARL) The Kissinger experience: American policy in the Middle East. New York, [1975]. pp. 189.

PRANGER (ROBERT JOHN) and TAHTINEN (DALE R.) Nuclear threat in the Middle East. Washington, 1975. pp. 57. (American Enterprise Institute for Public Policy Research. Foreign Affairs Studies. 23)

— — **Europe.**

ADAMS (DAVID KEITH) F[ranklin] D[elano] R[oosevelt], the New Deal and Europe; an inaugural lecture...given in the University of Keele, 23rd October 1973. Keele, [1974]. pp. 22.

MELANDRI (PIERRE) Les Etats-Unis et le "défi" européen, 1955-1958. Paris, [1975]. pp. 220. bibliog. (Paris. Université de Paris I (Panthéon- Sorbonne). Publications. Nouvelle Série. Recherches. 19)

CONFERENCE ON AMERICAN FOREIGN POLICY AND THE NEW EUROPE, BLACKSBURG, 1974. Changes in European relations: (proceedings of the conference); edited by James A. Kuhlman and Louis J. Mensonides. Leyden, 1976. pp. 214. (East-West Foundation. East-West Perspectives. 1)

LANGLEY (LESTER D.) Struggle for the American Mediterranean: United States- European rivalry in the Gulf-Caribbean, 1776-1904. Athens, Ga., [1976]. pp. 226. bibliog.

— — **Europe, Eastern.**

LUNDESTAD (GEIR) The American non-policy towards Eastern Europe, 1943-1947: universalism in an area not of essential interest to the United States. Tromsö, [1975]. pp. 654. bibliog.

— — **France.**

ZAHNISER (MARVIN R.) Uncertain friendship: American-French diplomatic relations through the cold war. New York, [1975]. pp. 314. bibliog.

— — **Germany.**

POETTERING (HANS GERT) Adenauers Sicherheitspolitik, 1955-1963: ein Beitrag zum deutsch-amerikanischen Verhältnis. Düsseldorf, [1975]. pp. 240. bibliog. (Bonn. Universität. Seminar für Politische Wissenschaft. Bonner Schriften zur Politik und Zeitgeschichte. 10)

— — **Haiti.**

HEALY (DAVID F.) Gunboat diplomacy in the Wilson era: the U.S. Navy in Haiti, 1915-1916. Madison, Wis., 1976. pp. 268. bibliog.

— — **Indonesia.**

CALDWELL (MALCOLM) ed. Ten years' military terror in Indonesia. Nottingham, 1975. pp. 295.

— — **Israel.**

GOLAN (MATTI) The secret conversations of Henry Kissinger: step-by-step diplomacy in the Middle East;...translated by Ruth Geyra Stern and Sol Stern. New York, [1976]. pp. 280.

— — **Korea.**

BALDWIN (FRANK) ed. Without parallel: the American-Korean relationship since 1945. New York, [1974]. pp. 376.

NOBLE (HAROLD JOYCE) Embassy at war;...edited with an introduction by Frank Baldwin. Seattle, [1975]. pp. 328. (Columbia University. East Asian Institute. Studies)

— — **Mexico.**

BRACK (GENE M.) Mexico views manifest destiny, 1821-1846: an essay on the origins of the Mexican war. Albuquerque, N.M., [1975]. pp. 194. bibliog.

— — **Micronesia.**

McHENRY (DONALD F.) Micronesia: trust betrayed: altruism vs. self interest in American foreign policy. New York, [1975]. pp. 260. bibliog.

— — **Pacific, The.**

WU (YUAN-LI) U.S. policy and strategic interests in the western Pacific. New York, [1975]. pp. 214.

— — **Persian Gulf.**

NAKHLEH (EMILE A.) Arab-American relations in the Persian Gulf. Washington, [1975]. pp. 82. (American Enterprise Institute for Public Policy Research. Foreign Affairs Studies. No. 17)

— — **Philippine Islands.**

POMEROY (WILLIAM J.) An American made tragedy: neo-colonialism and dictatorship in the Philippines. New York, 1974. pp. 190. bibliog.

THOMPSON (W. SCOTT) Unequal partners: Philippine and Thai relations with the United States 1965-75. Lexington, [1975]. pp. 183.

— — **Puerto Rico.**

ALBIZU CAMPOS (PEDRO) La conciencia nacional puertorriqueña...; seleccion, introduccion y notas de Manuel Maldonado-Denis. Mexico, 1972. pp. 218.

— — **Russia.**

WILSON (JOAN HOFF) Ideology and economics: U.S. relations with the Soviet Union, 1918-1933. Columbia, Mo., 1974. pp. 192. bibliog.

BOLKHOVITINOV (NIKOLAI NIKOLAEVICH) Russko-amerikanskie otnosheniia, 1815-1832; Russian-American relations. Moskva, 1975. pp. 626. bibliog. With English table of contents.

PETROV (VLADIMIR) U.S.-Soviet detente: past and future. Washington, 1975. pp. 60. (American Enterprise Institute for Public Policy Research. Foreign Affairs Studies. 18)

UNITED STATES (Cont.)

DÉTENTE: (edited versions of interviews originally broadcast, in 1973-75, over Radio Free Europe); edited by G.R. Urban. London, 1976. pp. 368.

GRAY (COLIN S.) The Soviet-American arms race. Farnborough, Hants, [1976]. pp. 196.

INTERNATIONAL SLAVIC CONFERENCE, 1ST, BANFF, ALBERTA, 1974. From the cold war to detente; [selected papers from the conference]; edited by Peter J. Potichnyj [and] Jane P. Shapiro. New York, 1976. pp. 223.

— — Saudi Arabia.

NAKHLEH (EMILE A.) The United States and Saudi Arabia: a policy analysis. Washington, 1975. pp. 69. *(American Enterprise Institute for Public Policy Research. Foreign Affairs Studies. 26)*

— — Thailand.

THOMPSON (W. SCOTT) Unequal partners: Philippine and Thai relations with the United States 1965-75. Lexington, [1975]. pp. 183.

— — United Kingdom.

BURTON (DAVID H.) Theodore Roosevelt and his English correspondents: a special relationship of friends. Philadelphia, 1973. pp. 70. *bibliog. (American Philosophical Society. Transactions. New Series. vol. 63, part 2)*

JENKINS (BRIAN) Britain and the war for the Union. Montreal, 1974 in progress. *bibliog.*

KNEER (WARREN G.) Great Britain and the Caribbean, 1901-1913: a study in Anglo-American relations. Michigan, [1975]. pp. 242. *bibliog.*

A TUG of loyalties: Anglo-American relations, 1765-85; edited by Esmond Wright. London, 1975. pp. 92. *(London. University. Institute of United States Studies. Monographs. 2) Lectures delivered at a colloquium at the Institute of United States Studies, University of London, 1972.*

WRIGHT (JAMES LEITCH) Britain and the American frontier, 1783-1815. Athens, Ga., [1975]. pp. 251. *bibliog.*

CONTRAST and connection: bicentennial essays in Anglo-American history; edited by H.C. Allen and Roger Thompson. London, 1976. pp. 373.

FERRIS (NORMAN B.) Desperate diplomacy: William H. Seward's foreign policy, 1861. Knoxville, [1976]. pp. 265. *bibliog.*

— — Vietnam.

BROWN (WELDON AMZY) Prelude to disaster: the American role in Vietnam, 1940-1963. Port Washington, 1975. pp. 278. *bibliog.*

— Foreign relations administration.

ESTERLINE (JOHN H.) and BLACK (ROBERT B.) Inside foreign policy: the Department of State political system and its subsystems. Palo Alto, Calif., 1975. pp. 271. *bibliog.*

BALL (GEORGE W.) Diplomacy for a crowded world: an American foreign policy. Boston, [Mass.], [1976]. pp. 356.

— Full employment policies.

GARTNER (ALAN) and others, eds. A full employment program for the 1970s. New York, 1976. pp. 144. *bibliog. Reprinted from various periodicals.*

— Government publications — Bibliography.

MONTHLY CATALOG OF UNITED STATES GOVERNMENT PUBLICATIONS: [with Superintendent of Documents' classification numbers added]; issued by the Superintendent of Documents. m., Ja 1895 - Je 1924 Washington D.C. *Subsequent issues of Monthly Catalog received as part of the U.S. deposit collection from July 1924 to date.*

LU (JOSEPH K.) compiler. U.S. government publications relating to the social sciences: a selected annotated guide. Beverly Hills, [1975]. pp. 260.

— Government publications (State governments).

PARISH (DAVID W.) compiler. State government reference publications: an annotated bibliography. Littleton, Co., 1974. pp. 237.

— Historiography.

KRAUS (MICHAEL) The writing of American history. Norman, 1953, repr. 1968. pp. 387.

SWIERENGA (ROBERT P.) ed. Quantification in American history: theory and research. New York, 1970. pp. 417. *bibliog.*

BILLIAS (GEORGE ATHAN) and GROB (GERALD N.) eds. American history: retrospect and prospect. New York, [1971]. pp. 471.

— History.

The HOFSTADTER aegis: a memorial; edited by Stanley Elkins and Eric McKitrick. New York, 1974. pp. 386,xi. *bibliogs.*

— — Sources.

MORRIS (ROBERT) 1734-1806. The papers of Robert Morris 1781-1784; E. James Ferguson, editor. [Pittsburgh, 1973 in progress].

JENSEN (MERRILL MONROE) and BECKER (ROBERT A.) eds. The documentary history of the first federal elections, 1788-1790. Madison, 1976 in progress.

— — 1607-1783, Colonial period.

RISJORD (NORMAN K.) Forging the American republic, 1760-1815. Reading, Mass., [1973]. pp. 400. *bibliog.*

ROGERS (ALAN) Historian. Empire and liberty: American resistance to British authority, 1755-1763. Berkeley, 1974. pp. 205. *bibliog.*

— — 1775-1783, Revolution.

A TUG of loyalties: Anglo-American relations, 1765-85; edited by Esmond Wright. London, 1975. pp. 92. *(London. University. Institute of United States Studies. Monographs. 2) Lectures delivered at a colloquium at the Institute of United States Studies, University of London, 1972.*

The AMERICAN Revolution: explorations in the history of American radicalism; edited by Alfred F. Young. DeKalb, Ill., 1976. pp. 481.

SHY (JOHN WILLARD) A people numerous and armed: reflections on the military struggle for American independence. New York, 1976. pp. 304.

WRIGHT (ESMOND) The War of American Independence. London, [1976]. pp. 46. *bibliog. (Historical Association. General Series. G.87)*

— — — Causes.

DERRY (JOHN WESLEY) English politics and the American Revolution. London, 1976. pp. 215. *bibliog.*

— — — French participation.

DULL (JONATHAN R.) The French navy and American independence: a study of arms and diplomacy, 1774-1787. Princeton, [1975]. pp. 437. *bibliog.*

— — — Naval operations.

DULL (JONATHAN R.) The French navy and American independence: a study of arms and diplomacy, 1774-1787. Princeton, [1975]. pp. 437. *bibliog.*

— — 1783-1865.

ROSSITER (CLINTON L.) The American quest, 1790-1860: an emerging nation in search of identity, unity, and modernity. New York, [1971]. pp. 396. *bibliog.*

RISJORD (NORMAN K.) Forging the American republic, 1760-1815. Reading, Mass., [1973]. pp. 400. *bibliog.*

CURTIS (JAMES C.) Andrew Jackson and the search for vindication. Boston, Mass., [1976]. pp. 194. *bibliog.*

— — 1789-1802, Constitutional period.

KOHN (RICHARD H.) Eagle and sword: the Federalists and the creation of the military establishment in America, 1783-1802. New York, [1975]. pp. 443. *bibliog.*

— — 1815-1861.

DENNISON (GEORGE M.) The Dorr War: Republicanism on trial, 1831-1861. Lexington, Ky., [1967]. pp. 250. *bibliog.*

— — 1845-1848, War with Mexico.

BRACK (GENE M.) Mexico views manifest destiny, 1821-1846: an essay on the origins of the Mexican war. Albuquerque, N.M., [1975]. pp. 194. *bibliog.*

— — 1861-1865, Civil War.

JENKINS (BRIAN) Britain and the war for the Union. Montreal, 1974 in progress. *bibliog.*

— — — Causes.

POTTER (DAVID MORRIS) The impending crisis, 1848-1861; completed and edited by Don E. Fehrenbacher. New York, [1976]. pp. 638. *bibliog.*

— — — Foreign public opinion.

FERRIS (NORMAN B.) Desperate diplomacy: William H. Seward's foreign policy, 1861. Knoxville, [1976]. pp. 265. *bibliog.*

— — — Negroes.

GERTEIS (LOUIS S.) From contraband to freedman: federal policy toward Southern blacks, 1861-1865. Westport, Conn., 1973. pp. 255. *bibliog.*

DEGLER (CARL N.) The other South: southern dissenters in the nineteenth century. New York, 1975. pp. 392. *bibliog.*

— — — Personal narratives.

CONKLIN (HENRY) 1832-1915. Through "Poverty's Vale": a hardscrabble boyhood in upstate New York, 1832-1862;...edited with an introduction by Wendell Tripp. Syracuse, N.Y., 1974. pp. 264.

— — 1898, War of.

LINDERMAN (GERALD F.) The mirror of war: American society and the Spanish-American War. Ann Arbor, [1974]. pp. 227.

— — 1900— .

BERNSTEIN (BARTON J.) and MATUSOW (ALLEN J.) eds. Twentieth century America: recent interpretations. 2nd ed. New York, [1972]. pp. 582. *bibliogs.*

NASH (GERALD D.) The American West in the twentieth-century: a short history of an urban oasis. Englewood Cliffs, [1973]. pp. 312. *bibliog.*

CHRISTIE (JEAN OGILVY) and DINNERSTEIN (LEONARD) eds. Decisions and revisions: interpretations of twentieth-century American history. New York, 1975. pp. 371. *bibliogs.*

— — 1945—

ROLAND (CHARLES P.) The improbable era: the South since World War II. Lexington, Ky., [1975]. pp. 228. *bibliog.*

— Industries.

KUDLIŃSKI (ROMUALD) Strukturalne podstawy monopolu w przemyśle USA. Warszawa, 1963. pp. 232. *bibliog.*

CONROY (MICHAEL E.) Regional economic growth: diversification and control. New York, 1975. pp. 163. *bibliog.*

STERNLIEB (GEORGE S.) and HUGHES (JAMES W.) eds. Post-industrial America: metropolitan decline and inter-regional job shifts. New Brunswick, [1975]. pp. 267

UNITED STATES(Cont.)

— Intellectual life.

DIGGINS (JOHN P.) Up from communism: conservative odysseys in American intellectual history. New York, [1975]. pp. 522.

LODGE (GEORGE CABOT) The new American ideology: how the ideological basis of legitimate authority in America is being radically transformed, etc. New York, 1976. pp. 350,xv.

MAY (HENRY FARNHAM) The enlightenment in America. New York, 1976. pp. 419.

The PURSUIT of knowledge in the early American republic: American scientific and learned societies from colonial times to the Civil War; edited by Alexandra Oleson and Sanborn C. Brown. Baltimore, [1976]. pp. 372. *Papers from a workshop held by the American Academy of Arts and Sciences in Cape Newagen, 1973.*

— Learned institutions and societies.

The PURSUIT of knowledge in the early American republic: American scientific and learned societies from colonial times to the Civil War; edited by Alexandra Oleson and Sanborn C. Brown. Baltimore, [1976]. pp. 372. *Papers from a workshop held by the American Academy of Arts and Sciences in Cape Newagen, 1973.*

— Marine Corps.

BINKIN (MARTIN) and RECORD (JEFFREY) Where does the Marine Corps go from here?. Washington, [1976]. pp. 93. *(Brookings Institution. Studies in Defense Policy)*

— Military policy.

SANDERS (RALPH) The politics of defense analysis. New York, [1973]. pp. 361.

DONOVAN (JOHN C.) The cold warriors: a policy-making elite. Lexington, Mass., [1974]. pp. 294.

KAHAN (JEROME H.) Security in the nuclear age: developing U.S. strategic arms policy. Washington, D.C., [1975]. pp. 361.

LISTVINOV (IURII NIKOLAEVICH) Obychnoe oruzhie v iadernom veke: amerikanskie kontseptsii vedeniia lokal'nykh voin. Moskva, 1975. pp. 143.

CENTER FOR DEFENSE INFORMATION. Current issues in U.S. defense policy; edited by David Thomas Johnson [and] Barry R. Schneider. New York, 1976. pp. 254.

— Moral conditions.

BLUMENTHAL (MONICA D.) and others. More about justifying violence: methodological studies of attitudes and behavior. Ann Arbor, 1975. pp. 401. *bibliog.*

— Nationalism.

ROSSITER (CLINTON L.) The American quest, 1790-1860: an emerging nation in search of identity, unity, and modernity. New York, [1971]. pp. 396. *bibliog.*

— Officials and employees.

AUSTIN (LEWIS) Saints and samurai: the political culture of the American and Japanese elites. New Haven, 1975. pp. 197. *(Yale University. Yale Studies in Political Science. 27)*

PUBLIC SECTOR LABOR RELATIONS CONFERENCE BOARD. Annual Conference, 3rd, University of Maryland, 1973. Challenges in public sector labor relations; editor, Paul A. Weinstein. College Park, Md., [1975]. pp. 121. *(Public Sector Labor Relations Conference Board. Publications. No. 2)*

SEIDMAN (LAURENCE S.) The design of federal employment programs. Lexington, Mass., [1975]. pp. 202. *bibliog.*

WEITZMAN (JOAN) The scope of bargaining in public employment. New York, 1975. pp. 384. *bibliog.*

MELTSNER (ARNOLD J.) Policy analysts in the bureaucracy. Berkeley, Calif., [1976]. pp. 310.

— Politics and government.

FOX (GEORGE TOWNSEND) American journals...1831-1868; editor, Bernard Crick. London, [1961]. 4 vols. *(British Association for American Studies. British Records relating to America in Microform. Series B) Microfilm of manuscript: 1 reel. No part of the contents may be published without the consent of the Librarian, South Shields Public Library.*

SAMSON (LEON) Toward a united front: a philosophy for American workers. New York, [1933]. pp. 276.

BUCHANAN (PATRICK J.) Conservative votes, liberal victories: why the right has failed. New York, [1975]. pp. 184.

CROZIER (MICHEL) and others. The crisis of democracy...; report on the governability of democracies to the Trilateral Commission. [New York], 1975. pp. 211.

DOMHOFF (G. WILLIAM) ed. New directions in power structure research. Eugene, Ore., 1975. pp. 264. *(Insurgent Sociologist, The. vol. 5, no.3)*

GRAHAM (HUGH DAVIS) ed. American politics and government: party, ideology, and reform in American history. New York, [1975]. pp. 351. *bibliog.*

LEES (JOHN DAVID) The political system of the United States. new ed. London, 1975. pp. 378. *bibliog.*

MORROW (WILLIAM L.) Public administration: politics and the political system. New York, [1975]. pp. 272. *bibliog.*

SHAPIRO (H.R.) The bureaucratic state: party bureaucracy and the decline of democracy in America. New York, [1975]. pp. 366. *bibliogs.*

WHITE (MICHAEL J.) and others, eds. Management and policy science in American government: problems and prospects. Lexington, Mass., [1975]. pp. 319.

The RISING South;...edited by Donald R. Noble and Joab L. Thomas. Alabama, [1976 in progress].

AMERICAN ACADEMY OF POLITICAL AND SOCIAL SCIENCE. Annals. vol. 426. Bientennial conference on the constitution: a report to the Academy; special editor of this volume: Marvin E. Wolfgang. Philadelphia, 1976. pp. 281. *bibliog.*

GRIFFITH (ERNEST STACEY) The American system of government. 3rd ed. London, 1976. pp. 204. *Text of 5th American ed.*

IPPOLITO (DENNIS S.) and others. Public opinion and responsible democracy. Englewood Cliffs, N.J., [1976]. pp. 330. *bibliog.*

VILE (MAURICE JOHN CRAWLEY) Politics in the U.S.A. rev. ed. London, 1976. pp. 318. *bibliog.*

— — Bibliography.

VOSE (CLEMENT ELLERY) A guide to library sources in political science: American government. Washington, [1975]. pp. 135. *bibliogs.(American Political Science Association. Division of Educational Affairs. Instructional Resource Monographs. No.1)*

— — 1783-1865.

STEWART (DONALD HENDERSON) The opposition press of the Federalist period. Albany, [1969]. pp. 957. *bibliog.*

JENSEN (MERRILL MONROE) and BECKER (ROBERT A.) eds. The documentary history of the first federal elections, 1788-1790. Madison, 1976 in progress.

— — 1815-1861.

CRENSON (MATTHEW A.) The federal machine: beginnings of bureaucracy in Jacksonian America. Baltimore, [1975]. pp. 186. *bibliog.*

MAY (ERNEST RICHARD) The making of the Monroe doctrine. Cambridge, Mass., 1975. pp. 306. *bibliog.*

SMITH (ELBERT N.) The presidency of James Buchanan. Lawrence, Kan., [1975]. pp. 225. *bibliog.*

— — 1865-1898.

BENEDICT (MICHAEL LES) A compromise of principle: Congressional Republicans and reconstruction, 1863-1869. New York, [1974]. pp. 493. *bibliog.*

MARTÍ (JOSÉ) Inside the monster...; writings on the United States and American imperialism; translated by Elinor Randall...; edited, with an introduction and notes, by Philip S. Foner. New York, [1975]. pp. 386.

GROSSMAN (LAWRENCE) The Democratic Party and the negro: northern and national politics, 1868-92. Urbana, [1976]. pp. 212. *bibliog.*

— — 1898-1945.

BROESAMLE (JOHN J.) William Gibbs McAdoo: a passion for change, 1863-1917. Port Washington, N.Y., 1973. pp. 304. *bibliog.*

MORGAN (ARTHUR ERNEST) The making of the TVA. Buffalo, 1974. pp. 205.

BEST (GARY DEAN) The politics of American individualism: Herbert Hoover in transition, 1918-1921. Westport, Conn., 1975. pp. 202. *bibliog.*

BRAEMAN (JOHN) and others, eds. The New Deal. Columbus, Ohio, 1975. 2 vols.

INGALLS (ROBERT P.) Herbert H. Lehman and New York's Little New Deal. New York, 1975. pp. 287. *bibliog.*

RYLEY (THOMAS W.) A little group of willful men: a study of congressional-presidential authority. Port Washington, N.Y., 1975. pp. 198. *bibliog.*

SUTTON (ANTONY C.) Wall Street and FDR. New Rochelle, [1975]. pp. 200. *bibliog.*

BLUM (JOHN MORTON) V was for victory: politics and American culture during World War II. New York, [1976]. pp. 372.

MURRAY (ROBERT KEITH) The 103rd ballot: Democrats and the disaster in Madison Square Garden. New York, [1976]. pp. 336. *bibliog.*

PARMAN (DONALD L.) The Navajos and the New Deal. New Haven, 1976. pp. 316. *bibliog.*

SOMBART (WERNER) Why is there no socialism in the United States?;...translated by Patricia M. Hocking and C.T. Husbands; edited and with an introductory essay by C.T. Husbands, etc. London, 1976. pp. 187. *bibliog.*

— — 1900— .

IAKOVLEV (NIKOLAI NIKOLAEVICH) Prestupivshie gran'. Moskva, 1970. pp. 352.

EKIRCH (ARTHUR ALPHONSE) Progressivism in America: a study of the era from Theodore Roosevelt to Woodrow Wilson. New York, 1974.pp. 308. *bibliog.*

KARP (WALTER) Indispensable enemies: the politics of misrule in America. Baltimore, 1974. pp. 324.

CHRISTIE (JEAN OGILVY) and DINNERSTEIN (LEONARD) eds. Decisions and revisions: interpretations of twentieth-century American history. New York, 1975. pp. 371. *bibliogs.*

LADD (EVERETT CARLL) and HADLEY (CHARLES D.) Transformations of the American party system: political coalitions from the New Deal to the 1970s. New York, [1975]. pp. 371.

WEINSTEIN (JAMES) Ambiguous legacy: the Left in American politics. New York, 1975. pp. 179.

KRICKUS (RICHARD) Pursuing the American dream: white ethnics and the new populism. Bloomington, 1976. pp. 424.

— — 1945— .

THEOHARIS (ATHAN G.) Seeds of repression: Harry S.Truman and the origins of McCarthyism. Chicago, 1971. pp. 238.

UNITED STATES (Cont.)

FISHEL (JEFF) Party and opposition: congressional challengers in American politics. New York, [1973]. pp. 254. *bibliog.*

GOLDSTON (ROBERT) The American nightmare: Senator Joseph McCarthy and the politics of hate. Indianapolis, [1973]. pp. 202. *bibliog.*

COMMITTEE FOR ECONOMIC DEVELOPMENT. Research and Policy Committee. Program Committee. Restoring confidence in the political process. New York, [1974]. pp. 20. *(Committee for Economic Development. Research and Policy Committee. Statements on National Policy)*

FOR Dirk Struik: scientific, historical and political essays in honor of Dirk J. Struik; edited by R.S. Cohen [and others]. Dordrecht, [1974]. pp. 652. *bibliogs. (Boston Colloquium for the Philosophy of Science. Boston Studies in the Philosophy of Science. vol.15)*

PARENTI (MICHAEL) Democracy for the few. New York, [1974]. pp. 307.

STEWART (JOHN G.) One last chance: the Democratic Party, 1974-76. New York, 1974. pp. 208.

BARTLEY (NUMAN V.) and GRAHAM (HUGH DAVIS) Southern politics and the second reconstruction. Baltimore, [1975]. pp. 233. *bibliog.*

EVANS (MEDFORD STANTON) Clear and present dangers: a conservative view of America's government. New York, [1975]. pp. 433.

GILMOUR (ROBERT S.) and LAMB (ROBERT B.) Political alienation in contemporary America. New York, [1975]. pp. 198.

HAMILTON (RICHARD F.) Restraining myths: critical studies of U.S. social structure and politics. New York, [1975]. pp. 296.

ISOLATION or interdependence?: today's choices for tomorrow's world; (papers...prepared for a conference at the University of Chicago...1974); edited by Morton A. Kaplan. New York, [1975]. pp. 254. *bibliog.*

NAYLOR (THOMAS H.) and CLOTFELTER (JAMES) Strategies for change in the South. Chapel Hill, [1975]. pp. 316.

PEIRCE (NEAL R.) The Border South States: people, politics and power in the five Border South States. New York, [1975]. pp. 415. *bibliog.*

PYNN (RONALD E.) ed. Watergate and the American political process. New York, 1975. pp. 246.

REICHARD (GARY W.) The reaffirmation of Republicanism: Eisenhower and the eighty-third Congress. Knoxville, Tenn., [1975]. pp. 303. *bibliog.*

SALE (KIRKPATRICK) Power shift: the rise of the southern rim and its challenge to the eastern establishment. New York, [1975]. pp. 362.

SCHLESINGER (STEPHEN C.) The new reformers: forces for change in American politics. Boston, Mass., 1975. pp. 238.

BLACK (EARL) Southern governors and civil rights: racial segregation as a campaign issue in the Second Reconstruction. Cambridge, Mass., 1976. pp. 408.

COLSON (CHARLES W.) Born again. London, [1976]. pp. 350.

FANNING (LOUIS A.) Betrayal in Vietnam. New Rochelle, N.Y., [1976]. pp. 256. *bibliog.*

FRIED (RICHARD M.) Men against McCarthy. New York, 1976. pp. 428. *bibliog.*

GOLDWATER (BARRY MORRIS) The coming breakpoint. New York, [1976]. pp. 184.

GRANTHAM (DEWEY WESLEY) The United States since 1945: the ordeal of power. New York, [1976]. pp. 310. *bibliogs.*

GUTTMAN (DANIEL) and WILLNER (BARRY) The shadow government: the government's multi-billion-dollar giveaway of its decision-making powers to private management consultants, "experts" and think tanks. New York, [1976]. pp. 354.

LAMBRO (DONALD) The conscience of a young conservative. New Rochelle, N.Y., [1976]. pp. 125.

MAILER (NORMAN) Some honorable men: political conventions 1960-1972. Boston, 1976. pp. 499.

NASH (GEORGE H.) The conservative intellectual movement in America since 1945. New York, [1976]. pp. 463. *bibliog.*

PETERS (CHARLES) and FALLOWS (JAMES M.) eds. Inside the system. 3rd ed. New York, 1976. pp. 339.

REEVES (RICHARD) A Ford, not a Lincoln: the decline of American political leadership. London, 1976. pp. 191.

RICHARDSON (ELLIOT L.) The creative balance: government, politics and the individual in America's third century. New York, [1976]. pp. 390.

RUBIN (RICHARD L.) Party dynamics: the Democratic coalition and the politics of change. New York, 1976. pp. 203.

WRIGHT (JAMES D.) The dissent of the governed: alienation and democracy in America. New York, 1976. pp. 329. *bibliog.*

— **Population.**

POLITICAL issues in U.S. population policy: [papers from a postdoctoral institute held at the University of North Carolina in 1973]; edited by Virginia Gray [and] Elihu Bergman. Lexington, Mass., [1974]. pp. 212.

BARSBY (STEVE L.) and COX (DENNIS R.) Interstate migration of the elderly: an economic analysis. Lexington, Mass., [1975]. pp. 149. *bibliog.*

EDMONSTON (BARRY) Population distribution in American cities. Lexington, Mass., [1975]. pp. 156. *bibliog.*

STERNLIEB (GEORGE S.) and HUGHES (JAMES W.) eds. Post-industrial America: metropolitan decline and inter-regional job shifts. New Brunswick, [1975]. pp. 267.

TURCHI (BOONE A.) The demand for children: the economics of fertility in the United States. Cambridge, Mass., [1975]. pp. 238. *bibliog.*

— **Presidents.**

HARGROVE (ERWIN C.) The power of the modern presidency. New York, [1974]. pp. 353. *bibliog.*

NOVAK (MICHAEL) Choosing our king: powerful symbols in presidential politics. New York, [1974]. pp. 324. *bibliog.*

CONGRESS against the president; (edited by Harvey C. Mansfield). New York, 1975. pp. 200. *Includes essays discussed at a conference sponsored by the Academy of Political Science at Columbia University in 1975.*

— — **Election.**

NOVAK (MICHAEL) Choosing our king: powerful symbols in presidential politics. New York, [1974]. pp. 324. *bibliog.*

The POLITICS of representation: the Democratic Convention 1972; [by] Denis G. Sullivan [and others]. New York, [1974]. pp. 152.

HADLEY (ARTHUR TWINING) 1924- . The invisible primary. Englewood Cliffs, [1976]. pp. 317.

KEECH (WILLIAM ROBERTSON) and MATTHEWS (DONALD ROWE) The party's choice. Washington, [1976]. pp. 258. *(Brookings Institution. Studies in Presidential Selection)*

MAILER (NORMAN) Some honorable men: political conventions 1960-1972. Boston, 1976. pp. 499.

MENDELSOHN (HAROLD) and O'KEEFE (GARRETT J.) The people choose a president: influences on voter decision making. New York, 1976. pp. 251. *bibliog.*

— — **Powers and duties.**

FISHER (LOUIS) Presidential spending power. Princeton, [1975]. pp. 345.

CORWIN (EDWARD SAMUEL) Presidential power and the constitution: essays...; edited with an introduction by Richard Loss. Ithaca, 1976. pp. 185. *bibliog.*

— **Public lands.**

ROBINSON (GLEN O.) The Forest Service: (a study in public land management). Baltimore, [1975]. pp. 337.

— **Race question.**

ROSE (PETER ISAAC) and others, eds. Through different eyes: black and white perspectives on American race relations. New York, 1973. pp. 453. *bibliog.*

ALLEN (ROBERT L.) 1942- , and ALLEN (PAMELA PARKER) Reluctant reformers: racism and social reform movements in the United States. Washington, D.C., 1974. pp. 324.

GINSBERG (YONA) Jews in a changing neighborhood: the study of Mattapan. New York, [1975]. pp. 214. *bibliog.*

KNOPF (TERRY ANN) Rumors, race and riots. New Brunswick, [1975]. pp. 398.

RACISM and inequality: the policy alternatives; edited by Harrell R. Rodgers. San Francisco, [1975]. pp. 220.

YETMAN (NORMAN R.) and STEELE (C. HOY) eds. Majority and minority: the dynamics of racial and ethnic relations. 2nd ed. Boston, Mass., 1975. pp. 640. *bibliogs.*

EISINGER (PETER K.) Patterns of interracial politics: conflict and cooperation in the city. New York, [1976]. pp. 202. *(Wisconsin University, Madison. Institute for Research on Poverty. Monograph Series)*

KATZ (PHYLLIS A.) ed. Towards the elimination of racism. New York, [1976]. pp. 444. *bibligs. Sponsored by the Society for the Psychological Study of Social Issues.*

KRICKUS (RICHARD) Pursuing the American dream: white ethnics and the new populism. Bloomington, 1976. pp. 424.

— — **Bibliography.**

OBUDHO (CONSTANCE E.) Black-white racial attitudes: an annotated bibliography. Westport, Conn., 1976. pp. 180.

— — **Economic aspects.**

SOWELL (THOMAS) Race and economics. New York, [1975] repr. 1976. pp. 276.

— **Relations (general) with Chile.**

HOROWITZ (IRVING LOUIS) ed. The rise and fall of Project Camelot: studies in the relationship between social science and practical politics. rev. ed. Cambridge, Mass., [1974]. pp. 409.

— **Relations (general) with China.**

FAIRBANK (JOHN KING) Chinese-American interactions: a historical summary. New Brunswick, [1975]. pp. 90. *bibliog. (University of Puget Sound. Brown and Haley Lectures. 1974)*

FAIRBANK (JOHN KING) China perceived: images and policies in Chinese-American relations. London, 1976. pp. 254.

— **Relations (general) with Japan.**

JOHNSON (SHEILA K.) American attitudes toward Japan, 1941-1975. Washington, 1975. pp. 114. *(American Enterprise Institute for Public Policy Research and Stanford University. Hoover Institution on War, Revolution and Peace. AEI-Hoover Policy Studies. 15)*

MUTUAL images: essays in American-Japanese relations [given at a conference held on Kauai, Hawaii in 1972] (by Priscilla A. Clapp [and others]); edited by Akira Iriye. Cambridge, Mass., 1975. pp. 304. *(Harvard University. Harvard Studies in American-East Asian Relations. 7)*

— **Relations (general) with Latin America.**

WELLS (ALAN FRANK) Picture-tube imperialism?: the impact of U.S. television on Latin America. Maryknoll, [1972]. pp. 197. *bibliog.*

— **Relations (general) with Puerto Rico.**

CLARK (TRUMAN R.) Puerto Rico and the United States, 1917-1933. [Pittsburgh, 1975]. pp. 238. *bibliog.*

— **Relations (general) with Spain.**

VAZQUEZ MONTALBAN (MANUEL) La penetracion americana en España. Madrid, [1974]. pp. 439.

— **Relations (general) with the United Kingdom.**

CONTRAST and connection: bicentennial essays in Anglo-American history; edited by H.C. Allen and Roger Thompson. London, 1976. pp. 373.

— **Relations (military) with Latin America.**

ETCHISON (DON L.) The United States and militarism in Central America. New York, 1975. pp. 150. *bibliog.*

— **Religion.**

BOLES (JOHN B.) The great revival, 1787-1805: (the origin of the southern evangelical mind). Lexington, Ky., [1972]. pp. 236. *bibliog.*

BRUCE (DICKSON D.) And they all sang hallelujah: plain-folk camp-meeting religion, 1800-1845. Knoxville, Tenn., [1974]. pp. 155. *bibliog.*

The RISE of adventism: religion and society in mid-nineteenth- century America; Edwin S. Gaustad, editor. New York, [1974]. pp. 329. *bibliog.*

— **Rural conditions.**

BOWERS (WILLIAM L.) The country life movement in America, 1900-1920. Port Washington, N.Y., 1974. pp. 189. *bibliog.*

SMITH (THOMAS LYNN) Studies of the great rural tap roots of urban poverty in the United States. New York, [1974]. pp. 144.

LAMB (RICHARD) 1943- . Metropolitan impacts of rural America. Chicago, 1975. pp. 196. *bibliog. (Chicago. University. Department of Geography. Research Papers. No. 162)*

LOOMIS (CHARLES PRICE) and BEEGLE (JOSEPH ALLAN) A strategy for rural change. New York, [1975]. pp. 525.

— **Social conditions.**

ALLEN (ROBERT L.) 1942- , and ALLEN (PAMELA PARKER) Reluctant reformers: racism and social reform movements in the United States. Washington, D.C., 1974. pp. 324.

REED (JOHN SHELTON) The enduring South: subcultural persistence in mass society. Chapel Hill, [1974]. pp. 135. *bibliog.*

BRAEMAN (JOHN) and others, eds. The New Deal. Columbus, Ohio, 1975. 2 vols.

COONTZ (STEPHANIE) and FRANK (CARL) eds. Life in capitalist America: private profit and social decay; [by] Stephanie Coontz [and others]. New York, [1975]. pp. 285. *(Reprinted from International Socialist Review, 1971-74)*

HELMER (JOHN) Drugs and minority oppression. New York, [1975]. pp. 192.

HOULT (THOMAS FORD) ed. Social justice and its enemies. New York, [1975]. pp. 584. *bibliog.*

INCIARDI (JAMES A.) and SIEGAL (HARVEY A.) compilers. Emerging social issues: a sociological perspective. New York, 1975. pp. 204. *bibliogs.*

KRUEGER (MARLIS) and SILVERT (FRIEDA) Dissent denied: the technocratic response to protest. New York, [1975]. pp. 194.

LEMASTERS (E.E.) Blue-collar aristocrats: life-styles at a working-class tavern. Madison, Wis., 1975. pp. 218.

MARTÍ (JOSÉ) Inside the monster...; writings on the United States and American imperialism; translated by Elinor Randall...; edited, with an introduction and notes, by Philip S. Foner. New York, [1975]. pp. 386.

NAYLOR (THOMAS H.) and CLOTFELTER (JAMES) Strategies for change in the South. Chapel Hill, [1975]. pp. 316.

ROGOW (ARNOLD A.) The dying of the light: a searching look at America today. New York, [1975]. pp. 384. *bibliog.*

STERNLIEB (GEORGE S.) and HUGHES (JAMES W.) eds. Post-industrial America: metropolitan decline and inter- regional job shifts. New Brunswick, [1975]. pp. 267.

CAMPBELL (ALBERT ANGUS) and others. The quality of American life: perceptions, evaluations and satisfactions. New York, [1976]. pp. 583. *bibliog.*

FAIRLIE (HENRY) The spoiled child of the Western world: the miscarriage of the American idea in our time. New York, 1976. pp. 350.

SOMBART (WERNER) Why is there no socialism in the United States?;...translated by Patricia M. Hocking and C.T. Husbands; edited and with an introductory essay by C.T. Husbands, etc. London, 1976. pp. 187. *bibliog.*

WESTBY (DAVID L.) The clouded vision: the student movement in the United States in the 1960s. Lewisburg, [1976]. pp. 291. *bibliog.*

WRIGHT (JAMES D.) The dissent of the governed: alienation and democracy in America. New York, 1976. pp. 329. *bibliog.*

— — **Bibliography.**

MARK (CHARLES) and MARK (PAULA F.) Sociology of America: a guide to information sources. Detroit, [1976]. pp. 454.

— **Social history.**

LINDERMAN (GERALD F.) The mirror of war: American society and the Spanish-American War. Ann Arbor, [1974]. pp. 227.

ZILG (GERARD COLBY) Du Pont: behind the nylon curtain. Englewood Cliffs, [1974]. pp. 623.

FINLAY (JOHN L.) Canada in the North Atlantic triangle: two centuries of social change. Toronto, 1975. pp. 343. *bibliog.*

GALAMBOS (LOUIS) The public image of big business in America, 1880-1940: a quantitative study in social change;...with the assistance of Barbara Barrow Spence. Baltimore, [1975]. pp. 324.

GUTMAN (HERBERT GEORGE) Work, culture and society in industrializing America: essays in American working-class and social history. New York, 1976. pp. 343, xvi. *Reprinted from various sources.*

JONES (MALDWYN ALLEN) Destination America. London, [1976]. pp. 256. *bibliog.*

— **Social life and customs.**

FOX (GEORGE TOWNSEND) American journals...1831-1868; editor, Bernard Crick. London, [1961]. 4 vols. *(British Association for American Studies. British Records relating to America in Microform. Series B) Microfilm of manuscript: 1 reel. No part of the contents may be published without the consent of the Librarian, South Shields Public Library.*

JACOBS (GLENN) ed. The participant observer. New York, [1970]. pp. 302.

BLUM (JOHN MORTON) V was for victory: politics and American culture during World War II. New York, [1976]. pp. 372.

SCITOVSKY (TIBOR) the Younger. The joyless economy: an inquiry into human satisfaction and consumer dissatisfaction. New York, 1976. pp. 310.

— **Social policy.**

DOLBEARE (KENNETH M.) ed. Public policy evaluation;...with a section on crime control evaluation edited by John A. Gardiner. Beverly Hills, [1975]. pp. 286.

ETHICAL and legal issues of social experimentation: [based on a conference convened by the Brookings Panel on Social Experimentation in 1973]; contributors, Alice M. Rivlin [and others]; (editors Alice M. Rivlin [and] P. Michael Timpane). Washington, [1975]. pp. 188. *(Brookings Institution. Brookings Studies in Social Experimentation)*

FEAGIN (JOE R.) Subordinating the poor: welfare and American beliefs. Englewood Cliffs, N.J., [1975]. pp. 180.

HAUGE (GABRIEL) The quality of citizenship. New York, [1975]. pp. 13.

JAMES (DOROTHY BUCKTON) Analyzing poverty policy. Lexington, Mass., [1975]. pp. 259.

SCHORR (PHILIP) Planned relocation. Lexington, Mass., [1975]. pp. 227. *bibliog.*

TUSSING (A. DALE) Poverty in a dual economy. New York, [1975]. pp. 229. *bibliogs.*

GRAHAM (OTIS L.) Toward a planned society: from Roosevelt to Nixon. New York, 1976. pp. 357. *bibliog.*

HARRINGTON (MICHAEL) b. 1928. The twilight of capitalism. New York, [1976]. pp. 446. *bibliog.*

HEIDENHEIMER (ARNOLD JOSEPH) and others. Comparative public policy: the politics of social choice in Europe and America. London, 1976. pp. 296.

JANOWITZ (MORRIS) Social control of the welfare state. New York, [1976]. pp. 170. *bibliog.*

LAMBRO (DONALD) The conscience of a young conservative. New Rochelle, N.Y., [1976]. pp. 125.

LEVITAN (SAR A.) and TAGGART (ROBERT) The promise of greatness. Cambridge, Mass., 1976. pp. 316.

STRATEGIC perspectives on social policy; editors: John E. Tropman [and others]. New York, [1976]. pp. 367. *bibliogs.*

WILLIAMS (WALTER) Dr., and ELMORE (RICHARD F.) eds. Social program implementation. New York, [1976]. pp. 299. *bibliog.*

UNITIZED CARGO SYSTEMS.

BERTA (ESPERO) and BERGMANN (ALEXANDER) Le container et l'Europe. Lausanne, 1973. pp. 134. *bibliog. (Lausanne. Université. Centre de Recherches Européennes. Publications. 6. Etudes Sectorielles)*

UNIVERSITIES AND COLLEGES.

STEPHENS (MICHAEL D.) and RODERICK (GORDON W.) eds. Universities for a changing world: the role of the university in the later twentieth century. Newton Abbot, [1975]. pp. 221.

UNIVERSITIES in the western world; edited by Paul Seabury. New York, [1975]. pp. 303. *Papers from a conference convened in Venice, 1973, by the International Council on the Future of the University.*

— **Administration.**

INSTITUTIONAL management in higher education: report of a conference...[held in Paris, 2-5 November, 1971]. [Paris], Organisation for Economic Co-operation and Development, 1972. pp. 67. *(Centre for Educational Research and Innovation. [Studies in Institutional Management in Higher Education])*

UNIVERSITIES AND COLLEGES.(Cont.)

— Curricula.

ENVIRONMENTAL education at university level: trends and data; part of this report is based on the results of a workshop on environmental education at university level...Tours...4th to 8th April, 1971, (organised) by CERI, etc. [Paris], Organisation for Economic Co-operation and Development, 1973. pp. 320.

— Finance.

VERRY (DONALD WILLIAM) and DAVIES (BLEDDYN PRYCE) University costs and outputs. Amsterdam, 1976. pp. 277. *bibliog.*

— Law and legislation — United States.

GLADIEUX (LAWRENCE E.) and WOLANIN (THOMAS R.) Congress and the colleges: the national politics of higher education. Lexington, Mass., [1976]. pp. 273.

— Teachers.

See TEACHERS.

— Canada.

HURTUBISE (RENÉ) and ROWAT (DONALD CAMERON) L'université, la société et le gouvernement: rapport de la Commission d'étude sur les relations entre les universités et les gouvernements; commissaires, René Hurtubise, Donald C. Rowat. Ottawa, 1970. pp. 268. *bibliog.*

— — Employees.

CANADA. Statistics Canada. Educational staff in public trade schools and similar institutions. a., 1971/72- Ottawa. *In English and French.*

— — Quebec (Province).

LAVALLEE (ANDRE) Québec contre Montréal: la querelle universitaire, 1876-1891. Montréal, 1974. pp. 261. *bibliog.*

— Germany.

GERMANY (BUNDESREPUBLIK). Wissenschaftsrat. 1974. Empfehlungen zum vierten Rahmenplan für den Hochschulbau 1975 1978. [Cologne?], 1974. 4 vols.(in 2).

WEBER (MAX) Max Weber on universities: the power of the state and the dignity of the academic calling in imperial Germany; translated, edited and with an introductory note by Edward Shils. Chicago, 1974. pp. 62. *(Reprinted from Minerva, vol. 11, no.4, October 1973)*

GERMANY (BUNDESREPUBLIK). Wissenschaftsrat. Empfehlungen zum fünften Rahmenplan für den Hochschulbau 1976-1979. Köln, 1975 in progress.

— Italy.

CRISI politica e riforma dell'università: atti del convegno regionale del PCI del Lazio, Roma 5-6 luglio 1974. Roma, 1975. pp. 210.

— Mexico — Statistics.

MEXICO CITY. Universidad Nacional Autonoma de Mexico. Instituto de Investigaciones Sociales. Primer censo nacional universitario, 1949. Mexico, 1953. pp. 518.

— Spain.

ALVAREZ DE MORALES (ANTONIO) Genesis de la universidad española contemporanea. Madrid, 1972. pp. 765. *bibliog. (Instituto de Estudios Administrativos. Estudios de Historia de la Administracion.[8])*

KAGAN (RICHARD L.) Students and society in early modern Spain. Baltimore, [1974]. pp. 278. *bibliog.*

— United Kingdom.

COMMITTEE OF VICE-CHANCELLORS AND PRINCIPALS OF THE UNIVERSITIES OF THE UNITED KINGDOM. University development in the 1970s. [London], 1970. pp. 19.

LONDON. University. University College, and London School of Economics and Political Science. Joint Unit for Planning Research. Networks of urban activities: internal and external linkages in an urban university. [London], 1971. 2 vols. (in 1). *bibliog.*

FAIRBAIRNS (ZOE) Study war no more: military involvement in British universities and colleges. London, [1974]. pp. 32. *bibliog.*

The UNIVERSITIES and applied research: their relevance to social and industrial needs; [proceedings of a symposium of the Research and Development Society held in London in 1974]. London, [1974]. pp. 90.

— — Finance.

PICKFORD (MICHAEL) University expansion and finance. London, 1975. pp. 237. *bibliog.*

— — Graduate work.

RUDD (ERNEST) The highest education: a study of graduate education in Britain. London, 1975. pp. 198. *bibliog.*

— — Commonwealth — Directories.

ASSOCIATION OF COMMONWEALTH UNIVERSITIES. Directory of education and training resources in the developing countries of the Commonwealth: a guide to institutions at the post-secondary level; edited by the Association of Commonwealth Universities for the Commonwealth Fund for Technical Co- operation. London, Commonwealth Secretariat, 1974. pp. 430.

— United States.

UNIVERSITIES in the urban crisis; Thomas P. Murphy, editor. New York, [1975]. pp. 418. *bibliog.*

— — Administration.

COMMITTEE FOR ECONOMIC DEVELOPMENT. Research and Policy Committee. Statements on National Policy. The management and financing of colleges. New York, 1973. pp. 95.

RICHMAN (BARRY M.) and FARMER (RICHARD N.) Leadership, goals, and power in higher education: (a contingency and open-systems approach to effective management). San Francisco, 1974. pp. 364. *bibliog.*

CYERT (RICHARD MICHAEL) The management of nonprofit organizations, with emphasis on universities: (lectures delivered at Hofstra University on the occasion of the inauguration of Robert L. Payton as president; responses by William R. Dill [and others]). Farnborough, Hants, [1975]. pp. 190.

MAUER (GEORGE J.) ed. Crises in campus management: case studies in the administration of colleges and universities. New York, 1976. pp. 266. *bibliog.*

— — Admission.

O'NEIL (ROBERT M.) Discriminating against discrimination: preferential admissions and the DeFunis case. Bloomington, [1975]. pp. 271. *bibliog.*

— — Finance.

COMMITTEE FOR ECONOMIC DEVELOPMENT. Research and Policy Committee. Statements on National Policy. The management and financing of colleges. New York, 1973. pp. 95.

— Uruguay.

Los MARXISTAS-leninistas y el COSUPEN. [Montevideo?, 1969?]. pp. 14.

UNIVERSITY COLLEGE OF CAPE COAST.

GHANA. Commission of Enquiry into the University College of Cape Coast. 1969. Report; [P.E.N.K. Archer, chairman]. [Accra, 1969?]. pp. 318. *Contains corrigenda pages 243,245,246,247. Bound with the White Paper on the report.*

GHANA. 1971. White Paper on the Commission of Enquiry into the University College of Cape Coast. [Accra], 1971. pp. 12. *(W[hite] P[apers]. 1971. No.5) Bound with the report.*

UNJUST ENRICHMENT

— Poland.

OHANOWICZ (ALFRED) Niesłuszne wzbogacenie. Warszawa, 1956. pp. 463. *bibliog.*

UNTOUCHABLES.

OUDEN (J.H.B. DEN) De onaanraakbaren van Konkunad: een onderzoek naar de positieverandering van de scheduled castes in een dorp van het district Coimbatore, India. Wageningen, 1975 in progress. *(Wageningen. Landbouwhogeschool. Mededelingen. 75-11) With English summary.*

HIRO (DILIP) The Untouchables of India. London, 1975. pp. 16. *bibliog. (Minority Rights Group. Reports. No. 26)*

UNWIN FAMILY.

UNWIN (PHILIP) The printing Unwins: a short history of Unwin Brothers: the Gresham Press. 1826-1976. London, 1976. pp. 159. *bibliog.*

UPPER ADIGE

— Nationalism.

SCHAFFERER (KARL) and EULER (ALOIS) Süd-Tirol erlebt, erlitten: eine Dokumentation;... eingeleitet und herausgegeben von Robert H. Drechsler. Wien, 1975. pp. 231.

TOSCANO (MARIO) Alto Adige-South Tyrol: Italy's frontier with the German world;...edited by George A. Carbone. Baltimore, [1975]. pp. 283.

DRECHSLER (ROBERT H.) Georg Klotz: der Schicksalsweg des Südtiroler Schützenmajors, 1919-1976; Dokumentation. Wien, 1976. pp. 299.

EULER (ALOIS) Michael Gamper: Hirte und Herold von Südtirol; eine Dokumentation...; herausgegeben von Robert H. Drechsler. Wien, 1976. pp. 265.

UPPER AUSTRIA

— Economic history.

PISECKY (FRANZ) Wirtschaft, Land und Kammer in Oberösterreich, 1851-1976. Linz, 1976 in progress.

UPPER SILESIAN QUESTION.

COMITE REPRESENTANT LES PARTIS ALLEMANDS DU TERRITOIRE INDUSTRIEL DE LA MORAVIE ET SILESIE DE L'EST. Mémoire concernant la future organisation politique du territoire industriel de la Moravie et Silésie de l'Est. Teschen, [1919?]. pp. 27.

AUERBACH (BERTRAND) Conférence sur la Haute-Silésie faite à Nancy le 16 décembre 1919. Gliwice, [imprint], 1920. pp. 24.

UPPER VOLTA

— Economic conditions.

WASUNGU (PASCAL) Enquête sur les effets de la sécheresse et les mouvements de population en Haute-Volta, 16 février - 30 mars 1974: rapport, 2 avril 1974. Abidjan, United Nations, 1974. 1 vol. (various pagings).

— Emigration and immigration.

WASUNGU (PASCAL) Enquête sur les effets de la sécheresse et les mouvements de population en Haute-Volta, 16 février - 30 mars 1974: rapport, 2 avril 1974. Abidjan, United Nations, 1974. 1 vol. (various pagings).

URAL REGION

— Economic history.

URAL'SKII GOSUDARSTVENNYI UNIVERSITET. Uchenye Zapiski. no. 120. Seriia Istoricheskaia. vyp. no.23. Iz istorii partiinykh organizatsii Urala: sbornik statei. Sverdlovsk, 1971. pp. 192.

GOLUBTSOV (VADIM SERGEEVICH) Chernaia metallurgiia Urala v pervye gody Sovetskoi vlasti, 1917-1923 gg. Moskva, 1975. pp. 230.

— Industries.

PROZOROV (VITALII PETROVICH) Khimicheskaia promyshlennost' Urala v gody dovoennykh piatiletok: iz istorii bor'by partiinykh organizatsii Urala za osushchestvlenie leninskoi politiki sotsialisticheskoi industrializatsii strany. Sverdlovsk, 1969. pp. 76.

— Politics and government.

REVOLIUTSIONNO-osvoboditel'noe dvizhenie v XIX-XX vv. v Povolzh'e i Priural'e. Kazan', 1974. pp. 115.

— Social history.

KUL'TURA i byt gorniakov i metallurgov Nizhnego Tagila, 1917- 1970. Moskva, 1974. 7p. 319.

URANIUM INDUSTRY

— Canada.

URANIUM and thorium in Canada: resources, production and potential; by R.M. Williams [and others]. Ottawa, 1971. pp. 28. *(Canada. Mineral Resources Division. Mineral [Information] Bulletins. 117)*

URBAN ECONOMICS.

CONROY (MICHAEL E.) The challenge of urban economic development: goals, possibilities and policies for improving the economic structure of cities. Lexington, Mass., [1975]. pp. 132. *bibliog.*

HEUER (HANS) Urban economist. Sozioökonomische Bestimmungsfaktoren der Stadtentwicklung. Stuttgart, [1975]. pp. 491. *bibliog. (Deutsches Institut für Urbanistik. Schriften. Band 50)*

PRESCOTT (JAMES RUSSELL) and LEWIS (W. CRIS) Urban-regional economic growth and policy. Ann Arbor, [1975]. pp. 220. *bibliogs.*

SMITH (WALLACE FRANCIS) Urban development: the process and the problems. Berkeley, Calif., [1975]. pp. 381. *bibliogs.*

BUTTON (K.J.) Urban economics: theory and policy. London, 1976. pp. 218. *bibliogs.*

URBAN RENEWAL

— United Kingdom — Citizen participation.

ROBERTSON (IAN) Community self-surveys in urban renewal. [Manchester, 1976]. pp. 140. *bibliog. (Manchester. University. Department of Adult Education. Manchester Monographs. 4)*

— United States.

BINGHAM (RICHARD D.) Public housing and urban renewal: an analysis of federal-local relations. New York, 1975. pp. 255. *bibliog.*

MODERNIZING the central city: new towns intown...and beyond; [by] Harvey S. Perloff [and others]. Cambridge, Mass., [1975]. pp. 414. *bibliogs.*

STONE (CLARENCE NATHAN) Economic growth and neighborhood discontent: system bias in the urban renewal program of Atlanta. Chapel Hill, [1976]. pp. 256. *bibliog.*

URBAN TRANSPORTATION.

DOMENCICH (THOMAS A.) and McFADDEN (DANIEL) Urban travel demand: a behavioral analysis; a Charles River Associates research study. Amsterdam, 1975. pp. 215. *bibliog.*

TOMAZINIS (ANTHONY R.) Productivity, efficiency, and quality in urban transportation systems. Lexington, Mass., [1975]. pp. 237. *bibliog.*

— Mathematical models.

STOPHER (PETER R.) and MEYBURG (ARNIM H.) Urban transportation modeling and planning. Lexington, Mass., [1975]. pp. 345.

— Brazil.

FOURACRE (P.R.) The development of public transport in Curitiba, Brazil. Crowthorne, 1975. pp. 17. *bibliog. (U.K. Transport and Road Research Laboratory. Supplementary Reports. 197 UC)*

— Hong Kong.

HONG KONG. Transport Department. Research and Development Section. 1975. North Point - Kwun Tong: vehicular ferry service. [Hong Kong], 1975. pp. 18. *(Studies Reports. No. 75/3)*

— United Kingdom.

ROYAL AUTOMOBILE CLUB. Traffic and the environment and Urban transport planning; memoranda of evidence...to the Greater London Council and to the Expenditure Committee...House of Commons. London, [1973]. pp. 13.

ADVANCED urban transport; [by] Ian Black [and others]. Farnborough, Hants, [1975]. pp. 212.

URBAN TRANSPORTATION POLICY

— South Africa.

SOUTH AFRICA. Ministry of Transport. 1975. White Paper on the report of the Committee of Inquiry into Urban Transport Facilities in the Republic, RP 60/74, the Driessen report. [Pretoria], 1975. pp. 17,18. *(South Africa. W[hite] P[aper] Series). 1975. [No.] V) In English and Afrikaans.*

— United Kingdom.

GREY (ALEXANDER) Urban fares policy. Farnborough, Hants., [1975]. pp. 160.

— — Tyne and Wear.

TYNE AND WEAR. County Council. Transport policies and programme. a., 1976/77- Newcastle-upon-Tyne.

— United States.

OWEN (WILFRED) Transportation for cities: the role of federal policy. Washington, D.C., [1976]. pp. 70.

URBANIZATION.

CURIE (JACQUES) Le devenir des travailleurs d'origine agricole: contribution à l'étude de la transformation des conduites de travail. Paris, 1975. pp. 529. *bibliog. Thèse présentée devant l'Université de Toulouse-le-Mirail.*

GOLDSTEIN (SIDNEY) and SLY (DAVID F.) eds. Basic data needed for the study of urbanization. Dolhain, [1975]. pp. 100. *bibliogs. (International Union for the Scientific Study of Population. Committee on Urbanization and Population Redistribution. Working Papers. 1)*

GOLDSTEIN (SIDNEY) and SLY (DAVID F.) eds. The measurement of urbanization and projection of urban population. Dolhain, [1975]. pp. 224. *bibliogs. (International Union for the Scientific Study of Population. Committee on Urbanization and Population Redistribution. Working Papers. 2)*

INTERNATIONAL UNION OF LOCAL AUTHORITIES. [Publications]. 106. New patterns of urbanization. The Hague, 1975. pp. 122.

— America, Latin.

HARDOY (JORGE) ed. Urbanization in Latin America: approaches and issues. Garden City, N.Y., 1975. pp. 456.

— Brazil.

COSTA (MANOEL AUGUSTO) Urbanization and migration in Brazil, with particular reference to trends since 1940; [Ph.D. (London) thesis]. 1975. pp. 298. *bibliog. Typescript: unpublished. This thesis is the property of London University and may not be removed from the Library.*

— Europe.

INTERNATIONAL GEOGRAPHICAL UNION. European Regional Conference, Budapest, 1972. Urbanization in Europe: selected papers in English, German and French; edited by Béla Sárfalvi. Budapest, 1975. pp. 313.

— Papua New Guinea.

REW (ALAN) Social images and process in urban New Guinea: a study of Port Moresby. St. Paul, [1974]. pp. 262. *bibliog. (American Ethnological Society. Monographs. 57)*

— Russia.

BATER (JAMES H.) St. Petersburg: industrialization and change. London, 1976. pp. 174. *bibliog.*

— United States.

BLUMIN (STUART M.) The urban threshold: growth and change in a nineteenth-century American community. Chicago, 1976. pp. 298. *bibliog.*

URUGUAY

— Economic conditions.

WEINSTEIN (MARTIN) Uruguay: the politics of failure. Westport, Conn., 1975. pp. 190. *bibliog.*

— Politics and government.

Los MARXISTAS-leninistas y el COSUPEN. [Montevideo?, 1969?]. pp. 14.

WEINSTEIN (MARTIN) Uruguay: the politics of failure. Westport, Conn., 1975. pp. 190. *bibliog.*

— Social conditions.

WEINSTEIN (MARTIN) Uruguay: the politics of failure. Westport, Conn., 1975. pp. 190. *bibliog.*

USED MACHINERY.

JAMES (DILMUS DELANO) The economic feasibility of employing used machinery in less developed countries. 1970. pp. 303. *bibliog. Ph.D. (Michigan State University) thesis: unpublished. Microfilm of typescript: 1 reel.*

USTASA.

VODINELIĆ (VLADIMIR) 10 verzija više jedna jednako istina: zapisi o Bonskom i Stockholmskom procesu ustaškim teroristima. Split, 1973. pp. 236.

USTIURT.

See USTYURT.

USTYURT DESERT.

VIKTOROV (SERGEI VASIL'EVICH) Pustynia Ustiurt i voprosy ee osvoeniia: The Ustyurt Desert and problems of the reclamation. Moskva, 1971. pp. 134. *bibliog. (Moskovskoe Obshchestvo Ispytatelei Prirody. Trudy. t.44) With brief English summary.*

UTILITARIANISM.

MILL (JOHN STUART) John Stuart Mill on politics and society; selected and edited by Geraint L. Williams. London, 1976. pp. 412. *bibliog.*

UTILITY THEORY.

FISHBURN (PETER C.) Utility theory for decision making. New York, [1970]. pp. 234. *bibliog. (Operations Research Society of America. Publications in Operations Research. No.18)*

UTILITY THEORY.(Cont.)

ANDERS (HANS DIETER) and others. Zum Bewertungsproblem im Sozialismus. Berlin, 1974. pp. 120. *(Akademie der Wissenschaften der DDR. Zentralinstitut für Wirtschaftswissenschaften. Forschungsberichte. Nr.12)*

RESEARCH CONFERENCE ON SUBJECTIVE PROBABILITY, UTILITY AND DECISION MAKING, 4TH, ROME, 1973. Utility, probability, and human decision making: selected proceedings...; edited by Dirk Wendt and Charles Vlek. Dordrecht, [1975]. pp. 418. *bibliogs.*

UTOPIAS.

GILISON (JEROME MARTIN) The Soviet image of utopia. Baltimore, [1975]. PP. 192.

BAUMAN (ZYGMUNT) Socialism: the active utopia. London, 1976. pp. 150.

UTTAR PRADESH

— Population.

INDIA. Census, 1971. Series 21. Uttar Pradesh: a portrait of population; [by] D.M. Sinha. [Delhi, 1973]. pp. 228. *bibliog.*

UZBEKISTAN

— Constitutional history.

GOSUDARSTVENNOE stroitel'stvo i pravo v Uzbekskoi SSR. Tashkent, 1974. pp. 366.

— Economic conditions.

PROIZVODITEL'NYE sily Uzbekistana i perspektivy ikh razvitiia. 2nd ed. Tashkent, 1974. pp. 367.

— Economic history.

KUDRIAKOV (VLADIMIR MIKHAILOVICH) Za pod"em narodnogo khoziaistva: opyt rukovodstva Kompartii Uzbekistana khoziaistvennym stroitel'stvom v gody semiletki, 1959- 1965 gg. Tashkent, 1969. pp. 192.

ALIMOV (IBRAGIM ABDUGAPPAROVICH) Uzbekskoe dekhkanstvo na puti k sotsializmu: sotsial'no-ekonomicheskie preobrazovaniia v uzbekskom kishlake v 1921-1925 gg. Tashkent, 1974. pp. 239. *bibliog.*

— Economic policy.

PROIZVODITEL'NYE sily Uzbekistana i perspektivy ikh razvitiia. 2nd ed. Tashkent, 1974. pp. 367.

— History.

ISTORIIA Uzbekskoi SSR s drevneishikh vremen do nashikh dnei. Tashkent, 1974. pp. 583. *bibliog.*

— Politics and government.

BRATSTVO narodov i internatsional'noe vospitanie: [materialy respublikanskoi nauchno-teoreticheskoi konferentsii "Torzhestvo leninskikh idei bratstva narodov i internatsional'noe vospitanie trudiashchikhsia"]. Tashkent, 1974. pp. 266.

VACCINATION.

ROBERTSON (JOHN MACKINNON) The truth about vaccination. Bradford, [1897]. pp. 7. *(Papers for the People. No.8)*

VAGRANCY.

EUROPEAN COURT OF HUMAN RIGHTS. Publications. Series A: Judgments and Decisions. [A12]. ...De Wilde, Ooms and Versyp cases; "vagrancy" cases. 1. Decision of 28th May 1970. 2. Judgment of 18th November 1970; question of procedure. 3. Judgment of 18th June 1971. Strasbourg, Council of Europe, 1971. pp. 75 [bis].

EUROPEAN COURT OF HUMAN RIGHTS. Publications. Series B: Pleadings, Oral Arguments and Documents.[B10]. "De Wilde, Ooms and Versyp" cases: "vagrancy" cases, 1969-1971. Strasbourg, Council of Europe, 1971. pp. 405 [bis], 407-474. *In English and French.*

EUROPEAN COURT OF HUMAN RIGHTS. Publications. Series A: Judgments and Decisions. [A] 14. ...De Wilde, Ooms and Versyp cases: "vagrancy" cases; judgment of 10 March 1972; question of the application of Article 50 of the Convention. Strasbourg, Council of Europe, 1972. pp. 22 [bis]. *In English and French.*

EUROPEAN COURT OF HUMAN RIGHTS. Publications. Series B: Pleadings, Oral Arguments and Documents. [B12]. "De Wilde, Ooms and Versyp" cases: "vagrancy" cases; question of the application of Article 50 of the Convention, (1971-1972). Strasbourg, Council of Europe, 1973. pp. 97 [bis], 99-126. *In English and French.*

— South Africa.

NATIONAL INSTITUTE FOR CRIME PREVENTION AND REHABILITATION OF OFFENDERS [SOUTH AFRICA]. "Vagrancy": a limited study of "vagrants" in the metropolitan area of Cape Town; (with Annexure: a legal fact paper on vagrancy and related offences). [Cape Town, 1974]. fo. 14, 11.

— United Kingdom.

NATIONAL COUNCIL FOR CIVIL LIBERTIES. Vagrancy: an archaic law. London, 1975. pp. 16.

VALENCIA, SPAIN (REGION)

— Economic conditions.

NI desarrollo regional, ni ordenacion del territorio: el caso valenciano; informe dirigido por Mario Gaviria. Madrid, [1974]. pp. 445.

— Industries.

NI desarrollo regional, ni ordenacion del territorio: el caso valenciano; informe dirigido por Mario Gaviria. Madrid, [1974]. pp. 445.

VALENCIA, VENEZUELA

— Politics and government.

CANNON (MARK W.) and others. Urban government for Valencia, Venezuela. New York, 1973. pp. 152. *bibliog. (Institute of Public Administration, New York. International Urban Studies. No. 9).*

VALENTINOV (NIKOLAI VLADISLAVOVICH) pseud.

VALENTINOV (NIKOLAI VLADISLAVOVICH) pseud. [i.e. Nikolai Vladislavovich VOL'SKII] Novaia ekonomicheskaia politika i krizis partii posle smerti Lenina: gody raboty v VSNKh vo vremia NEP; vospominaniia....; The new economic policy and the Party crisis after the death of Lenin: reminiscences of my work at the VSNKh during the NEP; edited by J. Bunyan and V. Butenko, etc. Stanford, 1971. pp. 256.

VALERO (HELENA).

[VALERO (HELENA)] Yanoáma: the narrative of a white girl kidnapped by Amazonian Indians; as told to Ettore Biocca;...translated from the Italian by Dennis Rhodes. New York, 1970 repr. 1971. pp. 382. *bibliog.*

VALOIS (GEORGES) pseud.

GUCHET (YVES) Georges Valois: l'Action Française, le Faisceau, la République Syndicale. Paris, [1975]. pp. 249. *bibliog.*

VALUE.

RUBIN (ISAAK IL'ICH) Essays on Marx's theory of value; translated by Miloš Samardźya and Fredy Perlman from the third edition...1928. Montréal, [1968]. pp. 275.

CHAO (TZU-YUAN) Neue Arbeitswerttheorie: der Weg nach Utopia;...aus dem Chinesischen übertragen von Christian Gries in Zusammenarbeit mit dem Autor. Hamburg, [1974]. pp. 173. *With English summary.*

El DEBATE cubano sobre el funcionamiento de la ley del valor en el socialismo; ([by] Ernesto "Che" Guevara [and others]) Barcelona, 1974. pp. 357.

AGAFONOV (ALEKSANDR KONSTANTINOVICH) Tovarnoe proizvodstvo i zakon stoimosti pri sotsializme. Kiev, 1975. pp. 240. *bibliog.*

MARGLIN (STEPHEN ALAN) Value and price in the labour-surplus economy. Oxford, 1976. pp. 252. *bibliog.*

PAQUIN (LLOYD TURNER) Problems in the foundations of monetary theory. 1976. fo. 187. *bibliog. Typescript. Ph. D. (London) thesis : unpublished. This thesis is the property of London University and may not be removed from the Library.*

— Mathematical models.

BAISCH (HELMUT) Wert, Preis und Allokation: eine Verallgemeinerung des Marxschen Reproduktionsmodells. Meisenheim am Glan, 1976. pp. 318. *bibliog. With English summary.*

VAMBE (LAWRENCE).

VAMBE (LAWRENCE) From Rhodesia to Zimbabwe. Pittsburgh, 1976. pp. 290.

VANDALISM.

GRAYSON (LESLEY) Vandalism on housing estates. [London], Greater London Council, 1975. pp. 8. *bibliog. (London Topics. No. 7)*

VARIABLES (MATHEMATICS).

KOOYMAN (M.A.) Dummy variables in econometrics. Tilburg, 1976. pp. 197. *(Tilburg. Katholieke Hogeschool. Tilburg Institute of Economics. Tilburg Studies on Economics. 14)*

VEGETABLES

— United Kingdom — Marketing.

HINTON (WILFRED LYNN) Marketing vegetables from store...; a study of investment and import saving. Cambridge, 1975. pp. 38. *(Cambridge. University. Department of Land Economy. Agricultural Economics Unit. Occasional Papers. No. 19)*

VEGETARIANISM.

WYNNE-TYSON (JON) Food for a future: the ecological priority of a humane diet. London, 1975. pp. 183. *bibliog.*

VENEZUELA

— Census.

VENEZUELA. Census, 1971. X censo de poblacion y vivienda: resumen nacional; [volume series]. Caracas, 1974 in progress.

— Economic history — Sources.

NUÑEZ (ENRIQUE BERNARDO) ed. Cacao; ensayo y prologo de Orlando Araujo. Caracas, 1972. pp. 565. *(Banco Central de Venezuela. Coleccion Cuatricentenario de Caracas. 9) A collection of documents.*

— Foreign relations — Curaçao.

GOSLINGA (CORNELIS CH.) Curaçao and Guzmán Blanco: a case study of small power politics in the Caribbean. 's-Gravenhage, 1975. pp. 143. *bibliog. (Instituut voor Taal-, Land- en Volkenkunde. Verhandelingen. [Deel] 76)*

— Industries.

PLAZA (SALVADOR DE LA) Estructuras de integracion nacional. Caracas, [1959? repr.] 1973. pp. 238. *Articles published in El Nacional, 1958-1959.*

— Manufactures.

KARLSSON (WEINE) Manufacturing in Venezuela: studies on development and location. Stockholm, 1975. pp. 240. *bibliog. (Latinamerika-Institutet. Skrifter. Serie A: Monografier. 2)*

— Politics and government.

KOLB (GLEN L.) Democracy and dictatorship in Venezuela, 1945-1958. [New London, Conn., 1974]. pp. 228. bibliog. (Connecticut College. Monographs. No. 10)

— Population.

VENEZUELA. Direccion General de Estadistica. 1975. XIX encuesta nacional de hogares por muestreo [1974]: datos generales de la poblacion y de las viviendas. Caracas, 1975. pp. 292.

VENICE.

VENEZIA e i problemi dell'ambiente: studio e impiego de modelli matematici; [research papers produced in collaboration by the Centro di Ricerca of IBM Italia and the Laboratorio per lo Studio della Dinamica delle Grandi Masse of the Consiglio Nazionale delle Ricerche]. Bologna, [1975]. pp. 360.

— Commerce.

CIRIACONO (SALVATORE) Olio ed ebrei nella Repubblica veneta del Settecento. Venezia, 1975. pp. 208. (Deputazione di Storia Patria per le Venezie. Miscellanea di Studi e Memorie. vol. 16)

— Economic history.

RAPP (RICHARD TILDEN) Industry and economic decline in seventeenth-century Venice. Cambridge, Mass., 1976. pp. 195. bibliog. (Harvard University. Harvard Historical Monographs. 69)

VENSTRE.

See LIBERAL PARTY — Denmark.

VEREINSTAG DEUTSCHER ARBEITERVEREINE.

PETRY (LOTHAR) Die Erste Internationale in der Berliner Arbeiterbewegung. Erlangen, 1975. pp. 381. bibliog.

VERRI (PIETRO) Conte.

NUCCIO (OSCAR) Economisti italiani del XVIII secolo: Ferdinando Galiani, Antonio Genovesi, Pietro Verri, Francesco Mengotti. Roma, 1974. pp. 286.

VERSAILLES, TREATY OF, JUNE 28, 1919 (GERMANY).

FERRERO (GUGLIELMO) Die Tragödie des Friedens: von Versailles zur Ruhr; (berechtigte Übersetzung aus dem Italienischen von B. Pritchard). Jena, 1923. pp. 207. Collection of essays and articles, mainly from the journal "Secolo", 1918-23, and some unpublished material.

HESSE (ALBERT HERMANN) Die Wirkungen des Friedens von Versailles auf die Wirtschaft des deutschen Ostens. Jena, 1930. pp. 62.

PAJEWSKI (JANUSZ) ed. Problem polsko-niemiecki w Traktacie Wersalskim; praca zbiorowa pod redakcja J. Pajewskiego, etc. Poznań, 1963. pp. 652. bibliog. (Poznań. Instytut Zachodni. Dzieje Polskiej Granicy Zachodniej. 3)

VERSYP (EDGARD).

EUROPEAN COURT OF HUMAN RIGHTS. Publications. Series A: Judgments and Decisions. [A12]. ...De Wilde, Ooms and Versyp cases; "vagrancy" cases. 1. Decision of 28th May 1970. 2. Judgment of 18th November 1970; question of procedure. 3. Judgment of 18th June 1971. Strasbourg, Council of Europe, 1971. pp. 75 [bis].

EUROPEAN COURT OF HUMAN RIGHTS. Publications. Series B: Pleadings, Oral Arguments and Documents.[B10]. "De Wilde, Ooms and Versyp" cases: "vagrancy" cases, 1969-1971. Strasbourg, Council of Europe, 1971. pp. 405 [bis], 407-474. In English and French.

EUROPEAN COURT OF HUMAN RIGHTS. Publications. Series A: Judgments and Decisions. [A] 14. ...De Wilde, Ooms and Versyp cases: "vagrancy" cases; judgment of 10 March 1972; question of the application of Article 50 of the Convention. Strasbourg, Council of Europe, 1972. pp. 22 [bis]. In English and French.

EUROPEAN COURT OF HUMAN RIGHTS. Publications. Series B: Pleadings, Oral Arguments and Documents. [B12]. "De Wilde, Ooms and Versyp" cases: "vagrancy" cases; question of the application of Article 50 of the Convention, (1971-1972). Strasbourg, Council of Europe, 1973. pp. 97 [bis], 99-126. In English and French.

VERWOERD (HENDRIK FRENSCH).

SCHOEMAN (B.M.) Die sluipmoord op Dr. Verwoerd. Pretoria, 1975. pp. 148.

VICO (GIAMBATTISTA).

BERLIN (Sir ISAIAH) Vico and Herder: two studies in the history of ideas. London, 1976. pp. 228.

VICTORIA, AUSTRALIA

— Economic conditions.

MEREDITH MEMORIAL LECTURES. 1972. Victoria: one society?. Bundoora, Victoria, 1972. 7 pts. Lecture by I.A.H. Turner on Trade unions and the community not published.

— Emigration and immigration.

AUSTRALIA. Migrant Task Force Committee, Victoria. 1973. Recommendations to the Minister for Immigration, 30th June 1973; chairman: H.J. Garrick. [Melbourne, 1973]. fo. 77. Photocopy.

— Legislative Assembly — Elections.

HUGHES (COLIN ANFIELD) and GRAHAM (BRUCE DESMOND) Voting for the Victorian Legislative Assembly. Canberra, 1975. pp. 468. Supplement to the same authors' A handbook of Australian government and politics, 1890-1964, to which it also contains corrigenda.

— Social conditions.

MEREDITH MEMORIAL LECTURES. 1972. Victoria: one society?. Bundoora, Victoria, 1972. 7 pts. Lecture by I.A.H. Turner on Trade unions and the community not published.

VIENNA

— Börse.

BALTZAREK (FRANZ) Die Geschichte der Wiener Börse: öffentliche Finanzen und privates Kapital im Spiegel einer österreichischen Wirtschaftsinstitution. Wien, 1973. pp. 173. bibliog. (Österreichische Akademie der wissenschaften. Kommission für Wirtschafts-, Sozial- und Stadtgeschichte. Veröffentlichungen. 1)

— Population.

SLUPETZKY (WERNER) Bevölkerungsentwicklung im Raum Wien, 1951-1961-1971. Wien, [1974]. pp. 59.

— Social history.

BOTZ (GERHARD) Wohnungspolitik und Judendeportation in Wien, 1938 bis 1945: zur Funktion des Antisemitismus als Ersatz nationalsozialistischer Sozialpolitik. Wien, 1975. pp. 200. bibliog. (Salzburg. Universität. Historisches Institut. Veröffentlichungen. 13)

VIETNAM

— Foreign relations — Canada.

CANADA. Department of External Affairs. 1973. Viet-nam: Canada's approach to participation in the International Commission of Control and Supervision, October 25, 1972-March 27, 1973. [Ottawa], 1973. pp. 51. In English and French.

— — China.

MURASHEVA (GALINA FEDOROVNA) V'etnamo-kitaiskie otnosheniia XVII-XIX vv. Moskva, 1973. pp. 158. bibliog.

LOESCHER (GILBURT DAMIAN) National liberation war in South Vietnam: the perceptions and policies of China and North Vietnam, 1954-1969; [Ph.D. (London) thesis]. 1975. fo. 421. bibliog. Typescript: unpublished. This thesis is the property of London University and may not be removed from the Library.

— — Russia.

ISAEV (MIKHAIL PETROVICH) and CHERNYSHEV (AL'BERT SERGEEVICH) Sovetsko-v'etnamskie otnosheniia. Moskva, 1975. pp. 327.

— — United States.

BROWN (WELDON AMZY) Prelude to disaster: the American role in Vietnam, 1940-1963. Port Washington, 1975. pp. 278. bibliog.

— History.

SHIBATA (SHINGO) Lessons of the Vietnam war: philosophical considerations on the Vietnam revolution. Amsterdam, 1973. pp. 228.

LÊ (NICOLE DOMINIQUE) Les missions-étrangères et la pénétration française au Viêt-Nam. Paris, [1975]. pp. 228. bibliog. (Nice. Université. Faculté des Lettres et Sciences Humaines. Institut d'Etudes et de Recherches Interethniques et Interculturelles. Publications. 5)

WOODSIDE (ALEXANDER BARTON) Community and revolution in modern Vietnam. Boston, [Mass., 1976]. pp. 351. bibliog.

— Nationalism.

HEMERY (DANIEL) Révolutionnaires vietnamiens et pouvoir colonial en Indochine: communistes, trotskystes, nationlistes à Saigon de 1932 à 1937. Paris, 1975. pp. 524. bibliog.

DUIKER (WILLIAM J.) The rise of nationalism in Vietnam, 1900-1941. Ithaca, N.Y., 1976. pp. 313. bibliog.

— Politics and government.

HEMERY (DANIEL) Révolutionnaires vietnamiens et pouvoir colonial en Indochine: communistes, trotskystes, nationlistes à Saigon de 1932 à 1937. Paris, 1975. pp. 524. bibliog.

LOESCHER (GILBURT DAMIAN) National liberation war in South Vietnam: the perceptions and policies of China and North Vietnam, 1954-1969; [Ph.D. (London) thesis]. 1975. fo. 421. bibliog. Typescript: unpublished. This thesis is the property of London University and may not be removed from the Library.

WOODSIDE (ALEXANDER BARTON) Community and revolution in modern Vietnam. Boston, [Mass., 1976]. pp. 351. bibliog.

— Social conditions.

WOODSIDE (ALEXANDER BARTON) Community and revolution in modern Vietnam. Boston, [Mass., 1976]. pp. 351. bibliog.

VIETNAMESE WARS, 1945-1975.

NO more armaments for no more Vietnams; [anonymous typescript letter sent to United States student bodies, foreign embassies and sociology departments of British universities]. Upton by Chester, 1970. 1 vol. (unpaged).

ELLSBERG (DANIEL) Papers on the war. New York, [1972]. pp. 309.

SHIBATA (SHINGO) Lessons of the Vietnam war: philosophical considerations on the Vietnam revolution. Amsterdam, 1973. pp. 228.

VIETNAMESE WARS, 1945-1975.(Cont.)

LOESCHER (GILBERT DAMIAN) National liberation war in South Vietnam: the perceptions and policies of China and North Vietnam, 1954-1969; [Ph.D. (London) thesis]. 1975. fo. 421. *bibliog.* Typescript: unpublished. This thesis is the property of London University and may not be removed from the Library.

O'BALLANCE (EDGAR) The wars in Vietnam, 1954-1973. London, 1975. pp. 204.

— **Conscientious objectors.**

DAMICO (ALFONSO J.) Democracy and the case for amnesty. Gainesville, Fla., 1975. pp. 78. *(Florida University. Monographs. Social Sciences. No. 55)*

— **Economic aspects — United States.**

LAKE (ANTHONY) ed. The Vietnam legacy: the war, American society and the future of American foreign policy. New York, 1976. pp. 440.

STEVENS (ROBERT WARREN) Vain hopes, grim realities: the economic consequences of the Vietnam war. New York, 1976. pp. 229.

— **Environmental aspects.**

WESTING (ARTHUR) Ecological consequences of the second Indochina war. Stockholm, [1976]. pp. 119. *bibliog.* *(Stockholm International Peace Research Institute. SIPRI [Monographs])*

— **Peace.**

CANADA. Department of External Affairs. 1973. Viet-nam: Canada's approach to participation in the International Commission of Control and Supervision, October 25, 1972-March 27, 1973. [Ottawa], 1973. pp. 51. *In English and French.*

PORTER (GARETH) A peace denied: the United States, Vietnam, and the Paris agreement. Bloomington, [1975]. pp. 357.

— **Personal narratives, Vietnamese.**

NGUYEN KHAI. Ceux de Conco. Hanoi, 1966. pp. 115.

— **Social aspects — United States.**

LAKE (ANTHONY) ed. The Vietnam legacy: the war, American society and the future of American foreign policy. New York, 1976. pp. 440.

— **United States.**

BROWN (WELDON AMZY) Prelude to disaster: the American role in Vietnam, 1940-1963. Port Washington, 1975. pp. 278. *bibliog.*

LAW and responsibility in warfare: the Vietnam experience; (papers and discussions from a special meeting of the American Society of International Law in October 1971); edited by Peter D. Trooboff. Chapel Hill, N.C., [1975]. pp. 280.

PORTER (GARETH) A peace denied: the United States, Vietnam, and the Paris agreement. Bloomington, [1975]. pp. 357.

BROWN (WELDON AMZY) The last chopper: the denouement of the American role in Vietnam, 1963-1975. Port Washington, N.Y., 1976. pp. 371. *bibliog.*

DEITCHMAN (SEYMOUR J.) The best-laid schemes: a tale of social research and bureaucracy. Cambridge, Mass., [1976]. pp. 483. *bibliog.*

FANNING (LOUIS A.) Betrayal in Vietnam. New Rochelle, N.Y., [1976]. pp. 256. *bibliog.*

VIGILANCE COMMITTEES.

BROWN (RICHARD MAXWELL) Strain of violence: historical studies of American violence and vigilantism. New York, 1975. pp. 397.

BURROWS (WILLIAM E.) Vigilante! New York, [1976]. pp. 311. *bibliog.*

VIGILANTE politics; [by] Dane Archer [and others]; H. Jon Rosenbaum and Peter C. Sederberg, editors. [Philadelphia], 1976. pp. 292.

VILLAGE COMMUNITIES

— **India.**

MAYER (ADRIAN CURTIS) Caste and kinship in central India: a village and its region. Berkeley, [1960] repr. 1966. pp. 295. *bibliog.*

— **Russia.**

ALEKSANDROV (VADIM ALEKSANDROVICH) Sel'skaia obshchina v Rossii, XVII - nachalo XIX v. Moskva, 1976. pp. 323.

— **Tanzania.**

AWITI (ADHU) The development of ujamaa villages and the peasant question in Iringa district: a study outline. Dar es Salaam, 1973. pp. 48. *bibliog.* *(Dar es Salaam. University. Economic Research Bureau. ERB Papers. 73.4)*

RAIKES (PHILIP L.) Economic evaluation criteria for ujamaa villages. Dar es Salaam, 1973. pp. 36. *bibliog.* *(Dar es Salaam. University. Economic Research Bureau. ERB Papers. 73. 3)*

CAPLAN (ANN PATRICIA) Choice and constraint in a Swahili community: property, hierarchy and cognatic descent on the east African coast. London, 1975. pp. 162. *bibliog.*

VILLAGES

— **Bibliography.**

[ROBERTSON (JOHN HENRY)] compiler. Labour utilization: an annotated bibliography of village studies; compiled by John Connell [pseud.]...; prepared for the International Labour Office within the framework of the World Employment Programme. [Brighton], University of Sussex, Institute of Development Studies, 1975. pp. 305.

— **Cambodia.**

MARTEL (GABRIELLE) Lovea, village des environs d'Angkor: aspects démographiques, économiques et sociologiques du monde rural cambodgien dans la province de Siem-Réap. Paris, 1975. pp. 359. *(Ecole Française d'Extrême-Orient. Publications. vol. 98)*

— **Denmark.**

TO byer i Odsherred...;[by] (Gunnar Viby Mogensen) [and others]. København, 1975. pp. 70. *(Socialforskningsinstituttet. Meddelelser. 12)* With English summary.

— **France.**

GAROFALO (YOLANDE) and WARNIER (BERTRAND) Un village, paysage et développement: [Avernes]. Paris, La Documentation Française, 1974. pp. 75.

— **Germany.**

GOLDE (GUENTER) Catholics and Protestants: agricultural modernization in two German villages. New York, [1975]. pp. 198. *bibliog.*

DEENEN (BERND VAN) and ZUREK (ERNST) Die Wirksamkeit zinsverbilligter Mittel in der Dorferneuerung: ein Beitrag zur Darlehenspolitik der Deutschen Siedlungs- und Landesrentenbank. Bonn, 1976. pp. 195. *(Forschungsgesellschaft für Agrarpolitik und Agrarsoziologie. [Publications]. 229)*

KNAUDT (NORBERT) Berufswahl und Berufsmobilität der Erwerbstätigen in zehn ehemals kleinbäuerlichen Dörfern der Bundesrepublik Deutschland, 1952 und 1972. Bonn, 1976. pp. 204. *bibliog.* *(Forschungsgesellschaft für Agrarpolitik und Agrarsoziologie. [Publications]. 231)*

SCHUY (WILLY) Landgemeinden im Wirkungsbereich der Regionalentwicklung und Raumordnung; dargestellt am Beispiel zehn ehemals kleinbäuerlicher Dörfer der Bundesrepublik Deutschland im Zeitraum 1952/1972. Bonn, 1976. pp. 236. *bibliog.* *(Forschungsgesellschaft für Agrarpolitik und Agrarsoziologie. [Publications]. 233)*

— **India — Bombay.**

MANN (HAROLD HART) and others. Land and labour in a Deccan village. London, 1917. pp. 184. *(Bombay (City). University. Economic Series. No. 1)*

— — **Haryana.**

MILLER (D.B.) From hierarchy to stratification: changing patterns of social inequality in a north Indian village. Delhi, 1975. pp. 229. *bibliog.*

— — **Rajasthan.**

CHAKRAVARTI (ANAND) Contradiction and change: emerging patterns of authority in a Rajasthan village. Delhi, 1975. pp. 234. *bibliog.*

— **Nigeria.**

BARRETT (STANLEY R.) Two villages on stilts: economic and family change in Nigeria. New York, [1974]. pp. 112. *bibliog.*

— **Switzerland.**

FRIEDL (JOHN) Kippel: a changing village in the Alps. New York, [1974]. pp. 129. *bibliog.*

— **United Kingdom.**

RAFTIS (J. AMBROSE) Warboys: two hundred years in the life of an English mediaeval village. Toronto, 1974. pp. 267. *bibliog.* *(Pontifical Institute of Mediaeval Studies. Studies and Texts. 29)*

CHAMBERLAIN (MARY) Fenwomen: a portrait of women in an English village. London, 1975. pp. 186.

DARLEY (GILLIAN) Villages of vision. London, 1975. pp. 152. *bibliog.*

VILLEINAGE

— **Russia.**

PANEIAKH (VIKTOR MOISEEVICH) Kholopstvo v XVI - nachale XVII veka. Leningrad, 1975. pp. 267.

VILLIERS (CHARLES PELHAM).

HENDERSON (WILLIAM OTTO) Charles Pelham Villiers and the repeal of the Corn Laws. [Manchester, 1975]. pp. 81.

VINCI (LEONARDO DA).

AMERICAN ASSOCIATION FOR THE ADVANCEMENT OF SCIENCE. Section L. Annual Meeting, 1969. Philosophical foundations of science: proceedings...; edited by Raymond J. Seeger and Robert S. Cohen. Dordrecht, [1974]. pp. 545. *bibliogs.* *(Boston Colloquium for the Philosophy of Science. Boston Studies in the Philosophy of Science. vol.11)*

VIOLENCE.

GREGORY (FRANK E.C.) Protest and violence: the police response: a comparative analysis of democratic methods. London, 1976. pp. 15. *(Institute for the Study of Conflict. Conflict Studies. No. 75)*

— **America, Latin.**

DUFF (ERNEST A.) and McCAMANT (JOHN F.) Violence and repression in Latin America: a quantitative and historical analysis. New York, [1976]. pp. 322. *bibliog.*

— **Curaçao.**

ANDERSON (WILLIAM AVERETTE) and DYNES (RUSSELL ROWE) Social movements, violence and change: the May Movement in Curaçao. Columbus, Ohio, [1975]. pp. 175. *bibliog.*

— **United States.**

BLUMENTHAL (MONICA D.) and others. More about justifying violence: methodological studies of attitudes and behavior. Ann Arbor, 1975. pp. 401. *bibliog.*

BROWN (RICHARD MAXWELL) Strain of violence: historical studies of American violence and vigilantism. New York, 1975. pp. 397.

DEWITT (HOWARD A.) Images of ethnic and radical violence in California politics, 1917- 1930: a survey. San Francisco, 1975. pp. 136. *bibliog.*

VIOLENCE IN TELEVISION.

CATER (DOUGLASS) and STRICKLAND (STEPHEN P.) TV violence and the child: the evolution and fate of the Surgeon General's report. New York, [1975]. pp. 167.

VIOLENT DEATHS

— Yugoslavia.

YUGOSLAVIA. Savezni Zavod za Statistiku. Studije, Analize i Prikazi. 70. Nasilne smrti u SFR Jugoslaviji, 1950-1970; Deaths by violence in SFR Yugoslavia, 1950-1970; [by] Andjelija Plavec. Beograd, 1974. pp. 103.

VISUAL PERCEPTION.

ZUSNE (LEONARD) Visual perception of form. New York, 1970. pp. 547. *bibliogs.*

VITAL STATISTICS.

HOEM (JAN M.) Two articles on the interpretation of vital rates, etc. Oslo, 1972. pp. 319-327,454-468. *bibliog.* (Norway. Statistiske Centralbyrå. Artikler. Nr. 46) Reprinted from Theoretical Population Biology, vol. 2, nos. 3 and 4.

— Bibliography.

MEUNIER (MARIE THERESE) compiler. Bibliographie des tables de mortalité: Europe et pays anglo- saxons d'outre-mer, 1960-1973;...sous la direction de Jacques Vallin. Paris, Institut National d'Etudes Démographiques, 1974. pp. 53, 4.

VITICULTURE

— Switzerland.

VEREIN FÜR WIRTSCHAFTSHISTORISCHE STUDIEN. Schweizer Pioniere der Wirtschaft und Technik. 29. Herman Müller-Thurgau, 1850-1927...und weitere Pioniere der Qualitätsverbesserung des Weins und der unvergorenen Trauben- und Obstsäfte; von Robert Fritzsche [and others]. Zürich, 1974. pp. 131. *bibliog.*

VITTORIO (GIUSEPPE DI).

PISTILLO (MICHELE) Giuseppe Di Vittorio, 1924-1944: la lotta contro il fascismo e per l'unità sindacale. Roma, 1975. pp. 479.

VLADIMIR (OBLAST')

— History — 1917-1921, Revolution.

SOVETY Vladimirskoi gubernii v period podgotovki i razvitiia Velikoi Oktiabr'skoi sotsialisticheskoi revoliutsii, 1917-1918 gg.: sbornik statei. Vladimir, 1969. pp. 71.

VLADIVOSTOK

— History.

SMITH (CANFIELD F.) Vladivostok under red and white rule: revolution and counterrevolution in the Russian Far East, 1920-1922. Seattle, [1975]. pp. 304. *bibliog.* (Washington State University. Institute for Comparative and Foreign Area Studies. Publications on Russia and Eastern Europe. No.6)

VOCABULARY.

WILLIAMS (RAYMOND) Keywords: a vocabulary of culture and society. London, [1976]. pp. 286. *bibliog.*

VOCATIONAL EDUCATION

— Israel.

ISRAEL. Department for Youth and Vocational Education. 1967. Vocational education in Israel; [by] Perez F. Harburger. Jerusalem, 1967. pp. 51.

— Norway.

NORWAY. Statistiske Centralbyrå. Utdanningsstatistikk: videregående skoler: Educational statistics: upper secondary schools. a., 1973/74- Oslo. *[in Norwegian and English]. Supersedes NORWAY. Statistiske Centralbyrå. Utdanningsstatistikk: fag- og yrkesskoler og høgskoler and NORWAY. Statistiske Centralbyrå. Utdanningsstatistikk: folkehøgskolar, realskolar og gymnas.*

— Russia.

RUSSIA (USSR). Ministerstvo Vysshego i Srednego Spetsial'nogo Obrazovaniia. Nauchno-Tekhnicheskii Sovet. Sektsiia Narodonaseleniia. Narodonaselenie. 9. Obrazovatel'naia i sotsial'no-professional'naia struktura naseleniia SSSR. Moskva, 1975. pp. 103. *With English table of contents.*

— United Kingdom — Commonwealth — Directories.

ASSOCIATION OF COMMONWEALTH UNIVERSITIES. Directory of education and training resources in the developing countries of the Commonwealth: a guide to institutions at the post-secondary level; edited by the Association of Commonwealth Universities for the Commonwealth Fund for Technical Co- operation. London, Commonwealth Secretariat, 1974. pp. 430.

— United States.

NATIONAL PLANNING ASSOCIATION. Reports. No. 144. Priorities for planning in vocational education: alternatives for the 1970s; by Leonard A. Lecht. Washington, 1975. pp. 44.

WILMS (WELLFORD W.) Public and proprietary vocational training: a study of effectiveness. Lexington, Mass., [1975]. pp. 190, 17. *bibliog.*

— Yugoslavia.

BREKIĆ (JOVO) ed. Samoupravna koncepcija razvitka kadrova: kadrologijski apekti usklađivanja obrazovanja, zapošljavanja i profesionalnog razvoja kadrova, etc. Zagreb, 1975. pp. 262. *bibliog. With English summary.*

VOCATIONAL GUIDANCE

— United Kingdom.

MILLER (RUTH) Careers for girls. 4th ed. Harmondsworth, 1975. pp. 477.

— United States.

CULL (JOHN G.) and HARDY (RICHARD E.) eds. Career guidance for black adolescents: a guide to selected professional occupations. Springfield, Ill., [1975]. pp. 148. *bibliogs.*

VOCATIONAL INTERESTS

— United States.

TILLERY (DALE) and KILDEGAARD (THEODORE C.) Educational goals, attitudes and behaviors: a comparative study of high school seniors. Cambridge, Mass., [1973]. pp. 251. *bibliog.*

VOCATIONAL REHABILITATION

— Hong Kong.

HONG KONG. Working Party on Vocational Training for the Disabled. 1971. Report; [Tsau Tsor-yan, chairman]. Hong Kong, 1970[or rather 1971]. pp. 36.

VOJVODINA

— Constitution.

USTAV Socijalističke Republike Srbije; Ustav Socijalističke Autonomne Pokrajine Vojvodine; Ustav Socijalističke Autonomne Pokrajine Kosova; sa ustavnim zakonima i registrima pojmova. Beograd, 1974. pp. 750. *In Cyrillic.*

VOLGA BASIN

— Economic history.

OCHERKI po istorii sotsialisticheskogo stroitel'stva v Povolzh'e. Kazan', 1974. pp. 120.

— Industries.

NAIAKSHIN (KUZ'MA IAKOVLEVICH) ed. Istoriia industrializatsii Srednego Povolzh'ia, 1926-1941 gg. Kuibyshev, 1974. pp. 541.

— Politics and government.

REVOLIUTSIONNO-osvoboditel'noe dvizhenie v XIX-XX vv. v Povolzh'e i Priural'e. Kazan', 1974. pp. 115.

VOLGOGRAD (OBLAST')

— Statistics.

VOLGOGRAD (OBLAST'). Statisticheskoe Upravlenie. Narodnoe khoziaistvo Volgogradskoi oblasti v 1966-1971 gg.: statisticheskii sbornik. Saratov, 1973. pp. 290.

VOLLMER (AUGUST).

CARTE (GENE E.) and CARTE (ELAINE H.) Police reform in the United States: the era of August Vollmer, 1905-1932. Berkeley, [1975]. pp. 137. *bibliog.*

VOL'SKII (NIKOLAI VLADISLAVOVICH).

See VALENTINOV (NIKOLAI VLADISLAVOVICH) pseud.

VOLTAIRE (FRANÇOIS MARIE AROUET DE).

STUDIES ON VOLTAIRE AND THE EIGHTEENTH CENTURY. vol. 143. Banbury, 1975. pp. 195. *Miscellaneous essays.*

MEYER (HENRY) Voltaire on war and peace. Banbury, 1976. pp. 202. *bibliog. (Studies on Voltaire and the Eighteenth Century. vol. 144)*

ROUSSEAU (ANDRE MICHEL) L'Angleterre et Voltaire. Oxford, 1976. 3 vols. *bibliog. (Studies on Voltaire and the Eighteenth Century. vol 145-147)*

VOLUNTEER WORKERS IN JUVENILE COURTS

— United States.

EXPERIMENT in a juvenile court: a study of a program of volunteers working with juvenile probationers; by Robert J. Berger [and others]. Ann Arbor, 1975. 1 vol. (various pagings). *bibliog.*

VOLUNTEER WORKERS IN SOCIAL SERVICE.

VOLUNTARY action research, 1973; edited by David Horton Smith. Lexington, Mass., [1973]. pp. 406. *bibliogs.*

VOLUNTARY action research, 1974: the nature of voluntary action around the world; edited by David Horton Smith. Lexington, Mass., [1974]. pp. 323. *bibliogs.*

— United Kingdom.

SEMINAR ON FINANCING THE VOLUNTARY SECTOR, LONDON, 1974. Seminar on financing the voluntary sector: (note of discussion . [London], Voluntary Services Unit, Home Office, [1975 . pp. 23.

VOLUNTEER CENTRE. Current research involving the community in meeting social need. Berkhamsted, [1975]. pp. 13.

VOLYN (OBLAST')

— Statistics.

VOLYN (OBLAST'). Statystychne Upravlinnia. Volyns'ka oblast' za roky Radians'koï vlady, 1940-1966 rr. : statystychnyi zbirnyk. L'viv, 1969. pp. 314.

VON NEUMANN (JOHN).

STEINMETZ (VOLKER) Zur Existenz von Wachstumsgleichgewichten in Wachstumsmodellen vom von Neumannschen Typ. Meisenheim am Glan, [1972]. pp. 100. *bibliog.*

VOROSHILOV (KLIMENT EFREMOVICH).

AKSHINSKII (VASILII SEMENOVICH) Kliment Efremovich Voroshilov: biograficheskii ocherk. Moskva, 1974. pp. 287. *bibliog.*

VOROSHILOVGRAD (OBLAST')

— Statistics.

VOROSHILOVGRAD (OBLAST'). Statisticheskoe Upravlenie. Narodnoe khoziaistvo Voroshilovgradskoi oblasti: statisticheskii sbornik. Donetsk, 1971. pp. 166.

VOTERS, REGISTRATION OF

— United Kingdom.

SEWELL (RICHARD CLARKE) A manual of the law and practice of registration of voters, in England and Wales under the 2 Wm. IV. c. 45, more especially adapted to the use of local committees, and persons engaged in the courts of the revising barristers. London, Saunders and Benning, 1835. pp. ii,111.

— United States.

SMOLKA (RICHARD G.) Registering voters by mail: the Maryland and New Jersey experience. Washington, D.C., 1975. pp. 85. *(American Enterprise Institute for Public Policy Research. Domestic Affairs Studies. 30)*

VOTING.

NEWLAND (ROBERT A.) Only half a democracy: why X-voting fails and how the single transferable vote works. 2nd ed. London, 1975. pp. 26. *bibliog.*

NEWLAND (ROBERT A.) Electoral systems. London, [1976]. pp. 25. *bibliog.*

TULLOCK (GORDON) The vote motive: an essay in the economics of politics with applications to the British economy...with a British commentary by Morris Perlman. London, 1976. pp. 88. *bibliogs. (Institute of Economic Affairs. Hobart Paperbacks. 9.)*

WORKSHOP ON PARTICIPATION, VOTING, AND PARTY COMPETITION, STRASBOURG, 1974. Party identification and beyond: representations of voting and party competition; edited by Ian Budge [and others]. London, [1976]. pp. 393. *bibliogs.*

— Chile.

LOPEZ PINTOR (RAFAEL) Algunos aspectos de la participacion politica en Chile. Santiago de Chile, 1969. pp. 54.

— European Economic Community countries.

LAKEMAN (ENID) Nine democracies: electoral systems of th countries of the European Economic Community. 2nd ed. London, 1975. pp. 24. *bibliog.*

— Germany.

SCHMIDT (RUDI) and others, eds. Das Blockwahlsystem in der SPD: zur Herrschaftstechnik des Parteiapparates. Hamburg, [1970]. pp. 112.

TROITZSCH (KLAUS G.) Sozialstruktur und Wählerverhalten:...dargestellt am Beispiel der Wahlen in Hamburg von 1949 bis 1974. Meisenheim am Glan, 1976. pp. 142. *bibliog.*

— — Bibliography.

SCHUMACHER (MARTIN) compiler. Wahlen und Abstimmungen, 1918-1933: eine Bibliographie zur Statistik und Analyse der politischen Wahlen in der Weimarer Republik. Düsseldorf, [1976]. pp. 155.

— Philippine Islands.

LANDÉ (CARL HERMAN) Southern Tagalog voting, 1946-1963: political behavior in a Philippine region. DeKalb, Ill.] 1973. pp. 159. *(NorthernIllinois University. Center for Southeast Asian Studies. Special Reports. No. 7)*

— Sweden.

GUSTAFSSON (GÖRAN) Partistyrka och partistyrkeförskjutningar: förändringar i svenskt väljarbeteende under 1960-talet belysta genom data på kommunnivå. Lund, 1974. pp. 308. *bibliog. With English summary.*

— United Kingdom.

HIRST (DEREK) The representative of the people?: voters and voting in England under the early Stuarts. Cambridge, 1975. pp. 306. *bibliog.*

NEWLAND (ROBERT A.) Electing the United Kingdom Parliament. London, 1976. pp. 16. *bibliog.*

ROGALY (JOE) Parliament for the people: a handbook of electoral reform. London, 1976. pp. 181. *bibliog.*

— — Scotland.

GILMOUR (JAMES) Ph.D. Participation by representation: the case for STV in Scotland. London, 1974. pp. 8.

GILMOUR (JAMES) Ph.D. and WOODWARD-NUTT (JAMES) Electing the Scottish Assembly. London, 1975. pp. 36. *bibliog.*

— United States.

HEITZMANN (WILLIAM RAY) American Jewish voting behavior: a history and analysis. San Francisco, 1975. pp. 121. *bibliog.*

NIE (NORMAN H.) and others. The changing American voter. Cambridge, Mass., 1976. pp. 399.

VOTING RESEARCH.

BUSTEED (M.A.) Geography and voting behaviour. London, 1975. pp. 60. *bibliog.*

VOZNESENSKII (NIKOLAI ALEKSEEVICH).

KOLOTOV (VASILII VASIL'EVICH) Nikolai Alekseevich Voznesenskii. Moskva, 1974. pp. 351.

VUTRESHNA MAKEDONSKA REVOLIUTSIONNA ORGANIZATSIIA.

ZOGRAFSKI (TODOR G.) and ZOGRAFSKI (DIMČE A.) KPJ i VMRO (Obedineta) vo Vardarska Makedonija vo periodot 1920-1930. Skopje, 1974. pp. 292.

WADIA (B.P.).

MASANI (MINOCHEHER RUSTOM) Indian trade unions and society: B.P. Wadia's vision and the reality. Bangalore, 1974. pp. 26. *(Indian Institute of World Culture. Transactions. No. 45)*

WAGE-PRICE POLICY.

RALL (WILHELM) Zur Wirksamkeit der Einkommenspolitik. Tübingen, 1975. pp. 273. *bibliog. (Tübingen. Universität. Fachbereich Wirtschaftswissenschaft. Tübinger Wirtschaftswissenschaftliche Abhandlungen. Band 20)*

CARNEGIE-ROCHESTER CONFERENCE ON PUBLIC POLICY. 1973, November Conference. The economics of price and wage controls: [papers and discussions from the conference]; editors Karl Brunner [and] Allan H. Meltzer. Amsterdam, 1976. pp. 304. *bibliogs. (Journal of Monetary Economics. Carnegie- Rochester Conference Series on Public Policy. vol. 2)*

The ILLUSION of wage and price control: essays on inflation, its causes and its cures; contributors...David Laidler [and others]; Michael Walker, editor. Vancouver, 1976. pp. 236.

— Australia.

NILAND (JOHN R.) and ISAAC (JOSEPH EZRA) eds. Australian labour economics: readings. [2nd ed.] Melbourne, 1975. pp. 676. *bibliogs.*

— Botswana.

BOTSWANA. 1973. Jobs past, present and future: national policy on incomes, employment, prices, and profits. [Gaborone, 1973?]. pp. (7).

— Canada.

WOOD (W.DONALD) and KUMAR (PRADEEP) eds. Canadian perspectives on wage-price guidelines: a book of readings. Kingston, Ont., 1976. pp. 404. *bibliog.*

— Fiji Islands.

FIJI. Prices and Incomes Board. 1975. Fighting inflation in Fiji: an account of the work of the Prices and Incomes Board during the year ended 30th June, 1974. Suva, 1975. pp. 70.

FIJI. Prices and Incomes Board. 1975. Inflation in Fiji: a further account of the work of the Prices and Incomes Board. Suva, [1975]. pp. 46.

FIJI. Prices and Incomes Board. 1975. A report covering the three months ended 30th June, 1975. [Suva, 1975]. pp. 4.

— United Kingdom.

U.K. National Board for Prices and Incomes. 1969. 100 PIB reports, summarised. [ondon], 1969. pp. 140.

LABOUR RESEARCH DEPARTMENT. LRD guide to the 6 limit. London, [1975]. 1 folded leaf.

SENDALL (WILFRID) Government, parliament and industry: when is a statutory wage policy not one?: the riddle to appease the Left. London, 1975. pp. 4.

WARD (SUE) and POND (CHRIS) The £6 trap. London, 1975. fo. 6. *(Low Pay Unit. Low Pay Papers. No. 6)*

CONFEDERATION OF BRITISH INDUSTRY. The counter-inflation policy: pay: the second year, 1 August 1976 to 31 July 1977: practical guidance. London, 1976. pp. 12.

FABIAN SOCIETY. Fabian Tracts. [No.] 442. A positive incomes policy; [by] William Brown [and] Keith Sisson. London, 1976. pp. 18.

— United States.

The ECONOMY and phase IV; (an AEI round table held on 19 July 1973...[in] Washington); Paul W. McCracken, moderator, etc. Washington, [1973]. pp. 36. *(American Enterprise Institute for Public Policy Research. Round Tables)*

GOODWIN (CRAUFURD D. W.) ed. Exhortation and controls: the search for a wage-price policy, 1945-1971. Washington, D.C., [1975]. pp. 432. *bibliog. (Brookings Institution. Studies in Wage-Price Policy)*

KRAFT (JOHN) and ROBERTS (BLAINE) eds. Wage and price controls: the U.S. experiment. New York, 1975. pp. 149.

MILLS (DANIEL QUINN) Government, labor, and inflation: wage stabilization in the United States. Chicago, [1975]. pp. 331.

MITCHELL (DANIEL J.B.) The future of American wage controls. Los Angeles, 1975. pp. 9. *(California University. Institute of Industrial Relations. [Southern Division]. Reprints. No. 248) Reprinted from California Management Review, vol. 17 no. 1.*

WAGES.

MEANS (DAVID MACGREGOR) Industrial freedom. New York, 1897. pp. 248.

LAWLER (EDWARD E.) Pay and organizational effectiveness: a psychological view. New York, [1971]. pp. 318. *bibliog.*

WAGES.

Un DEBAT sur l'échange inégal: salaires, sous-développement, impérialisme; [by] Arghiri Emmanuel [and others]; traduit de l'italien par M.C. Paoletti et A. Benaneti. Paris, 1975. pp. 160.

BREDEMEIER (WILLI) Lohnbestimmung durch organisationspolitische Grössen. Berlin, [1976]. pp. 375. *bibliog.*

— Minimum wage — India — Bombay.

REPORT of the Committee under the Minimum Wages Act, 1948, in respect of employment under local authorities; [Champaklal G. Modi, chairman]. Bombay, Government Central Press, 1955. pp. 24.

— — Uganda.

UGANDA. Minimum Wages Advisory Board. 1964. Report;...under the chairmanship of Shafiq Arain. Entebbe, [1964]. pp. 32.

— — United Kingdom.

HOWELL (RALPH FREDERIC) Why work?: a challenge to the Chancellor. London, 1976. pp. 39. *(Conservative Political Centre. [Publications]. No. 582)*

— Australia.

NILAND (JOHN R.) and ISAAC (JOSEPH EZRA) eds. Australian labour economics: readings. [2nd ed.] Melbourne, 1975. pp. 676. *bibliogs.*

— Botswana.

BOTSWANA. Central Statistics Office. Employment survey. a., 1973 (4th)- Gaborone.

— Canada.

KUMAR (PRADEEP) Relative wage differentials in Canadian industries. Kingston, 1974. pp. 83. *bibliog (Kingston, Ontario. Queen's University. Industrial Relations Centre. Research and Current Issues Series. No. 25)*

CANADA. Statistics Canada. Farm Wages in Canada. irreg., Current issues only kept. [Ottawa]. *In English and French.*

— Denmark.

CHRISTENSEN (JØRGEN PETER) Lønudviklingen inden for dansk håndvaerk og industri, 1870-1914. København, 1975. 2 vols. (in 1). *bibliog. (Københavns Universitet. Økonomiske Institut. Studier. Nr. 22)*

— European Economic Community countries.

STEWART (MARGARET) Employment conditions in Europe. 2nd ed. Epping, Essex, 1976. pp. 249. *bibliog.*

— France.

FRANCE. Institut National de la Statistique et des Etudes Economiques. Les salaires dans l'industrie, le commerce et les services. a., 1970- Paris. *1969 separately catalogued.*

FRANCE. Centre d'Etude des Revenus et des Coûts. 1972. Les disparités sectorielles de salaires en France et en Allemagne: un essai d'explication. Paris, 1972. pp. 102. *(Documents. No. 14)*

MURTEIRA (MARIA MANUELA MARTINS) Analise dos salarios reais em França, Portugal e Alemanha. Lisboa, 1974. pp. 83. *(Portugal. Ministerio do Trabalho. Gabinete de Planeamento. Serie Estudos. 27)*

— Germany.

LIEFMANN (ROBERT) Arbeitslöhne und Unternehmergewinne nach dem Kriege. Stuttgart, 1919. pp. 24.

GOTHEIN (GEORG) Der grosse Irrtum der deutschen Lohnpolitik. 2nd ed. Berlin, 1929. pp. 96.

GERMANY (BUNDESREPUBLIK). Statistisches Bundesamt. Preise, Löhne, Wirtschaftsrechnungen. Reihe 17. Gehalts- und Lohnstrukturerhebungen. Wiesbaden, 1963 in progress.

FRANCE. Centre d'Etude des Revenus et des Coûts. 1972. Les disparités sectorielles de salaires en France et en Allemagne: un essai d'explication. Paris, 1972. pp. 102. *(Documents. No. 14)*

MURTEIRA (MARIA MANUELA MARTINS) Analise dos salarios reais em França, Portugal e Alemanha. Lisboa, 1974. pp. 83. *(Portugal. Ministerio do Trabalho. Gabinete de Planeamento. Serie Estudos. 27)*

BERGMANN (JOACHIM E.) and others. Gewerkschaften in der Bundesrepublik: gewerkschaftliche Lohnpolitik zwischen Mitgliederinteressen und ökonomischen Systemzwängen. Frankfurt, [1975]. pp. 439. *bibliog. (Frankfurt am Main. Universität. Institut für Sozialforschung. Studienreihe. Band 1)*

PFROMM (HANS ADAM) Konflikte solidarischer Lohnpolitik: zur ökonomischen und sozialen Problematik tarifpolitischer Lohnstrukturnivellierung. Göttingen, [1975]. pp. 156. *bibliog. (Kommission für Wirtschaftlichen und Sozialen Wandel. Schriften. 55)*

— — North Rhine—Westphalia.

NORTH RHINE-WESTPHALIA. Landesamt für Datenverarbeitung und Statistik. Beiträge zur Statistik des Landes Nordrhein- Westfalen. Hefte 334-335. Die Verdiensthältnisse in der gewerblichen Wirtschaft und im Dienstleistungsbereich in Nordrhein-Westfalen, 1972:... Gehalts- und Lohnstrukturerhebung, 1972. Düsseldorf, 1975. 2 vols.

— India.

INDIA. Labour Bureau. 1974. Wage fixation in industry and agriculture in India. [Delhi, 1974]. pp. 106.

DAYAL (SAHAB) Promise of industrial peace in India: the role of the industrial wage board. Kensington, N.S.W., 1975. pp. 26. *(New South Wales, University of. Department of Industrial Relations. Working Papers. 2/1975)*

FONSECA (ALOYSIUS JOSEPH) Wage issues in a developing economy: the Indian experience. Bombay, 1975. pp. 264.

— Italy.

SELLA (DOMENICO) Salari e lavoro nell'edilizia lombarda durante il secolo XVII. Pavia, 1968. pp. 168. *With summaries in English and French.*

COMITATO PER IL SALARIO AL LAVORO DOMESTICO DI PADOVA. Le operaie della casa; a cura del Collettivo Internazionale Femminista. Venezia, 1975. pp. 78. *(Collettivo Internazionale Femminista. Salario al Lavoro Domestico: Strategia Internazionale.1)*

— Netherlands.

RAAD VOOR HET MIDDEN- EN KLEINBEDRIJF. Advies gewaardeerd ondernemersloon. 's-Gravenhage, 1975. pp. 25. *([Publikaties]. 1975, no.2)*

HEIDE (H. TER) Overleg en strijd: recente ontwikkelingen in de Nederlandse loonpolitiek. Leiden, 1976. pp. 72.

— Poland.

KUCZYŃSKI (MARIAN) Płace w przedsiębiorstwie przemysłowym. 2nd ed. Warszawa, 1958. pp. 87.

— Portugal.

PORTUGAL. Ministerio do Trabalho. Gabinete de Estudos, Planeamento e Organização. Relatorio de conjuntura. q., 1974 (no.4)- Lisboa.

ALMEIDA (MARIA HENRIQUETA DE) Factores determinantes das diferenciações salariais inter- industrias. Lisboa, 1974. pp. 77. *(Portugal. Ministerio do Trabalho. Gabinete de Planeamento. Serie Estudos. 21) With abstracts in English, French and German.*

CARVALHO (ODETE ESTEVES DE) Remunerações femininas e diferenciações salariais entre mulheres e homens em 1970: estudo analitico. Lisboa, 1974. pp. 92. *(Portugal. Ministerio do Trabalho. Gabinete de Planeamento. Serie Estudos. 23) With abstracts in English, French and German.*

MURTEIRA (MARIA MANUELA MARTINS) Analise dos salarios reais em França, Portugal e Alemanha. Lisboa, 1974. pp. 83. *(Portugal. Ministerio do Trabalho. Gabinete de Planeamento. Serie Estudos. 27)*

— Russia.

RUSSIA (U.S.S.R.). Sovet Ministrov. Gosudarstvennyi Komitet po Voprosam Truda i Zarabotnoi Platy. Biulleten'. m., 1962- , with gap (1967: 3). Moskva.

KOROTKOV (VASILII FEDOROVICH) Oplata truda rabotnikov organizatsii snabzheniia i zagotovok. Moskva, 1969. pp. 72.

SHKURKO (SERGEI IVANOVICH) Sovershenstvovanie form i sistem zarabotnoi platy. Moskva, 1975. pp. 231.

VOLKOV (A.P.) and others, eds. Arbeit und Arbeitslohn in der UdSSR. Berlin, [1976]. pp. 495.

— Saint Lucia.

REPORT of the Commission appointed by His Excellency the Governor to enquire into the stoppage of work at the sugar factories in St. Lucia in March, 1952 and into the adequacy of the existing wage-fixing machinery in that colony; Sir Clement Malone, chairman. [Castries, 1952]. pp. 81.

REPORT of the Commission appointed by His Excellency the Acting Governor to investigate the causes of the stoppage of work in the sugar industry during March and April, 1957, the wage structure, the terms and conditions of employment and other matters relating to all the foregoing in the industry in St. Lucia; Sir Donald Jackson, chairman. [Castries, 1957]. fo. (36).

— South Africa.

GREST (JEREMY) African wages in Grahamstown: a survey. Johannesburg, 1974. pp. 17.

— Swaziland.

SWAZILAND. Central Statistical Office. Employment and wages. a., 1970/71(3rd)- [Mbabane].

— Sweden.

HART (HORST) and OTTER (CASTEN VON) Lönebildningen på arbetsplatsen. [Stockholm, 1973]. pp. 176. *(Institutet för Social Forskning. Skrifter. 3) With English summary.*

NYSTRÖM (LENNART) Löner och priser. [Stockholm, 1973]. pp. 64.

EDGREN (JAN) With varying success: a Swedish experiment in wage systems and shop floor organization. Stockholm, [1974]. pp. 100.

— Tasmania.

TASMANIA. Commonwealth Bureau of Statistics. Tasmanian Office. Labour, wages and prices. a., 1973/74- Hobart.

— Turkey.

HIÇ (MÜKERREM) Employment and wages in the automotive and other assembly industries in Turkey. Istanbul, 1974. pp. 58. *(Istanbul. Üniversitesi. Iktisat Fakültesi. Institute of Economic Development. Yayınları. No. 23)*

— United Kingdom.

NATIONAL UNION OF MINEWORKERS. Handbook on the wage structure of the coalmining industry. n.p., 1955-1967. 1 vol. (looseleaf.) *Cover title only.*

NASIŁOWSKI (MIECZYSŁAW) Udział płac w dochodzie narodowym USA i Anglii. Warszawa, 1962. pp. 235. *bibliog. With English and Russian summaries.*

SISSON (KEITH) Industrial relations in Fleet Street: a study in pay structure. Oxford, [1975]. pp. 185. *(Warwick Studies in Industrial Relations)*

PANITCH (LEO VICTOR) Social democracy and industrial militancy: the Labour Party, the trade unions and incomes policy, 1945-1974. Cambridge, 1976. pp. 318.

WAGES.(Cont.)

ROBINSON (OLIVE) and WALLACE (JOHN) Pay and employment in retailing. Farnborough, Hants, [1976]. pp. 177.

WINYARD (STEVE) Policing low wages: a study of the wages inspectorate. London, 1976. pp. 39. *(Low Pay Unit. Low Pay Pamphlets. No.4)*

— United States.

NASIŁOWSKI (MIECZYSŁAW) Udział płac w dochodzie narodowym USA i Anglii. Warszawa, 1962. pp. 235. *bibliog. With English and Russian summaries.*

STOKES (HOUSTON H.) and others. Unemployment and adjustment in the labor market: a comparison between the regional and national responses. Chicago, 1975. pp. 125. *bibliog. (Chicago. University. Department of Geography. Research Papers. No. 177)*

WAGES AND PRODUCTIVITY

— South Africa.

ORPEN (CHRISTOPHER) Productivity and black workers in South Africa. Cape Town, [1976]. pp. 283. *bibliog.*

WALES

— Economic policy.

BALLARD (PAUL H.) and JONES (ERASTUS) ed. The valleys call: a self-examination by people of the South Wales valleys during the 'Year of the valleys, 1974'. Ferndale, Mid-Glam., 1975. pp. 498.

— Industries.

U. K. Welsh Office. 1976. The index of industrial production for Wales. Cardiff, 1976. pp. 29. *(Occasional Papers. No. 3)*

— Nationalism.

HEARNE (DERRICK K.) The rise of the Welsh republic: towards a Welsh theory of government. Talybont, Dyfed, 1975. pp. 207.

— Politics and government.

LIBERAL PARTY. Machinery of Government Panel. Our declining democracy; ...evidence to the Privy Council on the government's White Paper: Our changing democracy. London, [1976]. pp. 14. *(Liberal Publication Department. Study Papers. No. 2) White Paper published as Cmnd. 6348, British Parliamentary Papers, Session 1975-76.*

— Religion.

REES (D. BEN) Chapels in the valley: a study in the sociology of Welsh nonconformity. Upton, Wirral, [1975]. pp. 222. *bibliog.*

— Social policy.

BALLARD (PAUL H.) and JONES (ERASTUS) ed. The valleys call: a self-examination by people of the South Wales valleys during the 'Year of the valleys, 1974'. Ferndale, Mid-Glam., 1975. pp. 498.

WALL STREET.

STONE (JAMES M.) One way for Wall Street: a view of the future of the securities industry. Boston, 1975. pp. 187.

SUTTON (ANTONY C.) Wall Street and FDR. New Rochelle, [1975]. pp. 200. *bibliog.*

WALLACE (HENRY AGARD).

WALKER (J. SAMUEL) Henry A. Wallace and American foreign policy. Westport, Conn., 1976. pp. 224.

WALLACHIA

— Economic history.

CHIROT (DANIEL) Social change in a peripheral society: the creation of a Balkan colony. New York, [1976]. pp. 179. *bibliog.*

— Politics and government.

CHIROT (DANIEL) Social change in a peripheral society: the creation of a Balkan colony. New York, [1976]. pp. 179. *bibliog.*

— Social history.

CHIROT (DANIEL) Social change in a peripheral society: the creation of a Balkan colony. New York, [1976]. pp. 179. *bibliog.*

WALRAS (LEON).

HILDENBRAND (WERNER) and KIRMAN (A.P.) Introduction to equilibrium analysis: variations on themes by Edgeworth and Walras. Amsterdam, 1976. pp. 216. *bibliog.*

WANDSWORTH

— Officials and employees.

SHERMAN (ALFRED V.) Waste in Wandsworth: how direct labour squanders ratepayers' money and the nation's resources. London, [1976?]. pp. 14.

WAR.

LUTOSŁAWSKI (WINCENTY) Wojna wszechświatowa: jej odległe przyczyny i skutki. Lwów, 1920. pp. xx,273.

WORLD PEACE CONGRESS. Permanent Committee. Guerre ou paix. Paris, [1949?]. pp. 15.

FAIRBAIRNS (ZOE) Study war no more: military involvement in British universities and colleges. London, [1974]. pp. 32. *bibliog.*

PFISTER (JAMES W.) The compulsion to war: a quantitative exploration of remote international relations. Beverly Hills, [1974]. pp. 82. *bibliog.*

STOESSINGER (JOHN GEORGE) Why nations go to war. London, [1974]. pp. 230.

RUMMEL (RUDOLPH JOSEPH) Understanding conflict and war. *New York, [1975 in progress].*

JOHNSON (JAMES TURNER) Ideology, reason, and the limitation of war: religious and secular concepts, 1200-1740. Princeton, 1975. pp. 291. *bibliog.*

KARDELJ (EDVARD) Nacija i medjunarodni odnosi: [a collection of articles]. Beograd, 1975. pp. 249.

MIDLARSKY (MANUS I.) On war: political violence in the international system. New York, [1975]. pp. 229.

SPENCE (JOHN EDWARD) 'War is too serious...'; an inaugural lecture delivered in the University of Leicester, 22 February 1975. Leicester, 1975. pp. 22.

STARR (HARVEY) Coalitions and future war: a dyadic study of cooperation and conflict. London, [1975]. pp. 70. *bibliog.*

HOWARD (MICHAEL ELIOT) War in European history. London, 1976. pp. 165. *bibliog.*

— Economic aspects.

TULLOCK (GORDON) The social dilemma: the economics of war and revolution. Blacksburg, [1974]. pp. 143. *(Virginia Polytechnic Institute and State University. Center for the Study of Public Choice. Public Choice Society Book and Monograph Series)*

WAR, economy and the military mind; edited by Geoffrey Best and Andrew Wheatcroft. London, 1976. pp. 136.

— Moral aspects.

ROBERTSON (JOHN MACKINNON) The blood tax. Bradford, [1896]. pp. 7. *(Papers for the People. No. 4)*

WAR (INTERNATIONAL LAW).

LAW and responsibility in warfare: the Vietnam experience; (papers and discussions from a special meeting of the American Society of International Law in October 1971; edited by Peter D. Trooboff. Chapel Hill, N.C., [1975]. pp. 280.

MELZER (YEHUDA) Concepts of just war. Leyden, 1975. pp. 190. *bibliog.*

MILLER (RICHARD IRWIN) ed. The law of war. Lexington, Mass., [1975]. pp. 329.

HULL (ROGER H.) The Irish triangle: conflict in Northern Ireland. Princeton, [1976]. pp. 312. *bibliog.*

RÖLING (BERNARD VICTOR ALOYSIUS) and ŠUKOVIĆ (OLGA) The law of war and dubious weapons. Stockholm, [1976]. pp. 78. *bibliog.*

WAR, MARITIME (INTERNATIONAL LAW).

O'CONNELL (DANIEL PATRICK) The influence of law on sea power. Manchester, [1975]. pp. 204. *bibliog. (Manchester. University. Melland Schill Lectures. [1974])*

WAR AND CIVILIZATION.

NELSON (KEITH L.) ed. The impact of war on American life: the twentieth-century experience. New York, [1971]. pp. 395. *bibliog.*

WAR AND EMERGENCY POWERS

— United States.

AMERICAN SOCIETY OF INTERNATIONAL LAW. Panel on the Constitution and the Conduct of Foreign Policy. The constitution and the conduct of foreign policy: an inquiry by a panel of the...Society...; edited by Francis O. Wilcox [and] Richard A. Frank. New York, [1976]. pp. 145.

WAR AND SOCIALISM.

HEINEMANN (HUGO) Die sozialistischen Errungenschaften der Kriegszeit. Chemnitz, [1914]. pp. 16.

ROCKER (RUDOLF) Die Waffen niederc' Die Hämmer nieder: Rede... gehalten auf der Reichs-Konferenz der Rüstungsarbeiter Deutschlands, abgehalten vom 18. bis 22. März 1919 in Erfurt. Berlin, [1919]. pp. 16. *Also published in Erfurt under the title Keine Kriegswaffen mehr!'*

CONFEDERATION GENERALE DU TRAVAIL SYNDICALISTE REVOLUTIONNAIRE. Brochures. No. 1. Le syndicalisme et la guerre. [Paris, imprint], [192-!. pp. 14.

MILITANT SOCIALIST INTERNATIONAL. Les ouvriers devant la guerre. London, 1936. pp. 64.

SIGEL (ROBERT) Die Lensch-Cunow-Haenisch-Gruppe: eine Studie zum rechten Flügel der SPD im Ersten Weltkrieg. Berlin, [1976]. pp. 177. *bibliog. (Munich. Universität. Institut für Bayerische Geschichte. Beiträge zu einer Historischen Strukturanalyse Bayerns im Industriezeitalter. Band 14)*

WAR AND SOCIETY.

INTERNATIONAL CONGRESS OF ANTHROPOLOGICAL AND ETHNOLOGICAL SCIENCES. 9th Congress, 1973. War, its causes and correlates: [papers from the Congress]; editor[s] Martin A. Nettleship [and others]. The Hague, [1975]. pp. 813. *bibliogs.*

WILLEQUET (JACQUES) The science of polemology at the University of Brussels. Brussels, Ministry of Foreign Affairs, External Trade and Cooperation in Development, 1975. pp. 44. *(Memo from Belgium. No. 167)*

WAR CRIMES

— Trials — Germany.

KLAFKOWSKI (ALFONS) Zasady Norymberskie a rozwój prawa międzynarodowego. Warszawa, 1966. pp. 58.

LEBEDEVA (NATALIIA SERGEEVNA) Podgotovka Niurnbergskogo protsessa. Moskva, 1975. pp. 238. *bibliog.*

WAR IN LITERATURE.

MEYER (HENRY) Voltaire on war and peace. Banbury, 1976. pp. 202. *bibliog. (Studies on Voltaire and the Eighteenth Century. vol. 144)*

WAR OF THE LEAGUE OF AUGSBURG, 1688-1677.

CARTER (WILLIAM) Clothier. The usurpations of France upon the trade of the woollen manufacture of England briefly hinted at; being the effects of thirty years observations...; or, A caution to England to improve a season now put into her hand, to secure herself. London, printed for R. Baldwin, 1695. pp. 30. *p.1 bled. Wing 678.*

WAR RELIEF.

CIVIL wars and the politics of international relief: Africa, South Asia, and the Caribbean; edited by Morris Davis. New York, 1975. pp. 109.

WARBOYS, HUNTINGDONSHIRE

— History.

RAFTIS (J. AMBROSE) Warboys: two hundred years in the life of an English mediaeval village. Toronto, 1974. pp. 267. *bibliog. (Pontifical Institute of Mediaeval Studies. Studies and Texts. 29)*

WARD (LESTER FRANK).

HOFSTADTER (RICHARD) Social Darwinism in American thought. rev. ed. New York, 1959 repr. 1969. pp. 248. *bibliog.*

WAREHOUSE MANAGEMENT.

ECONOMIC DEVELOPMENT COMMITTEE FOR THE DISTRIBUTIVE TRADES. Finding the better way: a wholesaler's guide to improved labour utilisation. London, H.M.S.O., 1973. pp. 121.

WAREHOUSES

— United Kingdom.

TALBOT (M.F.) Warehouse traffic generation study: pilot survey. London, [1974]. pp. 101. *(London. Greater London Council. Department of Planning and Transportation. Research Memoranda. 400)*

WARNKE (HANS).

MUEHLSTAEDT (HERBERT) Hans Warnke, ein Kommunist. Rostock, 1975. pp. 216.

WARRAU INDIANS.

SUAREZ (MARIA MATILDE) Terminologia, alianza matrimonial y cambio en la sociedad Warao. Caracas, 1972. pp. 110. *bibliog. (Universidad Catolica Andres Bello. Instituto de Investigaciones Historicas. Seminario de Lenguas Indigenas. Serie Lenguas Indigenas de Venezuela. 9)*

WARREN, PENNSYLVANIA

— Economic history.

WEBER (MICHAEL P.) Social change in an industrial town: patterns of progress in Warren, Pennsylvania, from Civil War to World War I. University Park, Pa., [1976]. pp. 185.

— Social history.

WEBER (MICHAEL P.) Social change in an industrial town: patterns of progress in Warren, Pennsylvania, from Civil War to World War I. University Park, Pa., [1976]. pp. 185.

WARSAW

— Growth.

CIECHOCIŃSKA (MARIA) Problemy ludnościowe aglomeracji warszawskiej. Warszawa, 1975. pp. 250.

— History — Chronology.

BARTOSZEWSKI (WŁADYSŁAW) 1859 dni Warszawy. Kraków, 1974. pp. 835. *bibliog.*

— Social conditions.

WĘCŁAWOWICZ (GRZEGORZ) Struktura przestrzeni społeczno-gospodarczej Warszawy w latach 1931 i 1970 w świetle analizy czynnikowej. Wrocław, 1975. pp. 120. *bibliog. (Polska Akademia Nauk. Instytut Geografii. Prace Geograficzne. Nr.116) With Russian and English summaries.*

— Social history.

BRZEZIŃSKI (BOGDAN) Klasa robotnicza Warszawy, 1944-1949. Warszawa, 1975. pp. 279.

WARSAW (PROVINCE)

— Population.

RAKOWSKI (WITOLD) Procesy urbanizacji wsi: na przykładzie Woj. Warszawskiego. Warszawa, 1975. pp. 142. *(Polska Akademia Nauk. Komitet Przestrzennego Zagospodarowania Kraju. Studia. t.50) With Russian and English summaries.*

WARSAW, PACT OF, 1955.

RUSSIA (USSR). Ministerstvo Inostrannykh Del. 1975. Organizatsiia Varshavskogo Dogovora, 1955-1975: dokumenty i materialy. Moskva, 1975. pp. 192.

WASHINGTON, D.C. — Biography.

[PEARSON (DREW) and ALLEN (ROBERT SHARON)] Washington merry-go-round. New York, 1931. pp. 366.

— Social life and customs.

[PEARSON (DREW) and ALLEN (ROBERT SHARON)] Washington merry-go-round. New York, 1931. pp. 366.

WASTE LANDS

— United Kingdom.

U.K. Planning, Regional and Countryside Directorate. 1975. Results of the 1974 survey of derelict and despoiled land in England. London, 1975. 3 pts.(in 1 vol.).

WILSON (HUGH) AND WOMERSLEY (LEWIS) Firm, and TYM (ROGER) AND ASSOCIATES. Inner area study: Liverpool: vacant land. [London], Department of the Environment, [1976]. pp. 32.

— — Wales.

U.K. Welsh Office. Planning Services Division. 1975. The derelict land survey of Wales, 1971-1972. [Cardiff?], 1975. pp. 94.

WELSH COUNCIL. Derelict land in Wales. [Cardiff], 1976. pp. 53. *Map in end pocket.*

WASTE PAPER

— United Kingdom — Recycling.

CAMDEN FRIENDS OF THE EARTH. A critical analysis of the Camden Works Department report on paper salvage in Camden. London, 1974. pp. 13.

WATER

— Economic aspects — United Kingdom.

NATIONAL WATER COUNCIL [U.K.]. Paying for water: a discussion of economic and financial policies for the water services. London, 1976. pp. 42.

— Laws and legislation — Russia — Turkmenistan.

TURKMENISTAN. Statutes, etc. 1973. Vodnyi kodeks Turkmenskoi SSR: ofitsial'nyi tekst. Ashkabad, 1973. pp. 50.

— — South Africa.

SOUTH AFRICA. Parliament. House of Assembly. Select Committee on the Water Amendment Bill. 1969. Report (with Proceedings) (S.C.4-1969). in SOUTH AFRICA. Parliament. House of Assembly. Select Committee reports.

— Pollution — Law and legislation — European Economic Community countries.

AMENDOLA (GIANFRANCO) La normativa ambientale nei paesi della Comunità europea: acque, inquinamento atmosferico. Milano, 1975. pp. 254.

— — — United States.

LIEBER (HARVEY) and ROSINOFF (BRUCE) Federalism and clean waters: the 1972 Water Pollution Control Act. Lexington, Mass., [1975]. pp. 288.

— — America, North.

BLACK (WILLIAM ALEXANDER) The view from Water Street. Ottawa, 1973. pp. 43. *bibliog. (Canada. Inland Waters Directorate. Social Science Series. No. 2)*

WATER CONSUMPTION

— United Kingdom.

U.K. Central Water Planning Unit. 1976. Analysis of trends in public water supply. Reading, 1976. pp. 24.

WATER DISTRICTS

— United Kingdom.

INLAND WATERWAYS AMENITY ADVISORY COUNCIL [U.K.]. Observations on the Review of the water industry in England and Wales: the government consultative document. London, [1976]. pp. (39).

WESSEX WATER AUTHORITY. Review of the water industry in England and Wales: comments... on the consultative document issued in March 1976. [Bristol, 1976]. pp. 28.

WATER MILLS

— United Kingdom.

DILWORTH (DOUGLAS A.) The Tame mills of Staffordshire. London, 1976. pp. 212. *bibliog.*

WATER POWER ELECTRIC PLANTS.

— Canada.

RICHARDSON (BOYCE) Strangers devour the land: a chronicle of the assault upon the last coherent hunting culture in North America, the Cree Indians of northern Quebec, and their vast primeval homelands. New York, 1976. pp. 342,xiii.

— Nigeria.

NIGER DAMS AUTHORITY. Annual report and accounts. a., 1969/70- Lagos.

WATER QUALITY MANAGEMENT

— Costs — Canada — Quebec.

TATE (DONALD M.) Economic and financial aspects of wastewater treatment in the Yamaska river basin, Quebec. Ottawa, 1972 [or rather 1973]. pp. 20. *(Canada. Inland Waters Directorate. Social Science Series. No. 3)*

— Canada.

MACKENZIE BASIN INTERGOVERNMENTAL LIAISON COMMITTEE.Report. a., 1974(1st)- Ottawa.

MITCHELL (BRUCE) ed. Institutional arrangements for water management: Canadian experiences. Waterloo, Ont., [1975]. pp. 285. *(University of Waterloo, [Ontario]. Department of Geography. Publication Series. No. 5)*

— — New Brunswick.

NEW BRUNSWICK. Saint John River Basin Board. Annual report. a., 1972/1973 (3rd)- Fredericton. *In English and French.*

— United Kingdom.

U.K. Central Water Planning Unit. Annual report. a., 1974/5 (1st)- Reading.

WATER QUALITY MANAGEMENT(Cont.)

LONDON. University. London School of Economics and Political Science. Department of Geography. Non-sequential water quality project. London, 1975 in progress.

WATER RESOURCES DEVELOPMENT.

ECONOMIC modeling for water policy evaluation; editors, R.M. Thrall [and others]. Amsterdam, 1976. pp. 261. *bibliogs. Selected papers from the TIMS/ORSA meeting held in San Juan, Puerto Rico, 1974.*

— Bibliography.

FOOD AND AGRICULTURE ORGANIZATION. Documentation Center. 1973. Water for agriculture: annotated bibliography; author and subject index; FAO publications and documents 1945-Sep. 1973. (DC/Sp.27). [Rome, 1973]. 1 vol. (various pagings). *In various languages.*

— Mathematical models.

ECONOMIC modeling for water policy evaluation; editors, R.M. Thrall [and others]. Amsterdam, 1976. pp. 261. *bibliogs. Selected papers from the TIMS/ORSA meeting held in San Juan, Puerto Rico, 1974.*

— Canada.

MACKENZIE BASIN INTERGOVERNMENTAL LIAISON COMMITTEE.Report. a., 1974(1st)- Ottawa.

MITCHELL (BRUCE) ed. Institutional arrangements for water management: Canadian experiences. Waterloo, Ont., [1975]. pp. 285. *(University of Waterloo, [Ontario]. Department of Geography. Publication Series. No. 5)*

NEW BRUNSWICK. Saint John River Basin Board. Annual report. a., 1972/1973 (3rd)- Fredericton. *In English and French.*

— Russia.

PROBLEMY ispol'zovaniia i okhrany vodnykh resursov. [vyp.1]. Minsk, 1972. pp. 276. *bibliog. For vyp.2 see PROBLEMY okhrany i ispol'zovaniia vod.*

PROBLEMY okhrany i ispol'zovaniia vod. [vyp.2]. Khar'kov, 1973. pp. 191. *With English table of contents. For vyp.1 see PROBLEMY ispol'zovaniia i okhrany vodnykh resursov.*

PROBLEMY okhrany i ispol'zovaniia vod. vyp.3. Khar'kov, 1973. pp. 204. *With English table of contents.*

— United Kingdom.

NATIONAL WATER COUNCIL [U.K.]. Annual report and accounts. a., 1974/75(1st)- London.

U.K. Central Water Planning Unit. Annual report. a., 1974/5 (1st)- Reading.

INLAND WATERWAYS AMENITY ADVISORY COUNCIL [U.K.]. Water shortages on British Waterways Board system: a report to the Secretary of State for the Environment. [London], 1974. fo. 6.

NATIONAL WATER COUNCIL [U.K.]. Views of the...Council on the Water Resources Board report Water resources in England and Wales. London, [1975]. pp. 20.

— United States.

FIELD (DONALD R.) and others, eds. Water and community development: social and economic perspectives. Ann Arbor, [1974]. pp. 302. *bibliogs.*

— — New Jersey — Mathematical models.

GREENBERG (MICHAEL R.) and HORDON (ROBERT M.) Water supply planning: a case study and systems analysis. New Brunswick, N.J., [1976]. pp. 166.

— — Pennsylvania.

STRONG (ANN LOUISE) Private property and the public interest: the Brandywine experience. Baltimore, [1975]. pp. 206. *(Johns Hopkins University. Center for Metropolitan Planning and Research. Johns Hopkins Studies in Urban Affairs)*

WATER REUSE.

MATHIEU (HERVE) L'eau et les déchets urbains. [Paris, 1972]. pp. 131. *bibliog.*

WATER RIGHTS.

— Canada.

QUINN (FRANK J.) Area-of-origin protectionism in western waters. Ottawa, 1973. pp. 95. *bibliog. (Canada. Inland Waters Directorate. Social Science Series. No. 6)*

— United States.

QUINN (FRANK J.) Area-of-origin protectionism in western waters. Ottawa, 1973. pp. 95. *bibliog. (Canada. Inland Waters Directorate. Social Science Series. No. 6)*

WATER SUPPLY.

MATHIEU (HERVE) L'eau et les déchets urbains. [Paris, 1972]. pp. 131. *bibliog.*

— Canada.

MACKENZIE BASIN INTERGOVERNMENTAL LIAISON COMMITTEE.Report. a., 1974(1st)- Ottawa.

— — New Brunswick.

NEW BRUNSWICK. Saint John River Basin Board. Annual report. a., 1972/1973 (3rd)- Fredericton. *In English and French.*

— St. Helena.

KITCHING (JOHN) The water resources of St. Helena. St. Helena, 1954. fo. 30. *bibliog.*

— United Kingdom.

NATIONAL WATER COUNCIL [U.K.]. Annual report and accounts. a., 1974/75(1st)- London.

U.K. Central Water Planning Unit. Annual report. a., 1974/5 (1st)- Reading.

INLAND WATERWAYS AMENITY ADVISORY COUNCIL [U.K.]. Water shortages on British Waterways Board system: a report to the Secretary of State for the Environment. [London], 1974. fo. 6.

NATIONAL WATER COUNCIL [U.K.]. Views of the...Council on the Water Resources Board report Water resources in England and Wales. London, [1975]. pp. 20.

WATER DATA UNIT [U.K.]. Water demand in England and Wales 1973. Reading, 1975. pp. 11. *(Technical Memoranda. No. 2)*

— — Bibliography.

U.K. Department of the Environment. Library. 1972. Water supply. London, [1972]. pp. 8. *(Bibliographies. No. 157)*

— United States — New Jersey — Mathematical models.

GREENBERG (MICHAEL R.) and HORDON (ROBERT M.) Water supply planning: a case study and systems analysis. New Brunswick, N.J., [1976]. pp. 166.

WATER SUPPLY, RURAL

— United States.

WARNER (DENNIS) and DAJANI (JARIR S.) Water and sewer development in rural America: a study of community impacts. Lexington, Mass., [1975]. pp. 128. *bibliog.*

WATERGATE AFFAIR, 1972— .

PYNN (RONALD E.) ed. Watergate and the American political process. New York, 1975. pp. 246.

COLSON (CHARLES W.) Born again. London, [1976]. pp. 350.

WOODWARD (BOB) and BERNSTEIN (CARL) The final days. London, 1976. pp. 476.

WATERWAYS.

INTERNATIONAL navigable waterways: financial and legal aspects of their improvement and maintenance; report on the symposium held at Buenos Aires from 30 November to 4 December, 1970; based on the discussions...and the working papers prepared by Richard Baxter [and others]. New York, United Nations Institute for Training and Research, 1975. pp. 253. *(UNITAR Studies. No.6.)*

WAYNE STATE UNIVERSITY

— Monteith College.

RIESMAN (DAVID) and others. Academic values and mass education. New York, 1970, repr. 1975. pp. 331. *bibliog.*

WEALTH

— France.

LEON (PIERRE) Géographie de la fortune et structures sociales à Lyon au XIXe siècle, 1815-1914;...avec la collaboration de Simone Gellibert [and others]. Lyon, [1974]. pp. 440. *bibliog. (Lyons. Université de Lyon II. Centre d'Histoire Economique et Sociale de la Région Lyonnaise. [Publications]. 4)*

— Germany.

EHRENBERG (HERBERT) and STREICHAN (PETER) eds. Dokumente zur Vermögenspolitik. Bonn-Bad Godesberg, [1974]. pp. 127. *bibliog.*

ARMBRUSTER (BERNT) Transformationsprobleme im Spätkapitalismus: zur Dialektik spätkapitalistischer Reformpolitik am Beispiel der "Vermögensbildung in Arbeitnehmerhand". Heidelberg, 1975. pp. 278. *bibliog. Inauguraldissertation, Wirtschafts- und Sozialwissenschaftliche Fakultät, Universität Heidelberg.*

MUECKL (WOLFGANG J.) Vermögenspolitische Konzepte in der Bundesrepublik Deutschland: Analyse der Ziele, Mittel und Wirkungen. Göttingen, [1975]. pp. 112. *bibliog. (Kommission für Wirtschaftlichen und Sozialen Wandel. Schriften. 34)*

SCHILLERT (ULLRICH) Gewinne als Quelle der Vermögenspolitik?: die Belastbarkeit der Unternehmensgewinne durch vermögenspolitische Massnahmen. Berlin, [1976]. pp. 270. *bibliog.*

— — Saxony.

FUHRMANN (ERICH) Das Volksvermögen und Volkseinkommen des Königreichs Sachsen. Leipzig, 1914. pp. 60. *bibliog.*

— India.

INDIA. Committee on Taxation of Agricultural Wealth and Income. 1972. Report; [K.N. Raj, chairman]. [Delhi?], 1972. pp. 169.

— United Kingdom — Scotland.

HARRISON (ALAN J.) The distribution of personal wealth in Scotland. Glasgow, [1975]. pp. 17. *bibliog. (Glasgow. University of Strathclyde. Fraser of Allander Institute for Research on the Scottish Economy. Research Monographs No. 1)*

— United States.

SALE (KIRKPATRICK) Power shift: the rise of the southern rim and its challenge to the eastern establishment. New York, [1975]. pp. 362.

SOLTOW (LEE) Men and wealth in the United States, 1850-1870. New Haven, 1975. pp. 206.

THUROW (LESTER C.) Generating inequality. London, [1975]. pp. 258.

LEBERGOTT (STANLEY) The American economy: income, wealth and want. Princeton, N.J., [1976]. pp. 382.

WEAPONS SYSTEMS.

CENTER FOR DEFENSE INFORMATION. Current issues in U.S. defense policy; edited by David Thomas Johnson [and] Barry R. Schneider. New York, 1976. pp. 254.

WEAVERS

— Poland.

MARCZAK (JÓZEF) Z pracy i 'zycia wlókniarzy. Warszawa, 1976. pp. 200. *bibliog.*

— Silesia.

PEUCKERT (WILL ERICH) and FUCHS (ERICH) Die schlesischen Weber. Darmstadt, [1971]. pp. 210,135. *The second part of the book consists of etchings by Erich Fuchs.*

WEBB (WALTER PRESCOTT).

ESSAYS on Walter Prescott Webb; by Joe B. Frantz [and others];...edited by Kenneth R. Philp and Elliott West. Austin, [1976]. pp. 123. *(Texas University. Walter Prescott Webb Memorial Lectures. 10)*

TOBIN (GREGORY M.) The making of a history: Walter Prescott Webb and the Great Plains. Austin, Tx., [1976]. pp. 184. *bibliog.*

WEBER (MAX).

TURNER (BRYAN S.) Weber and Islam: a critical study. London, 1974. pp. 212.

LEWIS (JOHN) B.Sc., Ph.D. Max Weber and value-free sociology: a Marxist critique. London, 1975. pp. 192. *bibliog.*

BURGER (THOMAS) Max Weber's theory of concept formation: history, laws, and ide types. Durham, N.C., 1976. pp. 231. *bibliog.*

HANSEN (DONALD ANDREW) An invitation to critical sociology: involvement, criticism, exploration. New York, [1976]. pp. 258. *bibliog.*

WEHNER (HERBERT).

KLOENNE (ARNO) ed. Machte Wehner die SPD kaputt?: eine Dokumentation über den Identitätsverlust der bundesdeutschen Sozialdemokratie. Landshut, 1975. pp. 276.

WEIGHTS AND MEASURES

— Russia — Ukraine.

SYDORENKO (OLENA FEDORIVNA) Istorychna metrolohiia Livoberezhnoï Ukraïny XVIII st. Kyïv, 1975. pp. 160.

WELFARE ECONOMICS.

KOHN (ROBERT E.) Air pollution control: welfare economic interpretation. Lexington, [1975]. pp. 155. *bibliog.*

SELF (PETER J.O.) Econocrats and the policy process: the politics and philosophy of cost-benefit analysis. London, 1975. pp. 212.

BRITISH ASSOCIATION FOR THE ADVANCEMENT OF SCIENCE. Section F. Meeting, 1975. Economics and equality: (papers...); edited by Rt. Hon. Aubrey Jones. Deddington, Oxford, 1976. pp. 164. *bibliogs.*

MEADE (JAMES EDWARD) The just economy:...being volume four of Principles of political economy. London, 1976. pp. 247.

WELFARE STATE.

WILENSKY (HAROLD L.) The welfare state and equality: structural and ideological roots of public expenditures. Berkeley, [1975]. pp. 151. *bibliog.*

JANOWITZ (MORRIS) Social control of the welfare state. New York, [1976]. pp. 170. *bibliog.*

JORDAN (WILLIAM) Freedom and the welfare state. London, 1976. pp. 224.

ROBSON (WILLIAM ALEXANDER) Welfare state and welfare society: illusion and reality. London, 1976. pp. 184.

WELFARE WORK IN INDUSTRY

— United States.

HESKES (DEBORAH A.) Supportive services for disadvantaged workers and trainees. Ithaca, N.Y., 1973. pp. 56. *bibliog. (Cornell University. New York State School of Industrial and Labor Relations. Key Issue Series. No. 12)*

BRANDES (STUART D.) American welfare capitalism, 1880-1940. Chicago, 1976. pp. 210. *bibliog.*

WELSH IN PATAGONIA.

WILLIAMS (GLYN) The desert and the dream: a study of Welsh colonization in Chubut, 1865-1915. Cardiff, 1975. pp. 230. *bibliog.*

WEMHOFF (KARL HEINZ).

EUROPEAN COURT OF HUMAN RIGHTS. Publications. Series A: Judgments and Decisions. [A7]. ..."Wemhoff" case; judgment of 27th June 1968. Strasbourg, Council of Europe, 1968. pp. 40 [bis]. *In English and French.*

EUROPEAN COURT OF HUMAN RIGHTS. Publications. Series B: Pleadings, Oral Arguments and Documents. [B5]. "Wemhoff" case, (1969). Strasbourg, Council of Europe, 1969. pp. 301[bis], 302-361. *In English and French.*

WENDS.

MĚTŠK (FRIDO) Die Stellung der Sorben in de territorialen Verwaltungsgliederung des deutschen Feudalismus...ein Beitrag zur Rechts- und Verfassungsgeschichte des deutschen Feudalismus im Sorbenland. Bautzen, 1968. pp. 171. *(Deutsche Akademie der Wissenschaften zu Berlin. Institut für Sorbische Volksforschung in Bautzen. Schriftenreihe. 43)*

CYŻ (BENO) Die DDR und die Sorben: eine Dokumenation zur Nationalitätenpolitik in der DDR. Bautzen, [1969]. pp. 543. *bibliog.*

WERTHEIM.

ZOLL (RALF) Wertheim III: Kommunalpolitik und Machtstruktur. München, [1974]. pp. 304. *bibliog.*

WEST BROMWICH

— Civic improvement.

The BEECHES road area study: a potential housing action area; [by] Pat Niner [and others]. Birmingham, 1975. pp. 136, 22. *(Birmingham. University. Centre for Urban and Regional Studies. Research Memoranda. No. 49)*

WEST INDIANS IN THE UNITED KINGDOM.

COMMUNITY RELATIONS COMMISSION. Research summaries on the under fives: a critical guide to research on West Indian children under five in Britain. London, [1975]. 1 pamphlet(various pagings).

FIGUEROA (PETER EUGENE) West Indian school-leavers in London: a sociological study in ten schools in a London borough, 1966-1967; [Ph.D. (London) thesis]. 1974 (or rather 1975). fo. 541. *bibliog. Typescript: unpublished. This thesis is the property of London University and may not be removed from the Library.*

WEST INDIANS IN THE UNITED STATES.

DOMINGUEZ (VIRGINIA R.) From neighbor to stranger: the dilemma of Caribbean peoples in the United States. New Haven, Conn., [1975]. pp. 177. *bibliog. (Yale University. Antilles Research Program. Occasional Papers. 5)*

WEST INDIES

— Census.

COMMONWEALTH CARIBBEAN. Census, 1970. 1970 population census of the Commonwealth Caribbean, 7 April and 25 October, etc. Kingston, 1973 in progress.

— Economic history.

GREEN (WILLIAM A.) British slave emancipation: the sugar colonies and the great experiment, 1830-1865. Oxford, 1976. pp. 449. *bibliog.*

— Population.

WELLS (ROBERT V.) The population of the British colonies in America before 1776: a survey of census data. Princeton, [1975]. pp. 342. *bibliog.*

— Social history.

GREEN (WILLIAM A.) British slave emancipation: the sugar colonies and the great experiment, 1830-1865. Oxford, 1976. pp. 449. *bibliog.*

WEST YORKSHIRE

— Economic policy.

WEST YORKSHIRE. Metropolitan County Council. West Yorkshire structure plan. Annual statement. a., 1975(1st)- Wakefield.

WESTERLAND

— Economic conditions.

BIENERT (FRANK) Zur Bestimmung der ökonomischen Auswirkungen des Fremdenverkehrs...: eine empirische Fallstudie, dargestellt am Beispiel der Stadt Westerland auf Sylt. Berlin, 1974. pp. 287. *bibliog. Inaugural-Dissertation zur Erlangung des Grades eines Doktors der Wirtschaftswissenschaften der Freien Universität Berlin.*

WESTERN AUSTRALIA

— Emigration and immigration.

AUSTRALIA. Migrant Task Force Committee, Western Australia. 1973. Initial report to the Minister for Immigration; chairman: Joe Berinson. [Perth, 1973]. fo. 10.

WESTERN TOWNSHIP

— Social conditions.

BRINDLEY (MARIANNE) Western Coloured Township: problems of an urban slum. Johannesburg, 1976. pp. 110. *bibliog.*

WESTLAND

— History.

MAY (PHILIP ROSS) ed. Miners and militants: politics in Westland, 1865-1918: six essays. Christchurch, N.Z., 1975. pp. 174. *(Christchurch, New Zealand. University of Canterbury. Publications. No.21)*

— Politics and government.

MAY (PHILIP ROSS) ed. Miners and militants: politics in Westland, 1865-1918: six essays. Christchurch, N.Z., 1975. pp. 174. *(Christchurch, New Zealand. University of Canterbury. Publications. No.21)*

WESTMINSTER

— Transit systems.

WESTMINSTER. Department of Architecture and Planning. Westminster Development Plan Publications. Topic Papers. T 3. Transport. [London], 1975. pp. 160.

WESTON (RICHARD) 1st Earl of Portland.

ALEXANDER (MICHAEL VAN CLEAVE) Charles I's Lord Treasurer: Sir Richard Weston, Earl of Portland, 1577-1635. London, 1975. pp. 261.

WESTPHALEN (JOHANN LUDWIG VON).

MONZ (HEINZ) and others. Zur Persönlichkeit von Marx' Schwiegervater Johann Ludwig von Westphalen. Trier, [1973]. pp. 166. (Karl-Marx-Haus. Schriften. 9)

WESTPHALEN (LUDWIG VON).

See **WESTPHALEN (JOHANN LUDWIG VON).**

WESTPHALEN FAMILY.

MONZ (HEINZ) and others. Zur Persönlichkeit von Marx' Schwiegervater Johann Ludwig von Westphalen. Trier, [1973]. pp. 166. (Karl-Marx-Haus. Schriften. 9)

WHALING.

VAMPLEN (WRAY) Salvesen of Leith. Edinburgh, 1975. pp. 311.

WHEAT

— Australia.

AUSTRALIA. Bureau of Agricultural Economics. 1975. The Australian wheatgrowing industry: an economic survey, 1972- 1973. Canberra, 1975. pp. 96.

— Canada.

CANADA. Department of Agriculture. 1968. Winter wheat production in western Canada; [by] M.N. Grant [and others]. rev. ed. [Ottawa], 1968. pp. 14. (Publications. 1056)

— Pakistan.

KHAN (MAHMOOD HASAN) The economics of the green revolution in Pakistan. New York, 1975. pp. 226.

WHIG PARTY (UNITED KINGDOM).

MILLER (KARL) Cockburn's millennium. London, 1975. pp. 322.

THOMPSON (EDWARD PALMER) Whigs and hunters: the origin of the Black Act. London, 1975. pp. 313.

WHISKY

— United Kingdom — Scotland.

HOUSE (JACK) Pride of Perth: the story of Arthur Bell and Sons Ltd., Scotch Whisky distillers. London, 1976. pp. 135.

WHITE RUSSIA

— Constitutional history.

KRUTALEVICH (VADIM ANDREEVICH) Rozhdenie Belorusskoi Sovetskoi Respubliki: na puti k provozglasheniiu respubliki. Oktiabr' 1917 - dekabr' 1918 g.; redaktory A.F. Khatskevich, I.A. Iukho. Minsk, 1975. pp. 335.

— Economic history.

DRITS (V.I.) ed. Razvitie ekonomiki Belorussii v 1928-1941 gg. Minsk, 1975. pp. 317.

ROSMAN (IOSIF SAMUILOVICH) Kompartiia Belorussii v bor'be za uprochenie sotsialisticheskogo obshchestva v predvoennye gody, 1938 - iiun' 1941 gg. Minsk, 1975. pp. 351.

VOPROSY istorii KPSS: nekotorye voprosy organizatorskoi i ideologicheskoi deiatel'nosti KPSS; na materialakh Belorusskoi SSR; mezhvedomstvennyi sbornik 4. Minsk, 1975. pp. 238.

— Executive departments.

PETRIKOV (PETR TIKHONOVICH) Revkomy Belorussii. Minsk, 1975. pp. 287.

— Industries.

ZHIGALOV (V.N.) and others, eds. Industrializatsiia Belorusskoi SSR, 1926-1941 gg.: sbornik dokumentov i materialov. Minsk, 1975. pp. 467.

— Politics and government.

RAVNOPOLETS (LIUDMILA SILOVNA) Iz istorii izdaniia i rasprostraneniia proizvedenii V.I. Lenina v Belorussii. Moskva, 1974. pp. 159.

— Statistics, Vital.

SHAKHOT'KO (LIUDMILA PETROVNA) Rozhdaemost' v Belorussii: sotsial'no-ekonomicheskie voprosy. Minsk, 1975. pp. 167. bibliog.

WHOLE AND PARTS (PHILOSOPHY).

CHATTOPADHYAY(DEBIPRASAD) Individuals and societies: a methodological inquiry. 2nd ed. Calcutta, 1975. pp. 281. bibliog.

WHOLESALE TRADE

— Information storage and retrieval systems.

See **INFORMATION STORAGE AND RETRIEVAL SYSTEMS — Wholesale trade.**

— Canada.

CANADA. Statistics Canada. Merchandising businesses survey: wholsale merchants. a., 1973 (1st)- Ottawa. [In English and French]

— Finland.

FINLAND. Tilastokeskus. Tukku- ja vähittäiskaupan tasetilasto. ..: Statistics of profit and loss and balance sheet accounts of wholesale and retail trade. a., 1972- Helsinki. In Finnish with notes and headings in Swedish and English.

— France.

FRANCE. Direction Générale du Commerce Intérieur et des Prix. Service du Commerce. Les centres commerciaux de gros:...document d'orientation...à la suite du colloque organisé...par la Chambre de Commerce et d'Industrie de Nantes, au mois de décembre 1970. Paris, 1971. pp. 73.

— India — Goa, Daman and Diu.

GOA, DAMAN AND DIU. Bureau of Economics, Statistics and Evaluation. 1974. A pilot survey of distributive trade. Panaji, [1974]. pp. 107.

— Ireland (Republic).

EIRE. Central Statistics Office. 1975. Summary results for retail and wholesale trade, census of distribution, 1971. Dublin, 1975. pp. 48.

— New Zealand.

NEW ZEALAND. Department of Statistics. 1975- . Census of distribution, 1972-73: (statistical bulletins). Wellington, 1975 in progress.

— Norway.

NORWAY. Statistiske Centralbyrå. 1974. Regnskapsanalyse: industri og engroshandel, etc. Oslo, 1974. pp. 131. (Statistiske Analyser. 12) With summary in English.

— Portugal.

RAMOS (ANTONIO BRITO) O emprego no sector terciario metropolitano: tentativas de localização do crescimento. Lisboa, 1974. pp. 103. (Portugal. Ministerio do Trabalho. Gabinete de Planeamento. Serie Estudos. 24) With abstracts in English, French and German.

— Russia.

KOROTKOV (VASILII FEDOROVICH) Oplata truda rabotnikov organizatsii snabzheniia i zagotovok. Moskva, 1969. pp. 72.

— South Africa.

SOUTH AFRICA. Bureau of Statistics. 1976- . Census of wholesale and retail trade, 1970-71. [Pretoria, 1976 in progress]. (Reports. No. 04-11-02, etc.) In English and Afrikaans.

— United Kingdom.

ECONOMIC DEVELOPMENT COMMITTEE FOR THE DISTRIBUTIVE TRADES. Profitability and liquidity in the distributive trades: an examination of financial data in selected sectors; based on a report prepared for the Distributive Trades EDC by Whitefield Associates and Company. London, National Economic Development Office, 1975. pp. 123.

WILLAN (THOMAS STUART) The inland trade: studies in English internal trade in the sixteenth and seventeenth centuries. Manchester, [1976]. pp. 154.

WIDOWS.

GLICK (IRA OSCAR) and others. The first year of bereavement. New York, [1974]. pp. 311.

WIFE BEATING.

KEMP (MARTIN) and others. Battered women and the law. rev. ed. London, 1975. pp. 31. bibliog. (Interaction Advisory Service. Handbooks. 3)

WILDBERG

— Economic history.

MANTEL (JOACHIM) Wildberg: eine Studie zur wirtschaftlichen und sozialen Entwicklung der Stadt, etc. Stuttgart, 1974. pp. 166. bibliog. (Kommission für Geschichtliche Landeskunde in Baden-Württemberg. Veröffentlichungen. Reihe B: Forschungen. 80.Band)

WILDE (JACQUES DE).

EUROPEAN COURT OF HUMAN RIGHTS. Publications. Series A: Judgments and Decisions. [A12]. ...De Wilde, Ooms and Versyp cases; "vagrancy" cases. 1. Decision of 28th May 1970. 2. Judgment of 18th November 1970; question of procedure. 3. Judgment of 18th June 1971. Strasbourg, Council of Europe, 1971. pp. 75 [bis].

EUROPEAN COURT OF HUMAN RIGHTS. Publications. Series B: Pleadings, Oral Arguments and Documents.[B10]. "De Wilde, Ooms and Versyp" cases: "vagrancy" cases, 1969-1971. Strasbourg, Council of Europe, 1971. pp. 405 [bis], 407-474. In English and French.

EUROPEAN COURT OF HUMAN RIGHTS. Publications. Series A: Judgments and Decisions. [A] 14. ...De Wilde, Ooms and Versyp cases: "vagrancy" cases; judgment of 10 March 1972; question of the application of Article 50 of the Convention. Strasbourg, Council of Europe, 1972. pp. 22 [bis]. In English and French.

EUROPEAN COURT OF HUMAN RIGHTS. Publications. Series B: Pleadings, Oral Arguments and Documents. [B12]. "De Wilde, Ooms and Versyp" cases: "vagrancy" cases; question of the application of Article 50 of the Convention, (1971-1972). Strasbourg, Council of Europe, 1973. pp. 97 [bis], 99-126. In English and French.

WILDERNESS AREAS.

CICCHETTI (CHARLES J.) and SMITH (VINCENT KERRY) The costs of congestion: an econometric analysis of wilderness recreation. Cambridge, Mass., [1976]. pp. 112. bibliog.

SMITH (V. KERRY) and KRUTILLA (JOHN V.) Structure and properties of a wilderness travel simulator: an application to the Spanish Peaks area. Baltimore, [1976]. pp. 173. bibliogs.

WILLIAM TYNDALE JUNIOR AND INFANTS SCHOOLS.

AULD (ROBIN ERNEST) The William Tyndale Junior and Infants Schools: report of the public inquiry...into the teaching, organization and management of the William Tyndale Junior and Infants Schools, Islington, London, N.1. London, Inner London Education Authority, 1976. 1 vol. (various pagings).

WILLIAM Tyndale: the teachers' story; [by] Terry Ellis [and others]. London, 1976. pp. 171.

WILLS

— United Kingdom.

EMMISON (FREDERICK GEORGE) Elizabethan life: home, work and land; from Essex wills and sessions and manorial records. Chelmsford, 1976. pp. 364. *(Essex. Records Committee. Essex Record Office Publications. No. 69)*

WILSON (JOSEPH).

WILSON (JOSEPH) b. 1833. Joseph Wilson: his life and work. London, [1923?]. pp. 89.

WILSON (THOMAS WOODROW) President of the United States.

IAKOVLEV (NIKOLAI NIKOLAEVICH) Prestupivshie gran'. Moskva, 1970. pp. 352.

WINE AND WINE MAKING

— France.

BERT (PIERRE) In vino veritas: l'affaire des vins de Bordeaux. Paris, [1975]. pp. 244.

WINNIPEG

— Growth.

ARTIBISE (ALAN F.J.) Winnipeg: a social history of urban growth, 1874-1914. Montreal, 1975. pp. 382. *bibliog.*

— History.

ARTIBISE (ALAN F.J.) Winnipeg: a social history of urban growth, 1874-1914. Montreal, 1975. pp. 382. *bibliog.*

— Politics and government.

MANITOBA. Local Government Boundaries Commission. 1970. Provisional plan for the boundaries and structure of local government units within the Metropolitan Winnipeg area and its additional zone; [R.G. Smellie, chairman]. [Winnipeg], 1970. pp. 347.

WIRE INDUSTRY

— United Kingdom.

JENKINS (MICK) Time and motion strike, Manchester, 1934-7: the wiredrawers' struggle against the Bedoux system at Richard Johnson's. London, 1974. pp. 34. *(Communist Party of Great Britain. History Group. Our History. No. 60)*

WIRTSCHAFTLICHE AUFBAU-VEREINIGUNG.

WINGE (SÖREN) Die Wirtschaftliche Aufbau-Vereinigung, WAV, 1945-53: Entwicklung und Politik einer "undoktrinären" politischen Partei in der Bundesrepublik in der ersten Nachkriegszeit. Uppsala, 1976. pp. 251. *bibliog.* (Uppsala. Universitet. Historiska Institutionen. Studia Historica Upsaliensia. 78)

WIT AND HUMOUR.

CHAPMAN (ANTHONY J.) and FOOT (HUGH C.) eds. Humour and laughter: theory, research and applications. London, [1976]. pp. 348. *bibliogs.*

WITTGENSTEIN (LUDWIG).

FOGELIN (ROBERT J.) Wittgenstein. London, 1976. pp. 223. *bibliog.*

WIVES.

OAKLEY (ANN) The sociology of housework. [London, 1974]. pp. 242.

WODAK (WALTER).

WODAK (WALTER) Diplomatie zwischen Ost und West. Graz, [1976]. pp. 235. *(Österreichische Gesellschaft für Aussenpolitik und Internationale Beziehungen. Österreichische Diplomaten)* Collection of lectures and essays, in German or English. Includes correspondence with Karl Renner.

WOHLIN (NILS RICHARD).

HAGÅRD (BIRGER) Nils Wohlin: konservativ centerpolitiker. [Stockholm?, 1976]. pp. 467. *bibliog.* Akademisk avhandling, filosofie doktorsgrad, Stockholms Universitet.

WOLFENDEN (JOHN FREDERICK) Baron Wolfenden.

WOLFENDEN (JOHN FREDERICK) Baron Wolfenden. Turning points: the memoirs of Lord Wolfenden. London, 1976. pp. 186.

WOLSFELD

— Social history.

HERRIG (GERTRUD) Ländliche Nahrung im Strukturwandel des 20. Jahrhunderts: Untersuchungen im Westeifeler Reliktgebiet am Beispiel der Gemeinde Wolsfeld. Meisenheim am Glan, 1974. pp. 239. *bibliog.*

WOMEN.

ROSALDO (MICHELLE ZIMBALIST) and LAMPHERE (LOUISE)eds. Woman, culture and society. Stanford, [1974]. pp. 352. *bibliog.*

INTERNATIONAL CONGRESS OF ANTHROPOLOGICAL AND ETHNOLOGICAL SCIENCES. 9th Congress, 1973. Women cross-culturally: change and challenge; [papers from the Congress]; editor Ruby Rohrlich-Leavitt. The Hague, [1975]. pp. 669. *bibliogs.*

PERCEIVING women; edited by Shirley Ardener. London, 1975. pp. 167. *bibliog.*

— Employment.

SZALAI (SANDOR) The situation of women in the United Nations: a report based on the proceedings of the Colloquium of Senior United Nations Officials held on 4-6 July 1972 at Schloss Hernstein (Austria). [New York], United Nations Institute for Training and Research, 1973. pp. 49. *(Research Reports. No. 18)*

CURTHOYS (ANN) and others, eds. Women at work. Canberra, 1975. pp. 161.

— — America.

SYMPOSIUM ON EQUALITY OF OPPORTUNITY IN EMPLOYMENT IN THE AMERICAN REGION, PANAMA, 1973. Equality of opportunity in employment in the American region: problems and policies; report and documents of a regional symposium [held at] Panama, 1-12 October 1973. Geneva, International Labour Office, 1974. pp. 133.

— — Australia.

AUSTRALIA. Women's Bureau. 1974. The role of women in the economy: background information, Australia; (O.E.C.D. study). Canberra, 1974. pp. 181. *(Women and Work. No. 12)*

CURTHOYS (ANN) and others, eds. Women at work. Canberra, 1975. pp. 161.

— — Canada — Ontario.

WOMEN at work: Ontario, 1850-1930; (edited by Janice Acton [and others]). Toronto, [1974]. pp. 405. *bibliog.*

— — France.

FRANCE. Comité du Travail Féminin. 1973. Le rôle des femmes dans l'économie: synthèse du rapport de la France à l'O.C.D.E. Paris, 1973. fo. 31.

FRANCE. Comité du Travail Féminin. 1974. Le Comité du Travail Féminin. [Paris], 1974. pp. (8). *bibliog.*

FRANCE. Comité du Travail Féminin. 1974. La situation de l'emploi féminin en mars 1974. Paris, 1974. fo. 18,7.

COLIN (MADELEINE) Ce n'est pas d'aujourd'hui: femmes, syndicats, luttes de classe. Paris, [1975]. pp. 247.

FRANCE. Comité du Travail Féminin. 1975. Committee on Women's Work. Paris, 1975. fo. 5.

— — Germany.

ZETKIN (CLARA) Zu den Anfängen der proletarischen Frauenbewegung in Deutschland. Berlin, 1956. pp. 31. *bibliog.* (Institut für Marxismus-Leninismus (Berlin). Beiträge zur Geschichte und Theorie der Arbeiterbewegung. Heft 4) Originally published in the Neue-Welt-Kalender für 1906.

STIEGLER (BARBARA) Die Mitbestimmung der Arbeiterin: Frauen zwischen traditioneller Familienbindung und gewerkschaftlichem Engagement im Betrieb; ein Beitrag zur Psychologie der Arbeiterin. Bonn-Bad Godesberg, [1976]. pp. 227, 10 . *bibliog.* (Friedrich-Ebert-Stiftung. Forschungsinstitut. Schriftenreihe. Band 123)

— — Hungary.

HUNGARY. Központi Statisztikai Hivatal. 1961. A dolgozó nők a munkahelyen és otthon. Budapest, 1961. pp. 30.

— — India.

INDIA. Labour Bureau. 1975. Women in industry. [Delhi, 1975]. pp. 246.

— — Italy.

COMITATO PER IL SALARIO AL LAVORO DOMESTICO DI PADOVA. Le operaie della casa; a cura del Collettivo Internazionale Femminista. Venezia, 1975. pp. 78. *(Collettivo Internazionale Femminista. Salario al Lavoro Domestico: Strategia Internazionale.1)*

— — New Zealand.

MANUFACTURING DEVELOPMENT COUNCIL [NEW ZEALAND]. Women in manufacturing industry; report. [Wellington, 1973]. pp. 71.

— — Nigeria.

LUCAS (DAVID WILLIAM) The participation of women in the Nigerian labour force since the 1950's with particular reference to Lagos. 1975. fo. 324. *bibliog.* Typescript. Includes two reprints from periodicals. Ph.D.(London) thesis: unpublished. This thesis is the property of London University and may not be removed from the Library.

— — Poland.

OLĘDZKA (ANNA) Kobieta: budżet czasu, praca wielozmianowa. Warszawa, 1975. pp. 176. *bibliog.*

PRZEDPELSKI (MIECZYSŁAW) Struktura zatrudnienia kobiet w Polsce Ludowej. Warszawa, 1975. pp. 267. *bibliog.*

— — Portugal.

CARVALHO (ODETE ESTEVES DE) Remunerações femininas e diferenciações salariais entre mulheres e homens em 1970: estudo analítico. Lisboa, 1974. pp. 92. *(Portugal. Ministerio do Trabalho. Gabinete de Planeamento. Serie Estudos. 23)* With abstracts in English, French and German.

— — Russia.

SACKS (MICHAEL PAUL) Women's work in Soviet Russia: continuity in the midst of change. New York, [1976]. pp. 221. *bibliog.*

— — Switzerland.

GALLI (BEATRICE) Die Schweizerfrau im Handels- und Bureauberuf. Bern, 1934. pp. 122. *bibliog.*

WOMEN.(Cont.)

— — United Kingdom.

HUTCHINS (ELIZABETH LEIGH) [Correspondence about women's employment in Lancashire. 1914]. 12 letters. *Manuscript.*

DANGER! : women at work; report of a conference organised by the National Council for Civil Liberties [London]...1974; edited by Patricia Hewitt. London, [1974]. pp. 54. *bibliog.*

STEWART (VALERIE) Women in industry; [written for the Institute of Manpower Studies]. [London], 1974. pp. 33. *bibliog.*

LONDON. Greater London Council. Inner London Education Authority. Standing Committee on Careers Opportunities for Women and Girls. A report. London, [1975]. pp. 47.

CHIPLIN (BRIAN) and SLOANE (PETER J.) Sex discrimination in the labour market. London, 1976. pp. 161.

RAPOPORT (RHONA) and RAPOPORT (ROBERT NORMAN) Dual-career families re-examined: new integrations of work and family. [2nd ed.] London, 1976. pp. 382. *bibliog. Title of first edition: Dual-career families.*

— — United States.

ANGRIST (SHIRLEY S.) and ALMQUIST (ELIZABETH M.) Careers and contingencies: how college women juggle with gender. New York, [1975]. pp. 269. *bibliog.*

CARNEGIE COUNCIL ON POLICY STUDIES IN HIGHER EDUCATION. Making affirmative action work in higher education: an analysis of institutional and federal policies with recommendations. San Francisco, 1975. pp. 272. *bibliog.*

CONFERENCE ON LABOR MARKET SEGMENTATION, HARVARD UNIVERSITY, 1973. Labor market segmentation: [papers presented at the conference]; edited by Richard C. Edwards [and others]. Lexington, Mass., [1975]. pp. 297. *bibliogs.*

KREPS (JUANITA MORRIS) and CLARK (ROBERT) Sex, age, and work: the changing composition of the labor force. Baltimore, [1975]. pp. 95. *bibliog.*

MEDNICK (MARTHA TAMARA SHUCH) and others, eds. Women and achievement: social and motivational analyses. Washington, [1975]. pp. 447. *bibliogs.*

WOMEN in the professions; edited by Laurily Keir Epstein. Farnborough, Hants, [1975]. pp. 142. *Papers from a conference held at Washington University, St. Louis, Apr. 1975; sponsored by Monticello College Foundation and Washington University.*

BROWNLEE (W. ELLIOT) and BROWNLEE (MARY M.) Women in the American economy: a documentary history, 1675 to 1929. New Haven, 1976. pp. 350.

— History.

MATTHIASSON (CAROLYN J.) ed. Many sisters: women in cross-cultural perspective. New York, [1974]. pp. 443. *bibliogs.*

BRANCA (PATRICIA) Silent sisterhood: middle class women in the Victorian home. London, [1975]. pp. 170. *bibliog.*

DECKARD (BARBARA SINCLAIR) The women's movement: political, socioeconomic, and psychological issues. New York, [1975]. pp. 450. *bibliog.*

POWER (EILEEN EDNA LE POER) Medieval women;...edited by M.M. Postan. Cambridge, 1975 repr. 1976. pp. 112. *bibliog.*

WORLD COUNCIL OF CHURCHES: Consultation on Sexism in the 1970s, West Berlin, 1974. Discrimination against women: (sexism in the 1970s): [report of the consultation]. Geneva, [1975]. pp. 150.

BROWNLEE (W. ELLIOT) and BROWNLEE (MARY M.) Women in the American economy: a documentary history, 1675 to 1929. New Haven, 1976. pp. 350.

PESCATELLO (ANN M.) Power and pawn: the female in Iberian families, societies, and cultures. Westport, Conn., 1976. pp. 281. *bibliog. (Council on Intercultural and Comparative Studies. Contributions in Intercultural and Comparative Studies. No. 1)*

ZARETSKY (ELI) Capitalism, the family and personal life. London, 1976. pp. 156.

— Legal status, laws, etc.

WOMEN in the world: a comparative study; [edited by] Lynne B. Iglitzin, Ruth Ross. Santa Barbara, [1976]. pp. 427. *Papers from seminar meetings sponsored jointly by the Department of Political Science of the University of California, Santa Barbara and the Center for the Study of Democratic Institutions.*

— — Australia — Queensland.

QUEENSLAND. Commission of Inquiry into the Status of Women in Queensland. 1974. Report and recommendations; [A.G. Demack, chairman]. (A.1- 1974). Brisbane, 1974. pp. 34.

— — Colombia.

AMEZQUITA DE ALMEYDA (JOSEFINA) Law and the status of Colombian women. Medford, Mass., 1975. pp. 64. *(Tufts University. Fletcher School of Law and Diplomacy. Law and Population Monograph Series. No.32)*

— — France.

FRANCE. Comité du Travail Féminin. 1974. L'évolution de la situation des femmes dans la société française. Paris, 1974. fo. 28.

FRANCE. Comité du Travail Féminin. 1975. The social evolution of the status of women in France: a report [prepared for a conference organized by the] (Conseil Franco- Britannique) [on] (the status of women) [held at] (Saint-Germain-en-Laye, 11-13 April, 1975). [Paris], 1975. fo. 26.

— — Germany, Eastern.

GERMANY (DEUTSCHE DEMOKRATISCHE REPUBLIK). Statutes, etc. 1950-1975. Staatliche Dokumente zur Förderung der Frau in der Deutschen Demokratischen Republik: Gesetzesdokumentation; (Zusammenstellung und Bearbeitung, Heinz Adomeit). 2nd ed. Berlin, Staatsverlag der Deutschen Demokratischen Republik, 1975. pp. 410.

— — United Kingdom.

GILL (TESS) and COOTE (ANNA) Battered women: how to use the law. London, 1975. pp. 23.

HEWITT (PATRICIA) Rights for women: a guide to the Sex Discrimination Act, the Equal Pay Act, paid maternity leave, pension schemes and unfair dismissal. London, [1975]. pp. 98.

— Psychology.

MILLER (JEAN BAKER) ed. Psychoanalysis and women. Harmondsworth, 1973, repr. 1974. pp. 415. *bibliog.*

— Rights of women.

See WOMEN'S RIGHTS.

— Social conditions.

KEY (ELLEN KAROLINA SOFIA) The woman movement;...translated by Mamah Bouton Borthwick, with an introduction by Havelock Ellis. New York, 1912; Westport, Conn., 1976. pp. 224. *Facsimile reprint.*

SCHIRMACHER (KAETHE) The modern woman's rights movement: a historical survey; translated from the second German edition by Carl Conrad Eckhardt. New York, 1912; Westport, Conn., 1976. pp. 280.

DELL (FLOYD) Women as world builders: studies in modern feminism. Chicago, 1913. pp. 104.

ROSALDO (MICHELLE ZIMBALIST) and LAMPHERE (LOUISE)eds. Woman, culture and society. Stanford, [1974]. pp. 352. *bibliog.*

ROSENBERG (MARIE BAROVIC) and BERGSTROM (LEN V.) compilers. Women and society: a critical review of the literature with a selected annotated bibliography. Beverly Hills, [1975]. pp. 354. *bibliogs.*

ALLENDORF (MARLIS) Women in socialist society; English version by Ruth Michaelis- Jena and Patrick Murray. Leipzig, [1976]. pp. 219. *bibliog.*

BRITISH SOCIOLOGICAL ASSOCIATION. Annual Conference, 1974. Sexual divisions and society: process and change; [papers presented at the conference]; edited by Diana Leonard Barker and Sheila Allen. London, 1976. pp. 286. *bibliogs. (British Sociological Association. Explorations in Sociology. 6)*

EVANS (RICHARD J.) The feminist movement in Germany, 1894-1933. London, [1976]. pp. 310. *bibliog.*

MITCHELL (JULIET) and OAKLEY (ANN) eds. The rights and wrongs of women. Harmondsworth, 1976. pp. 438.

WOMEN in the world: a comparative study; [edited by] Lynne B. Iglitzin, Ruth Ross. Santa Barbara, [1976]. pp. 427. *Papers from seminar meetings sponsored jointly by the Department of Political Science of the University of California, Santa Barbara and the Center for the Study of Democratic Institutions.*

— Societies and clubs.

FORBES (ELIZABETH LAMONT) With enthusiasm and faith: history of the Canadian Federation of Business and Professional Women's Clubs...1930-1972. [Ottawa], 1974. pp. 170.

— Suffrage — France.

BRIMO (ALBERT) Les femmes françaises face au pouvoir politique. Paris, [1975]. pp. 131. *bibliog.*

— — United Kingdom.

ROBERTSON (JOHN MACKINNON) The vote for women. Bradford, [1897]. pp. 8. *(Papers for the People. No. 7)*

SUFFRAGE ANNUAL AND WOMEN'S WHO'S WHO, THE; edited by A.J.R. a. 1913. London.

MACKENZIE (MIDGE) Shoulder to shoulder: a documentary. Harmondsworth, 1975. pp. 338,iii. *bibliog.*

— — United States.

FULLER (PAUL E.) Laura Clay and the woman's rights movement. Lexington, Ky., [1975]. pp. 217. *bibliog.*

RAEBURN (ANTONIA) The suffragette view. Newton Abbot, [1976]. pp. 96.

— Africa.

WOMEN in Africa: studies in social and economic change; edited by Nancy J. Hafkin and Edna G. Bay. Stanford, 1976. pp. 306. *bibliog. A project of the Committee of the African Studies Association.*

— Algeria.

ALGERIA. Ministère de l'Information. 1969. The Algerian women. [Algiers, 1969?]. pp. 86.

— America, Latin.

SEX and class in Latin America; edited by June Nash and Helen Icken Safa. New York, 1976. pp. 330. *bibliogs. Papers from a conference sponsored by American Council of Learned Societies and Social Science Research Council. Joint Committee on Latin American Studies.*

— Arab Countries.

DEARDEN (ANNE) ed. Arab women. London, 1975. pp. 20. *bibliog. (Minority Rights Group. Reports. No. 27)*

— Australia.

CURTHOYS (ANN) and others, eds. Women at work. Canberra, 1975. pp. 161.

WOMEN AND SOCIALISM.

— **Austria.**

KLUCSARITS (RICHARD) and KUERBISCH (FRIEDRICH G.) eds. Arbeiterinnen kämpfen um ihr Recht: autobiographische Texte. ..in Deutschland, Österreich und der Schweiz des 19. und 20. Jahrhunderts. Wuppertal, [1975]. pp. 390. *bibliog.*

WEINZIERL (ERIKA) Emanzipation?: österreichische Frauen im 20. Jahrhundert. Wien, [1975]. pp. 212.

— **Brazil.**

MURPHY (YOLANDA) and MURPHY (ROBERT FRANCIS) Women of the forest. New York, 1974. pp. 236. *bibliog.*

— **Canada.**

FORBES (ELIZABETH LAMONT) With enthusiasm and faith: history of the Canadian Federation of Business and Professional Women's Clubs...1930-1972. [Ottawa], 1974. pp. 170.

— — **Bibliography.**

HOULE (GHISLAINE) La femme et la société québécoise. Montréal, Bibliothèque Nationale du Québec, Centre Bibliographique, 1975. pp. 228. *(Bibliographies Québécoises. No. 1)*

— **Caribbean Area.**

CARIBBEAN REGIONAL SEMINAR ON THE ROLE OF WOMEN IN THE SEVENTIES, GRENADA, 1975. Women in the seventies; report. [London], Commonwealth Secretariat, [1976]. pp. 65.

— **China.**

O'SULLIVAN (SUE) The moon for dinner: changing relations: women in China. London, 1975. pp. 46. *bibliog.*

WOMEN in Chinese society; edited by Margery Wolf and Roxane Witke. Stanford, 1975. pp. 315. *(American Council of Learned Societies and Social Science Research Council. Joint Committee on Contemporary China. Subcommittee on Research on Chinese Society. Studies in Chinese Society) Papers of a conference held in San Francisco in 1973.*

DAVIN (DELIA) Woman-work: women and the party in revolutionary China. Oxford, 1976. pp. 244. *bibliog.*

— — **Bibliography.**

COMMONWEALTH BUREAU OF AGRICULTURAL ECONOMICS. Women in Chinese society; compiled by Diana Martin. [Farnham Royal, 1974]. pp. 22. *(Annotated Bibliographies. No. 28)*

— **Denmark.**

RAPPORT om betydningen for ligestillingen i Danmark mellem maend og kvinder af en dansk indtraeden i de Europaeiske Faellesskaber; [report of a working group]. [Copenhagen, 1971]. pp. 22.

— **Europe, Eastern.**

FRANCE. Direction de la Documentation. La Documentation Française. Notes et Etudes Documentaires. No. 4,092. La condition féminine en Europe de l'Est; [par Mireille Lemaresquier et Thomas Schreiber]. Paris, 1974. pp. 28. *bibliog.*

— **France.**

UNION DES FEMMES FRANÇAISES. Congrès National, 1er, 1945. Les droits et les devoirs de la femme; ([by] Claudine Michaut); Les femmes françaises et l'Armée; ([by] Françoise Leclercq); Pour venger nos morts donnons la vie; ([by] Elisabeth de la Bourdonnaye). Paris, [1945]. pp. 46. *Not to be consulted without the permission of the Superintendent of Readers' Services.*

UNION DES FEMMES FRANÇAISES. Conférence Nationale, 1946. Issy-les-Moulineaux. Par notre travail et notre union assurons le bonheur et la sécurité de nos foyers dans une France grande et démocratique: rapport présenté par Yvonne Dumont à la conférence, etc. Paris, 1946. pp. 32.

FRANCE. Comité du Travail Féminin. 1973. Le rôle des femmes dans l'économie: synthèse du rapport de la France à l'O.C.D.E. Paris, 1973. fo. 31.

FRANCE. Comité du Travail Féminin. 1974. L'évolution de la situation des femmes dans la société française. Paris, 1974. fo. 28.

FRANCE. Comité du Travail Féminin. 1975. The social evolution of the status of women in France: a report [prepared for a conference organized by the] (Conseil Franco- Britannique) [on] (the status of women) [held at] (Saint-Germain-en-Laye, 11-13 April, 1975). [Paris], 1975. fo. 26.

FRANCE. French Embassy, London. Service de Presse et d'Information. 1975. Women in France. London, 1975. pp. 12. *bibliog. (France: facts, figures. A/107/3/75)*

— **Germany.**

ZETKIN (CLARA) Zu den Anfängen der proletarischen Frauenbewegung in Deutschland. Berlin, 1956. pp. 31. *bibliog. (Institut für Marxismus-Leninismus (Berlin). Beiträge zur Geschichte und Theorie der Arbeiterbewegung. Heft 4) Originally published in the Neue-Welt-Kalender für 1906.*

WERKKREIS LITERATUR DER ARBEITSWELT. Liebe Kollegin: Texte zur Emanzipation der Frau in der Bundesrepublik; herausgegeben von Britta Noeske [and others]. Frankfurt am Main, 1973 repr. 1975. pp. 170. *bibliog.*

DOKUMENTE der revolutionären deutschen Arbeiterbewegung zur Frauenfrage, 1848-1974: Auswahl; ([selected by] Hans- Jürgen Arendt [and others]). Leipzig, 1975. pp. 312.

KLUCSARITS (RICHARD) and KUERBISCH (FRIEDRICH G.) eds. Arbeiterinnen kämpfen um ihr Recht: autobiographische Texte. ..in Deutschland, Österreich und der Schweiz des 19. und 20. Jahrhunderts. Wuppertal, [1975]. pp. 390. *bibliog.*

STEPHENSON (JILL) Women in Nazi society. London, 1975. pp. 223. *bibliog.*

EVANS (RICHARD J.) The feminist movement in Germany, 1894-1933. London, [1976]. pp. 310. *bibliog.*

STERN (CAROLA) ed. Was haben die Parteien für die Frauen getan?; mit Beiträgen von Gerda Hollunder [and others]. Reinbek bei Hamburg, 1976. pp. 122. *bibliog.*

— — **Bibliography.**

GERMANY (BUNDESREPUBLIK). Deutscher Bundestag. Wissenschaftliche Dienste. 1974. Die Situation der Frau in Deutschland: Auswahlbibliographie; Nachtrag zur 3. erweiterten Auflage; [compiled by Hildegard Geissler]. Bonn, 1974. pp. 35. *(Bibliographien. 39)*

— **Germany, Eastern.**

DOKUMENTE der revolutionären deutschen Arbeiterbewegung zur Frauenfrage, 1848-1974: Auswahl; ([selected by] Hans- Jürgen Arendt [and others]). Leipzig, 1975. pp. 312.

— **India.**

ROY (MANISHA) Bengali women. Chicago, 1975. pp. 205. *bibliog.*

— **Israel.**

TIGER (LIONEL SAMUEL) and SHEPHER (JOSEPH) Women in the kibbutz. New York, [1975]. pp. 334. *bibliog.*

— **Poland.**

DZIĘCIELSKA-MACHNIKOWSKA (STEFANIA) ed. Kobieta w rozwijającym się społeczeństwie socjalistycznym. Łódź, 1975. pp. 182.

— **Russia.**

PORTER (CATHY) Fathers and daughters: Russian women in revolution. London, 1976. pp. 309. *bibliog.*

SACKS (MICHAEL PAUL) Women's work in Soviet Russia: continuity in the midst of change. New York, [1976]. pp. 221. *bibliog.*

— — **Lithuania — Statistics.**

LITHUANIA. Tsentral'noe Statisticheskoe Upravlenie. 1975. Zhenshchiny Litovskoi SSR: kratkii statisticheskii sbornik. Vil'nius, 1975. pp. 113.

— **Somali Republic.**

SOMALI REPUBLIC. Ministry of Information and National Guidance. 1974. The role of our socialist women: an active role in nation- building. Mogadishu, 1974. pp. 45.

— **Switzerland.**

KLUCSARITS (RICHARD) and KUERBISCH (FRIEDRICH G.) eds. Arbeiterinnen kämpfen um ihr Recht: autobiographische Texte. ..in Deutschland, Österreich und der Schweiz des 19. und 20. Jahrhunderts. Wuppertal, [1975]. pp. 390. *bibliog.*

— **Underdeveloped areas.**

See UNDERDEVELOPED AREAS — Women.

— **United Kingdom.**

COMMUNIST PARTY OF BRITAIN (MARXIST-LENINIST). Women in class struggle. [London, 1973?]. pp. 14.

BRANCA (PATRICIA) Silent sisterhood: middle class women in the Victorian home. London, [1975]. pp. 170. *bibliog.*

CHAMBERLAIN (MARY) Fenwomen: a portrait of women in an English village. London, 1975. pp. 186.

CRISHNA (SEETHA) Girls of Asian origin in Britain. London, [1975]. pp. 45.

JESSEL (PENELOPE) The ascent of women. London, [1975]. pp. 11. *(Liberal Party. Strategy 2,000. 1st Series. No. 7)*

— **United States.**

WOMEN and public policy: a humanistic perspective: [papers of a symposium held at the University of Iowa in 1973]; Mildred H. Lavin and Clara H. Oleson editors. Iowa City, 1974. pp. 147. *bibliogs.*

DECKARD (BARBARA SINCLAIR) The women's movement: political, socioeconomic, and psychological issues. New York, [1975]. pp. 450. *bibliog.*

FREEMAN (JO) The politics of women's liberation: a case study of an emerging social movement and its relation to the policy process. New York, [1975]. pp. 268. *bibliog.*

WOMEN in the professions; edited by Laurily Keir Epstein. Farnborough, Hants, [1975]. pp. 142. *Papers from a conference held at Washington University, St. Louis, Apr. 1975; sponsored by Monticello College Foundation and Washington University.*

BROWNLEE (W. ELLIOT) and BROWNLEE (MARY M.) Women in the American economy: a documentary history, 1675 to 1929. New Haven, 1976. pp. 350.

WOMEN, MOHAMMEDAN.

MERNISSI (FATIMA) Beyond the veil: male-female dynamics in a modern Muslim society. New York, [1975]. pp. 132. *bibliog.*

WOMEN AND SOCIALISM.

COMMUNIST PARTY OF BRITAIN (MARXIST-LENINIST). Women in class struggle. [London, 1973?]. pp. 14.

INSTITUT FÜR MARXISTISCHE STUDIEN UND FORSCHUNGEN. Arbeiterbewegung und Frauenemanzipation, 1889 bis 1933. Frankfurt/Main, 1973. pp. 209. *(Neudrucke zur Sozialistischen Theorie und Gewerkschaftspraxis. Band 3)*

WOMEN AND SOCIALISM.(Cont.)

BOELKE (GUNDULA) Die Wandlung der Frauenemanzipationsbewegung von Marx bis zur Rätebewegung. Hamburg, 1975. pp. 78.

DOKUMENTE der revolutionären deutschen Arbeiterbewegung zur Frauenfrage, 1848-1974: Auswahl; ([selected by] Hans- Jürgen Arendt [and others]). Leipzig, 1975. pp. 312.

DZIĘCIELSKA-MACHNIKOWSKA (STEFANIA) ed. Kobieta w rozwijającym się społeczeństwie socjalistycznym. Łódź, 1975. pp. 182.

KLUCSARITS (RICHARD) and KUERBISCH (FRIEDRICH G.) eds. Arbeiterinnen kämpfen um ihr Recht: autobiographische Texte. ..in Deutschland, Österreich und der Schweiz des 19. und 20. Jahrhunderts. Wuppertal, [1975]. pp. 390. *bibliog.*

ALLENDORF (MARLIS) Women in socialist society; English version by Ruth Michaelis- Jena and Patrick Murray. Leipzig, [1976]. pp. 219. *bibliog.*

WOMEN ENGINEERS

— France.

PESLOÜAN (GENEVIEVE DE) Qui sont les femmes ingénieurs en France?. Paris, [1974]. pp. 183. *bibliog.* *(Rouen. Université. Publications. 25)*

WOMEN IN BUSINESS.

BARTOL (KATHRYN M.) Male and female leaders in small work groups: an empirical study of satisfaction, performance and perceptions of leader behavior. East Lansing, 1973. pp. 154. *bibliog.* *(Michigan State University. MSU Business Studies)*

— Canada.

FORBES (ELIZABETH LAMONT) With enthusiasm and faith: history of the Canadian Federation of Business and Professional Women's Clubs...1930-1972. [Ottawa], 1974. pp. 170.

WOMEN IN POLITICS

— Germany.

HELLWIG (RENATE) Frauen verändern die Politik: eine gesellschaftspolitische Streitschrift. Stuttgart, [1975]. pp. 113.

BERGER (LIESELOTTE) and others. Frauen ins Parlament?: von den Schwierigkeiten, gleichberechtigt zu sein. Reinbek bei Hamburg, 1976. pp. 91.

GERMANY (BUNDESREPUBLIK). Deutscher Bundestag. Wissenschaftliche Dienste. 1976. Parlamentarierinnen in deutschen Parlamenten, 1919-1976; [edited by Edith Dalades]. Bonn, 1976. pp. 274. *(Materialien. 42)*

WOMEN IN PUBLIC LIFE.

FRANCE. Comité du Travail Féminin. 1974. Les femmes aux postes de direction de la fonction publique: rapport...; avec la collaboration de Geneviève M. Bécane- Pascaud. Paris, 1974. fo. 19.

WOMEN IN THE CIVIL SERVICE.

KRANZ (HARRY) The participatory bureaucracy: women and minorities in a more representative public service. Lexington, Mass., [1976]. pp. 244.

WOMEN IN TRADE UNIONS

— France.

COLIN (MADELEINE) Ce n'est pas d'aujourd'hui: femmes, syndicats, luttes de classe. Paris, [1975]. pp. 247.

— Germany.

STIEGLER (BARBARA) Die Mitbestimmung der Arbeiterin: Frauen zwischen traditioneller Familienbindung und gewerkschaftlichem Engagement im Betrieb; ein Beitrag zur Psychologie der Arbeiterin. Bonn-Bad Godesberg, [1976]. pp. 227, 10 . *bibliog.* *(Friedrich-Ebert-Stiftung. Forschungsinstitut. Schriftenreihe. Band 123)*

— United Kingdom.

DANGER! : women at work; report of a conference organised by the National Council for Civil Liberties [London]...1974; edited by Patricia Hewitt. London, [1974]. pp. 54. *bibliog.*

WOMEN JOURNALISTS

— United States.

GELFMAN (JUDITH S.) Women in television news. New York, 1976. pp. 186. *bibliog.*

WOMEN TEACHERS.

WOMEN in academia: evolving policies toward equal opportunities; edited by Elga Wasserman [and others]. New York, 1975. pp. 169. *bibliog.* Based on a symposium held at the 138th annual meeting of the American Association for the Advancement of Science in Philadelphia on December 30, 1971.

WOMEN'S LIBERATION MOVEMENT.

See FEMINISM.

WOMEN'S RIGHTS.

SCHIRMACHER (KAETHE) The modern woman's rights movement: a historical survey; translated from the second German edition by Carl Conrad Eckhardt. New York, 1912; Westport, Conn., 1976. pp. 280.

FROGER-DOUDEMENT (RAOUL) ed. Que veulent donc ces féministes?: opinions et arguments émis depuis cinq cents ans par les "précurseuses" et militantes notoires. Paris, 1926. pp. 74.

INSTITUT FÜR MARXISTISCHE STUDIEN UND FORSCHUNGEN. Arbeiterbewegung und Frauenemanzipation, 1889 bis 1933. Frankfurt/Main, 1973. pp. 209. *(Neudrucke zur Sozialistischen Theorie und Gewerkschaftspraxis. Band 3)*

BOELKE (GUNDULA) Die Wandlung der Frauenemanzipationsbewegung von Marx bis zur Rätebewegung. Hamburg, 1975. pp. 78.

KLUCSARITS (RICHARD) and KUERBISCH (FRIEDRICH G.) eds. Arbeiterinnen kämpfen um ihr Recht: autobiographische Texte. ..in Deutschland, Österreich und der Schweiz des 19. und 20. Jahrhunderts. Wuppertal, [1975]. pp. 390. *bibliog.*

LARSEN (CHERYL BETH) The United Nations Convention on the Political Rights of Women, 1952: a political analysis of its origin, negotiation and effects. 1975. fo. 229. *bibliog.* Typescript. Ph.D. (London) thesis: unpublished. This thesis is the property of London University and may not be removed from the Library.

WOMEN'S LIBERATION CAMPAIGN FOR LEGAL AND FINANCIAL INDEPENDENCE. The demand for independence. London, 1975. pp. 8.

YATES (GAYLE GRAHAM) What women want: the ideas of the movement. Cambridge, Mass., 1975. pp. 230. *bibliog.*

MITCHELL (JULIET) and OAKLEY (ANN) eds. The rights and wrongs of women. Harmondsworth, 1976. pp. 438.

— America.

SYMPOSIUM ON EQUALITY OF OPPORTUNITY IN EMPLOYMENT IN THE AMERICAN REGION, PANAMA, 1973. Equality of opportunity in employment in the American region: problems and policies; report and documents of a regional symposium [held at] Panama, 1-12 October 1973. Geneva, International Labour Office, 1974. pp. 133.

— Germany.

DOKUMENTE der revolutionären deutschen Arbeiterbewegung zur Frauenfrage, 1848-1974: Auswahl; ([selected by] Hans- Jürgen Arendt [and others]). Leipzig, 1975. pp. 312.

STERN (CAROLA) ed. Was haben die Parteien für die Frauen getan?; mit Beiträgen von Gerda Hollunder [and others]. Reinbek bei Hamburg, 1976. pp. 122. *bibliog.*

— Norway.

JUSS og juks: en arbeidsbok i likestilling; ([by] Tove Stang Dahl [and others]). Oslo, [1975]. pp. 82.

— Switzerland.

WOODTLI (SUSANNA) Gleichberechtigung: der Kampf um die politischen Rechte der Frau in der Schweiz. Frauenfeld, [1975]. pp. 271. *bibliog.*

— United Kingdom.

HEWITT (PATRICIA) Rights for women: a guide to the Sex Discrimination Act, the Equal Pay Act, paid maternity leave, pension schemes and unfair dismissal. London, [1975]. pp. 98.

JESSEL (PENELOPE) The ascent of women. London, [1975]. pp. 11. *(Liberal Party. Strategy 2,000. 1st Series. No. 7)*

— United States.

FLEXNER (ELEANOR) Century of struggle: the woman's rights movement in the United States. rev. ed. Cambridge, Mass., 1975. pp. 405.

CHAPMAN (JANE ROBERTS) ed. Economic independence for women: the Foundation for Equal Rights. Beverly Hills, [1976]. pp. 281. *bibliogs.* *(Center for Women Policy Studies. Sage Yearbooks in Women's Policy Studies. vol.1)*

WOOD AS FUEL.

EARL (D.E.) Forest energy and economic development. Oxford, 1975. pp. 128. *bibliog.*

WOOD-PULP INDUSTRY.

— Canada — New Brunswick.

NEW BRUNSWICK. 1972. Provincial position on matters relating to the report of the Industrial Inquiry Commission on the Pulp and Paper Industry in New Brunswick. [Fredericton, 1972]. fo.,11.

WOOD—USING INDUSTRIES

— Australia.

CONACHER (A.J.) Environment-industry conflict: the Manjimup woodchip industry proposal, southwestern Australia. Nedlands, 1975. pp. 43. *(Western Australia, University of. Department of Geography. Geowest. No. 4)*

— France.

FRANCE. Comité des Industries du Bois et de l'Ameublement. 1971. Préparation du VIe Plan...: rapport. [Paris], 1971. pp. 103.

— Russia.

NOVIKOV (L.I.) and KHARIN (IURII ANDREEVICH) Zavod v puti. Volgograd, 1970. pp. 116.

NEKOTORYE voprosy sotsialisticheskogo stroitel'stva i formirovaniia rabochego klassa SSSR v predvoennye gody. Murmansk, 1971. pp. 250. *(Leningrad. Leningradskii Gosudarstvennyi Pedagogicheskii Institut. Uchenye Zapiski. t.329)*

WOODWORKERS

— United Kingdom.

COHEN (MAX) 1911- . What nobody told the foreman. [London?], 1953. pp. 218. *The autobiography of a woodworker.*

WOOL

— Grading.

DOUGLAS (STEPHEN ARNOLD S.) and McINTYRE (GEORGE ARCHIBALD) A comparison of subjective and objective estimation of yield and fineness of greasy wool. [Canberra, 1970]. pp. 67. *(Australia. Bureau of Agricultural Economics. Wool Economic Research Reports. No. 20)*

AUSTRALIA. Bureau of Agricultural Economics. 1971. The economics of wool classing; (prepared by R.B. Whan). Canberra, 1971. pp. 68. *(Wool Economic Research Reports. No. 21)*

— Testing.

DOUGLAS (STEPHEN ARNOLD S.) and McINTYRE (GEORGE ARCHIBALD) A comparison of subjective and objective estimation of yield and fineness of greasy wool. [Canberra, 1970]. pp. 67. *(Australia. Bureau of Agricultural Economics. Wool Economic Research Reports. No. 20)*

WOOL TRADE AND INDUSTRY

— Australia.

AUSTRALIA. Bureau of Agricultural Economics. 1971. A study of supply relationships in the Australian sheep and wool industry; (by J.M. Malecky). Canberra, 1971. pp. 98. *(Wool Economic Research Reports. No. 19)*

AUSTRALIAN WOOL CORPORATION. The marketing of Australian wool; a report. [Canberra], 1973. pp. 121.

— — Mathematical models.

OSBORN (DENISE RAE) Time series analysis and dynamic specification in econometric models, with an application to the Australian wool market. 1975. fo. 251. bibliog. Typescript. Ph.D. (London) thesis: unpublished. *This thesis is the property of London University and may not be removed from the Library.*

— India.

INDIA. Labour Bureau. 1975. Report on survey of labour conditions in woollen factories in India, 1971. [Delhi, 1975]. pp. 96.

— United Kingdom.

REASONS for a limited exportation of wooll. [Oxford], 1677. pp. 24. *Wing 483.*

CARTER (WILLIAM) Clothier. The usurpations of France upon the trade of the woollen manufacture of England briefly hinted at; being the effects of thirty years observations...; or, A caution to England to improve a season now put into her hand, to secure herself. London, printed for R. Baldwin, 1695. pp. 30. *p.1 bled. Wing 678.*

— United States.

AUSTRALIA. Bureau of Agricultural Economics. 1970. End uses of fibres in the U.S.A.; (by J.L. Sault). Canberra, 1970. pp. 96. *(Wool Economic Research Reports. No. 18)*

WOOLLEN AND WORSTED MANUFACTURE

— Japan.

AUSTRALIA. Bureau of Agricultural Economics. 1969. The structure of the Japanese wool textile industry; (by Kyoko Sheridan). Canberra, 1969. pp. 58. *(Wool Economic Research Reports. No. 16)*

— United Kingdom.

[STEELE (Sir RICHARD)] The spinster: in defence of the woollen manufactures, to be continued occasionally. Numb.1. London, J. Roberts, 1719. pp. 16.

ECONOMIC DEVELOPMENT COMMITTEE FOR THE WOOL TEXTILE INDUSTRY. Finance and profitability in the wool textile industry. a., 1970-71/1972-73- London.

JENKINS (D.T.) The West Riding wool textile industry 1770-1835: a study of fixed capital formation. Edington, 1975. pp. 336. *bibliog. (Pasold Research Fund. Pasold Occasional Papers. vol. 4)*

WORK.

EISENSTAEDTER (JULIUS) Im Schweisse deines Angesichtes: eine Einführung in die gesellschaftliche Organisation der Arbeit. Jena, 1927. pp. 96. *(Urania: kulturpolitische Monatshefte über Natur und Gesellschaft. Jahrgang 1926/27. Buchbeigaben. 2)*

DENMARK. Arbejdsmiljøgruppen. Rapporter. København, 1973 in progress.

FAROUK (A.) and ALI (MUHAMMAD) The hardworking poor: a survey on how people use their time in Bangladesh. Dacca, 1975. 1 vol. (various pagings).

JOB demands and worker health: main effects and occupational differences; [by] Robert D. Caplan [and others]. [Washington, D.C.,] 1975. pp. 342. *bibliog. (United States. National Institute for Occupational Safety and Health. Research Reports)*

— Psychological aspects.

SHAMIR (BOAS) A study of working environments and attitudes to work of employees in a number of British hotels. 1975. fo.304. *bibliog.* Typescript. Ph.D. (London) thesis: unpublished. *This thesis is the property of London University and may not be removed from the Library.*

WARR (PETER B.) and WALL (TOBY) Work and well-being. Harmondsworth, 1975. pp. 220. *bibliog.*

GOLDMANN (ROBERT B.) A work experiment: six Americans in a Swedish plant. New York, [1976]. pp. 48.

MEAKIN (DAVID) Man and work: literature and culture in industrial society. London, 1976. pp. 215. *bibliog.*

WORK DESIGN.

KLEIN (LISL) New forms of work organisation. Cambridge, 1976. pp. 106. *bibliog.*

WORK ENVIRONMENT.

JOBS and the environment; contributions to a conference [held in 1975 by the Southeast London branches of the Socialist Environment and Resources Association and the Institute for Workers' Control] by Pat Kinnersly [and] Mike Cooley; edited by Jeremy Dale and Tony Emerson. Leeds, [1976]. pp. 15.

WORK RELIEF

— Germany.

MEYER (PAUL) Syndikus. Die Notstandsarbeiten und ihre Probleme: ein Beitrag zur Frage der Bekämpfung der Arbeitslosigkeit. Jena, 1914. pp. 112. *bibliog. (Jena. Universität. Staatswissenschaftliches Seminar. Abhandlungen. 13. Band, 4.Heft)*

— United States.

ABOUD (GRACE) Hiring and training the disadvantaged for public employment. Ithaca, N.Y., 1973. pp. 45. *bibliog. (Cornell University. New York State School of Industrial and Labor Relations. Key Issue Series. No. 11)*

WORKMEN'S COMPENSATION

— Canada — Newfoundland and Labrador.

NEWFOUNDLAND. Royal Commission on Matters pertaining to the Relationships of the Workmen's Compensation Board with the Employees, 1972. Report; [Hugh O'Neill, commissioner]. [St. John's, 1973]. pp. 32.

— United Kingdom.

UNITED KINGDOM. Statutes, etc. 1906. 6 Edw. 7. ch. 58. Workmen's Compensation Act, 1906. The law of workmen's compensation, with notes. London, [1907]. pp. 24.

— United States.

MARTIN (ROLLAND A.) Occupational disability: causes, prediction, prevention. Springfield, Ill., [1975]. pp. 206. *bibliog.*

WORKS COUNCILS.

NIKOLIĆ (MILOS) Razvoj ideje radničkog samoupravljanja. Subotica, 1973. pp. 173.

SUPEK (RUDI) Participacija, radnička kontrola i samoupravljanje: prilog povijesnom kontinuitetu jedne ideje. Zagreb, 1974. pp. 204. *bibliog.*

— Algeria.

KOULYTCHIZKY (SERGE) L'autogestion, l'homme et l'état: l'expérience algérienne. Paris, [1974]. pp. 482. *bibliog. (Paris. Ecole Pratique des Hautes Etudes. Section des Sciences Economiques et Sociales. Recherches Coopératives. 6)*

MAHSAS (AHMED) L'autogestion en Algérie: données politiques de ses premières étapes et de son application. Paris, [1975]. pp. 297.

— Russia.

DROBIZHEV (VLADIMIR ZINOV'EVICH) ed. Rabochii kontrol' i natsionalizatsiia promyshlennosti Novgorodskoi gubernii v 1917-1921 gg.: sbornik dokumentov i materialov. Leningrad, 1974. pp. 136.

— South Africa.

NATTRASS (JILL) and DUNCAN (IAN G.) A study of employers' attitudes towards African worker representation. Durban, 1975. pp. 36. *(Natal University. Department of Economics. Black/White Income Gap Project. Interim Research Project. No.1)*

— Yugoslavia.

MARKOVIĆ (DRAGAN) and others. Factories to their workers: chronicle about workers' management in Yugoslavia;...foreword: Svetozar Vukmanović-Tempo; (translated by Radmila Pavlović). Belgrade, 1965. pp. 291. *bibliog.*

VELJIĆ (ANDJELKO) Društveno samoupravljanje u Jugoslaviji: novi oblik demokratije. Sarajevo, 1973. pp. 246. *bibliog.*

DAŠIĆ (DAVID) Sistem i politika cena u uslovima socijalističkog samoupravljanja. Beograd, 1974. pp. 209. *bibliog.*

BREKIĆ (JOVO) ed. Samoupravna koncepcija razvitka kadrova: kadrologijski apekti usklađivanja obrazovanja, zapošljavanja i profesionalnog razvoja kadrova, etc. Zagreb, 1975. pp. 262. *bibliog. With English summary.*

ĆALIĆ (DUŠAN) Aktualni problemi razvoja samoupravnog društva u SFRJ. Zagreb, [1975?]. pp. 174.

GORUPIĆ (DRAGO) Osnovna i složena organizacija udruženog rada u privredi. Zagreb, 1975. pp. iii,136.

PETKOVSKI (BORO) Radnička klasa i samoupravljanje: prilog izučavanju razvoja radničke klase i procesa samoupravnog odlučivanja. Beograd, 1975. pp. 228.

DENITCH (BOGDAN DENIS) The legitimation of a revolution: the Yugoslav case. New Haven, 1976. pp. 254. *bibliog.*

— — Congresses.

KONGRES SAMOUPRAVLJAČA JUGOSLAVIJE, 2-i, 1971. Drugi kongres samoupravljača Jugoslavije. Beograd, 1971. 2 vols. (in 1).

WORLD HEALTH ORGANIZATION

— Officials and employees.

BEIGBEDER (YVES) La représentation du personnel à l'Organisation Mondiale de la Santé, et dans les principales institutions spécialisées des Nations Unies ayant leur siège en Europe. Paris, 1975. pp. 289. *bibliog.*

WORLD POLITICS.

UNITED STATES. Department of State. 1918-19. The Inquiry handbooks. Wilmington, 1974. 20 vols. *bibliogs. Reprint of documents originally published in Washington, 1918-19.*

WORLD POLITICS.(Cont.)

BRANDT (WILLY) Peace: writings and speeches of the Nobel Peace Prize winner, 1971. Bonn-Bad Godesberg, 1971. pp. 165.

FRELEK (RYSZARD) Historia zimnej wojny. Warszawa, 1971. pp. 178. *bibliog.*

MODELSKI (JERZY ALEKSANDER) ed. Multinational corporations and world order. Beverly Hills, [1973]. pp. 160. *bibliogs.*

BOELL (HEINRICH) Neue politische und literarische Schriften [1967-1972]. Köln, 1973. pp. 285. *bibliog.*

BABICI (ION) Boevaia antifashistskaia solidarnost', 1933-1939 gg.; (perevod s rumynskogo Natalii i Konstantina Unguru). Bukharest, 1974. pp. 244. *(Academia de Ştiinţe Sociale şi Politice a Republicii Socialiste România. Bibliotheca Historica Romaniae. Studies. 49)*

HERMANSSON (CARL HENRIK) För socialismen: (artiklar och tal, 1964-74). Stockholm, 1974. pp. 279.

KOTHARI (RAJNI) Footsteps into the future: diagnosis of the present world and a design for an alternative. Amsterdam, [1974]. pp. 173. *(Institute for World Order. Preferred Worlds for the 1990's)*

LEE (DWIGHT ERWIN) Europe's crucial years: the diplomatic background of World War I, 1902-1914. Hanover, N.H., 1974. pp. 482. *bibliog.*

SIPOLS (VILNIS IANOVICH) Sovetskii Soiuz v bor'be za mir i bezopasnost', 1933-1939. Moskva, 1974. pp. 428.

STOESSINGER (JOHN GEORGE) Why nations go to war. London, [1974]. pp. 230.

HUREWITZ (JACOB COLEMAN) ed. The Middle East and North Africa in world politics: a documentary record. 2nd ed. New Haven, 1975 in progress.

BARNSBY (GEORGE) 1945: year of victory. London, 1975. pp. 37. *bibliog. (Communist Party of Great Britain. History Group. Our History. No. 62)*

BRANDT (WILLY) and others. Briefe und Gespräche, 1972 bis 1975. Frankfurt, [1975]. pp. 133.

CLINE (RAY S.) World power assessment: a calculus of strategic drift. Boulder, Col., [1975]. pp. 173.

CUNY CONFERENCE ON HISTORY AND POLITICS, 1ST, NEW YORK, 1974. Detente in historical perspective;...[proceedings of the] conference...; [edited by] George Schwab...[and] Henry Friedlander, etc. New York, [1975]. pp. 171.

GRIFFITH (WILLIAM E.) ed. The world and the great-power triangles. Cambridge, Mass., [1975]. pp. 480. *(Massachusetts Institute of Technology. Center for International Studies. Studies in Communism, Revisionism, and Revolution. 21)*

HILSMAN (ROGER) The crouching future: international politics and U.S. foreign policy; a forecast. Garden City, N.Y. 1975. pp. 666.

IMLAY (ROBERT) The fragile peace: a short history of the cold war and its aftermath. London, [1975]. pp. 176.

L'IPOTESI del tripolarismo: Stati Uniti, URSS e Cina; a cura di Franco Soglian. Bari, [1975]. pp. 428. *(Milan. Istituto per gli Studi di Politica Internazionale. Saggi di Storia Contemporanea. 1)*

KINTNER (WILLIAM ROSCOE) and SICHERMAN (HARVEY) Technology and international politics: the crisis of wishing. Lexington, [1975]. pp. 177. *(Foreign Policy Research Institute. Book Series)*

LIEBKNECHT (WILHELM PHILIPP MARTIN CHRISTIAN LUDWIG) Leitartikel und Beiträge in der Osnabrücker Zeitung, 1864- 1866; herausgegeben von Georg Eckert. Hildesheim, 1975. pp. 794. *(Historische Kommission für Niedersachsen und Bremen. Veröffentlichungen. 35)*

A NEW world order?; [by] Cyril E. Black [and others]; [papers presented at the first of a series of Princeton University conferences held in 1974]. Princeton, 1975. pp. 87. *(Princeton University. Center of International Studies. World Order Studies Program. Occasional Papers. No. 1)*

OCHERKI mezhdunarodnykh otnoshenii v Iuzhnoi, Iugo-Vostochnoi Azii i na Dal'nem Vostoke posle vtoroi mirovoi voiny, 1945- 1955. Moskva, 1975. pp. 400.

THORBECKE (WILLIAM JOHAN RUDOLF) Mankind at the crossroads: an enquiry into the causes of the global predicaments and the means to overcome them. Leyden, 1975. pp. 217.

ZHURKIN (VITALII VLADIMIROVICH) SSHA i mezhdunarodno-politicheskie krizisy. Moskva, 1975. pp. 326. *bibliog.*

BRANDT (WILLY) Begegnungen und Einsichten: die Jahre 1960-1975. Hamburg, 1976. pp. 655.

CHOUCRI (NAZLI) and FERRARO (VINCENT) International politics of energy interdependence: the case of petroleum. Lexington, Mass., [1976]. pp. 250. *bibliog.*

DÉTENTE: (edited versions of interviews originally broadcast, in 1973-75, over Radio Free Europe); edited by G.R. Urban. London, 1976. pp. 368.

EVANS (DOUGLAS) and BODY (RICHARD) eds. Freedom and stability in the world economy. London, 1976. pp. 117.

GENRI (ERNST) Novye zametki po istorii sovremennosti. Moskva, 1976. pp. 435.

INTERNATIONAL organisations in world politics: yearbook, 1975; edited by Avi Shlaim. London, 1976. pp. 226.

MANSBACH (RICHARD W.) and others. The web of world politics: nonstate actors in the global system. Englewood Cliffs, [1976]. pp. 326.

MARKS (SALLY JEAN) The illusion of peace: international relations in Europe, 1918- 1933. London, [1976]. pp. 184. *bibliog.*

MIKDASHI (ZUHAYR) The international politics of natural resources. Ithaca, 1976. pp. 214.

PADELFORD (NORMAN JUDSON) and others. The dynamics of international politics. 3rd ed. New York, [1976]. pp. 603. *bibliogs.*

UNION OF INTERNATIONAL ASSOCIATIONS and MANKIND 2000. Year-book of world problems and human potential: a framework for representation of perceptions of interlinked networks of world problems, etc. Brussels, 1976. pp. 1136. *bibliogs.*

WORLD politics: an introduction; [edited by] James Rosenau [and others]. New York, [1976]. pp. 754.

— **Bibliography.**

SAINSBURY (KEITH) International history 1939-1970: a select bibliography. London, 1973. pp. 55. *(Historical Association. Helps for Students of History. No. 86)*

— **Congresses.**

VOSHCHENKOV (KONSTANTIN PAVLOVICH) SSSR v bor'be za mir: mezhdunarodnye konferentsii, 1944-1974 gg. ; obshchaia redaktsiia i predislovie...B.G. Trukhanovskogo. Moskva, 1975. pp. 255.

— **Periodicals.**

WINOCK (MICHEL) Histoire politique de la revue Esprit, 1930-1950. Paris, [1975]. pp. 447. *bibliog.*

— **Sources.**

CONFERENCE ON THE NATIONAL ARCHIVES AND FOREIGN RELATIONS RESEARCH, WASHINGTON, 1969. The National Archives and foreign relations research: (papers and proceedings of the Conference...sponsored by the National Archives and Records Service); edited by Milton O. Gustafson. Athens, Ohio, [1974]. pp. 292. *(United States. National Archives. National Archives Conferences. vol. 4)*

FERRELL (ROBERT H.) ed. America in a divided world, 1945-1972; [documents]. New York, [1975]. pp. 353. *bibliog.*

— **Study and teaching.**

GUNN (ANGUS M.) Man on the earth: teacher resource book for: population pressure in Indonesia: problems of industrialization in Eurasia: power blocs in Eurasia. Toronto, 1974. pp. 51.

WORLD WAR, 1939-1945.

BARNSBY (GEORGE) 1945: year of victory. London, 1975. pp. 37. *bibliog. (Communist Party of Great Britain. History Group. Our History. No. 62)*

MICHEL (HENRI) The Second World War; translated by Douglas Parmée. London, 1975. pp. 947. *bibliog.*

— **Aerial operations.**

HARRISSON (TOM) Living through the blitz. London, 1976. pp. 372. *bibliog.*

— **Aerial operations, German.**

SCHAETZ (LUDWIG) Schüler-Soldaten: die Geschichte der Luftwaffenhelfer im zweiten Weltkrieg. 2nd ed. Darmstadt, 1974. pp. 160. *bibliog.*

— **Blockades.**

ROCKBERGER (NICOLAUS) Göteborgstrafiken: svensk lejdtrafik under andra världskriget. Stockholm, 1973. pp. 332. *bibliog. With English summary.*

— **Campaigns — Africa, North.**

FUNK (ARTHUR LAYTON) The politics of Torch: the allied landings and the Algiers putsch, 1942. Lawrence, Kan., [1974]. pp. 322. *bibliog.*

— — **Caucasus.**

GRECHKO (ANDREI ANTONOVICH) Bitva za Kavkaz. 2nd ed. Moskva, 1973. pp. 494, (xxiii).

— — **Eastern.**

ANTONOV (VLADIMIR SEMENOVICH) Put' k Berlinu. Moskva, 1975. pp. 374.

— — **Greece.**

OLSHAUSEN (KLAUS) Zwischenspiel auf dem Balkan: die deutsche Politik gegenüber Jugoslawien und Griechenland von März bis Juli 1941. Stuttgart, 1973. pp. 375. *bibliog. (Militärgeschichtliches Forschungsamt. Beiträge zur Militär- und Kriegsgeschichte. Band 14) 7 maps in end pocket.*

CRUICKSHANK (CHARLES GREIG) Greece, 1940-1941. London, 1976. pp. 206. *bibliog.*

— — **Mediterranean.**

HENRICI (ECKHARD) Die deutsche Kriegführung und das Mittelmeer in den Jahren 1940 bis 1943. 1954. pp. 171. *bibliog. Ph.D.(Heidelberg) thesis: unpublished. Microfilm of typescript: 1 reel.*

— — **Poland.**

POLSKI SZTAB GŁOWNY W LONDYNIE. Komisja Historyczna. Polskie Siły Zbrojne w drugiej wojnie światowej. t.3. Armia Krajowa. Londyn, 1950. pp. 972.

ZAŁUSKI (ZBIGNIEW) Finał 1945: materiały do bilansu. 2nd ed. Warszawa, [1965]. pp. 155.

— — **Romania.**

ANTOSIAK (ALEKSEI VARFOLOMEEVICH) V boiakh za svobodu Rumynii. Moskva, 1974. pp. 288. *bibliog. With Romanian table of contents.*

— — **Russia.**

ANDERS (WŁADYSŁAW) Klęska Hitlera w Rosji, 1941-1945. 2nd ed. Londyn, 1972. pp. 205. *bibliog.*

REINHARDT (KLAUS) Die Wende vor Moskau: das Scheitern der Strategie Hitlers im Winter 1941/42. Stuttgart, 1972. pp. 355. *bibliog. (Militärgeschichtliches Forschungsamt. Beiträge zur Militär- und Kriegsgeschichte. Band 13) 7 maps in end pocket.*

WORLD WAR, 1939-1945.

ANFILOV (VIKTOR ALEKSANDROVICH) Proval "blitskriga". Moskva, 1974. pp. 616.

KOZLOV (NIKOLAI DMITRIEVICH) and ZAITSEV (ALEKSEI DMITRIEVICH) Srazhaiushchaiasia partiia. Moskva, 1975. pp. 271.

— — Syria.

MOCKLER (ANTHONY) Our enemies the French: being an account of the war fought between the French and the British, Syria 1941. London, 1976. pp. 252.

— — Yugoslavia.

OLSHAUSEN (KLAUS) Zwischenspiel auf dem Balkan: die deutsche Politik gegenüber Jugoslawien und Griechenland von März bis Juli 1941. Stuttgart, 1973. pp. 375. bibliog. (Militärgeschichtliches Forschungsamt. Beiträge zur Militär- und Kriegsgeschichte. Band 14) 7 maps in end pocket.

— Catholic Church.

KLEIN (CHARLES) Pie XII face aux Nazis. Paris, [1975]. pp. 250.

— Causes.

THOENE (KARIN) Entwicklungsstadien und Zweiter Weltkrieg: ein wirtschaftswissenschaftlicher Beitrag zur Frage der Kriegsursachen. Berlin, [1974]. pp. 106. bibliog.

OFFNER (ARNOLD A.) The origins of the Second World War: American foreign policy and world politics, 1917-1941. New York, 1975. pp. 268. bibliog.

SYWOTTEK (JUTTA) Mobilmachung für den totalen Krieg: die propagandistische Vorbereitung der deutschen Bevölkerung auf den Zweiten Weltkrieg. Opladen, [1976]. pp. 398. bibliog. (Hamburg. Hansische Universität. Studien zur Modernen Geschichte. Band 18)

— Chronology.

IZ khroniki istoricheskikh dnei, 1 maia 1944 - 6 marta 1945 gg.; (perevod s rumynskogo Ally Lazia). Bukharest, 1974. pp. 251. (Academia de Ştiinţe Sociale şi Politice a Republicii Socialiste România. Bibliotheca Historica Romaniae. Studies. 48)

— — Romania.

DIN cronica unor zile istorice. [Bucureşti, 1972?]. pp. 239.

— Civilian relief — United Kingdom.

U.K. [Cabinet Office]. History of the Second World War: United Kingdom Civil Series. Problems of social policy; by Richard M. Titmuss. rev. ed. London, 1976. pp. 632. Confidential version with full source references.

— Collaborationists — France.

AZEMA (JEAN PIERRE) La collaboration, 1940-1944. [Paris, 1975]. pp. 152. bibliog.

TUCKER (WILLIAM RAYBURN) The fascist ego: a political biography of Robert Brasillach. Berkeley, 1975. pp. 331. bibliog.

— Congresses.

VYSOTSKII (VIKTOR NIKOLAEVICH) Meropriiatie "Terminal", Potsdam, 1945. Moskva, 1975. pp. 206.

— Conscript labour — Germany.

ŁUCZAK (CZESŁAW) compiler. Poło'zenie polskich robotników przymusowych w Rzeszy, 1939- 1945: wybór źródeł, etc. Poznań, 1975. pp. cvi, 358. (Poznań. Instytut Zachodni. Documenta Occupationis. 9) Documents in the original German, with Polish, Russian, English and German introductions.

— Diplomatic history.

FUNK (ARTHUR LAYTON) The politics of Torch: the allied landings and the Algiers putsch, 1942. Lawrence, Kan., [1974]. pp. 322. bibliog.

BEREZHKOV (VALENTIN MIKHAILOVICH) Rozhdenie koalitsii. Moskva, 1975. pp. 248.

CUFF (ROBERT D.) and GRANATSTEIN (JACK LAWRENCE) Canadian-American relations in wartime: from the Great War to the cold war. Toronto, 1975. pp. 205.

FISCHER (ALEXANDER) Sowjetische Deutschlandpolitik im Zweiten Weltkrieg, 1941-1945. Stuttgart, 1975. pp. 252. bibliog. (Institut für Zeitgeschichte. Studien zur Zeitgeschichte)

HARRIMAN (WILLIAM AVERELL) and ABEL (ELIE) Special envoy to Churchill and Stalin, 1941-1946. New York, [1975]. pp. 595.

LUNDESTAD (GEIR) The American non-policy towards Eastern Europe, 1943-1947: universalism in an area not of essential interest to the United States. Tromsö, [1975]. pp. 654. bibliog.

RUHL (KLAUS JOERG) Spanien im Zweiten Weltkrieg: Franco, die Falange und das "Dritte Reich". Hamburg, 1975. pp. 414. bibliog. With English summary.

SHERWIN (MARTIN J.) A world destroyed: the atomic bomb and the grand alliance. New York, 1975. pp. 326. bibliog.

BARKER (ELISABETH) British policy in south-east Europe in the Second World War. London, 1976. pp. 320. bibliog.

— Economic aspects.

THOENE (KARIN) Entwicklungsstadien und Zweiter Weltkrieg: ein wirtschaftswissenschaftlicher Beitrag zur Frage der Kriegsursachen. Berlin, [1974]. pp. 106. bibliog.

— — Germany.

BAGEL-BOHLAN (ANJA E.) Hitlers industrielle Kriegsvorbereitung, 1936 bis 1939. Koblenz, [1975]. pp. 143. bibliog. (Arbeitskreis für Wehrforschung. Beiträge zur Wehrforschung. Band 24)

— — Russia.

POSPELOV (PETR NIKOLAEVICH) ed. Sovetskii tyl v Velikoi Otechestvennoi voine. Moskva, 1974. 2 vols. bibliog.

LIKHOMANOV (MIKHAIL IVANOVICH) Khoziaistvenno-organizatorskaia rabota partii v derevne v pervyi period Velikoi Otechestvennoi voiny, 1941-1942 gg. Leningrad, 1975. pp. 136.

— — Sweden.

ROCKBERGER (NICOLAUS) Göteborgstrafiken: svensk lejdtrafik under andra världskriget. Stockholm, 1973. pp. 332. bibliog. With English summary.

MÄNSSON (OLLE) Industriell beredskap: om ekonomisk försvarsplanering inför andra världskriget. Stockholm, 1976. pp. 269. bibliog. With English summary.

— — United Kingdom.

U.K.[Cabinet Office]. History of the Second World War: United Kingdom Civil Series. Agriculture; by Keith A.H.Murray. rev. ed. London, 1975. pp. 430. Confidential version with full source references.

U.K. [Cabinet Office]. History of the Second World War: United Kingdom Civil Series. British war economy; by W.K. Hancock and M.M. Gowing. rev. ed. London, 1975. pp. 634. Confidential version with full source references.

U.K. [Cabinet Office]. History of the Second World War: United Kingdom Civil Series. British war production; by M.M. Postan. rev. ed. London, 1975. pp. 553. Confidential version with full source references.

— Evacuation of civilians.

U.K. [Cabinet Office]. History of the Second World War: United Kingdom Civil Series. Problems of social policy; by Richard M. Titmuss. rev. ed. London, 1976. pp. 632. Confidential version with full source references.

— Finance — Sweden.

NYGREN (INGEMAR) Svensk kreditmarknad under freds- och beredskapstid, 1935-1945. Göteborg, 1974. pp. 303. bibliog. (Göteborgs Universitet. Ekonomisk-Historiska Institutionen. Meddelanden. 30)

— Jews.

DAWIDOWICZ (LUCY S.) The war against the Jews, 1933-1945. London, [1975]. pp. 460. bibliog.

SAKOWSKA (RUTA) Ludzie z dzielnicy zamkniętej: 'zydzi w Warszawie w okresie hitlerowskiej okupacji październik 1939 - marzec 1943. Warszawa, 1975. pp. 399. bibliog. With English and Russian tables of contents.

— Negroes.

WYNN (NEIL A.) The Afro-American and the second world war. London, 1976. pp. 183. bibliog.

— Peace.

ALLEN (LOUIS) The end of the war in Asia. London, 1976. pp. 306. bibliog.

MISGELD (KLAUS) Die "Internationale Gruppe demokratischer Sozialisten" in Stockholm, 1942-1945: zur sozialistischen Friedensdiskussion während des Zweiten Weltkrieges. Uppsala, 1976. pp. 212. bibliog. (Uppsala. Universitet. Historiska Institutionen. Studia Historica Upsaliensia. 79)

— Periodicals — Indexes.

HEINTZ (GEORG) compiler. Index des "Freien/Neuen Deutschland", Mexico, 1941-1946. [Worms, 1975]. pp. 110.

— Personal narratives, Polish.

BRZESKA (MARIA) Through a woman's eyes: life in Poland under the German occupation. London, [1944?]. pp. 92.

KOCHANOWICZ (TADEUSZ) Na wojennej emigracji: wspomnienia z lat 1942-1944. Warszawa, 1975. pp. 303.

— Pictorial works.

VELIKAIA Otechestvennaia voina, 1941-1945, v fotografiiakh i kinodokumentakh. Moskva, 1975 in progress.

— Propaganda.

KIRCHNER (KLAUS) Flugblattpropaganda im 2. Weltkrieg: Europa. München, [1972]. pp. 37. bibliog. With English summary.

CREMIEUX-BRILHAC (JEAN LOUIS) ed. Les voix de la liberté: ici Londres, 1940-1944;...; avant- propos de Jean Marin. [Paris], Documentation Française, 1975-76. 5 vols.

— Psychological aspects.

DICKS (HENRY VICTOR) The German deserter: a pyschological study. London, 1944. pp. 30. (U.K. War Office. Directorate of Army Psychiatry. Research Memoranda. No. 45/03/9)

DICKS (HENRY VICTOR) German political attitudes: an analysis and forecast of likely reactions confronting the Allies in occupied Germany. London, 1944. pp. 13. (U.K. War Office. Directorate of Army Psychiatry. Research Memoranda. No.45/03/11)

— Public opinion — Germany.

DICKS (HENRY VICTOR) German political attitudes: an analysis and forecast of likely reactions confronting the Allies in occupied Germany. London, 1944. pp. 13. (U.K. War Office. Directorate of Army Psychiatry. Research Memoranda. No.45/03/11)

— Refugees.

SKWARKO (KRYSTYNA) The invited...: the story of 733 Polish children who grew up in New Zealand. Wellington, N.Z., [1974]. 1 vol. (unpaged).

WORLD WAR, 1939-1945.(Cont.)

— Secret service.

BROWN (ANTHONY CAVE) Bodyguard of lies. London, 1976. pp. 947. *bibliog.*

— Sources.

CHUVASHSKAIA ASSR v period Velikoi Otechestvennoi voiny, iiun' 1941-1945 gg.: sbornik dokumentov i materialov. Cheboksary, 1975. pp. 528.

SOVETSKAIA Armeniia v gody Velikoi Otechestvennoi voiny, 1941- 1945: sbornik dokumentov i materialov. Erevan, 1975. pp. 838.

POLONSKY (ANTONY) ed. The great powers and the Polish question, 1941-45: a documentary study in cold war origins. London, 1976. pp. 282.

— Supplies.

MEIER-DOERNBERG (WILHELM) Die Ölversorgung der Kriegsmarine, 1935 bis 1945. Freiburg, 1973. pp. 111. *bibliog. (Militärgeschichtliches Forschungsamt. Einzelschriften zur Militärischen Geschichte des Zweiten Weltkrieges. 11)*

BAGEL-BOHLAN (ANJA E.) Hitlers industrielle Kriegsvorbereitung, 1936 bis 1939. Koblenz, [1975]. pp. 143. *bibliog. (Arbeitskreis für Wehrforschung. Beiträge zur Wehrforschung. Band 24)*

— Territorial questions — Denmark.

NOACK (JOHAN PETER) Det tyske mindretal i Nordslesvig under besaettelsen. [Copenhagen, 1975]. pp. 213. *bibliog. (Dansk Udenrigspolitisk Institut. Skrifter. 6)*

— — Italy.

SUCCESSFUL negotiation: Trieste 1954; an appraisal by the five participants; edited by John C. Campbell. Princeton, [1976]. pp. 181.

— — Poland.

POLONSKY (ANTONY) ed. The great powers and the Polish question, 1941-45: a documentary study in cold war origins. London, 1976. pp. 282.

— Transportation.

KREIDLER (EUGEN) Die Eisenbahnen im Machtbereich der Achsenmächte während des Zweiten Weltkrieges: Einsatz und Leistung für die Wehrmacht und Kriegswirtschaft. Göttingen, [1975]. pp. 440. *bibliog. (Arbeitskreis für Wehrforschung. Studien und Dokumente zur Geschichte des Zweiten Weltkrieges. Band 15)*

— Underground movements.

MACKSEY (KENNETH J.) The partisans of Europe in World War II. London, [1975]. pp. 271. *bibliog.*

— — Austria.

HINDELS (JOSEF) Österreichs Gewerkschaften im Widerstand, 1934-1945. Wien, [1976]. pp. 435. *bibliog.*

— — Denmark.

CHRISTMAS MØLLER (JOHN) Londonbreve:...korrespondance med hjemlandet, 1942-1945; udgivet af Jørgen Haestrup. [Copenhagen, 1974]. pp. 262.

— — France.

KNIGHT (FRIDA) The French resistance, 1940 to 1944. London, 1975. pp. 242. *bibliog.*

— — Italy.

BRANDIRALI (ALDO) and BOTTINO (GIANMARIO) La linea politica dei comunisti nella Resistenza e nel dopoguerra, 1943-1953. Milano, [1974]. pp. 291. *bibliog.*

CANOVA (F.) and others. Lotta di liberazione nella Bassa Modenese. Modena, [1974]. pp. 419. *bibliog.*

ARBIZZANI (LUIGI) Guerra, nazifascismo, lotta di liberazione nel Bolognese, luglio 1943-aprile 1945: fotostoria. Bologna, 1975. pp. 179.

BARBIERI (ORAZIO) Ponti sull'Arno: la Resistenza a Firenze. 3rd ed. Roma, 1975. pp. 307.

LUTI (GIORGIO) and ROMAGNOLI (SERGIO) eds. L'Italia partigiana: antologia. Milano, [1975]. pp. 379. *bibliog.*

— — Poland.

ZAŁUSKI (ZBIGNIEW) Czterdziesty czwarty: wydarzenia, obserwacje, refleksje. [Warszawa], 1968. pp. 538.

HOPPE (JAN) Wspomnienia, przyczynki, refleksje. Londyn, 1972. pp. 395.

BARTOSZEWSKI (WŁADYSŁAW) 1859 dni Warszawy. Kraków, 1974. pp. 835. *bibliog.*

GÓRA (WŁADYSŁAW) and OKĘCKI (STANISŁAW) Za nasza i wasza wolność: Für unsere und eure Freiheit: deutsche Antifaschisten im polnischen Widerstandskampf; herausgegeben von Reinhold Jeske; (von Norbert Rösler und Eduard Ullmann ins Deutsche übersetzt). Berlin, [1975]. pp. 562. *bibliog. In German.*

PRZYGOŃSKI (ANTONI) Z zagadnień strategii frontu narodowego PPR, 1942-1945. Warszawa, 1976. pp. 400. *bibliog.*

— — Russia — Lithuania.

DAUMANTAS (JUOZAS) pseud. [i.e. Juozas LUKŠA]. Fighters for freedom: Lithuanian partisans versus the U.S.S.R., 1944-1947. New York, [1975]. pp. 254.

— — — White Russia.

PODPOL'NYE partiinye organy Kompartii Belorussii v gody Velikoi Otechestvennoi voiny, 1941-1944: kratkie svedeniia ob organizatsii, strukture i sostave. Minsk, 1975. pp. 270.

— — Yugoslavia — Macedonian Republic.

IVANOVSKI (VLADO A.) Osloboditelnata vojna vo Zapadna Makedonija, 1941-1944. Skopje, 1973. pp. 362. *bibliog.*

— Africa, West.

MARDER (ARTHUR JACOB) Operation 'Menace': the Dakar expedition and the Dudley North affair. London, 1976. pp. 289.

— Asia.

ALLEN (LOUIS) The end of the war in Asia. London, 1976. pp. 306. *bibliog.*

— Balkan States.

BARKER (ELISABETH) British policy in south-east Europe in the Second World War. London, 1976. pp. 320. *bibliog.*

— Bulgaria.

MILLER (MARSHALL LEE) Bulgaria during the Second World War. Stanford, 1975. pp. 290. *bibliog.*

— Canada.

CANADA. Commissioner on the Canadian Expeditionary Force to the Crown Colony of Hong Kong. 1942. Report on the Canadian expeditionary force to the crown colony of Hong Kong; by Right Hon. Sir Lyman P. Duff. Ottawa, 1942. pp. 61.

GRANATSTEIN (J.L.) Canada's war: the politics of the Mackenzie King government, 1939-1945. Toronto, 1975. pp. 436.

— Denmark.

TORELL (ULF) Hjälp till Danmark: militära och politiska förbindelser, 1943-1945. Stockholm, 1973. pp. 385. *bibliog. With English summary.*

PETROW (RICHARD) The bitter years: the invasion and occupation of Denmark and Norway, April 1940-May 1945. London, [1975]. pp. 403. *bibliog.*

— East (Near East).

SCHROEDER (BERND PHILIPP) Deutschland und der Mittlere Osten im Zweiten Weltkrieg. Göttingen, [1975]. pp. 310. *bibliog. (Arbeitskreis für Wehrforschung. Studien und Dokumente zur Geschichte des Zweiten Weltkrieges. Band 16)* 3 maps in end pocket.

— Europe, Eastern.

BARKER (ELISABETH) British policy in south-east Europe in the Second World War. London, 1976. pp. 320. *bibliog.*

— France.

CREMIEUX-BRILHAC (JEAN LOUIS) ed. Les voix de la liberté: ici Londres, 1940-1944;...; avant- propos de Jean Marin. [Paris], Documentation Française, 1975-76. 5 vols.

COINTET (JEAN PAUL) La France Libre. [Paris], 1975. pp. 135. *bibliog.*

— Germany.

HENRICI (ECKHARD) Die deutsche Kriegführung und das Mittelmeer in den Jahren 1940 bis 1943. 1954. pp. 171. *bibliog.* Ph.D.(Heidelberg) thesis: unpublished. Microfilm of typescript: 1 reel.

ENGEL (GERHARD) Heeresadjutant bei Hitler, 1938-1943: Aufzeichnungen des Majors Engel; herausgegeben und kommentiert von Hildegard von Kotze. Stuttgart, [1974]. pp. 158. *bibliog. (Vierteljahrshefte für Zeitgeschichte. Schriftenreihe. Nr. 29)*

FISCHER (ALEXANDER) Sowjetische Deutschlandpolitik im Zweiten Weltkrieg, 1941-1945. Stuttgart, 1975. pp. 252. *bibliog. (Institut für Zeitgeschichte. Studien zur Zeitgeschichte)*

SCHROEDER (BERND PHILIPP) Deutschland und der Mittlere Osten im Zweiten Weltkrieg. Göttingen, [1975]. pp. 310. *bibliog. (Arbeitskreis für Wehrforschung. Studien und Dokumente zur Geschichte des Zweiten Weltkrieges. Band 16)* 3 maps in end pocket.

— Greece.

CRUICKSHANK (CHARLES GREIG) Greece, 1940-1941. London, 1976. pp. 206. *bibliog.*

— Hong Kong.

CANADA. Commissioner on the Canadian Expeditionary Force to the Crown Colony of Hong Kong. 1942. Report on the Canadian expeditionary force to the crown colony of Hong Kong; by Right Hon. Sir Lyman P. Duff. Ottawa, 1942. pp. 61.

— India.

CORR (GERARD H.) The war of the springing tigers. London, 1975. pp. 200. *bibliog.*

— Japan.

LEBRA (JOYCE CHAPMAN) ed. Japan's Greater East Asia Co-Prosperity Sphere in World War II: selected readings and documents. Kuala Lumpur, 1975. pp. 212. *bibliog.*

ALLEN (LOUIS) The end of the war in Asia. London, 1976. pp. 306. *bibliog.*

CRISIS and controversy: essays in honour of A.J.P. Taylor; edited by Alan Sked and Chris Cook. london, 1976. pp. 198.

— Norway.

PETROW (RICHARD) The bitter years: the invasion and occupation of Denmark and Norway, April 1940-May 1945. London, [1975]. pp. 403. *bibliog.*

— Poland.

DURACZYŃSKI (EUGENIUSZ) Wojna i okupacja, wrzesień 1939- kwiecień 1943. Warszawa, 1974. pp. 492. *bibliog.*

— **Romania.**

IZ khroniki istoricheskikh dnei, 1 maia 1944 - 6 marta 1945 gg.; (perevod s rumynskogo Ally Lazia) Bukharest, 1974. pp. 251. *(Academia de Științe Sociale și Politice a Republicii Socialiste România. Bibliotheca Historica Romaniae. Studies. 48)*

— **Russia.**

VELIKAIA Otechestvennaia voina, 1941-1945, v fotografiiakh i kinodokumentakh. Moskva, 1975 in progress.

ERICKSON (JOHN) The road to Stalingrad. London, [1975]. pp. 594. *bibliog. (Stalin's war with Germany. vol.1)*

FISCHER (ALEXANDER) Sowjetische Deutschlandpolitik im Zweiten Weltkrieg, 1941-1945. Stuttgart, 1975. pp. 252. *bibliog. (Institut für Zeitgeschichte. Studien zur Zeitgeschichte)*

— — **Armenia.**

SOVETSKAIA Armeniia v gody Velikoi Otechestvennoi voiny, 1941- 1945: sbornik dokumentov i materialov. Erevan, 1975. pp. 838.

— — **Azerbaijan.**

MADATOV (GARASH ALIEVICH) Azerbaidzhan v Velikoi Otechestvennoi voine. Baku, 1975. pp. 406. *bibliog.*

— — **Chuvash Republic.**

CHUVASHSKAIA ASSR v period Velikoi Otechestvennoi voiny, iiun' 1941-1945 gg.: sbornik dokumentov i materialov. Cheboksary, 1975. pp. 528.

— — **Karelia.**

KARELIIA v gody Velikoi Otechestvennoi voiny, 1941-1945: dokumenty, materialy. Petrozavodsk, 1975. pp. 447.

— — **Moldavian Republic.**

MOLDAVSKAIA SSR v Velikoi Otechestvennoi voine Sovetskogo Soiuza. Kishinev, 1975 in progress.

— — **Ukraine.**

UKRAINSKAIA SSR v Velikoi Otechestvennoi voine Sovetskogo Soiuza, 1941-1945 gg.; perevod s ukrainskogo iazyka. 2nd (i.e. 1st Russian) ed. Kiev, 1975. 3 vols.

— **Spain.**

RUHL (KLAUS JOERG) Spanien im Zweiten Weltkrieg: Franco, die Falange und das "Dritte Reich". Hamburg, 1975. pp. 414. *bibliog. With English summary.*

— **Sweden.**

UHLIN (ÅKE) Februarikrisen 1942: svensk säkerhetspolitik och militär planering, 1941-1942. Stockholm, 1972. pp. 265. *bibliog. With English summary.*

ÅMARK (KLAS) Makt eller moral: svensk offentlig debatt om internationell politik och svensk utrikes- och försvarspolitik 1938-1939. Stockholm, 1973. pp. 324. *bibliog. With English summary.*

ERLANDER (TAGE) 1940-1949. Stockholm, [1973]. pp. 406.

TORELL (ULF) Hjälp till Danmark: militära och politiska förbindelser, 1943-1945. Stockholm, 1973. pp. 385. *bibliog. With English summary.*

ZETTERBERG (KENT) Liberalism i kris: (Folkpartiet, 1939-1945). Stockholm, 1975. pp. 428. *bibliog. With English summary.*

— **United Kingdom.**

U.K. [Cabinet Office]. History of the Second World War: United Kingdom Civil Series. Statistical digest of the war; prepared in the Central Statistical Office. London, 1951 repr. 1975. pp. 248.

ADDISON (PAUL) The road to 1945: British politics and the Second World War. London, 1975. pp. 334. *bibliog.*

BURRIDGE (TREVOR D.) British Labour and Hitler's war. London, 1976. pp. 206. *bibliog.*

HARRISSON (TOM) Living through the blitz. London, 1976. pp. 372. *bibliog.*

U.K. [Cabinet Office]. History of the Second World War: United Kingdom Civil Series. Problems of social policy; by Richard M. Titmuss. rev. ed. London, 1976. pp. 632. *Confidential version with full source references.*

— **United States.**

SHERWIN (MARTIN J.) A world destroyed: the atomic bomb and the grand alliance. New York, 1975. pp. 326. *bibliog.*

BLUM (JOHN MORTON) V was for victory: politics and American culture during World War II. New York, [1976]. pp. 372.

WORTH.

FEATHER (NORMAN T.) Values in education and society. New York, [1975]. pp. 350. *bibliog.*

WOYTINSKY (WLADIMIR SAVELEVICH).

SCHNEIDER (MICHAEL) Das Arbeitsbeschaffungsprogramm des ADGB: zur gewerkschaftlichen Politik in der Endphase der Weimarer Republik; mit einer Einführung von George Garvy. Bonn-Bad Godesberg, [1975]. pp. 271. *bibliog. (Friedrich-Ebert-Stiftung. Forschungsinstitut. Schriftenreihe. Band 120) With English introduction.*

WRIGHT (GEORG HENRIK VON).

ESSAYS on explanation and understanding: studies in the foundations of humanities and social sciences; edited by Juha Manninen and Raimo Tuomela. Dordrecht, [1976]. pp. 440. *bibliogs. Includes papers from the International Colloquium on Explanation and Understanding, Helsinki, 1974.*

WUERTTEMBERG

— **Commerce.**

SEYBOLD (GERHARD) Württembergs Industrie und Aussenhandel vom Ende der napoleonischen Kriege bis zum Deutschen Zollverein. Stuttgart, 1974. pp. 177. *bibliog. (Kommission für Geschichtliche Landeskunde in Baden-Württemberg. Veröffentlichungen. Reihe B: Forschungen. 74.Band)*

— **Economic history.**

SEYBOLD (GERHARD) Württembergs Industrie und Aussenhandel vom Ende der napoleonischen Kriege bis zum Deutschen Zollverein. Stuttgart, 1974. pp. 177. *bibliog. (Kommission für Geschichtliche Landeskunde in Baden-Württemberg. Veröffentlichungen. Reihe B: Forschungen. 74.Band)*

— **Emigration and immigration.**

HACKER (WERNER) Auswanderungen aus dem nördlichen Bodenseeraum im 17. und 18. Jahrhundert; archivalisch dokumentiert. Singen, 1975. pp. 400. *bibliog. (Verein für Geschichte des Hegaus. Hegau- Bibliothek. Band 29)*

— **History.**

SAUER (PAUL) Württemberg in der Zeit des Nationalsozialismus. Ulm, 1975. pp. 519. *bibliog.*

— **Politics and government.**

HUNT (JAMES CLARK) The People's Party in Württemberg and southern Germany, 1890-1914: the possibilities of democratic politics. Stuttgart, [1975]. pp. 203. *bibliog.*

WUPPERTAL

— **Politics and government.**

BUSE (DIETER K.) ed. Parteiagitation und Wahlkreisvertretung: eine Dokumentation über Friedrich Ebert und seinen Reichstagswahlkreis Elberfeld-Barmen, 1910-1918. Bonn-Bad Godesberg, [1975]. pp. 135. *(Archiv für Sozialgeschichte. Beihefte. 3)*

XHOSA.

See XOSA.

XOSA.

SCHEUB (HAROLD) The Xhosa ntsomi. Oxford, 1975. pp. 446. *bibliog.*

YAKUTIA

— **History.**

IVANOV (VASILII FEDOTOVICH) Istoriko-etnograficheskoe izuchenie Iakutii XVII-XVIII vv. Moskva, 1974. pp. 287. *bibliog.*

YALE UNIVERSITY.

TAFT (JOHN) Mayday at Yale; a case study in student radicalism. Boulder, Co., 1976. pp. 224.

YANOAMA INDIANS.

[VALERO (HELENA)] Yanoáma: the narrative of a white girl kidnapped by Amazonian Indians; as told to Ettore Biocca;...translated from the Italian by Dennis Rhodes. New York, 1970 repr. 1971. pp. 382. *bibliog.*

CHAGNON (NAPOLEON A.) Studying the Y,nomamö. New York, [1974]. pp. 270. *bibliog.*

LIZOT (JACQUES) Le cercle des feux: faits et dits des Indiens yanomami. Paris, [1976]. pp. 253. *bibliog.*

YANOMAMO INDIANS.

See YANOAMA INDIANS.

YANONAMI INDIANS.

See YANOAMA INDIANS.

YAP

— **Politics and government.**

LINGENFELTER (SHERWOOD GALEN) Yap: political leadership and culture change in an island society. Honolulu, [1975]. pp. 270. *bibliog.*

— **Social conditions.**

LINGENFELTER (SHERWOOD GALEN) Yap: political leadership and culture change in an island society. Honolulu, [1975]. pp. 270. *bibliog.*

YOMBE (AFRICAN PEOPLE).

BOND (GEORGE CLEMENT) The politics of change in a Zambian community. Chicago, 1976. pp. 178. *bibliog.*

YORKSHIRE

— **Economic conditions.**

U.K. Department of Industry. Yorkshire and Humberside Regional Office. 1975. Yorkshire and Humberside: centre of Britain. [Leeds, 1975]. pp. 12.

YORUBAS.

ASIWAJU (ANTHONY IJAOLA) Western Yorubaland under European rule, 1889-1945: a comparative analysis of French and British colonialism. London, 1976. pp. 303. *bibliog.*

YOUNG (ARTHUR).

YOUNG (ARTHUR) F.R.S. Arthur Young and his times; edited by G.E. Mingay. London, 1975. pp. 264. *bibliog. Selections with introduction and commentary.*

YOUNG (THOMAS).

YOUNG (THOMAS).

WORRALL (JOHN) The 19th century revolution in optics: a case study in the interaction between philosophy of science and history and sociology of science. 1975 [or rather 1976]. fo. 277. *bibliog.* Typescript. Ph.D. (London) thesis: unpublished. This thesis is the property of London University and may not be removed from the Library.

YOUNG COMMUNIST LEAGUE

— Russia.

UCHENYE ZAPISKI KAFEDR OBSHCHESTVENNYKH NAUK VUZOV LENINGRADA. Istoriia KPSS. vyp.9. Istoriia KPSS. Leningrad, 1969. pp. 158.

SLAVNYI put' Leninskogo komsomola. Moskva, 1974. 2 vols.

VSESOIUZNYI LENINSKII KOMMUNISTICHESKII SOIUZ MOLODEZHI. Tsentral'nyi Komitet. Dokumenty TsK VLKSM, 1973. Moskva, 1974. pp. 254.

VSESOIUZNYI LENINSKII KOMMUNISTICHESKII SOIUZ MOLODEZHI. Ustav Vsesoiuznogo Leninskogo Kommunisticheskogo Soiuza Molodezhi: priniat XIV s″ezdom VLKSM. Moskva, 1974. pp. 32.

ZUBKOV (VADIM ALEKSANDROVICH) and PEDAN (STANISLAV ANDREEVICH) Leninskii komsomol v gody vosstanovleniia narodnogo khoziaistva, 1921-1925 gg.: ocherki istoriografii. Leningrad, 1975. pp. 127.

— — Congresses.

VSESOIUZNYI LENINSKII KOMMUNISTICHESII SOIUZ MOLODEZHI. S″ezd, 17- yi, 1974. XVII s″ezd Vsesoiuznogo Leninskogo Kommunisticheskogo Soiuza Molodezhi 23-27 aprelia 1974 goda: stenograficheskii otchet. Moskva, 1975. 2 vols.

— — Daghestan.

KICHEV (MAGOMED IBRAGIMOVICH) Ocherki komsomola Dagestana, 1920-1932 gg. Makhachkala, 1970. pp. 140.

— — Ukraine.

LENINSKII KOMMUNISTICHESKII SOIUZ MOLODEZHI UKRAINY. Tsentral'nyi Komitet. LKSM Ukraïny v tsyfrakh i faktakh: dovidnyk. Kyïv, 1974. pp. 207.

KOVALEV (IVAN IAKOVLEVICH) Komsomol i oborona Rodiny, 1921-1941 gg.: na materialakh Ukrainy. Kiev, 1975. pp. 207.

— — White Russia.

OCHERKI istorii Leninskogo komsomola Belorussii. Minsk, 1975. pp. 534.

YOUTH.

WESTHUES (KENNETH) Society's shadow: studies in the sociology of countercultures. Toronto, [1972]. pp. 223. *bibliog.*

ANDEMICAEL (BERHANYKUN) and MURDOCH (ANTHONY J.) eds. International youth organizations and the United Nations;... contributions by Louis Simon [and others]. New York, United Nations Institute for Training and Research, 1973. pp. 95. *bibliog.* (Research Reports. No. 17)

HAMILTON-SMITH (ELERY) Evaluation of social development programmes: a handbook for evaluation with special reference to youth work; (prepared for the Commonwealth Secretariat). London, Commonwealth Secretariat, [1974]. pp. 75. *bibliog.*

IKONNIKOVA (SVETLANA NIKOLAEVNA) Molodezh': sotsiologicheskii i sotsial'no-psikhologocheskii analiz. Leningrad, 1974. pp. 166.

— Employment — Africa, Subsaharan.

SYMPOSIUM ON UNEMPLOYED YOUTH, DAR-ES-SALAAM, 1962. Symposium...[held] 25-29 September, 1962: reports and recommendations. Lagos, 1962. 1 vol.(looseleaf.) *In English and French.*

— — Australia.

AUSTRALIAN COUNCIL OF TRADE UNIONS. Survey of young workers. Canberra, Australian Government Publishing Service, 1975. pp. 42.

— — Caribbean Area.

CARIBBEAN SYMPOSIUM ON EMPLOYMENT STRATEGIES AND PROGRAMMES, BARBADOS, 1975. The young unemployed: a Caribbean development problem. London, Commonwealth Secretariat, [1976]. pp. 112. *bibliog.*

— — Sri Lanka.

MARGA INSTITUTE. Marga Seminar Papers. 1. Youth, land and employment: [selected papers from a series of seminars held by the Marga Institute]. Colombo, 1974. pp. 185.

— — United States.

LEVITAN (SAR A.) and JOHNSTON (BENJAMIN H.) The Job Corps: a social experiment that works. Baltimore, [1975]. pp. 118.

— Africa, Subsaharan.

WORKSHOP ON NATIONAL YOUTH PROGRAMMES AND NATIONAL SERVICE, ACCRA, 1975. Youth for development: an African perspective; report. London, Commonwealth Secretariat, [1975]. pp. 203.

— France.

ETUDES SOCIALES NORD AFRICAINES. Cahiers Nord-Africains. No. 45. Les jeunes Nord-Africains en Métropole. Amsterdam, 1971. pp. 56.

CAMILLERI (CARMEL) and TAPIA (CLAUDE) Jeunesse française et groupes sociaux après Mai 1968: enquêtes sur des populations universitaires et scolaires de Paris et de province. Paris, 1974. pp. 183. (Centre National de la Recherche Scientifique. *Monographies Françaises de Psychologie.* 27)

TABARD (NICOLE) and others. Besoins et aspirations des familles et des jeunes. [Paris], 1974. pp. 512. (Caisse Nationale des Allocations Familiales. *Etudes.* [16])

— Germany.

ENGELHARDT (VICTOR) Die deutsche Jugendbewegung als kulturhistorisches Phänomen. Berlin, 1923. pp. 131. *bibliog.*

SCHELLENBERGER (BARBARA) Katholische Jugend und Drittes Reich: eine Geschichte des Katholischen Jungmännerverbandes, 1933-1939, etc. Mainz, [1975]. pp. 202. *bibliog.* (Kommission für Zeitgeschichte. *Veröffentlichungen. Reihe B: Forschungen. Band 17*)

NIKLES (BRUNO W.) Jugendpolitik in der Bundesrepublik Deutschland: Entwicklungen, Merkmale, Orientierungen. Opladen, 1976. pp. 244. *bibliog.*

— — Political activity.

BUTTERWEGGE (CHRISTOPH) Jungsozialisten und SPD, etc. Hamburg, [1975]. pp. 157.

STACHURA (PETER D.) Nazi youth in the Weimar Republic. Santa Barbara, [1975]. pp. 301. *bibliog.*

PULTE (PETER) ed. Politische Jugendorganisationen: Programmatik, Beschlüsse, Forderungen und Thesen von Jungsozialisten, Junger Union, Jungdemokraten. 2nd ed. Leverkusen, [1976]. pp. 356. *bibliog.*

— Germany, Eastern — Political activity.

GROTEWOHL (OTTO) Jugend und Partei: (aus einer Rede...des Parteivorstandes der SED, 20 und 21. Juli 1949). Berlin, [1949]. pp. 23.

— Japan — Political activity.

MASSEY (JOSEPH A.) Youth and politics in Japan. Lexington, Mass., [1976]. pp. 233. *bibliog.*

— Netherlands.

LANDELIJK WERKERS OVERLEG. Projekten Jongeren Zonder Werk. Afvaljeugd 15 tot 25 jaar: ons eigen werkboek om de politiek van regeringen en parlement mee door te lichten. 's-Hertogenbosch, 1974 repr. 1975. pp. 116.

LANDELIJK WERKERS OVERLEG. Projekten Jongeren Zonder Werk. Werklozenverzet het explosieve vervolg op Afvaljeugd, samengesteld door en voor werklozen. 's-Hertogenbosch, 1975. pp. 118-262.

RINSAMPESSY (ELIAS P.) De mogelijke gronden van agressie onder Molukse jongeren geplaatst in het kader van de integratieproblematiek. Utrecht, 1975. pp. 76. *bibliog.*

— Nigeria.

NIGERIA. National Youth Service Corps. 1974. Report on the orientation programme 1973-74. Lagos, 1974. pp. 34.

— Norway.

BEFRING (EDVARD) Ungdom i et bysamfunn: en socialpedagogisk studie av Oslo-ungdom. Oslo, 1973 repr. 1975. pp. 413. *bibliog.*

— Poland.

ZWIĄZEK Walki Młodych: materiały i dokumenty. Warszawa, 1953. pp. 576.

KACZOR (STANISŁAW) W dru'zynie harcerskiej: o niektórych problemach pracy wychowawczej. Warszawa, 1954. pp. 119.

— Russia — Caucasus — Political activity.

OGANDZHANIAN (SHAGEN BAGRATOVICH) Revoliutsionnoe dvizhenie molodezhi Zakavkaz'ia, 1890-ye gg. - 1917 g. Erevan, 1975. pp. 298.

— Somali Republic.

SOMALI REPUBLIC. Ministry of Information and National Guidance. 1974. The revolutionary generation of tomorrow: youth, sports and manpower. Mogadishu, 1974. pp. 72.

— Sri Lanka.

SRI LANKA. National Youth Service Council. 1970. Youth service plan. [Colombo, 1970?]. pp. 24.

— Underdeveloped areas.

See UNDERDEVELOPED AREAS — Youth.

— United Kingdom.

TUC YOUTH CONFERENCE, LONDON, 1975. Trade union youth in conference; report of the...conference. London, [1975]. pp. 55.

WORKING class youth culture; edited by Geoff Mungham and Geoff Pearson. London, 1976. pp. 167. *bibliog. A collection of essays, some of which were originally given as papers to a conference on 'Working Class Culture' at University College, Cardiff in 1973.*

— — Recreation.

CUMBRIA COMMUNITY DEVELOPMENT PROJECT. The report of a study of the needs of young people in Cleator Moor with particular reference to their leisure time; [by] Alan Tweedie [and others]. Cleator Moor, 1973 repr. 1974. pp. 91.

— United States.

FAMILY socialization and the adolescent: determinants of self- concept, conformity, religiosity, and counterculture values; [by] Darwin L. Thomas [and others]. Lexington, Mass., [1974]. pp. 181. *bibliog.*

YUGOSLAVIA

— Commerce.

YUGOSLAVIA. Savezni Zavod za Statistiku. Studije, Analize i Prikazi. 72. Medjusobni odnosi privrednih delatnosti SFR Jugoslavije u 1970. godini: uvoz po delatnostima porekla i namene; Inter-industry relations of the economy of the SFRY in 1970: imports by industries of origin and destination. Beograd, 1975. pp. 32. *With English summary and captions to tables.*

— Constitution.

KARDELJ (EDVARD) Osnovni uzroci i pravci ustavnih promena. Beograd, 1973. pp. 119.

— Defences.

ROBERTS (EDWARD ADAM) Nations in arms: the theory and practice of territorial defence. London, 1976. pp. 288.

— Economic conditions.

BELGIUM. Office Belge du Commerce Extérieur. 1972. Yougoslavie. Bruxelles, 1972. pp. 67. *(Un Marché. 8)*

YUGOSLAVIA. Savezni Zavod za Statistiku. Studije, Analize i Prikazi. 67. Porast stanovništva u periodu 1961-1971, odnosno, odlazak na privremeni rad u inostranstvo i neki indikatori ekonomske razvijenosti opština; Increase of population in the period 1961- 1971 and our workers on temporary work abroad and some indicators of economic development of communes; [by] Nikola Marković. Beograd, 1974. pp. 94. *bibliog. With English summary.*

AKTUELNI problemi privrednih kretanja i ekonomske politike Jugoslavije. Zagreb, 1975. pp. 132.

ČALIĆ (DUŠAN) Aktualni problemi razvoja samoupravnog društva u SFRJ. Zagreb, [1975?]. pp. 174.

GORUPIĆ (DRAGO) Osnovna i složena organizacija udruženog rada u privredi. Zagreb, 1975. pp. iii,136.

— — Mathematical models.

BABIĆ (MATE) Ekonometrijski model jugoslavenske privrede. Zagreb, 1974. pp. 95. *bibliog.*

— — Statistics.

YUGOSLAVIA. Savezni Zavod za Statistiku. Studije, Analize i Prikazi. 71. Medjusobni odnosi privrednih delatnosti SFR Jugoslavije u 1970. godini; Inter-industry relations of the economy of the SFRY in 1970. Beograd, 1975. pp. 55. *With English summary and captions to tables.*

— Economic policy.

YUGOSLAVIA. Savezna Skupština. Sekretarijat za Informativnu Službu. 1966. Osnove ekonomske politike u 1967. i mere za njeno sprovodjenje. Beograd, 1966. pp. 103. *(Biblioteka Savezne Skupstine, kolo 3, sv. 12)*

AKTUELNI problemi privrednih kretanja i ekonomske politike Jugoslavije. Zagreb, 1975. pp. 132.

DENITCH (BOGDAN DENIS) The legitimation of a revolution: the Yugoslav case. New Haven, 1976. pp. 254. *bibliog.*

— Foreign relations — Europe, Eastern.

GASTEYGER (CURT) ed. Die feindlichen Brüder: Jugoslawiens neuer Konflikt mit dem Ostblock, 1958; ein Dokumentenband, etc. Bern, 1960. pp. 315. *bibliog. (Schweizerisches Ost-Institut. Schriftenreihe. Reihe Dokumente. Heft 2)*

— — Italy.

SUCCESSFUL negotiation: Trieste 1954; an appraisal by the five participants; edited by John C. Campbell. Princeton, [1976]. pp. 181.

— — Russia.

O neistinitim i nepravednim optužbama protiv naše Partije i naše zemlje. Beograd, 1948. pp. 62. *Articles reprinted from "Borba", Oct. 2, 3 and 4, 1948. In Cyrillic.*

CLISSOLD (STEPHEN) ed. Yugoslavia and the Soviet Union, 1939-1973: a documentary survey. London, 1975. pp. 318.

ŠTRBAC (ČEDOMIR) Jugoslavija i odnosi izmedju socijalističkih zemalja: sukob KPJ i Informbiroa. Beograd, 1975. pp. 231. *bibliog. With English and Russian summaries.*

— History — 1941-1945, Axis occupation.

OLSHAUSEN (KLAUS) Zwischenspiel auf dem Balkan: die deutsche Politik gegenüber Jugoslawien und Griechenland von März bis Juli 1941. Stuttgart, 1973. pp. 375. *bibliog. (Militärgeschichtliches Forschungsamt. Beiträge zur Militär- und Kriegsgeschichte. Band 14) 7 maps in end pocket.*

— Industries.

YUGOSLAVIA. Savezni Zavod za Statistiku. Studije, Analize i Prikazi. 72. Medjusobni odnosi privrednih delatnosti SFR Jugoslavije u 1970. godini: uvoz po delatnostima porekla i namene; Inter-industry relations of the economy of the SFRY in 1970: imports by industries of origin and destination. Beograd, 1975. pp. 32. *With English summary and captions to tables.*

YUGOSLAVIA. Savezni Zavod za Statistiku. Studije, Analize i Prikazi. 74. Uporedjenje jugoslovenske i madjarske industrije: produktivnost rada i struktura industrije, 1960-1970; Comparison between the Yugoslav and Hungarian industry: labour productivity and structure of industry, 1960-1970. Beograd, 1975. pp. 68. *With English summary.*

— Learned institutions and societies.

PAREŽANIN (RATKO) Za Balkansko jedinstvo: osnivanje, program i rad Balkanskog Instituta u Beogradu, 1934-1941. Minhen, 1976. pp. 121.

— Nationalism.

DIMITRIJEVIĆ (MITA) Mi i Hrvati: hrvatsko pitanje, 1914-1939: Sporazum sa Hrvatima. Beograd, 1939. pp. 252. *In Cyrillic.*

KARDELJ (EDVARD) Nacija i medjunarodni odnosi: [a collection of articles]. Beograd, 1975. pp. 249.

BERTSCH (GARY K.) Values and community in multi-national Yugoslavia. New York, 1976. pp. 160. *(East European Quarterly. East European Monographs. 17)*

— Politics and government.

VELJIĆ (ANDJELKO) Društveno samoupravljanje u Jugoslaviji: novi oblik demokratije. Sarajevo, 1973. pp. 246. *bibliog.*

BERTSCH (GARY K.) Value change and political community: the multinational Czechoslovak, Soviet, and Yugoslav cases. Beverly Hills, [1974]. pp. 60. *bibliog.*

BERTSCH (GARY K.) Values and community in multi-national Yugoslavia. New York, 1976. pp. 160. *(East European Quarterly. East European Monographs. 17)*

DENITCH (BOGDAN DENIS) The legitimation of a revolution: the Yugoslav case. New Haven, 1976. pp. 254. *bibliog.*

SINGLETON (FREDERICK BERNARD) Twentieth-century Yugoslavia. London, 1976. pp. 346. *bibliog.*

— Population.

KRAKER (ANA) Gesetz über den Schwangerschaftsabbruch und die rückläufige Entwicklung des Geburtenüberschusses in Jugoslawien; herausgegeben von Hans Harmsen. Hamburg, 1972. pp. 52. *(Akademie für Staatsmedizin in Hamburg. Zur Entwicklung und Organisation des Gesundheitswesens in Sowjetrussland, in Osteuropäischen Volksdemokratien und in der DDR. Band 58)*

INSTITUT DRUŠTVENIH NAUKA. Centar za Demografko Istraživanje. The population of Yugoslavia. Belgrade, 1974. pp. 95. *(Committee for International Coordination of National Research in Demography. C.I.C.R.E.D. Series)*

RUSSIA (USSR). Ministerstvo Vysshego i Srednego Spetsial'nogo Obrazovaniia. Nauchno-Tekhnicheskii Sovet. Sektsiia Narodonaseleniia. Narodonaselenie. 5. Demograficheskii analiz rozhdaemosti. Moskva, 1974. pp. 112. *With English table of contents.*

YUGOSLAVIA. Savezni Zavod za Statistiku. Studije, Analize i Prikazi. 67. Porast stanovništva u periodu 1961-1971, odnosno, odlazak na privremeni rad u inostranstvo i neki indikatori ekonomske razvijenosti opština; Increase of population in the period 1961- 1971 and our workers on temporary work abroad and some indicators of economic development of communes; [by] Nikola Marković. Beograd, 1974. pp. 94. *bibliog. With English summary.*

— Relations (general) with Czechoslovakia.

PAULOVÁ (MILADA) Tajný výbor Maffie a spolupráce s Jihoslovany v letech 1916-1918. Praha, 1968. pp. 626. *bibliog.*

— Savezna Skupstina.

ANTIFAŠISTIČKO VIJEĆE NARODNOG OSLOBODJENJA JUGOSLAVIJE. Treće zasedanje Antifašističkog Veća narodnog oslobodjenja Jugolavije; Zasedanje Privremene narodne skupštine, 7-26 avgust 1945: stenografske beleške. Beograd, [1945?]. pp. 708. *In Cyrillic.*

— Skupstina.

See — Savezna Skupstina.

— Social conditions.

GLIGORIĆ (VELIBOR) Hronika jednog doba. Beograd, 1965. pp. 286. *Articles originally published in Vreme and Politika, 1931-36. In Cyrillic.*

— Social policy.

YUGOSLAVIA. Savezna Skupština. Sekretarijat za Informativnu Službu. 1972. Društveni plan Jugoslavije za period od 1971. do 1975. godine. [Beograd, 1972]. pp. 103. *(Biblioteka Savezne Skupštine. kolo 9, sv.3)*

— Statistics.

YUGOSLAVIA. Savezni Zavod za Statistiku. 1969. Jugoslavija izmedju VIII i IX kongresa SKJ, 1964-1968: statistički podaci. Beograd, 1969. pp. 119.

— Statistics, Vital.

YUGOSLAVIA. Savezni Zavod za Statistiku. Studije, Analize i Prikazi. 70. Nasilne smrti u SFR Jugoslaviji, 1950-1970; Deaths by violence in SFR Yugoslavia, 1950-1970; [by] Andjelija Plavec. Beograd, 1974. pp. 103.

YUGOSLAVIA. Savezni Zavod za Statistiku. Studije, Analize i Prikazi. 75. Smrtnost od raka u većim gradovima, 1968-1969; Deaths caused by malignant neoplasm in major towns, 1968-1969; [by] Nevena Stojkov. Beograd, 1975. pp. 71. *With English summary.*

YUGOSLAVS IN FOREIGN COUNTRIES.

YUGOSLAVIA. Savezni Zavod za Statistiku. Studije, Analize i Prikazi. 67. Porast stanovništva u periodu 1961-1971, odnosno, odlazak na privremeni rad u inostranstvo i neki indikatori ekonomske razvijenosti opština; Increase of population in the period 1961- 1971 and our workers on temporary work abroad and some indicators of economic development of communes; [by] Nikola Marković. Beograd, 1974. pp. 94. *bibliog. With English summary.*

YVELINES (DEPARTMENT).

FRANCE. Direction de la Documentation. La Documentation Française. Notes et Etudes Documentaires. Nos. 4,171-4, 172-4,173. Les départements français. 78. Yvelines, région parisienne; rédigé sous la direction de Jean Brenas par Philippe Cayla]. Paris, 1975. pp. 96. *Map in end pocket.*

ZADRUGA.

COMMUNAL families in the Balkans: the zadruga: essays by Philip E. Mosely and essays in his honor; edited by Robert F. Byrnes. Notre Dame, Indiana, [1976]. pp. 285. *bibliog. (Notre Dame. University. Committee on International Relations. International Studies)*

ZAGÓRSKI-OSTOJA (WLODZIMIERZ).

RAWICZ (JERZY) Generał Zagórski zaginął...: z tajemnic lat międzywojennych. [Warszawa, 1963]. pp. 376.

ZAIRE

— Census.

ZAIRE. Institut National de la Statistique. 1971. Recueil des rapports et totaux: calculés à partir des résultats officiels du Recensement de la population de la R.D.C. en 1970. [Kinshasa, 1971?]. fo. 94.

— Economic conditions.

MATON (J.G.) De input-output tabel als instrument van sociaal-economische analyse in een dualistische huishouding, met een proeve van toepassing op de economie van Ituri. Gent, [c. 1965]. fo. 233. *bibliog.*

— History.

DAYAL (RAJESHWAR) Mission for Hammarskjold: the Congo crisis. London, 1976. pp. 335. *bibliog.*

— — Sources.

CARR-GOMM (HUBERT WILLIAM CULLING) [Recollections of Parliament and letters from Winston S. Churchill. 1903-29]. 1 piece. *Manuscript, typescript.*

— Politics and government.

DAYAL (RAJESHWAR) Mission for Hammarskjold: the Congo crisis. London, 1976. pp. 335. *bibliog.*

ZAMBIA.

ZAMBIA. Information Services. 1974. Zambia, 1964-1974: ten years of achievement. [Lusaka, 1974?]. pp. 76.

— Economic conditions.

ZAMBIA. Development Planning Division. 1975. Mid-term review of the second national development plan: performance of the Zambian economy, 1972-1974. Lusaka, 1974 [or rather 1975]. pp. 144.

— Industries.

ENTERPRISE: the Indeco jl.; (pd. by the Industrial Development Corporation of Zambia. q., 1969- . Lusaka.

ZAMBIA. Central Statistical Office. 1971. Index of industrial production, new series: 1969 [equals] 100. Lusaka, 1971. pp. 29.

— Officials and employees — Salaries, allowances, etc.

ZAMBIA. 1966. Report on the Grading Structure and Salaries Commission: Whelan report: digest of government's attitude to the report. Lusaka, 1966. pp. (3). *(Government Papers. 1966. No. 2) Bound with the Report.*

ZAMBIA. Grading Structure and Salaries Commission. 1966. Report of the Commission appointed to review the grading structure of the civil service, the salary scales of the civil service, etc.; [F.J. Whelan, sole commissioner]. Lusaka, 1966. pp. 78. *Bound with Digest of government's attitude to the report.*

— Politics and government.

SKLAR (RICHARD L.) Corporate power in an African state: the political impact of multinational mining companies in Zambia. Berkeley, 1975. pp. 245. *bibliog.*

BOND (GEORGE CLEMENT) The politics of change in a Zambian community. Chicago, 1976. pp. 178. *bibliog.*

— Social conditions.

ZAMBIA. Development Planning Division. 1975. Mid-term review of the second national development plan: performance of the Zambian economy, 1972-1974. Lusaka, 1974 [or rather 1975]. pp. 144.

ZÁPOTOCKY (ANTONÍN)

— Bibliography.

HRBATOVÁ (ANEŽKA) compiler. Antonín Zápotocký: bibliografie. Praha, 1974 in progress.

ZEIDLER—KORNMANN (HEINZ).

EUROPEAN COMMISSION OF HUMAN RIGHTS. 1968. The Zeidler-Kornmann case: (Application No. 2686/65 by Heinz Zeidler-Kornmann against the Federal Republic of Germany). Strasbourg, Council of Europe, 1968. pp. 120.

ZELLWEGER (ALFRED).

VEREIN FÜR WIRTSCHAFTSHISTORISCHE STUDIEN. Schweizer Pioniere der Wirtschaft und Technik. 28. Alfred Zellweger, Uster, 1855-1916; Hans Blumer-Ris, Freiburg, 1902-1953; von Hans Rudolf Schmid. Zürich, 1975. pp. 113. *bibliog.*

ZENTRUMSPARTEI.

See CENTRE PARTIES — Germany.

ZHITOMIR

— Social history.

ARNDT (NIKOLAUS) Die Shitomirer Arndts: eine Familienchronik auf dem Hintergrund hundertfünfzigjähriger Geschichte der westlichen Ukraine. Würzburg, [1970]. pp. 151. *bibliog.*

ZJEDNOCZONE STRONNICTWO LUDOWE.

JUSZKIEWICZ (ALEKSANDER) and OZGA-MICHALSKI (JÓZEF) Zjednoczone Stronnictwo Ludowe w walce o podniesienie produkcji rolnej. Warszawa, 1953. pp. 54.

WYCECH (CZESŁAW) Podstawowe zagadnienia społeczno-polityczne ruchu ludowego. [Warszawa], 1958. pp. 87.

ZONING

— United States.

BERGMAN (EDWARD M.) Eliminating exclusionary zoning: reconciling workplace and residence in suburban areas. Cambridge, Mass., [1974]. pp. 307. *bibliog.*

LINOWES (R. ROBERT) and ALLENSWORTH (DONALD TRUDEAU) The states and land-use control. New York, 1975. pp. 243.

RICHARDSON (DAN K.) The cost of environmental protection: regulating housing development in the coastal zone. New Brunswick, N.J., [1976]. pp. 219. *bibliog.*

SIEGAN (BERNARD H.) Other people's property. Lexington, Mass., [1976]. pp. 147.

URBAN growth management through development timing; [by] David J. Brower [and others]. New York, 1976. pp. 153.

ZUBATOV (SERGEI VASIL'EVICH).

SCHNEIDERMAN (JEREMIAH) Sergei Zubatov and revolutionary marxism: the struggle for the working class in tsarist Russia. Ithaca, N.Y., 1976. pp. 401. *bibliog.*

ZWINGLI (ULRICH).

CLAASSEN (WALTER) Schweizer Bauernpolitik im Zeitalter Ulrich Zwinglis. Berlin, 1899. pp. 168. *bibliog. (Zeitschrift für Social- und Wirthschaftsgeschichte. Ergänzungshefte: Socialgeschichtliche Forschungen. Heft 4)*

ZYBLIKIEWICZ (MIKOLAJ).

DZIKOWSKA (IRENA HOMOLA) Mikołaj Zyblikiewicz, 1823-1887. Wrocław, 1964. pp. 193. *(Polska Akademia Nauk. Oddział w Krakowie. Komisja Nauk Historycznych. Prace. Nr.10)*

List of subject headings used in the Bibliography arranged under topics

TABLE OF SUBJECT SUB-DIVISIONS

SUBJECT SUB-DIVISIONS UNDER NAMES OF CONTINENTS, COUNTRIES, STATES OR TOWNS

Works on the following subjects, if confined to a particular geographical area, are entered not under subject, but under the name of the country, etc., with the subject sub-division.

Air force
Annexation
Antiquities
Appropriations and expenditures
Armed forces
Army

Bibliography
Bio-bibliography
Biography
Boundaries

Capital
Census
Centennial celebrations, etc.
Charters, grants, privileges
Church history
Civilization
Claims
Climate
Clubs
Colonies
Colonization
Commerce
Commercial policy
Commercial treaties
Constitution
Constitutional conventions
Constitutional history
Constitutional laws
Courts and courtiers

Defences
Description and travel
Dictionaries and encyclopaedias
Diplomatic and consular service
Directories
Discovery and exploration

Economic conditions
Economic history
Economic integration
Economic policy
Emigration and immigration

Executive departments
Exiles

Fairs
Famines
Foreign economic relations
Foreign opinion
Foreign population
Foreign relations
Foreign relations—Treaties
Foreign relations administration

Gazeteers
Genealogy
Gentry
Government property
Government publications
Government vessels
Governors

Historic houses, etc.
Historical geography
History
History, Local
History, Military
History, Naval

Industries
Intellectual life
International status

Kings and rulers

Languages
Learned institutions and societies

Manufactures
Maps
Military policy
Militia
Moral conditions

Nationalism
Native races

Navy
Neutrality
Nobility

Occupations
Officials and employees

Parliament (Congress, Nationalrat, etc.)
Peerage
Politics and government
Population
Presidents
Public buildings
Public lands
Public works

Race question
Registers
Relations (general) with (country)
Relations (military) with (country)
Religion
Religion and mythology
Rural conditions

Sanitary affairs
Seal
Semi-centennial celebrations, etc.
Social conditions
Social history
Social life and customs
Social policy
Statistics
Statistics, Medical
Statistics, Vital
Surveys

Territorial expansion
Territories and possessions
Tornadoes

Vice-Presidents
Voting registers

Year-books

SUBJECT SUB-DIVISIONS USED ONLY UNDER NAMES OF CITIES OR TOWNS

Works on the following matters, if confined to a particular region or country, are entered under the subject, with local sub-division; if confined to a particular city or town, under the name of the city or town, with subject sub-division.

Almshouses and workhouses
Ambulance service
Amusements

Benevolent and moral institutions and societies
Bridges
Buildings

Cemeteries
Charities
Civic improvement
Clubs

Description
Docks

Earthquake
Evening and continuation schools
Exhibitions
Fires and fire prevention

Fortifications

Gilds
Growth

Harbour
Hospitals
Hotels, taverns, etc.

Libraries
Lodging-houses

Markets
Massacre
Music-halls (Variety-theatres, cabarets, etc.)

Office buildings

Parks
Police
Poor
Port

Porters
Prisons and reformatories
Public laundries

Rapid transit
Recreation areas
Recreational activities
Riots

Schools
Sewerage
Stock Exchange (Beurs, Bourse, etc.)
Street cleaning
Streets
Suburbs and environs
Synagogues

Theatres
Transit systems

Water-supply

BIOGRAPHY

AGRICULTURE (including ANIMAL AND PLANT INDUSTRIES)

General.

AGRICULTURAL ADMINISTRATION
AGRICULTURAL COLLEGES
AGRICULTURAL CREDIT
AGRICULTURAL EDUCATION
AGRICULTURAL ESTIMATING AND REPORTING
AGRICULTURAL EXPERIMENT STATIONS
AGRICULTURAL EXTENSION WORK
AGRICULTURAL GEOGRAPHY
AGRICULTURAL INNOVATIONS.
AGRICULTURAL LAWS AND LEGISLATION
AGRICULTURAL MACHINERY
AGRICULTURAL RESEARCH
AGRICULTURAL SOCIETIES
AGRICULTURAL SURPLUS
AGRICULTURAL WAGES
AGRICULTURAL WASTES
AGRICULTURE.
AGRICULTURE, COOPERATIVE.
AGRICULTURE AND STATE.
ANIMAL INDUSTRY
ANIMAL PRODUCTS
ARTIFICIAL INSEMINATION.
BANANA TRADE
CATTLE BREEDING
CATTLE TRADE
CONSOLIDATION OF LAND HOLDINGS
CROFTERS.
CROP YIELDS
CROPS AND CLIMATE
DAIRY PRODUCTS
DAIRYING
FARM BUILDINGS
FARM INCOME
FARM LIFE
FARM MANAGEMENT.
FARM MECHANIZATION
FARM PRODUCE.
FARMERS
FARMS
FARMS, COLLECTIVE
FERTILIZERS AND MANURES.
FIELD CROPS
FOREST PRODUCTS
FORESTRY LAW AND LEGISLATION
FORESTRY RESEARCH
FORESTS AND FORESTRY.
GRAIN AS FEEDING STUFF.
HILL FARMING
HORTICULTURAL PRODUCTS
HORTICULTURE
IRRIGATION
LAND REFORM
METEOROLOGY, AGRICULTURAL
MIGRANT AGRICULTURAL LABOURERS
MILK SUPPLY.
PART-TIME FARMING
PASTURES
PHOSPHATIC FERTILIZERS.
POULTRY RESEARCH
PRODUCE TRADE.
RECLAMATION OF LAND.
SERICULTURE
SHEEP RANCHES
SMALL HOLDINGS
SOIL SURVEYS
SOILS.
STATE FARMS
STOCK AND STOCK BREEDING
STOCK-RANGES.
SUGAR GROWING.
SWINE BREEDING
VITICULTURE

Particular animals and animal products.

BEEF.
BEEF CATTLE
BIRDS
CATTLE
HIDES AND SKINS.
MEAT
POULTRY
SHEEP
SWINE
WOOL

Particular crops and plant products.

ASPARAGUS.
COCA.
COFFEE
FRUIT JUICES.
HAY
JUTE
MAIZE
MELONS.
OILSEEDS.
PAPAIN.
PEANUTS.
POTATOES
RAPESEED.
RICE
SUGAR.
TEA.
TIMBER
TOBACCO.
TOMATOES
TREES
VEGETABLES
WHEAT

Fisheries.

FISH MEAL.
FISHERIES.
FISHERY LAW AND LEGISLATION
FISHERY MANAGEMENT
FISHING BOATS
HERRING-FISHERIES
WHALING.

BIBLIOGRAPHY AND GENERAL WORKS.

ABBREVIATIONS.
ACRONYMS.
ANTIQUARIAN BOOKSELLERS
ARCHIVES
BIBLIOGRAPHY
BIBLIOGRAPHY, NATIONAL
BOOK SELECTION.
BOOKS
CATALOGUES, LIBRARY.
CATALOGUES, PUBLISHERS
CATALOGUES, UNION.
CLASSIFICATION, LIBRARY OF CONGRESS.
CORPORATE ENTRY (CATALOGUING).
CYBERNETICS.
DATA LIBRARIES.
DIARIES
DIRECTORIES.
ENCYCLOPAEDIAS AND DICTIONARIES
GOVERNMENT PUBLICATIONS
INFORMATION SCIENCE.
INFORMATION SERVICES
INFORMATION STORAGE AND RETRIEVAL SYSTEMS.
INFORMATION THEORY.
INTERLIBRARY LOANS
LIBRARIANS
LIBRARIES
LIBRARIES, NATIONAL
LIBRARIES, PRIVATE
LIBRARIES, SPECIAL
LIBRARY ADMINISTRATION.
LIBRARY FINANCE.
LIBRARY LEGISLATION
LIBRARY PLANNING.
LIBRARY SCIENCE
MACHINE-READABLE BIBLIOGRAPHIC DATA.
MANUSCRIPTS
MARC SYSTEM
MICROFILMS.
MUSEUMS
PAMPHLETS.
PERIODICALS
PLAY.
PRINTING
PRINTING, PUBLIC
PUBLISHERS AND PUBLISHING.
SOCIETY FOR THE DIFFUSION OF USEFUL KNOWLEDGE.
SUBJECT HEADINGS

BIOGRAPHY.

ADENAUER (KONRAD).
ALBIZU CAMPOS (PEDRO).
ALLARDT (HELMUT).
ALLISON (R. BRUCE).
ALTHUSSER (LOUIS).
AMIN (IDI).
ANDERSON (AGNES ALEXANDRINA) Lady.
ANDERSON (Sir ROBERT).
ANDREOTTI (GIULIO).
ANDRIEUX (LOUIS).
ANNUNZIO (GABRIELE D').
ANSON (HAROLD).
ARAGO (DOMINIQUE FRANÇOIS JEAN).
ARENDARENKO (GEORGII ALEKSEEVICH).
ARENDT (HANNAH).
ARISTOTLE.
ARMAND (EMILE) pseud.
ARMAND (INESSA FEDOROVNA).
ARNDT FAMILY.
ASHTON (THOMAS SOUTHCLIFFE).
ASQUITH (HERBERT HENRY) 1st Earl of Oxford and Asquith.
ATATÜRK (KEMÂL).
ATKINSON (Sir HARRY ALBERT).
ATTERBURY (FRANCIS) Bishop of Rochester.
AYERS (BRADLEY EARL).
BACULARD D'ARNAUD (FRANÇOIS THOMAS MARIE).
BAKUNIN (MIKHAIL ALEKSANDROVICH).
BALBO (CESARE).
BAMBERGER (LUDWIG).
BARCLAY (Sir RODERICK EDWARD).
BARNES (RON).
BARTHOU (LOUIS).
BARTOSZEWSKI (WŁADYSŁAW)
BATA (THOMAS).
BEBEL (AUGUST).
BECK (JÓZEF).
BECKER (RAYMOND DE).
BELINSKII (VISSARION GRIGOR'EVICH).
BENEDICT (RUTH FULTON).
BERKMAN (ALEXANDER).
BERNASCHEK (RICHARD).
BERRYER (PIERRE ANTOINE).
BERT (PIERRE).
BERTIE (FRANCIS LEVESON) 1st Viscount Bertie of Thame.
BESTEIRO FERNANDEZ (JULIAN).
BEVIN (ERNEST).
BHENGU (NICHOLAS).
BIOGRAPHY.
BISMARCK-SCHOENHAUSEN (OTTO EDUARD LEOPOLD VON) Prince.

BIOGRAPHY(Cont.)

BLAGODATOV (ALEKSEI VASIL'EVICH).
BLANC (JEAN JOSEPH LOUIS).
BLUMER-RIS (HANS).
BLUNT (WILFRED SCAWEN).
BOBEK (PAWEŁ).
BOECKLER (HANS).
BÓJNOWSKI (LUCYAN).
BORDING (KRISTEN MORTENSEN).
BOSE (SUBHAS CHANDRA).
BOTEV (KHRISTO).
BOULDING (KENNETH EWART).
BOURGUIBA (HABIB).
BRANDT (WILLY).
BRANTING (GEORG).
BRANTING (HJALMAR).
BRASILLACH (ROBERT).
BRAUN (OTTO).
BREZHNEV (LEONID IL'ICH).
BRODOWICZ (JÓZEF MACIEJ).
BROWDER (EARL RUSSELL).
BRUENING (HEINRICH).
BRUPBACHER (FRITZ).
BUBER (MARTIN).
BUCA (EDWARD).
BUCHANAN (JAMES) President of the United States.
BULL (ODD).
BURKE (EDMUND).
BURNS (Sir GEORGE).
BUSEK (ERHARD).
BUTLER (CHRISTINA VIOLET).
BUTLER (JOSEPHINE ELIZABETH).
BYRON (GEORGE GORDON NOEL) 6th Baron Byron.
CALLAGHAN (JAMES).
CAMPBELL (JAMES DUNCAN).
CAMPBELL-BANNERMAN (Sir HENRY).
CANNING (GEORGE).
CANNON (JAMES PATRICK).
CAPODISTRIA (JOHN) Count.
CARDANO (GIROLAMO).
CARDENAS (LAZARO).
CARDOSO (FERNANDO HENRIQUE).
CARITAT (MARIE JEAN ANTOINE NICOLAS) Marquis de Condorcet.
CARNAP (RUDOLF).
CASAS (BARTOLOMÉ DE LAS) Bishop of Chiapa.
CASEMENT (Sir ROGER DAVID).
CASTELO BRANCO (HUMBERTO DE ALENCAR).
CATHERINE II, Empress of Russia.
CATTANEO (CARLO).
CECIL (ROBERT ARTHUR TALBOT GASCOYNE) 3rd Marquess of Salisbury
CHABAN-DELMAS (JACQUES).
CHARLES V, Emperor of Germany.
CHAVEZ (CESAR).
CHEREPNIN (LEV VLADIMIROVICH).
CHERNYSHEVSKII (NIKOLAI GAVRILOVICH).
CHICHERIN (BORIS NIKOLAEVICH).
CHOMSKY (NOAM).
CHORNOVIL (VIACHESLAV MAKSYMOVYCH).
CHOWNITZ (JULIAN FEODOR JOSEPH).
CHRISTIAN VIII, King of Denmark.
CHRISTMAS MØLLER (JOHN).
CHULALONGKORN, King of Thailand.
CHURCHILL (JOHN) 1st Duke of Marlborough.
CHURCHILL (Sir WINSTON LEONARD SPENCER).
CLARK (Sir GEORGE NORMAN).
CLAUSEWITZ (CARL VON).
CLAY (LAURA).
CLIVE (ROBERT) Baron Clive.
CLOWER (ROBERT W.).
COBB (CULLY ALTON).
COBDEN (RICHARD).
COCKBURN (HENRY) Lord Cockburn.
CODREANU (CORNELIU ZELEA).
COHEN (MORRIS RAPHAEL)
COHN-BENDIT (DANIEL).
COKE (Sir EDWARD).
COKE (THOMAS WILLIAM) 1st Earl of Leicester of Holkham.
COLLINGWOOD (ROBIN GEORGE).
COLSON (CHARLES W.).
COMTE (ISIDORE AUGUSTE MARIE FRANÇOIS XAVIER).
CONKLIN (HENRY).
COOMBS (CHARLES A.).
COOPER (ANTHONY ASHLEY) 7th Earl of Shaftesbury.
COSTA (JOAQUIN).
CREMIEUX (ISAAC ADOLPHE).
CROCE (BENEDETTO).
CROSSMAN (RICHARD HOWARD STAFFORD).
CROWE (Sir EYRE).
CUNNINGHAM-REID (ALEC STRATFORD).
CUNNINGHAME-GRAHAM (ROBERT BONTINE).
DAHLSTRÖM (HANS).
DANQUAH (JOSEPH BOAKYE).
DARBY FAMILY.
DECLERCQ (GILBERT).
DE COSMOS (AMOR).
DEFUNIS (MARCO).
DEGRELLE (LEON).
DELČEV (GOCE).
DELCOURT (EMILE).
DERING (Sir EDWARD).
DEWEY (JOHN).
DIAZ (PORFIRIO).
DIEFENBAKER (JOHN GEORGE).
DIMITROV (GEORGI).
DIMOV (DIMITUR).
DOBRACZYŃSKI (JAN).
DOERING (WOLFGANG).
DOHERTY (JOHN).
DORR (THOMAS WILSON).
DOUGLAS (THOMAS CLEMENT).
DREES (WILLEM).
DRUZHININ (NIKOLAI MIKHAILOVICH).
DU BOIS (WILLIAM EDWARD BURGHARDT).
DU PONT FAMILY.
DUDLEY (JOHN) 1st Duke of Northumberland.
DUHEM (PIERRE).
DUPUY (FERNAND).
DURKHEIM (EMILE).
DUTTWEILER (GOTTLIEB).
DUVAL (CLEMENT).
DWORKIN (EUZEBIUSZ).
EBERT (FRIEDRICH).
EDEN (ROBERT ANTHONY) 1st Earl of Avon.
EDGEWORTH (FRANCIS YSIDRO).
EINAUDI (LUIGI).
EISENHOWER (DWIGHT DAVID) President of the United States.
ENGELS (FRIEDRICH).
EPICURUS.
ERICKSEN (EPHRAIM EDWARD).
ERLANDER (TAGE).
ERLER (FRITZ).
ERSKINE (Hon. HENRY).
FABRI (FRIEDRICH).
FEDOROV (IVAN).
FERMAT (PIERRE DE).
FISCHER (FRITZ).
FISHER (Sir NORMAN FENWICK WARREN).
FLETCHER (CALVIN).
FLORENCOURT FAMILY.
FORD (GERALD RUDOLPH) President of the United States.
FORD (HENRY).
FOREST (EVA).
FOURIER (FRANÇOIS CHARLES MARIE).
FOXWELL (HERBERT SOMERTON).
FRAGA IRIBARNE (MANUEL).
FRANCIS FERDINAND, Archduke of Austria.
FRANCO BAHAMONDE (FRANCISCO).
FRANK (HANS).
FREDERICK II, King of Prussia.
FRESNEL (AUGUSTIN JEAN).
FREUD (SIGMUND).
GAJ (LJUDEVIT).
GALBRAITH (JOHN KENNETH).
GALIANI (FERDINANDO).
GALLAGHER (JOHN).
GAMPER (MICHAEL).
GANDHI (MOHANDAS KARAMCHAND).
GARAUDY (ROGER).
GARRATT (VERO W.)
GARVEY (MARCUS).
GAULLE (CHARLES DE).
GENOVESI (ANTONIO).
GENTILE (GIOVANNI).
GEORGE VI, King of Great Britain and Ireland.
GEORGE (DAVID LLOYD) 1st Earl Lloyd George.
GERHARDSEN (EINAR).
GERMANI (GINO).
GERVINUS (GEORG GOTTFRIED).
GESELL (SILVIO)
GODOLPHIN (SIDNEY) 1st Earl of Godolphin.
GODWIN (MARY).
GOLDER (SIDNEY ELMER).
GOLDMAN (EMMA).
GOLDMAN (PIERRE).
GOMPERS (SAMUEL).
GONZALEZ CASANOVA (PABLO).
GORBACHEVSKII (IVAN IVANOVICH).
GOR'KII (MAKSIM) pseud.
GOSNAT (VENISE).
GOULD (Sir RONALD).
GRAMSCI (ANTONIO).
GRANT (STAN).
GREAVES (HAROLD RICHARD GORING).
GREGORY (Sir THEODOR EMANUEL GUGENHEIM.
GRIGORENKO (PETR GRIGOR'EVICH).
GRUEN (KARL).
GSCHWIND (STEFAN).
GUEVARA (ERNESTO).
GUZMAN BLANCO (ANTONIO).
GWIAZDOWICZ (MICHAŁ).
HABERMAS (JUERGEN).
HAILE SELASSIE I, Emperor of Ethiopia.
HALDANE (ELIZABETH SANDERSON).
HAMILTON (ALEXANDER).
HAMMARSKJÖLD (DAG).
HARRIMAN (WILLIAM AVERELL).
HARRINGTON (JAMES).
HARRISON (THOMAS RUSSELL).
HART (Sir ROBERT).
HAYEK (FRIEDRICH AUGUST).
HEBRANG (ANDRIJA).
HECHT (ROBERT).
HEFNER (HUGH MARSTON).
HEGEL (GEORG WILHELM FRIEDRICH).
HEINE (HEINRICH).
HEMPEL (CARL GUSTAV).
HERDER (JOHANN GOTTFRIED VON).
HERTZOG (JAMES BARRY MUNNIK).
HERWEGH (GEORG).
HEUSS (THEODOR).
HILLEBRAND (OSWALD).
HITLER (ADOLF).
HLINKA (ANDREJ).
HOBBES (THOMAS).
HOBSON (JOHN ATKINSON).
HOHOFF (WILHELM).
HOLTROP (MARIUS WILHELM).
HOLYOAKE (GEORGE JACOB).
HOOVER (HERBERT CLARK) President of the United States.
HOPPE (JAN).
HORA (JOSEF).
HORTHY (MIKLÓS) Regent of Hungary.
HUME (DAVID).

BIOGRAPHY (Cont.)

HUYSMANS (CAMILLE).
IMLAY (GILBERT).
JACKSON (ANDREW) President of the United States.
JACKSON (GEORGE LESTER).
JACOB (ILSE).
JACOBY (JOHANN).
JALON (CESAR).
JASPER (ALBERT STANLEY).
JAURES (JEAN).
JOHANSEN (HANS).
JOHNSON (LYNDON BAINES) President of the United States.
JOLIOT-CURIE (JEAN FRÉDÉRIC).
JONES (MARY HARRIS).
KÁDÁR (JÁNOS).
KALECKI (MICHAŁ).
KALININ (MIKHAIL IVANOVICH).
KALLER (MAXIMILIAN).
KANT (IMMANUEL).
KARAMZIN (NIKOLAI MIKHAILOVICH).
KAUNDA (KENNETH DAVID).
KEKKONEN (URHO KALEVA).
KENNEDY (JOHN FITZGERALD) President of the United States.
KENNEDY (ROBERT FRANCIS).
KEYNES (JOHN MAYNARD) 1st Baron Keynes.
KHRUSHCHEV (NIKITA SERGEEVICH).
KIM (IL-SUNG).
KING (WILLIAM LYON MACKENZIE).
KIRKBRIDE (Sir ALEC).
KISELEV (PAVEL DMITRIEVICH).
KISSINGER (HENRY ALFRED).
KLEJNER (ISRAEL).
KLIUCHEVSKII (VASILII OSIPOVICH).
KLOTZ (GEORG).
KNIES (CARL GUSTAV ADOLF).
KNIGHT (WILLIAM).
KOCHANOWICZ (TADEUSZ).
KOEPLINGER (RUDOLF).
KOLLONTAI (ALEKSANDRA MIKHAILOVNA).
KONARSKI (SZYMON).
KORANYI (KAROL)
KREBS (ALBERT).
KROPOTKIN (PETR ALEKSEEVICH) Prince.
KRUGER (STEPHANUS JOHANNES PAULUS).
KUEHLMANN (MIRA VON).
KUN (BÉLA).
KUZNETSOV (EDUARD SAMUILOVICH).
LABRIOLA (ANTONIO).
LA FOLLETTE (ROBERT MARION) the Elder.
LA HAYE (LOUIS MARIE DE) Vicomte de Cormenin.
LAM (JAN).
LAMB (WILLIAM) 2nd Viscount Melbourne.
LAMPSON (MILES WEDDERBURN) 1st Baron Killearn.
LANGE (FRIEDRICH ALBERT).
LANGSDORF (GRIGORII IVANOVICH).
LAVROV (PETR LAVROVICH).
LAW (JOHN).
LAWLESS (GERARD RICHARD).
LAWRENCE (THOMAS EDWARD).
LAZO (SERGEI GEORGIEVICH).
LEHMAN (HERBERT HENRY).
LEIJONHUFVUD (AXEL).
LELEWEL (JOACHIM).
LENIN (VLADIMIR IL'ICH).
LESSNER (FRIEDRICH).
LEVER (WILLIAM HESKETH) 1st Viscount Leverhulme.
LEVI-STRAUSS (CLAUDE).
LEVSKI (VASIL).
LIBELT (KAROL).
LIEBKNECHT (KARL).
LIEBKNECHT (WILHELM PHILIPP MARTIN CHRISTIAN LUDWIG).

LINDSAY (MICHAEL FRANCIS MORRIS) 2nd Baron Lindsay.
LIST (GEORG FRIEDRICH).
LIU (SHAO-CH'I).
LOCKE (JOHN).
LOHRENZ (WILHELM).
LONSDALE (JOHN) 1737-1807.
LORENZONI (JULIO).
LOUIS XIV, King of France.
LOWE (ROBERT) 1st Viscount Sherbrooke.
LUCRETIUS CARUS (TITUS).
LUKÀCS (GEORG).
LUMLEY (E.K.).
LUNIN (MIKHAIL SERGEEVICH).
LUNN (Sir HENRY SIMPSON).
LUSTY (Sir ROBERT FRITH).
LUXEMBURG (ROSA).
McADOO (WILLIAM GIBBS).
MACARTHUR (DOUGLAS).
McCARTHY (JOSEPH RAYMOND).
MACCHIAVELLI (NICCOLÒ).
McCRACKEN (ELIZABETH C.).
MAČEK (VLADKO).
McEWAN (TOM).
MACKINDER (Sir HALFORD JOHN).
MAKHNO (NESTOR).
MALRAUX (ANDRE).
MANDEVILLE (BERNARD DE).
MANETTI (CESARE).
MANTOUX (ETIENNE).
MAO (TSE-TUNG).
MARCHLEWSKI (JULIAN BALTAZAR).
MARCUSE (HERBERT).
MARGAI (Sir MILTON AUGUSTUS STRIEBY).
MARIAŃSKA (ANIELA).
MARITAIN (JACQUES).
MARK (KARL).
MARKOVIĆ (SVETOZAR).
MARQUART (FRANK).
MARSHALL (ALFRED).
MARTI (JOSE).
MARX (JENNY).
MARX (KARL).
MARX FAMILY.
MASARYK (JAN).
MASARYK (THOMAS GARRIGUE).
MASIUTKO (MYKHAILO SAVOVYCH).
MASSIE (ROBERT) the Younger.
MASSIE (ROBERT K.).
MASSIE (SUZANNE).
MATZNETTER (OTTO).
MAURIN (JOAQUIN).
MAZZINI (GIUSEPPE).
MEAD (GEORGE HERBERT).
MEDVEDEV (ZHORES ALEKSANDROVICH).
MENDÈS-FRANCE (PIERRE).
MENGOTTI (FRANCESCO) Conte.
MERLEAU-PONTY (MAURICE).
MERTON (ROBERT KING).
METTERNICH-WINNEBURG (CLEMENS WENZESLAUS NEPOMUK LOTHAR VON) Prince.
MICHAEL III, Voyvode of Wallachia.
MICHELSEN (CHRISTIAN).
MICKIEWICZ (ADAM).
MILL (JOHN STUART).
MILNER (ALFRED) 1st Viscount Milner.
MINKOV (SVETOSLAV).
MINTS (ISAAK IZRAILEVICH).
MITTERRAND (FRANÇOIS).
MORGAN (ARTHUR ERNEST).
MORGAN (LEWIS HENRY).
MOROZ (VALENTYN IAKOVYCH).
MORRIS (ROBERT).
MUELLER (JOSEF).
MUELLER-THURGAU (HERMANN).
MUIR (THOMAS).
MUMFORD (LEWIS).
MUSSOLINI (BENITO).

MYRDAL (GUNNAR)
MZILIKAZI, King of the Matabele.
NABOKOV (VLADIMIR DMITRIEVICH).
NADER (RALPH).
NAPOLEON I, Emperor of the French.
NAPOLEON III, Emperor of the French.
NASSER (GAMAL ABDEL).
NATANSON (MARK ANDREEVICH).
N'DONGO (SALLY).
NECHAEV (SERGEI GENNADIEVICH).
NEHRU (JAWAHARLAL).
NESSELRODE (KARL ROBERT VON) Graf.
NEUMEISTER (FRITZ).
NICHOLSON (JOHN).
NICOLE (LEON).
NIEBUHR (REINHOLD).
NIETZSCHE (FRIEDRICH WILHELM).
NITTI (FRANCESCO SAVERIO).
NIXON (RICHARD MILHOUS) President of the United States.
NOBLE (HAROLD JOYCE).
NORRIS (WILLIAM).
NORTH (Sir DUDLEY BURTON NAPIER).
NORTH (FREDERICK) 2nd Earl of Guilford.
NOVOSEL'SKII (ALEKSEI ANDREEVICH).
NOVOTNÝ (ANTONÍN).
NOWOTKO (MARCELI).
NOZHIN (NIKOLAI DMITRIEVICH).
NYERERE (JULIUS KAMBARAGE).
O'BRIEN (WILLIAM).
OGAREV (NIKOLAI PLATONOVICH).
OLMSTED (FREDERICK LAW).
OOMS (FRANZ).
OPPENHEIMER (JULIUS ROBERT).
ORTEGA Y GASSET (JOSE).
OYEWOLE (FOLA).
OZERNYI (MYKHAILO DMYTROVYCH).
PALMER (THOMAS FYSCHE).
PANIN (DIMITRII MIKHAILOVICH).
PANIN (NIKITA IVANOVICH).
PASCAL (BLAISE).
PAUL (Sir GEORGE ONESIPHORUS).
PEARSON (LESTER BOWLES).
PEARSON (WEETMAN DICKINSON) 1st Viscount Cowdray.
PEFFER (WILLIAM ALFRED).
PEREZ JIMENEZ (MARCOS).
PERHAM (Dame MARGERY FREDA).
PERON (JUAN DOMINGO).
PÉTAIN (HENRI PHILIPPE BÉNONI OMER JOSEPH).
PETRA'YCKI (LEON).
PHILIP II, King of Spain.
PIAGET (JEAN).
PICKERSGILL (JOHN WHITNEY).
PIECK (WILHELM).
PIL'NIAK (BORIS ANDREEVICH).
PITT (WILLIAM) Earl of Chatham.
PIUS XII, Pope.
PLEKHANOV (GEORGII VALENTINOVICH).
PLIMSOLL (SAMUEL).
PLISCHKE (OSKAR).
PLYUSHCH (LEONID).
POLLITT (HARRY).
POMPIDOU (GEORGES).
POPPER (JULIO).
POPPER (Sir KARL RAIMUND).
POUGET (EMILE).
POUND (EZRA).
PRAGIER (ADAM).
PRESTES (LUIS CARLOS).
PROUDHON (PIERRE JOSEPH).
QUESNAY (FRANÇOIS).
QUINE (WILLARD VAN ORMAN).
RADCHENKO (STEPAN IVANOVICH).
RADCLIFFE (Sir JOSEPH).
RADEV (SIMEON).
RADISHCHEV (ALEKSANDR NIKOLAEVICH).
RAKOVSKII (KHRISTIAN GEORGIEVICH).
RAWLS (JOHN).

BIOGRAPHY (Cont.)

RAZGON (IZRAIL' MENDELEEVICH).
REMY (BERNARD).
RICKERT (HEINRICH).
RIEL (LOUIS DAVID).
RIESSER (GABRIEL).
RINGEISEN (MICHAEL).
RIQUETTI (VICTOR) Marquis de Mirabeau.
RIZA SHAH PAHLAVI, Shah of Iran.
ROBESPIERRE (FRANÇOIS MAXIMILIEN JOSEPH ISIDORE).
ROBINSON (Sir HENRY AUGUSTUS).
ROBINSON (RONALD EDWARD)
ROCAFUERTE (VICENTE).
RODO (JOSE ENRIQUE).
ROEPKE (WILHELM).
ROOSEVELT (FRANKLIN DELANO) President of the United States.
ROOSEVELT (THEODORE) President of the United States.
ROSA (JOAO GUIMARÃES).
ROSAS (JUAN MANUEL DE).
ROSCHER (WILHELM).
ROSE (WILLIAM JOHN).
ROSSI (ERNESTO).
ROTSHTEIN (FEDOR ARONOVICH).
ROUSSEAU (JEAN JACQUES).
ROWELL (NEWTON WESLEY).
ROYER (JEAN).
ROZEN (ANDREI EVGEN'EVICH) Baron.
RUPPRECHT (ADOLF).
ST. LAURENT (LOUIS STEPHEN).
SAINT-SIMON (CLAUDE HENRI DE) Comte.
SANCHEZ-ALBORNOZ (CLAUDIO).
SANCTIS (GAETANO DE).
SARAN (MARY).
SARTRE (JEAN PAUL).
SAUD FAMILY.
SCHAFFERER (KARL).
SCHAPERA (ISAAC).
SCHARFFENBERG FAMILY.
SCHEFFLER (HEINRICH).
SCHMIDT (FOLKE).
SCHOENERER (GEORG VON).
SCHRUEBBERS (HUBERT).
SCHULZE (FIETE).
SCHWAB (CHARLES MICHAEL).
SECONDAT (CHARLES LOUIS DE) Baron de Montesquieu.
SEEMANN (KLAUS).
SÉGUY (GEORGES).
SELIGER (JOSEF).
SEPÚLVEDA (JUAN GINÉS DE).
SEWARD (WILLIAM HENRY).
SEYDOUX (FRANÇOIS).
SHAW (GEORGE BERNARD).
SHEVCHENKO (TARAS GRIGOR'EVICH).
SMITH (ADAM).
SMITH (FREDERICK EDWIN) 1st Earl of Birkenhead.
SMUTS (JAN CHRISTIAAN).
SOEKARNO (ACHMED).
SOHN-RETHEL (ALFRED).
SOLZHENITSYN (ALEKSANDR ISAEVICH).
SOMERS (JOHN) Baron Somers.
SOREL (GEORGES).
SOSNKOWSKI (KAZIMIERZ).
SPASOWICZ (WŁODZIMIERZ).
SPENCER (HERBERT).
SPINOZA (BENEDICTUS DE).
SPRINGER (AXEL).
SRAFFA (PIERO).
STALIN (IOSIF VISSARIONOVICH).
STAUNING (THORVALD AUGUST MARINUS).
STEEN (JOHANNES VILHELM).
STEFFEN (JOCHEN).
STEFFENS (JOSEPH LINCOLN).
STEPHEN (Sir LESLIE).
STEVENSON (ADLAI EWING).
STEWART (HENRY ROBERT) Viscount Castlereagh, 2nd Marquess of Londonderry.

STOEGMUELLER (ERNST).
STOIANOV (ZAKHARII).
STRAUSS (FRANZ JOSEF).
SUKLOVA (MARIIA).
SUMNER (WILLIAM GRAHAM).
SUZMAN (HELEN).
SYMONDS (JOHN).
SZÉCHENYI (ISTVÁN) Gróf.
SZENDE (STEFAN).
TALEV (DIMITUR).
TALMADGE (EUGENE).
TAUS (JOSEF).
TAYLOR (CATHERINE).
TELLER (EDWARD).
TELLEWOYAN (ZUBARYEA AKOI).
THIEL (ERNEST JACQUES).
THOMAS [BECKET], Saint, Archbishop of Canterbury.
THOREZ (MAURICE).
THUGUTT (STANISŁAW).
TKACHEV (PETR NIKITICH).
TODOROV (KOSTA).
TOGLIATTI (PALMIRO).
TOLBERT (WILLIAM RICHARD).
TOURE (SEKOU).
TREITSCHKE (HEINRICH VON).
TREVIRANUS (GOTTFRIED REINHOLD).
TROTSKII (LEV DAVYDOVICH).
TRUMAN (HARRY S.), President of the United States.
TRUMBIĆ (ANTE).
TSAFENDAS (DEMITRIOS).
TUBMAN (WILLIAM VACANARAT SHADRACH).
TUVERI (GIOVANNI BATTISTA).
ULČ (OTTO).
UNWIN FAMILY.
VALENTINOV (NIKOLAI VLADISLAVOVICH) pseud.
VALERO (HELENA).
VALOIS (GEORGES) pseud.
VAMBE (LAWRENCE).
VERRI (PIETRO) Conte.
VERSYP (EDGARD).
VERWOERD (HENDRIK FRENSCH).
VICO (GIAMBATTISTA).
VILLIERS (CHARLES PELHAM).
VINCI (LEONARDO DA).
VITTORIO (GIUSEPPE DI).
VOLLMER (AUGUST).
VOLTAIRE (FRANÇOIS MARIE AROUET DE).
VON NEUMANN (JOHN).
VOROSHILOV (KLIMENT EFREMOVICH).
VOZNESENSKII (NIKOLAI ALEKSEEVICH).
WADIA (B.P.)
WALLACE (HENRY AGARD).
WALRAS (LEON).
WARD (LESTER FRANK).
WARNKE (HANS).
WEBB (WALTER PRESCOTT).
WEBER (MAX).
WEHNER (HERBERT).
WEMHOFF (KARL HEINZ).
WESTON (RICHARD) 1st Earl of Portland.
WESTPHALEN (JOHANN LUDWIG VON).
WESTPHALEN FAMILY.
WILDE (JACQUES DE).
WILSON (JOSEPH)
WILSON (THOMAS WOODROW) President of the United States.
WITTGENSTEIN (LUDWIG).
WODAK (WALTER).
WOHLIN (NILS RICHARD).
WOLFENDEN (JOHN FREDERICK) Baron Wolfenden.
WOYTINSKY (WLADIMIR SAVELEVICH).
WRIGHT (GEORG HENRIK VON).
YOUNG (ARTHUR).
YOUNG (THOMAS).
ZAGÓRSKI-OSTOJA (WŁODZIMIERZ).

ZÁPOTOCKÝ (ANTONÍN)
ZEIDLER-KORNMANN (HEINZ).
ZELLWEGER (ALFRED).
ZUBATOV (SERGEI VASIL'EVICH).
ZWINGLI (ULRICH).
ZYBLIKIEWICZ (MIKOŁAJ).

COMMERCE AND INDUSTRY.

General.

ACCOUNTING.
ADVERTISING.
ADVERTISING AGENCIES
AGED AS CONSUMERS
APPRENTICES
ARBITRATION, INDUSTRIAL.
ASSEMBLY-LINE METHODS.
AUDITING.
BIG BUSINESS
BOOKKEEPING.
BUSINESS
BUSINESS AND POLITICS.
BUSINESS CYCLES.
BUSINESS EDUCATION
BUSINESS ETHICS.
BUSINESS FORECASTING.
BUSINESS RELOCATION
CENTRAL AMERICAN COMMON MARKET.
CHAMBERS OF COMMERCE
COLONIAL COMPANIES.
COMMERCE.
COMMERCIAL FINANCE COMPANIES
COMMERCIAL POLICY.
COMMERCIAL PRODUCTS.
COMMERCIAL STATISTICS.
COMMERCIAL VEHICLES.
COMMODITY CONTROL.
COMMODITY EXCHANGES.
COMMUNICATION IN MANAGEMENT
CONSOLIDATION AND MERGER OF CORPORATIONS.
CONSUMER PROTECTION.
CONSUMERS.
CONTRACTS
CONTRACTS, LETTING OF
COOPERATION.
COOPERATIVE SOCIETIES.
CORPORATIONS.
CORPORATIONS, AMERICAN.
CORPORATIONS, FOREIGN
CORPORATIONS, NON-PROFIT
CORPORATIONS, PUBLIC.
CORPORATIONS, SWEDISH
DANGEROUS GOODS
DECENTRALIZATION IN MANAGEMENT
DESIGN, INDUSTRIAL
DIVERSIFICATION IN INDUSTRY
DUMPING (COMMERCIAL POLICY).
EAST-WEST TRADE (1945-).
EFFICIENCY, INDUSTRIAL.
EMPLOYEE-MANAGEMENT RELATIONS IN GOVERNMENT
EMPLOYEES, DISMISSAL OF
EMPLOYEES, TRAINING OF.
EMPLOYEES' REPRESENTATION IN MANAGEMENT.
EMPLOYERS' ASSOCIATIONS
EMPLOYMENT AGENCIES
EMPLOYMENT FORECASTING
EMPLOYMENT MANAGEMENT.
ENERGY CONSERVATION.
ENERGY CONSUMPTION.
ENERGY POLICY.
EUROPEAN FREE TRADE ASSOCIATION.
EXPORT CREDIT
FACTORY SYSTEM
FAIRNESS.
FIRMS.
FOOD PRICES
FOREIGN TRADE PROMOTION

COMMERCE AND INDUSTRY

FOREIGN TRADE REGULATION.
FRANCHISES (RETAIL TRADE)
FUEL
GOVERNMENT BUSINESS ENTERPRISES.
IMPORT QUOTAS
INCENTIVES IN INDUSTRY.
INDUSTRIAL ACCIDENTS
INDUSTRIAL BUILDINGS
INDUSTRIAL CONCENTRATION.
INDUSTRIAL DISTRICTS
INDUSTRIAL EQUIPMENT
INDUSTRIAL HOUSING
INDUSTRIAL HYGIENE
INDUSTRIAL MANAGEMENT.
INDUSTRIAL MANAGEMENT AND INFLATION.
INDUSTRIAL ORGANIZATION.
INDUSTRIAL PROJECT MANAGEMENT.
INDUSTRIAL PROMOTION
INDUSTRIAL PUBLICITY.
INDUSTRIAL RELATIONS.
INDUSTRIAL SAFETY
INDUSTRIALIZATION.
INDUSTRIES, LOCATION OF.
INDUSTRIES, SIZE OF.
INDUSTRY.
INDUSTRY AND EDUCATION.
INDUSTRY AND STATE.
INSTALMENT PLAN
INTERNATIONAL BUSINESS ENTERPRISES.
INTERVIEWING IN MARKETING RESEARCH.
INVENTIONS.
INVENTORIES
JOINT ADVENTURES
JOURNALISM, COMMERCIAL
LATIN AMERICAN FREE TRADE ASSOCIATION.
LICENCES
MACHINERY IN INDUSTRY.
MANAGEMENT.
MANAGEMENT GAMES.
MANAGEMENT INFORMATION SYSTEMS.
MANAGERIAL ECONOMICS.
MARKET SURVEYS
MARKETING.
MARKETING MANAGEMENT.
MARKETING RESEARCH
MARKETS
MEDIATION AND CONCILIATION, INDUSTRIAL
MINE SAFETY
MINORITY BUSINESS ENTERPRISES
NEGOTIATION.
NEGROES AS CONSUMERS
NEW PRODUCTS.
OCCUPATIONAL MOBILITY.
OCCUPATIONAL TRAINING
OCCUPATIONS.
OCCUPATIONS AND RACE.
OFFICE BUILDINGS.
OFFICES.
OPERATIONS RESEARCH.
ORGANIZATION OF THE PETROLEUM EXPORTING COUNTRIES.
PANPACIFIC RELATIONS.
PATENTS
POOR AS CONSUMERS
POWER RESOURCES.
PRODUCTION MANAGEMENT.
PRODUCTION PLANNING.
PRODUCTIVITY.
PROFESSIONS
PROMOTIONS.
PUBLIC UTILITIES.
QUALITY CONTROL.
RADIO ADVERTISING
RAW MATERIALS.
RECRUITING OF EMPLOYEES.
REPLACEMENT OF INDUSTRIAL EQUIPMENT.

RESEARCH, INDUSTRIAL.
RESEARCH AND DEVELOPMENT CONTRACTS
RETAIL TRADE.
SELF SERVICE STORES
SERVICE INDUSTRIES.
SHOPPING
SHOPPING CENTRES
SHOPPING MALLS
SMALL BUSINESS
STANDARDIZATION
STORES, RETAIL.
SUPERMARKETS
TECHNICIANS IN INDUSTRY
TELEVISION IN ADVERTISING.
TIME ALLOCATION.
TRADE REGULATION
TURNOVER (BUSINESS)
UNITED NATIONS CONFERENCE ON TRADE AND DEVELOPMENT.
VOCATIONAL GUIDANCE
VOCATIONAL INTERESTS
WAREHOUSE MANAGEMENT.
WAREHOUSES
WELFARE WORK IN INDUSTRY
WHOLESALE TRADE
WOOD AS FUEL.
WORK DESIGN.
WORK ENVIRONMENT.
WORK RELIEF
WORKMEN'S COMPENSATION

Occupations and professions.

ACTING AS A PROFESSION.
AGRICULTURAL LABOURERS
ARTISANS
AUTOMOBILE INDUSTRY WORKERS.
BANKERS
BANKING AS A PROFESSION.
BUSINESS CONSULTANTS
BUSINESSMEN
CAPITALISTS AND FINANCIERS
CARPENTERS
CHEMISTS
CHIMNEY-SWEEPS
CIVIL ENGINEERS
CLERKS
CLOTHING WORKERS
COAL MINERS
CONSTRUCTION WORKERS
DAIRY WORKERS
DENTISTS
DIPLOMATS, AMERICAN.
DIPLOMATS, BRITISH
DIPLOMATS, CHINESE.
DIPLOMATS, FRENCH
DIPLOMATS, JAPANESE.
DIRECTORS OF CORPORATIONS
DOCK WORKERS
ECONOMISTS.
ELECTRIC INDUSTRY WORKERS
ELECTRONIC DATA PROCESSING PERSONNEL.
ELECTRONIC INDUSTRY WORKERS
EMPLOYEE TRAINING DIRECTORS
ENGINEERING AS A PROFESSION.
ENGINEERS
EXECUTIVES
FISHERMEN
GOLD MINERS
HOSIERY WORKERS
IRON AND STEEL WORKERS
JUDGES
JUTE INDUSTRY WORKERS
LAWYERS
MEDICAL PERSONNEL
MEDICINE AS A PROFESSION.
MERCHANTS, BELGIAN.
MERCHANTS, BRITISH.
MERCHANTS, EUROPEAN.

MERCHANTS, FRENCH.
MERCHANTS, GERMAN.
MERCHANTS, SCOTTISH.
METAL WORKERS
MIGRANT AGRICULTURAL LABOURERS
MILITARY SERVICE AS A PROFESSION.
MINERS.
MOTOR TRUCK DRIVERS.
NEGRO EXECUTIVES.
NURSES AND NURSING
PAPER INDUSTRY WORKERS
PETROLEUM WORKERS
PHYSICAL THERAPISTS
PHYSICIANS
PHYSICIANS (GENERAL PRACTICE)
PHYSICIANS, FOREIGN
PLASTICS WORKERS
POLITICAL SCIENTISTS.
POTTERS
PRINTERS
REAL ESTATE AGENTS
SCIENTISTS
SERVANTS
SHIPBUILDING WORKERS
SOCIAL WORK AS A PROFESSION.
SOCIOLOGY AS A PROFESSION.
SUGAR WORKERS
TEACHERS
TECHNOLOGISTS
TEXTILE WORKERS
TINKERS
TRANSPORT WORKERS
WEAVERS
WOMEN ENGINEERS
WOMEN IN BUSINESS.
WOMEN IN POLITICS.
WOMEN JOURNALISTS
WOMEN TEACHERS.
WOODWORKERS

Particular trades and industries.

AEROPLANE INDUSTRY AND TRADE
AEROSPACE INDUSTRIES
ALUMINIUM INDUSTRY AND TRADE
ASBESTOS INDUSTRY
ATOMIC ENERGY INDUSTRIES.
ATOMIC POWER PLANTS
AUTOMOBILE INDUSTRY AND TRADE
BANANA TRADE
BICYCLE INDUSTRY
BOOK INDUSTRIES AND TRADE.
BOOKSELLERS AND BOOKSELLING.
BREWING INDUSTRIES
BUILDING TRADES
BUILDINGS, PREFABRICATED.
CATERERS AND CATERING
CATTLE TRADE
CHEMICAL INDUSTRIES.
CHEMICAL PLANTS
CHEMICALS
CIVIL ENGINEERING
CLOTHING TRADE
COAL.
COAL MINE WASTE.
COAL MINES AND MINING
COAL TRADE
COCOA TRADE
COFFEE TRADE
COMPUTER INDUSTRY.
COMPUTERS.
CONSTRUCTION INDUSTRY.
COPPER INDUSTRY AND TRADE.
COPPER MINES AND MINING.
COPROLITES.
COTTAGE INDUSTRIES
COTTON GROWING AND MANUFACTURE
COTTON TRADE.
DIAMONDS.
DIESEL MOTOR INDUSTRY
DRUG TRADE (PHARMACEUTICAL)

COMMERCE AND INDUSTRY (Cont.)

DYE INDUSTRY
ELECTRIC CONTRACTING
ELECTRIC INDUSTRIES
ELECTRIC POWER-PLANTS
ELECTRICITY SUPPLY
ELECTRONIC DATA PROCESSING.
ELECTRONIC DATA PROCESSING DEPARTMENTS.
ELECTRONIC DIGITAL COMPUTERS.
ELECTRONIC INDUSTRIES
ENGINEERING
FERTILIZER INDUSTRY
FIBRES.
FIBRES, SYNTHETIC.
FOOD.
FOOD INDUSTRY AND TRADE
FOOD RESEARCH
FOOD SUPPLY.
FUEL TRADE
FUR TRADE
FURNITURE INDUSTRY AND TRADE
GAS, NATURAL.
GAS, NATURAL, IN SUBMERGED LANDS
GAS INDUSTRY
GLASS INDUSTRY AND TRADE
GLUCOSE INDUSTRY
GOLD MINES AND MINING
GOLDSMITHERY
GRAIN TRADE.
GROCERY TRADE
HOTELS, TAVERNS, ETC.
HOUSEHOLD APPLIANCES.
IRON INDUSTRY AND TRADE
LEAD MINES AND MINING
LEATHER INDUSTRY AND TRADE
LIGNITE
LINEN
MACHINE PARTS.
MACHINERY
MEAT INDUSTRY AND TRADE
METAL TRADE
METAL WORK
METALLURGY
MILK SUPPLY.
MILK TRADE
MINERAL INDUSTRIES.
MINES AND MINERAL RESOURCES.
MINING CORPORATIONS.
MINING INDUSTRY AND FINANCE
MOTOR CYCLES
MOVING PICTURE INDUSTRY
MUNITIONS.
NEWSPAPER PUBLISHING.
NICKEL INDUSTRY
OLIVE INDUSTRY AND TRADE
OPEN-CAST MINING
PAPER MAKING AND TRADE
PET INDUSTRY
PETROL.
PETROLEUM.
PETROLEUM CHEMICALS INDUSTRY
PETROLEUM IN SUBMERGED LANDS.
PETROLEUM INDUSTRY AND TRADE.
PETROLEUM PRODUCTS
PETROLEUM REFINERIES.
PHOSPHATE INDUSTRY
PHOTOGRAPHIC INDUSTRY
PLASTICS IN PACKAGING.
PLASTICS INDUSTRY AND TRADE
POTASH INDUSTRY AND TRADE
PRODUCE TRADE.
PUBLISHERS AND PUBLISHING.
REAL ESTATE BUSINESS
RUBBER INDUSTRY AND TRADE
SALT INDUSTRY AND TRADE
SHIPBUILDING
SILK MANUFACTURE AND TRADE
SLATE INDUSTRY
SODA INDUSTRY
STEAM ENGINES.
STEEL INDUSTRY AND TRADE.
STEEL-WORKS
SUGAR TRADE.
TEA TRADE.
TEXTILE FIBRES, SYNTHETIC
TEXTILE INDUSTRY AND FABRICS
TIN
TIN CONTAINERS.
TIN INDUSTRY
TIN MINES AND MINING.
TOBACCO MANUFACTURE AND TRADE
TOURISTS.
TYPEWRITER INDUSTRY
TYRES
URANIUM INDUSTRY
USED MACHINERY.
WATER DISTRICTS
WATER MILLS
WATER-POWER ELECTRIC PLANTS
WHISKY
WINE AND WINE MAKING
WIRE INDUSTRY
WOOD-PULP INDUSTRY
WOOD-USING INDUSTRIES
WOOL TRADE AND INDUSTRY
WOOLLEN AND WORSTED MANUFACTURE

ECONOMICS.

see also AGRICULTURE; COMMERCE AND INDUSTRY; FINANCE; TRANSPORT

ABILITY, INFLUENCE OF AGE ON
AGE AND EMPLOYMENT
AIR
ALIEN LABOUR
BARTER
BOYCOTT
CAPITALISM.
CASUAL LABOUR
CHRISTIANITY AND ECONOMICS.
CHURCH AND ECONOMICS.
CHURCH AND LABOUR
CIVIL SERVICE PENSIONS
COLLECTIVE BARGAINING.
COLLECTIVE LABOUR AGREEMENTS
COMMUNISM.
COMPETITION.
COMPETITION, INTERNATIONAL.
COMPETITION, UNFAIR
CONSUMPTION (ECONOMICS)
CONTRACT LABOUR
CONVICT LABOUR
CO-PARTNERSHIP.
COST AND STANDARD OF LIVING.
COST CONTROL.
COST EFFECTIVENESS.
COSTS, INDUSTRIAL
COUNCIL FOR MUTUAL ECONOMIC ASSISTANCE.
CRISES.
DEPRECIATION ALLOWANCES.
DISCRIMINATION IN EMPLOYMENT
DISTRIBUTION (ECONOMIC THEORY).
DIVISION OF LABOUR.
DOMESTIC ECONOMY.
EAST AFRICAN COMMUNITY.
EAST GHOR CANAL PROJECT.
ECONOMIC ASSISTANCE.
ECONOMIC ASSISTANCE, AMERICAN.
ECONOMIC ASSISTANCE, BRITISH.
ECONOMIC ASSISTANCE, CANADIAN.
ECONOMIC ASSISTANCE, CHINESE.
ECONOMIC ASSISTANCE, COMMUNIST.
ECONOMIC ASSISTANCE, DOMESTIC
ECONOMIC ASSISTANCE, DUTCH.
ECONOMIC ASSISTANCE, GERMAN.
ECONOMIC ASSISTANCE, JAPANESE.
ECONOMIC ASSISTANCE, RUSSIAN.
ECONOMIC ASSISTANCE IN AFRICA.
ECONOMIC ASSISTANCE IN ASIA.
ECONOMIC ASSISTANCE IN LIBERIA.
ECONOMIC ASSISTANCE IN RUSSIA.
ECONOMIC ASSISTANCE IN THAILAND.
ECONOMIC CONDITIONS.
ECONOMIC DEVELOPMENT.
ECONOMIC FORECASTING.
ECONOMIC HISTORY.
ECONOMIC INDICATORS
ECONOMIC LEGISLATION
ECONOMIC POLICY.
ECONOMIC STABILIZATION.
ECONOMIC ZONING
ECONOMICS.
ECONOMICS, COMPARATIVE.
ECONOMICS, MATHEMATICAL.
ECONOMICS, PRIMITIVE.
ECONOMIES OF SCALE.
EIGHT HOUR MOVEMENT.
EMPLOYMENT (ECONOMIC THEORY).
ENTREPRENEUR.
ENVIRONMENTAL POLICY.
ENVIRONMENTAL POLICY RESEARCH
EQUAL PAY FOR EQUAL WORK.
EQUILIBRIUM (ECONOMICS).
EUROPEAN ECONOMIC COMMUNITY.
EXTERNALITIES (ECONOMICS).
FAMILY ALLOWANCES
FOOD CONSUMPTION
FREE TRADE AND PROTECTION.
GENERAL AGREEMENT ON TARIFFS AND TRADE.
GENERAL STRIKE, UNITED KINGDOM, 1926.
GEOGRAPHY, ECONOMIC.
GOVERNMENT MONOPOLIES.
GOVERNMENT OWNERSHIP
GOVERNMENT PURCHASING
GRIEVANCE PROCEDURES
GROSS DOMESTIC PRODUCT
GROSS NATIONAL PRODUCT.
HOME LABOUR
HOME OWNERSHIP.
HOURS OF LABOUR.
HOUSING.
HOUSING, COOPERATIVE
HOUSING, RURAL
HOUSING FOR PHYSICALLY HANDICAPPED
HOUSING MANAGEMENT.
HOUSING SUBSIDIES
HUMAN CAPITAL
INCOME.
INCOME DISTRIBUTION.
INCOME MAINTENANCE PROGRAMMES
INDEX NUMBERS (ECONOMICS).
INDEXATION (ECONOMICS).
INDUSTRIAL ORGANIZATION (ECONOMIC THEORY).
INFORMATION THEORY IN ECONOMICS.
INTERINDUSTRY ECONOMICS.
INTERNATIONAL ECONOMIC INTEGRATION.
INTERNATIONAL ECONOMIC RELATIONS.
JOB ANALYSIS.
JOB EVALUATION.
JOB SATISFACTION.
LABOUR AND LABOURING CLASSES.
LABOUR CONTRACT
LABOUR COSTS
LABOUR DISCIPLINE
LABOUR DISPUTES
LABOUR ECONOMICS.
LABOUR MOBILITY
LABOUR POLICY
LABOUR SUPPLY.
LABOUR TURNOVER
LAND.
LAND, NATIONALIZATION OF
LAND REFORM
LAND TENURE.
LEASES

LIQUIDITY (ECONOMICS).
MALTHUSIANISM.
MANPOWER POLICY.
MARXIAN ECONOMICS.
MATERNITY LEAVE
MEDICAL CARE, COST OF.
MIGRANT LABOUR.
MONOPOLIES.
OLIGOPOLIES.
ORGANISATION FOR ECONOMIC
  COOPERATION AND DEVELOPMENT.
PART-TIME EMPLOYMENT
PENSIONS
PENSIONS, MILITARY
PHYSIOCRATS.
POLLUTION.
POPULATION.
POPULATION POLICY.
POPULATION RESEARCH.
PRICE INDEXES.
PRICE MAINTENANCE
PRICE REGULATION.
PRICES.
PRODUCTION (ECONOMIC THEORY)
PRODUCTION FUNCTIONS (ECONOMIC
  THEORY).
PRODUCTIVITY (ECONOMIC THEORY).
PROFIT.
PROFIT SHARING
PROPERTY.
PUBLIC HOUSING
PURCHASING POWER.
REAL PROPERTY
REGIONAL ECONOMICS.
RENT
RENT (ECONOMIC THEORY).
RENT CONTROL
RESTRAINT OF TRADE
RIGHT TO LABOUR.
RISK.
SALARIED EMPLOYEES
SEASONAL LABOUR
SELF-EMPLOYED
SEX DISCRIMINATION IN EMPLOYMENT
SHOP STEWARDS
SIT DOWN STRIKES
SKILLED LABOUR
SOCIALIST COMPETITION.
SPACE IN ECONOMICS.
STRIKES AND LOCKOUTS
SUBSIDIES.
SUPPLEMENTARY EMPLOYMENT
SUPPLY AND DEMAND
SYSTEM ANALYSIS.
TECHNICAL ASSISTANCE.
TECHNICAL ASSISTANCE, AMERICAN.
TECHNICAL ASSISTANCE, CHINESE
TECHNICAL ASSISTANCE, JAPANESE.
TECHNICAL ASSISTANCE, RUSSIAN.
TECHNICAL ASSISTANCE IN EAST
  AFRICA.
TECHNICAL ASSISTANCE IN PAKISTAN.
TECHNOCRACY.
TEMPORARY EMPLOYMENT
TIME AND ECONOMIC REACTIONS.
TRADE AND PROFESSIONAL
  ASSOCIATIONS
TRADE UNIONS.
TRADE UNIONS, CATHOLIC
TRADE UNIONS AND COMMUNISM.
TRADE UNIONS AND FOREIGN POLICY
TRANSFER PRICING.
TRUSTS, INDUSTRIAL.
UNDERDEVELOPED AREAS.
UNEMPLOYED.
UNEMPLOYMENT, TECHNOLOGICAL.
UNITED NATIONS ECONOMIC
  COMMISSION FOR EUROPE.
URBAN ECONOMICS.
UTILITY THEORY.
VALUE.
WAGE-PRICE POLICY.

WAGES.
WAGES AND PRODUCTIVITY
WEALTH
WELFARE ECONOMICS.
WOMEN IN TRADE UNIONS
WORK.
WORKS COUNCILS.

EDUCATION.

General.

AFRICAN STUDIES.
AFRO-AMERICAN STUDIES.
AGRICULTURAL COLLEGES
AGRICULTURAL EDUCATION
BUSINESS EDUCATION
CHINESE STUDIES
CHURCH SCHOOLS
CLASSROOM MANAGEMENT.
COLLEGE DROPOUTS
COMMUNIST EDUCATION.
COMMUNITY AND SCHOOL.
COMPUTER ASSISTED INSTRUCTION
CREATIVE ABILITY.
DEGREES, ACADEMIC
DISCRIMINATION IN EDUCATION
DISSERTATIONS, ACADEMIC
DOMESTIC EDUCATION
EDUCATION.
EDUCATION, COOPERATIVE
EDUCATION, ELEMENTARY
EDUCATION, HIGHER.
EDUCATION, HUMANISTIC
EDUCATION, PRESCHOOL
EDUCATION, SECONDARY
EDUCATION AND STATE
EDUCATION OF ADULTS
EDUCATION OF THE AGED
EDUCATION OF WOMEN.
EDUCATIONAL ASSISTANCE.
EDUCATIONAL EQUALIZATION.
EDUCATIONAL EXCHANGES.
EDUCATIONAL INNOVATIONS.
EDUCATIONAL LAW AND LEGISLATION
EDUCATIONAL PLANNING.
EDUCATIONAL PSYCHOLOGY.
EDUCATIONAL RESEARCH
EDUCATIONAL SOCIOLOGY.
EDUCATIONAL TECHNOLOGY.
EDUCATIONAL TESTS AND
  MEASUREMENTS.
ELECTRONIC DATA PROCESSING IN
  VOCATIONAL GUIDANCE.
EXAMINATIONS
EXCHANGE OF PERSONS PROGRAMMES.
FEDERAL AID TO HIGHER EDUCATION
GRADUATES
GROUP WORK IN EDUCATION.
HALLS OF RESIDENCE.
HANDICAPPED CHILDREN
HEALTH EDUCATION.
HIGH SCHOOLS
HIGHER EDUCATION AND STATE
HUMANITIES
ILLITERACY.
INDUSTRY AND EDUCATION.
INTELLECTUALS
INTERDISCIPLINARY APPROACH IN
  EDUCATION.
LEARNING, PSYCHOLOGY OF.
LEARNING AND SCHOLARSHIP.
LECTURES AND LECTURING.
MILITARY EDUCATION
MORAL EDUCATION
NEGRO STUDENTS.
ORIENTAL STUDIES
PERSONNEL SERVICE IN EDUCATION
PLAY SCHOOLS.
PROFESSIONAL EDUCATION
READING.

RELIGIOUS EDUCATION
SCHOLARS, AMERICAN.
SCHOOL ATTENDANCE
SCHOOL CHILDREN.
SCHOOL DISTRICTS
SCHOOL ENVIRONMENT.
SCHOOL INTEGRATION
SCHOOL MANAGEMENT AND
  ORGANIZATION.
SCHOOL SOCIAL WORK
SCHOOLS
SEGREGATION IN EDUCATION
SEX INSTRUCTION.
SOCIAL WORK EDUCATION.
SOCIALISM AND EDUCATION.
STUDENT AID
STUDENT ASPIRATIONS
STUDENT EVALUATION OF TEACHERS.
STUDENT PARTICIPATION IN
  ADMINISTRATION
STUDENT UNIONS.
STUDENTS
STUDENTS, FOREIGN
STUDENTS, PART-TIME
STUDENTS' SOCIETIES
STUDENTS' SOCIOECONOMIC STATUS
TEACHERS, TRAINING OF
TEACHERS' UNIONS
TEACHING.
TEACHING, FREEDOM OF
TECHNICAL EDUCATION
UKRAINIAN STUDIES.
UNIVERSITIES AND COLLEGES.
VOCATIONAL EDUCATION

Educational institutions.

BERLIN FREE UNIVERSITY.
BRADFORD UNIVERSITY.
CENTRE FOR EDUCATIONAL RESEARCH
  AND INNOVATION.
COPENHAGEN UNIVERSITY.
CRAIGIE COLLEGE OF EDUCATION, AYR.
DAR ES SALAAM TECHNICAL COLLEGE.
HARROW SCHOOL.
HARVARD UNIVERSITY.
IBADAN UNIVERSITY.
INSTITUCION LIBRE DE ENSEÑANZA.
LANCASTER UNIVERSITY.
LATYMER SCHOOL, EDMONTON.
LONDON UNIVERSITY
MANCHESTER UNIVERSITY.
MANNHEIM UNIVERSITY.
MIDHURST GRAMMAR SCHOOL.
OAKLAND UNIVERSITY.
OPEN UNIVERSITY.
READING UNIVERSITY.
UNIVERSITY COLLEGE OF CAPE COAST.
WAYNE STATE UNIVERSITY
WILLIAM TYNDALE JUNIOR AND
  INFANTS SCHOOLS.
YALE UNIVERSITY.

FINANCE.

General.

AGRICULTURAL CREDIT
ANNUITIES
BALANCE OF PAYMENTS.
BANK HOLDING COMPANIES
BANK INVESTMENTS.
BANK LOANS
BANKRUPTCY.
BANKS AND BANKING.
BANKS AND BANKING, COOPERATIVE
BANKS AND BANKING, INTERNATIONAL.
BANKS AND BANKING, TRADE UNION
BILLS OF EXCHANGE
BRAIN DRAIN.

FINANCE (Cont.)

BROKERS
BUDGET.
BUDGET IN BUSINESS.
BUILDING AND LOAN ASSOCIATIONS
CAPITAL.
CAPITAL BUDGET.
CAPITAL GAINS TAX
CAPITAL INVESTMENTS.
CAPITAL MOVEMENTS.
CASH FLOW.
CHEQUES
COINAGE
CONSUMER CREDIT
COST ACCOUNTING.
CREDIT
CUSTOMS ADMINISTRATION
CUSTOMS UNIONS.
DEBT
DEBTS, PUBLIC
DEFLATION (FINANCE)
DEVELOPMENT BANKS
DEVELOPMENT CREDIT CORPORATIONS
DIVIDENDS
DOLLAR.
EUROBOND MARKET.
EURODOLLAR MARKET.
EXPENDITURES, PUBLIC.
EXPORT CREDIT
FEES, PROFESSIONAL
FINANCE.
FINANCE, PERSONAL.
FINANCIAL INSTITUTIONS
FINANCIAL INSTITUTIONS, INTERNATIONAL.
FINANCIAL STATEMENTS.
FLOW OF FUNDS
FOREIGN EXCHANGE.
FRIENDLY SOCIETIES.
FUND RAISING.
GOLD CLAUSE.
GOLD STANDARD.
GOVERNMENT LENDING
GUARANTEED ANNUAL INCOME
INCOME TAX.
INFLATION (FINANCE).
INHERITANCE AND TRANSFER TAX
INSTITUTE OF BANKERS.
INSURANCE.
INSURANCE, ACCIDENT.
INSURANCE, AGRICULTURAL
INSURANCE, AUTOMOBILE
INSURANCE, CREDIT
INSURANCE, HEALTH
INSURANCE, LIFE.
INSURANCE, MARINE
INSURANCE, MATERNITY
INSURANCE, SOCIAL.
INSURANCE, UNEMPLOYMENT.
INSURANCE COMPANIES
INTERGOVERNMENTAL FISCAL RELATIONS
INTERGOVERNMENTAL TAX RELATIONS
INTERNATIONAL FINANCE.
INTERNATIONAL MONETARY FUND.
INVESTMENT BANKING
INVESTMENT OF PUBLIC FUNDS
INVESTMENTS.
INVESTMENTS, AMERICAN.
INVESTMENTS, ARAB
INVESTMENTS, BRITISH.
INVESTMENTS, DUTCH
INVESTMENTS, FOREIGN.
INVESTMENTS, SCOTTISH
LOANS, BRITISH
LOANS, FOREIGN.
LOCAL BUDGETS
LOCAL FINANCE.
LOCAL TAXATION
MEDICAL FEES
MONETARY UNIONS.
MONEY.
MORTGAGE LOANS
MORTGAGES
MUNICIPAL BUDGETS
MUNICIPAL FINANCE
NATIONAL INCOME.
PLATE
POUND, BRITISH.
PROFITS TAX.
PROGRAMME BUDGETING
PROPERTY TAX.
REAL ESTATE INVESTMENT
REAL PROPERTY TAX
REINSURANCE.
RETIREMENT INCOME
SAVING AND INVESTMENT.
SAVINGS BANKS
SINGLE TAX.
SOCIAL CREDIT.
SPECIAL DRAWING RIGHTS.
SPECULATION.
STOCK EXCHANGE
STOCKHOLDERS
STOCKS.
SYNDICATES (FINANCE)
TARIFFS
TAX ADMINISTRATION
TAX EVASION.
TAX PLANNING
TAXATION.
TAXATION, DOUBLE
TITHES
TURNOVER TAX
WALL STREET.

Banks, exchanges, etc.

ASIAN DEVELOPMENT BANK.
BANCO CENTRAL DE LA REPUBLICA ARGENTINA.
BANCO CENTRAL DE VENEZUELA.
BANK OF ENGLAND.
BANK OF JAMAICA.
BANQUE NATIONALE DE BELGIQUE.
GOSUDARSTVENNYI BANK SSSR.
INTERNATIONAL BANK FOR RECONSTRUCTION AND DEVELOPMENT.
REICHSBANK.

GEOGRAPHY, GEOLOGY AND METEOROLOGY.

General.

AERIAL PHOTOGRAPHY IN GEOGRAPHY.
AERIAL PHOTOGRAPHY IN GEOLOGY.
AGRICULTURAL GEOGRAPHY
AIR
ANTHROPOGEOGRAPHY.
ARID REGIONS
CENTRAL PLACES.
CHILTERN SOCIETY.
CITIES AND TOWNS.
CLIMATIC GEOMORPHOLOGY.
CLIMATOLOGY.
COASTAL ZONE MANAGEMENT
COASTS
COMMONS.
CONSERVATION OF NATURAL RESOURCES.
CROPS AND CLIMATE
DISCOVERIES (IN GEOGRAPHY)
DROUGHTS
ECOLOGY.
ENVIRONMENTAL ENGINEERING.
ENVIRONMENTAL POLICY.
ENVIRONMENTAL POLICY RESEARCH
ENVIRONMENTAL PROTECTION.
EROSION
ESTUARIES.
EUROPEAN ECONOMIC COMMUNITY ASSOCIATED COUNTRIES.
EVAPORATION (METEOROLOGY).
EXPLORERS
GEOGRAPHERS.
GEOGRAPHERS, MOHAMMEDAN.
GEOGRAPHICAL DISTRIBUTION OF ANIMALS AND PLANTS.
GEOGRAPHICAL PERCEPTION.
GEOGRAPHY
GEOGRAPHY, ECONOMIC.
GEOGRAPHY, POLITICAL.
GEOLOGY
GEOPOLITICS.
GLACIAL EPOCH
GREEN BELTS
HEATH ECOLOGY.
HUMAN ECOLOGY.
HUMAN ENGINEERING.
HYDROLOGY.
ISLANDS.
LAND.
LANDSCAPE.
LANDSCAPE ARCHITECTURE.
LANDSCAPE PROTECTION.
MAPS.
METEOROLOGY, AGRICULTURAL
MOUNTAINS
NAMES, GEOGRAPHICAL
NATURAL RESOURCES.
NEW TOWNS.
OCEAN BOTTOM.
PALAEONTOLOGY
PHOTOGRAPHY, AERIAL.
PHYSICAL GEOGRAPHY
POLAR REGIONS.
POLLUTION.
PRAIRIES.
RADIOACTIVE POLLUTION.
RECLAMATION OF LAND.
REGIONAL PLANNING.
RESIDENTIAL MOBILITY
SOIL EROSION
SOILS.
STEPPES.
STREAM MEASUREMENTS
TUNDRAS.
URBAN RENEWAL
URBANIZATION.
WASTE LANDS
WASTE PAPER
WATER
WATER CONSUMPTION
WATER QUALITY MANAGEMENT
WATER RESOURCES DEVELOPMENT.
WATER SUPPLY.
WATER SUPPLY, RURAL
WILDERNESS AREAS.
ZONING

Rocks, minerals, etc.

ANHYDRITE
CLAY
GYPSUM
PHOSPHORUS.
QUARTZ

Individual countries and places

Africa

ABIDJAN
ACHOLI
AFRICA.
AFRICA, CENTRAL
AFRICA, EAST
AFRICA, NORTH.
AFRICA, SUBSAHARAN
AFRICA, WEST

GEOGRAPHY, GEOLOGY AND METEOROLOGY

ALGERIA
ANGOLA
ARAB COUNTRIES
BLANTYRE
BOTSWANA
BUKOBA DISTRICT
CAIRO
CAMEROUN.
CHAD
CISKEI.
COMORO ARCHIPELAGO
CONGO (BRAZZAVILLE)
DAHOMEY
DEIR EL MEDINEH
DURBAN
EGYPT
ETHIOPIA
GAMBIA
GHANA.
GOMBE EMIRATE
GUINEA
GUINEA-BISSAU
IVORY COAST
KABYLIA
KARAGWE KINGDOM
KENYA
LESOTHO
LIBERIA
LIBYA.
LILONGWE
LOFA COUNTY, LIBERIA
MADAGASCAR
MALAWI
MALI (REPUBLIC).
MAURITIUS.
MOROCCO
MOZAMBIQUE
NAIROBI
NIGER
NIGERIA
NYERI
RHODESIA.
RWANDA
SAHEL
ST. HELENA
SAINT-LOUIS, SENEGAL
SALE
SASOLBURG, ORANGE FREE STATE
SEKONDI-TAKORADI
SELEBI-PIKWE
SENEGAL
SENEGAMBIA
SEYCHELLES
SHABA
SIDI LAHCEN.
SIERRA LEONE
SOMALI REPUBLIC
SOUTH AFRICA
SOUTH WEST AFRICA
SPANISH SAHARA.
SUDAN
SWAZILAND
TANZANIA
TOGO
TRANSKEI.
TRANSVAAL
TUNISIA
UGANDA
UPPER VOLTA
WESTERN TOWNSHIP
ZAIRE
ZAMBIA.

America, Latin.

AMAZON VALLEY
AMERICA
AMERICA, LATIN.
ANTIGUA
ARGENTINE REPUBLIC
BELIZE
BOLIVIA
BRASILIA.
BRAZIL
BRITISH VIRGIN ISLANDS
BUENOS AIRES
CARACAS
CARIBBEAN AREA
CAYMAN ISLANDS
CHILE
CHOLULA
CIUDAD JUAREZ
COLOMBIA
CORDOBA, ARGENTINE REPUBLIC
  (PROVINCE)
CUBA
CURAÇAO
CUZCO (PERU)
DOMINICA
DOMINICAN REPUBLIC
ECUADOR
FALKLAND ISLANDS
GUADELOUPE.
GUATEMALA
GUAYAQUIL (PROVINCE)
GULF OF MEXICO
GUYANA
HAITI
HONDURAS
HUEYAPAN
JAMAICA
KINGSTON, JAMAICA
LIMA
MANTARO VALLEY
MAR DEL PLATA
MARTIN GARCIA ISLAND.
MEXICO
MEXICO CITY
NETHERLANDS ANTILLES
NEW SPAIN (VICEROYALTY)
NICARAGUA
OAXACA VALLEY
OTAVALO VALLEY.
PANAMA
PARAGUAY
PERU
PORT ANTONIO, JAMAICA
PUERTO RICO
RIO DE JANEIRO
RIO GRANDE DO SUL
SAINT LUCIA
ST. VINCENT
SALVADOR
SOUFRIERE
TIERRA DEL FUEGO.
TRINIDAD AND TOBAGO
URUGUAY
VALENCIA, VENEZUELA
VENEZUELA
WEST INDIES

America, North.

ALASKA
ALBERTA
ALL HALLOW'S PARISH, MARYLAND
AMERICA
AMERICA, NORTH.
APPALACHIAN MOUNTAINS
ARIZONA
ATLANTA, GEORGIA
BOSTON, MASSACHUSETTS
BRITISH COLUMBIA
CALIFORNIA
CANADA
CHICAGO
CLEVELAND, OHIO
COOK COUNTY, ILLINOIS
DETROIT
ELLIS ISLAND
FLORIDA
GARDINER DAM.
GEORGIA (UNITED STATES)
GREAT LAKES.
GREAT PLAINS
GREENLAND
HAMILTON, ONTARIO
INDIANAPOLIS
KINGSTON, NEW YORK
LABRADOR
LOS ANGELES
MAINE
MANITOBA
MARYLAND
MASSACHUSETTS
MICHIGAN
MILWAUKEE
MISSISSIPPI VALLEY
MONTANA
MONTREAL
NEBRASKA
NEW ENGLAND
NEW HAMPSHIRE
NEW JERSEY
NEW YORK (CITY)
NEW YORK (STATE)
NEWFOUNDLAND
NEWFOUNDLAND AND LABRADOR
NORTH-WEST TERRITORIES
NOVA SCOTIA
OAKLAND, CALIFORNIA
ONTARIO
OTTAWA
PEACE RIVER
PEEKSKILL, NEW YORK
PHILADELPHIA
PITTSBURGH
QUEBEC
QUEBEC (PROVINCE)
RHODE ISLAND
SAN FRANCISCO
SANTA CLARA COUNTY
SASKATCHEWAN
SOUTH BEND, INDIANA
SOUTH SASKATCHEWAN RIVER.
TECUMSEH, ONTARIO
TENNESSEE
TEXAS
TORONTO
UNITED STATES
WARREN, PENNSYLVANIA
WASHINGTON, D.C.
WINNIPEG

Asia.

ADEN
AFGHANISTAN
AMBOINA
AMUR (OBLAST')
ANDHRA
ANDHRA PRADESH
ARAB COUNTRIES
ARMENIA
ASIA
ASIA, SOUTHEAST.
AZERBAIJAN
BAHRAIN
BALUCHISTAN
BANGLADESH.
BENGAL
BENGAL, WEST
BIHAR
BRUNEI
BUKHARA
BURMA.
BURYAT REPUBLIC
CAMBODIA
CHILIYING.
CHINA
CHITA (OBLAST')
CYPRUS
DELHI

GEOGRAPHY, GEOLOGY AND METEOROLOGY(Cont.)

EAST (FAR EAST)
EAST (NEAR EAST)
FAR EASTERN REPUBLIC
GOA, DAMAN AND DIU
GOLODNAIA STEP'.
GUJARAT
HONG KONG.
HUA KOK, THAILAND
INDIA
INDIAN OCEAN REGION.
INDONESIA
IRAN
IRAQ
ISRAEL
JAPAN.
JOGJAKARTA
JOHORE
JORDAN
JORDAN VALLEY.
KARAKALPAK REPUBLIC
KARIYA
KASTAMONU
KAZAKSTAN
KELANTAN
KERALA
KIRGHIZIA
KOREA.
KUALA LUMPUR
KUMAON
KUWAIT
LEBANON
LOVEA, CAMBODIA.
MADHYA PRADESH
MADRAS
MADRAS (CITY)
MADRAS PRESIDENCY
MAHARASHTRA
MALAYA
MALAYSIA
MALDIVE ISLANDS
MALPE
MANGALORE
MONGOLIA.
MYSORE
NEPAL
OMAN
ORISSA
PAKISTAN
PALESTINE
PAMIR
PERSIAN GULF
PHILIPPINE ISLANDS
QATAR
REUNION ISLAND
RUSSIA
RUSSIA (RSFSR)
SAUDI ARABIA
SIBERIA
SINGAPORE
SOVIET CENTRAL ASIA
SOVIET FAR EAST
SRI LANKA
SYRIA
TAIWAN
TAJIKISTAN.
THAILAND
TOKYO.
TRAVANCORE
TURKESTAN
TURKEY
TURKMENISTAN
TUVA
UNITED ARAB EMIRATES
USTYURT DESERT.
UTTAR PRADESH
UZBEKISTAN
VIETNAM
VLADIVOSTOK
YAKUTIA

Australia and Oceania.

ADELAIDE
AUSTRALASIA
AUSTRALIA
FIJI ISLANDS
GILBERT AND ELLICE ISLANDS COLONY
HAWAIIAN ISLANDS
MARSHALL ISLANDS
MICRONESIA
NEW SOUTH WALES
NEW ZEALAND
PACIFIC, THE
PAPUA NEW GUINEA
PORT MORESBY
QUEENSLAND
SABAH
SARAWAK
SOUTH AUSTRALIA
TASMANIA
TIMOR
VICTORIA, AUSTRALIA
WESTERN AUSTRALIA
WESTLAND
YAP

Europe.

AARHUS
ABKHAZIA
ABRUZZI E MOLISE
ABRUZZO
AIX-EN-PROVENCE.
ALBANIA
ALSACE.
AMIENS.
ANDORRA.
ANGERS
ANTWERP
APPENZELL
ARKHANGEL'SK (OBLAST')
ASBEST.
ASTRAKHAN'
ASTRAKHAN' (OBLAST')
ASTURIAS
ATHENS
AUSTRIA
AUSTRIA-HUNGARY
AVERNES.
AZORES
BADEN
BALKAN STATES
BALTIC, THE
BALTIC STATES
BARCELONA
BASQUE PROVINCES
BAVARIA
BAYONNE.
BELGIUM
BERGSLAGEN
BERLIN
BESSARABIA
BIESZCZADY.
BOLOGNA (PROVINCE)
BOSNIA
BRANDENBURG
BREMEN
BREST
BRUSSELS.
BUKOVINA
BULGARIA
BURGUNDY
BYGDEÅ
CAEN
CASTELLAMMARE DI STABIA
CATALONIA
CAUCASUS
CHAMPAGNE-ARDENNE
CHERNIGOV (OBLAST')
CHUVASH REPUBLIC
CIESZYN

COLOGNE
COPENHAGEN
CORSICA
CÔTES-DU-NORD.
CRACOW
CRACOW (PROVINCE)
CRETE
CRIMEA
CROATIA
CZECHOSLOVAKIA
DAGHESTAN
DANUBE, RIVER
DENMARK
DRÔME (DEPARTMENT).
EAST PRUSSIA
ELBEUF.
ESTONIA
ETANG DE BERRE.
EUROPE
EUROPE, EASTERN
EUROPEAN ECONOMIC COMMUNITY
   COUNTRIES.
FINLAND
FINSTERWOLDE
FJAERLAND, NORWAY
FLENSBURG
FLORENCE
FOS.
FRANCE
FRIULI
FUENTERRABIA, SPAIN
GALICIA (EASTERN EUROPE)
GALICIA (SPAIN)
GALWAY
GÄVLE
GDAŃSK
GENEVA (CANTON)
GEORGIA
GERMANY
GERMANY, EASTERN.
GHENT
GIBRALTAR
GOR'KII (OBLAST')
GOTHENBURG
GRAESTED, DENMARK.
GRAUBUENDEN
GREECE
GROSSRAMING
GUERNICA
GUIPUZCOA
HAGUE
HALLE
HALMSTAD
HAMBURG
HEILBRONN
HESSE
HOLSTEBRO
HUNGARY
ICELAND
IRELAND (REPUBLIC)
ITALY
IVANO-FRANKOVSK (OBLAST')
JURA
KALININGRAD
KALININGRAD (OBLAST')
KALMYK REPUBLIC
KARELIA
KAZAN'
KERGARADEC
KHARKOV (OBLAST')
KHMEL'NITSKII (OBLAST')
KIELCE (PROVINCE)
KIPPEL
KIROV (OBLAST')
KONKUNAD
KOSOVO
KUIBYSHEV
KUIBYSHEV (OBLAST')
KURPIE
LA SPEZIA (PROVINCE)
LATVIA
LENINGRAD

HISTORY

LENINGRAD (OBLAST')
LIECHTENSTEIN.
LIGURIA
LITHUANIA
LIVONIA
ŁÓDŹ
ŁÓDŹ (PROVINCE)
LOIRE (DEPARTMENT).
ŁOM'ZA
LORRAINE
LOWER SAXONY
LUEBECK
LUXEMBOURG
LYONS.
MACEDONIA
MACEDONIAN REPUBLIC
MADEIRA
MADRID
MAIN, RIVER
MAINZ
MALMÖ
MALTA
MARSEILLES
MATERA (PROVINCE)
MECHLIN
MEDITERRANEAN
MNIKÓW.
MODENA (PROVINCE)
MOLDAVIA
MOLDAVIAN REPUBLIC
MONACO.
MONTECASTELLO DI VIBIO
MONTICELLI
MORDVINIAN REPUBLIC
MOSCOW
MUNICH
NAPLES
NETHERLANDS
NIŠ
NORMANDY
NORRKÖPING
NORTH RHINE-WESTPHALIA
NORTH SEA.
NORWAY
NOVGOROD (OBLAST')
NOWA HUTA
NUREMBERG
OBERHAUSEN
ÖREBRO LÄN
OREL (OBLAST')
ORLEANS.
OSLO
OSNABRUECK
PADUA (PROVINCE)
PARIS.
PARIS (REGION)
PARMA AND PIACENZA (DUCHY)
PAYS DE LA LOIRE
PENZA (OBLAST')
PERM' (OBLAST')
PERUGIA (PROVINCE)
PISA
PLOZÉVET
POLAND.
POLTAVA (OBLAST')
PORTUGAL
POZNAŃ
POZNAŃ (PROVINCE)
PROVENCE
PROVENCE-CÔTE D'AZUR
PRUSSIA
REGION CENTRE
RHINE
RHINE PROVINCE
RHÔNE (DEPARTMENT).
ROMANIA
ROUEN.
ROVNO (OBLAST')
RUHR
RUSSIA
RUSSIA (RSFSR)
RUTHENIA

SAARLAND
ST. GALL (CANTON)
SALZBURG (STATE)
SAN MARINO.
SARDINIA
SAXONY
SCANDINAVIA
SCHAFFHAUSEN (CANTON)
SCHLESWIG-HOLSTEIN
SERBIA
SEVILLE (PROVINCE)
SICILY
SILESIA
SLOVAKIA
SMOLENSK (OBLAST')
SOFIA
SOGN OG FJORDANE, NORWAY
SOLINGEN
SOLOTHURN
SOVIET NORTH
SPAIN
STRALSUND
SUNNMØRE
SWABIA
SWEDEN
SWITZERLAND.
TALLIN
TAMBOV (OBLAST')
TEREK
THURINGIA
TINN
TOFTLUND
TRANSYLVANIA
TRIER
TRIESTE
TULA (OBLAST')
TURIN
UDMURT REPUBLIC
UKRAINE
UKRAINE, WESTERN
UMBRIA
UPPER ADIGE
UPPER AUSTRIA
URAL REGION
VALENCIA, SPAIN (REGION)
VENICE.
VIENNA
VLADIMIR (OBLAST')
VOJVODINA
VOLGA BASIN
VOLGOGRAD (OBLAST')
VOLYN (OBLAST')
VOROSHILOVGRAD (OBLAST')
WALLACHIA
WARSAW
WARSAW (PROVINCE)
WERTHEIM.
WESTERLAND
WHITE RUSSIA
WILDBERG
WOLSFELD
WUERTTEMBERG
WUPPERTAL
YUGOSLAVIA
YVELINES (DEPARTMENT).
ZHITOMIR

United Kingdom.

AFAN VALLEY
BARTON BLOUNT, DERBYSHIRE
BEDFORDSHIRE
BELFAST
BIRMINGHAM
BRADFORD
BRIGHTON
BRISTOL
BUCKINGHAMSHIRE
CAMDEN
CANNING TOWN
CLEATOR MOOR

COALBROOKDALE
CORNWALL
COVENTRY
CUMBERLAND
DEVONSHIRE
DONCASTER
DURHAM (CITY)
DURHAM (COUNTY)
EAST ANGLIA.
EAST SUSSEX
EDINBURGH
ESSEX
GLASGOW
GOLTHO, LINCOLNSHIRE
GUERNSEY
HACKNEY
HAMPSHIRE
HORNCASTLE
HOXTON
HULL
HUMBERSIDE
IRELAND
IRELAND, NORTHERN
ISLE OF MAN
ISLE OF WIGHT
KENT
KIRKLEES
LAMBETH
LANCASHIRE
LEICESTER
LIVERPOOL
LONDON
LONDONDERRY
LUTON
MANCHESTER
MERSEYSIDE
NEW WINDSOR
NEWCASTLE-UPON-TYNE
NORTHUMBERLAND
NOTTINGHAM
PEAK NATIONAL PARK.
PORTSMOUTH
PRESTON
PUTNEY
READING.
RIPON
ST. KILDA
SCOTLAND
SHEFFIELD
SHETLAND ISLANDS
SHROPSHIRE
SKYE
SNOWDONIA
SOMERSET
SOUTHAMPTON
SOUTHWARK
STAFFORDSHIRE
SUSSEX
SWINDON
TAYSIDE
TEESSIDE
THAMES, RIVER.
TYNEMOUTH
UNITED KINGDOM
WALES
WANDSWORTH
WARBOYS, HUNTINGDONSHIRE
WEST BROMWICH
WEST YORKSHIRE
WESTMINSTER
YORKSHIRE

HISTORY.

General.

ACQUISITION OF TERRITORY.
ARCHAEOLOGY, INDUSTRIAL
ARTS AND HISTORY.
CHRONOLOGY, HISTORICAL.
CHURCH HISTORY.

HISTORY (Cont.)

CIVIL WAR.
CIVILIZATION.
CIVILIZATION, ANCIENT.
CIVILIZATION, MODERN.
CIVILIZATION, ORIENTAL.
CIVILIZATION, SLAVIC.
COLONIAL COMPANIES.
CONSTITUTIONAL HISTORY.
ECONOMIC HISTORY.
FEUDALISM.
HISTORIANS
HISTORICAL RESEARCH.
HISTORIOGRAPHY.
HISTORY
HISTORY, MODERN
HISTORY, UNIVERSAL.
IRON AGE.
LAND SETTLEMENT
LAND TENURE.
MONUMENTS
MOVING PICTURES IN HISTORIOGRAPHY.
PEASANT UPRISINGS.
SERFDOM
SOCIAL HISTORY.
TALL BUILDINGS.
TWENTIETH CENTURY
TWENTY-FIRST CENTURY
VILLEINAGE
WILLS

International (including wars).

CHINESE-JAPANESE WAR, 1937-1945.
DIDGORA MOUNTAIN, GEORGIA, BATTLE OF, 1121.
EUROPEAN WAR, 1914-1918.
GENEVA CONVENTIONS.
INDOSOVIET TREATY OF PEACE, FRIENDSHIP AND COOPERATION, 1971.
ISRAEL-ARAB CONFLICT, 1948- .
ISRAEL-ARAB WAR, 1967.
ISRAEL-ARAB WAR, 1973.
ITALO-ETHIOPIAN WAR, 1935-1936.
KOREAN WAR, 1950-1953.
LEAFLETS DROPPED FROM AIRCRAFT.
LONDON, TREATY OF, 1915.
MOSCOW, BATTLE OF, 1941-1942.
MUNICH FOUR POWER AGREEMENT, 1938.
PEASANTS' WAR, 1524-1525.
PORTSMOUTH, TREATY OF, 1905.
RAPALLO, TREATY OF, 1922.
RECONSTRUCTION (1939-1951).
RUSSO-FINNISH WAR, 1939-1940.
RUSSO-TURKISH WAR, 1877-1878.
SCHLESWIG-HOLSTEIN WAR, 1864.
SPANISH SUCCESSION, WAR OF, 1701-1714.
SUEZ CANAL.
VERSAILLES, TREATY OF, JUNE 28, 1919 (GERMANY).
VIETNAMESE WARS, 1945-1975.
WAR OF THE LEAGUE OF AUGSBURG, 1688-1697.
WARSAW, PACT OF, 1955.
WORLD WAR, 1939-1945.

American territories.

CONFEDERATE STATES OF AMERICA
CRISTERO REBELLION, 1926-1929.
CUBAN MISSILE CRISIS, OCTOBER 1962.
FREEDMEN IN THE UNITED STATES.
FRONTIER AND PIONEER LIFE
RECONSTRUCTION (UNITED STATES).
RED RIVER REBELLION, 1869-1870.
RIEL REBELLION, 1885.

Asiatic territories.

ARMENIAN QUESTION.
EASTERN QUESTION (FAR EAST).
EASTERN QUESTION (NEAR EAST).
INDIA-PAKISTAN CONFLICT, 1971.
KOREAN REUNIFICATION QUESTION (1945-).

European territories.

ALSACE-LORRAINE QUESTION.
ANSCHLUSS MOVEMENT, 1918-1938.
BERLIN QUESTION (1945-).
EASTERN QUESTION (BALKAN).
EMIGRES.
GERMAN REUNIFICATION QUESTION (1949-).
GREECE, ANCIENT
HANSA TOWNS.
HANSEATIC LEAGUE.
HOLY ROMAN EMPIRE
MACEDONIAN QUESTION.
MOSCOW TRIALS, 1936-1937.
POLISH QUESTION.
REFORMATION.
RENAISSANCE.
ROME, ANCIENT
SCHLESWIG-HOLSTEIN QUESTION.
UPPER SILESIAN QUESTION.

United Kingdom.

BOYNE, BATTLE OF THE, 1690.
CARTULARIES.
CHARTISM.
GENERAL STRIKE, UNITED KINGDOM, 1926.
HOME RULE
IRISH QUESTION.
LEVELLERS.
LUDDITES.
"MANCHESTER MASSACRE", 1819.
MANORIAL COURTS
MANORIAL EXTENTS.

Colonial companies.

JALUIT-GESELLSCHAFT.
SWEDISH EAST INDIA COMPANY.

LANGUAGE, LITERATURE AND THE ARTS.

Language.

APHASIA.
ATHAPASKAN LANGUAGES.
BILINGUALISM.
CYRILLIC ALPHABET.
DISCOURSE ANALYSIS.
ENGLISH LANGUAGE
ENGLISH LANGUAGE IN AFRICA.
ENGLISH LANGUAGE IN THE UNITED STATES
FINNISH LANGUAGE
FRENCH LANGUAGE
GENERATIVE GRAMMAR.
GERMAN LANGUAGE
GRAMMAR, COMPARATIVE AND GENERAL.
GREEK LANGUAGE
HUNGARIAN LANGUAGE IN THE UNITED STATES.
KECHUA LANGUAGE.
LANGUAGE AND LANGUAGES.
LANGUAGES
LINGUISTIC ANALYSIS (LINGUISTICS).
LINGUISTICS.
MEANING.
NEGRO ENGLISH DIALECTS.
NEUROPSYCHOLOGY.
PRIVATE LANGUAGE PROBLEM.
PSYCHOLINGUISTICS.
SEMANTICS.
SEMANTICS, COMPARATIVE.
SOCIOLINGUISTICS.
SPEECH.
SPEECH, DISORDERS OF.
SPEECH AND SOCIAL STATUS.
VOCABULARY.

Literature.

AMERICAN LITERATURE
AMERICAN NEWSPAPERS.
AMERICAN PERIODICALS.
AUTHORS.
AUTHORS, LABOURING CLASS.
AUTHORS, RUSSIAN.
BULGARIAN LITERATURE.
CHEREMISSIAN LITERATURE
COMMUNISM AND LITERATURE.
CRITICISM.
DANISH NEWSPAPERS.
DIDACTIC LITERATURE, ROMANIAN.
ENGLISH LITERATURE
ENGLISH NEWSPAPERS.
FINNISH NEWSPAPERS.
FOREIGN NEWS.
FRENCH CANADIAN PERIODICALS.
FRENCH PERIODICALS.
GEORGIAN PERIODICALS.
GERMAN LITERATURE
GERMAN NEWSPAPERS.
GERMAN PERIODICALS.
GOVERNMENT AND THE PRESS
HEROES IN LITERATURE.
HOMER.
INTERNATIONAL UNION OF REVOLUTIONARY WRITERS.
ITALIAN PERIODICALS.
JOURNALISM
LITERATURE
LITERATURE, IMMORAL.
LITERATURE, MODERN
LITERATURE AND REVOLUTIONS.
LITERATURE AND SOCIETY.
LITERATURE AND STATE.
MEXICO IN LITERATURE
NEWSPAPERS
NORWEGIAN LITERATURE
NOVELISTS, FRENCH.
OBITUARIES
PEACE IN LITERATURE.
POLISH LITERATURE.
POLISH PERIODICALS.
POLITICAL POETRY, ENGLISH.
POLITICAL POETRY, IRISH.
POLITICAL SATIRE, AMERICAN.
POLITICS IN LITERATURE.
PRESS
RADIO JOURNALISM.
RHODESIAN NEWSPAPERS.
RUSSIAN FICTION
RUSSIAN LITERATURE
RUSSIAN NEWSPAPERS.
SATIRE, GERMAN.
SATIRE, POLISH.
SILESIAN PERIODICALS.
UNDERGROUND LITERATURE
WAR IN LITERATURE.

The Arts.

AESTHETICS.
ARCHITECTURE
ARCHITECTURE, DOMESTIC

ARCHITECTURE AND SOCIETY.
ART
ART, BULGARIAN.
ART AND SOCIETY.
ART PATRONAGE
ARTS
ARTS AND HISTORY.
CARICATURES AND CARTOONS
COMMUNISM AND MUSIC.
COMMUNISM AND THE ARTS.
FOLK MUSIC, AFRICAN
HISTORICAL FILMS.
MUSIC AND SOCIETY.
NATIONAL SONGS, CANADIAN.
ORATORY.
POLITICAL BALLADS AND SONGS, SWEDISH.
POLITICS IN MOVING PICTURES.
STATE ENCOURAGEMENT OF SCIENCE, LITERATURE AND ART
THEATRE

LAW (including INTERNATIONAL LAW).

General.

APPELLATE PROCEDURE
ATTORNEYS-GENERAL
BAIL
BAILIFFS
COMMON LAW
CONFIDENTIAL COMMUNICATIONS
CONTEMPT OF COURT
COURT RECORDS
COURTS.
CUSTOMARY LAW
EUROPEAN COMMITTEE ON LEGAL CO-OPERATION.
IDENTIFICATION
JUDGMENTS, DECLARATORY.
JUDICIAL ASSISTANCE
JUDICIAL DISCRETION
JUDICIAL REVIEW
JUDICIAL STATISTICS
JURISPRUDENCE.
JUSTICE.
JUSTICE, ADMINISTRATION OF.
JUSTICE AND POLITICS
JUSTICES OF THE PEACE
JUVENILE COURTS
LAW.
LAW, COMPARATIVE.
LAW AND ETHICS.
LAW AND POLITICS.
LAW AND SOCIALISM.
LAW ENFORCEMENT.
LAW REFORM.
LAW REPORTS, DIGESTS, ETC.
LEGAL AID.
LEGAL COMPOSITION.
LEGAL ETHICS
NATURAL LAW.
NOTARIES
PROCEDURE (LAW)
RESPONDEAT SUPERIOR.
RESPONSIBILITY, LEGAL
RULE OF LAW
SEX AND LAW.
SEX DISCRIMINATION AGAINST WOMEN
SEX DISCRIMINATION IN EDUCATION
SEX DISCRIMINATION IN EMPLOYMENT
SOCIAL LEGISLATION
SOCIOLOGICAL JURISPRUDENCE.
TECHNOLOGY AND LAW.
TRIALS

Public law.

ABUSE OF ADMINISTRATIVE POWER
ADMINISTRATIVE COURTS
ADMINISTRATIVE DISCRETION
ADMINISTRATIVE LAW
AGRICULTURAL LAWS AND LEGISLATION
AMNESTY.
ARREST
BUILDING LAWS
CITY PLANNING AND REDEVELOPMENT LAW
COMPENSATION (LAW)
ECONOMIC LEGISLATION
EDUCATIONAL LAW AND LEGISLATION
ELECTION LAW
EMIGRATION AND IMMIGRATION LAW
EMINENT DOMAIN
ENVIRONMENTAL LAW.
FISHERY LAW AND LEGISLATION
FOOD LAW AND LEGISLATION
FORESTRY LAW AND LEGISLATION
HABEAS CORPUS
INTERNAL REVENUE LAW
LEGISLATION.
LEGISLATIVE BODIES.
LEGISLATIVE POWER
MENTAL HEALTH LAWS
MILITARY LAW
PEOPLE (CONSTITUTIONAL LAW)
POLITICAL CRIMES AND OFFENCES
POLITICAL QUESTIONS AND JUDICIAL POWER
POOR LAWS
PRESS LAW.
PUBLIC INTEREST.
REPEAL OF LEGISLATION
TRAFFIC REGULATIONS
TREASON
WATER

Civil law and procedure.

ACCIDENT LAW
ACTIONS AND DEFENCES
ADMINISTRATION OF ESTATES
AGE (LAW)
CHARITABLE USES, TRUSTS AND FOUNDATIONS.
CIVIL LAW.
CIVIL PROCEDURE
COMPENSATION (LAW)
DAMAGES
DIVORCE
DOMESTIC RELATIONS.
EQUITY
EXECUTIONS (LAW)
INHERITANCE AND SUCCESSION.
INTELLECTUAL PROPERTY
JURISTIC PERSONS
LAND TITLES
LANDLORD AND TENANT
LIBEL AND SLANDER
MARRIAGE LAW
MATRIMONIAL ACTIONS
MORTMAIN
NEGLIGENCE
OBLIGATIONS (LAW)
PATERNITY
PERSONAL INJURIES
PERSONAL PROPERTY
PLEADING
REAL COVENANTS
REAL PROPERTY
SUPPORT (DOMESTIC RELATIONS)
TORTS
UNJUST ENRICHMENT

Commercial, industrial and labour laws.

AGENCY (LAW)
ARBITRATION AND AWARD
AUTHORS AND PUBLISHERS
BANKING LAW
BANKRUPTCY.
BUSINESS LAW
COMMERCIAL CRIMES
COMMERCIAL LAW
CONTRACTS
CONTRACTS, LETTING OF
COPYHOLD.
COPYRIGHT
CORN LAWS
CORPORATION LAW
DELIVERY OF GOODS (LAW)
FACTORY LAWS AND LEGISLATION
INDUSTRIAL LAWS AND LEGISLATION
INSURANCE LAW.
LABOUR LAWS AND LEGISLATION.
LETTERS OF CREDIT
MASTER AND SERVANT
MOTOR TRUCKS
NEGOTIABLE INSTRUMENTS
OIL AND GAS LEASES
PARTNERSHIP
PATENT LAWS AND LEGISLATION
PETROLEUM LAW AND LEGISLATION
PROFESSIONAL STANDARDS REVIEW ORGANIZATIONS (MEDICINE)

Criminal law and procedure.

ACCOMPLICES
ARREST
ASSAULT AND BATTERY
CRIMINAL ACT
CRIMINAL INVESTIGATION
CRIMINAL JUSTICE, ADMINISTRATION OF.
CRIMINAL LAW
CRIMINAL LIABILITY
CRIMINAL PROCEDURE
DEFENCE (CRIMINAL PROCEDURE)
DRUG ABUSE AND CRIME
EVIDENCE, CRIMINAL
EVIDENCE, DOCUMENTARY.
EXTORTION
GUILT.
PAROLE
PUBLIC PROSECUTORS
REPARATION
TRIALS (MURDER)
TRIALS (POLITICAL CRIMES AND OFFENCES)
TRIALS (ROBBERY)
TRIALS (TREASON)

Foreign law.

LAW, MOHAMMEDAN.

Conflict of laws, civil and criminal.

INTERNATIONAL LAW, PRIVATE
JUDGMENTS, FOREIGN

International law.

AGGRESSION (INTERNATIONAL LAW).
ATOMIC WEAPONS (INTERNATIONAL LAW).
BOUNDARIES.
COLONIES (INTERNATIONAL LAW).
CONTRACTS (INTERNATIONAL LAW).
CONTRACTS, MARITIME
COURT OF JUSTICE OF THE EUROPEAN COMMUNITIES.
CRIMINAL LIABILITY (INTERNATIONAL LAW).
EXTRADITION
INTERNATIONAL AND MUNICIPAL LAW

LAW (Cont.)

INTERNATIONAL LAW.
INTERVENTION (INTERNATIONAL LAW).
JURISDICTION (INTERNATIONAL LAW).
LABOUR LAWS AND LEGISLATION, INTERNATIONAL.
MARINE RESOURCES
MARITIME LAW.
PACIFIC SETTLEMENT OF INTERNATIONAL DISPUTES.
PASSPORTS.
PATENTS (INTERNATIONAL LAW).
PERSONS (INTERNATIONAL LAW).
RECOGNITION (INTERNATIONAL LAW).
SANCTIONS (INTERNATIONAL LAW).
TERRITORIAL WATERS.
TREATIES.
WAR (INTERNATIONAL LAW).
WAR, MARITIME (INTERNATIONAL LAW).

MATHEMATICS AND STATISTICS.

ALGEBRAIC NUMBER THEORY.
ALGORITHMS.
ANALYSIS OF VARIANCE.
CALCULATING MACHINES.
CALCULUS, OPERATIONAL.
CLUSTER ANALYSIS.
COBOL (COMPUTER PROGRAM LANGUAGE).
COMBINATORIAL ANALYSIS.
COMMERCIAL STATISTICS.
COMPILING (ELECTRONIC COMPUTERS).
COMPUTER ASSISTED INSTRUCTION
COMPUTER GRAPHICS.
COMPUTER INPUT-OUTPUT EQUIPMENT.
COMPUTER INTERFACES.
COMPUTER NETWORKS.
COMPUTER SIMULATION.
COMPUTER STORAGE DEVICES.
COMPUTERS.
CRIMINAL STATISTICS.
CYBERNETICS.
DATA BASE MANAGEMENT.
DATA STRUCTURES (COMPUTER SCIENCE).
DEBUGGING IN COMPUTER SCIENCE.
DECIMAL SYSTEM.
DECISION LOGIC TABLES.
DEMOGRAPHY.
DIFFERENTIAL EQUATIONS, PARTIAL.
DIFFERENTIAL GAMES.
DIGITAL COMPUTER SIMULATION.
DISTANCE GEOMETRY.
ECONOMICS, MATHEMATICAL.
ELECTRONIC DIGITAL COMPUTERS.
ESTIMATION THEORY.
EXPERIMENTAL DESIGN.
FILE ORGANIZATION (COMPUTER SCIENCE).
FIXED POINT THEOREMS (TOPOLOGY).
FUNCTIONAL ANALYSIS.
GAMES, THEORY OF.
GEOMETRY, ALGEBRAIC.
GEOMETRY, DIFFERENTIAL.
GRAPH THEORY.
HILBERT SPACE.
IBM 370 (computers).
INTEGER PROGRAMMING.
INTEGRALS, STOCHASTIC.
INTERACTIVE COMPUTER SYSTEMS.
K-THEORY.
LATTICE THEORY.
LINEAR OPERATORS.
LINEAR PROGRAMMING.
LINEAR TOPOLOGICAL SPACES.
LIST PROCESSING (ELECTRONIC COMPUTERS).
MACRO PROCESSORS.
MATHEMATICAL ANALYSIS.
MATHEMATICAL MODELS.
MATHEMATICAL OPTIMIZATION.
MATHEMATICS.
MATRICES.
MATRIX INVERSION.
MENSURATION.
MORTALITY.
MULTIVARIATE ANALYSIS.
NUMERICAL ANALYSIS.
OPERATIONS RESEARCH.
PARTITIONS (MATHEMATICS).
PERMUTATIONS.
PERP (COMPUTER PROGRAM).
POPULATION FORECASTING.
PRIVACY, RIGHT OF.
PROBABILITIES.
PROGRAMMING (ELECTRONIC COMPUTERS).
PROGRAMMING (MATHEMATICS).
PROGRAMMING LANGUAGES (ELECTRONIC COMPUTERS).
QUEUEING THEORY.
REAL-TIME DATA PROCESSING.
RECURSIVE PROGRAMMING.
REGISTERS OF BIRTH, ETC.
REGRESSION ANALYSIS.
SAMPLING (STATISTICS).
SET THEORY.
SIMULATION METHODS.
SOFTWARE COMPATIBILITY.
SORTING (ELECTRONIC COMPUTERS).
STATISTICS
STOCHASTIC DIFFERENTIAL EQUATIONS.
STOCHASTIC PROCESSES.
SYSTEM ANALYSIS.
SYSTEM THEORY.
SYSTEMS ENGINEERING.
TIME SERIES ANALYSIS.
TIME-SHARING COMPUTER SYSTEMS.
TOPOLOGY.
VARIABLES (MATHEMATICS).
VITAL STATISTICS.
WEIGHTS AND MEASURES

MILITARY AND NAVAL SCIENCE.

AERONAUTICS, MILITARY
ARMAMENTS.
ARMED FORCES.
ARSENALS
ATOMIC BOMB
ATOMIC WEAPONS.
BATTLES.
BIOLOGICAL WARFARE.
BOMBERS.
BORDER PATROLS
CHEMICAL WARFARE.
DEFENCES, NATIONAL.
DESERTION, MILITARY
EXSERVICEMEN
GENERALS.
GUERRILLA WARFARE.
INDIAN NATIONAL ARMY.
MILITARISM
MILITARY ART AND SCIENCE.
MILITARY EDUCATION
MILITARY LAW
MILITARY OFFENCES
MILITARY POLICY.
MILITARY SERVICE, COMPULSORY
MILITARY SERVICE AS A PROFESSION.
MUNITIONS.
MUTINY
NAVAL ART AND SCIENCE.
NAVIES.
PENSIONS, MILITARY
PRISONERS OF WAR.
REQUISITIONS, MILITARY
SEA POWER.
SOCIOLOGY, MILITARY.
SOLDIERS
STRATEGY.
WAR.
WEAPONS SYSTEMS.

PHILOSOPHY AND RELIGION.

Philosophy.

BUSINESS ETHICS.
CAUSATION.
CHRISTIAN ETHICS.
COMMUNIST ETHICS.
CONDUCT OF LIFE.
COSMOLOGY.
ENLIGHTENMENT.
ETHICS.
EXISTENTIALISM.
HERMENEUTICS.
IDEALISM.
IDEOLOGY.
JUDGMENT (ETHICS).
KNOWLEDGE, THEORY OF.
LAW AND ETHICS.
LEGAL ETHICS.
LOGIC.
LOGIC, SYMBOLIC AND MATHEMATICAL.
LOGICAL POSITIVISM.
MATERIALISM.
MEANING.
MEANING (PHILOSOPHY).
METHODOLOGY.
MORAL EDUCATION.
ONTOLOGY.
PHENOMENOLOGY.
PHILOSOPHERS
PHILOSOPHICAL ANTHROPOLOGY.
PHILOSOPHY.
PHILOSOPHY, AMERICAN.
PHILOSOPHY, ANCIENT.
PHILOSOPHY, ARMENIAN.
PHILOSOPHY, BULGARIAN.
PHILOSOPHY, FRENCH.
PHILOSOPHY, GERMAN.
PHILOSOPHY, MODERN.
PHILOSOPHY, RUSSIAN.
PHILOSOPHY, SCOTTISH.
PHILOSOPHY, SPANISH.
PHILOSOPHY, YUGOSLAV.
POSITIVISM.
PRAGMATICS.
RATIONALISM.
REASON.
RESPONSIBILITY.
SCEPTICISM.
SOCIAL SCIENCES AND ETHICS.
SOCIALISM AND ETHICS.
SOCIALIST ETHICS.
SPACE AND TIME.
UTILITARIANISM.
WHOLE AND PARTS (PHILOSOPHY).

Religion.

ADVENTISTS.
ANTICLERICALISM
ANTISEMITISM.
ATHEISM.
BROTHERHOODS.
CATHOLIC CHURCH
CATHOLIC CHURCH IN FRANCE.
CATHOLIC CHURCH IN GERMANY.
CATHOLIC CHURCH IN ITALY.
CATHOLIC CHURCH IN PERU.
CATHOLIC CHURCH IN POLAND.
CATHOLIC CHURCH IN RUSSIA.
CATHOLIC CHURCH IN THE UNITED STATES.
CATHOLICS IN FRANCE.
CATHOLICS IN GERMANY.
CATHOLICS IN ITALY.
CATHOLICS IN THE UNITED KINGDOM.

CATHOLICS IN THE UNITED STATES.
CHRISTIAN ETHICS.
CHRISTIAN LIFE.
CHRISTIANITY.
CHRISTIANITY AND ECONOMICS.
CHRISTIANITY AND INTERNATIONAL AFFAIRS.
CHRISTIANITY AND OTHER RELIGIONS.
CHRISTIANITY AND POLITICS.
CHURCH AND ECONOMICS.
CHURCH AND LABOUR
CHURCH AND RACE PROBLEMS
CHURCH AND SOCIAL PROBLEMS.
CHURCH AND STATE.
CHURCH AND STATE IN CANADA.
CHURCH AND STATE IN FRANCE.
CHURCH AND STATE IN GERMANY.
CHURCH AND STATE IN IRELAND.
CHURCH AND STATE IN ITALY.
CHURCH AND STATE IN MEXICO.
CHURCH AND STATE IN POLAND.
CHURCH AND STATE IN RUSSIA.
CHURCH AND STATE IN SPAIN.
CHURCH AND STATE IN THE UKRAINE.
CHURCH AND STATE IN THE UNITED KINGDOM.
CHURCH AND STATE IN THE UNITED STATES.
CHURCH HISTORY.
CHURCH LANDS
CHURCH OF ENGLAND
CHURCH PROPERTY
CHURCH SCHOOLS
CHURCH WORK WITH THE DEAF.
CHURCH WORK WITH YOUTH
CHURCHES
CITY MISSIONS
CLERGY
COMMUNISM AND CHRISTIANITY.
COMMUNISM AND RELIGION.
COMMUNISM AND ZIONISM.
CONFUCIUS AND CONFUCIANISM.
CORPORATIONS, RELIGIOUS
COVENANTERS.
DISSENTERS, RELIGIOUS
DOMINICANS IN SILESIA.
EVANGELICAL REVIVAL.
FRIENDS, SOCIETY OF.
GIFTS, SPIRITUAL.
GOD.
JEHOVAH'S WITNESSES.
JUDAISM AND SOCIAL PROBLEMS.
LUTHERAN CHURCH IN SWEDEN.
LUTHERANS IN GERMANY.
LUTHERANS IN THE ARGENTINE REPUBLIC.
MENNONITES IN CANADA.
MENNONITES IN KANSAS.
MISSIONS
MISSIONS, CANADIAN.
MISSIONS, FRENCH.
MODERNISM
MOHAMMEDANISM.
MOHAMMEDANS IN BOSNIA.
MOHAMMEDANS IN INDIA.
MOHAMMEDANS IN KIRGHIZIA.
MONASTERIES
MORMONS AND MORMONISM.
NEGRO CHURCHES.
OPUS DEI.
ORTHODOX EASTERN CHURCH, RUSSIAN.
PAGANISM.
PENTECOSTAL CHURCHES
PERSECUTION.
PRESS, CATHOLIC
PROTESTANTS IN CHILE.
PROTESTANTS IN FRANCE.
PROTESTANTS IN NORTHERN IRELAND.
PROTESTANTS IN THE ARGENTINE REPUBLIC.
PURITANS.
REFORMATION.
RELIGION.
RELIGION AND SCIENCE.
RELIGION AND SOCIOLOGY.
RELIGIONS.
RELIGIOUS EDUCATION
RELIGIOUS LIBERTY
SCIENTOLOGY.
SECTS.
SECULARISM.
SERMONS, ENGLISH.
SISTERHOODS.
SOCIALISM, CHRISTIAN.
SOCIALISM AND CATHOLIC CHURCH.
SOCIALISM AND RELIGION.
SOCIOLOGY, CHRISTIAN.
THEOLOGY, PURITAN
TRADE UNIONS, CATHOLIC

POLITICAL SCIENCE, POLITICS AND GOVERNMENT.

General.

ADMINISTRATION.
ADMINISTRATIVE AGENCIES
ADMINISTRATIVE AND POLITICAL DIVISIONS
ALIENS
ALLEGIANCE.
ALLIANCES.
ANARCHISM AND ANARCHISTS.
ANTICOMMUNIST MOVEMENTS.
ARBITRATION, INTERNATIONAL
ASSASSINATION
ATOMIC WEAPONS AND DISARMAMENT.
AUTARCHY.
AUTHORITY.
AUTONOMY.
BRIBERY
BUREAUCRACY.
BUSINESS AND POLITICS.
CAMPAIGN FUNDS.
CAMPAIGN MANAGEMENT.
CENSORSHIP
CENTRE PARTIES
CHRISTIANITY AND INTERNATIONAL AFFAIRS.
CHRISTIANITY AND POLITICS.
CHURCH AND STATE.
CITIZENSHIP.
CIVICS, EAST AFRICAN.
CIVICS, GERMAN.
CIVIL RIGHTS.
CIVIL SERVICE.
CIVIL SUPREMACY OVER THE MILITARY.
COALITION GOVERNMENTS.
COLONIES.
COLONIES IN AFRICA.
COLONIES IN THE FAR EAST.
COMMUNICATION IN POLITICS.
COMMUNISM.
COMMUNISM AND CHRISTIANITY.
COMMUNISM AND LITERATURE.
COMMUNISM AND MUSIC.
COMMUNISM AND RELIGION.
COMMUNISM AND SOCIAL SCIENCES.
COMMUNISM AND THE ARTS.
COMMUNISM AND ZIONISM.
COMMUNIST EDUCATION
COMMUNIST PARTY PURGES.
COMMUNIST REVISIONISM.
COMMUNIST STATE.
COMMUNIST STRATEGY.
COMMUNISTIC SETTLEMENTS.
COMMUNITY LEADERSHIP.
COMMUNITY POWER.
CONCENTRATION CAMPS
CONFLICT OF INTERESTS (PUBLIC OFFICE).
CONSCIENTIOUS OBJECTORS.
CONSERVATISM.
CONSTITUTIONAL HISTORY.
CONSTITUTIONS.
CONSTITUTIONS, STATE
CORPORATE STATE.
CORRUPTION (IN POLITICS).
COUPS D'ÉTAT.
DECENTRALIZATION IN GOVERNMENT.
DECISION-MAKING IN PUBLIC ADMINISTRATION.
DELEGATION OF POWERS
DEMOCRACY.
DEMONSTRATIONS
DESPOTISM.
DETENTE.
DETENTION OF PERSONS
DICTATORSHIP OF THE PROLETARIAT.
DIPLOMACY.
DIPLOMATIC DOCUMENTS.
DIPLOMATIC PRIVILEGES AND IMMUNITIES.
DISARMAMENT.
ELECTIONS.
ELITE.
EMPLOYEE-MANAGEMENT RELATIONS IN GOVERNMENT
EQUALITY.
EUROPEAN FEDERATION.
EXECUTIVE ADVISORY BODIES
EXECUTIVE POWER.
EXECUTIVE PRIVILEGE (GOVERNMENT INFORMATION)
FASCISM.
FEDERAL-CITY RELATIONS
FEDERAL GOVERNMENT.
FIRE-DEPARTMENTS
FREEDOM OF ASSOCIATION
FREEDOM OF INFORMATION
GEOGRAPHY, POLITICAL.
GEOPOLITICS.
GOVERNMENT, COMPARATIVE.
GOVERNMENT ADVERTISING
GOVERNMENT AND THE PRESS
GOVERNMENT CONSULTANTS
GOVERNMENT EXECUTIVES
GOVERNMENT INFORMATION
GOVERNMENT PUBLICITY
GOVERNMENTAL INVESTIGATIONS
GUERRILLAS
HIGHER EDUCATION AND STATE
HOME RULE
IMPERIALISM.
INDEPENDENT REGULATORY COMMISSIONS
INDUSTRY AND STATE.
INSURGENCY
INTELLIGENCE SERVICE
INTERNAL SECURITY
INTERNATIONAL AGENCIES.
INTERNATIONAL AGENCIES IN AFRICA
INTERNATIONAL AGENCIES IN EASTERN EUROPE.
INTERNATIONAL AGENCIES IN EUROPE.
INTERNATIONAL AGENCIES IN SWITZERLAND.
INTERNATIONAL BROADCASTING.
INTERNATIONAL COOPERATION.
INTERNATIONAL OFFICIALS AND EMPLOYEES.
INTERNATIONAL ORGANIZATION.
INTERNATIONAL RELATIONS.
INTERNATIONALISM.
JUSTICE AND POLITICS
LAW AND POLITICS.
LAW AND SOCIALISM.
LEADERSHIP.
LEFT AND RIGHT (POLITICAL SCIENCE).
LEGISLATORS.
LEGITIMACY OF GOVERNMENTS.
LIBERALISM.
LIBERTY.
LIBERTY OF INFORMATION

POLITICAL SCIENCE, POLITICS AND GOVERNMENT (Cont.)

LIBERTY OF SPEECH
LIBERTY OF THE PRESS.
LITERATURE AND REVOLUTIONS.
LITERATURE AND STATE.
LOBBYISTS
LOCAL GOVERNMENT.
LOCAL GOVERNMENT OFFICIALS AND EMPLOYEES
MANDATES
MARXISM.
MAYORS
MEDIATION, INTERNATIONAL.
MEDICINE AND STATE
METROPOLITAN GOVERNMENT
MINISTERIAL RESPONSIBILITY
MINORITIES.
MISCONDUCT IN OFFICE
MONARCHY, BRITISH.
MUNICIPAL GOVERNMENT
MUNICIPAL OWNERSHIP
MUNICIPAL POWERS AND SERVICES BEYOND CORPORATE LIMITS
MUNICIPAL RESEARCH.
MUNICIPAL SERVICES
NATIONALISM.
NATIONALISM AND SOCIALISM.
NEUTRALITY.
NONVIOLENCE.
OLIGARCHY.
OMBUDSMAN.
OPPOSITION (POLITICAL SCIENCE).
ORATORY.
PACIFIC SETTLEMENT OF INTERNATIONAL DISPUTES.
PACIFISM.
PANPACIFIC RELATIONS.
PARTY AFFILIATION.
PATRIOTISM
PEACE.
PEACE SOCIETIES.
PEASANT UPRISINGS.
PEOPLE'S DEMOCRACIES.
PLEBISCITE
POLICE, POLITICAL AND SECRET
POLICY SCIENCES.
POLITICAL CONVENTIONS.
POLITICAL CRIMES AND OFFENCES
POLITICAL ETHICS.
POLITICAL PARTICIPATION.
POLITICAL PARTIES.
POLITICAL PRISONERS
POLITICAL PSYCHOLOGY.
POLITICAL SCIENCE.
POLITICAL SOCIALIZATION.
POLITICAL SOCIOLOGY.
POLITICS, PRACTICAL.
POLITICS IN LITERATURE.
POPULATION TRANSFER
PRESS, LABOUR
PRESS AND POLITICS
PRESSURE GROUPS
PRIME MINISTERS
PROPORTIONAL REPRESENTATION
PUBLIC OFFICERS.
RADIO IN POLITICS
RADIO IN PROPAGANDA.
RAILWAYS AND STATE
REFERENDUM
REFUGEES.
REFUGEES, AUSTRIAN.
REFUGEES, GERMAN.
REFUGEES, POLITICAL.
REFUGEES, SPANISH.
REFUGEES IN BELGIUM.
REFUGEES IN EASTERN GERMANY.
REFUGEES IN EUROPE.
REFUGEES IN FRANCE.
REFUGEES IN GERMANY.
REFUGEES IN MEXICO
REFUGEES IN SWEDEN.
REFUGEES IN THE UNITED KINGDOM.
REGIONALISM.

REGIONALISM (INTERNATIONAL ORGANIZATION).
RELIGIOUS LIBERTY
REPRESENTATIVE GOVERNMENT AND REPRESENTATION.
REVOLUTIONISTS.
REVOLUTIONS.
RIGHT AND LEFT (POLITICAL SCIENCE).
RIGHT OF REPLY
SCIENCE AND STATE.
SECRET SOCIETIES
SECURITY, INTERNATIONAL.
SEDITION
SELF-DETERMINATION, NATIONAL.
SEPARATION OF POWERS
SIGNS AND SYMBOLS
SLAVOPHILISM.
SOCIAL SCIENCES AND STATE
SOCIALISM.
SOCIALISM, CHRISTIAN.
SOCIALISM AND CATHOLIC CHURCH.
SOCIALISM AND EDUCATION.
SOCIALISM AND ETHICS.
SOCIALISM AND RELIGION.
SOCIALISM AND YOUTH.
SOCIALIST ETHICS.
SOCIALISTS
SOVIETS
SPECIAL DISTRICTS
STATE, THE.
STATE ENCOURAGEMENT OF SCIENCE, LITERATURE AND ART
STATE GOVERNMENTS
STATE SUCCESSION.
STATES, NEW.
STATES, SMALL.
STATESMEN.
SUBVERSIVE ACTIVITIES.
SUFFRAGE
SYMBOLISM.
SYNDICALISM.
TECHNOLOGY AND STATE.
TELEVISION IN POLITICS
TERRORISM.
TOLERATION.
TORTURE.
TRADE UNIONS AND COMMUNISM.
TRADE UNIONS AND FOREIGN POLICY
TREASON
TREATIES.
TREATY-MAKING POWER
TRUST TERRITORIES.
UTOPIAS.
VIOLENCE.
VOTERS, REGISTRATION OF
VOTING.
VOTING RESEARCH.
WAR
WAR AND EMERGENCY POWERS
WAR AND SOCIALISM.
WAR CRIMES
WAR RELIEF.
WOMEN AND SOCIALISM.
WOMEN IN THE CIVIL SERVICE.
WOMEN'S RIGHTS.
WORLD POLITICS.

Particular countries, nationalities, parties, organizations, etc.

ACTION FRANÇAISE.
ALIANZA NACIONAL (PERU).
ALLGEMEINER DEUTSCHER ARBEITERVEREIN.
ANTIFAŠISTIČKO VIJEĆE NARODNOG OSLOBODJENJA JUGOSLAVIJE.
ANTINAZI MOVEMENT.
ASOCIACION CATOLICA NACIONAL DE PROPAGANDISTAS.
ASSOCIATION SULLY.
ATLANTIC COMMUNITY.

BAATH PARTY.
BLACK NATIONALISM
CARLISTS.
CHURCH AND STATE IN CANADA.
CHURCH AND STATE IN FRANCE.
CHURCH AND STATE IN GERMANY.
CHURCH AND STATE IN IRELAND.
CHURCH AND STATE IN ITALY.
CHURCH AND STATE IN MEXICO.
CHURCH AND STATE IN POLAND.
CHURCH AND STATE IN RUSSIA.
CHURCH AND STATE IN SPAIN.
CHURCH AND STATE IN THE UKRAINE.
CHURCH AND STATE IN THE UNITED KINGDOM.
CHURCH AND STATE IN THE UNITED STATES.
COMMONWEALTH DEVELOPMENT CORPORATION.
COMMUNIST COUNTRIES
COMMUNIST PARTIES.
COMMUNIST PARTY
COMMUNISTS
CONSERVATIVE PARTY (CANADA).
CONSERVATIVE PARTY (UNITED KINGDOM).
CONVENTION PEOPLE'S PARTY.
DECEMBRISTS.
DEMOCRATIC PARTY (UNITED STATES).
DEUTSCHE VOLKSPARTEI.
EUROPEAN COMMISSION OF HUMAN RIGHTS.
EUROPEAN COMMITTEE ON LEGAL CO-OPERATION.
EUROPEAN COMMUNITIES.
EUROPEAN CONVENTION ON HUMAN RIGHTS.
EUROPEAN FREE TRADE ASSOCIATION.
EUROPEAN PARLIAMENT.
FABIAN SOCIETY.
FEDERAL PARTY.
FÉDÉRATION NATIONALE DES RÉPUBLICAINS INDÉPENDENTS.
FENIANS.
FLEMISH MOVEMENT.
FREIE DEMOKRATISCHE PARTEI.
FREISINNING-DEMOKRATISCHE PARTEI DES KANTONS SOLOTHURN.
FRENTE PORTUGAL LIVRE.
HRVATSKA SELJACKA STRANKA.
INDIAN NATIONAL CONGRESS.
INTERNATIONAL, THE.
INTERNATIONAL SOCIALISTS.
INTERNATIONAL UNION OF REVOLUTIONARY WRITERS.
JACOBINS.
JACOBITES.
JEWISH-ARAB RELATIONS.
LABOUR PARTY
LATIN AMERICAN FREE TRADE ASSOCIATION.
LEAGUE OF ARAB STATES.
LEAGUE OF NATIONS.
LIBERAL PARTY
LIBERAL UNIONIST PARTY.
LONDON MUNICIPAL SOCIETY.
LOYALTY-SECURITY PROGRAM, 1947- .
LUD POLSKI (1835-1846).
MONROE DOCTRINE.
MOUVEMENT NATIONAL DES QUEBECOIS.
MOVIMENTO DAS FORÇAS ARMADAS.
MOVIMIENTO DE LA IZQUIERDA REVOLUCIONARIA.
MOVIMIENTO NACIONALISTA REVOLUCIONARIO.
NARODOWA PARTIA ROBOTNICZA.
NATIONAL LIBERAL PARTY (GERMANY).
NATIONAL PARTY (SOUTH AFRICA).
NATIONAL SOCIALISM.
NORDISK RÅD.

PUBLIC HEALTH AND MEDICINE

NORTH ATLANTIC TREATY ORGANIZATION.
OBÓZ ZJEDNOCZENIA NARODOWEGO.
OESTERREICHISCHE VOLKSPARTEI.
ORGANIZATION OF AFRICAN UNITY.
ORGANIZATION OF AMERICAN STATES.
OSVOBOZHDENIE TRUDA.
PALESTINE LIBERATION ARMY.
PALESTINE LIBERATION ORGANIZATION.
PANAFRICANISM.
PANGERMANISM.
PARTI CONGOLAIS DU TRAVAIL.
PARTI SOCIALISTE UNIFIE.
PARTIDO ACCION NACIONAL.
PARTIDO AFRICANO DA INDEPENDENCIA DA GUINE E CABOVERDE.
PARTIDO NACIONALISTA (PUERTO RICO).
PARTIIA "NARODNOGO PRAVA".
PARTITO D'AZIONE.
PARTITO DI UNITÀ PROLETARIA PER IL COMUNISMO.
PARTITO POPOLARE ITALIANO.
POLITICAL BALLADS AND SONGS, SWEDISH.
POLITICAL POETRY, ENGLISH.
POLITICAL POETRY, IRISH.
POLITICAL SATIRE, AMERICAN.
POLSKIE STRONNICTWO LUDOWE.
POPULAR FRONTS.
POPULISM IN BRAZIL.
POPULISM IN LATIN AMERICA.
POPULISM IN MEXICO.
POPULISM IN POLAND.
POPULISM IN RUSSIA.
POPULISM IN THE ARGENTINE REPUBLIC.
POPULISM IN THE UKRAINE.
POPULISM IN THE UNITED STATES.
PROGRESSIVE PARTY (SOUTH AFRICA).
PROGRESSIVISM (U.S. POLITICS).
PROPAGANDA, AMERICAN.
PROPAGANDA, COMMUNIST.
PROPAGANDA, GERMAN.
PROPAGANDA, INTERNATIONAL.
PROPAGANDA, ITALIAN.
PROPAGANDA, RUSSIAN.
RADICALISM IN FRANCE.
RADICALISM IN GERMANY.
RADICALISM IN ITALY
RADICALISM IN POLAND.
RADICALISM IN RUSSIA.
RADICALISM IN THE UNITED KINGDOM.
RADICALISM IN THE UNITED STATES.
REPUBLICAN PARTY (UNITED STATES).
REVOLUTIONISTS, BRITISH.
REVOLUTIONISTS, INDIAN.
REVOLUTIONISTS, JEWISH.
REVOLUTIONISTS, LATIN AMERICAN.
REVOLUTIONISTS, POLISH.
REVOLUTIONISTS, RUSSIAN.
SCANDINAVIANISM.
SECTIONALISM (UNITED STATES).
SOCIAL DEMOCRATIC PARTY (DENMARK).
SOCIAL DEMOCRATIC PARTY (GERMANY).
SOCIAL DEMOCRATIC PARTY (POLAND).
SOCIAL DEMOCRATIC PARTY (RUSSIA).
SOCIAL DEMOCRATIC PARTY (RUSSIA) (MENSHEVIKS)
SOCIAL DEMOCRATIC PARTY (SWEDEN).
SOCIAL DEMOCRATIC PARTY (YUGOSLAVIA).
SOCIALISM IN AFRICA.
SOCIALISM IN AUSTRIA.
SOCIALISM IN AUSTRIA-HUNGARY.
SOCIALISM IN BELGIUM.
SOCIALISM IN CHILE.
SOCIALISM IN CHINA.
SOCIALISM IN CUBA.
SOCIALISM IN CZECHOSLOVAKIA.
SOCIALISM IN DENMARK.
SOCIALISM IN ETHIOPIA.
SOCIALISM IN EUROPE.
SOCIALISM IN FRANCE.
SOCIALISM IN GERMANY.
SOCIALISM IN GHANA.
SOCIALISM IN INDIA.
SOCIALISM IN ITALY.
SOCIALISM IN KOREA.
SOCIALISM IN LATIN AMERICA.
SOCIALISM IN POLAND.
SOCIALISM IN PORTUGAL.
SOCIALISM IN RUSSIA.
SOCIALISM IN SCOTLAND.
SOCIALISM IN SERBIA.
SOCIALISM IN SILESIA.
SOCIALISM IN SPAIN.
SOCIALISM IN SWEDEN.
SOCIALISM IN SWITZERLAND.
SOCIALISM IN TANZANIA.
SOCIALISM IN THE ARGENTINE REPUBLIC.
SOCIALISM IN THE CONGO (BRAZZAVILLE).
SOCIALISM IN THE NETHERLANDS.
SOCIALISM IN THE UKRAINE.
SOCIALISM IN THE UNITED KINGDOM.
SOCIALISM IN THE UNITED STATES.
SOCIALISM IN WHITE RUSSIA.
SOCIALISM IN YUGOSLAVIA.
SOCIALIST PARTY (ARGENTINE REPUBLIC).
SOCIALIST PARTY (AUSTRIA).
SOCIALIST PARTY (CHILE).
SOCIALIST PARTY (FRANCE).
SOCIALIST PARTY (ITALY).
SOCIALIST PARTY (POLAND).
SOCIALIST PARTY (SWITZERLAND).
SOCIALIST PARTY (UNITED KINGDOM).
SOCIALIST WORKERS PARTY (UNITED STATES).
SOCIALIST-REVOLUTIONARY PARTY (RUSSIA).
SOCIJALISTIČKI SAVEZ RADNOG NARODA SRBIJE
SOUTH PACIFIC COMMISSION.
STRONNICTWO LUDOWE.
TANGANYIKA AFRICAN NATIONAL UNION.
TENNESSEE VALLEY AUTHORITY.
TORIES, ENGLISH.
TOWARZYSTWO DEMOKRATYCZNE POLSKIE.
ULSTER UNIONIST PARTY.
UNABHAENGIGE SOZIALDEMOKRATISCHE PARTEI DEUTSCHLANDS.
UNIDAD POPULAR.
UNION LEAGUE OF PHILADELPHIA.
UNITED NATIONS.
UNITED SOUTH AFRICAN NATIONAL PARTY.
USTAŠA.
VEREINSTAG DEUTSCHER ARBEITERVEREINE.
VUTRESHNA MAKEDONSKA REVOLIUTSIONNA ORGANIZATSIIA.
WATERGATE AFFAIR, 1972- .
WHIG PARTY (UNITED KINGDOM).
WIRTSCHAFTLICHE AUFBAU-VEREINIGUNG.
YOUNG COMMUNIST LEAGUE
ZJEDNOCZONE STRONNICTWO LUDOWE.

PSYCHOLOGY.

ACHIEVEMENT MOTIVATION.
ADOLESCENT PSYCHOLOGY
ADULTHOOD.
AGGRESSIVENESS (PSYCHOLOGY).
AGING.
ANGER.
ANIMAL INTELLIGENCE.
ANIMALS, HABITS AND BEHAVIOUR OF.
ANTIPATHIES AND PREJUDICES.
ANXIETY.
ARTIFICIAL INTELLIGENCE.
ATTENTION.
ATTITUDE (PSYCHOLOGY).
ATTITUDE CHANGE.
BEHAVIOUR MODIFICATION.
BEHAVIOUR THERAPY.
BELIEF AND DOUBT.
BEREAVEMENT.
CHANGE (PSYCHOLOGY).
CHILD PSYCHOLOGY.
COGNITION.
COGNITION (CHILD PSYCHOLOGY).
CONFLICT (PSYCHOLOGY).
CONFORMITY
CONSCIOUSNESS.
CRIMINAL BEHAVIOUR, PREDICTION OF.
CRIMINAL PSYCHOLOGY.
CRISIS INTERVENTION (PSYCHIATRY).
CROWDING STRESS.
DECISION-MAKING.
DECISION-MAKING IN PUBLIC ADMINISTRATION.
DEVELOPMENTAL PSYCHOLOGY.
EDUCATIONAL PSYCHOLOGY.
EMOTION.
ENVIRONMENTAL PSYCHOLOGY.
ETHNIC ATTITUDES.
FAMILY PSYCHOTHERAPY.
GAZE
GEOGRAPHICAL PERCEPTION.
GROUP PSYCHOTHERAPY.
GUILT.
HUMAN BEHAVIOUR.
HUMAN INFORMATION PROCESSING.
INTELLECT.
JUDGMENT.
LAUGHTER.
LEARNING, PSYCHOLOGY OF.
MEMORY.
METAPHYSICS.
MOTIVATION (PSYCHOLOGY).
NEUROCHEMISTRY.
NEUROPSYCHOLOGY.
OPTICAL PATTERN RECOGNITION.
PERCEPTION.
PERSONALITY.
PERSONALITY TESTS.
POLITICAL PSYCHOLOGY.
PRISON PSYCHOLOGY.
PSYCHIATRY.
PSYCHOANALYSIS.
PSYCHOLINGUISTICS.
PSYCHOLOGICAL RESEARCH.
PSYCHOLOGY.
PSYCHOLOGY, EXPERIMENTAL.
PSYCHOLOGY, FORENSIC.
PSYCHOLOGY, INDUSTRIAL.
PSYCHOLOGY, PHYSIOLOGICAL.
PSYCHOSES.
PSYCHOTHERAPY.
PSYCHOTROPIC DRUGS.
REASONING.
RECOGNITION (PSYCHOLOGY).
RECOLLECTION (PSYCHOLOGY).
SCALE ANALYSIS (PSYCHOLOGY).
SELF.
SELF-EVALUATION.
SOCIAL PSYCHOLOGY.
THOUGHT AND THINKING.
TRAVEL.
VISUAL PERCEPTION.
WIT AND HUMOUR.
WORK.

PUBLIC HEALTH AND MEDICINE (Cont.)

PUBLIC HEALTH AND MEDICINE.

ABORTION.
ACCIDENTS.
BIRTH CONTROL.
BIRTH CONTROL CLINICS
BLOOD
CANCER
CARDIOVASCULAR SYSTEM
CHILD GUIDANCE CLINICS
CHILD PSYCHIATRY.
CHRONICALLY ILL.
CITY NOISE
COCAINE.
COCAINE HABIT.
COMMUNICABLE DISEASES
COMMUNITY HEALTH SERVICES.
COMMUNITY HEALTH SERVICES FOR CHILDREN
COMMUNITY HEALTH SERVICES FOR THE AGED
COMMUNITY MENTAL HEALTH SERVICES
CORONARY HEART DISEASE.
DEAF
DEATH
DENTAL CARE
DIET
DRINKING WATER
DRUG ABUSE.
DRUGS.
DRUGS AND MINORITIES
DRUGS AND YOUTH.
EMERGENCY MEDICAL SERVICES
ENVIRONMENTAL HEALTH.
EUGENICS.
FETUS, DEATH OF THE.
FOOD.
FOOD LAW AND LEGISLATION
GOITRE
HAEMOPHILIA.
HANDICAPPED
HANDICAPPED CHILDREN
HEALTH ATTITUDES.
HEALTH CARE TEAMS
HEALTH EDUCATION.
HEALTH SERVICES ADMINISTRATION
HEALTH SURVEYS.
HOME ACCIDENTS
HOSPITALS.
HUMAN EXPERIMENTATION IN MEDICINE.
HYGIENE.
HYGIENE, PUBLIC.
INDUSTRIAL ACCIDENTS
INDUSTRIAL HYGIENE
INDUSTRIAL SAFETY
INFANTS
INFANTS (NEW-BORN)
KIDNEYS
LIFE EXPECTANCY.
LUNGS
MALNUTRITION.
MATERNAL AND INFANT WELFARE
MEDICAL CARE.
MEDICAL CARE, COST OF.
MEDICAL CENTRES
MEDICAL COOPERATION.
MEDICAL ECONOMICS.
MEDICAL FEES
MEDICAL INNOVATIONS
MEDICAL POLICY
MEDICAL RESEARCH
MEDICINE.
MEDICINE, PREVENTIVE.
MEDICINE, PSYCHOSOMATIC.
MEDICINE, RURAL
MEDICINE, STATE
MEDICINE AND STATE
MENTAL HEALTH LAWS
MENTAL HEALTH SERVICES
MENTAL HYGIENE.
MENTAL ILLNESS.
MENTALLY HANDICAPPED CHILDREN
MENTALLY ILL
MORTALITY.
NARCOTIC ADDICTS
NARCOTIC HABIT.
NURSES AND NURSING
NUTRITION.
NUTRITION POLICY
NUTRITION SURVEYS
OCCUPATIONAL MORTALITY
OIL POLLUTION OF RIVERS, HARBOURS, ETC.
OLD AGE
OPTICS.
PHARMACEUTICAL RESEARCH.
PHYSICAL EDUCATION AND TRAINING.
PHYSICALLY HANDICAPPED
PHYSICALLY HANDICAPPED CHILDREN
PHYSIOLOGY
PREGNANCY.
PRENATAL INFLUENCES.
PSYCHIATRIC HOSPITALS
PSYCHIATRY.
PSYCHOLOGY, PHYSIOLOGICAL.
PSYCHOTHERAPY.
PSYCHOTROPIC DRUGS.
PUBLIC HEALTH RESEARCH.
REFUSE AND REFUSE DISPOSAL.
REHABILITATION.
ROAD ACCIDENTS
RURAL HEALTH SERVICES
SEWAGE DISPOSAL
SEWERAGE, RURAL
SICK.
SMOKE PREVENTION.
SMOKING.
SOCIAL MEDICINE.
SPEECH, DISORDERS OF.
STERILIZATION (BIRTH CONTROL).
STRESS (PHYSIOLOGY).
THALIDOMIDE.
TOBACCO HABIT.
TYPHOID FEVER
VACCINATION.
VEGETARIANISM.
WATER QUALITY MANAGEMENT
WORLD HEALTH ORGANIZATION

SCIENCE AND TECHNOLOGY.

AGRICULTURAL INNOVATIONS.
AMMONIA
ASTRONAUTICS
ASTRONOMY.
ATOMIC ENERGY.
ATOMIC POWER.
AUTOMATION.
BIOLOGICAL WARFARE.
BIOLOGY.
BOTANY
BRAIN.
CHEMICAL WARFARE.
DIFFUSION OF INNOVATIONS.
EDUCATIONAL TECHNOLOGY.
ENVIRONMENTAL ENGINEERING.
EVOLUTION.
FORECASTING.
GENETICS
GROUND-EFFECT MACHINES.
NEUROCHEMISTRY.
PETROLEUM ENGINEERING.
RELIGION AND SCIENCE.
RESEARCH
SCIENCE
SCIENCE AND STATE.
TECHNOLOGICAL FORECASTING.
TECHNOLOGICAL INNOVATIONS.
TECHNOLOGISTS
TECHNOLOGY.
TECHNOLOGY AND CIVILIZATION.
TECHNOLOGY AND LAW.
TECHNOLOGY AND STATE.
TECHNOLOGY TRANSFER.
WATER REUSE.

SOCIOLOGY, ANTHROPOLOGY AND ETHNOLOGY.

General.

ABOLITIONISTS.
ACCULTURATION.
ACTION RESEARCH.
ADOLESCENCE.
AGE AND EMPLOYMENT
ALCOHOLICS
ALCOHOLISM.
ALCOHOLISM AND CRIME.
ALIENATION (SOCIAL PSYCHOLOGY).
ALMSHOUSES AND WORKHOUSES
ANTHROPOLOGY.
ANTHROPOMETRY.
ANTISEMITISM.
APARTMENT HOUSES
ARCHITECTURE AND SOCIETY.
ART AND SOCIETY.
ASSOCIATION OF CHILD CARE OFFICERS.
ASSOCIATIONS, INSTITUTIONS, ETC.
ASTRONAUTICS AND CIVILIZATION.
ATHLETIC CLUBS
BOYS.
BRITISH BROADCASTING CORPORATION.
BROADCASTING POLICY
BROKEN HOMES.
CAMP-MEETINGS.
CARAVANS (AUTOMOBILE TRAILERS).
CASTE
CHARITIES
CHILD DEVELOPMENT.
CHILD WELFARE
CHILDREN
CHILDREN IN CHINA.
CHILDREN IN FRANCE.
CHILDREN IN GERMANY.
CHILDREN IN NIGERIA.
CHILDREN IN THE UNITED KINGDOM.
CHILDREN OF IMMIGRANTS
CHILDREN OF WORKING MOTHERS.
CHURCH AND RACE PROBLEMS.
CHURCH AND SOCIAL PROBLEMS.
CHURCH WORK WITH THE DEAF.
CHURCH WORK WITH YOUTH
CITIES AND TOWNS.
CITIZENS' ADVICE BUREAUX.
CLANS AND CLAN SYSTEM.
COCAINE HABIT.
COLLECTIVE SETTLEMENTS
COMITE PERMANENT INTER-ETATS DE LUTTE CONTRE LA SECHERESSE DANS LE SAHEL.
COMMUNICATION.
COMMUNISM AND SOCIAL SCIENCES.
COMMUNITY.
COMMUNITY AND SCHOOL.
COMMUNITY CENTRES
COMMUNITY DEVELOPMENT.
COMMUNITY HEALTH SERVICES FOR CHILDREN
COMMUNITY HEALTH SERVICES FOR THE AGED
COMMUNITY LIFE.
COMMUNITY ORGANIZATION.
CONJUGAL VIOLENCE.
CONVERSATION.
CORPORAL PUNISHMENT.
COSTUME
COUNSELLING.
COUNTRY HOMES
COURTSHIP.
CRIME AND CRIMINALS.

SOCIOLOGY, ANTHROPOLOGY AND ETHNOLOGY

CRIME PREVENTION.
CRIMINAL ANTHROPOLOGY.
CRIMINAL STATISTICS.
CRUELTY TO CHILDREN.
CULTURE.
DAY NURSERIES
DELINQUENT WOMEN
DEVIANT BEHAVIOUR.
DISASTER RELIEF
DISCRIMINATION.
DISCRIMINATION IN HOUSING
DISSENTERS
DIVORCE
DIVORCEES.
DRINKING AND ROAD ACCIDENTS
DRINKING CUSTOMS
DRUG ABUSE.
DRUG ABUSE AND CRIME
DRUGS.
DRUGS AND MINORITIES
DRUGS AND YOUTH.
DWELLINGS
EDUCATIONAL SOCIOLOGY.
ELECTRIC ALARMS.
ELITE.
EMIGRATION AND IMMIGRATION.
ENDOWMENTS
EQUALITY.
ETHNIC ATTITUDES.
ETHNIC GROUPS.
ETHNICITY.
ETHNOLOGY.
EVALUATION RESEARCH (SOCIAL ACTION PROGRAMMES).
EVOLUTION.
EXCHANGE OF PERSONS PROGRAMMES.
EXILES
EXSERVICEMEN
FAMILY.
FAMILY LIFE EDUCATION.
FAMILY SIZE.
FAMILY SOCIAL WORK
FAMINES.
FATHER SEPARATED CHILDREN.
FATHERS.
FECUNDITY.
FEMINISM.
FOLK LORE
FOOD HABITS
FOOD RELIEF.
FOOTBALL
FOSTER HOME CARE
FOUNDLINGS
FREE LOVE.
FREEMASONS
FRIENDSHIP.
FUNCTIONAL ANALYSIS (SOCIAL SCIENCES).
GAMBLING.
GARDEN CITIES
GAY LIBERATION MOVEMENT.
GIRLS.
GRANDSTANDS
GROUP RELATIONS TRAINING.
HALFWAY HOUSES.
HANDICAPPED
HANDICAPPED CHILDREN
HEROIN.
HEROIN HABIT.
HIGH-RISE APARTMENT BUILDINGS
HISTORICAL SOCIOLOGY.
HOLIDAYS
HOMOSEXUALITY.
HOUSING FOR PHYSICALLY HANDICAPPED
HOUSING MANAGEMENT.
HUMAN ECOLOGY.
HUMAN ENGINEERING.
HUMAN EVOLUTION.
HUNTING, PRIMITIVE
HUSBAND AND WIFE
ILLEGITIMACY.

INCOME MAINTENANCE PROGRAMMES
INDIANS, TREATMENT OF.
INDIVIDUALISM.
INDUSTRIAL SOCIOLOGY.
INFANTICIDE.
INFANTS
INFANTS (NEW-BORN)
INSANE, CRIMINAL AND DANGEROUS
INSTITUTIONAL CARE
INTERCULTURAL COMMUNICATION.
INTERNATIONAL RELIEF.
INTERPERSONAL RELATIONS.
INTERVIEWING.
JUDAISM AND SOCIAL PROBLEMS.
JUVENILE COURTS
JUVENILE DELINQUENCY.
KINGSTON PENITENTIARY.
KINSHIP.
KNOWLEDGE, SOCIOLOGY OF.
LEADERSHIP.
LEISURE.
LIQUOR HABIT
LIQUOR PROBLEM.
LITERATURE AND SOCIETY.
LOTTERIES
MAGNETIC RECORDERS AND RECORDING.
MAN.
MAN, PREHISTORIC
MAN, PRIMITIVE.
MARIHUANA.
MARRIAGE.
MARRIAGE, MIXED.
MASS MEDIA
MASS MEDIA AND RACE PROBLEMS
MASS SOCIETY.
MENTALLY HANDICAPPED
MENTALLY HANDICAPPED CHILDREN
MENTALLY ILL
METROPOLITAN AREAS
MIDDLE CLASSES
MOTHERS
MOUNT CARMEL CENTRE.
MOVING PICTURES
MUGGING
MURDER
MUSIC AND SOCIETY.
MYTHOLOGY, GREEK.
NARCOTIC ADDICTS
NARCOTIC HABIT.
NARCOTICS.
NARCOTICS, CONTROL OF.
NATIONAL CHARACTERISTICS, AMERICAN.
NATIONAL CHARACTERISTICS, EUROPEAN.
NATIONAL CHARACTERISTICS, GERMAN.
NATIONAL CHARACTERISTICS, IRISH.
NATIONAL CHARACTERISTICS, JAPANESE.
NATIONAL CHARACTERISTICS, PORTUGUESE.
NATIONAL CHARACTERISTICS, SPANISH.
NEGRO FAMILIES.
NEGRO YOUTH
NEIGHBOURHOOD.
NEIGHBOURLINESS.
NEW TOWNS.
NEW YEAR.
NOMADS
NONVERBAL COMMUNICATION.
OCCUPATIONS AND RACE.
OLD AGE
OLD AGE ASSISTANCE
OLD AGE HOMES
OLD AGE PENSIONS.
ORGANIZATION.
ORGANIZED CRIME
OUTDOOR RECREATION.
PACKAGE TOURS
PARENT AND CHILD.
PEASANTRY.

PENAL INSTITUTIONS
PHILOSOPHICAL ANTHROPOLOGY.
PHYSICAL EDUCATION AND TRAINING.
PHYSICALLY HANDICAPPED
PHYSICALLY HANDICAPPED CHILDREN
PLANNING.
PLANTATION LIFE.
PLAY.
PLAY SCHOOLS.
PLAYGROUNDS
PLURALISM (SOCIAL SCIENCES).
POLICE.
POLITICAL SOCIALIZATION.
POLITICAL SOCIOLOGY.
POOR
POOR LAWS
POPULATION GENETICS.
POVERTY.
POVERTY.
POWER (SOCIAL SCIENCES).
PRESTIGE.
PRISON RIOTS
PRISONERS
PRISONS
PROBATION
PROBATION SYSTEM
PROBLEM CHILDREN
PROBLEM FAMILY
PROGRESS.
PROSTITUTION
PSYCHIATRIC SOCIAL WORK
PUBLIC HOUSING
PUBLIC OPINION
PUBLIC OPINION POLLS.
PUBLIC RELATIONS.
PUNISHMENT.
RACE.
RACE DISCRIMINATION.
RACE PROBLEMS.
RACETRACKS (HORSE-RACING)
RADIO AUDIENCES
RECIDIVISTS
RECREATION.
RECREATION AREAS
RECREATION RESEARCH.
REFORMATORIES
REGIONAL PLANNING.
REHABILITATION, RURAL
REHABILITATION COUNSELLING.
REHABILITATION OF CRIMINALS.
REHABILITATION OF JUVENILE DELINQUENTS
REHABILITATION RESEARCH.
RELIGION AND SOCIOLOGY.
RELOCATION (HOUSING)
REMAND HOMES
RESIDENTIAL MOBILITY
RETIREMENT.
RETIREMENT, PLACES OF
RIOTS
RITES AND CEREMONIES.
ROLE CONFLICT.
RUMOUR.
RURAL POOR
RURAL YOUTH
RURAL-URBAN MIGRATION.
SATISFACTION.
SCHOOL SOCIAL WORK
SEASIDE RESORTS.
SECRET SOCIETIES
SEGREGATION IN EDUCATION
SEGREGATION IN SPORTS.
SELF-HELP GROUPS.
SEMIGROUPS.
SEX.
SEX AND LAW.
SEX CUSTOMS.
SEX DIFFERENCES.
SEX DISCRIMINATION
SEX DISCRIMINATION AGAINST WOMEN
SEX DISCRIMINATION IN EDUCATION
SEX ROLE.

SOCIOLOGY, ANTHROPOLOGY AND ETHNOLOGY(Cont.)

SEXUAL BEHAVIOUR IN ANIMALS.
SEXUAL ETHICS
SINGLE PARENT FAMILY.
SINGLE PEOPLE
SLAVE TRADE.
SLAVERY
SLAVERY IN AMERICA.
SLAVERY IN CUBA.
SLAVERY IN LATIN AMERICA.
SLAVERY IN MEXICO.
SLAVERY IN THE CARIBBEAN AREA.
SLAVERY IN THE UNITED KINGDOM
SLAVERY IN THE UNITED STATES.
SLAVERY IN THE WEST INDIES
SLUMS
SMALL GROUPS.
SNUFF.
SOCCER
SOCIAL ACTION.
SOCIAL CASE WORK.
SOCIAL CHANGE.
SOCIAL CLASSES.
SOCIAL CONFLICT.
SOCIAL CONTROL.
SOCIAL EXCHANGE.
SOCIAL GROUP WORK.
SOCIAL GROUPS.
SOCIAL HISTORY.
SOCIAL INDICATORS.
SOCIAL INTERACTION.
SOCIAL ISOLATION.
SOCIAL JUSTICE.
SOCIAL LEGISLATION
SOCIAL MOBILITY.
SOCIAL MOVEMENTS.
SOCIAL PARTICIPATION.
SOCIAL PERCEPTION.
SOCIAL POLICY.
SOCIAL PREDICTION.
SOCIAL PROBLEMS.
SOCIAL PSYCHIATRY.
SOCIAL PSYCHOLOGY.
SOCIAL REFORMERS
SOCIAL SCIENCE RESEARCH.
SOCIAL SCIENCES.
SOCIAL SCIENCES AND ETHICS.
SOCIAL SCIENCES AND STATE
SOCIAL SCIENTISTS
SOCIAL SERVICE.
SOCIAL SETTLEMENTS.
SOCIAL STABILITY.
SOCIAL STATUS.
SOCIAL SURVEYS.
SOCIAL SYSTEMS.
SOCIAL VALUES.
SOCIAL WORK EDUCATION.
SOCIAL WORK WITH CHILDREN
SOCIAL WORK WITH DELINQUENTS AND CRIMINALS
SOCIAL WORK WITH THE HOMELESS
SOCIAL WORK WITH YOUTH
SOCIAL WORKERS
SOCIALISM AND YOUTH.
SOCIALIZATION.
SOCIALLY HANDICAPPED.
SOCIALLY HANDICAPPED CHILDREN
SOCIALLY HANDICAPPED YOUTH
SOCIOLINGUISTICS.
SOCIOLOGICAL JURISPRUDENCE.
SOCIOLOGICAL RESEARCH.
SOCIOLOGISTS.
SOCIOLOGY.
SOCIOLOGY, CHRISTIAN.
SOCIOLOGY, MILITARY.
SOCIOLOGY, RURAL.
SOCIOLOGY, URBAN.
SOLIDARITY.
SPEECH AND SOCIAL STATUS.
SPORTS
SPORTS BETTING.
SQUATTERS
STEALING.

STRUCTURALISM.
STUDENTS' SOCIOECONOMIC STATUS
SUBURBS
SUICIDE.
SUMMER HOMES
SUNDERLAND FOOTBALL CLUB.
SUPERVISION OF SOCIAL WORKERS.
SYMBOLISM.
TELEVISION AND CHILDREN.
TELEVISION AUDIENCES
TELEVISION BROADCASTING
TELEVISION BROADCASTING OF NEWS
TELEVISION CRITICISM.
TELEVISION PROGRAMMES, PUBLIC SERVICE.
TIME ALLOCATION SURVEYS
TOBACCO HABIT.
TRAMPS
TRIBES AND TRIBAL SYSTEM
TRUTH.
UNDERDEVELOPED AREAS.
UNTOUCHABLES.
URBAN RENEWAL
URBANIZATION.
VAGRANCY.
VANDALISM.
VIGILANCE COMMITTEES.
VILLAGE COMMUNITIES
VILLAGES
VIOLENCE.
VIOLENCE IN TELEVISION.
VIOLENT DEATHS
VOCATIONAL REHABILITATION
VOLUNTEER WORKERS IN JUVENILE COURTS
VOLUNTEER WORKERS IN SOCIAL SERVICE.
WAR AND CIVILIZATION.
WAR AND SOCIETY.
WATER-RIGHTS
WELFARE STATE.
WIDOWS.
WIFE BEATING.
WILDERNESS AREAS.
WIVES.
WOMEN.
WOMEN, MOHAMMEDAN.
WOMEN AND SOCIALISM.
WOMEN IN BUSINESS.
WOMEN IN POLITICS.
WOMEN IN PUBLIC LIFE.
WOMEN IN THE CIVIL SERVICE.
WOMEN IN TRADE UNIONS
WOMEN'S LIBERATION MOVEMENT.
WOMEN'S RIGHTS.
WORTH.
YOUTH.
ZADRUGA.

Particular races, tribes and nationalities.

ABANYAMBO (AFRICAN PEOPLE).
AFRICANS IN THE UNITED KINGDOM.
AKWE-SHAVANTE INDIANS.
ALGERIANS IN FRANCE.
APINAGE INDIANS.
ARAUCANIAN INDIANS.
ARHUACO INDIANS.
ARMENIANS IN THE CRIMEA.
ARMENIANS IN TURKEY.
ASIATICS IN THE UNITED KINGDOM.
AUSTRALIAN ABORIGINES.
AUSTRIANS IN THE UNITED KINGDOM.
BANTUS.
BEDOUINS.
BOLIVIANS IN FOREIGN COUNTRIES.
BRITISH IN INDIA.
BRITISH IN SOUTH AFRICA.
CANADIANS IN RUSSIA.
CARIB INDIANS.
CAYAPA INDIANS.

CHINESE IN CANADA.
CHINESE IN FOREIGN COUNTRIES.
CHINESE IN NEW ZEALAND.
CHINESE IN THE UNITED KINGDOM.
CHOCTAW INDIANS
COLOURED PEOPLE (SOUTH AFRICA).
CORITANI.
CREE INDIANS.
CREOLES.
CROATS IN THE UNITED STATES.
CZECHOSLOVAKS IN RUSSIA.
DOMINICANS (DOMINICAN REPUBLIC) IN THE UNITED STATES.
DUTCH IN THE UNITED STATES.
EAST INDIANS IN COMMONWEALTH COUNTRIES.
EAST INDIANS IN NATAL.
EAST INDIANS IN THE UNITED KINGDOM.
EAST INDIANS IN UGANDA.
ENGLISH
ESKIMOS
FINNS IN THE UNITED STATES.
FRENCH CANADIANS.
FRENCH IN ALGERIA.
FRENCH IN BOSNIA.
FRENCH IN BRAZIL.
GERMANS IN BRAZIL.
GERMANS IN CANADA.
GERMANS IN CZECHOSLOVAKIA.
GERMANS IN DENMARK.
GERMANS IN EASTERN EUROPE.
GERMANS IN ESTONIA.
GERMANS IN LATVIA.
GERMANS IN MEXICO
GERMANS IN POLAND.
GERMANS IN SILESIA.
GERMANS IN SUBSAHARAN AFRICA.
GERMANS IN THE BALTIC STATES.
GERMANS IN THE UKRAINE.
GERMANS IN THE UNITED STATES.
GIPSIES
GREEKS IN AUSTRALIA.
GREEKS IN EUROPE.
GREEKS IN THE UNITED STATES.
GUAJIRO INDIANS.
GUARANI INDIANS.
GUAYAQUI INDIANS
GURUNGS.
HAYA (AFRICAN TRIBE).
IBOS.
IDOMAS.
INCAS.
INDIANS
INDIANS OF CENTRAL AMERICA
INDIANS OF MEXICO.
INDIANS OF NORTH AMERICA
INDIANS OF SOUTH AMERICA.
IRISH.
IRISH IN NEW ZEALAND.
IRISH IN THE UNITED STATES.
ITALIANS IN AUSTRALIA
ITALIANS IN BRAZIL.
ITALIANS IN POLAND.
ITALIANS IN THE UNITED STATES.
JALE (PAPUAN PEOPLE).
JAPANESE.
JAPANESE IN CHINA.
JAPANESE IN THE UNITED STATES.
JEWS.
JEWS IN AUSTRIA.
JEWS IN EUROPE.
JEWS IN GERMANY.
JEWS IN ITALY.
JEWS IN POLAND.
JEWS IN RUSSIA.
JEWS IN THE UNITED KINGDOM.
JEWS IN THE UNITED STATES.
JUCHEN (TRIBE).
KAINGANGUE INDIANS.
KAMBAS.
KASHINAUA INDIANS.

TRANSPORT AND COMMUNICATIONS

KECHUA INDIANS.
KEREBE (BANTU PEOPLE).
KIKUYUS.
LATIN AMERICANS IN THE UNITED STATES.
LATVIANS IN FOREIGN COUNTRIES.
LEBANESE IN SIERRA LEONE.
LUNDA (BANTU TRIBE).
MACEDONIANS IN GREECE.
MALTESE IN THE UNITED KINGDOM.
MAORIS.
MASAI.
MATABELE.
MAYAS.
MAZAHUA INDIANS.
MBUNDU (AFRICAN PEOPLE).
MEXICANS IN THE UNITED STATES.
MIAO PEOPLE.
MOLUCCANS IN THE NETHERLANDS.
MUNDURUCU INDIANS.
NAIRS.
NAVAHO INDIANS.
NEGRO RACE
NEGROES.
NEGROES IN COLOMBIA.
NEGROES IN CUBA.
NEGROES IN ECUADOR.
NEGROES IN LATIN AMERICA.
NEGROES IN RHODESIA.
NEGROES IN SOUTH AFRICA.
NEGROES IN SOUTH WEST AFRICA.
NEGROES IN THE ARGENTINE REPUBLIC.
NEGROES IN URUGUAY.
NIKA (BANTU TRIBE).
OSSETIANS.
OWAMBO
PAKISTANIS IN SCOTLAND.
PAKISTANIS IN THE UNITED KINGDOM.
PALESTINIAN ARABS
PATHANS.
PIAROA INDIANS.
POLES IN BRAZIL.
POLES IN FOREIGN COUNTRIES.
POLES IN GERMANY.
POLES IN HUNGARY.
POLES IN NEW ZEALAND.
POLES IN RUSSIA.
POLES IN THE UNITED KINGDOM.
POLES IN THE UNITED STATES.
PUERTO RICANS IN THE UNITED STATES.
RAMAPO MOUNTAIN PEOPLE.
REGNI.
RUSSIANS IN CHINA.
RUSSIANS IN NORTH AMERICA.
RUSSIANS IN THE NEAR EAST.
RUSSIANS IN THE UKRAINE.
SEMINOLE INDIANS.
SENEGALESE IN FRANCE.
ŠERENTE INDIANS.
SIQINIQMIUT (ESKIMO TRIBE).
SLAVS.
SLOVENES IN CARINTHIA.
SPANIARDS IN MEXICO.
SWEDES IN BRAZIL.
SWEDES IN THE ARGENTINE REPUBLIC.
SWEDES IN THE UNITED STATES.
TAPIRAPE INDIANS.
TAQRAMIUT (ESKIMO TRIBE).
TOUCOULEURS.
TURKMENS IN IRAN.
TURKS IN EUROPE.
TRUMAÍ INDIANS.
UKRAINIANS IN THE UNITED KINGDOM.
ULAD STUT (ARAB TRIBE).
WARRAU INDIANS.
WELSH IN PATAGONIA.
WENDS.
WEST INDIANS IN THE UNITED KINGDOM.
WEST INDIANS IN THE UNITED STATES.
XOSA.

YANOAMA INDIANS.
YOMBE (AFRICAN PEOPLE).
YORUBAS.
YUGOSLAVS IN FOREIGN COUNTRIES.

TRANSPORT AND COMMUNICATIONS.

General.

AERONAUTICS
AERONAUTICS, COMMERCIAL.
AEROPLANES
AIR LINES
AIR TRAVEL.
AIRPORTS
ARTIFICIAL SATELLITES IN TELECOMMUNICATION.
AUTOMOBILE DRIVERS' LICENCES
AUTOMOBILE GRAVEYARDS.
AUTOMOBILE PARKING
AUTOMOBILES
BOATMEN
CAB AND OMNIBUS SERVICE
CANALS
CITY TRAFFIC
COACHING
COMMERCIAL VEHICLES.
COMMUNICATION AND TRAFFIC
COMMUNITY ANTENNA TELEVISION
COMMUTING
COMPUTER NETWORKS.
CONCORDE (JET TRANSPORTS).
DATA TRANSMISSION SYSTEMS.
DOCKS
DRINKING AND ROAD ACCIDENTS
FERRIES
FISHING BOATS
FOOTBRIDGES
FREIGHT AND FREIGHTAGE
GARAGES
GROUND-EFFECT MACHINES.
HARBOURS
INLAND NAVIGATION.
INTERNATIONAL TELECOMMUNICATION SATELLITE ORGANIZATION.
LEAFLETS DROPPED FROM AIRCRAFT.
LIGHTHOUSES.
LOCAL TRANSIT
MERCHANT MARINE
MOTOR BUS LINES
MOTOR TRUCKS
MOTOR VEHICLES
OIL SPILLS
ORIGIN AND DESTINATION TRAFFIC SURVEYS
PEDESTRIAN CROSSINGS.
PEDESTRIANS
PETROLEUM SHIPPING TERMINALS
POSTAL SERVICE
RADIO
RADIO BROADCASTING
RAILWAYS
RAILWAYS, LOCAL AND LIGHT
RAILWAYS AND STATE
ROAD ACCIDENTS
ROAD CONSTRUCTION
ROAD MACHINERY.
ROAD SAFETY
ROADS
ROADS, ROMAN
SHIPPING
SHIPS
STEAMBOAT LINES
TANK-VESSELS
TELECOMMUNICATION.
TELEGRAPH
TELEPHONE
TELEVISION
TOLL ROADS
TRAFFIC ASSIGNMENT
TRAFFIC ENGINEERING

TRAFFIC ESTIMATION
TRAFFIC NOISE
TRAFFIC REGULATIONS
TRAFFIC SURVEYS
TRANSPORTATION.
TRANSPORTATION, AUTOMOTIVE
TRANSPORTATION, PRIMITIVE.
TRANSPORTATION AND STATE
TRANSPORTATION PLANNING
UNITIZED CARGO SYSTEMS.
URBAN TRANSPORTATION.
URBAN TRANSPORTATION POLICY
WATERWAYS.

Individual undertakings, etc.

CANADIAN PACIFIC RAILWAY.
EAST GHOR CANAL PROJECT.
NORTH EASTERN RAILWAY.
RADIO AUSTRALIA.

Ref.
Z
7161
L84
v.34
1976

MAY 9 1978